STANDARD DEDUCTION

Filing Status	2002 Amount
Married individuals filing joint returns and surviving spouses	$7,850
Heads of households	6,900
Unmarried individuals (other than surviving spouses and heads of households)	4,700
Married individuals filing separate return	3,925
Additional standard deductions for the aged and the blind	
Individual who is married and surviving spouses	900*
Individual who is unmarried and not a surviving spouse	1,150*
Taxpayer claimed as dependent on another taxpayer's return	750

*These amounts are $1,800 and $2,300, respectively, for a taxpayer who is both aged and blind.

Personal Exemption 2002: $3,000 *Reduction in personal and dependency exemptions:* The personal and dependency exemption deductions are reduced or eliminated for certain high-income taxpayers. When a taxpayer's AGI exceeds the "phaseout begins after" amount described below, the deduction is reduced by 2% for each $2,500 (or fraction thereof) by which AGI exceeds such amount. For married persons filing separately, the exemption deduction is reduced by 2% for each $1,250 (or fraction thereof) by which AGI exceeds the "phaseout begins after" amount. The personal exemption deduction amount cannot be reduced below zero. The phaseout ranges are:

Filing Status	*Phaseout Begins After*	*Phaseout Completed After*
Married individuals filing joint return and surviving spouses	$206,000	$328,500
Heads of households	171,650	294,150
Unmarried taxpayers (other than surviving spouses and heads of households)	137,300	259,800
Married individuals filing separate returns	103,000	164,250

Itemized Deductions

The itemized deductions that are otherwise deductible for the tax year are reduced by the lesser of (1) 3% of the excess of AGI over a threshold amount, or (2) 80% of the amount of itemized deductions otherwise deductible for the tax year excluding medical expenses, investment interest expense, casualty losses, and wagering losses to the extent of wagering gains. The threshold amount for the 2002 tax year is $137,300 (except for married individuals filing separate returns for which it is $68,650).

PRENTICE HALL'S FEDERAL TAXATION 2003

Comprehensive

PRENTICE HALL'S FEDERAL TAXATION 2003

Comprehensive

EDITORS

THOMAS R. POPE
University of Kentucky

KENNETH E. ANDERSON
University of Tennessee

JOHN L. KRAMER
University of Florida

CONTRIBUTING AUTHORS

D. DALE BANDY
University of Central Florida

N. ALLEN FORD
University of Kansas

ANNA C. FOWLER
University of Texas at Austin

ROBERT L. GARDNER
Brigham Young University

RICHARD J. JOSEPH
University of Texas at Austin

SUSAN L. NORDHAUSER
University of Texas at San Antonio

MICHAEL S. SCHADEWALD
University of Wisconsin—Milwaukee

Upper Saddle River, NJ 07458

Acquisitions Editor: Alana Bradley
Editor-in-Chief: PJ Boardman
Assistant Editor: Beth Ann Romph
Editorial Assistant: Jane Avery
Marketing Manager: Beth Toland
Managing Editor (Production): John Roberts
Production Editor: Renata Butera
Production Assistant: Dianne Falcone
Permissions Coordinator: Suzanne Grappi
Associate Director, Manufacturing: Vincent Scelta
Production Manager: Arnold Vila
Manufacturing Buyer: Vincent Scelta
Design Manager: Patricia Smythe
Interior Design: BB&K Design Inc.
Cover Design: Steven Frim
Cover Illustration/Photo: Digital Imagery © 2002 PhotoDisk, Inc.
Composition: Black Dot Graphics
Printer/Binder: Courier-Kendalville

Credits and acknowledgments borrowed from other sources and reproduced, with permission, in this textbook appear on appropriate page within the text.

Pearson Education LTD.
Pearson Education Australia PTY, Limited
Pearson Education Singapore, Pte. Ltd
Pearson Education North Asia Ltd
Pearson Education, Canada, Ltd
Pearson Educación de Mexico, S.A. de C.V.
Pearson Education–Japan
Pearson Education Malaysia, Pte. Ltd

10 9 8 7 6 5 4 3 2 1
ISBN 0-13-064733-0
ISBN 0-13-064735-7 (IE)
ISBN 0-13-064732-2 (Looseleaf)

Overview

Preface xxvii

Individuals

CHAPTER 1 An Introduction to Taxation 1-1
CHAPTER 2 Determination of Tax 2-1
CHAPTER 3 Gross Income: Inclusions 3-1
CHAPTER 4 Gross Income: Exclusions 4-1
CHAPTER 5 Property Transactions: Capital Gains and Losses 5-1
CHAPTER 6 Deductions and Losses 6-1
CHAPTER 7 Itemized Deductions 7-1
CHAPTER 8 Losses and Bad Debts 8-1
CHAPTER 9 Employee Expenses and Deferred Compensation 9-1
CHAPTER 10 Depreciation, Cost Recovery, Amortization, and Depletion 10-1
CHAPTER 11 Accounting Periods and Methods 11-1
CHAPTER 12 Property Transactions: Nontaxable Exchanges 12-1
CHAPTER 13 Property Transactions: Section 1231 and Recapture 13-1
CHAPTER 14 Special Tax Computation Methods, Tax Credits, and Payment of Tax 14-1

Corporations

CHAPTER 1 Tax Research 1-1
CHAPTER 2 Corporate Formations and Capital Structure 2-1
CHAPTER 3 The Corporate Income Tax 3-1
CHAPTER 4 Corporate Nonliquidating Distributions 4-1
CHAPTER 5 Other Corporate Tax Levies 5-1
CHAPTER 6 Corporate Liquidating Distributions 6-1
CHAPTER 7 Corporate Acquisitions and Reorganizations 7-1
CHAPTER 8 Consolidated Tax Returns 8-1
CHAPTER 9 Partnership Formation and Operation 9-1
CHAPTER 10 Special Partnership Issues 10-1
CHAPTER 11 S Corporations 11-1
CHAPTER 12 The Gift Tax 12-1
CHAPTER 13 The Estate Tax 13-1
CHAPTER 14 Income Taxation of Trusts and Estates 14-1
CHAPTER 15 Administrative Procedures 15-1

TABLES	2000 Tax Tables and Rate Schedules T-1
APPENDIX A	Tax Research Working Paper File A-1
APPENDIX B	Tax Forms B-1
APPENDIX C	MACRS and ACRS Tables C-1
APPENDIX D	Glossary D-1
APPENDIX E	Statements on Standards for Tax Services E-1
APPENDIX F	Comparison of Tax Attributes for C Corporations, Partnerships, and S Corporations F-1
APPENDIX G	Credit for State Death Taxes G-1
APPENDIX H	Actuarial Tables H-1
APPENDIX I	Index of Code Sections I-1
APPENDIX J	Index of Treasury Regulations J-1
APPENDIX K	Index of Government Promulgations K-1
APPENDIX L	Index of Court Cases L-1
APPENDIX M	Subject Index M-1

CONTENTS

PREFACE xxvii

INDIVIDUALS

CHAPTER 1
▶ AN INTRODUCTION TO TAXATION 1-1

History of Taxation in the United States 1-2
- Early Periods 1-2
- Revenue Acts From 1913 to the Present 1-3
- Revenue Sources 1-3

Types of Tax Rate Structures 1-4
- The Structure of Individual Income Tax Rates 1-4
- The Structure of Corporate Tax Rates 1-5
- Marginal, Average, and Effective Tax Rates for Taxpayers 1-5
- Determination of Taxable Income and Tax Due 1-7

Other Types of Taxes 1-7
- State and Local Income and Franchise Taxes 1-7
- Wealth Transfer Taxes 1-8
- Other Types of Taxes 1-11

Criteria for a Tax Structure 1-12
- Equity 1-12
- Certainty 1-13
- Convenience 1-13
- Economy 1-13

Objectives of the Federal Income Tax Law 1-14
- Economic Objectives 1-14
- Encouragement of Certain Activities and Industries 1-14
- Social Objectives 1-15

Entities in the Federal Income Tax System 1-15
- Taxpaying Entities 1-15
- Flow-Through Entities 1-16

Tax Law Sources 1-18

Enactment of A Tax Law 1-18
- Steps in the Legislative Process 1-18

Administration of the Tax Law and Tax Practice Issues 1-20
- Organization of the Internal Revenue Service 1-20
- Enforcement Procedures 1-21
- Selection of Returns for Audit 1-21
- Statute of Limitations 1-22
- Interest 1-22
- Penalties 1-22
- Administrative Appeal Procedures 1-23

Components of A Tax Practice 1-23
- Tax Compliance and Procedure 1-23
- Tax Research 1-23
- Tax Planning and Consulting 1-24
- Financial Planning 1-24

Computer Applications in Tax Practice 1-25
- Tax Return Preparation 1-25
- Tax Planning Applications 1-25
- Tax Research Applications 1-25

Problem Materials 1-26
- Discussion Questions 1-26
- Problems 1-28
- Tax Strategy Problem 1-29
- Case Study Problem 1-30
- Research Problem 1-30

CHAPTER 2
▶ DETERMINATION OF TAX 2-1

Formula for Individual Income Tax 2-2
- Basic Formula 2-2
- Definitions 2-3
- Tax Formula Illustrated 2-6

Deductions from Adjusted Gross Income 2-7
- Itemized Deductions 2-7
- Standard Deduction 2-10
- Personal Exemptions 2-12
- Dependency Exemptions 2-13
- Child Credit 2-18

Determining The Amount of Tax 2-19
- Filing Status 2-19
- Joint Return 2-20
- Surviving Spouse 2-20
- Head of Household 2-21
- Single Taxpayer 2-22
- Married Filing a Separate Return 2-22
- Abandoned Spouse 2-22
- Dependents with Unearned Income 2-23

Business Income and Business Entities 2-25

Treatment of Capital Gains and Losses 2-27
- Definition of Capital Assets 2-28
- Shifting Income Between Family Members 2-28
- Tax Treatment of Gains and Losses 2-28

Tax Planning Considerations 2-28
Splitting Income 2-29
Maximizing Itemized Deductions 2-29
Filing Joint or Separate Returns 2-29

Compliance and Procedural 2-31
Who Must File 2-31
Due Dates for Filing Return 2-32
Use of Forms 1040, 1040ez, And 1040a 2-32
System for Reporting Income 2-32

Problem Materials 2-33
Discussion Questions 2-33
Issue Identification Questions 2-33
Problems 2-34
Tax Strategy Problems 2-38
Tax Form/Return Preparation Problems 2-39
Case Study Problems 2-39
Tax Research Problems 2-40

CHAPTER 3
▶ GROSS INCOME: INCLUSIONS 3-1

Economic and Accounting Concepts of Income 3-2
Economic Concept 3-2
Accounting Concept 3-2

Tax Concept of Income 3-3
Administrative Convenience 3-3
Wherewithal to Pay 3-4
Gross Income Defined 3-4

To Whom Is Income Taxable? 3-6
Assignment of Income 3-6
Allocating Income Between Married People 3-6
Income of Minor Children 3-8

When Is Income Taxable? 3-8
Cash Method 3-8
Accrual Method 3-11
Hybrid Method 3-12

Items of Gross Income: Sec. 61(a) 3-13
Compensation 3-13
Business Income 3-13
Gains from Dealings in Property 3-13
Interest 3-13
Rents and Royalties 3-15
Dividends 3-16
Alimony and Separate Maintenance Payments 3-17
Pensions and Annuities 3-19
Income from Life Insurance and Endowment Contracts 3-21
Income from Discharge of Indebtedness 3-22
Income Passed Through to Taxpayer 3-22

Other Items of Gross Income 3-22
Prizes, Awards, Gambling Winnings, and Treasure Finds 3-22
Illegal Income 3-23
Unemployment Compensation 3-23
Social Security Benefits 3-23
Insurance Proceeds and Court Awards 3-24
Recovery of Previously Deducted Amounts 3-25
Claim of Right 3-26

Tax Planning Considerations 3-27
Shifting Income 3-27
Alimony 3-27
Prepaid Income 3-27
Taxable, Tax-Exempt, or Tax-Deferred Bonds 3-28
Reporting Savings Bond Interest 3-28
Deferred Compensation Arrangements 3-29

Compliance and Procedural Considerations 3-29

Problem Materials 3-30
Discussion Questions 3-30
Issue Identification Questions 3-33
Problems 3-34
Comprehensive Problems 3-37
Tax Strategy Problems 3-37
Tax Form/Return Preparation Problems 3-38
Case Study Problems 3-38
Tax Research Problem 3-39

CHAPTER 4
▶ GROSS INCOME: EXCLUSIONS 4-1

tems that are not Income 4-2
Unrealized Income 4-2
Self-Help Income 4-3
Rental Value of Personal-use Property 4-3
Selling Price of Property 4-3

Major Statutory Exclusions 4-4
Gifts and Inheritances 4-4
Life Insurance Proceeds 4-5
Adoption Expenses 4-6
Awards for Meritorious Achievement 4-7
Scholarships and Fellowships 4-7
Distributions from Qualified Tuition Programs 4-8
Payments for Injury and Sickness 4-8
Employee Fringe Benefits 4-10
Foreign-Earned Income Exclusion 4-18
Income from The Discharge of a Debt 4-19
Exclusion for Gain from Small Business Stock 4-20
Other Exclusions 4-21

Tax Planning Considerations 4-21
Employee Fringe Benefits 4-21
Self-Help and Use of Personally Owned Property 4-23

Compliance and Procedural Considerations 4-23

Problem Materials 4-24

Discussion Questions 4-24
Issue Identification Questions 4-25
Problems 4-25
Comprehensive Problem 4-29
Tax Strategy Problems 4-29
Tax Form/Return Preparation Problems 4-30
Case Study Problems 4-30
Tax Research Problems 4-31

CHAPTER 5
▶ PROPERTY TRANSACTIONS: CAPITAL GAINS AND LOSSES 5-1

Determination of Gain or Loss 5-2

Realized Gain or Loss 5-2
Recognized Gain or Loss 5-4

Basis Considerations 5-5

Cost of Acquired Property 5-5
Property Received as a Gift: Gifts After 1921 5-6
Property Received from A Decedent 5-8
Property Converted from Personal Use to Business Use 5-9
Allocation of Basis 5-10

Definition of A Capital Asset 5-13

Influence of the Courts 5-13
Other IRC Provisions Relevant to Capital Gains and Losses 5-14

Tax Treatment for Capital Gains and Losses of Noncorporate Taxpayers 5-16

Capital Gains 5-16
Adjusted Net Capital Gains (ANCG) 5-17
Capital Losses 5-18

Tax Treatment of Capital Gains and Losses: Corporate Taxpayers 5-20

Sale or Exchange 5-21

Retirement of Debt Instruments 5-22
Worthless Securities 5-22
Options 5-24
Patents 5-25
Franchises, Trademarks, and Trade Names 5-26
Lease Cancellation Payments 5-27

Holding Period 5-28

Property Received as a Gift 5-28
Property Received from A Decedent 5-29
Nontaxable Exchanges 5-29
Receipt of Nontaxable Stock Dividends and Stock Rights 5-29

Preferential Treatment for Net Capital Gains 5-30

Mobility of Capital 5-30
Mitigation of the Effects of Inflation and The Progressive Tax System 5-30
Lower the Cost of Capital 5-31

Tax Planning Considerations 5-31

Selection of Property to Transfer By Gift 5-31
Selection of Property to Transfer at Time of Death 5-32

Compliance and Procedural Considerations 5-33

Documentation of Basis 5-33
Reporting of Capital Gains and Losses on Schedule D 5-33

Problem Materials 5-36

Discussion Questions 5-36
Issue Identification Questions 5-37
Problems 5-38
Comprehensive Problem 5-42
Tax Strategy Problems 5-43
Tax Form/Return Preparation Problems 5-43
Case Study Problems 5-44
Tax Research Problems 5-45

CHAPTER 6
▶ DEDUCTIONS AND LOSSES 6-1

For Versus from Adjusted Gross Income (AGI) Classification 6-3

Criteria for Deducting Business and Investment Expenses 6-4

Business or Investment Requirement 6-5
Ordinary Expense 6-7
Necessary Expense 6-8
Reasonable Expense 6-8
Expenses and Losses must be Incurred By the Taxpayer 6-9

General Restrictions on The Deductibility of Expenses 6-10

Capitalization Versus Expense Deduction 6-10
Expenses Related to Exempt Income 6-11
Expenditures That Are Contrary to Public Policy 6-12
Other Expenditures That Are Specifically Disallowed 6-14

Proper Substantiation Requirement 6-16

When an Expense Is Deductible 6-18

Cash Method 6-18
Accrual Method 6-20

Special Disallowance Rules 6-22

Wash Sales 6-22
Transactions Between Related Parties 6-25
Hobby Losses 6-28
Vacation Home 6-31
Expenses of An Office in the Home 6-34

Tax Planning Considerations 6-35

Hobby Losses 6-35
Unreasonable Compensation 6-35
Timing of Deductions 6-36

Compliance and Procedural Considerations 6-36
- Proper Classification of Deductions 6-36
- Proper Substantiation 6-37
- Business Versus Hobby 6-37

Problem Materials 6-37
- Discussion Questions 6-37
- Issue Identification Questions 6-39
- Problems 6-39
- Comprehensive Problem 6-45
- Tax Strategy Problems 6-45
- Tax Form/Return Preparation Problems 6-46
- Case Study Problems 6-48
- Tax Research Problem 6-48

CHAPTER 7
▶ ITEMIZED DEDUCTIONS 7-1

Medical Expenses 7-2
- Qualified Individuals 7-2
- Qualified Medical Expenses 7-3
- Amount and Timing of Deduction 7-6

Taxes 7-9
- Definition of A Tax 7-9
- Deductible Taxes 7-9
- Nondeductible Taxes 7-9
- State and Local Income Taxes 7-10
- Personal Property Taxes 7-10
- Real Estate Taxes 7-10
- General Sales Tax 7-11
- Self-Employment Tax 7-11

Interest 7-12
- Definition of Interest 7-12
- Classification of Interest Expense 7-12
- Timing of the Interest Deduction 7-19

Charitable Contributions 7-21
- Qualifying Organization 7-21
- Type of Property Contributed 7-22
- Deduction Limitations 7-24
- Application of Carryovers 7-25
- Special Rules for Charitable Contributions Made By Corporations 7-26
- Summary of Deduction Limitations 7-26

Casualty and Theft Losses 7-28

Miscellaneous Itemized Deductions 7-28
- Certain Employee Expenses 7-28
- Expenses to Produce Income 7-28
- Cost of Tax Advice 7-28

Reduction of Certain Itemized Deductions 7-29

Tax Planning Considerations 7-30
- Medical Expense Deduction 7-30
- Interest Expense Deduction 7-31
- Deduction for Charitable Contributions 7-32

Compliance and Procedural Considerations 7-33
- Medical Expenses 7-33
- Contribution of Property 7-33
- Charitable Contributions 7-33
- Taxes 7-36

Problem Materials 7-37
- Discussion Questions 7-37
- Issue Identification Questions 7-38
- Problems 7-38
- Comprehensive Problem 7-42
- Tax Strategy Problems 7-43
- Tax Form/Return Preparation Problems 7-43
- Case Study Problems 7-45
- Tax Research Problems 7-45

CHAPTER 8
▶ LOSSES AND BAD DEBTS 8-1

Transactions that may Result in Losses 8-2
- Sale or Exchange of Property 8-2
- Expropriated, Seized, or Confiscated Property 8-3
- Abandoned Property 8-3
- Worthless Securities 8-3
- Demolition of Property 8-4

Classifying the Loss on The Taxpayer's Tax Return 8-4
- Ordinary Versus Capital Loss 8-5
- Disallowance Possibilities 8-6

Passive Losses 8-7
- Computation of Passive Losses and Credits 8-7
- Carryovers 8-8
- Definition of A Passive Activity 8-10
- Taxpayers Subject to Passive Loss Rules 8-12
- Publicly Traded Partnerships 8-13
- Rental Real Estate Trade or Business 8-14
- Other Rental Real Estate Activities 8-15

Casualty and Theft Losses 8-17
- Casualty Defined 8-17
- Theft Defined 8-19
- Deductible Amount of Casualty Loss 8-19
- Limitations on Personal-use Property 8-20
- Netting Casualty Gains and Losses on Personal-use Property 8-21
- Casualty Gains and Losses Attributable to Business and Investment Property 8-22
- When Losses Are Deductible 8-22

Bad Debts 8-24
- Bona Fide Debtor-Creditor Relationship 8-24
- Taxpayer's Basis in the Debt 8-25
- Debt must be Worthless 8-26

Nonbusiness Bad Debts 8-26
Business Bad Debts 8-28
Accounting for the Business Bad Debt 8-28
Recovery of Bad Debts 8-28
Deposits in Insolvent Financial Institutions 8-28

Net Operating Losses 8-29
Computing the Net Operating Loss 8-30
Carryback and Carryover Periods 8-33
Recomputation of Taxable Income in the Carryover Year 8-33

Tax Planning Considerations 8-34
Bad Debts 8-34
Casualties 8-34
Net Operating Losses 8-35

Compliance and Procedural Consideration 8-35
Worthless Securities 8-35

Problem Materials 8-36
Discussion Questions 8-36
Issue Identification Questions 8-37
Problems 8-38
Tax Strategy Problems 8-42
Tax Form/Return Preparation Problems 8-43
Case Study Problems 8-44
Tax Research Problem 8-45

CHAPTER 9
▶ EMPLOYEE EXPENSES AND DEFERRED COMPENSATION 9-1

Classification of Employee Expenses 9-2
Nature of the Employment Relationship 9-2
Limitations on Unreimbursed Employee Expenses 9-3

Travel Expenses 9-4
Deductibility of Travel Expenses 9-4
Definition of Travel Expenses 9-5
General Qualification Requirements 9-6
Business Versus Pleasure 9-7
Foreign Travel 9-8
Additional Limitations on Travel Expenses 9-8

Transportation Expenses 9-9
Definition and Classification 9-9
Treatment of Automobile Expenses 9-10
Reimbursement of Automobile Expenses 9-12

Entertainment Expenses 9-12
50% Disallowance for Meal and Entertainment Expenses 9-12
Classification of Expenses 9-13
Business Meals 9-14
Entertainment Facilities and Club Dues 9-15
Business Gifts 9-15
Limitations on Entertainment Tickets 9-16

Reimbursed Employee Business Expenses 9-16

Moving Expenses 9-18
Expense Classification 9-19
Definition of Moving Expenses 9-19
Treatment of Employer Reimbursements 9-20

Education Expenses 9-20
Classification of Education Expenses 9-21
General Requirements for a Deduction 9-21

Office in Home Expenses 9-23
General Requirements for a Deduction 9-23
Deduction and Limitations 9-25

Deferred Compensation 9-26
Qualified Pension and Profit-Sharing Plans 9-27
Qualification Requirements for a Qualified Plan 9-28
Tax Treatment to Employees and Employers 9-29
Nonqualified Plans 9-30
Employee Stock Options 9-32
Plans for Self-employed Individuals 9-36
Individual Retirement Accounts (IRAs) 9-36
Traditional IRA 9-36
Roth IRA 9-38
Coverdell Education Savings Account 9-40
Simplified Employee Pensions 9-41
Simple Retirement Plans 9-42

Tax Planning Considerations 9-42
Moving Expenses 9-42
Providing Nontaxable Compensation to Employees 9-43
Rollover of Traditional IRA to Roth IRA 9-43

Compliance and Procedural Considerations 9-43
Stantiating Travel and Entertainment Expenses 9-43
Reporting Employee Business Expenses 9-44
Reporting Moving Expenses 9-47
Reporting Office in Home Expenses 9-47
Qualification of Pension and Profit-sharing Plans 9-47

Problem Materials 9-48
Discussion Questions 9-48
Issue Identification Questions 9-51
Problems 9-51
Comprehensive Problem 9-58
Tax Strategy Problem 9-59
Tax Form/Return Preparation Problems 9-60
Case Study Problems 9-61
Tax Research Problem 9-62

CHAPTER 10
▶ DEPRECIATION, COST RECOVERY, AMORTIZATION, AND DEPLETION 10-1

Depreciation and Cost Recovery 10-2
General Considerations 10-2
Depreciation Methods 10-4

Section 179 Expensing Election 10-9
MACRs Restrictions 10-10

Amortization 10-13
Sec. 197 Intangibles 10-13
Research and Experimental Expenditures 10-16

Depletion, Intangible Drilling and Development Costs 10-18
Depletion Methods 10-18
Treatment of Intangible Drilling and Development Costs 10-20

Tax Planning Considerations 10-21
Alternative Depreciation System Under MACRS 10-21
IDCs: Capitalization Versus Expensing Election 10-21
Use of Units of Production Depreciation 10-22
Structuring a Business Combination 10-22

Compliance and Procedural Considerations 10-22
IDC Election Procedures 10-22
Reporting Cost Recovery, Depreciation, Depletion, and Amortization Deductions 10-23
Research and Experimental Expenditures 10-23

Problem Materials 10-23
Discussion Questions 10-23
Issue Identification Questions 10-29
Problems 10-30
Comprehensive Problem 10-33
Strategy Problem 10-34
Case Study Problem 10-35
Tax Form/Return Preparation Problems 10-35
Tax Research Problem 10-36

CHAPTER 11
▶ ACCOUNTING PERIODS AND METHODS 11-1

Accounting Periods 11-2
Required Payments and Fiscal Years 11-3
Changes in the Accounting Period 11-4
Returns for Periods of Less Than 12 Months 11-5

Overall Accounting Methods 11-7
Cash Receipts and Disbursements Method 11-7
Accrual Method 11-9
Hybrid Method 11-10

Inventories 11-11
Determination of Inventory Cost 11-11

Special Accounting Methods 11-15
Long-Term Contracts 11-15
Installment Sales Method 11-17
Deferred Payment Sales 11-21

Imputed Interest 11-22
Imputed Interest Computation 11-23
Accrual of Interest 11-23
Gift, Shareholder, and Other Loans 11-24

Change in Accounting Methods 11-25
Amount of Change 11-26
Reporting the Amount of the Change 11-27
Obtaining IRS Consent 11-27

Tax Planning Considerations 11-28
Accounting Periods 11-28
Accounting Methods 11-28
Installment Sales 11-28

Compliance and Procedural Considerations 11-28
Reporting Installment Sales on Form 6252 11-28
Procedures for Changing to LIFO 11-30

Problem Materials 11-30
Discussion Questions 11-30
Issue Identification Questions 11-31
Problems 11-31
Comprehensive Problem 11-34
Tax Form/Return Preparation Problem 11-35
Tax Strategy Problems 11-35
Case Study Problems 11-35
Tax Research Problems 11-36

CHAPTER 12
▶ PROPERTY TRANSACTIONS: NONTAXABLE EXCHANGES 12-1

Like-kind Exchanges 12-2
Like-Kind Property Defined 12-2
A Direct Exchange Must Occur 12-5
Three-Party Exchanges 12-5
Receipt of Boot 12-6
Basis of Property Received 12-7
Exchanges Between Related Parties 12-8
Transfer of Non-Like-Kind Property 12-9
Holding Period for Property Received 12-9

Involuntary Conversions 12-10
Involuntary Conversion Defined 12-11
Tax Treatment of Gain Due to Involuntary Conversion Into Boot 12-12
Tax Treatment of Gain Due to an Involuntary Conversion Directly Into Similar Property 12-13
Replacement Property 12-13
Obtaining Replacement Property 12-15
Time Requirements for Replacement 12-15

Sale of Principal Residence 12-16
Principal Residence Defined 12-18
Sale of More Than One Principal Residence Within a Two-Year Period 12-19
Involuntary Conversion of a Principal Residence 12-20

Tax Planning Considerations 12-21
Avoiding the Like-kind Exchange Provisions 12-21
Sale of A Principal Residence 12-22

Reporting of Involuntary Conversions 12-23

Compliance and Procedural Considerations 12-23

Reporting of Sale or Exchange of a Principal Residence 12-24

Problem Materials 12-24

Discussion Questions 12-24
Issue Identification Questions 12-25
Problems 12-26
Comprehensive Problem 12-30
Tax Strategy Problem 12-30
Tax Form/Return Preparation Problems 12-31
Case Study Problems 12-32
Tax Research Problems 12-32

CHAPTER 13

▶ PROPERTY TRANSACTIONS: SECTION 1231 AND RECAPTURE 13-1

History of Sec. 1231 13-2

Overview of Basic Tax Treatment for Sec. 1231 13-3

Net Gains 13-3
Net Losses 13-3
Tax Rate for Net Sec. 1231 Gain 13-4

Section 1231 Property 13-5

Section 1231 Property Defined 13-5
Real or Depreciable Property Used in Trade or Business 13-5

Involuntary Conversions 13-6

Condemnations 13-6
Other Involuntary Conversions 13-7

Procedure for Sec. 1231 Treatment 13-7

Recapture Provisions of Sec. 1245 13-8

Purpose of Sec. 1245 13-9

Recapture Provisions of Sec. 1250 13-11

Purpose of Sec. 1250 13-11
Section 1250 Property Defined 13-11
Unrecaptured Section 1250 Gain 13-12
Recapture Rules for Residential Rental Property 13-13
Residential Rental Property that is Recovery Property 13-13
Recapture Rules for Nonresidential Real Estate 13-14
Low-Income Housing 13-15

Additional Recapture for Corporations 13-15

Summary of Sec. 1231, 1245 and 1250 Gains 13-16

Recapture Provisions-Other Applications 13-17

Gifts of Property Subject to Recapture 13-17
Transfer of Property Subject to Recapture At Death 13-18
Charitable Contributions 13-18
Like-Kind Exchanges 13-18
Involuntary Conversions 13-19
Installment Sales 13-19
Section 179 Expensing Election 13-20
Conservation and Land Clearing Expenditures 13-20
Intangible Drilling Costs and Depletion 13-21
Gain on Sale of Depreciable Property Between Related Parties 13-21

Tax Planning Considerations 13-22

Avoiding the Recapture Provisions 13-23

Compliance and Procedural Considerations 13-24

Reporting Sec. 1231 Gains and Losses on Form 4797 13-24
Reporting Gains Recaptured As Ordinary Income on Form 4797 13-25
Reporting Casualty or Theft Gain or Loss on Form 4684 13-25

Problem Materials 13-25

Discussion Questions 13-25
Issue Identification Questions 13-30
Problems 13-30
Comprehensive Problem 13-35
Tax Strategy Problems 13-35
Tax Form/Return Preparation Problems 13-36
Case Study Problems 13-37
Tax Research Problem 13-37

CHAPTER 14

▶ SPECIAL TAX COMPUTATION METHODS, TAX CREDITS, AND PAYMENT OF TAX 14-1

Alternative Minimum Tax 14-2

Computational Aspects 14-2
Tax Preference Items 14-3
Amt Adjustments 14-4
Summary Illustration of the AMT Computation 14-6

Self-Employment Tax 14-7

Computing the Tax 14-7
What Constitutes Self-Employment Income 14-8

Overview of Tax Credits 14-9

Use and Importance of Tax Credits 14-9
Value of a Credit Versus a Deduction 14-9
Classification of Credits 14-9

Personal Tax Credits 14-10

Child Tax Credit 14-10
Child and Dependent Care Credit 14-11
Tax Credit for the Elderly and Disabled 14-12
Adoption Credit 14-13
Hope Scholarship Credit 14-14
Lifetime Learning Credit 14-15
Qualified Retirement Savings Contributions Credit 14-16
Limitation on Personal Credits 14-17

Miscellaneous Credits 14-17
Foreign Tax Credit 14-17

General Business Credits 14-18
Credit for Increasing Research Activities 14-18
Disabled Access Credit 14-19
Tax Credit for Rehabilitation Expenditures 14-19
Business Energy Credits 14-20
Work Opportunity Credit 14-20
Welfare-to-Work Credit 14-21
Empowerment Zone Employment Credit 14-21
Limitation Based Upon Tax Liability 14-22

Refundable Credits 14-22
Earned Income Credit 14-22

Payment of Taxes 14-24
Withholding of Taxes 14-25
Estimated Tax Payments 14-27

Tax Planning Considerations 14-29
Avoiding the Alternative Minimum Tax 14-29
Avoiding the Underpayment Penalty for Estimated Tax 14-29
Cash-Flow Considerations 14-30
Use of General Business Tax Credits 14-30
Foreign Tax Credits and The Foreign Earned Income Exclusion 14-30
Child and Dependent Care Credit 14-31

Compliance and Procedural Considerations 14-32
Alternative Minimum Tax Filing Procedures 14-32
Withholding and Estimated Tax 14-32
General Business Tax Credits 14-32
Personal Tax Credits 14-32

Problem Materials 14-33
Discussion Questions 14-33
Issue Identification Questions 14-35
Problems 14-35
Comprehensive Problem 14-40
Tax Strategy Problem 14-41
Tax Form/Return Preparation Problems 14-41
Case Study Problems 14-42
Tax Research Problem 14-42

CORPORATIONS

CHAPTER 1
▶ TAX RESEARCH 1-1

Overview of Tax Research 1-2

Steps in the Tax Research Process 1-3

Importance of the Facts to the Tax Consequences 1-5
Ability to Create a Factual Situation Favoring the Taxpayer 1-6

The Sources of Tax Law 1-7
The Legislative Process 1-7
The Internal Revenue Code 1-8
Treasury Regulations 1-8
Administrative Interpretations 1-11
Judicial Decisions 1-14
Tax Treaties 1-24
Tax Periodicals 1-24

Tax Services 1-25
United States Tax Reporter 1-25
Standard Federal Tax Reporter 1-26
Federal Tax Coordinator 2d 1-26
Law of Federal Income Taxation (Mertens) 1-27
Tax Management Portfolios 1-27
CCH Federal Tax Service 1-28

Citators 1-28
CCH Citator 1-28
Research Institute of America Citator 2nd Series 1-31

Computers as a Research Tool 1-34

Statements on Standards for Tax Services 1-35

Problem Materials 1-38

Sample Work Papers and Client Letter 1-38
Discussion Questions 1-38
Problems 1-40
Comprehensive Problem 1-43
Tax Strategy Problem 1-43
Case Study Problem 1-43
Tax Research Problems 1-43

CHAPTER 2
▶ CORPORATE FORMATIONS AND CAPITAL STRUCTURE 2-1

Organization Forms Available 2-2
Sole Proprietorships 2-2
Partnerships 2-3
Corporations 2-5
Limited Liability Companies 2-7
Limited Liability Partnerships 2-7

Check-the-box Regulations 2-8

Tax Considerations in Forming a Corporation 2-9

Legal Requirements for Forming a Corporation 2-9

Section 351: Deferring Gain or Loss Upon Incorporation 2-12
The Property Requirement 2-12
The Control Requirement 2-13
The Stock Requirement 2-16
Effect of Sec. 351 on the Transferors 2-16
Tax Consequences to Transferee Corporation 2-20
Assumption of the Transferorus Liabilities 2-21
Other Considerations in a Sec. 351 Exchange 2-24

Choice of Capital Structure 2-26
Characterization of Obligations as Debt or Equity Capital 2-26
Debt Capital 2-27
Equity Capital 2-28
Capital Contributions By Shareholders 2-28

Worthlessness of Stock or Debt Obligations 2-30
Capital Contributions By Nonshareholders 2-30
Securities 2-30
Unsecured Debt Obligations 2-32

Tax Planning Considerations 2-33
Avoiding Sec. 351 2-33

Compliance and Procedural Considerations 2-35
Reporting Requirements Under Sec. 351 2-35

Problem Materials 2-35
Discussion Questions 2-35
Issue Identification Questions 2-36
Problems 2-37
Comprehensive Problem 2-41
Tax Strategy Problem 2-42
Case Study Problems 2-42
Tax Research Problems 2-43

CHAPTER 3

▶ THE CORPORATE INCOME TAX 3-1

Corporate Elections 3-2
Choosing a Calendar or Fiscal Year 3-2
Accounting Methods 3-4

General Formula for Determining the Corporate Tax Liability 3-5

Computing a Corporationus Taxable Income 3-5
Sales and Exchanges of Property 3-6
Business Expenses 3-7
Special Deductions 3-12
Exceptions for Closely-held Corporations 3-18

Computing a Corporationus Income Tax Liability 3-20
General Rules 3-20
Personal Service Corporations 3-22

Controlled Groups of Corporations 3-22
Why Special Rules Are Needed 3-22
What Is a Controlled Group 3-23
Application of the Controlled Group Test 3-26
Special Rules Applying to Controlled Groups 3-26
Consolidated Tax Returns 3-27

Tax Planning Considerations 3-28
Compensation Planning for Shareholder-Employees 3-28
Special Election to Allocate Reduced Tax Rate Benefits 3-29
Using Nol Carryovers and Carrybacks 3-31

Compliance and Procedural Considerations 3-31
Estimated Taxes 3-31
Requirements for Filing and Paying Taxes 3-34
When the Return must be Filed 3-35
Tax Return Schedules 3-35

Problem Materials 3-38
Discussion Questions 3-38
Issue Identification Questions 3-39
Problems 3-39
Comprehensive Problem 3-45
Tax Strategy Problem 3-46
Tax Form/Return Preparation Problem 3-46
Case Study Problems 3-47
Tax Research Problems 3-48

CHAPTER 4

▶ CORPORATE NONLIQUIDATING DISTRIBUTIONS 4-1

Nonliquidating Distributions in General 4-2
Current Earnings and Profits 4-3
Distinction Between Current and Accumulated E&P 4-6

Earnings and Profits (E&P) 4-3

Nonliquidating Property Distributions 4-8
Consequences of Nonliquidating Property Distributions to the Shareholders 4-8
Consequences of Property Distributions to the Distributing Corporation 4-9
Constructive Dividends 4-11

Stock Dividends and Stock Rights 4-13
Tax-free Stock Dividends 4-14
Tax-free Stock Rights 4-15
Effect of Nontaxable Stock Dividends on the Distributing Corporation 4-16
Taxable Stock Dividends and Stock Rights 4-16

Stock Redemptions 4-16
Effect of the Redemption on the Shareholder 4-17
Attribution Rules 4-18
Substantially Disproportionate Redemptions 4-20
Complete Termination of the Shareholderus Interest 4-21
Redemptions Not Essentially Equivalent to A Dividend 4-23
Partial Liquidations 4-24
Redemptions to Pay Death Taxes 4-25
Effect of Redemptions on The Distributing Corporation 4-27

Preferred Stock Bailouts 4-28
Sec. 306 Stock Defined 4-28
Dispositions of Sec. 306 Stock 4-29
Redemptions of Sec. 306 Stock 4-29
Exceptions to Sec. 306 Treatment 4-30

Stock Redemptions By Related Corporations 4-30
Brother-sister Corporations 4-30
Parent-subsidiary Corporations 4-32

Tax Planningconsiderations 4-33
Avoiding Unreasonable Compensation 4-33
Bootstrap Acquisitions 4-34
Timing of Distributions 4-35

Compliance and Procedural Considerations 4-36
Corporate Reporting of Nondividend Distributions 4-36
Agreement to Terminate Interest Under Sec. 302(b)(3) 4-36

Problem Materials 4-37
Discussion Questions 4-37
Issue Identification Questions 4-38
Problems 4-39
Comprehensive Problem 4-45
Tax Strategy Problem 4-46
Case Study Problems 4-46
Tax Research Problems 4-46

CHAPTER 5
▶ OTHER CORPORATE TAX LEVIES 5-1

The Corporate Alternative Minimum Tax 5-2
The General Formula 5-2
Definitions 5-4
Tax Preference Items 5-6
Adjustments to Taxable Income 5-7
Adjusted Current Earnings (Ace) Adjustment 5-9
Minimum Tax Credit 5-13
Tax Credits and the AMT 5-14

Personal Holding Company Tax 5-15
Personal Holding Company Defined 5-16
Stock Ownership Requirement 5-16
Passive Income Requirement 5-16
Determining the PHC Penalty Tax 5-21
Avoiding the PHC Designation and Tax Liability By Making Dividend Distributions 5-22
PHC Tax Calculation 5-23

Accumulated Earnings Tax 5-24
Corporations Subject to the Penalty Tax 5-24
Proving a Tax-Avoidance Purpose 5-25
Evidence Concerning the Reasonableness of an Earnings Accumulation 5-26
Determining the Accumulated Earnings Tax Liability 5-31
Accumulated Earnings Tax Calculation 5-33

Tax Planning Considerations 5-35
Special Amt Elections 5-35
Eliminating the ACE Adjustment 5-35
Avoiding the Personal Holding Company Tax 5-36
Avoiding the Accumulated Earnings Tax 5-36

Compliance and Procedural Considerations 5-37
Alternative Minimum Tax 5-37
Personal Holding Company Tax 5-37
Accumulated Earnings Tax 5-37

Problem Materials 5-38
Discussion Questions 5-38
Issue Identification Questions 5-41
Problems 5-41
Comprehensive Problem 5-47
Tax Strategy Problem 5-48
Tax Form/Return Preparation Problem 5-48
Case Study Problems 5-49
Tax Research Problems 5-50

CHAPTER 6
▶ CORPORATE LIQUIDATING DISTRIBUTIONS 6-1

Overview of Corporate Liquidations 6-2
The Shareholder 6-2
The Corporation 6-3
Definition of a Complete Liquidation 6-3

General Liquidation Rules 6-5
Effects of Liquidating on the Shareholders 6-5
Effects of Liquidating on the Liquidating Corporation 6-6

Liquidation of a Controlled Subsidiary Corporation 6-10
Requirements 6-10
Effects of Liquidating on the Shareholders 6-11
Effects of Liquidating on the Subsidiary Corporation 6-13

Special Shareholder Reporting Issues 6-14
Partially Liquidating Distributions 6-14
Subsequent Assessments Against the Shareholders 6-15
Open Versus Closed Transactions 6-15
Installment Obligationsreceived By a Shareholder 6-15

Special Corporate Reporting Issues 6-16
Expenses of the Liquidation 6-16
Treatment of Net Operating Losses 6-16

Recognition of Gain or Loss When Property Is Distributed in Retirement of Debt 6-17
General Rule 6-17
Satisfaction of the Subsidiaryus Debt Obligations 6-17

Tax Planning Considerations 6-18
Timing the Liquidation Transaction 6-18
Recognition of Ordinary Losses When a Liquidation Occurs 6-18
Obtaining 80% Ownership to Achieve Sec. 332 Benefits 6-19
Avoiding Sec. 332 to Recognize Losses 6-19

Compliance and Procedural Considerations 6-20
General Liquidation Procedures 6-20
Section 332 Liquidations 6-20

Plan of Liquidation 6-21

Problem Materials 6-21
Discussion Questions 6-21
Issue Identification Questions 6-23
Problems 6-23
Comprehensive Problem 6-29
Tax Strategy Problem 6-30
Case Study Problems 6-31
Tax Research Problems 6-32

CHAPTER 7
▶ CORPORATE ACQUISITIONS AND REORGANIZATIONS 7-1

Taxable Acquisition Transactions 7-2
Asset Acquisitions 7-2
Stock Acquisitions 7-4

Comparison of Taxable and Tax-free Acquisitions 7-11
Taxable and Tax-Free Asset Acquisitions 7-11
Comparison of Taxable and Tax-Free Stock Acquisitions 7-12

Types of Reorganizations 7-15

Tax Consequences of Reorganizations 7-16
Target or Transferor Corporation 7-16
Acquiring or Transferee Corporation 7-17
Shareholders and Security Holders 7-18

Acquisitive Reorganizations 7-21
Type A Reorganization 7-21
Type C Reorganization 7-28
Type D Reorganization 7-30
Type B Reorganization 7-31
Type G Reorganization 7-35

Divisive Reorganizations 7-35
Divisive Type D Reorganization 7-37
Type G Divisive Reorganization 7-41

Other Reorganization Transactions 7-41
Type E Reorganization 7-41
Type F Reorganization 7-43

Judicial Restrictions on The Use of Corporate Reorganizations 7-43
Continuity of Proprietary Interest 7-43
Continuity of Business Enterprise 7-44
Business Purpose Requirement 7-45
Step Transaction Doctrine 7-45

Tax Attributes 7-46
Assumption of Tax Attributes 7-46
Limitation on Use of Tax Attributes 7-47

Tax Planning Considerations 7-49
Why Use a Reorganization Instead of a Taxable Transaction? 7-49
Avoiding the Reorganization Provisions 7-50

Compliance and Procedural Considerations 7-51
Section 338 Election 7-51
Plan of Reorganization 7-51
Party to a Reorganization 7-51
Ruling Requests 7-51

Problem Materials 7-52
Discussion Questions 7-52
Issue Identification Questions 7-53
Problems 7-54
Comprehensive Problem 7-61
Tax Strategy Problems 7-62
Case Study Problems 7-63
Tax Research Problems 7-64

CHAPTER 8
▶ CONSOLIDATED TAX RETURNS 8-1

Source of the Consolidated Tax Return Rules 8-2

Definition of an Affiliated Group 8-2
Requirements 8-2
Comparison with Controlled Group Definitions 8-4

Should a Consolidated Return Be Filed? 8-4
Advantages of Filing a Consolidated Tax Return 8-4
Disadvantages of Filing a Consolidated Tax Return 8-5

Consolidated Taxable Income 8-5
Income Included in the Consolidated Tax Return 8-7
Affiliated Group Elections 8-8
Termination of the Affiliated Group 8-8

Computation of the Affiliated Groupus Tax Liability 8-9
Regular Tax Liability 8-9
Corporate Alternative Minimum Tax Liability 8-10
Consolidated Tax Credits 8-10

Intercompany Transactions 8-11
Property Transactions 8-12
Other Intercompany Transactions 8-18

Dividends Received By Group Members 8-21
Exclusion Procedure 8-21
Consolidated Dividends-Received Deduction 8-21

Consolidated Charitable Contributions Deduction 8-22

Net Operating Losses (NOLs) 8-23
Current Year NOLs 8-23
Carrybacks and Carryforwards of Consolidated NOLs 8-24
Carryback of Consolidated NOL to Separate Return Year 8-24
Carryforward of Consolidated NOL to Separate Return Year 8-26
Special Loss Limitations 8-27

Consolidated Capital Gains and Losses 8-32
Section 1231 Gains and Losses 8-32
Capital Gains and Losses 8-32

Stock Basis Adjustments 8-33

Tax Planning Considerations 8-35
100% Dividends-Received Deduction Election 8-35
Estimated Tax Payments 8-35

Compliance and Procedural Considerations 8-36
The Basic Election and Return 8-36
Parent Corporation as Agent for the Affiliated Group 8-37
Liability for Taxes Due 8-38

Problem Materials 8-38
Discussion Questions 8-38
Issue Identification Questions 8-40
Problems 8-41
Comprehensive Problem 8-46
Tax Strategy Problem 8-46
Tax Form/Return Preparation Problem 8-46
Case Study Problems 8-48
Tax Research Problems 8-48

CHAPTER 9
▶ **PARTNERSHIP FORMATION AND OPERATION 9-1**

Definition of a Partnership 9-2
General and Limited Partnerships 9-2

Overview of Taxation of Partnership Income 9-4
Partnership Profits and Losses 9-4
The Partnerus Basis 9-4
Partnership Distributions 9-5

Tax Implications of Formation of a Partnership 9-5
Contribution of Property 9-5
Contribution of Services 9-10
Organizational and Syndication Expenditures 9-12

Partnership Elections 9-12
Partnership Tax Year 9-12
Other Partnership Elections 9-15

Partnership Reporting of Income 9-16
Partnership Taxable Income 9-16
Separately Stated Items 9-16
Partnership Ordinary Income 9-17

Partner Reporting of Income 9-17
Partnerus Distributive Share 9-17
Special Allocations 9-18

Basis for Partnership Interest 9-21
Beginning Basis 9-21
Effects of Liabilities 9-21
Effects of Operations 9-23

Special Loss Limitations 9-24
At-Risk Loss Limitation 9-24
Passive Activity Limitations 9-26

Transactions Between a Partner and the Partnership 9-26
Sales of Property 9-26
Guaranteed Payments 9-27

Family Partnerships 9-29
Capital Ownership 9-29
Donor-Donee Allocations of Income 9-30

Tax Planning Considerations 9-30
Timing of Loss Recognition 9-30

Compliance and Procedural Considerations 9-31
Reporting to the IRS and the Partners 9-31
Irs Audit Procedures 9-32

Problem Materials 9-33
Discussion Questions 9-33
Issue Identification Questions 9-34
Problems 9-35
Comprehensive Problems 9-43
Tax Strategy Problem 9-43
Tax Form/Return Preparation Problem 9-44
Case Study Problems 9-45
Tax Research Problems 9-47

CHAPTER 10
▶ **SPECIAL PARTNERSHIP ISSUES 10-1**

Nonliquidating Distributions 10-2
Recognition of Gain 10-2
Basis Effects of Distributions 10-4
Holding Period and Character of Distributed Property 10-7

Nonliquidating Distributions with Sec. 751 10-7
Section 751 Assets Defined 10-7
Exchange of Sec. 751 Assets and Other Property 10-9

Terminating an Interest in A Partnership 10-11
Liquidating Distributions 10-12
Sale of a Partnership Interest 10-16
Retirement or Death of a Partner 10-19
Exchange of a Partnership Interest 10-20
Income Recognition and Transfers of a Partnership Interest 10-22
Termination of a Partnership 10-22
Mergers and Consolidations 10-25
Division of a Partnership 10-25

Optional Basis Adjustments 10-26
Optional Adjustment on Transfers 10-26
Optional Adjustment on Distributions 10-27

Special Forms of Partnerships 10-28
Tax Shelters and Limited Partnerships 10-28
Publicly Traded Partnerships 10-28
Limited Liability Companies 10-29
Limited Liability Partnerships 10-29
Electing Large Partnerships 10-30

Tax Planning Considerations 10-33
Liquidating Distribution or Sale to Partners 10-33

Problem Materials 10-34
Discussion Questions 10-34
Issue Identification Questions 10-35
Problems 10-36
Comprehensive Problems 10-45
Tax Strategy Problem 10-46
Case Study Problems 10-46
Tax Research Problems 10-48

CHAPTER 11
▶ S CORPORATIONS 11-1

Should an S Election Be Made? 11-3
Advantages of S Corporation Treatment 11-3
Disadvantages of S Corporation Treatment 11-3

S Corporation Requirements 11-4
Shareholder-Related Requirements 11-4
Corporation-Related Requirements 11-5

Election of S Corporation Status 11-7
Making the Election 11-8
Termination of the Election 11-9

S Corporation Operations 11-13
Taxable Year 11-13
Accounting Method Elections 11-14
Ordinary Income or Loss and Separately Stated Items 11-14
Special S Corporation Taxes 11-15

Taxation of the Shareholder 11-19
Income Allocation Procedures 11-19
Loss and Deduction Pass-Through to Shareholders 11-20
Family S Corporations 11-23

Basis Adjustments 11-24
Basis Adjustments to S Corporation Stock 11-24
Basis Adjustments to Shareholder Debt 11-25

S Corporation Distributions 11-27
Corporations Having No Earnings and Profits 11-27
Corporations Having Accumulated Earnings and Profits 11-28

Other Rules 11-32
Tax Preference Items and Other AMT Adjustments 11-32
Transactions Involving Shareholders and Other Related Parties 11-33
Fringe Benefits Paid to a Shareholder-employee 11-33

Tax Planning Considerations 11-34
Election to Allocate Income Based on the S Corporationus Accounting Methods 11-34
Increasing the Benefits from S Corporation Losses 11-35
Passive Income Requirements 11-36

Compliance and Procedural Considerations 11-37
Making the Election 11-37
Filing the Corporate Tax Return 11-37
Estimated Tax Payments 11-38
Consistency Rules 11-39
Sample S Corporation Tax Return 11-39

Problem Materials 11-39
Discussion Questions 11-39
Issue Identification Questions 11-41
Problems 11-41
Comprehensive Problems 11-48
Tax Strategy Problems 11-49
Tax Form/Return Preparation Problem 11-50
Case Study Problem 11-50
Tax Research Problems 11-50

CHAPTER 12
▶ THE GIFT TAX 12-1

Concept of Transfer Taxes 12-2
History and Purpose of Transfer Taxes 12-2

The Unified Transfer Tax System 12-3
Unified Rate Schedule 12-3
Impact of Taxable Gifts on Death Tax Base 12-3
Unified Credit 12-4

Gift Tax Formula 12-4
Determination of Gifts 12-4
Exclusions and Deductions 12-4
Gift-Splitting Election 12-5
Cumulative Nature of Gift Tax 12-6
Unified Credit 12-6

Transfers Subject to the Gift Tax 12-7
Transfers for Inadequate Consideration 12-7
Statutory Exemptions from the Gift Tax 12-8
Cessation of Donorus Dominion and Control 12-10
Valuation of Gifts 12-11
Gift Tax Consequences of Certain Transfers 12-13

Exclusions 12-16
Amount of the Exclusion 12-16
Present Interest Requirement 12-16

Gift Tax Deductions 12-18
Marital Deduction 12-19
Charitable Contribution Deduction 12-21

The Gift-splitting Election 12-22

Computation of the Gift Tax Liability 12-23
Effect of Previous Taxable Gifts 12-23
Effect of Previous Taxable Gifts 12-24

Comprehensive Illustration 12-25
Background Data 12-25
Calculation of Tax Liability 12-25

Basis Considerations for a Lifetime Giving Plan 12-26
Property Received By Gift 12-26
Property Received At Death 12-27

Below-market Loans: Gift and Income Tax Consequences 12-28
General Rules 12-28
De Minimis Rules 12-28

Tax Planning Considerations 12-29
Tax-saving Features of Inter Vivos Gifts 12-29
Negative Aspects of Gifts 12-30

Compliance and Procedural Considerations 12-30
Filing Requirements 12-30
Due Date 12-31
Gift-splitting Election 12-31
Liability for Tax 12-31
Determination of Value 12-31
Statute of Limitations 12-32

Problem Materials 12-33
Discussion Questions 12-33
Issue Identification Questions 12-34
Problems 12-34
Comprehensive Problem 12-37
Tax Strategy Problem 12-38
Tax Form/Return Preparation Problems 12-38
Case Study Problems 12-39
Tax Research Problems 12-39

CHAPTER 13
▶ THE ESTATE TAX 13-1

Estate Tax Formula 13-2
Gross Estate 13-2
Deductions 13-3
Adjusted Taxable Gifts and Tax Base 13-4
Tentative Tax on Estate Tax Base 13-4
Reduction for Post-1976 Gift Taxes 13-4
Unified Credit 13-5
Other Credits 13-5

The Gross Estate: Valuation 13-6
Date-of-Death Valuation 13-6
Alternate Valuation Date 13-7

The Gross Estate: Inclusions 13-8
Comparison of Gross Estate with Probate Estate 13-9
Property in Which the Decedent Had an Interest 13-10
Dower or Curtesy Rights 13-10
Transferor Provisions 13-10
Annuities and Other Retirement Benefits 13-13
Jointly Owned Property 13-14
General Powers of Appointment 13-15
Life Insurance 13-16
Consideration Offset 13-17
Recipient Spouseusinterest in QTIP Trust 13-17

Deductions 13-18
Debts and Funeral and Administration Expenses 13-18
Losses 13-19
Charitable Contribution Deduction 13-19
Marital Deduction 13-20
Deduction for Certain Interests in Family-Owned Businesses 13-22

Computation of Tax Liability 13-23
Taxable Estate and Tax Base 13-23
Tentative Tax and Reduction for Post-1976 Gift Taxes 13-23
Unified Credit 13-23
Other Credits 13-24

Comprehensive Illustration 13-25
Background Data 13-25
Calculation of Tax Liability 13-26

Liquidity Concerns 13-28
Deferral of Payment of Estate Taxes 13-28
Stock Redemptions to Pay Death Taxes 13-29
Special Use Valuation of Farm Realproperty 13-29

Generation-skipping Transfer Tax 13-30

Tax Planning Considerations 13-32
Use of Inter Vivos Gifts 13-32
Use of Exemption Equivalent 13-32
What Size Marital Deduction Is Best? 13-33
Use of Disclaimers 13-34
Role of Life Insurance 13-34
Qualifying the Estate for Installment Payments 13-34
Where to Deduct Administration Expenses 13-35

Compliance and Procedural Considerations 13-35
Filing Requirements 13-35
Due Date 13-36
Valuation 13-36
Election of Alternate Valuation Date 13-36
Documents to Be Included with Return 13-36

Problem Materials 13-37
Discussion Questions 13-37
Issue Identification Questions 13-38
Problems 13-38
Comprehensive Problems 13-42
Tax Strategy Problem 13-43
Tax Form/Return Preparation Problems 13-43
Case Study Problems 13-44
Tax Research Problems 13-45

CHAPTER 14
▶ INCOME TAXATION OF TRUSTS AND ESTATES 14-1

Basic Concepts 14-2
Inception of Trusts 14-2
Inception of Estates 14-2

Reasons for Creating Trusts 14-3
Basic Principles Offiduciary Taxation 14-3

Principles of Fiduciary Accounting 14-4
The Importance of Identifying Income and Principal 14-4
Effects of State Law or Terms of Trust Instrument 14-5
Principal and Income: The Uniform Act 14-5
Categorization of Depreciation 14-6

Formula for Taxable Income and Tax Liability 14-7
Gross Income 14-7
Deductions for Expenses 14-7
Distribution Deduction 14-9
Personal Exemption 14-9

Distributable Net Income 14-10
Credits 14-10
Significance of DNI 14-10
Definition of DNI 14-11
Manner of Computing DNI 14-11

Determining a Simple Trustus Taxable Income 14-13
Allocation of Expenses to Tax-exempt Income 14-14
Determination of Dni and the Distribution Deduction 14-15
Tax Treatment for Beneficiary 14-15
Short-Cut Approach to Proving Correctness of Taxable Income 14-16
Effect of a Net Operating Loss 14-16
Effect of a Net Capital Loss 14-16

Comprehensive Illustration: Determining a Simple Trustus Taxable Income 14-17
Background Data 14-17
Trusteeus Fee 14-18
Distribution Deduction and DNI 14-18
Trustus Taxable Income 14-18
Categorizing a Beneficiaryus Income 14-18

Determining Taxable Income for Complex Trusts and Estates 14-19
Determination of DNI and the Distribution Deduction 14-20
Tax Treatment for Beneficiary 14-21
Effect of a Net Operating Loss 14-24
Effect of a Net Capital Loss 14-24

Comprehensive Illustration: Determining a Complex Trustus Taxable Income 14-24
Background Data 14-24
Trusteeus Fee 14-25
Distribution Deduction and DNI 14-25
Trustus Taxable Income 14-26
Additional Observations 14-26

Income in Respect of a Decedent 14-27
Definition and Common Examples 14-27
Significance of IRD 14-28

Grantor Trust Provisions 14-30
Purpose and Effect 14-30
Revocable Trusts 14-31
Clifford Trusts 14-31
Post-1986 Reversionary Interest Trusts 14-31
Retention of Administrative Powers 14-32
Retention of Economic Benefits 14-32
Control of Others' Enjoyment 14-32

Tax Planning Considerations 14-34
Ability to Shift Income 14-34
Timing of Distributions 14-34
Property Distributions 14-34
Choice of Year-End for Estates 14-35
Deduction of Administration Expenses 14-35

Compliance and Procedural Considerations 14-35
Filing Requirements 14-35
Due Date for Return and Tax 14-36
Documents to Be Furnished to IRS 14-36
Sample Simple and Complex Trust Returns 14-36

Problem Materials 14-36
Discussion Questions 14-36
Issue Identification Questions 14-37
Problems 14-38
Comprehensive Problem 14-40
Tax Strategy Problem 14-41
Tax Form/Return Preparation Problems 14-41
Case Study Problems 14-42
Tax Research Problems 14-43

CHAPTER 15
▶ **ADMINISTRATIVE PROCEDURES 15-1**

Role of the Internal Revenue Service 15-2
Enforcement and Collection 15-2
Interpretation of the Statute 15-2
Organization of the IRS 15-3
Percentage of Returns Examined 15-3
Selection of Returns for Audit 15-5
Alternatives for a Taxpayer Whose Return Is Audited 15-7
90-Day Letter 15-9
Litigation 15-9

Audits of Tax Returns 15-3
Information to Be Included in Taxpayerus Request 15-11
Will the Irs Rule? 15-12
When Rulings Are Desirable 15-12

Requests for Rulings 15-11
Due Dates for Returns 15-13
Extensions 15-13
Due Dates for Payment of the Tax 15-13
Interest on Tax Not Timely Paid 15-14

Due Dates 15-13
Failure to File 15-16
Failure to Pay 15-18

Failure-to-file and Failure-to-pay Penalties 15-16
Payment Requirements 15-20
Penalty for Underpaying Estimated Taxes 15-21
Exceptions to the Penalty 15-22

Estimated Taxes 15-19
Negligence 15-22
Substantial Understatement 15-23
Civil Fraud 15-25
Criminal Fraud 15-26

Other More Severe Penalties 15-22
General Three-Year Rule 15-27
Six-Year Rule for Substantial Omissions 15-27
When No Return Is Filed 15-28
Other Exceptions to Three-Year Rule 15-28
Refund Claims 15-29

Statute of Limitations 15-26
Joint Returns 15-30
Transferee Liability 15-31

Liability for Tax 15-30
Statutory Provisions Concerning Tax Return Preparers 15-31
Rules of Circular 230 15-33
Tax Accounting and Tax Law 15-33
Accountant-Client Privilege 15-34

Tax Practice Issues 15-31

Problem Materials 15-35
Discussion Questions 15-35
Issue Identification Questions 15-36
Problems 15-37
Comprehensive Problem 15-39
Tax Strategy Problem 15-40
Case Study Problem 15-40
Tax Research Problems 15-40

TABLES

2000 Tax Tables and Rate Schedules T-1

APPENDICES

▶ APPENDIX A

Tax Research Working Paper File A-1

▶ APPENDIX B

Completed Tax Forms B-1

▶ APPENDIX C

MACRS and ACRS Tables C-1

▶ APPENDIX D

Glossary D-1

▶ APPENDIX E

Statements on Standards for Tax Services E-1

▶ APPENDIX F

Comparison of Tax Attributes for C Corporations, Partnerships, and S Corporations F-1

▶ APPENDIX G

Credit for State Death Taxes G-1

▶ APPENDIX H

Acturial Tables H-1

▶ APPENDIX I

Index of Code Sections I-1

▶ APPENDIX J

Index of Treasury Regulations J-1

▶ APPENDIX K

Index of Government Promulgations K-1

▶ APPENDIX L

Index of Court Cases L-1

▶ APPENDIX M

Subject Index M-1

ABOUT THE EDITORS

THOMAS R. POPE

Thomas R. Pope is the Ernst & Young Professor of Accounting and Director of the Master of Science in Accountancy Program at the University of Kentucky. He received a B.S. from the University of Louisville and an M.S. and DBA in business administration from the University of Kentucky. He teaches partnership and S corporation taxation, tax research and policy, and introductory taxation and has won outstanding teaching awards at the university, college, and school of accountancy levels. He has published articles in *The Tax Adviser, Taxes, The Accounting Review,* and a number of other journals.

Professor Pope's extensive professional experience includes eight years with Big Five accounting firms. Five of those years were with Ernst & Whinney (now part of Ernst & Young), including two years where he earned a position with their National Tax Department in Washington, D.C. He subsequently held the position of Senior Manager in charge of the Tax Department in Lexington, Kentucky. Professor Pope has also been a leader and speaker at professional tax conferences all over the United States and is active as a tax consultant.

KENNETH E. ANDERSON

Kenneth E. Anderson is a Distinguished Professor of Taxation at the University of Tennessee. He earned a B.B.A. from the University of Wisconsin-Milwaukee and subsequently attained the level of tax manager with Arthur Young & Company (now part of Ernst & Young). He then earned a Ph.D. from Indiana University. He teaches introductory taxation, corporate taxation, partnership taxation, tax research, and tax strategy, and has twice won the Beta Alpha Psi Outstanding Educator Award. Professor Anderson has published articles in *The Accounting Review, The Journal of the American Taxation Association, The Journal of Accountancy,* and a number of other journals.

JOHN L. KRAMER

John L. Kramer is the Arthur Andersen Professor of Accounting and Director of the Fisher School of Accounting at the University of Florida. He is a recipient of a Teaching Improvement Program award given by the University of Florida in 1994. He holds a Ph.D. in Business Administration, an M.B.A. from the University of Michigan (Ann Arbor), and a B.B.A. from the University of Michigan (Dearborn). He is a past-president of the American Taxation Association and the Florida Association of Accounting Educators, as well as a past editor of *The Journal of the American Taxation Association.* Professor Kramer has taught for the American Institute of CPAs, American Tax Institute of Europe, and a number of national and regional accounting firms. He is a frequent speaker at academic and professional conferences, as well as having served as an expert witness in a number of court cases. He has published more than 50 articles in *The Accounting Review, The Journal of the American Taxation Association, The Tax Adviser, The Journal of Taxation* and other academic and professional journals. Professor Kramer was an editor on the *Prentice Hall Federal Tax* series from 1989–2002.

ABOUT THE AUTHORS

D. DALE BANDY

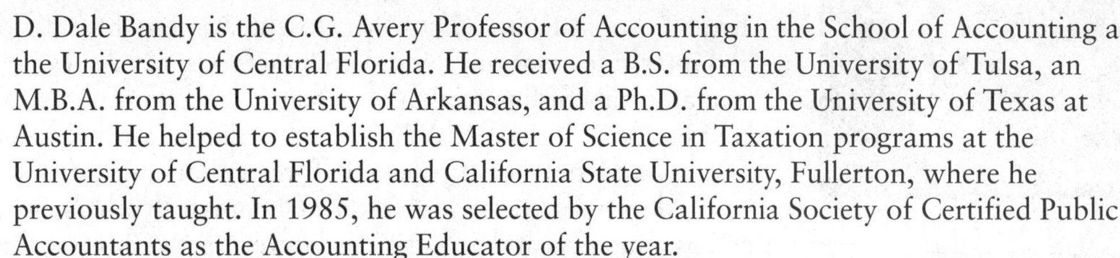

D. Dale Bandy is the C.G. Avery Professor of Accounting in the School of Accounting at the University of Central Florida. He received a B.S. from the University of Tulsa, an M.B.A. from the University of Arkansas, and a Ph.D. from the University of Texas at Austin. He helped to establish the Master of Science in Taxation programs at the University of Central Florida and California State University, Fullerton, where he previously taught. In 1985, he was selected by the California Society of Certified Public Accountants as the Accounting Educator of the year.

Professor Bandy has published 8 books and more than 30 articles in accounting and taxation. His articles have appeared in *Journal of Taxation, The Journal of Accountancy, Advances in Taxation, The Tax Adviser, CPA Journal, Management Accounting* and a number of other journals.

N. ALLEN FORD

N. Allen Ford is the Larry D. Homer/KPMG Peat Marwick Distinguished Teaching Professor of Professional Accounting at the University of Kansas. He received an undergraduate degree from Centenary College in Shreveport, Louisiana, and both the M.B.A. and Ph.D. in Business from the University of Arkansas. He has published more than 30 articles related to taxation, financial accounting, and accounting education in journals such as *The Accounting Review, The Journal of the American Taxation Association,* and *The Journal of Taxation.* He served as president of the American Taxation Association in 1979-80.

Professor Ford has received numerous teaching awards, at the college and university levels. In 1993, he received the Byron T. Shutz Award for Distinguished Teaching in Economics and Business. In 1996 he received the Ray N. Sommerfeld Outstanding Tax Educator Award, which is jointly sponsored by the American Taxation Association and Ernst & Young.

ANNA C. FOWLER

Anna C. Fowler is the John Arch White Professor in the Department of Accounting at the University of Texas at Austin. She received her B.S. in accounting from the University of Alabama and her M.B.A. and Ph.D. from the University of Texas at Austin. Active in the American Taxation Association, she has served on the editorial board of its journal and has held many positions, including president, within the organization. She is also active with the American Institute of CPAs and currently serves on the Executive committee of its Tax Division. Currently, Professor Fowler is a member of the Board of Trustees of the Educational Foundation of the Texas Society of CPAs. She has published a number of articles, most of which have dealt with estate planning or real estate transaction issues. She also is a frequent speaker before professional organizations on estate planning topics.

ROBERT L. GARDNER

Robert L. Gardner is the Robert J. Smith Professor of Accounting and the Associate Director of the School of Accountancy and Information Systems at Brigham Young University. He received a B.S. and M.B.A. from the University of Utah and a Ph.D. from the University of Texas at Austin. He has authored or coauthored two books and over 25 articles, and has received several teaching awards. Professor Gardner has served on the Board of Trustees of the American Taxation Association and served as President of the ATA in 1999-2000. He actively consults with several national CPA firms in their continuing education programs.

RICHARD J. JOSEPH

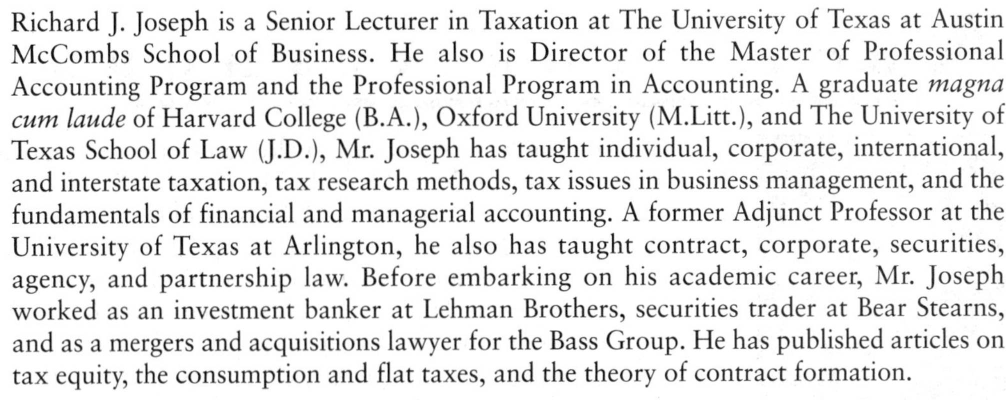

Richard J. Joseph is a Senior Lecturer in Taxation at The University of Texas at Austin McCombs School of Business. He also is Director of the Master of Professional Accounting Program and the Professional Program in Accounting. A graduate *magna cum laude* of Harvard College (B.A.), Oxford University (M.Litt.), and The University of Texas School of Law (J.D.), Mr. Joseph has taught individual, corporate, international, and interstate taxation, tax research methods, tax issues in business management, and the fundamentals of financial and managerial accounting. A former Adjunct Professor at the University of Texas at Arlington, he also has taught contract, corporate, securities, agency, and partnership law. Before embarking on his academic career, Mr. Joseph worked as an investment banker at Lehman Brothers, securities trader at Bear Stearns, and as a mergers and acquisitions lawyer for the Bass Group. He has published articles on tax equity, the consumption and flat taxes, and the theory of contract formation.

SUSAN L. NORDHAUSER

Susan L. Nordhauser is a Professor at the University of Texas at San Antonio. She received a B.A. from Cornell University, an M.S. from Purdue University, and a Ph.D. from the University of Texas at Austin. She has published many articles on taxation in journals including *The Journal of the American Taxation Association, The Accounting Review, The Tax Adviser,* and *The National Tax Journal.* Professor Nordhauser is the recipient of the 1992 Ernst & Young Tax Literature Award. She has served on the editorial board of several academic tax journals.

MICHAEL S. SCHADEWALD

Michael S. Schadewald is an Associate Professor of Accounting and Director of the Deloitte & Touche Center for Multistate Taxation at the University of Wisconsin-Milwaukee. He holds a Ph.D. from the University of Minnesota, an M.S. from the University of Wisconsin-Milwaukee, and a B.B.A. from the University of Wisconsin-Whitewater. He has co-authored a book on international taxation and has published over 30 articles in a number of accounting and tax journals, including *The Journal of the American Taxation Association, The Accounting Review, Contemporay Accounting Research*, and *The Journal of Taxation*. He serves on the editorial boards of *The Journal of the American Taxation Association, International Tax Journal, Issues in Accounting Education,* and *Journal of Accounting Education*. He has been awarded numerous research grants and fellowships by Big-Five accounting firms and has worked in the Milwaukee office of Arthur Young (now part of Ernst & Young) prior to entering academics.

PREFACE

Why is the Pope/Anderson/Kramer series the best choice for your students?

The Pope/Anderson/Kramer 2003 Series in Federal Taxation includes three volumes—available in both cloth and looseleaf formats—and is appropriate for use in any first course in federal taxation:

Federal Taxation 2003: Individuals
Federal Taxation 2003: Corporations, Partnerships, Estates, and Trusts
(the companion book to *Individuals*)
Federal Taxation 2003: Comprehensive
(includes 29 chapters; 14 chapters from *Individuals* and 15 chapters from *Corporations*)

The 2003 series represents the highest level of publisher service, author expertise, and unique learning resources for students, innovative technology, and supplements:

- ***Commitment to Early Publication Dates***
Prentice Hall has made a long-term commitment to publishing the annual Pope/Anderson/Kramer series texts on or before April 30 of each year. The ancillaries for each book will always be published well in advance of fall classes.

- ***FREE Online Standard Tax Course Available in WebCT, Blackboard, or CourseCompass***
You choose the platform and Prentice Hall provides the passcode to the course of your choice. A special ISBN is required, so please check with your Prentice Hall representative prior to ordering.

- ***JIT Custom Text***
Now you can create your own tax book using content drawn from the Pope/Anderson/Kramer series. You can even include your own materials. Ask your Prentice Hall representative for specific information on custom text procedures and policies or log onto www.prenhall.com/custombusiness to learn more about your options.

- ***NEW TaxACT 2001 Software Packaged with the Text for a Nominal Price***
This user-friendly tax preparation program includes more than 80 tax forms, schedules, and worksheets. TaxACT calculates returns and alerts the user to possible errors or entries. Specially created problems for students to use the software are available in Word documents on the Prentice Hall tax Web site, and solutions in TaxACT files are provided for faculty. Log onto www.prenhall.com/phtax to view the problems.

  A sample of this software is included with each Review Copy of *Individuals* and *Comprehensive* sent to faculty. It can be packaged with any version of the Pope/Anderson/Kramer series at a nominal price.

- ***Commitment to Service***
Prentice Hall's dedicated Accounting and Tax Hotline provides the highest level of service to accounting and tax faculty members (not available for students). Just call 1-800-227-1816. Faculty may also log onto www.prenhall.com/accounting to locate their Prentice Hall representative using our unique "Rep Locator" search feature.

Expert Insights—Unique Student Learning Features

What Would You Do in This Situation? Boxes

Unique to the Pope/Anderson/Kramer series, these boxes place students in a decision-making role. The boxes include many *current controversies* that are as yet unresolved or are currently being considered by the courts.

These boxes make extensive use of **Ethical Material** as they represent choices that may put the practitioner at odds with the client.

WHAT WOULD YOU DO IN THIS SITUATION?

INVENTORY VALUATION

Jack is a new tax client. He says he and his previous accountant did not get along very well. Jack owns an automobile dealership with sales of $12 million. He has provided you with most of the information you need to prepare his tax return, but he has not yet given you the year-end inventory value. You have completed much of the work on his return, but cannot complete it without the inventory figure. You have called Jack three times about the inventory. Each time he has interrupted, and asked you what his tax liability will be at alternative inventory levels. What problem do you see?

Stop & Think Boxes

These "speed bumps" encourage students to pause and apply what they have just learned. Solutions for each issue are provided in the box.

STOP & THINK

Question: When one company purchases the assets of another company, the purchasing company may acquire goodwill. Since purchased goodwill is a Sec. 197 intangible asset and may be amortized over 15 years, the determination of the cost of goodwill is important. How is the "cost" of goodwill determined when the purchasing company purchases many assets in the acquisition?

Solution: The IRS requires that taxpayers use the "residual method" as prescribed in Sec. 1060. Under this method, all of the assets except for goodwill are valued. The total value of these assets are then subtracted from the total purchase price and the residual value is the amount of the purchase price that is allocated to goodwill.

Unique Margin Notes

These provide an extensive series of learning tips for students and faculty. No other text can match the quantity, quality, or variety of these resources:

- Additional Comment
- Key Point
- Real World Examples
- Typical Misconceptions
- Ethical Points
- Self-Study Questions and Answers
- Book-to-Tax Accounting Comparison
- Historical Notes
- *New* Tax Strategy Tips

ETHICAL POINT

An employer must have a reasonable basis for treating a worker as an independent contractor or meet the general common law rules for determining whether an employer-employee relationship exists. Otherwise, the employer is liable for federal and state income tax withholding, FICA and FUTA taxes, interest, and penalties associated with the misclassification.

TAX STRATEGY TIP

Rather than having the corporation borrow money, an S corporation shareholder might consider borrowing money directly from the bank and then lending the loan proceeds to the corporation with the corporation guaranteeing the bank loan. In this way, the shareholder will obtain debt basis.

ADDITIONAL COMMENT

Stock purchased on which a dividend has been declared has an increased value. This value will drop when the dividend is paid. If the dividend is eligible for a dividends-received deduction and the drop in value also creates a capital loss, corporate shareholders could use this event as a tax planning device. To avoid this result, no dividends-received deduction is available for stock held 45 days or less.

Innovative Technology and Supplements

For Instructors

- ***New Course Organizer*** contains every print and technology ancillary that accompanies the Pope/Anderson/Kramer 2003 series. This feature makes it extremely easy for faculty to (1) customize any supplement; (2) access any supplement while using a computer; and (3) transport the entire package from home, to class, to office. **Free upon adoption.**
- ***Textbooks*** are available in traditional hardback and looseleaf editions or in **a new custom "JIT" format.** Ask your Prentice Hall representative, or log onto www.prenhall.com/custombusiness for more information.
- ***Instructor's Guide*** contains sample syllabi, instructor outlines, and notes on the end-of-chapter problems. It also contains all solutions to the tax form/tax return preparation problems, case studies, and research problems. It's also available as a password-protected download from the "Faculty Resources" on www.prenhall.com/phtax. Ask your Prentice Hall representative for your password.
- ***Solutions Manual*** contains solutions to discussion questions, problems, and comprehensive and tax strategy problems. It's also available as a password-protected download from the "Faculty Resources" on www.prenhall.com/phtax. Upon written request, Prentice Hall may grant permission for faculty to post solutions on a student-accessible site, provided that this is password-protected at the school.
- ***Testing.*** The **printed Test Bank** contains a wealth of true/false, multiple-choice, and calculative problems. **A Computerized Test Manager** program is available to adopters.
- ***PowerPoint slides*** include over 300 full-color electronic transparencies available for *Individuals* and *Corporations*. These are available on the Instructor Resource CD and on the Prentice Hall tax Web site where students and faculty have access to them.

Text Companion Web Site for Faculty and Students Available at www.prenhall.com/phtax

The Web site provides a wealth of FREE material to help students study and help faculty prepare for class.

1. Free Student Resources include

- True/False and Multiple-Choice Questions
- Current Events
- Internet Resources
- Tax Law Updates
- PowerPoint slides
- TaxACT Problems
- Online Chapters

2. Free Instructor Resources include

Downloadable supplements, PowerPoint slides, and solutions to the TaxACT Problems and the online cases (see your Prentice Hall representative for a password to access these tools). In a new partnership, Prentice Hall also gives faculty and students access to Tax Analyst's tacampus.org, a marvelous Tax Research database and search engine. Faculty log on with their special Prentice Hall password and create a password for their course and students.

3. Premium Student Resources include

Online "Study Guide"

Students check their understanding of chapter topics with a variety of computational problems, case study problems, and tax return preparation problems. Each quiz includes "hints," immediate scoring, graphical results reporter, explanation of incorrect answers, and the ability to e-mail results to a faculty member or other designated individual.

Online Tax Cases for *Individuals* and *Corporations*

"Life of Riley" Tax Cases require the student to research specific questions to complete the tax return for a given individual. These cases have been updated for 2001 forms. **"Endorphin USA" Tax Cases** require the student to research specific questions to complete the entire tax return for Endorphin USA as a C corporation, S corporation, or partnership.

ACKNOWLEDGMENTS

Our policy is to provide annual editions and to prepare timely updated supplements when major tax revisions occur. We are most appreciative of the suggestions made by outside reviewers because these extensive review procedures have been valuable to the authors and editors during the revision process. The editors gratefully acknowledge the contributions of W. Peter Salzarulo of Miami University of Ohio. His time and effort over the years helped to make the series what it is today.

We are grateful to the various graduate assistants, doctoral students, and colleagues who have reviewed the text and supplementary materials and checked solutions in order to maintain a high level of technical accuracy. In particular, we would like to acknowledge the following colleagues who assisted in the preparation of supplemental materials for this text:

Sally Baker	DeVry Institute of Technology—Kansas City
Arthur D. Cassill	University of North Carolina at Greensboro
Ann Burstein Cohen	SUNY—Buffalo
Priscilla Kenney (Supplements Coordinator)	University of Florida
Craig J. Langstraat	University of Memphis
Thomas Omer	University of Illinois at Chicago
Michael Schadewald	University of Wisconsin—Milwaukee
Caroline D. Strobel	University of South Carolina
Don Trippeer	East Carolina University
Ellen D. Cook	University of Louisiana—LaFayette
Richard Newmark	University of Northern Colorado
Pamela J. Legner	DeVry Institute of Technology—Addison

Thomas R. Pope
Kenneth E. Anderson
John L. Kramer

PRENTICE HALL'S FEDERAL TAXATION 2003

Comprehensive

CHAPTER 1

AN INTRODUCTION TO TAXATION

LEARNING OBJECTIVES

After studying this chapter, you should be able to

1. Discuss the history of taxation in the United States
2. Differentiate between the three types of tax rate structures
3. Describe the various types of taxes
4. Discuss what constitutes a "good" tax structure and the objectives of the federal income tax law
5. Describe the tax entities in the federal income tax system
6. Identify the various tax law sources and understand their implications for tax practice
7. Describe the legislative process for the enactment of the tax law
8. Describe the administrative procedures under the tax law
9. Describe the components of a tax practice and understand the importance of computer applications in taxation

CHAPTER OUTLINE

History of Taxation in the United States...1-2
Types of Tax Rate Structures...1-4
Other Types of Taxes...1-7
Criteria for a Tax Structure...1-12
Objectives of the Federal Income Tax Law...1-14
Entities in the Federal Income Tax System...1-15
Tax Law Sources...1-18
Enactment of a Tax Law...1-18
Administration of the Tax Law and Tax Practice Issues...1-20
Components of a Tax Practice...1-23
Computer Applications in Tax Practice...1-25

The federal tax system has a substantial effect on investor, business, and personal decisions in the United States. The following examples illustrate the impact of the tax law on various decisions in our society:

- A business decision about whether to invest in a new plant or equipment may depend, in part, on the existence of favorable tax provisions.
- An employee may decide to accept a new job because the prospective employer offers favorable tax-free fringe benefits or an attractive deferred compensation plan.
- An individual may decide to buy a principal residence rather than rent comparable property because of the availability of tax deductions for mortgage interest and real estate taxes.
- The terms of a property settlement agreement pursuant to a divorce decree may be structured to take into account the tax laws governing alimony and property settlements.

The purpose of this text is to provide an introduction to the study of federal income taxation as applicable to individuals. However, before discussing the specifics of the U.S. federal income tax law, it is helpful to have a broad conceptual understanding of the taxation process. This chapter provides an overview of the following topics:

- Historical developments of the federal tax system
- Types of taxes levied and structural considerations
- Objectives of the tax law
- Tax law sources and the legislative process
- Internal Revenue Service (IRS) collection, examination, and appeals processes
- The nature of tax practice, including computer applications and tax research

KEY POINT

In many situations, the use of the tax laws to influence human behavior is deliberate. As will be seen later in this chapter, tax laws are often used to achieve social and economic objectives.

HISTORY OF TAXATION IN THE UNITED STATES

OBJECTIVE 1

Discuss the history of taxation in the United States

EARLY PERIODS

The federal income tax is the dominant form of taxation in the United States. In addition, most states and some cities and counties also impose an income tax. Both corporations and individuals are subject to such taxes.

Before 1913 (the date of enactment of the modern-day federal income tax), the federal government relied predominantly on customs duties and excise taxes to finance its operations. The first federal income tax on individuals was enacted in 1861 to finance the Civil War but was repealed after the war. The federal income tax was reinstated in 1894, however, that tax was challenged in the courts because the U.S. Constitution required that an income tax be apportioned among the states in proportion to their populations. This type of tax system, which would be both impractical and difficult to administer, would mean that different tax rates would apply to individual taxpayers depending on their states of residence.

In 1895, the Supreme Court ruled that the tax was in violation of the U.S. Constitution.[1] Therefore, it was necessary to amend the U.S. Constitution to permit the passage of a federal income tax law. This was accomplished by the Sixteenth Amendment, which was ratified in 1913. The Sixteenth Amendment, while being an extraordinarily important amendment, consists of one sentence.

HISTORICAL NOTE

The reinstatement of the income tax in 1894 was the subject of heated political controversy. In general, the representatives in Congress from the agricultural South and West favored the income tax in lieu of customs duties. Representatives from the industrial eastern states were against the income tax and favored protective tariff legislation.

[1] *Pollock v. Farmers' Loan & Trust Co.*, 3 AFTR 2602, (USSC, 1895). Note, however, that a federal income tax on corporations that was enacted in 1909 was held to be constitutional because it was treated as an excise tax. See *Flint v. Stone Tracy Co.*, 3 AFTR 2834, (USSC, 1911).

Sixteenth Amendment to the Constitution of the United States

The Congress shall have power to lay and collect taxes on incomes, from whatever source derived, without apportionment among the several States, and without regard to any census or enumeration.

REVENUE ACTS FROM 1913 TO THE PRESENT

HISTORICAL NOTE

The Revenue Act of 1913 contained sixteen pages.

HISTORICAL NOTE

Before 1939, the tax laws were contained in the current revenue act, a reenactment of a prior revenue act plus amendments. In 1939, a permanent tax code was established; it was revised in 1954 and 1986.

The Revenue Act of 1913 imposed a flat 1% tax (with no exemptions) on a corporation's net income. The rate varied from 1% to 7% for individuals, depending on the individual's income level. However, very few individuals paid federal income taxes because a $3,000 personal exemption ($4,000 for married individuals) was permitted as an offset to taxable income. These amounts were greater than the incomes of most individuals in 1913.

Various amendments to the original law were passed between 1913 and 1939 as separate revenue acts. For example, a deduction for dependency exemptions was provided in 1917. In 1939, the separate revenue acts were codified into the Internal Revenue Code of 1939. A similar codification was accomplished in 1954. The 1954 codification, which was known as the Internal Revenue Code of 1954, included the elimination of many "deadwood" provisions, a rearrangement and clarification of numerous code sections, and the addition of major tax law changes. Whenever changes to the Internal Revenue Code (IRC) are made, the old language is deleted and the new language added. Thus, the statutes are organized as a single document, and a tax advisor does not have to read through the applicable parts of all previous tax bills to find the most current law. In 1986, major changes were made to the tax law, and the basic tax law was redesignated as the Internal Revenue Code of 1986.

The federal income tax became a "mass tax" on individuals during the early 1940s. This change was deemed necessary to finance the revenue needs of the federal government during World War II. In 1939, less than 6% of the U.S. population was subject to the federal income tax; by 1945, 74% of the population was taxed.[2] To accommodate the broadened tax base and to avoid significant tax collection problems, Congress enacted pay-as-you-go withholding in 1943.

A major characteristic of the federal income tax since its inception to today is the manner in which the tax law is changed or modified. The federal income tax is changed on an **incremental** basis rather than a complete revision basis. Under so-called incrementalism, when a change in the tax law is deemed necessary by Congress, the entire law is not changed but specific provisions of the tax law are added, changed, or deleted on an incremental basis. Thus, the federal income tax has been referred to as a "quiltwork" of tax laws, referring to the patchwork nature of the law. Without question, one of the principal reasons for the complexity of the federal income tax today is the incremental nature of the tax.

REVENUE SOURCES

ADDITIONAL COMMENT

In 1996, 119 million individual income tax returns were filed, and collections from individuals totaled $656 billion.

As mentioned earlier, the largest source of federal revenues is individual income taxes. Other major revenue sources include social security (FICA) taxes and corporate income taxes (see Table I1-1). Two notable trends from Table I1-1 are 1) the gradual increase in social security taxes from 1965 to 1999, and 2) the gradual decrease in corporate income taxes for the same period. Individual income taxes have slowly increasd during the thirty-year period.

[2] Richard Goode, *The Individual Income Tax* (Washington, DC: The Brookings Institution, 1964), pp. 2–4.

TYPICAL MISCONCEPTION

It is often assumed that the tax revenue from corporation income taxes is the largest source of tax revenue. However, the revenue generated from this tax represents approximately 11% of total federal revenues.

▼ **TABLE I1-1**
Breakdown of Federal Revenues

	1965	1975	1988	1999
Individual income taxes	43%	45%	44%	50%
Social insurance taxes and contribution	20	32	37	32
Corporation income taxes	23	15	10	10
Other	14	8	9	8
Total	100%	100%	100%	100%

Source: Council of Economic Advisors, *Economic Indicators* (Washington, DC: U.S. Government Printing Office, 1967, 1977, 2000).

TYPES OF TAX RATE STRUCTURES

OBJECTIVE 2

Differentiate between the three types of tax rate structures

THE STRUCTURE OF INDIVIDUAL INCOME TAX RATES

Virtually all tax structures are comprised of two basic parts: the **tax base** and the **tax rate.** The tax base is the amount to which the tax rate is applied to determine the tax due. For example, an individual's tax base for the federal income tax is *taxable income,* as defined and determined by the income tax law. Similarly, the tax base for the property tax is generally the fair market value of property subject to the tax. The tax rate is merely the percentage rate applied to the tax base.

Tax rates either may be progressive, proportional, or regressive. A **progressive rate** structure is one where the rate of tax increases as the tax base increases. The most notable tax that incorporates a progressive rate structure is the federal income tax. Thus, as a taxpayer's taxable income increases, a progressively higher rate of tax is applied. For 2002, the federal income tax rates for individuals begin at 10% and increase to 15%, 27%, 30%, 35% and 38.6% as a taxpayer's taxable income increases.[3] Examples I1-1 and I1-2 show how the progressive rate structure of the federal income tax operates.

ADDITIONAL COMMENT

In the 1950's, the top marginal tax rate for individual taxpayers reached 92%. This astonishingly high rate only applied to taxpayers with very high taxable incomes but is still an extremely confiscatory tax rate.

EXAMPLE I1-1 ▶ Alice, who is single, has $20,000 taxable income in 2002. Her federal income taxes for the year are $2,700 as the first $6,000 of taxable income is taxed at 10% and the remaining $14,000 at 15%. (For tax rates, see the inside front cover) Allen, who is also single, has taxable income of $40,000. A 10% rate applies to the first $6,000 of taxable income, 15% on the next $21,950 and a 27% rate applies to taxable income over $27,950. Thus, Allen's total tax is $7,146 [(0.10 × $6,000) + (0.15 × $21,950) + (0.27 × $12,050)]. If Allen's taxable income is $80,000, a 30% rate applies to $12,300 of his taxable income ($80,000 − $67,700) because the 30% rate applies to taxable income above $67,700 for a single individual and his total tax for the year is $18,315. Thus, the tax rates are progressive because the rate of tax increases as a taxpayer's taxable income increases. ◀

EXAMPLE I1-2 ▶ Assume the same facts as in Example I1-1 except that Alice has taxable income of $150,000. Of Alice's taxable income, $8,750 ($150,000 − $141,250) is subject to the 35% rate. Alternatively, assume that Allen has taxable income of $325,000. Of Allen's taxable income, $17,950 ($325,000 − $307,050) is subject to the top marginal rate of 38.6%. ◀

[3] See the inside front cover for the 2002 tax rates and Chapter I2 for a discussion of the computation procedures. 2001 rate schedules and tax tables are located immediately before Appendix A.

A **proportional tax** rate, sometimes called a **flat tax**, is one where the rate of tax is the same for all taxpayers, regardless of the level of their tax base. This type of tax rate is generally used for real estate taxes, state and local sales taxes, personal property taxes, customs duties, and excise taxes. A flat tax has been the subject of considerable discussion in the last couple of years and promises to be a highly controversial topic as the debate on federal income tax reform continues into the future.

EXAMPLE I1-3 ▶ Assume the same facts as in Example I1-1, except that a 17% tax rate applies to all amounts of taxable income. Based on the assumed flat tax rate structure, Alice's federal income tax is $3,400 on $20,000 of taxable income; Allen's tax is $6,800 on $40,000 of taxable income and $13,600 on $80,000 of taxable income. The tax rate is proportional because the 17% rate applies to both taxpayers without regard to their income level. As you can see, a proportional tax rate results in lower taxes for higher income taxpayers.[4] ◀

SELF-STUDY QUESTION

Assume a tax system with a tax of $1,000 on taxable income of $10,000 and a $1,500 tax on taxable income of $20,000. Is the tax rate system progressive, proportional, or regressive?

ANSWER

This tax system is regressive. Even though the amount of tax has increased, the rate of taxation has decreased from 10% on the first $10,000 of taxable income to 5% on the second $10,000 of taxable income.

A **regressive** tax rate decreases with an increase in the tax base (e.g., income). Regressive taxes, while not consistent with the fairness of the income tax,[5] are found in the United States. The social security (FICA) tax is regressive because a fixed rate of tax of 7.65% for both the employer and employee is levied up to a ceiling amount of $84,900 for 2002 ($80,400 in 2001). The employer and employee's FICA tax rate is only 1.45% for wages earned in excess of the ceiling amount. The sales tax, which is levied by many states, is also regressive when measured against the income base.

THE STRUCTURE OF CORPORATE TAX RATES

Corporations are separate entities and are subject to income tax. The federal corporate income tax reflects a stair-step pattern of progression that tends to benefit small corporations. The corporate rates, which have not changed for several years, are as follows:[6]

Taxable Income[7]	*Tax*
First $50,000	15% of taxable income
Over $50,000 but not over $75,000	$7,500 + 25% of taxable income over $50,000
Over $75,000 but not over $100,000	$13,750 + 34% of taxable income over $75,000
Over $100,000 but not over $335,000	$22,250 + 39% of taxable income over $100,000
Over $335,000	34% of taxable income
Over $10,000,000 but not over $15,000,000	$3,400,000 + 35% of taxable income over $10,000,000
Over $15,000,000 but not over $18,333,333	$5,150,000 + 38% over $15,000,000
Over $18,333,333	35% of taxable income

MARGINAL, AVERAGE, AND EFFECTIVE TAX RATES FOR TAXPAYERS

A taxpayer's **marginal tax rate** is the tax rate applied to an incremental amount of taxable income that is added to the tax base. The marginal tax rate concept is useful for planning because it measures the tax effect of a proposed transaction.

---

[4] This example assumes the same tax base (taxable income) for the flat tax as with the current federal tax. Most flat tax proposals allow few, if any, deductions and, therefore, would generate higher taxes than in the example.

[5] See the discussion of equity and fairness later in this chapter.

[6] For C corporations with taxable income over $100,000, the lower rates of tax on the first $75,000 of income are gradually phased out by applying a 5-percentage-point surtax on taxable income from $100,000 to $335,000 so that benefits of the favorable rates are eliminated once a corporation's taxable income reaches $335,000. Once taxable income exceeds $335,000 the tax equals 34% of taxable income. A 35% tax rate applies to taxable income in excess of $10 million. For corporations with taxable income in excess of $15 million, a 3 percentage-point-surtax applies to taxable income from $15 million to $18,333,333 to eliminate the lower 34% rate that applies to the first $10 million of taxable income.

[7] Also see the inside back cover for the 2002 corporation income tax rates.

EXAMPLE I1-4 ▶ Vania, who is single, is considering the purchase of a personal residence that will provide a $20,000 tax deduction for interest expense and real estate taxes in 2002. Vania's taxable income would be reduced from $90,000 to $70,000 if she purchases the residence. Because a 30% tax rate applies to taxable income from $70,000 to $90,000, Vania's marginal tax rate is 30%. Thus, Vania's tax savings from purchasing the personal residence would be $6,000 (0.30 × $20,000). ◀

ADDITIONAL COMMENT

One method of calculating economic income is to start with adjusted gross income (AGI), add back items of excludible income, such as tax-exempt bond interest, proceeds of life insurance policies, etc., and then deduct certain nondeductible business expenses, such as life insurance premiums, penalties and fines, etc.

While the marginal tax rate measures the tax rate applicable to the next $1 of income or deduction for a taxpayer, there are two other tax rates that are used primarily by tax policymakers: average tax rate and effective tax rate. The **average tax rate** is computed by dividing the total tax liability by the amount of taxable income. This represents the average rate of tax for each dollar of taxable income. For example, a single taxpayer with taxable income of $350,000 in 2002 would incur a total tax liability of $111,299. The taxpayer's marginal tax rate is 38.6%, but his average tax rate is 31.8% ($111,299/$350,000).

The **effective tax rate** is the total tax liability divided by total economic income. **Total economic income** includes all types of economic income that a taxpayer has for the year. Thus, economic income is much broader than taxable income and includes most types of excludible income, such as tax-exempt bond interest, and generally permits business deductions but not personal-type deductions. It should be pointed out that economic income is *not* statutorily defined and experts may disagree on a precise calculation. The basic purpose of calculating the effective tax rate is to provide a broad measure of taxpayers' ability to pay taxes. Accordingly, the effective tax rate mainly is used by tax policymakers to determine the fairness of the income tax system.

EXAMPLE I1-5 ▶ Amelia, who is single, has adjusted gross income of $40,000 and economic income of $55,000 in 2002. The difference is attributable to $15,000 of tax-exempt bond interest. If Amelia has deductions of $10,000, then her taxable income is $30,000, and her total tax is $4,446. Her average tax rate is 14.82% ($4,446 ÷ $30,000). Amelia's effective tax rate is 8.08% ($4,446 ÷ $55,000). Amelia's effective tax rate is considerably lower than her average tax rate because of her substantial amount of tax-exempt income. ◀

STOP & THINK

Question: Gwen, a single taxpayer, has seen her income climb to $200,000 in the current year. She wants a tax planner to help her reduce her tax liability. In planning for tax clients, tax professionals almost exclusively use the marginal tax rate in their analysis rather than the average tax rate. Why is the marginal tax rate much more important in the tax planning process than the average tax rate?

Solution: Because tax planning is done at the margin. A single taxpayer who has taxable income of $200,000 has a marginal tax rate of 35% (at 2002 rates), but an average tax rate of 28.63%, computed as follows:

Taxable income		$200,000
Tax on first $141,250 of taxable income		$36,690
Remaining taxable income	$58,750	
Times: Marginal tax rate	× 0.35	20,563
Total tax liability		$ 57,253

$$\text{Average tax rate} = \frac{\text{Total tax}}{\text{Taxable income}} = \frac{\$\ 57,253}{\$200,000} = 28.63\%$$

If a tax planner could reduce Gwen's taxable income by $10,000, Gwen's tax liability would decrease by $3,500 ($10,000 × 0.35). When the taxpayer wants to know how much she can save through tax planning, the appropriate marginal tax rate yields the answer.

Overall, effective federal income tax rates for individuals have changed little during the period 1979–1998,[8] amounting to 11% in 1997 as compared with 11.1% in 1979. However, for the highest 20% of households, the effective individual income tax rate rose to 16.4% in 1997 from 16.0% in 1979.

DETERMINATION OF TAXABLE INCOME AND TAX DUE

As will be discussed in later chapters, the federal income taxes imposed on all taxpayers (individuals, corporations, estates, and trusts) are based on the determination of taxable income. In general, taxable income is computed as follows:

ADDITIONAL COMMENT

In the determination of tax rates, one should consider the incidence of taxation that involves the issue of who really bears the burden of the tax. If a city raises the real property tax but landlords simply raise rents to pass on the higher taxes to their tenants, the tax burden is shifted. The concept has important implications in determining any kind of average or effective tax rate.

Total income (income from whatever source derived)	$xxx
Minus: Exclusions (specifically defined items, such as tax-exempt bond interest)	(xx)
Gross income	$xxx
Minus: Deductions (business expenses and itemized deductions)	(xx)
Exemptions (not applicable for corporations)	(xx)
Taxable income	$xxx
Times: Applicable tax rate	× .xx
Income tax before credits	$xxx
Minus: Tax credits	(xx)
Total tax liability	$xxx
Minus: Prepayments	(xx)
Balance due or refund	$xxx

Each different type of taxpayer (individuals, corporations, etc.) computes taxable income in a slightly different manner, but all use the general framework above. Individual taxpayers (Chapter I2) and corporation taxpayers (Chapter I16) are examined in this *Individuals* book (Chapter C3 of the *Comprehensive* edition). Corporations (in more detail), estates, and trusts are examined in *Prentice Hall's Federal Taxation: Corporations, Partnerships, Estates, and Trusts.*

OTHER TYPES OF TAXES

OBJECTIVE 3

Describe the various types of taxes

STATE AND LOCAL INCOME AND FRANCHISE TAXES

In addition to federal income taxes, many states and local jurisdictions impose income taxes on individuals and businesses. These state and local taxes have gradually increased over the years and currently represent a significant source of revenue for state and local governments but also represent a significant tax burden on taxpayers.

State and local income taxes vary greatly in both form and rates.[9] Only seven states do not impose an individual income tax.[10] In most instances, state income tax rates are mildly progressive and are based on an individual's federal adjusted gross income (AGI), with minor adjustments.[11] For example, a typical adjustment to a state income tax return is interest income on federal government bonds, which is subject to tax on the federal return but is generally not subject to state income taxes. Some states also allow a deduction for federal income taxes in the computation of taxable income for state income tax purposes.

---

[8] Congressional Budget Office, *Effective Federal Tax Rates 1979–1997* (Washington, DC: U.S. Government Printing Office, October, 2001), p. 148.

[9] For a thorough discussion of state and local taxes, see the chapter entitled *Multistate Income Taxation* that accompanies this textbook in electronic form on the Prentice Hall Federal Taxation 2002 webpage at www.prenhall.com/phtax.

[10] These states are Alaska, Florida, Nevada, South Dakota, Texas, Washington, and Wyoming. New Hampshire has an income tax that is levied only on dividend and interest income and Tennessee's income tax applies only to income from stocks and bonds.

[11] See Chapter I2 for a discussion of the AGI computation.

ADDITIONAL COMMENT

State income tax rates for individuals have increased significantly in the past twenty years. Thirty-three states now have marginal tax rates of 6% or higher.

States imposing a state income tax generally require the withholding of state income taxes and have established mandatory estimated tax payment procedures. The due date for filing state income tax returns generally coincides with the due date for the federal income tax returns (e.g., the fifteenth day of the fourth month following the close of the tax year for individuals).

Most states impose a corporate income tax, although in some instances the tax is called a **franchise tax.** Franchise taxes usually are based on a weighted-average formula consisting of net worth, income, and sales.

WEALTH TRANSFER TAXES

KEY POINT

The $11,000 annual exclusion is an important tax-planning tool for wealthy parents who want to transfer assets to their children and thereby minimize their gift and estate taxes. A husband and wife who have three children could transfer a maximum of $66,000 [($11,000 × 2) × 3] to their children each year without incurring any gift tax.

U.S. citizens are subject to taxation on certain transfers of property to another person. The tax law provides a unified transfer tax system that imposes a single tax on transfers of property taking place during an individual's lifetime (gifts) and at death (estates). (See the inside back cover of the text for the transfer tax rate schedules.) Formerly, the gift and estate tax laws were separate and distinct. The federal estate tax was initially enacted in 1916. The original gift tax law dates back to 1932. The gift tax was originally imposed to prevent widespread avoidance of the estate tax (e.g., taxpayers could make tax-free gifts of property before their death). Both the gift and estate taxes are wealth transfer taxes levied on the transfer of property and are based on the fair market value (FMV) of the transferred property on the date of the transfer. Below are brief descriptions of the gift tax and estate tax.

THE FEDERAL GIFT TAX. The **gift tax** is an excise tax that is imposed on the donor (not the donee) for transfers of property that are considered to be a taxable gift. A gift, generally speaking, is a transfer made gratuitously and with donative intent. However, the gift tax law has expanded the definition to include transfers that are not supported by full and adequate consideration.[12] To arrive at the amount of taxable gifts for the current year, a $11,000 annual exclusion is allowed per donee.[13] In addition, an unlimited marital deduction is allowed for transfers between spouses.[14] The formula for computing the gift tax is as follows:

FMV of all gifts made in the current year			$x,xxx
Minus:	Annual donee exclusions ($10,000 per donee)	$xx	
	Marital deduction for gifts to spouse	xx	
	Charitable contribution deduction	xx	(xxx)
Plus:	Taxable gifts for all prior years		xxx
Cumulative taxable gifts (tax base)			$x,xxx
Times:	Unified transfer tax rates		× .xx
Tentative tax on gift tax base			$ xxx
Minus:	Unified transfer taxes paid in prior years		(xx)
	Unified credit		(xx)
Unified transfer tax (gift tax) due in the current year			$ xx

ADDITIONAL COMMENT

The gift tax was enacted to make the estate tax more effective. Without a gift tax, estate taxes could be easily avoided by large gifts made before death.

Note that the gift tax is cumulative over the taxpayer's lifetime (i.e., the tax calculation for the current year includes the taxable gifts made in prior years). The detailed tax rules relating to the gift tax are covered in Chapter C12 in both *Prentice Hall's Federal Taxation: Corporations, Partnerships, Estates, and Trusts* and the *Comprehensive* volume. The following general concepts and rules for the federal gift tax are presented as background material for other chapters of this text dealing with individual taxpayers:

- Gifts between spouses are exempted from the gift tax due to the operation of an unlimited marital deduction.
- The primary liability for payment of the gift tax is imposed on the **donor.** The donee is contingently liable for payment of the gift tax in the event of nonpayment by the donor.

---

[12] Sec. 2512(b).

[13] Sec. 2503(b). The annual exclusion for gift tax purposes had been $10,000 for many years. However, for 2002 and later years, the inflation adjustment increases the exclusion to $11,000.

[14] Sec. 2523(a).

- A donor is permitted a $11,000 annual exclusion for gifts of a present interest to each donee.[15]
- Charitable contributions are effectively exempted from the gift tax because an unlimited deduction is allowed.
- The tax basis of the property to the donee is generally the donor's cost. It is the lesser of the donor's cost and the property's FMV on the date of the gift if the property is sold by the donee at a loss. (See Chapter I5 for a discussion of the gift tax basis rules.)
- A unified tax credit equivalent to a $1,000,000 deduction is available in 2002 and 2003 to offset any gift tax on taxable gifts that exceed the $11,000 annual exclusion.[16] The equivalent deduction increases to $1,500,000 in 2004 and 2005.

EXAMPLE I1-6 ▶ Antonio makes the following gifts in the year 2002:

- $25,000 cash gift to his wife
- $15,000 contribution to the United Way
- Gift of a personal automobile valued at $25,000 to his adult son
- Gift of a personal computer valued at $4,000 to a friend

The $25,000 gift to his wife is not taxed because of a $11,000 annual exclusion and a $14,000 tax exemption for transfers to spouses (i.e., the marital deduction). The $15,000 contribution to the United Way is also not taxed because of the $11,000 annual exclusion and the $4,000 deduction for charitable contributions. The $25,000 gift Antonio made to his son is reduced by the $11,000 annual exclusion to each donee, leaving a $14,000 taxable gift.[17] The $4,000 gift to the friend is not taxed because of the annual exclusion of up to $11,000 in gifts to a donee in a tax year. Thus, total taxable gifts for the current year subject to the unified transfer tax are $14,000. ◀

STOP & THINK *Question:* An important but frequently overlooked aspect of gift taxes is the interaction of gift taxes and income taxes. In many cases, gifts are made *primarily* for income tax purposes. Why would a gift be made for income tax purposes?

Solution: Gifts are frequently made to shift income from one family member to another family member who is in a lower marginal tax bracket. For example, assume Fran and Jan are married, have one 15-year-old son, earn $400,000 per year from their business, and generate $100,000 per year in dividends and interest from a substantial portfolio of stocks and bonds. With such a high level of income, Fran and Jan are in the 38.6% marginal tax bracket. If they make a gift of some of the stocks and bonds to their son, the dividends and interest attributable to the gift are taxed to the son at his marginal tax rate (maybe 15%). If the son's marginal tax rate is lower than 38.6%, the family unit reduces its overall income taxes.

THE FEDERAL ESTATE TAX. The **federal estate tax** is part of the unified transfer tax system that is based on the total property transfers an individual makes both during his or her lifetime and at death.

---

[15] A gift of a present interest is an interest that is already in existence and the donee is currently entitled to receive the income from the property. A gift of a future interest comes into being at some future date (e.g., property is transferred by gift to a trust in which the donee is not entitled to the income from the property until the donor dies) and is not eligible for the $11,000 annual exclusion.

[16] The new 2001 Tax Act increases the applicable exclusion amount to $1.5 million in 2004 and 2005, $2.0 million in 2006–2008, and $3.5 million in 2009. The estate tax is scheduled to be repealed in 2010 subject to sunset provisions which could reinstate the estate tax in 2011 to 2001 levels. Prior to the new 2001 Tax Act, the applicable exclusion amount was $675,000 in 2000 and 2001. For further details, see *Prentice Hall's Federal Taxation: Corporations, Partnerships, Estates and Trusts*, 2003 Edition, Chapter 12 and 13.

[17] This example assumes that the automobile is a gift rather than an obligation of support under state law and also assumes that Antonio's wife does not join with Antonio in electing to treat the gift to the son as having been made by both spouses (a gift-splitting election). In such event, donee exclusions of $22,000 (2 × $11,000) would be available, resulting in a taxable gift of only $3,000.

EXAMPLE I1-7 ▶ Amy dies during the current year. The formula for computing the estate tax on Amy's estate is as follows:

Gross estate (FMV of all property owned by the decedent at the date of death)		$xxx,xxx
Minus:	Deductions for funeral and administration expenses, debts of the decedent, charitable contributions, and the marital deduction for property transferred to a spouse	(x,xxx)
Taxable estate		$x,xxx
Plus:	Taxable gifts made after 1976	xx
Tax base		$x,xxx
Times:	Unified transfer tax rate(s)	× .xx
Tentative tax on estate tax base		$ xxx
Minus:	Tax credits (e.g., the unified tax credit equal to the tax on $1,000,000 in 2002 and 2003)	(xx)
Gift taxes paid after 1976		(xx)
Unified transfer tax (estate tax) due		$xx ◀

TYPICAL MISCONCEPTION

It is sometimes thought that the federal estate tax raises significant amounts of revenue, but it has not been a significant revenue producer since World War II. Only 86,000 estate tax returns were filed in 1996.

The estate tax rules are discussed in more detail in Chapter C13 in *Prentice Hall's Federal Taxation: Corporations, Partnerships, Estates, and Trusts* and in the *Comprehensive* volume. The following general rules are provided as background material for subsequent chapters of this text dealing with individual taxpayers:

- The decedent's property is valued at its FMV on the date of death unless the alternative valuation date (six months after the date of death) is elected. The alternative valuation date may be elected only if the aggregate value of the gross estate decreases during the six-month period following the date of death and the election results in a lower estate tax liability.
- The basis of the property received by the estate and by the decedent's heirs is the property's FMV on the date of death (or the alternate valuation date if it is elected).
- Property transferred to the decedent's spouse is exempt from the estate tax because of the estate tax marital deduction provision.

EXAMPLE I1-8 ▶ Barry died in 2002, leaving a $2,000,000 gross estate. One-half of the property is transferred to his wife, taxable gifts (after the gift tax annual exclusion) made after 1976 were $150,000, administrative and funeral expenses are $30,000, and debts of the decedent amount to $170,000. The estate tax due is computed as follows:

Gross estate		$2,000,000
Minus:	Marital deduction	(1,000,000)
	Funeral and administrative expenses	(30,000)
	Decedent's debts	(170,000)
Taxable estate		$ 800,000
Plus:	Taxable gifts made after 1976	150,000
Tax base		$ 950,000
Tentative tax on estate tax base		$ 326,300[a]
Minus:	Tax credits (unified tax credit)	(345,800)
Unified transfer tax due		$ —0— ◀

[a] $248,300 + (0.39 × $200,000)

Because of the generous credit and deduction provisions (e.g., the unified tax credit and the unlimited marital deduction), few estates are required to pay estate taxes. As can be seen above, the gross estate of the decedent was $2 million but no estate taxes were due primarily because of the large marital deduction and the unified credit. However, estate taxes rise quickly as is demonstrated below in Example I1-9.

EXAMPLE I1-9 ▶ Assume the same facts for Barry as in Example I1-8 except that Barry's gross estate is $3,000,000 rather than $1,000,000. The estate tax due is computed as follows:

Gross estate		$3,000,000
Minus:	Marital deduction	(1,500,000)
	Funeral and administrative expenses	(30,000)
	Decedent's debts	(170,000)
Taxable estate		$1,300,000
Plus:	Taxable gifts made after 1976	150,000
Tax base		$1,450,000
Tentative tax on estate tax base		$ 534,300
Minus:	Tax credits (unified tax credit)	(345,800)
Unified transfer tax due		$ 188,500 ◀

OTHER TYPES OF TAXES

ADDITIONAL COMMENT

Proposals to decrease reliance on the federal income tax have focused on a value added tax and selective energy taxes. A value added tax is a sales tax levied at each stage of production on the "value added."

Although this text focuses primarily on the federal income tax, some mention should be made of the following other types of taxes levied by federal, state, and local governments.

- **Property taxes** are based on the value of a taxpayer's property, which may include both real estate and personal property. Real estate taxes are a major source of revenue for local governments. In addition, some state and local governments levy a personal property tax on intangibles such as securities and tangible personal property (e.g., the value of a personal automobile).
- **Federal excise taxes** and **customs duties** on imported goods have declined in relative importance over the years but remain significant sources of revenue. Federal excise taxes are imposed on alcohol, tobacco, gasoline, telephone usage, production of oil and gas, and many other types of goods. Many state and local governments impose similar excise taxes on goods and services.

ADDITIONAL COMMENT

Anheuser-Busch Company ran a television commercial in 1990 during the deliberations on the Revenue Reconciliation Act of 1990 that asked viewers to call a toll-free telephone number to register their criticism of an increase in the excise tax on beer. The commercial asked viewers to "can the beer tax."

- **Sales taxes** are a major source of revenue for state and local governments. Sales taxes are imposed on retail sales of tangible personal property (e.g., clothing and automobiles). Some states also impose a sales tax on personal services (e.g., accounting and legal fees). Certain items often are exempt from the sales tax levy (e.g., food items or medicines), and the rates vary widely between individual state and local governments. Sales taxes are not deductible for federal income tax purposes unless incurred in a trade or business.
- **Employment taxes** include social security (**FICA**) and federal and state unemployment compensation taxes. If an individual is classified as an employee, the FICA tax that is imposed on the employee is comprised of two parts, 6.2% for old-age, survivors, and disability insurance (OASDI) and 1.45% for hospital insurance (HI), for a total of 7.65%. The OASDI portion is imposed on the first $84,900 (2002) of wages, whereas the HI portion has no ceiling. Both of these taxes are imposed on both the employer and employee. If an individual is self-employed, a self-employment tax is imposed at a 15.3% rate (12.4% for OASDI and 2.9% for HI) on the individual's self-employment income, with a ceiling on the OASDI portion of $84,900 (in 2002).[18] Similar to employees, there is no ceiling on the HI portion for self-employed individuals.

ADDITIONAL COMMENT

Revenue from employment taxes are indeed significant. In 1996, $491 billion in employment taxes were collected representing 36% of all Internal Revenue Service collections.

- Employers are required to pay federal and state unemployment taxes to fund the payment of unemployment benefits to former employees. The federal rate is 6.2% on the first $7,000 of wages for each employee in 2002.[19] However, a credit is granted for up to 5.4% of wages for taxes paid to the state government so that the actual amount paid to the federal government may be as low as 0.8%.[20] The amount of tax paid to the state depends on the employer's prior experience with respect to the frequency and amount of unemployment claims. In Kentucky, for example, the highest rate of unemployment tax imposed is 3% and this rate is subsequently adjusted down if the employer has a small number of unemployment claims.

The types of taxes and structural considerations that were previously discussed are summarized in Topic Review I1-1.

---

[18] Self-employed individuals receive an income tax deduction equal to 50% of taxes paid on their self-employment income and this deduction is also allowed to compute the amount of self-employment income (see Secs. 164(f) and 1402(a)(12) and Chapter I14).

[19] Sec. 3301.

[20] Sec. 3302. State unemployment taxes in some states are levied on tax bases above $7,000. For example, the wage base ceiling in North Carolina is $12,500 in 2001.

Topic Review I1-1

Types of Taxes and Tax Structure

Type of Tax	Tax Structure	Tax Base
Individuals:		
Federal income tax	Progressive	Gross income from all sources unless specifically excluded by law reduced by deductions and exemptions
State income tax	Progressive	Generally based on AGI for federal income tax purposes with adjustments
Federal gift tax	Progressive	FMV of all taxable gifts made during the tax year
Federal estate tax	Progressive	FMV of property owned at death plus taxable gifts made after 1976
Corporations:		
Federal corporate income tax	Progressive	Gross income from all sources unless specifically excluded by law reduced by deductions
State corporate income tax	Proportional or progressive	Federal corporate taxable income with adjustments
State franchise tax	Proportional	Usually based on a weighted-average formula consisting of net worth, income, and sales
Other Types of Taxes:		
Property taxes	Proportional	FMV of personal or real property
Excise taxes	Proportional	Customs and duties on imported and domestic goods from alcohol to telephone usage
Sales taxes	Proportional	Retail sales of tangible personal property or personal services
FICA and self-employment taxes	Regressive	Based on wages or self-employment income
Unemployment taxes	Regressive	Usually first $7,000 of an employee's wages

CRITERIA FOR A TAX STRUCTURE

OBJECTIVE 4

Discuss what constitutes a "good" tax structure and the objectives of the federal income tax law

Establishing criteria for a "good" tax structure was first attempted in 1776 by economist Adam Smith.[21] Smith's four "canons of taxation"—equity, certainty, convenience, and economy—are still used today when tax policy issues are discussed. Below is a discussion of these criteria and how they relate to income taxes as well as other taxes.

EQUITY

ADDITIONAL COMMENT

The Revenue Reconciliation Act of 1993 followed through on President Clinton's campaign promise to increase taxes on high-income taxpayers to correct perceived inequities resulting from the lowering of the top tax rates in the Tax Reform Act of 1986.

A rather obvious criteria for a good tax is that the tax be equitable or fair to taxpayers. However, equity or fairness is elusive because of the subjectivity of the concept. What one person may conclude is fair in a particular situation may be considered totally unfair by another person. In other words, fairness is relative in nature and is extremely difficult to measure. For example, the deductibility of mortgage interest on a taxpayer's home certainly seems to be a fair provision for taxpayers. However, for taxpayers who do not own a home but live in a rental apartment, the deductibility of mortgage interest may not be considered as fair because the renter cannot deduct any portion of the rent paid. In other types of situations, the federal tax law includes various measures to ensure that taxpayers are treated fairly. For example, a foreign tax credit is available to minimize the double taxation that would otherwise occur when U.S. taxpayers earn income in a foreign coun-

[21] Adam Smith, *The Wealth of Nations* (New York: Random House, Modern Library, 1937), pp. 777–779.

try that is taxed by both the United States and the country in which it is earned. (See the glossary at the end of this volume for a definition of tax credits and Chapter I14 for a discussion of the foreign tax credit.) Two aspects of equity are commonly discussed in the tax policy literature, **horizontal equity** and **vertical equity.** Horizontal equity refers to the notion that similarly situated taxpayers should be treated equally. Thus, two taxpayers who each have income of $50,000 should both pay the same amount of tax. Vertical equity, on the other hand, implies that taxpayers who are not similarly situated should be treated differently. Thus, if Taxpayer A has income of $50,000 and Taxpayer B has income of $20,000, Taxpayers A and B should not pay the same amount of income tax. Vertical equity provides that the incidence of taxation should be borne by those who have the **ability to pay** the tax, based on income or wealth. The progressive rate structure is founded on the vertical equity premise.

CERTAINTY

KEY POINT

Using retroactive dates for changes in the tax law does not help to accomplish the objective of certainty. For example, the effective date of the increase in the top tax rate was made retroactive to January 1, 1993, in tax legislation signed by President Clinton on August 19, 1993. This retroactive tax increase was unpopular with high-income taxpayers.

A certain tax (1) ensures a stable source of government operating revenues, and (2) provides taxpayers with some degree of certainty concerning the amount of their annual tax liability. A tax that is simple to understand and administer provides certainty for taxpayers. For many years, our income tax laws have been criticized as being overly complex and difficult to administer. Consider the remarks of a noted tax authority at a conference on federal income tax simplification:

> Tax advisers—at least some tax advisers—are saying that the income tax system is not working. They are saying that they don't know what the law provides, that the IRS does not know what the law provides, that taxpayers are not abiding by the law they don't know.[22]

While the above statement is over 20 years old, it is certainly still viable today. This uncertainty in the tax law causes frequent disputes between taxpayers and the IRS and has resulted in extensive litigation.

ADDITIONAL COMMENT

Humorist Jim Boren has proposed a constitutional amendment that would require any retroactive tax increases to be followed by retroactive elections for president, vice president and all members of Congress.

The federal tax system has made some attempts to provide certainty for taxpayers. For example, the IRS issues advance rulings to taxpayers, which provides some assurance concerning the tax consequences of a proposed transaction for the taxpayer who requests the ruling. The taxpayer may rely on the ruling if the transaction is completed in accordance with the terms of the ruling request. For example, if a merger of two corporations is being considered, the transaction can be structured so that the shareholders and the corporations do not recognize gain or loss. If a favorable ruling is received and the transaction is completed as planned, the IRS cannot later assert that the merger does not qualify for tax-free treatment.

CONVENIENCE

A tax law should be easily assessed, collected, and administered. Taxpayers should not be overly burdened with the maintenance of records and compliance considerations (preparation of their tax returns, payment of their taxes, and so on). One of the reasons that the sales tax is such a popular form of tax for state and local governments is that it is convenient for taxpayers to pay and for the government to collect. The consumer need not complete a tax return or keep detailed records.

ECONOMY

ADDITIONAL COMMENT

For tax year 1999, 55% of all individual tax returns were prepared by paid tax-return preparers. This compares with 48% of returns prepared by paid return preparers in 1990.

An economical tax structure should require only minimal compliance and administrative costs. The IRS collection costs, amounting to less than 0.5% of revenues, are minimal relative to the total collections of revenues from the federal income tax. Estimates of taxpayer compliance costs are less certain. One indicator of total compliance costs for taxpayers is the demand for tax professionals. Tax practice has been and continues to be one of the fastest growing areas in public accounting firms. Most large corporations also

[22] Sidney L. Roberts, "The Viewpoint of the Tax Adviser: An Overview of Simplification," *Tax Adviser,* January 1979, p. 32.

maintain sizable tax departments that engage in tax research, compliance, and planning activities. In addition, many commercial tax return preparer services are available to assist taxpayers who have relatively uncomplicated tax returns.

Fortune 500 companies spend over $1 billion annually complying with the tax laws, according to a study commissioned by the IRS.[23] The survey found that about 55% of the cost of compliance goes to pay in-house staff and about 16% goes to outside firms. The federal income tax system accounts for about 70% of this cost. State and local income tax compliance accounts for the remaining 30%. The companies surveyed said that the largest share of their tax compliance costs was for filing tax returns.

A more difficult question is whether the tax structure is economical in terms of taxpayer compliance. The issues of tax avoidance and tax evasion are becoming increasingly more important. The General Accounting Office (GAO) reported that two-thirds of tax returns are out of compliance, resulting in net income being underreported by 25 percent.[24]

OBJECTIVES OF THE FEDERAL INCOME TAX LAW

The primary objective of the federal income tax law is to raise revenues for government operations. In recent years, the federal government has broadened its use of the tax laws to accomplish various economic and social policy objectives.

ECONOMIC OBJECTIVES

The federal income tax law is used as a fiscal policy tool to stimulate private investment, reduce unemployment, and mitigate the effects of inflation on the economy. Consider the following example: Tax credits for businesses operating in distressed urban and rural areas (empowerment zones) are allowed to provide economic revitalization of such areas. This is a clear example of using the federal income tax law to stimulate private investment in specific areas.

Many items in the tax law are adjusted for inflation by using the consumer price index, including the tax brackets, personal and dependency exemptions, and standard deduction amounts. These inflation adjustments provide relief for individual taxpayers who would otherwise be subject to increased taxes due to the effects of inflation. (See Chapter I2 for a discussion of the tax computation for individuals.)

ENCOURAGEMENT OF CERTAIN ACTIVITIES AND INDUSTRIES

ADDITIONAL COMMENT

Among the provisions in the tax law that are designed to enhance the level of health care are the deductibility of medical expenses, deductibility of charitable contributions to hospitals, and exclusion of fringe benefits provided by employers for medical insurance premiums and medical care.

The federal income tax law also attempts to stimulate and encourage certain activities, specialized industries, and small businesses. One such example is the encouragement of research activities by permitting an immediate write-off of expenses and a special tax credit for increasing research and experimental costs. Special incentives are also provided to the oil and gas industry through percentage depletion allowances and an election to deduct intangible drilling costs.

Certain favorable tax provisions are provided for small businesses, including reduced corporate tax rates of 15% on the first $50,000 of taxable income and 25% for the next $25,000 of taxable income. Favorable ordinary loss (instead of capital loss) deductions are granted to individual investors who sell their small business corporation stock at a loss, provided that certain requirements are met.[25] In addition, noncorporate investors may exclude up to 50% of the gain realized from the disposition of qualified small business stock issued after August 10, 1993 if the stock is held for more than five years.[26]

---

[23] Joel Slemrod and Marsha Blumenthal, "Measuring Taxpayer Burden and Attitudes for Large Corporations: Report to the Coordinated Examination Program of the IRS," *Tax Notes*, December 20, 1993, p. 1422.

[24] News Report. "Compliance Said to Be Poor Among Sole Proprietorships," *Tax Notes*, December 12, 1994, p. 1328.

[25] Sec. 1244.

[26] Sec. 1202.

ADDITIONAL COMMENT

Deductible contributions made by self-employed individuals to their retirement plan (Keogh plans) totaled $8.8 billion in 1996. Charitable deductions totaled over $84.2 billion that same year.

SOCIAL OBJECTIVES

The tax law attempts to encourage or discourage certain socially desirable or undersirable activities. For example:

- Special tax-favored pension and profit-sharing plans have been created for employees and self-employed individuals to supplement the social security retirement system.
- Charitable contributions are deductible to encourage individuals to contribute to charitable organizations.
- The claiming of a deduction for illegal bribes, fines, and penalties has been prohibited to discourage activities that are contrary to public policy.

EXAMPLE I1-10 ▶ Able Corporation establishes a qualified pension plan for its employees whereby it makes all of the annual contributions to the plan. Able's contributions to the pension trust are currently deductible and not includible in the employee's gross income until the pension payments are distributed during their retirement years. Earnings on the contributed funds also are nontaxable until such amounts are distributed to the employees. ◀

EXAMPLE I1-11 ▶ Anita contributes $10,000 annually to her church, which is a qualified charitable organization. Anita's marginal tax rate is 27%. Her after-tax cost of contributing to the church is only $7,300 [$10,000 – (0.27 × $10,000)]. ◀

EXAMPLE I1-12 ▶ Ace Trucking Company incurs $10,000 in fines imposed by local and state governments for overloading its trucks during the current tax year. The fines are not deductible because the activity is contrary to public policy. ◀

The tax law objectives previously discussed are highlighted in Topic Review I1-2.

ENTITIES IN THE FEDERAL INCOME TAX SYSTEM

The federal income tax law levies taxes on taxpayers. However, not all entities that file income tax returns pay income taxes. For example, a partnership is required to file a tax return but does not pay any income tax because the income (or loss) of the partnership is allocated to the partners and they report the income or loss on their tax returns. Therefore, the various entities in the federal income tax system may be classified into two general categories, *taxpaying entities* and *flow-through entities*.[27] Taxpaying entities generally are required to pay income taxes on their taxable income. Flow-through entities, on the other hand, generally do not directly pay income taxes but merely pass the income on to a taxpaying entity. The major entities in each category are as follows:

Taxpaying Entities	*Flow-through Entities*
Individuals	Sole proprietorship
C corporations (regular corporations)	Partnerships
	S corporations
	Limited Liability Company (LLC) or Limited Liability Partnership (LLP)
	Trusts

TAXPAYING ENTITIES

INDIVIDUALS. Individual taxpayers are the principal taxpaying entities in the federal income tax system. Since the taxation of individuals is the focus of this textbook, we will not discuss individuals here.

[27] Some entities have characteristics of both categories of entities, including certain types of trusts and S corporations.

Topic Review I1-2

Objectives of the Tax Law

OBJECTIVE	EXAMPLE
Stimulate investment	Provide a tax credit for the purchase of business equipment
Prevent taxpayers from paying a higher percentage of their income in personal income taxes due to inflation (bracket creep)	Index the tax rates, standard deduction, and personal and dependency exemptions for inflation
Encourage research activities that will in turn strengthen the competitiveness of U.S. companies	Allow research expenditures to be written off in the year incurred and offer a tax credit for increasing research and experimental costs
Encourage venture capital for small businesses	Reduce corporate income tax rates on the first $75,000 of taxable income. Allow businesses to immediately expense $24,000 (2002) of certain depreciable business assets acquired each year.
Encourage social objectives	Provide a tax deduction for charitable contributions; provide favorable tax treatment for contributions to qualified pension plans

C CORPORATIONS. C corporations, many times referred to as regular corporations, are entities that are subject to so-called double taxation. Double taxation results from the corporation paying income tax on its taxable income and shareholders paying income tax on any dividends received from the corporation. Thus, the same corporate income is subjected to taxation twice—once at the corporate level and second at the shareholder level. For many years, much tax planning has been directed at trying to so arrange the tax affairs of a C coporation to avoid double taxation.

A C corporation is required to file annually a tax return using Form 1120. The corporation's taxable income is subject to taxation at graduated tax rates ranging from 15% to 35% (see the inside back cover for corporation income tax rates). Corporation's must report most of its income for income tax purposes but also are allowed to deduct virtually all ordinary and necessary expenses to arrive at taxable income.

EXAMPLE I1-13 ▶ During the current year, Crimson Corporation generated gross income of $1,500,000 and had ordinary and necessary deductions of $900,000, resulting in taxable income of $600,000. Crimson would be subject to corporation income taxes of $204,000 (see corporation tax rate schedule). Crimson also paid $200,000 of dividends to shareholders during the current year. The dividends are not deductible by Crimson and are taxable to the shareholders, possibly at the highest individual rate of 38.6%. The double taxation of the $600,000 is an onerous amount of tax. ◀

EXAMPLE I1-14 ▶ If, in Example I1-13, the shareholders are also employees of the Crimson Corporation, the double taxation could be avoided if the $200,000 was paid in the form of salaries rather than dividends. In this case, the $200,000 would be deductible by the corporation resulting in taxable income of $400,000 and tax of $136,000. Crimson would realize $68,000 of tax savings. The $200,000 would still be taxable to the shareholders. Since this technique seemingly is so simple to save significant income taxes, the tax law contains a number of tax rules that may reclassify salaries to employee/shareholders as dividends. See Chapter I16 of this text or Chapters C2-6 of the *Comprehensive* volume. ◀

FLOW-THROUGH ENTITIES

SOLE PROPRIETORSHIP. A sole proprietorship is the simplest form of business entity as there are no formal requirements to form such an entity. The net income earned by the proprietor is reported on Schedule C of Form 1040. Thus, the income of the sole proprietorship merely flows to the proprietor's individual tax return. The net income of the sole proprietorship is subject to income tax only once (at the individual level) but is also subject to self-employment tax (Social security and Medicare taxes).

PARTNERSHIPS. A partnership is the classic flow-through entity in that the income or loss of the partnership is allocated to the partners who report the income and pay tax on their tax returns. The partnership is really just a reporting entity as no income tax is paid by the partnership. Thus, the partnership form of the organization is not subject to double taxation. Partnerships report the income and deductions on Form 1065. However, the fact that partnerships are subject to unlimited liability is a major drawback of the partnership form.

EXAMPLE I1-15 ▶ Billy and Bob form the Billy-Bob Partnership as equal partners. During the current year, Billy-Bob earns net income of $300,000. The partnership is not subject to income taxation on the $300,000. On Form 1065, the partnership allocates $150,000 each to Billy and Bob, who report this amount on their individual income tax returns. ◀

S CORPORATIONS. S corporations (often referred to as Subchapter S corporations) are actual corporations pursuant to state law. The corporation is classified as an S corporation under the tax law if an election is made to the Internal Revenue Service. Basically, an S corporation is treated like a partnership for federal income tax purposes. Thus, the income or loss of the S corporation is allocated to the shareholders and reported on their individual tax returns. The corporation itself is not subject to tax. S corporations must file Form 1120S. While S corporations and partnerships appear to be nearly identical for federal income tax purposes, there are some significant differences. These differences are discussed later in this textbook as well as the other Prentice Hall textbooks.

LLC/LLP. Limited liability companies (LLCs) are the newest type of entity and are extremely popular as a form of organization. Basically, an LLC is a legal entity under state law that provides limited liability to its owners. Owners of an LLC are referred to as members. The principal tax advantage of LLCs is that they generally are treated as partnerships for tax purposes. Thus, the popularity of LLC's can be attributed to the fact that the members have limited liability and are only subject to a single level of taxation. Limited liability partnerships (LLPs) are slightly different than LLCs in that limited liability is not provided to a partner who commits an act of negligence or misconduct. However, limited liability is provided to all the other partners. LLP's are frequently used by professional service partnerships, such as public accounting firms. If an LLC or LLP is classified as a partnership, it files a Form 1065.

TRUSTS. Trusts are somewhat of a hybrid entity in that they may either be a taxpaying entity or flow-through entity. Also, there are a number of different types of trusts, so the discussion here is very general in nature. Trusts typically are subject to income taxation on all of its net income that is *not* distributed to the beneficiaries. The portion of net income that is distributed to beneficiaries is taxed to the beneficiaries. One drawback to the use of trusts is that the income tax rates are extremely progressive, reaching the 38.6% bracket when the taxable income of the trust reaches $9,200 in 2002. Trusts use Form 1041 to file its tax information.

EXAMPLE I1-16 ▶ Ben establishes a trust for the benefit of his daughter. The principal amount of the trust is $500,000 and is projected to earn approximately 10% per year. In the current year, the trust earned $50,000 of investment income and had $5,000 of expenses. If the trust did not make any distributions during the year to the daughter, the entire $45,000 (less a small exemption) would be subject to income taxation to the trust. Much of the taxable income would be subject to taxation at the 38.6% rate. Alternatively, if the trust distributed the entire $45,000 to the daughter, she would report the $45,000 on her individual tax return. Assuming she does not have significant other income, she would most likely be in the 27% marginal tax bracket. The trust's taxable income would be zero and would have no income tax liability. ◀

TAX LAW SOURCES

OBJECTIVE 5

Identify the various tax law sources and understand their implications for tax practice

The solution to any tax question may only be resolved by reference to tax law sources (also referred to as tax law authority). Tax law sources are generated from all three branches of the federal government, i.e., legislative, executive, and judicial. The principal sources of tax law are as follows:

Branch	*Tax Law Source*
Legislative	Internal Revenue Code
	Congressional Committee Reports
Executive (Administrative)	Income Tax Regulations
	Revenue Rulings
	Revenue Procedures
	Letter Rulings
Judicial	Court Decisions

ADDITIONAL COMMENT

Knowledge of tax law sources could be considered the most important topic in this book. It is similar to the old Chinese proverb that states that if you give a person a fish you have fed him for one day, but if you teach a person how to fish you have fed him for the rest of his life. By analogy, if a person has a knowledge of the tax law sources, he or she should be able to locate the answers to tax questions throughout his or her career.

A thorough knowledge of the various sources above as well as the relative weights attached to each source is vital to tax professionals. Because of the vast volume of tax law sources, the ability to "find the answer" to a tax question is of fundamental importance. In addition, the evaluation of the weight (or importance) of different sources of authority is also crucial in arriving at a proper conclusion. For example, a decision of the U.S. Supreme Court on a tax matter would certainly carry more weight than a Revenue Ruling issued by the Internal Revenue Service.

Clearly, the most authoritative source of tax law is the Internal Revenue Code, which is the tax law passed by Congress. However, Congress is not capable of anticipating every type of transaction that taxpayers might engage, so most of the statutes in the Code contain very general language. Because of the general language contained in the Code, both administrative and judicial interpretations are necessary to apply the tax law to specific situations and transactions. Thus, the regulations and rulings of the IRS and the decisions of the courts are an integral part of the federal income tax law. For a detailed discussion of tax law sources, see Chapter I15 (Chapter C1 of the *Comprehensive* edition). Topic Review I1-3 provides an overview of the tax law sources.

ENACTMENT OF A TAX LAW

OBJECTIVE 6

Describe the legislative process for the enactment of the tax law

Under the U.S. Constitution, the House of Representatives is responsible for initiating new tax legislation. However, tax bills may also originate in the Senate as riders to nontax legislative proposals. Often, major tax proposals are initiated by the President and accompanied by a Treasury Department study or proposal, and then introduced into Congress by one or more representatives from the President's political party.

ADDITIONAL COMMENT

In 2001, the chairman of the House Ways and Means Committee was Rep. William Thomas of California, and the chairman of the Senate Finance Committee was Sen. Max Baucus of Montana.

STEPS IN THE LEGISLATIVE PROCESS

The specific steps in the legislative process are discussed below and are summarized in Table I1-2. These steps typically include:

1. A tax bill is introduced in the House of Representatives and is referred to the House Ways and Means Committee.
2. The proposal is considered by the House Ways and Means Committee, and public hearings are held. Testimony may be given by members of professional groups such as the American Institute of CPAs and the American Bar Association and from various special-interest groups.
3. The tax bill is voted on by the House Ways and Means Committee and, if approved, is forwarded to the House of Representatives for a vote. Amendments to the bill from individual members of the House of Representatives are generally not allowed.

Topic Review I1-3

Tax Law Sources

Source	Key Points	Weight of Authority
LEGISLATIVE		
Internal Revenue Code	Contains provisions governing income, estate and gift, employment, alcohol, tobacco, and excise taxes.	Serves as the highest legislative authority for tax research, planning, and compliance activities.
ADMINISTRATIVE		
Treasury Regulations	Represents interpretations of the tax code by the Secretary of the Treasury. Regulations may be initially issued in proposed, temporary, and final form and are interpretative or legislative.	Legislative regulations have a higher degree of authority than interpretative regulations. Proposed regulations do not have authoritative weight.
IRS Rulings	The IRS issues Revenue Rulings (letter rulings or published rulings), Revenue Procedures, Information Releases, and Technical Advice Memoranda.	These pronouncements reflect the IRS's interpretation of the law and do not have the same level of scope and authority as Treasury Regulations.
JUDICIAL		
Judicial doctrines	Judicial doctrines are concepts that have evolved from Supreme Court cases that are used by the courts to decide tax issues. Examples include substance over form, tax benefit rule, and constructive receipt.	Judicial doctrines that evolve from Supreme Court cases have substantial weight of authority because a finding authority because a finding the force and effect of law.
Judicial interpretations	Tax cases are initially considered by a trial court (i.e., the Tax Court, a Federal district court, or the U.S. Court of Federal Claims). Either the taxpayer or the IRS may appeal to an appeals court. A final appeal is to the U.S. Supreme Court.	A trial court must abide by the precedents set by the court of appeals of the same jurisdiction. An appeals court is not required to follow the decisions of another court of appeals. A Supreme Court decision must be followed by the IRS, taxpayers, and the lower courts.

▼ TABLE I1-2
Steps in the Legislative Process

1. Treasury studies prepared on needed tax reform
2. President makes proposals to Congress
3. House Ways and Means Committee prepares House bill
4. Approval of House bill by the House of Representatives
5. Senate Finance Committee prepares Senate bill
6. Approval of Senate bill by the Senate
7. Compromise bill approved by a Joint Conference Committee
8. Approval of Joint Conference Committee bill by both the House and Senate
9. Approval or veto of legislation by the President
10. New tax law and amendments incorporated into the Code

4. If passed by the House, the bill is forwarded to the Senate for consideration by the Senate Finance Committee, and public hearings are held.
5. The tax bill approved by the Senate Finance Committee may be substantially different from the House of Representatives' version.
6. The Senate Finance Committee reports the Senate bill to the Senate for consideration. The Senate generally permits amendments (e.g., new provisions) to be offered on the Senate floor.
7. If approved by the Senate, both the Senate and House bills are sent to a Joint Conference Committee consisting of an equal number of members from the Senate and the House of Representatives.
8. The Senate and House bills are reconciled in the Joint Conference Committee. This process of reconciliation generally involves substantial compromise if the provisions of both bills are different. A final bill is then resubmitted to the House and Senate for approval.
9. If the Joint Conference Committee bill is approved by the House and Senate, it is sent to the President for approval or veto.
10. A presidential veto may be overturned if a two-thirds majority vote is obtained in both the House and Senate.
11. Committee reports are prepared by the staffs of the House Ways and Means Committee, the Senate Finance Committee, and the Joint Conference Committee as the bill progresses through Congress. These reports help to explain the new law before the Treasury Department drafts regulations on the tax law changes as well as to explain the intent of Congress for passing the new law.

ADDITIONAL COMMENT

The corridors near Congress's tax-writing rooms are called "Gucci Gulch," so named for the designer clothing worn by many of the lobbyists who congregate there when a tax bill is being considered.

HISTORICAL NOTE

The only practicing CPA ever elected to the U.S. Congress is Joe Dio Guardi. He was elected in 1984 from Westchester County, New York.

ADMINISTRATION OF THE TAX LAW AND TAX PRACTICE ISSUES

ORGANIZATION OF THE INTERNAL REVENUE SERVICE

OBJECTIVE 7

Describe the administrative procedures under the tax law

The **IRS** is the branch of the Treasury Department that is responsible for administering the federal tax law. It is organized on a national, regional, district, and service center basis. The responsibilities and functions of the various administrative branches include the following:

- The Commissioner of Internal Revenue, appointed by the President, is the chief officer of the IRS. This individual is supported by the Chief Counsel's office, which is responsible for preparing the government's case for litigation of tax disputes.
- The National Office includes a deputy commissioner, a series of assistants to the commissioner, a chief inspector, and a chief counsel. A significant responsibility of the National Office is to process ruling requests and to prepare revenue procedures that assist taxpayers with compliance matters.
- Regional commissioners in the four IRS regions are responsible for the settlement of administrative appeals for disputed tax deficiencies.
- District directors supervise the performance of IRS audits and collection of delinquent taxes in 33 districts.
- Ten service centers perform tax return processing work. They also select tax returns for audit.

In 1998, the IRS Restructuring and Reform Act of 1998 (Act) was enacted with a major objective of reforming the manner in which the IRS administers the tax system. The taxpaying public has been increasingly crititcal of the IRS, especially in the allegedly insensitive and strong-arm tactics used against taxpayers. Therefore, the Act places a greater emphasis on serving the public and meeting taxpayer needs. While the Act mandates substantial organizational and operational changes to the IRS, only time will tell if this legislation will be successful. Details of the Act are outside the scope of this textbook.

ADDITIONAL COMMENT

A survey of members of the American Institute of CPAs found that more than half of the 1,036 members who responded had an unfavorable opinion of the IRS, unchanged from a survey of three years prior. However, the accountants gave the IRS good marks for courtesy and a willingness to solve problems.

ENFORCEMENT PROCEDURES

All tax returns are initially checked for mathematical accuracy and items that are clearly erroneous. The Form W-2 amounts (e.g., wages, and so on), Form 1099 information return amounts (e.g., relating to dividend and interest payments, and so on) and other forms filed with the IRS are checked against the amounts reported on the tax return. If differences are noted, the IRS Center merely sends the taxpayer a bill for the corrected amount of tax and a statement of the differences. In some instances, the difference is due to a classification error by the IRS, and the additional assessment can be resolved by written correspondence. A refund check may be sent to the taxpayer if an overpayment of tax has been made.

EXAMPLE I1-17 ▶ Bart is an author of books and properly reports royalties on Schedule C (Profit or Loss from Business). The IRS computer matching of the Form 1099 information returns from the publishing companies incorrectly assumes that the royalties should be reported on Schedule E (Supplemental Income and Loss). If the IRS sends the taxpayer a statement of the difference and an adjusted tax bill, this matter (including the abatement of added tax, interest, and penalties) should be resolved by correspondence with the IRS. ◀

ADDITIONAL COMMENT

Individuals may call 800-366-4484 to report misconduct of IRS employees.

SELECTION OF RETURNS FOR AUDIT

The U.S. tax system is based on self-assessment and voluntary compliance. However, enforcement by the IRS is essential to maintain the integrity of the tax system. The IRS uses both computers and experienced personnel to select returns for examination. With respect to the use of the computer, a **Discriminant Function System (DIF)** is used to classify returns to be selected for audit. The DIF system generates a "score" for a return based on the potential for the return to generate additional tax revenue. After returns are scored under the DIF system, the returns are manually screened by experienced IRS personnel who decide which returns warrant further examination. In the aggregate, less than 1% of all individual returns are selected for examination each year. Some examples of situations where individuals are more likely to be audited include the following:

- Investments and trade or business expenses that produce significant tax losses
- Itemized deductions exceeding an average amount for the person's income level
- Filing of a refund claim by a taxpayer who has been previously audited, where substantial tax deficiencies have been assessed
- Individuals who are self-employed with substantial business income or income from a profession (e.g., a medical doctor)

ADDITIONAL COMMENT

A special task force has recommended that the percentage of returns audited be increased to 2.5%. Many individuals feel that the probability of being audited is so low as to be disregarded.

ETHICAL POINT

A CPA should not recommend a position to a client that exploits the IRS audit selection process.

AUDIT PROCEDURES. Audits of most individuals are handled through an **office audit procedure** in an office of the IRS. In most cases, an individual is asked to substantiate a particular deduction, credit, or income item (e.g., charitable contributions that appear to be excessive). The office audit procedure does not involve a complete audit of all items on the return.

EXAMPLE I1-18 ▶ Brad obtains a divorce during the current year and reports a $30,000 deduction for alimony. The IRS may conduct an office audit to ascertain whether the amount is properly deductible as alimony and does not represent a disguised property settlement to Brad's ex-wife. Brad may be asked to submit verification (e.g., a property settlement agreement between the spouses that designates the payments as alimony). ◀

KEY POINT

A taxpayer may appear on his or her own behalf before the IRS during an audit. An attorney or CPA in good standing is authorized to practice before the IRS upon the filing of a written statement that he or she is currently so qualified and is authorized to represent the taxpayer.

A **field audit procedure** often is used for corporations and individuals engaged in a trade or business. A field audit generally is broader in scope than the office audit (e.g., several items on the tax return may be reviewed). A field audit usually is conducted at the taxpayer's place of business or the office of his or her tax advisor.

Most large corporations are subject to annual audits. The year under audit may be several years prior to the current year because the corporation often will waive the statute of limitations pending the resolution of disputed issues.

STATUTE OF LIMITATIONS

REAL-WORLD EXAMPLE

Based on an IRS audit, the Mustang Ranch, Nevada's most famous legal bordello, was assessed some $13 million in taxes. When the amount owed could not be paid, the IRS sold the property to recoup the taxes.

Most taxpayers feel a sense of relief after they have prepared their income tax return and have mailed it to the IRS. However, the filing of the tax return is not necessarily the end of the story for that particular taxable year. It is possible, of course, that the IRS may select their tax return for audit after the return has been initially processed or a taxpayer may have filed an amended return to correct an error or omission.

Both the IRS and taxpayers can make corrections to a return after it has been originally filed. Fortunately, both only have a limited time period in which to make such corrections. This time period is called the **statute of limitations** and prevents either the taxpayer or the IRS from changing a filed tax return after the time period has expired. The general rule for the statute of limitations is three years from the later of the date the tax return was actually filed or its due date.[28] However, a six-year statute of limitations applies if the taxpayer omits items of gross income that in total exceed 25% of the gross income reported on the return.[29] The statute of limitations remains open indefinitely if a fraudulent return is filed or if no return is filed.[30]

EXAMPLE I1-19 ▶ Betty, a calendar-year taxpayer, is audited by the IRS in February 2002 for the tax year 1999. During the course of the audit, the IRS proposes additional tax for 1999 because Betty failed to substantiate certain travel and entertainment expense deductions. During the course of the audit, the IRS discovers that Betty failed to file a tax return for 1997, and in 1998 an item of gross income amounting to $26,000 was not reported. Gross income reported on the 1998 return was $72,000. Assuming Betty's 1999 return was filed on or before its due date (April 15, 2000), the IRS may assess a deficiency for 1999 because the three-year statute of limitations will not expire until April 15, 2003. A deficiency also may be assessed for the 1998 return because a six-year statute of limitations applies since the omission is more than 25% of the gross income reported on the return. A deficiency also may be assessed for 1997 as there is no statute of limitations for fraud. ◀

INTEREST

ADDITIONAL COMMENT

More than 150 penalties can be imposed on taxpayers. In fact, applying the penalties has become so complicated that the IRS is currently considering ways to consolidate and simplify them.

Interest accrues on both assessments of additional tax due and on refunds that the taxpayer receives from the government.[31] No interest is paid on a tax refund if the amount is refunded by the IRS within 45 days of the day prescribed for filing the return (e.g., April 15) determined without regard to extensions.[32] If a return is filed after the filing date, no interest is paid if the refund is made within 45 days of the date the return was filed.

EXAMPLE I1-20 ▶ Beverly, a calendar-year taxpayer, files her 2001 tax return on February 1, 2002, and requests a $500 refund. No interest accrues on the refund amount if the IRS sends the refund check to Beverly within 45 days of the due date (i.e., April 15, 2002). ◀

PENALTIES

ADDITIONAL COMMENT

In addition to the penalties listed on this page, the government also assesses penalties for civil fraud and criminal fraud. Criminal fraud carries a maximum penalty of $100,000, a prison sentence of up to five years, or both.

Various nondeductible penalties are imposed on the net tax due for failure to comply, including

- ▶ A penalty of 5% per month (or fraction thereof) subject to a maximum of 25% for failure to file a tax return[33]
- ▶ A penalty of 0.5% per month (or fraction thereof) up to a maximum of 25% for failure to pay the tax that is due[34]

---

[28] Secs. 6501(a) and (b)(1). Similar rules apply to claims for a refund filed by the taxpayer. Section 6511(a) requires that a refund claim be filed within three years of the date the return was filed or within two years of the date the tax was paid, whichever is later.

[29] Sec. 6501(e). See also *Stephen G. Colestock*, 102 T.C. 380 (1994), where the Tax Court ruled that the extended six-year limitation period applied to a married couple's entire tax liability for the tax year at issue, not just to items that constituted substantial omissions of gross income. Thus, the IRS was able to assert an increased deficiency and additional penalties attributable to a disallowed depreciation deduction.

[30] Sec. 6501(c).

[31] Sec. 6621(a). The rate is adjusted four times a year by the Treasury Department based on the current interest rate for short-term federal obligations. The interest rate individual taxpayers must pay to the IRS on underpayments of tax is the federal short-term rate plus three percentage points. The interest rate paid to taxpayers on overpayments of tax is the federal short-term rate plus two percentage points. The annual interest rate on noncorporate underpayments and overpayments for the period July 1, 2001 through December 31, 2001 was 7%.

[32] Sec. 6611(e).

[33] Sec. 6651(a)(1). The penalty assessed may be very small in some instances even though the taxpayer owes a large tax bill for the year because penalties are imposed on the net tax due. The percentages are increased to 15% per month (or fraction thereof) up to a maximum of 75% if the penalty is for fraudulent failure to file under Sec. 6651(f).

[34] Sec. 6651(a)(2). If the failure to file penalty (5%) and the failure to pay the tax penalty (0.5%) are both applicable, the failure to file penalty is reduced by the failure to pay penalty per Sec. 6651(c)(1). Further, the penalty is increased to 1% per month after the IRS notifies the taxpayer that it will levy on the taxpayer's assets.

- An accuracy-related penalty of 20% of the underpayment for items such as negligence or disregard of rules or regulations, any substantial understatement of income tax, or any substantial misstatement of valuation.[35]
- A 75% penalty for fraud[36]
- A penalty based on the current interest rate for underpayment of estimated taxes[37]

ADDITIONAL COMMENT

Pete Rose, major league baseball's all-time hit leader, was sent to prison in 1990 for income tax evasion.

ADMINISTRATIVE APPEAL PROCEDURES

If an IRS agent issues a deficiency assessment, the taxpayer may make an appeal to the IRS Appeals Division. Some disputes involve a gray area (e.g., a situation where some courts have held for the IRS whereas other courts have held for the taxpayer on facts that are similar to the disputed issue). In such a case, the taxpayer may be able to negotiate a compromise settlement (e.g., a percentage of the disputed tax amount plus interest and penalties) with the Appeals Division based on the "hazards of litigation" (i.e., the probability of winning or losing the case if it is litigated).

COMPONENTS OF A TAX PRACTICE

OBJECTIVE 8

Describe the components of a tax practice and understand the basic tax research process and computer applications

Tax practice is a rapidly growing field that provides substantial opportunities for tax specialists in public accounting, law, and industry. The tasks performed by a tax professional may range from the preparation of a simple Form 1040 for an individual to the conduct of tax research and planning for highly complex business situations. Tax practice consists of the following activities:

- Tax compliance and procedure (i.e., tax return preparation and representation of a client in administrative proceedings before the IRS)
- Tax research
- Tax planning and consulting
- Financial planning

TYPICAL MISCONCEPTION

Many people believe that a tax practitioner should serve in the capacity of a neutral, unbiased expert. They tend to forget that tax practitioners are being paid to represent their clients' interests. A tax practitioner may sometimes recommend a position that is defensible, but where the weight of authority is on the side of the IRS.

TAX COMPLIANCE AND PROCEDURE

Preparation of tax returns is a significant component of tax practice. Tax practitioners often prepare federal, state, and local tax returns for individuals, corporations, estates, trusts, and so on. In larger corporations, the tax return preparation (i.e., compliance) function usually is performed by a company's internal tax department staff. In such a case, a CPA or other tax practitioner may assist the client with the tax research and planning aspects of their tax practice, and may even review their return before it is filed.

An important part of tax practice consists of assisting the client in negotiations with the IRS. If a client is audited, the practitioner acts as the client's representative in discussions with the IRS agent. If a tax deficiency is assessed, the practitioner assists the client if an administrative appeal is contemplated with the IRS's Appellate Division. In most instances, an attorney is retained if litigation is being considered.

TAX RESEARCH

Tax research is the search for the best possible defensibly correct solution to a problem involving either a completed transaction (e.g., a sale of property) or a proposed transaction (e.g., a proposed merger of two corporations). Research involves each of the following steps:

[35] Sec. 6662.
[36] Sec. 6663.
[37] Sec. 6654.

SELF-STUDY QUESTION

Do large national CPA firms generally stress the importance of tax research in connection with tax-return preparation or tax planning?

ANSWER

The large CPA firms emphasize their skills in tax planning. Sometimes a slight alteration of a proposed transaction can save the client substantial tax dollars. This is high-value-added work and can be billed at premium rates.

- Determine the facts.
- Identify the issue(s).
- Identify and analyze the tax law sources (i.e., code provisions, Treasury Regulations, administrative rulings, and court cases).
- Evaluate nontax (e.g., business) implications.
- Solve the problem.
- Communicate the findings to the client.

Tax research may be conducted in connection with tax return preparation, tax planning, or procedural activities. A more thorough discussion of tax research is presented in Chapter I15.

TAX PLANNING AND CONSULTING

Tax planning involves the process of structuring one's affairs so as to minimize the amount of taxes *and* maximize the after-tax return. Thus, optimal tax planning is *not* to just pay the least amount of tax but to maximize after-tax cash flows. A text on tax research and planning has delineated the following tax planning principles:[38]

- Keep sufficient records.
- Forecast the effect of future events.
- Support the plan with a sound business purpose.
- Base the plan on sound legal authorities.
- Do not carry a good plan too far.
- Make the plan flexible.
- Integrate the tax plan with other factors in decision making.
- Conduct research to learn whether a similar plan has previously proved unsuccessful (e.g., a court case involving similar facts may have upheld the IRS's position).
- Consider the "maximum" risk exposure of the client (e.g., if the plan is subsequently challenged by the IRS and the tax treatment is disallowed, what is the economic impact upon the taxpayer?).
- Consider the effect of timing (e.g., whether it is more beneficial to take a deduction in one year versus another).
- Shape the plan to the client's needs and desires.

ADDITIONAL COMMENT

Several national accounting firms have divided their tax departments into two basic groups, consulting and compliance. The tax consultants work with clients in tax planning and consulting matters and do not prepare tax returns. Tax returns are prepared by the compliance staff.

CPAs and attorneys frequently are engaged by their clients to perform consulting services to optimize the client's tax situation. For example, a major corporation client is considering the acquisition of a major international corporation and wants to make sure that the tax implications of such an acquisition are properly managed. The CPA will be engaged to perform a thorough review of the transaction to ensure that the client is fully aware of the tax results of the acquisition, and possibly may request an advance ruling from the IRS.

Because of the importance of planning in tax practice, subsequent chapters in this text include a separate section on tax planning to discuss issues that are related to the topical coverage. These tax planning principles should be kept in mind when attempting to use the tax planning recommendations. Also, a systematic approach to tax planning developed by two noted tax academicians, Myron Scholes and Mark Wolfson, is discussed in Chapter I18.

FINANCIAL PLANNING

A relatively new field for tax professionals is that of financial planning for individual clients. Since taxes are an integral part of any financial plan and since a tax specialist regularly meets with his or her clients (filing returns and other tax matters), the area of finan-

[38] Fred W. Norwood et al., *Federal Taxation: Research, Planning, and Procedures,* 2nd ed. (Englewood Cliffs, NJ: Prentice Hall, 1979), pp. 215–216.

cial planning has become increasingly a part of tax practice. The typical steps in performing a financial planning engagement include the following steps:

- Determine the client's financial goals and objectives
- Review the client's insurance coverage for adequacy and appropriateness
- Recommend an investment strategy, including risk analysis and asset allocation
- Review tax returns to ensure that, through proper tax planning, the client is maximizing his or her after-tax cash flow
- Review the client's retirement plans to assure compliance with the law and possible new alternatives
- Review all documents related to estate and gift planning and work with the client's attorney to minimize all transfer taxes and fulfill the client's objectives.

COMPUTER APPLICATIONS IN TAX PRACTICE

KEY POINT

The use of computers has become very important in tax practice ranging from tax return preparation to tax research. It is essential that students having an interest in taxation develop advanced computer skills.

TAX RETURN PREPARATION

To prepare tax returns, most tax practitioners purchase tax preparation software from companies such as Commerce Clearing House or Intuit. This software allows the preparation of accurate and professional-looking tax returns. A word of caution, however, is in order. As with any computer software, the preparation of tax returns using the computer requires as much knowledge and expertise from the preparer as doing the returns by hand. A recent trend in tax return preparation is the **electronic filing** of tax returns, i.e., a "paperless" tax return. Taxpayers send their returns electronically to the IRS for processing, thereby saving enormous amounts of paper and, perhaps, reducing human error. Computerized tax return software, *Tax Cut,* is available for use with this textbook.

ADDITIONAL COMMENT

The Volunteer Income Tax Assistance (VITA) program sponsored by the IRS is aimed at taxpayers who need help with their federal return but cannot afford to pay for the assistance. Many college students put their textbook knowledge to work through VITA programs.

TAX PLANNING APPLICATIONS

Performing tax planning for clients involves the evaluation of alternative courses of action. This evaluation process can be very time-consuming because of the tax calculations necessary to arrive at an optimal solution. The computer has become an essential tool in this process because of the speed in which the tax calculations can be made. Many tax professionals now use sophisticated software to perform tax planning for their clients. A prime example of the use of the computer in tax planning has been in deciding whether a taxpayer should invest in a Roth Individual Retirement Account (Roth IRA) or a regular IRA (see Chapter I9 for more details on IRAs). There are many factors to consider, including current and projected tax rates, current and projected level of income, etc. With the computer, a tax professional can vary the assumptions and create a number of alternatives within a relatively short period of time. To perform this task by hand would require an enormous commitment of time. As with most aspects of life, the impact of the computer on tax planning has been highly significant and will only increase in the future.

TAX RESEARCH APPLICATIONS

ADDITIONAL COMMENT

When performing LEXIS research, the researcher need not be concerned with how an editor might have indexed a court case because the LEXIS research is performed independently. Every word of virtually every case is available in the LEXIS service.

Computerized information-retrieval systems are used in tax research and are rapidly replacing books as the principal source of tax-related information. There are three types of computerized information-retrieval systems: (1) electronic or "on-line" services, (2) CD-ROM services, and (3) Internet services. As to on-line services, the oldest and most well-known data base is LEXIS, which was developed by Mead Data Central. The database for these computerized systems contains in full text the same tax law sources (e.g., cases, rulings, committee reports, regulations, and commentary and analysis) that are included in a manual tax service. The system is entered by using a keyword or phrase or by entering a Code section number or case name. Researchers need to be imaginative in thinking of search requests; a computerized system will not locate an authority unless it contains the exact wording the researcher specifies, even though it contains synonymous terms.

EXAMPLE I1-21 ▶ A researcher is interested in whether a certain expenditure for clothing is deductible under Sec. 162 as a uniform expense. The researcher might instruct the computer to retrieve all cases containing the words "uniform" and "Sec. 162" in close proximity to each other. This search will turn up only cases containing those words. Cases using the words "work clothing" will not be retrieved. A more comprehensive search will take place if the researcher instructs the computerized system to look for either "uniform" or "work clothing" within close proximity to "Sec. 162." ◀

ADDITIONAL COMMENT

Using LEXIS, a tax researcher even has the ability to find decisions in which a particular judge concurred or dissented.

A number of tax services, including CCH's *Federal Tax Service,* RIA's *Federal Tax Coordinator 2d (RIA On Point),* CCH's *Standard Federal Tax Reporter (CCH Access)* and BNA's *Tax Management Portfolios* are available on CD-ROM (compact disc read-only memory). The materials are organized the same as in the paper services. The CD-ROMs generally are updated monthly. Information is retrieved from the CD-ROMs by typing key words into the computer. For example, one may locate the index on the disk, consult the index, and then refer to the portion of the disk that discusses the tax consequences of a related issue. The disks, of course, allow pages and pages of information to be stored in practically no space and avoid the need to file new pages. Extensive material is available on the CCH *"Access"* CD-ROM. For example, the CD-ROM product includes *Standard Federal Tax Reporter, State Tax Reports,* letter rulings and IRS positions, Revenue Rulings and Revenue Procedures, IRS publications, tax forms and instructions, and court cases dating back to 1913. Tax-oriented periodicals often provide reviews of computer-based or CD-ROM research products.[39]

Another source of tax materials that is destined to become even more useful and important are materials on the Internet.[40] The principal Internet services are RIA's *Checkpoint* and CCH's *Tax Internet Research Network*. These commercial Internet services contain a wide range of materials available to tax researchers who subscribe to the service. In addition, the IRS has a home page (www.irs.ustreas.gov) that taxpayers can access for forms, publications, and other related materials. All of the major accounting firms and many other tax organizations have home pages that allow users to access a myriad of tax information.

PROBLEM MATERIALS

DISCUSSION QUESTIONS

I1-1 The Supreme Court in 1895 ruled that the income tax was unconstitutional because the tax needed to be apportioned among the states in proportion to their populations. Why would the requirement of proportionality be so difficult to administer?

I1-2 Why was pay-as-you-go withholding needed in 1943?

I1-3 Congressman Patrick indicates that he is opposed to new tax legislative proposals that call for a flat tax rate that are currently being considered by Congress because the new taxing structure would not be in accord with our traditional practice of taxing those who have the ability to pay the tax. Discuss the position of the congressman, giving consideration to tax rate structures (e.g., progressive, proportional, and regressive) and the concept of equity.

I1-4 The Governor of your state stated in a recent political speech that he has never supported any income tax increases as the tax rates have remained at the same level during his entire term of office. Yet, you believe that you are paying more tax this year than in previous years even though your income has not increased. How can both you and the Governor be correct? In other words, is it possible for the government to raise taxes without raising tax rates?

---

[39] See Editorial Staff, "CD-ROM Research Products Reviewed by Practitioners," *The Journal of Taxation,* July 1994, pp. 28–38. Also, for a thorough discussion of computerized tax research, see William A. Raabe, Gerald E. Whittenburg, and John C. Bost, *West's Federal Tax Research,* 5th Ed. (Minneapolis/St. Paul, MN: West Publishing Co., 2000), Chapters 13 and 14.

[40] For a guide to tax information on the internet, link to the website of the American Taxation Association at www.atasection.org under Tax Directories.

I1-5 Carmen has computed that her average tax rate is 18% and her marginal tax rate is 27% for the current year. She is considering whether to make a charitable contribution to her church before the end of the tax year. Which tax rate is of greater significance in measuring the tax effect for her decision? Explain.

I1-6 Why are the gift and estate taxes called wealth transfer taxes? What is the tax base for computing each of these taxes?

I1-7 Cathy, who is single, makes gifts of $15,000 to each of her two children.
a. Is Cathy or her children primarily liable for the gift tax on the two gifts?
b. If Cathy has never made a taxable gift in prior years, is a gift tax due on the two gifts?

I1-8 Carlos inherits 100 shares of Allied Corporation stock from his father. The stock cost his father $8,000 and had a $10,000 FMV on the date of his father's death. The alternate valuation date was not elected. What is Carlos's tax basis for the Allied stock when it is received from the estate?

I1-9 Most estates are not subject to the federal estate tax.
a. Why is this the case?
b. Do you believe most estates should be subject to the federal estate tax?

I1-10 Indicate which of the following taxes are generally progressive, proportional, or regressive:
a. State income taxes
b. Federal estate tax
c. Corporate state franchise tax
d. Property taxes
e. State sales taxes

I1-11 Carolyn operates a small business as a sole proprietor (unincorporated). Carolyn is considering operating the business as a corporation because of nontax advantages (e.g., limited liability and ability to raise outside capital). From the standpoint of paying Social Security taxes, would the total Social Security taxes increase or decrease if the business is incorporated? Why?

I1-12 The three different levels of government (federal, state, and local) must impose taxes to carry out their functions. For each of the types of taxes below, discuss which level of government primarily uses that type of tax.
a. Property taxes
b. Excise taxes
c. Sales taxes
d. Income taxes
e. Employment taxes

I1-13 A "good" tax structure has four characteristics.
a. Briefly discuss the four characteristics.
b. Using the four characteristics, evaluate the following tax structures:
1. Federal income tax
2. State sales tax
3. Local ad valorem property tax

I1-14 Two commonly-recognized measures of the fairness of an income tax structure are "horizontal equity" and "vertical equity."
a. Discuss what is meant by horizontal equity and vertical equity as it pertains to the income tax.
b. Why is it so difficult to design a "fair" tax structure?

I1-15 The primary objective of the federal income tax law is to raise revenue. What are its secondary objectives?

I1-16 If the objectives of the federal tax system are multifaceted and include raising revenues, providing investment incentives, encouraging certain industries, and meeting desired social objectives, is it possible to achieve a simplified tax system? Explain.

I1-17 Distinguish between *taxpaying entities* and *flow-through entities* from the standpoint of the federal income tax law.

I1-18 Discuss what is meant by the term "double taxation" of corporations. Develop an example of double taxation using a corporation and shareholder.

I1-19 Limited liability companies (LLCs) are very popular today as a form of organization. Assume a client asks you to explain what this new type of organization is all about. Prepare a brief description of the federal income tax aspects of LLCs.

I1-20 Why is a thorough knowledge of sources of tax law so important for a professional person who works in the tax area?

I1-21 The Internal Revenue Code is the most authoritative source of income tax law. In trying to resolve an income tax question, however, a tax researcher also consults administrative rulings (Income Tax Regulations, Revenue Rulings, etc.) and court decisions. Why wouldn't the tax researcher just consult the Code since it is the highest authority? Similarly, why is there a need for administrative rulings and court decisions?

I1-22 Congressional committee reports are an important source of information concerning the legislative enactment of tax law.
a. Name the three Congressional committee reports that are issued in connection with a new tax bill.
b. Of what importance are Congressional committee reports to tax practitioners?

I1-23 What is the primary service function provided by the National Office of the IRS?

I1-24 What types of taxpayers are more likely to be audited by the IRS?

I1-25 Anya is concerned that she will be audited by the IRS.
a. Under what circumstances is it possible that the IRS will review each line item on her tax return?
b. Is it likely that all items on Anya's return will be audited?

I1-26 a. What does the term "hazards of litigation" mean in the context of taxation?
b. Why would the IRS or a taxpayer settle or compromise a case based on the "hazards of litigation"?

I1-27 If a taxpayer files his or her tax return and receives a tax refund from the IRS, does this mean that the IRS feels that the return is correct and will not be subject to audit?

I1-28 State the statute of limitations for transactions involving:
a. Fraud (e.g., failure to file a tax return)
b. Disallowance of tax deduction items
c. The omission of rental income equal to greater than 25% of the taxpayer's gross income

I1-29 In reference to tax research, what is meant by *the best possible defensibly correct solution?*

I1-30 The profession of tax practice involves four principal areas of activity. Discuss these four areas.

I1-31 Many tax professionals have moved into the field of financial planning for their clients.
a. How do taxes impact financial planning for a client?
b. Why do tax professionals have a perfect opportunity to perform financial planning for their clients?

I1-32 Is the principal goal of tax planning to absolutely minimize the amount of taxes that a taxpayer must pay?

I1-33 Explain how a computer can assist a tax practitioner in tax planning activities and making complex tax calculations.

PROBLEMS

I1-34 *Tax Rates.* Latesha, a single taxpayer, had the following income and deductions for the tax year 2002:

INCOME:	Salary	$ 60,000
	Business Income	25,000
	Dividends from stocks	10,000
	Tax-exempt bond interest	5,000
	TOTAL INCOME	100,000
DEDUCTIONS:	Business expenses	$ 9,800
	Itemized deductions	20,000
	Personal exemption	3,000
	TOTAL DEDUCTIONS	32,800

a. Compute Latesha's taxable income and federal tax liability for 2002.
b. Compute Latesha's marginal, average, and effective tax rates.
c. For tax planning purposes, which of the three rates in b. is the most important?

I1-35 *Marginal Tax Rate.* Jill and George are married and file a joint return. They expect to have $350,000 of taxable income in the next year and are considering whether to purchase a personal residence that would provide additional tax deductions of $80,000 for mortgage interest and real estate taxes.
a. What is their marginal tax rate for purposes of making this decision? (Ignore the effects of a phase-out of personal exemptions and itemized deductions (see Chapters I2 and I7, respectively).
b. What is the tax savings if the residence is acquired?

I1-36 *Gift Tax.* Chuck, a married taxpayer, makes the following gifts during the current year (2002): $20,000 to his church, $30,000 to his daughter, and $25,000 to his wife.
a. What is the amount of Chuck's taxable gifts for the current year (assuming that he does not elect to split the gifts with his spouse).
b. How would your answer to Part a change if a gift-splitting election were made?

I1-37 *Estate Tax.* Clay dies in 2002 and has a gross estate valued at $1,800,000. Six months after his death, the gross assets are valued at $2,000,000. The estate incurs funeral and administration expenses of $125,000. It also has debts amounting to $75,000, and Clay bequeaths $500,000 of the property to his wife. During his life Clay made no taxable gifts.
a. What is the amount of Clay's taxable estate?
b. What is the tax base for computing Clay's estate tax?
c. What is the amount of estate tax owed if the tentative estate tax (before credits) is $386,800?

d. Alternatively, if, six months after his death, the gross assets in Clay's estate declined in value to $1,500,000, can the administrator of Clay's estate elect the alternate valuation date? What are the important factors that the administrator should consider as to whether the alternate valuation date should be elected?

I1-38 ***Comparison of Tax Entities.***

a. Keith Thomas began a new consulting business in January 1, 2002. He organized the business as a C corporation, KT Inc. During 2002, the corporation was reasonably successful and generated revenues of $1,050,000. KT, Inc. had operating expenses of $800,000 before any payments to Keith. During 2002, KT, Inc. paid dividends to Keith in the amount of $250,000. Assume that Keith had other income (interest, dividends, etc.) of $30,000, itemized deductions of $40,000, is married (wife has no income) and has no children. Compute the total tax liability of KT, Inc. and Keith for 2002. Ignore any phaseouts of itemized deductions or personal exemptions.
b. Instead of organizing the consulting business as a C corporation, assume Keith organized the business as a limited liability company, KT, LLC. KT, LLC made a distribution of $250,000 to Keith during 2002. Compute the total tax liability of KT, LLC and Keith for 2002. Ignore any phaseouts of itemized deductions or personal exemptions.

I1-39 ***Interest and Penalties.*** In 2001, Paul, who is single, has a comfortable salary from his job as well as income from his investment portfolio. However, he is habitually late in filing his federal income tax return. He did not file his 2001 income tax return until November 30, 2002 (due date was April 15, 2002) and no extensions of time to file the return were filed. Below are amounts from his 2001 return:

Taxable income	$140,000
Total tax liability on taxable income	38,080
Total federal tax withheld from his salary	30,000

Paul sent a check with his return to the IRS for the balance due of $8,080. He is relieved that he has completed his filing requirement for 2001 *and* has met his financial obligation to the government for 2001.

Has Paul met *all* of his financial obligations to the IRS for 2001? If not, what additional amounts will Paul be liable to pay to the IRS?

I1-40 ***IRS Audits.*** Which of the following individuals is most likely to be audited:

a. Connie has a $20,000 net loss from her unincorporated business (a cattle ranch). She also received a $200,000 salary as an executive of a corporation.
b. Craig has AGI of $20,000 from wages and uses the standard deduction.
c. Dale fails to report $120 of dividends from a stock investment. His taxable income is $40,000 and he has no other unusually large itemized deductions or business expenses. A Form 1099 is reported to the IRS.

I1-41 ***Statute of Limitations.*** In April 2002, Dan is audited by the IRS for the year 2000. During the course of the audit, the agent discovers that Dan's deductions for business travel and entertainment are unsubstantiated and a $600 deficiency assessment is proposed for 2000. The agent also discovers that Dan failed to report $40,000 of gross business income on his 1998 return. Gross income of $60,000 was reported in 1998. The agent also discovers that Dan failed to file a tax return in 1997.

Will the statute of limitations prevent the IRS from issuing a deficiency assessment for 2000, 1998, or 1997? Explain.

TAX STRATEGY PROBLEM

I1-42 Pedro Bourbone is the founder and owner of a highly successful small business and, over the past several years, has accumulated a significant amount of personal wealth. His portfolio of stocks and bonds is worth nearly $5,000,000 and generates income from dividends and interest of nearly $250,000 per year. With his salary from the business and his dividends and interest, Pedro has taxable income of approximately $600,000 per year and is clearly in the top individual marginal tax bracket. Pedro is married and has three children, ages 16, 14, and 12. Neither his wife nor his children are employed and have no income. Pedro has come to you as his CPA to discuss ways to reduce his individual tax liability as well as to discuss the potential estate tax upon his death. You mention the possibility of making gifts each year to his children. Explain how annual gifts to his children will reduce both his income during lifetime and his estate tax at death.

CASE STUDY PROBLEM

I1-43 John Gemstone, a wealthy client, has recently been audited by the IRS. The agent has questioned the following deduction items on Mr. Gemstone's tax return for the year under review:

- A $10,000 loss deduction on the rental of his beach cottage.
- A $20,000 charitable contribution deduction for the donation of a painting to a local art museum. The agent has questioned whether the painting is overvalued.
- A $15,000 loss deduction from the operation of a cattle breeding ranch. The agent is concerned that the ranch is not a legitimate business (i.e., is a hobby).

Your supervisor has requested that you represent Mr. Gemstone in his discussions with the IRS.

a. What additional questions should you ask Mr. Gemstone in an attempt to substantiate the deductibility of the above items?

b. What tax research procedures might be applied to build the best possible case for your client?

RESEARCH PROBLEM

I1-44 Read the following two cases and explain why the Supreme Court reached different conclusions for cases involving similar facts and issues:

- *CIR v. Court Holding Co.*, 33 AFTR 593, 45-1 USTC ¶9215 (USSC, 1945)
- *U.S. v. Cumberland Public Service Co.*, 38 AFTR 978, 50-1 USTC ¶9129 (USSC, 1950)

CHAPTER 2

DETERMINATION OF TAX

LEARNING OBJECTIVES

After studying this chapter, you should be able to

1. Use the tax formula to compute an individual's taxable income
2. Determine the amount allowable for the standard deduction
3. Determine the amount and the correct number of personal and dependency exemptions
4. Determine the amount of child credit
5. Determine the filing status of individuals
6. Explain the tax formula for corporations
7. Explain the basic concepts of property transactions

CHAPTER OUTLINE

Formula for Individual Income Tax...2-2
Deductions from Adjusted Gross Income...2-7
Determining the Amount of Tax...2-18
Corporate Tax Formula and Rates ...2-24
Treatment of Capital Gains and Losses...2-26
Tax Planning Considerations...2-28
Compliance and Procedural Considerations...2-31

Each year, over 100 million individuals and married couples file tax forms on which they compute their federal income tax. The income tax is imposed "on the taxable income of every individual."[1] The amount of tax actually owed by an individual taxpayer is determined by applying a complex set of rules that together make up the income tax law. To understand the income tax, it is necessary to study the basic formula on which the income tax computation is based. Therefore, this chapter introduces the income tax formula and begins the development of its components. Because the income tax formula constitutes the basis of the income tax, most of the remainder of this book is an expansion of the formula. In addition to individual taxpayers, about 5 million corporations and 2 million partnerships file returns each year. These entities are discussed later in this chapter.

FORMULA FOR INDIVIDUAL INCOME TAX

OBJECTIVE 1

Use the tax formula to compute an individual's taxable income

BASIC FORMULA

Most individuals compute their income tax by using the formula illustrated in Table I2-1. The formula itself appears rather simple. However, the complexity of the income tax results from the intricate rules that must be applied in order to arrive at the amounts that enter into the formula.

The tax formula is incorporated into the income tax form. The tax formula illustrated in Table I2-1 can be compared with Form 1040, which is reproduced in Figure I2-1. Some differences exist between the tax formula below and the tax form itself. For example, taxpayers generally are not required to report exclusions (nontaxable income) on their tax returns. One exception does require taxpayers to disclose tax-exempt interest income. A number of separate schedules are used to report various types of income. For example, income from a sole proprietorship is reported on Schedule C where gross income from the business is reduced by related expenses which are deductions for AGI. Only the net income from the business actually appears on Form 1040. Also, Form 1040 is used to collect other taxes such as the self-employment tax. Hence, a line is provided for that tax on Form 1040. The main reason for differences between the formula and the form is administrative convenience. That is, there is no reason to require taxpayers to disclose income if the income is not subject to tax, it is simplier to report business income on a separate schedule, and it is convenient to collect other taxes on the same tax form.

ADDITIONAL COMMENT

"There is one difference between a tax collector and a taxidermist—the taxidermist leaves the hide." This is a quote from Mortimer Caplan, former Director of the Bureau of Internal Revenue, *Time,* Feb. 1, 1963.

ADDITIONAL COMMENT

The IRS estimates that the average taxpayer will spend 3 hours and 59 minutes for just preparing a Form 1040. When the estimated time for recordkeeping, learning about the law, and sending the form is added to the preparation time, the total time estimate jumps to 9 hours and 54 minutes. Each additional form and schedule adds even more time.

ADDITIONAL COMMENT

Comedian Jay Leno's explanation as to why the IRS calls it Form 1040 was, "For every $50 you earn, you get $10 and they get $40."

▼ TABLE I2-1
Tax Formula for Individuals

Income from whatever source derived	$xxx,xxx
Minus: Exclusions	(xxx)
Gross income	$ xx,xxx
Minus: Deductions for adjusted gross income	(xxx)
Adjusted gross income	$ x,xxx
Minus: Deductions from adjusted gross income:	
Greater of itemized deductions or the standard deduction	(xx)
Personal and dependency exemptions	(xx)
Taxable income	$ x,xxx
Times: Tax rate or rates (from tax table or schedule)	
Gross tax	$ xx
Minus: Credits and prepayments	(x)
Net tax payable or refund due	$ xx

[1] Sec. 1.

ADDITIONAL COMMENT

The Revenue Reconciliation Act of 1993 contains a provision that increased the amount of the checkoff for the Presidential Election Campaign Fund from $1 to $3. The amount was increased because too few individuals were using the checkoff and a shortfall in the fund was projected for the 1996 election cycle. The checkoff can be found on Form 1040 below the address section.

Examination of the formula reveals terms such as *gross income, exclusions, adjusted gross income, exemptions, gross tax,* and *credits*. These terms and others that make up the formula are defined below.

DEFINITIONS

INCOME. The term **income** includes both taxable and nontaxable income. Although the term is not specifically defined in the tax law, it does include income from any source.[2] Its meaning is close to that of the term **revenue**. However, it does not include a "return of capital." Thus, in the case of the sale of property, only the gain, not the entire sales proceeds, is viewed as income. This view extends to the sale of inventory, where gross profit is viewed as income, as opposed to the sale price. Also, no income results from any receipts received from borrowed funds.

TYPICAL MISCONCEPTION

It is easy to confuse an exclusion with a deduction. An exclusion is a source of income that is omitted from the tax base, whereas a deduction is an expense that is subtracted in arriving at taxable income. Both have the effect of reducing taxable income.

EXCLUSION. Not all income is taxable. An **exclusion** is any item of income that the tax law says is not taxable. Congress, over the years, has specifically excluded certain types of income from taxation for various social, economic, and political reasons. Chapter I4 discusses specific exclusions and the reasons for their existence. Table I2-2 contains a sample of the major exclusions from gross income.

ADDITIONAL COMMENT

One common exclusion, interest on state and local government bonds, must be reported on the tax return in amount only. It is not added to the other income items. In 1996, this reported tax-exempt interest totaled $49 billion.

GROSS INCOME. **Gross income** is income reduced by exclusions. In other words, it is income from taxable sources and is reported on the return (excluded income need not be disclosed). Section 61(a) contains a partial list of items of gross income. The items listed in Sec. 61(a) are shown in Table I2-3. Note, however, that Sec. 61(a) states that unless otherwise provided, "gross income means all income from whatever source derived, including (but not limited to)" the listed items of income. Thus, even though an item is omitted from the list does not necessarily mean that the item is excluded. For example, illegal income, although omitted from the list, is taxable.[3]

▼ TABLE I2-2
Major Exclusions

Gifts and inheritances
Life insurance proceeds
Welfare and certain other transfer payments
Certain scholarships and fellowships
Certain payments for injury and sickness
- Personal physical injury settlements
- Worker's compensation
- Medical expense reimbursements

Certain employee fringe benefits
- Health plan premiums
- Group term life insurance premiums (limited)
- Meals and lodging
- Employee discounts
- Dependent care

Certain foreign-earned income
Interest on state and local government bonds
Certain interest of Series EE bonds
Certain improvements by lessee to lessor's property
Child support payments
Property settlements pursuant to a divorce
Gain from the sale of a personal residence (limited)

[2] Sec. 61(a).

[3] *U.S. v. Manley S. Sullivan*, 6 AFTR 6753, 1 USTC ¶236 (USSC, 1927).

▼ **TABLE I2-3**
Gross Income Items Listed in Sec. 61(a)

Compensation for services, including fees, commissions, fringe benefits, and similar items
Gross income derived from business
Gains derived from dealings in property
Interest
Rents
Royalties
Dividends
Alimony and separate maintenance payments
Annuities
Income from life insurance and endowment contracts
Pensions
Income from the discharge of indebtedness
Distributive share of partnership gross income
Income in respect of a decedent
Income from an interest in an estate or trust

DEDUCTIONS FOR ADJUSTED GROSS INCOME. In general, taxpayers may deduct expenses that are specifically allowed by the tax law. Allowable deductions include business-type expenses, investment expenses, or personal expenses that are specifically provided for in the IRC, such as charitable contributions. Purely personal expenses generally are not deductible.

Deductions fall into two categories for individual taxpayers: deductions *for* adjusted gross income and deductions *from* adjusted gross income. In general, **deductions for adjusted gross income** are expenses connected with a trade or business. For the most part, **deductions from adjusted gross income** are personal expenses that Congress has chosen to allow. This classification scheme, however, is not always followed. For example, alimony paid, which is not a business expense, is a deduction *for* adjusted gross income. Table I2-4 contains a partial list of deductions *for* adjusted gross income that is taken from Sec. 62. Deductions for adjusted gross income are discussed further in Chapter I6 of this textbook.

ADDITIONAL COMMENT

In 1996, there were 42.6 million tax returns filed with AGI under $15,000, and 1.5 million returns filed with AGI over $200,000.

ADJUSTED GROSS INCOME. **Adjusted gross income (AGI)** is a measure of income that falls between gross income and taxable income. AGI is important because it is used in numerous other tax computations, especially to impose limitations. For example, AGI is used to establish floors for the medical deduction and casualty loss deduction and to establish a ceiling for the charitable contribution deduction.

ADDITIONAL COMMENT

In 1996, total AGI on all individual tax returns filed was just over $4.5 trillion, an increase of 8.9% from the previous year.

DEDUCTIONS FROM ADJUSTED GROSS INCOME. Section 62 lists deductions *for* AGI (see Table I2-4). Thus, any allowable deduction not listed in Sec. 62 is a deduction *from* AGI. The two categories of deductions *from* adjusted gross income are (1) itemized deductions or the standard deduction and (2) personal and dependency exemptions.[4] Deductions from AGI are discussed further in Chapter I7 of this textbook.

ITEMIZED DEDUCTIONS AND THE STANDARD DEDUCTION. As mentioned above, taxpayers generally cannot deduct personal expenses.[5] Congress, however, allows taxpayers to deduct specified personal expenses such as charitable contributions and medical expenses. In addition, taxpayers are allowed to itemize expenses related to the production or collection of income, the management of property held for the production of income, and the determination, collection, or refund of any tax.[6]

ADDITIONAL COMMENT

Itemized deductions were claimed on 29.3% of all returns filed in 1996 and amounted to 56.8% of all standard and itemized deductions.

[4] Sec. 63.
[5] Sec. 262.
[6] Sec. 212.

▼ **TABLE I2-4**

Deductions for Adjusted Gross Income Listed in Sec. 62

Trade and business deductions
Reimbursed employee expenses and certain expenses of performing artists
Losses from the sale or exchange of property
Deductions attributable to rents and royalties
Certain deductions of life tenants and income beneficiaries of property
Contributions to retirement plans (Keoghs and IRAs) and certain distributions
Penalties forfeited because of premature withdrawal of funds from time savings accounts
*One-half of self-employment taxes paid
*Portion of health insurance costs incurred by a self-employed person
Alimony
Moving expenses
Certain required repayments of supplemental unemployment compensation
Jury duty pay remitted to an individual's employer
Certain environmental expenditures (reforestation and clean fuel)
Interest on education loans
Contribution to medical savings account

*Though not actually mentioned in Sec. 62, self-employment taxes and health insurance costs of self-employed persons are defind by Secs. 164(f) and 162(l) respectively as trade or business deductions thereby indirectly enabling taxpayers to deduct portions of these amounts for AGI.

HISTORICAL NOTE

In 1986, when parents were required merely to list the names of their children to claim them as a dependent, 77 million children were claimed. In 1987, when taxpayers were required to list children's Social Security numbers to prove that the exemptions were valid, the number of children claimed as dependents decreased to 70 million.

HISTORICAL NOTE

As recently as 1986, the highest marginal tax rate was 50%, and as recently as 1981, it was 70%.

Taxpayers have the choice of claiming either itemized deductions or the standard deduction. The amount of the standard deduction varies depending on the taxpayer's filing status, age, and vision. As a practical matter, for most taxpayers the standard deduction is greater than the total itemized deductions. Taxpayers with small amounts of deductible expenses do not itemize and, in fact, do not have to keep records of medical expenses and other itemized deductions. The relationship between itemized deductions and the standard deduction is discussed later in this chapter.

PERSONAL AND DEPENDENCY EXEMPTIONS. A **personal exemption** generally is allowed for each taxpayer and his or her spouse and an additional dependency exemption is permitted for each dependent. Both personal and dependency exemptions are equal to $2,900 in 2001 and $3,000 in 2002. The amount of an exemption is adjusted annually for increases in the cost of living.

TAXABLE INCOME. **Taxable income** is adjusted gross income reduced by deductions *from* AGI. It is the amount of income that is taxed.

TAX RATES AND GROSS TAX. Tax rates are the percentage rates, set by Congress, at which income is taxed. Lower individual tax rates are being phased in through 2006. The previous five tax brackets that ranged from 15% to 39.6% are being replaced by six tax brackets that range from 10% to 35%.

2000	15%, 28%, 31%, 36%, and 39.6%
2001	10%, 15%, 27.5%, 30.5%, 35.5%, and 39.1%
2002 and 2003	10%, 15%, 27%, 30%, 35%, and 38.6%
2004 and 2005	10%, 15%, 26%, 29%, 34%, and 37.6%
2006 and later	10%, 15%, 25%, 28%, 33%, and 35%

The 10% tax bracket added in 2001 is intended to reduce the tax burden on lower income taxpayers. The width of 15% tax bracket is scheduled to increase for married couples between 2005 and 2008. It will eventually be twice as wide as the 15% tax bracket for single taxpayers. Taxpayers compute their tax by multiplying the percentage rates found in the tax rate schedules times taxable income. However, most taxpayers simply look in

▼ **TABLE I2-5**
Partial List of Tax Credits

Refundable
- Withholding from wages and back-up withholding
- Estimated tax payments
- Overpayment of prior year's tax
- Excess Social Security taxes paid
- Nonhighway-use gasoline tax
- Earned income credit
- Regulated investment company credit
- Payments made with extension request
- Child credit (in some cases)

Nonrefundable
- Adoption expense credit
- Credit for the elderly and disabled
- Foreign tax credit
- Child and dependent care credit
- Business energy credit
- Qualified electric vehicle credit
- Research and experimentation credit
- Low-income housing credit
- Building rehabilitation credit
- Hope and lifetime learning credits

tax table to find their gross tax. These two alternatives are discussed in more detail later in this chapter. The gross tax is the amount of tax determined by this process.

SELF-STUDY QUESTION

If a taxpayer is in the 28% marginal tax bracket, would he or she prefer $100 of tax credits or $300 of tax deductions?

ANSWER

The taxpayer would prefer the $100 of tax credits. The $300 of deductions will result in a tax savings of $84 ($300 × .28), whereas the $100 of credits would result in a tax savings of $100.

CREDITS AND PREPAYMENTS. **Tax credits**, which include prepayments, are amounts that can be subtracted from the gross tax to arrive at the net tax due or refund due. Credits may be classified as either refundable or nonrefundable tax credits. **Refundable tax credits** are allowed to reduce a taxpayer's tax liability to zero and, if some credit still remains, are refundable (paid) by the government to the taxpayer. Prepayments of tax, which are amounts paid to the government during the year through means such as withholding from wages, and selected other items are classified as **refundable tax credits. Nonrefundable tax credits** are allowances that have been created by Congress for various social, economic, and political reasons such as the child and dependent care credit. Nonrefundable tax credits can be subtracted from the tax and may reduce the tax liability to zero. However, if the nonrefundable credits exceed the tax liability, none of the excess will be paid to the taxpayer. A partial list of refundable and nonrefundable tax credits can be found in Table I2-5.

TAX FORMULA ILLUSTRATED

The following example illustrates the tax formula and Form 1040 for the tax year 2001.

EXAMPLE I2-1 ▶ The following facts relate to Larry S. and Jane V. Lane for 2001. Betty is their 9 year-old dependent daughter.

Salary	$75,000
Interest Income:	
Taxable	1,000
Exempt	500
Individual Retirement Account (IRA) contribution	2,000
Itemized deductions	12,300
Personal and dependency exemptions (3 × $2,900)	8,700
Federal income taxes withheld from salary	8,500

Their tax is computed as follows:

Income:		
Salary		$75,000
Taxable interest		1,000
Exempt interest		500
Total		$76,500
Minus: Exclusion:		
Exempt interest		(500)
Gross income		$76,000
Minus: Deductions for AGI:		
IRA contribution		(2,000)
Adjusted gross income		$74,000
Minus: Deductions from AGI:		
Itemized deductions		(12,300)
Personal and dependency exemptions		(8,700)
Taxable income		$53,000
Gross tax (2001 tax table)		$8,932
Minus: Credits and prepayments		
Child credit	(600)	
Federal income tax withheld	(8,500)	(9,100)
Tax refund		$168 ◀

This tax is also computed on Form 1040 (see Figure I2-1). Note that certain additional information, such as the taxpayers' address and Social Security numbers, also is included on the return.

DEDUCTIONS FROM ADJUSTED GROSS INCOME

ITEMIZED DEDUCTIONS

Itemized deductions are claimed only if the total of such expenses exceeds the standard deduction. Here, consideration is given to which expenses may be itemized and the relationship between itemized deductions and the standard deduction.

ADDITIONAL COMMENT

Of the total itemized deductions reported in 1996, interest paid in the amount of $227.6 billion comprised the largest portion at 39.1%. Taxes paid came in second with 34.8% of total itemized deductions.

DEDUCTIBLE ITEMS. Congress allows taxpayers to itemize specified personal expenses. These specified expenses include medical expenses, taxes, investment and residential interest, charitable contributions, casualty and theft losses, and employee expenses. In addition, taxpayers are allowed to itemize expenses related to the production or collection of nonbusiness income, the management of property held for the production of income, and the determination, collection, or refund of any tax. A partial list of itemized deductions is found in Table I2-6.

ADDITIONAL COMMENT

The phase-out of itemized deductions for taxpayers in the 36% tax bracket effectively raises their marginal tax rate by 1.08% which could be considered a hidden tax rate.

ITEMIZED DEDUCTION FLOORS. There are four adjusted gross income floors associated with itemized deductions. AGI floors represent amounts in which the deduction is allowable only if it exceeds the floor amount. Three of the floors apply to specific categories of itemized deductions; the remaining floor applies to total itemized deductions. The floors based on AGI are as follows:

- Medical expenses: only medical expenses over 7.5% of AGI of are deductible.
- Casualty losses: only casualty losses in excess of 10% of AGI are deductible.
- Miscellaneous itemized deductions: only miscellaneous itemized deductions in excess of 2% of AGI are deductible.

Form **1040** Department of the Treasury—Internal Revenue Service
U.S. Individual Income Tax Return **2001** (99) IRS Use Only—Do not write or staple in this space.

For the year Jan. 1–Dec. 31, 2001, or other tax year beginning , 2001, ending , 20 OMB No. 1545-0074

Label

(See instructions on page 19.)

Use the IRS label. Otherwise, please print or type.

LABEL HERE

Your first name and initial	Last name	Your social security number
Larry S.	Lane	123 45 6789
If a joint return, spouse's first name and initial	Last name	Spouse's social security number
Jane V.	Lane	987 65 4321
Home address (number and street). If you have a P.O. box, see page 19.	Apt. no.	
116 E. Edwards		
City, town or post office, state, and ZIP code. If you have a foreign address, see page 19.		
Lubbock Texas		

▲ **Important!** ▲ You **must** enter your SSN(s) above.

Presidential Election Campaign (See page 19.) ▶ **Note.** Checking "Yes" will not change your tax or reduce your refund. Do you, or your spouse if filing a joint return, want $3 to go to this fund? ▶

You: ☐ Yes ☒ No   Spouse: ☐ Yes ☒ No

Filing Status

Check only one box.

1 ☐ Single
2 ☒ Married filing joint return (even if only one had income)
3 ☐ Married filing separate return. Enter spouse's social security no. above and full name here. ▶
4 ☐ Head of household (with qualifying person). (See page 19.) If the qualifying person is a child but not your dependent, enter this child's name here. ▶
5 ☐ Qualifying widow(er) with dependent child (year spouse died ▶). (See page 19.)

Exemptions

6a ☒ **Yourself.** If your parent (or someone else) can claim you as a dependent on his or her tax return, **do not** check box 6a

b ☒ **Spouse**

No. of boxes checked on 6a and 6b: 2

c **Dependents:**

(1) First name Last name	(2) Dependent's social security number	(3) Dependent's relationship to you	(4) ✓ if qualifying child for child tax credit (see page 20)
Betty Lane	125 25 7774		☑
			☐
			☐
			☐
			☐
			☐

If more than six dependents, see page 20.

No. of your children on 6c who:
- lived with you: 1
- did not live with you due to divorce or separation (see page 20):

Dependents on 6c not entered above:

d Total number of exemptions claimed — Add numbers entered on lines above ▶ **3**

Income

Attach Forms W-2 and W-2G here. Also attach Form(s) 1099-R if tax was withheld.

If you did not get a W-2, see page 21.

Enclose, but do not attach, any payment. Also, please use **Form 1040-V.**

7	Wages, salaries, tips, etc. Attach Form(s) W-2		75,000
8a	**Taxable** interest. Attach Schedule B if required		1,000
b	**Tax-exempt** interest. **Do not** include on line 8a	8b 500	
9	Ordinary dividends. Attach Schedule B if required		
10	Taxable refunds, credits, or offsets of state and local income taxes (see page 22)		
11	Alimony received		
12	Business income or (loss). Attach Schedule C or C-EZ		
13	Capital gain or (loss). Attach Schedule D if required. If not required, check here ▶ ☐		
14	Other gains or (losses). Attach Form 4797		
15a	Total IRA distributions 15a	b Taxable amount (see page 23)	15b
16a	Total pensions and annuities 16a	b Taxable amount (see page 23)	16b
17	Rental real estate, royalties, partnerships, S corporations, trusts, etc. Attach Schedule E		
18	Farm income or (loss). Attach Schedule F		
19	Unemployment compensation		
20a	Social security benefits 20a	b Taxable amount (see page 25)	20b
21	Other income. List type and amount (see page 27)		
22	Add the amounts in the far right column for lines 7 through 21. This is your **total income** ▶		76,000

Adjusted Gross Income

23	IRA deduction (see page 27)	23 2,000	
24	Student loan interest deduction (see page 28)	24	
25	Archer MSA deduction. Attach Form 8853	25	
26	Moving expenses. Attach Form 3903	26	
27	One-half of self-employment tax. Attach Schedule SE	27	
28	Self-employed health insurance deduction (see page 30)	28	
29	Self-employed SEP, SIMPLE, and qualified plans	29	
30	Penalty on early withdrawal of savings	30	
31a	Alimony paid b Recipient's SSN ▶	31a	
32	Add lines 23 through 31a		2,000
33	Subtract line 32 from line 22. This is your **adjusted gross income** ▶		74,000

For Disclosure, Privacy Act, and Paperwork Reduction Act Notice, see page 72. Cat. No. 11320B Form **1040** (2001)

FIGURE I2-1 ▶ FORM 1040

Tax and Credits

Standard Deduction for—
- People who checked any box on line 35a or 35b **or** who can be claimed as a dependent, see page 31.
- All others:

Single, $4,550
Head of household, $6,650
Married filing jointly or Qualifying widow(er), $7,600
Married filing separately, $3,800

Line	Description	Line	Amount	Line	Amount
34	Amount from line 33 (adjusted gross income)			34	74,000
35a	Check if: ☐ **You** were 65 or older, ☐ Blind; ☐ **Spouse** was 65 or older, ☐ Blind. Add the number of boxes checked above and enter the total here ▶ 35a ☐				
b	If you are married filing separately and your spouse itemizes deductions, or you were a dual-status alien, see page 31 and check here ▶ 35b ☐				
36	**Itemized deductions** (from Schedule A) **or** your **standard deduction** (see left margin)			36	12,300
37	Subtract line 36 from line 34			37	61,700
38	If line 34 is $99,725 or less, multiply $2,900 by the total number of exemptions claimed on line 6d. If line 34 is over $99,725, see the worksheet on page 32			38	8,700
39	**Taxable income.** Subtract line 38 from line 37. If line 38 is more than line 37, enter -0-			39	53,000
40	**Tax** (see page 33). Check if any tax is from **a** ☐ Form(s) 8814 **b** ☐ Form 4972			40	8,932
41	**Alternative minimum tax** (see page 34). Attach Form 6251			41	
42	Add lines 40 and 41 ▶			42	8,932
43	Foreign tax credit. Attach Form 1116 if required	43			
44	Credit for child and dependent care expenses. Attach Form 2441	44			
45	Credit for the elderly or the disabled. Attach Schedule R	45			
46	Education credits. Attach Form 8863	46			
47	Rate reduction credit. See the worksheet on page 36	47			
48	Child tax credit (see page 37)	48	600		
49	Adoption credit. Attach Form 8839	49			
50	Other credits from: **a** ☐ Form 3800 **b** ☐ Form 8396 **c** ☐ Form 8801 **d** ☐ Form (specify) ______	50			
51	Add lines 43 through 50. These are your **total credits**			51	600
52	Subtract line 51 from line 42. If line 51 is more than line 42, enter -0- ▶			52	8,332

Other Taxes

53	Self-employment tax. Attach Schedule SE	53	
54	Social security and Medicare tax on tip income not reported to employer. Attach Form 4137	54	
55	Tax on qualified plans, including IRAs, and other tax-favored accounts. Attach Form 5329 if required	55	
56	Advance earned income credit payments from Form(s) W-2	56	
57	Household employment taxes. Attach Schedule H	57	
58	Add lines 52 through 57. This is your **total tax** ▶	58	8,332

Payments

If you have a qualifying child, attach Schedule EIC.

Line	Description	Line	Amount	Line	Amount
59	Federal income tax withheld from Forms W-2 and 1099	59	8,500		
60	2001 estimated tax payments and amount applied from 2000 return	60			
61a	**Earned income credit (EIC)**	61a			
b	Nontaxable earned income 61b				
62	Excess social security and RRTA tax withheld (see page 51)	62			
63	Additional child tax credit. Attach Form 8812	63			
64	Amount paid with request for extension to file (see page 51)	64			
65	Other payments. Check if from **a** ☐ Form 2439 **b** ☐ Form 4136	65			
66	Add lines 59, 60, 61a, and 62 through 65. These are your **total payments** ▶			66	8,500

Refund

Direct deposit? See page 51 and fill in 68b, 68c, and 68d.

Line	Description	Line	Amount	Line	Amount
67	If line 66 is more than line 58, subtract line 58 from line 66. This is the amount you **overpaid**			67	168
68a	Amount of line 67 you want **refunded to you** ▶			68a	168
▶ b	Routing number ▶ **c** Type: ☐ Checking ☐ Savings				
▶ d	Account number				
69	Amount of line 67 you want **applied to your 2002 estimated tax** ▶	69			

Amount You Owe

Line	Description	Line	Amount	Line	Amount
70	**Amount you owe.** Subtract line 66 from line 58. For details on how to pay, see page 52 ▶			70	
71	Estimated tax penalty. Also include on line 70	71			

Third Party Designee

Do you want to allow another person to discuss this return with the IRS (see page 53)? ☐ **Yes.** Complete the following. ☐ **No**

Designee's name ▶ Phone no. ▶ ( ) Personal identification number (PIN) ▶

Sign Here

Joint return? See page 19. Keep a copy for your records.

Under penalties of perjury, I declare that I have examined this return and accompanying schedules and statements, and to the best of my knowledge and belief, they are true, correct, and complete. Declaration of preparer (other than taxpayer) is based on all information of which preparer has any knowledge.

Your signature	Date	Your occupation	Daytime phone number
Larry S. Lane	4-15-01	Attorney	(555) 555-1212
Spouse's signature. If a joint return, both must sign.	**Date**	**Spouse's occupation**	
Jane V Lane	4-15-01	Student	

Paid Preparer's Use Only

Preparer's signature	Date	Check if self-employed ☐	Preparer's SSN or PTIN
Firm's name (or yours if self-employed), address, and ZIP code		EIN	
		Phone no. ( )	

Form **1040** (2001)

FIGURE 12-1 ▶ FORM 1040 (CONTINUED)

▼ **TABLE I2-6**
Partial List of Itemized Deductions

Medical expenses (over 7.5% of adjusted gross income)
Certain taxes
  State, local, and foreign income and real property taxes
  State and local personal property taxes
Residential interest and investment interest (limited)
Charitable contributions (limited)
Casualty and theft losses (over 10% of adjusted gross income)
Miscellaneous deductions (over 2% of adjusted gross income)
  Employee expenses (e.g., professional and union dues, professional publications, travel, transportation, education, job hunting, office-in-home, special clothing, and 50% of entertainment expenses)
  Expenses for producing investment income (e.g., accounting and legal fees, safe deposit rental, fees paid to an IRA custodian)
  Tax advice and tax return preparation and related costs
Other miscellaneous deductions
  Federal estate tax attributable to income in respect of a decedent
  Gambling losses to the extent of winnings
  Amortization of bond premium
  Amounts restored under claim of right

- High income taxpayers: higher income taxpayers must reduce total itemized deductions by 3% of their AGI over $137,300 in 2002 ($132,950 in 2001).[7] The amount for married persons filing separate returns is $68,650 in 2002 ($66,475 in 2001). This floor is scheduled to be phased-out between 2006 and 2010.

These floors are discussed in more detail in Chapter I7.

EXAMPLE I2-2 ▶ John and Jane file a joint tax return and report AGI of $150,000. Their itemized deductions include $14,000 of medical expenses and home mortgage interest of $10,000. The AGI floor reduces the medical expense deduction to $2,750 [$14,000 − (0.075 × $150,000)]. Total itemized deductions before the overall reduction is $12,750 ($2,750 + $10,000). This amount must be reduced by $381 [($150,000 − $137,300) × 0.03] as a result of the overall floor for itemized deductions. Thus, the total itemized deductions allowed would be $12,369 ($12,750 − $381). ◀

OBJECTIVE 2

Determine the amount allowable for the standard deduction

STANDARD DEDUCTION

Itemized deductions are claimed only if the total amount of such deductions exceeds the standard deduction. The **standard deduction** is an amount set by Congress. It varies depending on the taxpayer's filing status, age, and vision.

KEY POINT

The dollar amount of the standard deduction generally increases each year because it is indexed to the rate of inflation.

Filing Status	*Standard Deduction* 2001	2002
Single individual other than heads of households	$4,550	$4,700
Married couples filing joint returns and surviving spouses	7,600	7,850
Married people filing separate returns	3,800	3,925
Heads of households	6,650	6,900

The differences between the 2001 and 2002 amounts represent adjustments for the increase in the cost of living. The standard deduction for married couples is scheduled to

[7] The reduction in the itemized deductions cannot exceed 80% of the total itemized deductions other than medical expenses, investment interest expenses, casualty losses, and wagering losses. (See Chapter I7 for a discussion of the 80% overall limitation.)

increase between 2005 and 2009 so that it will be double the standard deduction for single taxpayers.

In 2002, a married taxpayer's standard deduction is increased by $900 if he or she is elderly or blind ($1,800 if the taxpayer is elderly *and* blind) or has a spouse who is elderly or blind (for a maximum possible increase of $3,600 for a married couple). If an unmarried taxpayer is elderly or blind, his or her standard deduction is increased by $1,150 ($2,300 if the taxpayer is elderly *and* blind). Thus, in 2002, a single taxpayer, age 65 and not blind, is entitled to a $5,850 standard deduction. Two special rules relating to age and blindness are noted below.

- The increase in the standard deduction for elderly taxpayers is available if the taxpayer turns 65 during the tax year. It is interesting that a taxpayer is considered to be age 65 on the day before his or her sixty-fifth birthday. Thus, a taxpayer who reaches age 65 on January 1 of a year is deemed to have reached age 65 on December 31 of the preceding year. The adjustment is allowed on the final return of a deceased taxpayer only if he or she reached age 65 before death.
- The IRC defines blindness as corrected vision in the better eye of no better than 20/200 or a field of no greater than 20 degrees. Vision is determined as of the last day of the tax year or, in the case of a deceased taxpayer, as of the date of death.

The standard deduction simplifies the computation of taxable income. As previously noted, for most taxpayers the standard deduction is greater than total itemized deductions. Those taxpayers do not itemize and, in fact, do not even have to keep records of medical expenses and other itemized deductions.

Who actually itemizes and who does not? High-income taxpayers are more likely to itemize than low-income taxpayers simply because they incur more expenses that can be itemized. This is true even though the AGI floors (previously discussed) affect high-income taxpayers more than low-income taxpayers. Another characteristic of taxpayers who generally itemize their deductions are individuals who own their homes and incur home mortgage expenses and property taxes. These two expenses are deductible and alone usually exceed the standard deduction.

EXAMPLE I2-3 ▶ In 2002, Joan is single, and a homeowner who incurs property taxes on her home of $2,000, makes charitable contributions of $500, and pays mortgage interest of $4,000. Joan's adjusted gross income is $30,000. Her taxable income is computed as follows:

Adjusted gross income			$30,000
Minus:	Itemized deductions:		
	Charitable contributions	$ 500	
	Property taxes	2,000	
	Mortgage interest	4,000	(6,500)
Minus:	Personal exemption		(3,000)
Taxable income			$20,500 ◀

Joan would itemize her deductions because they ($6,500) are greater than her standard deduction ($4,700).

EXAMPLE I2-4 ▶ Assume the same facts as in Example I2-3 except that Joan is not a homeowner. Thus, she has no property taxes or mortgage interest but does pay rent of $600 per month for an apartment. Her taxable income is computed as follows:

Adjusted gross income		$30,000
Minus:	Standard deduction	(4,700)
Minus:	Personal exemption	(3,000)
Taxable income		$22,300 ◀

Joan would use the standard deduction because it ($4,700) is greater than her itemized deduction ($500). Rent paid for a personal apartment is not deductible.

LOSS OF THE STANDARD DEDUCTION. Congress decided that a few taxpayers should not be permitted to use the standard deduction as they possibly would receive an unintended tax benefit.[8] The standard deduction is unavailable to three categories of taxpayers:

- An individual filing a return for a period less than twelve months because of a change in accounting period.
- A married taxpayer filing a separate return in instances where the other spouse itemizes.
- Nonresident aliens.

To illustrate why Congress does not permit certain taxpayers to claim the standard deduction, consider what could happen if a married couple files separate returns but only one spouse itemizes. On a separate return in 2002 when the standard deduction is $3,925, one spouse could claim all itemized deductions while the other uses the standard deduction.

EXAMPLE I2-5 ▶ Clay and Joy, a married couple, have incomes of $15,000 and $14,000, respectively. Their itemized deductions total $4,500. They would claim a $7,850 standard deduction on a joint return. If Clay filed a separate return and claimed all of the deductions, his itemized deductions of $4,500 would be greater than the $3,925 standard deduction. If Joy could claim the standard deduction on her return, their total deductions would equal $8,425 ($4,500 + $3,925). The law, however, requires that either they both itemize or they both use the standard deduction. ◀

Limitation on the Standard Deduction. A special rule applies to any individual for whom the dependency exemption is allowable to another taxpayer. In 2002, the standard deduction of the dependent is limited to the greater of 1) the dependent's earned income plus $250, or 2) $750 (unchanged from 2001). The purpose of this limitation is to prevent parents from shifting unearned income, such as interest and dividends, to their children and avoid paying tax on such income. Without this rule, children could use the standard deduction to offset income from interest and dividends.

EXAMPLE I2-6 ▶ Webb and Beth are married, in the 35% marginal tax rate bracket, and have one son, Vincent, age 15. Vincent has no income and is claimed as a dependent by his parents. Webb and Beth transfer stocks and bonds to Vincent that earn $3,000 in dividends and interest. Their goal is to shift the $3,000 of income to Vincent to utilize his standard deduction. However, since Vincent is claimed as a dependent by his parents on their return, Vincent's standard deduction is limited to $750, i.e., the *greater* of $750 or his earned income plus $250 ($0 + $250). ◀

EXAMPLE I2-7 ▶ Assume the same facts as in Example I2-6 except Vincent has a part-time job and earns $2,000 in wages. Vincent's standard deduction would be $2,250 ($2,000 + $250). Alternatively, if Vincent's wages were $5,000, his standard deduction would be $4,700 (the maximum for a single individual). ◀

OBJECTIVE 3

Determine the amount and the correct number of personal and dependency exemptions

PERSONAL EXEMPTIONS

In general, taxpayers cannot deduct personal expenses except for certain itemized deductions that are specifically authorized under the tax law. Congress has recognized the need to protect a small amount of income from tax in order to allow the taxpayer to meet personal expenses. Thus, almost every individual taxpayer is allowed a personal exemption of $2,900 in 2001 and $3,000 in 2002. Because there are two taxpayers on a joint return filed by a married couple, they are allowed two personal exemptions. In addition, if a married person files a separate return, the taxpayer can claim a personal exemption for his or her spouse if the spouse has no gross income during the year and the spouse is not the dependent of another taxpayer.[9]

Under current law, only one exemption is allowed for each person. Therefore, if an individual can be claimed as a dependent by another person, that individual is not entitled to a personal exemption on his or her own return. Despite the loss of the personal exemption, most dependents owe little or no tax. Since a person who may be claimed as a dependent typically has a very low amount of income, such person can usually offset his or her income by the standard deduction.

[8] Sec. 63(c)(6).

[9] Sec. 151(b).

DEPENDENCY EXEMPTIONS

ADDITIONAL COMMENT

One should forsake any preconceived notions as to what constitutes a dependent before examining the dependency tests.

KEY POINT

For someone to be claimed as a dependent, *all* five dependency tests must be satisfied.

In addition to claiming one personal exemption, an individual also may claim an exemption for each dependent. An individual qualifies as a dependent only if he or she **meets all five** of the following tests:[10]

- Support: The taxpayer must provide over 50% of the dependent's support.
- Gross income: The dependent's gross income must be less than the amount of the exemption. However, a taxpayer's children who are either, (1) full-time students and under age 24 or (2) under the age of 19, are exempt from this requirement.
- Joint return: In general, a married dependent cannot file a joint return.
- Relationship: Dependents must either be related to the taxpayer or reside with the taxpayer.
- Citizenship: Dependents must be U.S. citizens, residents, or nationals or they must reside in Canada or Mexico.

The full exemption is available for dependents who are born or die during the year. No exemption is available for unborn or stillborn children. All dependents must have social security numbers, and the numbers must be correctly reported on the taxpayer's return.[11] The five tests are discussed below.

SUPPORT TEST. The taxpayer normally must provide over one-half of the dependent's financial support during the year. Support includes amounts spent by the taxpayer, the dependent, and other individuals. Welfare[12] and Social Security benefits[13] spent on support count even if they are excluded from gross income.

EXAMPLE I2-8 ▶ Tarer provided $3,000 of support for his mother, Mary. Tarer's sister provided $1,000. Mary spent $4,500 of her savings for her own support. Because Mary provided at least one-half of her own support, she cannot be claimed as a dependent. ◀

EXAMPLE I2-9 ▶ George's father received Social Security benefits of $6,600, of which $1,800 were deposited into a savings account. He spent the remaining $4,800 on food, clothing, and lodging. George spent $5,600 to support his father. George meets the support test because the amount saved is not counted in the support test. ◀

ADDITIONAL COMMENT

A TV set bought by a parent for his 12-year-old child and set up in her bedroom was considered support. (Rev. Rul. 77-282, 1977-2 CB 52.) A power lawn mower, however, bought by a parent of a 13-year-old child was not considered support. The parent had assigned the child the job of mowing the lawn, and the power mower was intended to make the job more palatable. The lawn mower was considered a family item that benefits all members of the household. (Rev. Rul. 77-282, 1977-2 CB 52.)

Support includes amounts spent for food, clothing, shelter, medical and dental care, education, and the like.[14] Support is not limited to these items.[15] Support does not include the value of services rendered by the taxpayer to the dependent.[16] A scholarship received by a son or daughter[17] is not counted as support in deciding whether a parent provided over one half of the child's support.[18] Also, the IRS and the courts have excluded various other expenses from support.[19]

Generally, the amount of support equals the cost of the item, but in the case of support provided in a noncash form, such as lodging, the amount of support equals the fair market value or fair rental value. The cost of an item such as a television or an automobile is included in support if the item actually is support.[20]

---

[10] Sec. 152.

[11] Sec. 151(e). The IRS has the authority to disallow dependency exemptions for otherwise qualified dependents without social security numbers and with incorrectly reported social security numbers. A missing or incorrectly reported social security number may also bar an otherwise eligible individual from claiming head-of-household filing status.

[12] Rev. Rul. 71-468, 1971-2 C.B. 115.

[13] Rev. Ruls. 57-344, 1957-2 C.B. 112, and 58-419, 1958-2 C.B. 57.

[14] Reg. Sec. 1.152-1(a)(2)(i).

[15] Examples of other items that have been held to be support include church contributions (Rev. Rul. 58-67, 1958-1 C.B. 62), telephone (*William K. Price, III*, 1961 PH T.C. Memo ¶61,173, 20 TCM 886), medical insurance premiums (*James Edward Parker*, 1959 PH T.C. Memo ¶52,182, 18 TCM 800), child care (*Marvin D. Tucker*, 1957 PH T.C. Memo ¶57,118, 16 TCM 488), toys (*Loren S. Brumber*, 1952 PH T.C. Memo ¶52,087, 11 TCM 289), and vacations (*George R. Melat*, 1953 PH T.C. Memo ¶53,141, 12 TCM 443).

[16] *Frank Markarian v. CIR.*, 16 AFTR 2d 5785, 65-2 USTC ¶9699 (7th Cir., 1965).

[17] Including adopted children, stepchildren, and foster children (if the foster children live with the taxpayer for the entire year).

[18] Sec. 152(d).

[19] Examples of items that have been excluded are funeral expenses (Rev. Rul. 65-307, 1965-2 C.B. 40), taxes (Rev. Rul. 58-67, 1958-1 C.B. 62), a rifle, lawn mower, boat insurance (*Harriet C. Flower v. U.S.*, 52 AFTR 1383, 57-1 USTC ¶9655 (D.C. Pa., 1957)), and life insurance premiums (*John F. Miller*, 1959 PH T.C. Memo ¶59,155, 18 TCM 673).

[20] Rev. Rul. 77-282, 1977-2 C.B. 52.

EXAMPLE I2-10 ▶ Vicki's mother lives with her. Vicki purchased clothing for her mother costing $800, and provided her with a room that Vicki estimates she could have rented for $2,800. Vicki spent $2,500 for groceries she shared with her mother and $1,200 for utilities. In addition, Vicki purchased a television for $750 that she placed in the living room. Vicki and her mother both used the television. Vicki's support for her mother, at a minimum, includes:

Clothing	$ 800
Rental value of room	2,800
Food	1,250
Total	$4,850

Whether a portion of the utilities could be included in support would depend on whether the rental rate for the room included utilities. The fact that the mother used the television set probably would not be sufficient to cause its cost to be viewed as support. On the other hand, if the television set was a gift to the mother, was placed in her room, and was used exclusively by her, the cost probably would qualify as support. ◀

If a taxpayer contributes a lump sum for the support of two or more individuals, the amount is allocated between the individuals on a pro rata basis unless proof exists to the contrary.[21]

EXAMPLE I2-11 ▶ Jaime pays rent of $6,000 for an apartment occupied by his sisters Alice, Beth, and Cindy. Alice spends $3,000 toward her own support, Beth spends $1,000, and Cindy spends $1,000. Jaime is assumed to have provided $2,000 of support for each sister. Thus, assuming the other four tests are met, Jaime can claim exemptions for Beth and Cindy, but not for Alice. ◀

SELF-STUDY QUESTION

A parent provides $4,000 of support for his 17-year-old son. The son earns $5,000 during the year but only spends $3,000 for his own support. Will the parent be considered to have provided over 50% of the son's support?

ANSWER

Yes; only the amount actually spent by the son is taken into account.

While a taxpayer normally must provide over one-half of a dependent's support, there are two exceptions to this general rule:

- ▶ A multiple support declaration permits one member of a group of taxpayers who collectively provide over 50% of an individual's support to claim the dependency exemption.
- ▶ Special rules determine which parent will receive dependency exemptions for children in the case of a divorce.

Often several people contribute to the support of a dependent. Under normal rules, no one would be able to claim a dependency exemption unless one member of the group provided over one-half of the total support. However, when the group provides over one-half of the support of an individual but no one member of the group provides over one-half of the support, eligible members of the group are allowed to designate one group member to claim the exemption. Each eligible member (other than the taxpayer receiving the exemption) must complete a Multiple Support Declaration (Form 2120, shown on page I2-15) stating that he or she will not claim a dependency exemption under these rules. An eligible member is one who contributes more than 10% of the dependent's support and meet all requirements for claiming a dependency exemption except the support requirement.[22]

EXAMPLE I2-12 ▶ John T. Abel lives alone. His support comes from the following sources:

Andy (son)	$ 400
Gabe (son)	2,800
Mable (daughter)	2,000
Betty (friend)	2,800
Total	$8,000

Either Gabe or Mable can claim a dependency exemption if the other completes Form 2120. Andy cannot claim the exemption because he did not provide over 10% of John's support. Betty cannot claim a dependency exemption because she is not related and John does not live with her. For this reason, Andy and Betty need not complete Form 2120. A completed Form 2120 is illustrated in Figure I2-2. ◀

---

[21] Rev. Rul. 64-222, 1964-2 C.B. 47.

[22] Sec. 152(c).

Form **2120** (Rev. November 2000)
Department of the Treasury Internal Revenue Service

Multiple Support Declaration

▶ Attach to Form 1040 or Form 1040A of person claiming the dependent.

OMB No. 1545-0071
Attachment Sequence No. **114**

Name of person claiming the dependent: Gabe I. Abel
Social security number: 123 45 6789

During the calendar year .... , I paid over 10% of the support of:

John T. Abel
Name of person supported

I could have claimed this person as a dependent except that I did not pay over half of his or her support. I understand that this person is being claimed as a dependent on the Federal income tax return of:

Gabe I. Abel
Name of person claiming the dependent

111 W. Baker St. Lawrence, N.J. 08649
Address of person claiming the dependent

I agree not to claim this person as a dependent on my Federal income tax return for any tax year that began in the above calendar year.

Mabel B. Abel
Your signature

222 11 0001
Your social security number

402 N. Lable Lane
Address (number, street, apt. no.)

4-15-02
Date

Lawrence, N.J. 08649
City, state, and ZIP code

FIGURE I2-2 ▶ FORM 2120

ADDITIONAL COMMENT
Form 8332 may be completed each year by the custodial parent to relinquish the dependency exemption for only that year, or it may be completed once relinquishing the exemption for all future years.

As noted, special rules determine which parent will receive dependency exemptions for children in the case of a divorce or separation.[23] These rules are intended to avoid disputes over which parent provided more than one-half of a child's support. Generally, the parent who has custody of a child for the greater part of the year is entitled to the dependency exemption even if he or she did not provide over one-half of the child's support.[24]

The noncustodial parent may claim the dependency exemption only if the custodial parent agrees in writing. The signed statement must be attached to the noncustodial parent's return each year in which the exemption is claimed. Form 8332 may be used for this purpose. In the case of a divorce or separation, the custodial spouse probably would be reluctant to relinquish the dependency exemption for a child. A noncustodial parent, however, might be able to negotiate the exemption in exchange for increased child support payments.

EXAMPLE I2-13 ▶ Hal and Pam obtain a divorce under the terms of which Pam receives custody of their son. Hal is ordered to pay $600 per month of child support. In absence of a written agreement to the contrary, Pam will receive the dependency exemption for the child. ◀

EXAMPLE I2-14 ▶ Assume the same facts as in Example I2-13 except that Pam negotiates child support payments of $800 per month and agrees in writing to allow Hal to claim the dependency exemption for the child. The written agreement will enable Hal to claim the dependency exemption for the child. ◀

EXAMPLE I2-15 ▶ Andy and Beth obtain a divorce under the terms of which they share custody of their daughter. Whoever has custody for the greater part of the year receives the dependency exemption for the daughter unless they agree otherwise in writing. ◀

---

[23] Including adopted children, stepchildren, and foster children (if the foster children live with the taxpayer for the entire year).

[24] This assumes that together the parents provided over one-half of the support, that no multiple support agreement is in effect, that together the parents had custody of the child for over one-half of the year, and that the parents were divorced, separated, or lived apart for the last half of the year (Sec. 152(e)).

GROSS INCOME TEST. Generally, a dependent's gross income must be less than the amount of the dependency exemption ($3,000 in 2002). The statutory definition of gross income is used in applying this limitation. Therefore, nontaxable scholarships, tax-exempt bond interest, and nontaxable Social Security benefits are not considered, but salary, taxable interest, and rent are considered in deciding whether the person meets this test.

An important exception applies to the gross income test. The gross income test is waived for a child[25] of the taxpayer who is either under age 19, or if a full-time student, under age 24. A child is considered to be a student if he or she is in full-time attendance at a qualified educational institution during at least five months of the year. To be full-time, a student must carry the number of hours or courses the educational institution requires a student to take to be considered full-time. Note, however, that this is only an exception to the gross income test. Therefore, a self-supporting student cannot be claimed as a dependent by his or her parents. Such a student fails the support test.

EXAMPLE I2-16 ▶ Jim, age 22, is a college student and receives more than half of his support from his parents. Jim earned $6,000 from a summer job. Even though Jim earned more than the dependency exemption amount of $3,000 (2002), his parents may claim him as a dependent because the gross income test is waived and all of the other tests are met. Jim, of course, would not be able to claim himself on his own return.

One of the important details of this test is that the dependent must be a *child* of the taxpayer. Thus, if Jim was supported by his aunt and uncle (rather than his parents), the aunt and uncle could not claim Jim because the gross income test is not met. ◀

JOINT RETURN TEST. Generally, a taxpayer may not claim a dependency exemption for a married dependent who files a joint return. However, a taxpayer is entitled to the exemption if the dependent files a joint return solely to claim a refund of tax withheld (i.e., there is no tax on the joint return and there would have been no tax on two separate returns).[26] It is important for married dependents to weigh the taxes that would be saved by the family from an exemption against the taxes that would be saved by filing a joint return. Depending on the circumstances, either alternative may be more beneficial.

TYPICAL MISCONCEPTION

It is sometimes incorrectly believed that in order to claim someone as a dependent, the person must in all cases reside in the home of the taxpayer. They do not always realize that residency is a substitute for the relationship test.

RELATIONSHIP TEST. To be claimed as a dependent, a person either must be related to the taxpayer or reside with the taxpayer for the entire tax year.[27] Both immediate family and extended family relationships meet this test. Immediate family relationships include those based on blood, adoption, or marriage, and extended family relationships include only those based on blood or adoption.

Immediate family relationships include

- ▶ Parents (including adoptive parents, stepparents, mother-in-law, and father-in-law)
- ▶ Siblings (including adoptive siblings, stepbrothers, stepsisters, brothers-in-law, sisters-in-law, half brothers, and half sisters)
- ▶ Children (including adoptive children, stepchildren, sons-in-law, daughters-in-law, and foster children who live with the taxpayer for the entire year)

Extended family relationships include

- ▶ Grandparents and their ancestors
- ▶ Grandchildren and their descendants
- ▶ Aunts and uncles (or more specifically, a brother or sister of the mother or father of the taxpayer)
- ▶ Nephews and nieces (or more specifically, a son or daughter of a brother or sister of the taxpayer)

---

[25] Including adopted children, stepchildren, and foster children (if the foster children live with the taxpayer for the entire year).

[26] Rev. Ruls. 54-567, 1954-2 C.B. 108, and 65-34, 1965-1 C.B. 86. The theory is that the taxpayer is filing a claim for refund and not actually filing a tax return.

[27] The relationship between the taxpayer and the dependent cannot violate a local law (Sec. 152(b)(5)). The exemption has been disallowed where the relationship constituted "cohabitation" and was illegal in the state (*Cassius L. Peacock, III,*, 1978 PH T.C. Memo ¶78,030, 37 TCM 177).

EXAMPLE I2-17 ▶ Jesse supports three people: Tina, an unrelated child who lives with him; his cousin Judy, who lives in another state; and his mother Vicki, who lives in her own home. Jesse can claim two dependency exemptions: one for Tina, who lives with Jesse (a person who lives with the taxpayer need not be related) and one for his mother. Jesse cannot claim a dependency exemption for Judy (cousins do not meet the relationship test). ◀

On a joint return the dependent needs to be related to only one spouse.[28] Once established, an immediate family relationship is not terminated by death or divorce.

EXAMPLE I2-18 ▶ Ken and Lisa support Lisa's mother and claim her as a dependent on a joint return. Following Lisa's death, Ken continues to support Lisa's mother. Lisa's mother continues to be Ken's mother-in-law and can be claimed as a dependent by Ken. On the other hand, if Ken and Lisa had been supporting Lisa's niece, Ken would not be entitled to a dependency exemption. Although she would continue to be Ken's niece, she is not his niece by blood and cannot be claimed as a dependent unless she resides with Ken. ◀

SELF-STUDY QUESTION

Beth's mother, who is a U.S. citizen, has moved to France to spend her retirement years. She has retained her U.S. citizenship, but she is now a resident of France. Is it possible for Beth to claim her mother as a dependent?

ANSWER

Yes, the mother need only be a U.S. citizen.

CITIZENSHIP TEST. A dependent must be a U.S. citizen,[29] national,[30] or resident,[31] or be a resident of Canada or Mexico. The citizenship or residence test need only be met for part of the year.

PHASE-OUT OF PERSONAL AND DEPENDENCY EXEMPTIONS. Both personal and dependency exemptions are phased out for high-income taxpayers. Exemptions are phased out at a rate of 2% for each $2,500 ($1,250 for married people filing separate returns), or fraction thereof, of adjusted gross income above thresholds shown below. Thus, the entire amount of a taxpayer's personal and dependency exemptions will phase-out when his adjusted gross income exceeds the threshold amount by $122,500 ($61,250 on separate returns). Below are the phase-out amounts for 2002:[32]

	Phase-Out Begins	*Phase-Out Ends (More Than)*
Single	$137,300	$259,800
Joint return	206,000	328,500
Head of household	171,650	294,150
Married, filing separately	103,000	164,250

EXAMPLE I2-19 ▶ In 2002, Lee, a single taxpayer with no dependents, reports AGI of $143,050. The usual amount of the personal exemption of $3,000 is reduced by 6% to $2,820 ($5,750 excess AGI ÷ $2,500 = 2.3 which is rounded to 3; 3 × 2% = 6%). ◀

Note that the phase-out begins when the taxpayer's adjusted gross income *exceeds* the threshold. Thus, a single taxpayer with AGI of exactly $137,300 is entitled to the full amount of his or her personal and dependency exemptions, whereas a single taxpayer with AGI of $137,301 is entitled to only 98% of his or her personal and dependency exemptions.

STOP & THINK *Question:* Jack and Leslie, who have four dependent children, are in the process of getting a divorce. Leslie is a surgeon and earns a net income of $400,000 per year from her medical practice. Jack is a pilot and earns a salary of $140,000. The only other source of income is $20,000 of income from interest and dividends which is divided equally. One major stumbling block in structuring the divorce settlement is deciding which person will

[28] Reg. Sec. 1.152-2(d).

[29] U.S. citizens living in foreign countries can claim dependency exemptions for adopted children even if the children are not U.S. citizens.

[30] A U.S. national is an individual born in an outlying possession such as American Samoa.

[31] A resident is a person who is not a U.S. citizen and who is legally residing in the United States with intent to stay here permanently (see Sec. 7701(b)).

[32] Sec. 151(d). The thresholds are adjusted for inflation. In 2001, the phase-out began at $132,950 for single taxpayers, $199,450 for a joint return, $166,200 for a head of household, and $99,725 for a married individual filing a separate return.

be allowed to claim the children as dependents. Either Jack or Leslie will qualify under the income tax rules to claim any or all of the children and both will qualify for head-of-household filing status. The attorneys have come to you for advice. From an income tax standpoint, which parent would benefit the most from being able to claim the children in 2002, or should they each claim two of the children?

Solution: Since Leslie's income is well above the 2002 phase-out limit for personal and dependency exemptions ($294,150), she would not receive any tax benefit from claiming any or all of the children for income tax purposes. Jack, on the other hand, will get a tax benefit from the dependency exemptions because the phase-out amounts for a taxpayer filing as head of household begin at $171,650 and his AGI is only $150,000 ($140,000 + $10,000). Therefore, for income tax purposes only, Jack should claim the four children since he will receive a tax benefit from the dependency exemptions, whereas Leslie would receive no tax benefit if she claimed the children because her AGI is so high that her deduction for personal and dependency exemptions would be zero.

The rules for deducting personal and dependency exemptions are summarized in Topic Review I2-1.

The phase-out of personal and dependency exemptions is scheduled for elimination. During 2006 and 2007, only two-thirds of exemptions will be subject to the phase-out. During 2008 and 2009, only one-third of exemptions will be subject to the phase-out. The phase-out ends in 2010.

OBJECTIVE 4

Determine the amount of child credit

CHILD CREDIT

Under Sec. 24 of the IRC, individual taxpayers may claim a "child credit" of $600 for each qualifying child. The credit is scheduled to increase to $700 in 2005, $800 for 2009, and $1,000 in 2010. The credit is reduced by $50 for each $1,000 (or fraction thereof) by which the taxpayer's modified adjusted gross income exceeds a threshold amount ($110,000 on joint returns, $75,000 for single taxpayers, and $55,000 for married persons filing separate returns). These thresholds are not indexed for inflation. Modified adjusted gross income is AGI plus any amounts excluded from gross income under Secs. 911, 931, and 933 which relate to certain foreign earned income and possession's income. To qualify for the credit, a child must be a U.S. citizen, national, or resident under the age of 17 who qualifies as the taxpayer's dependent, and who is the taxpayer's descendent, stepchild, or foster child. See Chapter I14 for more information regarding the child credit.

ADDITIONAL COMMENT

There are now two credits that have similar names: the child credit and the child and dependent care credit. They are quite different in how the credit amounts are computed and which dependents qualify.

EXAMPLE I2-20 ▶ Jane and Bill have two eligible dependent children and a modified AGI of $120,300. They have excess AGI of $10,300 ($120,300 − $110,000) and are entitled to a credit of $650 [(2 × $600) − (11 × $50)]. ◀

Topic Review I2-1

Personal and Dependency Exemptions

EXEMPTIONS IN GENERAL

- One exemption is available for each taxpayer (except when the taxpayer is the dependent of another) and for each dependent.
- The amount of each exemption, which is adjusted annually for inflation, is $2,900 in 2001 and $3,000 in 2002.
- Exemptions are phased out for high-income taxpayers. For example, on a joint return the phase-out begins when the couple's adjusted gross income exceeds $206,000 and is completed when AGI reaches $328,500.

DEPENDENCY EXEMPTIONS

- One exemption is allowed for each dependent. As noted above, the exemptions are phased out for higher-income taxpayers.
- Five conditions must be met for each dependency exemption. The dependent must be supported by the taxpayer, must meet a gross income test, generally must not file a joint return, must be related to the taxpayer (or live with the taxpayer), and must meet a citizenship or residence test.

DETERMINING THE AMOUNT OF TAX

Once taxable income has been computed, the next step is to determine the gross tax. Most individuals determine the amount of gross tax by looking in the tax table (See page T-2 after Chapter I18 in *Individuals* volume or after Chapter C15 in the *Comprehensive* volume.). This method allows the taxpayer to arrive at the gross tax without the need for multiplication and, therefore, simplifies the computation and reduces the number of errors. Individuals are required to use the tax table unless taxable income exceeds the maximum income in the table (currently $100,000), or if the taxpayer files a short period return on account of a change in the annual accounting period.

Taxpayers who cannot use the tax table instead use the tax rate schedule (located after Chapter I18 and on the inside cover of the text). Taxpayers using the tax rate schedule must actually compute the tax.

EXAMPLE I2-21 ▶ Liz is single and has taxable income of $48,210 in 2001. Liz's tax is determined by reference to the tax table for single taxpayers. (At the time of this writing, the 2001 tax table was the most recent available.) The tax from the table is $9,881. ◀

EXAMPLE I2-22 ▶ Jack and Pam are married, file a joint tax return, and have taxable income of $105,000 in 2002. They will use the tax rate schedule to compute their tax. The tax is computed as follows:

Tax on $46,700	$ 6,405
Tax on remaining $58,300 at 0.27	15,741
Gross tax	$22,146 ◀

OBJECTIVE 5

Determine the filing status of individuals

FILING STATUS

In 2002, there are six tax brackets applicable to individual taxpayers: 10%, 15%, 27%, 30%, 35%, and 38.6%. These rates are progressive in that as a taxpayer's income increases, the taxpayer moves into higher tax brackets. The income level at which higher tax brackets begin depends on the taxpayer's filing status. There are five different filing statuses but only four rate schedules and/or tax tables because married couples filing jointly and certain surviving spouses use the same rate schedule or tax table. The five filing statuses are

- Married filing jointly
- Surviving spouse
- Head of household
- Single
- Married filing separately

KEY POINT

Currently the highest tax rates are those for married filing separately, and the lowest are those for married filing jointly.

SELF-STUDY QUESTION

If Congress were to adopt a truly proportional tax system, would it be necessary to have the four different tax rate schedules?

ANSWER

No, in a proportional tax system, there is no need for different rate schedules because all taxable income would be taxed at the same rate.

Before 1948, one rate schedule was used by all taxpayers. If a husband and wife both had income, each filed a return. This treatment was deemed to be unfair because various states allocated income between spouses differently. Some states used a community property law system while other states used a common law system. Today, only a few states continue to use the community property law system.[33]

In general, community property law allocates community income equally between a husband and wife, regardless of which spouse actually earns the income. In other states, income belongs to the spouse who produces the income. With a progressive tax system, placing income on one return instead of two can result in a much greater tax. For this reason, couples residing in noncommunity property states often paid more tax than their counterparts who resided in community property states. In 1948, Congress developed the joint-rate schedule to rectify this problem. Unmarried taxpayers who headed families felt they also should receive tax relief because they shared their incomes with their families.

[33] Several states had either adopted or had begun to adopt community property laws in order to reduce the federal taxes paid by their residents. After the joint rate schedule was created, states without a tradition of community property law returned to common law. For a more detailed discussion of community property states, see page I3-6.

So, in 1957, Congress created a rate schedule for heads of households. Below is a discussion of who is covered by each filing status.

JOINT RETURN

A *joint return* can be filed by a man and woman if they meet certain tests.

- They must be legally married as of the last day of the tax year.[34] Whether a couple is married depends on the laws of the state of residence.[35] Couples in the process of a divorce are still considered married until the date the divorce becomes final. A couple need not be living together in order to file a joint return. A joint return can be filed if one spouse dies during the year as long as the survivor does not remarry before the year-end. The executor of the estate must agree to the filing of a joint return.
- They must have the same tax year-end (except in the case of death).
- Both the husband and wife must be U.S. citizens or residents. An exception allows a joint return if the nonresident alien spouse agrees to report all of his or her income on the return.[36]

STOP & THINK

Question: Some couples who get married may find their tax liabilities increase even if their combined incomes remain unchanged. Others find that their tax liabilities decrease. Explain why taxes increase for some couples, but decrease for others.

Solution: Couples who marry ordinarily move from two returns where incomes are taxed using the rate schedule for single individuals to one return where the combined incomes are taxed using the joint rate schedule. The less progressive joint rate schedule results in a lower tax if one spouse had most of the income because more of that spouse's income is taxed at lower rates. However, when the husband and wife had approximately equal incomes, their combined incomes are taxed at higher rates on one joint return. Even though the rate schedule for married couples is the least progressive of the individual rate schedules, the combined tax is higher because the second income is added to the first and taxed at higher rates. This increased tax is called the "marriage penalty." As noted, the width of 15% tax bracket is scheduled to increase for married couples between 2005 and 2008, somewhat reducing the "marriage penalty." In addition, the standard deduction for married couples is scheduled to increase between 2005 and 2009 so that it will be double the standard deduction for single taxpayers.

ADDITIONAL COMMENT

Since marital status for the entire year is determined on the last day of the year, some couples actually plan for their wedding to occur on December 31 or January 1. In general, if only one person has income, the wedding should take place on December 31. If both have income, a January 1 wedding is best (for tax purposes).

SURVIVING SPOUSE

A widow or widower can file a joint return for the year his or her spouse dies if the widow or widower does not remarry. For the two years after the year of death, the widow or widower can file as a surviving spouse only if he or she meets specific conditions. The **surviving spouse** (sometimes called a qualifying widow or widower) must[37]

- Have not remarried as of the year end in which surviving spouse status is claimed.
- Be a U.S. citizen or resident.
- Have qualified to file a joint return in the year of death.
- Have at least one dependent child[38] living at home during the entire year and the taxpayer must pay over half of the expenses of the home.

In the year of death, a joint return can be filed. On the joint return, the income of the deceased spouse (earned before death) and the survivor are both reported. Personal exemptions are allowed for both spouses. In the two years following death, surviving spouse sta-

KEY POINT

The surviving-spouse provision entitles the taxpayer to the lower joint return tax rate schedule and to the higher joint return standard deduction.

[34] Sec. 6013.

[35] Thus, common law marriages recognized by the state of residence are covered. On the other hand, an annulled marriage is viewed as never having been valid. Thus, such a couple cannot file a joint return.

[36] Nonresident aliens are taxed only on income earned in the United States. If a joint return is filed by a U.S. citizen and his or her foreign spouse, they would receive the benefit of the low rate schedule, even though only the U.S. citizen reported income on the return. Thus, to file a joint return, the couple must agree to report both incomes (Sec. 6013(g)).

[37] Sec. 2(a).

[38] Includes an adopted child, a stepchild, or a foster child.

tus can be claimed only if the conditions outlined above are met. Only the surviving spouse's income is reported and, of course, no personal exemption is available for the deceased spouse. What the two situations have in common is that in both instances, the taxpayer can use the more favorable joint rate schedule and standard deduction amount.

EXAMPLE I2-23 ▶ Connie and Carl are married and have no dependent children. Carl dies in 2002. Connie can file a joint return, even though her husband died before the end of the year. Alternatively, Connie can file as a married individual filing a separate return. In 2003, however, Connie must file as a single taxpayer since she has no dependent children who would qualify her as a surviving spouse or a head of household. Alternatively, if Connie and Carl had dependent children, Connie could file as a surviving spouse for 2003 and 2004 and use the joint return rate schedules. ◀

STOP & THINK

Question: Most recently widowed individuals do not qualify for surviving spouse status. Why?

Solution: Most individuals are widowed late in life after their children are grown and have left home. As having a dependent child is a requirement for surviving spouse status, these individuals do not qualify for the special lower tax rate. Such individuals may ordinarily file a joint return in the year of the spouse's death.

ADDITIONAL COMMENT

Due in part by the high divorce rate in this country, the number of head-of-household returns has increased. In 1975, only 6% of all returns had the filing status of head-of-household. In 1996, that number was 14%, or 16.5 million returns.

HEAD OF HOUSEHOLD

A second rate schedule or tax table is available to a head of household. The head of household rates are higher than those applicable to married taxpayers filing jointly and surviving spouses, but lower than those applicable to other single taxpayers. To claim head-of-household status, a taxpayer must meet all of the following conditions:[39]

- Be unmarried as of the last day of the tax year. Exceptions apply to individuals married to nonresident aliens[40] and to abandoned spouses.[41] An individual cannot claim head-of-household status in the year his or her spouse died. Such individuals must file a joint return or a separate return.
- Not be a surviving spouse.
- Be a U.S. citizen or resident.
- Pay over half of the costs of maintaining as his or her home a household in which a dependent relative lives for more than half of the tax year. The dependency exemption cannot be based on a multiple support agreement. There are two special rules. First, a taxpayer with a dependent parent qualifies even if the parent does not live with the taxpayer. Second, an unmarried descendant who lives with the taxpayer,[42] need not be the taxpayer's dependent.

The second exception often comes into play in cases of divorced parents. As noted earlier in the chapter, a written agreement can give the dependency exemption to the noncustodial parent. This exception may allow the custodial parent to still claim head-of-household status.

EXAMPLE I2-24 ▶ Brad and Ellen divorce. Ellen receives custody of their child, and Brad is ordered by the court to pay child support of $6,000 per year. Ellen agrees in writing to allow Brad to claim the dependency exemption for the child. If Ellen maintains the home in which she and her child live, she can claim head-of-household status even though the child is Brad's dependent. ◀

As noted, the taxpayer must pay over half of the costs of maintaining the household. These expenses include property taxes, mortgage interest, rent, utility charges, upkeep

[39] Sec. 2(b).

[40] Specifically, this refers to an individual married to a nonresident alien if he or she meets the remaining head-of-household requirements.

[41] Abandoned spouse rules are discussed under a separate heading later in this chapter.

[42] Includes an adopted child, stepchild, and a descendant of a natural or adopted child.

ADDITIONAL COMMENT

In 1996, approximately 20 married couples filed joint returns for every married couple that filed separately.

and repairs, property insurance, and food consumed on the premises. Such costs do not include clothing, education, medical treatment, vacations, life insurance, transportation, or the value of services provided by the taxpayer.[43]

SINGLE TAXPAYER

An unmarried individual who does not qualify as a surviving spouse or a head of household must file as a single taxpayer. The tax rates are higher than those that apply to other unmarried taxpayers.

EXAMPLE I2-25 ▶ Becky, a single taxpayer with no dependents, files her first tax return. She will file as a single taxpayer. ◀

KEY POINT

Several disadvantages are associated with the filing of separate returns by married individuals. For example, a taxpayer may lose all or part of the benefits of the deduction for individual retirement accounts, the child care credit, and the earned income credit.

MARRIED FILING A SEPARATE RETURN

Married individuals who choose to file separate returns must use the separate rate schedule. The rates on this schedule are higher than other individual rate schedules. The implications of joint returns versus separate returns are discussed later in this chapter.

EXAMPLE I2-26 ▶ On December 31, Rose marries Joe. Because they were married before the year ended, they may elect to file jointly. Alternatively, they may file separate returns with each using the rate schedule applicable to separate returns. ◀

The filing requirements for individuals are summarized in Topic Review I2-2.

KEY POINT

When one thinks of a person who would qualify as an abandoned spouse, one thinks of a person in dire financial condition. If no relief were granted, this person would be required to use the married filing separately tax rate schedule, which contains the highest rates.

ABANDONED SPOUSE

The particular rate schedule a taxpayer uses can have a great impact on the amount of tax. Without any special rule, an abandoned spouse would be required to file using the rate schedules for a married person filing separately. Congress has provided relief for taxpayers in this situation if they can meet certain conditions. A married individual can claim head-of-household status if [44]

- ▶ The taxpayer lived apart from his or her spouse for the last six months of the year.
- ▶ The taxpayer pays over half of the cost of maintaining a household in which the taxpayer and a dependent son or daughter live for over half of the year.[45]
- ▶ The taxpayer is a U.S. citizen or resident.

Topic Review I2-2

Filing Status and Requirements

Filing Status	Must Maintain Household	Must Have Dependent	Marital Status	Must Be Citizen	Tax Rates
Joint	No requirement	No	Married	Yes	Lowest rates, but two incomes are combined
Surviving spouse	Yes	Yes, son or daughter	Widowed in prior or second prior year	Yes	Uses same schedule as married couple filing joint return
Head of household	Yes	Generally, yes	Generally, single	Yes	Intermediate tax rates
Single	No requirement	No	Single	No	Highest tax rates for unmarried taxpayers
Separate	No requirement	No	Married	No	Highest tax rates

[43] Reg. Sec. 1.2-2(d).
[44] Sec. 2(c).
[45] Includes adopted child, stepchild, and foster child.

The requirement that the taxpayer have a dependent child is met if a taxpayer who is otherwise qualified to claim the child as a dependent signs an agreement that allows the child's noncustodial parent to claim the dependency exemption for the child.[46]

EXAMPLE I2-27 ▶ In October, Bob and Gail decide to separate. Gail supports their children after the separation and pays the costs of maintaining their home. Gail cannot claim abandoned spouse status because Bob lived with her for over one-half of the year. If she had obtained a divorce before the end of the year, she could have filed as a head of household. In the absence of a divorce, Gail must file a separate return, unless both Bob and Gail agree to file a joint return. ◀

EXAMPLE I2-28 ▶ Assume the same facts as in Example I2-27 except that Gail continues to support her children and pay household expenses during the next year. She can file as a head of household even if she has not obtained a divorce. ◀

DEPENDENTS WITH UNEARNED INCOME

In the past, taxpayers in high tax brackets were able to reduce their tax liability by shifting income to children and other dependents. Under prior law, no tax was due if the income was less than the dependent's personal exemption and standard deduction. Even if the shifted income was greater than these amounts, there was a tax savings if the dependent was in a low tax bracket. Under current law, three rules apply that curtail the advantages of shifting income to dependents:

- ▶ Dependents do not receive a personal exemption on their own returns.
- ▶ A dependent's standard deduction is reduced to the greater of $750 or the dependent's earned income (such as salary) plus $250.
- ▶ The tax on the net unearned income (such as dividends and interest) of a child under age 14 is figured by reference to the parents' tax rate if it is higher than the child's.

KEY POINT

Children under the age of 14 will not have their net unearned income tax at their parents' tax rate until the children's unearned income exceeds $1,500.

The first two rules have been discussed previously in this chapter. The third rule is discussed below.

EXAMPLE I2-29 ▶ In 2002, Tim is a self-supporting 18-year-old who received $2,000 of dividends and $900 from a part-time summer job. He is entitled to the regular standard deduction and a personal exemption because his parents may not claim him as a dependent (does not meet the support test). Tim owes no tax as these deductions exceed his income. ◀

EXAMPLE I2-30 ▶ Assume the same facts as in Example I2-29 except that Tim is a dependent of his parents, and they are in the 27% tax bracket. Because Tim is a dependent, he is not entitled to a personal exemption. Tim's standard deduction is limited to the greater of $750 or his earned income plus $250 (but not more than $4,700). Because his earned income is $900, the standard deduction is $1,150 ($900 + $250). Therefore, Tim's taxable income is $1,750 ($2,900 AGI − $1,150 standard deduction). Since Tim is over age 13, he is not subject to the kiddie tax on his unearned income and his regular tax rate (10%) is used. The tax is $175 (0.10 × $1,750). ◀

Under the third rule, often called the kiddie tax, part of the **net unearned income** of a dependent child under age 14 is taxed at the child's rate, and part at the parents' marginal tax rate if that rate is higher than the child's. This tax can be computed following a three-step process:

1. Compute the child's taxable income in the normal fashion for dependents as discussed earlier in this chapter.
2. Compute the child's net unearned income:

Unearned income (described below)	$XXX
Less: Statutory deduction of $750	(XXX)

[46] Sec. 152(e).

WHAT WOULD YOU DO IN THIS SITUATION?

CHOICE OF RATE SCHEDULES

Jane Brown married Jim four years ago. Two years ago Jim lost his job. After looking for work for several months, Jim left town to look for work, and Jane has not heard from him. Jim's brother told Jane that he had heard that Jim lived in Texas, but a friend said he heard that Jim had been killed in an automobile accident.

Jane went back to school and completed a program as an medical technician. She returned to work this year, and she earned $35,000. She has asked you to prepare her tax return this year. She has asked you whether she should file as a single taxpayer, married person filing separately, or as a married person filing jointly. Because she has had a low income until recently, she has taken no legal steps to resolve her status. What should she do?

Less: Greater of	
a. $750 of standard deduction, or	
b. Itemized deductions directly connected with the production of the unearned income.	(XXX)
Equals: Net unearned income	$XXX

3. Compute the child's tax:

Net unearned income times parents' marginal tax rate	$XXX
Plus: Difference between taxable income and net unearned income times child's tax rate	XXX
Equals: Child's total tax	$XXX

Unearned income is the child's investment income including dividends, taxable interest, capital gains, rents, royalties and other income that is not earned income (such as salary).[47]

EXAMPLE I2-31 ▶ Assume the same facts as in Example I2-30 except that Tim is age 13. His standard deduction is still $1,150 and his taxable income is also $1,750. Since Tim is under age 14, a portion of his unearned income may be subject to tax at his parents' 27% rate. The computation of Tim's tax is as follows:

1. Compute Tim's taxable income:		
Wages		$ 900
Dividends		2,000
Adjusted gross income		$2,900
Standard deduction	$1,150	
Personal exemption	0	1,150
Taxable income		$1,750
2. Compute Tim's net unearned income:		
Unearned income: Dividends		$2,000
Statutory deduction		(750)
Portion of standard deduction		(750)
Net unearned income		$ 500
3. Compute Tim's tax		
Tax on net unearned income: $500 × 27%		$ 135
Tax on taxable income minus net unearned income: ($1,750 − $500) × 10%		125
Total income tax		$ 260 ◀

[47] Sec. 1(g)(4).

In figuring the tax where the parents file separate returns, the tax rate of the parent with the greater taxable income is used. If the parents are divorced, the parent with custody is the relevant parent.

Parents of a child under age 14 may elect to include the child's dividend and interest income on their own return.[48] This rule eliminates the need to file a tax return for the child. To be eligible for the election, the child's gross income must come solely from dividends and interest, and such income must not exceed $7,500. Furthermore, there can be no withholding or estimated payment using the child's Social Security number.[49]

BUSINESS INCOME AND BUSINESS ENTITIES

OBJECTIVE 6

Explain the tax formula for corporations

ADDITIONAL COMMENT

In 1996, there were 4.8 million corporate tax returns filed.

KEY POINT

The tax formula for C corporations differs from the tax formula for individuals in several important respects. The corporate tax formula does not contain an adjusted gross income figure, personal and dependency exemptions, or the standard deduction.

How business income is reported depends on the type of entity that produces the income. Proprietors report their business income on Schedule C of Form 1040 (Schedule F in the case of farmers). The income is taxed on the proprietor's Form 1040 along with any other income the taxpayer may have. Approximately 17 million taxpayers report income on Schedule C each year.

Corporations are divided into two groups: C Corporations and S Corporations. **C corporations**, also called **regular corporations**, are treated as separate entities for tax purposes and pay income taxes on the corporation's taxable income. Shareholders are taxed on dividends they receive from a C corporation but are not taxed on the corporation's undistributed income. Approximately 2 million corporations file the regular corporate return, Form 1120, each year.

The tax formula for C corporations is presented in Table I2-7 on page I2-26. The major difference between the formulas for individual and corporate taxpayers is the fact that there is only one category of deductions for corporations. Personal expenses do not come into consideration. Therefore, there are no itemized deductions, standard deductions, or personal exemptions. The tax rates applicable to C corporations are as follows:[50]

Taxable Income	*Tax*
First $50,000	15% of taxable income
Over $50,000, but not over $75,000	$7,500 + 25% of taxable income over $50,000
Over $75,000, but not over $100,000	$13,750 + 34% of taxable income over $75,000
Over $100,000, but not over $335,000	$22,250 + 39% of taxable income over $100,000
Over $335,000, but not over $10,000,000	$113,900 + 34% of taxable income over $335,000
Over $10,000,000, but not over $15,000,000	$3,400,000 + 35% of taxable income over $10,000,000
Over $15,000,000, but not over $18,333,333	$5,150,000 + 38% of taxable income over $15,000,000
Over $18,333,333	$6,416,667 + 35% of taxable income over $18,333,333

Note that the corporate tax rates reflect a stair-step pattern of progression, with the two highest rates of 39% and 38% in the middle of the progression. The benefits of the two lowest tax rates of 15% and 25% are completely eliminated by the application of the 39%

[48] Sec. 1(g)(7).

[49] Parents may use Form 8814, Parents' Election to Report Child's Interest and Dividends. If the child's income from dividends and interest is between $750 and $1,500, the child's tax is 10% of the income over $750. If the income is over $1,500, the child's tax is computed by multiplying the parents' tax rate times the child's income over $1,500 and adding $75. For example, if the child's dividend income is $2,000 and the parents' tax bracket is 27%, the child's tax is $210 [0.27 × ($2,000 − $1,500) + $75].

[50] Income of certain personal service corporations is taxed at a flat rate of 35%.

▼ **TABLE I2-7**
Tax Formula for C Corporations

Income from whatever source derived	$xxx
Minus: Exclusions	(xxx)
Gross income	$xxx
Minus: Deductions	(xxx)
Taxable income	$xxx
Times: Tax rates	× .xx
Gross tax	$xxx
Minus: Credits and prepayments	(xxx)
Net tax payable or refund due	$xxx

tax rate to taxable income between $100,000 and $335,000. Likewise, the benefit of the 34% tax rate on taxable income between $335,000 and $10,000,000 is eliminated by the application of a 38% tax rate on taxable income between $15,000,000 and $18,333,333.

The second group of corporations, **S corporations**, generally are not treated as separate entities for tax purposes. They are referred to as flow-through entities. S corporation shareholders are required to report their respective shares of the S corporation's income on their individual tax returns even if the income is not distributed. All shareholders must agree to the S corporation election when it is made. S corporations must also meet a series of conditions, such as having 75 or fewer shareholders. S corporations report ordinary income and special items separately and shareholders in turn report their respective shares of the ordinary income and of each special item. Approximately 3 million corporations file S corporation returns, Form 1120S, each year.

In one sense, there is no formula to compute an S corporation's taxable income because the corporation normally does not pay a tax. S corporations do file returns, but the returns are more informational in nature, much like tax returns of a partnership. A residual income total, known as ordinary income, is computed on the return. Special items, such as capital gains and losses and charitable contributions, are kept separate from the ordinary income amount. This is because every item that would receive special treatment on a shareholder's return is passed through to the shareholder with its status intact. Each shareholder reports his or her share of the ordinary income and his or her share of each special item. Losses pass through and generally can be deducted by shareholders up to their respective bases in the corporation's stock. The deductibility of losses is also subject to other rules, such as the at-risk and passive activity loss rules, and are covered in Chapter I8.

Partnerships, like S corporations, are flow-through entities for tax purposes. Partners report their respective shares of the partnership's income on their tax returns even if the income is not distributed. Approximately 2 million partnerships file returns, Form 1065, each year. Like S corporations, partnerships report ordinary income and special items separately and the partners report their respective shares of the ordinary income and of each special item. Losses also pass through and generally can be deducted by partners on their individual returns.

EXAMPLE I2-32 ▶ Jane is starting Jane's Computer Services and is considering alternative organizational forms. She anticipates the business will earn $100,000 from operations before compensating her for her services and before charitable contributions. Jane, who is single, has $3,000 of income from other sources and other itemized deductions of $11,000. Her compensation for services will be $50,000. Charitable contributions to be made by the business are expected to be $4,000. Other distributions to her from the business are expected to be $15,000. Compare her current income tax assuming she operates the business as a proprietorship, an S corporation, and a C corporation. Ignore payroll and other taxes.

	Proprietorship	S Corporation	C Corporation
Business Income			
Operating income	$100,000	$100,000	$100,000
Compensation paid to Jane		(50,000)	(50,000)
Contributions			(4,000)
Net	$100,000	$ 50,000	$ 46,000
Corporate income tax			$ 6,900
Jane's Income			
Business income (above)	$100,000	$ 50,000	
Compensation (above)		$ 50,000	$ 50,000
Dividends			15,000
Other income	3,000	3,000	3,000
Adjusted Gross Income	$103,000	$103,000	$ 68,000
Contributions	$ 4,000	$ 4,000	
Other itemized deductions	11,000	11,000	11,000
Personal exemption	3,000	3,000	3,000
Taxable income	$ 85,000	$ 85,000	$ 54,000
Individual income tax	$ 19,815	$ 19,815	$ 10,926
Total tax	$ 19,815	$ 19,815	$ 17,826

As shown, Jane's total current income tax will be lower if she chooses to operate her business as a C corporation even though the $15,000 paid to her as a dividend is taxed twice—once inside the corporation when it is earned and again on Jane's return. The reason the total tax is lower is because the $31,000 of income retained by the corporation is taxed at the corporation's marginal tax rate of 15% instead of being taxed at Jane's marginal rates of 27% and 30%. The savings will be lost in the future if the corporation distributes the retained income as a dividend. That distribution will be reported by Jane and taxed at her marginal rate at that time. Clearly, if the plans are to distribute the $31,000 in the near future, it is desirable to operate as a proprietorship or an S corporation so that the distribution can be made without any future tax.

Self-employment taxes and social security taxes would also be considered when an organizational form is selected for a new business. Although detailed consideration of these taxes is covered in Chapter I14, it is noted here that the self-employment tax, which generally applies to the proprietorship and partnership forms of doing business, would be greater than the social security tax which would apply only to the wages paid to Jane by the S and C corporations. Given the facts in this case, Jane might judge the proprietorship organizational form less favorably when these taxes are taken into consideration. Jane should consider these taxes along with other taxes (e.g., state and local taxes) and other nontax factors such as liability protection before making a final decision. ◀

The detailed rules of C corporations are covered in Chapter I16 while S corporations and Partnerships are covered in Chapter I17 of the *Individuals* volume. All three are covered more extensively in the *Corporations, Partnerships, Estates, and Trusts* volume and the *Comprehensive* volume.

TREATMENT OF CAPITAL GAINS AND LOSSES

OBJECTIVE 7

Explain the basic concepts of property transactions

Capital gains and losses have been accorded favored tax treatment since 1922. Favored tax treatment essentially means that capital gains are taxed at a lower rate than is ordinary income. A purpose of the special rules is to distinguish capital appreciation from gains attributable to ordinary business transactions and speculation. This goal is accomplished by defining capital assets to not include certain business property (e.g., inventory and trade receivables) and by requiring taxpayers to hold capital assets for minimum time periods in order to benefit from the lower rates that are available to capital gains.

The discussion below is intended as a brief introduction to capital gains and losses. A detailed discussion of this topic is contained in Chapter I5.

HISTORICAL NOTE

Net capital gains reported on individual income tax returns dropped from nearly $300 billion in 1986 to about $133 billion in 1987. The latter amount was more in line with 1984 and 1985. The large amount reported in 1986 was due to the fact that a 60% long-term capital gain deduction was available to individuals in 1986, but was repealed as of December 31, 1986. Many taxpayers sold capital assets to take advantage of the lower effective rates that existed in 1986.

DEFINITION OF *CAPITAL ASSETS*

A **capital gain** or **loss** is the gain or loss from the sale or exchange of a capital asset. Unfortunately, the tax law merely states what is not a capital asset. In other words, **capital assets** are assets other than those listed in Sec. 1221. A detailed discussion is found in Chapter I5. Here we simply note the categories of properties included on the list, which are thereby excluded from capital asset status are inventory, trade receivables, certain properties created by the efforts of the taxpayer (such as works of art), depreciable business property and business land, and certain government publications. All other assets are considered capital assets and include investment property (such as stocks and bonds) and personal use property (such as personal residence or automobile). As noted, a purpose of the rules applicable to capital gains and losses is to distinguish capital appreciation from gains derived from ordinary business operations. The profit from the sale of inventory and trade receivables is viewed as business profit as opposed to capital appreciation. Thus, a gain realized by an artist on the sale of one of his or her own works is ordinary income from personal services. However, gain from the sale of artwork held as an investment or for personal-use would be treated as a capital gain.

ADDITIONAL COMMENT

The amount of net capital gains reported on 1996 tax returns totaled $245 billion, an increase of 50.5% from 1995.

TAX TREATMENT OF GAINS AND LOSSES

Capital gains and losses are divided into long-term (associated with property held over one year) and short-term (associated with property held one year or less). Individual taxpayers pay a maximum 20% tax on a net long-term capital gain (a 10% tax in the case of individuals who are in the 15% tax bracket). A net short-term capital gain is taxed at the same rate as other income.

On the other hand, individuals who suffer net capital losses can deduct only up to $3,000 of the losses from other income. A net capital loss in excess of $3,000 can be carried over and offset against future capital gains or, subject to the $3,000 limitation, deducted from other income.

TAX PLANNING CONSIDERATIONS

SHIFTING INCOME BETWEEN FAMILY MEMBERS

Because of the progressive tax system, families often can reduce their taxes by **shifting income** to family members who are in lower tax brackets.

EXAMPLE I2-33 ▶ Mary, who is in the 35% tax bracket, shifted $5,000 of income to her 22-year-old son, Steve by making a gift of a 10%, $50,000 corporate bond. Steve had no income as he suffered a business loss. In absence of the shift, 35% of the income would have gone for taxes. There is no tax on Steve's return because the income is offset by his loss. ◀

EXAMPLE I2-34 ▶ Farouk, who is in the 35% tax bracket, shifted $2,000 of income to his 18-year-old daughter, Dana, who is in the 10% tax bracket. The tax savings from the shift is $500 [(0.35 × $2,000) – (0.10 × $2,000)]. ◀

ADDITIONAL COMMENT

All 50 states have enacted laws that simplify the procedures for making gifts to minors. This type of law, which in most states is called the Uniform Gifts to Minors Act, is especially important when making gifts of securities.

As noted earlier in this chapter, the net unearned income of children under the age of 14 is taxed at their parents' tax rate. Hence, a shifting of income to young children is often an ineffective method of minimizing tax.

Shifting income must be distinguished from assigning income. Earned income is taxed to the person who produces it. Income from property is taxed to the person who owns the property. Ordering income to be paid to another is an assignment of income that does not change who is taxed on the income. Normally, in the case of income from property, ownership of the property must be transferred in order to shift the income.

EXAMPLE I2-35 ▶ John owns stock in Valley Corporation. John orders the corporation to pay this year's dividends to his daughter. John will be taxed on the income even though he has assigned it to another person. ◀

EXAMPLE I2-36 ▶ Kay owns stock in Valley Corporation. Kay gives the stock to her 17-year-old son. Future dividends on Valley stock will be taxed to the son instead of to Kay. ◀

Individuals often are unwilling to give property away completely. As a result, personal preference may limit the amount of tax planning that is possible.

SPLITTING INCOME

Splitting income consists of creating additional taxable entities, especially corporations, in order to reduce an individual's effective tax rate.

EXAMPLE I2-37 ▶ Tom is a taxpayer in the 35% tax bracket and is involved in a variety of businesses. One business has been producing $20,000 of income per year for several years. Tom incorporates the business. The first $50,000 of a corporation's income is taxed at a 15% rate. Thus, the tax on the income is reduced by $4,000 [(0.35 × $20,000) − (0.15 × $20,000)]. ◀

The creation of a new corporate entity to split income is not always desirable because the corporation's income will be taxed to the shareholder as a dividend if it is distributed. In addition, if income is allowed to accumulate in a corporation indefinitely, it may be subject to the accumulated earnings tax.[51]

KEY POINT

The ability to maximize itemized deductions by the timing of expenditures is somewhat limited. The two most significant items that would lend themselves to such a strategy are property taxes and charitable contributions. Prepaid interest is not deductible until accrued.

MAXIMIZING ITEMIZED DEDUCTIONS

Timing expenditures properly often can increase deductions. In general, cash-basis taxpayers deduct expenses in the year paid. If itemized deductions are less than the standard deduction, the taxpayer will receive no tax benefit from the deductions. A taxpayer in that situation could defer some payments or accelerate others to maximize expenses in one year, thereby creating a sufficient amount of deductions in that year.

EXAMPLE I2-38 ▶ Jean's property taxes are due on January 1 of each year. Jean is a single, cash-basis, calendar-year taxpayer. Itemized deductions other than property taxes total $2,000 in each year. Jean pays the 2002 property taxes of $1,600 on January 1, 2002 and the 2003 property taxes of $1,600 on December 31, 2002. In the absence of doubling up, Jean would not be able to itemize in either year. The itemized deductions of $3,600 ($2,000 + $1,600) would be less than the standard deduction of $4,700. By doubling up, Jean has itemized deductions of $5,200 ($2,000 + $1,600 + $1,600) in 2002. ◀

Medical expenses are deductible only to the extent they exceed 7.5% of a taxpayer's AGI. In situations where medical expenses are just under 7.5% of AGI, taxpayers may be able to create a deduction by doubling up.

EXAMPLE I2-39 ▶ Troy's AGI is $20,000. So far in 2002, Troy's medical expenses have totaled $1,300. Troy has received a bill from his dentist for $500 that is due January 15, 2003. By paying the bill in 2002, Troy will have a deduction for medical expenses of $300 [$1,300 + $500 − (0.075 × $20,000)]. This assumes that Troy's other itemized deductions exceed the standard deduction.[52] ◀

FILING JOINT OR SEPARATE RETURNS

FACTORS TO BE CONSIDERED. In general, married couples may file either joint or separate returns. As noted earlier, if one spouse has significantly more than half of their combined income, filing separately will increase the couple's total income tax. Because of the potential tax saving from a joint return and because it is simpler to prepare one return than two, most married couples file jointly.

---

[51] Amounts accumulated in a corporation in excess of $250,000 may be subject to this tax. However, amounts accumulated for business purposes are exempt. This subject is discussed briefly in Chapter I16 and extensively in *Prentice Hall's Federal Taxation: Corporations, Partnerships, Estates and Trusts.*

[52] For a discussion of restrictions on the deductibility of prepaid medical expenses, see Chapter I7.

It should be noted that the joint return is not always preferred. Separate returns may result in increased deductions. Because only one spouse's income is reported on a separate return, medical expenses are more likely to exceed the 7.5% of adjusted gross income floor if one spouse incurs most of the medical expenses. Similarly, casualty losses involving personal-use assets, which are allowable only to the extent that they exceed 10% of AGI, may be deductible on separate returns.

One significant impact of the joint return is the joint income tax liability. Both the husband and wife may be liable for taxes owed on a joint return. This could be a major problem if a couple separates or divorces after filing a return.

EXAMPLE I2-40 ▶ Jim and Pat file a joint return. They are both informed as to the relevant information pertaining to the return. The next year they separate, and Jim moves out of town without leaving a forwarding address. The IRS audits their joint return and disallows $400 of charitable contributions deducted on the original return. Pat may be held responsible for the additional taxes owed. The IRS does not have to attempt to locate Jim in order to collect the tax. ◀

ETHICAL POINT

Because innocent spouse rules are strict, it may sometimes be safer to file a separate return than run the risk of being held responsible for the acts of another.

INNOCENT SPOUSE PROVISION. When married couples file a joint return, each spouse generally is liable for the entire tax and any penalties imposed.[53] This is the case even if all of the income was earned by one spouse. This rule could prove unfair in some instances, especially where one spouse concealed information from the other. For that reason, the Code contains an **innocent spouse** provision. An innocent spouse is relieved of the liability for tax on unreported income if:

- The amount is attributable to erroneous items of the other spouse.
- The innocent spouse did not know and had no reason to know that there was such an understatement of tax.
- Under the circumstances, it would be inequitable to hold the innocent spouse liable for the understatement.
- The innocent spouse elects relief within two years after the IRS begins collection activities.[54]

EXAMPLE I2-41 ▶ Dan and Joy file a joint return. Dan traveled much of the time and Joy had little information as to his whereabouts or income. Joy worked and her own salary was the sole source of her support. Their return was audited by the IRS. The audit disclosed that Dan had not reported income from a job he had held for several months during the year. In this situation, Joy may be able to use the innocent spouse provision in order to avoid being held liable for the tax on the unreported income. ◀

The election is permitted when the innocent spouse was aware of the understatement, but did not know or have reason to know the extent of the understatement. Relief is limited to the related portion of the understatement attributable to the "unknown" amounts.

SEPARATE LIABILITY ELECTION. Couples who file joint returns and are subsequently divorced, widowed, or separated may make a separate liability election. An electing spouse is liable only for the portion of any understatement attributable to him or her.

EXAMPLE I2-42 ▶ Al and Ann divorce after filing a joint return. An IRS examination of the return reveals $20,000 of unreported income attributable to Al and $10,000 of unallowable deductions attributable to Ann. Together, these amounts result in an understatement of their tax by $9,000. If Ann can establish that she was unaware of Al's unreported income, she can make a separate liability election. She will be liable only for $3,000 of tax as she is responsible for only one third of the understatement. The allocation would not be different because only part of the deductions were disallowed because of an AGI floor. ◀

---

[53] Sec. 6013(d)(3).

[54] Sec. 6015(b).

The election must be made within two years after the IRS begins collections efforts. The election may be made by both spouses. The election is invalid if the spouse responsible for the errors transfers assets to the "innocent" spouse in an effort to avoid payment.

ELECTING TO CHANGE TO A JOINT RETURN. In general, a husband and wife who file separate returns for a given year may elect to change to a joint return by filing an amended joint return. This change is permitted after the due date but must occur within three years of the due date including extensions. Taxpayers may not change from a joint return to separate returns after the due date.[55]

COMPLIANCE AND PROCEDURAL CONSIDERATIONS

WHO MUST FILE

ADDITIONAL COMMENT

The IRS is encouraging nonfilers (i.e., individuals and businesses who should have filed previous tax returns but did not) to come forward. The IRS estimates that there were 6 million nonfilers in 1990 alone.

ADDITIONAL COMMENT

A file-by-telephone system has been tested in some states in the last few years. The filers dial a toll-free telephone number and enter tax return data with a touch-tone telephone. While the taxpayer is still on the line, the IRS calculates any refund or tax due. The taxpayers then mail a signed Form 1040-TEL.

ADDITIONAL COMMENT

The IRS is required to impound tax refunds to help other agencies collect overdue student loans, child support, etc. However, the IRS found that people whose refunds were offset in 1985 and 1986 were far more likely than others to file no returns in the next two years or to file returns without paying all they owed.

Whether an individual must file a tax return is based on the amount of the individual's gross income.[56] The fact that the individual owes no tax does not mean that a return need not be filed. The gross income filing levels are as follows:[57]

	2001	*2002*
Single	$ 7,450	$ 7,700
Single (65 or over)	8,550	8,850
Married, filing jointly	13,400	13,850
Married, filing jointly (one spouse 65 or over)	14,300	14,750
Married, filing jointly (both 65 or over)	15,200	15,650
Surviving spouse	10,500	10,850
Surviving spouse (65 or over)	11,600	12,000
Married, filing separately	2,900	3,000
Married, living separately from spouse at year-end	2,900	3,000
Head of household	9,550	9,900
Head of household (65 or over)	10,650	11,050

There are three situations where taxpayers must file even if the gross income is less than the amounts shown above:

- Taxpayers who receive advance payments of the earned income credit (see Chapter I14) must file regardless of their income levels.
- Taxpayers with net self-employment income of $400 or more must file regardless of their total gross income.
- Taxpayers who can be claimed as a dependent by another must file if they have either unearned income over $750 or total gross income over the standard deduction.

In general, taxpayers must file if their gross income equals or exceeds the sum of the personal exemption and the standard deduction (including the additional standard deduction due to age but not blindness). The blindness allowance and dependency exemptions are not considered. If the disallowance of the standard deduction rules apply, the standard deduction is ignored in determining whether taxpayers must file.

EXAMPLE I2-43 ▶ In 2002, Carol is a single, self-supporting taxpayer with no dependents. Carol must file if her gross income is $7,700 or greater ($4,700 + $3,000). ◀

[55] Reg. Sec. 1.6013-1(a). However, a couple who filed a joint return whose marriage is later annulled must file amended returns as singles (Rev. Rul. 76-255, 1976-2 C.B. 40).

[56] *Gross income* has its usual meaning except that the gain excluded from the sale of a personal residence and excluded foreign earned income are included (Sec. 6012(c)).

[57] Sec. 6012(a)(1).

KEY POINT

It is possible that a taxpayer may be required to file an income tax return but still have no tax liability.

DUE DATES FOR FILING RETURN

An individual taxpayer must file on or before the fifteenth day of the fourth month following the close of his or her tax year.[58] For calendar-year taxpayers, the due date is April 15. If the due date falls on a Saturday, Sunday, or a legal holiday, the due date is the next day that is not a Saturday, Sunday, or holiday.[59]

An automatic four-month extension of time to file is given to taxpayers who file Form 4868 by the due date for the return. This is an extension to file the return, not an extension of the time to pay the tax. The taxpayer must estimate the amount of tax due and pay it with Form 4868.[60] Taxpayers who are unable to file their returns within the four-month extension period may request an additional two month extension of time by timely filing Form 2688.

ADDITIONAL COMMENT

In 1996, 66 million returns were filed on Form 1040, 23 million on Form 1040A, and 21 million on Form 1040EZ.

USE OF FORMS 1040, 1040EZ, AND 1040A

The primary individual tax return is Form 1040. Complicated returns often involve many additional forms and schedules. Two shorter forms are available to taxpayers with less-complicated tax returns. Form 1040EZ is available to single taxpayers and married individuals who file a joint return. Such taxpayers must have taxable income of less than $50,000 and claim no dependents. To use Form 1040EZ, the taxpayer's income must consist of salary and wages plus no more than $400 of taxable interest income. No deductions (other than the standard deduction) or credits (other than withholding from salary and wages) can be taken on the return.

Form 1040A is available to taxpayers who have somewhat more involved returns. Form 1040A can be used by taxpayers claiming any number of exemptions or any filing status. Salary, wages, dividends, interest, pension and annuity income, and unemployment compensation can be reported on Form 1040A. Taxpayers may deduct IRA contributions. Taxpayers may also claim credits for withholding, child care, and earned income.

SELF-STUDY QUESTION

It is sometimes said that the hallmark of the U.S. federal income tax system is voluntary compliance. With so much information being reported to the IRS, how voluntary is the system?

ANSWER

The system is not very voluntary with respect to income subject to reporting. But some sources of income, such as income from self-employment, are not subject to reporting by a third party. Also, the IRS would have to audit a tax return to verify most of the deductions.

SYSTEM FOR REPORTING INCOME

There is a significant and expanding relationship between computers, tax returns, the taxpayer identification system, and information returns. The IRS keeps records based on taxpayer identification numbers. Individual taxpayers report information based on Social Security numbers, whereas employer identification numbers (EIN) are used by corporations, other taxpayers, and tax-exempt entities. Individuals who employ others have both a Social Security number and an employer identification number.

Employers, banks, stockbrokers, savings and loans, and so on report payments they make to others along with the payee's identification number. Today, the IRS computers match much of the reported information with tax returns, using the taxpayer identification number as the cross-reference. The need for accurate information returns is obvious. Some major information returns are listed below:

Basic Form	*Type of Payment*	*Required if Amount Equals or Exceeds*
1099-R	Pensions and annuities	$600
W-2	Salary, wages, etc.	600
1099-DIV	Dividends	10
1099-INT	Interest	600[61]
1099-B	Sale of a security	All
1099-G	Unemployment compensation, tax refunds, etc.	10
1099-MISC	Rent, royalties, etc.	600
1099-R	Total lump-sum distributions from retirement plans	600[62]

This information-reporting system makes it more difficult for taxpayers to avoid IRS detection if they omit income from their returns.

[58] Sec. 6072(a).
[59] Sec. 7503.
[60] Reg. Sec. 1.6081-4(a)(1)-(5)-(5).
[61] For banks and corporations the amount is $10.
[62] Except that all IRA distributions must be reported.

PROBLEM MATERIALS

DISCUSSION QUESTIONS

I2-1 a. The tax law refers to gross income, yet the term gross income is not found on Form 1040. Explain.
b. Why is it important to understand the concept of gross income even though the term is not found on Form 1040?

I2-2 Explain the distinction between income and gross income.

I2-3 a. Explain the distinction between a deduction and a credit.
b. Which is worth more, a $10 deduction or a $10 credit?
c. Explain the difference between refundable and nonrefundable credits.

I2-4 List the five conditions that must be met in order to claim a dependency exemption. Briefly explain each one.

I2-5 a. Briefly explain the concept of support.
b. If a taxpayer provides 50% or less of another person's support, is it possible for the taxpayer to claim a dependency exemption? Explain.
c. Does support include the value of an automobile? Explain.

I2-6 Under what circumstances must a taxpayer use a rate schedule instead of a tax table?

I2-7 a. What determines who must file a tax return?
b. Is an individual required to file a tax return if he or she owes no tax?

I2-8 Many homeowners itemize deductions while many renters claim the standard deduction. Explain.

I2-9 Tax rules are often very precise. For example, a taxpayer must ordinarily provide "over 50%" of another person's support in order to claim a dependency exemption. Why is the threshold "over 50%" as opposed to "50% or more."

I2-10 What is the normal due date for the return of a calendar-year individual taxpayer? What happens to the due date if it falls on a Saturday, Sunday, or holiday?

I2-11 Why are there five filing statuses but only four rate schedules?

I2-12 Can tax-exempt income qualify as support? Explain.

I2-13 Can a scholarship qualify as support?

I2-14 Explain the purpose of the multiple support agreement.

I2-15 Summarize the rules that explain which parent receives the dependency exemption for children in cases of divorce.

I2-16 What conditions must be met by a married couple before they can file a joint return?

I2-17 Explain what is meant by the phrase *maintain a household.*

I2-18 Under what circumstances, if any, can a married person file as a head of household?

I2-19 a. Explain the principal difference in the tax treatment of an S corporation and a C corporation.
b. Why would a C corporation be used if an S corporation is generally exempt from tax?

I2-20 Income earned by C corporations is taxed twice, once when the income is earned and again when it is distributed. If so, how is it possible that operating a business as a C corporation can reduce taxes.

I2-21 a. What assets are excluded from capital asset status?
b. Are capital gains given favorable tax treatment?
c. What is the significance of an asset being classified as a capital asset?
d. Are capital losses deductible?

I2-22 Is there any tax advantage for an individual who has held an appreciated capital asset for eleven months to delay the sale of the asset? Explain.

I2-23 a. Explain the difference between income splitting and income shifting.
b. Why are taxpayers interested in shifting income from one tax return to another within the same family or economic unit?
c. Is there a relationship between the tax on unearned income of a minor and taxpayers who attempt to shift income?

I2-24 a. Who is liable for additional taxes on a joint return?
b. Why is this so important?

I2-25 Can couples change from joint returns to separate returns? Separate to joint?

ISSUE IDENTIFICATION QUESTIONS

I2-26 This year, Yung Tseng, a U.S. citizen, supported his nephew who is attending school in the United States. Yung is a U.S. citizen, but his nephew is a citizen of Hong Kong. The nephew has a student visa, but he hopes to become a permanent U. S. resident. Other family members hope to come to the U.S. What issues must be considered by Yung?

I2-27 Joan's parents were killed in an automobile accident late last year, and she moved in with her sister Joy. Their brother, Ed, provides $300 per month to help with Joan's expenses. Joy provides Joan with a room and she also pays some of Joan's expenses such as clothing and meals. Joan has no source of support other than Joy and Ed. What issues should Joy and Ed consider?

I2-28 Carmen and Carlos, who have filed joint tax returns for several years, separated this year. Carlos works in construction and is often paid in cash. Carlos says he only worked a few weeks this year and made $11,000. In prior years he made approximately $35,000 per year, and Carmen is surprised that his income is so low this year. Carmen received a salary of $38,000 as a medical laboratory technician. They have no dependents and claim the standard deduction. What tax issues should Carmen and Carlos consider?

I2-29 Jane and Bill have lived in a home Bill inherited from his parents. Their son Jim lives with them. Bill and Jane obtain a divorce during the current year. Under the terms of the divorce, Jane receives possession of the home for a period of five years and custody of Jim. Bill is obligated to furnish over one-half of the cost of the maintenance, taxes, and insurance on the home and pay $6,000 of child support per year. Bill lives in an apartment. What tax issues should Jane and Bill consider?

PROBLEMS

I2-30 *Computation of Tax.* The following information relates to two married couples:

	Lanes	*Waynes*
Salary (earned by one spouse)	$20,000	$110,000
Interest income	1,000	7,000
IRA contribution	2,000	0
Itemized deductions	8,000	10,000
Exemptions	6,000	6,000
Withholding	850	21,000

Compute the 2002 tax due or refund due for each couple. Assume that the itemized deductions have been reduced by the applicable floors.

I2-31 ***Dependency Exemptions.*** Anna, age 65, who lives with her unmarried son, Mario, received $7,000, which was used for her support during the year. The sources of support were as follows:

Social Security benefits	$1,500
Mario	2,600
Caroline, an unrelated friend	800
Doug, Anna's son	500
Elaine, Anna's sister	1,600
Total	$7,000

a. Who might be able to claim Anna as a dependent?
b. What must be done before Mario can claim the exemption?
c. Can anyone claim head-of-household status based on Anna's dependency exemption? Explain.
d. Can Mario claim an old age allowance for his mother? Explain.

I2-32 ***Computation of Taxable Income.*** The following information for 2002 relates to Tom, a single taxpayer, age 18:

Salary	$1,800
Interest income	1,600
Itemized deductions	600

a. Compute Tom's taxable income assuming he is self-supporting.
b. Compute Tom's taxable income assuming he is a dependent of his parents.

I2-33 ***Joint Versus Separate Returns.*** Carl and Carol have salaries of $14,000 and $22,000, respectively. Their itemized deductions total $5,000. They are married and both are under age 65.
a. Compute their taxable income assuming they file jointly.
b. Compute their taxable incomes assuming they file separate returns and that Carol claims all of the itemized deductions.

I2-34 ***Joint Versus Separate Returns.*** Hal attended school much of 2002, during which time he was supported by his parents. Hal married Ruth in December 2002. Hal graduated and commenced work in 2003. Ruth worked during 2002 and earned $18,000. Hal's only income was $800 of interest. Hal's parents are in the 30% tax bracket. Thus, claiming Hal as a dependent would save them $900 (0.30 × $3,000) of taxes.

a. Compute Hal and Ruth's gross tax if they file a joint return.

b. Compute Ruth's gross tax if she files a separate return in order to allow Hal's parents to claim him as a dependent.

c. Which alternative would be better for the family? In other words, will filing a joint return save Hal and Ruth more than $900?

I2-35 ***Dependency Exemptions.*** Wes and Tina are a married couple and provide financial assistance to several persons during the current year. For the situations below, determine whether the individuals qualify as dependency exemptions for Wes and Tina. In all of the situations below, assume that any dependency tests not mentioned have been met.

a. Brian is age 24 and Wes and Tina's son. He is a full-time student and lives in an apartment near campus. Wes and Tina provide over 50% of his support. Brian works as a waiter and earned $3,800.

b. Same as a. except that Brian is a part-time student.

c. Sherry is age 22 and Wes and Tina's daughter. She is a full-time student and lives in the college dormitory. Wes and Tina provide over 50% of her support. Sherry works part-time as a bookkeeper and earned $3,800.

d. Same as c. except that Sherry is a part-time student.

e. Granny, age 82, is Tina's grandmother and lives with Wes and Tina. During the current year, Granny's only sources of income were her Social Security of $4,800 and interest on U.S. bonds of $3,800. Granny uses her income to pay for 40% of her total support, Wes and Tina provide the remainder of Granny's support.

f. Wes and Tina provide 75% of the support for Charley, age 5, who lives with Tina's brother, Bob and his wife. Charley's parents were tragically killed in an accident two years ago and Bob and his wife are taking care of Charley in their home awaiting adoption proceedings. However, Bob does not have the financial resources to care for Charley on his own and Wes and Tina provide the above funds to help support Charley.

I2-36 ***Dependency Exemption and Child Credit: Divorced Parents.*** Joe and Joan divorce during the current year. Joan receives custody of their three children. Joe agrees to pay $2,000 of child support for each child.

a. Assuming no written agreement, who will receive the dependency exemption and child credit for the children? Explain.

b. Would it make any difference if Joe could prove that he provided over one-half of the support for each child?

I2-37 ***Filing Status, Dependency Exemptions and Child Credit.*** For the following taxpayers, indicate which tax form should be used, the applicable filing status, and the number of personal and dependency exemptions available, and the number of children who qualify for the child credit.

a. Arnie is a single college student who earned $7,700 working part-time. He had $200 of interest income and received $1,000 of support from his parents.

b. Buddy is a single college student who earned $7,700 working part-time. He had $600 of interest income and received $1,000 of support from his parents.

c. Cindy is divorced and received $6,000 of alimony from her former husband and earned $12,000 working as a secretary. She also received $1,800 of child support for her son who lives with her. According to a written agreement, her former husband is entitled to receive the dependency exemption.

d. Debbie is a widow, age 68, who receives a pension of $8,000, nontaxable social security benefits of $8,000, and interest of $4,000. She has no dependents.

e. Edith is married, but her husband left her two years ago and she has not seen him since. Edith supported herself and her daughter, age 6. She paid all household expenses. Her income of $16,000 consisted of a salary of $15,200 and interest of $800.

I2-38 ***Marriage and Taxes.*** Bill and Mary plan to marry in December 2002. Bill's salary is $32,000 and he owns his own residence. His itemized deductions total $9,000. Mary's salary is $36,000. Her itemized deductions total only $1,600 as she does not own her own residence. For purposes of this problem, assume 2003 tax rates, exemptions, and standard deductions are the same as 2002.

a. What will their tax be if they marry before year-end and file a joint return?

b. What will their combined taxes be for the year if they delay the marriage until 2003?
c. What factors contribute to the difference in taxes?

I2-39 *Dependency Exemptions and Child Credit.* How many dependency exemptions are the following taxpayers entitled to, assuming the people involved are U.S. citizens? Which dependents qualify for child credit?
a. Andrew supports his cousin Mary, who does not live with him. Mary has no income and is single.
b. Bob and his wife are filing a joint return. Bob provided over one-half of his father's support. The father received Social Security benefits of $6,000 and taxable interest income of $800. The father is single and does not live with them.
c. Clay provides 60% of his single daughter's support. She earned $3,000 while attending school during the year as a full-time student. She is 22 years old.
d. Dave provided 30% of his mother's support and she provided 55% of her own support. Dave's brother provided the remainder. The brother agreed to sign a multiple support agreement.

I2-40 *Amount of Personal Exemptions and Child Credit.* Juan and Maria are married and have two young children. Their adjusted gross income in 2002 is $280,000 and have itemized deductions of $38,000.
a. Assuming they can validly claim four personal and dependency exemptions, what is the amount of their personal and dependency exemptions that they will subtract in arriving at taxable income?
b. What is the amount of their child credit?

I2-41 *Filing Requirement.* Which of the following taxpayers must file a 2002 return?
a. Amy, age 19 and single, has $7,050 of wages, $300 of interest, and $350 of self-employment income.
b. Betty, age 67 and single, has a taxable pension of $4,100 and Social Security benefits of $6,200.
c. Chris, age 15 and single, is a dependent of his parents. Chris has earned income of $1,600 and interest of $400.
d. Dawn, age 15 and single, is a dependent of her parents. She has earned income of $400 and interest of $1,600.
e. Doug, age 25, and his wife are separated. He earned $3,400 while attending school during the year.

I2-42 *Head of Household.* In the following situations, indicate whether the taxpayer qualifies as a head of household.
a. Allen is divorced from his wife. He maintains a household for himself and his dependent mother.
b. Beth is divorced from her husband. She maintains a home for herself and supports an elderly aunt who lives in a retirement home.
c. Cindy was widowed last year. She maintains a household for herself and her dependent daughter, who lived with her during the year.
d. Dick is not divorced, but lived apart from his wife for the entire year. He maintains a household for himself and his dependent daughter. He does not receive any financial support from his wife.

I2-43 *Filing Status.* For the following independent situations, determine the optimum filing status for the years in question.
a. Wayne and Celia had been married for 24 years when Wayne died in an accident in October, 2000. Celia and her son, Wally, age 21 in 2000, continued to live at home in 2000, 2001, 2002, and 2003. Wally worked part-time (earning $5,000 in each of the four years) and attended the University on a part-time basis. Celia provided more than 50% of Wally's support for all four years. What is Celia's filing status for 2000, 2001, 2002, and 2003?
b. Juanita is a single parent who in 2002 maintained a household for her unmarried son Josh, age 19. Josh graduated from high school in 2001 and has not decided whether to attend college. Thus, in 2002, Josh worked full-time and earned $9,000. Juanita provided approximately 40% of Josh's support in 2002 but provided all the expenses of maintaining the household. What is Juanita's filing status for 2002?
c. Gomer and Gertrude are married and have one dependent son in 2002. In April, 2002, Gomer left Gertrude a note informing her that he needed his freedom and he was leaving her. As of December 31, 2002, Gertrude had not seen nor heard a word from

Gomer since April. Gertrude fully supported her son and completely maintained the household. What is Gertrude's filing status in 2002 assuming she was still legally married at December 31, 2002?

I2-44 *Computation of Taxable Income.* Jim and Pat are married and file jointly. In 2002, Jim earned a salary of $46,000. Pat is self-employed. Her gross business income was $49,000 and her business expenses totaled $24,000. Each contributed $2,000 to a deductible IRA. Their itemized deductions total $10,000. Compute Parts a, b, and c without regard to self-employment tax.

a. Compute their gross income.
b. Compute their adjusted gross income.
c. Compute their taxable income assuming they have a dependent daughter.

I2-45 *Itemized or Standard Deduction.* Jan, a single taxpayer, has adjusted gross income of $250,000, home mortgage interest of $4,000, and charitable contributions of $3,000. Should she itemize her deductions or claim the standard deduction?

I2-46 *Kiddie Tax.* Debbie is 16 years old and a dependent of her parents. She earns $4,300 working part-time and receives $1,600 interest on savings. She saves both the salary and interest. What is her taxable income? Would her taxable income or tax be different if Debbie were 13 years old?

I2-47 *Personal and Dependency Exemptions.* Determine the number of personal and dependency exemptions in each of the following situations. Assume any condition for a dependency exemption not mentioned is met.

a. Ann supports her mother, who lives in her own apartment.
b. Barry supports his aunt and her husband, who live in their own apartment.
c. Charles and his two brothers help support their mother. Each contributed $3,000 toward her support. She received a taxable pension of $4,000 and used the money to pay some of her own expenses.
d. Dave provided $3,000 of support for his sister. She received $6,000 of social security benefits which she used to pay part of her own expenses.
e. Ed, who is a dependent of his parents, files a return and reports his earnings from a summer job.

I2-48 *Computation of Tax, Standard Deduction, and Kiddie Tax.* Anthony and Latrisha are married and have two sons, James, age 16 and Jonas, age 13. Both sons are properly claimed as dependents. Anthony and Latrisha's taxable income is $130,000 in 2002 and they file a joint return. Both James and Jonas had part-time jobs as well as some unearned income. Below is a summary of their total income.

	James	*Jonas*
Wages	$2,800	$ 400
Dividends from stocks	1,800	2,000

Compute the taxable income and tax liability for James and Jonas.

I2-49 *Computation of Tax.*

a. Compute the tax on $120,000 of taxable income for the following taxpayers for the tax year 2002:
   - S corporation
   - C corporation
   - A married couple filing a joint return
   - A single taxpayer
b. Alternatively from above, assume a corporation is owned 100% by Joe Smith and that Joe also is an employee of the corporation. The corporation has taxable income *before* any salary payments of $120,000. What would be the tax liability to both the corporation and Joe under the following independent scenarios:
   - The corporation is an S corporation, paid Joe a salary of $50,000 and distributed the remaining $70,000 to Joe as a distribution during the year. Without regard to the salary, Joe has other gross income of $10,000, itemized deductions of $12,000, is married and files a joint return with his wife. They have no children.
   - The corporation is a C corporation and the facts are the same as with the S corporation above. The $70,000 distribution to Joe is considered to be a dividend.

I2-50 *Child Credit.* In 2002, Lana a single taxpayer with AGI of $85,400 claims exemptions for three dependent children, all under age 17. What is the amount of her child credit?

I2-51 *Capital Gains and Losses.* Bob and Anna are in the 35% tax bracket for ordinary income and the 20% bracket for capital gains. They have owned several blocks of stock for many years. They are considering the sale of two blocks of stock. The sale of one block would produce a gain of $10,000. The sale of the other would produce a loss of $15,000. For purposes of this problem, ignore personal exemptions, itemized deductions and other phase-outs. They have no other gains or losses this year.

a. How much tax will they save if they sell the block of stock that produces a loss?
b. How much additional tax will they pay if they sell the block of stock that produces a gain?
c. What will be the impact on their taxes if they sell both blocks of stock?

I2-52 *Timing of Deductions.* Virginia is a cash-basis, calendar-year taxpayer. Her salary is $20,000, and she is single. She plans to purchase a residence in 2003. She anticipates her property taxes and interest will total $7,200. Each year, Virginia contributes approximately $1,000 to charity. Her other itemized deductions total approximately $800. For purposes of this problem, assume 2003 tax rates, exemptions, and standard deductions are the same as 2002.

a. What will her gross tax be in 2002 and 2003 if she contributes $1,000 to charity in each year?
b. What will her gross tax be in 2002 and 2003 if she contributes $2,000 to charity in 2002 but makes no contribution in 2003?
c. What will her gross tax be in 2002 and 2003 if she makes no contribution in 2001 but contributes $2,000 in 2003?
d. Alternative c results in a lower tax than either a or b. Why?

I2-53 *Tax Forms and Filing Status.* Which tax form is used by the following individuals?

a. Anita is single, age 68, and has a salary of $22,000 and interest of $300.
b. Betty owns an apartment complex that produced rental income of $36,000. Expenses totaled $38,500.
c. Clay's wife died last year. He qualifies as a surviving spouse. His salary is $24,000.
d. Donna is a head of household. Her salary is $17,000 and she has $200 of interest income.

I2-54 *Computation of Tax.* Maria is a single taxpayer. Her salary is $51,000. Maria realized a short-term capital loss of $5,000. Her itemized deductions total $4,000.

a. Compute Maria's adjusted gross income.
b. Compute her taxable income.
c. Compute her tax liability.

I2-55 *Kiddie Tax.* Ralph and Tina (husband and wife) transferred taxable bonds worth $20,000 to Pam, their 12-year-old daughter. Pam received $1,800 of interest on the bonds in the current year. Ralph and Tina have a combined taxable income of $51,000.

a. Compute Ralph and Tina's gross tax. Assume they do not include Pam's income on their return.
b. Can Ralph and Tina claim a child credit for Pam?
c. Compute Pam's taxable income and gross tax.
d. What would be Pam's tax if she were age 16?

I2-56 *Filing Status.* Assume Gail is a wealthy widow whose husband died last year. Her dependent daughter lives with her for the entire year. Gail has dividend and interest income totaling $370,000 and she pays property taxes and home mortgage interest totaling $20,000.

a. What filing status applies to Gail?
b. Compute her taxable income and gross tax.
c. Assume that Gail does not have a daughter. What is Gail's filing status?
d. Compute Gail's taxable income and gross tax assuming she does not have a daughter.

TAX STRATEGY PROBLEMS

I2-57 Jack is starting a business that he expects to produce $60,000 of income this year before compensating Jack for his services. He has $1,000 of other income and itemized deductions totaling $10,000. He wants to know whether he should incorporate or operate the business as a proprietorship. If a corporation is formed, he wants to know whether he should make an S election. If he incorporates, the corporation will pay Jack a salary of $40,000. He expects to distribute an additional $5,000 of corporate profits to himself each year. Jack is single.

Required: Which organizational form, proprietorship, S corporation, or C corporation, will produce the lowest total current income tax liability for Jack and his business? Ignore payroll and other taxes.

I2-58 Andrea, who is in the 30% tax bracket, is interested in reducing her taxes. She is considering several alternatives. For each alternative listed below, indicate how much tax, if any, she would save?

a. Give $2,000 to a charity. Assume she itemizes.
b. Give $2,000 to a charity. Assume she does not itemize.
c. Make a gift of bonds valued at $8,000 yielding $600 of interest annually to her 15-year-old daughter who has no other income.
d. Sell the bonds from part c for $8,000 and buy tax exempt bonds yielding $400.

TAX FORM/RETURN PREPARATION PROBLEMS

I2-59 Aida Petosa (SSN 123-45-6789) is the 12-year-old daughter of Alfredo Petosa (Soc. Sec. no. 987-65-4321). Her only income is $2,800 of interest on savings. Alfredo qualifies as a head of household, and his taxable income is $52,000. Compute her tax using Form 8615.

I2-60 James S. (SSN 123-45-6789) and Lulu B. Watson (SSN 987-65-4321) reside at 999 E. North Street, Richmond, Virginia 23174. They have one dependent child, Waldo, age 4 (SSN 123-45-4321) and they are both under 65 years old. They do not wish to take advantage of the presidential election campaign check-off. Other relevant information includes

James's salary as a mechanic	$19,000
Lulu's salary as a teacher	24,000
Interest (First National Bank)	1,100
Withholding	4,000

Complete their Form 1040A.

I2-61 John R. Lane (SSN 123-44-6666) lives at 1010 Ipsen Street, Yorba Linda, California 90102. John, a single taxpayer, age 66, provided 100% of his cousin's support. The cousin lives in Arizona. He wants to take advantage of the presidential election campaign check-off. John is an accountant. Other relevant information includes

Salary	$20,000
Taxable pension	30,000
Interest income	300
IRA deduction	2,000
Itemized deductions (from Schedule A)	6,000
Withholding	8,000

Assume that the supplemental Schedule A has already been completed. Complete Form 1040.

CASE STUDY PROBLEMS

I2-62 Bala and Ann purchased as investments three identical parcels of land over a several-year period. Two years ago they gave one parcel to their daughter, Kim, who is now age 12. They have an offer from an investor who is interested in acquiring all three parcels. The buyer is able to purchase only two of the parcels now, but wants to purchase the third parcel two or three years from now, when he expects to have available funds to acquire the property. Because they paid different prices for the parcels, the sales will result in different amounts of gains and losses. The sale of one parcel owned by Bala and Ann will result in a $20,000 gain and the sale of the other parcel will result in a $28,000 loss. The sale of the parcel owned by Kim will result in a $19,000 gain. Kim has no other income and does not expect any significant income for several years. Bala and Ann, however, are in the 30% tax bracket. They do not have any other capital gains this year. Which two properties would you recommend that they sell this year? Why?

I2-63 Larry and Sue separated at the end of the year. Larry has asked Sue to sign a joint income tax return for the year because he feels that the tax will be lower on a joint return. Larry and Sue both work. Sue received a salary of $25,000 and Larry's salary was $20,000. Larry works as a waiter at a local restaurant and received tips. The restaurant asked Larry to indicate the amount of tips he received so that they could report the information to the IRS. Larry reported to the employer that the tips amounted to $3,000, but Sue believes that the amount was probably $6,000 to $10,000. They do not have enough expenses to itemize. Sue has asked you what are the advantages and risks of filing a joint return.

TAX RESEARCH PROBLEMS

I2-64 Ed has supported his stepdaughter, her husband, and their child since his wife's death three years ago. Ed promised his late wife that he would support her daughter from a former marriage and her daughter's husband until they both finished college. They live in another state, and meet gross income filing requirements. Is Ed entitled to dependency exemptions for the three individuals?

A partial list of research sources is

- Sec. 152
- Reg. Sec. 1.152-2
- *Desio Barbetti,* 9 T.C. 1097 (1947)

I2-65 Bob and Sue were expecting a baby in January, but Sue was rushed to the hospital in December. She delivered the baby but it died the first night. Are Bob and Sue entitled to a dependency exemption for the baby?

Research sources include Rev. Rul. 73-156, 1973-1 C.B. 58.

I2-66 Larry has severe vision problems and, in the past, he has claimed the additional standard deduction available to blind taxpayers. This year Larry's doctor prescribed a new type of contact lens that greatly improved his vision. Naturally, Larry was elated, but unfortunately new problems developed. He suffered severe pain, infection, and ulcers from wearing the new lens. The doctor recommended that he remove the lens and after several weeks his eyes healed. The doctor told him that he could wear the contacts again, but only for brief time periods, or the problems would recur. Can Larry claim the additional standard deduction available to blind taxpayers?

Research sources include *Emanuel Hollman,* 38 T.C. 251 (1963).

GROSS INCOME: INCLUSIONS

LEARNING OBJECTIVES

After studying this chapter, you should be able to

1. Explain the difference between the economic, accounting, and tax concepts of income
2. Explain the principles used to determine who is taxed on a particular item of income
3. Determine when a particular item of income is taxable under both the cash and accrual methods of reporting
4. Apply the rules of Sec. 61(a) to determine whether items such as compensation, dividends, alimony, and pensions are taxable

CHAPTER OUTLINE

Economic and Accounting Concepts of Income...3-2
Tax Concept of Income...3-3
To Whom Is Income Taxable?...3-6
When Is Income Taxable?...3-8
Items of Gross Income: Sec. 61(a)...3-13
Other Items of Gross Income...3-22
Tax Planning Considerations...3-27
Compliance and Procedural Considerations...3-29

Computation of an individual's income tax liability begins with the determination of income. Although the meaning of the term *income* has long been debated by economists, accountants, tax specialists, and politicians, no universally operational definition has been accepted.

The Sixteenth Amendment to the Constitution gave Congress the power to tax "income from whatever source derived." To ensure the constitutionality of the income tax, this phrase is incorporated in Sec. 61(a), where **gross income** is defined as follows: "Except as otherwise provided . . . gross income means all income from whatever source derived."

This chapter examines the concept of income for the purpose of determining what items of income are taxable. Chapter I4 considers items of income that are excluded from gross income. As noted in Chapter I2, many provisions in the tax law are created by a process of political compromise. Thus, there is no single explanation of why certain items are taxable and others are not. For this reason, determining whether a particular item of income is taxable often proves difficult.

ECONOMIC AND ACCOUNTING CONCEPTS OF INCOME

OBJECTIVE 1

Explain the difference between the economic, accounting, and tax concepts of income

ECONOMIC CONCEPT

In economics, *income* is defined as the amount an individual could consume during a period and remain as well off at the end of the period as he or she was at the beginning of the period. To the economist, therefore, income includes both the wealth that flows to the individual and changes in the value of the individual's store of wealth. Or, more simply, income equals consumption plus the change in wealth.

EXAMPLE I3-1 ▶ Alice earned a salary of $40,000. She consumed $30,000 of food, clothing, housing, medical care, and other goods and services. Assets owned by Alice were worth $100,000 at the beginning of the year. Her assets, including $10,000 of salary that was saved, were worth $115,000 at the end of the year. Her liabilities did not change during the year. Alice's economic income is $45,000 [$30,000 + ($115,000 − $100,000)]. ◀

Under the economist's definition, unrealized gains, as well as gifts and inheritances, are income. Furthermore, the economist adjusts for inflation in measuring income. An individual has no income to the extent that an increase in the measured value of property is caused by a decrease in the value of the measuring unit. In other words, inflation does not increase wealth and, therefore, does not cause an individual to be better off.

ACCOUNTING CONCEPT

In accounting, income is measured by a transaction approach. Accountants usually measure income when it is *realized* in a transaction. Values measured by transactions are relatively objective as accountants recognize (i.e., report) income, expenses, gains, and losses that have been realized as a result of a completed transaction. Accountants believe that the economic concept of income is too subjective to be used as a basis for financial reporting and, therefore, have traditionally used historical costs in measuring income instead of using unconfirmed estimates of changes in market value. In accounting, the meaning of the term *realization* is critical to the income measurement process. *Realization* generally results upon the occurrence of two events, (1) a change in the form or substance of a taxpayer's property (or phrased another way, a severance of the economic interest in the property), and (2) a transaction with a second party. Thus, if a taxpayer sells some property for cash, a realization has clearly occurred, i.e., the property has been changed to cash and the transaction was with a second party. Conversely, the mere increase in value of property owned by a taxpayer will not result in the realization of income because there has been no change in the form of the property and no transaction with a second party.

EXAMPLE I3-2 ▶ Assume the same facts as in Example I3-1. The amount consumed by Alice, the increase in the value of the property owned by her, and inflation are all ignored by the accountant in measuring her income. Only when she sells or otherwise disposes of the assets that have increased in value will the accountant recognize the gain. Thus, Alice's accounting income is $40,000. ◀

TAX CONCEPT OF INCOME

The income tax law essentially has adopted the accountant's concept of income rather than the economist's. The reasons for this generally relate to matters of administrative convenience and the wherewithal-to-pay concept. However, as we will see later, there are many differences between income for tax purposes and accounting income.

In general, three conditions must be met for amounts to be taxable.

- There must be economic benefit. The economic benefit is not limited to cash payments. Employees who receive a company's stock, rather than cash, are receiving an economic benefit. Taxpayers benefit even if they direct that payments be made to other persons. As a result, employees cannot avoid being taxed on their earnings by ordering that their salaries be paid to creditors or family members.
- The income must be realized. In general, realization occurs when the earning process is complete and a transaction with another party takes place that permits an objective measure of the income. This objective measurement increases "administrative convenience" which is discussed below. Unlike financial accounting, there are many exceptions that result in income being reported when the taxpayer receives payment even if that is at a time other than when the earning process is complete. These exceptions result in taxes being owed when the taxpayer has the "wherewithal to pay" (see below). Taxpayers who use the "cash method" of reporting, discussed later in the chapter, are normally taxed when payment is received.
- The income must be recognized. Some items of income are not taxable because of special provisions in the tax law. For example, certain real estate exchanges and corporate reorganizations are not taxable because of statutory nonrecognition rules. In such cases, the taxpayer receives a lower basis in replacement property, and that often means the income is recognized when the replacement property is sold. The tax law also contains exclusions that exempt specific types of income such as scholarships, inheritances, and municipal bond interest. Within statutory limitations, taxpayers are never taxed on such items of income.

ADMINISTRATIVE CONVENIENCE

The economic concept of income is considered to be too subjective to be used as a basis for determining income taxes. The need for objectivity in taxation is evident. If taxpayers were required to report increases in value as income, some individuals would certainly understate values to reduce their tax liabilities. The IRS and even the most honest taxpayer often would disagree over values and, as a result, the tax system would be extremely difficult to administer. The disputes over valuation issues would be constant, and the courts would be burdened with added litigation. This problem is evidenced by the few situations where valuations are required in the determination of tax. For example, taxpayers who contribute property to charity usually can deduct the value of the property. The courts are continuously having to resolve disputes between taxpayers and the IRS over the value of such contributions. Furthermore, in the case of certain large contributions of property, taxpayers are required to attach to their returns appraisals of the contributed property. Recently, penalties were added to the law for persons who substantially overvalue contributions.

In some instances, objectivity is achieved at the price of equity. For example, a taxpayer who owns land that has substantially declined in value generally cannot recognize the decline in value until it is realized through a disposition of the land. Similarly, an increase in value, no matter how large, is not taxed until a sale or exchange of the property has occurred. A taxpayer with a modest salary may feel that it is unfair that he or she is taxed on the salary while another person is not taxed on unrealized gains amounting to millions of dollars. As noted above, however, it would be practically impossible to fairly and consistantly administer an income tax law that was based on values.

WHEREWITHAL TO PAY

KEY POINT

Section 446(a) states that taxable income shall be computed under the method of accounting on the basis of which the taxpayer regularly computes his or her income in keeping his or her books. This provision would seem to require that tax accounting rules would conform to financial accounting rules. However, as will be seen later in this and other chapters, there are many differences.

The wherewithal-to-pay concept holds that tax should be collected when the taxpayer is in the best position to pay the tax. A taxpayer who sells property and collects the cash is in a better position to pay the tax than a taxpayer who owns property that is merely increasing in value without a sale.

This concept is the rationale for several tax provisions. For example, the tax law allows a cash-basis taxpayer who sells property on the installment basis to report the gain as the installment payments are collected, rather than at the time of the sale. Losses, on the other hand, cannot be reported on the installment basis, as the wherewithal-to-pay is not an issue. The concept is also used to justify differences between the tax law and financial accounting principles. Prepaid income is not income from an accounting standpoint until it is earned. The tax law, however, takes the position that prepaid income is subject to taxation at the time it is collected, rather than as it is earned. At the time of collection, the taxpayer clearly has the cash available to pay the tax. If the tax were deferred until the income is earned, the taxpayer may no longer have the cash.

GROSS INCOME DEFINED

KEY POINT

Congress has not adopted any particular concept or theory of income for tax purposes. Except as specifically limited by statute, the definition of income is broad and general.

Section 61(a) provides the following general definition and listing of income items:

> General Definition.—Except as otherwise provided in this subtitle, gross income means all income from whatever source derived, including (but not limited to) the following items:
>
> 1. Compensation for services, including fees, commissions, fringe benefits, and similar items
> 2. Gross income derived from business
> 3. Gains derived from dealings in property
> 4. Interest
> 5. Rents
> 6. Royalties
> 7. Dividends
> 8. Alimony and separate maintenance payments
> 9. Annuities
> 10. Income from life insurance and endowment contracts
> 11. Pensions
> 12. Income from discharge of indebtedness
> 13. Distributive share of partnership gross income
> 14. Income in respect of a decedent
> 15. Income from an interest in an estate or trust

SELF-STUDY QUESTION

Why should taxpayers who are using the cash method of accounting be required to include in gross income the value of property or services received?

ANSWER

If taxpayers were not required to include the value of property or services received in gross income, many taxpayers would arrange their financial affairs so that they would receive property or services instead of cash.

This definition certainly is not all-inclusive. For example, it does not indicate whether specific items of income such as insurance settlements, gambling winnings, or illegal income are taxable. One point is apparent: The phrase *[e]xcept as otherwise provided* means that all sources of income are presumed to be taxable unless there is a specific exclusion in the income tax law. The IRS does not have to prove that an item of income is taxable. Rather, the taxpayer must prove that the item of income is excluded. Thus, gambling winnings and illegal income are taxable simply because no specific provisions in the tax law exclude such amounts from taxation.

FORM OF RECEIPT. Gross income is not limited to amounts received in the form of cash. According to Reg. Sec. 1.61-1(a), income may be "realized in any form, whether in money, property, or services." The important question is whether the taxpayer receives an economic benefit. This rule covers barter transactions which are direct exchanges of property and services. Each party to the transaction is taxed on the value of the property or services received in the exchange. In general, the cost basis of property given up in a barter transaction can be subtracted from the value of the property received in arriving at the taxable amount.

EXAMPLE I3-3 ▶ King Corporation transfers 1,000 shares of its stock to its president. The stock has no restrictions and is part of the president's compensation. The president must include the value of the stock in gross income. ◀

EXAMPLE I3-4 ▶ Ali, an attorney, performs legal services for Paul, a painter, in exchange for Paul's promise to paint Ali's residence. Each taxpayer realizes income equal to the value of services received when the services are performed. Thus, Ali must report income in an amount equal to the value of the painting services provided by Paul. Paul must report the value of Ali's legal services. These amounts, assuming an arms-length transaction, should be the same. ◀

EXAMPLE I3-5 ▶ USA Corporation distributes an automobile to Vicki, a shareholder, in lieu of a cash dividend. Vicki must report the value of the automobile as dividend income. ◀

EXAMPLE I3-6 ▶ Len has fallen behind on loan payments due to a bank. The bank obtains a court order requiring Len's employer to pay part of Len's wages directly to the bank. Len will be taxed on the full wages even though a portion goes directly to the bank. ◀

EXAMPLE I3-7 ▶ Wayne borrowed $3,000 from his employer. The employer awarded year-end bonuses to other employees but told Wayne that the debt was being forgiven in lieu of a bonus. Wayne must include the $3,000 in income. ◀

STOP & THINK

Question: As noted, income is taxable even if it is paid in a form other than cash. What problem does this treatment produce for the IRS and taxpayers?

Solution: Two major problems are created: valuation and enforcement. First, it is necessary to determine the market value of property and services when income is received in a form other than cash. Determining values can be difficult. Second, enforcement by the IRS is made much more difficult because such income is not documented by canceled checks, credit card receipts, or other records. Thus, as demonstrated in Example I3-4 above, many of these so-called "traded services" are not reported as income. This evasion of income represents billions of lost tax revenues to the government.

INDIRECT ECONOMIC BENEFIT. As indicated earlier, the issue of taxability of income often depends on whether the taxpayer receives an economic benefit. In general, if a taxpayer benefits from an item, it is taxable. Frequently, however, an employer may make an expenditure in which its employees may incidentally or indirectly benefit. For example,

- Security guards patrol an employer's plant, protecting both the employer's property and the employees. The employees receive an indirect benefit for the protection provided by the security guards.
- An employer requires employees to undergo an annual checkup, the cost of which is paid by the employer.
- An employer provides protective clothing worn by employees while on the job.
- A shipping company provides sleeping accommodations to sailors while ships are at sea.
- A company requires certain employees to wear shoes manufactured by the company and provide regular reports on the quality of the shoes.

It is now well-established that taxpayers may exclude such indirect benefits from gross income. This judicially-developed rule holds that an expenditure is excludible if it is made in order to serve the business needs of the employer and any benefit to the employee is secondary and incidental.

Congress also has established rules dealing with situations where expenditures are made primarily to benefit employees. While expenditures made by employers that primarily benefit employees are generally taxable, there are instances whereby such expenditures are not taxable. These rules, which are discussed in Chapters I4 and I9, permit employees to exclude certain fringe benefits (such as employee discounts) from gross income.

TO WHOM IS INCOME TAXABLE?

OBJECTIVE 2

Explain the principles used to determine who is taxed on a particular item of income

KEY POINT

The law makes a clear distinction between an assignment of income and an assignment of income-producing property. The income is taxable to the assignor in the former case, but where there is a bona fide gift of property the income is taxable to the assignee.

ADDITIONAL COMMENT

The community property states are generally located in the western or southwestern United States. Generally these states were settled by immigrants from France and Spain, and their state laws reflect this fact. The common law is derived from English common law.

ADDITIONAL COMMENT

Community property laws are sometimes difficult to generalize. Depending on the specific law within a community property state, one-half of estimated taxes paid by one spouse may or may not be used by the other spouse on a separate return.

Once it is established that income is taxable, it is necessary to determine to whom it is taxable. Although such determinations are usually easy, there are circumstances where income is not necessarily taxed to the person who receives it. If physical receipt of income was the only test, a family might reduce or eliminate its income tax by having income paid to children and other members who are in low tax brackets or have no tax liability.

ASSIGNMENT OF INCOME

In 1930, the Supreme Court held in a landmark case, *Lucas v. Earl,* that an individual is taxed on the earnings from his or her personal services.[1] Specifically, the Supreme Court held that a husband was taxed on the earnings from his law practice, even though he had signed a legally enforceable agreement with his wife that the earnings would be shared equally. An agreement to assign income does not permit a person to avoid being taxed on the income. The Court used the previously developed analogy that likens income to the fruit and capital to the tree.[2] Accordingly, the fruit (income) could not be attributed to a tree other than the one on which it grew.

In 1940, the Supreme Court, in *Helvering v. Horst,* extended the assignment of income doctrine to income from property.[3] In this case, the taxpayer detached interest coupons from bonds and gave the coupons to his son. The son collected the interest and reported it on his own return. The Supreme Court held that the taxpayer was taxed on the interest income because he owned the bonds. This holding leads to a basic rule that the income from property is taxed to the owner of the property. To transfer the income from property, the taxpayer must transfer ownership of the property itself.[4]

Although married couples may file joint returns today, this privilege did not become available until 1948. Assignment of income is an issue today when other individuals such as parents and children are involved, and it can still be an issue with married couples if they file separate returns.

ALLOCATING INCOME BETWEEN MARRIED PEOPLE

For federal income tax purposes, income is allocated between a husband and wife depending on the state of residence. Forty-two states follow a common law property system, whereas eight states[5] use a community property system. Under common law, income is generally taxed to the individual who earns the income, either through labor or capital. Thus, in the case of a married couple, if the wife owns stock in her separate name and receives dividends from such stock, the income is taxed entirely to the wife. Generally, the only **joint income** in a common law state is income from jointly owned property.[6]

In community property states, income may be either separate or community. **Community income** is considered to belong equally to the spouses. In all community property states, the income from the personal efforts of either spouse is considered to belong

[1] *Lucas v. Earl,* 8 AFTR 10287, 2 USTC ¶496 (USSC, 1930).

[2] The analogy had been used some ten years earlier in *Eisner v. Myrtle H. Macomber,* 3 AFTR 3020, 1 USTC ¶32 (USSC, 1920). The court originally used the analogy in efforts to distinguish income from capital.

[3] *Helvering v. Horst,* 24 AFTR 1058, 40-2 USTC ¶9787 (USSC, 1940).

[4] A series of rather specific rules allocates income between the former and current owner when income-producing property is transferred. For example, in the case of bonds transferred by gift, the IRS has ruled that interest must be allocated based on the number of days the bonds were held by each owner during the interest period (Rev. Rul. 72-312, 1972-1 C.B. 22). A similar allocation must be made if bonds are sold (Rev. Rul. 72-224, 1972-1 C.B. 30).

[5] The states are Arizona, California, Idaho, Louisiana, Nevada, New Mexico, Texas, and Washington. Wisconsin's marital property law, though not providing for community property, is basically the same as community property.

[6] Historically, tenancy by the entirety, a form of joint ownership between spouses, allocated all income to the husband. Today, the laws of many states allocate income from property held in tenancy by the entirety equally between the spouses.

equally to the spouses. Furthermore, income from community property is considered to be community income. Thus, if a wife's salary is used to purchase stock, subsequent dividends are community income.

Couples can have separate property even in community property states. **Separate property** consists of all property owned before marriage and gifts and inheritances acquired after marriage. Whether income from separate property is community or separate depends on the state. In Idaho, Louisiana, and Texas, income from separate property is community income. In Arizona, California, Nevada, New Mexico, and Washington, such income is separate income.

EXAMPLE I3-8 ▶ A husband and wife file separate returns. The husband's salary is $40,000 and the wife's salary is $48,000. The wife received $1,000 of dividends on stock she had inherited from her parents. Interest of $1,200 was received on bonds that were purchased from the husband's salary. They received $2,600 in rent from farm land that they purchased jointly. The income would be allocated, depending on the state of residence, as follows:

California (Community Property State)	*Husband*	*Wife*
Salary	$44,000	$44,000
Dividends		1,000
Interest	600	600
Rent	1,300	1,300
Total	$45,900	$46,900
Texas (Community Property State)		
Salary	$44,000	$44,000
Dividends	500	500
Interest	600	600
Rent	1,300	1,300
Total	$46,400	$46,400
Pennsylvania (Common Law State)		
Salary	$40,000	$48,000
Dividends		1,000
Interest	1,200	
Rent	1,300	1,300
Total	$42,500	$50,300 ◀

These rules are important if couples file separate returns. The community income rules can prove to be a problem if one spouse conceals income from the other. Normally, each spouse is expected to report one-half of all community income. This treatment is inequitable if one spouse is not aware that the community income was earned. Special rules excuse an innocent spouse who fails to report community income on a separate return, provided that the spouse had no knowledge or reason to know of the item and, as a result, the inclusion of the community income would be inequitable.[7] A corresponding provision permits the IRS to include the entire amount in the income of the other spouse.[8]

STOP & THINK *Question:* The tax treatment of income earned in a common law state versus a community property state can be very inconsistent. As noted, the Supreme Court, in *Lucas v. Earl*, decided that a husband was taxed on all his income even though he agreed to share that income with his wife. Nevertheless, community income in a community property state is divided equally between husbands and wives even if one spouse earned all of the income. Why the tax distinction?

Solution: Lucas v. Earl dealt with a case in a common law state where the husband was legally entitled to the income, but decided to divide it with his wife. In community property states, couples are legally obligated to share their incomes. The federal income tax law respects the different property law systems of the states and taxes the income of per-

[7] Sec. 66(b).

[8] Sec. 66(c).

sons based on state law. It would be unfairly burdensome to tax individuals on income to which they never had any legal right.

INCOME OF MINOR CHILDREN

As noted earlier, whether a husband or wife is taxed on income is determined by state law. However, earnings of a minor child are taxed to the child regardless of the state's property law system. Therefore, earnings of a child from either personal services (compensation) or from property (dividends, interest, rents, etc.) are taxed to the child, not the child's parents. As noted in Chapter I2, the unearned income of a child under age 14 may be taxed at the parents' tax rate if it is higher than the child's rate. Alternatively, the parents may elect to include the child's unearned income on their return. In the case of spouses, the spouse who has a legal right to such income determines who is taxed on it. In the case of children, however, the individual who earned the income determines who is taxed on it.

WHEN IS INCOME TAXABLE?

OBJECTIVE 3

Determine when a particular item of income is taxable under both the cash and accrual methods of reporting

The year in which income is taxed depends on the taxpayer's accounting method. The three primary overall accounting methods are the **cash receipts and disbursements method,** the **accrual method**, and the **hybrid method.** While taxpayers have the right to choose a method of accounting, the chosen method still must clearly reflect income as determined by the IRS. The IRS has the power to change the accounting method used by a taxpayer if, in the opinion of the IRS, the method being used does not clearly reflect income. Further, the Regulations require taxpayers to use the accrual method for determining purchases and sales when a taxpayer maintains an inventory.[9] However, the IRS recently ruled that taxpayers whose annual gross receipts for the three prior years averaged $1 million or less are exempt from the requirement and may use the cash method.[10] This exception for small taxpayers is discussed in more detail below.

KEY POINT

Neither the IRC nor the Regulations define the terms *accounting* and *accounting method.*

Section 448 requires C corporations (and partnerships with corporate partners), tax shelters, and certain trusts to use the accrual method of accounting. Qualified personal service corporations, certain types of farms, and entities with average gross receipts under $5 million are exempt from the requirement.

Once an accounting method has been adopted, it cannot be changed without permission of the IRS. See Chapter I11.

CASH METHOD

ADDITIONAL COMMENT

Taxpayers engaged in more than one trade or business may use a different method of accounting for each separate trade or business.

ADDITIONAL COMMENT

The use of the cash receipts and disbursements method of accounting gives the taxpayer some control over the timing of the recognition of income and deductions. It also has the advantage of simplicity.

The **cash receipts and disbursements method** of accounting is used by most individual taxpayers and most small businesses. (See Chapter I11 for a more complete discussion of who is permitted to use the cash method.) Under this method, income is reported in the year the taxpayer actually or constructively receives the income rather than in the year the income is earned. The income can be received by the taxpayer or the taxpayer's agent and be in the form of cash, other property, or services.[11] In the case of property or services, the amount included in income is the value of the property or services. An accounts receivable or other unsupported promise to pay is considered to have no value under the cash method and, as a result, no income is recognized until the receivable is collected. Topic Review I3-1 summarizes when various types of income are reported.

The fact that prepaid income is usually taxed when received, rather than when earned, often results in a mismatching of income and expenses.

EXAMPLE I3-9 ▶ In December of the current year, Troy, who owns an apartment building, collects the first and last months' rent from the tenant. Troy must report two months' rent in the current year. The

---

[9] Reg. Sec. 1.446-1(c)(2)(i).

[10] Rev. Proc. 2000-22, 2000-01 C.B. 1008. This exception is referred to as the *small taxpayer exception.*

[11] An agent can be an employee, relative, or other person authorized to receive the income.

Topic Review I3-1

When Income Is Taxable

Item	Cash Basis	Accrual Basis
Compensation	Year actually or constructively received.	Year earned or year received if prepaid.
Interest	Year actually or constructively received.	Year accrued or year received if prepaid.
Discount on Series E or EE Bonds	Choice of reporting interest as it accrues or at maturity.	Year accrued.
Dividends	Year actually or constructively received.	Year actually or constructively received.
Rent	Year actually or constructively received (does not apply to a deposit).	Year accrued or year received if prepaid (year accrued if services are associated, e.g., in a hotel or motel) (does not apply to a deposit).
Services (maintenance contracts, dance lessons, etc.)	Year actually or constructively received.	Year accrued or year received if prepaid except that a taxpayer may report the income as it accrues if all the services are to be performed by the end of the next tax year.
Sale of goods	The cash method cannot be used to report sale of goods if inventories are an income-producing factor.	Year of sale or year cash is received if prepaid except may elect to report in year of sale if goods are not on hand, amount received is less than cost of item, and same accounting method is used for financial accounting.
Subscriptions (newspapers, magazines, etc.)	Year actually or constructively received.	Year earned or year cash is received, if prepaid, except may elect to report income as newspaper, etc., is published.
Memberships (automobile clubs, etc.)	Year actually or constructively received.	Year earned or year received if prepaid (certain nonstock corporations may elect to report prepaid amounts over the membership period, if the period covers three years or less).
Sale of property (other than stock)	Year actually or constructively received.	Year transaction is completed (e.g., the close of escrow in case of sale of real estate).
Sale of stock	Year transaction is executed.	Year transaction is executed.

actual expenses associated with the last month's rental are not incurred until the last month. However, Troy must report two months' income this year, but may only deduct one month's expenses. ◀

ADDITIONAL COMMENT

There is no recognized doctrine of constructive payment.

Reporting prepaid income can have harsh results because it is not offset by related deductions. If the income is taxed before the expenses are incurred, the taxpayer may not have enough cash to pay the expenses when they are incurred.[12] This burden is mitigated, in part, by Treasury Regulations and Revenue Procedures discussed in this chapter (e.g., the treatment of prepaid income, page I3-11).

REAL-WORLD EXAMPLE

Paul Hornung, a former football player with the Green Bay Packers, was awarded an automobile in 1961 for being the outstanding player in the NFL championship game, but he did not actually receive it until 1962. He attempted to invoke the constructive receipt doctrine and report the income in 1961. The court held that he could not claim constructive receipt because the car was not set aside in the year of the award. *Paul V. Hornung*, 47 T.C. 428 (1967).

CONSTRUCTIVE RECEIPT. As noted, a cash-basis taxpayer must report income in the year in which it is actually or constructively received. Constructive receipt means that the income is made available to the taxpayer so that he may draw upon it at any time. However, income is not constructively received if the taxpayer's control of its receipt is subject to substantial limitations or restrictions. This rule prevents taxpayers from deferring income that is otherwise available by merely "turning their backs" on it. A taxpayer cannot defer income recognition by refusing to accept payment until a later taxable year.

Examples of constructive receipt where taxpayers are required to report taxable income even though no cash is actually received include:

[12] This mismatching of income and expenses affects both cash and accrual basis taxpayers.

- A check received after banking hours[13]
- Interest credited to a bank savings account[14]
- Bond interest coupons that have matured but have not been redeemed[15]
- Salary available to an employee who does not accept payment[16]

An amount is not considered to be constructively received if:

- It is subject to substantial limitations or restrictions.
- The payor does not have the funds necessary to make payment.
- The amount is unavailable to the taxpayer.

EXAMPLE I3-10 ▶ Beth owns an ordinary life insurance policy with a cash surrender value. She need not report any income as the cash surrender value increases because the requirement that she cancel the policy in order to collect the cash surrender value constitutes a substantial restriction. If she cancels the policy, she reports as income the difference between the cash surrender value collected and net premiums paid. ◀

EXAMPLE I3-11 ▶ Cathy has received a paycheck from her employer but has been told to hold the check until the employer has sufficient funds to cover the payroll. Cathy need not report the amount of the check as income until funds are deposited to the employer's account. ◀

EXAMPLE I3-12 ▶ On December 2, 2002, Dan sold land for $100,000, payable on February 2, 2003. During the negotiations, the buyer offered to pay cash. Because the parties did not agree to a cash transaction, there was no constructive receipt in 2002. Under the terms of the sale, funds were not available at the time of sale. Thus, Dan is permitted to defer the recognition of income under the contract since the contract is made before the income is earned. ◀

HISTORICAL NOTE

Series EE bonds, officially known as United States Energy Savings Bonds, have been offered for sale since January 1, 1980.

EXCEPTIONS. There are exceptions to the basic rule that cash-basis taxpayers report income when it is actually or constructively received.

- The interest on Series E and Series EE U.S. savings bonds need not be reported until the final maturity date, which varies but may be as long as forty years after the date of issue, and can be deferred even longer if the bonds are exchanged within one year of the final maturity date for Series HH U.S. savings bonds.[17] Many taxpayers purchase bonds with a maturity date that occurs after retirement when the taxpayers expect to be in a lower tax bracket.

EXAMPLE I3-13 ▶ Tenisha purchased a Series EE U.S. savings bond in the current year for $2,500 that matures in 10 years. The bond will not pay any interest until the bond matures; at maturity, the bond will be worth $5,000. Tenisha is not required to report any interest income for tax purposes until the bond matures. At maturity, when Tenisha receives the $5,000, she will report $2,500 of interest income. If she desires to defer the interest further, she could exchange her Series EE bond for a Series HH bond within one year. ◀

- Special rules also apply to farmers and ranchers. Farmers may report crop insurance proceeds in the year following receipt if the crop would have ordinarily been sold in the following year. Ranchers who sell livestock on account of a drought, flood, or other weather related condition may delay reporting income until the following year if they can establish that the livestock sale would otherwise have taken place in a later tax year.[18] These rules help taxpayers avoid a bunching of income into one year.
- Small taxpayer exception for inventories. In 2000, the IRS issued Rev. Proc. 2000-22, 2000-1 C.B. 1008, whereby taxpayers who have average annual gross receipts of $1 million or less for the prior three years are exempt from maintaining inventories and

---

[13] *Charles F. Kahler*, 18 T.C. 31 (1952).
[14] Reg. Sec. 1.451-2(b).
[15] Ibid.
[16] *James J. Cooney*, 18 T.C. 883 (1952).
[17] Series E bonds were issued prior to 1980; Series EE bonds were issued after 1979. The interest on the Series HH bonds is taxable as received.
[18] Recognizing the volatile nature of farming and ranching, Congress established a special averaging technique for farmers and ranchers, effective in 1998. Electing farmers and ranchers compute their tax on the average income for the current and three preceding years. Sec. 1301.

may use the cash method. This ruling was widely interpreted to mean that small taxpayers did not need to account for inventories and could deduct the amount of their purchases in the year of payment. However, the IRS recently issued Rev. Proc. 2001-10, I.R.B. 2001-2, whereby it was clarified that the small taxpayer exception will only allow small taxpayers to deduct purchases of inventory in the year of purchase if (1) the inventory purchases are paid for by the end of the year, and (2) the inventory is actually sold in such year. The effect of this new ruling basically is to eliminate the small taxpayer exception with respect to inventories.

EXAMPLE I3-14 ▶ The Cheryl Corporation began a new retail business in the current year and had sales of $400,000. The corporation had year end accounts receivable of $15,000 and purchased $240,000 of merchandise during the year. At year-end, the corporation had not paid for $30,000 of the merchandise it had purchased and has $50,000 of inventory on hand at the end of the year. The corporation had paid operating expenses of $140,000 during the year. As the average gross receipts are less than $1 million, the corporation can use either the cash or accrual method. The corporation's income computed under both methods is as follows:

		Accrual		*Cash*
Sales		$400,000		$385,000
Purchases	$240,000		$210,000	
Ending inventory	50,000		20,000*	
Cost of sales		190,000		190,000
Gross profit		210,000		195,000
Expenses		140,000		140,000
Net income		$ 70,000		$ 55,000

*$50,000 − $30,000 = $20,000

The difference between the accrual and cash methods is that the sales are not reported under the cash method until such sales are actually collected. Thus, the corporation does not include year-end receivables in this year's income. The year-end receivables will be reported when the receivables are collected in later taxable years.

As can be seen above, the cost of sales under both the accrual and cash methods are the same. This is because under Rev. Proc. 2001-10, taxpayers may not deduct inventory unless it is both paid for by year-end and sold. Since $30,000 was not paid for by year-end, it is not deductible and the purchases under the cash method are $30,000 less than under the accrual method. The ending inventory under the cash method is the physical inventory of $50,000 reduced by the $30,000 of inventory on hand that has not been paid for by year-end. ◀

REAL-WORLD EXAMPLE

The Ninth Circuit Court of Appeals has held that "markers" customers gave to a gambling casino to evidence their indebtedness to the casino required accrual even though the receivables were legally unenforceable under state law. The court found that there need only be a "reasonable expectancy" that payment would be made. *Flamingo Resort, Inc. v. U.S.*, 50 AFTR 2d 82-502, 82-1 USTC ¶9136 (9th Cir., 1982).

ACCRUAL METHOD

Taxpayers using the accrual method of accounting generally report income in the year it is earned. Income is considered to have been earned when all the events have occurred that fix the right to receive the income and when the amount of income can be determined with reasonable accuracy.[19] In the case of a sale of property, income normally accrues when title passes to the buyer.[20] Income from services accrues as the services are performed.

PREPAID INCOME. A major exception to the normal operation of the accrual method is the rules applicable to the receipt of prepaid income. Prepaid income is generally taxable in the year of receipt. For example, if a lender receives January interest in the preceding December, it is taxable in the year received, whether the lender uses the cash or accrual method. This treatment, of course, differs from financial accounting, where the interest would be reported as it accrues.

Two important exceptions to the general rule are worth noting. Accrual-basis taxpayers may defer recognizing income in the case of certain advance payments for *goods* and

[19] Reg. Sec. 1.451-1(a).

[20] Regulation Sec. 1.446-1(c)(1)(ii), however, does permit taxpayers the right to accrue income from the sale of inventory when the goods are shipped, when the product is delivered or accepted, or when title passes, as long as the method is consistently used.

in the case of certain advance payments for *services* to be rendered. A taxpayer may defer advance payments for goods (inventory) if the taxpayer's method of accounting for the sale is the same for tax and financial accounting purposes.[21]

Under Rev. Proc. 71-21, a taxpayer may defer advance payments for services if the payments are for services to be performed before the end of the tax year following the year of receipt.[22] Such payments may be reported as the services are performed, e.g., the taxpayer may allocate the payment received over the current and succeeding years. The rule is not available if a payment covers a time period that extends beyond the end of the tax year following the year of receipt. The rule can be applied to a variety of services such as dance lessons, maintenance contracts (but not warranties included in the sales price of a product), and rent (if services are associated with the rent, as with a hotel or motel).

EXAMPLE I3-15 ▶

REAL-WORLD EXAMPLE

A dance studio using the accrual method was required to include in taxable income all advance payments for lessons in the form of cash and negotiable notes, plus contract installments due but remaining unpaid at year end. *Mark E. Schlude v. CIR,* 11 AFTR 2d 751, 63-1 USTC ¶9284 (USSC, 1963).

Bear Corporation, an accrual-basis taxpayer that uses the calendar year as its tax year, sells computer courses under contracts ranging from three months to two years. The contracts covered by Rev. Proc. 71-21 vary depending on the month of sale. For example, contracts sold in July for a term of longer than 18 months are not covered by the rule, and all income must be reported for these contracts in the year of the sale. Assume Bear Corporation sold three contracts in July 2002: one for three months costing $90, one for one year costing $300, and one for two years costing $500. Income would be recognized as follows:

Length of Contract	*2002*	*2003*
3 months	$ 90	
12 months	150	$150
24 months	500	

◀

HYBRID METHOD

The **hybrid method** of accounting is a combination of the cash and accrual methods. Under the hybrid method, some items of income or expense are reported under the cash basis and others are reported under the accrual method. The method is most often encountered in small businesses that maintain inventories and are required to use the accrual method of accounting for purchases and sales of goods. Such businesses often prefer to use the cash method of reporting for other items because the cash method is simpler and may provide greater flexibility for tax planning. A taxpayer using the hybrid method of accounting would use the accrual method with respect to purchases and sales of goods but would use the cash method in computing all other items of income and expenses.

STOP & THINK

Question: Taxpayers who are eligible to use the cash method often choose the cash method of reporting income over the accrual method. Why is the cash method generally more favorable for income tax purposes?

Solution: Taxpayers who have the option frequently choose the cash method over the accrual method because it is simpler, offers greater tax planning opportunity, and results in taxes being owed when income is actually received. The cash method is simpler because taxpayers are not required to make the complex accruals associated with the accrual method. Planning opportunities are greater because cash basis taxpayers can deduct expenses when paid thereby allowing taxpayers to control their tax liability. Under the accrual method, prepaid expenses are not deductible when paid, but must be deducted over the periods benefitted. Finally, cash basis taxpayers do not have to pay taxes until they receive the money. Under the accrual method, income is reported when it is earned even if it has not been received. As a result, accrual basis taxpayers sometimes have to pay the tax before they actually receive the income they have earned.

[21] Reg. Sec. 1.451-5.

[22] 1971-2 C.B. 549.

ITEMS OF GROSS INCOME: SEC. 61(a)

OBJECTIVE 4

Apply the rules of Sec. 61(a) to determine whether items such as compensation, dividends, alimony, and pensions are taxable

Section 61(a), quoted earlier in this chapter, states that gross income includes, but is not limited to, fifteen specifically listed types of income. Several of these items are discussed below.

COMPENSATION

Compensation is payment for personal services. It includes salaries, wages, fees, commissions, tips, bonuses, and specialized forms of compensation such as director's fees, jury fees, and marriage fees received by clergymen. What the compensation is called, how it is computed, the form and frequency of payment, and whether the compensation is subject to withholding is of little significance. Similarly, the fact that the services are part-time, one-time, seasonal, or temporary is immaterial.

There are exclusions, however, for a variety of employer-provided fringe benefits such as group term life insurance premiums, health and accident insurance premiums, employee discounts, contributions to retirement plans, and free parking. In addition, there is a limited exclusion applicable to foreign-earned income. Both fringe benefits and the foreign-earned income exclusion are discussed in Chapter I4.

ADDITIONAL COMMENT

Salaries and wages constituted 74.4% of total AGI reported in 1996.

BUSINESS INCOME

The term *gross income* usually refers to the total amount received from a particular source. In the case of businesses that provide services (e.g., accounting and law), the gross business income is the total amount received. In the case of manufacturing, merchandising, and mining, however, gross income is total sales less the cost of goods sold. Thus, gross income for tax purposes is comparable to gross profit for financial accounting purposes.

The cost of goods sold is, in effect, treated as a return of capital. Chapter I4 discusses a well-established tax concept that a return of capital is not income and, therefore, cannot be subject to the income tax. Chapter I11 discusses how inventories are valued.

SELF-STUDY QUESTION

A retail company had sales of $1,000,000 and the following costs: goods sold, $400,000, salaries, $200,000, and rent and other expenses, $100,000. What is the company's gross income?

ANSWER

The gross income is $600,000. The sales figure is reduced by the cost of goods sold.

GAINS FROM DEALINGS IN PROPERTY

Gains realized from property transactions are included in gross income unless a nonrecognition rule applies. As is true with business inventories, taxpayers may deduct the cost of property in order to arrive at the gain from a property transaction.[23] The tax law contains over 30 nonrecognition rules, which allow taxpayers to postpone the recognition of gains and losses from certain types of property transactions. In a few instances, these rules allow taxpayers to permanently exclude gains from gross income.[24]

Losses are not offset against gains in computing gross income. Rather, most losses are deductions *for* adjusted gross income. Furthermore, net capital losses for individuals are subject to provisions that limit the amount that can be deducted from other income to $3,000 per year. Losses from the sale or disposition of an asset held for personal use are not deductible.

INTEREST

Interest is compensation for the use of money. Taxable interest includes interest on bank deposits, corporate bonds, mortgages, life insurance policies, tax refunds, most U.S. government obligations,[25] and foreign government obligations.[26] Nontaxable interest is discussed below.

TYPICAL MISCONCEPTION

It is sometimes mistakenly assumed that interest paid on federal obligations such as Treasury bonds, notes, and bills will also qualify for tax exemption.

TAX-EXEMPT INTEREST. Since the inception of the federal income tax in 1913, interest on obligations of states, territories, and U.S. possessions and their political subdivisions

[23] Note that *business income* and *gains from dealings in property* are overlapping terms. The gross profit from the sale of inventory is actually both business income and a gain from a property transaction. Typically, however, the phrase *gains from dealings in property* may be assumed to mean gains from dealings in property other than inventory, so as to avoid confusion.

[24] For example, Sec. 121 allows taxpayers to exclude a limited amount of gain from a sale of a personal residence.

[25] The interest on many federal obligations issued before March 1, 1942 is tax exempt.

[26] Reg. Sec. 1.61-7.

ADDITIONAL COMMENT

Many tax advisers consider the exclusion of interest on municipal bonds to be one of the few remaining tax shelters. As a result, municipal bond funds have flourished in recent years.

ADDITIONAL COMMENT

The doctrine of intergovernmental immunity also results in most states exempting from taxation income received from U.S. obligations.

KEY POINT

The exclusion is available only to an individual who purchased the bond after reaching age 24. The exclusion is not available to an individual who owns a bond that was purchased by another individual, other than a spouse. Therefore, the exclusion is not allowable if bonds are purchased by a parent and put in the name of a child.

SELF-STUDY QUESTION

Young parents, whose annual income is currently $45,000, begin a regular program of purchasing Series EE savings bonds for their 8-year-old daughter's college education. Is there any risk that when the bonds are redeemed the interest income will not be excludable?

ANSWER

Yes, the parents' income may increase over the years to such an extent that the interest exclusion will not be available.

has been tax exempt.[27] Bonds issued by school districts, port authorities, toll road commissions, counties, and fire districts have been held to be tax exempt. In addition, Sec. 501(c)(3) organizations may issue up to $150 million of tax-exempt bonds. Such organizations include private universities, hospitals, churches, and similar nonprofit organizations.

As noted above, this exclusion does not extend to interest paid on most U.S. government obligations or foreign government obligations, nor does the exclusion exempt from taxation gains from the sale of state or local government bonds or interest on tax refunds paid by state and municipal governments.

There has always been some uncertainty as to whether the federal government could tax interest on state and local government obligations. The basic question is whether taxing these obligations would violate the doctrine of intergovernmental immunity in that the tax would reduce the ability of state and local governments to finance their operations because taxable bonds usually pay a higher rate of interest than tax-exempt bonds. The belief that taxing state and local government interest is unconstitutional is no longer widely held. While there have been efforts to tax interest on state and local bonds, the only changes have been to limit the use of bonds for private activities,[28] federally insured loans,[29] and arbitrage.[30]

SERIES EE SAVINGS BOND EXCLUSION. Taxpayers may purchase and eventually redeem Series EE bonds tax-free if they use the proceeds to pay certain college expenses for themselves, a spouse, or dependents.[31]

To qualify for the exclusion:

- The bonds must be purchased after 1989 by an individual who is age 24 or older at the time of the purchase.
- The bonds must be purchased by the owner and cannot be a gift to the owner.
- The receipts from the bond redemption must be used for tuition and fees, which are first reduced by tax-exempt scholarships, veterans benefits, Hope and Lifetime Learning credits, and other similar amounts.[32]
- Married couples living together must file a joint return to obtain the exclusion.

The full amount of interest is excluded only if the combined amount of principal and interest received during the year does not exceed the net qualified educational expenses (tuition and fees reduced by exempt scholarships, etc.), and the taxpayer's 2002 modified adjusted gross income is not over $57,600 ($86,400 for married individuals filing a joint return). The exclusion is fully phased-out for taxpayers whose 2002 modified AGI is more than $72,600 ($116,400 for married individuals filing a joint return).[33]

If the net qualified education expenses are less than the total principal and interest, a portion of the interest is excluded based on the ratio of the qualified educational expenses to the total principal and interest. The tentative exclusion is equal to

$$\text{Series EE interest} \times \frac{\text{Net qualified educational expenses}}{\text{Series EE interest} + \text{Principal}}$$

EXAMPLE I3-16 ▶ In 2002, Lois redeems Series EE bonds and receives $6,000, consisting of $1,875 of interest and $4,125 of principal. Assume that the net qualifying education expenses total $4,800. Lois's educational expenses equal 80% of the total amount received ($4,800 ÷ $6,000). Thus, her exclusion is limited to $1,500 (0.80 × $1,875). ◀

[27] Sec. 103(a)(1).

[28] Interest from state and local bonds issued for private activities such as the construction of sports facilities, convention centers, and industrial park sites is taxable. A limited amount of tax-exempt bonds can be issued each year by a state for "qualified" private activities such as airport construction, redevelopment, and student loans. The limit is the greater of $150 million or $50 per resident (Sec. 146(d)). The $150 million is scheduled to increase gradually to $225 million in 2007. Though exempt from regular income tax, interest from these "qualified" private activity bonds is subject to the alternative minimum tax (see Chapter I14).

[29] Sec. 149(b).

[30] Sec. 148. Interest from state or local government bonds issued for the purpose of using the proceeds to buy higher-yield investments is taxable. Such bonds are called arbitrage bonds.

[31] Sec. 135(c).

[32] The exclusion is not permitted for amounts paid for sports, games, or hobbies unless they are part of a degree program (Sec. 135(c)(2)(B)).

[33] Each of these amounts is adjusted annually for inflation. In 2001, the phase-out started at $55,750 ($83,650 on joint returns) and ended at $70,750 ($113,650 on joint returns).

ADDITIONAL COMMENT

A child born today will require about $100,000 for a four-year college education. If interest rates are around 6%, one would have to save about $245 a month until the child entered school to be able to pay this amount.

As noted, the amount of the exclusion is further reduced if modified adjusted gross income exceeds a $57,600 threshold ($86,400 for married individuals filing a joint return). Modified adjusted gross income includes the interest from education savings bonds and certain otherwise excludable foreign income.[34] The reduction is computed as follows:

$$\text{Otherwise excludable amount} \times \frac{\text{Excess modified AGI}}{\$15{,}000\ (\$30{,}000 \text{ for joint filers})}$$

EXAMPLE I3-17 ▶ Assume the same facts as in Example I3-16. Also assume that Lois is single and has other adjusted gross income of $60,725. Lois's otherwise available exclusion of $1,500 is reduced by $500 to $1,000. This reduction is computed by dividing the excess modified AGI of $5,000 ($60,725 + $1,875 − $57,600) by $15,000 and multiplying the result by $1,500. ◀

RENTS AND ROYALTIES

Amounts received as rents or royalties are included in gross income. As noted earlier, prepaid rent is taxable when received. Security deposits, which are refundable to tenants upon the expiration of a lease, are not included in gross income. The deposit is included in gross income only if it is not refunded upon the expiration of the lease.

EXAMPLE I3-18 ▶ In December 2002, Buddy rents an apartment to Gary. Buddy receives the first and last months' rent plus a security deposit of $500. Buddy must include in 2002 gross income both the first and last months' rent. Assume that Gary moves out of the apartment in 2004 and Buddy keeps $300 of the security deposit to cover repairs costing $200 and five days' unpaid rent, which amounts to $100. In 2004, Buddy would include the $300 in gross income and could deduct $200 for repairs. ◀

Royalties from copyrights, patents, and oil, gas, and mineral rights are all taxable as ordinary income. **Royalties** are proceeds paid to an owner by others who do business under some right belonging to the owner. Amounts received by a lessor to cancel, amend, or modify a lease also are taxable.

STOP & THINK

Question: Financial accounting contains extensive rules distinguishing "operating leases" from "capital leases." The IRC has no such rules. While the tax law does require the capitalization of leases that are in substance a purchase of the asset, most authority relating to the distinction comes from court cases. Why doesn't the tax law adopt specific rules relating to leased property?

Solution: The financial accounting rules that require businesses to capitalize some leases were established because of concern that long-term lease commitments represented unrecorded liabilities. The unrecorded liabilities distort a company's balance sheet, but may not distort reported income. Since the tax law is concerned with the reporting of income rather than the balance sheet, neither Congress nor the Treasury Department has seen the need to adopt leasing rules like those in financial accounting.

IMPROVEMENTS BY LESSEES. Improvements made by a lessee that increase the value of leased property are included in the lessor's income only if the improvements are made in lieu of paying rent or if rent is reduced because of the improvements. In such situations, the lessor must include the fair market value (FMV) of the improvement in gross income when it is made to the property.[35]

[34] Specifically, modified adjusted gross income includes amounts that qualify for the foreign earned income exclusion (Sec. 911), the exclusion for possession's income (Sec. 931), and the exclusion for income from Puerto Rico (Sec. 933). The limitation is determined after taking the partial exclusion for Social Security benefits and railroad retirement (Sec. 86), claiming the allowable deduction for retirement contributions (Sec. 219), and applying the passive loss limitation (Sec. 469).

[35] Reg. Sec. 1.109-1.

EXAMPLE I3-19 ▶ Rita rents an apartment to Anna. The apartment normally would rent for $500 per month, but Rita agrees to accept $200 per month for the first year if Anna builds a block wall around the property. Rita estimates that she would have to pay someone $3,000 to build the wall. Rita is accepting reduced rent and must report gross income of $3,000 when the wall is added to the property. The $3,000 could be added to Rita's basis in the property and should qualify as a depreciable asset. ◀

Improvements not made in lieu of rent are not income to the lessor. No adjustment is made to the lessor's basis in the property and, therefore, no depreciation is allowable. Gain or loss is recognized only when the property is disposed of.[36] Whether the improvements are in lieu of rent depends on the intent of the parties. This determination is based on the facts of the particular situation. The rental rate, the terms of the rental agreement, and whether the improvements have an estimated useful life exceeding the term of the lease may all be indications of intent.

ADDITIONAL COMMENT

Shareholders of closely held corporations generally do not want to receive dividends from their corporations. The reason? They are taxed as ordinary income and the corporation does not receive a tax deduction for the payments.

DIVIDENDS

Distributions to shareholders are taxable as dividends only to the extent they are made from either the corporation's current earnings and profits (a concept similar, although not identical, to current year's net income for financial accounting purposes) or accumulated earnings and profits (a concept similar, although not identical, to beginning of the year retained earnings).[37] Earnings and profits are discussed in Chapter I16 and in greater depth in *Prentice Hall's Federal Taxation: Corporations, Partnerships, Estates & Trusts* text and the *Comprehensive* volume. Distributions in excess of current and accumulated earnings and profits are treated as a nontaxable recovery of capital. Such distributions reduce the shareholder's basis in the stock. Distributions in excess of the basis of the stock are classified as capital gains.

EXAMPLE I3-20 ▶ Liz is the sole shareholder in Atlantic Corporation and has owned the stock for five years. The basis of her stock is $50,000. Atlantic distributes $40,000 to Liz. Accumulated earnings and profits at the beginning of the year equal $25,000, and current earnings and profits equal $10,000. Liz will report $35,000 of taxable dividend income and a nontaxable return of capital equal to $5,000. In addition, Liz must reduce her basis in the stock by $5,000. Alternatively, if the distribution to Liz were $100,000, she would report $35,000 of taxable dividend income, $50,000 as a nontaxable return of capital, and a $15,000 long-term capital gain. ◀

STOCK DIVIDENDS. A **stock dividend** is a distribution by a corporation to its shareholders of the corporation's own stock. In 1920, the Supreme Court held that simple stock dividends could not be taxed because they were not income.[38] More precisely, income had not been realized because there was no real change in the taxpayer's interest or the risks faced by the taxpayer. Over the years, however, the exclusion for stock dividends has been narrowed. If a shareholder has the option of receiving either cash or stock, the shareholder is taxed even if he or she opts to receive stock. The option to receive cash constitutes constructive receipt of the cash. Today, many other features of a stock dividend may cause it to be taxed. For example, a distribution in which preferred stock is distributed to some common shareholders and common stock is distributed to others is taxable.[39] The recipient of a taxable stock dividend includes the value of the stock received in gross income, and that amount becomes the basis of the shares received.

ADDITIONAL COMMENT

Many mutual funds do not want their shareholders to have a large tax bill on the undistributed capital gains allocated among the shareholders. Some mutual funds will sell stocks in the portfolio that can be sold at a loss to offset gains incurred earlier in the year.

A nontaxable stock dividend has no effect on a shareholder's income in the year received. The basis of the old shares is allocated between the old shares and the new shares. Furthermore, the holding period for the new shares starts on the same date as the holding period of the old.

---

[36] Reg. Sec. 1.1019-1.

[37] Sec. 316(a). The federal income tax became effective on March 1, 1913. Thus, income accumulated before that date can still be distributed on a tax-exempt basis.

[38] *Eisner v. Myrtle H. Macomber,* 3 AFTR 3020, 1 USTC ¶32 (USSC, 1920).

[39] Reg. Sec. 1.305-4.

EXAMPLE I3-21 ▶ Carol purchases 100 shares of Mesa Corporation stock for $1,100 (or $11 per share). Carol receives 10 shares of Mesa stock as a nontaxable stock dividend. After the dividend, Carol owns 110 shares of stock with a total basis of $1,100 (or $10 per share). All of the stock is assumed to have been acquired at the time of the original purchase. ◀

REAL-WORLD EXAMPLE

In the 1989 trial of Leona Helmsley, the billionaire hotel queen, it was disclosed that she had billed her companies for millions of dollars in personal items. The items ranged from a $12.99 girdle to a $1 million limestone-and-marble pool enclosure at her estate. She was sentenced to four years in prison and fined $7.1 million. The amounts paid to her by her companies represented constructive dividends.

CAPITAL GAIN DIVIDENDS. A **capital gain dividend** is a distribution by a regulated investment company (commonly called a *mutual fund*) of capital gains realized from the sale of investments in the fund. Such dividends also include any undistributed capital gains allocated to shareholders by such companies.[40] Capital gain dividends are long-term regardless of how long the shareholder has owned the stock of the regulated investment company.

CONSTRUCTIVE DIVIDENDS. In many corporations, the same individuals are both shareholders and employees. A corporation may not deduct dividends paid to shareholders but is permitted to deduct reasonable compensation. Questions are often raised as to whether amounts reported as compensation are really disguised dividends. If an amount called compensation is unreasonably high, it will be disallowed and reclassified as a dividend.[41] Often the reasonableness of compensation is determined by comparing the compensation paid to the employee-shareholders with amounts paid to others performing similar services.

EXAMPLE I3-22 ▶ Carmen owns 100% of the stock in Florida Corporation and receives a $400,000 salary for serving as president. The corporation reports no taxable income and pays no dividends. Presidents of similar companies received salaries ranging from $75,000 to $160,000. The IRS probably would disallow a portion of Carmen's salary as unreasonable. The disallowed portion would be treated as a dividend. ◀

ADDITIONAL COMMENT

In one case, the taxpayer, who was also the president and principal shareholder, diverted cash from vending and pinball machines at his truck stops/restaurants to his personal use. The IRS's position was that these diverted cash amounts were a constructive dividend. *Hagaman v. Com.*, 69 AFTR 2d 92-906 (1992, CA6).

Constructive dividends are not limited to shareholder-employee compensation payments but may include situations where the shareholder also is a landlord (e.g., property is rented to the corporation at an amount greater than its fair rental value). A shareholder also may receive a constructive dividend because of a creditor or vendor relationship. It is not necessary that a dividend be formally declared or that distributions be in proportion to stock holdings. **Constructive dividends** are often distributions that are intended to result in a deduction to the corporation and taxable income (such as compensation) to the shareholder.[42] Other constructive dividends are intended to produce a nonreportable benefit to the shareholder,[43] or even result in a deduction to the corporation without income to the shareholder.[44]

ALIMONY AND SEPARATE MAINTENANCE PAYMENTS

Any payment pursuant to a divorce or legal separation must be classified as one of the following for tax purposes:

(1) Alimony;

(2) Child support; or

(3) Property settlement.

The treatment of a payment depends on its classification. Alimony is deductible by the payor spouse and taxable to the payee spouse. Neither child support payments nor property settlements have any tax ramifications, that is, they are not subject to tax to the payee spouse nor deductible by the payor spouse.

Example I3-23 demonstrates the significant difference in taxation that can occur when a payment is classified as either alimony or a property settlement.

---

[40] Sec. 852(b).

[41] Sec. 162(a)(1).

[42] Other examples include excessive royalties (*Peterson & Pegau Baking Co.*, 2 B.T.A. 637 (1925)) and rent (*Limericks, Inc. v. CIR*, 36 AFTR 649, 48-1 USTC ¶9146 (5th Cir., 1948)).

[43] Examples include bargain sales of corporate assets to shareholders (*J. E. Timberlake v. CIR*, 30 AFTR 583, 42-2 USTC ¶9822 (4th Cir., 1942)), redemptions of a shareholder's stock (Sec. 302), and loans to shareholders that are actually dividends (*George Blood Enterprises, Inc.*, 1976 PH T.C. Memo ¶76,102, 35 TCM 436).

[44] Examples include paying an employee's personal expenses (*The Lang Chevrolet Co.*, 1967 PH T.C. Memo ¶67,212, 26 TCM 1054) and purchasing assets for an employee's use (*Joseph Morgenstern*, 1955 PH T.C. Memo ¶55,086, 14 TCM 282).

EXAMPLE I3-23 ▶ Helen earned $500,000 and, as a result of her divorce, she was required to pay William $250,000. If the payment were viewed as a property settlement, Helen could not deduct any of the $250,000 payment and William would not be required to include the payment in his income. However, if the $250,000 were viewed as alimony, Helen could deduct the full amount in computing her adjusted gross income. William would report the $250,000 as alimony income. ◀

ADDITIONAL COMMENT

Child-support payments are not treated as alimony and are neither deductible by the payor spouse nor includible in income of the payee spouse.

ADDITIONAL COMMENT

If any amount specified in the divorce instrument will be reduced due to the happening of a contingency relating to a child or reduced at a time that can clearly be associated with such contingency, the amount of the reduction is treated as child support.

ETHICAL POINT

Tax consultants who advise divorcing couples may face an ethical dilemma because advice that benefits one spouse may be detrimental to the other, and because of the need to maintain confidential client relationships.

The tax law has rather specific rules that distinguish alimony, child support, and property settlements. Under current law, in order to be treated as **alimony**, payments must meet all of the following requirements:[45]

- ▶ Be made in cash (not property)
- ▶ Be made pursuant to a divorce, separation, or a written agreement between the spouses
- ▶ Terminate at the death of the payee
- ▶ Not be designated as being other than alimony (e.g., child support)
- ▶ Be made between people who are living in separate households

These rules are summarized in Topic Review I3-2. Certain aspects of these rules will be discussed further.

A **property settlement** is a division of property pursuant to a divorce. In general, each spouse is entitled to the property brought into the marriage and a share of the property accumulated during marriage.[46] A division of property does not result in any income to either spouse, nor does either spouse receive a tax deduction. The basis of property received by either spouse as a result of the divorce or separation remains unchanged.

EXAMPLE I3-24 ▶ As a result of a divorce, Dawn receives stock that she had purchased with her former husband during their marriage. They had purchased the stock for $12,000. At the time of the divorce, the stock was worth $14,000. Neither Dawn nor her former husband reports income from the transfer of the stock because the stock was acquired as a property settlement. If Dawn subsequently sold the stock for $15,000, she would report a $3,000 gain. ◀

Topic Review I3-2

Tax Rules for Alimony

TREATMENT OF RECIPIENT

The recipient of alimony must include the amounts received in gross income. Property settlements and child support payments are not taxable.

TREATMENT OF PAYOR

The payor of alimony may deduct amounts paid *for* adjusted gross income. Property settlements and child support payments are not deductible.

APPLICABLE TO

Payments must be pursuant to a divorce, separation, or a written agreement between spouses.

REQUIREMENTS

Spouses must be living in separate households. Payments must be in the form of cash paid to (or for the benefit of) a spouse or former spouse. Payments must terminate at the death of the payee. Payments may not be designated as being other than alimony (such as child support or a property settlement).

RECAPTURE

If the amount of payments declines in the second or third year, a portion of the early payments may have to be recaptured as income by the payor. The payee may deduct the same recaptured amount.

---

[45] Before 1942, alimony was not deductible (*Gould v. Gould*, 3 AFTR 2958, 1 USTC ¶13 (USSC, 1917)). The original rules were revised in 1984 and again in 1986. Prior rules apply to earlier divorces unless both spouses elect to apply current rules.

[46] How the property accumulated during marriage is divided may be determined by an agreement of the parties, or if they are unable to agree, on a basis of state law.

One unusual rule found in the current law that relates to alimony is the so-called **recapture provision.** This provision was established to prevent a large property settlement that might take place after a divorce from being treated as alimony so as to produce a deduction for the payor. In essence, the concept of recapture in connection with a divorce means that the payor of the alimony (who has taken a deduction for such amounts in prior years) must report the recapture amount in his or her income. The payee (who has reported the income in prior years) receives a deduction for the recaptured amount. This recapture occurs because the payments that originally were reported as alimony are being reclassified as property settlements.

Recapture occurs if payments decrease sharply in either the second or third year. Specifically, the amount of second-year alimony recaptured is equal to the second-year alimony reduced by the total of $15,000 plus the third-year alimony. The amount of first-year alimony recaptured is equal to the first-year alimony reduced by the total of $15,000 plus the average alimony paid in the second year (reduced by the recapture for that year) and the third year. The calculation of recapture for both the first and second years is shown below.

$$R_2 = A_2 - (\$15{,}000 + A_3)$$

$$R_1 = A_1 - [\$15{,}000 + (A_2 + A_3 - R_2)/2)]$$

A_i = Alimony paid in first (A_1), second (A_2), and third year (A_3) respectvely.

R_i = Recaptured alimony from the first (R_1) and second year (R_2) respectively.

Both first- and second-year amounts are recaptured by requiring the payor to report the excess as income (and allowing the payee to deduct the same amount) in the third year. Recapture is not required if payments cease because of the death of either spouse or remarriage of the recipient.

EXAMPLE I3-25 ▶ As a result of their divorce, Hal is ordered to pay to Rose $100,000 alimony in 2002 and $20,000 per year thereafter until her death or remarriage. Hal must recapture the amount of the decrease that exceeds $35,000, or $65,000 ($100,000 – $20,000 – $15,000). The $65,000 of alimony in 2002 must be reported by Hal as income during 2004. Also, Rose may deduct the $65,000 *for* AGI in 2004. ◀

EXAMPLE I3-26 ▶ As a result of their separation, Mary agrees to pay Tom $20,000 per year. The payments are to cease if Tom remarries. In the year after the agreement is reached, Tom remarries and Mary discontinues the payments. No recapture is required because the payments are contingent on the remarriage of the recipient and the payments have been discontinued because of the occurrence of this contingency. ◀

PENSIONS AND ANNUITIES

ADDITIONAL COMMENT

The three largest sources of non-wage income in 1996, in rank order, were net capital gains, pensions and annuities, and business and professional net income.

An **annuity** is a series of regular payments that will continue for a fixed period of time or until the death of the recipient. Taxpayers occasionally purchase annuities from insurance companies to provide a source of funds during retirement years. The insurance company may agree to make payments to the insured for the remainder of the insured's life. The retired individual is assured of a steady flow of funds for life. The price paid for the annuity represents its cost. The insured taxpayer is permitted to recover this cost tax-free.

Individuals receiving an annuity are permitted to exclude their cost, but are taxed on the remaining portion of the annuity. The following steps can be followed to determine the nontaxable portion of the annuity:

ADDITIONAL COMMENT

The expected return is limited to amounts receivable as an annuity. It does not include amounts that may be paid after death, nor does it include anticipated dividends.

- ▶ Determine the **expected return multiple.** This multiple is the number of years that the annuity is expected to continue and may be a stated term, say ten years, or it may be for the remainder of the taxpayer's life. In the latter situation, the expected return multiple (life expectancy) is determined by referring to a table (see Table I3-1) developed by the IRS.
- ▶ Determine the **expected return.** This return is computed by multiplying the amount of the annual payment by the expected return multiple.

▼ **TABLE I3-1**
Ordinary Life Annuities (One Life) Expected Return Multiple

Age	Multiple	Age	Multiple	Age	Multiple
5	76.6	42	40.6	79	10.0
6	75.6	43	39.6	80	9.5
7	74.7	44	38.7	81	8.9
8	73.7	45	37.7	82	8.4
9	72.7	46	36.8	83	7.9
10	71.7	47	35.9	84	7.4
11	70.7	48	34.9	85	6.9
12	69.7	49	34.0	86	6.5
13	68.8	50	33.1	87	6.1
14	67.8	51	32.2	88	5.7
15	66.8	52	31.3	89	5.3
16	65.8	53	30.4	90	5.0
17	64.8	54	29.5	91	4.7
18	63.9	55	28.6	92	4.4
19	62.9	56	27.7	93	4.1
20	61.9	57	26.8	94	3.9
21	60.9	58	25.9	95	3.7
22	59.9	59	25.0	96	3.4
23	59.0	60	24.2	97	3.2
24	58.0	61	23.3	98	3.0
25	57.0	62	22.5	99	2.8
26	56.0	63	21.6	100	2.7
27	55.1	64	20.8	101	2.5
28	54.1	65	20.0	102	2.3
29	53.1	66	19.2	103	2.1
30	52.2	67	18.4	104	1.9
31	51.2	68	17.6	105	1.8
32	50.2	69	16.8	106	1.6
33	49.3	70	16.0	107	1.4
34	48.3	71	15.3	108	1.3
35	47.3	72	14.6	109	1.1
36	46.4	73	13.9	110	1.0
37	45.4	74	13.2	111	.9
38	44.4	75	12.5	112	.8
39	43.5	76	11.9	113	.7
40	42.5	77	11.2	114	.6
41	41.5	78	10.6	115	.5

Source: Reg. Sec. 1.72-9 Table V.
Note: This table should be used if any or all investments were made on or after July 1, 1986. If all investments were made before July 1, 1986, use Reg. Sec. 1.72-9 Table I (not shown).

- Determine the **exclusion ratio.** This ratio is computed by dividing the investment in the contract (its cost) by the expected return (from above).
- Determine the **current year's exclusion.** This exclusion is computed by multiplying the exclusion ratio (from above) times the amount received during the year.

EXAMPLE I3-27 ▶ David, age 65, purchases an annuity for $30,000. Under the terms of the annuity, David is to receive $300 per month ($3,600 per year) for the rest of his life.

- The expected return multiple is 20.0. The multiple is obtained from Table I3-1.
- The expected return is $72,000 (20.0 × $3,600).
- The exclusion ratio is 0.417 ($30,000 ÷ $72,000).
- The exclusion is $1,500 (0.417 × $3,600). ◀

After the entire cost of an annuity has been recovered, the full amount of all future payments is taxable. On the other hand, if an individual dies before recovering the entire cost, the remaining unrecovered cost can be deducted as an itemized deduction on that individual's final return. Insurance companies and businesses with retirement plans compute the taxable portion of annuities and report the amounts to recipients on Form 1099.

KEY POINT

The simplified method is used only for annuity distributions from qualified retirement plans. All other annuity distributions are taxed in accordance with the general rules above.

SIMPLIFIED METHOD FOR QUALIFIED RETIREMENT PLAN ANNUITIES. Distributions from pensions and other qualified retirement plans are often paid in the form of an annuity. Both the employer and the employee often contribute funds to plans during the years of employment. When an employee retires, the amounts contributed and income accumulated thereon become available to the retired employee. In some cases, the retired employee has the option of receiving a lump-sum payment or an annuity. The employee's cost is limited to amounts contributed (usually through withholding) by the employee that were previously taxed to the employee. The employee may recover this cost tax-free. The employee's cost does not include employer contributions.

A simplified method is now used to determine the taxable portion of an annuity paid from a qualified retirement plan (such as a pension). Under the simplified method, the nontaxable portion of each annuity payment is equal to the employee's investment in the annuity divided by the number of anticipated payments as determined from the following table:

Age of Primary Annuitant on the Start Date	*Number of Anticipated Payments*
55 and under	360
56-60	310
61-65	260
66-70	210
71 and over	160

EXAMPLE I3-28 ▶ Jack, age 62, retires, and receives a $1,000 per month annuity from his employer's qualified pension plan. Jack contributed $65,000 to the plan prior to his retirement. Under the simplified method, Jack would exclude $250 per month as a return of capital. This is calculated by dividing $65,000 by 260 anticipated payments. ◀

If payments are paid other than monthly, the number of anticipated payments is adjusted accordingly. Thus, if payments are made quarterly, the number from the table is divided by four.

KEY POINT

Under current law, a taxpayer must generally pay tax on a portion of each withdrawal made before the normal starting date of the annuity.

ADVANCE PAYMENTS. Many pensions contain provisions that allow taxpayers to withdraw amounts before the normal starting date. Under current law, an amount withdrawn from a pension before the starting date is considered to be in part a recovery of the employee's contributions and part a recovery of the employer's contributions.[47] After all contributions have been withdrawn, additional withdrawals are fully taxable. In addition to being subject to the regular income tax, any amount withdrawn may also be subject to a 10% nondeductible penalty. The penalty is not applicable to certain taxpayers, such as one who is age 59½ or older. This early withdrawal penalty is discussed in more detail in Chapter I9.

EXAMPLE I3-29 ▶ Dick, age 45 and in good health, withdrew $2,000 from a pension plan during the current year. No exception exempts Dick from the 10% penalty. Dick had contributed $40,000 to the plan, and his employer had contributed $60,000. Dick must include $1,200 (0.60 × $2,000) in income. Because no exception applies, Dick must also pay an additional penalty of $120 (0.10 × $1,200). The penalty is not deductible by Dick. ◀

INCOME FROM LIFE INSURANCE AND ENDOWMENT CONTRACTS

The face amount of life insurance received because of the death of the insured is not taxable. If the proceeds are left with the insurance company and as a result earn interest, the interest payments are taxable. (See Chapter I4 for a detailed discussion of life insurance and endowment contracts.)

[47] Sec. 72(e).

INCOME FROM DISCHARGE OF INDEBTEDNESS

In general, the forgiveness of debt is a taxable event. The person who owed the money must report the amount forgiven as income unless one of several exceptions found in the tax law applies. These exceptions are discussed in Chapter I4.

INCOME PASSED THROUGH TO TAXPAYER

Generally, entities are subject to income tax based on the amount of taxable income. Corporations, as an example, are subject to income taxation. However, certain types of entities are not subject to income taxation as the taxable income is taxed directly to the owners of the entity rather than the entity itself. Such entities are referred to as "flow-through entities." Section 61 specifically lists three such instances: the distributive share of a partnership's income, income in respect of a decedent, and income from an interest in an estate or trust. Though not mentioned in Sec. 61, similar treatment is accorded S corporation income. In each case, the income that is produced by the entity merely flows through to the owner or beneficiary of such entity. The rules can be summarized as follows:

KEY POINT

The pass-through of income by a partnership can create a situation known as phantom income. In this situation, a partner is required to report income on his or her individual tax return, but the partner may not have received a cash distribution from the partnership.

- Each partner reports his or her share of the partnership's income. Each partner deducts his or her share of the partnership's expenses. The income and deductions are reported by the partners whether or not any amount is actually distributed by the partnership during the year.
- Income in respect of a decedent is income earned by an individual before death that is paid to another after the death. For example, salary earned by a husband who uses the cash method of accounting before his death in an automobile accident may be paid to his widow after the accident. The recipient, in this case the widow, is taxed on the income if it has not been taxed to the decedent before his death.
- Income earned by estates and trusts is subject to taxation.[48] However, distributions to beneficiaries are deductible by estates and trusts and are taxable to the beneficiaries. Thus, if a trust had a net income of $20,000 and distributed $15,000 to the beneficiary of the trust, the trust would be taxed on $5,000 and $15,000 would be taxed to the beneficiary. The income taxation of estates and trusts is covered more fully in *Prentice Hall's Federal Taxation: Corporations, Partnerships, Estates, and Trusts.*
- S corporations are taxed much like partnerships. Each shareholder in the corporation is taxed on his or her proportionate share of the corporation's income whether or not the income is actually distributed.

OTHER ITEMS OF GROSS INCOME

The preceding discussions considered items of gross income specifically listed in Sec. 61(a). However, the fact that an item of income is listed in Sec. 61(a) does not necessarily cause it to be taxable. Rather, the condition that causes an item of income to be taxable is that it is not specifically excluded. Some items of gross income not mentioned in Sec. 61(a) are discussed below.

PRIZES, AWARDS, GAMBLING WINNINGS, AND TREASURE FINDS

In general, prizes, awards, gambling winnings, and treasure finds are taxable.[49] Winnings in contests, competitions, and quiz shows as well as awards from an employer to an employee in recognition of some achievement in connection with his or her employment

[48] Note the distinction between income in respect of a decedent and the income of an estate. Income in respect of a decedent is the income earned before death that was never taxed to the decedent. An example would be interest that was accrued but unpaid at death. Income of an estate is income earned after death that is paid to the estate. An example would be interest that accrues after the decedent's death.

[49] Exclusions for scholarships and fellowships and a limited exclusion for prizes awarded for scientific, charitable, or similar meritorious achievements are discussed in Chapter I4.

are taxable.[50] The amount to be included in gross income is the fair market value of the goods or services received. Total gambling winnings must be included in gross income.[51] This includes proceeds from lotteries, raffles, sweepstakes, and the like. Gambling losses (up to the amount of the current year's winnings) are allowable as an itemized deduction.[52] The Regulations state that a treasure find constitutes gross income to the extent of its value in the year in which it is reduced to undisputed possession.[53]

EXAMPLE I3-30 ▶ Several years ago, Colleen purchased a used piano at an auction for $15. In the current year, she finds $4,500 of currency hidden in the piano. Colleen must report the $4,500 as income in the current year.[54] ◀

REAL-WORLD EXAMPLE

An accountant collected from a client money that was to be used to pay the client's taxes. Then the accountant appropriated the money for his own use. The accountant was held to have received unreported income. *Richard A. Reeves,* 1977 PH T.C. Memo ¶ 77,114, 36 TCM 500.

ILLEGAL INCOME

Income from illegal activities is taxable.[55] Some people find this part of the tax law surprising, but this fact serves as the basis for many criminal convictions given that few criminals report their illegal income. For example, Al Capone was convicted of income tax evasion, not bootlegging or other crimes. It is not necessary to prove that an individual had illegal income, but merely that the individual had income that was not reported.

Individuals have used varied defenses against this rule. One taxpayer was successful in convincing the Supreme Court that he should not be taxed on embezzlement gains because he had an unconditional obligation to repay the amount embezzled,[56] but the Supreme Court reversed this position in a later case.[57] The court concluded that although an obligation to repay existed, the taxpayer had no "consensual recognition" (intent) to repay. In addition to embezzlement of funds, the courts have held that a kidnapper's ransom was taxable,[58] along with profits from bookmaking,[59] card playing,[60] forgery,[61] stealing,[62] bank robbery,[63] sale of narcotics,[64] illegal sale of liquor,[65] and bribes.[66] (See Chapter I6 for a discussion of related deductions.)

ADDITIONAL COMMENT

Welfare payments are not normally required to be included in gross income. However, if the welfare payments are fraudulently received under state or federal assistance programs, they must be included in the recipient's gross income.

UNEMPLOYMENT COMPENSATION

For many years, unemployment compensation was excluded from gross income. In 1978, Congress changed the law to tax unemployment compensation because these benefits are a substitute for taxable wages. Initially, unemployment compensation was taxable only if adjusted gross income exceeded certain base amounts. However, beginning in 1987, all unemployment compensation is now fully taxable for both government-financed programs and employer-financed benefits.

SOCIAL SECURITY BENEFITS

Social Security benefits were excluded from gross income until 1984. Between 1984 and 1993, up to 50% of Social Security benefits were taxable. Beginning in 1994, up to 85% of Social Security benefits may be taxable. Under Sec. 86, the portion of Social Security benefits that are taxable depends on the taxpayer's provisional income and filing status. *Provisional income* is computed using the following formula:

Adjusted gross income (excluding Social Security benefits)	$xx,xxx
Plus: Tax-exempt interest	x,xxx
Excluded foreign income	x,xxx
50% of Social Security benefits	x,xxx
Provisional income	$xx,xxx

[50] Sec. 74 and Reg. Sec. 1.74-1.
[51] *U.S. v. Manley S. Sullivan,* 6 AFTR 6753, 1 USTC ¶236 (USSC, 1927).
[52] Sec. 165(d).
[53] Reg. Sec. 1.61-14(a).
[54] *Ermenegildo Cesarini v. U.S.,* 26 AFTR 2d 5107, 70-2 USTC ¶9509 (6th Cir., 1970).
[55] Reg. 1.61-14(a).
[56] *CIR v. Laird Wilcox,* 34 AFTR 811, 46-1 USTC ¶9188 (USSC, 1946).
[57] *Eugene C. James v. U.S.,* 7 AFTR 2d 1361, 61-1 USTC ¶9449 (USSC, 1961).
[58] *Murray Humphreys v. CIR,* 28 AFTR 1030, 42-1 USTC ¶9237 (7th Cir., 1942).
[59] *James P. McKenna,* 1 B.T.A. 326 (1925).
[60] *L. Weiner,* 10 B.T.A. 905 (1928).
[61] *Cass Sunstein,* 1966 PH T.C. Memo ¶66,043, 25 TCM 247.
[62] *Mathias Schira v. CIR,* 50 AFTR 1404, 57-1 USTC ¶9413 (6th Cir., 1957).
[63] *Gary Ayers,* 1978 PH T.C. Memo ¶78,341, 37 TCM 1415.
[64] *Antonino Farina v. McMahon,* 2 AFTR 2d 5918, 58-2 USTC ¶9938 (D.C. N.Y., 1958).
[65] *U.S. v. Manley S. Sullivan,* 6 AFTR 6753, 1 USTC ¶236 (USSC, 1927).
[66] *U.S. v. Patrick Commerford,* 12 AFTR 364, 1933 CCH ¶9255 (2nd Cir., 1933).

REAL-WORLD EXAMPLE

The requirement that tax-exempt income be included in determining the taxable portion of Social Security benefits has been challenged on the basis that such provision is unconstitutional. However, the court held that this provision placed only an indirect burden on the governmental unit that issued the tax-exempt bonds, which was not protected by the intergovernmental immunity doctrine. *H.J. Goldin v. Baker,* 59 AFTR 2d 87-444, 87-1 USTC ¶9128, (2nd Cir., 1987).

MARRIED FILING SEPARATELY. In the case of a married person filing separately, taxable Social Security benefits are equal to the lesser of

- 85% of Social Security benefits, or
- 85% of provisional income

MARRIED FILING JOINTLY. For married couples filing jointly, the computation of the taxable portion of Social Security benefits is as follows:

- If provisional income is $32,000 or less, no Social Security benefits are taxable.
- If provisional income is over $32,000 (but not over $44,000), taxable Social Security benefits equal the lesser of:
  50% of the Social Security benefits, or
  50% of the excess of provisional income over $32,000
- If provisional income is over $44,000, taxable Social Security benefits are equal to the lesser of:
  85% of the Social Security benefits, or
  85% of provisional income over $44,000, plus the lesser of (1) $6,000 or (2) 50% of Social Security benefits.

SINGLE TAXPAYERS. For single taxpayers, the computation of the taxable portion of Social Security benefits is as follows:

- If provisional income is $25,000 or less, no Social Security benefits are taxable.
- If provisional income is over $25,000 (but not over $34,000), taxable Social Security benefits are equal to the lesser of:
  50% of the Social Security benefits, or
  50% of the excess of provisional income over $25,000
- If provisional income is over $34,000, taxable Social Security benefits are equal to the lesser of:
  85% of the Social Security benefits, or
  85% of provisional income over $34,000, plus the lesser of (1) $4,500 or (2) 50% of Social Security benefits

EXAMPLE I3-31 ▶ Holly is a single taxpayer with a taxable pension of $22,000, tax-exempt interest of $10,000, and Social Security benefits of $8,000. Her provisional income is $36,000, determined as follows:

Adjusted gross income	$22,000
Plus: Tax-exempt interest	10,000
50% of Social Security benefits	4,000
Provisional income	$36,000

The taxable Social Security benefits are equal to $5,700, which is the lesser of $6,800 (0.85 × $8,000) or $5,700 ($1,700* + the lesser of $4,500 or $4,000**).

*($36,000 provisional income − $34,000 threshold) × 0.85.
**50% of the Social Security benefits. ◀

The result of the computation excludes from gross income the Social Security benefits received by lower-income individuals but taxes a portion (up to 85%) of the benefits received by taxpayers with higher incomes.

ADDITIONAL COMMENT

For a 65-year-old taxpayer who retired in 1994, the maximum monthly individual Social Security benefit was $1,148.

The term **Social Security benefits** refers to basic monthly retirement and disability benefits paid under Social Security and also to tier-one railroad retirement benefits. It does not include supplementary Medicare benefits that cover the cost of doctors' services and other medical benefits.

INSURANCE PROCEEDS AND COURT AWARDS

In general, insurance proceeds and court awards are taxable. Two exceptions are accident and health insurance benefits and the face amount of life insurance. (See Chapter I4 for a discussion of these benefits.)

Insurance proceeds or court awards received because of the destruction of property are included in gross income only to the extent that the proceeds exceed the adjusted basis of the property. Involuntary conversion provisions permit taxpayers to avoid being taxed if they reinvest the proceeds in a qualified replacement property.[67] If the proceeds are less than the property's adjusted basis, they reduce the amount of any deductible loss. Proceeds of insurance guarding against loss of profits because of a casualty are taxable.[68] Similarly, if a taxpayer had to sue a customer to collect income owed to the taxpayer, the amount collected is taxable just as it would have been had the taxpayer collected the income without going to court.

EXAMPLE I3-32 ▶ Gulf Corporation's factory was destroyed by fire. Gulf Corporation collected insurance of $400,000, which equaled its basis in the building, and $250,000 for the profits lost during the time the company was rebuilding its factory. The $400,000 is not taxable because it constitutes a recovery of the basis of the factory. The $250,000 is taxable because it represents lost income. Recall that the income would have been taxable had it been earned by the company from regular operations. ◀

Although few exclusions are designed specifically for insurance proceeds or court awards, such amounts may be covered by other, more general exclusions. For example, Sec. 104(a)(2) excludes "damages (other than punitive damages) received . . . on account of personal physical injuries or sickness." Thus, amounts collected because of physical injury suffered in an automobile accident are excluded (See Chapter I4).

RECOVERY OF PREVIOUSLY DEDUCTED AMOUNTS

On occasion, a taxpayer may deduct an amount in one year but recover the amount in a subsequent year. In general, the amount recovered must be included in the gross income in the year it is recovered. Cash-basis taxpayers encounter this situation more often than accrual-basis taxpayers because their expenses are generally deductible in the year they are paid. If the amount was overpaid, the taxpayer can anticipate a refund.

EXAMPLE I3-33 ▶ During 2002, Cindy's employer withheld $1,000 from her wages for state income taxes. She claimed the $1,000 as an itemized deduction on her 2002 federal income tax return. Her itemized deductions totaled $12,000. On her 2002 state income tax return, her state income tax was only $800. As a result, Cindy received a $200 refund from the state in 2003. Because Cindy deducted the full $1,000 in 2002, she must report the $200 refund as income on her 2003 federal income tax return. ◀

Any recovery of a previously deducted amount may lead to income recognition. Recovery, however, is often associated with expenses such as state income taxes or bad debts deducted in one year but recovered in a later year, medical expenses deducted in one year but reimbursed by insurance in a later year, casualty losses deducted in one year but reimbursed by court award or insurance in a later year, and deductions for amounts paid by check where the payee never cashed the check.

Several related rules should be noted:

- ▶ If the refund or other recovery occurs in the same year, the refund or recovery reduces the deduction and is not reported as income.
- ▶ Interest on the amount refunded is taxable and is not subject to the tax benefit rule (discussed below).
- ▶ The character of the income reported in the year of repayment is dependent on the type of deduction previously reported. For instance, if the taxpayer deducted a short-term capital loss in one year, the subsequent recovery would be a short-term capital gain.[69]

[67] The involuntary conversion provisions are discussed in Chapter I12.

[68] *Oppenheim's Inc. v. Kavanagh*, 39 AFTR 468, 50-1 USTC ¶9249 (D.C.-Mich., 1950).

[69] *F. Donald Arrowsmith Exr. v. CIR*, 42 AFTR 649, 52-2 USTC ¶9527 (USSC, 1952).

TAX BENEFIT RULE. As noted above, a taxpayer who recovers an amount deducted in a previous year must report as gross income the amount recovered. The amount recovered need not be included in income, however, if the taxpayer received no tax benefit. A tax benefit occurs only if the deduction reduced the tax for the year.[70]

EXAMPLE I3-34 ▶ In 2002, Jack's employer withheld $1,200 from his wages for state income tax. Jack claimed the $1,200 as an itemized deduction on his 2002 federal income tax return. Because of a variety of losses incurred by Jack, he reported a negative taxable income of $32,000 during 2002. The state refunded the $1,200 during 2003. Jack will not have to report the $1,200 as gross income on his federal return. He would have owed no federal income tax in 2002 even without the deduction for state income taxes. Therefore, Jack received no tax benefit from the deduction. ◀

REAL-WORLD EXAMPLE

An attorney collected fees from clients of his employer. Because the attorney and his employer were engaged in a dispute over ownership of the money, he deposited the disputed amount in a trust account. The attorney was taxable on the amounts in the year received because he had control over the funds under the claim of right doctrine. *Edward J. Costello, Jr.*, 1985 PH T.C. Memo ¶85,571, 50 TCM 1463.

Tax benefit may be absent in other situations. For example, a taxpayer's total itemized deductions may have been less than the standard deduction, or the expense may have been less than the applicable floor. To illustrate, medical expenses can be deducted only to the extent that they exceed 7.5% of adjusted gross income. If a taxpayer does not deduct medical expenses because they are less than the floor, the taxpayer does not have to report a subsequent reimbursement of the expense as income. If only a portion of an expense produces a tax benefit, only that portion has to be reported as income.

EXAMPLE I3-35 ▶ In 2002, Chris, an unmarried individual, had $1,350 withheld from her wages for state income tax. Her itemized deductions consisted of state income taxes of $1,350 and charitable contributions of $3,500. Her itemized deductions exceed the standard deduction by $150 ($1,350 + $3,500 − $4,700). If Chris received a state income tax refund of $200 in 2003 she must report only $150 as gross income in 2003. She benefited only from $150 of the deduction and so that is all she has to report as income. ◀

CLAIM OF RIGHT

Sometimes taxpayers receive disputed amounts. For example, a contractor may receive payment on a job when the quality of the work is being questioned by the customer, a salesperson may receive commissions when there is a question as to whether the sales are final, or a litigant may receive a court award even though the case is on appeal. Under the claim of right doctrine, the recipient of a disputed amount must include the amount received in gross income as long as the use of the funds is unrestricted.

EXAMPLE I3-36 ▶ Jane wins a court case against a customer requiring the customer to pay her $10,000. The customer is unhappy with the result of the case and indicates that he plans to appeal, but pays the $10,000 to avoid interest on the amount in the event he loses the appeal. Jane must include the $10,000 in gross income even though she will have to repay the amount if she loses the appeal. ◀

EXAMPLE I3-37 ▶ Assume the same facts as in Example I3-36 except that the $10,000 is placed in escrow by the court awaiting the outcome of the appeal. Jane does not have to report the amount as she does not have use of the funds. ◀

Of course, taxpayers may be required to repay the disputed amount in a subsequent year. Such taxpayers may deduct the previously reported amount in the year of repayment. The taxes saved from such a deduction, however, may be considerably less than the original tax. If the repayment is over $3,000, taxpayers have the option of reducing the current tax by the tax paid in the prior year or years on the repaid amount.[71]

EXAMPLE I3-38 ▶ Assume the same facts as in Example I3-36, except that after reporting the disputed $10,000 Jane loses the appeal and must repay the $10,000 to her customer. If Jane was in the 28% tax bracket when she reported the disputed amount, she would have paid a $2,800 (0.28 × $10,000) tax on the disputed amount. If she were in the 15% bracket when she made the

[70] Sec. 111.

[71] Sec. 1341.

repayment, she would recover only $1,500 by deducting the $10,000. Because the amount exceeds $3,000, Jane has the option of determining her current year's tax by deducting from the tax she would otherwise pay the $2,800 tax she paid in the earlier year. This credit is allowed in lieu of receiving a deduction of $10,000. ◀

TAX PLANNING CONSIDERATIONS

KEY POINT

The advantage of shifting income to children has been increased since the revision of the tax rate schedules in 1993. The highest and lowest marginal tax rates in 1992 were 31% and 15%, respectively. In 1993 and in subsequent years, the highest and lowest marginal rates are 39.6% and 15%, respectively.

SHIFTING INCOME

A family can reduce its taxes by shifting income from family members who are in high tax brackets (e.g., parents) to family members who are in low tax brackets (e.g., children). Assignment of income rules prevent shifting from being done by merely redirecting the payment. Thus, a father cannot avoid a tax on his salary by ordering his employer to pay the salary to his daughter. Nevertheless, income can be shifted by transferring ownership of the property. For example, children may own stock in the family business. Dividends on the stock are taxed to the children. In the case of a child under age 14, however, the parents' (as opposed to the child's) tax rate applies to unearned income in excess of $1,500. Series EE bonds may prove useful to avoid the kiddie tax because the interest is deferred until the bond is redeemed or matures. The maturity date, of course, may be after the child reaches age 14. Another shifting technique is for the child to work for the family business and be paid a reasonable salary. Such income is taxed at the child's tax rate, even if the child is under 14 years old, and can be offset by the child's own standard deduction.

Shifting of income is constrained by several factors. As noted, the assignment of income doctrine limits transfers. Reasonableness limitations constrain compensation and other payments. Furthermore, outright gifts of property are subject to gift taxes. Also, individuals are reluctant to transfer wealth to children for a variety of personal reasons. However, the tax saving potential of shifting income is often so great as to prompt many well-to-do families to use available shifting techniques.

ALIMONY

Whether payments made in connection with a divorce or separation are classified as alimony is of major tax significance. Such classification results in a deduction for the payor and income to the payee. Alimony is actually one way to shift income.

EXAMPLE I3-39 ▶ Tony, who has a 36% marginal tax rate, makes payments of $40,000 to his former wife. If it is deductible as alimony, Tony will save $14,400 (0.36 × $40,000) a year in federal income taxes. The amount of tax that the former wife must pay depends on how much other income she has and whether she has deductions that reduce the tax. Her tax might be even higher than her former husband's or as little as zero. ◀

ADDITIONAL COMMENT

In 1996, $5.4 billion of alimony paid was reported as a deduction, while only $4.6 billion was reported as taxable income.

Two points are clear. One is that both parties should understand the implication of having amounts treated as alimony. Second, the designation of the payments as alimony may be beneficial to both parties. The payor will, of course, benefit from a tax deduction. The payee may benefit because the payor may agree to make larger alimony payments since the payments are tax deductible.

PREPAID INCOME

As explained earlier in this chapter, prepaid income is generally taxable when received. This accelerated recognition of income may be a significant disadvantage to the taxpayer if the related expenses are incurred in a later tax year. Thus, tax planning for prepaid amounts is essential.

EXAMPLE I3-40 ▶ Phil owns an apartment complex and requires tenants to pay the first and last months' rent before they move in. Rita, on the other hand, owns an apartment complex and requires tenants to pay the first month's rent and a refundable deposit (which equals one month's rent).

Although the full amount received by Phil is taxable when it is received, only one-half of the amount received by Rita is taxable when it is received. Rita is required to refund the deposit, assuming the tenant vacates leaving the property in good condition and having paid all rent. Therefore, the deposit is not taxable. ◀

HISTORICAL NOTE

In 1954 Congress passed Sec. 452, allowing deferral of certain prepaid income, but in 1955 Congress retroactively repealed this section.

Taxpayers receiving advance payments in connection with services may be able to meet the requirements of Rev. Proc. 71-21 (discussed earlier in the chapter); taxpayers receiving advance payments associated with the sale of merchandise may be able to meet the requirements of Reg. Sec. 1.451-5 (also discussed in this chapter). Also, special rules exist for subscription income, membership fees, crop insurance proceeds, and drought sales of livestock, all of which allow taxpayers to defer recognizing income.

TAXABLE, TAX-EXEMPT, OR TAX-DEFERRED BONDS

Which should a taxpayer choose: taxable bonds, tax-exempt bonds, or tax-deferred bonds? The answer depends on the relative interest rates and the taxpayer's current and future tax brackets. **Taxable bonds** yield the highest return, but the interest is taxable. **Tax-exempt bonds** yield a lower return. **Tax-deferred bonds** generally yield a return somewhere close to that of taxable bonds. Interest on U.S. Series EE savings bonds is tax exempt if it is used for educational purposes and if other requirements of Sec. 135 are met (see the discussion earlier in this chapter). If these conditions are not met, the tax is deferred until the bonds are redeemed. The taxpayer may be in a lower bracket when the tax is eventually paid, and in the meantime, the interest that will eventually go to pay taxes is earning additional income.

The decision between taxable and exempt bonds is a rather easy one if the risk of the investments is assumed to be approximately equal. A taxpayer should invest in exempt bonds instead of taxable bonds if the interest on the exempt bonds is greater than the interest on the taxable bonds multiplied by 1 minus the taxpayer's marginal tax bracket (expressed as a decimal). Stated in a formula, this means invest in tax-exempt bonds if

$$\text{Return on the tax-exempt bonds} > \text{Return on the taxable bonds} \times (1 - \text{Marginal tax bracket})$$

EXAMPLE I3-41 ▶ Robert's marginal tax bracket is 30% and he is trying to decide between tax-exempt bonds, which pay 6% interest, and taxable bonds paying 8% interest. Robert should invest in the exempt bonds because 6% is greater than 5.6% [0.08 × (1 − 0.30)]. ◀

SELF-STUDY QUESTION

The highest marginal tax rate is currently 39.6%, but it was 31% in 1992. Assume that interest rates on taxable bonds have remained constant at 10% since 1992. Considering only the effect of the tax rates, is the rate of interest on tax-exempt bonds likely to have fallen, risen, or remained the same?

ANSWER

Everything else being equal, one would expect the spread between taxable and nontaxable bonds to have widened. A taxpayer having a marginal tax rate of 31% would be indifferent between a taxable bond yielding 10% and a tax-exempt bond yielding 6.9%. However, if the marginal tax rate is 39.6%, the yield on the tax-exempt bond would have to decline to 6.04% for the taxpayer to remain indifferent.

Comparison of taxable bonds or exempt bonds to tax-deferred bonds is more complicated. As noted, the advantages of the tax-deferred bonds are twofold. First, the taxpayer may be in a lower tax bracket when the tax is paid (e.g., taxpayers who plan to redeem the bonds after retirement). Second, the amount that will eventually go to pay the tax earns income until the tax must be paid. Although the computation is not covered here, it is noted that taxpayers who anticipate that they will be in lower tax brackets and who plan to leave funds invested for several years may benefit from choosing Series EE U.S. savings bonds over taxable bonds. See Chapter I18 in the *Individuals* text for a further discussion of taxable, tax exempt, and tax deferred investments.

REPORTING SAVINGS BOND INTEREST

It may be desirable to purchase Series EE bonds in the child's name despite the fact that such interest is subject to the kiddie tax (see Chapter I2). This is because there is no income tax as long as the child's annual income is less than $700. However, even if a child is not otherwise required to file a return, it is necessary to report interest on Series EE bonds annually by filing a tax return.[72] Taxpayers who have not been reporting savings bond interest annually may change to annual reporting, but are required to report both current and previously accrued interest in the year of the change.[73]

[72] *Philip Apkin*, 86 T.C. 692 (1986).

[73] Reg. Sec. 1.454-1(a)(4), Ex. (1).

Taxpayers who report savings bond interest annually are allowed to change to the deferral method without IRS approval.[74] This is particularly useful where the decision to report interest currently was made before the imposition of the kiddie tax. Taxpayers who make this election are bound by it for five years.

DEFERRED COMPENSATION ARRANGEMENTS

Deferred compensation plans can be used as a means of avoiding the constructive receipt of income. Although income is normally taxable when the funds become available to the taxpayer, an advance contractual agreement can produce different results. Corporate executives, professional athletes, and others often sign agreements providing for compensation to be paid at future dates. Such agreements can produce tax savings because the recipients expect to be in a lower tax bracket. Because the arrangements are advance contractual agreements, the deferral of income does not constitute taxpayers "turning their backs" on the income.

EXAMPLE I3-42 ▶ Alonzo, a 35-year-old professional basketball player, signs a contract specifying that he will be paid $400,000 per year for ten years even if he does not play. Because of his age, both Alonzo and the team recognize that he will probably play for one or two more years. If the agreement had specified that he was to receive a salary of $1,300,000 per year for two years, most of the income would have been taxed at the highest rates. By spreading the amount over a longer period, Alonzo pays tax at lower rates on much of the income. Alonzo is compensated for the delayed payment by receiving a larger total amount [i.e., $4 million ($400,000 × 10 years) versus $2.6 million ($1.3 million × 2 years)]. ◀

COMPLIANCE AND PROCEDURAL CONSIDERATIONS

ADDITIONAL COMMENT

The dollar amount of tax-exempt interest income is recorded on Form 1040, line 8b, but is not included in the tax base. The IRS requires the reporting of this type of income probably because it may affect the taxability of Social Security benefits.

Form 1040 lists various types of income. Some items of income (wages, tax refunds, alimony, pensions and annuities, unemployment compensation, Social Security benefits, and other income) are listed directly on Form 1040. Most expenses related to these items of income are deducted as miscellaneous itemized deductions on Schedule A.

Most other types of income (and related deductions) are reported on special schedules.

Topic Review I3-3 summarizes the procedures for reporting income, and related deductions.

EXAMPLE I3-43 ▶ John J. Alexander has several items of income and related deductions:

KEY POINT

The amount labeled "total income" on line 22 of Form 1040 is not gross income, adjusted gross income, or taxable income.

Salary		$40,000
Deductible alimony payments		6,000
Taxable interest		300
Dividends:	Ford Motor Co.	150
	Omaha Mutual Fund ($120 is a return of capital distribution and $50 is a capital gain dividend)	600
Rent income (depreciation, interest, repairs, and other related expenses total $8,000)		11,000

The reporting of these items of income is illustrated on page 1 of Form 1040 (Figure I3-1) and on Schedule B of Form 1040 (Figure I3-2). Salary and interest (because the interest is less than $400) are entered directly on Form 1040. Note that on Schedule B, the capital gain distribution and the nontaxable distribution are subtracted in arriving at reported dividends. Rental income would be entered on Schedule E (not illustrated), and the net income after deducting related expenses is transferred to Form 1040. Alimony received and alimony payments are reported on page 1 of Form 1040. ◀

[74] Rev. Proc. 89-46, 1989-2 C.B. 597.

Topic Review I3-3

Reporting of Income

Type of Income	Reported On	Related Deductions Are Claimed On
Wages, salaries, tips, etc.	Form 1040	Schedule A and various other forms: moving, Form 3903; travel, transportation, etc., Form 2106
Interest	Form 1040 (if less than $400), otherwise Schedule B	Schedule A (miscellaneous deductions if any, e.g., safe deposit box fees)
Dividends	Form 1040 (if less than $400), otherwise Schedule B	Schedule A (miscellaneous deductions if any, e.g., safe deposit box fees)
Refund of state or local income taxes	Form 1040 (instructions contain a worksheet)	Schedule A (miscellaneous deductions if any, e.g., fee paid for tax advice)
Alimony	Form 1040	Schedule A (miscellaneous deduction, if any, e.g., legal fee associated with alimony)
Business income	Schedule C or C-EZ (net income or loss is transferred to Form 1040)	Schedule C or C-EZ (e.g., depreciation, advertising, repairs)
Capital gains	Schedule D	Schedule D (capital losses) or Schedule A (investment expenses)
Supplemental gains	Form 4797	Form 4797 (e.g., ordinary losses)
Pensions and annuities	Form 1040 (instructions contain a worksheet)	Generally no related deductions
Rents, royalties, partnerships, S corporations, estates, trusts, etc.	Schedule E	Schedule E
Farm income	Schedule F	Schedule F
Unemployment compensation	Form 1040	Generally no related deductions
Social Security benefits	Form 1040 (instructions contain a worksheet)	Generally no related deductions
Other income	Form 1040	Schedule A (miscellaneous deductions, if any)

Problem Materials

Discussion Questions

I3-1 What phrase is found in both the Sixteenth Amendment to the Constitution and Sec. 61(a)?

I3-2 Contrast the accounting and economic concepts of income.

I3-3 Why does the tax concept of income more closely resemble the accounting concept of income than the economic concept?

I3-4 Explain the meaning of the term *wherewithal to pay* as it applies to taxation.

I3-5 If a loan is repaid, the lender does not have to include the repayment in gross income. There is no exclusion in the tax law that permits taxpayers to omit such amounts from gross income. How can this be explained?

I3-6 A landlord who receives prepaid rent is required to report that amount as gross income when the payment is received. Why would Congress choose to do this? What problem does this create for the taxpayer?

I3-7 Office space is often rented without carpet, wall covering, or window covering. Furthermore, many rental agreements specify that these improvements cannot be removed by a tenant if removal causes any damage to the property. What issue does this raise?

I3-8 Does the fact that an item of income is paid in a form other than cash mean it is nontaxable? Explain.

I3-9 Explain the significance of *Lucas v. Earl* and *Helvering v. Horst.*

I3-10 Under present-day tax law, community property rules are followed in allocating income between husband and wife. Is this consistent with *Lucas v. Earl?* Explain.

I3-11 Ricardo owns a small unincorporated business. His 15-year-old daughter Jane works in the business on a part-time basis and was paid wages of $3,000 during the current year. Who is taxed on the child's earnings: Jane or her father? Explain.

Form **1040** Department of the Treasury—Internal Revenue Service
U.S. Individual Income Tax Return **2001** (99) IRS Use Only—Do not write or staple in this space.

For the year Jan. 1–Dec. 31, 2001, or other tax year beginning , 2001, ending , 20 OMB No. 1545-0074

Label (See instructions on page 19.) **Use the IRS label.** Otherwise, please print or type.	LABEL HERE	
Your first name and initial: John J.	Last name: Alexander	Your social security number: 123 45 6789
If a joint return, spouse's first name and initial	Last name	Spouse's social security number
Home address (number and street). If you have a P.O. box, see page 19.: 41 Oak St.	Apt. no.	▲ **Important!** ▲ You **must** enter your SSN(s) above.
City, town or post office, state, and ZIP code. If you have a foreign address, see page 19.: Orlando, Florida 32816		

Presidential Election Campaign (See page 19.) ▶ **Note.** Checking "Yes" will not change your tax or reduce your refund. Do you, or your spouse if filing a joint return, want $3 to go to this fund? ▶ You: ☐ Yes ☒ No Spouse: ☐ Yes ☐ No

Filing Status

Check only one box.

1 ☑ Single
2 ☐ Married filing joint return (even if only one had income)
3 ☐ Married filing separate return. Enter spouse's social security no. above and full name here. ▶
4 ☐ Head of household (with qualifying person). (See page 19.) If the qualifying person is a child but not your dependent, enter this child's name here. ▶
5 ☐ Qualifying widow(er) with dependent child (year spouse died ▶). (See page 19.)

Exemptions

6a ☒ **Yourself.** If your parent (or someone else) can claim you as a dependent on his or her tax return, **do not** check box 6a — No. of boxes checked on 6a and 6b: 1
b ☐ **Spouse**
c **Dependents:**

(1) First name	Last name	(2) Dependent's social security number	(3) Dependent's relationship to you	(4) ✓ if qualifying child for child tax credit (see page 20)
				☐
				☐
				☐
				☐
				☐
				☐

If more than six dependents, see page 20.

No. of your children on 6c who: • lived with you • did not live with you due to divorce or separation (see page 20) Dependents on 6c not entered above

d Total number of exemptions claimed — Add numbers entered on lines above ▶ 1

Income

Attach Forms W-2 and W-2G here. Also attach Form(s) 1099-R if tax was withheld.

If you did not get a W-2, see page 21.

Enclose, but do not attach, any payment. Also, please use Form 1040-V.

7	Wages, salaries, tips, etc. Attach Form(s) W-2	7	40,000
8a	**Taxable** interest. Attach Schedule B if required	8a	300
b	**Tax-exempt** interest. **Do not** include on line 8a — 8b		
9	Ordinary dividends. Attach Schedule B if required	9	580
10	Taxable refunds, credits, or offsets of state and local income taxes (see page 22)	10	
11	Alimony received	11	
12	Business income or (loss). Attach Schedule C or C-EZ	12	
13	Capital gain or (loss). Attach Schedule D if required. If not required, check here ▶ ☑	13	50
14	Other gains or (losses). Attach Form 4797	14	
15a	Total IRA distributions 15a — b Taxable amount (see page 23)	15b	
16a	Total pensions and annuities 16a — b Taxable amount (see page 23)	16b	
17	Rental real estate, royalties, partnerships, S corporations, trusts, etc. Attach Schedule E	17	3,000
18	Farm income or (loss). Attach Schedule F	18	
19	Unemployment compensation	19	
20a	Social security benefits 20a — b Taxable amount (see page 25)	20b	
21	Other income. List type and amount (see page 27)	21	
22	Add the amounts in the far right column for lines 7 through 21. This is your **total income** ▶	22	43,930

Adjusted Gross Income

23	IRA deduction (see page 27)	23			
24	Student loan interest deduction (see page 28)	24			
25	Archer MSA deduction. Attach Form 8853	25			
26	Moving expenses. Attach Form 3903	26			
27	One-half of self-employment tax. Attach Schedule SE	27			
28	Self-employed health insurance deduction (see page 30)	28			
29	Self-employed SEP, SIMPLE, and qualified plans	29			
30	Penalty on early withdrawal of savings	30			
31a	Alimony paid b Recipient's SSN ▶ 987 65 4321	31a	6,000		
32	Add lines 23 through 31a			32	6,000
33	Subtract line 32 from line 22. This is your **adjusted gross income** ▶			33	37,930

For Disclosure, Privacy Act, and Paperwork Reduction Act Notice, see page 72. Cat. No. 11320B Form **1040** (2001)

FIGURE 13-1 ▶ FORM 1040 (PAGE 1)

Name(s) shown on Form 1040. Do not enter name and social security number if shown on other side.
John J. Alexander

Your social security number: 123 45 6789

Schedule B—Interest and Ordinary Dividends

Attachment Sequence No. 08

Part I Interest

(See page B-1 and the instructions for Form 1040, line 8a.)

Note. If you received a Form 1099-INT, Form 1099-OID, or substitute statement from a brokerage firm, list the firm's name as the payer and enter the total interest shown on that form.

			Amount
1	List name of payer. If any interest is from a seller-financed mortgage and the buyer used the property as a personal residence, see page B-1 and list this interest first. Also, show that buyer's social security number and address ▶	1	
2	Add the amounts on line 1	2	
3	Excludable interest on series EE and I U.S. savings bonds issued after 1989 from Form 8815, line 14. You **must** attach Form 8815	3	
4	Subtract line 3 from line 2. Enter the result here and on Form 1040, line 8a ▶	4	

Note. If line 4 is over $400, you must complete Part III.

Part II Ordinary Dividends

(See page B-1 and the instructions for Form 1040, line 9.)

Note. If you received a Form 1099-DIV or substitute statement from a brokerage firm, list the firm's name as the payer and enter the ordinary dividends shown on that form.

			Amount
5	List name of payer. Include only ordinary dividends. If you received any capital gain distributions, see the instructions for Form 1040, line 13 ▶	5	
	Ford Motor Company		150
	Omaha Mutual Fund		430
6	Add the amounts on line 5. Enter the total here and on Form 1040, line 9 ▶	6	580

Note. If line 6 is over $400, you must complete Part III.

Part III Foreign Accounts and Trusts

(See page B-2.)

You must complete this part if you **(a)** had over $400 of taxable interest or ordinary dividends; **(b)** had a foreign account; or **(c)** received a distribution from, or were a grantor of, or a transferor to, a foreign trust.

		Yes	No
7a	At any time during 2001, did you have an interest in or a signature or other authority over a financial account in a foreign country, such as a bank account, securities account, or other financial account? See page B-2 for exceptions and filing requirements for Form TD F 90-22.1		X
b	If "Yes," enter the name of the foreign country ▶		
8	During 2001, did you receive a distribution from, or were you the grantor of, or transferor to, a foreign trust? If "Yes," you may have to file Form 3520. See page B-2		X

For Paperwork Reduction Act Notice, see Form 1040 instructions. **Schedule B (Form 1040) 2001**

FIGURE 13-2 ▶ SCHEDULES A & B (PAGE 2)

I3-12 Define the term *constructive receipt.* Explain its importance.

I3-13 Explain three restrictions on the concept of constructive receipt.

I3-14 When is income considered to be earned by an accrual-basis taxpayer?

I3-15 a. Explain the difference between the treatment of prepaid income under the tax law and under financial accounting.
b. Why are the two treatments so different?
c. What problem does this treatment create for taxpayers?

I3-16 Under what conditions is an accrual-basis taxpayer allowed to defer reporting amounts received in the advance of the delivery of goods?

I3-17 Under what conditions is an accrual-basis taxpayer allowed to defer reporting advance payments received for services?

I3-18 a. Is the interest received from government obligations taxable? Explain.
b. What impact does the fact that some bond interest is tax exempt have on interest rates?
c. Is an investor always better off buying tax-exempt bonds? Explain.

I3-19 Are improvements made by a lessee to a lessor's property included in the income of the lessor?

I3-20 Explain the relationship between dividends and earnings and profits.

I3-21 On what basis did the Supreme Court in *Eisner v. Macomber* decide that stock dividends are nontaxable?

I3-22 What is the significance of a constructive dividend?

I3-23 Explain the importance of the distinction between alimony and a property settlement.

I3-24 a. Are items of income not listed in Sec. 61 taxable? Explain.
b. Because there is no specific exclusion for unrealized income, why is it not taxable?
c. Can income be realized even when a cash-method taxpayer does not receive cash?
d. Does a cash basis taxpayer realize income upon the receipt of a note?

I3-25 a. Briefly explain the tax benefit rule.
b. Is a taxpayer required to report the reimbursement of a medical expense by insurance as income if the reimbursement is received in the year following the year of the expenditure?

I3-26 What opportunities are available for a taxpayer to defer the recognition of certain types of prepaid income? That is, what advice could you give someone who wishes to defer the reporting of prepaid income?

I3-27 Taxpayers who deduct an expense one year but recover it the next year are required to include the recovered amount in gross income. The tax benefit rule provides relief if the original deduction did not result in any tax savings. Does this rule provide relief to taxpayers who are in a higher tax bracket in the year they recover the previously deducted expense?

I3-28 George, a wealthy investor, is uncertain whether he should invest in taxable or tax-exempt bonds. What tax and nontax factors should he consider?

I3-29 Do you agree or disagree with the following statement: A taxpayer should not have to report income when debt is forgiven because the taxpayer receives nothing. Explain.

I3-30 Jack and June are retired and receive $10,000 of social security benefits and taxable pensions totaling $25,000. They have been offered $20,000 for a automobile that they restored after they retired. They did most of the restoration work themselves and the sale will result in a gain of $12,000. What tax issues should Jack and June consider?

ISSUE IDENTIFICATION QUESTIONS

I3-31 State Construction Company is owned equally by Andy, Bill, and Charlie. Andy works in the corporation full-time, and Bill and Charlie work elsewhere. When Andy left his previous job to work for State, he signed a contract specifying that he would receive a salary of $50,000 per year. This year, Andy felt that the company could expand if it purchased more equipment, and he offered to delay receiving $20,000 of his salary so the funds could be used to purchase the equipment. Bill and Charlie agreed, and the equipment was purchased. It is expected that State will have enough cash to pay Andy by early March of next year. What tax issues should Andy consider?

I3-32 Lisa and her daughter Jane are equal shareholders is Lisa's Flooring, Inc. Lisa founded the corporation and was the sole owner for over twenty years. The company is very successful and Lisa has accumulated a fairly large estate. When Jane turned age twenty-five last year, Lisa gave her half of the corporation's stock. The gift was properly reported on Lisa's gift tax return. Both Lisa and Jane now work full-time for the corporation. Lisa received a salary of $55,000 per year before Jane started working for the company. After Jane started working, Lisa reduced her salary to $15,000 and started paying Jane a salary of $50,000. Lisa indicates that she still makes most major decisions in the company, but she hopes that Jane will play a more important role as she becomes more familiar with the company. What tax issues should Lisa and the corporation consider?

I3-33 Larry's Art Gallery sells oil paintings, lithographs, and bronzes to collectors and corporations. Customers often come to Larry looking for special pieces. In order to meet customer needs, Larry often accepts orders and then travels looking for the desired item, which he purchases and delivers to the customer. The pieces are expensive, and Larry requires customers to demonstrate their sincerity by providing deposits. If it turns out that the item costs more than expected, Larry contacts the buyer and asks for additional funds. If the item costs less than expected, Larry refunds the excess amount. Also, Larry sometimes returns amounts he received in advance because he is unable to find what the customer wants. What tax issues should Larry's Art Gallery consider?

PROBLEMS

I3-34 *Noncash Compensation.* For each of the following items indicate, whether the individual taxpayer must include any amount in gross income.

a. Employees of Eastside Bookstore are given their birthdays off with pay.
b. Westside Hardware, Inc. gave each employee 10 shares of Westside stock worth $100 per share in lieu of a cash bonus.
c. Employees of Northside Manufacturing were allowed to take home the company's old computers when the company purchased new ones.

I3-35 *Constructive Receipt.* Which of the following constitutes constructive receipt?

a. A salary check received at 6:00 p.m. on December 31, after all the banks have closed.
b. A rent check, received on December 30 by the manager of an apartment complex. The manager normally collects the rent for the owner. The owner was out of town.
c. A paycheck received on December 29 that was not honored by the bank because the employer's account did not have sufficient funds.
d. A check received on December 30. The check was postdated January 2 of the following year.
e. A check received on January 2. The check had been mailed on December 30.

I3-36 *Cash and Accrual Methods.* Carmen opens a retail store. Her sales during the first year are $600,000, of which $30,000 has not been collected at year-end. Her purchases are $400,000. She still owes $20,000 to her suppliers, and at year-end she has $50,000 of inventory on hand. She incurred operating expenses of $160,000. At year-end she has not paid $15,000 of the expenses.

a. Compute her net income from the business assuming she elects the accrual method.
b. Compute her net income from the business assuming she elects the cash method.
c. Would paying the $15,000 she owes for operating expenses before year-end change her net income under accrual method of reporting? under the cash method?

I3-37 *Series EE Bond Interest.* In 1998, Harry and Mary purchased Series EE bonds, and in 2002 redeemed the bonds, receiving $500 of interest and $1,500 of principal. Their income from other sources totaled $30,000. They paid $2,200 in tuition and fees for their dependent daughter. Their daughter is a qualified student at State University.

a. How much of the Series EE bond interest is excludable?
b. Assuming that the daughter received a $1,000 scholarship, how much of the interest is excludable? Ignore any tax credits that might be available.
c. Assuming the daughter received the $1,000 scholarship and that the parents' income from other sources is $91,900, how much of the interest is excludable?

I3-38 *Alimony.* As a result of their divorce, Fred agrees to pay alimony to Tammy of $20,000 per year. The payments are to cease in the event of Fred's or Tammy's death or in the event of Tammy's remarriage. In addition, Tammy is to receive their residence, which cost them $100,000 but is worth $140,000.

a. Does the fact that Tammy receives the residence at the time of the divorce mean that there is a reduction in alimony, which will lead to Fred having to recapture an amount in the subsequent year?
b. How will the $20,000 payments be treated by Fred and Tammy?
c. Would recapture of the payments be necessary if payment ceased because of Tammy's remarriage?
d. What is Tammy's basis in the residence?

I3-39 *Constructive Dividend.* Brad owns a successful corporation that has substantial earnings and profits. During the year, the following payments were made by the corporation:

a. Salary of $250,000 to Brad. Officers in other corporations performing similar services receive between $50,000 and $85,000.
b. Rent of $25,000 to Brad. The rent is paid in connection with an office building owned by Brad and used by the corporation. Similar buildings rent for about the same amount.
c. Salary of $5,000 to Brad's daughter, who worked for the company full-time during the summer and part-time during the rest of the year while she attended high school.
d. Alimony of $40,000 to Brad's former wife. Although Brad was personally obligated to make the payments, he used corporation funds to make the payments.

Discuss the likelihood of these payments being treated as constructive dividends. If a payment is deemed to be a constructive dividend, indicate how such a payment will be treated.

I3-40 *Constructive Dividend.* Which of the following would likely be a constructive dividend?
a. An unreasonable salary paid to a shareholder.
b. An unreasonable salary paid to the daughter of a shareholder.
c. A sale of a corporation's asset to a shareholder at fair market value.
d. A payment by a corporation of a shareholder's debts.
e. A payment by a corporation of a shareholder's personal expenses.

I3-41 *Prepaid Rent.* Stan rented an office building to Clay for $3,000 per month. On December 29, 2001, Stan received a deposit of $4,000 in addition to the first and last months' rent. Occupancy began on January 2, 2002. On July 15, 2002, Clay closed his business and filed for bankruptcy. Stan had collected rent for February, March, and April on the first of each month. Stan had received May rent on May 10, but collected no payments afterwards. Stan withheld $800 from the deposit because of damage to the property and $1,500 for unpaid rent. He refunded the balance of the deposit to Clay. What amount would Stan report as gross income for 2001? for 2002?

I3-42 *Rental Income.* Ed owns Oak Knoll Apartments. During the year, Fred, a tenant, moved to another state. Fred paid Ed $1,000 to cancel the two-year lease he had signed. Ed subsequently rented the unit to Wayne. Wayne paid the first and last months' rents of $800 each and a security deposit of $500. Ed also owns a building that is used as a health club. The club has signed a fifteen-year lease at an annual rental of $17,000. The owner of the club requested that Ed install a swimming pool on the property. Ed declined to do so. The owner of the club finally constructed the pool himself at a cost of $15,000. What amount must Ed include in gross income?

I3-43 *Gross Income.* Susan's salary is $44,000 and she received dividends of $600. She received a statement from SJ partnership indicating that her share of the partnership's income was $4,000. The partnership distributed $1,000 to her during the year and $600 after year-end. She won $2,000 in the state lottery and spent $50 on lottery tickets. Which amounts are taxable?

I3-44 *Interest Income.* Holly inherited $10,000 of City of Atlanta bonds in February. In March, she received interest of $500, and in April she sold the bonds at a $200 gain. Holly redeemed Series E U.S. savings bonds that she had purchased several years ago. The accumulated interest totaled $800. Holly received $300 of interest on bonds issued by the City of Quebec, Canada. What amount, if any, of gross income must Holly report?

I3-45 *Annuity Income.* Tim retired during the current year at age 58. He purchased an annuity from American National Life Company for $40,000. The annuity pays Tim $500 per month for life.
a. Compute Tim's annual exclusion.
b. How much income will Tim report each year after reaching age 84?

I3-46 *Pension Income.* Beth turns 65 and retires from her position as a garment worker. She immediately began receiving a monthly pension for the remainder of her life of $300 from a qualified retirement plan. Over the years she worked, Beth made $13,104 of nondeductible contributions to the pension fund through withholding. How much must Beth report as income from the pension during the current year?

I3-47 *Social Security Benefits.* Dan and Diana file a joint return. Dan earned $30,000 during the year before losing his job. He subsequently received unemployment compensation of $1,000. Diana received Social Security benefits of $5,000.
a. Determine the taxable portion of the Social Security benefits.

b. What is the taxable portion of the Social Security benefits if Dan earned $45,000 before losing his job?

I3-48 *Social Security Benefits.* Lucia is a 69-year-old single individual who receives a taxable pension of $10,000 per year and Social Security benefits of $7,000. Lucia is considering the possibility of selling stock she has owned for years and using the funds to purchase a summer home. She will realize a gain of $20,000 when she sells the stock, which has been paying $1,000 of dividends each year. Lucia says her brother recommended that she sell half of the stock this year and half next year because selling all of the stock at once would affect the tax treatment of her Social Security benefits.

a. Compute her AGI under the assumption she sells all of the stock now after receiving $1,000 dividends from the stock.
b. Repeat the computation under the assumption she sells only half of the stock this year and also receives $1,000 dividends from the stock.

I3-49 *Social Security Benefits.* Bob received a salary of $27,000 before he retired in October of this year. After he retired, he received social security benefits of $3,000 during the year. What amount, if any, of the social security benefits are taxable for the year?

I3-50 *Adjusted Gross Income.* Amir, who is single, retired from his job this year. He received a salary of $25,000 for the portion of the year that he worked, tax-exempt interest of $3,000, and dividends from domestic corporations of $2,700. On September 1, he began receiving monthly pension payments of $1,000 and Social Security payments of $600. Assume an exclusion ratio of 40% for the pension. Amir owns a duplex that he rents to others. He received rent of $12,000 and incurred $17,000 of expenses related to the duplex. He continued to actively manage the property after he retired from his job. Compute Amir's adjusted gross income.

I3-51 *Recovery of Previously Deducted Expense.* In 2003, Fred received a $1,000 refund of state income taxes withheld from his salary during 2002. For each of the following cases, indicate whether Fred must include any portion of the refund in his 2003 gross income.

a. Fred did not itemize during 2002.
b. Fred does not itemize during 2003.
c. Fred uses the accrual method for determining his deduction for state income taxes.
d. Fred suffered a net loss during 2002 of $20,000.
e. Fred suffered a net loss during 2003 of $20,000.
f. Fred's itemized deductions during 2003 exceeded the standard deduction by $400.

I3-52 *Recovery of Previously Deducted Expense.* As the result of unexpected surgery, Jan incurred $14,000 of medical expenses in 2002. At the end of 2002, her medical insurance had paid only $5,000. Jan anticipates that the company will eventually pay an additional $7,000 of the bill. Because her AGI is $30,000 and there is a 7.5% floor for medical deductions, Jan can deduct medical expenses over $2,250. Her other itemized deductions exceed the standard deduction.

a. If Jan pays the balance of the $9,000 medical expenses before the end of the year, can she claim a deduction in 2002?
b. If she is reimbursed $7,000 in 2003, how will the reimbursement be treated?

I3-53 *Court Awards and Insurance Settlements.* What amount, if any, must be included in gross income by the following taxpayers?

a. Ann received $2,000 from her insurance company when her automobile which cost $3,000 was stolen.
b. Barry received $3,000 from his brother. Barry had initiated a lawsuit against his brother in an effort to recover $3,000 he had previously loaned to him. The brother paid Barry back before the case was tried, and Barry dropped the lawsuit.
c. Carry, an accountant, sued a client in order to collect her fee for doing tax work. Would Carry's accounting method make any difference?
d. Dave has incurred $6,000 of medical expenses so far this year. He paid $400 of the expenses himself. His insurance company paid $4,000 of the expenses. The hospital is suing Dave and the insurance company for the balance, $1,600.

I3-54 *Claim of Right.* USA Corporation hired Jesse to install a computer system for the company and paid him $8,000 for the work. USA soon realized that there were problems with the system and asked Jesse to refund the payment. At the end of the year the dispute had not been resolved. Jesse is in the 28% tax bracket in the year he did the original work.

During the next year, when he is in the 15% tax bracket, Jesse refunds the $8,000 to USA.
a. Is the original payment taxable to Jesse when he receives it?
b. What options are available to Jesse when he repays the $8,000?
c. What option would have been available to Jesse if he had been asked to repay only $2,000?

I3-55 *Tax Planning.* Bart and Kesha are in the 35% tax bracket. They are interested in reducing the taxes they pay each year. They are currently considering several alternatives. For each of the following alternatives, indicate how much tax, if any, they would save.
a. Make a gift of bonds valued at $5,000 that yield $400 per year interest to their 14-year-old daughter, who has no other income.
b. Sell the bonds from Part a rather than give them to their daughter, and buy tax-exempt bonds that pay 6%. Assume the bonds can be sold for $5,000.
c. Give $1,000 cash to a charity. Assume they itemize deductions.
d. Pay their daughter a salary of $10,000 for services rendered in their unincorporated business.

I3-56 ***Series EE Bond Interest and Kiddie Tax.*** In 2002, Ken and Lynn paid $5,000 to purchase Series EE bonds in the name of their 11-year-old son. The son has no other income, and they are in the 30% tax bracket. The taxable interest during the first year will be $400 if an election is made to accrue the interest on an annual basis.
a. Will the child owe any tax on the bond interest?
b. Does the son need to file a tax return?
c. What are the tax consequences in 2002 and subsequent years if annual gifts are made to their son?

COMPREHENSIVE PROBLEMS

I3-57 Matt and Sandy reside in a community property state. Matt left home in April 2002 because of disputes with his wife, Sandy. Subsequently, Matt earned $15,000. Before leaving home in April, Matt earned $3,000. Sandy was unaware of Matt's whereabouts or his earnings after he left home. The $3,000 earned by Matt before he left home was spent on food, housing, and other items shared by Matt and Sandy. Matt and Sandy have one child, who lived with Sandy after the husband left home.
a. Is any portion of Matt's earnings after he left home taxable to Sandy?
b. What filing status is applicable to Sandy if she filed a return?
c. How much income would Sandy be required to report if she filed?
d. Is Sandy required to file?

I3-58 During 2002, Gary earned $57,000 as an executive. Gary, who is single, supported his half sister, who lives in a nursing home. Gary received the following interest: $400 on City of Los Angeles bonds, $200 on a money market account, and $2,100 on a loan made to his brother.

Gary spent one week serving on a jury and received $50.

Gary received a refund of federal income taxes withheld during the prior year of $1,200 and a state income tax refund of $140. Gary had itemized deductions last year of $8,000.

Gary received dividends on Ace Corporation of $1,000 and on Tray Corporation of $1,400. Gary's itemized deductions equal $9,000, and withholding for federal income taxes is $10,000. Compute Gary's tax due or refund due for 2002.

TAX STRATEGY PROBLEMS

I3-59 Kamal is starting a new business in 2002 which will operate as an S corporation. This means that income earned by the corporation will be reported by shareholders even if they do not receive distributions. Kamal has $100,000 of income from other sources, and itemized deductions totaling $15,000. He expects that the new business will produce $30,000 of income each year. He is considering giving his son Rashid 20% of the stock in the corporation. Rashid is age 16, and is Kamal's dependent. Rashid's only other income is $2,000 of interest. Neither Kamal nor Rashid will be employed by the corporation. Which alternative will produce a lower income tax liability—having all stock owned by Kamal or having Kamal own 80% of the stock and Rashid own 20%. Assume Kamal's filing status is head of household and Rashid is single and ignore other taxes.

I3-60 Assume that it is December 31, and that Jake is considering making a $1,000 charitable contribution. Jake currently is in the 35% tax bracket, but expects that his tax bracket will be 26% next year. How much more will the deduction for the contribution be worth if it is made today compared to next year?

TAX FORM/RETURN PREPARATION PROBLEMS

I3-61 Sally W. Emanual had the following dividends and interest during the current year:

Acorn Corporation bond interest		$ 700
City of Boston bonds interest		1,000
Camp Bank interest		250
Jet Corporation dividend		300
North Mutual fund		
Capital gain distribution	100	
Ordinary dividend	150	
Nontaxable distribution	200	450
Blue Corporation foreign dividend		250

Additional information pertaining to Sally Emanual includes

Salary	$32,000
Rent income	12,000
Expenses related to rent income	14,000
Pension benefits	8,000
Alimony paid to Sally	4,000

The taxable portion of the pension is $7,000. Sally actively participates in the rental activity. Other relevant information includes

Address: 430 Rumsey Place, West Falls, California 92699
Occupation: Credit manager
Social Security number: 123-45-4321
Marital status: Single

Complete Sally's Schedule B and page 1 of her Form 1040. Assume Schedule E has already been prepared.

CASE STUDY PROBLEMS

I3-62 Jim and Linda are your tax clients. They were divorced two years ago, and the divorce decree stated that Jim was to make monthly payments to Linda. The court designated $300 per month as alimony and $200 per month as child support, or a total of $6,000 per year. Jim has been unemployed for much of the year and paid Linda $2,000 that he said was for child support. In addition, Jim transferred the title to a three-year-old automobile with a $4,000 FMV and basis of $7,000 in exchange for her promise not to pursue any claim she has against him for the unpaid child support and alimony. Does Linda have to report any alimony and is Jim entitled to an alimony deduction? Draft a memo for the file that discusses the tax consequences for both Jim and Linda.

I3-63 John and Mary (your clients) have two small children and are looking for ways to help fund the children's college education. They have heard that Series EE bonds are a tax-favored way of saving and have requested your opinion on the tax consequences. They have asked your opinion regarding the relative advantages of purchasing Series EE bonds in their names versus the children's names. John and Mary have indicated that they expect to have a high level of income in the future and that their children may receive other income sources from future inheritances. Prepare a client memo making recommendations about the tax consequences of Series EE bond investments for John and Mary.

I3-64 Lee and Jane have been your firm's clients for most of the twenty years they have been married. Recently Lee came to you and said that he and Jane are obtaining a divorce, and he wants you to help him with some of the tax and financial issues that may come up during the divorce. The next day, Jane called asking you for the same assistance. What ethical issues do you see in this case? What possible conflicts may arise if you represent both Lee and Jane?

TAX RESEARCH PROBLEM

I3-65 William owns a building that is leased to Lester's Machine Shop. Lester requests that William rewire the building for new equipment Lester plans to purchase. The wiring would cost about $4,000, but would not increase the value of the building because its only use is in connection with the specialized equipment. Rather than lose Lester as a lessee, William agrees to forgo one month's rent of $1,000 if Lester will pay for the wiring. Because Lester does not want to move, he agrees. What amount, if any, must William include in gross income?

A partial list of research sources is

- Sec. 109
- Reg. Sec. 1.109-1
- *CIR v. Grace H. Cunningham,* 2 AFTR 2d 5511, 58-2 USTC ¶9771 (9th Cir., 1958)

CHAPTER 4

GROSS INCOME: EXCLUSIONS

LEARNING OBJECTIVES

After studying this chapter, you should be able to

1. Explain the conditions that must exist for an item to be excluded from gross income
2. Determine whether an item is income
3. Decide whether specific exclusions are available
4. Understand employment-related fringe benefit exclusion items

CHAPTER OUTLINE

Items That Are Not Income...4-2
Major Statutory Exclusions...4-4
Tax Planning Consideration...4-21
Compliance and Procedural Considerations...4-23

Chapter I3 discussed specific items that must be included in gross income. This chapter considers items that are excluded from gross income. Under Sec. 61(a), all items of income are taxable unless specifically excluded. Taxpayers who wish to avoid being taxed have two basic alternatives. One approach is to establish that the item is not income. If an item is not income (e.g., if it is a return of capital), it is not subject to the income tax. The second approach is to establish that a specific exclusion applies to the item of income.

EXAMPLE I4-1 ▶ Matt borrowed $10,000 from the bank. Although Matt received $10,000, it is not income because he is obligated to repay the amount borrowed. No specific statutory authority states that borrowed funds are excluded from taxation. Presumably, the fact that borrowed funds are not income is considered to be both fundamental and obvious. ◀

KEY POINT

Given the sweeping definition of *income,* it is generally difficult to establish that an item is not income.

EXAMPLE I4-2 ▶ Sheila enrolled in State University. The university awarded her a $1,000 tuition scholarship because of her high admission test scores and grades. Section 117 excludes such scholarships from gross income. As a result, Sheila need not report the scholarship as income. ◀

OBJECTIVE 1

Explain the conditions that must exist for an item to be excluded from gross income

The major source of exclusions are those specific items contained in the IRC. These exclusions have evolved over the years and were enacted by Congress for a variety of reasons, including social and economic objectives.

Another source of exclusions are referred to as *administrative exclusions*. Exclusions exist because specific provisions in the Internal Revenue Code allow them. While the IRS has no authority to create exclusions, the IRS does have the authority to interpret the meaning of the Code. A liberal interpretation of the statute by the IRS may result in a broad definition of what constitutes an exclusion, and such a broad definition may reasonably be termed an administrative exclusion. For example, Sec. 102 excludes gifts received from gross income. The IRS has followed the practice of excluding certain welfare benefits from gross income, presumably because such benefits may be viewed as gifts.[1] The IRS could take the position that welfare benefits are not gifts. That position would no doubt be challenged in the courts.

The term *judicial exclusions* should be considered in the same vein. Although the courts cannot create exclusions, they can interpret the statute and decide whether a particular item is covered by a statutory exclusion.

REAL-WORLD EXAMPLE

Grants made to Native Americans by the federal government under the Indian Financing Act of 1974 to expand Native American–owned economic enterprises are excludable from gross income. Rev. Rul. 77-77, 1977-1 C.B. 11.

ITEMS THAT ARE NOT INCOME

OBJECTIVE 2

Determine whether an item is income

As noted above, some items are not income and, therefore, are not subject to the income tax. In addition to amounts obtained by a loan (discussed above), four other items are not considered income:

- Unrealized income
- Self-help income
- Rental value of personal-use property
- Gross selling price of property (as opposed to the profit or gain earned on the sale)

UNREALIZED INCOME

Income that is not realized is not subject to income taxation. Thus, if a taxpayer owns stock in a company and the stock increases in value but the taxpayer does not sell the stock, no taxable income is realized.

This issue of the taxability of unrealized income was addressed over 80 years ago in *Eisner v. Macomber,* where the Supreme Court held that a stock dividend cannot be taxed

TYPICAL MISCONCEPTION

It is sometimes erroneously assumed that severance pay, embezzlement proceeds, gambling winnings, hobby income, prizes, rewards, and tips are not taxable.

[1] For example, see Rev. Rul. 57-102, 1957-1 C.B. 26, which excludes from gross income public assistance payments to blind persons.

because the taxpayer had "received nothing that answers the definition of income within the meaning of the Sixteenth Amendment."[2] An ordinary stock dividend does not alter the existing proportionate ownership interest of any stockholder, nor does it increase the value of the individual's holdings. In effect, the court concluded that realization must occur before income is recognized. Although narrowed by subsequent legislation and litigation, ordinary stock dividends continue to be excluded from gross income even today. Perhaps more important, *Eisner v. Macomber* established realization as a criterion for the recognition of income.

SELF-HELP INCOME

TYPICAL MISCONCEPTION

When a taxpayer purchases an older house and remodels the kitchen or makes other improvements, there is a tendency to assume correctly that the taxpayer has no income from this activity, but it is often incorrectly assumed that the basis of the house can be increased by the value of the taxpayer's labor.

Although self-help income is considered as income by economists, it is not recognized as income by the IRS or by the courts. Taxpayers commonly benefit from activities such as painting their own homes or repairing their own automobiles. If a taxpayer hires someone else to do the work, the taxpayer has to earn the income, pay tax on such income, and use the after-tax income to pay for the work. In either case, the taxpayer receives the same economic benefit, but the economic benefit derived from self-help is not included in the taxpayer's gross income.

This situation should be contrasted with taxable exchanges of services. A mechanic might agree to repair a painter's automobile in exchange for the painter's promise to paint the mechanic's home. In this instance, when the parties exchange services, each party realizes income equal to the value of the services received.

STOP & THINK

Question: The discussion of self-help income refers to an exchange of services between two individuals, such as a painter and a mechanic. How can a taxable barter transaction be distinguished from an act of friendship which is repaid?

Solution: When one person helps another without any promise of repayment, the act of kindness does not represent an exchange and is not taxable. Friends help one another from time to time without contractual reciprocity. As a result, such acts are not taxable. The distinction between a taxable barter exchange and acts of friendship is not always easy to make.

RENTAL VALUE OF PERSONAL-USE PROPERTY

ADDITIONAL COMMENT

The tax situation of a homeowner is quite different than that of someone who lives in an apartment. The failure to include the rental value of the home as income in addition to the deduction of mortgage interest and property taxes favors homeowners.

Taxpayers are not taxed on the rental value of personally owned property. For example, taxpayers who own their own home receive the economic benefit of occupancy without being taxed on the rental value of the property. It would be very difficult to keep records and value benefits obtained from self-help and the personal use of property. For that reason, no significant effort has ever been made to tax such benefits.[3]

SELLING PRICE OF PROPERTY

If property is sold at a gain, the gain and not the entire sales price is taxable. Because the basic principle is almost universally accepted, the Supreme Court has never had to rule directly on whether the entire sale proceeds could be taxed. The IRS and the courts seemed to accept the basic principle even before the rule became part of the statute.[4] The primary reason for this principle (often referred to as the "recovery of capital" principle) is that a portion of the selling price represents a return of capital to the seller.

---

[2] 3 AFTR 3020, 1 USTC ¶32 (USSC, 1920).

[3] In 1928, the government tried unsuccessfully to tax the value of produce grown and consumed by a farmer (*Homer P. Morris,* 9 B.T.A. 1273 (1928)). The court stated, "To include the value of such products [would be to] in effect include in income something which Congress did not intend should be so regarded." The court did not explain how or why it reached this conclusion. In 1957, the IRS successfully disallowed the deduction of expenses incurred in raising such produce (*Robert L. Nowland v. CIR,* 51 AFTR 423, 57-1 USTC ¶9684 (4th Cir., 1957)).

[4] Section 202(a) of the Revenue Act of 1924 is the predecessor of current Sec. 1001(a), which describes that only the gain portion of the sale proceeds is included in gross income. S. Rept. No. 398, 68th Cong., 1st Sess., p. 10 (1924) states that Sec. 202(a) sets forth general rules to be used in the computation of gain or loss. The Senate report further states that the provision "merely embodies in the law the present construction by the Department and the courts of the existing law."

MAJOR STATUTORY EXCLUSIONS

OBJECTIVE 3

Decide whether specific exclusions are available

While Congress has created statutory exclusions for a variety of reasons, most exclusions have been enacted for reasons of social policy or reasons of incentive. The concept of social policy, that is, a concept of social generosity or benevolence, has prompted the government to exclude items such as:

- Gifts and inheritances (Sec. 102)
- Life insurance proceeds (Sec. 101)
- Public assistance payments
- Qualified adoption expenses (Sec. 137)
- Payments for personal physical sickness and injury (Sec. 104)
- Discharge of indebtedness during bankruptcy or insolvency (Sec. 108)
- Gain on sale of personal residence (Sec. 121)
- Partial exclusions for Social Security benefits (Sec. 86)

ADDITIONAL COMMENT

Tax expenditure estimates measure the decreases in individual and corporate income tax liabilities that result from provisions in income tax laws and regulations that provide economic incentives or tax relief to particular kinds of taxpayers.

Other exclusions may be explained in terms of economic incentive, that is, the government's desire to encourage or reward a particular type of behavior.

- Awards for meritorious achievement (Sec. 74(b))
- Various employee fringe benefits (Secs. 79, 105, 106, 124, 125, 129, 132)
- Partial exclusion for scholarships (Sec. 117)
- Foreign-earned income (Sec. 911)
- Interest on state and local government obligations (Sec. 103)

Other reasons may exist for some of the exclusions listed above. For example, one reason income from the discharge of indebtedness during bankruptcy is excluded from gross income is the fact that such taxpayers would be unlikely to have the resources needed to pay the tax. (See Chapter I3 for a discussion of tax-exempt interest and Social Security benefits, and Chapter I12 for the treatment of gain on the sale of a personal residence.)

GIFTS AND INHERITANCES

TYPICAL MISCONCEPTION

Some people still believe that gifts above the gift exclusion amount of $10,000 are taxable to the donees. They are not since the Code specifically exempts all gifts, regardless of the amount. The donor may, however, depending on the circumstances, pay a gift tax.

Congress has excluded the value of gifts and inheritances received from gross income since the inception of the income tax in 1913. Section 102 excludes the value of property received during the life of the donor (***inter vivos* gifts**) and transfers at death (**testamentary transfers**—bequests, devises, and inheritances).[5] The recipient of such property is taxed on the income produced by the property after the transfer.[6] It should be noted that a donor, under the assignment of income doctrine, cannot avoid the income tax by making a gift of income. To avoid paying tax on income, a donor must make a gift of the underlying property to the donee.

EXAMPLE I4-3 ▶ Stan owns stock in a corporation and orders the corporation to pay dividends on the stock to his daughter. Even though his daughter received the dividends, Stan must include the dividends in his gross income. Stan could avoid being taxed on future dividends by giving the stock to his daughter before the dividend. ◀

It is often difficult to distinguish gifts, which are not included in the recipient's gross income, from other transfers, which are taxable. Gifts sometimes closely resemble prizes and awards.[7]

EXAMPLE I4-4 ▶ Tina received a free automobile for being the ten millionth paying guest at an amusement park. The automobile is not considered a gift but a prize and is taxable to Tina. ◀

[5] Although excluded from gross income, such transfers may be subject to the gift tax or the estate tax which are imposed on the transferor.

[6] Reg. Sec. 1.102-1.

[7] Recall that under Sec. 74 (discussed in Chapter I3) most prizes and awards are taxable.

Also, some payments made to employees by employers may resemble gifts.

EXAMPLE I4-5 ▶ At Christmas, Red Corporation paid $500 to each employee who had been with the company for more than five years. These payments are not considered gifts for tax purposes and are taxable to the employees. ◀

REAL-WORLD EXAMPLE

Amounts received by a dealer from players in the operation of a gambling casino were not excludable as gifts even though impulsive generosity or superstition may be the dominant motive. The amounts were similar to tips, which are taxable. *Louis R. Tomburello,* 86 T.C. 540 (1986).

Whether a transfer is a gift depends on the intent of the donor. A donor is expected to be motivated by love, affection, kindness, sympathy, generosity, admiration, or similar emotions. In the two preceding examples, the transfers probably were made for business motives and not necessarily for donative reasons. Thus, the automobile is a taxable prize, and the amounts paid to employees represent taxable awards for services rendered, but see the discussion of Sec. 274 later in this chapter.

Transfers of money or property between family members frequently create problems of classification. For example, assume a father, who owns a business, hires his 10-year old son to work in the business. Is the payment to the son a salary (and, therefore, deductible by the business) or is it really just a gift from the father to the son? The answer depends on the true value of the services performed by the son. If the son truly performs services that are commensurate with the salary paid, the payment may properly be classified as a salary. On the other hand, if the son is paid an amount that exceeds the value of the services, the excess amount will be treated as a gift.

LIFE INSURANCE PROCEEDS

Life insurance proceeds paid to a beneficiary because of the insured person's death are not taxable.[8] The exclusion applies whether the proceeds are paid in a lump sum or in installments. Amounts received in excess of the face amount of the policy usually are taxable as interest.

EXAMPLE I4-6 ▶ Buddy is the beneficiary of a $100,000 insurance policy on his mother's life. Upon her death, he elects to receive $13,000 per year for ten years instead of the lump sum. He receives $10,000 per year tax-free ($100,000 ÷ 10), but the remaining $3,000 per year is taxable as interest. ◀

EXAMPLE I4-7 ▶ Assume the same facts as in Example I4-6, except that Buddy elects to receive the full $100,000 face amount upon his mother's death. None of the $100,000 is taxable. ◀

The exclusion exists because life insurance benefits closely resemble inheritances, which are not taxable.

There is one exception that may result in a portion of the face amount of a life insurance policy being included in gross income.[9] The life insurance exclusion generally is not available if the insurance policy is obtained by the beneficiary in exchange for valuable consideration from a person other than the insurance company. For example, an individual may purchase an existing life insurance policy for cash from another individual. In this situation, the exclusion for death benefits is limited to the consideration paid plus the premiums or other sums subsequently paid by the buyer.

EXAMPLE I4-8 ▶ Kwame is the owner and beneficiary of a $100,000 policy on the life of his father. Kwame sells the policy to his brother Anwar for $10,000. Anwar subsequently pays premiums of $12,000. Upon his father's death, Anwar must include $78,000 [$100,000 − ($10,000 + $12,000)] in gross income. However, if Kwame gave the policy to his brother, all of the proceeds would be excluded from gross income because the gift of the policy does not constitute valuable consideration. ◀

ADDITIONAL COMMENT

The proceeds of a life insurance policy payable to named beneficiaries can be excluded from the federal estate tax when the decedent does not possess any incidents of ownership. This provision and the exclusion from gross income of life insurance proceeds underscore the favored position of life insurance.

The proceeds are excludable under the general exclusion for life insurance proceeds if the beneficiary's basis is found by reference to the transferor's basis (as would be true in the case of a gift), or if the policy is transferred to the insured, the insured's partner, a partnership that includes the insured, or a corporation in which the insured is a shareholder or officer.

[8] Sec. 101(a).

[9] Sec. 101(a)(2).

SELF-STUDY QUESTION

A corporation acquires a life insurance policy on the president of the corporation, and the corporation is named as the beneficiary of the policy. Are the insurance premiums deductible?

ANSWER

No, the premiums are not deductible because any costs incurred to produce tax-exempt income are nondeductible.

SURRENDER OR SALE OF POLICY. The exclusion for life insurance is available for amounts payable by reason of the death of the insured. In general, if a life policy is sold or surrendered for a lump sum before the death of the insured, the amount received is taxable to the extent that it exceeds the net premiums paid.[10] On the other hand, no loss is recognized if a life insurance policy is surrendered before maturity and premiums paid exceed the cash surrender value.[11]

"Accelerated death benefits" may be excluded from gross income. Accelerated death benefits include payments made to a terminally ill person and periodic payments made to a chronically ill person. A person is terminally ill if a physician certifies that he is reasonably likely to die within 24 months. A person is chronically ill if he has a disability requiring long-term care (e.g., nursing home care). In general, the exclusion for periodic payments made to a chronically ill person is limited to the greater of $210 per day ($200 per day in 2001), or the actual cost of such care. The exclusion covers amounts received from the insurance provider or from a "viatical settlement provider" (i.e., person in the business of providing accelerated death benefits).

EXAMPLE I4-9 ▶ Harry has been diagnosed with AIDS and is expected to live less than a year. Harry is covered by a life insurance policy with a $100,000 face amount. The insurance company offers terminally ill individuals the option of receiving 75% of the policy face amount. If Harry accepts the settlement, the amount he receives is excludable from gross income because he is a terminally ill individual. ◀

EXAMPLE I4-10 ▶ Mary suffered a severe stroke and has been admitted to a nursing home where she is expected to remain for the rest of her life. She is certified by a licensed health care practitioner as being a "chronically ill individual." Her nursing home expenses amount to $160 per day. Mary has elected to receive $180 per day from a $200,000 face amount life insurance policy as accelerated death benefits. Because she is a chronically ill individual, Mary may exclude the full amount she receives as it is less than daily limitation of $210 established by law. ◀

DIVIDENDS ON LIFE INSURANCE AND ENDOWMENT POLICIES. Dividends on life insurance and endowment policies are normally not taxable because they are considered to be a partial return of premiums paid. The dividends are taxable to the extent that the total dividends received exceed the total premiums paid. Also, if dividends are left with the insurance company and earn interest, the interest is taxable.

ADOPTION EXPENSES

Congress provides tax benefits for qualified adoption expenses in the form of tax credits (see Chapter I14) or an exclusion for amounts paid pursuant to an adoption assistance plan created by an employer. An employee is allowed a $10,000 per child exclusion from gross income for qualified adoption expenses paid by an employer under an adoption assistance program.[12] The exclusion is phased-out ratably for taxpayers with modified adjusted gross income of $150,000 to $190,000.

Qualified adoption expenses include adoption fees, court costs, attorney fees, and other expenses related to an adoption. An adoption assistance program is a separate written plan of an employer, exclusively for the benefit of its employees, to provide adoption assistance.

EXAMPLE I4-11 ▶ Reggie and Rhonda are married, have AGI of $165,000, and adopt a child. Rhonda's employer maintains a written adoption assistance program. They spend $12,000 during the year in connection with the adoption, all of which is paid by Rhonda's employer pursuant to the plan. Reggie and Rhonda must include in their gross income an amount of $5,750, computed as follows:

---

[10] Sec. 72(e)(2). In some instances where distributions are made before the recipient reaches age 59½, a 10% penalty applies (see Sec. 72(q)).

[11] *London Shoe Co. v. CIR.*, 16 AFTR 1398, 35-2 USTC ¶9664 (2nd Cir., 1935).

[12] Sec. 137.

Total adoption expenses paid from the plan	$12,000
Maximum exclusion	10,000
Phase-out percentage [$15,000/($190,000 − $150,000)]	37.5%
Reduction in exclusion	3,750
Exclusion amount ($10,000 − $3,750)	6,250
Amount includible in gross income ($12,000 − $6,250)	5,750

◀

In general, the exclusion cannot exceed the amount of qualified expenses. However, in the case of the adoption of a child with special needs, the exclusion is $10,000 and not limited to the actual expenses incurred.

EXAMPLE I4-12 ▶ Assume the same facts as in the previous example except that the amount of adoption expenses paid totaled $4,000. The exclusion would be limited to $4,000 except in the case of an adoption of a child with special needs in which case the exclusion would be $6,250. Even though Reggie and Rhonda only spent $4,000, they are allowed an exclusion of $10,000. Since their AGI is over $150,000, the $10,000 exclusion is reduced to $6,250. ◀

ADDITIONAL COMMENT

Notice that to exclude awards for meritorious achievement, the award must not come into the possession of the taxpayer.

AWARDS FOR MERITORIOUS ACHIEVEMENT

As noted in Chapter I3, prizes and awards generally are taxable. An exception is applicable to awards and prizes made for religious, charitable, scientific, educational, artistic, literary, or civic achievement if the recipient:

- Was selected without action on his or her part to enter the contest or the proceeding,
- Does not have to perform substantial future services as a condition to receiving the prize or award, and

- Designates that the payor is to pay the amount of the award to either a government unit or a charitable organization.[13]

The recipient of such an award normally would owe no tax if he or she collected the proceeds and then contributed the proceeds to a charity because the gift would qualify as a deductible charitable contribution. However, the exclusion changes AGI and thereby affects other computations. Also, this rule is beneficial in situations where the taxpayer could not deduct the full amount of the award because of the limitation on the charitable contribution deduction (generally 50% of AGI; see Chapter I7) or in the case of a small award to a taxpayer who does not itemize.

ADDITIONAL COMMENT

Athletic scholarships for fees, books, and supplies awarded by a university to students who are expected, but not required, to participate in a particular sport can be excludable.

KEY POINT

The exclusion for scholarships does not include amounts received for room, board, and laundry.

SCHOLARSHIPS AND FELLOWSHIPS

Subject to certain limitations, scholarships are excluded from gross income.[14] A scholarship is an amount paid or allowed to a student, whether an undergraduate or graduate, to aid degree-seeking individuals.

The exclusion for scholarships is limited to the amount of the scholarship used for *qualified tuition and related expenses*. Qualified tuition and related expenses typically include tuition and fees, books, supplies, and equipment required for courses of instruction at an educational organization. The value of services and accommodations supplied such as room, board, and laundry are not excluded. The exclusion for scholarships does not extend to salary paid for services even if all candidates for a particular degree are required to perform the services.[15]

EXAMPLE I4-13 ▶ Becky is awarded a $5,000 per year scholarship by State University. Becky spends $3,000 of the scholarship for tuition, books, and supplies, and $2,000 is for room and board. In addition, Becky works part-time on campus and earns $4,000, which covers the rest of her room and board and other expenses. Becky is taxed on the $2,000 of the scholarship spent for room and board and $4,000 of salary earned from her part-time job. ◀

---

[13] Sec. 74.

[14] Sec. 117.

[15] Scholarships may need to be reviewed to determine whether the amount constitutes compensation. A "scholarship" awarded to the winner of a televised beauty pageant by a profit-making corporation was ruled to be compensation for performing subsequent services for the corporation (Rev. Rul. 68-20, 1968-1 C.B. 55). An employer-paid "scholarship" was held to be compensation in a situation where the employee was on leave and was required to return to work after finishing the degree (*Richard E. Johnson v. Bingler*, 23 AFTR 2d 69-1212, 69-1 USTC ¶9348 (USSC, 1969)). However, in Ltr. Rul. 9526020 (September 10, 1995) the IRS ruled that grants to law students are not taxable even if they are conditioned upon the students agreeing to practice upon graduation in public, nonprofit, or other low paying sectors.

DISTRIBUTIONS FROM QUALIFIED TUITION PROGRAMS

To assist students (and/or their families) in meeting costs of higher education, Congress has expanded the income tax provisions dealing with *qualified tuition plans*, or so-called "Section 529 plans." Basically, amounts are put into a qualified tuition plan (QTP) on behalf of a designated beneficiary and these amounts grow tax-free while in the QTP. The amounts may be withdrawn tax-free by the beneficiary if the amounts are used for qualified higher education expenses, including tuition, books, fees, and room and board. Room and board is a qualified higher education expense only if the beneficiary is at least a half-time student. The principal reason that these plans are so useful is that there is no income limitation for such plans. Therefore, a taxpayer who has a very high income could invest amounts into a QTP for his children and obtain the tax benefits.

QTP plans, formerly called Qualified State Tuition Plans, may be maintained either by state governments or private universities.[16] These plans are classified into two basic types, (1) a plan whereby tuition credits are purchased today to be used by the beneficiary in the future, or (2) a plan whereby amounts are put into a qualified fund, invested in mutual funds or similar investments, and then used to pay the higher education expenses of the beneficiary. Private universities only may offer the second type of plan. A QTP, while typically set up by parents or grandparents of the designated beneficiary, may be set up and funded by anyone interested in the child's college education.

As mentioned above, for the distributions from a QTP to be excluded, the amounts must be used for qualified higher education expenses. If a distribution is made from the QTP to the beneficiary and any portion of such distribution is not used for qualified expenses, the portion not used for qualified expenses must be included in the beneficiary's gross income and is also subject to a 10% penalty.

EXAMPLE I4-14 ▶ David VonAlmond, a high income taxpayer, lives in Kentucky and has two children, ages 10 and 8. Kentucky offers a Qualified Tuition Program and David establishes a separate QTP for each of his children and invests $5,000 into each account. The money is invested by the state of Kentucky into a mutual fund investment. The $5,000 is considered as a gift by David to each of his children, but since the annual exclusion for gift tax purposes is $11,000, no gift tax is due. David plans on putting $5,000 into each of his children's accounts for the next several years. The amounts in the QTP grow tax-free. When the children begin attending college, distributions may be made to the children to pay for their college education expenses and no taxes will be due on such distributions as long as the distributions do not exceed the amount of qualified higher education expenses. If any amounts are distributed and not used for qualified education expenses, the amounts must be included in the income of the children and subject to a 10% penalty. ◀

There are several other important considerations in QTP's, including:

- A valuable feature of QTP's is the ability to change beneficiaries in the future without any tax consequences as long as the new beneficiary is a member of the family of the original beneficiary. Members of the family are very broadly defined and include all of the relationships for determining a dependency exemption as well as a first cousin.
- The exclusion permitted under Sec. 529 must be reduced by any amounts used to claim the HOPE credit or the lifetime learning credit.[17]
- The amounts transferred into a QTP are treated as a gift by the transferor to the designated beneficiary and, when combined with other gifts, are generally limited to $11,000 per year for each beneficiary.

PAYMENTS FOR INJURY AND SICKNESS

Sec. 104(a) excludes from gross income the "amount of any damages (other than punitive damages) . . . received . . . on account of personal physical injuries or physical sickness." Thus, for example, a taxpayer may exclude an insurance settlement for physical injury

[16] Under prior law, for tax years beginning on or before December 31, 2001, Section 529 plans could only be established and maintained by the states. Under the new 2001 Tax Act, for taxable years beginning after December 31, 2001, such plans can be established and maintained by eligible private institutions.

[17] Sec. 529(c)(3)(B)(v). These credits are discussed in Chapter I14 of this textbook.

that resulted from an automobile accident. The exclusion does not cover amounts awarded for nonphysical injuries (such as a damaged reputation or libel) except that taxpayers may exclude reimbursements for medical expenses related to nonphysical injuries.

EXAMPLE I4-15 ▶ After she was denied a promotion, Jane sued her employer claiming sex discrimination. She was awarded $5,000 to cover the medical bills she incurred because of the related emotional distress, $20,000 to punish her employer for discrimination, and $10,000 to compensate her for lost wages. The $5,000 awarded to cover medical bills is excluded from gross income, but not the amounts awarded as punitive damages or lost wages. ◀

The exclusion under Sec 104(a) applies to damages received because of emotional distress in only two situations: (1) when the payments are for medical expenses related to the emotional distress, and (2) when the payments are for emotional distress *attributable* to a physical injury (including physical injury suffered by another person).

Sometimes, victims are awarded amounts that are intended to punish the guilty party. These so called "punitive damages" are taxable even when they are awarded for physical injuries.

EXAMPLE I4-16 ▶ Mary was injured in an automobile accident caused by another driver. Mary's daughter, Sarah, was in the automobile, but she was not physically injured. The other driver's insurance company was required by a court to pay Mary $10,000 to cover medical bills relating to her injuries, $5,000 to compensate her for emotional distress caused by the injuries and 15,000 of punitive damages. Sarah was paid $3,000 to compensate her for distress caused by her witnessing her mother's injuries. Only the $15,000 of punitive damages are taxable to Mary as the other amounts are compensatory damages related to her physical injuries. Sarah's damage award of $3,000 is also excludable. ◀

Sec. 104(a)(3) excludes from gross income amounts collected under an accident and health insurance policy purchased by the taxpayer, even if the benefits are a substitute for lost income. In addition, Sec. 101 specifies that benefits received under a qualified long term care insurance contract may be excluded from gross income, but limits the exclusion to the greater of $210 per day ($200 per day in 2001) or the actual cost of such care.[18] Such policies pay for nursing home and other types of long term care. If the benefits exceed the actual cost of such care, but are less than $210 per day, no portion of the benefits is taxable.

EXAMPLE I4-17 ▶ Chuck purchased a disability income policy from an insurance company. Chuck subsequently suffered a heart attack. Under the terms of the policy, Chuck received $1,000 per month for the five months he was unable to work. The amounts received are not taxable, even though the payments are a substitute for the wages lost due to the illness. ◀

This exclusion is not applicable if the accident and health benefits are provided by the taxpayer's employer.[19]

EXAMPLE I4-18 ▶ Assume the same facts as in Example I4-17 except that Chuck's employer paid the premiums on the policy. The amounts received by Chuck are taxable. ◀

EXAMPLE I4-19 ▶ Ruth suffered a serious stroke and was admitted to a nursing home. During the year, she was in a nursing home for 140 days. Nursing home charges, physician fees and other related expenses totaled $22,050.

Under Ruth's long-term care insurance contract, she received reimbursements of $24,000. The reimbursements are not includible in Ruth's gross income because the amounts are less than the allowed exclusion amount of $29,400 (140 days × $210). This exclusion applies even though she was reimbursed more than her actual costs. Alternatively, if the reimbursements had been $30,000, she would be required to report $600 ($30,000 − $29,400) as gross income. ◀

---

[18] Sec. 101.

[19] A limited credit is available to taxpayers who receive such benefits. See Chapter I14 for a discussion of the credit for the elderly and disabled.

If the cost of the coverage is shared by the employer and the taxpayer, a portion of the benefits is taxable. For example, if the employer paid one-half of the premiums, one-half of the benefits would be taxable. The principal reason for the different tax treatment is that employer-paid coverage represents a tax-free employee fringe benefit, whereas employee-paid premiums are from after-tax dollars.

In the case of an award intended to reimburse the taxpayer for medical expenses, it follows that the taxpayer cannot deduct the reimbursed medical expenses.[20] If the award exceeds the actual expense, it is not taxable except in the case of employer-financed accident and health insurance.[21]

State worker's compensation laws establish fixed amounts to be paid to employees suffering specific job-related injuries. Section 104(a)(1) specifically excludes worker's compensation from gross income, even though the payments are intended, in part, to reimburse injured workers for loss of future income and even if the injuries are nonphysical.

EMPLOYEE FRINGE BENEFITS

OBJECTIVE 4

Understand employment-related fringe benefit exclusion items

In general, employee compensation is taxable regardless of the form it takes. Nevertheless, the tax law encourages certain types of fringe benefits by allowing an employer to deduct the cost of the benefit, by permitting the employee to exclude the benefit from gross income, or by permitting both the employer deduction and an employee exclusion. Employee fringe benefits subject to special rules include employee insurance, Sec. 132 benefits, meals and lodging, dependent care, and cafeteria plans. These fringe benefits are discussed below.

ADDITIONAL COMMENT

Many companies provide health care benefits to retired employees. However, due to mounting medical insurance bills, a rising retiree population, and an FASB rule that requires firms to recognize the associated liability, a number of companies are requiring retired workers to pick up a larger portion of their medical costs.

EMPLOYER-PAID INSURANCE. Employers commonly provide group insurance coverage for employees. In general, employers may deduct the premiums paid for life, health, accident, and disability insurance. Normally an employee does not have to include in gross income premiums paid on his or her behalf for health, accident, and disability insurance. Special rules applicable to life insurance premiums are discussed below.

Benefits received from medical, health, and group term life insurance coverage generally are excluded from an employee's gross income. Benefits received from a disability policy are normally taxable, but may qualify for the credit for the elderly and disabled (see Chapter I14). The tax treatments of employer-financed and taxpayer-financed insurance coverage are compared in Topic Review I4-1.

In general, premiums paid by an employer on behalf of employees are deductible. However, medical premiums including long-term health insurance premiums paid by self-employed individuals are subject to special tax treatment. In 2002, a self-employed individual may deduct 70% of the *medical* premiums attributable to coverage as a business expense.[22] These business expenses are allowed as a deduction for adjusted gross income (see Chapter I6 for a discussion of classification of deductions for individuals). The self-employed taxpayer may deduct the remaining medical premiums as a medical expense if his total medical expenses exceed 7.5% of the AGI reported on his individual return.

ADDITIONAL COMMENT

The tax expenditure estimate associated with the exclusion of contributions by employers for medical insurance premiums and medical care for the period 1994–1998 is $213 billion.

The rules relating to accident and health insurance are more generous than those for some other types of benefits. Under Sec. 106, employers can deduct insurance premiums and employees need not report the premiums as income. This is true even if the insurance is offered only to officers and other highly compensated employees.

KEY POINT

The nondiscrimination requirements for self-insured accident and health plans are designed to ensure that such plans do not discriminate against rank-and-file workers.

Some employers provide self-insured accident and health plans to employees. Under such plans the employer pays employee medical expenses directly rather than paying insurance premiums. Such plans are subject to nondiscrimination requirements. *Discrimination* is defined in terms of an eligibility test (whether a sufficient number of non–highly compensated employees are covered) and benefits (whether non–highly compensated employees receive benefits comparable to highly compensated employees). Highly compensated employees include the five highest-paid officers, greater-than-10%

[20] See Chapter I3 for a discussion of the reimbursement of an expense deducted in a preceding year.

[21] Sec. 105(a).

[22] Sec. 162(l). The deductible portion of such premiums is 60% in 1999, 2000, and 2001, 70% in 2002, and 100% thereafter. In addition, the amount of long-term care insurance premiums eligible to be deducted by self-employed persons are subject to the limitations in Sec. 213(d)(10).

Topic Review I4-1

Treatment of Insurance

	Premiums Paid by Employer	Premiums Paid by Employee
Medical and health Premiums	Premiums not included in employee's gross income. Premiums deductible by employer.	Premiums deductible as medical expense subject to 7.5% of AGI limitation.
Benefits	Excluded from employee's gross income except when benefits exceed actual expenses.	Excluded from gross income.
Disability Premiums	Premiums not included in employee's gross income. Premiums deductible by employer.	Not deductible.
Benefits	Included in employee's gross income. May qualify for credit for elderly and disabled.	Excluded from gross income.
Life insurance Premiums	Included in employee's gross income (except for limited exclusion applicable to group term life insurance). Premiums deductible by employer (assuming employer is not the beneficiary).	Not deductible.
Benefits	Excluded from gross income.	Excluded from gross income.

shareholders, and highest-paid 25% of other employees.[23] If a plan discriminates in favor of highly compensated employees, these employees must include in gross income any medical reimbursements they receive that are not available to other employees.

ADDITIONAL COMMENT

The Economic Strategy Institute estimates that domestic auto producers have to pay about $400 per car to cover their health care and pension costs.

In general, life insurance premiums paid by an employer on an employee's behalf are deductible by the employer and are includable in the employee's gross income.[24] A limited exception is applicable to group term life insurance coverage. In general, premiums attributable to the first $50,000 of group term life insurance coverage may be excluded from an employee's gross income.[25] To qualify group term life insurance premiums for the exclusion, broad coverage of employees is required. Though somewhat different, the rules may be compared to those associated with self-insurance coverage.[26] The amount of coverage can vary between employees as long as the coverage bears a uniform relationship to each employee's compensation.

EXAMPLE I4-20 ▶ Data Corporation provides group term life insurance coverage for each full-time employee. The coverage is equal to one year's compensation. The arrangement constitutes a qualified group term life insurance plan. ◀

TYPICAL MISCONCEPTION

Many individuals erroneously believe that all life insurance coverage provided by employers is exempt from income.

The group term life insurance exclusion is available only for employees, whether active or retired. Thus, proprietors and partners are not employees and, therefore, the premiums paid on their behalf are not deductible.

In the case of coverage that exceeds $50,000, employees must include in gross income the amount established by the Regulations. (See Table I4-1)

EXAMPLE I4-21 ▶ USA Corporation provides Joy, age 61, with $150,000 of group term life insurance coverage. Joy must include in gross income $792, an amount determined by reference to Table I4-1 [($100,000/$1,000 × $.66) × 12 = $792]. ◀

---

[23] Sec. 105(h)(5).

[24] If the employer is the beneficiary of the policy, the employee receives no economic benefit and, as a result, need not include the premiums in gross income. Such premium payments would not be deductible by the employer. Subsequent benefits would not be included in the employer's gross income.

[25] Sec. 79(a).

[26] For example, the rules refer to "key employees" as opposed to highly compensated employees. The term *key employee* is somewhat narrower in scope.

▼ **TABLE I4-1**
Uniform One-Month Group Term Premiums for $1,000 of Life Insurance Coverage

Employee's age	Premiums
Under 25	$0.05
25 to 29	.06
30 to 34	.08
35 to 39	.09
40 to 44	.10
45 to 49	.15
50 to 54	.23
55 to 59	.43
60 to 64	.66
65 to 69	1.27
70 and above	2.06

Source: Reg. Sec. 1.79-3(d)(2).

The amount that must otherwise be included in an employee's gross income is reduced by any premiums paid by the employee.

If group term life insurance coverage discriminates in favor of key employees, each key employee must include in gross income the greater of the premiums paid on his or her behalf or the amount determined based on Table I4-1 without any exclusion for the first $50,000 of coverage.

STOP & THINK

Question: Does the fact that employers can provide health insurance and group term life insurance to employees on a tax-favored basis mean that such benefits should be provided to all employees? Explain.

Solution: No. Providing such benefits to all employees may be inefficient. Some employees have other health coverage (e.g., coverage through a spouse's employer). Employees with no dependents may not want life insurance coverage. As a result, employers who provide all employees with such benefits may be spending money on coverage that some employees neither want nor need. A cafeteria plan, discussed later in this chapter, is often a more efficient option. Such plans permit employees to choose either cash or from a menu of tax-favored benefits.

HISTORICAL NOTE

A limited exclusion from income for unemployment compensation was repealed in the Tax Reform Act of 1986.

SECTION 132 FRINGE BENEFITS. It has become common for employers to provide employees with such diverse benefits as free parking, membership in professional organizations, and small discounts on products sold by the employer. Section 132 was added to the IRC in 1984 to clarify whether certain types of benefits are taxable. Section 132 lists six types of fringe benefits that may be excluded from an employee's gross income (see Topic Review I4-2). Any costs incurred by an employer to provide the specified benefits are deductible under Sec. 162 if they meet the "ordinary and necessary" test of that section.[27] Benefits covered by Sec. 132 include:

- ▶ No-additional-cost benefits (e.g., a hotel employee's use of a vacant hotel room)
- ▶ Qualified employee discounts (e.g., discounts on merchandise sold by the employer)
- ▶ Working condition benefits (e.g., membership fees in professional organizations paid by an employer)

[27] See Chapter I6 for a discussion of Sec. 162 and its requirements. Section 274 does provide one exception to the general rule. The costs of maintaining recreational facilities (such as swimming pools) are not deductible if the facilities are made available on a discriminatory basis (e.g., only officers may use the facilities).

Topic Review I4-2

Summary of Sec. 132 Fringe Benefits

Section	Benefit	May Be Made Available To	Comments
132(b)	No-additional-cost (e.g., telephone, unused hotel rooms for hotel employees, unused airline seats for airline employees)	Employees, spouses, dependents, and retirees	The services must be of the same types that are sold to customers and in the line of business in which the employee works. Discrimination is prohibited.
132(c)	Qualified employee discounts	Employees, spouses, dependents, and retirees	Discounts on services limited to 20%. Discounts on merchandise are limited to the employer's gross profit percentage. No discount is permitted on real estate, stock, or other investment type property. Discrimination is prohibited.
132(d)	Working condition (e.g., free magazines, out-placement, and memberships)	Employees	Discrimination is permitted. Special rules apply to tuition reductions for employees of educational institutions and to an auto salesperson's demonstrator.
132(e)	De minimis (e.g., free coffee, holiday turkeys, or use of company eating facilities)	Employees	Eating facilities must be made available on a nondiscriminatory basis.
132(f)	Qualified transportation fringes (e.g., transit passes, tokens, and parking)	Employees	Limited in 2002 to $185 per month for parking and $100 per month for other transportation fringes.
132(j)(4)	Recreation and athletic facilities (e.g., gyms, pools, saunas, tennis courts)	Employees, spouses, dependents, and retirees.	If discrimination is present, employer loses deduction.

ADDITIONAL COMMENT

The nondiscrimination rules do not apply to working condition fringe benefits. For example, if a corporation makes bodyguards available only to key officers, the working condition fringe benefit exclusion would still apply.

- ▶ De minimis benefits (e.g., coffee provided by the employer)
- ▶ Qualified transportation and parking fringes (transportation benefits [e.g., transit passes, tokens, and vouchers] limited to $100 per month in 2002 and $65 per month in 2001 and parking, limited to $185 per month in 2002 and $180 per month in 2001)
- ▶ Athletic facilities (e.g., employer-owned tennis courts used by employees)

No-additional-cost benefits are limited to services, as opposed to property. Common examples of no-additional-cost benefits include the use of vacant hotel rooms by hotel employees and standby air flights provided to airline employees. The employer may not incur substantial additional costs, including forgone revenue, in providing the services to the employee. Thus, a hotel may allow employees to stay in vacant hotel rooms even though the hotel incurs additional utility and laundry costs as a result of the stay. However, the hotel cannot allow the employees to stay in lieu of paying guests. No-additional-cost benefits are limited to services provided to employees, their spouses, dependent children, and to retired and disabled employees. The term employee includes partners who perform services for a partnership. In addition, the benefits may be extended, on a reciprocal basis, to employees of other companies in the same line of business.

Employers may permit employees to purchase goods and services at a discount from the price charged regular customers. In the case of services, the discount is limited to 20% of the price charged regular customers. In the case of property, the discount is limited to the company's gross profit percent. No discounts are permitted on real property or investment property (e.g., houses or stocks). Further, the discounts must be from the same line of business in which the employee works. The discounts may be provided to the same persons as no-additional-cost benefits except that the discounts may not be provided on a reciprocal basis to employees of companies in the same line of business.

Discrimination is prohibited with respect to certain benefits. The benefits must be made available to employees in general rather than to highly compensated employees only. (See Topic Review I4-2 for specific rules.)

SELF-STUDY QUESTION

Western Airlines and Central Airlines have a reciprocal agreement that permits employees of the other airline to travel for free on a standby basis. Stan, an employee of Western Airlines, takes a free flight on Central Airlines that would have cost $800. What is Stan's income?

ANSWER

None, reciprocal agreements with regard to no-additional-cost services are permitted.

EMPLOYEE AWARDS. As noted earlier, it is often difficult to distinguish between gifts and awards. The de minimis rule mentioned above permits employers to make small gifts such as a holiday turkey or a watch at retirement without the employee having to include the value of the gift in gross income. The employer is entitled to a deduction for the cost of such gifts.

Section 74 provides a similar rule for **employee achievement awards** and **qualified plan awards.**[28] Such awards must be in the form of tangible personal property other than cash and must be based on safety records or length of service. Employee achievement awards are limited to $400 for any one employee during the year. Furthermore, the awards must be presented as part of a meaningful presentation and awarded under circumstances that do not create a significant likelihood of the payment being disguised compensation. Qualified plan awards must be granted under a written plan and may not discriminate in favor of highly compensated employees. The average cost of qualified plan awards is limited to $400, but individual awards can be as large as $1,600.

- An award for length of service cannot qualify under the IRC if it is received during the employee's first five years of employment or if the employee has received a length-of-service award during the year or any of the preceding four years.
- No more than 10% of an employer's eligible employees may receive an excludable safety achievement award during any year. Eligible employees are employees whose positions involve significant safety concerns.

EXAMPLE I4-22 ▶ Each year, USA Corporation presents length-of-service awards to employees who have been with the company five, ten, fifteen, or twenty years. The presentations are made at a luncheon sponsored by the company and include gifts such as desk clocks, briefcases, and watches, none of which cost more than $400. The awards, which qualify as employee achievement awards, are deductible by USA Corporation and are not taxable as income to USA's employees. ◀

Gifts to employees that do not qualify as employee achievement awards or qualified plan awards can be excluded by the employee only if the awards can be excluded as de minimis amounts under Sec. 132(e).

MEALS AND LODGING. Section 119 provides a limited exclusion for the value of meals and lodging that are provided to employees at either no cost or a reduced cost.

- Meals provided by an employer may be excluded from an employee's gross income if they are furnished on the employer's premises and for the convenience of the employer.
- Lodging provided by an employer may be excluded from an employee's gross income if it is furnished on the employer's premises and for the convenience of the employer, and the employee is required to accept the lodging as a condition of employment.

REAL-WORLD EXAMPLE

Many university presidents are furnished with personal residences, the value of which they can generally exclude from gross income.

The requirement that meals and lodging be furnished on the premises of the employer refers to the employee's place of employment.[29] In one case, the Tax Court held that the business premises requirement was met in a situation where a hotel manager lived in a residence across the street from the hotel he managed.[30]

---

[28] Sec. 74(c). The definitions and requirements for employee achievement awards and qualified plan awards are contained in Sec. 274(j).

[29] Reg. Sec. 1.119-1(c)(1).

[30] *Jack B. Lindeman*, 60 T.C. 609 (1973).

REAL-WORLD EXAMPLE

A brewery provided houses on the business premises to officers. The value of the houses was excludable because it was important to have the officers available for around-the-clock operations of the business. *Adolph Coors Co.,* 1968 PH T.C. Memo ¶68, 256, 27 TCM 1351.

The convenience of the employer test considers whether a substantial noncompensatory business reason exists for providing the meals or lodging. Thus, the test is met if the owner of an apartment complex furnishes a unit to the manager of the complex because it is necessary to have the manager present on the premises even when he or she is off duty.

The value of lodging cannot be excluded from gross income unless the employee is required to accept the lodging as a condition of employment. This requirement is not met if the employee has a choice of accepting the lodging or receiving a cash allowance. Furthermore, meal allowances do not qualify for the exclusion because the employer does not actually provide the meal.[31] Section 132 (discussed earlier in this chapter) provides a de minimis exception. Some employers provide supper money to employees who must work overtime. If such benefits are occasionally provided to employees, the amount is excludable from the employees' gross income.

EXAMPLE I4-23 ▶ A hospital maintains a cafeteria that is used by employees, patients, and visitors. Employees are provided free meals while on duty in order to be available for emergency calls. Since the meals are provided on the employer's premises and for the convenience of the employer, the value of the meals are excluded from the employees' gross income. ◀

EXAMPLE I4-24 ▶ A state highway patrol organization provides its officers with a daily meal allowance to compensate them for meals eaten while they are on duty. Officers typically eat their meals at the restaurant of their choice. Because the officers receive cash instead of meals, the amount provided must be included in the officers' gross income. ◀

EXAMPLE I4-25 ▶ A large corporation requires five of its employees to work overtime two evenings each year when the company takes inventory. The corporation gives each of the employees a small amount to cover the cost of the dinner for the two evenings. The amounts constitute supper money and are excluded from the employees' gross income. ◀

Section 119 provides that if employees can exclude the value of meals from gross income, the employer can deduct the full cost of the meal. Further, if more than half of the employees who receive meals meet the "convenience of the employer" test, then all employees who receive meals can exclude the value from gross income.

deduction

MEALS AND ENTERTAINMENT. One obvious question is whether employees who are reimbursed by their employers when they entertain customers must include the reimbursement in gross income. If they must include the reimbursement in gross income, can they deduct the cost of the entertainment and meals? Assuming conditions for deductibility are met, the tax law clearly allows 50% of the cost of entertaining customers to be deducted (discussed in Chapter I9). Can the employee deduct the meals and entertainment that he personally consumes?

EXAMPLE I4-26 ▶ Joe is a sales representative for Zero Corporation. As a part of his regular duties, Joe buys lunch for Wayne, a Zero Corporation customer. Fifty percent of the cost of Wayne's meal is deductible either by Joe if he pays for the luncheon without being reimbursed by his employer, or by the Zero Corporation if it reimburses Joe for the cost. Can Joe deduct 50% of the cost of his own meal if he pays for it and is not reimbursed? If Zero pays for the meal, must Joe include in his gross income the cost of his own lunch? ◀

In the above question, Joe apparently can deduct the portion of the luncheon that applies to himself. While this issue is not clearcut, the IRS has indicated in Rev. Rul. 63-144 that it will not pursue the issue except where taxpayers claim deductions for substantial amounts of personal expenses.[32] In any case, it is an accepted practice today for taxpayers to deduct 50% of the total cost of a meal (taxpayer and customer) unless the practice is considered abusive.[33]

---

[31] *CIR v. Robert J. Kowalski,* 40 AFTR 2d 77-6128, 77-2 USTC ¶9748 (USSC, 1977).

[32] Rev. Rul. 63-144, 1963-2 C.B. 129.

[33] See, however, *Richard A. Sutter,* 21 T.C. 170 (1953), where the Tax Court ruled that business meals, entertainment, etc. for one's own self are inherently personal and nondeductible. *Sutter* has been cited and upheld some 50 times.

WHAT WOULD YOU DO IN THIS SITUATION?

FRINGE BENEFIT

National Boats manufactures pleasure boats sold to consumers. The boats range in price from $40,000 to $1,500,000. Jake is the president of National Boats. The company provides Jake with one of its more expensive boats. The company pays for fuel, insurance, and other costs, and deducts these expenses along with depreciation on the boat. The company states that Jake is responsible for testing and for demonstrating the boat to possible customers. Jake has had the same boat for two years, and the company plans to provide him with a new boat next month.

You asked Jake how often he uses the boat. He indicated that he uses it once or twice each month on weekends, except during the winter. You asked him who accompanies him, and what types of testing he conducts. He seemed reluctant to answer the question, but acknowledged that his family often accompanies him on the boat, and said that he tests it during ordinary operations to determine how it performs. He added that potential customers who have also accompanied him included neighbors and friends. What tax issues do you see?

EMPLOYEE DEATH BENEFITS. Occasionally, an employer may make payments to the family or friends of an employee who dies. In some instances, the payments might be viewed as a gift made for reasons such as the financial need of the family, kindness, or charity. Alternatively, the amount might constitute a payment of compensation based on the past services of the deceased employee. Gifts are, of course, excluded from gross income, whereas compensation is taxable. The treatment of payments made to the family or other beneficiaries of the employee's estate is determined by the following rules:

- Payments for past services (such as bonuses, accrued wages, and unused vacation pay) are taxable as income to the family and are deductible by the employer. The important issue is whether the employee would have received this amount had he or she lived. If the employer was legally obligated to make the payment at the time of the employee's death, the payments are taxable to the recipient.
- Other amounts may be either taxable compensation or excludable gifts depending on the facts and circumstances. If the amount is a gift, it is not deductible by the employer. If the amount is taxable income to the deceased employee's family, it is deductible by the employer.

In determining whether the amount is taxable, the courts have considered such factors as whether the employer derived benefit from the payment, whether the employee had been fully compensated, and whether the payment was made to the family and not to the estate. The Supreme Court stated, "The most critical consideration [in determining whether a transfer is a gift] is the transferor's 'intention.'"[34] Although the case did not deal with death benefits, it did establish the importance of motive in determining whether a payment is a gift. Thus, the transfer should be made for reasons such as kindness, sympathy, generosity, affection, or admiration.

It should be noted that it is more difficult to establish that a payment is a gift in situations where the payments are made to persons owning stock in the corporation making the payment. Such payments may be construed as constructive dividends, which are not deductible by the corporation but are taxable income to the recipients.[35]

ADDITIONAL COMMENT

The $5,000 limit was placed on the exclusion for dependent care assistance programs because it was thought to be inequitable to provide an unlimited dependent care exclusion but a limited child care credit for people who pay their own child care expenses.

DEPENDENT CARE. **Dependent care assistance programs** are employer-financed programs that provide care for an employee's children or other dependents. An employee may exclude up to $5,000 of assistance each year ($2,500 for a married individual filing a separate return).The care must be of a type that, if paid by the employee, would qualify for the dependent care credit. Furthermore, the credit is scaled down if the employee

---

[34] *CIR* v. *Mose Duberstein*, 5 AFTR 2d 1626, 60-2 USTC ¶9515 (USSC, 1960).

[35] *Ernest L. Poyner* v. *CIR*, 9 AFTR 2d 1151, 62-1 USTC ¶9387 (4th Cir., 1962).

ADDITIONAL COMMENT

The classification of an employee as highly compensated is made on the basis of the facts and circumstances of each case. Any officers and shareholders owning more than 5% of the stock are classified as highly compensated employees.

receives benefits under the employer's plan. (See Chapter I14 for a discussion of the child and dependent care rules.) The program cannot discriminate in favor of highly compensated employees or their dependents.[36]

EDUCATIONAL ASSISTANCE. Under Sec. 127 educational assistance plans, employers pay employee educational costs. Employees may exclude from gross income annual payments of up to $5,250. The exclusion applies to payments for tuition and similar amounts, fees, books, supplies, and equipment.

ADDITIONAL COMMENT

About half of the large employers in the United States offer flexible spending accounts.

CAFETERIA PLANS. **Cafeteria plans**, also called flexible spending accounts, are plans that offer employees the option of choosing cash or statutory nontaxable fringe benefits (such as group term life insurance, medical insurance, adoption expenses, child care, etc.). If the employee chooses cash, the cash is taxable. However, if the employee chooses a statutory nontaxable fringe benefit, the value of the benefit is excluded from gross income.[37] In other words, the fact that the employee could have chosen cash does not cause the fringe benefit to be taxed. The plan cannot discriminate in favor of highly compensated employees or their dependents or spouses.[38] Employer plans may specify what benefits are offered and may limit the amount of benefits individual employees may receive.

ADDITIONAL COMMENT

While the main benefit of a cafeteria plan is to offer tax-free choices to employees, the plan must also offer at least one taxable benefit.

Some plans supplement wages; others are wage reduction plans. In supplemental wage plans, employer funds are used to pay fringe benefits. In the case of wage reduction plans, employees elect to receive reduced wages in exchange for the fringe benefits. In both cases, employees receive benefits without being taxed on them.

Employers often allow employees to use such funds to pay medical expenses. Typically, the plans supplement medical insurance, and funds are used to pay dental bills and other medical expenses not covered by regular insurance. In general, employees annually elect to set-aside funds to pay medical expenses, and the employer pays the expenses using the set aside funds. One problem with the agreements is that they are binding for one year. As a result, the employee loses the funds if the actual medical expenses are less than the amount set aside. Employers, on the other hand, are obligated to pay expenses up to the agreed amount even if the full amount has not yet been withheld from the employee's wages. Thus, the employer may lose money if an employee terminates employment after incurring the designated amount of medical expenses but before the full amount is withheld.

ADVANTAGE OF FRINGE BENEFITS. The major advantage of taking fringe benefits (such as those described above) in lieu of a cash payment is the fact that employees do not have to use after-tax income to obtain the product or service.

EXAMPLE I4-27 ▶ Dan, an employee of Central Corporation, has a $40,000 life insurance policy and pays the premiums out of his salary. Since his salary is taxable, the premiums are paid on an after-tax basis. Kay, an employee for Western Corporation, is covered by a $40,000 group term life insurance policy financed by Western Corporation. Western Corporation pays the premiums on the policy. Because the premiums are excludable, Kay does not have to report the premiums as income. ◀

EXAMPLE I4-28 ▶ John's employer establishes a cafeteria plan which allows each employee to set aside up to $5,000 for health insurance premiums and medical reimbursements. John, whose salary has been $30,000, agrees to a salary reduction of $4,000 of which $2,500 is to cover his health insurance premiums and $1,500 is available to reimburse his medical expenses. Under the arrangement, John's salary is reduced to $26,000 for tax purposes. Neither the health insurance coverage nor the medical expense reimbursement is taxable. During the year, John incurs $1,400 of medical expenses not covered by insurance. He receives a reimbursement for all of the expenses. His employer retains the remaining $100. Alternatively, if the medical expenses were $1,800, John would receive a reimbursement of $1,500 and he must pay the remaining $300 of expenses out of after-tax salary dollars. ◀

---

[36] Sec. 129.

[37] Long-term care insurance (sometimes called nursing home insurance) can be offered to employees on a tax-favored basis, but that benefit cannot be offered as part of a flexible spending account.

[38] Sec. 125.

STOP & THINK

Question: Employers and employees both pay FICA taxes on salaries. Fringe benefits such as health insurance are exempt from both income taxes and FICA taxes. What is the tax effect of an employee's decision to elect health insurance coverage in exchange for a reduced salary?

Solution: The employee's income and FICA taxes are both lowered. The employer is permitted an income tax deduction for either the salary payment or the payment of the health insurance premium. The employer's FICA tax is reduced because the health insurance benefit also is exempt from that tax.

INTEREST-FREE LOANS. One benefit that was often used in the past was interest-free loans to employees. The advantage of this type of transaction was diminished by the Tax Reform Act of 1984. Under present law, interest must generally be imputed on interest-free loans. (See Chapter I11 for a detailed discussion of rules applicable to interest-free loans.)

ADDITIONAL COMMENT

Many U.S. embassies and consulates in foreign countries provide income tax assistance.

ADDITIONAL COMMENT

Foreign-earned income does not include amounts paid to an employee of the U.S. government or any U.S. government agency or instrumentality.

FOREIGN-EARNED INCOME EXCLUSION

In general, the income of U.S. citizens is subject to the U.S. income tax even if the income is derived from sources outside the United States. The foreign income of U.S. citizens also may be taxed by the host country possibly leading to a substantial double tax on the same income. The double tax is mitigated by a **foreign tax credit.** Subject to limitations, U.S. citizens may subtract from their U.S. income tax liability the income taxes they pay to foreign countries. (See Chapter I14 for a discussion of foreign tax credit.)

In the case of foreign-earned income, individuals have available the alternative option in 2002 of excluding the first $80,000 of foreign-earned income from gross income.[39] The *exclusion* is available in lieu of the foreign tax credit. If both a husband and wife have foreign-earned income, each may claim an exclusion. Community property rules are ignored in determining the amount of the exclusion. Thus, if only one spouse has foreign-earned income, only one exclusion is available. The principal reasons for the exclusion are to encourage U.S. businesses to operate in foreign countries and to hire U.S. citizens and resident aliens to manage the businesses. The hope is that such operations will improve the balance of payments. Taxpayers who elect the exclusion in one year may switch to the foreign tax credit in any subsequent year. Taxpayers who change from the exclusion to the credit may not reelect the exclusion before the sixth tax year after the tax year in which the change was made.[40] The IRS can waive the six-year limitation in special situations (such as an individual employee changing the location of his or her foreign employment).

TYPICAL MISCONCEPTION

A taxpayer must be present in one or more foreign countries for 330 days during a period of twelve consecutive months, rather than 330 days during a calendar year.

Foreign-earned income includes an individual's earnings from personal services rendered in a foreign country. The place where the services are performed determines whether earned income is foreign or U.S. source income. If an individual is engaged in a trade or business in which both personal services and capital are material income-producing factors, no more than 30% of the net profits from the business may be excluded.[41] Furthermore, pensions, annuities, salary paid by the U.S. government, and deferred compensation do not qualify for the exclusion.[42]

To qualify for the foreign-earned income exclusion, the taxpayer must either be a bona fide resident of one or more foreign countries for an entire taxable year, or be present in one or more foreign countries for 330 days during a period of 12 consecutive months.[43] The exclusion limitation for a year must be prorated if the taxpayer is not present in, or a resident of, a foreign country or countries for the entire year.

EXAMPLE I4-29 ▶ Sondra is given a temporary assignment to work in foreign country T. She arrives in T on October 19, 2002 and leaves on October 1, 2003. Although Sondra does not establish a permanent

[39] Sec. 911(b)(2). The foreign earned income exclusion was, for many years, $70,000. Beginning in 1998 the exclusion increased $2,000 per year reaching $80,000 in 2002. It is scheduled to remain at $80,000 until 2008 when the exclusion will be indexed for inflation.

[40] Sec. 911(e)(2).

[41] Sec. 911(d)(2)(B).

[42] Sec. 911(b)(1)(B).

[43] Sec. 911(d).

residence in T, she is present in T for at least 330 days out of a twelve-month period beginning on October 20, 2002. Thus, 73 days fall in 2002 and the rest in 2003. Sondra's exclusion for 2002 is limited to $16,000 [(73 ÷ 365) × $80,000]. She may exclude $16,000 or the income she earns in foreign country T during 2002, whichever is less. ◀

Deductions directly attributable to the excluded foreign-earned income are disallowed. Expenses attributable to foreign-earned income must be allocated if foreign-earned income exceeds the exclusion. The disallowed portion is determined by multiplying the total amount of such expenses by the ratio of excluded earned income over total foreign-earned income.

EXAMPLE I4-30 ▶ Connie earned $120,000 during 2002 while employed in a foreign country for the entire year. She is entitled to an exclusion of $80,000. Connie incurred $12,000 of travel, transportation, and other deductible expenses attributable to the foreign-earned income. She may deduct only $4,000 of such expenses because $8,000 [($80,000 ÷ $120,000) × $12,000] is allocated to the excluded income and, therefore, not deductible. The $4,000 is classified as a miscellaneous itemized deduction and subject to the 2% of AGI floor associated with such deductions. ◀

U.S. citizens working in foreign countries must often pay more for housing than they would pay in the United States. Therefore, an additional exclusion from gross income is available for housing costs that exceed 16% of the salary paid government employees in Step 1 of grade GS-14. This GS-14 grade is used to establish a standard for taxpayers in general.

EXAMPLE I4-31 ▶ Wayne is employed in Tokyo, Japan, and earns a salary of $120,000. His housing costs are $32,000 for the year and are reasonable considering the high cost of living in Tokyo. Assume that 16% of the GS-14 (Step 1) salary is $10,557. Wayne can exclude $101,443 from gross income [($80,000 + ($32,000 − $10,557)]. ◀

INCOME FROM THE DISCHARGE OF A DEBT

If debt of a taxpayer is cancelled or forgiven, the taxpayer may have to include the cancelled amount in gross income. It is important to distinguish a debt cancellation from a gift, a bequest, or a renegotiation of the purchase price.

EXAMPLE I4-32 ▶ Farouk loaned his daughter $4,000 to help her purchase an automobile. Several months after she purchased the automobile, but before she repaid the $4,000, Farouk's daughter married. Farouk told his daughter that he was "tearing up" the $4,000 note as a wedding present. In this instance, the amount forgiven would constitute an excludable gift and would not be taxable as income to the daughter. ◀

EXAMPLE I4-33 ▶ Clay purchased a used automobile from a dealer for $6,000. He paid $2,000 down and agreed to pay the balance of $4,000 over three years. After Clay purchased the automobile, he determined that it was defective. Clay tried to return the automobile, but the automobile dealer refused. Clay threatened to sue the dealer. To resolve the problem, the dealer offered to reduce the balance due on the purchase-money debt from $4,000 to $2,500. Clay agreed. The transaction constitutes a reduction in the purchase price of the automobile. Clay will not recognize any income, but must reduce the basis in his automobile from $6,000 to $4,500. ◀

EXAMPLE I4-34 ▶ Blue Corporation issued bonds for $1,000 when interest rates were low. After a few years, interest rates increased and the bond price declined to $850. Blue Corporation purchased the bonds on the open market. Blue will recognize $150 of income from the discharge of indebtedness. ◀

EXAMPLE I4-35 ▶ Indy Coal Company has seen its business decline during the past two years. The Company has a significant amount of bank debt that was incurred over the years to fund its coal operations. In order to maintain its operations, Indy entered into an agreement with the bank whereby the bank agreed to cancel 50% of Indy's debt. Assuming Indy was solvent at the time of the cancellation, Indy must report the discharge of indebtedness as gross income. ◀

STOP & THINK *Question:* In Example I4-35, the bank agreed to cancel 50% of Indy Coal Company's debt. Why would a lender agree to unilaterally cancel a borrower's debt?

Solution: A bank might cancel a portion of a borrower's debt in order to protect the remaining portion of the debt. If the debt forced the company into bankruptcy, the bank may be able to collect none or only a small percentage of the debt. If the cancellation would help stabilize Indy, the bank may be able to collect at least 50% of the debt. Further, if Indy becomes a viable company in the years ahead, the bank will have a good customer to earn profits in the future.

REAL-WORLD EXAMPLE

A taxpayer purchased and retired its own bonds. The purchase resulted in a gain because the bonds were payable in British pounds, which had been devalued. The gain was excludable. *Kentucky & Indiana Terminal Railroad Co. v. U.S.*, 13 AFTR 2d 1148, 64-1 USTC ¶9374 (6th Cir., 1964).

The enforceability of a debt under state law may also determine whether the forgiveness results in income. For example, one case held that the forgiveness of a gambling debt was not included in gross income where the debt was unenforceable under state law.[44]

DISCHARGE IN BANKRUPTCY AND INSOLVENCY. Section 61(a)(12) indicates that gross income includes income from the discharge of an indebtedness. Section 108, on the other hand, provides for the following exceptions where the discharge of an indebtedness is not taxable:

- The discharge occurs in bankruptcy.
- The discharge occurs when the taxpayer is insolvent.

These exceptions are intended to allow a "fresh start" for bankrupt and other financially troubled taxpayers. Since a taxpayer is not required to include the discharge in gross income, he is required to reduce certain tax attributes. For example, if the taxpayer has a net operating loss carryover, the NOL carryover must be reduced by the excluded discharge.

KEY POINT

A discharge of debt in bankruptcy does not generate income.

If a debt is reduced during bankruptcy proceedings, the taxpayer recognizes no income even if the reduction in debt exceeds the available tax attributes. In the case of an insolvent taxpayer, no income is recognized as long as the taxpayer is insolvent after the reduction in debt takes place. A taxpayer is insolvent if the debts owed by the taxpayer exceed the FMV of assets owned. Thus, an insolvent taxpayer reduces the tax attributes to the point of solvency. From that point on, any reduction in debt results in the recognition of income even if all tax attributes have not been offset.

ADDITIONAL COMMENT

Also excludable is the income from the cancellation of a student loan pursuant to a provision under which part of the debt is discharged due to working for a period of time in certain professions for a broad class of employers.

STUDENT LOAN FORGIVENESS. Under Sec. 108(f)(2), the discharge of certain student loans is excluded from gross income if the discharge is contingent on the individual's performing certain public services. The loans must have been made by governmental, educational, or charitable organizations, and the loan proceeds must have been used to pay the cost of attending an educational institution or used to refinance outstanding student loans. Further, the loan forgiveness must be contingent upon the individual's working for a specified time period in certain professions, and the services must normally be performed for someone other than the lender.

EXAMPLE I4-36 ▶ Lee borrowed $60,000 from the federal government to attend medical school. Under the terms of the loan, $20,000 of debt is forgiven for each year she practices medicine in designated low-income neighborhoods. Lee does not have to include the debt forgiveness in gross income. ◀

EXCLUSION FOR GAIN FROM SMALL BUSINESS STOCK

Noncorporate taxpayers may exclude up to 50% of the gain realized on the disposition of qualified small business stock issued after August 10, 1993, if the stock is held for more than five years.[45] The remaining gain is taxed at a rate not greater than 28% resulting in a maximum effective rate of 14%. For each issuer of qualified small business stock, there is a limit on the amount of gain a taxpayer may exclude. The amount of gain eligible for the exclusion may not exceed the greater of $10 million, reduced by amounts previously

---

[44] *David Zarin v. CIR*, 66 AFTR 2d 90-5679, 90-2 USTC ¶50,530 (3rd Cir., 1990).

[45] Sec. 1202(a). The exclusion is 60% in the case of empowerment zone stock acquired after December 21, 2000.

excluded for gains on the company's stock, or ten times the taxpayer's aggregate adjusted basis of the stock disposed of during the year.[46] When measuring the taxpayer's aggregate basis for the stock to determine the maximum amount of gain to exclude, the fair market value of the assets contributed to the corporation is used.

EXAMPLE I4-37 ▶ Dennis contributed property with a basis of $1,000,000 and an FMV of $4,000,000 to a qualified small business corporation for all of its common stock. If he sells one-half of the stock after five years for $14,000,000, he may exclude $6,750,000 of the $13,500,000 ($14,000,000 − $500,000) realized gain. The maximum gain eligible for the exclusion is the greater of $10,000,000 or $20,000,000 [10 times the $2,000,000 basis ($4,000,000 FMV × 0.50) of the stock sold]. Thus, none of the $13,500,000 realized gain is subject to the limitation. ◀

Moreover, taxpayers do not have to recognize any gain if they reinvest the proceeds from the sale of small business stock in other small business stock within 60 days of the sale. Gain is recognized only to the extent that the amount realized from the sale exceeds the cost of the replacement stock. The basis of the replacement stock is reduced by the amount of gain not recognized. To qualify for the replacement provision the original stock must have been held for over 6 months.

EXAMPLE I4-38 ▶ Assume the same facts as in Example I4-37, except that Dennis purchases $13,000,000 of small business investment stock within 60 days. Dennis is taxed only on $1,000,000 ($14,000,000 − $13,000,000) of his $13,500,000 realized gain. Dennis' basis for the new stock, however, is $500,000 ($13,000,000 cost of the new stock − $12,500,000 portion of the gain that is not taxed). ◀

A corporation may issue qualified small business stock only if the corporation is a C corporation that is not an excluded corporation with an aggregate adjusted basis of not more than $50 million of gross assets, and at least 80% of the value of its assets must be used in the active conduct of one or more qualified trades or businesses.[47]

OTHER EXCLUSIONS

The tax law contains other exclusions that are either covered elsewhere in the text or are of limited application. Table I4-2 lists several such exclusions.

TAX PLANNING CONSIDERATIONS

EMPLOYEE FRINGE BENEFITS

ADDITIONAL COMMENT

A case can be made for the desirability of encouraging employers to provide health insurance and other fringe benefits. However, these provisions may contribute to increases in the cost of insurance and medical care.

The tax law encourages certain forms of fringe benefits by allowing an employer to deduct the cost of the benefit while permitting the employee to exclude the benefit from gross income. This deduction does not represent an income tax advantage to the employer because compensation, whether in the form of cash or nontaxable fringe benefits, is deductible if reasonable in amount. While employees receive the greatest income tax benefit from the exclusion of fringe benefits from gross income, employers receive a small benefit from the fact that fringe benefits are not subject to Social Security and Medicare taxes.

EXAMPLE I4-39 ▶ USA Company has decided to offer $20,000 of group term life insurance coverage for each of its employees at an average annual premium cost of $100 per employee. Tim, an employee of USA Corporation, is in the 15% tax bracket. Because USA is offering a nontaxable fringe benefit, Tim will owe no additional income tax. If Tim had received a salary increase of $100, he would have had to pay an additional income tax of $15 (0.15 × $100). The remaining $85 of after-tax income would probably not have been sufficient to obtain the same amount of life insurance coverage. ◀

---

46 Sec. 1202(b)(1).

47 Secs. 1202(d) and (e). Excluded corporations are those engaged in providing professional services (e.g., law and health), financial services (e.g., banking and insurance), hospitality (e.g., hotels and restaurants), farming, and mining and oil and gas production.

▼ **TABLE I4-2**
Other Exclusions

Section	Applies to	Comments
121	Gain from sale of personal residence	Taxpayers may exclude up to $250,000 ($500,000 in the case of a married couple filing a joint return) of gain from the sale of a personal residence. (See Chapter I12 for a detailed discussion of this provision.)
101(h)	Annuities paid to survivors of public safety officers	Annuities paid to survivors of public safety officers, such as firefighters and police officers, killed in the line of duty are excluded.
104(a) 112 134	Military disability pay Combat pay Military housing allowance	Military personnel may exclude disability pay, combat pay (noncommissioned personnel only), and housing allowances.
107	Housing allowance for ministers	Ministers may exclude either the rental value of their homes or a rental allowance if provided in connection with their religious duties.
119	Campus housing	A limited exclusion is provided to employees of educational institutions when they are provided with on campus housing.
131	Foster care payments	Certain allowances received by foster care providers are excluded from gross income.
162(o)	Rural letter carrier's allowance	Rural letter carriers may exclude the "equipment maintenance allowance" they receive for the use of their personal automobiles in delivering the mail. They receive no deduction for the use of their automobiles.
408A(d)	Roth IRA distributions	Qualified distributions from Roth IRAs are excluded from gross income (see Chapter I9 for a detailed discussion of the provisions.)
530(d)	Education IRA distributions	Qualified distributions from Education IRAs are excluded from gross income (see Chapter I9 for a detailed discussion of this provision.)
988(e)	Personal foreign currency gains	Individuals are excused from recognizing gain on the disposition of foreign currency in any personal transaction, provided that the gain does not exceed $200.

Excluding fringe benefits from gross income favors employees who are subject to higher tax rates.

EXAMPLE I4-40 ▶ Assume the same facts as in Example I4-39 except that Tim is in the 35% tax rate. Tim would save $35 (0.35 × $100) of taxes by receiving the group term life insurance coverage instead of the $100 salary increase. ◀

ADDITIONAL COMMENT

Fringe benefits offered by potential employers are important consideration factors when weighing total compensation packages.

It is not always desirable for employers to offer nontaxable fringe benefits. Some employees are not interested in certain benefits. For example, in the case of married couples where both spouses are employed, it is not necessary for both employers to provide medical insurance coverage for both spouses. Alternatively, single employees may not feel the need for group term life insurance and employees with no children are uninterested in employer-provided child care.

To avoid providing fringe benefits that are unneeded or unwanted, many employers have turned to cafeteria plans. Under cafeteria plans, employees may select from a list of nontaxable fringe benefits. On the other hand, employees who so choose may receive cash in lieu of some or all of the nontaxable benefits. Thus, each employee selects what he or she wants most. One common result is that high-tax-rate employees select the nontaxable fringe benefits, whereas other employees choose to receive cash.

SELF-HELP AND USE OF PERSONALLY OWNED PROPERTY

As noted earlier in this chapter, self-help income and income derived from the use of personal property are not taxable. Thus, self-help and personal ownership of property are favored by the tax system. Taxpayers who rent their personal residences cannot deduct rental payments, but taxpayers who own their residences do not pay rent and may deduct interest and real estate taxes as itemized deductions. Thus, the tax law encourages ownership of personal residences.

Effective tax planning necessitates weighing the tax incentives with other nontax factors. Taxpayers with little accumulated funds may find it difficult to purchase a residence despite the availability of tax incentives. Taxpayers who move frequently may find that transaction costs such as real estate commissions and other closing costs are greater than the tax benefits obtained from home ownership. Other factors such as the personal preference of the taxpayer and anticipated inflation rates must also be considered.

Self-help must be viewed in the same way. Taxpayers who are deciding whether to paint their own residences or hire someone else to do it must consider factors such as personal preference and the amount of income that could be produced if the time were spent working at an activity that produces taxable income.

COMPLIANCE AND PROCEDURAL CONSIDERATIONS

ADDITIONAL COMMENT

Taxpayers filing Form 1040 are asked to report any tax-exempt interest income on line 8b.

Taxpayers are usually not required to disclose excluded income on their tax returns. For example, a taxpayer who receives a tax-exempt scholarship need not disclose that income on his or her tax return. An exception is provided for tax-exempt interest and Social Security benefits, which must be disclosed on the tax return. If a taxpayer's only income is from tax-exempt sources, the taxpayer need not file a tax return. Whether an individual must file a return is based on the amount of the individual's gross income for the year (see Chapter I2).

This chapter considers the taxability of various fringe benefits. The rules regarding the need for an employer to withhold federal income taxes or to report a payment on an employee's Form W-2 (Statement of Income Tax Withheld on Wages) closely parallel the gross income rules. (See Chapter I14 for a discussion of these reporting requirements.) In general, if a fringe benefit is nontaxable, employers do not withhold from the benefit, nor do they report the benefit on the employee's W-2 at year-end. On the other hand, if the benefit is taxable, it is subject to withholding and is reported on the employee's W-2 at year-end. Thus, employers do not withhold for nontaxable meals and lodging provided to employees[48] or a moving expense reimbursement if the expenses are deductible.[49] Similarly, no withholding is required for the following fringe benefits if they are nontaxable: scholarships and fellowships covered by Sec. 117, dependent care covered by Sec. 129, and miscellaneous fringes covered by Sec. 132.

There are exceptions to this basic system. Certain fringe benefits are not subject to withholding even if the benefits are taxable. These include group-term life insurance coverage and medical expense reimbursements.

In general, fringe benefits which are exempt from the income tax are also exempt from Social Security and Medicare taxes. For example, medical insurance coverage and group term life coverage of up to $50,000 can be provided to employees without either the employer or the employee owing any Social Security or Medicare taxes on the premiums. This is true if the employee elects the benefits instead of cash salary under a cafeteria plan.

Employers who are obligated to withhold from employee wages are subject to penalty if they fail to withhold, fail to provide employees with correct W-2s, or fail to correctly report the compensation and withholding information to the IRS.[50] In general, the failure to report

---

[48] Reg. Sec. 31.3401(a)-1(b)(9).

[49] See Sec. 3401 for withholding requirements for numerous special situations.

[50] Secs. 6672, 6674, and 6721 respectively.

wages and withholding to either employees or the IRS is subject to penalty generally equal to $50 per failure. The failure to withhold can result in a penalty equal to 100% of the amount that should have been withheld. The penalty can be imposed on the employer and other people, such as officers or accountants, who are responsible for withholding.

Occasionally, employees do not want employers to withhold taxes from their wages. Officers or others who choose not to withhold from employee wages face an extremely burdensome penalty, particularly if a large number of employees are involved. Therefore, it is important that employers comply with withholding requirements. One closely related issue is whether an individual is an employee subject to withholding or an independent contractor, as only employee wages are subject to withholding (see Chapter I14).

PROBLEM MATERIALS

DISCUSSION QUESTIONS

I4-1 What is meant by the terms *administrative exclusion* and *judicial exclusion*?

I4-2 There is no specific statutory exclusion for welfare benefits. Nevertheless, the IRS has ruled that such benefits are not taxable. Is this within the authority of the IRS?

I4-3 What was the issue in the tax case *Eisner* v. *Macomber*? Why is the case important?

I4-4 Most exclusions exist for one of two reasons. What are those reasons? Give examples of exclusions that exist for each.

I4-5
a. If a gift of property is made, who is taxed on income produced by the property?
b. How can interfamily gifts reduce a family's total tax liability?

I4-6
a. What role does intent play in determining whether a transfer is a gift and therefore not subject to the income tax?
b. Are tips received by employees from customers excludable from gross income as gifts? Explain.

I4-7 What is the tax significance of the face amount of a life insurance policy?

I4-8 What conditions must be met for an award to qualify for an exclusion under Sec. 74?

I4-9 Which of the requirements for the Sec. 74 awards exclusion most severely limits its use? Does the exclusion benefit taxpayers more if they itemize their deductions or use the standard deduction?

I4-10
a. Define the term *scholarship* as it is used in Sec. 117.
b. If a scholarship covers room and board, is it excludable?
c. If an employer provides a scholarship to an employee who is on leave of absence, is that scholarship taxable?
d. Is the amount paid by a university to students for services excludable from the students' gross income?

I4-11 What special rules are applicable to non–degree candidates who receive scholarships?

I4-12 Is the personal injury exclusion found in Sec. 104 limited to physical injury? Explain.

I4-13 Answer the following questions relative to employer-financed medical and health, disability, and life insurance plans.
a. May employers deduct premiums paid on employee insurance?
b. Do employees have to include such premiums in gross income?
c. Are benefits paid to the employee included in the employee's gross income?

I4-14 Special rules are applicable in situations where group term life insurance coverage exceeds $50,000. How are key employees treated?

I4-15
a. What are the six major types of fringe benefits covered by Sec. 132?
b. What tax advantage is offered relative to such benefits?
c. Are such benefits available to employees only or may the benefits also be offered to spouses, dependents, and retirees?
d. Is discrimination prohibited relative to Sec. 132 benefits?
e. What is the tax impact on the employer and employees if an employer's plan is discriminatory?

I4-16 What conditions must be met if an employee is to exclude meals and lodging furnished by an employer?

I4-17 The president and vice president of USA Corporation receive benefits that are unavailable to other employees. These benefits include free parking, payment of monthly expenses in a local club, discounts on products sold by the corporation, and payment of premiums on a whole life insurance policy. Which of the benefits must be included in the gross income of the president and vice president?

I4-18 Are the same fringe benefits that are available to employees also available to self-employed individuals?

I4-19 If an employee takes a customer to lunch and discusses business, can the employee deduct 50% of the meal for both the customer and himself? Explain.

I4-20 Are distributions from a qualified state tuition program taxable?

I4-21 What types of income qualify for the foreign-earned income exclusion?

I4-22 Are taxpayers who claim the foreign-earned income exclusion entitled to deduct expenses incurred in producing that income? Explain.

I4-23 a. Why is it important to distinguish debt cancellation from a gift, bequest, or renegotiation of a purchase price?
b. What happens to the basis of an asset if the taxpayer renegotiates its purchase price?

I4-24 a. Under what conditions is the discharge of indebtedness not taxable?
b. If a father forgives a daughter's debt to him, is she required to include such amount in her gross income?

I4-25 Bankrupt and insolvent taxpayers do not recognize income if debt is discharged. They must, however, reduce specified tax attributes. What is involved?

I4-26 Are employee awards taxable? Explain.

I4-27 Why are cafeteria plans helpful in the design of an employee benefit plan that provides nontaxable fringe benefits?

I4-28 Both high-income and low-income employees are covered by cafeteria plans. Under such plans, all employees may select from a list of nontaxable fringe benefits or they may elect to receive cash in lieu of these benefits.
a. Which group of employees is more likely to choose nontaxable fringe benefits in lieu of cash? Explain.
b. Is this result desirable from a social or economic point of view? Explain.

ISSUE IDENTIFICATION QUESTIONS

I4-29 Luke, who retired this year, lives in a four-plex owned by Julie. Luke's income decreased when he retired, and he now has difficulty paying his rent. Julie offered to reduce Luke's rent if he would agree to mow the lawn, wash windows, and provide other maintenance services. Luke accepted, and Julie reduced the monthly rental from $650 to $300. What are the tax issues that should be considered by Luke and Julie?

I4-30 Mildred worked as a maid for 27 years in the home of Larry and Kay. When she retired, they presented her with a check for $25,000, indicating that it was a way of showing their appreciation for her years of loyal service. What tax issues should Mildred and her employer consider?

I4-31 Troy Department Stores offers employees discounts on merchandise carried in the store. Newly hired employees receive a 10% discount. The discount rate increases 1% each year until employees have 20 years of service when the discount rate is capped at 30%. What tax issues should Troy and the employees consider?

I4-32 Jerry works in the human resources department of Ajax Corporation. One of his responsibilities is to interview prospective employees. Two or three days each week, Jerry takes a prospective employee to lunch, and Ajax reimburses him for the cost of the meals. What tax issues should Jerry and Ajax Corporation consider?

PROBLEMS

I4-33 *Self-Help Income.* In which of the following situations would the taxpayer realize taxable income?
a. A mechanic performs work on his own automobile. The mechanic would have charged a customer $400 for doing the same work.
b. A mechanic repairs his neighbor's personal automobile. In exchange, the neighbor, an accountant, agrees to prepare the mechanic's tax return. The services performed are each worth $200.
c. A mechanic repairs his daughter's automobile without any charge.

I4-34 *Excludable Gifts.* Which of the following would constitute excludable gifts?
a. Alice appeared on a TV quiz show and received a prize of $500.
b. Bart received $500 from his employer because he developed an idea that reduced the employer's production costs.

c. Chuck borrowed $500 from his mother in order to finance his last year in college. Upon his graduation, Chuck's mother told him he did not have to repay the $500. She intended the $500 to be a graduation present.

I4-35 ***Life Insurance Proceeds.*** Don is the beneficiary of a $50,000 insurance policy on the life of his mother, Anna. To date, Anna has paid premiums of $16,000. What amount of gross income must be reported in each of the following cases.

a. Anna elects to cancel the policy and receives $20,000, the cash surrender value of the policy.
b. Anna dies and Don receives the face amount of the policy, $50,000.
c. Anna dies and Don elects to receive $15,000 per year for four years.

I4-36 ***Transfer of Life Insurance.*** Ed is the beneficiary of a $20,000 insurance policy on the life of his mother. Because Ed needs funds, he sells the policy to his sister, Amy, for $6,000. Amy subsequently pays premiums of $8,000.

a. How much income must Amy report if she collects the face value of the policy upon the death of her mother?
b. Would Amy have to report any income if her brother had given her the policy? Assume the only payment she made was $8,000 for the premiums.

I4-37 ***Settlement of Life Insurance Policy.*** Sue is age 73 and has a great deal of difficulty living independently as she suffers from severe rheumatoid arthritis. She is covered by a $400,000 life insurance policy, and her children are named as her beneficiaries. Because of her health, Sue decides to live in a nursing home, but she does not have enough income to pay her nursing home bills which are expected to total $42,000 per year. The insurance company offers disabled individuals the option of either a reduced settlement on their policies or an annuity. Given Sue's age and health she has the option of receiving $3,200 per month or a lump sum payment of $225,000. To date, Sue has paid $80,000 in premiums on the policy.

a. How much income must Sue report if she chooses the lump sum settlement?
b. How much income must Sue report if she elects the annuity?
c. How much income would Sue have to report if her nursing home bills amounted to only $36,000 per year?

I4-38 ***Insurance Policy Dividends.*** Hank carries a $100,000 insurance policy on his life. Premiums paid over the years total $8,000. Dividends on the policy have totaled $6,000. Hank has left the dividends on the policy with the insurance company. During the current year, the insurance company credited $600 of interest on the accumulated dividends to Hank's account.

a. How much income is Hank obligated to report in connection with the policy?
b. Would it make any difference if the accumulated dividends equaled $9,000 instead of $6,000?

I4-39 ***Prizes and Awards.*** For each of the following, indicate whether the amount is taxable:

a. Peggy won $4,000 in the state lottery.
b. Jane won a $500 prize for her entry in a poetry contest.
c. Linda was awarded $2,000 when she was selected as "Teacher of the Year" by the local school district.

I4-40 ***Scholarships.*** For each of the following, indicate the amount that must be included in the taxpayer's gross income:

a. Larry was given a $1,500 tuition scholarship to attend Eastern Law School. In addition, Eastern paid Larry $4,000 per year to work part-time in the campus bookstore.
b. Marty received a $10,000 football scholarship for attending Northern University. The scholarship covered tuition, room and board, laundry, and books. Four thousand dollars of the scholarship was designated for room and board and laundry. It was understood that Marty would participate in the school's intercollegiate football program, but Marty was not required to do so.
c. Western School of Nursing requires all third-year students to work twenty hours per week at an affiliated hospital. Each student is paid $6 per hour. Nancy, a third-year student, earned $6,000 during the year.

I4-41 ***Research Grant.*** Otto is a biology professor at State University. The university gave Otto a sabbatical leave to study the surface of the flatworm. During the year he received a salary of $50,000 which is less than his regular salary of $56,000. Otto also received a grant to cover expenses associated with the study. The grant was $2,000 as were his related expenses. Otto also incurred memberships and other employment related expenses totaling $1,000. How much must Otto include in gross income.

I4-42 ***Payments for Personal Injury.*** Determine which of the following payments for sickness and injury must be included in the taxpayer's gross income.

a. Pat was injured in an automobile accident. The other driver's insurance company paid him $2,000 to cover medical expenses and a compensatory amount of $4,000 for pain and suffering.
b. A newspaper article stated that Quincy had been convicted of tax evasion. Quincy, in fact, had never been accused of tax evasion. He sued and won a compensatory settlement of $4,000 from the newspaper.
c. Rob, who pays the cost of a commercial disability income policy, fell and injured his back. He was unable to work for six months. The insurance company paid him $1,800 per month during the time he was unable to work.
d. Steve fell and injured his knee. He was unable to work for four months. His employer-financed disability income policy paid Steve $1,600 per month during the time he was unable to work.
e. Ted suffered a stroke. He was unable to work for five months. His employer continued to pay Ted his salary of $1,700 per month during the time he was unable to work.

I4-43 ***Employee Benefits.*** Ursula is employed by USA Corporation. USA Corporation provides medical and health, disability, and group term life insurance coverage for its employees. Premiums attributable to Ursula were as follows:

Medical and health	$1,800
Disability	300
Group term life (face amount is $40,000)	200

During the year, Ursula suffered a heart attack and subsequently died. Before her death, Ursula collected $14,000 as a reimbursement for medical expenses and $5,000 of disability income. Upon her death, Ursula's husband collected the $40,000 face value of the life insurance policy.

a. What amount can USA Corporation deduct for premiums attributable to Ursula?
b. How much must Ursula include in income relative to the premiums paid?
c. How much must Ursula include in income relative to the insurance benefits?
d. How much must Ursula's widower include in income?

I4-44 ***Group Term Life Insurance.*** Data Corporation has four employees and provides group term life insurance coverage for all four employees. Coverage is nondiscriminatory and is as follows:

Employee	*Age*	*Key Employee*	*Coverage*	*Actual Premiums*
Andy	62	yes	$200,000	$4,000
Bob	52	yes	40,000	700
Cindy	33	no	80,000	600
Damitria	33	no	40,000	300

a. How much may Data Corporation deduct for group term life insurance premiums?
b. How much income must be reported by each employee?

I4-45 ***Life Insurance Proceeds.*** Joe is the beneficiary of a life insurance policy taken out by his father several years ago. Joe's father died this year and Joe has the option of receiving $100,000 cash or electing to receive $14,000 per year for the remainder of his life. Joe is now 65. Joe's father paid $32,000 in premiums over the years.

a. How much must Joe include in gross income this year if he elects to accept the $100,000 face amount?
b. How much must be included in Joe's gross income this year if he elects to receive installment payments?

I4-46 ***Employee Benefits.*** Al flies for AAA Airlines. AAA provides its employees with several fringe benefits. Al and his family are allowed to fly on a space-available basis on AAA Airline. Tickets used by Al and his family during the year are worth $2,000. AAA paid for a subscription to two magazines published for pilots. The subscriptions totaled $80. The airline paid for Al's meals and lodging while he was away from home overnight in connection with his job. Such meals and lodging cost AAA $10,000. Although Al could not eat while flying, he was allowed to drink coffee provided by the airline. The coffee was worth about $50. AAA provided Al with free parking, which is valued at $100 per month. The airline treated Al and his family to a one-week all-expenses-paid vacation at a resort near his home. This benefit was awarded because of Al's outstanding safety record. The value of the vacation was $2,300. Which of these benefits are taxable to Al?

I4-47 *Employee Benefits.* Jet Corporation is involved in the purchase and rental of several large apartment complexes. Questions have been raised about the treatment of several items pertaining to Jet Corporation and its employees. Jet Corporation employs a manager for each complex. The manager is required to occupy a unit in the complex in order to be available at all hours. The average rental value of the units is $7,800 per year. The corporation's president finds that it is beneficial to the corporation if he entertains bankers and others with whom Jet does business. He does such entertaining about once each month and the corporation pays the cost. Business is discussed at the meals. The cost for the year of such entertaining was $600, and about one-third of the cost was attributable to meals consumed by the president.

Each year as the company closes its books, the controller and certain other members of the accounting staff must work overtime. The company pays each employee supper money totaling $25 during this period.

The corporation's vice president is expected to travel on business-related matters to visit various properties owned by the corporation. Because of the distances involved, the vice president must stay away from home several nights. Total meals and lodging incurred on the trips total $3,000, most of which is attributable to the vice president himself.

Which amounts are deductible by the corporation? Which are taxable to the employee?

I4-48 *Death Benefits.* After a brief illness, Bill died. Bill's employer paid $20,000 to his widow. The corporation sent along a letter with the check indicating that $5,000 represented payment for Bill's accrued vacation days and back wages. The balance was being awarded in recognition of Bill's many years of loyal service. The company was obligated to pay the accrued vacation days and back wages, but the balance was discretionary.

a. Is the employer entitled to deduct the $20,000 paid to Bill's widow?
b. Is Bill's widow required to include the $20,000 in her gross income?

I4-49 *Foreign-Earned Income Exclusion.* For each of the following cases, indicate the amount of the foreign-earned income exclusion. (Disregard the effect of exemptions for certain allowances under Sec. 912.)

a. Sam, a U.S. citizen, is an assistant to the ambassador to Spain. Sam lives and works in Spain. His salary of $40,000 is paid by the U.S. government.
b. Jim, a U.S. citizen, owns an unincorporated oil drilling company that operates in Argentina, where he resides. The business is heavily dependent on equipment owned by Jim. His profit for the year totaled $100,000.
c. Ken, a U.S. citizen, works for a large Japanese corporation. Ken is employed in the United States, but must travel to Japan several times each year. During the current year he spent sixty days in Japan. This is typical of most years. His salary is $45,000.

I4-50 *Foreign-Earned Income Exclusion.* On January 5, Rita left the United States for Germany, where she had accepted an appointment as vice president of foreign operations. Her employer, USA Corporation, told her the assignment would last about two years. Rita decided not to establish a permanent residence in Germany because her assignment was for only two years. Her salary for the year is $240,000. Rita incurred travel, transportation, and other related expenses totaling $6,000, none of which is reimbursed.

a. What is Rita's foreign-earned income exclusion?
b. How much may she deduct for travel and transportation?

I4-51 *Discharge of Debt.* During bankruptcy, USA Corporation debt was reduced from $780,000 to $400,000. USA Corporation's assets are valued at $500,000. USA's NOL carryover was $400,000.

a. Is USA Corporation required to report any income from the discharge of its debts?
b. Which tax attributes are reduced and by how much? Assume USA does not make any special elections when reducing its attributes.

I4-52 *Discharge of Debt.* Old Corporation has suffered losses for several years, and its debts total $500,000; Old's assets are valued at only $380,000. Old's creditors agree to reduce Old's debts by one-half in order to permit the corporation to continue to operate. Old's NOL carryover is $150,000.

a. What impact does the reduction in debt have on Old's NOL?
b. Is Old required to report any income?

I4-53 *Court and Insurance Awards.* Determine whether the following items represent taxable income.

a. As the result of an age discrimination suit, Pat received a cash settlement of $40,000. One-half of the settlement represented wages lost by Pat as a result of the discrimination and the balance represented an award based on personal injury.
b. Matt sued the local newspaper for a story that reported he was affiliated with organized crime. The court awarded him $50,000 of libel damages.
c. Pam was injured in an automobile accident and received $10,000 from an employer-sponsored disability policy. In addition, her employer-financed medical insurance policy reimbursed her for $15,000 of medical expenses.

I4-54 *Cafeteria Plan.* Jangyoun is a married taxpayer with a dependent 4-year-old daughter. His employer offers a flexible spending account under which he can choose to receive cash or, alternatively, choose from certain fringe benefits. These benefits include health insurance that costs $2,500 and child care that costs $2,600. Assume Jangyoun is in the 30% tax bracket.

a. How much would Jangyoun save in income taxes if he chooses to participate in the employer's health insurance plan? Assume that he does not have sufficient medical expenses to itemize his deductions.
b. Would you recommend that Jangyoun participate in the employer's health insurance plan if his wife's employer already provides comparable health insurance coverage for the family?
c. Would you recommend that Jangyoun participate in the employer-provided child care option if he has the alternative option of claiming a child care credit of $480.

I4-55 *Exclusion of Gain from Small Business Stock.* Jose acquired 1,000 shares of Acorn Corporation common stock by transferring property with an adjusted basis of $1,000,000 and fair market value of $4,000,000 for 100% of the stock. Acorn is a qualified small business corporation. After six years, Jose sells all of the Acorn Corporation common stock for $16,000,000.

a. What is the amount of gain that may be excluded from Jose's gross income?
b. What would your answer be if the fair market value of the Acorn stock were only $1,000,000 upon its issue?
c. What would your answer be if the stock were sold after two years?
d. Can Jose avoid recognizing gain by purchasing replacement stock?

COMPREHENSIVE PROBLEM

I4-56 Pat was divorced from her husband in 1997. During the current year she received alimony of $18,000 and child support of $4,000 for her 11-year old son, who lives with her. Her former husband had asked her to sign an agreement giving him the dependency exemption for the child but she declined to do so. After the divorce she accepted a position as a teacher in the local school district. During the current year she received a salary of $22,000. The school district paid her medical insurance premiums of $1,900 and provided her with group term life insurance coverage of $40,000. The premiums attributable to her coverage equaled $160. During her marriage, Pat's parents loaned her $8,000 to help with the down payment on her home. Her parents told her this year that they understand her financial problems and that they were cancelling the balance on the loan, which was $5,000. They did so because they wanted to help their only daughter.

Pat received dividends from National Motor Company of $4,600 and interest on State of California bonds of $2,850.

Pat sold her personal automobile for $2,800 because she needed a larger car. The automobile had cost $8,000. She purchased a new auto for $11,000. Pat had itemized deductions of $8,600. Assume her withholding and estimated payments total $8,000. Compute her taxable income for the current year.

TAX STRATEGY PROBLEMS

I4-57 Sally owns a small C corporation that has provided health insurance coverage for Sally and the company's three other employees. The insurance coverage for Sally and the three employees is individual coverage, not family coverage. Sally's own family coverage is through a separate private policy. She pays the premiums out of after-tax dollars. Sally's salary is $40,000 and the salary for the other three employees averages $30,000. The premiums on the health insurance policy average $2,000 per employee per year. The provider recently informed Sally that the premiums will increase to $2,500 per employee. The spouses of her two married employees have coverage through their employers. The third employee has announced that he will marry soon and would very much like to have family health insurance coverage. The insurance provider says that family coverage will approximately double the premiums. Sally is finding the cost of providing medical insurance coverage particularly burdensome for her small business. What planning suggestions can you offer?

I4-58 Maria was planning to paint the interior of her apartment over a three-day weekend. Her employer asked her to work all three days and will pay her $600 overtime. She called a professional painter who offered to do the job for $500. He is willing to use the paint she has already purchased. Maria is in the 30% tax bracket. Will she be better off financially to work the overtime and pay the painter or to turn down the overtime and do the work herself? What other factors should she consider?

TAX FORM/RETURN PREPARATION PROBLEMS

I4-59 A. J. Paige, Social Security number 111-22-3333, is the vice president of marketing (Japan) for International Industries, Inc. (III). III is headquartered at 123 Main Street, Los Angeles, California 92601. A. J., who is single, accepted the position and became a resident of Japan on July 8 of last year. Her business address is 86 Sano, Tokyo, Japan. A. J.'s visa permits her to stay in Japan indefinitely. Her only trips to the United States in the current year were for vacations (August 2 to 16 and December 21 to 28). A. J.'s contract specifies that her appointment is to last indefinitely, but states that III is to pay her $4,000 per year to cover the cost of two vacation trips to the United States. Her salary is $140,000, out of which she pays rent on an apartment of $28,000 per year. A. J. has no family or residence in the United States. She paid an income tax in Japan of $23,500. Complete a Form 2555 for the current year.

I4-60 Alice Johnson, Social Security number 222-23-3334, is a single mother of two children, Jack and Jill, ages 15 and 17, respectively, and is employed as a secretary by State University of Florida. She has the following items pertaining to her income tax return for the current year:

- Received a $20,000 salary from her employer, who withheld $4,000 federal income tax.
- Received a gift of 1,000 shares of Ace Corporation stock with a $100,000 FMV from her mother. She also received $4,000 of cash dividends from the Ace Corporation.
- Received $1,000 of interest income on bonds issued by the City of Tampa.
- Received a stock dividend (qualifying under Sec. 305) of 50 shares of Ace Corporation stock with a $5,000 FMV.
- Alice's employer paid $2,000 of medical and health insurance premiums on her behalf.
- Maintains a household for herself and two children and provides more than 50% of their support. In the prior year, however, she entered into an agreement with her ex-husband that provided that he is entitled to the dependency exemptions for the children.
- Received $12,000 alimony and $6,000 child support from her ex-husband (Charlie Johnson).
- State University provided $60,000 of group term life insurance. Alice is 42 years old and is not a key employee. Assume the table in the text is applicable all year.
- Received a $1,000 cash award from her employer for being designated the Secretary of the Year.
- Total itemized deductions are $7,000.

Complete Form 1040 and accompanying schedules for Alice Johnson's federal income tax return for the current year.

CASE STUDY PROBLEMS

I4-61 Able Corporation is a closely held company engaged in the manufacture and retail sales of automotive parts. Able maintains a qualified pension plan for its employees but has not offered nontaxable fringe benefits.

You are a tax consultant for the company who has been asked to prepare suggestions for the adoption of an employee fringe benefit plan. Your discussions with the client's chief financial officer reveal the following:

- Employees currently pay their own premiums for medical and health insurance.
- No group term life insurance is provided.
- The company owns a vacant building that could easily be converted to a parking garage.
- Many of the employees purchase automobile parts from the company's retail outlets and pay retail price.
- The president of the corporation would like to provide a dependent care assistance program under Sec. 129 for its employees.

Required: Prepare a client memo that recommends the adoption of an employee fringe benefit program. Your recommendations should discuss the pros and cons of different types of nontaxable fringe benefits.

I4-62 Jay Corporation owns several automobile dealerships. This year, the corporation initiated a policy of giving the top salesperson at each dealership a free vacation trip to Florida. The president believes that this is an effective sales incentive. The cost of the vacations is deductible by the corporation as compensation paid to employees, and is taxable to the recipients. Nevertheless, the president objects to reporting the value of the vacations as income on the W-2s of the recipients and to withholding taxes from wages for the value of the trips. He feels that this undermines the effectiveness of the incentive. What are the implications of this behavior for the corporation and the president?

TAX RESEARCH PROBLEMS

I4-63 Ann is a graduate economics student at State University. State University awarded her a $1,000 scholarship. In addition, Ann works as a half-time teaching assistant in the Economics Department at State University. For her services she is paid $7,000 per year and her tuition is waived. Her tuition would be $8,000 were it not for the waiver. Ann paid $500 for her books and supplies and she incurred living expenses of $7,400. Determine how much gross income Ann must report.

A partial list of research sources is

- Sec. 117(d)
- Prop. Reg. 1.117-6(d)(5)

I4-64 Kim leased an office building to USA Corporation under a ten-year lease specifying that at the end of the lease USA had to return the building to its original condition if any modifications were made. USA changed the interior of the building, and at the end of the lease USA paid Kim $30,000 instead of making the required repairs. Does Kim have to include the payment in gross income?

A partial list of research sources is

- Sec. 109
- *Boston Fish Market Corp.*, 57 T.C. 884 (1972)
- *Sirbo Holdings Inc. v. CIR*, 31 AFTR 2d 73-1005, 73-1 USTC ¶9312 (2nd Cir., 1973)

I4-65 As a result of a fire damaging their residence, the Taylors must stay in a motel for five weeks while their home is being restored. They pay $2,000 for the room and $500 for meals. Their homeowner's policy pays $2,500 to reimburse them for the cost. They estimate that during the five-week period they would normally spend $300 for meals. Is the reimbursement taxable?

A partial list of research sources is

- Sec. 123
- Reg. Sec. 1.123-1

I4-66 Bold Corporation paid $25 to each full-time employee at year end in recognition of the holidays. Bold Corporation is interested in whether the amounts are taxable income to its employees, and whether the company can deduct the amounts.

A partial list of research sources is

- Sec. 74(c), 102, 132(c), and 274(b)
- Reg. Sec. 1.132-6(e)(1)
- *Hallmark Cards, Inc.* v *U.S.*, 9 AFTR2d 391, 62-1 USTC ¶9162 (DC-Mo, 1961).
- Rev. Rul. 59-58, 1959-1 CB 17.

5

CHAPTER

PROPERTY TRANSACTIONS: CAPITAL GAINS AND LOSSES

LEARNING OBJECTIVES

After studying this chapter, you should be able to

1. Determine the realized gain or loss from the sale or other disposition of property
2. Determine the amount realized from the sale or other disposition of property
3. Determine the basis of property
4. Distinguish between capital assets and other assets
5. Understand how capital gains and losses affect taxable income
6. Recognize when a sale or exchange has occurred
7. Determine the holding period for an asset when a sale or disposition occurs

CHAPTER OUTLINE

Determination of Gain or Loss...5-2
Basis Considerations...5-5
Definition of a Capital Asset...5-13
Tax Treatment for Capital Gains and Losses of Noncorporate Taxpayers...5-16
Tax Treatment of Capital Gains and Losses: Corporate Taxpayers...5-20
Sale or Exchange...5-21
Holding Period...5-28
Preferential Treatment for Net Capital Gains...5-30
Tax Planning Considerations...5-31
Compliance and Procedural Considerations...5-33

Gross income includes "gains derived from dealings in property,"[1] and certain "losses from sale or exchange of property"[2] are allowed as deductions from gross income to determine adjusted gross income. All recognized gains and losses must eventually be classified either as *capital* or *ordinary.* Before 1987, long-term capital gains (LTCGs) generally were taxed at lower rates than ordinary gains or short-term capital gains (STCGs).[3] The Tax Reform Act of 1986 substantially eliminated the difference in tax treatment for capital gain income and ordinary income. However, as tax rates have increased since 1986, Congress has again created preferential treatment for capital gains for certain taxpayers.

For tax years beginning after 1990, the maximum tax rate imposed on net capital gains (the excess of net long-term capital gain (NLTCG) over net short-term capital loss (NSTCL)) recognized by noncorporate taxpayers is 28%. This benefit for net LTCG was increased with the passage of the Taxpayer Relief Act of 1997, which enacted major changes in the tax treatment of capital gains. Net capital gain (NCG) is still defined as the excess of NLTCG over NSTCL, but taxpayers must now compute adjusted net capital gain (ANCG) which might be taxed at rates of 8%, 10%, 18%, or 20%. Because the maximum tax rate on ordinary income is currently 38.6% (2002), noncorporate taxpayers can benefit by having a gain classified as LTCG.

HISTORICAL NOTE

A preferential tax rate on capital gains was included in the tax law from 1921 until 1987. A modest preferential rate was reintroduced in 1991, with capital gains for noncorporate taxpayers being subject to a maximum 28% tax rate and ordinary income being subject to a maximum tax rate of 31%. The capital gains differential became more significant in 1993 when the highest marginal rate was increased to 39.6%.

Capital losses must be offset against capital gains, and net capital losses are subjected to restrictions on their deductibility. Thus, most taxpayers prefer to have losses classified as ordinary instead of capital.

Most property transactions have tax consequences to the taxpayer. For example, when a sale, exchange, or abandonment occurs, the taxpayer must determine the realized gain or loss, the portion of the realized gain or loss that must be recognized (if any), and the character of the gain or loss. This chapter focuses on determining the realized gain or loss and the portion of the recognized gain or loss that is classified as capital or ordinary. When classifying a recognized gain or loss, (i.e., the gain or loss actually reported on the taxpayer's tax return) three important questions must be considered:

- What type of property has been sold or exchanged?
- When has a sale or exchange occurred?
- When did the holding period for the property commence?

In this chapter, these three questions are considered as well as difficulties associated with determining the basis of the property sold or exchanged and the amount of realized gains or losses.

DETERMINATION OF GAIN OR LOSS

OBJECTIVE 1

Determine the realized gain or loss from the sale or other disposition of property

REALIZED GAIN OR LOSS

To determine the **realized gain** or **loss**, the amount realized from the sale or exchange of property is compared with the adjusted basis of that property. A gain is realized when the amount realized is greater than the basis, and a loss is realized when the amount realized is less than the basis of the property.[4]

EXAMPLE I5-1 ▶ Jack sells an asset with an adjusted basis of $10,000 to Judy for $14,000. Because the amount realized is greater than the basis, Jack has a realized gain of $4,000 ($14,000 – $10,000). ◀

Despite the fact that most transfers of property involve a sale, gains and losses may also be realized on certain other types of dispositions of property, such as exchanges, condemnations, casualties, thefts, bond retirements, and corporate distributions. However, gains and losses are generally not realized when property is disposed of by gift or bequest.

---

[1] Sec. 61(a)(3).
[2] Sec. 62(a)(3).
[3] See page I5-28 and below for a discussion of the holding period for capital assets. A capital gain or loss is long-term or short-term depending on the length of time the asset has been held by the taxpayer.
[4] Sec. 1001(a).

EXAMPLE I5-2 ▶ Alice owns land that is held for investment and has a basis of $20,000. The land is taken by the city by right of eminent domain, and she receives a payment of $30,000 for the land. This condemnation is treated as a sale or disposition, and Alice's realized gain is $10,000 ($30,000 − $20,000). ◀

EXAMPLE I5-3 ▶ Two years ago, Bob purchased stock of a newly formed corporation for $10,000. During the current year, he receives a $12,000 distribution, constituting a return of capital, from the corporation. This distribution is treated as a sale. Therefore, Bob has a realized gain of $2,000 ($12,000 − $10,000). Bob's basis for the stock is now zero because his basis of $10,000 has been recovered. ◀

For a sale or other disposition to occur, there must be an identifiable event. Mere changes in the value of property are not normally recognized as a disposition for purposes of determining a realized gain or loss.

STUDY AID

Students should pay close attention to the technical terms used in tax law. For example, the similar sounding terms of "realized gain" and "recognized gain" are often different dollar amounts for the sale of an asset.

Many reasons exist for not taxing unrealized gains and losses that arise due to a mere change in value. The Treasury Regulations state that "A loss is not ordinarily sustained prior to the sale or other disposition of the property, for the reason that until such sale or other disposition occurs there remains the possibility that the taxpayer may recover or recoup the adjusted basis of the property."[5] Because of administrative difficulties associated with determining FMV, disputes with the Internal Revenue Service would be greatly increased if unrealized gains were taxed and unrealized losses were allowed as deductions. In addition, payment of tax on income is generally required only when a taxpayer has the wherewithal to pay the tax (e.g., the taxpayer has received cash from the sale or other disposition of property and can therefore pay the tax on the gain).

AMOUNT REALIZED. The **amount realized** from a sale or other disposition of property is the sum of any money received plus the FMV of all other property received.

EXAMPLE I5-4 ▶ Tony sells land to Rita for $15,000 in cash and a machine having a $3,000 FMV. The amount realized by Tony is $18,000 ($15,000 + $3,000). ◀

OBJECTIVE 2

Determine the amount realized from the sale or other disposition of property

From a practical standpoint, the determination of FMV is a question of fact and often creates considerable controversy between taxpayers and the IRS. **Fair market value (FMV)** is "the price at which property would change hands between a willing buyer and a willing seller, neither being under any compulsion to buy or sell."[6] In some cases, the FMV of the asset given in the exchange may be easier to determine than the FMV of the property received. In those cases, the FMV of the property given may be used to measure the amount realized. If a buyer assumes the seller's liability or takes the property subject to the debt, the courts have included the amount of the liability when determining the amount realized.[7]

EXAMPLE I5-5 ▶ Anna exchanges land subject to a liability of $20,000 for $35,000 of stock owned by Mario. Mario takes the property subject to the liability. The amount realized by Anna is $55,000 ($35,000 + $20,000 liability assumed by Mario). If Anna's adjusted basis for the land exchanged is $42,000, her realized gain is $13,000 ($55,000 amount realized − $42,000 adjusted basis). ◀

In the above example, Anna receives stock with a $35,000 FMV and is relieved of a $20,000 debt. Mario's taking the property subject to the debt is equivalent to providing Anna with cash of $20,000. Thus, the amount realized by Anna is $55,000.

Generally, selling expenses such as sales commissions and advertising incurred in order to sell or dispose of the property reduce the amount realized.

EXAMPLE I5-6 ▶ Doug sells stock of Laser Corporation, which has a cost basis of $10,000, for $17,000. Doug pays a sales commission of $300 to sell the stock. The amount realized by Doug is $16,700 ($17,000 − $300) and he has a realized gain of $6,700 ($16,700 − $10,000). ◀

---

[5] Reg. Sec. 1.1001-1(c)(1).

[6] *CIR v. Homer H. Marshman*, 5 AFTR 2d 1528, 60-2 USTC ¶9484 (6th Cir., 1960).

[7] *Beulah B. Crane v. CIR*, 35 AFTR 776, 47-1 USTC ¶9217 (USSC, 1947).

TYPICAL MISCONCEPTION

The difference between the assumption of a liability and the taking of the property subject to the debt is sometimes confusing. The latter means that the lender can satisfy the debt only by repossessing the property. In the former case, where the buyer assumes the debt, the lender can satisfy the debt by repossessing the property and by going after other assets of the buyer.

ADJUSTED BASIS. The initial adjusted basis of property depends on how the property is acquired (e.g., by purchase, gift, or inheritance). Most property is acquired by purchase and therefore its initial basis is the cost of the property. However, if property is acquired from a decedent, its basis to the estate or heir is its FMV either at the date of death or, if the alternate valuation date is elected, six months from the date of death. The rules for determining the adjusted basis are discussed in subsequent sections of this chapter. Once the initial basis is determined, it may be adjusted upward or downward. Capital additions (also called capital expenditures) are expenditures that add to the value or prolong the life of property or adapt the property to a new or different use. Capital additions increase the basis. Capital recoveries, such as the deductions for casualty losses, cost recovery, and depreciation, reduce the basis. A property's adjusted basis can be determined by the following equation:

ETHICAL POINT

The taxpayer may have lost records relating to the basis of the assets acquired many years earlier. In that case, the CPA can accept estimates of the missing data made by the taxpayer.

Initial basis
\+ Capital additions (e.g., new porch for a building)
− Capital recoveries (e.g., depreciation deduction)
= Adjusted basis

Capital expenditures are distinguished from expenditures that are deductible as ordinary and necessary business expenses. For example, the cost of repairing a roof may be a deductible expense, whereas the cost of replacing a roof is a capital addition. It is sometimes difficult to determine whether an item is a capital expenditure or a business expense. Because of the preference for an immediate tax deduction, taxpayers normally prefer to classify expenditures as expenses rather than as capital expenditures.

EXAMPLE I5-7 ▶ Ellen pays $2,500 for a major overhaul of an automobile used in her trade or business. The $2,500 is capitalized as part of the automobile's cost rather than deducted as a repair expense. ◀

Capital recoveries reduce the adjusted basis. The most common form of capital recovery is the deduction for depreciation or cost recovery. As discussed in Chapter I10, the accelerated cost recovery system (ACRS) provides a deduction for cost recovery and applies to most property placed in service after December 31, 1980, and before 1987. A modified ACRS form of depreciation (MACRS) is mandatory for most tangible depreciable property placed in service after 1986.

EXAMPLE I5-8 ▶ Jeremy paid $100,000 for equipment two years ago and has claimed depreciation deductions of $37,000 for the two years. The cost of repairs during the same period was $6,000. At the end of the two-year period, the property's adjusted basis is $63,000 ($100,000 − $37,000). The amount spent for repairs does not affect the basis. ◀

ADDITIONAL COMMENT

In addition to depreciation, other capital recoveries that reduce the adjusted basis of property include depletion, amortization, corporate distributions that are a return of basis, compensation or awards for involuntary conversions, deductible casualty losses, insurance reimbursements, and cash rebates received by a purchaser.

RECOVERY OF BASIS DOCTRINE. The **recovery of basis doctrine** states that taxpayers are allowed to recover the basis of an asset without being taxed because such amounts are a return of capital that the taxpayer has invested in the property. If a taxpayer receives a $12,000 return of capital distribution from a corporation when the taxpayer's basis for its investment in the corporation's stock is $10,000, the first $10,000 received represents a recovery of basis and only the $2,000 excess amount is treated as a gain realized on a sale or exchange of the stock investment. In many cases, basis is recovered in the form of a deduction for depreciation, cost recovery, or a casualty loss.

TYPICAL MISCONCEPTION

It is sometimes incorrectly believed that all realized gains and losses are recognized for tax purposes. Although most realized gains are recognized, some realized losses are not. For example, losses on the sale or exchange of property held for personal use cannot be recognized.

RECOGNIZED GAIN OR LOSS

Realized gain or loss represents the difference between the amount realized and the adjusted basis when a sale or exchange occurs. The amount of gain or loss that is actually reported on the tax return is the **recognized gain or loss.** In some instances, gain or loss is not recognized due to special provisions in the tax law (e.g., a gain or loss may be deferred or a loss may be disallowed).

Losses are generally deductible if they are incurred in carrying on a trade or business, incurred in an activity engaged in for profit, and casualty and theft losses. Realized losses on the sale or exchange of assets held for personal use are not recognized for tax purposes. Therefore, a taxpayer who incurs a loss on the sale or exchange of a personal-use asset does not fully recover the basis. As explained in Chapter I8, realized losses on personal-use assets may be recognized to some extent if the property is disposed of by casualty or theft.

EXAMPLE I5-9 ▶ Ralph purchases a personal residence for $60,000. Deductions for depreciation are not allowed because the asset is not used in a trade or business or held for the production of income. If Ralph sells the house for $55,000, the realized loss of $5,000 is not deductible, and he recovers only $55,000 of his original $60,000 basis. ◀

BASIS CONSIDERATIONS

OBJECTIVE 3

Determine the basis of property

COST OF ACQUIRED PROPERTY

In most cases, the basis of property is its cost. Cost is the amount paid for the property in cash or the FMV of other property given in the exchange. Any costs of acquiring the property and preparing the property for use are included in the cost of the property.

EXAMPLE I5-10 ▶ Penny purchases equipment for $15,000 and pays delivery costs of $300. Installation costs of $250 are also incurred. The cost of the equipment is $15,550 ($15,000 + $300 + $250). ◀

Funds borrowed and used to pay for an asset are included in the cost. Obligations of the seller that are assumed by the buyer increase the asset's cost.

EXAMPLE I5-11 ▶ Peggy purchases an asset by paying cash of $40,000 and signs a note payable to the seller for $60,000. She also assumes a lien against the property in the amount of $2,000. Her basis for the asset is its cost of $102,000 ($40,000 + $60,000 + $2,000). The amount realized by the seller is $102,000. ◀

UNIFORM CAPITALIZATION RULES. Before 1987, taxpayers often had a degree of flexibility with respect to capitalizing or expensing certain costs. The Tax Reform Act of 1986 created one set of capitalization rules applicable to all taxpayers and all types of activities. These uniform capitalization rules, which apply principally to inventory, are provided in Sec. 263A and discussed in Chapter I11.

The uniform capitalization rules also affect property other than inventory if the property is used in a taxpayer's trade or business or in an activity engaged in for profit. Taxes paid or accrued in connection with the acquisition of property are included as part of the cost of the acquired property. Taxes paid or accrued in connection with the disposition of property reduce the amount realized on the disposition.[8]

ADDITIONAL COMMENT

The sales tax is a good example of a tax that would be paid in connection with the acquisition of property.

EXAMPLE I5-12 ▶ The Compact Corporation owns and operates a funeral home. The corporation purchases a hearse for $30,000 and pays sales taxes of $1,500. The cost basis for the hearse is $31,500 ($30,000 + $1,500). ◀

CAPITALIZATION OF INTEREST. Interest on debt paid or incurred during the production period to finance production expenditures incurred to construct, build, install, manufacture, develop, or improve real or tangible personal property must be capitalized.[9] The real or tangible personal property must have "a long useful life, an estimated production period exceeding two years, or an estimated production period exceeding one year and a cost exceeding $1,000,000."[10] Property has a long useful life if it is real property or property with a class life of at least 20 years. The production period starts when "production of the property begins and ends when the property is ready to be placed in service or is ready to be held for sale."[11]

EXAMPLE I5-13 ▶ The Indiana Corporation started construction of a $3 million motel on July 1, 2001, and borrowed an amount equal to the motel's construction costs. The motel is completed and ready for

[8] Sec. 164(a).
[9] Sec. 263A(f).
[10] Sec. 263A(f)(1)(B).
[11] Sec. 263A(f)(4)(B).

service on October 1, 2002. Interest incurred for the construction loan for the period from July 1, 2001 through October 1, 2002, is included in the motel's cost. The capitalized interest cost is depreciated over the motel's recovery period (see Chapter I10). ◀

ADDITIONAL COMMENT

If a stockholder leaves his or her stock with a broker in street name, the stockholder can specifically identify the shares sold by simply informing the broker which shares he or she wishes to sell. The date basis of the shares sold should appear on the confirmation from the broker.

IDENTIFICATION PROBLEMS. In most cases, the adjusted basis of property is easily identified with the property that is sold. However, problems occur when property is homogenous in nature such as when an investor owns several blocks of common stock of the same corporation that are purchased on different dates at different prices. The Regulations require the taxpayer to adequately identify the particular stock that is sold or exchanged.[12] Many investors allow brokers to hold their stock in street name (i.e., the brokerage firm holds title to the stock certificates) and thus do not make a physical transfer of securities. Such investors need to be careful to provide specific instructions to the broker as to which securities should be sold. If the stock sold or exchanged is not adequately identified, the first-in, first-out (FIFO) method must be used to identify the stock.[13] With the FIFO method, the stock sold or exchanged is presumed to come from the first lot or lots acquired.

EXAMPLE I5-14 ▶ Tammy purchased 300 shares of the Acme Corporation stock last year:

Month Acquired	*Size of Block*	*Basis*
January	100 shares	$4,000
May	100	5,000
October	100	6,000

In March of the current year Tammy sells 120 shares of the stock for $5,160. If Tammy specifically identifies the stock sold as being all of the stock purchased in October and 20 shares purchased in May, her realized loss is $1,840 [$5,160 − ($6,000 + $1,000)]. ◀

If Tammy did not specifically identify the stock that is sold, the FIFO method is used, and her realized gain is $160 [$5,160 − ($4,000 + $1,000)].

Owners of shares of mutual funds have more choices when determining the basis of shares sold. In addition to FIFO and specific identification, they may use an average cost method.

EXAMPLE I5-15 ▶ Colin purchased 100 shares of Bluejay Mutual Fund on May 10, 19Y1, for $1,000, and has been reinvesting dividends. On December 20, 19Y3, he sells 115 shares.

ADDITIONAL COMMENT

Because of the difficulty and complexity of tracking basis of shares in a mutual fund, the average cost method is widely used by taxpayers.

	Amount	*No. of Shares*
Purchase May 10, 19Y1	$1,000	100
Reinvested Dividend Nov. 1, 19Y1	125	10
Reinvested Dividends Nov. 1, 19Y2	140	7
Reinvested Dividends Nov. 1, 19Y3	185	8
	1,450	125
		$11.60 Average Cost

His basis for the 115 shares sold is $1,225 with FIFO, $1,334 (115 × $11.60) with average cost and could be as high as $1,350 with specific identification. Note that if he sells the shares obtained with the reinvested dividends in 19Y3, part of the gain or loss is short-term. ◀

PROPERTY RECEIVED AS A GIFT: GIFTS AFTER 1921

The basis of property received as a gift is generally the same as the donor's basis.[14] If the FMV of the property at time of the gift is less than the donor's basis, the donee may have to use one basis if the property is subsequently disposed of at a gain and another if the property is disposed of at a loss. As discussed later in this chapter, the basis may be increased by a portion or all of the gift tax paid because of the transfer.

---

[12] Reg. Sec. 1.1012-1(c)(1).

[13] For mutual fund investors, the IRS has authorized the use of FIFO, specific identification, or two average cost basis methods if only a portion of the fund shares is redeemed or sold. (See Reg. Sec. 1.1012-1(e) and Chapter I17).

[14] Sec. 1015(a).

ADDITIONAL COMMENT

Upon receipt of property from a relative, one should inquire as to its basis at that time. It might be years later that the asset is sold and the information about the donor's basis may be lost or forgotten.

Current rules for determining the donee's basis for property received as a gift are a function of the relationship between the FMV of the property at the time the gift is made and the donor's basis. If the FMV is equal to or greater than the donor's basis, the donee's basis is the same as the donor's basis for all purposes. However, if the FMV is less than the donor's basis, the donee has a dual basis for the property, that is, a basis for loss and a basis for gain. If the donee later transfers the property at a loss, the donee's basis is the property's FMV at the time of the gift (basis for loss). However, if the donee transfers the property at a gain, the donee's basis is the same as the donor's basis (basis for gain).

EXAMPLE I5-16 ▶ Kevin makes a gift of property with a basis of $350 to Janet when it has a $425 FMV. If Janet sells the property for $450, she has a realized gain of $100 ($450 − $350). If Janet sells the property for $330, she has a realized loss of $20 ($330 − $350). Because the FMV of the property at the time of the gift is more than the donor's basis, the donee's basis is $350 for determining both gain and loss. ◀

The following example illustrates the scenario when a taxpayer has a dual basis. The basis for determining a gain is different from the basis for determining a loss.

EXAMPLE I5-17 ▶ Chuck makes a gift of property with a basis of $600 to Maggie when the property has a $500 FMV. Maggie's basis for the property is $600 if the property is sold at a gain (i.e., for more than $600), but the basis is $500 if the property is sold at a loss (i.e., for less than $500). If the property is sold for $500 or more but not more than $600, no gain or loss is recognized. ◀

ADDITIONAL COMMENT

If Maggie in Example I5-17 sells the land for $750, she has a $150 gain. If she sells the land for $400, she has a $100 loss and there is no gain or loss if she sells the land for $560.

TAX STRATEGY TIP

Donors generally should not make gifts of property that have declined in value below original cost. Since the donee's basis will be the property's fair market value, the loss will never be recognized.

The dual basis rules were designed to prevent tax-avoidance schemes. Taxpayers are prevented from shifting unrealized losses to another taxpayer by making gifts of such "loss" property. For example, a low-income taxpayer who owns property that has depreciated in value might transfer the property by gift to a high-income taxpayer who would receive greater tax benefit from the deduction of the loss upon the subsequent sale of the property. The loss basis rules prevent the donee from recognizing a loss on the sale of the property because the basis for loss is the lesser of the donor's basis or FMV on the date of the gift.

EFFECT OF GIFT TAX ON BASIS. If the donor pays a gift tax on the transfer of property, the donee's basis may be increased. This increase occurs only if the FMV of the property exceeds the donor's basis on the date of the gift. For taxable gifts after 1976, the increase in the donee's basis is equal to a pro rata portion of the gift tax that is attributable to the unrealized appreciation in the property. The amount of the addition to the donee's basis is determined as follows:[15]

KEY POINT

No gift tax can be added to the basis of the property if the donor's basis is greater than the FMV of the property.

$$\text{Gift tax paid} \times \frac{\text{FMV at time of the gift} - \text{Donor's basis}}{\text{Amount of the gift}}$$

The amount of the gift is the FMV of the property less the amount of the annual exclusion.[16]

EXAMPLE I5-18 ▶ During the current year, Cindy makes one gift of property with a $21,000 basis to Jessie when the property has a $61,000 FMV. Cindy pays a gift tax of $20,500. The amount of the gift is $50,000 ($61,000 − $11,000). Thus, 80% [($61,000 − $21,000)/$50,000] of the gift tax is added to Jessie's basis. Jessie's basis for the property for determining both gain and loss is $37,400 [$21,000 + (0.80 × $20,500)]. ◀

EXAMPLE I5-19 ▶ During the current year, Sally makes a gift of property with a basis of $50,000 to Troy when the property has a $40,000 FMV. Sally pays a gift tax of $1,000. Troy's basis for the property is not affected by the gift tax paid by Sally because the FMV is less than the donor's basis at the time of the gift. Troy's basis for the property is $50,000 to determine gain and $40,000 to determine loss. ◀

---

[15] Sec. 1015(d)(6).

[16] Sec. 1015(d)(2) and Sec. 2503(b). For 2002, the annual exclusion for gifts has been increased to $11,000. Before 2002, an annual exclusion of $10,000 per year was allowed for each donee. See Chapter I1 for a limited discussion of the annual exclusion and Chapter C12 of the *Corporations, Partnerships, Estates, and Trusts* and *Comprehensive* volumes for a more detailed discussion.

STOP & THINK *Question:* Pete wants to make a gift of either ABC common stock (basis of $44,000 and FMV of $50,000) or XYZ common stock (basis of $73,000 and FMV of $50,000) to his nephew. Pete and his nephew have the same tax rate. Which stock should he give to his nephew?

Solution: Pete should give the ABC stock to his nephew because the nephew's basis for determining a gain or loss is $44,000 plus a portion of any gift tax Pete pays. The nephew's basis for XYZ common stock is $50,000 to determine a loss and $73,000 to determine a gain. If the nephew sells XYZ stock for less than $73,000, no loss is recognized and thus some of the basis is not used. Note that Pete would have a $23,000 loss if he sells the XYZ stock for $50,000. Furthermore, the nephew's basis for the XYZ stock is not increased if Pete has to pay a gift tax on the $40,000 taxable gift.

PROPERTY RECEIVED FROM A DECEDENT

The basis of property received from a decedent is generally the FMV of the property at the date of the decedent's death or an alternate valuation date.[17] This can result in either a step up (increase) or step down (decrease) in basis.

EXAMPLE I5-20 ▶ Patrick inherits property having an $80,000 FMV on the date of the decedent's death. The decedent's basis in the property is $47,000. The executor of the estate does not elect the alternate valuation date. Patrick's basis for the property is $80,000. ◀

EXAMPLE I5-21 ▶ Dianna inherits property having a $60,000 FMV at the date of the decedent's death. The decedent's basis in the property is $72,000. The alternate valuation date is not elected. Dianna's basis for the property is $60,000. ◀

REAL-WORLD EXAMPLE

The alternate valuation date was used in valuing the estates of many individuals owning large portfolios of common stocks who died shortly before the stock market crash in October 1987.

Instead of using the FMV on the date of death to determine the estate tax, the executor of the estate may elect to use the FMV on the alternate valuation date. The alternate valuation date is generally six months after the date of death. If the alternate valuation date is elected, the basis for all of the assets in the estate is their FMV on that date unless the property is distributed by the estate to the heirs or is sold before the alternate valuation date. If the alternate valuation date is used, property distributed or sold after the date of the decedent's death and before the alternate valuation date has a basis equal to its FMV on the date of distribution or the date it is disposed of.[18]

If the estate is small enough that an estate tax return is not required, the value of the property on the alternate valuation date may not be used.[19]

EXAMPLE I5-22 ▶ Marilyn inherits all of the property owned by an individual who dies in April, when the property has a $100,000 FMV. The value of the property six months later is $90,000. Because of the size of the estate, no estate tax is due. The alternate valuation date may not be used, and Marilyn's basis for the property is $100,000. Note that Marilyn does not want the alternate valuation date to be used because her basis would be $90,000 instead of $100,000. ◀

As noted above, the basis of the property to the estate and the heirs can be affected if the alternate valuation date is used to value the estate's assets. The alternate valuation date may be elected only if the value of the gross estate and the amount of estate tax after credits are reduced as a result of using the alternate valuation date.[20] This means that the aggregate value of the assets determined by using the alternate valuation date may be used only if the total value of the assets has decreased during the six-month period.

EXAMPLE I5-23 ▶ Helmut inherits all of the property owned by an individual who dies in March when the FMV of the property is $900,000. Six months after the date of death, the property has a $950,000 FMV.

---

[17] Sec. 1014(a).

[18] Sec. 2032(a).

[19] Rev. Rul. 56-60, 1956-1 C.B. 443. For a decedent dying after 2000 and in 2001 or 2002, Sec. 6018(a) requires an estate tax return to be filed if the gross estate exceeds $1,000,000.

[20] Credits available include the unified transfer tax credit and possibly credits for state death taxes, gift taxes, foreign death taxes, and the credit for taxes on prior transfers.

The property is distributed to Helmut in December. Use of the alternate valuation date is not permitted because the value of the gross estate has increased. Therefore, his basis in the property is $900,000, the FMV on the date of death. ◀

An executor may elect to use the alternate valuation date to reduce the estate taxes owed by the estate. However, the income tax basis of the property included in the estate is also reduced for the heirs who inherit the property.

EXAMPLE I5-24 ▶ Michelle inherits property with a $900,000 FMV at the date of the decedent's death. Because the FMV of the property on the alternate valuation date (six months after the date of the decedent's death) is $850,000, the executor of the estate elects to use $850,000 to value the property for estate tax purposes. Michelle's basis for the property is thus $850,000 instead of $900,000. ◀

COMMUNITY PROPERTY. If the decedent and the decedent's spouse own property under community property laws,[21] one-half of the property is included in the decedent's estate and its basis to the surviving spouse is its FMV.[22] The Internal Revenue Code also provides that the surviving spouse's one-half share of the community property is adjusted to the FMV.[23] In effect, the surviving spouse's share of the community property is considered to have passed from the decedent.

EXAMPLE I5-25 ▶ Matt and Jane, a married couple, live in Texas, a community property state, and jointly own land as community property that cost $110,000. The land has an $800,000 FMV when Jane dies, leaving all of her property to Matt. His basis for the entire property is $800,000. ◀

In a common law state, only one-half of the jointly owned property is included in the decedent's estate and is adjusted to its FMV. The survivor's share of the jointly held property is not adjusted.

EXAMPLE I5-26 ▶ Barry and Maria, a married couple, live in Iowa, a common law state, and jointly own land that cost $200,000. The property has a $700,000 FMV when Barry dies, leaving all of his property to Maria. Her basis for the land is $450,000 [$100,000 + (0.50 × $700,000)]. ◀

PROPERTY CONVERTED FROM PERSONAL USE TO BUSINESS USE

ADDITIONAL COMMENT

It is important to estimate the FMV of property at the time the property is converted from personal use to business use.

Often, taxpayers who own personal-use assets convert these assets to an income-producing use or for use in a trade or business. When this conversion occurs, the property's basis must be determined. The basis for computing depreciation is the lower of the FMV or the adjusted basis of the property at the time the asset is transferred from personal use to an income-producing use or for use in a trade or business.[24] This rule prevents taxpayers from obtaining the benefits of depreciation to the extent that the property has declined in value during the period that it is held for personal use.

EXAMPLE I5-27 ▶ Olga owns a boat that cost $2,000 and is used for personal enjoyment. At a time when the boat has a $1,400 FMV, Olga transfers the boat to her business of operating a marina. The basis for depreciation is $1,400 because the FMV is less than Olga's adjusted basis at the time of conversion to business use. The $600 decline ($2,000 − $1,400) that occurred while Olga used the boat for personal use may not be deducted as depreciation. ◀

REAL-WORLD EXAMPLE

A taxpayer sold a personal residence to a purchaser, and the purchaser rented the property from the taxpayer until financing could be secured. The rental agreement was executed simultaneously with the sales agreement and was incidental to the sale. The taxpayer was not permitted to recognize any loss on the sale because the property was never converted to rental property. *Henry B. Dawson*, 1972 PH T.C. Memo 31 TCM 5.

If the boat's FMV in Example I5-27 is more than $2,000, the basis for depreciation is $2,000 because the FMV is higher than its adjusted basis at the time the asset is transferred to business use.

If a personal-use asset is transferred to business use when its FMV is less than its adjusted basis, the basis for determining a loss on a subsequent sale or disposition of the property is its FMV on the date of the conversion to business use less any depreciation taken before the disposition.[25]

---

[21] Community property states are Arizona, California, Idaho, Louisiana, New Mexico, Nevada, Texas, and Washington. Wisconsin has a marital property law that is basically the same as community property.

[22] Sec. 1014(a).

[23] Sec. 1014(b)(6).

[24] Reg. Sec. 1.167(g)-1.

[25] Reg. Sec. 1.165-9(b)(2).

EXAMPLE I5-28 ▶ Susanna purchased a personal residence for $50,000 and subsequently converted the property to rental property. At the time of the conversion, the property had a $46,000 FMV. Assume depreciation of $20,700 has been deducted when the property is sold for $21,000. The basis of the property at the time of the sale is $25,300 ($46,000 − $20,700). Thus, her loss on the sale is $4,300 ($21,000 − $25,300). ◀

The rule for determining the basis, that is, lower of adjusted basis or FMV, applies only to the sale of converted property at a loss. The basis for determining gain is its adjusted basis at the time of conversion less any depreciation taken before the disposition.

EXAMPLE I5-29 ▶ Assume the same facts as in Example I5-28, except that the property is sold for $31,000 instead of $21,000. The basis of the property is $29,300 ($50,000 − $20,700) and her gain is $1,700 ($31,000 − $29,300). ◀

Without the rule for determining basis of personal-use property converted to business property, taxpayers would have an incentive to convert nonbusiness assets that have declined in value to business use before selling the asset to convert nondeductible losses into deductible losses.

EXAMPLE I5-30 ▶ Craig owns a personal-use asset with a basis of $80,000 and a $50,000 FMV. If he sells the asset for its FMV, the $30,000 loss ($50,000 − $80,000) is not deductible because losses on the sale of personal-use assets are not deductible. If Craig converts the asset to business use and then immediately sells the asset for $50,000, no loss is realized because the basis of the asset for purposes of determining loss is $50,000, the FMV when property was converted. ◀

REAL-WORLD EXAMPLE

A taxpayer purchased a group of lots and allocated the total cost evenly among the lots. The court, however, held that more cost should be allocated to the waterfront lots than to the interior lots. *Biscayne Bay Islands Co.*, 23 B.T.A. 731 (1931).

ALLOCATION OF BASIS

When property is obtained in one transaction and portions of the property are subsequently disposed of at different times, the basis of the property is allocated to the different portions of the property. Gain or loss is computed at the time of disposal for each portion. If one purchases a 20-acre tract of land and later sells the entire tract, an allocation of basis is not needed. However if the taxpayer divides the property into smaller tracts of land for resale, the cost of the 20-acre tract must be allocated among the smaller tracts of land.

BASKET PURCHASE. If more than one asset is acquired in a single purchase transaction (i.e., a basket purchase), the cost must be apportioned to the various assets acquired. The allocation is based on the relative FMVs of the assets.

EXAMPLE I5-31 ▶ Kelly purchases a duplex for $80,000 to use as a rental property. The land has a $15,000 FMV, and the building has a $65,000 FMV. Kelly's bases for the land and the building are $15,000 and $65,000, respectively. ◀

SELF-STUDY QUESTION

If Kelly in Example I5-31 paid $2,000 for the cost of a title search and other costs that must be capitalized, what is the basis of the land and building?

ANSWER

Land $15,375
Building $66,625

Because no depreciation deduction is allowed for land, taxpayers tend to favor a liberal allocation of the total purchase price to the building. Appraisals or other measures of FMV may be used to make the allocation.

COMMON COSTS. As in the case of financial accounting, common costs incurred to obtain or prepare an asset for service must be capitalized and allocated to the basis of the individual assets.

EXAMPLE I5-32 ▶ Priscilla acquires three machines for $60,000, which have FMVs of $30,000, $20,000, and $10,000, respectively. Costs of delivery amount to $2,000, and costs to install the three machines amount to $1,000. The total installation and delivery costs of $3,000 are allocated to each of the three machines based on their FMVs.

The allocation of the $3,000 of common costs occurs as follows:

$$\text{Machine No. 1:}\quad \frac{\$30{,}000 \text{ FMV}}{\$30{,}000 + \$20{,}000 + \$10{,}000} \times \$3{,}000 = \$1{,}500$$

$$\text{Machine No. 2:}\quad \frac{\$20{,}000 \text{ FMV}}{\$30{,}000 + \$20{,}000 + \$10{,}000} \times \$3{,}000 = \$1{,}000$$

$$\text{Machine No. 3: } \frac{\$10{,}000 \text{ FMV}}{\$30{,}000 + \$20{,}000 + \$10{,}000} \times \$3{,}000 = \$500$$

The bases for each of the three machines are $31,500, $21,000, and $10,500, respectively. ◀

NONTAXABLE STOCK DIVIDENDS RECEIVED. If a nontaxable stock dividend is received, a portion of the basis of the stock on which the stock dividend is received is allocated to the new shares received from the stock dividend.[26] The cost basis of the previously acquired shares is then reduced by the amount of basis that is allocated to the stock dividend shares. If the stock received as a stock dividend is the same type as the stock owned before the dividend, the total basis of the stock owned before the dividend is allocated equally to all shares now owned.

EXAMPLE I5-33 ▶ Wayne owns 1,000 shares of Bell Corporation common stock with a $44,000 basis. Wayne receives a nontaxable 10% common stock dividend and now owns 1,100 shares of common stock. The basis for each share of common stock is now $40 ($44,000 ÷ 1,100). ◀

If the stock received as a stock dividend is not the same type as the stock owned before the dividend, the allocation is based on relative FMVs.

EXAMPLE I5-34 ▶ Stacey owns 500 shares of Montana Corporation common stock with a $60,000 basis. She receives a nontaxable stock dividend payable in 50 shares of preferred stock. At time of the distribution, the common stock has a $40,000 FMV ($80 × 500 shares), and the preferred stock has a $10,000 FMV ($200 × 50 shares). After the distribution, Stacey owns 50 shares of preferred stock with a basis of $12,000 [($10,000 ÷ $50,000) × $60,000]. Thus, $12,000 of the basis of the common stock is allocated to the preferred stock and the basis of the common stock is reduced from $60,000 to $48,000. ◀

KEY POINT

Corporations issue stock rights to shareholders so that the shareholders will be able to maintain their same proportional ownership in the corporation. This is called the preemptive right.

NONTAXABLE STOCK RIGHTS RECEIVED. Stock rights represent rights to acquire shares of a specified corporation's stock at a specific exercise price when certain conditions are met. The exercise price is usually less than the market price when the stock rights are issued. Stock rights may be distributed to employees as compensation, and they are often issued to shareholders to encourage them to purchase more stock, thereby providing more capital for the corporation.

If the FMV of nontaxable stock rights received is less than 15% of the FMV of the stock, the basis of the stock rights is zero unless the taxpayer elects to allocate the basis between the stock rights and the stock owned before distribution of the stock rights.[27]

EXAMPLE I5-35 ▶ Tina owns 100 shares of Bear Corporation common stock with a $27,000 basis and a $50,000 FMV. She receives 100 nontaxable stock rights with a total FMV of $4,000. Because the FMV of the stock rights is less than 15% of the FMV of the stock (0.15 × $50,000 = $7,500), the basis of the stock rights is zero unless Tina elects to make an allocation. ◀

REAL-WORLD EXAMPLE

In 1993, United States Cellular Corporation issued one right for each common share held. Each whole right entitled the holder to buy one common share for $33.

If in Example I5-35, Tina elects to allocate the basis of $27,000 between the stock rights and the stock, the basis of the rights is $2,000 ([$4,000 ÷ $54,000] × $27,000) and the basis of the stock is $25,000 ([$50,000 ÷ $54,000] × $27,000).

The decision to allocate the basis affects the gain or loss realized on the sale or disposition of the stock rights because the basis of the rights is zero unless an allocation is made. Furthermore, the basis of any stock acquired by exercising the rights is affected by whether or not a portion of the basis is allocated to the rights. The basis of stock acquired by exercising the stock rights is the amount paid plus the basis of the stock rights exercised.

EXAMPLE I5-36 ▶ George receives 10 stock rights as a nontaxable distribution, and no basis is allocated to the stock rights. With each stock right, George may acquire one share of stock for $20. If he exercises all 10 stock rights, the new stock acquired has a basis of $200 ($20 × 10 shares). If George sells all 10 stock rights for $135, he has a realized gain of $135 ($135 − 0). ◀

---

[26] Sec. 307(a).

[27] Sec. 307(b)(1).

If the FMV of a nontaxable stock right received is equal to or greater than 15% of the FMV of the stock, the basis of the stock owned before the distribution must be allocated between the stock and the stock rights.

EXAMPLE I5-37 ▶ Helen owns 100 shares of NMO common stock with a $14,000 basis and a $30,000 FMV. She receives 100 stock rights with a total FMV of $5,000. Because the FMV of the stock rights is at least 15% of the FMV of the stock, the $14,000 basis must be allocated between the stock rights and the stock. The basis of the stock rights is $2,000 [($5,000 ÷ $35,000) × $14,000] and the basis of the stock is $12,000 [($30,000 ÷ $35,000) × $14,000]. ◀

A recipient of stock rights generally has three courses of action. The stock rights can be sold or exchanged, in which case the basis allocated to the stock rights, if any, is used to determine the gain or loss. The stock rights may be exercised, and any basis allocated to the rights is added to the purchase price of the acquired stock. The stock rights may be allowed to expire, in which case no loss is recognized, and any basis allocated to the rights is reallocated back to the stock. If the stock rights received in Example I5-37 expire without being exercised, Helen does not recognize a loss and the basis of her 100 shares of common stock is $14,000.

Property basis rules are highlighted in Topic Review I5-1.

Topic Review I5-1

Property Basis Rules

METHOD ACQUIRED	BASIS OF THE ACQUIRED PROPERTY
1. Acquired by direct purchase	1. Basis includes the amount paid for the property, costs of preparing the property for use, obligations of the seller that are assumed by the buyer, and liabilities to which the property is subject.
2. Acquired as a gift. (a) FMV on the date of the gift is equal to or greater than the donor's basis (b) FMV on the date of the gift is less than the donor's basis	2. (a) The donee's basis is the same as the donor's basis plus a pro rata portion of the gift tax attributable to the property's unrealized appreciation at the time of the gift. (b) The donee's gain basis is the donor's basis and the loss basis is FMV. No increase for any gift tax paid.
3. Received from a decedent (a) Alternative valuation date is not elected (b) Alternative valuation date is elected	3. (a) The basis is its FMV on the date of death. (b) The basis of nondistributed property is its FMV on the alternative valuation date. If the property is distributed or sold before this date, its basis is FMV on the date of sale or distribution.
4. Converted from personal to business use	4. The basis for a loss (as well as for depreciation) is the lesser of its adjusted basis or FMV at the date of conversion. The basis for a gain is its adjusted basis at the date of conversion.
5. Nontaxable stock dividend	5. Basis of the stock dividend shares includes a pro rata portion of the adjusted basis of the underlying shares owned.
6. Nontaxable stock right	6. If the FMV of the rights is less than 15% of the stock's FMV, the basis of the rights is zero unless an election is made to allocate basis. Basis of the underlying stock is allocated to the rights based on the respective FMV's of the stock and the rights.

DEFINITION OF A CAPITAL ASSET

OBJECTIVE 4

Distinguish between capital assets and other assets

Instead of defining capital assets, Sec. 1221 provides a list of properties that are **not** capital assets. Thus, a capital asset is any property owned by a taxpayer *other* than the types of property specified in Sec. 1221. Property which is not a capital asset includes the following:

1. Inventory or property held primarily for sale to customers in the ordinary course of a trade or business.
2. Property used in the trade or business and subject to the allowance for depreciation provided in Sec. 167 or real property used in a trade or business. (As explained in Chapter I13, these properties are referred to as *Sec. 1231 assets* if held by the taxpayer more than one year.)
3. Accounts or notes receivable acquired in the ordinary course of a trade or business for services rendered or from the sale of property described in item 1.
4. Other assets including
   a. A letter, memorandum, or similar property held by a taxpayer for whom such property was prepared or produced.
   b. A copyright; a literary, musical, or artistic composition; a letter or memorandum; or similar property held by a taxpayer whose personal efforts created such property or whose basis in the property for determining a gain is determined by reference to the basis of such property in the hands of one who created the property or one for whom such property was prepared or produced.
   c. A U.S. government publication held by a taxpayer who receives the publication by any means other than a purchase at the price the publication is offered for sale to the public.
   d. A U.S. government publication held by a taxpayer whose basis in the property for determining a gain is determined by reference to the basis of such property in the hands of a taxpayer in item 4c (e.g., certain property received by gift).

TYPICAL MISCONCEPTION

It is common in financial accounting classes to include property used in a trade or business in the definition of a capital asset. For example, factory buildings, machinery, trucks, and office buildings would be defined as capital assets. However, such items are not capital assets for tax purposes.

EXAMPLE I5-38 ▶ Maxine owns a building used in her business. Other business assets include equipment, inventory, and accounts receivable. None of the assets are classified as capital assets. ◀

Chapter I13 provides an in-depth discussion of business assets such as buildings, land, and equipment. Although these items are not capital assets, Sec. 1231 provides in many cases that the gain on the sale or exchange of such an asset is eventually taxed as LTCG.

EXAMPLE I5-39 ▶ Eric owns an automobile that is held for personal use and also owns a copyright for a book he has written. Because the copyright is held by the taxpayer whose personal efforts created the property, it is not a capital asset. The automobile held for personal use is a capital asset. ◀

SELF-STUDY QUESTION

Doug owns a personal residence, an automobile, 100 shares of Ford Motor Company, and a poem he wrote for his girlfriend. Which of these assets are capital assets?

ANSWER

All of the items are capital assets except the poem, which is a literary composition.

By analyzing Examples I5-38 and I5-39, one can conclude that the classification of an asset is often determined by its use. An automobile used in a trade or business is not a capital asset but is considered a capital asset when it is held for personal use. Examples of assets that qualify as capital assets include a personal residence, land held for personal use, and investments in stocks and bonds. In addition, certain types of assets are specifically given capital asset status, such as patents, franchises, etc. These and other special assets are discussed later in this chapter.

INFLUENCE OF THE COURTS

In *Corn Products Refining Co.*, the Supreme Court rendered a landmark decision when it determined that the sale of futures contracts related to the purchase of raw materials resulted in ordinary rather than capital gains and losses.[28] The Corn Products Company, a

[28] *Corn Products Refining Co. v. CIR*, 47 AFTR 1789, 55-2 USTC ¶9746 (USSC, 1955).

ADDITIONAL COMMENT

If an asset such as an automobile is used in part in a trade or business and in part for personal use, then the business part of the car is not a capital asset, but the other part is a capital asset.

ETHICAL POINT

A CPA should not prepare or sign a tax return for a client unless the position or issue has (1) a realistic possibility of being sustained on its merits, or (2) is not frivolous and is adequately disclosed in the return.

manufacturer of products made from grain corn, purchased futures contracts for corn to ensure an adequate supply of raw materials. While delivery of the corn was accepted when needed for manufacturing operations, unneeded contracts were later sold. Corn Products contended that any gains or losses on the sale of the unneeded contracts should be capital gains and losses because futures contracts are customarily viewed as security investments, which qualify as capital assets. The Supreme Court held that these transactions represented an integral part of the business for the purpose of protecting the company's manufacturing operations and that the gains and losses should, therefore, be ordinary in nature.

Although the *Corn Products* doctrine has been interpreted as creating a nonstatutory exception to the definition of a capital asset when the asset is purchased for business purposes, the Supreme Court ruled in the 1988 *Arkansas Best Corporation* case that the motivation for acquiring assets is irrelevant to the question of whether assets are capital assets. Arkansas Best, a bank holding company, sold shares of a bank's stock that had been acquired for the purpose of protecting its business reputation. Relying on the *Corn Products* doctrine, the company deducted the loss as ordinary. The Supreme Court ruled that the loss was a capital loss because the stock is within the broad definition of the term *capital asset* in Sec. 1221 and is outside the classes of property that are excluded from capital-asset status.[29] *Arkansas Best* apparently limits the application of *Corn Products* to hedging transactions that are an integral part of a taxpayer's system of acquiring inventory.

OTHER IRC PROVISIONS RELEVANT TO CAPITAL GAINS AND LOSSES

A number of IRC sections provide special treatment for certain types of assets and transactions. For example, loss on the sale or exchange of certain small business stock that qualifies as Sec. 1244 stock is treated as an ordinary loss rather than a capital loss to the extent of $50,000 per year ($100,000 if the taxpayer is married and files a joint return).[30]

ADDITIONAL COMMENT

For purposes of Sec. 1236, a security is defined as any share of stock in any corporation, note, bond, debenture, or evidence of indebtedness, or any evidence of an interest in or right to subscribe to or purchase any of the above.

DEALERS IN SECURITIES. Normally, a security dealer's gain on the sale or exchange of securities is ordinary income. Section 1236 provides an exception for dealers in securities if the dealer clearly identifies that the property is held for investment. This act of identification must occur before the close of the day on which the security is acquired, and the security must not be held primarily for sale to customers in the ordinary course of the dealer's trade or business at any time after the close of the day of purchase.

EXAMPLE I5-40 ▶ Allyson, a dealer in securities, purchases Cook Corporation stock on April 8, and identifies the stock as being held for investment on that date. Four months later, Allyson sells the stock. Any gain or loss recognized due to the sale is capital gain or loss. ◀

Once a dealer clearly identifies a security as being held for investment, any loss on the sale or exchange of the security is treated as a capital loss.

EXAMPLE I5-41 ▶ Kris, a dealer in securities, purchases Boston Corporation stock and clearly identifies the stock as being held for investment on the date of purchase. Eight months later, the security is removed from the investment account and held as inventory. If the security is later sold at a gain, the gain is an ordinary gain. However, if the stock is sold at a loss, the loss is a capital loss. ◀

For tax years ending on or after December 31, 1993, securities dealers must use the mark-to-market method for their inventory of securities. Securities must be valued at FMV at the end of each taxable year. Dealers in securities recognize gain or loss each year as if the security is sold on the last day of the tax year. Gains and losses are generally treated as ordinary rather than capital. Gains or losses due to adjustments in subsequent years or resulting from the sale of the security must be adjusted to reflect gains and losses already taken into account when determining taxable income.[31]

---

[29] *Arkansas Best Corporation v. CIR*, 61 AFTR 2d 88-655, 88-1 USTC ¶9210 (USSC, 1988).

[30] Secs. 1244(a) and (b). (See Chapter I8 for additional discussion on small business corporation stock losses.)

[31] Sec. 475. The mark-to-market rule also applies to some securities that are not inventory, but does not apply to any security that is held for investment and certain other transactions (see Sec. 475(b)).

EXAMPLE I5-42 ▶ Jim Spikes, a dealer in securities and calendar-year taxpayer, purchases a security for inventory on October 10, 2002, for $10,000 and sells the security for $18,000 on July 1, 2003. The security's FMV on December 31, 2002 is $15,000. Jim recognizes $5,000 of ordinary income in 2002 and $3,000 of ordinary income in 2003. ◀

REAL PROPERTY SUBDIVIDED FOR SALE. A taxpayer who engages in regular sales of real estate is considered to be a dealer, and any gain or loss recognized is ordinary gain or loss rather than capital gain or loss. A special relief provision is provided in Sec. 1237 for nondealer, noncorporate taxpayers who subdivide a tract of real property into lots (two or more pieces of real property are considered to be a tract if they are contiguous). Part or all of the gain on the sale of the lots may be treated as a capital gain if the following provisions of Sec. 1237 are satisfied:

ADDITIONAL COMMENT

The conversion of an apartment building into condominiums does not qualify under Sec. 1237, even if the property has been held for five years and no substantial improvements have been made.

- During the year of sale, the noncorporate taxpayer must not hold any other real property primarily for sale in the ordinary course of business.
- Unless the property is acquired by inheritance or devise, the lots sold must be held by the taxpayer for a period of at least five years.
- No substantial improvement may be made by the taxpayer while holding the lots if the improvement substantially enhances the value of the lot.[32]
- The tract or any lot may not have been previously held primarily for sale to customers in the ordinary course of the taxpayer's trade or business unless such tract at that time was covered by Sec. 1237.

The primary advantage of Sec. 1237 is that potential controversy with the IRS is avoided as to whether a taxpayer who subdivides investment property is a dealer. Section 1237 does not apply to losses. Such losses are capital losses if the property is held for investment purposes, or ordinary losses if the taxpayer is a dealer.

If the Sec. 1237 requirements are satisfied, all gain on the sale of the first five lots may be capital gain. Starting in the tax year during which the sixth lot is sold, 5% of the selling price for all lots sold in that year and succeeding years is ordinary income.

EXAMPLE I5-43 ▶ Jean subdivides a tract of land held as an investment into seven lots, and all requirements of Sec. 1237 are satisfied. The lots have a fair market value of $10,000 each and have a basis of $4,000. Jean incurs no selling expenses and sells four lots in 2002 and three lots in 2003. In 2002, all of the $24,000 [4 lots × ($10,000 − $4,000)] gain is capital gain. In 2003, the year in which the sixth lot is sold, $1,500 of the gain is ordinary income [0.05 × ($10,000 × 3 lots)], and the remaining $16,500 {[3 lots × ($10,000 − $4,000)] − $1,500} gain is capital gain. ◀

EXAMPLE I5-44 ▶ Assume the same facts as in Example I5-43, except that all seven lots are sold in 2002. The amount of ordinary income recognized is $3,500 [0.05 × ($10,000 × 7 lots)], and the remaining $38,500 {[7 lots × ($10,000 − $4,000)] − $3,500} gain is capital gain. ◀

ADDITIONAL COMMENT

If a taxpayer sells any lots from a tract and does not sell any others for a period of five years, the remaining property is considered a new tract.

Based on Examples I5-43 and I5-44, the advantage of selling no more than five lots in the first year should be apparent. Expenditures incurred to sell or exchange the lots are also treated favorably because they are first applied against the portion of the gain treated as ordinary income. Because selling expenses (e.g., commissions) are often equal to or greater than 5% of the selling price, this offset against ordinary income may result in the elimination of the ordinary income portion of the gain. Selling expenses in excess of the gain taxed as ordinary income reduce the amount realized on the sale or exchange.

NONBUSINESS BAD DEBT. Although the topic of bad debts is discussed in Chapter I8, it is important to note that bad debt losses from nonbusiness debts are deductible only as short-term capital losses (STCLs).[33] This treatment applies regardless of when the debt occurred. A nonbusiness bad debt is deductible only in the year in which the debt becomes totally worthless.

---

[32] Certain improvements are not treated as substantial under Sec. 1237(b)(3) if the lot is held for at least ten years.

[33] Sec. 166(d)(1)(B).

EXAMPLE I5-45 ▶ Two years ago, Alice loaned $4,000 to a friend. During the current year, the friend declares bankruptcy and the debt is entirely worthless. Assuming that Alice has no other gains and losses from the sale or exchange of capital assets during the year, she deducts $3,000 in determining adjusted gross income (AGI) and has a STCL carry forward of $1,000. ◀

TAX TREATMENT FOR CAPITAL GAINS AND LOSSES OF NONCORPORATE TAXPAYERS

OBJECTIVE 5

Understand how capital gains and losses affect taxable income

To recognize capital gain or loss, it is necessary to have a sale or exchange of a capital asset. Once it is determined that a capital gain or loss has been realized and is to be recognized, it is necessary to classify the gains and losses as either short-term or long-term. If the asset is held for one year or less, the gain or loss is classified as a short-term capital gain (STCG) or a short-term capital loss (STCL). If the capital asset is held for more than one year, the gain or loss is classified as a long-term capital gain (LTCG) or long-term capital loss (LTCL).[34]

CAPITAL GAINS

ADDITIONAL COMMENT

1996 was a good year for taxpayers owning capital assets. Total net capital gains reported that year were $245.9 billion, up 50.5% from 1995. Net capital losses were $8.8 billion, down 8.0%.

Net capital gain (NCG), which may receive favorable tax treatment, is defined as the excess of net long-term capital gain over net short-term capital loss.[35] NCG may be taxed at 8%, 10%, 18%, 20%, 25% or 28%. Part or all of NCG may be adjusted net capital gain (ANCG). ANCG, which is explained later, is subject to the lower rates of 10% and 20%. ANCG may be taxed at rates as low as 8% or 18% for tax years beginning after December 31, 2000, if the holding period is more than five years.[36]

To compute net capital gain, first determine all STCGs, STCLs, LTCGs, LTCLs, and then net gains and losses as described below.

NET SHORT-TERM CAPITAL GAIN. If total STCGs for the tax year exceed total STCLs for that year, the excess is defined as net short-term capital gain (NSTCG). As discussed later, NSTCG may be offset by net long-term capital loss (NLTCL).

EXAMPLE I5-46 ▶ Hal has two transactions involving the sale of capital assets during the year. As a result of those transactions, he has a STCG of $4,000 and a STCL of $3,000. Hal's NSTCG is $1,000 ($4,000 – $3,000), and his AGI increases by $1,000. His gross income increases by $4,000, and he is entitled to a $3,000 deduction for AGI. ◀

NET LONG-TERM CAPITAL GAIN. If the total LTCGs for the tax year exceed the total LTCLs for that year, the excess is defined as net long-term capital gain (NLTCG). As indicated earlier, a NCG exists when NLTCG exceeds net short-term capital loss (NSTCL).

EXAMPLE I5-47 ▶ Clay has two transactions involving the sale of capital assets during the year. As a result of the transactions, he has a LTCG of $4,000 and a LTCL of $3,000. Clay has a NLTCG and a net capital gain of $1,000. His AGI increases by $1,000. ◀

EXAMPLE I5-48 ▶ Linda has four transactions involving the sale of capital assets during the year. As a result of the transactions, she has a STCG of $5,000, a STCL of $7,000, a LTCG of $10,000, and a LTCL of $2,000. After the initial netting of short-term and long-term gains and losses, Linda has a NSTCL of $2,000 ($7,000 – $5,000) and a NLTCG of $8,000 ($10,000 – $2,000). Because the NLTCG exceeds the NSTCL by $6,000 ($8,000 – $2,000), her NCG is $6,000. ◀

---

[34] While the Taxpayer Relief Act of 1997 reduced the rates for most LTCGs, it increased the required holding period to more than 18 months to be eligible for the lower rates of 10% and 20%. During the last few months of 1997, gain resulting from the sale of a capital asset might be taxed at many different rates depending on whether or not the holding period is one year or less, more than one year but not more than 18 months, or more than 18 months. These changes in the law dramatically increased the complexity associated with the taxation of capital gains. The 1998 Restructuring and Reform Act eliminated the more than 18-month holding period requirement for tax years ending after 1997 and returned to the more than one year requirement to be LTCG.

[35] Sec. 1222(11).

[36] Sec. 1(h).

LOWER RATES FOR ADJUSTED NET CAPITAL GAIN (ANCG). The new rates of 20% and 10% apply to ANCG recognized for sales after May 6, 1997, and the rate to use depends upon the taxpayer's tax bracket. The maximum rate for ANCG recognized by noncorporate taxpayers (individuals, estates and trusts) is 20% unless the taxpayer's regular tax rate is 15%. Taxpayers whose rate is 15% are subject to a rate of only 10% on ANCG.[37]

EXAMPLE I5-49 ▶ Sandy is single with taxable income of $100,000 without considering the sale of Merck stock during the current year for $15,000. The stock was purchased four years earlier for $3,000. Sandy has $12,000 of NLTCG which is ANCG taxed at 20%. ◀

EXAMPLE I5-50 ▶ Assume the same facts as in Example I5-49 except Sandy's taxable income without the capital gain is $11,400. The $12,000 ANCG is taxed at 10% because her taxable income is less than the $27,950 that is subject to the 15% rate.

Computation of the tax becomes more complicated if the ANCG causes taxable income to exceed the amount subject to the 15% tax rate, i.e., $27,950 for a single taxpayer. If a single taxpayer has taxable income of $30,000 that includes $9,000 of ANCG, the taxpayer's tax is determined as follows:

Tax on $21,000 (taxable income without the ANCG)	$2,850	($6,000 × 10%) + ($15,000 × 15%)
+ Tax on $6,950 ($27,950 − $21,000) of the ANCG at 10%	695	($6,950 × 10%)
+ Tax on $2,050 ($9,000 − $6,950) at 20% because the taxable income is greater than $27,950.	410	($2,050 × 20%)
Total tax	$3,955	

◀

SELF-STUDY QUESTION

Mary sells common stock for a gain of $10,000 on December 29, 2002. The settlement date, or date that Mary will receive the proceeds from the stockbroker, is January 2, 2003. Will Mary report the gain on her 2002 or 2003 tax return?

ANSWER

Mary is required to report the gain in the year of the sale (2002). Losses are also recognized in the year of sale.

ADJUSTED NET CAPITAL GAINS (ANCG)

ANCG is NCG without regard to:

1. 28-percent rate gain and
2. unrecaptured section 1250 gain.[38]

The term *28-percent rate gain* is the sum of collectibles gain and section 1202 gain over the sum of collectibles loss, NSTCL and LTCL carried forward from a preceding year.

For many taxpayers, NCG and ANCG will be the same amount. Collectibles gain is explained below. Section 1202 gain refers to the 50% exclusion of net capital gain discussed in Chapter I4 and below. Unrecaptured Sec. 1250 gain which is taxed at a maximum rate of 25% may occur when a building is sold and is explained in Chapter I13.

COLLECTIBLES GAIN. As a general rule, gains resulting from the sale of collectibles such as artwork, rugs, antiques, stamps and most coins are not taxed at the lower tax rates of 10% and 20% but may be taxed at a maximum rate of 28%. Recall that NCG is reduced by collectibles gains to determine ANCG.

EXAMPLE I5-51 ▶ Danny, whose tax rate is 35%, purchased Bowling common stock and antique chairs for investment on March 10, 2000. He sells the assets in April of 2002 and has a gain of $8,000 on the sale of the stock and $10,000 on the sale of the antique chairs. His NLTCG is $18,000, and his NCG is $18,000. His ANCG is $8,000 since $10,000 of the NCG is a collectibles gain. His tax on the capital gains is $4,400 [(20% × $8,000) + (28% × $10,000)] ◀

SEC. 1202 GAIN. As explained in Chapter I4, Sec. 1202 provides that noncorporate taxpayers may exclude 50% of the gain resulting from the sale or exchange of qualified small business stock (QSBS) issued after August 10, 1993, if the stock is held for more than five years. A corporation may have QSBS only if the corporation is a C corporation and at least 80% of the value of its assets must be used in the active conduct of one or more qualified trades or businesses.[39]

[37] Sec. 1(h).
[38] Sec. 1(h)(4).
[39] Sec. 1202.

Normally, the excluded gain is 50% of any gain resulting from the sale or exchange of QSBS held for more than five years and the remaining half of the gain is taxed at a maximum rate of 28%. However, the excluded gain may be less than 50% of the gain, because the amount of gain that may be excluded by a taxpayer for one corporation is 50% of the greater of $10,000,000 or ten times the aggregate basis of the qualified stock. If gain on the sale of QSBS is $11.4 million and $5 million of the gain is excluded, $5 million of the gain is taxed at 28% and the remaining $1.4 million gain is taxed at 20%.

EXAMPLE I5-52 ▶ Raef purchased $200,000 of newly issued Monona common stock on October 1, 1997. On December 15, 2002, he sells the stock for $4 million, resulting in a $3.8 million gain. He excludes $1.9 million of the gain, and the remaining $1.9 million of gain is Sec. 1202 gain taxed at 28%. ◀

EXAMPLE I5-53 ▶ Matthew, whose tax rate is 30%, has the following capital gains this year:

STCG	$10,000
LTCG (artwork)	12,000
LTCG (stock of AT&T)	17,000
LTCG (QSBS held more than five years)	45,000

Matthew may exclude $22,500 of the $45,000 Sec. 1202 gain. His NCG is $51,500 ($12,000 + $17,000 + $22,500). His ANCG is $17,000. The increase in his tax is $16,060. [30%($10,000) + 28%($12,000) + 20%($17,000) + 28%($22,500)] ◀

ADDITIONAL COMMENT

If Raef's gain in Example 5-52 is $12 million, he excludes $5 million, $5 million of the gain is taxed at 28%, and $2 million is taxed at 20%.

CAPITAL LOSSES

To have a capital loss, one must sell or exchange the capital asset for an amount less than its adjusted basis. As in the case of capital gains, the one-year period is used to determine whether the capital loss is short-term or long-term.

NET SHORT-TERM CAPITAL LOSS. If total STCLs for the tax year exceed total STCGs for that year, the excess is defined as a net short-term capital loss (NSTCL). As indicated above, the NSTCL is first offset against any NLTCG to determine the net capital gain.

If the NSTCL exceeds the NLTCG, the capital loss may be offset, in part, against other income. The NSTCL may be deducted in full (i.e., on a dollar-for-dollar basis) against a noncorporate taxpayer's ordinary income for amounts up to $3,000 in any one year.[40]

EXAMPLE I5-54 ▶ Bob has gross income of $60,000 before considering capital gains and losses. If Bob has a NLTCG of $10,000 and a NSTCL of $15,000, he has $5,000 of NSTCL in excess of NLTCG and may deduct $3,000 of the losses from gross income. Assuming no other deductions for AGI, Bob's AGI is $57,000 ($60,000 − $3,000). ◀

ADDITIONAL COMMENT

A husband and wife filing a joint return may use capital losses carried forward from years when they were single. Also, a divorced couple may use capital losses carried forward from a joint return year to their single returns.

In Example I5-54, $10,000 of the NSTCL is used to offset the $10,000 of NLTCG, and $3,000 of the NSTCL is used to reduce ordinary income. However, $2,000 of the loss is not used. This net capital loss is carried forward for an indefinite number of years.[41] The loss retains its original character and will be treated as a STCL occurring in the subsequent year. If a taxpayer dies with an unused capital loss carryover, it expires.

EXAMPLE I5-55 ▶ Last year, Milt had a NSTCL of $8,000 and a NLTCG of $2,600. The netting of short-term and long-term gains and losses resulted in a $5,400 excess of NSTCL over NLTCG, and $3,000 of this amount was offset against ordinary income. Milt's NSTCL carryforward is $2,400. During the current year he sells a capital asset and generates a STCG of $800. His NSTCL is $1,600 ($2,400 − $800), and the loss is offset against $1,600 of ordinary income. ◀

REAL-WORLD EXAMPLE

In 1975 an amendment was added to a tax bill in the House Ways and Means Committee that would have permitted individuals to take a three-year carryback for capital losses. When *The Wall Street Journal* disclosed that the provision would provide Ross Perot with a $15 million tax break, the amendment was defeated.

NET LONG-TERM CAPITAL LOSS. If total LTCLs for the tax year exceed total LTCGs for the year, the excess is defined as net long-term capital loss (NLTCL). If there is both a NSTCG and a NLTCL, the NLTCL is initially offset against the NSTCG on a dollar-for-dollar basis. If the NLTCL exceeds the NSTCG, the excess is offset against ordinary income on a dollar-for-dollar basis up to $3,000 per year.

---

[40] Sec. 1211(b). A $1,500 limitation applies to a married individual filing a separate return.

[41] Sec. 1212(b) and Reg. Sec. 1.1212-1(b).

EXAMPLE I5-56 ▶ In the current year, Gordon has a NLTCL of $9,000 and a NSTCG of $2,000. He must use $2,000 of the NLTCL to offset the $2,000 NSTCG, and then use $3,000 of the $7,000 ($9,000 − $2,000) NLTCL to offset $3,000 of ordinary income. Gordon's carryforward of NLTCL is $4,000 [$9,000 − ($2,000 + $3,000)]. This amount is treated as a LTCL in subsequent years. ◀

If an individual has both NSTCL and NLTCL, the NSTCL is offset against ordinary income first, regardless of when the transactions occur during the year.

EXAMPLE I5-57 ▶ In the current year, Beth has a NSTCL of $2,800 and a NLTCL of $2,000. The entire NSTCL is offset initially against $2,800 of ordinary income on a dollar-for-dollar basis. Because capital losses can be offset against only $3,000 of ordinary income, $200 of NLTCL is used to offset $200 ($3,000 − $2,800) of ordinary income. The NLTCL carryover to the next year is $1,800 ($2,000 − $200). ◀

TAX STRATEGY TIP

Taxpayers who have realized capital gains during the tax year should consider selling securities with a loss during the same year. The losses can be offset against the gains and tax savings result.

CAPITAL LOSSES APPLIED TO CAPITAL GAINS BY GROUPS. Taxpayers separate their LTCGs and LTCLs into three tax rate groups: (1) 28% group, (2) 25% group, and (3) the 20% group. The 28% group includes capital gains and losses when the capital asset is a collectible held more than one year and half of the gain from the sale of QSBS held for more than five years. The 25% group consists of unrecaptured Sec. 1250 gain discussed in Chapter I13, and there are no losses for this group. The 20% or 10% group, depending upon the taxpayer's tax rate, includes capital gains and losses when the holding period is more than one year and the capital asset is not a collectible or Sec. 1202 small business stock.

When a taxpayer has NSTCL and NLTCG, the NSTCL is first offset against NLTCG from the 28% group, then the 25% group and finally the 20% (or 10%) group. This treatment of NSTCL is favorable for taxpayers. Note that a taxpayer could have NLTCLs in one group, except the 25% group, and NLTCGs in another group. A net loss from the 28% group is first offset against gains in the 25% group then net gains in the 20% (or 10%) group. A net loss from the 20% group is first offset against net gains in the 28% group then gains in the 25% group.[42]

EXAMPLE I5-58 ▶ Leroy, whose tax rate is 35%, has NSTCL of $20,000, a $25,000 LTCG from the sale of a rare stamp held 16 months and a $18,000 LTCG from the sale of stock held for three years. The $20,000 NSTCL is offset against $20,000 of the collectibles gain in the 28% group. Leroy's tax liability increases by $5,000 [($5,000 × 28%) + ($18,000 × 20%)]. ◀

EXAMPLE I5-59 ▶ Elizabeth, whose tax rate is 35%, has a $32,000 LTCL from the sale of stock held for four years and the following capital gains:

NSTCG	$40,000
LTCG from sale of collectible	$30,000
LTCG in the 25% group (unrecaptured Sec. 1250 gain)	$10,000

The $32,000 LTCL is offset first against $30,000 of the LTCG in the 28% group and $2,000 of the unrecaptured Sec. 1250 gain. ◀

ADDITIONAL COMMENT

If Elizabeth in Example I5-59 also had a $9,000 LTCG from the sale of stock held for two years, she would only be able to offset $23,000 of the LTCG in the 28% group.

STOP & THINK *Question:* Srinija has a salary of $100,000. If she sells a non-personal use asset during the year and has a $40,000 loss, why is it important that the asset not be a capital asset?

Solution: Only $3,000 of a $40,000 capital loss is used as a deduction to reduce her gross income each year. Her AGI is $97,000 if the asset is a capital asset, and she has a $37,000 capital loss carryforward. All of the $40,000 loss is used to reduce her gross income if the asset is not a capital asset and her AGI is $60,000. It is possible that Srinija might not care whether or not the asset is a capital asset if she has capital gains that could be reduced by capital losses. If the asset is a personal-use asset, the loss is not deductible regardless of whether or not it is a capital asset.

---

42 Notice 97-59, I.R.B. 1997-45

TAX TREATMENT FOR NET CAPITAL GAIN. Congress eliminated preferential tax rates on NCG in 1986 but did provide some preferential treatment in 1990 when the maximum rate on NCG was reduced to 28%.[43] However, this tax reduction only benefited taxpayers whose tax rate exceeded 28%. The change in 1997 to rates as low as 10% benefits all noncorporate taxpayers if they hold the capital asset for more than one year. The new lower rates should make taxpayers more interested in having capital gain income instead of ordinary income. Investors are likely to have an increased preference for growth stocks as opposed to stocks with high dividends.

Taxpayers who own mutual funds must recognize their share of capital gains even if no distributions are received. Many mutual fund shareholders reinvest their distributions instead of withdrawing assets from the mutual fund. Mutual funds must classify the gains as short-term or long-term, and long-term gains will need to be separated by rate groups. When shareholders of a mutual fund recognize their share of capital gains when no distribution is actually received, the basis for their shares is increased.

EXAMPLE I5-60 ▶ Eunice, whose tax rate is 35%, is a shareholder of Canyon Mutual Fund. The basis for her shares is $23,000. At the end of the current year, she received a statement from Canyon indicating her share of the following: dividend income, $200; STCG, $300; 28-percent rate gain, $1,000; and ANCG of $1,500. The increase in her taxes as a result of her ownership of the mutual shares is $755 [($500 × 35%) + ($1,000 × 28%) + ($1,500 × 20%)]. The basis for her shares of Canyon Mutual Fund is $26,000. ◀

TAX TREATMENT OF CAPITAL GAINS AND LOSSES: CORPORATE TAXPAYERS

Most topics covered in this chapter concerning capital gains and losses, including the classification of an asset as a capital asset, rules for determining holding periods, and the procedure for offsetting capital losses against capital gains, apply to both corporate and noncorporate taxpayers. However, a major difference is that the lower tax rates of 10%, 20%, 25% and 28% on net capital gain for noncorporate taxpayers do not apply to corporations. A second significant difference relates to the treatment of capital losses: Unlike the noncorporate taxpayer, who may offset capital losses against ordinary income up to $3,000, corporations may offset capital losses only against capital gains. Corporate taxpayers may carry capital losses back to each of the three preceding tax years (the earliest of the three tax years first and then to the next two years) and forward for five years to offset capital gains in such years. When a corporate taxpayer carries a loss back to a preceding year or forward to a following year, the loss is treated as a STCL.[44]

EXAMPLE I5-61 ▶ The Peach Corporation has income from operations of $200,000, a NSTCG of $40,000, and a NLTCL of $56,000 during the current year. The $40,000 NSTCG is offset by $40,000 NLTCL. The remaining $16,000 of NSTCL may not be offset against the $200,000 of other income but may be carried back three years and then forward five years to offset capital gains arising in these years. If Peach has NLTCG and/or NSTCG in the previous three years, a refund of taxes paid during those years will be received during the current year. ◀

NEW MAXIMUM RATE ON NET CAPITAL GAIN FOR CORPORATIONS. While the House proposed a reduction in the corporate tax rate on net capital gain, the proposal was rejected although a maximum rate of 35% was created for net capital gain for tax years ending after 1997. Corporations apply a maximum rate of 35% to the corporation's net capital gain.[45] Given the present tax rates for corporations, the existence of the 35% alternative rate for net capital gain will have little benefit.

[43] For years prior to 1990, a myriad of rules have applied. Prior to 1987, noncorporate taxpayers received a deduction from gross income equal to 60% of the taxpayer's net capital gain. For years 1987-1990, net capital gains were subject to tax at ordinary income rates.

[44] Sec. 1212(a).

[45] Sec. 1201.

Topic Review I5-2

Comparison of Corporate and Noncorporate Taxpayers: Capital Gains and Losses

	NONCORPORATE	CORPORATE
A statutory maximum tax rate applicable to net capital gain	Yes, 10%, 20%, 25% and 28%	Yes, but rate is 35%
Offset of net capital losses against ordinary income	Yes, up to $3,000	No
Carryback of capital losses	No	Yes, three years as STCLs
Carryforward of capital losses	Yes, indefinitely	Yes, five years as STCLs

Topic Review I5-2 summarizes the principal differences in the tax treatment of capital gains and losses for corporate and noncorporate taxpayers.

STOP & THINK *Question:* Most taxpayers believe that if they have a long-term capital gain, their income taxes will be less on the LTCG than on their other ordinary income. Explain why all taxpayers do not have a tax savings from a net capital gain.

Solution: Noncorporate taxpayers whose marginal tax rate is 28% or less will not have a reduction in taxes if the LTCG is gain from the sale of a collectible, or the recognized half of the gain from the sale of qualified small business stock under Sec. 1202. Also, corporations are not eligible for the lower rates available to noncorporate taxpayers and pay taxes on NLTCG at the same rate as ordinary income except the rate may not exceed 35% on the NLTCG.

SALE OR EXCHANGE

OBJECTIVE 6

Recognize when a sale or exchange has occurred

As previously indicated, capital gains and losses result from the sale or exchange of capital assets. Although Sec. 1222 does not define a sale or an exchange, a **sale** is generally considered to be a transaction where one receives cash or the equivalent of cash, including the assumption of one's debt. An **exchange** is a transaction where one receives a reciprocal transfer of property, as distinguished from a transaction where one receives only cash or a cash equivalent.[46]

EXAMPLE I5-62 ▶ Two years ago, Bart acquired 100 shares of Alaska Corporation common stock for $12,000 to hold as an investment. Bart sells 50 shares of the stock to Sandy for $10,000 and transfers the other 50 shares to Gail in exchange for land that has a $10,000 FMV. In each transaction, Bart realizes a $4,000 ($10,000 − $6,000) LTCG due to the sale or exchange of a capital asset. The transfer to Sandy qualifies as a sale, and the transfer to Gail qualifies as an exchange. ◀

TYPICAL MISCONCEPTION

Because the carryover for net operating losses is 20 years, it is sometimes erroneously assumed that the carryover for corporate capital losses is also 20 years instead of five years.

To qualify as a sale or exchange, the transaction must be bona fide. Transactions between related parties such as family members are closely scrutinized. For example, a sale of property on credit to a relative may be a disguised gift if there is no intention of collecting the debt. If this is the case, a subsequent bad debt deduction due to the debt's worthlessness is disallowed. In some instances, the Code specifically states that a particular transaction or event either qualifies or does not qualify for sale or exchange treatment. For example, the holder of an option who fails to exercise such an option treats the lapse of the option as a sale or exchange.[47] However, abandonment of property is generally not deemed to be a sale or exchange.[48]

---

[46] Reg. Sec. 1.1002-1(d).

[47] Sec. 1234(b) and Reg. Sec. 1.1234-1(b).

[48] Reg. Secs. 1.165-2 and 1.167(a)-8.

WORTHLESS SECURITIES

ADDITIONAL COMMENT

The worthlessness of a security is treated as a sale or exchange so that the taxpayer is not forced to arrange for someone to buy the security for a token amount.

If a security that is a capital asset becomes worthless during the year, Sec. 165(g)(1) specifies that any loss is treated as a loss from the sale or exchange of a capital asset on the last day of the tax year. The term includes stock, a stock option, and "a bond, debenture, note or certificate, or other evidence of indebtedness, issued by a corporation or by a government or political division thereof, with interest coupons or in registered form."[49] Whether a security has become worthless during the year is a question of fact, and the taxpayer has the burden of proof to show evidence of worthlessness.[50]

EXAMPLE I5-63 ▶ Charlotte purchased $40,000 of bonds issued by the Jet Corporation in March 2001. In February 2002, Jet is declared bankrupt, and its bonds are worthless. Charlotte has a LTCL of $40,000 because the bonds have become worthless and are deemed to have been sold on the last day of 2002. The more-than-one-year holding period requirement is satisfied by the last day of 2002. ◀

REAL-WORLD EXAMPLE

A corporation owned 76% of the stock of a Mexican company. The corporation later acquired the remaining 24% of the stock, allegedly for the purpose of avoiding interference by minority shareholders. Later the corporation claimed an ordinary loss on the worthless Mexican stock because it owned at least 80% of the stock. The Court treated the loss as a capital loss because the acquisition of the remaining stock was without a business purpose. *Hunter Mfg. Co.*, 21 T.C. 424 (1953).

SECURITIES IN AFFILIATED CORPORATIONS. If the security that becomes worthless is a security in a domestic affiliated corporation owned by a corporate taxpayer, the worthless security is not considered a capital asset. Thus, a corporate taxpayer's loss due to owning worthless securities in an affiliated corporation is treated as an ordinary loss. Because capital losses are of only limited benefit to corporate taxpayers, the classification of the loss as ordinary is preferable.

To qualify as an affiliated corporation, the parent corporation must own at least 80% of the voting power of all classes of stock and at least 80% of each class of nonvoting stock. The subsidiary corporation must be engaged in the active conduct of an operating business as opposed to being a passive investment company (i.e., more than 90% of its aggregate gross receipts must be from sources other than passive types of income such as royalties, dividends, and interest).[51]

EXAMPLE I5-64 ▶ Ace Corporation owns 80% of all classes of stock issued by the same Jet Corporation described in Example I5-63. Jet Corporation is actively engaged in an operating business and has no income from passive investments before being declared bankrupt. Ace's loss from its worthless stock investment is an ordinary loss instead of a capital loss because Jet is an affiliated corporation. Ace owns at least 80% of all classes of Jet's stock and more than 90% of Jet's gross receipts are from sources other than passive types of income. ◀

RETIREMENT OF DEBT INSTRUMENTS

Generally, the collection of a debt is not a sale or an exchange. However, if a debt instrument is retired, amounts received by the holder are treated as being received in an exchange.[52] Debt instruments include bonds, debentures, notes, certificates, and other evidences of indebtedness.

EXAMPLE I5-65 ▶ In 1997 the Rocket Corporation issued $50,000 of five-year, interest-bearing bonds that were purchased by Elaine as an investment for $49,800. Elaine receives $50,000 at maturity in 2002. Retirement of the debt instrument is an exchange, and the $200 gain is a LTCG.[53] ◀

Although Congress has provided that retirements of debt instruments are treated as exchanges, Congress is not willing to allow taxpayers to convert large amounts of potential ordinary interest income into capital gain by purchasing debt instruments at a substantial discount. As illustrated in Example I5-65, a small amount of bond discount is sometimes converted to capital gain. However, if the discount is large enough to be classified as original issue discount, the discount must be amortized and included in gross income for each day the debt instrument is held. Original issue discount (OID) is defined as "the excess (if any) of the stated redemption price at maturity over the issue price.[54]

---

[49] Sec. 165(g)(2).

[50] *Minnie K. Young v. CIR*, 28 AFTR 365, 41-2 USTC ¶9744 (2nd Cir., 1941).

[51] Sec. 165(g)(3).

[52] Sec. 1271(a).

[53] If Rocket Corporation issued the bonds with the intention of calling the bonds before maturity, Sec. 1271(a)(2) treats the gain as ordinary income.

[54] Sec. 1273(a)(1).

EXAMPLE I5-66 ▶ On January 1, 2002, Connie purchases $100,000 of the City Corporation's newly issued bonds for $85,000. The bonds mature in 20 years. In 2002 and in subsequent years Connie must annually recognize as interest income a portion of the $15,000 of OID. ◀

The OID is considered to be zero if the amount of discount "is less than ¼ of 1% of the stated redemption price at maturity, multiplied by the number of complete years to maturity."[55] In Example I5-63, the $200 discount is not OID because it is less than $625 (0.0025 × $50,000 × 5 years). If Connie pays more than $95,000 for the bonds in Example I5-66, the OID is zero.

ADDITIONAL COMMENT

Two different types of bonds are sold at a discount: original issue discount (OID) bonds and market discount bonds. OID bonds are issued at a discount, whereas market discount bonds have market discount resulting from a rise in interest rates after the issuance of the bonds.

ORIGINAL ISSUE DISCOUNT. Instead of spreading the OID ratably over the life of the bond, amortization of the discount is based on an interest amortization method. This method is called the **constant interest rate method.** The total amount of interest income is determined by multiplying the interest yield to maturity by the adjusted issue price. With this method of amortizing the discount, the amount of OID amortized increases for each year the bond is held. In Example I5-66, Connie recognizes a larger amount of interest income in 2003 than in 2002 due to amortization of the OID.

The daily portion of the OID for any accrual period is "determined by allocating to each day in any accrual period its ratable portion to the increase during such accrual period in the adjusted issue price of the debt instrument."[56] The increase in the adjusted issue price for any accrual period is shown below.

REAL-WORLD EXAMPLE

Time Warner has issued zero coupon bonds, which are a type of OID bonds. These bonds mature in year 2013 and in late 2000 traded at 108.

$$\text{Increase in the adjusted issue price} = \left[\text{Adjusted issue price at the beginning of the accrual period} \times \text{Yield to maturity}\right] - \text{Interest payments during the accrual period}$$

EXAMPLE I5-67 ▶ On June 30, 2002, Fred purchases a 10%, $10,000 corporate bond for $9,264. The bond is issued on June 30, 2002, and matures in five years. Interest is paid semiannually, and the effective yield to maturity is 12% compounded semiannually. In 2002, Fred recognizes interest income of $556, as illustrated in Table I5-1. The adjusted issue price as of January 1, 2003 is $9,320. This is the sum of the issue price plus any amounts of OID includible in the income of any holder since the date of issue. ◀

KEY POINT

The owner of an OID bond is normally required to accrue interest income each year.

If a debt instrument is sold or exchanged before maturity, part of the original issue discount is included in the seller's income. The amount to be included depends on the number of days the debt instrument is owned by the seller within the accrual period.

EXAMPLE I5-68 ▶ Assume the same facts as in Example I5-67, except that Fred sells the corporate bond to Carolyn on February 24, 2004 (the 55th day in the accrual period). Fred must include $20 [(55 days ÷ 181 days in the accrual period) × $67] of accrued interest for the period of January 1, 2004 to February 24, 2004 in income for 2004. Fred's basis for the bond increases by $20. Thus, his basis for determining a gain or loss is $9,462 ($9,442 + $20). ◀

MARKET DISCOUNT BONDS PURCHASED AFTER APRIL 30, 1993. The sale or exchange of a market discount bond may result in part or all of the gain being classified as ordinary income. The Revenue Reconciliation Act of 1993 substantially increased the number of bonds subject to the market discount provisions.[57] A market discount bond is a bond that is acquired in the bond market at a discount. Market discount is the excess of the stated redemption price of the bond at maturity over the taxpayer's basis for such bond immediately after it is acquired.

---

[55] Sec. 1273(a)(3).

[56] Sec. 1272(a)(3).

[57] Ordinary income treatment for accrued market discount does not apply to owners of taxable market discount bonds issued on or before July 18, 1984 if the bonds were acquired before May 1, 1993. Owners of tax-exempt bonds are not required to accrue market discount if the bonds were acquired before May 1, 1993 (regardless of the issue date).

▼ **TABLE I5-1**
Computation for Interest Income in Examples I5-65 and I5-66

	Interest Received (1)	Amortization of Original Issue Discount (2)	Interest Income (3) = (1) + (2)	Taxpayer's Basis for the Bond
6-30-02				$ 9,264
12-31-02	$ 500	$ 56[a]	$ 556	9,320[b]
6-30-03	500	59	559	9,379
12-31-03	500	63	563	9,442
6-30-04	500	67	567	9,509
12-31-04	500	71	571	9,580
6-30-05	500	75	575	9,655
12-31-05	500	79	579	9,734
6-30-06	500	84	584	9,818
12-31-06	500	89	589	9,907
6-30-07	500	93[c]	593	10,000
	$5,000	$736	$5,736	

[a] 6% × $9,264 − $500 = $56.
[b] $9,264 + $56 = $9,320.
[c] This figure is adjusted for rounding.

EXAMPLE I5-69 ▶ On January 1, Stephano purchased $100,000 of 8%, 20-year bonds for $82,000. The bonds were issued at par by the Solar Corporation two years ago on January 1. The bonds are market discount bonds. ◀

Similar to original issue discount, there is a de minimis rule for determining market discount. Market discount is zero if the discount is less than ¼ of 1% of the stated redemption price of the bond at maturity multiplied by the number of complete years to maturity.[58] If Stephano had paid $95,500 or more for the Solar Corporation bonds in Example I5-69, the bonds would not be market discount bonds.[59]

Gain realized on disposition of the market discount bond is ordinary income to the extent of the accrued market discount.[60] The ratable accrual method (straight line method computed on a daily basis) is used to determine the amount of the accrued market discount recognized as ordinary income.[61] The market discount is allocated on the basis of the number of days the taxpayer held the bond relative to the number of days between the acquisition date and maturity date.

EXAMPLE I5-70 ▶ Assume the same facts as in Example I5-69 except that Stephano sells the bonds to Kimberly three years later for $86,400. $3,000 (3/18 × $18,000) of the $4,400 ($86,400 − $82,000) gain is ordinary income and the remaining gain is LTCG. If Stephano sold the bond for more than $82,000 but less than $85,000, all of the gain is ordinary income. The entire $18,000 gain is ordinary income if the bond is held to maturity. ◀

ADDITIONAL COMMENT

An option is a contract in which the owner of property agrees with a potential buyer that the potential buyer has the right to buy the property at a fixed price within a certain period of time.

OPTIONS

The owner of an option to buy property may sell the option, exercise the option, or allow the option to expire. If the option is exercised, the amount paid for the option is added to the purchase price of the property acquired.[62]

---

[58] Sec. 1278(a)(2)(C).
[59] $100,000 × .25% × 18 years = $4,500.
[60] Sec. 1276(a)(1).
[61] Sec. 1276(b)(1). A taxpayer may elect to use the constant interest rate method (see Sec. 1276(b)(2)).
[62] Rev. Rul. 58-234, 1958-1 C.B. 279.

EXAMPLE I5-71 ▶ On August 5, 2002, Len pays $600 for an option to acquire 100 shares of Hill Corporation common stock for $80 per share at any time before December 20, 2002. Len exercises the option on November 15, 2002 and pays $8,000 for the stock. Len's basis for the 100 shares of Hill is $8,600, ($8,000 + $600), and the stock's holding period begins on November 15, 2002. ◀

ADDITIONAL COMMENT

The Wall Street Journal publishes daily a list of all call and put options traded on the Chicago Board, the American Stock Exchange, and other exchanges where these options are traded.

When an option is sold or allowed to expire, a sale or exchange has occurred and gain or loss is therefore recognized.[63] The character of the underlying property determines whether the gain or loss from the sale or expiration of the option is capital or ordinary in nature. If the optioned property is a capital asset, the option is treated as a capital asset and capital gain or loss is recognized on the sale or exchange.

EXAMPLE I5-72 ▶ On March 2, 2002, Holly pays $270 for an option to acquire 100 shares of Arkansas Corporation stock for $30 per share at any time before December 10, 2002. As a result of an increase in the market value of the Arkansas stock, the market price of the option increases and Holly sells the option for $600 on August 2, 2002. Because the Arkansas stock is a capital asset in the hands of Holly, the option is a capital asset and she must recognize a STCG of $330 ($600 − $270). ◀

EXAMPLE I5-73 ▶ On October 12, 2001, Mary paid $400 for an option to acquire 100 shares of Portland Corporation stock for $50 per share at any time before February 19, 2002. The price never exceeds $50 before February 19, 2002, and Mary does not exercise the option. Because the option expires, Mary recognizes a STCL of $400 in 2002. ◀

SELF-STUDY QUESTION

Marc writes a call option on stock owned by him and receives $800 on November 1, 2001. The value of the stock declines and the option is allowed to expire on February 15, 2002. When does Marc recognize the $800 gain?

ANSWER

Marc recognizes the gain in 2002 when the transaction is completed.

Transactions in which taxpayers purchase or write options to buy (calls) are quite common today. An investor who anticipates that the market value of a stock or security (e.g., common stock) will increase during the next few months may purchase a call option instead of actually buying the stock. As indicated above, the tax treatment for the option depends on whether the call is exercised, sold, or expires. Someone, however, must be willing to write a call on the stock. Typically an owner of the same stock will write a call option. The writer of the call receives a payment for granting the right to purchase the stock at a fixed price within a given period of time.

If the call is exercised, the writer of the call adds the amount received for the call to the sales price to determine the amount realized.[64] If the call is not exercised within the given time period and thus expires, the writer retains the amount received for the option and recognizes a STCG. The gain is short-term even if the option is written and held for more than a year.

EXAMPLE I5-74 ▶ Sam owns 100 shares of Madison Corporation common stock, which he purchased on May 1, 1995, for $4,000. On November 8, 2002, Sam writes a call that gives Joan, an investor, the option to purchase Sam's 100 shares of Madison stock at $60 per share any time before April 19, 2003. The current market price of Madison stock is $56 per share, and Sam receives $520 for writing the call. If the call is exercised, Sam has a LTCG of $2,520 [($6,000 + $520) − $4,000]. If the call is not exercised and expires on April 19, 2003, Sam must recognize a STCG of $520 in 2003. ◀

EXAMPLE I5-75 ▶ Assume the same facts as in Example I5-74, but consider instead the tax treatment for Joan, the holder of the call. If Joan exercises the call, the basis of the stock is $6,520 ($6,000 + $520). If she does not exercise the call, a STCL of $520 is recognized. If Joan sells the call, the amount received is compared with her basis in the call ($520) to compute Joan's gain or loss. ◀

KEY POINT

A copyright held by a taxpayer whose personal efforts created it is omitted from the definition of a capital asset. However, a patent can be considered a capital asset. In effect, the tax law could be said to favor individuals whose efforts lead to scientific or technological advancement.

PATENTS

To encourage technological progress and to clarify whether a transfer of rights to a patent is capital gain or ordinary income, Congress created Sec. 1235, which allows the holder of a patent to treat the gain resulting from the transfer of all substantial rights in a patent as LTCG. This tax treatment is more favorable than that accorded to producers of artistic, literary, and musical works, who receive ordinary rather than capital gain from the sale of their works.

---

[63] Sec. 1234(a).

[64] Rev. Rul. 58-234, 1958-1 C.B. 279.

REQUIREMENTS FOR CAPITAL GAIN TREATMENT. Section 1235 provides that the transfer of all substantial rights to a patent by the holder of the patent is treated as a sale or exchange of a capital asset that has been held long-term. Thus, long-term capital gain is recognized on the transfer of a patent regardless of its holding period or the character of the asset. Favorable long-term capital gain treatment applies even if the transferor of the patent receives periodic payments contingent on the productivity, use, or disposition of the property transferred.[65]

EXAMPLE I5-76 ▶ Clay invents a small utensil used to peel shrimp. He has a patent on the utensil and transfers all rights to the patent to a manufacturing company. Clay receives $100,000 plus 40 cents per utensil sold. Because Sec. 1235 applies, the total of the lump-sum payment and the royalty payments received less his cost basis for the patent is recognized as a LTCG. ◀

SUBSTANTIAL RIGHTS. The principal requirement in Sec. 1235 is that the holder must transfer all substantial rights to the patent. The Regulations state that the circumstances of the whole transaction should be considered in determining whether all substantial rights to a patent have been transferred.[66] All substantial rights have not been transferred if the patent rights of the purchaser are limited geographically within the country of issuance or the rights are for a period less than a patent's remaining life.

EXAMPLE I5-77 ▶ Bruce, an inventor, transfers one of his U.S. patents on a manufacturing process to a manufacturer located in Utah. The manufacturer's rights to use the patent are limited to the state of Utah. Because the use of the patent is limited to a geographical area, all substantial rights have not been transferred, and Sec. 1235 does not apply. Payments received for the use of the patent are royalties and taxed as ordinary income. ◀

DEFINITION OF A HOLDER. Long-term capital gain treatment applies only to a holder of the patent rights. For purposes of Sec. 1235, a holder is an individual whose efforts created the property or an individual who acquires the patent rights from the creator for valuable consideration before the property covered by the patent is placed in service or used. Furthermore, the acquiring individual may not be related to the creator or be the creator's employer.

Section 1235 may not be used by corporate taxpayers because corporations are not permitted to be classified as holders. Although a partnership is not permitted to be a holder, individual partners may qualify as holders to the extent of the partner's interest in the patent owned by the partnership.

EXAMPLE I5-78 ▶ Joy purchases a patent from Martin, whose efforts created the patent. The purchase occurs before the property is placed in service or used. Joy and Martin are unrelated individuals, and Joy is not Martin's employer. For purposes of Sec. 1235, both Joy and Martin qualify as holders. ◀

ADDITIONAL COMMENT

The scope of Sec. 1253 is very broad. A franchise "includes an agreement which gives one of the parties to the agreement the right to distribute, sell, or provide goods, services, or facilities within a specified area."

REAL-WORLD EXAMPLE

Shaquille O'Neal, the NBA star of the Orlando Magic, has obtained a trademark on his nickname, Shaq. The trademark covers nearly 200 products including athletic shoes, cake decorations, bathroom tissue, bathtub toys, and kites.

FRANCHISES, TRADEMARKS, AND TRADE NAMES

Before the enactment of Sec. 1253, significant uncertainty existed as to whether the transfer of a franchise, trademark, or trade name should be treated as a sale or exchange or as a licensing agreement. If the transfer is tantamount to a sale of the property, payments received should be treated by the transferor as a return of capital and capital gain, and the transferee should be required to capitalize and amortize such payments. However, if the transfer represents a licensing agreement, the transferor should recognize ordinary income and the transferee should receive an ordinary deduction for such payments.

Section 1253, which applies to the granting of a franchise, trademark, or trade name, as well as renewals and transfers to third parties, attempts to resolve the uncertainty by stating, "A transfer of a franchise, trademark, or trade name shall not be treated as a sale or exchange of a capital asset if the transferor retains any significant power, right, or continuing interest with respect to the subject matter of the franchise, trademark, or trade name."[67]

[65] Sec. 1235(a).

[66] Reg. Sec. 1.1235-2(b).

[67] Sec. 1253(a). Section 1253(e) prevents the basic Sec. 1253 rules from applying to the transfer of a professional sports franchise.

The IRC provides examples of some rights that are to be considered a "significant power, right, or continuing interest."[68] These rights include the right to

- Disapprove of any assignment.
- Terminate the agreement at will.
- Prescribe standards of quality for products, product services, and facilities.
- Require the exclusive selling or advertising of the transferor's products or services.
- Require the transferee to purchase substantially all of its supplies and equipment from the transferor.

If the transferor does not retain any significant power, right, or continuing interest in the property, the transferor treats the transfer as a sale of the franchise and has the benefits of capital gain treatment. However, any amounts received that are contingent on the productivity, use, or disposition of such property must be treated as ordinary income by the transferor.

EXAMPLE I5-79 ▶ Rose, who owns a franchise with a basis of $100,000, transfers the franchise to Ruth and retains no significant power, right, or continuing interest. Rose receives a $250,000 down payment when the agreement is signed and annual payments for five years equal to 10% of all sales in excess of $2,000,000. Rose has a capital gain of $150,000 with respect to the initial payment, but all of the payments received during the next five years will be ordinary income because they are contingent payments. ◀

Under Sec. 1253, the transferee may deduct payments that are contingent on the productivity, use, or disposition of such property as business expenses. Generally, other payments are capitalized and amortized over a period of 15 years.[69] In practice, payments received for the transfer of a franchise are generally treated as ordinary income to the transferor and are deductible by the transferee because in most franchise agreements the transferor desires to maintain significant powers, rights, or continuing interests in the franchise operation. Also, in many instances the payments are, in part, predicated on the success of the franchised business and are, therefore, established as contingent payments.

REAL-WORLD EXAMPLE

A taxpayer sold a building with the purchaser paying $500,000 and the lessee of the building paying $60,000 under a separate agreement to cancel the lease. The $60,000 was treated as ordinary income because no "sale or exchange" of the property occurred in return for the lessee's $60,000 payment. *Gary Gurvey v. U.S.*, 57 AFTR 2d. 86-1062, 86-1 USTC ¶9260 (D.C. Ill., 1986).

LEASE CANCELLATION PAYMENTS

A lease arrangement may be terminated before the lease period expires, and a lease cancellation payment may be made as consideration for the other party's agreement to terminate the lease. Either a lessor or a lessee may receive such a payment because the payment is normally made by the person who wants to cancel the lease. The tax treatment may differ significantly depending on which party is the recipient.

PAYMENTS RECEIVED BY LESSOR. The Supreme Court has ruled that lease cancellation payments received by a lessor are treated as ordinary income on the basis that the payments represent a substitute for rent.[70] Lease cancellation payments are included in the lessor's income in the year received, even if the lessor uses an accrual method.[71]

PAYMENTS RECEIVED BY LESSEE. Payments received by a lessee for canceling a lease are considered amounts received in exchange for the lease.[72] If the lease is a capital asset, any gain or loss is a capital gain or loss.

EXAMPLE I5-80 ▶ Jim has a three-year lease on a house used as his personal residence. The lessor has an opportunity to sell the house and has agreed to pay $1,000 to Jim to cancel the lease. Assuming that Jim has no basis in the lease, the gain of $1,000 is capital gain because the lease is a capital asset. ◀

---

[68] Sec. 1253(b)(2).
[69] Sec. 197(a).
[70] *Walter M. Hort v. CIR*, 25 AFTR 1207, 41-1 USTC ¶9354 (USSC, 1941).
[71] *Farrelly-Walsh, Inc.*, 13 B.T.A. 923 (1928).
[72] Sec. 1241.

HOLDING PERIOD

OBJECTIVE 7

Determine the holding period for an asset when a sale or disposition occurs

The length of time an asset is held before it is disposed of (i.e., the *holding period*) is an important factor in determining whether any gain or loss resulting from the disposition of a capital asset is treated as long-term or short-term. To be classified as a long-term capital gain or loss, the capital asset must be held more than one year.[73] To determine the holding period, the day of acquisition is excluded and the disposal date is included.[74]

If the date of disposition is the same date as the date of acquisition, but a year later, the asset is considered to have been held for only one year. If the property is held for an additional day, the holding period is more than one year.

EXAMPLE I5-81 ▶ Arnie purchased a capital asset on April 20, 2001, and sells the asset at a gain on April 21, 2002. The gain is classified as a LTCG. If the asset is sold on or before April 20, 2002, the gain is a STCG. ◀

ADDITIONAL COMMENT

When determining the holding period for marketable securities, it is important to use the "trade" dates, not the "settlement" dates.

The fact that all months do not have the same number of days is not a factor in determining the one-year period. Acquisitions made on the last day of any month must be held until the first day of the thirteenth subsequent month in order to have been held for more than one year.

EXAMPLE I5-82 ▶ Alford sells stock held as an investment and recognizes a gain. If the capital asset was purchased on May 31, 2001, the gain is LTCG subject to the 20% or 10% rate if the asset is sold on or after June 1, 2002. If sold on or before May 31, 2002, the new 20% and 10% rates do not apply. ◀

ADDITIONAL COMMENT

One June 1, 1995, the Securities and Exchange Commission adopted a new set of rules that will require investors who purchase or sell securities to deliver the funds to pay for the securities or deliver the certificates to be sold within three days of when the order is placed. Formerly, investors had five days to deliver funds or certificates.

HOLDING PERIOD OF MORE THAN FIVE YEARS. Even lower rates may apply if the capital asset is sold after December 31, 2000, when the holding period is more than five years. This "qualified 5-year gain" that would normally be taxed at 10% is taxed at 8%, and the "qualified 5-year gain" that would normally be taxed at 20% is taxed at 18%.[75]

The beginning of the five-year holding period differs depending on the taxpayer's normal tax rate. If the taxpayer's tax rate is more than 15%, the lower 18% rate applies only if the asset is acquired after December 31, 2000, and the asset's holding period is more than five years. These taxpayers may elect to have property acquired before 2001 treated as acquired on January 1, 2001, if they elect to have a deemed sale of the asset. Any appreciation as of January 1, 2001, is recognized as a gain and taxes on the gain must be paid. Any loss from the deemed sale is not recognized.

EXAMPLE I5-83 ▶ Judd, whose tax rate is at least 27%, purchased a capital asset on June 22, 2000, for $10,000. On January 1, 2001, the asset's FMV is $12,000. If Judd sells the asset on July 13, 2006, for $50,000, the $40,000 gain is taxed at 20%. If Judd elects to recognize a $2,000 gain on January 1, 2001, his $38,000 gain in 2006 is taxed at 18%. ◀

If the taxpayer's tax rate is 15%, the capital asset may be purchased before January 1, 2001, and the holding period for the five-year requirement starts when the asset is purchased. If Judd's tax rate in the above example is 15%, the gain is taxed at 8% if the asset is sold on or after June 23, 2005.

PROPERTY RECEIVED AS A GIFT

If a person receives property as a gift and uses the donor's basis to determine the gain or loss from a sale or exchange, the donor's holding period is added to the donee's holding period.[76] In other words, the donee's holding period includes the donor's holding period. If, however, the donee's basis is the FMV of the property on the date of the gift, the donee's holding period starts on the date of the gift. This situation occurs when the FMV

[73] Sec. 1222. A six-month holding period was applied to property acquired after June 27, 1984 and before January 1, 1988.

[74] *H. M. Hooper*, 26 B.T.A. 758 (1932), and Rev. Rul. 70-598, 1970-2 C.B. 168.

[75] Sec. 1(h)(2).

[76] Sec. 1223(1) and Reg. Sec. 1.1223-1(b).

is less than the donor's basis on the date of the gift and the property is subsequently sold at a loss.

EXAMPLE I5-84 ▶ Cindy receives a capital asset as a gift from Marc on July 4, 2002, when the asset has a $4,000 FMV. Marc acquired the property on April 12, 2002, for $3,400. If Cindy sells the asset after April 12, 2003, any gain or loss is LTCG or LTCL. Cindy's basis is the donor's cost because the FMV of the property is higher than the donor's basis on the date of the gift. Because Cindy takes Marc's basis, Marc's holding period is included. ◀

EXAMPLE I5-85 ▶ Roy receives a capital asset as a gift from Diane on September 12, 2002, when the asset has a $6,000 FMV. Diane acquired the asset on July 1, 2001, for $6,500. If the asset is sold at a gain (i.e., for more than $6,500), Roy's holding period starts on July 1, 2001, the date when Diane acquired the property, because the donor's basis of $6,500 is used by Roy to compute the gain. If the asset is sold at a loss (i.e., for less than $6,000), Roy's holding period does not start until the date of the gift, September 12, 2002, because Roy's basis is the $6,000 FMV. The FMV is used to compute the loss because it is less than the donor's basis on the date of the gift. ◀

ADDITIONAL COMMENT

The provision permitting the holding period of property received from a decedent to be deemed to be long-term is a rule of convenience. It is not necessary to try to determine when the decedent actually acquired the property.

PROPERTY RECEIVED FROM A DECEDENT

The holding period of property received from a decedent is always deemed to be long-term. If the person who receives the property from the decedent sells the property within one year after the decedent's death, the property is considered to be held for more than one year.[77]

EXAMPLE I5-86 ▶ The executor of Paul's estate sells certain securities for $41,000 on September 2, 2002, which are valued in the estate at their FMV of $40,000 on June 5, 2002, the date of Paul's death. The estate has a LTCG of $1,000 because the securities are considered to have been held long-term. The gain is taxed at 20% or 10%. ◀

ADDITIONAL COMMENT

The like-kind exchange rules under Sec. 1031 allow taxpayers to trade certain types of business and investment properties with no tax consequences arising from the exchange.

NONTAXABLE EXCHANGES

In a nontaxable exchange, the basis of the property received is determined by taking into account the basis of the property given in the exchange. If the properties are capital assets or Sec. 1231 assets, the holding period of the property received includes the holding period of the surrendered property.[78] In essence, the holding period of the property given up in a tax-free exchange is tacked on to the holding period of the property received in the exchange.

RECEIPT OF NONTAXABLE STOCK DIVIDENDS AND STOCK RIGHTS

If a shareholder receives nontaxable stock dividends or stock rights, the holding period of the stock received as a dividend or the stock rights received includes the holding period for the stock owned by the shareholder.[79] However, if the stock rights are exercised, the holding period for the stock purchased begins with the date of exercise.

EXAMPLE I5-87 ▶ As a result of owning Circle Corporation stock acquired three years ago, Paula receives nontaxable stock rights on June 5, 2002. Any gain or loss on the sale of the rights is long-term, regardless of whether any basis is allocated to the rights, because the holding period of the rights includes the holding period of the stock. ◀

EXAMPLE I5-88 ▶ Assume the same facts as in Example I5-85, except that the stock rights are exercised on August 20, 2002. The holding period for the newly acquired Circle stock begins on the date of exercise. ◀

STOP & THINK

Question: Carter owns 500 shares of Okoboji, Inc. (current market price of $310) with a basis of $101,500 acquired three years ago. In May of the current year, she receives 500 stock rights and exercises those rights that entitle her to purchase 500 shares of Okoboji at $300 per share. The current market price of the stock right is $40 per right. She plans

[77] Sec. 1223(11).
[78] Sec. 1223(1).
[79] Sec. 1223(5) and Reg. Sec. 1.1223-1(e).

to sell the 500 shares obtained by exercising the stock rights in January when she expects the market price to be $350 per share. Why should she elect to allocate basis to the stock rights?

Solution: If she does not allocate basis, her STCG will be $25,000 ($175,000 − $150,000). If she allocates basis to the stock rights, the basis of the 500 shares obtained when she exercises the rights is $161,600 ($150,000 + $11,600), and her STCG will be $13,400 ($175,000 − $161,600). Note that Carter might benefit by waiting a few months before selling because the gain might then be LTCG. She could also sell the original 500 shares and have a LTCG of $73,500 or $85,100.

PREFERENTIAL TREATMENT FOR NET CAPITAL GAINS

HISTORICAL NOTE

In part the preferential treatment of net capital gains was repealed in the Tax Reform Act of 1986 because Congress believed that the reduction of individual tax rates on such forms of capital income as business profits, interest, dividends, and short-term capital gains eliminated the need for a reduced rate for net capital gains.

Preferential treatment for capital gains was first created by the Revenue Act of 1921, which became effective on January 1, 1922. Despite almost continuous controversy concerning the need for preferential treatment, some form of preferential treatment for capital gains has existed since 1922. The range of controversy concerning the need for preferential tax treatment for capital gains is wide. Some maintain that capital gains do not represent income and should not be taxed, whereas others maintain that capital gains are no different from any other type of income and should be taxed accordingly.[80] A few of the most common arguments are discussed below.

MOBILITY OF CAPITAL

Without some form of preferential treatment, taxpayers who own appreciated capital assets may be unwilling to sell or exchange the asset if high tax rates exist, despite the presence of more attractive investment opportunities. In essence, the taxpayer may be "locked in" to holding an appreciated capital asset instead of shifting resources to more profitable investments.

EXAMPLE I5-89 ▶ Carmen owns Missouri Corporation stock with a $4,000 basis and a $20,000 FMV. She anticipates that the future after-tax annual return will be 10% on the Missouri stock and 12% on Kansas Corporation stock that has a similar level of risk. Assume her marginal tax rate is 50% (without consideration of favorable capital gain rates or deductions). Without preferential treatment of capital gains, Carmen will have to pay a tax of $8,000 ($16,000 × 0.50) on the sale of the Missouri stock and will have only $12,000 ($20,000 − $8,000) to invest in the Kansas stock. With a 12% return, she will receive an investment return of only $1,440 ($12,000 × 0.12), as compared with $2,000 ($20,000 × 0.10) if she maintains the investment in the Missouri stock. ◀

The "locked-in" effect is reduced if tax rates are lowered. The justification for eliminating the special 60% deduction for long-term capital gains after 1986 was due to a significant reduction in the top marginal tax rate applicable to ordinary income.

MITIGATION OF THE EFFECTS OF INFLATION AND THE PROGRESSIVE TAX SYSTEM

Because the tax laws do not generally reflect the effect of changes in purchasing power due to inflation, the sale or exchange of a capital asset may produce inequitable results. In fact, taxes may have to be paid even where a transaction results in an inflation-adjusted loss.

EXAMPLE I5-90 ▶ Beverly purchased a capital asset nine years ago for $100,000. If the asset is sold today for $180,000 and the general price level has increased by 100% during the nine-year period, Beverly will have a taxable gain of $80,000, despite suffering an inflation-adjusted loss of $20,000 [$180,000 sale price − ($100,000 × 200%)]. ◀

[80] Walter J. Blum, "A Handy Summary of the Capital Gains Argument," *Taxes—The Tax Magazine*, 35 (April 1957), pp. 247–66.

ADDITIONAL COMMENT

The American Assembly at Columbia University, in its final report on *Reforming and Simplifying the Federal Tax System* issued in 1985, recommends that capital gains be taxed as ordinary income if they are adjusted for inflation.

With a progressive tax system, the failure to adjust for inflation creates an even greater distortion. However, it should be noted that this distortion applies to all assets, not just capital assets.

LOWER THE COST OF CAPITAL

By reducing the tax rate on capital gains, investors are more willing to provide businesses with capital and the cost of capital is reduced. A lower cost of capital encourages capital formation to create more jobs and improve our competitive position in the global economy. Reducing the cost of capital is particularly important for the formation and growth of small business.

TAX PLANNING CONSIDERATIONS

SELECTION OF PROPERTY TO TRANSFER BY GIFT

Many tax reasons exist for making gifts of property, although the donor may incur a gift tax liability if the gift is a taxable gift. For example, taxpayers may give income-producing property to a taxpayer subject to a lower tax rate, or property expected to appreciate in the future may be given away to reduce estate taxes. Individuals may annually give property of $11,000[81] or less to a donee without making a taxable gift.[82]

EXAMPLE I5-91 ▶ Maya, who is single, owns marketable securities with a $6,200 basis and $10,400 FMV. She makes gifts of the marketable securities to Phil and cash of $11,000 to Roy. Because of the $11,000 annual exclusion per donee, Maya's gifts are not taxable gifts. ◀

EXAMPLE I5-92 ▶ Harry, who is single, makes a gift of land with a $241,000 basis and a $931,000 FMV to Rita. Harry's taxable gift is $920,000 ($931,000 − $11,000), and he incurs a gift tax liability. Rita's basis is $241,000 + 75% of the gift tax paid by Harry [($931,000 − $241,000)/$920,000 = 75%]. ◀

Individuals often reduce future estate taxes by making gifts. By using the annual exclusion, an individual may reduce future estate taxes and avoid the gift tax.

EXAMPLE I5-93 ▶ Christine owns only one asset—cash of $900,000—and has no liabilities. In December of the current year, she gives $11,000 to each of her five grandchildren. Because of the $11,000 annual exclusion per donee, Christine's gifts are not taxable gifts. By making the gifts, she reduces her potential gross estate by $55,000 (5 × $11,000). ◀

ADDITIONAL COMMENT

A husband and wife can each make a $11,000 gift to their daughter, enabling her to receive a total of $22,000 annually without the parents incurring a gift tax.

The selection of which property to give is important if one is attempting to reduce future estate taxes. It is generally preferable to make gifts of properties that are expected to significantly increase in value during the postgift period before the donor's death. Any increases in value after the date of the gift are not included in the donor's gross estate.

EXAMPLE I5-94 ▶ In 1994, Hal owned Sun Corporation stock with a $100,000 FMV and Union Corporation stock with a $100,000 FMV. Hal expected the Sun stock to increase in value at a moderate rate and the Union stock to increase at a substantial rate. In 1994, Hal made a gift of the Union stock to Dana. Hal's taxable gift in 1994 was $90,000 ($100,000 − $10,000). Hal dies in the current year when the FMVs of the Sun and Union stocks are $180,000 and $425,000, respectively. The postgift appreciation of $325,000 ($425,000 − $100,000) is not included in Hal's gross estate. By giving the Union stock instead of the Sun stock in 1994, Hal reduces his gross estate by $245,000. ◀

Gifts are often made for income tax purposes to shift income to other family members who are in a lower income tax bracket than the donor.

---

[81] Before 2002, the annual exclusion was $10,000.

[82] Sec. 2503(b).

EXAMPLE I5-95 ▶ In 2002, Anne has a marginal tax rate of 27% and owns Atlantic Corporation bonds, which have a $5,000 basis and $8,000 FMV. The bonds pay interest of $900 per year. If Anne gives the bonds to her dependent child, the interest income is shifted to the child. If the child has no other income, the child's taxable income is $150 ($900 − $750 standard deduction), and the child's marginal tax rate is 10%. The gift results in an annual income tax savings to the family unit of $228 [(0.27 × $900) − (0.10 × $150)]. The rate of tax that is imposed may be the parent's rate (see Chapter I2) if the child is less than 14 years old and has net unearned income in excess of $1,500.

In addition to shifting the interest income, Anne has also shifted a potential gain of $3,000. The child's basis for the bonds is $5,000 because the donee takes the donor's basis when the FMV of the property at the time of the gift is greater than the donor's basis. No gain is recognized by Anne when the gift is made, and a future sale of the property by the child may be taxed at a lower income tax rate. ◀

Although gifts of appreciated property may generate desirable income tax benefits, it is not usually advantageous to make a gift of property that has an FMV less than its basis because the donee's basis for determining a loss is the FMV. The excess of the donor's basis over the FMV at the time of the gift may never generate any tax benefit for the donor or the donee. Therefore, the donor should sell the asset and make a gift of the proceeds if the loss on the sale is deductible.

EXAMPLE I5-96 ▶ Bob owns Red Corporation stock with an $8,000 basis and $6,000 FMV, which is held as an investment. Bob wishes to make a graduation gift of the marketable securities to Angela, although he expects her to sell the stock and purchase a car. If Angela sells the stock for $6,000, no gain or loss is recognized because her loss basis for the stock is $6,000. In addition, no loss is recognized by Bob on the gift of the stock to Angela. Instead of giving the stock, Bob should sell it to recognize a $2,000 capital loss and then give the proceeds from the sale to Angela. ◀

SELF-STUDY QUESTION

Doug owns IBM Corporation shares, which have a $50,000 FMV and basis of $75,000. Doug makes a deathbed telephone call to his stockbroker and sells the IBM shares. Assuming that Doug is in the 30% bracket and had no other capital gains or losses, calculate the tax savings associated with the sale.

ANSWER

Doug saves $900 ($3,000 × 0.30). It should be noted that the loss is limited to $3,000; if Doug dies, the unused capital loss of $22,000 is lost.

The effect of gift taxes paid by the donor on the donee's basis for property received is another reason why it may be more advantageous to give appreciated property rather than property with an FMV less than its basis. A portion of the gift taxes paid as a result of giving appreciated property is added to the property's basis. However, payment of gift taxes due to the gift of property that has an FMV less than its basis does not result in an increase in the donee's basis.

SELECTION OF PROPERTY TO TRANSFER AT TIME OF DEATH

An integral part of gift and estate planning is the selection of property to be transferred to family members and others both during the taxpayer's lifetime and upon death. Usually, taxpayers find it advantageous to retain highly appreciated property in their estates and transfer such property at death to the taxpayer's heirs because the basis of the inherited property will be increased to its FMV at the date of death (or six months from the date of death if the alternate valuation date is elected). Of course, the impact of gift and estate taxes also play a major role in this planning process.

Investment and business assets that have declined in value (i.e., the FMV is less than the basis) should normally be sold before death to obtain an income tax deduction for the loss. If the property is not sold or otherwise disposed of before death, the basis of the inherited property is reduced to its FMV.

EXAMPLE I5-97 ▶ Paul owns two farms of similar size and quality. Each farm has a $500,000 FMV. Paul's basis for the first farm is $100,000, and his basis for the second farm is $430,000. Eventually, Paul plans for both farms to be owned by Roberta. However, he would like to transfer ownership of one farm now and retain the other farm until his death. Paul should make a gift of the second farm and transfer the first farm to Roberta upon his death because the second farm has appreciated less in value. When Paul dies and devises the first farm to Roberta, she will have a basis for the property equal to its FMV at the date of death even though Paul's basis is only $100,000. ◀

COMPLIANCE AND PROCEDURAL CONSIDERATIONS

KEY POINT

Many taxpayers do not maintain adequate records that can be used to document the basis of their most important asset, their personal residence. For example, taxpayers can increase the basis of their residence if they have the driveway paved or add a new room or porch.

DOCUMENTATION OF BASIS

The importance of being able to determine and document the basis of assets acquired by a taxpayer cannot be overemphasized. Accurate records of asset acquisitions, dispositions, and adjustments to basis are essential. When more than one asset is acquired at the same time, the amount paid must be allocated among the assets acquired based on their relative FMVs. Subsequent adjustments to basis, such as those due to capital improvements and depreciation deductions, must be documented.

Because the basis of property can be determined by reference to another person's basis for that asset (e.g., gifts), taxpayers should be particularly aware of obtaining documentation for that basis at the time of the transfer. In the case of a gift, the taxpayer's basis may be affected by any gift tax paid by the donor. A copy of the donor's gift tax return is useful in documenting the upward adjustment to the donor's basis in determining the donee's basis.

Taxpayers who inherit property may use the decedent's federal Estate Tax Return (Form 706) to determine the FMV at the time of the decedent's death or FMV as of the alternate valuation date. However, the appraised value used for estate tax purposes is only presumptively correct for basis purposes. Although the FMVs used to determine the estate tax are typically used to determine basis, neither the taxpayer nor the IRS is barred from using an FMV for basis purposes that differs from the values used for the estate tax return.[83]

REPORTING OF CAPITAL GAINS AND LOSSES ON SCHEDULE D

Capital gains and losses are reported by individuals on Schedule D, which is then attached to Form 1040. Part I is used to report short-term capital gains and losses, and Part II is used to report long-term capital gains and losses. In Part II, a separate column is provided for NCG that is taxed at 28%. Part III is a summary of Parts I and II, while computation of the tax liability is presented in Part IV. Because of the different rates that may apply to NCG, 21 lines are used to compute the tax and furthermore a worksheet must be used if the taxpayer has unrecaptured Sec. 1250 gain (see line 19). The total tax is then entered on line 40 of page 2 of Form 1040. Because of different rates that apply to NCG, Schedule D is now one of the most difficult forms for taxpayers to prepare.

Capital gains due to installment sales are first reported on a separate form before being included on Schedule D. The taxpayer's share of capital gains and losses from partnerships, S corporations, and fiduciaries is reported in Parts I and II on lines 5 and 12. The carryover of capital losses is also included in Parts I and II on lines 6 and 14.

A filled-in copy of Schedule D is shown in Figure I5-1. It includes the computations relating to the information in Example I5-98.

EXAMPLE I5-98 ▶ Virgil Brady uses the following information to prepare his Schedule D for 2001. He sold 200 shares of Tennis Corporation stock for $13,000 on June 20, 2001. The shares were purchased on October 2, 2000 for $8,700. He has an STCL carryforward from 2000 of $8,200. He sold a piano for $4,000 on May 30, 2001. The piano was purchased on April 12, 1991 for $2,500 and used by his two sons.

Virgil has an STCG of $4,300 that is offset by the $8,200 of STCL carryforward on line 6. His NSTCL of $3,900 ($8,200 − $4,300) is shown on line 7. His $1,500 LTCG as a result of the sale of the piano is on line 8. Because this is his only sale of a capital asset held more than one year, his NLTCG on line 16 is $1,500.

On line 17, the NSTCL of $3,900 and NLTCG of $1,500 are combined and shown on line 17 as $2,400. This net capital loss of $2,400 is recorded on line 18 and is deducted on line 13 of Form 1040. ◀

---

[83] Rev. Rul. 54-97, 1954-1 C.B. 113 and *Achille F. Ford v. U.S.*, 5 AFTR 2d 1157, 60-1 USTC ¶9375 (Ct. Cls., 1960).

SCHEDULE D (Form 1040)

Department of the Treasury Internal Revenue Service (99)

Capital Gains and Losses

▶ Attach to Form 1040. ▶ See Instructions for Schedule D (Form 1040).

▶ Use Schedule D-1 to list additional transactions for lines 1 and 8.

OMB No. 1545-0074

2001

Attachment Sequence No. **12**

Name(s) shown on Form 1040: Virgil Brady

Your social security number: 444 44 4444

Part I **Short-Term Capital Gains and Losses—Assets Held One Year or Less**

(a) Description of property (Example: 100 sh. XYZ Co.)	(b) Date acquired (Mo., day, yr.)	(c) Date sold (Mo., day, yr.)	(d) Sales price (see page D-5 of the instructions)	(e) Cost or other basis (see page D-5 of the instructions)	(f) Gain or (loss) Subtract (e) from (d)
1 200 Tennis Corp.	10-2-00	6-20-01	13,000	8,700	4,300
2 Enter your short-term totals, if any, from Schedule D-1, line 2 . . . . **2**					
3 **Total short-term sales price amounts.** Add lines 1 and 2 in column (d) **3**					
4 Short-term gain from Form 6252 and short-term gain or (loss) from Forms 4684, 6781, and 8824 . . . **4**					
5 Net short-term gain or (loss) from partnerships, S corporations, estates, and trusts from Schedule(s) K-1 . . . **5**					
6 Short-term capital loss carryover. Enter the amount, if any, from line 8 of your 2000 Capital Loss Carryover Worksheet . . . **6**					(8,200)
7 **Net short-term capital gain or (loss).** Combine lines 1 through 6 in column (f). **7**					(3,900)

Part II **Long-Term Capital Gains and Losses—Assets Held More Than One Year**

(a) Description of property (Example: 100 sh. XYZ Co.)	(b) Date acquired (Mo., day, yr.)	(c) Date sold (Mo., day, yr.)	(d) Sales price (see page D-5 of the instructions)	(e) Cost or other basis (see page D-5 of the instructions)	(f) Gain or (loss) Subtract (e) from (d)	(g) 28% rate gain or (loss) * (see instr. below)
8 Piano	4-12-91	5-30-01	4,000	2,500	1,500	
9 Enter your long-term totals, if any, from Schedule D-1, line 9 . . . . **9**						
10 **Total long-term sales price amounts.** Add lines 8 and 9 in column (d) **10**						
11 Gain from Form 4797, Part I; long-term gain from Forms 2439 and 6252; and long-term gain or (loss) from Forms 4684, 6781, and 8824 . . . **11**						
12 Net long-term gain or (loss) from partnerships, S corporations, estates, and trusts from Schedule(s) K-1 . . . **12**						
13 Capital gain distributions. See page D-1 of the instructions . . . **13**						
14 Long-term capital loss carryover. Enter in both columns (f) and (g) the amount, if any, from line 13 of your 2000 Capital Loss Carryover Worksheet . . . **14**					( )	( )
15 Combine lines 8 through 14 in column (g) . . . **15**						
16 **Net long-term capital gain or (loss).** Combine lines 8 through 14 in column (f) **16** **Next:** Go to Part III on the back.					1,500	

* **28% rate gain or loss** includes **all** "collectibles gains and losses" (as defined on page D-6 of the instructions) and up to 50% of the eligible gain on qualified small business stock (see page D-4 of the instructions).

For Paperwork Reduction Act Notice, see Form 1040 instructions. Cat. No. 11338H **Schedule D (Form 1040) 2001**

FIGURE I5-1 ▶ PARTS I–II OF SCHEDULE D FOR EXAMPLE I5-97

Part III **Taxable Gain or Deductible Loss**

17 Combine lines 7 and 16 and enter the result. If a loss, go to line 18. If a gain, enter the gain on Form 1040, line 13, and complete Form 1040 through line 39 . . . . **17** (2,400)

Next: • If both lines 16 and 17 are gains **and** Form 1040, line 39, is more than zero, complete Part IV below.
• Otherwise, skip the rest of Schedule D and complete Form 1040.

18 If line 17 is a loss, enter here and on Form 1040, line 13, the **smaller** of **(a)** that loss or **(b)** ($3,000) (or, if married filing separately, ($1,500)). Then complete Form 1040 through line 37 **18** (2,400)

Next: • If the loss on line 17 is more than the loss on line 18 **or** if Form 1040, line 37, is less than zero, skip **Part IV** below and complete the **Capital Loss Carryover Worksheet** on page D-6 of the instructions before completing the rest of Form 1040.
• Otherwise, skip **Part IV** below and complete the rest of Form 1040.

Part IV **Tax Computation Using Maximum Capital Gains Rates**

19 Enter your unrecaptured section 1250 gain, if any, from line 17 of the worksheet on page D-7 of the instructions **19**

If line 15 or line 19 is more than zero, complete the worksheet on page D-9 of the instructions to figure the amount to enter on lines 22, 29, and 40 below, and skip all other lines below. Otherwise, go to line 20.

20 Enter your taxable income from Form 1040, line 39 . . . . . . **20**

21 Enter the **smaller** of line 16 or line 17 of Schedule D **21**

22 If you are deducting investment interest expense on Form 4952, enter the amount from Form 4952, line 4e. Otherwise, enter -0- **22**

23 Subtract line 22 from line 21. If zero or less, enter -0- **23**

24 Subtract line 23 from line 20. If zero or less, enter -0- **24**

25 Figure the tax on the amount on line 24. Use the Tax Table or Tax Rate Schedules, whichever applies **25**

26 Enter the **smaller** of:
• The amount on line 20 **or**
• $45,200 if married filing jointly or qualifying widow(er); $27,050 if single; $36,250 if head of household; or $22,600 if married filing separately } . . . **26**

If line 26 is greater than line 24, go to line 27. Otherwise, skip lines 27 through 33 and go to line 34.

27 Enter the amount from line 24 . . . . **27**

28 Subtract line 27 from line 26. If zero or less, enter -0- and go to line 34 **28**

29 Enter your qualified 5-year gain, if any, from line 7 of the worksheet on page D-8 . . . **29**

30 Enter the **smaller** of line 28 or line 29 . . . . **30**

31 Multiply line 30 by 8% (.08) **31**

32 Subtract line 30 from line 28 . . . . **32**

33 Multiply line 32 by 10% (.10) **33**

If the amounts on lines 23 and 28 are the same, skip lines 34 through 37 and go to line 38.

34 Enter the **smaller** of line 20 or line 23 . . . . **34**

35 Enter the amount from line 28 (if line 28 is blank, enter -0-) . . . **35**

36 Subtract line 35 from line 34 . . . . **36**

37 Multiply line 36 by 20% (.20) **37**

38 Add lines 25, 31, 33, and 37 . . . . **38**

39 Figure the tax on the amount on line 20. Use the Tax Table or Tax Rate Schedules, whichever applies **39**

40 **Tax on all taxable income (including capital gains).** Enter the **smaller** of line 38 or line 39 here and on Form 1040, line 40 . . . . **40**

Schedule D (Form 1040) 2001

FIGURE I5-1 ▶ PARTS III–IV OF SCHEDULE D FOR EXAMPLE I5-90

To improve taxpayer compliance with respect to the reporting of sales and exchanges, every person doing business as a broker is required to furnish the government with information pertaining to each customer, including gross proceeds due to any sales or exchanges.[84] The Tax Reform Act of 1986 extended this requirement to real estate brokers and defined the term *real estate broker* as meaning "any of the following persons involved in a real estate transaction in the following order: the person responsible for closing the transaction, the mortgage lender, the seller's broker, or the buyer's broker."[85] The information provided by the broker to the government must be reported to each customer on Form 1099-B. Taxpayers must use Schedule D to reconcile amounts shown on Form 1099-B with the taxpayer's income tax return. Starting in 1997, all investors who receive LTCGs distributions from mutual funds are required to file Schedule D.

PROBLEM MATERIALS

DISCUSSION QUESTIONS

I5-1 What problem may exist in determining the amount realized for an investor who exchanges common stock of a publicly traded corporation for a used building? How is the problem likely to be resolved?

I5-2 In 1992 Ellen purchased a house for $60,000 to use as her personal residence. She paid $12,000 and borrowed $48,000 from the local savings and loan company. In 1995 she paid $10,000 to add a room to the house. In 1997 she paid $625 to have the house painted and $800 for built-in bookshelves. As of January 1 of the current year, she has reduced the $48,000 mortgage to $44,300. What is her basis for the house?

I5-3 Vincent pays $20,000 for equipment to use in his trade or business. He pays sales tax of $800 as a result of the purchase. Must the $800 sales tax be capitalized as part of the purchase price?

I5-4 Sergio owns 200 shares of Palm Corporation common stock, purchased during the prior year: 100 shares on July 5, for $9,000; and 100 shares on October 15, for $12,000. When Sergio sells 50 shares for $8,000 on July 18 of the current year, he does not identify the particular shares sold. Determine the amount and character of the gain.

I5-5 On August 5 of the current year, David receives stock of Western Corporation as a gift from his grandfather, who acquired the stock on January 15, 1987. Under what conditions would David's holding period start on

a. August 5 of the current year?
b. January 15, 1987?

I5-6 Jim inherits property (a capital asset) from his brother, who dies in March of the current year, when the property has a $1,900,000 FMV. This property is the only property included in his brother's gross estate and there is a taxable estate. The FMV of the property as of the alternate valuation date is $1,700,000.

a. Why might the executor of the brother's estate elect to use the alternate valuation date to value the property?
b. Why might Jim prefer the executor to use FMV at time of the death to value the property?
c. If the marginal estate tax rate is 37% and Jim's marginal income tax rate is 27%, which value should the executor use?

I5-7 Martha owns 500 shares of Columbus Corporation common stock at the beginning of the year with a basis of $82,500. During the year, Columbus declares and pays a 10% nontaxable stock dividend. What is her basis for each of the 50 shares received?

I5-8 Mario owns 2,000 shares of Nevada Corporation common stock at the beginning of the year. His basis for the stock is $38,880. During the year, Nevada declares and pays a stock dividend. After the dividend, Mario's basis for each share of stock owned is $18. What is the percentage dividend paid by Nevada?

I5-9 A corporate taxpayer plans to build a $6 million office building during the next 18 months. How must the corporation treat the interest on debt paid or incurred during the production period?

I5-10 Andy owns an appliance store where he has merchandise such as refrigerators for sale. Roger, a bachelor, owns a refrigerator, which he uses in his apartment for personal use. For which individual is the refrigerator a capital asset?

I5-11 Why did the Supreme Court rule in the *Corn Products* case that a gain due to the sale of futures contracts is ordinary income instead of capital gain?

---

[84] Sec. 6045(a).

[85] Sec. 6045(c).

I5-12 When is the gain on the sale or exchange of securities by a dealer in securities classified as capital gain?

I5-13 In 1982, Florence purchased 30 acres of land. She has not used the land for business purposes or made any substantial improvements to the property. During the current year, she subdivides the land into 15 lots and advertises the lots for sale. She sells four lots at a gain.
a. What is the character of the gain on the sale of the four lots?
b. Explain how the basis of each lot would be determined.

I5-14 Amy has LTCGs that are taxed at different tax rates, 20%, 25% and 28%. She also has NSTCLs that amount to less than her NLTCG. The procedure for offsetting the NSTCL against the LTCGs is favorable to her. Explain.

I5-15 Four years ago, Susan loaned $7,000 to her friend Joe. During the current year, the $7,000 loan is considered worthless. Explain how Susan should treat the worthless debt for tax purposes.

I5-16 Why did the Supreme Court rule in *Arkansas Best* that the stock of a corporation purchased by the taxpayer to protect the taxpayer's business reputation was a capital asset?

I5-17 The effective tax rate on gain of $1,000,000 resulting from the sale of qualified small business stock held more than five years is 14%. Do you agree or disagree? Explain.

I5-18 Nancy and the Minor Corporation own bonds of the East Corporation. Minor Corporation owns 80% of the stock of East Corporation. East Corporation has declared bankruptcy this year, and bondholders will receive only 26% of the face value of the debt. Explain why the loss is a capital loss for Nancy but an ordinary loss for the Minor Corporation.

I5-19 On January 1 of the current year, the Orange Corporation issues $500,000 of 11%, 20-year bonds for $480,000. Determine the amount of original issue discount, if any.

I5-20 Today, Juanita purchases a 15-year, 7% bond of the Sunflower Corporation issued four years ago at par. She purchases the bond as an investment at a discount from the par value. If she sells the bonds two years from now, explain why some or all of the gain may be ordinary income.

I5-21 Judy just obtained a patent on a new product she has developed. Bell Corporation wishes to market the product and will pay 12% of all future sales of the product to Judy. How can she be sure that the payments received will be treated as a long-term capital gain?

I5-22 When is the transferor of a franchise unable to treat the transfer as a sale or an exchange of a capital asset?

I5-23 How does a lessor treat payments received for canceling a lease?

I5-24 What is the first day that an individual could sell a capital asset purchased on March 31, 2002 and have a holding period of more than one year?

I5-25 Phil, a cash-basis taxpayer, sells the following marketable securities, which are capital assets during 2002. Determine whether the gains or losses are long-term or short-term. Also determine the net capital gain and adjusted net capital gain for 2002.

Capital Asset	*Basis*	*Date Acquired*	*Trade Date in 2002*	*Sales Price*
A	$40,000	Feb. 10, 2001	Aug. 12	$52,000
B	20,000	Dec. 5, 2001	May 2	17,000
C	30,000	Apr. 9, 2000	Dec. 10	37,400

I5-26 How might the current treatment of capital losses discourage an individual investor from purchasing stock of a high-risk, start-up company?

I5-27 An individual taxpayer has realized a $40,000 loss on the sale of an asset that had a holding period of eight months. Explain why the taxpayer may be indifferent as to whether the asset is a capital asset.

I5-28 If Pam transfers an asset to Fred and the asset is subject to a liability that is assumed by Fred, how does Fred's assumption of the liability affect the amount realized by Pam? How does Fred's assumption of the liability affect his basis for the property?

ISSUE IDENTIFICATION QUESTIONS

I5-29 Acorn Corporation, a company that purchases malt barley from farmers and sells it to brewers, is interested in determining whether a new variety of barley will grow successfully in the Pacific Northwest. The corporation has acquired the seed from Europe and will conduct the experiments with the cooperation of farmers in the area. If the experiments prove successful, Acorn will sell the remaining seed to the farmers. What tax issues should Acorn Corporation consider?

I5-30 Lisa and John are in the business of breeding beavers to produce fur for sale. They recently purchased a pair of breeding beavers for $30,000 from XUN, Inc. and agreed to pay interest at 10% each year for five years. After the five-year period, they could pay the debt by delivering seven beavers to XUN, Inc. provided that each beaver was at least nine months old. Identify the tax issues involved in this situation.

I5-31 Mike, a real estate broker in California, recently inherited a farm from his deceased uncle and plans to sell the farm to the first available buyer. His uncle purchased the property 12 years ago for $600,000. The FMV of the farm on the date of the uncle's death was $500,000. Mike sells the farm for $520,000 seven months after his uncle's death. What tax issues should Mike consider?

I5-32 Sylvia, a dentist with a marginal tax rate of 38.6% and excellent skills as a carpenter, started the construction of a house that she planned to give to her son as a surprise when he returned from Saudia Arabia, where he is serving in the military. She began construction on March 23, 2001, and finished the house on July 10, 2002, at a total cost of $70,000. Her son is expected to be home on September 1, 2002.

On July 30, 2002, Roscoe offered Sylvia $145,000 for the house and Sylvia considered the offer to be so attractive that she accepted it. She decided that she could purchase a suitable home for her son for about $100,000. What tax issues should Sylvia consider?

PROBLEMS

I5-33 ***Amount Realized.*** Tracy owns a nondepreciable capital asset held for investment. The asset was purchased for $150,000 six years earlier and is now subject to a $45,000 liability. During the current year, Tracy transfers the asset to Tim in exchange for $74,000 cash and a new automobile with a $40,000 FMV to be used by Tracy for personal use; Tim assumes the $45,000 liability. Determine the amount of Tracy's LTCG or LTCL.

I5-34 ***Basis of Property Received as a Gift.*** Doug receives a duplex as a gift from his uncle. The uncle's basis for the duplex and land is $90,000. At the time of the gift, the land and building have FMVs of $40,000 and $80,000, respectively. No gift tax is paid by Doug's uncle at the time of the gift.

a. To determine gain, what is Doug's basis for the land?
b. To determine gain, what is Doug's basis for the building?
c. Will the basis of the land and building be the same as in Parts a and b for purposes of determining a loss?

I5-35 ***Sale of Property Received as a Gift.*** During the current year, Stan sells a tract of land for $800,000. The property was received as a gift from Maxine on March 10, 1987, when the property had a $310,000 FMV. The taxable gift was $300,000. Maxine purchased the property on April 12, 1980, for $110,000. At the time of the gift, Maxine paid a gift tax of $12,000. In order to sell the property, Stan paid a sales commission of $16,000.

a. What is Stan's realized gain on the sale?
b. How would your answer to Part a change, if at all, if the FMV of the gift property was $85,000 as of the date of the gift?

I5-36 ***Sale of Asset Received as a Gift and Inheritance.*** Bud receives 200 shares of Georgia Corporation stock from his uncle on July 20, 2001, when the stock has a $45,000 FMV. The taxable gift is $45,000, since his uncle made another gift to Bud for $10,000 in January. The uncle pays a gift tax of $1,500. The uncle paid $30,000 for the stock on April 12, 1995.

Without considering the transactions below, Bud has AGI of $25,000 in 2001. No other transactions involving capital assets occur during the year. Analyze each transaction below, independent of the others, and determine Bud's AGI in each case.

a. He sells the stock on October 12, 2003, for $48,000.
b. He sells the stock on October 12, 2003, for $28,000.
c. He sells the stock on December 16, 2002, for $42,000.

I5-37 ***Basis of Property Converted from Personal Use.*** Irene owns a truck costing $15,000 and used for personal activities. The truck has a $9,600 FMV when it is transferred to her business, which is operated as a sole proprietorship.

a. What is the basis of the truck for determining depreciation?
b. What is Irene's realized gain or loss if the truck is sold for $5,000 after claiming depreciation of $4,000?

I5-38 ***Sale of Assets Received as a Gift and Inherited.*** Daniel receives 400 shares of A&M Corporation stock from his aunt on May 20, 2002, as a gift when the stock has a $60,000 FMV. His aunt purchased the stock in 1999 for $42,000. The taxable gift is $60,000 because she made earlier gifts to Daniel during 2002 and used the annual exclusion. She paid a gift tax of $11,000 on the gift of A&M stock to Daniel.

Daniel also inherited 300 shares of Longhorn Corporation preferred stock when his uncle died on November 12, 2002, when the stock's FMV was $30,000. His uncle purchased the stock in 1990 for $27,600. Determine the gain or loss on the sale of A & M and Longhorn stock on December 15, 2002 under each alternative situation below.

a. A & M stock was sold for $62,600, and Longhorn stock was sold for $30,750.
b. A & M stock was sold for $58,200, and Longhorn stock was sold for $28,650.
c. Assume the same as in (a) except his aunt purchased A & M stock for $51,000 and his uncle purchased Longhorn stock for $31,200.

I5-39 ***Personal-use Property Converted to Rental Property.*** Tally owns a house that she has been living in for eight years. She purchased the house in 1990 for $245,000 and the FMV today is $200,000. She is moving into her friend's house and has decided to convert her residence to rental property. Assume 20% of the property's value is allocated to land.

a. What is the basis of the house for depreciation?
b. If she claims depreciation of $15,000 and sells the property six years later for $260,000 (20% allocated to land), determine the gain on the sale of the building and gain on the sale of the land.
c. If the FMV is $290,000 when she converts the house to rental property instead of $200,000, what is the basis of the house for depreciation?

I5-40 ***Stock Rights.*** Kathleen owns 500 shares of Buda Corporation common stock which was purchased on March 20, 1999, for $48,000. On October 10 of the current year, she receives a distribution of 500 stock rights. Each stock right has a $20 FMV and the FMV of the Buda common stock is $100 per share. With each stock right, she may acquire one share of Buda common stock for $95.

a. How much gross income must Kathleen recognize?
b. What is the basis of each stock right received?
c. If she sells the 500 stock rights for $10,600, what is her gain?
d. If she exercises the 500 stock rights on November 10, what is the basis of the 500 shares she receives and when does the holding period for those shares start?

I5-41 ***Stock Rights.*** Martha Lou owns 100 shares of Atlanta Corporation common stock. She purchased the stock on July 25, 1986, for $4,000. On May 2 of the current year, she receives a nontaxable distribution of 100 stock rights. Each stock right has a $10 FMV, and the FMV of the Atlanta common stock is $70 per share. With each stock right, Martha Lou may acquire one share of Atlanta common for $68 per share. Assuming that she elects to allocate basis to the stock rights, answer the following:

a. What is the basis allocated to the stock rights?
b. If she sells the stock rights on June 10 for $1,080, what are the amount and character of the recognized gain?
c. If she exercises the stock rights on May 14, what is the basis of the 100 shares purchased and when does the holding period start?
d. If she does not elect to allocate basis to the stock rights, what are the amount and character of the gain if she sells the stock rights on June 10 for $1,080?

I5-42 ***Real Property Subdivided for Sale.*** Beth acquired only one tract of land seven years ago as an investment. In order to sell the land at a higher price, she decides to subdivide it into 20 lots. She pays for improvements such as clearing and leveling, but the improvements are not considered to be substantial. Each lot has a basis of $2,000, and a selling price of $6,000. Selling expenses of $480 were incurred to sell two lots last year. This year, ten lots are sold, and selling expenses amount to $1,900. How much ordinary income and capital gain must be recognized in the prior and current year?

I5-43 ***Marginal Tax Rates.*** Mr. and Mrs Dunbar have taxable income of $145,000. Consider the following independent cases where capital gains are recognized and determine the marginal tax rate for the capital gain in each case. Ignore the effect of increasing AGI on deductions.

CASE A - $10,000 gain from sale of Storm Lake common stock held for seven months.
CASE B - $10,000 gain from sale of antique clock held for six years.
CASE C - $10,000 gain from sale of Ames preferred stock held for three years.

I5-44 ***Netting Gains and Losses*** Trisha, whose tax rate is 35%, sells the following capital assets in 2002 with gains and losses as shown:

Asset	*Gain or (Loss)*	*Holding Period*
A	$15,000	15 months
B	7,000	20 months
C	(3,000)	14 months

a. Determine Trisha's increase in tax liability as a result of the three sales. All assets are stock held for investment. Ignore the effect of increasing AGI on deductions and phase-out amounts.
b. Determine her increase in tax liability if the holding period for asset B is 8 months.
c. Determine her increase in tax liability if the holding periods are the same as in (a) but asset B is an antique clock.

I5-45 *Computing the Tax.* Donna files as a head of household in 2002 and has taxable income of $90,000, including the sale of a stock held as an investment for two years at a gain of $20,000. Only one asset was sold during the year and Donna does not have any capital loss carryovers.
a. What is the amount of Donna's tax liability?
b. What is the amount of Donna's tax liability if the stock is held for 11 months?

I5-46 *Computing the Tax.* Wayne is single and has no dependents. Without considering his $11,000 adjusted net capital gain (ANCG) his taxable income in 2002 is as follows:

AGI		$137,300
Home mortgage interest	$22,250	
State and local income taxes	8,000	
Charitable contributions	7,000	
Personal exemption	3,000	40,250
Taxable income		$97,050

a. What is Wayne's tax liability without the ANCG?
b. What is Wayne's tax liability with the ANCG?

I5-47 *Computing the Sales Price.* An investor in a 28% tax bracket owns land that is a capital asset with a $70,000 basis and a holding period of three years. The investor wishes to sell the asset at a price high enough so that he will have $120,000 in cash after paying the taxes. What is the minimum price which the investor could accept?

I5-48 *Capital Gains and Losses.* Consider the four independent situations below for an unmarried individual, and analyze the effects of the capital gains and losses on the individual's AGI. For each case, determine AGI after considering the capital gains and losses.

	Situation 1	*Situation 2*	*Situation 3*	*Situation 4*
AGI (excluding property transactions)	$40,000	$50,000	$60,000	$70,000
STCG	6,000	2,000	5,000	6,000
STCL	2,000	5,000	4,000	15,000
LTCG	3,500	15,000	10,000	9,000
LTCL	2,500	4,000	12,000	4,000

I5-49 *Capital Losses.* To better understand the rules for offsetting capital losses and how to treat capital losses carried forward, analyze the following data for an unmarried individual for the period 1999 through 2002. No capital loss carryforwards are included in the figures. For each year, determine AGI and the capital losses to be carried forward to a later tax year.

	1999	*2000*	*2001*	*2002*
AGI (excluding property transactions)	$40,000	$50,000	$60,000	$70,000
STCG	4,000	5,000	7,000	10,000
STCL	9,000	3,000	5,000	12,000
LTCG	6,000	10,000	2,200	6,000
LTCL	5,000	21,000	1,000	9,500
AGI (including property transactions)	______	______	______	______
STCL to be carried forward	______	______	______	______
LTCL to be carried forward	______	______	______	______

I5-50 *Character of Loss.* The Michigan Corporation owns 20% of the Wolverine Corporation. The Wolverine stock was acquired eight years ago to ensure a steady supply of raw materials. Michigan also owns 30% of Spartan Corporation and 85% of Huron Corporation.

Stock in both corporations was acquired more than ten years ago for investment purposes. During the current year, Wolverine, Spartan, and Huron are deemed bankrupt, and the stocks are considered worthless. Describe how Michigan should treat its losses.

I5-51 *Original Issue Discount.* On December 31, 2001, Phil purchased $20,000 of newly issued bonds of Texas Corporation for $16,568. The bonds are dated December 31, 2001. The bonds are 9%, 10-year bonds paying interest semiannually on June 30 and December 31. The bonds are priced to yield 12% compounded semiannually.

a. What is the amount of the original issue discount?
b. For the first semiannual period, what is the amount of the original issue discount Phil must recognize as ordinary income?
c. What is the total amount of interest income Phil must recognize in 2002?
d. What is Phil's basis for the bonds as of December 31, 2002?

I5-52 On January 1, 2000, Swen paid $184,000 for $200,000 of the 8%, 20-year bonds of Penn Corporation, issued on January 1, 1996, at par. The bonds are held as an investment. Determine the gain and the character of the gain if the bonds are sold on January 1, 2002 for

a. $191,000
b. $185,750
c. $183,000

I5-53 *Capital Gains and Losses.* During 2002, Gary receives a $50,000 salary and has no deductions for AGI. In 2001, Gary had a $5,000 STCL and no other capital losses or capital gains. Consider the following sales and determine Gary's AGI for 2002.

- An automobile purchased in 1997 for $10,800 and held for personal use is sold for $7,000.
- On April 10, 2002, stock held for investment is sold for $21,000. The stock was acquired on November 20, 2001, for $9,300.

I5-54 *Call Options.* On February 10, 2002, Gail purchases 20 calls on Red Corporation for $250 per call. Each call represents an option to buy 100 shares of Red stock at $42 per share any time before November 25, 2002. Compute the gain or loss recognized, and determine whether the gain or loss is long-term or short-term for Gail in the following situations:

a. The 20 calls are sold on May 15, 2002, for $310 per call.
b. The calls are not exercised but allowed to expire.
c. The calls are exercised on July 15, 2002 and the 2,000 shares of Red Corporation stock are sold on July 20, 2003, for $50 per share.

I5-55 *Call Writing.* Dan owns 500 shares of Rocket Corporation common stock. The stock was acquired two years ago for $30 per share. On October 2, 2002, Dan writes five calls on the stock, which represent options to buy the 500 shares of Rocket at $75 per share. For each call, Dan receives $210. The calls expire on June 22, 2003. Consider the following transactions and describe the tax treatment for Dan:

a. The five calls are exercised on December 4, 2002.
b. The calls are not exercised and allowed to expire.

I5-56 *Corporate Capital Gains and Losses.* Determine the taxable income for the Columbia Corporation for the following independent cases:

Case	*Income from Operations*	*STCG (NSTCL)*	*NLTCG (NLTCL)*
A	$110,000	$30,000	$44,000
B	100,000	(50,000)	65,000
C	80,000	(37,000)	30,000
D	90,000	(15,000)	(9,000)

I5-57 *Original Issue Discount.* On January 1, 2001, Sean purchased an 8%, $100,000 corporate bond for $92,277. The bond was issued on January 1, 2001 and matures on January 1, 2006. Interest is paid semiannually, and the effective yield to maturity is 10% compounded semiannually. On July 1, 2002, Sean sells the bond for $95,949. A schedule of interest amortization for the bond is shown in Table I5-2 on page 5-42.

a. How much interest income must Sean recognize in 2001?
b. How much interest income must Sean recognize in 2002?
c. How much gain must Sean recognize in 2002 on the sale of the bond?

▼ **TABLE I5-2**
Interest Amortization for Problem I5-57

	Interest Received (1)	Amortization of Discount (2)	Interest Income (3) = (1) + (2)
6-30-01	$4,000	$614	$4,614
12-31-00	4,000	645	4,645
6-30-01	4,000	677	4,677
12-31-01	4,000	711	4,711
6-30-02	4,000	747	4,747
12-31-02	4,000	783	4,783
6-30-03	4,000	823	4,823
12-31-03	4,000	864	4,864
6-30-04	4,000	907	4,907
12-31-07	4,000	952	4,952

I5-58 *Capital Gains and Losses.* Martha has $40,000 AGI without considering the following information. During the year, she incurs a LTCL of $10,000 and has a gain of $14,000 due to the sale of a capital asset held for more than a year.

a. If the $14,000 gain is not properly classified as a LTCG (i.e., is improperly treated as an ordinary gain), determine Martha's AGI.
b. If the $14,000 gain is properly classified as a LTCG, determine her AGI.
c. If Martha has a $2,500 STCL carryover from earlier years, how would the answers to Parts a and b be affected?

I5-59 *Capital Gains and Losses.* Without considering the following capital gains and losses, Charlene has taxable income of $140,000 and a marginal tax rate of 36%. During the year, she sold stock held for nine months at a gain of $10,000; stock held for three years at a gain of $15,000; and a collectible asset held for six years at a gain of $20,000. Ignore the effect of the gains on any threshold amounts and assume that her marginal tax rate of 36% does not change.

a. What is her taxable income after considering the three gains and the increase in her tax liability?
b. In addition to the above three sales, assume that she sells another asset and has a STCL of $14,000. What is her taxable income after considering the four transactions and the increase in her tax liability as a result of the four transactions?
c. In addition to the above three sales in a., assume that she sells another collectible asset held seven years as an investment and has a $27,000 capital loss. What is her taxable income after considering the four transactions and the increase in her tax liability?

I5-60 *Corporate Capital Gains and Losses.* In 1997, the City Corporation sold a capital asset and incurred a $40,000 LTCL that was carried forward to subsequent years. That sale was the only sale of a capital asset that City had made until 2002, when City sells a capital asset and recognizes a STCG of $53,000. Without considering the STCG from the sale, City's taxable income is $250,000.

a. Determine the corporation's NSTCG for 2002.
b. Determine the corporation's 2002 taxable income.
c. If the sale of the asset in 1997 had occurred in 1996, determine the corporation's 2002 taxable income.

COMPREHENSIVE PROBLEM

I5-61 Betty incurs the following transactions during the current year. Without considering the transactions, her 2002 AGI is $40,000. Analyze the transactions and answer the questions below:

- On March 10, 2002, she sells a painting for $2,000. Betty is the artist, and she completed the painting in 1997. Her basis for the painting is $50.

- On June 18, 2002, she receives $28,500 from the sale of stock purchased by her uncle in 1992 for $10,000, which she inherits on February 20, 2002, as a result of her uncle's death. The stock's FMV on that date is $30,000.
- On July 30, 2002, she sells land for $25,000 that was received as a gift from her brother on April 8, 2002, when the land's FMV was $30,000. Her brother purchased the land for $43,000 on October 12, 1994. No gift tax was paid.

a. What is her NSTCL or NSTCG?
b. What is her NLTCL or NLTCG?
c. What is the effect of capital gains and losses on her AGI?
d. What is her capital loss carryforward to 2003?

TAX STRATEGY PROBLEMS

I5-62 Dale purchased Blue Corporation stock four years ago for $1,000 as an investment. He intended to hold the stock until funds were needed to help pay for his daughter's college education. Today the stock has a $6,500 FMV and Dale decides to sell the stock and give the proceeds, less any taxes paid on the sale, to Tammy, his 18-year-old daughter. Dale's marginal tax rate is 30% and Tammy's marginal tax rate is 15%. Tammy has no other gross income and receives more than half of her support from Dale.
a. What advice would you give to Dale?
b. What is the cash savings if Dale follows your advice?

I5-63 Calvin, whose tax rate is 40% is considering two alternative investments on January 1, 20Y1. He can purchase $100,000 of 10% bonds due in five years or purchase $100,000 of Hobbes, Inc. common stock. The bonds are issued at par, pay interest annually on December 31, and mature at the end of five years. Interest received can be reinvested at 10%. Assume that he knows with relative certainty that the value of the stock will increase 8% each year (i.e., the value of the Hobbes stock will be $108,000 at the end of 20Y1) and the interest and principal for the bonds will be paid as scheduled. On December 31, 20Y5, he will sell the stock or receive the bond principal plus the last interest payment. Which alternative should Calvin select if he wants to have the greater amount of money as of January 1, 20Y6? Provide supporting information for your answer.

I5-64 On December 20 of the current year, Winneld has decided to sell all of the stock that she owns and reinvest the proceeds in state of Minnesota bonds. Without considering the sales, her gross income is expected to exceed $400,000 this year and in future years. Information about the stocks are provided below:

Corporation	*FMV*	*Basis*	*Holding Period*
Viking, Inc.	$190,000	$140,000	7 months
Twins, Inc.	200,000	255,000	4 years
Timberwolves, Inc.	382,000	300,000	3 years

She is willing to sell some of the stock this year and the remaining stock next year if it is more advantageous to spread the sales over two years. Assume that the FMV of the stock will not change during the next 30 days, her regular tax rate is 35% and ignore the effect of a sale on threshold amounts.

Determine the tax effect for each of the following alternatives and advise Winneld.
a. Sell all stock this year.
b. Sell Twins and Timberwolves this year and Viking next year.
c. Sell Viking and Twins this year and Timberwolves next year.

TAX FORM/RETURN PREPARATION PROBLEMS

I5-65 Given the following information for Jane Cole, complete Schedule D of Form 1040 through Part III.

- Stock options, which she purchases on February 14 of the current year for $850, expire on October 1.
- On July 1, she sells for $1,500 her personal-use automobile acquired on March 31, 1990 for $8,000.
- On August 16, she sells for $3,100 her stock of York Corporation purchased as an investment on February 16, for $1,600.

- On March 15, she sells for $5,600 an antique brass bed, a gift from her grandmother on January 10, 1988, when its FMV was $1,600. The bed was purchased by her grandmother on April 2, 1979 for $1,800.
- She has a STCL carryover of $250 from last year.

I5-66 Spencer Duck (SSN 277-31-7264) is single and his eight-year-old son, Mitch, lives with him nine months of the year in a rented condominium at 321 Hickory Drive in Ames, Iowa. Mitch lives with his mother, Spencer's ex-wife, during the summer months. His mother provides more than half of Mitch's support and Spencer has agreed to allow her to claim Mitch as her dependent. Spencer has a salary of $34,000 and itemized deductions of $4,000. Taxes withheld during the year amount to $7,000. On July 14 of the current year, he sold the following assets:

- Land was sold for $35,000. The land was received as a property settlement on January 10, 1996, when the land's FMV amounted to $30,000. His ex-wife's basis for the land, purchased on January 10, 1985, was $18,600.
- A personal-use computer acquired on March 2 last year for $4,000 was sold for $2,480.
- A membership card for a prestigious country club was sold for $8,500. The card was acquired on October 10, 1993, for $6,000.
- Marketable securities held as an investment were sold for $20,000. The securities were inherited from his uncle, who died on March 10 of the current year when FMV of the securities was $21,000. The uncle purchased the securities on May 10, 1990, for $10,700.

In addition to the above sales, Spencer received a $100 refund of state income taxes paid last year. Spencer used the standard deduction last year to compute his tax liability. Prepare Form 1040 and Schedule D for the current year.

CASE STUDY PROBLEMS

I5-67 As a political consultant for an aspiring politician, you have been hired to evaluate the following statements that pertain to capital gains and losses. Evaluate the statement and provide at least a one-paragraph explanation of each statement. As you prepare your answer, consider the fact that the aspiring politician does not have much knowledge about taxation.

a. The tax on capital gains is considered a voluntary tax.
b. The tax treatment for capital gains and losses after 1986 and before 1991 made it disadvantageous for individuals to sell or exchange capital assets as opposed to selling or exchanging assets that are not capital assets.
c. On October 22, 1986, the Tax Reform Act of 1986 was passed, which eliminated the 60% of net capital gain deduction (i.e., an individual taxpayer with $10,000 of net capital gain was entitled to a $6,000 deduction when computing AGI) before January 1, 1987. Many state governments enjoyed a substantial increase in 1986 tax revenue.
d. High-income taxpayers receive the most benefit from preferential treatment for capital gains.

I5-68 Your client, Apex Corporation, entered into an agreement with an executive to purchase his personal residence at its current FMV in the event that his employment is terminated by the company during a five-year period. The executive's job was terminated before the end of the five-year period and Apex acquired the house for $500,000. Due to a downturn in the real estate market, a $200,000 loss was incurred by the company upon the resale of the house. The chief financial officer of Apex insists that the loss be characterized as ordinary, based on the *Corn Products* doctrine. Your research into this matter reveals that the weight of authority heavily favors capital loss treatment (i.e., case law based on facts identical to the above issue held that the loss was capital rather than ordinary). You therefore conclude that the client's position does not have a realistic possibility of being sustained administratively or judicially on its merits if challenged by the IRS. What responsibility do you have as a tax practitioner relative to preparing the client's tax return and rendering continuing tax consulting services to the client? (See the Section *Statements on Standards for Tax Services* in Chapter I1 for a discussion of these issues.)

TAX RESEARCH PROBLEMS

I5-69 Tom Williams is an equal partner in a partnership with the Kansas Corporation. Williams, an inventor, produced a new process while working for the partnership, which has been patented by the partnership. Before making any use of the patent, the partnership entered into a contract granting all rights to use the process for the life of the patent to the Mason Manufacturing Co.

The time between receiving the patent and entering into the contract with Mason amounted to eight months. Mason agreed to pay 0.3% of all sales revenue generated by products produced as a result of the process. If Mason fails to make payments on a timely basis, Mason's right to use the process is forfeited and the agreement between the partnership and Mason is canceled. Will any of the proceeds collected qualify as LTCG under Sec. 1235?

A partial list of research sources is

- Reg. Sec. 1.1235-2
- *George N. Soffron,* 35 T.C. 787 (1961)

I5-70 Lynette, a famous basketball player, is considering the possibility of transferring the sole right to use her name to promote basketball shoes produced and sold by the NIK Corporation. NIK will pay $2 million to obtain the right to use Lynette's name for the next 40 years. NIK may use the name on the shoes and as a part of any of the company's advertisements for basketball shoes. If Lynette signs the contract and receives the $2 million payment, will she have to recognize capital gain or ordinary income?

A partial list of research sources is

- Sec. 1221
- Rev. Rul. 65-261, 1965-2 C.B. 281

I5-71 Jack, a tenured university professor, has been a malcontent for many years at Rockport University. The university has recently offered to pay $200,000 to Jack if he will relinquish his tenure position and resign. Jack is of the opinion that tenure is an intangible capital asset and the $200,000 received for release of the tenure should be a long-term capital gain. Explain why you agree or disagree

A partial list of research sources is

- *Harry M. Flower,* 61 T.C. 140 (1973)
- *Estelle Goldman,* 1975 PH T.C. Memo ¶75,138, 34 TCM 639

I5-72 Web Baker was hired three years ago by the Berry Corporation to serve as CEO for the company. As part of his employment contract, the corporation had agreed to purchase his residence at FMV in the event the company decided to fire him. Last year, Berry, unsatisfied with Web's performance, fired him and purchased the residence for $350,000. Berry immediately listed the house with a real estate agency. Soon after the purchase, the real estate market in the area experienced a serious decline, especially in higher-priced homes. Berry sold the house this year for $270,000 and paid selling expenses of $12,000. How should the Berry Corporation treat the $92,000 loss?

A partial list of research sources is

- Sec. 1221
- Rev. Rul. 82-204, 1982-2 C.B. 192
- *Azar Nut Co. v. CIR,* 67 AFTR 2d 91-987, 91-1 USTC ¶50,257 (5th Cir., 1991)

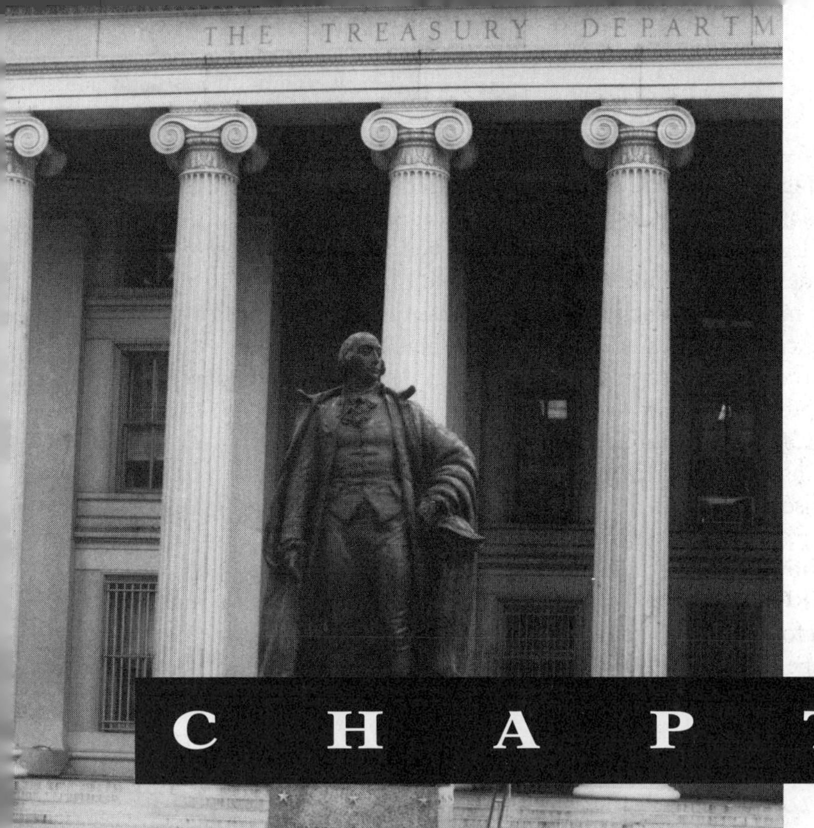

6

CHAPTER

DEDUCTIONS AND LOSSES

LEARNING OBJECTIVES

After studying this chapter, you should be able to

1. Distinguish between deductions *for* and *from* AGI
2. Discuss the criteria for deducting business and investment expenses
3. List the substantiation requirements for deducting travel and entertainment expenses
4. Explain the timing of deductions under both the cash and accrual methods of accounting
5. Explain the tax consequences of wash sales
6. Explain the tax consequences of transactions between related parties
7. Discuss the criteria for determining whether an activity is a hobby or a trade or business
8. Determine the tax consequences of vacation homes

CHAPTER OUTLINE

For versus From Adjusted Gross Income (AGI) Classification...6-3
Criteria for Deducting Business and Investment Expenses...6-4
General Restrictions on the Deductibility of Expenses...6-10
Proper Substantiation Requirement...6-16
When an Expense is Deductible...6-18
Special Disallowance Rules...6-22
Tax Planning Considerations...6-35
Compliance and Procedural Considerations...6-36

The next five chapters (I6–I10) deal with deductions. As you recall from Chapters I3 and I4, the principles governing the reporting of income are based on an "all inclusive" system of taxation; that is, gross income includes all items of income unless specifically excluded by statute. In contrast, deductions or losses are not allowed for tax purposes unless the statute specifically provides for the deduction. For example, a taxpayer who pays medical expenses during the year may deduct such expenses because the statute specifically allows for the deduction of medical expenses under Sec. 213 of the IRC.

Chapter I6 discusses the general requirements for the deductibility of taxpayer expenditures and losses. Chapter I7 deals with itemized deductions of individual taxpayers, such as medical expenses, taxes, charitable contributions, interest expense and other miscellaneous deductions. Chapter I8 covers two major areas, the deductibility of losses and bad debts. Chapter I9 discusses employee compensation and expenses, and Chapter I10 discusses tax depreciation, amortization, and depletion.

As was mentioned above, expenditures are deductible only if specifically allowed by the IRC. However, the IRC cannot possibly specify *every* deductible expense that a taxpayer might incur. Therefore, the IRC contains a framework for analyzing the nature of an expenditure. If the expenditure meets the criteria developed in the framework, the item is deductible. This framework provides for three general categories of deductions:

(1) Expenses incurred in connection with a **trade or business** (Sec. 162);
(2) Expenses incurred in connection with the **production of income** (Sec. 212);
(3) Other types of expenses that fall within specific provisions of the IRC, such as personal expenditures for medical expenses, taxes, certain types of interest expense, etc.

The first two categories of deductions, trade or business (Sec. 162) and production of income expenses (Sec. 212), are those incurred in connection with profit-motivated activities. The IRC does not attempt to specify every conceivable type of deductible expense under these two categories. Rather, the IRC sets forth general guidelines for deductibility. Any expense incurred in connection with a trade or business or for the production of income is deductible if it falls within these general guidelines and is not specifically excluded from deductibility by the IRC. For example, although the IRC does not specifically provide for the deductibility of utilities or maintenance and repairs, these expenditures are deductible if incurred in a profit-motivated activity. These general guidelines are discussed later in this chapter.

A trade or business, as discussed below, is a business activity of the taxpayer. Deductible expenses related to the production of income include expenses incurred for the following:

- Production or collection of income
- Management, conservation, or maintenance of property held for the production of income
- Determination, collection, or refund of any tax

As will be discussed later, the distinction between a trade or business and the production of income is important because it can affect both the amount and type of the deduction. Expenses incurred in both types of activities must meet additional standards of deductibility; that is, they must also be ordinary, necessary, and reasonable in the context of the activity in which they are incurred. Losses incurred in either type of activity are deductible.

Section 262 also provides, in general, that no deduction is allowed for any personal, living, or family expenses. However, the tax law does specifically provide for the deductibility of certain personal expenditures or losses. For example, casualty losses (subject to specific limitations) are allowed for personal-use property. Taxpayers may also deduct personal expenditures for certain types of interest, taxes, medical expenses, alimony, and retirement savings if the expenditures meet strict requirements. These deductions and losses for personal expenditures are discussed in Chapters I7, I8, and I9.

FOR VERSUS FROM ADJUSTED GROSS INCOME (AGI) CLASSIFICATION

OBJECTIVE 1

Distinguish between deductions for and from AGI

As demonstrated in Chapter I2, the tax formula for individuals divides all allowable business, investment, and personal deductions into the following two categories:

- Deductions subtracted from gross income in order to calculate adjusted gross income (*for* AGI deductions)
- Deductions subtracted from AGI to arrive at the amount of taxable income (*from* AGI deductions)

Section 62 specifically identifies deductions *for* AGI. All other deductions for individuals are deductions *from* AGI. The more common *for* AGI deductions include the following, subject to certain limitations:

- All allowable expenses incurred in a taxpayer's trade or business, but not including an employee's unreimbursed business expenses
- Employee business expenses that are reimbursed by the employer
- Losses from the sale or exchange of trade, business, or investment property
- Expenses attributable to the production of rent or royalty income
- Moving expenses
- Contributions to certain pension, profit-sharing, or retirement plan arrangements
- Penalties paid to a bank or other savings institution because of the early withdrawal of funds from a certificate of deposit or time savings account
- Alimony
- Interest paid by certain individuals on qualified educational loans
- Higher education expenses
- Contributions to qualified Archer medical savings accounts
- One-half of the self-employment tax imposed on self-employed individuals and 70% of health insurance costs paid by such individuals (see Chapter I14).[1]

KEY POINT

Many *for* AGI deductions are either expenses incurred in a trade or business or investment expenses or losses. Most of the deductible personal expenses are deductible *from* AGI.

For individuals, the distinction between deductions *for* AGI and *from* AGI is critical for two reasons. First, as explained in Chapter I2, the tax formula allows individuals to deduct the greater of the standard deduction or the total of the *from* AGI (itemized) deductions in arriving at taxable income. A taxpayer does not benefit from these deductions if the total for the year does not exceed the standard deduction. Second, certain itemized deductions for taxpayers with adjusted gross income over certain levels are phased out and lost. However, this phase-out of itemized deductions for higher income individuals is gradually eliminated starting in 2006, and will be completely eliminated after 2009. (See Chapter I7 for a discussion of these limits.) *For* AGI deductions, on the other hand, reduce AGI (and consequently taxable income), even if the standard deduction is used in computing taxable income. The concept of AGI has no application to corporations, estates, or trusts.

EXAMPLE I6-1 ▶ Brad, a single individual with no dependents, incurs $1,500 of deductible expenses and earns $30,000 in gross income during 2002. If the expenses are all deductions *from* AGI, Brad's taxable income is $22,300 (i.e., Brad receives a $3,000 deduction for his personal exemption and a $4,700 standard deduction). Brad receives no direct tax benefit from the expenses because they do not exceed the standard deduction. However, if the $1,500 of expenses are all deductions *for* AGI, Brad's taxable income is $20,800. In this latter case, Brad receives a full tax benefit from the expenses.

[1] Sections 62, 162(l) and 164(f). This 70% increases to 100% for 2003 and beyond. Other deductions *for* AGI include deductions for depreciation and depletion for life tenants and income beneficiaries of property, a portion of certain lump-sum distributions from qualified pension plans, reforestation expenses, required repayments of supplemental unemployment compensation benefits, certain expenses incurred for clean-fuel vehicles and refueling property, and jury duty pay that is remitted to an employer.

	Deductions from AGI	Deductions for AGI
Gross income	$30,000	$30,000
Minus: *For* AGI deductions	0	(1,500)
AGI	$30,000	$28,500
Minus: Standard deduction	(4,700)	(4,700)
Personal exemption	(3,000)	(3,000)
Taxable income	$22,300	$20,800 ◀

KEY POINT

For many individuals, the benefit of a *from* AGI deduction is lost because that particular deduction is less than its applicable limit or, the total of the itemized deductions is less than the standard deduction. Furthermore, certain itemized deductions of taxpayers with AGI over certain levels are phased out.

A second important reason for the proper classification of deductions is that AGI helps establish limits on certain deductions *from* AGI, such as medical expenses, casualty losses, charitable contributions, and miscellaneous itemized deductions. For example, an individual may deduct certain miscellaneous itemized deductions only to the extent that the sum of these deductions for the year exceeds 2% of the individual's AGI. These expenses include unreimbursed employee business expenses,[2] expenses incurred to produce investment income,[3] and the cost of tax advice and tax return preparation (see Chapter I7). A taxpayer may deduct medical expenses only to the extent their total exceeds 7.5% of the individual's AGI for the year. Individual taxpayers must first reduce casualty losses on personal-use property by $100 per casualty event. After this reduction, casualty losses are deductible only to the extent that the sum exceeds 10% of the individual's AGI. The deduction for charitable contributions, on the other hand, may not exceed 50% of the taxpayer's AGI. (See Chapter I7 for a discussion of these deductions and their limits.)

Deductions *for* AGI are generally located in two places on the tax return. First, some deductions *for* AGI appear on the front page of Form 1040 (lines 23–31a). These deductions include such items as moving expenses, alimony paid, student loan interest, and higher education expenses. Second, other deductions appear on separate schedules, including Schedule C (Profit or Loss from Business), Schedule E (Supplemental Income or Loss), or Schedule F (Profit or Loss from Farming). The profit or loss from these schedules carry over to the front page of Form 1040 as part of gross income. Thus, the deductions on these schedules are deductions *for* AGI. Figure I2-1 (Chapter I2) contains the front page of Form 1040.

CRITERIA FOR DEDUCTING BUSINESS AND INVESTMENT EXPENSES

OBJECTIVE 2

Discuss the criteria for deducting business and investment expenses

Business and investment expenses are deductible only if certain requirements are met. Thus, deductible business or investment expenses must be:

- Related to a profit-motivated activity of the taxpayer (i.e., a business or investment activity rather than a personal expenditure)
- Ordinary
- Necessary
- Reasonable in amount
- Properly documented (discussed later in the chapter under the heading Proper Substantiation Requirement), and
- An expense of the taxpayer (not someone else's expense)

Furthermore, as discussed later in this chapter under the heading General Restrictions on the Deductibility of Expenses, even if the requirements for deductibility above are met,

[2] These expenses include unreimbursed expenditures for travel and transportation, supplies, special clothing or uniforms, union dues, and subscriptions to trade journals. Reimbursed employee expenses are deductible *for* AGI and thus, are deductible in full. See Chapter I9.

[3] These expenses include rental fees for safe deposit boxes used to hold investment property, subscriptions to investment journals, bank service charges on checking accounts used in an investment or income-producing activity, and fees paid for consulting advice. Expenses incurred in an investment or income-producing activity that generates either rental or royalty income are deductions *for* AGI.

taxpayers may not deduct expenditures meeting certain criteria. Thus, an expenditure is not deductible if it is

- ► A capital expenditure
- ► Related to tax-exempt income
- ► Illegal or in violation of public policy, or
- ► Specifically disallowed by the tax law.

These criteria and related matters are discussed later.

BUSINESS OR INVESTMENT REQUIREMENT

Except for a few personal expenses, all deductible expenditures or losses must be incurred in a profit-motivated activity. For individuals, most of these expenses are deductible either under Sec. 162 as an expense incurred in a trade or business or under Sec. 212 as an expense incurred for the production of income or for the maintenance and conservation of income-producing property (an investment activity). Thus, the requirement of an activity being profit-motivated is really two-pronged: (1) a determination whether an expenditure is incurred in an activity engaged in for profit, and (2) a distinction between a trade or business and an investment activity.

REAL WORLD EXAMPLE

A taxpayer attempted to deduct treasure-hunting costs as a business expense, but the court concluded that there was no profit motive. The taxpayer kept no business records, the time spent was negligible and appeared to be recreational in nature, and no income was produced from the activity. *William J. Hezel*, 1985 PH T.C. Memo ¶85,010, 49 TCM 458.

ACTIVITY ENGAGED IN FOR PROFIT. This first part of the test classifies the expense as having been incurred in either a profit-motivated activity or a personal activity. Classifying expenses as either profit-motivated or personal can be quite difficult. For example, is the activity of coin collecting a hobby that is personal in nature, a profit-motivated business, or an investment activity? No single objective test is available. Rather, one must examine all the facts and circumstances surrounding the activity in which the expense is incurred. These factors, as well as other issues dealing with the determination of whether or not a particular activity is profit-motivated, are examined in more detail later in this chapter in the section entitled Hobby Losses.

TRADE OR BUSINESS VERSUS INVESTMENT CLASSIFICATION. The second part of the profit-motive test is the determination of whether a particular activity is a trade or business of the taxpayer or only an investment. This distinction is important for several reasons. First, a loss on the sale of the assets used in the activity may be an ordinary loss if the activity is a trade or business.[4] If it is an investment activity, however, the loss is classified as a capital loss which, as explained in Chapter I5, receives different treatment. Second, this distinction may control whether an expense of the activity is a deduction *for* AGI or a deduction *from* AGI. In general, expenses incurred in a trade or business are deductions *for* AGI whereas investment expenses other than those incurred to produce rents and royalties are deductions *from* AGI. Finally, under Sec. 179, taxpayers may currently deduct up to $24,000 each year (increasing to $25,000 in 2003 and thereafter) of tangible personal property purchased during the year for use in a trade or business. However, taxpayers must capitalize and depreciate the same expenditures over several years if they are incurred in an investment activity rather than in a trade or business. (See Chapter I10 for a discussion of the Sec. 179 current deduction for capital expenditures.)

EXAMPLE I6-2 ► Robin is a self-employed financial consultant. She meets daily with a variety of clients to discuss their investments. Because she must keep abreast of the latest market quotes and strategies, Robin subscribes to several trade publications, newsletters, and quote services. She also purchased a $4,000 computer to be used exclusively in her consulting business. The expenses incurred for these publications and services are deductions *for* AGI because Robin incurred them in her consulting business. Furthermore, she can currently deduct the $4,000 paid for the computer under the special rules of Sec. 179 because it is a business asset. ◄

On the other hand, expenses incurred in an investment activity, other than those incurred to produce rents and royalties, are miscellaneous itemized deductions *from* AGI and are deductible only to the extent that they exceed 2% of AGI (see Chapter I7).

---

[4] Under Sec. 1231, the exact treatment depends on the total gains and losses from such property for the year. See Chapter I13 for a discussion of Sec. 1231.

EXAMPLE I6-3 ▶ Steve is a wealthy attorney who invests in the stock market and keeps abreast of the latest market quotes and strategies by subscribing to several trade publications and newsletters. He also purchased a computer to use exclusively for tracking his investments. Steve generally spends a few hours each day studying this information and analyzing his portfolio. The subscription expenses are deductions *from* AGI because they are incurred in an investment (rather than a business) activity and do not relate to the production of rents and royalties. Furthermore, Steve cannot currently deduct the entire cost of the computer but must depreciate the cost over a period of five years. The deductibility of all of the above items depends on whether Steve's total miscellaneous itemized deductions exceed 2% of his AGI and whether Steve itemizes his deductions instead of using the standard deduction. ◀

ADDITIONAL COMMENT

A trade or business is an activity with a profit motive and some type of economic activity. An investment activity requires a profit motive but does not require economic activity.

Despite these important differences in treatment, the distinction between an investment activity and a trade or business is not always clear. Neither the IRC nor the Treasury Regulations provide a precise definition of what constitutes a trade or business. Judicial law provides some guidelines. In one of the first cases dealing with the issue, the Supreme Court stated that the carrying on of a trade or business involves "holding one's self out to others as engaged in the selling of goods or services."[5]

Later, another Supreme Court case emphasized that one must examine all the surrounding facts and circumstances to determine the underlying nature of an activity.[6] In that case, the taxpayer owned a large portfolio of stocks, bonds, and real estate. The taxpayer's holdings were so large that he rented offices and hired employees to help him manage the properties. The Court, however, regarded these activities as investment activities despite the size of the holdings and the amount of work and effort involved because the taxpayer merely kept records and collected interest and dividends from his securities. Other cases, however, indicate that a taxpayer who invests in stocks and bonds may be considered to be in a business if he or she frequently buys and sells securities in order to make a short-term profit on the daily swings in the market.

LEGAL AND ACCOUNTING FEES. Taxpayers may generally deduct legal and accounting fees if the fees are incurred in the regular conduct of a trade or business or for the production of income. Taxpayers may also deduct fees incurred for the determination, collection, or refund of any tax. As mentioned previously, trade or business expenses and expenses incurred in producing rents and royalties are deductible *for* AGI. Likewise, fees paid for the determination, collection, or refund of any tax are deductible *for* AGI if they are allocable to the taxpayer's trade or business or to the production of rents and royalties. These expenses include fees paid to prepare a taxpayer's Schedule C (Profit or Loss from Business), Part I of Schedule E (Supplemental Income and Loss, which is used to report rental and royalty income), and Schedule F (farm income and expenses).[7] Other tax related fees are deductible *from* AGI as miscellaneous itemized deductions, subject to the 2% of AGI limitation.

Taxpayers may not deduct legal expenses incurred for personal purposes. Likewise, taxpayers may not deduct legal fees incurred in the acquisition of property. Instead, these expenses must be capitalized and added to the cost of the property.

EXAMPLE I6-4 ▶ During the current year, Lia pays legal and accounting fees for the following:

Services rendered with regard to a contract dispute in Lia's business	$ 8,000
Services rendered in resolving a federal tax deficiency relating to Lia's business	2,500
Tax return preparation fees:	
Allocable to preparation of Schedule C	1,600
Allocable to preparation of Schedules A and B and to the remainder of Form 1040	400
Legal fees incident to a divorce	1,200
Total	$13,700

[5] *Deputy v. Pierre S. DuPont*, 23 AFTR 808, 40-1 USTC ¶9161 (USSC, 1940).

[6] *Eugene Higgins v. CIR*, 25 AFTR 1160, 41-1 USTC ¶9233 (USSC, 1941). See also *Chang H. Liang*, 23 T.C. 1040 (1955), and *Ralph E. Purvis v. CIR*, 37 AFTR 2d 76-968, 76-1 USTC ¶9270 (9th Cir., 1976); and *Samuel B. Levin v. U.S.*, 43 AFTR 2d 79-612, 79-1 USTC ¶9331 (ct. Cls., 1979).

[7] Rev. Rul. 92-29, 1992-1 C.B. 20.

Lia may deduct $12,100 ($8,000 + $2,500 + $1,600) *for* AGI. The remaining $400 of tax preparation fees are deductible *from* AGI as a miscellaneous itemized deduction subject to the 2% of AGI limitation. The legal fees incident to the divorce are personal expenses and generally are not deductible. However, Lia could take a partial deduction *from* AGI as a miscellaneous itemized deduction to the extent that the legal fees relate to giving tax advice incident to the divorce. ◀

In certain cases, taxpayers may deduct legal expenses incurred in defending one's reputation or in defending against criminal charges. In these situations, however, the legal action must have a direct relationship to the taxpayer's business or income-producing activity. In criminal proceedings, the Supreme Court has held that as long as the expenses are business expenses, they are deductible, even if the taxpayer is convicted.[8]

EXAMPLE I6-5 ▶ Mario is engaged in the business of underwriting and selling securities to the public. In the current year, Mario is charged and convicted on criminal charges of securities fraud. The conviction is appealed, but the conviction is upheld. Mario incurs $80,000 in attorney's fees in the unsuccessful defense. In this case, the legal expenses are directly related to Mario's business. Additionally, they are ordinary and necessary. Despite Mario's conviction, the attorney's fees are deductible. ◀

ORDINARY EXPENSE

Another requirement for deductibility is that a business or investment expense must be **ordinary**. Although the IRC does not provide either a definition or an application of this requirement, the Treasury Regulations under Sec. 212 indicate that for an expense to be ordinary it must be reasonable in amount and it must bear a reasonable and proximate relationship to the income-producing activity or property. This means that more than a remote connection must exist between the expense and the anticipated income. It does not mean that the property must be producing income currently.

EXAMPLE I6-6 ▶ Ahmed purchases a plot of land, on which there is an old vacant warehouse. Ahmed anticipates making a long-run profit from the investment because the value of the land is expected to appreciate eventually due to commercial development in the area. To help cover the costs of holding the property, Ahmed plans to rent storage space in the warehouse. During the current year, Ahmed incurs the following expenses, although he is unable to rent the warehouse:

Expenses	*Amount*
Property taxes	$1,000
Interest	4,000
Insurance	800
Utilities	200

All of these expenditures qualify as ordinary deductible expenses under Sec. 212 because they bear a reasonable and proximate relationship to the income Ahmed hopes to obtain, even though he generated no income from the property during the year. However, Ahmed might not be able to deduct them all in the current year because of the passive loss limitations explained in Chapter I8. ◀

ADDITIONAL COMMENT

A General Accounting Office report finds that tax cheating is widespread among self-employed taxpayers. These workers represent only 13% of all taxpayers, but account for approximately 40% of all underreported individual income. The report identified truckers as one of the least compliant groups.

The Supreme Court has ruled that for an expense to be ordinary it must be customary or usual in the context of a particular industry or business community.[9] Thus, an expenditure may be ordinary in the context of one type of business, but not in the context of another.

EXAMPLE I6-7 ▶ For many years, Hank has been an officer in Green Corporation, which is engaged in the grain business. Green Corporation purchases its grain from various suppliers. Last year, Green Corporation went bankrupt and was relieved from having to pay off its debts to its suppliers. In the current year, Hank enters into a contract to act as a commissioned agent to purchase grain for

---

[8] *CIR v. Walter F. Tellier*, 17 AFTR 2d 633, 66-1 USTC ¶9319 (USSC, 1966).

[9] *Thomas H. Welch v. Helvering*, 12 AFTR 1456, 3 USTC ¶1164 (USSC, 1933) and *Deputy v. Pierre S. DuPont*, 23 AFTR 808, 40-1 USTC ¶9161 (USSC, 1940).

Green Corporation. To reestablish a relationship with suppliers whom Hank knew previously, Hank decides to pay off as many of Green Corporation's debts as he can. Hank is under no legal obligation to do so. Hank's payments are not ordinary. Rather, they are extraordinary expenditures made for goodwill to establish Hank in a new trade or business, and they must be capitalized. ◀

An expense may be ordinary with respect to a taxpayer even though that taxpayer encounters it only once.

EXAMPLE I6-8 ▶ For several years, Donna has been engaged in the business of making and selling false teeth. Most of the advertisements, orders, and deliveries of the teeth are done through the mail. During the current year, the post office judged that some of the advertisements were false. As a result, a fraud order is issued under which the post office stamps "Fraudulent" on all letters addressed to Donna, and then returns them to the senders. In an unsuccessful suit to prevent the post office from continuing this practice, Donna expends $25,000 in lawyer's fees. These fees are ordinary business expenses because they are incurred in an action that normally or ordinarily would be taken under the circumstances. ◀

The Supreme Court has also indicated that the term *ordinary* in this context refers to an expenditure that is currently deductible rather than an expenditure that must be capitalized.[10]

REAL WORLD EXAMPLE

Payments made by a corporation to an individual who was a 50% shareholder were necessary in order to prevent him from interfering in the management of the business and damaging the corporation's reputation. *Fairmont Homes, Inc.*, 1983 PH T.C. Memo ¶83,209, 45 TCM 1340.

NECESSARY EXPENSE

In addition to being ordinary, a deductible investment or business expense must also be **necessary**. The Supreme Court has indicated that an expense is considered necessary if it is "appropriate and helpful" in the taxpayer's business.[11] To meet this appropriate or helpful standard, an expenditure need not be necessary in the sense that it is indispensable. Rather, the test is whether a reasonable or prudent businessperson would incur the same expenditure under similar circumstances.

EXAMPLE I6-9 ▶ The expenditures in Example I6-7 (the payment of debts from a former business) and Example I6-8 (the payment of legal fees) are both necessary because they are appropriate and helpful in each case. However, the expenditure in Example I6-7 is not ordinary and, therefore, is not deductible. The expenditure in Example I6-8 is deductible because it meets both tests. ◀

REASONABLE EXPENSE

Section 162 and Treasury Regulations under Sec. 212 provide that in order to be deductible the expense must be reasonable. Problems with meeting this standard generally arise when salaries are paid to an individual who is both a shareholder and an employee in a closely held business. In this situation, a controlling shareholder of a corporation receives a payment, characterized as salary, that the IRS asserts is too large for the services rendered.

EXAMPLE I6-10 ▶ Brian, the controlling shareholder and an employee of Central Corporation, receives an annual salary of $650,000 from the corporation. Based on several factors, such as the size of Central Corporation's total operations and a comparison of salary received by officers of comparably sized corporations, the IRS contends that Brian's salary should be no higher than $300,000. If Central successfully defends the $650,000 salary, the corporation is able to deduct the full amount as salary expense. If the defense is not successful, the excess $350,000 is considered a dividend to the extent of earnings and profits, and no deduction is available to Central Corporation for this amount. In either event, Brian must take the full $650,000 into income. (See the Tax Planning Considerations section in this chapter for a discussion of the use of a payback agreement in these situations.) ◀

In an attempt to link executive compensation to productivity and business performance and to discourage a common practice of increasing executive compensation despite

---

[10] *CIR v. S. B. Heininger,* 31 AFTR 783, 44-1 USTC ¶9109 (USSC, 1943). See also *CIR v. Walter F. Tellier,* 17 AFTR 2d 633, 66-1 USTC ¶9319 (USSC, 1966).

[11] *Thomas H. Welch v. Helvering,* 12 AFTR 1456, 3 USTC ¶1164 (USSC, 1933).

KEY POINT

Since the Sec. 162(m) compensation deduction limit applies only to publicly-held corporations, privately-held corporations are faced with the general reasonableness standard which looks at the particular facts and circumstances.

declines in business performance, Congress enacted Sec. 162(m) that disallows a deduction for certain employee compensation that exceeds a yearly amount of $1 million. This limit applies to compensation payable by a publicly held corporation to the corporation's chief executive officer and its four highest compensated officers for the taxable year. Compensation based on commissions or other performance goals is not subject to this limitation.

The tests for determining whether a business or investment expense is deductible are summarized in Topic Review I6-1.

EXPENSES AND LOSSES MUST BE INCURRED BY THE TAXPAYER

Generally, taxpayers may not take a deduction for a loss or expense of another person. Thus, a deduction is allowed only for the taxpayer's own losses and expenses. This requirement prevents taxpayers from engaging in manipulative schemes.

EXAMPLE I6-11 ▶ April and Bruce, the elderly parents of Carol, live in their own home. They have little income and Carol must help support them. During the current year, the interest and property taxes due on April and Bruce's home total $2,000. April and Bruce file a joint return. They have no other expenses that qualify as itemized deductions. Thus, April and Bruce plan to use the standard deduction, and the benefit of the $2,000 expenditure for interest and taxes will be lost. In an attempt to take advantage of a deduction that otherwise would be lost, Carol pays the interest and taxes out of her business. Carol's business cannot deduct these payments because they are not a liability of the business. ◀

ADDITIONAL COMMENT

When one taxpayer pays the expenses of another, neither taxpayer is entitled to the deduction.

This general rule applies to all types of expenditures, whether incurred in a trade or business, an investment activity, or a personal activity for which deductions are allowed. There is one exception: under Sec. 213 taxpayers may take a deduction for medical expenses paid on behalf of a dependent. Medical expenses are also deductible if they are paid for a person who would qualify as a dependent except for the fact that the gross income test is not met (see Chapter I2).

EXAMPLE I6-12 ▶ During the current year, Dan incurs $3,400 in deductible medical expenses. Dan is not a full-time student and is not under age 19 but is otherwise supported by Tom, his father. Dan's gross income for the year is $15,000. If Tom pays Dan's medical expenses, Tom may deduct the expenses as an itemized deduction (subject to the 7.5% of AGI limitation) even though Tom may not take a dependency exemption for Dan. ◀

Topic Review I6-1

Tests for Deductibility as a Business or Investment Expense

Test	Application
Ordinary	▶ Based on the facts and circumstances. ▶ Reasonable and proximate relationship to the activity. ▶ Customary or usual in context of the industry. ▶ Need not be encountered by the taxpayer more than once.
Necessary	▶ Based on the facts and circumstances. ▶ Appropriate and helpful. ▶ Need not be indispensable. ▶ Would a reasonable or prudent businessperson incur the same expense?
Reasonable	▶ Based on the facts and circumstances. ▶ Applies to all business and investment expenses. ▶ Compensation paid to an owner-employee of a small corporation is the most commonly contested area. ▶ Compensation in excess of $1 million payable by a publicly held corporation to its key executives may not be deductible.

GENERAL RESTRICTIONS ON THE DEDUCTIBILITY OF EXPENSES

As mentioned earlier on page I6-4, certain types of expenditures are not deductible. These types of expenditures fall within certain categories which are discussed below.

CAPITALIZATION VERSUS EXPENSE DEDUCTION

GENERAL CAPITALIZATION REQUIREMENTS. Under Sec. 263, a taxpayer may not take a current deduction for capital expenditures. Generally, expenses that add to the value of, substantially prolong the useful life of, or change the use of the property are considered **capital expenditures**. Thus, capital expenditures include the cost of acquiring or constructing buildings, machinery, equipment, furniture, and any similar property that has a useful life that extends substantially beyond the end of the tax year. Taxpayers must also capitalize the cost of goodwill purchased in connection with the acquisition of the assets of a going concern.[12] (See Chapter I10 for a discussion of the amortization of goodwill.)

Some assets, such as buildings, machinery, equipment, furniture and fixtures, purchased goodwill, and customer lists are depreciable or amortizable and may provide deductions that are spread over more than one tax year. Others, such as land, stock, and partnership interests, are neither depreciable nor amortizable and the taxpayer must wait until the asset is sold or disposed of to recover its cost. In some instances, it is difficult to ascertain whether an asset is eligible for depreciation or amortization. For example, the Tax Court has held that antique violin bows and an antique bass violin are depreciable property, overriding the IRS's arguments that they should not be depreciable because they were actually appreciating in value and it was impossible to determine their useful life.[13]

Maintenance and repair expenditures that only keep an asset in a normal operating condition are deductible if they do not increase the value or prolong the useful life of the asset. Distinguishing between a currently deductible expenditure and a capital expenditure can be difficult because expenditures for normal maintenance and repair can cost more than a capital improvement. Normal maintenance and repair may also increase the value of an asset. In one Tax Court case, the court held that expenditures incurred in replacing support beams and floor joists to shore up a sagging floor were deductible, whereas the court held that the cost of placing a new floor over an old one was a capital expenditure.[14] A tax advisor must examine all of the facts and circumstances to determine whether the expenditures constitute part of an overall plan of improvement or a change in use of the asset.

ADDITIONAL COMMENT

Some provisions permit taxpayers to depreciate or amortize capital expenditures over a relatively short period of time. For example, there is a rapid write-off available for pollution control facilities under Sec. 169 and for organization costs of corporations under Sec. 248.

ELECTION TO DEDUCT CURRENTLY. Taxpayers sometimes may elect a current deduction for certain capital expenditures. Taxpayers often prefer a current deduction over capitalizing and depreciating an asset because of the time value of money. Some expenditures that taxpayers may elect to deduct currently[15] include

- Cost of fertilizers incurred by farmers
- Cost of soil and water conservation incurred by farmers
- Intangible drilling costs incurred in drilling oil and gas wells
- Costs for tertiary injectants
- Costs for certain mining development projects

---

[12] Reg. Sec. 1.263(a)-2(h). See also *Indopco, Inc., v. CIR*, 69 AFTR 2d 92-694, 92-1 USTC ¶50,113 (USSC, 1992), where expenses incurred by a corporation that was the target of a "friendly" takeover were held to be nondeductible capital expenditures because they provided long-term benefits to the corporation. In this case, the Supreme Court held that these long-term benefits do not need to be associated with a specific identifiable asset.

[13] *Richard L. Simon*, 103 T.C. 247 (1994) and *Brian P. Liddle*, 76 AFTR 2d 95-6255, 95-2 USTC ¶50,488 (3rd Cir., 1959). The IRS has stated it will not follow these decisions. See AOD 96-9, 7/15/96.

[14] Reg. Sec. 1.162-4. *See also Standard Fruit Product Co.*, 1949 PH T.C. Memo ¶49,207, 8 TCM 733.

[15] See Secs. 180, 175, 263(c), 193, 616, 190, and 174.

BOOK-TAX COMPARISON

Although for tax purposes a taxpayer may elect to deduct these capital expenditures, for book purposes capital expenditures must still be capitalized and depreciated or amortized. This difference in treatment gives rise to a book-tax adjustment.

- Costs incurred to remove architectural and transportation barriers to the handicapped and elderly
- Costs for certain qualified research and experimental expenditures

Taxpayers may also elect to deduct certain amounts each year for the purchase of qualified tangible personal property used in a trade or business instead of depreciating the property over its useful life. This deduction is limited to $24,000 in 2002 and $25,000 in 2003 and thereafter. This election under Sec. 179 is examined in chapter I10.

CAPITALIZATION OF DEDUCTION ITEMS. The exceptions mentioned above provide a current deduction for expenditures that are normally capital in nature. Conversely, Section 266 provides for the capitalization of certain expenses that are normally deductible. Section 266 is elective and applies to the following items:

- Annual property taxes, interest on a mortgage, and other carrying charges incurred on unimproved and unproductive real estate.
- Annual property taxes, interest, employment taxes, and other necessary expenses incurred for the development, improvement, or construction of real property, up to the time the development or construction is completed. For these expenses to be capitalized, the real property may be either improved or unimproved, productive or unproductive.
- Interest and employment taxes incurred in transporting and installing personalty (as opposed to realty) up to the time when the property is first put into use by the taxpayer.

A taxpayer may make a new election to capitalize the expenses on unimproved and unproductive real estate each year.

EXAMPLE I6-13 ▶ During 2002 and 2003, Nancy pays property taxes of $5,000 on a piece of land. During 2002, the land is vacant and unproductive. In 2003, Nancy uses the land as a parking lot, generating $7,000 in income. Nancy can elect to capitalize the taxes in 2002 because the property is both unimproved and unproductive. In 2003, however, the land is productive, and Nancy cannot elect to capitalize the taxes. Because the expenses relate to the production of rental income, they are deductible *for* AGI. If the land remains unproductive during 2003, Nancy can elect to capitalize the taxes paid in 2003. However, the election is optional and need not be made for 2003 merely because it is made in 2002. ◀

For the development or construction of real property, an election to capitalize the other expenses incurred during the development or construction period remains in effect for that year and for all subsequent years until the end of the construction period. However, a taxpayer may make the election on each new project separately.

EXAMPLE I6-14 ▶ During the current year, Paul begins construction of an office building and a hotel. Paul incurs $20,000 in property taxes during the construction of the office building and $12,000 for the hotel. The election to capitalize the taxes on the office building does not bind Paul to make the same election with respect to the taxes on the hotel. ◀

SELF-STUDY QUESTION

Chuck borrows $100,000 at a 10% rate of interest and invests the $100,000 in exempt bonds yielding 8%. Chuck is in the 27% tax bracket. Calculate what Chuck's cash flow on these transactions would be on an after-tax basis if expenses related to exempt income were deductible.

ANSWER

Chuck has $8,000 of exempt income and $10,000 of interest expense. However, if the interest expense were deductible, its after-tax cost would be $7,300 ($10,000 − 2,700). Chuck's cash flow would be $700 ($8,000 − $7,300) on an unsound economic investment.

If a taxpayer elects to capitalize this type of expense under Sec. 266, it is added to the basis of the property to which it pertains. If the property is depreciable, a deduction is allowed for the expenses as the property is depreciated. Taxpayers are motivated to make this election if they have large net operating loss (NOL) carryovers, or if they expect to be in a significantly higher tax rate in future years and thus feel that the benefit of the deduction is greater in the future.

Under Sec. 263A, certain taxpayers must capitalize certain costs into inventory instead of taking a current deduction. (See Chapter I11 for a discussion of inventories.)

EXPENSES RELATED TO EXEMPT INCOME

Under Sec. 265, taxpayers may not deduct any expense allocated or related to tax-exempt income. The purpose of this disallowance is to prevent a double tax benefit to the taxpayer.

BOOK-TAX COMPARISON

For book purposes, tax-exempt income and related expenses are included in the calculation of net income. For tax purposes, they are excluded from gross income.

The IRC specifically disallows interest expense on debt the taxpayer incurs in order to purchase or carry tax-exempt securities. Thus, the disallowance depends on the taxpayer's intended use of the loan proceeds. Intent is generally determined by an examination of all the facts and circumstances surrounding the transaction. Intent to carry the tax-exempt securities is shown if the tax-exempt securities are used as collateral in securing a loan.[16] If an individual who holds tax-exempt securities later incurs some debt, no disallowance will occur if the debt is incurred to finance personal items (e.g., a mortgage on a personal residence). However, if a taxpayer incurs the debt to finance an investment, a portion of the interest is generally disallowed. Even though the interest is not incurred to carry tax-exempt securities, it still may not be deductible. For example, if a taxpayer incurs interest on personal debt, it is not deductible. (See Chapter I7 for a discussion of limitations on the deductibility of personal interest.)

EXAMPLE I6-15 ▶ Sam, an individual, has invested $80,000 in Gold Corporation stock, $120,000 in real estate, and $50,000 in tax-exempt municipal bonds. During the current year, Sam borrows $70,000 for the purpose of investing in a limited partnership. For the year, he pays $6,000 interest on the loan. Under these circumstances, the IRS will presume that Sam has incurred a portion of the debt in order to carry the tax-exempt securities and will disallow a portion of the deduction. Sam may overcome that presumption if he can show that he could not have sold the tax-exempt securities. He cannot overcome this presumption if he can show only that the sale of the bonds would have resulted in a loss. If Sam instead borrowed the money to purchase a personal residence, the IRS probably would not attempt to disallow the deduction. (See Chapter I7 for a discussion of restrictions on the deductibility of interest for personal residences.) ◀

EXPENDITURES THAT ARE CONTRARY TO PUBLIC POLICY

Certain expenditures, even though incurred in a profit-motivated activity, may not be deductible if the payment itself is illegal or if the payment is a penalty or fine resulting from an illegal act. These nondeductible expenses generally fall within one of the following categories:

- Illegal payments to government officials or employees
- Other illegal payments
- Kickbacks, rebates, and bribes under Medicare and Medicaid
- Payments of fines and penalties
- Payment of treble damages under the federal antitrust laws

REAL-WORLD EXAMPLE

A subcontractor involved with the construction of a new shopping mall made kickbacks to the supervisor of the primary contractor. The kickbacks were deductible because they were not illegal, and the kickbacks were also ordinary and necessary because the subcontractor would not have been able to continue to work if the kickbacks had not been made. *Raymond Bertolini Trucking Co. v. CIR* 54 AFTR 2d 84-5413, 1984-2 USTC ¶9591 (6th Cir., 1984).

BRIBES AND KICKBACKS. Under Sec. 162(c)(1), any illegal bribe or kickback made to any official or employee of a government is not deductible. This applies to payments made to

- Federal officials and employees
- State, local, and foreign government officials and employees
- Officials and employees of an agency of a government

EXAMPLE I6-16 ▶ During February of the current year, Road Corporation enters into a contract with the State of Iowa to construct a five-mile stretch of a new highway. Under the terms of the contract, Road Corporation must complete the project by October 22 of the current year. If it is not completed and accepted by Iowa on or before that date, Iowa will fine Road Corporation $5,000 per day for every day after that date until the project is accepted. By October 20, the project foreman realizes that the company will not make the deadline if it complies with all the requirements imposed by the state inspector assigned to the project. To avoid the fine, the foreman arranges for the inspector to "look the other way" on several of the requirements in exchange for a payment of $8,000. Because this payment constitutes an illegal bribe to a government official, the payment is not deductible. ◀

[16] Rev. Proc. 72-18, 1972-1 C.B. 740. *See also Wisconsin Cheeseman, Inc. v. U.S.*, 21 AFTR 2d 383, 68-1 USTC ¶9145 (7th Cir., 1968).

Taxpayers may not deduct illegal payments to officials or employees of a foreign government if the payment is unlawful under the Foreign Corrupt Practices Act of 1977, unless such payments constitute a normal way of doing business in that country. In all cases, the burden rests on the government to prove the illegality of the payment.

Illegal bribes, kickbacks, and other illegal payments made to people other than a government official or employee are nondeductible if they are illegal under a federal law that subjects the payor to a criminal penalty or loss of the privilege of doing business. In addition, illegal payments under a state law imposing the same penalties are nondeductible if the state law is generally enforced. Here, the definition of a kickback includes a payment for referring a client, patient, or customer.

ETHICAL POINT

A CPA discovers that a client included fines and penalties in a miscellaneous expense section of a previously filed tax return. The CPA should recommend the filing of an amended return. However, the CPA is not obligated to inform the IRS, and the CPA may not do so without the client's permission, except where required by law.

The courts and the IRS have made a distinction between an illegal nondeductible kickback and a rebate of the purchase price. If the rebate is made directly to the purchaser by the seller, it is considered an adjustment to the selling price and, as such, is an *exclusion* (rather than a deduction) from gross income.[17] The distinction between the two payments seems to be that the rebate is actually negotiated as part of the selling price.

Section 162(c)(3) specifically disallows a deduction for any kickback, rebate, or bribe under Medicare and Medicaid. Disallowed amounts include payments made by physicians or by suppliers and providers of goods and services who receive payment under the Social Security Act or a federally funded state plan. Unlike payments to foreign government or nongovernment employees and officials, these payments need not be illegal under federal or state law.

STOP & THINK

Question: Queen, Inc. is engaged in the ship and boat repair business. Since the competition is very tough, Queen generally kicks back approximately 10% of any repair bill to any ship captain who brings his ship to Queen for repairs. Queen's customers include individual owners of large ocean-going yachts and fishing boats, as well as government vessels owned by state, federal, and foreign governments. During the current year, Queen paid $80,000 in kickbacks to the captains of privately-owned yachts and boats, $40,000 to the owners of privately-owned vessels, and $100,000 to the captains of state, federal, and foreign government vessels. The crews of these government vessels are government employees. What is the proper tax treatment of these payments?

Solution: The $40,000 in kickbacks paid directly to the owners of the privately-owned vessels are treated as merely a rebate in the price of the services and reduces Queen's gross income, unless the payments could result in the imposition of a criminal penalty or loss of the privilege of doing business. The kickbacks paid to the captains of the state and federal vessels are not deductible because they are paid to employees of state and federal governments. The kickbacks paid to the captains of the privately-owned vessels are not deductible if they are illegal and subject the payor to a criminal penalty or loss of the privilege to do business. Likewise, the payments to the captains of the foreign vessels are not deductible if the payments are unlawful under the Foreign Corrupt Practices Act.

FINES AND PENALTIES. Section 162(f) of the IRC also disallows a deduction for the payment of any fine or penalty paid to a government because of the violation of a law.

Furthermore, it disallows a deduction for two-thirds of any payment for damages made as a result of a conviction (or a guilty or no-contest plea) in an action regarding a criminal violation of the federal antitrust laws.[18]

EXAMPLE I6-17 ▶ During the current year, the United States files criminal and civil actions against Allen, the president of Able Corporation, and Betty, the president of Bell Corporation, for conspiring to fix and maintain prices of electrical transformers. Both Allen and Betty enter pleas of no contest, and the appropriate judgments are entered. Subsequent to this action, Circle Corporation sues both Able and Bell Corporations for treble damages of $300,000. In settlement, Able and Bell Corporations each pay Circle Corporation $75,000. The maximum that Able and Bell Corporations may each deduct is $25,000 ($75,000 ÷ 3). ◀

[17] Rev. Rul. 82-149, 1982-2 C.B. 56.

[18] Sec. 162(g).

EXPENSES RELATING TO AN ILLEGAL ACTIVITY. Interestingly, although the payment of an illegal bribe or kickback and the payment of a fine or penalty as the result of an illegal act are both nondeductible, expenses incurred in an illegal activity are generally deductible if they are ordinary, necessary, and reasonable and the income from the illegal activity is also reported.[19]

EXAMPLE I6-18 ▶ Fred owns and operates a small financial services business involved in the sale of securities and the lending of money. Fred often sells securities to customers in other states. However, because he did not register the business with the appropriate state or federal authorities, the operation of the business is illegal. During the current year, Fred incurs the following expenses:

Interest	$ 20,000
Salaries	140,000
Depreciation	7,000
Printing	5,000
Bribe to employee of state securities commission	12,000
Total	$184,000

If Fred reports the income from this activity, the deductible expenses for the year total $172,000. The illegal payment of $12,000 to the government employee is not deductible. ◀

One exception to this general rule exists. Section 280E disallows a deduction for expenses incurred in an illegal business of trafficking or dealing in drugs.

OTHER EXPENDITURES THAT ARE SPECIFICALLY DISALLOWED

The IRC also specifically disallows deductions for certain other expenses, even though they might meet all the requirements mentioned previously. These include political contributions and lobbying expenses and, in certain situations, business start-up expenses.

POLITICAL CONTRIBUTIONS AND LOBBYING EXPENSES. Political contributions and lobbying expenses constitute one general category of disallowed expenses. Taxpayers may not deduct expenditures made in connection with the following:

- Influencing legislation
- Participating or intervening in any political campaign of any candidate for public office
- Attempting to influence the general public with respect to elections, legislative matters, or referendums
- Communicating directly with the President, Vice President, and certain other federal employees and officials

Sec. 162(e) also denies a deduction for contributions to tax-exempt organizations that carry on lobbying activities if a principal purpose of the contribution is to obtain a deduction for what otherwise would have been disallowed. Furthermore, the IRC disallows payments made for advertising in a convention or any other program if any part of the proceeds of the publication will directly or indirectly benefit a specific political party or candidate.[20]

Taxpayers may deduct lobbying expenses incurred to influence legislation on a local level if the legislation is of direct interest to the taxpayer's business. Local legislation includes actions by a legislative body of any political subdivision of a state (e.g., city or county council), but does not include any state or federal action. These deductible expenditures include expenses of communicating with or dues paid to an organization of which the taxpayer is a member. For administrative convenience, the deduction disallowance does not apply to any in-house expenditure attributable to such activities as long as the total of such expenditures for the taxable year does not exceed $2,000. In-house expendi-

[19] *CIR v. Neil Sullivan, et al.*, 1 AFTR 2d 1158, 58-1 USTC ¶9368 (USSC, 1958).

[20] Sec. 276(a). Nondeductible political contributions also include payments for admission to a dinner or program where the proceeds will benefit a party or candidate, or admission to an inaugural ball, party, or concert if the activity is identified with a political party or candidate.

tures are expenses incurred directly by the taxpayer other than amounts paid to a professional lobbyist or dues that are allocable to lobbying. Additionally, the deduction disallowance does not apply to taxpayers engaged in the business of lobbying.

EXAMPLE I6-19 ▶ Kate is the senior partner of a large New York law firm. During the year, she flies to Washington, D.C., to testify before a Congressional subcommittee with regard to proposed changes in the Social Security taxes imposed on employers. Such changes directly affect her business because they affect the amount of taxes she must pay on behalf of her employees. Kate's ordinary and necessary expenses incurred with respect to the trip are not deductible because the expenses were incurred to influence federal rather than local legislation. ◀

If the legislation cannot reasonably be expected to directly affect the taxpayer's trade or business, the expenses are not deductible.

EXAMPLE I6-20 ▶ Kate is the owner of a real estate company in Chicago. The city of Chicago has proposed legislation to increase the hotel room tax. Kate spends time researching and traveling to speak to the Chicago City Council regarding this legislation. Kate's lobbying expenses are not deductible. While they are used to influence legislation on the local level, they are not of direct interest to her business. ◀

BUSINESS INVESTIGATION AND PREOPENING EXPENSES. Section 195 of the IRC also specifically disallows a current deduction for business start-up expenditures. Instead, these expenses are capitalized and are subject to amortization if an election is made to amortize the start-up costs over a period of not less than 60 months starting with the month in which the new business begins. Start-up expenditures specifically include three types of expenditures:

- *Business investigation expenses.* These expenses are costs a taxpayer incurs in reviewing and analyzing a prospective business before deciding whether to acquire or create it. The key here is that the taxpayer incurs the expenses before making a decision. These expenses include such items as analyses and surveys of markets, traffic patterns, products, labor supplies, and distribution facilities.
- *Preopening or start-up costs.* Preopening or start-up costs are expenses incurred after a taxpayer decides to acquire or create a business but before the business activity itself has started. These costs include expenditures for training employees; advertising; securing supplies, distributors, and potential customers; and expenditures for professional services in setting up the business's books and records. These costs are incurred by a taxpayer who is not engaged in any existing business or is engaged in a business that is unrelated to the business being acquired or created.
- *Expenses incurred in connection with an investment activity.* These expenses are costs incurred in connection with an investment activity that the taxpayer anticipates will become an active trade or business.

ADDITIONAL COMMENT

Costs incurred in connection with the issuance of stock or securities do not qualify as start-up costs. These costs are charged to Paid in Capital.

As defined by Sec. 195, start-up expenditures do not include these same types of expenses when they are incurred by a taxpayer who is already engaged in a business similar to the new one being created or acquired. In such a case, the taxpayer may deduct these expenditures currently because they are incurred in the taxpayer's existing business. Figure I6-1 provides a flowchart to assist in properly classifying these types of expenditures.

STOP & THINK

Question: Shauna works in an automobile manufacturing plant in Detroit, Michigan. In January of the current year, she took a two-week vacation in order to fly to Orlando, Florida. While in Orlando, she spent some time investigating the possibility of opening a store in nearby Coco Beach. In total, she spent $800 on airfare, $1,500 on hotels and food, $300 on equipment rentals, and $300 on a car rental. In addition to spending time on the beach talking to people and checking out the rental equipment, she also spent some time talking to shop owners and real estate agents. After some analysis, however, Shauna has decided to keep her job in Detroit. What is the proper tax treatment for these expenditures?

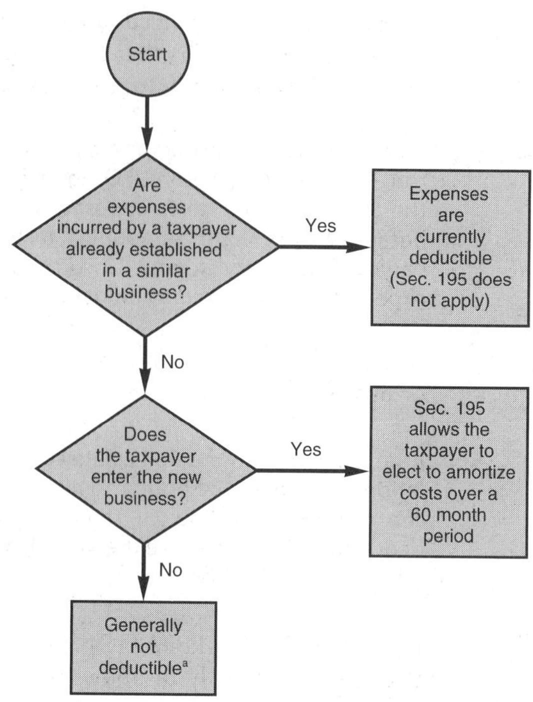

[a] Rev. Rul. 57-418, 1957-2 C.B. 143 and Rev. Rul. 77-254, 1977-2 C.B. 63; *Morton Frank*, 20 T.C. 511 (1953).

FIGURE I6-1 ▶ DEDUCTIBILITY OF BUSINESS INVESTIGATION AND START-UP COSTS

Solution: In general, Sec. 162 of the IRC allows a deduction for expenses incurred in a business. Expenses incurred before the business starts are not incurred in a business and thus are not deductible under Sec. 162. However, under Sec. 195 certain expenditures such as business investigation expenses and start-up costs can be capitalized and amortized over a 60-month period, beginning with the month in which the new business begins. Unfortunately Shauna did not open the new business. Thus, she may not deduct or amortize any of these expenses.

Topic Review I6-2 summarizes the restrictions on the deductibility of these items.

PROPER SUBSTANTIATION REQUIREMENT

OBJECTIVE 3

List the substantiation requirements that must be met to deduct travel and entertainment expenses

Generally, the burden of proving the existence of a deduction or loss falls on the taxpayer. Thus, a taxpayer must properly substantiate all deductible expenses. Because the IRS may audit a return and request proof, taxpayers should retain items such as receipts, cancelled checks, and paid bills. Occasionally, the courts will allow a deduction that is not properly substantiated by the taxpayer if an expenditure clearly has been made. In these cases, the amount of the deduction is estimated based on all the facts and circumstances. This procedure is known as the *Cohan* rule and derives its name from a court case in which the judge allowed a deduction for an estimated amount of certain expenses.[21] The most prudent course of action, of course, is to retain proper documentation rather than to rely upon the *Cohan* rule.

---

[21] *George M. Cohan v. CIR*, 8 AFTR 10552, 2 USTC ¶489 (2nd Cir., 1930). Interestingly, the *Cohan* case dealt with travel and entertainment expenses. Because of the subsequent enactment of Sec. 274(d), the *Cohan* rule may not be used to deduct entertainment expenses. It is still effective for other types of expenses.

Topic Review I6-2

Restrictions on the Deductibility of Expense Items

Item	Restrictions Imposed
1. Capital expenditures	The general rule is that the expenditure is not currently deductible if its life extends beyond the end of the year. Special elections are available to currently deduct certain capital expenditures (e.g., research and experimental costs under Sec. 174; and limited amounts per year for acquisitions of tangible personal property used in a trade or business under Sec. 179).
2. Carrying charges	An election may be made under Sec. 266 to capitalize certain expenses that are normally deductible such as property and employment taxes, interest, and carrying charges on unimproved unproductive real estate.
3. Expenses related to tax exempt income	Expenses such as interest incurred on debt used to purchase or carry tax-exempt securities are disallowed under Sec. 265.
4. Expenditures contrary to public policy	Such expenditures are generally not deductible. Examples include bribes and kickbacks, fines and penalties, and expenses of an illegal activity involved with trafficking or dealing in drugs.
5. Legal and accounting fees	Legal and accounting fees can be either *for* AGI deductible business expenses, nondeductible personal use expenditures, or *from* AGI fees incurred in the determination of any tax (e.g., tax return preparation fees).
6. Political contributions and lobby expenses	The general rule is that such items are not deductible (e.g., costs of influencing public opinion), but there are certain exceptions (e.g., costs of appearing before local legislative bodies on topics directly related to the taxpayer's business).
7. Business investigation and preopening expenses	The following rules apply: a. Currently deductible if the taxpayer is already engaged in a similar business. b. Not deductible if the taxpayer is not currently engaged in a similar business and does not enter the new business. c. Amortized over 60 months if the taxpayer enters the new business and makes an election. d. Deductible if expenditures constitute specific items such as legal expenses incurred in drafting purchase documents in an unsuccessful attempt to acquire a specific business. However, general investigation expenditures in search of a new business are not deductible.

EXAMPLE I6-21 ▶ In April of the current year, Terry took his tax records to a CPA to have his prior year's income tax return prepared. As part of the return, the CPA attached a supplemental schedule listing all of Terry's items of income and expense. After the return was prepared and filed, Terry's records were stolen. Upon audit two years later, the IRS disallowed Terry's deductions because he had no records to substantiate the expenses. When the case was litigated, the court allowed deductions for an estimated amount of expenses under the *Cohan* rule because of the list that was attached to Terry's return and because the court believed that Terry had testified honestly in his own behalf.[22] ◀

HISTORICAL NOTE

Justice Learned Hand, in permitting a deduction for unsubstantiated amounts in *George M. Cohan v. CIR*, 8 AFTR 10552, 2 USTC ¶489 (2nd Cir, 1930), wrote "absolute certainty in such matters is usually impossible and it is not necessary; the Board should make as close an approximation as it can, bearing heavily if it chooses on the taxpayer whose inexactitude is of his own making."

Additionally, Sections 274 and 280F provide specific and more stringent recordkeeping requirements for travel, entertainment, business gifts, computers, and vehicles used for transportation. In these cases no deduction may be taken unless the taxpayer substantiates the expenditure by either an adequate record or sufficient evidence that corroborates the taxpayer's statement. This substantiation may take the form of account books, diaries, logs, receipts and paid bills, trip sheets, expense reports, and statements of witnesses. The information that must be substantiated includes the following:

- Amount of the expense
- Time and place of the travel or entertainment
- Date and description of the gift
- Business purpose of the expenditure

[22] *Layard M. White*, 1980 PH T.C. Memo ¶80,582, 41 TCM 671.

- Business relationship to the taxpayer of the person entertained or of the person who received the gift

The *Cohan* rule may not be used for these types of expenses. (See Chapter I9 for a more complete discussion regarding the deductibility of these types of expenses.)

WHEN AN EXPENSE IS DEDUCTIBLE

OBJECTIVE 4

Explain when deductions may be taken under both the cash and accrual methods of accounting

Because taxable income generally is measured on an annual basis, the question of when a particular expense is deductible is especially important. The answer to this question largely depends on the taxpayer's method of accounting.[23] The most common methods include the following:

- Cash receipts and disbursements method (cash method)
- Accrual method
- Hybrid method (a combination of the cash and accrual methods where some items are accounted for on the cash method and other items are accounted for on the accrual method)

ADDITIONAL COMMENT

Section 446(b) provides that in cases where no method of accounting has been regularly used or if the method used does not clearly reflect income, then the computation of taxable income is to be made under a method that, in the opinion of the IRS, does clearly reflect income.

Taxpayers normally use the same method for computing taxable income that they use in keeping their financial accounting records. However, except for the use of the last-in, first-out (LIFO) method of accounting for inventory, the tax law does not generally require conformity. For example, many companies use the straight-line depreciation method for financial accounting purposes and the modified accelerated cost recovery system (MACRS) for tax purposes. This difference in depreciation methods, of course, results in a book-tax adjustment.

CASH METHOD

Under the **cash method of accounting**, expenses are deductible when they are actually paid. As long as it is subsequently honored, payment by check is considered a cash payment in the year the check is mailed or delivered, even if it is delivered so late on the last day of the year that the payee could not have cashed it.[24] If a check is mailed near the end of the year, the taxpayer must have evidence that the check was mailed in the year in which the deduction is claimed. Furthermore, the use of a credit card to satisfy an obligation is considered a cash payment at the time of the charge rather than at the time the charge is paid.

A mere promise to pay, or the issuance of a note payable, does not constitute a payment under the cash method. Thus, a charge on an open account with a creditor is not deductible until cash is actually transferred in satisfaction of the charge.

EXAMPLE I6-22 ▶ Peter, a calendar-year taxpayer, is the sole owner of a plumbing repair business. The business uses the cash method of accounting. Under an arrangement with one of his suppliers, Peter and his employees can pick up supplies at any time during the month by merely signing for them. At the end of the month, the supplier sends Peter a bill for the charges. Peter always pays the bill in full during the following month. In December of the current year, Peter charges $1,500 for supplies. During the same month Peter purchases a plumbing fixture for $250 from another supplier. Peter uses his charge card at the time of purchase. Peter may deduct the $250 during the current year. However, the $1,500 charged on the open account is deductible when paid in the following year. ◀

[23] Methods of accounting as they relate to the reporting of income are discussed in Chapter I3. Methods of accounting as they relate to deductibility of expenses and losses are covered in this chapter. For an overall discussion of accounting methods, see Chapter I11.

[24] *CIR v. Estate of M. A. Bradley*, 10 AFTR 1405, 3 USTC ¶904 (6th Cir., 1932) and *Charles F. Kahler*, 18 T.C. 31 (1952).

PREPAID EXPENSES. In general, a capital expenditure or the prepayment of expenses by a cash method taxpayer does not result in a current deduction if the expenditure creates an asset having a useful life that extends substantially beyond the close of the tax year. This can occur when a taxpayer makes expenditures for prepaid rent, services, or interest. However, in the case of prepaid rent, a circuit court of appeals decision has held that a current deduction may be taken for the entire amount of an expenditure if the period covered by the prepayment does not exceed one year and the taxpayer is obligated to make the prepayment.[25]

EXAMPLE I6-23 ▶ On November 1 of the current year, Twyla enters into a lease arrangement with Rashad to rent Rashad's office space for the following 36 months. By prepaying the rent for the entire 36-month period, Twyla is able to obtain a favorable monthly lease payment of $800. This prepayment creates an asset (a leasehold) with a useful life that extends substantially beyond the end of the taxable year. Thus, only $1,600 ($800 × 2 months) of the total payment is deductible in the current year. The rest must be capitalized and amortized over the life of the lease. However, assume that under the terms of the lease, Twyla is obligated to make three annual payments of $9,600 each November 1 for the subsequent 12 months. On November 1 of the current year, Twyla pays Rashad $9,600 for the first 12-month period. Because Twyla is obligated to make the prepayment and the period covered by the prepayment does not exceed one year, the entire $9,600 is deductible in the current year using the reasoning of the previously cited circuit court decision. ◀

PREPAID INTEREST. The IRC requires that prepaid interest expense be deducted over the period of the loan to which the interest charge is allocated.[26] Receipt of a discounted loan does not represent prepaid interest expense. Instead, the interest is deemed to be paid as the loan is repaid.

EXAMPLE I6-24 ▶ During the current year, Richelle borrows $1,000 from the bank for use in her business. Richelle uses the cash method of accounting in her business. Under the terms of the loan, the bank discounts the loan by $80, paying Richelle $920. When the loan comes due in the following year, however, Richelle is to repay the full $1,000. Richelle cannot deduct the $80 of interest expense until she repays the loan in the following year. ◀

REAL-WORLD EXAMPLE

A taxpayer made an overpayment of the federal income tax in 1975. In 1979, the IRS offset the overpayment against interest the taxpayer owed to the IRS. The Tax Court held that the interest expense was deductible in 1979 rather than in 1975. *Saverio Eboli*, 93 T.C. 123 (1989).

Taxpayers often prepay interest in the form of points. A point is one percent of the loan amount. Thus, the payment of two points on a $100,000 loan amounts to $2,000. While points must generally be amortized over the life of the loan, points paid in connection with the purchase or improvement of a principal residence may be deductible when paid. According to the IRS, points paid in connection with the purchase (but not the improvement) of a principal residence are automatically deductible in the year paid if the following four requirements are met:

- the closing agreement clearly designates the amounts as points
- the amount is computed as a percentage of the amount borrowed
- the charging of points is an established business practice in the geographic area, and
- the points are paid in connection with the purchase of the taxpayer's principal residence which is used to secure the loan.[27]

REAL LIFE EXAMPLE

The mortgage company will, at the end of the year, mail to the taxpayer a Form 1098 which shows the amount of interest and points paid.

Although points paid on loans incurred to *improve* the taxpayer's principal residence do not fall under this safe harbor rule, they still are currently deductible if the loan is secured by the residence, the payment of points is an established business practice in the geographic area in which it is incurred, and the amount of the prepayment does not exceed the amount generally charged.

[25] *Martin J. Zaninovich v. CIR*, 45 AFTR 2d 80-1442, 80-1 USTC ¶9342 (9th Cir., 1980) and *Bonaire Development Co. v. CIR*, 50 AFTR 2d 82-5167, 82-2 USTC ¶9428 (9th Cir., 1982). See also *Stephen A. Keller v. CIR*, 53 AFTR 2d 84-663, 84-1 USTC ¶9194 (8th Cir., 1984).

[26] Sec. 461(g).

[27] Rev. Proc. 94-27, I.R.B. 94-15, 17. As explained in Chapter I7, acquisition indebtedness incurred to acquire a personal residence is limited to $1,000,000. Hence, points that are allocated to the loan principal in excess of this limit are not deductible either.

A taxpayer may not currently deduct points paid to refinance a mortgage on a principal residence because the points are not paid in connection with the purchase or improvement of the taxpayer's residence.[28]

EXAMPLE I6-25 ▶ During the current year, Pam purchases a principal residence for $150,000, paying $50,000 down and financing the remainder with a 20-year mortgage secured by the property. Pam must make monthly payments on the mortgage. At the closing, Pam must pay three points as a loan origination fee. Because these points are paid in connection with the purchase of a principal residence, Pam may deduct $3,000 ($100,000 × 0.03) as interest expense during the current year. In addition, Pam may also deduct the interest portion of each monthly payment made during the year. On the other hand, assume that Pam takes out the $100,000 loan in order to refinance her home at a lower interest rate. The $3,000 prepaid interest is not currently deductible. Instead, Pam must deduct the interest ratably over the term of the loan. Thus, Pam may deduct an additional $12.50 ($3,000 ÷ 240 payments) interest expense for each payment that she makes during the year. ◀

If a home is sold and the refinanced mortgage is paid off, any unamortized portion of the points is deductible in the year of repayment. Points paid by the seller are treated as incurred by the purchaser, and therefore are currently deductible by the purchaser if the other requirements are met and they are subtracted from the purchase price of the residence.[29]

The cash method of accounting provides some degree of flexibility to taxpayers because, under this method, taxpayers can generally deduct expenses when paid rather than when accrued. Thus, subject to the limitations mentioned above with regard to prepaid expenses, taxpayers may to some degree accelerate or defer deductions from one year to another by merely accelerating or deferring payment. However, the IRC imposes limitations on the use of the cash method. For example, taxpayers must account for inventories under the accrual method.[30] Furthermore, under Sec. 448, most C corporations (corporations that have not elected Subchapter S status), partnerships that have a C corporation as a partner, and tax shelters may not use the cash method. However, the IRC makes exceptions to this general rule for personal service corporations, small businesses with average annual gross receipts of $5 million or less, and businesses involved in the farming and timber businesses. (See Chapter I11 for a complete discussion of the different accounting methods that may be used for computing taxable income.)

ACCRUAL METHOD

An **accrual method** taxpayer deducts expenses in the period in which they accrue. Generally, items accrue when the transaction meets both an **all-events test** and an **economic performance test**.[31]

ALL-EVENTS TEST. The all-events test is met when both of the following occur:

- The existence of a liability is established.
- The amount of the liability is determined with reasonable accuracy.

EXAMPLE I6-26 ▶ During the current year, Phil provides services for Louis. Louis uses the accrual method of accounting. Phil claims that Louis owes $10,000 for the services. Louis admits owing Phil $6,000, but contests the remaining $4,000. Because the amount of the liability can be accurately established only with respect to $6,000, Louis can deduct only that amount. If Louis pays the full $10,000, he may deduct the full amount in the year of payment, even though the contested amount ($4,000) is not resolved until a subsequent taxable year.[32] If Phil loses the lawsuit and

[28] Rev. Rul. 87-22, 1987-1 C.B. 146, and Rev. Proc. 87-15, 1987-1 C.B. 624. However, the Eighth Circuit has allowed a current deduction for points paid upon the refinancing of a mortgage loan because the original loan was merely a "bridge" or temporary loan until permanent financing could be arranged. See *James R. Huntsman v. CIR*, 66 AFTR 2d 90-5020, 90-2 USTC ¶50,340 (8th Cir., 1990).

[29] Rev. Proc. 94-27, I.R.B. 94-15, 17.

[30] However, taxpayers with average annual gross receipts of $1 million or less are not required to use the accrual method of accounting for inventories. See Rev. Proc. 2000-22, IRB 2000-22, 1008. Taxpayers who must use the accrual method for inventories may also use the hybrid method, which requires the accrual method for cost of goods sold but permits the cash method for all other expenses.

[31] Reg. Sec. 1.461-1(a)(2) and Sec. 461(h).

[32] Reg. Sec. 1.461-2(a)(1).

repays Louis the $4,000, Louis will include that amount in income in the year of repayment under the tax benefit rule (see Chapter I11). ◀

Because of the all-events test, taxpayers may not deduct additions to reserves for estimated expenses such as warranty expenses. Instead, the taxpayer deducts the expenses in the year in which such work is actually performed.

EXAMPLE I6-27 ▶ Best Corporation uses the accrual method of accounting and is engaged in the business of painting and rustproofing automobiles. Best Corporation provides a 5-year warranty for new vehicles and a 2-year warranty for used vehicles. Best Corp. extends the warranty only to the person who owns the car at the time the car is painted. Furthermore, in order to keep the warranty in force, the customer must present the vehicle to Best Corporation for inspection each year. The warranty is void if the vehicle is involved in an accident. Even though for financial accounting purposes Best Corporation may provide a reserve for estimated warranty expenses and deduct a reasonable addition to the reserve on an annual basis, no income tax deduction is allowed until the warranty work is actually done. ◀

ECONOMIC PERFORMANCE TEST. To be currently deductible under the accrual method, an expense must also meet an economic performance test. Exactly when economic performance is deemed to have occurred depends on the type of transaction. Table I6-1 contains a listing of various types of transactions that may arise and identifies when economic performance is deemed to have occurred under Sec. 461(h).

EXAMPLE I6-28 ▶ On December 20 of the current year, Chris, an accrual method taxpayer, enters into a binding contract with Pat to have Pat clean and paint the exterior of Chris's business building. Under the terms of the contract, Pat is to do the work in March of the following year. The total cost of the job is $4,000. Chris pays 10% down at the time the contract is signed. Because the job is not to be done until the following year, economic performance has not occurred in the current year and Chris may not deduct any portion of the expense in the current year. ◀

HISTORICAL NOTE

The economic performance test was added by Congress in the Tax Reform Act of 1984. Congress was concerned that in some situations taxpayers could deduct expenses currently, but the actual cash expenditure might not be made for several years. Taking a current deduction in such situations overstated the real cost because the time value of money was ignored.

An exception to the economic performance test provides that taxpayers may take a current deduction for recurring liabilities if all of the following occur:

- ▶ The all-events test is met during the year.
- ▶ Economic performance of the item occurs within the shorter of 8½ months after the close of the tax year, or a reasonable period after the close of the tax year.
- ▶ The expense is recurring and the taxpayer consistently treats the item as incurred in the tax year.
- ▶ Either the item is not material or the accrual of the item in the tax year results in a more proper matching against income than accruing the item in the tax year in which economic performance occurs.

This exception for recurring liabilities is available for the first four types of transactions identified in Table I6-1, but may not be used for the last type of transaction in the table.

EXAMPLE I6-29 ▶ Dawn is a calendar-year, accrual method taxpayer. Every year at the end of October, Dawn enters into a contract with Sam to provide snow removal services for the parking lots at Dawn's business. This contract extends for five months through the end of March of the following year. Because the all-events test is met (the liability is fixed), the expense recurs every year, economic performance occurs within the requisite period of time, and the item is not material, Dawn may deduct the entire expense in the year in which the contract is signed. ◀

A special rule under Sec. 461(c) applies to real property taxes. Under this provision, a taxpayer may elect to accrue real property taxes ratably over the period to which the taxes relate. Once made, this election may not be changed without permission from the IRS.

EXAMPLE I6-30 ▶ Under the law of State X, the lien date for real property taxes for calendar year 2002 is January 1, 2002. The tax is payable in full on November 30, 2002. Alpha Corp. is an accrual method taxpayer that has a January 31 fiscal year-end. On January 1, 2002, real property taxes of $100,000 are assessed against a building Alpha Corp. owns. Alpha pays the taxes on November 30, 2002.

▼ **TABLE I6-1**
When Economic Performance Is Deemed to Have Occurred

Event That Gives Rise to Liability	When Economic Performance Is Deemed to Have Occurred (i.e. when the accrual method taxpayer may take the deduction)
Another person provides the taxpayer with property or services	When the property or services are actually provided[a]
Taxpayer uses property	As the property is used[a]
Taxpayer must provide property or services to another person	As the taxpayer provides property or services to the other person[b]
Taxpayer must make payments to another, including payments for rebates and refunds, awards or prizes, insurance or service contracts, and taxes.	As payments to the other person are made
Taxpayer must make payments to another person because of a tort, breach of contract, violation of law, or injury claim under a worker's compensation act	As payments to the other person are made

[a] Economic performance may be deemed to have occurred at the earlier date of payment if the taxpayer reasonably expects the property or services to be provided within 3½ months after the payment is made. Reg. Sec. 1.461-4(d)(6)(ii).
[b] Economic performance may also occur as the taxpayer incurs costs in connection with the obligation to provide the property or services. Reg. Sec. 1.461-4(d)(4)(i).

If Alpha does not make the election to use the ratable accrual method, none of the payment is deductible in Alpha's fiscal year ending January 31, 2002 because the payment date is more than 8½ months after the January 31, 2002 year-end.

On the other hand, if Alpha makes the election, it may deduct $8,333 ($100,000 × 1⁄12) in its fiscal year that ends January 31, 2002 and $91,667 ($100,000 × 11⁄12) in its fiscal year that ends January 31, 2003.

If the taxes are due and paid on September 30, 2002, Alpha would be better off not making the ratable accrual election. In this case, the recurring item exception applies because the payment is made within 8½ months of Alpha's 2002 fiscal year-end. Thus, if Alpha does not make the election, all of the $100,000 is deductible in the fiscal year ending on January 31, 2002. ◀

The rules for determining when an expense is deductible are presented in Topic Review I6-3.

SPECIAL DISALLOWANCE RULES

OBJECTIVE 5

Explain the tax consequences of wash sales

In addition to the general rules of deductibility mentioned above, certain types of transactions are subject to further limitations and disallowances. These include transactions known as wash sales, transactions between related persons, gambling losses, losses associated with an activity determined to be a hobby, expenses of renting a vacation home, and expenses of an office in the taxpayer's home. These special disallowance rules are discussed below.

WASH SALES

Section 1091 disallows losses incurred on wash sales of stock or securities in the year of sale. For purposes of Sec. 1091, a **wash sale** occurs when

- ▶ A taxpayer realizes a loss on the sale of stock or securities, and

Topic Review I6-3

When an Expense Is Deductible

Cash Method: Deductible When Paid

Payment Is Made When

- Cash or other property is transferred.
- A check is delivered or mailed.
- An item is charged on a credit card.

  Note: A mere promise to pay or delivery of a note payable is not considered payment.

Prepaid Expenses

- Generally are deductible over the period covered.
- Deductible when paid if the period covered does not exceed one year.
- Prepaid interest is generally deductible ratably over the period covered by the loan.
- Points are deductible when paid if:
  - —The loan is used to purchase or improve the taxpayer's principal residence.
  - —The loan is secured by the residence.
  - —Points are established business practice in the geographical area.
  - —The points do not exceed the amount generally charged.
  - —For points paid to purchase a principal residence, the closing agreement clearly designates the amounts as points and the amount must be computed as a percentage of the amount borrowed.

Accrual Method: Deductible When Accrued

In General

- The accrual method must be used for inventories (except for taxpayers with average annual gross receipts of $1 million or less).
- Accrual occurs when both all-events test and economic performance have been met.

All-Events Test

- The existence of a liability is established and
- The amount of the liability is determined.

Economic Performance

- When economic performance is deemed to occur depends on the transaction involved (see Table I6-1).
- May be deemed to occur in the year the all-events test is met if all of the following tests are met:
  - —Actual economic performance occurs within the shorter of:
    8½ months after taxable year or a reasonable period after the taxable year.
  - —The expense is recurring and is treated consistently from year to year.
  - —Either:
    The item is immaterial or
    Deducting the expense in the year the all-events test is met results in a more proper matching of income and deductions.

- The taxpayer acquires "substantially identical" stock or securities within a 61-day period of time that extends from 30 days before the date of sale to 30 days after the date of sale.[33]

Thus, the purpose of the wash sale rule is to prevent taxpayers from generating artificial tax losses in situations where taxpayers do not intend to reduce their holdings in the stock or securities that are sold.

EXAMPLE I6-31 ▶ Leslie realizes $10,000 in short-term capital gains (STCGs) through dealings in the stock market during the current year. Realizing that STCGs are fully includible in gross income unless they are offset against realized capital losses, Leslie analyzes her portfolio to determine whether she owns any stocks that have declined in value. She finds that the FMV of her Edison Corporation common stock is only $8,000, even though she originally purchased it for $16,000. Despite this

[33] Here the term *acquire* includes an acquisition of the stock either by purchase or in a taxable exchange. The term *stock or securities* includes contracts or options to acquire or sell stock or securities (see Sec. 1091(a)).

paper loss on the stock, Leslie feels that Edison Corporation is still a good investment and wants to retain the stock. If Leslie attempts to take advantage of the paper loss on the Edison stock by selling the stock she owns and repurchasing a similar number of shares of Edison common stock within the 61-day period, the loss is disallowed. ◀

SELF-STUDY QUESTION

During 1997, you bought 100 shares of X stock on each of three occasions. You paid $158 a share for the first block of 100 shares, $100 a share for the second block, and $95 a share for the third block. On December 23, 2002, you sold 300 shares of X stock for $125 a share. On January 6, 2003, you bought 250 shares of identical X stock. Can you deduct the loss realized on the first block of stock?

ANSWER

You cannot deduct the loss of $33 a share on the first block because within 30 days after the date of sale you bought 250 identical shares of X stock. In addition, you cannot reduce the gain realized on the sale of the second and third blocks of stock by this loss.

At times, taxpayers may attempt to circumvent the wash sale provisions through either a sham transaction or an indirect repurchase of the securities. If this is the case, the wash sale provisions still prevent the recognition of the loss. The Supreme Court has held that losses on sales of stock by a husband were disallowed when the stockbroker was instructed to purchase the same number of shares in his wife's name.[34]

In some instances a taxpayer may be tempted to circumvent the wash sale provisions by merely delaying the repurchase of the substantially identical stock. This tactic should work as long as a written agreement to repurchase the stock does not exist at the time of the sale or at any time within the 61-day period mandated by the Sec. 1091 wash sale provisions. If such an agreement is made, the courts will disallow the loss, even though the actual purchase does not occur within the 61-day period.[35]

In certain cases, taxpayers may still recognize losses on transactions that literally fall within the wash sale requirements. For example, a taxpayer may purchase stock and then sell a portion of those shares within 30 days where the intent is merely to reduce the stock holdings. Taken together, these two transactions meet the tests of Sec. 1091. However, because the purpose of the sale is to reduce the taxpayer's holdings rather than to generate an artificial tax loss, the loss on the sale is allowed.[36] Section 1091 also does not apply to losses realized in the ordinary course of business by a dealer in stock or securities.

If fewer shares of stock are acquired within the 61-day period than were disposed of, only a proportionate amount of the total loss is disallowed.

EXAMPLE I6-32 ▶ Several years ago, Henry purchased 100 shares of New Corporation common stock for $2,000 ($20 per share). On July 2 of the current year, Henry sells all 100 shares for $1,000. On July 30 of the current year, Henry purchases 75 shares (three-fourths of the original shares) of New Corporation common stock. As a result of the reacquisition, three-fourths of the total loss ($750) is disallowed. Henry recognizes the remaining $250 loss. ◀

SUBSTANTIALLY IDENTICAL STOCK OR SECURITIES. Only the acquisition of substantially identical stock or securities will cause a disallowance of the loss. The IRC and the Treasury Regulations do not define the term *substantially identical*. Judicial and administrative rulings have held that bonds issued by the same corporation generally are not considered substantially identical if they differ in terms (e.g., interest rate and term to maturity). However, bonds of the same corporation that differ only in their maturity dates (e.g., the bonds do not come due for 16 years and mature within a few months of each other) have been held to be substantially identical. The preferred stock of a corporation generally is not considered substantially identical to the common stock of the same corporation.[37]

BASIS OF STOCK. If a loss is disallowed because of the wash sale provisions, the basis of the acquired stock that causes the nonrecognition is increased to reflect the disallowance. This increase means that the disallowed loss is merely postponed and will eventually be recognized either in the form of a reduced gain or an increased loss upon the subsequent sale or disposition of the stock that causes the loss disallowance. Because the amount of the increase in basis is equal to the postponed loss, the taxpayer eventually recovers the cost of the original shares of stock. If there has been more than one purchase of replacement stock and the amount of stock purchased within the 61-day period

---

[34] *John P. McWilliams v. CIR*, 35 AFTR 1184, 47-1 USTC ¶9289 (USSC, 1947).

[35] Rev. Rul. 72-225, 1972-1 C.B. 59, and *Frank Stein*, 1977 PH T.C. Memo ¶77,241, 36 TCM 992.

[36] Rev. Rul. 56-602, 1956-2 C.B. 527.

[37] *Marie Hanlin, Executrix v. CIR*, 39-2 USTC ¶9783 (3d Cir., 1939). However, the IRS held in Rev. Rul. 77-201, 1977-1 C.B. 250, that the convertible preferred stock of a corporation is substantially identical to its common stock if the preferred stock has the same voting rights and is subject to the same dividend restrictions as the common stock, is unrestricted as to its convertibility, and sells at relatively the same price (taking into consideration the conversion ratio).

exceeds the stock that is sold, the stock that is deemed to have caused the disallowance of the loss is accounted for chronologically. The holding period of the replacement stock includes the period of time the taxpayer held the stock that was sold.

EXAMPLE I6-33 ▶ Ingrid enters into the following transactions with regard to Pacific Corporation common stock:

Date	*Transaction*	*Amount*
January 4, 1993	Purchases 600 shares	$30,000
October 2, 2002	Purchases 400 shares	10,000
October 12, 2002	Sells original 600 shares	12,000
October 20, 2002	Purchases 200 shares	5,000
October 25, 2002	Purchases 300 shares	8,400

Because Ingrid purchases more than 600 shares within the 61-day period before and after the date of sale (the purchases made on October 2, 20, and 25), the entire loss of $18,000 ($30,000 − $12,000) is postponed. Four hundred shares (two-thirds of the number of shares sold) are purchased on October 2 and 200 shares (one-third) are purchased on October 20. Thus, the basis of the 400 shares of stock purchased on October 2 is $22,000 [$10,000 purchase price + ($18,000 disallowed loss × 0.667)]. The basis of the 200 shares of stock purchased on October 20 is $11,000 [$5,000 + ($18,000 disallowed loss × 0.333)]. Both of these blocks of stock have a holding period that starts on January 4, 1993.[38] The basis of the 300 shares of stock purchased on October 25 is its purchase price of $8,400. Its holding period begins on October 25. ◀

STOP & THINK

Question: With regard to his investments in the stock market, the current year has been like a roller coaster ride for Doug. He now wants to do some year-end tax planning. For the year to date, he has realized a net gain of $12,000 on his stock investments. Although some of his current stock holdings have unrealized losses, he feels that they are excellent investments that will provide excellent returns in the next year or two. His stock broker has suggested that he sell enough of his holdings to realize a $12,000 loss (to offset the $12,000 capital gain) and then simply repurchase some of the stock. What advice would you give Doug as he discusses this strategy with his broker?

Solution: By realizing $12,000 in capital losses this year, Doug may be able to offset the capital gains he has already recognized. In order to recognize these losses, however, he must make sure that the wash sale provisions do not apply. Thus, he must either 1) purchase stock of different corporations or 2) delay the repurchase of the same issue of stock for at least 31 days after the date of sale. Since Doug is happy with his current investments, perhaps the second strategy is the best. Of course, other non-tax issues must also be considered. For example, does Doug think that the prices will go up quickly within the next 30 days? If so, he may lose out on some significant gains while he is waiting to repurchase the stock. Additionally, the transaction costs (such as commissions) must also be considered.

TRANSACTIONS BETWEEN RELATED PARTIES

OBJECTIVE 6

Explain the tax consequences of transactions between related parties

Section 267 places transactions between certain related parties under special scrutiny because of the potential for tax abuse. For example, a taxpayer could sell a piece of property at a loss to a wholly owned corporation. Without any restrictions on the deductibility of the loss, the individual could recognize the loss while still retaining effective control of the property. Under Sec. 267, related taxpayers may not take current deductions on two specific types of transactions between them. These transactions are

- Losses on sales of property
- Accrued expenses that remain unpaid at the end of the tax year

[38] An asset's holding period is important in determining whether subsequent gain or loss on the asset is long-term or short-term gain or loss. This is explained further in Chapter I5.

ADDITIONAL COMMENT

Section 267 does not define the word property, but the IRS and the courts have given it a broad meaning.

RELATED PARTIES DEFINED. Section 267 defines the following relationships as related parties:

- Individuals and their families. The term family includes an individual's spouse, brothers and sisters (including half-brothers and half-sisters), ancestors, and lineal descendants.
- An individual and a corporation in which the individual owns more than 50% of the value of the outstanding stock.
- Various relationships between grantors, beneficiaries, and fiduciaries of a trust or trusts, or between the fiduciary of a trust and a corporation if certain ownership requirements are met.
- A corporation and a partnership if the same persons own more than 50% in value of the stock of the corporation and more than 50% of the partnership.
- Two corporations if the same persons own more than 50% in value of the outstanding stock of both corporations and at least one of the corporations is an S corporation.
- Other complex relationships involving trusts, corporations and individuals.

TAX STRATEGY TIP

The related party rules many times cause the tax consequences to be different than what was expected. Be sure that your clients provide all details to you ahead of time when relatives are involved in the transaction. You might be able to help structure the transaction in a way that meets your client's expectations.

Several of these relationships depend on an individual's ownership of a corporation. For example, if a taxpayer does not own more than 50% of a corporation's stock, the individual and the corporation are not related, and a loss on the sale of business or investment property between the two is deductible. Occasionally, individuals might attempt to circumvent the related party rules by dispersing the ownership of a corporation (e.g., among close family members) while retaining economic control. To prevent these tactics, Sec. 267 contains constructive ownership rules whereby a taxpayer is deemed to own stock owned by certain other persons. These constructive ownership rules are as follows:

- Stock owned by an individual's family is treated as owned by the individual. Here the definition of *family* is the same as that of *related parties* (i.e. spouse, brothers and sisters, ancestors, and lineal descendants).
- Stock owned by a corporation, partnership, estate, or trust is treated as owned proportionately by the shareholders, partners, or beneficiaries.
- If an individual partner in a partnership owns (or is treated as owning) stock in a corporation, the individual is treated as owning any stock of that corporation owned by any other partner in the partnership. This does not occur, however, if the only stock the individual owns (or is considered to own) is what his or her family owns.[39]
- Stock ownership that is attributed to a shareholder or partner from an entity can be reattributed to another taxpayer under any of the constructive ownership rules. However, stock ownership attributed to a taxpayer under the family or partner rules cannot be reattributed.

These rules are illustrated by the following examples:

EXAMPLE I6-34 ▶ Alice and Beth are equal partners in the AB Partnership. Beth owns 60% of First Corporation's stock, and Craig, Alice's husband, owns the other 40%. The ownership of the partnership and the corporation is demonstrated in Figure I6-2. Under the constructive ownership rules, Alice is considered to own Craig's 40% of the First Corporation stock. Alice is not considered to own the First Corporation stock owned by her partner, Beth, because the only First Corporation stock Alice owns (or is considered to own) is that owned by her husband. If Alice sells property at a loss to First Corporation, the loss is recognized because Alice does not directly or constructively own more than 50% of the First Corporation stock. ◀

EXAMPLE I6-35 ▶ Assume the same facts as in Example I6-34, except that the First Corporation stock is owned 50% by the AB Partnership and 25% each by Beth and Craig. The ownership of the partnership and the corporation is shown in Figure I6-3. In addition to Craig's 25%, Alice is considered to own 50% of the stock owned by the AB Partnership because of her 50% ownership in AB. The other half of AB's stock ownership is attributed to her partner, Beth. However, Alice is also

---

[39] Reg. Sec. 1.267(c)-1(b), Exs. (2) and (3).

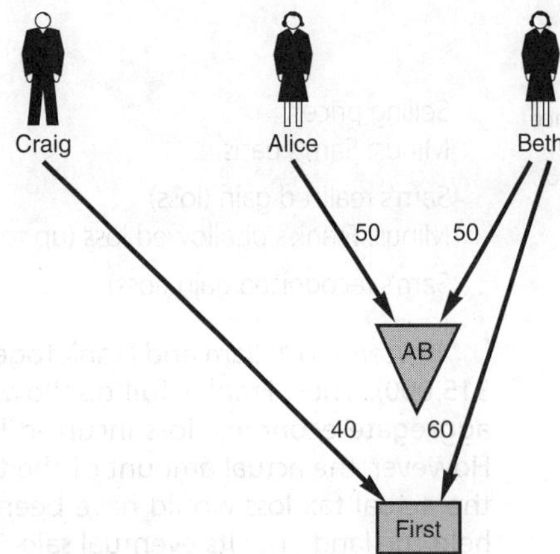

FIGURE I6-2 ▶ ILLUSTRATION FOR EXAMPLE I6-34

treated as owning the First Corporation stock Beth owns both actually and constructively (50%). Thus, Alice is treated as owning 100% of the First Corporation stock. In this case, Alice will not be able to recognize a loss on the sale of property to First Corporation. ◀

DISALLOWED LOSSES. If a loss is disallowed under Sec. 267, the original seller of the property receives no tax deduction. The disallowed loss has no effect on the purchaser's basis. The cost basis to the purchaser is equal to the amount paid for the property. However, partial relief is provided because on a subsequent sale of the property, the related purchaser may reduce the recognized gain by the amount of the disallowed loss. This offsetting of a subsequent gain is available only to the related person who originally purchased the property. If the disallowed loss is larger than the subsequent gain, or if the purchaser sells the property at a loss, no deduction is allowed for the unused loss. This may result in a partial disallowance of an overall economic loss for the related parties because there is no upward basis adjustment for the previously disallowed loss (as is the case for a wash sale).

EXAMPLE I6-36 ▶ Assume three separate scenarios in which Sam sells a tract of land during the current year. In each case assume that Sam purchased the land from his father, Frank, for $10,000. Frank's basis at the time of the original sale was $15,000 in each case. Thus, Frank's $5,000 loss on each land sale was disallowed.

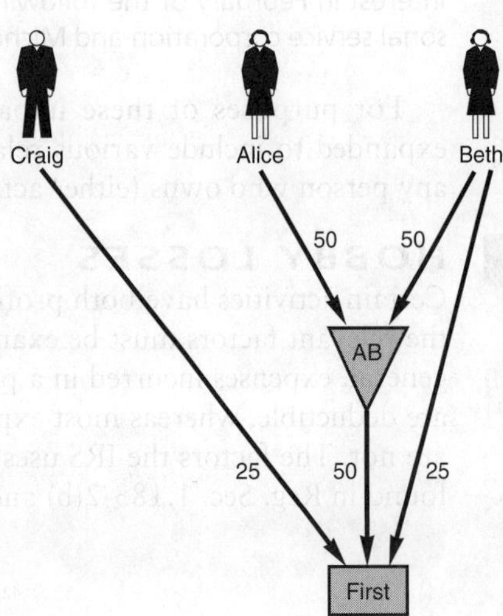

FIGURE I6-3 ▶ ILLUSTRATION FOR EXAMPLE I6-35

KEY POINT

The loss disallowance rule for related parties is more severe compared to the loss disallowance rule on wash sales. In a related party transaction, it is possible to lose the tax benefit of all or a portion of the economic loss.

	Scenario 1	Scenario 2	Scenario 3
Selling price	$17,000	$12,000	$ 8,000
Minus: Sam's basis	(10,000)	(10,000)	(10,000)
Sam's realized gain (loss)	$ 7,000	$ 2,000	$(2,000)
Minus: Frank's disallowed loss (up to Sam's gain)	(5,000)	(2,000)	—0—
Sam's recognized gain (loss)	$2,000	—0—	($2,000)

In Scenario 1, Sam and Frank together have incurred an aggregate gain of $2,000 ($17,000 – $15,000). Thus, Frank's full disallowed loss reduces Sam's subsequent gain. In Scenario 2, the aggregate economic loss incurred by Sam and Frank is actually $3,000 ($12,000 – $15,000). However, the actual amount of the tax loss recognized for Sam and Frank is zero. In Scenario 3, the actual tax loss would have been $7,000 ($8,000 – $15,000) instead of $2,000 if Frank had held the land until its eventual sale. ◀

A similar rule found in Sec. 707(b)(1) disallows losses between a partner and a partnership in which the partner owns directly or indirectly over 50% of the partnership and between two partnerships in which the same people own directly or indirectly over 50% in each partnership. The constructive ownership rules of Sec. 267 apply here in determining ownership (see *Prentice Hall's Federal Taxation: Corporations, Partnerships, Estates, and Trusts* text or the *Comprehensive* volume).

KEY POINT

The effect of Sec. 267 with respect to unpaid expenses is to place an accrual method taxpayer on the cash method for amounts owed to a related cash method taxpayer.

UNPAID EXPENSES. Under Sec. 267, a related obligor of any unpaid expenses must defer the deduction for those expenses until the year in which the related payee recognizes the amount as income. In effect, this rule prevents an accrual-method taxpayer from taking a deduction for an unpaid expense in the earlier year of accrual while the related cash-method taxpayer recognizes the payment as income in the subsequent year.

For unpaid expenses, the definition of *related parties* in Sec. 267 is expanded to include a personal-service corporation and any employee-owner.[40] A personal-service corporation is one whose principal activity is the performance of personal services that are substantially performed by employee-owners. An employee-owner is an employee who owns any of the outstanding stock of the personal-service corporation.[41]

EXAMPLE I6-37 ▶ Michelle owns 100% of the outstanding stock of Hill Corporation. Michelle is a cash method taxpayer and Hill Corporation is an accrual method taxpayer. Both taxpayers are calendar-year taxpayers. In a bona fide transaction, Hill borrows some funds from Michelle. By the end of the current year, $8,000 interest had accrued on the loan. However, Hill Corporation does not pay the interest to Michelle until February of the following year. Because Michelle is a cash method taxpayer, she reports the interest income when she receives it in the following year. Although Hill is an accrual method taxpayer, it must defer the deduction for the interest expense until it pays the interest in February of the following year. The results are the same if Hill Corporation is a personal service corporation and Michelle is an employee and owns only 20% of the Hill stock. ◀

For purposes of these unpaid expenses, the definition of *related parties* is also expanded to include various relationships involving partnerships or S corporations and any person who owns (either actually or constructively) any interest in these entities.[42]

OBJECTIVE 7

Discuss the criteria used to determine whether an activity is a hobby or a trade or business

HOBBY LOSSES

Certain activities have both profit-motivated and personal attributes. In these cases all of the relevant factors must be examined to determine the tax status of the activity since, in general, expenses incurred in a profit-motivated activity such as a business or investment are deductible, whereas most expenses associated with personal activities such as hobbies are not. The factors the IRS uses to determine whether an activity is profit-motivated are found in Reg. Sec. 1.183-2(b) and include the following:

---

[40] Sec. 267(a)(2).

[41] Secs. 269A(b) and 441(i)(2). In determining the ownership of an employee-owner, the constructive ownership rules of Sec. 318 as modified by Sec. 441(i)(2) are used. These rules differ substantially from the constructive ownership rules of Sec. 267.

[42] Sec. 267(e). A discussion of these modifications is beyond the scope of this book.

- Whether the taxpayer conducts the activity in a businesslike manner
- The expertise of the taxpayer or the taxpayer's advisors
- The time and effort expended by the taxpayer in carrying on the activity
- Whether the assets used in the activity are expected to appreciate in value
- The taxpayer's success in carrying on other similar activities
- The taxpayer's history of income or losses with respect to the activity
- The amount of occasional profits, if any, that are earned
- The taxpayer's financial status
- Any elements of personal pleasure or recreation the activity might involve

ADDITIONAL COMMENT

Many of the court cases dealing with profit motive under Sec. 183 are ranch and farm cases. In fact, Sec. 183, now titled "Activities Not Engaged in for Profit" was originally titled "Farm Losses, etc." in the Tax Reform Act of 1969.

No one of these factors is determinative. In fact, the IRS also may consider other factors not listed. Furthermore, the IRS does not make a determination by merely counting the number of factors that are present. Instead, the decision depends on an examination of all the factors together. The IRS can, therefore, make the decision on a more subjective basis than the taxpayer might like. If the IRS asserts that an activity is a personal one (i.e., a hobby) rather than a business or investment, the burden of proof rests on the taxpayer to prove otherwise.

EXAMPLE I6-38 ▶ Paula, a successful attorney with an annual income of $200,000, also enjoys raising and training quarter horses. She generally spends 5 to 6 hours each week training, showing, or racing the horses. Over the last 4 years her winnings from shows and races have amounted to $16,000. Over that same period, she has generated an additional $8,000 of income from stud fees and the sale of colts. Often the horses are used to take Paula's family or friends riding. In addition, Paula often participates in equestrian clinics and demonstrations for 4-H Clubs and other similar groups. Paula employs a high school student to feed the horses each day and to clean the stalls weekly. Paula also hires a professional horse trainer for 4 hours each week to help her train the horses.

In this case, several factors such as the level of earnings, the hiring of professional help, and the amount of time spent in the activity might indicate that Paula is engaged in a business. Other factors, such as the time spent riding with family and friends, the voluntary clinics and demonstrations, and the small amount of revenue generated as compared with Paula's other income, support the position that Paula merely has a hobby of raising horses. ◀

In cases where a clear profit motive cannot be shown under the factors mentioned above, the Code provides a test whereby an activity may be presumed to be one engaged in for profit. This test is met if the activity shows a profit for any three years during a consecutive five-year period. The five-year period consists of the year in question plus the previous four years.[43] This presumption is rebuttable (i.e., if the taxpayer meets the test, the burden of proof is shifted to the IRS to show that the activity *is not* profit motivated). Otherwise, the taxpayer would be required to prove that the activity *is* profit-motivated.

KEY POINT

Section 183(d) primarily serves to shift the burden of proof from the taxpayer to the IRS.

If the activity is determined to be a business, the taxpayer may deduct all qualified business expenses from the gross income, even if a net loss results.[44] However, if the activity is determined to be a hobby, the expenses are generally deductible as a miscellaneous itemized deduction but only to the extent of the gross income from the activity. A net loss may not be reported from the activity if it is a hobby.

EXAMPLE I6-39 ▶ Lorenzo, a stockbroker, enjoys raising pedigreed poodles. Although he mainly raises them for recreation and relaxation after work, Lorenzo periodically sells some of his poodles. Lorenzo reports $850 in income and $2,900 in expenses from the activity on his 2002 tax return. Upon auditing Lorenzo's 2002 return, the IRS disallowed the expenses in excess of the income, arguing that the activity is a hobby rather than a business or investment. If Lorenzo can prove that he realized a profit from the poodle-raising operation for any three years from 1998 through 2002 inclusive, the presumption will be made that the poodles are raised for a profit and not

---

[43] Sec. 183(d). If the major part of the activity involves breeding, training, showing, or racing horses, the five-year period is extended to a seven-year period, and a profit must be shown in only two, rather than three, of the years covered by that seven-year period.

[44] If the activity is a passive activity, the loss may be suspended. See Chapter I8 for a discussion of the passive loss rules.

for recreation. The IRS then has the burden of proof to show that the activity is really a hobby. If Lorenzo cannot show a profit for three years out of the five-year period, he must rely on the factors mentioned in the Treasury Regulations to convince the IRS and/or the courts that the activity is a business.

If Lorenzo's poodle-raising activity is determined to be a business, Lorenzo would report a net loss of $2,050 ($2,900 expenses − $850 income), assuming the loss is not incurred in a passive activity (see Chapter I8). If the activity is determined to be a hobby, however, Lorenzo may deduct only $850 of the expenses (up to the amount of the gross income) as an itemized deduction. As explained later, these expenses must be deducted in a certain order. The remaining expenses are not allowed as tax deductions. ◀

ADDITIONAL COMMENT

Gross income from an activity not engaged in for profit is defined to include the total gains from the sale, exchange, or other disposition of property, and all other gross receipts derived from such activity. Cost of goods sold can be deducted from gross receipts to calculate gross income.

DEDUCTIBLE EXPENSES. Some hobby activities generate gross income, even though profit is not a primary motive for the activity. In such situations, Sec. 183 allows the taxpayer to deduct the expenses related to the hobby, but only to the extent of the gross income from the hobby. Furthermore, a hobby-related expense is deductible only if it would have been deductible if incurred in a trade or business or an investment activity.

In essence, a taxpayer may deduct all the hobby-related expenses as long as there is enough gross income from the activity to cover the expenses. However, a hobby cannot generate a tax loss that is then used to offset a taxpayer's other types of income.

ORDER OF THE DEDUCTIONS. If the hobby expenses exceed the amount of gross income generated by the hobby, the expenses must be deducted against the gross income in the following order:

- Tier 1: Expenses that may be deducted even though they are not incurred in a trade or business (e.g., itemized deductions such as taxes, certain interest, and casualty losses)
- Tier 2: Other expenses of the hobby that could have been deducted if they had been incurred in a profit-motivated activity, but which do not reduce the tax basis of any of the assets used in the hobby (e.g., utilities and maintenance expenses)
- Tier 3: The expenses of the hobby that could have been deducted if incurred in a profit-motivated activity and that reduce the basis of the hobby's assets (e.g., depreciation on fixed assets used in the hobby)[45]

To the extent that the expenses are taken as deductions against the gross income of the activity, they are deductions *from* AGI and are deductible only if the taxpayer has itemized deductions in excess of the standard deduction. The tier 1 expenses are reported in their respective sections on Schedule A of Form 1040. The tier 2 and tier 3 expenses allocated to the hobby are treated as miscellaneous itemized deductions and are, therefore, deductible only to the extent that they exceed 2% of AGI (see Chapter I7). Gross income from a hobby is reported as other income on Form 1040. If gross income is not sufficient to cover all of the tier 1 expenses, the excess tier 1 expenses may also be deducted as itemized deductions on Schedule A of Form 1040 because these expenses are allowed in any event. Any remaining expenses in the other two tiers are disallowed and may not be carried over to a subsequent year.

ADDITIONAL COMMENT

Hobby expenses are subject to the 2% of AGI limitation on miscellaneous itemized deductions. However, if the hobby expense is one that is deductible whether or not incurred in an income producing activity, such as real property taxes on a home, it is fully deductible.

If depreciation expense is disallowed, it is not necessary to reduce the cost basis of the asset to the extent of the disallowance.

EXAMPLE I6-40 ▶ Lynn raises various plants and flowers in a small greenhouse constructed specifically for that purpose. During the current year, Lynn reports gross income from the greenhouse activities of $1,700. Lynn also incurs the following expenses:

Property taxes on the greenhouse	$1,150
Utilities	300
Depreciation (assuming the activity is considered a business.)	800

If the greenhouse activity is considered to be a hobby rather than a business, the deductions Lynn may take are computed as follows:

[45] Reg. Sec. 1.183-1(b).

REAL LIFE EXAMPLE

Good records are very important in establishing the existence of a business rather than a hobby. A taxpayer, who owned and operated an apple orchard, asserted that he maintained sufficient business records, consisting of bank deposit slips, check stubs, and tax forms. A separate bank account was also maintained. But the taxpayer did not present any production records for the apple orchard. In fact, at trial, the taxpayer was not even certain of the exact number of trees in the orchard. Thus, the court found that due to the limited records, the taxpayer's activity was considered to be a hobby rather than a business. *Zdun,* TC Memo 1998-296 (1998).

Income From greenhouse		$1,700
Tier 1 Expenses:		
Property taxes	$1,150	
Tier 2 Expenses:		
Utilities	300	
Tier 3 Expenses:		
Depreciation[a]	250	$1,700
Total		$0

[a]Limited to greenhouse income remaining after accounting for the Tier 1 and Tier 2 expenses. ◀

VACATION HOME

Because owning a second home or dwelling unit may have both personal and profit-motivated attributes, deductions for expenses related to the rental of a vacation home that is also used as a residence by the taxpayer may be disallowed or limited by Sec. 280A.

OBJECTIVE 8

Determine the tax consequences of vacation homes

RESIDENCE DEFINED. For the restrictive rules of Sec. 280A to apply, the property must be a dwelling unit that qualifies as the taxpayer's residence. As used in this context, the term *dwelling unit* is quite expansive. Property such as boats and mobile homes may be considered dwelling units. The determining factor is whether the property provides shelter and accommodations for eating and sleeping.[46] Thus, a mini-motorhome that contains the appropriate accommodations has been held to be a dwelling unit subject to the rules and limitations of Sec. 280A. The fact that the unit is small and cramped is disregarded.

A dwelling unit is considered to be used by the taxpayer as a residence if the number of days during which the taxpayer uses the property for personal use throughout the year exceeds the greater of the following:

- 14 days, or
- 10% of the number of days during the year that the property is rented at a fair rental[47]

SELF-STUDY QUESTION

What is the maximum number of days during a year that a taxpayer may use a property for personal use and not have it considered to be used as a residence?

ANSWER

If a property was rented for 332 days it could be used by the taxpayer for 33 days and not be considered a residence.

EXAMPLE I6-41 ▶ Sarah owns a houseboat on Lake Powell that she personally uses for 21 days out of the year. During the year she also rents out the boat for a total of 300 days. Even though Sarah's personal use exceeds 14 days during the year, the houseboat is not considered a residence under Sec. 280A because Sarah's personal use does not exceed 30 days during the year (10% of the 300 rental days for the year). ◀

For purposes of the residence test, a day of personal use includes any day that the property is used

- For personal purposes by the taxpayer or the taxpayer's family. *Family* is defined here as including a taxpayer's spouse, brothers and sisters, ancestors, and lineal descendants.[48]
- By any individual under a reciprocal-use arrangement.[49]
- By any individual who does not pay a fair rental for the use of the property.[50]

Despite the family-use rule, if a taxpayer rents property at a fair rental to a family member who uses the property as a principal residence, such use does not constitute personal use by the taxpayer.

[46] *Ronald L. Haberkorn,* 75 T.C. 259 (1980), and *John O. Loughlin v. U.S.,* 50 AFTR 2d 82-5827, 82-2 USTC ¶9543 (D.C. Minn., 1982).

[47] Sec. 280A(d)(1). In certain cases, this residence test might be met when a taxpayer uses a property as his or her principal residence for part of the year and rents the property for the rest of the year. This could occur, for example, when a taxpayer moves from his or her home and turns the old residence into a rental unit. In such a case, special rules prevent the home from being classified as a residence under Sec. 280A, thus preventing the application of the limitations.

[48] Under Sec. 280A(d)(2), a day during which the taxpayer spends substantially full time on repairs and maintenance does not count as a personal-use day.

[49] Sec. 280A(d)(2)(B). A reciprocal-use arrangement is one whereby another person uses the taxpayer's property in exchange for the taxpayer's use of the other person's property.

[50] Sec. 280A(d)(2)(C). Exactly what constitutes a fair rental must be determined by an examination of all the associated facts and circumstances.

EXAMPLE I6-42 ▶ During the current year, Peggy purchases a small house as an investment and rents the property to Stan, her married son, who uses the property as his principal residence. Peggy's son pays her a fair rental for the property. Because Stan uses the property as his principal residence and pays Peggy a fair rental for the property, Stan's personal use of the property does not constitute personal use by Peggy. Thus, the rules of Sec. 280A do not apply to limit the expenses that Peggy may deduct. ◀

KEY POINT

A second home is classified as either rental property, a residence, or some combination of the two. If it is classified as some combination of rental property and a residence, the expenses of the property must be allocated between the two categories.

ALLOCATION OF EXPENSES. Expenses related to the property must be allocated between personal use and rental use. Generally, no deduction is allowed for expenses that are allocable to personal use. However, qualified mortgage interest and real estate taxes are deductible even when allocated to personal use because such expenses are deductible on personal residences.[51] Expenses allocated to the rental use are deductible under Sec. 280A, but only to the extent of the gross income generated by the property. The property may not generate a loss that is used to reduce other income of the taxpayer. Expenses that are not deductible because they exceed the gross income from the property may be carried over to the subsequent year and taken as a deduction, limited to the gross income of that year.[52] Expenses that are allocated to the rental use of the property and deducted against the gross income must be taken in the same order (explained previously) that the expenses under the hobby loss rules of Sec. 183 are deducted. Example I6-40 illustrates these rules.

Allocation Formula. In allocating expenses between the personal use and the rental use of the property, the following formula is used:[53]

$$\text{Rental use expenses} = \frac{\text{Number of rental days}}{\text{Total number of days used}} \times \begin{array}{c}\text{Total expenses}\\ \text{for the year}\end{array}$$

The denominator of the allocation fraction is the sum of the days the property is rented plus the days that the property is used for personal purposes. The days when the property is not used are not included in the formula.

Some courts have modified the allocation formula by allowing the use of the total number of days in the year as the denominator for qualified residential interest and taxes.[54] Use of this ratio allocates less interest and taxes to the rental use, allowing more of the other expenses to be deducted against the rental income. Subject to limitations, the interest and taxes not allocated to the rental use are still deductible as itemized deductions. Example I6-43 uses the allocation formula that has been sanctioned by the courts.

EXAMPLE I6-43 ▶ Joan owns a cabin near the local ski resort. During the year, Joan and Joan's family use the cabin a total of 25 days. The cabin is also rented to out-of-state skiers for a total of 50 days during the year, generating rental income of $10,000. Joan incurs the following expenses:

Expense	*Amount*
Property taxes	$1,500
Interest on mortgage	3,000
Utilities	2,000
Insurance	1,500
Security and snow removal	2,500

Joan would have been entitled to $12,000 depreciation if the property had been entirely rental property held for investment. However, because the property is also used for personal purposes, the amount of deductions (for AGI) Joan may take with respect to the property during the year is as follows:

[51] No deduction is allowed for interest incurred with respect to a personal residence if the debt on which the interest is paid is not secured by the property or the taxpayer has not chosen the property as a second residence for purposes of deducting the interest as qualified residential interest (see Chapter I7). For purposes of the discussion and examples used here, the assumption is made that the interest qualifies as qualified residential interest.

[52] Sec. 280A(c)(5)(B). The expenses that are carried over to the subsequent year are deductible to the extent of the property's gross income of that year, even though the property is not used by the taxpayer as a residence during that year.

[53] Sec. 280A(e)(1).

[54] *Dorance D. Bolton v. CIR*, 51 AFTR 2d 83-305, 82-2 USTC ¶9699 (9th Cir., 1982). See also *Edith G. McKinney v. CIR*, 52 AFTR 2d 83-6281, 83-2 USTC ¶9655 (10th Cir., 1983).

SELF-STUDY QUESTION

Assume that a taxpayer rents his cabin to an individual who occupies it on a Saturday afternoon. Two weeks later the tenant leaves the cabin on a Saturday morning. Has the cabin been rented for more than 14 days?

ANSWER

No, although the tenant was on the premises for 15 calendar days, he is treated as having rented the property for only 14 days.

Item	*Calculation*	*Amount*
Rental income		$10,000
Interest and taxes	$\$4,500 \times \frac{50}{365}$	(616)[a]
All other expenses except depreciation	$\$6,000 \times \frac{50}{75}$	(4,000)
Depreciation	$\$12,000 \times \frac{50}{75}$	(5,384)[b]
Net income from property		$0

The income and these expenses are reported on Schedule E. Thus, the expenses allocated to the rental use are *for* AGI deductions. In addition to the deductions above, Joan may also deduct $3,884 ($4,500 − $616) interest and taxes as itemized deductions on Schedule A if the interest is qualified residence interest (see Chapter I7) and her total itemized deductions exceed her standard deduction.

[a] Under the approach favored by the IRS, $3,000 ($4,500 × 50/75) of interest and taxes would be used to offset the gross income and only $3,000 of depreciation would be deductible.

[b] $8,000 of the depreciation is allocated to the rental use (50/75 × $12,000). Since the deduction for depreciation is limited to $5,384, the additional $2,616 ($8,000 − $5,384) can be carried over and deducted in the next year if the gross income of that year is sufficient to cover all the expenses allocable to the rental use. If there had been sufficient gross income, Joan could have taken $8,000 depreciation. ◀

NOMINAL NUMBER OF RENTAL DAYS. If a property qualifies as a taxpayer's residence under Sec. 280A and it is rented for less than 15 days during the year, the law takes the approach that the property is completely personal in nature. As such, no rental income is included in gross income and no expenses may be deducted. However, expenses such as qualified residential interest and taxes may still be deducted as itemized deductions. (See Chapter I7 for a discussion of the limitations on interest.)

EXAMPLE I6-44 ▶ Assume the same facts as in Example I6-43, except that during the year Joan rents the cabin out for only 12 days and the amount of rental income is $2,400. The cabin qualifies as Joan's residence because her personal use exceeds 14 days. Because the cabin is rented for less than 15 days during the year, Joan may only take itemized deductions of $4,500 for the qualified residential interest and taxes. She may not deduct the other expenses. In addition, she does not include the $2,400 in gross income. ◀

KEY POINT

Assume that a taxpayer owns a beachfront condo. The taxpayer personally uses the condo for only 12 days during the year and rents the property for 35 days. Section 280A does not apply because the taxpayer has not used the property for over 14 days. However, if the taxpayer cannot demonstrate a profit motive, it may still be treated as a hobby. If so, the deductibility of the expenses allocated to the rental use is limited to the gross income generated by the property. Furthermore, the interest allocated to the personal use of the property is not deductible as qualified residential interest (see Chapter I7).

NOMINAL NUMBER OF PERSONAL USE DAYS. If a taxpayer does not have enough personal use days during the year to qualify the property as a residence (i.e., the personal use is not more than the greater of 14 days or 10% of the rental days), the Sec. 280A rules and limitations do not apply. If the owner demonstrates a profit motive, the property is treated as rental property. On the other hand, if the property does not qualify as either rental property or as the taxpayer's residence, the property is considered a hobby. Under these circumstances, the expenses must still be allocated between the rental use and the personal use. The taxpayer treats the taxes allocated to the personal use as itemized deductions. None of the interest allocated to the personal use is deductible because it is not qualified residential interest. (See Chapter I7 for a discussion of the deductibility of personal interest and qualified residential interest.) Tier 2 and 3 expenses allocated to the personal use are not deductible. The income from the property and all of the expenses allocated to the rental use are reported on Schedule E of Form 1040. As such, the expenses are *for* AGI deductions. Any net income or loss from the property is subject to the passive loss rules, which may limit the deductibility of any losses from the property (see Chapter I8). The rules of Sec. 280A regarding the rental of property are summarized in Figure I6-4.

EXAMPLE I6-45 ▶ Assume the same facts as in Example I6-43 except that Joan and her family use the cabin only 10 days during the year and rent it out for 65 days of the year. Joan may take the following deductions with respect to the property during the year:

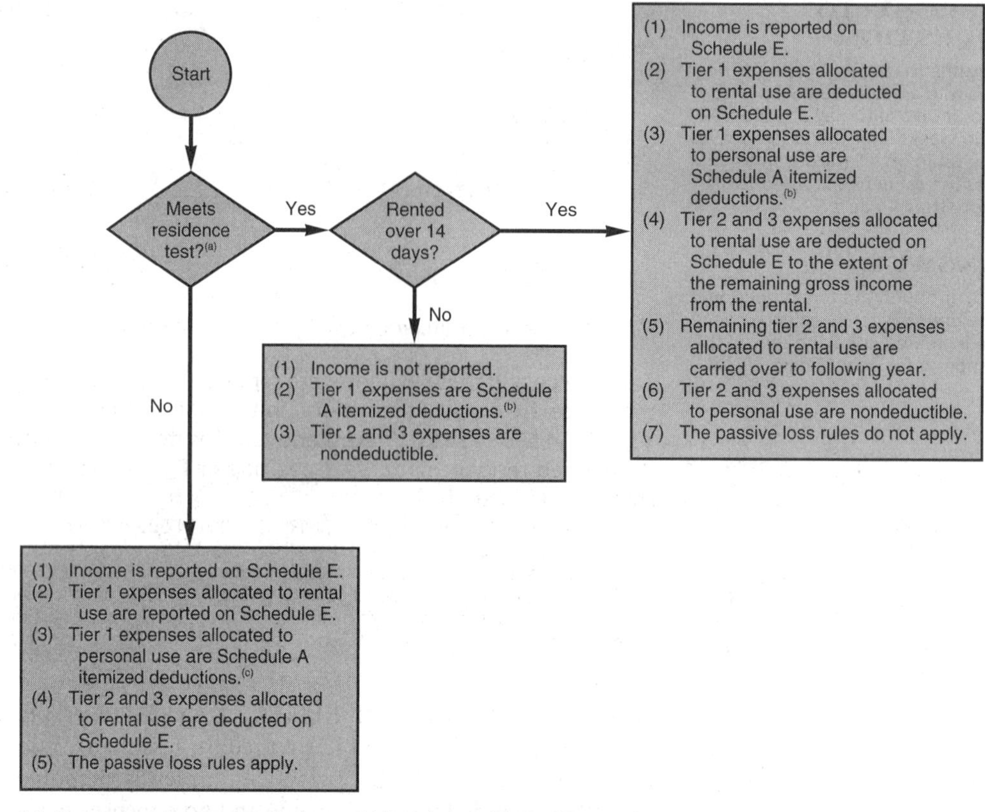

(a) Personal use is more than the larger of (1) 14 days or (2) 10% of rental days.
(b) In order for the interest to be deductible, it must be "qualified residence interest" (See Chapter 7).
(c) In order for the interest to be deductible as qualified residence, the property must not have been rented at all during the year (see Chapter 7).

FIGURE I6-4 ▶ SECTION 280A: LIMITATION OF DEDUCTIONS ON RENTAL OF RESIDENTIAL PROPERTY

	Calculation	*Amount*
Rental income		$10,000
Interest	$\$3,000 \times \frac{65}{365}$	(535)[a]
Taxes	$\$1,500 \times \frac{65}{365}$	(267)[a]
Other expenses	$\$6,000 \times \frac{65}{75}$	(5,200)
Depreciation	$\$12,000 \times \frac{65}{75}$	(3,998)[b]
	Total	$ 0

[a] Under the approach favored by the IRS, $3,900 ($4,500 × 65/75) of interest and taxes would have been allocated to the rental use. Joan would treat the remaining $1,233 in taxes ($1,500 − $267) as an itemized deduction. However, Joan may not deduct the remaining $2,465 ($3,000 − $535) interest because it does not qualify as deductible residential interest.
[b] A total of $10,400 depreciation is allocated to the rental use ($12,000 × 65/75). Since the deduction is limited to $3,998, the additional $6,402 ($10,400 − $3,998) can be carried over and deducted in the next year if the gross income of that year is sufficient to cover all the expenses allocable to the rental use. ◀

EXPENSES OF AN OFFICE IN THE HOME

Unless the taxpayer meets certain strictly imposed requirements, Sec. 280A disallows any deduction for home office expenses. In general, for a taxpayer to deduct office-in-home expenses, the office must have been regularly and exclusively used as either of the following:

- The principal place of business for a trade or business of the taxpayer; or
- A place where the taxpayer meets or deals with clients in the normal course of business

The term "principal place of business" includes a home office used by the taxpayer for administrative or management activities of the business if no other fixed location exists where the taxpayer conducts these administrative or managerial activities.

For employees to take a deduction for home office expenses, the use must also have been for the convenience of the employer. In addition, a separate structure not attached to the taxpayer's house may qualify if regularly and exclusively used in connection with the taxpayer's business. (See Chapter I9 for a comprehensive discussion of these rules.)

TAX PLANNING CONSIDERATIONS

HOBBY LOSSES

ETHICAL POINT

In some cases it is difficult to ascertain whether an activity is a trade or business or a hobby. A CPA should not prepare or sign a tax return unless he or she in good faith believes that the return takes a position that has a realistic possibility of being sustained on its merits.

Deductions for expenses incurred in a hobby activity are limited to the gross income generated by the hobby for the year. However, if the gross income exceeds the deductions from the activity in at least three out of five consecutive years, (two out of seven for activities involving the breeding, training, showing, or racing of horses) the activity is presumed to be a business, and the limits on the deductibility of expenses do not apply. Thus, if possible, taxpayers should use care in timing the realization of items of income and expense. For example, if an activity has shown a profit in only two out of the previous four years, a taxpayer may consider accelerating some of the income into the fifth year or deferring some of the expenses of the activity into the following year. Under the cash method of accounting, this can be done by delaying payment for some of the expenses or accelerating income-generating transactions. Note that meeting the three-out-of-five-year test does not automatically ensure the activity will be treated as a business. It merely compels the IRS to prove the activity is *not* a business. Under these circumstances, the IRS may be less inclined to challenge the deductions.

UNREASONABLE COMPENSATION

If the IRS feels that a salary payment to an officer of a corporation is excessive, it will often recharacterize the excess portion as a dividend. If that happens, the corporation cannot deduct the full amount of the salary payment. To prevent a potential future disallowance, the parties may enter into a payback or hedge agreement, which provides that

WHAT WOULD YOU DO IN THIS SITUATION?

SERIOUS WINE OR HOBBY LOSS?

Mr. Bouteilles Gerbeuses has been your longtime tax client. He has amassed an impressive portfolio of real estate, securities, and joint venture investments. His net worth is substantial.

Despite all his material well-being, Mr. Gerbeuses wants to take on a new challenge—that of producing fine wines. He has not had any formal wine training but he has decided to start his own winery, named *Cuvée de Prestige*. He will pattern it after the great wine houses of Europe.

He already owns several hundred acres of agriculturally zoned land in the wine producing region of the Noir Valley. It happens to adjoin his home in the Wemadeit Country Club and Retirement Resort subdivision. He anticipates a life of semi-retirement by engaging in the art of malolactic fermentation and blending of his *blanc de blancs* and *pinot noir* grapes into his own estate wine. He expects his start-up capital investment to be over $5 million and does not expect the first harvest to take place for at least seven years after the initial planting of grape vines. He expects to offset any losses by his other income.

Assuming Mr. Gerbeuses comes to you for tax advice on his new wine venture, what tax and ethical issues should be considered?

the employee must return to the corporation any payment held to be excessive. Under such an agreement, the employee receives a *for* AGI deduction for any amount he or she repays to the corporation. This deduction is available in the year of repayment. A payback agreement must meet the following requirements to be effective:

- It must be entered into before the payment is actually made.
- It must legally obligate the employee to repay the excess amount.[55]

The IRS may take the position that the existence of the payback agreement itself is evidence that the compensation is excessive. This situation may be avoided if the payback agreement is included in the general corporate bylaws rather than in a specific contract with a particular employee.[56]

TIMING OF DEDUCTIONS

Because of the time value of money, taxpayers generally prefer to deduct an expenditure as a current expense rather than capitalize it. If an expenditure is required to be capitalized, the deductions (e.g., for depreciation or amortization) are spread over several years. In addition, some capital expenditures (e.g., land) are not subject to depreciation or amortization. In some situations, however, the taxpayer may prefer to capitalize rather than expense a particular item. For example, if a taxpayer has net operating losses (NOLs) that are about to expire, a current deduction may prevent the use of these losses.[57]

In some cases it is difficult to determine whether an item should be treated as a capital expenditure or a deduction item (e.g., certain repairs may in the aggregate be treated as a capital expenditure). In addition, certain types of expenditures, such as those for research and experimentation, may be either capitalized (subject to amortization) or expensed at the election of the taxpayer. A tax practitioner should give consideration to the taxpayer's tax situation when this decision is made. In making this decision, taxpayers and their advisors should consider NOL carryovers that might be expiring. They should also compare their current marginal tax rate with their anticipated future marginal tax rate.

COMPLIANCE AND PROCEDURAL CONSIDERATIONS

SELF-STUDY QUESTION

A professor in the Department of Accounting also teaches continuing education courses for the state CPA society as a sole proprietor. If she is a member of the state CPA society, are her dues deductible on Schedule C or as an itemized deduction?

ANSWER

Certainly, she would prefer to have the dues deductible on Schedule C so that they will not be subject to the 2% limit on miscellaneous itemized deductions. This question demonstrates the difficulty of classifying some deductions, and the answer probably depends on the primary reason for membership in the organization.

PROPER CLASSIFICATION OF DEDUCTIONS

Individuals report trade or business expenses on Schedule C (Profit or Loss from Business or Profession). It is similar to an income statement for business-related income and expenses. The net income computed on Schedule C is then included in gross income on Form 1040. Because business-related expenses are deducted in arriving at the taxable income from the business, these expenses are deductions *for* AGI. Similar treatment is given to expenses attributable to the production of rental and royalty income because they are reported on Schedule E, which is an income statement. The other deductions *for* AGI have specific lines on Form 1040 itself where they are deducted.[58] All of these deductions appear before line 33 (where AGI appears) of Form 1040.

Deductions *from* AGI are reported on Schedule A, where they are totaled and then transferred to Line 36 of Form 1040.

---

[55] *Vincent E. Oswald*, 49 T.C. 645 (1968); and *J. G. Pahl*, 67 T.C. 286 (1976). See also *Ernest H. Berger*, 37 T.C. 1026 (1962).

[56] *Charles Schneider and Co. v. CIR*, 34 AFTR 2d 74-5422, 74-2 USTC ¶9563 (8th Cir., 1974). *See also Plastics Universal Corp.*, 1979 PH T.C. Memo ¶79,355, 39 TCM 32. Additionally, some taxpayers have been successful in defending their current level of compensation where they proved that they had been undercompensated in prior years. See *Acme Construction Co., Inc.*, 1995 RIA T.C. Memo ¶95,600, 69 TCM 1596.

[57] A NOL arises when business expenses exceed business income for a year. This excess can be carried to another year (generally back two years and forward twenty years) and is deducted against the income of that year. If the years to which the NOL is carried do not have enough income, the NOL is lost when the carryover period expires. See Chapter I8 for a discussion of NOLs.

[58] Some of these expenses, such as employee business expenses (Form 2106) and moving expenses (Form 3903), are summarized on separate forms. These separate forms, however, are not net income statements in the same sense that Schedules C and E are.

ADDITIONAL COMMENT

When a taxpayer elects to defer the determination of whether a particular activity is engaged in for profit, the statute of limitations is automatically extended for all years in the postponement period. However, the automatic extension applies only to items that might be disallowed under the hobby loss rules.

PROPER SUBSTANTIATION

The burden of proving the deductibility of any expense generally rests on the taxpayer. This has always been the case. However, in recent years Congress and the IRS have become increasingly concerned about the propriety of many deductions. In the case of travel and entertainment expenses, the Code states that no deduction may be taken for an expense that is not properly documented. This documentation must include the amount of the expense, the time and place of the travel or entertainment activity, the business purpose, and the business relationship of the people entertained.

BUSINESS VERSUS HOBBY

Self-employed individuals who claim a home office deduction on Schedule C must attach Form 8829, which is used to allocate direct and indirect expenses to the appropriate use. Form 8829 need not be filed by employees who claim home office expenses on Form 2106.

When an activity has both profit-making and personal attributes, the burden is normally on the taxpayer to prove that the activity is a business. However, if a taxpayer can show that the activity has generated a profit in at least three out of five consecutive years (two out of seven for activities involving the breeding, training, showing, and racing of horses), the burden of proof shifts to the IRS. Because the statute of limitations generally runs three years after the filing of a return for any particular year (i.e., for audit purposes the year is closed and the IRS cannot assess any tax deficiency for that year), a potential problem exists for taxpayers who want to rely on this presumption during the first year or two of an activity's life. In these cases, the taxpayer may elect to defer the determination of whether the presumption applies until the fifth (seventh) year of operation. The election keeps the year in question open with respect to that activity until sufficient years have passed that the presumptive test may be applied. If the taxpayer subsequently does not meet the presumptive test, the IRS can still assess a deficiency for that activity for the prior year, because the year is still open. A taxpayer makes the election by filing Form 5213 (Election to Postpone Determination as to Whether the Presumption That an Activity Is Engaged In for Profit Applies) within three years after the due date for the year in which the taxpayer first engages in the activity.

PROBLEM MATERIALS

DISCUSSION QUESTIONS

I6-1 Why is the distinction between deductions *for* AGI and deductions *from* AGI important for individuals?

I6-2 Sam owns a small house that he rents out to students attending the local university. Are the expenses associated with the rental unit deductions *for* or *from* AGI?

I6-3 During the year, Sara sold a capital asset at a loss of $2,000. She had held the asset as an investment. Is her deduction for this capital loss a deduction *for* or a deduction *from* AGI?

I6-4 Discuss the difference in tax treatment between reimbursed employee business expenses and unreimbursed employee business expenses.

I6-5 For the current year, Mario a single individual with no dependents, receives income of $55,000 and incurs deductible expenses of $9,000.

a. What is Mario's taxable income assuming that the expenses are deductions *for* AGI.

b. What is Mario's taxable income assuming that the expenses are miscellaneous itemized deductions *from* AGI.

I6-6 Deductible business or investment expenses must be related to a profit-motivated activity.

a. What are the factors used in determining whether an activity is profit-motivated?

b. Why are these factors so important in making this determination?

I6-7 If an activity does not generate a profit in three out of five consecutive years, is it automatically deemed to be a hobby? Why or why not?

I6-8 Because expenses incurred both in a business and for the production of investment income are deductible, why is it important to determine in which category a particular activity falls?

I6-9 In order for a business expense to be deductible it must be *ordinary, necessary,* and *reasonable.* Explain what these terms mean.

I6-10 What are the criteria for distinguishing between a deductible expense and a capital expenditure?

I6-11 Why are expenses related to tax-exempt income disallowed?

I6-12 Under what circumstances may a taxpayer deduct an illegal bribe or kickback?

I6-13 Michelle pays a CPA $400 for the preparation of her federal income tax return. Michelle's only sources of income are her salary from employment and interest and dividends from her investments.

a. Is this a deductible expense? If so, is it a deduction *for* or *from* AGI?

b. Assume the same facts as in Part a except that in addition to her salary and investment and dividend income, Michelle also owns a small business. Of the $400 fee paid to the CPA, $250 is for the preparation of her Schedule C (Profit or Loss from Business). How much, if any, of the $400 is a deductible expense? Identify it as either *for* or *from* AGI.

I6-14 Jennifer flies to her state capital to lobby the legislature to build a proposed highway that is planned to run through the area where her business is located.

a. What part, if any, of her expenses are deductible?

b. Would it make a difference if the proposed road were a city road rather than a state highway, and Jennifer lobbied her local government?

c. Assume the same facts in Part a except that Jennifer's total expenses are $1,500. Are these expenses deductible?

I6-15 During November and December of last year, Tom incurred the following expenses in investigating the feasibility of opening a new restaurant in town:

Expenses to do a market survey	$3,000
Expenses to identify potential suppliers of goods	$2,000
Expenses to identify a proper location	$1,000

Explain the proper treatment of these expenses under the following scenarios:

a. Tom already owns another restaurant in town and is wanting to expand. Tom opens the new restaurant in February of the current year.

b. Tom is tiring of his current job as an outside salesperson and wants to go into business for himself. He opens the restaurant in February of the current year.

c. Tom is tiring of his current job as an outside salesperson and wants to go into business for himself. However, after getting the results of the investigations back, he decides against opening a restaurant.

I6-16 What documentation is required in order for a travel or entertainment expense to be deductible?

I6-17 Under what circumstances can prepaid expenses be deducted in the year of payment by a taxpayer using the cash method of accounting?

I6-18 Under what circumstances would a taxpayer use both the cash method and the accrual method of accounting at the same time?

I6-19 Whether the economic performance test is satisfied depends on the type of transaction and whether the transaction is recurring.

a. When does economic performance occur for a taxpayer who must provide property or services to another person?

b. When does economic performance occur when another person provides the taxpayer with property or services?

c. Explain the exception to the economic performance test for recurring liabilities.

I6-20 Why did Congress enact the wash sale provisions?

I6-21 The wash sale rules disallow a loss in the year of sale when substantially identical stock or securities are acquired by the taxpayer within a 61-day period. What types of stock or securities are considered substantially identical?

I6-22 Under Sec. 267, current deductions may not be taken for certain transactions between related parties.

a. Who is considered a member of a taxpayer's family under the related party transaction rules of Sec. 267?

b. Identify some of the other relationships that are considered related parties for purposes of Sec. 267. Why are these other relationships included in the definition?

I6-23 Under the related party rules of Sec. 267, why has Congress imposed the concept of constructive ownership?

I6-24 If property is sold at a loss to a related taxpayer, under what circumstances can at least partial benefit be derived from the disallowed loss?

I6-25 Assume that Jill is engaged in painting as a hobby. During the year, she earns $1,000 from sales of her paintings and incurs $2,500 expenses for supplies and lessons. Jill's salary from her job is $70,000. What is the tax treatment of the hobby income and expenses?

I6-26 Under Sec. 280A, what constitutes personal use of a vacation home by the taxpayer?

I6-27 Under Sec. 280A, how are expenses allocated to the rental use of a vacation home? In what order must the expenses be deducted against the gross income of the property?

I6-28 Under Sec. 280A, how will a taxpayer report the income and expenses of a vacation home if it is rented out for only 12 days during the year?

ISSUE IDENTIFICATION QUESTIONS

I6-29 David, a CPA for a large accounting firm, works 10- to 12-hour days. As a requirement for his position, he must attend social events to recruit new clients. He also has private clients in his unincorporated professional practice. David purchased exercise equipment for $3,000. He works out on the equipment to maintain his stamina and good health that enables him to carry such a heavy workload. What tax issues should David consider?

I6-30 Gus, a football player who was renegotiating his contract with the Denver Broncos, paid his ex-girlfriend $25,000 to drop a sexual assault complaint against him and keep the matter confidential. The Broncos stated that if criminal charges were filed and made public, they would terminate his employment. What tax issues should Gus consider?

I6-31 Kathleen pays $3,000 mortgage interest on the home that she and her husband live in. Kathleen and her husband live with Molly, Kathleen's mother. The title to the home is in Kathleen's name. However, the mortgage is Molly's obligation. Kathleen claims Molly as her dependent on her current tax return. What tax issues should Kathleen consider?

I6-32 Katie and Alan are avid boaters and water skiers. They also enjoy parasailing. This year, they started a new parasailing venture to give rides to patrons. Katie and Alan are both employed full-time in other pursuits, but they take patrons out during the summer months, on weekends and holidays. Alan has attended classes on boat operation and parasailing instruction. Katie and Alan have owned a boat for four years, but because of the heavy usage this summer, they replaced their old boat in July. They plan on replacing their boat with a new one every two years now. They use their boat in the parasailing activity and for recreational purposes. This year, Katie and Alan earned $5,400 from chartering activities and incurred $11,600 of expenses associated with their boating and parasailing. What tax issues should Katie and Alan consider?

PROBLEMS

I6-33 ***For or From AGI Deductions.*** Roberta ia an accountant employed by a local firm. During the year, Roberta incurs the following unreimbursed expenses:

Item	*Amount*
Travel to client locations	$750
Subscriptions to professional journals	215
Taking potential clients to lunch	400
Photocopying	60

a. Identify which of these expenses are deductible and the amount that is deductible. Indicate whether they are deductible *for* or *from* AGI.

b. Would the answers to Part a change if the accounting firm reimburses Roberta for these expenses?

c. Assume all of the same facts as in Part a, except that Roberta is self-employed. Identify which of the expenses are deductible, and indicate whether they are deductions *for* or *from* AGI.

I6-34 ***From AGI Deductions.*** During the current year, Brandon, an individual who is married with 2 minor children, incurred the following deductible expenses (before any limitations are applied):

Medical expenses	$12,000
Real estate taxes	4,000
Interest on a principal residence	6,300
Charitable contributions	2,500
Net personal casualty losses (already reduced by the $100 limit)	3,000
Miscellaneous itemized deductions	2,800

Brandon's AGI for the current year is $120,000. What is Brandon's taxable income?

I6-35 ***For vs. From AGI.*** During the current year, Kent, a single taxpayer, reports the following items of income and expense:

Income:	
Salary	$150,000
Dividends from Alta Corporation	800
Interest income from a savings account	1,500
Rental income from a small apartment she owns	8,000
Expenses:	
Medical	6,000
Interest on a principal residence	7,000
Real property taxes on the principal residence	4,300
Charitable contributions	4,000
Casualty loss - personal	6,100
Miscellaneous itemized deductions	1,200
Loss from the sale of Delta Corporation stock (held for two years)	2,000
Expenses incurred on the rental apartment:	
Maintenance	500
Property taxes	1,000
Utilities	2,400
Depreciation	1,700
Insurance	800
Alimony payments	10,000

Assuming all of these items are deductible and that the amounts are before any limitations, what is Kent's taxable income for the year?

I6-36 *Capitalization Versus Expense.* Lavonne incurs the following expenditures on an apartment building she owns:

Item	*Amount*
Replace the roof	$25,000
Repaint the exterior	7,000
Install new locks	1,500
Replace broken windows	1,200
Replace crumbling sidewalks and stairs	7,000

Discuss the proper tax treatment for these expenditures.

I6-37 *Political Contributions and Lobbying Expenses.* Sam is a sole proprietor who owns several apartment complexes and office buildings. The leasing and managing of these buildings constitutes Sam's only business activity. During the current year Sam incurred the following:

- $900 in airfare and lodging incurred on a trip to Washington, D.C. The purpose of the trip was to protest proposed tax rate increases for individuals and corporations.
- $700 for renting space on billboards along the highway. The billboards express his concern regarding pending legislation that would significantly increase property taxes.
- $500 in airfare and hotel bills incurred on a trip to the state capital. The purpose of the trip was to meet with the legislative subcommittee on property taxation.
- $50 for a subscription to a political newsletter published by a national political party.
- $150 in making a presentation to the county council protesting a proposed increase in the property tax levy.

a. What is the total amount Sam may deduct because of these expenditures?
b. Assume all the same facts as in Part a except that the expenses for the trip to the state capital are only $300 instead of $500. What amount may Sam deduct because of these expenditures?

I6-38 *Legal and Accounting Expenses.* During the current year, Sam from Problem I6-37 incurs the following expenses. Which of these expenditures are deductible? Are they *for* or *from* AGI deductions?

a. $200 in attorney's fees for title searches on a new property Sam has acquired.
b. $450 in legal fees in an action brought to collect back rents.
c. $500 to his CPA for the preparation of his federal income tax return. $400 is for the preparation of Schedule C (Profit or Loss from Business).
d. $300 in attorney's fees for drafting a will.

e. $250 in attorney's fees in an unsuccessful attempt to prevent the city from rezoning the area of the city where several of his office buildings are located.

I6-39 ***Illegal Payments.*** Damian is engaged in the business of purchasing and importing carpets from Iran. Importing these carpets from Iran is illegal. Following is a list of income and expense items for the year:

Item	*Amount*
Sales	$750,000
Cost of goods sold	270,000
Salaries	75,000
Freight	22,500
Bribes to customs officials	30,000
Lease payments on warehouses	15,000
Interest expense	12,000

a. What is Damian's taxable income from the illegal business activity?
b. Assume the same facts as in Part a except that Damian's business consists of buying and selling marijuana and cocaine. What is Damian's taxable income from this illegal business activity?

I6-40 ***Illegal Payments.*** Indicate whether Glenda can deduct the $5,000 payment in each of the following independent situations.
a. Glenda is a supplier of medical supplies. In order to secure a large sales contract to the regional Veterans Administration Hospital, Glenda makes a gift of $5,000 to the hospital's purchasing agent. The payment is illegal under state law.
b. Assume the same facts as in Part a, except that the payment is made to the purchasing agent of a government-owned hospital in Brazil.
c. Assume the same facts in Part a, except that the payment is made to the purchasing agent of a privately owned hospital in Idaho.

I6-41 ***Business Investigation Expenditures.*** During January and February of the current year, Mario incurs $3,000 in travel, feasibility studies, and legal expenses to investigate the feasibility of opening a new entertainment gallery in one of the new suburban malls in town. Mario already owns two other entertainment galleries in other malls in town.
a. What is the proper tax treatment of these expenses if Mario decides not to open the new gallery?
b. What is the proper tax treatment of these expenses if Mario decides to open the new gallery?

I6-42 ***Business Investigation Expenditures.*** Assume the same facts as in Problem I6-41, except that Mario does *not* already own the other entertainment galleries.
a. What is the proper tax treatment of these expenses if Mario does not open the new gallery?
b. What is the proper tax treatment of these expenses if Mario decides to open the new gallery on May 1 of the current year?

I6-43 ***Timing of Expense Recognition.*** Solutions Corporation, a computer vendor and consulting company, uses the accrual method of accounting. Its tax year is the calendar year. The following are three of the corporation's transactions during the current year:
1. Solutions Corporation hired a contractor to remodel its sales floor. The contractor completed the remodeling on November 30. On December 15, Solutions received a $21,000 bill from the contractor. Solutions immediately contacted the contractor to contest the $8,000 labor charge included in the total bill, which Solutions claims should only be $7,000. Solutions made no payment on the bill.
2. Solutions offers a 2-year warranty on all of its computer systems. For sales of computers in the current year, it paid $11,500 to service warranties during the current tax year, and it expects to pay $12,000 to fulfill the remaining warranty obligations next year.
3. Every year, Solutions offers a series of six trade seminars from November 1 through March 31. It receives all registration fees from participants by October 1, before the seminars begin. As of December 31, two of the six seminars are completed, and the next seminar is scheduled for January 14-15. The expenses incurred in performing the seminars are routine each year. On the first of each month from November through March, Solutions pays the $625 monthly rent for the seminar location. On

September 16, Solutions signs a contract with the seminar teacher, a computers expert and excellent public speaker. The contract requires Solutions to pay the teacher $900 after each seminar, a total of $5,400. On October 3, Solutions signs a contract with a local printing company, which will provide text materials for the seminars. Solutions pays the printer $350 after each seminar's materials are delivered the day before the seminar.

Required:

a. How should Solutions Corporation treat these transactions? What rules apply?
b. How would your answer change if Solutions Corporation were a cash-method taxpayer.

I6-44 ***Prepaid Expenses.*** Pamela, an engineering consultant, is self-employed and uses the cash method of accounting. Compute the amount of Pamela's current year deductions for the following transactions:

a. On November 1 of the current year, she entered into a lease to rent some office space for five years. The lease agreement states that the lease payments are $12,000 per year, payable in advance each November 1 for the following 12-month period. Under the terms of the lease, Pamela is required to pay a $5,000 deposit, refundable upon the termination of the lease.
b. On December 1 of the current year, Pamela also renewed her malpractice insurance, paying $18,000 for the three-year contract.
c. On December 31 of the current year, Pamela mailed out a check for $5,000 for drafting services performed for her by an individual who lives in another city.
d. On December 31, she also picked up $700 worth of stationery and other office supplies. Pamela has an open charge account with the office supply company, which bills Pamela monthly for charges made during the year.
e. Finally, on December 31, Pamela picked up some work that a local printing company had done for her, which amounted to $1,000. She charged the $1,000 with her business credit card.

I6-45 ***Prepaid Interest.*** During the current year, Richard and Alisha, a married couple who use the cash method of accounting, purchased a principal residence for $320,000. They paid $40,000 down and financed the remaining $280,000 of the purchase price with a 30-year mortgage. At the closing, they also paid $500 for an appraisal, $500 for a title search, and 1.5 points representing additional interest over the term of the loan. At the end of the year, Richard and Alisha received a statement from the mortgage company indicating that $12,000 of their total monthly payments made during the year represents interest and $1,000 is a reduction of the principal balance.

a. What is the total amount Richard and Alisha may deduct in the current year arising from the purchase and ownership of their home?
b. What is the treatment of the other items that are not deductible?

I6-46 ***Wash Sales.*** Boyd owns 500 shares of Atwood Corporation common stock. Boyd purchased the 500 shares on April 17, 1994 for $10,000. On December 8, 2001, Boyd sells all 500 shares for $5,000. On January 2, 2002, Boyd buys 250 shares of Atwood Corporation common stock for $2,500 and 50 shares of Atwood Corporation preferred stock for $1,000. The preferred stock is nonvoting, nonconvertible.

a. What is Boyd's realized and recognized loss on the December 8 sale of stock?
b. What is Boyd's basis and the holding periods of the stock?

I6-47 ***Wash Sales.*** Vicki owns 1,000 shares of Western Corporation common stock, which she purchased on March 8, 1994, for $12,000. On October 3, 2002, she purchases an additional 300 shares for $3,000. On October 12, 2002, she sells the original 1,000 shares for $8,500. On November 1, 2002, she purchases an additional 500 shares for $4,000.

a. What is Vicki's recognized gain or loss as a result of the sale on October 12, 2002?
b. What are the basis and the holding period of the stock Vicki continues to hold?
c. How would your answers to Parts a and b change if the stock Vicki purchases during 2002 is Western nonvoting, nonconvertible, preferred stock instead of Western common stock?

I6-48 ***Constructive Ownership.*** During the current year, Troy sells land to Berry Corporation for $165,000. Troy purchased the land in 1998 for $170,000. The Berry Corporation is owned as follows:

Owner	*Percentage Ownership*
Troy	20%
Jimmy (Troy's cousin)	15%
Jimmy's father (Troy's uncle)	35%
Angie (Troy's wife)	10%
Nicole (Angie's Sister)	25%

Troy and Jimmy are equal partners in a separate entity, TJ Partnership.
a. What is Troy's ownership (actual and constructive) in Berry Corporation?
b. What is the amount of loss Troy may recognize?
c. How would your answers to Parts a and b change if TJ Partnership owned 25%, instead of Nicole?

I6-49 ***Constructive Ownership.*** PIB Partnership is owned 20% by Shore, 40% by Steve, and 40% by Thann. Burnham, Inc. is owned 70% by PIB Partnership, 10% by Ralph, 10% by Thann, and 10% by Shore. Ralph and Thann are brothers. All other individuals are unrelated. During the current year, Ralph sold a piece of land to Burnham, Inc. for $90,000. Ralph originally purchased the land as an investment a few years ago for $100,000.
a. How much of the loss may Ralph recognize?
b. Now assume all the same facts except that the sale occurred between Thann and Burnham, Inc. How much of the loss may Thann recognize?
c. Now assume the same facts as in b. except that Burnham, Inc. is owned 60% by Shore and 40% by Ralph. Thann sells the land to Burnham, Inc. How much of the loss may Thann recognize?

I6-50 ***Related Party Transactions.*** Sally is an attorney who computes her taxable income using the cash method of accounting. Sage Corporation, owned 40% by Sally's brother, 40% by her cousin, and 20% by her grandmother, uses the accrual method of accounting. Sally is a calendar-year taxpayer, whereas Sage Corporation's fiscal year ends on January 31. During 2002, Sally does some consulting work for Sage Corporation for a fee of $10,000. The work is completed on December 15 and Sage receives Sally's invoice on that date. For each of the following assumptions, answer the following questions: During which tax year must Sally report the income? During which tax year must Sage Corporation deduct the expense?
a. The payment to Sally is made on December 27, 2002.
b. The payment to Sally is made on January 12, 2003.
c. The payment to Sally is made on February 3, 2003.

I6-51 ***Related Party Transactions.*** During the current year, Delta Corporation sells a tract of land for $80,000. The sale is made to Shirley, Delta Corporation's sole shareholder. Delta Corporation originally purchased the land five years earlier for $95,000.
a. What is the amount of gain or loss that Delta Corporation will recognize on the sale during the current year?
b. Assume that in the following year, Shirley sells the land for $85,000. What is the amount of gain or loss Shirley will recognize? What are the tax consequences to Delta Corporation upon the subsequent sale by Shirley?
c. Assume that in the following year, Shirley sells the land for $70,000. What is the amount of gain or loss Shirley will recognize?
d. Assume that in the following year, Shirley sells the land for $105,000. What is the amount of gain or loss Shirley will recognize?

I6-52 ***Hobby Loss Presumptive Rule.*** Rachel Schutz is a high school English teacher. In her spare time, she likes to make her own body lotion, lip-gloss, and bath and shower gel. She uses the bath products herself and gives them to her friends and relatives as gifts. In 2001, Rachel started attending arts and crafts festivals to sell her products three or four times a year, and she hands out her business card so her customers can buy directly from her by phone or email. In 2001, Rachel reported a net loss of $375 from the activity. In 2002, she reported a loss of $460. Rachel is audited for the year 2002, and the agent disallows the $460 loss. Rachel is pretty sure she will make a profit on her sales in 2003, and she assumes she will continue to make a profit after 2003. Rachel is not sure that she can prove that her activity is not a hobby right now. What can she do to avoid proving that her loss is not a hobby loss?

I6-53 ***Hobby Loss Presumptive Rule.*** Emily is an interior decorator who does consulting work for several furniture stores. Additionally, she has been designing and creating rubber stamps for the past several years. She sells the stamps to local stationary and novelty shops. Emily has reported the following net income or loss from the rubber stamp activity:

Year	*Net Income (Loss)*
1997	300
1998	(900)
1999	(400)
2000	600
2001	(550)
2002	(800)

Emily is audited for the year 2002, and the agent disallows the $800 loss. Can Emily make an election for 2002 to keep the year open in anticipation of meeting the presumptive rule for the year? Why or why not?

I6-54 ***Hobby Losses.*** Chuck, a dentist, raises prize rabbits for breeding and showing purposes. Assume that the activity is determined to be a hobby. During the year the activity generates the following items of income and expense:

Item	*Amount*
Sale of rabbits for breeding stock	$800
Prizes and awards	300
Property taxes on rabbit hutches	300
Feed	600
Veterinary fees	500
Depreciation on rabbit hutches	300

a. What is the total amount of deductions Chuck may take during the year with respect to the rabbit raising activities?
b. Identify which expenses may be deducted and indicate whether they are deductions *for* or *from* AGI.
c. By what amount is the cost basis of the rabbit hutches to be reduced for the year?

I6-55 ***Hobby Losses.*** Assume the same facts as in Problem I6-54, except that the income from the sale of rabbits is $1,200.
a. What is the total amount of deductions Chuck may take during the year with respect to the rabbit raising activities?
b. Identify which expenses may be deducted and indicate whether they are deductions *for* or *from* AGI.
c. By what amount is the cost basis of the rabbit hutches to be reduced for the year?

I6-56 ***Rental of Vacation Home.*** During the current year, Kim incurs the following expenses with respect to her beachfront condominium in Hawaii:

Item	*Amount*
Insurance	$ 500
Repairs and maintenance	700
Interest on mortgage	3,000
Property taxes	1,000
Utilities	800

In addition to the expenses listed above, Kim could have deducted a total of $8,000 depreciation if the property had been acquired only for investment purposes. During the year, Kim uses the condominium 20 days for vacation. She also rented it out for a total of 60 days during the year, generating a total gross income of $9,000.
a. What is the total amount of deductions for and from AGI that Kim may take during the current year with respect to the condominium?
b. What is the effect on the basis of the condominium?

I6-57 ***Rental of Vacation Home.*** Assume all of the same facts as in Problem I6-56, except that during the year Kim rents the condominium a total of 14 days. How does Kim report the income and deductions from the property?

COMPREHENSIVE PROBLEM

I6-58 Bryce, a bank official, is married and files a joint return. During 2002 he engages in the following activities and transactions:

a. Being an avid fisherman, Bryce develops an expertise in tying flies. At times during the year, he is asked to conduct fly-tying demonstrations, for which he is paid a small fee. He also periodically sells flies that he makes. Income generated from these activities during the year is $2,500. The expenses for the year associated with Bryce's fly-tying activity include $125 personal property taxes on a small trailer that he uses exclusively for this purpose, $2,900 in supplies, $270 in repairs on the trailer, and $200 in gasoline for traveling to the demonstrations.
b. Bryce sells a small building lot to his brother for $40,000. Bryce purchased the lot four years ago for $47,000, hoping to make a profit.
c. Bryce enters into the following stock transactions: (None of the stock qualifies as small business stock).

Date	*Transaction*
March 22	Purchases 100 shares of Silver Corporation common stock for $2,800
April 5	Sells 200 shares of Gold Corporation common stock for $8,000. The stock was originally purchased two years ago for $5,000.
April 15	Sells 200 shares of Silver Corporation common stock for $5,400. The stock was originally purchased three years ago for $9,400.
May 20	Sells 100 shares of United Corporation common stock for $12,000. The stock was originally purchased five years ago for $10,000.

d. Bryce's salary for the year is $115,000. In addition to the items above, he also incurs $5,000 in other miscellaneous deductible itemized expenses.

Answer the following questions regarding Bryce's activities for the year.

1. Compute Bryce's taxable income for the year.
2. What is Bryce's basis in the Silver stock he continues to own?

TAX STRATEGY PROBLEMS

I6-59 Danielle Anderson, your client and a cash method taxpayer, works full time at a music store located in a mall. She assists the manager in buying decisions, serves customers on the sales floor, and plays music to draw in customers. On the weekends, she plays in various orchestras, working as an independent contractor. She does not work under a business name, maintain an office, or maintain a separate bank account for her performing activities. She always pays her bills as soon as possible, well before the bill due date. In prior years, she has taken every allowable deduction related to the performing activities. Prior year returns show the following taxable income on her Schedule C:

1999	(5,000)
2000	2,100
2001	3,000
2002	(1,800)

Danielle has come to you on December 12, 2003. She understands that the IRS can deny losses generated by her performing business if it determines the business is actually a hobby. Because of the uncertainty of the entertainment industry, she will likely continue to generate profits in some years and losses in others. Still, she continues the activities with the intent to earn a profit.

Danielle routinely sends bills to orchestra clients at the end of the month for work she performed during the month. Most of her clients, including the Springville Orchestra, send payment within ten days of when they receive her bill.

The following is a summary of the business' financial position for 2003 as of 12/20/2003:

Income received to date:	9,000
General Expenses paid to date:	9,200

Other items:	
Bill for refurbishing work on cello, due 1/2/2004	300
Newspaper bill for monthly advertisement, due 1/14/2004	200
Printer bill for business cards, due 1/5/2004	500
Meals eaten while in transit to performance locations	150
Income for 12/3/2003 performance with the Springville Orchestra	1,000

What will you recommend to your client? What issues must you address? What actions will you take to ensure the most favorable tax outcome possible? What advice, if any, will you give your client for the future?

I6-60 Peter Baumann, your client, wants to sell a printing press to Chamberlain Corporation for $50,000. Pete has used the press in his business for two years and its adjusted basis is $90,000. The Coxmann Partnership, Chloe International, Inc., Watts, Inc., and Raleigh Corporation own Chamberlain Corporation equally. Pete and Emily Cox each own 50% of the Coxmann Partnership. Emily owns 70% of Chloe International, Inc., and Pete's sister Susan owns the other 30%. Pete's brother, Brian, owns 100% of Watts, Inc. And, Wade and Catherine Chamberlain, friends of Pete, own Raleigh Corporation equally. Peter wants to know what the tax consequences will be if he sells the printing press to Chamberlain Corporation. In a memo to Pete, explain any tax consequences of the proposed sale and any alternatives that would provide a better result.

TAX FORM/RETURN PREPARATION PROBLEMS

I6-61 Dave Stevens, age 34, is a self-employed physical therapist. His wife Sarah, age 31, teaches English as a Second Language at a local language school. Dave's social security number is 417-46-9403. Sarah's social security number is 528-95-6271. Sarah and Dave have three children—Andrew, age 8; Isaac, age 6; and Mira, age 3. The children's social security numbers are respectively 377-83-2836, 377-64-7283, and 377-17-1415. They live at 12637 Pheasant Run, West Bend, Oregon 74658. They paid $8,900 in qualified residence interest and $2,400 in property taxes on their home. They also had cash charitable contributions of $14,000. They had no other itemized deductions. Sarah and Dave earned interest on CDs of $3,200. Sarah's salary for the year is $32,000, from which $9,600 in federal income tax and $1,400 in state income tax were withheld. Dave's office is located at Suite 402, 942 Woodview Drive, Portland, Oregon 74624, and his employer ID number is 22-7584904. Dave has been practicing for 4 years, and he uses the cash method of accounting. During the current year, Dave recorded the following items of income:

Revenue from patient visits	$300,000
Interest earned on the office checking balance	225

The following expenses were recorded on the office books:

Property taxes on the office	$4,500
Mortgage interest on the office	12,000
Depreciation on the office	4,500
Malpractice insurance	37,500
Utilities	3,750
Office staff salaries	51,000
Rent payments on equipment	15,000
Office magazine subscriptions	150
Office supplies	24,000
Medical journals	330

Prepare Dave and Sarah's tax return (Form 1040, Schedules A, B, C, and SE) for the current year.

I6-62 Lyle and Kaye James are married, have two minor children, Jessica age 8 and Jerron age 4, and are filing a joint tax return in the current year. They are both employed. Lyle and Kaye, ages 38 and 37, respectively, have combined salaries of $240,000 from which $42,000 of federal income tax and $10,000 of state income tax are withheld. Lyle and Kaye own two homes. Their primary residence is located at 11620 N. Mount Ave., New

Haven, Connecticut 22222, and their vacation home is on the beach in Fort Lauderdale, Florida. They often rent their vacation home to supplement their income. The following items are related to the James' ownership of the two homes:

Item	*New Haven*	*Fort Lauderdale*
Rental income	$ —	$15,000
Qualified residence interest	7,200	5,000
Property taxes	1,400	1,000
Utilities	1,000	1,300
Repairs	200	300
Depreciation	0	3,500
Advertising	0	200
Insurance	1,500	1,500

The James used their Fort Lauderdale home 20 days during the year. They rented the vacation home 60 days during the year. The James have no other income or expense items. Lyle and Kaye's Social Security numbers are 111-22-3333 and 444-55-6666, respectively. Jessica and Jerron's social security numbers are 123-45-6789 and 888-99-1010.

File the James' income tax return Form 1040, Schedules A and E using the currently available forms and rates.

I6-63 Chris, age 56, and Scarlet Lindsay, age 54, are married and are filing jointly in the current year. Their social security numbers are 123-45-6789 and 987-65-4321, respectively. Chris's salary for the year is $97,000, from which $19,000 of federal income tax and $4,000 of state income tax were withheld. Scarlet is the sole owner of Scarlet Used & Vintage Books, a proprietorship that supplements the couple's income. The store is located at 450 W. Center Street, Kaysville, Ohio 11111. Scarlet reports the following income and expenses related to her business operation:

Revenues	$50,000
Cost of goods sold	10,000
City business license	400
Yellow pages advertisement	40
Depreciation on store	3,500
Real estate tax on store	1,000
Supplies	500
Wages & salaries	15,000

Scarlet subscribes to the following journals:

Book Archivist Monthly	$50
Wall Street Journal	150
Money Magazine	45
Reader's Digest	60
U.S. News & World Report	55

Chris and Scarlet jointly purchase stock in various corporations and make the following transactions in the current year: (None of the stock qualifies as small business stock).

Date	*Transaction*	*Price Paid/Sold*
2/15	Bought 50 shares of Lake common stock (own no other Lake stock)	$1,000
5/14	Bought 100 shares of Bass common stock (own no other Bass stock)	3,000
5/24	Sold 25 shares of Lake common stock	500
5/27	Bought 50 shares of Lake common stock	900
	Sold 50 shares of Bass common stock	1,750
7/12	Bought 100 shares of Bass common stock	2,800

During the year, Chris and Scarlet receive dividend income of $600 from Biggs, Inc. and taxable interest income of $400 from American Bank, make political contributions of $300, and pay $50 for use of a safety deposit box to store certain documents Scarlet needs in her business.

Chris and Scarlet own only one home at 237 E. 100 N., Kaysville, Ohio 11111. Their deductible mortgage interest for the year is $9,000 and their real estate tax is $2,300. Chris and Scarlet filed their state income tax return for the prior year in April of this year and paid an additional $400 of state income tax. In April of the current year, they also paid $180 to a CPA for preparing their federal and state income tax returns for the prior year, $100 of which was for the preparation of Scarlet's Schedule C.

Chris and Scarlet have no other deductions.

Prepare Chris and Scarlet's tax return (Form 1040, Schedules A, C, D, and SE) for the current year.

CASE STUDY PROBLEMS

I6-64 John and Kathy Brown have just been audited and the IRS agent disallowed the business loss they claimed in 2000. The agent asserted that the activity was a hobby, not a business.

John and Kathy live in Rochester, New York, near Lake Ontario. Kathy is a CPA and John was formerly employed by an insurance firm. John's firm moved in 1995 and John resolved not to move to the firm's new location. Instead of seeking other employment John felt he could supplement his income by using his fishing expertise. He had been an avid fisherman for 15 years and he owned a large Chris-Craft fly-bridge which he chartered to paying parties.

In 1996 Kathy and John developed a business plan, established a bank account for the charter activities, developed a bookkeeping system, and acquired insurance to cover the boat and the passengers. John fulfilled all the requirements to receive a U.S. Coast Guard operating license, a New York sport trolling license, and a seller's permit. These licenses and permits were necessary to legally operate a charter boat. 1996 was the first year of their activity.

John advertised in local papers and regional sport fishing magazines. He usually had three or four half-day paying parties each week. John spent at least one day maintaining and repairing his boat. Kathy usually accompanied John on charters three or four times each year.

John's charter activity was unprofitable the first two years. In 1998, John and Kathy restructured the activity to improve profitability. The restructuring included increasing advertising, participating in outdoor shows, and negotiating small contracts with local businesses. After the restructuring, the activity provided a small profit in 1998 and 1999.

In 2000 John started working with another insurance company in the area on a full-time basis. Even though he returned to the insurance business, John normally took two paying parties and one nonpaying, promotional party each week throughout the fishing season. John's costs unexpectedly increased and he lost $8,000 in the activity during 2000. John and Kathy deducted the entire loss on Schedule C of their 2000 tax return.

Required: Prepare a memo to the Browns recommending what position they should take and why. Show the logic used in arriving at your recommendation.

TAX RESEARCH PROBLEM

I6-65 Richard Penn lives in Harrisburg, Pennsylvania. Richard is the president of an architectural firm. Richard has become known throughout the community for excellent work and honesty in his business dealings. Richard believes his reputation is an integral part of the success of the firm.

Oil was found recently in the area around Harrisburg and some geologists believed the reserves were large. A few well-respected businesspeople organized Oil Company to develop a few wells. Although some oil was being extracted, the oil corporation lacked capital to develop the oil fields to their expected potential. After reading the geologists' report, Richard felt that Oil Company was a good investment; therefore, he acquired 25% of the company. A short time after Richard's acquisition, the price of foreign oil decreased sharply. The drop in foreign oil prices caused Oil Company to be unprofitable due to its high production costs. Three months later Oil Company filed bankruptcy.

The bankruptcy proceedings were reported in the local newspaper. Many of Oil Company's creditors were real estate developers that engaged Richard's architectural firm to provide designs. After Oil Company declared bankruptcy the architectural firm's business noticeably decreased.

Richard felt the decline in business was related to the bankruptcy of Oil Company. Richard convinced his partner to use the accumulated earnings of the firm to repay all the creditors of Oil Company.

Richard has asked you whether his firm can deduct the expenses of repaying Oil Company's creditors. After completing your research explain to Richard why the expenses are or are not deductible.

A partial list of research sources is as follows:

- Sec. 162
- *Thomas H. Welch v. Helvering,* 12 AFTR 1456, 3 USTC ¶1164 (USSC, 1933)
- *William A. Thompson, Jr.,* 1983 PH T.C. Memo ¶83,487, 46 TCM 1109

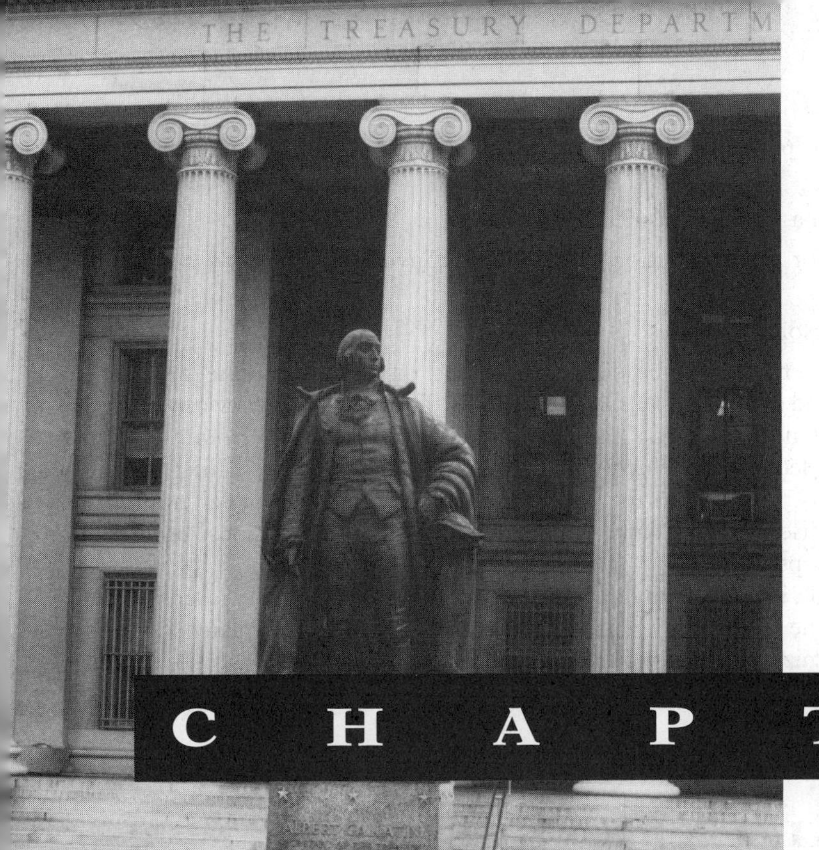

7

CHAPTER

ITEMIZED DEDUCTIONS

LEARNING OBJECTIVES

After studying this chapter, you should be able to

1. Identify qualified medical expenses and compute the medical expense deduction
2. Determine the timing of a medical expense deduction and the effect of a reimbursement
3. Identify taxes that are deductible as itemized deductions
4. Identify different types of interest deductions
5. Compute the amount of investment interest deduction
6. Compute the deduction for qualified residence interest
7. Compute the amount of a charitable contribution deduction and identify limitations
8. Identify certain miscellaneous itemized deductions subject to the 2% of AGI limit
9. Compute total itemized deductions for a taxpayer who is subject to the itemized deduction phase-out.

CHAPTER OUTLINE

Medical Expenses...7-2
Taxes...7-9
Interest...7-12
Charitable Contributions...7-21
Casualty and Theft Losses...7-28
Miscellaneous Itemized Deductions...7-28
Reduction of Certain Itemized Deductions...7-29
Tax Planning Considerations...7-30
Compliance and Procedural Considerations...7-33

As explained in Chapter I6, most deductible expenses for individuals fit into three general categories:

- Expenses incurred in a trade or business
- Expenses incurred for the production of income (an investment activity) or for tax advice
- Certain specified personal expenses

Once an expense is determined to be deductible based on the above categories, the expense must be classified as either *for* AGI or *from* AGI. The distinction between *for* and *from* AGI was discussed in Chapter I6. This chapter focuses on deductions *from* AGI, also referred to as **itemized deductions**, which include medical expenses, taxes, interest, and charitable contributions. Other itemized deductions, such as unreimbursed employee business expenses, are discussed in Chapter I9 and casualty losses on personal-use property are discussed in Chapter I8.

In arriving at taxable income, individuals may subtract from AGI the larger of the standard deduction or the sum of all itemized deductions. However, as explained later in this chapter, certain itemized deductions are reduced if a taxpayer's AGI exceeds certain limits.

MEDICAL EXPENSES

Medical expenses, which comprise one category of deductible personal expenditures, are deductible because Congress felt that excessive medical expenses might ultimately affect a taxpayer's ability to pay his or her federal income tax. However, under Sec. 213, taxpayers may deduct medical expenses only to the extent the expenses exceed 7.5% of the taxpayer's AGI. To qualify as a medical expense deduction, the expenditure must be incurred for the medical care of a qualified individual. Taxpayers may not take a deduction for medical expenses to the extent the expenses are reimbursed (i.e., compensated for by insurance or otherwise).

QUALIFIED INDIVIDUALS

To deduct medical expenses, taxpayers must pay the expenses on behalf of themselves, their spouses, or their dependents.

TAXPAYER'S DEPENDENT. Deductible medical expenses include those paid on behalf of a taxpayer's dependent as well as on behalf of a person for whom the taxpayer could take a dependency exemption except for the failure to meet the gross income or joint return tests.[1]

EXAMPLE I7-1 ▶

In March of the current year, Jean's son, Steve, is involved in an automobile accident. Steve is 25 years old at the time of the accident and has worked full-time for part of the year, earning a total of $10,000. Because Steve has no medical insurance and cannot pay the medical bills or support himself as a result of the accident, Jean pays Steve's medical expenses and supports him for the rest of the year. Because Jean provides over one-half of Steve's support for the year and Steve, except for the gross income test, otherwise qualifies as Jean's dependent, Jean may deduct the medical expenses she pays on his behalf. Jean may not claim a dependency exemption for Steve because the gross income test is not satisfied. ◀

KEY POINT

Medical expenses are deductible for a person who satisfies only the support, relationship, and citizenship dependency tests.

CHILDREN OF DIVORCED PARENTS. As long as one divorced parent is entitled to the dependency exemption under Sec. 152(e), the parent who pays medical expenses on behalf of the children may deduct the expenses. The parent taking the medical expense deduction need not be the parent who is entitled to the dependency exemption.

---

[1] Sec. 152. See Chapter I2 for the tests that must be met to claim another individual as a dependent.

QUALIFIED MEDICAL EXPENSES

OBJECTIVE 1

Identify qualified medical expenses and compute the medical expense deduction

The **medical expense deduction** is available only for expenditures paid for medical care. Section 213 defines *medical care* as amounts paid for

- The diagnosis, cure, mitigation, treatment, or prevention of disease
- The purpose of affecting any structure or function of the body
- Transportation primarily for and essential to the first two items listed above
- Qualified long-term care services
- Insurance covering all of the items listed above

DIAGNOSIS, CURE, MITIGATION, TREATMENT, OR PREVENTION OF DISEASE. Although the term *medical expense* is not precisely defined, it is clear that medical expenses are deductible only if they are paid for procedures or treatments that are legal in the locality in which they are performed. For example, taxpayers may not deduct expenditures for controlled substances.[2] The definition of medical care includes preventive measures such as routine physical and dental examinations. However, other expenses should be "confined strictly to expenses incurred primarily for the prevention or alleviation of a physical or mental defect or illness." Thus, unless they are for routine physical or dental examinations, the expenditures must be for the purpose of curing a specific ailment rather than related to the general health of an individual. This determination is especially critical when the expenditures in question are for items such as vacations, weight loss programs, or stop smoking programs. Such expenses may or may not be incurred for a specific ailment.

ADDITIONAL COMMENT

One cannot deduct the cost of nonprescription medicine (except insulin), toothpaste, toiletries, maternity clothes, diaper service, or funeral expenses.

EXAMPLE I7-2 ▶ Helmut is nervous and irritable because of pressures at work and begins to suffer angina symptoms. In order to relax and get away from it all, he takes an ocean cruise around the world. Helmut's angina symptoms ease while he is on the cruise. However, the Tax Court held that a cruise is not a proven medical necessity because Helmut's physician did not specifically prescribe it. Although the cruise was beneficial to Helmut's general health, it was not deductible.[3] ◀

EXAMPLE I7-3 ▶ Dave enrolls in a weight reduction program on the advice of two doctors who prescribe the program as a means of relieving his obesity, hypertension, and certain hearing problems. In a private letter ruling, the IRS held that these expenses qualify as deductible medical expenditures because they are incurred for specific medical conditions.[4] ◀

Although receipt of a doctor's recommendation for incurring the cost appears to lend a great deal of weight to deductibility, it is not always sufficient. For example, a taxpayer could not deduct the cost of dancing lessons for an emotionally disturbed child, even though the lessons proved to be beneficial and were recommended by a physician. Likewise, a taxpayer suffering from arthritis could not deduct the cost of ballroom dance lessons, even though the lessons were recommended by a doctor. On the other hand, the IRS has ruled that the cost of a clarinet and clarinet lessons was deductible when recommended by an orthodontist to correct a malocclusion of a child's teeth.[5] In short, determining the deductibility of certain expenditures can be difficult.

Range of Deductible Medical Services. According to the Treasury Regulations, typical medical expenses include payments for a wide range of medical, dental, and other diagnostic and healing services. Thus, taxpayers may deduct payments to licensed or certified medical professionals such as general practitioners, obstetricians, surgeons, ophthalmologists, opticians, dentists, and orthodontists. Furthermore, deductible medical expenditures include payments for medical services rendered by individuals such as chiropractors, osteopaths, and psychotherapists who may or may not be required to be licensed or certi-

---

[2] Reg. Sec. 1.213-1(e)(1)(ii). See also Rev. Rul. 97-9, I.R.B. 1997-9.

[3] *Daniel E. Mizl*, 1980 PH T.C. Memo ¶80,227, 40 TCM 552. Even if the taxpayer's physician had prescribed the trip, it still may not have been deductible. See Reg. Sec. 1.213-1(e)(1)(ii).

[4] Ltr. Rul. 8004111 (October 31, 1979).

[5] *John J. Thoene*, 33 T.C. 62 (1959), *Rose C. France v. CIR*, 50 AFTR 2d 82-5504, 1982-1 USTC ¶9225 (6th Cir., 1982), and Rev. Rul. 62-210, 1962-2 C.B. 89.

fied.[6] Taxpayers may deduct payments to Christian Science practitioners as well as acupuncture treatment if the treatment is received for a specific medical purpose.[7] Qualified medical expenses also include payment for hospital services, nursing services, laboratory fees, X-rays, artificial teeth or limbs, ambulance hire, eyeglasses, and prescribed medicines and insulin. Nondeductible expenses include expenditures for nonprescription medicines, drugs, vitamins, and other types of health foods that improve the individual's general health.

To deduct costs incurred for schools and camps, the taxpayer must show that the facility is equipped with the appropriate medical equipment and is regularly engaged in providing medical services. For example, expenses a taxpayer incurred to send his mentally handicapped son to a school with a special curriculum for such children was held to be deductible. Similarly, a taxpayer was allowed to deduct the cost of sending a child with psychiatric problems to a school specializing in learning disorders. However, taxpayers generally may not deduct the cost of sending children with special medical problems to schools or camps that do not have the proper equipment, facilities, or curriculum for such problems.

TYPICAL MISCONCEPTION

Taxpayers tend to define qualifying medical expenses too narrowly. This may be caused, in part, by comparison with expense reimbursement limitation policies of health insurance companies.

MEDICAL PROCEDURES AFFECTING ANY FUNCTION OR STRUCTURE OF THE BODY. Deductible medical expenditures also include payments for services affecting any function or structure of the body, even though no specific illness or disease exists. Thus, qualifying medical expenses include expenditures for such items as physical therapy, obstetrical services, eyeglasses, dental examinations and cleaning, and hearing aids. Under Sec. 213, cosmetic surgery or any other similar procedure does not qualify as a medical expense unless such surgery is necessary to correct a deformity arising from a congenital abnormality, a personal injury resulting from an accident or trauma, or a disfiguring disease. Cosmetic surgery is defined as any procedure undertaken to improve a person's appearance that does not meaningfully promote the proper function of the body or prevent or treat an illness or disease.

TRANSPORTATION ESSENTIAL TO MEDICAL CARE. Taxpayers may deduct transportation expenses that are incurred primarily for and essential to qualified medical care. Thus, taxpayers may deduct actual out-of-pocket automobile expenditures, taxis, airfare, ambulance fees, and other forms of transportation if the travel is for medical reasons. However, no deduction is allowed if the travel is undertaken for recreational purposes or for the general improvement of the taxpayer's health.

In lieu of the actual cost of the use of an automobile, the IRS allows a deduction of 13 cents for each mile that the automobile is driven for medical reasons. In addition to this standard mileage rate, taxpayers may also deduct the cost of tolls and parking.

Certain courts have held that the cost of meals and lodging while en route to a medical facility is part of deductible travel costs incurred for medical purposes. However, taxpayers may not deduct the cost of meals eaten on trips that are too short to warrant a stop for meals. Additionally, taxpayers may deduct only 50% of the cost of meals. (See Chapter I9 for a discussion of the 50% disallowance rule for meals and entertainment.) The IRC limits the potential deduction for the cost of lodging to $50 per night. Furthermore, lodging expenses qualify as medical expenditures only if the travel is primarily for and essential to medical care, the medical care is provided in a licensed hospital (or a facility that is related or equivalent to a licensed hospital), and there is no significant element of personal pleasure or recreation in the travel. The $50 limitation on lodging is imposed on a per-individual basis. Thus, if the patient is unable to travel alone, an additional $50 per night may be deducted for the lodging costs of a nurse, parent, or spouse.

---

[6] Reg. Sec. 1.213-1(e)(1) and Rev. Rul. 63-91, 1963-1 C.B. 54. See also Ltr. Rul. 8919009 (February 6, 1989) where a pregnant woman was entitled to a deduction for the cost of childbirth classes to the extent that they prepared her for the childbirth. However, the cost of the classes where she received instructions on the care of the unborn child represented a flat fee that allowed a coach to attend the class with the taxpayer. Thus, one-half of the fee was deemed attributable to the coach and was not allowed as a qualified medical expense.

[7] Rev. Rul. 72-593, 1972-2 C.B. 180 and IRS Special Ruling, February 2, 1943.

Qualified Long-Term Care. Taxpayers may also deduct expenditures for qualified long-term care as medical expenses subject to the 7.5% of AGI limitation. Long-term care is defined as medical services required by a chronically ill individual which are provided under a prescribed plan of care. Under Sec. 7702B, such items include expenditures for diagnostic, preventive, therapeutic, curing, treating, mitigating, rehabilitative, and personal care services. A chronically ill individual generally is someone who, for a period of at least 90 days, cannot perform at least two daily living tasks such as eating, toileting (including continence), bathing, or dressing.

Expenditures for long-term care insurance premiums also qualify as medical deductions, subject to an annual limit based upon the age of an individual.[8]

CAPITAL EXPENDITURES FOR MEDICAL CARE. Generally, taxpayers may not deduct capital expenditures for federal income tax purposes. For assets used in a trade or business or held for the production of income, taxpayers must recover such costs through depreciation, cost recovery, or amortization. Capital expenditures incurred for personal medical purposes are not depreciable or amortizable. However, a current deduction is available when the capital expenditure is made to acquire an asset primarily for the medical care of the taxpayer, the taxpayer's spouse, or the taxpayer's dependents. To qualify as a deduction, the expenditure must be incurred as a medical necessity for primary use by the individual in need of medical treatment, and the expenditure must be reasonable in amount. Deductible capital expenditures for medical care are classified into three categories:[9]

- ▶ Expenditures that relate only to the sick or handicapped person, not to the permanent improvement or betterment of the taxpayer's property (e.g., eyeglasses, dogs or other animals that assist the blind or the deaf, artificial teeth and limbs, wheelchairs, crutches, and portable air conditioners purchased for the sole use of a sick person)
- ▶ Expenditures that permanently improve or better the taxpayer's property as well as provide medical care (e.g., a swimming pool installed in the home of an individual suffering from arthritis)
- ▶ Expenditures to remove structural barriers in the home of a physically handicapped individual such as costs of constructing entrance ramps, widening doorways and halls, lowering kitchen cabinets, adding railings, etc.

REAL-WORLD EXAMPLE

The cost of installing an elevator in the home upon the recommendation of a physician to help a patient with a heart condition was deductible to the extent that it did not increase the value of the home. *James E. Berry v. Wiseman*, 2 AFTR 2d 6015, 58-2 USTC ¶9870 (D.C. Okla., 1958).

Capital expenditures that relate only to the sick person (the first category) are fully deductible in the year paid. Expenditures that improve the residence (the second category) are deductible only to the extent that the amount of the expenditure exceeds the increase in the fair market value (FMV) of the residence brought about by the capital expenditure. Expenditures to remove physical barriers in the home of a physically handicapped individual (the third category) are deductible in full (i.e., the increase in the home's value is deemed to be zero). In addition, any costs of operating or maintaining the assets in all three categories are deductible as long as the medical reason for the capital expenditure continues to exist.[10] The deductibility of all of the above expenditures are subject to the 7.5% floor.

EXAMPLE I7-4 ▶ During the current year, Rita is injured in an industrial accident. As a result, she sustains a chronic disabling leg injury, which requires her to spend much time in a wheelchair. Rita's physician recommends that a swimming pool be installed in her backyard and that she devote several hours each day to physical exercise. During the year, Rita makes the following expenditures:

Wheelchair	$ 2,500
Swimming pool	27,000
Operation and maintenance of the pool	1,800
Entrance ramp and door modification	5,000

[8] For 2002, if the individual is 40 years of age or less, the annual deductible limit for the premiums is $240. For individuals over 40 but less than 50 the limit is $450. For those over 50 but less than 60 the limit is $900; over 60 but less than 70 the limit is $2,390; and over 70 the limit is $2,990.

[9] Reg. Sec. 1.213-1(e)(1)(iii) and H. Rept. No. 99-841, 99th Cong., 2d Sess. p. II-22 (1986).

[10] Rev. Rul. 87-106, 1987-2 C.B. 67.

REAL-WORLD EXAMPLE

Taxpayers made nonrefundable advance payments required as a condition for an institution's future acceptance of their handicapped child for lifetime care in the event that taxpayers could not care for child. The amounts paid were deductible as expenses for medical care in the year paid. Rev. Rul. 75-303, 1975-2 C.B. 87. This current deduction for prepaid amounts is only available for certain lifetime care expenditures incurred in situations described in this ruling. Rev. Rul. 93-72, I.R.B. 1993-34,7.

A qualified appraiser estimates that the swimming pool increases the value of Rita's home by only $20,000. Rita's medical expenses for the year include $2,500 for the wheelchair, $7,000 for the swimming pool (the excess of the cost of the pool over the increase in the FMV of the home), $1,800 for the operation and maintenance of the pool, and $5,000 for the ramp and door modification. ◀

COSTS OF LIVING IN INSTITUTIONS. The entire cost of in-patient hospital care, including meals and lodging, qualifies as a medical expense. However, if an individual is in an institution other than a hospital (e.g., a nursing home or a special school for the handicapped), the deductibility of the costs involved depends on the facts of the particular case. If the principal reason for the taxpayer's presence in an institution is the need for and availability of the medical care furnished by that institution, the entire costs of meals, lodging, and other services necessary for furnishing the medical care are qualified medical expenditures.

ADDITIONAL COMMENT

A taxpayer cannot deduct the 1.45% Medicare (hospital insurance benefits) tax that is withheld from wages as part of the Social Security tax.

MEDICAL INSURANCE PREMIUMS. Qualified medical expenses also include all premiums paid for medical insurance, including premiums paid for supplementary medical insurance for the aged under the Social Security Act and premiums paid for qualified long-term care insurance contracts. In many cases, taxpayers pay premiums for insurance coverage that extends beyond mere medical care. For example, in addition to the standard medical care coverage, an insurance policy may provide coverage for loss of income or loss of life, limb, or sight. In such cases, a deduction is allowed for the medical care portion of the premium only if the cost of each type of insurance is either separately stated in the contract or is furnished to the policyholder by the insurance company in a separate statement.[11]

EXAMPLE I7-5 ▶ Each month Malazia pays $300 for an insurance policy under which she is reimbursed for any doctor or hospital charges she incurs. In addition, the policy will pay two-thirds of her regular salary each month if she becomes disabled. Finally, the policy will pay her $10,000 for the loss of any limb. At the end of the year, her insurance company issues a statement that allocates two-thirds of the premiums to the medical insurance coverage. Malazia's medical care expenditure is $2,400 ($300 × 12 × 0.667). ◀

If a taxpayer pays the premiums attributable to an individual or group medical insurance plan, the payments are deductible as medical expenses which in most cases are itemized deductions. However, in 2002 self-employed individuals may deduct 70% of these amounts as deductions *for* AGI, and in 2003 and thereafter they may deduct 100% for AGI. The remainder is deductible as an itemized deduction. Any amounts paid by the taxpayer's employer are excluded from the employee's gross income and are not includible in the taxpayer's medical expenses.[12]

The deduction for medical savings accounts established for employees is discussed in Chapter I9.

AMOUNT AND TIMING OF DEDUCTION

OBJECTIVE 2

Determine the timing of a medical expense deduction and the effect of a reimbursement

The amount and timing of the allowable medical expense deduction depend on when the medical expenses are actually paid, the taxpayer's AGI, and whether any reimbursement is received for the medical expenses.

TIMING OF THE PAYMENT. In general, taxpayers may deduct medical expenses only in the year they actually pay the expenses. This rule applies regardless of the taxpayer's method of accounting or when the event that caused the expenditure occurs.[13] Thus, if medical care is received during the year but remains unpaid as of the end of the year, taxpayers must defer the deduction for that care until the year they pay for the medical care. If the obligation is charged on a credit card, payment is deemed to have been made on the

[11] Sec. 213(d). See also Rev. Ruls. 66-216, 1966-2 C.B. 100, and 79-175, 1979-1 C.B. 117.

[12] Sections 162 and 106.

[13] Reg. Sec. 1.213-1(a)(1). However, medical expenses paid within one year from the day following the taxpayer's death are treated as paid at the time they are incurred (see Sec. 213(c)).

date of the charge, not on the later date when the credit card balance is paid. Conversely, if medical care is prepaid, the deduction is deferred until the year the care is actually rendered unless there is a legal obligation to prepay or unless the prepayment is a requirement for the receipt of the medical care.[14]

LIMITATION ON AMOUNT DEDUCTIBLE. As previously noted, a medical expense deduction is allowed only for the years in which the taxpayer itemizes his or her deductions and the taxpayer's expenditures for medical care exceed 7.5% of AGI.

EXAMPLE I7-6 ▶ During the current year, Kelly incurs qualified medical expenditures of $3,000. Her AGI for the year is $30,000. After subtracting the floor, she has $750 ($3,000 − [0.075 × $30,000]) of deductible medical expenses. These medical expenses are added to Kelly's other itemized deductions to determine whether they exceed the standard deduction. ◀

SELF-STUDY QUESTION

Why does the IRS not require that the taxpayer file an amended return when a reimbursement is received in a later year?

ANSWER

The administrative burden on the IRS of processing additional returns would be too great.

MEDICAL INSURANCE REIMBURSEMENTS. Taxpayers may only deduct unreimbursed medical expenditures. It does not matter whether the reimbursement is from an insurance plan purchased from an insurance company, a medical reimbursement plan of an employer, or a payment resulting from litigation.

If the taxpayer receives reimbursement in the same year the medical expenses are paid, the deduction is reduced by the amount of the reimbursement. If a taxpayer receives a reimbursement in a year subsequent to the year of payment, the taxpayer must include the reimbursement in gross income for the year the payment is received to the extent that the taxpayer derived a tax benefit from the deduction in the previous year. If the taxpayer did not take a deduction in the prior year, the taxpayer doesn't need to report the reimbursement as income. This may occur because the taxpayer's total itemized deductions do not exceed the standard deduction or because the taxpayer's total medical expenses do not exceed 7.5% of AGI. If a deduction was taken in the prior year, however, the taxpayer must report as income the lesser of the amount of the reimbursement or the amount by which the taxable income of the prior year was reduced because of medical expenses.

EXAMPLE I7-7 ▶ During 2002, Diane, a single taxpayer under age 65, reports the following items of income and expense:

AGI	$35,000
Total qualified medical expenses	3,500
Itemized deductions other than medical	3,900

Diane's taxable income for 2002 is calculated as follows:

AGI			$35,000
Reduction: larger of itemized deductions or standard deduction			
Medical expenses	$3,500		
Minus: 7.5% of AGI	(2,625)	875	
Other itemized deductions		3,900	
Total itemized deductions		$4,775	
Standard deduction		$4,700	(4,775)
Personal exemption			(3,000)
Taxable income			$27,225

If during 2003 Diane receives a reimbursement of $1,000 for medical expenses incurred the prior year, she must include $75 ($4,775 − $4,700) in gross income for 2003 (the amount of the tax benefit from the medical expense deduction for the prior year). This amount can be calculated by comparing the actual taxable income for 2002 with what would have been the 2002 taxable income if the reimbursement had been received that year.

[14] Rev. Rul. 78-39, 1978-1 C.B. 73 and *Robert M. Rose v. CIR*, 26 AFTR 2d 70-5653, 70-2 USTC ¶9646 (5th Cir., 1970). See also Rev. Rul. 93-72, Rev. Rul. 1993-2 C.B. 77, Rev. Rul. 75-302, 1975-2 C.B. 86, and Rev. Rul. 75-303, 1975-2 C.B. 87.

AGI			$35,000
Reduction: larger of itemized deductions or standard deduction			
Medical expenses	$3,500		
Minus: Reimbursement	(1,000)		
7.5% of AGI	(2,625)		
Excess medical expenses		0	
Plus: Other itemized deductions		3,900	
Total itemized deductions		$3,900	
Standard deduction		$4,700	(4,700)
Personal exemption			(3,000)
Taxable income (assuming reimbursement was received in 2002)			$27,300
Minus: Actual 2002 taxable income			(27,225)
Tax benefit			$ 75◀

Topic Review I7-1 highlights the principal requirements for the medical expense deduction previously discussed.

STOP & THINK

Question: Vince and Diane are married and file a joint tax return. For the current year they estimate their AGI at $100,000. They also estimate their itemized deductions for taxes, interest, and charitable contributions total $9,000. Up to the current date they have incurred $7,000 in deductible medical expenses. For several months they have been considering laser surgery on Diane's eyes. The total expenditure for the operations will be $4,000 and is not covered by their medical insurance. Since they already have spent so much this year on medical expenses and they do not anticipate such large expenses next year they are considering delaying the eye operation until next year. They estimate next year's AGI to be approximately $110,000. Does this decision make sense from a tax point of view?

Solution: From a tax point of view, Diane should consider having and paying for the operation this year. If so, $4,000 is added to the prior $7,000 medical expenditures for a total of $11,000 for the year. After applying the 7.5% of AGI limitation, $3,500 [$11,000 − ($100,000 × 0.075)] of the medical expenses is deductible. If they wait until next year and if their estimates are correct, none of the medical expenses in either year are deductible because of the 7.5% of AGI limitation.

Topic Review I7-1

Medical Expense Deductions

Items	Deduction Rules and Limitations
Qualifying expenditures	(a) Expenditures for the diagnosis, cure, mitigation, treatment, or prevention of disease and qualified long-term care. (b) Transportation at $0.13 per mile and lodging limited to $50 per-night, per-person, and 50% of meals. (c) Medical and qualified long-term care insurance premiums. (d) Capital expenditures (subject to specific limitations).
Qualifying individuals	Taxpayer, spouse, dependents, and children of divorced parents even if not dependent.
Amount and timing of the deduction	Deduct in the year paid unless prepayment is required or there is a legal obligation to pay. Medical expenses are subject to a 7.5% of AGI nondeductible limitation.
Treatment of insurance reimbursements	The deduction is reduced if the reimbursement is received in the year of payment. Reimbursements received in a subsequent year are included in gross income of the year received if tax benefit was received in the earlier year.

TAXES

OBJECTIVE 3

Identify taxes that are deductible as itemized deductions

Section 164 provides taxpayers with a federal income tax deduction for specifically listed taxes that are paid or accrued during the taxable year. Generally, cash-method taxpayers are entitled to the deduction when the taxes are paid, whereas taxpayers using the accrual method deduct taxes in the year they accrue. Other taxes are specifically listed as nondeductible. To be deductible as a tax, the assessment in question must be a tax rather than a fee or charge imposed by a government for providing specific goods or services.

ADDITIONAL COMMENT

In 1998, the deduction for taxes represented 36.1% of the total dollar amount of itemized deductions, making it the second largest itemized deduction.

DEFINITION OF A TAX

A **tax** is a mandatory assessment levied under the authority of a political entity for the purpose of raising revenue to be used for public or governmental purposes. Thus, fees, assessments, or fines imposed for specific privileges or services are not deductible as taxes under Sec. 164. These nontax items include

- Vehicle registration and inspection fees
- Registration tags for pets
- Toll charges for highways and bridges
- Parking meter charges
- Charges for sewer, water, and other services
- Special assessments against real estate for items such as sidewalks, lighting, and streets

However, if taxpayers incur these nontax fees and charges in a business or income-producing activity, these items may be either capitalized or deducted as ordinary and necessary business expenses or ordinary and necessary expenses incurred for the production of income.

DEDUCTIBLE TAXES

The following taxes are specifically deductible under Sec. 164:

- State, local, and foreign real property taxes
- State and local personal property taxes if based on value
- State, local, and foreign income, war profits, and excess profits taxes
- Other state, local, and foreign taxes that are paid or incurred in either a trade or business or an income-producing activity

All of these taxes are imposed by a government body other than the federal government. Federal taxes other than the generation-skipping transfer tax are not deductible for federal income tax purposes.[15] However, federal customs and excise taxes incurred in the taxpayer's business or income-producing activity are deductible as ordinary and necessary expenses under Secs. 162 or 212. Likewise, the *employer's* portion of federal Social Security taxes and federal and state unemployment taxes are deductible by the employer as ordinary and necessary business expenses if the employee works in the employer's business or income-producing activity.

SELF-STUDY QUESTION

Would a taxpayer normally prefer to deduct foreign taxes or take a foreign tax credit?

ANSWER

Normally the foreign tax credit is better because a credit provides a direct dollar-for-dollar reduction of the tax liability rather than a reduction of taxable income.

NONDEDUCTIBLE TAXES

The following taxes are not deductible under Sec. 164:

- Federal income taxes
- Federal estate, inheritance, legacy, succession, and gift taxes
- Federal import or tariff duties and excise taxes unless incurred in the taxpayer's business or for the production of income
- Employee's portion of Social Security and other payroll taxes
- State and local sales taxes and state inheritance, legacy, succession, and gift taxes

---

[15] The generation-skipping transfer tax is imposed by the United States on certain distributions from a trust (see Sec. 2601). Furthermore, under Sec. 691(c) a taxpayer who includes income in respect of a decedent in taxable income may deduct estate tax attributable to that amount.

- Foreign income taxes if the taxpayer elects to take the taxes as a credit against his or her federal income tax liability
- Property taxes on real estate to the extent the taxes are treated as imposed on another taxpayer

BOOK-TAX DIFFERENCE

For financial accounting purposes, all taxes are deducted in arriving at net income after taxes. However, for tax purposes, only certain taxes are deductible.

STATE AND LOCAL INCOME TAXES

For individuals, state and local income taxes are normally an itemized (*from* AGI) deduction. Thus, a taxpayer does not receive any federal income tax benefit if these taxes, in addition to the other itemized deductions, do not exceed the standard deduction. Cash-method taxpayers deduct all state and local income taxes paid or withheld during the year even if the taxes are attributable to another tax year.

EXAMPLE I7-8 ▶ During 2002, Rita had $1,500 in state income taxes withheld from her salary. On April 15, 2003, Rita pays an additional $400 when she files her 2002 state income tax return. On her 2002 federal income tax return, Rita may deduct the $1,500 in state income taxes withheld from her salary during 2002 as an itemized deduction. The $400 that Rita pays on April 15, 2003 is deductible on her 2003 federal income tax return, even though the liability relates to her 2002 state income tax return. ◀

ADDITIONAL COMMENT

Every state except Alaska, Florida, Nevada, South Dakota, Texas, Washington, and Wyoming has some type of income tax.

If a taxpayer receives a refund of state income taxes deducted in a prior year, the taxpayer must include the refund as income in the year of the refund to the extent the taxpayer received a tax benefit from the prior deduction. This calculation is done in the same way the tax benefit from a medical expense reimbursement was calculated in Example I7-7.

PERSONAL PROPERTY TAXES

Many state and local governments impose personal property taxes. For individuals, the key issue is whether the levy is a deductible tax under Sec. 164 or a nondeductible fee. To qualify as a deductible personal property tax, the levy must meet two basic tests:

- The tax must be an ad valorem tax on personal property. In other words, the amount of the tax is determined by the property's value rather than some other measure such as a vehicle's weight or model year.
- The tax must be imposed on an annual basis, even if it is not collected annually.[16]

If a personal property tax is based partly on value and partly on some other basis, only the ad valorem portion is deductible.

EXAMPLE I7-9 ▶ Banner County imposes on all passenger automobiles a property tax of 1% of value plus 20 cents per hundredweight. Clay's automobile has a value of $10,000 and weighs 1,500 pounds. Clay may deduct $100 ($10,000 × 0.01) under Sec. 164. Clay may not deduct the remaining $300 (1,500 × 0.20) under Sec. 164; however, he may deduct it as an ordinary business expense if the automobile is used in his business. ◀

ADDITIONAL COMMENT

Several states impose a tax on the value of a taxpayer's investment portfolio. This is an example of a deductible intangible personal property tax.

For individuals, personal property taxes are *from* AGI (itemized) deductions unless they are incurred in an individual's trade or business or for the production of rental income.

REAL ESTATE TAXES

Apportionment of Taxes. When real estate is sold during the year, the federal income tax deduction for property taxes imposed on that real estate is allocated between the seller and the purchaser based on the amount of time each taxpayer owns the property during the real property tax year. The real property tax year may or may not coincide with the taxpayer's tax year. The apportionment, based on the number of days each party holds the property during the real property tax year of sale, assumes that the purchaser owns the property on the date of the sale. This apportionment is mandatory for all taxpayers even

[16] Reg. Sec. 1.164-3(c).

though one of the parties (i.e., the purchaser or seller) may have actually paid the entire property tax bill. The party who actually pays the taxes (either the buyer or the seller) deducts his or her share of the taxes in the year the taxes are paid unless an election is made under Sec. 461(c) to accrue the taxes. The tax consequences do not depend on who actually pays the real estate taxes or whether the real estate taxes are prorated under the agreement.

EXAMPLE I7-10 ▶ The real property tax year for Bannock County is the calendar year. Property taxes for a particular real property tax year become a lien against the property as of June 30 of that year, and the owner of the property on that date becomes liable for the tax. However, the taxes are not payable until February 28 of the subsequent year. On May 30 of the current (non-leap) year, Sandy, a cash-method taxpayer, sells a building to Roger, who is also a cash-method taxpayer. The real estate taxes on the property for the current year are $1,095. Although Roger is liable for the payment of the tax, Sandy is treated as having paid $447 ($1,095 × 149/365 [the numerator of 149 is the number of days from January 1 through May 29 and the denominator is the entire real property tax year]) on the date of the sale. Roger may deduct his share of the taxes, equaling $648 ($1,095 × 216/365), in the subsequent year (i.e., the year during which Roger actually pays the full amount of property tax due of $1,095). On the other hand, if the taxes become a lien against the property on April 1, Sandy is the owner of the building on that date and, since she is liable for the tax, she will be the one who actually pays the tax. Under these circumstances, the result is the same (i.e. Sandy deducts $447 and Roger deducts $648) except that Roger may take the $648 deduction in the year of sale rather than in the year of payment. ◀

ADDITIONAL COMMENT

Delinquent taxes of the seller that are paid by the buyer as part of the contract price are not deductible.

Generally, the sales agreement provides for the proper apportionment of property taxes between the buyer and seller. Thus, in the closing statement, the amount of the taxes apportioned to each party generally is stated separately from the selling price of the property.[17]

TYPICAL MISCONCEPTION

Taxpayers often fail to differentiate between assessments for new construction and for repairs. For example, an assessment for street repairs is deductible, but an assessment for the construction of a new street is not deductible.

REAL PROPERTY ASSESSMENTS FOR LOCAL BENEFITS. Local governments often make assessments against real estate for the purpose of funding local improvements. These assessments may be for such items as street improvements, sidewalks, lighting, drainage, and sewer improvements. If the tax is assessed only against the property that benefits from the improvement, it is not deductible, even though the general public may also be incidentally benefited.[18] Such assessments are capitalized as part of the property's adjusted basis.

Real property taxes incurred on personal-use assets, such as a personal residence, are deductible *from* AGI. Real property taxes incurred on business property or property held for the production of rental income are deductions *for* AGI.

GENERAL SALES TAX

Before 1987, Sec. 164 allowed a deduction for sales taxes. However, that deduction was eliminated by the Tax Reform Act of 1986 for 1987 and subsequent years. Instead, the sales tax is treated as part of the purchase price of the property, increasing its basis.

SELF-EMPLOYMENT TAX

Self-employed individuals pay a tax on their self-employment income in lieu of the payment of a Social Security payroll tax on salary. The self-employment tax rate and total amount of tax are equal to the combined employee and employer Social Security tax (i.e., 12.4% with a ceiling of $84,900 in 2002; and no ceiling for the 2.9% additional Medicare hospital insurance premium for self-employed individuals). However, self-employed individuals may deduct one-half of the self-employment taxes paid as a *for* AGI deduction.[19]

[17] However, if the agreement does not provide for an apportionment of taxes, the seller's gain or loss on the sale (and the purchaser's basis in the property) must be adjusted either upward or downward, depending on which party actually pays the taxes.

[18] Reg. Sec. 1.164-4. However, if the assessment against the local benefits is made for maintenance, repair, or interest charges on the benefits, the assessment is deductible. The burden of proof to show how much of the assessment is deductible falls on the taxpayer (see Sec. 164(c)(1)).

[19] Sec. 164(f). (See Chapter I14 for a discussion of the self-employment tax.)

INTEREST

OBJECTIVE 4

Identify different types of interest deductions

ADDITIONAL COMMENT

In 1998, the deduction for interest paid represented 39.8% of the total dollar amount of itemized deductions, making it the largest itemized deduction.

In years past, taxpayers could deduct virtually all interest paid or accrued in the taxable year. Gradually, however, Congress has enacted numerous exceptions into the tax law rendering several types of interest nondeductible. For example, individuals may not deduct personal interest expense, such as interest paid on personal credit cards, automobile loans, etc. Interest incurred in connection with a trade or business is always deductible. Thus, to determine the amount of interest expense deduction, taxpayers must properly classify their interest expense for the year. The interest expense categories include the following:

- Active trade or business
- Passive activity
- Investment
- Personal
- Qualified residence
- Student loan

DEFINITION OF INTEREST

Interest is defined as "compensation for the use or forbearance of money."[20] Thus, finance charges, carrying charges, loan discounts, premiums, loan origination fees, and points are all considered interest if they represent a cost for the use of money.

CHARGE FOR SERVICES. In addition to interest, borrowers may incur other charges in connection with borrowing money. These service charges include fees for appraisals, title searches, bank service charges, and the annual service charge on credit cards. Unless incurred in a trade or business, these expenses are not deductible because they all represent nondeductible personal expenses. As explained in the section in this chapter entitled Personal Interest, although finance charges on credit cards represent interest rather than service costs, they likewise are not deductible unless incurred in a trade or business.

BANK SERVICE CHARGES AND FINANCE CHARGES. Bank service charges on checking accounts are nondeductible expenses for services rendered rather than interest. The annual service charge on credit cards is also a charge for services rather than interest. However, finance charges on credit cards are interest. Late payments charged by public utilities are interest expense because they are not incurred for any specific service.[21] Of course, if these expenses are incurred in a trade or business, they are deductible.

KEY POINT

The classification of interest expense depends on the use to which the borrowed money is put, not on the nature of the property used to secure the loan.

CLASSIFICATION OF INTEREST EXPENSE

The deductibility of interest generally depends on the purpose for which the indebtedness is incurred because interest incurred in certain activities is subject to limitation and disallowance. For example, interest expense incurred in the taxpayer's active business is deductible in full against the business income (a deduction *for* AGI, taken on Schedule C), whereas interest expense allocated to the purchase of the taxpayer's residence is subject to the limitations applicable to that type of interest and is an itemized deduction (a deduction *from* AGI). In general, other than certain interest on a personal residence, taxpayers may not deduct interest allocated to personal-use expenditures.

Pursuant to the Treasury Regulations, taxpayers must allocate interest expense to the different interest expense categories by identifying the use of the borrowed money. Property used as collateral in securing the debt normally has no bearing on the allocation of the interest expense.[22]

[20] *Deputy v. Pierre S. DuPont*, 23 AFTR 808, 40-1 USTC ¶9161 (USSC, 1940).
[21] Rev. Rul. 73-136, 1973-1 C.B. 68 and Rev. Rul. 74-187, 1974-1 C.B. 48. However, interest on a credit card or interest charged by a public utility is not deductible if it is personal interest.
[22] Temp. Reg. Sec. 1.163-8T. The major exception to this rule deals with home equity loans where the funds borrowed may be used for any purpose. Home equity loans are discussed later in this chapter.

EXAMPLE I7-11 ▶ Cathy pledges some stock and securities as collateral for a $30,000 loan. She then purchases an automobile with the proceeds of the loan. The automobile is used 100% of the time for personal use. Even though the collateral for the loan is investment property, the interest expense is allocated to a personal-use asset and is not deductible. ◀

If the taxpayer deposits borrowed funds in a bank rather than spending them immediately, the deposit is considered an investment, and the interest on the loan is investment interest until the funds are withdrawn and expended. Then, the interest expense is allocated to the category for which the expenditure is made, regardless of when the interest expense for the debt is actually paid. This reallocation occurs as of the date the check is written on the account, as long as the check is delivered or mailed within a reasonable period of time.[23]

EXAMPLE I7-12 ▶ On March 1 of the current year, José borrows $100,000 and immediately deposits the funds into an account that contains no other funds. José makes no additional deposits nor payments. On May 1 of the current year, he withdraws $40,000 from the account and purchases a sailboat to be used for personal purposes. On July 1, José withdraws an additional $50,000 and purchases a passive activity. For the current year, the interest expense on the loan is categorized as follows: from March 1 through April 30, all of the expense is investment interest expense. 40% ($40,000/$100,000) of the interest expense attributable to the period May 1 through June 30 is classified as personal interest and the remainder is investment interest. The interest expense attributable to the period from July 1 to the end of the year is classified as 40% personal interest, 50% passive activity interest, and 10% investment interest. ◀

If both borrowed and personal funds are mingled in the same account, expenditures from that account are treated as coming first from the borrowed funds.[24]

EXAMPLE I7-13 ▶ On April 1 of the current year, Diane borrows $30,000 and deposits it into a checking account that contains $10,000 of personal funds. On May 1 of the current year, Diane purchases a passive activity for $15,000, and on June 1 she purchases a personal automobile for $20,000. The $15,000 expended for the passive activity on May 1 is treated as coming from the borrowed funds. Thus, as of that date, one-half of the interest expense on the debt is reallocated from investment interest to passive activity interest. $15,000 of the funds expended for the personal automobile on June 1 is treated as coming from the borrowed funds, and the remaining $5,000 is treated as coming from the personal funds. Thus, as of June 1, the remaining interest expense on the debt is reallocated to personal interest. ◀

When a debt is repaid, the repayment is allocated to the expenditures made with that debt in the following order: (1) personal expenditures, (2) investment expenditures and passive activity expenditures other than rental real estate, (3) passive activity expenditures in rental real estate, and (4) trade or business expenditures.

ACTIVE TRADE OR BUSINESS. Generally, a taxpayer may deduct without limit any interest expense incurred in the taxpayer's active trade or business. As explained in Chapter I6, the determination of whether a particular activity constitutes a trade or business or an investment depends on an examination of all the relevant facts and circumstances. For individuals, estates, trusts, and certain corporations, however, it is not sufficient that the interest be incurred in the taxpayer's trade or business. In addition, the taxpayer must *materially participate* in the business. If not, the activity is considered passive, and losses from the activity (including the interest expense) are subject to the passive loss limitation rules (see Chapter I8 for a discussion of these rules). Interest incurred in an active trade or business is a deduction *for* AGI.

[23] Temp. Reg. Sec. 1.163-8T(c). If during any one month several expenditures are made from an account, the taxpayer may elect to treat all the expenditures as if made on the first day of the month. However, this election is made on each account separately and is available only for accounts where the borrowed funds are already in the account as of the first day of the month. If the funds are not in the account as of the first day of the month, the expenditures may be treated as made on the date that the borrowed funds are deposited in the account. See Temp. Reg. Sec. 1.163-8T(c)(4)(iv).

[24] Temp. Reg. Sec. 1.163-8T(c)(4)(ii). However, if an expenditure is made out of the mingled funds within 15 days of the deposit of the borrowed funds into the account, the taxpayer may designate the expenditure to which the borrowed funds are allocated.

PASSIVE ACTIVITY. Individuals, estates, trusts, and certain corporations that incur losses from passive activities are subject to the passive loss limitation rules explained in Chapter I8. These rules prevent taxpayers from offsetting passive activity losses against other types of income such as salary, interest, dividends, and income from an active business. Taxpayers must include interest expense attributable to the passive activity in computing the net income or loss generated from the activity, and thus may not be able to deduct the interest under these limitation rules (see Chapter I8 for a discussion of these rules).

OBJECTIVE 5

Compute the amount of investment interest deduction

INVESTMENT INTEREST. Individuals and other noncorporate taxpayers are limited on the deductibility of interest expense attributable to investments. Without any limitation, high-income taxpayers could realize significant tax savings by borrowing money to invest in assets that are appreciating in value but produce little or no current income. This would enable the taxpayer to offset current highly taxed income with a current interest deduction, while deferring the taxable income from the investment until it is sold at a later date. This technique also would enable taxpayers to increase their future capital gain income and reduce their current ordinary income. This procedure is favorable to taxpayers because the tax on capital gains is, in many cases, less than the tax on ordinary income.

Because of these concerns, Sec. 163(d) limits the current deduction for investment interest expense to the taxpayer's net investment income for the taxable year. Any investment interest expense disallowed as a current deduction is carried over and treated as investment interest expense incurred in the following year.

EXAMPLE I7-14 ▶ In the current year, Rita earns $27,000 in net investment income and incurs $40,000 of investment interest expense. Rita's interest expense deduction for the year is limited to $27,000, the amount of her net investment income.

The remaining investment interest expense of $13,000 ($40,000 − $27,000) may be carried over and deducted in a subsequent year. This carryover amount is treated as paid or accrued in the subsequent year and is subject to the disallowance rules that pertain to the subsequent year. ◀

Investment Interest. **Investment interest** is interest expense on indebtedness properly allocable to property held for investment. This includes property that generates portfolio types of income such as interest, dividends, annuities, and royalties. It does not include business interest, personal interest, qualified residence interest, or interest incurred in connection with any activity that is determined to be passive. Under Sec. 469, all rental activities are deemed to be passive (see Chapter I8 for a discussion of the passive loss limitation rules). Thus, interest incurred in owning and renting property is subject to the passive loss limitation rather than the investment interest limitation.

Investment interest also does not include interest expense incurred to purchase or carry tax-exempt securities. This interest is not deductible at all. Without this disallowance, a taxpayer could, in certain circumstances, actually borrow funds at a higher rate of interest than the rate at which they were reinvested, while still generating a positive net cash flow because the government would be subsidizing the transaction through the interest deduction on the borrowings.

Net Investment Income. For purposes of the investment interest limitation, the term **net investment income** means the excess of the taxpayer's investment income over investment expenses. Investment income is gross income from property held for investment, including items such as dividends, interest, annuities, and royalties (if not earned in a trade or business). Investment income also includes net gain (all gains minus all losses) on the sale of investment property, but only to the extent that the net gain exceeds the net capital gain (net long-term capital gains in excess of net short-term capital losses). Stated another way, net short-term capital gains are included in the definition of net investment income.

As explained in Chapter I5, net capital gain is generally taxed at a 20% maximum rate. Including net capital gain in the definition of investment income would increase the amount of deductible investment interest expense, which might offset other income that is taxed at higher rates. Thus, generally, net capital gain attributable to the disposition of property held for investment is excluded from the definition of investment income.

However, net capital gain from the disposition of investment property is included in the definition to the extent that the taxpayer elects to subject the gain from the disposition of investment property to the regular tax rates.[25] Gains on business and personal-use property are not included in the calculation of investment income.

EXAMPLE I7-15 ▶ During the current year, Michael incurs $15,000 investment interest expense, earns $7,000 of dividends and $3,000 interest income. He also reports the following gains and losses from the sale of stocks and bonds during the year:

Short-term capital gains	$4,000
Short-term capital losses	(3,000)
Long-term capital gains	5,000
Long-term capital losses	(2,000)

Considering all of Michael's other income and deductions for the year, assume that he is subject to a 38.6% marginal tax rate. Michael's net capital gain is $3,000 (net long-term capital gain of $3,000 in excess of net short-term capital losses of $0). He also has a $1,000 ($4,000 − $3,000) net short-term capital gain. Thus, of his total capital gain of $4,000 ($9,000 of total gains − $5,000 of total losses), only $1,000 ($4,000 net gain − $3,000 net capital gain) is included in investment income. If Michael does not make an election, his investment income is $11,000 ($10,000 of dividends and interest plus $1,000 net short-term capital gain). He may deduct $11,000 of the investment interest expense in the current year. The excess investment interest for the current year of $4,000 ($15,000 − $11,000) is carried over to the next year. The $3,000 net capital gain is subject to the 20% ceiling tax rate on net capital gain. If Michael makes the election, his investment income is $14,000 (the $3,000 net capital gain is included), and he may deduct $14,000 of the investment interest expense. Thus, only $1,000 ($15,000 − $14,000) of investment interest expense is not currently deductible and is carried over to the next year. However, his $3,000 net capital gain is subject to the 38.6% ordinary income tax rate. ◀

ADDITIONAL COMMENT

Investment expenses are those which are deductible on the tax return, after the 2% limitation.

Investment expenses include all deductions (except interest) that are directly connected with the production of investment income. These expenses include rental fees for safe-deposit boxes, fees for investment counsel,[26] and subscriptions to investment and financial planning journals. As explained later in this chapter (see the section of this chapter titled Miscellaneous Itemized Deductions), these investment expenses are deductible only to the extent they exceed 2% of the taxpayer's AGI for the year. Only the investment expenses remaining after application of this limitation are used in computing the net investment income. Furthermore, in computing the amount of the disallowed investment expenses, the 2% of AGI limitation is applied to the noninvestment expenses first.[27] Any remaining 2% of AGI limitation is then used to reduce the noninterest investment expenses.

EXAMPLE I7-16 ▶ Kevin's AGI for the current year is $200,000. Included in his AGI is $175,000 salary and $25,000 of investment income. In earning the investment income, Kevin paid investment interest expense of $33,000. He also incurred the following expenditures subject to the 2% of AGI limitation:

Investment expenses:	
Subscriptions to investment journals	$ 700
Investment counseling	2,000
Safe-deposit box rental	300
Noninvestment expenses:	
Unreimbursed employee business expenses	1,500
Tax return preparation fees (non–business-related)	500

Kevin's investment interest expense deduction for the year is computed by first determining the deductible investment expenses (other than interest) and the net investment income.

[25] Secs. 1(h)(3) and 163(d)(4)(B).

[26] Sec. 163(d)(4)(C). Not included here are commissions for the sale or purchase of investment property. A commission paid on the purchase of property is added to the purchase price (and the basis) of the property. A commission paid on the sale of property reduces the amount realized.

[27] H. Rept. No. 99-841, 99th Cong., 2d Sess., pp. II-153 and 154 (1986). The noninvestment expenses subject to the 2% of AGI limitation include unreimbursed employee business expenses, hobby expenses up to the income from the hobby, and tax return preparation fees.

Investment expenses:			
Subscriptions		$ 700	
Investment counseling		2,000	
Safe-deposit box rental		300	$3,000
Disallowed by the 2% limitation:			
2% of AGI ($200,000 × 0.02)	$4,000		
Unreimbursed employee expenses	(1,500)		
Tax return preparation fees	(500)		
Investment expenses (remainder of 2% limit allocated to investment expenses)			(2,000)
Deductible investment expenses			$1,000
Net investment income ($25,000 − $1,000)			$24,000

The investment interest expense deduction is limited to $24,000. The remaining investment interest of $9,000 ($33,000 − $24,000) is carried over and deducted in a subsequent year (subject to the disallowance rules that pertain to the subsequent year). ◀

OBJECTIVE 6

Compute the deduction for qualified residence interest

PERSONAL INTEREST. In general, the tax law does not allow a deduction for interest expense on debt incurred for personal purposes. Thus, taxpayers may not deduct interest on credit cards, car loans, and consumer debt. However, if certain requirements are met, taxpayers may deduct interest on debt to acquire a personal residence as well as interest on certain student loans.

ADDITIONAL COMMENT

Banks and other financial institutions that receive mortgage interest from homeowners are required to report interest of $600 or more to the IRS and to the homeowners on Form 1098.

QUALIFIED RESIDENCE INTEREST. Subject to certain limitations discussed below, individuals may deduct **qualified residence interest.** To be qualified residence interest, the interest payment must be either acquisition indebtedness or home equity indebtedness with respect to a qualified residence of the taxpayer. In all cases the debt must be secured by the residence.[28] A qualified residence (discussed below) may consist of the taxpayer's principal residence and a second residence.

Acquisition Indebtedness. Acquisition indebtedness is any debt that is secured by the residence and is incurred in acquiring, constructing, or substantially improving the qualified residence. Debt may be treated as qualified acquisition indebtedness if the residence is acquired within 90 days before or after the date that the debt is incurred. In the case of the construction or substantial improvement of a residence, debt incurred before the completion of the construction or improvement can qualify as acquisition debt to the extent of construction expenditures that are made no more than 24 months before the date the debt is incurred. Furthermore, debt incurred after construction is complete and within 90 days of the completion date may qualify as acquisition indebtedness to the extent of any construction expenditures made within the 24-month period ending on the date the debt is incurred.[29] As payments of principal are made on the loan, the amount of acquisition debt is reduced and cannot be increased unless the residence is substantially improved. Acquisition indebtedness may be refinanced (and therefore treated as acquisition indebtedness) to the extent that the principal amount of the refinancing does not exceed the principal amount of the acquisition debt immediately before the refinancing.

EXAMPLE I7-17 ▶ Kay acquired a personal residence in 1993 for $100,000 and borrowed $85,000 on a mortgage that was secured by the property. In the current year the principal balance of the mortgage has been reduced to $60,000. Kay's acquisition indebtedness in the current year is only $60,000 and

[28] Sec. 163(h). If the loan is not secured by the residence, it does not qualify. In one instance the taxpayer agreed to purchase her ex-husband's interest in their residence. The terms of the sale were $10,000 down plus an unsecured $25,000 note. In a private ruling, the IRS ruled that because the note was not secured by the residence, the interest on the note was not qualified residence interest. (See Ltr. Rul. 8752010 September 18, 1987). However, if under any state or local homestead law the security interest is ineffective or unenforceable, the interest expense still qualifies as qualified residence interest. See Sec. 163(h)(4)(C). In another letter ruling the taxpayer borrowed money to purchase a residence securing the debt by pledging stock and bonds. Here also, the IRS denied the deduction because the loan was not secured by the residence. (See Ltr. Rul. 8906031 November 10, 1988).

[29] Notice 88-74, 1988-2 C.B. 385.

cannot be increased above $60,000 (except by indebtedness incurred to substantially improve the residence). If she refinances the existing mortgage in the current year and the refinanced debt is $70,000, only $60,000 (the principal balance of the existing acquisition indebtedness) qualifies as acquisition indebtedness. ◀

Qualified acquisition indebtedness is limited to $1,000,000 ($500,000 for a married individual filing a separate return). Qualified acquisition indebtedness incurred before October 13, 1987 (pre-October 13, 1987 indebtedness) is not subject to any limitation. However, the aggregate amount of pre-October 13, 1987 indebtedness reduces the $1,000,000 limitation on the indebtedness incurred after October 13, 1987.

ADDITIONAL COMMENT

Many banks, in attempting to generate new loan business, have heavily advertised the tax advantages of home equity indebtedness.

Home Equity Indebtedness. Taxpayers may also deduct interest incurred on home equity indebtedness (so-called home equity loans). Subject to certain limits, home equity indebtedness is any indebtedness (other than acquisition indebtedness) that is secured by a qualified residence of the taxpayer. The proceeds of the loan may be used for any purpose (including purchasing or improving a qualified residence), as long as the loan is secured by the taxpayer's qualified residence. However, home equity indebtedness is limited to the lesser of:

- The FMV of the qualified residence in excess of the acquisition indebtedness with respect to that residence, or
- $100,000 ($50,000 for a married individual filing a separate return)

The $1,000,000 limit on acquisition indebtedness and the $100,000 limit on home equity indebtedness are two separate limits. The maximum amount of indebtedness on which a taxpayer may deduct qualified residence interest is generally limited to $1,100,000 if an individual has $100,000 or more equity in the property.

EXAMPLE I7-18 ▶ On April 23 of the current year, Kesha borrows $125,000 to purchase a new sailboat. The loan is secured by her personal residence. On that date, the outstanding balance on the original debt Kesha incurred to purchase the residence is $400,000 and the FMV of the residence is $900,000. The original debt is also secured by Kesha's residence. Kesha may deduct the interest paid on the $400,000 of acquisition indebtedness, plus the interest paid on $100,000 of the home equity loan. The interest on $25,000 ($125,000 − $100,000) is treated as personal interest and is, therefore, not deductible. The home equity loan is limited to the lesser of $100,000 or the FMV of the residence in excess of the outstanding acquisition indebtedness (the lesser of $100,000 or ($900,000 − $400,000)). ◀

Points Paid as Qualified Residence Interest. Often taxpayers must pay **points** on real estate debt. A point is equal to 1% of the loan amount. Thus, two points paid on a $60,000 mortgage equal $1,200 ($60,000 × .02). Points often represent prepaid interest because the stated rate of interest for the loan is lower than the current rate of interest. Generally, prepaid interest paid in the form of points must be capitalized and amortized over the life of the loan. However, points paid on a loan incurred to purchase the taxpayer's principal residence (acquisition indebtedness) are automatically deductible when paid if certain requirements are met. The IRS has also indicated that points paid on Veteran Administration (VA) and Fedeal Home Administration (FHA) loans are also currently deductible as interest if they are clearly designated as points incurred in connection with the indebtedness.[30]

EXAMPLE I7-19 ▶ During the current year, Kevin and Donna purchase a new home for $300,000, putting $100,000 down and borrowing $200,000. At the closing, they are required to pay one and one-half points as a loan discount in connection with the loan, which is secured by a mortgage against the home. The practice of charging points is an established business practice where they live.

[30] These requirements, mentioned in Chapter I6, are as follows: The points must be paid in connection with the purchase (not the improvement) of the taxpayer's principal residence, the closing agreement must clearly designate the amounts as points paid in connection with the acquisition debt, the amount must be computed as a percentage of the amount borrowed, the points must conform with established business practices, and the loan must be secured by the residence. Rev. Proc. 94-27, I.R.B. 94-15, 17. See also Rev. Proc. 92-12A, 1992-1 C.B. 664.

These points represent prepaid interest on the purchase of a principal residence. Thus, in addition to the interest portion of every payment they make during the year, Kevin and Donna may also deduct $3,000 ($200,000 × 0.015) as interest paid during the year of purchase. ◀

Taxpayers must capitalize points paid on a loan to purchase property other than a principal residence or for refinancing a mortgage on a principal residence. If the property is business, investment, or a qualified residence (the taxpayer's principal residence and one other that the taxpayer chooses) the taxpayers may amortize the points over the life of the loan.[31]

In order for the points to be currently deductible, the purchaser of the principal residence (borrower) must have paid for them with unborrowed funds. However, amounts provided by the borrower as down payments, escrow deposits, earnest money, or other funds are treated as paid for the points. Furthermore, as long as the borrower provides sufficient funds in these other categories, he or she is treated as having paid the points even if the seller has paid for them on behalf of the borrower.[32]

Qualified Residence. For any tax year, a taxpayer may have two qualified residences:

- Taxpayer's principal residence
- One other residence selected by the taxpayer, with regard to which the taxpayer meets the residence test of Sec. 280A(d)(1).

In order to meet this residence test, the taxpayer must have personally used the property more than the greater of 14 days or 10% of any rental days during the year.[33]

EXAMPLE I7-20 ▶

Fred owns a lakeside cabin that he uses for vacations. He also rents the cabin out to others when he is not using it. During the year Fred rents the cabin out at a fair rental for 90 days. Fred personally uses the cabin for a total of 22 days. Because Fred's personal use for the year (22 days) exceeds 14 days [the greater of 14 days or 9 days (10% of the rental days)], the cabin qualifies as his residence for purposes of deducting qualified residence interest for the year. ◀

ADDITIONAL COMMENT

Whether property is a residence for tax purposes is determined based on all the facts and circumstances, including the good faith of the taxpayer. A residence generally includes a house, condominium, mobile home, boat, or house trailer, that contains sleeping space and toilet and cooking facilities. Treas. Reg. § 1.163-10T(p)(3)(ii).

Despite the residence test, the taxpayer may select a property that has not been rented by the taxpayer at any time during the year as the second residence on which qualified residence interest may be deducted.

STOP & THINK

Question: Jana is about to purchase a new sport utility vehicle for $35,000. If she pays $5,000 down, the dealer is prepared to offer her a loan for the remaining $30,000 at 8% interest. In investigating other possible sources of funds, she found out that her brokerage firm would lend her the $30,000 at 9% interest if she pledged her stock as collateral. At her local credit union, she found that she could borrow the $30,000 at 10% interest if she took out a home equity loan by using her home as security. Jana is confused about which loan she should take.

Solution: The best way to analyze this problem is to compare the after-tax interest rates of the loans. Jana may not deduct the interest paid to the car dealer because it is personal interest. Thus, its after-tax interest rate remains at 8%. Furthermore, even though Jana uses her stock holdings as collateral, the interest on the loan from the brokerage firm is non-deductible personal interest because the proceeds of the loan are used to purchase personal property rather than investment property. Its after-tax interest rate remains at 9%. Only the interest on the home equity loan from the credit union is potentially

---

[31] Rev. Rul. 87-22, 1987-1 C.B. 146, and Rev. Proc. 87-15, 1987-1 C.B. 624. The 8th Circuit Court of Appeals has held in one case that points paid on refinancing a "bridge" or temporary loan are currently deductible. *James R. Huntsman v. CIR*, 66 AFTR 2d 90-5020, 90-2 USTC ¶ 50,340 (8th Cir., 1990) rev'g 91 TC 57 (1988). However, the IRS has announced that it will not follow *Huntsman* in circuits other than the circuit in which the case was decided (IRS Action on Decision CC-1991-02, Feb. 11, 1991).

[32] Reg. Sec. 1.6050H-1(f)(3). See also Rev. Proc. 94-27, I.R.B. 94-15, 17.

[33] Sec. 280A(d)(1). Use by the taxpayer's family, as defined in Sec. 267(c)(4), other individuals under a reciprocal-use arrangement, and anyone when a fair rental is not charged is counted as a day of personal use by the taxpayer (see Sec. 280A(d)(2) and Chapter I6).

deductible. This depends, of course, on the amount of Jana's total itemized deductions. Assuming that Jana's total itemized deductions exceed the standard deduction and that Jana is in the 30.0% marginal tax bracket, the after-tax interest rate of the home equity loan drops from 10% to 7.0% [10% × (1 − 0.30)].

STUDENT LOAN INTEREST. If certain requirements are met, individuals may take a *for* AGI deduction for interest paid on qualified education loans. The maximum annual interest deduction for qualified student loans is $2,500. Furthermore, the deduction is phased out ratably for individuals with modified AGI of $50,000 to $65,000 ($100,000 to $115,000 for individuals filing joint returns).[34]

EXAMPLE I7-21 ▶ During 2002, Ryan paid a total of $1,800 in interest on a loan incurred for qualified education expenses. Ryan is single and reports modified AGI of $59,000 for the year. Since his modified AGI of $59,000 is $9,000 greater than $50,000, the total potential deduction of $2,500 is reduced by 60% ($9,000/$15,000). Ryan may take a *for* AGI deduction of $1,000. ◀

To qualify for this deduction, the interest must be payable on a loan incurred solely to pay qualified higher education expenses. If a taxpayer takes out a loan to pay for higher education expenses and for other purposes, none of the interest on the loan qualifies. Higher education expenses include tuition, fees, books and equipment, and room and board incurred during a time the taxpayer, the taxpayer's spouse, or the taxpayer's dependent is a student at a qualified higher education institution on at least a half-time basis. However, these qualified expenditures are reduced by amounts excluded from income under an employer educational assistance program or from United States savings bonds, as well as any scholarship or allowance that is excluded from income. Furthermore, to prevent a double deduction, the tax law allows no deduction to an individual for whom a dependency exemption may be taken on another's tax return or for any amount that is deductible under any other provision of the Code.

TIMING OF THE INTEREST DEDUCTION

Section 163 allows a deduction for all interest paid or accrued during the tax year. This generally means that cash-method taxpayers deduct interest in the year it is paid, whereas accrual-method taxpayers deduct interest as it accrues. However, the IRC makes exceptions to this general rule.

ADDITIONAL COMMENT

Points paid on the refinancing of an existing mortgage must be written off over the life of the new mortgage.

PREPAID INTEREST. If a cash method taxpayer prepays interest and the prepayment relates to a loan that extends beyond the end of the tax year, generally the payment must be capitalized and amortized over the periods to which the interest relates (i.e., the accrual method is applied to cash method taxpayers). As previously discussed, the law makes one exception to this rule involving interest paid in the form of points charged in connection with the purchase or improvement of the taxpayer's principal residence. If these points represent prepaid interest, the taxpayer may deduct them in the year paid.[35]

INTEREST PAID WITH LOAN PROCEEDS. Assuming the interest is otherwise deductible, if an individual borrows money from a third party rather than from the original lending institution and uses the funds to make a payment on a previously outstanding loan, the individual generally may deduct the interest portion of the payment. However, if the taxpayer borrows the funds used to pay the interest on the first loan from the same lender to whom the interest is due, and either the purpose of the second loan is to pay the

[34] Modified AGI includes certain excluded income from Guam, American Samoa, or Puerto Rico, as well as any income excluded under the foreign earned income provisions. Furthermore, the deduction for qualified tuition and related expenses is not allowed.

[35] Sec. 461(g). In order for the exception to apply, the home must be used to secure the loan, and the charging of points must be an established business practice in the area where the loan is granted. (See the discussion of the deductibility of points in this chapter under the heading Definition of *Interest* as well as the discussion in Chapter I6.)

interest on the first, or the borrower does not have unrestricted control of the funds, then the borrower may not deduct the interest.[36]

DISCOUNTED NOTES. Lending institutions often discount notes. In effect, the borrower pays the interest by repaying more money than is received when the note is signed. A cash method taxpayer can deduct this interest at the time the note is repaid, whereas an accrual method taxpayer must deduct the interest as it accrues over the term of the loan.

EXAMPLE I7-22 ▶ On December 1, 2002, Stan borrows $1,000 from his credit union to use in his business. Under the terms of the contract, Stan actually receives $970 but is required to repay $1,000 on February 28, 2003 (three months later). Because Stan is a cash method taxpayer, he may deduct the full $30 interest in 2003 when the note is repaid. If he were an accrual method taxpayer, he could deduct $10 ($30 × 0.333) in 2002, and $20 ($30 × 0.667) in 2003. ◀

TYPICAL MISCONCEPTION

Taxpayers sometimes mistakenly assume that any interest paid on loans between related taxpayers is not deductible. However, if the taxpayers are not governed by the Sec. 267 limitation and the interest is paid on a bona fide loan, it is deductible.

INTEREST OWED TO A RELATED PARTY BY AN ACCRUAL METHOD TAXPAYER. One of the purposes of Sec. 267 is to require related cash method lenders and accrual method borrowers to report the results of their joint transaction in the same year. Thus, an accrual method taxpayer must defer the deduction for any expense (including interest) accrued until the year in which the expense is actually paid and is reported as income by a cash method creditor who is related to the debtor. Section 267 also disallows losses on the sale of property between related parties. The disallowance of such losses is discussed in Chapter I6.

The relationships covered by this rule are quite extensive. Some of the more common relationships include the following:

- ▶ Members of a family (defined as an individual's brothers, sisters, spouse, ancestors, and lineal descendants)
- ▶ An individual and a C corporation in which the individual owns directly or indirectly more than 50% of the outstanding stock
- ▶ A corporation and a partnership which are both over 50% owned directly or indirectly by the same people
- ▶ A partnership and any partner of the partnership
- ▶ An S Corporation and any shareholder of the S Corporation[37]

EXAMPLE I7-23 ▶ During the current year, Lisa, a cash method taxpayer, loans some money to her 100%-owned corporation, which uses the accrual method of accounting. As of December 31 of the current year, the corporation owes Lisa $3,000 in interest. However, because of a shortage of funds, the corporation does not actually pay the interest until February 15 of the following year. Despite the fact that the corporation uses the accrual method of accounting, the corporation cannot deduct the $3,000 until the corporation actually pays the interest to Lisa in the subsequent year. The result would be the same if the corporation were an S Corporation even if Lisa owned 50% or less of the outstanding stock. ◀

IMPUTED INTEREST. Under certain circumstances, if a taxpayer charges less than an adequate rate of interest, the IRS is authorized to impute an interest charge. This may cause the lender to have additional interest income and the borrower to have additional interest expense. The deductibility of this imputed interest expense depends on how the expense is classified (i.e. personal, investment, etc.). (See Chapter I11 for a discussion of imputed interest.)

The rules for deducting various types of interest are summarized in Topic Review I7-2.

---

[36] *H. C. Franklin v. CIR*, 50 AFTR 2d 82-5551, 82-2 USTC ¶9532 (5th Cir., 1982) and *Newton A. Burgess*, 8 T.C. 47 (1947). See also *Norman W. Menz*, 80 T.C. 1174 (1983). The IRS has also announced that it will disallow a deduction for interest paid with funds obtained through a second loan from the same lender (see IRS News Release 83-93, July 6, 1983).

[37] Secs. 267(b) and (e). The list of relationships is much more extensive than those mentioned. An S Corporation is one that meets certain requirements and has made an election to have its income taxed directly to its shareholders. A C Corporation is one that has not made an S election. (See Chapter C11 of the *Prentice Hall's Federal Taxation: Corporations, Partnerships, Estates, and Trusts* text or Chapter C11 of the *Prentice Hall's Federal Taxation: Comprehensive* text.)

Topic Review I7-2

Deductibility of Interest Expense

TYPE OF INTEREST	RULES
Business	Deductible in full as a *for* AGI deduction.
Passive	Subject to the passive loss limits (see Chapter I8).
Investment	Deductible as an itemized deduction to the extent of the taxpayer's net investment income for the year. Any amount not deductible is carried over to subsequent years.
Personal	Not deductible.
Qualified residence	(a) Must be attributable to debt secured by the taxpayer's principal residence and one other residence selected by the taxpayer. (b) Interest on up to $1,000,000 of home acquisition indebtedness is deductible as an itemized deduction. (c) Interest on home equity debt is deductible as an itemized deduction. Home equity debt is limited to the lesser of $100,000 or the excess of the FMV of the residence over the home acquisition indebtedness.
Student Loan Interest	(a) Payable on loan incurred to pay qualified higher education expenses. (b) Taken as a *for* AGI deduction. (c) Maximum deductible amount is $2,500. Amount is phased out ratably for AGI between $50,000 to $65,000 ($100,000 to $115,000 for married filing jointly).

CHARITABLE CONTRIBUTIONS

OBJECTIVE 7

Compute the amount of a charitable contribution deduction and identify limitations

ADDITIONAL COMMENT

In 1998, the deduction for charitable contributions totaled $105.3 billion which represented 16% of the total dollar amount of itemized deductions.

Under Sec. 170, corporations and individuals who itemize their deductions can deduct **charitable contributions** to qualified organizations. With the exception of certain contributions made by corporations (explained later in this chapter), taxpayers take the deduction in the year the contribution is made, regardless of the taxpayer's method of accounting. The amount of the deduction depends on the type of charity receiving the contribution, the type of property contributed, and the applicable limitations.

QUALIFYING ORGANIZATION

To deduct a contribution for federal income tax purposes, a taxpayer must make the contribution to or for the use of a qualified organization.[38] Contributions made directly to individuals, even though the individuals may be needy, are generally not deductible.[39] Under Sec. 170, qualified organizations include the following:

- The United States, the District of Columbia, a state or possession of the United States, or a political subdivision of a state or possession
- A corporation, trust, community chest, fund or foundation created or organized under the laws of the United States, a state, possession, or the District of Columbia[40]
- A post or organization of war veterans
- A domestic fraternal society, order, or association[41]
- Certain cemetery companies

Because of the restrictions and limitations examined later in this chapter, these qualifying organizations are further classified into public charities and private nonoperating foundations. Different restrictions and limitations apply to each type of organization.

---

[38] The Supreme Court has ruled that in order for a contribution to be for the use of a qualifying organization, the gift must be held either in a legally enforceable trust or in a similar legal arrangement. (See *U.S. v. Harold Davis*, 65 AFTR 2d 90-1051, 90-1 USTC ¶50,270 (USSC, 1990).)

[39] Under certain circumstances, a taxpayer may take a deduction (limited to $50 per month) for maintaining a student as a member of his or her household. The student may not be a dependent or relative of the taxpayer and must be placed in the taxpayer's home under an arrangement with a qualifying organization (see Sec. 170(g)).

[40] These organizations must be organized and operated exclusively for religious, charitable, scientific, literary, or educational purposes; to foster national or international amateur sports competition; or for the prevention of cruelty to children or animals.

[41] Furthermore, gifts to these organizations must be made by individuals and must be used exclusively for religious, charitable, scientific, literary, or educational purposes, or for the prevention of cruelty to children or animals.

REAL-WORLD EXAMPLE

The American Red Cross, Boy Scouts, United Fund, Goodwill, and Indiana University are examples of public charities.

Public charities include:

- Churches or a convention or association of churches
- Educational institutions that normally maintain a regular faculty, curriculum, and regularly enrolled students
- Organizations such as hospitals and medical schools whose principal function is medical care or medical education and research
- Government-supported organizations that exist to receive, hold, invest, and administer property for the benefit of a college or university
- Any qualified governmental unit
- Organizations that normally receive a substantial part of their support from either a governmental unit or the general public
- Certain private operating foundations[42]

Because several thousand organizations meet these requirements, the IRS publishes a list of many of the organizations that have applied for and received tax-exempt status.[43] Although this publication is frequently updated, an organization need not be listed in order to qualify.

SELF-STUDY QUESTION

Doug purchases an item having a FMV of $75 for $100 in a charity auction. How much can he deduct?

ANSWER

Doug can deduct only $25 because the cash paid must be reduced by the value of the property received.

TYPE OF PROPERTY CONTRIBUTED

If a taxpayer makes a contribution in cash, the amount of the deduction is easily determinable. However, if noncash property is donated, the amount of the contribution is not as easy to identify. In the case of noncash property, the amount of the donation depends on two factors: the type of property donated and the type of qualifying organization (public charity or private nonoperating foundation) to whom the property is given. Furthermore, a gift of property that consists of less than the donor's entire interest in the property is not usually considered a contribution of property. Thus, for example, no charitable contribution is made when an individual donates the use of a vacation home for a charitable fund-raising auction.[44]

CONTRIBUTION OF CAPITAL GAIN PROPERTY. In general, the amount of a donation of capital gain property is its FMV. Regulation Sec. 1.170A-1(c)(2) defines a property's FMV as the price at which the property would change hands between a willing buyer and a willing seller, neither being under any compulsion to buy or sell and both having reasonable knowledge of relevant facts. For purposes of charitable contributions, **capital gain property** is defined as property held over one year on which a long-term capital gain would be recognized if it were sold at its FMV on the date of the contribution. If a capital loss or a short-term capital gain would be recognized on the sale of the property, the property is considered to be ordinary income property for purposes of the charitable contribution deduction.

Contribution to a Private Nonoperating Foundation. The tax law provides an exception to this general rule for contributions of capital gain property to private nonoperating foundations. In general, a private nonoperating foundation is an organization that does not receive funding from the general public (e.g., the Carnegie Foundation). Private nonoperating foundations distribute funds to various charitable organizations that actually perform the charitable services. The amount of the contribution to a private nonoperating foundation is the property's FMV, reduced by the capital gain that would be recognized if the property were sold at its FMV on the date of the contribution. This means that generally the deductible amount of the contribution is the property's adjusted basis.[45]

---

[42] Sec. 170(b)(1)(E). The distinction between a private operating foundation and a private nonoperating foundation generally depends on the way the foundation spends or distributes its income and contributions. The details of this distinction are beyond the scope of this text.

[43] IRS, Pub. No. 78, Cumulative List of Organizations, 2000.

[44] Sec. 170(f)(3), Reg. Sec. 1.170A-7(a)(1) and Rev. Rul. 89-51, 1989-1 C.B. 89. Note, however, that certain transfers of partial interests in property do qualify (e.g., the contribution of certain remainder interests to a trust, the transfer of a remainder interest in a personal residence or a farm, or a contribution of an undivided interest in property). These exceptions are beyond the scope of this text.

[45] The amount of a contribution of appreciated stock made to a private nonoperating foundation remains at its FMV.

EXAMPLE I7-24 ▶ Betty purchases land in 1990 for $10,000. In the current year, she contributes the land to the United Way. At the time of the contribution, the FMV of the property is $25,000. Because the land is long-term capital gain property donated to a public charity, the amount of the contribution is $25,000 (its FMV).

On the other hand, if Betty donates the land to Cherry Foundation, a private nonoperating foundation, the amount of the contribution is $10,000 ($25,000 − $15,000 capital gain that would be recognized if the land were sold). ◀

TYPICAL MISCONCEPTION

Many people do not understand that the unrelated use restriction applies only to tangible personal property. A gift of shares of stock (intangible property) would not be a gift of unrelated use property where the stock is sold by the donee.

Unrelated Use Property. A second exception applies to capital gain property (that is also tangible personal property) contributed to a public charity and used by the organization for purposes unrelated to the charity's function. In such cases, the amount of the contribution deduction is equal to the property's FMV minus the capital gain that would be recognized if the property were sold at its FMV. This amount generally is the property's adjusted basis. Tangible property is all property that is not intangible property (e.g., property other than stock, securities, copyrights, patents, and so on). Personal property is all property other than real estate. The taxpayer is responsible for proving that the property was not put to unrelated use. However, a taxpayer meets this burden of proof if, at the time of the contribution, the taxpayer reasonably anticipates that the property will not be put to unrelated use. The immediate sale of the property by the charitable organization is considered to be a use unrelated to its tax-exempt purpose.

EXAMPLE I7-25 ▶ Laura purchases a painting for $3,000. Several years later she contributes the painting to a local college. The FMV of the painting is $5,000 at the time the property is contributed. The painting is both tangible personal property and capital gain property. The college places the painting in the library for display and study by art students. Because the college does not use the painting for purposes unrelated to its function as an educational institution, the amount of Laura's contribution is equal to its FMV ($5,000). On the other hand, if the college had sold the painting immediately after receiving it, the presumption is that the property's use was unrelated to the college's tax-exempt purpose. In this case, Laura's contribution is only $3000. ◀

CONTRIBUTION OF ORDINARY INCOME PROPERTY

General Rule. If ordinary income property is contributed to a charitable organization, the deduction is equal to the property's FMV minus the amount of gain that would be recognized if the property were sold at its FMV on the date of the contribution. In most cases, this deduction is equal to the property's adjusted basis. This rule applies regardless of the type of charitable organization to which the property is donated.

REAL-WORLD EXAMPLE

A retired congressman was not entitled to a charitable contribution of his papers because the papers were ordinary income property and had no basis. *James H. Morrison,* 71 T.C. 683 (1979).

For this purpose **ordinary income property** includes any property that would result in the recognition of income taxed at ordinary income rates if the property were sold. Thus, ordinary income property includes inventory, works of art or manuscripts created by the taxpayer, capital assets that have been held for one year or less, and Sec. 1231 property to the extent a sale would result in the recognition of ordinary income due to depreciation recapture.[46]

EXAMPLE I7-26 ▶ During the current year Bart purchases land as an investment for $10,000. Five months later he contributes the land to the United Way. At the time of the contribution the property's FMV is $15,000. The amount of Bart's contribution is $10,000 ($15,000 − [$15,000 − $10,000]) because he held the land for less than one year. ◀

EXAMPLE I7-27 ▶ Paul purchased a truck a few years ago for $20,000. During the current year, Paul donates the truck, which he used in his business, to a local community college. At the time of the contribution, the truck's adjusted basis is $5,000 and its FMV is $8,000. Because Paul would have recognized a $3,000 gain (all ordinary income under Sec. 1245) if the truck were sold at its FMV, the amount of the contribution is $5,000 ($8,000 − $3,000), which is equal to the truck's adjusted basis. ◀

---

[46] Reg. Secs. 1.170A-4(b)(1) and 1.170A-4(d). Sec. 1231 property includes property used in a trade or business that is subject to depreciation. If it is sold at a gain, part or all of the gain is treated as ordinary income. Any remaining gain is subject to the Sec. 1231 rules. (See Chapter I13 for an explanation of the depreciation recapture and Sec. 1231 rules.)

Donation of Inventory by a Corporation. Under certain circumstances, a corporation's donation of inventory to certain public charities gives rise to a contribution that is valued at more than the adjusted basis of the inventory. One exception is available if the inventory is to be used by the charity solely for the care of the ill, needy, or infants.[47] Another exception involves the donation of scientific equipment constructed by the taxpayer and donated to a college, university, or qualified research organization to be used for research, experimentation, or research training in the physical or biological sciences. A third exception is available for contributions of computer technology and equipment that is donated to public libraries and elementary and secondary schools.[48] In all three cases, the amount of the charitable contribution is the property's FMV, reduced by 50% of the ordinary income that would be recognized if the property were sold at its FMV. However, the amount of the contribution is limited to twice the basis of the property.

EXAMPLE I7-28 ▶ During the current year, Able Corporation, a manufacturer of medical supplies, donates some of its inventory to the American Red Cross. The Red Cross intends to use the inventory for the care of the needy and ill. At the time of the contribution, the FMV of the inventory is $10,000. Able's basis in the inventory is $3,000. Because this transaction qualifies under the exception, the amount of Able's contribution (before any limitations are applied) is $6,500 [$10,000 – (0.50 × $7,000)] but the actual amount of the contribution is limited to $6,000 (2 x the $3,000 basis in the property). ◀

REAL-WORLD EXAMPLE

The donation of blood is considered a personal nondeductible service.

CONTRIBUTION OF SERVICES. When a taxpayer renders services to a qualified charitable organization, the taxpayer may only deduct the unreimbursed expenses incurred incident to rendering the services. These items include out-of pocket transportation expenses, the cost of lodging and 50% of the cost of meals while away from home, and the cost of a uniform without general utility that is required to be worn in performing the donated services. The out-of-pocket expenses are deductible only if they are incurred by the taxpayer who actually renders the services to the charity. Taxpayers cannot take a deduction for expenses while away from home unless they experience no significant element of personal pleasure, recreation, or vacation in such travel. Instead of the actual costs of operating an automobile while performing the donated services, the law permits a deduction of 14 cents per mile.

EXAMPLE I7-29 ▶ During the current year, Tony spends a total of 100 hours developing an accounting system for the local council of the Boy Scouts of America. As an accountant, Tony earns $200 per hour. During the year, Tony also drives his car a total of 500 miles in performing the services for the Boy Scouts of America. If he uses the automatic mileage method to compute the amount of the charitable contribution, he can deduct $70 (0.14 × 500). No deduction is available for the value of 100 hours of Tony's contributed services. ◀

REAL-WORLD EXAMPLE

The cost of newspaper advertising, paper, pencils, and other supplies purchased by volunteers in connection with their involvement in the Volunteer Income Tax Assistance Program (VITA) is deductible. Rev. Rul. 80-45, 1980-1 C.B. 54.

Many employers allow employees to forgo vacation, sick, or personal leave in exchange for employer contributions to charity. On October 25, 2001, the IRS announced that businesses could deduct such charitable contributions as a business expense under Sec. 162. Furthermore, the IRS announced it would not require employees to report the contribution as income. This announcement, however, applies only to contributions made before January 1, 2003.[49]

DEDUCTION LIMITATIONS

OVERALL 50% LIMITATION. The charitable contribution deduction available for any tax year is subject to certain limitations. For individuals, the general overall limitation applicable to public charities is 50% of the taxpayer's AGI for the year. Any contributions in excess of the overall limitation may be carried forward and deducted in the subsequent 5 tax years. In addition, the tax law imposes further limitations on contributions of capital gain property to either a public charity or a private nonoperating foundation and all types of property contributions to private nonoperating foundations.

---

[47] Sec. 170(e). These charitable organizations are known as Sec. 501(c)(3) charities.

[48] Sec. 170(e)(6) Qualified donations can also be made to certain private foundations and other charitable organizations if the equipment is then contributed to one of the target organizations (schools and public libraries) within a specified period of time. In addition to inventory, this exception includes the donation of computer equipment that is no more than three years old.

[49] Notice 2001-69, 2001-46 I.R.B.

30% LIMITATION. Under certain circumstances, a special 30% of AGI limitation applies. Contributions of capital gain property (capital assets held over one year on which a gain would be realized if sold) to public charities are generally valued at the property's FMV, but are subject to an overall limit of 30% of AGI instead of a 50% limit. This limit does not apply, however, in the following situations:

KEY POINT

The generosity of Congress in permitting individuals to use FMV is tempered by the 30% of AGI limitation.

- Capital gain property (which is tangible personal property) donated to a public charity that does not put the property to its related use. In such cases, the amount of the contribution is scaled down by the capital gain that would be recognized if the property were sold.
- The taxpayer elects to reduce the amount of the charitable contribution deduction by the capital gain that would be recognized if the property were sold.

EXAMPLE I7-30 ▶ Joy donates a painting to the local university during a year in which she has AGI of $50,000. The painting, which cost $10,000 several years before, is valued at $30,000 at the time of the contribution. The university exhibits the painting in its art gallery. Because the painting is put to a use related to the university's purpose, the amount of Joy's contribution is $30,000. The amount of Joy's charitable deduction for the year, however, is limited to $15,000 (0.30 × $50,000 AGI) unless she elects to reduce the amount of the contribution by the long-term capital gain. ◀

The overall deduction limitation of 30% of AGI also applies to the contribution of all types of property other than capital gain property (e.g., cash and ordinary income property) to a private nonoperating foundation. However, the deductibility of certain contributions to this type of charity may be subject to even further restrictions.

20% LIMITATION ON CAPITAL GAIN PROPERTY CONTRIBUTED TO PRIVATE NONOPERATING FOUNDATIONS. Contributions of capital gain property to private nonoperating foundations are limited to the lesser of 20% of the taxpayer's AGI or 30% of the taxpayer's AGI, reduced by any contributions of capital gain property donated to a public charity.

CONTRIBUTIONS FOR ATHLETIC EVENTS. If a taxpayer makes a contribution to a college or university and in return receives the right to purchase tickets to athletic events, the taxpayer may deduct only 80% of the payment.

APPLYING THE DEDUCTION LIMITATIONS. Contributions subject only to the 50% of AGI limitation are accounted for before the contributions subject to the 30% of AGI limitation.

EXAMPLE I7-31 ▶ During a year when Ted's AGI is $70,000, he donates $22,000 to his church and $18,000 to a private nonoperating charity. The church contribution is initially subject to the 50% limitation and is fully deductible because the $22,000 contribution is less than the limitation amount of $35,000 (0.50 × $70,000). Ted's deduction for the contribution to the private nonoperating charity (a 30% charity) is limited to $13,000 (the lesser of the following three amounts):

The actual contribution	$18,000
The remaining 50% limitation after the contribution to Ted's church [(0.50 × $70,000) − $22,000]	$13,000
30% of AGI (0.30 × $70,000)	$21,000 ◀

APPLICATION OF CARRYOVERS

As noted earlier, any contributions that exceed the 50% limitation may be carried over and deducted in the subsequent five years. These carryovers are subject to the limitations that apply in subsequent years. Thus, carryovers may be deducted only to the extent that the limitation of the subsequent year exceeds the contributions made during that year.

TAX PLANNING

If a taxpayer has contribution carryovers that are about to expire, the taxpayer should consider reducing the current year's contribution so that the carryovers can be deducted.

These general rules also apply with regard to the special limitations. For example, if property subject to the 30% limitation is donated during the current year and the amount of the contribution exceeds the limitation, the excess may be carried over to the five subsequent years subject to the 30% limitation in the carryover years. In the carryover year, a deduction may be taken for the excess contribution to the extent that the 30% limitation of the subsequent year exceeds the amount of the property donated during the subsequent year subject to the 30% limitation. Excess contributions of property subject to the 20% limitation may also be carried over to the subsequent five years. This carryover is also subject to the special restrictions noted above for the 30% limitation. The carryovers are used in chronological order.

EXAMPLE I7-32 ▶ Assume that for the years 2000 through 2002, Joan reports AGI and makes charitable contributions in the following amounts:

	2000	*2001*	*2002*
AGI	$40,000	$40,000	$60,000
Cash contributions subject to the 50% of AGI limitation	25,000	23,000	24,000
50% of AGI limitation	20,000	20,000	30,000

The amount of the charitable contribution deduction for each year and the order in which the deduction and carryovers are used are as follows:

	2000	*2001*	*2002*
Amount of deduction	$20,000	$20,000	$30,000
Amount of carryover			
From 2000	5,000	5,000	0
From 2001		3,000	2,000 ◀

SPECIAL RULES FOR CHARITABLE CONTRIBUTIONS MADE BY CORPORATIONS

The rules governing charitable contributions made by corporations are generally the same as those pertaining to contributions made by individuals. However, certain differences do exist.

ETHICAL POINT

A tax practitioner should not be a party to the backdating of a Board of Director's authorization of a charitable contribution pledge so that the corporation may improperly deduct the contribution in the earlier year.

PLEDGES MADE BY AN ACCRUAL METHOD CORPORATION. Generally, taxpayers may only deduct actual contributions (not pledges) made during the tax year. This rule applies to both cash and accrual method taxpayers. A major exception to this general rule exists for accrual method corporations. Such corporations may elect to claim a charitable deduction for the year in which a pledge is made as long as the actual contribution is made by the fifteenth day of the third month following the close of the year in which the pledge is made.

LIMITATION APPLICABLE TO CORPORATIONS. Corporate charitable deductions are limited to 10% of the corporation's taxable income for the year. This amount is computed without regard to the dividends-received deduction, net operating loss or capital loss carrybacks, or any deduction for the charitable contribution itself. Excess contributions may be carried forward for five years and are deductible only if the current-year contributions are less than the current year's 10% limitation. The carryovers are used in chronological order.

SUMMARY OF DEDUCTION LIMITATIONS

The rules governing the deduction for charitable contributions are summarized in Topic Review I7-3.

STOP & THINK

Question: During the current year, Kim pledged to contribute $10,000 to both the Boy Scouts of America (BSA) and to a private nonoperating foundation. She wants to satisfy those pledges before the end of the year in order to take a deduction this year. She has enough cash to satisfy one of the pledges, but must either sell or donate some land in order to satisfy the other. The land she has in mind has a fair market value of $10,000 and a cost basis of $2,000. She purchased the land four years ago. Kim estimates that she will have AGI of $300,000 and will be in the 38.6% marginal tax bracket. Assuming that both charities would gladly accept either contribution, how should Kim satisfy these pledges?

Topic Review I7-3

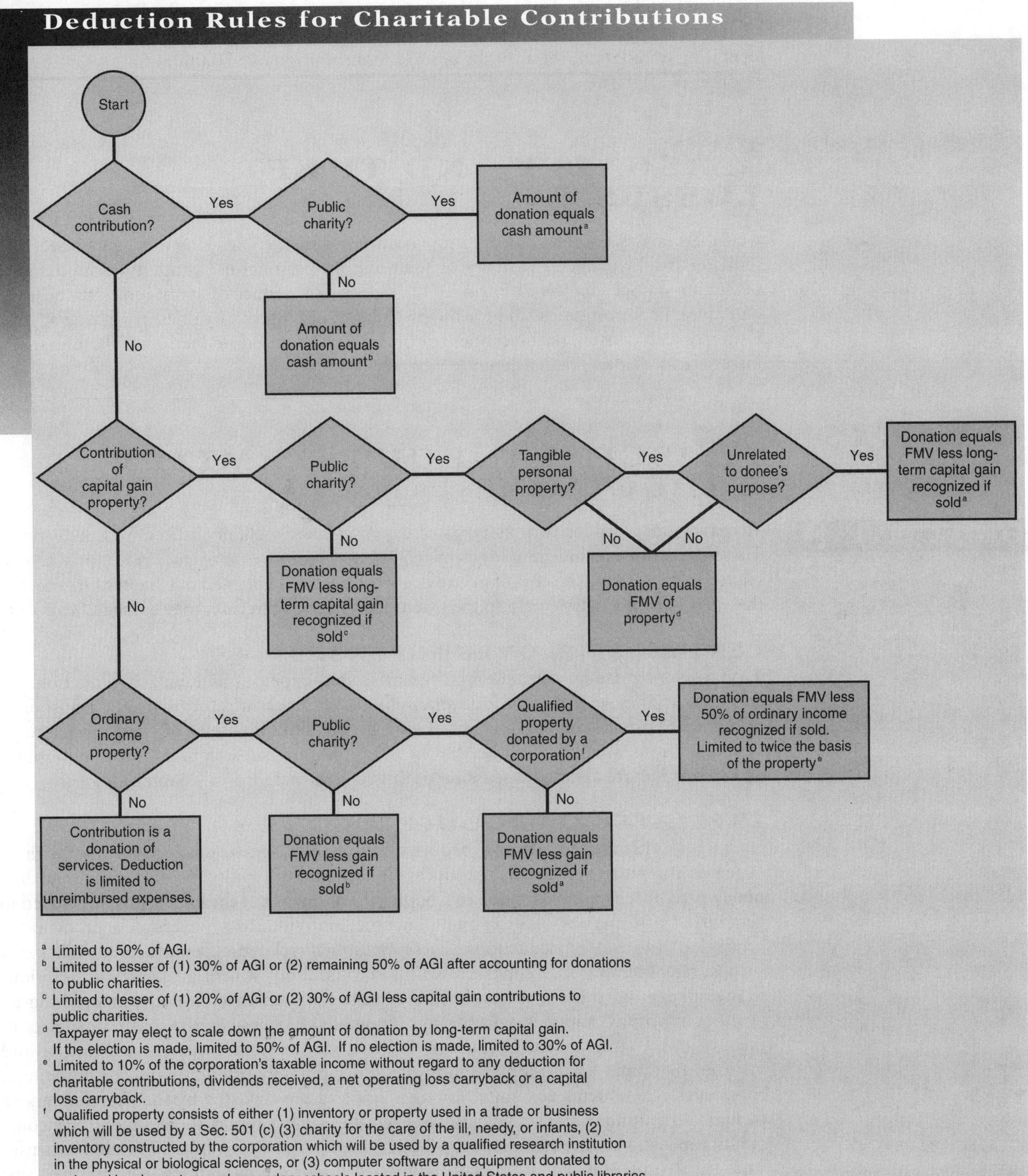

Solution: The amount of contribution of capital gain property to a public charity is the property's fair market value. Such contributions are subject to a 30% of AGI limitation. However, a contribution of capital gain property to a private non-operating private foundation is the property's fair market value, reduced by the gain that would be recognized if the property were sold (generally the property's basis). These contributions are subject to a 50% of AGI limitation. Since Kim's AGI for the year is so high, the limitations do not apply. Thus, Kim should contribute the land to the BSA and the cash to the private non-operating foundation, for a total charitable contribution of $20,000.

CASUALTY AND THEFT LOSSES

Generally, losses on personal-use property are not deductible. However, under Sec. 165 individuals may deduct a casualty or theft loss on personal-use property as an itemized deduction on Schedule A of Form 1040. Individuals deduct casualty losses on business and investment properties held for the production of rents or royalties in arriving at AGI. Other casualty losses on investment property are itemized deductions. These casualty losses are studied in greater depth in Chapter I8.

MISCELLANEOUS ITEMIZED DEDUCTIONS

OBJECTIVE 8

Identifying certain miscellaneous itemized deductions subject to the 2% of AGI limit

Taxpayers may deduct various types of expenses as miscellaneous itemized deductions. These deductions include employment-related expenses of employees, certain investment-related expenses, and the cost of tax advice. However, as explained in Chapter I9, generally these items are deductible only to the extent that, in the aggregate, they exceed 2% of AGI.

CERTAIN EMPLOYEE EXPENSES

Taxpayers may deduct certain employment-related expenses as itemized deductions on Schedule A. These expenses include *unreimbursed* expenditures for travel and transportation, dues to professional organizations, costs of job hunting, items of protective clothing or uniforms not suitable for everyday wear, union dues, subscriptions to trade journals, and so on. A more detailed discussion of this topic is included in Chapter I9.

EXPENSES TO PRODUCE INCOME

Under Sec. 212, individuals may deduct expenses incurred to produce income. If these expenses arise in an activity that produces either rental or royalty income, they are deductions *for* AGI (see the explanation in Chapter I6). However, if the expenses are incurred in generating other types of investment income, individual taxpayers deduct them on Schedule A as itemized deductions. These investment-related expenditures include items such as rental fees for safe-deposit boxes used to hold investment property, subscriptions to investment and trade journals, bank service charges on checking accounts used in an investment activity, and fees paid for consulting advice. These expenses are all subject to the 2% of AGI reduction. Certain investment income and expenses are earned and incurred by taxpayers in mutual funds and other publicly offered regulated investment companies. These items generally flow through and are reported by the shareholders or owners of the fund. Because typically these entities simply report the net income (income minus expenses) to the owners, Sec. 67(c)(2) exempts these investment-related expenses from the 2% of AGI limitation. Other types of flow-through entities (e.g., partnerships and S corporations) must report these expenses to their owners as separately stated items so that the 2% of AGI reduction may be applied to these expenses also.

ETHICAL POINT

If a client furnishes a handwritten list of his or her miscellaneous itemized deductions to a CPA, the CPA may in good faith rely on the information without verification. However, the CPA should not ignore the implications of information that is provided and should make reasonable inquiries if the information furnished appears to be incorrect, incomplete, or inconsistent.

COST OF TAX ADVICE

Section 212 provides individuals with a deduction for expenses incurred in connection with the determination, collection, or refund of any tax, including federal, state, local, and foreign income taxes as well as estate, gift, and inheritance taxes. These items include (1) tax return preparation fees, (2) appraisal fees incurred in determining the amount of a

REAL-WORLD EXAMPLE

A taxpayer claimed that it was necessary to take a leave of absence from his job in order to appear before the Tax Court, to type various legal papers, and to take notes during the trial. He was not allowed to deduct the so-called lost wages representing the amount of vacation time spent in defending the suit. *James P. Stuart,* 1987 PH T.C. Memo ¶87,386, 54 TCM 70.

casualty loss, certain capital improvements for a medical deduction, or the FMV of property donated to a qualified charity, (3) fees paid to an accountant for representation in a tax audit, (4) long-distance telephone calls responding to IRS questions, (4) costs of tax return preparation materials and books, and (5) legal fees incurred in planning the tax consequences dealing with estate planning. If an individual incurs these items in connection with the taxpayer's (1) trade or business (reported on Schedule C), (2) farm income (reported on Schedule F), or (3) an activity which produces rents or royalties (reported on Part I of Schedule E), they are *for* AGI deductions.[50] All other expenses incurred for tax advice are miscellaneous itemized deductions subject to the 2% of AGI limitation.

Fees that are not directly connected with the determination, collection, or refund of a tax or with the taxpayer's trade or business are personal expenses and are not deductible. Thus, legal fees incurred for drafting wills generally are not deductible. However, legal expenses incurred in tax fraud cases in connection with the filing of a fraudulent return generally are deductible.[51] Legal fees relating to a divorce generally are not deductible, unless they deal with tax-related items such as determining who will receive the exemption for dependent children. These fees are discussed in greater detail in Chapter I3.

REDUCTION OF CERTAIN ITEMIZED DEDUCTIONS

OBJECTIVE 9

Compute total itemized deductions for a taxpayer who is subject to the itemized deduction phase-out

ADDITIONAL COMMENT

The reduction in itemized deductions obscures the true marginal tax rate applicable to high-income taxpayers and can be thought of as a hidden tax rate.

Because of concerns with the budget deficit, Congress enacted Sec. 68 which provides for a reduction in the total amount of certain itemized deductions for high-income taxpayers.[52] This reduction applies only to individuals with AGI in excess of a certain threshold amount. This AGI threshold amount for 2002 is $137,300 ($68,650 for married people filing separate returns), and will be adjusted by an inflation factor for subsequent years. The reduction of the itemized deductions is 3% of the amount that the individual's AGI for the year exceeds the threshold amount. However, two limitations apply. First, the reduction in the itemized deductions cannot exceed 80% of the total itemized deductions other than medical expenses, investment interest, casualty losses, and wagering losses. Second, the 3% reduction is applied after taking into account the other limitations on itemized deductions (e.g., the 2% of AGI limitation on miscellaneous itemized deductions).

EXAMPLE I7-33 ▶ During 2002, John and Sue (a married couple filing a joint return) report AGI of $250,000. In addition, their itemized deductions consist of $10,000 charitable contributions, $4,000 real property taxes, and $8,000 state income taxes. Because their AGI exceeds $137,300, their itemized deductions for the year are limited to $18,619 ($22,000 − $3,381), computed as follows:

AGI	$250,000
Threshold	(137,300)
Excess	$112,700
Times: Reduction percentage	× 0.03
Potential reduction	$3,381
Limit to reduction:	
Charitable contributions	$ 10,000
Property taxes	4,000
State income taxes	8,000
Total	$ 22,000
Times: Limitation percentage	× 0.80
Overall limit on reduction	$17,600

The 80% limitation does not apply because the $3,381 reduction is less than $17,600. ◀

[50] Rev. Rul. 92-29, 1992-1 C.B. 20.

[51] Rev. Rul. 68-662, 1968-2 C.B. 69.

[52] However, in 2001, Congress authorized the elimination of these phase-outs, which will begin in 2006 and be complete in 2009.

EXAMPLE I7-34 ▶ Assume the same facts as Example I7-33 except that the $10,000 charitable contributions were instead medical expenses in excess of 7.5% of AGI and that the state income taxes were instead a deductible casualty loss (i.e., the amount in excess of the 10% of AGI limitation). Now John and Sue's allowable itemized deductions for the year are $18,800 ($22,000 − $3,200), computed as follows:

AGI	$250,000
Threshold	(137,300)
Excess	$112,700
Times: Reduction percentage	× 0.03
Potential reduction	$3,381
Limit to reduction:	
Real property taxes	$ 4,000
Times: Limitation percentage	× 0.80
Overall limit on reduction	$3,200 ◀

STOP & THINK *Question:* Joe is a general contractor who uses the cash method of accounting. He has been hired to do a job that will pay him $30,000. Under the terms of the agreement, Joe is to receive the full $30,000 when the job is complete. By December 15 of the current year, Joe estimates that the job can be completed with approximately seven more days of work. The person who hired Joe doesn't care if the job is completed in December of the current year or January of the subsequent year. Joe's AGI for the current year, excluding this job, will be $150,000. Joe and his wife, Kim, estimate that their state income taxes, residential interest, and charitable contributions for the current year total approximately $10,000. Because of a general economic slowdown, Joe estimates that his AGI for the subsequent year will be $90,000. What advice can you give Joe regarding when he should complete this job and collect the income?

Solution: For tax purposes, Joe should complete the job in January of the subsequent year for a couple of reasons. First, if their estimates are correct, Joe and Kim likely will be in the 30% marginal tax bracket for the current year and the 27% marginal tax bracket for the subsequent year. Second, if Joe is paid for the job in the current year, Joe and Kim's AGI will exceed the threshold amount, thus causing a reduction in their itemized deductions. This reduction increases their effective tax rate. On the other hand, if Joe and Kim report the $30,000 in income in the subsequent year, they will not have to reduce their itemized deductions of that year. Finally, since there is only a delay of a few days between collecting the income in the current year and delaying the collection into the subsequent year, present value issues regarding the receipt of the income don't need to be addressed.

TAX PLANNING CONSIDERATIONS

MEDICAL EXPENSE DEDUCTION

WORKING WITH THE 7.5% OF AGI FLOOR. As explained previously, a deduction for medical expenses is available to individuals only to the extent that those expenditures exceed 7.5% of the taxpayer's AGI for the year. Thus, many individuals find that no deduction is available, even though their medical expenses are relatively high. In these cases, taxpayers may obtain some benefit if they can bunch the medical expenses into one year. Orthodontic work, certain orthopedic treatment, noncosmetic elective surgery, and new eyeglasses are all examples of medical expenditures that may be either accelerated or delayed into a year in which other medical expenses are high or AGI is lower.

Generally, a deduction for medical expenses is allowed only in the year in which the expense is actually paid. The mere prepayment of future expenses usually does not accelerate the deduction. However, taxpayers may take a deduction in the earlier year of payment if there is a legal obligation to pay or if the prepayment is a requirement for the receipt of the medical care.[53] If the taxpayer has already received the medical treatment, but the taxpayer does not have sufficient cash to pay the bill, the taxpayer may preserve a deduction for the current year by either borrowing the cash to satisfy the bill or by using a credit card.

EXAMPLE I7-35 ▶ During the current year, Marty's estimated AGI is $50,000. Marty has already incurred $2,000 in medical expenses for himself and his family during the year. Because 7.5% of AGI for the year is $3,750, he receives no medical expense deduction. Marty plans to incur $4,000 in medical expenses for orthodontic work for his son next year. No other major medical expenses are anticipated, and Marty expects his AGI in the following year to remain the same. If these estimates are accurate, he will receive no medical deduction in either year. However, if the orthodontic work is started in the current year and Marty pays for the work, he will incur a total of $6,000 in medical expenses in the current year. Thus, $2,250 ($6,000 – $3,750) of the medical expenses may be deducted.

Mere prepayment in this case is not sufficient. Marty must have a portion of the orthodontic services performed in the earlier year. If he does not have sufficient cash to pay the bill in the current year, he could borrow the money or use a bank credit card.

KEY POINT

Even if the medical expenses exceed 7.5% of AGI the taxpayer may not benefit from the deduction if the medical expenses in addition to the other itemized deductions do not exceed the standard deduction.

MULTIPLE SUPPORT AGREEMENTS. An individual may deduct medical expenses incurred for him- or herself, his or her spouse, and any dependents. In cases where a multiple support agreement has been filed, the individual who is the subject of the agreement is treated as the dependent of the taxpayer who is entitled to the dependency exemption. Thus, to preserve the medical expense deduction, the taxpayer who is entitled to the dependency exemption should pay all medical expenditures for the dependent individual.

EXAMPLE I7-36 ▶ Amy, Bart, Clay, and Donna each provide 25% of the support of their father, Eric. Under the terms of a multiple support agreement, Bart, Clay, and Donna all agree to allow Amy to claim the dependency exemption with respect to Eric. During the year, $3,000 in medical expenses are incurred on Eric's behalf. If Amy pays these expenses, she may deduct them (subject to limitations). However, if Bart, Clay, or Donna pays these expenses, no one may claim the medical expenses as a deduction. ◀

INTEREST EXPENSE DEDUCTION

A taxpayer may deduct qualified residence interest incurred on a principal residence and one other qualified residence that is selected by the taxpayer. The taxpayer makes this choice annually. For the second residence to qualify, it must be used personally by the taxpayer for more than the greater of 14 days or 10% of the rental days during the year. If this test is met, however, the Sec. 280A limitations on the rental of vacation homes also apply. As explained in Chapter I6, under these rules, taxpayers must allocate expenses between the rental use and the personal use of the property. Taxpayers may deduct the expenses allocated to the rental use only to the extent of the rental income. Of the expenses allocated to the personal use, only the taxes and interest (if the residence is selected and if the loan is secured by the residence) are deductible as itemized deductions.

If the personal use by the taxpayer does not meet the test mentioned above, the interest allocated to the personal use cannot qualify as residence interest and it becomes nondeductible personal interest. Furthermore, the rental income and expenses allocated to the rental use of the property generally are subject to the passive loss rules (see Chapter I8). Under these rules, individuals generally can deduct losses generated from a passive activity only to the extent of the individual's passive income. Certain individuals, however, may deduct up to $25,000 of losses from the rental of real estate. Thus, the two alternatives and their consequences are as follows:

[53] *Robert M. Rose v. CIR*, 26 AFTR 2d 70-5653, 70-2 USTC ¶9646 (5th Cir., 1970). See also Rev. Ruls. 75-302, 1975-2 C.B. 86, and 75-303, 1975-2 C.B. 87, both clarified by Rev. Rul. 93-72, 1993-2 C.B. 77.

- Meet the test. No loss from the rental portion of the property may be deducted. However, the interest allocated to the personal use portion may be fully deductible as qualified residence interest.
- Do not meet the test. The interest allocated to the personal use portion is nondeductible personal interest. However, all of the passive loss from the rental portion is deductible against passive income. Furthermore, certain individuals may deduct up to $25,000 additional passive loss.

The alternative a taxpayer chooses depends on several factors, including the amount of the taxpayer's passive income, the total amount of itemized deductions, and whether the loan is secured by the vacation home, etc.

DEDUCTION FOR CHARITABLE CONTRIBUTIONS

SELF-STUDY QUESTION

What type of property lends itself to the "election to reduce"?

ANSWER

Property on which there is very little appreciation.

ELECTION TO REDUCE THE AMOUNT OF A CHARITABLE CONTRIBUTION. The election to reduce the contribution of capital gain property to public charities by the long-term capital gain that would be recognized if the property were sold is an annual election that applies to all capital gain property donated to public charities during the year. Because the election increases the ceiling limitation from 30% to 50%, under certain circumstances a taxpayer may actually receive a larger deduction for the year than would normally be available if the election were not made.

EXAMPLE I7-37 ▶ During the current year, Jane has AGI of $50,000. She donates a painting to the local university during the same year. The painting, valued at $30,000 at the time of contribution, cost her $25,000 several years before. The university displays the painting in its art museum. If Jane does not make the election, the amount of the contribution is equal to its FMV ($30,000). However, Jane's charitable contribution deduction for the year is limited to $15,000 ($50,000 × 0.30). If Jane makes the election to scale down the contribution amount, the deduction is reduced to $25,000 ($30,000 − $5,000 LTCG). The deduction limitation, however, increases to $25,000 for the year because the limitation is now based on 50% of AGI instead of 30%. In this case, Jane will receive a larger deduction for the year by making the election. However, the cost associated with this election is the loss of $5,000 of deduction because the total deduction is reduced from $30,000 to $25,000 if she makes the election. ◀

Many tax practitioners make this election only when preparing the taxpayer's final tax return. The taxpayer makes the election at this time because charitable contribution carryovers to the decedent's estate are not permitted.

ADDITIONAL COMMENT

To help determine the FMV of contributed property, taxpayers can read IRS Pub. No. 561, Determining the Value of Donated Property.

DONATION OF APPRECIATED CAPITAL GAIN PROPERTY. Instead of selling substantially appreciated capital gain property and donating the cash proceeds, the taxpayer should donate the property directly to charity. If property is donated in this way, the donor receives a deduction equal to the FMV of the property and does not recognize any taxable gain on the disposition.

EXAMPLE I7-38 ▶ Colleen wishes to satisfy a pledge of $100,000 made to a local university. She owns $100,000 worth of marketable securities purchased ten years ago for $30,000. Because the securities are marketable, the university is indifferent as to whether Colleen donates cash or the securities. Although her marginal tax rate is 38.6%, Colleen would be subject to a tax rate of 20% on the sale of the securities. She has enough AGI to be able to deduct the full contribution in the current year. The following chart summarizes the cash flows to Colleen under two different alternatives:

	Donate Securities	*Sell Securities and Donate Cash*
Proceeds of sale	0	$100,000
Tax on gain	0	(14,000)[a]
Cash payment to charity		(100,000)
Tax savings from the contribution deduction	$38,600[b]	38,600
Net tax benefit	$38,600	$24,600

[a] ($100,000 − $30,000) × 0.20 = $14,000.
[b] $100,000 × 0.386 = $38,600.

◀

In order to take a tax loss on business or investment property, a taxpayer should not donate property that has decreased in value. Rather, the property should be sold and the cash proceeds donated.

COMPLIANCE AND PROCEDURAL CONSIDERATIONS

MEDICAL EXPENSES

In certain cases, expenditures qualify as both a medical care expense and a dependent care expense (i.e., expenses for household and dependent care services that the taxpayer must pay to be gainfully employed). A taxpayer who incurs an expense that qualifies under both provisions may choose to take either a medical expense deduction or a tax credit under Sec. 21.[54] However, if a taxpayer takes a credit for these expenses, they are not deductible as medical expenses.

EXAMPLE I7-39 ▶ Joel's daughter, Debbie, is physically handicapped. As a result, Joel hires a nurse who provides daily care while he is at work. During the year, Joel pays the nurse a total of $3,000. This amount qualifies for both the dependent care credit and the medical expense deduction. If Joel takes the dependent care credit, the $3,000 may not be deducted as a medical expense. Because of the limitations imposed on each, the determination of which treatment is more advantageous depends on items such as the taxpayer's AGI, other medical expenses, and total itemized deductions. ◀

CONTRIBUTION OF PROPERTY

ADDITIONAL COMMENT

On Form 8283, the charitable organization is required to acknowledge receipt of the gift and to file an information return if the property is sold or disposed of within two years.

When property other than cash is donated to a qualifying charity, proper determination of the property's FMV is a critical issue. Because of actual and perceived abuses in this area, the IRS often scrutinizes and, if necessary, challenges the valuation of contributed property. This is especially true of property for which no published market quotes exist. If contributions of property exceed $500, the taxpayer must file Form 8283 (see Appendix B), which requires information about the type, location, holding period, basis, and FMV of the property. The taxpayer must also retain this information. If the noncash contributions exceed $5,000, the taxpayer must get an appraisal by a qualified appraiser and must submit an appraisal summary, signed by the appraiser and an authorized officer of the charitable organization, with Form 8283.[55] Taxpayers should keep a copy of completed Form 8283 and any attachments for their records. Publicly traded securities need not be appraised. Nonpublicly traded stock must be appraised only if its value exceeds $10,000.

REAL LIFE EXAMPLE

In one case the taxpayer, a CPA, failed to support a contribution with a qualified appraisal. As a result, his charitable deduction for art and printing supplies donated to a high school was denied. To substantiate the claimed $40,000 charitable deduction, the taxpayer submitted with Form 8283 an appraisal of the donated items made by the high school's principal. The principal, however, wasn't a "qualified appraiser." *D'Arcangelo*, TC Memo 1994-572 (1994).

CHARITABLE CONTRIBUTIONS

Individuals report their charitable contribution deductions on Schedule A of Form 1040. Out-of-pocket expenses and contributions by cash or check are all reported on line 15. All contributions of property are included on line 16. As previously mentioned, if noncash property contributions exceed $500, the taxpayer must attach Form 8283 (Noncash Charitable Contributions) to the return. The IRS has announced that if taxpayers do not attach Form 8283 to their tax returns in support of their noncash contributions, the deduction will be disallowed.[56]

[54] A credit of 30% of expenses for household and dependent care services is allowed if the dependent is under age 13 or a spouse or dependent who is mentally or physically incapable of caring for himself or herself. The credit is reduced 1% for every $2,000 (or portion thereof) of AGI over $10,000. (See the discussion on Personal Tax Credits in Chapter I14 for a more detailed explanation of the child and dependent care credit.)

[55] Reg. Sec. 1.170A-13(c). However, the requirement for an appraisal may be waived for contributions of inventory for the care of the ill, needy, or infants if the contribution is made by a closely held corporation or a personal service corporation. See Notice 89-56, 1989-1 C.B. 698.

[56] IRS Announcement 90-25, I.R.B. 1990-8, 25.

If the contribution is made in cash, the taxpayer must retain evidence of the donation by keeping a cancelled check or a receipt from the charitable organization. In the absence of a cancelled check or receipt, other reliable written records showing the charity's name and the date and amount of the contribution will be accepted. If the contribution is in the form of noncash property, the taxpayer is required to maintain records containing the

- Name and address of the charity to which the contribution was made
- Date and location of the contribution
- Description of the property
- FMV of the property
- Method of determining the property's FMV
- Signed copy of the appraisal report if an appraiser was used[57]

ADDITIONAL COMMENT

If the taxpayer's total deduction for art is $20,000 or more, he or she must include an 8 × 10 inch color photograph or a color transparency no smaller than 4 × 5 inches.

For charitable contributions of $250 or more, no deduction is allowed unless the contribution is substantiated by a contemporaneous, written acknowledgment by the donee organization. Separate payments generally are treated as separate contributions for purposes of applying the $250 threshold. This acknowledgment must contain the following information:

- The amount of cash and a description of any property contributed
- Whether or not the organization provided any goods or services in consideration for the cash or property received, including a description and good faith estimate of the value of any goods or services provided by the organization.

The acknowledgment is considered contemporaneous if it is obtained by the earlier of the date the taxpayer files a return for the year in question or the extended due date for filing such a return. This substantiation requirement is waived if the donee organization files a return that contains the required information.[58]

Additionally, certain disclosure requirements must be met by charitable organizations for a quid pro quo contribution in excess of $75. This $75 limit is applied separately on each transaction. A quid pro quo contribution is a transaction that is partly a contribution and partly a payment for goods and services. For such payments to be deductible, the donee organization must provide the donor with a written statement indicating

- That the amount of the deduction is limited to the excess of the cash and value of the contributed property over the value of the goods and services provided by the charitable organization.
- A good faith estimate of the value of the goods and services provided to the donor by the charitable organization.

Failure to make the required disclosure subjects the charitable organization to a $10 per contribution penalty unless the failure is due to reasonable cause. The penalty is capped at $5,000 per fund-raising event.[59]

EXAMPLE I7-40 ▶ During the current year, Peter Smith (Soc. Sec. no. 276-31-7242) reports AGI of $100,000. Smith also makes the following charitable contributions during the year:

- Smith performs voluntary dental work three days each month in rural areas of the state. Smith drives a total of 4,000 miles on these trips during the year.
- Smith makes the following contributions by cash or check: $750 to the city library, $2,000 to the United Way, $500 to a local community college, and $4,000 to his church.
- Smith contributes a tract of land to a small rural town. The town plans to erect a public library on the site. Smith purchased the land in 1986 for $5,000. Its appraised value at the time of the contribution is $8,000.

Smith's contributions are reported on the partially completed Schedule A shown in Figure I7-1. The out-of-pocket expenses of $560 (4,000 miles × $0.14) and the contributions by cash or

[57] Reg. Sec. 1.170A-13.
[58] Sec. 170(f)(8) and Reg. Sec. 1.170A-13(f).
[59] Sec. 6115.

SCHEDULES A&B (Form 1040)

Department of the Treasury
Internal Revenue Service (99)

Schedule A—Itemized Deductions

(Schedule B is on back)

▶ Attach to Form 1040. ▶ See Instructions for Schedules A and B (Form 1040).

OMB No. 1545-0074

2001

Attachment Sequence No. **07**

Name(s) shown on Form 1040: Peter Smith

Your social security number: 276 31 7242

Medical and Dental Expenses		**Caution.** Do not include expenses reimbursed or paid by others.				
	1	Medical and dental expenses (see page A-2)	1			
	2	Enter amount from Form 1040, line 34 [2]				
	3	Multiply line 2 above by 7.5% (.075)	3			
	4	Subtract line 3 from line 1. If line 3 is more than line 1, enter -0-			4	
Taxes You Paid (See page A-2.)	5	State and local income taxes	5			
	6	Real estate taxes (see page A-2)	6			
	7	Personal property taxes	7			
	8	Other taxes. List type and amount ▶	8			
	9	Add lines 5 through 8			9	
Interest You Paid (See page A-3.)	10	Home mortgage interest and points reported to you on Form 1098	10			
	11	Home mortgage interest not reported to you on Form 1098. If paid to the person from whom you bought the home, see page A-3 and show that person's name, identifying no., and address ▶	11			
Note. Personal interest is not deductible.	12	Points not reported to you on Form 1098. See page A-3 for special rules	12			
	13	Investment interest. Attach Form 4952 if required. (See page A-3.)	13			
	14	Add lines 10 through 13			14	
Gifts to Charity If you made a gift and got a benefit for it, see page A-4.	15	Gifts by cash or check. If you made any gift of $250 or more, see page A-4	15	7,810		
	16	Other than by cash or check. If any gift of $250 or more, see page A-4. You **must** attach Form 8283 if over $500	16	8,000		
	17	Carryover from prior year	17			
	18	Add lines 15 through 17			18	15,810 –
Casualty and Theft Losses	19	Casualty or theft loss(es). Attach Form 4684. (See page A-5.)			19	
Job Expenses and Most Other Miscellaneous Deductions	20	Unreimbursed employee expenses—job travel, union dues, job education, etc. You **must** attach Form 2106 or 2106-EZ if required. (See page A-5.) ▶	20			
	21	Tax preparation fees	21			
(See page A-5 for expenses to deduct here.)	22	Other expenses—investment, safe deposit box, etc. List type and amount ▶	22			
	23	Add lines 20 through 22	23			
	24	Enter amount from Form 1040, line 34 [24]				
	25	Multiply line 24 above by 2% (.02)	25			
	26	Subtract line 25 from line 23. If line 25 is more than line 23, enter -0-			26	
Other Miscellaneous Deductions	27	Other—from list on page A-6. List type and amount ▶			27	
Total Itemized Deductions	28	Is Form 1040, line 34, over $132,950 (over $66,475 if married filing separately)? ☐ **No.** Your deduction is not limited. Add the amounts in the far right column for lines 4 through 27. Also, enter this amount on Form 1040, line 36. ☐ **Yes.** Your deduction may be limited. See page A-6 for the amount to enter.			▶ 28	

For Paperwork Reduction Act Notice, see Form 1040 instructions. Cat. No. 11330X **Schedule A (Form 1040) 2001**

FIGURE I7-1 ▶ PARTIALLY COMPLETED SCHEDULE A

check of $7,250 (library, United Way, church, and community college) are totaled and reported on line 15. The property contribution of $8,000 is separately stated on line 16. Because Smith contributes property with a value exceeding $500, Form 8283, an appraisal summary, and signed statements by the qualified appraiser and an authorized official of the organization that received the property must be attached to the return. In addition, for the donations that separately exceed $250, Peter must obtain and retain written acknowledgments from the donee organizations in order for the contributions to be deductible. ◀

TAXES

Individuals generally report their deduction for property taxes on Schedule A of Form 1040. However, if the taxes are incurred in the taxpayer's business, they are reported on Schedule C. Taxes incurred for the production of rents and royalties are reported on Schedule E. Taxes incurred in the taxpayer's farming business are reported on Schedule F. State and local income taxes imposed on individuals are always reported on Schedule A, even if the individual is self-employed.

Real estate brokers are required to report any real estate tax allocable to the purchaser of a residence. (See the discussion in this chapter regarding the allocation of real estate taxes between the seller and buyer of a residence.)[60] This information is reported by the broker on Form 1099-S (Proceeds from Real Estate Transactions).

EXAMPLE I7-41 ▶ During the year, Andrea incurs $1,500 in property taxes on a two-family house. Andrea lives in one unit and rents out the other. She also pays $100 in registration fees and $600 in personal property taxes on her automobile, based on its value. Andrea uses the automobile 80% of the time in an unincorporated business. During the current year, she also pays $2,000 in state income taxes, all of which is attributable to her income of the prior year from the unincorporated business.

Because one-half of the real estate taxes are attributable to property used to produce rental income, $750 (0.50 × $1,500) is reported on Schedule E, and the remaining personal-use portion ($750) is reported on Schedule A. Because 80% of the use of the automobile is in Andrea's business, $80 (0.80 × $100) of the registration fee is deductible as a business expense on Schedule C. The remaining $20 is not deductible because the registration fee is not a tax. However, $480 (0.80 × $600) of the personal property tax on the automobile is deductible as a business expense on Schedule C. The remaining $120 is deductible as a tax on Schedule A. Finally, even though the tax is related to Andrea's business income, all $2,000 of the state income tax is reported on Schedule A. Because the state income tax is paid in the current year, it is deductible in the current year. ◀

WHAT WOULD YOU DO IN THIS SITUATION?

GIVING TO BOTH: GOODWILL AND THE IRS

Much has been written about abusive practices concerning the valuation of noncash property donated to qualified charities. Under Sec. 170, both corporations and individuals may deduct the FMV of property contributed to charitable organizations. Of course, a number of valuation and percentage limitations and carryover rules are applicable to both individual and corporate taxpayers.

Assume your clients, Mr. and Mrs. Nicholas Nice, come into your office on December 27 for some year-end tax planning. Your review of their tax situation indicates that they have made substantial donations of clothing and household goods to Goodwill Industries. They have obtained proper documentation for donations made during the year but do not know how to qualify for taking a charitable deduction vis-à-vis valuation, forms, and the like. They do know that their original cost basis in the donated goods was $15,000 and that the goods were in usable condition at the time of the donation. What tax and ethical issues should be considered?

---

[60] Sec. 6045(e)(4) and NOTICE 93-4, 1993-1 C.B. 295.

PROBLEM MATERIALS

DISCUSSION QUESTIONS

I7-1 a. A taxpayer may deduct medical expenses incurred on behalf of which people?
b. In the case of children of divorced parents, must the parent who is entitled to the dependency exemption pay the medical expenses of the child to ensure that the expenses are deductible? Explain.
c. Who should pay the medical expenses of an individual who is the subject of a multiple support agreement?

I7-2 What is the definition of medical care for purposes of the medical care deduction?

I7-3 a. What is the definition of cosmetic surgery under the Internal Revenue Code?
b. Is the cost of cosmetic surgery deductible as a medical expense? Explain.

I7-4 a. If a taxpayer must travel away from his or her home in order to obtain medical care, which en route costs, if any, are deductible as medical expenses?
b. Are there any limits imposed on the deductibility of these expenses?

I7-5 What are the rules dealing with the deductibility of the cost of meals and lodging incurred while away from home in order to receive medical treatment as an outpatient?

I7-6 a. Which types of capital expenditures incurred specifically for medical purposes are deductible?
b. What limitations, if any, are imposed on the deductibility of these expenditures?

I7-7 Bill, a plant manager, is suffering from a serious ulcer. Bill's doctor recommends that he spend three weeks fishing and hunting in the Colorado Rockies. Can Bill deduct the costs of the trip as a medical expense?

I7-8 In what cases are medical insurance premiums paid by an individual not deductible as qualified medical expenses?

I7-9 What is the limit placed on medical expense deductions? When can a deduction be taken for medical care? What if the medical care is prepaid?

I7-10 a. Which taxes are specifically deductible for federal income tax purposes under Sec. 164?
b. If a tax is not specifically listed in Sec. 164, under what circumstances may it still be deductible?

I7-11 If Susan overpays her state income tax due to excess withholdings, can she deduct the entire amount in the year withheld? When Susan receives a refund from the state how must she treat that refund for tax purposes?

I7-12 What is an ad valorem tax? If a tax that is levied on personal property is not an ad valorem tax, under what circumstances may it still be deductible?

I7-13 When real estate is sold during a year, why is it necessary that the real estate taxes on the property be apportioned between the buyer and seller?

I7-14 a. Identify the different categories of interest expense an individual may incur. How is the classification of the interest determined?
b. Are these different categories of interest deductible? If so, how?

I7-15 At times, the term *points* is used to refer to different types of charges. Define the term and describe when points are deductible.

I7-16 In which year or years are points (representing prepaid interest on a loan) deductible?

I7-17 Why does Sec. 267 impose a restriction on the deductibility of expenses accrued and payable by an accrual-method taxpayer to a related cash-method taxpayer?

I7-18 a. What is the amount of the annual limitation placed on the deductibility of investment interest expense?
b. Explain how net investment income is calculated.
c. Is any disallowed interest expense for the year allowable as a deduction in another year? If so, when?

I7-19 Explain what acquisition indebtedness and home equity indebtedness are with respect to a qualified residence of a taxpayer, and identify any limitations on the deductibility of interest expense on this indebtedness.

I7-20 Explain what a qualified residence is for purposes of qualified residence interest.

I7-21 Why is interest expense disallowed if it is incurred to purchase or carry tax-exempt obligations?

I7-22 When is interest generally deductible for cash-method taxpayers? Explain if the general rule applies to prepaid interest, interest paid with loan proceeds, discounted notes, and personal interest. If the general rule does not apply, explain when these interest expenses are deductible.

I7-23 a. For purposes of the charitable contribution deduction, what is capital gain property? Ordinary income property?
b. What is the significance of classifying property as either capital gain property or ordinary income property?

I7-24 How is the *amount* of a charitable contribution of capital gain property determined if it is donated to a private nonoperating foundation? How does this determination differ if capital gain property is donated to a public charity?

I7-25 May an individual who is married and files a joint return deduct any charitable contributions if the itemized deductions total $7,000 (of which $3,000 are qualified charitable contributions)?

I7-26 For individuals, what is the overall deduction limitation on charitable contributions? What is the limitation for corporations?

I7-27 If a taxpayer's charitable contributions for any tax year exceed the deduction limitations, may the excess contributions be deducted in another year? If so, in which years may they be deducted?

I7-28 How are charitable contribution deductions reported on the tax return for individuals? What reporting requirements must be met for the contribution of property?

I7-29 List some of the more common miscellaneous itemized deductions and identify any limitations that are imposed on the deductibility of these items.

I7-30 Certain itemized deductions of high-income taxpayers must be reduced. Which itemized deductions are subject to this reduction and when does the reduction apply?

ISSUE IDENTIFICATION QUESTIONS

I7-31 Wayne and Maria file a joint tax return on which they itemize their deductions and report AGI of $50,000. During the year they incurred $1,500 of medical expenses when Maria broke her leg. Furthermore, their dentist informed them that their daughter, Alicia, needs $3,000 of orthodontic work to correct her overbite. Wayne also needs a new pair of eyeglasses that will cost $300. What tax issues should Wayne and Maria consider?

I7-32 This year, Chuck took out a loan to purchase some raw land for investment. He paid $40,000 for the land, and he expects that within 5 years the land will be worth at least $75,000. Chuck is married, and his AGI for the year is $325,000. Chuck paid $4,300 in interest on the loan this year. Chuck has $2,600 in interest income and $1,300 in dividend income for the year. He plans to itemize his deductions, so he can use the interest expense to offset his investment income. What tax issues should Chuck consider?

I7-33 During the current year, George made contributions totaling $40,000 to an organization called the National Endowment for the Preservation of Liberty (NEPL). Later during the year, the NEPL started giving money to a political candidate to help with his campaign expenses. What tax issues should George consider?

I7-34 During the current year, Bob has AGI of $100,000. He donates stock to his church that was purchased two years ago for $55,000. The FMV of the stock is $60,000. Bob has $5,000 of unused excess contributions from a prior year. What tax issues should Bob consider?

PROBLEMS

I7-35 *Medical Expense Deduction.* During 2002, Angela sustains serious injuries from a snow-skiing accident. She incurs the following expenses:

Item	*Amount*
Doctor bills	$11,700
Hospital bills	9,400
Legal fees in suit against ski resort	3,000

Angela is single and has no dependents. During 2002, her salary is $58,000. She pays $600 in medical and dental insurance premiums, $2,750 in mortgage interest on her home, and $1,200 in interest on her car loan. Her health insurance provider reimburses her for $10,000 of the medical expenses. What is her 2002 taxable income?

I7-36 *Reimbursement of Previously Deducted Medical Expenses.* Assume the same facts as in Problem I7-35. In addition, assume that in 2003, Angela receives an additional $7,000 in a settlement of a lawsuit arising because of the snow-skiing accident. $4,000 of the settlement is to pay Angela's medical bills, and $3,000 is to reimburse her legal expenses. What is the proper tax treatment of this $7,000 settlement?

I7-37 *Medical Expense Deduction.* Dan lives in Duncan, a small town in Arizona. Because of a rare blood disease, Dan is required to take special medical treatments once a month. The closest place these treatments are available to Dan is in Phoenix, 200 miles away. The treatments are provided on an outpatient basis but require him to stay overnight in Phoenix. During the year, Dan makes 12 trips to Phoenix by automobile to receive the treatments. The motel he always stays in charges $85 per night. For the year, Dan also spends a total of $250 for meals on these trips. $100 of this $250 is spent while en route to Phoenix. What is the amount of Dan's qualified medical expenses for the year?

I7-38 *Medical Expense Deduction.* Chad is divorced and has custody of Brett, his 14-year-old son. Chad's ex-wife has custody of their daughter, Sara. During the year, Chad incurs $3,000 for orthodontic work for Sara to correct a severe overbite and $2,000 in unreimbursed medical expenses associated with Brett's broken leg. Chad also pays $900 in health insurance premiums. Both Brett and Sara are covered under Chad's medical insurance plan. In addition, Chad incurs $400 for prescription drugs and $1,000 in doctor bills for himself. Chad's AGI is $40,000. What is Chad's medical expense deduction for the year assuming that his other itemized deductions exceed the standard deduction?

I7-39 *Medical Expense Deduction.* In 2002, Charla, a single taxpayer with no dependents, was severely hurt in a farm accident. The accident left Charla's legs 85% paralyzed. After incurring $14,000 of medical expenses at the hospital, the doctor recommended that Charla install a pool at her home for therapy. The pool cost $25,000 to install and increased the value of her home by $22,000. She spent $930 maintaining the pool in 2002 and $1,060 in 2003. Charla also purchased a wheelchair on December 28, 2002 for $2,300, which she charged to her credit card. She paid her credit card bill on January 6, 2003. She also purchased a hospital bed for $3,800, but did not pay for the bed until 2003. Charla paid her physical therapist $4,000 for services to be performed in 2003. Charla paid $1,200 in medical insurance premiums in both 2002 and 2003. In 2003, the insurance company reimbursed Charla $9,000 for her hospital stay in 2002. Her AGI for 2002 and 2003 is $38,000 and $43,000, respectively, not considering any of the above items. Charla has no other itemized deductions in either year.

a. What is Charla's taxable income for 2002?
b. What is Charla's medical expense deduction for 2003? How does she treat the reimbursement?

I7-40 *Deduction of Taxes.* Joyce is a single, cash method taxpayer. On April 11, 2001, Joyce paid $120 with her 2000 state income tax return. During 2001, Joyce had $1,600 in state income taxes withheld. On April 13, 2002, Joyce paid $70 with her 2001 state tax return. During 2002, she had $1,850 in state income taxes withheld from her paycheck. Upon filing her 2002 tax return on April 15, 2003, she received a refund of $450 for excess state income taxes withheld. Joyce had total AGI in 2002 and 2003 of $51,000 and $53,500, respectively. In 2002, Joyce also paid $2,900 in qualified residence interest.

a. What is the amount of state income taxes Joyce may include as an itemized deduction for 2001?
b. What is the allowed itemized deduction for state income taxes for 2002?
c. What is her taxable income for 2002?
d. What is her AGI for 2003?

I7-41 Assume the same facts as Problem I7-40, but change the amount of Joyce's mortgage interest to $3,300.

a. What is her taxable income for 2002?
b. What is her AGI for 2003?

I7-42 *Deduction of Taxes.* Dawn, a single, cash method taxpayer, paid the following taxes in 2002: Dawn's employer withheld $5,400 for federal income taxes, $2,000 for state income taxes, and $3,800 for FICA from her 2002 paychecks. Dawn purchased a new car and paid $600 in sales tax and $70 for the license. The car's FMV was $20,000 and it weighed 3,000 pounds. The county also assessed a property tax on the car. The tax was 2% of its value and $10 per hundredweight. The car is used 100% of the time for personal purposes. Dawn sold her house on April 15, 2002. The county's property tax on the home for 2002 is $1,850, payable on February 1, 2003. Dawn's AGI for the year is $50,000 and her other itemized deductions exclusive of taxes are $4,000.

a. What is Dawn's deduction for taxes in 2002?
b. Where on Dawn's tax return should she report her deduction for taxes?

I7-43 *Apportionment of Real Estate Taxes.* On May 1 of the current year, Tara sells a building to Janet for $500,000. Tara's basis in the building is $300,000. The county in which the building is located has a real property tax year that ends on June 30. The taxes are payable by September 1 of that year. On September 1, Janet pays the annual property taxes of $6,000. Both Tara and Janet are calendar-year, cash method taxpayers. The closing agreement does not separately account for the property taxes.

a. What amount of real property taxes may Janet deduct in the current year?

b. What amount of real property taxes may Tara deduct in the current year?

c. If no apportionment on the real property taxes is made in the sales agreement, what is Tara's total selling price of the building? Janet's basis for the building?

I7-44 *Classification of Interest Expense.* On January 1 of the current year, Scott borrowed $80,000, pledging the assets of his business as collateral. He immediately deposited the money in an interest-bearing checking account. Scott already had $20,000 in this account. On April 1, Scott invests $75,000 in a limited real estate partnership. On July 1, he buys a new ski boat for $12,000. On August 1, he makes a $10,000 capital contribution to his unincorporated business. Scott repays $50,000 of the loan on November 30 of the current year. Classify Scott's interest expense for the year.

I7-45 *Investment Income and Deductions.* During 2002, Travis takes out a $40,000 loan, using stock he owns as collateral. He uses $10,000 to purchase a car, which he uses 100% for personal use. He uses the remaining funds to purchase stocks and bonds. He pays $3,200 interest on the loan. Travis also reports the following for the year:

AGI without any investment income	$150,000
State income taxes paid	8,400
Dividend income	10,000
Interest income	2,100
Investment expenses (exclusive of interest)	8,000
Net short term capital gains	7,300
Net long term capital gain	8,800

Travis is married and files a joint tax return. What is his net taxable income?

I7-46 *Qualified Residence Interest.* During the current year, Tina purchases a beachfront condominium for $600,000, paying $150,000 down and taking out a $450,000 mortgage, secured by the property. At the time of the purchase, the outstanding mortgage on her principal residence is $700,000. This debt is secured by the residence and the FMV of the principal residence is $1,400,000. She purchased the principal residence in 1994. What is the amount of qualified indebtedness on which Tina may deduct the interest payments?

I7-47 *Qualified Residence Interest.* Several years ago, Magdelena purchased a new residence for $300,000. Currently, the outstanding mortgage on the residence is $260,000. The current fair market value of the home is $330,000. Magdelena wants to borrow a sizeable sum of money to pay for the college education costs of her two children and believes the interest would be deductible if she takes out a home equity loan. For each of the independent situations below, determine the amount of the loan on which Magdelena may deduct the interest as qualified residence interest.

a. Magdelena borrows $50,000 as a home equity loan.

b. Magdelena borrows $80,000 as a home equity loan.

c. Alternatively, assume the current fair market value of her residence is $375,000 and she borrows $110,000 as a home equity loan.

d. Alternatively, assume the current outstanding balance of the mortgage Magdelena incurred to purchase the home is $1,200,000, the home's fair market value is $1,400,000, and she borrows $80,000 as a home equity loan.

I7-48 *Interest Between Related Parties.* Crown Corporation is an accrual method taxpayer owned 55% by Brett and 45% by Susie. Brett and Susie are good friends and have been business associates for several years. BJ Partnership is a cash method taxpayer, owned 40% by Brett and 60% by Jeremy, Brett's uncle. Both Crown Corporation and BJ Partnership are calendar year entities. On January 5 of the current year, Crown borrows $50,000 from BJ Partnership, and pays 8% interest on the loan. Crown must pay the interest on January first of next year.

a. What amount of interest expense can Crown Corporation deduct in the current year?

b. How would your answer change if Jeremy were Brett's brother, instead of his uncle?

I7-49 *Timing of Interest Deduction.* On April 1 of the current year, Henry borrows $12,000 from the bank for a year. Because the note is discounted for the interest charge and Henry receives proceeds of $10,200, he is required to repay the face amount of the loan

($12,000) in four equal quarterly payments beginning on July 1 of the current year. Henry is a cash method individual.

a. What is the amount of Henry's interest expense deduction in the current year with respect to this loan?
b. Assume the same facts except that the initial starting date when the repayments begin is April 1 of the following year. What is the amount of Henry's interest expense deduction in the current year?
c. Assume the same facts as in Part b, except that Henry is an accrual method taxpayer. What is the amount of his interest expense deduction in the current year?

I7-50 ***Itemized Deductions.*** During 2002, Doug incurs the following deductible expenses: $2,100 in state income taxes, $2,000 in local property taxes, $800 in medical expenses, and $1,500 in charitable contributions. He is single, has no dependents, and has $35,000 AGI for the year. What is the amount of Doug's taxable income?

I7-51 ***Computation of Taxable Income.*** During 2002, James, a single, cash method taxpayer incurred the following expenditures:

Qualified medical expenses	$ 8,000
Investment interest expense	16,000
Other investment activity expenses	15,000
Qualified residence interest	12,000
Interest on loan on personal auto	2,000
Charitable contributions	3,000
State income tax paid	7,000
Property taxes	4,000
Tax return preparation and consulting fees	5,000

James's income consisted of the following items:

Salary	$70,000
Interest and Dividend income	20,000
Long-term Capital gains	23,000
Long-term Capital losses	(15,000)

a. Compute James's taxable income for the year (assuming that he makes an election to have the net capital gain taxed at the regular tax rates).
b. What is James' investment interest carryover (if any)?

I7-52 ***Computation of Taxable Income.*** Assume all the same facts as in Problem I7-51 except that James's salary income is $150,000 instead of $70,000 and that he does not make the election. Compute James's taxable income for the year.

I7-53 ***Charitable Contributions: Services.*** Donna is an attorney who renders volunteer legal services to a Legal Aid Society, which provides legal advice to low-income individuals. The Legal Aid Society is a qualified charitable organization. During the current year she spends a total of 200 hours in this volunteer work. Her regular billing rate is $150 per hour. In addition, she spends a total of $800 in out-of-pocket costs in providing these services. She receives no compensation and is not reimbursed for her out-of-pocket costs. What is Donna's charitable contribution for the year because of these activities?

I7-54 ***Charitable Contribution Limitations.*** In each of the following independent cases, determine the amount of the charitable contribution and the limitation that would apply. In each case, assume that the donee is a qualified public charity.

a. Sharon donates a tract of land to a charitable organization. She has held the land for seven years. Her basis in the land is $10,000 and its FMV is $40,000.
b. Assume the same facts in Part a, except that Sharon has held the land for only 11 months and that its FMV is $23,000.
c. Jack purchases a historical document for $50,000. He donates the historical document to a charitable organization two years later. The organization plans to use it for research and study. Its FMV at the time of the donation is $100,000.
d. Assume the same facts in Part c, except that the organization plans to sell the document and put the money into an endowment fund.
e. Valerie donates some inventory to a charitable organization. The inventory is purchased for $500 and its FMV is $1,200 at the time of the donation. She held the inventory for seven months.

I7-55 *Charitable Contributions to Private Nonoperating Foundations.* Assume the same facts as Problem I7-54, except that the qualified organization is a private nonoperating foundation. Determine the amount of the charitable contribution for Parts a through e.

I7-56 *Charitable Contribution Limitations.* During the current year, Helen donates stock worth $50,000 to her local community college. Two years ago the stock cost Helen $40,000. Her AGI for the current year is $100,000. Beginning next year, the bulk of her income will be from tax-exempt municipal securities. Thus, she is not interested in any carryover of excess charitable contribution. What is the maximum charitable contribution deduction Helen may take this year?

I7-57 *Charitable Contribution Limitations.* During the current year, Melissa reports AGI of $200,000. As part of some estate planning, she donates $30,000 to her alma mater, Middle State University, and $65,000 to a private nonoperating foundation.

a. What is the amount of Melissa's charitable deduction for the current year?

b. Assume the same facts in a. except that she donates $45,000 to Middle State University.

I7-58 *Corporate Charitable Contributions.* Circle Corporation, an accrual method taxpayer, manufactures and sells mainframe computers. In January of the current year, Circle Corporation donates a mainframe that was part of its inventory to City College. City College will use the computer for physical science research. Circle's basis in the mainframe is $300,000. The computer's FMV is $650,000. On December 15 of the current year, Circle also pledged stock to the Red Cross and promised delivery of the stock by March 1 of the following year. The stock's FMV is $100,000 and Circle's adjusted basis in the stock is $50,000. Circle's taxable income (before deducting any charitable contributions) for the current year is $4,000,000.

a. What is the amount of Circle's charitable contribution for the current year?

b. How much of the contribution can Circle deduct in the current year and how much may be carried over, if any?

I7-59 *Charitable Contribution Carryovers.* Bonnie's charitable contributions and AGI for the past four years were as follows:

	1999	*2000*	*2001*	*2002*
AGI	$50,000	$55,000	$58,000	$60,000
Contributions subject to the 50% limitation	40,000	29,000	25,000	10,000

What is the amount of the charitable deduction for each year and the order in which the deduction and carryovers are used?

COMPREHENSIVE PROBLEM

I7-60 Tim and Monica Nelson are your newest tax clients. They provide you with the following information relating to their 2002 tax return:

1. Tim works as a pediatrician for the county hospital. The W-2 form he received from the hospital shows wages of $145,000 and state income tax withheld of $8,500.
2. Monica spends much of her time volunteering, but also works as a substitute teacher for the local schools. During the year, she spent 900 hours volunteering. When she doesn't volunteer, she earns $8.00 per hour working as a substitute. The W-2 form she received from the school district shows total wages of $3,888 and state income tax withheld of $85.
3. On April 13, the couple paid $250 in state taxes with their 2001 state income tax return.
4. On December 18, the Nelsons donated a small building to the Boy Scouts of America. They purchased the building three years ago for $80,000. A professional appraiser determined the fair market value of the home was $96,000 on December 12.
5. Tim and Monica both received corrective eye surgery, at a total cost of $3,000. They also paid $1,900 in health insurance premiums.
6. On June 1, the couple bought a car for $16,000, paying $4,000 down and borrowing $12,000. They paid $750 total interest on the loan in 2002.
7. On June 10, the Nelsons took out a home equity loan of $20,000 to expand their home. They paid $850 interest with their monthly payments on the loan.

8. The Nelsons paid $2,300 interest on their original home loan.
9. They sold stock in Cabinets, Inc. for $5,200, which they purchased for $7,900 in March of the current year. They also sold stock in The Outdoor Corporation for $12,500, which they purchased several years ago for $8,600.
10. Tim incurred the following expenses related to his profession, none of which were reimbursed by his employer:

Item	*Amount*
Subscriptions to medical journals	$400
American Medical Association (AMA) annual membership fee	250

11. During the year, the couple paid their former tax advisor $700 to prepare their prior year tax return.
12. The Nelsons do not have children, and they do not provide significant financial support to any family members.

Required: Compute the Nelsons' taxable income for 2002.

TAX STRATEGY PROBLEMS

I7-61 Dean makes a pledge of $30,000 to a local college. The college is willing to accept either cash or marketable securities in fulfillment of the pledge. Dean owns stock in Ajax Corporation worth $30,000. The stock was purchased five years ago for $10,000, Dean's marginal tax rate is 38.6%. Should Dean sell the stock and then donate the cash, or should he donate the stock directly? Compute the net tax benefit from each alternative and explain the difference.

I7-62 On December 5, 2003, Rebecca Ward, a single taxpayer, comes to you for tax advice. At the end of every year, she donates $3,800 to charity. She has no other itemized deductions. This year, she plans to make her charitable donation with stock. She presents you with the following information relating to her stock investments:

Corporation	*FMV on Dec. 1*	*Adjusted Basis*	*Date Purchased*
Sycamore	9,600	7,800	5/22/00
Oak	2,900	3,800	9/10/01
Redwood	5,400	4,900	6/15/03

Which stock should Rebecca donate to charity? What other tax advice would you give her?

TAX FORM/RETURN PREPARATION PROBLEMS

I7-63 Following is a list of information for Peter and Amy Jones for the current tax year. Pete and Amy are married and have three children, Aubrynne, Bryson, and Caden. They live at 1846 Joplin Way, Lakeville, MN 55022. Pete is a lawyer working for a Native American law firm. Amy works part-time in a genetic research lab. The Jones' Social Security numbers and ages are as follows:

Name	*S.S. No.*	*Age*
Peter	215-60-1989	32
Amy	301-60-2828	28
Aubrynne	713-84-5555	5
Bryson	714-87-2222	3
Caden	714-89-1684	1

Receipts

Pete's salary	$70,000
Amy's salary	32,000
Interest income on municipal bonds	2,400
Interest income on certificate of deposit (Universal Savings)	3,100
Dividends on GM stock	1,600

Disbursements

Eyeglasses and exam for Aubrynne	600
Orthodontic work for Bryson to correct a congenital defect	2,500
Medical insurance premiums	1,800
Withholding for state income taxes	7,200
Withholding for federal income taxes	16,000
State income taxes paid with last year's tax return (paid when the return was filed in the current year)	500
Property taxes on home	1,100
Property taxes on automobile	300
Interest on home	9,700
Interest on credit cards	200
Cash contribution to church	3,900

In addition to the above, Pete and Amy donate some stock to the local community college. The FMV of the stock at the date of the donation is $700. They purchased the stock 3 years before for $300.

Compute Pete and Amy's income tax liability for the current year using Form 1040, Schedules A and B, and Form 8283, if necessary.

I7-64 Kelly and Chanelle Chambers, ages 47 and 45, are married and live at 584 Thoreau Drive, Boston, MA 59483. Kelly's social security is 254-93-9483 and Chanelle's is 374-48-2938. The Chambers have two children; Emma, age 23, and Chet, age 19. Their social security numbers are 385-64-8496 and 385-68-9462, respectively. Emma is a single college student and earned $8,000 during the summer. Kelly and Chanelle help Emma through school by paying for her room, board, and tuition. Emma lives at home during the summer. Chet has a physical handicap and lives at home. He attends a local university and earned $4,000 working for a marketing firm.

Kelly is a commercial pilot for a small airline. His salary is $95,000, from which $19,000 of federal income tax and $8,000 of state income tax were withheld. Kelly also pays premiums for health, disability, and life insurance. $2,000 of the premium was for health insurance, $250 for disability, and $400 for life insurance.

Chanelle owns Alliance Networks, a sold proprietorship that does network consulting. During the year, Chanelle's gross revenues were $23,000. She incurred the following expenses in her business:

Liability insurance	$ 700
Software rental	5,400
Journals and magazines	150
Training seminars	1,200
Supplies	1,300
Donations to a political campaign fund	800

Kelly enjoys playing guitar and plays in a band. Kelly's band has developed a local following. This year, his gross revenues were $1,200 for playing shows and $700 on CD sales. He incurred the following expenses:

Studio rent expense	$1,300
Sound system repairs	200
CD production	500
New guitar and amplifier	800

Kelly's father passed away during the year. Kelly and Chantelle received $100,000 from the life insurance policy. Neither Kelly nor Chanelle paid any of the premiums.

Chanelle purchased 100 shares of Thurston Co. stock on May 1, 1991 for $1,000. Thurston Co. was declared bankrupt during the current year.

Chet's physician recommended that he see a physical therapist to help with his disability. Kelly paid the therapist $7,000 during the year because his insurance would not cover the bills.

Kelly and Chanelle went to Las Vegas and won $5,000 at the blackjack table. The next night, they lost $6,000.

Derek and Corinne gave $900 to their church and, during the year, they had the following other income and expenses:

Real estate taxes	$1,400
Property taxes on car (determined by value)	500
Home mortgage interest	9,000
Credit card finance charges	2,600
Tax return preparation fees ($600 is allocable to Corinne's business)	1,000
Sales tax on purchases during the year	6,200
Interest from a savings account	800
Interest from City of Boston Bonds	700
Dividend from 3M stock	400

Prepare Kelly and Chanelle's tax return Form 1040 and Schedules A, B, C, and SE for the current year.

CASE STUDY PROBLEMS

I7-65 Brian Brown, an executive at a manufacturing enterprise, comes to you on December 1 of the current year for tax advice. He has agreed to donate a small tract of land to the Rosepark Community College. The value of the land has been appraised at $53,000. Mr. Brown purchased the land 14 months ago for $50,000. Mr. Brown's estimated AGI for the current year is $100,000. He plans to retire next year and anticipates that his AGI will fall to $30,000 for all subsequent years. He does not anticipate making any additional large charitable contributions. He understands that there are special rules dealing with charitable contributions, and wants your advice in order to get the maximum overall tax benefit from his contribution. Because the college plans to use the property, selling the land is not an alternative. You are to prepare a letter to Mr. Brown explaining the tax consequences of the different alternatives. His address is 100 East Rosebrook, Mesa, Arizona 85203. For purposes of your analysis, assume that Mr. Brown is married and files a joint return. Also assume that Mr. Brown feels that an appropriate discount rate is 10%. In your analysis, use the tax rate schedules for the current year.

I7-66 For several years, you have prepared the tax return for Alpha Corporation, a closely held corporation engaged in manufacturing garden tools. On February 20 of the current year, Bill Johnson, the president of Alpha Corporation, delivered to your office the files and information necessary for you to prepare Alpha's tax return for the immediately preceding tax year. Included in this information were the minutes of all meetings held by Alpha's Board of Directors during the year in question.

Then on February 27, Bill stops by your office and hands you an "addendum" to the minutes of the director's meeting held December 15 of the tax year for which you are preparing the tax return. The addendum is dated the same day of the director's meeting, and authorizes a charitable contribution pledge of $20,000 to the local community college. With a wink and a big smile, Bill explains that the addendum had been misplaced. In reviewing the original minutes, you find no mention of a charitable contribution pledge.

What should you do? (See Appendix E and the *Statements on Standards for Tax Services* section in Chapter I15 (or C1 of *Comprehensive* volume) for a discussion of these issues.)

TAX RESEARCH PROBLEMS

I7-67 Mark Hancock is a self-employed attorney who operates his law practice as an unincorporated sole proprietorship. In 2002, the I.R.S. disallowed several business deductions he took in 1999 and 2000. In addition to paying the deficiency and assessed penalties, he also pays $18,000 in interest on the tax owed. Can he deduct that interest in the current year?

- Sec. 162, Sec. 163
- Reg. §1.163-9T
- *Kikalos v. Comm.*, 84 AFTR 2d 99-5933

I7-68 Last year Mr. Smith was involved in an automobile accident, severely injuring his legs. As part of a long-term rehabilitation process, his physician prescribes a daily routine of swimming. Because there is no readily available public facility nearby, Smith investigates the possibility of either building a pool in his own back yard or purchasing another home with a pool. In the current year he finds a new home with a pool and purchases it for $175,000. He then obtains some estimates and finds that it would cost approximately $20,000 to replace the pool in the home he has just purchased. He also obtains some real estate appraisals, which indicate that the existing pool increases the value of the home by only $8,000. During the current year, Smith also expends $500 in maintaining the pool and $1,800 in other medical expenses. What is the total amount of medical expenses he may claim in the current year? Smith's AGI for the year is $60,000.

A partial list of research sources is

- Sec. 213
- Reg. Sec. 1.213-1(e)(1)(iii)
- *Richard A. Polacsek,* 1981 PH T.C. Memo ¶81,569, 42 TCM 1289
- *Paul A. Lerew,* 1982 PH T.C. Memo ¶82,483, 44 TCM 918
- *Jacob H. Robbins,* 1982 PH T.C. Memo ¶82,565, 44 TCM 1254

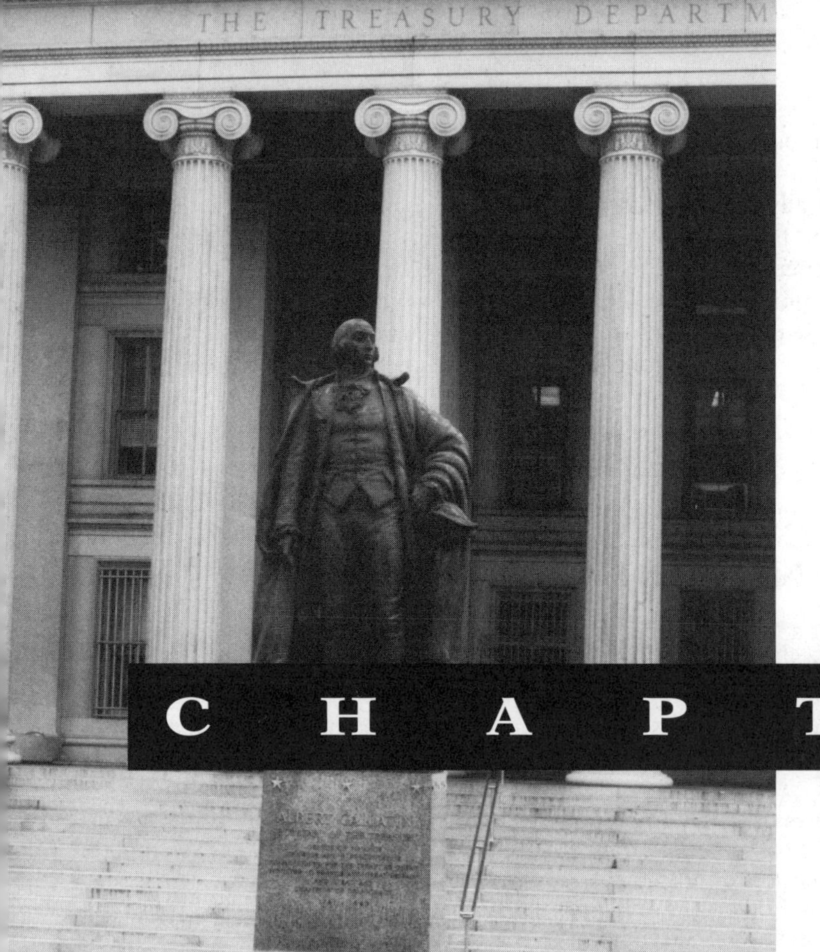

8

CHAPTER

LOSSES AND BAD DEBTS

LEARNING OBJECTIVES

After studying this chapter, you should be able to

1. Identify transactions that may result in losses
2. Determine the proper classification for losses
3. Calculate the suspended loss from passive activities
4. Identify what constitutes a passive activity loss
5. Determine when a taxpayer has materially participated in a passive activity
6. Identify and calculate the deduction for a casualty or theft loss
7. Compute the deduction for a bad debt
8. Compute a net operating loss deduction

CHAPTER OUTLINE

Transactions That May Result in Losses...8-2
Classifying the Loss on the Taxpayer's Tax Return...8-4
Passive Losses...8-7
Casualty and Theft Losses...8-17
Bad Debts...8-24
Net Operating Losses...8-29

Taxpayers often sustain losses on property that is sold, exchanged, or otherwise disposed of. If the taxpayer uses the property in a trade or business or holds the property for investment, the tax law generally provides a deduction for these losses. The tax law also provides a limited deduction for losses on personal-use property that is either stolen or damaged in a casualty. Other losses on personal-use property (e.g. a sale of a personal residence at a loss) are not deductible. A deduction is also provided for losses that taxpayers may incur because of uncollectible business or nonbusiness debts.

This chapter discusses the rules concerning with the deductibility of these types of losses.

TRANSACTIONS THAT MAY RESULT IN LOSSES

OBJECTIVE 1

Identify transactions that may result in losses

For taxpayers to deduct a loss on property, the loss must be both realized and recognized for tax purposes. Generally, *realization* occurs in a completed (closed) transaction evidenced by an identifiable event. Generally, taxpayers must recognize realized losses on business or investment property unless a specific provision holds otherwise (see pages I8-6 and I8-7).

EXAMPLE I8-1 ▶

Anita purchased 500 shares of Data Corporation stock for $10,000 on February 22 of the current year. By October 31 of the same year, the price of the stock declines to $8,000. Even though Anita realizes an economic loss on the stock, no realization event has occurred, and she may not deduct the $2,000 loss. However, if Anita sells the stock for $8,000 on October 31, she realizes the loss for tax purposes in the current year. ◀

ADDITIONAL COMMENT

If property is used partly for business and partly for personal use, the loss attributable to the business portion is deductible but the loss on the personal-use portion is not unless the loss was sustained in a casualty.

KEY POINT

Anticipated losses, including those for which reserves have been established, are not deductible.

Losses on property may arise in a variety of transactions, including

- Sale or exchange of the property
- Expropriation, seizure, confiscation, or condemnation of the property by a government
- Abandonment of the property
- Worthlessness of stock or securities
- Planned demolition of the property in order to construct other property in its place
- Destruction of the property by fire, storm, or other casualty
- Theft
- Deductible business expenses exceeding business income, giving rise to a net operating loss (NOL)

SALE OR EXCHANGE OF PROPERTY

The amount of the loss a taxpayer incurs in a sale or exchange of property equals the excess of the property's adjusted basis over the amount realized for the property.[1] The amount realized for the property equals the sum of the money received plus the fair market value (FMV) of any other property received in the transaction. If the property sold or exchanged is subject to a mortgage or other liability, the amount realized also includes the amount of the liability transferred to the buyer.[2] The treatment of any selling costs depends on the type of property being sold or exchanged. If the property is inventory (i.e. property normally held for sale in the taxpayer's business), the selling costs are deductible expenses in the year in which they are paid or incurred. However, if the sale involves property that is not normally held for sale by the taxpayer, the selling costs reduce the amount realized from the sale or exchange.

---

[1] Sec. 1001.

[2] *Beulah B. Crane v. CIR*, 35 AFTR 776, 47-1 USTC ¶9217 (USSC, 1947); and Reg. Sec. 1.1001-2.

EXAMPLE I8-2 ▶ Four years ago, Louis purchased a plot of land as an investment for $50,000. Unfortunately, local economic conditions worsened after the land was purchased, and its value declined to $35,000. Becoming discouraged, Louis sells the property in the current year. At the time of the sale, the land is subject to a $10,000 mortgage. The terms of the sale are $25,000 paid in cash with the purchaser assuming the mortgage. Louis also incurs $2,000 in sales commissions. The amount realized is $33,000 ($25,000 cash + $10,000 mortgage assumed by the buyer − $2,000 commissions). The loss on the sale is $17,000 ($50,000 basis − $33,000 amount realized). ◀

Taxpayers can only deduct losses they incur in the sale or exchange of property used in a trade or business or held for investment. Taxpayers cannot deduct losses they incur in the sale or exchange of personal-use property. Furthermore, the type of deduction a taxpayer may take for a loss realized on the sale or exchange of business or investment property depends on the type of property sold. For example, if the asset is a capital asset, the loss is a capital loss (see Chapter I5). If the sale is of property used in a trade or business (a Sec. 1231 asset), the type of loss depends on the total gain or loss realized on all the taxpayer's Sec. 1231 assets sold during the year (see Chapter I13). If the sale is of inventory, the loss is an ordinary loss.

EXPROPRIATED, SEIZED, OR CONFISCATED PROPERTY

A taxpayer may own property that is expropriated, seized, confiscated, or condemned by a government. In these cases, the taxpayer incurs a deductible loss if the property is used in a trade or business or is held for investment. However, the Tax Court has held that the confiscation, seizure, condemnation, or expropriation of property does not constitute a theft or a casualty. Rather, it is treated as a sale or exchange. Thus, no deductible loss arises if the seized property is personal-use property.[3] If the seized or condemned property is business or investment property, the classification of the loss depends on the type of property. (See the section in this chapter titled Classifying the Loss on the Taxpayer's Return.) A taxpayer may take the deduction only in the year in which the property is actually seized. It is irrelevant whether formal expropriation or nationalization occurs in a later year.[4] A taxpayer realizes gain if he or she receives compensation for the property in excess of its basis. Under certain circumstances, the taxpayer may defer this gain. (See Chapter I12 for a discussion of the nonrecognition of gain in an involuntary conversion.)

REAL-WORLD EXAMPLE

A taxpayer cannot deduct domestic confiscation losses, even if the property was used in business. For example, a taxpayer who had been engaged in the business of trafficking in marijuana was arrested. As a result of the arrest, the taxpayer's truck and horse trailer were confiscated. The taxpayer was not entitled to a loss deduction, because losses from illegal activities are disallowed under Sec. 165. *Bill D. Holt*, 69 T.C. 75 (1977). See also Sec. 280E.

ABANDONED PROPERTY

If a taxpayer's property becomes worthless or if it is not worth placing into a serviceable condition, the taxpayer may simply abandon the property. If the property still has basis, the taxpayer realizes a loss. The taxpayer may not deduct such losses if the property is personal-use property. However, the taxpayer may deduct business or investment property losses. Furthermore, because the abandonment of property is not a sale or exchange, the loss is an ordinary loss. The amount of the loss is the property's adjusted basis on the date of abandonment. The burden of proof to show that the property was actually abandoned rests with the taxpayer. If the property is depreciable (e.g., machinery and buildings), the taxpayer must actually physically abandon it to take the full amount of the loss.[5]

WORTHLESS SECURITIES

A taxpayer may take a deduction for securities that become completely worthless during the tax year.[6] Because the deduction is only available in the year the security actually becomes worthless, a major problem for both the taxpayer and the IRS is determining the year in which the security becomes worthless. A mere decline in value is not sufficient to create a deductible loss if the stock has any recognizable value. Furthermore, the sale of the stock for a nominal amount such as $1 does not necessarily establish that the stock became

[3] *William J. Powers*, 36 T.C. 1191 (1961).

[4] Rev. Rul. 62-197, 1962-2 C.B. 66 as modified by Rev. Rul. 69-498, 1969-2 C.B. 31. See also *Estate of Frank Fuchs v. CIR*, 24 AFTR 2d 69-5077, 69-2 USTC ¶9505 (2nd Cir., 1969).

[5] Reg. Sec. 1.167(a)-8(a)(4).

[6] For this purpose, a *security* is defined in Sec. 165(g)(2) as stock in a corporation, the right to subscribe for or receive a share of stock in a corporation, or a bond, debenture, note, or certificate of indebtedness issued by a corporation or a government either in registered form or with interest coupons. Promissory notes issued by a corporation are generally not securities.

worthless in the year of the sale. The burden of proof rests with the taxpayer to show that the security is completely worthless and that the security became worthless during the year.

Under Sec. 165, once the taxpayer determines the year of worthlessness, the taxpayer treats the loss as a loss from the sale of a capital asset on the last day of the tax year. Although this provision does not help in determining the year of worthlessness, it does establish a definite date for purposes of measuring whether the loss is short- or long-term. In some cases, this provision causes the loss to be long-term because the time period is extended to the end of the year in which the worthlessness occurs.

EXAMPLE I8-3 ▶ On February 20 of the current year, Control Corporation enters into bankruptcy with no possibility for the shareholders to receive anything of value. Because the amount of Control Corporation's outstanding liabilities exceeds the FMV of its assets on that date, the stock of the corporation becomes worthless. Janet, a calendar-year taxpayer, owns 500 shares of Control's common stock, which she had purchased for $10,000 through her broker on June 17 of the prior year. Under Sec. 165(g), she treats the loss as having arisen from the sale of a capital asset on the last day of the current year. Thus, Janet incurs a $10,000 long-term capital loss because the holding period for the stock is more than one year. On the other hand, if Janet had received the stock directly from Control Corporation in exchange for either money or other property, and if certain other requirements are met, the stock may qualify as Sec. 1244 stock. Individuals who sustain losses on Sec. 1244 stock receive ordinary loss treatment rather than capital loss treatment. (See the discussion in this chapter under the heading Losses on Sec. 1244 Stock.) ◀

Under certain circumstances, if a domestic corporation owns worthless securities of an affiliated corporation, the domestic corporation treats the loss as having arisen from the sale of a noncapital asset. This allows the corporation to treat the loss as an ordinary loss rather than as a capital loss.[7] For this exception to apply, the following percentage ownership requirements must be met:

- ▶ The domestic corporation that is deducting the loss must own at least 80% of the voting power of all classes of the affiliated corporation's stock (and 80% of all classes of nonvoting stock).
- ▶ More than 90% of the affiliated corporation's gross receipts for all its taxable years must be from nonpassive income.[8]

DEMOLITION OF PROPERTY

At times, taxpayers, intent on building their own facilities, purchase land that contains an existing structure that must first be removed. Taxpayers may also demolish a structure they currently use to construct new facilities. In both cases, taxpayers may not deduct any demolition costs or any loss sustained on account of the demolition. Instead, under Sec. 280B, taxpayers must add these amounts to the basis of the land on which the demolished structure was located.

CLASSIFYING THE LOSS ON THE TAXPAYER'S TAX RETURN

OBJECTIVE 2

Determine the proper classification for losses

If a loss is deductible, the taxpayer must determine whether the loss is an ordinary loss or a capital loss. In addition, individual taxpayers must also identify the amount as either a deduction *for* or *from* AGI.

[7] As explained in Chapter I5, the deductibility of capital losses is limited. For corporate taxpayers, capital losses must initially be offset against capital gains of the current year, and any excess loss is not deductible but must be carried back 3 years and forward for 5 years. Individuals may offset capital losses against capital gains and any excess loss is deductible up to $3,000 per year as an offset to ordinary income. Capital losses in excess of this amount for an individual are carried forward for an indefinite period. Thus, taxpayers generally prefer ordinary losses rather than capital losses.

[8] Sec. 165(g)(3). *Nonpassive income* includes all income other than royalties, rents, dividends, interest, annuities, and gains from the sale or exchange of stocks and securities.

ORDINARY VERSUS CAPITAL LOSS

Whether a deductible loss is ordinary or capital depends on the type of property involved and the transaction in which the loss is sustained. To incur a capital loss, a sale or exchange of a capital asset must occur. If both elements (i.e., a sale or exchange and a capital asset) are not present, the deduction is an ordinary loss. In general, all assets except inventory, notes and accounts receivable, and depreciable property and land used in a trade or business (i.e., property, plant, and machinery) are classified as **capital assets.**[9]

Because a casualty is not a sale or exchange, the destruction of a capital asset by a casualty creates an ordinary rather than a capital loss. Likewise, a deductible loss realized on the abandonment of property is an ordinary loss because an abandonment is not a sale or exchange.

EXAMPLE I8-4 ▶ On July 24 of the current year, Jermaine sells some investment property for $75,000. The property's adjusted basis is $85,000. The investment property is a capital asset. Jermaine realizes a $10,000 ($75,000 − $85,000) capital loss. If, instead, the property had been destroyed by fire and Jermaine had received $75,000 in insurance proceeds, the $10,000 loss would have been an ordinary loss since a casualty is not a sale or exchange. ◀

BOOK-TAX DIFFERENCE

For book purposes, it makes no difference if a gain or loss is ordinary or capital. The full amount of the loss is deductible. However, because corporations may not deduct a capital loss in excess of its capital gains for the year, a book-tax timing (temporary) difference may arise.

Certain transactions, though not actually constituting a sale or exchange, are treated as a sale or exchange. For example, if a security owned by an individual investor becomes worthless during the year, the individual treats the loss as a loss from the sale of a capital asset on the last day of the tax year, even though no sale actually occurs. Thus, the loss is a capital loss. Likewise, the seizure or condemnation of property is treated as a sale or exchange.

SECTION 1231 PROPERTY. Whether a loss on a particular transaction is treated as a capital loss may also depend on the gains and losses reported from other property transactions for the tax year. For instance, under Sec. 1231, taxpayers must net certain gains and losses together. If the Sec. 1231 gains exceed the Sec. 1231 losses, both the gains and losses are treated as long-term capital gains and losses. However, if the losses equal or exceed the gains, both the gains and the losses are treated as ordinary. **Section 1231 property** includes real property or depreciable property used in a trade or business that is held for more than one year. (See Chapter I13 for a discussion of the netting procedure under Sec. 1231.)

LOSSES ON SEC. 1244 STOCK. Taxpayers generally recognize capital gain or loss on the sale of stock or securities. The tax law provides an exception for losses from the sale or worthlessness of small business corporation (Sec. 1244) stock. Taxpayers may deduct these losses as ordinary losses up to a maximum of $50,000 per tax year ($100,000 for married taxpayers filing a joint return). Any remaining loss for the year is capital loss.

To qualify the loss as ordinary under Sec. 1244, the following requirements must be met:

- ▶ The stock must be owned by an individual or a partnership.
- ▶ The stock must have been originally issued by the corporation to the individual or to a partnership in which an individual is a partner.[10]
- ▶ The stock must be stock in a domestic (U.S.) corporation.
- ▶ The stock must have been issued for cash or property other than stock or securities. Stock issued for services rendered is not eligible for Sec. 1244 treatment.

---

[9] Sec. 1221. The definition of a capital asset is more fully examined in Chapter I5.

[10] Stock received in certain reorganizations of corporations in exchange for Sec. 1244 stock is also considered Sec. 1244 stock. Section 1244 does not apply to stock that the individual has received through other means such as purchase in a secondary market, exchange, gift, or inheritance.

- The corporation must not have derived over 50% of its gross receipts from passive income sources during the five tax years immediately preceding the year of sale or worthlessness.[11]
- The amount of money and property contributed to both capital and paid-in surplus may not exceed $1 million at the time the stock is issued.

Note that the last test listed above is made *at the time the stock is issued*. Thus, even though at the time the loss is realized the corporation has capital and paid-in surplus in excess of the $1 million limit, the individual may still report an ordinary loss as long as the test is met when the stock is issued.

STOP & THINK

Question: Tony, a single taxpayer, incorporated Waffle, Inc. three years ago by contributing $70,000 in exchange for the stock. Waffle, Inc. owns and operates a small restaurant. Unfortunately, Waffle, Inc.'s business never really became profitable. Tony has been trying to sell the Waffle, Inc. stock since July of last year, but because the corporation had become insolvent, he couldn't find any buyers. In February of the current year Waffle, Inc. was judged to be bankrupt. Tony didn't receive anything for his stock. What issues should Tony's tax advisor address with regard to the Waffle, Inc. stock?

Solution: Tony's tax advisor must determine (1) the amount of any realized loss, (2) the year in which the loss is recognized, and (3) the character of the realized loss. The Waffle, Inc. stock is considered a security under Sec. 165. Whenever a security becomes completely worthless and it is determined that the owner will receive nothing for it, the owner realizes a loss to the extent of the security's basis ($70,000). The loss is deemed to be realized in the year in which the security becomes worthless. While the stock was judged to be worthless by the bankruptcy court in February of the current year, the fact that Tony could not find any buyers last year because the corporation was insolvent may indicate that the stock really became worthless last year. This determination is important because its loss must be taken in the year in which the stock becomes worthless. Furthermore, the stock is deemed to become worthless on the last day of that year. Since Tony received the stock directly from the corporation in exchange for contributed cash, Waffles, Inc.'s gross receipts are from business operations, and the capitalization is less than $1,000,000, the stock qualifies as Sec. 1244 stock. Thus, $50,000 of the loss is characterized as ordinary loss. The remaining $20,000 is a long-term capital loss.

DISALLOWANCE POSSIBILITIES

Losses taxpayers incur in certain transactions and activities may be disallowed or deferred. These include

- Transfers of property to a controlled corporation in exchange for stock of the corporation (see the discussion in Chapter C2 of *Prentice Hall's Federal Taxation: Corporations, Partnerships, Estates, and Trusts* text and Chapter C2 of the *Comprehensive* volume)
- Exchanges of property for other property that is considered to be like-kind to the property given up (see the discussion in Chapter I12)
- Property sold to certain related parties (see the discussion in Chapter I6)
- Wash sale transactions (see the discussion in Chapter I6)
- Losses limited because the losses exceed the amount for which the taxpayer is at risk (see the discussion in Chapter C9 of *Prentice Hall's Federal Taxation: Corporations, Partnerships, Estates, and Trusts* text and Chapter C9 of the *Comprehensive* volume)

In addition, individuals and certain corporations may be limited on the amount of deductible losses because of the passive loss rules.

Topic Review I8-1 contains a summary of loss transactions.

---

[11] For this purpose, passive income sources include royalties, rents, dividends, interest, annuities, and sales or exchanges of stocks and securities. If the corporation has not been in existence for a full five years, the gross receipts test is applied to the shorter period. If the corporation has not been in existence for an entire taxable year, the test is applied to the time period up to the date of the loss (see Sec. 1244(c)(2)).

Topic Review I8-1

Transactions That May Result In Losses

TYPE OF TRANSACTION	RESULT
Sale or exchange	Taxpayers may not deduct a loss on personal-use property. The tax treatment of a loss on business or investment property depends on the type of property. Losses on capital assets result in capital losses. Losses on Sec. 1231 assets are subject to the Sec. 1231 netting rules discussed in Chapter I13.
Seizure, expropriation, confiscation, or condemnation	Treated as a sale or exchange.
Abandonment	Not treated as a sale or exchange. No deduction is allowed for a loss on personal-use property. Business or investment property is given ordinary loss treatment.
Worthless securities	Treated as a loss from the sale of the securities on the last day of the year in which the securities become worthless. This generally will result in a capital loss. However, if the requirements of Sec. 1244 are met, at least part of the loss may be treated as an ordinary loss. (See Sec. 1244 stock below.) A loss on worthless securities of an affiliated corporation results in an ordinary loss.
Demolition	No deductible loss is allowed. Instead, losses and costs of demolition are added to the basis of the land where the demolished structure was located.
Sec. 1244 stock	An ordinary loss is allowed for individuals up to $50,000 per year ($100,000 for married filing jointly). The remaining loss is capital. The stock must have been originally issued to the individual for property or cash, and the corporation must meet the requirements to be a small business corporation.

PASSIVE LOSSES

HISTORICAL NOTE

Before the passive activity loss limits became effective in 1987, most tax shelters were concentrated in the areas of real estate, oil and gas, equipment leasing, farming, motion pictures, timber, and research and development. Many tax shelters took advantage of liberal depreciation rules during the early 1980's such as the rapid depreciation of real estate over a 15-year period.

Before 1987, taxpayers were able to reduce their income tax liability on income from one business or investment activity with deductions, losses, and credits arising in another activity. Thus, taxpayers often invested in activities, called **tax shelters**, that would spin off tax deductions and credits. Many of these tax shelters were simply *passive investments* because they did not require the taxpayer's involvement or participation. In some situations, tax shelters had real economic substance i.e., a taxpayer's investment in this type of shelter was not based solely on the tax benefits that the activity generated. In many cases, however, tax shelters had no real economic substance other than the creation of deductions and credits that enabled taxpayers to reduce and sometimes eliminate the income tax liability from their other business activities. To prevent these perceived and real abuses, Congress enacted Sec. 469, which restricts the current use of losses and credits that arise in rental activities and in other activities in which the taxpayer does not materially participate. These activities are described as passive activities. (See the Definition of a Passive Activity section in this chapter for an extended discussion of what constitutes a passive activity.)

COMPUTATION OF PASSIVE LOSSES AND CREDITS

OBJECTIVE 3

Calculate the suspended loss from passive activities

In enacting the passive loss rules, Congress did not want to prevent taxpayers from currently deducting or using losses and credits generated in active business endeavors of the taxpayer. At the same time, Congress realized that certain investments (such as investments that generate interest or dividend income) normally give rise to taxable income, which could itself be sheltered by losses and credits that arise in other passive activities. Thus, Sec. 469 requires taxpayers to classify their income into three categories: *active income* (such as wages, salaries, and active business income), *portfolio (or investment) income,* and *passive income.* **Portfolio income** includes dividends, interest, annuities, and royalties (and allocable expenses and interest expense) that are not derived in the ordinary course of a trade or business. Gains and losses on property that produces these types of income also are included in portfolio income if the disposition of the property does not occur in the ordinary course of business.[12] Portfolio income becomes part of net investment income, which is used in computing the deduction limit for investment interest expense. (See Chapter I7 for a discussion of the investment interest expense limitation.)

PASSIVE INCOME AND LOSSES. Taxpayers compute income and loss in the passive category separately for each passive activity in which they have invested. In general, for any tax year, a taxpayer may use losses generated in one passive activity to offset income from other passive activities, but may not use them to offset either active or portfolio income.

EXAMPLE I8-5 ▶ During the year, Kasi, a CPA, reports $100,000 of active business income from his CPA practice. He also owns two passive activities. From activity A, he earned $10,000 of income, and from activity B, he incurred a $15,000 loss. Kasi may use $10,000 of the loss from activity B to offset the $10,000 of income from activity A. However, Kasi may not deduct the $5,000 excess loss from Activity B in the current year, even though he has $100,000 of active business income. ◀

CARRYOVERS

KEY POINT

Excess passive activity losses are not "lost" because they can be carried over to future years.

A taxpayer can carry over disallowed passive activity losses indefinitely and treat them as losses allocable to that passive activity in the following tax years. The taxpayer may use these losses, known as **suspended losses,** to offset passive activity income of the subsequent year, but generally may not offset other types of income. If a taxpayer has invested in several passive activities, and for the year some of the activities generate income while others generate losses, the loss carried over for each loss activity is a pro rata portion of the total passive loss for the year.

EXAMPLE I8-6 ▶ Tammy reports the following income and loss for the year:

Salary	$200,000
Loss from activity X	(40,000)
Loss from activity Y	(10,000)
Income from activity Z	30,000

X, Y, and Z are all passive activities. The losses generated in activities X and Y offset the income from activity Z, but none of the salary income is offset. Thus, Tammy has a net passive loss for the year of $20,000 ($40,000 + $10,000 − $30,000), which must be carried over to subsequent years. The amount of the carryover attributable to each activity is as follows:

Activity X: $$\$20,000 \times \frac{\$40,000}{\$50,000} = \$16,000$$

Activity Y: $$\$20,000 \times \frac{\$10,000}{\$50,000} = \$\ 4,000$$ ◀

TAXABLE DISPOSITION OF INTEREST IN A PASSIVE ACTIVITY. When a taxpayer disposes of a passive activity in a taxable transaction, the taxpayer can compute the economic gain or loss generated by the activity and can deduct the suspended losses of the activity against other income. However, the amount of the total net economic loss from the asset that is disposed of must first offset any passive income from other passive activities.[13]

EXAMPLE I8-7 ▶ During the current year, Pam realizes $6,000 of taxable income from activity A, $1,000 of loss from activity B, and $8,000 of taxable income from activity C. All three activities are passive activities with regard to Pam. In addition, $30,000 of passive losses from activity C are carried over from prior years. During the current year, Pam sells activity C for a $15,000 taxable gain. Pam reports salary income of $90,000 for the year. Because activity C is disposed of in a fully taxable transaction, Pam may deduct $2,000 of loss against the salary income:

[12] Sec. 469(e)(1). Gain or loss on property dispositions occurring in the ordinary course of business is either passive or active business income, depending on the taxpayer's level of involvement (i.e., material participation) in the activity.

[13] Sec. 469(g). Income from the activity for prior years may also be taken into account in arriving at the net income from all passive activities for the year if it is necessary to prevent avoidance of the passive loss rules.

Income for the year from C	$ 8,000	
Gain from the sale of C	15,000	
Suspended losses from C	(30,000)	
Total loss from C		($7,000)
Income for the year from A	$ 6,000	
Loss for the year from B	(1,000)	5,000
Pam's deduction against salary income		($2,000) ◀

BOOK-TAX DIFFERENCE

Since passive losses are not limited under financial accounting rules, the limitation and carryover of passive losses for tax purposes will create a timing (temporary) difference between book and tax. However, most taxpayers subject to the passive loss rules do not use financial accounting rules.

If the taxpayer sells the passive activity to a related party, the suspended loss is not deductible until the related party sells the activity to a nonrelated person. The definition of *related persons* includes spouse, brothers and sisters, ancestors, lineal descendants, and corporations or partnerships in which the individual has a greater than 50% ownership.[14]

Although the death of a taxpayer is not a taxable disposition of the asset, some of the suspended losses may be deducted when a taxpayer dies. The amount of the deduction allowed is the amount by which the suspended losses exceed the increase in basis of the property. These losses generally are deducted on the decedent's final income tax return. Any suspended losses up to the amount of the increase in basis are lost.[15]

EXAMPLE I8-8 ▶ At the time that John died during the current year, he owned passive activity property with an adjusted basis of $20,000 and a FMV of $35,000. There were $25,000 in suspended losses attributable to the property. Because the increase in the basis of the property is $15,000 ($35,000 − $20,000), $15,000 of the suspended losses are lost. However, $10,000 ($25,000 suspended losses − $15,000 increase in basis) of the suspended losses are deductible on John's final income tax return. ◀

In general, the suspended losses of a passive activity become deductible only when the taxpayer completely disposes of his or her interest in the activity. However, in Treasury Reg. 1.469-4(g) the government has stated that taxpayers may treat the disposition of a substantial part of an activity as the disposition of a separate activity. This treatment is only available, however, if the taxpayer can establish with reasonable certainty the amount of income, deductions, credits, and suspended losses and credits that are allocable to that part of the activity.

CARRYOVERS FROM A FORMER PASSIVE ACTIVITY. The determination of whether an activity is passive with respect to a taxpayer is made annually. Thus, an activity that previously was considered passive may not be passive with respect to the taxpayer for the current year. This is called a **former passive activity**. A taxpayer may deduct any loss carryover from a former passive activity against the current year's income of that activity even though the activity is not a passive activity in the current year. However, any suspended loss in excess of the activity's income for the year is still subject to the carryover limitations. Since the activity is no longer passive for the year, the current year's loss is deductible against active business income.

EXAMPLE I8-9 ▶ Kris owns activity A, which, for the immediately preceding tax year, was considered a passive activity with regard to Kris. $10,000 in losses from activity A were disallowed and carried over to the current year. Because of Kris' increased involvement in activity A in the current year, it is not considered passive with regard to Kris for that year. During the current year, activity A generates a $5,000 loss. During the current year, Kris also has an investment in activity B, a passive activity. Her share of activity B's income is $7,000. Kris reports $60,000 in salary. Because for the current year activity A is not a passive activity, the $5,000 current year loss is fully deductible against her salary. However, the $10,000 loss carryover from the prior year is deductible only against the $7,000 of income from passive activity B. The $3,000 ($10,000 − $7,000) excess is carried over to the subsequent year. ◀

[14] Other relationships described in Secs. 267(b) and 707(b) are also considered related parties for this purpose.

[15] Sec. 469(g)(2). Generally, the basis of inherited property is its FMV on the date of death (see Chapter I5).

Credits. Credits generated in a passive activity are also limited and may be used only against the portion of the tax liability that is attributable to passive income. This amount is determined by comparing the tax liability on all income for the year with the tax liability on all income excluding the passive income.

EXAMPLE I8-10 ▶ Dale invests in a passive activity. For the year, he must report $10,000 of taxable income from the passive activity. Dale's share of tax credits generated by the passive activity is $5,000. Assume Dale's precredit tax liability on all income (including the $10,000 from the passive activity) is $25,000, and his precredit tax liability on all income excluding the passive activity income is $22,000. He may use only $3,000 ($25,000 − $22,000) of the tax credits generated by the passive activity. The remaining $2,000 of tax credits is carried forward and may be used in a subsequent year against the portion of the tax liability attributable to passive activity income in that year. However, these credits may never offset any portion of the tax liability attributable to nonpassive activities. (See Chapter I14 for a discussion of credits and their carryovers.) ◀

OBJECTIVE 4

Identify what constitutes a passive activity loss

DEFINITION OF A PASSIVE ACTIVITY

The term *passive activity* includes any rental activity or any trade or business in which the taxpayer does not materially participate.[16] The definition of a passive activity is based on two critical elements: an identification of exactly what constitutes an activity and a determination of whether the taxpayer has materially participated in that activity.

IDENTIFICATION OF AN ACTIVITY. Identifying whether an activity is either passive or active becomes critical for several reasons. Whether a taxpayer materially participates in an activity is determined separately for each activity. A taxpayer may deduct suspended losses of a passive activity when the taxpayer's ownership of the activity is completely terminated. As explained in a subsequent section of this chapter, taxpayers may deduct currently up to $25,000 of passive losses from rental real estate activities. Thus, taxpayers must not combine losses from passive business and rental real estate activities into one activity.

The way taxpayers combine or separate operations into activities can significantly impact the deductibility of losses that are generated. Taxpayers may treat one or more activities as a single activity only if they constitute an "appropriate economic unit."[17] Although the taxpayer makes this determination by examining all the relevant facts and circumstances, the following factors are given the greatest weight:

ADDITIONAL COMMENT

Tax year 1991 gave a clearer review of the impact of the passive loss provisions that were enacted in 1986. Net losses of limited partnerships, the types that are used as tax shelters, declined to $16.7 billion in 1991 from $35.5 billion in 1986.

- Similarities and differences in the types of business
- The extent of common control
- The extent of common ownership
- The geographical location, and
- Any interdependencies between the operations (i.e. the extent to which they purchase or sell goods between the activities, have the same customers, are accounted for with a single set of books, etc.).

A taxpayer may treat more than one operation as a single activity, even if all of these factors do not apply. Furthermore, a taxpayer may use any reasonable method of applying the relevant facts and circumstances in grouping the activities.

EXAMPLE I8-11 ▶ Carla owns a bakery and a movie theater in each of two different shopping malls, one located in Baltimore and the other in Philadelphia. Depending on other relevant facts and circumstances, a reasonable grouping of the operations may result in any of the following:

[16] Secs. 469(c)(1) and (c)(2). Sec. 469(c)(6) also includes investment (production of income) activities under Sec. 212 as a passive activity. Section 469(j)(8) defines the term *rental activity* as any activity where payments are principally for the use of tangible property. Pursuant to the Regulations, there are six exceptions to this general rule. These exceptions include providing the use of tangible property where the average period of customer use is seven days or less, the average period of customer use is 30 days or less and significant personal services are provided by the owner in conjunction with the use of the property, extraordinary personal services are provided by the owner in conjunction with the use of the property, the rental of the property is incidental to a nonrental activity of the taxpayer, the property is customarily made available during defined business hours for nonexclusive use by various customers, or the property is provided for use in a nonrental activity conducted by a partnership, S corporation, or joint venture in which the taxpayer owns an interest. The details of these exceptions are beyond the scope of this text. See Reg. Sec. 1.469-1(e)(3)(iii).

[17] Reg. Sec. 1.469-4.

- One activity involving all four operations
- Two activities: a bakery activity and a theater activity
- Two activities: a Baltimore activity and a Philadelphia activity
- Four activities ◀

Under the Treasury Regulations, taxpayers apparently have some degree of flexibility in determining how different business operations are grouped into activities. However, once taxpayers establish the activities, they must be consistent in grouping their activities in subsequent years unless material changes in the facts and circumstances clearly make the groupings inappropriate.

In identifying separate activities, taxpayers generally may not group rental operations with trade or business operations. However, a combination is allowed if either the rental operation is insubstantial in relation to the business operation or vice versa. Unfortunately, the Treasury Regulations do not give any guidance with regard to what is insubstantial. Furthermore, because of the special rules dealing with real estate rental activities (explained later in this chapter), rental activities involving real estate may not be combined with rental activities involving personal property.

EXAMPLE I8-12 ▶ Sandy owns a building in which she (1) operates a restaurant and (2) leases out apartments to tenants. Generally the tenants sign apartment leases of one year or longer. Of the total gross income derived from the building, 15% comes from the apartment rentals and 85% comes from the restaurant operation. If the apartment rental operation is considered insubstantial in relation to the restaurant operation, the two may be combined into one activity. If it is not insubstantial, the two operations are considered two separate activities: a business activity and a rental real estate activity. ◀

Partnerships and S corporations (pass-through entities) must identify their business and rental activities by applying these rules at the partnership or S corporation level and then must report the results of their operations by activity to the partners or shareholders. Each partner or shareholder must then take these activities and, using these same rules, combine them where appropriate with operations conducted either directly or through other pass-through entities. In fact, many real estate passive activities are held as either partnerships or S corporations.

OBJECTIVE 5

Determine when a taxpayer has materially participated in a passive activity

MATERIAL PARTICIPATION. Once each activity is identified, taxpayers must determine whether the activity is passive or active. If the taxpayer does not **materially participate** in the activity, it is deemed to be a passive activity with respect to that taxpayer. Pursuant to the Treasury Regulations,[18] taxpayers materially participate in an activity if they meet at least one of the following tests:

- The individual participates in the activity for more than 500 hours during the year.
- The individual's participation in the activity for the year constitutes substantially all of the participation in the activity by all individuals, including individuals who do not own any interest in the activity.
- The individual participates in the activity for more than 100 hours during the year, and that participation is more than any other individual's participation for the year (including participation by individuals who do not own any interest in the activity).
- The individual participates in "significant participation activities" for an aggregate of more than 500 hours during the year.[19] Thus, an individual who spends over 100 hours each in several separate significant participation activities may aggregate the time spent in these activities in order to meet the 500-hour test.
- The individual materially participated in the activity in any five years during the immediately preceding ten taxable years. These five years need not be consecutive.

[18] Temp. Reg. Sec. 1.469-5T(a).

[19] A significant participation activity is a trade or business in which the individual participates for more than 100 hours during the year but for which the individual does not meet the material participation test alone (i.e., with respect to that activity, the individual does not meet one of the other material participation tests.). See Temp. Reg. Sec. 1.469-5T(c).

- The individual materially participated in the activity for any three years preceding the year in question, and the activity is a personal service activity.[20]
- The individual participates in the activity on a regular, continuous, and substantial basis during the year, taking into account all the relevant facts and circumstances.

ADDITIONAL COMMENT

A taxpayer may be a material participant in an activity one year and a passive investor the next year. A taxpayer must satisfy one of the material participation tests each year to be treated as a material participant.

Note that the first four tests are based on the number of hours the taxpayer spent in the activity during the current year. The fifth and sixth tests are based on the material participation of the taxpayer in prior years and are designed to prevent taxpayers from asserting that retirement income is passive and offsetting it with passive losses from tax shelters. To determine whether a taxpayer materially participates in an activity, the participation of the taxpayer's spouse is taken into account.

LIMITED PARTNERSHIPS. A limited partner has a limited liability for his or her investment in the partnership without assuming any active involvement; thus, the material participation test is not met and the limited partner's investment is generally considered passive. However, a limited partner can meet the material participation test if the individual meets either the 500 hour test or the fifth and sixth tests above (prior year tests). Rarely does a limited partner meet the material participation test because limited partners generally are not involved in the operation of the business. Thus, most income and deductions from limited partnerships are passive.

WORKING INTEREST IN AN OIL AND GAS PROPERTY. A working interest is an interest that is responsible for the cost of development or operation of the oil and gas property. This type of interest in an oil and gas property is not a passive activity as long as the taxpayer's liability in the interest is not limited. Thus, even though a taxpayer may not materially participate in the activity, the passive loss rules do not apply. This is so even if the taxpayer holds the interest through an entity such as a partnership.

TAXPAYERS SUBJECT TO PASSIVE LOSS RULES

The passive loss limitation rules apply to

- Individuals, estates, trusts
- Any closely held C corporation
- Any personal service corporation
- Certain publicly traded partnerships

Because the income and losses of partnerships and S corporations are taxed directly to the partners and shareholders, the passive loss rules do not apply to these entities.[21] Rather, the passive loss limitations apply directly at the partner or shareholder level. Thus, the situation may arise where one partner or shareholder is subject to the passive loss rules with regard to an activity conducted by the partnership or S corporation while the partners or shareholders are not.

Generally, regular corporations (i.e., C corporations) are not subject to the passive loss limitation rules. However, to prevent certain individuals from avoiding the passive loss rules through the use of a regular corporation, the rules do apply to closely held C corporations and personal service corporations.

ADDITIONAL COMMENT

Because a closely held C corporation's passive losses may offset its income from active business operations, some tax professionals advise their clients to transfer their investments that generate passive losses to their profitable corporations.

CLOSELY HELD C CORPORATIONS. The passive loss rules apply to closely held C corporations but only on a limited basis. A **closely held C corporation** is a C corporation where more than 50% of the stock is owned by five or fewer individuals at any time during the last half of the corporation's taxable year.[22] Without this special rule involving

[20] A personal service activity involves rendering personal services in the fields of health, law, engineering, architecture, accounting, actuarial science, performing arts, or consulting. It also includes any other trade or business in which capital is not a material income-producing factor. See Temp. Reg. Sec. 1.469-5T(d).

[21] An S corporation is a corporation that has elected for federal income tax purposes to be treated basically like a partnership. Thus, the income or losses and separately stated items of an S corporation flow through to the shareholders and are reported on their individual tax returns.

[22] Secs. 469(j)(1), 465(a)(1)(B), and 542(a)(2).

closely held C corporations, taxpayers would be motivated to transfer their investments (both portfolio investments and passive activities) to a C corporation where the portfolio income could be offset by the corporation's passive losses. Thus, as applied to a closely held C corporation, the passive loss rules prevent passive activity losses from offsetting portfolio income. However, a closely held C corporation's passive losses may offset its income from active business operations.

EXAMPLE I8-13 ▶ All of the outstanding stock of Delta Corporation is owned equally by individuals Allen and Beth. During the current year, Delta generates $15,000 taxable income from its active business operations. It also earns $10,000 of interest and dividends from investments and reports a $30,000 loss from a passive activity. Because Delta is a closely held C corporation, the $15,000 of taxable income from the active business is offset by $15,000 of the passive loss. However, the $10,000 of portfolio income may not be offset. Thus, for the current year, Delta reports $10,000 of taxable income from its portfolio income and has a $15,000 passive loss carryover. ◀

PERSONAL SERVICE CORPORATION. A **personal service corporation (PSC)** is a regular C corporation whose principal activity is the performance of personal services that are substantially performed by owner-employees.[23] However, a corporation is not a PSC unless owner-employees own more than 10% of the value of the stock. In contrast with a non-PSC closely held C corporation, the passive loss limitation rules apply in their entirety. If a corporation is both a PSC and a closely held C corporation, the more restrictive rules for PSCs apply. Thus, passive losses of a PSC may not offset the PSC's active business income or portfolio income.

MATERIAL PARTICIPATION BY PSCs AND CLOSELY HELD C CORPORATIONS. Special rules apply for determining whether closely held C corporations or PSCs materially participate in an activity. These corporations materially participate in an activity only if one or more shareholders who own more than 50% in value of the outstanding stock materially participate in the activity. In addition, a closely held C corporation (other than a PSC) materially participates in an activity if it meets *all* of the following tests with regard to an activity:

1. A substantial portion of the services of at least one full-time employee is in the active management of the activity.
2. A substantial portion of the services of at least three full-time nonowner employees is directly related to the activity.
3. The Sec. 162 business deductions of the activity exceed 15% of the activity's gross income for the period.[24]

PUBLICLY TRADED PARTNERSHIPS

In many cases, a **publicly traded partnership (PTP)** is treated for tax purposes as a corporation. For purposes of the passive loss rules, a PTP is defined as any partnership if interests in the partnership are either traded on an established securities market or readily tradable on a secondary market.[25] If a PTP is treated for tax purposes as a corporation, the passive loss rules generally do not apply. However, if a PTP meets certain gross income requirements, it may still be treated as a partnership, causing its items of income, loss, and credit to flow through to the partners.[26] If this is the case, the passive loss rules apply at the partner level separately to the flow through items from each PTP. Thus, partners treat losses from a PTP as separate from any other type of income (passive, active business, or

---

[23] Secs. 469(j)(2) and 269A(b)(1). For this purpose any employee who owns any stock of the corporation is an owner-employee. This stock ownership is determined by using the Sec. 318 constructive ownership rules as modified by Sec. 469(j)(2).

[24] Secs. 469(h)(4) and 465(c)(7). Tests 1 and 2 must be met for the 12-month period ending on the last day of the tax year. Test 3 must be met for the tax year. Furthermore, the Sec. 404 deductions are also included in the 15% of gross income test.

[25] Sec. 469(k)(2). See Chapter C10 of *Prentice Hall's Federal Taxation: Corporations, Partnerships, Estates, and Trusts* and Chapter C10 of the *Comprehensive* volume for a definition and discussion of publicly traded partnerships.

[26] Sec. 7704(c). For the taxable year and all preceding years beginning after Dec. 31, 1987, at least 90% of the PTP's gross income consists of dividends, interest, real property rents, income from certain gas, oil, mineral or timber activities, and gains from the sale of real estate or certain capital assets. Furthermore, certain other PTPs may also elect to continue to be treated as a partnership rather than as a corporation.

portfolio), and separate from any income from other PTPs. Partners can only carry these losses forward and offset them against income generated by that particular PTP in a subsequent year. Furthermore, a PTP loss may not offset any portfolio income that the PTP might generate. Any net income from PTPs is treated as portfolio income.

EXAMPLE I8-14 ▶ Mark owns interests in partnerships A and B, both of which are PTPs that are treated as partnerships. During the current year, Mark's share of the income from A is $2,000. Mark's share of B's loss is $1,200. B also generated some portfolio income. Mark's share of B's portfolio income is $800. The $1,200 loss from B may not offset any of B's $800 portfolio income. Furthermore, it may not offset any of the $2,000 income from A. The $2,000 income from A is treated as portfolio income. Thus, Mark reports $2,800 portfolio income and has a $1,200 suspended loss from B. In a subsequent year, Mark's share of any income from B can be offset by the $1,200 of suspended loss that is carried forward. ◀

Partners may deduct suspended losses from a PTP only in the year the partner disposes of his or her interest in the PTP. Partners do not recognize a loss in the year that the PTP itself sells a passive activity.

KEY POINT

Up to $25,000 of passive losses attributable to rental real estate can be deducted each year against income from nonpassive sources such as salary, interest, and dividends.

RENTAL REAL ESTATE TRADE OR BUSINESS

In general, rental activities are considered passive activities. However, the passive activity loss rules do not apply to certain taxpayers that are involved in real property trades or businesses. Instead, these activities are treated as active businesses. A real property trade or business involves the development, redevelopment, construction, reconstruction, acquisition, conversion, rental, operation, management, leasing, or brokering of real property.

This exception applies to taxpayers if both the following requirements are met:

- More than one-half of the personal services the taxpayer performs in all trades or businesses during the year are performed in real property trades or businesses in which the taxpayer materially participates.
- The taxpayer performs more than 750 hours of work during the taxable year in real property trades or businesses in which the taxpayer materially participates.

In meeting these tests, personal services a taxpayer renders in his or her capacity as an employee are not treated as performed in real property trades or businesses unless the employee owns at least 5% of the employer. Furthermore, for married taxpayers filing a joint return, the exception applies only if one of the spouses separately meets both requirements. The time spent in the activity by both spouses is used in determining whether or not the material participation test is met.

EXAMPLE I8-15 ▶ Anwar and Anya are married and file a joint return. Anwar's only job is renting and maintaining four large apartment complexes that he owns. Anwar and Anya manage the buildings themselves. During the current year, Anya spent 500 hours keeping records and corresponding with tenants. Anwar spent 700 hours during the year maintaining and repairing the apartments. Even though all of Anya and Anwar's personal services are connected with a real property trade or business in which they materially participate, this rental activity is considered passive because neither Anwar nor Anya alone spends more than 750 hours doing services related to the rental activity. ◀

For a closely held C corporation to meet this rental real estate business exception, the corporation must derive more than one-half of its gross receipts from real property businesses in which it materially participates.

Any deduction allowed under the previously discussed exception for taxpayers who are involved in real property trades or businesses is not taken into consideration in determining the taxpayer's AGI for purposes of the phase-out of the $25,000 deduction available for taxpayers who actively participate in a rental real estate activity. (See the following section in this chapter for a discussion of the $25,000 active participation exception.)

OTHER RENTAL REAL ESTATE ACTIVITIES

Many rental real estate activities are not considered rental real estate businesses, and are therefore subject to the passive loss rules. However, if an individual taxpayer meets certain requirements, the taxpayer still may deduct up to $25,000 of annual losses from these passive rental real estate activities against other income. To meet this exception, an individual must do both of the following:

- *Actively* participate in the activity[27]
- Own at least 10% of the value of the activity for the entire tax year

KEY POINT

Active participation is different from *material participation,* and is a lesser standard of involvement.

ACTIVE PARTICIPATION. A taxpayer can achieve *active participation*, as opposed to material participation, without regular, continuous, and material involvement in the activity and without meeting any of the material participation tests. However, the taxpayer still must participate in making management decisions or arranging for others to provide services in a significant and bona fide sense. This includes approving new tenants, deciding on rental terms, approving expenditures, and other similar decisions. Taxpayers may achieve active participation even if they hire a rental agent and others provide the services.[28] In general, a limited partner cannot participate actively in any activity of a limited partnership.

ADDITIONAL COMMENT

In calculating AGI to determine the amount of the $25,000 that is phased out, married taxpayers filing joint returns must include the income of both spouses. This provision results in a marriage penalty where both spouses have income.

LIMITATION ON DEDUCTION OF RENTAL REAL ESTATE LOSS. Taxpayers must first apply rental real estate losses against other net passive income for the year. Taxpayers may then reduce their portfolio or active business income by up to $25,000. The $25,000, however, is reduced by 50% of the taxpayer's AGI in excess of $100,000. For this purpose, AGI is determined without regard to any passive activity loss or to any loss allowable to taxpayers who materially participate in real property trades or businesses (e.g., a real estate developer). Thus, if a taxpayer has AGI of $150,000 or more, all of the rental real estate losses must be suspended and carried over with the taxpayer's other passive losses.

EXAMPLE I8-16 ▶ During the current year, Penny, a married individual who files a joint return, reports the following items of income and loss:

Salary income	$120,000
Activity A (passive)	15,000
Activity B (nonbusiness rental real estate)	(50,000)

Penny owns over 10% and actively participates in Activity B. Her AGI for the year is as follows:

Salary		$120,000
Passive income from Activity A	$15,000	
Minus: Passive loss from Activity B ($50,000, but limited to $15,000)	(15,000)	–0–
Minus: Maximum rental real estate loss (from Activity B)	$25,000	
Reduced by phase-out: [($120,000 – $100,000)× 0.50]	(10,000)	
Deductible amount (but not to exceed actual loss)		(15,000)
AGI		$105,000

Penny may deduct $30,000 of the loss from Activity B during the year ($15,000 as an offset to the passive income from Activity A + $15,000 deductible against portfolio or active business income). Penny has $20,000 ($50,000 – $30,000) of suspended passive losses from Activity B that are carried over to the following year. ◀

[27] In order for a deduction to be taken in the current year for a loss sustained in a prior year, the taxpayer must actively participate in the activity during both years. See Sec. 469(i)(1).

[28] S. Rept. No. 99-313, 99th Cong., 2d Sess., pp. 737–738 (1986). However, a lessor under a net lease will probably not be deemed to achieve active participation.

The $25,000 limit applies to the sum of both deductions and credits. Thus, in order to properly apply the limit, taxpayers must convert the credits into deduction equivalents. A *deduction equivalent* is an amount that if taken as a deduction, would reduce the tax liability by an amount equal to the credits. The amount of deduction equivalents can be computed by dividing the amount of the credit by the taxpayer's marginal tax rate. If the sum of the deductions and the deduction equivalents exceeds the $25,000 limit, the deductions are used first.

EXAMPLE I8-17 ▶ Hal owns over 10% and actively participates in activity A, which is a passive real estate rental activity. Hal's marginal tax rate is 27% and he has AGI of less than $100,000. For the year, activity A generates a $20,000 net loss and $10,000 in tax credits (which amounts to $37,037 in deduction equivalent {$10,000/.27}). After deducting the $20,000 net loss against his active business and portfolio income, Hal has a remaining real estate deduction under the limit of $5,000 ($25,000 − $20,000). Thus, Hal may use $1,350 ($5,000 × 0.27) of the credits. The remaining $8,650 ($10,000 − $1,350) of tax credits must be carried over to subsequent years. ◀

If deductions and credits exceeding the $25,000 limit arise from more than one passive activity, they must be allocated between the activities.

EXAMPLE I8-18 ▶ Mary has AGI of less than $100,000 and a 27% marginal tax rate. During the year she reports a $30,000 loss from activity A and a $10,000 loss from activity B. Additionally, activity A generates $5,000 of tax credits. Both activities A and B are passive real estate rental activities in which Mary actively participates and owns over 10% of each activity. The $25,000 deduction is first allocated to the losses. Because the sum of the losses ($40,000) exceeds the limit, the deductible loss must be allocated ratably between the activities as follows:

Activity A: $25,000 × $30,000 ÷ $40,000 = $18,750
Activity B: $25,000 × $10,000 ÷ $40,000 = $6,250

Activity A has an $11,250 ($30,000 − $18,750) suspended loss, and activity B has a $3,750 ($10,000 − $6,250) suspended loss. In addition, activity A has $5,000 of suspended tax credits. ◀

A summary of the passive activity loss rules is presented in Topic Review I8-2.

STOP & THINK

Question: Jana is a business woman who has successfully invested in various stock and bond funds. Now she is considering diversifying her holdings by investing in real estate. One of the alternatives she is considering is purchasing an interest in a limited partnership that invests in real estate. A friend is also urging Jana to go into a partnership with him in order to purchase a small office building they would rent out. Assume that the size of Jana's investment in the two alternatives would be exactly the same and that Jana estimates the economic results to be equivalent (e.g., she expects both to spin off equivalent losses for the first few years and then begin turning a profit.) What tax issues should Jana consider when making her investment decision?

Solution: In comparing alternatives such as these, of course, the most important considerations should be the non-tax factors such as cash flow from the investment, the capital appreciation of the assets, the marketability of the investment, and the risk. For example, as a limited partner, Jana will not personally be liable for debts of the partnership or lawsuits filed against the partnership. Purchase of the office building as a general partner with her friend will cause her to be personally liable. Additionally, in comparing these two alternatives, certain tax issues may come into play. Both alternatives are investments in rental real estate. However, Jana is not eligible to deduct up to $25,000 of the passive losses from the limited partnership because she will not actively participate in the partnership. On the other hand, if she is involved in management decisions regarding the office building, she will be actively participating and will be eligible for the $25,000 passive loss deduction exception. Of course, the benefit of this exception is phased out if her AGI exceeds $100,000.

Topic Review I8-2

Passive Losses

TOPIC	SUMMARY
Taxpayers covered	Individuals, estates, trusts, closely held C corporations, personal service corporations, certain publicly traded partnerships.
Definition	Any trade or business activity in which the taxpayer does not materially participate. Includes all rental activities except for certain rental real estate activities and exceptions contained in regulations. Does not include working interests in oil and gas property.
Limitation	Passive losses are deductible against passive income, but not against active or portfolio income. Disallowed losses are carried over to subsequent years (suspended losses). Losses must be accounted for separately by activity. Activities are identified by examining the taxpayer's undertakings.
Suspended losses	Must be allocated and attributed among the passive activities that generated the losses.
Disposition of interest	Suspended losses may be deducted in the year of a taxable disposition. For inherited property, suspended losses in excess of the increase in basis may be deducted on the final return of a decedent. Losses up to the amount of the basis increase are lost.
Material participation	Must be regular, continuous, and substantial. The regulations contain seven separate tests; four based on current-year participation; two based on participation in prior years; and one based on facts and circumstances.
Real property trades or businesses	Passive activity loss rules do not apply to taxpayers who materially participate in real property trade or business activities constituting more than 750 hours. Additionally, more than one-half of the taxpayer's personal services must be performed in real property trades or businesses in which the taxpayer materially participates.
Rental of real estate	Individuals may deduct losses up to $25,000 against active and portfolio income if they actively participate in the activity. This is a lesser standard than material participation, but the taxpayer must still participate in management decisions or arranging for others to provide services. The deduction phases out at a 50% rate for AGI in excess of $100,000.

CASUALTY AND THEFT LOSSES

OBJECTIVE 6

Identify and calculate the deduction for a casualty or theft loss

Taxpayers may deduct losses incurred in connection with business or investment property, but taxpayers generally are not allowed a deduction for losses on personal-use property. However, under Sec. 165, taxpayers may take a limited deduction if the loss on personal-use property arises from a fire, storm, shipwreck, other casualty, or theft. In other words, losses on personal-use property are deductible only if the loss results from a casualty. In order for an event to qualify as a casualty, the event must meet certain requirements.

CASUALTY DEFINED

According to the IRS, a deductible **casualty loss** is one that occurs in an identifiable event that is sudden, unexpected, or unusual.[29]

IDENTIFIABLE EVENT. Because the event that causes the loss must be *identifiable*, the act of losing or misplacing property is generally not considered a casualty.

However, in some cases, taxpayers have proven that the loss of property was the result of an identifiable event.

[29] IRS *Publication No. 547* (Nonbusiness Disasters, Casualties, and Thefts), 2000, p. 1.

EXAMPLE I8-19 ▶ One evening Troy and his wife, Lynn, go to the theater. Troy accidentally slams the car door on Lynn's hand. The impact breaks the flanges holding the diamond in her ring. As a result, the diamond falls from the ring and is lost. In this case, a deductible casualty loss has occurred.[30] ◀

KEY POINT

The taxpayer has the burden of proof to establish that a loss was caused by a casualty. The taxpayer should gather as much evidence as possible. Newspaper clippings, police reports, photographs, and insurance reports can be helpful in establishing the cause of the loss.

SUDDEN, UNEXPECTED, OR UNUSUAL EVENTS. According to the IRS, a *sudden event* is one that is swift, not gradual or progressive. An *unexpected event* is one that is ordinarily unanticipated and not intended. An *unusual event* is one that is not a day-to-day occurrence and that is not typical of the activity in which the taxpayer is engaged.

Thus, the IRS has ruled that a deductible casualty loss was sustained when a taxpayer went ice fishing and his automobile fell through the ice.[31] A taxpayer whose automobile was damaged as the result of an accident also sustained a deductible casualty loss. However, a taxpayer may not deduct losses incurred in an accident caused by the taxpayer's willful negligence or willful act.[32] Damage sustained as the result of an accident in an automobile race was held to be nondeductible because accidents occur often and are not unusual events in automobile races.[33]

ADDITIONAL COMMENT

Sudden, unexpected, or unusual events must also be accompanied by an external force. For example, a blown engine in an automobile is a sudden event but because no external force caused the event, the loss is not a casualty loss.

The following are a few examples of events that have been held to constitute a deductible casualty loss:

- Rust and water damage to furniture and carpets caused by the bursting of a water heater
- Damage to the exterior paint of a residence caused by a severe, sudden, and unexpected concentration of chemical fumes in the air
- Loss caused by fire (unless the taxpayer sets the fire, in which case no deduction is available)
- Damage to a building caused by an unusually large blast at a nearby quarry or a jet sonic boom[34]
- Death of trees just a few days after a sudden infestation of pine beetles[35]

The following are examples of events that have been held *not* to be a casualty:

- Water damage to the walls and ceiling of a taxpayer's personal residence as the result of the gradual deterioration of the roof[36]
- Trees dying because of gradual suffocation of the root systems
- The loss of trees and shrubs because of disease[37]
- Damage to carpet and clothing caused by moths and carpet beetles[38]
- Damage to a road due to freezing, thawing, and gradual deterioration[39]
- Damage to a residence caused by the gradual sinking of the land underneath the home[40]
- Damage caused by drought because it occurs through progressive deterioration
- The steady weakening of a building caused by normal wind and weather conditions
- The rusting and deterioration of a water heater[41]

ETHICAL POINT

A client loses his diamond ring while fishing and wants to deduct the loss as a casualty. The CPA should not sign the tax return unless he or she believes that the client's position has a realistic possibility of being sustained on its merits if challenged, which is doubtful in this situation.

[30] *John P. White*, 48 T.C. 430 (1967), *acq.* 1969-2 C.B. xxv. In another case, the taxpayer convinced the Tax Court to allow a deduction for a lost diamond, even though the taxpayer could not remember a specific blow to the ring. In this instance, the taxpayer obtained an expert witness to testify that the flanges of the ring were strong enough and in good enough repair that the loss of the diamond had to have been caused by a sudden, unexpected blow rather than by progressive deterioration.

[31] Rev. Rul. 69-88, 1969-1 C.B. 58.

[32] *Willie C. Robinson*, 1984 PH T.C. Memo ¶84,188, 47 TCM 1510 and Reg. Sec. 1.165-7(a)(3).

[33] Ltr. Rul. 8227010 (March 30, 1982) contains the above examples.

[34] *Ray Durden*, 3 T.C. 1 (1944), *acq.* 1944 C.B. 8 and Rev. Rul. 60-329, 1960-2 C.B. 67.

[35] Rev. Rul. 79-174, 1979-1 C.B. 99. See also *Charles A. Smithgall v. U.S.*, 47 AFTR 2d 81-695, 81-1 USTC ¶9121 (D.C.-Ga., 1980). However, the IRS has ruled in Ltr. Rul. 8544001 (July 12, 1985) that no casualty loss results when the time interval between the infestation and the death of the trees was too long.

[36] *Lauren Whiting*, 1975 PH T.C. Memo ¶75,038, 34 TCM 241.

[37] *William R. Miller*, 1970 PH T.C. Memo ¶70,167, 29 TCM 741 and Rev. Rul. 57-599, 1957-2 C.B. 142. See also *Howard F. Burns v. U.S.*, 6 AFTR 2d 6036, 61-1 USTC ¶9127 (6th Cir., 1960).

[38] Rev. Rul. 55-327, 1955-1 C.B. 25. See also *J. P. Meersman v. U.S.*, 18 AFTR 2d 6152, 67-1 USTC ¶9125 (6th Cir., 1966).

[39] *Howard Stacy*, 1970 PH T.C. Memo ¶70,127, 29 TCM 542. However, the breaking up of a road over a 4-month period because of extreme weather conditions was held to be a casualty. See *Emmett J. O'Connell v. U.S.*, 29 AFTR 2d 72-596, 72-1 USTC ¶9312, (D.C. Cal., 1972). See also *Stephen L. Shaffer*, 1983 PH T.C. Memo ¶83,677, 47 TCM 285.

[40] *Henry W. Berry*, 1969 PH T.C. Memo ¶69,162, 28 TCM 802. See also *David McDaniel*, 1980 PH T.C. Memo ¶80,557, 41 TCM 563.

[41] IRS *Publication No. 547* (Nonbusiness Disasters, Casualties, and Thefts), 2001, contains the above examples.

At times it is very difficult to determine under the particular facts whether the necessary incidents of suddenness, unexpectedness, or unusualness exist. For example, damage caused by the sudden infestation of pine beetles in some instances has been held to be a casualty, but in other instances it has not constituted a casualty.[42]

THEFT DEFINED

Under Sec. 165, a taxpayer may also deduct a loss sustained as the result of a theft. This includes theft of business, investment, or personal-use property. The Treasury Regulations state that "the term theft shall be deemed to include, but shall not necessarily be limited to, larceny, embezzlement, and robbery."[43] A determination whether other actions also constitute theft often depends on whether criminal intent is involved and the action is illegal under the state law where the action has occurred. Thus, the IRS has stated that blackmail, extortion, and kidnapping for ransom may also constitute theft.[44]

DEDUCTIBLE AMOUNT OF CASUALTY LOSS

The amount of a casualty loss deduction depends on the amount of the loss sustained, any insurance or other reimbursement received; and, in the case of personal-use property, the limitations imposed under the tax law.

MEASURING THE LOSS. In general, the amount of loss sustained in a casualty is the amount by which the property's FMV is reduced as a result of the casualty. This is measured by comparing the property's FMV immediately before and immediately after the casualty.[45] Any reduction in the FMV of the taxpayer's surrounding but undamaged property is disregarded.

EXAMPLE I8-20 ▶ Gail purchased a vacation home for $110,000. Shortly after she purchased the property, a mudslide completely destroyed several neighboring cabins. Gail's cabin sustained no damage. After the slide, an appraisal reveals that the FMV of the cabin has declined to $80,000 because of fears that other mudslides might occur. The $30,000 reduction in the FMV of the cabin does not constitute a deductible casualty loss. ◀

ADDITIONAL COMMENT

Taxpayers cannot deduct a loss unless they own the damaged property. Therefore, a taxpayer cannot deduct amounts he or she paid to another individual for damage he or she caused to the other individual's property.

Actual market value, not sentimental value, is used to compute the reduction in the FMV. Additionally, the cost of protecting property to prevent damage from a casualty is not a deductible loss.

If the property involved in the casualty is only partially destroyed, the amount of the loss is the lesser of the reduction in the property's FMV or the taxpayer's adjusted basis in the property.

EXAMPLE I8-21 ▶ Troy purchased a home for $25,000 several years ago. Through the years, the value of the home appreciated until it was appraised at $125,000 in the current year. Shortly after the appraisal, a flood sweeps through the area, severely damaging Troy's home and reducing its value to $90,000. Troy does not have any flood insurance. His loss is limited to the $25,000 basis in the home even though the economic loss is $35,000 ($125,000 − $90,000). ◀

TYPICAL MISCONCEPTION

Taxpayers sometimes think their loss should be based on the total economic loss rather than just the property's basis. Taxpayers should remember that they have not paid a tax on the appreciation in value and, therefore, should not be entitled to a deduction for a loss on the unrealized gain.

If business or investment property is totally destroyed in a casualty, the amount of the loss is the taxpayer's adjusted basis in the property, even if it is greater than the property's FMV. However, if personal-use property is totally destroyed, the amount of the loss is limited to the lesser of the reduction in the property's FMV or the property's adjusted basis.

---

42 Rev. Rul. 79-174, 1979-1 C.B. 99 and *George K. Notter,* 1985 PH T.C. Memo ¶85,391, 50 TCM 614. A graphic illustration of the controversy that may arise when determining whether an event is a casualty can be made by comparing the following two cases. In one case the taxpayer was washing dishes. Seeing a glass of water on the windowsill, he quickly dumped the contents down the drain and turned on the garbage disposal, not realizing that his wife's rings were in the glass. Damage to the rings in this case was deemed to be a casualty (*William H. Carpenter,* 1966 PH T.C. Memo ¶66,228, 25 TCM 1186). In the second case, the taxpayer gathered up some tissues from the night stand and flushed them down the toilet, not knowing that his wife's rings were wrapped in one of them. This event was held not to be a casualty (*W.J. Keenan, Jr. v. Bowers,* 39 AFTR 849, 50-2 USTC ¶9444 (D.C.-S.C., 1950)).

43 Reg. Sec. 1.165-8(d).

44 Rev. Rul. 72-112, 1972-1 C.B. 60 and IRS *Publication No. 547* (Nonbusiness Disasters, Casualties, and Thefts), 2001, p. 1.

45 Reg. Sec. 1.165-7(a)(2).

EXAMPLE I8-22 ▶ A machine that Beth uses in her business is completely destroyed by fire. At the time of the fire, the adjusted basis of the machine is $5,000 and its FMV is $3,000. Because the machine is business property, Beth's loss is $5,000. If the machine were a personal-use asset, the amount of the loss would be $3,000. ◀

Generally, taxpayers must establish the reduction in the FMV of the property by an appraisal. If an appraisal is difficult or impossible to obtain, the cost of the repairs may be used instead. All of the following requirements must be met before this alternative can be used:

- ▶ The repairs will bring the property back to its condition immediately before the casualty.
- ▶ The cost of the repairs is not excessive.
- ▶ The repairs do no more than repair the damage incurred in the casualty.
- ▶ The repairs do not increase the value of the property over its value immediately before the casualty.

If more than one property is destroyed in the same casualty, the taxpayer calculates the loss on each property separately.[46] Thus, the taxpayer compares each property's basis with the reduction in the FMV of that property, rather than aggregating the basis and FMV amounts for all the properties destroyed in the casualty.

If the taxpayer receives insurance or any other type of recovery, the taxpayer must reduce the amount of the loss by these amounts. In some cases these payments may actually exceed the taxpayer's basis in the property, causing the realization of a gain. If certain requirements are met, taxpayers may defer or exclude the recognition of these gains. (See the detailed discussion of involuntary conversions in Chapter I12.)

LIMITATIONS ON PERSONAL-USE PROPERTY

The amount a taxpayer may deduct for a casualty loss on personal-use property is subject to two limitations: the losses sustained in each separate casualty are reduced by $100, and the total amount of all net casualty losses for personal-use property is reduced by 10% of the taxpayer's AGI for the year. For property destroyed in the same casualty, only $100 is deducted from all the properties (i.e., $100 is not deducted from each separate property).

EXAMPLE I8-23 ▶ A windstorm blows over a large tree in front of Cathy's house, damaging the house and totally destroying her automobile. After the insurance reimbursement, the loss on the house amounts to $3,000, and the loss on the automobile is $2,500. Because the losses occur in the same casualty, the total amount of the loss is reduced to $5,400 ($3,000 + $2,500 − $100). If the damage to the car was sustained in a separate event such as an automobile accident, the total amount of the casualty losses incurred by Cathy during the year would have been $5,300 ($3,000 + $2,500 − $200). This $5,300 or $5,400 loss is then further reduced by 10% of Cathy's AGI for the year. ◀

EXAMPLE I8-24 ▶ As the result of a storm, Liz incurs a $4,500 casualty loss on personal-use property during the current year. She also sustains a $600 theft loss. Liz's AGI for the year is $50,000. She receives no tax deduction for the casualty and theft losses because they do not exceed the following limitations:

KEY POINT

Many taxpayers cannot deduct their casualty losses because of the $100 floor and 10% of AGI limitation.

	Storm	*Theft*	*Total*
Loss before limitations	$4,500	$600	$5,100
Minus: $100 floor	(100)	(100)	(200)
	$4,400	$500	$4,900
Minus: 10% of AGI (0.10 × $50,000)			(5,000)
Deductible loss			0 ◀

[46] Reg. Sec. 1.165-7(b)(2). For personal-use property, losses on real property and improvements to the property are computed in the aggregate. Thus, no separate basis need be apportioned to the improvements. See Reg. Secs. 1.165-7(b)(2)(ii) and 1.165-7(b)(3) Example (3).

ADDITIONAL COMMENT

Individuals sometimes fail to file insurance claims for damage to their personal automobile for fear that their insurance rates will increase, and hope instead to deduct the loss. In this situation, the taxpayer cannot deduct the loss.

Because of these limitations, many taxpayers who sustain casualty and theft losses on personal-use property do not receive a tax deduction. Furthermore, if the property is covered by insurance, the taxpayer cannot take a casualty loss deduction unless he or she timely files an insurance claim for the loss. This disallowance relates only to the portion of the loss that was covered by the insurance.

The rules concerning deductibility of losses described above are summarized as follows:

Result of Casualty		*Business*	*Investment*	*Personal-Use*
Total Destruction	Amount of Casualty[a]	Basis	Basis	Lesser of: basis or decline in FMV, reduced by $100 and 10% of AGI
	Type	For AGI	From AGI (For AGI if Rental)	From AGI
Partial Destruction	Amount of Casualty[a]	Lesser of: basis or decline in FMV	Lesser of: basis or decline in FMV	Lesser of: basis or decline in FMV, reduced by $100 and 10% of AGI
	Type	For AGI	From AGI (For AGI if Rental)	From AGI

[a]All amounts are first reduced by any insurance reimbursement.

NETTING CASUALTY GAINS AND LOSSES ON PERSONAL-USE PROPERTY

TYPICAL MISCONCEPTION

The concept of a gain on a casualty can be confusing. Nevertheless, if the insurance proceeds exceed the basis, a gain results.

Casualty gains and losses incurred during the year on personal-use assets are netted against each other. They are not combined with casualty gains and losses on business and investment property. For purposes of the netting process, the losses should be reduced by any insurance reimbursements and the $100 limitation, but not the 10% of AGI floor. If the gains exceed the losses for the year, all the gains and losses are treated as capital gains and losses.

EXAMPLE I8-25 ▶ During the current year, Pat incurs the following casualty gains and losses on personal-use assets. Assets W and X are destroyed in one casualty, and asset Y is destroyed in another. Pat acquired assets X and Y in the current year, whereas she acquired asset W several years ago.

Asset	*Reduction in FMV*	*Adjusted Basis*	*Insurance*	*Holding Period*
W	$10,000	$3,000	$10,000	More than 12 months
X	4,000	5,000	2,000	Less than one year
Y	2,000	3,000	0	Less than one year

Pat realizes a $7,000 ($10,000 − $3,000) gain on asset W because the insurance proceeds received for the asset exceed its basis. She realizes a $2,000 ($4,000 reduction in FMV − $2,000 insurance) loss on asset X. This loss is reduced to $1,900 because of the $100 reduction for personal casualty losses. She realizes a $2,000 loss on asset Y. Because this loss of $2,000 is realized as a result of the second casualty, the $100 limitation is deducted, resulting in a $1,900 loss from that casualty. Pat realizes a $3,200 [$7,000 − ($1,900 + $1,900)] net casualty gain for the year. Thus, the gain or loss on each asset is treated as a capital gain or loss. Pat must report a $7,000 long-term capital gain on asset W, a $1,900 short-term capital loss on asset X, and a $1,900 short-term capital loss on asset Y. ◀

If the casualty losses on personal-use property exceed the casualty gains for the year, the net loss is further reduced by 10% of AGI. The taxpayer performs all of these calculations (the netting process and reductions) on Form 4684. If any loss remains after the netting and reductions, the taxpayer reports the loss as an itemized deduction on Schedule A of Form 1040.

CASUALTY GAINS AND LOSSES ATTRIBUTABLE TO BUSINESS AND INVESTMENT PROPERTY

Taxpayers must net casualty gains and losses on business and investment property. (See Chapter I13 for a discussion of the netting procedure under Sec. 1231.) If the losses exceed the gains, the business losses and losses on investment property that generate rents or royalties are *for* AGI deductions. Losses on other investment property (e.g., the theft of a security) are itemized deductions but are not subject to the 2% of AGI floor or the 3% overall reduction of itemized deductions. Losses on business and investment property are not subject to the $100 or 10% of AGI limitations.

WHEN LOSSES ARE DEDUCTIBLE

In general, taxpayers must deduct casualty losses in the tax year in which the loss is sustained. In the following instances, however, taxpayers may deduct the loss in another year:

- Theft losses
- Insurance or other reimbursements that are reasonably expected to be received in a subsequent year
- Certain disaster losses (discussed later in this chapter)

THEFT. Taxpayers must deduct a theft loss in the tax year in which the theft is discovered. This rule is equitable and practical because a taxpayer may not discover a theft until a subsequent year.

EXAMPLE I8-26 ▶ Dale owns a hunting lodge in upstate New York. Sometime after his last trip to the lodge in November 2002, someone breaks into the lodge and steals several guns and paintings. Dale discovers the theft when he returns to the lodge on May 19, 2003. Dale's insurance does not cover the entire cost of the items. The loss is deductible in 2003, even though the theft may have occurred in 2002. ◀

REAL-WORLD EXAMPLE

A taxpayer had property confiscated by the Cuban government in 1960. The taxpayer left the country and could have filed for indemnity but did not because she expected to return. Later, the government took away the right of indemnity in 1961. Since she did not file for indemnity from the Cuban government when she had the chance, she was not allowed a casualty or theft loss. *Vila v. U.S.*, 23 AFTR2d 69-1311 (1969).

INSURANCE AND OTHER REIMBURSEMENTS. Taxpayers must subtract any reimbursement received as compensation for a loss in arriving at the amount of the loss. This is necessary even when the taxpayer has not yet received the reimbursement, as long as there is a reasonable prospect that it will be received in the future. Thus, no deduction is allowed in the year of loss if in that year a reasonable expectation of full recovery exists.[47] If full recovery is not anticipated, a loss may be deducted in the year the casualty occurs for the estimated unrecovered amount. As previously mentioned, no deduction is allowed to the extent the personal-use property is covered by insurance and the taxpayer does not file a timely insurance claim.

EXAMPLE I8-27 ▶ In December of the current year, Andrea suffers a $10,000 casualty loss when her personal automobile is struck by a city bus. Although she does not receive any reimbursement from the insurance company by December 31, she reasonably expects to recover the full amount. Andrea may not deduct a casualty loss in the current year. ◀

EXAMPLE I8-28 ▶ Assume the same facts as in Example I8-27, except that Andrea reasonably anticipates that her reimbursement from the insurance company will be only $7,000. In this case, her casualty loss in the current year is $3,000 (before reduction by the limitations). ◀

If the taxpayer does not receive the full amount of the anticipated recovery in the subsequent year, he or she may deduct the unrecovered portion. However, rather than filing an amended return for the year of loss, the taxpayer deducts the loss in the subsequent year. Thus in some cases, the income tax consequences for a single casualty loss may be spread over two years.

---

[47] Reg. Sec. 1.165-1(d)(2)(i).

EXAMPLE I8-29 ▶ During the current year, Javier's home is damaged by an exceptionally severe blast at a nearby stone quarry owned by Acme Corporation. Although the amount of the damage is properly appraised at $20,000, Javier can reasonably anticipate a recovery of only $15,000 from Acme Corporation at the end of the current year. He does not receive any recovery from Acme during the current year. Unfortunately, in the subsequent year Acme Corporation is declared bankrupt, and Javier does not receive any reimbursement. Javier's AGI is $40,000 in the current year and $45,000 in the subsequent year. During the current year, Javier may deduct $900 {$5,000 loss reasonably anticipated in the current year − [$100 limitation + (0.10 × $40,000)]}. In the subsequent year, Javier may deduct an additional casualty loss of $10,500 [$15,000 additional loss − (0.10 × $45,000)]. ◀

If a taxpayer receives a subsequent recovery for a loss that was previously deducted, the taxpayer includes the reimbursement in income in the year of recovery. The taxpayer does not file an amended return. However, the amount that the taxpayer must include in income is limited to the amount of tax benefit the taxpayer received for the previous deduction.

EXAMPLE I8-30 ▶ During the current year, Becky's automobile sustains $5,000 in damages when it is struck by another automobile. The driver of the other automobile is at fault and is uninsured, and Becky does not reasonably expect to recover any of the loss. Becky's AGI for the current year is $35,000. Becky deducts $1,400 ($5,000 loss − [$100 + $3,500]). During the subsequent year, the other driver reimburses Becky for the full amount of the damage. Because Becky received a tax benefit of only $1,400 for the loss in the year of the accident, she must only include $1,400 in gross income in the subsequent year, even though she receives a $5,000 reimbursement. Becky does not file an amended return for the year of the accident. ◀

REAL-WORLD EXAMPLE

In 1999, losses due to Hurricane Floyd in portions of North Carolina qualified as disaster losses.

DISASTER LOSSES. Under certain circumstances, a taxpayer may elect to deduct a casualty loss in the year preceding the year in which the loss actually occurs. This election is available to taxpayers who suffer losses attributable to a disaster that occurs in an area subsequently declared by the President of the United States as a disaster area.[48] Thus, an individual can elect to deduct a disaster loss occurring in 2003 on his or her 2002 tax return or report it in the regular way on his or her 2003 return. The taxpayer must file an amended return (Form 1040X) unless he or she has not filed the prior year's return when the disaster occurs. This allows taxpayers the possibility of receiving financial help from potential tax refunds by filing an amendment to the prior year's return.

Casualty loss deduction rules are summarized in Topic Review I8-3.

STOP & THINK

Question: Due to unusually heavy rainfall in the Pacific Northwest during the current year, many homes, roads and other property are destroyed. Because of the tremendous destruction, the President of the United States declares the area a disaster area. One of the properties totally destroyed in a mudslide is Jack's mountain cabin in Oregon. Jack uses the cabin exclusively for vacationing. The value of the cabin is $190,000. Unfortunately, the cabin is not insured against a mudslide. What issues must Jack consider in determining the year in which to take the casualty loss?

Solution: Since the property was destroyed in a disaster and is located in an area which the President subsequently declared as a disaster area, Jack may take the casualty deduction either in the year of the casualty or in the previous year. The year which is most beneficial is based on several factors. The destroyed property was personal use property, so the deduction is an itemized deduction subject to the 10% of AGI limitation. Thus, Jack should compare his estimated AGI for the current year with his AGI in the last year. He also should consider his other itemized deductions, including any other casualty losses. In addition, he should compare his marginal tax rates in the two years. Jack should also consider the time value of money, since by taking the deduction on his prior year return, he will receive the tax benefit earlier than if he takes the deduction on the current year return.

---

[48] Sec. 165(i). Additionally, the same treatment may apply under Sec. 165 to taxpayers who live in a disaster area and who are ordered by a state or local government to move from or relocate their residence because the disaster caused the residence to be unsafe. In order to qualify for this treatment, the order to move must come from the state or local government within 120 days of the date that the President determines the area to be a disaster area. If the property destroyed in a presidentially declared disaster area is the taxpayer's principal residence and the casualty results in a gain, a portion of the gain may be excluded if certain conditions are met (see Chapter I12).

Topic Review I8-3

Casualty Losses

TYPE OF PROPERTY	LIMITATION AND TREATMENT
Personal-use	The amount of the loss is the lesser of the property's adjusted basis or the reduction of the asset's FMV. This amount is reduced by any insurance reimbursement. If the insurance reimbursement exceeds the property's basis, a gain is realized. To the extent the property is insured, a claim must be filed or the loss is disallowed. The amount of loss incurred in each separate casualty event during the year is reduced by $100. All casualty gains and losses for the year are netted. If the gains exceed the losses, all gains and losses are treated as capital gains and losses. If the losses exceed the gains, the net loss is reduced by 10% of AGI. Any remaining loss is an itemized deduction.
Business or investment	If the property is totally destroyed, the amount of the loss is the adjusted basis of the property. If only partially destroyed, the amount of the loss is the lesser of the property's adjusted basis or the reduction of the asset's FMV. This amount is reduced by any insurance reimbursement. A gain is realized if the insurance reimbursement exceeds the property's basis. For property held one year or less, the losses and gains are ordinary losses and gains. For property held over one year, the casualty gains and losses for the year are netted. The treatment depends on the total of the taxpayer's other Sec. 1231 transactions (see Chapter I13). Business casualty losses and losses on investment property that generate rents or royalties are not subject to the $100 or 10% of AGI limitations.

BAD DEBTS

OBJECTIVE 7

Compute the deduction for a bad debt

In addition to losses on property, taxpayers may also sustain losses generated by uncollectible debts. In dealing with a deduction for **bad debts**, taxpayers must address the following requirements and issues:

- A bona fide debtor-creditor relationship must exist between the taxpayer and some other person or entity.
- The taxpayer must have basis in the debt.
- The debt must actually have become worthless during the year.
- The type and timing of a bad debt deduction depend on whether the debt is a business or nonbusiness bad debt.
- Generally, only the specific write-off method of accounting may be used in deducting the bad debt.
- A partial or complete recovery of a debt that was previously deducted may occur. In many cases a recovery of this type causes income recognition in the year of the recovery.

KEY POINT

The tax provisions that deal with deductions for losses and the tax provisions that deal with the deductions for bad debts are mutually exclusive, and an amount properly deductible as a loss cannot be deducted as a bad debt or visa versa.

BONA FIDE DEBTOR-CREDITOR RELATIONSHIP

Only items constituting bona fide debt are eligible to be deducted as a bad debt. A **bona fide debt** is one that arises from a valid and enforceable obligation to pay a fixed or determinable sum of money and results in a debtor-creditor relationship.[49]

RELATED-PARTY TRANSACTIONS. Determining whether a bona fide loan transaction has actually taken place is especially critical when the transaction is between the taxpayer and a family member or other related party (e.g., a controlled corporation). The taxpayer must carefully examine all the facts and circumstances surrounding the transaction because a gift does not constitute a debt. The taxpayer's intent is critical here. For example, if the taxpayer's intent is to provide property, cash, or services to someone else

KEY POINT

The fact that the debtor is a related party does not preclude deduction of a bad debt, but the taxpayer should be able to document the debt as being bona fide.

[49] Reg. Sec. 1.166-1(c).

without receiving any consideration in return, a gift—not a loan—has been made. Some tests used to determine the taxpayer's intent include the following:

- Does a note or other written instrument exist which evidences an obligation to repay?[50]
- Have the parties established a definite schedule of repayment?
- Is a reasonable rate of interest stated?
- Would a person who is unrelated to the debtor make the loan?[51]

EXAMPLE I8-31 ▶

REAL-WORLD EXAMPLE

Taxpayer advanced $8,500 to his son-in-law who operated a livestock auction barn. Taxpayer was entitled to a bad debt deduction upon default because notations on the checks indicated that they were loans and undisputed testimony indicated that repayment was to be made within 90 days. *Giffin A. Andrew,* 54 T.C. 239 (1970).

During the current year Maria loaned $20,000 to her son Sam, who used the money in his business. Although no written note or contract was signed, Sam orally promised to repay Maria as soon as his business became profitable. No rate of interest was stated. Unfortunately, the business failed and Sam went out of business in the subsequent year. He never repaid the loan principal or interest.

In this case, no valid debt exists because neither an interest rate nor a repayment schedule was established. An unrelated person would not have made a loan to Sam under these conditions. In addition, Maria does not receive any consideration in return for the "loan." Since the facts indicate that the transaction is actually a gift, Maria may not claim a bad debt deduction because of Sam's failure to repay. ◀

Tax advisers should also closely examine other related party transactions. For example, a loan from a shareholder to a controlled corporation may actually be an additional contribution to capital disguised as a loan. Thus, a transfer of cash by a shareholder who owns a controlling (i.e., more than 50%) interest in the stock of a corporation may indicate a capital contribution rather than a loan. Likewise, a loan from a corporation to a controlling shareholder may actually be a disguised dividend or a salary payment.

THIRD PARTY DEBT. Generally, a taxpayer may deduct a bad debt only when a debtor-creditor relationship exists. However, in some cases a taxpayer will guarantee or endorse someone else's obligation. If the taxpayer is forced to pay the third party's debt under the terms of the guarantee, the guarantor may actually be treated as the creditor. If the original debtor does not repay the taxpayer who guarantees and pays the debt, the guarantor may deduct the loss. Any accrued interest that the guarantor pays may also be deductible as a bad debt. However, the interest is not deductible as interest when paid by the guarantor because it accrued on someone else's debt. Here, too, the taxpayer's intent determines whether the guarantee and payment constitute a gift.

EXAMPLE I8-32 ▶

Ron is the sole shareholder and a full-time employee of Zip Corporation. For Zip Corporation to obtain a bank loan, Ron personally signs a guarantee that the loan would be repaid. Unfortunately, Zip Corporation defaults on the loan and Ron is required to repay the loan. In this case, Ron signed the guarantee to preserve his job and enhance his investment in Zip Corporation. Although Ron receives no direct consideration for having signed the note, he does receive indirect consideration in the form of continued job security and protection of his investment. Because the loan guarantee was motivated by a business or investment purpose, Ron may deduct the bad debt. ◀

TYPICAL MISCONCEPTION

Taxpayers sometimes mistakenly assume that a cash method taxpayer can take a bad debt deduction on a debt that arose from services rendered by the taxpayer.

TAXPAYER'S BASIS IN THE DEBT

For a bad debt to be deductible, the creditor must have basis in the debt. The taxpayer may acquire this basis in different ways. If a taxpayer loans money, the taxpayer's basis in the debt is the amount loaned. If the debt arises because the taxpayer provides property or

---

[50] A written note or other instrument is an evidence of a bona fide debtor-creditor relationship. However, if the note or other instrument is registered or has interest coupons and is issued by a corporation or a government, the bad debt provisions of Sec. 166 do not apply. Instead, the worthless security provisions of Sec. 165 (previously discussed) apply.

[51] *Jean C. Tyler v. Tomlinson,* 24 AFTR 2d 69-5426, 69-2 USTC ¶9559 (5th Cir., 1969). See also, *C. L. Hunt,* 1989 PH T.C. Memo ¶89,335, 57 TCM 919, where certain loans that the taxpayer made to his children were treated as bona fide loans, whereas others were treated as gifts. In that case, the children had been trading in silver futures and were required to make margin calls. Because they could not make the calls, the children's positions were involuntarily liquidated. Up to the date of the liquidation, the taxpayer had made loans to the children that were payable on demand and were subject to the prime rate of interest. These loans were evidenced by promissory notes. After the liquidation, the taxpayer continued to make loans to the children. However, these loans were not evidenced by notes. The loans up to the time of the liquidation were treated as bona fide loans and the subsequent loans were treated as gifts.

services for the other party, basis is established only if the taxpayer has previously included the FMV of the property or services in income. This often depends on the taxpayer's method of accounting. An accrual method taxpayer generally reports income in the year the services are performed or the property is provided. (See the discussion in Chapter I11.) Thus, an accrual method taxpayer has a basis in either a note receivable or an open account receivable equal to the amount included in gross income (i.e., the FMV of the services). A cash method taxpayer, however, reports income only in the year in which payment in the form of cash or property is received. Because a note constitutes the receipt of property, a cash method taxpayer reports income (and establishes basis) in the year the note is received. However, if the cash-method taxpayer does not receive a note and the receivable is an open account item, the taxpayer reports no income until the receivable is collected. Thus, the taxpayer has no basis in the receivable and does not receive a bad debt deduction if the receivable is not collected.

EXAMPLE I8-33 ▶ In October of the current year, Jim performs some legal services for Joy. Jim bills Joy for $1,000. Joy does not sign a note for the debt. As a cash method taxpayer, Jim does not include the $1,000 in his current year's income. After repeated efforts to collect the fee, Jim discovers in June of the subsequent year that Joy has left the city and cannot be found. Jim may not deduct a bad debt for the uncollected amount in the subsequent year because he has not taken the amount into income and he has no basis in the debt. If Joy had signed a note for the debt, Jim would have reported income in the current year in an amount equal to the note's FMV and could have deducted the loss when the note became uncollectible in the subsequent year. ◀

DEBT MUST BE WORTHLESS

To deduct a bad debt, the taxpayer must show that the debt is worthless. This determination is made by reference to all the pertinent evidence, including the general financial condition of the debtor and whether the debt is secured by collateral.

In proving the worthlessness of a debt, a taxpayer does not need to take legal action if the surrounding circumstances indicate that legal action probably would not result in the collection of the debt. By simply showing that legal action is not warranted, the taxpayer provides sufficient proof that the debt is worthless.[52] Indications that an unsecured debt is worthless include bankruptcy of the debtor, disappearance or death of a debtor, and repeated unsuccessful attempts at collection. Furthermore, if the surrounding circumstances warrant it, a taxpayer may deduct a worthless debt even before the debt comes due. As will be explained later in this chapter, a nonbusiness debt must be totally worthless before a deduction is allowed. However, a current deduction is allowed for a partially worthless business bad debt.

KEY POINT

Taxpayers must distinguish between business and nonbusiness bad debts because the tax treatment varies according to the type of debt.

NONBUSINESS BAD DEBTS

The distinction between a business bad debt and a nonbusiness bad debt is important because the character of the debt determines its tax treatment. A business bad debt gives rise to an ordinary deduction, whereas a nonbusiness bad debt is treated as a short-term capital loss. All loans made by a corporation are assumed to be associated with the corporation's business; therefore, the provisions for nonbusiness bad debts do not apply to corporations.

TYPICAL MISCONCEPTION

Assume that a taxpayer lends money to a friend to be used in the friend's business. If the friend does not repay the loan, the debt is a nonbusiness bad debt unless the taxpayer is in the business of lending money. This type of debt is occasionally improperly classified as a business debt.

DEFINITION OF A NONBUSINESS BAD DEBT. A *nonbusiness debt* is defined as any debt other than (1) a debt created or acquired in connection with a trade or business of the taxpayer, or (2) a debt the loss from the worthlessness of which is incurred in the taxpayer's trade or business. This determination depends on an examination of the facts and circumstances surrounding the debt in question.

A debt incurred in a taxpayer's business continues to be a business debt for that taxpayer even if, at the time the debt goes bad, the taxpayer has ceased conducting that particular business. This is situation (1) above. If another taxpayer acquires a business, any outstanding debt at the time the business is acquired continues to be business debt as long

[52] Reg. Sec. 1.166-2.

as the purchaser continues the business. This is situation (2) above. The debt is a nonbusiness debt if the person who owns the debt when it becomes worthless is not engaged in the business in which the debt is incurred either at the time the debt arose or when it becomes worthless.

EXAMPLE I8-34 ▶ Matt, an individual who uses the accrual method of accounting, is engaged in the grocery business. During 2002, he extends credit to Jeff on an open account. In 2003, Matt sells his business to Joan, but retains Jeff's account. Jeff's account becomes worthless in 2003. Even though Matt is no longer engaged in the grocery business at the time the debt becomes worthless, he may deduct the loss as a business bad debt in 2003. If Joan purchases Jeff's account upon acquiring the grocery business, Joan is entitled to a business bad debt deduction in 2003 because the debt was incurred in the trade or business in which Joan is currently engaged. ◀

ETHICAL POINT

A tax practitioner should serve as an advocate for his or her client. Thus, a tax practitioner may resolve doubt in favor of the client as long as reasonable support exists for his or her position.

In addition, classification as a business debt requires a proximate relationship between the debt and the taxpayer's business.[53] According to the Supreme Court, this relationship exists if a business motive is the taxpayer's dominant motivation in incurring the debt. This determination must be made on a case-by-case basis. For example, when an individual stockholder who is also an employee of the corporation loans money to the corporation, is the loan a business or nonbusiness debt? Because an employee is considered to be engaged in the business of working for a corporation, a loan made to the corporation in an attempt to protect the employment relationship may be held to be a business debt. However, if the individual's dominant motive is to protect his or her stock investment, the loan is a nonbusiness debt.[54]

EXAMPLE I8-35 ▶ Lisa is an individual engaged in the advertising business. If clients occasionally need additional funds to meet their cash-flow obligations, Lisa sometimes lends them money. Lisa's dominant motive for making the loans is to retain the clients. She has no ownership interests in these clients. Under these facts, if any of these loans becomes worthless, it would be considered a business bad debt.[55] ◀

TAX TREATMENT. Individuals deduct nonbusiness debts that become wholly worthless during the year as short-term capital losses. The length of time the debt is outstanding has no bearing on this treatment.

Individuals generally prefer an ordinary deduction over a short-term capital loss because the tax deduction attributable to net capital losses is limited to $3,000 each year. Any loss in excess of this limit is carried over to subsequent years to be included in the capital gain and loss netting process in those years (see Chapter I5).

EXAMPLE I8-36 ▶ During 2001, Kim loaned her friend $10,000. The friend used the funds to invest in commodities futures. The transaction had all the characteristics of a bona fide debt rather than a mere gift to a friend. Unfortunately, the commodities market prices declined, and Kim's friend incurred substantial losses. In 2002, Kim's friend declared personal bankruptcy and Kim was unable to collect any of the loan. Kim did not recognize any other capital gains or losses during 2002. The $10,000 bad debt loss recognized in 2002 is treated as a short-term capital loss. Thus, Kim may deduct only $3,000 in 2002. The remaining $7,000 is carried over indefinitely to 2003 and subsequent years. ◀

TYPICAL MISCONCEPTION

Partial worthlessness means that a debt is still partially recoverable. The term is sometimes erroneously applied to debt where there has been a partial recovery even though there is no prospect for further recovery.

PARTIAL WORTHLESSNESS. As previously noted, taxpayers may not deduct a partially worthless nonbusiness debt. Thus, a taxpayer cannot deduct a loss for a nonbusiness debt that is still partially recoverable during the year.

EXAMPLE I8-37 ▶ Gordon, an individual, made a $5,000, five-year interest-bearing loan to a small company in 2000. Gordon was not in the trade or business of making commercial loans. In 2002, Gordon received word from the attorney who was appointed trustee of the company that bankruptcy proceedings had been filed. The trustee indicated that, although final disposition of the case

---

[53] Reg. Sec. 1.166-5(b)(2).

[54] *John M. Trent v. CIR*, 7 AFTR 2d 1599, 61-2 USTC ¶9506 (2nd Cir., 1961). See also *Charles L. Hutchinson*, 1982 PH T.C. Memo ¶82,045, 43 TCM 440 and *U.S. v. Edna Generes*, 29 AFTR 2d 72-609, 72-1 USTC ¶9259 (USSC, 1972).

[55] *Stuart Bart*, 21 T.C. 880 (1954), *acq.* 1954-1 C.B. 3.

will not occur until 2003, Gordon can reasonably expect to receive only 20 cents for every $1 invested. Because this is a nonbusiness bad debt that is still partly recoverable in 2002, Gordon may not deduct the partial loss as a short-term capital loss in 2002. ◀

BUSINESS BAD DEBTS

The tax treatment of losses from business bad debts differs substantially from the treatment of nonbusiness bad debts. As previously discussed, a business bad debt provides an ordinary loss deduction. Furthermore, taxpayers may also deduct a business debt that has become only partially worthless during the year.

EXAMPLE I8-38 ▶ Assume the same facts as in Example I8-37 except that Gordon's loan is made for business reasons (e.g., to provide assistance to a customer in financial difficulty). Because 80% of the loan is reasonably expected to be unrecoverable during 2002, Gordon may deduct $4,000 (0.80 × $5,000) as an ordinary loss in 2002. In 2003, when Gordon receives the $500 settlement, he may deduct an additional $500 of ordinary loss. ◀

ACCOUNTING FOR THE BUSINESS BAD DEBT

BOOK-TAX DIFFERENCES

In general, for tax purposes, taxpayers can use only the specific write-off method of accounting for bad debts. However, a corporation or other taxpayer would probably be required to use the reserve method for financial reporting purposes. This book-tax difference is one of the most common so-called M-1 adjustments in filing a Form 1120 for corporate taxpayers.

In general, two basic methods are available to account for business bad debts: the specific write-off method and the reserve method. Except for certain specialized industries, however, taxpayers can use only the specific write-off method for tax purposes. Under the **specific write-off method**, the taxpayer deducts each bad debt individually as it becomes worthless and writes it off as an expense. Taxpayers use this method for (1) business bad debts that are either totally or partially worthless and (2) nonbusiness bad debts that are totally worthless. However, as previously noted, taxpayers take no deduction for partially worthless nonbusiness bad debts.

In the case of a partially worthless business bad debt, taxpayers may only deduct the worthless part of the debt. The taxpayer must prove to the satisfaction of the IRS the amount of the debt that has become worthless.

RECOVERY OF BAD DEBTS

A taxpayer may collect a debt that was previously written off for tax purposes. Since the taxpayer previously deducted the uncollectible debt, the taxpayer must report the recovery as income in the year it is collected. The amount of the income that must be reported depends on the tax benefit rule discussed in Chapter I4.

DEPOSITS IN INSOLVENT FINANCIAL INSTITUTIONS

KEY POINT

If a loss is treated as a casualty loss, it is subject to a $100 floor, and total net casualty losses for the year are deductible only to the extent that they exceed 10% of AGI.

At their election, qualified individuals may treat a loss on deposits in qualified bankrupt or insolvent financial institutions as a personal casualty loss in the year in which the individual can reasonably estimate the loss. The recognized loss is the difference between the taxpayer's basis in the deposit and a reasonable estimate of the amount that the taxpayer will receive. This treatment allows the individual an ordinary loss deduction, but subjects the loss to the personal casualty loss limitations. In lieu of this election, qualified individuals may elect to treat these losses as if they were incurred in a transaction entered into for profit (but not connected with a trade or business). This election is available only with respect to deposits that are not insured under federal law, and is limited to $20,000 ($10,000 if married and filing separately) per institution per year. This limitation is reduced by any insurance proceeds expected to be received under state law. This election also allows the individual an ordinary loss deduction but subjects the loss to the $20,000 limitation as well as the 2% of AGI floor on miscellaneous itemized deductions. If the taxpayer makes neither of these elections, the taxpayer may claim the loss as a nonbusiness bad debt (a capital loss) in the year of worthlessness or partial recovery, whichever comes last.

A qualified individual is any individual *except* one who

- Owns at least 1% of the outstanding stock of the financial institution
- Is an officer of the financial institution

► Is a relative of an officer or a 1% owner of the financial institution[56]

Qualified financial institutions include banks, federal or state chartered savings and loans and thrift institutions, and federal or state insured credit unions.

This election applies to all losses sustained by the individual in the same institution and cannot be revoked unless the taxpayer receives IRS permission.[57]

The treatment of business and nonbusiness bad debts is summarized in Topic Review I8-4.

NET OPERATING LOSSES

OBJECTIVE 8

Compute a net operating loss deduction

A **net operating loss** (NOL) under Sec. 172 generally involves only business income and expenses. An NOL occurs when taxable income for any year is negative because business expenses exceed business income. A deduction for the NOL arises when a taxpayer carries the NOL to a year in which the taxpayer has taxable income. Thus, an NOL for one year becomes a deduction against taxable income of another year. This is accomplished in one of two ways:

► The year's NOL is carried back and deducted from the income of a previous year. This procedure provides for a refund of some of the taxes previously paid for the prior year.

► The year's NOL is carried forward and deducted from the income of a subsequent year. This procedure provides a reduction in the taxable income of the subsequent year, thus reducing the tax liability associated with that year.

KEY POINT

If taxpayers were not entitled to a deduction for net operating losses, taxpayers would actually pay a tax on an amount that exceeded their economic income over a period of time. The NOL deduction permits taxpayers to offset taxable income with losses incurred in other years.

The NOL deduction is intended to mitigate the inequity caused by the interaction of the progressive rate structure and the requirement to report income on an annual basis. This inequity arises between taxpayers whose business income fluctuates widely from year to year and those whose business income remains relatively constant.

EXAMPLE I8-39 ► Julie and Ken are both married (not to each other) and both file a joint return with their respective spouses. Over a two-year period they both report a total of $140,000 in taxable income. However, Julie and her husband report $70,000 of taxable income each year; Ken and his wife report $200,000 of taxable income in the first year and a $60,000 loss in the second year. Without the NOL provisions, Julie would report a $25,392 ($12,696 + $12,696) total tax liability for the two years, whereas Ken would report a total tax liability of $51,813 (taxable income of $200,000).[58] However, Ken can carryback the $60,000 loss to recover a portion of the taxes paid on the $200,000 in the prior year. Based on 2002 rates, Ken would recover $19,402 of

Topic Review I8-4

Bad Debts

TYPE OF DEBT	RESULTS
Nonbusiness	Deductible as a short-term capital loss. Deductible only when the debt is totally worthless. The taxpayer must have basis in the debt.
Business	Deductible as an ordinary loss. Except for certain specialized exceptions, the specific write-off method must be used. The reserve method is not available. May deduct partial worthlessness. Must have basis in the debt.

[56] Sec. 165(l). A *relative* is defined as a sibling, spouse, aunt, uncle, nephew, niece, ancestor, or lineal descendant.

[57] The rules dealing with this special election are found in Notice 89-28, (1989-1 C.B. 667).

[58] Using the 2002 tax rate schedules.

the $51,813 paid, resulting in a net tax liability for both years of $32,411 ($51,813 − $19,402). Although the total tax liability over the two years for the two couples is still unequal, the ability to carryover NOL's provides some degree of fairness. ◀

COMPUTING THE NET OPERATING LOSS

The starting point in calculating an individual's NOL is generally taxable income. As mentioned earlier in this chapter, individuals may deduct three basic types of expenses to arrive at the amount of taxable income: business-related expenses, investment-related expenses, and certain personal expenses. The NOL, however, generally attempts to measure only the economic loss that occurs when business expenses exceed business income. Thus, taxpayers must make several adjustments to taxable income to arrive at the amount of the NOL for any particular year.[59] These include adjustments for an NOL deduction, a capital loss deduction, the deduction for personal exemptions, and the excess of nonbusiness deductions over nonbusiness income.

ADDITIONAL COMMENT

If taxpayers were permitted to calculate the NOL for the current year by including NOL carryovers from earlier years, they could possibly extend the carryover period beyond the statutorily established 20-year carryforward period.

ADD BACK ANY NOL DEDUCTION. Under certain circumstances, a taxpayer might have taken a deduction for an NOL arising from another tax year in computing the taxable loss for the current loss year. To allow this deduction to create or increase the NOL of the current loss year would provide an unwarranted benefit. Thus, taxable income for the current loss year must be increased for this deduction.

ADD BACK ANY CAPITAL LOSS DEDUCTION. To compute taxable income, individuals may deduct up to a maximum of $3,000 capital losses in excess of capital gains in any year. Any capital loss in excess of this limit can be carried over and deducted in a subsequent tax year, subject to the same limitation. Because capital losses have their separate carryover provisions, taxpayers must add back any deduction associated with these losses to taxable income to arrive at the NOL for the current loss year. To make this adjustment, the taxpayer must follow several steps:

Step 1: A taxpayer must separate nonbusiness capital gains and losses from business capital gains and losses. The nonbusiness gains and losses are then netted, while the business gains and losses are netted separately.

Step 2: If the nonbusiness capital gains exceed the nonbusiness capital losses, the excess, along with other types of nonbusiness income, is first used to offset any nonbusiness ordinary deductions. Any nonbusiness capital gain remaining is then used to offset any business capital loss in excess of the business capital gain for the year.[60]

Step 3: If both groups of transactions result in net losses, the capital loss deduction provided by these transactions must be added back. For purposes of the NOL, no deduction is allowed for either business or nonbusiness net capital losses.

Step 4: If the taxpayer's nonbusiness capital losses exceed the nonbusiness capital gains, the losses may not be offset against the taxpayer's excess business capital gains. Allowing this offset would provide an indirect deduction for a nonbusiness economic loss.[61]

EXAMPLE I8-40 ▶ During the current year, Nils recognizes a short-term capital loss of $10,000 on the sale of an investment capital asset. He also recognizes a $5,000 long-term capital gain on the sale of a business capital asset. For taxable income purposes, the loss is netted against the gain, leaving a $5,000 net short-term capital loss. This loss provides a $3,000 deduction from taxable income, with the remaining $2,000 being carried forward to the following year. To compute the NOL, however, none of the $10,000 nonbusiness capital loss is deductible. Thus, the $3,000 deduction as well as the $5,000 loss that offset the business capital gain must be added back. ◀

---

[59] In the case of a corporation, these adjustments are minor.

[60] Reg. Sec. 1.172-3. If the nonbusiness deductions exceed the nonbusiness income, the excess is added back. This adjustment is discussed later in the chapter.

[61] Sec. 172(d)(2). Note that all deductible nonbusiness capital losses involve investment property because capital losses on personal-use assets are not deductible in arriving at taxable income. To make the adjustment for any capital loss, the exclusion under Sec. 1202 for gains from small business stock is not allowed (see Chapter I5).

ADD BACK THE DEDUCTION FOR PERSONAL EXEMPTIONS. Because the deduction for personal and dependency exemptions is strictly a personal deduction, it must be added back to arrive at the year's NOL.

ADDITIONAL COMMENT

An excess of nonbusiness deductions over nonbusiness income cannot increase the NOL. However, an excess of nonbusiness income over nonbusiness expenses can reduce the NOL.

ADD BACK EXCESS OF NONBUSINESS DEDUCTIONS OVER NONBUSINESS INCOME. Because nonbusiness deductions do not reflect an economic loss from business, they are not deductible in arriving at the NOL. However, these deductions do offset any nonbusiness income reported during the year. Nonbusiness income includes sources of income such as dividends and interest, as well as nonbusiness capital gains in excess of nonbusiness capital losses. Wages and salary, even if they are earned in part-time employment, are considered business income. Nonbusiness deductions include itemized deductions such as charitable contributions, medical expenses, and nonbusiness interest and taxes. Casualty losses on personal-use assets, however, are treated as business losses and are excluded from this adjustment.[62] If a taxpayer does not have itemized deductions in excess of the standard deduction, the standard deduction is used as the amount of the nonbusiness deductions.

Following are several independent examples demonstrating these required adjustments. In each case, assume that Nancy is a single taxpayer.

EXAMPLE I8-41 ▶ During 2002, Nancy, who is single, reports the following taxable income:

Gross income from business		$123,000	
Minus: Business expenses		(147,000)	($24,000)
Plus: Interest income			700
Dividend income			400
AGI			($22,900)
Minus: Greater of itemized deductions or standard deduction:			
Interest expense		$6,000	
Taxes		4,000	
Casualty loss (reduced by the $100 floor)		1,000	
Total itemized deductions		$11,000	
		or	
Standard deduction		4,700	(11,000)
Minus: Personal exemption			(3,000)
Taxable income			($36,900)

Nancy's NOL for the year is computed as follows:

Taxable income			($36,900)
Nonbusiness deductions:			
Itemized deductions	$11,000		
Minus: Casualty loss	(1,000)	$10,000	
Minus: Nonbusiness income:			
Interest	$700		
Dividends	400	(1,100)	
Plus: Excess of nonbusiness deductions over nonbusiness income			8,900
Plus: Personal exemption			3,000
Net operating loss			($25,000)[a] ◀

[a]Note that the NOL equals the total of the $24,000 net business loss and the $1,000 casualty loss.

[62] Sec. 172(d)(4)(C).

EXAMPLE I8-42 ▶ **During 2002, Nancy, who is single, reports the following taxable income:**

Gross income from business		$123,000	
Minus: Business expenses		(147,000)	($24,000)
Plus: Interest income			700
Dividend income			400
AGI			($22,900)
Minus: Greater of itemized deductions or standard deduction:			
Interest expense		$ 2,000	
		or	
Standard deduction		4,700	(4,700)
Minus: Personal exemption			(3,000)
Taxable income			($30,600)

Nancy's NOL for the year is computed as follows:

Taxable income			($30,600)
Nonbusiness deductions:			
Standard deduction		$4,700	
Minus: Nonbusiness income:			
Interest	$700		
Dividends	400	(1,100)	
Plus: Excess of nonbusiness deductions over nonbusiness income			3,600
Plus: Personal exemption			3,000
Net operating loss			($24,000)[a] ◀

[a]Note that the NOL equals the net business loss for the year.

EXAMPLE I8-43 ▶ **During 2002, Nancy, who is single, reports the following taxable income:**

Gross income from business		$123,000	
Minus Business expenses		(147,000)	($24,000)
Plus: Interest income			700
Dividend income			400
Salary			6,000
Nonbusiness LTCG			10,000
AGI			($6,900)
Minus: Greater of itemized deductions or standard deduction:			
Interest expense		$ 6,000	
Taxes		4,000	
Casualty (reduced by the $100 floor)		1,000	
Total itemized deductions		$11,000	
		or	
Standard deduction		4,700	(11,000)
Minus: Personal exemption			(3,000)
Taxable income			($20,900)

Nancy's NOL for the year is computed as follows:

Taxable income			($20,900)
Plus: Nonbusiness deductions:			
Itemized deductions	$11,000		
Minus: Casualty loss	(1,000)	$10,000	
Minus: Nonbusiness income:			
Interest	$700		
Dividends	400		
LTCG	10,000	(11,100)	
Excess of nonbusiness deductions over nonbusiness income			0

Plus:	Personal exemption	3,000
Net operating loss		($17,900)[a] ◀

[a]Note that the NOL can also be calculated as follows:

Loss from business	($24,000)
Salary	6,000
Casualty loss	(1,000)
Excess of nonbusiness income ($11,100) over nonbusiness deductions ($10,000)	1,100
NOL	($17,900)

CARRYBACK AND CARRYOVER PERIODS

Under Sec. 172, an NOL is initially carried back for two years and is deductible as an offset to the taxable income of the carryback years. Except as noted below, taxpayers must carry the loss back first. If any loss remains, taxpayers may then carry it forward for a period of 20 years.[63] Furthermore, in both the carryback and carryforward periods, the loss must be deducted from the years in chronological order. Thus, if an NOL is sustained in 2002, it first must be carried to 2000, then to 2001, followed by 2003, 2004, and so on until the loss is completely used. Any NOL that is not used during the carryover period expires and is of no further tax benefit.

If the NOL is carried back to a prior year, the taxpayer must file for a refund of taxes previously paid. If the NOL deduction is carried forward, it reduces the taxable income and the tax liability for the carryover year.

ADDITIONAL COMMENT

An election to forgo the carryback period for the NOL of any year is irrevocable.

ELECTION TO FORGO CARRYBACK PERIOD. A taxpayer may elect not to carryback the NOL, but to carry the loss forward. This election, which is made with respect to the entire carryback period, does not extend the carryforward period beyond 20 years. This allows a taxpayer some degree of flexibility in using the NOL deduction to the greatest advantage. (See the Tax Planning Considerations section in this chapter for a discussion of this topic.)

LOSS CARRYOVERS FROM TWO OR MORE YEARS. At times, a taxpayer might have NOL carryovers that are incurred in two or more taxable years. Often these losses are carried to the same years in the carryover period. If such is the case, the loss of the earliest year is always completely used first before deducting any of the loss incurred in a subsequent year. Because of the limited carryover period, this rule is beneficial to the taxpayer.

RECOMPUTATION OF TAXABLE INCOME IN THE CARRYOVER YEAR

When the taxpayer carries back the NOL deduction to a prior year, the taxpayer must recompute that year's taxable income. Because the NOL is attributable to a taxpayer's trade or business, it is deductible *for* AGI. As a result, the recomputation of taxable income for the carryback year may affect the deductible amount of certain itemized deductions because some of the deductions (e.g., the deductions for medical expenses, charitable contributions, and casualty losses) are limited or measured by reference to the taxpayer's AGI. All of these deductions except the deduction for charitable contributions must be recomputed using the reduced AGI amount.[64]

Once the taxpayer determines the tax refund for the carryback year, the taxpayer must calculate the amount of the NOL available to be deducted in subsequent carryover years. This is done by adjusting the recomputed income of the prior carryover year. Although certain differences exist, these adjustments are similar to those mentioned above.

The rules for computing and deducting NOLs are presented in Topic Review I8-5.

[63] For NOLs arising in a farming business, in a qualified small business attributable to a Presidentially declared disaster, or in a casualty or theft sustained by an individual, the carry back period is extended to three years. These NOLs are taken after the regular NOL. Certain "specified liability losses" are entitled to a 10-year carryback. Sec. 172(b)(1)(C) and (f).

[64] Reg. Sec. 1.172-5(a)(3)(ii).

Topic Review I8-5

Net Operating Losses

ITEM	RULES
Computation of NOL (adjustments to taxable income)	Add back any NOL deduction carried to the current year. Add back any capital loss deduction. Add back the deduction for personal and dependency exemptions. Add back the excess of nonbusiness deductions over nonbusiness income. For this purpose, casualty losses on personal-use property are treated as business losses.
Carryover period	May be carried back two years and forward twenty years. (certain exceptions apply) Must be carried to the carryover years in chronological order: first carried back to the second prior year, then to the first prior year, then to the first succeeding year, etc. An election may be made to forgo the carryback. This does not extend the carryforward period. If losses from two or more years are carried to the same year, the losses from the earliest year are completely used first.

TAX PLANNING CONSIDERATIONS

BAD DEBTS

KEY POINT

If uncertainty exists as to the year in which a debt became worthless, the issue may not be settled within the normal three-year statute of limitations. For this reason, a taxpayer may claim a deduction for a worthless debt at any time within seven years.

To deduct a bad debt, a taxpayer must show that the debt is worthless. At times the IRS might assert that the debt being written off is either not yet worthless or that it became worthless in a previous year. If the taxpayer is unable to overcome the IRS's assertion concerning the year of worthlessness, the taxpayer might be barred from filing an amended return for the prior year because of the statute of limitations.[65] Thus, taxpayers should carefully document all efforts at collection and other facts that show the debt is worthless.

As previously mentioned, a third-party guarantor of a loan who is required to repay the debt may, under certain circumstances, be entitled to a bad debt deduction. The guarantor must demonstrate that he or she received reasonable consideration in the form of cash or property in exchange for guaranteeing the debt. If the taxpayer does not receive proper consideration, the guarantee and subsequent payment of the loan by the guarantor is considered to be a gift rather than a loan. Reasonable consideration is also deemed to be received if the taxpayer enters into the agreement for a good faith business purpose or in accordance with normal business practice. However, if the taxpayer guarantees the debt of a spouse or a relative, the taxpayer must receive the consideration in the form of cash or property.

In the case of an outright loan between related taxpayers, the lender should always make sure to retain proper documentation to substantiate the fact that the transaction is a loan. If the taxpayer does not keep such documentation, the IRS may assert that the transaction is a gift.

CASUALTIES

A deduction is allowed for stolen property, but no deduction is allowed for lost property. Thus, taxpayers should always carefully document losses of property through theft (e.g., the filing of police reports or claims with the taxpayer's insurance company). In addition, pictures and written appraisals may be helpful to prove the amount of the loss.

[65] However, the statute of limitations for claims for a refund or credit because of a bad debt is extended from three years to seven years under Sec. 6511(d)(1), thus giving the taxpayer additional time if this is the case.

ADDITIONAL COMMENT

Normally, a taxpayer would want to carry back the NOL because he or she will receive a refund in a short time period by filing the amended return. The carryover of the NOL involves waiting for a year or more to receive a tax benefit.

NET OPERATING LOSSES

If a taxpayer incurs a net operating loss, the taxpayer should carefully analyze whether to elect to forgo the carryback period. Situations under which a taxpayer might elect to only carry the loss deduction forward include the following:

- A taxpayer might anticipate being in a higher marginal tax rate in future years than in the carryback years. If such is the case, the value of the deduction is higher in the carryforward years than in the carryback years. Taxpayers should consider, however, cash flows and the time value of money (e.g., the tax benefits from a refund of taxes are immediately available only if the NOL is carried back).
- General business and other tax credits that are nonrefundable (i.e., the credits are limited to the tax liability or some percentage thereof) may be reduced or eliminated for the carryback years because these credits must be recomputed based on the adjusted tax liability after applying the NOL carryback. (See Chapter 14 for a discussion of tax credits.)

COMPLIANCE AND PROCEDURAL CONSIDERATIONS

ADDITIONAL COMMENT

Instant access for downloading Federal income tax forms, instructions, publications, etc. is available on the World Wide Web (http://www.irs.ustreas.gov).

CASUALTY LOSSES

If a taxpayer sustains a casualty loss in a location that the President of the United States declares a disaster area, he or she may make an election to deduct the loss in the year preceeding the year in which the loss occurred. A taxpayer makes this election by either filing the return for the previous year and including the loss in that year (if the return has not already been filed) or filing an amended return or claim for refund for that year.[66] The return should clearly include all the following information:

- That the election is being made
- The date of the disaster giving rise to the loss
- The city, county, and state in which the damaged property is located

The taxpayer must make the election before the due date of the return for the year in which the disaster actually occurs. Although the Regulations state that the election may not be revoked more than 90 days after it is made, the Tax Court has held that this part of the Regulation is invalid.[67]

NET OPERATING LOSSES

When a taxpayer carries an NOL deduction back to a prior year, the taxpayer claims a refund of taxes by either filing an amended return on Form 1040X or filing for a quick refund on Form 1045. Corporations use Form 1139. If the taxpayer uses Form 1045, the IRS must act on the application for refund within 90 days of the later of the date of the application and the last day of the month in which the return of the loss year must be filed.[68] A taxpayer must file Form 1045 within one year after the end of the year in which the NOL arose. The taxpayer must attach additional information such as pages 1 and 2 of Form 1040 for the year of loss, a copy of the application for an extension of time to file the return for the year of loss, and copies of forms or schedules for items refigured in the carryback years.

WORTHLESS SECURITIES

As explained earlier in this chapter, securities that become worthless during the taxable year are deemed to have become worthless on the last day of the year. In many cases, this treatment causes the loss to be treated as a long-term capital loss. If the loss from the worthless security is long term, the taxpayer reports it in Part II of Schedule D (Form 1040) along with the other long-term gains and losses for the year. The taxpayer reports short-term capital losses in Part I of Schedule D.

66 Reg. Sec. 1.165-11(e).

67 *Chester Matheson*, 74 T.C. 836 (1980), *acq.* 1981-2 C.B. 2.

68 IRS, *Instructions for Filing Form 1045*, Revised, 2001.

WHAT WOULD YOU DO IN THIS SITUATION?

A client comes to you with an idea to treat a loan that he made to one of his children two years ago as a bad debt. The loan is evidenced by a properly executed note with stated interest and payment dates. However, the client has not collected any loan payments or interest during the two-year period. The child is insolvent and has declared bankruptcy. Before leaving your office, the client also mentions in passing that the child is in London on vacation with other members of the family and will stay in Europe for six weeks. What would you do about classifying this loan as a bad debt?

PROBLEM MATERIALS

DISCUSSION QUESTIONS

I8-1 What is the closed transaction doctrine, and why does it exist for purposes of recognizing a loss realized on holding property?

I8-2 When property is disposed of, what factors influence the amount of the deductible loss?

I8-3 Describe the usual tax consequences that apply to a worthless security.

I8-4 Under what circumstances will a loss that is realized on a worthless security not be treated as a capital loss?

I8-5 What two general requirements must be met for a transaction to result in a capital loss?

I8-6 What requirements must be met for stock to be considered Sec. 1244 stock?

I8-7 What tax treatment applies to gains and losses on Sec. 1244 stock?

I8-8 Describe a situation where a loss on the sale of business or investment property is not currently deductible, and explain why.

I8-9
a. What is a passive activity?
b. Who is subject to the passive loss limitation rules?

I8-10
a. For purposes of the passive loss rules, what is a closely held C corporation?
b. In what way do the passive loss rules differ from the regular passive loss rules when applied to closely held C corporations?

I8-11 Why is it important to identify exactly what constitutes an activity for purposes of the passive activity rules?

I8-12
a. If a taxpayer is involved in several different business operations during the year, how is the determination made as to how many activities these operations constitute for purposes of the passive activity loss rules?
b. Can a business operation and a rental operation ever be combined into one activity? Explain.

I8-13 Which of the following activities are considered passive for the year? Explain. Consider each situation independently.
a. Laura owns a rental unit that she rents out to students. The rental unit is Laura's only business and she spends approximately 875 hours per year managing, collecting the rent, advertising, and performing minor repairs. At times she must hire professionals such as plumbers to do the maintenance. Is the rental unit a passive activity with respect to Laura?
b. Kami is a medical doctor who works four days a week in a medical practice that she and five other doctors formed. Last year she and her partners formed another partnership that owns and operates a medical lab. The lab employs ten technicians, one of whom also acts as manager. During the year Kami spent 120 hours in meetings, reviewing records, etc., for the lab. Is the lab a passive activity with respect to Kami?
c. Assume the same facts in part b. In addition, assume that the same group of doctors have formed two other partnerships. One is a medical supply partnership. Kami spent 150 hours working for this partnership. The medical supply partnership has five full-time employees. Kami also spent 250 hours during the year working for the other partnership. This partnership specializes in providing medical services to individuals from out of town who are staying at local hotels and motels. This partnership hires two full-time and six part-time nurses. Are the lab and the two other partnerships passive activities with respect to Kami?

I8-14 Explain the difference between materially participating and actively participating in an activity. When is the active participation test used?

I8-15
a. What requirements must be met in order for a taxpayer to deduct up to $25,000 of passive losses from rental real estate activities against active and portfolio income?

b. What requirements must be met in order for a real estate rental activity to be considered a real estate business that is not subject to the passive loss rules?

I8-16 Are the suspended losses under the passive loss rules lost forever? Explain.

I8-17 What tests must be met to qualify a loss as deductible under the casualty loss provisions? Discuss the application of each of these tests.

I8-18 Explain how a taxable gain on property can be realized because of a casualty event such as a fire or theft. How are these gains treated?

I8-19 During the current year, Rulon's toilet overflowed because of a mechanical problem. Rulon was outside playing croquet, and by the time he returned inside, the water had flooded the basement, causing damage to the carpet, walls, and ceiling. The cost of repairing the damage was $9,000. Rulon has homeowners insurance that will cover half of the damage. However, because he has already had claims this year, Rulon does not want to report the incident to his insurance company for fear of a large increase in insurance rates. Instead, Rulon wants to deduct the loss as a casualty loss on his tax return. His AGI for this year is $50,000, and he has other itemized deductions of $6,000. Rulon is widowed. What amount of the casualty loss may he deduct?

I8-20 Compare and contrast the computational rules for deducting casualty losses on personal-use property with casualty losses incurred on business or investment property.

I8-21 Under what circumstances may a loss arising from a casualty or theft be deducted in a year other than the year in which the loss occurs?

I8-22 For individuals, how are casualty losses on personal-use property reported on the tax return? How are casualty losses on business property reported?

I8-23 Is the $100 floor on personal-use casualty losses imposed on each individual loss item if more than one item of property is destroyed in a single casualty? Is the floor imposed before or after the casualty gains are netted against the casualty losses?

I8-24 Steve loans $50,000 to his best friend, John. John uses the money to open a pizza parlor next to the local high school. Three years later, when John still owed Steve $15,000, John closed the pizza parlor and declared bankruptcy. Discuss the appropriate tax treatment for Steve.

I8-25 Dana is an attorney who specializes in family law. She uses the cash method of accounting and is a calendar-year taxpayer. During the current year, she represented a client in a lawsuit and billed the client $5,000 for her services. Although she made repeated attempts during the current and subsequent year, Dana was unable to collect the outstanding receivable. Finally in November of the subsequent year she found out that the individual has moved without leaving any forwarding address. Dana's attempts to locate the individual were futile. What is the amount of deduction that Dana may take with respect to this bad debt?

I8-26 Under what circumstances may a taxpayer deduct a bad debt even though another party to the transaction is the creditor?

I8-27 What is the definition of a nonbusiness debt? What is the character of the deduction for a nonbusiness bad debt?

I8-28 a. What alternatives do individuals have in deducting a loss on a deposit in a qualified financial institution?

b. Explain when it might be better to elect one over the other.

I8-29 A taxpayer collects a debt that was previously written off as a bad debt. What tax consequences arise if the recovery is received in a subsequent tax year?

I8-30 What is an NOL deduction, and why is it allowed?

I8-31 List the adjustments to an individual taxpayer's negative taxable income amount that must be made in computing an NOL for the year. What is the underlying rationale for requiring these adjustments for individuals?

I8-32 a. What is the NOL carryback and carryover period?

b. Does a taxpayer have any choice in deciding the years to which the NOL should be carried?

c. Explain the circumstances under which a taxpayer might elect not to use the regular carryback or carryover period.

I8-33 Can a casualty loss on a personal-use asset create or increase an NOL? Explain.

I8-34 If an NOL is carried back to a prior year, what adjustments must be made to the prior year's taxable income? What are the possible results of the adjustments?

ISSUE IDENTIFICATION QUESTIONS

I8-35 On January 12 of the current year, Barney Corporation, a publicly-held corporation, files bankruptcy. During the bankruptcy proceedings it is determined that creditors will only receive 10% of what they are owed and that the shareholders will receive nothing. Sheryl, a calendar-year taxpayer, purchased 1,000 shares of Barney Corporation common stock for $7,000 on February 22 of the prior year. What tax issues should Sheryl consider?

I8-36 Five years ago, Cora incorporated Gold, Inc., by contributing $80,000 and receiving 100% of the Gold common stock. Cora is single. Gold, Inc. experienced financial difficulties. On December 22 of the current year, Cora sold all of her Gold, Inc. stock for $5,000. What tax issues should Cora consider?

I8-37 In a rage because of personal difficulties, Evan drove recklessly and crashed his automobile doing $8,000 damage. Fortunately, no one was injured. Since Evan received two speeding tickets during the past year, he is concerned about losing his insurance if he files an insurance claim. What tax issues should Evan consider?

I8-38 Dan, a full-time employee of Beta, Inc., also owns 10% of its outstanding stock. The other 90% is owned by his three brothers. During the year, the president of Beta came to Dan, expressing grave concern about whether the company had the financial resources to remain in business. He mentioned specifically that a bank was threatening to force Beta to file bankruptcy if it didn't repay its $100,000 loan in full. After some negotiation, Dan agreed to loan Beta the $100,000 for one year until permanent financing could be obtained. A reasonable interest rate was set and a payment schedule was documented. Unfortunately, business did not improve, Beta discontinued its business and did not repay the loan. What tax issues should Dan consider?

PROBLEMS

I8-39 *Sec. 1244 Losses.* During the current year, Karen sells her entire interest in Central Corporation common stock for $22,000. She is the sole shareholder, and originally organized the corporation several years ago by contributing $89,000 in exchange for her stock, which qualifies as Sec. 1244 stock. Since its incorporation, Central has been involved in the manufacture of items that protect personal computers from static electricity. Unfortunately, this market is extremely competitive, and Central Corporation incurs substantial losses throughout its existence.

a. Assuming Karen is single, what are the amount and the character of the loss recognized on the sale of the Central Corporation stock?
b. Assuming Karen is married and files a joint return, what are the amount and the character of the loss recognized on the sale of the Central Corporation stock?
c. How would your answer to Part a change if Karen had originally purchased the stock from another shareholder rather than organizing the corporation?
d. How might Karen have structured the transaction in Part a to receive a greater tax advantage?

I8-40 *Amount and Character of Loss Transactions.* On October 4 of the current year, Madison Corporation files for bankruptcy. At the time, it estimates that the total FMV of its assets are $450,000, whereas the total amount of its outstanding debt amounts to $700,000. Madison has been engaged for several years in a gold mining operation in Montana.

a. At the time of the bankruptcy Madison is owned 100% by Barry, who purchased the stock from an investor for $150,000 several years ago. Barry is married and files a joint return. What are the amount and character of the loss sustained by Barry upon Madison's bankruptcy?
b. How would your answer to Part a change if Barry originally organized Madison Corporation capitalizing it with $150,000? Madison Corporation qualifies as a small business corporation.
c. How would your answer to Part a change if Barry were a corporation instead of an individual?
d. How would your answer to Part b change if Barry were a corporation instead of an individual?

I8-41 *Character of Losses.* Five years ago, Leonard and his sister formed Quilt Corp., a quilt manufacturing corporation. At that time, Leonard contributed $40,000 to the corporation in exchange for 50% of its stock. During the current year, Leonard needed some cash to purchase a boat, so he sold half of his interest in Quilt Corp. for $18,000. He also sold stock in the following companies for the amounts indicated:

Corporation	*Sales Proceeds*	*Adjusted Basis*	*When Acquired*
Rapids	$12,000	$ 8,000	3 years ago
Sandstorm	15,000	17,000	2 years ago
Tsunami	9,000	2,000	9 months ago
Volcano	41,000	33,000	6 years ago
Waterfall	23,000	25,500	4 months ago

During the year Leonard hired a collection agency to collect a $5,000 debt he made to an old friend, which was due in full on January 1 of the current year. The agency found no trace of his friend. Also during the year, Tornado Corporation, in which he owns stock, went bankrupt. His investment was worth $11,500 on January 1, he purchased it 6 years ago for $10,300, and he expects to receive only $3,200 in redemption of his stock. Finally, Leonard's salary for the year was $62,000 for his work as a bank officer.

a. What are the net gains and losses of the above items?
b. What is Leonard's AGI for the year?

I8-42 ***Passive Losses.*** In the current year Alice reports $150,000 of salary income, $20,000 of income from activity X, and $35,000 and $15,000 losses from activities Y and Z, respectively. All three activities are passive with respect to Alice and are purchased during the current year. What is the amount of loss that may be deducted and that must be carried over with respect to each of these activities?

I8-43 ***Passive Losses.*** In the current year Clay reports income and losses from the following activities:

Activity X	$ 28,000
Activity Y	(10,000)
Activity Z	(20,000)
Salary	100,000

Activities X, Y, and Z are all passive with respect to Clay. Activity Z has $40,000 in passive losses which are carried over from the prior year. In the current year Clay sells activity Z for a taxable gain of $30,000.

a. What is the amount of loss that Clay may deduct and that must be carried over in the current year?
b. Based solely on the amounts above, compute Clay's AGI for the current year.

I8-44 ***Passive Losses: Rental Real Estate.*** During the current year, Irene, a married individual who files a joint return, reports the following items of income and loss:

Salary	$130,000
Activity X (passive)	10,000
Activity Y (nontrade or business rental real estate)	(30,000)
Activity Z (nontrade or business rental real estate)	(20,000)

Irene actively participates in activities Y and Z and owns 100% of both Y and Z.

a. What is Irene's AGI for the year?
b. What is the amount of losses that may be deducted and must be carried over with respect to each activity?

I8-45 ***Passive Losses.*** In 2001, Mark purchased two separate activities. Information regarding these activities for 2001 and 2002 is as follows:

	2001			2002	
Activity	*Status*	*Income (Loss)*	*Activity*	*Status*	*Income (Loss)*
A	Passive	($24,000)	A	Active	$10,000
B	Passive	(8,000)	B	Passive	20,000

The 2001 losses were suspended losses for that year. During 2002, Mark also reports salary income of $120,000 and interest and dividend income of $20,000. Compute the amount (if any) of losses attributable to activities A and B that are deductible in 2002 and any suspended losses carried to 2003.

I8-46 ***Passive Losses.*** During the current year, Juan has AGI of $125,000 before taking into account any passive activity losses. He also actively participates and owns 100% of activity A, which is a real estate rental activity. For the year, activity A generates a net loss of $6,000 and $3,000 in tax credits. Juan is in the 30% tax bracket. What is the amount of suspended loss and credit from activity A that must be carried to subsequent years?

I8-47 ***Passive Losses.*** In 2002, Julie, a single individual, reported the following items of income and deduction:

Salary	$126,000
Dividend income	14,000
Long-term capital gain from sales of stock	22,000
Short-term capital losses from sales of stock	(17,000)
Loss from a passive real estate activity	(20,000)

Interest expense on loan to purchase stock	(21,000)
Qualified residence interest on residence	(12,000)
Charitable contributions	(8,000)
Property taxes on residence	(5,000)
Tax return preparation fees	(2,500)
Unreimbursed employee business expenses	(2,000)

Julie owns 100% and is an active participant in the real estate activity. What is Julie's taxable income in 2002?

I8-48 *Casualty Losses.* Tony is a carpenter who owns his own furniture manufacturing business. During the current year, vandals broke into the workshop, damaged several pieces of equipment, stole his delivery truck, and stole his personal automobile, which he often kept in the workshop garage. The asset descriptions and related values are as follows:

Asset	*FMV Before Casualty*	*FMV After Casualty*	*Cost to Repair/Replace*	*Adjusted Basis*	*Insurance Proceeds*
Equipment A	$12,300	$4,000	$ 8,700	$ 9,000	$ 3,700
Equipment B	8,100	0	9,000	3,000	7,800
Equipment C	Not Available	Not Available	13,800	15,300	11,400
Delivery Truck	18,000	0	32,000	17,500	16,000
Automobile	15,000	0	12,000	28,000	12,000

Although he could not obtain its fair market value after the casualties, Troy decided to repair rather than replace Equipment C.

Before considering any deductions because of these casualties, Troy's AGI is $80,000. What deductions may Tony take relating to the vandalism?

I8-49 *Theft Losses.* On December 17 of the current year, Kelly's business office safe is burglarized. The theft is discovered a few days after the burglary. $3,000 cash for the cash registers is stolen. A diamond necklace and a ring that Kelly frequently wore are also stolen. The necklace cost Kelly $2,300 many years ago and is insured for its $6,000 FMV. Kelly purchased the ring for $3,000 just two weeks before the burglary. Unfortunately, the ring and the cash are not insured. Kelly's AGI for the year, not including the items noted above, is $70,000.

a. What is Kelly's deductible theft loss in the current year?

b. What is Kelly's deductible theft loss in the current year if the theft is not discovered until January of the following year?

I8-50 *Casualty Losses: Year of Deduction.* Jerry sprayed all of the landscaping around his house with a pesticide in June 2002. Shortly thereafter, all of the trees and shrubs unaccountably died. The FMV and the adjusted basis of the plants were $15,000. Later that year, the pesticide manufacturer announced a recall of the particular batch of pesticide that Jerry used. It also announced a program whereby consumers would be repaid for any damage caused by the improper mixture. Jerry is single and reports $38,000 AGI in 2002 and $42,000 in 2003.

a. Assume that in 2002 Jerry files a claim for his losses and receives notification that payment of $15,000 will be received in 2002. Jerry receives full payment for the damage in 2003. How should the loss and the reimbursement be reported?

b. How will your answer to Part a change if in 2003 the manufacturer files bankruptcy and Jerry receives $1,500 in total and final payment for his claim?

c. How will your answer to Part a change if the announcement and the reimbursement do not occur until late in 2003, after Jerry has already filed his tax return for 2002?

I8-51 *Personal-Use Casualty Losses.* In the current year Ned completely destroys his personal automobile (purchased two years earlier for $28,000) in a traffic accident. Fortunately none of the occupants are injured. The FMV of the car before the accident is $18,000; after the accident it is worthless. Ned receives a $14,000 settlement from the insurance company. Later in the same year his house is burglarized and several antiques are stolen. The antiques were purchased a number of years earlier for $8,000. Their value at the time of the theft is estimated at $12,000. They are not insured. Ned's AGI for the current year is $60,000. What is the amount of Ned's deductible casualty loss in the current year, assuming the thefts are discovered in the same year?

I8-52 *Casualty Losses.* During 2002, Pam incurred the following casualty losses:

Asset	*FMV Before*	*FMV After*	*Basis*	*Insurance*
Business 1	$18,000	$ 0	$15,000	$ 4,000
Business 2	25,000	10,000	8,000	3,000
Business 3	20,000	0	18,000	19,000
Personal 1	12,000	0	20,000	2,000
Personal 2	8,000	5,000	10,000	0
Personal 3	9,000	0	6,000	8,000

All of the items were destroyed in the same casualty. Before considering the casualty items, Pam reports business income of $80,000, qualified residential interest of $6,000 property taxes on her personal residence of $2,000, and charitable contributions of $4,000. Compute Pam's taxable income for 2002. Pam is single.

I8-53 ***Business Bad Debt.*** Elaine is a physician who uses the cash method of accounting for tax purposes. During the current year, Elaine bills Ralph $1,200 for office visits and outpatient surgery. Unfortunately, unknown to Elaine, Ralph moves away leaving no payment and no forwarding address. What is the amount of Elaine's bad debt deduction with respect to Ralph's debt?

I8-54 ***Nonbusiness Bad Debt.*** During 2001, Becky loans her brother Ken $5,000, which he intends to use to establish a small business. Because Ken has no other assets and needs cash to expand the business, the agreement provides that Ken will repay the debt if (and when) sufficient funds are generated from the business. No interest rate is agreed upon. The business is unsuccessful, and Ken is forced to file for bankruptcy in 2002. By the end of 2002, it is estimated that the creditors will receive only 20% of the amount owed. In 2003 the bankruptcy proceedings are closed, and the creditors receive 10% of the amount due on the debt. What is Becky's bad debt deduction for 2002? For 2003?

I8-55 ***Bad Debt Deduction.*** Assume the same facts as in Problem I8-54, except that Becky and Ken are not related and that under the terms of the loan Ken agrees to repay Becky the $5,000 plus interest (at a reasonable stated rate) over a five-year period. What is Becky's bad debt deduction for 2002? For 2003?

I8-56 ***Net Operating Loss Deduction.*** Michelle and Mark are married and file a joint return. Michelle owns an unincorporated dental practice. Mark works part-time as a high school math teacher, and spends the remainder of his time caring for their one daughter. During the current year, they report the following items:

Mark's salary	$18,000
Interest earned on savings account	1,200
Interest paid on personal residence	7,100
Itemized deductions for state and local taxes	3,400
Items relating to Michelle's dental practice	
Revenues	65,000
Payroll and salary expense	49,000
Supplies	17,000
Rent	16,400
Advertising	4,600
Depreciation	8,100

a. What is Michelle and Mark's taxable income or loss for the year?
b. What is Michelle and Mark's NOL for the year?

I8-57 ***Net Operating Loss Deduction.*** Assume the same facts as in Problem I8-56, except in addition to the other itemized deductions Michelle and Mark suffer a $4,500 deductible casualty loss (after limitations).
a. What is Michelle and Mark's taxable income or loss for the year?
b. What is Michelle and Mark's NOL for the year?

I8-58 ***Net Operating Loss Deduction.*** Assume the same facts as in Problem I8-56, except instead of $3,400 itemized deduction for state and local taxes, Michelle and Mark have a $3,400 deductible casualty loss (after limitations).
a. What is Michelle and Mark's taxable income or loss for the year?
b. What is Michelle and Mark's NOL for the year?

I8-59 ***Net Operating Loss.*** During the year, Karen, a single taxpayer, reports the following income and expense items relating to her interior design business:

Revenues	$52,000
Cost of goods sold	41,000
Advertising	3,300
Office supplies	1,700
Rent	13,800
Contract labor	28,000

Karen also worked part-time during the year, earning $13,500. She reports a long-term capital gain of $4,200, and a short-term capital loss of $3,800. Her itemized deductions total $5,200.

a. What is Karen's taxable income or loss for the year?
b. What is Karen's NOL for the year?

TAX STRATEGY PROBLEMS

I8-60 In 1998, Annie Cook and several family members formed Treehouse Rentals, Inc., in Denver, Colorado. Treehouse is a closely-held C corporation engaged in the rental real estate business. Treehouse properly classifies its activities as passive. In 1999, 2000, 2001 the corporation generated net passive losses of $380,000, $145,000, and $194,000, respectively, all of which were properly suspended.

Effective January 2002, Treehouse elected to be taxed as an S Corporation. Also during 2002, Treehouse sold two pieces of rental real estate property. The suspended losses related to these properties were $63,000 and $112,000.

How should Treehouse treat the disposition of the rental properties in 2002?

- Sec. 469, Sec. 1371
- TAM 9628002
- *St. Charles Investment Co. v. Comm.* 86 AFTR 2d 2000-6882

I8-61 Jace Seaton is a single taxpayer living in Eugene, Oregon. From 1996-2001, he worked as the CEO of Wengren & Jeffers, a local architectural firm. In 2001, he left the firm to start his own company. On October 25, 2002, he formed Seaton & Associates, a Limited Liability Company (LLC) under Oregon law.

Upon forming the LLC, Jace received an 80% interest in the company. Two other architects, Maria Juarez and Jaman Turhoon, each received a 10% interest in the company. Jace provided all necessary capital, whereas Maria and Jamal provided experience and a commitment to work for the company. Seaton & Associates chose to be taxed as a partnership for federal income tax purposes.

During 2002, Jace worked approximately 215 hours for Seaton & Associates, and received compensation of $7,200. Maria and Jamal each worked approximately 600 hours each, and each received compensation of $16,000. In 2002, the company generated a net loss of $530,000.

How should the LLC members, particularly Jace, treat the loss generated in 2002?

- Reg. 1.469-5T
- *Gregg v. U.S.* 87 AFTR 2d 2001-337

I8-62 On November 15, Alex and Deanna Kent come to you for tax advice. The Kents, a married couple that files a joint tax return, own a rental home in Southern California. From January-November 1 of the current year, they rented out the home for 210 days. Since they live in Minnesota, they are considering staying in their rental home from December 10-31. If they do not stay in the home during that period, it will sit vacant. They ask you if this decision would have any tax consequences. They also provide you with the following information for the year:

Rental home income and expenses:	
Rental income	$12,000
Mortgage interest	12,400
Management fees	1,200
Utilities	2,300
Property taxes	4,300

Other income and expenses:

Deanna's salary	75,000
Alex's salary	65,000
Passive income (from an investment in a limited partnership)	1,000
Mortgage interest	7,800
Charitable contributions	14,200
Medical expenses	8,100
Property taxes	2,900
State income taxes	9,700

What do you recommend to the Kents?

I8-63 Jim had $100,000 in deposits in a savings account at a bank in Page, Arizona. The bank collapsed and Jim did not receive anything for his deposits. The bank was chartered by the state of Arizona and was not insured by federal law. Jim is not sure what his options are in deducting this loss on his tax return. What can Jim do to take advantage of this loss on his tax return? He has an AGI of $110,000 and no capital gains for the current year.

TAX FORM/RETURN PREPARATION PROBLEMS

I8-64 Heather and Nikolay Laubert are married and file a joint income tax return. Their address is 3847 Jackdaw Path, Madison, WI 58493. Nikolay's social security number is 968-84-8532, and Heather's is 498-65-5432. Nikolay is a mechanical engineer, and Heather is a highly renowned speech therapist. She is self-employed. They report all their income and expenses on the cash method. For 2001, they report the following items of income and expense:

Gross receipts from Heather's business	$110,000
Rent on Heather's office	12,000
Receivables written off during the year (received in Heather's business)	1,300
Subscriptions to linguistic journals for Heather	250
Salary for Heather's secretary-receptionist	22,000
Nikolay's salary	78,000
Qualified medical expenses	12,000
Property taxes on their personal residence	4,200
State income tax refund received this year (the tax benefit was received in the prior year from the state income tax deduction)	400
State income taxes withheld on Nikolay's salary	4,600
Federal income taxes withheld on Nikolay's salary	12,000
Heather's estimated tax payments	20,000
Interest paid on residence	11,000
Income tax preparation fee for the prior year's return paid this year ($500 is allocated to preparation of Schedule C)	940

Heather and Nikolay sold the following assets:

Asset	*Acquired*	*Sold*	*Sales Price*	*Cost*
KNA stock	2/15/99	3/13/01	$14,000	$ 8,000
AEN stock	3/2/01	7/7/01	20,000	22,000
KLN stock	6/8/99	4/10/01	13,000	17,000
Motorcycle	5/3/97	9/12/01	2,500	6,000

Heather owned the KLN stock and sold it to her brother, Jacob. Heather and Nikolay used the motorcycle for personal recreation.

In addition to the items above, they donate Miner Corporation stock to their church. The FMV of the stock on the date it is donated (8/18/01) is $6,200. It cost $2,700 when purchased on 3/12/90. Heather and Nikolay's home is burglarized during the year. The burglar stole an entertainment system (FMV $3,500; cost $5,000), an antique diamond ring and pendant (FMV $12,000; cost $10,000), and a painting (FMV $1,500; cost $1,300). The insurance company pays $1,500 for the entertainment system, $4,000 for the jewelry, and $500 for the painting. Complete Heather and Nikolay's Form 1040, Schedules A, C, D, and SE, Form 4684, and Form 8283.

I8-65 Kara and Brandon Arnold are married and file a joint return. Their Social Security numbers are 587-64-5235 and 588-54-8623, respectively. Kara and Brandon have one son, Henry, age 3. His social security is 587-45-3197. They live at 356 Welcome Lane, Woodbury, WA 84653. They report their income on the cash method. During 2001, they report the following items:

Salary	$103,000
Interest income from money market accounts	600
Dividend income from Davis Corp. stock	700
Cash contributions to church	6,000
Rental of a condominium in Lutsen:	
Rental income (30 days)	12,000
Interest expense	7,000
Property taxes	3,200
Maintenance	1,700
Depreciation (entire year)	7,500
Insurance	2,000
Days of personal use	16

During the year the following events also occur:

a. In 1999, Brandon had loaned a friend $3,000 to help pay medical bills. During 2001, he discovers that his "friend" has skipped town.

b. On June 20, 2001, Brandon sells Kim Corporation stock for $16,000. He purchased the stock on December 12, 1998 for $22,000.

c. On September 19, 2001, Kara discovers that the penny stock of Roberts, Inc. she purchased on January 2 of the prior year is completely worthless. She paid $5,000 for the stock.

d. Instead of accepting the $60 the repairperson offers for their old dishwasher, they donate it to Goodwill on November 21, 2001. They purchased the dishwasher for $750 on March 30, 1996. The new dishwasher cost $900.

e. Kara and Brandon purchased a new residence for $250,000. As part of the closing costs, they pay two points, or $3,800 on the $200,000 mortgage, which is interest rather than loan processing fees. This payment enables them to obtain a more favorable interest rate for the term of the loan. They also paid $8,400 in interest on their mortgage on their personal residence.

f. They paid $4,100 in property taxes on their residence and $7,500 in state income taxes.

g. On July 20, 2001 Kara and Brandon donated an antique automobile to the local community college. The value of the automobile was $10,200. They bought the car November 10, 1997 for $1,000 and fixed it up themselves. They estimate that they put in approximately $6,000 worth of labor into the project. The college auctioned the car for $9,700.

h. $16,450 in federal income tax was withheld during the year.

Complete Kara and Brandon's Form 1040, Schedules A, B, D, and E, Form 4684, and Form 8283.

CASE STUDY PROBLEMS

I8-66 Dr. John Brown is a physician who expects to make $150,000 this year from his medical practice. In addition, Dr. Brown expects to receive $10,000 dividends and interest income.

Last year, on the advice of a friend, Dr. Brown invested $100,000 in Limited, a limited partnership. He spends no time working for Limited. Limited's operations did not turn out exactly as planned, and Dr. Brown's share of Limited's losses last year amounted to $15,000. Dr. Brown has already been informed that his share of Limited's losses this year will be $10,000.

In January of the current year, Dr. Brown set up his own laboratory. Originally he intended to have the lab only do the work for his own practice, but other physicians in the area were impressed with the quick turnaround and convenience that the lab provided, and began sending their work. This year Dr. Brown estimates that the lab will generate $30,000 of taxable income. The work in the lab is done by 2 full-time qualified laboratory technicians. A part-time bookkeeper is hired to keep the books. Dr. Brown has spent

320 hours to date establishing and managing the lab. He plans to hire another technician, who will also manage the lab so that it can operate on its own.

In November, Dr. Brown calls you requesting some tax advice. Specifically, he would like to know what actions he should take before the end of the year in order to reduce his tax liability for the current year.

Write a memo to Dr. Brown, detailing your suggestions. His address is: Dr. John Brown, 444 Physician's Drive, Suite 100, Anytown, USA, 88888.

I8-67 In preparing the tax return for one of your clients, Jack Johnson, you notice that he has listed a deduction for a large business bad debt. Jack explains that the loan was made to his corporate employer when the corporation was experiencing extreme cash flow difficulties. In fact, Jack was very concerned at the time he made the loan that the corporation would go bankrupt. This would have been extremely bad, because not only would he have lost his job, but he also would have lost the $80,000 he had invested in the common stock of the corporation.

You know that if the loan is a business loan Jack will receive an ordinary deduction. However, if the loan is a nonbusiness debt, it becomes a short-term capital loss (and Jack can only currently deduct $3,000).

After thoroughly reviewing all of the facts you do a complete search of the relevant judicial and administrative authority. There you find that the courts are split as to whether under these circumstances the loan should be treated as a business or nonbusiness bad debt.

What position should you take on Jack's federal income tax return? (See the *Statements on Standards for Tax Services* section in Chapter I15 and Appendix E for a discussion of this issue.)

TAX RESEARCH PROBLEM

I8-68 Early in 2002, Kay meets Dan through a business associate. Dan tells Kay that he is directing a business venture that purchases poorly managed restaurants in order to turn them around and make them profitable. Dan mentions that he is currently involved in acquiring a real "gold mine" but needs to raise additional cash in order to purchase it. On the strength of Dan's representations, Kay loans Dan $30,000 for the venture. An agreement is written up between Kay and Dan, wherein Dan agrees to repay Kay the entire amount over a 5-year period plus 14% interest per annum on the unpaid balance. Later in the year, however, Kay discovers that Dan had never intended to purchase the restaurant and, in fact, had used most of the money for his own benefit. Upon making this discovery, Kay sues Dan for recovery of the money, alleging that Dan falsely, fraudulently, and deceitfully represented that the money would be invested and repaid, in order to cheat and defraud Kay out of her money. Unfortunately for Kay, she is never able to recover any amount of the loan. Discuss the tax treatment that Kay may claim with regard to the loss.

A partial list of research sources is

- *Robert S. Gerstell,* 46 T.C. 161 (1966)
- *Michele Monteleone,* 34 T.C. 688 (1960)

9

CHAPTER

EMPLOYEE EXPENSES AND DEFERRED COMPENSATION

LEARNING OBJECTIVES

After studying this chapter, you should be able to

1. Determine the proper classification and deductibility of travel and transportation expenses
2. Determine the proper deductible amount for entertainment expenses under the 50% disallowance rule
3. Identify deductible moving expenses and determine the amount and year of deductibility
4. Describe the requirements for deducting education expenses
5. Determine whether the expenses of an office in home meet the requirements for deductibility and apply the gross income limitations
6. Discuss the tax treatment and requirements for various deferred compensation arrangements

CHAPTER OUTLINE

Classification of Employee Expenses...9-2
Travel Expenses...9-4
Transportation Expenses...9-9
Entertainment Expenses...9-12
Reimbursed Employee Business Expenses...9-16
Moving Expenses...9-18
Education Expenses...9-20
Office in Home Expenses...9-23
Deferred Compensation...9-26
Tax Planning Considerations...9-42
Compliance and Procedural Considerations...9-43

This chapter discusses the tax consequences that arise from two types of expenditures:

- Expenditures incurred by an employee in connection with his or her job
- Deferred compensation payments made to employees

Employees routinely incur expenses in connection with their jobs, such as travel, entertainment, professional journals, etc. The tax law considers **employee expenses** to be incurred in connection with a trade or business and therefore, are deductible under Sec. 162. However, employee expenses are subject to a myriad of special rules and limitations. Because of the large number of taxpayers who are employees and importance of the topic, this chapter discusses the rules as well as tax planning opportunities.

Deferred compensation refers to methods of compensating employees that are based on their current service but the actual payments are deferred until future periods. Deferred compensation arrangements are very popular and widely used in business. The two principal types of deferred compensation methods are qualified plans and nonqualified plans. Qualified plans, such as pension and profit-sharing plans, have very favorable tax benefits but also impose strict eligibility and coverage requirements. Nonqualified plans, while not as tax advantageous as qualified plans, are very useful for highly compensated employees. Both of these types of deferred compensation arrangements are discussed later in this chapter.

CLASSIFICATION OF EMPLOYEE EXPENSES

ADDITIONAL COMMENT

"The income tax has made more liars out of the American people than golf has. Even when you make a tax form on the level, you don't know when its through if you are a crook or a martyr." Will Rogers.

Employee expenses, for purposes of the tax law, are divided into two classifications: *reimbursed* employee expenses and *unreimbursed* employee expenses. Reimbursed employee expenses are expenses incurred by the employee that are reimbursed by the employer. IRC Section 62(a)(2) provides that an employee may deduct reimbursed employee expenses *for* AGI. This presumes, of course, that the employee has included the reimbursement in his gross income. Unreimbursed employee expenses are generally deductible by employees, but are deductible *from* AGI.

Some of the more frequently encountered employee expenses discussed in this chapter include

- Travel
- Transportation
- Moving
- Entertainment
- Education
- Office in home

Each of these types of employee expenses are discussed later in this chapter.

NATURE OF THE EMPLOYMENT RELATIONSHIP

KEY POINT

The business expenses of a self-employed individual and the reimbursed business expenses of an employee are deductible *for* AGI. The unreimbursed business expenses of an employee are deductible *from* AGI.

An individual who provides services for another person or entity may be classified either as an employee or as a self-employed individual (also referred to as an independent contractor). If the individual is classified as self-employed, expenses are deductible *for* AGI under Sec. 162, and are reported on Schedule C of Form 1040. Conversely, expenses of employees are deductible either *for* or *from* AGI depending on whether such expenses are reimbursed or unreimbursed (see discussion above). In addition to the deductibility of expenses, the proper classification is also important due to employment taxes, such as social security taxes. As is discussed below, self-employed taxpayers must pay both the employee and employer share of social security taxes.

EMPLOYER-EMPLOYEE RELATIONSHIP DEFINED. The Treasury Regulations provide that an employer-employee relationship generally exists where the employer has the right to control and direct the individual who provides services with regard to the end result and the means by which the result is accomplished.[1]

EXAMPLE I9-1 ▶ Carmen is a nurse who assists a group of doctors in a clinic. Carmen is under the direct supervision of the doctors and is told what procedures to perform and when to perform them. Therefore, Carmen is classified as an employee. ◀

EXAMPLE I9-2 ▶ Carol is a live-in nurse who is paid by the patient and receives instructions from the patient's doctor regarding such items as medications and diet. Carol is directly responsible for the delivery of nursing care and is in control of the end result. Thus, Carol is self-employed. ◀

ADDITIONAL COMMENT

Anyone in a trade or business making payments of $600 or more to an independent contractor during a year must file Form 1099-MISC.

IMPORTANCE OF PROPER CLASSIFICATION. As mentioned above, proper classification is important both to employers and employees. If an individual is classified as an employee, the employer must match the Social Security and Medicare taxes that are paid by the employee. In addition, employers are generally liable for unemployment taxes for its employees. Thus, an employer must pay these employment taxes to the government in addition to the wages, which means that the cost of an employee generally is higher than for a non-employee. If an individual is determined to *not* be an employee, the individual is considered to be self-employed (also called an independent contractor). Amounts paid to a self-employed individual are not considered to be wages and the payor is not responsible for any employment taxes. However, the self-employed individual must pay both the employee and employer portions of Social Security and Medicare taxes. This tax is referred to as the self-employment tax. As can be seen from the above discussion, employment taxes are shifted from the employer to the self-employed individual if the individual is not considered to be an employee.

Individuals may prefer to be classified as employees because the employee portion of the Social Security and Medicare taxes (7.65% in 2002) is only one-half of the self-employment tax rate (15.3% in 2002). Of the 7.65%, 6.2% (12.4% for self-employed individuals) is for the old age, survivors and disability insurance (OASDI) portion of the FICA tax and is assessed on a maximum income amount of $84,900 (2002). The remaining 1.45% (2.9% for self-employed individuals) portion of the FICA tax is for hospital insurance and has no ceiling limitation.[2]

LITIGATION ISSUES AND ADMINISTRATIVE ENFORCEMENT. The determination as to whether an individual who performs services is either an employee or an independent contractor has been a major area of contention between the IRS and taxpayers. In Rev. Rul. 87-41, 1987-1 CB 296, the IRS enumerated 20 factors as guides for determining whether an individual is an employee or an independent contractor. These factors are designed to help determine whether the person or persons for whom the services are performed exercises sufficient **control** over the individual for such individual to be classified as an employee. Some of the factors include; instructions, set hours of work, work on employer's premises, and method of payment (hourly versus commission, for example).

Substantial litigation has occurred in the interpretation of these factors. For example, truck drivers who were owner-operators and were engaged under contract by an interstate trucking company were considered independent contractors because they selected their own routes and were paid a percentage of the company's receipts for shipment.[3] However, drivers for a moving van company were considered employees because the company exercised control over their assignments.[4]

KEY POINT

Even if the employee expenses exceed 2% of AGI, the employee may not derive a tax benefit if the deductible employee expenses, when added to the other itemized deductions, do not exceed the standard deduction.

LIMITATIONS ON UNREIMBURSED EMPLOYEE EXPENSES

2% NONDEDUCTIBLE FLOOR. IRC Section 67 imposes a nondeductible floor of 2% of AGI to the following types of itemized deductions:

---

[1] Reg. Sec. 31.3401(c)-1(b).

[2] For years before 1994, a ceiling limitation applied to earnings and self-employment income subject to the hospital insurance portion of the FICA tax ($135,000 in 1993). See Chapter I14 for a discussion of these rules.

[3] Rev. Rul. 76-226, 1976-1 CB 332

[4] *R. N. Smith v. U.S.*, 78-1 USTC ¶9263 (CA-5, 1978).

ADDITIONAL COMMENT

Unreimbursed employee business expenses are reported by the taxpayer first on Form 2106, then carried to Schedule A as a miscellaneous itemized deduction.

1) Unreimbursed employee business expenses,

2) Investment expenses, and

3) Other miscellaneous itemized deductions (i.e., tax return preparation fees)

All of these types of expenses are referred to as **miscellaneous itemized deductions** in Sec. 67.[5] Unreimbursed employee expenses that are classified as miscellaneous itemized deductions include

TAX STRATEGY TIP

For taxpayers who typically do not have enough miscellaneous itemized deductions to get over the 2% floor, "bunching" of expenses in a particular year may allow some of the expenses to be deducted.

- The cost and maintenance of special clothing (e.g., uniforms for an airline pilot)
- Job-hunting expenses for seeking employment in the same trade or business (e.g., employment agency fees)
- Professional journals, professional dues, union dues, small tools and supplies.

Investment expenses include expenses connected with the earning of investment income, such as publications and safe deposit box rentals. Other miscellaneous itemized deductions include items such as fees for tax return preparation and appraisal fees for charitable contributions.

EXAMPLE I9-3 ▶

Charles incurs $3,000 unreimbursed employee expenses in 2002. Charles also incurs $1,000 of investment counseling fees and $500 for the preparation of his 2001 tax return and pays these amounts in 2002. Charles's AGI is $100,000. The total of miscellaneous itemized deductions is $4,500 ($3,000 + $1,000 + $500). Charles is limited to a $2,500 itemized deduction ($4,500 − $2,000) because of the application of the 2% nondeductible floor (0.02 × $100,000 AGI = $2,000). ◀

SELF-STUDY QUESTION

Before the Tax Reform Act of 1986, unreimbursed employee business expenses were not subject to the 2% nondeductible floor. Why did Congress decide to subject these expenses to this floor?

EXCEPTIONS TO THE 2% FLOOR. The 2% floor only applies to certain miscellaneous itemized deductions. Thus, most itemized deductions, such as charitable contributions, mortgage interest and real estate taxes on a principal residence, are not subject to the 2% nondeductible floor.

EXAMPLE I9-4 ▶

In the current year Carmelia, who is single, incurs $1,500 of unreimbursed employee expenses, $3,000 of charitable contributions, and $4,000 of mortgage interest and real estate taxes on her principal residence. She has no other miscellaneous itemized deductions or investment expenses, and her AGI is $100,000. The $1,500 of employee expenses are not deductible because the 2% nondeductible floor ($2,000 in this case) is higher than the $1,500 of expenses. The $3,000 of charitable contributions and $4,000 of mortgage interest and real estate taxes are fully deductible as itemized deductions because Carmelia's total itemized deductions of $7,000 exceed the standard deduction amount ($4,700 for a single taxpayer in 2002). The charitable contributions, mortgage interest, and real estate taxes are not subject to the 2% nondeductible floor. ◀

ANSWER

Prior law required extensive recordkeeping with regard to items that were commonly small expenditures. These small amounts presented significant administrative and enforcement problems for the IRS. The use of a floor also takes into account the fact that some expenses are sufficiently personal in nature that they might be incurred apart from any business activities.

TRAVEL EXPENSES

OBJECTIVE 1

Determine the proper classification and deductibility of travel and transportation expenses

DEDUCTIBILITY OF TRAVEL EXPENSES

The deductibility of travel expenses depends on the nature of the expenditure and whether the employee receives a reimbursement from the employer. The following rules apply to the deductibility of travel expenses.

- If the taxpayer is engaged in a trade or business as a self-employed individual or is engaged in an activity for the production of rental and royalty income, the travel-related expenditures are deductible *for* AGI and the 2% nondeductible floor is not applicable.

[5] The 2% disallowance applies before considering the 3% scale down of total itemized deductions under Sec. 68 for upper-income individuals with AGI in excess of $137,300 (2002). See Chapter I7 for a discussion of these rules. The 2% floor does not apply to certain other miscellaneous itemized deductions, including impairment-related work expenses for handicapped employees, amortizable bond premiums, certain short sale expenses, terminated annuity payments, and gambling losses to the extent of winnings.

- If the taxpayer is an employee and incurs travel expenses in connection with his job, the expenses are deductible either *for* AGI or *from* AGI depending on whether the expenses are reimbursed by the employer.
- Personal travel expenses are not deductible.

REIMBURSED EXPENSES: If business travel expenses are reimbursed and the reimbursement is included in the employee's gross income, the expenses are deductible *for* AGI.

UNREIMBURSED EXPENSES: Generally, if business travel expenses are not reimbursed by the taxpayer's employer, the expenses are a deduction *from* AGI subject to the 2% floor.

The tax rules for reporting reimbursed and unreimbursed employee business expenses are discussed in more detail later in this chapter. Table I9-1 illustrates these tax consequences.

ADDITIONAL COMMENT

Before 1987, travel and transportation costs were deductible *for* AGI whereas most other unreimbursed employee business expenses were deductible *from* AGI. Congress changed the law to move unreimbursed travel and transportation costs to deductions *from* AGI to make them conform to the other business expenses. All of these expenses constitute costs of earning income.

DEFINITION OF TRAVEL EXPENSES

Travel expenses include transportation, meals, lodging, and other reasonable and necessary expenses incurred by a taxpayer while "away from home" in the pursuit of a trade or business or an employment-related activity. The term *travel expense* is more broadly defined in the IRC than is the term **transportation expense**. If an individual is not away from home, expenses related to local transportation are classified as transportation expenses rather than travel expenses. Transportation expenses for employees are deductible under certain conditions and are discussed later in this chapter.

EXAMPLE I9-5 ▶ Ahmed is away from home overnight on a job-related business trip and incurs air fare, hotel, and taxi fares amounting to $800. Because Ahmed is away from home, the $800 is deductible as travel expenses. ◀

EXAMPLE I9-6 ▶ Charlotte uses her personal automobile to make deliveries of company products to customers in the same local area of her employer's place of business. Charlotte's automobile expenses are classified as transportation expenses (rather than travel expenses) because she was not away from home when they were incurred. As is discussed later in this chapter, transportation expenses are deductible but are subject to strict recordkeeping rules. If Charlotte stopped to eat lunch alone during her delivery activities, the meals are not deductible as they are neither travel nor transportation expenses. ◀

▼ TABLE I9-1
Classification of Travel Expenses

Situation Facts	Tax Treatment: Deductible *for* AGI	Tax Treatment: Deductible *from* AGI	Tax Treatment: Not Deductible
1. Cindy is a self-employed attorney who incurs travel expenses related to her business.	X[a]		
2. Jose, who lives in Dallas, is the owner of several apartment buildings in Denver. Periodically he travels to Denver to inspect and manage the properties.	X[a]		
3. Clay is an employee who is required to travel to company facilities throughout the U.S. in the conduct of his management responsibilities. Clay is not reimbursed by his employer.		X[b]	
4. Same as Situation 3, except that Clay is fully reimbursed by his employer and includes the reimbursement in his gross income.	X[a]		
5. Colleen is a student who travels to her parents' home during the holidays.			X

[a] The 2% nondeductible floor is not applicable.
[b] The 2% nondeductible floor is applicable and the expenses are only deductible in excess of the floor.

HISTORICAL NOTE

The partial disallowance of business meals (and entertainment) was enacted because Congress believed that prior law had not focused sufficiently on the personal consumption element of deductible business meal and entertainment expenses. Congress felt that taxpayers who could arrange business settings for personal consumption were unfairly receiving a federal tax subsidy for such consumption.

TYPICAL MISCONCEPTION

There is a tendency to erroneously assume that a taxpayer's tax home is the location of the primary personal residence.

REAL-WORLD EXAMPLE

A taxpayer was employed by a traveling circus with headquarters in Chicago. The Tax Court held that the taxpayer's home was wherever he happened to be with the circus. Therefore, the cost of his meals and lodging was not deductible. *Nat Lewis,* 1954 PH T.C. Memo ¶54,233, 13 TCM 1167.

GENERAL QUALIFICATION REQUIREMENTS

To qualify as a travel expense deduction, the following requirements must be met:

- The purpose of the trip must be connected with a trade or business or be employment-related (e.g., personal vacation trips or commuting to and from a job location are nondeductible personal expenses).[6]
- The taxpayer must be away from his tax home overnight or for a sufficient duration to require sleep or rest before returning home.

AWAY-FROM-TAX-HOME REQUIREMENT. Travel expenses are deductible if the taxpayer is temporarily away from his tax home overnight. While this seems simple enough, there has been considerable debate as to what the words actually mean. There are three important aspects of determining the deductibility of travel expenses; (1) where is the taxpayer's home, (2) how is *temporarily* distinguished from *indefinite* or *permanent*, and (3) how the term "overnight" is interpreted.

Taxpayer's home: The IRS's position is that a person's tax home is the location of his principal place of employment regardless of where the family residence is maintained. Thus, a taxpayer who works permanently or for an indefinite period of time away from his or her family residence is *not* considered to be away from home and, therefore, travel expenses are not deductible. In this situation, the taxpayer's *tax home* is considered to be his work location.

Temporary vs Indefinite: The determination of whether a taxpayer is away from home temporarily or indefinitely is based upon the length of time the taxpayer is at such location. Work assignments of more than one year are treated as indefinite.[7] Work assignments for one year or less are classified as either temporary or indefinite depending on the facts and circumstances of each case. If an employee is reassigned only for a temporary period, then his tax home does not change and the travel expenses are deductible. However, if the assignment is for an indefinite period, the individual's tax home shifts to the new location. The following bulleted items and examples are taken from Rev. Rul. 93-86[8] and are used to illustrate the IRS's position concerning whether a taxpayer is away from home temporarily for purposes of deducting travel expenses:

- A taxpayer accepts away from home employment where it is realistically expected that the work will be completed in six months. The actual employment period lasts ten months. Because the employment period is realistically expected to last (and does in fact last) for one year or less, the IRS's position is that the employment is temporary and the taxpayer's travel expenses are deductible.
- A taxpayer accepts away from home employment where it is realistically expected that the work will be completed in 18 months but the work is actually completed in ten months. In such case the IRS's position is that the employment is treated as indefinite, regardless of whether it actually exceeds one year or not.
- A taxpayer accepts away from home employment where it is realistically expected that the work will be completed in nine months. After eight months the taxpayer is asked to remain for seven more months or a total period of more than one year. Based on these facts, the IRS's position is that the employment is temporary for eight months and the travel expenses are deductible for the eight-month period. The job is considered indefinite for the remaining seven months and no travel expense deduction is allowed for the travel expenses during this period.

Overnight test: To satisfy the overnight test, a taxpayer must show that it was reasonable for him to need and to obtain sleep or rest during release time on such trips in order to meet the demands of his job.[9] Generally, costs of meals on one-day business

---

[6] Travel expenses incurred in the production or collection of income are also deductible from AGI under Sec. 212(1), even though the travel is not connected with employment or with the conduct of a trade or business. See Rev. Rul. 84-113, 1984-2 C.B. 60.

[7] Sec. 162(a). See also Rev. Rul. 99-7, 1999-1 C.B. 361.

[8] Rev. Rul. 93-86, 1993-2 C.B. 71.

[9] Rev. Rul. 75-168, 1975-1 C.B. 58.

trips are not deductible since the taxpayer was not away from home overnight. The Supreme Court held that a taxpayer who took short rest stops on long one-day business trips was not allowed to deduct his meals.[10] However, whether it is reasonable to need sleep or rest depends on the specific circumstances. A railroad conductor was allowed to deduct lodging, meals, and tips incurred during a six-hour layover on a total trip of 16 hours.[11]

SELF-STUDY QUESTION

A student accepts employment in another state during his summer vacation. Would the cost of his meals and lodging at the job location be deductible?

ANSWER

No, the student did not travel to the job because of the employer's business needs. *Peter F. Janss v. CIR*, 2 AFTR 2d. 5927, 58-2 USTC ¶9873 (8th Cir., 1958).

BUSINESS VERSUS PLEASURE

Travel expenses are deductible only if they are incurred in the pursuit of a trade or business activity or are related to the taxpayer's employment. Thus, if a taxpayer takes a trip that is primarily personal in nature but some business is transacted, the only deductions allowed are those that are directly related to the business activity.[12] In such event, all of the traveling expenses to and from the destination are treated as nondeductible personal expenditures. However, if the trip is *primarily related* to business or employment, all of the traveling expenses to and from the destination are deductible, and meals and lodging, local transportation, and incidental expenses are allocated to the business and personal activities respectively. In effect, an all-or-nothing approach is applied to the deductibility of traveling expenses to and from the destination depending upon the primary purpose for making the trip.

In determining the primary purpose for a trip, the amount of time spent on personal activities compared to the time spent on business activities is an important factor. However, the fact that a taxpayer may spend slightly more time on personal activities than business activities will not automatically prohibit the deductibility of the transportation expenses to and from the destination. The taxpayer must clearly show that the purpose of the trip was *primarily business.*

EXAMPLE I9-7 ▶ Dana travels to New York on a business trip for her employer. She is not reimbursed for the travel expenses. Dana spends three days in business meetings and vacations for two days. Because the trip is primarily business, the traveling expenses to and from the destination (e.g., airfare) are fully deductible by Dana. If Dana's meals, lodging, and incidental expenses amount to \$100 per day, only \$300 (\$100 × 3 business days) of such travel expenses is also deductible. The deductible business meal expenses are reduced by 50%, and the total amount of deductible travel expenses are subject to the nondeductible 2% floor on miscellaneous itemized deductions. A proration of the meals, lodging, and incidental expenses based on the number of days may not be appropriate if the expenses are uneven or are directly related to either business or personal activities. ◀

EXAMPLE I9-8 ▶ Assume that the facts in Example I9-7 are reversed (i.e., that two days are employment-related and three days are personal). Because more time was spent on personal activities, the general rule would hold that the trip is primarily personal and the traveling expenses to and from the destination are not deductible. Thus, only \$200 (\$100 × two business days) of travel expenses related to meals, lodging, and incidental expenses are deductible (subject to the limitations previously discussed). None of the traveling expenses to and from the destination (i.e., the airfare) are deductible. ◀

EXAMPLE I9-9 ▶ Carroll, who lives and works in St. Louis, is required by his employer to attend a sales meeting in San Francisco. The meeting lasts two days. Carroll decides to take three days of vacation and sightsee in the San Francisco area. Even though Carroll spent more days on personal activities than business activities, Carroll's airfare would be deductible if he can clearly show that the primary purpose of the trip was business. ◀

---

[10] *Correll v. U.S.*, 389 U.S. 299 (1968).

[11] *Williams v. Patterson*, 286 F2d 333 (5th Cir. 1961) and Rev. Rul. 75-170, 1975-1 C.B. 60.

[12] Reg. Sec. 1.162-2(b)(1).

REAL-WORLD EXAMPLE

A movie executive's wife accompanied him on business trips in the U.S. and abroad. She helped promote the movie company's image of a "family-type movie company." She also helped arrange his personal schedule. A deduction for her costs was allowed. *U.S. v. Roy O. Disney*, 24 AFTR 2d 69-5123, 69-2 USTC ¶9494 (9th Cir., 1969). However, as a result of the Revenue Reconciliation Act of 1993, the wife's travel costs would no longer be deductible unless she were an employee.

The IRS has ruled that the incremental expenses of an additional night's lodging and an additional day's meals that are incurred to obtain "excursion" air fare rates with respect to employees whose business travel extends over Saturday night are deductible business expenses.[13] The reimbursement for these expenses is deductible by the employer (subject to the 50% disallowance for meals). The employer is not required to report the reimbursement on the employee's Form W-2 as gross income or withhold employment taxes.

Stringent rules are applied if the taxpayer is accompanied by family members because of the likelihood that the trip is primarily for personal reasons. No deduction is permitted for travel expenses of a spouse or dependent (or other person accompanying the taxpayer) unless the person is an employee, the travel is for a bona fide business purpose, and the expenses would be otherwise deductible.[14]

FOREIGN TRAVEL

Due to the potential for abuse, special rules apply to foreign travel and foreign convention expenses.[15] Travel expenses related to foreign conventions, seminars, or similar types of meetings are disallowed unless it can be shown that the meeting is directly related to the taxpayer's trade or business (including employment) activity and that it is reasonable for the meeting to be held outside North America. In addition, complex expense allocation rules are applied to business trips made outside the United States.[16]

SELF-STUDY QUESTION

Would the cost of going on a safari in Africa be deductible if the taxpayer were in the business of selling guns?

ANSWER

In an actual case, the Court held that the safari expenses were not sufficiently connected to the taxpayer's gun-selling business. Therefore, the safari costs were not deductible. *Vincent W. Eckel*, 1974 PH T.C. Memo ¶74,033, 33 TCM 147.

ADDITIONAL LIMITATIONS ON TRAVEL EXPENSES

IRC Section 274 also provides several limitations on the deductibility of certain types of travel expenses, including the following:

- Travel deductions are disallowed if the expenses are deductible only as a form of education. For example, a French language professor cannot deduct travel expenses to France if the purpose of the trip is to maintain a general familiarity with the French language and customs.
- Deductions allowed for luxury water travel (i.e., ocean liners, cruise ships, or other forms of water transportation) are limited to twice the highest per diem amount allowable for a day of domestic travel by employees in the executive branch of the federal government.
- Travel deductions to attend a convention, seminar, or meeting are not allowed if they are related to income-producing activities coming under Sec. 212. Expenses to attend a convention, seminar, or meeting are deductible if directly connected with a taxpayer's trade or business. However, expenses to attend such meetings on a U.S. cruise ship are deductible but only to a maximum amount of $2,000.

EXAMPLE I9-10 ▶ Dawn travels on a cruise ship to attend a business meeting in Bermuda. The round-trip cost of the cruise is $4,000, and the travel is for a period of four days. If the daily per diem amount is $150 for a government employee, the travel expenses related to the cruise ship are limited to $1,200 ($300 per day × 4 days travel). ◀

EXAMPLE I9-11 ▶ Danielle is an investor in the stock market who attends investment counseling seminars. During the current year, she incurs $4,000 travel expenses to attend the seminars. None of the travel expenses are deductible because the expenses are related to income-producing activities coming under Sec. 212. If Danielle was employed as a stockbroker (rather than an investor) and attended investment seminars, her travel expenses would be deductible. ◀

---

13 Ltr. Rul. 9237014 (June 10, 1992).

14 Sec. 274(m)(3).

15 Secs. 274(c) and (h).

16 Reg. Sec. 1.274-4. No allocation of total expenses is made to the personal-use (nondeductible) element if an individual is away from home for seven days or less or if less than 25% of the time is devoted to personal purposes. In all other cases, all of the foreign travel expenses (including transportation costs) must be apportioned between business and personal activities based on the relative percentage of time devoted to each activity.

TRANSPORTATION EXPENSES

The deductibility and classification of transportation expenses also depends on the nature of the expenditure, as follows:

- Trade or business-related transportation expenses are deductible *for* AGI and are not subject to specific limitations.
- Transportation expenses related to the production of rental and royalty income (e.g., an owner-investor in rental properties) are deductible *for* AGI and are not subject to specific limitations.
- Reimbursed employee transportation expenses are deductible *for* AGI (assuming that an adequate accounting is made to the employer, see discussion of reimbursed employee business expenses on page I9-16).
- Unreimbursed employee transportation expenses are deductible *from* AGI as itemized deductions subject to the 2% nondeductible floor for miscellaneous itemized deductions.
- Commuting expenses are nondeductible personal expenses.

DEFINITION AND CLASSIFICATION

KEY POINT

The primary difference between travel expenses and transportation expenses for tax purposes is that travel expenses are broad in nature and include transportation, lodging, meals, and other necessary expenses, whereas transportation expenses include only the cost of transportation.

Transportation costs include taxi fares, automobile expenses, airfares, tolls, parking fees, and so on incurred in a trade or business or employment-related activity. Generally speaking, transportation costs are those incurred for "local transportation" and are not treated as travel expenses because the away from home requirements have not been met. The cost of commuting to and from an employee's job location are nondeductible personal expenditures regardless of the length of the trip. Both unreimbursed employment-related travel and transportation expenses for employees are subject to the 2% floor on miscellaneous itemized deductions. If a reimbursement is received, such expenses would be deductible *for* AGI.

EXAMPLE I9-12 ▶ Eurie's employer requires her to call on several customers at different locations in the metropolitan area during the course of the workday. Her transportation expenses (e.g., auto expenses, tolls, and parking) are deductible as transportation expenses because they are related to providing services as an employee. If Eurie is required to travel away from home overnight, the transportation costs are included with meals and lodging and deducted as a travel expense. In either situation, the unreimbursed employment-related expenses are treated as miscellaneous itemized deductions and are subject to the 2% nondeductible floor limitation. If the expenses were reimbursed by Eurie's employer and an adequate accounting is made to the employer, the expenses would be deductible *for* AGI. ◀

EXAMPLE I9-13 ▶ David accepts a permanent job with a company located 80 miles from his principal residence. He decides not to move to the new location. None of David's transportation costs are deductible because they are personal commuting expenses. (Note: Because the job is a permanent assignment, it is for an indefinite period rather than a temporary period and the transportation expenses are not deductible as travel expenses.) ◀

ADDITIONAL COMMENT

The IRS takes the position that the hauling of equipment, tools, etc., in an automobile for business purposes does not make the commuting expenses deductible. This position is based on the Supreme Court's decision in *Donald W. Fausner v. CIR,* 32 AFTR 2d 73-5202, 73-2 USTC ¶9515 (USSC, 1973). The Court held that it was not possible to allocate the automobile expenses between nondeductible commuting expenses and deductible business expenses. However, if the taxpayer incurs additional costs, such as in renting a trailer, these additional costs are deductible.

The following exceptions or unusual circumstances should be noted:

- Transportation expenses incurred to go from one job to another are deductible if an employee has more than one job. If the employee goes home between jobs, the deduction is only the amount it would have cost him to go directly from the first location to the second.[17]
- Certain transportation expenses related to income-producing activities are deductible under Sec. 212. Expenses are deductible *for* AGI if they are related to the production of rental or royalty income; expenses connected with other investment-related activities are deductible as miscellaneous itemized deductions subject to the 2% floor.

---

[17] IRS, *Publication No. 917* (Business Use of a Car), 2001, p. 3

- Transportation expenses related to medical treatment may be deductible from AGI as a medical expense (subject to the limitations on the deductibility of medical expenses discussed in Chapter I7).
- Transportation expenses related to charitable activities may be deductible as a charitable contribution (subject to the limitations on the deductibility of charitable contributions discussed in Chapter I7).
- Transportation expenses incurred in going between the taxpayer's residence and a temporary work location outside the metropolitan area are deductible.[18] Further, assuming a taxpayer has at least one regular work location (such as his primary office location), transportation expenses are deductible in going between the taxpayer's residence and a temporary work location, regardless of the distance.[19] Thus, a CPA who is employed by a CPA firm and who maintains a regular work location (e.g., an office is provided at the CPA firm work location) may deduct transportation expenses for trips from home to clients in the metropolitan area. Unreimbursed transportation costs for an employee are deductible *from* AGI as unreimbursed employee expenses that are subject to the 2% nondeductible floor. Transportation expenses for a self-employed individual are deductible *for* AGI.

EXAMPLE I9-14 ▶ As shown in Figure I9-1 below, Dick has two jobs that are 10 miles apart. Dick lives 5 miles from the first job site and 8 miles from the second job site. If Dick drives directly from Job 1 to Job 2, he may deduct the automobile costs associated with the 10-mile trip. If he goes home from the first job before driving to the second job, the deduction is still limited to 10 miles, even though he actually travels 13 miles. ◀

EXAMPLE I9-15 ▶ Diana owns a duplex, which she rents to tenants. She periodically drives from her place of business to this income-producing property to collect the rents and to inspect the property. The transportation expenses are deductible *for* AGI as an expense related to the production of rental income under Sec. 212. ◀

EXAMPLE I9-16 ▶ Donna, an accountant who is employed by a CPA firm, travels from her home to an audit client located in the local metropolitan area. The firm maintains an office for Donna at their business location. She is not reimbursed for her transportation costs. The transportation costs are deductible *from* AGI as unreimbursed employee expenses that are subject to the 2% nondeductible floor. If Donna were instead a self-employed CPA operating a business from her home, her transportation expenses would be deductible *for* AGI. ◀

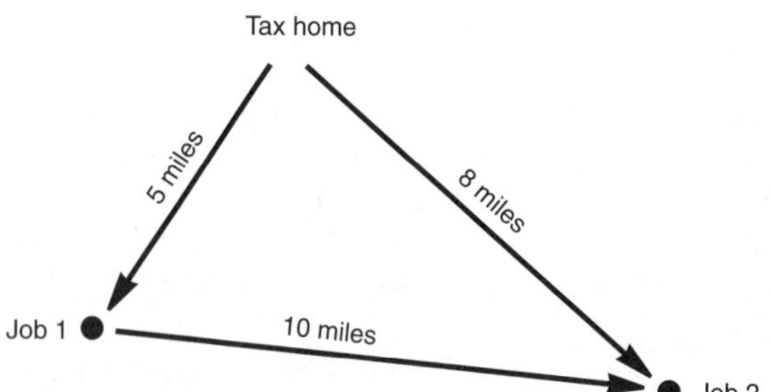

FIGURE I9-1 ▶ ILLUSTRATION FOR EXAMPLE I9-14

TREATMENT OF AUTOMOBILE EXPENSES

An employee or self-employed person may deduct actual automobile expenses, including gas, oil, repairs, depreciation, interest, property taxes, license fees, insurance, and so on based on the percentage of business miles to total miles. Detailed records to support the expenses are necessary in order to properly claim the deduction. To help reduce the burden of detailed recordkeeping, an alternative method, the standard mileage rate method, is available to taxpayers.

---

[18] Rev. Rul. 99-7, 1999-1 C.B. 361.

[19] Ibid.

The standard mileage rate method permits a deduction based on a standard mileage rate of 36.5 cents per mile for the year 2002.[20] Parking and tolls for business purposes are allowed as an addition to this deduction as well as interest expense on an automobile loan and personal property taxes on the automobile. The following restrictions apply when the standard mileage rate is used:

- The standard mileage rate method cannot be used if two or more automobiles are used simultaneously for business purposes.
- If a taxpayer changes from the standard mileage rate method rate in one year to the actual expense method in a later year, the basis of the used automobile must be reduced by 15 cents per mile for 2001 and 2002 (14 cents for 2000, 12 cents per mile for years 1997–1999) for any year or years in which the standard mileage rate method was used. The modified accelerated cost-recovery system (MACRS) rules (discussed in Chapter I10) cannot be used for computing depreciation in the year of the change and for the remaining useful life of the automobile. In such case, only the straight-line method under the alternative depreciation system (ADS) may be used (see Chapter I10).
- A change to the standard mileage rate method is not allowed for an automobile that was previously depreciated under the MACRS rules or where an election was made under Sec. 179 to expense part or all of the automobile's cost in the year of acquisition. (See Chapter I10 for a discussion of the Sec. 179 election.)
- The actual expense method is based on the ratio of business or employment-related miles to total miles. (See Chapter I10 for a discussion of specific restrictions on the computation of depreciation where mixed business- and personal-use automobiles are acquired.)

ADDITIONAL COMMENT

It should be remembered that in many cases the taxpayer can choose between the automatic mileage method and calculating the actual costs of operating the car. Although the automatic mileage method has the advantage of convenience, a calculation of the actual costs might produce a larger deduction.

STOP & THINK

Question: Assume a taxpayer uses his car (original cost, $20,000) in his business, drives a total of 25,000 miles per year, and can substantiate 80% of the mileage as business use. In general, will the taxpayer benefit more from the standard mileage method of deducting automobile expenses or from the actual expenses method?

Solution: In general, the actual expenses method will yield a higher deduction. The AAA (American Automobile Association) estimates that it costs approximately $0.50 per mile to operate a car in the United States. Therefore, the actual cost of operating the automobile would be approximately $12,500 (25,000 miles × $0.50). The deductible amount for tax purposes would be 80% of $12,500, or $10,000 for the actual expense method. Compare this amount with the standard mileage amount of $7,300 (25,000 miles × 80% business usage × $0.365/mile) and the actual expenses method yields a higher deduction. Of course, each individual situation is different and the actual results can vary based on circumstances, such as the amount of repairs, depreciation, and so on.

EXAMPLE I9-17 ▶ Danielle owns two automobiles that are used at the same time in her small unincorporated business. One automobile is driven by an employee of the business and Danielle drives the other vehicle for business use. Danielle cannot use the standard mileage rate method for either automobile because both cars are used in the business simultaneously. ◀

EXAMPLE I9-18 ▶ Doug acquired an automobile for use in his unincorporated business in 2000 and used the standard mileage rate method in 2000 and 2001. If the actual expense method is used for 2002 and later years, the automobile's adjusted basis (for depreciation purposes) must be reduced by 14 cents per mile for its 2000 business usage and 15 cents for its 2001 usage. Thus, if the automobile originally cost $20,000 in 2000 and was used 10,000 miles for business purposes during the initial year and 15,000 miles in 2001, the adjusted basis for computing depreciation in 2002 is reduced to $16,350 [$20,000 − (0.14 × 10,000) + (0.15 × 15,000)]. The remaining $16,350 basis must be depreciated using straight-line depreciation over the automobile's estimated useful life if the actual expense method is used. ◀

---

[20] Rev. Proc. 2001-54. For the taxable year 2001, the standard mileage rate was 34.5 cents per mile.

EXAMPLE I9-19 ▶ Edith uses her automobile 50% of the time for business and employment-related use and 50% for personal use. These percentages are substantiated by records that document the total usage for the automobile. During 2002, Edith drives 3,000 miles per month or a total of 36,000 miles for the year. If the standard mileage rate method is used, she can deduct $6,570 [(0.365 × 36,000 miles) × 50%] for the business and employment-related use. Additionally, Edith may deduct any business-related parking fees and tolls. ◀

KEY POINT

The Tax Reform Act of 1984 imposed a "contemporaneous" records test for substantiating expenses for automobiles and certain other activities. Public outcry caused Congress to repeal this requirement in 1985. Now the business use of an automobile can be substantiated either by keeping adequate records or by sufficient corroborating evidence, oral or written.

REIMBURSEMENT OF AUTOMOBILE EXPENSES

An employee is entitled to deduct actual automobile expenses (or amounts derived under the standard mileage rate method if applicable) in excess of reimbursed amounts received from the employer. The computation is made on Form 2106 (Employee Business Expenses) and is reported on Schedule A of Form 1040.

EXAMPLE I9-20 ▶ Elizabeth, who makes an adequate accounting to her employer, receives a $2,000 (20,000 miles at 10 cents per mile) reimbursement in 2002 for employment-related business miles. She incurs the following expenses related to both business and personal use:

Gas and oil	$4,400
Repairs and maintenance	2,700
Depreciation	3,000
Insurance	1,900
Total	$12,000

Elizabeth also spent $100 on parking fees and tolls that were all related to business. Elizabeth drives a total of 32,000 miles during the year. Thus, 62.5% (20,000 ÷ 32,000) of the $12,000 in automobile expenses is deductible. After subtracting the employer's $2,000 reimbursement, Elizabeth may deduct $5,600 [($12,000 × 0.625) + 100 − $2,000] as a miscellaneous itemized deduction (subject to the 2% nondeductible floor). Alternatively, if 2002 is the first year she used the car in her business, she could have claimed a deduction using the standard mileage rate method. In this case the $7,600 ($7,500 + 100) of actual expenses is greater than the $7,400 permitted under the standard mileage rate method [(32,000 miles × 62.5% × $0.365) + $100 business-related tolls]. ◀

ADDITIONAL COMMENT

The kind of written record that could corroborate the business use of an automobile would include account books, diaries, logs, trip sheets, expense reports, or written statements from witnesses.

ENTERTAINMENT EXPENSES

OBJECTIVE 2

Determine the proper deductible amount for entertainment expenses under the 50% disallowance rule

Entertainment of business customers and clients is a routine and, in many cases, an essential practice in business. Because entertainment expenses are considered ordinary and necessary practices of a business, they are deductible under either Sec. 162 or Sec. 212. However, the nature of entertainment expenses lend themselves to abuse by taxpayers. There certainly is an element of personal pleasure in taking a client to a hockey game or a Philharmonic orchestra performance and allowing taxpayers to deduct such expenses creates serious enforcement problems for the IRS.

For the reasons above, Congress enacted Sec. 274, which is strictly a disallowance section and contains classification rules, restrictive tests, and specific recordkeeping requirements. To deduct entertainment expenses, taxpayers must first show that the expenditure qualifies for a deduction under Sec. 162 (trade or business expense) or Sec. 212 (investment-type expense). Then the various requirements of Sec. 274 must be adhered to in order for an entertainment expense to be deductible. Over the years, Congress has continued to tighten the rules for the deductibility of entertainment expenses.

50% DISALLOWANCE FOR MEAL AND ENTERTAINMENT EXPENSES

Sec. 274(n) provides that any expense incurred for either business meals or entertainment must be reduced by 50%.[21] Business meals may be deductible either as travel expenses or

[21] For pre-1994 tax years, the disallowance was 20%.

as entertainment, depending on the nature of the expenditure. In either case, the 50% limit applies to the cost of food and beverages including tips and taxes but is not applicable to transportation expenses incurred going to and from a business meal. Further, any portion of a business meal that is considered lavish or extravagant is disallowed.[22] In such a situation, the 50% reduction rule is applied to the allowable portion of the business meal.

EXAMPLE I9-21 ▶ Krishna, a self-employed individual, pays $80 for a business meal plus $4 sales tax and a $16 tip. The total cost of the meal is $100. If $40 of the meal is considered lavish or extravagant, Krishna could deduct $30 ($60 × 0.50). ◀

If an employee incurs entertainment or business meal expenses that are fully reimbursed by the employer, it is the employer rather than the employee who is limited to a deduction for 50% of the expenses. Assuming the reimbursement is made pursuant to an accountable plan (see discussion later in this chapter), the employee would not include the reimbursement in income and would not be allowed a deduction.

EXAMPLE I9-22 ▶ Gordon incurs employment-related entertainment expenses of $1,000 and is fully reimbursed by his employer pursuant to an accountable plan. The employer may deduct $500 [$1,000 − ($1,000 × 0.50)] of entertainment expenses. Gordon would not include the $1,000 reimbursement in gross income and would not be allowed to deduct the $1,000 as a deduction. Thus, there is no overall tax effect to Gordon. ◀

ADDITIONAL COMMENT

Entertainment expenses are not considered "directly related" if there are substantial distractions. Therefore, if a meeting takes place at a sporting event, theater, or night club, the entertainment cannot be "directly related." This type of entertainment could qualify as an "associated with" expense. An example of a "directly related" expense would be the costs related to a hospitality room at a convention.

CLASSIFICATION OF EXPENSES

If an individual is engaged in a trade or business (but not as an employee), allowable entertainment expenses are deductible *for* AGI. Employees, however, may deduct entertainment expenses only as a miscellaneous itemized deduction (subject to the 2% nondeductible floor) unless the expenses are reimbursed. The tax rules for reimbursements of employee business expenses are discussed more fully later in this chapter.

EXAMPLE I9-23 ▶ Helen is a self-employed attorney who entertains clients and prospective clients. To the extent that these expenditures meet the Sec. 274 requirements, they are deductible by Helen as a *for* AGI expense on Schedule C of Form 1040 because Helen is engaged in a trade or business activity. The entertainment expenses are subject to the 50% limit but are not subject to the 2% nondeductible floor because the entertainment is deductible when determining AGI as a trade or business expense. ◀

CRITERIA FOR DEDUCTION. To be deductible as an entertainment expense, an expenditure must be either **directly related** to the active conduct of a trade or business or **associated with** the active conduct of a trade or business. Different restrictions apply to each of these categories. The Regulations under Sec. 274 provide the substantive rules for the two types of entertainment expenses.

"Directly Related" Expenses. To meet the requirements for a "directly related" **entertainment expense**, some business benefit must be expected from the business conducted other than goodwill and the expense must be incurred in a clear business setting (i.e., where there are no substantial distractions). In other words, business in anticipation of a business benefit must actually be conducted during the entertainment period.

ADDITIONAL COMMENT

With respect to the "associated with" type of expense, there is *no* requirement that the business discussion last for any specified period, or that more time be devoted to business than to entertainment.

"Associated With" Expenses. To qualify an expense as an "associated with" entertainment expenditure, the taxpayer must show a clear business purpose, such as obtaining new business or encouraging the continuation of an existing business relationship. An added restriction is placed on "associated with" entertainment in that the entertainment must directly precede or follow a bona fide business discussion. This means that the entertainment generally must occur on the same day that business is discussed.

EXAMPLE I9-24 ▶ Holly is a lawyer who hosts a birthday party in her home. Most of the guests are law partners or clients. No formal business discussions are conducted either before or immediately following

[22] Sec. 274(k).

the party. The expenditures for the birthday party are not deductible because they do not meet either the "directly related" or "associated with" tests. ◀

REAL WORLD EXAMPLE

One common way business people document a business meal is to write on the back of the credit card receipt the other person(s) at the meal and the topic discussed. Then all of the necessary substantiation requirements are present on the one piece of paper: date, time, place, amount, people present, and business discussed.

Substantiation Requirements. In addition to both the directly related and associated with requirements, Sec. 274 imposes stringent substantiation requirements for entertainment expenses. In order to deduct entertainment expenses, taxpayers are required to substantiate each expenditure for which a deduction is claimed. Lack of documentation alone will cause the disallowance of a deduction.

BUSINESS MEALS

Business meals related to travel or entertainment activities are subject to the same business-connection requirements as other types of entertainment expenses. Thus, an entertainment deduction is allowed only if the meal meets the "directly related" or "associated with" tests previously discussed. In addition, the expense must not be lavish or extravagant under the circumstances, and the taxpayer (or an employee of the taxpayer) must generally be present when the food or beverages are furnished. These requirements do not apply to a business meal associated with travel where the taxpayer claims a deduction only for his or her own expenses.

EXAMPLE I9-25 ▶ Hank is a salesman for a manufacturing supply company. Hank meets Harold, a purchasing agent who is a substantial customer, for lunch during a normal business day. Business is actually conducted during the lunch, and the lunch expenses are not lavish or extravagant under the circumstances. Hank is fully reimbursed by his employer for the $30 lunch expenses after an adequate accounting of the expenses is submitted. The business meal qualifies as "directly related" entertainment because the entertainment involved the actual conduct of business where some business benefit is reasonably expected and a business discussion was conducted during the meal. Hank's employer may deduct $15 ($30 × 0.50) of entertainment expenses because the meal was not lavish or extravagant. ◀

EXAMPLE I9-26 ▶ Assume the same facts as in Example I9-25, except that the purchasing agent is a prospective customer and no business is actually discussed either during, directly preceding, or immediately following the meal. Thus, no deduction is allowed because no business is discussed either before, during, or after the meal. ◀

The Regulations provide that the surroundings in which food or beverages are furnished must be in an atmosphere where there are no substantial distractions to the discussion (e.g., a floor show).[23]

WHAT WOULD YOU DO IN THIS SITUATION?

You have recently acquired a new individual tax client, Joe Windsack, who is a manufacturer's representative for a local tool and die company. You have been engaged by Windsack to prepare his individual income tax return for the current year. Before the current tax year is over, you are at a party where Windsack is also a guest. You overhear Windsack bragging to a group of people that he substantially reduces his income tax liability by overstating meal and entertainment expenses. He indicated that he overstates the deductions in several ways, (1) when he goes out to lunch or dinner that is personal in nature, such as with his family, he always uses a credit card and fictitiously writes the name of a client or prospective client on the charge card receipt, (2) when he goes out to lunch with several colleagues from his office (not business related), he charges the entire amount on his credit card (for everyone at the table), collects the cash from his colleagues for the cost of their meals, and then writes the entire amount off as a business-related meal, and (3) whenever he goes to any entertainment event, such as a ballgame, he always says that he took a client to the game with him and deducts the cost of the ticket as a business expense. When Windsack brings his tax information to you a couple of months later and you see a substantial amount of meal and entertainment expenses, what should you do?

[23] Reg. Sec. 1.274-2(f)(2)(i)(b).

EXAMPLE I9-27 ▶ Harry is a salesman who takes a customer to a local nightclub to watch a floor show and to have a few drinks. No business is discussed either before, during, or after the entertainment. The expenses for the beverages and floor show are not deductible because neither of the business meal requirements are met (i.e., the floor show produced substantial distractions, and no business was discussed). Even if business was actually discussed, no deduction would be allowed because there were substantial distractions. ◀

ENTERTAINMENT FACILITIES AND CLUB DUES

KEY POINT

Subject to a very few exceptions, no deduction is permitted for costs related to yachts, swimming pools, fishing camps, tennis courts, bowling alleys, vacation resorts, etc. This highly visible type of entertainment contributed to the public perception that the tax system was unfair.

No deduction is permitted for costs (e.g., depreciation, maintenance, repairs, and so on) related to the maintenance of facilities that are used for entertainment, amusement, or recreation. Facilities include yachts, hunting lodges, beach cottages, and so on.

No deduction is permitted for any type of club dues (including business, social, athletic, luncheon, and sporting clubs, as well as airline and hotel clubs).[24] Professional, civic and public service organizations (e.g., business leagues, trade associations, chambers of commerce, boards of trade, and real estate boards) are generally not subject to the dues disallowance rules. Initiation fees that are paid only upon joining a club are treated as nondeductible capital expenditures. While club dues are not deductible, other business expenses (e.g., business meals) are deductible if the general requirements for entertainment deductions are met.

EXAMPLE I9-28 ▶ Heidi is a self-employed CPA who entertains clients at her country club. Her club expenses include the following:

Annual dues	$4,000
Meal and entertainment charges related to business use	3,000
Personal-use meal charges	2,500
Initiation fee	10,000
Total expenses	$19,500

The only expense that is deductible is 50% of the specific business charges relating to the meals and entertainment. Thus, Heidi may deduct $1,500 ($3,000 × 0.50) *for* AGI as a business expense because she is a self-employed CPA. ◀

BUSINESS GIFTS

Business gifts are subject to an annual ceiling amount of $25 per donee.[25] Amounts in excess of the $25 limit per donee are disallowed. The following rules and exceptions apply to determine the business gift deduction:

- Multiple gifts to each donee are aggregated for purposes of applying the $25 per donee annual limitation. Husbands and wives and other family members are treated as a single donee.
- Husbands and wives who make gifts to a particular donee are treated as a single taxpayer and are subject to a single $25 limit.
- Incidental costs such as gift wrapping, mailing, and delivery of gifts and certain imprinted gift items costing $4 or less are excluded.
- Employee achievement awards made for length of service or safety that are under $400 per individual are excluded.[26]
- A gift from an employee to his or her supervisor does not qualify as a business gift because such gifts are personal rather than business related and are, therefore, not deductible.

EXAMPLE I9-29 ▶ Jack, an employee, makes the following gifts during the year, none of which are reimbursed by his employer:

---

[24] Sec. 274(a)(3).

[25] Sec. 274(b)(1).

[26] Sec. 274(j). The total limit including both qualified and nonqualified plan awards is $1,600 per individual (see Chapter I4).

REAL-WORLD EXAMPLE

A taxpayer who had deducted the full cost of two wedding gifts, both of which were in excess of $25 apiece, was able to deduct only $25 for each gift. *Jack R. Howard,* 1981 PH T.C. Memo ¶81,250, 41 TCM 1554.

Jack's immediate supervisor	$20
Jack's secretary	15
Jeff (a customer of Jack's)	24
Jeff's wife (a noncustomer)	26
Gift-wrapping for the gift to Jeff	6
Total	$91

Jack's total deduction for business gifts is $46 ($15 + $25 + $6) and is classified as a miscellaneous itemized deduction subject to the 2% nondeductible floor because Jack is an employee. The $20 gift to Jack's immediate supervisor is not deductible. The gifts of $24 and $26 to Jeff and Jeff's wife must be aggregated and are limited to $25. The gift-wrapping charge is fully deductible because it is an incidental cost. ◀

LIMITATIONS ON ENTERTAINMENT TICKETS

In addition to the general 50% meals and entertainment limitation, the cost of a ticket for any entertainment activity or facility is limited to the ticket's face value. Thus, the 50% limit applies to the face value of the ticket. Further restrictions are placed on the rental of skyboxes that are leased for more than one event.[27]

EXAMPLE I9-30 ▶ Able Corporation acquires four tickets to a football game for $500 that are used for entertaining customers. The face amount of the tickets is only $100. Able's deduction for entertainment is initially limited to the $100 face value of the tickets. The deductible amount is $50 ($100 × 0.50) after applying the 50% limit on entertainment expenses. ◀

REIMBURSED EMPLOYEE BUSINESS EXPENSES

The tax treatment of reimbursements received by an employee from his employer for employment-related expenses depends upon whether the reimbursement is made pursuant to an **accountable** or **nonaccountable** plan. An accountable plan is a reimbursement arrangement that meets both of the following two tests.[28]

ADDITIONAL COMMENT

While reimbursed business expenses under an accountable plan are technically deductions for AGI, they do not actually appear on the employee's tax return as a deduction. This is because the reimbursement itself is not included on the Form W-2.

1. Substantiation—the employee must make an adequate accounting of expenses to his employer, which means that each business expense must be substantiated (an expense report, for example); and
2. Return of excess reimbursement—within a reasonable period of time, the employee is required to return to the employer any portion of the reimbursement in excess of the substantiated expenses.

If both of these tests are not met, all amounts paid to an employee are treated as paid under a nonaccountable plan.

ACCOUNTABLE PLAN. Under an accountable plan, reimbursements are excluded from the employee's gross income and the expenses are not deductible by the employee. Because of this netting of reimbursement and expense, nothing is reported on the employee's return. In the event, however, that an excess reimbursement is not returned to the employer, the excess reimbursement is included in the employee's gross income.

EXAMPLE I9-31 ▶ Antoine is an employee of the Bluechip Corporation, which maintains an accountable plan for purposes of reimbursing employee expenses. During the current year, Antoine went on a busi-

[27] Sec. 274(l)(2). The cost of a skybox is disallowed to the extent that it exceeds the cost of the highest-priced nonluxury box seat tickets multiplied by the number of seats in the skybox (e.g., if a skybox contains 30 seats and the cost of the highest-priced nonluxury box seat for a particular event is $40, the deduction for the skybox is limited to $1,200 ($40 × 30). The deduction would be also reduced by the 50% limitation applicable to entertainment expenses.

[28] Reg. Sec. 1.62-2(c).

ness trip and incurred $1,500 of expenses as follows: airfare, $800; lodging, $450; meals, $200; and tips, $50. Bluechip reimbursed him $1,500. Because the reimbursement is pursuant to an accountable plan, Antoine will not include the $1,500 reimbursement in his gross income and he is not allowed to deduct any of the business expenses. ◀

EXAMPLE I9-32 ▶ Using the same facts as in Example I9-31, assume Bluechip advanced Antoine $1,800 for his business trip and his expenses were the same as above. If Antoine returned the excess $300 to Bluechip within a reasonable period of time, the result would be the same as in Example I9-31. However, if Antoine did not return the excess reimbursement (even though he is required to under the terms of the plan), Antoine must include the $300 in his gross income. ◀

If an employee receives a reimbursement that is not as much as his expenses, a proration is required.

EXAMPLE I9-33 ▶ Fred, an employee, incurs employment-related expenses of $4,500 consisting of $1,200 business meals, $1,800 local transportation, and $1,500 entertainment of customers. He receives a $3,000 reimbursement from his employer that is intended to cover all of the expenses. Since the reimbursement is less than the amount of expenses, Fred must prorate the expenses as follows:

Expense	*Total Amount*	*Reimbursed Expense* [a]	*Unreimbursed Expense*
Business meals	$1,200	$ 800	$ 400
Local transportation	1,800	1,200	600
Entertainment	1,500	1,000	500
Total	$4,500	$3,000	$1,500

The reimbursed expenses of $3,000 are not deductible by Fred and the $3,000 reimbursement is not reportable as income. The $1,500 of unreimbursed expenses are deductible *from* AGI (subject to 2% of AGI) as follows:

Business meals ($400 × 50%)	$200
Local transportation	600
Entertainment ($500 × 50%)	250
	$1,050

[a]Reimbursements are allocated to each expense category on a prorata basis. For example, the $800 for business meals is computed, $\frac{\$1,200}{\$4,500} \times \$3,000$. ◀

KEY POINT

Why does the government require reimbursements from nonaccountable plans to be included in the employee's gross income? Because these types of plans are often referred to as "expense accounts paid to employees as additional compensation."

NONACCOUNTABLE PLAN. Under a nonaccountable plan, reimbursements are included in the employee's gross income and the expenses are deductible by the employee as miscellaneous itemized deductions, subject to the 2% of AGI floor and the 50% disallowance for meals and entertainment expenses.

EXAMPLE I9-34 ▶ Use the same facts as in Example I9-31 except that Bluechip does not require its employees to submit an accounting of expenses incurred. Bluechip's plan is a nonaccountable plan. Antoine must include the $1,500 in his gross income and may deduct the expenses as miscellaneous itemized deductions, subject to the 2% of AGI floor, in the amount of $1,400 [$800 + 450 + (200 × 50%) + 50]. ◀

PER DIEM ALLOWANCES FOR MEALS AND LODGING. The IRS permits employers and employees to use optional "per diem allowances" for meals and lodging expenses in lieu of actual expenses. The use of per diem allowances is intended to simplify the burden of keeping detailed records for taxpayers who incur significant travel expenses. Special tables have been issued by the IRS that provide fixed per diem amounts for lodging as well as meals and incidental expenses (M&IE). The per diem allowances vary in amount depending on the city in which the travel took place. The tables list many cities in the United States as well as many cities in foreign countries. Thus, a taxpayer must only substantiate the time, place, and business purpose of the trip and then is permitted to use the per diem allowances. The per diem system is permitted only for payments under an accountable plan, the expenses must be reasonably expected to be incurred, and the amount of expenses should be in reasonable proximity to the expected actual expense amount.[29] A full discussion of this topic is outside the scope of this textbook.

EXAMPLE I9-35 ▶ Peyton Boying is an employee of UT, Inc. UT, Inc. maintains an accountable plan for reimbursing employees for their business expenses. Peyton travels extensively in the United States for business purposes. Instead of requiring Peyton to keep actual records of his travel expenses, UT, Inc. reimburses Peyton the per diem amounts as allowed by the IRS. Assuming Peyton traveled exclusively in low-cost localities (see footnote below) and was away from home for 100 days, UT, Inc. could reimburse Peyton in the amount of $12,500 (100 days × $125) without the necessity of Peyton keeping detailed records of his actual travel expenses. The amount that Peyton actually spent is irrelevant as the IRS will accept the per diem amounts. ◀

Table I9-2 summarizes the concepts relating to employee business expenses and reimbursements.

▼ TABLE I9-2
Treatment of Employee Reimbursements

TYPE OF PLAN	TAX EFFECT
ACCOUNTABLE PLAN	
Reimbursement = Expense	No effect, amounts are netted and not reported on employee's return.
Reimbursement > Expense	Not permissible under plan, but should it occur, excess reimbursement is included in employee's gross income.
Reimbursement < Expense	Expenses are prorated to amount of reimbursement. Reimbursed expenses–no effect; Unreimbursed expenses are deductible as miscellaneous itemized deductions subject to 2% of AGI
NONACCOUNTABLE PLAN	
Reimbursements	Always included in employee's gross income.
Expenses	Deductible as miscellaneous itemized deductions subject to 2% of AGI.

MOVING EXPENSES

ADDITIONAL COMMENT

In 1996, moving expenses deducted on tax returns totaled $1.6 billion.

Moving expenses are generally nondeductible personal expenditures. However, Sec. 217 allows a limited deduction for moving expenses for employees and self-employed people. The underlying rationale for this deduction is that such moves are similar to business expenditures because they are either employment-related or connected with a trade or business.

EXAMPLE I9-36 ▶ Ken retires from his job and moves from Ohio to Arizona. His moving expenses are nondeductible personal expenditures because the move is not employment-related and he is not moving to look for a new job. ◀

[29] The IRS tables for per diem allowances paid on or after October 1, 2001 may be found in Rev. Proc. 2001-47, September 28, 2001. The rate for high-cost localities (specifically identified by the IRS) is $204 per day (including $42 for M&IE); low-cost localities are $125 per day (including $34 for M&IE). Further, self-employed individuals who are not reimbursed for their travel expenses may use the M&IE rate, but must substantiate lodging with actual receipts.

OBJECTIVE 3

Identify deductible moving expenses and determine the amount and year of deductibility

Two conditions must be met for a moving expense to be deductible:[30]

- *Distance requirement.* The new job location must be at least 50 miles farther from the taxpayer's old residence than the old residence was from the former place of employment. If an individual has no former place of employment, the new job must be at least 50 miles from the old residence.
- *Time requirement.* A new or transferred employee must be employed on a full-time basis at the new location for at least 39 weeks during the 12-month period immediately following the move. More stringent requirements must be met by self-employed people who either work as an employee at the new location or continue to be self-employed. Such individuals are subject to a 78-week minimum work period during the first two years following the move. At least 39 of the 78 weeks must be in the first 12-month period. A waiver of the time requirements is permitted for both employees and self-employed individuals if the taxpayer becomes disabled, dies, or is involuntarily terminated (other than for willful misconduct). Unemployed or retired individuals are generally not able to deduct moving expenses because they do not meet the 39 or 78 week test.

ADDITIONAL COMMENT

The time requirement test ensures that taxpayers cannot use temporary jobs as a pretext for deducting the cost of moving for personal reasons.

EXAMPLE I9-37 ▶ Ellen is employed by the Able Company in Dallas, Texas. She lives 30 miles from her place of employment in Dallas. If Ellen accepts a new job in Houston, the new job location is 270 miles from her former residence in Dallas. The 50-mile distance requirement is satisfied because the distance from her old residence to her new job in Houston exceeds the distance from her old residence to her old job by 240 miles (270 − 30). In addition, to meet the time requirement, Ellen must be employed on a full-time basis in Houston for at least 39 weeks during the 12-month period immediately following the move. ◀

EXAMPLE I9-38 ▶ Assume the same facts as in Example I9-37, except that Ellen accepts a new job and moves to a new residence in a small town outside of Dallas. Her new job location is 55 miles from her former residence. The 50-mile distance requirement is not met because the distance from her old residence to her new job is 55 miles and the distance from her old residence to her old job is 30 miles; thus, the excess distance is only 25 miles. ◀

ADDITIONAL COMMENT

The individual need not be employed at the location that he or she is leaving. For example, a graduating college student who has not been employed for the most recent four years could deduct moving costs if the distance requirement is satisfied and if he or she has been employed at the *new* location for the minimum time period.

EXPENSE CLASSIFICATION

Moving expenses of an employee or a self-employed individual are deductible *for* AGI.[31] Thus, a taxpayer may receive a tax benefit from the deduction of moving expenses even if the standard deduction is used in lieu of itemizing deductions.

DEFINITION OF MOVING EXPENSES

DIRECT MOVING EXPENSES. Only direct moving expenses are deductible. These expenses are deductible without limit as long as they are reasonable in amount and include:

- The cost of moving household goods and personal effects from the former residence to the new residence (e.g., moving van).
- The cost of traveling (including lodging but excluding meals) from the former residence to the new residence. If the trip is by personal automobile, a deduction of 13 cents per mile (or actual expenses) is allowed for each automobile that is driven.

KEY POINT

The standard mileage rate for purposes of the moving expense deduction is only 13 cents per mile, compared to the 2002 standard business mileage rate of 36.5 cents per mile.

The expenses of moving household goods and personal effects do not include storage charges in excess of 30 days, penalties for breaking leases, mortgage penalties, expenses of refitting drapes, or losses on deposits and club memberships.[32]

EXAMPLE I9-39 ▶ Gail, a resident of California and a college student in that state, graduates from college and accepts a new position with an accounting firm in Atlanta. Thus, Gail is an employee of the Atlanta firm. Because the move meets the distance requirement (i.e., more than 50 miles), Gail

[30] The requirements for deducting moving expenses are contained in Sec. 217 and the Treasury Regulations thereunder.

[31] Sec. 62(a)(15). For years before 1994 moving expenses were deductible *from* AGI as an itemized deduction (not subject to the 2% nondeductible floor).

[32] Reg. Sec. 1.217-2(b)(3). In-transit storage charges for up to 30 consecutive days are allowable moving expenses.

qualifies for the deduction if she also meets the 39-week time requirement. Gail incurs the following expenses pursuant to the move: moving van, $1,200; lodging en route, $400; automobile expenses, $325 (2,500 miles × $0.13 cents per mile); and tolls and parking, $25. Assuming these expenses are reasonable, they qualify as direct moving expenses and are deductible without limitation. The cost of any meals incurred by Gail en route is not deductible. ◀

Otherwise allowable expenses of any individual other than the taxpayer are taken into account only if the individual has both the former residence and the new residence as his principal place of abode and is a member of the taxpayer's household.

EXAMPLE I9-40 ▶ Assume the same facts as in Example I9-39 except that Gail's son Paul is a member of her household. Additional automobile expenses (including tolls and parking) of $275 are incurred during the move because Paul owns an automobile which is driven to the new location. The $275 of additional automobile expenses are deductible as moving expenses because Paul is a member of Gail's household and his principal place of abode includes both the former and the new residences. ◀

KEY POINT

Indirect moving expenses are not deductible after December 31, 1993. In the Revenue Reconciliation Act of 1993, Congress eliminated the deduction for costs associated with pre-move househunting trips, temporary quarters, and selling the old residence. Congress felt that a deduction was not justified for expenses that were not directly related to the move.

NONDEDUCTIBLE INDIRECT MOVING EXPENSES. In addition to the disallowed moving expenses previously discussed (e.g., meals en route, storage charges etc.), the following indirect or moving-related expense items are not deductible:[33]

- Househunting trips including meals, lodging, and transportation.
- Temporary living expenses at the new job location.
- Qualified expenses related to a sale, purchase, or lease of a residence (e.g., attorney's fees, points, or payments to a lessor to cancel a lease).

TREATMENT OF EMPLOYER REIMBURSEMENTS

Moving expense reimbursements made by an employer, either paid directly or through reimbursement, are excluded from the employee's gross income as a qualified fringe benefit under Sec. 132 to the extent that the expenses meet the requirements for deductibility (i.e., the reimbursement is for moving expenses that are otherwise deductible under Sec. 217). Moving expense reimbursements must be included in gross income if the employee actually deducted the expenses in a prior tax year or if the expenses are otherwise not deductible under Sec. 217.[34]

EXAMPLE I9-41 ▶ In 2002, Ralph incurs $2,400 of moving expenses related to moving household effects and traveling to his new residence. He also incurs $2,600 of nondeductible moving-related expenses (e.g., househunting trips and temporary living expenses). Ralph receives a $5,000 reimbursement from his employer. Of the total reimbursement, $2,400 is excluded from gross income as a Sec. 132 fringe benefit. However, $2,600 of the reimbursement for nondeductible moving-related expenses is included in Ralph's gross income under Sec. 82. None of the $2,400 of moving expenses may be deducted by Ralph because they were reimbursed by his employer. ◀

EDUCATION EXPENSES

OBJECTIVE 4

Describe the requirements for deducting education expenses

Generally, education expenses are considered personal expenses and, therefore, are not deductible despite the obvious benefits that accrue to society from the pursuit of such activities. However, education expenses that are necessary in the pursuit of an employment-related or trade or business activity are deductible. It would be inequitable if such educational expenditures were not deductible because they are incurred to produce income from employment or business activities. Educational expenses incurred by employees or self-employed individuals may be contrasted with scholarship and fellow-

[33] Before 1994, indirect moving expenses were deductible subject to a $1,500 limit for househunting trips and temporary living expenses and a $3,000 overall limitation was applied to all indirect moving expenses.

[34] Sec. 82 and Sec. 132(g).

ADDITIONAL COMMENT

Attendance at a convention or professional meeting is one of the most common deductible education expenses. Almost every profession or occupation has its own society or association. Often these organizations sponsor local, regional, or national meetings. Training sessions or other types of educational activities are normally included on the program.

ship grants under Sec. 117 and educational assistance payments under Sec. 127 made by employers. Both of these latter types of payments generally can be excluded from gross income. (See Chapter I4 for a discussion of scholarship and fellowship grants and educational assistance payments.) Further, several recent provisions have been enacted to provide individuals with some reductions in taxation for education expenses. The primary two provisions are in the form of tax credits, the HOPE Scholarship Credit and the Lifetime Learning Credit. Both of these credits are discussed in Chapter I14. Finally, a new type of Individual Retirement Account for education was also created, this new IRA is discussed later in this chapter.

The discussion below focuses on the deductibility of education expenses. The other tax incentives for education are discussed elsewhere in the textbook.

CLASSIFICATION OF EDUCATION EXPENSES

Depending on the nature of the education-related activity, educational expenses may be either personal and nondeductible, deductible *for* AGI, deductible *from* AGI (as a miscellaneous itemized deduction), or reimbursed by an employer and excluded from gross income. Table I9-3 illustrates the tax consequences that are accorded to various types of education expenses depending on the facts and circumstances and the type of expenditure for each case.

GENERAL REQUIREMENTS FOR A DEDUCTION

An employee may generally deduct education expenses if either of the following two requirements are met:[35]

TYPICAL MISCONCEPTION

Education costs include more than the cost of books, tuition, registration fees, and supplies. Transportation costs and travel costs are also included.

- ▶ The expenditure is incurred to maintain or improve skills required by the individual in his or her employment, trade, or business; or
- ▶ The expenditure is incurred to meet requirements imposed by law or by the employer for retention of employment, rank, or compensation rate.

▼ TABLE I9-3

Classification and Tax Treatment of Educational Expenses

Situation Facts	Classification and Tax Treatment
▶ Jeremy is a college student who is not classified as an employee and is pursuing a general course of study.	▶ The expenses are nondeductible personal expenditures regardless of whether Jeremy or his parents pay them.
▶ Irene is an employee who incurs certain employment-related educational expenses including travel, transportation, tuition, and books. Her expenses are not reimbursed by her employer.	▶ If the expenses meet the two general deduction requirements, the education expenses are deductible *from* AGI as a miscellaneous itemized deduction (subject to the 2% nondeductible floor).
▶ Jesse is an employee who receives educational assistance payments from his employer to reimburse him certain educational expenses incurred in attending college at the undergraduate level.	▶ Educational assistance payments up to $5,250 per year are excluded from Jesse's gross income and are deductible by the employer as trade or business expenses if the requirements of Sec. 127 are met.[36]
▶ Jackie is a self-employed CPA who incurs education expenses including travel, transportation, books, registration fees, and so on to attend a continuing education conference.	▶ All of the education expenses are deductible *for* AGI as trade or business expenses.
▶ Jim is an employee who incurs education expenses for a continuing education course related to his employment, and the expenses are reimbursed by the employer.	▶ The reimbursement is deductible by the employer as a trade or business expense. There is no tax effect to the employee because the education expenses are offset by the reimbursement.

[35] Reg. Sec. 1.162-5

[36] The Sec. 127 exclusion is applicable for expenses paid by an employer for courses taken by employees. Qualified expenses include tuition, fees, and related expenses. Both undergraduate and graduate-level c the exclusion.

ETHICAL POINT

A client asks advice from his CPA as to whether certain educational expenses are deductible. The CPA should inform the client that the advice reflects professional judgment based on an existing situation. The CPA should use cautionary language to the effect that the advice is based on facts as stated and authorities that are subject to change.

Even if one of the two requirements above are met, education expenses are not deductible if:

- The education is required to meet minimum educational requirements for qualification in the taxpayer's employment; or
- The education qualifies the taxpayer for a new trade or business (or employment activity).

The deductibility of education expenses has been a frequent source of controversy and litigation because of the uncertainty in interpreting the above Regulations. The principal area of disagreement has been the interpretation of the term "qualifies the taxpayer for a new trade or business." If a taxpayer undertakes education and that education will *qualify* her for a new trade or business, then her expenses will not be deductible. For example, several courts have disallowed deductions to IRS agents and accountants for educational expenses incurred in obtaining a law degree, even though such training would be helpful in the taxpayer's employment.[37] The courts reasoned that the taxpayers were qualifying for a new profession (i.e., the practice of law). However, the IRS has ruled that a practicing dentist may deduct educational expenses in becoming an orthodontist under the theory that a dentist becoming an orthodontist is not a new trade or business.[38]

STOP & THINK

Question: The Regulations clearly provide that if the education "qualifies" a taxpayer for a new trade or business, the cost of such education is not deductible. If taken to the extreme, could the IRS argue that *any* course would qualify an individual for a new trade or business? For example, if a person took a basket weaving course, could not the IRS argue that the person is now qualified for the new trade or business of basket weaving? How can a taxpayer support his position that the education does not qualify him for a new trade or business in order to meet the deductibility requirements?

Solution: This is a difficult question and many commentators have written that the Regulations are unfairly harsh toward taxpayers. The courts have required that the IRS be "reasonable" in its interpretations of qualification of a new trade or business. The best way for a taxpayer to support his position is to find a case where the facts are approximately the same as the taxpayer's and where the court has upheld the taxpayer's position in that case.

ADDITIONAL COMMENT

The same course could be deductible as a qualified educational expense or not depending on the particular situation of the student. For example, a CPA enrolled in a taxation course to update his or her tax knowledge could deduct the expense. On the other hand, a non-CPA taking the course as part of a series of courses meeting the requirements to sit for the CPA exam could not deduct the expense. The CPA has already met the minimum education requirements for the profession and the non-CPA has not.

Generally, a taxpayer must be employed or self-employed to be eligible for an education expense deduction. However, some courts have permitted individuals to qualify if they are unemployed for a temporary period.[39] School teachers have generally qualified for an education expense deduction in situations where the public school system requires advanced education courses as a condition for retention of employment or renewal of a teaching certificate or where state law imposes similar requirements. However, college instructors who are working on a doctorate in a college where the Ph.D. is the minimum degree for holding a permanent position generally have not been permitted to deduct the expenditures made to obtain the degree.[40]

EXAMPLE I9-42 ▶ Jane is a self-employed dentist who incurs education expenses attending a continuing education conference on new techniques in her field. Such expenditures are incurred to maintain or improve her skills as a practicing dentist (a trade or business activity). All of her educational expenses are deductible *for* AGI because Jane is engaged in a trade or business activity. ◀

EXAMPLE I9-43 ▶ Juan is a business executive who incurs education expenses in the pursuit of an MBA degree in management. None of the expenses are reimbursed by Juan's employer. The expenses are deductible because they are incurred to maintain or improve Juan's skills as a manager and do not qualify Juan for a new trade or business. All of Juan's education expenses (e.g., travel,

---

[37] *Jeffry L. Weiler*, 54 T.C. 398 (1970).

[38] Rev. Rul. 74-78, 1974-1 C.B. 44.

[39] *Robert J. Picknally*, 1977 PH T.C. Memo ¶77,321, 36 TCM 1292. The IRS conceded that a deduction may be warranted in periods where the cessation of business activity was for periods of a year or less (Rev. Rul. 68-591, 1968-2 C.B. 73).

[40] *Kenneth C. Davis*, 65 T.C. 1014 (1976).

transportation, tuition, books, and word processing) are deductible *from* AGI as a miscellaneous itemized deduction (subject to the 2% nondeductible floor). ◀

EXAMPLE I9-44 ▶ Janet is a high school teacher who is required by state law to complete a specified number of additional graduate courses to renew her provisional teaching certificate. None of the expenses are reimbursed by Janet's employer. The educational expenses are deductible *from* AGI as a miscellaneous itemized deduction (subject to the 2% nondeductible floor) because the expenditures are incurred to meet the requirements imposed by law to retain her job and do not qualify her for a new trade or business. ◀

EXAMPLE I9-45 ▶ Jean is an accountant with a public accounting firm who incurs expenses in connection with taking the CPA examination (e.g., CPA review course fees, travel, and transportation). None of the expenses are reimbursed by Jean's employer. Even though the expenditures may improve her employment-related skills, they are not deductible because they are incurred to meet the minimum educational standards for qualification in Jean's accounting position.[41] ◀

EXAMPLE I9-46 ▶ Joy is a tax accountant who incurs expenses to obtain a law degree. Despite the fact that the law school courses may be helpful to Joy to maintain or improve her skills as a tax practitioner, such expenses are not deductible because the taxpayer is qualifying for a new trade or business. If Joy were not a degree candidate at the law school and merely took a few tax law courses for continuing education, the educational expenses would be deductible because they are incurred to maintain or improve Joy's skills as a tax specialist and do not qualify her for a new trade or business. In such a case, the expenses are deductible *for* AGI if Joy is self-employed and *from* AGI as a miscellaneous itemized deduction (subject to the 2% nondeductible floor) if Joy is an employee. ◀

KEY POINT

The deduction for travel expenses is not permitted if the travel itself is the educational activity. Therefore, a high school teacher who teaches Spanish cannot deduct expenses incurred in living in Madrid during the summer.

OFFICE IN HOME EXPENSES

OBJECTIVE 5

Determine whether the expenses of an office in home meet the requirements for deductibility and apply the gross income limitations

Employees or self-employed individuals who use a portion of their home for trade or business or employment-related activities should be entitled to a deduction because the property is used for trade or business or employment-related activities. However, it is often difficult to determine whether a taxpayer is using a portion of the home for business or personal use.

For over twenty years, there has been an ongoing controversy in the tax law as to the deductibility of office in home expenses. Because of the possibility of abuse by taxpayers, the IRC, Treasury Regulations, and the courts[42] have been extremely strict as to who qualifies to deduct office in home expenses. In order to promote fairness and consistency in the tax law, Congress, effective for tax years beginning after December 31, 1998, liberalized the definition of an office in home that qualifies for a tax deduction.

GENERAL REQUIREMENTS FOR A DEDUCTION

Employees and self-employed individuals are permitted to deduct office in home expenses only if the office is exclusively used on a regular basis under any of the following conditions:

- The office is used as the principal place of business for *any* trade or business of the taxpayer;
- The office is used as a place for meeting or dealing with patients, clients, or customers in the normal course of business; or
- If the office in home is located in a separate structure which is not attached to the dwelling unit, the office is used in connection with the taxpayer's trade or business.[43]

In addition to meeting any of these tests, an employee further must prove that the exclusive use is for the convenience of the *employer*. It is not enough that it is merely appropriate or helpful to the employee.

ADDITIONAL COMMENT

Approximately 24 million individuals, or 23% of the work force, work at least part-time at home.

REAL-WORLD EXAMPLE

Most teachers have been denied a home office deduction because the home office is not the principal place of business. Also, most teachers cannot demonstrate that their office in the home is for the convenience of the employer because the employer typically provides an office at the school.

---

[41] Rev. Rul. 69-292, 1969-1 C.B. 84.

[42] See, for example, *CIR v. Nader E. Soliman,* 71 AFTR2d 93-463, 93-1 USTC 50,014 (USSC, 1993).

[43] Sec. 280A(c)(1).

The first condition above has caused the major controversy in this area. Taxpayers are required to prove that the office is used exclusively as the "principal place of business". Under prior law, the principal place of business was interpreted to mean the "most important or significant place for the business", or more precisely, where the primary services were performed. Thus, a physician who performed medical services at a hospital but maintained an office in home to perform administrative duties was not allowed a deduction for the office because the principal place of business was interpreted to be the hospital.

EXAMPLE I9-47 ▶ In the *Soliman* case, Dr. Soliman was a self-employed anesthesiologist who performed medical services at three hospitals, none of which provided him with an office. He spent approximately two hours per day in his office in home where he maintained patient records and correspondence and he performed billing procedures. The office was not used as a place for meeting with or dealing with patients, clients, or customers in the normal course of his business. The U.S. Supreme Court denied a deduction for Dr. Soliman's office in home because it concluded that the essence of professional service rendered by the doctor was the actual medical treatment in the hospitals. A second factor considered by the court was the amount of time spent at the office relative to the total work effort. The effect of this case was to deny a deduction for an office in home for any type of taxpayer in a trade or business where the primary services were performed outside of the office (such as plumbers, electricians). This case was highly criticized. ◀

To combat the perceived unfairness of the *Soliman* case, Congress expanded the definition of "principal place of business" for tax years beginning after December 31, 1998. An office in home now qualifies as a taxpayer's principal place of business if:

1. the office is used by the taxpayer for *administrative or management* activities of the taxpayer's trade or business, and
2. there is no other fixed location of the trade or business where the taxpayer conducts substantial administrative or management activities of the trade or business.[44]

KEY POINT

The office-in-home deduction is available only where the office is being used for trade or business purposes. No deduction is permitted if the office is used to carry on investment activities.

Thus, the new law essentially allows a deduction for an office in home even though the taxpayer provides his primary service away from the office. The above tests are clearly intended for self-employed taxpayers. However, they also apply to employees except that the additional "convenience of the employer" test will still apply.

EXAMPLE I9-48 ▶ David is a self-employed electrician who performs his electrical services at the location of his customers. He also maintains an office where he does his administrative and management duties. David is permitted a deduction for an office in home even though his primary duties of providing electrical services are performed away from his office. ◀

EXAMPLE I9-49 ▶ Barbara is an employee of DRK, Inc. and is provided with an office on DRK's premises. However, Barbara's job requires significant administrative work after normal working hours and she prefers to perform these duties in her office at home. Barbara may not deduct the costs of her office in home because she uses her office at home for *her* convenience, not her employer's convenience. ◀

As can be seen from the discussion above, the deduction for an office in home is generally restricted to self-employed taxpayers and employees who are not provided with an office by their employer. If a self-employed taxpayer maintains an office in home, the expenses are deductible *for* AGI. Employees must deduct the office in home expenses as miscellaneous itemized deductions, subject to the 2% nondeductible floor.

---

[44] Ibid. For years before 1999, this new definition of principal place of business does not apply. Thus, the restrictive rules promulgated by *Soliman* apply to these years.

DEDUCTION AND LIMITATIONS

The deduction for home office expenses is computed using the following two categories of expenses:

1. Expenses directly related to the office, and
2. Expenses indirectly related to the office.

Direct expenses include operating expenses (supplies, etc.) that are used in the business as well as other expenses that relate solely to the office, such as painting and wallpaper. Indirect expenses are the prorata share of expenses that benefit the entire house or apartment, such as mortgage interest (or rent), real estate taxes, insurance, utilities, and maintenance. The office in the home expense is the sum of the direct expenses plus the prorata share (generally based on square footage) of indirect expenses.

EXAMPLE I9-50 ▶ Julie works as a full-time employee for a local company. She also operates a mail order business out of her home and maintains an office in her home that is used exclusively for business. The size of her home in total is 2,400 square feet and her office is 300 square feet. During the current year, the following expenses were incurred in connection with the office in her home:

Painting of office	$ 600
Decorations in office	900
Mortgage interest (total)	3,200
Real estate taxes (total)	1,800
Insurance (total)	600
Utilities (total)	2,400
Depreciation (total)	800

TAX STRATEGY TIP

When a taxpayer depreciates his office in the home, the office becomes business property. Upon the sale of the residence, the portion of the sale price attributable to the office will not be eligible for the sale of principal residence exclusion. Therefore, taxpayers might consider only deducting direct expenses of an office-in-home to preserve the exclusion.

Julie's home office expense for the current year would be computed as follows:

Direct expenses:		
Painting	$600	
Decorations	900	$1,500
Indirect expenses:		
Mortgage interest	3,200	
Real estate taxes	1,800	
Insurance	600	
Utilities	2,400	
Depreciation	800	
	8,800	
Business percentage (300/2,400)	12.5%	1,100
Total expense for office in home		$2,600

◀

TYPICAL MISCONCEPTION

Where a taxpayer is not entitled to an office-in-home deduction, the taxpayer can still deduct directly related business expenses (e.g., the cost of office supplies, and an MACRS deduction on filing cabinets and other equipment).

The total allowable office in home expenses may not exceed the taxpayer's gross income from the business (or rental) activity.[45] This ceiling limitation on otherwise qualifying office in home deductions is intended to prevent taxpayers from recognizing tax losses if the business (or rental) activity does not produce sufficient amounts of gross income. Expenses disallowed because of the gross income limitation can be carried forward but are subject to the gross income limitation in the later year and are subject to specific ordering rules.[46]

Employee expense classifications and deduction limitations are summarized in Topic Review I9-1.

[45] Sec. 280A(c)(5).

[46] See Prop. Reg. Sec. 1.280A-2 for the ordering rules. These rules are similar, but not identical to the ordering rules for hobby losses under Sec. 183.

Topic Review I9-1

Classification and Deductibility of Employee Expenses

Type of Expenditure	50% Disallowance	For or From AGI	Other Limitations
Miscellaneous itemized deductions	Applies to unreimbursed meals and entertainment	*From* AGI	Subject to 2% of AGI nondeductible floor.
Reimbursed travel expenses (adequate accounting is made)	Applies to the employer for meals portion of the travel only	*For* AGI	2% of AGI nondeductible floor applies only to employee expenses that exceed the reimbursement.
Unreimbursed travel expenses	Applies to meals portion of travel only	*From* AGI	Subject to the 2% of AGI nondeductible floor. Employee must be away from his or her tax home overnight.
Automobile expenses	Not applicable	*From* AGI	Subject to the 2% of AGI nondeductible floor. The standard mileage rate method may be used.
Moving expenses	Not applicable because meals are not deductible	*For* AGI;	Indirect moving-related expenses are not deductible.
Entertainment expenses	Applies to all entertainment expenses	*From* AGI	Subject to the 2% of AGI non-deductible floor. Club dues and initiation fees are not deductible.
Education expenses	Applies to meal portion of education expenses	*From* AGI	Qualifying expenses are subject to the 2% of AGI nondeductible floor.
Office-in-home	Not applicable	*From* AGI; If trade- or business-related, the expenses are for AGI	Employment-related expenses (other than real estate taxes and interest) are subject to the 2% of AGI nondeductible floor. Gross income limitations apply to allowable expenses.

DEFERRED COMPENSATION

OBJECTIVE 6

Discuss the tax treatment and requirements for various deferred compensation arrangements

Various types of benefit plans providing favorable tax treatment are available to employees and self-employed individuals. These tax benefits are provided to stimulate savings accumulations for retirement as a supplement to the social security system. Favorable tax consequences generally include the following benefits:

- Deferral of taxes on amounts contributed to retirement plans until the individual retires or receives a distribution from the plan;
- An immediate deduction for contributions to qualified retirement plans for the employer or self-employed individual;
- Deferral of taxation on income earned on retirement plan assets;

The following types of *deferred compensation arrangements* are discussed here:

- Qualified pension and profit-sharing plans;
- Nonqualified deferred compensation arrangements, including restricted property and employee stock option plans;
- Self-employed (H.R. 10) retirement plans and individual retirement accounts (IRAs).

QUALIFIED PENSION AND PROFIT-SHARING PLANS

ADDITIONAL COMMENT

The Staff of the Joint Committee on Taxation estimates the revenue loss resulting from the deferral of taxes on contributions and earnings for qualified pension and profit-sharing plans for the period from 1994 through 1998 will approximate $311.1 billion. The provision is designed to encourage employers to establish pension plans for their employees. The employer receives a deduction for the contribution, but the employee is not taxed currently. The repeal of this provision would substantially reduce the budget deficit.

The federal tax law provides favorable tax benefits for *qualified* pension and profit-sharing plans. A **qualified plan** is one that must meet strict requirements, such as not discriminating in favor of highly compensated individuals, be formed and operated for the exclusive benefit of employees, and meet specified vesting and funding requirements. In a qualified plan, both the employer and employee receive significant tax benefits, as follows:

EMPLOYER: receives an immediate tax deduction for pension and profit-sharing contributions made on behalf of employees.

EMPLOYEE: is not taxed on either employer or employee contributions or earnings of the plan assets until funds are withdrawn from the plan at retirement.[47]

TYPES OF PLANS. Qualified plans[48] include

- Pension plans
- Profit-sharing plans (including Sec. 401(k) plans)
- Stock bonus plans, including employee stock ownership plans (ESOPs)

Pension Plans. The features that distinguish a *qualified pension plan* include the following:

- Systematic and definite payments are made to a pension trust (without regard to profits) based on formulas or actuarial methods.
- A pension plan may provide for incidental benefits such as disability, death, or medical insurance benefits.

A pension plan may be either contributory or non-contributory. Under a **non-contributory pension plan**, the contributions are made solely by the employer. Under a **contributory pension plan**, the employee also makes voluntary contributions that supplement those made by the employer.

Pension plans may also be either defined benefit plans or defined contribution plans. In a **defined contribution pension plan**, a separate account is established for each participant and fixed amounts are contributed based on a specific formula (e.g., a specified percentage of compensation). The retirement benefits are based on the value of a participant's account (including the amount of earnings that accrue to the account) at the time of retirement.

EXAMPLE I9-51 ▶ Alabama Corporation establishes a qualified pension plan for its employees that provides for employer contributions equal to 8% of each participant's salary. Retirement payments to each participant are based on the amount of accumulated benefits in the employee's account at the retirement date. The pension plan is a defined contribution plan, because the contribution rate is based on a specific and fixed percentage of compensation. ◀

KEY POINT

All qualified plans can be classified into two broad categories. They are either defined contribution plans or defined benefit plans. An understanding of the distinction between these two broad categories is important because some rules will apply to one type of plan but not the other.

Defined benefit plans establish a contribution formula based on actuarial techniques that are sufficient to fund a fixed benefit amount to be paid upon retirement. For example, a defined benefit plan might provide fixed retirement benefits equal to 40% of an employee's average salary for the five years before retirement.

A distinguishing feature of a defined benefit plan is that forfeitures of unvested amounts (e.g., due to employee resignations) must be used to reduce the employer contributions that would otherwise be made under the plan. In a defined contribution plan, however, the forfeitures related to unvested amounts may either be reallocated to the other participants in a nondiscriminatory manner or used to reduce future employer contributions.

---

[47] An employee may not be liable for federal income taxes but may be subject to Social Security taxes and possibly local or city income taxes.

[48] Qualified plans are generally covered in Secs. 401-416 of the IRC.

Profit-Sharing Plans. A qualified **profit-sharing plan** may also be established by an employer in addition to, or in lieu of, a qualified pension plan arrangement. Profit-sharing plans include the following distinguishing features:

- A definite, predetermined formula must be used to allocate employer contributions to individual employees and to establish benefit payments.
- Annual employer contributions are not required, but substantial and recurring contributions must be made to satisfy the requirement that the plan be permanent.
- Employees may be given the option to receive cash that is fully taxable as current compensation or to defer taxation on employer contributions by having such amounts contributed to the profit-sharing trust. Plans of this type are called Sec. 401(k) plans.[49]
- Forfeitures arising under the plan may be reallocated to the remaining participants to increase their profit-sharing benefits, provided that certain nondiscrimination requirements are met.
- Lump-sum payments made to an employee before retirement may be provided following a prescribed period for the vesting of such amounts.
- Incidental benefits such as disability, death, or medical insurance may also be provided in a profit-sharing arrangement.

Stock Bonus Plan. A **stock bonus plan** is a special type of defined contribution plan whereby the investments of the plan are in the employer-company's own stock. The employer makes its contribution to the trust either in cash or in stock. If in cash, the amounts are invested in the company's stock. The stock is allocated and subsequently distributed to the participants. Stock bonus plan requirements are similar to profit-sharing plans. An **employee stock ownership plan (ESOP)** is a type of qualified stock bonus plan.[50] An ESOP, funded by a combination of employer and employee contributions and plan loans, invest primarily in employer stock. The stock is held for the benefit of the employees. ESOPs are attractive because the employer is allowed to reduce taxable income by deducting any dividends that are paid to the participants (or their beneficiaries) in the year such amounts are paid and are taxable to the participant. For employer securities acquired by the ESOP, the dividends-paid deduction is limited to dividends paid on employer stock acquired with an ESOP loan.

ADDITIONAL COMMENT

The tax law with respect to qualified pension and profit-sharing plans is extremely complex. A detailed study of these provisions is beyond the scope of this text.

QUALIFICATION REQUIREMENTS FOR A QUALIFIED PLAN

Qualified pension, profit-sharing, and stock bonus plans must meet complex qualification rules and requirements to achieve and maintain their favored qualifying status. A summary of the important requirements are discussed below.

- Section 401(a) requires that the plan must be for the employee's exclusive benefit. For example, the trust must follow prudent investment rules to ensure that the pension benefits will accrue for the employees' benefit.
- The plan may not discriminate in favor of highly compensated employees. Highly compensated employees are employees who meet either of two tests, (1) own more than 5% of the corporation's stock in either the current or prior year, or (2) receive compensation of greater than $90,000 in the prior year.[51]
- Contributions and plan benefits must bear a uniform relationship to the compensation payments made to covered employees. For example, if contributions for the benefit of the participants are based on a fixed percentage of the employee's compensation (e.g., 4%), the plan should not be disqualified despite the fact that the contributions for highly-compensated employees are greater on an actual dollar basis than those for lower paid individuals.

---

[49] Sec. 401(k).

[50] Secs. 409(a) and 4975(e)(7).

[51] Sec. 414(q). The $90,000 amount is subject to annual indexing for inflation. Alternatively, an employer may elect to define a highly-compensated group as employees earning more than $90,000 *and* the top 20% group of employees based on compensation.

- Certain coverage requirements that are expressed in terms of a portion of the employees covered by the plan must be met.
- An employee's right to receive benefits from the employer's contributions must vest (i.e., become nonforfeitable) after a certain period or number of years of employment. The vesting requirement is intended to ensure that a significant percentage of employees will eventually receive retirement benefits. Employer-provided benefits must be 100% vested after 3 years of service.[52] In all cases, any employee contributions to the plan must vest immediately.

EXAMPLE I9-52 ▶ Ken is a participant in a noncontributory qualified pension plan that provides for no vesting until an employee completes three years of service. Ken terminates his employment with the company after two years of service. Because Ken has not met the minimum vesting requirements, he is not entitled to receive any of the employer contributions that are made on his behalf. If the plan adopted the alternative vesting schedule (see footnote 52 below), 20% of the employer-provided benefits would be vested at the time of his termination and would provide Ken with future retirement benefits. ◀

ADDITIONAL COMMENT

Most employees choose to contribute amounts to their qualified retirement plans on a pre-tax basis because of the time value of money. A current deduction (and the related tax savings) is more valuable than a deduction at retirement.

TAX TREATMENT TO EMPLOYEES AND EMPLOYERS

Employer contributions to a qualified plan are immediately deductible (subject to specific limitations on contribution amounts), and earnings on pension fund investments are tax-exempt to the plan. Amounts paid into a plan by or for an employee are not taxable until the pension payments are received, normally at retirement. At the election of the employee, amounts may be treated as having been made from either pre-tax or after-tax earnings. If amounts contributed to a qualified plan by an employee are made on a pre-tax basis, the taxable portion of the employee's earnings is reduced by the contribution amount. This has the effect of permitting a deduction for the contribution amount. When amounts are withdrawn at retirement, the entire distribution is subject to taxation.

EXAMPLE I9-53 ▶ Larry is an employee of Cisco Corporation, which maintains a Sec. 401(k) plan. Larry contributes 5% of his gross salary into the plan on a pre-tax basis. During the current year, Larry's gross salary is $80,000 so his Sec. 401(k) contribution is $4,000. Since Larry's contribution is made on a pre-tax basis, his taxable salary for the current year will be $76,000. In effect, Larry is able to deduct the $4,000 from his salary in the current year. When Larry retires and begins withdrawing amounts from the plan, the entire amount withdrawn will be subject to income taxation. ◀

Conversely, an employee may elect to contribute to a qualified plan on an after-tax basis. If, in Example I9-53, Larry contributed to the Sec. 401(k) plan on an after-tax basis, his taxable salary would have been $80,000. The $4,000 contributed to the plan is treated as an investment in the plan and is considered a tax-free return of capital when this amount is withdrawn at retirement.[53]

EMPLOYEE RETIREMENT PAYMENTS. An employee's retirement benefits are generally taxed under the Sec. 72 annuity rules (see Chapter I3). If the plan is noncontributory (i.e., no employee contributions are made to the plan), all of the pension benefits when received by the employee are fully taxable. If the plan is contributory, the taxability depends on whether the employee's contributions were made on a pre-tax or after-tax basis. If the contributions were made on a pre-tax basis, *all* retirement payments received by the employee are taxable. Alternatively, if the contributions were made on an after-tax basis, each payment is treated, in part, as a tax-free return of the employee's contributions and the remainder is taxable. The excluded portion is based on the ratio of the employee's investment in the contract to the expected return under the contract. However, the total

[52] Sec. 411(a). An alternative vesting schedule may also be used that provides for 20% vesting each year beginning in the second year of service. Thus, after a total of six years of service, an employee would be 100% vested.

[53] Amounts contributed to a qualified plan on an after-tax basis are treated as an investment in the contract under the annuity rules of Sec. 72. Amounts withdrawn during retirement are taxed under the general rules of Sec. 72. See Chapter I3 for a discussion of taxation of annuities.

amount that may be excluded is limited to the amount of the employee's contributions to the plan. If the employee dies before the entire investment in the contract is recovered, the unrecovered amount is allowed as an itemized deduction in the year of death.

EXAMPLE I9-54 ▶ Kevin retires in 2002 and receives annuity payments for life from his employer's qualified pension plan of $24,000 per year beginning in 2003. Kevin's investment in the contract (represented by his contributions made on an after-tax basis) is $100,000, and the total expected return (based on his life expectancy) is $300,000. The exclusion ratio is one-third, so that $8,000 ($24,000 × 0.333) is excluded from Kevin's income and $16,000 ($24,000 − $8,000) is taxable in 2003. After Kevin receives payments for 12.5 years, his investment in the contract is recovered ($8,000 × 12.5 = $100,000), and all subsequent payments are fully taxable. (See Chapter I3 for a discussion of the annuity formula and related rules.) ◀

ADDITIONAL COMMENT

Many individuals have the option of taking their retirement savings from traditional pensions, profit-sharing plans, and 401(k)s as a lump sum or an annuity. Those who want to take a lump-sum distribution can delay taxes by transferring the money directly into a tax-deferred IRA.

If an employee age 59½ or older receives a lump-sum distribution from a qualified plan, a five-year forward income-averaging technique was generally available through 1999 to mitigate the effects of receiving a large amount of income in the year of the distribution.[54]

LIMITATION ON EMPLOYER CONTRIBUTIONS. The Code places limitations on (1) amounts an employer may contribute to qualified pension, profit-sharing, and stock bonus plans and (2) amounts that the employer may deduct:

- Defined contribution plan contributions in 2002 are limited to the lesser of $40,000 or 100% of the employee's compensation.[55]
- Defined benefit plans are restricted to an annual benefit to an employee equal to the lesser of $160,000 for 2002 or 100% of the participant's average compensation for the highest three years.[56]
- An overall maximum annual employer deduction of 25% of compensation paid or accrued to plan participants is placed on defined contribution, profit-sharing and stock bonus plans.[57] If an employer has more than one type of qualified plan (e.g., a defined benefit pension plan and a profit-sharing plan), a maximum deduction of 25% of compensation is allowed.

KEY POINT

For purposes of the limitation on employer contributions, all defined contribution plans maintained by one employer are treated as a single defined contribution plan. Furthermore, under some circumstances a group of employers can be treated as a single employer.

The distinguishing features and major requirements for qualified pension and profit-sharing plans are summarized in Topic Review I9-2.

NONQUALIFIED PLANS

KEY POINT

Although the nonqualified plans are not subject to the same restrictions imposed upon qualified plans, they do not receive the same tax benefits as are available under qualified plans. For example, the employer may not be able to deduct amounts that are set aside or placed in an escrow account.

Nonqualified deferred compensation plans are often used by employers to provide incentives or supplementary retirement benefits for executives. Common forms of nonqualified plans include the following:

- An unfunded, nonforfeitable promise to pay fixed amounts of compensation in future periods.[58]
- Restricted property plans involving property transfers (usually in the form of the employer-company stock), where the property transferred is subject to a substantial risk of forfeiture and is nontransferable.[59]

DISTINGUISHING CHARACTERISTICS OF NONQUALIFIED PLANS. Nonqualified plans are not subject to the same restrictions imposed on qualified plans (such as the nondiscrimination and vesting rules), although nonqualified plans may have some vesting rules. Thus, such plans are particularly suitable for use in executive compensation plan-

[54] Sec. 402(e). Under the Small Business Act of 1996, the five-year forward averaging provision was repealed for tax years beginning after December 31, 1999.

[55] Sec. 415(c). The deduction limit for 2001 was limited to the lesser of $35,000 or 25% of the employee's compensation. The 2001 Tax Act increased both the dollar amount and the percentage of the employee's compensation. In addition, individuals over 50 years of age are now eligible to contribute extra amounts into their plans. The amount of the so-called "catch-up contributions" depend on the type of plan.

[56] Sec. 415(b)(1). The benefit amount for 2001 was $140,000. These amounts are subject to indexing each year. The increase to $160,000 was made by the 2001 Tax Act.

[57] Sec. 404(a)(3)(A).

[58] Rev. Rul. 60-31, 1960-1 C.B. 174.

[59] Sec. 83.

Topic Review I9-2

Qualified Pension and Profit-Sharing Plans

Distinguishing Features and Major Requirements

- Employer contributions and earnings on contributed amounts are not taxed to employees until distributed or made available. The contributions are immediately deductible by the employer.
- Pension plans can be established as either defined contribution or defined benefit plans in which systematic and definite payments are made to a pension trust. Incidental benefits (e.g., death and disability payments) can be provided under the plan.
- Profit-sharing plans require the use of a predetermined allocation formula and substantial and recurring contributions must be made although annual employer contributions are not required and the contributions need not be based on profits. Section 401(k) plans can be established where employees have the option to receive cash or to have such amounts contributed to the profit-sharing trust. The employer may also establish an ESOP where the plan is funded by a contribution of the employer's stock.
- Qualified plans must be created for the employees' exclusive benefit.
- The plans may not discriminate in favor of highly compensated employees.
- Contributions and plan benefits must bear a uniform relationship to the compensation of covered employees.
- Minimum vesting requirements must be met (e.g., 100% vesting after five years).
- Employee benefits are taxed under the Sec. 72 annuity rules.
- Total employer contributions to the plan are subject to specific ceiling limitations.

ning. In general, nonqualified plans impose certain restrictions on the outright transfer of the plan's benefits to the employee. This avoids immediate taxation under the constructive receipt doctrine, which does not apply if the benefits are not yet credited, set apart, or made available so that the employee may draw on them. The amount is taxed to the employee upon the lapse of such restrictions, and the employer receives a corresponding deduction in the same year.

UNFUNDED DEFERRED COMPENSATION PLANS. **Unfunded deferred compensation plans** are often used to compensate highly compensated employees who desire to defer the recognition of income until future periods (e.g., a professional athlete or a business executive who receives a signing bonus may prefer to defer the recognition of income from the bonus). In general, if the promise to make the compensation payment in a future period is nonforfeitable, the agreement must not be funded (e.g., the transfer of assets to a trust for the employee's benefit) or evidenced by a negotiable note. The employer, however, may establish an *escrow account* on behalf of the employee. Such an account is used to accumulate and invest the deferred compensation amounts. If the requirements for deferral are met, the employee is taxed when the amounts are actually paid or made available, and the employer receives a corresponding deduction in the same year.[60]

EXAMPLE I9-55 ▶ In 2002, Kelly signs an employment contract to play professional football for the Chicago Skyhawks. The contract includes a $500,000 signing bonus that is payable in five annual installments beginning in 2008. The bonus agreement is nonforfeitable and is unfunded. The Skyhawks have agreed to place sufficient amounts of money into an escrow account to fund the future payments to Kelly. None of the $500,000 bonus is deductible by the employer or taxable to Kelly when the agreement is signed in 2002. The Skyhawks do not receive a deduction for any amounts that are deposited into the escrow account during the 2002–2007 period. In 2008, Kelly receives $100,000 taxable compensation (interest, if any, that accrued and was paid to Kelly is also taxable) upon receipt of the initial payment, and the Skyhawks receive a corresponding tax deduction. ◀

RESTRICTED PROPERTY PLANS. **Restricted property plans** are used to attract and retain key executives. Under such arrangements, the executive generally obtains an ownership interest (i.e., stock) in the corporation. Restricted property plans are governed by

[60] Reg. Sec. 1.451-2(a).

the income recognition rules contained in Sec. 83. Under these rules, the receipt of restricted property in exchange for services rendered is not taxable if the property is nontransferable and subject to a substantial risk of forfeiture.

The employee is treated as receiving taxable compensation based on the amount of the property's fair market value (FMV) (less any amount paid for the property) at the earlier of the time the property is no longer subject to a substantial risk of forfeiture or is transferable. The employer receives a corresponding compensation deduction at the same time the income is taxed to the employee.

EXAMPLE I9-56 ▶ In the current year, Allied Corporation transfers 1,000 shares of its common stock to employee Karen as compensation pursuant to a restricted property plan. The FMV of the Allied stock is $10 per share on the transfer date. The restricted property agreement provides that the stock is nontransferable by Karen until the year 2006 (i.e., Karen cannot sell the stock to outsiders until year 2006). The stock is also subject to the restriction that if Karen voluntarily leaves the company before the year 2006, she must transfer the shares back to the company and will receive no benefit from the stock other than from the receipt of dividends. The FMV of the stock is $100 per share in year 2006 when the forfeiture and nontransferability restrictions lapse. Because the stock is both nontransferable and subject to a substantial risk of forfeiture from the issue date to year 2006, the tax consequences from the stock transfer are deferred for both Karen and Allied Corporation until the lapse of the nontransferability or forfeiture restrictions in year 2006. In year 2006, Karen must report ordinary (compensation) income of $100,000 ($100 × 1,000 shares), and Allied Corporation is entitled to a corresponding compensation deduction of the same amount. Karen is taxed currently on the dividends she receives because they are not subject to any restrictions. ◀

KEY POINT

If an employee makes the election to be taxed immediately, he or she should be aware of the adverse consequences of leaving the company before the forfeiture restrictions lapse. The employee will not receive the property, and no deduction is allowed on the forfeiture.

Election to Be Taxed Immediately. An exception which permits an employee to elect (within 30 days after the receipt of restricted property) to recognize income immediately upon receipt of the restricted property is provided in Sec. 83(b). If the election is made, the employer is entitled to a corresponding deduction at the time the income is taxed to the employee. This election is frequently made when the fair market value of the restricted property is expected to increase significantly in the future and the future gain would be taxed as long-term capital gain. Because the current rate of tax on long-term capital gains has been reduced to 20%, one would expect that more taxpayers would make the Sec. 83(b) election.

EXAMPLE I9-57 ▶ Assume the same facts as Example I9-56, except that Karen elects to recognize income on the transfer date. Karen must include $10,000 ($10 × 1,000 shares) in gross income as compensation in the current year, and Allied Corporation is entitled to a corresponding deduction in the same year. Karen will report no income in 2006 when the restrictions lapse and her basis in the Allied Corporation stock remains at $10,000. If Karen sells the stock for $100,000 in the year 2006 after the restrictions lapse, Karen reports a $90,000 ($100,000 − $10,000) long-term capital gain on the sale.[61] If Karen voluntarily leaves the company before the forfeiture restrictions lapse, no deduction is allowed when the forfeiture occurs, despite the fact that Karen is previously taxed on the stock's value on the transfer date (i.e., $10,000 of income is recognized by Karen in the current year). In such event, Allied Corporation must include $10,000 in gross income in the year of the forfeiture (i.e., the amount of the deduction that is taken in the year of the transfer to the extent of any previous tax benefit). ◀

Nonqualified plan features and requirements are summarized in Topic Review I9-3.

EMPLOYEE STOCK OPTIONS

Stock option plans are used by corporate employers to attract and retain key management employees. Both stock option and restricted property arrangements using the employer's stock permit the executive to receive a proprietary interest in the corporation. Thus, an executive may identify more closely with shareholder interests and the firm's long-run

[61] Sec. 1223. The holding period originates on the day following the transfer date because Karen made the election to be taxed immediately under Sec. 83(b).

Topic Review I9-3

Nonqualified Plans

DISTINGUISHING FEATURES AND MAJOR REQUIREMENTS

1. The employee is taxed upon the lapse of restrictions imposed on the availability or withdrawal of funds and the employer receives a corresponding deduction in the same year.
2. Nonqualified plans may discriminate in favor of highly compensated employees and no minimum vesting rules are required.
3. Restricted property (usually employer stock) may be offered to executives where the incidents of taxation are deferred if the property is nontransferable and subject to a substantial risk of forfeiture. An election may be made under Sec. 83(b) to recognize income immediately upon the receipt of the restricted property.
4. Restrictions must be imposed to avoid immediate taxation to the employee under the constructive receipt doctrine.
5. To avoid immediate taxation, restricted property plans must be both nonforfeitable and subject to a substantial risk of forfeiture.

profit-maximization goals. The tax law currently includes two types of stock-option arrangements: the incentive stock option and the nonqualified stock option.[62] Each type is treated differently for tax purposes.

As will be seen in the discussions below, both types of plans have their respective advantages and disadvantages. Incentive stock option arrangements generally are preferred when long-term capital gain rates are low as compared to ordinary income rates. Thus, because the long-term capital gain rate has been decreased to 20% and marginal tax rates for ordinary income are rather high (38.6%), interest should increase in incentive stock option arrangements. However, an employer is more favorably treated under the nonqualified stock-option rules (i.e., the employer receives a tax deduction for the compensation related to a nonqualified stock option but does not receive a corresponding deduction if an incentive stock-option plan is adopted) and may therefore still prefer to continue to use nonqualified stock options.

KEY POINT

The incentive stock option has the disadvantage of not providing a compensation deduction for the employer. Before January 1, 1987, this disadvantage was offset by the fact that the employee was eligible for a 60% long-term capital gain deduction. With the repeal of the long-term capital gain deduction, the incentive stock option lost much of its appeal. However, the maximum 20% tax rate for net long-term capital gains may help to increase the popularity of incentive stock options.

INCENTIVE STOCK OPTION PLANS.

Employer Requirements. An **incentive stock option (ISO)** must meet the following plan or employer requirements:[63]

- The option price must be equal to or greater than the stock's FMV on the option's grant date.
- The option must be granted within ten years of the date the plan is adopted, and the employee must exercise the option within ten years of the grant date.
- The option must be both exercisable only by the employee and nontransferable except in the event of death.
- The employee cannot own more than 10% of the voting power of the employer corporation's stock immediately before the option's grant date.
- The total FMV of the stock options that become exercisable to an employee in any given year may not exceed $100,000 (e.g., an employee can be granted ISOs to acquire $200,000 of stock in one year, provided that no more than $100,000 is exercisable in any given year).
- Other procedural requirements must be met (e.g., shareholder approval of the plan).

KEY POINT

Incentive stock options can be a valuable tax planning tool because the earliest that they are generally taxed is when they are exercised. Also, when an employee realizes profits from stock options those profits in certain cases may qualify as capital gains.

Employee Requirements. In addition to the above plan requirements, the employee must meet the following requirements:

- The employee must not dispose of the stock within two years of the option's grant date nor within one year after the option's exercise date.

---

[62] The incentive stock option rules are provided in Sec. 422, whereas the rules governing nonqualified stock options are contained in Reg. Sec. 1.83-7.

[63] Sec. 422.

- The employee must be employed by the issuing company on the grant date and continue such employment until within three months before the exercise date.

If an employee meets the requirements listed above, no tax consequences occur on the grant date or the exercise date. However, the excess of the FMV over the option price on the exercise date is a tax preference item for purposes of the alternative minimum tax (see Chapter I14). When the employee sells the optioned stock, a long-term capital gain or loss is recognized. If the employee meets the two requirements, the employer does not receive a corresponding compensation deduction. If the requirements are not met, the option is treated as a nonqualified stock option.

EXAMPLE I9-58 ▶ American Corporation grants an incentive stock option to Kay, an employee, on January 1, 2002. The option price is $100, and the FMV of the American stock is also $100 on the grant date. The option permits Kay to purchase 100 shares of American stock. Kay exercises the option on June 30, 2004, when the stock's FMV is $400. Kay sells the 100 shares of American stock on January 1, 2006, for $500 per share. Because Kay holds the stock for the required period (at least two years from the grant date and one year from the exercise date) and because Kay is employed by American Corporation on the grant date and within three months before the exercise date, all of the requirements for an ISO have been met. No income is recognized on the grant date or the exercise date, although $30,000 [($400 − $100) × 100 shares] is a tax preference item for the alternative minimum tax in 2004. Kay recognizes a $40,000 [($500 − $100) × 100 shares] long-term capital gain on the sale date in 2006. American Corporation is not entitled to a compensation deduction in 2006 or in any other year. ◀

EXAMPLE I9-59 ▶ Assume the same facts as Example I9-58, except that Kay disposes of the stock on August 1, 2004, thus violating the one-year holding period requirement. Kay must recognize ordinary income on the sale date equal to the spread between the option price and the exercise price, or $30,000 [($400 − $100) × 100 shares]. The $30,000 spread between the FMV and the option price is no longer a tax preference item because the option ceases to qualify as an ISO. American Corporation can claim a $30,000 compensation deduction in 2004. Kay also recognizes a $10,000 [($500 − $400 adjusted basis) × 100 shares] short-term capital gain on the sale date, which represents the appreciation of the stock from the exercise date to the sale date. The gain is short-term because the holding period from the exercise date to the sale date does not exceed one year. ◀

KEY POINT

With ISO the employee does not recognize income when the option is exercised; income is recognized only when the stock is sold. With nonqualified stock options, income is recognized when the option is exercised or on the grant date and when the stock is sold at a gain.

NONQUALIFIED STOCK OPTION PLANS. Stock options that do not meet the plan requirements for incentive stock options are referred to as **nonqualified stock options**. The tax treatment of nonqualified stock options depends on whether the option has a **readily ascertainable fair market value** (e.g., whether the option is traded on an established options exchange).

Readily Ascertainable Fair Market Value. If a nonqualified stock option has a readily ascertainable FMV (e.g., the option is traded on an established options exchange), the employee recognizes ordinary income on the grant date equal to the difference between the stock's FMV and the option's exercise price. The employer receives a compensation deduction on the grant date equal to the same amount of income that is recognized by the employee. In such case, no tax consequences occur on the date the option is exercised, and the employee recognizes capital gain or loss upon the sale or disposition of the stock.

No Readily Ascertainable Fair Market Value. If a nonqualified stock option has no readily ascertainable FMV, no tax consequences occur on the grant date. On the exercise date the employee recognizes ordinary income equal to the spread between the FMV of the stock and the option price, and the employer receives a corresponding compensation deduction. When the stock option is exercised, the employee's basis in the stock is equal to the option price plus the amount reported as ordinary income on the exercise date. Capital gain or loss is recognized upon the subsequent sale of the stock by the employee.

The alternative minimum tax does not apply to nonqualified stock options regardless of whether the option has a readily ascertainable FMV. Table I9-4 illustrates the tax consequences to employees and employers for such options.

▼ TABLE I9-4
Taxation of Nonqualified Stock Options

Situation Facts	Readily Ascertainable FMV	No Readily Ascertainable FMV
Grant date: On January 1, 2002, Kim is granted a nonqualified stock option to purchase 100 shares of stock from Apple Corporation (Kim's employer) at $90 per share. The stock's FMV is $100 on the grant date.	Ordinary income of $1,000 is recognized [($100 − $90) × 100 shares] by Kim in 2002. Apple Corporation receives a corresponding $1,000 compensation deduction in 2002.	No tax consequences to Kim or Apple Corporation.
Exercise date: On January 31, 2003, Kim exercises the option and acquires the 100 shares of Apple Corporation stock for the $90 option price when the FMV is $190.	No tax consequences to Kim or Apple Corporation.	Kim recognizes ordinary income in 2003 of $10,000 [($190 − $90) × 100 shares], and Apple Corporation receives a $10,000 compensation deduction.
Sale date: On February 1, 2004, Kim sells the stock for $200 per share and realizes $20,000 ($200 × 100 shares).	Kim recognizes a $10,000 ($20,000 − $10,000 basis) long-term capital gain.[a]	Kim recognizes a $1,000 ($20,000 − $19,000 basis) long-term capital gain.[b]

[a] Kim's basis includes the amount paid for the optioned stock of $9,000 plus ordinary income of $1,000 recognized on the grant date. Kim's holding period commences on the January 1, 2002 grant date for determining whether the gain is long-term.
[b] Kim's basis includes the $9,000 paid for the option stock plus the $10,000 ordinary income recognized on the exercise date. Kim's holding period commences on the January 31, 2003 exercise date for determining whether the gain is long-term.

As illustrated in Table I9-4, Kim reports a total gain of $11,000 from the option transaction under both circumstances. However, the character of her profit (i.e., ordinary income or capital gain) and the timing of the profit recognition (i.e., grant date or exercise date) depends on whether the option's FMV is readily ascertainable.

The distinguishing features and major requirements for employee stock options are summarized in Topic Review I9-4.

Topic Review I9-4

Employee Stock Options

Distinguishing Features and Major Requirements

- For an incentive stock option (ISO) plan no tax consequences occur on the grant or the exercise date (except for the recognition of a tax preference item under the AMT provisions on the exercise date). Capital gain or loss is recognized by the employee upon the sale or exchange of the stock. No deduction is allowed to the employer.
- ISOs and nonqualified stock options may be issued to highly compensated employees without regard to nondiscrimination rules.
- If a nonqualified stock option has a readily ascertainable FMV, the employee recognizes ordinary income equal to the spread between the FMV of the stock and the option price on the grant date and the employer receives a corresponding deduction. If the option has no readily ascertainable FMV, income is recognized on the exercise date equal to the spread between the FMV of the stock and the option price and a corresponding deduction is available to the employer.
- For an ISO, the option price must be equal to or greater than the FMV of the stock on the grant date, employees cannot own more than 10% of the voting power of the employer's stock, and restrictions are placed on the total FMV of stock options that may be issued.
- To qualify under the ISO rules, a two-year holding period from the grant date is required (and at least one year after the exercise date) and the employee must continue to be employed by the company until within three months of the exercise date.

ADDITIONAL COMMENT

If you are self-employed and establish a Keogh plan, you must include any employees in the plan.

PLANS FOR SELF-EMPLOYED INDIVIDUALS

Self-employed individuals, such as sole proprietors and partners who practice a trade or business, are not classified as employees and are subject to special retirement plan rules known as **H.R. 10 plans** (also called **Keogh plans**). Retirement plans of self-employed people are generally subject to the same contribution and benefit limitations as other qualified corporate plans. An employee who is covered under a qualified pension or profit-sharing plan for wages earned as an employee and who is also self-employed may establish an H.R. 10 plan for earned income derived from self-employment activities.

KEY POINT

Keogh plans can be either defined benefit or defined contribution plans. Many individuals avoid the defined benefit type of Keogh plan due to the extra paperwork and administrative costs.

For a **defined contribution H.R. 10 plan**, a self-employed individual in 2002 may contribute the smaller of $40,000 or 100% of earned income from the self-employment activity.[64] *Earned income* refers to net earnings from self-employment. To compute the limitations for 2002, only $200,000 of earned income may be taken into account for any one individual.[65] Earned income is reduced by the contribution made on behalf of the self-employed individual.

EXAMPLE I9-60 ▶ Larry is a self-employed CPA whose 2002 net earnings from his trade or business (before the H.R. 10 plan contribution but after the deduction for one-half of the self-employment taxes paid under Sec. 164(f) [see Chapter I14]) is $100,000. Larry may contribute $40,000 to the plan for 2002. Larry must also provide coverage for all of his eligible full-time employees under the general rules provided in the law for qualified plans (e.g., nondiscrimination, vesting, and so on).[66] If Larry's earned income for 2002 was only $28,000 rather than $100,000, his deduction would be limited to $28,000. ◀

KEY POINT

A Keogh plan must be created no later than the last day of your tax year.

An H.R. 10 plan must be established before the end of the tax year, but contributions may be made up to the due date for the tax return (including extensions). All H.R. 10 pension contributions made by a self-employed individual for *employees* are deductible for AGI on Schedule C. The H.R. 10 contribution for the self-employed individual is deductible *for* AGI on page 1 of Form 1040.

INDIVIDUAL RETIREMENT ACCOUNTS (IRAS)

Under current law, there are three types of IRA's that are available to taxpayers:

- ▶ Traditional IRA
- ▶ Roth IRA
- ▶ Coverdell Education Savings Account IRA

REAL WORLD EXAMPLE

The IRA savings provisions were originally enacted in 1974 to provide a tax-favored retirement savings arrangement to individuals who were not covered under a qualified plan. Beginning in 1982, Congress extended IRA availability to all taxpayers. It was hoped that the extended availability would increase the level of savings and provide a discretionary retirement savings plan that was uniformly available. However, Congress in the Tax Reform Act of 1986 restricted the availability of IRAs because there was no discernible impact on aggregate personal savings.

The Roth IRA and Coverdell IRA were both created in 1997 and were effective beginning in 1998. Prior to July 26, 2001, the Coverdell Education Savings Account was called an Education Individual Retirement Account.[67]

TRADITIONAL IRA

Traditional IRAs have been in the law for nearly 25 years and taxpayers may make either deductible or nondeductible contributions to the IRA. A contribution to a traditional IRA that is deductible has two principal benefits, (1) the amount contributed to the IRA (maximum $3,000 per year) is deductible on the taxpayer's return,[68] and (2) the income earned on the investments in the IRA is not subject to current taxation. However, when amounts are withdrawn from the IRA at retirement, such amounts are fully subject to taxation. Nondeductible contributions to a traditional IRA may not be deducted on the taxpayer's return, but such contributions are not subject to taxation when withdrawn from the IRA. While contributions are not subject to taxation, any earnings are subject to taxation when withdrawn.

---

[64] Sec. 415(c)(1). The 25% deduction limit also applies if the defined contribution plan is a profit sharing plan.

[65] Secs. 401(a)(17) and 404(l). The ceiling in 2001 was $170,000.

[66] Sec. 401(d).

[67] The Coverdell Education Savings Account was named after the late Senator Paul Coverdell of Georgia.

[68] The 2001 Tax Act increased the deductible amount to an IRA to $3,000 for 2002–2004, $4,000 for 2005–2007, and $5,000 in 2008 and future years. After 2008, the deductible amount will be indexed for inflation. Prior to 2002, the deductible amount was $2,000. In addition, individuals over 50 years of age are now eligible to contribute an extra $500 into their IRA in years 2002–2005 (increasing to $1,000 in 2006 and future years). These extra amounts are referred to as "catch-up contributions."

Individuals may make deductible contributions equal to the lesser of $3,000 or 100% of compensation only if either of the following conditions exists:

- The individual is *not* an active participant in an employer-sponsored retirement plan, including tax-sheltered annuities, government plans, simplified employee pension plans, and H.R. 10 plans; or
- Individuals who are active participants in an employer-sponsored retirement plan must have an AGI equal to or below the following applicable dollar limits for 2002:[69] $34,000 for an unmarried taxpayer; $54,000 for a married couple filing a joint return; zero for a married individual filing separately. If an individual has AGI above these amounts, the deductible IRA contribution amounts are phased out on a pro rata basis as AGI increases from $34,000 to $44,000 for unmarried taxpayers and from $54,000 to $64,000 for married taxpayers filing a joint return.

EXAMPLE I9-61 ▶ Laura is an unmarried taxpayer who is not an active participant in an employer-sponsored retirement plan or other qualified plan. In 2002, Laura's AGI is $60,000, consisting of earned income from wages. Laura is not subject to the dollar limitation because she is not an active participant in a qualified plan and may, therefore, contribute and deduct up to $3,000 to a traditional IRA. Laura's AGI is reduced to $57,000 ($60,000 − $3,000) because the amount is deductible *for* AGI. ◀

EXAMPLE I9-62 ▶ Judy is an unmarried taxpayer who is an active participant in her employer's qualified retirement plan. In 2002, Judy's AGI is $40,000, consisting of earned income from wages of $35,000 and interest and dividends of $5,000. Since she is an active participant in a qualified plan and her AGI is over $34,000, her deductible contribution to a traditional IRA is subject to the phaseout. Since the ceiling amount is exceeded by $6,000 ($40,000 − $34,000), the maximum IRA contribution is reduced by 60% ($6,000/$10,000). Thus, the maximum that Judy can contribute and deduct to her IRA in 2002 is $1,200 ($3,000 − $1,800). ◀

ADDITIONAL COMMENT

Banks, savings and loan associations, insurance companies, and stock brokerage firms make IRAs available to taxpayers. Usually, the amounts are invested in long-term savings accounts. However, self-directed plans are offered by some stock brokerage firms. In this type of IRA, the taxpayer can specify how the contributions will be invested.

If a taxpayer's AGI exceeds the above limits, the taxpayer may make a nondeductible contribution of up to $3,000 to a traditional IRA. The benefit of making a nondeductible contribution to an IRA is that the earnings of the IRA investments grow tax-free. Thus, even though the *earnings* of the nondeductible IRA will be taxed when distributed, the ability to allow investments to compound before-tax is a major advantage for taxpayers. However, as will be seen in the discussion of Roth IRAs below, if a taxpayer can qualify for a Roth IRA rather than a traditional nondeductible IRA, the choice clearly favors a Roth IRA. The maximum amount of a nondeductible contribution that may be made to a traditional IRA is $3,000 minus the amount that is allowed as a deduction. Also, a taxpayer may elect for all of his contributions to be nondeductible even though the contributions are otherwise eligible to be deducted.

EXAMPLE I9-63 ▶ Using the same facts as in Example I9-62, Judy is permitted to make a nondeductible contribution to her IRA of $1,800 ($3,000 − $1,200). She also could elect to designate all $3,000 as a nondeductible contribution even though she is eligible to deduct the $1,200. ◀

Two special rules apply to married couples relative to traditional IRAs. First, if only one spouse is employed and this working spouse is otherwise eligible to make IRA contributions, the nonworking spouse may contribute up to $3,000 per year to an IRA (a so-called spousal IRA). Thus, a total of $6,000 may be deductible by a married couple ($3,000 to each spouse's IRA) even though only one spouse has earned income. It should be noted that even though only the working spouse must have earned income, such working spouse must have at least $6,000 of earned income in order to contribute $6,000 to the two IRAs. Second, if one spouse is covered under a qualified retirement plan but the other spouse is not covered, the non-covered spouse may contribute to a traditional deductible IRA. However, the contribution to a traditional deductible IRA is phased out at adjusted gross incomes between $150,000 and $160,000.

---

[69] Sec. 219(g). The phaseout limits for unmarried individuals increase from $34,000 in 2002 to $40,000 in 2003 and gradually phasing up to $50,000 by 2005. For married taxpayers filing a joint return, the $54,000 limit in 2002 increases to $60,000 in 2003 and gradually phases up to $80,000 by 2007.

EXAMPLE I9-64 ▶ Gary and Babs are a married couple. Gary is covered under a qualified retirement plan at his job and earned $170,000 in 2002. Babs is employed as a secretary and earned $10,000. They file a joint return, have interest and dividend income of $20,000, and their AGI, therefore, is $200,000. Neither Gary nor Babs is entitled to deduct contributions to a traditional IRA because their AGI exceeds $160,000. However, both Gary and Babs are allowed to make nondeductible contributions of $3,000 each to the IRA. ◀

EXAMPLE I9-65 ▶ Assume the same facts as in Example I9-64 but that Gary's income is $100,000 and their AGI is $130,000. Babs may contribute and deduct $3,000 to a traditional IRA because their AGI is less than $150,000. However, Gary may not make a deductible contribution because he is covered under a qualified plan and their AGI exceeds $54,000. Gary is permitted to make a $3,000 contribution to a nondeductible IRA. ◀

ADDITIONAL COMMENT

A contribution to an IRA for the year 2001 can be made as late as the due date for filing the 2002 return.

The following significant tax rules apply to traditional IRAs:

- An IRA plan may be established between the end of the tax year and the due date for the tax return (not including any extensions that are permitted). Any deductible contributions made during this time are treated as a deduction for the prior year. Contributions are deductible if made by the due date for the tax return (i.e., contributions for 2002 must be made no later than April 15, 2003). Contributions to nondeductible IRAs also must be made by April 15th of the following year.
- Distributions from a traditional IRA are taxed under the annuity rules in Sec. 72. Normally distributions from an IRA are fully subject to taxation. However, if nondeductible contributions are made to an IRA, these amounts would represent the investment in the contract in calculating the exclusion ratio.
- Withdrawals by a participant before age 59½ are both includible in income and subject to a nondeductible 10% penalty tax.[70]
- Withdrawals must begin no later than April 1 of the year following the end of the tax year in which the individual reaches age 70½. IRA contributions that were deducted over the years on the taxpayer's returns are fully taxable as ordinary income when the amounts are distributed.
- A nondeductible 6% penalty is levied on excess contributions to an IRA.[71]

ADDITIONAL COMMENT

Some financial advisers recommend the following approach when someone can only afford to have limited amounts set aside for retirement. Have pre-tax dollars withheld from salary up to the employer-matching amount in 401(k) plans, then place $3,000 in a Roth IRA. This maximizes employer contributions and places the maximum amount allowable into the much favored Roth IRA.

ROTH IRA

The Roth IRA[72] is a relatively new type of IRA that is referred to as a "backloaded IRA" because the tax benefits come at the end, not at the beginning, of the IRA. Contributions to a Roth IRA are nondeductible but all distributions from the IRA, including earnings, are nontaxable. The maximum amount that may be contributed to a Roth IRA is $3,000. However, taxpayers who are eligible for both a Roth IRA and a traditional IRA, may only contribute a total of $3,000 to both types of IRAs. As with traditional IRAs, Roth IRAs are also subject to AGI phaseout limitations, although the limitation amounts are higher that with traditional IRAs. Roth IRAs are available for tax years beginning after December 31, 1997.

All taxpayers may contribute up to $3,000 to a Roth IRA, however, this amount is phased out for single taxpayers if their AGI is between $95,000 and $110,000 ($150,000 and $160,000 for married couples filing a joint return). The principal advantage of the Roth IRA is the nontaxability of qualified distributions. One requirement of a qualified distribution is that the distribution must meet a five year holding period. More specifically, the distribution may not be made before the end of the five-tax-year period beginning with the first tax year for which a contribution was made to the Roth IRA. In addition to satisfying the five-year test, a qualifying distribution must also meet one of the following:

---

70 Sec. 72(t). The amount subject to the 10% penalty is the portion of the amount that must be included in gross income. Exceptions to the 10% penalty are provided in the event of death, disability, and certain non-lump-sum distributions. The TRA 1997 also added two additional exceptions, (1) withdrawals used to pay qualified higher education costs for taxpayer, spouse, children or grandchildren, and (2) up to $10,000 to buy or build the principal residence for a "first time homebuyer".

71 Sec. 4973(b).

72 Sec. 408A.

- made on or after the date on which the individual attains age 59½,
- made to a beneficiary (or the individual's estate) on or after the individual's death,
- attributable to the individual being disabled, or
- a distribution for first-time homebuyer expenses (maximum of $10,000).

An important aspect of distributions from a Roth IRA is a special ordering rule for determining the taxability of nonqualifying withdrawals. Under this rule, distributions are treated as being made from contributions first and, thus, are nontaxable. After all contributions have been withdrawn, any remaining amounts are considered taxable and subject to the 10% penalty.

EXAMPLE I9-66 ▶ Ray and Sandy are married and Ray is covered under his employer's qualified retirement plan. Their AGI on a joint return is $130,000. Ray can contribute $3,000 to a Roth IRA. Alternatively, however, if their AGI was $156,000, Ray would be limited to a maximum contribution of $1,200. Since their AGI exceeds the threshold of $150,000 by $6,000, the $3,000 contribution is reduced by 60% ($6000/$10,000), or $1,800. ◀

EXAMPLE I9-67 ▶ Bob, age 60 in 2001, contributes $3,000 each year to a Roth IRA in 2002, 2003, and 2004. On November 30, 2006, the value of the Roth IRA is $9,000. Bob has experienced some financial setbacks and needs to withdraw the money from the Roth IRA. If Bob withdraws $6,000 in 2006 and waits until January, 2007 to withdraw the remaining $3,000, none of the distributions are taxable. This result occurs because the first $6,000 is treated as coming from contributions. The remaining $3,000 is nontaxable because Bob has met the five-year test and is over age 59½. Conversely, if Bob withdraws the entire $9,000 in 2006, $3,000 must be included in his income because the five-year test was not met. ◀

A final aspect of Roth IRAs is the ability to "rollover" funds from an existing deductible IRA into a Roth IRA. However, since the taxpayer received a deduction for the contribution into the deductible IRA, any rollover amount must be included in gross income in the year the rollover occurred. More specifically, if a taxpayer's AGI does not exceed $100,000 and does not file as married filing separately, the taxpayer is eligible to rollover any amount of funds from a deductible IRA into a Roth IRA. Such rollover amount is includible in the taxpayer's income, but is not subject to the 10% penalty for early withdrawals. If the rollover was made before January 1, 1999, individuals could have elected to include the amounts in gross income ratably over a four-year period beginning with the year of rollover.

EXAMPLE I9-68 ▶ Mikael has a traditional IRA that has a balance of $60,000 on June 30, 2002. He is single and has AGI of $80,000. Mikael is eligible to rollover the $60,000 to a Roth IRA. If he completes the rollover in 2002, he will be required to include the $60,000 in his gross income for 2002. He is not subject to the 10% early withdrawal penalty on such rollover. ◀

TAX STRATEGY TIP

Because of the tax-deferral of income within a Roth IRA and the ability to withdraw amounts at retirement tax-free, the Roth IRA generally is superior to a traditional IRA for younger taxpayers. Once a taxpayer reaches 50 years of age, the two types of IRAs become more equal.

Below is a discussion of some of the important tax rules for Roth IRAs:

- Like traditional IRAs, Roth IRAs must be established by the due date of the tax return (not including extensions). Similarly, contributions to a Roth IRA also must be made by the due date of the return (i.e., April 15, 2003 for 2002 contributions).
- Contributions to a Roth IRA are never deductible.
- Contributions to a Roth IRA are subject to special modified AGI limitations.
- Contributions to a Roth IRA can be made after the owner has reached age 70½. Similarly, no distributions are required at any age from a Roth IRA. (Remember: owners of traditional IRAs must begin taking distributions in the year after the taxpayer has reached age 70½).
- Withdrawals from a Roth IRA are not taxable if such withdrawals are "qualified distributions." If a withdrawal is not a qualified distribution, the amount is taxed under special ordering rules and subject to the 10% penalty.
- A taxpayer whose AGI is $100,000 or less may rollover his traditional IRA to a Roth IRA. However, the total amount rolled over from a traditional deductible IRA must be included in the taxpayer's gross income.

STOP & THINK *Question:* Both nondeductible contributions to a traditional IRA and contributions to a Roth IRA are similar in the sense that neither provide a tax deduction at the date of contribution. Which of the two types would be most advantageous to taxpayers?

Solution: Clearly, if a taxpayer qualifies for a Roth IRA, that type of IRA is superior to a nondeductible contribution to a traditional IRA. The reason is that distributions from a Roth IRA are totally excluded from gross income while only the principal portion of nondeductible contributions to a traditional IRA are excludable. In other words, the earnings generated in a Roth IRA are excluded from gross income whereas earnings associated with nondeductible contributions to a traditional IRA are subject to taxation. Generally, a nondeductible contribution to a traditional IRA will not be advantageous unless the taxpayer's AGI exceeds $160,000.

For a discussion of the decision whether to invest in a traditional deductible IRA or a Roth IRA, see the Tax Planning Considerations later in this chapter. Also, for a more detailed analysis including computations, see Chapter I18 of this *Individuals* textbook.

Topic Review I9-5 contains a table which summarizes the eligibility rules for traditional and Roth IRAs.

Topic Review I9-5

Traditional and Roth IRAs—Eligibility

If 2002 AGI Is	Eligible For IRA (Joint Returns)				
	Traditional IRA (Deductible)			Roth IRA	Traditional IRA (Nondeductible)*
	A	B	C		
Up to $54,000	Yes	Yes	Yes	Yes	Yes
$54,000–$64,000	Yes	Partially	Yes	Yes	Yes
$64,000–$150,000	Yes	No	Yes	Yes	Yes
$150,000–$160,000	Yes	No	Partially	Partially	Yes
Over $160,000	Yes	No	No	No	Yes

A If neither spouse is an active participant in an employer-sponsored plan
B For the IRA of a spouse who is an active participant in an employer-sponsored plan
C For the IRA of a spouse who is not an active participant in an employer-sponsored plan.

* If AGI is not above $160,000, a nondeductible IRA will not be advantageous.

COVERDELL EDUCATION SAVINGS ACCOUNT

ADDITIONAL COMMENT

Any number of people may contribute funds to a Coverdell Education Savings Account for one child. But all of the contributions may not total more than $2,00 for that child.

A special type of IRA, referred to as an Education IRA, was established in 1997 to specifically assist low and middle-income taxpayers with higher education expenses. As mentioned previously, the Education IRA was renamed the Coverdell Education Savings Account (CESA) in 2001. The 2001 Tax Act significantly increased the attractiveness of this type of plan in the following principal ways beginning in 2002:

- Increased the annual contribution into such plan from $500 to $2,000.
- CESAs may now be used for elementary and secondary education expenses as well as for higher education expenses, and
- Taxpayers may claim either the HOPE scholarship credit or lifetime learning credit as well as excluding distributions from a CESA in the same year.

A contributor can make a *nondeductible* contribution of up to $2,000 per year into a CESA for a designated beneficiary until the beneficiary reaches age 18.[73] The contributor need not be related to the beneficiary and there is no limit on the number of CESAs that

[73] Sec. 530. The 2001 Tax Act allows contributions to continue past age 18 for a special needs beneficiary, Sec. 530(b)(1).

can be set up by a contributor. Distributions to the beneficiary are excluded from gross income provided the distribution does not exceed the *qualified education expenses* of the designated beneficiary during the taxable year. Qualified education expenses include tuition, fees, books, supplies, equipment, and room and board. In the case of elementary and secondary education expenses, qualified education expenses include academic tutoring and Internet access fees. Distributions in any tax year in excess of qualified education expenses are includible in the gross income of the beneficiary and subject to a 10% penalty.

Similar to other IRA-type accounts, there are phaseout limits based on the contributor's AGI. The $2,000 annual contribution is phased out for married taxpayers filing joint returns with AGI from $190,000 to $220,000 ($95,000 to $110,000 for other taxpayers). In addition, if the taxpayer claims either the HOPE scholarship credit or the lifetime learning credit, the education expenses used for these credits must reduce the qualified expenses for exclusion from a CESA.

EXAMPLE I9-69 ▶ Lee and Patsy are married and have two young grandchildren. To assist the grandchildren with their future education expenses, they set up a CESA for each child in 2002 and plan to deposit $2,000 in both accounts. Their AGI for 2002 is $202,000. Because their AGI exceeds $190,000, they are limited to putting $1,200 [$2,000 – $2,000($202,000 – $190,000)/$30,000)] into the accounts in 2002. In the future, the children can withdraw amounts tax-free from their CESA to pay for qualified education expenses for elementary, secondary, or higher education. ◀

EXAMPLE I9-70 ▶ Craig Shaw is about to enter State University as a freshman and plans to withdraw amounts from his CESA to help pay his expenses. His expenses for the Fall Semester, 19X1 are as follows:

Tuition and fees	$2,200
Books	500
Supplies	300
Room and board	2,400
Total	$5,400

Craig's parents plan on paying Craig's tuition and fees and Craig will pay the remaining $3,200 from his CESA. Craig qualifies as a dependent of his parents for the tax year. Craig's parents plan on claiming the HOPE scholarship credit. Craig is not required to include the $3,200 in his gross income in 19X1 as his qualified education expenses are at least $3,200. The qualified education expenses in 19X1 for purposes of excluding amounts withdrawn from the CESA are $3,900 ($5,400 – $1,500). Qualified education expenses for a designated beneficiary must be reduced for amounts taken into account in determining the HOPE scholarship credit and the lifetime learning credit. Since Craig's parents will use $1,500 of the $2,200 to claim the HOPE credit, the qualified education expenses must be reduced by such amount. ◀

SIMPLIFIED EMPLOYEE PENSIONS

Due to the administrative complexity associated with qualified pension and profit-sharing plans, small businesses often establish simplified employee pension (SEP) plans for their employees. In a SEP, the employer makes contributions to the IRAs of its employees.[74] The following is a summary of the tax rules that apply to a SEP:

- ▶ The employer receives an immediate tax deduction for contributions made under the plan. The annual deductible contributions for each participant are limited to the lesser of 25% of the participant's compensation (up to a ceiling of $200,000) and the dollar limitations for defined contribution plans.[75]
- ▶ Contributions are treated as being made on the last day of the tax year if they are made by the due date of the tax return (including extensions).
- ▶ Employer contributions must be nondiscriminatory.
- ▶ Distributions from a SEP are subject to taxation based on the IRA rules (previously discussed) including the penalty tax for premature distributions.

[74] Sec. 408(k).

[75] Sec. 404(h)(1).

► A self-employed person (i.e., a partner or sole proprietor) may establish a SEP rather than using an H.R. 10 plan arrangement because of reduced administrative complexity associated with a SEP.

SIMPLE RETIREMENT PLANS

Another more recent type of retirement savings plan for small businesses is called the savings incentive match plan for employees (SIMPLE).[76] This type of plan can be adopted by employers who have 100 or fewer employees who received at least $5,000 in compensation from the employer in the preceding year. A SIMPLE plan may be set up either as an IRA for each employee or part of a qualified cash or deferred arrangement (401(k) plan). Essentially, employees are allowed to make elective contributions in 2002 of up to $7,000 ($6,500 in 2001) per year and employers are required to make matching contributions.

The unique features of the SIMPLE plans are (1) that elective contributions by employees must be matched by the employer or the employer has the option of making nonelective contributions, (2) that all contributions to an employee's SIMPLE account must be fully vested and (3) the SIMPLE plans are not subject to the special nondiscrimination rules generally applicable to qualified plans. This last feature is important in that there is no requirement that a set number of employees *participate* in the plan, the only requirement is that all employees who had $5,000 in compensation in the previous year and are reasonably expected to have $5,000 in compensation in the current year must be eligible to participate.

TAX PLANNING CONSIDERATIONS

MOVING EXPENSES

To be eligible for the moving expense deduction, the moving expenses must be paid in connection with the commencement of work by the taxpayer as a full-time employee or self-employed individual. Therefore, it is important to secure full-time employment or to carry on a trade or business as a self-employed individual at the new location. Taxpayers who are approaching retirement are eligible for a moving expense deduction only if they continue to work in the new location before their actual retirement (e.g., 39 weeks in the 12-month period following the move).

EXAMPLE I9-71 ► Louis decides to quit his job and return to school as a full-time graduate student. Louis incurs substantial long-distance moving expenses that would otherwise be deductible to relocate to the university where the education is to be taken. No deduction is allowed unless Louis is employed on a full-time basis or is engaged in a self-employment activity at the new location. ◄

REIMBURSED AMOUNTS. Moving expense reimbursements are often greater than the amounts allowable as a deduction. This is caused by the common practice of reimbursing nondeductible items (e.g., an employer may reimburse an employee for the cost of certain indirect moving expenses such as househunting trips, which do not qualify as deductible moving expenses). This results in an increase in the employee's gross income to the extent of the excess reimbursement. From a tax planning standpoint, the employer may provide an additional payment to compensate the employee for the additional tax cost associated with the move (commonly referred to as a "gross-up").

EXAMPLE I9-72 ► Austin Corporation has a policy of reimbursing transferred employees for 30% of their moving reimbursement that exceeds their deductible expenses to cover the federal and state tax costs associated with the excess reimbursement. Kathy, an employee, is transferred by the company to a new job location and incurs $6,000 of deductible moving expenses and receives an $8,000 reimbursement. Austin also will make an additional payment to Kathy of $600 (0.30 × $2,000) to cover the additional federal and state income tax costs. Kathy must include $2,600 ($2,000 + $600) of the reimbursement in gross income. ◄

[76] Sec. 408(p).

PROVIDING NONTAXABLE COMPENSATION TO EMPLOYEES

Employers should consider the tax consequences to employees when changes in fringe benefit and deferred compensation arrangements are evaluated. For example, it is preferable for an employer to pay for fringe benefit items such as group term life insurance (up to $50,000 in coverage), health and accident insurance, employee parking, and so on rather than to give cash raises of a comparable amount. Such payments are nontaxable to the employee up to certain limits, whereas a comparable salary increase is fully taxable. Both types of payments are deductible by the employer.

REAL WORLD EXAMPLE

Banks and other financial institutions in their ads sometimes compare the accumulated wealth in an IRA to the accumulated wealth in a fully taxable investment. Although the IRA is generally advantageous, the ads sometimes overstate the advantages because they fail to deduct the tax that will be paid when amounts are withdrawn from the IRA.

Consideration should also be given to increased deferred compensation benefit programs for employees, particularly highly compensated individuals. The use of nonqualified deferred compensation plans, restricted property, and stock options result in tax deferrals and may result in the eventual recognition of capital gains that may be used to offset capital losses or that are taxed at a maximum 20% marginal tax rate.

All eligible employees should consider establishing an individual retirement account (IRA) because of the available tax deferral benefits. Even if a premature withdrawal (i.e., before age 59½ occurs), the time value of the deferred benefits for the plan contributions and the earnings may be greater than the penalty tax imposed.

ROLLOVER OF TRADITIONAL IRA TO ROTH IRA

Taxpayers have the ability to rollover amounts from a traditional IRA to a Roth IRA. However, if such a rollover is made, the taxpayer must include the amount in gross income in the year of the rollover. If the rollover was made before January 1, 1999, the taxpayer could have included the amount in gross income on a ratable basis over four years. The principal benefit of the rollover is that once the amounts are in the Roth IRA, no further taxes are due on these amounts upon distribution (assuming the five-year test is met). The essential question, therefore, is whether it is advantageous to rollover amounts from a traditional IRA to a Roth IRA and pay the tax now or keep the traditional IRA intact and pay the tax when regular distributions are made.

The decision rests on several factors, including (1) the marginal tax rate at retirement, (2) age of taxpayer, and (3) payment of tax from rollover from post-tax funds. First, if a taxpayer's marginal tax rate at retirement is expected to be lower than the current tax rate, a rollover may not be advantageous. Second, younger taxpayers are more likely to benefit from a rollover because they have more years to accumulate earnings tax-free and may be in a lower tax bracket today than at retirement. Finally, if the taxes that accrue from the rollover must be paid from the rollover funds, a rollover will probably not be in the taxpayer's favor. In other words, taxpayers should have sufficient funds from other sources to pay the tax, then the entire amount of rollover into the Roth IRA will have maximum ability to grow on a tax-free basis.

Each case must be analyzed based on the unique factors of that particular situation. However, for most taxpayers, it is generally advantageous to rollover funds from a traditional IRA to a Roth IRA. Of course, as is pointed out earlier in this chapter, the individual must have AGI of $100,000 or less (before the rollover distribution) to qualify for the rollover.

COMPLIANCE AND PROCEDURAL CONSIDERATIONS

KEY POINT

It is extremely important to be able to substantiate travel and entertainment expenses. The *Cohan* Rule that permits a reasonable deduction when substantiation is lacking does not apply to travel and entertainment expenses (see Chapter I6).

SUBSTANTIATING TRAVEL AND ENTERTAINMENT EXPENSES

Travel and entertainment expenses are disallowed if the taxpayer does not maintain adequate records or documentary proof of the expenditures.[77] Normally, documentation includes expense statements (diary or account book) and proof of the amount, time, place, and business purpose. Strict substantiation rules are enacted in the law to curb widespread abuses in the so-called expense account living practices engaged in by some taxpayers.

[77] Sec. 274(d).

To make compliance easier, the IRS formulated the following administrative procedural rules:

- If an employee makes an adequate accounting of the expenditures to the employer, it is not necessary to submit a detailed statement on the employee's tax return unless the expenses exceed the reimbursements.
- The standard mileage rate may be used to compute automobile expenses in lieu of actual expenses and is reported on Form 2106 (Employee Business Expenses).
- Taxpayers may elect an optional method for computing deductions for business travel and meal expenses in lieu of using actual costs. If a per diem allowance is paid by an employer in lieu of reimbursing actual expenses, the reimbursement is deemed to be substantiated if it does not exceed a federal per diem rate for the travel locality. In lieu of using actual expenses an employee or self-employed individual may use the applicable federal per diem rate. The taxpayer must still provide documentation of time, place, and business purpose for the expenditures.

ETHICAL POINT

The CPA has a responsibility to make sure that proper documentation has been furnished by the taxpayer to substantiate travel and entertainment expenses according to the provisions in Sec. 274(d). The CPA cannot rely on the use of estimates for these expenses despite the fact that the *AICPA's Statements on Responsibilities in Tax Practice No. 4* (see Appendix E) permits the use of estimates if it is impractical to obtain exact data and the estimated amounts appear to be reasonable.

REPORTING EMPLOYEE BUSINESS EXPENSES

Form 2106 (Employee Business Expenses) is used to report employee business expenses (see Appendix B). Part I of Form 2106 is a recap of travel and transportation expenses. Part II includes a computation of automobile expenses using either actual expenses or the standard rate mileage method. Employer reimbursements must be included in the employee's wages on Form W-2 if an adequate accounting of the expenses is not made. Employer withholding of federal income tax is also required for nonaccountable plan reimbursements. Form 2106-EZ may be used by employees who do not receive an employer reimbursement, and where the standard mileage rate is used for the current year and for the year the taxpayer's automobile was first placed in service.

Moving expenses are reported on Form 3903 (Moving Expenses) instead of Form 2106 because they are treated differently from other employee expenses (e.g., unreimbursed moving expenses are deductible *for* AGI). Expenses such as entertainment, union dues, business gifts, and education expenses are reported on Schedule A of Form 1040 as itemized deductions (see Appendix B).

A filled-in copy of Form 2106 is shown in Figure I9-2. It includes the computations relating to the information in Example I9-73.

EXAMPLE I9-73 ▶ Eric Graber, SSN 231-54-9876, is single and employed as a salesman by the Houston Corporation. Eric is required to use his personal automobile for employment-related business. He uses only one automobile for business purposes. During 2001, Eric drives his automobile 80% of the time for business use and incurs the following total expenses:

Gas and oil	$3,000
Repairs	600
Depreciation	2,300
Insurance	1,400
Parking and tolls (all business related)	250
Total	$7,550

ADDITIONAL COMMENT

Many of the provisions related to employee business expenses are very complex. It has been said of the general complexity of the tax law that: "If Patrick Henry thought taxation without representation was bad, he should have seen taxation with representation."

During the year, Eric drives a total of 30,000 miles, of which 24,000 are business miles. Of the 6,000 personal miles, 2,000 miles are commuting to and from work. Eric receives a reimbursement of 15 cents per business mile from his employer. Eric also incurred $4,000 of unreimbursed employment-related travel and entertainment expenses. These expenses include the following:

Airfare	$2,500
Car rental	250
Business meals at which business was discussed	150
Laundry	100
Lodging	200
Entertainment of customers	800
Total	$4,000

Form **2106**

Department of the Treasury Internal Revenue Service (99)

Employee Business Expenses

▶ See separate instructions.

▶ Attach to Form 1040.

OMB No. 1545-0139

2001

Attachment Sequence No. **54**

Your name	Occupation in which you incurred expenses	Social security number
Eric Grabar	Salesman	231 54 9876

Part I Employee Business Expenses and Reimbursements

Step 1 Enter Your Expenses		**Column A** Other Than Meals and Entertainment	**Column B** Meals and Entertainment
1 Vehicle expense from line 22 or line 29. (Rural mail carriers: See instructions.)	1	8,280	
2 Parking fees, tolls, and transportation, including train, bus, etc., that **did not** involve overnight travel or commuting to and from work	2	250	
3 Travel expense while away from home overnight, including lodging, airplane, car rental, etc. **Do not** include meals and entertainment	3	3,050	
4 Business expenses not included on lines 1 through 3. **Do not** include meals and entertainment	4		
5 Meals and entertainment expenses (see instructions)	5		950
6 **Total expenses.** In Column A, add lines 1 through 4 and enter the result. In Column B, enter the amount from line 5	6	11,580	950

Note: *If you were not reimbursed for any expenses in Step 1, skip line 7 and enter the amount from line 6 on line 8.*

Step 2 Enter Reimbursements Received From Your Employer for Expenses Listed in Step 1			
7 Enter reimbursements received from your employer that were **not** reported to you in box 1 of Form W-2. Include any reimbursements reported under code "L" in box 12 of your Form W-2 (see instructions)	7	3,600	

Step 3 Figure Expenses To Deduct on Schedule A (Form 1040)

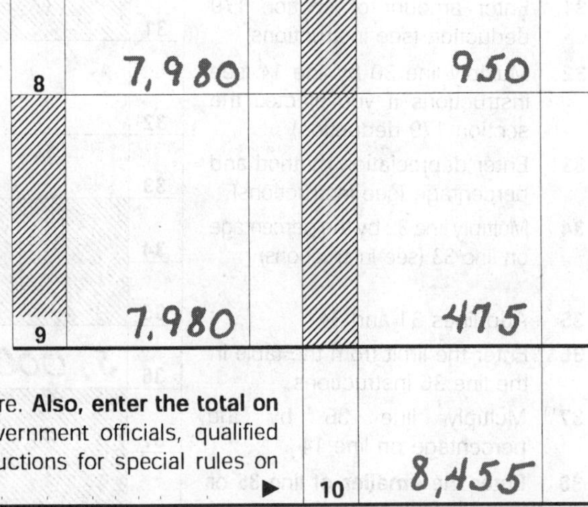

8 Subtract line 7 from line 6. If zero or less, enter -0-. However, if line 7 is greater than line 6 in Column A, report the excess as income on Form 1040, line 7	8	7,980	950
Note: *If **both columns** of line 8 are zero, you cannot deduct employee business expenses. Stop here and attach Form 2106 to your return.*			
9 In Column A, enter the amount from line 8. In Column B, multiply line 8 by 50% (.50). (Employees subject to Department of Transportation (DOT) hours of service limits: Multiply meal expenses by 60% (.60) instead of 50%. For details, see instructions.)	9	7,980	475

10 Add the amounts on line 9 of both columns and enter the total here. **Also, enter the total on Schedule A (Form 1040), line 20.** (Fee-basis state or local government officials, qualified performing artists, and individuals with disabilities: See the instructions for special rules on where to enter the total.) ▶ 10 8,455

For Paperwork Reduction Act Notice, see instructions. Cat. No. 11700N Form **2106** (2001)

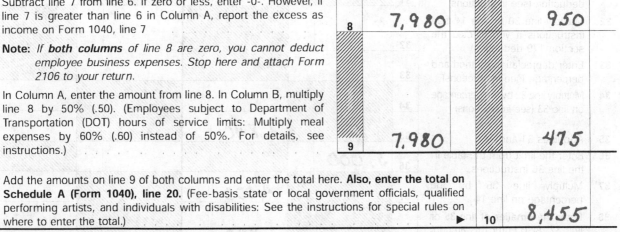

FIGURE I9-2 ▶ PAGE 1 OF FORM 2106 FOR EXAMPLE I9-72

Part II Vehicle Expenses

Section A—General Information (You must complete this section if you are claiming vehicle expenses.)

			(a) Vehicle 1	(b) Vehicle 2
11	Enter the date the vehicle was placed in service	11	/ /	/ /
12	Total miles the vehicle was driven during 2001	12	30,000 miles	miles
13	Business miles included on line 12	13	24,000 miles	miles
14	Percent of business use. Divide line 13 by line 12	14	80 %	%
15	Average daily roundtrip commuting distance	15	8 miles	miles
16	Commuting miles included on line 12	16	2,000 miles	miles
17	Other miles. Add lines 13 and 16 and subtract the total from line 12	17	4,000 miles	miles

18 Do you (or your spouse) have another vehicle available for personal use? ☒ Yes ☐ No

19 Was your vehicle available for personal use during off-duty hours? ☐ Yes ☐ No

20 Do you have evidence to support your deduction? ☒ Yes ☐ No

21 If "Yes," is the evidence written? ☒ Yes ☐ No

Section B—Standard Mileage Rate (See the instructions for Part II to find out whether to complete this section or Section C.)

22	Multiply line 13 by 34½¢ (.345)	22	8,280

Section C—Actual Expenses

			(a) Vehicle 1		(b) Vehicle 2	
23	Gasoline, oil, repairs, vehicle insurance, etc.	23		5,000		
24a	Vehicle rentals	24a				
b	Inclusion amount (see instructions)	24b				
c	Subtract line 24b from line 24a	24c				
25	Value of employer-provided vehicle (applies only if 100% of annual lease value was included on Form W-2—see instructions)	25				
26	Add lines 23, 24c, and 25	26		5,000		
27	Multiply line 26 by the percentage on line 14	27		4,000		
28	Depreciation. Enter amount from line 38 below	28		1,840		
29	Add lines 27 and 28. Enter total here and on line 1	29		5,840		

Section D—Depreciation of Vehicles (Use this section only if you owned the vehicle and are completing Section C for the vehicle.)

			(a) Vehicle 1		(b) Vehicle 2	
30	Enter cost or other basis (see instructions)	30				
31	Enter amount of section 179 deduction (see instructions)	31				
32	Multiply line 30 by line 14 (see instructions if you elected the section 179 deduction)	32				
33	Enter depreciation method and percentage (see instructions)	33				
34	Multiply line 32 by the percentage on line 33 (see instructions)	34				
35	Add lines 31 and 34	35		1,840		
36	Enter the limit from the table in the line 36 instructions	36	5,000			
37	Multiply line 36 by the percentage on line 14	37		4,000		
38	Enter the **smaller** of line 35 or line 37. Also enter this amount on line 28 above	38		1,840		

Form **2106** (2001)

FIGURE I9-2 ▶ PAGE 2 OF FORM 2106 FOR EXAMPLE I9-72

Step 1, line 1: Vehicle expense (24,000 × $0.345)	$8,280
Step 2, line 7: (24,000 miles × $0.15)	$3,600
Section C, line 23: Actual Expenses:	
Gas and oil	$3,000
Repairs	600
Insurance	1,400
Total	$5,000
Section C, line 28: Depreciation ($2,300 × .80)	$1,840 ◀

REPORTING MOVING EXPENSES

Employer reimbursements for qualifying moving expenses reduce the otherwise deductible amount for the employee. Reimbursements for nondeductible moving expenses are included in gross income and should be included in total wages on the employee's Form W-2 and reported on page 1 (line 7) of Form 1040. Employers should complete Form 4782 (Employee Moving Expense Information) which summarizes the moving expense payments made to the employee and to third parties. The form is provided to an employee to properly report his moving expenses and reimbursements. Form 3903 (Moving Expenses) is used to compute the allowable moving expenses and is attached to the employee's tax return (see Appendix B). Moving expenses are deductible *for* AGI on line 26 of page 1 of the 2001 Form 1040. Moving expenses are not subject to federal income tax withholding if it is reasonable to believe that an employee will be entitled to a deduction for such amounts. Reimbursements in excess of the deductible amounts, however, are subject to the withholding of income and social security taxes.

KEY POINT

If a taxpayer who is an employee moves in early December, the earliest that the 39-week test could be met would be early September of the following year. This is well after the April 15 due date for the individual return. The taxpayer may nevertheless deduct the moving expenses in the earlier year.

A taxpayer may deduct moving expenses, even though the tests for qualification have not been met (e.g., the 39-week test). If the individual subsequently fails to satisfy the requirements, gross income for the subsequent year must be increased by the previous tax benefit.[78] Another alternative is to wait until the tests have been met and then file an amended return (Form 1040X–see Appendix B) for the prior year.

REPORTING OFFICE IN HOME EXPENSES

Form 8829 (Expenses for Business Use of Your Home) must be used to figure the allowable expenses for business use that are reported on Schedule C (Profit or Loss from Business) and the carryover of any nondeductible amounts from prior years. Form 4562 (Depreciation and Amortization) must also be used to compute depreciation on the office portion of the residence. These tax forms are reproduced in Appendix B.

QUALIFICATION OF PENSION AND PROFIT-SHARING PLANS

The reporting requirements to establish and maintain a qualified pension or profit-sharing plan are too complex for this text. However, it should be noted that it is generally advisable for a taxpayer to obtain advance approval of the plan from the district director of the IRS by requesting a determination letter that all requirements for qualification have been met. A new determination letter should generally be requested when any material (e.g., substantial) modification is made to a plan. Material changes are frequently required when major tax legislation is enacted. In addition, several reports must be filed with the IRS and the U.S. Department of Labor.

[78] Secs. 217(d)(2) and (3).

PROBLEM MATERIALS

DISCUSSION QUESTIONS

I9-1 Why is it important to distinguish whether an individual is an employee or an independent contractor (self-employed)?

I9-2 Matt, a CPA, is employed full-time as a tax accountant for a major company. He also operates a small tax practice in his spare time. Matt incurs local transportation and unreimbursed travel expenses for both his employment and business activities. How does Matt report these expenses on his tax return?

I9-3 Determine whether the following expenses are either deductible *for* AGI or *from* AGI or nondeductible on an employee's return. Indicate whether the expenses are subject to the 2% nondeductible floor for miscellaneous itemized deductions and whether the 50% meals and entertainment deduction limit applies.

a. Reimbursed business meals (an adequate accounting is made to the employer and any excess reimbursement must be repaid)
b. Automobile expenses associated with commuting to and from work
c. Legal expenses incurred to prepare the taxpayer's income tax return
d. Unreimbursed travel and transportation expenses (including meals)
e. Unreimbursed entertainment expenses
f. Qualified moving expenses of an employee
g. Education-related expenses involving tuition and books

I9-4 Which of the following deduction items are subject to the 2% nondeductible floor applicable to miscellaneous itemized deductions?

a. Investment counseling fees
b. Fees for tax return preparation
c. Unreimbursed professional dues for an employee
d. Gambling losses
e. Interest on a personal residence
f. Unreimbursed employee travel expenses
g. Reimbursed employee travel expenses (an adequate accounting is made to the employer and any excess reimbursement must be re-paid)
h. Safe-deposit box rental expenses for an investor

I9-5 In each of the following cases involving travel expenses, indicate how each item is reported on the taxpayer's tax return. Include any limitations that might affect its deductibility.

a. Marilyn, who lives in Houston, owns several apartments in Denver. To supervise the management of these properties, Marilyn incurs travel expenses including airfare, lodging, and meals while traveling to and from the apartment site.
b. Marc is an employee who incurs travel expenses as a salesperson. The expenses are fully reimbursed by his employer after an adequate accounting has been made.
c. Assume the same facts as in Part b, except that the expenses are not reimbursed.
d. Kay is a self-employed attorney who incurs travel expenses (including meals) to prepare a court case in a nearby city.

I9-6 Kelly is an employee who incurs $2,000 of business meal expenses in connection with business entertainment and travel, none of which are reimbursed by her employer. $500 of the business meal costs are lavish or extravagant. How much can Kelly deduct before applying the 2% nondeductible floor on miscellaneous itemized deductions?

I9-7 Latoya is a college professor who takes a nine-month leave of absence from her employment at a college in Ohio and accepts a visiting professorship (temporary assignment) at a college in Texas. Latoya leaves her husband and children in Ohio and incurs the following expenses in connection with the temporary assignment:

Airfare to and from the temporary assignment	$ 1,000
Living expenses in the new location (including meals of $1,000)	8,000
Personal clothing	1,500
Total	$10,500

a. Which (if any) of these items can Latoya deduct?
b. Would your answer to a. change if Latoya, after completing the nine month assignment, resigned her position in Ohio and accepted a full-time assignment with the college in Texas?

I9-8 Louie is a full-time employee for a retail company and also an investor in real estate in his spare time. In the current year, Louie incurs $2,500 of travel expenses and $1,000 in registration fees related to attending real estate investment seminars. He deducts the expenses on his income tax return as a *for* AGI expense related to the production of income. Are the travel expenses and registration fees deductible? Should they be classified as *for* AGI or *from* AGI?

I9-9 If an employee receives a specific monthly amount from his or her employer as a reimbursement for employment-related entertainment, travel, and transportation expenses, why is it necessary to allocate a portion of the total reimbursement to each expense category?

I9-10 If an employee receives a reimbursement of 15 cents a mile from her employer for employment-related transportation expenses, is the employee permitted to deduct the difference between the standard mileage rate and the reimbursement rate as an unreimbursed employee expense? What other alternative is available for claiming the transportation deduction?

I9-11 If an employee (or self-employed individual) uses the standard mileage rate method for the year in which an automobile is acquired, may the actual expense method be used in a subsequent year? If so, what restrictions are imposed (if any) on depreciation methods? What adjustments to basis are required?

I9-12 What reporting procedures should be followed by an employee who deducts unreimbursed employee expenses on his or her tax return?

I9-13 Discuss the reporting procedures that should be followed by an employee to report employment-related expenses on his or her tax return under the following conditions:

a. Expenses are less than reimbursements, and no accounting is made to the employer.

b. Expenses equal reimbursements, and an adequate accounting is made to the employer.

c. Expenses exceed reimbursements, and an adequate accounting is made to the employer.

d. Expenses are less than reimbursements. An adequate accounting is made to the employer and the employee is required to repay any excess amount.

I9-14 Why were distance and time requirements legislated as conditions for eligibility for a moving expense deduction?

I9-15 Does it matter whether a moving expense is incurred by an employee, a self-employed individual, or an unemployed person?

I9-16 Len incurs $2,000 of deductible moving expenses in the current year and is fully reimbursed by his employer in the same year.

a. How are the expense deduction and the reimbursement reported on Len's tax return if he uses the standard deduction?

b. What tax consequences occur if the reimbursement is $2,000 but only $1,200 of the $2,000 of moving expenses are tax deductible?

I9-17 Why are strict recordkeeping requirements required for the deduction of entertainment expenses?

I9-18 Louis incurs "directly related" entertainment expenses of $4,000, but he is reimbursed by his employer for only $3,000 after an adequate accounting is made.

a. How are these amounts reported on Louis's tax return?

b. What are the tax consequences if Louis is unable to provide adequate documentation of the expenditures during the course of an IRS audit of his tax return?

I9-19 Latesha is a self-employed attorney who entertains clients and potential clients in her home.

a. What requirements must be met to qualify the outlays as deductible entertainment expenses?

b. If the expenses qualify, are they classified as "directly related" or "associated with" entertainment?

I9-20 Liz is an employee who entertains customers. In the current year, Liz incurs $6,000 in business meal expenses that are connected with entertainment. Liz's expenses are not lavish or extravagant. She itemizes her deductions in the current year.

a. If none of these expenses are reimbursed by Liz's employer, what amounts are deductible and how are they classified?

b. How are these amounts reported by Liz and her employer if all of her expenses are reimbursed and an adequate accounting is made by Liz?

I9-21 Atlantic Corporation provides a cafeteria for its employees. The meal charges are set at a sufficiently high level that the employees are not taxed on the subsidized eating facilities. Are Atlantic's cafeteria-related costs subject to the 50% disallowance for business meals?

I9-22 Lynn is a salesperson who entertains clients at business luncheons. A business relationship exists for the entertainment, and there is a reasonable expectation of business benefit. However, no business discussions are generally conducted before, during, or immediately following the meals. Do the business meal expenditures qualify as entertainment expenses?

I9-23 If an individual belongs to a country club and uses the facility primarily for business entertainment of customers, what portion of the club dues is deductible?

I9-24 Bass Corporation purchases 10 tickets to the Super Bowl in January 2002 for entertaining its customers. Due to unusually high demand, the tickets have to be purchased from scalpers for $6,000 (10 × $600). The face value of the tickets is only $900 (10 × $90). What amount is deductible by Bass in 2002?

I9-25 a. Discuss the two requirements for an employee expense reimbursement plan to be treated as an accountable plan.

b. How are expenses and reimbursements treated under an accountable plan?

c. How are expenses and reimbursements treated under a nonaccountable plan?

I9-26 Martin is a tax accountant employed by a public accounting firm. He incurs the following expenses:

CPA review course	$ 400
Law school tuition and books	4,000
Accounting continuing education course (travel, fees, and transportation (including meals of $200)	600
Total	$5,000

Martin is a degree candidate at the law school. Which (if any) of these expenditures qualify as deductible education expenses? How are they reported?

I9-27 Why are public school teachers generally allowed a deduction for education expenses related to graduate school or advanced courses?

I9-28 Discuss whether each of the following individuals is entitled to an office-in-home deduction:
a. Maggie is a self-employed management consultant who maintains an office in her home exclusively used for client meetings and other business-related activities. Maggie has no other place of business and her office is the most significant place for her business. She has substantial income from the consulting practice.
b. Marty is a college professor who writes research papers for academic journals in his office at home which is used exclusively for this purpose. Although Marty has an office at his place of employment, he finds it very convenient to maintain an office at home to avoid distractions from students and colleagues. Marty receives no income from the publication of the research articles for the year in question.
c. Bobby operates his own sole proprietorship as an electrician. He maintains an office at home where he keeps his books, takes phone calls from customers, and does the payroll for his five employees. All of his electrical work is done at the location of his customers.

I9-29 Compare and contrast the tax advantages accruing to employers and employees from the establishment of a qualified pension or profit-sharing plan versus a nonqualified deferred compensation arrangement (e.g., a restricted property plan).

I9-30 What is the difference between a defined benefit pension plan and a defined contribution pension plan?

I9-31 Austin Corporation is proposing the establishment of a pension plan that will cover only employees with salaries in excess of $100,000. No other employees are covered under comparable qualified plans. What problems (if any) do you envision regarding the plan's qualification with the IRS?

I9-32 Babson Corporation is proposing the creation of a qualified profit-sharing plan for its employees. The proposed plan provides for vesting of employer contributions after 20 years because the company wants to discourage employee turnover and does not feel that short-term employees should qualify for benefits. Will this plan qualify? Why or why not?

I9-33 Explain how distributions from a qualified pension plan, which are made in the form of annuity payments, are reported by an employee under the following circumstances:
a. No employee contributions are made to the plan.
b. The pension plan provides for matching employee contributions.

I9-34 Discuss the limitations and restrictions that the Code places on employer contributions to qualified pension and profit-sharing plans.

I9-35 Why are nonqualified deferred compensation plans particularly well-suited for use in executive compensation arrangements?

I9-36 If a newly formed corporation is considering going public and anticipates substantial future appreciation in its stock, would it be advisable for an executive receiving restricted property to elect to recognize income immediately under Sec. 83(b)? Contrast the tax consequences of a restricted property arrangement for both the employer and employee when this election is made versus when it is not made. Consider the effect of the subsequent lapsing of the restrictions and the employee's sale of the stock.

I9-37 List and discuss the qualification requirements for an incentive stock option plan (ISO). Describe the advantages and disadvantages of ISOs compared to nonqualified stock option plans.

I9-38 What difference does it make if a nonqualified stock option has a readily ascertainable FMV on the grant date?

I9-39 Is a self-employed individual, who is also employed and covered by an employer's qualified pension plan, eligible to establish an H.R. 10 or an SEP plan on his or her self-employment income?

I9-40 What limitations are placed on self-employed individuals for contributions made to defined contribution H.R. 10 plans? Must self-employed individuals cover their full-time employees if an H.R. 10 plan is established?

I9-41 Would you be more favorably inclined to advise a 50-year-old individual or a 30-year-old individual to establish a traditional deductible IRA? Why? A traditional nondeductible IRA? Why? Consider any tax problems involved if the IRA funds are needed before age 59½.

I9-42 Discuss the essential differences between a traditional IRA and a Roth IRA.

I9-43 Would it generally be advisable for a 30-year-old individual to invest in a traditional deductible IRA or a Roth IRA?

I9-44 Your client, Charley Long, age 40, has requested your advice with respect to his IRA. He has a traditional IRA with a balance of $80,000 and his current AGI is $50,000. He expects his income to increase slightly when he retires at age 65. Charley has been reading about Roth IRAs and wants your advice as to whether he should rollover the $80,000 from his traditional IRA into a Roth IRA. He has sufficient outside money to pay any taxes due on the rollover. What advice would you give Charley?

I9-45 Sally, who is single and age 40, has previously made deductible IRA contributions for years before 1987 but has not been eligible to make deductible IRA contributions since that time because she is covered under her employer's plan. Her AGI is $60,000. She is interested in making IRA contributions in the current year, what advice would you give her?

I9-46 The Coverdell Education Savings Account (CESA), formerly named the Education IRA, was significantly enhanced by the 2001 Tax Act. What are the principal ways the CESA has been improved over the old Education IRA?

I9-47 The owner of an unincorporated small business is considering whether to establish a simplified employee pension (SEP) plan for its employees.

a. What nontax factors might make an SEP attractive as an alternative to establishing a qualified pension or profit-sharing plan?

b. Is the owner of the small business eligible to make contributions on his or her behalf to the SEP?

ISSUE IDENTIFICATION QUESTIONS

I9-48 Georgia is an executive who recently completed an assignment with her employer at an away-from-home location. It was realistically expected that the assignment would be completed in 15 months but the actual time period was only 11 months. Georgia incurred $15,000 of away-from-home expenses during the 11-month period none of which were reimbursed by her employer. What tax issues should Georgia consider?

I9-49 Jeremy is an executive for Columbia Corporation, which is going through a restructuring of its corporate headquarters operations. Columbia has offered to relocate Jeremy from its New York headquarters to its divisional operation in South Carolina and will reimburse him for both direct and indirect moving expenses. What tax issues should Jeremy consider?

I9-50 Juan, a self-employed medical doctor, maintains an office in his home where he maintains patient records and performs billing procedures. Most of his time is spent visiting patients and performing surgical procedures in the operating room at several local hospitals. Juan intends to deduct his expenses of his office in his home. What tax issues should Juan consider?

I9-51 David is on the audit staff of a national accounting firm. He has been with the firm for three years and is a CPA. David has applied and been accepted into a prestigious MBA program. The program is two years in duration. David has decided to resign from the accounting firm even though the firm has indicated that it would very much like David to return to work for the firm after he receives his MBA degree. David is somewhat interested in returning to public accounting but will certainly look at all of his options when he completes the program. David wants to deduct his education expenses, what are the relevant tax issues in this case?

PROBLEMS

I9-52 *Employment-Related Expenses.* Mike incurs the following employment-related expenses in the current year:

Actual automobile expenses	$ 2,500
Moving expenses (deductible under Sec. 217)	4,000
Entertainment expenses	1,500
Travel expenses (including $500 of business meals)	2,500
Professional dues and subscriptions	500
Total	$11,000

Mike's AGI is $120,000 before the above expenses are deducted. None of the expenses listed above are reimbursed by Mike's employer. He has no other miscellaneous itemized deductions and does not use the standard deduction.

a. What is the amount of Mike's deduction for employment-related expenses?

b. How are these items reported in Mike's tax return?

I9-53 *Travel and Entertainment.* Monique is a self-employed manufacturer's representative who solicits business for clients and receives a commission based on sales. She incurs the following expenditures during the current year:

Airfare and lodging while away from home overnight	$ 4,000
Business meals while traveling at which business is discussed	1,000
Local transportation costs for automobile, parking, tolls, etc. (business-related)	2,000
Commuting expenses	1,000
Local entertainment of customers	2,000
Total	$10,000

a. Which of the expenditures listed above (if any) are deductible by Monique?
b. Are each of these items classified as *for* AGI or *from* AGI deductions?
c. How would your answers to Parts a and b change if Monique were an employee rather than self-employed and none of the expenses were reimbursed by her employer?

I9-54 ***Unreimbursed Employee Expenses.*** In the current year Mary incurs $3,600 of unreimbursed employment-related travel and entertainment expenses. These expenses include the following:

Airfare	$1,500
Taxi fare	100
Meals eaten alone while away from home on business	300
Laundry	50
Lodging	650
Business meals with customers at which business is discussed	500
Entertainment of customers	500
Total	$3,600

Mary also pays $1,000 of investment counseling fees and $500 of tax return preparation fees in the current year. Mary's AGI is $70,000.
a. What is the total amount of Mary's deductible expenses?
b. Are the deductible expenses classified as *for* AGI or *from* AGI?

I9-55 ***Travel Expenses.*** Marilyn is a business executive who accepts a temporary out-of-town assignment in Atlanta for a period of ten months. Marilyn leaves her husband and children in Miami and rents an apartment in Atlanta during the ten-month period. Marilyn incurs the following expenses, none of which are reimbursed by her employer:

Airfare to and from Atlanta	$ 800
Airfare for weekend trips to visit her family	8,000
Apartment rent	10,000
Meals in Atlanta	8,500
Entertainment of customers	2,000
Total	$29,300

a. Which of the expenditures listed above (if any) are deductible by Marilyn (before any limitations are applied)?
b. Are each of these expenditures classified as *for* AGI or *from* AGI deductions?
c. If Marilyn's AGI is $120,000, what is the amount of the deduction for the expenditures?
d. Do the tax consequences change if Marilyn's assignment is for a period of more than one year and is for an indefinite period rather than a temporary period?
e. Do the tax consequences in Parts a through c change if it was realistically expected that the work would be completed in ten months but after the ten-month period Marilyn is asked to continue for seven more months and if an additional $10,000 of travel expenses are incurred during the extended period?

I9-56 ***Business/Personal Travel Expenses.*** In the current year Mike's AGI is $50,000. Mike has no miscellaneous itemized deductions other than the employment-related expenses on the list below. Mike attends a professional trade association convention in Los Angeles. He spends three days at the meeting and two days vacationing before the meeting. Mike was unable to obtain excursion airfare rates (i.e., staying over a Saturday night) despite the fact that he was on vacation immediately before the meeting. Mike's total expenses, of which the business-related expenses are fully reimbursed by his employer after an adequate accounting is made, include the following:

Airfare	$ 450
Meals ($50 per day)	250
Hotel ($100 per day)	500
Entertainment of customers (business is discussed)	500
Total	$1,700

a. How much can Mike deduct for employment-related expenses?
b. How is the reimbursement reported on Mike's tax return?
c. Is the reimbursement fully deductible by Mike's employer?

I9-57 ***Employment-Related Expenses and Reimbursements.*** Maxine incurs the following employment-related business expenses in the current year:

Professional dues and subscriptions	$1,000
Airfare and lodging	2,000
Local transportation for employment-related business activities	1,000
Customer entertainment (business lunches where business is discussed)	1,000
Total	$5,000

After making an adequate accounting of the expenses, Maxine receives a fixed reimbursement of $3,000 from her employer. Assume that Maxine's AGI is $60,000, she has other miscellaneous itemized deductions of $1,000, and she does not use the standard deduction.
a. What amount of the expenses are deductible by Maxine?
b. Are each of these expenditures classified as *for* AGI or *from* AGI deductions?
c. How would your answers to Parts a and b change if Maxine instead received a $6,000 reimbursement?

I9-58 ***Miscellaneous Itemized Deductions.*** In the current year, Melissa, a single employee whose AGI is $100,000 before any of the items below, incurs the following expenses:

Safe deposit box rental for investments	$ 100
Tax return preparation fees	500
Moving expenses (deductible under Sec. 217)	2,000
Mortgage interest on Melissa's principal residence	12,000
Real estate taxes on Melissa's principal residence	1,800
Unreimbursed employment-related expenses (other than business meals and entertainment)	6,000
Unreimbursed employment-related expenses for business meals and entertainment (business is discussed)	1,200
Total	$23,600

a. What is the amount of Melissa's total miscellaneous itemized deductions (after deducting the 2% floor)?
b. What is the amount of Melissa's total itemized deductions?
c. What is the amount of Melissa's total itemized deductions if her AGI, after all adjustments above, is instead $150,000?

I9-59 ***Transportation Expenses.*** Jose, an employee of a law firm, maintains an office at the principal business location of his firm. He frequently travels from his home to client locations within and outside the metropolitan area. Jose is not reimbursed for his transportation expenses and has incurred the following:

Transportation expenses associated with trips to clients within the metropolitan area	$2,000
Transportation expenses associated with trips to clients located outside the metropolitan area	3,000
Total	$5,000

a. What is the amount of Jose's deduction for transportation expenses?
b. How is the deduction reported on Jose's tax return?
c. What is the amount of Jose's deduction for transportation expenses and its classification if he is self-employed and operates his office from his home? Assume that the requirements of Sec. 280A are satisfied.

I9-60 *Auto Expenses.* Michelle is an employee who must use her personal automobile for employment-related business trips. During 2002, Michelle drives her car 60% for business use and incurs the following total expenses (100% use of car):

Gas and oil	$4,000
Repairs	400
Depreciation	4,900
Insurance and license fees	1,300
Parking and tolls (business related)	100
Total	$10,700

Michelle drives 20,000 business miles during 2002 and receives a reimbursement of 10 cents per mile from her employer. Assume that the 2% nondeductible floor on miscellaneous itemized deductions is not applicable and that an adequate accounting is made to Michelle's employer.
a. What amount is deductible if Michelle elects to use the standard mileage method?
b. What amount is deductible if Michelle uses the actual cost method?
c. Can taxpayers switch back and forth between the mileage and actual methods each year?

I9-61 *Entertainment Expenses.* Milt, a self-employed attorney, incurs the following expenses in the current year:

Dues paid to the local chamber of commerce	$ 1,000
Business lunches for clients and prospective clients (Milt does not believe in conducting business discussions during lunch)	4,000
Entertainment of professional associates in his home (immediately following business meetings)	2,000
Country club dues (the club is used exclusively for business)	2,500
Entertainment of clients and prospective clients at the country club (meals and drinks)	1,500
Total	$11,000

a. Which of the expenditures listed above (if any) are deductible by Milt?
b. Are each of these items classified as *for* AGI or *from* AGI deductions?

I9-62 *Entertainment Expenses.* Beach Corporation purchases tickets to sporting events and uses them to entertain customers. In the current year Beach Corporation purchases the following tickets:

100 tickets to football games (face value of the tickets is $3,600)	$6,000
A skybox rented for six athletic events (seating capacity of the skybox is 30, and the highest price of a nonluxury box seat is $40)	18,000

What amount of the entertainment expenses is deductible in the current year?

I9-63 *Reimbursed Employee Expenses.* Latrisha is an employee of the Cooper Company and incurs significant employment-related expenses. During the current year, she incurred the following expenses in connection with her job:

Travel: Airfare	$ 5,850
Lodging	1,800
Meals	1,200
Entertainment of customers	2,400
Total	$11,250

a. Determine the amount of deductible expenses for both Latrisha and the Cooper Company and, for Latrisha, whether they are deductible *for* AGI or *from* AGI assuming Cooper Company maintains an accountable plan for employee expense reimbursements, if the reimbursements are alternatively:

1. $11,250
2. $9,000
3. $14,000

b. What would be the result in a. for each of the three situations if the plan was a nonaccountable plan?

I9-64 *Moving Expenses.* Michael graduates from New York University and on February 1, 2002 accepts a position with a public accounting firm in Chicago. Michael is a resident of New York. In March, Michael travels to Chicago to locate a house and starts to work in June. He incurs the following expenses, none of which are reimbursed by the public accounting firm:

Automobile expense enroute (1,000 miles at 13 cents per mile-standard mileage rate)	$ 130
Cost of meals en route	100
Househunting trip travel expenses	1,400
Moving van expenses	3,970
Commission on the sale of Michael's New York condominium	3,500
Points paid to acquire a mortgage on Michael's new residence in Chicago	1,000
Temporary living expenses for one week in Chicago (hotel and $100 in meals)	400
Expenses incurred in decorating the new residence	500
Total expenses	$11,000

a. What is Michael's moving expense deduction?
b. How are the deductible expenses classified on Michael's tax return?
c. How would your answer to Part a change if all of Michael's expenses were reimbursed by his employer?

I9-65 *Education Expenses.* For each of the following independent situations, determine whether any of the expenditures qualify as deductible education expenses. Are the expenditures classified as *for* AGI or *from* AGI deductions?

a. Law school tuition and books for an IRS agent who is pursuing a law degree: $2,000.
b. Continuing professional accounting education expenses of $1,900 for a self-employed CPA: travel, $1,000 (including $200 meals); registration fees, $800; books, $100.
c. MBA education expenses totaling $5,000 for a business executive of a major corporation: tuition, $4,000; transportation, $800; and books, $200.
d. Tuition and books acquired for graduate education courses required under state law for a schoolteacher in order to renew a provisional certificate: $1,000.
e. Bar review courses for a recent law school graduate: $1,000.

I9-66 *Office-in-Home.* Nancy is a self-employed artist who uses 10% of her residence as a studio. The studio portion is used exclusively for business and is frequented by customers on a regular basis. Nancy also uses her den as an office (10% of the total floor space of her home) to prepare bills and keep records. However, the den is also used by her children as a TV room. Nancy's income from the sale of the artwork amounts to $40,000 in the current year. She also incurs $2,000 of expenses directly related to the business other than home office expenses (e.g., art supplies and selling expenses). Nancy incurs the following expenses in the current year related to her residence:

Real estate taxes	$ 2,000
Mortgage interest	5,000
Insurance	500
Depreciation	3,500
Repairs and utilities	1,000
Total	$12,000

a. Which of the expenditures above (if any) are deductible? Are they *for* AGI or *from* AGI deductions?
b. Would your answer to Part a change if Nancy's income from painting were only $2,500 for the year? What is the amount of the office-in-home deduction and the amount of the carryover (if any) of the unused deductions? (Assume that Nancy is not subject to the hobby loss restrictions.)

I9-67 Darrell is a self-employed consultant who uses 15% of his home exclusively as an office. Darrell operates completely out of his home office and makes all of his appointments from the office as well as keeping his books and records in the office. Darrell's gross income from his consulting business is $60,000 in 2002. He incurs $6,000 of expenses that are directly-related to his business, such as computer and office supplies. Below are expenses that relate to Darrell's residence for 2002:

Real estate taxes	$ 4,000
Mortgage interest	6,000
Insurance	1,000
Depreciation	4,000
Repairs and utilities	1,000
Total	$16,000

a. Which of the above expenditures (if any) are deductible? Are they *for* AGI or *from* AGI deductions?
b. How would your answer change if Darrell was an employee of a consulting company and maintained an office at home in order to take work home with him so he did not have to spend so many hours at his consulting company office?

I9-68 ***Deferred Compensation Plan Requirements.*** Identify whether each of the following plan features is associated with a qualified pension plan, a qualified profit-sharing plan, an employee stock ownership plan, a nonqualifed plan, or none of these plans.
a. Annual employer contributions are not required, but substantial and recurring contributions must be made based on a predetermined formula.
b. Annual, systematic, and definite employer contributions are required without regard to profits but based on actuarial methods.
c. Forfeitures must be used to reduce contributions that would otherwise be made under the plan.
d. The plan may discriminate in favor of highly compensated individuals.
e. The trust is funded with the contribution of employer stock, which is subsequently distributed to employees.

I9-69 ***Taxability of Pension Payments.*** Pat is a participant in a qualified pension plan. She retires on January 1, 2002 at age 63, and receives pension payments beginning in January 2002. Her pension payments, which will be received monthly for life, amounts to $1,000 per month. Pat contributed $30,000 to the pension plan on a pre-tax basis, and the number of anticipated payments based on Pat's age of 63 years in 260 months (see IRS table in Chapter I3) from the date she starts receiving payments.
a. What gross income will Pat recognize in 2002 and each year thereafter?
b. How would your answer to Part a change if Pat made contributions to the plan on an after-tax basis?
c. If, in part b., Pat dies in December 2003 after receiving pension payments for two full years, what tax consequences occur in the year of death?

I9-70 ***Restricted Property.*** In 2002, Bear Corporation transfers 100 shares of its stock to its employee Patrick. The stock is valued at $10 per share on the issue date. The stock is subject to the following restrictions:

- Patrick cannot transfer the stock by sale or other disposition (except in the event of death) for a five-year period.
- The stock must be forfeited to Bear Corporation if Patrick voluntarily terminates his employment with the company within a five-year period.

In year 2007, the Bear stock is worth $100 per share when the restrictions expire.
a. Assuming that no Sec. 83(b) election is made, what are the tax consequences to Patrick and Bear Corporation in 2002?
b. What are the tax consequences to Patrick and Bear Corporation if Patrick makes a valid Sec. 83(b) election in 2002?
c. What are the tax consequences to Patrick and Bear Corporation if Patrick forfeits the stock back to the company in 2003 when the stock is worth $20 per share if an election was made under Sec. 83(b)? What would happen if no Sec. 83(b) election were made?
d. What are the tax consequences to Patrick and Bear Corporation upon the lapse of the restrictions in year 2007 if an election has been made under Sec. 83(b)? What would the results be if no Sec. 83(b) election were made?

e. What are the tax consequences to Patrick and Bear Corporation if Patrick sells the Bear stock in year 2008 for $120 per share if a Sec. 83(b) election is made? if no Sec. 83(b) election is made?

I9-71 *IRAs.* On February 15, 2003, Phong, who is single and age 30, establishes an IRA and contributes $3,000 to the account. Phong's adjusted gross income is $38,000 in both 2002 and 2003. Phong is an active participant in an employer-sponsored retirement plan.
a. What amount of the contribution is deductible? In what year is it deductible?
b. How is the deduction (if any) reported (i.e., *for* AGI or *from* AGI)?
c. What tax treatment is accorded to Phong if he withdraws the $3,000 contribution from the IRA in 2004 due to a need for cash to make a down payment for a new car.
d. How would your answer to Part a change, if at all, if Phong were not an active participant in an employer-sponsored retirement plan?
e. How would your answer to Part a change if Phong were married and files a joint return with his spouse, who has no earned income? (Assume their combined AGI is $45,000.)

I9-72 *IRAs.* Phil, age 30, is married and files a joint return with his spouse. On February 15, 2003, Phil establishes an IRA for himself and a spousal IRA for his spouse with a $6,000 contribution, $3,000 for himself and $3,000 for his wife. Phil's spouse earns $1,000 in 2002 from a part-time job, and their combined AGI is $40,000. Neither Phil nor his spouse is an active participant in an employer-sponsored retirement plan.
a. What amount of the contribution is deductible?
b. To what year does the contribution apply? (Assume that an election is made to treat Phil's spouse as having no compensation.)
c. Is the deduction reported as *for* AGI or *from* AGI?
d. How would your answer to Part a change, if at all, if Phil and his spouse were active participants in an employer-sponsored retirement plan?
e. If a portion of the contribution is nondeductible in Part d, is it possible for Phil to make a deductible and a nondeductible contribution in the same year? Explain.
f. How would your answer to Part a change if Phil and his spouse's combined AGI were $70,000 in 2002 and 2003 and Phil were an active participant in an employer-sponsored retirement plan?

I9-73 ***Roth IRA.*** Chatham Mae is single, age 35, and wants to make a contribution to an IRA for the year ended December 31, 2002. She is an active participant in a qualified retirement plan sponsored by her employer. Her AGI for 2002 is $100,000 before considering any IRA contribution.
a. What type of IRA, if any, is Chatham Mae eligible to make a contribution for 2002? If she is eligible to contribute to an IRA, what is the maximum amount that she can contribute?
b. Assume Chatham Mae makes contributions of $2,000 per year for six years to a Roth IRA. In 2008, she withdraws $15,000 to payoff her car loan. Her financial advisor suggested she withdraw the money from the IRA for two major reasons, (1) to eliminate her debt, and (2) no tax would be due on distributions from a Roth IRA after five years. Chatham Mae wants to verify the accuracy of her advisor's advice. What would be the tax consequences of this withdrawal? Alternatively, what if Chatham Mae withdrew the $15,000 to purchase a house (she is a first-time homebuyer)?
c. Alternatively to b. above, assume Chatham Mae has a traditional deductible IRA that has a balance of $50,000. She has been able to deduct all of her contributions to the IRA in prior years. Her financial advisor has recommended that she rollover the funds from her traditional IRA to a Roth IRA in 2002. What are the tax consequences of this rollover in 2002?

I9-74 ***Coverdell Education Savings Accounts.*** Jack and Katie have five grandchildren, ages 19, 16, 15, 12, and 10. They have established Coverdell Education Savings Accounts (CESA) for each of the grandchildren and would like to contribute the maximum amount allowable to each CESA for the 2002 taxable year. Jack and Katie's AGI for 2002 is $196,000.
a. How much can Jack and Katie contribute to each grandchild's CESA in 2002?
a. Assume that the 19-year old granddaughter is a freshman in college and makes a withdrawal of $7,000 from her CESA during the year 2002. Her college expenses for 2002 were as follows:

Tuition	$1,500
Room and board	2,500
Books and supplies	500

The extra amount withdrawn was used a down payment on a car that the granddaughter purchased during the year. She needed the car in order to drive to school rather than having to either ride the bus or ride with a friend. What are the tax consequences of the $7,000 distribution to the granddaughter?

I9-75 *H.R. 10 Plans.* Paula is a self-employed doctor who is considering whether to establish a defined contribution H.R. 10 plan. Paula's only employee is a full-time nurse who has been employed by Paula for seven years. Paula's net earnings from self-employment (before the H.R. 10 plan contribution but after the deduction for one-half of self-employment taxes paid) is expected to be $100,000 during the current year and in future years.

a. If the H.R. 10 plan is established, what is the maximum amount Paula can contribute for the nurse's benefit?
b. What is the maximum amount Paula can contribute for herself? Is the amount reported as a *for* AGI or *from* AGI deduction?
c. Is Paula's nurse required to be included in the plan?
d. What are the tax consequences if Paula makes a premature withdrawal from the plan before reaching age 59½?

I9-76 *Stock Options.* Bell Corporation grants an incentive stock option to Peggy, an employee, on January 1, 2002, when the option price and FMV of the Bell stock is $80. The option entitles Peggy to buy 10 shares of Bell stock. Peggy exercises the option and acquires the stock on April 1, 2004, when the stock's FMV is $100. Peggy, while still employed by the Bell Corporation, sells the stock on May 1, 2006, for $120 per share.

a. What are the tax consequences to Peggy and Bell Corporation on the following dates: January 1, 2002; April 1, 2004; and May 1, 2006? (Assume all incentive stock option qualification requirements are met.)
b. How would your answer to Part a change if Peggy instead sold the Bell stock for $120 per share on May 1, 2004?

I9-77 *Stock Options.* Bender Corporation grants a nonqualified stock option to Penny, an employee, on January 1, 2002 that entitled Penny to acquire 10 shares of Bender stock at $80 per share. On this date, the stock has a $100 FMV and the option has a readily ascertainable FMV. Penny exercises the option on January 1, 2003 (when the FMV of the stock is $150) and acquires 10 shares of the stock for $80 per share. Penny later sells the Bender stock on January 1, 2005, for $200 per share.

a. What are the tax consequences to Penny and Bender Corporation on the following dates: January 1, 2002; January 1, 2003; and January 1, 2005?
b. How would your answer to Part a change if the Bender stock were instead closely-held and the option had no readily ascertainable FMV?

COMPREHENSIVE PROBLEM

I9-78 Dan and Cheryl are married, file a joint return, and have no children. Dan is a pharmaceutical salesman and Cheryl is a nurse at a local hospital. Dan's SSN is 400-20-1000 and Cheryl's SSN is 200-40-8000 and they reside at 2033 Palmetto Drive, Nashville, TN 28034. Dan is paid according to commissions from sales, however, his compensation is subject to withholding of income and payroll taxes. He also maintains an office in his home as the pharmaceutical company does not have an office in Nashville and when he is not traveling. Dan operates his business from his home office. During 2002, Dan earned total compensation from his job of $125,000, on which $24,000 of federal income taxes were withheld, $5,264 of OASDI, and $3,625 of Medicare taxes. No state income taxes were withheld. Cheryl earned a salary during 2002 of $45,400, on which federal taxes withheld were $6,500, OASDI of $2,815, and Medicare taxes of $1,317.

During 2002, Dan and Cheryl had interest income from corporate bonds and bank accounts of $1,450 and dividends from stocks of $5,950. Dan also actively trades stocks and had the following results for 2002:

LTCG	$4,900
LTCL	(3,200)
STCG	0
STCL	(7,800)

He had no capital loss carryovers from previous years.

Dan does a considerable amount of travel in connection with his job. He uses his own car and is reimbursed $0.20 per business mile. During 2002, Dan drove his car a total of 38,000 miles, of which 32,000 were business-related. He also had parking fees and tolls during the year of $280. Dan uses the mileage method for deducting auto expenses. Dan also had the following travel expenses during the year:

Hotel	$4,200
Meals	820
Entertainment of customers	1,080
Tips	100
Laundry and cleaning	150
	$6,350

Dan was reimbursed for the travel expenses by his employer, pursuant to an accountable plan, in the amount of $5,080.

Dan's expenses in connection with his office in the home were as follows:

Office supplies	$ 290
Telephone (separate line)	1,100
Utilities (entire house)	3,400
Homeowners insurance	600
Interest and property taxes (see below for totals)	
Repairs and maintenance (entire house)	800

Dan's office is 300 square feet and the total square footage of the house is 3,000 square feet. Dan and Cheryl purchased the house on June 12, 1995 for $280,000, of which $40,000 is attributable to the land.

Cheryl incurred several expenses in connection with her nursing job. She paid $450 in professional dues, $200 in professional journals, and $350 for uniforms.

Dan and Cheryl had the following other expenditures during the year:

Health insurance premiums		$ 4,400
Doctor bills		470
Real estate taxes on home		2,200
Personal property taxes		400
Mortgage interest		15,600
Charitable contributions—cash		9,000
Charitable contributions—GE stock		
FMV	$12,000	
Adjusted basis	2,000	
Tax preparation fees		750

Compute Dan and Cheryl's income tax liability for 2002.

TAX STRATEGY PROBLEM

I9-79 Paul Price is the President and majority stockholder of Lightmore Communications, Inc. Lightmore is a C corporation and has been extremely successful over the past 20 years. Paul travels extensively in connection with the business to meet with existing and prospective clients. Paul's wife, Laura, would be helpful to Paul in his business entertaining if she could accompany him on many of his business trips and, furthermore, she was unable to go on these trips in the past because of their children at home. Their youngest child is in college and Laura's duties at home have diminished. During the current year, Laura has made a number of trips with Paul, but after conferring with the company's tax advisor, had been informed that Laura's expenses would not be deductible for tax purposes. The tax advisor suggested the possibility of putting Laura on the Lightmore payroll as an employee.

a. Would Laura's travel expenses be deductible if she was an employee of the corporation?

b. What other benefits would be available to Laura if she was an employee of the corporation?

c. Are there any detriments to putting Laura on the payroll?

TAX FORM/RETURN PREPARATION PROBLEMS

I9-80 In the current year Dennis Johnson (SSN 277-33-7263) incurs the following unreimbursed employee business expenses:

Airplane and taxi fares	$ 4,000
Lodging away from home	5,000
Meals while away from home	1,000
Automobile expenses (related to 100% of the use of his personal automobile):	
Gasoline and oil	1,500
Repairs	500
Insurance	400
Depreciation	1,500
Parking and tolls (includes both business and personal use)	100
Total	$14,000

Johnson receives a $7,800 reimbursement for the travel expenses. He did not receive any reimbursement for the auto expenses. He uses his personal automobile 80% for business use. Total business miles amount to 20,000. Johnson's AGI is $40,000, and he has no other miscellaneous itemized deductions.

a. Calculate Johnson's expense deduction using Form 2106 (Employee Business Expenses) based on actual automobile expenses and other employee business expenses.
b. Calculate Johnson's expense deduction using the standard mileage rate method and other employee business expenses. (Assume that none of the restrictions on the use of the standard mileage rate method are applicable.)

I9-81 George Large (SSN 414-33-5688) and his wife Marge Large (SSN 555-81-9495), want you to prepare their income tax return based on the information below:

George Large worked as a salesman for Toyboat, Inc. He received a salary of $50,000 ($6,000 of income taxes withheld) plus an additional $5,000 to cover his employee business expenses. George must make an adequate accounting to his employer and return any excess reimbursement. Additionally, Toyboat provides George with medical insurance worth $3,500 per year. George drove his car 20,000 miles during the year. His log indicates that 17,000 miles were for sales calls to prospective customers at the customers' offices. George uses the standard mileage rate method. George is a professional basketball fan. He purchased two season tickets for a total of $2,000. He takes a customer to every game, and they usually discuss business at the games. George also takes clients to business lunches. His log indicates that he spent $1,500 on these business meals. George also took a five-day trip to the Toyboat headquarters in Musty, Ohio. He was so well-prepared that he finished his business in three days, so he spent the other two days sightseeing. He had the following expenses during each day of his trip:

Airfare	$200
Lodging	$85/day
Meals	$50/day
Taxicabs	$20/day

Marge Large is self-employed. She repairs rubber toy boats in the basement of their home, which is 25% of the house's square footage. She had the following income and expenses:

Income from rubber toy boat repairs	$12,000
Cost of materials	5,000
Contract labor	3,500
Long-distance phone calls (business)	500

The Large's home cost a total of $150,000, of which the cost of the land was $20,000. The FMV of the house is $225,000. The house is depreciable over a 39 year recovery period. The Larges incurred other expenses:

Utility bills for the house	$2,000
Real estate taxes	2,500
Mortgage interest	4,500
Cash charitable contributions	2,500

Prepare Form 1040, Schedules A and C for Form 1040, and Form 2106 for the 2001 year. (Assume no depreciation for this problem and that no estimated taxes were paid by the Larges.)

CASE STUDY PROBLEMS

I9-82 Ajax Corporation is a young high-growth company engaged in the manufacture and distribution of automotive parts. Its common stock has doubled in value since the company was listed on the NASDAQ exchange about two years ago. Ajax currently has a high debt/equity ratio due to the issuance of debt to finance its capital expansion needs. Despite rapid growth in assets and profitability, Ajax has severe cash flow problems and a poor working capital ratio. The company urgently needs to attract new executives to the organization and to provide financial incentives to existing top management because of recent turnover and high growth. Approximately 55% of the common stock is owned by Andrew Ajax, who is the CEO, and his immediate family. None of the other officers own stock in the company.

You are a tax consultant for the company who has been asked to prepare suggestions after reviewing the compensation system. Your discussions with several top management individuals reveal the following aspects of corporate strategy and philosophy:

- The company needs to expand the equity capital base because of its concern for the high risk caused by large amounts of debt.
- Improvement in cash flow and liquidity would enhance its stock price and enable the company to continue its high growth rate.
- Top management feels that employee loyalty and productivity would be improved if all employees owned some stock in the company. The company currently offers a qualified pension plan to its employees and executives that provides only minimal pension benefits. No other deferred compensation or bonus arrangements are currently being offered.
- Andrew Ajax feels that the top management group should own a substantial amount of Ajax stock to ensure that the interests of management correspond with the shareholder interests (i.e., the maximization of shareholder wealth).

The following types of compensation arrangements have been discussed:

- Sec. 401(k) and ESOP plans for employees.
- Encourage all employees and executives to independently fund their retirement needs beyond any Social Security benefits by establishing IRA plans.
- Provide restricted property arrangements (using Ajax stock) to attract new top level executives and to retain existing executives.
- Offer nonqualified or incentive stock options to existing and new executives.

Required: Prepare a client memo that recommends revisions to Ajax Corporation's existing compensation system for both its employee and executive groups. Your recommendations should discuss the pros and cons of different deferred compensation arrangements and should consider both tax and nontax factors.

I9-83 Steve is part owner and manager of a small manufacturing company that makes keypads for alarm systems. The keypads are sold to several different alarm companies throughout the country. Steve must travel to several cities each year to meet with current customers and to attract new business. When you meet with Steve to obtain information to prepare his current year tax return, he tells you that he has spent about $5,000 during the current year on airfare and taking his customers out to dinner to discuss business. Because he took most of his trips in the summer and fall, and it is now April of the following year, Steve cannot remember the exact time and places of the business dinners and did not retain any receipts for the cash used to pay the bills. However he remembers the names of the customers he went to see and the business topics that were discussed. As Steve's tax consultant, what is your responsibility regarding the treatment of the travel and entertainment expenses under the mandates of the AICPA's *Statements on Standards for Tax Services?* Prepare a client letter explaining to Steve the requirements under Sec. 274(d) for sufficient substantiation of travel and entertainment expenses. (See the *Statements on Standards for Tax Services* section in Chapter I15 for a discussion of these issues and Appendix E.)

TAX RESEARCH PROBLEM

I9-84 Charley Long is a truck driver, the 18-wheeler variety. He works for Fishy Co., a seafood company in Mobile, Alabama, and drives a company truck. Charley's job entails leaving Mobile at 4:00 PM each day (five days per week) and delivering fresh fish to restaurants and wholesale fish distributors in Mississippi and Louisiana. His last stop, in Lafayette, Louisiana, is generally around 12:00 midnight. It normally takes Charley about five hours to get back to Mobile.

Charley's routine is varied. Sometimes, he drives straight back to Mobile from Lafayette. On other occasions, he will pull off at a truck stop and sleep in his cab before returning to Mobile. His cab is equipped with sleeping facilities, although small and sparse. Finally, on other occasions, Charley will spend the night in a motel along the road. The Fishy Co. has no preference as to what Charley does and has given him permission to either drive back or stay overnight. However, the company does not reimburse him for his food and lodging expenses.

When Charley drives straight back to Mobile, Charley will eat one meal. When he sleeps overnight (either in his cab or in a motel) he will eat two meals, a late dinner and breakfast. He spends an average of $6.00 for dinner and $4.00 for breakfast. The cost of his motel averages $50.00 per night. When Charley sleeps in the cab, he generally sleeps about 4-5 hours and then drives on to Mobile.

During the current year, Charley incurred the following expenses:

Meals incurred on nonstop trips	$ 900
Meals incurred when: slept in cab	600
slept in motel	400
Lodging	2,000
TOTAL	$3,900

The IRS has disallowed all of the above expenses on the grounds that they are not bona fide travel expenses but personal expenses. Would you advise Charley to contest this issue?

A partial list of research sources is:

- Sec. 162(a)(2) and Reg. Sec. 1.162-2(a)
- *U.S. v. Correll,* 389 U.S. 299 (1967)
- *Williams v. Patterson,* 286 F.2d 333 (5th Cir. 1961)
- Rev. Rul. 75-168, 1975-1 C.B. 58 and Rev. Rul. 75-432, 1975-2 C.B. 60

10

CHAPTER

DEPRECIATION, COST RECOVERY, AMORTIZATION, AND DEPLETION

LEARNING OBJECTIVES

After studying this chapter, you should be able to

1. Understand the general concepts of tax depreciation
2. Classify property and calculate depreciation under the MACRS rules
3. Calculate amortization for intangible assets and understand the difference between amortizable and non-amortizable assets
4. Apply cost and percentage depletion methods and understand the treatment for intangible drilling costs

CHAPTER OUTLINE

Depreciation and Cost Recovery...10-2
Amortization...10-13
Depletion, Intangible Drilling and Development Costs...10-18
Tax Planning Considerations...10-21
Compliance and Procedural Considerations...10-22

The tax law allows taxpayers to deduct a reasonable allowance for the exhaustion, wear and tear, and obsolescence of property used in a trade or business or held for the production of income.[1] The purpose of allowing a depreciation deduction is to enable taxpayers to recover the cost of an asset under the return of capital doctrine. Depreciation, therefore, is the systematic allocation of the cost of an asset over its estimated economic life. *Depreciation* relates to deductions for most tangible property, *amortization* relates to deductions for intangible property, and *depletion* relates to deductions for natural resources (oil and gas, coal, etc.). While the concepts of depreciation, amortization, and depletion are similar to those in financial accounting, the income tax rules are unique. This chapter discusses the income tax rules relating to depreciation, amortization, and depletion.

DEPRECIATION AND COST RECOVERY

GENERAL CONSIDERATIONS

TYPICAL MISCONCEPTION
It is easy to forget that the depreciation or cost-recovery system that applies to any one asset is the system that was in effect when the property was placed in service. Property acquired in 1986 is not affected by the MACRS rules that became effective in 1987.

Taxpayers must use specific depreciation methods depending on *when* an asset is placed into service. Three separate depreciation and cost recovery systems are currently in place. These three distinct systems are the result of tax law changes in 1981 and 1986. The systems that taxpayers must use are as follows:

- Property placed into service after December 31, 1986

  Taxpayers must use the Modified Accelerated Cost Recovery System (MACRS) as provided in Sec. 168.
- Property placed into service after December 31, 1980 and before January 1, 1987

  Taxpayers must use the Accelerated Cost Recovery System (ACRS) as provided in Sec. 168.
- Property placed into service prior to 1981

  Taxpayers must use the rules contained in Sec. 167 and these rules basically follow financial accounting principles.

REAL-WORLD EXAMPLE
Harrah's Club in Reno, Nevada, restores antique autos and displays them. The restoration costs cannot be depreciated because the autos have an indefinite life as museum pieces. *Harrah's Club v. U.S.,* 43 AFTR 2d 79-745, 81-2 USTC ¶9677 (Ct. Cls., 1981).

The primary emphasis in this chapter is placed upon the MACRS rules because most assets placed into service before 1987 are now fully depreciable.

HISTORICAL NOTE
Before 1954, except for the limited use of a declining-balance method, taxpayers were required to use the straight-line method.

The terms *depreciation* and *cost recovery* are used interchangeably in this text. The rules in Sec. 167 (or pre-ACRS) and the MACRS rules under Sec. 168 both refer to depreciation. However, the deduction under ACRS is referred to as cost recovery. In 1981, Congress initiated the original ACRS system to achieve a number of objectives, including a stimulus for private investment, improving business productivity, simplifying taxpayer compliance, and facilitating IRS administration of the tax law. Therefore, less importance was placed on the financial accounting concept of matching costs and revenues, which is the primary theory that governed the Sec. 167 depreciation rules. The primary objective of Congress in 1981 was to allow businesses and investors to recover the cost of capitalized expenditures over a period of time that is substantially shorter than the property's economic useful life. Thus, the term *cost recovery* rather than *depreciation* was used under the ACRS system. The post-1986 MACRS rules more closely follow the concept of economic useful life and, therefore, the MACRS rules refer to depreciation rather than cost recovery.

ADDITIONAL COMMENT
Property is considered to be "placed in service" when it is in a condition or state of readiness and is available for a specifically assigned function. This can be important in attempting to determine the first year that a depreciation deduction is available.

COMMON RULES OF ALL SYSTEMS. Regardless of the particular system of depreciation that is required to be used (i.e., MACRS, ACRS, etc.), there are certain rules that are common to all systems of depreciation. These common rules are discussed below.

- As discussed above, depreciation may only be claimed on property used in a trade or business or for the production of income. Thus, personal-use assets, such as a personal-use automobile or the taxpayer's personal residence, are not depreciable.

[1] Sec. 167(a).

- No depreciation is permitted for land or other assets that have an indefinite life. Assets such as works of art are generally not depreciable.
- Depreciation for the first year is permitted only in the year the asset is placed into service. For example, a taxpayer may purchase a depreciable asset in December, 2001, but not place it into service until January, 2002. In this case, depreciation is not allowed until 2002.
- Regardless of the depreciation system, consistency is required. Taxpayers must consistently use the method selected in the year the asset was placed into service unless a change of accounting method is requested from the IRS.
- The basis of the property being depreciated must be reduced by the amount of depreciation that is allowable for each taxable year. An important aspect of depreciation is determining the amount of depreciation that is *allowed* and *allowable*. The depreciation allowed is the actual depreciation that is claimed by the taxpayer for a particular taxable year. Allowable depreciation is the amount of depreciation to be claimed under the tax law by using the slowest possible method (i.e., straight-line using the longest permissible recovery period). If a taxpayer does not take any depreciation during a particular year, the basis of the property must be reduced by the amount of depreciation that should have been taken during the year (i.e., the allowable depreciation).

EXAMPLE I10-1 ► Maria acquires a machine in the current year for $50,000 to be used in her business and elects straight-line depreciation under MACRS. The machine is classified as seven-year property for tax purposes. Maria properly takes depreciation in the first two years the asset is used in her business in the amount of $10,714 ($3,571 in Year 1 assuming the half-year convention and $7,143 in Year 2). However, because of a net operating loss in Year 3, Maria did not take any depreciation on the tax return. The allowable depreciation in Year 3 was $7,143. Even though Maria did not claim the $7,143 of depreciation in Year 3, the basis of the machine must still be reduced by that amount. Thus, at the end of Year 3, the basis of the machine would be $32,143 ($50,000 minus the allowable accumulated depreciation of $17,857). This is the case even though she did not actually claim any depreciation in Year 3. Obviously, Maria should amend her tax return for Year 3 and claim the allowable depreciation. This would increase her net operating loss for Year 3 which either can be carried back two years or forward 20 years. ◄

ADDITIONAL COMMENT

A case held that a professional musician could depreciate a nineteenth-century violin bow. The IRS had argued the bow had an indeterminate life but because the taxpayer played the violin, there was "wear and tear" on the bow and depreciation was allowed. *Simon v. Comm.*, 95-2 USTC ¶50,552 (CA-2, 1995).

TYPES OF PROPERTY. Before examining the depreciation rules, it is necessary to define certain terms relating to the various types of property. For both property law and income tax purposes, there are two basic types of property, tangible and intangible. **Tangible property** refers to property that has physical substance, such as land, buildings, natural resources, equipment, etc. **Intangible property** refers to property that does not have physical substance, such as goodwill, patents, and stocks and bonds. The cost of tangible property (other than land, of course) is systematically written off through depreciation or depletion. Natural resources, such as oil and gas reserves, are recovered through depletion. Intangible property is written off through amortization.

Tangible property is further classified as either real property or personal property. **Real property** (often referred to as real estate or realty) is defined as land or any structure permanently attached to the land, such as buildings. **Personal property** is any tangible property that is not real property, and includes items such as equipment, vehicles, furniture, etc. It is important to distinguish between personal property and personal-use property. **Personal-use property** is any property, tangible or intangible, real or personal, that is used by the taxpayer for his own personal use rather than in a trade or business or for the production of income.

ADDITIONAL COMMENT

The IRS issued a private letter ruling that required an airline to capitalize engine overhauls rather than expensing such amounts in the current year. The IRS position requires capitalization because the overhauls involve replacement or reconditioning of a large portion of the engine's parts. This ruling has been severely criticized by the airlines industry, saying that the decision could negatively impact passenger safety.

CAPITALIZATION VERSUS EXPENSE. A frequent dilemma for taxpayers is whether an expenditure should either be capitalized (and depreciated) or expensed entirely in the current year. As is discussed in Chapter I6, if an expenditure either improves the efficiency of an asset or extends the life of an asset beyond the end of the year, the expenditure should generally be capitalized. However, most taxpayers have established materiality limits in order to justify the expensing of small expenditures that technically should be considered a capital expenditure. Since the capitalization-expense decision many times is subjective in nature, disputes between the IRS and taxpayers are common.

CONVERSION OF PERSONAL-USE PROPERTY. If personal-use property is either converted to business use or held for the production of income (e.g., a rental house), the property's basis for depreciation purposes is the lesser of its adjusted basis or its fair market value (FMV) determined as of the conversion date.[2] This lower of cost or market rule is intended to prevent taxpayers from depreciating the portion of the cost that represents a nondeductible loss on a personal-use asset.

EXAMPLE I10-2 ▶ Marty acquires a personal residence for $115,000 in 1999. In 2002, he converts the property to rental use because he is unable to sell the house due to a depressed local real estate market. The property's FMV is only $100,000 when it is converted to rental status in 2002. The $15,000 ($115,000 − $100,000) decline in value represents a nondeductible personal loss and is not depreciable. The depreciable basis is $100,000 (minus the portion of the property's FMV that represents land that is not depreciable). ◀

OBJECTIVE 1

Classify property and calculate depreciation under the MACRS rules.

DEPRECIATION METHODS

As mentioned previously, the method of depreciation required for income tax purposes depends on the date the asset was placed into service. Assets placed into service prior to 1987 must use the old depreciation methods that were in place during those years.[3] For assets placed into service after 1986, the MACRS system of depreciation is required for most assets. There are several unique features of the MACRS system that are different from depreciation methods used for financial accounting purposes. These features include the following:

- Salvage value is not considered in the computation of the depreciation amount.
- Specific asset classes are used. Both tangible personal property and real property must be placed into specific asset classes, based on the type of property. Asset classes merely refer to the number of years over which the asset must be depreciated.
- Fewer depreciation methods are used and the methods are built into the MACRS tables. Both accelerated and straight-line methods are used in MACRS, however, accelerated methods are not permissible for real property. The MACRS tables are summarized in Appendix C.
- The term "convention" in the tax law refers to the assumption as to when an asset is either placed into service or disposed of and is used extensively in the MACRS system. The **half-year convention** generally is required for all tangible personal property and assumes that all asset acquisitions or dispositions are made at the midpoint of the tax year, regardless of when the actual acquisition or disposition is made. For real estate, the **mid-month convention** is used and assumes that all asset acquisitions or dispositions are made at the midpoint of the month in which the transaction occurs.

EXAMPLE I10-3 ▶ Ted, a calendar-year taxpayer, purchases a machine for his business on March 10, 2002. For depreciation purposes, under the half-year convention, the machine is treated as if it were placed into service on July 1, 2002 and one-half year's depreciation is allowable in 2002. The half-year convention assumes all asset acquisitions and dispositions occur at the midpoint of the tax year. ◀

EXAMPLE I10-4 ▶ Bob, a calendar-year taxpayer, purchases a building for his business on March 5, 2002. For depreciation purposes, under the mid-month convention, the building is treated as if it were placed into service on March 15, 2002 and 9½ months of depreciation is allowable in 2002. ◀

TANGIBLE PERSONAL PROPERTY: CLASSIFICATION AND RECOVERY RATES. Tangible personal property, such as equipment, furniture, computers, etc., generally are

[2] Reg. Sec. 1.167(g)-1.

[3] For assets placed into service between 1981 and 1986, taxpayers were required to use the ACRS method; for assets placed into service before 1981, a pre-ACRS method was required. The pre-ACRS methods more closely resemble depreciation methods used for financial statement purposes.

depreciable under MACRS if used in a trade or business or held for the production of income. Certain types of property are *excluded* from being depreciated under MACRS,[4] including:

- Property depreciated under a method not expressed in terms of years, such as the units of production method, and the taxpayer elects to not depreciate the property under MACRS;
- Intangible assets, such as goodwill or copyrights;
- Films, video tapes, or sound recordings.

For property depreciated under MACRS, each property acquired must be classified into one of six categories and depreciation computed using the percentages contained in Table I10-1. The classification of assets is based upon the determination of a class life from a listing of assets published by the IRS.[5]

The following classifications apply to personal property placed in service after December 31, 1986 under the MACRS system.[6]

ADDITIONAL COMMENT

The depreciable life of an automobile has been extended from 3 years to 5 years under the MACRS rules.

KEY POINT

Most depreciable personal property is classified as 7-year property under MACRS.

- 3-Year — Property with a class life of 4 years or less, including tractor units, race horses over 12 years old, and special tools.
- 5-Year — Property with a a class life of more than 4 years but less than 10 years including automobiles, light and heavy-duty, general purpose trucks, computers, and research and experimental (R&E) equipment.
- 7-Year — Property with a class life of 10 years or more but less than 16 years, including office furniture and equipment, horses, single-purpose agricultural or horticultural structures, and property with no class life and not classified elsewhere. Most types of machinery are included in this class.
- 10-Year — Property with a class life of more than 16 years, but less than 20 years, including barges, vessels, and petroleum and food processing equipment.
- 15-Year — Property with a class life of more than 20 years, but less than 25 years, including billboards, service station buildings, and land improvements.
- 20-Year — Property with a class life of 25 or more years, including utilities and sewers.

KEY POINT

Remember that salvage value is not taken into consideration under the MACRS system.

The depreciation rates for the 3-year, 5-year, and 7-year recovery classes are provided in Table I10-1 (See also Table 1 in Appendix C). The rates in Table I10-1 are based on the 200% DB method switching to straight-line when it yields a larger amount. A half-year convention is used in the year of acquisition and zero salvage value is assumed. In the year of disposition, the amount calculated from the table must be reduced by one-half in order to properly apply the half-year convention.

EXAMPLE I10-5 ▶ In March, 2002, Mary acquires and places into service a business machine which cost \$20,000. The machinery has a 7-year recovery period under the MACRS rules. The depreciation deduction for 2002 is \$2,858 (0.1429 × \$20,000). The rate that is applied from Table I10-1 (0.1429) is based on the 200% DB method and assumes a half-year convention and zero salvage value. The MACRS depreciation deduction for the year of acquisition can also be computed by applying the accelerated depreciation rate (using the half-year convention) to the basis of the assets. Thus the depreciation deduction for 2002 is \$2,857 (\$20,000 ÷ 7 years × 200% DB × 0.50 year). Minor differences between the two calculations are due to rounding. ◀

KEY POINT

Remember, the mid-quarter convention does *not* apply to real property.

Use of the Mid-Quarter Convention. As mentioned previously, the MACRS system generally requires the use of the half-year convention. However, the MACRS system requires the use of the **mid-quarter convention** if the aggregate basis of all *personal property* placed in service during the last three months of the year exceeds 40% of the cost of all personal property placed in service during the tax year.[7] Therefore, if the test is met, the mid-quarter convention must be used instead of the half-year convention and special mid-quar-

---

[4] Sec. 168(f).

[5] To determine the class life of assets, see Rev. Proc. 87-56, modified by Rev. Proc. 88-22, which sets forth the class life of property for depreciation purposes.

[6] Sec. 168(e)(1).

[7] Sec. 168(d)(3). The IRS has recently announced that taxpayers whose third or fourth quarter includes September 11, 2001, the taxpayer may elect to apply the half-year convention to all property placed in service during the 2001 taxable year, Cumulative Bulletin Notice 2001-74, November 9, 2001, expanding Cumulative Bulletin Notice 2001-70, October 18, 2001.

SELF-STUDY QUESTION

In Table I10-1, how has the 0.2000 first-year cost recovery rate for five-year property been calculated?

ANSWER

The 0.2000 rate is calculated by multiplying the double declining-balance rate of 0.4000 by ½ year of depreciation.

▼ **TABLE I10-1**
MACRS Rates for Tangible Personal Property (using half-year convention)

Recovery Year	Recovery Classes 3-Year	5-Year	7-Year
1	0.3333	0.2000	0.1429
2	0.4445	0.3200	0.2449
3	0.1481	0.1920	0.1749
4	0.0741	0.1152	0.1249
5	—	0.1152	0.0893
6	—	0.0576	0.0892
7	—	—	0.0893
8	—	—	0.0446

Source: Table 1 of Rev. Proc. 87-57, 1987-2 C.B. 687.

ter tables must be used to compute depreciation under this convention. (See Tables 2-5 in Appendix C). Property placed in service and disposed of during the same tax year is not taken into account.[8] Also, property expensed under Sec. 179 is excluded in computing the 40% test for the applicability of the mid-quarter convention.[9]

The 40% rule prevents taxpayers from using the half-year convention and thereby obtaining one-half year's depreciation in the year of acquisition when a substantial portion of the assets are acquired during the last quarter of the tax year.

EXAMPLE I10-6 ▶ Michael, a calendar-year taxpayer, acquires 5-year tangible personal property in 2002 and places it in service on the following schedule:

Date Placed in Service	*Acquisition Cost*
January 20	$100,000
April 18	200,000
November 5	300,000
Total	$600,000

Because more than 40% of the property acquired during the year is placed in service in the last three months ($300,000/$600,000 = 50%), the mid-quarter convention will apply for all property placed in service during the year. (See Tables 2 through 5 in Appendix C for the percentages that are used to make this calculation.)

Property Placed in Service	*Year 1 Depreciation*	
January 20	$100,000 × 35% =	$ 35,000
April 18	200,000 × 25% =	50,000
November 5	300,000 × 5% =	15,000
Total	$600,000	$100,000

Note that if the half-year convention had been applied in this example, $120,000 (0.2000 × $600,000) of depreciation could have been claimed. Generally, if larger depreciation deductions are desired, care should be exercised on asset acquisitions to prevent the application of the mid-quarter convention. ◀

STOP & THINK *Question:* A common misconception of the mid-quarter convention is that it always yields a smaller depreciation deduction than the half-year convention. Consider the following situation where a business has placed into service the following assets (all 7-year property under MACRS) during the current year:

[8] Sec. 168(d)(3)(B) and Reg. Sec. 1.168(d)-1(b)(3).

[9] PLR 9126014 (March 29, 1991). Section 179 is discussed later in this chapter.

February	$300,000
June	10,000
November	200,000

The business needs an additional $10,000 of equipment (also 7-year property) in the current year, but the purchase could be delayed until early January of the next year. Assuming the business wants to *maximize* its depreciation deduction in the current year, should the business purchase the additional $10,000 of equipment in the current year or delay the purchase until next year?

Solution: The business should purchase the equipment in the current year even though it will require the use of the mid-quarter convention.

Mid-quarter Test

Currently (before the purchase): $200,000/$510,000 = 39.2%

With the purchase: $210,000/$520,000 = 40.4%

Therefore, if the business purchases the additional $10,000 in the current year, the mid-quarter convention will apply. The depreciation for the current year assuming the purchase is made is:

First quarter:	$300,000 × 25% =	$75,000
Second quarter:	10,000 × 17.85% =	1,785
Fourth quarter:	210,000 × 3.57% =	7,497
TOTAL		$84,282

If the purchase *was not* made in the current year, the depreciation that would result under the half-year convention is $72,879 ($510,000 × 14.29%). (The mid-quarter convention produces a higher depreciation deduction even if the half-year convention is computed on $520,000, i.e., $520,000 × 14.29% = $74,308). In this situation, the mid-quarter convention actually maximizes depreciation for the current year. You should notice that the mid-quarter convention yields more than the half-year convention for the reason that virtually all of the equipment that was purchased (other than the fourth quarter) was in the first quarter and this equipment is depreciated using a 25% rate versus a 14.29% rate under the half-year convention.

ADDITIONAL POINT
You must manually make the adjustment for the depreciation factor found in the MACRS table for assets sold during the year.

Year of Disposition. The MACRS system allows depreciation to be taken in the year of disposition using the same convention that applied on acquisition (e.g., half-year, mid-month, or mid-quarter convention). Therefore, if property is disposed of during the year in which the half-year convention is applicable, the depreciation for the year of disposition will be one-half of the amount computed by using the table percentages.

EXAMPLE I10-7 ▶ Assume the same facts as in Example I10-6, except that the equipment purchased on April 18 is disposed of on August 14 in the following year. The mid-quarter convention must be used because it is used in the year of acquisition. Thus, $37,500 of depreciation is claimed in the year of disposition [($200,000 × 0.30) × (7.5 ÷ 12)]. (See Table 3 in Appendix C.) ◀

EXAMPLE I10-8 ▶ Michelle acquires machinery in 2001 that qualifies as seven-year MACRS property and has a $100,000 basis for depreciation. The half-year convention is applied in the year of acquisition. In December 2002 the machinery is sold. Michelle's depreciation deduction in 2002 is $12,245 [$100,000 × (0.2449 × 0.50)] for the equipment (see Table I10-1). ◀

KEY POINT
All depreciable real property can be classified in one of two classes residential rental or nonresidential, real property.

REAL PROPERTY: CLASSIFICATION AND RECOVERY RATES. The MACRS recovery periods that apply to real property placed in service in years after 1986 are as follows:

- Residential rental property: 27.5 years
- Nonresidential real property: 39 years[10]

[10] Sec. 168(c)(1). A 31.5-year recovery period applied to nonresidential real property placed in service on or after January 1, 1987 and before May 13, 1993.

Depreciation must be calculated using the straight-line method. A mid-month convention is used in the year of acquisition and in the year of disposition. The tables for computing depreciation for real property are located in Tables 7, 8 and 9 in Appendix C.

EXAMPLE I10-9 ▶ On October 4, 2002, Husker, Inc. acquired an office building to relocate its rapidly-growing staff. The property was purchased for $1,500,000, of which $200,000 was allocated to the underlying land. Since the property is nonresidential real property, it is classified as 39-year property. Using Table 9 in Appendix C, the depreciation percentage is 0.535%, and the depreciation deduction for the year 2002, using the mid-month convention, is $5,506 ($1,300,000 × .00535 × 9.5/12). ◀

ADDITIONAL COMMENT

The recovery period for nonresidential real property was extended from 31.5 years to 39 years in 1993 to offset the revenue loss from liberalizing the passive activity loss rules affecting real estate.

KEY POINT

Depreciable real property placed in service after 1986 must be depreciated using the straight-line method.

ADDITIONAL COMMENT

For purposes of determining whether at least 80% of the gross rental income is rental income from dwelling units, a taxpayer living in any part of the building includes the fair rental value of his unit in the gross rental income.

A common transaction for taxpayers owning buildings is the depreciation of subsequent capital improvements. Capital improvements are depreciated over the full life of the improvement, not over the remaining life of the building. Thus, the cost of a new roof on an office building must be depreciated over 39 years even though the building may have been placed into service several years ago.

Real properties are divided into two categories: residential rental property and nonresidential real property. **Residential rental property** is defined as property from which at least 80% of the gross rental income is rental income from dwelling units.[11] Dwelling units include houses, apartments, and manufactured homes that are used for residential purposes but not hotels, motels, or other establishments for transient use. Nonresidential real property is any real property other than residential rental property.

STRAIGHT-LINE (METHOD) ELECTION UNDER MACRS. Instead of using the accelerated methods previously described under the MACRS rules, taxpayers may elect to use the straight-line method for tangible personal property. If the straight-line election is made, the taxpayer must use either the same depreciation period or an extended period based on the alternative depreciation system, as discussed below.[12]

ALTERNATIVE DEPRECIATION SYSTEM. The MACRS system provides an alternative depreciation system (ADS) that is required for certain property and is also available for all other depreciable assets if the taxpayer so elects.[13] The principal type of property for which the ADS is *required* is any tangible property which is used predominantly outside the United States. The recovery periods are specified under the ADS and, many times, are longer than the recovery periods under MACRS. Under the ADS, assets must be depreciated using the class life as set forth in Rev. Proc. 87-56. Personal property with no specific class life is assigned a 12-year life and real property is assigned a 40-year life. Further, the ADS requires the use of the straight-line method with a half-year, mid-quarter, or mid-month convention, whichever is applicable. The election of the ADS is generally made by taxpayers who want to use the straight-line method over a longer recovery period. These taxpayers frequently have net operating losses or are subject to the alternative minimum tax (see Chapter I14 for a discussion of the alternative minimum tax).

The ADS generally is an elective provision made on a year-by-year basis. Once the election is made for specified property, it is irrevocable. Also, for personal property, the ADS election applies to all property within a class (all five-year property, for example); for real property, the ADS election may be made on an individual property basis.

EXAMPLE I10-10 ▶ In May, 2002, Bob Roaster purchased an office building for $300,000 ($50,000 allocated to the land) as rental property. Because he has substantial net operating losses from other business ventures, Roaster elects to depreciate the building using the ADS. Depreciation expense for 2002, using the mid-month convention and a 40-year life is $3,906 ($250,000 ÷ 40 years × 7.5/12). If Roaster had not elected the ADS, his depreciation would have been $4,013 [$250,000 × .01605 (from Table 9, Appendix C)]. The difference is small because the recovery period is 39 years under regular MACRS and 40 years under the ADS. ◀

[11] Secs. 168(e)(2)(A).

[12] Sec. 168(g)(7).

[13] Sec. 168(g). See Tables 10–12 in Appendix C.

Topic Review I10-1

Comparison of MACRS and ADS

	MACRS	ADS
Recovery Periods:		
Automobiles	5 years	5 years
Computers	5 years	5 years
Office furniture and equipment	7 years	10 years
Residential rental property	27.5 years	40 years
Nonresidential real property	31.5 or 39 years	40 years
Conventions:		
Personal property	Half-year or mid-quarter[a]	Half-year or mid-quarter[a]
Real property	Mid-month	Mid-month
Depreciation in year of sale:		
Personal property	Yes	Yes
Real property	Yes	Yes

[a] If more than 40% of personal property is placed in service during the last quarter of year.

The alternative depreciation system is also used to compute earnings and profits (E&P) for a corporation and to compute the alternative minimum tax for both individuals and corporations (see Chapter I14).

A comparison of the ACRS and MACRS rules is presented in Topic Review I10-1.

SECTION 179 EXPENSING ELECTION

ADDITIONAL COMMENT

In the case of a partnership, the partnership and each partner are individually subject to the annual $20,000 limitation.

In lieu of capitalizing the cost of new or used tangible personal business property, taxpayers may elect to expense up to $24,000 (2002) of the acquisition cost as an ordinary deduction in the year of acquisition.[14] To qualify for the deduction, the property must actually be placed into service during the year. The immediate expensing election is not applicable to real estate. The election is made on an annual basis, and the taxpayer must select the assets to which the $24,000 write-off applies. The MACRS rules apply to any residual amount of an asset's cost that is not expensed under Sec. 179.

The amount that may be expensed under Sec. 179 was increased in 1997 as follows:

▼ TABLE I10-2

Section 179 Expense Amounts

Tax Year Beginning In	Maximum Sec. 179 Expense
1996	$17,500
1997	18,000
1998	18,500
1999	19,000
2000	20,000
2001	24,000
2002	24,000
2003 and after	25,000

[14] Sec. 179. The amount was increased from $10,000 to $17,500 for property placed in service in tax years beginning after December 31, 1992 and before January 1, 1997.

EXAMPLE I10-11 ▶ Tanya acquires and places into service a business machine (tangible personal property qualifying under Sec. 179) for $36,000 in July 2002. The machine has a 7-year MACRS recovery period. Tanya elects to immediately expense $24,000 of the asset's cost under Sec. 179. Tanya's remaining basis for calculating the MACRS depreciation deduction is $12,000 ($36,000 − $24,000). Tanya's 2002 regular depreciation allowance is $1,715 ($12,000 × 0.1429). Tanya's total depreciation deductions for 2002 are $25,715 ($24,000 expensed under Sec. 179 + $1,715 MACRS depreciation). ◀

The following limitations and special rules apply to the Sec. 179 election:

- The property must be purchased for use in an active trade or business as distinguished from property that is acquired for the production of income (e.g., personal property used in a rental activity held by an investor does not qualify).
- The property cannot be acquired from a related party under Sec. 267 or by gift or inheritance.
- The Sec. 179 tax benefits are recaptured if the property is no longer predominantly used in a trade or business (e.g., the property is converted to personal use) at any time.[15] In the year of recapture, the taxpayer must include in gross income the amount previously expensed reduced by the amount of depreciation that would have been allowed for the period the property was held for business use.[16]
- If the total cost of qualified property placed into service during the year is more than $200,000, the $24,000 ceiling is reduced on a dollar-for-dollar basis by the excess amount. Thus, no deduction is permitted for the 2002 tax year in which $224,000 or more of Sec. 179 property is placed into service.
- A second limitation on the total Sec. 179 deduction is that it cannot exceed the taxpayer's taxable income (before deducting the Sec. 179 expense) from the trade or business.[17] Any acquisition cost that is unable to be deducted because of the limitation based on taxable income is carried forward for an unlimited number of years and is added to the other amounts eligible for the Sec. 179 deduction in the future year. The carryover amount is subject to the taxable income limitation in the carryover year.

ADDITIONAL COMMENT

Married taxpayers who file separate tax returns are each entitled to a maximum $12,000 ($24,000 ÷ 2) limitation under Sec. 179.

SELF-STUDY QUESTION

Are corporations entitled to the election to expense up to $24,000 under Sec. 179?

ANSWER

Yes, but larger corporations will not receive the benefit from it because the ceiling is reduced when the cost of qualified property exceeds $200,000.

EXAMPLE I10-12 ▶ Pam owns an unincorporated manufacturing business. In 2002, she purchases and places in service $213,000 of qualifying equipment for use in her business. Pam's taxable income from the business (before deducting any Sec. 179 amount) is $4,000. The $24,000 ceiling amount is initially reduced by $13,000 ($213,000 − $200,000) to reflect the fact that the qualified property placed in service during the year exceeded $200,000. The remaining $11,000 Sec. 179 deduction is further reduced by $7,000 ($11,000 − $4,000) to reflect the taxable income limitation. Pam's Sec. 179 deduction is $4,000; $7,000 is available for use as a carryover to 2003. The cost basis of the equipment for MACRS purposes is reduced by $11,000 in 2002 despite the fact that only $4,000 was immediately deductible under Sec. 179. ◀

ETHICAL POINT

The personal use of a corporate automobile by a shareholder-employee may be a constructive dividend. Personal use by a non-shareholder-employee results in additional taxable compensation to the employee and may present an ethical dilemma for the tax consultant.

MACRS RESTRICTIONS

PERSONAL-USE ASSETS. The personal use portion of an asset's cost is not depreciable. For example, if a taxpayer owns a duplex and uses one unit as a personal residence, only the portion of the unit that is rented to tenants qualifies for depreciation.

LISTED PROPERTY RULES. Because Congress was concerned about taxpayers claiming large depreciation deductions (using accelerated methods) on certain types of assets that are conducive to mixed business/personal use, restrictions are placed on assets that are classified as *listed property.* Listed property includes automobiles, computers and peripheral equipment, cellular telephones, and property generally used for purposes of entertainment, recreation, or amusement (for example, a video recorder). If a listed property's business usage is greater than 50% of its total usage, the taxpayer may use the regular MACRS tables for the business-use portion of the asset's cost. However, if the busi-

---

[15] Sec. 179(d)(10).

[16] Reg. Sec. 1.179-1(e).

[17] Sec. 179(b)(3). Under Reg. Sec. 1.179-2(c)(5)(iv), employees are considered to be engaged in the active conduct of the trade or business from their employment. Thus, a small business person who is also an employee may include wages and salary derived from employment in determining taxable income for purposes of this limitation. Such amounts are considered derived from the conduct of a trade or business. For an individual, taxable income is also computed without regard to the deduction for one-half of self-employment taxes paid under Sec. 164(f) (see Chapter I14).

ness use is 50% or less, the taxpayer must use the alternative depreciation system (e.g., five-year straight-line cost recovery period for automobiles and computers).

EXAMPLE I10-13 ▶ Patrick acquires an automobile for $10,000 in June 2002. It is used 60% for business. The depreciation deduction on the business-use portion of the automobile's cost is based on the MACRS system and five-year recovery class because the automobile is predominantly used in business (i.e., more than 50%). The MACRS depreciation allowance in 2002 is $1,200 ($10,000 × 0.20 MACRS rate × 0.60 business percentage use). See Table I10-1 for the MACRS rate. ◀

EXAMPLE I10-14 ▶ Paula acquires an automobile for $10,000 in 2002. It is used only 40% for business. Paula must use the alternative depreciation system (ADS) to claim depreciation allowances on the business portion of the automobile. The business portion is $4,000 ($10,000 × 0.40). Paula's depreciation allowance in 2002 is $400 [($4,000 ÷ 5 years) × 0.50] the half-year convention. ◀

ADDITIONAL COMMENT

The restrictions on automobiles were enacted in 1984 because of a concern that the tax system was underwriting the acquisition of automobiles whose cost and luxury far exceeded what was required for business needs.

Additional restrictions apply to employees who acquire listed property (e.g., an automobile, personal computer, etc.) for use in employment-related activities. In addition to the "more than 50% test," the use must be for the convenience of the employer and be required as a condition of employment.[18] This rule is strictly interpreted by the IRS.

EXAMPLE I10-15 ▶ Raul, a college professor, acquired a personal computer for use at home. He used the computer 60% of the time on teaching- and research-related activities associated with his job. The remaining usage was for personal activities. Raul's employer finds that it is helpful for employees to own a personal computer but does not require them to purchase a computer as a condition of employment. Raul meets the first requirement (i.e., the 60% business usage is greater than the 50% threshold). However, the second requirement for employees (that the use must be for the convenience of the employer and required as a condition of employment) is not met. Thus, no depreciation may be taken because the employment-related use is not deemed to be business use. ◀

ADDITIONAL COMMENT

An automobile for purposes of the listed property restrictions is defined as any 4-wheeled vehicle manufactured primarily for use on public streets and rated at 6,000 pounds or less unloaded gross vehicle weight. At one time the Jeep Wagoneer was advertised as not being subject to the listed property limitation or luxury automobile limitation because its weight was slightly over the weight limit. Ambulances, hearses, and taxis are excluded.

RECAPTURE OF EXCESS COST-RECOVERY DEDUCTIONS. For listed property, if the MACRS rules were used and the business-use percentage decreases to 50% or less in a subsequent year, the property is subject to depreciation recapture. The depreciation deductions for all years are recomputed using the alternative depreciation system. The excess depreciation that has been taken is recaptured as ordinary income by including the excess amount in the taxpayer's gross income in the year the business-use percentage first falls to 50% or below.[19] Once the business use falls to 50% or below, the alternative depreciation system must be used for the current year and for all subsequent years, even if the business-use percentage increases to more than 50% in a subsequent year.

EXAMPLE I10-16 ▶ Peggy, a self-employed attorney, acquires an automobile in 2002 for $10,000. The automobile's business usage is 60% in 2002 but declines to 40% in 2003. In 2002, Peggy is eligible to use the regular MACRS depreciation rates because the business use was greater than 50%. The MACRS deduction in 2002 is $1,200 ($10,000 cost × 0.60 business use × 0.20). The straight-line depreciation method using the five-year life specified for the alternative depreciation system and the half-year convention would have resulted in a deduction of only $600 [($10,000 cost × 0.60 business use ÷ 5 years) × 0.50 year] in 2002. Thus, $600 ($1,200 − $600) of the previously claimed depreciation is recaptured as ordinary income in 2003. Peggy's depreciation deduction for 2003 and subsequent years is limited to the straight-line method and a five-year recovery period. Her depreciation deduction for 2003 is $800 [($10,000 cost × 0.40 business use) ÷ 5 years]. ◀

ADDITIONAL COMMENT

The limitations on luxury automobiles mean that the depreciation deductions are limited during the normal five-year recovery period on business automobiles costing more than $15,300 (for 2002).

LIMITATIONS ON LUXURY AUTOMOBILES. Additional MACRS depreciation deduction restrictions are placed on the purchase of so-called luxury automobiles.[20] The limitations apply even if such automobiles are used 100% of the time for business. The MACRS depreciation for automobiles placed into service in 2002 is subject to a $3,060

---

[18] Sec. 280F(d)(3). Any other property used for transportation (e.g., a pickup truck) qualifies as listed property if the nature of the property lends itself to personal use. See Sec. 280F(b)(4).

[19] Sec. 280F(b)(3).

[20] Sec. 280F. The term "luxury automobile" may be an overstatement as the limitations apply to automobiles acquired in 2002 which cost in excess of $15,300.

ceiling limitation for the first year, $4,900 for the second year, $2,950 for the third year, and $1,775 for each succeeding year in the recovery period.[21] In the years following the end of the depreciation period (e.g., in year six and subsequent years), additional depreciation up to $1,775 per year is allowed in taxable years commencing after the end of the recovery period until the business use portion of the automobile is fully depreciated. Luxury automobile limitations for the past several years are contained in Table 6 of Appendix C. These amounts are adjusted for inflation each year. These ceilings are reduced by the percentage of personal use and also apply to amounts that are expensed under Sec. 179. The effect of these ceilings is to extend the basic MACRS depreciation period from six to seven years or longer depending on the automobile's acquisition cost.

EXAMPLE I10-17 ▶ Phil acquires an automobile for $20,000 in 2002. The automobile is used 80% for business and 20% for personal activities during the year. Table I10-3 lists the depreciation amounts for a six-

TYPICAL MISCONCEPTION

It is sometimes mistakenly believed that the $24,000 expensing allowance can be used to boost the first-year write-off on luxury automobiles.

▼ **TABLE I10-3**

Depreciation Amounts for Example I10-17

	MACRS Deduction Before Limitation	Ceiling Limit	Deduction Allowed
2002			
Regular calculation			
($20,000 × 0.80 × 0.20)	$3,200		
Ceiling limit			
($3,060 × 0.80)		$2,448	$2,448
2003			
Regular calculation			
($20,000 × 0.80 × 0.32)	5,120		
Ceiling limit			
($4,900 × 0.80)		3,920	3,920
2004			
Regular calculation			
($20,000 × 0.80 × 0.192)	3,072		
Ceiling limit			
($2,950 × 0.80)		2,360	2,360
2005			
Regular calculation			
($20,000 × 0.80 × 0.1152)	1,843		
Ceiling limit			
($1,775 × 0.80)		1,420	1,420
2006			
Regular calculation			
($20,000 × 0.80 × 0.1152)	1,843		
Ceiling limit			
($1,775 × 0.80)		1,420	1,420
2007			
Regular calculation			
($20,000 × 0.80 × 0.0576)	922		
Ceiling limit			
($1,775 × 0.80)		1,420	922
2008 and later years until fully depreciated			
Ceiling limit			
($1,775 × 0.80)		1,420	1,420

[21] Sec. 280F(a)(2). The ceiling imitation for the first year includes any amounts that are immediately written off under Sec. 179. The Sec. 280F limitations restrict the deductibility of lease payments for automobiles in the same way that depreciation is restricted.

year period, assuming that the 80% business use continues for the life of the automobile and that no amount is expensed under Sec. 179. At the end of the regular six-year depreciation period, the unrecovered cost in the business use portion of the automobile may be recovered in year 2008 and succeeding years at an annual rate not to exceed $1,420 ($1,775 × 0.80). ◀

ADDITIONAL COMMENT

The amount that can be deducted for leased automobiles is also limited.

ADDITIONAL COMPUTATIONS FOR LEASED LUXURY AUTOMOBILES. If a taxpayer leases an automobile for business purposes, the deduction for rental payments is reduced to reflect the limitations on depreciation deductions that are imposed on owners of automobiles under Sec. 280F. If these restrictions were not applied to leased automobiles, the limitations could be avoided by leasing instead of purchasing an automobile. The leasing restriction is accomplished by requiring taxpayers to include in their gross income an "inclusion amount" obtained from an IRS table.[22] This amount is based on the automobile's FMV and the tax year in which the lease commences, and is prorated for the percentage of business use and number of days used during the year. A partial lease inclusion table is provided in Table 17 in Appendix C.

EXAMPLE I10-18 ▶ On April 1, 2001 Jim leases and places into service an automobile with a FMV of $40,000. Business use is 60%. The "inclusion amount" for the initial year of the lease (2001) from the IRS lease inclusion table is $198 (see table in Appendix C). This amount is prorated for the number of days the automobile is leased (275/365) and is then multiplied by the percentage of business use (60%). Jim is entitled to deduct 60% of the lease payments but must include $90 [($198 × 275/365) × 60%] in his gross income for the current year. In 2002, the second year of the lease, the inclusion amount is $433. Thus, Jim must include $260 ($433 × 60%) in his gross income for the second year. Subsequent years follow the same procedures. ◀

Special elections and restrictions are summarized in Topic Review I10-2.

AMORTIZATION

OBJECTIVE 2

Calculate amortization for intangible assets and understand the difference between amortizable and non-amortizable assets

An amortization deduction is allowed for a variety of intangible assets. While the amortization period varies greatly depending on the type of asset, a characteristic of all intangible assets is that they are amortized on a *straight-line basis*. The major intangible assets that may be amortized are as follows:

- Goodwill and Other Purchased Intangibles, Sec. 197
- Research and Experimental Expenditures, Sec. 174
- Computer software
- Start-up Expenditures, Sec. 195
- Organizational Expenditures, Sec. 248
- Pollution Control Facilities, Sec. 169

Several of the above intangibles are discussed below.

ADDITIONAL COMMENT

The only way goodwill will appear on a balance sheet is if the business was purchased.

SEC. 197 INTANGIBLES

Sec. 197 was enacted in 1993 to provide greater certainty as to the amortization of many acquired intangible assets and to specifically allow the amortization of *purchased goodwill*. An amortization deduction is permitted for certain acquired Sec. 197 intangible assets. The amortization is deducted on a ratable basis over a 15-year period beginning with the month of acquisition.[23] In general, Sec. 197 applies only to intangible assets that are *acquired* in connection with the conduct of a trade or business or an activity engaged in for the production of income. For example, Sec. 197 does not apply to an intangible asset that is internally created by the taxpayer, such as a patent resulting from the taxpayer's

---

[22] The latest lease inclusion table at the date of printing of this textbook is contained in Rev. Proc. 2001-19 I.R.B. 2001-9, 732. The luxury depreciation amounts for 2002 are based on changes to the Consumer Price Index.

[23] Sec. 197(a).

Topic Review I10-2

Special Elections and Restrictions

SECTION 179 EXPENSING ELECTION

Deduction: $24,000 for 2002 on the purchase of new or used tangible personal business property used in the conduct of a trade or business.

Limitations:

Asset purchases: The $24,000 limit is reduced by the excess of qualified purchases over $200,000.

Taxable income limitation: Limited to taxable income before the Sec. 179 deduction.

Basis reduction: The depreciable basis is reduced by the amount of the Sec. 179 deduction.

Recapture: Occurs when the asset is no longer predominantly used in a trade or business.

The recapture amount equals the excess of the Sec. 179 expense amount minus the amount that would have been claimed as depreciation if no Sec. 179 election were made.

BUSINESS USE RESTRICTION

Listed property: Business use must be more than 50% to use the regular MACRS rules. If business use is less than 50%, the alternative depreciation system's straight-line method must be used.

Recapture: If business use falls below 50%, the taxpayer must recompute depreciation using the alternative depreciation system's straight-line method and recapture the difference between the prior depreciation taken and straight-line depreciation. The straight-line method is continued for the remaining useful life even if business use subsequently exceeds 50%.

LUXURY AUTOMOBILE LIMITATIONS

Sum of depreciation and Sec. 179 expense limits:

	2001 and 2002
1st year	$3,060
2nd year	4,900
3rd year	2,950
4th and later years	1,775

LEASED LUXURY AUTOMOBILE LIMITATIONS

An "inclusion amount" is added to gross income based on the automobile's FMV on the date placed in service to approximate the depreciation restrictions. Special tables that are revised annually are used to calculate the inclusion amount. A partial lease inclusion table is provided in Appendix C.

research and development lab. Internally-created patents and copyrights both have definite and limited lives and are therefore amortizable over the defined period.[24] Internally created patents are generally amortized over 17 years; internally created copyrights over 28 years.

EXAMPLE I10-19 ▶ On January 1, 2002, Central Corporation receives patent approval on an internally created process improvement. Legal costs associated with the patent are $100,000 and the patent has a legal life of 17 years. The patent does not qualify as a Sec. 197 intangible. The patent has a definite and limited life and is amortizable ratably over its legal life of 17 years beginning with the month of its creation. ◀

ADDITIONAL COMMENT

In the 1993 *Newark Morning Ledger Co. v. U.S.* case the U.S. Supreme Court held that a taxpayer could depreciate intangible assets if the asset could be valued and if it had a limited life. The case was a victory for taxpayers but promised disputes over valuation of intangibles. To eliminate potential battles, Congress in the Revenue Reconciliation Act of 1993 required a 15-year amortization of certain intangible assets such as goodwill, information base, know-how, customer lists, etc.

DEFINITION OF A SEC. 197 INTANGIBLE ASSET. Sec. 197 intangibles (i.e., intangible assets that are subject to 15-year ratable amortization) include the following:

▶ Goodwill and going concern value. Conceptually, goodwill is an intangible asset that is neither separately identified or valued but possesses characteristics that allow a business to earn greater returns than would be possible without such characteristics. The characteristics that make-up goodwill include many items, such as valued employees, superior management team, loyal customer base, strategic location, etc. For income tax purposes, however, goodwill is determined in a much more practical manner. **Goodwill** is defined as the value of a trade or business that is attributable to the expectancy of continued customer patronage, whether due to the name or reputation of the trade or

[24] Reg. Sec. 1.167(a)-3.

business or to any other factor.[25] Going concern value is the added value that attaches to acquired property because it is an integral part of a going concern.

- Intangible assets relating to the workforce, information base, know-how, customers, suppliers, or similar items, (e.g., the portion of the purchase price of an acquired business that is attributable to an existing employment contract for a key employee) may be amortized over a 15-year period. An example of an information base intangible would be a customer list. Know-how related intangibles include patents, copyrights, formulas, and processes.
- Licenses, permits, or other rights granted by a governmental unit or agency (e.g., the capitalized cost of acquiring a radio broadcasting license).
- Covenants not to compete. A covenant not to compete represents an agreement between a buyer and seller of a business that the seller (i.e., the selling corporation and/or its shareholders) will not compete with the buyer for a limited period. The covenant may also be limited to a geographic area. A covenant not to compete must be amortized over 15 years even though the agreement was only for five years.[26]
- Franchises, trademarks, and tradenames. A franchise includes any agreement that gives one of the parties the right to distribute, sell, or provide goods, services, or facilities, within a specified area.

EXAMPLE I10-20 ▶ During the current year, Chicago Corporation acquires all of the net assets of Coastal Corporation for $1,000,000. The following intangible assets are included in the purchase agreement:

Assets	*Acquisition Cost*
Goodwill and going concern value	$100,000
Licenses	55,000
Patents	45,000
Covenant not to compete for five years	100,000

All of the intangible assets above qualify as Sec. 197 intangible assets and are amortizable on a ratable basis over 15 years beginning with the month of the acquisition. This 15-year amortization period applies to the convenant not to compete even though the convenant is only for five years. ◀

STOP & THINK *Question:* When one company purchases the assets of another company, the purchasing company may acquire goodwill. Since purchased goodwill is a Sec. 197 intangible asset and may be amortized over 15 years, the determination of the cost of goodwill is important. How is the "cost" of goodwill determined when the purchasing company purchases many assets in the acquisition?

Solution: The IRS requires that taxpayers use the "residual method" as prescribed in Sec. 1060. Under this method, all of the assets except for goodwill are valued. The total value of these assets are then subtracted from the total purchase price and the residual value is the amount of the purchase price that is allocated to goodwill.

ADDITIONAL COMMENT

Sec. 1231 generally allows gains to be treated as long-term capital gains and losses to be deducted as ordinary losses. Sec. 1245 requires gains to be classified as ordinary income to the extent depreciation, amortization or depletion was claimed as an ordinary deduction in prior periods. (See Chapter I13).

CLASSIFICATION AND DISPOSITION OF INTANGIBLE ASSETS. A Sec. 197 intangible asset is treated as depreciable property so that Sec. 1231 treatment is accorded the disposition if the intangible asset is held for more than one year.[27] Gain from the disposition of a Sec. 197 intangible is subject to depreciation recapture under Sec. 1245 (see Chapter I13).[28] A loss on the disposition of a Sec. 197 intangible asset, however, is not deductible if other intangibles acquired in the same asset acquisition of a trade or business are retained. In such case, the bases of the retained Sec. 197 intangibles are increased by the unrecognized loss.[29]

[25] Reg. Sec. 1.197-2(b)(1).
[26] Frontier Chevrolet Co., 116 T.C., No. 23 (2001).
[27] Sec. 197(f)(7).
[28] Sec. 1245(a)(2)(C).
[29] Sec. 197(f)(1).

EXAMPLE I10-21 ▶ Assume the same facts as in Example I10-20 except that after five years the covenant not to compete expires when its adjusted basis is $66,667 [$100,000 − (0.333 × $100,000)]. The loss is not deductible and the $66,667 disallowed loss is allocated to the retained Sec. 197 assets based on their respective FMVs. ◀

EXAMPLE I10-22 ▶ Assume the same facts as in Example I10-21 except that after one year the patent is sold for $50,000. In the initial year, $3,000 of amortization was deducted. The recognized gain is $8,000 ($50,000 − $42,000) and $3,000 of the gain is recaptured as ordinary income under Sec. 1245. The remaining $5,000 of gain is classified as Sec. 1231 gain. ◀

RESEARCH AND EXPERIMENTAL EXPENDITURES

TYPICAL MISCONCEPTION

It is sometimes mistakenly believed that if a company constructs a new building to be used entirely as a research facility, the entire cost of the building can be expensed. However, the expensing election applies only to the depreciation allowances on the building.

In general, research and experimental (R&E) expenditures, as defined in Sec. 174, include experimental and laboratory costs incidental to the development of a product.[30] Sec. 174 was enacted to clarify the income tax treatment of research and experimental expenditures. Without statutory guidance, the decision to either capitalize or currently expense such expenditures would be in doubt. The Regulations define items that do and do not qualify as research and experimental expenditures. These items are summarized in Table I10-4. For income tax purposes, the following alternatives are available for R&E expenditures:

- ▶ Expense in the year paid or incurred
- ▶ Defer and amortize the costs as a ratable deduction over a period of 60 months or more
- ▶ Capitalize and write off the costs only when the research project is abandoned or is worthless[31]

A taxpayer must make an election to expense or defer and amortize the costs in the initial year the R&E expenditures are incurred. If no election is made, the costs must be capitalized. The taxpayer must continue to use the same accounting method for the R&E expenditures unless IRS approval to change methods is obtained.

The following points are significant regarding the computation of the deduction for R&E expenditures:

- ▶ Most taxpayers elect to expense the R&E expenditures because they prefer the immediate tax benefit.

▼ TABLE I10-4
Research and Experimental Expenditures

Items That Qualify	Items That Do Not Qualify[a]
▶ Costs incident to the development of an experimental or pilot model, a plant process, a product, a formula, an invention	▶ Expenditures for ordinary testing or inspection of materials or products for quality control purposes
▶ Costs associated with product improvements	▶ Efficiency surveys and management studies
▶ Costs of obtaining a patent, such as attorney fees	▶ Marketing research, advertising, and so on
▶ Research contracted to others	▶ Cost of acquiring another person's patent, model, production, or process
▶ Depreciation or cost-recovery amounts attributable to capitalized R&E items (e.g., research laboratory and equipment)	▶ Research incurred in connection with literary, historical, or similar projects

[a] Certain of these expenses may be deductible as trade or business expenses under Sec. 162, subject to amortization under Sec. 197, or treated as start-up expenditures under Sec. 195.

[30] Reg. Sec. 1.174-2(a)(2). The Regulations define the term "product" to include any pilot model, formula, invention, technique, patent, or similar product.

[31] Sec. 174.

- The deferral and amortization method is desirable if the taxpayer is currently in a low tax rate situation or expects initial NOLs during a start-up period.
- If the deferral and amortization method is used, the amortization period of 60 or more months commences with the month in which the benefits from the expenditures are first realized.
- R&E expenses include depreciation allowances related to capitalized expenditures. Thus, if the deferral and amortization method is used, depreciation allowances are deferred as part of the R&E expenditures that are amortized over a period of at least 60 months. Capital expenditures made in connection with R&E activities cannot be expensed when they are incurred merely because an election to expense R&E costs are made.
- A 20% tax credit applies to certain incremental research expenditures, even if they are immediately expensed under Sec. 174. (See Chapter I14 for a discussion of the research activities credit.)

EXAMPLE I10-23 ▶ In 2002 Control Corporation leases a research laboratory to develop new products and to improve existing products. Control Corporation, a calendar-year taxpayer that uses the accrual method of accounting, incurs the following expenditures during 2002:

Laboratory supplies and materials	$ 40,000
Laboratory equipment	60,000[a]
Utilities and rent	50,000
Salaries	50,000
Total expenditures	$200,000

[a] The MACRS recovery period is 5 years at a 20% rate for the initial year.

REAL-WORLD EXAMPLE

An airline company made payments to an aircraft manufacturer to help defray the cost of designing, developing, producing, and testing a supersonic transport prototype aircraft. These payments were considered R&E expenditures. Rev. Rul. 69-484, 1969-2 C.B. 38.

Assume the benefits from the R&E expenditures are first realized in January, 2003. If Control Corporation elects to expense the R&E expenditures, the deduction in 2002 is $152,000 ($40,000 laboratory supplies and materials + $12,000 depreciation on the equipment + $50,000 utilities and rent + $50,000 salaries). If the deferral and amortization method is elected, none of the expenditures above are deductible in 2002 because the benefits of the R&E activities are not first realized until January, 2003. If the 60-month minimum amortization period is elected, the monthly amortization commencing in January, 2003 is $2,533 ($152,000 ÷ 60 months). The $48,000 ($60,000 − $12,000) of laboratory equipment cost is depreciated over the remaining MACRS recovery period beginning in 2003. ◀

COMPUTER SOFTWARE

The amortization or depreciation of computer software depends on the nature of the software and how it is acquired. Basically, computer software is either developed by the taxpayer or purchased or leased from an outside party.

DEVELOPED COMPUTER SOFTWARE The cost of developing computer software that is considered research and development is treated under Sec. 174 of the IRC. Thus, such software costs may either be expensed in the year the costs are incurred or, if the taxpayer so elects, amortize the costs over 60 months beginning with the month in which the taxpayer first realizes benefits from such expenditures. If the costs incurred to develop the software are not considered research and development costs (e.g., the software is not in the experimental stage), such costs should be depreciated on a straight line basis over 36 months beginning with the date the software is placed in service.[32]

ACQUIRED COMPUTER SOFTWARE Computer software that is purchased generally may be depreciated in two alternative ways; (1) if the software is included in the cost of the computer hardware, the software does not have to be separately stated as long as the taxpayer consistently follows this treatment and, therefore, the computer and software would be depreciated together under MACRS over five years, or (2) if the software is purchased separately, the software must be depreciated on a straight line basis over 36

[32] Sec. 167(f)(1) and Rev. Proc. 2000-50, I.R.B. 2000-52, 24.

months. An exception to these rules occurs if computer software is purchased in connection with the acquisition of a number of assets of an existing trade or business. In this case, the computer software is considered to be a Sec. 197 intangible and must be amortized over a period of 15 years.[33]

EXAMPLE I10-24 ▶ Morris Corporation purchased all these assets of an existing trade or business on April 1, 2002 for $1,000,000. Included in the assets that Morris Corporation purchased was some computer software that the corporation intends to use in its business. The software is specialized for use by Morris Corporation. Based on relative fair market values, the computer software is allocated a cost of $63,000. The software is considered a Sec. 197 intangible and would be amortized over 15 years beginning in the month of acquisition. For the eight month period in calendar year 2002, Morris Corporation's amortization deduction would be $2,800 ($63,000/15 years × 8/12). ◀

EXAMPLE I10-25 ▶ Using the same facts as in Example I10-24, if Morris Corporation alternatively purchased computer software on April 1, 2002 (not in connection with an asset acquisition) for $63,000, the software would not be considered a Sec. 197 intangible and would be depreciable under Sec. 167(f) on a straight line basis over a period of 36 months. Therefore, in 2002, Morris Corporation's depreciation deduction would be $14,000 ($63,000/36 × 8 months). ◀

LEASED OR LICENSED COMPUTER SOFTWARE Computer software that is leased or licensed for use in the taxpayer's trade or business generally is deductible in full in the year paid.[34]

DEPLETION, INTANGIBLE DRILLING AND DEVELOPMENT COSTS

OBJECTIVE 3

Apply cost and percentage depletion methods and understand the treatment for intangible drilling costs

The exploration, development, and operation of oil and gas properties require an outlay of various types of expenditures. These expenditures must be properly classified to determine the correct income tax treatment of such expenditures. Below are the four major types of expenditures of an oil and gas property and their income tax treatment.

- Payments for the mineral interest. These costs are capitalized and recovered through depletion.
- Intangible drilling and development costs (e.g., labor and other operating costs to clear land, erect a derrick, and drill the well). Taxpayers elect to either capitalize or immediately write off these expenditures.
- Tangible asset costs (e.g., machinery, pipe). These expenditures must be capitalized and depreciated under the MACRS rules.
- Operating costs after the well is producing. These expenditures are deductible under Sec. 162 as ordinary and necessary business expenses.

KEY POINT

A depletion deduction is available in the case of mines, oil and gas wells, other natural resources, and timber. However, the percentage depletion method is not available in the case of timber.

DEPLETION METHODS

Depletion is similar to depreciation but refers to natural resources, such as oil and gas, timber, and coal. Depletion is the using up of natural resources by the process of mining (coal, for example) or drilling (oil and gas) and is calculated under the **cost depletion method** or the **percentage depletion method** for each period. The method that is used in any year is the one that results in the largest deduction. Thus, percentage depletion may be used in one year and cost depletion may be used in the following year.

[33] Sec. 197(e)(3)(A). If the computer software acquired in an asset acquisition is software that is readily available for purchase by the general public, such software would not be considered a Sec. 197 intangible. See Sec. 197(e)(3)(A)(i).

[34] Reg. Sec. 1.162-11 and Rev. Proc. 2000-50, I.R.B. 2000-52, 24.

Depletion is allowed to the taxpayer who has an **economic interest** in the property. The person who typically has an economic interest in the property is the owner of the natural resource (i.e., the oil, gas, coal, etc.). Thus, depletion may be claimed by the persons who either own the natural resource property or retain a royalty interest. A mining company that only mines coal from a property and does not own (or lease) the underlying coal is not considered to hold an economic interest and, therefore, is not allowed a depletion deduction. The landowner who owns the coal would be entitled to the depletion deduction.

ADDITIONAL COMMENT

Note that a taxpayer must use the greater of cost depletion or percentage depletion. If percentage depletion is used, the adjusted basis of the property is reduced by the percentage depletion amount.

COST DEPLETION METHOD. The cost depletion method is similar to the units-of-production method of depreciation. The adjusted basis of the asset is divided by the estimated recoverable units to arrive at a per-unit depletion cost. This per-unit cost is then multiplied by the number of units sold to determine the cost depletion deduction.[35] If percentage depletion is used in any one year because it is greater than the cost depletion amount, the property's adjusted basis for purposes of determining cost depletion in the following year and the gain or loss on disposition of the property is reduced by the amount of percentage depletion claimed. If the original estimate of recoverable units is subsequently determined to be incorrect, the per-unit cost depletion rate must be revised and used on a prospective basis to determine cost depletion in future years.[36] It is not proper to file an amended return for the years in which the incorrect estimated unit cost was used.

EXAMPLE I10-26 ▶ Ralph acquires an oil and gas property interest for $100,000 in 2002. The estimate of recoverable units is 10,000 barrels of oil. The per-unit cost depletion amount is $10 ($100,000 ÷ 10,000). If 3,000 units are produced and 2,000 units are sold in 2002, the cost depletion amount is $20,000 (2,000 units × $10 per unit). If cost depletion is used because it exceeds the percentage depletion amount, the cost basis of the property is reduced to $80,000 ($100,000 − $20,000) at the beginning of 2003. If the estimate of remaining recoverable units is revised downward from 8,000 units in 2003 (10,000 − 2,000 units sold in 2002) to 5,000 units (including the 1,000 barrels produced but not sold in 2002), the property's $80,000 adjusted basis is divided by 5,000 units to arrive at a new per-unit cost depletion amount of $16 for 2003. This process is continued each year until the cost of the oil and gas property interest is fully depleted. ◀

REAL-WORLD EXAMPLE

Taxpayers are entitled to a depletion deduction if they have an economic interest in the property. This economic interest may be in the form of a royalty interest where a landowner receives a certain amount per unit extracted from her land, such as $10 for each barrel of oil. The landowner would be entitled to a depletion deduction based on the royalty income received.

PERCENTAGE DEPLETION METHOD. Percentage depletion generally offers substantial tax benefits for taxpayers in the natural resources industry. The purpose of allowing percentage depletion is to encourage persons to invest and/or operate in an industry that is both capital intensive and high risk but is also vital to our national interests. Percentage depletion may be used by taxpayers for a wide variety of natural resources, such as oil and gas, coal, gold, etc. However, the percentage depletion method has not been available to *large* oil and gas producers since 1974, but is still available to *small* oil and gas producers and royalty owners under a specific exemption in the law.[37] Percentage depletion is computed by multiplying the percentage depletion rate times the gross income from the property. However, the depletion amount may not exceed 50% of the taxable income from the property before depletion is deducted (100% for oil and gas properties).[38] Percentage depletion may not be calculated on any lease bonus, advance royalty, or other amount payable without regard to production from the property.

When using either cost depletion or percentage depletion, the amount of the depletion deduction reduces the basis of the natural resource property. Once the basis of depletable property has been reduced to zero, a taxpayer may no longer claim depreciation using the cost depletion method. However, the taxpayer may continue to claim percentage depletion, even though subsequent percentage depletion will not reduce the basis of the property below zero. It should be apparent that percentage depletion is a very advantageous method because the amount of depletion that is allowed over the life of the property may exceed the property's cost.[39]

---

35 Sec. 612.

36 Sec. 611(a).

37 Sec. 613A(c). To be classified as a small oil and gas producer or royalty owner, the maximum depletable quantity is based on average daily production of not more than 1,000 barrels of oil or 6 million cubic feet of natural gas.

38 Sec. 613(a).

39 Depletion in excess of the adjusted basis of the property is a tax preference item under Sec. 57(a)(1).

Percentage depletion rates vary by the type of mineral. Depletion rates for selected minerals are as follows:

Mineral	*Depletion Rate*
Oil and gas	15%[40]
Coal, asbestos	10%
Gold, silver, copper, iron ore	15%
Sulphur and uranium	22%
Gravel, stone	5%

EXAMPLE I10-27 ▶ Carmen acquires an oil and gas property interest for $400,000 in the current year with 200,000 barrels of estimated recoverable oil. During the year, 10,000 barrels of oil are sold for $250,000. Intangible drilling and development costs amount to $100,000 and are expensed in the current year. Other expenses are $50,000. Cost depletion is $20,000 (10,000 × $2) in the current year. The computation of percentage depletion is as follows:

(1) Percentage depletion before taxable income limitation $250,000 × 0.15	$ 37,500
(2) Taxable income ceiling:	
Gross income	$250,000
Minus: Intangible drilling costs	(100,000)
Other expenses	(50,000)
Taxable income before depletion	$100,000
(3) Percentage depletion (lesser of (1) or (2))	$37,500

Carmen's depletion deduction is $37,500 because the percentage depletion amount is greater than the $20,000 of cost depletion. The adjusted basis of the property is reduced by $37,500, the amount of depletion actually claimed. ◀

HISTORICAL NOTE

An Arab oil embargo to the United States in 1973 created a situation where oil prices increased significantly. Consequently, most domestic U.S. oil producers reported huge profits. This situation contributed to the repeal of the percentage depletion allowance for large oil and gas producers.

KEY POINT

The use of the percentage depletion method permits recovery of more than the cost of the property.

TREATMENT OF INTANGIBLE DRILLING AND DEVELOPMENT COSTS

Intangible drilling and development costs (IDCs) may either be deducted as an expense or capitalized.[41] IDCs apply only to oil, gas, and geothermal wells and basically include all expenditures, other than the acquisition costs of the underlying property, that are incurred for the drilling and preparation of wells. If the IDCs are capitalized, the amounts are added to the property's basis for determining cost depletion, and the costs are written off through cost depletion. For a well that is nonproductive (i.e., a dry hole), an ordinary loss is allowed for any IDC costs that have been capitalized and not recovered through depletion. The amount of depletion claimed in a tax year equals the greater of the percentage depletion and cost depletion amounts. If IDCs are capitalized and cost depletion is thereby increased, little or no tax benefit may result because the percentage depletion may still produce a greater deduction than cost depletion. Therefore, it is generally preferable to expense the IDCs if the percentage depletion is expected to be more than the cost depletion and is used to compute the depletion allowance.

EXAMPLE I10-28 ▶ Penny acquires certain rights to oil and gas property in the current year for $1,000,000. In the current year Penny incurs $300,000 of IDCs. If the IDCs are capitalized, the basis for cost depletion purposes is $1,300,000. Assume that the cost depletion amounts are $100,000 in the current year if the IDCs are expensed and $130,000 if IDCs are capitalized. If the percentage depletion amount is $150,000, percentage depletion will be used because it is greater than either of the cost depletion amounts. Thus, the expensing of the IDCs permits the taxpayer to deduct the entire $300,000 of IDCs in the current year plus $150,000 of percentage depletion. ◀

---

[40] For small producers and royalty owners of oil and gas properties, there is a further limitation: the percentage depletion deduction may not exceed 65% of taxable income from all sources before the depletion deduction, Sec. 631A(d)(1).

[41] Sec. 263(c).

TAX PLANNING CONSIDERATIONS

ADDITIONAL COMMENT

A taxpayer who is attempting to report a profit in three out of five years in an attempt to avoid the hobby loss rules might want to use the alternative depreciation system.

ALTERNATIVE DEPRECIATION SYSTEM UNDER MACRS

In some instances, it may be preferable to elect to use the alternative depreciation system rather than the regular MACRS rules. For example, a taxpayer who anticipates losses during the next few years or who currently has NOL carryovers may elect to use the alternative depreciation system, which employs the straight-line method of depreciation over a longer recovery period.

EXAMPLE I10-29 ▶ Delta Corporation has substantial NOL carryovers that will expire if not used during the next few years. Delta Corporation anticipates it will not have taxable income for each of the next seven years if the regular MACRS rules are used to depreciate its fixed asset additions. In the current year, Delta Corporation acquires new machinery and equipment at a cost of $100,000. Depreciation deductions using the MACRS rules and a seven-year recovery period are $14,290 (0.1429 × $100,000). Depreciation deductions under the straight-line method using the alternative depreciation system (a 12-year life) and the half-year convention are only $4,167 [($100,000 ÷ 12 years) × 0.50 year]. The alternative depreciation system election increases taxable income in the current year by $10,123 and allows Delta Corporation to offset additional loss carryovers (which might otherwise expire) against this income amount. ◀

KEY POINT

In general, the option to capitalize or to expense applies only to drilling or development expenditures having no salvage value. For example, the cost of oil well pumps, oil storage tanks, and pipe lines would not be eligible for immediate expensing.

IDCs: CAPITALIZATION VERSUS EXPENSING ELECTION

Although most taxpayers elect to expense intangible drilling costs (IDCs), sometimes capitalization and amortization are preferable because of the effect of IDCs on the depletion deduction.

If IDCs are expensed, taxable income from the property is reduced. This may result in a smaller percentage depletion deduction because the percentage depletion claimed is limited to 100% of pre-depletion taxable income.

EXAMPLE I10-30 ▶ Gross income from an oil and gas property is $500,000. Expenses of $450,000 are incurred including $200,000 of IDCs. The percentage depletion deduction (before the 100% limitation) is $75,000 (0.15 × $500,000). The percentage depletion limitation is $50,000 (1.00 × $50,000

WHAT WOULD YOU DO IN THIS SITUATION?

Your CPA firm has a long-standing tax client named Widgets R Us, Incorporated (WRU). WRU has been a worldwide leader in widget technology for years and continues to expand its global market share of Class A Crystal Widgets through a substantial program of basic research and development of widget crystallization processes. You have always advised WRU as to which of these expenditures qualify as research and experimental (R&E) expenditures. In addition, you have always given timely advice as to when to expense rather than capitalize these expenditures.

You are having your monthly tax conference with Ms. Ima Worthmore, president of WRU, and Mr. Stan Cunning, tax counsel of WMU, and Ms. Worthmore relates to you a conversation she had with the local manager of a competitor CPA firm, Ms. Ruth Less. Ms Less told Ms. Worthmore that she had discovered that WRU was one of the top spenders on research and development in the area and that her firm was "certified" to practice before the IRS and had experienced great success in gaining better R&E write-offs for comparable firms. Ms. Less went on to say that, "For you, for this one year only, we offer to prepare your tax returns on a contingent basis. We promise to save you at least $1 million dollars from what you are now paying the IRS through our better use of R&E write-offs and our fee will only be 30% of the tax savings!"

Ms. Worthmore was excited that WRU might pay considerably less taxes under the plan of Ruth Less and is somewhat perturbed at you because you had not brought this tax opportunity to her attention. She wants your firm to provide her with a counteroffer. How do you ethically respond to your client's request to match or better Ms. Ruth Less' proposal?

net income before depletion). Thus, the percentage depletion that is allowed is limited to the lesser of the percentage depletion earned ($75,000) or the limitation ($50,000), or $50,000. If the IDCs are capitalized, the percentage depletion deduction limitation is $250,000 (1.00 × $250,000 net income before depletion) and the taxpayer could claim the full $75,000 of percentage depletion earned. ◀

If the IDCs are capitalized, the property's basis for cost depletion purposes is increased and the IDCs are amortized as part of the cost depletion. However, if cost depletion is less than percentage depletion, the benefits from IDC amortization may be lost because percentage depletion is used.

EXAMPLE I10-31 ▶ Assume the same facts as in Example I10-30, except that the IDCs are capitalized and assume that cost depletion is increased from $20,000 to $45,000 due to the capitalization of the IDCs. Because percentage depletion is $75,000 and cost depletion is only $45,000, percentage depletion is used and the benefits from capitalizing IDCs (i.e., $25,000 increase in cost depletion) are lost. The election to capitalize the IDCs did result in an increase in the amount of percentage depletion from $50,000 to $75,000. ◀

USE OF UNITS OF PRODUCTION DEPRECIATION

Many times, the MACRS depreciation system requires taxpayers to use a recovery period that is much longer than the actual useful life of the asset. For example, assume a taxpayer uses a machine in her business that is required to be classified as 7-year property under MACRS. However, the machine is operated 24 hours a day, seven days a week and will completely wear out in two years. The use of the 7-year recovery period substantially understates the depreciation for the machine. Under Sec. 168(f), taxpayers may exclude property from the MACRS system if the property is depreciated under the unit-of-production method or any other method not expressed in terms of years. Therefore, if a taxpayer can express the useful life of the machine in terms of some other base than years (such as machine hours, units produced, etc.), it may be possible for the taxpayer to depreciate the machine over a much shorter period than the seven years required under MACRS.

STRUCTURING A BUSINESS COMBINATION

REAL-WORLD EXAMPLE

A taxpayer purchased a business that owned retail franchises. It was the opinion of the IRS that the amounts paid in excess of the value of the net assets represented a nondepreciable "indivisible asset." However, the taxpayer was able to show that retail franchises have limited useful lives, and was able to amortize the excess costs. *Super Food Services, Inc. v. U.S.*, 24 AFTR 2d 69-5309, 69-2 USTC ¶ 9558 (7th Cir., 1969).

Tax planning needs to be conducted to ensure favorable tax consequences for the acquiring company if the assets of the acquired company are purchased as part of a business combination. The sales agreement must specify the amounts that have been paid for the tangible depreciable and nondepreciable assets and the intangible assets and the reporting requirements of Sec. 1060 must be complied with. Under the requirements of Sec. 1060, both the transferor and the transferee are bound by their written agreement as to the allocation of the purchase price to individual assets unless the IRS determines that such allocation is not appropriate. The amounts paid for the tangible assets should be documented by appraisals and evidence of negotiations between the buyer and seller. Within reason, the purchaser should attempt to allocate as much of the total price to the tangible depreciable assets. The purchaser should also consider allocating part of the purchase price to amortizable Sec. 197 intangible assets such as goodwill, a covenant not to compete, patents, copyrights, licenses, and customer lists because such asset costs are recovered over a 15-year period.

COMPLIANCE AND PROCEDURAL CONSIDERATIONS

IDC ELECTION PROCEDURES

The IDC election is made in the initial year that the expenditures are incurred. No formal statement or form is required. The expensing election is made by merely deducting the IDCs on the tax return.[42] If the costs are capitalized, cost depletion merely reflects the capitalized IDC costs.

[42] Reg. Sec. 1.612-4(d).

REPORTING COST RECOVERY, DEPRECIATION, DEPLETION, AND AMORTIZATION DEDUCTIONS

If an individual is engaged in a trade or business as a sole proprietor, depreciation, cost recovery, depletion, and amortization deductions are initially computed and reported on Form 4562 (Depreciation and Amortization) and the totals are then carried to Schedule C. Depletion and depreciation on rental properties are reported on Schedule E instead of Schedule C if the taxpayer is an investor. Depreciation on employee business property is reported on Form 2106. Separate Form 4562s are required for each different activity.

The election to expense property under Sec. 179 is made by claiming the deduction on Part I of Form 4562. The taxpayer must specify the items of property and the portion of the cost for each asset being expensed. Form 4562 is not required of individuals and non-corporate taxpayers (including S corporations) when filing their 2001 tax returns if the depreciation deduction is for assets, other than listed property, placed in service before 2001. In such cases, the depreciation deduction is entered directly on Form 1040 or other equivalent tax forms. However, even though a Form 4562 may not be required to be filed with the return, detailed depreciation records must still be maintained by the taxpayers to support the deduction.

EXAMPLE I10-32 ▶ George Jones, SSN 277-32-6542, is a building trade contractor who owns the following properties:

- Specialized utility repair truck (5-year property that is not listed property under Sec. 280F(d)(4)), costing $20,000, acquired on February 15, 2001. The election to expense under Sec. 179 is made for $1,000.
- Office equipment (7-year property), costing $23,000, acquired on May 10, 2001. The election to expense under Sec. 179 is made for $20,000.
- Patent, costing $10,000, that was acquired on June 1, 2001 when it had a remaining legal life of 17 years.
- ACRS deduction for assets placed into service before 1987 is $2,000.
- MACRS deduction for assets placed into service before 2001 is $8,000.

Jones has taxable income (before the Sec. 179 deduction and the deduction for one-half of self-employment taxes paid under Sec. 164(f)) of $60,000. The cost-recovery, depreciation, and amortization amounts are reported on Form 4562 and Schedule C, respectively, and are shown in Figures I10-1 and I10-2. ◀

RESEARCH AND EXPERIMENTAL EXPENDITURES

ADDITIONAL COMMENT

Once the election to expense R&E expenditures has been made, it is applicable to all R&E expenditures paid or incurred in the current year and all subsequent years.

The election to expense or to defer R&E expenditures is made by attaching a statement to the tax return for the first tax year in which the expenditures are incurred.[43] As previously discussed in the text, the capitalization method is not an election and applies only if no election is made in the initial year. Once a method has been adopted, the taxpayer is required to obtain the permission of the IRS to change to another method.

PROBLEM MATERIALS

DISCUSSION QUESTIONS

I10-1 Which of the following assets are subject to either amortization, depreciation, or cost recovery? Explain.

a. An automobile held for personal use.
b. Excess amounts paid in a business combination that are attributable to goodwill.
c. Excess amounts paid in a business combination that are attributable to customer lists that have a limited useful life.
d. A patent that has been created internally and has a legal life of 17 years.
e. Land that is being held for investment purposes.
f. A covenant not to compete which is entered into by the buyer and seller of a business.

I10-2 Rick is a sole proprietor who has a small business that is currently operating at a loss. He would like to discontinue depreciating the fixed assets of the

[43] Reg. Sec. 1.174-3(b)(1).

Form **4562** | Department of the Treasury, Internal Revenue Service (99)

Depreciation and Amortization
(Including Information on Listed Property)

▶ See separate instructions. ▶ Attach this form to your return.

OMB No. 1545-0172 | **2001** | Attachment Sequence No. **67**

Name(s) shown on return	Business or activity to which this form relates	Identifying number
George Jones	Building Trade Contractor	277-32-6542

Part I — Election To Expense Certain Tangible Property Under Section 179
Note: *If you have any "listed property," complete Part V before you complete Part I.*

1	Maximum dollar limitation. If an enterprise zone business, see page 2 of the instructions	1	$24,000
2	Total cost of section 179 property placed in service (see page 2 of the instructions)	2	43,000
3	Threshold cost of section 179 property before reduction in limitation	3	$200,000
4	Reduction in limitation. Subtract line 3 from line 2. If zero or less, enter -0-	4	-0-
5	Dollar limitation for tax year. Subtract line 4 from line 1. If zero or less, enter -0-. If married filing separately, see page 2 of the instructions	5	24,000

	(a) Description of property	(b) Cost (business use only)	(c) Elected cost
6	Office Equipment	23,000	23,000
	Truck	20,000	1,000

7	Listed property. Enter amount from line 27	7	
8	Total elected cost of section 179 property. Add amounts in column (c), lines 6 and 7	8	24,000
9	Tentative deduction. Enter the smaller of line 5 or line 8	9	24,000
10	Carryover of disallowed deduction from 2000 (see page 3 of the instructions).	10	
11	Business income limitation. Enter the smaller of business income (not less than zero) or line 5 (see instructions)	11	24,000
12	Section 179 expense deduction. Add lines 9 and 10, but do not enter more than line 11	12	24,000
13	Carryover of disallowed deduction to 2002. Add lines 9 and 10, less line 12 ▶	13	

Note: *Do not use Part II or Part III below for listed property (automobiles, certain other vehicles, cellular telephones, certain computers, or property used for entertainment, recreation, or amusement). Instead, use Part V for listed property.*

Part II — MACRS Depreciation for Assets Placed in Service Only During Your 2001 Tax Year (Do not include listed property.**)**

Section A—General Asset Account Election

14 If you are making the election under section 168(i)(4) to group any assets placed in service during the tax year into one or more general asset accounts, check this box. See page 3 of the instructions ▶ ☐

Section B—General Depreciation System (GDS) (See page 3 of the instructions.)

(a) Classification of property	(b) Month and year placed in service	(c) Basis for depreciation (business/investment use only—see instructions)	(d) Recovery period	(e) Convention	(f) Method	(g) Depreciation deduction
15a 3-year property						
b 5-year property		19,000	5 yr.	HY	MACRS	3,800
c 7-year property						
d 10-year property						
e 15-year property						
f 20-year property						
g 25-year property			25 yrs.		S/L	
h Residential rental property			27.5 yrs.	MM	S/L	
			27.5 yrs.	MM	S/L	
i Nonresidential real property			39 yrs.	MM	S/L	
				MM	S/L	

Section C—Alternative Depreciation System (ADS) (See page 5 of the instructions.)

(a)	(b)	(c)	(d)	(e)	(f)	(g)
16a Class life					S/L	
b 12-year			12 yrs.		S/L	
c 40-year			40 yrs.	MM	S/L	

Part III — Other Depreciation (Do not include listed property.**)** (See instructions beginning on page 5.)

17	GDS and ADS deductions for assets placed in service in tax years beginning before 2001	17	8,000
18	Property subject to section 168(f)(1) election	18	
19	ACRS and other depreciation	19	2,000

Part IV — Summary (See page 6 of the instructions.)

20	Listed property. Enter amount from line 26	20	
21	**Total.** Add deductions from line 12, lines 15 and 16 in column (g), and lines 17 through 20. Enter here and on the appropriate lines of your return. Partnerships and S corporations—see instructions	21	37,800
22	For assets shown above and placed in service during the current year, enter the portion of the basis attributable to section 263A costs	22	

For Paperwork Reduction Act Notice, see page 9 of the instructions. Cat. No. 12906N Form **4562** (2001)

FIGURE I10-1 ▶ FORM 4562

Part V **Listed Property** (Include automobiles, certain other vehicles, cellular telephones, certain computers, and property used for entertainment, recreation, or amusement.)

Note: *For any vehicle for which you are using the standard mileage rate or deducting lease expense, complete* ***only*** *23a, 23b, columns (a) through (c) of Section A, all of Section B, and Section C if applicable.*

Section A—Depreciation and Other Information (Caution: *See page 7 of the instructions for limits for passenger automobiles.)*

23a Do you have evidence to support the business/investment use claimed? ☐ **Yes** ☐ **No** **23b** If "Yes," is the evidence written? ☐ **Yes** ☐ **No**

(a) Type of property (list vehicles first)	(b) Date placed in service	(c) Business/ investment use percentage	(d) Cost or other basis	(e) Basis for depreciation (business/investment use only)	(f) Recovery period	(g) Method/ Convention	(h) Depreciation deduction	(i) Elected section 179 cost
24 Property used more than 50% in a qualified business use (see page 6 of the instructions):								
		%						
		%						
		%						
25 Property used 50% or less in a qualified business use (see page 6 of the instructions):								
		%				S/L -		
		%				S/L -		
		%				S/L -		

26 Add amounts in column (h). Enter the total here and on line 20, page 1 . . . . **26**

27 Add amounts in column (i). Enter the total here and on line 7, page 1 . . . . **27**

Section B—Information on Use of Vehicles

Complete this section for vehicles used by a sole proprietor, partner, or other "more than 5% owner," or related person.
If you provided vehicles to your employees, first answer the questions in Section C to see if you meet an exception to completing this section for those vehicles.

	(a) Vehicle 1		(b) Vehicle 2		(c) Vehicle 3		(d) Vehicle 4		(e) Vehicle 5		(f) Vehicle 6	
28 Total business/investment miles driven during the year (**do not** include commuting miles—see page 2 of the instructions)												
29 Total commuting miles driven during the year												
30 Total other personal (noncommuting) miles driven												
31 Total miles driven during the year. Add lines 28 through 30 . . .												
	Yes	**No**	**Yes**	**No**	**Yes**	**No**	**Yes**	**No**	**Yes**	**No**	**Yes**	**No**
32 Was the vehicle available for personal use during off-duty hours?												
33 Was the vehicle used primarily by a more than 5% owner or related person?												
34 Is another vehicle available for personal use?												

Section C—Questions for Employers Who Provide Vehicles for Use by Their Employees

Answer these questions to determine if you meet an exception to completing Section B for vehicles used by employees who **are not** more than 5% owners or related persons (see page 8 of the instructions).

	Yes	**No**
35 Do you maintain a written policy statement that prohibits all personal use of vehicles, including commuting, by your employees?		
36 Do you maintain a written policy statement that prohibits personal use of vehicles, except commuting, by your employees? See page 8 of the instructions for vehicles used by corporate officers, directors, or 1% or more owners		
37 Do you treat all use of vehicles by employees as personal use?		
38 Do you provide more than five vehicles to your employees, obtain information from your employees about the use of the vehicles, and retain the information received?		
39 Do you meet the requirements concerning qualified automobile demonstration use? (See page 8 of the instructions.) . .		

Note: *If your answer to 35, 36, 37, 38, or 39 is "Yes," do not complete Section B for the covered vehicles.*

Part VI **Amortization**

(a) Description of costs	(b) Date amortization begins	(c) Amortizable amount	(d) Code section	(e) Amortization period or percentage	(f) Amortization for this year
40 Amortization of costs that begins during your 2001 tax year (see instructions beginning on page 8):					
Patent	6-1-2001	10,000	167	17yr	343
41 Amortization of costs that began before your 2001 tax year				**41**	
42 **Total.** Add amounts in column (f). See page 9 of the instructions for where to report . .				**42**	343

Form **4562** (2001)

FIGURE I10-2 ▶ FORM 4562 (CONTINUED)

SCHEDULE C (Form 1040)

Department of the Treasury Internal Revenue Service (99)

Profit or Loss From Business

(Sole Proprietorship)

▶ Partnerships, joint ventures, etc., must file Form 1065 or Form 1065-B.

▶ Attach to Form 1040 or Form 1041. ▶ See Instructions for Schedule C (Form 1040).

OMB No. 1545-0074

2001

Attachment Sequence No. **09**

Name of proprietor: George Jones | Social security number (SSN): 277 32 6542

A Principal business or profession, including product or service (see page C-1 of the instructions): Building Trade Contractor

B Enter code from pages C-7 & 8 ▶

C Business name. If no separate business name, leave blank.

D Employer ID number (EIN), if any

E Business address (including suite or room no.) ▶ 1998 Natchamp Blvd
City, town or post office, state, and ZIP code: Lexington, KY 40506

F Accounting method: (1) ☑ Cash (2) ☐ Accrual (3) ☐ Other (specify) ▶

G Did you "materially participate" in the operation of this business during 2001? If "No," see page C-2 for limit on losses ☐ Yes ☐ No

H If you started or acquired this business during 2001, check here ▶ ☐

Part I Income

1	Gross receipts or sales. **Caution.** If this income was reported to you on Form W-2 and the "Statutory employee" box on that form was checked, see page C-2 and check here ▶ ☐	1	
2	Returns and allowances	2	
3	Subtract line 2 from line 1	3	
4	Cost of goods sold (from line 42 on page 2)	4	
5	**Gross profit.** Subtract line 4 from line 3	5	
6	Other income, including Federal and state gasoline or fuel tax credit or refund (see page C-3)	6	
7	**Gross income.** Add lines 5 and 6 ▶	7	

Part II Expenses. Enter expenses for business use of your home only on line 30.

8	Advertising	8		19	Pension and profit-sharing plans	19	
9	Bad debts from sales or services (see page C-3)	9		20	Rent or lease (see page C-4):		
				a	Vehicles, machinery, and equipment	20a	
10	Car and truck expenses (see page C-3)	10		b	Other business property	20b	
11	Commissions and fees	11		21	Repairs and maintenance	21	
12	Depletion	12		22	Supplies (not included in Part III)	22	
				23	Taxes and licenses	23	
13	Depreciation and section 179 expense deduction (not included in Part III) (see page C-3)	13	37,800	24	Travel, meals, and entertainment:		
				a	Travel	24a	
14	Employee benefit programs (other than on line 19)	14		b	Meals and entertainment		
15	Insurance (other than health)	15		c	Enter nondeductible amount included on line 24b (see page C-5)		
16	Interest:						
a	Mortgage (paid to banks, etc.)	16a		d	Subtract line 24c from line 24b	24d	
b	Other	16b		25	Utilities	25	
17	Legal and professional services	17		26	Wages (less employment credits)	26	
18	Office expense	18		27	Other expenses (from line 48 on page 2)	27	343

28	**Total expenses** before expenses for business use of home. Add lines 8 through 27 in columns ▶	28	
29	Tentative profit (loss). Subtract line 28 from line 7	29	
30	Expenses for business use of your home. Attach **Form 8829**	30	
31	**Net profit or (loss).** Subtract line 30 from line 29. • If a profit, enter on **Form 1040, line 12,** and **also** on **Schedule SE, line 2** (statutory employees, see page C-5). Estates and trusts, enter on Form 1041, line 3. • If a loss, you **must** go to line 32.	31	
32	If you have a loss, check the box that describes your investment in this activity (see page C-6). • If you checked 32a, enter the loss on **Form 1040, line 12,** and **also** on **Schedule SE, line 2** (statutory employees, see page C-5). Estates and trusts, enter on Form 1041, line 3. • If you checked 32b, you **must** attach **Form 6198.**	32a ☐ All investment is at risk. 32b ☐ Some investment is not at risk.	

For Paperwork Reduction Act Notice, see Form 1040 instructions. Cat. No. 11334P **Schedule C (Form 1040) 2001**

FIGURE I10-3 ▶ FORM 1040, SCHEDULE C

Part III **Cost of Goods Sold** (see page C-6)

33 Method(s) used to value closing inventory: a ☐ Cost b ☐ Lower of cost or market c ☐ Other (attach explanation)

34 Was there any change in determining quantities, costs, or valuations between opening and closing inventory? If "Yes," attach explanation ☐ Yes ☐ No

35	Inventory at beginning of year. If different from last year's closing inventory, attach explanation	35	
36	Purchases less cost of items withdrawn for personal use	36	
37	Cost of labor. Do not include any amounts paid to yourself	37	
38	Materials and supplies	38	
39	Other costs	39	
40	Add lines 35 through 39	40	
41	Inventory at end of year	41	
42	**Cost of goods sold.** Subtract line 41 from line 40. Enter the result here and on page 1, line 4	42	

Part IV **Information on Your Vehicle.** Complete this part **only** if you are claiming car or truck expenses on line 10 and are not required to file Form 4562 for this business. See the instructions for line 13 on page C-3 to find out if you must file.

43 When did you place your vehicle in service for business purposes? (month, day, year) ▶ ____ / ____ / ____

44 Of the total number of miles you drove your vehicle during 2001, enter the number of miles you used your vehicle for:

a Business ________ b Commuting ________ c Other ________

45 Do you (or your spouse) have another vehicle available for personal use? ☐ Yes ☐ No

46 Was your vehicle available for personal use during off-duty hours? ☐ Yes ☐ No

47a Do you have evidence to support your deduction? ☐ Yes ☐ No

b If "Yes," is the evidence written? ☐ Yes ☐ No

Part V **Other Expenses.** List below business expenses not included on lines 8–26 or line 30.

Patent Amortization	343
48 Total other expenses. Enter here and on page 1, line 27 — 48	343

Schedule C (Form 1040) 2001

FIGURE I10-4 ▶ FORM 1040, SCHEDULE C (CONTINUED)

business for the next few years in order to carry the deductions over to a future period. What tax consequences would result if Rick implements the plan to discontinue depreciation and then sells some of the depreciable assets several years later?

I10-3 Rita acquired a personal residence two years ago for $120,000. In the current year she purchases another residence and attempts to sell her former residence. Due to depressed housing conditions in the town where she used to live, Rita is unable to sell the house. Her former residence is now being offered for sale at $100,000 (its current FMV according to real estate appraisal experts). Rita has decided to rent the house rather than "give it away." She states that renting the house on a permanent basis will permit her to write off the original $120,000 investment over its useful life and to, therefore, recoup her investment. What restrictions in the tax law may prevent her from accomplishing this objective? Explain.

I10-4 Daytona Corporation, a manufacturing corporation, acquires the following business assets in the current year:

- Furniture
- Plumbing fixtures
- Land
- Goodwill and a trademark acquired in the acquisition of a business
- Automobile
- Heavy truck
- Machinery
- Building used in manufacturing activities

a. Which of the assets above are eligible for depreciation under the MACRS rules or amortization under Sec. 197?

b. What recovery period should be used for each of the assets above that come under the MACRS rules or under Sec. 197?

I10-5 Robert, a sole proprietor who uses the calendar year as his tax year, acquires a business machine on August 30, 2002 for $10,000 and sells certain business equipment on the same date for $2,000. No other property was acquired in 2002. The equipment that is sold was acquired on January 5, 1998 for $20,000.

a. What amount (if any) of depreciation deductions should be allowed under MACRS for the newly acquired machine and for the equipment that is sold in 2002 assuming both assets are 7-year property and the expensing election under Sec. 179 was not made.

b. How would your answer in a. change if the business machine was acquired on December 1, 2002 rather than August 30, 2002?

I10-6 Is a depreciation deduction allowed under the MACRS rules for depreciable real estate (used in a business or held for investment) in the year the property is sold? If so, explain how it is calculated.

I10-7 Jose is considering acquiring a new luxury automobile costing $44,000 that will be used 100% in his business. The salesperson at the automobile dealership states that Jose will be entitled to both of the following tax benefits in the initial year (2002):

- A deduction for $24,000 of the acquisition cost under Sec. 179.
- A $4,000 ($20,000 × 0.20) MACRS depreciation deduction.

a. Are the salesperson's assertions relative to the tax benefits accurate? Explain.

b. How would your answer to Part a differ (if any) if the automobile were used only 60% for business purposes?

c. How would your answer to Part a differ (if any) if Jose instead was to lease the automobile?

I10-8 Explain why the straight-line MACRS method (using the ADS) might be preferable over the regular MACRS method under the following circumstances:

a. Ray incurs NOLs in his business for a number of years and has NOL carryovers he would like to use.

b. Rhonda's marginal tax rate is 15% but is expected to increase to 36% in three years.

I10-9 Rudy is considering whether to make the election under Sec. 179 to expense $24,000 (2002) of the acquisition cost related to certain fixed asset additions. What advantages are associated with the Sec. 179 election?

I10-10 Your client is a self-employed attorney who is considering the purchase of a $25,000 automobile that will be used 80% of the time for business and a $4,000 personal computer that will be used 100% of the time for business, but is located in his home.

a. What depreciation methods and recovery periods may be used under MACRS for the automobile and the personal computer?

b. How would your answer to Part a change if your client were an employee and the computer and automobile were not required as a condition of employment?

c. What tax consequences occur in Part a if the business use of the personal computer or the automobile decreases to 50% or less in a succeeding year? Explain.

I10-11 Sarah enters into a three-year lease of an automobile in March of the current year that is used exclusively in her business. The automobile's FMV was $40,000 at the inception of the lease. Sarah made ten monthly lease payments of $600 each during the current year. Is Sarah able to avoid the luxury automobile restrictions on depreciation by leasing instead of purchasing the automobile? Explain. (The inclusion amount for Sarah's automobile under the current Rev. Proc. is $202.)

I10-12 What difference does it make for income tax purposes whether an intangible asset (1) is acquired in connection with a business acquisition, (2) is acquired by the purchase of an individual asset (e.g., a patent), or (3) is created internally? Explain.

I10-13 In January of the current year, Park Corporation incurs $34,000 of legal costs associated with the obtaining of a patent that was developed internally and has a legal life of 17 years. Park also acquired for cash the net assets of Central Corporation on January 1, for $1,000,000. The following assets are specified in the purchase agreement:

Land	$200,000
Goodwill and going concern value	100,000
Covenant not to compete	50,000
Licenses	125,000
Customer lists	25,000
Inventory	100,000
Equipment and other tangible depreciable business assets	400,000
Total	$1,000,000

a. What tax treatment should be accorded the intangible assets?
b. Assuming that you were advising Park Corporation during the negotiations before the drafting of the purchase agreement, what suggestions would you make regarding the allocation of the total purchase price to the individual assets? How could the purchase price of individual assets be substantiated?

I10-14 Why do most taxpayers prefer to currently expense research and experimental expenditures?

I10-15 In a business combination, why does the buyer generally prefer to allocate as much of the purchase price to short-lived depreciable assets, ordinary assets such as inventory, and Sec. 197 intangible assets?

I10-16 Explain the difference between cost depletion and percentage depletion. Which of these two methods will generally provide the largest deduction?

I10-17 Simon acquires an interest in an oil property for $50,000. Intangible drilling costs (IDCs) in the initial year are $10,000. Cost depletion is $5,000 if the IDCs are expensed and $6,000 if the costs are capitalized. Percentage depletion is $15,000 if the IDCs are expensed and $20,000 if the costs are capitalized. The difference in the percentage depletion amounts is due to the 100% taxable income limitation.
a. What method (i.e., immediate write-off or capitalization and amortization) should be elected for the treatment of the IDCs in the initial year if Simon wants to maximize his deductions?
b. Why are intangible drilling costs expensed by most taxpayers?

ISSUE IDENTIFICATION QUESTIONS

I10-18 Georgia Corporation acquires a business automobile for $30,000 on December 31 of the current year but does not actually place the automobile into service until January 1 of the following year. What tax issues should Georgia Corporation consider?

I10-19 Paula is planning to acquire by purchase or by lease a $50,000 luxury automobile. She anticipates that the business use will be 60% for the first two years but will decline to 40% in years three through five. Currently, Paula's marginal tax rate is 15% but she anticipates that her marginal tax rate will be 36% after a few years. What tax issues should Paula consider relative to the decision to purchase or lease the automobile?

I10-20 In the current year Coastal Corporation acquires all of the net assets of Acorn Corporation for $2,000,000. The purchase agreement allocated the following amounts to the individual assets and liabilities:

Land and building	$1,400,000
Accounts receivable	200,000
Inventory	300,000
Goodwill	400,000
Patents (remaining legal life of ten years)	100,000
Covenant not to compete	200,000
Liabilities	(600,000)
Total	$2,000,000

What tax issues should Coastal Corporation consider relative to the asset acquisitions?

I10-21 Weiskopf, a sole proprietor and a calendar-year taxpayer, purchased $100,000 of equipment during the current year, as follows:

	Cost	*Recovery Period*
March 1	$25,000	7 years
September 18	$40,000	7 years
October 2	$35,000	5 years

Weiskopf's CPA, to maximize the depreciation deduction, elected to take Sec. 179 depreciation on the March 1 property of $24,000. What tax issue should be considered with respect to the total depreciation deduction for the current year?

PROBLEMS

I10-22 ***Allowed Versus Allowable Depreciation.*** Sandy acquires business machinery (which qualifies as 7-year MACRS property) on July 15, 2000 for $10,000. In 2000, Sandy claims a $1,429 depreciation deduction, but Sandy fails to claim any depreciation deduction in 2001 or 2002. The machine is sold on July 1, 2002 for $6,000.

a. What is the adjusted basis of the machine on the sale date?
b. How much gain or loss is recognized on the sale of the machine?

I10-23 ***Conversion of Personal Asset to Business Use.*** Sid purchased an automobile for personal use on January 18, 2000 for $10,000. On January 1, 2002, Sid starts a small business and begins to use the automobile exclusively in the business. The automobile's FMV on this date is $6,000. MACRS depreciation deductions are taken in 2002 based on a 5-year recovery period.

a. What is the automobile's basis for depreciation purposes when converted to business use in 2002?
b. What is Sid's depreciation deduction in 2002?

I10-24 ***MACRS Depreciation.*** Small Corporation acquires and places in service the following business assets in 2002 (no other assets were placed in service during the year):

- Light truck costing $10,000 (on December 15) with a 5-year MACRS recovery period
- Machinery costing $50,000 (on February 1) with a 7-year MACRS recovery period
- Land costing $60,000 (on July 1)
- Building costing $100,000 (on December 1) with a 39-year MACRS recovery period
- Equipment costing $40,000 (acquired on December 24, but not placed in service until January of the following year) with a 5-year MACRS recovery period

a. What is the MACRS depreciation deduction for each asset in 2002 (assume Sec. 179 was not elected for any asset)?
b. What is the MACRS deduction for each asset in 2002 if the machinery is instead acquired on November 1?
c. Assume the facts in Part a. If Small Corporation sells the machinery on June 15, 2004 and sells the building on October 20, 2004, compute the depreciation deductions for 2003 and 2004 and the adjusted basis for these two assets at the respective dates of sale.

I10-25 ***MACRS Depreciation.*** Ted is in the real estate business and owns rental property. On May 12, 2002, Ted purchased a small apartment building for $180,000. In addition, Ted purchased 5-year recovery period personal property costing $30,000 on April 1, 2002, and 7-year recovery period personal property costing $40,000 on November 1 of 2002. (Assume that Ted does not elect the Sec. 179 expensing election and uses the MACRS rules.) What is the amount of the MACRS depreciation deduction for each asset in 2002 and 2003?

I10-26 ***Sec. 179 Expensing Election and MACRS Depreciation.*** Tish acquires and places in service a business machine with a 7-year MACRS recovery period in July 2002. The machine costs $30,000, and Tish elects to expense the maximum amount allowable under Sec. 179. The total cost of qualifying property placed in service during the year amounts to $214,000. Tish's taxable income (before deducting the Sec. 179 amount and one-half of self-employment taxes paid) is $4,000.

a. What is the amount Tish can deduct under Sec. 179 in 2002?
b. What is the amount of MACRS depreciation deduction for the machine in 2002?

I10-27 ***ACRS and MACRS Dispositions.*** Tampa Corporation disposes of the following assets in 2002:

	Date Acquired	*Date Sold*	*Original Cost Basis*	*Depreciation/ Cost-Recovery Method*	*Recovery Period (Years)*	*Sales Price*
Auto	1/1/99	12/1/02[a]	9,000	MACRS	5	1,200
Equipment	1/6/99	9/1/02[a]	20,000	MACRS	7	9,500
Building	4/1/86	12/10/02	100,000	ACRS	19	240,000

[a] Assume that the half-year convention was used in the year of acquisition and Sec. 179 expense election was not made.

a. What is the amount of cost recovery or depreciation deduction for each asset in 2002?
b. Compute the gain or loss on each asset that was sold in 2002.

I10-28 ***Sec. 179 and MACRS Depreciation.*** Thad acquires a machine for use in his business on April 1, 2002 for $32,000. The MACRS rules with a 7-year recovery period are used, and Thad elects to expense $24,000 of the acquisition cost under Sec. 179.

a. What is the machine's basis for regular depreciation purposes and the depreciation deduction in 2002?
b. Assume Thad depreciates the machine in 2002 and 2003 and then sells the machine on October 5, 2004 for $15,000. Compute Thad's depreciation deductions for 2002 and 2004, the adjusted basis of the machine on October 5, 2004, and the gain or loss on the sale.

I10-29 ***Sec. 179 and Mid-Quarter Convention.*** Todd acquired two pieces of equipment for use in his business during the year as follows:

Item	*Date Acquired*	*Recovery Period*	*Cost*
Equipment A	April, 2002	5-year	$50,000
Equipment B	November, 2002	7-year	$50,000

Todd elects to expense $24,000 of the acquisition cost under Sec. 179 and wants to maximize the amount of depreciation for the year. Compute Todd's depreciation in order to yield the highest depreciation possible. (Hint: The mid-quarter convention is calculated after taking Sec. 179 on any asset or assets)

I10-30 ***Straight-Line Depreciation.*** Long Corporation has been unprofitable for several years and has substantial NOL carryovers. Therefore, the company policy has been to use the straight-line MACRS rules for property acquisitions. The following assets are acquired, held, or sold in 2002:

	Date Acquired	*Date Sold*	*Original Cost Basis*	*Selling Price*	*Depreciation Method*	*Recovery Period (Years)*
Equipment	6/1/02	—	$40,000	—	SL	7
Light truck	7/1/99	12/1/02	30,000	$12,000	SL	5
Furniture	3/1/00	—	10,000	—	SL	7
Automobile	7/1/00	12/1/02	12,000	10,000	SL	5

Assume the expensing election under Sec. 179 is not made.

a. What is the depreciation deduction for each asset in 2002?
b. What amount of gain or loss is recognized on the properties sold in 2002?

I10-31 ***Mixed Personal/Business Use.*** Trish, a self-employed CPA and calendar-year taxpayer, acquires an automobile and a personal computer in 2002. Pertinent data include the following:

Asset	*Date Acquired*	*Original Cost Basis*	*Portion of Business Usage*	*Sec. 179 Election*
Automobile	1/2/02	$11,000	60%	No
Personal computer	7/1/02	4,000	40%	No

For each asset calculate the MACRS current year depreciation deduction.

I10-32 ***Employee Listed Property.*** Assume the same facts as in Problem I10-31, except that Trish is an employee and uses the automobile and personal computer on employment-related activities. While both assets are helpful to Trish in performing her job duties, her employer does not require employees to purchase a car or a personal computer as a condition of employment. What is the amount of depreciation for each asset?

I10-33 *Recapture of Depreciation Deductions Due to Personal Use.* Tammy acquires an automobile for $10,000 on July 1, 2000. She uses the automobile partially for business purposes during the 2000–2002 period. The percentage of business use is as follows: 2000–70%; 2001–70%; 2002–40%. The MACRS rules with a 5-year recovery period are used for all years.

a. What is the amount of the MACRS depreciation deduction for 2000? 2001? 2002?
b. What is the amount of recapture of previously claimed depreciation deductions (if any) that must take place in 2002?

I10-34 *Luxury Auto Limitations.* Lutz Corporation acquires a luxury automobile on July 1, 2002 for $20,000 that is used 100% for business-use. The Sec. 179 expensing election is not made but the company chooses to claim the maximum amount of MACRS depreciation deductions available. What is the depreciation deduction amount for 2002, 2003, 2004, and any subsequent years?

I10-35 *Luxury Auto Limitations.* Tracy acquires a luxury automobile on March 1, 2002, that is used 80% of the time in his business and 20% of the time for personal use. The automobile cost $30,000, and no amounts are expensed under Sec. 179. What is the depreciation amount for 2002–2004 and any subsequent years?

I10-36 *Luxury Auto Limitations—Leasing.* Troy enters into a 3-year lease of a luxury auto on January 1, 2001, for use 80% in business and 20% for personal use. The FMV of the automobile at the inception of the lease is $40,500 and twelve monthly lease payments of $600 were made in 2001 and 2002.

a. What is the amount of lease payments that are deductible in 2001 and 2002?
b. What portion, if any, of the "inclusion amount" must be included in gross income in 2001 and 2002?
c. How would your answers to Parts a and b change if the FMV of the auto were instead $15,000 and the monthly lease payments were $200.

I10-37 *Goodwill.* On January 1 of the current year, Palm Corporation acquires the net assets of Vicki's unincorporated business for $600,000. The tangible net assets have a $300,000 book value and $400,000 FMV. The purchase agreement states that Vicki will not compete with Palm Corporation by starting a new business in the same area for a period of five years. The stated consideration received by Vicki for the covenant not to compete is $50,000. Other intangible assets included in the purchase agreement are as follows:

- Goodwill: $70,000
- Patents (12-year remaining legal life): $30,000
- Customer list: $50,000

a. How would Vicki's assets be recorded for tax purposes by Palm Corporation?
b. What is the amortization amount for each intangible asset in the current year?

I10-38 *R&E Expenditures.* Park Corporation incurs the following costs in the initial year of doing business:

Materials and supplies for research laboratory	$ 80,000
Utilities and depreciation on research laboratory and equipment	40,000
Costs of acquiring another person's patent for a new product	20,000
Market research salaries for surveys relative to proposed new products	60,000
Labor and supplies for quality control tests	50,000
Research costs subcontracted to a local university	35,000
Total	$285,000

Park's controller states that all of these costs are qualifying R&E expenditures and that the company policy is to expense such amounts for tax purposes in the year they are incurred. Which of these expenditures are deductible as R&E costs under Sec. 174?

I10-39 *R&E Expenditures.* In 2002, Phoenix Corporation acquires a new research facility and hires several scientists to develop new products. No new products are developed until 2003, although the following expenditures were incurred in 2002:

Laboratory materials	$ 40,000
Research salaries	80,000
Overhead attributable to the research facility	30,000
R&E equipment placed into service (5-year MACRS recovery period)	100,000
Total	$250,000

a. What is Phoenix Corporation's deduction for R&E expenditures in 2002 and 2003 if the expensing method is elected?
b. How would your answer to Part a change if the deferral and amortization method were elected and the amortization period were 60 months?

I10-40 ***Computer Software.*** The Phillips Corporation, a construction company that specializes in home construction, uses special computer software to schedule its jobs and keep track of job costs and uses generic software for bookkeeping and spreadsheet analysis. During 2002, Phillips Corporation had the following transactions relating to computer software:

- The corporation purchased a new computer system on May 12, 2002 for $15,000. The system included computer hardware and built-in computer software valued at $3,000. The corporation has never separated computer software from the hardware in prior years when a computer system was purchased.
- The corporation separately purchased new bookkeeping software on September 1, 2002 for $5,760.
- On June 1, 2002, Phillips Corporation acquired another home building company to strengthen its position in higher-priced homes. The total purchase price was $700,000 and the allocation to specific assets was as follows:

Equipment	$500,000
Goodwill	150,000
Computer software	50,000

What amount can the Phillips Corporation deduct in 2002 with respect to computer software?

I10-41 ***Cost Depletion.*** Tina acquires an oil and gas property interest for $200,000 in the current year. The following information about current year operations is supplied for purposes of computing the amount of Tina's depletion and IDC deductions:

Estimated recoverable units	20,000
Units produced	6,000
Units sold	4,000
IDCs	$20,000
Percentage depletion (after limitations)	$25,000

a. What is the cost depletion amount if the IDCs are expensed?
b. What is the cost depletion amount if the IDCs are capitalized?
c. How much depletion is deducted on the tax return?
d. Should the IDCs be capitalized or expensed? Explain.

I10-42 ***Percentage Depletion.*** Tony has owned an oil and gas property for a number of years. The following information is provided about the property's operations in the current year:

Gross income	$500,000
Minus: Expenses (including IDCs of $100,000)	(300,000)
Taxable income (before depletion)	$200,000
Cost depletion (if IDCs are expensed)	$ 20,000
Cost depletion (if IDCs are capitalized)	$ 30,000

a. What is the percentage depletion amount if the IDCs are expensed?
b. What is the percentage depletion amount if the IDCs are capitalized?
c. What is the depletion deduction amount assuming that the IDCs are expensed?
d. Based on the information above, which method should be used for the IDCs? Explain.

COMPREHENSIVE PROBLEM

I10-43 John and Ellen Brite (SSN 265-32-1497 and 571-07-7345, respectively) own an unincorporated specialty electrical lighting retail store, Brite-On. Brite-On had the following assets on January 1, 2001:

Assets	*Cost*
Building purchased April 1, 1994	$100,000
7-year recovery period equipment purchased January 10, 1997	30,000
Inventory valued using FIFO method:	
Inventory: 4,000 light bulbs	$5/bulb

The Brites purchased a competitor's store on March 1, 2001 for $107,000. The purchase price included the following:

	FMV
Store building	$60,000
Land	18,000
5-year recovery period equipment	11,000
Inventory: 3,000 light bulbs	$6/bulb

On June 30, 2001 the Brites sold the 7-year recovery period equipment for $12,000. Brite-On leased a $30,000 car for $500/month beginning on January 1, 2001. The car is used 100% for business and the car was driven 14,000 miles during the year. Brite-On sold 8,000 light bulbs at $15/bulb during the year. Also, Brite-On made additional purchases of 4,000 light bulbs in August and September, 2001 at $7/bulb. Brite-On had the following revenues (in addition to the sales of light bulbs) and additional expenses:

Service revenues	$40,000
Interest on business loans	4,000
Auto expenses (gas, oil, etc.)	3,800
Taxes and licenses	3,300
Utilities	2,800

John and Ellen also had some personal expenses:

Medical bills	$ 4,500
Real property taxes	3,800
Home mortgage interest	9,000
Charitable contributions (cash)	600

They had interest income on a bank savings account of $275. John and Ellen made four $5,000 quarterly estimated tax payments.

Additional Facts:

- Assume that an election is made under Sec. 179 to expense the cost of the 5-year equipment that was acquired in 2001.
- The latest IRS lease inclusion table requires the Brites to include $119 in their gross income due to the leased automobile restrictions.

Compute the Brite's taxable income for 2001.

TAX STRATEGY PROBLEM

I10-44 Stan Bushart works as a customer representative for a large corporation. Stan's job entails traveling to meet with customers and uses his personal car 100% for business use. In 2001, Stan has decided to acquire a new car and is trying to decide whether to buy or lease the car. After bargaining with several car dealers, Stan has agreed to a price of $30,000 for the car. If he buys the car, he will borrow the entire $30,000 at an annual interest rate of 8% and pay monthly payments over 60 months. If he leases the car, his lease payment will be $450 per month for 60 months with a residual amount of $10,000 at the end of the lease. Therefore, Stan will pay the $450 each month for 60 months and at the end of the lease, has the option of purchasing the car for $10,000. For income tax purposes, assume a lease inclusion amount of $400 per year and Stan's marginal income tax rate is 31%. From a financial standpoint, is Stan better off leasing or buying the car?

For purposes of your analysis, if Stan purchases the car, assume he sells the car for $10,000 at the end of five years. If he leases the car, assume he merely turns the car in at the end of the lease.

TAX FORM/RETURN PREPARATION PROBLEMS

I10-45 Thom Jones (SSN 277-31-7253) is an unincorporated manufacturer of widgets. He uses the LCM method to value his inventory and has the following transactions during the year:

Sales (less returns and allowances)	$800,000
Costs of goods sold	500,000
Office expenses	10,000
Depreciation and Sec. 179 deduction (see the schedule below)	
Legal services	4,000
Salary expenses	36,000
Travel expenses	30,000
Repairs	20,000

Mr. Jones's depreciation schedule is as follows:

Office furniture held for business use is purchased on April 15, 2001 and an election is made to expense the maximum amount possible under Sec. 179.	$30,000
Depreciation on other recovery property acquired and placed into service on August 1, 2001:	
5-year recovery period property (computers-not listed property)	6,000
7-year recovery period property (equipment)	14,000
Depreciation on assets purchased prior to 2001	28,000

Complete Form 4562 and Schedule C of Form 1040 for 2001 for Mr. Jones.

I10-46 Using the facts in Problem I10-43, complete 2001 Form 1040, Schedules A and C, and Forms 4562 and 4797.

CASE STUDY PROBLEM

I10-47 Able Corporation is a manufacturer of electrical lighting fixtures. Able is currently negotiating with Ralph Johnson, the owner of an unincorporated business, to acquire his retail electrical lighting sales business. Johnson's assets that are to be acquired include the following:

Assets	*Adjusted Basis*	*FMV*
Inventory of electrical fixtures	$ 30,000	$ 50,000
Store buildings	80,000	100,000
Land	40,000	100,000
Equipment: 7-year recovery period	30,000	50,000
Equipment: 5-year recovery period	60,000	100,000
Total	$240,000	$400,000

Mr. Johnson indicates that a total purchase price of $1,000,000 in cash is warranted for the business because of its high profitability and strategic locations and Able has agreed that the business is worth $1,000,000. Despite the fact that both parties attribute the excess payment to be for goodwill, Able would prefer that the $600,000 excess amount be designated as a 5-year covenant not to compete so that he can amortize the excess over a 5-year period.

You are a tax consultant for Able who has been asked to make recommendations as to the structuring of the purchase agreement and the amounts to be assigned to individual assets. Prepare a client memo to reflect your recommendations.

I10-48 The Margate Corporation acquired an automobile with an acquisition cost of $30,000 for use in its business in 2000. During this time, Margate Corporation was experiencing a seasonal decline in sales. Several employees were laid off and the automobile was not immediately needed for any of the sales personnel. Instead of letting the new automobile sit in the corporate lot, the president decided to permit a corporate officer to use the automobile for personal use. The officer used the automobile in 2000 and 2001 only. In 2002, Margate Corporation has hired you as their new CPA (tax consultant). You learn about the officer's personal use of the corporate automobile that took place for the two prior years without proper accounting of the automobile to the IRS. As Margate Corporation's tax consultant, what actions (if any) should you take regarding the proper treatment of the automobile? What are your responsibilities as a CPA regarding this matter under the rules of the AICPA's *SSTS* No. 6? (See the *Statements on Standards for Tax Services (SSTS)* section in Chapter I15 and Appendix E for a discussion of *SSTS* No. 6.)

TAX RESEARCH PROBLEM

I10-49 The Mumme Corporation is a very successful and profitable manufacturing corporation. The corporation just completed the construction of new corporate offices, primarily for its top executives. The president and founder of the corporation, Mr. Timothy Couch, is an avid collector of artwork and has instructed that the lobby and selected offices be decorated with rare collections of art. These expensive works of art were purchased by the corporation in accordance with Couch's directives. Couch justified the purchase of these artworks on the premise that (1) they are excellent investments and should increase in value in the future, (2) they provide an appropriate and impressive office atmosphere when current and prospective customers visit the corporation's offices, and (3) the artwork is depreciable property and the corporation will be able to take sizable writeoffs against its income. The Financial Vice-President of the corporation has requested your advice as to whether the works of art are, in fact, depreciable property. Prepare a research memorandum for the Financial Vice-President on this issue.

A partial list of research sources is provided below.

- *Rev. Rul. 68-232,* 1968-1 C .B. 70
- *Shauna C. Clinger,* 60 T.C.M. 598 (1990).
- *Simon v. Comr.,* 103 T.C. 247 (1994), *aff'd,* 95-2 USTC ¶50,552 (2d Cir. 1995) *nonacq*. 1996-2 C.B.I.
- *Liddle v. Comr.,* 103 T.C. 285 (1994), *aff'd,* 95-2 USTC ¶50,488 (3rd Cir. 1995)

CHAPTER 11

ACCOUNTING PERIODS AND METHODS

LEARNING OBJECTIVES

After studying this chapter, you should be able to

1. Explain the rules for adopting and changing an accounting period
2. Explain the differences among cash, accrual, and hybrid accounting
3. Determine whether specific costs must be included in inventory
4. Determine the amount of income to be reported from a long-term contract
5. Compute the gain to be reported from an installment sale
6. Compute the amount of imputed interest in a transaction
7. Determine the tax treatment of duplications and omissions that result from changes of accounting methods

CHAPTER OUTLINE

Accounting Periods...11-2
Overall Accounting Methods...11-7
Inventories...11-11
Special Accounting Methods...11-15
Imputed Interest...11-22
Change in Accounting Methods...11-26
Tax Planning Considerations...11-28
Compliance and Procedural Considerations...11-30

An **accounting method** is a system of rules and procedures that is used to determine the year in which income and expenses are reported for tax purposes. The accounting methods used in computing income for tax purposes generally must be the same as those used in keeping the taxpayer's books and records and determine *when* income and expenses are reported, not whether they are reported. Although the accounting methods used by a taxpayer do not necessarily affect the amount of income reported over the life of a business, they do affect the tax burden in two ways. First, selecting the appropriate accounting method can accelerate deductions or defer income recognition in order to postpone tax payments, and second, because of the progressive tax rate structure, taxpayers can save taxes by spreading income over several accounting periods rather than having income bunched into one period.

EXAMPLE I11-1 ▶ Jane, a taxpayer using the cash method of accounting, has a 27% marginal tax rate for 2002 and expects to have a 15% marginal tax rate in 2003. Jane plans to make a charitable contribution of $1,000 in January 2003. A contribution in 2003 will reduce Jane's tax by $150 (0.15 × $1,000), whereas a contribution in 2002 will reduce Jane's tax by $270 (0.27 × $1,000). Obviously Jane may wish to accelerate the contribution in order to reduce her tax liability. ◀

ACCOUNTING PERIODS

OBJECTIVE 1

Explain the rules for adopting and changing an accounting period

Taxable income is computed on the basis of the taxpayer's annual **accounting period**, which is ordinarily 12 months (either a calendar year or a fiscal year). A **fiscal year** is a 12-month period that ends on the last day of any month other than December. The tax year must coincide with the year used to keep the taxpayer's books and records. Taxpayers who do not have books (e.g., an individual with wage income) must use the calendar year.[1] A taxpayer with a seasonal business may find a fiscal year to be advantageous. During the slow season, inventories may be lower and employees are available to take inventory and perform other accounting duties associated with the year-end. The tax year is elected on the first tax return that is filed by a taxpayer and cannot be changed without consent from the IRS.[2]

A partnership generally must use the same tax year of the partners who own the majority (greater than 50%) of partnership income and capital. If a majority of partners do not have the same year, the partnership must use the tax year of its principal partners (those with more than a 5% interest in the partnership). If the principal partners do not have the same tax year, the partnership must use the taxable year that results in the least aggregate deferral of income to the partners.[3] An exception is made for partnerships that can establish to the satisfaction of the IRS a business purpose for having a different year.

The purpose of the strict rules for selecting accounting periods is to prevent partners from deferring partnership income by choosing a different tax year for the partnership. For example, calendar-year partners might select a partnership year that ends on January 31. Because partnership income is considered to be earned by the partners on the last day of the partnership's tax year, reporting the profits would thus be deferred 11 months because the partnership year ends after the partner's year. (See the section entitled Required Payments and Fiscal Years in this chapter for further discussion of the calendar-year requirement.)

A similar rule generally requires S corporations and personal service corporations to adopt a calendar year unless the corporation has a business purpose for electing a fiscal year.[4] Taxpayers willing to make required payments or distributions may choose a fiscal year. (See the Required Payments and Fiscal Years section in this chapter.)

STOP & THINK *Question:* The tax rules related to accounting periods essentially require most partnerships, S corporations, and personal service corporations to report on the calendar

[1] Sec. 441(g).
[2] Reg. Sec. 1.441-1(b)(4).
[3] Temp. Reg. Sec. 1.706-1T.
[4] Sec. 1378(a).

year basis. Of course, almost all individual taxpayers also report on the calendar year basis. What impact does this have on accountants?

Solution: The principal impact is a compression of tax compliance work into the "accounting busy season." A substantial portion of auditing and other accounting work also takes place shortly after the year end. As a result, these services are also compressed into the accounting busy season. The accounting profession has sought to have these tax rules changed, but has, at least so far, been unsuccessful.

An improper election to use a fiscal year automatically places the taxpayer on the calendar year.[5] Thus, if the first return is filed late because of oversight, the option to choose a fiscal year is lost.

EXAMPLE I11-2 ▶ City Corporation receives its charter in 2000 but does not begin operations until 2002. Tax returns are required for 2000 and 2001 as well as for 2002. Timely returns are not filed because the City's officers are unaware that returns must be filed for inactive corporations. Thus, City Corporation must use the calendar year. City Corporation may petition the IRS for approval to use a fiscal year. ◀

ADDITIONAL COMMENT
The use of a 52-53-week year aids in budgetary matters and statistical comparisons because a four-week period, unlike a calendar month, is a uniform, fixed period.

REAL-WORLD EXAMPLE
Merrill Lynch & Company uses a 52-53-week year ending on the last Friday in December.

TYPICAL MISCONCEPTION
It is sometimes mistakenly believed that a tax year can end on a day in the middle of the month.

While most tax years end on the last day of a month, the tax law allows taxpayers to use a tax year that always ends on the same day of the week, such as the last Friday in October. This means that the tax years will vary in length between 52 and 53 weeks. Taxpayers who regularly keep their books over a period that varies from 52 to 53 weeks may elect the same period for tax purposes. A 52-53-week taxable year must end either the last time a particular day occurs during a calendar month (e.g., the last Friday in October) or the occurrence of the particular day that is closest to the end of a calendar month (e.g., the Saturday closest to the end of November).[6] Under the first alternative, the year may end as many as six days before the end of the month, but must end within the month. Under the second alternative, the year may end as many as three days before or after the end of the month.

The 52-53-week year is especially useful to businesses with inventories. For example, a manufacturer might choose a 52-53-week year that ends on the last Friday in December to permit inventory to be taken over the weekend without interfering with the company's manufacturing activity. Similarly, wage accruals would be eliminated for a company with a weekly payroll if the payroll period always ends on Friday.

Although the 52-53-week year may actually end on a day other than the last day of the month, it is treated as ending on the last day of the calendar month for "effective date" changes in the tax law that would otherwise coincide with the year-end.

EXAMPLE I11-3 ▶ Eagle Corporation has adopted a 52-53-week year. Eagle's tax year begins on December 29, 2002. Assume that a new tax rate schedule applies to tax years beginning after December 31, 2002. The new tax rate schedule is applicable to Eagle because, in the absence of the 52-53-week year, its tax period would have started on January 1, 2003. ◀

REQUIRED PAYMENTS AND FISCAL YEARS

Virtually all C corporations (other than personal service corporations) have flexibility in choosing an accounting period. Other taxpayers, such as partnerships and S corporations, may use a fiscal year if they have an acceptable business purpose. However, most of these businesses are unable to meet the rather rigid business purpose requirements outlined by the IRS. As a result, these businesses report using the calendar year concentrating most tax work during the early months of the year. Concern over this problem led Congress to enact Sec. 444 which allows partnerships, S corporations, and personal service corporations (such as incorporated medical practices) to elect a taxable year that results in a tax deferral of three months or less (e.g., a partnership with calendar-year partners may elect a September 30 year end). This is called the **Sec. 444 election**. Furthermore, partnerships,

---

[5] *Q.A. Calhoun v. U.S.*, 33 AFTR 2d 74-305, 74-1 USTC ¶9104 (D.C. Va., 1973).

[6] Sec. 441(f).

S corporations, and personal service corporations may continue using the fiscal year they were using when the current law was passed in 1986 even if that fiscal year results in a deferral beyond three months.

ADDITIONAL COMMENT

The American Institute of Certified Public Accountants and accounting firms lobbied extensively for the provision that permits partnerships, S corporations, and personal service corporations to continue to use a fiscal year if annual required payments are made.

Partnerships and S corporations making the Sec. 444 election, however, must make annual required payments by April 15 of the following year. The purpose of the required payment is to offset the tax deferral advantage obtained when fiscal years are used.

The amount of the required payment is determined by multiplying the maximum tax rate for individuals plus 1% (i.e., 39.6% in 2002) times the previous year's taxable income times a deferral ratio.[7] The deferral ratio is equal to the number of months in the deferral period divided by the number of months in the taxable year. An adjustment is made for deductible amounts distributed to the owners during the year. If the amount due is $500 or less, no payment is required.

EXAMPLE I11-4 ▶ ABC Partnership begins operations on October 1, 2002 and elects a September 30 year-end under Sec. 444. The partnership's net income for the fiscal year ended September 30, 2003 is $100,000. ABC must make a required payment of $9,900 ($100,000 × 39.6% × 3⁄12) on or before April 15, 2004. ◀

The owners of businesses making such payments do not claim a credit for the amount paid. Instead, the partnership or S Corporation subtracts the previous year's required payment from the current year's required payment. If the result is negative, then the entity is entitled to a refund.

EXAMPLE I11-5 ▶ Assume the same facts as in Example I11-4 except that ABC Partnership's required payment for the year ended September 30, 2004 is $6,000. ABC is entitled to a refund of the difference of $3,900 ($9,900 − $6,000). ◀

Personal service corporations may elect a fiscal year if they make minimum distributions to shareholders during the deferral period.[8] Personal service corporations are incorporated medical practices and other similar businesses owned by individuals who provide their services through the corporation. In general, the rules prevent a distribution pattern that creates a tax deferral. This is achieved by requiring that the deductible payments made to owners during the deferral period be at a rate no lower than during the previous fiscal year.

EXAMPLE I11-6 ▶ Austin, Inc. is a personal service corporation of attorneys with a fiscal year ending September 30. For the year ended September 30, 2002 the company earned a profit of $480,000 before any salary payments to the owners. The entire profit, however, was paid out as wages to the owners, resulting in a taxable income of zero. To avoid penalty, Austin must pay salaries to its owners of no less than $120,000 ($480,000 × 3⁄12) during the period October 1, 2002 to December 31, 2002. ◀

An option allows personal service corporations to compute the amount of the minimum distribution by using a three-year average of income and distributions.

CHANGES IN THE ACCOUNTING PERIOD

KEY POINT

The use of a natural business year helps in the matching of revenue and expense because the business is normally in a maximum state of liquidity and the problems associated with making estimates involving uncompleted transactions are reduced to a minimum.

Once adopted, an accounting period cannot normally be changed without approval of the IRS.[9] The IRS will usually approve a change only if the taxpayer can establish a substantial business purpose for the change (e.g., changing to a natural business year).[10] A natural business year ends at or soon after the peak income earning period (e.g., the natural business year for a department store that has a seasonal holiday business may be on January 31). A business without a peak income period may not be able to establish a natural business year and may, therefore, be precluded from changing its tax year. In general, at least 25% of revenues must occur during the last two months of the year in order to qualify as a natural business year.

---

[7] Sec. 7519(b).

[8] Sec. 280H(k).

[9] Sec. 442.

[10] Rev. Proc. 74-33, 1974-2 C.B. 489 and Rev. Proc. 87-32, 1989-2 C.B. 32.

EXAMPLE I11-7 ▶ USA Department Store's sales reach their peak during the holiday season in December. During January the department store further reduces its inventory through storewide clearance sales. USA elects a "natural" business year-end of January 31 because its inventory levels are lowest at the end of January. Also, USA meets the prescribed test because at least 25% of its revenues for the year occur in December and January. ◀

REAL-WORLD EXAMPLE

J.C. Penney, K mart, and Wal-Mart all use an accounting period ending January 31.

In a few instances IRS approval is not required to change to another accounting period.

- A newly married person may change tax years to conform to that of his or her spouse so that a joint return may be filed. The election must be made in either the first or second year after the marriage date.[11]
- A change to a 52-53-week year that ends with reference to the same calendar month in which the former tax year ended.[12]
- A taxpayer who erroneously files tax returns using an accounting period other than that on which his or her books are kept is not required to obtain permission to file returns for later years based on the way the books are kept.[13]
- A corporation meeting the following specified conditions may change without IRS approval: (1) There has been no change in its accounting period within the past ten calendar years, (2) the resulting year does not have a net operating loss (NOL), (3) the taxable income for the resulting short tax year when annualized is at least 90% of the taxable income for the preceding full tax year, and (4) there is no change in status of the corporation (such as an S corporation election).[14]
- An existing partnership can change its tax year without prior approval if the partners with a majority interest have the same tax year to which the partnership changes or if all principal partners who do not have such a tax year concurrently change to such a tax year.[15]

There is one instance, however, when a change in tax years is required: A subsidiary corporation filing a consolidated return with its parent corporation must change its accounting period to conform with its parent's tax year.

Application for permission to change accounting periods is made on Form 1128, Application for Change in Accounting Period, on or before the due date of the return including extensions. The application must be sent to the Commissioner of the IRS, Washington, D.C.

The IRS may establish certain conditions for the taxpayer to meet before it approves the change to a new tax year. For example, the IRS has ruled that if the short period that results from a change involves a NOL greater than $50,000, the taxpayer may have to forgo a carryback of the loss.[16]

RETURNS FOR PERIODS OF LESS THAN 12 MONTHS

Most income tax returns cover an accounting period of 12 months. On two occasions, however, a taxpayer's accounting period may be less than 12 months: when the taxpayer's first or final return is filed and when the taxpayer changes accounting periods.

Taxpayers filing an initial tax return and executors filing a taxpayer's final return or corporations filing their last return are not required to annualize the year's income, nor are personal exemptions or tax credits prorated. These returns are prepared and filed, and taxes are paid as though they are returns for a 12-month period ending on the last day of the short period. An exception permits the final return of a decedent to be filed as though the decedent lived throughout the entire tax year.[17]

---

[11] Reg. Sec. 1.442-1(e). A statement should be attached to the resulting short period return indicating that the change is being made.

[12] Reg. Sec. 1.441-2(c)(2). A statement should be attached to the first return filed under the election indicating that the change is being made.

[13] Rev. Rul. 58-256, 1959-1 C.B. 215.

[14] Reg. Sec. 1.442-1(c). A statement should be attached to the return indicating that each condition is met.

[15] Reg. Sec. 1.442-1(b)(2).

[16] Rev. Proc. 2000-11, 2000-1 C.B. 309.

[17] Reg. Sec. 1.443-1(a)(2).

EXAMPLE I11-8 ▶ ABC Partnership, which has filed its returns on a calendar-year basis, terminates on June 30, 2002. ABC's final return is due on October 15, 2002. ◀

EXAMPLE I11-9 ▶ Joy, a single individual who has filed her returns on a calendar-year basis, dies on June 30, 2002. Joy's final return is due on April 15, 2003. ◀

Taxpayers who change from one accounting period to another must annualize their income for the resulting short period. This prevents income earned during the resulting short period from being taxed at lower rates. Income is annualized as follows:

1. Determine modified taxable income. Individuals must compute their taxable income for the short period by itemizing their deductions (i.e., the standard deduction is not allowed) and personal and dependency exemptions must be prorated.[18]
2. Multiply modified taxable income by the following fraction:

$$\frac{12}{\text{Number of months in short period}}$$

3. Compute the tax on the resulting taxable income using the appropriate tax rate schedule.
4. Multiply the resulting tax by the following fraction:

$$\frac{\text{Number of months in short period}}{12}$$

EXAMPLE I11-10 ▶ Pat, a single taxpayer, obtains permission to change from a calendar year to a fiscal year ending on June 30, 2002. During the six months ending June 30, 2002, Pat earns $25,000 and has $5,000 in itemized deductions.[19]

Gross Income	$25,000
Minus: Itemized deductions	(5,000)
Personal exemption [(6 ÷ 12) × $3,000]	(1,500)
Modified taxable income	$18,500
Annualized income [(12 ÷ 6) × $18,500]	$37,000
Tax on annualized income	$ 6,336
Current tax [(6 ÷ 12) × $6,336]	$ 3,168 ◀

Topic Review I11-1 summarizes the available accounting periods and the rules for changing accounting periods.

STOP & THINK *Question:* Why are taxpayers required to annualize when they change tax years? What provision of the tax law creates this need?

Solution: A change of tax years results in a shortened filing period during the period the change takes place. For example, a taxpayer who changes from a calendar year to a June 30 year end reports income for only a 6-month period on the first return following the change. Less income is reported, and that income would be taxed at lower rates without annualization. Annualization is necessary because of the progressive tax rate structure.

[18] The exemptions are prorated as follows: exemptions × (number of months in the short period ÷ 12).

[19] An alternative method to compute the tax is provided in Sec. 443(b)(2) and Reg. Sec. 1.443-1(b)(2) whereby the taxpayer can elect to compute the tax for a 12-month period beginning on the first day of the short period and then convert the tax to a short-period tax.

Topic Review I11-1

Accounting Periods and Changes

AVAILABLE YEARS

- Available tax years include the calendar year, a fiscal year (a year that ends on the last day of any month other than December), and a 52-53-week year (a year that always ends on the same day of the week).
- A partnership must use the tax year of its partners unless the partnership can establish a satisfactory business purpose for having a different year or if the partnership makes required payments.
- Similar rules generally require S corporations and personal service corporations to adopt a calendar year unless the corporation has a business purpose for electing a fiscal year. Taxpayers willing to make required payments or distributions may choose a fiscal year ending on September 30, October 31, or November 30.

CHANGE IN ACCOUNTING PERIODS

- Once adopted, an accounting period normally cannot be changed without approval by the IRS. The IRS is more likely to approve a change to a natural business year. In general, at least 25% of revenues must occur during the last two months of the year in order to qualify as a natural business year.
- Taxpayers who change from one accounting period to another must annualize their income for the resulting short period. This prevents income earned during the resulting short period from being taxed at lower rates.

OVERALL ACCOUNTING METHODS

OBJECTIVE 2

Explain the difference between cash, accrual, accounting and hybrid accounting

A taxpayer's method of accounting determines the year in which income is reported and expenses are deducted. Taxable income must be computed using the method of accounting regularly used by the taxpayer in keeping his or her books if that method clearly reflects income.[20] Permissible overall accounting methods are

- Cash receipts and disbursements method (often called the cash method of accounting)
- Accrual method
- A combination of the first two methods, often called the hybrid method

KEY POINT

The Code provides the IRS with broad powers in ascertaining whether the taxpayer's accounting method clearly reflects income. It entitles the IRS to more than the usual presumption of correctness.

New taxpayers may generally choose any of the accounting methods listed above. However, the accrual method must be used for sales and cost of goods sold if inventories are an income-producing factor to the business. Exceptions permit businesses with inventories to use the cash method if their average annual gross receipts for the three preceding years do not exceed $1 million ($10 million if the taxpayer's principal business is not the sale of inventory).[21] The fact that an overall accounting method is used in one trade or business does not mean that the same method must be used in a second trade or business or for nonbusiness income and deductions.

EXAMPLE I11-11 ▶ Troy, a practicing CPA, also owns an appliance store. The fact that Troy uses the accrual method of reporting income from the appliance store, where inventories are an income-producing factor, does not preclude Troy from using the cash method to report income from his service-based accounting practice. Troy could also use the cash method for reporting nonbusiness income (such as dividends) and nonbusiness expenses (such as itemized deductions). ◀

REAL-WORLD EXAMPLE

It has been held that the cash method of accounting can be used where inventories are inconsequential. *Michael Drazen,* 34 T.C. 1070 (1960).

The term *method of accounting* is used to include not only overall methods of accounting listed above but also the accounting treatment of any item.[22]

CASH RECEIPTS AND DISBURSEMENTS METHOD

Most individuals and service businesses use the cash receipts and disbursements method of accounting. Taxpayers cannot use the cash method in a business for sales and cost of goods

[20] Sec. 446.

[21] Rev. Proc. 2000-22, 2000-1 C.B. 1008. This Revenue Procedure has been modified and superseded by Rev. Proc. 2001-10, I.R.B. 2001-2, 272 and Notice 2001-76, I.R.B. 2001-52, 613.

[22] Reg. Sec. 1.446-1(a)(1). Examples of accounting methods for specific items include Sec. 174, relating to research and experimentation expenses; Sec. 451, relating to reporting income from long-term contracts; and Sec. 453, relating to reporting income from installment sales.

sold if inventories are an income-producing factor.[23] However, as noted above, businesses with inventories are permitted to use the cash method if their average annual gross receipts for the three preceding tax years do not exceed $1 million. (See discussion of small taxpayer exception and Rev. Proc. 2001-10 in Chapter I3) C corporations and partnerships with a corporate partner may use the cash method only if their average annual gross receipts for the three preceding tax years do not exceed $5 million or if the business meets the requirements associated with providing personal services (i.e., if it is owned by professionals who are using the business to provide professional services).[24] Thus, a law or accounting firm can use the cash method even if its average receipts exceed $5 million.

Under the cash receipts and disbursements method of accounting, a taxpayer is required to report income for the tax year in which payments are actually or constructively received. While it might seem that receipts under the cash method of accounting should only be recognized if the taxpayer receives cash, this is not the case. The Regulations clearly provide that gross income under the cash method includes cash, property, or services.[25] Thus, if a CPA accepts a set of golf clubs as payment from a client for services rendered, the CPA must include the fair market value of the golf clubs in his gross income. However, an accounts receivable or other unsupported promise to pay is considered to have no value and, as a result, no income is recognized until the receivable is collected. Expenses are deducted in the year paid. Because the recognition of expense is measured by the flow of cash, a taxpayer can determine the year in which an expense is deductible by choosing when to make the payment. Individual taxpayers do not have the same opportunity to determine the year in which income is recognized, because the constructive receipt rule requires taxpayers to recognize income if a payment is available, even if actual payment has not been received. (See Chapter I3 for a discussion of constructive receipt.)

KEY POINT

A taxpayer using the cash method is entitled to certain deductions that do not involve current year cash disbursements, such as depreciation, depletion, and losses.

CAPITALIZATION REQUIREMENTS FOR CASH-METHOD TAXPAYERS. Taxpayers who use the cash receipts and disbursements method are required to capitalize fixed assets and to recover the cost through depreciation or amortization. The Regulations state that prepaid expenses must be capitalized and deducted over the life of the asset if the life of the asset extends substantially beyond the end of the tax year.[26] Typically, capitalization is required only if the life of the asset extends beyond the close of the tax year following the year of payment.[27]

EXAMPLE I11-12 ▶ On July 1, 2002, Acme Corporation, a cash basis, calendar-year taxpayer, pays an insurance premium of $3,000 for a policy that is effective July 1, 2002 to June 30, 2003. The full $3,000 is deductible in 2002. ◀

EXAMPLE I11-13 ▶ Assume the same facts as in Example I11-12, except that the premium covers a three-year period beginning July 1, 2002 and ending June 30, 2005. Acme Corporation may deduct $500 in 2002, $1,000 in 2003 and 2004, and $500 in 2005. ◀

One notable exception to the one-year rule denies a deduction for prepaid interest. Cash-method taxpayers must capitalize such amounts and allocate interest over the prepayment period. A special rule allows homeowners to deduct points paid on a mortgage used to buy or improve a personal residence. The payment must be an established business practice in the area and not exceed amounts generally charged for such home loans. (See Chapter I7 for a discussion of the deductibility of points.)

To be deductible, a payment must be more than just a refundable deposit. A taxpayer who has an option of cancelling delivery and receiving a refund of amounts prepaid is not normally entitled to deduct the amount of the deposit.

Payments can be made either by a check that is honored in due course or by the use of a credit card.[28] Payment by credit card is considered to be the equivalent of borrowing

---

[23] Reg. Sec. 1.471-1. However, Sec. 448(b) permits farmers to use the cash method even though they have inventories. Sec. 448(a) denies tax shelters the right to use the cash method even if they do not have inventories.

[24] Secs. 448(b) and (c).

[25] Reg. Sec. 1.446-1(c)(1)(i).

[26] Reg. Sec. 1.461-1(a)(1).

[27] *Bonaire Development Co.*, 76 T.C. 789 (1981), and *Martin J. Zaninovich v. CIR*, 45 AFTR 2d 80-1442, 80-1 USTC ¶9342 (9th Cir., 1980).

[28] Rev. Rul. 78-39, 1978-1 C.B. 73.

funds to pay the expense. However, a taxpayer's note is not the equivalent of cash, so if a cash method taxpayer gives a note in payment, he or she cannot take the deduction until the note is paid, even if the note is secured by collateral.[29]

ACCRUAL METHOD

There are two tests used to determine when an item of income must be reported or an expense deducted: the **all-events test** and the **economic performance test**.

ADDITIONAL COMMENT

The phrase *reasonable accuracy* means that approximate amounts are ascertainable. Although the word *accuracy* means exactness or precision, when it is used with the word *reasonable* it implies something less than an exact amount.

ALL-EVENTS TEST. An accrual-method taxpayer reports an item of income when "all events" have occurred that fix the taxpayer's right to receive the item of income and the amount can be determined with reasonable accuracy.[30] Similarly, an expense is deductible when all events have occurred that establish the fact of the liability and the amount of the expense can be determined with reasonable accuracy. For deductions, the all-events test is not satisfied until economic performance has taken place.

ECONOMIC PERFORMANCE TEST. Economic performance (of services or property to be provided to a taxpayer) occurs when the property or services are actually provided by the other party.

EXAMPLE I11-14 ▶ The owner of a professional football team provides medical benefits for injured players through insurance coverage. Economic performance occurs over the term of the policy rather than when the team enters into a binding contract with the insurance company or during the season when the player earns the right to medical benefits. Thus, a one-year premium is deductible over the year of the insurance coverage rather than over the term of the player's contract under which the benefit is earned. ◀

Similarly, if a taxpayer is obligated to provide property or services, economic performance occurs in the year the taxpayer provides the property or service.

EXAMPLE I11-15 ▶ Assume the same facts as in Example I11-14 except that medical benefits are required under the terms of a player's contract. Also, the team decides to pay medical costs directly. Economic performance occurs as the team actually provides the benefits. Thus, the deduction is permitted only as medical care is provided. ◀

REAL-WORLD EXAMPLE

Before the economic performance test was added to the tax law, a company engaged in strip mining coal was able to deduct the future land reclamation costs as the coal was mined because the liability was certain and the cost could be estimated. *Ohio River Collieries*, 77 T.C. 1369 (1981).

The requirement that economic performance take place before a deduction is allowed is waived if all of the following five conditions are met:

- The all-events test, without regard to economic performance, is satisfied.
- Economic performance occurs within a reasonable period (but in no event more than 8½ months) after the close of the tax year.
- The item is recurring in nature, and the taxpayer consistently treats items of the same type as incurred in the tax year in which the all-events test is met.
- The taxpayer is not a tax shelter.
- Either the amount is not material or the earlier accrual of the item results in a better matching of income and expense.[31]

EXAMPLE I11-16 ▶ To promote sales, Bass Corporation (a used car sales company) offers coupons to customers for three free car washes. Bass purchases the coupons from a local car wash. The coupons must be used within six months after the purchase of an automobile. If Bass uses the cash method, it could deduct the cost of the coupons at the time the payment for the coupons is made to the car wash. Under the accrual method and assuming the five conditions listed above are met, Bass could deduct the cost of the coupons as they are given to customers (instead of having to wait until the coupons are used). ◀

---

[29] *Frank D. Quinn Exec. v. CIR*, 24 AFTR 927, 40-1 USTC ¶9403 (5th Cir., 1940).

[30] Reg. Sec. 1.451-1(a). See Chapter I3 for a discussion of the all-events test as it applies to gross income.

[31] Sec. 461(h).

TYPICAL MISCONCEPTION

It is sometimes mistakenly believed that taxpayers can deduct warranty expenses and bad debts using the allowance method instead of the direct write-off method.

Reserves for items such as product warranty expense are commonly encountered in financial accounting. The all-events and economic performance tests prevent the use of such reserves for tax purposes. This is because the amount of such expense is not usually determinable with sufficient accuracy. Under prior law, taxpayers were permitted to use the allowance method for bad debts, but that method is no longer allowed for tax purposes.

HYBRID METHOD

Taxpayers may use a combination of accounting methods as long as income is clearly reflected. Taxpayers with inventories are required to use the accrual method to report sales and purchases if their average gross receipts for the three preceding years exceeds $1 million. These taxpayers may use the cash method to report other items of income and expense. To ensure that income is clearly reflected, certain restrictions have been placed on combining accounting methods.

KEY POINT

A taxpayer who uses the cash method in computing gross income from his or her business must use the cash method in computing expenses of such business.

Taxpayers who use the cash method of accounting in determining gross income from a trade or business must use the cash method for determining expenses of the same trade or business. Similarly, taxpayers who use the accrual method of accounting for expenses must use the accrual method in computing gross income from the trade or business.

The basic rules relating to accounting methods, the all-events test, and economic performance are summarized in Topic Review I11-2.

STOP & THINK

Question: If an accountant does tax work for an automobile dealer, in exchange for free use of an automobile, does the accountant have to report any income? Does it make a difference whether the accountant uses the automobile in her business? When is any taxable income reported?

Solution: The rental value of the automobile must be included in gross income. If the automobile is used in the accountant's business, a portion of the rental value is deductible as a business expense. Although it is not entirely clear, it seems that an accrual basis accountant would report income as tax services are provided to the dealer. A cash basis taxpayer would report income over the time the automobile is used.

Topic Review I11-2

Accounting Methods

AVAILABLE METHODS

- Permissible overall accounting methods are the cash receipts and disbursements method, the accrual method, and the hybrid method.
- The cash method is available to taxpayers without inventories and to taxpayers with inventories whose average gross receipts during the three preceding years was $1 million or less. C corporations whose average gross receipts fall between $1 and $5 million thresholds may use the cash method if they do not have inventories. C corporations (other than personal service corporations) may not use the cash method if their average gross receipts in the three preceding tax years exceed $5 million.

ALL-EVENTS TEST AND ECONOMIC PERFORMANCE TEST

- An accrual-method taxpayer reports an item of income when all events have occurred that fix the taxpayer's right to receive the item of income and when the amount of the item can be determined with reasonable accuracy.
- An expense is deductible when all events have occurred that establish that there is a liability and when the amount of the expense can be determined with reasonable accuracy. The all-events test is not satisfied until economic performance has taken place.
- Economic performance takes place when property or services are actually provided.

INVENTORIES

OBJECTIVE 3

Determine whether specific costs must be included in inventory

KEY POINT

Taxpayers cannot always use inventory methods for tax purposes that conform with generally accepted accounting principles.

In general, manufacturing and merchandising companies are required to use the accrual method of accounting for purchases and sales of merchandise. The inventory method used by a taxpayer must conform to the best accounting practice in the trade or business, and it must clearly reflect income. However, best accounting practices (synonymous with generally accepted accounting principles) and clear reflection of income (which is determined by the IRS) occasionally conflict. The Supreme Court has held that the standard of clear reflection of income prevails in a case where the two standards conflict. In the *Thor Power Tool Co.* case, the company wrote off the cost of obsolete parts for both tax and financial accounting purposes even though the parts were kept on hand and their selling price was not reduced.[32] Regulation Sec. 1.471-4(b) states that obsolete or other slow-moving inventory cannot be written down unless the selling price is also reduced.

Although the company's practice conformed with generally accepted accounting principles, it did not, according to the Supreme Court, clearly reflect income. Hence, generally accepted accounting principles are used only when the Regulations do not specify the treatment of an item or, alternatively, when the Regulations provide more than one alternative accounting method.

Taxpayers who value inventory at cost may write down goods that are not salable at their normal price (e.g., damaged, obsolete, or shopworn goods) only after the selling price has been reduced. Items may be valued at a bona fide selling price reduced by the direct cost of disposal.[33] The option to write down this type of merchandise is available even if the taxpayers use the LIFO inventory method.

EXAMPLE I11-17 ▶ Stone Corporation publishes books for small academic audiences in Sanskrit and other ancient languages. There is typically one printing of a few hundred or perhaps a thousand copies of each book. Stone may sell a few copies a year of each book. Only after several years can the Corporation determine whether they will ever sell all copies of a given work. Based upon the *Thor Power Tool Co.* case, Stone Corporation cannot write off unsold copies unless they are destroyed or otherwise disposed of, and they cannot write down unsold copies unless the selling price is reduced below cost. ◀

KEY POINT

The uniform capitalization rules, included in the Tax Reform Act of 1986, require the capitalization of significant overhead costs that previously were expensed.

DETERMINATION OF INVENTORY COST

Inventories may be valued at either cost or at the lower of cost or market value. Taxpayers who use the LIFO inventory valuation method (discussed later in this chapter) may not use the lower of cost or market method. In the case of merchandise purchased, cost is the invoice price less trade discounts, plus freight and other handling charges.

ETHICAL POINT

The UNICAP rules must be followed by taxpayers. To bring a business into compliance with these rules, the taxpayer may need to make certain estimates. SRTP No. 4 provides that a CPA may use a client's estimates if such use is generally acceptable or if it is impractical to obtain exact data. If a change in the overhead application rate is contemplated, it may be desirable to request IRS approval.

Unlike financial accounting, purchasing costs (e.g., salaries of purchasing agents), warehousing costs, packaging, and administrative costs related to these functions must be allocated between cost of goods sold and inventory. The costs that must be included in inventory are found in Sec. 263A and are referred to as the Uniform Capitalization rules (UNICAP). This requirement is applicable only to taxpayers whose average gross receipts for the three preceding years exceed $10 million.[34]

In the case of goods manufactured by the taxpayer, cost is determined by using the UNICAP rules, which may be thought of as an expanded version of the full absorption costing method. Thus, direct costing and prime costing are not acceptable inventory methods. Direct labor and materials along with manufacturing overhead must be included in inventory. Under UNICAP, the following overhead items are included in inventory:

- ▶ Factory repairs and maintenance, utilities, rent, insurance, small tools, and depreciation (including the excess of tax depreciation over accounting depreciation)
- ▶ Factory administration and officers' salaries related to production
- ▶ Taxes (other than the income tax)

---

[32] *Thor Power Tool Co. v. CIR*, 43 AFTR 2d 79-362, 79-1 USTC ¶9139 (USSC, 1979).

[33] Reg. Sec. 1.471-2(c).

[34] Sec. 263A(b)(2)(B).

- Quality control and inspection
- Rework, scrap, and spoilage
- Current and past service costs of pension and profit-sharing plans
- Service support such as purchasing, payroll, and warehousing costs

Nonmanufacturing costs (e.g., advertising, selling, and research and experimental costs) are not required to be included in inventory. Interest must be inventoried if the property is real property, long-lived property, or property requiring more than two years (one year in the case of property costing more than $1 million) to produce.

KEY POINT

Identifying the appropriate additional overhead costs to capitalize can be confusing and extremely time consuming.

The main difference between full absorption costing traditionally used for financial accounting purposes and UNICAP costing required for tax purposes is that UNICAP expands the list of overhead costs to include certain indirect costs that have not always been included in overhead for financial accounting purposes. For example, for financial accounting purposes, the costs of operating payroll and personnel departments have sometimes been considered sufficiently indirect or remote to justify omitting them from manufacturing overhead. This is true even though much of the effort of the payroll and personnel departments may be directed toward manufacturing operations. For simplicity and other reasons, overhead costs included in inventory for financial purposes are often limited to those incurred in the factory. UNICAP requires that costs associated with these departments be allocated between manufacturing and nonmanufacturing functions (e.g., sales, advertising, research and experimentation).

EXAMPLE I11-18 ▶ Best Corporation manufactures traditional style rocking chairs in a small factory with 34 employees. The office staff consists of four employees who handle payroll, receivables, hiring, and other office responsibilities. The sales staff includes three employees who travel the region selling to furniture and craft stores. The remaining 27 employees all work in the factory. Under UNICAP, factory costs including the wages of the 27 factory workers are generally all manufacturing costs. The costs associated with the sales staff are not manufacturing costs. This would include their compensation along with related costs such as travel. Office expenses including the wages paid to the four office workers can be allocated between manufacturing overhead and sales. Reasonable allocation methods are acceptable. One possibility might be to allocate office overhead between sales and manufacturing on a basis as simple as the number of employees in sales (3) and the number in manufacturing (27). Thus, 90% of the cost of the office operation could be treated as manufacturing-related and 10% sales-related. In such case, 90% of the office expenses would be allocated to manufacturing and 10% deducted as a period cost (i.e., selling expenses). The office expenses allocated to manufacturing would in turn be allocated between cost of sales and ending inventory. This allocation could be done on a basis as simple as multiplying the allocated office expenses by the number of chairs in ending inventory and dividing by the total number of chairs made during the year. ◀

A manufacturer may use standard costs to value inventory if any significant variance is reallocated pro rata to ending inventory and cost of goods sold.[35] Taxpayers may determine inventory costs by the following methods: specific identification method; first-in, first-out method (FIFO); last-in, first-out method (LIFO); or average cost method. A few taxpayers, such as an automobile or large appliance dealer, may find it practical to determine the specific cost of items in inventory. Most taxpayers, however, must rely on a flow of goods assumption (e.g., FIFO or LIFO). A discussion of the LIFO method is presented below.

LIFO METHOD. Many taxpayers use the LIFO cost flow assumption because, during inflationary periods, LIFO normally results in the lowest inventory value and hence the lowest taxable income. Once LIFO has been elected for tax purposes, the taxpayer's financial reports must also be prepared using LIFO.[36] This requirement to conform financial reporting often discourages companies from electing LIFO because lower earnings must be reported to shareholders. However, taxpayers may make footnote disclosure of the amount

[35] Reg. Sec. 1.471-11(d)(3).

[36] Sec. 472(c).

of net income that would have been reported under FIFO or other inventory methods.[37] Taxpayers may adopt LIFO by attaching a completed Form 970 (or by a statement acceptable to the IRS) to the return for the tax year in which the method is first used.

STOP & THINK

Question: As noted, many publicly held companies do not use LIFO inventory valuation. This is, in part, attributed to the fact that LIFO ordinarily results in lower reported income for accounting purposes than FIFO, and management prefers to report higher profits. Many small, closely-held companies also use FIFO even though their earnings are not reported to the public. Why wouldn't closely-held companies use LIFO?

Solution: There are a variety of reasons. Some businesses are very interested in how their financial statements look to banks and other lenders and to potential investors. In some industries, such as electronics, FIFO may actually provide lower inventory values. Also, LIFO cannot be used with lower of cost or market. As a result, some businesses may elect FIFO to be eligible to use lower of cost or market.

Perhaps, however, the main reason is that LIFO is more complex, and small businesses prefer to simplify their accounting. The advent of computers, accounting software, and bar codes may be having some impact on inventory valuation choices. Nevertheless, many accounting packages only track units on hand and sales revenue. They do not track inventory value (cost). Thus, the company must assign a value to inventory at year end, and the complexity of LIFO remains a deterrent.

REAL-WORLD EXAMPLE

An automobile dealer, using the dollar-value LIFO method in maintaining its inventory, was required to use one pool for new automobiles and a separate pool for new trucks. *Fox Chevrolet, Inc.*, 76 T.C. 708 (1981).

Recordkeeping under LIFO can be cumbersome. For this reason, taxpayers are permitted to determine inventories using "dollar-value" pools and government price indexes rather than by maintaining a record of actual costs.[38] Retailers use appropriate categories in the Consumer Price Index; other taxpayers use categories in the Producer Price Index. Taxpayers using the index method must divide their inventories into one or more pools (groups of similar items). Thus, a department store might create separate pools for automobile parts, appliances, clothing, furniture, and other products. Dividing inventory into pools can be critical because of the different inflation rates associated with various goods and because, if a particular pool is depleted, the taxpayer loses the right to use the lower prices associated with past layers. An important exception permits taxpayers with average annual gross receipts of $5 million or less for the current and two preceding tax years to use the **simplified LIFO method.**[39] The simplified LIFO method uses a single LIFO pool, thereby avoiding problems with multiple pools.

EXAMPLE I11-19 ▶

In 2002 King Department Store changes its inventory method from FIFO to LIFO. Because King's gross receipts have never exceeded $5 million, the simplified LIFO method is available. King's year-end inventories under FIFO are as follows:

2001	$100,000
2002	$130,000

Assume the 2001 price index is 120% and the 2002 index is 125%. King must convert its 2002 inventory to 2001 prices.

$$\frac{120\%}{125\%} \times \$130{,}000 = \$124{,}800$$

A base period inventory of $100,000 is established. The increase in inventory (the 2002 layer) is valued at 2002 prices.

Base inventory (2001)	$100,000
Plus: 2002 layer [(125% ÷ 120%) × ($124,800 − $100,000)]	25,833
2002 ending inventory	$125,833

Assume the 2003 inventory valued under FIFO is $136,000 and the 2003 price index is 130%. The 2003 inventory is converted to 2001 prices.

[37] Reg. Sec. 1.472-2(e).
[38] Sec. 472(f).
[39] Sec. 474(c).

$$\frac{120\%}{130\%} \times \$136{,}000 = \$125{,}538$$

The 2003 increase in inventory (the 2003 layer) is valued at 2003 prices.

Base inventory (2000)	$100,000
2002 layer	25,833
2003 layer	800[a]
2003 ending inventory	$126,633

[a] [(130% ÷ 120%) × ($125,538 − $124,800)].

◀

ADDITIONAL COMMENT

For tax purposes the lower of cost or market method must ordinarily be applied to each separate inventory item, but for financial accounting purposes it can be applied using an aggregate approach.

LOWER OF COST OR MARKET METHOD. Inventory may be valued at the **lower of cost or market.** This option is available to all taxpayers other than those who determine cost using the LIFO method.[40] The term *market* refers to replacement cost. On the date an inventory is valued, the replacement cost of each item in the inventory is compared with its cost. The lower figure is used as the inventory value. The lower of cost or market method must ordinarily be applied to each separate item in the inventory.

Recall the *Thor Power Tool,* case (discussed earlier in this chapter) in which the Supreme Court distinguished market value from expected selling price. **Market value** is the price at which the taxpayer can replace the goods in question. Replacement cost is used in the lower of cost or market determination. Obsolete or other slow-moving inventory can be written down below replacement cost only if the selling price has been reduced.

CYCLE INVENTORY VALUATION. Computer technology, including bar codes and software developments, enables businesses to maintain real-time perpetual inventory records. Many businesses, especially those with multiple locations, do not attempt to count all inventory items on the last day of the taxable period. Instead they count inventory following a scheduled cycle. At year-end, businesses adjust quantities shown in perpetual records for shrinkage since the most recent physical count utilizing estimates based on past experiences. The IRS challenged this practice unsuccessfully arguing that the adjustments failed the "all events" test which requires that amounts must be determined with reasonable accuracy.[41] In midst of the litigation, Congress specifically permitted the method in instances where "the taxpayer makes proper adjustment to such inventories and its estimation method [for] actual shrinkage."[42]

WHAT WOULD YOU DO IN THIS SITUATION?

INVENTORY VALUATION

Jack is a new tax client. He says he and his previous accountant did not get along very well. Jack owns an automobile dealership with sales of $12 million. He has provided you with most of the information you need to prepare his tax return, but he has not yet given you the year-end inventory value. You have completed much of the work on his return, but cannot complete it without the inventory figure. You have called Jack three times about the inventory. Each time he has interrupted, and asked you what his tax liability will be at alternative inventory levels. What problem do you see?

[40] Reg. Secs. 1.471-2(b) and (c).

[41] *Wal-Mart Stores Inc. v. CIR*, 82 AFTR 2d 5601, 98-2 USTC ¶50,645 (8th Cir., 1998), *Dayton Hudson Corp. v. CIR*, 82 AFTR 2d 5610, 98-2 USTC ¶50,644 (8th Cir., 1998), and *Kroger Co.*, 1997 RIA T.C. Memo ¶97,002, 73 TCM 1637.

[42] Sec. 471(b).

SPECIAL ACCOUNTING METHODS

The term *method of accounting* is used to include not only overall methods of accounting (i.e., cash, accrual, and hybrid) but also the accounting treatment of specific items. Special rules have been established for two types of transactions that cover long periods of time. One rule applies to installment sales (a sale in which final payment is not received until a subsequent tax year) and a separate set of rules applies to long-term contracts (construction and similar contracts that are not completed in the same year they are started). These special rules permit taxpayers to report income from this type of transaction when they have the wherewithal to pay the tax (i.e., the year in which payment is received).

LONG-TERM CONTRACTS

OBJECTIVE 4

Determine the amount of income to be reported from a long-term contract

Long-term contracts include building, installation, construction, or manufacturing contracts that are not completed in the same tax year in which they began.[43] A manufacturing contract is long-term only if the contract involves the manufacture of either a unique item not normally carried in finished goods inventory or items that normally require more than 12 calendar months to complete. Contracts for services (architectural, accounting, legal, and so on) do not qualify for long-term contract treatment.[44]

EXAMPLE I11-20 ▶ Diamond Corporation manufactures two types of airplanes: small, general aviation planes that require approximately six months to complete and large jet aircrafts sold to airlines that require two years to complete. Diamond maintains an inventory of the small planes but manufactures the large planes to contract specification. Diamond can use long-term contract accounting only for the large planes. Assume Diamond also offers aircraft design assistance to the government and others who seek such services. The long-term contract method of accounting is not available for such services. ◀

HISTORICAL NOTE

The use of the completed contract method was severely restricted in the Tax Reform Act of 1986 because Congress found that several large corporations, particularly those with large defense contracts, had significant deferred taxes attributable to this method. Many of these companies had extremely low or negative tax rates for several years.

ADDITIONAL COMMENT

In general, a construction contract must involve what has historically been thought of as construction which includes erecting buildings, building dams, roads, and power plants.

The accounting method selected by a taxpayer must be used for all long-term contracts in the same trade or business.[45] In general, the income and expenses associated with long-term contracts may be accounted for by using either the **percentage of completion method** or the **modified percentage of completion method.** In limited instances (explained below), taxpayers may use the **completed contract method.** Under the percentage of completion method, income from a project is reported in installments as the work progresses. Under the completed contract method, income from a project is recognized upon completion of the contract. The modified percentage of completion method is a hybrid that combines two methods (discussed below). Alternatively, taxpayers may use any other accounting method (e.g., the accrual method) that clearly reflects income.

COSTS SUBJECT TO LONG-TERM CONTRACT RULES. Direct contract costs are subject to the long-term contract rules. Labor, materials, and overhead costs must be allocated to the contract and accounted for accordingly. Thus, under the completed contract method, such costs are capitalized and deducted from revenue in the year the contract is completed. Selling, marketing and advertising expenses, expenses for unsuccessful bids and proposals, and research and development costs not associated with a specific contract may be deducted currently.

In general, administrative overhead must be allocated to long-term contracts. (See the earlier list of overhead items that must be included in inventory.) This is not required of taxpayers (other than homebuilders) using the completed contract method, but as noted below, the use of the completed contract method is limited.

As previously mentioned, interest must be capitalized if the property being produced is real property, long-lived property, or property requiring more than two years (one year in

[43] Reg. Sec. 1.451-3(b).

[44] Rev. Proc. 71-21, 1971-2 C.B. 549, does establish rules for service contracts that extend into the year following the receipt of payment. These rules are discussed in Chapter I3.

[45] Reg. Sec. 1.451-3(a)(1).

the case of property costing more than $1 million) to produce. Interest costs directly attributable to a contract and those that could have been avoided if contract costs had not been incurred must be allocated to long-term contracts.

COMPLETED CONTRACT METHOD. Under the completed contract method of accounting, income from a contract is reported in the taxable year in which the contract is completed. This is true without regard to whether the contract price is collected in advance, upon completion of the contract, or in installments. Costs associated with the contract are accumulated in a work-in-progress account and deducted upon completion. Several courts are in conflict with regard to determining when a contract is completed. Some courts have required total completion and acceptance of the contract.[46] Other courts have held the contract to have been completed when the only work remaining consists of correcting minor defects or furnishing incidental parts.[47]

The use of the completed contract method may only be used in two limited circumstances. First, the method can be used by smaller companies (those whose average gross receipts for the three preceding tax years is $10 million or less) for construction contracts that are expected to take two years or less to complete and second, for home construction contracts.[48] It cannot be used by larger companies for manufacturing, or for other long-term contracts other than construction or for construction contracts expected to last longer than two years.

KEY POINT

In general, taxpayers with long-term contracts must compute income under the percentage of completion method for contracts entered into after July 10, 1989.

PERCENTAGE OF COMPLETION METHOD. Under the percentage of completion method of reporting income, the taxpayer reports a percentage of the gross income from a long-term contract based on the portion of work that has been completed. The portion of the total contract price reported in a given year is determined by multiplying the total contract price by the percentage of work completed in the year. The percentage is determined by dividing current year costs by the expected total costs.

KEY POINT

After a taxpayer has adopted an accounting method for long-term contracts, he or she must continue to use that method unless permission to change methods is granted.

MODIFIED PERCENTAGE OF COMPLETION METHOD. At the beginning of a contract, it is difficult to estimate total costs. For this reason, taxpayers may elect to defer reporting any income from a contract until they have incurred at least 10% of the estimated total cost.[49] This is called the modified percentage of completion method. Under this method, if a contract has just been started as of the end of the year, the taxpayer does not have to estimate the profit on the contract during that year. The next year the taxpayer will report profit on all work that has been completed, including work done during the first year. Of course, this assumes that at least 10% of the work has been completed as of the end of the taxable year. If more than 10% of the costs are incurred during the first year, the modified percentage of completion method is identical to the regular percentage of completion method.

The completed contract method, the percentage of completion method, and the modified percentage of completion method are compared in Example I11-21.

EXAMPLE I11-21 ▶ In 2002, a contractor enters into a contract to construct a bridge for $1,400,000. At the outset, the contractor estimates that it will cost $1,200,000 to build the bridge. Actual costs in 2002 are $540,000 (45% of the $1,200,000 total estimated costs). Actual costs in 2003 are less than expected and amount to $600,000. The profits reported in both years of the contract are illustrated below.

	2002	2003
Completed contract		
Revenue	0	$1,400,000
Costs incurred	0	(1,140,000)
Gross profit	0	$ 260,000

[46] *E. E. Black Limited v. Alsup*, 45 AFTR 1345, 54-1 USTC ¶9340 (9th Cir., 1954), and *Thompson-King-Tate, Inc. v. U.S.*, 8 AFTR 2d 5920, 62-1 USTC ¶9116 (6th Cir., 1961).

[47] *Ehret-Day Co.*, 2 T.C. 25 (1943), and *Nathan Wohlfeld*, 1958 PH T.C. Memo ¶58,128, 17 TCM 677.

[48] Sec. 460(e).

[49] Sec. 460(a).

Percentage of completion		
Revenue	$630,000[a]	$770,000[b]
Costs incurred	(540,000)	(600,000)
Gross profit	$ 90,000	$170,000

[a] 540,000/1,200,000 × $1,400,000 = $630,000.
[b] $1,400,000 − $630,000 = $770,000.

In Example I11-21, the modified percentage of completion method results in the same income being reported each year as the percentage of completion method because more than 10% of the estimated costs were incurred during the first year. Note that the completed contract method defers reporting income until the contract is completed, causing all income from the project to be reported in a single year. Thus, the tax is deferred but the taxpayer may end up being taxed at higher rates. As noted, the completed contract is available only for home construction contracts and to certain smaller contractors for projects of two years or less.

LOOK-BACK INTEREST. Certain contracts (or portions of a contract) accounted for under either the regular or modified percentage of completion method are subject to a **look-back interest** adjustment. When a contract is completed, a computation is made to determine whether the tax paid each year during the contract is more or less than the tax that would have been paid if the actual total cost of the contract had been used rather than the estimated cost.[50] Interest is paid on any additional tax that would have been paid. The taxpayer receives interest on any additional tax that was paid.

Look-back interest is applicable only to contracts completed more than two years after the commencement date. Furthermore, look-back interest is applicable only if the contract price equals or exceeds either 1% of the taxpayer's average gross receipts for the three taxable years preceding the taxable year the contract was entered into or $1 million.[51]

Taxpayers may elect a "de minimis" exception to the "look-back" interest computation. If elected, the exception is applicable to all contracts completed within a year, and the election to use the exception can be revoked only with IRS approval. Under the exception, if income reported each year on a contract is within 10% of the recomputed "look-back income," no interest computation is made for the contract. Whether reported income is within 10% of recomputed income is determined separately for each completed contract.

EXAMPLE I11-22 ▶ The contractor in Example I11-21 is exempt from the look-back rule because the contract is completed within two years after the commencement date. On the other hand, if the contract took more than two years to complete, interest would be owed on the underpaid taxes for the first and subsequent contract years. The underreported income for the first year would be $33,158 [($260,000 profit × $540,000 first year's costs ÷ $1,140,000 total costs) − $90,000 first year reported income]. Assuming a 35% tax bracket, the underpaid tax for the first year is $11,605. Upon completion of the contract, interest would be paid on this amount and underpaid taxes for other years. Even if elected, the "de-minimis" exception would be inapplicable as the reported income in the first year of the contract ($90,000) is not within 10% of the income that would have been reported if actual costs had been used in the computation ($123,158 = $33,158 + $90,000). ◀

INSTALLMENT SALES METHOD

OBJECTIVE 5

Compute the gain to be reported from an installment sale

In general, the gain or loss from the sale of property is reported in the year the property is sold. If the sales proceeds are collected in years after the sale, the taxpayer may find it difficult to pay the tax on the entire amount of the gain in the year of sale. To reduce the burden, the tax law permits taxpayers to spread the gain from installment sales over the collection period. The installment method is applicable only to gains and is used to report income from an installment transaction unless the taxpayer elects not to use the install-

[50] Sec. 460(b)(3).

[51] Sec. 460(b)(3).

KEY POINT

The installment sales method allows either a cash or an accrual method taxpayer to spread the gain from the sale of property over the period during which payments are received.

ment method. An **installment sale** is any disposition of property where at least one payment is received after the close of the taxable year in which the disposition occurs. The installment method is *not* applicable to sales:

- inventory, or
- marketable securities[52]

SELF-STUDY QUESTION

A taxpayer sells 100 shares of Ford Motor Company stock for a gain of $800 on December 30, 2001. The taxpayer received the proceeds from the sale from the stockbroker on January 5, 2002. Can the taxpayer use the installment sales method?

ANSWER

No, the method is not applicable to sales of publicly traded property.

TYPICAL MISCONCEPTION

The selling price is sometimes confused with the contract price.

COMPUTATIONS UNDER SEC. 453. Income under the installment sales method is computed as follows:

STEP 1: Compute the gross profit from the sale.

Selling price	$xx,xxx
Minus: Adjusted basis	(x,xxx)
Selling expenses	(x,xxx)
Depreciation recapture[53]	(x,xxx)
Gross profit	$ x,xxx

STEP 2: Determine the contract price.

Contract price (greater of the gross profit from above or the selling price reduced by any existing mortgage assumed or acquired by the purchaser)	$xx,xxx

STEP 3: Compute the gross profit percentage.

$$\text{Gross profit percentage} = \frac{\text{Gross profit}}{\text{Contract price}} = xx\%$$

STEP 4: Compute the gain to be reported in the year of sale.

Collections of principal received during year (exclusive of interest)	$xx,xxx
Plus: Excess mortgage (if any)[a]	x,xxx
Total $xx,xxx	
Times: Gross profit percentage	× xx%
Net gain recognized in year of sale	$ x,xxx
Plus: Depreciation recapture	x,xxx
Gain reported in year of sale	$ x,xxx

STEP 5: Compute the gain to be reported in subsequent years.

Collections of principal received	$ x,xxx
Times: Gross profit percent	× xx%
Gain reported in each of the subsequent years	$ x,xxx

[a] Mortgage − Basis − Selling expense − Depreciation recapture = Excess mortgage.

ADDITIONAL COMMENT

On the sale of a capital asset a taxpayer might elect not to use the installment sales method and report the entire gain in the year of sale if he or she has capital losses that could be used to offset the gain.

Note that depreciation recapture (see Chapter I13) must be reported in the year of the sale even if no payment is received.

EXAMPLE I11-23 ▶ Gina, a cash basis taxpayer, sells equipment for $200,000. The equipment originally cost $70,000, and $10,000 of MACRS depreciation has been deducted before the sale. The $10,000 of depreciation must be recaptured as ordinary income under Sec. 1245. The buyer assumes the existing mortgage of $50,000, pays $10,000 down, and agrees to pay $10,000 per year for 14 years plus interest at a rate acceptable to the IRS. Selling expenses are $13,000. Using the steps listed above, calculations are made as follows:

[52] Sec. 453(b)(2) and (k).

[53] For a discussion of depreciation recapture, see Chapter I13.

STEP 1: Compute the gross profit from the sale.

Selling price	$200,000
Minus: Adjusted basis	(60,000)
Selling expenses	(13,000)
Depreciation recapture	(10,000)
Gross profit	$117,000

STEP 2: Determine the contract price.

Greater of gross profit of $117,000 or selling price minus mortgage assumed by purchaser ($150,000 = $200,000 − $50,000)	$150,000

STEP 3: Compute the gross profit percentage.

$$\text{Gross profit percentage} = \frac{\text{Gross profit (\$117,000)}}{\text{Contract price (\$150,000)}} = 78\%$$

STEP 4: Compute the gain to be reported in the year of sale.

Principal received during year	$ 10,000
Plus: Excess mortgage	0
Total amount realized	$ 10,000
Times: Gross profit percentage	
Gross profit	$ 7,800
Plus: Depreciation recapture	10,000
Gain reported in year of sale	$ 17,800

STEP 5: Compute the gain to be reported in subsequent years.

Principal received	$ 10,000
Times: Gross profit percentage	× 78%
Gain reported in each subsequent year	$ 7,800

Thus, the total gain reported is $127,000 [$17,800 + ($7,800 × 14)]. This is equal to the gross profit of $117,000 (which is the amount of Sec. 1231 gain reported on the sale) plus the $10,000 of depreciation recapture). As a cash basis taxpayer Gina will report the interest income as it is collected. See Figure I11-1 at the end of this chapter which illustrates this computation on Form 6252, Installment Sale Income. ◀

REAL-WORLD EXAMPLE

When an installment obligation is assigned as collateral for a loan, the transaction is treated as a disposition of the obligation. Rev. Rul. 65-185, 1965-2 C.B. 153.

DISPOSITION OF INSTALLMENT OBLIGATIONS. A taxpayer who sells property on the installment basis may decide not to hold the obligation until maturity. For example, the holder may sell the obligation to a financial institution for the purpose of raising cash. Alternatively, the holder may not be able to collect the full amount of the installments because of the inability of the buyer to make payments. Thus, the holder must determine the adjusted basis of the obligation in order to compute the gain or loss realized on the disposition. The adjusted basis of an installment obligation is equal to the face amount of the obligation reduced by the gross profit that would be realized if the holder collects the face amount of the obligation. In general, this means the adjusted basis of an obligation is equal to

$$\text{Face amount} \times (100\% - \text{Gross profit percentage})$$

EXAMPLE I11-24 ▶ Assume the same facts as in Example I11-23 except that Gina immediately sells a single $10,000 installment to a bank for $9,700. Gina reports a gain of $7,500 computed as follows:

Selling price	$9,700
Minus: Adjusted basis of installment	(2,200)[a]
Recognized gain	$7,500

[a]$10,000 face amount × (100% − 78% gross profit percentage) = $2,200

Gina would have reported a gain of $7,800 had she decided not to sell the installment but to collect the face amount. Because the obligation is discounted by $300 ($10,000 − $9,700), the reported gain is reduced by $300. If the installment had not been sold immediately, the bank would probably also pay to Gina an amount for the accrued interest. In such a situation Gina would report the gain from the sale and the accrued interest as income. ◀

EXAMPLE I11-25 ▶ Assume that Gina in Example I11-24 is unable to collect the final $10,000 installment because the individual who purchases the property declares bankruptcy. Gina would be entitled to a bad debt deduction of $2,200, the basis of the installment. Gina does not receive a bad debt deduction for the accrued interest because the interest has not been included in her gross income. ◀

KEY POINT

A donor of property does not normally recognize gain, but a gift of certain installment obligations causes the recognition of gain.

Certain dispositions of installment obligations, such as gifts, are taxable events.[54] The main objective of this rule is to prevent income from being shifted from one taxpayer to another. Thus, if a corporation distributes an installment obligation as a dividend or if a father gives his daughter an installment obligation, gain or loss is recognized. In general, the gain or loss recognized is equal to the difference between the FMV of the obligation and its adjusted basis. In the case of a gift, the gain recognized is equal to the difference between the face of the obligation and its adjusted basis. However, certain exceptions to this rule exist. Transfers to controlled corporations under Sec. 351, certain corporate reorganizations and liquidations, transfers on the taxpayer's death, transfers incident to divorce, distributions by partnerships, and contributions of capital to a partnership are exceptions to this rule. In these cases, the recipients of the obligations report income when the installments are collected.

REPOSSESSIONS OF PROPERTY SOLD ON THE INSTALLMENT BASIS. In general, the repossession of property sold on the installment basis is a taxable event. The gain or loss recognized is generally equal to the difference between the value of the repossessed property (reduced by any costs incurred as a result of the repossession) and the adjusted basis of any remaining installment obligations.

EXAMPLE I11-26 ▶ Yuji sells stock of a non–publicly traded corporation with a $7,000 adjusted basis for $10,000. Yuji receives a $1,000 down payment, and the balance of $9,000 is due the following year. In the year of the sale Yuji reports a capital gain of $300 (0.30 × $1,000) under the installment method of accounting. Yuji is unable to collect the $9,000 note, and after incurring legal fees of $500, he repossesses the stock. When Yuji repossesses the stock it is worth $8,700. The adjusted basis of the note is $6,300 (0.70 × $9,000). Yuji must report a capital gain of $1,900 ($8,700 − $500 − $6,300). The basis of the stock to Yuji is its FMV at the time it is repossessed ($8,700). ◀

The amount of gain recognized from the repossession of real property is limited to the lesser of (1) the gross profit in the remaining installments reduced by the costs incurred as a result of the repossession or (2) the cash and FMV of other property received from the buyer in excess of the gain previously recognized.[55] In the case of the repossession of either real or personal property, the gain or loss retains the same character as the gain or loss on the original sale.

EXAMPLE I11-27 ▶ Assume the same facts as in Example I11-26, except that the property sold is land. Yuji reports a capital gain of $700, which is the lesser of $2,200 [(0.30 × $9,000)− $500] or $700 ($1,000 − $300). The basis of the land is $7,500 [$9,000 − (0.30 × $9,000) unrealized profit + $700 gain previously recognized + $500 legal fees]. ◀

INSTALLMENT SALES FOR MORE THAN $150,000. Special rules apply to nondealers who sell property for more than $150,000. The special rules do not apply to sales of personal use property, to sales of property used or produced in the trade or business of farming, or to sales of timeshares or residential lots.

First, if the taxpayer borrows funds using the installment obligations as security, the amount borrowed is treated as a payment received on the installment obligation.[56] This

[54] Sec. 453B(a).
[55] Sec. 1038.
[56] Sec. 453A(d).

prevents the taxpayer from using the installment method to defer tax and yet obtain cash by borrowing against the installment obligation. Second, if the installment method is used, interest must be paid to the government on the deferred tax.[57] This rule, however, applies only to deferred principal payments over $5 million.[58]

KEY POINT

Installment sales between related parties cannot be used to defer the recognition of gain by the original owner when the related purchaser receives cash.

INSTALLMENT SALES BETWEEN RELATED PERSONS. Installment sales between related persons are subject to the same rules as other installment sales except when the property is resold by the related purchaser. The primary purpose of the resale rule is to prevent the original owner from deferring gain recognition by selling the property to a related person who, in turn, resells the property.

Sec 453(e) requires the first seller to treat amounts received by the related person (second seller) as having been personally received. Thus, the first seller would be required to report the gain in the year (or years) in which proceeds are received by the second seller. This acceleration provision is applicable only if the resale takes place within two years of the initial sale. For purposes of Sec. 453(e), the term *related person* includes a spouse, children, grandchildren, and parents. Controlled corporations, partnerships, estates, and trusts are also covered.

DEFERRED PAYMENT SALES

The installment sale rules are not applicable to all sales involving future payments. The installment method cannot be used when the sale of property produces a loss. Also a taxpayer can elect out of the installment method when a sale results in a gain. The manner in which these transactions are reported depends on the taxpayer's accounting method. For accrual method taxpayers, the total *amount receivable* from the buyer (exclusive of interest) is treated as part of the amount realized. Thus, the entire gain or loss is reported in the year of sale. For cash method taxpayers, the FMV of the installment obligation is treated as part of the amount realized in the year of sale. The amount realized, however, cannot be considered to be less than the FMV of the property sold minus any other consideration received (e.g., cash).[59]

EXAMPLE I11-28 ▶ USA Corporation, an accrual method taxpayer, sells land for $100,000. USA receives $50,000 down and a $50,000 note payable in 12 months plus 14% interest. Assume the basis of the land is $80,000 and that it is a capital asset. Because of the buyer's poor credit, the value of the note is only $45,000. USA affirmatively elects not to report the installment sale on the installment method. USA reports a capital gain of $20,000 ($100,000 − $80,000). If USA collects the face of the note at maturity, no additional gain or loss is recognized. If USA sells the note for $45,000, a $5,000 capital loss is recognized. ◀

EXAMPLE I11-29 ▶ Assume the same facts as in Example I11-28, except that USA is a cash method taxpayer. If the FMV of the land is $100,000 (the stated selling price), the treatment of the transaction is exactly the same as it is using the accrual method. If the FMV of the land is assumed to be $95,000 (cash received plus FMV of the note received), USA recognizes a $15,000 ($95,000 − $80,000) capital gain in the year of the sale. If USA collects the face of the note at maturity, $5,000 of ordinary income is recognized. If USA sells the note for $45,000, no gain or loss is recognized. ◀

ADDITIONAL COMMENT

A contingent payment sale is a sale or other disposition of property in which the aggregate selling price cannot be determined by the close of the tax year in which the sale took place.

INDETERMINATE MARKET VALUE. In certain transactions, the value of obligations received cannot be determined (e.g., a mineral interest is sold for an amount equal to 10% of the value of future production). Under the Regulations, the value of obligations with an **indeterminate market value** is assumed to be no lower than the value of the property sold less the value of other property received.[60] Hence, if the value of property sold is determinable, the recognized gain equals the excess of the value of the property sold over its basis. On occasion, however, neither the value of the obligation received nor the value of property sold can be determined.

Temporary regulations specify how these types of transactions are to be treated.[61] The basic rules relating to special accounting methods are summarized in Topic Review I11-3.

---

[57] The interest computation is described in Sec. 453A(c).
[58] Sec. 453A(b)(2)(B).
[59] Temp. Reg. Sec. 15A.453-1(d)(2)(ii)(A).
[60] Reg. Sec. 1.453-1(d)(3)(iii).
[61] Temp. Reg. Sec. 15A.453-1(c).

Topic Review I11-3

Special Accounting Methods

LONG-TERM CONTRACTS

- Long-term contracts include building, installation, construction, or manufacturing contracts that are not completed in the same tax year in which they are entered into. A manufacturing contract is long-term only if the contract involves the manufacture of either a unique item not normally carried in inventory or an item that normally requires more than 12 calendar months to complete.
- Long-term contracts may be reported under the regular or the modified percentage of completion method. Under both methods income is reported as work is completed, except that under the modified percentage of completion method no income is reported until at least 10% of the work is completed.
- The completed contract method is available only for home construction contracts, for construction contracts expected to take two years or less to complete, and for use by smaller companies (those whose average gross receipts for the three preceding tax years are $10 million or less).

INSTALLMENT METHOD

- Under the installment method gain is reported as the sales proceeds are collected. The installment method is generally not available for sales of inventory or publicly traded property. Furthermore, the method is available only for gains.
- Gain is reported as sales proceeds are collected. However, both depreciation recapture and any mortgage in excess of basis must be reported in the year of sale. Gain recognition is also accelerated in certain situations if the seller borrows against the installment obligation or if a related buyer resells the property within two years.

IMPUTED INTEREST

OBJECTIVE 6

Compute the amount of imputed interest in a transaction

KEY POINT

Imputed interest is important because it alters the amount of gain on the sale and causes an interest expense deduction for the buyer and interest income for the seller.

TYPICAL MISCONCEPTION

Some people mistakenly assumed that the imputed interest rules do not apply if the property is sold for a loss.

Before the enactment of Sec. 1274 and the amendment of Sec. 483, property could be sold on an installment basis in a contract providing for little or no interest. Instead of charging interest, the seller charged a higher price for the property. If the property sold was a capital asset, the result of the arrangement was to reduce the interest income reported by the seller and to increase the amount of favorably taxed capital gain. Sections 483 and 1274 now *impute* interest in a deferred payment contract where no interest or a low rate of interest is provided. Another impact of the **imputed interest rules** on sellers is to reallocate payments received between interest (which is fully taxable) and principal (only the gain portion of which is taxable). The result is often an increase in the income reported in early years and a decrease in later years. The rules are generally applicable to both buyers and sellers. In certain instances, the buyer may want interest to be imputed in order to increase his interest deduction in early years.

The following transactions are exempt from the imputed interest rules:

- Debt subject to original issue discount provisions (basically bonds issued for less than face where amortization of the discount is required under Sec. 1274, see Chapter I5)
- Sales of property for $3,000 or less
- Any sales where all of the payments are due within six months
- Sales of patents to the extent the payment is contingent on the use or disposition of the patent
- Certain carrying charges for personal property or educational services covered by Sec. 163(b) when the interest charge cannot be ascertained
- Charges for the purchase of personal-use property (purchaser only)[62]

---

[62] Sec. 483(d). The rule lowers the basis of a personal-use asset in order to increase any gain on the future sale of the property.

EXAMPLE I11-30 ▶ Joan is involved in several transactions during the current year. No interest is stated on any of the transactions. The terms of the transactions and the applicability of the imputed interest rules are summarized below:

Transaction	*Imputation of Interest*
Purchases furniture costing $8,000 for her residence. Full price is payable within four months.	Not applicable because property is for personal use. Also, all payments are due within six months.
Sells a boat for $2,000. Payment is due in a year.	Not applicable because sales price is not more than $3,000.
Sells land for $100,000. Payment is due in five years.	Interest must be imputed because no exception is applicable.
Purchases a newly issued bond for $650 (face of $1,000).	Not applicable because transaction is subject to the original issue discount rules in Sec. 1274. Also, the price is not more than $3,000. ◀

IMPUTED INTEREST COMPUTATION

In order to avoid the imputation of interest, the stated interest rate must be at least equal to 100% of the applicable federal rate (110% of the applicable federal rate in the case of sale–lease back arrangements). Lower rates are specified for two types of transactions: (1) If the stated principal amount for qualified debt obligations that are issued in exchange for property under Sec. 1274A does not exceed $2,800,000, the interest rate is limited to 9% compounded semiannually; and (2) the interest rate is limited to 6% compounded semiannually in the case of sales of land between related individuals (unless the sales price exceeds $500,000).

The **applicable federal rate** is determined monthly and is based on the rate paid by the federal government on borrowed funds. The rate varies with the terms of the loan. Loans are divided into short-term (not over three years), mid-term (over three years but not over nine years), and long-term (over nine years).

EXAMPLE I11-31 ▶ Kasi sells land for $100,000 to Bill, an unrelated person. The sales price is to be paid to Kasi at the end of five years in a single installment with no stated interest. Kasi paid $60,000 for the land. Assume the current federal rate is 10%. Because the amount of the stated principal is less than $2,800,000, interest is imputed at a rate not to exceed 9% compounded semiannually. As a result, the effective rate is 9.2025% (9% compounded semiannually), and the present value factor is .64393 ($1 \div 1.092025^5$). Thus, the present value of the final payment is $64,393 (0.64393 × $100,000). Kasi reports a $4,393 ($64,393 – $60,000) gain on the sale of the land and $35,607 ($100,000 – $64,393) interest income instead of a $40,000 gain and no interest income. The buyer is treated as incurring $35,607 in interest and has a $64,393 basis in the land. Whether the interest is deductible depends on a variety of other factors (see Chapter I7). ◀

ACCRUAL OF INTEREST

ADDITIONAL COMMENT

The $2,000,000 limit on the stated principal is subject to inflation adjustments for calendar years beginning after 1989.

Is imputed interest reported under the cash or the accrual method? In other words, is imputed interest reported when it accrues or when it is paid? In general, imputed interest is reported as it accrues. However, there are some major exceptions, as follows:

- ▶ Sales of personal residences
- ▶ Most sales of farms for $1 million or less
- ▶ Sales involving aggregate payments of $250,000 or less
- ▶ Sales of land between related persons unless the sales price exceeds $500,000[63]

In addition, if the borrower and lender jointly elect, and if the stated principal does not exceed $2,000,000, accrual of interest is not required. This election is not available if the lender is an accrual method taxpayer or a dealer with respect to the property sold or exchanged.[64]

[63] Sec. 1274(c)(4).

EXAMPLE I11-32 ▶ Assume the same facts as in Example I11-31. Because the aggregate payments do not exceed $250,000, the transaction is exempt from the requirement that interest be accrued. As a result, Kasi reports interest income and Bill reports interest expense in the fifth year when the final payment is made on the transaction. Under the installment method, $4,393 gain on the sale is recognized in the fifth year. ◀

GIFT, SHAREHOLDER, AND OTHER LOANS

Imputed interest rules are not limited to installment transactions. Sec. 7872 applies to transactions involving related parties whose taxes are lowered as a result of low interest or interest-free loans. These situations include

- *Gift loans.* For example, parents in higher tax brackets may loan money to their children without charging interest. If the children invest the borrowed money and are taxed on the income at a lower rate, the family has reduced its total tax liability in the absence of imputed interest rules.
- *Corporation shareholder loans.* In the absence of imputed interest rules, taxes may be saved by a corporation that makes an interest-free loan to a shareholder. If the corporation had invested the money and paid out the resulting income as a dividend, it would have first been taxed on the profit. By making the interest-free loan, the corporation could, in the absence of imputed interest rules, reduce its taxes by avoiding the otherwise taxable income.
- *Compensation-related loans.* Employers may loan money to employees without charging interest. Without the requirement to impute interest, this could produce tax savings if the employer was unable to deduct additional compensation because of the reasonable compensation limitation or if the employee was unable to deduct the interest, say, because the borrowed funds were used to purchase personal use property.
- *Other tax avoidance loans.* Any other low-interest or interest-free loan that produces tax savings may be subject to the imputed interest rules. For example, a club may offer its members a choice of either paying dues or making a large refundable deposit. The club can invest the money and earn interest perhaps equal to the dues. In the absence of imputed interest rules, the member avoids taxes by not having to report the income that would have been earned if the member personally invested the funds. The club is indifferent between the alternatives because both the dues and the interest income are taxable.

In general, interest is imputed on the above loans by applying the applicable federal rates discussed earlier. The resulting interest income is taxable to the lender. Whether the interest expense is deductible by the borrower is determined by applying the usual interest deduction rules (see Chapter I7).

The imputation process involves a second step. The lender is treated as returning the imputed interest to the borrower. This is necessary because the interest was not actually paid. For example, in the case of a gift loan, the lender is treated as giving the imputed interest back to the borrower. This would not normally have income tax implications, but if the imputed interest were large enough, it could result in a gift tax. In the case of the corporation-shareholder loan, the corporation is treated as paying the imputed interest back to the shareholder as a dividend. Typically, this does not increase the corporation's tax, but it results in the recognition of dividend income to the shareholder. For compensation-related loans, the second step is to impute compensation paid by the employer and received by the employee. The compensation is taxable to the employee and, if reasonable in amount, is deductible by the employer.

There are several important exceptions intended to limit the application of imputed interest in situations where tax avoidance may be immaterial:

- Interest is not imputed on gift loans between two individuals totaling $10,000 or less, except when the borrowed funds are used to purchase income-producing property.
- If the gift loans between two individuals total $100,000 or less, the imputed interest is limited to the borrower's "net investment income" as defined by Sec. 163(d)(4). (See

[64] Sec. 1274A(c).

Chapter I7 for a discussion of net investment income). If the net investment income is $1,000 or less, it is not necessary to impute interest.

- Interest is not imputed on compensation-related and corporate shareholder loans totaling $10,000 or less.

These exceptions do not apply when tax avoidance is one of the principal purposes of the loans.

EXAMPLE I11-33 ▶ Linda made interest-free gift loans to each of her four children: Andy, Bob, Cathy, and Donna. Andy borrowed $9,000 to purchase an automobile. Bob borrowed $25,000 to buy stock. Bob's net investment income is $800. Cathy also borrowed $25,000 to buy stock, but her net investment income is $1,100. Donna borrowed $120,000 to purchase a residence, and her net investment income is $500. Tax avoidance is not a motive for any of the loans. Imputation of interest is not required for the loans to Andy or Bob. The loan to Andy is exempt because the amount is less than $10,000, and the loan to Bob is exempt because his net investment income is under $1,000. Imputation of interest is required for the loans to Cathy and Donna. In the case of Cathy, the amount of imputed interest is limited to her net investment income of $1,100. The imputed interest for Donna, however, is not limited to her net investment income because the amount of the loan is over $100,000. ◀

The imputed interest rules are summarized in Topic Review I11-4.

CHANGE IN ACCOUNTING METHODS

In general, a new taxpayer elects an accounting method by simply applying the selected method when computing income for the initial tax return.[65] If a particular item does not occur in the first year, the accounting method is elected the first year in which the item occurs.

EXAMPLE I11-34 ▶ Gordon opened a beauty shop several years ago. Because he had no inventory, no inventory method was selected. In the current year, Gordon expanded his business to offer beauty supplies to his customers. Gordon can delay electing the FIFO inventory method until the current year, the first year in which he has an inventory. ◀

Topic Review I11-4

Imputed Interest

PURPOSE

The imputed interest rules are intended to prevent taxpayers from reducing their taxes by charging little or no interest on installment payment transactions and loans.

APPLIES TO

In most cases applies to both parties, the debtor and the creditor. The result is to impute interest income to the lender and interest expense to the borrower. Several exceptions exempt small transactions from imputed interest. For example, sales involving payments of $3,000 or less are generally exempt as are loans of less than $10,000.

RATE

Interest is imputed at the applicable federal rate if the stated interest rate is lower. The applicable federal rate is the rate the federal government pays on borrowed funds and is determined monthly. In general, the current rate at the time of the transaction is used throughout the term of the loan. The rate varies with the term of the loan. Loans are divided into short-term (not over three years), mid-term (over three years but not over nine years), and long-term (over nine years).

[65] Reg. Sec. 1.446-1(e)(1).

OBJECTIVE 7

Determine the tax treatment of duplications and omissions that result from changes of accounting methods

In general, once an accounting method is chosen, it cannot be changed without IRS approval. There are a few exceptions. For example, taxpayers may adopt the LIFO inventory method without prior IRS approval.[66] Once such methods are adopted, however, they cannot be changed without IRS approval.

As previously noted, the term *accounting method* indicates not only the overall accounting method used by the taxpayer, but also the treatment of any item of income or deduction.[67] A change of accounting methods should not be confused with the correction of an error. Errors include mathematical mistakes, posting errors, deductions of the wrong amount for an expense, omission of an item of taxable income, or incorrect computation of a credit. An error is normally corrected by filing an amended return for the tax year or years in which the error occurs. In general, there is a three-year statute of limitations on the correction of errors. After three years, the tax year is closed and changes cannot be made.[68]

REAL-WORLD EXAMPLE

The write-down of soil aggregate to its market value by a paving company was a change in accounting method rather than the mere correction of an accounting error. The soil aggregate was included in its election to adopt the LIFO inventory method, and the use of this method required that the soil aggregate be included at cost regardless of market value. *First National Bank of Gainesville, Trustee*, 88 T.C. 1069 (1987).

REAL-WORLD EXAMPLE

An extension of time to file the application for change of accounting method was granted because of the death of the accountant in charge of filing the application. Rev. Rul. 79-417, 1979-2 C.B. 202.

Taxpayers wishing to change accounting methods must file Form 3115 with the IRS in Washington, DC on or before the due date of the tax return including extensions. A duplicate copy of Form 3115 must be filed with the tax return for the year. A taxpayer who amends the original income tax return within six months of its due date may request a change of accounting methods with the amended return.[69]

In general, taxpayers initiate a change in accounting methods from an incorrect to a correct method are exempt from penalty and from retroactive application of the new reporting method. Although changes in accounting methods require IRS approval, the IRS states that approval will automatically be granted for a wide variety of changes if the taxpayer meets specific requirements that include proper filing of both Form 3115 and the current year's tax return, agreeing to take into account the Sec. 481(a) adjustment (as described below), not being under examination, and not having changed the same method of accounting within the last four years.[70] Although the IRS retains the right to again change any method of accounting adopted under these procedures it states that such changes will not be retroactive except in rare or unusual circumstances. Examples of situations where retroactive application may occur include misstatement or omission of material facts, change in material facts, and changes in applicable authority.

AMOUNT OF CHANGE

A change in accounting methods usually results in duplications or omissions of items of income or expense.

EXAMPLE I11-35 ▶ Bonnie, a practicing CPA, has been reporting income using the cash method. In the current year, Bonnie obtains permission to change to the accrual method. At the beginning of the current year, Bonnie has $80,000 of receivables that have not been reported in prior years. The receivables were not reported in prior years because they were not collected. Although the receivables are collected in the current year, they are not taxable because, under the accrual method, Bonnie now reports income as it is earned and the income is not earned in the current year. In this case, the income was earned in prior years.

Also, assume Bonnie has accounts payable of $15,000 at the beginning of the current year. The accounts payable were not deducted in prior years because the expenses had not been paid. Furthermore, the accounts payable are not deductible in the current year even if they are paid. This is because the expenses were incurred in prior years. Obviously, the IRS expects to collect the tax on the $80,000 of receivables, and Bonnie is entitled to deduct the $15,000 of payables. In the absence of any special provision, both amounts would be omitted from the computation of taxable income. If the change is from the accrual method to the cash method,

---

[66] A taxpayer may adopt LIFO by merely determining year-end inventory by that method and attaching Form 970 to the tax return for the year (Reg. Sec. 1.472-3(a)).

[67] Reg. Sec. 1.446-1(e)(2)(ii)(b).

[68] Exceptions are applicable when the taxpayer omits from the return an amount of income that is over 25% of the gross income stated on the return (6 years) or where fraud occurs (no limitation).

[69] The extension will be granted if the taxpayer (a) files the original income tax return on time, (b) uses the new method of accounting on the amended return, (c) attaches the application to change methods to the amended return, (d) files a copy of the application with the national office no later than when the original is filed with the amended return, and (e) writes at the top of the application "FILED PURSUANT TO §301.9100-2." Rev. Proc. 99-49, 1999-2, C.B. 725.

[70] 1997-2 C.B. 455.

both amounts would be reported twice (in the year prior to the change because they had accrued and in the year of the change because they are collected or paid). Thus, a special provision is also needed for duplications. ◀

REPORTING THE AMOUNT OF THE CHANGE

The net amount of the change must be taken into account.[71] A positive adjustment is added to income, whereas a negative adjustment is subtracted from income. This adjustment can, of course, be made in the year of the change. If the amount is small, recognizing the full amount of the net adjustment in the year of the change is both simple and equitable. Reporting a large positive adjustment in one year could push the taxpayer into a higher marginal tax bracket and result in a significant tax increase. Because the extra income is due to changing accounting methods, not increasing cash flows, the taxpayer may not have the wherewithal to pay the additional tax.

As a result, there are alternative methods that may be used to report the amount of the change. The methods that are available depend on whether the change is voluntary (a change that is initiated by the taxpayer) or involuntary (a change from an unacceptable to an acceptable method that is required by the IRS).

In the case of an involuntary change, several alternative methods are available to the IRS.[72]

In the case of voluntary changes, taxpayers must agree to report the adjustment over a period not to exceed four years. When the amount of the adjustment is $25,000 or less, taxpayers may elect to include the full amount in the current year.[73] In the case of a change spread over four years, equal portions of the change are reported in each of the four years beginning with the year of the change.

EXAMPLE I11-36 ▶ In 2002 Diana obtains permission to change from the accrual to the cash method of reporting income. The change results in a $30,000 negative adjustment to income. The IRS requires Diana to spread the adjustment over four years. As a result, she may deduct $7,500 in 2002 and $7,500 per year through year 2005. Note that because the amount of the adjustment is spread over the current and future years, the tax savings associated with the deduction are deferred. ◀

In general, the amount of the adjustment cannot be spread over a period longer than the method being changed has been used.

OBTAINING IRS CONSENT

REAL-WORLD EXAMPLE

A pipeline company was required to capitalize reconditioning costs on its natural gas pipelines instead of expensing these costs. *Mountain Fuel Supply Co. v. U.S.*, 28 AFTR 2d 71-5833, 71-2 USTC ¶9681 (10th Cir., 1971).

Most changes in accounting method require IRS approval. Sec. 446(e) states that a taxpayer changing the method of accounting "on the basis of which he regularly computes his income in keeping his books" must obtain consent before computing taxable income under the new method. This implies that a taxpayer who has been computing taxable income on a method other than that used in computing book income does not need approval to conform the computation of taxable income to the method regularly used on the taxpayer's books. This conclusion is supported by Sec. 441(a), which requires that the same method of accounting be used in computing taxable income as is used in keeping the books. The alternative might be to require the taxpayer to conform his or her book accounting method with the tax accounting method. The answer may well be in how one defines "books." The IRS has ruled that a reconciliation of taxable income with accounting income was a part of the taxpayer's auxiliary records.[74] Hence, the taxpayer was using the same accounting method for book and tax reporting. As a result, a taxpayer who changes the method of accounting used for financial reporting may not be required to change the method of accounting used for tax reporting as long as financial income and book income are reconciled.

[71] Sec. 481.

[72] Sec. 481(a), (b)(1), (b)(2), and (c).

[73] Rev. Rul. 97-37, 1997-2 C.B. 455.

[74] Rev. Rul. 58-601, 1958-2 C.B. 81.

TAX PLANNING CONSIDERATIONS

ACCOUNTING PERIODS

KEY POINT

C corporations and estates have more flexibility than S corporations and partnerships in the selection of a tax year.

New corporations often routinely adopt a calendar year. Consideration should be given, however, to adopting a tax year for the initial reporting period that ends before the amount of taxable income exceeds the amount that is taxed at the lowest tax rates (e.g., when taxable income is $50,000 or less). This is less critical for a corporation suffering losses because the NOLs may be carried forward for a 20-year period.

In the past, taxpayers were able to defer income by selecting different tax years for partners and partnerships or S corporations and shareholders. Current law limits this opportunity. Nevertheless, partnerships and S corporations may adopt a tax year that differs from that of their owners if that year qualifies as a natural business year (i.e., at least 25% of revenues occur during the last two months of the year). Furthermore, deferral is possible in the case of estates, because they are not subject to similar restrictions on the choice of tax years.

ACCOUNTING METHODS

KEY POINT

The election to use an accounting method is made by filing the first tax return on the basis of that method.

New businesses should consider the tax implications of electing an accounting method. For example, taxpayers may benefit from the LIFO inventory method because LIFO typically reduces gross profit and defers the payment of taxes during inflationary periods. Similarly, service companies usually choose the cash method of reporting income because it permits receivables to be reported when collected rather than when the income is earned. Choosing an accounting method requires an understanding not only of the available accounting methods, but also the nature of the taxpayer's business. Will a specific election be to the tax advantage of the taxpayer? LIFO inventory is often recommended because, during inflationary periods, it tends to reduce inventory values and increase the cost of goods sold. In certain industries, such as the computer industry, however, costs are declining, and LIFO actually may result in a higher inventory value.

In other industries, inventories may fluctuate widely from one year to the next because of changing demand, shortages of materials, strikes, or other causes. LIFO layers may have to be depleted simply to continue business operations. This can cause one of two things to happen: (1) incurring extra recordkeeping costs of LIFO for little or no benefit because the inventories are depleted before they produce significant tax deferrals or (2) depleting low-cost layers from years past, resulting in a substantial increase in taxable income in the year of occurrence.

INSTALLMENT SALES

Taxpayers normally choose the installment method of reporting income from casual sales of property. By spreading the gain from a sale over more than one tax year, the taxpayer normally remains in lower tax brackets and defers the tax. A taxpayer with low current taxable income may elect not to use the installment sale method in order to take advantage of the lower current tax rates.

COMPLIANCE AND PROCEDURAL CONSIDERATIONS

REPORTING INSTALLMENT SALES ON FORM 6252

Form 6252 (Installment Sale Income) is used to report income under the installment method from sales of real property and casual sales of personal property other than inventory. Figure I11-1 illustrates how an installment sale transaction is reported. The illustration is based on Example I11-23. A separate Form 6252 is normally used for each installment sale. Form 6252 is used in the year of the sale and any year in which the taxpayer receives a payment from the sale. Taxpayers who do not wish to use the installment method may report the transaction on either Schedule D or on Form 4797.

Form **6252**

Department of the Treasury
Internal Revenue Service

Installment Sale Income

▶ Attach to your tax return.

▶ Use a separate form for each sale or other disposition of property on the installment method.

OMB No. 1545-0228

2001

Attachment Sequence No. **79**

Name(s) shown on return: Gina Green

Identifying number: 123-45-6789

1 Description of property ▶ Equipment

2a Date acquired (month, day, year) ▶ 7/01/99 **b** Date sold (month, day, year) ▶ 8/31/01

3 Was the property sold to a related party (see instructions) after May 14, 1980? If "No," skip line 4 ☐ Yes ☒ No

4 Was the property you sold to a related party a marketable security? If "Yes," complete Part III. If "No," complete Part III for the year of sale and the 2 years after the year of sale ☐ Yes ☒ No

Part I **Gross Profit and Contract Price.** Complete this part for the year of sale only.

5	Selling price including mortgages and other debts. **Do not** include interest whether stated or unstated		200,000
6	Mortgages, debts, and other liabilities the buyer assumed or took the property subject to (see instructions)	50,000	
7	Subtract line 6 from line 5	150,000	
8	Cost or other basis of property sold	70,000	
9	Depreciation allowed or allowable	10,000	
10	Adjusted basis. Subtract line 9 from line 8	60,000	
11	Commissions and other expenses of sale	13,000	
12	Income recapture from Form 4797, Part III (see instructions)	10,000	
13	Add lines 10, 11, and 12		83,000
14	Subtract line 13 from line 5. If zero or less, **do not** complete the rest of this form (see instructions)		117,000
15	If the property described on line 1 above was your main home, enter the amount of your excluded gain (see instructions). Otherwise, enter -0-		
16	**Gross profit.** Subtract line 15 from line 14		117,000
17	Subtract line 13 from line 6. If zero or less, enter -0-		-0-
18	**Contract price.** Add line 7 and line 17		150,000

Part II **Installment Sale Income.** Complete this part for the year of sale **and** any year you receive a payment or have certain debts you must treat as a payment on installment obligations.

19	Gross profit percentage. Divide line 16 by line 18. For years after the year of sale, see instructions		78%
20	If this is the year of sale, enter the amount from line 17. Otherwise, enter -0-		-0-
21	Payments received during year (see instructions). **Do not** include interest, whether stated or unstated		10,000
22	Add lines 20 and 21		10,000
23	Payments received in prior years (see instructions). **Do not** include interest, whether stated or unstated		
24	**Installment sale income.** Multiply line 22 by line 19		7,800
25	Enter the part of line 24 that is ordinary income under the recapture rules (see instructions)		10,000
26	Subtract line 25 from line 24. Enter here and on Schedule D or Form 4797 (see instructions)		17,800

Part III **Related Party Installment Sale Income. Do not** complete if you received the final payment this tax year.

27 Name, address, and taxpayer identifying number of related party

28 Did the related party resell or dispose of the property ("second disposition") during this tax year? ☐ Yes ☐ No

29 **If the answer to question 28 is "Yes," complete lines 30 through 37 below unless one of the following conditions is met. Check the box that applies.**

a ☐ The second disposition was more than 2 years after the first disposition (other than dispositions of marketable securities). If this box is checked, enter the date of disposition (month, day, year) ▶ / /

b ☐ The first disposition was a sale or exchange of stock to the issuing corporation.

c ☐ The second disposition was an involuntary conversion and the threat of conversion occurred after the first disposition.

d ☐ The second disposition occurred after the death of the original seller or buyer.

e ☐ It can be established to the satisfaction of the Internal Revenue Service that tax avoidance was not a principal purpose for either of the dispositions. If this box is checked, attach an explanation (see instructions).

30	Selling price of property sold by related party	
31	Enter contract price from line 18 for year of first sale	
32	Enter the **smaller** of line 30 or line 31	
33	Total payments received by the end of your 2001 tax year (see instructions)	
34	Subtract line 33 from line 32. If zero or less, enter -0-	
35	Multiply line 34 by the gross profit percentage on line 19 for year of first sale	
36	Enter the part of line 35 that is ordinary income under the recapture rules (see instructions)	
37	Subtract line 36 from line 35. Enter here and on Schedule D or Form 4797 (see instructions)	

For Paperwork Reduction Act Notice, see page 4. Cat. No. 13601R Form **6252** (2001)

FIGURE I11-1 ▶ REPORTING INSTALLMENT SALE INCOME ON FORM 6252 (BASED ON EXAMPLE I11-23)

PROCEDURES FOR CHANGING TO LIFO

The LIFO method may be adopted in the initial year that inventories are maintained by merely using the method in that year. In addition, advance approval (e.g., within 180 days following the start of the year) from the IRS is not required for an adoption of the LIFO method in the initial year that inventories are maintained on the LIFO method. However, Form 970 should be filed along with the taxpayer's tax return for the year of the change.[75] The application must include an analysis of the beginning and ending inventories. Further, if a taxpayer is changing to the LIFO method from another method (e.g., FIFO), advance approval from the IRS is also not required. Form 970 must be filed with the return and the beginning inventory for LIFO purposes is the same as under the former inventory method.[76]

If the former inventory is valued based on the lower of cost or market (LCM) method, an adjustment is required to restate the beginning inventory to cost because the LCM method cannot be used under LIFO. Generally, the beginning LIFO inventory is the same as the closing inventory for the prior year, except for the required restatement of previous writedowns to market. This adjustment to the beginning inventory can be spread ratably over the year of the change and the next two years.[77]

EXAMPLE I11-37 ▶ Delaware Corporation elects to change to the LIFO inventory method for 2002. In 2001 Delaware's inventories are valued using the LCM method based on the FIFO cost-flow assumption. The FIFO cost for the ending inventory in 2001 is $50,000, and its LCM amount is $35,000. The initial inventory for 2002 under LIFO must be restated to its cost, or $50,000. The $15,000 ($50,000 cost − $35,000 LCM value) difference can be included in taxable income over the current year and next two years. $5,000 is added to taxable income in 2002, 2003, and 2004. ◀

PROBLEM MATERIALS

DISCUSSION QUESTIONS

I11-1 Do accounting rules determine the amount of income to be reported by a taxpayer?

I11-2 How does a taxpayer's tax accounting method affect the amount of tax paid?

I11-3 Most individuals use the calendar year as their tax year. What requirement, if any, in the tax law causes this?

I11-4 Why is it desirable for a new taxpayer to select an appropriate tax year?

I11-5 What restrictions apply to partnerships selecting a tax year?

I11-6 Does a similar restriction apply to S corporations? Explain.

I11-7 How could the 52-53 week year prove to be beneficial to taxpayers? Explain.

I11-8 Under what circumstances can an individual taxpayer change tax years without IRS approval?

I11-9 Is there any instance in which a change in tax years is required? Explain.

I11-10
a. In what situations will a tax year cover a period of less than 12 months?
b. Under what conditions is a taxpayer required to annualize income?
c. Does annualizing income increase or decrease the taxpayer's tax liability? Explain.

I11-11 When is a final tax return due for an individual who uses a calendar year and who dies during the year?

I11-12
a. Is it correct to say that businesses with inventories must use the accrual method?
b. What other restrictions apply to taxpayers who are choosing an overall tax accounting method?
c. Why is the cash method usually preferred to the accrual method?

I11-13
a. Does the term *method of accounting* refer only to overall methods of accounting? Explain.
b. Does a taxpayer's accounting method affect the total amount of income reported over an extended time period?
c. How can the use of an accounting method affect the total amount of tax paid over time?

I11-14
a. When are expenses deductible by a cash method taxpayer?
b. Are the rules that determine when interest is deductible by a cash method taxpayer the same as for other expenses?

[75] An acceptable election is considered to have been made even if Form 970 is not filed as long as all of the information required by Reg. Sec. 1.472-3(a) is provided by the taxpayer.

[76] Reg. Sec. 1.472-2(c).

[77] Sec. 472(d).

c. Is a cash method taxpayer subject to the same rules for depreciable assets as accrual method taxpayers?

I11-15 Who may use the completed contract method of reporting income from long-term contracts?

I11-16 When is a cash method taxpayer allowed to deduct deposits?

I11-17 What constitutes a payment in determining when a cash-basis taxpayer is entitled to deduct an expense?

I11-18 What is meant by economic performance?

I11-19 What conditions must be met if the economic performance test is to be waived for an accrual-method taxpayer?

I11-20 When is an accrual method taxpayer permitted to deduct estimated expenses? Explain.

I11-21 What is the significance of the *Thor Power Tool Co.* decision?

I11-22 a. How are overhead costs treated in determining a manufacturing company's inventory?
b. Do retailers have a similar rule?
c. Are these rules the same as for financial accounting? If not, explain.

I11-23 What transactions are subject to the long-term contract method of reporting?

I11-24 a. What conditions must be met in order to use the installment method?
b. Why would a taxpayer elect not to use the installment method?

I11-25 What is the impact of having the entire gain on an installment sale consist of ordinary income from depreciation recapture?

I11-26 What impact does the gifting of an installment obligation have on the donor?

I11-27 What treatment is given to an installment sale involving related people?

I11-28 What is the primary impact of the imputed interest rules on installment sales?

I11-29 What changes in accounting method can be made without IRS approval?

I11-30 Can the IRS require a taxpayer to change accounting methods?

I11-31 Explain the purpose of the four-year method used in computing the tax resulting from a net adjustment due to a change in accounting methods.

I11-32 If a taxpayer changes the method of accounting used for financial reporting purposes, must the taxpayer also change his or her method of accounting for tax purposes?

ISSUE IDENTIFICATION QUESTIONS

I11-33 Judy's Cars, Inc. sells collectible automobiles to consumers. She employs the specific identification inventory valuation method. Prices are negotiated by Judy and individual customers. Judy accepts trade-ins when she sells an automobile. Judy negotiates the allowance for trade with the customer. Occasionally, Judy finds that it can take two or three years to sell a given automobile. Judy now has four automobiles that she has held for over two years. She expects to eventually sell those automobiles, but expects that they will sell for less than their original cost. What tax issues should Judy consider?

I11-34 Lana operates a real estate appraisal service business in a small town serving local lenders. After noting that lenders must pay to bring in a surveyor from out of town, she completes a course and obtains a surveyor's license that enables her to provide this service also. She now provides both services as a proprietor. What tax issues should Lana consider?

I11-35 John owns a small farm on a lake. A local developer offers John $400,000 cash for his farm. The developer believes John's farm will be very attractive to home buyers because it is on a lake. After John turns down the initial offer, the developer offers to pay John $250,000 plus an amount equal to 10% of the selling price for the homes that are developed and sold. Identify the tax issues John should consider if he accepts the offer.

I11-36 Lee is starting a small lawn service. On the advice of his accountant, Lee has formed a corporation and made an S corporation election. The accountant has asked Lee to consider electing a fiscal year ending on the last day in February. The accountant pointed out that Lee's business is likely to slow down in the winter. Also, the accountant indicated that the February year end would permit the accountant to do Lee's accounting work after the busy season in accounting is over. What tax issues should Lee consider?

PROBLEMS

I11-37 *Allowable Taxable Year.* For each of the following cases, indicate whether the taxpayer has selected an allowable tax year in an initial year. If the year selected is not acceptable, indicate what an acceptable year would be.
a. A corporation selects a January 15 year-end.
b. A corporation selects a March 31 year-end.

c. A corporation selects a year that ends on the last Friday in March.
d. A partnership selects a year that ends on December 31 and has three equal partners whose years end on March 31, April 30, and June 30.
e. An S corporation selects a December 31 year-end.

I11-38 *Change in Accounting Period.* In which of the following instances is a taxpayer permitted to change accounting periods without IRS approval?
a. A calendar-year taxpayer who wishes to change to a year that ends on the last Friday in December.
b. ABC Partnership has filed its tax return using a fiscal-year ending on March 31 for over 40 years. The partnership wishes to change to a calendar year-end that coincides with its partners' year-end.
c. Iowa Corporation, a newly acquired subsidiary, wishes to change its year-end to coincide with its parent.

I11-39 *Annualization.* Each of the following cases involves a taxable year of less than 12 months. In which situations is annualization required?
a. A new corporation formed in September elects a calendar year.
b. A calendar-year individual dies on June 15.
c. Jean, who has been using a calendar year, marries Hank, a fiscal-year taxpayer. Soon after the marriage, Jean changes her tax year to coincide with her husband's tax year.
d. A calendar-year corporation liquidates on April 20.

I11-40 *Short Period Return.* Lavanya, a single taxpayer, is a practicing accountant. She obtains permission to change her tax year from the calendar year to a year ending July 31. Her practice income for the seven months ending July 31 is $40,000. In addition, Lavanya has $3,000 of interest income and $6,250 of itemized deductions. She is entitled to one exemption. What is her tax for the short period?

I11-41 *Cash Basis Expenses.* How much of the following expenses are currently deductible by a cash basis taxpayer?
a. Medical prescriptions costing $20 paid by credit card (medical expenses already exceed the 7.5% of AGI floor).
b. Prepaid interest (not related to points) of $200 on a residential loan.
c. Taxpayer borrows $300 from the bank to make a charitable contribution. The $300 is paid to the charitable organization before the end of the tax year.
d. Taxpayer gives a note to his church indicating an intent to contribute $300.
e. A calendar-year individual mails a check for $200 to his church on December 31. The check is postmarked December 31 and clears the bank on January 4.

I11-42 *Economic Performance.* In light of the economic performance requirement, how much is deductible by the following accrual-basis corporate taxpayers in 2002?
a. Camp Corporation sells products with a one-year warranty. In 2002 Camp estimates that the warranty costs on products sold during the year will amount to $80,000. In 2001 Camp performs $38,000 of warranty work on products sold during 2001 and $36,000 of warranty work on products sold in 2002.
b. Data Corporation agrees to pay $10,000 per year for two years to a software developer. The developer has completed all work on the software and delivers the product to Data before the end of 2002.
c. In 2002 Palm Corporation pays $5,000 to a supplier to guarantee delivery of raw materials. The $5,000 is refundable if Palm decides not to acquire the materials.
d. In 2002 North Corporation pays a $1,000 security deposit on space it rents for a new office. In addition, North pays 2002 rent of $18,000. The security deposit is refundable if the property is returned in good condition.

I11-43 *Manufacturing Inventory.* Which of the following costs must be included in inventory by a manufacturing company?
a. Raw materials
b. Advertising
c. Payroll taxes for factory employees
d. Research and experimental costs
e. Factory insurance
f. Repairs to factory equipment
g. Factory utility costs
h. Factory rent

I11-44 ***Single Pool LIFO.*** Prime Corporation begins operations in late 2002. Prime decides to use the single pool LIFO method. Year-end inventories under FIFO are as follows:

2002	$110,000
2003	134,000
2004	125,000

The price index for 2002 is 130%; for 2003, 134%; and 2004, 140%. What are 2003 and 2004 inventories?

I11-45 ***Installment Sale.*** In 2002 Ace Construction Company sells a used crane to Go Construction Company. The crane, which cost $87,000 in 1994, sells for $80,000. Ace has deducted the entire cost of the crane under MACRS depreciation. Ace receives $20,000 down and is to receive $20,000 per year plus 10% interest for four years. Under the Sec. 1245 depreciation recapture rules, the entire gain is taxable as ordinary income. There is no applicable installment obligation. How much of the gain is taxable in 2002? 2003?

I11-46 ***Inventory Method.*** Zap Company manufactures computer hard drives. The cost of hard drives has been declining for years. Sales totaled $4,000,000 last year. Zap's ending inventory was valued at $300,000 under FIFO. The company's new president is trying to cut taxes and asks you whether the company should switch to LIFO. What do you recommend?

I11-47 ***Installment Sales.*** First Company sold the following assets during the year. Indicate whether First Company can use the installment method to report each transaction. If not, how is the transaction reported? Assume First Company is an accrual basis taxpayer.

a. First Company sold stock in a publicly held company costing $35,000. First Company received a $20,000 down payment and is to receive $20,000 per year for two years plus interest.
b. First Company sold land costing $150,000. First Company received a $20,000 down payment and is to receive $20,000 per year for five years plus interest.
c. First Company initiated credit sales of merchandise. The company previously sold merchandise only to cash customers. Cash sales this year totaled $4,000,000. Credit sales totaled $500,000. At year end, First Company has receivables of $100,000. The company expects to collect only $85,000 of the current receivables.

I11-48 ***Installment Sale.*** On December 31, 2002, Dan sells unlisted stock with a cost of $14,000 for $20,000. Dan collects $5,000 down and is scheduled to receive $5,000 per year for three years plus interest at a rate acceptable to the IRS.

a. How much gain must Dan recognize in 2002? Assume Dan uses the installment method to report the gain.
b. In early January 2003, Dan sells the three installments for a total of $13,800. How much gain or loss must Dan recognize from the sale?

I11-49 ***Repossession.*** Lina, an attorney, sold an antique rug for $45,000 that had been in her home. The rug cost Lina $12,000 several years ago. Lina collected $15,000 down and received a one-year interest bearing note for the balance. She is unable to collect the balance, and after incurring court costs of $500, she repossesses the rug. The rug is damaged when she recovers it and is now worth only $30,000.

a. How much gain must Lina report in the year of the sale?
b. How much gain, in any, must Lina report in the year she repossesses the rug?
c. What is the basis of the rug after the repossession?

I11-50 ***Deferred Payment Sale.*** Joe sells land with a $60,000 adjusted basis for $42,000. He incurs selling expenses of $2,000. The land is subject to a $10,000 mortgage. The buyer, who assumes the mortgage, pays $8,000 down and agrees to pay Joe $8,000 per year for three years plus interest. The installment obligations are worth $24,000.

a. How much gain or loss does Joe report in the year of the sale?
b. When does Joe report the interest income from the sale?
c. Does Joe report gain or loss when he collects the installment payments

I11-51 ***Imputed Interest.*** On January 30, 2002, Amy sells land to Bob for a stated price of $200,000. The full $200,000 is payable on January 30, 2004. No interest is stated. Amy, a cash-method taxpayer, purchased the land in 1998 for $130,000.

a. How much interest income must be reported by Amy on the sale? Assume a 9% rate compounded semiannually. The present value factor is 0.83856.
b. In what year is the interest reported?
c. How much gain is reported by Amy on the sale?

d. In what year is the gain reported?
e. What is Bob's basis in the land?

I11-52 *Change of Accounting Method.* Dana owns a retail store and is a cash method taxpayer. She changes to the accrual method in 2003. Dana's business income for 2003 is $30,000 computed on the accrual method. Her books show the following:

	December 31, 2002	*December 31, 2003*
Accounts receivable	$ 6,000	$ 5,300
Accounts payable	15,200	11,800
Inventory	12,000	12,400

a. What adjustment is necessary to Dana's income?
b. How should Dana report the adjustment?

I11-53 *Required Payment.* BCD Partnership has, for many years, had a March 31 year end. The Partnership's net income for the fiscal year ended March 31, 2003 is $400,000. Because of its fiscal year, BCD has $100,000 on deposit with the IRS from 2002.
a. How much must BCD add to the deposit?
b. When must BCD make the addition?
c. Will the partners receive any credit for the deposit? That is, are they permitted to treat the amount as estimated payments?

I11-54 *Change to LIFO.* Lance Corporation's management has asked whether they may change their inventory valuation method to LIFO. They now report their inventory using FIFO. If they can change, how would they go about it? How is the related adjustment handled?

I11-55 *Imputed Interest.* Jane loans $80,000 to John, her son, to permit him to purchase a principal residence. The loan principal is secured by John's residence, but the agreement does not specify any interest. The applicable federal rate for the year is 8%. John's net investment income is $800.
a. How much interest is imputed on the loan each year?
b. Assume that the amount of the loan is $125,000. How much interest is imputed on the loan?
c. Is John allowed to deduct the imputed interest?
d. What other tax implications are there for the loan?

I11-56 *Long-Term Contract.* King Construction Company is engaged in a road construction contract to build a highway over a three-year period. King will receive $11,200,000 for building five miles of highway. King estimates that it will incur $10,000,000 of costs before the contract is completed. As of the end of the first year King incurred $3,000,000 of costs allocated to the contract.
a. How much income from the contract must King report during the first year?
b. Assume King incurs an additional $5,000,000 of costs during the second year. How much income is reported during that year?
c. Assume that King incurs an additional $2,500,000 of costs in the third and final year of the contract. How much does King report during the third year?
d. Will King receive or pay look-back interest? Explain.

COMPREHENSIVE PROBLEM

I11-57 Dan turned age 65 and retired this year. He owned and operated a tugboat in the local harbor before his retirement. The boat cost $100,000 when he purchased it two years ago. A tugboat is 10-year property. Dan deducted $10,000 of depreciation on the boat the year he purchased it and he deducted $18,000 of depreciation last year. He sold the tugboat in November of this year for $90,000 collecting an $18,000 down payment. The buyer agreed to pay 8% interest annually on the unpaid balance and to pay $18,000 annually for four years toward the principal. The four $18,000 principal payments and related interest payments begin next year. Dan received $72,000 of business income and incurred other business expenses of $30,000 this year before he retired. He received Social Security benefits of $2,000 and withdrew $10,000 from a regular IRA account. He contributed $4,000 to his church, paid real property taxes of $2,000, and home mortgage interest of $6,500. Dan paid $200 of state income taxes when he filed last year's return earlier this year and he made estimated state income tax payments of $800 during the this year and $220 after year end. In addition, Dan made federal estimated payments of $8,000. Dan is a single, cash basis taxpayer. Ignore self-employment taxes.

a. Compute the depreciation for the current year on the tugboat.
b. Compute the amount of gain to be reported currently on the sale of the tugboat. Assume that Dan wants to use the installment method if it can be used. The accumulated depreciation on the tugboat is subject to Sec. 1245 depreciation recapture and must be reported currently.
c. How much interest, if any, must Dan report this year.
d. What is the income from the business, excluding the gain on the sale of the tugboat.
e. What is Dan's AGI.
f. What is the amount of Dan's itemized deductions.
g. What is Dan's taxable income.

TAX STRATEGY PROBLEMS

I11-58 Leon has a substantial portfolio of stocks and bonds as well as cash from some bonds that have recently matured. He has been looking at investing $200,000 in corporate bonds that pay 7% interest. The $14,000 of annual interest would be used to pay his 18 year old son's tuition at State University. A friend suggested that Leon loan the money "interest free" to his son, a student who has no other income. The son would then invest the $200,000 in the corporate bonds and use the $14,000 interest to pay his tuition. Leon is in the 30% tax bracket. Would such a strategy reduce his family's tax? Assume the applicable federal rate is 6.5%.

I11-59 Linda is selling land she has owned for many years. The land cost $80,000 and will sell for $200,000. The buyer has offered to pay $100,000 down and pay the balance next year plus interest at 8%. Assume that Linda's after tax rate of return on investments is 10%. Would she be better off receiving the installment payments or receiving cash? Assume her ordinary income is taxed at 30% and that long-term capital gains are taxed at 20%.

TAX FORM/RETURN PREPARATION PROBLEM

I11-60 Barbara B. Kuhn (SSN 987-65-4321) purchases a fourplex on January 8, 1998 for $175,000. She allocates $25,000 of the cost to the land, and she deducts MACRS depreciation totaling $16,364. Barbara sells the fourplex on January 6, 2001, for $225,000. The buyer assumes the existing mortgage of $180,000, pays $15,000 down, and agrees to pay $15,000 per year for two years plus 12% interest. Barbara incurs selling expenses of $18,000. Complete Form 6252.

CASE STUDY PROBLEMS

I11-61 Lavonne just completed medical school and residency. She plans to open her medical practice soon. She is not familiar with the intricacies of accounting methods and periods. On advice of her attorney, she plans to form a professional corporation (a form of organization permitted under the laws of most states that does not have the usual limited liability found with business corporations, but is taxed as a corporation). She has asked you whether she should elect a fiscal year and whether she should use the cash or accrual method of reporting income. Discuss whether the options are available to her and the implications of available choices.

I11-62 Don owns an office building that he purchased several years ago. He purchased the building for $400,000, allocated $280,000 of the purchase price to the structure, and over the years properly deducted $110,000 of depreciation. The depreciation will have to be recaptured as ordinary income on the sale. There is a $90,000 mortgage on the property. Don has an offer to purchase the building from an individual who says he will pay $100,000 down and $100,000 per year for five years. There is no mention of interest. As the mortgage is nonassumable, Don will pay off the mortgage using most of the down payment. Don is age 61, and proceeds from the sale along with a pension from his employer will provide for his retirement. Don plans to retire next year. He currently has a 28% marginal tax rate. Discuss the tax implications of the sale. Is there anything Don can do to improve his situation?

I11-63 Troy Tools manufactures over one hundred different hand tools used by mechanics, carpenters, and plumbers. Troy's cost accounting system has always been very simple. The costs allocated to inventory have included only materials, direct labor, and factory overhead. Other overhead costs such as costs of the personnel department, purchasing, payroll, and computer services have never been treated as manufacturing overhead even though many of the activities of the departments relate to the manufacturing operations.

You are preparing Troy's tax return for the first time and determine that the company is not following the uniform capitalization rules prescribed in the tax law. You have explained to the company's president that there is a problem, and she is reluctant to change accounting methods. She says allocating these costs to the many products the company makes will be a time-consuming and expensive process. She feels that the cost of determining the additional amounts to include in inventory under the uniform capitalization rules will probably be more than the additional tax that the company will pay. What is the appropriate way to handle this situation? (See the *Statements on Standards for Tax Services* section in Chapter I15 for a discussion of these issues.)

TAX RESEARCH PROBLEMS

I11-64 Eagle and Hill Corporations discuss the terms of a land sale in December 2002, and they agree to a price of $230,000. Eagle wants to use the installment sale method, but is not sure Hill is a reliable borrower. As a result, Eagle requires Hill to place the entire purchase price in escrow to be released in five yearly installments by the escrow agent. Is the installment method available to Eagle?

A partial list of research sources is

- Rev. Rul. 77-294, 1977-2 C.B. 173
- Rev. Rul. 79-91, 1979-1 C.B. 179
- *H. O. Williams v. U.S.*, 46 AFTR 1725, 55-1 USTC ¶9220 (5th Cir., 1955)

I11-65 Texas Corporation disassembles old automobiles for the purpose of reselling their components (i.e., different types of metals, plastics, rubber, and other materials). Texas sells some of the items for scrap, but must pay to dispose of environmentally hazardous plastics and rubber. At year-end, Texas Corporation has a difficult time determining the cost of the individual parts that are stacked in piles. In fact, it would be very expensive to even weigh some of the materials on hand. Texas has followed the practice of having two experienced employees estimate the weight of different stacks and then pricing them based on quotes found in trade journals. If Texas must pay to dispose of an item, it is assigned a value of zero. In other words, Texas does not value its inventory using standard FIFO or LIFO methods. Is such a practice acceptable?

A partial list of research sources is

- Reg. Secs. 1.471-2(a) and 1.471-3(d)
- *Morrie Chaitlen*, 1978 PH T.C. Memo ¶78,006, 37 TCM 17
- *Justus & Parker Co.*, 13 BTA 127 (1928)

I11-66 Apple Corporation has never been audited before the current year. An audit is now needed from a CPA because the company is in a rapid expansion period and is planning to issue stock to the public in a secondary offering. A CPA firm has been doing preliminary evaluations of the Apple Corporation's accounts and records. One major problem involves the valuation of inventory under GAAP. Apple Corporation has been valuing its inventory under the cost method and no write-downs have been made for obsolescence. A review of the inventory indicates that obsolescence and excess spare parts in the inventory are two major problems. The CPA states that for GAAP the company will be required to write down its inventory by 25% of its stated amount, or $100,000, and charge this amount against net income from operations for the current period. Otherwise, a "clean opinion" will not be rendered. The company controller asks your advice regarding the tax consequences from the obsolescence and spare parts inventory write-downs for the current year and the procedures for changing to the LCM method for tax purposes. Apple Corporation is on a calendar year, and the date of your contact with the company is December 1 of the current year.

A partial list of research sources is

- Secs. 446 and 471
- Reg. Secs. 1.446-1(e)(3), 1.471-2 and 1.471-4
- *American Liberty Pipe Line Co. v. CIR,*, 32 AFTR 1099, 44-2 USTC ¶9408 (5th Cir., 1944)
- *Thor Power Tool Co. v. CIR*, 43 AFTR 2d 79-362,79-1 USTC ¶9139 (USSC, 1979)

12

CHAPTER

PROPERTY TRANSACTIONS: NONTAXABLE EXCHANGES

LEARNING OBJECTIVES

After studying this chapter, you should be able to

1. Understand the tax consequences arising from a like-kind exchange
2. Determine the basis of property received in a like-kind exchange
3. Determine whether gain from an involuntary conversion may be deferred
4. Determine the basis of replacement property in an involuntary conversion
5. Determine when a gain resulting from the sale of a principal residence is excluded

CHAPTER OUTLINE

Like-Kind Exchanges...12-2
Involuntary Conversions...12-10
Sale of Principal Residence...12-16

Taxpayers who sell or exchange property for an amount greater or less than their basis in that property have a realized gain or loss on the sale or exchange. Almost any transfer of property is treated as a sale or other disposition (see Chapter I5). The realized gain or loss must be recognized unless a specific Code section provides for nonrecognition treatment. If the realized gain or loss is not recognized at the time of the transaction, the nonrecognized gain or loss may be deferred in some cases and excluded in others.

The general rules related to the computation of realized and recognized gains or losses are covered in Chapter I5. This chapter discusses three of the most common transactions that may result in *nonrecognition* of a realized gain or loss:

- Like-kind exchanges under Sec. 1031 (deferred gain or loss)
- Involuntary conversions under Sec. 1033 (deferred gain)
- Sales of a personal residence under Sec. 121 (excluded gain)

KEY POINT

The transactions examined in this chapter override the normal rule that provides for the recognition of realized gains and realized losses on property used in a business or held for investment.

Nonrecognition of gain treatment for like-kind exchanges, involuntary conversions, and the sale of a residence may be partially justified by the fact that taxpayers may lack the wherewithal to pay the tax despite the existence of a realized gain. For example, a taxpayer who realizes a gain due to an involuntary conversion of property (damage from fire, storm, etc.) may have to use the amount received to replace the converted property.

A typical requirement in a nontaxable exchange is that the taxpayer is required to maintain a continuing investment in comparable property (e.g., a building is exchanged for another building). In essence, a change in form rather than a change in substance occurs.

A transaction generally considered to be nontaxable may be taxable in part. In a like-kind exchange, for example, the taxpayer may also receive money or property that is not like–kind property. If non-like-kind property or money is received, the realized gain is taxable to the extent of the sum of the money and the fair market value (FMV) of the non–like-kind property received.[1]

LIKE-KIND EXCHANGES

OBJECTIVE 1

Understand the tax consequences arising from a like-kind exchange

Section 1031(a) provides that "No gain or loss shall be recognized on the exchange of property held for productive use in a trade or business or for investment if such property is exchanged solely for property of like-kind which is to be held either for productive use in a trade or business or for investment."[2]

In a **like-kind exchange**, both the property transferred and the property received must be held either for productive use in the trade or business or for investment.

EXAMPLE I12-1 ▶ Tom owns land used in his trade or business. He exchanges the land for other land, which is to be held for investment. No gain or loss is recognized by Tom because he has exchanged property used in a trade or business for like-kind property to be held for investment. ◀

EXAMPLE I12-2 ▶ Dawn's automobile is held only for personal use. She exchanges the automobile, which has a $10,000 basis, for stock of AT&T with a $12,000 FMV. The stock will be held for investment. A $2,000 gain is recognized because the automobile is not used in Dawn's trade or business or held for investment. The exchange is not a like-kind exchange because neither personal-use assets nor stock qualify as like-kind property. ◀

REAL-WORLD EXAMPLE

An exchange or trade of professional football player contracts qualifies as a like-kind exchange. Rev. Rul. 71-137, 1971-1 C.B. 104.

Section 1031 is not an elective provision. If the exchange qualifies as a like-kind exchange, nonrecognition of gain or loss is mandatory. To qualify for like-kind exchange treatment, a direct exchange must occur and the property exchanged must be like-kind. A taxpayer who prefers to recognize a loss on an exchange must structure the transaction to avoid having the exchange qualify as a like-kind exchange.

ADDITIONAL COMMENT

The mandatory nonrecognition of loss under Sec. 1031 can be avoided by selling the old property in one transaction and buying the new property in a separate, unrelated transaction.

LIKE-KIND PROPERTY DEFINED

CHARACTER OF THE PROPERTY. To be a nontaxable exchange under Sec. 1031, the property exchanged must be like-kind. The Treasury Regulations specify that "the words

[1] Sec. 1031(b).

[2] Sec. 1031(a).

'like-kind' have reference to the nature or character of the property and not to its grade or quality."[3] Thus, exchanges of real property qualify even if the properties are dissimiliar.

EXAMPLE I12-3 ▶ Eric owns an apartment building held for investment. Eric exchanges the building for farmland to be used in his trade or business. The exchange is a like-kind exchange because both the building and the farmland are classified as real property and both properties are used either in business or held for investment. ◀

EXAMPLE I12-4 ▶ Trail Corporation exchanges improved real estate for unimproved real estate, both of which are held for investment. The exchange is a like-kind exchange.[4] ◀

ADDITIONAL COMMENT

Real property is often referred to as real estate.

LOCATION OF THE PROPERTY. Transfers of real property located in the U.S. and real property located outside the U.S. after July 9, 1989, are not like-kind exchanges. Exchanges of personal property predominantly used in the United States and personal property used outside of the United States that occur after June 8, 1997, are not like-kind exchanges. To determine where the property is predominantly used, the two-year period ending on the date the property is exchanged is analyzed. For property received, the location of predominant use is determined by analyzing the use during the two-year property after the property is received.

PROPERTY MUST BE THE SAME CLASS. An exchange is not a like-kind exchange when property of one class is exchanged for property of a different kind or class.[5] For example, if real property is exchanged for personal property (or vice versa), no like-kind exchange occurs.[6]

EXAMPLE I12-5 ▶ Gail exchanges an office building with a $400,000 adjusted basis for an airplane with a $580,000 FMV to be used in business. This is not a like-kind exchange because the office building is real property and the airplane is personal property. Gail must recognize a $180,000 ($580,000 − $400,000) gain. ◀

EXAMPLE I12-6 ▶ Gary exchanges a business truck for another truck to use in his business. This is an exchange of like-kind property. ◀

ADDITIONAL COMMENT

The rules in the Regulations dealing with exchanges of personal property are not interpreted as liberally as the rules relating to real property.

PROPERTY OF A LIKE CLASS. The Treasury Regulations provide that personal property of a **like class** meets the definition of *like-kind*.[7] Like class property is defined as depreciable tangible personal properties within the same General Asset Class or within the same Product Class.[8] Property within a General Asset Class consists of depreciable tangible personal property described in one of the asset classes provided in Rev. Proc. 87-56 for depreciation.[9] Some of the General Asset Classes are as follows:

- ▶ Office furniture, fixtures, and equipment (Asset Class 00.11)
- ▶ Information systems such as computers and peripheral equipment (Asset Class 00.12)
- ▶ Automobiles and taxis (Asset Class 00.22)
- ▶ Buses (Asset Class 00.23)
- ▶ Light general purpose trucks (Asset Class 00.231)
- ▶ Heavy general purpose trucks (Asset Class 00.242)
- ▶ Vessels, barges, tugs, and similar water-transportation equipment except those used in marine construction (Asset Class 00.28)

For purposes of the like-kind exchange provisions, a single property may not be classified in more than one General Asset Class or more than one Product Class. Furthermore, property in any General Asset Class may not be classified in a Product Class. A property's General Asset Class or Product Class is determined as of the exchange date.

---

[3] Reg. Sec. 1.1031(a)-1(b).
[4] *Ibid.*
[5] *Ibid.*
[6] Real property includes land and property attached to land in a relatively permanent manner. Personal property that is affixed to real property in a relatively permanent manner is a fixture and is considered part of the real property. Personal property is all property that is not real property or a fixture.
[7] Reg. Sec. 1.1031(a)-2.
[8] Reg. Sec. 1.1031(a)-2(b).
[9] 1987-2 C.B. 674.

EXAMPLE I12-7 ▶ Wint transfers a personal computer used in his trade or business for a printer to be used in his trade or business. The exchange is a like-kind exchange because both properties are in the same General Asset Class (00.12). ◀

EXAMPLE I12-8 ▶ Renee transfers an airplane (Asset Class 00.21) that she uses in her trade or business for a heavy general purpose truck to use in her trade or business. The properties are not of a like class because they are in different General Asset Classes. The heavy general purpose truck is in Asset Class 00.242. ◀

Example I12-8 is taken from the Treasury Regulations, which further state: "Because each of the properties is within a General Asset Class, the properties may not be classified within a Product Class. The airplane and heavy general purpose truck are also not of a like kind. Therefore, the exchange does not qualify for nonrecognition of gain or loss under Sec. 1031."[10]

If two properties are not within a General Asset Class, it still may be possible to be considered like-kind if the properties are within the same Product Class. Property in a Product Class consists of depreciable tangible personal property listed in a 4-digit product class in Division D of the ***Standard Industrial Classification (SIC)*** codes set forth in the *Standard Industrial Classification Manual.*[11] The Regulations state that an exchange of a grader for a scrapper is an exchange of properties of like class because neither property is in a General Asset Class and both properties are listed in the same Product Class (SIC code 3533).[12]

There are no like classes for intangible personal property, nondepreciable personal property, or personal property held for investment. To have a like-kind exchange of property held for investment, the property must be exchanged for like-kind property. To determine whether an exchange of intangible personal property is a like-kind exchange, one must consider the type of right involved as well as the underlying property to which the intangible property relates. An exchange of a copyright for a novel for a copyright on a different novel is a like-kind exchange, but the exchange of a copyright on a novel for a copyright on a song is not a like-kind exchange.[13]

ADDITIONAL COMMENT

An exchange can be a like-kind exchange for one party to the transaction but not qualify as a like-kind exchange for the other party.

NON–LIKE-KIND PROPERTY EXCHANGES. An exchange of inventory or securities does not qualify as a like-kind exchange.[14]

EXAMPLE I12-9 ▶ Antonio, a dealer in farm equipment, exchanges a new combine for other property in the same General Asset Class to be used in Antonio's trade or business. Because Antonio is a dealer, the new combine is inventory and the exchange does not qualify as a like-kind exchange. ◀

EXAMPLE I12-10 ▶ Nancy owns Able Corporation stock as an investment. Nancy exchanges the stock for antiques to be held as investments. This exchange is taxable because stock does not qualify as like-kind property. ◀

In most cases, to qualify as a like-kind exchange of personal property, the property must be nearly identical. For example, livestock of different sexes are not like-kind property.[15] An exchange of gold bullion held for investment for silver bullion held for investment is not a like-kind exchange. Silver and gold are intrinsically different metals and primarily are used in different ways.[16] Currency exchanges are not like-kind exchanges,[17] and the exchange of a partnership interest for an interest in another partnership is not a like-kind exchange.[18]

---

[10] Reg. Sec. 1.1031(a)-2(b)(7) Ex. 2.

[11] Reg. Sec. 1.1031(a)-2(b)(3).

[12] Reg. Sec. 1.1031(a)-2(b)(7) Ex. 3.

[13] Reg. Sec. 1.1031(a)-2(c)(1).

[14] Sec. 1031(a)(2). An exchange of stock is not a like-kind exchange. However, an exchange of stock is a nontaxable exchange if the exchange is related to a tax-free reorganization.

[15] Sec. 1031(e).

[16] Rev. Rul. 82-166, 1982-2 C.B. 190.

[17] Rev. Rul. 74-7, 1974-1 C.B. 198.

[18] Sec. 1031(a)(2).

EXCHANGE OF SECURITIES. The like-kind exchange rules do not apply to stocks, bonds, or notes.[19] However, Sec. 1036 provides that no gain or loss is recognized on the exchange of common stock for common stock or preferred stock for preferred stock in the same corporation. Sec. 1036 applies even if voting common stock is exchanged for nonvoting common stock of the same corporation. The nontaxable exchange of stock of the same corporation may be between two stockholders or a stockholder and the corporation.[20]

Section 1036 does not apply to exchanges of common stock for preferred stock; stock for bonds of same corporation, or any kind of stock in different corporations.

EXAMPLE I12-11 ▶ Kelly owns common stock of Best Corporation. Best issues class B common stock to Kelly in exchange for her common stock. No gain or loss is recognized because this is an exchange of common stock for common stock in the same corporation. If Best issues its preferred stock for Kelly's common stock, Kelly will have a recognized gain or loss unless there is a tax-free reorganization. ◀

EXAMPLE I12-12 ▶ Shirley owns 100 shares of Top Corporation common stock. The stock has a $40,000 adjusted basis and a $50,000 FMV. Bob owns 100 shares of Star Corporation common stock with a $50,000 FMV. If Shirley and Bob exchange their stock, the exchange is taxable, and Shirley has a $10,000 ($50,000 − $40,000) recognized gain. The exchange is neither a like-kind exchange nor an exchange of stock for stock of the same corporation. ◀

A DIRECT EXCHANGE MUST OCCUR

To qualify as a like-kind exchange, a direct exchange of property must occur.[21] Thus, the sale of property and the subsequent purchase of like-kind property does not qualify as a like-kind exchange unless the two transactions are interdependent.

EXAMPLE I12-13 ▶ Karen sells a lathe used in her business to Rashad for an amount greater than the lathe's adjusted basis. After the sale, Karen purchases another lathe from David. The gain is recognized because these two transactions do not qualify as an exchange of like-kind property. ◀

A sale and a subsequent purchase may be treated as an exchange if the two transactions are interdependent. The IRS indicates that a nontaxable exchange may exist when the taxpayer sells property to a dealer and then purchases like-kind property from the same dealer.[22]

THREE-PARTY EXCHANGES

The typical two-party exchange is not always practical. If both parties do not own like-kind property that meets each other's needs, a three-party exchange might be necessary. A three- party exchange is also useful when the taxpayer is willing to exchange property for like-kind property but is not willing to sell the property to a prospective buyer. The taxpayer's unwillingness to sell the property may be motivated by the desire to avoid an immediate tax on a gain resulting from the sale of the property. Therefore, the taxpayer may arrange to have the prospective buyer purchase property from a third party that fulfills the taxpayer's needs. The three-party exchange can be an effective way of allowing the taxpayer to consummate a like-kind exchange.

EXAMPLE I12-14 ▶ Kathy owns a farm in Nebraska, which Dick offers to purchase. Kathy is not willing to sell the farm but is willing to exchange the farm for an apartment complex in Arizona. The complex is available for sale. Dick purchases the apartment complex in Arizona from Allyson and transfers it to Kathy in exchange for Kathy's farm. The farm and the apartment complex each have a $900,000 FMV. For Kathy, the transaction qualifies as a like-kind exchange because it is a direct exchange of business real property (the farm) for investment real estate (the apartment complex). For Dick, the exchange is not a like-kind exchange. ◀

KEY POINT

Transfers of property in a three-party exchange must be part of a single, integrated plan. It is important that the taxpayers can show their intent to enter into a like-kind exchange even though contractual interdependence is not necessary to the finding of an exchange.

In the example above, the exchange is convenient for all the parties. However, it is not always this convenient to execute a three-party exchange. For example, Kathy may want

[19] Reg. Sec. 1.1031(a)-1(a)(1)(ii).
[20] Reg. Sec. 1.1036-1(a).
[21] Sec. 1031(a).
[22] Rev. Rul. 61-119, 1961-1 C.B. 395.

to own an apartment complex in Arizona, but the property she prefers may not be currently available. In this case, a nonsimultaneous exchange may occur.

TAX STRATEGY TIP

Deferred like-kind exchanges are typically used for real estate transactions. A taxpayer who has highly appreciated real estate can use a deferred, three-party, like-kind exchange to exchange the highly appreciated real estate for other real estate that is more desirable to him.

NONSIMULTANEOUS EXCHANGE. A nonsimultaneous exchange is treated as a like-kind exchange if the exchange is completed within a specified time period. The property to be received in the exchange must be identified within 45 days after the date of the transfer of the property relinquished in the exchange. The replacement property must be received within the earlier of 180 days after the date the taxpayer transfers the property relinquished in the exchange or the due date for filing a return (including extensions) for the year in which the transfer of the relinquished property occurs.[23]

EXAMPLE I12-15 ▶ On May 5, 2002, Joal transfers property to Lauren, who transfers cash to an escrow agent. The escrow agent is to purchase suitable like-kind property for Joal. Joal does not have actual or constructive receipt of the cash during the delayed period. To be a like-kind exchange for Joal, the suitable like-kind property must be identified by June 19, 2002 (45 days after the transfer) and Joal must receive the property by November 1, 2002 (180 days after the transfer). ◀

EXAMPLE I12-16 ▶ Assume the same facts as Example I12-15 except that the transfer by Joal occurs on November 10, 2002. To be a like-kind exchange for Joal, the suitable like-kind property must be identified by December 25, 2002 and Joal must receive the property by April 15, 2002 unless Joal files an automatic four-month extension for the filing of his return (i.e., the due date is extended until August 15, 2003). In such a case, the property must be received no later than 180 days following the transfer of the property relinquished in the exchange, or by May 8, 2003 (i.e., 180 days after November 10, 2002). ◀

RECEIPT OF BOOT

TYPICAL MISCONCEPTION

In calculating the amount of gain to be recognized when boot is received, it is important not to apply financial accounting principles, which use a proportionate approach.

Taxpayers who want to exchange property do not always own property of equal value. To complete the exchange, non–like-kind property or money may be given or received. Cash and non–like-kind property constitute **boot**.

Gain is recognized to the extent of the boot received. However, the amount of recognized gain is limited to the amount of the taxpayer's realized gain.[24] In effect, the realized gain serves as a ceiling for the amount of the recognized gain. The receipt of boot as part of a nontaxable exchange does not cause a realized loss to be recognized.[25]

EXAMPLE I12-17 ▶ Mario exchanges business equipment with a $50,000 adjusted basis for $10,000 cash and business equipment with a $65,000 FMV. The realized gain is $25,000 ($75,000 − $50,000). Because the $10,000 of boot received is less than the $25,000 of realized gain, the recognized gain is $10,000. ◀

EXAMPLE I12-18 ▶ Mary exchanges business equipment with a $70,000 adjusted basis for $20,000 cash and business equipment with a $65,000 FMV. Her realized gain is $15,000 ($85,000 − $70,000). Because the $20,000 of boot received is more than the $15,000 of realized gain, only $15,000 of gain is recognized. ◀

TYPICAL MISCONCEPTION

It is possible to erroneously assume that the receipt of boot causes the recognition of loss.

Taxing part or all of the gain when cash is received in like-kind exchanges is consistent with the wherewithal-to-pay concept. However, boot may not always be in the form of a liquid asset. If non-like-kind property other than cash is received as boot, the amount of the boot is the property's FMV.

EXAMPLE I12-19 ▶ Jane exchanges land held as an investment with a $70,000 basis for other land with a $100,000 FMV and a motorcycle with a $2,000 FMV. The acquired land is to be held for investment, and the motorcycle is for personal use. Personal-use property is non-like-kind property and constitutes boot. The realized gain is $32,000 [($100,000 + $2,000) − $70,000]. The amount of boot received is equal to the FMV of the motorcycle. The recognized gain is $2,000, the lesser of the amount of boot received ($2,000) or the realized gain ($32,000). ◀

---

[23] Secs. 1031(a)(3)(A) and (B).
[24] Sec. 1031(b).
[25] Sec. 1031(c).

EXAMPLE I12-20 ▶ Assume the same facts in Example I12-19 except that Jane uses the motorcycle in a business. The motorcycle is boot, and a $2,000 gain is still recognized because the exchange of real property for personal property is not a like-kind exchange. ◀

SELF-STUDY QUESTION

Why is the relief of a liability treated as if one has received cash?

ANSWER

If it were not treated as such, a taxpayer could receive cash shortly before the exchange by borrowing from a bank, using the property as collateral. Then, if the taxpayer is relieved of the debt in the like-kind exchange, he or she would still have the cash without having paid a tax on the gain.

PROPERTY TRANSFERS INVOLVING LIABILITIES. If a liability is assumed (or the property is taken subject to a liability), the amount of the liability is considered money received by the taxpayer on the exchange.[26] One who assumes the debt or takes the property subject to a liability is treated as having paid cash, while the party that is relieved of the debt is treated as having received cash. If each party assumes a liability of the other party, only the net liability given or received is treated as boot.[27]

EXAMPLE I12-21 ▶ Mary exchanges land with a $550,000 FMV that is used in her business for Doug's building, which has a $450,000 FMV. Mary's basis in the land is $400,000, and the land is subject to a liability of $100,000, which Doug assumes. Mary's realized gain is $150,000 [($450,000 + $100,000) − $400,000]. Because assumption of the $100,000 liability is treated as boot, Mary recognizes a $100,000 gain. ◀

EXAMPLE I12-22 ▶ Matt owns an office building with a $700,000 basis, which is subject to a liability of $200,000. Susan owns an apartment complex with a $900,000 FMV, which is subject to a $150,000 liability. Matt and Susan exchange buildings and assume the related liabilities. Matt's realized gain is $250,000 [($900,000 + $200,000) − ($700,000 + $150,000)]. Matt receives boot of $50,000 ($200,000 − $150,000) and recognizes a $50,000 gain. ◀

BASIS OF PROPERTY RECEIVED

OBJECTIVE 2

Determine the basis of property received in a like-kind exchange

LIKE-KIND PROPERTY RECEIVED. The basis of property received in a nontaxable exchange is equal to the adjusted basis of the property exchanged increased by gain recognized and reduced by any boot received or loss recognized on the exchange.[28]

$$\text{Basis of property received in a nontaxable exchange} = \text{Basis of property exchanged} - \text{Boot received} + \text{Gain recognized} - \text{Loss recognized}^{29}$$

EXAMPLE I12-23 ▶ Chuck, who is in the business of racing horses, exchanges a racehorse with a $30,000 basis for $10,000 cash and a trotter with an $80,000 FMV. Chuck's realized gain is $60,000 [($80,000 + $10,000) − $30,000], and $10,000 of the gain is recognized because the boot received is less than the realized gain. Chuck's basis for the replacement property (i.e., the trotter) is $30,000 ($30,000 basis of property exchanged − $10,000 of boot received + $10,000 of gain recognized). ◀

ADDITIONAL COMMENT

In effect the formula used to calculate the basis of the new property involves nothing more than journalizing the transaction and adjusting the basis of the new property by an amount needed to make the entry balance.

The basis of the like-kind property received can also be computed by subtracting the unrecognized gain from its FMV or by adding the unrecognized loss to its FMV. Chuck's $30,000 basis for the trotter in Example I12-23 may be computed by subtracting the $50,000 of unrecognized gain from the $80,000 FMV.

EXAMPLE I12-24 ▶ Pam, who operates a circus, exchanges an elephant with a $15,000 basis for $3,000 cash and a tiger with a $10,000 FMV. The $2,000 realized loss [($10,000 + $3,000) − $15,000] is not recognized. The receipt of boot does not cause a realized loss to be recognized. Pam's basis for the replacement property (i.e., the tiger) is $12,000 ($15,000 basis of property exchanged − $3,000 boot received). ◀

KEY POINT

The basis adjustment is the mechanism that ensures that gain or loss is temporarily postponed rather than permanently excluded.

As indicated earlier, realized gains and losses resulting from nontaxable exchanges are deferred. This deferral is reflected in the basis of property received and is illustrated in the

---

[26] Sec. 1031(d). If a liability is assumed, the taxpayer agrees to pay the debt. If property is taken subject to the liability, the taxpayer is responsible for the debt only to the extent that the property could be used to pay the debt.

[27] Reg. Sec. 1.1031(b)-1(c).

[28] Sec. 1031(d).

[29] A loss is recognized only when the taxpayer transfers boot with a basis greater than its FMV. Transfers of non–like-kind property (i.e. boot) are discussed in a separate section of this chapter.

two preceding examples. In Example I12-23, the $50,000 ($60,000 − $10,000) unrecognized gain may be recognized when the trotter is sold or exchanged in a taxable transaction, because the basis of the replacement property is less than its FMV by the amount of the deferred gain. For example, if the trotter is sold in a taxable transaction for its $80,000 FMV, the $50,000 ($80,000 − $30,000 basis) of previously unrecognized gain would be recognized. In Example I12-24, the $2,000 unrecognized loss is reflected in the basis of the tiger. If Pam sells the tiger for its $10,000 FMV, a $2,000 loss ($10,000 − $12,000 basis) is recognized.

If more than one item of like-kind property is received, the basis is allocated among the properties in proportion to their relative FMVs on the date of the exchange.

EXAMPLE I12-25 ▶ Saul, who operates a zoo, exchanges a boa constrictor with a $300 basis for a python with a $400 FMV and an anaconda with a $600 FMV. The $700 realized gain [($400 + $600) − $300] is not recognized. The total bases of the properties received is $300. This amount is allocated to the properties (i.e., the python and the anaconda) based on their relative FMVs. Saul's basis for the python is $120 [($400 ÷ $1,000) × $300], and the basis for the anaconda is $180 [($600 ÷ $1,000) × $300]. ◀

NON–LIKE-KIND PROPERTY RECEIVED. The basis of non–like-kind property received is "an amount equivalent to its FMV at the date of the exchange."[30]

EXAMPLE I12-26 ▶ Steve exchanges a punch press with a $20,000 adjusted basis for a press brake with a $50,000 FMV and $5,000 of marketable securities. Steve's realized gain is $35,000 [($50,000 + $5,000) − $20,000], and $5,000 of the realized gain is recognized due to the receipt of boot. Steve's basis for the marketable securities is $5,000, and the basis for the press brake is $20,000 ($20,000 basis of property exchanged − $5,000 boot received + $5,000 gain recognized). ◀

KEY POINT

Steve had basis of $20,000 before the exchange. Since he recognized gain of $5,000, the total basis of the two assets should be $25,000.

STOP & THINK *Question:* Chris Reedy owns 40 houses that he uses as rental property. All houses have a FMV greater than their adjusted basis. Chris wishes to diversify his investments and is considering selling ten of his houses and using the proceeds to purchase other types of investment assets such as stocks, bonds, commercial parking lots and land near town that he expects to increase in value. He asks you for advice.

Solution: If he sells the ten houses, he will have a gain and must pay taxes on the gain. He could defer the gain by exchanging the houses for like-kind property. Stocks and bonds are not like-kind property, but the commercial parking lots and the land should qualify as like-kind property, therefore the tax law encourages him to exchange the houses for the commercial parking lot and/or the land.

ADDITIONAL COMMENT

The running of the two-year holding period is suspended during any period in which the property holder's risk of loss is substantially diminished.

EXCHANGES BETWEEN RELATED PARTIES

Prior to 1990, related taxpayers could often use the like-kind exchange provisions to lower taxes because the tax basis for the property received is determined by the basis of the property exchanged. Related taxpayers could take advantage of the shift in tax basis to transfer a gain on a subsequent sale to a related party.[31] However, exchanges of property between related parties are not like-kind exchanges under current law if either party disposes of the property within two years of the exchange. Any gain resulting from the original exchange is recognized in the year of the subsequent disposition.[32] Dispositions due to death or involuntary conversion, or for non–tax avoidance purposes are disregarded.[33]

EXAMPLE I12-27 ▶ Melon Corporation, which is 100% owned by Linda, owned land with a basis of $200,000 that was held for investment. Rick wanted to purchase the land for $900,000. Linda owned an office building with a basis of $750,000 and a FMV of $900,000. Instead of selling the land to Rick, Melon Corporation exchanged the land for Linda's office building in December, 2001.

[30] Reg. Sec. 1.1031(d)-1(c).

[31] The definition of *related parties* is the same as those for Sec. 267(a) which is discussed in Chapter I6, and includes brothers, sisters, parents, children, and corporations where the taxpayer owns at least 50% in value. See Sec. 1031(f)(3).

[32] Sec. 1031(f)(1)(C).

[33] Secs. 1031(f)(2).

ADDITIONAL COMMENT

If Linda in Example 12-27 sells the land to Rick for $910,000, she has a $150,000 recognized gain on the exchange and a $10,000 recognized gain on the sale.

Two months later, Linda sells the land to Rick for $900,000. The exchange of the land for the office building is not a like-kind exchange because one of the related parties disposes of the property within two years of the exchange. In 2002, Melon's recognized gain on the exchange of the land is $700,000 ($900,000 − $200,000) and Linda's recognized gain on the exchange of the office building is $150,000 ($900,000 − $750,000). Because Linda's basis for the land is now $900,000, no gain is recognized on the sale of the land to Rick. ◀

If the parties in Example I12-27 were not related, a like-kind exchange occurred in 2001 and Linda's gain on the sale of the land to Rick is $150,000 ($900,000 − $750,000). Of course, the exchange is not a like-kind exchange if Linda does not hold the land for investment or for use in her trade or business after receiving it from Melon.

TRANSFER OF NON–LIKE-KIND PROPERTY

In all of the preceding examples that include a transfer of boot, the transferor (i.e., the taxpayer) received boot. If the taxpayer transfers non–like-kind property, gain or loss equal to the difference between the FMV and the adjusted basis of the non–like-kind property surrendered must be recognized. However, if the non–like-kind property is a personal use asset, the loss is not recognized.

EXAMPLE I12-28 ▶ Shirley exchanges land with a $30,000 basis and marketable securities with a $10,000 basis to David for land with a $60,000 FMV in a transaction that otherwise qualifies as a like-kind exchange. The FMV of the marketable securities and the land surrendered by Shirley is $14,000 and $46,000 respectively. Because the non–like-kind property that Shirley transfers has a FMV greater than its basis, she recognizes $4,000 ($14,000 − $10,000) of gain. Shirley's basis for the land received is $44,000 ($30,000 + $10,000 + $4,000), which is the basis of both assets exchanged plus the gain recognized on the exchange. ◀

EXAMPLE I12-29 ▶ Paul exchanges timberland held as an investment for undeveloped land with a $200,000 FMV. Paul's basis for the timberland is $125,000. His tractor with a $6,000 basis and a $4,000 FMV is also transferred. Because the non–like-kind property (i.e., the tractor) that Paul transfers has a FMV less than its basis, he recognizes a $2,000 ($4,000 − $6,000) loss. Paul's basis for the undeveloped land is $129,000 ($125,000 + $6,000 − $2,000). ◀

In Example I12-29, Paul recognizes a loss on the non–like-kind property he surrenders, despite receiving property in the aggregate with a FMV greater than the total adjusted basis of the transferred assets. Paul is actually making two exchanges. His exchange of timberland with a basis of $125,000 for undeveloped land with a $196,000 FMV is a like-kind exchange, but his exchange of the tractor with a basis of $6,000 for undeveloped land with a $4,000 FMV is a taxable exchange. In Example I12-30, Ed also makes two exchanges. He has a realized and recognized gain as well as a realized but unrecognized loss.

EXAMPLE I12-30 ▶ Ed owns equipment used in business with a $20,000 adjusted basis and a $15,000 FMV and marketable securities with a $10,000 basis and an $18,000 FMV. Ed exchanges the marketable securities and the equipment for business equipment in the same General Asset Class with a $33,000 FMV. Although the net realized gain is $3,000 [$33,000 − ($20,000 + $10,000)], Ed recognizes an $8,000 gain because he has transferred non–like-kind property with a $10,000 basis and an $18,000 FMV. The $5,000 realized loss on the transfer of equipment is not recognized due to the nonrecognition of gain or loss rules of Sec. 1031. Ed's basis for the equipment received is $38,000 ($20,000 + $10,000 + $8,000). ◀

KEY POINT

A taxpayer who exchanges like-kind property and non-like-kind property is actually making two exchanges.

ADDITIONAL COMMENT

The holding period is relevant only when the asset is a capital asset or a Sec. 1231 asset.

HOLDING PERIOD FOR PROPERTY RECEIVED

LIKE-KIND PROPERTY. The holding period of like-kind property received in a nontaxable exchange includes the holding period of the property exchanged if the like-kind property surrendered is a capital asset or an asset that is Sec. 1231 property. In essence, the holding period of the property exchanged carries over to the holding period of the like-kind property received.[34] The rule regarding the holding period carryover is consistent with the notion of a continuing investment in the underlying property that has been transferred.

[34] Sec. 1223(1) and Reg. Sec. 1.1223-1(a).

BOOT. The holding period for the boot property received begins the day after the date of the exchange.[35]

EXAMPLE I12-31 ▶ Mario owns a Van Gogh painting he acquired on May 1, 1991 as an investment. He exchanges the painting on April 10, 2002, for a Picasso sculpture and marketable securities to be held as investments. The holding period for the sculpture begins on May 1, 1991, and the holding period for the marketable securities starts on April 11, 2002. ◀

The like-kind exchange provisions are summarized in Topic Review I12-1.

Topic Review I12-1

Section 1031—Like-Kind Exchanges

- Gains and losses are not recognized for like-kind exchanges.
- Nonrecognition of gains and losses is mandatory if the exchange is a like-kind exchange.
- Section 1031 applies to exchanges of property used in a trade or business or held for investment.
- Property exchanged and received must be like-kind.
- Subject to certain time constraints, a nonsimultaneous exchange may qualify as a like-kind exchange.
- Some gain may be recognized if the taxpayer receives or gives non–like-kind property (boot) in an otherwise like-kind exchange.
- A loss may be recognized if the taxpayer transfers non–like-kind property (boot) in an otherwise like-kind exchange.
- The basis of property received in an exchange is the basis of the property exchanged less the boot received plus the gain recognized and less any loss recognized.
- The nonrecognized gain or loss is deferred.
- The holding period of like-kind property received includes the holding period of the property exchanged.

INVOLUNTARY CONVERSIONS

OBJECTIVE 3

Determine whether gain from an involuntary conversion may be deferred

KEY POINT

Unlike the like-kind exchange provisions which are mandatory, the involuntary conversion provisions are elective. Further, the involuntary conversion rules apply only to gains, not losses.

Taxpayers who realize a gain due to the involuntary conversion of property may elect to defer recognition of the entire gain if qualifying replacement property is acquired within a specified time period at a cost equal to or greater than the amount realized from the involuntary conversion. No gain is recognized if the property is converted "into property similar or related in service or use to the property so converted."[36]

The opportunity provided in Sec. 1033 to defer recognition of the gain reflects the fact that the taxpayer maintains a continuing investment and may lack the wherewithal to pay the tax on the gain that would otherwise be recognized. Furthermore, the involuntary conversion is beyond the taxpayer's control.

Note that the gain is deferred, not excluded. The basis of the replacement property is the property's cost reduced by the amount of gain deferred. The tax treatment for an involuntary conversion is similar to the tax treatment of a like-kind exchange.

EXAMPLE I12-32 ▶ Lenea's warehouse with a $500,000 basis is destroyed by a hurricane. She collects $650,000 from the insurance company and purchases a new warehouse for $720,000. Lenea may elect to defer recognition of the $150,000 gain ($650,000 – $500,000). If the election is made, the basis of the new warehouse is $570,000 ($720,000 – $150,000). The $150,000 gain is merely deferred rather than excluded, because an immediate sale of the replacement property at its $720,000 FMV results in a recognized gain equal to the deferred gain on the involuntarily converted property. For example, if the new warehouse is sold for $720,000, the recognized gain is $150,000 ($720,000 – $570,000). ◀

ADDITIONAL COMMENT

Property involved in an involuntary conversion need not be used in a trade or business or held for investment to qualify for the deferral of gain.

[35] Sec. 1223 and Reg. Sec. 1.1223-1(a).

[36] Sec. 1033(a)(1).

TYPICAL MISCONCEPTION
Occasionally, taxpayers fail to realize that Sec. 1033 applies only to gains, not losses.

Section 1033 does not apply to losses realized from an involuntary conversion. A taxpayer may not elect to defer recognition of a loss resulting from an involuntary conversion.

EXAMPLE I12-33 ▶ Barry's offshore drilling rig with an $800,000 basis is destroyed by a typhoon. He collects $700,000 from the insurance company and purchases a new drilling rig for $760,000. The $100,000 loss ($700,000 − $800,000) is recognized as a casualty loss, and the basis of the new drilling rig is its purchase price of $760,000. ◀

INVOLUNTARY CONVERSION DEFINED

ADDITIONAL COMMENT
Typically, an involuntary conversion consists of either a casualty or a condemnation.

For Sec. 1033 to apply, property must be compulsorily or involuntarily converted into money or other property. An **involuntary conversion** may be due to theft, seizure, requisition, condemnation, or destruction of the property. The destruction of the property may be complete or partial.[37] For purposes of Sec. 1033, destruction of property does not have to meet the "suddenness" test if the cause of destruction otherwise falls within the general concept of a casualty.[38]

An involuntary conversion occurs when a governmental unit exercises its power of eminent domain to acquire the taxpayer's property without the taxpayer's consent. Furthermore, the threat or imminence of requisition or condemnation of property may permit a taxpayer to defer recognition of gain from the sale or exchange of property under the involuntary conversion rules. Taxpayers who transfer property due to such a threat must be careful to confirm that a decision to acquire their property for public use has been made.[39] Written confirmation of potential condemnation is particularly helpful.[40]

EXAMPLE I12-34 ▶ Bruce owns an automobile dealership near a state university campus. On a number of occasions, the president of the university expressed an interest in acquiring Bruce's property for additional parking space. The president is not certain about the availability of funds for the purchase, and the university is reluctant to have the property condemned for its use. Based on the university's interest in the property, Bruce sells the property to the Jet Corporation. The threat or imminence of conversion does not exist merely because the property is being considered for acquisition. The sale does not constitute an involuntary conversion.[41] ◀

THREAT OF CONDEMNATION. If a threat of condemnation exists and the taxpayer has reasonable grounds to believe that the property will be condemned, Sec. 1033 applies even if the taxpayer sells the property to an entity other than the governmental unit that is threatening to condemn the property.[42]

EXAMPLE I12-35 ▶ At its regular meeting on Tuesday night, the city commission authorized the city attorney to start the process of condemning two lots owned by Beth for use as a public park. On Wednesday afternoon, Beth sells the two lots to Marty at a gain. The sale of property to Marty is an involuntary conversion, and Beth may elect to defer recognition of the gain if she satisfies the Sec. 1033 requirements. ◀

ADDITIONAL COMMENT
If the property in Example I12-35 is later condemned, Marty may be able to defer part or all of the gain.

CONVERSION MUST BE INVOLUNTARY. The conversion must be involuntary. For example, an involuntary conversion does not occur when a taxpayer pays someone to set fire to his or her building.[43] An involuntary conversion also does not occur when a taxpayer who is developing a subdivision, reserves certain property for a school site, and later sells the property to the school district under condemnation proceedings. In this situation, the taxpayer was required to reserve property for a school site in order to receive zoning approval for development of the subdivision.[44]

---

37 Reg. Sec. 1.1033(a)-1.
38 Rev. Rul. 59-102, 1959-1 C.B. 200.
39 Rev. Rul. 63-221, 1963-2 C.B. 332, and *Joseph P. Balistrieri*, 1979 PH T.C. Memo ¶79,115, 38 TCM 526.
40 Rev. Rul. 63-221, 1963-2 C.B. 332.
41 *Forest City Chevrolet*, 1977 PH T.C. Memo ¶77,187, 36 TCM 768.
42 Rev. Rul. 81-180, 1981-2 C.B. 161, and *Creative Solutions, Inc. v. U.S.*, 12 AFTR 2d 5229, 1963-2 USTC ¶9615 (5th Cir., 1963).
43 Rev. Rul. 82-74, 1982-1 C.B. 110.
44 Rev. Rul. 69-654, 1969-2 C.B. 162.

REAL-WORLD EXAMPLE

Because of mounting losses and declining property values, a taxpayer decided to burn down his building to collect the fire insurance proceeds. Although the building was converted into money (insurance proceeds) as a result of its destruction, this conversion was not involuntary within the meaning of Sec. 1033. Rev. Rul. 82-74, 1982-1 C.B. 110.

Although the typical involuntary conversion generally results from a casualty or condemnation, Sec. 1033 provides that certain transactions involving livestock are to be treated as involuntary conversions.[45] For example, the destruction or sale of livestock because of disease is an involuntary conversion.

TAX TREATMENT OF GAIN DUE TO INVOLUNTARY CONVERSION INTO BOOT

Gain may be deferred if the property is involuntarily converted into money or property that is not similar or related in service or use to the converted property.[46] The taxpayer must make a proper replacement of the converted property within a specific time period and elect to defer the gain.

REALIZED GAIN. The taxpayer's realized gain is the excess of the amount received due to the involuntary conversion over the adjusted basis of the property converted. The total award or proceeds received are reduced by expenses incurred to determine the amount realized (e.g., attorney's fees incurred in connection with determining the settlement to be received from a condemnation). If the payment of the award or proceeds is delayed, any amounts paid as interest are not included in determining the amount realized.[47] Amounts received as interest on an award for property condemned are taxed as ordinary income even if the interest is paid by a state or political subdivision.[48]

EXAMPLE I12-36 ▶ Richard's property with a $100,000 basis is condemned by the city of Phoenix. Richard receives a $190,000 award and pays $1,000 legal expenses for representation at the condemnation proceedings and $800 for an appraisal of the property. The amount realized is $188,200 [$190,000 – ($1,000 + $800)]. The gain realized is $88,200 ($188,200 – $100,000). Part or all of the realized gain may be deferred if the requirements of Sec. 1033 are satisfied and an election is made to defer the gain. ◀

ADDITIONAL COMMENT

The gain recognized is limited to the lesser of the gain realized or the excess of the amount realized from the conversion over the cost of the qualified replacement property.

GAIN RECOGNIZED. To defer the entire gain, the taxpayer must purchase replacement property with a cost equal to or greater than the amount realized from the involuntary conversion. If the replacement property is purchased for an amount less than the amount realized, that portion of the realized gain that is equal to the excess of the amount realized from the conversion over the cost of the replacement property must be recognized.[49]

EXAMPLE I12-37 ▶ Bob owns a restaurant with a $200,000 basis. The restaurant is destroyed by fire, and he receives $300,000 from the insurance company. Bob's realized gain is $100,000 ($300,000 – $200,000). He purchases another restaurant for $275,000. Bob may elect to defer $75,000 of the gain under Sec. 1033; $25,000 ($300,000 – $275,000) of Bob's gain must be recognized because he failed to reinvest all of the $300,000 insurance proceeds in a suitable replacement property. ◀

EXAMPLE I12-38 ▶ Stacey owns a racehorse with a $450,000 basis used for breeding purposes. The racehorse is killed by lightning, and she collects $800,000 from the insurance company. Stacey's realized gain is $350,000 ($800,000 – $450,000). She purchases another racehorse for $430,000. The entire $350,000 of gain is recognized, because the amount realized from the involuntary conversion exceeds the cost of the replacement property by $370,000 ($800,000 – $430,000) which is more than the realized gain. ◀

OBJECTIVE 4

Determine the basis of replacement property in an involuntary conversion

BASIS OF REPLACEMENT PROPERTY. If replacement property is purchased, the basis of the replacement property is its cost less any deferred gain. If the taxpayer elects to defer the gain, the holding period of the replacement property includes the holding period of the converted property.[50]

---

[45] Secs. 1033(d) and (e). If a taxpayer sells or exchanges more livestock than normal because of a drought, the sale or exchange of the excess amount is treated as an involuntary conversion. The livestock must be other than poultry and be held by the taxpayer for draft, breeding, or dairy purposes.

[46] Sec. 1033(a)(2).

[47] *Flushingside Realty & Construction Co.*, 1943 PH T.C. Memo ¶43,286, 2 TCM 259.

[48] *Spencer D. Stewart* v. *CIR.*, 52 AFTR 2d 83-5885, 83-2 USTC ¶9573 (9th Cir., 1983).

[49] Sec. 1033(a)(2)(A).

[50] Sec. 1223(1)(A).

EXAMPLE I12-39 ▶ Tracy owns a yacht that is held for personal use and has a $20,000 basis. The yacht is destroyed by a storm, and Tracy collects $24,000 from the insurance company. She purchases a new $35,000 yacht for personal use and elects to defer the $4,000 ($24,000 − $20,000) gain. The basis of the new yacht is $31,000 ($35,000 − $4,000). The holding period for the new yacht includes the holding period of the yacht that was destroyed. ◀

SEVERANCE DAMAGES. If a portion of the taxpayer's property is condemned, the taxpayer may receive **severance damages** as compensation for a decline in the value of the retained property. For example, if access to the retained property becomes difficult or if the property is exposed to greater damage from flooding or erosion, its value may decline.

The IRS considers severance damages to be "analogous to the proceeds of property insurance; they represent compensation for damages to the property."[51] Amounts received as severance damages reduce the basis of the retained property, and any amount received in excess of the property's basis is treated as gain.[52]

EXAMPLE I12-40 ▶ Cindy owns a 500-acre farm with a $200 basis per acre ($100,000 basis). The state condemns ten acres across the northwest corner of her farm to build a major highway. Cindy receives a condemnation award of $500 per acre for the ten acres. The highway separates the farm into a 25-acre tract and a 465-acre tract. Because her ability to efficiently use the 25-acre tract for farming is reduced, the state pays additional severance damages of $90 per acre for the 25 acres. Cindy's gain realized from condemnation of the ten acres is $3,000 [$5,000 − ($200 × 10 acres)]. The $2,250 ($90 × 25 acres) of severance damages reduce the basis of the 25-acre tract from $5,000 ($200 × 25 acres) to $2,750 [($200 × 25) − $2,250]. The reduction in basis is applied solely to the 25 acres because of its decline in value as farmland. ◀

REAL-WORLD EXAMPLE

Seven of the 18 holes of a golf course were condemned. Although 11 holes remained, it was anticipated that the course would have to be reduced to 9 holes. Therefore, $21,000 of the condemnation award was allocated to severance damages to reflect the decline in value of the two lost holes. *Marco S. Marinello Associates, Inc.*, 1975 PH T.C. Memo ¶75,078, 34 TCM 392.

The Sec. 1033 provisions concerning nonrecognition of gain may apply to severance damages. For instance, if severance damages are used to restore the retained property, only that portion of severance damages not spent for restoration reduces the basis of the retained property. A taxpayer who uses severance damages to purchase adjacent farmland to replace the portion of the farm condemned may use Sec. 1033 to defer a gain due to the receipt of the severance damages.[53]

TAX TREATMENT OF GAIN DUE TO AN INVOLUNTARY CONVERSION DIRECTLY INTO SIMILAR PROPERTY

ADDITIONAL COMMENT

The direct conversion of property into similar property is rarely encountered.

Nonrecognition of gain is mandatory if property is involuntarily converted directly into similar property rather than money.[54] The basis of the replacement property is the same as the basis of the converted property, and the holding period for the converted property carries over to the replacement property.[55]

EXAMPLE I12-41 ▶ Ed's farm with a $200,000 basis is condemned by the state. The state transfers other farmland with a $280,000 FMV to Ed. The $80,000 ($280,000 − $200,000) of realized gain is not recognized, and the basis of the farmland received is $200,000. Nonrecognition of gain is mandatory. Direct conversions are rarely encountered because the usual payment procedure for insurance companies and governmental agencies involves a payment of cash. ◀

REPLACEMENT PROPERTY

To qualify for nonrecognition of gain due to an involuntary conversion, the taxpayer must acquire qualified replacement property. With some exceptions, the **replacement property** must be "similar or related in service or use to the property so converted."[56] Taxpayers who own and use the property must use the functional use test although

[51] Rev. Rul. 53-271, 1953-2 C.B. 36.
[52] Rev. Rul. 68-37, 1968-1 C.B. 359.
[53] Rev. Ruls. 69-240, 1969-1 C.B. 199, 73-35, 1973-1 C.B. 367, and 83-49, 1983-1 C.B. 191.
[54] Sec. 1033(a).
[55] Sec. 1033(b).
[56] Secs. 1033(a)(2)(A) and 1033(f). The replacement of property requirement is modified when proceeds from the involuntary conversion of livestock may not be reinvested in property similar or related in use to the converted livestock because of soil contamination or other environmental contamination. Sec. 1033(f) permits the livestock to be replaced with other property, including real property, used for farming purposes.

replacement may be made with like-kind property in certain cases. A taxpayer who owns and leases the property that is involuntarily converted may use the taxpayer-use test.

FUNCTIONAL-USE TEST. The **functional-use test** is more restrictive than the like-kind test. To be considered similar or related in service or use, the replacement property must be functionally the same as the converted property. For example, the exchange of a business building for land used in business qualifies as a like-kind exchange. Replacing a building with land does not qualify as replacement property under the involuntary conversion rules. The building must be replaced with a building that is functionally the same as the converted building.

EXAMPLE I12-42 ▶ Julie owns a movie theater that is destroyed by fire. She uses the insurance proceeds to purchase a skating rink. The converted property has not been replaced with property that is similar or related in service or use under the functional-use test. The election to defer gain under Sec. 1033 is not available. ◀

REAL-WORLD EXAMPLE

The replacement of bowling alleys destroyed in a fire with a recreational billiards center did not pass the functional-use test. Rev. Rul. 76-319, 1976-2 C.B. 242.

REPLACEMENT WITH LIKE-KIND PROPERTY. If real property held for productive use in a trade or business or for investment is **condemned**, a proper replacement may be made by acquiring like-kind property.[57] This exception to the functional use test applies only to real property used in a trade or business or held for investment but not to real property held as inventory.

EXAMPLE I12-43 ▶ Ken owns a building used in his business that is condemned by the state to widen a highway. He uses the proceeds to purchase land to be held for investment. The land is a qualified replacement property because the condemned building is real property used in a trade or business, and the like-kind exchange rule may be applied to the condemnation. ◀

EXAMPLE I12-44 ▶ Assume the same facts as in Example I12-43 except that the building is destroyed by a violent windstorm. Ken's purchase of the investment land is not qualified replacement property because the more flexible like-kind exchange rules apply only to condemnations. He must purchase property with the same functional use as the business building. ◀

REAL-WORLD EXAMPLE

A nursery with its trees and shrubs was condemned, and the taxpayer replaced the condemned property with land and greenhouses. The replacement was considered to have been made with like-kind property. *Evert Asjes, Jr.*, 74 T.C. 1005 (1980).

If business or investment property is involuntarily converted as a result of a Presidentially declared disaster after 1994, the taxpayer may replace the property with any tangible property that is held for productive use in a trade or business.

TAXPAYER-USE TEST. The **taxpayer-use test** applies to the involuntary conversion of rental property owned by an investor. This test permits greater flexibility than the functional use test. The principal requirement is that the owner-investor must lease out the replacement property that is acquired. However, the lessee is not required to use the leased property for the same functional use.[58]

EXAMPLE I12-45 ▶ Sally owns an apartment complex that is rented to college students. The apartment complex is destroyed by fire. She uses the insurance proceeds to purchase a medical building that is leased to physicians. This is a qualified replacement property by Sally under the taxpayer-use test, and the gain, if any, may be deferred if an election is made under Sec. 1033. ◀

STOP & THINK *Question:* Greg Stacey's motel is destroyed by fire on March 10 of the current year. The basis of the property is $400,000 and he receives $2,000,000 from the insurance company. Greg is concerned about the possibility of having to pay income tax on the $1,600,000 gain and is aware of the tax rules relating to involuntary conversions. Greg is considering replacing the destroyed motel by building either a new motel or an ice skating rink on the vacant lot. The cost of a new motel or an ice skating rink is expected to be $2,500,000, and he expects to borrow 60% of the cost. What tax advice would you give him?

---

[57] Sec. 1033(g)(1).

[58] Rev. Rul. 64-237, 1964-2 C.B. 319.

REAL-WORLD EXAMPLE

Taxpayer owned land and a warehouse held for rental purposes. Upon the condemnation of this property, taxpayer invested the proceeds in a gas station on land already owned by the taxpayer which was also held for rental purposes. The taxpayer-use test applied, and the taxpayer was able to defer the gain. Rev. Rul. 71-41, 1971-1 C.B. 223.

Solution: Greg may defer the $1,600,000 gain if the involuntary conversion requirements are met and he makes a proper election. The principal issue in this case is whether the replacement property is considered to be "similar in service or use" to the converted property. Because the functional-use test is applicable in this case, an ice skating rink is not similar property and the gain of $1,600,000 must be recognized. Conversely, the new motel is similar property and, since Greg is reinvesting an amount greater than $2,000,000, none of the gain is recognized. His basis in the new motel is $900,000 ($2,500,000 − deferred gain of $1,600,000). The fact that he borrows money and does not spend the $2,000,000 insurance proceeds does not prevent him from electing to defer the gain. The tax requirement is only that he must reinvest an amount equal to or greater than the $2,000,000 insurance proceeds. In this case, the tax law clearly encourages the taxpayer to build a new motel rather than an ice skating rink.

OBTAINING REPLACEMENT PROPERTY

The general rule is that the taxpayer must purchase the replacement property.[59] Taxpayers may purchase replacement property indirectly by purchasing control (i.e., 80% or more of the stock) of a corporation that owns the replacement property.[60] However, this exception is not applicable to the purchase of like-kind property to replace condemned real property used in a trade or business or held for investment.[61]

EXAMPLE I12-46 ▶ Hank's airplane, used in business, is hijacked and taken to a foreign country. He uses the insurance proceeds to purchase 80% of the Fast Corporation stock. Fast Corporation owns an airplane which is qualified replacement property. The involuntary conversion requirements are satisfied if Hank elects to defer any gain realized. ◀

EXAMPLE I12-47 ▶ Lynn's farm is condemned by the state for public use. She uses the proceeds to purchase 80% of Vermont Corporation stock. Vermont Corporation owns eight parking lots. A qualified replacement property has not been obtained through the stock purchase because the parking lots are not functionally the same as the farm. ◀

TIME REQUIREMENTS FOR REPLACEMENT

TYPICAL MISCONCEPTION

The first taxable year in which any part of the gain on the conversion is realized is the year in which the insurance proceeds are received not the year in which the involuntary conversion took place.

To qualify for nonrecognition of gain treatment, the converted property must be replaced within a specified time period. The general rule is that the period begins with the date of disposition of the converted property and ends "two years after the close of the first taxable year in which any part of the gain upon the conversion is realized."[62] If the involuntary conversion is due to condemnation or requisition, or the threat of such, the replacement period begins on the date of the threat or imminence of the requisition or condemnation. The replacement period may be extended by obtaining permission from the IRS.[63]

EXAMPLE I12-48 ▶ On December 8, 2002, Craig's business property was destroyed by fire. Craig receives insurance proceeds in 2003 and elects to defer recognition of the gain. He must replace the property between December 8, 2002, and December 31, 2005. The two-year time period includes 2005 because the gain is realized when the insurance proceeds are received in 2003. ◀

KEY POINT

The replacement period is three years instead of two years on the condemnation of real property used in a business or held for investment.

The replacement period is longer if the involuntary conversion is due to the condemnation of real property (excluding inventory) held for productive use in a trade or business or for investment. The replacement period ends three years after the close of the first tax year in which any part of the gain is realized.[64] This provision for a longer replacement period applies to the same type of real property that may be replaced with like-kind property.

---

[59] To qualify as a purchase of property or stock under Sec. 1033(a)(2)(A)(ii), the unadjusted basis of the property or stock must be its cost within the meaning of Sec. 1012 without considering the basis adjustment for the deferred gain. Property acquired by inheritance, gift, or a nontaxable exchange does not qualify as replacement property (see Reg. Sec. 1.1033(a)-2(c)(4)).

[60] Sec. 1033(a)(2)(A) and Reg. Sec. 1.1033(a)-2(c).

[61] Sec. 1033(g)(2).

[62] Sec. 1033(a)(2)(B).

[63] Sec. 1033(a)(2)(B)(ii).

[64] Sec. 1033(g)(4).

EXAMPLE I12-49 ▶ Beth owns a building used in her dry cleaning business. In 2002, the state condemns the building and awards Beth an amount greater than the adjusted basis of the building. Beth may replace the property with like-kind property, and the replacement period ends on December 31, 2005. ◀

The involuntary conversion rules are summarized in Topic Review I12-2.

Topic Review I12-2

Section 1033: Involuntary Conversions

1. Section 1033 applies only to gains, not losses.
2. Nonrecognition of gain under Section 1033 is elective. (Nonrecognition of gain is mandatory in a direct conversion, but direct conversions seldom occur.)
3. Section 1033 applies to involuntary conversions of all types of properties.
4. Some gain may be recognized if the taxpayer replaces the involuntarily converted property with property that costs less than the amount realized in the involuntary conversion.
5. The nonrecognized gain is deferred.
6. The basis of property acquired to replace the involuntarily converted property is the cost of the property less the deferred gain.
7. Property acquired to replace the involuntarily converted property generally must be functionally related property.
8. The required replacement period generally begins with the date of disposition of the converted property and ends two years after the close of the first taxable year in which any part of the gain on the conversion is realized. (A three-year period applies to condemnations of real property used in a trade or business or held for the production of income.)

SALE OF PRINCIPAL RESIDENCE

OBJECTIVE 5

Determine when a gain resulting from the sale of a principal residence is excluded

Congress uses the tax law to encourage home ownership in many ways: (1) Real estate taxes and interest on a mortgage used to acquire a principal or second residence are deductible (see Chapter I7), (2) part or all of the interest on home equity debt may be deductible and (3) taxpayers may elect to exclude up to $250,000 ($500,000 on a joint return) of gain from the sale of a principal residence.

Individuals who sell or exchange their personal residence after May 6, 1997, may exclude up to $250,000 of gain if it was owned and occupied as a principal residence for at least two years of the five-year period before the sale or exchange. A married couple may exclude up to $500,000 when filing jointly if both meet the use test, at least one meets the ownership test and neither spouse is ineligible for the exclusion because he or she sold or exchanged a residence within the last two years.[65]

The Sec. 121 exclusion is available regardless of age, and taxpayers do not have to purchase a replacement residence. Any gain not excluded is capital gain because a personal residence is a capital asset. A loss on the sale or exchange of a personal residence is not deductible because the residence is personal-use property.[66]

EXAMPLE I12-50 ▶ Maki, who is single and 35 years old, sells her principal residence that she purchased four years ago and realizes a $230,000 gain. Maki may exclude the entire gain regardless of her age or whether she purchases a new principal residence. ◀

EXAMPLE I12-51 ▶ Assume the same facts as in Example I12-50 except the realized gain is $320,000. Maki may exclude $250,000 and recognize a $70,000 LTCG. ◀

---

[65] Sec. 121(a) and (b).

[66] Reg. Secs. 1.165-9(a) and 1.262-1b)(4).

EXAMPLE I12-52 ▶ Assume the same facts as in Example I12-51 except Maki is married to Yixin, and they have owned and occupied the residence for the last four years. They may exclude the entire $320,000 gain. ◀

ADDITIONAL COMMENT

The elimination of taxes on up to $500,000 of gain from the sale of a personal residence has been a great benefit for many taxpayers who had very large built-in gains.

KEY POINT

The reason that recordkeeping will be reduced is the sales price for most homes is less than $250,000 ($500,000 on a joint return). If the sale price is less than $250,000, clearly no taxable gain would result and no records are necessary to prove the basis of the home.

Prior to the Taxpayer Relief Act of 1997, taxpayers could defer gain resulting from sale of a personal residence if they purchased another principal residence within two years at a cost greater than the adjusted sales price. Taxpayers who were at least 55-years-old could exclude up to $125,000 of gain resulting from the sale of a personal residence. The deferral provision of Sec. 1034 has been repealed; the exclusion has been increased to $250,000 or $500,000; and taxpayers may exclude gain regardless of age.

Today, the rules for excluding gain resulting from the sale of a personal residence are more favorable for most taxpayers than the old rules because Congress wanted to eliminate the need for homeowners to maintain records for long periods of time. However, taxpayers who expect to sell their homes for more than $250,000, or $500,000 if a joint return is filed, still need to maintain records. Also, taxpayers who convert their personal residence to business property or rental property will need to know the property's correct adjusted basis to compute depreciation.

DETERMINING THE REALIZED GAIN. Gain realized is the excess of the amount realized over the property's adjusted basis.[67] The amount realized on the sale of the property is equal to the selling price less selling expenses.[68] Selling expenses include commissions, advertising, deed preparation costs, and legal expenses incurred in connection with the sale.[69]

EXAMPLE I12-53 ▶ Kirby sells his personal residence, which has a $100,000 basis, to Maxine. To make the sale, Kirby pays a $7,000 sales commission and incurs $800 of legal costs. Maxine pays $30,000 cash and assumes Kirby's $90,000 mortgage. The amount realized is $112,200 [($30,000 + $90,000) − ($7,000 + $800)]. The realized gain is $12,200 ($112,200 − $100,000). ◀

ADJUSTED BASIS OF RESIDENCE. The original basis of a principal residence is a function of how the residence is obtained. It could be purchased, received as a gift or inherited. The cost of a residence includes all amounts attributable to the acquisition including commissions and other purchasing expenses paid to acquire the residence.[70] Capital improvements, but not repairs, increase the adjusted basis of the residence. The costs of adding a room, installing an air conditioning system, finishing a basement and landscaping are capital improvements. Expenses incurred to protect the taxpayer's title in the residence are also capitalized. Under Sec. 1034 which was repealed in 1997, a taxpayer who deferred gain on the sale of a principal residence was required to reduce the basis of the replacement residence by the amount of the deferred gain.[71]

EXAMPLE I12-54 ▶ In 1996, Susan paid $200,000 to purchase a new residence. She paid a realtor $4,000 to help locate the house and paid legal fees of $1,200 to make certain that the seller had legal title to the property. As a result of the purchase, she deferred a gain of $50,000 from the sale a former residence in 1995. In 1997, she added a new porch to the house at a cost of $6,000 and installed central air conditioning at a cost of $5,200. Since purchasing the house, she has paid $1,500 for repairs. The adjusted basis of her house is $166,400 [$200,000 + $4,000 + $1,200 − $50,000 +$6,000 + $5,200]. ◀

REAL-WORLD EXAMPLE

An unmarried taxpayer plans to make good use of the multiple exclusion allowance. He has purchased two houses; one to live in and one to use as rental property. After a certain number of years he will sell his personal residence and move into the rental house. After at least two more years he will then sell the second house. Except for the gain due to depreciation on the rental house, the gain from both houses will be tax-free up to $250,000 each.

MULTIPLE USE OF THE EXCLUSION. Previously under Sec. 121, a taxpayer was limited to the exclusion once in their lifetime. A married taxpayer whose spouse had taken the exclusion could not use the exclusion even if the taxpayer filed as married filing separately. The exclusion is now determined on an individual basis. An individual may claim the exclusion even if the individual's spouse used the exclusion within the past two years. Also, for a married couple filing a joint return when each spouse maintains a separate

[67] Reg. Sec. 1.1034-1(b)(5).
[68] Reg. Sec. 1.1034-1(b)(4).
[69] Reg. Sec. 1.1034-1(b)(4)(i).
[70] Reg. Sec. 1.1034-1(c)(4).
[71] Sec. 1034(e).

principal residence, the $250,000 exclusion is available for the sale or exchange of each spouse's principal residence.

EXAMPLE I12-55 ▶ Krista who has owned and used a house as her principal residence for the last seven years marries Eric in January of 2001. Eric sold his residence in October of 2001 and excluded a $145,000 gain. Krista sells her residence in December of 2002 and realizes a gain of $378,000. She may exclude $250,000 of the gain.

Assuming that Krista and Eric use her residence in the above example for a two-year period starting in January 2002, they could exclude up to $500,000 if she waits to sell the house until January, 2004. ◀

PRINCIPAL RESIDENCE DEFINED

For Sec. 121 to apply, taxpayers must sell property that qualifies as their principal residence. Whether property is used as the taxpayer's principal residence is determined on a case-by-case basis.[72]

EXAMPLE I12-56 ▶ Len, a 40-year-old college professor, owns and occupies a house in Oklahoma. During the summer, he lives in a cabin in Idaho. After owning the cabin for eight years, Len sells it for $50,000 and realizes a gain. Gain on the sale of the cabin in Idaho must be recognized because Len's principal residence is in Oklahoma. ◀

KEY POINT

A taxpayer may own two or more residences, but only one of them qualifies as the principal residence.

Condominium apartments, houseboats, and housetrailers may qualify as principal residences.[73] Stock held by a tenant-stockholder in a cooperative housing corporation is a principal residence if the dwelling that the taxpayer is entitled to occupy as a stockholder is used as his or her principal residence.[74]

DETERMINING WHETHER THE PROPERTY IS THE TAXPAYER'S PRINCIPAL RESIDENCE. To qualify for the favorable tax treatment provided by Sec. 121, the residence must be the taxpayer's principal residence.[75] Controversy often exists as to whether a residence qualifies as the taxpayer's principal residence, and the IRS will not issue rulings or determination letters concerning whether property qualifies under Secs. 121.[76]

Property that is not being used as a principal residence when sold may have lost its character as the taxpayer's residence. A taxpayer's residence that is abandoned before its sale does not qualify as the taxpayer's principal residence.[77] In a case where taxpayers had not occupied their residence for more than ten years, the court ruled that the residence was not their principal residence. The taxpayers were in the process of remodeling the property when they received and accepted an unsolicited offer.[78]

KEY POINT

A residence can be rented and retain its designation as the taxpayer's principal residence. However, the taxpayer should be able to show that he or she was trying to sell the property.

While attempting to sell the residence, the taxpayer may rent the property to another party. This action may jeopardize the taxpayer's ability to exclude the gain, although temporary rental before the sale does not always indicate a conversion to business use.[79]

EXAMPLE I12-57 ▶ In December 2001, Sandy discovered that her "dream house" was available for purchase. Sandy purchased the house and immediately occupied it as her new principal residence. She lives in a college town and knows that the market for housing becomes active in the spring. She lists her vacated house for sale with a realtor and agrees to allow two college students to rent the property on a month-to-month basis. Sandy retains the right to show the house to prospective buyers while the students are tenants. In April 2002, she sells the property. Because the conversion to rental property status is temporary, the residence is still Sandy's principal residence. ◀

ADDITIONAL COMMENT

When a residence retains its designation as the principal residence, the taxpayer may deduct depreciation and other rental expenses during the rental period.

If rental of the property constitutes abandonment of the residence, it is no longer the taxpayer's principal residence.

---

[72] Reg. Sec. 1.1034-1(c)(3). Even though Sec. 1034 has been repealed, the definition of a *principal residence* is still contained in the Treasury Regulations under Sec. 1034.

[73] Rev. Rul. 64-31, 1964-1 C.B. 300.

[74] Reg. Sec. 1.1034-1(c)(3).

[75] Sec. 121(a).

[76] Rev. Proc. 92-3, 1992-1 C.B. 561.

[77] *William C. Stolk* v. *CIR*, 13 AFTR 2d 535, 64-1 USTC ¶9228 (2nd Cir., 1964).

[78] *Ann K. Demeter*, 1971 PH T.C. Memo ¶71,209, 30 TCM 863.

[79] Rev. Rul. 78-146, 1978-1 C.B. 260.

EXAMPLE I12-58 ▶ In 1996, Sam and his wife moved from their residence in New Orleans to a home in Mobile. After renting the house in New Orleans for six years, they sell it in 2002. Section 121 will not apply to the sale of the residence in New Orleans because the extended rental period constitutes an abandonment of the principal residence.[80] ◀

ADDITIONAL COMMENT

The taxpayer does not have to be occupying the old residence at the date of sale. The taxpayer may have already moved to a new residence and be renting the old residence temporarily before its sale.

SALE OF MORE THAN ONE PRINCIPAL RESIDENCE WITHIN A TWO-YEAR PERIOD

The new exclusion provided by Sec. 121 applies to only one sale or exchange every two years. A portion of the gain may be excluded in certain circumstances even if the two-year requirement is not satisfied.

If a principal residence is sold within two years of a previous sale or exchange of a residence, part of the gain may be excluded if the sale or exchange is due to a change in employment, health or unforseen circumstances. The portion of the gain excluded is based on a ratio with a denominator of 730 days and the numerator being the shorter of:

1) the period during which the ownership and use tests were met during the five-year period ending on the date of sale, or

2) the period of time after the date of the most recent prior sale or exchange for which the exclusion applied until the date of the current sale or exchange.[81]

The amount excluded is $250,000 or $500,000 times the above ratio.

EXAMPLE I12-59 ▶ Winnie, who is single, sold her principal residence in Detroit on November 1, 2002, and excluded the $127,000 gain because she owned and used the residence for two of the last five years. Winnie purchased another residence in Cleveland on October 1, 2002, that she occupies until June 12, 2003, when she receives a job offer from a new employer in Dallas. She moves to Dallas on June 12 and rents a townhouse. She sells the residence in Cleveland on November 15, 2003, and realizes a gain of $40,000. Winnie may exclude all of the gain because (254/730) of $250,000 is more than the $40,000 realized gain. She owns and uses the residence in Cleveland for 254 days, and the period between the sale of the residence in Detroit and the sale in Cleveland is 379 days. ◀

ADDITIONAL COMMENT

If Winnie's gain in Example I2-59 is $100,000, she may exclude $86,986 (254/730 × $250,000).

OWNERSHIP AND USE TESTS If a principal residence is sold before satisfying the ownership and use tests, part of the gain may be excluded if the sale is due to a change in employment, health, or unforseen circumstances. The portion of the gain excluded is determined by multiplying the amount of the exclusion (i.e., $250,000 or $500,000) by a fraction whose numerator is the number of days the use and ownership tests were met and the denominator is 730 days.

EXAMPLE I12-60 ▶ Tim, a single taxpayer who purchased his home on January 1, 2002, for $500,000, recently became ill and sells his home in order to move closer to a relative who can care for him. Tim sells his principal residence on September 14, 2002, for $620,000 realizing a gain of $120,000. Because he owned and occupied the residence for 256 days and the sale was due to a change in his health, he may exclude $87,671 ($250,000 × 256/730) ◀

For purposes of the two-year ownership rule, a taxpayer's period of ownership includes the period during which the taxpayer's deceased spouse owned the residence. When a taxpayer receives a residence from a spouse or an ex-spouse incident to a divorce, the taxpayer's period of owning the property includes the time the residence was owned by the spouse or ex-spouse.[82]

EXAMPLE I12-61 ▶ Sachie receives an $800,000 residence owned for six years by, Richard, her former spouse as part of a divorce settlement. Richard's basis for the residence is $430,000. They lived in the house for five years prior to the divorce. Three months after transfer of the residence to Sachie, she sells it for $825,000, and $250,000 of her $395,000 realized gain is excluded. Sachie must recognize a $145,000 LTCG. Sachie's period of ownership includes the six years Richard owned the residence. ◀

---

80 *Rene A. Stiegler, Jr.*, 1964 PH T.C. Memo ¶64,057, 23 TCM 412.

81 Sec. 121(c).

82 Sec. 121(d)(2) and (3).

STOP & THINK *Question:* Rebecca's uncle told her that she could purchase his house for $150,000 in five years provided that she could pay at least $30,000 of the purchase price in cash. Rebecca has $15,000 and is considering two alternative methods to obtain the remaining $15,000 in five years. The first alternative is to purchase $15,000 of non-dividend paying stock that she expects to increase in value to $30,000 within five years. The second alternative is to purchase an $80,000 residence by paying $15,000 and borrowing $65,000. Payments on the mortgage will be interest only for five years and amount to $450 per month. Insurance, property taxes and other home ownership expenses average $90 per month. She expects the house to be worth $95,000 at the end of five years. She will rent an apartment for $540 per month if she buys the stock. Ignoring transaction costs and assuming that she does not itemize deductions, should Rebecca purchase the stock or the house?

Solution: The $15,000 gain resulting from sale of the stock is LTCG and probably taxed at 20%. If the rate is 20%, she must pay taxes of $3,000 and has only $27,000 available to purchase her uncle's house. She will have a gain of $15,000 if she sells the house but the gain is excluded. She has $30,000 of cash and is able to buy her uncle's house. The tax law encourages Rebecca to buy a principal residence.

INVOLUNTARY CONVERSION OF A PRINCIPAL RESIDENCE

Ordinarily, the involuntary conversion of a principal residence is governed by Sec. 1033, discussed earlier in this chapter. A gain due to an involuntary conversion of a personal residence may be deferred if the requirements of Sec. 1033 are satisfied. The functional use test must be satisfied regardless of the type of involuntary conversion.

For purposes of Sec. 121, the destruction, theft, seizure, requisition, or condemnation of property is treated as a sale.[83] Thus, taxpayers may exclude a gain of up to $250,000 or $500,000 due to the involuntary conversion of a principal residence if the use and ownership test is satisfied. Taxpayers normally prefer to exclude gain if the use and ownership tests are satisfied rather than defer gain under the involuntary conversion provisions.

If taxpayers make a proper and timely replacement of the residence subject to the involuntary conversion, gain may be excluded up to $250,000, or $500,000, and the remaining gain may be deferred. For purposes of applying the involuntary conversion provisions, the amount realized due to the involuntary conversion is reduced by any gain excluded under Sec. 121.[84]

EXAMPLE I12-62 ▶ The Koch's principal residence, with an adjusted basis of $200,000, has been used and owned by them for nine years. The house is destroyed by a hurricane and the Kochs receive insurance proceeds of $820,000. Four months later, they purchase another residence for $900,000. The Kochs have a realized gain of $620,000 and may exclude $500,000 under Sec. 121. The remaining $120,000 gain may be deferred and the basis of their replacement residence is $780,000 ($900,000 – $120,000). ◀

Because the amount realized is reduced by the gain excluded, the Kochs could have deferred the $120,000 gain in the above example by investing $320,000 in a replacement residence.

If gain due to the involuntary conversion of a principal residence is deferred under Sec. 1033, the holding period of the replacement residence includes the holding period of the converted property for purposes of satisfying the use and ownership tests of Sec. 121.[85] The Kochs satisfy the use and ownership requirements for Sec. 121 with respect to their new residence in Example I12-62 because gain is deferred under Sec. 1033.

A loss due to a condemnation of a personal residence is not recognized. If the loss is due to a casualty, the loss is deductible and is treated like other casualty losses of nonbusiness property (see Chapter I8).

---

[83] Sec. 121(d)(5)(A).
[84] Sec. 121(d)(5)(B).
[85] Sec. 121(d)(8).

ADDITIONAL COMMENT

Because of the tremendous damage and hardships produced by Hurricane Andrew in Florida and the flooding of the Mississippi River, Congress responded with substantial tax relief for taxpayers who received insurance proceeds for damaged personal property, and made the favorable tax treatment retroactive to disasters after August 31, 1991.

PRESIDENTIALLY DECLARED DISASTER OF A PRINCIPAL RESIDENCE. Special treatment is provided when a taxpayer's principal residence or any of its contents is compulsorily or involuntarily converted and the residence is located in an area which is determined by the President to be in an area that warrants assistance by the federal government under the Disaster Relief and Emergency Assistance Act. Part of the gain resulting from the receipt of insurance proceeds is excluded if the President's declaration is after August 31, 1991.[86]

No gain is recognized due to the receipt of insurance proceeds for damaged personal property located in the residence if the property was unscheduled property for the purpose of such insurance. Although proceeds received for property that is not separately scheduled are excluded from gross income, other proceeds received, including those received for scheduled property, are treated as being received as a common fund for a single item of property. Separately scheduled property typically consists of items such as computers, jewelry, artwork, and pianos.

EXAMPLE I12-63 ▶ Nora's principal residence, with an adjusted basis of $70,000, was destroyed by a flood in May 2002. The area was declared by the President to be a federal disaster area. All of the contents of her home, including a Steinway grand piano with a basis of $25,000 and a FMV of $30,000, were destroyed. Nora received the following payments from the insurance company in July 2002: $200,000 for the house, $25,000 for personal property contents with an adjusted basis of $15,000, and $30,000 for the piano, which was separately scheduled property in the insurance policy. The $10,000 ($25,000 − $15,000) gain on the unscheduled personal property is excluded from gross income. The $135,000 gain attributable to the house and the piano is excluded under Sec. 121. ◀

TAX PLANNING CONSIDERATIONS

AVOIDING THE LIKE-KIND EXCHANGE PROVISIONS

In some cases, a taxpayer may prefer a taxable exchange to a nontaxable like-kind exchange. For instance, if the gain is taxed as a capital gain and the taxpayer has capital losses to offset the gain, the taxpayer may prefer to recognize the gain during the current year. If gain on the exchange is recognized instead of deferred, the basis of the property received in the exchange is higher.

EXAMPLE I12-64 ▶ Connie owns land with a $20,000 basis. The land is held as an investment. Connie exchanges the land for a duplex with a $100,000 FMV. Because the exchange qualifies as a like-kind exchange, no gain is recognized and Connie's basis for the duplex is $20,000. If the exchange does not qualify as a like-kind exchange (e.g., the land is a personal-use asset), Connie recognizes an $80,000 capital gain. Connie's basis for the duplex is $100,000. The basis of the duplex, except for the portion allocable to land, is eligible for depreciation. ◀

If an exchange qualifies as a like-kind exchange, no loss on the exchange is recognized. A taxpayer who prefers to recognize a loss should avoid making a like-kind exchange. It may be advantageous to sell the property to recognize the loss and then purchase the replacement asset in two independent transactions. If the sale and purchase transactions are with the same party, the IRS may maintain that the like-kind exchange rules apply because the two transactions are in substance a like-kind exchange (i.e., the judicial doctrine of substance over form might be applied).

---

[86] Sec. 1033(h)(1)(A) The Revenue Reconciliation Act of 1993 granted retroactive tax relief for taxpayers because of the mass destruction in Florida caused by Hurricane Andrew and the flooding in several midwest states that occurred in 1993.

SALE OF A PRINCIPAL RESIDENCE

ELECTION PROVISION. When the requirements of Sec. 121 are satisfied, gain is excluded unless the taxpayer elects not to have Sec. 121 apply.[87] It is unlikely that a taxpayer will ever have an incentive to elect not to apply Sec. 121.

IDENTIFYING THE PRINCIPAL RESIDENCE. In view of the advantages of excluding gain on the sale of a principal residence, a taxpayer contemplating a sale should satisfy all requirements of Sec. 121. A taxpayer who owns and occupies more than one residence may have difficulty identifying the principal residence. The *principal residence* is the one that the taxpayer occupies most of the time.[88]

EXAMPLE I12-65 ▶ Paula, a business consultant, owns residences in Boston and Philadelphia. She plans to sell both residences in two years and purchase a new residence in California. The Boston residence has a FMV that is $200,000 greater than its basis. The residence in Philadelphia has not appreciated. Paula should plan her activities in a manner that will allow her to occupy the Boston residence more than the Philadelphia residence so the Boston residence will qualify as her principal residence. ◀

PROPERTY CONVERTED TO BUSINESS USE. If a residence is converted to business use at the time of the sale, it does not qualify as a principal residence.[89] A principal residence converted to business use may subsequently become the taxpayer's principal residence if the business use is discontinued for a period of time.[90]

EXAMPLE I12-66 ▶ Brad, a college professor, uses 20% of his residence as an office from 1975 until 2002. Brad deducted expenses related to the office portion of the residence for the years 1975 through 1980. After 1980, no deduction was allowed because Brad no longer met the eligibility requirements for an office-in-home deduction. (See Chapter I9 for a discussion of the office-in-home deduction.) If Brad sold the property before 1981, only 80% of the property would have qualified as a principal residence and 20% would be considered business property. Alternatively, if he sells the residence in 2002, he may exclude up to $250,000 of gain. The entire residence is considered to be his principal residence because the business use has been discontinued. The basis of the residence is reduced by the depreciation allowed from 1975 through 1980. ◀

The Taxpayer Relief Act of 1997 created a major change for the sale of a principal residence when depreciation has been allowed or allowable for periods attributable to periods after May 6, 1997. Only the gain in excess of the amount of depreciation after May 6, 1997, is eligible to be excluded under Sec. 121.[91]

Note that under the new law, a taxpayer such as Brad in Example I12-66 will not be able to exclude all of the gain under Sec. 121 if depreciation was allowed after May 6, 1997, even if the residence is being used solely as a residence at the time of sale.

EXAMPLE I12-67 ▶ Ilena purchased a residence on June 1, 1997, for $150,000 and uses 20% of the residence as an office for her consulting business until she sells the residence in November of the current year for $200,000. She must treat the transaction as the sale of two assets and may exclude the $40,000 gain on the sale of the residence ($160,000 − $120,000). Because 20% of the house is not being used as a principal residence, the gain on the portion of the house used for the consulting business must be recognized. The amount of the gain is $40,000 less the adjusted basis which is $30,000 less depreciation allowed. ◀

EXAMPLE I12-68 ▶ Bobbi purchased a house in 1986 and used it as her principal residence until March 1, 1997, when she rented the house to the Allens while she lived with her mother. On November 1, 2001, the Allens' lease expired and she moved back into the house. She sells the house on July 12, 2002, and realizes a gain of $210,000. She may not exclude any of the gain because she has not used the property as her principal residence for two of the last five years. ◀

---

[87] Sec. 121(f).
[88] Rev. Rul. 77-298, 1977-2 C.B. 308.
[89] Reg. Sec. 1.1034-1(a)(3)(ii).
[90] Rev. Rul. 82-26, 1982-1 C.B. 114.
[91] Sec. 121(d)(6).

EXAMPLE I12-69 ▶ Assume the same facts as in I12-68 except that Bobbi sells the house on December 12, 2003. Because she has used the property as her principal residence for two of the last five years, she may exclude the excess of the $210,000 gain over depreciation allowed after May 6, 1997. ◀

COMPLIANCE AND PROCEDURAL CONSIDERATIONS

REPORTING OF INVOLUNTARY CONVERSIONS

ADDITIONAL COMMENT

The failure to include gain from an involuntary conversion in gross income is deemed to be an election even though the details are not reported.

The election to defer recognition of the gain from an involuntary conversion is made by not reporting the gain as income for the first year in which gain is realized. All details pertaining to the involuntary conversion (including those relating to the replacement of the converted property) should be reported for the taxable year or years in which any of the gain is realized.[92]

A taxpayer who elects to defer recognition of the gain but does not make a proper replacement of the property within the required period of time must file an amended return for the year or years for which the election was made. An amended return may be needed if the cost of the replacement property is less than expected at the time of the election. All details pertaining to the replacement of converted property must be reported in the year in which replacement occurs.[93]

EXAMPLE I12-70 ▶ Bob's property, with a $40,000 adjusted basis, was destroyed by a storm in 2001. Bob received $45,000 insurance proceeds in 2001 and planned to purchase property similar to the converted property in 2002 at a cost of $47,000. Bob elected to defer recognition of the gain in 2000. In 2002 the replacement property is purchased for $44,500. Bob must file an amended return for 2001 and recognize a $500 ($45,000 − $44,500) gain. ◀

ADDITIONAL COMMENT

The replacement period may be extended if special permission is obtained from the IRS.

A taxpayer who either is ineligible or does not want to defer the gain must report the gain in the usual manner. If a taxpayer does not elect to defer the gain in the year the gain is realized and the replacement period has not expired, a subsequent election may be made. In such an event, a refund claim should be filed for the tax year in which the gain was realized and previously recognized.[94]

Taxpayers who do not initially elect to defer the gain from an involuntary conversion may later make the election, but the election may not subsequently be revoked. The Tax Court has ruled that the Treasury Regulations allow the filing of an amended return for a year in which the election is made only if proper replacement is not made within the specified time period or the replacement is made at a cost lower than anticipated at the time of the election.[95] The IRS takes the position that taxpayers who designate qualifying property as replacement property may not later designate other qualifying property as the replacement property.[96]

EXAMPLE I12-71 ▶ In 2000 Troy collected $200,000 from an insurance company as the result of the destruction of rental property with a $140,000 basis. He made the election to defer the gain realized in 2000 and attached a supporting schedule of details regarding the involuntary conversion including a designation of replacement property to be acquired in 2001. In 2001 Troy purchased the designated replacement rental property for $225,000. In 2002 Troy purchases other rental property for $400,000 and now wants to designate that property as the replacement property for the property destroyed in 2000. Troy may not designate the property acquired in 2002 as the replacement property because the rental property purchased in 2001 was already designated as such. ◀

92 Reg. Sec. 1.1033(a)-2(c)(2).
93 *Ibid.*
94 *Ibid.*
95 *John McShain*, 65 T.C. 686 (1976).
96 Rev. Rul. 83-39, 1983-1 C.B. 190.

REPORTING OF SALE OR EXCHANGE OF A PRINCIPAL RESIDENCE

Taxpayers only have to report the sale if any of the gain is not excluded. If the taxpayer does not qualify to exclude all of the gain or elects not to exclude the gain, the entire gain realized is reported on Schedule D either on line 1, if residence is held for one year or less, or on line 8. On the line below where the entire gain is shown, the taxpayer should indicate on the following line the amount of the gain that is being excluded as a loss (i.e., show in parentheses).

Publication 523, Selling Your Home provides the following worksheet that may be used to determine if any gain is recognized. If the taxpayer has to utilize the exceptions to the two-year ownership and use tests, a different worksheet is provided.

Worksheet 2. **Gain (or Loss), Exclusion, and Taxable Gain**

Part 1–Gain (or Loss) on Sale		
1.	Selling price of home	______
2.	Selling expenses.	______
3.	Subtract line 2 from line 1	______
4.	Adjusted basis of home sold. (From Worksheet 1, line 15.)	______
5.	Subtract line 4 from line 3. This is the **gain (or loss)** on the sale. If this is a loss, stop here	______
Part 2–Exclusion and Taxable Gain		
6.	Maximum exclusion. (See *Amount of Exclusion* in this chapter.)	______
7.	Enter any depreciation claimed on the property for periods after May 6, 1997. If none, enter zero	______
8.	Subtract line 7 from line 5. (If the result is less than zero, enter zero.)	______
9.	Subtract line 7 from line 6	______
10.	Enter the smaller of line 8 or 9. This is your exclusion. If you are reporting the sale on the installment method, enter this amount on line 15 of Form 6252	______
11.	Subtract line 10 from line 5. This is your taxable gain. Report it on Schedule D (Form 1040) as described under *Reporting the Gain* in this chapter. If the amount on this line is zero, do not report the sale or exclusion on your tax return	______

PROBLEM MATERIALS

DISCUSSION QUESTIONS

I12-1 Evaluate the following statement: The underlying rationale for the nonrecognition of a gain or loss resulting from a like-kind exchange is that the exchange constitutes a liquidation of the taxpayer's investment.

I12-2 Why might a taxpayer want to avoid having an exchange qualify as a like-kind exchange?

I12-3 Debbie owns office equipment with a basis of $300,000 acquired on May 10, 1995. Debbie exchanges the equipment for other office equipment owned by Doug on July 23, 2002. Doug's equipment has an FMV of $500,000. Both Debbie and Doug use the equipment in their businesses.

a. What is Debbie's basis for the office equipment received in the exchange and when does the holding period start for that equipment?

b. If Debbie and Doug are related taxpayers, explain what action could occur that would cause the exchange not to qualify as a like-kind exchange.

I12-4 Kay owns equipment used in her business and exchanges the equipment for other like-kind equipment and marketable securities.

a. Will Kay's recognized gain ever exceed the realized gain?

b. Will Kay's recognized gain ever exceed the FMV of the marketable securities?

c. What is the basis of the marketable securities received?

d. When does the holding period of the marketable securities begin?

I12-5 Demetrius sells word processing equipment used in his business to Edith. He then purchases new word processing equipment from Zip Corporation.

a. Do the sale and purchase qualify as a like-kind exchange?

b. When may a sale and a subsequent purchase be treated as a like-kind exchange?

I12-6 When determining whether property qualifies as like-kind property, is the quality or grade of the property considered?

I12-7 What is personal property of a like class that meets the definition of like-kind?

I12-8 When does a nonsimultaneous exchange qualify as a like-kind exchange?

I12-9 Burke is anxious to purchase land owned by Kim for use in his trade or business. Kim's basis for the land is $150,000 and Burke has offered to pay $800,000 if she will sell within the next 10 days. Kim is interested in selling but wants to avoid recognizing gain. What advice would you give?

I12-10 Lanny wants to purchase a farm owned by Jane, but Jane does not want to recognize a gain on the transfer of the appreciated property. Explain how a three-party exchange might be used to allow Lanny to obtain the farm without Jane having to recognize a gain.

I12-11 Does the receipt of boot in a transaction that otherwise qualifies as a like-kind exchange always cause the exchange to be at least partially taxable?

I12-12 When must a taxpayer who gives boot recognize a gain or loss?

I12-13 What is the justification for Sec. 1033, which allows a taxpayer to elect to defer a gain resulting from an involuntary conversion? May a taxpayer elect under Sec. 1033 to defer recognition of a loss resulting from an involuntary conversion?

I12-14 Must property be actually condemned for the conversion of property to be classified as an involuntary conversion? Explain.

I12-15 What are severance damages? What is the tax treatment for severance damages received if the taxpayer does not use the severance damages to restore the retained property?

I12-16 The functional use test is often used to determine whether the replacement property is similar or related in service or use to the property converted. Explain the functional use test.

I12-17 In what situations may a gain due to an involuntary conversion of real property be deferred if like-kind property is purchased to replace the converted property?

I12-18 Prior to the Taxpayer Relief Act of 1997, taxpayers could defer a gain on the sale of a principal residence sold before May 7, 1997, if they purchased and occupied a new principal residence within two years before or after the sale and the cost of the new residence was at least equal to the adjusted sales price of the old residence. Some taxpayers who were at least 55 years old had a once-in-a-lifetime exclusion up to $125,000 if they owned and used the property as a principal residence for at least three years of the five-year-period ending on the date of sale. Discuss why current law with respect to the sale of a personal residence is more favorable than the law prior to the Taxpayer Relief Act of 1997.

I12-19 One reason Congress expanded the exclusion of gain on the sale of a principal residence and eliminated the deferral provision was to eliminate the need for many taxpayers to keep records of capital improvements that increase the basis of their residence. Why might taxpayers still need to maintain such records to substantiate the adjusted basis of their principal residence?

I12-20 Steve maintains that the cost of wallpapering his three-bedroom house is a capital expenditure while Martha maintains that the cost of wallpapering her three-bedroom house is an expense. Steve uses his house as his personal residence while Martha's house is rental property. Explain why Steve and Martha view the cost of wallpapering differently.

I12-21 The Nelsons purchased a new residence in 1988 for $200,000 from David who owned and used the residence as rental property. When the Nelsons wanted to purchase the property, it was being rented to tenants who had four months remaining on their lease. The Nelsons paid the tenants $1,000 to relinquish the lease and vacant the property. They deferred a $70,000 gain on the sale of a principal residence on December 10, 1987. In 1990, they added a family room to the house at a cost of $45,300. In 1994, they suffered hail damage to the roof and received $6,000 from the insurance company. They did not repair the damaged roof, and no casualty loss was allowed. What is their adjusted basis for the house today?

I12-22 What requirements must be satisfied by an unmarried taxpayer under Sec. 121 to be eligible for the election to exclude a gain up to $250,000 on the sale or exchange of a principal residence?

ISSUE IDENTIFICATION QUESTIONS

I12-23 John owns 25% of the ABC Partnership and Jane owns 25% of the XYZ Partnership. The ABC Partnership owns a farm and produces corn and the XYZ Partnership owns a farm and produces soybeans. John and Jane agree to exchange their partnership interests. What tax issues should John and Jane consider?

I12-24 Chauvin Oil Corporation operates primarily in the United States and owns an offshore drilling rig with an adjusted basis of $400,000 that it uses near Louisiana. Chauvin, Inc. exchanges the rig for a new rig with a FMV of $1,000,000, and Chauvin also pays $250,000. Chauvin plans to expand its drilling operations to offshore sites near Finland. What tax issues should the Chauvin Corporation consider?

I12-25 Jaharta, Inc. owns land used for truck farming and cattle raising. The California Division of Highways condemned 36 acres of Jaharta's land to build a new highway. Jaharta owned a 50% interest in property being used for apricot, prune, and walnut orchards. Jaharta used the proceeds received as a result of the condemnation to purchase the remaining interest in the property being used for orchards.

PROBLEMS

I12-26 *Like-Kind Property.* Which of the following exchanges qualify as like-kind exchanges under Sec. 1031?

a. Acme Corporation stock held for investment purposes for Mesa Corporation stock also held for investment purposes
b. A motel used in a trade or business for an apartment complex held for investment
c. A pecan orchard in Texas used in a trade or business for an orange grove in Florida used in a trade or business
d. A one-third interest in a general partnership for a one-fourth interest in a limited partnership
e. Inventory for equipment used in a trade or business
f. Unimproved land held as an investment for a warehouse used in a trade or business
g. An automobile used as a personal-use asset for marketable securities held for investment

I12-27 *Like-Kind Property.* Which of the following exchanges qualify as like-kind exchanges under Sec. 1031?

a. A motel in Texas for a motel in Italy
b. An office building held for investment for an airplane to be used in the taxpayer's business
c. Land held for investment for marketable securities held for investment
d. Land held for investment for a farm to be used in the taxpayer's business

I12-28 *Like-Kind Exchange: Boot.* Determine the realized gain or loss, the recognized gain or loss, and the basis of the equipment received for the following like-kind exchanges:

Basis of Equipment Exchanged	*FMV of Boot Received*	*FMV of Equipment Received*
$40,000	$-0-	$75,000
50,000	10,000	70,000
60,000	25,000	65,000
70,000	30,000	60,000
80,000	20,000	50,000

I12-29 *Like-Kind Exchange: Personal Property.* Beach Corporation owns a computer with a $30,000 adjusted basis. The computer is used in the company's trade or business. What is the realized and recognized gain or loss for each of the following independent transactions?

a. The computer is exchanged for a used computer with a $70,000 FMV plus $12,000 cash.
b. The computer is exchanged for a used computer with a $18,000 FMV plus $7,000 cash.
c. The computer is exchanged for marketable securities with a $61,000 FMV.

I12-30 *Like-Kind Exchange: Personal Property.* Boise Corporation exchanges a machine with a $14,000 basis for a new machine with an $18,000 FMV and $3,000 cash. The machines are used in Boise's business and are in the same General Asset Class.

a. What are Boise Corporation's recognized gain and the basis for the new machine?
b. How would your answer to Part a change if the corporation's machine is also subject to a $6,000 liability, and the liability is assumed by the other party?

I12-31 *Exchange of Personal Property.* Lithuania Corporation operates a ferry service and owns four barges. Lithuania exchanges one of the barges with an adjusted basis of $350,000 for a used smaller barge with a FMV of $444,000 and a $26,000 computer. Without considering the exchange, Lithuania Corporation's taxable income is $700,000.

a. What is the realized gain on the exchange?
b. What is the recognized gain?

c. What is the basis of the new barge?
d. What is the basis of the computer?
e. Assume that the recognized gain is $26,000 and the gain is not capital gain. What is the increase in Lithuania's tax liability as a result of the exchange?

I12-32 ***Like-Kind Exchange: Liabilities.*** Paul owns a building used in his business with an adjusted basis of $400,000 and an $750,000 FMV. He exchanges the building for a building owned by David. David's building has a $950,000 FMV but is subject to a $200,000 liability. Paul assumes David's liability and uses David's building in his business.
a. What is Paul's realized gain?
b. What is Paul's recognized gain?
c. What is Paul's basis for the building received?

I12-33 ***Like-Kind Exchange: Liabilities.*** Helmut exchanges his apartment complex for Heidi's farm, and the exchange qualifies as a like-kind exchange. Helmut's adjusted basis for the apartment complex is $600,000 and the complex is subject to a $180,000 liability. The FMV of Heidi's farm is $770,000 and the farm is subject to a $100,000 liability. Each asset is transferred subject to the liability. What is Helmut's recognized gain and the basis of the new farm?

I12-34 ***Like-Kind Exchange: Liabilities.*** Sheila owns land with a basis of $100,000 and FMV of $220,000. The land is subject to an $80,000 liability. Sheila plans to exchange the land for land owned by Tony that has a $250,000 FMV but is subject to a liability of $150,000. Sheila plans to assume Tony's debt and Tony will assume her $80,000 debt. Because the exchange is not of equal value, how much cash must Tony transfer to equalize the exchange?

I12-35 ***Like-Kind Exchange: Transfer of Boot.*** Wayne exchanges unimproved land with a $50,000 basis and marketable securities with a $10,000 basis for an eight-unit apartment building having a $150,000 FMV. The land and marketable securities are held by Wayne as investments, and the apartment building is held as an investment. The marketable securities have a $25,000 FMV. What is his realized gain, recognized gain, and the basis for the apartment building?

I12-36 ***Like-Kind Exchange: Related Parties.*** Bob owns a duplex used as rental property. The duplex has a basis of $86,000 and $300,000 FMV. He transfers the duplex to Cindy, his sister, in exchange for a triplex that she owns. The triplex has a basis of $279,000 and a $300,000 FMV. Two months after the exchange, Cindy sells the duplex to a business associate for $312,000.
a. What is Bob's realized and recognized gain on the exchange?
b. What is Cindy's realized and recognized gain on the exchange?

I12-37 ***Like-Kind Exchange: Related Parties.*** Assume the same facts as in I12-36 except Cindy sells the duplex to a nonrelated individual more than two years after the exchange with Bob. Ignore any changes in adjusted basis due to depreciation that would have occurred after the exchange.
a. What is Bob's realized and recognized gain on the exchange?
b. What is Cindy's realized and recognized gain on the exchange?
c. What is Cindy's realized and recognized gain on the sale?

I12-38 ***Involuntary Conversion.*** Duke Corporation owns an office building with a $400,000 adjusted basis. The building is destroyed by a tornado. The insurance company paid $750,000 as compensation for the loss. Eight months after the loss, Duke uses the insurance proceeds and other funds to acquire a new office building for $682,000 and machinery for one of the company's plants at a $90,000 cost. Assuming that Duke elects to defer as much of the gain as possible, what is the recognized gain, the basis for the new office building, and the basis for the machinery acquired?

I12-39 ***Involuntary Conversion: Replacement Period.*** The Madison Corporation paid $3,000 for several acres of land in 1993 to use in its business. The land is condemned and taken by the state in March 2002. The company receives $25,000 from the state. Whenever possible, the corporation elects to minimize taxable income. For each of the following independent cases, what is the recognized gain or loss in 2002 on the conversion and the tax basis of the replacement property (whenever the property is replaced)?
a. The land will not be replaced.
b. Replacement land will be purchased in July 2003 for $22,500.
c. Replacement land will be purchased in July 2004 for $28,500.
d. Replacement land will be purchased in July 2005 for $23,600.

I12-40 *Involuntary Conversion of Real Property.* On April 27, 2002, an office building owned by Newark Corporation, an offshore drilling company that is a calendar-year taxpayer, is destroyed by a hurricane. The basis of the office building is $600,000, and the corporation receives $840,000 from the insurance company.

a. To defer the entire gain due to the involuntary conversion, what amount must the corporation pay for replacement property?
b. To defer the gain due to the involuntary conversion, by what date must the corporation replace the converted property?
c. If Newark replaces the office building by purchasing a 900,000 gallon storage tank at an $810,000 cost, may it defer any of the gain due to the involuntary conversion?
d. How would your answers to Parts b and c change if the office building had been condemned by the state? Explain.

I12-41 *Involuntary Conversion: Different Methods of Replacement.* On September 3, 2002, Federal Corporation's warehouse is totally destroyed by fire. $800,000 of insurance proceeds are received, and the realized gain is $300,000. Whenever possible, Federal elects to defer gains. For each of the following independent situations, what is the amount of gain recognized? Explain why the gain is not deferred, if applicable.

a. On October 23, 2002, Federal purchases a warehouse for $770,000.
b. On February 4, 2003, Federal purchases 100% of the Park Corporation, which owns a warehouse. Federal pays $895,000 for the stock.
c. On March 10, 2003, Federal receives a capital contribution from its majority shareholder. The shareholder transfers a warehouse to the corporation. The warehouse's FMV is $975,000. The shareholder's basis in the warehouse is $635,000.
d. On November 20, 2004, Federal purchases an apartment complex for $900,000.
e. On March 26, 2005, Federal purchases a warehouse for $888,000.

I12-42 *Severance Damages.* Twelve years ago, Marilyn purchased two lots in an undeveloped subdivision as an investment. Each lot has a $10,000 basis and a $40,000 FMV when the city condemns one lot for use as a municipal sewage treatment plant. As a result of the condemnation, Marilyn receives $40,000 from the city. Because the value of the other lot is reduced, the city pays $7,500 severance damages. She does not plan to replace the condemned lot.

a. What is her recognized gain due to the condemnation?
b. What is her recognized gain from the receipt of the severance damages?
c. What is her basis for the lot she continues to own?

I12-43 *Sale of a Principal Residence.* Marc, age 45, sells his personal residence on May 15, 2002, for $70,000. He pays $5,000 in selling expenses and $600 in repair expenses. He has lived in the residence since 1980, when he purchased it for $40,000. In 1984, he paid $4,000 to install central air conditioning. If Marc purchases a new principal residence in December of the current year for $62,000, what is the realized gain, recognized gain, and the basis for the new residence?

I12-44 *Sale of a Principal Residence.* Mr. and Mrs. Rusbarsky purchased a residence on June 12, 1999, for $200,000. On March 12, 2002, they sell the residence for $300,000, and selling expenses amount to $11,000. They purchase another house in a new subdivision for $275,000. Determine the gain realized and recognized.

I12-45 *Sale of a Principal Residence.* On January 10, 2002, Kirsten married Joe. Joe sold his personal residence on October 25, 2001, and excluded the entire gain of $175,000. Although they had originally planned to live in the house that Kirsten had received as a gift from her parents in 1993, they decided to purchase a larger house, and Kirsten sold her house and realized a $370,000 gain.

a. If they file a joint return, how much of the $370,000 gain may be excluded?
b. If Kirsten files as married filing separately, how much of the $370,000 gain may be excluded?

I12-46 *Involuntary Conversion of Principal Residence.* Mr. and Mrs. Mahan own and live in a house, with an adjusted basis of $200,000, that was purchased in 1994. The house is destroyed by a tornado on March 10 of the current year, and the Mahans receive insurance proceeds of $275,000. They purchase another residence for $322,000 four months later.

a. May they exclude the $75,000 gain, and if so, what is the basis of the residence purchased in July?
b. May they defer the $75,000 gain, and if so, what is the basis of the residence purchased in July?

I12-47 *Sale of a Principal Residence.* Mr. and Mrs. Kitchens purchased their first home in Ohio for $135,000 on October 1, 2001. Because Mr. Kitchens' employer transferred him to Utah, they sold the house for $160,000 on January 10, 2002. How much of the gain is recognized?

I12-48 *Sale of a Principal Residence.* Prior to the Taxpayer Relief Act of 1997, taxpayers could defer a gain on the sale of a principal residence sold before May 7, 1997. To defer all of the gain, the taxpayer had to make a timely purchase of a replacement residence that cost more than the adjusted sales price of the residence sold. The basis of the replacement residence was reduced by the gain deferred.

Answer the following questions to demonstrate why Beverley and George might prefer the law prior to the Taxpayer Relief Act if they sell their principal residence for $900,000, with an adjusted basis of $200,000. Selling expenses of $20,000 were paid. They owned and occupied the home for 20 years and file a joint return. The amount realized is equal to the adjusted sales price, and they purchase a new residence for $1,000,000 two weeks after the sale.

a. Under current law, what is the gain recognized and the basis of their new residence?
b. If the sale had occurred prior to May 7, 1997, what is the gain recognized and the basis of their new residence?
c. Which law might they prefer?

I12-49 *Definition of a Principal Residence.* Ken's parents lived with him until 2000 in a house on 23rd Street purchased by Ken in 1999 for $30,000. In 2000 Ken married Beth and moved to a rented apartment. In 2002 they purchase a house on 42nd Street for $90,000 and Ken sells the house on 23rd Street for $60,000 when his parents move into a nursing home. Ken pays $4,000 selling expenses and $1,000 repair expenses. How much of the realized gain on the sale of the house on 23rd Street is recognized?

I12-50 *Sale of a Principal Residence: Rental Property.* For the last several years, Mr. and Mrs. Cockrell have rented their furnished basement to local college students. When determining their taxable income each year, they have deducted a portion of the utilities, property taxes, interest, and depreciation based on the fact that 15% of the house is used for rental purposes. The original basis of the property is $100,000, and depreciation of $4,000 has been allowed on the rental portion of the property. During the current year, Mr. and Mrs. Cockrell sell the house for $300,000. No selling expenses or fixing-up expenses are incurred. They plan to purchase a new principal residence and will no longer rent any portion of their house to college students.

a. What is the amount realized on the sale of the principal residence?
b. What is the realized and recognized gain on the sale of the principal residence?
c. What is the amount realized on the sale of the portion of the residence not considered to be the principal residence?
d. What is the realized and recognized gain on the sale of the portion of the residence not considered to be the principal residence?

I12-51 *Multiple Sales of a Principal Residence.* Consider the following information for Mr. and Mrs. Di Palma:

- On June 10, 2001, they sold their principal residence for $80,000 and incur $6,000 of selling expenses. The basis of the residence, acquired in 1993, is $50,000.
- On June 25, 2001, they purchased a new principal residence for $90,000 and occupied it immediately.
- May 10, 2002, they purchase their neighbor's residence for $115,000 and occupy the residence immediately.
- August 29, 2002, they sell the residence purchased on June 25, 2001, for $148,000. They pay $7,000 of selling expenses.

a. What is the realized gain on the sale of the residence in 2001?
b. What is the recognized gain on the sale of the residence in 2001?
c. What is the realized gain on the sale of the residence in 2002?
d. What is the recognized gain on the sale of the residence in 2002?

I12-52 *Multiple Sales of a Principal Residence.* Consider the following information for Mr. and Mrs. Gomez:

- On May 26, 2001, they sold their principal residence, acquired in 1992, for $200,000. They paid $8,000 of selling expenses. Their basis in the residence was $70,000.
- On July 25, 2001, they purchased a new principal residence for $250,000.

- On June 2, 2002, Mr. Gomez, a bank officer, is transferred to another bank in the northern part of the state and they vacate their house.
- On July 1, 2002, they purchase a new principal residence for $420,000.
- On October 6, 2002, they sell the residence that was purchased on July 25, 2001 for $520,000. They pay $30,000 of selling expenses.

a. What is the realized gain on the sale of the residence in 2001?
b. What is the recognized gain on the sale of the residence in 2001?
c. What is the realized gain on the sale of the residence in 2002?
d. What is the recognized gain on the sale of the residence in 2002?

COMPREHENSIVE PROBLEM

I12-53 Paden, who is single and has been employed as an accountant for 27 years with Harper, Inc., lost his job due to company downsizing. His last day of employment is July 31, 2002, and Harper provides a $9,000 severance payment. The severance payments are based on an employee's time of employment. During the year, Paden received a salary from Harper of $36,000. Harper also paid $1,500 of Paden's medical insurance premiums.

In May, 2002, Paden, who had always wanted to be associated with a football team, applied for the head coaching job at Hawk University in Iowa and, much to his surprise, received the job beginning on August 1. In June and July, Paden paid $4,500 to take courses in sports management at the local university. Hawk University is substantially short of funding and Paden paid $2,000 for entertainment expenses related to his job and $500 for supplies. No reimbursement was received.

His salary from Hawk is $4,000 per month payable at the end of each month. His salary for December was not received until January 6, 2003.

On August 1, he sold his house for $329,000 and paid a sales commission of $14,000. He inherited the house 20 years ago when his mother died. Her basis for the house was $37,000 and the FMV when she died was $50,000. Property taxes for the 2002 calendar year amount to $3,600, and property taxes were apportioned at the closing. Property taxes are payable on October 1. He paid $12,000 of interest on home equity debt of $150,000.

To move to Iowa, he drove 154 miles and spent $25 for meals during the trip. Movers charged $4,150 to move his household items. He purchased a new house in Iowa for $150,000 on August 15 and borrowed $110,000. He also agreed to pay all property taxes for 2001. Real property taxes for the home in Iowa will be paid on January 30, 2003 and amount to $1,500. Interest on the $110,000 debt during the current year is $1,475. To obtain the loan, Paden paid points of $1,000.

He contributed common stock (basis of $1,000 and FMV of $6,000) held as an investment for three years to Hawk University and cash of $1,765 to the First United Methodist Church. He paid personal property taxes of $435 for his car.

Paden sold 200 shares of Dell Corporation stock on April 10 for $100 per share. His basis was $145 per share. On May 1, he purchased 300 shares of Dell at $89 per share.

Determine:

1. Gross income without considering the sale of his house or the Dell Corporation stock.
2. Recognized gain due to the sale of his house.
3. Net capital gain
4. Adjusted gross income
5. Total amount of itemized deductions
6. Taxable income
7. Basis of his house in Iowa
8. If the sales price for his home was $470,000 instead of $370,000, would his taxable income increase by more than $100,000. If yes, explain.

TAX STRATEGY PROBLEM

I12-54 *Sale of a Principal Residence.* Ray and Ellie have each owned a principal residence for more than five years. Ray's residence has an adjusted basis of $100,000 and a FMV of $325,000, while Ellie's residence has an adjusted basis of $300,000 and a FMV of $490,000. They plan to marry and will purchase another house.

a. Should they sell their houses before the marriage in order to minimize their taxes?
b. Will your answer to part a change if the FMV of Ellie's house is $690,000.
c. In part b, what tax strategy should Ray and Ellie consider?

TAX FORM/RETURN PREPARATION PROBLEMS

I12-55 On October 29, 2001, Miss Joan Seely (SSN 123-45-6789) sells her principal residence for $150,000 cash. She purchased the residence on May 12, 1994 for $85,000. She spent $12,000 for capital improvements in 1995. To help sell the house, she pays $300 on October 2, 2001, for minor repairs made on that date. The realtor's commission amounts to $7,500. On February 3, 2002, she purchases a new principal residence for $130,000. Her old residence is never rented out or used for business. Complete the worksheet on page I12-24 for Miss Seely for 2001.

I12-56 At the beginning of the current year, Donna Harp was employed as a cinematographer by Farah Movie, Inc., a motion picture company in Los Angeles, California. In June, she accepted a new job with Ocala Production in Orlando, Florida. Donna is single and her social security number is 223-77-6793. She sold her house in California on August 10 for $500,000. She paid a $14,000 sales commission. The house was acquired on March 23, 1987, for $140,000.

The cost of transporting her household goods and personal effects from California to Orlando amounted to $2,350. To travel from California to Florida, she paid travel and lodging costs of $370 and $100 for meals.

On July 15, she purchased a house for $270,000 on 1225 Minnie Lane in Orlando. To purchase the house, she incurred a 20-year mortgage for $170,000. To obtain the loan, she paid points of $3,400. The $3,600 of property taxes for the house in Orlando were prorated with $1,950 being apportioned to the seller and $1,650 being apportioned to the buyer. In December of the current year she paid $3,600 for property taxes.

Other information related to her return:

Salary from Farah Movie, Inc.	$30,000
Salary from Ocala Production, Inc.	70,000
Federal income taxes withheld by Farah	6,000
Federal income taxes withheld by Ocala	22,000
FICA taxes withheld by Farah	2,295
FICA taxes withheld by Ocala	5,355
Dividend income	10,000
Interest paid for mortgage:	
Home in California	6,780
Home in Orlando	3,800
Property taxes paid in California	4,100
Sales taxes paid in California and Florida	3,125
State income taxes paid in California	2,900
Interest income from Sun National Bank	1,800

Prepare Form 1040 including Schedules A, B, and D and Form 3903.

I12-57 Jim Sarowski (SSN 344-77-9255) is 70 years old and single. He received social security benefits of $16,000. He works part-time as a greeter at a local discount store and received wages of $7,300. Federal income taxes of $250 were withheld from his salary. Jim lives at Rt. 7 in Daingerfield, Texas.

In March of the current year, he purchased a duplex at 2006 Tennessee Street to use as rental property for $100,000, with 20% of the price allocated to land. During the current year, he had the following receipts and expenditures with respect to the duplex:

Rent receipts	$8,800
Interest paid	5,900
Property taxes	1,400
Insurance	800
Maintenance	300

Other expenditures during the current year:

Contributions to the church	$2,600
Personal property taxes	225
Sales tax	345

On July 24 of the current year, he exchanged ten acres of land for a car with a $16,500 FMV to be held for personal use. The land was purchased on November 22, 1991, for $18,000 as an investment. Because of some pollution problems in the area, the value of the land declined.

On December 1 of the current year, he sold his residence, which had been his home for 30 years, for $475,000. Sales commissions of $16,000 were paid, and the adjusted basis for his home is $110,000. He plans to rent an apartment and does not plan to purchase another home. His only other sale of a principal residence occurred 32 years ago.

Prepare Forms 1040 and 4562 and Schedules D and E.

CASE STUDY PROBLEMS

I12-58 The Electric Corporation, a publicly held corporation, owns land with a $1,600,000 basis that is being held for investment. The company is considering exchanging the land for two assets owned by the Quail Corporation: land with a FMV of $3,000,000 and marketable securities with a $1,000,000 FMV. Both assets will be held by the Electric Corporation for investment, although the corporation is considering the possibility of developing the land and building residential houses. The president of the corporation has hired you to prepare a report explaining how the exchange will affect the corporation's reported net income and its tax liability. The corporation has a tax rate of 34%.

TAX RESEARCH PROBLEMS

I12-59 For the last nine years, Mr. and Mrs. Orchard live in a residence located on eight acres. In January of the current year they sell the home and two acres of land. The purchaser of the residence does not wish to own the entire eight acres of land. In December they sell the remaining 6 acres of land to another individual for $60,000. The house and the land have never been used by the Orchards in a trade or business or held for investment. The realized gains resulting from the two sales are computed as follows:

	House and Two Acres January Sales	*Eight Acres December Sale*
Selling price	$140,000	$60,000
Minus: selling expenses	(8,000)	(3,000)
Amount realized	$132,000	$57,000
Minus: Basis	(80,000)	(18,000)
Realized gain	$ 52,000	$39,000

In March they purchase a new residence for $225,000. As a result of the sales described above, what is the amount of realized gain that must be recognized during the current year?

A partial list of research sources is

- Sec. 1034
- Reg. Sec. 1.1034-1(c)(3)
- Rev. Rul. 76-541, 1976-2 C.B. 246

I12-60 George, age 68, decides to retire from farming and is considering selling his farm. The farm has a $100,000 basis and a $400,000 FMV. George's two sons are not interested in farming. Both sons have large families and would like to own houses suitable for their needs. The Iowa Corporation is willing to purchase George's farm. George's tax advisor suggests that Iowa Corporation should buy the two houses the sons want to own for $400,000 and then exchange the houses for George's farm. After the exchange, George could make a gift of the houses to the sons.

a. If the transactions are executed as suggested by the tax advisor, George's recognized gain will be $300,000. The transaction does not qualify as a like-kind exchange. Explain why.

b. George wants the exchange to qualify as a like-kind exchange and still help his sons obtain the houses. What advice do you have for him?

A partial list of research sources is

- *Dollie H. Click*, 78 T.C. 225 (1982)
- *Fred S. Wagensen*, 74 T.C. 653 (1980)

CHAPTER 13

PROPERTY TRANSACTIONS: SECTION 1231 AND RECAPTURE

LEARNING OBJECTIVES

After studying this chapter, you should be able to

1. Identify Sec. 1231 property
2. Understand the tax treatment for Sec. 1231 transactions
3. Apply the recapture provisions of Sec. 1245
4. Apply the recapture provisions of Sec. 1250
5. Describe other recapture applications

CHAPTER OUTLINE

History of Sec. 1231...13-2
Overview of Basic Tax Treatment for Sec. 1231...13-3
Section 1231 Property...13-5
Involuntary Conversions...13-6
Procedure for Sec. 1231 Treatment...13-7
Recapture Provisions of Sec. 1245...13-8
Recapture Provisions of Sec. 1250...13-11
Additional Recapture for Corporations...13-15
Recapture Provisions—Other Applications...13-17
Tax Planning Considerations...13-22
Compliance and Procedural Considerations...13-24

Chapter I5 states that all recognized gains and losses must eventually be designated as either capital or ordinary. However, gains or losses on certain types of property are designated as Sec. 1231 gains or losses, which are given preferential treatment under the tax law. Ordinary loss treatment is accorded to a net Sec. 1231 loss, which is defined as the excess of Sec. 1231 losses over Sec. 1231 gains.[1] Net Sec. 1231 gain, which is the excess of Sec. 1231 gains over Sec. 1231 losses, is generally treated as long-term capital gain.[2] However, as with many provisions of the tax law, the preferential treatment of Sec. 1231 gains has been gradually diminished, principally by the so-called "depreciation recapture rules" and the five-year lookback rule. This chapter discusses the important rules dealing with Sec. 1231 gains and losses and depreciation recapture.

HISTORY OF SEC. 1231

During the depressed economy of the early and mid-1930s, business property was classified as a capital asset. Many business properties were worth less than their adjusted basis. Instead of selling business properties, taxpayers found it advantageous to retain assets that had declined in value because they could recover the full cost as depreciation. Capital losses had only limited deductibility during this period. To encourage the mobility of capital (i.e., the replacement of business fixed assets), the Revenue Act of 1938 added business property to the list of properties not considered to be capital assets.

KEY POINT

If a taxpayer has gains, it is preferable to have the gains treated as capital gains; if a taxpayer has losses, it is preferable to have the losses treated as ordinary losses. Because Sec. 1231 property receives the preferable treatment for both net gains and losses, it has been said that this property enjoys the best of both worlds.

During the period from 1938 to 1942, gains and losses on the sale or exchange of business property were treated as ordinary gains and losses. Favorable capital gain treatment was eliminated and taxpayers with appreciated business properties were reluctant to sell the assets because of the high tax cost. This restriction on the mobility of capital was more significant than usual because business assets had to be shifted into industries that were more heavily involved in the production of military goods. Furthermore, taxpayers were often forced to recognize ordinary gains because the government used the condemnation process to obtain business property for the war effort. In 1942, Congress created the predecessor of Sec. 1231, which allowed taxpayers to treat net gains from the sale of business property as capital gains and net losses as ordinary losses. Before 1987, only 40% of an individual's net capital gain might be subject to tax because of the 60% long-term capital gain deduction.

The Tax Reform Act of 1986 eliminated the 60% long-term capital gain deduction for net long-term capital gains. Favorable long-term capital gain treatment was reinstated into the tax law in 1991 in the form of a 28% maximum tax rate applying to net capital gains for noncorporate taxpayers. The Taxpayer Relief Act of 1997 significantly increased the preferential tax treatment by reducing the maximum rate to 20% for net capital gain that is adjusted net capital gain. However, to qualify for the 20% rate, the holding period was increased to greater than 18 months. Finally, the IRS Restructuring and Reform Act of 1998 eliminated the more than 18-month holding period requirement.

It may also be advantageous to have gains classified as capital or Sec. 1231 if taxpayers have capital losses or capital loss carryovers because of the limitations imposed on the deductibility of capital losses. Furthermore, there are other situations where it may be important for the property to be Sec. 1231 property (e.g., a contribution of appreciated property to a charitable organization).

---

[1] Secs. 1231(c)(4) and (a)(2).
[2] Secs. 1231(c)(3) and (a)(1). There are several exceptions to this rule that are covered later in this chapter.

OVERVIEW OF BASIC TAX TREATMENT FOR SEC. 1231

NET GAINS

At the end of the tax year, Sec. 1231 gains are netted against Sec. 1231 losses. If the overall result is a net Sec. 1231 gain, the gains and losses are treated as long-term capital gains (LTCGs) and long-term capital losses (LTCLs) respectively.[3] For the sake of expediency, it is often stated that a net Sec. 1231 gain is treated as a LTCG. For tax years beginning after 1984, however, a portion or all of the net Sec. 1231 gain may be treated as ordinary income because of a special five-year lookback rule (see discussion below).

EXAMPLE I13-1 ▶ Dawn owns a business that has $20,000 of Sec. 1231 gains and $12,000 of Sec. 1231 losses during the current year. Because the Sec. 1231 gains exceed the Sec. 1231 losses, the gains and losses are treated as LTCGs and LTCLs. After the gains and losses are offset, there is an $8,000 net long-term capital gain (NLTCG). ◀

EXAMPLE I13-2 ▶ Assume the same facts as in Example I13-1 except that Dawn also recognizes a $7,000 LTCG from the sale of a capital asset. After considering the $8,000 net Sec. 1231 gain, which is treated as a LTCG, Dawn has a $15,000 NLTCG ($8,000 + $7,000). ◀

NET LOSSES

If the netting of Sec. 1231 gains and losses at the end of the year results in a net Sec. 1231 loss, the Sec. 1231 gains and losses are treated as ordinary gains and losses.[4] For expediency, it is often stated that the net Sec. 1231 loss is treated as an ordinary loss.

EXAMPLE I13-3 ▶ David owns an unincorporated business and has $30,000 of Sec. 1231 gains and $40,000 of Sec. 1231 losses in the current year. Because the losses exceed the gains, they are treated as ordinary losses and gains. ◀

EXAMPLE I13-4 ▶ Assume the same facts as in Example I13-3 except that David receives a $37,000 salary as a corporate employee. David has no other income, losses, or deductions affecting his adjusted gross income (AGI). The Sec. 1231 gains and losses are treated as ordinary gains and losses, and David's AGI is $27,000 ($37,000 salary − $10,000 of ordinary loss). The $40,000 of ordinary losses offsets the $30,000 of ordinary gains and $10,000 of David's salary. ◀

TYPICAL MISCONCEPTION

It is sometimes erroneously thought that each Sec. 1231 gain should be treated as a LTCG and each Sec. 1231 loss as an ordinary loss. However all Sec. 1231 gains and losses must be combined to determine whether the Sec. 1231 gains and losses are LTCGs and LTCLs or ordinary gains and losses.

One important advantage of Sec. 1231 is illustrated in Example I13-4. Because the Sec. 1231 gains and losses are treated as ordinary, the $10,000 net Sec. 1231 loss is fully deductible in the current year. If the gains and losses were classified as long-term capital gains and losses, David would have a $10,000 NLTCL. Only $3,000 of the $10,000 NLTCL would have been deductible against David's other income. As explained in Chapter I5, only $3,000 of net capital losses may be deducted from non-capital gain income per year.

ADDITIONAL COMMENT

A taxpayer's share of a Sec. 1231 loss from a partnership or S Corporation may be subject to the passive activity loss rules.

FIVE-YEAR LOOKBACK RULE The Tax Reform Act of 1984 reduced the benefits of Sec. 1231. For tax years beginning after 1984, any net Sec. 1231 gain is ordinary gain to the extent of any nonrecaptured net Sec. 1231 losses from the previous five years.[5] This provision is referred to as the *five-year lookback rule*. In essence, net Sec. 1231 losses previously deducted as ordinary losses are recaptured by changing what would otherwise be a LTCG into ordinary income.

EXAMPLE I13-5 ▶ In 2002, Craig recognizes $25,000 of Sec. 1231 gains and $15,000 of Sec. 1231 losses. In 1998, Craig reported $14,000 of Sec. 1231 losses and no Sec. 1231 gains. No other Sec. 1231 gains or losses were recognized by Craig during the 1999–2001 period. The $10,000 ($25,000 − $15,000) of net Sec. 1231 gain in 2002 is treated as ordinary income due to the $14,000 of nonrecaptured net Sec. 1231 losses. ◀

[3] Sec. 1231(a)(1).
[4] Sec. 1231(a)(2).
[5] Sec. 1231(c)(1).

HISTORICAL NOTE

Congress reduced the benefits of Sec. 1231 by requiring the recapture of any nonrecaptured net Sec. 1231 loss. This recapture is required because taxpayers have a certain amount of control over the timing of the recognition of Sec. 1231 gains or losses. Taxpayers had attempted to recognize Sec. 1231 losses in one year and Sec. 1231 gains in another year to avoid the netting process.

To determine the amount of nonrecaptured net Sec. 1231 losses, compare the aggregate amount of net Sec. 1231 losses for the most recent preceding five tax years with the amount of such losses recaptured as ordinary income for those preceding tax years. The excess of the aggregate amount of net Sec. 1231 losses over the previously recaptured loss is the nonrecaptured net Sec. 1231 loss. In Example I13-5, $4,000 of nonrecaptured net Sec. 1231 losses remain that can be recaptured in 2003. In 2003, the preceding five-year period includes 1998 through 2002.

TAX RATE FOR NET SEC. 1231 GAIN

In general, Sec. 1231 gains are taxed similarly to the taxation of net long-term capital gains. Thus, a Sec. 1231 gain will be subject to a maximum tax rate of 20% (or 10% if the taxpayer's regular tax rate is 15%). Sec. 1231 property must have a holding period of more than one year. Recall from Chapter 5 that adjusted net capital gain (ANCG) is net capital gain (NCG) determined *without* regard to:

(1) the 28% rate gain, and

(2) unrecaptured section 1250 gain–taxed at no more than 25% as explained later.

ANCG might be taxed at 20% or 10%.[6] If Sec. 1231 property is sold at a gain, the Sec. 1231 gain is LTCG if there are no Sec. 1231 losses or nonrecaptured Sec. 1231 losses. However, all or part of this gain is unrecaptured Section 1250 gain if the asset is a building. Thus, net Sec. 1231 gain might be taxed today at 10%, 15%, 20% or 25% depending on the taxpayer's tax rate and whether or not the gain is unrecaptured section 1250 gain.

EXAMPLE I13-6 ▶ Savannah, whose tax rate is 30%, sells land at a gain of $10,000 and other land at a gain of $15,000. Both tracts of land qualify as Sec. 1231 property. She has no other transactions involving capital assets or 1231 property and no nonrecaptured Sec. 1231 losses. Savanah has net Sec. 1231 gain of $25,000 that is NLTCG and her NCG is $25,000. Her ANCG is $25,000 taxed at a rate of 20%. ◀

EXAMPLE I13-7 ▶ Assume the same facts as in Example 13-6 except Savannah also has a $7,000 loss from the sale of a third tract of land that is Sec. 1231 property. Her net Sec. 1231 gain is $18,000. Her NCG is $18,000 and her ANCG is $18,000 taxed at a rate of 20%. ◀

EXAMPLE I13-8 ▶ Grace, whose tax rate is 15%, sells land that is Sec. 1231 property at a gain of $2,000. She has no other transactions involving capital assets or 1231 property and no nonrecaptured Sec. 1231 losses. The $2,000 gain is taxed at 10%. ◀

ADDITIONAL COMMENT

The Sec. 1231 property in Examples I13-6, I13-7 and I13-8 is land and none of the gain is unrecaptured Section 1250 gain.

APPLYING THE FIVE-YEAR LOOKBACK RULE. As explained earlier, net Sec. 1231 gain is ordinary income to the extent of nonrecaptured Sec. 1231 losses. Net Sec. 1231 gain is recharacterized as ordinary income under the five-year lookback rule in the following order:

(1) Net Sec. 1231 gain in the 25% group (unrecaptured Sec. 1250 gain)
(2) Net Sec. 1231 gain in the 20% group

EXAMPLE I13-9 ▶ Chris has nonrecaptured net Sec. 1231 losses of $20,000 at the beginning of the current year when he recognizes gains from the sale of two assets used in his trade or business and held more than one year. Asset #1 has a $14,000 gain and the entire gain is unrecaptured Sec. 1250 gain. Asset #2 has a Sec. 1231 gain of $15,000. All of the gain resulting from the sale of asset #1 is ordinary income and $6,000 of the gain from the sale of asset #2 is ordinary income because of the five-year lookback rule. The remaining $9,000 gain from the sale of asset #2 is taxed at 20%, or possibly 10%. ◀

[6] The rates could be as low as 18% or 8% for tax years beginning after Dec. 31, 2000, if the holding period is more than five years.

SECTION 1231 PROPERTY

OBJECTIVE 1

Identify Sec. 1231 property

SECTION 1231 PROPERTY DEFINED

Section 1231 property includes the following types of property:

- Real property or depreciable property used in a trade or business that is held for more than one year.
- Timber, coal, or domestic iron ore.
- Livestock.
- Unharvested crops.

Each of these types of Sec. 1231 assets are discussed below.

REAL OR DEPRECIABLE PROPERTY USED IN TRADE OR BUSINESS

KEY POINT

Inventory, free publications of the U.S. government, and copyrights, literary, musical, or artistic compositions are not capital assets.

As noted in Chapter I5, the Code does not provide a definition of a capital asset. Instead, Sec. 1221 provides a list of noncapital assets. This list includes both depreciable property and real property used in a trade or business.[7] These properties are treated as Sec. 1231 properties if held for more than one year. Depreciable property and real property used in a trade or business and held for **one year or less** are neither capital assets nor Sec. 1231 property. Any gain or loss resulting from the disposition of such assets is ordinary.

EXAMPLE I13-10 ▶ The Prime Corporation owns land held as an investment and land used as an employee parking lot. The land held as an investment is a capital asset. The land used as a parking lot is real property used in a trade or business and is not a capital asset. The land used as a parking lot is a Sec. 1231 asset if held for more than one year. ◀

EXAMPLE I13-11 ▶ Dale, a self-employed plumber, owns an automobile held for personal use and a truck used in his trade. The automobile is a capital asset because it is held for personal use, but the truck is a Sec. 1231 asset if held for more than one year. As described later, a portion or all of any gain realized on the sale of the truck may be taxed as ordinary income due to the Sec. 1245 depreciation recapture provisions. ◀

KEY POINT

Only property used in a trade or business is included in the definition of Sec. 1231 property. Gains and losses on property held for investment may be included only if the result of a condemnation or casualty.

Certain types of property do not qualify as Sec. 1231 property, even if used in a trade or business. For example, inventory is not Sec. 1231 property. Thus, a sale of inventory results in ordinary gain or loss. Publications of the U.S. Government received other than by purchase at its regular sale price; a copyright; literary, musical, or artistic compositions; letters or memorandums; or similar properties held by certain taxpayers are not classified as Sec. 1231 property.[8]

EXAMPLE I13-12 ▶ Carl, who owns a recording studio, writes a musical composition to be sold to a record company. Because the musical composition is created by the personal efforts of the taxpayer, the musical composition is not Sec. 1231 property, and the sale results in ordinary gain from the sale of an ordinary asset. ◀

REAL-WORLD EXAMPLE

Christmas trees can be included in the definition of Sec. 1231 property, and this opportunity to convert ordinary income into capital gains has resulted in the use of Christmas tree tax shelters.

TIMBER. Section 631 allows taxpayers to elect to treat the cutting of timber as a sale or exchange of such timber. To be eligible to make this election, the taxpayer must own the timber or hold the contract right on the first day of the year and for more than one year. Furthermore, the timber must be cut for sale or for use in the taxpayer's trade or business.[9]

The gain or loss is determined by comparing the timber's adjusted basis for depletion with its fair market value (FMV) on the first day of the tax year in which it is cut. If the timber is eventually sold for more or less than its FMV (determined on the first day of the year the timber is cut), the difference is ordinary gain or loss.

---

[7] Sec.1221(2).
[8] Sec. 1231(b)(1).
[9] Sec. 631(a) and Reg. Sec. 1.631-1.

EXAMPLE I13-13 ▶ Vermont Corporation owns timber with a $60,000 basis for depletion. The timber, acquired four years ago, is cut during the current year for use in the corporation's business. The FMV of the timber on the first day of the current year is $200,000. Vermont Corporation may elect to treat the cutting of the timber as a sale or exchange and recognize a $140,000 ($200,000 – $60,000) gain. ◀

SELF-STUDY QUESTION

Is the possible inclusion of timber and coal or domestic iron ore in the definition of Sec. 1231 property favorable to the taxpayers who produce these items?

ANSWER

Yes, it can result in income being taxed at rates applicable for long-term capital gain instead of ordinary income from the sale of inventory.

If the election is made to treat the cutting of timber as a sale or exchange, the timber is considered Sec. 1231 property.[10] Thus, the $140,000 of gain in Example I13-13 is a Sec. 1231 gain. If the taxpayer does not make the election, the character of any gain or loss depends on whether the timber is held for sale in the ordinary course of the taxpayer's trade or business, held for investment, or held for use in a trade or business.

COAL OR DOMESTIC IRON ORE. An owner who disposes of coal (including lignite) or domestic iron ore while retaining an economic interest in it must treat the disposal as a sale.[11] The coal or iron ore is considered Sec. 1231 property.[12] The owner must own and retain an economic interest in the coal or iron ore in place.[13] An economic interest is owned when one acquires by investment any interest in mineral in place and seeks a return of capital from income derived from the extraction of the mineral.[14]

ADDITIONAL COMMENT

Livestock includes cattle, hogs, horses, mules, donkeys, sheep, goats, fur-bearing animals, and other mammals, but excludes poultry, fish, frogs, and reptiles.

LIVESTOCK. Livestock held by the taxpayer for draft, breeding, dairy, or sporting purposes is considered Sec. 1231 property if held for 12 months or more from the date of acquisition. However, cattle and horses must be held for 24 months or more from the date of acquisition to qualify as Sec. 1231 property.[15]

ADDITIONAL COMMENT

The treatment of unharvested crops as a Sec. 1231 asset is largely a rule of convenience. If the taxpayer were not permitted to treat the crops in this fashion, it would be necessary to allocate the selling price between the land and crops.

UNHARVESTED CROPS AND LAND. An unharvested crop growing on land used in a trade or business is considered Sec. 1231 property if the crop and the land are both sold at the same time to the same person and the land is held more than one year.[16] Section 1231 does not apply to the sale or exchange of an unharvested crop if the taxpayer retains any right or option to reacquire the land.[17]

If Sec. 1231 applies to the sale or exchange of an unharvested crop sold with the land, no deductions are allowed for expenses attributable to the production of the unharvested crop.[18] Instead, costs of producing the crop must be capitalized.

INVOLUNTARY CONVERSIONS

Gains and losses from involuntary conversions of property used in a trade or business generally are classified as Sec. 1231 gains and losses. Involuntary conversions of capital assets that are held in connection with a trade or business or in a transaction entered into for profit also generally qualify for Sec. 1231 treatment. The property that is involuntarily converted must be held for more than one year. Certain involuntary conversions are treated differently for income tax purposes. For example, the tax rules are different for condemnations and casualties, even though both are involuntary conversions of property.

CONDEMNATIONS

Gains and losses resulting from condemnations of Sec. 1231 property and capital assets held more than one year are classified as Sec. 1231 gains and losses. As indicated above, the capital assets must be held in connection with a trade or business or with a transaction entered into for profit.[19]

10 Sec. 1231(b)(2) and Reg. Sec. 1.631-1(d)(4).
11 Sec. 631(c) and Reg. Sec. 1.631-3(a)(1).
12 Sec. 1231(b)(2) and Reg. Sec. 1.631-3(a)(2).
13 Reg. Sec. 1.631-3(b)(4).
14 Reg. Sec. 1.611-1(b)(1).
15 Sec. 1231(b)(3).
16 Sec. 1231(b)(4) and Reg. Secs. 1.1231-1(c)(5) and 1(f).
17 Reg. Sec. 1.1231-1(f).
18 Sec. 268 and Reg. Sec. 1.268-1.
19 Secs. 1231(a)(3)(A) and (4)(B).

EXAMPLE I13-14 ▶ Kathryn owns land with a $20,000 basis and a $30,000 FMV as well as a capital asset with a $40,000 basis and a $26,000 FMV. Both assets are used in her trade or business and have been held for more than one year. As a result of the state exercising its powers of requisition or condemnation, Kathryn is required to transfer both properties to the state for cash equal to their FMVs. No other transfers of assets occur during the current year. The $10,000 gain due to condemnation of the land is a Sec. 1231 gain and the $14,000 loss due to condemnation of the capital asset is a Sec. 1231 loss. ◀

OTHER INVOLUNTARY CONVERSIONS

TYPICAL MISCONCEPTION

The inclusion of gains and losses from condemnations in the netting of the other involuntary conversions is a common error.

Gains or losses resulting from an involuntary conversion arising from fire, storm, shipwreck, other casualty, or theft are not classified as Sec. 1231 gains or losses if the recognized losses from such conversions exceed the recognized gains.[20] In such a case, the involuntary conversions are treated as ordinary gains and losses. However, if the gains from such involuntary conversions exceed the losses, both are classified as Sec. 1231 gains and losses.

EXAMPLE I13-15 ▶ Jose owns equipment having a $50,000 basis and a $42,000 FMV and a building having a $30,000 basis and a $35,000 FMV which are used in Jose's trade or business. The straight-line method of depreciation is used for the building. Both assets are held for more than a year. As a result of a fire, both assets are destroyed, and Jose collects insurance proceeds equal to the assets' FMV. No other transfers of assets occur during the current year. Because the $8,000 ($42,000 − $50,000) recognized loss exceeds the $5,000 ($35,000 − $30,000) recognized gain, the recognized loss and gain are both treated as ordinary. ◀

PROCEDURE FOR SEC. 1231 TREATMENT

OBJECTIVE 2

Understand the tax treatment for Sec. 1231 transactions

After determining the recognized gains and losses from transfers of property qualifying for Sec. 1231 treatment, it is necessary to determine whether any gain must be recaptured as ordinary income under Secs. 1245 and 1250. The recaptured gain, discussed later in this chapter, is not eligible for Sec. 1231 treatment. After eliminating the gain recaptured as ordinary income due to the recapture of depreciation, the procedure for analyzing Sec. 1231 transactions is as follows:

STEP 1. Determine all gains and losses resulting from casualties or thefts of Sec. 1231 property and non–personal-use capital assets held for more than one year. Gains and losses are netted and treated as Sec. 1231 gains and losses if the gains exceed the losses.

If the losses exceed the gains, both are treated as ordinary losses and gains and do not, therefore, enter into the Sec. 1231 netting procedure. Recall from Chapter I8 that business casualty losses are deductible *for* AGI and other casualty losses are deductible *from* AGI.

KEY POINT

Gains that are recaptured under Secs. 1245 and 1250 are not eligible for Sec. 1231 treatment.

STEP 2. Combine the following gains and losses to determine whether Sec. 1231 gains exceed Sec. 1231 losses or vice versa:

- Net casualty and theft gains resulting from Step 1, if any
- Gains and losses resulting from the sale or exchange of Sec. 1231 property
- Gains and losses resulting from the condemnation of Sec. 1231 property and non–personal-use capital assets held more than one year.

If a net Sec. 1231 loss is the result, the losses and gains are treated as ordinary losses and gains. If a net Sec. 1231 gain is the result, the gains and losses are treated as LTCGs and LTCLs, although a portion or all of the capital gain may be recaptured as ordinary income as outlined in Step 3 (five-year lookback rule) below.

[20] Sec. 1231(a)(4)(C).

STEP 3. If a net Sec. 1231 gain is the result of Step 2, determine if the taxpayer has any nonrecaptured net Sec. 1231 losses. Nonrecaptured net Sec. 1231 losses are the excess of aggregate net Sec. 1231 losses for the preceding five years over losses previously recaptured as ordinary income due to the recapture provision of Sec. 1231. Net Sec. 1231 gains to the extent of any nonrecaptured net Sec. 1231 losses are treated as ordinary income. Sec. 1231 gain that is unrecaptured Sec. 1250 gain is first treated as ordinary income to the extent of nonrecaptured net Sec. 1231 losses. Any net Sec. 1231 gain in excess of nonrecaptured net Sec. 1231 loss is treated as a LTCG.

EXAMPLE I13-16 ▶ The following gains and losses pertain to Danielle's business assets that qualify as Sec. 1231 property. Danielle does not have any nonrecaptured net Sec. 1231 losses from previous years, and the portion of gain recaptured as ordinary income due to the depreciation recapture provisions has been eliminated.

Gain due to an insurance reimbursement for fire damage	$10,000
Loss due to condemnation	19,000
Gain due to the sale of Sec. 1231 property	22,000

The $10,000 casualty gain is classified as a Sec. 1231 gain because gains resulting from casualties or thefts of Sec. 1231 property exceed losses. Danielle has $32,000 ($10,000 + $22,000) of Sec. 1231 gains and a $19,000 Sec. 1231 loss. Danielle's $13,000 net Sec. 1231 gain is treated as a LTCG. No portion of the $13,000 LTCG is recaptured as ordinary income because Danielle does not have any nonrecaptured net Sec. 1231 losses during the preceding five-year period. ◀

EXAMPLE I13-17 ▶ Assume the same facts as in Example I13-16 except that Danielle has a $10,000 loss because of the fire instead of a $10,000 gain. The $10,000 casualty loss is an ordinary loss, not a Sec. 1231 loss because losses resulting from casualties or thefts of Sec. 1231 property exceed gains. Because the loss is a business loss, it is deductible *for* AGI. Due to the $19,000 condemnation loss and the $22,000 of Sec. 1231 gain, she has a $3,000 net Sec. 1231 gain that is treated as a LTCG. ◀

EXAMPLE I13-18 ▶ The following gains and losses recognized in 2002 pertain to Fred's business assets that were held for more than one year. The assets qualify as Sec. 1231 property.

Gain due to an insurance reimbursement for a casualty	$15,000
Gain due to a condemnation	25,000
Loss due to the sale of Sec. 1231 property	12,000

A summary of Fred's net Sec. 1231 gains and losses for the previous five-year period is as follows:

Year	*Sec. 1231 Gain*	*Sec. 1231 Loss*	*Cumulative Nonrecaptured Net Sec. 1231 Losses (from 5 Prior Years)*
1997	$ 5,000		—0—
1998		$2,000	$2,000
1999		6,000	8,000
2000	13,000		—0—
2001		9,000	9,000

The $15,000 gain due to the insurance reimbursement for a casualty is treated as a Sec. 1231 gain. The $25,000 gain from the condemnation is also a Sec. 1231 gain. Fred's net Sec. 1231 gain in 2002 is $28,000 [($15,000 + $25,000) − $12,000]. However, $9,000 of the Sec. 1231 gain is recaptured as ordinary income due to the $9,000 of nonrecaptured Sec. 1231 loss from 2001. The remaining $19,000 of net Sec. 1231 gain is a LTCG. ◀

RECAPTURE PROVISIONS OF SEC. 1245

OBJECTIVE 3

Apply the recapture provisions of Sec. 1245

In 1962, Congress enacted Sec. 1245, which substantially reduced the advantages of Sec. 1231. A gain from the disposition of Sec. 1245 property is treated as ordinary income to the extent of the total amount of depreciation (or cost-recovery) deductions allowed since January 1, 1962. The gain recaptured as ordinary income cannot exceed the amount of the realized gain.

EXAMPLE I13-19 ▶ Adobe Corporation sells equipment used in its trade or business for $95,000. The equipment was acquired several years ago for $110,000 and is Sec. 1245 property.[21] The equipment's adjusted basis is $60,000 because $50,000 of depreciation was deducted. The entire $35,000 ($95,000 – $60,000) gain is treated as ordinary income because the total amount of depreciation taken ($50,000) is greater than the $35,000 realized gain. ◀

TYPICAL MISCONCEPTION

It is sometimes thought that only tangible property is subject to Sec. 1245 recapture. In fact, both tangible and intangible personal property are included.

The recapture provisions of Sec. 1245 apply to the total amount of depreciation (or cost recovery) allowed or allowable for Sec. 1245 property. It makes no difference which method of depreciation is used.[22]

Generally, the entire gain from the disposition of Sec. 1245 property is recaptured as ordinary income because the total amount of depreciation (or cost recovery) is greater than the gain realized. A portion of the gain will receive Sec. 1231 treatment if the realized gain exceeds total depreciation or cost recovery.

EXAMPLE I13-20 ▶ Assume the same facts as in Example I13-19 except that the asset is sold for $117,000. Because the $57,000 ($117,000 – $60,000) realized gain is greater than the $50,000 of total depreciation, $50,000 of the gain is ordinary income and the remaining $7,000 is a Sec. 1231 gain. ◀

PURPOSE OF SEC. 1245

ADDITIONAL COMMENT

Section 1245 does not apply to losses because in these cases the taxpayers have taken too little depreciation rather than too much depreciation.

The purpose of Sec. 1245 is to eliminate any advantage taxpayers would have if they were able to reduce ordinary income by deducting depreciation and subsequently receive Sec. 1231 treatment when the asset was sold. For individuals, Sec. 1245 recapture prevents net Sec. 1231 gain from being treated as LTCG and being taxed at a maximum 20% rate. An increase in the maximum tax rates for high-income individuals in 1993 and subsequent years from 31% to 36% or 39.6% increased the negative effect of the Sec. 1245 recapture provisions for such individuals. The conversion of Sec. 1231 gain to Sec. 1245 ordinary income also prevents taxpayers from possibly using capital losses.

EXAMPLE I13-21 ▶ During the current year, Coastal Corporation has capital losses of $50,000 and no capital gains for the current year or the preceding three years. The corporation owns equipment purchased several years ago for $90,000, and depreciation deductions of $48,000 have been allowed. If Coastal sells the equipment for $72,000, the entire $30,000 ($72,000 – $42,000) gain, which is due to the depreciation deductions, is Sec. 1245 ordinary income. Without Sec. 1245, the $30,000 gain is a Sec. 1231 gain that could be offset by $30,000 of the corporation's capital loss. ◀

KEY POINT

On the sale of Sec. 1245 property, a portion of the gain is treated as Sec. 1231 gain only if the property is sold for more than the original cost. This is very unlikely for factory equipment, trucks, office equipment, and other Sec. 1245 property.

Note that Sec. 1245 does not apply to losses. If Coastal Corporation sells the equipment in Example I13-21 for $40,000, a $2,000 ($40,000 – $42,000 basis) Sec. 1231 loss is recognized.

KEY POINT

Property must be depreciable or amortizable to be considered Sec. 1245 property.

SECTION 1245 PROPERTY. **Section 1245 property** is certain property subject to depreciation and, in some cases, amortization. The most common example of Sec. 1245 property is depreciable personal property such as equipment. Automobiles, livestock, railroad grading, and single-purpose agricultural or horticultural structures are Sec. 1245 properties as well as intangible assets that are subject to amortization under Sec. 197 (see Chapter I10).[23] Except for certain buildings placed in service after 1980 and before 1987, buildings and structural components are generally not Sec. 1245 property.[24]

EXAMPLE I13-22 ▶ Buckeye Corporation owns the following assets acquired before 1981: equipment, a patent, an office building (including structural components), and land. The equipment and patent are Sec. 1245 property. The office building and the land are not Sec. 1245 property. ◀

---

[21] Throughout this chapter, property is considered to be placed in service when it is purchased or acquired. The term *Sec. 1245 property* is used here to refer to either recovery property under the ACRS or MACRS rules or nonrecovery property that falls outside of the ACRS or MACRS rules.

[22] As explained later in this chapter, the method of cost recovery used determines whether certain real property is treated as Sec. 1245 recovery property.

[23] Sec. 1245(a)(3).

[24] Sec. 1245(a)(3)(B)(i). Tangible real property "used as an integral part of the manufacturing, production, extraction, or furnishing of transportation, communication, electrical energy, gas, water, or sewage disposal services" is Sec. 1245 property.

REAL WORLD EXAMPLE

Pipelines, electric transmission towers, blast furnaces, greenhouses, and oil tanks are examples of real property that are included in the definition of Sec. 1245 property.

In many cases, taxpayers are allowed preferential treatment with respect to amortizing certain costs. For example, taxpayers may elect to expense up to $15,000 of the cost of making any business facility more accessible to handicapped and elderly people,[25] or to amortize pollution control facilities over 60 months[26] and reforestation expenditures over 84 months.[27] If taxpayers have amortized the costs of any real property under the special provisions, Sec. 1245 applies to the gain resulting from the disposition of such property.[28]

If taxpayers elect to expense certain depreciable property under Sec. 179, the amount deducted is treated as a depreciation deduction for purposes of the Sec. 1245 recapture provisions.[29]

EXAMPLE I13-23 ▶ Compact Corporation purchased $90,000 of 5-year equipment on March 10, 2001, and elected to expense $20,000 of the cost under Sec. 179. Compact sells the equipment on July 30, 2002, for $95,000. Regular depreciation allowed under MACRS for 2001 and 2002 is $14,000 and $11,200 (½ year) respectively. The adjusted basis of the equipment on the date of sale is $44,800 ($90,000 – $20,000 – $25,200 depreciation). The realized gain is $50,200 ($95,000 – $44,800), and $45,200 ($20,000 + $25,200) of the gain is Sec. 1245 ordinary income. The remaining $5,000 is Sec. 1231 gain. ◀

TYPICAL MISCONCEPTION

The categorization of nonresidential real estate acquired between 1981 and 1986 on which an accelerated depreciation method was used, as Sec. 1250 property rather than as Sec. 1245 property is a common error.

APPLICATION OF SEC. 1245 TO NONRESIDENTIAL REAL ESTATE. Most real property is not affected by Sec. 1245. However, Sec. 1245 does apply to nonresidential real estate that qualified as recovery property under the ACRS rules (i.e., placed in service after 1980 and before 1987) unless the taxpayer elected to use the straight-line method of cost recovery.[30] Section 1245 does not apply to nonresidential real estate acquired after 1986, because only straight-line depreciation may be used for nonresidential real estate acquired after 1986 (see Chapter I10).

EXAMPLE I13-24 ▶ Brad sells the following two warehouses during the current year:

KEY POINT

Taxpayers acquiring nonresidential real property between 1981 and 1986 were confronted with choosing between straight-line ACRS and ACRS using the statutory rates. In making the decision, these taxpayers should have considered the number of years the property would be held, the estimated selling price, the present value of the additional depreciation deductions, and any preferential treatment for net capital gains.

	Warehouse 1	*Warehouse 2*
Year of purchase	1985	1985
Cost*	$720,000	$900,000
Cost recovery—straight line ACRS	570,000	
Cost recovery—ACRS statutory rates (accelerated)		730,000
Adjusted basis	150,000	170,000
Selling price	700,000	800,000

*does not consider the cost of land

Both warehouses were placed in service after 1980 and before 1987 and qualify as recovery property under ACRS. The $550,000 ($700,000 – $150,000) gain on the sale of Warehouse 1 is a Sec. 1231 gain. Section 1245 does not apply because the straight-line method of cost recovery is used. Section 1245 applies to the sale of Warehouse 2 because ACRS is used and the property is nonresidential real estate placed in service after 1980 and before 1987. Therefore, the $630,000 ($800,000 – $170,000) gain is ordinary income because the $630,000 gain is less than the $730,000 total ACRS cost-recovery allowance. ◀

If the properties in Example I13-24 were acquired before 1981 or after 1986, they would not be subject to the Sec. 1245 recapture rules regardless of the method of depreciation used. However, nonresidential real estate (e.g., a warehouse) acquired after 1963 and before 1981 is subject to the Sec. 1250 recapture rules, and a portion of the gain from its disposition may be treated as ordinary income.

The Sec. 1245 recapture rules are summarized in Topic Review I13-1.

[25] Sec. 190.
[26] Sec. 169(a).
[27] Sec. 194(a).
[28] Sec. 1245(a)(3)(C). The Sec. 1245 rules recapture amortization deductions claimed on real property under Secs. 169, 179, 185, 188, 190, 193 and 194.
[29] Sec. 1245(a)(2)(C). The maximum amount deductible under Sec. 179 is $24,000 in 2002 and 2003 and $25,000 after 2003.
[30] Sec. 1245(a)(5), before being eliminated by the Tax Reform Act of 1986.

Topic Review I13-1

Section 1245 Recapture

- Section 1245 affects the character of the gain, not the amount of gain.
- Section 1245 does not apply to assets sold or exchanged at a loss.
- Section 1245 ordinary income is never more than the realized gain.
- Section 1245 recapture applies to the total depreciation or amortization allowed or allowable but not more than the realized gain.
- Section 1245 property includes depreciable personal property and amortizable intangible assets (e.g., a patent).
- Section 1245 property includes nonresidential real estate placed in service after 1980 and before 1987 under the ACRS rules **unless** the taxpayer elected to use the straight-line method of cost recovery.
- Section 1245 does not apply to any buildings placed in service after 1986.

RECAPTURE PROVISIONS OF SEC. 1250

OBJECTIVE 4

Apply the recapture provisions of Sec. 1250

In 1964, Sec. 1250 was enacted to extend the recapture concept to include most depreciable real property. Unlike Sec. 1245, where the recapture is based upon the total amount of depreciation (or cost recovery) allowed, Sec. 1250 applies solely to additional depreciation. **Additional depreciation,** also referred to as **excess depreciation,** is the excess of the actual amount of accelerated depreciation (or cost-recovery deductions under ACRS) over the amount of depreciation that would be deductible under the straight-line method. For property held a year or less, additional depreciation is the total amount of depreciation taken on the property.[31] Although Sec. 1250 was enacted in 1964, it is no longer necessary to consider additional depreciation for pre-1970 years.[32]

PURPOSE OF SEC. 1250

Section 1250 has the effect of converting a portion of the Sec. 1231 gain into ordinary income when real property is sold or exchanged. The incremental benefits from using accelerated depreciation or ACRS cost recovery may be recaptured when the property is sold. Noncorporate taxpayers can avoid Sec. 1250 recapture by either using the straight-line method of depreciation or cost recovery or holding the Sec. 1250 property for its entire useful life or recovery period.

When the Sec. 1250 recapture rules are applied solely to the additional depreciation amount instead of total depreciation claimed (as is the case for Sec. 1245 property), real property that is not Sec. 1245 property gets more favorable treatment. Despite a number of changes making Sec. 1250 more restrictive, Sec. 1250 still affords taxpayers more favorable tax treatment than Sec. 1245.

SECTION 1250 PROPERTY DEFINED

ADDITIONAL COMMENT

Elevators and escalators were defined as Sec. 1245 property if placed in service before 1987, but as Sec. 1250 property if placed in service after 1986.

Section 1250 **property** is any depreciable real property other than Sec. 1245 property and includes the following:[33]

- All other depreciable real property except nonresidential real estate that qualifies as recovery property (i.e., placed in service after 1980 and before 1987) unless the straight-line method of cost recovery is elected
- Low-income housing
- Depreciable residential rental property

---

[31] Sec. 1250(b)(1).

[32] Recapture of additional depreciation allowed before 1970 is avoided under Sec. 1250(a)(3) if the property is held for more than ten years.

[33] Sec. 1250(c).

KEY POINT

An apartment building is the most common type of property classified as residential real estate.

For noncorporate taxpayers depreciation recapture is not required on real property placed in service after 1986 because such property must be depreciated under the straight-line modified ACRS rules.[34]

EXAMPLE I13-25 ▶ Frances sells an office building during the current year for $800,000. The office building was purchased in 1980 for $700,000* and depreciation of $500,000 has been allowed using an accelerated method of depreciation. If the straight-line method was used, depreciation would be $420,000. The office building is Sec. 1250 property. Her realized gain is $600,000 and $80,000 is Sec. 1250 ordinary income due to excess depreciation. The remaining $520,000 gain is Sec. 1231 gain. ◀

*does not consider the cost of land

As explained below, $420,000 of the gain in Example 13-25 is taxed at 25% and $100,000 is taxed at 20% if there are no Sec. 1231 losses, unrecaptured Sec. 1231 losses, and no capital gains and losses from other transactions. Recall from Chapter 5 that the tax rate on LTCG may be 20% or 10%.

UNRECAPTURED SECTION 1250 GAIN

For sales of real property after May 6, 1997, some or all of the Sec. 1231 gain may be LTCG that is unrecaptured Sec. 1250 gain taxed at a rate of 25%. Unrecaptured Sec. 1250 gain is the amount of LTCG, not otherwise treated as ordinary income, which would be taxed as ordinary if Sec. 1250 provided for the recapture of all depreciation and not just additional depreciation. When a taxpayer sells Sec. 1250 property at a gain, any gain due to excess depreciation is ordinary income. Any remaining gain is Sec. 1231 gain and may be LTCG, however any of the LTCG due to depreciation other than excess depreciation is unrecaptured Sec. 1250 gain.

An individual taxpayer who uses straight-line depreciation for Sec. 1250 property does not have any additional depreciation that would be recaptured as ordinary gain under Sec. 1250. Today however, all of the Sec. 1231 gain to the extent of straight-line depreciation is unrecaptured Sec. 1250 gain subject to a maximum tax rate of 25%. In Example 13-25, $420,000 of the gain is unrecaptured Sec. 1250 gain because $420,000 more of the gain would be taxed as ordinary income if all depreciation had been recaptured.

EXAMPLE I13-26 ▶ Linnie owns a building used in her trade or business that was placed in service in 1987. She has no Sec. 1231 losses, nonrecaptured Sec. 1231 losses or capital gains and losses. The building cost $400,000* and depreciation-to-date amounts to $160,000. If she sells the building for $350,000, her $110,000 gain ($350,000−$240,000) is Sec. 1231 gain and there is no depreciation recapture under Sec. 1250 because straight-line depreciation was allowed. ◀

*does not consider the cost of land

SELF-STUDY QUESTION

In Example I13-24, how much of the $550,000 Sec. 1231 gain resulting from the sale of warehouse #1 is unrecaptured Sec. 1250 gain?

ANSWER

All $550,000

The $110,000 Sec. 1231 gain in the above example is LTCG and is taxed at a rate of 25% because it is unrecaptured Sec. 1250 gain.

Prior to the Taxpayer Relief Act of 1997, the $110,000 gain recognized by Linnie was subject to a maximum rate of 28%. Although the law was changed to lower the rate on capital gains to 20% or even 10%, Congress did not extend such favorable treatment to real property subject to depreciation. The maximum rate was reduced from 28% to 25%, not to 20%.

EXAMPLE I13-27 ▶ Assume the same facts as above except Linnie sells the building for $500,000. Her Sec. 1231 gain is $260,000 ($500,000−$240,000), and $160,000 of the gain is taxed at 25% because it is unrecaptured Sec. 1250 gain. The remaining $100,000 of gain is taxed at 20%. ◀

[34] As explained in the Additional Recapture for Corporations section for this chapter, corporations may have depreciation recapture under Sec. 291(a) despite the use of straight-line depreciation.

ADDITIONAL COMMENT

When a building is sold at a gain, different tax rates might apply to portions of the gain: rate for ordinary income, 25% for unrecaptured Sec. 1250 gain and 20% (or 10%) for ANCG.

RECAPTURE RULES FOR RESIDENTIAL RENTAL PROPERTY

All residential rental property is Sec. 1250 property. For a building or structure to qualify as residential rental property, 80% or more of the gross rental income from the building or structure must be rental income from dwelling units. Residential rental property does not include any unit in a hotel, motel, inn, or other establishment if more than one-half of the units are used on a transient basis.[35]

For depreciable residential rental property, Sec. 1250 recapture as ordinary income applies only to **additional depreciation** allowed after 1975.

EXAMPLE I13-28 ▶ Buddy sells an apartment complex used as residential rental property and placed in service on January 1, 1976. The cost of the apartment complex is $900,000*, and the complex is sold on January 1, 2002, for $700,000. Depreciation claimed by Buddy on the property is as follows:

Time Period	*Depreciation Allowed*	*Straight-Line Depreciation*	*Additional Depreciation*
Jan. 1, 1976–Jan. 1, 2002	$800,000	$710,000	$90,000

On the date of sale, the adjusted basis of the apartment is $100,000 ($900,000 − $800,000) and the realized gain is $600,000 ($700,000 − $100,000). All $90,000 of additional depreciation allowed is recaptured as ordinary income because the additional depreciation is less than the realized gain. The remaining $510,000 ($600,000 − $90,000) of gain is a Sec. 1231 gain, that is taxed at 25% because it is unrecaptured Sec. 1250 gain. ◀

ADDITIONAL COMMENT

If the selling price in Example 13-28 is $172,000, all of the gain is Sec. 1250 ordinary income.

Selling Price	$172,000
Adjusted Basis	100,000
Realized Gain	$ 72,000
Ordinary Gain	$ 72,000

RESIDENTIAL RENTAL PROPERTY THAT IS RECOVERY PROPERTY

For residential rental property that is cost-recovery property (i.e., property placed in service after 1980 and before 1987), all of the **additional depreciation** is recaptured as ordinary income to the extent of gain. Additional depreciation is the excess of the ACRS deduction using the percentages provided in the ACRS tables over a hypothetical cost recovery amount based upon the straight-line ACRS method using the length of the recovery period (i.e., 15, 18, or 19 years).

EXAMPLE I13-29 ▶ Joel purchased depreciable residential rental property for $800,000 ($100,000 is for land) on January 1, 1986. The property is 19-year recovery property and accelerated cost recovery was used. Joel sells the property for $980,000 ($180,000 for land) during the current year.

Cost Recovery Deductions Allowed	*Cost Recovery with Straight-Line*	*Additional Depreciation*
$610,400	$589,500	$20,900

Joel's realized gain on the sale of the building is $710,400 [$800,000 − ($700,000 − $610,400)] and $20,900 is recaptured as Sec. 1250 ordinary income. The remaining $689,500 of gain is Sec. 1231 gain. $589,500 may be taxed at 25% because it is unrecaptured Sec. 1250 gain. The $80,000 gain on sale of land is Sec. 1231 gain and may be taxed at 20%. $100,000 ($689,500 − $589,500) of the gain on sale of the building may also be taxed at 20%. ◀

There is a difference between Sec. 1250 ordinary income and unrecaptured Sec. 1250 gain. Sec. 1250 ordinary income could be taxed at 38.6% for noncorporate taxpayers while unrecaptured Sec. 1250 gain is LTCG taxed at a maximum rate of 25%. To have unrecaptured Sec. 1250 gain, the property must have a holding period greater than one year.

EXAMPLE I13-30 ▶ Kim, whose tax rate is 35%, owns an office building purchased for $1,000,000* on April 10 of last year. The building is sold on March 28 of the current year for $990,000 when its adjusted basis is $966,850. The $23,150 gain is not Sec. 1231 gain and none of the gain is unrecaptured Sec. 1250 gain because the holding period is not more than one year. The $23,150 gain is ordinary taxed at 35%. If the holding period was more than one year, the Sec. 1231 gain of $23,150 is LTCG that is unrecaptured Sec. 1250 gain taxed at 25%. ◀

*does not consider the cost of land

[35] Reg. Sec. 1.167(j)-3(b)(1)(i).

RECAPTURE RULES FOR NONRESIDENTIAL REAL ESTATE

Depreciable nonresidential real property is Sec. 1250 property except when the property is placed in service after 1980 and before 1987 and accelerated cost recovery was allowed. If the property is placed in service after 1980 and before 1987, the property is Sec. 1245 property if accelerated cost recovery is used.[36] There is no depreciation recapture if the noncorporate taxpayer elected to use the straight-line method of cost recovery[37] for nonresidential ACRS property.[38]

EXAMPLE I13-31 ▶ The AB partnership purchased an office building in 1981 and a warehouse in 1982. The statutory percentages provided in the ACRS table are used to determine cost-recovery deductions for the office building. The straight-line method is used to determine cost-recovery deductions for the warehouse. The office building is subject to the Sec. 1245 recapture rules, and the warehouse is Sec. 1250 property. Even though the warehouse is Sec. 1250 property, the gain realized on the sale is Sec. 1231 gain because the straight-line ACRS method was used. However, the Sec. 1231 gain realized on the sale at the warehouse is unrecaptured Sec. 1250 gain to the extent of depreciation allowed, if the warehouse is sold after May 6, 1997. ◀

PRE-ACRS NONRESIDENTIAL REAL ESTATE. All additional depreciation allowed after December 31, 1969, is subject to recapture as ordinary income under Sec. 1250.[39] The recaptured amount is limited to the realized gain.

EXAMPLE I13-32 ▶ Wayne sells his manufacturing plant during the current year. The plant was purchased in 1972 for use in his business. Additional depreciation (excess of accelerated depreciation under ACRS over straight-line) of $375,000 has been taken on the building. Information pertaining to the sale is as follows:

	Original Cost	*Total Depreciation*	*Adjusted Basis*	*Selling Price*
Plant	$3,000,000	$2,400,000	$600,000	$1,100,000
Land	300,000		300,000	900,000

The realized gain from the sale of the plant is $500,000 ($1,100,000 − $600,000) and $375,000 of the gain is recaptured as ordinary income under Sec. 1250. The remaining $125,000 of gain is Sec. 1231 gain taxed at 25% because it is unrecaptured Sec. 1250 gain. The $600,000 of realized gain from the sale of the land is a Sec. 1231 gain. ◀

EXAMPLE I13-33 ▶ Assume the same facts as in Example I13-32 except that the selling price of the plant is $850,000. All of the $250,000 realized gain ($850,000 − $600,000) is recaptured as ordinary income because the $375,000 of additional depreciation is greater than the $250,000 of realized gain. ◀

TYPICAL MISCONCEPTION

It is easy to forget that the amount recaptured as ordinary income under either Sec. 1245 or Sec. 1250 can never exceed the realized gain.

RECAPTURE FOR ACRS NONRESIDENTIAL REAL ESTATE. Section 1245 applies to nonresidential real property (1) if ACRS statutory rates were used to determine the cost-recovery deductions (as opposed to straight-line rates) and (2) if the property was placed in service after December 31, 1980, and before January 1, 1987. For Sec. 1245 recovery property, all gain to the extent of the lesser of the gain realized or the cost recovery deductions claimed is ordinary income. If the straight-line method of cost recovery is elected, the property is Sec. 1250 and none of the cost-recovery deductions are recaptured under Sec. 1250.[40]

---

[36] Sec. 1245(a)(5), before amendment by the Tax Reform Act of 1986.

[37] The cost of 18-year recovery property may be recovered under Sec. 168(b)(3)(A) over a period of 18, 35, or 45 years.

[38] Sec. 1245(a)(5)(C), before being repealed by the Tax Reform Act of 1986.

[39] Secs. 1250(a)(1)(B)(v) and (a)(2)(B)(v).

[40] An exception is provided for corporate taxpayers under Sec. 291 (See the Additional Recapture for Corporations section in this chapter.)

EXAMPLE I13-34 ▶ Larry owns the following two buildings that are used in his business. Both buildings were purchased in 1985 and qualify as recovery property under the ACRS rules. Larry uses the ACRS statutory rates to determine cost-recovery deductions for Building 1 and the straight-line method for Building 2.

	Original Cost	*Cost-Recovery Deductions*	*Adjusted Basis*
Building 1	$1,000,000	$420,000	$580,000
Building 2 (SL)	1,000,000	300,000	700,000

If Building 1 is sold for $1,200,000, the realized gain is $620,000 ($1,200,000 – $580,000). Section 1245 applies, and $420,000 is recaptured as ordinary income. The remaining $200,000 is Sec. 1231 gain. If Building 2 is sold for $1,200,000, the realized gain is $500,000 ($1,200,000 – $700,000). None of the gain is Sec. 1245 ordinary income because the straight-line cost recovery method is used, and Sec. 1245 does not apply unless the ACRS statutory rates are used. $300,000 of the Sec. 1231 gain realized on the sale of Building 2 is unrecaptured Sec. 1250 gain, thus $300,000 may be taxed at 25%, and $200,000 at 20%. ◀

SELF-STUDY QUESTION

If the asset in Example I13-29 is an office building, how much ordinary income must Joel recognize?

ANSWER

$610,400.
The office building is Sec. 1245 property. Joel must recognize ordinary income of $610,400 and a $100,000 Sec. 1231 gain.

LOW-INCOME HOUSING

Congress has provided incentives for the construction and rehabilitation of low-income housing. For tax years after 1986, a low-income housing credit is available to owners of qualified low-income housing projects.[41]

The depreciation recapture provisions of Sec. 1250 also favor low-income housing. The recapture percentage applied to the amount of additional depreciation allowed for low-income housing after 1975 is 100% less one percentage point for each full month the property is held for more than 100 months.[42] If the low-income housing unit is held for 16 years and 8 months, none of the additional depreciation is subject to recapture as ordinary income.

The Sec. 1250 recapture rules for noncorporate taxpayers are summarized in Topic Review I13-2.

ADDITIONAL RECAPTURE FOR CORPORATIONS

KEY POINT

Section 291 has no effect on Sec. 1245 property because gain is already recaptured to the extent of all depreciation.

ADDITIONAL COMMENT

Corporations are subject to an additional 20% depreciation recapture rule under Sec. 291 on sales of Sec. 1250 property.

Corporations are subject to additional recapture rules under Sec. 291 if depreciable real estate is sold or otherwise disposed of. This recapture is in addition to the normal recapture rules under Sec. 1250. The additional ordinary income that is recaptured effectively reduces the amount of the Sec. 1231 gain.

The additional recapture amount under Sec. 291 is equal to 20% of the difference between the amount that would be recaptured if the property was Sec. 1245 property and actual recapture amount under Sec. 1250.[43]

EXAMPLE I13-35 ▶ In 1980 Orlando Corporation purchased an office building for $500,000* for use in its business. The building is sold during the current year for $480,000. Total depreciation allowed for the building is $245,000. Total depreciation of $160,000 would have been allowed if the straight-line method of depreciation has been used. The property's adjusted basis is $255,000 ($500,000 – $245,000) and the realized gain is $225,000 ($480,000 – $255,000). Under Sec. 1250, the ordinary income recaptured amount is equal to 100% of the additional depreciation, which is $85,000 ($245,000 – $160,000). Under Sec. 1245, the ordinary income recapture amount would be $225,000. The amount of Sec. 1250 ordinary income under Sec. 291 is $28,000 [0.20 × ($225,000 – $85,000)]. To summarize, the total amount recaptured as Sec. 1250 ordinary income is $113,000 ($85,000 + $28,000) and the Sec. 1231 gain is $112,000 ($225,000 – $113,000). ◀

*does not consider the cost of land

SELF-STUDY QUESTION

If the taxpayer in Example I13-35 is a noncorporate taxpayer, how much of the gain is Sec. 1250 ordinary income?

ANSWER

$85,000

[41] Sec. 42.
[42] Secs. 1250(a)(1)(B)(i), (ii), (iii), and (iv).
[43] Sec. 291(a)(1).

Topic Review I13-2

Section 1250 Recapture for Noncorporate Taxpayers

- Section 1250 affects the character of the gain, not the amount of gain.
- Section 1250 does not apply to assets sold or exchanged at a loss.
- Section 1250 ordinary income is never more than the realized gain.
- Section 1250 ordinary income is never more than the *additional* depreciation allowed. (Note, that this statement is not true for corporate taxpayers.)
- Section 1250 property includes depreciable real property unless the real property is nonresidential real estate placed in service in 1980 and before 1987 under the ACRS rules and the straight-line method is not elected.
- Section 1250 ordinary income does not exist if the straight-line method of depreciation is used. (Note that this statement is not true for corporate taxpayers because of the additional recapture requirements under Sec. 291.)

EXAMPLE I13-36 ▶ Pacific Corporation purchased an office building in 1981 for $800,000* for use in its trade or business. The building is sold during the current year for $850,000. Pacific elected to use the straight-line method of cost recovery and $800,000 cost-recovery deductions have been allowed. The realized gain is $850,000 ($850,000 – 0). Because there is no excess depreciation, none of the gain is ordinary income under Sec. 1250 if Sec. 291 is not considered. If the building were instead Sec. 1245 recovery property, $800,000 of the gain would be treated as ordinary income. The amount of Sec. 1250 ordinary income under Sec. 291 is $160,000 [0.20 × ($800,000 – $0)]. The remaining $640,000 ($800,000 – $160,000) gain is Sec. 1231 gain. ◀

*does not consider the cost of land

SELF-STUDY QUESTION

If the taxpayer in Example I13-36 was a noncorporate taxpayer, how much of the gain is Sec. 1250 ordinary income?

ANSWER

Zero

For corporations, none of the Sec. 1231 gain is unrecaptured Sec. 1250 gain.

SUMMARY OF SEC. 1231, 1245 AND 1250 GAINS

Sec. 1231 property is depreciable property and nondepreciable real property used in one's trade or business and held for more than one year. Net Sec. 1231 gain, the excess of Sec. 1231 gain over Sec. 1231 loss, is LTCG unless the five-year lookback rule applies in which case the gain is ordinary to the extent of the nonrecaptured net Sec. 1231 loss. Net Sec. 1231 loss, the excess of Sec. 1231 loss over Sec. 1231 gain, is ordinary.

Sec. 1245 applies to depreciable personal property and amortizable intangible assets. It also applies to certain nonresidential real property placed in service during ACRS if accelerated cost recovery is used. Gain to the extent of depreciation is ordinary income. All of the gain resulting from the sale of Sec. 1245 property is ordinary income unless the asset is sold for more than its original basis.

Sec. 1250 property is depreciable real property, and gain is ordinary income to the extent of additional depreciation, the excess of accelerated depreciation over straight-line. After 1986, the straight-line method must be used for real property and thus noncorporate taxpayers will not have any Sec. 1250 ordinary income on the sale of depreciable real property placed in service after 1986. Unfortunately, Congress made the sale and exchange of buildings more complicated in 1997 when it created the concept of unrecaptured Sec. 1250 gain that is taxed at 25%. When a noncorporate taxpayer sells depreciated buildings at a gain, any gain to the extent of straight-line depreciation is Sec. 1231 gain but is taxed at 25% because it is unrecaptured Sec. 1250 gain.

To further illustrate Sec. 1231, 1245 and 1250, refer to Topic Review I13-3 where a noncorporate taxpayer with a 38.6% tax rate sells various assets during the current year. Each asset was purchased in 1995 and the selling price is $450,000 for each of the first three assets. All assets are used in a trade or business. There are no other gains and losses and no unrecaptured Sec. 1231 losses.

Topic Review I13-3

Section 1231, 1245 and 1250—Comparison of Various Assets

The taxpayer is a noncorporate taxpayer with a 38.6% tax rate who sells each of the first three assets for $450,000. Each asset was purchased in 1995 and is used in a trade or business. There are no other gains and losses and no nonrecaptured Sec. 1231 losses.

	Original Basis	Adjusted Basis	Tax Treatment
1. Land	$400,000	$400,000	$50,000 Sec. 1231 gain taxed at 20%
2. Equipment	600,000	400,000	$50,000 Sec. 1245 ordinary income taxed at 38.6%. All gain is due to depreciation.
3. Building	500,000	400,000	$50,000 Sec. 1231 gain which is unrecaptured Sec. 1250 gain taxed at 25%
For assets 4, 5 & 6, assume the selling price is $700,000.			
4. Land	$400,000	$400,000	$300,000 Sec. 1231 gain taxed at 20%
5. Equipment	600,000	400,000	$200,000 Sec. 1245 ordinary income taxed at 38.6% and $100,000 Sec. 1231 gain taxed at 20%
6. Building	500,000	400,000	$300,000 Sec. 1231 gain with $200,000 taxed at 20% and $100,000 of unrecaptured Sec. 1250 gain taxed at 25%

Recapture Provisions—Other Applications

OBJECTIVE 5

Describe other recapture applications

The Secs. 1245 and 1250 recapture provisions take precedence over other provisions of the tax law.[44] Unless an exception or limitation is specifically stated in Secs. 1245 or 1250, gain is recognized under Secs. 1245 or 1250 despite the existence of provisions elsewhere in the Code that allow nonrecognition of gain.[45]

Gifts of Property Subject to Recapture

A gift of appreciated depreciable property does not result in the recapture of depreciation or cost-recovery deductions under Secs. 1245 or 1250.[46] The donee must consider the recapture potential when disposing of the property. The recapture amount for the donee is computed by including the recaptured amount attributable to the donor.[47]

EXAMPLE I13-37 ▶ Ashley makes a gift of equipment with an $8,200 FMV to Helmut. Ashley paid $10,000 for the equipment and deducted $4,000 of depreciation before making the gift. Ashley does not have to recapture any depreciation when making the gift. Helmut's basis for the equipment is $6,000 and the potential depreciation recapture carries over to Helmut. ◀

EXAMPLE I13-38 ▶ Assume the same facts as in Example I13-37 except that Helmut uses the equipment in a trade or business, deducts $1,500 of depreciation, and sells the equipment for $7,100. When determining the amount of depreciation subject to recapture, Helmut must also consider the depreciation allowed to Ashley. The entire $2,600 [$7,100 – ($6,000 – $1,500)] of gain is recaptured as ordinary income because it is less than the $5,500 ($4,000 + $1,500) of depreciation claimed. ◀

---

[44] Secs. 1245(d) and 1250(i).

[45] Reg. Secs. 1.1245-6(a) and 1.1250-1(c)(1).

[46] Secs. 1245(b)(1) and 1250(d)(1).

[47] Reg. Secs. 1.1245-2(a)(4) and 1.1250-2(d).

ADDITIONAL COMMENT

If the taxpayer in Topic Review I13-3 is a corporation, the character of the gain is the same for assets 1, 2, 4 and 5. For asset 3, $10,000 of the gain is Sec. 1250 ordinary income under Sec. 291 and $40,000 is Sec. 1231 gain. For asset 6, $20,000 is Sec. 1250 ordinary income under Sec. 291 and $280,000 is Sec. 1231 gain.

TRANSFER OF PROPERTY SUBJECT TO RECAPTURE AT DEATH

The transfer of appreciated property at death does not cause a recapture of depreciation deductions to the decedent's estate under Secs. 1245 and 1250.[48] In addition, recapture potential does not carry over to the person who receives the property from the decedent.

EXAMPLE I13-39 ▶

KEY POINT

Death is one of the few ways to avoid the recapture provisions.

Nancy dies while owning a building with a $900,000 FMV. The building is Sec. 1245 property acquired in 1985 for $800,000* on which cost-recovery deductions of $745,000 have been claimed. Pam inherits the building from Nancy. Pam's basis for the building is $900,000, and the $745,000 of cost-recovery deductions are not recaptured. If Pam immediately sells the building, there is no depreciation recapture attributable to the $745,000 of cost-recovery deductions taken by the decedent. ◀

*does not include cost of land

CHARITABLE CONTRIBUTIONS

As discussed in Chapter I7, the deduction for a charitable contribution of ordinary income property is generally limited to its adjusted basis (i.e., the amount of the contribution deduction is equal to the FMV of the property less the amount of gain that would not have been LTCG [or Sec. 1231 gain] if the contributed property had been sold by the taxpayer at its FMV).[49] Thus, the contribution deduction for recapture property is generally scaled down to reflect the ordinary income that would be recognized if the property were sold rather than contributed to the charity.

EXAMPLE I13-40 ▶

Ralph makes a gift of an organ to a church. The organ is used in Ralph's trade or business and has a $6,300 FMV. Ralph paid $10,000 for the organ, and $8,000 depreciation has been claimed. If the organ were sold for its $6,300 FMV, the realized and recognized gain would be $4,300 ($6,300 − $2,000) and all of the gain would be ordinary income due to the recapture of depreciation under Sec. 1245. The charitable contribution deduction is limited to $2,000 ($6,300 − $4,300), because none of the $4,300 gain would be taxed as a LTCG if the organ were sold. ◀

ADDITIONAL COMMENT

If the FMV of the organ in Example I13-40 is $11,000, the charitable contribution deduction is limited to $3,000, the $11,000 FMV less $8,000. If the organ is sold for $11,000, $8,000 of the gain is ordinary income.

LIKE-KIND EXCHANGES

A taxpayer who receives boot (i.e., non–like-kind property) in a transaction that otherwise qualifies as a like-kind exchange recognizes gain equal to the lesser of the realized gain and the amount of boot received. If the property is Sec. 1245 or 1250 property, the gain is first considered to be ordinary income up to the maximum amount of the gain that is subject to the recapture provisions.

EXAMPLE I13-41 ▶

REAL-WORLD EXAMPLE

A taxpayer's exchange of yachts used for business was a nontaxable transaction under Sec. 1031. Because no gain was recognized on the transaction, no gain could be subject to the recapture rules. *J. Wade Harris,* 1975 PH T.C. Memo ¶75,276, 34 TCM 1192.

Virginia owns a duplex that is residential rental property. The duplex cost $300,000* in 1979 and has a $140,000 adjusted basis. Additional depreciation of $22,000 has been deducted. Virginia exchanges the duplex for a four-unit apartment building with a $250,000 FMV and $25,000 in cash. Gain realized on the exchange is $135,000 [($250,000 + $25,000) − $140,000)], and the recognized gain is $25,000. Gain recognized is the lesser of the $25,000 boot received or the $135,000 of gain realized. Because additional depreciation is recaptured as ordinary income under Sec. 1250, $22,000 of the gain is ordinary income and $3,000 of the gain is Sec. 1231 gain which may be taxed at 25% because it is unrecaptured Sec. 1250 gain. ◀

*does not include cost of land

If gain is not recognized in a like-kind exchange, the recapture potential carries over to the replacement property (i.e., any recapture potential associated with the property exchanged attaches to the property received in the exchange).[50]

[48] Secs. 1245(b)(2) and 1250(d)(2).
[49] Sec. 170(e)(1)(A).
[50] Reg. Sec. 1.1245-2(c)(4).

EXAMPLE I13-42 ▶ Melissa owns a Chevrolet pickup truck used in her trade or business that cost $10,000 and has a $6,000 adjusted basis due to $4,000 in depreciation deductions she has claimed. The truck is exchanged for a Ford pickup truck with a $9,000 FMV. The Ford truck is used in Melissa's business. Melissa does not recognize any portion of the $3,000 realized gain because the exchange qualifies as a like-kind exchange and no boot is received. Her basis for the Ford truck is $6,000 (i.e., a substituted basis).

After deducting $2,000 of depreciation, Melissa sells the Ford truck for $7,300. All of the recognized gain of $3,300 ($7,300 – $4,000) is ordinary income. The depreciation recapture amount under Sec. 1245 is equal to the total $6,000 in depreciation (including $4,000 on the Chevrolet pickup truck) but the recognized gain is only $3,300.[51] ◀

INVOLUNTARY CONVERSIONS

If an involuntary conversion of Sec. 1245 property occurs and all or a portion of the gain is not recognized,[52] the amount of gain that is considered to be Sec. 1245 ordinary income is limited. Ordinary income under Sec. 1245 may not exceed the sum of (1) the recognized gain and (2) the FMV of acquired property that is not Sec. 1245 property but is qualifying property under Sec. 1033.[53] A similar provision exists for the involuntary conversion of Sec. 1250 property.[54]

EXAMPLE I13-43 ▶ The Ryan Corporation's printing equipment with original cost of $600,000 and adjusted basis of $200,000 is destroyed by fire. Ryan, Inc. receives $550,000 of insurance proceeds and purchases $510,000 of printing equipment. If the corporation elects to defer gain, it must recognize a $40,000 gain which is Sec. 1245 ordinary income. The basis of the printing equipment acquired is $200,000. ◀

REAL-WORLD EXAMPLE

Taxpayer received insurance proceeds in excess of the adjusted basis of a business automobile upon the destruction of the auto in an accident. The taxpayer did not use Sec. 1033 to defer the gain and the court held that the gain was subject to recapture under Sec. 1245. *Anthony Astone*, 1983 PH T.C. Memo ¶83,747, 47 TCM 632.

INSTALLMENT SALES

As discussed in Chapter I11, gain resulting from an installment sale is generally recognized as payments are received. Thus, the gain may be spread over more than one accounting period. An installment sale of depreciable property may result in all of the recaptured gain being taxed in the year of the sale.[55] Recapture income is "the aggregate amount which would be treated as ordinary income under Sec. 1245 or 1250 for the taxable year of the disposition if all payments to be received were received in the taxable year of disposition."[56] Recapture income must be recognized in the year of sale, even if no payments are received.

EXAMPLE I13-44 ▶ Pat owns equipment with a $100,000 acquisition cost and a $42,000 adjusted basis. Depreciation of $58,000 has been allowed. During the current year, Pat sells the property for $30,000 cash and a $60,000 ten-year interest-bearing note. The realized gain is $48,000 ($90,000 – $42,000), and the recapture income amount is $48,000 (the lesser of total depreciation deductions of $58,000 or the $48,000 of realized gain). The $48,000 of gain is all recognized as ordinary income in the current year, despite the fact that the transaction qualifies as an installment sale and only $30,000 of cash is received in the year of sale. ◀

KEY POINT

In the case of an installment sale of Sec. 1245 or 1250 property, it is possible to report a large taxable gain even though the taxpayer has not yet received the cash to pay the tax on such gain.

If gain realized from the installment sale exceeds the recapture income, the excess gain is reported under the installment method.[57] The amount of recapture income recognized is added to the adjusted basis to determine the gross profit ratio.

EXAMPLE I13-45 ▶ Bob owns an office building acquired for $700,000* in 1986 and subject to the Sec. 1245 recapture rules. After claiming $560,000 of cost recovery deductions, Bob sells the building to Judy in 2002 for $1,000,000. Bob receives $200,000 in cash and an $800,000 interest-bearing note. The note is to be paid with annual principal payments of $100,000 beginning in 2003. The total amount of realized gain is $860,000 ($1,000,000 – $140,000). In 2002, Bob recognizes $560,000 of Sec. 1245 ordinary income. The gross profit ratio is determined by adding $560,000 recapture income to the $140,000 basis. The gross profit ratio is 30% [($1,000,000 – $700,000) ÷

SELF-STUDY QUESTION

What method of cost recovery is Bob using in Example I13-45?

---

[51] Reg. Sec. 1.1245-2(a)(4).

[52] As discussed in Chapter I12, one may elect to defer recognition of the gain if the Sec. 1033 requirements are satisfied.

[53] Sec. 1245(b)(4) and Reg. Sec. 1.1245-4(d)(1).

[54] Sec. 1250(d)(4) and Reg. Sec. 1.1250-3(d).

[55] Sec. 453(i)(1).

[56] Sec. 453(i)(2).

[57] Sec. 453(i)(1)(B).0.

WHAT WOULD YOU DO IN THIS SITUATION?

You recently graduated with an advanced degree in taxation and have accepted a job with a CPA firm in the tax department. One of the firm's clients, a wealthy individual, was in need of cash and decided to sell some assets to raise the cash. The client asked the firm to advise him, from a tax standpoint, which assets he should sell. The client is in the 38.6% tax bracket. You suggested in a written memo that the client sell one of the client's jet airplanes. The plane you recommended to be sold had originally cost $16 million and now had an adjusted basis of $6 million. A buyer had offered to buy the plane for $12 million on the installment basis, paying $4 million per year for three years plus interest at 9%. The principal reason for selling that particular plane is that it would raise $12 million over three years, but the tax could be spread over three years by using the installment sale method. The client took your advice and sold the plane in the current year.

Later, when preparing the client's tax return, you realize that depreciation recapture must be recognized in the year of sale, even if the property is sold under the installment sale method. Thus, *all* of the gain on the sale of the plane must be recognized in the year of sale, not spread over three years. You go to your manager and tell him about your major mistake. Your manager, who reviewed your original memo, indicates that he thinks that the two of you should not tell anyone about the mistake as it will negatively impact both of your careers. The manager thinks that because the client has such a large amount of income, reporting the entire gain on the sale of the plane on the client's return might not be detected by the client. Thus, the manager instructs you to prepare the current year return with the entire $6 million of gain and not tell anyone about the mistake. What should you do in this situation?

ANSWER

Accelerated cost recovery. The office building is subject to Sec. 1245 recapture.

$1,000,000]. In addition to recognizing $560,000 of ordinary income, Bob recognizes $60,000 (0.30 × $200,000) Sec. 1231 gain in 2002 because a $200,000 cash down payment was received in the year of the sale. In 2003 and in each subsequent year, $30,000 (0.30 × $100,000) of Sec. 1231 gain is recognized as the cash payments on the principal are received. ◀

*does not include cost of land

SECTION 179 EXPENSING ELECTION

In lieu of capitalizing the cost of new or used tangible personal business property, taxpayers may elect to expense up to $24,000 of the acquisition cost in 2001 and 2002[58] (see Chapter I10). If the property is subsequently converted to nonbusiness use, previous tax benefits derived from the immediate expensing election must be recaptured and added to the taxpayer's gross income in the year of the conversion.[59] The recaptured amount equals the difference between the amount expensed under Sec. 179 and the total depreciation that would otherwise have been claimed for the period of business use.

EXAMPLE I13-46 ▶ Joel purchased business equipment last year for $18,100 and elected to expense the entire amount under Sec. 179. In the current year, he converts the equipment to nonbusiness use. Depreciation of $3,620 (0.20 × $18,100) based on a five-year recovery period under the MACRS rules would have been allowed during the period the equipment was held for business use if Joel had not elected to expense the $18,100 cost. Joel must include $14,480 ($18,100 − $3,620) in his gross income for the current year. This amount represents the previous tax benefit obtained from the immediate expensing election. ◀

CONSERVATION AND LAND CLEARING EXPENDITURES

Taxpayers engaged in the business of farming may deduct expenditures paid or incurred during the taxable year for soil and water conservation or the prevention of erosion. The expenditures must be made with respect to land used in farming and would be capital expenditures except for this provision.[60]

The deductions for conservation expenditures may be partially or fully recaptured as ordinary income if the farmland is disposed of before the land is held for more than nine

[58] Secs. 179(a) and (b)(1).
[59] Sec. 179(d)(10) and Reg. Sec. 1.179-1(e).
[60] Sec. 175(a).

KEY POINT

There is no recapture of conservation costs if the farmland is held for at least 10 years.

years.[61] The amount of deductions recaptured as ordinary income under Sec. 1252 is a percentage of the aggregate deductions allowed for conservation expenditures. The amount of ordinary income recognized under Sec. 1252 is limited to the lesser of the taxpayer's realized gain or the applicable recapture percentage times the total conservation expenditures.

The recapture percentage is 100% if the farmland is disposed of within five years after the date it is acquired. The percentage declines by 20 percentage points for each additional year the property is held. If the land is disposed of after being held for more than nine years, none of the expenses are recaptured.[62]

EXAMPLE I13-47 ▶ Paula owns farmland with a $400,000 basis. She has deducted $50,000 for soil and water conservation expenditures. After farming the land for six years and five months, Paula sells the land for $520,000. The realized gain is $120,000 ($520,000 − $400,000) and the recapture percentage is 60%, because the farmland is disposed of within the seventh year after it was acquired. The amount of ordinary income due to recapture under Sec. 1252 is $30,000, the lesser of the $120,000 realized gain or the $30,000 (0.60 × $50,000) recapture amount. ◀

INTANGIBLE DRILLING COSTS AND DEPLETION

ADDITIONAL COMMENT

Intangible drilling and development costs represent the major cost of operations and can provide investors with working interests in oil and gas properties with a first-year write-off of substantially all of their investment.

Taxpayers may elect to either expense or capitalize intangible drilling and development costs (IDC).[63] If the election to expense is not made, the costs are capitalized and recovered through additional cost depletion deductions. Intangible drilling and development costs include "all expenditures made by an operator for wages, fuel, repairs, hauling, supplies, etc., incident to and necessary for the drilling of wells and the preparation of wells for the production of oil or gas."[64]

Part or all of the gain from the sale of oil and gas properties may be recaptured as ordinary income due to the recapture of the IDC deduction and the deduction for depletion. However, the amount of ordinary income recognized from the recapture of IDC and depletion is limited to the gain realized from the disposition of the property.[65]

EXAMPLE I13-48 ▶ In 1997 Marty purchased undeveloped property for the purpose of drilling for oil and gas. Intangible drilling and development costs of $400,000 were paid in 1997. Marty elected to expense the IDC. During the current year, Marty sells the property and realizes a $900,000 gain. $300,000 of cost depletion was allowed. Marty must recognize $700,000 of ordinary income because of the recapture of IDC ($400,000) and the recapture of depletion ($300,000). The remaining $200,000 ($900,000 − $700,000) gain is Sec. 1231 gain. ◀

EXAMPLE I13-49 ▶ In 1998 Tina acquired oil and gas properties for $700,000. During 1998, she elected to expense $200,000 of IDC. Total depletion allowed was $80,000. During the current year, Tina sells the property for $840,000 and realizes a $220,000 [($840,000 − ($700,000 − $80,000)] gain. The amount of ordinary income due to recapture is $220,000, because both IDC and depletion must be recaptured only to the extent of the gain. ◀

GAIN ON SALE OF DEPRECIABLE PROPERTY BETWEEN RELATED PARTIES

All gain recognized on the sale or exchange of property between related parties is ordinary income if the property is subject to depreciation in the hands of the transferee (i.e., the person who purchases the property). The sale or exchange may be direct or indirect.[66]

EXAMPLE I13-50 ▶ Phil owns a building with a $500,000 adjusted basis and $800,000 FMV. The building, which cost $700,000, is used in his business, and the straight-line method of depreciation is used. $200,000 of depreciation deductions were allowed. If the building is sold to Phil's 100%-owned corporation for $800,000, the $300,000 realized gain ($800,000 − $500,000) is treated as ordinary income under Sec. 1239, because the property is subject to depreciation in the hands of the transferee and the corporation and Phil are related parties. ◀

---

[61] Sec. 1252(a)(1).
[62] Sec. 1252(a)(3).
[63] Sec. 263(c).
[64] Reg. Sec. 1.612-4(a).
[65] Sec. 1254(a)(1).
[66] Sec. 1239(a).

A sale or exchange of property could be subject to depreciation recapture under Sec. 1245 or 1250 as well as the Sec. 1239 related party rules. If so, recapture under Sec. 1245 or 1250 is considered before recapture under Sec. 1239.[67]

EXAMPLE I13-51 ▶ Assume the same facts as in Example I13-50 except that Phil sells equipment to the corporation instead of a building. All of the $300,000 realized gain is treated as ordinary income. The recapture amount under Sec. 1245 is $200,000, and Sec. 1239 applies to the remaining $100,000 gain. ◀

REAL-WORLD EXAMPLE

A taxpayer sold a secret formula for typing correction fluid to a corporation that was a related party. The gain on the sale was treated as a capital gain, not as ordinary income under Sec. 1239, because the secret formula was not depreciable. *Bette C. Graham v. U.S.*, 43 AFTR 2d 79-1013, 79-1 USTC ¶9274 (D.C. Tx., 1979).

PURPOSE OF SEC. 1239. Without Sec. 1239, a taxpayer could transfer appreciated depreciable property to a related party and recognize a Sec. 1231 gain on the sale. Net Sec. 1231 gain is treated as LTCG. The related purchaser of the property would receive a step up in the depreciation basis of the property to its FMV and be able to claim a larger amount of depreciation. In Example I13-50, Phil might prefer to recognize a $300,000 Sec. 1231 gain if the 100%-owned corporation was able to obtain a step-up in the property's basis to $800,000. Because Sec. 1239 applies, Phil must recognize $300,000 of ordinary income rather than Sec. 1231 gain. This rule prevents an individual taxpayer from receiving favorable Sec. 1231 gain treatment and prevents all taxpayers having large capital loss carryovers from using a related party to recognize a Sec. 1231 or capital gain which can be offset against their capital losses.

RELATED PARTIES. A person is related (1) to any corporation if the individual owns (directly or indirectly) more than 50% of the value of the outstanding stock and (2) to any partnership in which the person has a capital or profits interest of more than 50%.[68] Constructive ownership rules apply when determining whether the person owns more than 50% of the corporation or has more than a 50% interest in the partnership. Thus, an individual is considered to own stock that is owned by other family members and related entities (e.g., corporations, partnerships, estates, and trusts).

EXAMPLE I13-52 ▶ Tony sells a truck, which he has used for nonbusiness purposes, to the Able Corporation for $15,000. The truck's adjusted basis is $12,000 on the date of the sale.

Tony owns 30% of the Able stock and his spouse owns 40% of the Able stock. Tony and Able are related parties because Tony is deemed to own 70% of the Able stock under the constructive ownership rules and $3,000 of ordinary income must be recognized under Sec. 1239 unless the overriding recapture rules of Sec. 1245 apply. ◀

A person is related to any trust in which such a person or the person's spouse is a beneficiary.[69] Section 1239 also applies to a sale or exchange of depreciable property between two corporations if the same individual owns more than 50% of each corporation.[70]

TAX PLANNING CONSIDERATIONS

For noncorporate taxpayers, net Sec. 1231 gains are generally preferable to ordinary gains because of the possible lower tax rate applicable to net capital gains. The tax rate could be 10%, 15%, 20% or 25%. For corporate taxpayers, however, after 1986 it usually does not make any difference whether a gain is classified as Sec. 1231 or ordinary unless the corporation has capital losses. Corporations do have a 35% alternative tax rate on net capital gains.

[67] Reg. Sec. 1.1245-6(f).
[68] Sec. 1239(c).
[69] Sec. 1239(b)(2).
[70] Rev. Rul. 79-157, 1979-1 C.B. 281.

EXAMPLE I13-53 ▶ Western Corporation has taxable income of $550,000 without considering the sale of equipment for $400,000 during the current year. The equipment originally cost $500,000 and has a $350,000 adjusted basis after deducting depreciation. The corporation has no other gains and losses during the year or any capital loss carryovers from previous years. For Western Corporation, it does not make any difference whether the gain is Sec. 1245 ordinary income or Sec. 1231 gain. The effect on the corporation's taxable income and tax liability is the same regardless of how the gain is classified. ◀

The avoidance of the recapture provisions is important to both corporate and noncorporate taxpayers if capital loss carryovers exist. For example, if Western Corporation has a capital loss carryforward of $40,000 in Example I13-53, the corporation's taxable income is increased by $10,000 ($50,000 − $40,000) if the $50,000 gain is Sec. 1231 gain. However, because the gain is Sec. 1245 ordinary income, the corporation's taxable income is increased by $50,000. The $40,000 capital loss carryforward is not deductible unless it can be offset by a capital gain or a net Sec. 1231 gain.

AVOIDING THE RECAPTURE PROVISIONS

In view of the pervasiveness of the recapture provisions discussed in this chapter, recapture is difficult to avoid. In some cases, recapture can be avoided by holding the property a specific length of time before disposing of it (e.g., the recapture of conservation and land clearing expenses can be avoided by holding the farmland for more than nine years).[71] Contributing appreciated property to a qualified charitable organization cannot be used to circumvent the recapture provisions because in such case the amount of the charitable contribution is reduced by the amount of the gain that would not be a LTCG if the property were sold by the taxpayer.[72]

Although it is often difficult to avoid the recapture provisions, taxpayers may dispose of the property and defer recapture if the disposition is a nontaxable exchange. In a like-kind exchange where no boot is received, the recapture potential is carried over to the property received in the exchange. In a tax-free incorporation under Sec. 351, the recapture potential is transferred to the corporation receiving the recapture property. Sec. 351 is discussed in Chapter I16. Recapture may also be avoided in situations involving a transfer of property to a partnership in exchange for a partnership interest.

Proper timing of the asset's disposition may be advantageous. Disposition may be delayed until the taxpayer's tax rate is low or the property can be sold in the same year that the taxpayer has an NOL that is about to expire.

Taxpayers can shift the recapture potential to other taxpayers by making a gift of property subject to recapture. The recapture potential remains with the property and must be considered when the donee disposes of the property.

RESIDENTIAL RENTAL PROPERTY. Noncorporate taxpayers can avoid the recapture provisions for residential rental property by using the straight-line method of depreciation.[73] The recapture provisions do not apply to residential rental property acquired after 1986 because only the straight-line depreciation method may be used. Recapture can also be avoided if the asset is fully depreciated at the date of disposal because no additional depreciation or cost recovery exists.

EXAMPLE I13-54 ▶ Vincent owns a building used as residential rental property. The building was purchased before 1981 and is not ACRS recovery property. Vincent could avoid depreciation recapture at the time of disposing of the asset by using the straight-line method of depreciation. If Vincent uses an accelerated method of depreciation, recapture is avoided if the disposition does not occur until the asset is fully depreciated. ◀

EXAMPLE I13-55 ▶ Assume the same facts as in Example I13-54 except that Vincent purchased the building after 1980 and before 1987 and the building is ACRS recovery property. Vincent could avoid recapturing cost recovery deductions when he disposes of the asset by using the straight-line method

---

[71] Sec. 1252(a)(1).
[72] Sec. 170(e)(1)(A).
[73] Corporate taxpayers must consider Sec. 291(a). (See the Additional Recapture for Corporations section in this chapter.)

of cost recovery. If Vincent uses the accelerated method of cost recovery and disposes of the residential rental property at a gain, he cannot avoid recapture unless the asset's cost is fully recovered (i.e., no additional cost recovery exists). ◀

KEY POINT

For noncorporate taxpayers, there is no recapture on either residential or nonresidential real property placed in service after 1986 because the property can be depreciated only by using the straight-line method.

NONRESIDENTIAL REAL PROPERTY. For noncorporate taxpayers, the Sec. 1250 recapture provisions do not apply to nonresidential real property acquired after 1986 because only the straight-line method may be used. However, to avoid recapture on the disposition of appreciated nonresidential real property acquired after 1980 and before 1987 noncorporate taxpayers must use the straight-line method of depreciation. Nonresidential real property acquired before 1987, which is recovery property subject to ACRS, is subject to the Sec. 1245 recapture rules unless the straight-line method is used. If the accelerated method of cost recovery is used, recapture cannot be avoided by waiting until the asset's cost is fully recovered before disposing of the asset.

EXAMPLE I13-56 ▶ Christine purchased an office building in 1982 for $225,000* for use in her trade or business. The property is ACRS recovery property, and she uses the accelerated method to compute the cost-recovery deductions. Cost-recovery deductions taken before the sale of the building amount to $225,000. If she sells the building for $250,000, $225,000 of the $250,000 ($250,000 − 0) realized gain is recaptured as ordinary income under Sec. 1245. The remaining gain of $25,000 is Sec. 1231 gain. Recapture could have been avoided if Christine had instead used the straight-line method of cost recovery. If the straight-line method were used instead, she would report a smaller realized gain, all of which is Sec. 1231 gain. ◀

*does not include cost of land

TRANSFER PROPERTY AT DEATH. One of the most effective ways to avoid the recapture provisions is to transfer the property at death. No recapture occurs at the time of the transfer, and the basis of property received from a decedent is generally the FMV of the property at the date of the decedent's death.[74] The property's recapture potential does not carry over to the beneficiary as in the case of a gift made to a donee.

COMPLIANCE AND PROCEDURAL CONSIDERATIONS

ADDITIONAL COMMENT

Form 4797 has four major parts. In completing this form one should normally begin with Part III on page 2, where the recapture is calculated. Note that the total amount recaptured from line 31 is carried forward to Part II, where it is combined with other ordinary gains and losses. Any unrecaptured gain from line 32 is carried forward to Part I, where it is netted with other Sec. 1231 gains and losses.

Form 4797, Supplemental Schedule of Gains and Losses, is used to report gains and losses from sales or exchanges of assets used in a trade or business (see Figures I13-1 through I13-3). The form is also used to report gains or losses resulting from involuntary conversions, other than casualties or thefts, of property used in the trade or business and capital assets held more than a year. If gains or losses due to casualties or thefts of property used in a trade or business or property held to produce income are recognized, they are reported on Form 4684, Casualties and Thefts (see Figure I13-3). If such casualties or thefts occur, Form 4684 is prepared either before or at the same time as Form 4797.

REPORTING SEC. 1231 GAINS AND LOSSES ON FORM 4797

Part I of Form 4797, which is reproduced in Figure I13-1, is used to report gains and losses resulting from

- The sale or exchange of Sec. 1231 property
- An involuntary conversion, other than a casualty or theft, of Sec. 1231 property
- An involuntary conversion, other than a casualty or theft, of capital assets held more than one year and used to produce income.

As indicated on lines 3 through 6 in Part I of Form 4797, gains and losses recorded on other forms and in Part III of Form 4797 are reported in Part I. The netting of Sec. 1231 gains and losses occurs in Part I of Form 4797. All gains and losses are recorded in column (g). If line 7(g) has a loss, Sec. 1231 losses exceed Sec. 1231 gains and the net loss is

[74] Sec. 1014(a).

reported on line 11 as ordinary loss. If there is no nonrecaptured net section 1231 losses, the amount on line 7(g) is transferred to Schedule D. If the taxpayer does have nonrecaptured net Sec. 1231 losses, that amount is reported on line 8. Gains reported on line 7(g) will be recharacterized as ordinary income to the extent of the nonrecaptured net Sec. 1231 losses and reported as ordinary income on line 12.

Ordinary gains and losses recognized including those recorded on other forms and in Parts I and III of Form 4797 are reported on lines 11 through 17 in Part II of Form 4797.

REPORTING GAINS RECAPTURED AS ORDINARY INCOME ON FORM 4797

Part III of Form 4797, reproduced in Figure I13-2, is used to determine and report ordinary income due to the recapture provisions of Secs. 1245, 1250, 1252, 1254, and 1255. Part III is completed before Parts I and II. To illustrate the use of Part III, assume an individual sells equipment (7-year recovery) used in a trade or business for $60,000 on April 30, 2001. The equipment cost $58,000 on March 10, 1999 and depreciation deductions through the date of sale of $27,565 were allowed. The $29,565 ($60,000 – $30,435) total gain is reported on line 24. The $3,000 of depreciation allowed is reported on lines 25(a) and also on (b) because the depreciation allowed is less than the realized gain. On line 30, total gains resulting from the sale of all properties ($29,565 in this illustration) reported in Part III are combined. The total amount of ordinary income due to the recapture provisions ($27,565 in this illustration) is reported on line 31 and then reported as ordinary income on line 13 in Part II. The excess of the gain over the amount of ordinary income is reported on line 32. The portion of this gain not due to casualty or theft ($2,000 in this illustration) is a Sec. 1231 gain and is reported on line 6 of Part I of Form 4797. If any of the gain is due to casualty or theft, that portion of the gain is reported on Section B of Form 4684.

REPORTING CASUALTY OR THEFT GAIN OR LOSS ON FORM 4684

Section A of Form 4684 is used to report gains and losses resulting from a casualty or theft of personal-use property. These gains and losses are not Sec. 1231 transactions, and Sec. A of Form 4684 is not discussed in this chapter.

Section B of Form 4684, reproduced in Figure I13-3, is used to report gains and losses resulting from a casualty or theft of property used in a trade or business or held for the production of income. Note that a separate Part I is used for each different casualty or theft. Gains are reported on line 22, and losses are reported on line 27. For properties held a year or less, the gains and losses are reported on lines 29 through 32 of Part II. These gains and losses are either recorded as ordinary gains and losses on line 14 of Part II of Form 4797 or as itemized deductions on Schedule A of Form 1040.

For properties held more than a year, the gains and losses are reported on lines 33 and 34. If gains exceed losses, the net gain is reported on line 39 and then on line 3 of Part I of Form 4797 (i.e., the gains and losses are treated as Sec. 1231 gains and losses). If the losses exceed the gains, all or part of the gains and losses are reported as ordinary in Part II of Form 4797 and/or on Schedule A of Form 1040.

PROBLEM MATERIALS

DISCUSSION QUESTIONS

I13-1 Explain how the gain on the sale or exchange of land could be classified as either ordinary income, a Sec. 1231 gain, or a LTCG, depending on the facts and circumstances.

I13-2 Why were taxpayers reluctant to sell appreciated business property between 1938 and 1942? What effect did this reluctance have on the tax law?

I13-3 Alice owns timber, purchased six years ago, with an adjusted basis of $50,000. The timber is cut for use in her furniture business on October 1, when the FMV of the timber is $200,000. The FMV of the timber on January 1 is $190,000. May Alice treat any of the gain as Sec. 1231 gain? If so, how much?

Form **4797**

Department of the Treasury
Internal Revenue Service (99)

Sales of Business Property

(Also Involuntary Conversions and Recapture Amounts Under Sections 179 and 280F(b)(2))

▶ Attach to your tax return. ▶ See separate instructions.

OMB No. 1545-0184

2001

Attachment Sequence No. 27

Name(s) shown on return | Identifying number

1	Enter the gross proceeds from sales or exchanges reported to you for 2001 on Form(s) 1099-B or 1099-S (or substitute statement) that you are including on line 2, 10, or 20 (see instructions)	1	

Part I Sales or Exchanges of Property Used in a Trade or Business and Involuntary Conversions From Other Than Casualty or Theft—Most Property Held More Than 1 Year (See instructions.)

	(a) Description of property	(b) Date acquired (mo., day, yr.)	(c) Date sold (mo., day, yr.)	(d) Gross sales price	(e) Depreciation allowed or allowable since acquisition	(f) Cost or other basis, plus improvements and expense of sale	(g) Gain or (loss) Subtract (f) from the sum of (d) and (e)
2							

3	Gain, if any, from Form 4684, line 39	3	
4	Section 1231 gain from installment sales from Form 6252, line 26 or 37	4	
5	Section 1231 gain or (loss) from like-kind exchanges from Form 8824	5	
6	Gain, if any, from line 32, from other than casualty or theft	6	2,000
7	Combine lines 2 through 6. Enter the gain or (loss) here and on the appropriate line as follows:	7	2,000

Partnerships (except electing large partnerships). Report the gain or (loss) following the instructions for Form 1065, Schedule K, line 6. Skip lines 8, 9, 11, and 12 below.

S corporations. Report the gain or (loss) following the instructions for Form 1120S, Schedule K, lines 5 and 6. Skip lines 8, 9, 11, and 12 below, unless line 7 is a gain and the S corporation is subject to the capital gains tax.

All others. If line 7 is zero or a loss, enter the amount from line 7 on line 11 below and skip lines 8 and 9. If line 7 is a gain and you did not have any prior year section 1231 losses, or they were recaptured in an earlier year, enter the gain from line 7 as a long-term capital gain on Schedule D and skip lines 8, 9, 11, and 12 below.

8	Nonrecaptured net section 1231 losses from prior years (see instructions)	8	
9	Subtract line 8 from line 7. If zero or less, enter -0-. Also enter on the appropriate line as follows (see instructions):	9	

S corporations. Enter any gain from line 9 on Schedule D (Form 1120S), line 15, and skip lines 11 and 12 below.

All others. If line 9 is zero, enter the gain from line 7 on line 12 below. If line 9 is more than zero, enter the amount from line 8 on line 12 below, and enter the gain from line 9 as a long-term capital gain on Schedule D.

Part II Ordinary Gains and Losses

10 Ordinary gains and losses not included on lines 11 through 17 (include property held 1 year or less):

11	Loss, if any, from line 7	11	( )
12	Gain, if any, from line 7 or amount from line 8, if applicable	12	
13	Gain, if any, from line 31	13	27,565
14	Net gain or (loss) from Form 4684, lines 31 and 38a	14	
15	Ordinary gain from installment sales from Form 6252, line 25 or 36	15	
16	Ordinary gain or (loss) from like-kind exchanges from Form 8824	16	
17	Recapture of section 179 expense deduction for partners and S corporation shareholders from property dispositions by partnerships and S corporations (see instructions)	17	
18	Combine lines 10 through 17. Enter the gain or (loss) here and on the appropriate line as follows:	18	27,565

a **For all except individual returns.** Enter the gain or (loss) from line 18 on the return being filed.

b **For individual returns:**

(1)	If the loss on line 11 includes a loss from Form 4684, line 35, column (b)(ii), enter that part of the loss here. Enter the part of the loss from income-producing property on Schedule A (Form 1040), line 27, and the part of the loss from property used as an employee on Schedule A (Form 1040), line 22. Identify as from "Form 4797, line 18b(1)." See instructions	18b(1)	
(2)	Redetermine the gain or (loss) on line 18 excluding the loss, if any, on line 18b(1). Enter here and on Form 1040, line 14	18b(2)	27,565

For Paperwork Reduction Act Notice, see page 7 of the instructions. Cat. No. 13086I Form **4797** (2001)

FIGURE I13-1 ▶ PART I AND PART II OF FORM 4797

Part III Gain From Disposition of Property Under Sections 1245, 1250, 1252, 1254, and 1255

19 (a) Description of section 1245, 1250, 1252, 1254, or 1255 property:	(b) Date acquired (mo., day, yr.)	(c) Date sold (mo., day, yr.)
A Equipment	3·10·99	4·30·01
B		
C		
D		

These columns relate to the properties on lines 19A through 19D. ▶		Property A	Property B	Property C	Property D
20 Gross sales price (**Note:** *See line 1 before completing.*)	20	60,000			
21 Cost or other basis plus expense of sale	21	58,000			
22 Depreciation (or depletion) allowed or allowable	22	27,565			
23 Adjusted basis. Subtract line 22 from line 21	23	30,435			
24 Total gain. Subtract line 23 from line 20	24	29,565			
25 **If section 1245 property:**					
a Depreciation allowed or allowable from line 22	25a	27,565			
b Enter the **smaller** of line 24 or 25a	25b	27,565			
26 **If section 1250 property:** If straight line depreciation was used, enter -0- on line 26g, except for a corporation subject to section 291.					
a Additional depreciation after 1975 (see instructions)	26a				
b Applicable percentage multiplied by the **smaller** of line 24 or line 26a (see instructions)	26b				
c Subtract line 26a from line 24. If residential rental property **or** line 24 is not more than line 26a, skip lines 26d and 26e	26c				
d Additional depreciation after 1969 and before 1976	26d				
e Enter the **smaller** of line 26c or 26d	26e				
f Section 291 amount (corporations only)	26f				
g Add lines 26b, 26e, and 26f	26g				
27 **If section 1252 property:** Skip this section if you did not dispose of farmland or if this form is being completed for a partnership (other than an electing large partnership).					
a Soil, water, and land clearing expenses	27a				
b Line 27a multiplied by applicable percentage (see instructions)	27b				
c Enter the **smaller** of line 24 or 27b	27c				
28 **If section 1254 property:**					
a Intangible drilling and development costs, expenditures for development of mines and other natural deposits, and mining exploration costs (see instructions)	28a				
b Enter the **smaller** of line 24 or 28a	28b				
29 **If section 1255 property:**					
a Applicable percentage of payments excluded from income under section 126 (see instructions)	29a				
b Enter the **smaller** of line 24 or 29a (see instructions)	29b				

Summary of Part III Gains. Complete property columns A through D through line 29b before going to line 30.

30 Total gains for all properties. Add property columns A through D, line 24	30	29,565
31 Add property columns A through D, lines 25b, 26g, 27c, 28b, and 29b. Enter here and on line 13	31	27,565
32 Subtract line 31 from line 30. Enter the portion from casualty or theft on Form 4684, line 33. Enter the portion from other than casualty or theft on Form 4797, line 6	32	2,000

Part IV Recapture Amounts Under Sections 179 and 280F(b)(2) When Business Use Drops to 50% or Less (See instructions.)

		(a) Section 179	(b) Section 280F(b)(2)
33 Section 179 expense deduction or depreciation allowable in prior years	33		
34 Recomputed depreciation. See instructions	34		
35 Recapture amount. Subtract line 34 from line 33. See the instructions for where to report	35		

Form **4797** (2001)

FIGURE I13-2 ▶ PART III OF FORM 4797

Name(s) shown on tax return. Do not enter name and identifying number if shown on other side. | **Identifying number**

SECTION B—Business and Income-Producing Property

Part I Casualty or Theft Gain or Loss (Use a separate Part I for each casualty or theft.)

19 Description of properties (show type, location, and date acquired for each):

Property **A** ....

Property **B** ....

Property **C** ....

Property **D** ....

		Properties (Use a separate column for each property lost or damaged from the same casualty or theft.)			
		A	**B**	**C**	**D**
20 Cost or adjusted basis of each property	**20**				
21 Insurance or other reimbursement (whether or not you filed a claim). See the instructions for line 3	**21**				
Note: *If line 20 is **more** than line 21, skip line 22.*					
22 Gain from casualty or theft. If line 21 is **more** than line 20, enter the difference here and on line 29 or line 34, column (c), except as provided in the instructions for line 33. Also, skip lines 23 through 27 for that column. See the instructions for line 4 if line 21 includes insurance or other reimbursement you did not claim, or you received payment for your loss in a later tax year	**22**				
23 Fair market value **before** casualty or theft	**23**				
24 Fair market value **after** casualty or theft	**24**				
25 Subtract line 24 from line 23	**25**				
26 Enter the **smaller** of line 20 or line 25	**26**				
Note: *If the property was totally destroyed by casualty or lost from theft, enter on line 26 the amount from line 20.*					
27 Subtract line 21 from line 26. If zero or less, enter -0-	**27**				

28 Casualty or theft loss. Add the amounts on line 27. Enter the total here and on line 29 **or** line 34 (see instructions). **28**

Part II Summary of Gains and Losses (from separate Parts I)

(a) Identify casualty or theft		(b) Losses from casualties or thefts		(c) Gains from casualties or thefts includible in income
		(i) Trade, business, rental or royalty property	(ii) Income-producing and employee property	
Casualty or Theft of Property Held One Year or Less				
29		( )	( )	
		( )	( )	
30 Totals. Add the amounts on line 29	**30**	( )	( )	
31 Combine line 30, columns (b)(i) and (c). Enter the net gain or (loss) here and on Form 4797, line 14. If Form 4797 is not otherwise required, see instructions			**31**	
32 Enter the amount from line 30, column (b)(ii) here. Individuals, enter the amount from income-producing property on Schedule A (Form 1040), line 27, and enter the amount from property used as an employee on Schedule A (Form 1040), line 22. Estates and trusts, partnerships, and S corporations, see instructions			**32**	
Casualty or Theft of Property Held More Than One Year				
33 Casualty or theft gains from Form 4797, line 32			**33**	
34		( )	( )	
		( )	( )	
35 Total losses. Add amounts on line 34, columns (b)(i) and (b)(ii)	**35**	( )	( )	
36 Total gains. Add lines 33 and 34, column (c)			**36**	
37 Add amounts on line 35, columns (b)(i) and (b)(ii)			**37**	
38 If the loss on line 37 is **more** than the gain on line 36:				
a Combine line 35, column (b)(i) and line 36, and enter the net gain or (loss) here. Partnerships (except electing large partnerships) and S corporations, see the note below. All others, enter this amount on Form 4797, line 14. If Form 4797 is not otherwise required, see instructions			**38a**	
b Enter the amount from line 35, column (b)(ii) here. Individuals, enter the amount from income-producing property on Schedule A (Form 1040), line 27, and enter the amount from property used as an employee on Schedule A (Form 1040), line 22. Estates and trusts, enter on the "Other deductions" line of your tax return. Partnerships (except electing large partnerships) and S corporations, see the note below. Electing large partnerships, enter on Form 1065-B, Part II, line 11			**38b**	
39 If the loss on line 37 is **less** than or **equal** to the gain on line 36, combine lines 36 and 37 and enter here. Partnerships (except electing large partnerships), see the note below. All others, enter this amount on Form 4797, line 3			**39**	

Note: *Partnerships, enter the amount from line 38a, 38b, or line 39 on Form 1065, Schedule K, line 7. S corporations, enter the amount from line 38a or 38b on Form 1120S, Schedule K, line 6.*

Form **4684** (2001)

FIGURE I13-3 ▶ SECTION B OF FORM 4684

I13-4 Explain how the gain from an involuntary conversion of business property held more than one year is taxed if the involuntary conversion is the result of a condemnation. Explain the tax treatment if the involuntary conversion is due to a casualty.

I13-5 When is livestock considered Sec. 1231 property?

I13-6 When is a net Sec. 1231 gain treated as ordinary income?

I13-7 Carlie has a Sec. 1231 gain of $10,000 and no Sec. 1231 losses during the current year. Explain why the gain might be taxed at (a) 20%, (b) 35%, (c) 25%, or (d) 10%.

I13-8 Why is it unlikely that gains due to the sale of equipment will be treated as Sec. 1231 gains?

I13-9 Hank sells equipment used in a trade or business for $25,000. The equipment costs $30,000 and has an adjusted basis of $25,500. Why is it important to know the holding period?

I13-10 Jackie purchases equipment during the current year for $800,000 that has a seven-year MACRS recovery period. She expects to sell the property after three years. Jackie anticipates that her marginal tax rate in the year of sale will be significantly higher than her current marginal tax rate. Why might it be advantageous for her to use the straight-line method of depreciation?

I13-11 Karen purchased a computer three years ago for $15,300 to use exclusively in her business. She expensed the entire cost of the computer under Sec. 179. If she sells the computer during the current year for $3,721, what is the amount and character of her recognized gain?

I13-12 Sheila owns a motel that is used in a trade or business. If she sells the motel, the gain will be Sec. 1245 ordinary income. During what period of time was the motel placed into service?

I13-13 How may a taxpayer avoid having additional depreciation?

I13-14 Marty sells his fully depreciated building at a gain to an unrelated party. The building is purchased before 1981. Is any of the gain taxed as ordinary income?

I13-15 Which of the following assets (assume all assets have a holding period of more than one year) do not qualify as Sec. 1231 property: inventory, a pig held for breeding, land used as a parking lot for customers, and marketable securities?

I13-16 When is an office building subject to the depreciation recapture rules of Sec. 1245?

I13-17 Does a building that is 60% rented for residential use and 40% for commercial use qualify as residential rental property?

I13-18 Roger owns an apartment complex with a FMV of $2 million. If he sells the apartment complex, $700,000 of the gain is ordinary income. If he dies before selling the apartment complex and his estate sells the property for $2 million, how much ordinary income must the estate recognize?

I13-19 Rashad owns a duplex used 100% as residential rental property. Under what conditions, if any, will any gain that he recognizes be Sec. 1245 ordinary income?

I13-20 John and Karen are unrelated individuals. John sold land that is Sec. 1231 property held for three years and recognized a $50,000 gain. Karen sold a building that is Sec. 1231 property held for three years and recognized a $50,000 gain. Straight-line depreciation was used. John and Karen both have a 30% tax rate, no other transactions involving capital assets or 1231 assets, and no nonrecaptured Sec. 1231 losses. Except for the sales of different assets, their tax situation is exactly the same. As a result of selling his Sec. 1231 property, will John pay more, less or the same amount of taxes than Karen as a result of selling her Sec. 1231 property? Explain.

I13-21 Why may a corporation recognize a greater amount of ordinary income due to the sale of Sec. 1250 property than a noncorporate taxpayer?

I13-22 Assume a taxpayer sells equipment used in a trade or business for a gain that is less than the depreciation allowed. If the taxpayer is a corporation, will a greater amount of Sec. 1245 income be recognized than if the taxpayer is an individual? Explain.

I13-23 Dale owns business equipment with a $100,000 FMV and an adjusted basis of $60,000. The property was originally acquired for $150,000. Which one of the following transactions would result in recognition of $40,000 ordinary income by Dale due to the depreciation recapture rules of Sec. 1245?

a. He makes a gift of the property to a daughter.

b. He contributes the property to a qualified charitable organization.

c. He disposes of the equipment in an installment sale and receives $10,000 cash in the year of sale.

I13-24 Carlos owns an office building with a $700,000 acquisition cost, a $250,000 adjusted basis, and a $500,000 FMV. The office building was acquired before 1981, and additional depreciation amounts to $110,000. Carlos makes a gift of the building to a charitable organization. What is the amount of his charitable contribution deduction?

I13-25 Ted owns a warehouse that cost $650,000 in 1984 and is subject to depreciation recapture under Sec. 1245. The warehouse, which has an adjusted basis of $300,000, is destroyed by a tornado and Ted receives $510,000 from the insurance company. Within nine months, he pays $450,000 for a new warehouse and an election is made to defer the gain under Sec. 1033. What is the amount and character of Ted's recognized gain?

I13-26 When a taxpayer disposes of oil, gas, or geothermal property, part or all of the gain may be recaptured as ordinary income. Explain how the recapture amount is determined for oil and gas and geothermal properties.

I13-27 William owns two appreciated assets, land and a building, which have been used in his trade or business for several years. The straight-line method of depreciation is used for the building. If he sells the two assets to his 100%-owned corporation, will William have to recognize any ordinary income? Explain.

ISSUE IDENTIFICATION QUESTIONS

I13-28 Six years ago Joelle started raising chinchillas. She separates her chinchillas into two groups, a breeding group and a market group. During the year, she had the following sales of chinchillas from her market group: 400 to producers of fur products; 100 to pet stores; and 25 to individuals to use as pets. From her breeding stock, she sold six chinchillas to Rebecca, an individual who is starting a chinchilla ranch, and five to Fur Pelts, a producer of fur products. All 11 chinchillas from the breeding group have been held for at least 22 months, and the five sold to Fur Pelts were poor performers.

I13-29 Green Acres, Inc. owns 1,400 acres adjacent to land owned by the U.S. government. The government, wanting to sell timber from its land, had to assure prospective bidders of access to the timber. The government entered into an agreement with Green Acres for a logging road easement across land owned by Green Acres. The government agreed to pay $2 per thousand board feet of timber removed up to a maximum of $130,000. Bidders for the rights to obtain the government's timber had to agree to pay the fee to Green Acres as part of their bids for the timber. Stanley Lumberyard, Inc. provided the highest bid and paid $80,000 to Green Acres during the first year of cutting and removing the timber and $50,000 during the second year. What tax issues should Green Acres and Stanley Lumberyard consider?

I13-30 Sarah, who has been in the business of erecting, maintaining, and renting outdoor advertising displays for 18 years, has an offer to purchase her business. Two basic types of advertising displays are used in her business: structure X and structure Y. Structure X consists of a single sign face nailed to a wooden support frame and attached to wooden poles 30 feet long. Its structure is rather easy to dismantle and move from one location to another. In contrast, structure Y is a permanent sign that is designed to withstand winds of up to 100 miles per hour. None of the Structure Y signs have ever been moved. What tax issues should Sarah consider?

I13-31 Sylvester owns and operates an unincorporated pizza business that delivers pizza to customers. Three years ago, he acquired an automobile for $10,000 to provide delivery service. Recently, Sylvester hired an employee who prefers to use his personal automobile to make the deliveries. Thus, Sylvester decided to permit his 18-year old daughter to use the automobile for her personal use. The automobile's adjusted basis is $3,080 and its FMV is $4,700. What tax issues should Sylvester consider?

PROBLEMS

I13-32 *Sec. 1231, 1245, and 1250 Transactions.* All assets listed below have been held for more than one year. Which assets might be classified as Sec. 1231, Sec. 1245, or Sec. 1250 property? An asset may be classified as more than one type of property.

a. Land on which a factory is located
b. Equipment used in the factory
c. Raw materials inventory
d. Patent purchased to allow use of a manufacturing process
e. Land held primarily for sale
f. Factory building acquired in 1986 (the straight-line ACRS recovery method is used)

I13-33 *Sec. 1231 Gains and Losses.* Vivian's AGI is $40,000 without considering the gains and losses below. Determine her revised AGI after the inclusion of any applicable gains or losses for the following independent cases. Assume she has no unrecaptured net Sec. 1231 losses at the beginning of the year.

	Case A	*Case B*	*Case C*	*Case D*
Sec. 1231 gain	$15,000	$10,000	$30,000	$ 5,000
Sec. 1231 loss	5,000	18,000	38,000	12,000
LTCG	—0—	—0—	4,000	—0—
LTCL	—0—	—0—	—0—	4,200

I13-34 *Sec. 1231 Gains and Losses.* Edith, who has no other sales or exchanges and no nonrecaptured Sec. 1231 losses, sells three tracts of land that are used in her trade or business. Her regular income tax rate is 35%.
Asset #1–$14,000 gain and holding period of 20 months
Asset #2–$17,000 loss and holding period of 25 months
Asset #3–$ 5,000 gain and holding period of 13 months
a. What is the increase in her taxes as a result of the three sales?
b. If the holding period for Asset #2 is nine months, what is the decrease in her taxes as a result of the three sales?

I13-35 *Sec. 1231 Transactions.* Which of the following transactions or events is treated as a Sec. 1231 gain or loss? Assume all assets are held for more than one year.
a. Theft of uninsured diamond ring, with an $800 basis and a $1,000 FMV.
b. Gain due to condemnation of land used in business.
c. Loss on the sale of a warehouse.
d. Gain on the sale of equipment. The gain recognized amounts to $4,000 and the depreciation deductions allowed amount to $10,000.

I13-36 *Capital Loss Versus Sec. 1231 Loss.* Vicki has an AGI of $60,000 without considering the sale of a nondepreciable asset for $23,000. The asset was acquired six years ago and has an adjusted basis of $35,000. She has no other sales or exchanges. Determine her AGI for the following independent situations:
a. The asset is a capital asset.
b. The asset is Sec. 1231 property.

I13-37 *Ordinary Income Versus Sec. 1231 Gain.* At the beginning of 2002, Silver Corporation has a $95,000 capital loss carryforward from 2001. During 2002, the corporation sells land, held for four years, and realizes a $80,000 gain. Silver has no unrecaptured Sec. 1231 losses, and it made no other sales during the current year. Determine the amount of capital loss carryforward that Silver can use in 2002 if
a. The land is Sec. 1231 property.
b. The land is not a capital asset or Sec. 1231 property.

I13-38 *Sec. 1231 Transactions.* During the current year, Sean's office building is destroyed by fire. After collecting the insurance proceeds, Sean has a $50,000 recognized gain. The building was acquired in 1978, and the straight-line method of depreciation has been used. He does not plan to acquire a replacement building. Consider the following independent cases and determine his net capital gain. For each case, include the $50,000 casualty gain described above.
a. Land used in his trade or business and held more than a year is condemned by the state. The recognized gain is $60,000.
b. Assume the same facts as in Part a, except the condemnation results in a $60,000 loss.
c. An apartment building used as residential rental property and held more than one year is destroyed by a sudden, unexpected mudslide. The building is not insured, and the loss amounts to $200,000.

I13-39 *Nonrecaptured Net Sec. 1231 Losses.* Consider the following summary of Sec. 1231 gains and losses recognized by Janet during the period 1997–2001. If Janet has no capital gains and losses during the six-year period, determine her net capital gain for each year.

	Sec. 1231 Gains	*Sec. 1231 Losses*
1997	$ 9,000	$ 7,000
1998	20,000	24,000
1999	12,000	19,000
2000	9,000	4,000
2001	25,000	13,200
2002	10,000	17,000

I13-40 *Nonrecaptured Net Sec. 1231 Losses.* Dillion has a tax rate of 30% and $40,000 of net nonrecaptured Sec. 1231 losses at the start of the year. During the year, he recognizes a Sec. 1231 gain of $53,000 from the sale of land. As a result of the sale, how much does Dillion's tax liability increase?

I13-41 *Sec. 1245.* The Pear Corporation owns equipment with a $300,000 adjusted basis. The equipment was purchased six years ago for $650,000. If Pear sells the equipment for the selling prices given in the three independent cases below, what are the amount and character of Pear's recognized gain or loss?

Case	*Selling Price*
A	$407,000
B	790,000
C	245,000

I13-42 *Sec. 1245.* Elizabeth owns equipment that cost $500,000 and has an adjusted basis of $230,000. If the straight-line method of depreciation had been used, the adjusted basis would be $300,000.

a. What is the maximum selling price that she could sell the equipment for without having to recognize Sec. 1245 ordinary income?
b. If she sold the equipment and had to recognize $61,000 of Sec. 1245 ordinary income, what was the selling price?

I13-43 *Sale of Business and Personal-Use Property.* Arnie, a college student, purchased a new truck in 2000 for $6,000. He used the truck 70% of the time as a distributor for the local newspaper and 30% of the time for personal use. The truck has a five-year recovery period, and he claimed depreciation deductions of $840 in 2000 and $1,344 in 2001. Arnie sells the truck on June 20, 2002, for $3,000.

a. What is the amount of allowable depreciation in 2002?
b. What are the amount and character of Arnie's realized and recognized gain or loss?

I13-44 *Like-Kind Exchange of Sec. 1245 Property.* General Corporation owns equipment which cost $70,000 and has a $44,000 adjusted basis. General exchanges the equipment for other equipment with a $42,000 FMV and marketable securities with a $30,000 FMV. Determine the following:

a. Realized gain
b. Recognized gain
c. Gain treated as ordinary income
d. Gain treated as Sec. 1231 gain
e. Basis of marketable securities received
f. Basis of equipment received

I13-45 *Like-Kind Exchange of Sec. 1245 Property.* Leroy owns a truck used in his trade or business that cost $50,000 and has an adjusted basis of $34,000. The truck is exchanged for a new truck that is like-kind property with a FMV of $40,000. Prior to selling the new truck two years later, Leroy is allowed depreciation of $13,000 for the new truck. Determine:

a. Gain realized on the exchange?
b. Gain recognized on the exchange?
c. Basis of truck received?
d. Gain recognized, and the character of the gain, if the sales price of the truck is $41,000?
e. Gain recognized, and the character of the gain, if the sale price of the truck is $52,000?

I13-46 *Purpose of Sec. 1245.* Assume the year is 1986 when noncorporate taxpayers are allowed to deduct 60% of net capital gains to determine their AGI. Martin owns equipment used in his trade or business that was purchased in 1979 for $200,000. Allowed depreciation deductions amount to $160,000. Martin sells the equipment in 1986 for $110,000. No other sales or exchanges are made in 1986 or the preceding five years.

a. Determine the increase in Martin's 1986 AGI as a result of the sale if Sec. 1245 did not exist.
b. Given that Sec. 1245 does exist, what is the increase in his AGI as a result of the sale?
c. How would your answers to Parts a and b change if the asset were sold in 2002?

I13-47 *Secs. 1231 and 1250.* Charles owns an office building and land that are used in his trade or business. The office building and land were acquired in 1978 for $800,000 and

$100,000, respectively. During the current year, the properties are sold for $900,000 with 20% of the selling price being allocated to the land. The assets as shown on the taxpayer's books before their sale are as follows:

Building	$800,000	
Accumulated depreciation	590,000[a]	$210,000
Land		100,000

[a] If the straight-line method of depreciation had been used, the accumulated depreciation would be $440,000.

a. What is the recognized gain due to the sale of the building?
b. What is the character of the recognized gain due to the sale of the building?
c. What is the recognized gain and character of the gain due to the sale of the land?
d. If the taxpayer is a corporation, how will the answers to Parts a–c change?

I13-48 ***Secs. 1231, 1245 and Unrecaptured Sec. 1250.*** Brigham is single, in the 30% marginal income tax bracket, and has the sales or exchanges below. At the beginning of the year, he has nonrecaptured net Sec. 1231 losses of $10,000. Determine the increase or decrease in Brigham's tax liability as a result of the following independent sales or exchanges.
a. Sells equipment used in his trade or business for $40,000. The equipment was purchased for $100,000 and depreciation allowed amounts to $72,000.
b. Sells land used in his trade or business for $80,000. The land was purchased four years ago for $61,000.
c. He sells a building used in his trade or business for $163,000. The building was purchased in 1988 for $250,000 and depreciation allowed amounts to $110,000.
d. Same as (c) except he sells the building for $127,000.

I13-49 ***Sec. 1250.*** Ken purchased an office building on January 1, 1980, for $360,000 (40-year life and a $32,000 salvage value) and he elected to use the sum-of-the-years' digits method of depreciation. Prior to 1981, salvage value was considered when computing depreciation. Total depreciation allowed at the time of sale is $259,600. If the building is sold on January 1, 2002, for $340,000, what is the amount of gain recognized and the character of the gain?

I13-50 ***Sec. 1250.*** Assume the same facts as Problem I13-49 except that the taxpayer is a corporation instead of an individual. What is the amount and character of the corporation's recognized gain or loss?

I13-51 ***Sec. 1250 Residential Rental Property.*** Assume the same facts as Problem I13-49 except that the building is an apartment complex that qualifies as residential rental property. What is the amount and character of Ken's recognized gain or loss?

I13-52 ***Sec. 1250 Residential Rental Property.*** Assume the same facts as in Problem I13-50 except that the building is an apartment complex that qualifies as residential rental property. What is the amount and character of the corporation's recognized gain or loss?

I13-53 ***Sec. 1250 Residential Rental Property.*** Jesse owns a duplex that he uses as residential rental property. The duplex cost $100,000 in 1986, and 10% of the cost was allocated to the land. Total cost-recovery deductions allowed amount to $81,000. The statutory percentages were used to compute cost-recovery deductions. If the straight-line method of cost recovery were used instead, $76,000 of cost-recovery deductions would have been allowed.
a. What is the amount of recognized gain and the character of the gain if Jesse sells the duplex for $125,000?
b. What is the amount of recognized gain in the year of sale and the character of the gain if Jesse sells the property under the installment sale method? Terms of the installment sale are as follows: $25,000 in the year of sale and a $100,000 note to be paid in four annual payments. The note is an interest-bearing note at the market rate of interest.

I13-54 ***Sec. 1250.*** Rosemary owns an office building placed in service before 1981 that cost $625,000 and has an adjusted basis of $227,000. If the straight-line method of depreciation were used, the adjusted basis would be $300,000.
a. What is the maximum selling price that she could sell the building for without having to recognize Sec. 1250 ordinary income?
b. If she sold the building and had to recognize $51,000 of Sec. 1250 ordinary income, what was the selling price?

I13-55 Consider three office buildings placed in service as shown below and answer the following true-false questions. Assume all assets are sold by a noncorporate taxpayer at a gain and there are no other sales or exchanges or nonrecaptured Sec. 1231 loss unless told otherwise. None of the buildings are fully depreciated when sold.

	Placed in Service
Building #1	Before 1981
Building #2	After 1980 and before 1987
Building #3	After 1986

1. Some or all of the gain on sale of #1 is ordinary if accelerated depreciation was used.
2. If the straight-line method of depreciation was used for #1, some or all of the gain may be taxed at 25%.
3. Gain on the sale of #2 could be Sec. 1245 ordinary income.
4. Gain on the sale of #2 could be Sec. 1231 gain.
5. Part of the gain on the sale of #2 could be Sec. 1245 ordinary income and part could be Sec. 1231 gain.
6. If the straight-line method of depreciation was used for #2, some or all of the gain may be taxed at 25%.
7. Some or all of the gain on the sale of #3 could be Sec. 1245 ordinary income.
8. Some or all of the gain on the sale of #3 could be taxed at 25%.
9. Some of the gain on the sale of #3 could be Sec. 1250 ordinary income.
10. If the taxpayer has a nonrecaptured Sec. 1231 loss of $30,000 and the gain on the sale of #3 is $40,000, all $40,000 of the gain is taxed as ordinary income.

I13-56 Assume the same facts as in Problem 55 except the taxpayer is a corporate taxpayer and answer the ten true-false questions.

I13-57 *Secs. 1231 and 1250.* Molly sells an apartment complex for $4,500,000 with 10% of the price allocated to land. The apartment complex was purchased in 1991. She has no other sales or exchanges during the year and no nonrecaptured net Sec. 1231 losses. Information about the assets at the time of sale is:

	Building	*Land*
Original Cost	$2,700,000	$300,000
Accumulated Depreciation	1,000,000	0

a. What is the recognized gain on the sale of the building and the character of the gain?
b. What is the recognized gain on the sale of the land and the character of the gain?
c. How much of the Sec. 1231 gain is taxed at 25%?
d. If Molly has NSTCL of $50,000, will the capital loss reduce the Sec. 1231 gain taxed at 25% or 20%?

I13-58 *Secs. 1231 and 1250 for Corporate Taxpayer.* Assume the same facts as in Problem I13-57 except the taxpayer is a corporation instead of an individual.
a. What is the recognized gain on the sale of the building and the character of the gain?
b. What is the recognized gain on the sale of the land and the character of the gain?
c. How much of the Sec. 1231 gain is taxed at 25%?

I13-59 *Recapture of Soil and Water Conservation Expenditures.* Bob owns farmland with a $600,000 basis, and he elects to expense $100,000 of expenditures incurred for soil and water conservation purposes. After farming for seven years and four months, Bob sells the farmland for $825,000.
a. What is the amount of the recognized gain and the character of the gain?
b. What is the amount of recognized gain and the character of the gain if the farmland is sold for $615,000?

I13-60 *Recapture of Intangible Drilling Costs.* Jeremy purchased undeveloped oil and gas property in 1994 and paid $300,000 for intangible drilling and development costs. He elected to expense the intangible drilling and development costs in 1994. During the current year, Jeremy sells the property, which has an $800,000 adjusted basis, for $900,000. What is the amount of gain treated as ordinary income under Sec. 1254 because of the election to expense intangible drilling and development costs?

I13-61 ***Recapture of Intangible Drilling Costs and Depletion.*** In 1997, Jack purchased undeveloped oil and gas property for $900,000 and paid $170,000 for intangible drilling and development costs. He elected to expense the intangible drilling and development costs. During the current year he sells the property for $950,000 when the property's adjusted basis is $700,000. Depletion of $200,000 was allowed on the property.

a. What is the realized gain and how much of the gain is ordinary income?
b. For Jack to have a Sec. 1231 gain, the selling price must exceed what amount?

I13-62 ***Related Party Transactions.*** Ed operates a storage business as a sole proprietorship and owns the following assets acquired in 1977:

Warehouse	$400,000	
Minus: Accumulated depreciation (straight-line method)	(230,000)	
Adjusted basis		$170,000
Land		65,000

The FMV of the warehouse and the land are $500,000 and $200,000, respectively. Ed owns 75% of the stock of the Crane Corporation. If he sells the two assets to Crane at a price equal to the FMV of the assets, determine the following:

a. Recognized gain due to sale of the building and character of the gain.
b. Recognized gain due to the sale of the land and character of the gain.

COMPREHENSIVE PROBLEM

I13-63 Betty is in the business of breeding and racing horses. Except for the transactions below, she has no other sales or exchanges and she has no unrecaptured Sec. 1231 losses. Consider the following transactions that occur during the year:

- A building with an adjusted basis of $300,000 is destroyed by fire. Insurance proceeds of $500,000 are received, but Betty does not plan to replace the building. The building was built 12 years ago at a cost of $430,000 and straight-line depreciation has been used. The building was used to provide lodging for her employees.
- Four acres of the farm are condemned by the state to widen the highway and Betty receives $50,000. The adjusted basis of the four acres is $15,000 and the land was inherited from her mother 15 years ago. She does not plan to purchase additional land.
- A racehorse purchased four years ago for $200,000 was sold for $550,000. Total depreciation allowed using the straight-line method amounts to $160,000.
- Equipment purchased three years ago for $200,000 is exchanged for $100,000 of IBM common stock. The adjusted basis of the equipment is $120,000. If straight-line depreciation had been used, the adjusted basis would be $152,000.
- A pony, with an adjusted basis of $20,000 and FMV of $35,000, that her daughter uses only for personal use is injured while attempting a jump. Because of the injury, the uninsured pony has to be destroyed by a veterinarian.

a. What amount of Sec. 1245 ordinary income must be recognized?
b. What amount of Sec. 1250 ordinary income must be recognized?
c. Will the loss resulting from the destruction of her daughter's pony be used to determine net Sec. 1231 gains or losses?
d. After all of the netting of gains or losses is completed, will the gain resulting from the involuntary conversion of the building be treated as LTCG?
e. What is the amount of the net Sec. 1231 gain or loss?
f. What is the amount of her unrecaptured Sec. 1250 gain?

TAX STRATEGY PROBLEMS

I13-64 Russ has never recognized any Sec. 1231 gains or losses. In December 2002, Russ is considering the sale of two Sec. 1231 assets. The sale of one asset will result in a $20,000 Sec. 1231 gain while the sale of the other asset will result in a $20,000 Sec. 1231 loss. Russ has no other capital or Sec. 1231 gains and losses in 2002 and does not expect to have any other capital or Sec. 1231 gains and losses in 2002. He is aware that it might be advantageous to recognize the Sec. 1231 gain and the Sec. 1231 loss in different tax years. However, he does not know whether he should recognize the Sec. 1231 gain in 2002 and the Sec. 1231 loss in 2003 or vice versa. His marginal tax rate for each year is expected to be 31%. Advise the taxpayer with respect to these two alternatives:

a. Recognize the $20,000 Sec. 1231 loss in 2002 and the $20,000 Sec. 1231 gain in 2003.
b. Recognize the $20,000 Sec. 1231 gain in 2002 and the $20,000 Sec. 1231 loss in 2003.

I13-65 Holly has recognized a $9,000 STCL. She has no other recognized capital gains and losses in 2002. She is considering the sale of a Sec. 1231 asset held for four years at a $5,000 gain in 2002. She had not recognized any Sec. 1231 losses during the previous five years and does not expect to have any other Sec. 1231 transactions in 2002. Her marginal tax rate for 2002 is 31%. What is the amount of increase in her 2002 taxes if Holly recognizes the $5,000 Sec. 1231 gain in 2002?

TAX FORM/RETURN PREPARATION PROBLEMS

I13-66 George Buckner, Soc. Sec. no. 267-31-7251, sells an apartment building during the current year for $1,750,000. The building was purchased on January 1, 1978, for $2,000,000. An accelerated method of depreciation has been used, and depreciation of $1,140,000 has been taken. If the straight-line method of depreciation had been used, depreciation of $800,000 would have been allowed. The figures given above do not include the purchase price or the selling price of the land. Mr. Buckner's adjusted basis for the land is $200,000, and the sales price is $350,000. Mr. Buckner, who owns and operates a taxi business, sells one of the automobiles for $1,800. The automobile's adjusted basis is zero, and the original cost is $15,000. The automobile was purchased on April 25, 1995. Mr. Buckner has no other gains and losses during the year, and nonrecaptured net Sec. 1231 losses amount to $32,000. Prepare Form 4797 for the current year.

I13-67 Julie Hernandez is single and has no dependents. She operates a dairy farm and her social security number is 510-88-6387. She lives at 1325 Vermont Street in Costa, Florida. Consider the following information for her tax return for the current year:

- Schedule C was prepared by her accountant and the net profit from the dairy operations for the current year is $48,000.
- Itemized deductions amount to $3,185.
- Dividend income amounts to $280.
- State income tax refund received during the year is $125. She did not itemize her deductions last year.
- In June, a burglar broke into her house and stole the following two assets, which were acquired in 1987:

	Basis	*FMV*	*Insurance Proceeds Received*
Painting	$2,000	$10,000	$9,000
Sculpture	1,700	1,500	0

The following assets used in her business were sold during the year:

	Acquisition Date	*Original Cost*	*Depreciation to Date of Sale*	*Date of Sale*	*Selling Price*
Tractor	June 10, 1990	$25,000	$25,000	Oct. 20	$ 8,300
Barn	May 23, 1980	90,000	36,000[(a)]	May 13	87,000
Land	May 23, 1980	15,000	—0—	May 13	27,000
Cows	Sept. 7, 1998	20,000	13,000	Nov. 8	21,000

[(a)] $25,000 if the straight-line method had been used.

In August, three acres of the farm were taken by the state under the right of eminent domain for the purpose of building a highway. The basis of the three acres is $1,500 and the state paid the FMV, $22,000, on February 10. The farm was purchased on August 12, 1971.

Nonrecaptured net Section 1231 losses from the five most recent tax years preceding the current year amount to $7,000. Estimated taxes paid during the year amount to $32,000.

Prepare Forms 1040, 4684 Section A, 4797, and Schedule D for the current year. (Do not consider self-employment taxes discussed in Chapter I14.)

CASE STUDY PROBLEMS

I13-68 Your client, Kent Earl, whose tax rate is 39.6%, owns a bowling alley and has indicated that he wants to sell the business for $1,000,000 and purchase a minor league baseball franchise. His business consists of the following tangible assets:

	Acquisition Date	*Original Cost*	*Adjusted Basis*
Equipment	1987	$600,000	$150,000
Building	1978	900,000	400,000[a]
Land	1978	100,000	100,000
Inventory	Current year	50,000	50,000

[a] $480,000 if straight-line depreciation had been used.

Because you have another client, Tom Quick, who is interested in purchasing a business, you informed Tom of Kent's interest in selling. Tom wants to purchase the bowling alley, and the price sounds right to him. The bowling alley business has been very profitable in the last few years because Kent has developed a loyal group of customers by promoting bowling leagues during the week days and a special Saturday afternoon session for children in the elementary school grades. Kent and Tom have come to you and want to know how the transaction should be handled for the best tax results. You know, of course, that the $1,000,000 purchase price will have to be allocated among the assets and it will be necessary to estimate the FMV of all assets. Because FMV is often subjective, Kent and Tom recognize that some flexibility might exist in allocating the purchase price. For example, it might be just as easy to justify a FMV of $300,000 or $325,000 for the equipment.

a. What advice do you have for Kent with respect to the allocation (i.e., should he be interested in allocating more to some assets than others)? Explain the reasoning for your advice.

b. Would your advice to Kent be different if he had a large amount of capital losses and no nonrecaptured net Sec. 1231 losses?

c. What advice do you have for Tom with respect to the allocation (i.e., should he be interested in allocating more of the purchase price to some assets than to others)? Explain the reasoning for your advice.

d. What advantages might result from having Kent sign an agreement not to compete (i.e., operate a bowling alley)?

e. Should you have a concern about the ethical implications of advising both Kent and Tom?

I13-69 Assume the same facts as in Case Study Problem I13-68 except you have the following market values as a result of an appraisal:

Equipment	$ 250,000
Building	500,000
Land	140,000
Inventory	110,000
Total	$1,000,000

Tom insists that $150,000 of the purchase price should be allocated to inventory and $100,000 should be allocated to land. He refuses to complete the purchase unless the allocation is made as he requests. What action should you take with respect to Tom's request? (See Chapter I10 for a discussion of valuation issues in the purchase and sale of a business.)

TAX RESEARCH PROBLEM

I13-70 Berkeley Corporation has a policy of furnishing new automobiles to the athletic department of the local university. The automobiles are used for short periods of time by the extremely popular head basketball coach. When the automobiles are returned to Berkeley Corporation, they are sold to regular customers. The owner of Berkeley Corporation maintains that any such cars held for more than one year should qualify as Sec. 1231 property. Do you agree?

Research sources include

- Rev. Rul. 75-538, 1975-2 C.B. 34.

14

CHAPTER

SPECIAL TAX COMPUTATION METHODS, TAX CREDITS, AND PAYMENT OF TAX

LEARNING OBJECTIVES

After studying this chapter, you should be able to

1. Calculate the alternative minimum tax
2. Describe what constitutes self-employment income and compute the self-employment tax
3. Describe the various business and personal tax credits
4. Understand the mechanics of the federal withholding tax system and the requirements for making estimated tax payments

CHAPTER OUTLINE

Alternative Minimum Tax...14-2
Self-Employment Tax...14-7
Overview of Tax Credits...14-9
Personal Tax Credits...14-10
Miscellaneous Credits...14-17
General Business Credits...14-17
Refundable Credits...14-22
Payment of Taxes...14-24
Tax Planning Considerations...14-29
Compliance and Procedural Considerations...14-32

Chapter I2 discussed the basic tax computation for individuals using the tax table and tax rate schedules. This chapter completes the discussion of the tax computation by examining three principal topics:

1. Two special methods of tax computation, the alternative minimum tax and self-employment tax,
2. Various tax credits that are available to reduce a taxpayer's tax liability, and
3. Methods for payment of an individual's tax liability, including the pay-as-you-go withholding rules and estimated tax payment requirements.

ALTERNATIVE MINIMUM TAX

OBJECTIVE 1

Calculate the alternative minimum tax

Over the years, Congress has used the income tax law for a variety of purposes other than just the raising of revenue to fund government operations, such as enacting provisions to promote economic and social goals. As the number of special tax provisions increased, many taxpayers were able to carefully plan their financial affairs so as to use these special tax provisions to substantially reduce or eliminate their entire income tax liability. As a result, a new set of rules were implemented in 1969 to ensure that all taxpayers would pay at least a minimum amount of income tax. Thus was born what is known today as the **alternative minimum tax** (**AMT**).

The original minimum tax was referred to as an add-on minimum tax because it was added to the taxpayer's regular income tax liability. The amount of the tax was 10% times the taxpayer's tax preferences in excess of a $30,000 statutory exemption. The present AMT system, originally created in 1978, is no longer an add-on tax but is actually a separate and parallel tax system. Taxpayers are first required to compute their regular income tax liability and then compute their tax under the AMT system. The AMT system essentially requires taxpayers to adjust their regular taxable income by a number of adjustments and preferences, then subtract an exemption amount to arrive at the AMT base. The AMT base is then multiplied by the special AMT rates to compute the AMT. Taxpayers are required to pay the *greater* of (1) the regular income, or (2) the AMT.

The present AMT applies to individuals, corporations, estates, and trusts.[1] Most individual taxpayers are actually not subject to the AMT because their regular income tax is greater than the AMT. This is primarily caused because many taxpayers do not have substantial adjustments and preferences and the AMT exemption is liberal in amount (i.e., $49,000 for married individuals filing a joint return and $35,750 for single individuals).

EXAMPLE I14-1 ▶ Ricardo and Sue are married and file a joint return for the current year with taxable income of $30,000 and tax preferences and adjustments of $12,000 for AMT purposes. Their alternative minimum taxable income (AMTI) is $42,000 ($30,000 + $12,000), but the alternative minimum tax base is zero because of the $49,000 exemption. Thus, their tax liability is based on the regular tax computation and no AMT liability is owed. ◀

EXAMPLE I14-2 ▶ Assume the same facts for Ricardo and Sue above except that they have tax preferences and adjustments of $50,000. Their alternative minimum taxable income (AMTI) is $80,000 ($30,000 + $50,000). Their regular tax would be $4,500 ($30,000 × 15%). The total tax computed under the AMT system would be $8,060 ($80,000 minus the AMT exemption of $49,000 yields the AMT base of $31,000; $31,000 × AMT tax rate of 26% equals $8,060). Thus, Ricardo and Sue must pay $8,060 in tax since it is greater than their regular tax of $4,500. ◀

COMPUTATIONAL ASPECTS

The formula for computing the alternative minimum tax for individuals for the tax year is to apply a two-tiered graduated rate schedule to the AMT tax base. The tax base consists of the following items:[2]

[1] The AMT applicable to corporations is discussed in *Prentice Hall's Federal Taxation: Corporations, Partnerships, Estates, and Trusts* text and in the *Comprehensive* volume.

[2] Sec. 55(b)(1).

ADDITIONAL COMMENT

Some tax advisors recommend accelerating income into a year in which the taxpayer is subject to the AMT because the income will be taxed at a 26% or a 28% rate rather than a possibly higher rate in a later year.

TAXABLE INCOME
Plus: Tax preference items[3]
Plus: Personal and dependency exemptions
The standard deduction if the taxpayer does not itemize
Plus or minus: Adjustments required because different rules are used for calculating the alternative minimum taxable income as compared with taxable income (e.g., special AMT limitations on certain itemized deductions)

EQUALS: ALTERNATIVE MINIMUM TAXABLE INCOME (AMTI)
Minus: Exemption amount ($49,000 for a married couple filing a joint return and surviving spouses, $35,750 for single individuals, and $24,500 for a married individual filing separately). The exemption amount is reduced by 25% of AMTI in excess of $150,000 for a married couple filing a joint return and surviving spouses, $112,500 for single individuals, and $75,000 for a married individual filing separately.[4]

EQUALS: ALTERNATIVE MINIMUM TAX BASE
Times: Tax rate (26% of first $175,000; 28% of amounts in excess of $175,000)[5]

EQUALS: TENTATIVE MINIMUM TAX
Minus: Regular tax

EQUALS: ALTERNATIVE MINIMUM TAX

EXAMPLE I14-3 ▶ Rita, a single taxpayer, has taxable income of $138,200, a regular tax liability of $35,775, a positive AMT adjustment due to limitations on itemized deductions of $30,000, and tax preferences of $40,000 in 2002. Rita's alternative minimum tax for 2002 is calculated as follows:

KEY POINT

For purposes of the alternative minimum tax, no deduction is allowed for personal exemptions or the standard deduction.

Taxable income	$138,200
Plus: Tax preferences	40,000
Plus: Personal exemption	3,000
Plus: Adjustments related to itemized deductions	30,000
Alternative minimum taxable income	$211,200
Minus: Exemption	(11,075)[a]
Alternative minimum tax base	$200,125
Tax on first $175,000: $175,000 × 0.26 =	$ 45,500
Tax on excess over $175,000: $25,125 × 0.28 =	$7,035
Tentative minimum tax	$ 52,535
Minus: Regular tax	(35,775)
Alternative minimum tax	$ 16,760

ADDITIONAL COMMENT

In the Revenue Reconciliation Act of 1993, Congress created a two-tier alternative minimum tax schedule in order to make the individual income tax system more progressive.

Rita will pay a total of $52,535 ($35,775 regular tax + $16,760 AMT).

[a] $35,750 − [0.25 × ($211,200 − $112,500)]. ◀

TAX PREFERENCE ITEMS

ADDITIONAL COMMENT

Most taxpayers will not have tax preference items. Over the years, tax preference items have diminished in importance while adjustments create most AMT.

Tax preferences are certain provisions in the Internal Revenue Code (IRC) granting favorable treatment to taxpayers. For example, accelerated depreciation allowed for real property placed in service before 1987 is a tax preference item. (See Chapter I10 for a discussion of ACRS depreciation.) To compute the tax base for the AMT, the tax preferences designated in Sec. 57 must be added to taxable income. Some of the most common tax preference items include the following:

[3] Sec. 57.

[4] Sec. 55(d)(3). These exemption amounts were increased by the Economic Growth and Tax Relief Reconciliation Act of 2001 effective for tax years beginning in 2001 through 2004. For tax years beginning in 2005, the exemption amounts are scheduled to revert back to the amounts effective in 2000, which were $45,000, $33,750, and $22,500 respectively.

[5] The AMT rate on net capital gains has been reduced from the 26%/28% rates to 20%/10% to correspond with the reduction in rates on net capital gains for regular tax purposes. This reduction is effective for tax years ending after May 6,1997.

- Excess of accelerated depreciation (or ACRS cost recovery) claimed over a hypothetical straight-line depreciation amount for real property placed in service before 1987 computed on an item-by-item basis.
- Tax-exempt interest on certain private activity bonds. In general, private activity bonds are state or local bonds that are issued to help finance a private business.
- Exclusion of gain on the sale of certain small business stock. The exclusion is 28% of the gain on the disposition of qualified small business stock under Sec. 1202[6] (See Chapter I15).

It should be noted, however, that not all items receiving preferential treatment are tax preference items. For example, most municipal bond interest income is exempt from the federal income tax but is not a tax preference item. Only tax-exempt interest on private activity bonds (e.g., bonds issued by a municipality to fund certain nongovernmental activities such as industrial parks) issued after August 7, 1986 are subject to the AMT.

EXAMPLE I14-4 ▶ Richard, a single taxpayer, has the following tax preference items for the current year:

- $15,000 ACRS cost-recovery deduction on real property placed in service before 1987 and held for investment. The straight-line ACRS deduction would have been $10,000.
- $10,000 of tax-exempt interest on private activity bonds.

Richard's total tax preferences are $15,000, consisting of $5,000 excess cost recovery deductions and $10,000 tax-exempt interest on the private activity bonds. ◀

As one can see from the discussion above, most taxpayers will have little, if any, tax preferences.

AMT ADJUSTMENTS

ADDITIONAL COMMENT

Some tax advisors recommend that cash basis taxpayers prepay their local property taxes or state income taxes before the end of the year in order to reduce the current year's tax liability. However, if the taxpayer is subject to the AMT, this may not be a valid strategy.

As previously discussed, AMTI equals taxable income as modified by certain adjustments and increased by tax preference items. For most individual taxpayers AMT adjustments represent itemized deductions that are not allowed in computing AMTI or timing differences relating to the deferral of income or the acceleration of deductions under the regular tax rules. These adjustments generally increase the AMT tax base, although the AMT tax base may be reduced when the timing differences reverse. Some of the more important adjustments are discussed below.

LIMITATION ON ITEMIZED DEDUCTIONS. Only certain itemized deductions are allowed in computing AMTI. Additionally, the standard deduction is not allowed if an individual does not itemize deductions. The following items are deductible for AMT purposes:

- Casualty and theft losses in excess of 10% of AGI
- Charitable contributions (but not in excess of the 20%, 30%, and 50% of AGI limitation amounts)
- Medical expenses in excess of 10% of AGI (a 7.5% ceiling applies to the regular tax computation)
- Qualified housing interest and certain other interest up to the amount of qualified net investment income included in the AMT base
- Estate tax deduction on income in respect of a decedent
- Gambling losses

Some of the more significant itemized deductions that are not deductible for the AMT include miscellaneous itemized deductions (e.g., unreimbursed employee expenses), state, local, and foreign income taxes, and real and personal property taxes. The 3% reduction of itemized deductions of high-income taxpayers does not apply to the AMT.

---

[6] Sec. 57(a)(7). The 28% rate was formerly 42%. For stock acquired after December 31, 2000, the 42% rate is reduced to 28%.

EXAMPLE I14-5 ▶ Robin, a single taxpayer, has AGI of $100,000 and the following itemized deductions in 2002:

Charitable contributions	4,000
Medical expenses in excess of 7.5% of AGI ($10,000 actual expenses − $7,500)	2,500
Mortgage interest on Robin's personal residence	18,500
Real estate taxes	4,000
State income taxes	6,000
Personal casualty loss, net of insurance, in excess of 10% of AGI ($22,000 actual loss − $10,000) and $100 floor	$12,000

From the information above, Robin's taxable income is $50,000 ($100,000 minus itemized deductions and personal exemption of $3,000). Assume she also has $20,000 of tax preferences for AMT purposes. Robin's AMT adjustments for disallowed itemized deductions include $2,500 of medical expenses, because the 10% AMT limitation eliminates the medical expense deduction [$10,000 − (0.10 × $100,000 AGI) = $0] and $10,000 of real estate and state income taxes ($4,000 + $6,000). Thus, Robin's total AMT adjustment for disallowed itemized deductions is $12,500 ($2,500 + $10,000). Robin's AMTI is $85,500 ($50,000 taxable income + $20,000 tax preferences + $12,500 disallowed itemized deductions + her $3,000 personal exemption). ◀

AMT ADJUSTMENTS DUE TO TIMING DIFFERENCES. Other adjustments are required when the rules for calculating taxable income permit the taxpayer to temporarily defer the recognition of income or to accelerate deductions. This temporary benefit is caused by applying different accounting methods that result in timing differences when income or expenses are recognized. The most common AMT adjustments for individuals that represent timing differences include:

- For real property placed in service after 1986 and before January 1, 1999, the difference between the MACRS depreciation claimed using the property's actual recovery period and a hypothetical straight-line depreciation amount calculated using a 40-year life (see Chapter I10 for a discussion of the alternative depreciation system).[7]
- For personal property placed in service after 1986, the difference between the MACRS deduction and the amount determined by using the 150% declining balance method under the alternative depreciation system with a switch to the straight-line method.[8]
- For research and experimental (R&E) expenditures, the difference between the amount expensed and the deduction that would have been allowed if the expenditures were capitalized and amortized over a ten-year period.[9]

EXAMPLE I14-6 ▶ Rob has the following AMT adjustments caused by timing differences in 2002:

- Depreciation in 2002 on residential rental property costing $100,000 and placed in service in January, 1997 is $3,636 using the straight-line method, a 27½-year recovery period, and based on MACRS rules. The depreciation in 2002 for AMT purposes is $2,500 based on the straight-line method and a 40-year recovery period under the alternative depreciation system. Thus, the positive AMT adjustment is $1,136 ($3,636 − $2,500). (See footnote 7 for real property placed in service after December 31, 1998)
- Depreciation on an automobile used in business costing $10,000 and placed in service in 2002 is $2,000 based on the MACRS rules (i.e., 200% DB method, a half-year convention, and a five-year recovery period). The depreciation for AMT purposes is $1,500 based on the alternative depreciation system (i.e., 150% DB method, half-year convention and a five-year recovery period). Thus, the positive AMT adjustment is $500 ($2,000 − $1,500).
- R&E expenditures amounting to $50,000 are expensed in the current year. For AMT purposes, the R&E deduction would be $5,000 ($50,000 ÷ 10 years) since the expenditures are capitalized and amortized over a 10-year period. Thus, the positive AMT adjustment is $45,000 ($50,000 − $5,000).

Rob's total positive AMT adjustment to his taxable income in 2002 to arrive at AMTI is $46,636 ($1,136 + $500 + $45,000). ◀

ADDITIONAL COMMENT

For corporate taxpayers only, there is a 0.12% environmental tax imposed on the excess of the corporation's modified alternative minimum taxable income over $2 million.

[7] For real property being depreciated under the straight-line method and placed in service after 1998, the Taxpayer Relief Act of 1997 eliminates this adjustment.

[8] For personal property not being depreciated under the 200% declining balance method (i.e., 15-year and 20-year property) and placed into service after 1998, the Taxpayer Relief Act of 1997 effectively eliminates this adjustment for such property.

[9] Sec. 56(b)(2). However, this adjustment does not apply if the taxpayer materially participates in the activity, Sec. 56(b)(2)(D).

CREDIT THAT REDUCES THE AMT. As we will discuss later in this chapter, there are a number of credits that are allowed to reduce a taxpayer's regular tax liability. However, for purposes of the AMT, only two credits are allowed to reduce the tentative minimum tax: the foreign tax credit and the nonrefundable portion of the child credit.[10] The foreign tax credit that may be deducted from the AMT is a specially computed credit, called the "alternative minimum tax foreign tax credit" and basically is computed using the various amounts used in computing alternative minimum taxable income instead of taxable income. Thus, the AMT is likely to apply to a taxpayer who uses credits (other than the child and foreign tax credits) to reduce his regular tax liability.

STOP & THINK

Question: What are the most common characteristics of taxpayers who are subject to the AMT?

Solution: While each situation is certainly unique, there are certain taxpayers who are more likely to be subject to the AMT. First, taxpayers who have materially invested in real estate before January 1, 1999 are likely candidates for the AMT because they will have a large positive adjustment caused from the differences in depreciation. Second, as discussed above, taxpayers who use credits to reduce their regular tax liability may well be subject to the AMT because only the foreign tax credit can reduce the AMT. Third, taxpayers who have very large itemized deductions, primarily from large state and local taxes, may be subject to the AMT because state and local taxes are not deductible for AMT purposes.

AMT CREDIT. Under Sec. 53, taxpayers are allowed an AMT credit which can be used against their *regular tax liability.* Basically, if a taxpayer pays AMT in a taxable year, that amount of AMT is eligible to be used as a credit against the taxpayer's regular tax liability in a future year. While this may seem unusual at first glance, the underlying reasoning for the AMT credit is as follows: since the AMT is caused primarily by adjustments that will reverse in the future and the taxpayer will actually pay a higher regular tax in those future years, the imposition of a prior year AMT and the current year regular tax essentially would constitute double taxation. Thus, a taxpayer who has paid AMT in prior years, but is not subject to the AMT in the current year, may be entitled to an AMT credit against his regular tax liability in the current year.[11]

SUMMARY ILLUSTRATION OF THE AMT COMPUTATION

The AMT formula is illustrated in the following example:

EXAMPLE I14-7 ▶ Roger and Kate are married and file a joint return. They have the following items (including $25,000 in tax preference items from interest income earned on private activity bonds) that are used to compute taxable income in 2002:

Gross income:		
Salary		$ 60,000
Dividends and interest		10,000
Business income		30,000[a]
AGI		$100,000
Minus: Itemized deductions:		
State and local property taxes	$10,000	
Mortgage interest on their personal residence	12,000	
Charitable contributions	3,000	(25,000)
Minus: Personal and dependency exemptions ($3,000 × 2)		(6,000)
Taxable income		$ 69,000

[a] MACRS depreciation deductions of $70,000 on personal property placed in service after 1986 were claimed in arriving at business income. Only $50,000 of depreciation would be claimed under the alternative depreciation system using the 150% declining balance method.

ADDITIONAL COMMENT

In some circumstances, the AMT applies to unsuspecting taxpayers. In a recent case, *D.R. Klaussen*, TC Memo. 1998-241 (affd, CA-10), the taxpayers had 12 personal exemptions and were subject to the AMT even though they had no tax preferences or adjustments.

[10] The child credit, discussed later in this chapter and in Chapter I2, is $600 for each eligible child in 2001 through 2004 and increases to $1,000 by 2010.

[11] Detailed discussion of the rules for computing the AMT credit is beyond the scope of this book. See Sec. 53 for additional information.

Roger's AMT is computed as follows:

Taxable income			$ 69,000
Plus:	Tax preferences		25,000
	Personal and dependency exemptions		6,000
	AMT adjustments:		
	Excess depreciation ($70,000 − $50,000)	$20,000	
	State and local property taxes	10,000	30,000
AMTI			$130,000
Minus:	AMT exemption		(49,000)
Tax base			$ 81,000
Times:	Tax rate		× 0.26
Tentative minimum tax ($81,000 × 26%)			$ 21,060
Minus:	Regular tax (based on taxable income of $69,000)		(12,426)
Alternative minimum tax			$ 8,634[a]

[a] An AMT credit may be available in future years to offset any regular tax that is owed. However, the AMT credit applies only to the AMT that results from timing differences such as depreciation adjustments and not from exclusions (e.g., personal exemptions and taxes).

The total tax liability for Roger and Kate for 2002 is $21,060 ($12,426 + $8,634). ◀

SELF-EMPLOYMENT TAX

OBJECTIVE 2

Describe what constitutes self-employment income and compute the self-employment tax

Most individuals are classified as employees and are not subject to the self-employment tax. Employees are covered under the Federal Insurance Contributions Act (FICA) through the payment of payroll taxes. The employer must withhold the employee's share of the FICA tax and provide a matching amount. Employees are not subject to an additional employment tax upon the filing of their federal income tax return.

The self-employment tax is imposed to finance Social Security coverage for self-employed individuals. Thus, the distinction between a self-employed individual (often referred to as an independent contractor) and an employee is important because no employer FICA contribution is required if the payee is deemed to have independent contractor status. Independent contractors are subject to self-employment tax on the amount of net earnings from the self-employment activity. Employees who have a small business in addition to their regular employment (e.g., an accountant, who is an employee for a large corporation, also prepares tax returns in a sideline consulting practice) may be subject to the self-employment tax on the consulting income in addition to the FICA tax on wages.

ETHICAL POINT

An employer must have a reasonable basis for treating a worker as an independent contractor or meet the general common law rules for determining whether an employer-employee relationship exists. Otherwise, the employer is liable for federal and state income tax withholding, FICA and FUTA taxes, interest, and penalties associated with the misclassification.

COMPUTING THE TAX

Self-employed individuals are subject to the self-employment (SE) tax if their net earnings are $400 or more.[12] The SE tax rate is a total of 15.3%, comprised of 12.4% for old-age, survivors, and disability insurance (OASDI) up to a ceiling amount of $84,900 in 2002 ($80,400 in 2001), and 2.9% for hospital insurance (HI), commonly referred to as Medicare taxes. No ceiling amount applies to the HI portion. Note that the SE tax rates are exactly twice the rates for employees under FICA (e.g., 6.2% for OASDI up to a ceiling amount of $84,900 in 2002, and 1.45% for HI). For employee wages, the 6.2% and 1.45% (total of 7.65%) must be matched by the employer. This matching requirement for employers effectively equalizes Social Security taxes for employees and self-employed individuals.

One-half of the self-employment tax imposed is allowed as a *for* AGI deduction and is reported on page 1 of Form 1040.[13] Net earnings from self-employment are determined by multiplying self-employment income by 0.9235 (which is equivalent to 100% of self-employment income minus one-half of self-employment taxes, or 7.65%, resulting in net earnings from self-employment of 92.35%) to compute the amount that is subject to self-employment tax.

HISTORICAL NOTE

The ceiling amount on income from self-employment was $7,800 in 1971.

[12] Sec. 6017.

[13] Sec. 164(f).

EXAMPLE I14-8 ▶ Rose is a CPA and operates her practice as a sole proprietorship. She has $120,000 of earnings from self-employment in 2002. Her net earnings from self-employment is $110,820 ($120,000 × 0.9235). The OASDI portion of the tax is $10,528 ($84,900 × 0.124). The amount of self-employment income that is subject to the hospital insurance portion of the tax is $110,820 and the HI tax is $3,214 ($110,820 × 0.029). Thus, the total self-employment tax reported on Schedule SE is $13,742. Rose also receives a *for* AGI tax deduction of $6,871 ($13,742 × 0.50), which is reported on page 1 of Form 1040. ◀

ADDITIONAL COMMENT

The Revenue Reconciliation Act of 1993 eliminated the wage cap on the hospital insurance component of wages. Though presented as a tax increase for high-income individuals, it also increases the tax burden for employers of high-income individuals.

If an individual is an employee and also has income from self-employment, the tax base for computing the self-employment tax is reduced by the wages that are subject to the FICA tax. The self-employment tax base for the OASDI component is equal to the lesser of the primary ceiling ($84,900 in 2002) reduced by the FICA wages or the self-employment income multiplied by 0.9235.

EXAMPLE I14-9 ▶ Sandy receives wages as an employee of $35,000 in 2002 that are subject to FICA tax. In addition, Sandy has a small consulting practice that generates $10,000 of income from self-employment. The tentative tax base for computing the self-employment tax is $9,235 ($10,000 × 0.9235) net earnings from self-employment. Thus, the tax base for computing the OASDI portion of the tax is the lesser of $9,235 net earnings from self-employment or $49,900 ($84,900 ceiling − $35,000 FICA wages). Sandy's self-employment tax for the OASDI portion is $1,145 ($9,235 × 0.124) and the HI component is $268 ($9,235 × 0.029) The total amount of self-employment tax is therefore $1,413 ($1,145 + $268) and Sandy also receives a *for* AGI deduction of $707 ($1,413 × 0.50), which is reported on page 1 of Form 1040. ◀

EXAMPLE I14-10 ▶ Assume the same facts as in Example I14-9 except that Sandy's wages are $100,000. Sandy's taxable self-employment income for the OASDI portion of the tax is zero because her FICA wages exceed the $84,900 primary ceiling amount. However, she is subject to self-employment tax with respect to the HI portion. The tax base for the HI portion is the $9,235 net earnings from self-employment because no ceiling amount is applicable. The HI portion of the self-employment tax is $268 ($9,235 × 0.029) and Sandy also receives a *for* AGI deduction for $134 ($268 × 0.50). ◀

KEY POINT

In the case of married taxpayers filing joint returns, it is important on Schedule SE of Form 1040 to fill in the name and Social Security number of the spouse with the self-employment income. This information is used to establish benefit eligibility.

WHAT CONSTITUTES SELF-EMPLOYMENT INCOME

Individuals who carry on a trade or business as a proprietor or partnership are considered to render services as independent contractors and are, therefore, subject to the self-employment tax. If an individual has two separate self-employment activities, the *net* earnings from each activity are aggregated. However, where a husband and wife file a joint return and both have self-employment income, the self-employment tax must be computed separately.

EXAMPLE I14-11 ▶ Russ and Ruth are married and file a joint return. Russ has $13,000 net earnings from a consulting business and a $4,000 net loss from a retail store that is operated as a sole proprietorship. Ruth has wages of $50,000 from her employer that are subject to FICA taxes. Russ's net earnings from self-employment are $8,312 ($9,000 × 0.9235). No reduction in the self-employment tax base is allowed for Ruth's wages as an employee because Ruth is not self-employed and the tax is computed separately for Russ and Ruth. ◀

ADDITIONAL COMMENT

For some self-employed taxpayers, the amount of self-employment tax exceeds the amount of income tax for the year. For example, a married couple with two children and $17,000 of self-employment income would not owe any income tax, but would have a $2,402 (17,000 × .9235 × 15.3%) self-employment tax liability.

Among the items that constitute earnings that are subject to the self-employment tax are:

- Net earnings from a sole proprietorship
- Director's fees[14]
- Taxable research grants
- Distributive share of partnership income plus guaranteed payments from the partnership

The self-employment tax is computed on Schedule SE of Form 1040 (see Appendix B). The rules for computing the self-employment tax are summarized in Topic Review I14-1.

[14] Rev. Rul. 57-246, 1957-1 C.B. 338. It is a factual question whether an officer who also serves as a director is performing services as an employee or as an independent contractor. The courts have recognized that an individual can perform services as a director and also perform employment-related services but the director fees may be recharacterized by the courts if the fees are in reality compensation for services rendered as an employee. See *Peter H. Jacobs* 1993 RIA T.C. Memo ¶ 93, 570, 66 TCM 1470.

Topic Review I14-1

Self-Employment Tax Summary

- The self-employment tax is imposed on net earnings from self-employment over $400.
- The tax base for computing the self-employment tax is generally the amount of self-employment income multiplied by 0.9235.
- A $84,900 (2002) ceiling applies to the old age, survivors, and disability (OASDI) portion. However, no ceiling applies to the hospital insurance (HI) portion of the tax.
- Self-employment tax is computed separately for married individuals filing joint returns.
- One-half of the self-employment tax that is imposed is allowed as a business deduction *for* AGI.
- The self-employment tax rate is 15.3% which includes 12.4% for the OASDI portion and 2.9% for the hospital insurance (HI) portion.

OVERVIEW OF TAX CREDITS

OBJECTIVE 3

Describe the various business and personal tax credits

USE AND IMPORTANCE OF TAX CREDITS

Tax credits are often used by the federal government to implement tax policy objectives. For example, tax credits may help to increase employment, encourage energy conservation and research and experimental activities, encourage certain socially desired activities, and provide tax relief for low-income taxpayers. Tax credits are also used to mitigate the effects of double taxation on income from foreign countries. Thus, tax credits are an important part of the income tax law.

Credits may be classified into two broad categories, **nonrefundable** and **refundable.** Nonrefundable credits may only be used to offset a taxpayer's tax liability. Refundable credits, on the other hand, not only offset a taxpayer's tax liability but if the credits exceed the tax liability, the excess will be paid (refunded) directly to the taxpayer. Topic Review I14-2, located at the end of this section, provides a summary of selected tax credits and the rationale for their inclusion in the tax law. Note that most tax credits are nonrefundable. The principal refundable credits include taxes withheld on wages and the earned income credit.

VALUE OF A CREDIT VERSUS A DEDUCTION

Tax credits are extremely valuable for taxpayers as they reduce the tax liability on a dollar-for-dollar basis. This is in contrast to a tax deduction which reduces taxable income and the value of a tax deduction is limited to the taxpayer's marginal tax rate. Thus, tax deductions are more valuable to high-income taxpayers than lower-income taxpayers because their marginal tax rate is higher. Tax credits, however, benefit all taxpayers in the same amount regardless of their marginal tax rate.

EXAMPLE I14-12 ▶ Tasha and Sean are both single taxpayers and each have an $800 expenditure that qualifies for either a tax deduction or a 20% credit. Tasha is in the 15% marginal tax bracket while Sean is in the 35% marginal tax bracket. If the $800 is claimed as a tax deduction, Tasha would receive a tax benefit of $120 ($800 × 15%) whereas Sean would receive a tax benefit of $280 ($800 × 35%). Thus, higher income taxpayers realize greater benefits from the same amount of deduction because of the progressive nature of the federal income tax system. Conversely, if the credit is claimed, both Tasha and Sean would benefit equally as the $160 credit ($800 × 20%) would reduce each taxpayer's tax liability on a dollar-for-dollar basis. Thus, tax credits provide the same benefit to taxpayer's regardless of the applicable marginal tax bracket. In this case, Tasha would benefit more from the credit while Sean would benefit more from the tax deduction. ◀

ADDITIONAL COMMENT

The total amount of tax credits claimed by individual taxpayers increased by 14.9% in 1996.

CLASSIFICATION OF CREDITS

As mentioned earlier, credits may be classified into two general categories, refundable and nonrefundable credits. Table I14-1 lists and further classifies the various types of major credits available under the tax law. The reason why it is important to properly classify the credits is that limitations are imposed on credits depending on the classification.

▼ **TABLE I14-1**
CLASSIFICATION OF MAJOR TAX CREDITS

NONREFUNDABLE CREDITS

Personal Credits
- Child and dependent care credit – Sec. 21
- Credit for the elderly and disabled – Sec. 22
- Adoption credit – Sec. 23
- Child tax credit – Sec. 24
- Residential mortgage credit – Sec. 25
- HOPE scholarship credit – Sec. 25A
- Lifetime learning credit – Sec. 25A
- Qualified Retirement Savings Contributions Credit – Sec. 25B

Miscellaneous Credits
- Foreign tax credit – Sec. 27
- Nonconventional source fuel credit – Sec. 29
- Credit for qualified electric vehicles – Sec. 30

General Business Credits
- Research credit – Sec. 41
- Low income housing credit – Sec. 42
- Disabled access credit – Sec. 44
- Rehabilitation credit – Sec. 47
- Business energy credit – Sec. 48
- Work opportunity credit – Sec. 51
- Welfare-to-work credit – Sec. 51A
- Empowerment zone employment credit – Sec. 1396

REFUNDABLE CREDITS

- Tax withheld on wages – Sec. 31
- Earned income credit – Sec. 32

PERSONAL TAX CREDITS

As a result of tax legislation in the last few years, the number of personal tax credits has increased significantly. These credits are allowed as an offset against an individual's tax liability before all other nonrefundable credits (i.e., the miscellaneous credits and the general business credits).[15] Most of the personal tax credits have been enacted for social welfare rather than economic reasons. The more important personal tax credits are discussed below.

CHILD TAX CREDIT

Taxpayers are allowed a nonrefundable credit of $600 for each qualifying child under the age of 17.[16] The new 2001 Tax Act increases the child credit to $1,000, phased-in over ten years, beginning in 2001. The table below shows the increase of the child tax credit.

[15] Sec. 26. See detailed discussion below on limitation on personal credits. [16] Sec. 24.

Calendar Year	*Credit Amount Per Child*
2001–2004	$600
2005–2008	$700
2009	$800
2010 and thereafter	$1000

The credit is phased out when the taxpayer's modified AGI reaches $110,000 ($75,000 for single taxpayers and $55,000 for married taxpayers filing separately) at a rate of $50 for each $1,000, or fraction thereof, that modified AGI exceeds the above thresholds.

A qualifying child must be a dependent of the taxpayer and must be the taxpayer's son or daughter (or a descendent of either), a stepchild, or an eligible foster child. Further, the child must also be a U.S. citizen, a U.S. national, or a resident of the U.S.[17]

In general, the child tax credit is limited to the taxpayer's income tax liability. However, the new 2001 Tax Act has expanded the child credit to become refundable to the extent the taxpayer's earned income exceeds $10,300 (2002).

CHILD AND DEPENDENT CARE CREDIT

ADDITIONAL COMMENT

The dollar amount of the child and dependent care credit amounted to $2.5 billion in 1996.

The child and dependent care credit provides relief for taxpayers who incur child and dependent care expenses because of employment activities.[18] To qualify for the credit, an individual must meet two requirements: qualifying child or dependent care expenses must be incurred to enable the taxpayer to be gainfully employed, and the taxpayer must maintain a household for a dependent under age 13 or an incapacitated dependent or spouse.[19]

EXAMPLE I14-13 ▶ Tim and Tina are married and have two children under age 13. They incur child care expenses (e.g., a housekeeper and nurse) to enable both Tim and Tina to work on a full-time basis. The child care expenditures are eligible for the child and dependent care credit because Tim and Tina incurred the child care expenses to enable the taxpayers to be gainfully employed. Alternatively, if Tina was not employed but incurred the child care expenses to play tennis and other social activities, the expenditures would not be eligible for the child and dependent care credit. ◀

ADDITIONAL COMMENT

Qualifying child care expenses include amounts spent to send a child to nursery school or kindergarten, but not first grade.

QUALIFYING EMPLOYMENT-RELATED EXPENSES. Eligible expenses include amounts spent for housekeeping, nursing, cooking, baby-sitting, etc. in the taxpayer's home but do not include expenses for a chauffeur or gardener. If the child or dependent care is provided outside the home by a dependent care facility (e.g., a day care facility), the amounts will generally qualify only if the dependent care facility provides care for more than six individuals. Employment-related expenses do not include amounts paid for services outside of the taxpayer's household at a camp where the qualifying individual stays overnight. In addition, amounts paid for services outside of the taxpayer's household (e.g., adult day care) that are spent for the care of an incapacitated dependent or spouse qualify only if the individual lives in the taxpayer's home for at least eight hours a day.

EXAMPLE I14-14 ▶ Tony is divorced and has two children under age 13. He is employed and incurs child care expenses at a preschool nursery for one of the children. He also has a live-in nanny who provides housekeeping services and a gardener to care for his yard. The expenditures for the preschool nursery and the live-in nanny qualify because these services constitute eligible household services and care of a qualifying individual. However, the payments to the gardener do not constitute qualifying household services. ◀

The following special rules also apply:

- ▶ The maximum amount of child and dependent care expenses that qualify for the credit is $2,400 for one qualifying individual and $4,800 for two or more individuals.[20]

---

[17] Sec. 24(c).

[18] Sec. 21. The complete title of this credit is *Expenses for Household and Dependent Care Services Necessary for Gainful Employment.*

[19] Secs. 21(b)(1) and (e)(1). Maintaining a household means that the individual (or the individual and spouse if married) must provide over one-half of the cost of maintaining the home. Married individuals must generally file a joint return to obtain the credit.

[20] The 2001 Tax Act increases these amounts beginning in 2003 to $3,000 for one qualifying individual and $6,000 for two or more individuals.

These ceilings are reduced by the aggregate amount excludable from gross income due to the exclusion under Sec. 129 relating to dependent care assistance programs. No carryover is permitted for expenses that exceed these maximum amounts.

- Payments to a relative qualify unless the relative is a dependent or a child (under age 19) of the taxpayer.[21]
- The maximum child and dependent care expenses cannot exceed the individual's earned income. For married individuals, the limitation is applied to the earned income of the spouse with the smaller amount of earned income.
- A spouse who either is a full-time student or is incapacitated is deemed to have earned income of $200 per month.[22] The amount is increased to $400 per month if there are two or more qualifying individuals (e.g., children under age 13) in the household.

EXAMPLE I14-15 ▶ Troy and Tracy are married and incur qualifying child care expenses of $4,000 to take care of their two children, ages 1 and 3. Tracy's earned income is $20,000, and Troy's earned income from a part-time job is $3,000. The limitation on qualifying child care expenses is $3,000. Although the overall limitation of $4,800 is not exceeded, the earned income limitation applies because Troy's earned income ($3,000) is less than the child care expenses ($4,000). Therefore, the amount of eligible child-care expenses is limited to $3,000. ◀

KEY POINT

The percentage used to calculate the credit varies from 20% to 30% depending on the taxpayer's AGI.

COMPUTATION OF THE CREDIT RATE AND AMOUNT. The credit is 30% of the qualifying expenses (after the ceiling limitations of $2,400 or $4,800 have been applied).[23] However, the credit rate is reduced by one percentage point for each $2,000 (or fraction thereof) of adjusted gross income (AGI) in excess of $10,000 but goes no lower than 20%. The minimum credit (20%) is applied once a taxpayer's AGI exceeds $28,000.

EXAMPLE I14-16 ▶ Vincent and Vicki are married, file a joint return, and have three children under age 13. Vincent and Vicki's employment-related earnings are $25,000 and $10,000, respectively. Their AGI is $35,000. They incur $8,000 of child care expenses during the current year. The eligible child care expenses are limited to $4,800, because Vincent and Vicki have more than one child who is qualified and this limitation is less than Vicki's earned income or the actual expenses incurred. Because their AGI is greater than $28,000, the minimum 20% credit rate is applicable. The child and dependent care credit is $960 (0.20 × $4,800). ◀

DEPENDENT CARE ASSISTANCE. An employee may exclude amounts up to $5,000 from gross income for dependent care assistance payments made by the individual's employer and provided to the employee.[24] The exclusion amount is limited to the earned income of the employee (or in the case of a married taxpayer, the lesser of the employee's earned income or the earned income of the spouse). To avoid a double benefit, the otherwise eligible expenses for purposes of computing the child and dependent care credit are reduced by the amount of assistance that is excluded from gross income.[25]

EXAMPLE I14-17 ▶ Assume the same facts as in Example I14-16 except that Vincent was reimbursed $4,000 by his employer under a qualified dependent care assistance program and this amount was excluded from his gross income. Since $4,000 was excluded under a Sec. 129 qualified dependent care assistance program, expenses eligible for the child and dependent care credit must be reduced. Thus, the eligible child care expenses are reduced to $800 ($4,800 − $4,000) and the child care credit is $160 (0.20 × $800). ◀

ADDITIONAL COMMENT

The tax credit for the credit for the elderly or disabled has been declining in recent years and amounted to only $32 million in 1996, down 32% from 1995.

TAX CREDIT FOR THE ELDERLY AND DISABLED

A limited, personal, nonrefundable credit is provided for certain low-income elderly individuals who have attained age 65 before the end of the tax year and individuals who retired because of a permanent and total disability and who receive insubstantial Social Security benefits. Most elderly taxpayers are ineligible for the credit because they receive

---

[21] Sec. 21(e)(6).

[22] Sec. 21(d)(2). To qualify as a full-time student, the individual must enroll in an educational institution on a full-time basis for at least five calendar months of the year (Reg. Sec. 1.44A-2(b)(3)(B)(ii)).

[23] This percentage is increased to 35% beginning in 2003.

[24] Sec. 129. (See Chapter I4 for a discussion of the requirements for exclusion.)

[25] Sec. 21(c).

Social Security benefits in excess of the ceiling limitations that apply to the credit (e.g., an initial amount of $5,000 per year for a single taxpayer) or they have AGI amounts in excess of the limitations, which effectively reduces or eliminates the allowable credit.

The maximum credit is 15% times an initial amount of $5,000 ($7,500 for married individuals filing jointly if both spouses are 65 or older).[26] This initial amount is reduced by:

- Social Security, railroad retirement, or Veterans Administration pension or annuity benefits that are excluded from gross income
- One-half of AGI in excess of $7,500 for a single individual ($10,000 for married taxpayers filing a joint return).[27] All types of taxable income items are included in AGI (e.g., salaries, taxable pension and taxable Social Security benefits, and investment income).

EXAMPLE I14-18 ▶ Wayne and Tammy are both 67 years old and file a joint return. They have AGI of $11,000 and receive nontaxable Social Security payments of $3,000 during the current year. Their tax credit for the elderly is computed as follows:

Initial ceiling amount		$7,500
Minus: Nontaxable social security	$3,000	
One-half of AGI in excess of $10,000		
(0.50 × [$11,000 − $10,000])	500	(3,500)
Total credit base		$4,000
Times: Credit percentage		
Tax credit		$ 600

The $600 credit is allowed only to the extent that Wayne and Tammy's total personal tax credits do not exceed the actual tax due before credits. ◀

ADOPTION CREDIT

A nonrefundable credit is allowed for qualified adoption expenses. The amount of the credit in 2002 and future years is limited to a maximum of $10,000 (including a child with special needs) and generally is allowable in the year the adoption is finalized.[28] If adoption expenses are paid *prior* to the year the adoption is finalized, such expenses are not eligible until the year the adoption is finalized. If the adoption expenses are paid during or after the year the adoption is finalized, the credit is allowable in the year the expenses are paid or incurred. Further, there is a phase-out of the credit based on AGI. For taxpayers with AGI between $150,000 and $190,000, the credit is ratably phased out and is fully phased out when a taxpayer's AGI reaches $190,000.[29] Beginning in 2003, in the case of the adoption of a child with special needs, $10,000 is allowed as an adoption credit regardless of whether the taxpayer has qualified adoption expenses.

Qualified adoption expenses include reasonable and necessary adoption fees, court costs, attorney fees, and other expenses that are directly related to the legal adoption by the taxpayer of an eligible child. An eligible child is defined as a child who has not reached 18 years old when the adoption takes place or is physically or mentally incapable of self-care.

EXAMPLE I14-19 ▶ Oscar and Betty began adoption proceedings in June, 2002 to adopt an infant child. They incurred attorney fees and adoption agency fees in 2002 of $5,000. In 2003, they incurred an additional $7,000 of qualified adoption expenses when the adoption became final. Oscar and Betty's AGI in 2003 is $160,000. The adoption credit is allowable in 2003 in the amount of $7,500, computed as follows:

---

[26] Sec. 22(c)(2). The initial ceiling amount is $5,000 if one spouse filing a joint return is less than age 65 and the limitation is $3,750 for a married individual filing a separate return. Unless married individuals are living apart for the entire year, they must file a joint return in order to obtain the credit.

[27] The AGI ceiling is $5,000 for married individuals filing a separate return. To obtain the credit, however, a separate return can be filed only if both spouses live apart for the entire tax year.

[28] For tax years 1996–2001, the adoption credit was limited to $5,000 ($6,000 in the case of a child with special needs) and the credit was ratably phased out between $75,000 and $115,000 of adjusted gross income.

[29] For purposes of the phase-out of the credit, AGI must be modified. AGI for this purpose is determined without regard to the exclusions from gross income for foreign earned income under Sec. 911 and after the application of the rules relating to the taxation of Social Security, as well as selected other items. See Sec. 23.

Total qualified adoption expenses in 2002 and 2003	$12,000
Maximum credit	10,000
Phase-out percentage ($10,000/$40,000)	25%
Amount of credit disallowed	2,500
Amount of credit allowed ($10,000 − $2,500)	7,500

Oscar and Betty only can use $10,000 of expenses (maximum) and must claim the expenses in 2003, the year the adoption becomes final. Finally, the adoption is limited based upon the level of their AGI. ◀

The adoption credit for 2002 and later years is limited to the excess of the regular tax liability plus any AMT *over* the sum of the taxpayer's other nonrefundable credits. The portion of the credit which is limited may be carried forward for up to five years.

HOPE SCHOLARSHIP CREDIT

Two credits are available to assist taxpayers who incur higher education expenses for themselves, their spouses, and dependents. The two credits are the "HOPE scholarship credit" and the "lifetime learning credit".[30] The Hope scholarship credit (HOPE credit) is discussed first, then the lifetime learning credit is discussed.

Taxpayers are allowed up to a $1,500 credit for tuition and related expenses paid during the taxable year for each qualified student. Qualified tuition and related expenses include only tuition and fees required for enrollment and do not include books, room and board, student activity fees, and other expenses unrelated to an individual's academic course of instruction. The HOPE credit applies to expenses paid after December 31, 1997 for education furnished in academic periods beginning after such date. Below are a number of requirements and limitations that exist for the HOPE credit:

- The $1,500 credit is allowed only for a maximum of two years per student and is computed by taking 100% of the first $1,000 of tuition and fees *plus* 50% of the second $1,000 of tuition and fees.
- Qualified tuition and related expenses eligible for the HOPE credit are limited to the first two years of postsecondary education. The first two years of postsecondary education is measured at the *beginning* of the taxable year. If a student has not completed the first two years of postsecondary education by the beginning of the taxable year, qualified tuition and related fees are eligible for the HOPE credit. The first two years is determined based on whether the educational institution awards the student two years of academic credit at that institution.
- If a taxpayer pays qualified education expenses in one year but the expenses relate to an academic period that begins during January, February, or March of the next taxable year, the academic period is treated as beginning during the taxable year in which the payment is made. Thus, a payment of tuition in December, 2001 for the Spring Semester, 2002 (which begins in January, 2002) would be eligible for the HOPE credit in 2001.
- An eligible student must carry at least ½ of the normal full-time load for the course of study the student is pursuing.
- The HOPE credit is not available to any student who has been convicted of a federal or state felony offense for possession or distribution of a controlled substance as of the end of the taxable year for which the credit is claimed.
- Qualified tuition and related expenses eligible for the credit must be reduced by amounts received under other sections of the tax law, such as scholarships (Sec. 117), employer-sponsored educational reimbursement plans (Sec. 127), Education IRAs (Sec. 530), or other provisions of the tax law.
- The allowable credit (including both the HOPE credit and the lifetime learning credit) is reduced for taxpayers who have modified AGI above certain amounts. The phaseout for taxpayers filing joint returns for 2002 is $82,000 to $102,000 ($41,000 to

---

[30] Sec. 25A. Both credits are contained in Sec. 25A, the HOPE credit is specifically described in Sec. 25A(b) while the lifetime learning credit is described in Sec. 25A(c). The various definitions contained in Sec. 25A apply to both credits.

$51,000 for other taxpayers). The HOPE credit and lifetime learning credit are ratably phased-out for joint filers using the formula below:

$$\text{Sum of HOPE credit and lifetime learning credit} \times \frac{\text{Modified AGI - \$82,000}}{\text{\$20,000}}$$

For taxpayers other than joint filers, the $82,000 is replaced with $41,000 and the $20,000 is replaced with $10,000.

It is important to understand that the HOPE credit applies to each student. Thus, parents who have two children in their first two years of college may claim up to a $1,500 credit for each child.

ADDITIONAL COMMENT

The education expenses for the HOPE and lifetime learning credits must be incurred at an educational institution that is eligible to participate in Department of Education student aid programs.

LIFETIME LEARNING CREDIT

The lifetime learning credit is computed differently than the HOPE credit and is less restrictive, however, most of the definitions regarding eligible students and qualified expenses are identical with the HOPE credit. The credit is 20% of a maximum of $5,000 per year of qualified tuition and fees paid by the taxpayer for one or more eligible students. However, unlike the HOPE credit, the $5,000 limitation is imposed at the taxpayer level, not on a per student basis. Below are some important requirements for the lifetime learning credit.

- The definition of qualified tuition and related expenses are the same as for the HOPE credit above.
- The lifetime learning credit is available for an unlimited number of years and may be used for undergraduate, graduate, and professional degree expenses.
- The maximum amount of expenses eligible for the credit is $5,000, however, this amount increases to $10,000 in 2003 and later years.
- The lifetime learning credit applies only to expenses paid after June 30, 1998 for education furnished in academic periods beginning after such date.
- The lifetime learning credit and HOPE credit may not be taken in the same tax year with respect to the same student's tuition and related expenses, i.e., no doubling-up is permitted. For example, if Son A's tuition for the academic year is $10,000 and is used to claim $1,500 HOPE credit, none of the $10,000 may be used for the lifetime learning credit with respect to Son A. However, if Son B also has tuition expenses in the same tax year, either the lifetime learning credit or the HOPE credit is allowed for Son B.
- The lifetime learning credit may be claimed for any course (degree or nondegree)at a college or university that helps an individual acquire or improve their job skills, such as credit or noncredit courses that qualify as continuing professional education (CPE). Also, the requirement that a student take at least ½ of a full load does not apply to the lifetime learning credit.

EXAMPLE I14-20 ▶ Mark and Jane are married, file a joint return, and have three dependent children in college, Ron, Rhonda, and Ray. All three children attend State U. Mark and Jane's modified AGI is $85,000 in 2002 and the classification of each of the three children for each semester is as follows: Ron was a junior during the Spring Semester, 2002 and a senior in Fall Semester, 2002; Rhonda was a sophomore during the Spring Semester, 2002 and a junior in Fall Semester, 2002; Ray was in high school until the Fall Semester, 2002. Below are the expenses incurred in calendar year 2002 for the three children's college expenses:

		Spring Semester, 2002 (Paid in January, 2002)	**Fall Semester, 2002** (Paid in August, 2002)
Ron:	Tuition and fees	$1,500	$1,550
	Books	300	300
	Room and board	3,500	3,700
Rhonda:	Tuition and fees	1,500	1,550
	Books	275	325
	Room and board	4,000	4,200
Ray:	Tuition and fees		1,550
	Books		325
	Room and board		3,700

Mark and Jane are allowed to claim the HOPE credit and the lifetime learning credit for 2002 as follows:

HOPE credit: Only Rhonda and Ray qualify for the credit because the HOPE credit is limited to the first two years of postsecondary education. Rhonda qualifies because she has not completed two years of postsecondary education as of the beginning of the taxable year. Thus, the tentative HOPE credit is $2,775, $1,500 for Rhonda and $1,275 for Ray [100%($1,000) + 50%($1,550 − $1,000)]. Only tuition and fees qualify for the HOPE credit, the books and room and board are not qualified education expenses.

Lifetime learning credit: Ron qualifies for the credit. His tuition and fees for the year total $3,050 and the tentative lifetime learning credit is $610 [20% × ($3,050)]. Only tuition and fees qualify for the credit, the books and room and board are not qualified education expenses.

Since Mark and Jane have modified AGI above $82,000, the above credits of $4,660 ($4,050 + $610) are partially phased-out as follows:

$$\$4,660 \times \frac{\$85,000 - \$82,000}{\$20,000} = \$699$$

Thus, the total HOPE and lifetime learning credits for 2002 are $3,961 ($4,660 − $699). ◀

QUALIFIED RETIREMENT SAVINGS CONTRIBUTIONS CREDIT

To encourage low and middle income taxpayers to save for retirement, a *temporary* nonrefundable credit for contributions or deferrals to retirement savings plans has been established for tax years beginning after December 31, 2001.[31] This credit is in addition to the exclusion or deduction from gross income for contributions or deferrals that are otherwise allowable. The credit is scheduled to terminate after December 31, 2006.

The credit is computed by multiplying the amount contributed to a qualified retirement plan by an applicable percentage. The maximum amount to compute the credit for each eligible individual is $2,000 per year. The applicable percentage depends on the amount of the taxpayer's adjusted gross income as shown in the following table:

Adjusted Gross Income						
Joint Return		*Head of Household*		*All Other*		*Applicable Percentage*
Over	*Not Over*	*Over*	*Not Over*	*Over*	*Not Over*	
$ 0	$30,000	$ 0	$22,500	$ 0	$15,000	50
30,000	32,500	22,500	24,375	15,000	16,250	20
32,500	50,000	24,375	37,500	16,250	25,000	10
50,000	—	37,500	—	25,000	—	0

The qualified retirement savings contribution amounts for any tax year equals the sum of contributions or deferrals by the taxpayer to specified types of retirement plans, including IRAs (Roth and Traditional), 401(k) plans, 403(b) plans, and certain other plans. These amounts must be reduced for any distributions from such plans.

EXAMPLE I14-21 ▶ Steve is single and has AGI of $16,000 in 2002. During the year, he contributes $2,000 to his Roth IRA. Steve is eligible for the Qualified Retirement Savings Contributions Credit in the amount of $400 ($2,000 × 20%). The credit would be the same if he contributed $2,000 to a traditional IRA. In addition to the $400 credit, Steve also would be permitted to deduct the $2,000 contribution to the traditional IRA on his individual return. ◀

To be eligible for the credit, a taxpayer must be at least 18 years of age as of the close of the tax year, must not be claimed as a dependent on someone else's tax return, and must not be a full-time student as defined for purposes of the dependency exemption (full-time student for at least 5 calendar months).

[31] Sec. 25B.

LIMITATION ON PERSONAL CREDITS

Sec. 26 imposes limitations of the amount of nonrefundable personal credits for individual taxpayers (see Table I14-1 for a listing of such credits). For tax years beginning after December 31, 2001, nonrefundable personal credits, other than the *adoption credit*, the *child credit*, and the credit for *qualified retirement savings contributions*, may not exceed the excess of (1) the taxpayer's regular tax liability for the taxable year, over (2) the tentative minimum tax for the taxable year.[32] The tax liability limitation rules for the adoption credit, the child tax credit, and the qualified retirement savings credit are contained in the IRC sections applicable to those credits.

MISCELLANEOUS CREDITS

The miscellaneous credits, with the exception of the foreign tax credit, are specialized types of tax credits. For this reason, only the foreign tax credit is discussed in this textbook.

KEY POINT

The foreign tax credit is available only on income, war profits, and excess profits taxes or taxes paid in lieu of such taxes. It is sometimes difficult to determine whether a particular foreign tax falls into the qualifying category.

FOREIGN TAX CREDIT

U.S. citizens, resident aliens, and U.S. corporations are subject to U.S. taxation on their worldwide income.[33] To reduce double taxation, the tax law provides a foreign tax credit for income taxes paid or accrued to a foreign country or a U.S. possession.[34]

Taxpayers may elect to take a deduction for the taxes paid or accrued in lieu of a foreign tax credit.[35] In general, the foreign tax credit results in a greater tax benefit because (as previously discussed) a credit is fully offset against the tax liability, while a deduction merely reduces taxable income.

ADDITIONAL COMMENT

In 1996, 2.1 million tax returns claimed $3.1 billion in foreign tax credits.

Computation of Allowable Credit. The **foreign tax credit** amount equals the lesser of the foreign taxes paid or accrued in the tax year or the portion of the U.S. income tax liability attributable to the income earned in all foreign countries.[36] This limitation, which restricts the claiming of foreign tax credit if the effective foreign tax rate on the foreign earnings exceeds the effective U.S. tax rate on these earnings, may result in double taxation if the unused credit cannot be used as a carryback or carryover (see discussion under the next heading). The foreign tax credit limitation is based on the following formula:

$$\frac{\text{Foreign source taxable income}}{\text{Worldwide taxable income}} \times \text{U.S. income tax before credits} = \text{Foreign tax credit limitation}$$

EXAMPLE I14-22 ▶ Edison Corporation has $200,000 U.S. source taxable income and $100,000 of foreign source taxable income from country A. Total worldwide taxable income is $300,000 ($200,000 + $100,000). Country A levies a total of $40,000 in foreign income taxes upon the foreign source taxable income (i.e., a 40% effective tax rate). The U.S. tax before credits is $100,250 on the $300,000 of taxable income. Using the formula given above, the overall foreign tax credit limitation is computed as follows:[37]

$$\frac{\$100{,}000}{\$300{,}000} \times \$100{,}250 = \$33{,}417$$

---

[32] The limitations for nonrefundable personal credits for individual taxpayers for years prior to 2002 were subject to special rules that are not detailed in this textbook.

[33] Certain exceptions are provided by treaty agreements between the United States and foreign countries whereby certain types of foreign-source income may be exempt from taxation in the foreign country.

[34] Under Sec. 911, U.S. citizens and resident aliens may elect to exclude from gross income up to $80,000 (2002 and thereafter) of foreign-earned income and certain housing cost amounts. The foreign taxes that are attributable to the excluded income cannot be taken as a credit. (See Chapter I4 for a discussion of these exclusions.)

[35] Sec. 164(a)(3).

[36] Sec. 904.

[37] Certain types of income may have a separate foreign tax credit limitation. These types of income include passive income, high withholding tax interest, financial services income, shipping income, dividends from noncontrolled foreign (Sec. 902) corporations, dividends from domestic international sales corporations (DISCs), and foreign trade income from a foreign sales corporation. See Chapter C16 of *Prentice Hall's Federal Taxation: Corporations, Partnerships, Estates, and Trusts* for a more detailed discussion of these separate limitations.

Because the foreign tax payments ($40,000) exceed the U.S. tax attributable to the foreign source income ($33,417), the limitation applies. Thus, $6,583 ($40,000 − $33,417) of foreign tax credit cannot be used in the current year. ◀

STOP & THINK *Question:* Since a credit is generally much more valuable than a deduction, under what circumstances would it be more beneficial for a taxpayer to take a deduction for foreign taxes in lieu of the foreign tax credit?

Solution: If a taxpayer has foreign source taxable income from one country and an equal loss from another foreign country, the foreign tax credit limitation is zero because the net foreign source taxable income is zero. Because none of the taxes paid in the foreign country in which taxable income was produced can be claimed as a credit, the taxpayer may choose to deduct them unless the credits are carried back or forward.

Treatment of Unused Credits. Unused foreign tax credits are carried back two years and then forward for five years to years where the limitation is not exceeded (i.e., the foreign tax payment is lower than the U.S. taxes attributable to the foreign source income in the carryback or carryover years). The unused credits are lost if they are not used by the end of the five-year carryover period.

GENERAL BUSINESS CREDITS

The tax credits commonly available to businesses are grouped into a special credit category called the **general business credit** and are summarized in Table I14-1 on page 14-10. The general business credits are combined for the purpose of computing an overall dollar limitation on their use because these credits are nonrefundable. The general business credit may not exceed the *net income tax* minus the greater of the tentative minimum tax or 25% of the *net regular tax liability* above $25,000.[38] If the general business credits exceed the tax limits, effective for tax years beginning after December 31,1997, they may be carried back one year and carried forward 20 years.[39]

During the carryover years, the unused credits from prior years are first applied (commencing with the earliest carryover year) before the current year credits that are earned are used (i.e., a first-in, first-out [FIFO] method is applied). This method permits the use of credits from the earliest of the carryover years and may prevent such carryovers from expiring.

EXAMPLE I14-23 ▶ Eastern Corporation has unused general business tax credits of $10,000 in 2001 that are carried forward to 2002. Eastern earns $5,000 of additional credits in 2002 and has a $12,000 limitation. The $12,000 of credits that are used consist of the $10,000 carryover from 2001 and $2,000 from 2002. The remaining $3,000 ($5,000 − $2,000) of 2002 credits are carried forward to 2003. ◀

The more important general business credits are discussed below.

CREDIT FOR INCREASING RESEARCH ACTIVITIES

HISTORICAL NOTE

The research credit was enacted in 1981 because Congress was concerned about the substantial relative decline in total U.S. expenditures for research and development.

The tax law provides two means of encouraging research and experimental activities: (1) research and experimental expenditures may be either deducted immediately or capitalized and amortized over a period of 60 months or more under Sec. 174 (see Chapter I10 for a discussion of these rules) or (2) a tax credit for qualified research expenses is available under Sec. 41. Before July 1, 1995, the research credit was allowed in an amount equal to the sum of:

[38] Sec. 38(c). The term *net income tax* is the sum of the regular tax plus the alternative minimum tax reduced by other nonrefundable credits. The term *net regular tax liability* means the regular tax liability reduced by nonrefundable credits. See Example I14-27 for an example of this calculation.

[39] For tax years prior to 1998, the carryback period was three years and the carryforward period was 15 years.

- 20% of qualified research expenses incurred in a tax year in excess of a base amount[40] for that tax year, plus
- 20% of basic research payments in excess of a base amount for that year.

The tax law allows taxpayers to elect to compute the credit in two alternative ways: (1) in a manner substantially similar to the law that existed prior to July 1, 1995, or (2) to elect to compute the credit under an alternative method that employs a three-tiered credit regime with reduced credit rates and fixed-based percentages. The second alternative is intended to benefit taxpayers whose base amount has gotten very high because of dramatically higher sales. Because the computation of the research credit is very complex, the details are not presented in this textbook. Readers are directed to Sec. 41 for additional details. The research credit is scheduled to expire on June 30, 2004.[41]

DISABLED ACCESS CREDIT

A nonrefundable tax credit is available to eligible small businesses for expenditures incurred to make existing business facilities accessible to disabled individuals. Eligible access expenditures include payments for the purpose of removing architectural, communication, physical or transportation barriers that prevent a business from being accessible or usable by disabled individuals. Expenditures made in connection with new construction are not eligible for the credit. The disabled access credit is equal to 50% of eligible expenditures that exceed $250 but do not exceed $10,250.[42] Thus, the annual credit limitation is $5,000. The basis of the property is reduced by the allowable credit. An eligible small business is any business that either (1) had gross receipts of $1 million or less in the preceding year or, (2) in the case of a business failing the first test, had no more than 30 full-time employees in the preceding year and makes a timely election to claim the credit.

EXAMPLE I14-24 ▶ Crane Corporation had 14 employees during the preceding tax year and $2 million of gross receipts. During the current year, Crane installed concrete access ramps at a total cost of $14,000. Crane is an eligible small business because the company had 30 or fewer full-time employees during the preceding year even though its gross receipts exceed the threshold amount (i.e., $1 million). Only $10,000 of eligible expenditures qualify for the credit, thereby limiting the credit to $5,000 ($10,000 × 0.50). The depreciable basis of the property is reduced by the credit amount to $9,000 ($14,000 − $5,000). ◀

The disabled access credit is also one of the items included in the general business credit. Thus, the limitation is based on the taxpayer's tax liability, and the carryback and carryover of excess credits are governed by the Sec. 38 rules.

TAX CREDIT FOR REHABILITATION EXPENDITURES

Congress has provided incentives for the rehabilitation of older industrial and commercial buildings and certified historic structures. A credit for rehabilitation expenditures is available subject to the following special rules and qualification requirements:[43]

- The credit is 10% for structures that were originally placed in service before 1936 and 20% for certified historic structures.[44]
- The credit applies only to trade or business property and property held for investment that is depreciable. Residential rental property does not qualify unless the building is a certified historic structure.

REAL-WORLD EXAMPLE

Taxpayers incurred substantial rehabilitation expenditures on an old factory building, but the tax credit was not allowed because the taxpayers did not use the straight-line depreciation method. *Frank DeMarco*, 87 T.C. 518 (1986).

---

40 The base amount is defined in Sec. 41(c)(2) as the product of the fixed-base percentage and the taxpayer's average annual gross receipts for the four tax years before the current (credit) year. All taxpayers are limited to a minimum base amount that may not be less than 50% of the qualified research expenses for the current year. The fixed-based percentage is the ratio of the taxpayer's total qualified research expenses to its total gross receipts for a specified base period (see Sec. 41(c)(3)).

41 The research credit had expired effective June 30, 1999. However, the credit was retroactively restored and extended through June 30, 2004 by the Tax Relief Extension Act of 1999.

42 Sec. 44.

43 Sec. 47.

44 Secs. 47(a)(1) and (2). A certified historic structure must be certified by the Department of Treasury and must be located in a registered historic district or listed in the *National Register*.

- At least 75% of the external walls, including at least 50% utilization of external walls, and at least 75% of the building's internal structural framework must remain in place.[45]
- Straight-line depreciation generally must be used with the applicable Sec. 168 recovery periods with respect to rehabilitation expenditures. The regular MACRS depreciation rules apply to the portion of the property's basis that is not eligible for the credit.
- The basis of the property for depreciation is reduced by the full amount of the credit taken.[46]
- The rehabilitation expenditures must exceed the greater of the property's adjusted basis or $5,000.
- The rehabilitation credit is recaptured at a rate of 20% per year if there is an early disposition of the property.

EXAMPLE I14-25 ▶ During the current year, Ted rehabilitates a certified historic structure used in his business at a cost of $40,000. The adjusted basis of the certified historic structure is $38,000 at the time the property is rehabilitated. The property qualifies for the rehabilitation credit because

- It is used in Ted's trade or business and is depreciable.
- The property is a certified historic structure.
- The amount of the expenditure exceeds the greater of the property's $38,000 adjusted basis or the $5,000 statutory minimum.

The credit is $8,000 (0.20 × $40,000). The basis of the rehabilitation expenditures for depreciation purposes is reduced by the full amount of the credit to $32,000 ($40,000 − $8,000). If the property is disposed of after one year, $1,600 of the credit (0.20 × $8,000) is earned and $6,400 ($8,000 − $1,600) is recaptured. ◀

BUSINESS ENERGY CREDITS

To encourage energy conservation measures, additional credits are available to businesses that invest in energy-conserving properties (e.g., solar and geothermal property).[47] The business energy credit is 10%. The construction, reconstruction, or erection of the property must be completed by the taxpayer and its original use must commence with the taxpayer. This credit is part of the general business credit and is subject to the same limitations on deductibility and carryback and carryover rules as other general business credits.

WORK OPPORTUNITY CREDIT

ADDITIONAL COMMENT

The employer must receive or request the certification in writing no later than the employee's first day of work.

A work opportunity tax credit (WOTC) is available on an elective basis and is intended to reduce unemployment for individuals who are considered economically disadvantaged. The WOTC has been allowed to expire several times but has been repeatedly restored by Congress. The current WOTC is scheduled to expire for individuals beginning work after December 31, 2001.[48] This constant reshuffling of effective dates creates considerable uncertainty and complexity for taxpayers. However, Congress presumably wants to allow the credit on a year-by-year basis in order to evaluate its effectiveness in creating employment opportunities for economically disadvantaged individuals.

The WOTC includes the following targeted groups:[49]

(1) Qualified IV-A (Aid to Families with Dependent Children) recipient,
(2) Qualified veteran,
(3) Qualified ex-felon,
(4) High-risk youth,
(5) Vocational rehabilitation referral,
(6) Qualified summer youth employee,
(7) Qualified food stamp recipient, or
(8) Qualified SSI recipient.

[45] Sec. 47(c)(1)(A). The percentage requirements for rehabilitation do not apply to a certified historic structure.
[46] Sec. 50(c)(1).
[47] Sec. 48(a)(2).
[48] The Work Opportunity Credit has been extended several times over the past several years.
[49] Sec. 51.
[50] Sec. 51A.

The credit is 40% of the first $6,000 of qualified wages paid to employees hired from one or more of the eight targeted groups. The new credit imposes a minimum employment period for qualified employees: employment for at least 180 days (20 days for qualified summer youth employee) or completes at least 400 hours of service for the employer (120 hours for a qualified summer youth employee). For employees working fewer than 400 hours, but at least 120 hours, the credit is reduced to 25%. No credit is available for an employee who works less than 120 hours. To qualify for the credit, the employer must obtain a certification from a local jobs service office of a state employment security agency stating that the unemployed individual is a qualified member of a targeted group. Further, an employee is not eligible for the credit if such employee was formerly employed by the employer at any time (i.e., a rehire). A disadvantage associated with the WOTC is that the employer's deduction for wages must be reduced by the amount of the credit.

EXAMPLE I14-26 ▶ Jet Corporation hires two individuals in the current year, one a qualified ex-felon and the other a qualified food stamp recipient. Both individuals are properly certified by the state agency. One of the individuals is paid $8,000 of wages during the year, and the second individual is paid $4,000. The amount of wages eligible for the work opportunity credit is $10,000 ($6,000 ceiling limit for the first employee plus $4,000 actual wages paid to the second employee). The credit is $4,000 (40% × $10,000). Jet must reduce its $12,000 deduction for wages paid to the two individuals by $4,000 in the current year. ◀

The WOTC is one of the items included in the general business credit. Thus, the limitation is based on the taxpayer's tax liability, and the carryback and carryover of excess credits are governed by the Sec. 38 rules.

WELFARE-TO-WORK CREDIT

A new credit was enacted in 1997 to encourage employers to hire individuals who are on welfare.[50] The credit is 35% of the qualified of the qualified first-year wages plus 50% of the qualified second year wages for "long-term family assistance recipients" up to a maximum of $10,000 of wages during the applicable tax years. Thus, the maximum credits are $3,500 for the first year and $5,000 for the second year. First- and second-year wages refer to the periods beginning with the date employment begins. This credit expires for employees who begin work for the employer after December 31, 2001.[51]

Long term family assistance recipients generally include members of a family that has been receiving family assistance for at least the 18-month period ending on the hiring date or no more than two years after a family is no longer eligible for assistance because they have reached the maximum duration for such assistance. If an employer takes the welfare-to-work credit for a recipient, the employer is not permitted to claim the work opportunity credit under Sec. 51 for such recipient.

EMPOWERMENT ZONE EMPLOYMENT CREDIT

The empowerment zone employment credit is an attempt to provide economic revitalization of distressed urban and rural areas. Empowerment zones and enterprise zones that have a condition of pervasive poverty, unemployment, and general distress are designated by the Secretary of Housing and Urban Development and the Secretary of Agriculture.

Employers are eligible for a 20% tax credit on the first $15,000 of wages per employee including training and educational costs paid to full- and part-time employees who are residents of an empowerment zone provided that the employer's trade or business and the employee's principal place of abode are within the empowerment zone.[52]

Qualified wages do not include wages taken into account for purposes of the targeted jobs credit (discussed above). The empowerment zone employment credit is one of the items included in the general business credit and the employer's deduction for wages is also reduced by the amount of the credit.

---

[51] The welfare-to-work credit expired on June 30, 1999 but was restored retroactively to July 1, 1999 and extended through December 31, 2001 by the Tax Relief Extension Act of 1999.

[52] Sec. 1396.

EXAMPLE I14-27 ▶ Ace Corporation is located in a designated empowerment zone and employs two eligible individuals who reside in the empowerment zone. One of the individuals is paid $12,000 in wages (plus $4,000 of training expenses are incurred for the employee) and the second employee is paid $10,000 in wages. $15,000 of wages and training expenses for the first employee and $10,000 of wages for the second employee are qualified wages. The credit is $5,000 ($25,000 × 0.20). Ace Corporation must reduce its $26,000 deduction for wages and training expenses by $5,000 (the credit amount for the year). ◀

LIMITATION BASED UPON TAX LIABILITY

As mentioned previously on page I14-18, there is an overall dollar limitation of the general business credit based on the tax liability of the taxpayer. The general business credit may not exceed the *net income tax* minus the greater of the tentative minimum tax or 25% of the *net regular tax liability* above $25,000.[53] This complicated limitation is demonstrated in the example below.

EXAMPLE I14-28 ▶ Steve's general business tax credit includes a $40,000 research credit and a $10,000 work opportunity credit. Steve's regular tax liability (before credits) is $45,000, and his tentative minimum tax is $10,000 (thus, Steve is not subject to the AMT). Nonrefundable tax credits also include a $2,000 child and dependent care credit (a nonrefundable personal tax credit) and a $1,000 foreign tax credit. Steve's dollar limitation on the general business tax credit is initially limited by the amount of net income tax of $42,000 ($45,000 regular tax minus $3,000 other nonrefundable credits). This amount is reduced by the $10,000 tentative minimum tax because this amount is greater than the net regular tax ceiling of $4,250 [0.25 × ($45,000 regular tax − $3,000 nonrefundable credits − $25,000)]. Thus, the limitation upon the $50,000 of general business tax credits ($40,000 + $10,000) is $32,000 ($42,000 − $10,000). ◀

ADDITIONAL COMMENT

The general business credit fell from $4.8 billion in 1985 to $0.6 billion in 1996. The decrease is attributable to the phasing out in 1986 of the major component of the general business credit, the investment tax credit.

REFUNDABLE CREDITS

As mentioned earlier, refundable credits not only may offset a taxpayer's income tax liability but, if the refundable credits exceed the taxpayer's tax liability, such excess will be refunded by government to the taxpayer. The principal type of refundable credit is the earned income credit, which is discussed below.

EARNED INCOME CREDIT

ADDITIONAL COMMENT

The earned income credit was claimed on 19.7 million tax returns in 1996 and amounted to $29.4 billion. This compares with 14.4 million returns and $13.4 billion in 1992.

The earned income credit is refundable and, as such, the earned income credit is a special type of "negative income tax" or welfare benefit for certain low-income families. The credit is based on earned income that includes wages, salaries, tips, and other employee compensation plus net earnings from self-employment and is designed to encourage low-income individuals to become gainfully employed.[54] Earned income does not include any form of employee compensation that is not includible in the taxpayer's income for the year.

KEY POINT

The Revenue Reconciliation Act of 1993 dramatically increased the benefits available from the earned income credit, which follows President Clinton's campaign promise to provide tax relief to the working poor.

ELIGIBILITY RULES. The credit is available to individuals with qualifying children and to certain individuals without children if the earned income and AGI thresholds are met.[55] The earned income credit applies to married individuals only if a joint return is filed. Individuals without children are eligible only if the following requirements are met:

- ▶ The individual's principal place of abode is in the United States for more than one-half of the tax year.
- ▶ The individual (or spouse if married) is at least age 25 and not more than age 64 at the end of the tax year.
- ▶ The individual is not a dependent of another taxpayer for the tax year.[56]

---

[53] The limitation discussed above actually must be separated into two parts, (1) all general business credits other than the empowerment zone credit, and (2) the empowerment zone credit. See Sec. 38(c) for details.

[54] See Chapter I2 for a discussion of the relationship between the child tax credit and the earned income credit.

[55] Sec. 32(c). A qualifying child must be the taxpayer's child, stepchild, foster child, or a descendent of the taxpayer's child. The child must share the same principal place of abode with the taxpayer for more than one-half of the tax year and the child must be less than age 19 or be a full-time student under age 24 or be permanently and totally disabled.

[56] Sec. 32(c)(1)(A).

A taxpayer will become ineligible for the earned income credit if the taxpayer has excessive investment income. Excessive investment income is defined as disqualified income that exceeds $2,550 for the taxable year 2002 ($2,450 for 2001). Disqualified income includes:

1. Dividends;
2. Interest (both taxable and tax-free); and
3. Net rental income.
4. Capital gain net income.

COMPUTATION OF THE CREDIT AMOUNT. The earned income credit percentages and the maximum amount of earned income used to compute the credit for 2002 are summarized in Table I14-2. The basic percentage rate and the maximum amount of earned income used to compute the credit depend on the number of qualifying children (from none to two or more) and filing status. The maximum allowable credit is then reduced by a phase-out percentage (see Table I14-3).[57]

EXAMPLE I14-29 ▶ Vivian is not married, has one qualifying child, and is eligible for the earned income credit in 2002. In the current year, she has $15,400 of earned income from wages and $3,600 of alimony. The wages are considered earned income, the alimony is not earned income but is included in AGI. Vivian's AGI is $19,000. The tentative credit is $2,506 (0.34 × the first $7,370 of earned income). This amount is reduced by $876 [0.1598 × ($19,000 − $13,520)]. The allowable credit is therefore $1,630 ($2,506 − $876), and this amount is refundable to Vivian.[58] ◀

▼ TABLE I14-2
2002 Earned Income Credit Table

Number of Qualifying Children	Basic Percentage	Maximum Amount of Earned Income to Compute Credit	Maximum Tentative Credit
All taxpayers			
No children	7.65%	$ 4,910	$ 376
One child	34.0%	7,370	2,506
Two or more children	40.0%	10,350	4,140

▼ TABLE I14-3
2002 Earned Income Credit Phase-Out Table

Number of Qualifying Children	Phase-Out Begins at[a]	Phase-Out Percentage	Phase-Out Ends at
Married filing joint return			
No children	$ 7,150	7.65%	$12,060
One child	14,520	15.98%	30,201
Two or more children	14,520	21.06%	34,178
Other taxpayers			
No children	$ 6,150	7.65%	$11,060
One child	13,520	15.98%	29,201
Two or more children	13,520	21.06%	33,178

[a]Larger of AGI or earned income.

[57] The percentages are adjusted annually for inflation.

[58] Sec 32(b)(1). $19,000 is used in the formula because AGI of $19,000 is greater than $13,090 of earned income. In years prior to 2002, the phase-out computation used modified AGI. To attempt to simplify the earned income credit, AGI is now used.

Topic Review I14-2

Summary of Selected Tax Credits

Tax Credit Item	Rationale
PERSONAL CREDITS	
Child and dependent care credit	To provide equitable relief for parents and other individuals who are employed and who must incur expenses for household and dependent care services
Tax credit for the elderly	To provide tax relief for elderly taxpayers who are not substantially covered by the Social Security system
Adoption credit	To provide relief for taxpayers who incur expenses in the adoption of children
Child tax credit	To reduce the tax burden on families with dependent children.
Residential mortgage interest credit	To encourage qualified first-time home buyers to purchase a principal residence (this credit is not discussed in the text due to its limited applicability)
HOPE scholarship credit and lifetime learning credit	To assist students and families of students with the cost of postsecondary education.
Qualified Retirement Savings Contributions Credit	To encourage low and middle income taxpayers to save for retirement.
MISCELLANEOUS CREDITS	
Foreign tax credit	To mitigate the effects of double taxation on foreign source income
Qualified electrical vehicles credit[a]	To encourage energy conservation (this credit is not discussed in the text due to its limited applicability)
GENERAL BUSINESS CREDITS	
Credit for increasing research activities[a]	To encourage research and development activities to enhance our technological base
Low-income housing credit[a]	To encourage construction, rehabilitation, and ownership of qualified low-income housing projects (this credit is not discussed in the text due to its limited applicability)
Disabled access credit[a]	To encourage small businesses to provide access for disabled
Rehabilitation expenditure credit[a]	To encourage the rehabilitation of older buildings including certified historic structures
Business energy credits[a]	To encourage energy conservation measures and the use of fuel other than petroleum
Work opportunity[a]	To encourage employers to hire unemployed people from disadvantaged groups
Welfare-to-work[a]	To encourage employees to hire persons who are on welfare
Empowerment zone employment credit[a]	To reduce the level of unemployment in distressed urban and rural areas.
REFUNDABLE CREDITS	
Earned income credit	To provide special tax breaks for certain low-income individuals who have earned income (e.g., salary and wages) and dependent children or other incapacitated individuals living in the household

[a]Part of the general business credit.

PAYMENT OF TAXES

OBJECTIVE 4

Understand the mechanics of the federal withholding tax system and the requirements for making estimated tax payments.

The IRS collects federal income taxes during the year either through withholding on wages or quarterly estimated tax payments. If the withholdings and estimated taxes are less than the amount of tax computed on the tax return, the taxpayer must pay the balance of the tax due when the tax return is filed. If there has been an overpayment of tax, the taxpayer may either request a refund or choose to apply the overpayment to the following year's quarterly estimated taxes.

Substantial penalties are imposed if an employer fails to withhold federal income tax and pay such amounts to the IRS.[59] In addition, a taxpayer may be subject to a nondeductible penalty upon an underpayment of estimated tax.[60]

WITHHOLDING OF TAXES

REAL-WORLD EXAMPLE

A teacher claimed a credit for Social Security taxes that had been withheld from his salary. He believed that the Social Security tax was illegally withheld because he did not authorize the collection of the tax. The Tax Court held that the Social Security tax is mandatory for designated employees and does not allow a person to elect not to contribute. *Richard L. Feldman*, 1967 PH T.C. Memo ¶67,091, 26 TCM 444.

An employer must withhold federal income taxes and FICA taxes from an employee's wages. No withholdings are required if an employer-employee relationship does not exist (e.g., an individual who performs services as an independent contractor).Generally, unless a specific exemption is provided under the IRC, withholding is required on all forms of remuneration paid to an employee. Thus, salaries, fees, bonuses, dismissal payments, commissions, vacation pay, and taxable fringe benefits are subject to withholding.[61] Special rules include for the following:

- *More than one employer during the same year.* Each employer must withhold FICA and federal income taxes without regard to the fact that the employee has more than one employer. This requirement may result in an overwithholding of FICA taxes if the ceiling amount on the OASDI portion of the tax is exceeded. In the event of an overwithholding of FICA taxes, the employee may credit the excess amount as an additional payment of tax on line 62 on page 2 of Form 1040. However, the excess FICA contributions related to the matching employer contributions are not refundable or creditable against the tax liabilities of either employer.
- *Exemptions for certain employment activities.* Certain employees such as agricultural laborers, ministers, household employees, newspaper carriers under age 18, and tips of less than $20 per month from an employer are exempt from income tax withholding. Note, however, that the earnings of such individuals are fully taxable and that an employer may be liable for FICA tax payments on these earnings.[62]

HISTORICAL NOTE

The withholding of federal income taxes by employers began during World War II.

- *Special rules for supplemental wage payments.* If an employee receives supplemental wage payments (in addition to regular wage payments), the withholding amount is determined under either of two methods:[63]

  Concurrent payments—if the supplemental wages are included in the payment of regular wages, the tax is withheld as if the total was a single wage payment for the payroll period.

  Separate payments—if the supplementary wages are paid separately, the tax withheld is either a flat 28% or by aggregating the supplemental wage payment with wages paid within the same calendar year for the last preceding payroll period or the current payroll period.

Supplemental wages payments include items such as bonuses, commissions, overtime, accumulated sick pay, severance pay, awards, prizes, back pay, and retroactive pay increases.

- *Backup withholding.* Backup withholding rules were enacted to prevent abusive noncompliance situations, such as not providing a payor of a dividend with the payee's social security number. A 30% withholding rate is required on most types of payments that are reported on Form 1099 (e.g., interest, dividends, royalties, etc.) where a proper taxpayer identification number is not provided.
- *Other special rules.* There are many other special rules on withholding in certain circumstances, such as for fringe benefits, pension and annuity payments, etc.

WITHHOLDING ALLOWANCES AND METHODS. Every employee must file an employee's withholding allowance certificate (Form W-4), which lists the employee's mar-

[59] Sec. 3403. Employers are liable for payment of the full amount of withholdings that must be withheld and paid to the IRS. In addition, responsible individuals (e.g., corporate officers, directors, and consultants) may be held personally liable for payment of the tax. (See *Renate Schiff v. U.S.*, 69 AFTR 2d 92-804, 92-1 USTC ¶50,248 (D.C. NV, 1992), *Ted E. Tsouprake v. U.S.*, 69 AFTR 2d 92-821, 92-1 USTC ¶50,249 (D.C. FL, 1992), and *Ralph M. Guito, Jr. v. U.S.*, 67 AFTR 2d 91-1066, 92-1 USTC ¶ 50,231 (D.C. FL, 1991).

[60] Sec. 6654.

[61] Reg. Sec. 31.3401(a)-1(a)(2).

[62] Reg. Sec. 31.3401(a)(10)-1(a). An employer is liable for FICA tax payments for domestic servants if $1,200 or more is paid to an individual in any calendar year.

[63] Reg. Sec. 31.3402(g)-1(a).

ital status and number of withholding allowances and becomes the basic source of input for the computation of the amount to be withheld. If an employee's circumstances change (e.g., a married taxpayer is divorced or the amount of allowances claimed is reduced), an amended Form W-4 must be filed within 10 days. In general, the employee's Form W-4 is not sent to the IRS unless the number of withholding allowances exceeds 10 or an employee claims an exemption from withholding when his earnings are more than $200 per week.[64] This procedure is intended to prevent employees from avoiding the withholding of income tax on amounts that are otherwise due.

The following procedural rules apply to withholding:

- A $500 civil penalty is imposed for filing false statements (e.g., claiming excessive numbers of withholding allowances).[65]
- An employee may claim an exempt status on Form W-4 if he or she has no income tax liability in the prior year and anticipates none in the current year. High school or college students with jobs earning less than the minimum dollar amount required to file a tax return should take advantage of this exemption. Otherwise, it may be necessary to file a return to obtain a tax refund in the following year. In such a case, the student has, in effect, made an interest-free loan to the government.
- Income tax withholding tables result in a lower amount being withheld if the taxpayer is married.
- An individual may request that additional amounts be withheld if it is anticipated that taxes will be owed at the end of the year and the person does not want to make quarterly estimated payments. It is also possible to claim fewer withholding allowances in order to increase the amount withheld.
- Each additional withholding allowance that is claimed reduces the amount withheld.

REAL-WORLD EXAMPLE

It has been held that the employer's withholding of federal income taxes is not an improper taking of property without due process in violation of the Fifth Amendment. *Michael O. Campbell v. Amax Coal Co.*, 610 F.2d 701, 45 AFTR 2d 80-564, 80-1 USTC ¶9185 (10th Cir., 1980).

Withholding allowances on Form W-4 may be claimed for the same number of personal and dependency exemptions that will be taken on the employee's tax return for the year. An additional special withholding allowance that reflects the standard deduction may be claimed by a taxpayer who has one job or, if married, has a spouse who is unemployed.[66] Additional withholding allowances may be claimed if an individual who has deductions, losses, or credits from a wide variety of sources, including itemized deductions, alimony payments, moving expenses, and losses from a trade or business, rental property, or farm. Tables and a worksheet are provided to compute the amount of the additional withholding allowances.[67]

EXAMPLE I14-30 ▶ Sam and Sally are married and have three dependent children. They file a joint return. Sally is not employed, and Sam does not claim additional withholding allowances for unusually large deductions or tax credits. Sam may claim six allowances (two personal exemptions [for Sam and Sally]) plus three dependency exemptions plus one special withholding allowance to reflect the standard deduction). The special allowance is available because Sally is not employed and Sam has only one job. ◀

STOP & THINK

Question: Many taxpayers believe that they must claim the same number of withholding allowances for withholding purposes as the number of personal exemptions on their income tax return. Why is this not correct?

Solution: While the starting point for determining withholding allowances is taxpayer's marital status and number of personal exemptions, taxpayers are allowed to claim more or less withholding allowances based on their individual situations. According to the IRS, taxpayers may claim additional withholding allowances for two principal reasons: (1) a

[64] Reg. Sec. 31.3402(f)(2)-1.
[65] Sec. 6682(a).
[66] Sec. 3402(f)(1)(E).
[67] Married taxpayers who are both employed may allocate withholding allowances as they see fit as long as the same allowance is not claimed more than once.

taxpayer has high deductions, losses, or credits, or (2) an unmarried taxpayer qualifies for head of household filing status. The withholding tables are constructed by assuming that the taxpayer's deductions will be equal to the standard deduction. Therefore, if a taxpayer has much higher itemized deductions than the standard deduction, the withholding tables may prescribe too much tax to be withheld and the taxpayer would have a large refund at the end of the year. To alleviate this situation, taxpayers are allowed to claim additional withholding allowances so as to prevent a large overpayment. Similarly, the withholding tables only have two categories of marital status, single or married. Thus, if an unmarried taxpayer qualifies for the head of household status, the "single" withholding tables may cause over-withholding of tax.

COMPUTATION OF FEDERAL INCOME TAX WITHHELD. The computation of the amount to be withheld is made by using wage bracket tables or by an optional percentage method of withholding. Both methods produce approximately the same results. Wage bracket tables are available for daily, weekly, biweekly, and monthly payroll periods. Separate tables are used for single (including heads-of-household) and married individuals. The wage bracket table for married persons using a monthly payroll period for wages from $0 through $3,239.99 is located in the 2002 Tax Tables and Rate Schedules on page T-15.

EXAMPLE I14-31 ▶ Henry is married and claims six withholding allowances. His monthly salary is $3,000. The federal income tax withheld per month for 2002 using the wage bracket table on page T-15 is $155. ◀

ESTIMATED TAX PAYMENTS

ADDITIONAL COMMENT

The IRS does not mail reminder statements for the required quarterly estimated payments.

Certain types of income are not subject to withholding (e.g., investment income, rents, income from self-employment, and capital gains). Taxpayers who earn this type of income must make quarterly estimated tax payments.

The purpose of the estimated tax system is to ensure that all taxpayers have paid enough tax by the end of the tax year to cover most of their tax liability. Thus, estimated tax payments may also be required if insufficient tax is being withheld from an individual's salary, pension, or other income (although many taxpayers prefer to file an amended Form W-4 instead and request additional withholding amounts or reduce the number of withholding allowances). The amount of estimated tax is the taxpayer's tax liability

WHAT WOULD YOU DO IN THIS SITUATION?

THE NANNY TAX: DON'T PAY NOW, WORRY LATER

You are a CPA engaged in tax practice and one of your clients is Mr. Throckmorton D. Princeton IV, J.D. He is a senior partner in the prestigious employment litigation firm of Huey, Dewey and Fooey. Mr. Princeton is known for his ruthless style of litigation services.

Things were really rosy for Mr. Princeton until last week, when there was some speculation in the press about his being appointed to a cabinet-level position by the President. A TV news magazine show looked into Mr. Princeton's domestic worker situation. It appears that Mr. Princeton has long engaged in the practice of hiring part-time workers in his household to clean his house, tend to his gardens, walk his dogs, cook his meals, service his car, and nurse him when he is ill. All told, he used over twenty-five people at one time or another over the past year. These workers were all paid as little as possible, and all were asked to sign a contract with Mr. Princeton that declared that they were to be classified as independent contractors. The total amount paid out to these workers added up to $50,000. No payroll taxes of any kind were paid by Mr. Princeton, although he did file Forms 1099 with the IRS. What tax and ethical issues should be considered?

(including self-employment tax and alternative minimum tax) reduced by withholdings, tax credits, and any excess FICA amounts.[68]

ADDITIONAL COMMENT

Red Skelton on the IRS: "I get even with them. I send in an estimated tax form, but I don't sign it. If I've got to guess what I'm making, let them guess who's making it."

REQUIRED ESTIMATED TAX PAYMENTS. For calendar-year individuals, required quarterly payments are due by April 15, June 15, September 15 of the current year, and January 15 of the following year. The estimated tax payments must be the lesser of the following amounts to avoid the imposition of a penalty[69] on the underpaid amount:

- 90% of the tax liability shown on the return for the current year;
- 100% of the tax liability shown on the return for the prior year if the taxpayer's AGI for such prior year was $150,000 or less. If the taxpayer AGI is greater than $150,000, no penalty will be imposed if the taxpayer pays estimated tax payments in the current year equal to a percentage of the preceding year's income tax liability, as follows:

CURRENT YEAR	*PRECEDING YEAR*	*PERCENT OF PRECEDING YEAR'S INCOME TAX LIABILITY*
2001	2000	110%
2002	2001	112%

- 90% of the tax liability shown on the return for the current year computed on an annualized basis.

Further, no penalty is imposed if (1) the estimated tax for the current year is less than $500 or (2) the individual had no tax liability for the prior year.

It should be noted that no penalty is imposed for failure to file quarterly estimated tax payments, even though the IRC includes specific filing requirements. A penalty is imposed only if the taxpayer fails to meet the minimum payment requirements or one of the previously mentioned exceptions does not apply.

EXAMPLE I14-32 ▶ Sarah does not make quarterly estimated tax payments for 2002, even though she has a substantial amount of income not subject to withholding. Her taxable income in 2002 is $140,000. Her actual tax liability (including self-employment taxes and the alternative minimum tax) for 2002 is $40,000. Withholdings from her salary are $30,000. She pays the $10,000 balance due to the IRS with the filing of the 2002 return on April 3, 2003. Sarah's tax liability for 2001 was $27,000. There is no penalty for failure to make the quarterly estimated tax payments because she meets one or more of the exceptions relating to the minimum payment requirement. Although the first exception is not met because her $30,000 of withholdings (plus zero estimated tax payments) is less than 90% of her $40,000 tax liability for 2002 ($30,000 ÷ $40,000 = 75%), she meets the second exception because the $30,000 of withholdings is more than 100% of her $27,000 tax liability for 2001. If Sarah's AGI for 2001 was more than $150,000, the second exception safe harbor amount would be 112% (instead of 100%) of the prior year's tax or $30,240 ($27,000 × 1.12). Because the $30,000 of withholding is less than 112% of her $27,000 tax liability, Sarah would not meet the second exception and would be subject to the underpayment penalty. ◀

Form 2210 (see Appendix B) should be completed and submitted with the tax return if a possible underpayment of tax is indicated. This form is used to determine whether one of the exceptions is applicable and, if not, to compute the amount of the underpayment penalty. The actual computation of the underpayment penalty is not shown here because of the length and complexity of the rules. Topic Review I14-3 summarizes the withholding tax and estimated payment requirements.

[68] Excess FICA payments will occur if an employee has more than one employer during the year and the total FICA payments exceed in the aggregate the ceiling on FICA taxes.

[69] Sec. 6654.

Topic Review I14-3

Withholding Taxes and Estimated Payments

Withholding of Taxes

	FICA	Income Tax
When to withhold	All employee earnings up to $84,900 (in 2002) per employer. No ceiling applies to the 1.45% hospital insurance portion of the tax.	All employee wages, salaries, fees, bonuses, commissions, taxable fringe benefits, and so on.[a]
Amount to withhold	7.65% of FICA wages including 1.45% for the hospital insurance portion of the tax. 1.45% for amounts in excess of $84,900 is withheld from the employee's earnings.	Determined by using withholding tables or the percentage method based on an individual's filing status and number of exemptions.

[a]Exceptions are provided for certain nontaxable fringe benefits.

Estimated Tax Payments

- To avoid an underpayment penalty, the estimated tax payments and withholdings for the year must be equal to or exceed any one of the following:
  90% of the tax liability shown on the return for the current year, or 100% of the tax liability shown on the return for the prior year (112% if AGI for the prior year 2001 exceeds $150,000), or 90% of the tax liability shown on the return for the current year computed on an annualized basis.
- The underpayment penalty is not deductible for income tax purposes.
- Form 2210 should be completed and submitted with the tax return if an underpayment is indicated.

Tax Planning Considerations

Avoiding the Alternative Minimum Tax

KEY POINT

The alternative minimum tax can be avoided or its impact lessened by various tax strategies.

Taxpayers with substantial amounts of tax preference items and a corresponding low regular tax liability may be subject to the AMT. These taxpayers need to engage in tax planning in order to minimize or avoid the AMT. Because a liberal exemption is provided for most individuals (i.e., $45,000 for married individuals filing a joint return and $33,750 for single taxpayers and heads-of-households), the timing of certain income and deduction items may result in the full use of the exemption in each year. For example, planning to avoid the AMT may be accomplished by delaying the payment of certain itemized deductions (e.g., state and local taxes) that reduce the regular income tax but do not reduce the AMT. A cash method of accounting taxpayer who defers the payment of state income taxes into the following year triggers an increase in the regular tax for the current year. This increase can eliminate the AMT liability. However, it is necessary to consider the tax effects for both the current and following years because state income taxes are deductible for purposes of the regular tax calculation when the payment is made in the following year. This reduction may affect the AMT calculation in such a year and increase the amount of tax that is owed.

Certain tax-exempt investments generate additional tax preferences for the investor such as interest on private activity bonds. Before such investments are acquired, an investor should determine the impact on his or her AMT.

Avoiding the Underpayment Penalty for Estimated Tax

Many taxpayers find it difficult to estimate their taxes for the purposes of making quarterly estimated payments and are uncertain whether their withholdings and estimated tax will equal or exceed 90% or more of their actual tax liability for the year. A common planning technique to avoid a possible underpayment tax penalty is to make estimated tax payments and withholdings in an amount that is at least 100% (or 112%[70] if AGI was in excess of $150,000 for the prior year) of the actual tax liability for the prior year, thereby meeting one of the exceptions that prevents the underpayment penalty from being imposed. This technique is commonly referred to as a "safe estimate."

EXAMPLE I14-33 ▶ Yong expects his federal income tax withholdings to be $14,000 for 2002 and estimates that his income tax liability will be $24,000. Yong's actual federal income taxes in 2001 were $20,000. If estimated taxes of at least $6,000 are paid during the year, Yong's estimated taxes plus withholding will be at least 100% of his prior year's tax liability ($14,000 + $6,000 = $20,000) and no underpayment penalty is due despite the fact that there is a $4,000 ($24,000 – $20,000) balance due of the actual tax liability. If Yong's AGI was in excess of $150,000 for 2001, his estimated taxes plus withholding must be at least 112% of his 2000 tax liability or $22,400 (1.12 × $20,000) to avoid the underpayment penalty. Thus, his estimated tax payments must be at least $8,400. ◀

CASH-FLOW CONSIDERATIONS

KEY POINT

A taxpayer should avoid making estimated payments that exceed the actual tax liability because the taxpayer is making an interest-free loan to the IRS. Nevertheless, many taxpayers deliberately have excess amounts withheld from their wages or make excessive estimated payments in order to receive a refund. These taxpayers view this strategy as a forced saving plan.

Assuming that the underpayment penalty can be avoided, it is generally preferable to have an underpayment of tax to the government at the time for filing the return rather than to receive a refund resulting from an overpayment of tax. No interest is paid on a refund if the IRS pays the refund within 45 days from the later of the due date of the return or its filing date.[71] In addition, the IRS has, in effect, received an interest-free loan from the taxpayer during the period such overpayment is made. To avoid an overpayment, a taxpayer may file an amended W-4 form and claim additional withholding allowances if the requirements are met (e.g., the taxpayer has unusually large itemized deductions, tax credits, alimony payments, etc.).

If an individual anticipates that her estimated tax payments and withholdings are insufficient to avoid the underpayment penalty, it may be preferable to increase amounts withheld before the end of the tax year (e.g., amounts withheld in the fourth quarter) to avoid the penalty rather than to increase the estimated tax payments.[72] This technique may be advantageous because the penalty is calculated on a quarterly basis, and the withholdings are spread evenly over the year, despite the fact that such increased withholding amounts are paid near the end of the year. The end result is cash-flow savings to the taxpayer. Another way to avoid the underpayment penalty is to accelerate certain deductions (e.g., real estate taxes on a personal residence), by paying such amounts before the end of the tax year. Additionally, otherwise deductible contributions to an IRA made between the end of the tax year and the due date for the tax return may be treated as a deduction for the prior year, thereby avoiding the underpayment penalty (see Chapter I9).

USE OF GENERAL BUSINESS TAX CREDITS

Business tax credits (e.g., the disabled access credit and the work opportunity credit) are combined for the purpose of computing an overall limitation based on the taxpayer's tax liability. Also, an individual's personal tax credits (e.g., the child and dependent care credit) and the foreign tax credit are deducted from the tax liability before the limitations are applied to the general business tax credit. Similarly, the nonrefundable personal tax credits reduce the tax liability before the foreign tax credit limitation is applied. Therefore, it is necessary to consider the priority and interrelated aspects of these credits to ensure that a particular credit is fully used.

FOREIGN TAX CREDITS AND THE FOREIGN EARNED INCOME EXCLUSION

Individuals who accept foreign job assignments should consider the federal income tax implications because U.S. citizens are subject to U.S. tax on their worldwide income. Assuming that certain requirements and limitations are met, an individual may elect to take either a for-

[70] The 112% is applicable if the preceding year is 2001. If the preceding year is 2000, the percentage is 110%. See the text discussion for more details.

[71] Sec. 6611(e).

[72] To completely avoid the underpayment penalty, the tax law generally requires the estimated payments to be made equally on the four installment dates.

eign tax credit or a foreign-earned income exclusion of $80,000 (2002 and future years) with respect to salaries, allowances, and other forms of earned income that are earned while on extended non-U.S. assignments.[73] Any taxes that are paid or accrued with respect to the excluded income are not available as a foreign tax credit. In general, the exclusion is preferable if the effective foreign tax rate is less than the effective U.S. tax rate because the foreign tax credit that can be claimed does not equal the gross U.S. tax owed on the income. If the effective foreign tax rate on the earned income exceeds the effective U.S. tax rate, U.S. taxpayers ordinarily elect not to use the exclusion. Instead, the excess tax credits on earned income are used to offset the U.S. taxes owed on other types of foreign income. Detailed coverage of foreign tax credits and the exclusion is contained in Chapter C16 of the *Prentice Hall's Federal Taxation: Corporations, Partnerships, Estates and Trusts* text.

CHILD AND DEPENDENT CARE CREDIT

ADDITIONAL COMMENT

If the employer provides a child care assistance plan, the taxpayer may lose the benefit of the child and dependent care credit because it is necessary to reduce the amount of expenses eligible for the credit dollar-for-dollar by the amount excluded from gross income under the employer's child care plan.

The child and dependent care credit is increasingly important because a greater percentage of both spouses are now in the labor force as well as the large number of single parent families. Nonworking spouses who are considering employment should evaluate the tax consequences arising from the child and dependent care credit.

It should be noted that certain child and dependent care expenses may qualify as a medical expense (e.g., nursing care for a disabled dependent). Therefore, it is necessary to compare the marginal tax benefit from the additional child and dependent care credit with the marginal tax benefit from the additional medical expense deduction to determine whether the credit is worth more than the deduction. Expenditures in excess of the child and dependent care ceiling amounts ($2,400 for one child or dependent and $4,800 for two or more children or dependents) may also qualify as medical expenses.

EXAMPLE I14-34 ▶ Stacey, a single taxpayer, maintains a household for an incapacitated dependent parent and two children under age 13. Stacey has AGI from alimony of $20,000 and could earn an additional $15,000 working as a secretary. To enable Stacey to be employed, assume that she would incur $4,000 of eligible child care expenses for the children and an additional $4,000 of nursing expenses for the care of her disabled parent. Before considering the tax effects, Stacey's net increase in income from being employed would only be $7,000 ($15,000 earnings − $8,000 of child and dependent care expenses). The tax credit for child and dependent care expenses is $960 ($4,800 × 0.20). The rate is scaled down from 30% to 20% because Stacey's AGI is $35,000 (i.e., the credit rate is reduced by one percentage point for each $2,000 of AGI in excess of $10,000 until it reaches 20% when AGI exceeds $28,000). A portion of the qualified nursing care expenses (i.e., $8,000 − $4,800 = $3,200) that is not used as child and dependent care expenditures may be deducted as medical expenses if they exceed the 7.5% of AGI floor. If Stacey itemizes her deductions and has other medical expenses equal to or greater than 7.5% of AGI and has an average tax rate of 20%, the value of the additional medical deductions is $640 (0.20 × $3,200). Stacey's additional net cash flows from working are only $4,453, consisting of the following:

REAL WORLD EXAMPLE

Many taxpayers do not comply with the tax law when they hire people to care for their children. Zoe Baird withdrew as attorney general nominee when it was disclosed that she had hired illegal aliens to care for her children and had failed to withhold the FICA tax from the employee's wages and to pay the employer's FICA tax.

Gross earnings from employment		$15,000
Minus:	Federal income tax on earnings ($15,000 × 0.20)	(3,000)[a]
	Actual child and dependent care expenses	(8,000)
	FICA taxes (0.0765 × $15,000)	(1,147)
Plus:	Child and dependent care credit	960
	Medical expense tax benefit	640
Cash flow from employment		$ 4,453

[a] A 20% average tax rate was used because more than one tax rate is used to compute Stacey's tax liability.

Consideration should also be given to additional incremental work-related expenditures (e.g., clothing, meals, and commuting expenses) that are not deductible. The income tax and cash flow consequences arising from an employee assistance program for child care or medical expenses should also be considered if a plan is offered to employees. ◀

[73] Sec. 911(a). The foreign income exclusion requirements are discussed in Chapter I4.

COMPLIANCE AND PROCEDURAL CONSIDERATIONS

ALTERNATIVE MINIMUM TAX FILING PROCEDURES

Form 6251 is used by individuals to compute the AMT, and corporations must use Form 4626 (see Appendix B for both forms). Form 6251 must be completed and attached to an individual's tax return in any of the following situations:

- An AMT tax liability actually exists.
- The taxpayer has tax credits that are limited by the tentative minimum tax.
- The AMT base exceeds the exemption amounts and an individual has AMT adjustment or tax preference items.

IRS Publication 909 contains detailed information regarding filing considerations for individuals.

ADDITIONAL COMMENT

The Revenue Reconciliation Act of 1993 raised the AMT rate from 24% to 26% on the first $175,000 of AMTI over the exemption amount and 28% on amounts over $175,000. Because the rate on net capital gains was capped at 28%, taxpayers whose income is primarily from net capital gains are more likely to fall into an AMT position.

WITHHOLDING AND ESTIMATED TAX

Taxpayers who have income taxes withheld from wages, pensions, and so on should receive a Form W-2 (or Form 1099-R for pensions) by January 31. These forms should be attached to the tax return to substantiate the amount of the withholdings. If the form is incorrect, the taxpayer should request a corrected form from the payor.

If an individual makes quarterly estimated tax payments, Form 1040A or Form 1040EZ may not be used. Married individuals may make either joint estimated tax payments or separate estimated tax payments. If joint estimated tax payments are made and the married individuals subsequently file separate returns (e.g., in the case of a divorce that is pending or a divorce completed before the end of the year), the joint estimated tax payments are divided in proportion to each spouse's individual tax if no agreement is reached concerning an appropriate division.

EXAMPLE I14-35 ▶ Allen and Alice are married and make joint estimated tax payments during 2002 of $10,000. Allen and Alice are separated in February 2003 and Alice refuses to file a joint return with Allen for the tax year 2002. Allen's tax liability for 2002 on his separate return is $20,000 and Alice's tax liability on her separate return is $5,000. If no agreement is reached concerning the allocation of the joint estimated payments of $10,000, Alice is entitled to claim $2,000 of the estimated tax payments on her return [($5,000 ÷ $25,000) × $10,000]. The remaining $8,000 is apportioned to Allen. ◀

GENERAL BUSINESS TAX CREDITS

The computation of the business energy credit is made on Form 3468. Individuals must transfer the totals to page 2 of Form 1040. Form 3800 must be filed if any other general business credits are claimed.

PERSONAL TAX CREDITS

KEY POINT

The earned income credit is available even in cases where the taxpayer has no tax liability. The refund of taxes not even paid or incurred is often called a negative income tax.

Personal tax credits are reported on page 2 of Form 1040. These credits are deducted from the taxpayer's tax liability before other credits. The credits section on page 2 of Form 1040 limits the deduction for personal tax credits to the amount of the tax due. Form 2441 (see Appendix B) must be filed to claim the child and dependent care credit. Taxpayers who claim the child and dependent care credit must also include the care provider's name, address, and taxpayer identification number on their tax return. If the caregiver will not provide the required information, the taxpayer has the option to supply the name and address of the caregiver on Form 2441 and attach a statement explaining that the caregiver has refused to provide his or her identification number (TIN). Schedule R of Form 1040 (see Appendix B) is filed to claim the credit for the elderly. An elderly individual may elect to have the IRS compute the tax and the amount of the tax credit.[74]

---

[74] Sec. 6014. See Form 1040 instructions for more reporting details.

The earned income credit is refundable to an individual even if no tax is owed. The IRS will automatically compute the credit amount.[75] However, tax tables to assist in the process are included in IRS instructions to Forms 1040 and 1040A. Schedule EIC of Form 1040 (see Appendix B) is used to compute the credit if Form 1040 is used. If an individual expects to be eligible for the earned income credit, he or she can obtain advance payments of the credit amount by filing Form W-5 (Earned Income Credit Advance Payment Certificate) with his or her employer, who will increase the employee's pay by the amount of the credit. Individuals who receive advance payments must file Form 1040 or Form 1040A to obtain the credit even if they are not required to file a tax return. Taxpayers who are eligible for the earned income credit can not use Form 1040-EZ.

The foreign tax credit for individuals is computed on Form 1116 (see Appendix B). The foreign tax credit amount so determined is entered on page 2 of Form 1040.

PROBLEM MATERIALS

DISCUSSION QUESTIONS

I14-1 Why are most taxpayers not subject to the alternative minimum tax (AMT)?

I14-2 Does the AMT apply if an individual's tax liability as computed under the AMT rules is less than his or her regular tax amount?

I14-3 Which of the following are tax preference items for purposes of computing the individual AMT?
a. Net long-term capital gain
b. Excess depreciation for real property placed in service before 1987
c. Straight-line depreciation on residential real estate acquired in 1992
d. Appreciated element for charitable contributions of capital gain real property

I14-4 Which of the following are individual AMT adjustments?
a. Itemized deductions that are allowed for regular tax purposes but not allowed in computing AMTI
b. Excess of MACRS depreciation over depreciation computed under the alternative depreciation system for real property placed in service after 1986.
c. Excess of MACRS depreciation over depreciation computed under the alternative depreciation system for personal property placed in service after 1986
d. Tax-exempt interest earned on State of Michigan general revenue bonds.

I14-5 Which of the following itemized deductions are deductible when computing the alternative minimum tax for individuals?
a. Charitable contributions
b. Mortgage interest on a personal residence
c. State and local income taxes
d. Interest related to an investment in undeveloped land where the individual has no investment income
e. Medical expenses amounting to 8% of AGI

I14-6 Why are most individuals not subject to the self-employment tax?

I14-7 Tony, who is single and 58 years old, is considering early retirement. He currently has $70,000 salary and $50,000 of profits from a consulting business. What advice would you give Tony relative to the need to make Social Security tax payments if he retires and continues to be actively engaged as a consultant during his retirement?

I14-8 Theresa is a college professor who wants to work for a consulting firm during the summer. She will be working on special projects involving professional development programs. What advantages might accrue to the consulting firm if the engagement is set up as a consulting arrangement rather than an employment contract?

I14-9 Ted and Tina, a married couple, both have self-employment income and file a joint return in 2002. Ted has self-employment income of $20,000 and receives a $30,000 salary from his employer. Tina's has no salary and self-employment income of $10,000.
a. How much self-employment tax is due for Ted and Tina on a joint return?
b. How much, if any, of the self-employment tax payments may be deducted on Ted and Tina's income tax return?

I14-10 Discuss the underlying rationale for the following tax credit items:

[75] Sec. 6695(g) requires preparers to meet due diligence requirements with respect to the earned income credit (EIC). If the EIC is incorrectly computed or overlooked, the *preparer* could be subject to a $100 penalty.

a. Foreign tax credit
b. Research credit
c. Business energy credit
d. Work opportunity credit
e. Child and dependent care credit
f. Earned income credit
g. HOPE scholarship credit
h. Disabled access credit
i. Empowerment Zone employment credit
j. Adoption credit

I14-11 If Congress is considering a tax credit or deduction as an incentive to encourage certain activities, is a $40 tax credit more valuable than a $200 tax deduction for a taxpayer with a 15% marginal rate? a 27% marginal rate?

I14-12 What are the more significant tax credit items included in the computation of the general business tax credit?

I14-13 Discuss the limitations that have been imposed on the claiming of the general business tax credit including the following:
a. Overall ceiling limitation based on the tax liability
b. Priority of general business and personal credits
c. Carryback and carryover of unused credits (including the application of the FIFO method).

I14-14 Wayne is considering a foreign assignment for two years. He will earn approximately $90,000 in the foreign country and will be eligible for either the foreign tax credit or the earned income exclusion. The average tax rate on Wayne's earnings if fully taxable under U.S. law would be 30%. The average tax rate for the foreign salary is 20% under the foreign country's laws.
a. Discuss in general terms the computation of the foreign tax credit and its limitation.
b. Would Wayne be better off electing the foreign tax credit or the earned income exclusion? Explain.

I14-15 King Corporation is expanding its business and is planning to hire four additional employees at an annual labor cost of $12,000 each. What will the tax consequences be if King hires employees who are eligible for the work opportunity tax credit?

I14-16 Queen Corporation has been in business since 1979. During the preceding year the company had 25 full-time employees and gross receipts of $8,000,000. During the current year Queen spent $10,000 to install access ramps for disabled individuals. Is Queen Corporation eligible for the disabled access credit? If so, what is the credit amount and the basis reduction (if any) for the depreciable property?

I14-17 Discuss the special tax rules that apply to the tax credit for rehabilitation expenditures including the following:
a. Types of eligible expenditures
b. Applicable tax credit rates
c. Restrictions on depreciation methods
d. Calculation of basis for expenditures
e. Potential recapture of the credit

I14-18 What types of business property qualify for the business energy credit?

I14-19 What is the underlying reason for enactment of most of the personal tax credits?

I14-20 Discuss the difference between a refundable tax credit and a nonrefundable tax credit. Give at least one example of each type of credit.

I14-21 If an individual is unemployed and has no earned income, is it possible to receive a child and dependent care credit for otherwise qualifying child and dependent care expenses? Explain.

I14-22 Discuss the major differences between the HOPE scholarship credit and the lifetime learning credit. Include in your discussion the type of taxpayers that would likely qualify for each of the credits.

I14-23 What is the maximum child and dependent care credit available to an individual who has $6,000 of qualifying child care expenses and two or more qualifying children or incapacitated dependents?

I14-24 Vivian is a single taxpayer with two children who qualify for the child and dependent care credit. She incurred $5,000 of qualifying child care expenses during the current year. She also received $3,000 in reimbursements from her employer from a qualified employee dependent care assistance program. What is the maximum child and dependent care credit available to Vivian if her AGI is $21,000?

I14-25 The adoption credit is intended to assist taxpayers with the financial burden of adopting children.
a. Discuss how the credit is computed.
b. Why did Congress impose a phase-out of the credit for taxpayers based on AGI?

I14-26 Alice is a single mother, 37 years old, and has two qualifying children, ages 3 and 6. She receives $3,600 alimony and earns $9,000 in wages resulting in $12,600 of AGI in 2002. Is Alice eligible for the earned income credit? If so, is it possible for her to receive advance payments of the credit amounts rather than receiving a tax refund when the tax return is filed?

I14-27 Why are most elderly people unable to qualify for the tax credit for the elderly?

I14-28 If an employer fails to withhold federal income taxes and FICA taxes on wages or fails to make payment to the IRS, what adverse tax consequences may result? May corporate officers or other corporate officials be held responsible for the underpayment?

I14-29 Taxpayers are permitted to contribute money into qualified retirement plans and receive very favorable tax benefits. Now Congress has provided further incentives to contribute money into such plans by enacting the Qualified Retirement Savings Contributions Credit.
a. Why did Congress enact this credit when such contributions already receive favorable tax treatment?
b. Briefly describe how the credit is computed.

I14-30 Although Virginia is entitled to five personal and dependency exemptions, she claims only one withholding allowance on Form W-4.

a. Is it permissible to claim fewer allowances than an individual is entitled to?
b. Why would an individual claim fewer allowances?
c. Is it possible for Virginia to claim more than five withholding allowances?

I14-31 Mario is a college student who had no income tax liability in the prior year and expects to have no tax liability for the current year.

a. What steps should Mario take to avoid having amounts being withheld from his summer employment wages?
b. What are the cash-flow implications to Mario if the employer withholds federal income taxes?

I14-32 What is backup withholding? What is its purpose?

I14-33 In March 2002, Vincent anticipates that his actual tax liability for 2002 tax year will be $12,000 and that the federal income taxes withheld from his salary will be $9,000. Thus, when he files his 2002 income tax return in 2003, he will have a $3,000 balance due. His actual federal income tax liability for 2001 was $8,000 and his AGI for 2001 was less than $150,000.

a. Is Vincent required to make estimated tax payments in 2002?
b. If no estimated tax payments are made, will Vincent be subject to an underpayment penalty if the actual tax liability for the 2002 tax year is $12,000? Why or why not?
c. Will Vincent be subject to an underpayment penalty if his actual tax liability for 2002 is instead $25,000? Why?

I14-34 What tax planning strategy can you suggest to avoid the penalty for underpayment of estimated tax for an individual who has increasing levels of income each year and is uncertain regarding the amount of his or her estimated taxable income for any given year?

I14-35 From a cash-flow perspective, why is it generally preferable to have an underpayment of tax (assuming there is no underpayment penalty imposed) rather than an overpayment of tax?

I14-36 Why do many taxpayers intentionally overpay their tax through withholdings so as to obtain a tax refund?

ISSUE IDENTIFICATION QUESTIONS

I14-37 Daryl is an executive who has an annual salary of $120,000. He is considering early retirement so that he can pursue a career as a management consultant. Daryl estimates that he could earn approximately $80,000 annually from his consulting business. What tax issues should Daryl consider?

I14-38 Jennifer recently received a check for $30,000 and securities with an FMV of $200,000 from her former husband pursuant to a divorce. The $30,000 represents alimony and the securities were transferred pursuant to the property settlement. The property settlement is nontaxable to Jennifer. Assuming the alimony is taxable and no income taxes are being withheld, what tax issues should Jennifer consider?

I14-39 Coastal Corporation is planning an expansion of its production facilities and is considering whether to hire additional employees from economically disadvantaged groups so as to be able to avail itself of the targeted jobs credit. The company plant is not located in an Empowerment Zone. New employees are paid approximately $18,000 per year. If economically disadvantaged employees are hired, additional job training expenses of $5,000 per employee will be required. What tax issues should Coastal consider with regard to the hiring and training of its new employees?

PROBLEMS

I14-40 *AMT Computation.* William and Maria are a married couple, have no children, and report the following items in 2002:

Taxable income	$70,000
Tax preferences	20,000
AMT adjustments related to itemized deductions	30,000
Regular tax liability	12,696

a. What is William's AMT liability in the current year?
b. What is William's AMT liability in the current year if he is instead a single taxpayer and his regular tax liability is $15,315 rather than $12,696?

I14-41 *AMT Computation.* Jose, a single taxpayer with no dependents, has AGI of $180,000 and reports the following items in 2002:

Taxable income	$130,000
Tax preferences	40,000
AMT adjustments related to itemized deductions	30,000
Regular tax liability	33,315

What is Jose's AMT liability in the current year?

I14-42 *AMT Computation.* Harry and Mary Prodigious are married and have 12 children. With the large number of children, they live in a very austere manner. Harry works for a local engineering firm and earns a salary of $80,000 in 2002. Mary does not work outside the home. The only other income is interest and dividends in the amount of $3,000. They claim the standard deduction in filing their 2002 return and have no tax preferences or adjustments for purposes of the AMT.

a. Compute Harry and Mary's regular tax and AMT under the facts above.
b. Comment on the tax policy implications of your answer in a. above.

I14-43 *AMT Adjustments and Computation of Tax.* Allen, a single taxpayer, reports the following items on his 2002 federal income tax return:

Adjusted gross income	$75,000
Taxable income	48,000
Regular tax liability	9,306
Tax preferences	20,000
Itemized deductions including:	
Charitable contributions	7,500
Medical expenses (before AGI floor)	10,000
Mortgage interest on personal residence	10,000
State income taxes	5,000
Real estate taxes	8,000

a. What is the amount of Allen's AMT adjustments related to the itemized deductions?
b. What is Allen's AMT liability for the current year?

I14-44 *Self-Employment Tax.* In the current year, Amelia receives wages of $40,000 and net earnings from a small unincorporated business of $50,000.

a. What is the amount of Amelia's self-employment tax and *for* AGI deduction relative to her self-employment tax?
b. How would your answer to a. change if Amelia's wages were $70,000 rather than $40,000?

I14-45 *Self-Employment Tax.* Arnie and Angela are married and file a joint return in the current year. Arnie is a partner in a public accounting firm. His share of the partnership's income in the current year is $40,000, and he receives guaranteed payments of $30,000. Angela receives wages of $50,000 from a large corporation. What is each taxpayer's self-employment tax amount? (Hint: Guaranteed payments received from a partnership are considered self-employment income.)

I14-46 *Self-Employment Tax.* Anita, a single taxpayer, reports the following items for the current year:

Salary (subject to withholding)	$20,000
Income for serving on the Board of Directors for XYZ Corporation	10,000
Consulting income	10,000
Expenses related to consulting practice	(15,000)

a. What is the amount of Anita's self-employment tax?
b. How would your answer to Part a change if Anita's salary were instead $88,000?

I14-47 *Computation of Tax Credits.* Becky's tentative tax credits for the current year include the following:

Work opportunity credit	$ 1,000
Child and dependent care credit	960
Research credit	14,000
Business energy credit	600
Total	$16,560

Becky's regular tax liability before credits is $14,000. Assume that there is no alternative minimum tax liability.

a. What is the amount of allowable personal tax credits?
b. What is the amount of allowable business tax credits?
c. What treatment is accorded to the unused tax credits for the current year?

I14-48 ***Child and Dependent Care Credit.*** In each of the following independent situations, determine the amount of the child and dependent care tax credit. (Assume that both taxpayers are employed.)

a. Brad and Bonnie are married and file a joint return. Brad and Bonnie have earned income of $40,000 and $14,000, respectively. Their combined AGI is $52,000. They have two children ages 10 and 12 and employ a live-in nanny at an annual cost of $9,000.
b. Assume the same facts as in Part a, except that Brad and Bonnie employ Bonnie's mother as the live-in nanny. Bonnie's mother is not claimed as a dependent by her children.
c. Bruce is divorced and has two children ages 10 and 16. He has AGI and earned income of $27,000. Bruce incurs qualifying child care expenses of $8,000 during the year which were incurred equally for both children. Bruce's employer maintains an employee dependent care assistance program. $1,000 was paid to Bruce from this program and excluded from Bruce's gross income.
d. Buddy and Candice are married and file a joint return. Their combined AGI is $50,000. Buddy earns $46,000, and Candice's salary from a part-time job is $4,000. They incur $5,000 of qualifying child care expenses for a day-care facility for their two children, ages 2 and 4.

I14-49 ***Adoption Credit.*** Brad and Valerie decided to adopt a child and contacted an adoption agency in August 2001. After extensive interviews and other requirements (such as financial status, etc.), Brad and Valerie were approved as eligible parents to adopt a child. The agency indicated that it might take up to two years to find a proper match. In November, 2002, the adoption became final and Brad and Valerie adopted an infant daughter (not a special needs child). Below is a list of expenses that they incurred:

2001:	Agency fees (first installment)	$5,000
	Travel expenses for interviews, etc.	1,500
	Publications for prospective adoptive parents	300
	Legal fees connected with the adoption	1,000
	Kennel fees for dog while on adoption trips	250
2002:	Agency fees (final installment)	$3,000
	Travel expenses	400
	Court costs for adoption	200
	Kennel fees	100
	Nursery furniture (baby's room) and supplies	2,000

Brad and Valerie's AGI for 2001 was $70,000 and in 2002 was $90,000.

a. Compute Brad and Valerie's qualified adoption expenses for 2000 and 2001.
b. Compute Brad and Valerie's adoption credit. What year(s) may the credit be taken?
c. Would your answer to b. change if the adopted child was a special needs child?

I14-50 ***HOPE Scholarship Credit and Lifetime Learning Credit.*** John and Mary, a married couple who file a joint return, have two dependent children in college, Jeff and Brooke. Jeff attends Pepper College, a private, liberal arts college, and Brooke attends State U. During the calendar year 2002, Jeff was a sophomore during the Spring Semester, 2002 and a junior during the Fall Semester, 2002. Brooke was a freshman during the Fall Semester, 2002 and was in high school during the Spring Semester, 2002. Below are the college expenses paid by John and Mary for Jeff and Brooke during 2002:

	Spring Semester, 2002 (Paid in January, 2002)		Fall Semester, 2002 (Paid in August, 2002)	
	Jeff	*Brooke*	*Jeff*	*Brooke*
Tuition	$4,500		$4,800	$1,200
Laboratory fees	500		500	0
Student activity fees	100		100	100
Books	400		350	400
Room and board	3,000		3,200	3,500

a. Compute any education credits that John and Mary may claim in 2002 assuming that neither Jeff nor Brooke receive any type of financial assistance and John and Mary's modified AGI is less than $80,000.
b. Would your answer in a. change if Jeff received an academic scholarship of $2,500 for each semester in 2002?
c. How would your answer in a. change if John and Mary's modified AGI for 2002 was $90,000?
d. How would your answer in a. change if Jeff was a junior during the Spring Semester, 2002 and a senior during the Fall Semester, 2002?

I14-51 *Tax Credit for the Elderly.* Caroline, age 66 and single, receives the following income items for the current year:

Social Security payments	$ 3,000
Fully taxable pension	4,000
Dividend and interest income	4,500
Total	$11,500

Caroline's tax liability (before credits) is $300 in the current year.
a. What is Caroline's tentative tax credit for the elderly (before the tax liability limitation is applied) in the current year?
b. What is the amount of Caroline's allowable tax credit for the elderly in the current year?

I14-52 *Business Tax Credit Carrybacks and Carryovers.* In 2002, Large Corporation, which was incorporated in 1996, has an unused general business tax credit of $40,000 in 1999. The following schedule shows the amount of business tax credits earned and used for the period 1996–2002:

	Credits Earned During the Year	*Credit Limitation for the Carryback or Carryover Year*
1996	$40,000	$40,000
1997	30,000	40,000
1998	25,000	25,000
1999	60,000	20,000
2000	20,000	22,000
2001	15,000	20,000
2002	15,000	15,000

The excess credits for 1999 were carried back to 1997.
a. How much of the unused 1999 credit may be carried back to prior years?
b. What is the amount of the unused credit that is carried forward to 2000, 2001, 2002, and 2003? In what years are the credits used? Identify the tax years in which the credit carryovers are earned.

I14-53 *Foreign Tax Credit.* Laser Corporation, a U.S. corporation, has a foreign office that conducts business in France. Laser pays foreign taxes of $40,000 on foreign-source taxable income of $100,000. Its U.S.-source taxable income is $200,000, total U.S. taxable income of $300,000, and the total U.S. tax liability (before reductions for the foreign tax credit) is $100,250. What is Laser's foreign tax credit? What is Laser's foreign tax credit carryback or carryover?

I14-54 *Work Opportunity Credit.* Last Corporation hires two economically disadvantaged youths (qualified for the work opportunity credit) in August of the current year. Each employee receives $8,000 of wages in the current year. Salaries and wages paid to other employees in the current year are $50,000. Last Corporation has a regular tax liability of $50,000 in the current year before deducting its tax credits assuming the appropriate deduction is claimed for the youths' salaries. Its tentative minimum tax is $10,000. Business tax credits other than the work opportunity credit amount to $50,000 in the current year.
a. What is Last Corporation's tentative work opportunity credit (before limitations) in the current year?
b. What is Last Corporation's total general business credit that is used in the current year? What amount is available for carryover or carryback?
c. What is Last Corporation's deduction for salaries and wages paid to the two youths?

I14-55 *Empowerment Zone Employment Credit.* Acorn Corporation operates its business in an Empowerment Zone and John, one of its employees, lives in the zone. In the current year

John received $12,000 in wages. In addition, Acorn incurred $4,000 of training expenses related to John's employment.

a. What is Acorn Corporation's tentative Empowerment Zone credit (before any limitations on the general business credit are considered)?
b. What is Acorn Corporation's deduction for wages paid to John?

I14-56 ***Rehabilitation Tax Credit.*** Bob acquires a certified historic structure in the current year to be used as an office for his business. He pays $20,000 for the building (exclusive of the land) and spends $40,000 for renovation costs.

a. What is the rehabilitation tax credit (before limitations)?
b. What depreciation method(s) must be used for the property?
c. What is the basis of the building for MACRS depreciation purposes?

I14-57 ***Earned Income Credit.*** Carolyn is single and has a dependent child, age 6, who lived with her for the entire year. She has earned income of $12,000 of wages and $4,000 of alimony in the current year. Her AGI is $16,000.

a. What is Carolyn's tentative earned income credit (before the phase-out reduction is applied)?
b. What is Carolyn's allowable earned income credit?
c. If Carolyn has no income tax liability (before the earned income credit is subtracted), is she entitled to a tax refund in the current year?

I14-58 ***Earned Income Credit.*** Jose is single with no qualifying children. He has $7,800 of wages during the current year and is otherwise eligible for the earned income credit. Jose has $200 of interest income and no *for* AGI deductions. His AGI is $8,000.

a. What is Jose's tentative earned income credit before the phase-out reduction is applied?
b. What is Jose's allowable earned income credit?
c. If Jose has no income tax liability (before the earned income credit is subtracted), is he entitled to a refund for the current year?
d. Would your answer to b. change if Jose had dividend and interest income of $3,000 during the taxable year?

I14-59 ***Penalties for Nonpayment of Withholding and FICA Taxes.*** Lake Corporation has some severe cash-flow problems. You are the company's financial and tax consultant. The treasurer of the company has informed you that the company has failed to make FICA and federal income tax withholding payments for both the employer and employee contributions to the IRS for a period of approximately six months.

a. What advice can you give to the company treasurer regarding the nonpayment of taxes?
b. Can the liability for payment of the taxes extend to parties other than the corporation? Explain.

I14-60 ***Exemptions from Withholding.*** Which of the following categories of individuals or income are exempt from the federal withholding tax requirements?

a. Domestic servants
b. Independent contractors
c. Newspaper carriers over age 18
d. Bonuses
e. Commissions
f. Vacation pay
g. Tips under $20 per month from a single employer

I14-61 ***Withholding Exemptions.*** Barry is a college student who is employed as a waiter during the summer. He earns approximately $1,500 during the summer and estimates that he will not be required to file a tax return and will have no federal income tax liability. Last year, however, he made $6,000 and was required to file a return and pay $400 in taxes. Barry is single and is supported by his parents. He has no dependents and does not have any other sources of income or deductions.

a. Can Barry claim an exempt status on Form W-4 for withholding purposes?
b. Can Barry claim more than one exemption on Form W-4 (e.g., additional withholding allowances or the standard deduction allowance) to minimize the amount withheld? Explain.

I14-62 ***Witholding Allowances.*** Bart's spouse is not employed. They plan to file a joint return. Bart obtains a new job and is asked to fill out a Form W-4. His monthly gross earnings will be $3,000. Bart, who has four dependent children, can claim three additional withholding allowances because he is obligated to pay substantial alimony to his ex-wife.

a. What is the correct number of withholding allowances that he may claim on Form W-4?

b. What is the amount of federal income tax to be withheld using the wage bracket tables (see withholding table on page T-15)?
c. What disclosure procedures must Bart's employer follow if Bart claims more than ten allowances?

I14-63 *Estimated Tax Requirements.* Anna does not make quarterly estimated tax payments even though she has substantial amounts of income that are not subject to withholding. In 2001, Anna's tax liability was $18,000. This year, in 2002, Anna's actual tax liability is $30,000, although only $18,200 was withheld from her salary. Anna's AGI for 2001 was $135,000.
a. Is Anna subject to the underpayment penalty? Why?
b. If Anna's withholdings were only $15,000, would she be subject to the underpayment penalty? Why?
c. If Anna is subject to an underpayment penalty, can she deduct this amount as interest? Explain.

I14-64 *Estimated Tax Underpayment Penalty.* Anne's estimated tax payments for 2002 are $14,000 and her withholdings amount to $12,000. Anne's actual tax liability for 2001 and 2002 are $25,000 and $30,000, respectively. Her income is earned evenly throughout the current year. Anne's AGI for 2001 was $160,000. Is Anne subject to the underpayment penalty? Explain.

COMPREHENSIVE PROBLEM

I14-65 Mike Webb, married to Nancy Webb, is employed by a large pharmaceutical company and earns a salary. In addition, Mike is an entrepreneur at heart and has two small businesses on the side. One business is a consulting business where Mike provides financial and retirement assistance to pharmacists. The consulting business is doing very well. The other business involves the manufacture of Christmas novelties in China and reselling the products in gift shops in the U.S. This business, operated as a sole proprietorship, is struggling. However, Mike feels the Christmas novelty business has great potential. In 2002, Mike had the following information for tax purposes:

Salary			$140,000
Consulting practice:	Revenues	$65,000	
	Ordinary expenses	12,000	53,000
Sole proprietorship:	Revenues	$22,000	
	Ordinary Expenses	40,000	(18,000)
Interest and dividends (none tax-exempt)			12,000
LTCG		$24,000	
STCL		(4,000)	20,000
Itemized deductions:			
State and local taxes		$14,000	
Real estate taxes		5,000	
Mortgage interest on personal residence		10,000	
Charitable contributions		8,000	37,000
Child care expenses: Mike and his wife, Nancy, have two children, ages 13 and 11 and pay child care expenses of $3,000 per year for each child, for a total of $6,000. Nancy is not employed, but is a full-time student at University of South Carolina. She has gone back to school to get her degree in Accounting. Both children are dependents of Mike and Nancy.			
Federal income tax withheld from salary			28,000
Estimated taxes paid for 2002 during the year			12,000

Mike and Nancy's AGI in 2002 was $175,000 and actual federal income tax liability for 2001 was $35,000.

Compute Mike and Nancy's federal income tax liability for 2002, including self-employment taxes and AMT, if applicable. Also, are Mike and Nancy subject to any underpayment penalties for 2002?

TAX STRATEGY PROBLEM

I14-66 Mike and Linda Foley are married and file a joint income tax return. Mike is a lawyer and a partner in the firm of Foley & Looby, Attorneys at Law. Mike is a 50% partner in the firm along with his partner, John Looby who is the other 50% partner. Foley & Looby (F&L) currently rent office space in a prestigious building and pay rent of $6,000 per month or $72,000 per year for their 4,000 square foot office. Thus, the firm pays $18 per square foot per year. As no equity is being generated by paying rent, Mike and John are considering buying an office building. They have two buildings under consideration, as follows:

Building #1

Building #1 is a relatively new building and has 10,000 square feet of space. The new building can be purchased for a total price of $1,000,000. F&L would only use 4,000 square feet of the space and have other businesses that would rent the 6,000 from F&L for $15 per square foot per year. Maintenance costs would amount to approximately $10 per square foot per year. The building is in excellent condition and is ready to be moved in to immediately and would require very little other outlays by F&L.

Building #2

Building #2 is located in the downtown area in a certified historic district and would qualify as a certified historic structure. This building, nearly 80 years old, also has 10,000 square feet and, like Building #1, the other 6,000 square feet can be rented to other tenants at $15 per square foot per year. However, Building #2 is not in as good a condition as the above building. The purchase price of the building would be $600,000 and Mike and John estimated that approximately $400,000 would have to be invested in capital expenditures to make the building suitable for their business. After the significant capital expenditures, F&L estimate the maintenance costs to be similar to Building #1, or $10 per square foot per year.

Both buildings can be 100% financed at 8% annual interest rate for 15 years. The annual payment on the $1,000,000 mortgage would be $117,000. Also, assume both buildings will appreciate at a rate of 8% per year.

Mike Foley and John Looby have come to you as their financial and tax advisor to help them make the decision as to which building to purchase. If the buildings are equally desirable from a non-financial and non-tax standpoint, what is the best decision for Mike and John? That is, should they stay where they are and rent or purchase one of the two buildings? Assume both Mike and John are in the top 38.6% marginal tax bracket.

TAX FORM/RETURN PREPARATION PROBLEMS

I14-67 Warren (SSN 123-45-6789) and Alice (SSN 987-65-4321) Williams have the following tax credits for 2001:

General business credits	$12,140
Child and dependent care credit	960
Total	$13,100

Warren and Alice Williams have two children, 5 and 7, and incur $5,000 of qualifying child care expenses ($2,500 for day care and $2,500 for a nurse). Warren had earned income of $90,000; Alice's earned income was $25,000 and their AGI is $116,988. Their itemized deductions are $14,200, taxable income is $91,188, and regular tax liability (before credits) is $18,417. Disregard any limitations that might be imposed by the tentative minimum tax. Complete Form 2441, Form 3800 and the Tax Credits section on page 2 of Form 1040.

I14-68 Harold Milton (SSN 574-45-5477) is single and had the following income and deductions for 2001:

Salary	$177,000	State income taxes	18,000
Interest income	12,000	Mortgage interest expense on residence	19,000
Dividend income	3,000	Interest expense on car loan	3,000
IRA contribution	2,000	Real estate taxes on residence	2,000
Tax-exempt interest from private activity bonds issued in 1990	24,000	Miscellaneous deductions (before the 2% AGI floor)	7,000
Charitable contributions	27,000	Income taxes withheld	20,000
		Estimated tax payments ($2,500 per quarter)	10,000

Complete Milton's 2001 Form 1040, Schedule A, Form 6251 and Form 2210. Milton had AGI in 2000 of $200,000 and his 2000 income tax liability was $46,000. (Note: Milton is eligible to use the Short Method on Form 2210)

CASE STUDY PROBLEMS

I14-69 Barbara was divorced in 1999. However, the final property settlement and determination of alimony payments was not made until February, 2002 because of extended litigation. Barbara received a $20,000 payment of back alimony in March 2002 and will receive monthly alimony payments of $2,000 for the period April through December, 2002. Last year, in 2001, Barbara's income consisted of $15,000 salary and $2,000 of taxable interest income. She used the standard deduction and had no dependents. In 2001, Barbara's tax liability was $1,900. In 2002, she expects to continue working at an annual salary of $15,000 and will have $2,000 of interest income in 2002. Her federal income taxes withheld from her salary in 2002 will be $1,500. Her monthly alimony payments of $2,000 are also expected to continue for an indefinite period.

In early April 2002 Barbara requests your advice regarding the payment of quarterly estimated taxes for 2002. Prepare a memo to your client that discusses these requirements, including any possible penalties for not making quarterly payments and nontax issues such as cash-flow and investment income decisions.

I14-70 Chips-R-Us is a computer technology corporation that designs hardware and software for use in large businesses. The corporation regularly pays individuals to install programs and give advice to different companies that buy their software. In the current year, Simone, a computer expert, was sent to a customer of Chips-R-Us by the corporation to perform computer services. Simone is not a regular employee of the corporation and the corporation did not train Simone for the task. Simone keeps track of the time spent on the job at the customer and reports to the corporation, which pays Simone for her services. The corporation specifies the work to be done for their client. The corporation can also replace Simone with another individual if her work is not satisfactory. Chips-R-Us treats Simone as an independent contractor for employment tax purposes. In the current year the IRS challenges the corporation that it has failed to remit FICA taxes and income taxes that should have been withheld with respect to Simone's employment. Chips-R-Us refuses to pay the amount, stating that it is not required to do so because Simone is not an employee of the corporation. What will be the likely outcome of the IRS's decision concerning the status of Simone as an employee or independent contractor? Who may be liable for payment of the employment taxes, interest, and penalties to the government? What ethical responsibilities should be followed in the remittance of taxes on behalf of an employee?

TAX RESEARCH PROBLEM

I14-71 Lean Corporation was incorporated in 1981 by Bruce Smith, who has served as an officer and member of the Board of Directors. Carl Jones has served as the secretary-treasurer of the company as a convenience to his friend Bruce Smith. He acted as a part-time bookkeeper but did not run the everyday business affairs and paid only the bills he was instructed to pay. Carl was an authorized signatory for the corporate bank accounts but had no final control over expenditures.

Beginning in the last quarter of 2001, the company failed to pay all of the taxes withheld from employees and the employer's share of FICA taxes to the IRS. Despite this delinquency, the corporation continued to pay other creditors, including its employees, in preference to the IRS.

In January, 2002, Lean Corporation entered into an installment agreement with the IRS to keep current on its withholding taxes and to make payments on the past due balance until paid in full. The company subsequently defaulted on the agreement in April, 2002. During this period, Bruce Smith was serving as chief financial officer and was a member of the Board of Directors. He had the authority to make policy decisions. He was responsible for negotiating the installment agreement with the IRS and the decision to default on the agreement.

Who is liable for the penalty for the nonpayment of the payroll tax withholdings?

A partial list of research sources is

- Sec. 6672
- *Ernest W. Carlson v. U.S.*, 67 AFTR 2d 91-1104, 91-1 USTC ¶50,262 (D.C. UT, 1991)

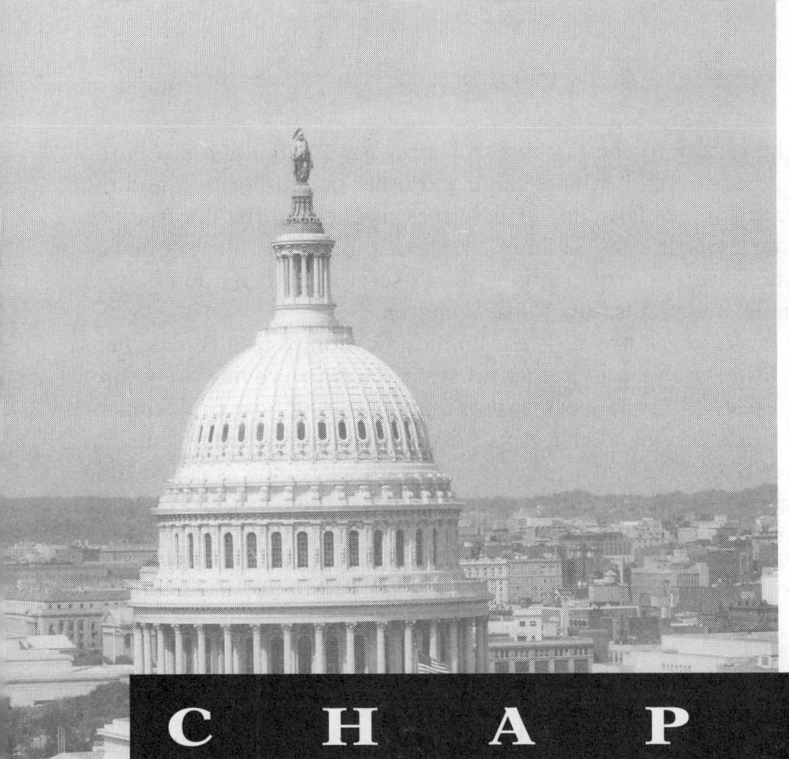

1

TAX RESEARCH

LEARNING OBJECTIVES

After studying this chapter, you should be able to

1. Describe the steps in the tax research process
2. Explain how the facts affect the tax consequences
3. Identify the sources of tax law and understand the authoritative value of each
4. Use tax services to research an issue
5. Use a citator to assess tax authorities
6. Understand the basics of computerized tax research
7. Understand the guidelines that CPAs in tax practice should follow
8. Prepare work papers and communications to clients

CHAPTER OUTLINE

Overview of Tax Research...1-2
Steps in the Tax Research Process...1-3
Importance of the Facts to the Tax Consequences...1-5
The Sources of Tax Law...1-7
Tax Services...1-25
Citators...1-28
Computers as a Research Tool...1-34
Statements on Standards for Tax Services...1-35
Sample Work Papers and Client Letter...1-38

This chapter introduces the reader to the tax research process. Its major focus is the sources of the tax law (i.e., the Internal Revenue Code and other tax authorities) and the relative weights given to each source. The chapter describes the steps in the tax research process and places particular emphasis on the importance of the facts to the tax consequences. It also describes the features of frequently used tax services and computer-based tax research resources. Finally, it explains how to use a citator.

The end product of the tax research process—the communication of results in a client letter—also is discussed. This text uses a hypothetical set of facts to provide a comprehensive illustration of the process. Sample work papers demonstrating how to document the results of the research efforts are included in Appendix A. In addition, a supplemental explanation of the computerized tax research process and available resources is available for download at *www.prenhall.com/phtax*. The text also discusses the American Institute of Certified Public Accountants' (AICPA's) *Statements on Standards for Tax Services,* which provide guidance for CPAs in tax practice. These statements are reproduced in Appendix E.

OVERVIEW OF TAX RESEARCH

Tax research is the process of solving a tax-related problem by applying tax law to a specific set of facts. Sometimes it involves researching several issues and often is conducted to determine tax policy. For example, policy-oriented research would determine the extent (if any) to which the amount contributed to charitable organizations would likely change if such contributions were no longer deductible. This type of tax research usually is performed by economists to assess the effects of government actions.

Tax research also is conducted to determine the tax consequences of specific transactions to a particular taxpayer. For example, client-oriented research would determine whether Smith Corporation could deduct a particular expenditure as a trade or business expense. This type of research generally is conducted by accounting and law firms for the benefit of their clients. This text considers only the latter type of research.

ADDITIONAL COMMENT

Closed-fact situations allow the tax advisor the least amount of flexibility. Because the facts are already established, the tax advisor must develop the best solution possible within certain predetermined constraints.

Client-oriented tax research is performed in one of two contexts:

1. **Closed-fact or tax compliance situations:** The client contacts the tax advisor after completing a transaction or while preparing a tax return. In such situations, the tax consequences can be costly because the facts cannot be modified to obtain more favorable results.

EXAMPLE C1-1 ▶ Tom informs Carol, his tax advisor, that on November 4 of the current year, he sold land held as an investment for $500,000 cash. His basis in the land was $50,000. On November 9, Tom reinvested the sales proceeds in another plot of investment land costing $500,000. This is a closed-fact situation. Tom wants to know the amount and the character of the gain (if any) he must recognize. Because Tom solicits the tax advisor's advice after the sale and reinvestment occur, the opportunity for tax planning is limited. For example, the opportunity to defer taxes by using a like-kind exchange or an installment sale has been lost. ◀

ADDITIONAL COMMENT

Open-fact or tax-planning situations give a tax advisor flexibility to structure transactions to accomplish the client's objectives. In this type of situation, a creative tax advisor can save taxpayers dollars through effective tax planning.

2. **Open-fact or tax-planning situations:** Before structuring or concluding a transaction, the client contacts the tax advisor to discuss tax planning opportunities. Tax-planning situations generally are more difficult and challenging because the tax advisor must bear in mind the client's tax and nontax objectives. Most clients will not engage in a transaction if it is inconsistent with their nontax objectives even though it minimizes their taxes

EXAMPLE C1-2 ▶ Diane seeks advice from Carol, her tax advisor, about how to minimize her estate taxes while passing the the greatest value of property to her descendants. Diane is a widow with three children and five grandchildren and at present owns property valued at $10 million. This is an open-fact situation. Carol could advise Diane to leave all but a few hundred thousand dollars of her property to a charitable organization so that her estate would owe no estate taxes. Although this recommendation would minimize Diane's estate taxes, Diane is likely to reject it because she wants her children or grandchildren to be her primary beneficiaries. Thus, reducing estate taxes to zero is inconsistent with her objective of allowing her descendants to receive as much after-tax wealth as possible. ◀

TAX STRATEGY TIP

Taxpayers should make investment decisions based on after-tax rates of return or after-tax cash flows.

When conducting research in a tax-planning context, the tax professional should keep a number of points in mind. First, the objective is not to minimize taxes per se but rather to maximize the after-tax return. For example, if the federal income tax rate is a constant 40%, an investor should not buy a tax-exempt bond yielding 5% when he or she could buy a corporate bond of equal risk that yields 9% before tax and 5.4% after tax. This is the case even though his or her explicit taxes (actual tax liability) would be minimized by investing in the tax-exempt bond.[1] Second, taxpayers do not engage in unilateral transactions; thus, the tax ramifications for all parties to the transaction are relevant. For example, in the executive compensation context, employees may prefer to receive incentive stock options (because income recognition is postponed until they sell the stock), but the employer may prefer to grant a different type of option (because he or she is entitled to no tax deduction with respect to incentive stock options). Thus, the employer might grant a different number of options if it uses one type of stock option as compensation versus another. Third, taxes are but one cost of doing business. In deciding where to locate a manufacturing plant, for example, factors more important to some businesses than the amount of state and local taxes paid might be the proximity to raw materials, good transportation systems, the cost of labor, the quantity of available skilled labor, and the quality of life in the area. Fourth, the time for tax planning is not restricted to the beginning date of an investment, contract, or other arrangement. Instead, the time extends throughout the life of the activity. As tax rules change or as business and economic environments change, the tax advisor needs to reevaluate whether the taxpayer should hold on to an investment and must consider the transaction costs of making changes.

ADDITIONAL COMMENT

It is important to consider nontax objectives as well as tax objectives. In many situations, the nontax considerations outweigh the tax considerations. Thus, the plan eventually adopted by a taxpayer may not always be the best when viewed strictly from a tax perspective.

One final note: the tax advisor should always bear in mind the financial accounting implications of proposed transactions. An answer that may be desirable from a tax perspective may not always be desirable from a financial accounting perspective. Though interrelated, the two fields of accounting have different orientations and different objectives. Tax accounting is oriented primarily to the Internal Revenue Service (IRS). Its objectives include calculating, reporting, and predicting one's tax liability according to legal principles. Financial accounting is oriented primarily to stockholders, creditors, managers, and employees. Its objectives include determining, reporting, and predicting a business's financial position and operating results according to Generally Accepted Accounting Principles. Success in any tax practice, especially at the managerial level, requires consideration of both sets of objectives and orientations.

STEPS IN THE TAX RESEARCH PROCESS

OBJECTIVE 1

Describe the steps in the tax research process

In both open- and closed-fact situations, the tax research process involves six basic steps:

1. Determine the facts.
2. Identify the issues (questions).
3. Locate the applicable authorities.
4. Evaluate the authorities and choose those to follow where the authorities conflict.
5. Analyze the facts in terms of the applicable authorities.
6. Communicate conclusions and recommendations to the client.

[1] For an excellent discussion of explicit and implicit taxes and tax planning see Myron S. Scholes, Mark A. Wolfson, Merle Erickson, Edward L. Maydew, and Terry Shevlin, *Taxes and Business Strategy,* Second Edition (Upper Saddle River, NJ: Prentice Hall Inc, 2001). See also Chapter I18 of the the *Individuals* volume. An example of an implicit tax is the excess of the before-tax earnings on a taxable bond over the risk-adjusted before-tax earnings on a tax-favored investment (e.g., a municipal bond).

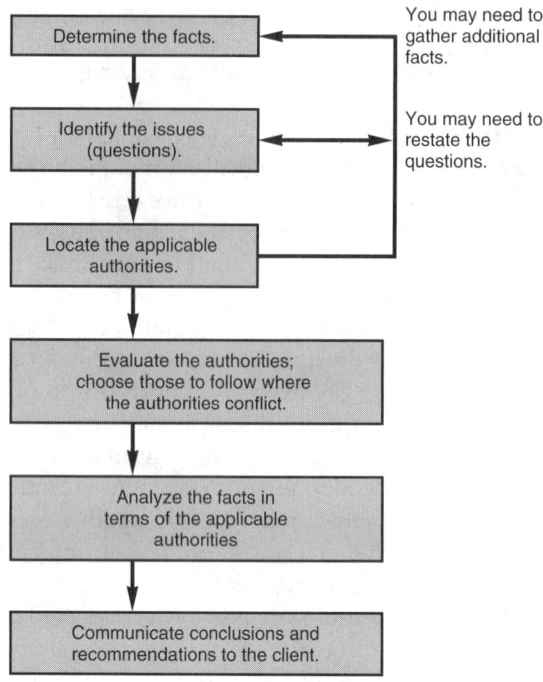

FIGURE C1-1 ▶ STEPS IN THE TAX RESEARCH PROCESS

ADDITIONAL COMMENT

The steps of tax research provide an excellent format for a written tax communication. For example, a good format for a client memo includes (1) statement of facts, (2) list of issues, (3) discussion of relevant authority, (4) analysis, and (5) recommendations to the client of appropriate actions based on the research results.

TYPICAL MISCONCEPTION

Many taxpayers think the tax law is all black and white. However, most tax research deals with gray areas. Ultimately, when confronted with tough issues, the ability to develop strategies that favor the taxpayer and then to find relevant authority to support those strategies will make a successful tax advisor.

Although the above outline suggests a lock-step procedure, the tax research process often is circular. That is, it does not always proceed step-by-step. Figure C1-1 illustrates a more accurate process, and Appendix A provides a comprehensive example of this process.

In a closed-fact situation, the facts have already occurred, and the tax advisor's task is to analyze them to determine the appropriate tax treatment. In an open-fact situation, by contrast, the facts have not yet occurred, and the tax advisor's task is to plan for them or shape them so as to produce a favorable tax result. The tax advisor performs the latter task by reviewing the relevant legal authorities, particularly court cases and IRS rulings, all the while taking into consideration the facts of those cases or rulings that produced favorable results compared with those that produced unfavorable results. For example, if a client wants to realize an ordinary loss (as opposed to a capital gain) from the sale of several plots of land, the tax advisor might consult cases involving similar land sales. The advisor might attempt to distinguish the facts of those cases in which the taxpayer realized an ordinary loss from the facts of those cases in which the taxpayer realized a capital gain. The advisor then might structure the transaction accordingly.

Often, the research pertains to a gray area (i.e., it involves a question for which no clearcut, unequivocally correct answer exists). In such situations, probing a related issue might lead to a solution pertinent to the central question. For example, in researching whether the taxpayer may deduct a loss as ordinary instead of capital, the tax advisor might research the related issue of whether the presence of an investment motive precludes classifying a loss as ordinary. The solution to the latter issue might be relevant to the question of whether the taxpayer may deduct the loss as ordinary.

Identifying the issue(s) to be researched often is the most difficult step in the tax research process. In some instances, the client defines the issue(s) for the tax advisor, such as where the client asks, "May I deduct the costs of a winter trip to Florida recommended by my physician?" In other instances, the tax advisor, after reviewing the documents submitted to him or her by the client, defines the issue(s) himself or herself. The ability to do so presupposes a firm grounding in tax law.[2]

[2] Often, in an employment context, supervisors define the questions to be researched and the authorities that might be relevant to the tax consequences.

Once the tax advisor locates the applicable legal authorities, he or she might have to turn to the client for additional information. Example C1-3 illustrates the point. The example assumes that all relevant tax authorities are in agreement.

EXAMPLE C1-3 ► Mark calls his tax advisor, Al, and states that (1) he incurred a loss on renting his beach cottage during the current year and (2) he wonders whether he may deduct the loss. He also states that he, his wife, and their minor child occupied the cottage only eight days during the current year.

This is the first time Al has dealt with the Sec. 280A vacation home rules. On reading Sec. 280A, Al learned that a loss is *not* deductible if the taxpayer used the residence for personal purposes for longer than the greater of (1) 14 days or (2) 10% of the number of days the unit was rented at a fair rental value. He also learned that the property is *deemed* to be used by the taxpayer for personal purposes on any days on which it is used by any member of his or her family (as defined in Sec. 267(c)(4)). The Sec. 267(c)(4) definition of family members includes brothers, sisters, spouse, ancestors, or lineal descendants (i.e., children and grandchildren).

Mark's eight-day use is not long enough to make the rental loss nondeductible. However, Al must inquire about the number of days, if any, Mark's brothers, sisters, or parents used the property. (He already knows about use by Mark, his spouse, and his lineal descendants.) In addition, Al must find out how many days the cottage was rented to other persons at a fair rental value. On obtaining such additional facts, Al proceeds to determine how to calculate the deductible expenses. Al then reaches his conclusion concerning the deductible loss, if any, and communicates it to Mark. This example assumes the passive activity and at-risk rules restricting a taxpayer's ability to deduct losses from real estate activities will not pose a problem for Mark. (See Chapter I8 of *Prentice Hall's Federal Taxation: Individuals* for a comprehensive discussion of these topics.) ◄

Many firms require that a researcher's conclusions be communicated to the client in writing. Members or employees of such firms can answer questions orally, but their oral conclusions must be followed up with a written communication. According to the AICPA's *Statements on Standards for Tax Services* (reproduced in Appendix E),

> Although oral advice may serve a client's needs appropriately in routine matters or in well-defined areas, written communications are recommended in important, unusual, or complicated transactions. The member may use judgment about whether, subsequently, to document oral advice in writing.[3]

IMPORTANCE OF THE FACTS TO THE TAX CONSEQUENCES

OBJECTIVE 2

Explain how the facts affect the tax consequences

Many terms and phrases used in the Internal Revenue Code (IRC) and other tax authorities are vague or ambiguous. Some of their provisions conflict or are difficult to reconcile, posing to the researcher the dilemma of deciding which rules are applicable and which tax results are proper. For example, as a condition to claiming another person as a dependent, the taxpayer must provide more than half of such person's support.[4] Neither the IRC nor the Treasury Regulations define "support." The lack of definition could be problematic. For example, if the taxpayer purchased a used automobile costing $5,000 for an elderly parent whose only source of income is $4,800 in Social Security benefits, the question of whether the expenditure constitutes support would arise. The tax advisor would have to consult court opinions, revenue rulings, and other IRS pronouncements to ascertain the legal meaning of the term "support." Only after a thorough research effort would the meaning of the term become clear.

In other instances, the legal language is quite clear, but a question arises as to whether the taxpayer's transaction conforms to the specific pattern of facts necessary to obtain a particular tax result. Ultimately, the peculiar facts of a transaction or event determine its tax consequences. A change in the facts can significantly change the consequences. Consider the following illustrations:

---

[3] AICPA, *Statement on Standards for Tax Services,* No. 8, "Form and Content of Advice to Clients," 2000, Para. 6.

[4] Sec. 152(a).

Illustration One

Facts: A holds stock, a capital asset, that he purchased two years ago at a cost of $1,000. He sells the stock to B for $920. What are the tax consequences to A?

Result: Under Sec. 1001, A realizes an $80 capital loss. He recognizes this loss in the current year. A must offset the loss against any capital gains recognized during the year. Any excess loss is deductible from ordinary income up to a $3,000 limit.

Change of Facts: A is B's son.

New Result: Under Sec. 267, A and B are related parties. Therefore, A may not recognize the realized loss. However, B may use the loss if she subsequently sells the stock at a gain.

Illustration Two

Facts: C donates ten acres of land that she purchased two years ago for $10,000 to State University. The fair market value (FMV) of the land on the date of the donation is $25,000. C's adjusted gross income is $100,000. What is C's charitable contribution deduction?

Result: Under Sec. 170, C is entitled to a $25,000 charitable contribution deduction (i.e., the FMV of the property unreduced by the unrealized long-term gain).

Change of Facts: C purchased the land 11 months ago.

New Result: Under the same IRC provision, C is entitled to only a $10,000 charitable contribution deduction (i.e., the FMV of the property reduced by the unrealized short-term gain).

Illustration Three

Facts: Acquiring Corporation pays Target Corporation's shareholders one million shares of Acquiring voting stock. In return, Target's shareholders tender 98% of their Target voting stock. The acquisition is for a bona fide business purpose. Acquiring continues Target's business. What are the tax consequences of the exchange to Target's shareholders?

Result: Under Sec. 368(a)(1)(B), Target's shareholders are not taxed on the exchange, which is solely for Acquiring voting stock.

Change of Facts: Acquiring purchases the remaining 2% of Target's shares with cash as part of the same transaction.

New Result: Under the same IRC provision, Target's shareholders are now taxed on the exchange, which is not solely for Acquiring voting stock.

ABILITY TO CREATE A FACTUAL SITUATION FAVORING THE TAXPAYER

TYPICAL MISCONCEPTION

Many taxpayers believe tax practitioners spend most of their time preparing tax returns. In reality, providing tax advice that accomplishes the taxpayer's objectives is one of the most important responsibilities of a tax advisor. This latter activity is tax consulting as compared to tax compliance.

Based his or her research, a tax advisor might recommend to a taxpayer how to structure a transaction or plan an event so as to increase the likelihood that related expenses will be deductible. For example, suppose a taxpayer is given a temporary task in a location (City Y) different from the location (City X) of his or her permanent employment. Suppose also that the taxpayer wants to deduct the meal and lodging expenses incurred in City Y as well as the cost of transportation thereto. To do so, the taxpayer must establish that City X is his or her tax home and that he or she temporarily works in City Y. (Section 162 provides that a taxpayer may deduct travel expenses while "away from home" on business. A taxpayer is deemed to be "away from home" if his or her employment at the new location does not exceed one year, i.e., it is "temporary.") Suppose the taxpayer wants to know the tax consequences of his or her working in City Y for ten months and then, within that ten-month period, finding permanent employment in City Y. What is tax research likely to reveal?

Tax research is likely to reveal an IRS ruling that states that, in such circumstances, the employment will be deemed to be temporary until the date on which the realistic expectation about the temporary nature of the assignment changes.[5] After this date, the employment will be deemed to be permanent, and travel expenses relating to it will be nondeductible. Based on this finding, the tax advisor might advise the taxpayer to postpone his or her permanent job search in City Y until the end of the ten-month period and simply treat his or her assignment as temporary. So doing would lengthen the period of time during which he or she is deemed to be "away from home" on business and thus increase the amount of meal, lodging, and transportation costs deductible as travel expenses.

[5] Rev. Rul. 93-86, 1993-2 C.B. 71.

THE SOURCES OF TAX LAW

OBJECTIVE 3

Identify the sources of tax law and understand the authoritative value of each

The language of the IRC is general; that is, it prescribes in generic terms the tax treatment of broad categories of transactions and events. The reason for the generality is that Congress can neither foresee nor provide for every detailed transaction or event. Even if it could, doing so would render the statute narrow in scope and inflexible in application. Accordingly, interpretations of the IRC—both administrative and judicial—are necessary. Administrative interpretations are provided by Treasury Regulations, revenue rulings, and revenue procedures. Judicial interpretations are presented in court opinions. The term *tax law* as used by most tax advisors encompasses administrative and judicial interpretations in addition to the IRC. It also includes the meaning conveyed in reports issued by Congressional committees involved in the legislative process.

THE LEGISLATIVE PROCESS

Tax legislation begins in the House of Representatives. Initially, a tax proposal is incorporated in a bill. The bill is referred to the House Ways and Means Committee, which is charged with reviewing all tax legislation. The Ways and Means Committee holds hearings in which interested parties, such as the Treasury Secretary and IRS Commissioner, testify. At the conclusion of the hearings, the Ways and Means Committee votes to approve or reject the measure. If approved, the bill goes to the House floor where it is debated by the full membership. If the House approves the measure, the bill moves to the Senate where it is taken up by the Senate Finance Committee. Like Ways and Means, the Finance Committee holds hearings in which Treasury officials, tax experts, and other interested parties testify. If the committee approves the measure, the bill goes to the Senate floor where it is debated by the full membership. Upon approval by the Senate, it is submitted to the President for his or her signature. If the President signs the measure, the bill becomes public law. If the President vetoes it, Congress can override the veto by at least a two-thirds majority vote in each chamber.

Generally, at each stage of the legislative process, the bill is subject to amendment. If amended, and if the House version differs from the Senate version, the bill is referred to a House-Senate conference committee.[6] This committee attempts to resolve the differences between the House and Senate versions. Ultimately, it submits a compromise version of the measure to each chamber for its approval. Such referrals are common. For example, in 1998 the House and Senate disagreed over what the taxpayer must do to shift the burden of proof to the IRS. The House proposed that the taxpayer assert a "reasonable dispute" regarding a taxable item. The Senate proposed that the taxpayer introduce "credible evidence" regarding the item. A conference committee was appointed to resolve the differences. This committee ultimately adopted the Senate proposal, which was later approved by both chambers.

ADDITIONAL COMMENT

Committee reports can be helpful in interpreting new legislation because they indicate the intent of Congress. With the proliferation of tax legislation, committee reports have become especially important because the Treasury Department often is unable to draft the needed regulations in a timely manner.

After approving major legislation, the Ways and Means Committee and Senate Finance Committee usually issue official reports. These reports, published by the U.S. Government Printing Office (GPO) as part of the *Cumulative Bulletin* and as separate documents, explain the committees' reasoning for approving (and/or amending) the legislation.[7] In addition, the GPO publishes both records of the committee hearings and transcripts of the floor debates. The records are published as separate House or Senate documents. The transcripts are incorporated in the *Congressional Record* for the day of the debate. In tax research, these records, reports, and transcripts are useful in deciphering the meaning of the statutory language. Where this language is ambiguous or vague, and the courts have not interpreted it, they can shed light on **Congressional intent**, i.e., what Congress *intended* by a particular term, phrase, or provision.

EXAMPLE C1-4 ▶ As mentioned earlier, in 1998 Congress passed legislation concerning shifting the burden of proof to the IRS. This legislation was codified in Sec. 7491. The question arises as to what constitutes "credible evidence." (Remember, the taxpayer must introduce "credible evidence" to

---

[6] The size of a conference committee can vary. It is made up of an equal number of members from the House and the Senate.

[7] The *Cumulative Bulletin* is described in the discussion of revenue rulings on page C1-12.

shift the burden of proof to the IRS). Section 7491 does not define the term. Because the provision is relatively new, few courts have had an opportunity to interpret what "credible evidence" means. In the absence of relevant statutory or judicial authority, the researcher might look to the committee reports to ascertain what Congress intended by the term. Senate Report No. 105-174 states that "credible evidence" means evidence of a quality, which, "after critical analysis, the court would find sufficient upon which to base a decision on the issue if no contrary evidence were submitted."[8] This language suggests that Congress intended the term to mean evidence of a kind sufficient to withstand judicial scrutiny. Such a meaning should be regarded as conclusive in the absence of other authority. ◀

ADDITIONAL COMMENT

According to Sheldon S. Cohen, in *The Wall Street Journal's* weekly tax column, a bound volume of the Internal Revenue Code in 1952 measured three-fourths of an inch thick. Treasury Regulations could fit in one bound volume measuring one-half of an inch thick. In 2001, a bound volume of the Internal Revenue Code measured over four inches thick, and Treasury Regulations fit into six bound volumes measuring around ten inches thick.

THE INTERNAL REVENUE CODE

The IRC, which comprises Title 26 of the United States Code, is the foundation of all tax law. First codified (i.e., organized into a single compilation of revenue statutes) in 1939, the tax law was recodified in 1954. The IRC was known as the Internal Revenue Code of 1954 until 1986, when its name was changed to the Internal Revenue Code of 1986. Whenever changes to the IRC are approved, the old language is deleted and new language added. Thus, the IRC is organized as an integrated document, and a researcher need not read through the applicable parts of all previous tax bills to find the current version of the law.

The IRC contains provisions dealing with income taxes, estate and gift taxes, employment taxes, alcohol and tobacco taxes, and other excise taxes. Organizationally, the IRC is subdivided into subtitles, chapters, subchapters, parts, subparts, sections, subsections, paragraphs, subparagraphs, and clauses. Subtitle A contains rules relating to income taxes, and Subtitle B deals with estate and gift taxes. A set of provisions concerned with one general area constitutes a subchapter. For example, the topics of corporate distributions and adjustments appear in Subchapter C, and topics concerning partners and partnerships appear in Subchapter K. Figure C1-2 presents the organizational scheme of the IRC.

A section is the organizational category to which tax advisors most often refer. For example, they speak of "Sec. 351 transactions," "Sec. 306 stock," and "Sec. 1231 gains and losses." Although a tax advisor need not know all the IRC sections, paragraphs, and parts, he or she must be familiar with the IRC's organizational scheme to read and interpret it correctly. The language of the IRC is replete with cross-references to titles, paragraphs, subparagraphs, and so on.

EXAMPLE C1-5 ▶ Section 7701, a definitional section, begins, "When used in this title . . ." and then provides a series of definitions. Thus, a definition in Sec. 7701 applies for all of Title 26; that is, it applies for purposes of the income tax, estate and gift tax, excise tax, and so on. ◀

EXAMPLE C1-6 ▶ Section 302(b)(3) allows taxpayers whose stock holdings are completely terminated in a redemption (a corporation's purchase of its stock from one of its shareholders) to receive capital gain treatment on the excess of the redemption proceeds over the stock's basis instead of ordinary income treatment on the entire proceeds. Section 302(c)(2)(A) states, "In the case of a distribution described in subsection (b)(3), section 318(a)(1) shall not apply if. . . ." Further, Sec. 302(c)(2)(C)(i) indicates "Subparagraph (A) shall not apply to a distribution to any entity unless. . . ." Thus, in determining whether a taxpayer will receive capital gain treatment for a stock redemption transaction, a tax advisor must be able to locate and interpret various cross-referenced IRC sections, subsections, paragraphs, subparagraphs, and clauses. ◀

TREASURY REGULATIONS

The Treasury Department issues regulations that expound upon the IRC. Treasury Regulations often contain examples with computations that assist in understanding the statutory language.[9]

Because of frequent statutory changes, the Treasury Department does not always update the regulations in a timely manner. Consequently, when consulting a regulation, a tax advisor should check its introductory or end note to determine when the regulation was adopted. If the regulation was adopted before the most recent revision of the applica-

---

[8] S. Rept. No. 105-174, 105th Cong., 1st Sess. (unpaginated) (1998).

[9] Treasury Regulations are formulated on the basis of Treasury Decisions (T.D.s) The numbers of the Treasury Decisions that form the basis of a Treasury Regulation usually are found in the notes at the end of the regulation.

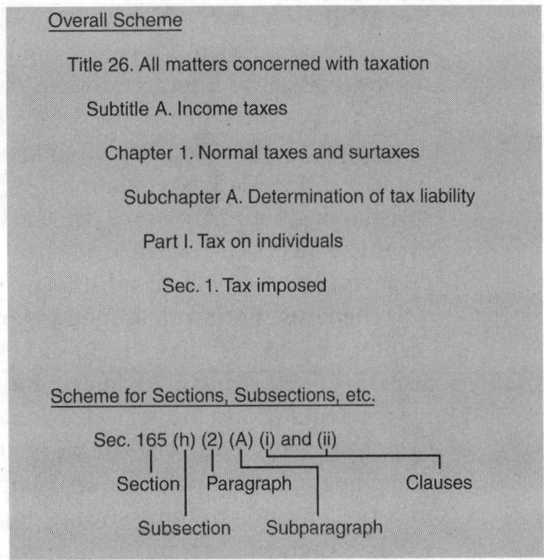

Overall Scheme
Title 26. All matters concerned with taxation
Subtitle A. Income taxes
Chapter 1. Normal taxes and surtaxes
Subchapter A. Determination of tax liability
Part I. Tax on individuals
Sec. 1. Tax imposed
Scheme for Sections, Subsections, etc.
Sec. 165 (h) (2) (A) (i) and (ii)
Section
Paragraph
Clauses
Subsection
Subparagraph

FIGURE C1-2 ▶ ORGANIZATIONAL SCHEME OF THE INTERNAL REVENUE CODE

ble IRC section, the regulation should be treated as authoritative to the extent consistent with the revision. Thus, for example, if a regulation issued before an IRC amendment specifies a dollar amount, and the amendment changed the dollar amount, the regulation should be regarded as authoritative in all respects except the dollar amount.

PROPOSED, TEMPORARY, AND FINAL REGULATIONS. Generally, Treasury Regulations are first issued to the public in proposed form. The public is given the opportunity to comment on them and suggest changes. Individuals most likely to comment are tax accountants and tax attorneys. Organizations such as the American Bar Association, the Tax Division of the AICPA, and the American Taxation Association also provide feedback on the regulations as proposed. In general, such comments suggest that the proposed treatment affects the taxpayer more adversely than what Congress anticipated. In drafting final regulations, the Treasury Department usually considers the remarks and somewhat modifies the regulations.

Proposed regulations are just that—proposed. Consequently, they carry no more weight than the arguments of the IRS in a court brief. They do, nonetheless, represent the Treasury Department's official interpretation of the IRC. In finalizing regulations, the Treasury Department generally responds to taxpayer comments concerning rules as proposed. If the response is favorable, it usually finalizes the rules with minor revisions. If the response is unfavorable, it finalizes them with major revisions or allows them to expire.

Immediately after a major statutory change, the Treasury Department often issues **temporary regulations** (which usually are effective upon publication) to guide taxpayers and their advisors on procedural or computational matters. For example, in 2001 the Treasury Department issued temporary regulations concerning information reporting for payments of qualified tuition expenses. In the same year, it issued temporary regulations prohibiting discrimination against beneficiaries based on a health factor. According to Sec. 7805, a temporary regulation expires within three years after the date of issuance. Also, a temporary regulation must be issued concurrently as a proposed regulation.

The Treasury Department drafts final regulations after the public has had an opportunity to comment on the proposed regulations. Most of the time, the final version of the regulation differs at least slightly from the proposed version. For changes to the IRC enacted after July 29, 1996, the Treasury Department generally is precluded from issuing regulations with retroactive effect. Final regulations, however, can be effective on the date proposed or the date on which the temporary regulations preceding them were published in the *Federal Register.*

INTERPRETATIVE AND LEGISLATIVE REGULATIONS. In addition to being classified as proposed, temporary, or final, Treasury Regulations are categorized as interpretative or legislative. **Interpretative regulations** are issued under the general authority of Sec. 7805 and, as the name implies, merely make the statutory language easier to understand and apply. In addition, they often provide illustrations as to how to perform various computations. **Legislative regulations**, by contrast, are written where Congress delegates its rule-making authority to the Treasury Department. Because Congress believes it lacks the expertise necessary to deal with a highly technical matter, it instructs the Treasury Department to articulate substantive tax principles relating to the matter.

Whenever the statute contains language such as "The Secretary shall prescribe such regulations as he may deem necessary" or "under regulations prescribed by the Secretary," the regulations interpreting such a statute are legislative. The consolidated tax return regulations are the clearest example of legislative regulations. In Sec. 1502, Congress delegated to the Treasury Department authority to issue regulations that determine the tax liability of a group of affiliated corporations filing a consolidated tax return. As a precondition to filing such a return, the corporations must consent to follow the consolidated return regulations.[10] Such consent generally precludes the corporations from arguing in court that the regulatory provisions should be overturned.

AUTHORITATIVE WEIGHT. Final regulations are presumed to be valid and to have almost the same authoritative weight as the IRC. Despite this presumption, taxpayers occasionally argue that a regulation is invalid and, consequently, should not be followed. A court will not conclude that an interpretative regulation is invalid unless, in its opinion, such regulation is "unreasonable and plainly inconsistent with the revenue statutes."[11] Thus, a court is unlikely to invalidate a legislative regulation because it recognizes that Congress has abdicated its rule-making authority with respect to such regulation to the Treasury Department. Nevertheless, the courts have invalidated legislative regulations where, in their opinion, the regulations exceeded the scope of power delegated to the Treasury Department,[12] were contrary to the statute,[13] or were unreasonable.[14]

KEY POINT

The older a Treasury Regulation becomes, the less likely a court is to invalidate the regulation. The legislative reenactment doctrine holds that if a regulation did not reflect the intent of Congress, lawmakers would have changed the statute in subsequent legislation to obtain their desired objectives.

In assessing the validity of Treasury Regulations, some courts apply the **legislative reenactment doctrine**. Under this doctrine, a regulation is deemed to receive Congressional approval whenever the statute under which the regulation was issued is reenacted without amendment.[15] Underlying this doctrine is the rationale that, if Congress believed that the regulation offered an erroneous interpretation of the statute, it would have amended the statute to conform to its belief. Congress's failure to amend the statute signifies approval of the regulation.[16] This doctrine is predicated upon the power of Congress under the Constitution to lay taxes. The power implies that, if Congress is dissatisfied with the manner in which either the executive or the judiciary have interpreted its tax statutes, it can invalidate these interpretations through new legislation.

STOP & THINK

Question: You are researching the manner in which a deduction is calculated. You consult the Treasury Regulations for guidance because the IRC states that the calculation is to be done "in a manner prescribed by the Secretary." After studying these authorities, you conclude that another way of doing the calculation arguably is correct under an intuitive approach. This approach would result in a lower tax liability for the client. Should you follow the Treasury Regulations or use the intuitive approach and argue that the regulations are invalid?

---

[10] Sec. 1501.

[11] *CIR v. South Texas Lumber Co.*, 36 AFTR 604, 48-1 USTC ¶5922 (USSC, 1948). In *U.S. v. Douglas B. Cartwright, Executor*, 31 AFTR 2d 73-1461, 73-1 USTC ¶12,926 (USSC, 1973), the Supreme Court concluded that a regulation dealing with the valuation of mutual fund shares for estate and gift tax purposes was invalid.

[12] *McDonald v. CIR*, 56 AFTR 2d 5318, 85-2 USTC ¶9494 (5th Cir., 1985).

[13] *Jeanese, Inc. v. U.S.*, 15 AFTR 2d 429, 65-1 USTC ¶9259 (9th Cir., 1965).

[14] *United States v. Vogel Fertilizer Co.*, 49 AFTR 2d 82-491, 82-1 USTC ¶9134 (USSC, 1982).

[15] *United States v. Homer O. Correll*, 20 AFTR 2d 5845, 68 USTC ¶9101 (USSC, 1967).

[16] One can rebut the presumption that Congress approved of the regulation by showing that Congress was unaware of the regulation when it reenacted the statute.

Solution: Because of the language "in a manner prescribed by the Secretary," the Treasury Regulations dealing with the calculation are legislative. Whenever it calls for legislative regulations, Congress explicitly authorizes the Treasury Department to write the "rules." Thus, such regulations are more difficult than interpretative regulations to be overturned by the courts. Grounds for overruling legislative regulations include exceeding the scope of the power that Congress delegated, being contrary to the statute, and being unreasonable. If based on your research, you do not believe the Treasury Regulations would be overturned by a court, you should follow them.

ADDITIONAL COMMENT

Citations serve two purposes in tax research: first, they substantiate propositions; second, they enable the reader to locate underlying authority.

CITATIONS. Citations to Treasury Regulations are relatively easy to understand. One or more numbers appear before a decimal place, and several numbers follow the decimal place. The numbers immediately following the decimal place indicate the IRC section being interpreted. The numbers preceding the decimal place indicate the general subject matter of the regulation. Numbers that often appear before the decimal place and their general subject matter are as follows:

Number	*General Subject Matter*
1	Income tax
20	Estate tax
25	Gift tax
301	Administrative and procedural matters
601	Procedural rules

The number following the IRC section number indicates the numerical sequence of the regulation, such as the fifth regulation. No relationship exists between this number and the subsection of the IRC being interpreted. An example of a citation to a final regulation is as follows:

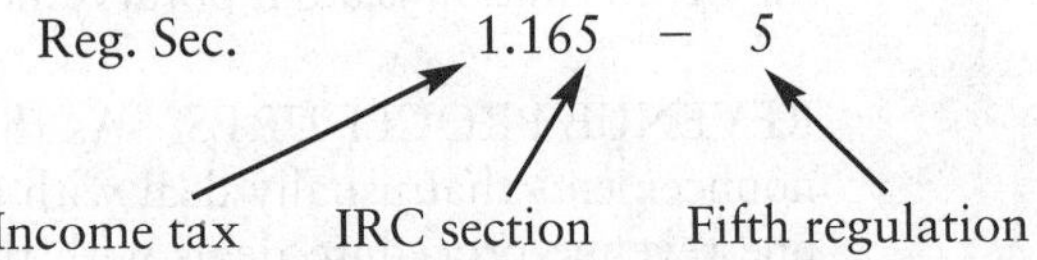

Citations to proposed or temporary regulations are in the same format. They are referenced as Prop. Reg. Sec. or Temp. Reg. Sec. For temporary regulations the numbering system following the IRC section number always begins with the number of the regulation and an upper case T (e.g., -1T).

Section 165 addresses the broad topic of losses and is accompanied by several regulations. According to its caption, the topic of Reg. Sec. 1.165-5 is worthless securities, which also is addressed in subsection (g) of IRC Sec. 165. Parenthetical information following the caption to this regulation indicates that the regulation was last amended December 6, 1972 by Treasury Decision (T.D.) 7224. Section 165(g) was last revised in 1991.

When referencing a regulation, the researcher should fine tune the citation as much as possible to indicate the precise wording that provides the basis for his or her conclusion. An example of such a detailed citation is Reg. Sec. 1.165-5(i), Ex. 2(i), which refers to paragraph (i) of Example 2, found in paragraph (i) of the fifth regulation interpreting Sec. 165.

ADMINISTRATIVE INTERPRETATIONS

TYPICAL MISCONCEPTION

Even though revenue rulings do not have the same weight as Treasury Regulations or court cases, one should not underestimate their importance. Because a revenue ruling is the official published position of the IRS, in audits the examining agent will place considerable weight on any applicable revenue rulings.

The IRS interprets the IRC through various pronouncements. These pronouncements generally are regarded as **administrative interpretations**. After consulting the IRC and the Treasury Regulations, tax advisors are likely next to consult these interpretations. Some of the most important of them are discussed below.

REVENUE RULINGS. In **revenue rulings**, the IRS indicates the tax consequences of a particular transaction in which several taxpayers might engage. For example, in a revenue ruling, the IRS might indicate whether the exchange of stock for stock derivatives in a corporate acquisition is tax-free.

The IRS issues more than 100 revenue rulings a year. These rulings do not rank as high in the hierarchy of authorities as do Treasury Regulations or federal court cases. They simply represent the IRS's view of the tax law. Taxpayers who do not follow a revenue ruling will not incur a substantial understatement penalty if they have substantial authority for different treatment.[17] Nonetheless, the IRS presumes that the tax treatment specified in a revenue ruling is correct. Consequently, if an examining agent discovers in an audit that a taxpayer did not adopt the position prescribed in a revenue ruling, the agent will contend that the taxpayer's tax liability should be adjusted to reflect that position.

Soon after it is issued, a revenue ruling appears in the weekly *Internal Revenue Bulletin* (cited as I.R.B.), published by the U.S. Government Printing Office (GPO). Revenue rulings later appear in the *Cumulative Bulletin* (cited as C.B.), a bound publication issued semiannually by the GPO. An example of a citation to a revenue ruling appearing in the *Cumulative Bulletin* is as follows:

Rev. Rul. 80-265, 1980-2 C.B. 378.

This is the 265th ruling issued in 1980, and it appears on page 378 of Volume 2 of the 1980 *Cumulative Bulletin.* Before the issuance of the appropriate volume of the *Cumulative Bulletin,* citations are given to the *Internal Revenue Bulletin.* An example of such a citation follows:

Rev. Rul. 98-1, I.R.B. 1998-2, 1.

The ruling is the first issued in 1998. It was published on page 1 of the *Internal Revenue Bulletin* for the second week of 1998. Once a revenue ruling is published in the *Cumulative Bulletin,* only the citation to the *Cumulative Bulletin* should be used. Thus, the I.R.B. citation is a temporary one.

REVENUE PROCEDURES. As the name suggests, **revenue procedures** are IRS pronouncements that usually deal with the procedural aspects of tax practice. For example, one revenue procedure deals with the manner in which tip income should be reported. Another revenue procedure describes the requirements for reproducing paper substitutes for informational returns such as Form 1099.

Revenue procedures are published first in the *Internal Revenue Bulletin* and later in the *Cumulative Bulletin.* An example of a citation to a revenue procedure appearing in the *Cumulative Bulletin* is as follows:

Rev. Proc. 97-19, 1997-1 C.B. 644.

This item was published in Volume 1 of the 1997 *Cumulative Bulletin* on page 644. It was the nineteenth revenue procedure issued in 1997.

In addition to revenue rulings and revenue procedures, the *Cumulative Bulletin* includes IRS notices, as well as texts of proposed regulations, treaties and tax conventions, committee reports, and U.S. Supreme Court decisions.

SELF-STUDY QUESTION

Are letter rulings of precedential value for third parties?

ANSWER

No. A letter ruling is binding only on the taxpayer to whom the ruling was issued. Nevertheless, letter rulings can be very useful to third parties because they provide insight as to the IRS's opinion about the tax consequences of various transactions.

LETTER RULINGS. **Letter rulings** are initiated by taxpayers who write and ask the IRS to explain the tax consequences of a particular transaction.[18] The IRS provides its explanation in the form of a letter ruling, that is, a personal response to the individual or corporation requesting an answer. Only the taxpayer to whom the ruling is addressed may rely on it as authority. Nevertheless, letter rulings are significant to other taxpayers and to tax advisors because they offer insight into the IRS's position on the tax treatment of particular transactions.

---

[17] Chapter C15 discusses in depth the authoritative support taxpayers and tax advisors should have for positions they adopt on a tax return.

[18] Chapter C15 further discusses letter rulings.

Originally the public did not have access to letter rulings issued to other taxpayers. As a result of Sec. 6110, enacted in 1976, letter rulings (with any confidential information deleted) are accessible to the general public and have been reproduced by the major tax services. An example of a citation to a letter ruling appears below:

Ltr. Rul. 200130006 (August 6, 2001).

The numbering system for letter rulings issued after 1999 consists of nine digits.[19] If issued before 2000, the letter ruling number contains seven digits because only the last two digits of the year are used. The first four digits (two if issued before 2000) indicate the year in which the ruling was made public, in this case, 2001. The next two digits denote the week in which it was made public, here the thirtieth. The last three numbers indicate the ruling for the week, here the sixth. The date in parentheses denotes the date of the ruling.

OTHER INTERPRETATIONS

ADDITIONAL COMMENT

A technical advice memorandum is published as a letter ruling. Whereas a taxpayer-requested letter ruling deals with prospective transactions, a technical advice memorandum deals with past or consummated transactions.

Technical Advice Memoranda. When the IRS audits a taxpayer's return on a complicated, technical matter, the IRS agent may refer the matter to the IRS national office in Washington, DC for technical advice concerning the appropriate tax treatment. The answer from the national office, in the form of a **technical advice memorandum**, is made available to the public as a letter ruling.[20] Researchers can recognize which letter rulings are technical advice memoranda because they generally begin with language such as, "In response to a request for technical advice. . . ." An example of a citation to a technical advice memorandum is as follows:

T.A.M. 9801001 (January 1, 1998).

This item represents the first technical advice memorandum issued in the first week of 1998. The memorandum is dated January 1, 1998.

Information Releases. If the IRS wants to disseminate information to the general public, it will issue an **information release**. Information releases are written in lay terms and are dispatched to thousands of newspapers throughout the country. The IRS, for example, may issue an information release to announce the standard mileage rate applicable to business travel. An example of a citation to an information release is as follows:

I.R. 86-70 (June 12, 1986).

This item signifies the seventieth information release issued in 1986. The release is dated June 12, 1986.

ADDITIONAL COMMENT

Announcements are used to summarize new tax legislation or publicize procedural matters. Announcements generally are aimed at tax practitioners and are "the equivalent of revenue rulings and revenue procedures" [Rev. Rul. , 1987-2 C.B. 287].

Announcements and Notices. The IRS also disseminates information to tax practitioners in the form of **announcements** and **notices**. These pronouncements generally are more technical than information releases, and they frequently address current tax developments. After a major tax act, and before the Treasury Department has had an opportunity to issue proposed or temporary regulations, the IRS may issue an announcement or notice to clarify the measure. The IRS is bound to follow the announcement or notice just as it is bound to follow a revenue procedure or revenue ruling. Examples of citations to announcements and notices are as follows:

Announcement 98-1, I.R.B. 1998-2, 38.
Notice 98-1, I.R.B. 1998-3, 42.

The first citation is to the first announcement issued in 1998. It can be found on page 38 of the second *Internal Revenue Bulletin* for 1998. The second citation is to the first notice issued in 1998. It can be found on page 42 of the third *Internal Revenue Bulletin* for 1998. While notices appear in both the *Internal Revenue Bulletin* and the *Cumulative Bulletin*, announcements appear only in the first of these publications.

---

[19] Sometimes a letter ruling is cited as PLR (private letter ruling) instead of Ltr. Rul.

[20] Technical advice memoranda are discussed further in Chapter C15.

JUDICIAL DECISIONS

Judicial decisions are an important source of tax law. Judges are reputed to be unbiased individuals who decide questions of fact (the existence of a fact or the occurrence of an event) or questions of law (the applicability of a legal principle or the proper interpretation of a legal term). Judges do not always agree on the tax consequences of a particular transaction or event. Therefore, tax advisors often must reach their conclusions against the background of conflicting judicial authorities. For example, a U.S. district court may disagree with the Tax Court on the deductibility of an expense. Likewise, one circuit court may disagree with another circuit court.

OVERVIEW OF THE COURT SYSTEM. In tax matters, there are three trial courts: the U.S. Tax Court, the U.S. Court of Federal Claims (formerly the U.S. Claims Court), and U.S. district courts. The taxpayer may begin litigation in any of the three. Court precedents are important in deciding where to begin litigation (see page C1-21 for a discussion of precedent). Also important is when the taxpayer must pay the deficiency the IRS contends is due. A taxpayer who wants to litigate either in a U.S. district court or in the U.S. Court of Federal Claims must first pay the deficiency. The taxpayer then files a claim for refund, which the IRS will deny. This denial must be followed by a suit for a refund of the taxes. If the taxpayer wins the refund suit, he or she receives a refund of the taxes in question plus interest. If the taxpayer begins litigation in the Tax Court, on the other hand, he or she need not pay the deficiency until the case has been decided. If the taxpayer loses in the Tax Court, he or she must pay the deficiency plus any interest and penalties.[21] A taxpayer who thinks that a jury trial would be especially favorable should litigate in a U.S. district court, the only forum where a jury trial is possible.

SELF-STUDY QUESTION

What are some of the factors that a taxpayer should consider when deciding in which court to file a tax-related claim?

ANSWER

(1) Each court's published precedent pertaining to the issue, (2) desirability of a jury trial, (3) tax expertise of each court, and (4) when the deficiency must be paid.

If a party loses at the trial court level, it can appeal the decision to a higher court. Appeals of Tax Court and U.S. district court decisions are made to the Court of Appeals for the taxpayer's circuit (i.e., geographical area). There are eleven numerical circuits plus the circuit for the District of Columbia. The map in Figure C1-3 shows the states that lie in the various circuits. California, for example, lies in the Ninth Circuit. When referring to these appellate courts, instead of saying, for example, "the Court of Appeals for the Ninth Circuit," one generally says "the Ninth Circuit." All decisions of the U.S. Court of Federal Claims are appealable to one court—the Court of Appeals for the Federal Circuit—irrespective of where the taxpayer resides or does business.[22] The only cases the Federal Circuit hears are those that originate in the U.S. Court of Federal Claims.

The party losing at the Court of Appeals level can petition the Supreme Court to hear the case by a **writ of certiorari.** If the Supreme Court agrees to consider the case, it grants certiorari.[23] If it refuses to consider the case, it denies certiorari. In recent years, the Court has granted certiorari in only about six to ten tax cases per year. Figure C1-4 and Table C1-1 provide an overview and summary of the court system with respect to tax matters.

THE U.S. TAX COURT. The U.S. Tax Court was created in 1942 as a successor to the Board of Tax Appeals. It is a court of national jurisdiction that hears only tax-related cases. All taxpayers, regardless of their state of residence or place of business, may litigate in the Tax Court. It has 19 judges, including one chief judge.[24] The President, with the consent of the Senate, appoints the judges for a 15-year term and may reappoint them for an additional term. The judges, specialists in tax-related matters, periodically travel to roughly 100 cities throughout the country to hear cases. In most instances, only one judge hears a case.

ADDITIONAL COMMENT

Because the Tax Court deals only with tax cases, it presumably has a higher level of tax expertise than do other courts. Tax Court judges are appointed by the President, in part, due to their considerable tax experience. In July 2001, the Tax Court judges faced a backlog of about 15,000 cases. This is an improvement over its 27,000 cases in 1998.

The Tax Court issues both regular and memorandum (memo) decisions. The chief judge decides whether to publish each opinion as a memo or regular decision. Generally, the first time the Tax Court decides a particular legal issue, its decision appears as a **regu-**

---

[21] Revenue Procedure 84-58, 1984-2, C.B. 501, provides procedures for taxpayers to make remittances or apply overpayments to stop the accrual of interest on deficiencies.

[22] The Court of Claims was reconstituted as the United States Court of Claims in 1982. In 1992, this court was renamed the U.S. Court of Federal Claims.

[23] The granting of certiorari signifies that the Supreme Court is granting an appellate review. The denial of certiorari does not necessarily mean that the Supreme Court agrees with the lower court's decision. It simply means the court has decided not to hear the case.

[24] The Tax Court also periodically appoints, depending on budgetary constraints, a number of trial judges and senior judges who hear cases and render decisions with the same authority as the regular Tax Court judges.

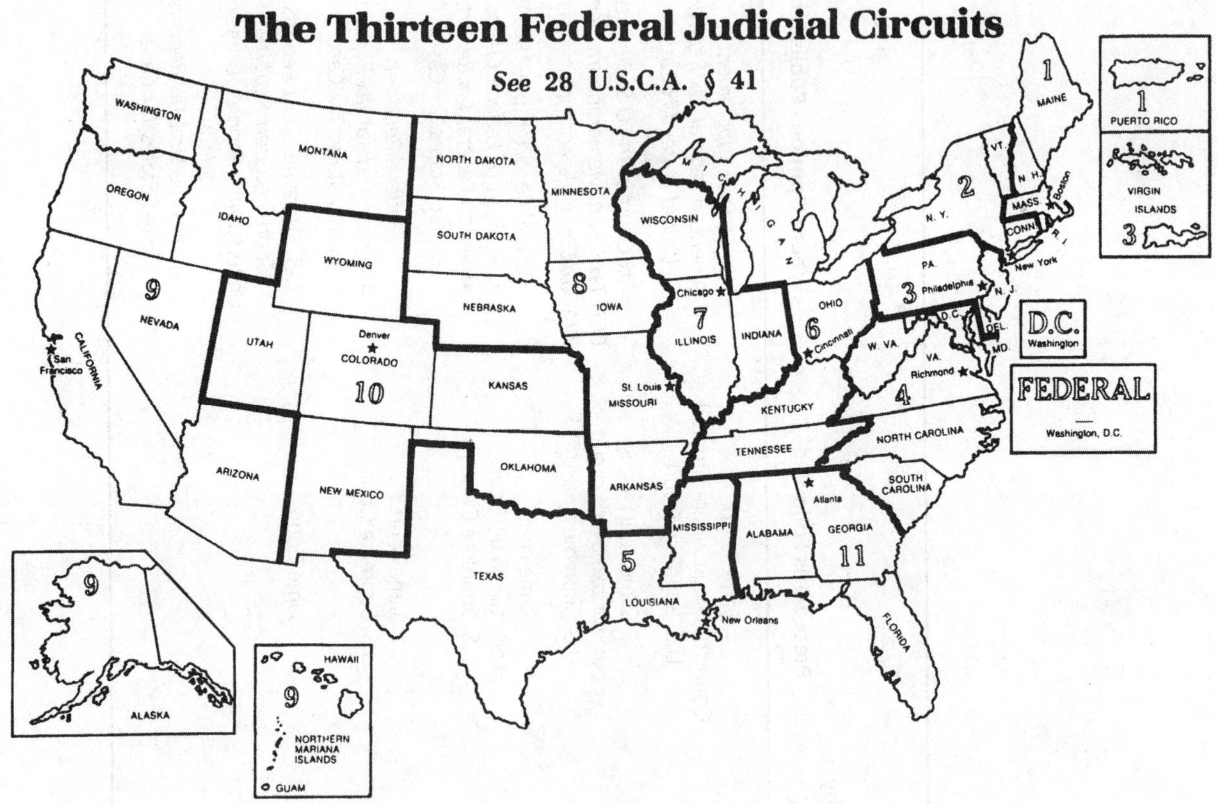

FIGURE C1-3 ▶ MAP OF THE GEOGRAPHICAL BOUNDARIES OF THE CIRCUIT COURTS OF APPEALS

Source: Reprinted with permission from *West's Federal Reporter,* Third Series, Copyright © by West Publishing Company.

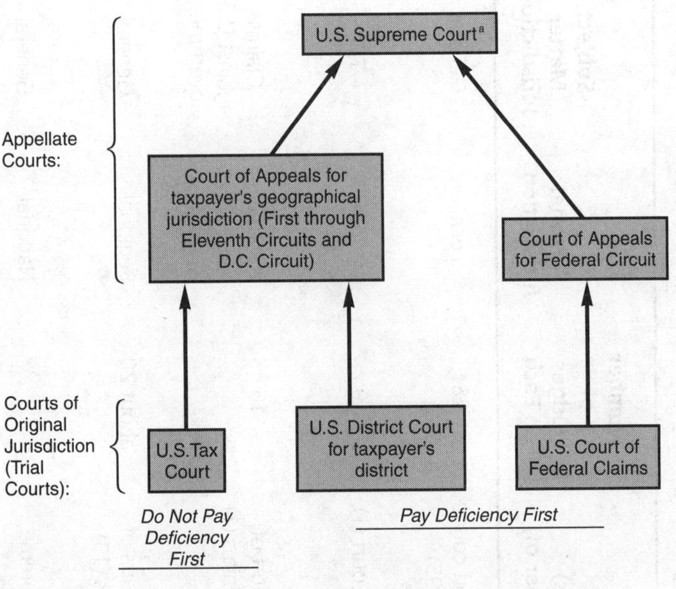

FIGURE C1-4 ▶ OVERVIEW OF COURT SYSTEM—TAX MATTERS

▼ TABLE C1-1

Summary of Court Sytem—Tax Matters

Court(s) (Number of)	Number of Judges on Each	Personal Jurisdiction	Subject Matter Jurisdiction	Determines Questions of Fact	Trial by Jury	Precedents Followed	Where Opinions Published
U.S. district courts (over 95)	1-28*	Local	General	Yes	Yes	Same court Court for circuit where situated U.S. Supreme Court	*Federal Supplement* *American Federal Tax Reports* *United States Tax Cases*
U.S. Tax Court (1)	19	National	Tax	Yes	No	Same court Court for taxpayer's circuit U.S. Supreme Court	*Tax Court of the U.S. Reports* *CCH Tax Court Memorandum Decisions* *RIA Tax Court Memorandum Decisions*
U.S. Court of Federal Claims (1)	16	National	Claims against U.S. Government	Yes	No	Same court Federal Circuit Court U.S. Supreme Court	*Federal Reporter* (pre-1982) *U.S. Court of Federal Claims* *American Federal Tax Reports* *United States Tax Cases*
U.S. Courts of Appeals (13)	about 20	Regional	General	No	No	Same court U.S. Supreme Court	*Federal Reporter* *American Federal Tax Reports* *United States Tax Cases*
U.S. Supreme Court (1)	9	National	General	No	No	Same Court	*U.S. Supreme Court Reports* *Supreme Court Reporter* *United States Reports, Lawyers' Editon* *American Federal Tax Reports* *United States Tax Cases*

*Although the number of judges assigned to each court varies, only one judge decides a case.

lar decision. Memo decisions usually deal with a factual variation of a previously-decided issue. Regular and memo decisions have the same precedential value.

At times, the chief judge determines that a particular case deals with an important matter that the entire Tax Court should consider. In such a situation, the words *reviewed by the court* will appear at the end of the majority opinion. Any concurring or dissenting opinions will appear after the majority opinion.[25]

Other language sometimes appearing at the end of a Tax Court opinion is *Entered under Rule 155*. These words signify that the court has reached a decision concerning the tax treatment of an item but has left computation of the deficiency to the two litigating parties.

SELF-STUDY QUESTION

What are some of the considerations for litigating under the small cases procedure of the Tax Court?

ANSWER

The small cases procedure gives the taxpayer the advantage of having his or her "day in court" without the expense of an attorney. But if the taxpayer loses, the decision cannot be appealed.

Small Cases Procedure. The Tax Court has a special policy concerning small cases. Taxpayers have the option of having their cases heard under the **small cases procedure** if the amount in question for a particular year does not exceed $50,000.[26] This procedure is less formal than the regular Tax Court procedure, and taxpayers can appear without an attorney.[27] The cases are heard by special commissioners instead of by one of the 19 Tax Court judges. For the losing party, a disadvantage of the small cases procedure is that the decision cannot be appealed. The opinions of the small case commissioners are not published and have no precedential value.

Acquiescence Policy. The IRS has adopted a policy of announcing whether, in future cases involving similar facts and similar issues, it will follow federal court decisions that are adverse to it. This policy is known as the IRS **acquiescence policy**. If the IRS wants taxpayers to know that it will follow an adverse decision in future cases involving similar facts and issues, it will announce its "acquiescence" in the decision. Conversely, if it wants taxpayers to know that it will not follow the decision, it will announce its "nonacquiescence." The IRS does not announce its acquiescence or nonacquiescence in every decision it loses.

ADDITIONAL COMMENT

The only cases with respect to which the IRS will consider publishing an acquiescence or nonacquiescence are decisions that the government loses. Because the majority of cases, particularly Tax Court cases, are won by the government, the IRS will potentially acquiescence in only a small number of cases.

The IRS publishes its acquiescences and nonacquiescences as "Actions on Decision" first in the *Internal Revenue Bulletin,* then in the *Cumulative Bulletin.* Before 1991, the IRS published acquiescences and nonacquiescences in regular Tax Court decisions only. In 1991, it broadened the scope of its policy to include adverse U.S. Claims Court, U.S. district court, and U.S. circuit court decisions.

In cases involving multiple issues, the IRS may acquiesce in some issues but not others. In decisions supported by extensive reasoning, it may acquiesce in the result but not rationale (*acq. in result*). Further, it may retroactively revoke an acquiescence or nonacquiescence. The footnotes to the relevant announcement in the *Internal Revenue Bulletin* and *Cumulative Bulletin* indicate the nature and extent of IRS acquiescences and nonacquiescences.

ADDITIONAL COMMENT

If a particular case is important, the chief judge will instruct the other judges to review the case. If a case is reviewed by the entire court, the phrase *reviewed by the court* is inserted immediately after the text of the majority opinion. A reviewed decision provides an opportunity for Tax Court judges to express their dissenting opinions.

These acquiescences and nonacquiescences are important for taxpayers. If a taxpayer bases his or her position on a decision in which the IRS has nonacquiesced, he or she can expect an IRS challenge in the event of an audit. In this situation, the taxpayer's only recourse may be litigation. On the other hand, if the taxpayer bases his or her position on a decision in which the IRS has acquiesced, he or she can expect little or no challenge. In either case, the examining agent will be bound by the IRS position.

Published Opinions and Citations. Regular Tax Court decisions are published by the U.S. Government Printing Office in a bound volume known as the *Tax Court of the United States Reports*. Soon after a decision is made public, it also is published by

---

[25] A judge who issues a concurring opinion agrees with the basic outcome of the majority's decision but not with its rationale. A judge who issues a dissenting opinion believes the majority reached an erroneous conclusion.

[26] Sec. 7463. The $50,000 amount includes penalties and additional taxes but excludes interest.

[27] Taxpayers can represent themselves in regular Tax Court proceedings also, even though they are not attorneys. Where taxpayers represent themselves, the words *pro se* appear after the taxpayer's name. The Tax Court is the only federal court before which non-attorneys, including CPAs, are allowed to practice.

Research Institute of America (RIA) and CCH Incorporated (CCH) in their looseleaf reporters of Tax Court decisions. An official citation to a Tax Court decision is as follows:[28]

J. Simpson Dean, 35 T.C. 1083 (1961).

The citation indicates that this case appears on page 1083 in Volume 35 of the official *Tax Court of the United States Reports* and that the case was decided in 1961.

Regular decisions of the Board of Tax Appeals (predecessor of the Tax Court) were published by the U.S. Government Printing Office in the *United States Board of Tax Appeals Reports* from 1924 to 1942. An example of a citation to a Board of Tax Appeals case is as follows:

J. W. Wells Lumber Co. Trust A., 44 B.T.A. 551 (1941).

This case is found in Volume 44 of the *United States Board of Tax Appeals Reports* on page 551. It is a 1941 decision.

ADDITIONAL COMMENT

Once the IRS has acquiesced in a federal court decision, other taxpayers generally will not need to litigate the same issue. However, the IRS can change its mind and revoke a previous acquiescence or nonacquiescence. References to acquiescences or nonacquiescences in federal court decisions can be found in the citators.

If the IRS has acquiesced or nonacquiesced in a federal court decision, the IRS's action should be denoted in the citation. At times, the IRS will not announce its acquiescence or nonacquiescence until several years after the date of the decision. An example of a citation to a decision in which the IRS has acquiesced is as follows:

Estate of John A. Moss, 74 T.C. 1239 (1980), *acq.* 1981-1 C.B. 2.

The case appears on page 1239 of Volume 74 of the *Tax Court of the United States Reports* and the acquiescence is reported on page 2 of Volume 1 of the 1981 *Cumulative Bulletin.* The IRS acquiesced to this 1980 decision in 1981. A citation to a decision in which the IRS has nonacquiesced is as follows:

Warren Jones Co., 60 T.C. 663 (1973), *nonacq.* 1980-1 C.B. 2.

The case appears on page 663 of Volume 60 of the *Tax Court of the United States Reports.* The nonacquiescence is reported on page 2 of Volume 1 of the 1980 *Cumulative Bulletin.* The IRS nonacquiesced in this 1973 decision in 1980.

Tax Court memo decisions are not published by the U.S. Government Printing Office. The decisions are available in bound form from RIA in *RIA T.C. Memorandum Decisions* and from CCH in *CCH Tax Court Memorandum Decisions.* In addition, soon after an opinion is issued, it is published in loose-leaf form by RIA and CCH. The following are citations to a Tax Court memo decision:

Edith G. McKinney, 1981 PH T.C. Memo ¶81,181, 41 TCM 1272.

KEY POINT

To access all Tax Court cases, a tax advisor must refer to two different publications. The regular opinions are found in the *Tax Court of the United States Reports,* published by the U.S. Government Printing Office, and the memo decisions are published by both RIA (formerly PH) and CCH in their own court reporters.

McKinney is found at Paragraph 81,181 of Prentice Hall's (now RIA's)[29] 1981 *PH T.C. Memorandum Decisions* reporter, and in Volume 41, page 1272, of CCH's *Tax Court Memorandum Decisions.* The 181 in the PH citation denotes that the case is the Tax Court's 181st memo decision of the year. A more recent citation is based on the same format but refers to RIA's memo decisions.

Paul F. Belloff, 1992 RIA T.C. Memo ¶92,346, 63 TCM 3150.

---

[28] In a citation to a Tax Court case, only the name of the plaintiff (taxpayer) is listed. The defendant is understood to be the Commissioner of Internal Revenue whose name usually is not shown in the citation. In cases litigated outside the Tax Court, the name of the plaintiff is listed first and the name of the defendant second. For non-Tax Court cases, the Commissioner of Internal Revenue is referred to as *CIR* in our footnotes and text.

[29] For several years the Prentice Hall Information Services division published its *Federal Taxes 2nd* tax service and a number of related publications, such as the *PH T.C. Memorandum Decisions*. Changes in ownership occurred, and in late 1991 Thomson Professional Publishing added the former Prentice Hall tax materials to the product line of its RIA tax publishing division. Some products such as the *PH T.C. Memorandum Decisions* still have the Prentice Hall name on the spine of older editions.

U.S. DISTRICT COURTS. Each state has at least one U.S. district court, and more populous states have more than one. Each district court is independent of the others and is thus free to issue its own decisions, subject to the precedential constraints discussed later in this chapter. Many different types of cases—not just tax cases—are heard in this forum. A district court is the only forum in which the taxpayer may have a jury decide questions of fact. Depending on the particular taxpayer and the circumstances involved, a jury trial might or might not be beneficial.[30]

District court decisions are officially reported in the *Federal Supplement* (cited as F. Supp.) published by West Publishing Co. (West). However, some decisions are not officially reported and are referred to as **unreported decisions**. Decisions by U.S. district courts on the topic of taxation also are published by RIA and CCH in secondary reporters that include only tax-related cases. RIA's reporter is called *American Federal Tax Reports* (cited as AFTR),[31] and CCH's reporter is known as *U.S. Tax Cases* (cited as USTC). Even though a case is not officially reported, it nevertheless may be published in the AFTR and USTC. An example of a complete citation to a U.S. district court decision is as follows:

> *Margie J. Thompson v. U.S.*, 429 F. Supp. 13, 39 AFTR 2d 77-1485, 77-1 USTC ¶9343 (DC Eastern District PA., 1977).

ADDITIONAL COMMENT

A citation, at a minimum, should contain the following information: (1) the name of the case, (2) the reporter that publishes the case along with both a volume and page (or paragraph) number, (3) the year the case was decided, and (4) the court that decided the case.

In the example above, the **primary citation** is to the *Federal Supplement*. The case appears on page 13 of Volume 429 of this reporter. **Secondary citations** are to *American Federal Tax Reports* and *U.S. Tax Cases*. The same case is found in Volume 39 of the second series of the AFTR, page 77-1485 (meaning page 1485 in the volume containing 1977 cases) and in Volume 1 of the 1977 USTC at Paragraph 9343. The parenthetical indicates that the case was decided in 1977 by the U.S. District Court for the Eastern District of Pennsylvania. Because some judicial decisions have greater precedential weight than others (e.g., a Supreme Court decision versus a district court decision), information relating to the identity of the adjudicating court is useful.

ADDITIONAL COMMENT

The U.S. Court of Federal Claims adjudicates claims (including suits to recover federal income taxes) against the U.S. Government. This court usually hears cases in Washington, D.C., but will hold sessions in other locations as the court deems necessary.

U.S. COURT OF FEDERAL CLAIMS. The U.S. Court of Federal Claims, another trial court that addresses tax matters, has nationwide jurisdiction. Originally, this court was named the U.S. Court of Claims (cited as Ct. Cl.), and its decisions were appealable to the U.S. Supreme Court only. In a restructuring, effective October 1, 1982, the reconstituted court was named the U.S. Claims Court (cited as Cl. Ct.), and its decisions became appealable to the Circuit Court of Appeals for the Federal Circuit. In October 1992, the court's name was again changed to the U.S. Court of Federal Claims (cited as Fed. Cl.).

Beginning in 1982, U.S. Claims Court decisions were reported officially in the *Claims Court Reporter*, published by West from 1982 to 1992.[32] An example of a citation to a U.S. Claims Court decision appears below:

> *Benjamin Raphan v. U.S.*, 3 Cl. Ct. 457, 52 AFTR 2d 83-5987, 83-2 USTC ¶9613 (1983).

The *Raphan* case appears on page 457 of Volume 3 of the *Claims Court Reporter*. Secondary citations are to Volume 52, page 83-5987 of the AFTR, second series, and to Volume 2 of the 1983 USTC in Paragraph 9613.

---

[30] Taxpayers prefer to have a jury trial if they think a jury will be sympathetic to their case.

[31] The *American Federal Tax Reports* (AFTR) is published in two series. The first series, which includes opinions issued up to 1957, is cited as AFTR. The second series, which includes opinions issued after 1957, is cited as AFTR 2d. The *Margie Thompson* decision cited as an illustration of a U.S. district court decision appears in the second *American Federal Tax Reports* series.

[32] Before the creation in 1982 of the U.S. Claims Court (and the *Claims Court Reporter*), the opinions of the U.S. Court of Claims were reported in either the *Federal Supplement* (F. Supp.) or the *Federal Reporter, Second Series* (F.2d). The *Federal Supplement* was the primary source of U.S. Court of Claims opinions from 1932 through January 19, 1960. From January 20, 1960, to October 1982, such opinions were reported in the *Federal Reporter, Second Series.*

Effective with the 1992 name change, decisions of the U.S. Court of Federal Claims are now reported in the *Federal Claims Reporter.* An example of a citation to an opinion published in this reporter is presented below:

> *Jeffrey G. Sharp v. U.S.*, 27 Fed. Cl. 52, 70 AFTR 2d 92-6040, 92-2 USTC ¶50,561 (1992).

The *Sharp* case appears on page 52 of Volume 27 of the *Federal Claims Reporter,* on page 6040 of the 70th volume of the AFTR, Second Series, and in Paragraph 50,561 of Volume 2 of the 1992 USTC reporter. Note that, even though the name of the reporter published by West has changed, the volume numbers continue in sequence as if there had been no name change.

CIRCUIT COURTS OF APPEALS. Trial court decisions are appealable by the losing party to the court of appeals for the circuit in which the litigation originated. Generally, if the case began in the Tax Court or a U.S. district court, the case is appealable to the circuit for the individual's residence as of the appeal date. For a corporation, the case is appealable to the circuit for the corporation's principal place of business. As mentioned above, the Federal Circuit handles all appeals of cases originating in the U.S. Court of Federal Claims.

There are 11 geographical circuits designated by numbers, the circuit for the District of Columbia, and the Federal Circuit. A map of the circuits and their jurisdictions appears in Figure C1-3, displayed earlier in this chapter. The 11 numbered circuits and the D.C. Circuit hear appeals of persons or firms from their locality. In October 1981, the Eleventh Circuit was created by moving Alabama, Georgia, and Florida from the Fifth to the new Eleventh Circuit. The Eleventh Circuit voluntarily adopted the policy that it will follow as precedent all decisions made by the Fifth Circuit during the time the states currently constituting the Eleventh Circuit were part of the Fifth Circuit.[33]

EXAMPLE C1-7 ▶ In the current year, the Eleventh Circuit first considered an issue in a case concerning a Florida taxpayer. In 1980, the Fifth Circuit had ruled on this issue in a case involving a Louisiana taxpayer. Because Florida was part of the Fifth Circuit in 1980, under the policy adopted by the Eleventh Circuit, it will follow the Fifth Circuit's earlier decision. Had the Fifth Circuit's decision been rendered in 1982—after the creation of the Eleventh Circuit—the Eleventh Circuit would not have been bound by the Fifth Circuit's decision. ◀

As the later discussion of precedential value points out, different circuits may reach different conclusions concerning the same issue.

Circuit court decisions—regardless of topic (e.g., civil rights, securities law, and taxation)—are now reported officially in the *Federal Reporter, Third Series* (cited as F.3d), published by West. The third series began in October 1993 after the volume number for the second series reached 999. The primary citation to a circuit court opinion should be to the *Federal Reporter*. Tax decisions of the circuit courts also appear in the *American Federal Tax Reports* and *U.S. Tax Cases*. Below is an example of a citation to a 1994 circuit court decision:

> *Leonard Greene v. U.S.*, 13 F.3d 577, 73 AFTR 2d 94-746, 94-1 USTC ¶50,022 (2nd Cir., 1994).

The *Greene* case appears on page 577 of Volume 13 of the *Federal Reporter, Third Series.* It also is reported in Volume 73, page 94-746 of the AFTR, second series, and in Volume 1, Paragraph 50,022, of the 1994 USTC. Parenthetical information indicates that the Second Circuit decided the case in 1994. (A *Federal Reporter, Second Series* citation can be found in footnote 33 of this chapter.)

---

[33] *Bonner v. City of Prichard*, 661 F.2d 1206 (11th Cir., 1981).

ADDITIONAL COMMENT

A judge is not required to follow judicial precedent beyond his or her jurisdiction. Thus, the Tax Court, the U.S. district courts, and the U.S. Court of Federal Claims are not required to follow the others' decisions, nor is a circuit court required to follow the decision of a different circuit court.

U.S. SUPREME COURT. Whichever party loses at the appellate court level can request that the U.S. Supreme Court hear the case. The Supreme Court, however, hears very few tax cases. Unless the circuits are divided on the proper treatment of a tax item, or the issue is deemed to be of great significance, the Supreme Court probably will not hear the case.[34] Supreme Court decisions are the law of the land and supersede earlier cases. As a practical matter, a Supreme Court ruling on an interpretation of the IRC has the same effect as if its interpretative language was added to the IRC. If Congress does not agree with the Court's interpretation, it can amend the statutory language to achieve a contrary result. From time to time, Congress has responded to Supreme Court decisions by amending the IRC.[35] If the Supreme Court declares a particular statute to be unconstitutional, the statute is invalid.

All Supreme Court decisions, regardless of the subject matter, are published in the *United States Supreme Court Reports* (cited as U.S.) by the U.S. Government Printing Office, the *Supreme Court Reporter* (cited as S.Ct.) by West, and the *United States Reports, Lawyers' Edition* (cited as L. Ed.) by Lawyer's Co-Operative Publishing Co. In addition, the AFTR and USTC reporters published by RIA and CCH, respectively, contain Supreme Court decisions concerned with taxation. An example of a citation to a Supreme Court opinion appears below:

U.S. v. Maclin P. Davis, 397 U.S. 301, 25 AFTR 2d 70-827, 70-1 USTC ¶9289 (1970).

According to the primary citation, this case appears in Volume 397, page 301, of the *United States Supreme Court Reports.* According to the secondary citation, it also is reported in Volume 25, page 70-827, of the AFTR, Second Series, and in Volume 1, Paragraph 9289, of the 1970 USTC.

SELF-STUDY QUESTION

Is it possible for the Tax Court to intentionally issue conflicting decisions?

ANSWER

Yes. If the Tax Court issues two decisions that are appealable to different circuit courts and these courts have previously reached different conclusions on the issue, the Tax Court follows the respective precedent in each circuit and issues conflicting decisions. This is a result of the *Golsen* Rule.

Table C1-2 provides a summary of how court decisions, revenue rulings, revenue procedures, and other administrative interpretations should be cited. Primary citations are to the reporters published by West or the U.S. Government Printing Office, and secondary citations are to the AFTR and USTC reporters.

PRECEDENTIAL VALUE OF VARIOUS DECISIONS.

Tax Court. The Tax Court is a court of national jurisdiction. Consequently, it generally rules uniformly for all taxpayers, regardless of their geographical location. It follows Supreme Court decisions and its own earlier decisions. It is not bound by cases decided by the U.S. Court of Federal Claims or a U.S. district court, even if the district court has jurisdiction over the taxpayer.

In 1970, the Tax Court adopted what has become known as the *Golsen* Rule.[36] Under the *Golsen* Rule, the Tax Court departs from its general policy of ruling uniformly for all taxpayers and instead follows the decisions of the court of appeals to which the case in question is appealable. Stated differently, the *Golsen* Rule holds that the Tax Court rules consistently with decisions of the court for the circuit where the taxpayer resides or does business.

EXAMPLE C1-8 ▶ In the year in which an issue was first litigated, the Tax Court decided that an expenditure was deductible. The government appealed the decision to the Tenth Circuit Court of Appeals and won a reversal. This is the only appellate decision regarding the issue. If and when the Tax Court encounters this issue again, it will hold, with one exception, that the expenditure is deductible. The exception applies to taxpayers in the Tenth Circuit. Under the *Golsen* Rule, these taxpayers will be denied the deduction. ◀

[34] *Vogel Fertilizer Co. v. U.S.*, 49 AFTR 2d 82-491, 82-1 USTC ¶9134 (USSC, 1982), is an example of a case the Supreme Court heard to settle a split in judicial authority. The Fifth Circuit, the Tax Court, and the Court of Claims had reached one conclusion on an issue, while the Second, Fourth, and Eighth Circuits had reached another.

[35] For an example of where Congress enacted legislation to achieve a result contrary to that of a Supreme Court decision, see *U.S. v. Marian A. Byrum,* 30 AFTR 2d 72-5811, 72-2 USTC ¶12,859 (USSC, 1972).

[36] The *Golsen* Rule is based on the decision in *Jack E. Golsen,* 54 T.C. 742 (1970).

▼ **TABLE C1-2**
Summary of Tax-related Primary Sources—Statutory and Administrative

Source Name	Publisher	Materials Provided	Citation Example
U.S. Code, Title 26	Government Printing Office	Internal Revenue Code	Sec. 441(b)
Code of Federal Regulations, Title 26	Government Printing Office	Treasury Regulations (final)	Reg. Sec. 1.461-1(c)
		Treasury Regulations (temporary)	Temp. Reg. Sec. 1.62-1T(e)
Internal Revenue Bulletin	Government Printing Office	Treasury Regulations (proposed)	Prop. Reg. Sec. 1.671-2(e)
		Treasury decisions	T.D. 8756 (January 12, 1998)
		Revenue rulings	Rev. Rul. 98-1, I.R.B. 1998-2, 1
		Revenue procedures	Rev. Proc. 97-37, I.R.B. 1997-33, 18
		Committee reports	S.Rept. No. 105-33, 105th Cong., 1st Sess., p. 308 (1997)
		Public laws	P.L. 105-34, Sec. 224(a), enacted August 6, 1997
		Announcements	Announcement 98-1, I.R.B. 1998-2, 38
		Notices	Notice 98-1, I.R.B. 1998-3, 42
Cumulative Bulletin	Government Printing Office	Treasury Regulations (proposed)	Prop. Reg. Sec. 1.671-2(e)
		Treasury decisions	T.D. 8756 (January 12, 1998)
		Revenue rulings	Rev. Rul. , 1974-1 C.B. 105
		Revenue procedures	Rev. Proc. 77-28, 1977-2 C.B. 537
		Committee reports	S.Rept. No. 105-33, 105th Cong., 1st Sess., p. 308 (1997)
		Public laws	P.L. 105-34, Sec. 224(a), enacted August 6, 1997
		Notices	Notice 88-74, 1988-2 C.B. 385

Summary of Tax-related Primary and Secondary Sources—Judicial

Reporter Name	Publisher	Decisions Published	Citation Example
U.S. Supreme Court Reports	Government Printing Office	U.S. Supreme Court	*U.S. v. Maclin P. Davis*, 397 U.S. 301 (1970)
Supreme Court Reports	West Publishing Company	U.S. Supreme Court	*U.S. v. Maclin P. Davis*, 90 S. Ct. 1041 (1970).
Federal Reporter (1st-3d Series)	West Publishing Company	U.S. Court of Appeal Pre-1982 Court of Claims	*Leonard Green v. U.S.*, 13 F.3d 577 (2nd Cir., 1994)
Federal Supplement Series	West Publishing Company	U.S. District Court	*Margie J. Thompson v. U.S.*, 429 F.Supp. 13 (DC Eastern District PA, 1977)
U.S. Court of Federal Claims	West Publishing Company	Court of Federal Claims	*Jeffery G. Sharp v. U.S.*, 27 Fed. Cl. 52 (1992)
Tax Court of the U.S. Reports	Government Printing Office	U.S. Tax Court regular	*Henry D. Duarte*, 44 T.C. 193 (1965), acq. 1967-2 C.B. 3
Tax Court Memorandum Decisions	CCH Incorporated	U.S. Tax Court memo	*Paul F. Beloff*, 63 TCM 3150 (1992).
RIA Tax Court Memorandum Decisions	Research Institute of America	U.S. Tax Court memo	*Paul F. Beloff*, 1992 RIA T.C. Memo ¶92,346.
American Federal Tax Reports	Research Institute of America	Tax: all federal courts except Tax Court	*U.S. v. Maclin P. Davis*, 25 AFTR 2d 70-827 (USSC, 1970)
U.S. Tax Cases	CCH Incorporated	Tax: all federal courts except Tax Court	*Ruddick Corp. v. U.S.*, 81-1 USTC ¶9343 (Ct. Cls., 1981)

U.S. District Court. Because each U.S. district court is independent of the other district courts, the decisions of each have precedential value only within its own jurisdiction (i.e., only with respect to subsequent cases brought before that court). District courts must follow decisions of the U.S. Supreme Court, the circuit court to which the case is appealable, and the district court's own earlier decisions on the same issue.

EXAMPLE C1-9 ▶ The U.S. District Court for Rhode Island, the Tax Court, and the Eleventh Circuit have ruled on a particular issue. Any U.S. district court within the Eleventh Circuit must follow that circuit's decision. Similarly, the U.S. District Court for Rhode Island must rule consistently with its previous ruling. Tax Court decisions are not binding on the district courts. Thus, all district courts other than the one for Rhode Island and those within the Eleventh Circuit are free to decide the issue independently. ◀

U.S. Court of Federal Claims. In adjudicating a dispute, the U.S. Court of Federal Claims must rule consistently with U.S. Supreme Court decisions, decisions of the Circuit Court of Appeals for the Federal Circuit, and its own earlier decisions, including those rendered when the court had a different name. It need not follow decisions of other circuit courts, the Tax Court, or U.S. district courts.

EXAMPLE C1-10 ▶ Assume the same facts as in Example C1-9. In a later year, the same issue is litigated in the U.S. Court of Federal Claims. This court is not bound by any of the authorities that have addressed the issue. Thus, it has complete flexibility to reach its own conclusion. ◀

Circuit Courts of Appeals. A circuit court is bound by U.S. Supreme Court decisions and its own earlier decisions. If neither the Supreme Court nor the circuit in question has already decided an issue, the circuit court has no precedent that it must follow, regardless of whether other circuits have ruled on the point. In such a situation, the circuit court is said to be writing on a clean slate. In issuing a decision, the judges may adopt the view expressed in another circuit's opinion if they deem it appropriate.

EXAMPLE C1-11 ▶ Assume the same facts as in Example C1-9. Any circuit other than the Eleventh would be writing on a clean slate if it adjudicated the same issue. After reviewing the Eleventh Circuit's decision, another circuit might or might not rule in the same way. ◀

In such a case of "first impression," when the court has had no precedent on which to base a decision, a tax practitioner might look at past opinions of the court to see which other judicial authority the court has found to be "persuasive."

Forum Shopping. Not surprisingly, courts often disagree as to the appropriate tax treatment of the same item. This disagreement gives rise to differing precedents within the various jurisdictions (what is called a "split in judicial authority"). Because taxpayers have the flexibility of choosing where to file a lawsuit, these circumstances afford them the opportunity to **forum shop.** Forum-shopping involves choosing where among the courts to file a lawsuit based on differing precedents.

An example of a split in judicial authority concerned the issue of when it became too late for the IRS to question the proper tax treatment of items that "flowed through" an S corporation's return to a shareholder's return. The key question was this: if the time for assessing a deficiency (statute of limitations) with respect to the corporation's, but not the shareholder's, return had expired, was the IRS precluded from collecting additional taxes from the shareholder? In *Kelley,*[37] the Ninth Circuit Court of Appeals ruled that the IRS would be barred from collecting additional taxes from the shareholder if the statute of limitations for the *S corporation's* return had expired. In *Bufferd,*[38] *Fehlhaber,*[39] and

[37] *Daniel M. Kelley v. CIR,* 64 AFTR 2d 89-5025, 89-1 USTC ¶9360 (9th Cir., 1989).

[38] *Sheldon B. Bufferd v. CIR,* 69 AFTR 2d 92-465, 92-1 USTC ¶50,031 (2nd Cir., 1992).

[39] *Robert Fehlhaber v. CIR,* 69 AFTR 2d 92-850, 92-1 USTC ¶50,131 (11th Cir., 1992).

Green,[40] three other circuit courts ruled that the IRS would be barred from collecting additional taxes from the shareholder if the statute of limitations for the *shareholder's* return had expired. The Supreme Court affirmed the *Bufferd*[41] case, establishing that the statute of limitations for the shareholder's return governed. This action brought about certainty and uniformity in the judicial system.

Dictum. At times, a court may comment on an issue or a set of facts not central to the case under review. A court's remark not essential to the determination of a disputed issue, and therefore not binding authority, is called *dictum.* An example of dictum is found in *Central Illinois Public Service Co.*[42] In this case, the U.S. Supreme Court addressed whether lunch reimbursements received by employees constitute wages subject to withholding. Justice Blackman remarked in passing that earnings in the form of interest, rents, and dividends are not wages. This remark is dictum because it is not essential to the determination of whether lunch reimbursements are wages subject to withholding. Although not authoritative, dictum may be cited by taxpayers to bolster an argument in favor of a particular tax result.

STOP & THINK

Question: You have been researching whether a certain amount received by your new client can be excluded from her gross income. The IRS is auditing the client's tax return for two years ago, which another firm prepared. In a similar case decided a few years ago, the Tax Court allowed an exclusion, but the IRS nonacquiesced in the decision. The case involved a taxpayer from the Fourth Circuit. Your client is a resident of Maine, which is in the First Circuit. Twelve years ago, in a case involving another taxpayer, the U.S. district court for the client's district ruled that this type of receipt is not excludable. No other precedent exists. To sustain an exclusion, must your client litigate? Explain. If your client litigates, in which trial court should she begin her litigation?

Solution: Because of its nonacquiescence, the IRS is likely to challenge your client's tax treatment. Thus, she may be compelled to litigate. She would not want to litigate in her U.S. district court because it would be bound by its earlier decision, which is unfavorable to taxpayers generally. A good place to begin would be the Tax Court because of its earlier pro-taxpayer position. No one can predict how the U.S. Court of Federal Claims would rule because no precedent that it must follow exists.

TAX TREATIES

ADDITIONAL COMMENT

A tax treaty carries the same authoritative weight as a statute. A tax advisor should be aware of provisions in tax treaties that will affect a taxpayer's worldwide tax liability.

The United States has concluded **tax treaties** with numerous foreign countries. These treaties address the avoidance of double taxation and other matters. A tax advisor addressing the U.S. tax consequences of a U.S. corporation's business operations in another country should determine whether a treaty exists between that country and the United States. If one does, the tax advisor should ascertain the applicable provisions of the treaty. (See Chapter C16 of this text for a more extensive discussion of treaties.)

TAX PERIODICALS

KEY POINT

Tax articles can be used to help *find* answers to tax questions. Where possible, the underlying statutory, administrative, or judicial sources referenced in the tax article should be cited as authority and not the author of the article. The courts and the IRS will place little, if any, reliance on mere editorial opinion.

Tax periodicals assist the researcher in tracing the development of, and in analyzing tax law. These periodicals are especially useful when they trace the legislative history of a recently enacted statute, and there is little or no administrative or judicial authority on point.

Tax experts write articles on recent court decisions, proposed regulations, new tax legislation, and other matters. Frequently, those who write articles of a highly technical nature are attorneys, accountants, or professors. Among the periodicals that provide in-depth coverage of tax-related developments are the following:

[40] *Charles T. Green v. CIR,* 70 AFTR 2d 92-5077, 92-2 USTC ¶50,340 (5th Cir., 1992).

[41] *Sheldon B. Bufferd v. CIR,* 71 AFTR 2d 93-573, 93-1 USTC ¶50,038 (USSC, 1993).

[42] *Central Illinois Public Service Co. v. CIR,* 41 AFTR 2d 78-718, 78-1 USTC ¶9254 (USSC, 1978).

The Journal of Taxation
The Tax Adviser
Practical Tax Strategies
Taxes—the Tax Magazine
Tax Law Review
Tax Notes
The Journal of Corporate Taxation
Business Entities
The Journal of Real Estate Taxation
The Review of Taxation of Individuals
Estate Planning

The first six journals are generalized; that is, they deal with a variety of topics. As their titles suggest, the next five are specialized; they deal with specific subjects. All these publications (other than *Tax Notes,* which is published weekly) are published either monthly or quarterly. Daily newsletters, such as the *Daily Tax Report,* published by the Bureau of National Affairs (BNA), are used by tax professionals when they need updates more timely than can be provided by monthly or quarterly publications.

Tax periodicals and tax services are secondary authorities. The IRC, Treasury Regulations, IRS pronouncements, and court opinions are primary authorities. In presenting research results, the tax advisor should always cite primary authorities.

TAX SERVICES

OBJECTIVE 4

Use tax services to research an issue

Various publishers provide multivolume commentaries on the tax law in what are familiarly referred to as **tax services.** Each tax service is encyclopedic in scope. Most come in looseleaf form so that information on current developments can be easily added. The organizational scheme of each service differs. Some are updated more frequently than others. Each has its own special features and unique way of presenting material. The best way to acquaint oneself with the various tax services is to use them in researching hypothetical or actual problems.

ADDITIONAL COMMENT

Tax services often are consulted at the beginning of the research process. A tax service helps identify the tax authorities pertaining to a particular tax issue. The actual tax authorities, and not the tax service, are generally cited as support for a particular tax position.

Organizationally, there are two types of tax services: "annotated" and "topical" (although this distinction has become somewhat blurred in the Internet version of these services). An **annotated tax service** is organized by IRC section. The IRC-arranged subdivisions of this service are likely to encompass several topics. A **topical tax service** is organized by broad topic. The topically-arranged subdivisions of this service are likely to encompass several IRC sections. The principal annotated tax services are the *United States Tax Reporter* and *Standard Federal Tax Reporter.* The main topical services are the *Federal Tax Coordinator 2d, Law of Federal Income Taxation (Mertens), Tax Management Portfolios, and CCH Federal Tax Service.* Each of these services is discussed below.

KEY POINT

Both the *United States Tax Reporter* and the *Standard Federal Tax Reporter* services are organized by IRC section. Many tax advisors find both of these services easy to use. The other major tax services are organized by topic.

UNITED STATES TAX REPORTER

The *United States Tax Reporter,* published by RIA, is a multivolume series devoted to income, estate, gift, and excise taxes. It is organized by IRC section number, i.e., its commentary begins with Sec. 1 of the IRC and proceeds in numerical order through the last section of the IRC. Researchers who know the number of the IRC section applicable to their problem can turn directly to the paragraphs that discuss that section. Each organizational part presents the text of the relevant IRC section, committee reports, Treasury Regulations, IRS pronouncements, and editorial explanations, all indexed according to IRC section number. Separate volumes contain an index and finding lists that reference explanatory paragraphs respectively by topic and by case name or IRS pronouncement. These resources enable the researcher to access this service in one of three ways: first, by IRC section number; second, by topic; and third, by citation.

One of the more salient features of this service (as well as the CCH service discussed below) are the annotations following the editorial explanations. These annotations consist of digests or summaries of IRS pronouncements and court opinions that interpret a particular IRC section. They are classified by subtopic and cite pertinent primary authorities.

The *United States Tax Reporter* is updated weekly. Information on recent developments is referenced in a table in Volume 16 and periodically moved into the main body of the text. To determine whether any recent developments impact a particular issue, the researcher should look in the table for references to the numbers of paragraphs that discuss the issue. The service includes, in addition to the recent developments volume, several volumes on the IRC and Treasury Regulations, a compilation of newly issued *American Federal Tax Reports* decisions, and practical aids such as tax rate, interest rate, and per diem rate tables. The computerized version of the *United States Tax Reporter* is available on RIA CHECKPOINT™.

STANDARD FEDERAL TAX REPORTER

REAL WORLD EXAMPLE

The 1913 CCH explanation of the federal tax law was a single 400-page volume. The current *Standard Federal Tax Reporter* is 25 volumes and over 95,000 pages in length.

CCH publishes the *Standard Federal Tax Reporter* (CCH service), also organized by IRC section number. Separate services devoted to income taxes, estate and gift taxes, and excise taxes are available. Like RIA's *United States Tax Reporter*, the CCH service compiles in its main volumes the text of the IRC, Treasury Regulations, editorial explanations, and annotations. Also like the RIA service, the CCH service includes a topical index and finding lists that reference explanatory paragraphs respectively by topic and by authority. Thus, like the *United States Tax Reporter*, the CCH service can be accessed by IRC section number, topic, and citation.[43]

The IRC volumes of the CCH service contain tables that cross-reference sections of the current IRC with other sections of the current IRC and with predecessor provisions of the 1954 IRC. The first of these tables enables the researcher to identify other sections of the current IRC that potentially impact a transaction or taxable event. The second table enables the researcher to trace the statutory history of a particular IRC provision. The IRC volumes also contain a comprehensive listing of committee reports organized by IRC section number. This listing enables the researcher to locate sources that suggest the legislative intent behind a particular IRC provision.

The CCH service issues weekly supplements on current developments. Until the end of the calendar year, when CCH publishes a new reporter series, it supplies periodic updates on court opinions and revenue rulings. Throughout the year, information on major developments, such as new tax legislation and Supreme Court decisions, is incorporated in the main body of the text. The Internet version of the CCH service is available on the CCH Internet Tax Research NetWork™.

FEDERAL TAX COORDINATOR 2d

ADDITIONAL COMMENT

The RIA *Federal Tax Coordinator 2d* service is a more voluminous service than either the *United States Tax Reporter* or *Standard Federal Tax Reporter* services because it has more editorial commentary. The *Federal Tax Coordinator 2d* updates are integrated into the main body of the text. The service is not replaced each year. By contrast, both the *United States Tax Reporter* and *Standard Federal Tax Reporter* services compile their updates in one volume. CCH issues a new *Standard Federal Tax Reporter service each year. The other services integrate the updates into the body of existing text at the beginning of each year.*

The *Federal Tax Coordinator 2d* (FTC service), also published by RIA, is a multivolume looseleaf publication organized by broad topic. It covers three major areas: income taxes, estate and gift taxes, and excise taxes. Unlike the annotated services, the FTC service presents its editorial commentary before excerpts of relevant IRC and Treasury Regulation sections. The latter excerpts are placed behind a tab titled Code & Regs within the same topical volume. The editorial commentary is heavily footnoted. The footnotes refer to court cases, revenue rulings, and other primary authorities that pertain to the topical discussion. An index volume references the numbers of paragraphs that discuss various topics. Cross-reference tables reference the numbers of paragraphs that discuss particular IRC sections, Treasury Regulations, IRS pronouncements, and court cases. Instead of providing a separate volume for new developments, the FTC service incorporates new developments information in the main body of the service.

A peculiar feature of the FTC service is its editorial notations, which suggest the practical implications of the tax principle under discussion. Among the notations are "*illustration*," which offers examples of how the principle is applied; "*caution*," which points to the risks associated with application; "*recommendation*," which suggests ways to minimize the risk; and "*observation*," which offers an editorial analysis of the principle.

---

[43] Examples of citations to these tax services are as follows: (2001) 6 *United States Tax Reporter* (RIA) ¶3025 and (2001) 8 *Std. Fed. Tax Rep.* (CCH) ¶21,966.02, where 6 and 8 represent the volume numbers, and the paragraph numbers refer to the cited passages in the volume. Because citations should be to primary authorities, citations to secondary authorities are rarely used.

One volume of the FTC service titled Practice Aids provides tools useful in tax practice. Other services provide similar tools. Such tools include Tax Savings Opportunity Checklists, designed to assist taxpayers in proceeding with business and personal transactions; a Current Legislation Table, which indicates the status of pending tax legislation; and an IRS Forms Table, which cross-references the numbers of IRS forms to those of paragraphs in the topical discussion; and tax calendars, tax schedules, sample client letters, and daily compound interest tables. Other volumes of the FTC service present the text of tax treaties, revenue rulings, revenue procedures, and proposed Treasury Regulations. A separate volume compiles issues of *Weekly Alert*, RIA's tax newsletter. The Internet version of the FTC service is available on RIA CHECKPOINT™.

LAW OF FEDERAL INCOME TAXATION (MERTENS)

The *Law of Federal Income Taxation,* published by the West Group, originally was edited by Merten's and is called "Mertens" by tax practitioners and in this text. Legalistic in orientation, Mertens deals only with federal income taxation. Its commentary is narrative in form and reads like a treatise. Mertens is highly regarded by tax accountants and tax lawyers. It is the only tax service cited by the U.S. judiciary with any regularity. The text of Mertens is heavily footnoted. The footnotes contain a wealth of information relating to the IRC, Treasury Regulations, IRS pronouncements, and court opinions.

Mertens includes several volumes devoted exclusively to Treasury Regulations and IRS pronouncements. These volumes contain the full text of *current* Treasury Regulations and IRS pronouncements (this text does not appear in the main commentary volumes), as well as the full text of *old* Treasury Regulations and IRS pronouncements. The old versions enable the researcher to reconstruct the state of the tax law in any given year. Such reconstruction is useful in three contexts: first, where the IRS audits a taxpayer's return for a previous year; second, where the researcher evaluates the effects of a transaction beginning in a previous year; and third, where the researcher analyzes a court opinion issued in a previous year.

Like the annotated services, Mertens contains a topical index and finding lists cross-referenced to the IRC, Treasury Regulations, IRS pronouncements, and court opinions. Its *Current Rulings Materials* volume includes a Code-Rulings Table that lists by IRC section the numbers of all post-1954 revenue rulings that interpret a particular section. The same volume also includes a Rulings Status Table that indicates the status of every post-1954 revenue ruling (i.e., whether the ruling has been revoked, modified, amplified, or otherwise impacted by an IRS decision).[44] Its *Current Materials* volume compiles issues of *Development and Highlights*, Mertens' monthly periodical. The Internet version of Mertens is available on WESTLAW™.

TAX MANAGEMENT PORTFOLIOS

ADDITIONAL COMMENT

The *Tax Management Portfolios* are popular with many tax advisors because they are very readable yet still provide a comprehensive discussion of the pertinent tax issues. However, because the published portfolios do not cover all areas of the tax law, another service may be necessary to supplement the gaps in the portfolio coverage.

BNA publishes over 200 booklets of specialized tax materials called *Tax Management Portfolios* (referred to as BNA portfolios by many practitioners and in this text). BNA portfolios are issued in three series: U.S. income; foreign income; and estates, gifts, and trusts. Each portfolio is prepared by a specialized tax practitioner. Thus, the particular slant of BNA portfolios is practical application, as opposed to the theoretical. In each portfolio, the author's discussion of a particular topic is found in the Detailed Analysis section. Here, provisions of the IRC and Treasury Regulations are explained, court opinions are analyzed, and transactional structures are proposed. The text of the Detailed Analysis is heavily footnoted. The footnotes cite and summarize relevant primary and secondary sources.

A noteworthy feature of each BNA portfolio is its Working Papers, which are tools designed to aid the practitioner in tax planning and compliance. Among such tools are tax-related checklists, IRS forms and instructions, computational worksheets, and draft legal documents. The Bibliography and References section at the back of each volume lists primary and secondary sources used by the author to prepare the portfolio. In this section,

[44] RIA and CCH services provide essentially the same information in different formats.

the researcher will find a listing of IRC sections, Treasury Regulations, IRS pronouncements, and court opinions that support the Detailed Analysis, as well as references to pertinent law review articles and tax treatises.

Unlike the other tax services, BNA portfolios do not contain finding lists indexed to court opinions or IRS pronouncements. On the other hand, they do contain a topical index, an IRC reference table, and an IRS forms index that cross-references the numbers of IRS forms to pertinent pages in the portfolios. Like CCH and RIA, BNA publishes a weekly newsletter as part of its tax service. The Internet version of BNA portfolios is available on LexisNexis™ and the BNA Tax Management Library.

CCH FEDERAL TAX SERVICE

The newest of the major tax services is the *CCH Federal Tax Service,* currently published by CCH and formerly published by Matthew Bender & Company. This service is a multivolume looseleaf publication that, like RIA's FTC service and Mertens, is organized by broad topic. Just like portfolios in the BNA service, chapters of the *CCH Federal Tax Service* are authored by tax practitioners and thus are practical in orientation.

The *CCH Federal Tax Service* does not compile sections of the IRC and Treasury Regulations in the same volumes as the topical analysis. Rather it publishes them in separate volumes devoted exclusively to the IRC and proposed, temporary, and final Treasury Regulations. A particular IRC section and its related Treasury Regulations are found in the same volume.

CCH periodically updates the *Federal Tax Service* to reflect current developments. As with its annotated tax service, CCH issues a weekly newsletter as part of this topical tax service. The Internet version of the *CCH Federal Tax Service* is available on the CCH Internet Tax Research NetWork™.

Figure C1-5 provides an overview of one approach for using the tax services to research a tax question.

CITATORS

OBJECTIVE 5

Use a citator to assess tax authorities

Citators serve two functions: first, they give a history of the case (e.g., if the case under analysis is an appeals court decision, the citator indicates the trial court that heard the case and whether the Supreme Court reviewed the case); and second, they list other authorities (e.g., cases and revenue rulings) that cite the case in question. The RIA citator is available separately from either of RIA's principal tax services.

CCH CITATOR

The CCH citator consists of two loose-leaf volumes, one for cases with names beginning with the letters A through M and the other for cases with names starting with the letters N through Z. In the CCH Internet Tax Research NetWork™, this information is integrated into one citator service. This citator analyzes every decision reported in CCH's *Standard Federal Tax Reporter,* its *Excise Tax Reporter,* and its *Federal Estate and Gift Tax Reporter* and selectively lists cases that cite the reported decision. (CCH editors decide which of these other cases influence the precedential weight of the reported decision.) With respect to rulings and other government promulgations, the Finding Lists section provides full histories of all actions affected by or affecting each pronouncement. For example, the list notes that a certain 1993 revenue ruling revokes a certain 1989 revenue ruling. An excerpt from the CCH citator appears in Figure C1-6.

Refer to Figure C1-6, and find the *Leonarda C. Diaz* case. The information in bold print with bullets to the left denotes that *Diaz* was a decision of the Second Circuit and the Tax Court and that the Second Circuit affirmed (upheld) the Tax Court's decision. The two cases listed beneath the Second Circuit decision (i.e., *Kuh* and *Damm*) cite the *Diaz* decision. The six cases listed beneath the Tax Court decision (i.e., *German, Jr., Orr, Zeidler, Schwerm, Wassenaar,* and *Toner*) cite the Tax Court's opinion in *Diaz.* The abbreviation *Dec.* appearing in some of the citations stands for *decision.* The CCH citator lists the decision numbers of the Tax Court cases.

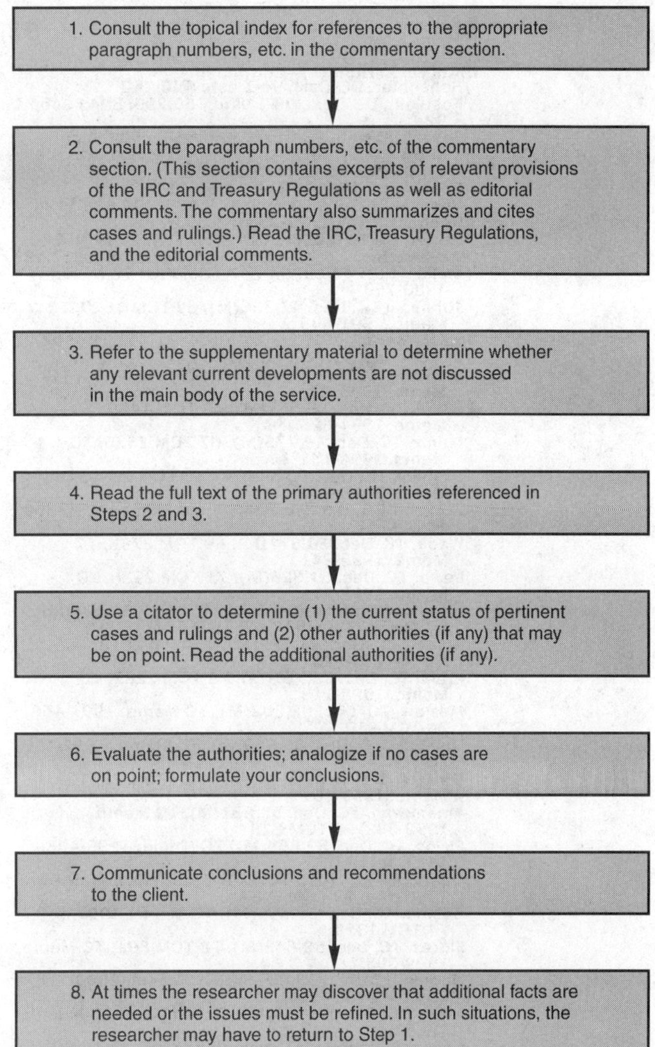

1. Consult the topical index for references to the appropriate paragraph numbers, etc. in the commentary section.
2. Consult the paragraph numbers, etc. of the commentary section. (This section contains excerpts of relevant provisions of the IRC and Treasury Regulations as well as editorial comments. The commentary also summarizes and cites cases and rulings.) Read the IRC, Treasury Regulations, and the editorial comments.
3. Refer to the supplementary material to determine whether any relevant current developments are not discussed in the main body of the service.
4. Read the full text of the primary authorities referenced in Steps 2 and 3.
5. Use a citator to determine (1) the current status of pertinent cases and rulings and (2) other authorities (if any) that may be on point. Read the additional authorities (if any).
6. Evaluate the authorities; analogize if no cases are on point; formulate your conclusions.
7. Communicate conclusions and recommendations to the client.
8. At times the researcher may discover that additional facts are needed or the issues must be refined. In such situations, the researcher may have to return to Step 1.

FIGURE C1-5 ▶ USE OF TAX SERVICES TO RESEARCH A TAX QUESTION

The main CCH citator volumes are published once a year. The first of these volumes contains a "Current Citator Table," which lists court decisions recently cited, as well as additional citing cases for court decisions previously cited. Citator updates are issued quarterly. The *Diaz* decision has not been cited in any opinion issued since 2001, the year in which the CCH citator was last published. The applicable page from the main citator table for the *Diaz* decision is reproduced here.

The entry "¶5504.20" appearing to the right of *Alfonso Diaz* denotes the number of the *Standard Federal Tax Reporter* paragraph that discusses the case. Usually, before consulting the citator, a researcher already would have read about this case in the paragraph and would have decided that it was relevant to his or her research. In such circumstances, the paragraph reference would not be particularly useful. In other circumstances, the reference would be useful. For example, if the researcher had heard about the case from a colleague and wanted to read more about it, he or she could readily locate the passage that discusses it.

The CCH citator lists cases even where they have not been cited in other cases. For example, refer to the entry for *Frank Diaz*. This Tax Court memo decision is listed among the cases analyzed, even though no other published decision has referred to it. Moreover, the citator indicates whether the IRS Commissioner has acquiesced or nonacquiesced in a Tax Court decision. For example, refer to the entry for *Alfonso Diaz*. Note that the first

DIA 93,334 ——CCH——

DiAndre, Anthony F.—continued
Schachter, DC-Calif, 94-1 USTC ¶ 50,242
Fostvedt, DC-Colo, 93-1 USTC ¶ 50,299, 824 FSupp 978
Jones, DC-Neb, 95-2 USTC ¶ 50,567, 898 FSupp 1360
May, DC-Mo, 95-2 USTC ¶ 50,605
Spence, DC-NM, 96-2 USTC ¶ 50,615
Spence, CA-10, 97-1 USTC ¶ 50,485, 114 F3d 1198
Roebuck, DC-NC, 99-2 USTC ¶ 50,627
Lester, CA-10, 2000-1 USTC ¶ 50,255, 208 F3d 226

DiAndrea, Inc. .... ¶ 16,233.25, 21,817.188
● **TC**—Dec. 40,697(M); 47 TCM 731; TC Memo. 1983-768
Johnson, TC, Dec. 47,836(M), 62 TCM 1629, TC Memo. 1991-645

Diaz, Alfonso .... ¶ 5504.20
● **TC**—Dec. 31,442; 58 TC 560; A. 1972-2 CB 2
Marrone, TC, Dec. 50,424(M), 69 TCM 1684, TC Memo. 1995-22
Sloan, TC, Dec. 50,305(M), 68 TCM 1489, TC Memo. 1994-628
Muniz, TC, Dec. 49,775(M), 67 TCM 2625, TC Memo. 1994-151
Drabiuk, TC, Dec. 50,692(M), 69 TCM 2890, TC Memo. 1995-260
Jackson, TC, Dec. 50,736(M), TC Memo. 1995-300, 70 TCM 12
Wada, TC, Dec. 50,672(M), 69 TCM 2793, TC Memo. 1995-241
Levin, TC, Dec. 51,326(M), 71 TCM 2938, TC Memo. 1996-211
American Underwriters, Inc., TC, Dec. 51,694(M), TC Memo. 1996-548, 72 TCM 1511
Solaas, TC, Dec. 52,529(M), 75 TCM 1613, TC Memo. 1998-25
Arcia, TC, Dec. 52,701(M), 75 TCM 2287, TC Memo. 1998-178
Maslow, TC, Dec. 52,302(M), TC Memo. 1997-466, 74 TCM 910
Neff Est., TC, Dec. 51,999(M), TC Memo. 1997-186, 73 TCM 2606
Swiatek, TC, Dec. 53,485(M), 78 TCM 223, TC Memo. 1999-257
Amankwah, TC, Dec. 53,631(M), TC Memo. 1999-382, 78 TCM 823
Fields, TC, Dec. 53,658(M), TC Memo. 1999-408, 78 TCM 1167
Quantum Co. Trust, TC, Dec. 53,867(M), TC Memo. 2000-149, 79 TCM 1964
Schirle, TC, Dec. 52,398(M), TC Memo. 1997-552, 74 TCM 1379
Flores, TC, Dec. 53,642(M), 78 TCM 891, TC Memo. 1999-393
Nissley, TC, Dec. 53,906(M), TC Memo. 2000-178, 79 TCM 2105
Kong, TC, Dec. 46,090(M), 58 TCM 378, TC Memo. 1989-560
Caglia, E. Bonnie, TC, Dec. 45,585(M), 57 TCM 1, TC Memo. 1989-143
Ettig, TC, Dec. 44,736(M), 55 TCM 720, TC Memo. 1988-182
Heller, TC, Dec. 44,083(M), 53 TCM 1486, TC Memo. 1987-376
Anastasato, TC, Dec. 43,309(M), 52 TCM 293, TC Memo. 1986-400
Stevenson, TC, Dec. 43,068(M), 51 TCM 1050, TC Memo. 1986-207
Wilhelm, TC, Dec. 42,813(M), 51 TCM 261, TC Memo. 1986-12
Branson, TC, Dec. 38,026(M), 42 TCM 281, TC Memo. 1981-338
Calloway, TC, Dec. 37,019(M), 40 TCM 495, TC Memo. 1980-211
Greenfield, TC, Dec. 35,253(M), 37 TCM 1082, TC Memo. 1978-251
Leong, TC, Dec. 34,232(M), 36 TCM 89, TC Memo. 1977-19
Dougherty, TC, Dec. 32,138, 60 TC 917
Hernandez, TC, Dec. 52,552(M), TC Memo. 1998-46, 75 TCM 1714
Reilly Est., TC, Dec. 37,691, 76 TC 369

Diaz, Antonio A. v. Southern Drilling Corp. .... ¶ 41,699.45
● **CA-5**—(aff'g unreported DC), 71-1 USTC ¶ 9236

Diaz, Enrique .. ¶ 33,538.43, 39,475.65, 39,585.63, 41,688.198
● **DC-Calif**—90-1 USTC ¶ 50,209
Van Camp & Bennion, P.S., DC-Wash, 96-2 USTC ¶ 50,438

Diaz, Frank .... ¶ 29,412.9911
● **TC**—Dec. 42,922(M); 51 TCM 594; TC Memo. 1986-98

Diaz, Greg, Acting County Recorder for the City and County of San Francisco (See Chase Manhattan Bank, N.A. v. City & County of San Francisco)

Diaz, Humberto (See Flicker, Marvin)

Diaz, Juan (See Setal, Manuel G.)

Diaz, Leonarda C. .... ¶ 8632.3876
● **CA-2**—(aff'g TC), 79-2 USTC ¶ 9473; 607 F2d 995
Kuh, TC, Dec. 40,461(M), 46 TCM 1405, TC Memo. 1983-572
Damm, TC, Dec. 37,861(M), 41 TCM 1359, TC Memo. 1981-203
● **TC**—Dec. 35,436; 70 TC 1067
German, Jr., TC, Dec. 48,867(M), 65 TCM 1931, TC Memo. 1993-59
Orr, TC, Dec. 48,532(M), 64 TCM 882, TC Memo. 1992-566
Zeidler, TC, Dec. 51,264(M), 71 TCM 2603, TC Memo. 1996-157
Schwerm, TC, Dec. 42,817(M), 51 TCM 270, TC Memo. 1986-16
Wassenaar, TC, Dec. 36,359, 72 TC 1195
Toner, TC, Dec. 35,877, 71 TC 772

Diaz, Miguel A. (See Powers (Belcher), Sandra L.)

Dibble, Leon N., Exr. .... ¶ 29,225.442
● **BTA**—Dec. 2320; 6 BTA 732; A. VI-2 CB 2

Dibble, Phillip A. .... ¶ 25,124.415
● **TC**—Dec. 41,602(M); 49 TCM 32; TC Memo. 1984-589
Ogden, CA-5, 86-1 USTC ¶ 9368, 788 F2d 252
Elrod, TC, Dec. 43,486, 87 TC 1046

Dibblee, Isabel K. .... ¶ 30,463.381, 43,840.26
● **SCt**—(rev'g CA-9), 36-1 USTC ¶ 9008; 296 US 102; 56 SCt 54
G.C.M. 19347 , 1938-1 CB 218
● **CA-9**—(aff'g BTA), 35-1 USTC ¶ 9128; 75 F2d 617
● **BTA**—Dec. 8415; 29 BTA 1070

DiBella, Michael (See New York State Division of the Lottery)

Di Benedetto, Frank R. .... ¶ 39,780.61
● **DC-RI**—75-1 USTC ¶ 9503
Carlucci, DC-NY, 93-1 USTC ¶ 50,211, 793 FSupp 482
Cook, DC-Pa, 91-1 USTC ¶ 50,284, 765 FSupp 217
Seachrist v. Riggs, DC-Va, 91-1 USTC ¶ 50,019
Continental Illinois Nat'l Bk. and Trust Co., Chicago, DC-Ill, 87-2 USTC ¶ 9442
Swift, DC-Conn, 86-1 USTC ¶ 9109, 614 FSupp 172
Rebelle, DC-La, 85-2 USTC ¶ 9493
Rebelle, III, DC-La, 84-2 USTC ¶ 9717, 588 FSupp 49
Moats, DC-Mo, 83-2 USTC ¶ 9735, 564 FSupp 1330
Garity, DC-Mich, 81-2 USTC ¶ 9598
Garity, DC-Mich, 80-1 USTC ¶ 9407
Hanhauser, DC-Pa, 80-1 USTC ¶ 9139, 85 FRD 89
Geiger, DC-Md, 78-1 USTC ¶ 9395

DiBenedetto, Jack F. ...... ¶ 41,318.15, 41,333.199
● **CA-8**—(aff'g unreported DC), 76-2 USTC ¶ 9705; 542 F2d 490
Vannelli, CA-8, 79-1 USTC ¶ 9257, 595 F2d 402

DiBernardo, Robert (See Grama, Nathan)

Di Bianco, Emilio v. Folson ... ¶ 5600.36, 32,578.26
● **DC-NY**—57-1 USTC ¶ 9544

Dible, Leonard F. .... ¶ 5800.18, 6662.962
● **TC**—Dec. 46,122(M); 58 TCM 556; TC Memo. 1989-589

Di Bona, Donald R. .... ¶ 7183.47
● **TC**—Dec. 29,149(M); 27 TCM 1055; TC Memo. 1968-214
Meehan, TC, Dec. 33,949, 66 TC 794
Jamieson, TC, Dec. 29,423, 51 TC 635

Di Borgo, Valerie N. P. .... ¶ 12,523.55
● **TC**—Dec. 20,609; 23 TC 76
DiLeonardo, TC, Dec. 53,836(M), TC Memo. 2000-120, 79 TCM 1820
Whittemore, CA-8, 67-2 USTC ¶ 9670, 383 F2d 824
Whittemore, DC-Mo, 66-2 USTC ¶ 9663, 257 FSupp 1008

Dibrell Bros., Inc. ...... (Expired Excess Profits Tax)
● **BTA**—Dec. 5801; 18 BTA 1046

Dibs, Albert N. . ¶ 8523.273, 11,700.636, 14,417.30
● **TC**—Dec. 30,247(M); 29 TCM 897; TC Memo. 1970-204

Dibsy, Julius ... ¶ 29,608.254, 39,560.34, 39,652.16
● **TC**—Dec. 50,930(M); 70 TCM 918; TC Memo. 1995-477
Lincoln, TC, Dec. 52,970(M), TC Memo. 1998-421, 76 TCM 926

DiCarlo, Stephen A. .... ¶ 2900.897, 11,700.636, 35,150.124, 39,475.23, 39,560.79, 39,651G.305, 39,790.22
● **TC**—Dec. 48,220(M); 63 TCM 3015; TC Memo. 1992-280
Freas, TC, Dec. 49,424(M), 66 TCM 1413, TC Memo. 1993-552

FIGURE C1-6 ▶ EXCERPT FROM THE CCH CITATOR

Tax Court citation is followed by a capital "A," then another citation. The "A" indicates that the IRS Commissioner acquiesced in the Tax Court decision. The second citation indicates that the Commissioner's acquiescence is found on page 2 of Volume 2 of the 1972 *Cumulative Bulletin.*

RESEARCH INSTITUTE OF AMERICA CITATOR 2nd SERIES

Like the CCH citator, the *Research Institute of America Citator 2nd Series*[45] (RIA citator) provides the history of each authority and lists the cases and rulings that have cited that authority. The RIA citator, however, conveys more information than does the CCH citator. This information includes the following:

1. Whether the citing cases comment favorably or unfavorably on the cited cases, or whether they can be distinguished from the cited cases.[46]
2. The specific issue(s) in the cited case that is (are) referenced by the citing authorities.

ADDITIONAL COMMENT

The history of a case may be easier to find in CCH because each of the courts that tried the case is listed in a single volume in boldface print.

In print form, the RIA citator (formerly, the Prentice Hall citator) consists of six hard-bound volumes and several cumulative supplements. The first hard-bound volume lists cases decided from 1863 through 1941; the second, cases decided from 1942 through September 30, 1948; the third, cases decided from October 1, 1948 through July 29, 1954; the fourth, cases decided from July 30, 1954 through December 15, 1977; the fifth, cases cited from December 15, 1977 through December 20, 1989; and the sixth, cases decided from January 4, 1990 to December 26, 1996. A softback cumulative supplement lists cases decided from January 2, 1997 to December 22, 2000. Each year, a revised annual supplement is published. Each month, a revised monthly supplement is published. In analyzing a 1945 case, a researcher should consult every cumulative supplement and every main volume except the first. In analyzing a 1980 case, the researcher should consult every cumulative supplement and the last two bound volumes. The Internet version of the RIA citator (i.e., in RIA CHECKPOINT™) integrates this information, thus allowing the researcher to consult only one citator source.

As mentioned earlier, the RIA citator reveals the manner in which the citing authorities comment on the case under analysis. The nature of the comment is indicated by symbols that appear to the left of the citing case names. The RIA citator also reveals the history of the case under analysis (i.e., whether it was affirmed, reversed, etc.)[47] This history is indicated by symbols that appear to the left of citations to the same case heard at different appellate levels (parallel citations). Figure C1-7 explains the meaning of the various symbols, which are spelled out in the computerized version.

The RIA citator is especially useful if the cited case deals with more than one issue. As previously mentioned, the citator reports the issue(s) addressed in the cited case that is (are) referenced in the citing authority. The numbers to the left of this authority denote the specific issue(s) referenced. These numbers correspond to headnotes before the opinion as it appears in *American Federal Tax Reports.* A **headnote** is an editorial summary of a particular point of case law. Headnotes appear in case reporters immediately before the text of the opinions authored by the judges.

An excerpt from the 1978–1989 citator volume appears in the first column of Figure C1-8. Refer to it and locate the Tax Court decision for *Leonarda C. Diaz.* All the cases that cite the decision after 1977 and through 1989 are listed. (*Diaz* was decided by the Tax Court in 1978, so no earlier references will be found.) *Diaz* has been cited with respect to its first and second AFTR headnotes. If there are other AFTR headnotes, the case has not been cited with respect to them.

---

[45] The *Research Institute of America Citator 2nd Series* is published currently by RIA. It originally was published by Prentice Hall's Information Services Division, which was acquired in 1990 by Maxwell Macmillan. *Prentice Hall* and/or *Maxwell Macmillan* appears on the spines and title pages of the older citators and will remain there because, unlike the CCH citator, the RIA citator is not republished each year.

[46] When a court distinguishes the facts of one case from those of an earlier case, it suggests that its departure from the earlier decision is justified because the facts of the two cases are different.

[47] If a case is *affirmed,* the decision of the lower court is upheld. *Reversed* means the higher court invalidated the decision of the lower court because it reached a conclusion different from that derived by the lower court. *Remanded* signifies that the higher court sent the case back to the lower court with instructions to address matters not earlier addressed.

FIGURE C1-7 ▶ ABBREVIATIONS USED IN RIA CITATOR 2ND SERIES

Source: Reproduced with permission from Research Institute of America, Inc.

SYMBOLS USED IN CITATOR COURT DECISIONS

Judicial History

- **a** — affirmed by a higher court (Note: When available, the official cite to the affirmance is provided; if the affirmance is by unpublished order or opinion, the date of the decision and the court deciding the case are provided.)
- **App auth** — appeal authorized by the Treasury
- **adptd** — magistrate judge's decision is accepted and adopted by district court
- **adptg** — district court accepts and adopts magistrate judge's decision
- **App** — appeal pending (Note: Later volumes may have to be consulted to determine if appeal was decided or dismissed.)
- **cert gr** — petition for certiorari was granted by the U.S. Supreme Court
- **d** — appeal dismissed by the court or withdrawn by the party filing the appeal
- **(G)** — following an appeal notation, this symbol indicates that it was the government filing the appeal
- **m** — the earlier decision has been modified by the higher court, or by a later decision.
- **r** — the decision of the lower court has been reversed on appeal
- **rc** — related case arising out of the same taxable event or concerning the same taxpayer
- **reh den** — rehearing has been denied by the same court in which the original case was heard
- **reinst** — a dismissed appeal has been reinstated by the appellate court and is under consideration again
- **remd** — the case has been remanded for proceedings consistent with the higher court decision
- **remg** — the cited case is remanding the earlier case
- **revg & remg** — the decision of the lower court has been reversed and remanded by a higher court on appeal
- **s** — same case or ruling
- **sa** — the cited case is affirming the earlier case
- **sm** — the cited case is modifying the earlier case
- **sr** — the cited case is reversing the earlier case
- **sx** — the cited case is an earlier proceeding in a case for which a petition for certiorari was denied
- **(T)** — an appeal was filed from the lower court decision by the taxpayer
- **vacd** — the lower court decision was vacated on appeal or by the original court on remand
- **vacg** — a higher court or the original court on remand has vacated the lower court decision
- **widrn** — the original opinion was withdrawn by the court
- **x** — petition for certiorari was denied by the U.S. Supreme Court
- **•** — Supreme Court cases are designated by a bold-faced bullet (•) before the case line for easy location

v

Certain notations appear at the end of the cited case line. These notations include:

- **(A) or acq** — the government has acquiesced in the reasoning or the result of the cited case
- **(NA) or nonacq** — the government has refused to acquiesce or to adopt the reasoning or the result of the cited case, and will challenge the position adopted if future proceedings arise on the same issue
- **on rem** — the case has been remanded by a higher court and the case cited is the resulting decision

Evaluation of Cited Cases

- **c** — the citing case court has adversely commented on the reasoning of the cited case, and has criticized the earlier decision
- **e** — the cited case is used favorably by the citing case court
- **f** — the reasoning of the court in the cited case is followed by the later decision
- **g** — the cited and citing cases are distinguished from each other on either facts or law
- **inap** — the citing case court has specifically indicated that the cited case does not apply to the situation stated in the citing case.
- **iv** — on all fours (both the cited and citing cases are virtually identical)
- **k** — the cited and citing case principles are reconciled
- ***l*** — the rationale of the cited case is limited to the facts or circumstances surrounding that case (this can occur frequently in situations in which there has been an intervening higher court decision or law change)
- **n** — the cited case was noted in a dissenting opinion
- **o** — the later case directly overrules the cited case (use of the evaluation is generally limited to situations in which the court notes that it is specifically overturning the cited case, and that the case will no longer be of any value)
- **q** — the decision of the cited case is questioned and its validity debated in relation to the citing case at issue

The evaluations used for the court decisions generally are followed by a number. That number refers to the headnoted issue in the American Federal Tax Reports (AFTR) or Tax Court decision to which the citing case relates. If the case is not directly on point with any headnote, a bracketed notation at the end of the citing case line directs the researcher to the page in the cited case on which the issue appears.

A blank may appear in the evaluation space. Generally, this means that the citing court didn't comment on any of the legal issues raised in the cited case.

vi

ADDITIONAL COMMENT

The RIA citator has the advantage of providing the most references for a cited case. This point is apparent when one compares RIA's six volumes plus supplements with CCH's two volumes. Also, RIA numbers each tax issue litigated in a court case. This coding allows the tax advisor to identify cases dealing with the specific issue being researched. For example, if the advisor is interested in the first issue in the *Leonarda Diaz* Tax Court decision, the citator reproduced in Figure C1-8 denotes five cases that deal specifically with issue 1 of which three follow the *Diaz* reasoning.

1978–1989
Citator Volume

DiANDREA, YOLANDA, TRANSFEREE, 1983 PH TC Memo ¶ 83,768 See DiAndrea, Inc.)
DIAZ, ALFONSO & MARIA de JESUS, 58 TC 560, ¶ 58.57 PH TC
Reilly, Peter W., Est. of, 76 TC 374, 76 PH TC 201 [See 58 TC 565, n. 2]
e—Greenfield, Stuart & Eileen, 1978 PH TC Memo 78-1070 [See 58 TC 564]
e—Calloway, Johnny T., 1980 PH TC Memo 80-952 [See 58 TC 564]
e—Branson, David L., 1981 PH TC Memo 81-1199 [See 58 TC 564, 565]
e—Cohen, Robert B. & Marilyn W., 1983 PH TC Memo 83-1042 [See 58 TC 564]
e—Patton, Luther R., 1985 PH TC Memo 85-629 [See 58 TC 564]
e—Malek, Theresa M. & Edward J., Sr., 1985 PH TC Memo 85-1905 [See 58 TC 574]
e—Wilhelm, Mary R., 1986 PH TC Memo 86-39 [See 58 TC 564]
e—Stevenson, Wayne E. & Marilyn J., 1986 PH TC Memo 86-866, 86-873 [See 58 TC 564]
e—Anastasato, Pano & Janice, 1986 PH TC Memo 86-1811 [See 58 TC 564]
e—Shih-Hsieh, Marilan, 1986 PH TC Memo 86-2429 [See 58 TC 562]
e—Heller, Jacob W. & Esther R., 1987 PH TC Memo 87-1881 [See 58 TC 562]
e—Ettig, Tobin R., 1988 PH TC Memo 88-953 [See 58 TC 564]
e—Belli, Melia, 1989 PH TC Memo 89-1950 [See 58 TC 564]
f-Kong, Young E. & Jeen K., 1989 PH TC Memo 89-2781 [See 58 TC 564-565]
e-1—Caglia, E. Bonnie, 1989 PH TC Memo 89-689
DIAZ, FRANK & AMPARO R., 1986 PH TC Memo ¶ 86,098
DIAZ, LEONARDA C., 70 TC 1067, ¶ 70.95 PH TC
a—Diaz, Leonarda C. v Comm., 44 AFTR2d 79-6027 (USCA 2)
e—Stazer, Alan K. & Katalin V., 1981 PH TC Memo 81-505 [See 70 TC 1076]
e—Damm, Marvin V. & Nina M., 1981 PH TC Memo 81-673 [See 70 TC 1074-1075]
e—Stuart, Ian & Maria, 1981 PH TC Memo 81-1311, 81-1312 [See 70 TC 1076]
e—Olsen, Randy B. & Deborah R., 1981 PH TC Memo 81-2409 [See 70 TC 1076]
f—Kuh, Johannes L. & Adriana, 1983 PH TC Memo 83-2311 [See 70 TC 1075, 1076]
f-1—Wassenaar, Paul R., 72 TC 1200, 72 PH TC 659
f-1—Browne, Alice Pauline, 73 TC 726, 73 PH TC 402 [See 70 TC 1074]
f-1—Rehe, William G. & Suzanne M., 1980 PH TC Memo 80-1426
g-1—Schwerm, Gerald & Joyce J., 1986 PH TC Memo 86-54, 86-55
e-1—Baist, George A. & Janice, 1988 PH TC Memo 88-2859
f-2—Toner, Linda M. Liberi, 71 TC 778, 779, 781, 71 PH TC 435, 436, 437 [See 70 TC 1075]
2—Toner, Linda M. Liberi, 71 TC 782, 783, 71 PH TC 437, 438
n-2—Toner, Linda M. Liberi, 71 TC 790, 71 PH TC 441
f-2—Robinson, Charles A. & Elaine M., 78 TC 552, 78 PH TC 290 [See 70 TC 1074]
2—Gruman, David T., 1982 PH TC Memo 82-1700 [See 70 TC 1074]
DIAZ, LEONARDA C. v COMM., 44 AFTR2d 79-6027 (USCA 2, 6-25-79)
sa—Diaz, Leonarda C., 70 TC 1067, ¶ 70.95 PH TC
e—Stazer, Alan K. & Katalin V., 1981 PH TC Memo 81-505
e—Damm, Marvin V. & Nina M., 1981 PH TC Memo 81-673
e—Olsen, Randy B. & Deborah R., 1981 PH TC Memo 81-2409
f—Kuh, Johannes L. & Adriana, 1983 PH TC Memo 83-2311
e—Malek, Theresa M. & Edward J., Sr., 1985 PH TC Memo 85-1905
f-1—Rehe, William G. & Suzanne M., 1980 PH TC Memo 80-1426
g-1—Schwerm, Gerald & Joyce J., 1986 PH TC Memo 86-54, 86-55
e-1—Baist, George A. & Janice, 1988 PH TC Memo 88-2859
DIAZ, MIGUEL A. & FELICIA N., 1981 PH TC Memo ¶ 81,069 (See Powers, Sandra L.)

1990–1996
Citator Volume

DiANDRE, ANTHONY F. v U.S., 70 AFTR 2d 92-5190, 968 F2d 1049, 92-2 USTC ¶ 50,373, (CA10, 7-7-92)
x—Metro Denver Maintenance Cleaning, Inc. v. U.S., 507 US 1029, 113 S Ct 1843, 123 L Ed 2d 468, (US, 4-19-93), (T)
e-1—Barnes, William R. v U.S., 73 AFTR 2d 94-1161, (CA3)
e-1—Fostvedt, Robert J. v U.S., 71 AFTR 2d 93-1573, 824 F Supp 983, (DC CO)
e-1—Jones, Terry L., et al v. U.S., et al, 74 AFTR 2d 94-6706, 869 F Supp 753, (DC NE), [Cited at 71 AFTR2d 93-1573, 824 F Supp 983]
g-1—Russell, Orval D. v. U.S., 75 AFTR 2d 95-496, (DC MI)
e-1—Stewart, Daniel v. U.S., 75 AFTR 2d 95-2250, 95-2251, (DC OH)
e-1—Jones, Terry L., et al v. U.S., et al, 76 AFTR 2d 95-6607, 95-6615, 898 F Supp 1373, 1380, (DC NE), [Cited at 71 AFTR2d 93-1573, 824 F Supp 983]
e-1—May, Joseph A. v. U.S., 76 AFTR 2d 95-7228, (DC MO)
e-1—Cassity, James v. Great Western Bank, 76 AFTR 2d 95-8035, (DC CA)
e-1—Spence, Raymond v. U.S., 78 AFTR 2d 96-5777, (DC NM)
DiANDREA, INC., 1983 PH TC Memo ¶ 83,768
e-1—Johnson, Peter A., 1991 TC Memo 91-3185
DIAZ, ALFONSO & MARIA de JESUS, 58 TC 560, ¶ 58.57 PH TC, (A), 1972-2 CB 2
Sanai, Farhin, 1990 PH TC Memo 90-2459, [See 58 TC 564-565]
e—Hawkins, Robert Lavon & Pamela, 1993 RIA TC Memo 93-2734, [See 58 TC 564]
e—Muniz, Rolando, 1994 RIA TC Memo 94-760, [See 58 TC 564]
e—Sloan, Lorin G., 1994 RIA TC Memo 94-3427, [See 58 TC 564]
e—Marrone, Anthony & Carol, 1995 RIA TC Memo 95-145, [See 58 TC 564]
e—Wada, Takeshi & Young Sook, 1995 RIA TC Memo 95-1532, [See 58 TC 564]
e—Drabiuk, Stanislaw & Jeanette, 1995 RIA TC Memo 95-1649, [See 58 TC 565]
e—Jackson, Sammy Lee, 1995 RIA TC Memo 95-1875, [See 58 TC 564]
e—Levin, Harris & Gayle, 1996 RIA TC Memo 96-1557, [See 58 TC 564]
e—American Underwriters Inc, 1996 RIA TC Memo 96-3980, [See 58 TC 564]
DIAZ, BARBARA E., 1990 PH TC Memo ¶ 90,559, (See Taylor, Barbara E.)
DIAZ, ENRIQUE v. U.S., 71A AFTR 2d 93-3563, 90-1 USTC ¶ 50209, (DC CA, 3/19/90)
g-1—Van Camp & Bennion, P.S. v. U.S., 78 AFTR 2d 96-5847, (DC WA)
DIAZ, LEONARDA C., 70 TC 1067, ¶ 70.95 PH TC
a—Diaz, Leonarda C. v Comm., 44 AFTR 2d 79-6027, 607 F2d 995, (CA2)
f—Wiertzema, Vance v U.S., 66 AFTR 2d 90-5371, 747 F Supp 1365, (DC ND), [See 70 TC 1074-1075]
e—Barboza, David, 1991 TC Memo 91-1905, [See 70 TC 1074]
e—Orr, J. Thomas, 1992 RIA TC Memo 92-2912, [See 70 TC 1073]
e—German, Harry, Jr. & Carol, 1993 RIA TC Memo 93-261—93-262, [See 70 TC 1074—1075]
e—Meredith, Judith R., 1993 RIA TC Memo 93-1247, [See 70 TC 1074, cited at 73 TC 726]
e—Holmes, Lynn J., 1993 RIA TC Memo 93-1978, [See 70 TC 1072—1073]
e—Kersey, Robert C., 1993 RIA TC Memo 93-3396, [See 70 TC 1072-1073]
e—Zeidler, Gerald L. & Joy M., 1996 RIA TC Memo 96-1151, [See 70 TC 1074, cited at 73 TC 726]
DIAZ, LEONARDA C. v COMM., 44 AFTR 2d 79-6027, 607 F2d 995, (CA2, 6-25-79)
e—Wiertzema, Vance v U.S., 66 AFTR 2d 90-5371, 747 F Supp 1363, (DC ND)
e—Zeidler, Gerald L. & Joy M., 1996 RIA TC Memo 96-1151
DiBENEDETTO, FRANK R. v U.S., 35 AFTR 2d 75-1502, 75-1 USTC ¶ 9503, (DC RI, 11-7-74)
e-1—Seachrist, Craig v Riggs, C.W., 67 AFTR 2d 91-453, (DC VA)
e-1—Cook, Dean A. v U.S., 68 AFTR 2d 91-5053—91-5056, 765 F Supp 219, 221, (DC PA)
e-1—Carlucci, Joseph P. v U.S., 70 AFTR 2d 92-6002, 793 F Supp 484, (DC NY)
e-1—Padalino, Vincent v. U.S., 71A AFTR 2d 93-3016, (DC NJ)

FIGURE C1-8 ▶ EXCERPTS FROM THE RIA CITATOR

The "a" on the first line beneath the name of the case indicates that the Tax Court's decision was affirmed by the Second Circuit. The Tax Court's opinion has been explained and followed in various cases, but it has not been cited in an unfavorable manner. Thus, its authoritative weight is substantial.

The Second Circuit's decision appears as a separate entry. The letters "sa" signify that the circuit court affirmed the Tax Court decision in the *Diaz* case. The cases that have cited the circuit court's opinion are listed under the entry for such opinion. The appellate decision has not been questioned or criticized; thus, its authority is relatively strong.

More recent references to *Leonarda C. Diaz* are reported in the 1990–96 citator volume (see Figure C1-8, Column 2). Nine additional cases cite the Tax Court decision[48]; two additional cases cite the Second Circuit Court decision. Recall that the CCH citator indicates that in 1972 the IRS Commissioner acquiesced in the Tax Court decision in *Alphonso Diaz*. This acquiescence is denoted by the capital "A," which appears after the citation to the same decision in the 1990–1996 citator volume.

No additional cases citing each of the Leonarda C. Diaz decisions are listed in the 1997–2001 cumulative supplements.

COMPUTERS AS A RESEARCH TOOL

OBJECTIVE 6

Understand the basics of computerized tax research

Tax professionals are increasingly using computers to conduct their tax-related research. Tax services are increasingly shifting their resources to media accessible by computer. With the technological advances in computer hardware and software, large databases are becoming more accessible and less costly. In the coming years, computer-assisted tax research will become an even more important tool for the tax advisor. A supplement to this chapter, which discusses this development, is available for download at *www.prenhall.com/phtax*. It also presents an overview of tax resources on the Internet.

In the major computerized tax services, most of the primary authorities discussed in this chapter appear as databases. Typically, each authority constitutes a separate database. Thus, the Internal Revenue Code constitutes a separate database, as do Treasury Regulations, revenue rulings, revenue procedures, and other IRS pronouncements. Supreme Court opinions constitute a separate database, as do opinions of the Tax Court, the U.S. district courts, the Court of Federal Claims, and the circuit courts. Likewise, most of the secondary authorities discussed in this chapter appear as databases. Some authorities, however, are found exclusively in one service, while others are found exclusively in another. For example, the *Standard Federal Tax Reporter, Federal Tax Service,* and CCH citator are found exclusively in the CCH Internet Tax Research Network. The *U.S. Tax Reporter, Federal Tax Coordinator 2d,* and RIA citator are found exclusively in RIA CHECKPOINT™. The basic features of the computerized and print sources generally are the same, with the following notable exceptions:

- Computerized sources have no finding lists. Cross referencing is facilitated through hyperlinks.
- Computerized sources have no cumulative supplements. New developments information is integrated into the main text.
- On computer, primary sources pertinent to explanatory paragraphs are accessible through hyperlink.
- On computer, citator symbols are explicitly spelled out.

---

48 The first listing under the citation to the Tax Court decision in *Leonarda C. Diaz* refers to the same case decided at the Second Circuit Court level.

STATEMENTS ON STANDARDS FOR TAX SERVICES

OBJECTIVE 7

Understand the guidelines that CPAs in tax practice should follow

Tax advisors confronted with ethical issues frequently turn to a professional organization for guidance. Although the guidelines set forth by such organizations are not *legally* enforceable, they carry significant moral weight, may be cited in a negligence lawsuit as the proper "standard of care" for tax practitioners, and may provide grounds for the termination or suspension of one's professional license. One such set of guidelines is the ***Statements on Standards for Tax Services*** (SSTSs),[49] issued by the American Institute of Certified Public Accountants (AICPA) and reproduced in Appendix E. Inspired by the principles of honesty and integrity, these guidelines define standards of ethical conduct for CPAs engaged in tax practice. In the words of the AICPA:

> In our view, practice standards are the hallmark of calling one's self a professional. Members should fulfill their responsibilities as professionals by instituting and maintaining standards against which their professional performance can be measured. The promulgation of practice standards also reinforces one of the core values of the AICPA Vision—that CPAs conduct themselves with honesty and integrity.[50]

The SSTSs differ in one important way from the AICPA's predecessor standards, *Statements on Responsibilites in Tax Practice,* in that the SSTSs are *professionally* enforceable; that is, they may be enforced through a disciplinary proceeding conducted by the AICPA, which may terminate or suspend a practitioner from AICPA membership.

Statement No. 1 defines the circumstances under which a CPA should (or should not) recommend a tax return position to a taxpayer. It also prescribes a course of conduct that the CPA should follow when making such a recommendation. Specifically,

- ▶ A member should not recommend that a tax return position be taken with respect to any item unless the member has a good-faith belief that the position has a realistic possibility of being sustained administratively or judicially on its merits if challenged . . .
- ▶ [A] member may recommend a tax return position that the member concludes is not frivolous so long as the member advises the taxpayer to appropriately disclose . . .
- ▶ When recommending tax return positions and when preparing or signing a return on which a tax return position is taken, a member should, when relevant, advise the taxpayer regarding potential penalty consequences of such tax return position and the opportunity, if any, to avoid such penalties through disclosure.

The "realistic possibility standard" set forth in Statement No. 1 parallels that of Sec. 6694. (For a discussion of the latter IRC section, see Chapter C15.) However, it differs from the IRC standard in that it allows as support for a tax return position well-reasoned articles or treatises, in addition to primary tax authorities. The IRC standard allows as support for a tax return position only primary tax authorities.

Statement No. 3 addresses (1) whether tax practitioners can reasonably rely on information supplied to them by the taxpayer, (2) when they have a duty to examine or verify such information, (3) when they have a duty to make inquiries of the taxpayer, and (4) what information they should consider in preparing a tax return. Specifically,

- ▶ In preparing or signing a return, a member may in good faith rely, without verification, on information furnished by the taxpayer or by third parties. However, a member should make reasonable inquiries if the information furnished appears to be incorrect, incomplete, or inconsistent either on its face or on the basis of other facts known to a member . . .

---

49 AICPA, *Statements on Standards for Tax Services*, 2000, effective October 31, 2000. The SSTSs supercede the AICPA's *Statements on Responsibilities in Tax Practice, 1991 Revision.*

50 Letter to AICPA members by David A. Lifson, Chair, AICPA Tax Executive Committee, and Gerald W. Padwe, Vice President, AICPA Taxation Section (April 18, 2000).

WHAT WOULD YOU DO IN THIS SITUATION?

Regal Enterprises and Macon Industries, unaffiliated corporations, have hired you to prepare their respective income tax returns. In preparing Regal's return, you notice that Regal has claimed a depreciation deduction for equipment purchased from Macon on February 22 at a cost of $2 million. In preparing Macon's return, you notice that Macon has reported sales proceeds of $1.5 million from the sale of equipment to Regal on February 22. One of the two figures must be incorrect. How do you proceed to correct it?

- If the tax law or regulations impose a condition with respect to the deductibility or other tax treatment of an item . . . a member should make appropriate inquiries to determine to the member's satisfaction whether such condition has been met.
- When preparing a tax return, a member should consider information actually known to that member from the tax return of another taxpayer if the information is relevant to that tax return and its consideration is necessary to properly prepare that tax return . . .

Note that the duty to verify arises only when taxpayer-provided information appears "strange" on its face. Otherwise, the tax practitioner has no duty to investigate taxpayer facts and circumstances.

Statement No. 4 defines the circumstances in which a tax practitioner may use estimates in the preparation of a tax return. In addition, it cautions the practitioner as to the manner in which he or she may use such estimates. Specifically,

- A member may advise on estimates used in the preparation of a tax return, but the taxpayer has the responsibility to provide the estimated data. Appraisals or valuations are not considered estimates . . .
- [A] member may use the taxpayer's estimates in the preparation of a tax return if it is not practical to obtain exact data and if the member determines that the estimates are reasonable based on the facts and circumstances known to the member. If the taxpayer's estimates are used, they should be presented in a manner that does not imply greater accuracy than exists.

Notwithstanding this Statement, the tax practitioner may not use estimates when such use is implicitly prohibited by the IRC. For example, Sec. 274(d) disallows deductions for certain expenses (e.g., meals and entertainment) unless the taxpayer can substantiate the expenses with adequate records or sufficient corroborating information. The documentation requirement effectively precludes the taxpayer from estimating such expenses and the practitioner from using such estimates.

Statement No. 6 defines a tax practitioner's duty when he or she becomes aware of (1) an error in the taxpayer's return, (2) the taxpayer's failure to file a required return, or (3) the taxpayer's failure to correct an error in a prior year's return. Specifically,

- A member should inform the taxpayer promptly upon becoming aware of an error in a previously filed return or upon becoming aware of a taxpayer's failure to file a required return. A member should recommend the corrective measures to be taken . . . The member is not obligated to inform the taxing authority, and a member may not do so without the taxpayer's permission, except when required by law.
- If a member is requested to prepare the current year's return and the taxpayer has not taken appropriate action to correct an error in a prior year's return, the member should consider whether to withdraw from preparing the return and whether to continue a professional or employment relationship with the taxpayer . . .

This Statement implies that the tax practitioner's primary duty is to the taxpayer, not the taxing authority. Furthermore, upon the taxpayer's failure to correct a tax-related error, the practitioner may exercise discretion in deciding whether or not to terminate the professional relationship.

Occasionally, the tax practitioner discovers a taxpayer error in the course of an administrative proceeding (e.g., an IRS audit or appeals conference). The practitioner may advise the client to disclose the error, and the taxpayer may refuse. Statement No. 7 provides guidance as to what to do in these situations. Specifically,

- If a member is representating a taxpayer in an administrative proceeding with respect to a return that contains an error of which the member is aware, the member should inform the taxpayer promptly upon becoming aware of the error. The member should recommend the corrective measures to be taken. . . . A member is neither obligated to inform the taxing authority nor allowed to do so without the taxpayer's permission, except where required by law.
- A member should request the taxpayer's agreement to disclose the error to the taxing authority. Lacking such agreement, the member should consider whether to withdraw from representing the taxpayer in the administrative proceeding and whether to continue a professional or employment relationship with the taxpayer.

Finally, Statement No. 8 addresses the quality of advice provided by the tax practitioner, what consequences presumably ensue from such advice, and whether the practitioner has a duty to update advice to reflect subsequent developments. Specifically,

- A member should use judgment to ensure that tax advice provided to a taxpayer reflect professional competence and appropriately serves the taxpayer's needs . . .
- A member should assume that tax advice provided to a taxpayer will affect the manner in which the matters or transactions considered would be reported on the taxpayer's tax returns . . .
- A member has no obligation to communicate with a taxpayer when subsequent developments affect advice previously provided with respect to significant matters except while assisting a taxpayer in implementing procedures or plans associated with the advice provided or when a member undertakes an obligation by specific agreement.

The Statement implies that practitioner-taxpayer dealings should be neither casual nor nonconsensual nor open-ended; rather, they should be professional, contractual, and definite.

From the foregoing emerges the following picture of the normative relationship between the tax advisor and his or her client: unlike an auditor, a tax advisor is an advocate. His or her primary duty is to the client, not the IRS. In fullfilling this duty, the advisor is bound by the highest standards of care. These standards include a good-faith belief that a tax return position has a realistic possibility of being sustained on its merits and on quality advice based on professional competence and client needs. Encompassed under the advisor's duty is the obligation to inform the client of the potential adverse consequences of a tax return position, how the client can avoid a penalty through disclosure, errors in a previously filed tax return, and corrective measures to be taken. Also encompassed is the obligation to determine by inquiry that the client satisfies conditions for taking a deduction, and to obtain information when material provided by the client appears incorrect, incomplete, or inconsistent. Excluded from the advisor's duty is the obligation to verify client-provided information when, based on the advisor's own knowledge, such information is not suspicious on its face. Also excluded is the obligation to update professional advice based on developments following its original conveyance. In preparing a tax return, the advisor may use estimates if obtaining concrete data is impractical and if the advisor determines that the estimates are reasonable. Although responsibility for providing the estimates resides with the client, responsibility for presenting them in a manner that does not imply undue accuracy resides with the advisor. Finally, the advisor may terminate a professional relationship if the client refuses to correct a tax-related error. On the other hand, unless legally bound, the advisor may not disclose the error to the IRS without the client's consent.

In addition to these obligations, the tax advisor has a strict duty of confidentiality to the client. Though not encompassed under the SSTSs, this duty is implied by the accountant-client privilege. (For a discussion of this privilege, see Chapter C15.)

STOP & THINK

Question: As described in the Stop & Think box on page C1-10, you are researching the manner in which a deduction is calculated. The IRC states that the calculation is to be made "in a manner prescribed by the Secretary." After studying the IRC, Treasury Regulations, and committee reports, you conclude that another way of doing the calculations is arguably correct under an intuitive approach. This approach would result in a lower tax liability for the client. According to the *Statements on Standards for Tax Services,* may you take a position contrary to final Treasury Regulations based on the argument that the regulations are not valid?

Solution: You should not take a position contrary to the Treasury Regulations unless you have a "good-faith belief that the position has a realistic possibility of being sustained administratively or judicially on its merits." However, you can take a position that does not meet the above standard, provided you adequately disclose the position and the position is not frivolous. Whether or not you have met the standard depends on all the facts and circumstances. Chapter C15 discusses tax return preparer positions contrary to the Treasury Regulations.

ADDITIONAL COMMENT

The underpayment penalty rules under Sec. 6662 impose a higher standard for disregarding a rule, such as a Treasury Regulation. Under these rules, the taxpayer must have a reasonable basis rather than a nonfrivolous position, in addition to disclosure.

SAMPLE WORK PAPERS AND CLIENT LETTER

OBJECTIVE 8

Prepare work papers and communications to clients

Appendix A presents a set of sample work papers, including a draft of a client letter and a memo to the file. The work papers indicate the issues to be researched, the authorities addressing the issues, and the researcher's conclusions concerning the appropriate tax treatment, with rationale therefor.

The format and other details of a set of work papers differ from firm to firm. The sample in this text offers general guidance concerning the content of work papers. In practice, work papers may include less detail.

PROBLEM MATERIALS

DISCUSSION QUESTIONS

C1-1 Explain the difference between closed-fact and open-fact situations.

C1-2 According the the AICPA's *Statements on Standards for Tax Services,* what duties does the tax practitioner owe the client?

C1-3 Explain what is encompassed by the term *tax law* as used by tax advisors.

C1-4 The U.S. Government Printing Office publishes both hearings on proposed legislation and committee reports. Distinguish between the two.

C1-5 Explain how committee reports can be used in tax research. What do they indicate?

C1-6 A friend notices that you are reading the Internal Revenue Code of 1986. Your friend inquires why you are consulting a 1986 publication, especially when tax laws change so frequently. What is your response?

C1-7 Does Title 26 contain statutory provisions dealing only with income taxation? Explain.

C1-8 Refer to IRC Sec. 301.
a. Which subsection discusses the general rule for the tax treatment of a property distribution?
b. Where should one look for exceptions to the general rule?
c. What type of Treasury Regulations would relate to subsection (e)?

C1-9 Why should tax researchers note the date on which a Treasury Regulation was adopted?

C1-10 a. Distinguish between proposed, temporary, and final Treasury Regulations.

b. Distinguish between interpretative and legislative Treasury Regulations.

C1-11 Which type of regulation is more difficult for a taxpayer to successfully challenge, and why?

C1-12 Explain the legislative reenactment doctrine.

C1-13 a. Discuss the authoritative weight of revenue rulings.
b. As a practical matter, what consequences are likely to ensue if a taxpayer does not follow a revenue ruling and the IRS audits his or her return?

C1-14 a. In which courts may litigation dealing with tax matters begin?
b. Discuss the factors that might be considered in deciding where to litigate.
c. Describe the appeals process in tax litigation.

C1-15 May a taxpayer appeal a case litigated under the Small Cases Procedure of the Tax Court?

C1-16 Explain whether the following decisions are of the same precedential value: (1) Tax Court regular decisions, (2) Tax Court memo decisions, (3) decisions under the Small Cases Procedures of the Tax Court.

C1-17 Does the IRS acquiesce in decisions of U.S. district courts?

C1-18 The decisions of which courts are reported in the AFTR 2d? In the USTC?

C1-19 Who publishes regular decisions of the Tax Court? Memo decisions?

C1-20 Explain the *Golsen* Rule. Give an example of its application.

C1-21 Assume that the only precedents relating to a particular issue are as follows:
Tax Court—decided for the taxpayer
Eighth Circuit Court of Appeals—decided for the taxpayer (affirming the Tax Court)
U.S. District Court for Eastern Louisiana—decided for the taxpayer
Fifth Circuit Court of Appeals—decided for the government (reversing the U.S. District Court of Eastern Louisiana)
a. Discuss the precedential value of the foregoing decisions for your client, who is a California resident.
b. If your client, a Texas resident, litigates in the Tax Court, how will the court rule? Explain.

C1-22 Which official publication(s) contain(s) the following:
a. Transcripts of Senate floor debates
b. IRS announcements
c. Tax Court regular opinions
d. Treasury decisions
e. U.S. district court opinions
f. Technical advice memoranda

C1-23 Under what circumstances might a tax advisor find the provisions of a tax treaty useful?

C1-24 Compare the print version of the tax services listed below (if they are found in your tax library) with respect to (a) how they are organized and (b) where current developments are reported.
a. *United States Tax Reporter*
b. *Standard Federal Tax Reporter*
c. *Federal Tax Coordinator 2d*
d. *Law of Federal Income Taxation* (Mertens)
e. BNA's *Tax Management Portfolios*
f. CCH's *Federal Tax Service*

C1-25 Indicate (1) which Internet tax service provides each of the following secondary sources and (2) whether the source is annotated or topical.
a. *Federal Tax Coordinator 2d*
b. Mertens
c. *BNA Tax Management Portfolios*
d. *Standard Federal Tax Reporter*
e. *United States Tax Reporter*

C1-26 What two functions does a citator serve?

C1-27 Describe two types of information that can be gleaned from citing cases in the RIA citator but not the CCH citator.

C1-28 Explain how your research approach might differ if you use the computerized version of a tax service instead of the print version (e.g., RIA or CCH).

C1-29 Compare the features of the electronic, CD-ROM, and Internet tax services. What are the relative advantages and disadvantages of each type of service? (In answering this question, consult the supplement to this chapter available for download at *www.prenhall.com/phtax.*)

C1-30 Compare the features of the computerized tax services with those of Internet sites maintained by noncommercial institutions. What are the relative advantages and disadvantages of each? Could the latter sites serve as a substitute for a commercial tax service? (In answering this question, consult the supplement to this chapter available for download at *www.prenhall.com/phtax.*)

C1-31 According to the *Statements on Standards for Tax Services*, what belief should a CPA have before taking a pro-taxpayer position on a tax return?

C1-32 Under the AICPA's *Statements on Standards for Tax Services*, what is the tax practitioner's professional duty in each of the following situations?
a. Client erroneously deducts $5,000 (instead of $500) on a previous year's tax return.
b. Client refuses to file an amended return to correct the deduction error.
c. Client informs tax practitioner that client incurred $200 in out-of-pocket office supplies expenses.
d. Client informs tax practitioner that client incurred $700 in business-related entertainment expenses.
e. Tax practitioner learns that the exemption amount for single taxpayers has been increased by $1,000. Client is a single taxpayer.

PROBLEMS

C1-33 *Interpretation of the IRC.* Under a divorce agreement executed in the current year, an ex-wife receives from her former husband cash of $25,000 per year for eight years. The agreement does not explicitly state that the payment is excludible from income.

a. Does the ex-wife have gross income? If so, how much?

b. Is the former husband entitled to a deduction? If so, is it for or from AGI?

Refer only to the IRC in answering this problem. Start with Sec. 71.

C1-34 *Interpretation of the IRC.* Refer to Sec. 385 and answer the questions below.

a. Whenever Treasury Regulations are issued under this section, what type are they likely to be: legislative or interpretative? Explain.

b. Assume Treasury Regulations under Sec. 385 have been finalized. Will they be relevant to estate tax matters? Explain.

C1-35 *Using the Cumulative Bulletin.* Consult any volume of the *Cumulative Bulletin.* In what order are revenue rulings arranged?

C1-36 *Using the Cumulative Bulletin.* Which IRC section(s) does Rev. Rul. 2001-29 interpret? (Hint: consult the official publication of the IRS.)

C1-37 *Using the Cumulative Bulletin.* Refer to the 1989-1 *Cumulative Bulletin.*

a. What time period does this bulletin cover?

b. What appears on page 1?

c. What items are found in Part I?

d. In what order are the items presented in Part I?

e. What items are found in Part II?

f. What items are found in Part III?

C1-38 *Using the Cumulative Bulletin.* Refer to the 1990-1 *Cumulative Bulletin.*

a. For the time period covered by the bulletin, in which cases did the IRS nonacquiesce?

b. What is the topic of Rev. Rul. 90-10?

c. Does this bulletin contain a revenue ruling that interprets Sec. 162? If so, specify.

C1-39 *Determination of Acquiescence.*

a. What official action did the IRS Commissioner take in 1986 concerning the Tax Court decision in *John McIntosh*? (Hint: consult the 1986-1 *Cumulative Bulletin.*)

b. Did this action concern *all* issues in the case? If not, explain. (Consult the headnote to the court opinion before answering this question.)

C1-40 *Determination of Acquiescence.*

a. What original action (acquiescence or nonacquiescence) did the IRS Commissioner take concerning *Streckfus Steamers, Inc.,* 19 T.C. 1 (1952)?

b. Was the action complete or partial?

c. Did the IRS Commissioner subsequently change his mind? If so, when?

C1-41 *Determination of Acquiescence.*

a. What original action (acquiescence or nonacquiescence) did the IRS Commissioner take concerning *Pittsburgh Milk Co.,* 26 T.C. 707 (1956)?

b. Did the IRS Commissioner subsequently change his mind? If so, when?

C1-42 *Evaluating a Case.* Look up *James E. Threlkeld,* 87 T.C. 1294 (1988), and answer the questions below.

a. Was the case reviewed by the court? If so, was the decision unanimous? Explain.

b. Was the decision entered under Rule 155?

c. Consult a citator. Was the case reviewed by an appellate court? If so, which one?

C1-43 *Evaluating a Case.* Look up *Bush Brothers & Co.,* 73 T.C. 424 (1979), and answer the questions below.

a. Was the case reviewed by the court? If so, was the decision unanimous? Explain.

b. Was the decision entered under Rule 155?

c. Consult a citator. Was the case reviewed by an appellate court? If so, which one?

C1-44 *Writing Citations.* Provide the proper citations (including both primary and secondary citations where applicable) for the authorities listed below. (For secondary citations, reference both the AFTR and USTC.)

a. *National Cash Register Co.,* a 6th Circuit Court decision

b. *Thomas M. Dragoun v. CIR,* a Tax Court memo decision

c. *John M. Grabinski v. U.S.,* a District Court of Minnesota decision

d. *John M. Grabinski v. U.S.*, an Eighth Circuit Court decision
e. *Rebekah Harkness*, a 1972 Court of Claims decision
f. *Hillsboro National Bank v. CIR*, a Supreme Court decision
g. Rev. Rul. 78-129

C1-45 ***Writing Citations.*** Provide the proper citations (including both primary and secondary citations where applicable) for the authorities listed below. (For secondary citations, reference both the AFTR and USTC.)
a. Rev. Rul. 99-7
b. *Frank H. Sullivan*, a Board of Tax Appeals decision
c. *Tate & Lyle, Inc.*, a 1994 Tax Court decision
d. *Ralph L. Rogers v. U.S.*, an Ohio District Court decision
e. *Norman Rodman v. CIR*, a Second Circuit Court decision

C1-46 ***Interpreting Citations.*** Indicate which courts decided the cases cited below. Also indicate on which pages and in which publications the authority is reported.
a. *Lloyd M. Shumaker v. CIR*, 648 F.2d 1198, 48 AFTR 2d 81-5353 (9th Cir., 1981)
b. *Xerox Corp. v. U.S.*, 14 Cl. Ct. 455, 88-1 USTC ¶9231 (1988)
c. *Real Estate Land Title & Trust Co. v. U.S.*, 309 U.S. 13, 23 AFTR 816 (USSC, 1940)
d. *J. B. Morris v. U.S.*, 441 F. Supp. 76, 41 AFTR 2d 78-335 (DC TX, 1977)
e. Rev. Rul. 83-3, 1983-1 C.B. 72
f. *Malone & Hyde, Inc. v. U.S.*, 568 F.2d 474, 78-1 USTC ¶9199 (6th Cir., 1978)

C1-47 ***Using a Tax Service.*** Use the topical index of the *United States Tax Reporter* to locate authorities dealing with the deductibility of the cost of a facelift.
a. In which paragraph(s) does the *United States Tax Reporter* summarize and cite these authorities?
b. List the authorities.
c. Have there been any recent non-statutory developments concerning the tax consequences of facelifts? (*Recent* suggests authorities appearing in the cross-reference section.)
d. May a taxpayer deduct the cost of a facelift paid for in the current year? Explain.

C1-48 ***Using a Tax Service.*** Refer to Reg. Sec. 1.302-1 at ¶3022 of the *United States Tax Reporter.* Does this Treasury Regulation reflect recent amendments to the IRC? Explain.

C1-49 ***Using a Tax Service.*** Use the topical index of the *Standard Federal Tax Reporter* to locate authorities dealing with whether termite damage qualifies for a casualty loss deduction.
a. In which paragraph(s) does the *Standard Federal Tax Reporter* summarize and cite these authorities?
b. List the authorities.
c. Have there been any recent developments concerning the tax consequences of termite damage? (*Recent* suggests authorities appearing in the cumulative index section.)

C1-50 ***Using a Tax Service.***
a. Locate in the *Standard Federal Tax Reporter* where Sec. 303(b)(2)(A) is reproduced. This provision states that Sec. 303(a) applies only if the stock in question meets a certain percentage test. What is the applicable percentage?
b. Locate Reg. Sec. 1.303-2(a) in the same service. Does this Treasury Regulation reflect recent amendments to the IRC with respect to the percentage test addressed in Part a? Explain.

C1-51 ***Using a Tax Service.*** The questions below deal with BNA's *Tax Management Portfolios.*
a. What is the number of the main portfolio that deals with tax-free exchanges under Sec. 1031?
b. On which page does a discussion of "boot" begin?
c. What are the purposes of Worksheets 1 and 5 of this portfolio?
d. Refer to the bibliography and references at the end of the portfolio. Indicate the numbers of the IRC sections listed as "secondarily" relevant.

C1-52 ***Using a Tax Service.*** This problem deals with Mertens' *Law of Federal Income Taxation.*
a. Refer to Volume 5. What general topics does it discuss?
b. Which section of Volume 5 discusses the principal methods of determining depreciation?
c. In Volume 5, what is the purpose of the yellow and white sheets appearing before the tab labeled "Text"?

d. Refer to the Ruling Status Table in the Current Rulings Materials volume. What is the current status of Rev. Ruls. 79-433 and 75-335?
e. Refer to the Code-Rulings Tables in the same volume. List the numbers (e.g., Rev. Rul. 84-88) of all 1984 revenue rulings and revenue procedures that interpret Sec. 121.

C1-53 *Using a Tax Service.* The questions below deal with RIA's *Federal Tax Coordinator 2d.*
a. Use the topical index to locate authorities dealing with the deductibility of the cost of work clothing by ministers (clergymen). List the authorities.
b. Where does this tax service report new developments?

C1-54 *Using a Tax Service.* Refer to the *United States Tax Reporter* and *Standard Federal Tax Reporter*. Then, for each tax reporter, answer the following questions.
a. In which volume is the index located?
b. Is the index arranged by topic or IRC section?
c. If all you know is an IRC section number, how do you locate additional authorities?
d. If all you know is the name of a court decision, how do you locate additional authorities?

C1-55 *Using a Citator.* Trace *Biltmore Homes, Inc.*, a 1960 Tax Court memo decision, in both the CCH and RIA citators.
a. According to the RIA citator, how many times has the Tax Court decision been cited by other courts on Headnote Number 5?
b. How many issues were involved in the trial court litigation? (Hint: refer to the case headnote numbers.)
c. Did an appellate court review the case? If so, which one?
d. According to the CCH citator, how many times has the Tax Court decision been cited by other courts?
e. According to the CCH citator, how many times has the circuit court decision been cited by other courts on Headnote Number 5?

C1-56 *Using a Citator.* Trace *Stephen Bolaris*, 776 F.2d 1428, in both the CCH and RIA citators.
a. According to the RIA citator, how many times has the Ninth Circuit's decision been cited?
b. Did the decision address more than one issue? Explain.
c. Was the decision ever cited unfavorably? Explain.
d. According to the CCH citator, how many times has the Ninth Circuit's decision been cited?
e. According to the CCH citator, how many times has the Tax Court's decision been cited on Headnote Number 1?

C1-57 *Interpreting a Case.* Refer to the *Holden Fuel Oil Company* case (31 TCM 184).
a. In which year was the case decided?
b. What controversy was litigated?
c. Who won the case?
d. Was the decision reviewed at the trial level?
e. Was the decision appealed?
f. Has the decision been cited in other cases?

C1-58 *Internet Research.* Access the IRS Internet site at *http://www.irs.gov* and answer the following questions: (In answering them, consult the supplement to this chapter available for download at *www.prenhall.com/phtax.*)
a. What types of tax-related documents are available on this site?
b. What tax-rate schedules are available on this site?

C1-59 *Internet Research.* Access the IRS Internet site at *http://www.irs.gov* and indicate the titles of the following IRS forms: (In so doing, consult the supplement to this chapter available for download at *www.prenhall.com/phtax.*)
a. Form 4506
b. Form 973
c. Form 8725

C1-60 *Internet Research.* Access the IRS Internet site at *http://www.irs.gov* and indicate the titles of the following state tax forms and publications: (In so doing, consult the supplement to this chapter available for download at *www.prenhall.com/phtax.*)
a. Minnesota Form M-3
b. Illinois Schedule CR
c. New York State Form CT-3-C

C1-61 ***Internet Research.*** Access Emory's *Federal Courts Finder* at *http://www.law.emory.edu/FEDCTS/* and answer the following questions: (In answering them, consult the supplement to this chapter available for download at *www.prenhall.com/phtax*.)

a. What is the historical timespan of the underlying databases?
b. In what ways can they be accessed?
c. What 1995 Eleventh Circuit Court decisions address the issue of the charitable deduction for estates?

COMPREHENSIVE PROBLEM

C1-62 Your client, a physician, recently purchased a yacht on which he flies a pennant with a medical emblem on it. He recently informed you that he purchased the yacht and flies the pennant to advertise his occupation and thus attract new patients. He has asked you if he may deduct as ordinary and necessary business expenses the costs of insuring and maintaining the yacht. In search of an answer, consult either CCH's *Standard Federal Tax Reporter* or RIA's *United States Tax Reporter* first in print, and then on computer (i.e., the CCH Internet Tax Research Network or RIA CHECKPOINT). Then compare the steps taken on each to find your answer.

TAX STRATEGY PROBLEM

C1-63 Your client, Home Products Universal (HPU), distributes home improvement products to independent retailers throughout the country. Its management wants to explore the possibility of opening its own home improvement centers. Accordingly, it commissions a consulting firm to conduct a feasibility study, which ultimately persuades HPU to expand into retail sales. The consulting firm bills HPU $150,000, which HPU deducts on its current year tax return. The IRS disputes the deduction, contending that, because the cost relates to entering a new business, it should be capitalized. HPU's management, on the other hand, firmly believes that, because the cost relates to expanding HPU's existing business, it should be deducted. In contemplating legal action against the IRS, HPU's management considers the state of judicial precedent: The federal court for HPU's district has ruled that the cost of expanding from distribution into retail sales should be capitalized. The appellate court for HPU's circuit has stated in *dictum* that, although in some circumstances switching from product distribution to product sales entails entering a new trade or business, improving customer access to one's existing products generally does not. The Federal Circuit Court has ruled that wholesale distribution and retail sales, even of the same product, constitute distinct businesses. In a case involving a taxpayer from another circuit, the Tax Court has ruled that such costs invariably should be capitalized. HPU's Chief Financial Officer approaches you with the question, "In which judicial forum should HPU file a lawsuit against the IRS: (1) U.S. district court, (2) the Tax Court, or (3) the U.S. Court of Federal Claims?" What do you tell her?

CASE STUDY PROBLEM

C1-64 A client, Mal Manley, fills out his client questionnaire for the previous year and on it provides information for the preparation of his individual income tax return. The IRS has never audited Mal's returns. Mal reports that he made over 100 relatively small cash contributions totaling $24,785 to charitable organizations. In the last few years, Mal's charitable contributions have averaged about $15,000 per year. For the previous year, Mal's adjusted gross income was roughly $350,000, about a 10% increase from the year before.

Required: According to the *Statements on Standards for Tax Services,* may you accept at face value Mal's information concerning his charitable contributions? Now assume that the IRS recently audited Mal's tax return for two years ago and denied 75% of that year's charitable contribution deduction because the deduction was not substantiated. Assume also that Mal indicates that, in the previous year, he contributed $25,000 (instead of $24,785). How does this change of fact affect your earlier decision?

TAX RESEARCH PROBLEMS

C1-65 In answering these questions, refer only to *Thomas A. Curtis, M.D., Inc.*, 1994 RIA TC Memo ¶94,015. The purpose of this question is to enhance your skills in interpreting the authorities that you locate in your research.

a. What general controversy was litigated in this case?
b. Which party—the taxpayer or the government—won?
c. Why is the corporation instead of Dr. and/or Ms. Curtis listed as the plaintiff?
d. What is the relationship between Ellen Barnert Curtis and Dr. Thomas A. Curtis?
e. Approximately how many hours a week did Ms. Curtis work, and what were her credentials?
f. For the fiscal year ended in 1989, what salary did the corporation pay Ms. Curtis? What amount did the court decide was reasonable?
g. What dividends did the corporation pay for its fiscal years ending in 1988 and 1989?
h. To which circuit would this decision be appealable?
i. According to *Curtis*, what five factors did the Ninth Circuit mention in *Elliotts, Inc.* as relevant in determining reasonable compensation?

C1-66 Josh contributes $5,000 toward the support of his widowed mother, aged 69. His mother, a U.S. citizen and resident, earns gross income of $2,000 and spends it all for her own support. In addition, Medicare pays $3,200 of her medical expenses. She does not receive support from sources other than those described above. Must the Medicare payments be included in the support that Josh's mother is deemed to provide for herself?

Prepare work papers and a client letter (to Josh) dealing with the issue.

C1-67 Amy owns a vacation cottage in Maine. She predicts that use of the cottage during the current year will be as follows:

By Amy, solely for vacation	12 days
By Amy, making repairs ten hours per day and vacationing the rest of the day	2 days
By her sister, who paid fair rental value	8 days
By her cousin, who paid fair rental value	4 days
By her friend, who paid a token amount of rent	2 days
By three families from the Northeast, who paid fair rental value for 40 days each	120 days
Not used	217 days

Calculate the ratio for allocating the following expenses to the rental income expected to be received from the cottage: interest, taxes, repairs, insurance, and depreciation. The ratio will be used to determine the amount of expenses that are deductible and, thus, Amy's taxable income for the year.

Prepare for the tax manager to whom you report work papers in which you address the manner of the calculation. Also, draft a memo to the file dealing with the results of your research.

C1-68 Look up *Summit Publishing Company,* 1990 PH T.C. Memo ¶90,288, 59 TCM 833, and *J.B.S. Enterprises,* 1991 PH T.C. Memo ¶91,254, 61 TCM 2829, and answer the following questions:
a. What was the principal issue in these cases?
b. What factors did the Tax Court consider in resolving the central issue?
c. How are the facts of these cases similar? How are they dissimilar?

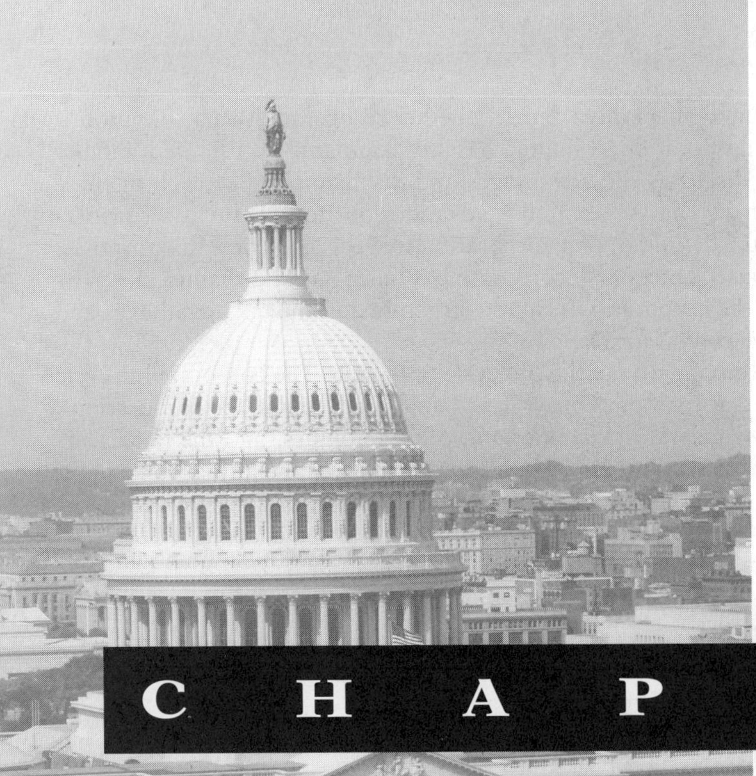

2

C H A P T E R

CORPORATE FORMATIONS AND CAPITAL STRUCTURE

LEARNING OBJECTIVES

After studying this chapter, you should be able to

1. Explain the tax advantages and disadvantages of using each of the alternative business forms
2. Determine check-the-box regulations as they pertain to partnerships, corporations, and trusts
3. Determine the legal requirements for forming a corporation
4. Explain the requirements for deferring gain or loss upon incorporation
5. Determine the tax consequences of alternative capital structures
6. Determine the tax consequences of worthless stock or debt obligations

CHAPTER OUTLINE

Organization Forms Available...2-2
Check-the-Box Regulations...2-8
Legal Requirements for Forming a Corporation...2-9
Tax Considerations in Forming a Corporation...2-9
Section 351: Deferring Gain or Loss Upon Incorporation...2-12
Choice of Capital Structure...2-26
Worthlessness of Stock or Debt Obligations...2-30
Tax Planning Considerations...2-33
Compliance and Procedural Considerations...2-35

When starting a business, its owners must decide whether to operate it as a sole proprietorship, a partnership, a corporation, a limited liability company, or a limited liability partnership. This chapter discusses the advantages and disadvantages of each of these business entities. Because many businesses find it advantageous to operate as a corporation, this chapter looks at the definition of a corporation for federal income tax purposes. It also discusses the tax consequences of incorporating a business. The chapter closes by looking at the selection of the corporation's capital structure and the tax advantages and disadvantages of alternative capital forms.

The corporate taxation discussion takes a life-cycle approach. The corporate life cycle starts in this chapter with its formation. Once formed and in operation, the corporation's taxable income (or loss), its federal income tax and other liabilities, and the tax consequences of any distributions to its shareholders must be determined. Finally, at some point the corporation may outlive its usefulness and be dissolved, thus ending the life of the corporation. The corporate life cycle is too complex to discuss in one chapter, however, so detailed coverage follows in Chapters C3 through C8.

ORGANIZATION FORMS AVAILABLE

OBJECTIVE 1

Explain the tax advantages and disadvantages of using each of the alternative business forms

Business can be conducted in several entities or forms including

- Sole proprietorships
- Partnerships
- Corporations
- Limited liability companies
- Limited liability partnerships

An overview of each entity form is presented below.

SELF-STUDY QUESTION

What is involved in reporting the activities of a sole proprietorship?

ANSWER

The income/loss of a sole proprietorship is reported on Schedule C. This schedule is simply a summary of the operating income and expense items of the sole proprietorship. The net income/loss then is carried to Form 1040 and included in the computation of the individual's taxable income.

SOLE PROPRIETORSHIPS

A **sole proprietorship** is a business owned by one individual and often is selected by individuals who are beginning a new business. It is not a separate entity. Thus, the proprietor owns all the business assets and reports income or loss from the sole proprietorship directly on his or her individual tax return. Specifically, the proprietor (owner) reports all the business's income and expenses for the year on Schedule C (Profit or Loss from Business) or Schedule C-EZ (Net Profit from Business) of Form 1040. A completed Schedule C is included in Appendix B, where a common set of facts (with minor modifications) illustrates the similarities and differences in the tax reporting process for a sole proprietorship, C corporation, partnership, and S corporation.

If the business is profitable, the profit is added to the proprietor's other income.

EXAMPLE C2-1 ▶ John is single and starts a new computer store, which he operates as a sole proprietorship. John reports a $15,000 profit from the store for his first year. Assuming he has enough income from other sources to be taxed at a 35% marginal tax rate, his tax on the $15,000 of profit from the new store is $5,250 (0.35 × $15,000).[1] ◀

If the business operates at a loss, the loss reduces the proprietor's taxable income and provides a tax savings.

EXAMPLE C2-2 ▶ Assume the same facts as in Example C2-1 except that John reports a $15,000 loss on his new computer store instead of a $15,000 profit. Assuming he still is taxed at a 35% marginal tax rate, the $15,000 loss on the new venture produces a $5,250 (0.35 × $15,000) tax savings. ◀

---

[1] The $15,000 Schedule C profit in Example C2-1 will increase adjusted gross income (AGI). The AGI level affects certain deduction calculations (e.g., medical, charitable contributions, and miscellaneous itemized) and may result in a taxable income increase different from the $15,000 AGI increase.

ADDITIONAL COMMENT

Although this chapter emphasizes the tax consequences of selecting the entity in which a business will be conducted, other issues often are more important in making such a decision. For example, the amount of legal liability assumed by an owner is important and can vary substantially among the different business entities.

TAX ADVANTAGES. The tax advantages of doing business as a sole proprietorship include

- The entity itself is not subject to taxation. The sole proprietor is taxed on any income at his or her marginal tax rate. The proprietor's marginal tax rate may be lower than a corporation's marginal tax rate that would be imposed on the same amount of income.
- The owner can contribute money to, or withdraw money from, the business without any tax consequences. Although the owner usually maintains separate books and records and a separate bank account for his or her business, the money in that bank account is still the owner's. The owner may withdraw money from or put money into the business bank account without any tax consequences. He or she also can contribute property to or withdraw property from the business without gain or loss recognition. However, the owner is taxed on the profits of the business whether those profits are retained in the business or withdrawn for the owner's use.
- Losses offset income from other sources such as interest, dividends, and any salary of the taxpayer and the taxpayer's spouse, subject to the passive loss limitations.

TAX DISADVANTAGES. The tax disadvantages of doing business as a sole proprietorship include

- The proprietor is taxed on all the profits when they are earned even if they are not withdrawn by him or her but are reinvested in the business. Shareholders, however, are taxed on a corporation's earnings only when those earnings are distributed. Corporate tax rates may be lower than those imposed on a sole proprietor.
- A sole proprietor is not considered an employee of the business. Therefore, the proprietor must pay self-employment taxes on the self-employment income derived from the business. This tax can be a disadvantage where the business profit is more than would be withdrawn as salary (and subject to the FICA taxes) if incorporated. In addition, some tax-exempt fringe benefits (e.g., full deductibility for premiums paid on accident and health insurance and premiums for group term life insurance) generally are not available to a sole proprietor.[2]
- A sole proprietor must use the same reporting period for both business and individual tax returns. Income cannot be deferred by choosing a fiscal year for the business that differs from the proprietor's own tax year.

PARTNERSHIPS

REAL WORLD EXAMPLE

The IRS estimates the following business entity returns to be filed for 2001:

Entity	Number
Partnership	2.29 million
C corporation	2.82 million
S corporation	3.11 million

A **partnership** is an unincorporated business carried on by two or more individuals or other entities. The partnership form often is used by friends or relatives who decide to go into business together and by groups of investors who want to share the profits and expenses of some type of business or investment such as a real estate project.

A partnership is a tax reporting, but not generally a taxpaying entity. The partnership acts as a conduit. Its income, expenses, losses, credits, and so on flow through to the partners who report those items on their own tax returns.

A partnership must file a tax return every year (Form 1065—U.S. Partnership Return of Income) to report the results of its operations. When the partnership return is filed, the preparer must send each partner a statement (Schedule K-1, Form 1065) that reports the partner's share of the partnership's income, expenses, losses, credits, and so on. The partners then must report these items on their individual tax returns. A completed Form 1065 is included in Appendix B.

Just as with a sole proprietorship, if the business is profitable, the partners' allocable shares of the profit are added to the partners' other income and taxed at the partners' marginal tax rates.

EXAMPLE C2-3 ► Bob is single and owns a 50% interest in the new BT Partnership, a calendar year entity. The BT Partnership reports $30,000 of profits for its first year. Bob's $15,000 share flows through to him

[2] Section 162(1) permits self-employed individuals to deduct a percentage of the health insurance costs incurred on behalf of themselves, their spouses, and their dependents as a trade or business expense. Excess health insurance costs may be deducted as an itemized deduction subject to the 7.5% of AGI limitation. The percentage allowed is 60% in 1999–2001, 70% in 2002, and 100% in 2003 and thereafter.

from the partnership. Assuming Bob is taxed at a 35% marginal tax rate on the additional income, his tax on his $15,000 share of partnership profits is $5,250 (0.35 × $15,000). Bob owes the $5,250 in taxes whether the BT Partnership distributes any of its profits to him or not. ◀

If a partnership reports a loss, the partners' allocable shares of the loss reduce the partners' other income and provide a tax savings based on the partners' marginal tax rates. The passive loss rules may limit these deductions to the partners. (See Chapter C9 of this book).

EXAMPLE C2-4 ▶ Assume the same facts as in Example C2-3 except that the BT Partnership reports a $30,000 loss for its first year instead of a profit. Assuming Bob is taxed at a 35% marginal tax rate, his $15,000 share of the first year loss produces a $5,250 (0.35 × $15,000) tax savings. ◀

A partnership can be either a general partnership or a limited partnership. In a general partnership, each partner has unlimited liability for partnership debts. Thus, these partners are at risk for more than their investment in the partnership. In a limited partnership, at least one partner must be a general partner, and at least one partner must be a limited partner. As in a general partnership, the general partners are liable for all partnership debts, but the limited partners are liable only to the extent of their investment plus any amount they commit to contribute to the partnership if called upon. Moreover, limited partners may not participate in the management of the partnership.

The tax advantages and disadvantages of doing business as a partnership are similar to those of a sole proprietorship and are presented below.

TAX ADVANTAGES. The tax advantages of doing business as a partnership are

- The partnership itself is exempt from taxation. The income of the partnership flows through and is taxed directly to the partners. Their individual tax rates may be lower than the corporate marginal tax rate on the same amount of taxable income.
- No double taxation is inherent in the partnership form. Profits are taxed only at the partner level when earned by the partnership. Additional taxes generally are not imposed on withdrawals made by the partners. With limited exceptions, partners can contribute money or property to the partnership or withdraw money or property from the partnership without gain or loss recognition.
- Losses can be used by partners to offset income from other sources, subject to limitations.
- A partner's basis in a partnership interest is increased by his or her share of partnership income. This basis adjustment reduces the amount of gain recognized when the partner sells his or her partnership interest, thereby preventing double taxation.

ADDITIONAL COMMENT

If two or more owners exist, a business cannot be conducted as a sole proprietorship. From a tax compliance and recordkeeping perspective, conducting a business as a partnership is more complicated than conducting the business as a sole proprietorship.

TAX DISADVANTAGES. The tax disadvantages of doing business as a partnership are

- All the partnership's profits are taxed to the partners when earned even if reinvested in the business. The partners' tax rates may be higher than the marginal tax rate that applies to a corporation.
- A partner is not considered an employee of the partnership. Therefore, partners must pay self-employment taxes on their share of the partnership's self-employment income. Some tax-exempt fringe benefits (e.g., full deductibility for premiums paid on accident and health insurance[3] and premiums for group term life insurance) are not available to the partners.
- Partners generally cannot defer income by choosing a fiscal year for the partnership that differs from the tax year of the partner(s) who own a majority interest in the partnership. However, if the partnership can establish a business purpose or if it makes a special election, the partnership can use a fiscal year.

Chapters C9 and C10 of this volume provide a detailed discussion of partnerships.

---

[3] Partners also are eligible to deduct a percentage of their health insurance costs in the same manner as a sole proprietor. See footnote 2 for details.

CORPORATIONS

Corporations can be divided into two categories. A regular corporation, or C corporation, is taxed annually on its earnings. These earnings are taxed to the corporation's shareholders when distributed as a dividend. A special S election also is available that permits a corporation's earnings to be taxed directly to its shareholders.

ADDITIONAL COMMENT

Unlike a sole proprietorship and a partnership, a C corporation is a separate taxpaying entity. This form can be an advantage because corporate rates start at 15%, which may be much lower than an individual shareholder's rate, which might be as high as 38.6% (in 2002).

C CORPORATIONS. A **C corporation** is a separate taxpaying entity taxed on its taxable income at rates ranging from 15% to 35%. A corporation must report all its income and expenses and compute its tax liability on Form 1120 (U.S. Corporation Income Tax Return). A completed Form 1120 is included in Appendix B. Shareholders are not taxed on the corporation's earnings unless they are distributed as dividends. Thus, income is taxed twice: first to the corporation and then to its shareholders when distributed as a dividend.

EXAMPLE C2-5 ▶

Jane owns 100% of York Corporation's stock. York reports taxable income of $50,000 for the year. The first $50,000 of taxable income is taxed at a 15% rate, so York pays a corporate income tax of $7,500 (0.15 × $50,000). If the corporation makes no distributions to Jane during the year, she pays no taxes on York's earnings. However, if York distributes its current after-tax earnings to Jane, she must pay tax on $42,500 ($50,000 − $7,500) of dividend income. Assuming she is in the 35% marginal tax bracket, the tax Jane pays on the dividend income is $14,875 (0.35 × $42,500). The total tax on York's $50,000 of profits is $22,375 ($7,500 paid by York + $14,875 paid by Jane). ◀

TAX STRATEGY TIP

If a shareholder is also an employee of the corporation, the corporation can avoid double taxation by paying a deductible salary instead of a dividend. The salary, however, must be reasonable in amount. See Chapter C3 for further discussion of this technique.

Even when a corporation does not distribute its profits, double taxation may occur. The profits are taxed to the corporation when they are earned. Then they may be taxed a second time (as capital gains) when the shareholder sells his or her stock or when the corporation liquidates.

EXAMPLE C2-6 ▶

On January 1 of the current year, Ken purchases 100% of York Corporation stock for $60,000. York Corporation reports taxable income of $50,000 in the current year, on which it pays tax of $7,500. The corporation distributes none of the remaining $42,500 to Ken. However, on January 1 of the next year, Ken sells his stock to Mary for $102,500 (his initial investment plus the current year's accumulated earnings). Ken must report a capital gain of $42,500 ($102,500 − $60,000). Thus, York's profit is taxed twice—once at the corporate level and again at the shareholder level when the stock is sold. ◀

TAX STRATEGY TIP

By having a corporation accumulate earnings instead of paying dividends, the shareholder converts current ordinary income into deferred capital gains. The corporation, however, must avoid the accumulated earnings tax (see Chapter C5).

Tax Advantages. The tax advantages of the C corporation form of doing business are

- Corporations (other than personal service corporations) are taxed at rates starting at 15%. Because a corporation is an entity independent of its owners, its marginal tax rate may be lower than the shareholder's marginal tax rate. A tax savings may result as long as the earnings are not distributed and taxed to both the shareholder and the corporation. As a result, more earnings may be available for reinvestment and the retirement of debt. This advantage is limited, however, by the accumulated earnings tax and the personal holding company tax (see Chapter C5 for a discussion of these two penalty taxes).
- Shareholders employed by their own corporation are treated as employees for tax purposes. As employees, they are eligible to receive deductible salary payments. With this technique, shareholder/employees can adjust their compensation (within limits) so that the income is taxed partly on the corporate return and partly on the individual returns, thereby minimizing their overall tax liability. In addition, they are entitled to tax-free fringe benefits (e.g., premiums paid on group term life insurance and accident and health insurance). The corporation can provide fringe benefits with *before-tax* dollars (instead of after-tax dollars). Sole proprietors and partners are not considered to be employees and, therefore, are ineligible for some benefits, although they are permitted to deduct a portion of their health insurance premiums.
- A C corporation can use a fiscal year instead of a calendar year as its reporting period. A fiscal year may enable a corporation to defer income to a later reporting period. A

personal service corporation, however, generally must use a calendar year as its tax year.[4]

- Special rules allow a 50% exclusion of gain realized on the sale or exchange of stock held more than five years if the C corporation meets certain requirements.

SELF-STUDY QUESTION

How are corporate earnings subject to double taxation?

ANSWER

Corporate earnings initially are taxed to the corporation. In addition, once these earnings are distributed to the shareholders (dividends), they are taxed again. Because the corporation does not receive a deduction for the distribution, these earnings have been taxed twice. Also, double taxation can occur when a shareholder sells his or her stock at a gain.

Tax Disadvantages. The tax disadvantages of the C corporation form of doing business are

- Double taxation of income occurs when the corporation distributes its earnings as dividends to shareholders or when shareholders sell or exchange their stock.
- Shareholders generally cannot withdraw money or property from the corporation without income recognition. A distribution of profits to a shareholder is taxable as a dividend to the shareholder if the corporation has sufficient earnings and profits (E&P).[5]
- Net operating losses provide no benefit in the year they are incurred. They can be carried back or carried forward to offset the corporation's income in other years. For corporations in the start-up phase of operations, these losses cannot provide any tax benefits until the corporation earns a profit in a subsequent year. Shareholders cannot use these losses to offset their income from other sources.
- Capital losses provide no benefit in the year they are incurred. They cannot offset any ordinary income of the corporation or of its shareholders. These losses must be carried back or carried forward to offset corporate capital gains reported in other years.

S CORPORATIONS. An **S corporation** is so designated because rules pertaining to this entity are located in Subchapter S of the IRC and allow S corporations to be treated as flow-through entities. Similar to partnerships, therefore, S corporations are not taxed, and income, deductions, losses, and credits flow through to the shareholders. These entities, however, still are corporations so that corporate tax rules apply to them unless overridden by the Subchapter S provisions. As with regular C corporations, the shareholders enjoy limited liability, but S corporations offer less flexibility than do partnerships. For example, the number and type of shareholders are limited, and the shareholders cannot agree to allocate income, deductions, losses, and credits in a way that differs from their proportionate ownership.

To achieve S corporation status, the corporation must file an election, and its shareholders must consent to that election. An S corporation files an information return, Form 1120S (U.S. Income Tax Return for an S Corporation), which reports the results of the corporation's operations and indicates the separate items of income, deductions, losses, and credits that flow through to the shareholders.

EXAMPLE C2-7 ▶ Chuck owns 50% of the stock of Maine Corporation, a qualifying S corporation that is a calendar year taxpayer. For its first year, Maine reports $30,000 of taxable income, all of it ordinary income. Maine pays no corporate income taxes. Chuck must pay taxes on his share of Maine's income, $15,000 (0.50 × $30,000), whether the corporation distributes it to him or not. If Chuck's marginal tax rate is 35%, he pays $5,250 (0.35 × $15,000) of tax on his additional income from Maine Corporation. If Maine instead reports a $30,000 loss, Chuck's $15,000 share of the loss reduces his tax liability by $5,250 (0.35 × $15,000). ◀

TAX STRATEGY TIP

If a corporation anticipates losses in its early years, it might consider operating as an S corporation (see Chapter C11) so that the losses pass through to the shareholders. When the corporation becomes profitable, it can revoke the S election if it wishes to accumulate earnings for growth.

Tax Advantages. The tax advantages of doing business as an S corporation are

- S corporations generally are exempt from taxation. Income flows through and is taxed to the shareholders. The shareholders' marginal tax rates may be lower than a C corporation's marginal tax rate.
- Losses flow through to shareholders and can be used to offset income earned from other sources unless limitations apply. This feature is particularly important to corporations just beginning their operations. (Passive loss and basis rules may limit loss deductions to shareholders. See Chapter C11).

[4] Sec. 441. See Chapter C3 for the special tax year restrictions applying to personal service corporations.

[5] The term *earnings and profits* is a technical term that represents the corporation's ability to pay a dividend. The term is discussed in Chapter C4.

- Because income, loss, and other pass through items retain their character when they flow through to the shareholders, individual shareholders are taxed on capital gains as though the individual earned the gains. An individual may be able to offset those gains with capital losses from other sources or have them taxed at the appropriate capital gain tax rate.
- Shareholders generally can contribute money to or withdraw money from an S corporation without gain recognition. Shareholders are taxed only on the annual income of the S corporation.
- Corporate profits are taxed only at the shareholder level. Generally, no additional taxes are imposed on distributions of profits to the S corporation's shareholders.
- A shareholder's basis in S corporation stock is increased by his or her share of the corporation's income. This basis adjustment reduces the shareholder's gain when he or she sells the S corporation stock, thereby preventing double taxation.

Tax Disadvantages. The tax disadvantages of doing business as an S corporation are

- Shareholders are taxed on all of an S corporation's current year profits whether those profits are distributed or not. If the shareholders' marginal tax rates exceed those for a C corporation, the capital available for reinvestment and debt retirement may be reduced.
- Tax-free corporate fringe benefits generally are not available to S corporation shareholders who are employed by the business.[6] Fringe benefits provided by an S corporation are deductible by the corporation and taxable to the shareholder. The S corporation's shareholder-employees are treated as employees for purposes of social security tax payments on their salary income.
- S corporations generally cannot defer income by choosing a fiscal year for the S corporation other than a calendar year unless the S corporation can establish a business purpose for a fiscal year or unless it makes a special election.

Chapter C11 of this volume discusses S corporations in detail. In addition, Appendix F contains a comparison of the tax rules for partnerships, C corporations, and S corporations.

ADDITIONAL COMMENT

All 50 states have adopted statutes allowing LLCs.

LIMITED LIABILITY COMPANIES

A **limited liability company** (LLC) combines the best features of a partnership and corporation even though it is neither. Specifically, it is taxed like a partnership while providing the limited liability of a corporation. Moreover, this limited liability extends to all the LLC's owners, called members. Thus, the LLC is similar to an unlimited partnership with no general partners. Unlike an S corporation, however, it can have an unlimited number of members who can be individuals, corporations, estates, and trusts. As discussed below, the LLC may elect to be taxed as either a corporation or a partnership under the check-the-box regulations. Assuming the LLC elects partnership treatment, it files Form 1065 (U.S. Partnership Return of Income). Nevertheless, the LLC is not legally a partnership; it just is taxed as one.

REAL WORLD EXAMPLE

All the Big 5 accounting firms have converted general partnerships into LLPs.

LIMITED LIABILITY PARTNERSHIPS

Many states also have statutes that allow a business to operate as a **limited liability partnership** (LLP). This partnership form is particularly attractive to professional service partnerships, such as public accounting firms. As a result, many firms have adopted the LLP form, primarily to limit legal liability. Under state LLP laws, partners are liable for their own acts and the acts of individuals under their direction. However, LLP partners are not liable for the negligence or misconduct of other partners. Thus, from a liability perspective, an LLP partner is like a limited partner with respect to other partners' acts but like a

[6] S corporation shareholders also are eligible to deduct a percentage of their health insurance costs in the same manner as a sole proprietor and partner. See footnote 2 for details.

general partner with respect to his or her own acts. Like a traditional partnership or an LLC, an LLP can elect to be treated as a corporation or a partnership under the check-the-box regulations. If it elects partnership treatment, it files Form 1065 (U.S. Partnership Return of Income).

CHECK-THE-BOX REGULATIONS

OBJECTIVE 2

Determine check-the-box regulations as they pertain to partnerships, corporations, and trusts

TAX STRATEGY TIP

When applying the federal check-the-box regulations, taxpayers also must check to see whether or not their state will treat the entity in a consistent manner.

Most unincorporated businesses can choose whether to be taxed as a partnership or a corporation. These rules are commonly referred to as the **check-the-box regulations.**

These regulations provide that an unincorporated business with two or more owners is treated as a partnership unless it elects to be taxed as a corporation. An unincorporated business with one owner is disregarded as a separate entity, and its income is taxed directly to the owner (i.e., on a Schedule C included as part of the individual owner's tax return unless it elects to be taxed as a corporation). This rule does not apply to corporations, trusts, or certain special entities such as Real Estate Investment Trusts, Real Estate Mortgage Investment Conduits, or Publicly Traded Partnerships.[7]

An eligible entity may affirmatively elect its classification on Form 8832 (Entity Classification Election). The election must be signed by each member of the entity, or any officer, manager, or member of the entity authorized to make the election. The election must include all required information, including the entity's taxpayer identification number. Taxpayers must specify the date on which an election will be effective. The effective date cannot be more than 75 days before or 12 months after the date entity files the election. A copy of the Form 8832 must be attached to the entity's tax return for the election year.

EXAMPLE C2-8 ▶ On January 10 of the current year, a group of ten individuals organizes an LLC to conduct a bookbinding business in Texas. In the current year, the LLC is an eligible entity under the check-the-box regulations and thus may elect (with the owners' signatures) to be taxed as a corporation. However, if the entity does not make an election to be taxed as a corporation, the LLC is treated as a partnership. ◀

EXAMPLE C2-9 ▶ Assume the same facts as in Example C2-8 except the LLC was created by a single individual. Because one individual organized the LLC and did not have the entity elect to be taxed as a corporation, the LLC is disregarded for tax purposes. Its income is taxed to the owner under the rules for a sole proprietorship. ◀

If an entity makes an election to change its classification, it cannot again change its classification by election during the 60 months following the effective date of the election.

The change made by an eligible entity from one classification to another may produce some tax consequences. The consequences of changing from a partnership to an LLC or an LLP are discussed in Chapter C10. An election by an LLC to be taxed as a corporation would cause the Sec. 351 corporate formation rules to apply. As discussed below, the corporate formation transaction generally will be tax-free. An election by an LLC to change from being taxed as a corporation to a sole proprietorship or partnership is treated as a corporate liquidation (see Chapter C6).[8]

---

[7] Reg. Sec. 301.7701-2(b)(8). Publicly traded partnerships are discussed in Chapter C10. Special check-the-box rules apply to foreign corporations. These rules are beyond the scope of this text.

[8] An alternative way for a corporation to be taxed as a flow-through entity is to make an election to be taxed as an S corporation. See Chapter C11.

LEGAL REQUIREMENTS FOR FORMING A CORPORATION

OBJECTIVE 3

Determine the legal requirements for forming a corporation

The legal requirements for forming a corporation depend on state law. These requirements may include

- A minimum amount of capital
- The filing of the articles of incorporation
- The granting of a corporate charter by the state
- The issuance of stock
- The payment of incorporation fees to the state

One of the first decisions owners must make when planning to form a corporation is selecting the state in which to incorporate the organization. A particular state may provide certain advantages to the corporation and/or its shareholders because its laws provide smaller legal capital minimums, a smaller incorporation fee, a lower annual franchise tax liability, or a lower corporate income tax liability. Most corporations, however, are incorporated in the state in which they initially conduct their primary business activities.

Regardless of which state the owners select, the laws of that state must be followed in the incorporation process. Normally, articles of incorporation must be filed with the appropriate state agency. The articles must contain such information as the name of the corporation, the purpose of the corporation, the amount and types of stock the corporation is authorized to issue, and the names of the individuals on the corporation's board of directors. The state charges a fee at the time of incorporation. In addition, the state may impose an annual franchise tax for the privilege of doing business as a corporation.

ADDITIONAL COMMENT

States are not consistent in how they tax corporations. Certain states have no state income taxes. Other states do not recognize an S election, thereby taxing an S corporation as a C corporation.

TAX CONSIDERATIONS IN FORMING A CORPORATION

Once a decision has been reached to use the corporate form for conducting a business, the investors must transfer money, property (e.g., equipment, furniture, inventory, and receivables), or services (e.g., accounting, legal, or architectural services) to the corporation in exchange for a debt or equity interest in the corporation. These transfers may have tax consequences to both the transferor and the corporation. For instance, an exchange of property for stock usually is a taxable exchange to the transferors.[9] However, if Sec. 351(a) (which considers certain transferred business assets to be "changed in form" rather than "disposed of") applies, any gain or loss realized on the exchange is deferred. Thus, the answers to the following questions must be considered carefully in relation to the tax consequences of incorporation:

- What property should be transferred to the corporation?
- What services should the transferors or third parties provide to the corporation?
- What liabilities should be transferred to the corporation in addition to the transferred property?
- How should the property be transferred to the corporation (e.g., sale, contribution to capital, or loan)?

Table C2-1 and Example C2-10 compare the tax consequences of taxable and tax-free asset transfers.

[9] Sec. 1001.

▼ **TABLE C2-1**
Overview of Corporate Formation Rules

Tax Treatment for:	Taxable Transaction	Tax-Free Transaction
Transferors:		
1. Gain realized	FMV of stock received Money received FMV of nonmoney boot property (including securities) received Amount of liabilities assumed by transferee corporation Minus: Adjusted basis of property transferred Realized gain (Sec. 1001(a))	Same as taxable transaction
2. Gain recognized	Transferors recognize the entire amount of realized gain (Sec. 1001(c)) Losses may be disallowed under related party rules (Sec. 267(a)(1)) Installment sale rules may apply to the gain (Sec. 453)	Transferors recognize none of the realized gain unless one of the following exceptions applies (Sec. 351(a)): a. Boot property is received (Sec. 351(b)) b. Liabilities having a nonbusiness or tax avoidance purpose are transferred to the corporation (Sec. 357(b)) c. Liabilities exceeding basis are transferred to the corporation (Sec. 357(c)) d. Services, certain corporate indebtednesses, and interest claims are transferred to the corporation (Sec. 351(d)) The installment method may defer recognition of gain when a shareholder receives a corporate note as boot (Sec. 453)
3. Basis of property received	FMV (Cost) (Sec. 1012)	Basis of property transferred to the corporation Plus: Gain recognized Minus: Money received (including liabilities treated as money) FMV of nonmoney boot property Total basis of stock received (Sec. 358(a)) Allocation of total stock basis is based on relative FMVs Basis of nonmoney boot property is its FMV
4. Holding period of property received	Day after the exchange date	Holding period for stock includes holding period of property transferred if received for Sec. 1231 property or capital assets (Sec. 1223); otherwise it is the day after the exchange date
Transferee Corporation:		
1. Gain recognized	The corporation recognizes no gain or loss on the receipt of money or other property in exchange for its stock (including treasury stock) (Sec. 1032)	Same except the corporation may recognize gain under Sec. 311 if it gives nonmoney boot property (Sec. 351(f))
2. Basis	FMV (Cost) (Sec. 1012)	Same as in transferor's hands plus any gain recognized by transferor (Sec. 362)
3. Holding period	Day after the exchange date	Carryover holding period from transferor applies regardless of the property's character (Sec. 1223(2))

EXAMPLE C2-10 ▶ Brad has operated a successful manufacturing business as a sole proprietorship for several years. For good business reasons, he decides to incorporate his business. Immediately preceding the formation of Block Corporation, the balance sheet for his sole proprietorship, which uses the accrual method of accounting, is as follows:

BOOK-TO-TAX ACCOUNTING COMPARISON

The IRC treats most corporate formations as nontaxable transactions. Property received in a corporate formation transaction generally is recorded on the tax books using the carryover basis rules. Services are recorded at their FMV. The financial accounting rules, however, record services and noncash property received for stock at either the FMV of the stock issued or the FMV of the noncash consideration received, whichever is more readily determinable.

		Adjusted Basis	*Fair Market Value*
Assets:			
Cash		$ 10,000	$ 10,000
Accounts receivable		15,000	15,000
Inventory		20,000	25,000
Equipment	$120,000		
Minus: Depreciation	(35,000)	85,000	100,000
Total		$130,000	$150,000
Liabilities and owner's equity:			
Accounts payable		$ 30,000	$ 30,000
Note payable on equipment		50,000	50,000
Owner's equity		50,000	70,000
Total		$130,000	$150,000

When Brad transfers the assets to Block Corporation in exchange for stock, he realizes a gain because the stock he receives has a value higher than his basis in those assets. If the transfer of these assets and liabilities to Block Corporation is a taxable event, Brad must recognize a $5,000 ordinary gain on the transfer of the inventory ($25,000 FMV – $20,000 basis) and, because of depreciation recapture, a $15,000 ordinary gain on the transfer of the equipment ($100,000 FMV – $85,000 basis). However, if the transaction meets the requirements of Sec. 351(a), the exchange is tax-free; Brad does not recognize any gain realized on the transfer of the assets and liabilities to the corporation. ◀

STOP & THINK *Question:* Joyce has been operating a business as a sole proprietorship for several years. She needs additional capital and wants to incorporate her business. The assets of her business (building, land, inventory, and so on) have a $400,000 adjusted basis and a $1.5 million FMV. Joyce is willing to exchange the assets for 1,500 shares of Ace Corporation stock each having a $1,000 fair market value. Bill and John are each willing to invest $500,000 in Joyce's business for 500 shares of stock. Why is Sec. 351 important to Joyce? Does it matter to Bill and John?

Solution: If not for Sec. 351, Joyce would recognize gain on the incorporation of her business. She has a $1.1 million ($1,500,000 – $400,000) realized gain on her contribution of the proprietorship's assets to a new corporation in exchange for 60% of its outstanding shares (1,500 ÷ [1,500 + 500 + 500] = 0.60). However, she recognizes none of this gain under Sec. 351. Section 351 does not affect Bill or John because each individual is simply purchasing 20% of the new corporation's stock for $500,000 cash. They do not realize or recognize any gain whether Sec. 351 applies or not.

If all exchanges of property for corporate stock were taxable, many business owners would find the tax cost of incorporating prohibitively expensive. In Example C2-10, for example, Brad would recognize a $20,000 gain on the exchange of his assets for the corporate stock.

A second problem is that losses also are realized in an exchange transaction. Therefore, taxpayers might be able to exchange loss property for stock and recognize the loss while maintaining an economic interest in the property through stock ownership.

Congress enacted Sec. 351 to respond to these two problems: to allow taxpayers to incorporate without incurring adverse tax consequences and to prevent taxpayers from recognizing losses while maintaining ownership of the loss assets indirectly through stock ownership.

SECTION 351: DEFERRING GAIN OR LOSS UPON INCORPORATION

OBJECTIVE 4

Explain the requirements for deferring gain or loss upon incorporation

Section 351(a) provides that transferors recognize no gain or loss when they transfer property to a corporation solely in exchange for the corporation's stock provided that, immediately after the exchange, the transferors are in control of the corporation. Section 351 does not apply to a transfer of property to an investment company, nor does it apply in certain bankruptcy cases.

This rule is based on the premise that, when property is transferred to a controlled corporation, the transferors merely have exchanged direct ownership for indirect ownership through a stock interest in the transferee corporation. In other words, the transferors have a continuity of interest in the transferred property. Furthermore, if all the shareholders receive is stock, they do not have any cash with which to pay any taxes. This scenario is an example of the "wherewithal-to-pay doctrine." If the transferors of property receive anything in addition to stock, such as cash or debt instruments, they do have the wherewithal to pay and may have to recognize some or all of their realized gain under Sec. 351(b).

TAX STRATEGY TIP

A transferor who wishes to recognize gain or loss must take steps to avoid Sec. 351 by failing at least one of its requirements or by engaging in sales transactions. See Tax Planning Considerations later in this chapter for details.

A transferor's gain or loss that goes unrecognized when Sec. 351 applies is not permanently exempt from taxation; it is only *deferred* until the shareholder sells or exchanges the stock received in the Sec. 351 exchange. Shareholders who receive stock in an exchange qualifying under Sec. 351 take a stock basis that reflects the deferred gain or loss. For example, if a shareholder recognizes no gain or loss, the stock basis equals the basis of property transferred less liabilities assumed by the corporation (see Table C2-1). Further discussion of this method appears later in this chapter. Under an alternative method, the stock basis can be calculated as follows: FMV of stock received minus any deferred gain (or plus any deferred loss). This latter approach highlights the deferral aspect inherent in this type of transaction. If the shareholder later sells the stock, he or she will recognize the deferred gain or loss because of the basis adjustment.

EXAMPLE C2-11 ▶ Assume the same facts as in Example C2-10. If Sec. 351 applies, Brad does not recognize the $20,000 realized gain ($15,000 gain on equipment + $5,000 gain on inventory) when he transfers the assets and liabilities of his sole proprietorship to Block Corporation. Under the alternative method, Brad's basis for the Block stock is decreased to reflect the deferred gain. Thus, Brad's basis in the Block stock is $50,000 ($70,000 FMV of Block stock − $20,000 deferred gain). If Brad later sells his stock for its $70,000 FMV, he will recognize the $20,000 gain at that time. ◀

The specific requirements for complete deferral of gain and loss under Sec. 351(a) are

- ▶ Property must be transferred to the corporation in an exchange transaction.
- ▶ The transferors of the property must be in control of the corporation immediately after the exchange.
- ▶ The transferors must receive stock of the transferee corporation in exchange for their property.

Each of these requirements is explained below.

THE PROPERTY REQUIREMENT

Nonrecognition of gain or loss applies only to transfers of property to a corporation in exchange for the corporation's stock. Section 351 does not define the term *property.* However, the courts and the government have defined the term *property* to include money and almost any other kind of property, including installment obligations, accounts receivable, inventory, equipment, patents and other intangibles representing "know how," trademarks, trade names, and computer software.[10]

[10] For an excellent discussion of the definition of *property,* see footnote 6 of *D. N. Stafford v. U.S.*, 45 AFTR 2d 80-785, 80-1 USTC ¶9218 (5th Cir., 1980).

Statutorily excluded from the property definition are[11]

- Services (such as legal or accounting services) rendered to the corporation in exchange for its stock
- Indebtedness of the transferee corporation not evidenced by a security
- Interest on an indebtedness of the transferee corporation that accrued on or after the beginning of the transferor's holding period for the debt

The first of these exclusions is perhaps the most important. A person receiving stock as compensation for services must recognize the stock's FMV as compensation (ordinary income) for tax purposes. In other words, an exchange of services for stock is a taxable transaction even if Sec. 351 applies to other property transfers.[12] A shareholder's basis in the stock received as compensation for services is the stock's FMV.

EXAMPLE C2-12 ▶ Amy and Bill form West Corporation. Amy exchanges cash and other property for 90 shares (90% of the outstanding shares) of West stock. The exchange is tax-free because Sec. 351(a) applies. Bill performs accounting services in exchange for ten shares of West stock worth $10,000. Bill's exchange is *not* tax-free under Sec. 351. Thus, Bill must recognize $10,000 of ordinary income—the FMV of the West stock received—as compensation for services. Bill's basis in the West stock received is $10,000, its FMV. ◀

THE CONTROL REQUIREMENT

Section 351 requires the transferors, as a group, to be in control of the transferee corporation immediately after the exchange. A transferor can be any type of tax entity (such as an individual, a partnership, another corporation, or a trust). Section 368(c) defines *control* as ownership of at least 80% of the total combined voting power of all classes of stock entitled to vote and at least 80% of the total number of shares of all other classes of stock (e.g., nonvoting preferred stock).[13] The minimum ownership levels for nonvoting stock apply to each class of stock rather than to the nonvoting stock in total.[14]

EXAMPLE C2-13 ▶ Dan exchanges property having a $22,000 adjusted basis and a $30,000 FMV for 60% of newly created Sun Corporation's single class of stock. Ed exchanges $20,000 cash for the remaining 40% of the Sun stock. The transaction qualifies under Sec. 351 because the transferors, Dan and Ed, together own at least 80% of the Sun stock immediately after the exchange. Therefore, Dan defers recognition of his $8,000 ($30,000 − $22,000) gain on the exchange. ◀

Because services do not qualify as property, stock received by a transferor in exchange for services does not count in determining whether the 80% control test has been met. Unless 80% of the corporation's stock is owned by the transferors who exchanged property for stock, Sec. 351 does not apply, and the entire transaction is taxable.

EXAMPLE C2-14 ▶ Dana exchanges property having an $18,000 adjusted basis and a $35,000 FMV for 70 shares of newly created York Corporation stock. Ellen exchanges legal services worth $15,000 for the remaining 30 shares of York stock. Because Ellen does not transfer any property to York Corporation, her stock is not counted for the control requirement. Only Dana transfers property to York and is counted for the control test. However, Dana is not in control of York immediately after the exchange because he owns only 70% of the York stock. Therefore, Sec. 351 does not apply to the transaction. Dana must recognize $17,000 ($35,000 − $18,000) of gain on the exchange. Dana's basis in his York stock is $35,000, its FMV. Ellen must recognize $15,000 of ordinary income, the FMV of the stock received for her services. The tax consequences to Ellen are the same whether Sec. 351 applies to Dana or not. Ellen's basis in her York stock is $15,000. ◀

If the property transferors own at least 80% of the stock after the exchange, Sec. 351 applies to them even though it does not apply to a transferor of services.

---

[11] Sec. 351(d).
[12] Secs. 61 and 83.
[13] In determining whether the 80% requirements are satisfied, the constructive ownership rules of Sec. 318 do not apply (see Rev. Rul. 56-613, 1956-2 C.B. 212). See Chapter C4 for an explanation of Sec. 318.
[14] Rev. Rul. 59-259, 1959-2 C.B. 115.

EXAMPLE C2-15 ▶ Assume the same facts as in Example C2-14, except a third individual, Fred, provides $35,000 of cash for 70 shares of York stock. Now Dana and Fred together own more than 80% of the York stock ($140 \div 170 = 0.82$). Therefore, Sec. 351 applies to the transaction. Neither Dana nor Fred recognizes any gain on the exchange. Ellen still must recognize $15,000 of ordinary income, the FMV of the stock she receives for her services. ◀

TRANSFERORS OF BOTH PROPERTY AND SERVICES. If a person transfers both services *and* property to a corporation in exchange for the corporation's stock, all the stock received by that person, including stock received in exchange for services, is counted in determining whether the property transferors have acquired control.[15]

EXAMPLE C2-16 ▶ Assume the same facts as in Example C2-14 except that, in addition to legal services worth $15,000, Ellen also contributes property worth at least $1,500. In such case, all of Ellen's stock counts in determining whether the 80% minimum stock ownership requirement has been met. Because Dana and Ellen together own 100% of the York stock, the exchange meets the control requirement of Sec. 351. Therefore, Dana recognizes no gain on the exchange. However, Ellen still must recognize $15,000 of ordinary income, the FMV of the stock received as compensation for services. ◀

When a person transfers both property and services in exchange for a corporation's stock, the property must be of more than nominal value for that person's stock to count toward the 80% control requirement.[16] The IRS generally requires that the FMV of the stock received for transferred property be at least 10% of the value of the stock received for services provided. If the value of the stock received for property is less than 10% of the value of the stock received for services provided, the IRS will not issue an advance ruling stating that the transaction meets the requirements of Sec. 351.[17]

EXAMPLE C2-17 ▶ Assume the same facts as in Example C2-16 except that Ellen contributes only $1,000 worth of property in addition to $15,000 of legal services. In such case, the IRS will not issue an advance ruling that the transaction meets the Sec. 351 requirements because the FMV of stock received for the property transferred ($1,000) is less than 10% of the value of the stock received for services provided ($\$1,500 = 0.10 \times \$15,000$). Because the transaction does not meet the IRS requirement for an advance ruling, the IRS probably will challenge the transaction if Ellen treats the transfer as qualifying under Sec. 351 and the IRS audits her tax return for the year of transfer. ◀

TRANSFERS TO EXISTING CORPORATIONS. Section 351 can apply to transfers to an existing corporation as well as transfers to a newly created corporation. The same requirements apply in both cases. Property must be transferred in exchange for stock, and the property transferors must be in control of the corporation immediately after the exchange.

EXAMPLE C2-18 ▶ Jack and Karen own 75 shares and 25 shares of Texas Corporation stock, respectively. Jack transfers property with a $15,000 adjusted basis and a $25,000 FMV to Texas Corporation in exchange for an additional 25 shares of Texas stock. Section 351 applies because, after the transaction, Jack owns 80% ($100 \div 125 = 0.80$) of the Texas stock and is in control of Texas Corporation. Therefore, Jack recognizes no gain on the exchange. ◀

If a shareholder transfers property to an existing corporation for additional stock but does not own at least 80% of the stock after the exchange, Sec. 351 does not apply. The 80% control requirement precludes many transfers of property to an existing corporation by a new shareholder from qualifying as tax-free. A transfer to an existing corporation is tax-free for a new shareholder only if an 80% interest in the corporation is acquired, or enough existing shareholders also transfer property to the corporation to permit the 80% requirement to be satisfied by the transferors as a group.

---

[15] Reg. Sec. 1.351-1(a)(2), Ex. (3).
[16] Reg. Sec. 1.351-1(a)(1)(ii).
[17] Rev. Proc. 77-37, 1977-2 C.B. 568, Sec. 3.07.

EXAMPLE C2-19 ▶ Alice owns all 100 shares of Local Corporation's stock, valued at $100,000. Beth owns property that has a $15,000 adjusted basis and a $100,000 FMV. Beth contributes the property to Local Corporation in exchange for 100 shares of newly issued Local stock. Section 351 does not apply because Beth owns only 50% of the Local stock after the exchange and is not in control of Local Corporation. Beth must recognize an $85,000 ($100,000 – $15,000) gain on the exchange. ◀

If an existing shareholder exchanges property for additional stock to help another shareholder qualify under Sec. 351, the stock received must be of more than nominal value.[18] For advance ruling purposes, the IRS requires that the value of the stock received for property transferred be at least 10% of the value of the stock already owned.[19]

EXAMPLE C2-20 ▶ Assume the same facts as in Example C2-19 except that Alice transfers additional property worth $10,000 for an additional ten shares of Local stock. Now Alice and Beth are both considered to be transferors, and Sec. 351 does apply. Neither Alice nor Beth recognizes any gain on the exchange. If Alice receives fewer than ten shares, the IRS will not issue an advance ruling that Sec. 351 applies to the exchange. ◀

STOP & THINK *Question:* Matthew and Michael each own 50 shares of Main Corporation stock having a $250,000 FMV. Matthew wants to transfer property with a $40,000 adjusted basis and a $100,000 FMV to Main Corporation for an additional 20 shares of Main stock. Can Matthew avoid recognizing $60,000 ($100,000 – $40,000) of gain on the transfer?

Solution: If Matthew simply exchanges the property for additional stock, he will have to recognize the gain. Section 351 will not apply because Matthew owns only 70 out of 120 outstanding shares (or 58.33%) of the Main stock immediately after the exchange.

Matthew can avoid recognizing gain in two ways:

1. Matthew can transfer sufficient property to Main Corporation to receive 150 additional shares (i.e., $750,000 worth of property) so that, after the exchange, he owns 80% (200 out of 250 shares) of the Main stock.
2. Alternatively, Matthew can avoid recognizing gain if Michael contributes sufficient property to be counted in the control group since, together, the two shareholders will own 100% of the Main stock. To count, Michael must contribute cash or other property worth at least $25,000, 10% of the $250,000 value of the Main stock that Michael already owns.

DISPROPORTIONATE EXCHANGES OF PROPERTY AND STOCK. Section 351 does not require that the value of the stock received by the transferors be proportional to the value of the property transferred. However, if the value of the stock received is *not* proportional to the value of the property transferred, the exchange must be treated in accordance with its true nature, that is, a proportional exchange followed by a gift, payment of compensation, or payment of a liability owed by one shareholder to another.[20] If the true nature of the transaction is a gift from one transferor to another transferor, for example, the donor is treated as though he or she received stock equal in value to the property contributed to the corporation and then gave some of the stock to the donee.

EXAMPLE C2-21 ▶ Don and his son John transfer property worth $75,000 (adjusted basis to Don of $42,000) and $25,000 (adjusted basis to John of $20,000), respectively, to newly formed Star Corporation in exchange for all 100 shares of Star stock. Don and John receive 25 and 75 shares of Star stock, respectively. Because Don and John are in control of Star Corporation immediately after the transaction, Sec. 351 applies, and they recognize no gain or loss on the exchange. However, because the stock was not received by Don and John in proportion to the FMV of their property contributions, it is likely that Don has received 75 shares of Star stock (worth $75,000) and made a gift of 50 shares of Star stock (worth $50,000) to John, thereby leaving Don with $25,000 of Star stock. If a gift in fact has been made, Don may be required to pay gift taxes on the gift to John. Don's basis in the 25 shares of Star stock is $14,000 [(25 ÷ 75) × $42,000 basis in the prop-

[18] Reg. Sec. 1.351-1(a)(1)(ii).

[19] Rev. Proc. 77-37, 1977-2 C.B. 568, Sec. 3.07.

[20] Reg. Sec. 1.351-1(b)(1).

erty transferred]. John's basis in the 75 shares is $48,000 [$20,000 basis in the property transferred by John + ($42,000 − $14,000) basis in the shares received from Don]. ◀

IMMEDIATELY AFTER THE EXCHANGE. Section 351 requires that the transferors be in control of the transferee corporation "immediately after the exchange." This requirement does not mean that all transferors must exchange their property for stock simultaneously. The exchanges must all be agreed to beforehand, and the agreement must be executed in an expeditious and orderly manner.[21]

EXAMPLE C2-22 ▶ Art, Beth, and Carlos agree to form New Corporation. Art and Beth each transfer noncash property worth $25,000 for one-third of the New stock. Carlos contributes $25,000 cash for one-third of the New stock. Art and Carlos exchange their property and cash, respectively, for stock on January 10. Beth exchanges her property for stock on March 3. Because all three of the exchanges are part of the same prearranged transaction, the Sec. 351 nonrecognition rules apply to all three exchanges. ◀

TAX STRATEGY TIP

If one shareholder has a prearranged plan to dispose of his or her stock, and the disposition drops the ownership of the transferor shareholders below the required 80% control, such disposition can disqualify the Sec. 351 transaction for all the shareholders. As a possible protection, all shareholders could provide a written representation that they do not currently have a plan to dispose of their stock.

Section 351 does not require the transferors to retain control of the transferee corporation for any specific length of time after the exchange takes place. Control is only required "immediately after the exchange." However, the transferors must not have a prearranged plan to dispose of their stock outside the group. If they have such an arrangement, they are not considered to be in control immediately after the exchange.[22]

EXAMPLE C2-23 ▶ Amir, Bill, and Carl form White Corporation. Each contributes appreciated property worth $25,000 for one-third of the White stock. Before the exchange, Amir arranges to sell his stock to Dana as soon as he receives it. This prearranged plan means that Amir, Bill, and Carl do *not* have control immediately after the exchange. Therefore, Sec. 351 does not apply to the transaction. ◀

THE STOCK REQUIREMENT

Under Sec. 351, transferors who exchange property solely for transferee corporation stock recognize no gain or loss. Stock for this purpose includes voting or nonvoting stock. However, nonqualified preferred stock is treated as boot.[23] Preferred stock means stock that is limited and preferred as to dividends and does not participate in corporate growth to any significant extent. Such preferred stock is nonqualified if:

- The shareholder can require the corporation to redeem the stock,
- The corporation is either required to redeem the stock or is likely to exercise a right to redeem the stock, or
- The dividend rate on the stock varies with interest rates, commodity prices, or other similar indices.

In addition, stock rights or stock warrants are not considered stock for purposes of Sec. 351.[24]

Topic Review C2-1 summarizes the major requirements to achieve a tax-free transfer under Sec. 351.

EFFECT OF SEC. 351 ON THE TRANSFERORS

If all Sec. 351 requirements are met, the transferors recognize no gain or loss on the exchange of their property for stock in the transferee corporation. The receipt of property other than stock does not completely disqualify the transaction from qualifying under Sec. 351. However, the receipt of such property may cause the transferors to recognize part or all of their realized gain under Sec. 351(b).

---

[21] Reg. Sec. 1.351-1(a)(1).

[22] Rev. Rul. 79-70, 1979-1 C.B. 144.

[23] Sec. 351(g). The nonqualified preferred stock rules apply to corporate formation transactions occurring after June 8, 1997.

[24] Reg. Sec. 1.351-1(a)(1)(ii).

Topic Review C2-1

Major Requirements of Sec. 351

1. Nonrecognition of gain or loss applies only to transfers of property in exchange for a corporation's stock. It does not apply to an exchange of services for stock.
2. The property transferors must be in control of the transferee corporation immediately after the exchange. Control means ownership of at least 80% of the voting power and 80% of the total number of shares of all other classes of stock. Stock disposed of after the exchange pursuant to a prearranged plan does not count toward control.
3. Nonrecognition applies only to an exchange of property for stock. If the transferor receives property other than stock, it is considered boot. The transferor recognizes gain to the extent of the lesser of the FMV of any boot received or the realized gain.

RECEIPT OF BOOT. If a transferor receives any money or property other than stock of the transferee corporation, the additional property is considered **boot.** Boot may include cash, notes, securities, or stock in another corporation. Upon receipt of boot, the transferor recognizes gain to the extent of the lesser of the transferor's realized gain or the FMV of the boot property received.[25] However, a transferor never recognizes a loss in an exchange qualifying under Sec. 351 whether boot is received or not.

The character of the boot gain recognized depends on the type of property transferred. For example, if the shareholder transfers a capital asset such as stock of another corporation, the recognized gain is a capital gain. If the shareholder transfers Sec. 1231 property, such as equipment or a building, the recognized gain is Sec. 1231 gain, except for any ordinary income recaptured under Sec. 1245 or 1250.[26] If the shareholder transfers inventory, the recognized gain is ordinary income. Note that depreciation recapture is *not* required unless the transferor receives boot and recognizes a gain on the depreciated property transferred.[27]

EXAMPLE C2-24 ▶ Pam, Rob, and Sam form East Corporation by transferring the following property.

		Property Transferred		
Transferor	*Asset*	*Transferor's Adj. Basis*	*FMV*	*Consideration Received*
Pam	Machinery	$10,000	$12,500	25 shares East stock
Rob	Land	18,000	25,000	40 shares East stock and $5,000 East note
Sam	Cash	17,500	17,500	35 shares East stock

The machinery and land are Sec. 1231 property and a capital asset, respectively. The transaction meets the requirements of Sec. 351 except that, in addition to East stock, Rob receives boot of $5,000 (the FMV of the note). Rob realizes a $7,000 ($25,000 − $18,000) gain on the exchange. Rob must recognize $5,000 of gain—the lesser of the $7,000 realized gain or the $5,000 boot received. The gain is a capital gain because the property transferred was a capital asset in Rob's hands. Pam realizes a $2,500 gain on her exchange of machinery for East stock. However, even though Pam might be required to recapture depreciation taken on the machinery as ordinary income if the machinery were sold or exchanged, Pam recognizes no gain on the exchange because Sec. 351 applies to the exchange and Pam did not receive any boot. Sam neither realizes nor recognizes any gain on his cash purchase of the East stock. ◀

ADDITIONAL COMMENT

If multiple assets were aggregated into one computation, any built-in losses would be netted against the gains. Such a result is inappropriate because losses cannot be recognized in a Sec. 351 transaction.

COMPUTING GAIN WHEN SEVERAL ASSETS ARE TRANSFERRED. If a shareholder transfers more than one asset, Rev. Rul. 68-55 adopts a "separate properties approach" for computing gain or loss.[28] The gain or loss realized and recognized is computed separately for each property transferred. The transferor is assumed to have received a proportionate share of the stock, securities, and boot for each property transferred based on the assets' relative FMVs.

---

[25] Sec. 351(b).

[26] Section 1239 also may require some gain to be characterized as ordinary income.

[27] Secs. 1245(b)(3) and 1250(c)(3).

[28] 1968-1 C.B. 140.

EXAMPLE C2-25 ▶ Joan transfers two properties to newly created North Corporation in a transaction qualifying under Sec. 351. The total FMV of the assets transferred is $100,000. The consideration received by Joan consists of $90,000 of North stock and $10,000 of North notes. The following summary shows how Joan determines her realized and recognized gain using the procedure outlined in Rev. Rul. 68-55.

	Asset 1	*Asset 2*	*Total*
Asset's FMV	$40,000	$60,000	$100,000
Percent of total FMV	40%	60%	100%
Consideration received in exchange for asset:			
Stock (Stock × percent of total FMV)	$36,000	$54,000	$ 90,000
Notes (Notes × percent of total FMV)	4,000	6,000	10,000
Total proceeds	$40,000	$60,000	$100,000
Minus: Adjusted basis	(65,000)	(25,000)	(90,000)
Realized gain (loss)	($25,000)	$35,000	$10,000
Boot received	$ 4,000	$ 6,000	$ 10,000
Recognized gain (loss)	None	$ 6,000	$ 6,000

Under the separate properties approach, the loss realized on the transfer of asset 1 does not offset the gain realized on the transfer of asset 2. Therefore, Joan recognizes only $6,000 of the total $10,000 realized gain, even though she receives $10,000 of boot. It may be advisable to sell asset 1 to North Corporation to recognize the loss. See, however, the possible loss limitation under Sec. 267 if Joan is a controlling shareholder (page C2-33). ◀

COMPUTING A SHAREHOLDER'S BASIS.

Boot Property. A transferor's basis for any boot property received is the property's FMV.[29]

Stock. A shareholder's adjusted basis for stock received in an exchange qualifying under Sec. 351 is computed as follows:[30]

Adjusted basis of property transferred to the corporation
Plus: Any gain recognized by the transferor
Minus: FMV of boot received from the corporation
Money received from the corporation
Amount of any liabilities assumed by the corporation

Adjusted basis of stock received

ADDITIONAL COMMENT

Because Sec. 351 is a deferral provision, any unrecognized gain must be reflected in the basis of the stock received by the transferor shareholder. This is accomplished by substituting the transferor's basis in the property given up (plus certain adjustments) for the basis of the stock received.

EXAMPLE C2-26 ▶ Bob transfers Sec. 1231 property acquired two years earlier having a $50,000 basis and an $80,000 FMV to South Corporation. Bob receives all 100 shares of South stock, having a $70,000 FMV, and a $10,000 90-day South note (boot property). Bob realizes a $30,000 gain on the exchange, computed as follows:

FMV of stock received	$70,000
Plus: FMV of 90-day note	10,000
Amount realized	$80,000
Minus: Adjusted basis of property transferred	(50,000)
Realized gain	$30,000

Bob's recognized gain is the lesser of the $30,000 realized gain or the $10,000 FMV of the boot property, resulting in $10,000 of Sec. 1231 gain. The Sec. 351 rules thus require Bob to defer $20,000 ($30,000 − $10,000) of gain. Bob's basis for the South stock is $50,000, computed as follows:

[29] Sec. 358(a)(2).

[30] Sec. 358(a)(1).

SELF-STUDY QUESTION

What is an alternative method for determining the basis of the assets received by the transferor shareholder? How is this method applied to Bob in Example C2-26?

ANSWER

The basis of all boot property is its FMV, and the basis of stock received is the stock's FMV minus any deferred gain or plus any deferred loss. Bob's stock basis under the alternative method is $50,000 ($70,000 FMV of stock – $20,000 deferred gain).

Adjusted basis of property transferred	$50,000
Plus: Gain recognized by Bob	10,000
Minus: FMV of boot received	(10,000)
Adjusted basis of stock to Bob	$50,000 ◀

If a transferor receives more than one class of stock, his or her basis for the stocks received must be allocated among the classes of stock received in accordance with their relative FMVs.[31]

EXAMPLE C2-27 ▶ Assume the same facts as in Example C2-26 except that Bob receives 100 shares of South common stock with a $45,000 FMV, 50 shares of South qualified preferred stock with a $25,000 FMV, and a 90-day South note with a $10,000 FMV. The recognized gain remains $10,000. The total adjusted basis of the stock is $50,000 ($50,000 basis of property transferred + $10,000 gain recognized – $10,000 FMV of boot received). This basis must be allocated between the common and preferred stock received in accordance with their relative FMVs, as follows:

$$\text{Basis of common stock} = \frac{\$45{,}000}{\$45{,}000 + \$25{,}000} \times \$50{,}000 = \$32{,}143$$

$$\text{Basis of preferred stock} = \frac{\$25{,}000}{\$45{,}000 + \$25{,}000} \times \$50{,}000 = \$17{,}857$$

Bob's basis for the note is $10,000, its FMV. ◀

TRANSFEROR'S HOLDING PERIOD. The transferor's holding period for any stock received in exchange for a capital asset or Sec. 1231 property includes the holding period of the property transferred.[32] If any other kind of property (e.g., inventory) is exchanged for the stock, the transferor's holding period for the stock received begins on the day after the exchange. The holding period for boot property begins on the day after the exchange.

EXAMPLE C2-28 ▶ Assume the same facts as in Example C2-26. Bob's holding period for the stock includes the time period he held the Sec. 1231 property. His holding period for the note starts on the day after the exchange. ◀

STOP & THINK *Question:* The holding period for stock received in exchange for a capital asset or Sec. 1231 asset includes the holding period of the transferred asset. The holding period for inventory or other assets begins on the day after the exchange. Why the difference?

Solution: Stock received in a Sec. 351 transaction generally is a capital asset. The holding period for the stock includes the transferred property's holding period if a sale of the asset would have meant recognizing a capital gain or loss. The holding period for the stock does not include the holding period for the asset if a sale of the transferred assets would have meant recognizing ordinary gain or loss (e.g., a sale of inventory). In the latter case, a sale of the stock within one year of the transfer date means recognizing a short-term capital gain or loss. For an individual shareholder, this outcome is not the same as recognizing an ordinary gain or loss from the inventory sale. Note that the gain is not eligible for the 20% tax rate for long-term capital gains until the stock has been held for at least one year.

Topic Review C2-2 summarizes the tax consequences of a Sec. 351 transaction to the transferor and the transferee corporation.

[31] Sec. 358(b)(1) and Reg. Sec. 1.358-2(b)(2).

[32] Sec. 1223(1). Revenue Ruling 85-164 (1985-2 C.B. 117) holds that a single share of stock may have two holding periods: a carryover holding period for the portion of such share received in exchange for a capital asset or a Sec. 1231 property and a holding period that begins on the day after the exchange for the portion of such share received for inventory or other property. The split holding period is relevant only if the transferor sells the stock received within one year of the transfer date.

Topic Review C2-2

Tax Consequences of a Sec. 351 Transaction

To Shareholders:

General Rules:
1. Transferors recognize no gain or loss when they exchange property for stock. Exception: A transferor recognizes gain equal to the lesser of the realized gain or the sum of any money received plus the FMV of any other boot property received. The character of the gain recognized depends on the type of property given up.
2. The basis of the stock received equals the adjusted basis of the property transferred plus the gain recognized minus the FMV of the boot property received minus any money received (including liabilities assumed or acquired by the transferee corporation).
3. The holding period of stock received for capital assets or Sec. 1231 property includes the holding period for the transferred property. The holding period of stock received for other property begins on the day after the exchange.

To Transferee Corporation:

General Rules:
1. A corporation recognizes no gain or loss when it exchanges its own stock for property or services.
2. The corporation's basis in any property received in a Sec. 351 exchange is the transferor's basis plus any gain recognized by the transferor.
3. The corporation's holding period for property received in a Sec. 351 exchange includes the transferor's holding period.

ADDITIONAL COMMENT

The nonrecognition rule for corporations that issue stock for property applies whether or not the transaction qualifies the transferor shareholder for Sec. 351 treatment.

TAX CONSEQUENCES TO TRANSFEREE CORPORATION

A corporation that issues stock or debt for property or services engages in an exchange, thereby requiring rules for determining the tax consequences of that exchange.

GAIN OR LOSS RECOGNIZED BY THE TRANSFEREE CORPORATION. Corporations recognize no gain or loss when they issue their own stock for property or services.[33] This rule applies whether the exchange is subject to Sec. 351 or not. It is irrelevant whether the corporation issues new stock or treasury stock.

EXAMPLE C2-29 ▶ West Corporation acquires 100 shares of treasury stock for $10,000. The next year, West reissues the 100 shares for land having a $15,000 FMV. West realizes a $5,000 ($15,000 − $10,000) gain on the exchange. The corporation, however, recognizes none of this gain. ◀

Corporations also recognize no gain or loss when they exchange their own debt instruments for property or services.

A corporation, however, must recognize gain (but not loss) if it transfers appreciated property to a transferor as part of a Sec. 351 exchange. The amount and character of the gain recognized are determined as though the property had been sold by the corporation immediately before the transfer.

EXAMPLE C2-30 ▶ Alice, who owns 100% of Ace Corporation, transfers to Ace land having a $100,000 FMV and a $60,000 adjusted basis. In return, Alice receives 75 additional shares of Ace common stock having a $75,000 FMV and Zero Corporation common stock having a $25,000 FMV. Ace's basis in the Zero stock, a capital asset, is $10,000. Alice realizes a $40,000 gain [($75,000 + $25,000) − $60,000] on the land transfer, of which $25,000 must be recognized. In addition, Ace Corporation recognizes a $15,000 capital gain ($25,000 − $10,000) when transferring the Zero stock to Alice. ◀

[33] Sec. 1032.

ADDITIONAL COMMENT

If a shareholder transfers built-in gain property in a Sec. 351 transaction, the built-in gain actually is duplicated. This duplication occurs because the transferee corporation assumes the potential gain through its carryover basis in the assets it receives, and the transferor shareholder assumes the potential gain through its substituted basis in the transferee corporation stock. A similar duplication occurs for built-in loss property. This result reflects the double taxation characteristic of C corporations.

TRANSFEREE CORPORATION'S BASIS FOR PROPERTY RECEIVED. A corporation that acquires property by issuing its stock in a transaction that is taxable to the transferor uses the property's acquisition cost (i.e., its FMV) as its basis for the property. However, if the exchange qualifies for nonrecognition treatment under Sec. 351 and is wholly or partially tax-free to the transferor, the corporation's basis for the property is computed as follows:[34]

Transferor's adjusted basis for property transferred to the corporation
Plus: Gain recognized by transferor

Transferee corporation's basis for property

The transferee corporation's holding period for property acquired in a transaction satisfying the Sec. 351 requirements includes the period of time the property was held by the transferor.[35] This general rule applies to all properties without regard to their character in the transferor's hands or the amount of gain recognized by the transferor.

EXAMPLE C2-31 ▶ Top Corporation issues 100 shares of its stock for land having a $15,000 FMV. Tina, who transferred the land, had $12,000 basis in the property. If the exchange satisfies the Sec. 351 requirements, Tina recognizes no gain on the exchange. Top Corporation's basis in the land is $12,000, the same basis that Tina had in the land. Top Corporation's holding period includes the period of time the land was held by Tina. However, if the exchange does *not* satisfy the Sec. 351 requirements, Tina must recognize $3,000 of gain. Top Corporation's basis in the land is its $15,000 acquisition cost. Its holding period for the land begins on the day after the acquisition date. ◀

ASSUMPTION OF THE TRANSFEROR'S LIABILITIES

When a shareholder transfers property to a controlled corporation, the corporation often assumes the transferor's liabilities as well. The question arises as to whether the transferee corporation's assumption of liabilities is equivalent to a cash payment to the transferor and, therefore, is boot. In many other kinds of transactions, the transferee's assumption of a transferor's liability is treated as a payment of cash to the transferor. For example, in a like-kind exchange, if a transferee assumes a transferor's liability, the transferor is treated as though he or she received a cash payment equal to the amount of the liability assumed. However, if a transaction satisfies the Sec. 351 requirements, the special rules of Sec. 357 apply, and the liability transfer is not treated as a cash payment.

GENERAL RULE—SEC. 357(a). The transferee corporation's assumption of liabilities in a property transfer qualifying under Sec. 351 is *not* considered to result in the receipt of money by the transferor. Therefore, the transferee corporation's assumption of liabilities does not cause the transferor to recognize part or all of his or her realized gain. The liabilities, however, are treated as money received for purposes of the transferor's stock basis calculation.[36]

EXAMPLE C2-32 ▶ Roy and Eduardo form Palm Corporation by transferring the following assets and liabilities:

Transferor	*Asset/ Liability*	*Transferor's Adj. Basis*	*FMV*	*Consideration Received*
Roy	Machinery	$15,000	$32,000	50 shares Palm stock
	Mortgage	8,000		Assumed by Palm
Eduardo	Cash	24,000	24,000	50 shares Palm stock

The transaction meets the requirements of Sec. 351. Roy's recognized gain is determined as follows:

[34] Sec. 362.
[35] Sec. 1223(2).
[36] Sec. 358(d)(1).

FMV of stock received	$24,000
Plus: Release from mortgage assumed by Palm	8,000
Amount realized	$32,000
Minus: Basis of machinery	(15,000)
Realized gain	$17,000
Boot received	$ -0-
Recognized gain	$ -0-

Roy recognizes none of this gain because Sec. 351 applies, and the mortgage assumption is not considered to be money paid to Roy. Eduardo recognizes no gain because he transferred only cash. Roy's stock basis is $7,000 ($15,000 basis of property transferred − $8,000 liability assumed by the corporation). Eduardo's stock basis is $24,000. ◀

ADDITIONAL COMMENT

If any of the assumed liabilities are created for tax avoidance purposes, *all* the assumed liabilities are tainted.

The general rule of Sec. 357(a) has two exceptions, however. These exceptions, discussed below, are (1) transfers made for the purpose of tax avoidance or that have no bona fide business purpose and (2) transfers where the liabilities assumed by the corporation exceed the total basis of property transferred by the transferor.

ETHICAL POINT

Information about any transferor liabilities assumed by the transferee corporation must be reported with the transferee and transferor's tax returns for the year of transfer (see page C2-35). Where a client asks a tax practitioner to ignore the fact that tax avoidance is the primary purpose for transferring a liability to a corporation, the tax practitioner must examine the ethical considerations of continuing to prepare returns and provide tax advice for the client.

TAX AVOIDANCE OR NO BONA FIDE BUSINESS PURPOSE—SEC. 357(b). All liabilities assumed by a controlled corporation *are* considered money received by the transferor (and, therefore, are considered boot) if the principal purpose of the transfer of any portion of such liabilities is to avoid tax or if the liability transfer has no bona fide business purpose.

Liabilities whose transfer might be considered to have tax avoidance as the principal purpose are those the transferor incurred shortly before transferring the property and liability to the corporation. Perhaps the most important factor in determining whether a tax avoidance purpose exists is the length of time between the incurrence of the liability and the transfer of the liability to the corporation.

The assumption of liabilities normally is considered to have a business purpose if the transferor incurred the liabilities in the normal course of business or in the course of acquiring business property. Examples of liabilities that have no business purpose and whose transfer would cause *all* liabilities transferred to be considered boot are personal obligations of the transferor, including a home mortgage or any other loans of a personal nature.

EXAMPLE C2-33 ▶ David owns land having a $100,000 FMV and a $60,000 adjusted basis. The land is not encumbered by any liabilities. To obtain cash for his personal use, David transfers the land to his wholly owned corporation in exchange for additional stock and $25,000 cash. Because the cash received is considered boot, David must recognize $25,000 of gain. Assume instead that David mortgages the land for $25,000 to obtain the needed cash. If shortly after obtaining the mortgage, David transfers the land and the mortgage to his corporation for additional stock, it appears that the transfer of the mortgage has no business purpose. Therefore, the $25,000 mortgage assumed by the corporation would be considered boot. David's recognized gain is the lesser of the boot received ($25,000) or his realized gain ($40,000), or $25,000. The special liability rule prevents David from obtaining cash with no boot recognition. ◀

LIABILITIES IN EXCESS OF BASIS—SEC. 357(c). Under Sec. 357(c), if the total amount of liabilities transferred to a controlled corporation by a transferor exceeds the total adjusted basis of all property transferred by such transferor, the excess liability is a gain taxable to the transferor. This rule applies regardless of whether the transferor realizes any gain or loss. The rule recognizes the fact that the transferor has received a benefit (in the form of a release from liabilities) that exceeds his or her original investment in the transferred property. Therefore, the excess amount is taxable. The character of the recognized gain depends on the type of property transferred to the corporation. The transferor's basis in any stock received is zero.

EXAMPLE C2-34 ▶ Judy transfers land, a capital asset, having a $70,000 adjusted basis and a $125,000 FMV and $10,000 cash to Duke Corporation in exchange for all its stock. Duke Corporation assumes the $100,000 mortgage on the land. The mortgage assumption has no tax-avoidance purpose and has the requisite business purpose. Although Judy does not receive any boot, Judy must recognize a $20,000 ($100,000 − $80,000) capital gain, the amount by which the liabilities assumed by Duke Corporation exceed the basis of the land and the cash transferred by Judy. Judy's basis for the Duke stock is zero, computed as follows:

Judy's basis in the land transferred		$ 70,000
Plus:	Cash transferred	10,000
	Gain recognized	20,000
Minus:	Boot received (i.e., liabilities assumed by Duke)	(100,000)
Judy's basis in the Duke stock		$ -0-

Note that, without the Sec. 357(c) requirement to recognize a $20,000 gain, Judy's basis in the Duke stock would be a negative $20,000 ($80,000 − $100,000). ◀

STOP & THINK *Question:* What are the fundamental differences between the liability exceptions of Sec. 357(b) and Sec. 357(c)?

Solution: Section 357(b) treats all "tainted" liabilities as boot so that gain recognition is the lesser of gain realized or the amount of boot. Excess liabilities under Sec. 357(c) are not treated as boot; they require gain recognition whether or not the transferor realizes any gain. Section 357(b) tends to be punitive in that the tax avoidance liabilities cause all the "offending" shareholder's transferred liabilities to be treated as boot even if some liabilities do not have a tax avoidance purpose. Section 357(c) is not intended to be punitive. Rather, it recognizes that the shareholder has received an economic benefit to the extent of excess liabilities, and it prevents a negative stock basis. In short, Section 357(b) deters or punishes tax avoidance behavior while Sec. 357(c) taxes an economic gain.

KEY POINT

Because of the "liabilities in excess of basis" exception, many cash basis transferor shareholders might inadvertently create recognized gain in a Sec. 351 transaction. However, a special exception exists that protects cash basis taxpayers. This exception provides that liabilities that would give rise to a deduction when paid are not treated as liabilities for purposes of Sec. 357(c).

LIABILITIES OF A TAXPAYER USING THE CASH METHOD OF ACCOUNTING—SEC. 357(c)(3). Special problems arise when a taxpayer using the cash or hybrid method of accounting transfers property and liabilities of an ongoing business to a corporation in a tax-free exchange under Sec. 351.[37] Quite often, the main assets transferred are accounts receivable having a zero basis. Liabilities usually are transferred as well. Consequently, the amount of liabilities transferred often exceeds the total basis (but not the FMV) of the property transferred.

Under Sec. 357(c), gain equal to the amount by which the liabilities assumed exceed the total basis of the property transferred would have to be recognized. However, a special exception to Sec. 357(c) provides that the term *liabilities* does *not* include any amount that (1) would give rise to a deduction when paid or (2) any amount payable under Sec. 736(a) (i.e., amounts payable to a retiring partner or to liquidate a deceased partner's interest). These amounts also are not considered liabilities for purposes of applying the Sec. 358 basis rules to determine the shareholder's basis for any stock items.[38] Therefore, they do not reduce the shareholder's basis in his or her stock.

EXAMPLE C2-35 ▶ Tracy operates an accounting practice as a sole proprietorship. She transfers the assets of her cash basis accounting practice to Prime Corporation in exchange for all the Prime stock. The items transferred are

[37] Sec. 357(c)(3).

[38] Sec. 358(d)(2).

Assets and Liabilities	*Adjusted Basis*	*FMV*
Cash	$ 5,000	$ 5,000
Furniture	5,000	8,000
Accounts receivable	–0–	50,000
Total	$10,000	$63,000
Accounts payable (expenses)	$ –0–	$25,000
Note payable (on office furniture)	2,000	2,000
Owner's equity	8,000	36,000
Total	$10,000	$63,000

If the accounts payable were considered liabilities, the $27,000 of liabilities transferred (i.e., the $25,000 of accounts payable and the $2,000 note payable) would exceed the $10,000 basis of the property transferred. However, because payment of the $25,000 of accounts payable gives rise to a deduction, they are not considered liabilities for purposes of applying Sec. 357(c). The $2,000 note payable *is* considered a liability because paying it would *not* give rise to a deduction. Thus, for purposes of applying Sec. 357(c), the total liabilities transferred to Prime Corporation amount to $2,000. Because that amount does not exceed the $10,000 total basis of the property transferred, Tracy recognizes no gain. Moreover, the accounts payable are not considered liabilities for purposes of computing Tracy's basis for the Prime stock. Therefore, Tracy's basis for her stock is $8,000 ($10,000 – $2,000). ◀

Topic Review C2-3 summarizes the liability assumption and acquisition rules of Sec. 357.

OTHER CONSIDERATIONS IN A SEC. 351 EXCHANGE

RECAPTURE OF DEPRECIATION. If a Sec. 351 exchange is completely nontaxable (i.e., the transferor receives no boot), no depreciation recapture is required.[39] Instead, the entire amount of the transferor's recapture potential transfers to the transferee corporation. Where the transferor recognizes part of the depreciation recapture as ordinary income (e.g., under Sec. 351(b)), the remaining recapture potential transfers to the transferee corporation. If the transferee corporation subsequently disposes of the property, it is subject to the depreciation recapture rules on all depreciation it has claimed plus the recapture potential transferred by the transferor.

Topic Review C2-3

Liability Assumption and Acquisition Rules of Sec. 357

1. *General Rule (Sec. 357(a)):* A transferee corporation's assumption of liabilities in a Sec. 351 exchange does not result in the receipt of money/boot by the shareholder for gain recognition purposes. The liabilities, however, are treated as money for purposes of determining the basis of the stock received.
2. *Exception 1 (Sec. 357(b)):* All liabilities assumed by a transferee corporation *are* considered money/boot received by the transferor if the principal purpose of the transfer of any of the liabilities is tax avoidance or if no bona fide business purpose exists for the transfer.
3. *Exception 2 (Sec. 357(c)):* If the total amount of liabilities assumed by a transferee corporation exceeds the total basis of property transferred, the transferor recognizes the excess liability amount as gain.
4. *Special Rule (Sec. 357(c)(3)):* For purposes of Exception 2, the term *liabilities* for a transferor using a cash or hybrid method of accounting does not include any amount that (a) would give rise to a deduction when paid or (b) is payable to a retiring partner or to liquidate a deceased partner's interest.

[39] Secs. 1245(b)(3) and 1250(d)(3).

EXAMPLE C2-36 ▶ Azeem transfers machinery having an $18,000 adjusted basis and a $35,000 FMV for all 100 shares of Wheel Corporation's stock. Before the transfer, Azeem used the machinery in his business. He originally paid $25,000 for the machinery and claimed $7,000 of depreciation before transferring the machinery. Azeem recaptures no depreciation on the transfer. Instead, the $7,000 recapture potential transfers to Wheel Corporation. After claiming an additional $2,000 of depreciation on the machinery, Wheel's basis in the machinery is $16,000. If Wheel Corporation now sells the machinery for $33,000, it must recognize a $17,000 ($33,000 – $16,000) gain on the sale. Of this gain, $9,000 is ordinary income recaptured under Sec. 1245. The remaining $8,000 is Sec. 1231 gain. ◀

COMPUTING DEPRECIATION. When a shareholder transfers depreciable property to a corporation in a nontaxable Sec. 351 exchange, and the shareholder has been depreciating the property, the corporation must continue to use the same depreciation method and recovery period with respect to the transferor's basis in the property.[40] For the year of the transfer, the depreciation must be allocated between the transferor and the transferee corporation according to the number of months the property was held by each. The transferee corporation is assumed to have held the property for the entire month in which the property was transferred.[41]

EXAMPLE C2-37 ▶ On June 10, 2001, Carla purchased a computer (five-year property for MACRS purposes) for $6,000, which she used in her sole proprietorship. She claimed $1,200 (0.20 × $6,000) of depreciation for 2001. On February 10, 2002, she transfers the computer and other assets of her sole proprietorship to King Corporation in exchange for King stock in a transfer qualifying under Sec. 351. Thus, she recognizes no gain or loss. King Corporation must use the same MACRS recovery period and method that Carla used. Depreciation for 2002 is $1,920 (0.32 × $6,000). That amount must be allocated between Carla and King Corporation. The computer is considered to have been held by Carla for one month and by King Corporation for 11 months (including the month of transfer). The 2002 depreciation claimed by Carla and King Corporation is calculated as follows:

Carla	$6,000 × 0.32 × 1/12 = $ 160
King Corporation	$6,000 × 0.32 × 11/12 = $1,760

King Corporation's basis in the computer is calculated as follows:

Original cost of computer	$6,000
Minus: 2001 depreciation taken by Carla	(1,200)
2002 depreciation taken by Carla	(160)
Adjusted basis on transfer date	$4,640

◀

If the transferee corporation's basis for the depreciable property exceeds the transferor's basis, the corporation treats the excess amount as a newly purchased MACRS property and uses the recovery period and method applicable to the type of property transferred.[42]

EXAMPLE C2-38 ▶ Assume the same facts as in Example C2-37 except that, in addition to King stock, Carla receives a King note and must recognize $1,000 of gain on the transfer of the computer. King Corporation's basis in the computer is calculated as follows:

Original cost	$6,000
Depreciation claimed by Carla	(1,360)
Adjusted basis on transfer date	$4,640
Plus: Gain recognized by Carla on transfer	1,000
Basis to King Corporation on transfer date	$5,640

The additional $1,000 of basis is depreciated as though it is a separate, newly purchased MACRS property. Thus, King claims depreciation of $200 (0.20 × $1,000) on this portion of the basis in addition to the $1,760 of depreciation on the $4,640 of carryover basis. ◀

40 Sec. 168(i)(7).
41 Prop. Reg. Secs. 1.168-5(b)(2)(i)(B) and 1.168-5(b)(4)(i).
42 Prop. Reg. Sec. 1.168-5(b)(7).

ASSIGNMENT OF INCOME DOCTRINE. The **assignment of income doctrine** is a judicial requirement that income be taxed to the person who earns it.[43] Income may not be assigned to another taxpayer. The question arises as to whether the assignment of income doctrine applies when a taxpayer using the cash method of accounting transfers uncollected accounts receivable to a corporation in a Sec. 351 exchange. The question is: who must recognize the income when it is collected—the taxpayer who transferred the receivable to the corporation before recognizing the earned income or the corporation that now owns and collects the receivable? The IRS has ruled that the doctrine does *not* apply in a Sec. 351 exchange if the transferor transfers substantially all the business assets and liabilities, and a business purpose exists for the transfer. Instead, the accounts receivable take a zero basis in the corporation's hands and are included in the corporation's income when collected.[44]

EXAMPLE C2-39 ▶ For good business reasons, Ruth, a lawyer who uses the cash method of accounting, transfers all the assets and liabilities of her legal practice to Legal Services Corporation in exchange for all of Legal Services' stock. The assets include $30,000 of accounts receivable related to earnings that Ruth has not included in her gross income. The assignment of income doctrine does not apply to the accounts receivable. Legal Services Corporation's basis in the receivables is zero, and the corporation includes the receivables in income as they are collected. ◀

Many cases have disputed whether a transferee corporation could deduct the accounts payable transferred to it in a nontaxable transfer.[45] Normally, expenses are deductible only by the party that incurred those liabilities in the course of its trade or business. However, the IRS has ruled that the transferee corporation may deduct the payments it makes to satisfy the transferred accounts payable even though they arose in the transferor's business.[46]

CHOICE OF CAPITAL STRUCTURE

OBJECTIVE 5

Determine the tax consequences of alternative capital structures

When a corporation is formed, decisions must be made as to the capital structure of the corporation. The corporation may derive its capital from shareholders, nonshareholders, and creditors. In exchange for their capital, shareholders may receive common stock or preferred stock; nonshareholders may receive benefits such as employment for a city's residents or special rates on products produced by the corporation; and creditors may receive long-term or short-term debt obligations. Each of these alternatives has tax consequences and other advantages and disadvantages for the shareholders, the creditors, and the corporation itself.

SELF-STUDY QUESTION

From a tax perspective, why is the distinction between debt and equity important?

ANSWER

Interest paid with respect to a debt instrument is deductible by the payor corporation. Dividends paid with respect to an equity instrument are not deductible by the payor corporation. Thus, the determination of whether an instrument is debt or equity can provide different results to the payor corporation.

CHARACTERIZATION OF OBLIGATIONS AS DEBT OR EQUITY CAPITAL

The tax laws provide a strong incentive for many corporations to use as much debt financing as possible (because of the deduction allowed for annual interest payments). Debt financing often resembles equity obligations (i.e., preferred stock), and the IRS and the courts have refused in some cases to accept the form of the obligation as controlling.[47] In some cases, obligations labeled as debt that possessed more characteristics of equity than debt have been reclassified as common or preferred stock. The courts have relied on no single factor in making this determination.

In 1969, Congress enacted Sec. 385 in an attempt to establish a workable standard for determining whether an obligation is debt or equity capital. Section 385 suggests that the following factors be taken into account in determining whether an amount advanced to a corporation should be characterized as debt or equity capital:

---

[43] See, for example, *Lucas v. Guy C. Earl*, 8 AFTR 10287, 2 USTC ¶496 (USSC, 1930).

[44] Rev. Rul. 80-198, 1980-2 C.B. 113.

[45] See, for example, *Wilford E. Thatcher v. CIR*, 37 AFTR 2d 76-1068, 76-1 USTC ¶9324 (9th Cir., 1976), and *John P. Bongiovanni v. CIR*, 31 AFTR 2d 73-409, 73-1 USTC ¶9133 (2nd Cir., 1972).

[46] Rev. Rul. 80-198, 1980-2 C.B. 113.

[47] See, for example, *Aqualane Shores, Inc. v. CIR*, 4 AFTR 2d 5346, 59-2 USTC ¶9632 (5th Cir., 1959) and *Sun Properties, Inc. v. U.S.*, 47 AFTR 273, 55-1 USTC ¶9261 (5th Cir., 1955).

HISTORICAL NOTE

The Treasury Department at one time issued proposed and final regulations covering Sec. 385. These regulations were the subject of so much criticism that the Treasury Department eventually withdrew them. The 1989 amendment to Sec. 385 makes it clear that Congress wants the Treasury Department to make another attempt at clarifying the debt-equity issue. So far, the Treasury Department has issued no "new" proposed or final regulations.

- Whether there is a written unconditional promise to pay on demand or on a specified date a certain sum of money in return for an adequate consideration in money or money's worth, and to pay a fixed rate of interest
- Whether the debt is subordinate to or preferred over other indebtedness of the corporation
- The ratio of debt to equity of the corporation
- Whether the debt is convertible into the stock of the corporation
- The relationship between holdings of stock in the corporation and holdings of the interest in question[48]

DEBT CAPITAL

Tax laws affect the use of debt capital (1) when the debt is issued; (2) annually as the interest is paid on the obligation; (3) and when the debt is satisfied, retired, or declared worthless. The tax implications for each of these three events are examined next.

ISSUANCE OF DEBT. Under Sec. 351, appreciated assets may be exchanged tax-free for stock provided the transferors have control of the transferee corporation immediately after the exchange. However, if the transferor exchanges assets for corporate debt instruments, whether part of the same transaction or not, the FMV of the debt received is treated as boot. Therefore, the transferor's receipt of debt may result in gain recognition.

WHEN INTEREST IS PAID. Interest paid on an indebtedness is deductible by the corporation in arriving at taxable income.[49] Moreover, a corporation is not subject to the limitations on interest deductions that apply to individual taxpayers (e.g., investment interest or personal interest limitations). Dividends paid on equity capital are not deductible.

If the corporation issues a debt instrument at a discount, Sec. 163(e) requires that the original issue discount be determined and amortized by the holder under the rules of Secs. 1272 through 1275. The debtor corporation amortizes the original issue discount over the life of the obligation and treats the discount as an additional cost of borrowing.[50] If the corporation repurchases its debt obligation for more than the issue price (plus any original issue discount deducted as interest), the corporation deducts the excess of the purchase price over the issue price (adjusted for any amortization of original issue discount) as interest expense.[51]

If the corporation issues the debt instrument at a premium, Sec. 171 permits the holder to elect to amortize the premium over the life of the obligation and treat the premium as a reduction in the interest income earned from the obligation. The debtor corporation must amortize the premium over the life of the obligation and report such amount as additional interest income.[52] Again, if the corporation repurchases the debt obligation at a price greater than the issue price (minus any premium reported as income), the corporation deducts the excess of the purchase price over the issue price (adjusted for any amortization of premium) as interest expense.[53]

WHEN AN INDEBTEDNESS IS SATISFIED. Generally, the repayment of an indebtedness is not considered an exchange transaction. Thus, an obligation repaid by a corporation does not result in a gain or loss being recognized by the creditor. However, Sec. 1271(a) considers amounts received by the holder of a debt instrument (e.g., note, bond, or debenture) at the time of its retirement to be received in exchange for the obligation. Thus, if the obligation is a capital asset in the holder's hands, the holder will recognize a capital gain or loss if the amount received in retirement of the obligation differs from its adjusted basis, unless the difference is due to original issue discount or market discount.

---

[48] See also the *O.H. Kruse Grain & Milling v. CIR* case (5 AFTR 2d 1544, 60-2 USTC ¶9490 (9th Cir., 1960)) which lists additional factors that the courts might consider.

[49] Sec. 163(a).

[50] Sec. 163(e).

[51] Reg. Sec. 1.163-7(c).

[52] Reg. Sec. 1.61-12(c)(2).

[53] Reg. Sec. 1.163-7(c).

EXAMPLE C2-40 ▶ Titan Corporation issues a ten-year obligation at its $1,000 face amount. Rick purchases the obligation for $1,000 on the issue date. Due to a decline in interest rates, Titan Corporation calls the obligation by paying $1,050 to each of the holders of the ten-year obligations. Rick will recognize a $50 capital gain on the repayment of the debt instrument. The premium paid by Titan Corporation is deductible as interest expense. ◀

ADDITIONAL COMMENT

Even though debt often is thought of as a preferred instrument because of the deductibility of the interest paid, the debt must be repaid at its maturity, whereas stock has no specified maturity date. Also, interest usually must be paid at regular intervals, whereas dividends do not have to be declared if sufficient funds are not available.

Table C2-2 presents a comparison of the tax advantages and disadvantages of using debt in the capital structure.

EQUITY CAPITAL

Equity capital issues come in a variety of forms. Some corporations have only a single class of stock, whereas others have a number of outstanding classes of stock. Reasons for the use of multiple classes of stock include

- Permitting the employees of family owned corporations to obtain an equity interest in the business while keeping voting control in the hands of the family members
- Permitting a **closely held corporation** to acquire outside financing from a corporate investor or wealthy individual who acquires a preferred stock interest and to enable the existing shareholders to retain their voting control by owning the common stock.

Because of the wide variety of situations that can occur and the unlimited number of equity forms that can be issued, it is impossible to list all the tax and nontax advantages of each type of equity form. Therefore, Table C2-3 lists some of the major tax advantages and disadvantages of common and preferred stock issues.

SELF-STUDY QUESTION

Does the transferee corporation recognize gain on the receipt of appreciated property from a shareholder?

ANSWER

No. A corporation does not recognize gain when it receives property from its shareholders, regardless of whether or not it exchanges its own stock. However, the transfer must qualify as a Sec. 351 exchange or the transaction will be taxable to the shareholders.

CAPITAL CONTRIBUTIONS BY SHAREHOLDERS

A corporation recognizes no income when it receives money or property as a capital contribution from a shareholder.[54] If the shareholders make voluntary pro rata payments to a corporation but do not receive any additional stock, the payments are regarded as an additional price paid for the stock already owned.[55] The shareholders' bases in their stock are increased by the amount of money contributed, plus the basis of any nonmoney property contributed and plus any gain recognized by the shareholders. The corporation's basis in any property received as a capital contribution from a shareholder equals the shareholder's basis plus any gain recognized by the shareholder.[56] Normally, the shareholders recognize no gain when they contribute property to a controlled corporation as a capital contribution.

▼ **TABLE C2-2**

Tax Advantages and Disadvantages of Using Debt in the Capital Structure

Advantages:

1. A corporation can deduct interest payments made on debt instruments.
2. Shareholders do not have to recognize income when an amount is received in repayment of debt as they would in the case of a stock redemption.

Disadvantages:

1. If a shareholder receives a debt instrument in exchange for property at the time the corporation is formed or later when the shareholder makes a capital contribution, the debt is considered boot and the realized gain must be recognized to the extent of the lesser of the boot received or the realized gain.
2. If debt becomes worthless or is sold at a loss, the loss generally is a nonbusiness bad debt (short-term capital loss) or a capital loss. Section 1244 ordinary loss treatment applies only to stock (see pages C2-31 and C2-32).

[54] Sec. 118(a).
[55] Reg. Sec. 1.118-1.
[56] Sec. 362(a).

▼ TABLE C2-3

Tax Advantages and Disadvantages of Using Stock in the Capital Structure

Advantages:

1. A 70%, 80%, or 100% dividends-received deduction is available for a corporate shareholder receiving dividends. A special deduction is not available for interest income (see Chapter C3).
2. A shareholder can receive common and preferred stock in a tax-free corporate formation qualifying under Sec. 351 or a tax-free reorganization qualifying under Sec. 368 without any need to recognize gain (see Chapters C2 and C7, respectively). Receipt of debt obligations in each of these two types of transactions generally triggers the recognition of gain by the shareholder.
3. Common and preferred stock can be distributed tax-free to the corporation's shareholders as a stock dividend. Some common and preferred stock distributions may be taxable as dividends under Sec. 305(b). Distributions of debt obligations of the distributing corporation are taxable as a dividend (see Chapter C4).
4. Common or preferred stock that the shareholder sells or exchanges or that becomes worthless is eligible for ordinary loss treatment under Sec. 1244 (see pages C2-31 and C2-32). The loss recognized on similar transactions involving debt obligations generally is a capital loss.
5. Section 1202 permits a 50% capital gains exclusion on the sale or exchange of qualified small business (C) corporation stock that has been held for more than five years.

Disadvantages:

1. Dividends are not deductible in determining a corporation's taxable income.
2. Redemption of common or preferred stock generally is taxable to the shareholders as a dividend. Under this general rule, none of the distribution offsets the shareholder's basis for the stock investment. Redemption of common and preferred stock by the issuing corporation is eligible for exchange treatment only in specific situations contained in Secs. 302 and 303 (see Chapter C4).
3. Preferred stock received by a shareholder as a tax-free stock dividend can be labeled Sec. 306 stock. Sale, exchange, or redemption of such stock can result in the recognition of ordinary income or dividend income instead of capital gains (see Chapter C4).

TYPICAL MISCONCEPTION

The characteristics of preferred stock can be similar to those of a debt security. Often, a regular dividend is required at a stated rate, much like what would be required with respect to a debt obligation. The holder of preferred stock, like a debt holder, may have preferred liquidation rights over holders of common stock. Also, it is not required that preferred stock possess voting rights. Thus, where preferred stock is concerned, the differences between debt and equity can be minimal.

EXAMPLE C2-41 ▶ Dot and Fred own equally all of Trail Corporation's stock, and each has a $50,000 basis in that stock. Later, as a voluntary contribution to capital, Dot contributes $40,000 in cash and Fred contributes property having a $25,000 basis and a $40,000 FMV. Trail Corporation recognizes no gross income because of the contributions. However, Dot's basis in her stock is increased to $90,000 ($50,000 + $40,000), and Fred's basis in his stock is increased to $75,000 ($50,000 + $25,000). Trail's basis in the property contributed by Fred is $25,000—the same as Fred's basis in the property. ◀

WHAT WOULD YOU DO IN THIS SITUATION?

You are a CPA who has a corporate client that wants to issue 100-year bonds. The corporation's CEO reads *The Wall Street Journal* regularly and has seen that similar bonds have been issued by a number of companies, including Coca-Cola and Disney. He touts the fact that the interest rate on these bonds is little more than 30-year U.S. Treasury Notes. In addition, the interest on the bonds will be deductible, whereas dividends paid on preferred or common stock would be nondeductible. You are concerned that the IRS may treat the bonds as equity because of the length of time they will be outstanding. If they are, the "interest" paid will be treated as dividends and will not be deductible.

Your CPA firm is acting as an advisor to your client with regard to the new bond issue. What advice would you give your client in this situation? When preparing its tax return if the new bonds are issued?

If a shareholder gratuitously forgives an indebtedness of the corporation, the transaction generally represents a contribution to the corporation's capital equal to the principal amount of the indebtedness. The determination of whether forgiveness of debt is a capital contribution is based on the facts and circumstances surrounding the situation.

CAPITAL CONTRIBUTIONS BY NONSHAREHOLDERS

BOOK-TO-TAX ACCOUNTING COMPARISON

The IRC requires capital contributions of property other than money made by a nonshareholder to be reported at a zero basis. Financial accounting rules, however, require donated capital to be reported at the FMV of the asset on the financial accounting books. Neither set of rules requires the property's value to be included in income.

Nonshareholders sometimes make capital contributions in the form of money or property. For example, a city government might contribute land to a corporation to induce the corporation to locate within the city and provide jobs for its citizens. Such contributions are excluded from gross income if the money or property contributed is neither a payment for goods or services rendered nor a subsidy to induce the corporation to limit production.[57]

If a nonshareholder contributes property other than money to a corporation, the basis of such property to the corporation is zero.[58] The zero basis assigned to the property prevents the transferee corporation from claiming either a depreciation or capital recovery deduction with respect to the contributed property.

If a nonshareholder contributes money, the basis of any property acquired with the money during a 12-month period beginning on the day the contribution was received is reduced by the amount of the contribution. This limits the corporation's deduction to the amount of funds it invested to purchase the property. The amount of any money received from nonshareholders not spent to purchase property during the 12-month period reduces the basis of any other property held by the corporation on the last day of the 12-month period.[59]

The basis reduction applies to the corporation's property in the following order:

1. Depreciable property
2. Amortizable property
3. Depletable property
4. All other property

A property's basis may not be reduced below zero as a result of these downward basis adjustments.

EXAMPLE C2-42 ▶ The City of San Antonio contributes $100,000 in cash and a tract of land having a $500,000 FMV to Circle Corporation to induce the company to locate there. Because of a downturn in Circle's business, it spends only $70,000 of the contributed funds in the next 12 months. Circle has no gross income on account of the contribution. Circle's bases in the land and the property purchased with the contributed funds are zero. The basis of Circle's remaining property must be reduced by the $30,000 ($100,000 − $70,000) contributed but not spent, starting with its depreciable property. ◀

WORTHLESSNESS OF STOCK OR DEBT OBLIGATIONS

OBJECTIVE 6

Determine the tax consequences of worthless stock or debt obligations

Investors who invest or lend money to a corporation usually intend to earn a profit and recover their investment. Unfortunately, some investments do not provide a good return and an investor may lose part or all of the investment. This section of the chapter examines the tax consequences of stock or debt becoming worthless.

SECURITIES

A debt or equity investment that is evidenced by a **security** and that becomes worthless results in a capital loss for the investor on the last day of the tax year in which worthlessness occurs. A security includes (1) a share of stock in the corporation; (2) a right to sub-

[57] Reg. Sec. 1.118-1.

[58] Sec. 362(c)(1).

[59] Sec. 362(c)(2).

TYPICAL MISCONCEPTION

Probably the most difficult aspect of deducting a loss on a worthless security is establishing that the security is actually worthless. A mere decline in value is not sufficient to create a loss. The burden of proof of establishing total worthlessness rests with the taxpayer.

scribe for, or the right to receive, a share of stock in the corporation; or (3) a bond, debenture, note, or other evidence of indebtedness issued by a corporation with interest coupons or in registered form.[60]

In some situations, investors can report an ordinary loss when a security becomes worthless. Investors who advance money to an unsuccessful corporation, either in the form of equity or debt capital, generally will find it advantageous if the loss is an ordinary deduction. Ordinary losses are not subject to the $3,000 annual limitation on capital losses, and ordinary losses are deductible against any ordinary income reported on the investor's tax return. Ordinary losses that produce an NOL on the investor's tax return can be carried back or forward under the general NOL rules. Situations permitting the deduction of an ordinary loss include

- *Securities that are noncapital assets.* Ordinary loss treatment results when a security that is a noncapital asset is sold or exchanged or becomes totally worthless. Securities fitting into this category include those held as inventory by a securities dealer.
- *Affiliated corporations.* A domestic corporation can claim an ordinary loss incurred in connection with any security of an affiliated corporation that becomes worthless during the tax year. The domestic corporation must own at least 80% of the total voting power of all classes of stock entitled to vote, and at least 80% of each class of nonvoting stock (other than stock limited and preferred as to dividends). At least 90% of the aggregate gross receipts of the loss corporation for all tax years must come from sources other than passive income.
- *Section 1244 stock.* Section 1244 permits a shareholder to claim an ordinary loss if qualifying stock issued by small business corporations is sold or exchanged or becomes worthless. Ordinary loss treatment is available only to an individual who sustains a loss and was issued the qualifying stock by an eligible small business corporation, or to an individual who was a partner in a partnership at the time the partnership acquired the stock from the issuing corporation and whose distributive share of partnership losses includes the loss sustained by the partnership on such stock. Thus, ordinary loss treatment is not available for stock inherited, received as a gift, or purchased from another shareholder. The ordinary loss is limited to $50,000 per year (or $100,000 if the taxpayer is married and files a joint return). Losses exceeding the dollar ceiling in any given year are considered capital losses.

SELF-STUDY QUESTION

Why would a shareholder want his or her stock to qualify as Sec. 1244 stock?

ANSWER

Section 1244 is a provision that may help the taxpayer but that can never hurt. If the Sec. 1244 requirements are satisfied, the individual shareholders of a small business corporation may treat losses from the sale or worthlessness of their stock as ordinary rather than capital losses. If the Sec. 1244 requirements are not satisfied, such losses generally are capital losses.

EXAMPLE C2-43 ▶ Tammy and her husband purchased 25% of the initial offering of Minor Corporation's single class of stock for $175,000. Minor Corporation is a qualifying small business corporation, and the Minor stock satisfies all the Sec. 1244 requirements. On September 1, 2000, Minor Corporation filed for bankruptcy. After substantial litigation, the shareholders are notified in 2002 that the Minor stock is worthless. Tammy and her husband can deduct $100,000 of their loss as an ordinary loss. The remaining $75,000 loss is a capital loss. ◀

If the stock is issued for property whose adjusted basis exceeds its FMV immediately before the exchange, the basis of the stock is reduced to the property's FMV for purposes of determining the amount of ordinary loss claimed under Sec. 1244.

EXAMPLE C2-44 ▶ Penny exchanges property having a $40,000 adjusted basis and a $32,000 FMV for 100 shares of Bear Corporation stock in a transaction qualifying under Sec. 351. The stock qualifies as Sec. 1244 stock. Penny's basis in her Bear stock is $40,000. However, for Sec. 1244 purposes only, her basis in the stock is the transferred property's FMV, or $32,000. If Penny sells the stock for $10,000, her recognized loss is $30,000 ($10,000 − $40,000). Her ordinary loss under Sec. 1244 is $22,000 ($10,000 − $32,000 Sec. 1244 basis). The remaining $8,000 loss is a capital loss. ◀

No special election is required to take advantage of Sec. 1244. Investors, however, should be aware of the special requirements that must be satisfied. Failure to satisfy any

[60] Sec. 165(g).

of these requirements will disqualify the stock from Sec. 1244 treatment and generally cause the shareholder's loss to be a capital loss. The special requirements include

- The issuing corporation must be a small business corporation at the time it issues the stock. A small business corporation is one whose aggregate money and other property received for stock is $1 million or less.[61]
- The stock must be issued for money or property (other than stock and securities).
- The issuing corporation must have derived more than 50% of its aggregate gross receipts from "active" sources (i.e., other than royalties, rents, dividends, interest, annuities, and gains on sales of stock and securities) during the five most recent tax years ending before the date on which the shareholder sells or exchanges the stock or the stock becomes worthless.

TAX STRATEGY TIP

If a shareholder contributes additional money or property to an existing corporation, he or she should be sure to receive additional stock in the exchange so that it will qualify for Sec. 1244 treatment if all requirements are met. If the shareholder does not receive additional stock, the increased basis of existing stock resulting from the capital contribution will not qualify for Sec. 1244 treatment.

If a shareholder contributes additional money or property to a corporation after acquiring Sec. 1244 stock, the amount of ordinary loss recognized upon the sale, exchange, or worthlessness of the Sec. 1244 stock is limited to the shareholder's capital contribution at the time the shares were issued.

UNSECURED DEBT OBLIGATIONS

Shareholders may lend money to the corporation in addition to their stock investment. The type of loss allowed if these advances are not repaid depends on the nature of the loan or advance. If the advance is treated as additional paid-in capital, the worthless security loss claimed by the shareholder for his or her stock investment is increased.

If the unpaid loan was not evidenced by a security (i.e., an unsecured debt obligation), it is either a business or nonbusiness bad debt. Under Sec. 166, nonbusiness bad debts receive less favorable tax treatment than do business bad debts. Nonbusiness bad debts are deductible only as short-term capital losses (up to the $3,000 annual limit for all capital losses) when the debt is determined to be totally worthless. Business bad debts are deductible as ordinary deductions without limit when they are either partially or totally worthless. The IRS generally treats a loan made by a shareholder to a corporation in connection with his or her stock investment as a nonbusiness activity.[62] It is simple to see why a shareholder might like to rebut this presumption and say that a business purpose exists for making the loan.

An advance made in connection with the shareholder's trade or business, such as a loan made to protect the shareholder's employment with the corporation, may be treated as an ordinary loss under the business bad debt rules. Regulation Sec. 1.166-5(b) indicates that whether the loss is treated as a business or nonbusiness bad debt depends on the taxpayer's motive for making the advance. The debt qualifies as a business bad debt should the necessary relationship between the loss and the conduct of the taxpayer's trade or business exist at the time the debt was created or acquired, or when the debt becomes worthless.

KEY POINT

In many closely held corporations, the shareholders are also employees. Thus, when a shareholder-employee makes a loan to the corporation, a question arises whether the loan is being made in the individual's capacity as an employee or a shareholder. The distinction is important because an employee loan that is worthless is entitled to ordinary loss treatment, whereas a shareholder loan that is worthless is treated as a nonbusiness bad debt (short-term capital loss).

In *U.S. v. Edna Generes*, the Supreme Court held that, when multiple motives exist for making an advance to a corporation, such as when a shareholder also is an employee of the corporation, the distinction between whether a business or nonbusiness loan exists is based on the "dominant motivation" for making the loan.[63] If only a "significant motivation" exists relating the debt and the taxpayer's trade or business, this motivation usually is insufficient to satisfy the proximate relationship required between the bad debt and the taxpayer's trade or business under Reg. Sec. 1.166-5(b) to have a business bad debt.

Factors that have proven to be important in making the business bad debt determination include the relative dollar amounts of the taxpayer's stock investment in the corporation, compensation from the corporation, and other compensation. A small salary and a large stock investment would indicate an investment purpose for making the loan. A large salary and a small stock investment would indicate a business purpose for making the loan. Because these factors are subjective in nature and because the dollars involved may be substantial, this issue still remains open to litigation.

---

[61] Regulation Sec. 1.1244(c)-2 provides special rules for designating which shares of stock are eligible for Sec. 1244 treatment when the corporation has issued more than $1 million of stock.

[62] The assumption is made here that the loan is not considered to be an additional capital contribution. In such a case, the Sec. 165 worthless security rules apply instead of the Sec. 166 bad debt rules.

[63] 29 AFTR 2d 72-609, 72-1 USTC ¶9259 (USSC, 1972).

EXAMPLE C2-45 ▶ Top Corporation employs Mary as its legal counsel. Her annual compensation from Top Corporation is $100,000. Top Corporation is experiencing financial problems, and Mary lends the corporation $50,000 in 2000 in an attempt to help it through its financial difficulties. Top Corporation subsequently declares bankruptcy, and in 2002 Mary and the other creditors receive 10 cents on each dollar they are owed. Mary's $45,000 ($50,000 × 0.90) loss is an ordinary loss and is fully deductible in the year she incurs the loss if she can prove that the dominant motivation for making the loan is in connection with her employment. If a significant relationship exists between Mary's loan and her investment in the Top stock, the loss probably will be a nonbusiness bad debt, of which only $3,000 can be deducted each year (assuming Mary has no capital gains). ◀

ADDITIONAL COMMENT

For the act of lending money to a corporation to be considered the taxpayer's trade or business, the taxpayer must show that he or she was individually in the business of seeking out, promoting, organizing, and financing business ventures. *Ronald L. Farrington v. CIR*, 65 AFTR 2d 90-617, 90-1 USTC ¶50,125 (DC, OK, 1990).

A loss sustained by a shareholder who acts as a guarantor on a loan made by a third party to the corporation generally is considered to be a nonbusiness bad debt. The loss can be claimed only to the extent the shareholder actually makes a payment to the third party and is unable to collect any amount due from the debtor corporation.[64]

TAX PLANNING CONSIDERATIONS

AVOIDING SEC. 351

Section 351 is not an elective provision. If its provisions are met, Sec. 351 applies even if the taxpayer does not want it to apply. Most often, taxpayers desire Sec. 351 treatment because it enables them to defer gains when transferring property to a corporation. In some cases, however, shareholders find it disadvantageous and seek to avoid it. Sometimes shareholders have gains or losses they want to recognize.

SELF-STUDY QUESTION

Which tax provisions may potentially limit a transferor shareholder from recognizing a loss on the transfer of property to a corporation?

ANSWER

Such transfer cannot be to a controlled corporation, or Sec. 351 will defer the loss. Even if Sec. 351 can be avoided, losses on sales between a corporation and a more than 50% shareholder are disallowed under Sec. 267. Thus, to recognize a loss on the sale of property, such shareholders must, directly or indirectly, own 50% or less of the transferee corporation's stock.

AVOIDING NONRECOGNITION OF LOSSES UNDER SEC. 351. If a shareholder transfers property to a corporation on which he or she has a loss, the shareholder may want to recognize the loss on the property so that income from other sources can be offset. However, the loss is not recognized if Sec. 351 applies to the transfer. The shareholder can recognize the loss only if Sec. 351 and the Sec. 267 related party rules do not apply to the exchange.

To avoid Sec. 351 entirely requires that one or more of its requirements not be met. The best way to accomplish this objective is to make sure that the transferors of property do not receive 80% of the voting stock.

Even if a shareholder avoids Sec. 351, he or she still may not be able to recognize the losses because of the Sec. 267 related party transaction rules. Under Sec. 267(a)(1), if the shareholder owns more than 50% of the corporation's stock, directly or indirectly, he or she cannot recognize any losses on an exchange of the property for the corporation's stock or other property.

Thus, to recognize a loss when exchanging property for stock, the shareholder must avoid both Sec. 351 and Sec. 267. If the transferors of property receive less than 80% of the voting stock of the corporation and the transferor of loss property does not own more than 50% of the corporate stock, the transferor of loss property may recognize the loss.

EXAMPLE C2-46 ▶ Lynn owns property that has a $100,000 basis and a $60,000 FMV. If Lynn transfers the property to White Corporation in a transaction qualifying under Sec. 351, she will not recognize the loss. It is postponed until she sells her White stock. If Sec. 351 does not apply, she may be able to recognize a $40,000 loss in the year she transfers the property. If Lynn receives 50% of the White stock in exchange for her property; and Cathy, an unrelated individual, receives 25% of the stock in exchange for $30,000 cash, and John, another unrelated individual, receives the remaining 25% of stock for services performed, Sec. 351 does not apply because transferors of

[64] Reg. Sec. 1.166-8(a).

property receive less than 80% of the stock. Moreover, Sec. 267 does not apply to the exchange because Lynn does not own more than 50% of the stock either directly or indirectly. Therefore, Lynn recognizes a $40,000 loss on the exchange of her property for the White stock. ◀

ADDITIONAL COMMENT

Any potential built-in gain on property transferred to the transferee corporation is duplicated because such gain may be recognized at the corporate level and at the shareholder level. This double taxation may be another reason for avoiding the nonrecognition of gain under Sec. 351.

AVOIDING NONRECOGNITION OF GAIN UNDER SEC. 351. Sometimes a transferor wants to recognize a gain when he or she transfers appreciated property to a corporation so that the transferee corporation has a higher basis in the transferred property. Some other possible reasons for wanting to recognize gain are as follows:

- The transferor's gain is capital gain that he or she can offset with capital losses from other sources.
- For 1997 and later years, individual long-term capital gains generally are taxed at a maximum 20% rate (18% if the taxpayer acquires capital assets in 2001 or later and holds them more than five years). This rate is below the 35% maximum marginal tax rate generally applicable to corporate capital gains.
- The corporation's marginal tax rate may be higher than the marginal tax rate applicable to a noncorporate transferor. In such case, it might be beneficial for the transferor to recognize gain on the transfer so that the corporation can obtain a higher basis in the property. A higher basis would either reduce the corporation's gain when it sells the property or allow the corporation to claim higher depreciation deductions on the property while it is using it.

A transferor who cannot recognize a gain on a transfer of appreciated property because of Sec. 351 may be able to avoid Sec. 351 and recognize the gain by using one of the following methods:

- The transferor can sell the property to the controlled corporation for cash, thereby avoiding Sec. 351 altogether.
- The transferor can sell the property to the controlled corporation for cash and debt. This method requires less cash than the previous method. However, the sale may be treated as a transfer coming under Sec. 351 if the debt instruments received are considered equity.[65]
- The transferor can sell the property to a third party for cash and have the third party transfer the property to the corporation for stock.
- The transferor can arrange to receive sufficient boot property so that, even if Sec. 351 applies to the transaction, he or she recognizes gain.
- The transferors can fail one or more of the Sec. 351 provisions. If the property transferors do not obtain control of the corporation (i.e., 80% of the voting stock), Sec. 351 does not apply, and they recognize gain.
- The transferors may transfer to the corporation either sufficient debt so that the debt exceeds the basis of all property transferred or debt that lacks a business purpose to trigger the gain recognition provisions of Secs. 357(b) or (c).

EXAMPLE C2-47 ▶ Jaime owns land purchased as an investment ten years ago for $100,000. The land is now worth $500,000. Jaime plans to transfer the land to Bell Corporation in exchange for all its stock. Bell Corporation will subdivide the land and sell individual parcels. Its gain on the land sales will be ordinary income. Jaime has a large capital loss in the current year and would like to recognize a capital gain on the transfer of the land to Bell Corporation. One way for Jaime to accomplish this objective is to transfer the land to Bell Corporation in exchange for all the Bell stock plus a note for $400,000. Because the note is boot, Jaime recognizes $400,000 of gain even though Sec. 351 applies to the exchange. However, if the note is due in a subsequent year, Jaime's gain recognition is postponed until collection unless she elects out of the installment method. ◀

---

[65] See, for example, *Aqualane Shores, Inc. v. CIR*, 4 AFTR 2d 5346, 59-2 USTC ¶9632 (5th Cir., 1959) and *Sun Properties, Inc. v. U.S.*, 47 AFTR 273, 55-1 USTC ¶9261 (5th Cir., 1955).

COMPLIANCE AND PROCEDURAL CONSIDERATIONS

REPORTING REQUIREMENTS UNDER SEC. 351[66]

Every person who receives stock or other property in an exchange qualifying under Sec. 351 must attach a statement to his or her tax return for the period that includes the date of the exchange. The statement must include all the facts pertinent to the exchange, including

ADDITIONAL COMMENT

The required information provided to the IRS by both the transferor-shareholders and the transferee corporation should be consistent. For example, the FMVs assigned to the stock and other properties included in the exchange should be the same for both sides of the transaction.

- A description of the property transferred and its adjusted basis to the transferor
- A description of the stock received in the exchange, including its kind, number of shares, and FMV
- A description of the securities received in the exchange, including principal amount, terms, and FMV
- The amount of money received
- A description of any other property received, including its FMV
- A statement on the liabilities transferred to the corporation, including the nature of the liabilities, when and why they were created, and the corporate business reason for their transfer

The transferee corporation must attach a statement to its tax return for the year in which the exchange took place. The statement must include

- A complete description of all property received from the transferors
- The adjusted basis of the property to the transferors
- A description of the stock issued to the transferors
- A description of the securities issued to the transferors
- The amount of money distributed to the transferors
- A description of any other property distributed to the transferors
- Information regarding the transferor's liabilities assumed by the corporation

PROBLEM MATERIALS

DISCUSSION QUESTIONS

C2-1 What entities or business forms are available for a new business? Explain the advantages and disadvantages of each.

C2-2 Alice and Bill plan to go into business together. They anticipate losses for the first two or three years, which they would like to use to offset income from other sources. They also are concerned about exposing their personal assets to the business liabilities. Advise Alice and Bill as to what business form would best satisfy their concern.

C2-3 Bruce and Bob organize Black LLC on May 10 of the current year. What is the default rule for the entity's tax classification? Are any alternative classification(s) available? If so, (1) how do Bruce and Bob elect the alternative classification(s) and (2) what are the tax consequences of electing an alternative classification?

C2-4 John and Wilbur form White Corporation on May 3 of the current year. What is the default rule for the entity's tax classification? Are any alternative classification(s) available? If so, (1) how do John and Wilbur elect the alternative classification(s) and (2) what are the tax consequences of electing an alternative classification?

C2-5 Barbara organizes Blue LLC on May 17 of the current year. What is the default rule for the entity's tax classification? Are any alternative classification(s) available? If so, (1) how does

[66] Reg. Sec. 1.351-3.

Barbara elect the alternative classification(s) and (2) what are the tax consequences of electing an alternative classification?

C2-6 Debate the following proposition: All corporate formation transactions should be treated as taxable events.

C2-7 What are the tax consequences of Sec. 351 for the transferor and transferee when property is transferred to a newly created corporation?

C2-8 What items are included in the property definition for purposes of Sec. 351(a)? What items are excluded from the property definition?

C2-9 How is the *control* requirement defined for purposes of Sec. 351(a)?

C2-10 Explain how the IRS has interpreted the phrase "in control immediately after the exchange" for purposes of a Sec. 351 exchange.

C2-11 John and Mary each exchange property worth $50,000 for 100 shares of New Corporation stock. Peter exchanges services for 98 shares of stock and $1,000 in money for two shares of stock. Does Sec. 351 apply to the exchange? Explain why or why not. What advice would you give the shareholders?

C2-12 Does Sec. 351 require shareholders to receive stock equal in value to the property transferred? Suppose Fred and Susan each transfer property worth $50,000 to Spade Corporation. Fred receives 25 shares of Spade stock and Susan receives 75 shares. Does Sec. 351 apply? Explain the tax consequences of the transaction.

C2-13 Can Sec. 351 apply to property transferred to an existing corporation? Suppose Ken and Lynn each own 50 shares of North Corporation stock. Ken transfers property worth $50,000 to North for an additional 25 shares of stock. Does Sec. 351 apply? Explain why or why not. If not, what can be done to make the transaction qualify?

C2-14 How are a transferor's basis and holding period for stocks and other property (boot) received in a Sec. 351 exchange determined? How does the transferee corporation's assumption of liabilities affect the transferor's basis for the stock?

C2-15 How are the transferee corporation's basis and holding period for property received in a Sec. 351 exchange determined?

C2-16 Under what circumstances is a corporation's assumption of liabilities considered boot in a Sec. 351 exchange?

C2-17 What factor(s) would the IRS likely use to determine whether a liability transferred by an individual to a corporation in a Sec. 351 transaction possessed the necessary business purpose to avoid being treated as boot under Sec. 357(b)?

C2-18 Mark transfers all the property of his sole proprietorship to newly formed Utah Corporation in exchange for all the Utah stock. Mark has claimed depreciation on some of the property. Under what circumstances is Mark required to recapture previously claimed depreciation deductions? How is the depreciation deduction calculated for the year of transfer? What happens if Utah Corporation sells the depreciable property?

C2-19 How does the assignment of income doctrine affect a Sec. 351 exchange?

C2-20 What factors did Congress mandate should be used in determining whether an indebtedness is classified as debt or equity for tax purposes?

C2-21 What are the advantages and disadvantages of using debt as part of a firm's capital structure?

C2-22 How are capital contributions by shareholders and nonshareholders treated by the recipient corporation?

C2-23 What are the advantages of qualifying for Sec. 1244 loss treatment when a stock investment becomes worthless? What requirements must be satisfied to take advantage of the Sec. 1244 benefits?

C2-24 What are the advantages of business bad debt treatment when a shareholder's loan or advance to a corporation cannot be repaid? How can one avoid having such a loss treated as a nonbusiness bad debt?

C2-25 Why might shareholders want to avoid Sec. 351? Explain three ways they can accomplish this.

C2-26 What are the reporting requirements under Sec. 351?

ISSUE IDENTIFICATION QUESTIONS

C2-27 Peter Jones has owned all 100 shares of Trenton Corporation's stock for the past five years. This year, Mary Smith contributes property with a $50,000 basis and an $80,000 FMV for 80 newly issued Trenton shares. At the same time, Peter contributes $15,000 in cash for 15 newly issued Trenton shares. What tax issues should Mary and Peter consider with respect to the stock acquisitions?

C2-28 Carl contributes equipment with a $50,000 adjusted basis and an $80,000 FMV to Cook Corporation for 50 of its 100 shares of stock. His son, Carl Jr., contributes $20,000 cash for the remaining 50 Cook shares. What tax issues should Carl and his son consider with respect to the stock acquisitions?

C2-29 Several years ago, Bill acquired 100 shares of Bold Corporation stock directly from the corporation for $100,000 in cash. This year, he sold the stock to Sam for $35,000. What tax issues should Bill consider with respect to the stock sale?

PROBLEMS

C2-30 ***Transfer of Property and Services to a Controlled Corporation.*** In 2002, Dick, Evan, and Fran form Triton Corporation. Dick contributes land (a capital asset) purchased in 2000 for $60,000 that has a $50,000 FMV in exchange for 50 shares of Triton stock. Evan contributes machinery (Sec. 1231 property) purchased in 1999 that has a $45,000 adjusted basis and a $30,000 FMV in exchange for 30 shares of Triton stock. Fran contributes services worth $20,000 in exchange for 20 shares of Triton stock.

a. What is the amount of Dick's recognized gain or loss?
b. What is Dick's basis in his Triton shares? When does his holding period begin?
c. What is the amount of Evan's recognized gain or loss?
d. What is Evan's basis in his Triton shares? When does his holding period begin?
e. How much income, if any, must Fran recognize?
f. What is Fran's basis in her Triton shares? When does her holding period begin?
g. What is Triton Corporation's basis in the land and the machinery? When does its holding period begin? How does Triton Corporation treat the amount paid to Fran for her services?

C2-31 ***Transfer of Property and Services to a Controlled Corporation.*** In 2002, Ed, Fran, and George form Jet Corporation. Ed contributes land purchased as an investment in 1998 for $15,000 that has a $35,000 FMV in exchange for 35 shares of Jet stock. Fran contributes machinery (Sec. 1231 property) purchased in 1998 and used in her business having a $45,000 adjusted basis and a $35,000 FMV in exchange for 35 shares of Jet stock. George contributes services worth $30,000 in exchange for 30 shares of Jet stock.

a. What is the amount of Ed's recognized gain or loss?
b. What is Ed's basis in his Jet shares? When does his holding period begin?
c. What is the amount of Fran's recognized gain or loss?
d. What is Fran's basis in her Jet shares? When does her holding period begin?
e. How much income, if any, must George recognize?
f. What is George's basis in his Jet shares? When does his holding period begin?
g. What is Jet Corporation's basis in the land and the machinery? When does its holding period begin? How does Jet Corporation treat the amount paid to George for his services?
h. How would your answers to Parts a through g change if George instead contributed $5,000 cash and services worth $25,000 for his 30 shares of Jet stock?

C2-32 ***Control Test.*** In which of the following independent situations is the Sec. 351 control requirement met?

a. Olive transfers property to Quick Corporation for 75% of Quick's stock, and Mary provides services to Quick Corporation for the remaining 25% of Quick's stock.
b. Pete transfers property to Target Corporation for 60% of Target's stock, and Robert transfers property worth $15,000 and performs services worth $25,000 for the remaining 40% of Target's stock.
c. Herb and his wife, Wilma, each have owned 50 of the 100 outstanding shares of Vast Corporation stock since it was formed three years ago. In the current year, their son, Sam, transfers property to Vast Corporation for 50 newly issued shares of Vast stock.
d. Charles and Ruth develop a plan to form Tiny Corporation. On June 3 of this year, Charles transfers property worth $50,000 for 50 shares of Tiny stock. On August 1, Ruth transfers $50,000 cash for 50 shares of Tiny stock.
e. Assume the same facts as in Part d except that Charles has a prearranged plan to sell 30 of his shares to Sam on October 1.

C2-33 ***Sec. 351 Requirements.*** To which of the following exchanges does Sec. 351 apply?

a. Fred exchanges property worth $50,000 and services worth $50,000 for 100 shares of New Corporation stock. Greta exchanges $100,000 cash for the remaining 100 shares of New stock.
b. Maureen exchanges property worth $2,000 and services worth $48,000 for 100 shares of Gemini Corporation stock. Norman exchanges property worth $50,000 for the remaining 100 shares of Gemini stock.

If the transaction does not comply with the Sec. 351 requirements, suggest ways in which the transaction can be made to comply.

C2-34 ***Sec. 351 Requirements.*** Al, Bob, and Carl form West Corporation with the following assets:

		Property Transferred		
Transferor	*Asset*	*Transferor's Basis*	*FMV*	*Shares Received by Transferor*
Al	Patent	–0–	$25,000	1,000 common
Bob	Cash	$25,000	25,000	250 preferred
Carl	Services	–0–	7,500	300 common

The common stock has voting rights. The preferred stock is nonvoting stock.

a. Does the transaction qualify as tax-free under Sec. 351? Explain the tax consequences of the transaction to Al, Bob, Carl, and West Corporation.

b. How would your answer to Part a change if Bob instead had received 200 shares of common stock and 200 shares of preferred stock?

c. How would your answer to Part a change if Carl instead had contributed $800 cash as well as services worth $6,700?

C2-35 ***Incorporating a Sole Proprietorship.*** Tom incorporates his sole proprietorship by transferring all its assets to newly formed Total Corporation for all 100 shares of Total stock, with a $125,000 FMV, and four $10,000 interest-bearing notes that mature consecutively on the first four anniversaries of the incorporation date. The assets transferred are

Assets		*Adjusted Basis*	*FMV*
Cash		$ 5,000	$ 5,000
Equipment	$130,000		
Minus: Accumulated depreciation	(70,000)	60,000	90,000
Building	$100,000		
Minus: Accumulated depreciation	(49,000)	51,000	40,000
Land		24,000	30,000
Total		$140,000	$165,000

a. What are the amount and character of Tom's recognized gain or loss?

b. What is Tom's basis in his Total stock and notes?

c. What is Total Corporation's basis in the property received from Tom?

C2-36 ***Transfer to an Existing Corporation.*** For the last five years, Ann and Fred each have owned 50 of the 100 outstanding shares of Zero Corporation's stock. Ann transfers land having a $10,000 basis and a $25,000 FMV to Zero Corporation for an additional 25 shares of Zero stock. Fred transfers $1,000 to Zero Corporation for one additional share of Zero stock. What amount of the gain or loss must Ann recognize on the exchange? If the transaction does not comply with the Sec. 351 requirements, suggest ways in which the transaction can be made to comply.

C2-37 ***Transfer to an Existing Corporation.*** For the last three years, Lucy and Marvin each have owned 50 of the 100 outstanding shares of Lucky Corporation's stock. Lucy transfers property that has an $8,000 basis and a $12,000 FMV to Lucky Corporation for an additional ten shares of Lucky stock. How much gain or loss must Lucy recognize on the exchange? If the transaction does not comply with the Sec. 351 requirements, suggest ways in which the transaction can be made to comply.

C2-38 ***Disproportionate Receipt of Stock.*** Jerry transfers property with a $28,000 adjusted basis and a $50,000 FMV to Texas Corporation for 75 shares of Texas stock. Frank, Jerry's father, transfers property with a $32,000 adjusted basis and a $50,000 FMV to Texas Corporation for the remaining 25 shares of Texas stock.

a. What is the amount of each transferor's recognized gain or loss?

b. What is Jerry's basis for his Texas stock?

c. What is Frank's basis for his Texas stock?

C2-39 ***Sec. 351: Boot Property Received.*** Sara transfers land (a capital asset) having a $30,000 adjusted basis to Temple Corporation in a transaction qualifying under Sec. 351. In exchange, Sara receives the following consideration:

Consideration	*FMV*
100 shares of Temple Corporation common stock	$100,000
50 shares of Temple Corporation qualified preferred stock	50,000
Temple Corporation note due in three years	20,000
Total	$170,000

a. What are the amount and character of Sara's recognized gain or loss?
b. What is Sara's basis for her common stock, preferred stock, and note?
c. What is Temple Corporation's basis for the land?

C2-40 ***Receipt of Bonds for Property.*** Joe, Karen, and Larry form Gray Corporation. Joe contributes land (a capital asset) having an $8,000 adjusted basis and a $15,000 FMV to Gray Corporation in exchange for a similar dollar amount of its ten-year bonds. Karen contributes equipment (a Sec. 1231 asset) having an $18,000 adjusted basis and a $25,000 FMV on which $10,000 of depreciation had previously been claimed for 50 shares of Gray stock. Larry contributes $25,000 cash for 50 shares of Gray stock.
a. What are the amount and character of Joe's, Karen's, and Larry's recognized gains or losses on the transactions?
b. What basis do Joe, Karen, and Larry take in the stock or bonds they receive?
c. What basis does Gray Corporation take in the land and equipment? What happens to the $10,000 of depreciation recapture potential on the equipment?

C2-41 ***Transfer of Depreciable Property.*** Nora transfers depreciable machinery that originally cost $18,000 and has a $15,000 adjusted basis to Needle Corporation in exchange for all 100 shares of Needle's stock, having an $18,000 FMV, and a three-year Needle Corporation note having a $4,000 FMV.
a. What are the amount and character of Nora's recognized gain or loss?
b. What are Nora's bases for the stock and note she received?
c. What is Needle Corporation's basis for the depreciable machinery received from Dana?

C2-42 ***Transfer of Personal Liabilities.*** Jim owns 80% of Gold Corporation's stock. He transfers a business automobile to Gold Corporation in exchange for additional Gold stock worth $5,000 and its assumption of his $1,000 debt on the automobile and his $2,000 education loan. The automobile originally cost Jim $12,000, has a $4,500 adjusted basis, and has an $8,000 FMV on the transfer date.
a. What are the amount and character of Jim's recognized gain or loss?
b. What is Jim's basis for his additional Gold shares?
c. When does Jim's holding period start for the additional shares?
d. What basis does Gold Corporation take in the automobile?

C2-43 ***Liabilities in Excess of Basis.*** Barbara transfers machinery that has a $15,000 basis and a $35,000 FMV and $10,000 in money to Moore Corporation in exchange for 50 shares of Moore stock. The machinery was used in Barbara's business, originally cost Barbara $50,000, and is subject to a $28,000 liability, which Moore Corporation assumes. Sam exchanges $17,000 cash for the remaining 50 shares of Moore stock.
a. What are the amount and character of Barbara's recognized gain or loss?
b. What is her basis in the Moore stock?
c. What is Moore Corporation's basis in the machinery?
d. What are the amount and character of Sam's recognized gain or loss?
e. What is Sam's basis in the Moore stock?
f. When do Barbara and Sam's holding periods for their stock begin?
g. How would your answers to Parts a through f change if Sam received $17,000 of Moore stock for legal services (instead of for money)?

C2-44 ***Transfer of Business Properties.*** Jerry transfers property that has a $32,000 adjusted basis and a $50,000 FMV to Emerald Corporation in exchange for all its stock worth $15,000, and for Emerald Corporation's assumption of a $35,000 mortgage on the property.
a. What is the amount of Jerry's recognized gain or loss?
b. What is Jerry's basis in his Silver stock?
c. What is Emerald Corporation's basis in the property?
d. How would your answers to Parts a through c change if the mortgage assumed by Emerald were $15,000 and the Emerald stock were worth $35,000?

C2-45 ***Incorporating a Cash Basis Proprietorship.*** Ted decides to incorporate his medical practice. He uses the cash method of accounting. On the date of incorporation, the practice has the following balance sheet:

	Basis	FMV
Assets:		
Cash	$ 5,000	$ 5,000
Accounts receivable	–0–	65,000
Equipment (net of $15,000 depreciation)	35,000	40,000
Total	$40,000	$110,000
Liabilities and Owner's Equity:		
Current liabilities	$ –0–	$ 35,000
Note payable on equipment	15,000	15,000
Owner's equity	25,000	60,000
Total	$40,000	$110,000

All the current liabilities would be deductible by Ted if he paid them. Ted transfers all the assets and liabilities to a professional corporation in exchange for all of its stock.

a. What are the amount and character of Ted's recognized gain or loss?
b. What is Ted's basis in the shares he receives?
c. What is the corporation's basis in the property it receives?
d. Who must recognize the income from the receivables when they are collected? Can the corporation obtain a deduction for the liabilities when they are paid?

C2-46 ***Transfer of Depreciable Property.*** On January 10, 2002, Mary transfers to Green Corporation a machine purchased on March 3, 1999, for $100,000. The machine has a $60,000 adjusted basis and a $110,000 FMV on the transfer date. Mary receives all 100 shares of Green stock, worth $100,000, and a two-year Green Corporation note worth $10,000.

a. What are the amount and character of Mary's recognized gain or loss?
b. What is Mary's basis in the stock and note? When does her holding period begin?
c. What are the amount and character of Green Corporation's gain or loss?
d. What is Green Corporation's basis for the machine? When does Green Corporation's holding period begin?

C2-47 ***Contribution to Capital by a Nonshareholder.*** The City of San Antonio donates land worth $500,000 to Ace Corporation to induce it to locate in San Antonio and provide 2,000 jobs for its citizens.

a. How much income, if any, must Ace Corporation report because of the land contribution?
b. What basis does the land have to Ace Corporation?
c. Assume the same facts except that the City of San Antonio also donated $100,000 cash to Ace Corporation, which the corporation used to pay a portion of the $250,000 cost of equipment that it purchased six months later. How much income, if any, must Ace Corporation report because of the cash contribution? What basis does the equipment that was purchased have to Ace Corporation?

C2-48 ***Choice of Capital Structure.*** Reggie transfers $500,000 in cash to newly formed Jackson Corporation for 100% of Jackson's stock. In the first year of operations, Jackson's taxable income before any payments to Reggie is $120,000. What total amount of taxable income must Reggie and Jackson Corporation each report in the following two scenarios?

a. Jackson Corporation distributes a $70,000 dividend to Reggie.
b. Assume that when Jackson Corporation was formed, Reggie transferred his $500,000 to the corporation for $250,000 of Jackson stock and $250,000 in Jackson notes payable in five annual installments of $50,000 plus 8% annual interest on the unpaid balance. During the current year, Jackson Corporation pays Reggie $50,000 in repayment of the first note plus $20,000 interest.

C2-49 ***Worthless Stock or Securities.*** Tom and Vicki, who are husband and wife and who file a joint tax return, each purchase one-half of the stock of Guest Corporation from Al, for which they each pay $75,000. Tom is employed full-time by Guest Corporation and is paid $100,000 in salary annually. Because of Guest Corporation's financial difficulties, Tom and Vicki each lend Guest Corporation an additional $25,000. The $25,000 is secured by registered bonds and is to be repaid in five years, with interest being charged at a rate acceptable to the IRS. Guest Corporation's financial difficulties continue, and it declares bankruptcy. Tom and Vicki receive nothing for their Guest stock or for their Guest Corporation bonds.

a. What are the amount and character of each shareholder's loss on the worthless stock and bonds?
b. How would your answer to Part a change if the liability were not secured by a bond?
c. How would your answer to Part a change if Tom and Vicki had each purchased their stock for $75,000 at the time Guest Corporation was formed?

C2-50 ***Worthless Stock.*** Duck Corporation is owned equally by Harry, Susan, and Big Corporation. Harry and Susan are both single. Harry, Tom, and Big Corporation, the original investors in Duck Corporation, each paid $125,000 for their Duck stock in 1994. Susan purchased her stock from Tom in 1997 for $175,000. No adjustments to basis occur after the stock acquisition date. Duck Corporation suffers some financial difficulties as the result of losing a large judgment in a lawsuit brought by a person who purchased a defective product, resulting in a serious personal injury. Duck Corporation files for bankruptcy, and all its assets ultimately are used to pay its creditors in 2002. What are the amount and character of each shareholder's loss?

C2-51 ***Sale of Sec. 1244 Stock.*** Lois, who is single, transfers property with an $80,000 basis and a $120,000 FMV to Water Corporation in exchange for all of Water's 100 shares of stock. The Water stock qualifies as Sec. 1244 stock. Two years later, Lois sells the stock for $28,000.
a. What are the amount and character of Lois's recognized gain or loss?
b. How would your answer to Part a change if the FMV of the property transferred were $70,000?

C2-52 ***Transfer of Sec. 1244 Stock.*** Assume the same facts as in Problem C2-51 except that Lois gave the Water stock to her daughter, Sue, six months after she received it. The stock had a $120,000 FMV when Lois received it and when she made the gift. Sue sold the stock two years later for $28,000. How is the loss treated for tax purposes?

C2-53 ***Avoiding Sec. 351 Treatment.*** Donna purchased land six years ago as an investment. The land cost her $150,000 and is now worth $480,000. Donna plans to transfer the land to Development Corporation. Development Corporation will subdivide the land and sell individual parcels. Development Corporation's profit on the land sales will be ordinary income.
a. What are the tax consequences of the asset transfer and land sales if Donna contributes the land to Development Corporation in exchange for all its stock?
b. What alternative methods can be used to structure the transaction to achieve better tax consequences? Assume Donna's marginal tax rate is 35%. Development Corporation's marginal tax rate is 34%.

COMPREHENSIVE PROBLEM

C2-54 On March 1 of the current year, Alice, Bob, Carla, and Dick form Bear Corporation with the following investments:

	Property Transferred			
Transferor	*Asset*	*Basis to Transferor*	*FMV*	*Number of Common Shares Issued*
Alice	Land	$12,000	$30,000	
	Building	38,000	70,000	400
	Mortgage on the land and building	60,000	60,000	
Bob	Equipment	25,000	40,000	300
Carla	Van	15,000	10,000	50
Dick	Accounting services	–0–	10,000	100

Alice purchased the land and building several years ago for $12,000 and $50,000, respectively. Alice has claimed straight-line depreciation on the building. Bob also receives a Bear Corporation note for $10,000 due in three years. The note bears interest at a rate acceptable to the IRS. Bob purchased the equipment three years ago for $50,000. Carla also receives $5,000 cash. Carla purchased the van two years ago for $20,000.
a. Does the transaction satisfy the requirements of Sec. 351?

b. What are the amount and character of the recognized gains or losses for Alice, Bob, Carla, Dick, and Bear Corporation?
c. What is each shareholder's basis for his or her Bear stock? When does the holding period for the stock begin?
d. What is Bear Corporation's basis for its property and services? When does its holding period begin for each property?

TAX STRATEGY PROBLEM

C2-55 Paula Green owns and operates the Green Thumb Nursery, a sole proprietorship. The business has assets with a $260,000 adjusted basis and a $500,000 FMV. Paula wants to expand into the landscaping business. She believes this expansion to be somewhat risky and therefore wants to incorporate so as not to put her personal assets at risk. Her friend, Mary Brown, is willing to invest $250,000 in the enterprise, so together they will have sufficient capital.

Although Green Thumb has been earning approximately $55,000 per year, Paula and Mary anticipate that, when the new landscaping business is launched, the new corporation will incur losses of $50,000 per year for the next two years. After that, they expect profits of at least $80,000 per year. Paula and Mary have approximately $50,000 of income from other sources.

They are considering the following alternative capital structures and elections:

a. Green Thumb Corporation issues 50 shares of common stock to Paula and 25 shares of common stock to Mary.
b. Green Thumb Corporation issues 50 shares of common stock to Paula and a $250,000 ten-year bond to Mary bearing interest at 8%
c. Green Thumb Corporation issues 40 shares of common stock to Paula plus a $100,000 ten-year bond bearing interest at 6% and 15 shares of common stock to Mary plus a $100,000 ten-year bond bearing interest at 6%.
d. Green Thumb Corporation issues 50 shares of common stock to Paula and 25 shares of preferred stock to Mary. The preferred stock is nonparticipating but pays a cumulative preferred dividend of 8% of its $250,000 stated value.

What are the advantages and disadvantages of each of these alternatives? What are the main considerations in choosing which alternative is best?

CASE STUDY PROBLEMS

C2-56 Bob Jones has approached you for advice. He has a small repair shop that he has run for several years as a sole proprietorship. The proprietorship has used the cash method of accounting and the calendar year as its tax year. He needs additional capital for expansion and knows two people who might be interested in investing in the business. One would like to work in the business. The other would be an investor only.

Bob wants to know what the tax consequences of incorporating his business are. His business assets include a small building, equipment, accounts receivable, and cash. Liabilities include a mortgage on the building and a small amount of accounts payable, which represent deductible expenses.

Required: Write a memorandum to Bob explaining the tax consequences of the incorporation. As part of your memorandum examine the possibility of having the corporation issue common and preferred stock and debt for the shareholders' property and money.

C2-57 Eric Wright operates a dry cleaning business as a sole proprietorship. The business operates in a building that Eric owns. Last year, he borrowed $150,000 by placing a mortgage on the building and the land on which the building sits. He used the money for a down payment on his personal residence and college expenses for his two children. He now wants to incorporate his business and transfer the building and the mortgage to his new corporation, along with other assets and some accounts payable. The amount of the unpaid mortgage balance will not exceed Eric's adjusted basis for the land and building at the time he transfers it to the corporation. Eric is aware that Sec. 357(b) is likely to apply to this transaction because no bona fide business purpose exists for the transfer of the mortgage, and the IRS probably will consider it to have been transferred for tax avoidance purposes. However, the client refuses to acknowledge this problem when you confront him about the situation. He maintains that many taxpayers play the audit lottery and that, in the event of an audit, this issue can be used as a bargaining ploy.

Required: What information about the transaction must accompany the transferor and transferee's tax returns for the year in which the transfer takes place? Discuss the ethical issues in the AICPA's *Statements on Standards for Tax Services No. 1, Tax Return Positions* (which can be found in Appendix E) as it relates to this situation. Should the tax practitioner act as an advocate for the client's position in this situation? Should the practitioner sign the return?

C2-58 You are a tax manager with Dewey, Cheatem, and Howe, a regional accounting firm. Peter Moon has been a client of your firm for a number of years. He asked your assistance in starting his new manufacturing corporation two years ago. Peter contributed $100,000 to purchase all 100 shares of Moon Corporation stock. The corporation borrowed an additional $400,000 from Third National Bank to purchase land, a building, and manufacturing equipment. Interest at a floating rate is being charged on the bank loan. The bank rate currently is 12%, and it has been no lower than 10.25%. Peter is a guarantor on the bank loans. In addition, Peter loaned the corporation $500,000 for working capital with interest being charged at a 5% rate. The loan is not secured by a note. None of the principal or current year interest has been paid. Upon your initial review of the work papers for Moon's current year tax return you become concerned about the high debt/equity ratio and whether the interest that has been incurred is deductible. What factors will the IRS use to determine whether the loans are in fact debt or equity? Do these factors appear to favor the IRS or the taxpayer?

TAX RESEARCH PROBLEMS

C2-59 Anne and Michael own and operate a mattress business. It has been quite successful, and they now have determined to take it public. They contribute all the assets of the business to newly formed Spring Corporation in exchange for 20% of the stock for each of them. The remaining 60% of the stock is issued to an underwriting company that will sell the stock to the public and keep 10% of the sales proceeds as a commission. Prepare a memorandum for your tax manager explaining whether or not this transaction meets the nonrecognition of gain or loss requirements of Sec. 351.

C2-60 Bob and Carl transfer property to Stone Corporation for 90% and 10% of the Stone stock, respectively. Pursuant to a binding agreement entered into before the transfer, Bob sells half of his stock to Carl. Prepare a memorandum for your tax manager explaining why Sec. 351 does or does not apply to this exchange. Your manager has suggested that, at a minimum, you consult the following resources:

- IRC Sec. 351
- Reg. Sec. 1.351-1

C2-61 In an exchange qualifying under Sec. 351, Greta receives 100 shares of White Corporation stock plus a contingent right to receive another 25 shares. The shares are contingent on the valuation of a patent contributed by Greta. The licensing of the patent is pending, and consequently the patent cannot be valued for several months. Prepare a memorandum for your tax manager explaining whether the contingent shares are considered "stock" for purposes of Sec. 351 and what tax consequences result from Greta's receipt of the actual and contingent shares of stock.

C2-62 Your clients, Lisa and Matthew, are planning to form Lima Corporation. Lisa will contribute $50,000 cash to Lima Corporation for 50 shares of its stock. Matthew will contribute land having a $35,000 adjusted basis and a $50,000 FMV to Lima Corporation for 50 shares of its stock. Lima Corporation will borrow additional capital from a bank and then will subdivide and sell the land. Prepare a draft memorandum for your tax manager's signature outlining the tax treatment for the corporate formation transaction. As part of your memorandum, compare the reporting of this transaction on the tax and financial accounting books.

References:

- IRC Sec. 351
- APB, *Opinions of the Accounting Principles Board No. 29* [Accounting for Nonmonetary Transactions]

C2-63 John plans to transfer the assets and liabilities of his business to Newco, a new corporation, in exchange for all of Newco's stock. The assets have a $250,000 basis and an $800,000 FMV. John also plans to transfer $475,000 of business liabilities (all business related). Can John avoid recognizing a $175,000 gain (the excess of liabilities transferred over the basis of assets tranferred) under Sec. 357(c) by transferring his personal promissory note for $175,000 to the corporation along with the assets and liabilities?

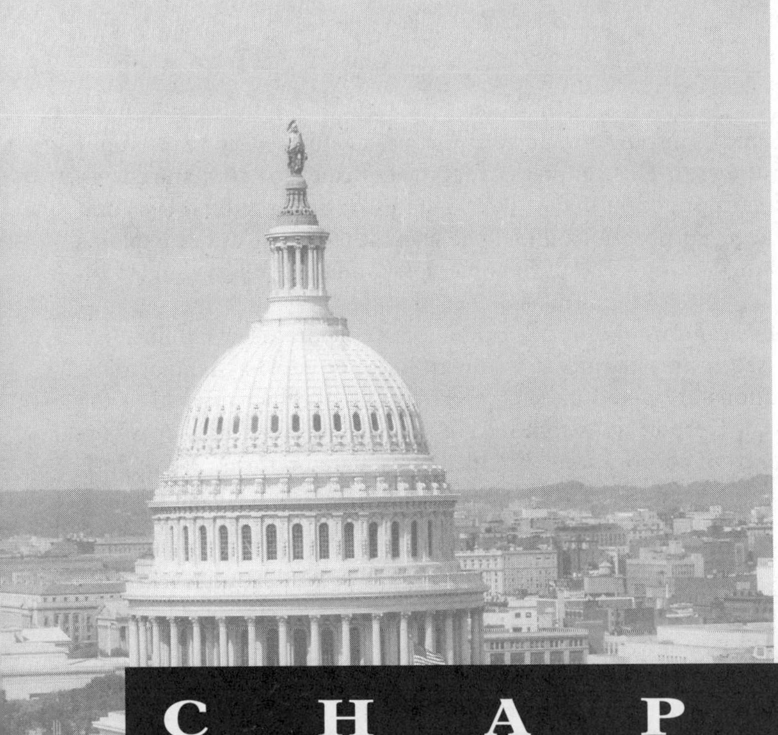

3

CHAPTER

THE CORPORATE INCOME TAX

LEARNING OBJECTIVES

After studying this chapter, you should be able to

1. Explain the requirements for selecting tax years and accounting methods
2. Compute a corporation's taxable income
3. Compute a corporation's income tax liability
4. Explain what a controlled group is and the tax consequences of being a controlled group
5. Explain how compensation planning can reduce taxes for corporations and their shareholders
6. Determine the requirements for paying corporate income taxes and filing a corporate tax return

CHAPTER OUTLINE

Corporate Elections...3-2
General Formula For Determining the Corporate Tax Liability...3-5
Computing a Corporation's Taxable Income...3-5
Computing a Corporation's Income Tax Liability...3-20
Controlled Groups Of Corporations...3-22
Tax Planning Considerations...3-28
Compliance and Procedural Considerations...3-31

A **corporation** is a separate taxpaying entity that must file a tax return every year, even if it has no income or loss for the year. This chapter covers the tax rules for **domestic corporations** (i.e., corporations incorporated in one of the 50 states or under federal law) and other entities taxed as domestic corporations under the check-the-box rules.[1] It explains the rules for determining a corporation's taxable income, loss, and tax liability and for filing corporate tax returns.

See Table C3-1 for the general formula for determining the corporate tax liability.

The corporations discussed in this chapter are sometimes referred to as regular or C corporations. Such corporations are taxed under the provisions of Subchapter C of the Internal Revenue Code (IRC). Corporations that have a special tax status include S corporations and affiliated groups of corporations that file consolidated returns. A comparison of the tax treatments of C corporations, S corporations, and partnerships appears in Appendix F.

CORPORATE ELECTIONS

OBJECTIVE 1

Explain the requirements for selecting tax years and accounting methods

When a corporation is formed, it must make certain elections. The corporation must select its **tax year**. It also must select its basic accounting method. These elections are made on the corporation's first tax return. They are important and should be considered carefully because, once made, they generally can be changed only with permission from the Internal Revenue Service (IRS).

CHOOSING A CALENDAR OR FISCAL YEAR

A new corporation may elect to use either a calendar year or a fiscal year as its accounting period. The corporation's tax year must be the same as the annual accounting period used for financial accounting purposes. The election is made by filing the corporation's first tax return for the selected period. A calendar year is a 12-month period ending on December 31. A fiscal year is a 12-month period ending on the last day of any month other than December. Examples of acceptable fiscal years are February 1, 2002 through January 31, 2003; and October 1, 2002 through September 30, 2003. A fiscal year that runs from September 16, 2002 through September 15, 2003 is not an acceptable tax year because it does not end on the last day of the month. The IRS will require a corporation using an unacceptable tax year to change to a calendar year.[2]

KEY POINT

Whereas partnerships and S corporations generally must adopt a calendar year, C corporations (other than personal service corporations) have the flexibility of adopting a fiscal year. The fiscal year must end on the last day of the month.

SHORT TAX PERIOD. A corporation's first tax year may not cover a full 12-month period. If, for example, a corporation begins business on March 10, 2002 and elects a fiscal year ending on September 30, its first tax year covers the period from March 10, 2002 through September 30, 2002. Its second tax year covers the period from October 1, 2002 through September 30, 2003. The corporation must file a **short-period tax return** for its first tax year.[3] From then on, its tax returns cover a full 12-month period. The last year of a corporation's life also may be a short period covering the period of time from the beginning of the last tax year through the date the corporation goes out of existence.

RESTRICTIONS ON ADOPTING A TAX YEAR. A corporation may be subject to restrictions in its choice of a tax year. An S corporation generally must use a calendar year (see Chapter C11). All members of an affiliated group filing a consolidated return must use the same tax year as the group's parent corporation (see Chapter C8).

A personal service corporation generally must use a calendar year as its tax year. This restriction prevents a personal service corporation with, for example, a January 31 year-end from distributing a large portion of its income that was earned during the February through December portion of 2002 to its calendar year shareholder-employees in January 2002, thereby deferring income largely earned in 2002 to 2003. A **personal service corpo-**

[1] Sec. 7701(a)(4). Corporations that are not classified as domestic are **foreign corporations**. Foreign corporations are taxed like domestic corporations if they conduct a trade or business in the United States.

[2] Sec. 441. Accounting periods of either 52 or 53 weeks that always end on the same day of the week (such as Friday) are also permitted under Sec. 441.

[3] Sec. 443(a)(2).

▼ TABLE C3-1
General Rules for Determining the Corporate Tax Liability

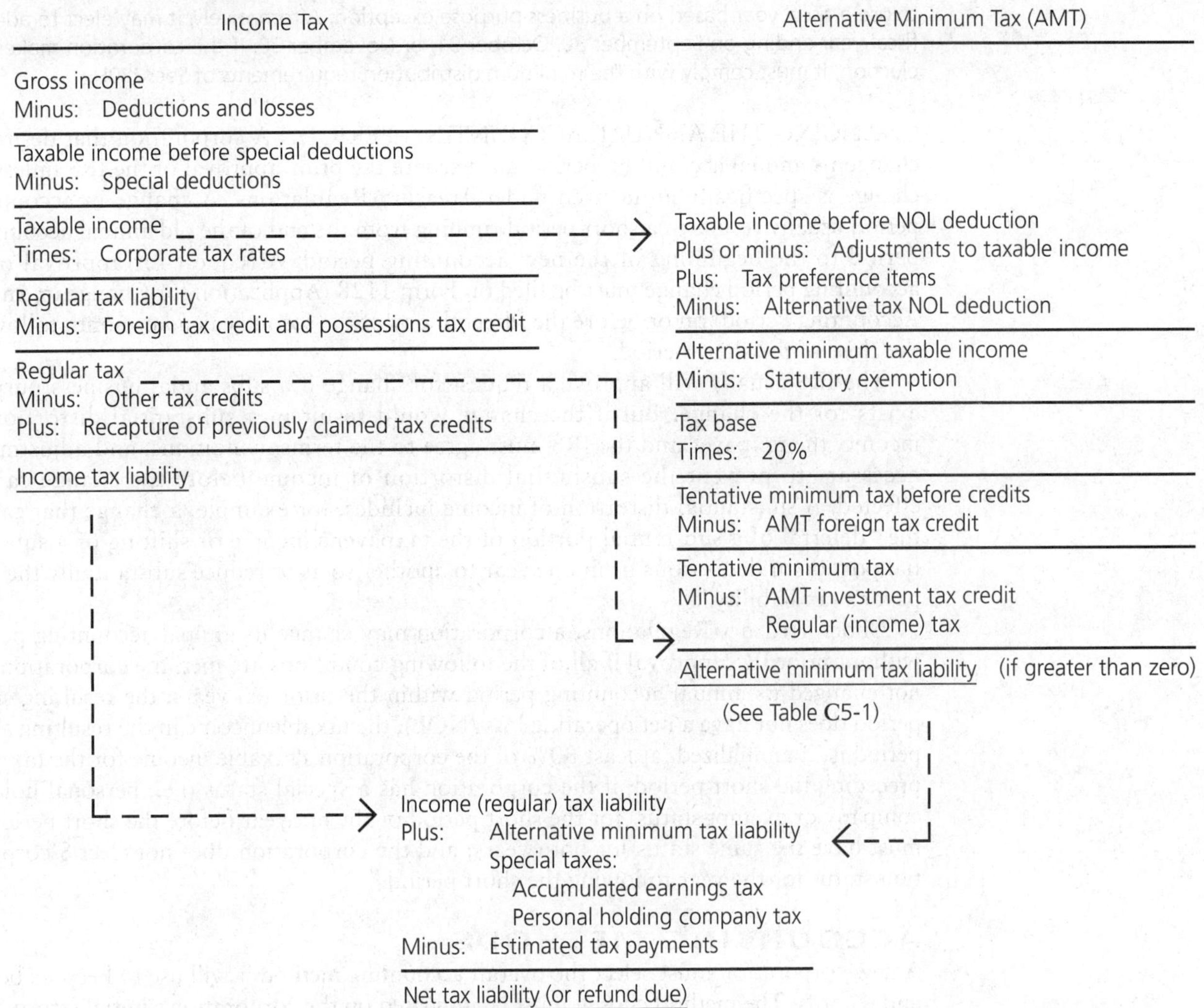

ration (PSC) is defined for this purpose as a corporation whose principal activity is the performance of personal services by its employee-owners who own more than 10% of the stock (by value) on any day of the year.[4]

A PSC is allowed to adopt a fiscal tax year if it can establish a business purpose for such a year. For example, it may be able to establish a natural business year and use that year as its tax year.[5] Deferral of income by shareholders is not an acceptable business purpose.

A PSC may elect to use certain fiscal years even when no business purpose exists.[6] Under this rule, a new PSC may elect to use a September 30, October 31, or November 30 year-end if it meets minimum distribution requirements to employee-owners during the deferral period. If it fails to meet these distribution requirements, the PSC's deduction for amounts paid to employee-owners may have to be deferred to the corporation's next fiscal year.[7]

[4] Sec. 441(i).

[5] The natural business year rule requires that the year-end used for tax purposes coincide with the end of the taxpayer's peak business period. (See the partnership and S corporation chapters and Rev. Proc. 87-32, 1987-2 C.B. 396, for a further explanation of this exception.)

[6] Sec. 444.

[7] Sec. 280H.

EXAMPLE C3-1 ▶ Cole Corporation is created by Alice and Bob, each of whom owns 50% of its stock. Alice and Bob use the calendar year as their tax year. Alice and Bob are both active in the business and are the corporation's primary employees. The new corporation performs engineering services for the automotive industry. Cole Corporation must use a calendar year as its tax year unless it qualifies to use a fiscal year based on a business purpose exception. Alternatively, it may elect to adopt a fiscal year ending on September 30, October 31, or November 30. If the corporation makes this election, it must comply with the minimum distribution requirements of Sec. 280H. ◀

CHANGING THE ANNUAL ACCOUNTING PERIOD. A corporation that desires to change its annual accounting period must secure the prior approval of the IRS unless the change is specifically authorized under Treasury Regulations. A change in accounting period usually results in a short period running from the end of the old annual accounting period to the beginning of the new accounting period. A request for approval of an accounting period change must be filed on Form 1128 (Application for Change in Annual Accounting Period) on or before the fifteenth day of the second calendar month following the close of the short period.

The IRS usually will approve a request for change if a substantial business purpose exists for the change. But if the change would result in a substantial distortion of income, the taxpayer and the IRS must agree to the terms, conditions, and adjustments necessary to prevent the substantial distortion of income before the change can be effected. A substantial distortion of income includes, for example, a change that causes the "deferral of a substantial portion of the taxpayer's income or shifting of a substantial portion of deductions from one year to another so as to reduce substantially the taxpayer's tax liability."[8]

Under Treasury Regulations, a corporation may change its annual accounting period without prior IRS approval if all of the following conditions are met: the corporation has not changed its annual accounting period within the prior ten years; the resulting short period does not have a net operating loss (NOL); the taxable income in the resulting short period is, if annualized, at least 80% of the corporation's taxable income for the tax year preceding the short period; if the corporation has a special status (i.e., personal holding company or exempt status) for the short period or the tax year before the short period, it must have the same status for both years; and the corporation does not elect S corporation status for the year following the short period.[9]

ACCOUNTING METHODS

A new corporation must select the overall **accounting method** it will use to keep its books and records. The method chosen must be indicated on the corporation's initial return. The three possible accounting methods are: accrual, cash, and hybrid.[10]

BOOK-TO-TAX ACCOUNTING COMPARISON

Treasury Regulations literally require taxpayers to use the same overall accounting method for book and tax purposes. However, the courts have allowed different methods if the taxpayer maintains adequate reconciling workpapers. The IRS has adopted the courts' position on this issue.

ACCRUAL METHOD. Under the accrual method, a corporation reports income when it has been earned and reports expenses when they have been incurred. A corporation must use this method unless it qualifies under one of the following exceptions:

- A qualified family farming corporation.[11]
- A qualified personal service corporation, which is a corporation substantially all of whose activities involve the performance of services in the fields of health, law, engineering, architecture, accounting, actuarial science, performing arts, or consulting; and substantially all of whose stock is held by current (or retired) employees performing the services listed above, their estates, or (for two years only) persons who inherited their stock from such employees.[12]

---

[8] Reg. Sec. 1.442-1(b)(1).

[9] Reg. Sec. 1.442-1(c).

[10] Sec. 446.

[11] Sec. 448. Certain family farming corporations having gross receipts of less than $25 million may use the cash method of accounting. Section 447 requires farming corporations with gross receipts over $25 million to use the accrual method of accounting.

[12] The personal service corporation definition for the tax year election [Sec. 441(i)] is different from the personal service corporation definition for the cash accounting method election [Sec. 448].

- Corporations that meet the $5 million gross receipts test for all prior tax years beginning after December 31, 1985. A corporation meets this test for any prior tax year if its average gross receipts for the three-year period ending with that prior tax year do not exceed $5 million. If the corporation was not in existence for the entire three-year period, the period during which the corporation *was* in existence may be used.
- S corporations.

ADDITIONAL COMMENT

Whereas partnerships and S corporations are generally allowed to be cash method taxpayers, most C corporations must use the accrual method of accounting. This restriction can prove inconvenient for many small corporations (with more than $5 million of gross receipts) that would rather use the less complicated cash method of accounting.

If a corporation meets one of the exceptions listed above, it may use either the accrual method or one of the following two methods.

CASH METHOD. Under the cash method, a corporation reports income when it is actually or constructively received and reports expenses when they are paid. Corporations in service industries such as engineering, medicine, law, and accounting generally use this method because they do not want to report their income until they actually receive payment. This method may not be used if inventories are a material income-producing factor. In such case, the corporation must use either the *accrual* method or the *hybrid* method of accounting.

HYBRID METHOD. Under the hybrid method, a corporation uses the accrual method of accounting for sales, cost of goods sold, inventories, accounts receivable, and accounts payable, and the cash method of accounting for all other income and expense items. Small businesses with inventories (e.g., retail stores) often use this method. Although they must use the accrual method of accounting for sales-related income and expense items, they often find the cash method less burdensome to use for other income and expense items, such as utilities, rents, salaries, and taxes.

General Formula for Determining the Corporate Tax Liability

Each year, C corporations are responsible for determining their corporate income (or regular) tax liability. In addition to the income tax, a C corporation may owe the corporate alternative minimum tax and possibly either the accumulated earnings tax or the personal holding company tax. A corporation's total tax liability equals the sum of its regular income tax liability plus the amount of any additional tax levy that it owes.

This chapter explains how to compute a corporation's income (or regular) tax liability. Chapter C5 explains the computation of the corporate alternative minimum tax, personal holding company tax, and accumulated earnings tax.

Computing a Corporation's Taxable Income

OBJECTIVE 2

Compute a corporation's taxable income

Like an individual, a corporation is a taxpaying entity with gross income and deductions. However, a number of differences arise between individual and corporate taxation as summarized in Figure C3-1. This section of the text expands on some of these items and discusses other tax aspects particular to corporations.

1. **Gross income:** Generally, the same gross income definition applies to individuals and corporations. Certain exclusions are available to individuals but not to corporations (e.g, fringe benefits); other exclusions are available to corporations but not to individuals (e.g., capital contributions).
2. **Deductions:** Individuals have above-the-line ("for" AGI), itemized ("from" AGI) deductions, and personal exemptions. Corporations do not compute AGI, and their deductions are presumed to be ordinary and necessary business expenses.
3. **Charitable contributions:** (a) Individuals are limited to 50% of AGI (30% for capital gain property). Corporations are limited to 10% of taxable income without regard to any dividends-received deductions, NOL and capital loss carrybacks, and the contribution deduction itself. (b) Individuals deduct a contribution only in the year in which it is made. Accrual basis corporations may deduct contributions in the year of accrual if the board of directors authorizes the contribution by the end of the tax year, and the corporation pays it by the fifteenth day of the third month of the next year.
4. **Depreciation recapture on Sec. 1250 property:** Individuals generally do not recapture depreciation under the MACRS rules since straight-line depreciation is used for real property. Corporations must recapture 20% of the excess of the amount that would be recaptured under Sec. 1245 over any amount recaptured under Sec. 1250.
5. **Dividends-received deduction:** Not available for individuals. Corporations receive a 70%, 80%, or 100% special deduction depending on the percentage of stock ownership.
6. **Net capital gains:** Individuals usually are taxed at a maximum rate of 20% (however, 10%, 25%, and 28% apply in special cases). Corporate capital gains are taxed at the regular corporate tax rates without any special rate ceiling.
7. **Capital losses:** Individuals can deduct $3,000 of net capital losses to offset ordinary income. Individual capital losses are carried over indefinitely. Corporations cannot offset any ordinary income with capital losses. However, capital losses can be carried back three years and forward five years and used to offset capital gains in those years.
8. **NOLs:** Individuals must make many adjustments to arrive at the NOL they are allowed to carry back or forward. A corporation's NOL is simply the excess of its deductions over its income for the year. In 1998 and later years, the NOL carries back two years and forward 20 years, or the corporation can elect to forgo the carryback and only carry the NOL forward.
9. **Tax rates:** Individual's tax rates range from 10% and 38.6% (in 2002). Corporate tax rates range from 15% to 39%.
10. **AMT:** Individual AMT rates are 26% or 28%. The corporate AMT rate is 20%. Corporations are subject to a special AMTI adjustment called the "Adjusted Current Earnings" (ACE) adjustment that does not apply to individuals.
11. **Passive Losses:** Passive loss rules apply to individuals, partners, S corporation shareholders, closely held C corporations, and PSCs. They do not apply to widely-held C corporations.
12. **Casualty losses:** Casualty losses are deductible in full by a corporation because all corporate casualty losses are considered to be business related. Moreover, they are not reduced by a $100 offset, nor are they restricted to losses exceeding 10% of AGI, as are an individual's nonbusiness casualty losses.

FIGURE C3-1 ▶ DIFFERENCES BETWEEN INDIVIDUAL AND CORPORATE TAXATION

SALES AND EXCHANGES OF PROPERTY

Sales and exchanges of property generally are treated the same way for corporations as they are for an individual. However, special rules apply to capital gains and losses, and corporations are subject to an additional 20% depreciation recapture rule under Sec. 291 on sales of Sec. 1250 property.

CAPITAL GAINS AND LOSSES. A corporation has a capital gain or loss if it sells or exchanges a capital asset. As with individuals, a corporation must net all of its capital gains and losses together to obtain its net capital gain or loss position.

Net Capital Gain. A corporation includes all its net capital gains (net long-term capital gains in excess of net short-term capital losses) for the tax year in gross income. Unlike with individuals, a corporation's capital gains receive no special tax treatment and are taxed in the same manner as any other ordinary income item.

EXAMPLE C3-2 ▶ Beta Corporation has a net capital gain of $40,000, gross profits on sales of $110,000, and deductible expenses of $28,000. Beta's gross income is $150,000 ($40,000 + $110,000). Its taxable income is $122,000 ($150,000 − $28,000). The $40,000 of net capital gain receives no special treatment and is taxed using the regular corporate tax rates described below. ◀

Net Capital Losses. If a corporation incurs a net capital loss, it cannot deduct the loss in the current year. A corporation's capital losses can offset only capital gains. They *never* can be used to offset the corporation's ordinary income.

A net capital loss must be carried back as a short-term capital loss to the three previous tax years and used to offset capital gains in the earliest year possible (i.e., the losses must be carried to the third previous year first). If the loss is not totally absorbed as a carryback, the remainder is carried forward as a short-term capital loss for five years. Any losses that remain unused at the end of the carryforward period are lost.

EXAMPLE C3-3 ▶ In 2002, East Corporation reports gross profits of $150,000, deductible expenses of $28,000, and a net capital loss of $10,000. East reported the following capital gain net income (excess of gains from sales or exchanges of capital assets over losses from such sales or exchanges) during 1999 through 2001:

Year	*Capital Gain Net Income*
1999	$6,000
2000	–0–
2001	3,000

East has gross income of $150,000 and taxable income of $122,000 ($150,000 – $28,000) for 2002. East also has a $10,000 net capital loss that carries back to 1999 first and offsets the $6,000 capital gain net income reported in that year. East receives a refund for the taxes paid on the $6,000 of capital gains in 1999. The $4,000 ($10,000 – $6,000) remainder of the loss carryback carries to 2001 and offsets East's $3,000 capital gain net income reported in that year. East still has a $1,000 net capital loss to carry forward to 2003. ◀

SELF-STUDY QUESTION

How does the use of a net capital loss differ for individual and corporate taxpayers?

ANSWER

Net capital losses are treated differently by individuals and corporations. Individuals may use up to $3,000 per year of net capital losses to offset ordinary income. They cannot carry back net capital losses but can carry net capital losses forward indefinitely. In contrast, corporations may not use any net capital losses to offset ordinary income, can carry net capital losses back three years, and can carry net capital losses forward for only five years.

SEC. 291: TAX BENEFIT RECAPTURE RULE. If a taxpayer sells Sec. 1250 property at a gain, Sec. 1250 requires that the taxpayer report the recognized gain as ordinary income to the extent the depreciation taken exceeds the depreciation that would have been allowed if the straight-line method had been used. This ordinary income is known as Sec. 1250 depreciation recapture. For individuals, any remaining gain is characterized as Sec. 1231 gain. However, corporations must recapture as ordinary income an additional amount equal to 20% of the additional ordinary income that would have been recognized had the property been Sec. 1245 property instead of Sec. 1250 property.

EXAMPLE C3-4 ▶ Texas Corporation purchased residential real estate in January 2000 for $125,000, of which $25,000 is allocated to the land and $100,000 to the building. Texas took straight-line MACRS depreciation deductions of $10,606 on the building in the years 2000 through 2002. In December 2002, Texas sells the property for $155,000, of which $45,000 is allocated to the land and $110,000 to the building. Texas has a $20,000 ($45,000 – $25,000) gain on the land sale, all of which is Sec. 1231 gain. This gain is not affected by Sec. 291 because land is not Sec. 1250 property. Texas has a $20,606 [$110,000 sales price – ($100,000 original cost – $10,606 depreciation)] gain on the sale of the building. If Texas were an individual taxpayer, the entire $20,606 recognized gain would be Sec. 1231 gain. But as a *corporate* taxpayer, $2,121 of gain must be reported as ordinary income. These amounts are summarized below:

	Land	Building	Total
Amount of gain:			
Sales price	$45,000	$110,000	$155,000
Minus: adjusted basis	(25,000)	(89,394)	(114,394)
Recognized gain	$20,000	$ 20,606	$ 40,606
Character of gain:			
Ordinary income	$ –0–	$ 2,121[a]	$ 2,121
Sec. 1231 gain	20,000	18,485	38,485
Recognized gain	$20,000	$ 20,606	$ 40,606

[a] 20% × lesser of $10,606 depreciation claimed or $20,606 recognized gain. ◀

ADDITIONAL COMMENT

Section 291 results in the recapture, as ordinary income, of an additional 20% of the gain on sales of Sec. 1250 property. This recapture requirement reduces the amount of net Sec.1231 gains that can be offset by corporate capital losses.

BUSINESS EXPENSES

Corporations may deduct most of the same type of business expenses that a sole proprietor may deduct on Schedule C (or Schedule C-EZ) of an individual return. Deductions are allowed for ordinary and necessary business expenses, including salaries paid to officers and other employees of the corporation, rent, repairs, insurance premiums, advertising, interest, taxes, losses on sales of inventory or other property, bad debts, and depreciation.[13]

No deductions are allowed for interest on amounts borrowed to purchase tax-exempt securities, illegal bribes or kickbacks, fines or penalties imposed by a government, or insurance premiums incurred to insure the lives of officers and employees when the corporation is the beneficiary.

TAX STRATEGY TIP

A corporation always should have a Sec. 248 election in place because, if the IRS later reclassifies deducted expenses as organizational expenditures, the corporation cannot make a retroactive election.

BOOK-TO-TAX ACCOUNTING COMPARISON

Most corporations amortize organizational expenditures for tax purposes over the minimum 60-month period. For financial accounting purposes, they are expensed currently under SOP 98-5, effective for financial statements issued after June 30, 1998.

ORGANIZATIONAL EXPENDITURES. When formed, a corporation may incur some organizational expenditures such as legal fees and accounting fees incident to the incorporation process. These expenditures must be capitalized. Unless the corporation makes an election under Sec. 248, however, these expenditures cannot be amortized because they have an unlimited life. A Sec. 248 election allows organizational expenditures to be amortized over a period of 60 or more months beginning with the month in which the corporation begins its business. The election must be made in a statement attached to the first return filed by the corporate entity. The return and statement must be filed no later than the due date of the tax return (including any permitted extensions). If an amortization election is not made, organizational expenditures cannot be deducted until the corporation is liquidated.

The election applies only to expenditures incurred before the end of the tax year in which the corporation begins business. A corporation begins business when it starts the business operations for which it was organized. In determining when an organizational expenditure has been incurred, it is irrelevant whether the corporation uses the cash or accrual method of accounting. Expenditures incurred *after* the first tax year has ended (e.g., legal expenses incurred to modify the corporate charter) must be capitalized and cannot be deducted until the corporation is liquidated.[14]

Organizational expenditures include any expenditure incident to the creation of the corporation; chargeable to the corporation's capital account; and of a character that, if expended incident to the creation of a corporation having a limited life, would be amortizable over that life.

Organizational expenditures include

- Legal services incident to the organization of the corporation (e.g., drafting the corporate charter and bylaws, minutes of organizational meetings, and terms of original stock certificates)
- Accounting services necessary to create the corporation
- Expenses of temporary directors and of organizational meetings of directors and stockholders
- Fees paid to the state of incorporation.[15]

WHAT WOULD YOU DO IN THIS SITUATION?

You are a CPA with a medium-size accounting firm. One of your corporate clients is an electrical contractor in New York City. The client is successful and had $10 million of sales last year. The contracts involve private and government electrical work. Among the corporation's expenses are $400,000 of kickbacks paid to people working for general contractors who award electrical subcontracts to the corporation, and $100,000 of payments made to individuals in the electricians' union. Technically, these payments are illegal. However, your client says that everyone in this business needs to pay kickbacks to obtain contracts and to have enough electricians to finish the projects in a timely manner. He maintains that it is impossible to stay in business without making these payments. Your client wants you to deduct these expenses. What are your options and responsibilities under the AICPA's *Statements on Standards for Tax Services? Treasury Department Circular 230?*

[13] Sec. 162.

[14] Reg. Sec. 1.248-1(a).

[15] Reg. Sec. 1.248-1(b)(2).

Organizational expenditures do not include any expenditures connected with issuing or selling the corporation's stock or other securities (e.g., commissions, professional fees, and printing costs) and expenditures related to the transfer of assets to the corporation.

EXAMPLE C3-5 ▶ Heart Corporation is incorporated on July 12 of the current year, starts in business on August 10, and elects a tax year ending on September 30. Heart incurs the following expenses during the current year while organizing the corporation:

Date	*Type of Expenditure*	*Amount*
June 10	Legal expenses to draft charter	$ 2,000
July 17	Commission to stockbroker for issuing and selling stock	40,000
July 18	Accounting fees to set up corporate books	2,400
July 20	Temporary directors' fees	1,000
August 25	Directors' fees	1,500
October 9	Legal fees to modify corporate charter	1,000

Heart's first tax year begins July 12 and ends on September 30. Heart may amortize organizational expenditures of $5,400. The legal expenses to modify the corporate charter may not be amortized because they were not incurred during the tax year in which Heart began to conduct its business. The commission for selling the Heart stock is treated as a reduction in the amount of Heart's paid-in capital. The directors' fees incurred in August are deducted as a trade or business expense under Sec. 162 because Heart had begun in business by that date. If Heart elects to amortize its organizational expenditures over 60 months, it deducts $90 ($5,400 ÷ 60) per month. Heart can claim a $180 deduction in its first tax year ($90 per month × 2 months).

The classification of expenses is summarized below.

			Type of Expenditure		
Date	*Expense*	*Amount*	*Organizational*	*Capital*	*Business*
6/10	Legal	$ 2,000	$2,000		
7/17	Commission	40,000		$40,000	
7/18	Accounting	2,400	2,400		
7/20	Directors' fees	1,000	1,000		
8/25	Directors' fees	1,500			$1,500
10/9	Legal	1,000		1,000	
	Total	$47,900	$5,400	$41,000	$1,500 ◀

If the corporation discontinues or disposes of the business before the end of the amortization period, it may deduct any remaining organizational expenditures as a loss.

START-UP EXPENDITURES. A distinction must be made between a corporation's organizational expenditures and its start-up expenditures. Start-up expenditures are ordinary and necessary business expenses paid or incurred by an individual or corporate taxpayer

- To investigate the creation or acquisition of an active trade or business
- To create an active trade or business
- To conduct an activity engaged in for profit or the production of income before the time the activity becomes an active trade or business

BOOK-TO-TAX ACCOUNTING COMPARISON

The capitalization of start-up expenses is required for tax purposes with amortization of the capitalized expenses permitted over 60 or more months. *Statement of Financial Accounting Standards No. 7* holds that the financial accounting practices and reporting standards used for development stage businesses should be no different for an established business. The two different sets of rules can lead to different reporting for tax and book purposes.

Examples of start-up expenditures include the costs incurred for a survey of potential markets; an analysis of available facilities; advertisements relating to opening the business; the training of employees; travel and other expenses for securing prospective distributors, suppliers, or customers; and the hiring of management personnel and outside consultants.

The expenditures must be such that, if they were incurred in connection with the operation of an existing active trade or business, they would be allowable as a deduction for the year in which they are paid or incurred. However, under Sec. 195, they must be capitalized.

Under Sec. 195, the corporation may elect to amortize start-up expenditures over a period of 60 or more months starting with the month in which an active trade or business begins. If the election is not made, the expenditures are capitalized and cannot be deducted until the corporation is liquidated. If the corporation discontinues or disposes of the business before the end of the amortization period, it may deduct any remaining start-up expenditures as a loss.

STOP & THINK

Question: What is the difference between an "organizational expenditure" and a "start-up" expenditure?

Solution: Organizational expenditures are outlays made in forming a corporation, such as fees paid to the state of incorporation for the corporate chapter and fees paid to an attorney to draft the documents needed to form the corporation. Start-up expenditures are outlays that otherwise would be deductible as "ordinary and necessary" business expenses but that are capitalized because they were incurred prior to the start of the corporation's business activities.

A corporation may elect to amortize both organizational expenditures and start-up expenditures over 60 or more months. Like a corporation, a partnership can capitalize and amortize its organizational and start-up expenditures, but not its syndication costs. A sole proprietorship may incur start-up expenditures that it can capitalize and amortize. However, sole proprietorships do not incur organizational expenditures.

LIMITATION ON DEDUCTIONS FOR ACCRUED COMPENSATION. If a corporation accrues an obligation to pay compensation, the payment must be made within 2½ months after the close of the corporation's tax year. Otherwise, the deduction cannot be taken until the year of payment.[16] The reason is that, if a payment is delayed beyond 2½ months, the IRS treats it as a deferred compensation plan. Deferred compensation cannot be deducted until the year payment is made and the recipient includes the payment in income.[17]

EXAMPLE C3-6 ▶ On December 10, 2002, Bell Corporation (a calendar year taxpayer) accrues an obligation for a $100,000 bonus to Marge, a sales representative who has had an outstanding year. Marge owns no Bell stock. Bell must make the payment by March 15, 2003. Otherwise, Bell Corporation cannot deduct the $100,000 on its 2002 tax return but must wait until the year it makes the payment. ◀

CHARITABLE CONTRIBUTIONS. The treatment of charitable contributions by individual and corporate taxpayers differs in three ways: the timing of the deduction, the amount of the deduction permitted for the contribution of certain nonmoney property, and the maximum deduction permitted in any given year.

Timing Of The Deduction. Corporations are allowed a deduction for contributions to qualified charitable organizations just as individuals are. Generally, the contribution must have been *paid* during the year (not just pledged) for a deduction to be allowed for a given year. A special rule applies to corporations using the accrual method of accounting (corporations using the cash or hybrid methods of accounting are not eligible).[18] These corporations may elect to treat part or all of a charitable contribution as having been made in the year in which it was accrued (instead of being deducted in the year paid) if

- ▶ The board of directors authorizes the contribution in the year it was accrued
- ▶ The corporation pays the contribution on or before the fifteenth day of the third month following the end of the accrual year.

The election is made by deducting the contribution on the corporation's tax return for the year it was accrued and attaching a copy of the board of director's resolution to the return. Any portion of the contribution for which the election is not made is deducted in the year it is paid.

EXAMPLE C3-7 ▶ Echo Corporation is a calendar year taxpayer using the accrual method of accounting. In 2002, its board of directors authorizes a $10,000 contribution to the Girl Scouts. Echo pays the contri-

[16] Temp. Reg. Sec. 1.404(b)-1T.
[17] Sec. 404(b).
[18] Sec. 170(a).

bution on March 10, 2003. Echo may elect to treat part or all of the contribution as having been paid in 2002. If the contribution is paid after March 15, 2003, it may not be deducted in 2002 but may be deducted in 2003. ◀

TAX STRATEGY TIP

The tax laws do not require a corporation to recognize a gain when it contributes appreciated property to a charitable organization. Thus, except for inventory and limited other properties, a corporation can deduct the FMV of its donation without having to recognize any appreciation in its gross income. On the other hand, a decline in the value of donated property is not deductible. Thus, the corporation should sell the loss property to recognize the loss and then donate the sales proceeds to the chariable organization.

Deducting Contributions Of Nonmonetary Property. If a taxpayer donates money to a qualified charitable organization, the amount of the charitable contribution deduction equals the amount of money donated. If the taxpayer donates property, the amount of the charitable contribution deduction generally equals the property's fair market value (FMV). However, special rules apply to donations of appreciated nonmonetary property known as ordinary income property and capital gain property.[19]

Ordinary income property is defined as property whose sale would have resulted in a gain other than a long-term capital gain (i.e., ordinary income or short-term capital gain). Examples of ordinary income property include investment property held for one year or less, inventory property, and property subject to recapture under Secs. 1245 and 1250. The deduction allowed for a donation of such property is limited to the property's FMV minus the amount of ordinary income or short-term capital gain that would have been recognized had the property been sold.

In three special cases, a corporate donor may deduct the donated property's adjusted basis plus one-half of the excess of the property's FMV over its adjusted basis (not to exceed twice the property's adjusted basis). This special rule applies to inventory if

1. The use of the property is related to the donee's exempt function, and it is used solely for the care of the ill, the needy, or infants;
2. The property is not transferred to the donee in exchange for money, other property, or services; and
3. The donor receives a statement from the charitable organization stating that conditions (1) and (2) will be complied with.

A similar rule applies to contributions of scientific research property if the taxpayer created the property and contributed it to a college, university, or tax-exempt scientific research organization for its use within two years of creating the property.

EXAMPLE C3-8 ▶ King Corporation donates inventory having a $26,000 adjusted basis and a $40,000 FMV to a qualified public charity. A $33,000 [$26,000 + (0.50 × $14,000)] deduction is allowed for the contribution of the inventory if the charitable organization will use the inventory for the care of the ill, needy, or infants, or if the donee is an educational institution or research organization that will use the scientific research property for research or experimentation. Otherwise, the deduction is limited to the property's $26,000 adjusted basis. If the inventory's FMV is instead $100,000 and the donation meets either of the two sets of requirements outlined above, the charitable contribution deduction is limited to $52,000, the lesser of the property's adjusted basis plus one-half of the appreciation [$63,000 = $26,000 + (0.50 × $74,000)] or twice the property's adjusted basis ($52,000 = $26,000 × 2). ◀

When a corporation donates appreciated property whose sale would result in long-term capital gain (also known as **capital gain property**) to a charitable organization, the amount of the contribution deduction generally equals the property's FMV. However, special restrictions apply if

- ▶ A corporation donates tangible personal property to a charitable organization and the organization's use of the property is unrelated to its tax-exempt purpose or
- ▶ A corporation donates appreciated property to certain private nonoperating foundations.[20]

In either case, the amount of the corporation's contribution is limited to the property's FMV minus the long-term capital gain that would have resulted from the property's sale.

EXAMPLE C3-9 ▶ Fox Corporation donates artwork to the MacNay Museum. The artwork, purchased two years earlier for $15,000, is worth $38,000 on the date of the gift. At the time of the donation, it is

---

[19] Sec. 170(e).

[20] Sec. 170(e)(5). The restriction on contributions of appreciated property to private nonoperating foundations does not apply to contributions of stock for which market quotations are readily available.

known that the MacNay Museum intends to sell the work to raise funds to conduct its activities. Fox's deduction for the gift is limited to $15,000. If the artwork is to be displayed by the MacNay Museum to be viewed by the public, the entire $38,000 deduction is permitted. Fox Corporation can avoid the loss of a portion of its charitable contribution deduction by placing restrictions on the sale or use of the property at the time it is donated. ◀

BOOK-TO-TAX ACCOUNTING COMPARISON

For financial accounting purposes, all charitable contributions can be claimed as an expense without regard to the amount of profits reported. Only the tax deduction for charitable contributions is limited.

Maximum Deduction Permitted. A limit applies to the amount of charitable contributions a corporation can deduct in a given year. The limit is calculated differently for corporations than for individuals. Contribution deductions by corporations are limited to 10% of adjusted taxable income. Adjusted taxable income is the corporation's taxable income computed without regard to any of the following:

- The charitable contribution deduction
- An NOL carryback
- A capital loss carryback
- Any dividends-received deduction[21]

Contributions that exceed the 10% limit are not deductible in the current year. Instead, they carry forward to the next five tax years. Any excess contributions not deducted within those five years are lost. The corporation may deduct excess contributions in the carryover year only after it deducts any contributions made in that year. The total charitable contribution deduction (including any deduction for contribution carryovers) is limited to 10% of the corporation's adjusted taxable income in the carryover year.[22]

EXAMPLE C3-10 ▶ Golf Corporation reports the following results in 2002 and 2003:

	2002	2003
Adjusted taxable income	$200,000	$300,000
Charitable contributions	35,000	25,000

Golf's 2002 contribution deduction is limited to $20,000 (0.10 × $200,000). Golf has a $15,000 ($35,000 − $20,000) contribution carryover to 2003. The 2003 contribution deduction is limited to $30,000 (0.10 × $300,000). Golf's deduction for 2003 is composed of the $25,000 donated in 2003 and $5,000 of the 2002 carryover. A $10,000 carryover from 2002 carries over to 2004, 2005, 2006, and 2007. ◀

Topic Review C3-1 summarizes the basic corporate charitable contribution deduction rules.

SPECIAL DEDUCTIONS

C corporations are allowed two special deductions: dividends-received deductions and NOL deductions.

BOOK-TO-TAX ACCOUNTING COMPARISON

Dividends are included in a corporation's financial accounting income, but no dividends-received deduction is permitted in determining a corporation's net income. The dividends-received deduction is avalable only when calculating taxable income.

DIVIDENDS-RECEIVED DEDUCTION. Any dividend a corporation receives because of owning stock in another corporation is included in its gross income. As was described in Chapter C2, the taxation of dividend payments to a shareholder generally results in double taxation. When the dividend payment is made to a corporate shareholder and the distributee corporation subsequently distributes these earnings to its shareholders, triple taxation of the earnings can result.

EXAMPLE C3-11 ▶ Adobe Corporation owns stock in Bell Corporation. Bell Corporation reports taxable income of $100,000 and pays federal income taxes on its income. Bell distributes its after-tax income to its shareholders. The dividend Adobe Corporation receives from Bell must be included in its gross income and, to the extent that it reports a profit for the year, Adobe will pay taxes on the dividend. Adobe Corporation distributes its remaining after-tax income to its shareholders. The shareholders must include Adobe's dividends in their gross income and generally end up paying federal income taxes on the distribution. Thus, Bell's income in this example is eventually taxed three times. ◀

[21] Sec. 170(b)(2).

[22] Sec. 170(d)(2).

Topic Review C3-1

Corporate Charitable Contribution Rules

1. Timing of the contribution deduction
   a. General rule: A deduction is allowed for contributions paid during the year.
   b. Accrual method of accounting corporations can accrue contributions approved by their board of directors prior to the end of the accrual year and paid within 2½ months of the end of the accrual year.
2. Amount of the contribution deduction
   a. General rule: A deduction is allowed for the amount of money and the FMV of other property donated.
   b. Exceptions for ordinary income property:
      1. If donated property would result in ordinary income or short-term capital gain being recognized if sold, the deduction is limited to the property's FMV minus this potential ordinary income or short-term capital gain. Thus, for gain property the deduction equals the property's cost or adjusted basis.
      2. Special rule: For donations of (1) inventory used for the care of the ill, needy, or infants or (2) scientific research property or computer technology and equipment to certain educational institutions, a corporate donor may deduct the property's basis plus one-half of the excess of the property's FMV over its adjusted basis. The deduction may not exceed twice the property's adjusted basis.
   c. Exceptions for capital gain property: If the corporation donates tangible personal property to a charitable organization for a use unrelated to its tax-exempt purpose, or the corporation donates appreciated property to a private nonoperating foundation, the corporation's contribution is limited to the property's FMV minus the long-term capital gain that would result if the property were sold.
3. Limitation on contribution deduction
   a. The contribution deduction is limited to 10% of the corporation's taxable income computed without regard to the charitable contribution deduction, any NOL or capital loss carryback, and any dividends-received deduction.
   b. Excess contributions carry forward for a five-year period.

To partially mitigate the effects of multiple taxation, corporations are allowed a **dividends-received deduction** for dividends received from other domestic corporations and from certain foreign corporations.

General Rule for Dividends-Received Deduction. Corporations that own less than 20% of the distributing corporation's stock may deduct 70% of the dividends received. If the shareholder corporation owns 20% or more of the distributing corporation's stock (both voting power and value) but less than 80% of such stock, it may deduct 80% of the dividends received.[23]

EXAMPLE C3-12 ▶ Hale Corporation reports the following results in the current year:

Gross income from operations	$300,000
Dividends from 15%-owned domestic corporation	100,000
Expenses	280,000

Hale's dividends-received deduction is $70,000 (0.70 × $100,000). Thus, Hale's taxable income is computed as follows:

Gross income	$400,000
Minus: Expenses	(280,000)
Taxable income before special deductions	$120,000
Minus: Dividends-received deduction	(70,000)
Taxable income	$50,000 ◀

Limitation on Dividends-Received Deduction. In the case of dividends received from corporations that are less than 20% owned, the deduction is limited to the lesser of 70% of dividends received or 70% of taxable income computed without regard to any NOL deduction, any capital loss carryback, or the dividends-received deduction itself.[24] In the case of dividends received from a 20% or more owned corporation, the dividends-

[23] Secs. 243(a) and (c).

[24] Sec. 246(b).

received deduction is limited to the lesser of 80% of dividends received or 80% of taxable income computed without regard to any NOL deduction, any capital loss carryback, or the dividends-received deduction itself.

EXAMPLE C3-13 ▶ Assume the same facts as in Example C3-12 except that Hale Corporation's expenses for the year are $310,000. Hale's taxable income before the dividends-received deduction is $90,000 ($300,000 + $100,000 − $310,000). The dividends-received deduction is limited to the lesser of 70% of dividends received ($70,000) or 70% of taxable income before the dividends-received deduction ($63,000 = $90,000 × 0.70). Thus, the dividends-received deduction is $63,000. Hale's taxable income is $27,000 ($90,000 − $63,000). ◀

A corporation that receives dividends eligible for both the 80% dividends-received deduction and the 70% dividends-received deduction must reduce taxable income by the aggregate amount of dividends eligible for the 80% deduction before computing the 70% deduction.

Exception to the Limitation. The taxable income limitation on the dividends-received deduction does not apply if, after taking into account the full dividends-received deduction, the corporation has an NOL for the year.

EXAMPLE C3-14 ▶ Assume the same facts as in Example C3-12 except that Hale Corporation's expenses for the year are $331,000. Hale's taxable income before the dividends-received deduction is $69,000 ($300,000 + $100,000 − $331,000). The tentative dividends-received deduction is $70,000 (0.70 × $100,000). Hale's dividends-received deduction is not restricted by the limitation of 70% of taxable income before the dividends-received deduction because, after taking into account the tentative $70,000 dividends-received deduction, the corporation has a $1,000 ($69,000 − $70,000) NOL for the year. ◀

The results of Examples C3-12, C3-13, and C3-14 are compared in the following table:

	Example C3-12	*Example C3-13*	*Example C3-14*
Gross income	$400,000	$400,000	$400,000
Minus: Expenses	(280,000)	(310,000)	(331,000)
Taxable income before special deductions	$120,000	$ 90,000	$ 69,000
Minus: Dividends-received deduction	(70,000)	(63,000)	(70,000)
Taxable income (NOL)	$ 50,000	$ 27,000	$ (1,000)

ADDITIONAL COMMENT

When the dividends-received deduction creates (or increases) an NOL, the corporation gets the full benefit of the deduction because it can carry back or carry forward the NOL.

The only case where the dividends-received deduction is not equal to the full 70% of the $100,000 dividend is Example C3-13. In that case, the deduction is limited to $63,000 because taxable income before special deductions is less than the $100,000 dividend *and* the full $70,000 deduction would not create an NOL. The special exception to the dividends-received deduction can create interesting situations. For example, the additional $21,000 of deductions incurred in Example C3-14 (as compared to Example C3-13) resulted in a $28,000 reduction in taxable income. Corporate taxpayers should be aware of these rules and consider deferring income or recognizing expenses to ensure being able to deduct the full 70% or 80% dividends-received deduction. If the taxable income limitation applies, the unused dividends-received deductions is lost.

TAX STRATEGY TIP

A corporation can avoid the dividends-received deduction limitation either by (1) increasing its taxable income before the dividends-received deduction so the limitation exceeds the tentative dividends-received deduction or (2) decreasing its taxable income before the dividends-received deduction so the tentative dividends-received deduction creates an NOL.

Members of an Affiliated Group. Members of an affiliated group of corporations can claim a 100% dividends-received deduction with respect to dividends received from other group members.[25] A group of corporations is affiliated if a parent corporation owns at least 80% of the stock (both voting power and value) of at least one subsidiary corporation and at least 80% of the stock (both voting power and value) of each other corpora-

[25] Sec. 243(a)(3).

tion is owned by other group members. The 100% dividends-received deduction is not subject to a taxable income limitation.[26]

Dividends Received from Foreign Corporations. The dividends-received deduction applies primarily to dividends received from domestic corporations. A dividends-received deduction is not allowed for dividends received from a foreign corporation because its income is not taxed by the U.S. government and, therefore, is not subject to the multiple taxation illustrated above.[27]

ADDITIONAL COMMENT

Stock purchased on which a dividend has been declared has an increased value. This value will drop when the dividend is paid. If the dividend is eligible for a dividends-received deduction and the drop in value also creates a capital loss, corporate shareholders could use this event as a tax planning device. To avoid this result, no dividends-received deduction is available for stock held 45 days or less.

Stock Held 45 Days or Less. A dividends-received deduction is not allowed to a corporation if it holds the dividend paying stock for less than 46 days during the 90-day period that begins 45 days before the stock becomes ex-dividend with respect to the dividend.[28] This rule prevents a corporation from claiming a dividends-received deduction if it purchases stock shortly before an ex-dividend date and sells the stock shortly thereafter. (The ex-dividend date is the first day on which a purchaser of stock is not entitled to a previously declared dividend.) Absent this rule, such a purchase and sale would allow the corporation to receive dividends at a low tax rate—a maximum of a 10.5% [(100% − 70%) × 0.35] effective tax rate—and to obtain a capital loss on the sale of stock that could offset capital gains taxed at a 35% tax rate.

EXAMPLE C3-15 ▶ Rose Corporation purchases 100 shares of Maine Corporation's stock (less than 1% of the outstanding stock) for $100,000 one day before Maine's ex-dividend date. Rose receives a $5,000 dividend on the stock. Rose sells the stock for $95,000 on the forty-fifth day *after* the dividend payment date. (Because the stock is worth $100,000 immediately before the $5,000 dividend is paid, the stock is worth $95,000 ($100,000 − $5,000) immediately after the dividend is paid.) The sale results in a $5,000 ($100,000 − $95,000) capital loss that may offset a $5,000 capital gain. The profit (loss) to Rose Corporation with and without the rule disallowing the dividends-received deduction on stock held less than 46 days is summarized below:

	If Deduction Is Allowed	*If Deduction Is Not Allowed*
Dividends	$5,000	$5,000
Minus: 35% tax on dividend	(525)[a]	(1,750)
Dividend (after taxes)	$4,475	$3,250
Capital loss	$5,000	$5,000
Minus: 35% tax savings on loss	(1,750)	(1,750)
Net loss on stock	$3,250	$3,250
Dividend (after taxes)	$4,475	$3,250
Minus: Net loss on stock	(3,250)	(3,250)
Net profit (loss)	$1,225	$ -0-

[a] [$5,000 − (0.70 × $5,000)] × 0.35 = $525

The profit is not available if Rose sells the stock shortly after receiving the dividend because Rose must hold the Maine stock for at least 46 days to obtain the dividends-received deduction. ◀

ADDITIONAL COMMENT

Borrowing money with deductible interest to purchase a tax-advantaged asset, such as stock eligible for the dividends-received deduction, is an example of "tax arbitrage." Many provisions in the IRC, such as the limits on debt-financial stock, are aimed at curtailing tax arbitrage transactions.

Debt-Financed Stock. The dividends-received deduction is not allowed to the extent the stock on which a dividend is paid is debt-financed (i.e., purchased with borrowed money).[29] This rule prevents a corporation from deducting interest paid on money borrowed to purchase the stock, while paying little or no tax on the dividends received on the stock.

EXAMPLE C3-16 ▶ Peach Corporation borrows $100,000 at a 10% interest rate to purchase 30% of Sun Corporation's stock. The Sun stock pays an $8,000 annual dividend. If a dividends-received

[26] Secs. 243(b)(5) and 1504.

[27] Sec. 245. A limited dividends-received deduction is allowed on dividends received from a foreign corporation that earns income by conducting a trade or business in the United States and, therefore, is subject to U.S. taxes.

[28] Sec. 246(c)(1).

[29] Sec. 246A.

deduction were allowed for this investment, Peach would have a net profit of $940 annually on owning the Sun stock even though the dividend received is less than the interest paid. The profit (loss) to Peach Corporation with and without the rule disallowing the dividends-received deduction on debt-financed stock is summarized below:

	If Deduction Is Allowed	*If Deduction Is Not Allowed*
Dividends	$ 8,000	$ 8,000
Minus: 35% tax on dividend	(560)[a]	(2,800)
Dividend (after taxes)	$ 7,440	$5,200
Interest paid	$10,000	$10,000
Minus: 35% tax savings on deduction	(3,500)	(3,500)
Net cost of borrowing	$ 6,500	$6,500
Dividend (after taxes)	$ 7,440	$ 5,200
Minus: net cost of borrowing	(6,500)	(6,500)
Net profit (loss)	$ 940	$(1,300)

[a] [$8,000 − (0.80 × $8,000)] × 0.35 = $560

This example illustrates how the rule disallowing the dividends-received deduction on debt-financed stock prevents corporations from making an after-tax profit by borrowing funds to purchase stocks paying dividends that are less than the cost of the borrowing. ◀

SELF-STUDY QUESTION

How does the calculation of an NOL differ for individual and corporate taxpayers?

ANSWER

An individual must make many adjustments to his or her taxable income to calculate his or her NOL. A corporation's NOL is simply the excess of its current deductions over its income.

NET OPERATING LOSSES (NOLs). If a corporation's deductions exceed its gross income for the year, the corporation has a **net operating loss (NOL)**. The NOL is the amount by which the corporation's deductions (including any dividends-received deduction) exceed its gross income.[30] In computing an NOL for a given year, no deduction is permitted for a carryover or carryback of an NOL from a preceding or succeeding year. However, unlike an individual's NOL, no other adjustments are required to compute a corporation's NOL.

A corporation's NOL carries back two years and carries forward 20 years. It carries to the earliest of the two preceding years first and offsets taxable income reported in that year. If the loss cannot be used in that year, it carries to the immediately preceding year, and then to the next 20 years in chronological order. The corporation may elect to forgo the carryback period entirely and instead carry the entire loss forward to the next 20 years.[31]

EXAMPLE C3-17 ▶ In 2002, Gray Corporation has gross income of $150,000 (including $100,000 from operations and $50,000 in dividends from a 30%-owned domestic corporation) and $180,000 of expenses. Gray has a $70,000 [$150,000 − $180,000 − (0.80 × $50,000)] NOL. The loss carries back to 2000 unless Gray elects to relinquish the carryback period. If Gray had $20,000 of taxable income in 2000, $20,000 of Gray's 2001 NOL offsets that income. Gray receives a refund of all taxes paid in 2000. Gray carries the remaining $50,000 of NOL from 2000 to 2001. ◀

A corporation might elect not to carry an NOL back because its income was taxed at a low marginal tax rate in the carryback period and the corporation anticipates income being taxed at a higher marginal tax rate in later years or because it used tax credit carryovers in the earlier year that were about to expire. The corporation must make this election for the entire carryback by the due date (including any permitted extensions) for filing the return for the year in which the corporation incurred the NOL. The corporation makes the election by checking a box on Form 1120 when it files the return. Once made for a tax year, the election is irrevocable.[32] However, if the corporation incurs an NOL in another year, the decision as to whether that NOL should be carried back is a separate decision. In other words, each year's NOL is treated separately and is subject to a separate election.

---

[30] Sec. 172(c).

[31] The two year carryback and 20-year carryforward applies to NOLs incurred in tax years beginning after August 5, 1997. The change does not apply to NOLs carried forward from earlier years. These NOLs are, in general, carried back three years and carried forward 15 years.

[32] Sec. 172(b)(3)(C).

To obtain a refund due to carrying an NOL back to a preceding year, a corporation must file either Form 1120X (Amended U.S. Corporation Income Tax Return) or Form 1139 (Corporation Application for a Tentative Refund).

THE SEQUENCING OF THE DEDUCTION CALCULATIONS. The rules for charitable contributions deductions, dividends-received deductions, and NOL deductions require that these deductions be taken in the correct sequence. Otherwise, the computation of these deductions may be incorrect. The correct order for taking deductions is

1. All deductions other than the charitable contributions deduction, the dividends-received deduction, and the NOL deduction
2. The charitable contributions deduction
3. The dividends-received deduction
4. The NOL deduction

As stated previously, the charitable contributions deduction is limited to 10% of taxable income before the charitable contributions deduction, any NOL or capital loss carryback, or any dividends-received deduction, but *after* any NOL carryover deduction. Once the charitable contributions deduction has been computed, any NOL carryover deduction must be added back and the charitable contributions deduction subtracted before the dividends-received deduction is computed and subtracted. Then the NOL deduction is subtracted.

EXAMPLE C3-18 ▶ East Corporation reports the following results:

Gross income from operations	$150,000
Dividends from 30%-owned domestic corporation	100,000
Operating expenses	100,000
Charitable contributions	30,000

In addition, East has a $40,000 NOL carryforward available. East's charitable contributions deduction is computed as follows:

Gross income from operations	$150,000
Plus: Dividends	100,000
Gross income	$250,000
Minus: Operating expenses	(100,000)
NOL carryforward	(40,000)
Base for calculation of the charitable contributions limitation	$110,000

East's charitable contributions deduction is limited to $11,000 (0.10 × $110,000). The $11,000 limitation means that East has a $19,000 ($30,000 − $11,000) excess contribution that carries forward for five years. East Corporation computes its taxable income as follows:

Gross income	$250,000
Minus: Operating expenses	(100,000)
Charitable contributions deduction	(11,000)
Taxable income before special deductions	$139,000
Minus: Dividends-received deduction	(80,000)
NOL carryover deduction	(40,000)
Taxable income	$ 19,000

East's dividends-received deduction is $80,000 (0.80 × $100,000). The entire NOL carryforward is deductible because taxable income before the NOL deduction is $59,000 ($139,000 − $80,000). ◀

Note that if an NOL is carried *back* from a later year, it is *not* taken into account in computing a corporation's charitable contributions limitation. In other words, the contribution deduction remains the same as it was in the year the return was filed.

EXAMPLE C3-19 ▶ Assume the same facts as in Example C3-17 except that East instead has a $40,000 NOL carryback from a later year. East's base for calculation of the charitable contributions limitation was computed as follows when the return was originally filed:

ADDITIONAL COMMENT

These computations in the carry-back year are done on an amended return or an application for refund.

Gross income from operations	$150,000
Plus: Dividends	100,000
Gross income	$250,000
Minus: Operating expenses	(100,000)
Base for calculation of the charitable contributions limitation	$150,000

East's charitable contributions deduction was limited to $15,000 (0.10 × $150,000). The $15,000 limitation means that East has a $15,000 ($30,000 − $15,000) contribution carryforward. East Corporation computes its taxable income after the NOL carryback as follows:

Gross income	$250,000
Minus: Operating expenses	(100,000)
Charitable contributions deduction	(15,000)
Taxable income before special deductions	$135,000
Minus: Dividends-received deduction	(80,000)
NOL carryback deduction	(40,000)
Taxable income as recomputed	$ 15,000

East's dividends-received deduction remains $80,000 as in the preceding example. The entire NOL carryback is deductible because taxable income before the NOL deduction was $55,000 ($135,000 − $80,000). ◀

STOP & THINK

Question: Why does a corporation's NOL or capital loss carryback not affect its charitable contribution deduction, but yet an NOL or capital loss carryforward must be taken into account when calculating its charitable contribution limition?

Solution: Remember that a carryback will affect a tax return for a prior year already filed. If a carryback had to be taken into account when calculating the charitable contribution deduction limitation in the prior year, it might change the amount of the allowable charitable contribution. This change in turn might affect other items such as the carryback year's dividends-received deduction and some later years' deductions as well. For example, assume Alpha Corporation has a $10,000 NOL in 2002 that it carries back to 2000. If the NOL were permitted to reduce Alpha's allowable charitable contribution for 2000 by $1,000, Alpha's dividends-received deduction for 2000 and its charitable contribution deductions for 2001 as well might change.

To avoid these complications, which might force Alpha to amend its tax returns from the carryback year (2000) to the current year (2002), the law states that carrybacks are not taken into account in calculating the charitable contribution deduction limitation. Also, in the prior year, management made its charitable contribution decisions without knowledge of future NOLs. Altering the result of those prior decisions with future events might be unfair.

EXCEPTIONS FOR CLOSELY-HELD CORPORATIONS

Congress has placed certain limits on certain transactions to prevent abuse in situations where a corporation is closely held. Some of these restrictions are explained below.

TRANSACTIONS BETWEEN A CORPORATION AND ITS SHAREHOLDERS. Special rules apply to transactions between a corporation and a controlling shareholder. Section 1239 may convert a capital gain realized on the sale of depreciable property between a corporation and a controlling shareholder into ordinary income. Section 267(a)(1) denies a deduction for losses realized on property sales between a corporation and a controlling shareholder. Section 267(a)(2) defers a deduction for accrued expenses and interest on certain transactions involving a corporation and a controlling shareholder.

In all three of the preceding situations, a controlling shareholder is defined as one who owns more than 50% (in value) of the corporation's stock.[33] In determining whether a

[33] Sec. 267(b)(2).

shareholder owns more than 50% of a corporation's stock, certain constructive stock ownership rules apply.[34] Under these rules, a shareholder is considered to own not only his or her own stock, but stock owned by family members (e.g., brothers, sisters, spouse, ancestors, and lineal descendants) and entities in which the shareholder has an ownership or beneficial interest (e.g., corporations, partnerships, trusts, and estates).

Gains on Sale or Exchange Transactions. If a controlling shareholder sells depreciable property to a controlled corporation (or vice versa) and the property is depreciable in the purchaser's hands, any gain on the sale is treated as ordinary income under Sec. 1239(a).

EXAMPLE C3-20 ▶ Ann owns all of Cape Corporation's stock. Ann sells a building to Cape Corporation and recognizes a $25,000 gain, which usually would be Sec. 1231 gain or Sec. 1250 gain (taxed at a maximum 20% or 25% tax rate, respectively). However, because Ann owns more than 50% of the Cape stock and the building is a depreciable property in Cape Corporation's hands, Sec. 1239 causes the entire $25,000 gain to be ordinary income to Ann. ◀

BOOK-TO-TAX ACCOUNTING COMPARISON

The denial of deductions for losses involving related party transactions is unique to the tax area. No similar disallowance rule is found in the financial accounting rules.

Losses on Sale or Exchange Transactions. Section 267(a)(1) denies a deduction for losses realized on a sale of property by a corporation to a controlling shareholder or on a sale of property by the controlling shareholder to the corporation. If the purchaser later sells the property to another party at a gain, the seller recognizes gain only to the extent that it exceeds the previously disallowed loss.[35] Should the purchaser instead sell the property at a loss, the disallowed loss is never recognized.

EXAMPLE C3-21 ▶ Hope Corporation sells an automobile to Juan, its sole shareholder, for $6,500. The corporation's adjusted basis for the automobile is $8,000. Hope realizes a $1,500 ($6,500 – $8,000) loss on the sale. Section 267(a)(1) disallows the loss to the corporation. If Juan later sells the auto for $8,500, he realizes a $2,000 ($8,500 – $6,500) gain. He recognizes only $500 of that gain, the amount by which his $2,000 gain exceeds the $1,500 loss previously disallowed to Hope Corporation. If Juan instead sells the auto for $7,500, he realizes a $1,000 ($7,500-$6,500) gain but recognizes no gain or loss. The previously disallowed loss reduces the gain to zero but may not create a loss. If Juan instead sells the auto for $4,000, he realizes and may be able to recognize a $2,500 ($4,000 – $6,500) loss. However, the $1,500 loss disallowed to Hope Corporation is permanently lost. ◀

KEY POINT

Section 267(a)(2) is primarily aimed at the situation involving an accrual method corporation that accrues compensation to a cash method shareholder-employee. This provision forces a matching of the income and expense recognition by deferring the deduction to the day the shareholder recognizes the income.

Corporation and Controlling Shareholder Using Different Accounting Methods. Section 267(a)(2) defers a deduction for accrued expenses or interest owed by a corporation to a controlling shareholder or by a controlling shareholder to a corporation when the two parties use different accounting methods and the payee will include the accrued expense as part of gross income at a date later than when the payer accrues the deduction. Under this rule, accrued expenses or interest owed by a corporation to a controlling shareholder may not be deducted until the day the shareholder includes the payment in gross income.

EXAMPLE C3-22 ▶ Hill Corporation uses the accrual method of accounting. Hill's sole shareholder, Ruth, uses the cash method of accounting. Both taxpayers use the calendar year as their tax year. The corporation accrues a $25,000 interest payment to Ruth on December 20, 2002. Hill Corporation makes the payment on March 20, 2003. Hill Corporation, however, cannot deduct the interest in 2002 but must wait until Ruth reports the income in 2003. Thus, the expense and income are matched. ◀

LOSS LIMITATION RULES

At-Risk Rules If five or fewer shareholders own more than 50% of the value of the outstanding stock of a C corporation at any time during the last half of the corporation's tax year, the corporation is subject to the at-risk rules.[36] In such case, the corporation's losses for any activity are deductible only to the extent the corporation is at risk for that activity

[34] Sec. 267(e)(3).
[35] Sec. 267(d).
[36] Sec. 465(a).

at the close of its tax year. Any losses not deductible because of the at-risk rules must be carried over and deducted in a succeeding year when the corporation's risk with respect to the activity has increased. (See Chapter C9 for additional discussion of the at-risk rules and the at-risk amount.)

Passive Activity Limitation Rules. Personal service corporations (PSCs) and **closely held C corporations** (those subject to the at-risk rules described above) may be subject to the **passive activity limitations.**[37] If a PSC does not meet the material participation requirements, its net **passive losses** and credits must be carried over to a year when it has **passive income.** In the case of closely held C corporations that do not meet material participation requirements, passive losses and credits are allowed to offset the corporation's net active income but not its portfolio income (i.e., interest, dividends, annuities, royalties, and capital gains on the sale of investment property).[38]

COMPUTING A CORPORATION'S INCOME TAX LIABILITY

OBJECTIVE 3

Compute a corporation's income tax liability

Once a corporation's taxable income has been computed, the next step is to compute the corporation's tax liability for the year. Table C3-2 outlines the steps for computing a corporation's regular (income) tax liability. This section explains the steps involved in arriving at a corporation's income tax liability in detail.

GENERAL RULES

REAL WORLD EXAMPLE

In 2000, the IRS collected $236 billion from corporations, which was 11.2% of the $2.1 trillion collected by the IRS.

All C corporations (other than members of controlled groups of corporations and personal service corporations) use the same tax rate schedule to compute their **regular tax** liability. These rates are shown below and are reproduced on the inside back cover.

Taxable Income Over	*But Not Over*	*The Tax Is*	*Of the Amount Over*
$ -0-	$50,000	15%	$ -0-
50,000	75,000	$7,500 + 25%	50,000
75,000	100,000	13,750 + 34%	75,000
100,000	335,000	22,250 + 39%	100,000
335,000	10,000,000	113,900 + 34%	335,000
10,000,000	15,000,000	3,400,000 + 35%	10,000,000
15,000,000	18,333,333	5,150,000 + 38%	15,000,000
18,333,333	—	6,416,667 + 35%	18,333,333

EXAMPLE C3-23 ▶ Copper Corporation reports taxable income of $100,000. Copper's regular tax liability is computed as follows:

Tax on first $50,000:	0.15 × $50,000 =	$7,500
Tax on second $25,000:	0.25 × 25,000 =	6,250
Tax on remaining $25,000:	0.34 × 25,000 =	8,500
Regular tax liability		$22,250

This tax liability also can be determined from the above tax rate schedule. ◀

If taxable income exceeds $100,000, a 5% surcharge applies to the corporation's taxable income exceeding $100,000. The maximum surcharge is $11,750. The surcharge phases out the lower graduated tax rates that apply to the first $75,000 of taxable income for corporations earning between $100,000 and $335,000 [$11,750 = ($335,000 − $100,000) × 0.05] of taxable income. The tax rates listed above incorporate the 5% sur-

[37] Secs. 469(a)(2)(B) and (C).

[38] Sec. 469(e)(2).

▼ **TABLE C3-2**
Computation of the Corporate Regular (Income) Tax Liability

Taxable income
Times: Income tax rates
Regular tax liability
Minus: Foreign tax credit (Sec. 27)
Regular tax
Minus: General business credit (Sec. 38)
Minimum tax credit (Sec. 53)
Nonconventional fuels production credit (Sec. 29)
Credit for qualified electric vehicles (Sec. 30)
Puerto Rican economic activity credit (Sec. 30A)
Nonhighway use of gasoline and special fuels credit (Sec. 34)
Plus: Recapture of previously claimed tax credits
Income tax liability

charge by imposing a 39% (34% + 5%) rate on taxable income from $100,000 to $335,000.

EXAMPLE C3-24 ▶ Delta Corporation has taxable income of $200,000. Delta's regular tax liability is computed as follows:

Tax on first $50,000:	0.15 × $ 50,000 =	$ 7,500
Tax on next $25,000:	0.25 × 25,000 =	6,250
Tax on remaining $125,000:	0.34 × 125,000 =	42,500
Surcharge (income over $100,000):	0.05 × 100,000 =	5,000
Regular tax liability		$61,250

Alternatively, from the above tax rate schedule, the tax is $22,250 + [0.39 × ($200,000 − $100,000)] = $61,250. ◀

If taxable income is at least $335,000 but less than $10 million, the corporation pays a flat 34% tax rate on all of its taxable income. A corporation whose income is at least $10 million but less than $15 million pays $3.4 million plus 35% of the income above $10 million.

EXAMPLE C3-25 ▶ Elgin Corporation has taxable income of $350,000. Elgin's regular tax liability is $119,000 (0.34 × $350,000). If Elgin's taxable income is instead $12 million, its tax liability is $4.1 million [$3,400,000 + (0.35 × $2,000,000)]. ◀

If a corporation's taxable income exceeds $15 million, a 3% surcharge applies to the corporation's taxable income exceeding $15 million (but not exceeding $18,333,333). The maximum surcharge is $100,000. The surcharge phases out the one percentage point lower rate (34% vs. 35%) that applies to the first $10 million of taxable income. A corporation whose taxable income exceeds $18,333,333 pays a flat 35% tax rate on all its taxable income.

STOP & THINK *Question:* Planner Corporation has an opportunity to realize $50,000 of additional income in either the current year or next year. Planner has some discretion as to the timing of this additional income. Not counting the additional income, Planner's current year taxable income is $200,000, and it expects next year's taxable income to be $500,000. In what year should Planner recognize the additional $50,000?

Solution: Even though Planner's current year taxable income is lower than next year's expected taxable income, Planner will have a lower marginal tax rate next year. The current year's marginal tax rate is 39% because Planner's taxable income is in the 5% surtax range (or 39% "bubble"). Next year's taxable income is beyond the 39% bubble and is in the flat 34% range. Thus, Planner can save $2,500 (0.05 × $50,000) in taxes by deferring the $50,000 until next year.

PERSONAL SERVICE CORPORATIONS

Personal service corporations are denied the benefit of the graduated corporate tax rates. Thus, all the income of personal service corporations is taxed at a flat 35% rate.

Section 448(d) defines a personal service corporation as a corporation that meets the following two tests:

- Substantially all of its activities involve the performance of services in the fields of health, law, engineering, architecture, accounting, actuarial science, performing arts, and consulting.
- Substantially all of its stock (by value) is held directly or indirectly by employees performing the services or retired employees who performed the services in the past, their estates, or persons who hold stock in the corporation by reason of the death of an employee or retired employee within the past two years.

This rule encourages employee-owners of personal service corporations to withdraw earnings from the corporation as deductible salary (rather than have the corporation retain them) or make an S election.

CONTROLLED GROUPS OF CORPORATIONS

OBJECTIVE 4

Explain what a controlled group is and the tax consequences of being a controlled group

Special tax rules apply to corporations under common control to prevent them from avoiding taxes that otherwise would be due. The rules apply to corporations that meet the definition of a controlled group of corporations. This section explains why special rules apply to controlled groups, how controlled groups are defined, and what special rules apply to controlled groups.

WHY SPECIAL RULES ARE NEEDED

Special controlled group rules prevent shareholders from using multiple corporations to avoid having corporate income taxed at a 35% rate. If these rules were not in effect, the owners of a corporation could allocate the corporation's income among two or more corporations and take advantage of the lower 15%, 25%, and 34% rates on the first $10 million of corporate income for each corporation.

The following example demonstrates how a group of shareholders could obtain a significant tax advantage by dividing a business enterprise among several corporate entities. Each corporation then would be able to take advantage of the graduated corporate tax rates. To prevent a group of shareholders from using multiple corporations to gain such tax advantages, Congress enacted laws that limit the tax benefits of multiple corporations.[39]

EXAMPLE C3-26 ▶ Axle Corporation has taxable income of $450,000. Axle's regular tax liability on that income is $153,000 (0.34 × $450,000). If Axle's taxable income could be divided equally among six corporations ($75,000 apiece), each corporation's federal income tax liability would be $13,750 [(0.15 × $50,000) + (0.25 × $25,000)], or a total regular tax liability of $82,500 for all the corporations. Thus, Axle could save $70,500 ($153,000 − $82,500) in federal income taxes. ◀

The law governing controlled corporations operates by requiring special treatment for two or more corporations controlled by the same shareholder or group of shareholders. The most important restrictions on a controlled group of corporations are that the group

[39] Secs. 1561 and 1563.

must share the benefits of the progressive corporate tax rate schedule and pay a 5% surcharge on the group's taxable income exceeding $100,000, up to a maximum surcharge of $11,750, and also pay a 3% surcharge on the group's taxable income exceeding $15 million, up to a maximum surcharge of $100,000.

EXAMPLE C3-27 ▶ White, Blue, Yellow, and Green Corporations belong to a controlled group. Each corporation has $100,000 of taxable income (a total of $400,000). Only one $50,000 amount is taxed at 15% and only one $25,000 amount is taxed at 25%. Furthermore, the group is subject to the maximum $11,750 surcharge because its total taxable income exceeds $335,000. This surcharge is levied on the group member(s) that received the benefit of the 15 and 25% rates. Therefore, the group's total regular tax liability is $136,000 (0.34 × $400,000), the same as though the entire $400,000 were earned by one corporation. ◀

WHAT IS A CONTROLLED GROUP?

A **controlled group** is comprised of two or more corporations owned directly or indirectly by the same shareholder or group of shareholders. Controlled groups fall into three categories: a parent-subsidiary controlled group, a brother-sister controlled group, and a combined controlled group. Each of these groups is subject to the limitations described above.

PARENT-SUBSIDIARY CONTROLLED GROUPS. In a **parent-subsidiary controlled group**, one corporation (the parent corporation) must own directly at least 80% of the voting power of all classes of voting stock, or 80% of the total value of all classes of stock, of a second corporation (the subsidiary corporation).[40] The group can contain more than one subsidiary corporation. If the parent corporation, the subsidiary corporation, or any other members of the controlled group in total own at least 80% of the voting power of all classes of voting stock, or 80% of the total value of all classes of stock, of another corporation, that other corporation also is included in the parent-subsidiary controlled group.

EXAMPLE C3-28 ▶ Parent Corporation owns 80% of Axle Corporation's single class of stock and 40% of Wheel Corporation's single class of stock. Axle Corporation also owns 40% of Wheel's stock. Parent, Axle, and Wheel are members of the same parent-subsidiary controlled group because Parent directly owns 80% of Axle's stock and therefore is its parent corporation, and Wheel's stock is 80% owned by Parent (40%) and Axle (40%). (See Figure C3-2.)

If Parent and Axle together owned only 70% of Wheel's stock and the remaining 30% was owned by an unrelated shareholder, Wheel would not be included in the parent-subsidiary group. The controlled group then would consist only of Parent and Axle Corporations. ◀

EXAMPLE C3-29 ▶ Beta Corporation owns 70% of Cove Corporation's single class of stock and 60% of Red Corporation's single class of stock. Blue Corporation owns the remaining stock of Cove Corporation (30%) and Red Corporation (40%). No combination of these corporations forms a parent-subsidiary group because there is no direct stock ownership by one corporation of at least 80% of any other corporation's stock. ◀

BROTHER-SISTER CONTROLLED GROUPS. A group of two or more corporations is a **brother-sister controlled group** if five or fewer individuals, trusts, or estates own

- At least 80% of the voting power of all classes of voting stock (or at least 80% of the total value of the outstanding stock) of each corporation, and
- More than 50% of the voting power of all classes of stock (or more than 50% of the total value of the outstanding stock) of each corporation, taking into account only the stock ownership that each person has that is common with respect to each corporation.[41] A shareholder's common ownership is the percentage of stock the shareholder

---

[40] Sec. 1563(a)(1). Section 1563(d)(1) requires that certain attribution rules apply to determine stock ownership for parent-subsidiary controlled groups. If any person has an option to acquire stock, such stock is considered to be owned by the person having the option. Certain types of stock are excluded by Sec. 1563(c) from the controlled group definition of stock.

[41] Sec. 1563(a)(2). Section 1563(d)(2) requires that certain attribution rules apply to determine stock ownership for brother-sister controlled groups. If any person has an option to acquire stock, such stock is considered to be owned by the person having the option. A proportionate amount of stock owned by a partnership, estate, or trust is attributed to partners having an interest of 5% or more in the capital or profits of the partnership or beneficiaries having a 5% or more actuarial interest in the estate or trust. A proportionate amount of stock owned by a corporation is attributed to shareholders owning 5% or more in value of the corporate stock. Family attribution rules also can cause an individual to be considered to own the stock of a spouse, child, grandchild, parent, or grandparent.

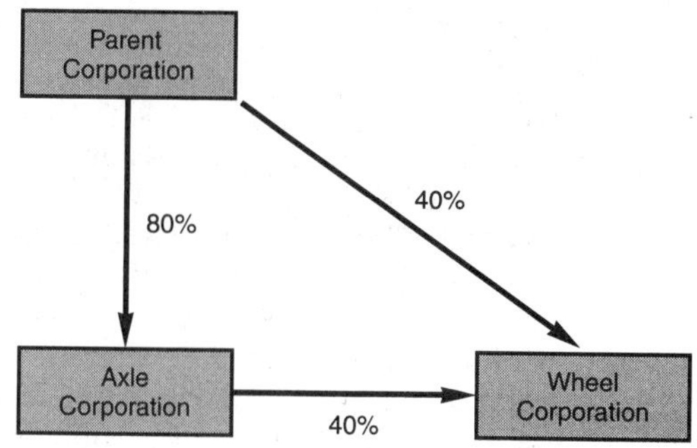

FIGURE C3-2 ▶ PARENT-SUBSIDIARY CONTROLLED GROUP (EXAMPLE C3-28)

owns that is common or identical in each of the corporations. If, for example, a shareholder owns 30% of New Corporation and 70% of Old Corporation, his or her common ownership is 30%.

Thus, it is not sufficient for five or fewer shareholders to own 80% or more of the stock of two corporations. The shareholders also must have more than 50% common ownership in the corporations for them to be brother-sister corporations.

EXAMPLE C3-30 ▶ North and South Corporations have only one class of stock outstanding, owned by the following individuals:

	Stock Ownership Percentages		
Shareholder	*North Corp.*	*South Corp.*	*Common Ownership*
Walt	30%	70%	30%
Gail	70%	30%	30%
Total	100%	100%	60%

Five or fewer individuals (Walt and Gail) own at least 80% (they own 100%) of each corporation's stock, and the same individuals own more than 50% (they own 60%) of each corporation's stock, taking into account only their common ownership in both corporations. Because both tests are satisfied, North and South Corporations are a brother-sister controlled group (see Figure C3-3). ◀

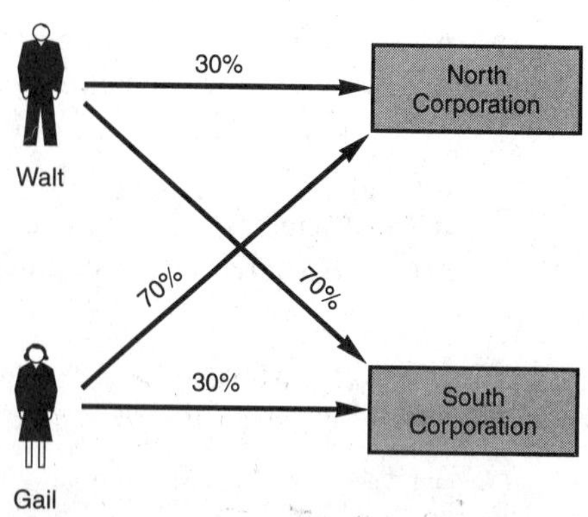

FIGURE C3-3 ▶ BROTHER-SISTER CONTROLLED GROUP (EXAMPLE C3-30)

EXAMPLE C3-31 ▶ East and West Corporations have only one class of stock outstanding, owned by the following individuals:

	Stock Ownership Percentages		
Shareholder	*East Corp.*	*West Corp.*	*Common Ownership*
Javier	80%	25%	25%
Sara	20%	75%	20%
Total	100%	100%	45%

Five or fewer individuals (Javier and Sara) own at least 80% (they own 100%) of each corporation's stock. However, those same individuals own only 45% of each corporation's stock, taking into account only their common ownership. Because the more-than-50% test is not satisfied, East and West Corporations are not a brother-sister controlled group. Because they are not members of a controlled group, each corporation is taxed on its own income without regard to the earnings of the other. ◀

TYPICAL MISCONCEPTION

The application of the 50% common ownership test for purposes of the brother-sister controlled group definition is confusing. Examples C3-30 and C3-31 illustrate a case when the 50% test is satisfied and one when it is not satisfied. Also note that both the 80% *and* the 50% tests must be satisfied for a brother-sister controlled group to exist.

An individual's stock ownership can be counted for the 80% test only if that individual owns stock in each and every corporation in the controlled group.[42]

EXAMPLE C3-32 ▶ Toy and Robot Corporations each have only a single class of stock outstanding, owned by the following individuals:

	Stock Ownership Percentages		
Shareholder	*Toy Corp.*	*Robot Corp.*	*Common Ownership*
Ali	50%	40%	40%
Beth	20%	60%	20%
Carol	30%	—	—
Total	100%	100%	60%

Carol's stock is not counted for purposes of Toy's 80% stock ownership requirement because she owns no stock in Robot Corporation. Only Ali and Beth's stock holdings are counted, and together they own only 70% of Toy Corporation's stock. Thus, the 80% test is failed, and Toy and Robot Corporations are *not* a brother-sister controlled group of corporations. ◀

COMBINED CONTROLLED GROUPS. A **combined controlled group** is comprised of three or more corporations meeting the following criteria:

- Each corporation is a member of a parent-subsidiary controlled group or a brother-sister controlled group
- At least one of the corporations is both the parent corporation of a parent-subsidiary controlled group and a member of a brother-sister controlled group.[43]

EXAMPLE C3-33 ▶ Able, Best, and Coast Corporations each have a single class of stock outstanding, owned by the following shareholders:

	Stock Ownership Percentages		
Shareholder	*Able Corp.*	*Coast Corp.*	*Best Corp.*
Art	50%	50%	—
Barbara	50%	50%	—
Able Corp.	—	—	100%

Able and Coast Corporations are a brother-sister controlled group because Art and Barbara satisfy both the 80% and 50% tests. Able and Best Corporations are a parent-subsidiary controlled group because Able owns all of Best's stock. Each of the three corporations is a member of either the parent-subsidiary controlled group (Able and Best) or the brother-sister controlled group (Able and Coast), and the parent corporation (Able) of the parent-subsidiary controlled group also is a member of the brother-sister controlled group. Therefore, Able, Best, and Coast Corporations are members of a combined controlled group (see Figure C3-4). ◀

KEY POINT

The combined controlled group definition does just what its name implies: It combines a parent-subsidiary controlled group and a brother-sister controlled group. Thus, instead of trying to apply the controlled group rules to two different groups, the combined group definition eliminates the issue by combining the groups into one controlled group.

[42] Reg. Sec. 1.1563-1(a)(3).

[43] Sec. 1563(a)(3).

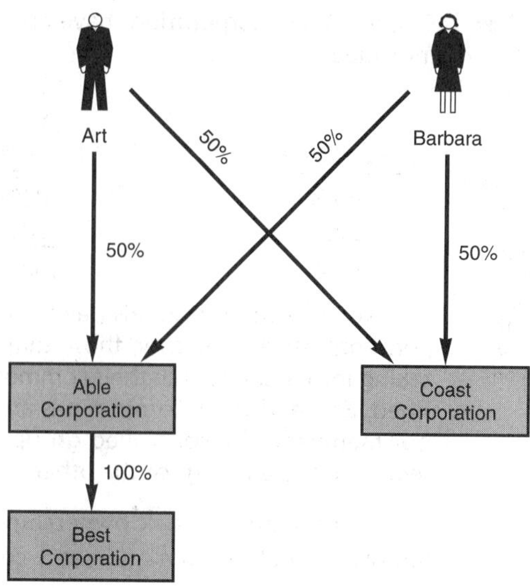

FIGURE C3-4 ▶ COMBINED CONTROLLED GROUP (EXAMPLE C3-33)

APPLICATION OF THE CONTROLLED GROUP TEST

The controlled group test generally is applied on December 31. A corporation is included in a controlled group if it is a group member on December 31 and has been a group member on at least one-half of the days in its tax year that precede December 31. A corporation that is not a group member on December 31 is considered a member for the tax year if it has been a group member on at least one-half the days in its tax year that precede December 31. Corporations are excluded from the controlled group if they were members for less than one-half of the days in their tax year that precede December 31 or if they retain certain special tax statuses such as being a tax-exempt corporation.

EXAMPLE C3-34 ▶ Ace and Copper Corporations are members of a parent-subsidiary controlled group of which Ace is the common parent corporation. Both corporations are calendar year taxpayers and have been group members for the entire year. They do not file a consolidated return. Bell Corporation, which has a fiscal year ending on August 31, becomes a group member on December 1, 2002. Although Bell is a group member on December 31, 2002, it has been a group member for less than half of the days in its tax year that precede December 31—only 30 of 121 days starting on September 1. Therefore, Bell is *not* a component member of the Ace-Copper controlled group for its tax year beginning on September 1, 2002. ◀

SPECIAL RULES APPLYING TO CONTROLLED GROUPS

As discussed earlier, if two or more corporations are members of a controlled group, the member corporations are limited to a total of $50,000 being taxed at 15%, $25,000 being taxed at 25%, and $9,925,000 million being taxed at 34%—the reduced tax rates found in Sec. 11(b).

TAX STRATEGY TIP

A controlled group of corporations should elect to apportion the tax benefits in a manner that will maximize the tax savings from the tax benefits. See Tax Planning Considerations later in this chapter for details.

In addition, a controlled group must apportion certain other tax benefits among its group members. Among the items requiring allocation are

- The $250,000 minimum accumulated earnings tax credit
- The $25,000 amount for general business tax credit limitation purposes
- The $40,000 statutory exemption for the alternative minimum tax
- The $20,000 (in 2001) of depreciable assets that can be expensed annually
- The $100,000 exemption for the 5% surcharge on taxable income and the $15 million exemption for the 3% surcharge on taxable income.

Furthermore, under Sec. 267(a)(1), no deduction is allowed for any loss on the sale or exchange of property between two members of the same controlled group. However, in contrast to losses between a corporation and controlling shareholder described earlier in this chapter, a loss realized on a transaction between members of a controlled group is deferred (instead of being disallowed). The selling member recognizes the entire deferred loss when the property that was sold or exchanged in the intragroup transaction is sold outside the controlled group. Under Sec. 267(a)(2), no deduction is allowed for certain accrued expenses or interest owed by one member of a controlled group to another member of the same controlled group when the two corporations use different accounting methods so that the payments would be reported in different tax years. (See page C3-19 for a detailed discussion of Sec. 267.) The Sec. 1239 rules that convert capital gain into ordinary income on depreciable property sales between related parties also apply to sales or exchanges involving two members of the same controlled group.

CONSOLIDATED TAX RETURNS

WHO CAN FILE A CONSOLIDATED RETURN. Some groups of related corporations (i.e., affiliated groups) may elect to file a single income tax return called a **consolidated tax return.** An **affiliated group** is one or more chains of includible corporations connected through stock ownership with a common parent,[44] but only if the following criteria are met:

TYPICAL MISCONCEPTION

The definitions of a parent-subsidiary controlled group and an affiliated group are similar, but not identical. For example, the 80% stock ownership test for controlled group purposes is satisfied if 80% of the voting power *or* 80% of the FMV of a corporation's stock is owned. For purposes of an affiliated group, 80% of both the voting power *and* the FMV of a corporation's stock must be owned.

- ▶ The common parent directly owns stock with at least 80% of the voting power and 80% of the value of at least one includible corporation.
- ▶ Stock with at least 80% of the voting power and 80% of the value of each other corporation included in the affiliated group is owned directly by one or more group members.[45]

Many parent-subsidiary controlled groups also qualify as affiliated groups and thus are eligible to file a consolidated return in place of separate tax returns for each corporation. The parent-subsidiary portion of a combined group also can file a consolidated tax return if it qualifies as an affiliated group. Brother-sister controlled groups, however, are not eligible to file consolidated returns because the requisite parent-subsidiary relationship does not exist.

An affiliated group makes the election to file a consolidated tax return by filing Form 1120, which includes all the income and expenses of each of its members. Each corporate member of the affiliated group must consent to the original election. Thereafter, any new member of the affiliated group is required to join in the return.

SELF-STUDY QUESTION

What is probably the most common reason for making a consolidated return election?

ANSWER

Filing consolidated returns allows the group to offset losses of one corporation against the profits of other members of the group.

ADVANTAGES OF FILING A CONSOLIDATED RETURN. A consolidated return is, in effect, one tax return for the entire affiliated group of corporations. The main advantages of filing a consolidated return are

- ▶ Profits of one member of the group can be offset against losses of another member of the group.
- ▶ Capital gains of one member of the group can be offset against capital losses of another member of the group.
- ▶ Profits or gains reported on intercompany transactions are deferred until a sale outside the group takes place (i.e., if one member sells property to another member, the gain is postponed until the member sells the property to someone outside the affiliated group).

If the group members file separate returns, members with NOLs or capital losses must either carry back these losses to earlier years or carry them forward to future years. Although the losses of one group member can offset the profits of another group member when the group files a consolidated return, some important limitations apply to the use of a member corporation's NOL. These limitations prevent one corporation from purchasing another corporation's NOL carryovers to offset its own taxable income or purchasing a profitable corporation to facilitate the use of its own NOL carryovers.

The following example illustrates the advantage of a consolidated return election.

EXAMPLE C3-35 ▶ Parent Corporation owns 100% of Subsidiary Corporation's stock. Parent reports $110,000 of taxable income, including a $10,000 capital gain. Subsidiary has a $100,000 NOL and a $10,000

[44] Includible corporations are those eligible to join in the consolidated tax return election under Sec. 1504(b).

[45] Sec. 1504(a).

capital loss. If Parent and Subsidiary file separate returns, Parent has a $26,150 [$22,250 + 0.39 × ($110,000 − $100,000)] tax liability. Subsidiary has no tax liability but may be able to use its $100,000 NOL and $10,000 capital loss to offset taxable income in other years. If Parent and Subsidiary file a consolidated return, the group's consolidated taxable income is zero and the group has no tax liability. By filing a consolidated return, the group saves $26,150 in taxes for the year. ◀

BOOK-TO-TAX ACCOUNTING COMPARISON

The corporations included in a consolidated tax return may differ from those included in consolidated financial statements.

DISADVANTAGES OF FILING A CONSOLIDATED RETURN. The main disadvantages of a consolidated return election are

- The election is binding on all subsequent tax years unless the IRS grants permission to discontinue filing consolidated returns or the affiliated group is terminated.
- Losses on intercompany transactions are deferred until a sale outside the group takes place.
- One member's Sec. 1231 losses are offset by another member's Sec. 1231 gains instead of being reported as an ordinary loss.
- Losses of an unprofitable member of the group may reduce the deduction or credit limitations of the group below what would be available had the members filed separate tax returns.
- Additional administrative costs may be incurred in maintaining the records needed to file a consolidated return.

Determining whether to make a consolidated tax return election is a complex decision because of the various advantages and disadvantages and because the election is so difficult to revoke once it is made.

TAX PLANNING CONSIDERATIONS

OBJECTIVE 5

Explain how compensation planning can reduce taxes for corporations and their shareholders

COMPENSATION PLANNING FOR SHAREHOLDER-EMPLOYEES

Compensation paid to a shareholder-employee in the form of salary carries with it the advantage of single taxation; that is, the salary is taxable to the employee and deductible by the corporation. A dividend payment, however, is taxed twice. The corporation is taxed on its income when earned, and the shareholder is taxed on the profits paid out in the form of dividends, which are nondeductible. Some owners of closely held corporations elect to be taxed under the rules of Subchapter S to avoid double taxation. Other owners of closely held corporations retain C corporation status to use the 15% and 25% marginal corporate tax rates and to benefit from tax-free fringe benefits such as health and accident insurance. These fringe benefits are nontaxable to the employee and deductible by the corporation. For both tax and nontax reasons, closely held corporations must determine the appropriate level of earnings to be withdrawn from the business in the form of salary and fringe benefits and the amount of earnings to be retained in the business.

ADVANTAGE OF SALARY PAYMENTS. If all corporate profits are paid out as salary and fringe benefit payments, double taxation is eliminated. However, the following considerations limit the tax planning opportunities available in the salary and fringe benefits area:

ADDITIONAL COMMENT

Reasonableness of a salary payment is a question of fact to be determined for each case. No formula can be used to determine a reasonable amount.

- Regulation Sec. 1.162-7(a) requires salary or fringe benefit payments to be reasonable in amount and to be paid for services rendered by the employee. If the IRS deems compensation to be unreasonable, it will characterize the payment as a dividend (see Chapter C4), which will result in double taxation. This restriction primarily affects closely held corporations.

- A corporation may not deduct compensation paid to an executive of a publicly traded corporation that exceeds $1 million. However, this limitation does not apply to compensation paid to an executive other than the corporation's top five officers, or to performance-based compensation.[46]
- A corporation is a tax-paying entity independent of its owners. The first $75,000 of a corporation's earnings is taxed at 15% and 25% corporate tax rates. These rates are lower than the marginal tax rate that may apply to an individual taxpayer and provides an incentive to retain some earnings in the corporation instead of paying them out as salaries. For large corporations, the 34% and 35% marginal tax rates for a C corporation are lower than the top individual tax rates and may permit larger accumulations of earnings for reinvestment and debt repayment if salary levels for shareholder-employees are kept low.
- A combined employee–employer social security tax rate of 15.30% applies in 2002. Employers and employees are each liable for 6.20% of old age security and disability insurance tax, or a total of 12.40% of the first $84,900 of wages for 2002. Employers and employees also are each liable for a 1.45% Medicare hospital insurance tax, for a total of 2.90% of all wages. In addition to these taxes, state and federal unemployment taxes may be imposed on a portion of the wages paid.

TAX STRATEGY TIP

A fringe benefit probably is the most cost effective form of compensation because the amount of the benefit is deductible by the employer and never taxed to the employee. Thus, where possible, fringe benefits are an excellent compensation planning tool. For closely held corporations, however, the tax savings to shareholder-employees are reduced because the fringe benefit must be offered to all employees without discrimination.

ADVANTAGE OF FRINGE BENEFITS. Fringe benefits provide two types of tax advantages: a tax deferral or an exclusion. Qualified pension, profit-sharing, and stock bonus plans provide a tax deferral; that is, the corporation's contribution to such a plan is not taxable to the employees when the contribution is made. Instead, the benefits from the plan are taxed to the employees when received. Other fringe benefits that closely held corporations commonly provide, such as group term life insurance, accident and health insurance, and disability insurance, are exempt from tax altogether; that is, the employee never is taxed on the value of these fringe benefits.

The value of fringe benefits is excluded from an employee's gross income. Thus, the marginal individual tax rate applicable to these employee benefits is zero. Conversion of salary into a fringe benefit provides tax savings for the shareholder-employee equal to the amount of the converted salary times the marginal individual tax rate, assuming the shareholder-employee could not purchase the same fringe benefit and deduct its cost on his or her individual tax return.

LIMITATION ON DEDUCTIBLE COMPENSATION PAYMENTS FOR SHAREHOLDER-EMPLOYEES. The amount of compensation that is reasonable for a shareholder-employee of a closely held corporation depends on the facts and circumstances of the situation. Any portion of compensation the IRS considers to be unreasonable is treated as a constructive dividend and subject to double taxation. The corporation bears the burden of proof to show that the amount of cash and deferred compensation plus fringe benefits paid to a shareholder-employee is reasonable. Further discussion on the tax consequences of paying an unreasonable amount of compensation is presented in Chapter C4.

SPECIAL ELECTION TO ALLOCATE REDUCED TAX RATE BENEFITS

A controlled group may elect to apportion the tax benefits of the 15%, 25%, and 34% tax rates to the member corporations in any manner it chooses. If the corporations elect no special apportionment plan, the $50,000, $25,000, and $9,925,000 amounts allocated to the three reduced tax rate brackets are divided equally among all the corporations in the group.[47] If a controlled group has one or more group members that report little or no taxable income, a special apportionment of the reduced tax benefits should be elected to obtain the full tax savings resulting from the reduced rates.

[46] Sec. 162(m).

[47] Sec. 1561(a).

EXAMPLE C3-36 ▶ North and South Corporations are members of the North-South controlled group. The corporations file separate tax returns for the current year and report the following results:

Corporation	*Taxable Income (NOL)*
North	$(25,000)
South	100,000

If they elect no special apportionment plan, North and South are limited to $25,000 each taxed at a 15% rate and to $12,500 each taxed at a 25% rate. The tax liability for each corporation is determined as follows:

Corporation	*Calculation*	*Tax*
North		$ –0–
South	15% tax bracket: 0.15 × $25,000	$ 3,750
	25% tax bracket: 0.25 × $12,500	3,125
	34% tax bracket: 0.34 × $62,500	21,250
	Subtotal for South Corporation	$28,125
Total for North-South controlled group		$28,125

If the corporations elect a special apportionment plan, the group may apportion the full $50,000 and $25,000 amounts for each of the reduced tax rate brackets to South Corporation. The tax liability for each corporation is determined as follows:

Corporation	*Calculation*	*Tax*
North		$ –0–
South	15% tax bracket: 0.15 × $50,000	$ 7,500
	25% tax bracket: 0.25 × $25,000	6,250
	34% tax bracket: 0.34 × $25,000	8,500
	Subtotal for South Corporation	$22,250
Total for North-South controlled group		$22,250

Use of the special apportionment election reduces the total tax liability for the North-South group by $5,875 ($28,125 – $22,250). ◀

If a controlled group's total taxable income exceeds $100,000 ($15 million), a 5% (3%) surcharge recaptures the benefits of the reduced tax rates. The component member (or members) that took advantage of the lower tax rates pays this additional tax.

EXAMPLE C3-37 ▶ Hill, Jet, and King Corporations are members of the Hill-Jet-King controlled group. The corporations file separate tax returns and report the following results:

Corporation	*Taxable Income*
Hill	$200,000
Jet	100,000
King	100,000
Total	$400,000

All the reduced tax rate benefits are allocated to Hill Corporation under a special apportionment plan. Hill's income tax is calculated as follows:

15% tax bracket: 0.15 × $50,000	$ 7,500
25% tax bracket: 0.25 × $25,000	6,250
34% tax bracket: 0.34 × $125,000	42,500
Surcharge	11,750
Hill's total tax liability	$68,000

Jet and King each have a regular tax liability of $34,000 (0.34 × $100,000). Thus, the group's total regular tax liability is $136,000 ($68,000 + $34,000 + $34,000). Because Hill, Jet, and King each report taxable income exceeding $75,000, the group would have the same total regular tax liability if the special apportionment plan apportioned all the tax benefit to Jet or King Corporation or divided it equally among the three corporations.[48] ◀

[48] A 3% surcharge applies if the controlled group's total taxable income exceeds $15 million. The recapture rule applies in a fashion similar to Example C3-37.

TAX STRATEGY TIP

A corporation may want to elect to forgo the NOL carryback when tax credit carryovers are being used in the earlier years. If the NOLs are carried back, the tax credits may expire. Thus, before deciding to carry back NOLs, the prior tax returns should be carefully examined to ensure that expiring tax credits do not exist.

USING NOL CARRYOVERS AND CARRYBACKS

When a corporation incurs an NOL for the year, it has two choices:

- Carry the NOL back to the second and first preceding years in that order, and then forward to the succeeding 20 years in chronological order until the NOL is exhausted.
- Forgo any carryback and just carry the NOL forward to the 20 succeeding years.

A corporation might elect to forgo an NOL carryback because it would offset income taxed at a low rate so that the tax refund obtained due to the NOL would not be as great as is anticipated if the NOL were carried forward instead.

EXAMPLE C3-38 ▶ Boyd Corporation incurs a $30,000 NOL in 2002. Boyd's 2000 taxable income was $50,000. If Boyd carries the NOL back to 2000, Boyd's tax refund is computed as follows:

Original tax on $50,000 (using 2000 rates)	$7,500
Minus: Recomputed tax on $20,000 [($50,000 − $30,000) × 0.15]	(3,000)
Tax refund	$4,500

ETHICAL POINT

When tax practitioners take on a new client, they should review the client's prior year tax returns and tax elections for accuracy and completeness. Tax matters arising in the current year, such as an NOL, can affect prior year tax returns prepared by another tax practitioner. Positions taken or errors discovered in a prior year return may have ethical consequences for a practitioner who takes on a new client.

If Boyd anticipates taxable income (after reduction for any NOL carryovers) of $75,000 or more in 2003, carrying the NOL forward will result in the entire loss offsetting taxable income that otherwise would be taxed at a 34% or higher marginal tax rate. The tax savings is computed as follows:

Tax on $105,000 of expected taxable income	$24,200
Minus: Tax on $75,000 ($105,000 − $30,000)	(13,750)
Tax savings in 2002	$10,450

Thus, if Boyd expects taxable income to be $105,000 in 2003, it might elect to forgo the NOL carryback and obtain the additional $5,950 ($10,450 − $4,500) tax benefit. Of course, by carrying the NOL over to 2003, Boyd loses the value of having the funds immediately available. However, the NOL may be used to reduce Boyd's estimated tax payments for 2003. If the corporation expects the NOL carryover benefit to occur at an appreciably distant point in the future, the corporation would have to determine the benefit's present value to make it comparable to a refund from an NOL carryback. ◀

COMPLIANCE AND PROCEDURAL CONSIDERATIONS

ESTIMATED TAXES

Every corporation that expects to owe more than $500 in tax for the current year must pay four installments of estimated tax, each equal to 25% of its required annual payment.[49] For corporations that are not large corporations (defined below), the required annual payment is the lesser of 100% of the tax shown on the return for the current year or 100% of the tax shown on the return for the preceding year. A corporation may not base its required estimated tax amount on the tax shown on the return for the preceding tax year if the preceding year tax return showed a zero tax liability.[50] The estimated tax amount is the sum of the corporation's income tax and alternative minimum tax liabilities that exceeds its tax credits. The amount of estimated tax due may be computed on Schedule 1120-W (Corporation Estimated Tax).

ESTIMATED TAX PAYMENT DATES. A calendar year corporation must deposit estimated tax payments in a Federal Reserve bank or authorized commercial bank on or before April 15th, June 15th, September 15th, and December 15th.[51] This schedule differs

[49] Sec. 6655.

[50] Rev. Rul. 92-54, 1992-2 C.B. 320.

[51] Sec. 6655(c)(2). Fiscal year taxpayers are required by Sec. 6655(i)(1) to deposit their taxes on or before the fifteenth day of the fourth, sixth, ninth, and twelfth month of their tax year.

from that of an individual taxpayer. The final estimated tax installment for a calendar year corporation is due in December of the tax year, rather than in January of the following tax year, as is the case for individual taxpayers.

EXAMPLE C3-39 ▶ Garden Corporation uses a calendar year as its tax year. For 2002, Garden expects to report the following results:

Regular tax	$119,000
Alternative minimum tax	25,000

Garden's 2002 estimated tax liability is $144,000 ($119,000 regular tax liability + $25,000 AMT liability). Garden's tax liability for 2001 was $120,000. Assuming Garden is not a large corporation, its required annual payment for 2002 is $120,000, the lesser of its 2001 liability ($120,000) or its 2002 tax return liability ($144,000). Garden will not incur any penalty if it deposits four equal installments of $30,000 ($120,000 ÷ 4) on or before April 15, June 17, September 16, and December 16, 2002. (June 15, 2002 falls on a Saturday making the second due date June 17, and September 15 and December 15 fall on Sundays making those due dates September 16 and December 16, respectively.) ◀

TYPICAL MISCONCEPTION

The easiest method of determining a corporation's estimated tax payments is to pay 100% of last year's tax liability. Unfortunately, for "large corporations," other than for its first quarterly payment, last year's tax liability is not an acceptable method of determining the required estimated tax payments. Also, last year's tax liability cannot be used if no tax liability existed in the prior year or if the corporation filed a short-year return for the prior year.

Different estimated tax payment rules are used for large corporations. A large corporation's required annual payment is 100% of the tax shown on the return for the current tax year. The estimated tax payments for a large corporation cannot be based on the prior year's tax liability, although a large corporation is allowed to base its first installment payment for the year on last year's tax liability. If a large corporation elects to base its first estimated tax payment on the prior year's liability, any shortfall between the required payment based on the current year's tax liability and the actual payment must be made up when the second payment is made.[52] A large corporation is one whose taxable income was $1 million or more in any of its three immediately preceding tax years. Controlled groups of corporations must allocate the $1 million amount among its group members.

EXAMPLE C3-40 ▶ Assume the same facts as in Example C3-39 except that Garden is a large corporation (i.e., it had more than $1 million of taxable income in 2000). Garden can base its first estimated tax payment on either 25% of its 2002 tax liability, or 25% of its 2001 tax liability. Garden should elect to use its 2001 tax liability as the basis for its first installment because it can reduce the needed payment from $36,000 (0.25 × $144,000) to $30,000 (0.25 × $120,000). However, it must recapture the shortfall of $6,000 ($36,000 − $30,000) when it pays its second installment. Therefore, the total second installment is $42,000 ($36,000 second installment + $6,000 recapture from first installment). ◀

SELF-STUDY QUESTION

What is the consequence of underpaying a corporation's estimated taxes?

ANSWER

A nondeductible penalty is assessed if estimated taxes are not timely paid. The amount of penalty depends on three factors: the underpayment rate in Sec. 6621, the amount of the underpayment, and the amount of time that lapses until payment is actually made.

PENALITES FOR UNDERPAYMENT OF ESTIMATED TAX. The IRS will assess a nondeductible penalty if a corporation does not deposit its required estimated tax installment on or before the due date for that installment. The penalty is the underpayment rate found in Sec. 6621 times the amount by which the installment(s) due by a payment date exceed the payment(s) actually made.[53] The penalty is owed from the payment due date for the installment until the earlier of the date the payment is actually made or the due date for the tax return (excluding extensions).

EXAMPLE C3-41 ▶ Globe Corporation is a calendar year taxpayer whose tax liability for 2001 was $100,000. Globe's tax liability for 2000 was $125,000. It should have made estimated tax payments of $25,000 ($100,000 ÷ 4) on or before April 16, June 15, September 17, and December 17, 2001. No penalty is assessed if Globe deposited at least $25,000 on or before each of the four dates. If, for example, a deposit of only $16,000 ($9,000 less than the required $25,000) was made on April 16, 2001, and the remaining $9,000 was not deposited before the due date for the 2001

[52] Sec. 6655(d)(2)(B). A revision to the required estimated tax payment amount also may be needed if the corporation is basing its quarterly payments on the current year's tax liability. Installments paid after the estimate of the current year's liability has been revised must take into account any shortage or excess in previous installment payments resulting from the change in the original estimate.

[53] Sec. 6621. This interest rate is the short-term federal rate as determined by the Secretary of the Treasury plus three percentage points. It is subject to change every three months. The interest rate for large corporations is the short-term federal rate plus five percentage points. This higher interest rate begins 30 days after the issuance of either a 30-day or 90-day deficiency notice.

return, Globe must pay a penalty at the Sec. 6621 rate on the $9,000 underpayment for the period of time from April 16, 2001 through March 15, 2002. The penalty is calculated on the completed Form 2220 in Appendix B (assuming $16,000 is paid in on each installment date). If Globe deposits $34,000 on the second installment date (June 15, 2001), so that a total of $50,000 has been paid by the due date for the second installment, the penalty runs only from April 16, 2001 through June 15, 2001. ◀

SPECIAL COMPUTATION METHODS. Corporations are allowed to use two special methods for calculating estimated tax installments:

- The annualized income method or
- The adjusted seasonal income method.

The Annualized Income Method. This method is useful if a corporation's income is likely to increase a great deal toward the end of the year. It allows a corporation to base its first and second quarterly estimated tax payments on its annualized taxable income for the first three months of the year. The corporation then must base its third payment on its annualized taxable income for the first six months of the year and its fourth payment must be based on annualized taxable income for the first nine months of the year. (Two other options for the number of months used for each installment are available.)

EXAMPLE C3-42 ▶ Erratic Corporation, a calendar year taxpayer, reports taxable income of: $10,000 in each of January, February, and March; $20,000 in each of April, May, and June; and $50,000 in each of the last six months of the current year. Its annualized income for the first three months is calculated as follows:

Taxable income from January through March	$30,000
Times: Annualization factor	× 12/3[a]
Annualized taxable income	$120,000

[a] Number of months in the tax year divided by number of months that have passed since the beginning of the tax year.

Erratic may base its first and second estimated tax payments on annualized taxable income of $120,000 (see calculation above). Its third installment is based on annualized taxable income of $180,000 ($90,000 taxable income for first six months × 12/6), and its fourth estimated tax payment is based on annualized taxable income of $320,000 ($240,000 taxable income for first nine months × 12/9). These calculations assume that Erratic uses the annualized method for all four installments. ◀

TAX STRATEGY TIP

Both the "annualized income exception" and the "adjusted seasonal income exception" are complicated computations. However, due to the large amounts of money involved in making corporate estimated tax payments along with the possible underpayment penalties, the time and effort spent in determining the least amount necessary for a required estimated tax payment are often worthwhile.

Taxable income for a period of less than 12 months (short period) is placed on an annual basis by (1) multiplying the taxable income for the short period by 12 and (2) dividing the resulting amount by the number of months in the short period.

A corporation may use the annualized income method for an installment payment only if it is less than the regular required installment. It must recapture any reduction in an earlier required installment resulting from use of the annualized income method by increasing the amount of the next installment that does not qualify for the annualized income method.

For small corporations, the best way to ensure that no penalty will be imposed for the underpayment of estimated tax is to make sure the current year's estimated tax payments are based on 100% of last year's tax. This approach is not possible, however, for large corporations or for corporations that did not owe any tax in the prior year or filed a short period tax return for the prior year. This approach also is not advisable if the corporation had a high tax liability in the prior year and expects a low tax liability in the current year.

Adjusted Seasonal Income Method. A corporation may base its installments on its adjusted seasonal income. This rule permits corporations that earn seasonal income to annualize their income by assuming income earned in the current year is earned in the same pattern as in preceding years. As in the case of the annualized income exception, the seasonal income exception may be used only if the resulting installment payment is less than the regular required installment. Once the exception no longer applies, any savings resulting from its use for prior installments must be recaptured.

REPORTING THE UNDERPAYMENT. A corporation reports its underpayment of estimated taxes and the amount of any penalty owed on Form 2220 (Underpayment of Estimated Tax by Corporations). A copy of a completed Form 2220 using the facts from Example C3-41 appears in Appendix B.

PAYING THE REMAINING TAX LIABILITY. A corporation must pay all of its remaining tax liability for the year when it files its corporate tax return. An extension of time to file the tax return does *not* extend the time to pay the tax liability. If any amount of tax is not paid by the original due date for the tax return, interest at the underpayment rate prescribed by Sec. 6621 must be paid from the due date until the tax is paid. In addition to interest, a penalty is assessed if the tax is not paid on time, and the corporation cannot show reasonable cause for the failure to pay. Reasonable cause is presumed if the corporation requests an extension of time to file its tax return and the amount of tax shown on the request for extension (Form 7004) or the amount of tax paid by the original due date of the return is at least 90% of the corporation's tax shown on its Form 1120.[54] A discussion of the failure-to-pay penalty and the interest calculation can be found in Chapter C15.

STOP & THINK

Question: Why does the tax law permit a corporation to use special methods such as the annualized income method to calculate its required estimated tax installments?

Solution: A large corporation whose income varies widely may not be able to estimate its taxable income for the year until late in the year, and it is not allowed to base its estimates on last year's income. If, for example, a calendar year corporation has an income of $100,000 per month during the first six months of its year, it may base its first two installments on a total taxable income of $1.2 million. But if its income unexpectedly increases to $500,000 per month in the seventh month, it would need to use the annualized method to avoid an underpayment penalty for the first two installments. Were it not for the ability to use the annualized method, the corporation would have no way to avoid an underpayment penalty even though it was impossible for the corporation to predict its taxable income for the year when it made the first two installment payments.

OBJECTIVE 6

Determine the requirements for paying corporate incomes taxes and filing a corporate tax return

REQUIREMENTS FOR FILING AND PAYING TAXES

A corporation must file a tax return even if it has no taxable income for the year.[55] If the corporation was not in existence for its entire annual accounting period (either calendar year or fiscal year), it must file a return for the part of the year during which it was in existence. A corporation is not in existence after it ceases business and dissolves, retaining no assets, even if, under state law, it is treated as continuing as a corporation for purposes of winding up its affairs.[56]

Corporations must use Form 1120 (U.S. Corporation Income Tax Return) or Form 1120-A (U.S. Corporation Short-Form Income Tax Return) to file their tax returns. A corporation is eligible to use Form 1120-A if the following requirements are satisfied:[57]

- The corporation's gross receipts must be under $500,000.
- Its total income must be under $500,000.
- Its total assets must be under $500,000.

A completed Form 1120 corporate income tax return is reproduced in Appendix B. A spreadsheet that converts book income into taxable income for the Johns and Lawrence business enterprise (introduced in Chapter C2) is presented with the C corporation tax return.

REAL WORLD EXAMPLE

The IRS estimates that, in 2001, 267,000 corporations will file Form 1120A compared to 2.4 million corporations that will file the regular Form 1120.

---

[54] Reg. Sec. 301.6651-1(c)(4).

[55] Sec. 6012(a)(2).

[56] Reg. Sec. 1.6012-2(a)(2).

[57] See the instructions to Form 1120-A for a series of additional requirements (e.g., the corporation is not filing its final return).

WHEN THE RETURN MUST BE FILED

Corporate returns must be filed by the fifteenth day of the third month following the close of the corporation's tax year.[58] A corporation can obtain an automatic six-month extension to file its tax return by filing Form 7004 (Application for Automatic Extension of Time to File Corporation Income Tax Return) by the original due date for the return. Corporations that fail to file a timely tax return are subject to the failure-to-file penalty. A discussion of this penalty is presented in Chapter C15.

EXAMPLE C3-43 ▶ Perry Corporation uses a fiscal year ending on September 30 as its tax year. Its corporate tax return for the year ending September 30, 2002 is due on or before December 16, 2002. If Perry files a Form 7004 by December 16, 2002, it can obtain an automatic extension of time to file until June 16, 2003. Assuming Perry expects its 2002 tax liability to be $72,000 and it has paid $68,000 in estimated tax during the year, it must pay an additional $4,000 to the IRS by December 16, 2002. A completed Form 7004 appears in Appendix B. ◀

Additional extensions beyond the automatic six-month period are not available. The IRS can rescind the extension period by mailing a ten-day notice to the corporation before the end of the six-month period.[59]

TAX RETURN SCHEDULES

SELF-STUDY QUESTION

Is the balance sheet required on Schedule L a tax balance sheet or a financial accounting balance sheet?

ANSWER

Schedule L requires a financial accounting balance sheet rather than a tax balance sheet. However, for many smaller corporations, the tax balance sheet is the same as the financial accounting balance sheet.

SCHEDULE L (OF FORM 1120): THE BALANCE SHEET. Form 1120 requires a balance sheet showing the financial accounting results at the beginning and end of the tax year. The balance sheets must be provided on Schedule L of Form 1120. Both forms also require the reconciliation of the corporation's financial accounting income (also known as *book income*) and its taxable income (before special deductions). The reconciliation must be provided on Schedule M-1 of Form 1120. Form 1120 also requires an analysis of the unappropriated retained earnings account on Schedule M-2.

SCHEDULE M-1 (OF FORM 1120): RECONCILIATION OF BOOK INCOME AND INCOME PER RETURN. A corporation's book income usually differs from the corporation's taxable income. These differences arise because

- ▶ Some book income is not taxable (e.g., tax-exempt interest)
- ▶ Some gross income is not reflected in book income for the current period (e.g., prepaid rent)
- ▶ Some financial accounting expenses are not deductible for tax purposes (e.g., federal income taxes)
- ▶ Some deductions allowed for tax purposes are not expenses in determining book income for the current period (e.g., asset costs expensed under Sec. 179)

BOOK-TO-TAX ACCOUNTING COMPARISON

The Internal Revenue Code and related authorities determine the treatment of items in the tax return while *Statement of Financial Accounting Standard No. 109, Accounting for Income Taxes,* dictates the treatment of tax items in the financial statements.

Some book income items that are nontaxable in the current year will never be taxed; some book expense items that are nondeductible in computing taxable income for the current year will never be deductible. These income and deduction items are called **permanent differences.** They include tax-exempt interest and IRS penalties.

Some book income items that are nontaxable in the current year will be taxed in a later year or were taxed in an earlier year. Some book expense items that are nondeductible in computing taxable income for the current year will be deductible in a later year or were deductible in an earlier year. These differences are called **temporary differences.** They include prepaid rent and charitable contributions exceeding the 10% of taxable income limitation. Both permanent and temporary differences appear on Schedule M-1.

The reconciliation of book income to taxable income starts with net book income. The result of the reconciliation is the corporation's taxable income before special deductions (e.g., NOL and dividends-received deductions).

The items that must be added to the book income amount to arrive at the reconciling figure are listed on the left side of Schedule M-1 and include

[58] Sec. 6072(b).

[59] Reg. Sec. 1.6081-3.

1. *Federal income tax expense.* This amount is deducted in arriving at book income but is not deductible for tax purposes.
2. *Excess of capital losses over capital gains.* This amount is deducted in arriving at book income but is not deductible for tax purposes. (The loss, however, may be carried back or forward and will "reverse" when used.)
3. *Income subject to tax but not recorded on the books this year.* This item includes prepayments received during the current year (e.g., prepaid rent or prepaid interest) that must be included in gross income during the current year but will be included in book income in a later year when earned.
4. *Expenses recorded on the books but not deductible for tax purposes this year.* Among the items included are
   a. Contributions exceeding the 10% of taxable income limitation
   b. Book depreciation expense exceeding that allowed for tax purposes
   c. Disallowed travel and entertainment costs (e.g., 50% nondeductible portion of meal and entertainment expenditures)
   d. Life insurance premiums on key personnel where the corporation is the beneficiary of the policy
   e. Interest payments on money borrowed to purchase tax-exempt securities
   f. Estimated costs of warranty service
   g. Political contributions

SELF-STUDY QUESTION

Why might the IRS be interested in reviewing a corporation's Schedule M-1?

ANSWER

Because the Schedule M-1 adjustments reconcile book income to taxable income, this schedule can prove illuminating to an IRS agent who is auditing a corporate return. Because Schedule M-1 highlights each departure from the financial accounting rules, the schedule sometimes helps the IRS identify tax issues that it may want to examine further.

The items that must be deducted from book income to arrive at the reconciling figure are listed on the right side of Schedule M-1 and include

1. *Income recorded on books this year that is not taxable in the current year.* Among the items included are
   a. Prepaid rent or interest received and reported for tax purposes in an earlier year but earned in the current year
   b. Life insurance proceeds received on the death of key personnel
   c. Tax-exempt interest
2. *Deductions or losses claimed in the tax return that do not reduce book income in the current year.* Among the items included are
   a. Depreciation, cost recovery deductions, and asset costs expensed under Sec. 179 that exceed the depreciation taken for book purposes.
   b. Charitable contribution carryovers from an earlier year deducted on this year's tax return
   c. Capital losses from another year used to offset capital gains on this year's tax return
   d. Amortization of organizational expenditures exceeding the amortization allowed for book purposes

The following example illustrates the reconciliation required on Schedule M-1:

EXAMPLE C3-44 ▶

BOOK-TO-TAX COMPARISON

Schedule M-1 adjustments highlight the fact that financial accounting and tax accounting differ in many ways. A review of Schedule M-1 is an excellent way to compare the financial accounting and tax accounting differences in a corporation.

Valley Corporation reports the following results:

Net income per books (after tax expense)	$121,700
Federal income tax expense per books	27,250
Prepaid rent	10,000
Net capital loss	10,750
Tax-exempt interest income	12,500
Insurance premiums on life of key employee where Valley is the beneficiary	800
Proceeds of insurance policy on life of key employee	50,000
Interest paid on loan to buy tax-exempt bonds	15,000
MACRS deductions exceeding book depreciation deduction (straight-line depreciation was used for book purposes)	2,000

Valley's Schedule M-1 reconciliation is shown in Figure C3-5.[60] ◀

[60] A worksheet for converting book income to taxable income for the sample Form 1120 return is provided in Appendix B with that return.

1	Net income (loss) per books	121,700	7	Income recorded on books this year not included on this return (itemize): Tax-exempt interest $ 12,500 Insurance proceeds 50,000	62,500
2	Federal income tax	27,250			
3	Excess of capital losses over capital gains	10,750			
4	Income subject to tax not recorded on books this year (itemize): Prepaid rent	10,000	8	Deductions on this return not charged against book income this year (itemize):	
5	Expenses recorded on books this year not deducted on this return (itemize):		a	Depreciation $ 2,000	
a	Depreciation $		b	Contributions carryover $	
b	Contributions carryover $				
c	Travel and entertainment $ Premiums on life insurance 800 Interest on loan 15,000	15,800			2,000
			9	Add lines 7 and 8	64,500
6	Add lines 1 through 5	185,500	10	Income (line 28, page 1)—line 6 less line 9	121,000

FIGURE C3-5 ▶ VALLEY CORPORATION'S FORM 1120 SCHEDULE M-1 (EXAMPLE C3-44)

SCHEDULE M-2 (OF FORM 1120). Schedule M-2 on Form 1120 requires an analysis of the changes in the unappropriated retained earnings account from the beginning of the year to the end of the year. The schedule supplies the IRS with information regarding dividends paid during the year and any special transactions that caused a change in retained earnings for the year.

Schedule M-2 starts with the balance in the unappropriated retained earnings account at the beginning of the year. The following items, which must be added to the beginning balance amount, are listed on the left side of the schedule:

- ▶ Net income per books
- ▶ Other increases (e.g., refund of federal income taxes paid in a prior year taken directly to the retained earnings account instead of used to reduce federal income tax expense)

The following items, which must be deducted from the beginning balance amount, are listed on the right side of the schedule:

- ▶ Dividends (e.g., cash or property)
- ▶ Other decreases (e.g., appropriation of retained earnings made during the tax year)

The result is the balance in the unappropriated retained earnings account at the end of the year.

ADDITIONAL COMMENT

Schedule M-2 requires an analysis of a corporation's retained earnings. Retained earnings is a financial accounting number that has little relevance to tax accounting. It would seem much more worthwhile for the IRS to require an analysis of a corporation's earnings and profits, which is an extremely important number in determining the taxation of a corporation and its shareholders.

EXAMPLE C3-45 ▶ In 2002, Beta Corporation reports net income and other capital account items as follows:

Unappropriated retained earnings, January 1, 2002	$400,000
Net income	350,000
Federal income tax refund for 2000	15,000
Cash dividends paid in 2002	250,000
Unappropriated retained earnings, December 31, 2002	515,000

Beta Corporation's Schedule M-2 is shown in Figure C3-6. ◀

Topic Review C3-2 summarizes the requirements for paying the taxes due and filing the corporate tax return.

Analysis of Unappropriated Retained Earnings per Books (Line 25, Schedule L)

1	Balance at beginning of year	400,000	5	Distributions: a Cash	250,000
2	Net income (loss) per books	350,000		b Stock	
3	Other increases (itemize):			c Property	
	Federal tax refund 2000	15,000	6	Other decreases (itemize):	
			7	Add lines 5 and 6	250,000
4	Add lines 1, 2, and 3	765,000	8	Balance at end of year (line 4 less line 7)	515,000

FIGURE C3-6 ▶ BETA CORPORATION'S FORM 1120 SCHEDULE M-2 (EXAMPLE C3-45)

Topic Review C3-2

Requirements for Paying Taxes Due and Filing Tax Returns

1. Estimated Tax Requirement
   a. Corporations that expect to owe more than $500 in tax for the current year must pay four installments of estimated tax, each equal to 25% of its required annual payment.
   b. Taxes for which estimated payments are required of a C corporation include regular tax and alternative minimum tax, minus any tax credits.
   c. If a corporation is not a large corporation, its required annual payment is the lesser of 100% of the tax shown on the current year's return or 100% of the tax shown on the preceding year's return.
   d. If a corporation is a large corporation, its required annual payment is 100% of the tax shown on the current year's return. Its first estimated tax payment may be based on the preceding year's tax liability, but any shortfall must be made up when the second installment is due.
   e. Special rules apply if the corporation bases its estimated tax payments on the annualized income or adjusted seasonal income methods.
2. Filing Requirements
   a. The corporate tax return is due by the fifteenth day of the third month after the end of the tax year.
   b. A corporate taxpayer may request an automatic six-month extension.

PROBLEM MATERIALS

DISCUSSION QUESTIONS

C3-1 High Corporation incorporates on May 1 and begins business on May 10 of the current year. What alternative tax years can High elect to report its initial year's income?

C3-2 Port Corporation wants to change its tax year from a calendar year to a fiscal year ending June 30. Port is a C corporation owned by 100 shareholders, none of whom own more than 5% of the stock. Can Port Corporation change its tax year? If so, how can the change be accomplished?

C3-3 Stan and Susan, two calendar year taxpayers, are starting a new business to manufacture and sell digital circuits. They intend to incorporate the business with $600,000 of their own capital and $2 million of equity capital obtained from other investors. The company expects to incur organizational and start-up expenditures of $100,000 in the first year. Inventories are a material income-producing factor. The company also expects to incur losses of $500,000 in the first two years of operations and substantial research and development expenses during the first three years. The company expects to break even in the third year and be profitable at the end of the fourth year, even though the nature of the digital circuit business will require continual research and development activities. What accounting methods and tax elections must Stan and Susan consider in their first year of operation? For each method/election, explain the possible alternatives and the advantages and disadvantages of each alternative.

C3-4 Compare the tax treatment of capital gains and losses by a corporation and by an individual.

C3-5 Explain the effect of the Sec. 291 recapture rule when a corporation sells depreciable real estate.

C3-6 What are organizational expenditures? How are they treated for tax purposes?

C3-7 What are start-up expenditures? How are they treated for tax purposes?

C3-8 Describe three ways in which the treatment of charitable contributions by individual and corporate taxpayers differ.

C3-9 Carver Corporation uses the accrual method of accounting and the calendar year as its tax year. Its board of directors authorizes a cash contribution on November 3, 2002 that the corporation pays on March 10, 2003. In what year(s) is it deductible? What happens if the contribution is not paid until April 20, 2003?

C3-10 Zero Corporation contributes inventory (computers) to State University for use in its mathematics program. The computers have a $1,225 cost basis and an $2,800 FMV. How much is Zero's charitable contribution deduction for the computers? (Ignore the 10% limit.)

C3-11 Why are corporations allowed a dividends-received deduction? What dividends are eligible for this special deduction?

C3-12 Why is a dividends-received deduction disallowed if the stock on which the dividend is paid is debt-financed?

C3-13 Crane Corporation incurs a $75,000 NOL in the current year. In which years can Crane Corporation use this NOL if it makes no special elections? When might a special election to forgo the carryback of the NOL be beneficial for Crane Corporation?

C3-14 What special restrictions apply to the deduction of a loss realized on the sale of property between a corporation and a shareholder who owns 60% of the corporation's stock? What restrictions apply to the deduction of expenses accrued by a corporation at year-end and owed to a cash method of accounting shareholder who owns 60% of the corporation's stock?

C3-15 Deer Corporation is a C corporation. Its taxable income for the current year is $200,000. What is Deer Corporation's income tax liability for the year?

C3-16 Budget Corporation is a personal service corporation. Its taxable income for the current year is $75,000. What is Budget Corporation's income tax liability for the year?

C3-17 Why do special restrictions on using the progressive corporate tax rates apply to controlled groups of corporations?

C3-18 Describe the three types of controlled groups.

C3-19 List five restrictions on the claiming of multiple tax benefits that apply to controlled groups of corporations.

C3-20 What are the major advantages and disadvantages of filing a consolidated tax return?

C3-21 What are the tax advantages of substituting fringe benefits for salary paid to a shareholder-employee?

C3-22 Explain the tax consequences to both the corporation and a shareholder-employee of an IRS determination that a portion of the compensation paid in a prior tax year exceeds the reasonable compensation limit.

C3-23 What is the advantage of a special apportionment plan for the benefits of the 15%, 25%, and 34% tax rates to members of a controlled group?

C3-24 What corporations must pay estimated taxes? When are the estimated tax payments due?

C3-25 What is a "large" corporation for purposes of the estimated tax rules? What special rules apply to such large corporations?

C3-26 What penalties are assessed for the underpayment of estimated taxes? The late payment of the remaining tax liability?

C3-27 Describe the situations in which a corporation must file a tax return.

C3-28 When is a corporate tax return due for a calendar-year taxpayer? What extension(s) of time in which to file the return are available?

C3-29 List four types of differences that can cause a corporation's book income to differ from its taxable income.

ISSUE IDENTIFICATION QUESTIONS

C3-30 X-Ray Corporation received a $100,000 dividend from Yancey Corporation this year. X-Ray owns 10% of the Yancey's single class of stock. What tax issues should X-Ray consider with respect to its dividend income?

C3-31 Williams Corporation sold a truck with an adjusted basis of $100,000 to Barbara for $80,000. Barbara owns 25% of the Williams stock. What tax issues should Williams and Barbara consider with respect to the sale/purchase?

C3-32 You are the CPA who prepares the tax returns for Don, his wife, Mary, and their two corporations. Don owns 100% of Pencil Corporation's stock. Pencil's current year taxable income is $100,000. Mary owns 100% of Eraser Corporation's stock. Eraser's current year taxable income is $150,000. Don and Mary file a joint federal income tax return. What issues should be considered with respect to the calculation of the three tax return liabilities?

C3-33 Rugby Corporation has a $50,000 NOL in the current year. Rugby's taxable income in each of the previous two years was $25,000. Rugby expects its taxable income for next year to exceed $400,000. What issues should be considered with respect to the use of the NOL?

PROBLEMS

C3-34 *Depreciation Recapture.* Young Corporation purchased residential real estate in 1998 for $225,000, of which $25,000 was allocated to the land and $200,000 was allocated to the building. Young took straight-line MACRS deductions of $30,000 during the years 1998–2002. In 2002, Young sells the property for $285,000, of which $60,000 is allocated to the land and $225,000 is allocated to the building. What are the amount and character of Young's recognized gain or loss on the sale?

C3-35 *Organizational and Start-up Expenditures.* Delta Corporation incorporates on January 7, begins business on July 10, and elects to have its initial tax year end on October 31. Delta incurs the following expenses between January and October related to its organization during the current year:

Date	Expenditure	Amount
January 30	Travel to investigate potential business site	$2,000
May 15	Legal expenses to draft corporate charter	2,500
May 30	Commissions to stockbroker for issuing and selling stock	4,000
May 30	Temporary directors' fees	2,500
June 1	Expense of transferring building to Delta	3,000
June 5	Accounting fees to set up corporate books	1,500
June 10	Training expenses for employees	5,000
June 15	Rent expense for June	1,000
July 15	Rent expense for July	1,000

a. What alternative treatments are available for Delta's expenditures?
b. What amount of organizational expenditures can Delta Corporation deduct on its first tax return for the fiscal year ending October 31?

C3-36 ***Charitable Contribution of Property.*** Yellow Corporation donates the following property to the State University:

- ABC Corporation stock purchased two years ago for $18,000. The stock, which is traded on a regional stock exchange, has a $25,000 FMV on the contribution date.
- Inventory with a $17,000 adjusted basis and a $22,000 FMV. The inventory is to be used for scientific research and qualifies under the special Sec. 170(e)(4) rules.
- An antique vase purchased two years ago for $10,000 and having an $18,000 FMV. State University plans to sell the vase to obtain funds for educational purposes.

Yellow Corporation's taxable income before any charitable contributions deduction, NOL or capital loss carryback, or dividends-received deduction is $250,000.
a. What is Yellow Corporation's charitable contributions deduction for the current year?
b. What is the amount of its charitable contributions carryover (if any)?

C3-37 ***Charitable Contributions of Property.*** Blue Corporation donates the following property to Johnson Elementary School:

- XYZ Corporation stock purchased two years ago for $25,000. The stock has a $16,000 FMV on the contribution date.
- Computer equipment built one year ago at a cost of $16,000. The equipment has a $50,000 FMV on the contribution date. Blue Corporation is not in the business of manufacturing computer equipment.
- PQR Corporation stock purchased six months ago for $12,000. The stock has an $18,000 FMV on the contribution date.

The stock contributions are to be used to renovate a classroom to be used as a computer laboratory. Blue Corporation's taxable income before any charitable contribution deduction, dividends-received deduction, or NOL or capital loss carryback is $400,000.
a. What is Blue Corporation's charitable contributions deduction for the current year?
b. What is the amount of Blue Corporation's charitable contribution carryback or carryover (if any)? In what years can they be used?

C3-38 ***Charitable Contribution Deduction Limitation.*** Zeta Corporation reports the following results for 2002 and 2003:

	2002	*2003*
Adjusted taxable income	$180,000	$125,000
Charitable contributions (cash)	20,000	12,000

The adjusted taxable income is before any charitable contributions deduction, NOL or capital loss carryback, or dividends-received deduction is claimed.
a. How much is Zeta Corporation's charitable contributions deduction in 2002? In 2003?
b. What is Zeta Corporation's contribution carryover to 2004, if any?

C3-39 ***Taxable Income Computation.*** Omega Corporation reports the following results for the current year:

Gross profits on sales	$120,000
Dividends from less-than-20%-owned domestic corporations	40,000
Operating expenses	100,000
Charitable contributions (cash)	11,000

a. What is Omega Corporation's charitable contributions deduction for the current year and its charitable contributions carryover to next year, if any?
b. What is Omega Corporation's taxable income for the current year?

C3-40 ***Dividends-Received Deduction.*** Theta Corporation reports the following results for the current year:

Gross profits on sales	$220,000
Dividends from less-than-20%-owned domestic corporations	100,000
Operating expenses	218,000

a. What is Theta Corporation's taxable income for the current year?
b. How would your answer to Part a change if Theta's operating expenses are instead $234,000?
c. How would your answer to Part a change if Theta's operating expenses are instead $252,000?

C3-41 ***Stock Held 45 Days or Less.*** Beta Corporation purchased 100 shares of Gamma Corporation common stock (less than 5% of the outstanding stock) two days before the ex-dividend date for $200,000. Beta receives a $10,000 cash dividend from Gamma. Beta sells the Gamma stock one week after purchasing it for $190,000. What are the tax consequences of these three events?

C3-42 ***Debt-financed Stock.*** Cheers Corporation borrowed $400,000 and used $100,000 of its cash to purchase 5,000 shares of Beer Corporation common stock (less than 5% of the outstanding Beer stock) at the beginning of the current year. Cheers paid $50,000 of interest on the debt this year. Cheers received a $40,000 cash dividend on the Beer stock on September 1 of the current year.
a. What is the amount that Cheers can deduct for the interest paid on the loan?
b. What is the amount of the dividends-received deduction that Cheers can claim with respect to the dividend?

C3-43 ***Net Operating Loss Carrybacks and Carryovers.*** In 2002, Ace Corporation reports gross income of $200,000 (including $150,000 of profit from its operations and $50,000 in dividends from less-than-20%-owned domestic corporations) and $220,000 of operating expenses. Ace's 2000 taxable income (all ordinary income) was $75,000, on which it paid taxes of $13,750.
a. What is Ace's NOL for 2002?
b. What is the amount of Ace's tax refund if the 2002 NOL is carried back to 2000?
c. Assume that Ace expects 2003's taxable income to be $400,000. What election could Ace make to increase the tax benefit from its NOL? What is the dollar amount of the expected benefit (if any)?

C3-44 ***Ordering of Deductions.*** Beta Corporation reports the following results for the current year:

Gross income from operations	$180,000
Dividends from less-than-20%-owned domestic corporations	100,000
Operating expenses	150,000
Charitable contributions	20,000

In addition, Beta has a $50,000 NOL carryover from the preceding tax year.
a. What is Beta's taxable income for the current year?
b. What carrybacks or carryovers are available to other tax years?

C3-45 ***Sale to a Related Party.*** Union Corporation sells a truck for $18,000 to Jane, who owns 70% of its stock. The truck has a $24,000 adjusted basis on the sale date. Jane sells the truck to an unrelated party, Mike, for $28,000 two years later after claiming $5,000 in depreciation.
a. What is Union Corporation's realized and recognized gain or loss on selling the truck?
b. What is Jane's realized and recognized gain or loss on selling the truck to Mike?
c. How would your answers to Part b change if Jane instead sold the truck for $10,000?

C3-46 ***Payment to a Cash Basis Employee/Shareholder.*** Value Corporation is a calendar year taxpayer that uses the accrual method of accounting. On December 10, 2002, Value accrues a bonus payment of $100,000 to Brett, its president and sole shareholder. Brett is a calendar year taxpayer who uses the cash method of accounting.
a. When can Value Corporation deduct the bonus if it is paid to Brett on March 13, 2003? On March 18, 2003?

b. How would your answers to Part a change if Brett were an employee of Value Corporation who owns no stock in the corporation?

C3-47 ***Capital Gains and Losses.*** Western Corporation reports the following results for the current year:

Gross profits on sales	$150,000
Long-term capital gain	8,000
Long-term capital loss	15,000
Short-term capital gain	10,000
Short-term capital loss	2,000
Operating expenses	41,000

a. What are Western's taxable income and income tax liability for the current year?
b. How would your answers to Part a change if Western Corporation's short-term capital loss is $5,000 instead of $2,000?

C3-48 ***Computing the Corporate Income Tax Liability.*** What is Beta Corporation's income tax liability assuming its taxable income is (a) $94,000, (b) $300,000, and (c) $600,000. How would your answers change if Beta Corporation were characterized as a personal service corporation?

C3-49 ***Computing the Corporate Income Tax Liability.*** Fawn Corporation, a C corporation, paid no dividends and had no capital gains or losses in the current year. What is its income tax liability assuming its taxable income for the year was
a. $50,000
b. $14,000,000
c. $18,000,000
d. $34,000,000

C3-50 ***Computing Taxable Income and Income Tax Liability.*** Pace Corporation reports the following results for the current year:

Gross profit on sales	$120,000
Long-term capital loss	10,000
Short-term capital loss	5,000
Dividends from 40%-owned domestic corporation	30,000
Operating expenses	65,000
Charitable contributions	10,000

a. What are Pace's taxable income and income tax liability?
b. What carrybacks and carryovers (if any) are available and to what years must they be carried?

C3-51 ***Computing Taxable Income and Income Tax Liability.*** Roper Corporation reports the following results for the current year:

Gross profits on sales	$80,000
Short-term capital gain	40,000
Long-term capital gain	25,000
Dividends from 25%-owned domestic corporation	15,000
NOL carryover from the preceding tax year	9,000
Operating expenses	45,000

What are Roper's taxable income and income tax liability?

C3-52 ***Controlled Groups.*** Which of the following groups constitute controlled groups? (Any stock not listed below is held by unrelated individuals each owning less than 1% of the outstanding stock.)
a. Judy owns 90% of the single classes of stock of Hot and Ice Corporations.
b. Jones and Kane Corporations each have only a single class of stock outstanding. The two controlling individual shareholders own the stock as follows:

	Stock Ownership Percentages	
Shareholder	*Jones Corp.*	*Kane Corp.*
Tom	60%	80%
Mary	30%	0%

c. Link, Model, and Name Corporations each have a single class of stock outstanding. The stock is owned as follows:

Shareholder	Model Corp.	Name Corp.
	Stock Ownership Percentages	
Link Corp.	80%	50%
Model Corp.		40%

Link Corporation's stock is widely held by over 1,000 shareholders, none of whom owns directly or indirectly more than 1% of Link's stock.

d. Oat, Peach, Rye, and Seed Corporations each have a single class of stock outstanding. The stock is owned as follows:

Shareholder	Oat Corp.	Peach Corp.	Rye Corp.	Seed Corp.
	Stock Ownership Percentages			
Bob	100%	90%		
Oat Corp.			80%	30%
Rye Corp.				60%

C3-53 ***Controlled Groups of Corporations.*** Sally owns 100% of the outstanding stock of Eta, Theta, Phi, and Gamma Corporations, each of which files a separate return for the current year. During the current year, the corporations report taxable income as follows:

Corporation	*Taxable Income*
Eta	$40,000
Theta	(25,000)
Phi	50,000
Gamma	10,000

a. What are each corporation's separate tax liabilities, assuming the corporations do not elect a special apportionment plan governing the reduced Sec. 11(b) corporate tax rates?

b. What are each corporation's separate tax liabilities, assuming the corporations make a special election for apportioning the Sec. 11(b) reduced corporate tax rates that minimizes the group's total tax liability?

C3-54 ***Compensation Planning.*** Marilyn owns all of Bell Corporation's stock. Bell Corporation is taxed as a C corporation and employs 40 people. Marilyn is married, has two dependent children, and files a joint tax return with her husband. In the past, Marilyn has not itemized her deductions. She projects that Bell Corporation will report $400,000 of pretax profits for the current year. Marilyn is considering five salary levels as follows:

Total Income	*Salary Paid to Marilyn*	*Earnings Retained by Bell Corporation*	*Tax Liability* Marilyn	*Tax Liability* Bell Corporation	*Tax Liability* Total
$400,000	$ –0–	$400,000			
400,000	$100,000	300,000			
400,000	200,000	200,000			
400,000	300,000	100,000			
400,000	400,000	–0–			

a. Determine the total tax liability for Marilyn and Bell Corporation for each of the five proposed salary levels. (Assume no other income for Marilyn's family, and assume that Marilyn and her husband claim the standard deduction)

b. What recommendations can you make about a salary level for Marilyn that will minimize the total tax liability? Assume salaries paid up to $400,000 are considered reasonable compensation.

c. What possible disadvantage could accrue to Marilyn if Bell Corporation retains funds in the business and distributes some of the accumulated earnings as a dividend in a later tax year?

C3-55 ***Fringe Benefits.*** Refer to the facts in Problem C3-54. Marilyn has read an article explaining the advantages of paying tax-free fringe benefits (e.g., premiums on group term life insurance, accident and health insurance, etc.) and having deferred compensation plans (e.g., qualified pension and profit-sharing plans). Provide Marilyn with information on the tax savings associated with converting $3,000 of her salary into tax-free fringe benefits. What additional costs might Bell Corporation incur if it adopts a fringe benefit plan?

C3-56 ***Estimated Tax Requirement.*** Zeta Corporation's taxable income for 2001 was $1.5 million, on which Zeta paid federal income taxes of $510,000. Zeta estimates calendar year

2002's taxable income to be $2 million, on which it will owe $680,000 in federal income taxes.

a. What are Zeta's minimum quarterly estimated tax payments for 2002 to avoid an underpayment penalty?
b. When is Zeta's 2002 tax return due?
c. When are any remaining taxes due? What amount of taxes are due when the return is filed assuming Zeta timely pays estimated tax payments equal to the amount determined in Part a?
d. If Zeta obtains an extension, when is its tax return due? Will the extension permit Zeta to delay making its final tax payments?

C3-57 ***Filing the Tax Return and Paying the Tax Liability.*** Wright Corporation's taxable income for calendar years 1999, 2000, and 2001 was $120,000, $150,000, and $100,000, respectively. Its total tax liability for 2001 was $22,250. Wright estimates that its 2002 taxable income will be $500,000, on which it will owe federal income taxes of $170,000. Taxable income in 2002 is assumed to be earned evenly throughout the year.

a. What are Wright's minimum quarterly estimated tax payments for 2002 to avoid an underpayment penalty?
b. When is Wright's 2002 tax return due?
c. When are any remaining taxes due? What amount of taxes are due when Wright files its return assuming it timely paid estimated tax payments equal to the amount determined in Part a?
d. How would your answer to Part a change if Wright's tax liability for 2001 were $200,000?

C3-58 ***Converting Book Income to Taxable Income.*** The following income and expense accounts appeared in the accounting records of Rocket Corporation, an accrual basis taxpayer, for the current calendar year.

	Book Income	
Account Title	*Debit*	*Credit*
Net sales		$ 3,000,000
Dividends		8,000 (1)
Interest		18,000 (2)
Gain on sale of stock		5,000 (3)
Key-man life insurance proceeds		100,000
Cost of goods sold	$2,000,000	
Salaries and wages	500,000	
Bad debts	13,000 (4)	
Payroll taxes	62,000	
Interest expense	12,000 (5)	
Charitable contributions	50,000 (6)	
Depreciation	60,000 (7)	
Other expenses	40,000 (8)	
Federal income taxes	96,000	
Net income	298,000	
Total	$3,131,000	$3,131,000

The following additional information applies.

1. Dividends were from Star Corporation, a 30%-owned domestic corporation.
2. Interest revenue consists of interest on corporate bonds, $15,000; and municipal bonds, $3,000.
3. The stock is a capital asset held for three years prior to sale.
4. Rocket Corporation uses the specific chargeoff method of accounting for bad debts.
5. Interest expense consists of $11,000 interest incurred on funds borrowed for working capital, and $1,000 interest on funds borrowed to purchase municipal bonds.
6. All contributions were paid in cash during the current year to State University.
7. Depreciation per books is calculated using the straight-line method. For income tax purposes, depreciation amounted to $85,000.
8. Other expenses include premiums of $5,000 on the key-person life insurance policy covering the Rocket Corporation's president, who died in December.

Required: Prepare a worksheet reconciling Rocket Corporation's book income with its taxable income (before special deductions). Six columns should be used—two (one debit and one credit) for each of the following three major headings: book income, Schedule M-

1 adjustments, and taxable income. (See sample worksheet with Form 1120 in Appendix B if you need assistance).

C3-59 ***Reconciling Book Income and Taxable Income.*** Zero Corporation reports the following results for the current year:

Net income per books (after taxes)	$33,000
Federal income tax per books	12,000
Tax-exempt interest income	6,000
Interest on loan to purchase tax-exempt bonds	8,000
MACRS depreciation exceeding book depreciation	3,000
Net capital loss	5,000
Insurance premium on life of corporate officer where Zero is the beneficiary	10,000
Excess charitable contributions carried over to next year	2,500

Prepare a reconciliation of Zero's taxable income before special deductions with its book income.

C3-60 ***Reconciling Unappropriated Retained Earnings.*** White Corporation's financial accounting records disclose the following results for the period ending December 31 of the current year:

Retained earnings balance on January 1	$246,500
Net income for year	259,574
Contingency reserve established on December 31	60,000
Cash dividend paid on July 23	23,000

What is White's unappropriated retained earnings balance on December 31 of the current year?

COMPREHENSIVE PROBLEM

C3-61 Jackson Corporation prepared the following *book* income statement for its year ended December 31, 2002:

Sales			$765,000
Minus: Cost of goods sold			(400,000)
Gross profit			$365,000
Plus:	Dividends received on Invest Corporation stock	$ 3,000	
	Gain on sale of Invest Corporation stock	30,000	
	Total dividends and gain		33,000
Minus:	Depreciation ($7,500 + $8,000)	$ 15,500	
	Charitable contributions	10,000	
	Other operating expenses	105,500	
	Loss on sale of Equipment 1	70,000	
	Federal income taxes per books	99,000	
	Total expenses and loss		(300,000)
Net income per books			$98,000

Information on equipment depreciation and sale:

Equipment 1:

- Acquired March 3, 2000 for $180,000
- For books: 12-year life; straight-line depreciation
- Sold February 17, 2002 for $80,000

Sales price				$ 80,000
Cost			$180,000	
Minus:	Depreciation for 2000 (½ year)	$ 7,500		
	Depreciation for 2001 ($180,000/12)	15,000		
	Depreciation for 2002 (½ year)	7,500		
	Total depreciation		(30,000)	
Book value at time of sale				(150,000)
Book loss on sale of Equipment 1				$(70,000)

- For tax: 7-year MACRS property for which the corporation made no Sec. 179 election in the acquisition year.

Equipment 2:

- Acquired February 16, 2002 for $192,000
- For books: 12-year life; straight-line depreciation
- Book depreciation in 2002: $192,000/12 × 0.5 = $8,000
- For tax: 7-year MACRS property for which the corporation makes the Sec. 179 election

Other information:

- Jackson Corporation has a $40,000 NOL carryover and a $6,000 capital loss carryover from last year.
- Jackson Corporation purchased the Invest Corporation stock (less than 20% owned) on June 21, 2000 for $25,000 and sold the stock on December 22, 2002 for $55,000.

Required:

a. For 2002, calculate Jackson Corporation's tax depreciation deduction for Equipment 1 and Equipment 2, and determine the tax loss on the sale of Equipment 1.
b. For 2002, calculate Jackson Corporation's taxable income and tax liability.
c. Prepare a schedule reconciling net income per books to taxable income before special deductions.

TAX STRATEGY PROBLEM

C3-62 Mike Barton owns Barton Products, Inc. The corporation has 30 employees. Barton Corporation expects $500,000 of net income before taxes in 2002. Mike is married and files a joint return with his wife, Elaine, who has no earnings of her own. They have one dependent son, Robert, who is 16 years old. Mike and Elaine have no other income and do not itemize. Mike's salary is $200,000 per year (already deducted in computing Barton Corporation's $500,000 net income).

a. Should Mike increase his salary from Barton to reduce the overall tax burden to himself and Barton Products? If so, by how much?
b. Should Barton employ Mike's wife for $50,000 rather than increase Mike's salary? Take into consideration employment taxes as well as federal income taxes.
c. How much would be saved in overall taxes if Barton employs Robert part-time for $20,000 per year?

TAX FORM/RETURN PREPARATION PROBLEM

C3-63 Packer Corporation, incorporated on January 3, 1992, is a calendar year taxpayer that uses the accrual method of accounting. Its employer identification number is 74-1234567. Its address is 1010 West Avenue, San Antonio, Texas 78213. Packer operates a bookstore. Bob Parks (social security number 000-45-3000) owns 100% of the single class of stock. Bob resides at 25 Ancient Bend, San Antonio, TX 78248. He receives $65,000 in salary from Packer in the current year. During the current year, Packer reports the following income and expense items:

Gross receipts		$595,000
Purchases		300,000
Salaries:	Officers	65,000
	Other employees	50,000
Rent payments		48,000
Taxes:	Payroll	9,000
	Franchise	250
Interest payments		250
Charitable contributions (cash)		8,000
Depreciation (see schedule below)		38,820
Advertising		15,000
Telephone		500
Utilities		17,080
Officer's life insurance premium (firm is the beneficiary)		1,500

Depreciation Schedule

Asset	*Cost*	*Prior Depreciation*	*Method*	*Current Year Depreciation*
Light truck	$ 20,000	$10,400	MACRS	$ 3,840
Fixtures	200,000	77,560	MACRS	34,980
Total	$220,000	$87,960		$38,820

A truck purchased seven years earlier for $8,000, which was fully depreciated using the regular MACRS tables, was sold on May 10 for $3,500. Packer uses the same depreciation method for tax and book purposes. The corporation made estimated tax payments on April 14, June 15, September 11, and December 15 of the current year of $2,000 each (total of $8,000). Its prior year tax liability was $8,000. Packer's balance sheet at the beginning and end of the current year is as follows:

Assets	*January 1*	*December 31*
Cash	$ 34,000	$ 32,420
Other current assets	-0-	48,075
Depreciable assets	228,000	220,000
Minus: Accumulated depreciation	(95,960)	(126,780)
Inventory	125,000	145,000
Total assets	$291,040	$318,715
Liabilities and Stockholders' Equity		
Accounts payable	$ 68,900	$ 39,475
Common stock	60,000	60,000
Retained earnings (unappropriated)	162,140	219,240
Total liabilities and equity	$291,040	$318,715

Packer Corporation uses the first-in, first-out inventory method. The corporation does not claim any deduction for expenses connected with entertainment facilities, living accommodations, or employees attending foreign conventions. The corporation does not own any stock in any other corporation and has no interest in or authority over any foreign bank account or other foreign assets. The corporation did not pay any dividends in the current year. The other current assets amount at year-end consists entirely of marketable securities. No NOL carryovers are available from prior tax years. In computing the year-end retained earnings balance, Packer expensed $8,000 of federal income taxes (i.e., the amount paid in estimated taxes during the year). Prepare Form 1120 for Packer Corporation for the current year.

CASE STUDY PROBLEMS

C3-64 Marquette Corporation, a tax client since its creation three years ago, has requested that you prepare a memorandum explaining its estimated tax requirements for 2003. The corporation is in the fabricated steel business. Its earnings have been growing each year. Marquette's taxable income for the last three tax years has been $500,000, $1.5 million, and $2.5 million, respectively. The Chief Financial Officer expects its taxable income in 2003 to be approximately $3 million.

Required: Prepare a one-page client memorandum explaining Marquette's estimated tax requirements for 2003, providing the necessary supporting authorities.

C3-65 Susan Smith accepted a new corporate client, Winter Park Corporation. One of Susan's tax managers conducted a review of Winter Park's prior year tax returns. The review revealed that an NOL for a prior tax year was incorrectly computed, resulting in an overstatement of NOL carrybacks and carryovers to prior tax years.

a. Assume the incorrect NOL calculation does not affect the current year's tax liability. What recommendations (if any) should be made to the new client?

b. Assume the IRS is currently auditing a prior year. What are Susan's responsibilities in this situation?

c. Assume that the NOL carryover is being carried to the current year and that Winter Park Corporation does not want to file amended tax returns to correct the error? What should Susan do in this case?

C3-66 The Chief Executive Officer of a client of your public accounting firm saw the following advertisement in *The Wall Street Journal:*

> DONATIONS WANTED
> The Center for Restoration of Waters
> A Nonprofit Research and Educational Organization
> Needs Donations—Autos, Boats, Real Estate, Etc.
> ALL DONATIONS ARE TAX-DEDUCTIBLE

Prepare a memorandum to your client Phil Nickelson explaining how the federal income tax laws regarding donations of cash, automobiles, boats, and real estate apply to corporate taxpayers.

TAX RESEARCH PROBLEMS

C3-67 Wicker Corporation makes estimated tax payments of $6,000 in 2001. On March 15, 2002, it files its 2001 tax return, showing a tax liability of $20,000, and it pays the balance of $14,000. On April 16, 2002, it discovers an error and files an amended return for 2001 showing a reduced tax liability of $8,000. Prepare a memorandum for your tax manager explaining whether Wicker Corporation can base its estimated tax payments for 2002 on the $8,000 tax liability for 2001, or must it use the $20,000 tax liability reported on its original return. Your manager has suggested that, at a minimum, you consult the following resources:

- IRC Sec. 6655(d)(1)
- Rev. Rul. 86-58, 1986-1 C.B. 365

C3-68 King Corporation is owned equally by three individuals: Alice, Bill, and Charles, who purchased King stock when King Corporation was created. King Corporation has used the cash method of accounting since its inception in 1988. Alice, Bill, and Charles operate an environmental engineering firm of 60 employees, which had gross receipts of $4 million in 2001. Gross receipts have grown by about 15% in each of the last three years and were just under $5 million in 2002. The 15% growth rate is expected to continue for at least five years. Outstanding accounts receivable average about $600,000 at the end of each month. Forty-four of the employees (including Alice, Bill, and Charles) are actively engaged in providing engineering services on a full-time basis. Sixteen of the employees serve in a clerical and support capacity (secretarial staff, accountants, etc.). Bill has read about special restrictions on the use of the cash method of accounting and requests information from you about the impact these rules might have on King Corporation's continued use of the cash method of accounting. Prepare a memorandum for your tax manager addressing the following issues: (1) If the corporation changes to the accrual method of accounting, what adjustments must it make? (2) Would an S election relieve King Corporation from having to make a change? (3) If the S election relieves King from having to make a change, what factors should enter into the decision about whether King should make an S election?

Your manager has suggested that, at a minimum, you should consult the following

- IRC Secs. 446 and 448
- Temp. Reg. Secs. 1.448-1T and -2T
- H. Rept. No. 99-841, 99th Cong., 2d Sess., pp. 285-289 (1986)

C3-69 James Bowen owns 100% of the Bowen Corporation stock. Bowen Corporation is a calendar year, accrual method of accounting taxpayer. During 2002, Bowen Corporation made three charitable contributions:

Donee	*Property Donated*	*FMV of Property*
State University	Bates Corporation Stock	$110,000
Red Cross	Cash	5,000
Girl Scouts	Pledge to pay cash	25,000

Bowen Corporation purchased the Bates Corporation stock three years ago for $30,000. Bowen holds a 28% interest, which is accounted for by using the equity method of accounting. The current carrying value for the Bates stock for book purposes is $47,300. The pledge to the Girl Scouts will be paid by check on March 1, 2003. Bowen

Corporation's taxable income for 2002 before any charitable contributions deduction, dividends-received deduction, or NOL or capital loss carryback is $600,000. Your tax manager has asked you to prepare a memorandum for your tax manager explaining how these transactions are to be treated for tax purposes and for accounting purposes. Your manager has suggested that, at a minimum, you should consult the following:

- IRC Sec. 170
- FASB, *Statement of Financial Accounting Standards No. 116*

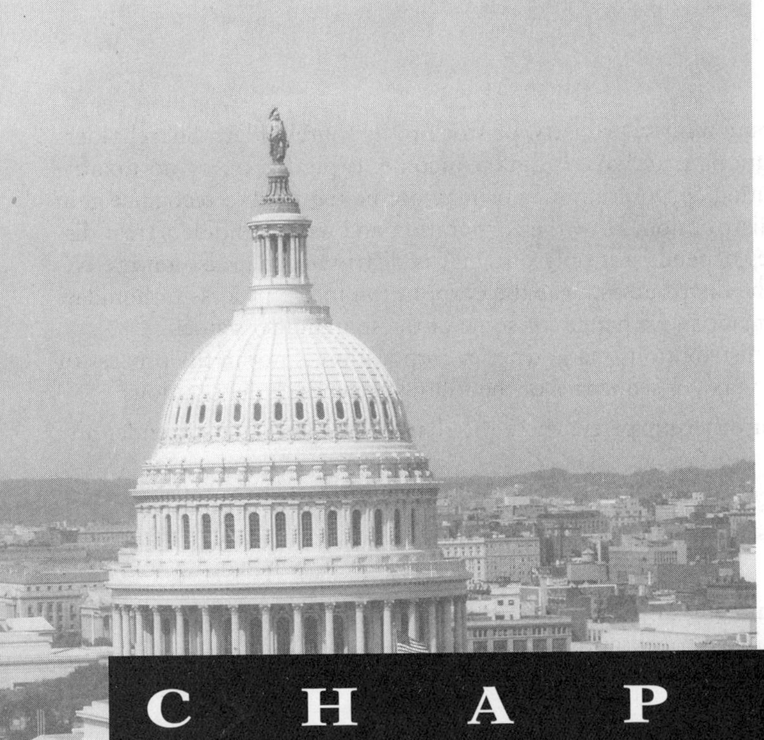

4

C H A P T E R

CORPORATE NONLIQUIDATING DISTRIBUTIONS

LEARNING OBJECTIVES

After studying this chapter, you should be able to

1. Explain how current E&P is calculated
2. Explain the difference between current and accumulated E&P
3. Determine the tax consequences of nonliquidating property distributions
4. Determine the tax consequences of stock dividends and distributions of stock rights
5. Distinguish between a stock redemption treated as a sale and one treated as a dividend
6. Explain the tax treatment for preferred stock bailouts
7. Determine when Sec. 304 applies to a stock sale and its tax consequences

CHAPTER OUTLINE

Nonliquidating Distributions in General...4-2
Earnings and Profits (E&P)...4-3
Nonliquidating Property Distributions...4-8
Stock Dividends and Stock Rights...4-13
Stock Redemptions...4-16
Preferred Stock Bailouts...4-28
Stock Redemptions By Related Corporations...4-30
Tax Planning Considerations...4-33
Compliance and Procedural Considerations...4-36

A corporation may distribute money, property, or stock to its shareholders. Shareholders who receive such distributions may have ordinary income, capital gain, or no taxable income at all. The distributing corporation may or may not be required to recognize gain or loss when making the distribution. How the corporation and its shareholders treat distributions for tax purposes depends not only on what is distributed but also on the circumstances surrounding the distribution. Was the corporation in the process of liquidating? Was the distribution made in exchange for some of the shareholder's stock?

This chapter discusses distributions made when a corporation is not in the process of liquidating. It discusses the tax consequences of the following types of distributions:

- Distributions of cash or other property where the shareholder does not surrender any stock
- Distributions of stock or rights to acquire stock of the distributing corporation
- Distributions of property in exchange for the corporation's own stock (i.e., stock redemptions)

Chapter C6 discusses **liquidating distributions**. Chapter C7 discusses distributions of the stock of a controlled subsidiary corporation.

NONLIQUIDATING DISTRIBUTIONS IN GENERAL

SELF-STUDY QUESTION

How does a shareholder classify a distribution for tax purposes?

ANSWER

Distributions are treated as follows: (1) dividends to the extent of corporate E&P, (2) return of capital to the extent of the shareholder's stock basis, and (3) gain from the sale of stock.

When a corporation makes a nonliquidating distribution to a shareholder, the shareholder must answer the following three questions:

- What is the amount of the distribution?
- To what extent is the amount distributed a dividend?
- What is the basis of the distributed property, and when does its holding period begin?

In addition, the distributing corporation must answer the following two questions:

- What are the amount and character of the gain or loss that the corporation must recognize on the distribution?
- What effect does the distribution have on the distributing corporation's E&P account?

A brief summary of the rules for determining the taxability of a distribution follows, along with a simple example.

Section 301 requires a shareholder to include in gross income the amount of any distribution from a corporation to the extent that it is a dividend. Section 316(a) defines a **dividend** as a distribution of property made by a corporation out of its earnings and profits (E&P). The term E&P is defined in the next section of this chapter. Section 317(a) defines **property** broadly to include money, securities, and any other property except stock or stock rights of the distributing corporation. Distributed amounts that exceed a corporation's E&P are treated as a return of capital that reduces the shareholder's basis in his or her stock (but not below zero). Excess distributions beyond the shareholder's basis are treated as gain from the sale of the stock. If the stock is a capital asset in the shareholder's hands, the gain is a capital gain.

EXAMPLE C4-1 ▶ On March 1, Gamma Corporation distributes $60,000 in cash to each of its two equal shareholders, Ellen and Bob. At the time of the distribution, Gamma's E&P is $80,000. Ellen's basis in her stock is $25,000, and Bob's basis in his stock is $10,000. Ellen and Bob each must recognize $40,000 (0.50 × $80,000) of dividend income. This portion of the distribution reduces Gamma's E&P to zero. The additional $20,000 that each shareholder receives is treated as a return of capital or capital gain as summarized in the table below.

	Ellen	*Bob*	*Total*
Distribution	$60,000	$60,000	$120,000
Dividend income[a]	(40,000)	(40,000)	(80,000)
Remaining distribution	$20,000	$20,000	$ 40,000
Return of capital[b]	(20,000)	(10,000)	(30,000)
Capital gain[c]	$ –0–	$10,000	$ 10,000

[a]Smaller of E&P allocable to the distribution or the amount of the distribution.
[b]Smaller of remaining distribution to shareholder or his or her stock basis.
[c]Any amount received that exceeds the shareholder's basis in his or her stock.

EARNINGS AND PROFITS (E&P)

TYPICAL MISCONCEPTION

Because E&P is such an important concept in many corporate transactions, one would assume that corporations know exactly what their E&P is. However, many corporations do not compute their E&P on a regular basis.

The term E&P is not specifically defined in the IRC. Its meaning must be inferred from its function in judicial decisions, Treasury Regulations, and some rules provided in the IRC regarding how certain transactions affect E&P.

E&P provides a measure of the corporation's economic ability to pay dividends to shareholders. Distributions are considered to come from the corporation's E&P unless the corporation can show that it has no E&P.

CURRENT EARNINGS AND PROFITS

E&P consists of two parts: current E&P and accumulated E&P. **Current E&P** is calculated annually as explained below. **Accumulated E&P** is the sum of undistributed current E&P balances for all previous years reduced by the sum of all previous current E&P deficits and any distributions that have been made out of accumulated E&P. Distributions come first from current E&P and then from accumulated E&P if current E&P is insufficient.

EXAMPLE C4-2 ▶ Zeta Corporation is formed in 1999. Its current E&P (or current E&P deficit) and distributions for each year through 2002 are as follows:

Year	*Current E&P (Deficit)*	*Distributions*
1999	$(10,000)	–0–
2000	15,000	–0–
2001	18,000	$9,000
2002	8,000	–0–

The $9,000 distribution is made from 2001's current E&P. At the beginning of 2002, Zeta's accumulated E&P is $14,000 (– $10,000 + $15,000 + $18,000 – $9,000). At the beginning of 2003, Zeta's accumulated E&P is $22,000 ($14,000 + $8,000). ◀

OBJECTIVE 1

Explain how current E&P is calculated

COMPUTING CURRENT E&P. Current E&P is computed on an annual basis at the end of each year. The starting point for computing current E&P is the corporation's taxable income or net operating loss (NOL) for the year. Taxable income or the NOL must be adjusted to obtain the corporation's economic income or loss (current E&P) for the year. For example, federal income taxes are deducted from taxable income when determining E&P. Because these taxes must be paid to the U.S. government, they reduce the amount available to pay dividends to shareholders. On the other hand, tax-exempt income must be added to taxable income (or the NOL) because, even though not taxable, it increases the corporation's ability to pay dividends.

A partial listing of the adjustments that must be made is presented in Table C4-1. Some of the adjustments that must be made to taxable income to derive current E&P are explained below.[1]

[1] The adjustments required are based on rules found in Sec. 312 and related Treasury Regulations.

▼ **TABLE C4-1**
Computation of Current E&P

Taxable income
Plus: *Income excluded from taxable income but included in E&P*
  Tax-exempt interest income
  Life insurance proceeds where the corporation is the beneficiary
  Recoveries of bad debts and other deductions from which the corporation received no tax benefit
  Federal income tax refunds from prior years
Plus: *Income deferred to a later year when computing taxable income but included in E&P in the current year*
  Deferred gain on installment sales is included in E&P in the year of sale
Plus or minus: *Income and deduction items that must be recomputed when computing E&P*
  Income on long-term contracts must be based on percentage of completion method rather than completed contract method
  Depreciation on personal and real property must be based on:
    The straight-line method for property other than MACRS or ACRS property
    A straight-line ACRS calculation with an extended recovery period for ACRS property
    The alternative depreciation system for MACRS property
  Excess of percentage depletion claimed over cost depletion
Plus: *Deductions that reduce taxable income but are not allowed in computing E&P*
  Dividends-received deduction
  NOL carryovers, charitable contribution carryovers, and capital loss carryovers used in the current year
Minus: *Expenses and losses that are not deductible in computing taxable income but that reduce E&P*
  Federal income taxes
  Life insurance premiums where the corporation is the beneficiary
  Excess capital losses that are not deductible
  Excess charitable contributions that are not deductible
  Expenses related to production of tax-exempt income
  Nondeductible losses on sales to related parties
  Nondeductible penalties and fines
  Nondeductible political contributions and lobbying expenses

Current E&P (or current E&P deficit)

INCOME EXCLUDED FROM TAXABLE INCOME BUT INCLUDED IN E&P. Although certain income is specifically excluded from taxable income, any income received by the corporation must be included in its E&P if it increases the corporation's ability to pay a dividend and is not a contribution to capital. Thus, a corporation's current E&P includes both tax-exempt interest income and life insurance proceeds. Current E&P also includes any recovery of an item deducted in a previous year if the deduction did not result in a tax benefit to the corporation and therefore was excluded from taxable income.

EXAMPLE C4-3 ▶ Ace Corporation deducted $10,000 of bad debts in 2001. Because Ace Corporation had an NOL in 2001 that it was unable to carry back or forward, it received no tax benefit from the deduction. Ace Corporation recovers $8,000 of the amount due in 2002. Ace excludes the $8,000 from its gross income for 2002 because it received no tax benefit from the bad debt deduction in 2001. However, Ace must add the $8,000 to its taxable income when determining current E&P for 2002 because the NOL reduced current E&P in 2001. ◀

INCOME DEFERRED TO A LATER YEAR WHEN COMPUTING TAXABLE INCOME BUT INCLUDED IN E&P IN THE CURRENT YEAR. Gains and losses on property transactions generally are included in E&P in the same year they are recognized for tax purposes. For example, gain deferred in a like-kind exchange is deferred for E&P purposes as well.

EXAMPLE C4-4 ▶ Stone Corporation exchanges investment property that has a $12,000 basis and an $18,000 fair market value (FMV) for investment property worth $17,000 and $1,000 cash. Stone recognizes a $1,000 gain on the like-kind exchange—the amount of boot received—and defers $5,000 of gain. Stone includes the recognized gain in taxable income and in current E&P. It does not include the deferred gain in taxable income or in current E&P. ◀

In the case of an installment sale, the entire gain must be included in current E&P in the year of the sale. This rule applies to sales made by dealers and nondealers.

EXAMPLE C4-5 ▶ In the current year, Tally Corporation sells land that has a $12,000 basis and a $20,000 FMV to Rick, an unrelated individual. Rick makes a $5,000 down payment this year and will pay Tally an additional $5,000 in each of the next three years, plus interest on the unpaid balance at a rate acceptable to the IRS. Tally's realized gain is $8,000 ($20,000 − $12,000). Using the nondealer installment sale rules, Tally recognizes its gain on the sale using the installment method of accounting. This year, Tally recognizes $2,000 of gain [($8,000 ÷ $20,000) × $5,000] in computing taxable income. All $8,000 of Tally's realized gain must be included in current E&P. In computing current E&P for this year, Tally's taxable income must be increased by $6,000. The remaining $6,000 of gain will be recognized over the next three years ($2,000 per year) as Tally collects the installments. E&P will have to be reduced by $2,000 in each of those years since all $8,000 was included in E&P in the current year. ◀

SELF-STUDY QUESTION

In computing taxable income and E&P, different depreciation methods are often used. What happens when the taxpayer sells such assets?

ANSWER

The taxpayer must calculate a gain/loss for taxable income and E&P purposes separately. This difference is an added complexity in making E&P calculations.

INCOME AND DEDUCTION ITEMS THAT MUST BE RECOMPUTED WHEN COMPUTING E&P. Some deductions must be computed differently for E&P purposes than they are for taxable income. Therefore, an adjustment must be made for the difference between the two computations.

- E&P must be computed using the percentage of completion method even if the corporation uses the completed contract method of accounting for tax purposes.
- Depreciation must be recomputed using the alternative depreciation system of Sec. 168(g). Property expensed under Sec. 179 is expensed ratably over a five-year period starting with the month in which it is deductible for Sec. 179 purposes. Other personal property must be depreciated over the property's class life and using a half-year convention. Real property must be depreciated over a 40-year period for E&P purposes using the straight-line method and mid-month convention.

EXAMPLE C4-6 ▶ In January 1999, Radon Corporation paid $5,000 for equipment with a ten-year class life. Radon expensed the entire cost of the equipment in 1999 under Sec. 179. Radon's depreciation deduction for E&P purposes is $1,000 ($5,000 ÷ 5) in each year from 1999 through 2003. ◀

- Cost depletion must be used for E&P purposes even if percentage depletion is used when computing taxable income.
- Intangible drilling costs must be capitalized and amortized over 60 months for E&P purposes.

ADDITIONAL COMMENT

Many corporations use retained earnings to measure the taxability of their dividend payments. Because retained earnings are based on financial accounting concepts, E&P may represent a different amount and may provide a different answer.

DEDUCTIONS THAT REDUCE TAXABLE INCOME BUT ARE NOT ALLOWED IN COMPUTING E&P. Some deductions claimed when computing taxable income are not allowed when computing current E&P.

- The dividends-received deduction is not permitted for E&P purposes because it does not reduce the corporation's ability to pay dividends. Therefore, it must be added back to taxable income to compute E&P.
- NOL carryovers, charitable contribution carryovers, and capital loss carryovers that reduce taxable income for the current year cannot be deducted when determining E&P. These losses or excess deductions reduce E&P in the year they are incurred.
- Amortization of organizational expenses is not permitted as a deduction for E&P purposes.

EXAMPLE C4-7 ▶ Thames Corporation's taxable income is $50,000 after deducting a $10,000 NOL carryover from two years ago and after claiming a $20,000 dividends-received deduction. Thames must add $30,000 to its taxable income to compute current E&P. The $10,000 NOL reduced E&P in the year it was incurred. ◀

EXPENSES AND LOSSES THAT ARE NOT DEDUCTIBLE IN COMPUTING TAXABLE INCOME BUT THAT REDUCE E&P. Some expenses and losses that are not deductible in computing taxable income are deductible when computing current E&P.

- Federal income taxes are not deductible when computing taxable income. For E&P purposes, federal income taxes are deductible in the year they accrue if the corporation uses the accrual method of accounting and in the year they are paid if the corporation uses the cash method of accounting.

EXAMPLE C4-8 ▶ Perch Corporation, which uses the accrual method of accounting, has taxable income of $100,000 on which it owes $22,250 of federal income taxes. In computing its current E&P, it must reduce taxable income by $22,250. ◀

- Charitable contributions are deductible in full for E&P purposes without regard to the 10% limitation on such deductions. Thus, when current E&P is computed, taxable income must be reduced by any charitable contributions disallowed because of the 10% limitation.

EXAMPLE C4-9 ▶ Dot Corporation has $25,000 of taxable income before any charitable contribution deduction. Dot contributed $10,000 to the Red Cross. Although Dot's contribution deduction is limited to $2,500 in computing taxable income because of the 10% of taxable income limitation on charitable contribution deductions, Dot deducts the entire $10,000 in computing current E&P. Therefore, $7,500 must be deducted from taxable income of $22,500 ($25,000 − $2,500) to compute current E&P. In a later year(s), when the $7,500 carryover is deducted in determining taxable income, it must be added to taxable income in arriving at current E&P. ◀

- Life insurance premiums paid on policies to insure the lives of key corporate personnel (net of any increase in the cash surrender value of the policy) are not deductible when computing taxable income but are deductible when computing E&P.
- Capital losses exceeding capital gains cannot be deducted when computing taxable income but are deductible when computing current E&P.
- Nondeductible expenses related to the production of tax-exempt income (e.g., interest charges to borrow money to purchase tax-exempt securities) are deductible when computing E&P.
- Losses on sales to related parties that are disallowed under Sec. 267 are deductible when computing E&P.
- Nondeductible fines, penalties, and political contributions are deductible for E&P purposes.

The adjustments listed in Table C4-1 and described above are only a partial list of the adjustments that must be made to taxable income to compute current E&P. The basic rule is that adjustments are made so that current E&P represents the corporation's economic ability to pay dividends out of its current earnings.

OBJECTIVE 2

Explain the difference between current and accumulated E&P

DISTINCTION BETWEEN CURRENT AND ACCUMULATED E&P

A distinction must be made between current and accumulated E&P. A nonliquidating distribution is classified as a dividend if it is deemed to come from either current or accumulated E&P. Corporate distributions are deemed to come from current E&P first and then from accumulated E&P only if current E&P is insufficient.[2] If current E&P is sufficient to cover all distributions made during the year, each distribution is treated as a taxable divi-

[2] The distinction between current and accumulated E&P is explained in Reg. Sec. 1.316-2.

dend. This rule applies even if the corporation has a deficit in accumulated E&P. Current E&P is computed on the last day of the tax year with no reduction for distributions made during the year.

EXAMPLE C4-10 ▶ At the beginning of the current year, Water Corporation has a $30,000 accumulated E&P deficit. For the year, Water reports current E&P of $15,000. Water distributes $10,000 to its shareholders during the current year. The $10,000 distribution is a taxable dividend to the shareholders because it comes from current E&P. At the beginning of the next tax year, Water has an accumulated E&P deficit of $25,000 (– $30,000 E&P deficit + $5,000 undistributed current E&P). ◀

TAX STRATEGY TIP

A corporation with an accumulated deficit and current E&P may want to postpone distributions to a later year to avoid dividend treatment in the current year. See Example C4-53 later in this chapter.

If distributions made during the year exceed current E&P, current E&P is allocated to those distributions on a pro rata basis regardless of when during the year the distributions were made. Distributions exceeding current E&P come from accumulated E&P (if any) in chronological order. Distributions exceeding current and accumulated E&P are a return of capital and reduce the shareholder's basis on a dollar-for-dollar basis. However, these distributions cannot create an E&P deficit. Deficits arise only because of losses. These rules are important if the stock changes hands during the year and total E&P is insufficient to cover all distributions.

EXAMPLE C4-11 ▶ At the beginning of the current year, Cole Corporation has $20,000 of accumulated E&P. For the current year, Cole's current E&P is $30,000. On April 10, Cole distributes $20,000 to Bob, its sole shareholder. On July 15, Cole distributes an additional $24,000 to Bob. On August 1, Bob sells all of his Cole stock to Lynn. On September 15, Cole distributes $36,000 to Lynn. Cole's current and accumulated E&P must be allocated to the three distributions made during the year as follows:

Date	*Distribution Amount*	*Current E&P*	*Accumulated E&P*	*Dividend Income*	*Return of Capital*
April 10	$20,000	$ 7,500	$12,500	$20,000	$ –0–
July 15	24,000	9,000	7,500	16,500	7,500
September 15	36,000	13,500	–0–	13,500	22,500
Total	$80,000	$30,000	$20,000	$50,000	$30,000

The current E&P allocated to the April 10 distribution is calculated as follows:

$$\$30{,}000 \text{ (Current E\&P)} \times \frac{\$20{,}000 \text{ (April 10 distribution)}}{\$80{,}000 \text{ (Total distributions)}}$$

Note that the total amount of dividends paid by Cole equals $50,000, the sum of $30,000 of current E&P and $20,000 of accumulated E&P. Current E&P is allocated to all three distributions on a pro rata basis, whereas accumulated E&P is allocated first to the April 10 distribution ($12,500). The remaining accumulated E&P is allocated to the July 15 distribution, so that none is available to allocate to the September 15 distribution. Thus, Bob's dividend income from Cole is $36,500 ($20,000 + $16,500). He also has a $7,500 return of capital that reduces his stock basis. Lynn's dividend income from Cole is $13,500. She also has a $22,500 return of capital payment that reduces her stock basis. Note that Bob cannot determine his gain on the stock sale until after the end of the year. He must wait until he knows how much of the two distributions he received reduced his stock basis. ◀

If the corporation has a current E&P deficit and an accumulated E&P deficit, none of the distributions are treated as dividends. Instead, all distributions are a return of capital until the basis of a shareholder's stock is reduced to zero. Any additional amounts received are taxable as a capital gain.

EXAMPLE C4-12 ▶ At the beginning of the current year, Rose Corporation has a $15,000 accumulated E&P deficit. Rose's current E&P deficit is $20,000. Rose distributes $10,000 on July 1. The distribution is not a dividend but is a return of capital and/or a capital gain for amounts exceeding the shareholder's stock basis. Rose's accumulated E&P deficit at January 1 of next year is $35,000 because the distribution did not come from E&P but represents a return of capital or a capital gain. ◀

SELF-STUDY QUESTION

When is E&P measured for purposes of determining whether a distribution is a dividend?

ANSWER

Usually at year-end. However, if a current deficit exists, the E&P available for measuring dividend income is determined at the distribution date.

If the corporation has a current E&P deficit and a positive accumulated E&P balance, it must net the two accounts at the time of the distribution to determine the amount of any distribution that comes from E&P.[3] The deficit in current E&P that has accrued up through the day before the distribution reduces the accumulated E&P balance on that date. If the balance remaining after the reduction is positive, the distribution is a dividend to the extent of the lesser of the distribution amount or the E&P balance. If the E&P balance is zero or negative, the distribution is a return of capital. If the actual deficit in current E&P to the date of distribution cannot be determined, the current E&P deficit is prorated on a daily basis to the day before the distribution date.

EXAMPLE C4-13 ▶ Assume the same facts as in Example C4-12 except that Rose Corporation has a $15,000 accumulated E&P balance. The current E&P deficit of $20,000 accrues on a daily basis unless information indicates otherwise. The amount of the July 1 distribution that is a dividend is calculated as follows:

Date	*Distribution Amount*	*Accumulated E&P*	*Dividend Income*	*Return of Capital*
Jan. 1	$ -0-	$15,000		
July 1	10,000	(9,918)[a]	$5,082	$4,918
Total	$10,000	$ 5,082[b]	$5,082	$4,918

[a]181/365 × ($20,000) = ($9,918)—the current E&P deficit accrued up to the distribution date.

[b]$15,000 − $9,918 = $5,082—accumulated E&P at beginning of year minus the current E&P deficit accrued up to the distribution date. ◀

STOP & THINK *Question:* Why is it necessary to keep separate balances for current and accumulated E&P?

Solution: If the total current and accumulated E&P is less than the total distributions made to the shareholders, E&P must be allocated to all distributions made during the year to determine the amount of each distribution that is a dividend. When no change in the shareholder's stock ownership occurs during the year and all distributions are proportional to stock ownership, an E&P allocation is needed only to track each shareholder's stock basis. Tracking E&P to individual distributions is necessary to determine the taxability of a particular distribution when a change in a shareholder's stock ownership occurs because current E&P is allocated on a pro rata basis and accumulated E&P is allocated chronologically. Therefore, distributions made early in a tax year may be more heavily taxed than are distributions made later in the year. On the other hand, current E&P deficits offset accumulated E&P balances. In such a situation, distributions made later in a tax year may be less heavily taxed than are distributions made earlier in the year.

NONLIQUIDATING PROPERTY DISTRIBUTIONS

OBJECTIVE 3

Determine the tax consequences of nonliquidating property distributions

CONSEQUENCES OF NONLIQUIDATING PROPERTY DISTRIBUTIONS TO THE SHAREHOLDERS

Property includes money, securities, and any other property except stock in the corporation making the distribution (or rights to acquire such stock).[4] When a corporation makes a property distribution to its shareholders, the following three questions must be answered:

- What is the amount of the distribution?
- To what extent is the amount distributed a dividend to the shareholder?

[3] Reg. Sec. 1.316-2(b).

[4] Sec. 317(a).

KEY POINT

The amount of the distribution is measured by the FMV of the property less liabilities assumed (but not below zero) because this net amount represents the real economic value received by the shareholder.

- What is the basis of the property to the shareholder, and when does its holding period begin?

For cash distributions, these questions are easy to answer. The distribution amount is the amount of cash distributed. This distribution is a dividend to the extent it comes from the corporation's current and accumulated E&P, and the E&P account is reduced by the cash dividend amount. The shareholder's basis in the cash received is its face amount. The distributing corporation recognizes no gain on the distribution of cash.

When the corporation distributes property such as land or inventory to a shareholder, these questions are more difficult to answer. Neither the amount of the distribution nor the basis of the property to the shareholder is immediately apparent. The corporation must recognize gain (but not loss) on the distribution, and the impact of the distribution on the corporation's E&P and the taxability of the distribution must be determined. The following sections explain the rules that govern the answers to these questions.

When the corporation distributes property to a shareholder, the amount of the distribution is the FMV of the property distributed.[5] The value is determined on the date of the distribution. The amount of any liability assumed by the shareholder in connection with the distribution, or to which the distributed property is subject, reduces the distribution amount. However, the distribution amount cannot be reduced below zero. The distribution amount is a dividend to the shareholder to the extent of the distributing corporation's E&P.

The shareholder's basis in any property received is the property's FMV. The basis is not reduced by any liabilities assumed by the shareholder or to which the property is subject.[6] The holding period of the property begins on the day after the distribution date. It does not include the holding period of the distributing corporation.

EXAMPLE C4-14 ▶

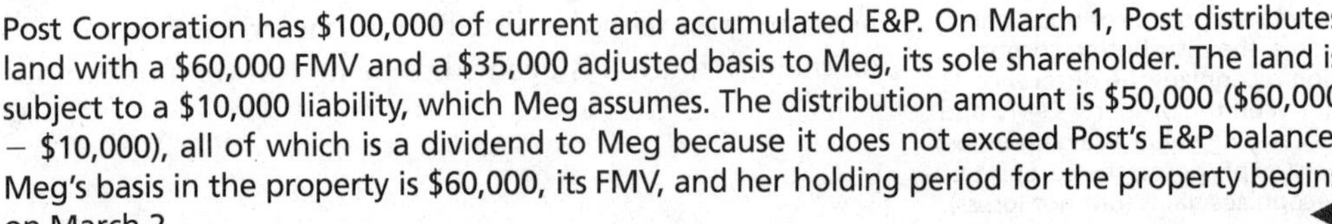

Post Corporation has $100,000 of current and accumulated E&P. On March 1, Post distributes land with a $60,000 FMV and a $35,000 adjusted basis to Meg, its sole shareholder. The land is subject to a $10,000 liability, which Meg assumes. The distribution amount is $50,000 ($60,000 − $10,000), all of which is a dividend to Meg because it does not exceed Post's E&P balance. Meg's basis in the property is $60,000, its FMV, and her holding period for the property begins on March 2. ◀

STOP & THINK

Question: Why do liabilities reduce the amount of income reported when a corporation makes a distribution to a shareholder, but do not reduce the shareholder's adjusted basis for the property?

Solution: The amount of a distribution to a shareholder is the property's FMV on the distribution date. In Example C4-14, Meg receives land worth $60,000 and also acquires the $10,000 debt, which she is obligated to pay. Therefore, the value of the distribution to Meg is the net amount that she receives, or $50,000 ($60,000 − $10,000). The adjusted basis of the land to Meg is $60,000, its FMV. This rule is the same as if Meg purchased the land for $60,000 but financed the purchase by borrowing $10,000. The basis of the land to Meg would still be its $60,000 FMV.

Topic Review C4-1 summarizes the tax consequences of a nonliquidating distribution to the shareholders.

CONSEQUENCES OF PROPERTY DISTRIBUTIONS TO THE DISTRIBUTING CORPORATION

KEY POINT

Property distributions may trigger income at both the shareholder and the distributing corporation level. This is another example of the double taxation that exists in our corporate tax system.

Two questions must be answered with respect to a corporation that distributes property:

- What amount and character of gain or loss must the distributing corporation recognize on the distribution?
- What effect does the distribution have on the corporation's E&P?

---

[5] Sec. 301(b).

[6] Sec. 301(d).

Topic Review C4-1

Tax Consequences of a Nonliquidating Distribution to the Shareholders

1. The amount of a distribution is the amount of money received plus the FMV of any nonmoney property received reduced by any liabilities assumed or acquired by the shareholder.
2. The distribution is a dividend to the extent of the distributing corporation's current and accumulated E&P. Any excess distribution is a return of capital that reduces the shareholder's stock basis (but not below zero). Any further excess distribution is a capital gain.
3. The shareholder's basis in the property received is its FMV.
4. The shareholder's holding period begins on the day after the distribution date.

CORPORATE GAIN OR LOSS ON PROPERTY DISTRIBUTIONS. When a corporation distributes property that has appreciated in value, the corporation must recognize gain as though the corporation had sold the property for its FMV. However, a corporation does not recognize any loss when it makes a nonliquidating distribution of property even if a sale of the property would have yielded a loss.[7]

EXAMPLE C4-15 ▶ Silver Corporation distributes land (a capital asset) worth $60,000 to Mark, a shareholder. The land has a $20,000 adjusted basis to Silver. Silver recognizes a $40,000 ($60,000 − $20,000) capital gain, as though Silver had sold the property. If the land instead has a $12,000 FMV, Silver recognizes no loss on the distribution. ◀

BOOK-TO-TAX ACCOUNTING COMPARISON

Divdends-in-kind are reported at their FMV by the distributing corporation for financial accounting (book) purposes. For book purposes, the distributing corporation recognizes the difference between the property's FMV and its carrying value as a gain or loss. For tax purposes, the corporation recognizes gains (but not losses).

If the distributed property is subject to a liability or the shareholder assumes a liability in connection with the distribution, the property's FMV for purposes of determining gain on the distribution is deemed to be no less than the amount of the liability.[8]

EXAMPLE C4-16 ▶ Assume the same facts as in Example C4-15 except that the land's FMV is instead $25,000, and the land is subject to a $35,000 mortgage. The land's FMV for gain recognition is $35,000 because it cannot be less than the amount of the liability. Thus, Silver Corporation's gain is $15,000 ($35,000 − $20,000), the amount by which the land's deemed FMV exceeds its basis.[9] ◀

TAX STRATEGY TIP

If possible, a corporation should avoid distributing property subject to a liability exceeding the property's FMV because of the potential gain recognition caused by the excess liability.

EFFECT OF PROPERTY DISTRIBUTIONS ON THE DISTRIBUTING CORPORATION'S E&P. Distributions have two effects on E&P:[10]

- When a corporation distributes appreciated property to its shareholders, it must increase E&P by the **E&P gain**, which is the excess of the property's FMV over its adjusted basis for E&P purposes. Because a property's **E&P adjusted basis** may differ from its tax basis (as discussed earlier in this chapter), this E&P gain may differ from the corporation's recognized tax gain upon distribution.
- If the E&P adjusted basis of the noncash asset distributed equals or exceeds its FMV, E&P is reduced by the asset's E&P adjusted basis. If the FMV of the asset distributed exceeds its E&P adjusted basis, E&P is reduced by the asset's FMV. In either case, the E&P reduction is net of any liability to which the asset is subject or that the shareholder assumes in connection with the distribution. E&P also is reduced by the income taxes incurred on the gain recognized, if any.[11]

---

[7] Sec. 311(a).

[8] Sec. 311(b)(2).

[9] Treatment at the shareholder level is not completely clear. Section 336(b), which Sec. 311(b)(2) makes applicable to nonliquidating distributions, specifically states that this liability rule applies only for determining the corporation's gain or loss. Thus, it does not seem to extend to Sec. 301(d), which requires the shareholder to take a FMV basis in the distributed property. Some commentators have suggested that the strict statutory interpretation of giving the shareholders the actual FMV basis, rather than the greater liability basis, produces an illogical result. (See B.C. Randall and D.N. Stewart, "Corporate Distributions: Handling Liabilities in Excess of the Fair Market Value of Property Remains Unresolved," *The Journal of Corporate Taxation*, 1992, pp. 55-64.) Also, given that the liability exceeds the distributed property's FMV, the shareholder's amount distributed should be zero, resulting in no dividend.

[10] Secs. 312(a) and (b).

[11] Secs. 312(a) and (c).

EXAMPLE C4-17 ▶ Brass Corporation distributes to its shareholder, Joan, property with a $25,000 tax adjusted basis, a $22,000 E&P adjusted basis, and a $40,000 FMV. The property is subject to a $12,000 mortgage, which Joan assumes. Brass recognizes a $15,000 ($40,000 FMV – $25,000 tax adjusted basis) gain on the distribution. Brass's E&P is increased by $18,000 ($40,000 FMV – $22,000 E&P adjusted basis) and is reduced by $28,000 ($40,000 FMV – $12,000 liability). E&P also is reduced by the amount of income taxes paid or accrued by Brass on the $15,000 gain. ◀

A special rule applies when a corporation distributes its own obligation (e.g., its notes, bonds, or debentures) to a shareholder. In such case, the distributing corporation's E&P is reduced by the principal amount of the obligation distributed.[12]

Topic Review C4-2 summarizes the tax consequences of a nonliquidating distribution to the distributing corporation.

CONSTRUCTIVE DIVIDENDS

A **constructive dividend** (or undeclared distribution) is an indirect payment made to a shareholder without the benefit of a formal declaration. Ordinarily, a corporate dividend payment is formally declared by the board of directors and is paid in cash or property on a specified date. A formal declaration is not required, however. Constructive dividends may be treated as dividends for income tax purposes even though they have not been formally authorized by the corporation's board of directors. It is not even necessary that the distribution be pro rata. Any economic benefit provided by a corporation to a shareholder may be treated as a constructive dividend to the shareholder.

Constructive dividends are most likely to arise in the context of a closely held corporation where the shareholders (or relatives of shareholders) and management groups overlap. In such situations, the dealings between the corporation and its shareholders are likely to be less structured and subject to less review than they would be in a publicly held corporation. However, constructive dividends can arise in a publicly held corporation as well.

INTENTIONAL EFFORTS TO AVOID DIVIDEND TREATMENT. Constructive dividends may arise from intentional attempts to bail out a corporation's E&P without subjecting it to taxation at the shareholder level or to obtain a deduction at the corporate level for distributions to shareholders that should not be deductible. If a corporation has sufficient E&P, dividend distributions are fully taxable to the shareholder but are not deductible by the distributing corporation. For example, shareholders may try to disguise a dividend as a salary payment. If successful, the payment is taxable to the shareholder-employee and is deductible by the distributing corporation as long as the amount is reasonable. Shareholders also may try to disguise a dividend as a loan to the shareholder. If successful, the payment is neither deductible by the corporation nor taxable to the share-

Topic Review C4-2

Tax Consequences of a Nonliquidating Distribution to the Distributing Corporation

1. A corporation must recognize gain when it distributes appreciated property as though the property had been sold for its FMV immediately before the distribution.
2. For gain recognition purposes, a property's FMV is deemed to be at least equal to any liability to which the property is subject or that the shareholder assumes in connection with the distribution.
3. A corporation recognizes no loss when it distributes property to its shareholders.
4. A corporation's E&P is increased by any E&P gain resulting from a distribution of appreciated property.
5. A corporation's E&P is reduced by (a) the amount of money distributed plus (b) the greater of the FMV or E&P adjusted basis of any nonmoney property distributed, minus (c) any liabilities to which the property is subject or that the shareholder assumes in connection with the distribution. E&P also is reduced by taxes paid or incurred on the corporation's recognized gain, if any.

[12] Sec. 312(a)(2).

ETHICAL POINT

A CPA should always be an advocate for his or her client if the question of whether a constructive dividend has been paid is in doubt (i.e., the facts and the law are sufficiently gray and the taxpayer's position has reasonable support).

holder. If the IRS reclassifies either payment as a dividend, it is taxable to the shareholder and nondeductible by the distributing corporation.

UNINTENTIONAL CONSTRUCTIVE DIVIDENDS. Some constructive dividends are unintentional. Shareholders may not realize that the benefits they receive from the corporation in which they own stock are actually taxable dividends until a tax consultant or the IRS examines the transactions. A transaction found to be a dividend rather than a salary payment, loan, and so on will be recast as a dividend. Appropriate adjustments must then be made to the corporation's and shareholder's books, which may increase the shareholder's taxable income (e.g., because the distribution is a dividend rather than a loan) or increase the distributing corporation's taxable income (i.e., because of reduced deductions). Transactions most likely to be recast and treated as dividends are summarized below.

ADDITIONAL COMMENT

The government requires that, when loans exist between a corporation and its shareholders, the loans must bear a reasonable interest rate. If a "below-market" interest rate loan exists, the IRS will impute a reasonable rate of interest (Sec. 7872).

LOANS TO SHAREHOLDERS. Loans to shareholders may be considered disguised dividends unless they are bona fide loans. Whether a loan is considered as bona fide ordinarily depends on the shareholder's intent when he or she makes the loan. To prove that the loan is bona fide (and to avoid having the loan treated as a dividend), the evidence must show that the shareholder intends to repay the loan. Evidence of an intent to repay includes

- Recording the loan on the corporate books
- Evidencing the loan by a written note
- Charging a reasonable rate of interest
- Scheduling regular payments of principal and interest

Evidence that the loan is *not* bona fide includes

- Maintaining a continuing "open account" loan to the shareholder (allowing the shareholder to borrow from the corporation whenever money is required and with no fixed schedule for repayment)
- Failing to charge interest on the loan
- Failing to enforce the payment of interest and principal
- Making advances in proportion to stockholdings
- Making advances to a controlling shareholder

If the corporation lends money to a shareholder and then, after a period of time, cancels the loan, the amount cancelled is treated as a dividend distribution under Sec. 301. If inadequate interest is charged, interest is imputed on the loan. The corporation will report interest income from the loan, and the shareholder may have a deduction for interest deemed paid. The imputed interest is treated as a dividend paid to the shareholder, thereby resulting in no offsetting deduction for the corporation.

SELF-STUDY QUESTION

Because both compensation and dividends are taxable to a shareholder-employee, why is there such concern regarding excessive compensation?

ANSWER

The concern is not at the shareholder-employee level, but rather at the paying corporation level. Compensation is deductible to the paying corporation, whereas dividend distributions are not deductible. Excess compensation paid to an individual who does not own stock in the corporation causes a loss of the corporate deduction, but generally creates no dividend income.

EXCESSIVE COMPENSATION PAID TO SHAREHOLDER-EMPLOYEES. Shareholders may receive compensation for services in the form of salary, bonus, or fringe benefits. Such compensation payments are deductible by the distributing corporation as long as they are ordinary and necessary expenses and are reasonable in amount. However, if the IRS finds them to be excessive, the excess amounts may be considered constructive dividends to the shareholders. In such cases, the payments are not deductible by the corporation, but they are still taxable to the shareholder as dividend income. There are no hard and fast rules as to when compensation is excessive. As a result, much controversy and many court cases have occurred in this area.

Reasonableness of compensation paid must be determined on a case-by-case basis. Some factors considered important in determining whether compensation is reasonable were cited in *Mayson Manufacturing Co.*, a 1949 Sixth Circuit Court of Appeals case.[13] These factors include the following:

[13] *Mayson Manufacturing Co. v. CIR*, 38 AFTR 1028, 49-2 USTC ¶9467 (6th Cir., 1949).

TAX STRATEGY TIP

Although controversial, paying salary instead of dividends to a shareholder-employee is good tax strategy as long as the salary is reasonable in amount. The tax benefit of the salary deduction usually will outweigh the additional costs of employment taxes (e.g., FICA) on the salary.

- The employee's qualifications
- The nature, extent, and scope of the employee's work
- The size of the business
- The complexities of the business
- A comparison of the salaries paid with the corporation's gross and net income
- The prevailing general economic conditions
- Whether the corporation has paid any dividends
- Compensation for comparable positions in comparable concerns
- The corporation's salary policy to its employees
- The amount of compensation paid to the particular employee in previous years
- The amount of compensation voted by the board of directors

EXCESSIVE COMPENSATION PAID TO SHAREHOLDERS FOR THE USE OF SHAREHOLDER PROPERTY. Like salary payments, payments to shareholders for the use of property (i.e., rents, interest, and royalties) are deductible by a corporation under Sec. 162(a) if they are ordinary, necessary, and reasonable in amount. To the extent they exceed the amounts that would have been paid to an unrelated party, the excess amount may be recast as a constructive dividend to the shareholder.

CORPORATE PAYMENTS FOR THE SHAREHOLDER'S BENEFIT. If a corporation pays a personal obligation of a shareholder, the amount of the payment may be treated as a constructive dividend to the shareholder. Such payments may include payment by the corporation of the shareholder's personal debt obligations, expenses in connection with the shareholder's personal residence, expenses incurred for the improvement of the shareholder's land and property, and debt obligations personally guaranteed by the shareholder.

If a corporate expenditure is disallowed as a deduction, it may be a constructive dividend to the shareholder if it provides the shareholder with an economic benefit. Examples of such constructive dividends are unsubstantiated travel and entertainment expenses, club dues, and automobile, airplane, and yacht expenses related to the shareholder-employee's personal use of the property.

BARGAIN PURCHASE OF CORPORATE PROPERTY. If a shareholder purchases corporate property at a price less than the property's FMV, the discount from the FMV may be a constructive dividend to the shareholder.

SHAREHOLDER USE OF CORPORATE PROPERTY. If a shareholder uses corporate property (such as a hunting lodge, yacht, or airplane) without paying adequate compensation to the corporation, the FMV of such use (minus any amounts paid) may be a constructive dividend to the shareholder.

STOCK DIVIDENDS AND STOCK RIGHTS

OBJECTIVE 4

Determine the tax consequences of stock dividends and distributions of stock rights

In 1919, the Supreme Court ruled in *Eisner v. Macomber* that a stock dividend was not income to the shareholder because it took nothing from the property of the corporation and added nothing to the property of the shareholder.[14] Subsequently, the Revenue Act of 1921 provided that stock dividends are nontaxable. This general rule still applies today, but Congress has enacted some exceptions to prevent perceived abuses.

Section 305(a) provides, "Except as otherwise provided in this section, gross income does not include the amount of any distribution of the stock of a corporation made by

[14] *Eisner v. Myrtle H. Macomber*, 3 AFTR 3020, 1 USTC ¶32 (USSC, 1919).

such corporation to its shareholders with respect to its stock." Thus, a distribution of additional common stock made with respect to a shareholder's common stock is a tax-free stock dividend. However, to circumvent tax-avoidance schemes fostered by the tax-free stock dividend rule, Sec. 305(b) provides for some exceptions.

TYPICAL MISCONCEPTION

Stock dividends generally are nontaxable as long as a shareholder's proportionate interests in the corporation do not increase. If a shareholder's stock interest increases, Sec. 305(b) causes the dividend to be taxable.

As a general rule, whenever a stock dividend changes or has the potential to change the shareholders' proportionate interests in the distributing corporation, the distribution is taxable. Taxable stock distributions include those where

- Any shareholder can elect to receive either stock of the distributing corporation or other property (e.g., money).
- Some shareholders receive property and other shareholders receive an increase in their proportionate interests in the distributing corporation's assets or E&P.
- Some holders of common stock receive preferred stock and others receive additional common stock.
- The distribution is on preferred stock unless it is merely a change in the conversion ratio of convertible preferred stock made to take into account a common stock dividend or a common stock split.
- Convertible preferred stock is distributed unless it can be established that the distribution will have no disproportionate effect.

The following example illustrates how these exceptions work.

EXAMPLE C4-18 ▶ Peach Corporation has $100,000 of current E&P. Two shareholders, Al and Beth, each own 100 of the 200 outstanding shares of Peach stock. Al has a high marginal tax rate and does not want any additional income in the current year. Beth has a low marginal tax rate and needs additional cash. Peach Corporation declares a dividend payable in stock or money. Each taxpayer can receive one share of Peach stock (valued at $100) or $100 in money for each share of Peach stock already owned. Al, who elects to receive stock, receives 100 additional shares of Peach stock. Beth, who elects to receive money, receives $10,000. Beth's distribution is taxable as a dividend. Absent any exceptions to Sec. 305, Al would have a nontaxable stock dividend because he chose to receive Peach stock. However, Al has received something of value. After the distribution, he owns two-thirds of the outstanding shares of Peach stock, whereas before the distribution he owned only one-half of the Peach stock. One of the exceptions to the general rule of Sec. 305(a) applies here, so that Al has a taxable stock dividend equal to the value of the additional shares he received. Even if both shareholders were to elect to receive stock, they each would have a taxable dividend because they had the option to receive cash. In this example, Al and Beth each have a $10,000 dividend. Al's basis in his new shares is $10,000, their FMV. His basis in his original shares is unchanged. Peach reduces its E&P by $20,000, the amount of the dividend to Al and Beth. ◀

TAX-FREE STOCK DIVIDENDS

If a **stock dividend** is nontaxable, the basis of the stock with respect to which the distribution was made must be allocated between the old and the new shares.[15] The holding period of the new shares includes the holding period of the old shares.[16]

If the old shares and the new shares are identical, the basis of each share is determined by dividing the basis of the old shares by the total number of shares held by the shareholder after the distribution.

EXAMPLE C4-19 ▶ Barbara owns 1,000 shares of Axle Corporation common stock with a $66,000 basis, or $66 per share. Barbara receives a nontaxable 10% common stock dividend and now owns 1,100 shares of common stock. The basis for each share of common stock is now $60 ($66,000 ÷ 1,100). ◀

If the old shares and the new shares are not identical, the allocation of the old shares' basis is based on the relative FMVs of the old and the new shares on the distribution date.

---

[15] Sec. 307(a) and Reg. Secs. 1.307-1 and -2.

[16] Sec. 1223(5).

EXAMPLE C4-20 ▶ Mark owns 1,000 shares of Axle Corporation common stock with a $60,000 basis. Mark receives a nontaxable stock dividend payable in preferred stock. At the time of the distribution, the common stock has a $90,000 FMV ($90 × 1,000 shares) and the preferred stock has a $10,000 FMV ($200 × 50 shares). After the distribution, Mark owns 50 shares of preferred stock with a basis of $6,000 [($10,000 ÷ $100,000) × $60,000]. Thus, $6,000 of the basis of the common stock is allocated to the preferred stock, and the basis of the common stock is reduced from $60,000 to $54,000. ◀

REAL WORD EXAMPLE

Tracking the effects of nontaxable dividends, stock splits, stock dividends, and stock rights distributions on the basis of a stock investment can be difficult and time consuming. A number of publishers offer reporters (such as CCH's *Capital Changes Reporter*) that provide a complete history of these four types of events for publicly traded companies. These reporters greatly simplify the making of stock basis calculations.

TAX-FREE STOCK RIGHTS

A distribution of **stock rights** is tax-free under Sec. 305 unless it changes, or has the potential to change, the shareholders' proportionate interests in the distributing corporation. The same exceptions to tax-free treatment for stock dividends enumerated in Sec. 305(b) also apply to distributions of stock rights.

If the value of the stock rights is less than 15% of the value of the stock with respect to which the rights were distributed (i.e., the underlying stock), the basis of the rights is zero unless the shareholder elects to allocate basis to those rights.[17] If the taxpayer plans to sell the rights, it might be desirable to allocate basis to the rights so as to minimize the amount of gain recognized on the sale. The election to allocate basis to the rights must be made in the form of a statement attached to the shareholder's return for the year in which the rights are received. The allocation is based on the relative FMVs of the stock and the stock rights. The holding period for the rights includes the holding period for the underlying stock.[18]

EXAMPLE C4-21 ▶ Linda owns 100 shares of Yale Corporation common stock with a $27,000 basis and a $50,000 FMV. Linda receives 100 nontaxable stock rights with a $4,000 FMV. Because the FMV of the stock rights is less than 15% of the FMV of the stock (0.15 × $50,000 = $7,500), the basis of the stock rights is zero unless Linda elects to make an allocation. Should Linda elect to allocate the $27,000 basis of the Yale common stock between the stock and the stock rights, the basis of the rights is $2,000 [($4,000 ÷ $54,000) × $27,000], and the basis of the stock is $25,000 ($27,000 − $2,000). ◀

If the value of the stock rights is 15% or more of the value of the underlying stock, the shareholder must allocate the basis of the underlying stock between the stock and the stock rights.

EXAMPLE C4-22 ▶ Kay owns 100 shares of Minor common stock with a $14,000 basis and a $30,000 FMV. Kay receives 100 stock rights with a total FMV of $5,000. Because the FMV of the stock rights is at least 15% of the stock's FMV (0.15 × $30,000 = $4,500), the $14,000 basis must be allocated between the stock rights and the stock. The basis of the stock rights is $2,000 [($5,000 ÷ $35,000) × $14,000], and the basis of the stock is $12,000 ($14,000 − $2,000). ◀

TYPICAL MISCONCEPTION

Taxpayers often get confused about what happens to a stock right. A stock right may be sold or exercised, which means the actual stock is acquired. If the rights are not sold or exercised, they eventually will lapse.

If the taxpayer sells the stock rights, gain or loss is measured by subtracting the allocated basis of the rights (if any) from the sale price. A shareholder cannot claim a loss for any basis assigned to stock rights when the rights lapse. If the rights lapse, the allocated basis is added back to the basis of the underlying stock. If the taxpayer exercises the rights, the basis allocated to the rights is added to the basis of the stock purchased with those rights.[19] The holding period for any stock acquired with the rights begins on the exercise date.[20]

EXAMPLE C4-23 ▶ Jeff receives ten stock rights in a nontaxable distribution. No basis is allocated to the stock rights. With each stock right, Jeff may acquire one share of Jackson stock for $20. If Jeff exercises all ten stock rights, the new Jackson stock acquired has a $200 (10 rights × $20) basis. If instead Jeff sells the ten rights for $30 each, he has a recognized gain of $300 [($30 × 10 rights) − 0 basis] on the sale. If the rights are permitted to lapse, Jeff can claim no loss. ◀

---

[17] Sec. 307(b)(1).
[18] Sec. 1223(5).
[19] Reg. Sec. 1.307-1(b).
[20] Sec. 1223(6).

EFFECT OF NONTAXABLE STOCK DIVIDENDS ON THE DISTRIBUTING CORPORATION

BOOK-TO-TAX ACCOUNTING COMPARISON

For financial accounting purposes, stock dividends reduce retained earnings. However, for tax purposes, nontaxable stock dividends have no effect on a corporation's E&P.

Nontaxable distributions of stock and stock rights have no effect on the distributing corporation. The corporation does not recognize gain or loss on the distribution, nor does any reduction in its E&P occur.[21]

TAXABLE STOCK DIVIDENDS AND STOCK RIGHTS

If a distribution of stock or stock rights is taxable, the distribution amount equals the FMV of the stock or stock rights on the distribution date. The distribution is treated the same as any other property distribution. It is a dividend to the extent it is made out of the distributing corporation's E&P. The basis of the stock or stock rights to the recipient shareholder is its FMV.[22] The holding period of the stock or stock rights begins on the day after the distribution date. No adjustment is made to the basis of the underlying stock with respect to which the distribution was made. The distributing corporation recognizes no gain or loss on the distribution,[23] and the corporation reduces its E&P by the FMV of the stock or stock rights on the distribution date.

STOCK REDEMPTIONS

OBJECTIVE 5

Distinguish between a stock redemption treated as a sale and one treated as a dividend

A **stock redemption** is defined as a corporation's acquisition of its own stock in exchange for property. The property exchanged may be money, securities, or any other property the corporation wants to use to acquire its own stock.[24] The corporation may cancel the acquired stock, retire it, or hold it as treasury stock.

A stock redemption may be desirable for many reasons:

- A shareholder may want to withdraw from a corporation and sell his or her stock. In such a case, the shareholder may prefer that the corporation, rather than an outsider, purchase the stock so that the remaining shareholders (who may be family members) retain complete control and ownership of the corporation after his or her withdrawal.
- A shareholder may be required to sell the stock back to the corporation by the terms of an agreement that he or she has entered into with the corporation.
- A shareholder may want to sell some stock to reduce his or her ownership in a corporation but may be unwilling or unable to sell that stock to outsiders. For example, no market may exist for the shares, or sales to outsiders may be restricted.
- A shareholder may want to withdraw some assets from a corporation before a sale of the business. A potential purchaser of the business may not be interested in acquiring all the assets of the business or able to pay the full value for the stock. A withdrawal of some assets by the seller in exchange for some of the stock allows the purchaser to acquire the remaining stock and business assets for a lower total price.
- After the death of a major shareholder, a corporation may have an agreement to purchase the decedent's stock from either the estate or a beneficiary to provide sufficient funds to pay estate and inheritance taxes and funeral and administrative expenses.
- Management may believe that its stock is selling at a low price and that the best use for the corporation's available cash would be to acquire the corporation's own stock on the open market.

Whatever the reason for the redemption, the shareholder must answer the following questions:

- What are the amount and character of the income, gain, or loss recognized as a result of the stock redemption?

[21] Secs. 311(a) and 312(d).

[22] Reg. Sec. 1.301-1(h)(2)(i).

[23] Sec. 311(a). Gain may be recognized when the shareholder can elect to receive either appreciated property or stock or stock rights of the distributing corporation.

[24] Sec. 317.

- What basis does the shareholder take in any property received in redemption of his or her stock?
- When does the holding period for the property received begin?
- What basis does the shareholder take for any stock of the distributing corporation that he or she holds after the redemption?

The distributing corporation must answer the following questions:

- What amount and character of gain or loss must the distributing corporation recognize when it uses property to redeem its stock?
- What effect does the redemption have on the corporation's E&P?[25]

EFFECT OF THE REDEMPTION ON THE SHAREHOLDER

KEY POINT

As far as a shareholder is concerned, the basic issue in a stock redemption is whether the redemption is treated as a dividend or a sale.

As a general rule, when a shareholder sells or exchanges stock in a corporation, any gain or loss on the transaction is treated as a capital gain or loss. In some cases, a redemption is treated the same as any other sale or exchange of stock. In other cases, the entire amount received by a shareholder in exchange for stock is treated as a dividend. The reason for this difference is that some redemptions more closely resemble a sale of stock to a third party, whereas others are essentially equivalent to a dividend. The following two examples illustrate the difference between a redemption treated as a dividend distribution and a redemption treated as a sale or exchange.

EXAMPLE C4-24 ▶ John owns all 100 outstanding shares of Tango Corporation stock. John's basis for his stock is \$50,000. Tango has E&P of \$100,000. If Tango redeems 25 of John's shares for \$85,000, John still owns all the Tango stock. Because John's ownership of Tango Corporation is not affected by the redemption, the redemption is equivalent to a dividend, and John is deemed to have received an \$85,000 dividend. ◀

EXAMPLE C4-25 ▶ Carol has owned three of the 1,000 outstanding shares of Water Corporation's stock for two years. Her basis in the stock is \$1,000. Water Corporation has E&P of \$100,000. If Water redeems all three of Carol's shares for \$5,000, Carol has a \$4,000 (\$5,000 − \$1,000) capital gain. She is in essentially the same position as though she had sold the stock to a third party. She has received \$5,000 for her stock and has no further ownership interest in Water Corporation. This redemption is treated the same as any other sale or exchange because it terminates her interest in the corporation. It is not equivalent to a dividend. ◀

Example C4-24 is an extreme case that clearly should be treated as a dividend to the shareholder. Example C4-25 is an extreme case that clearly should be treated as a sale of stock by the shareholder. Many cases, however, fall in between, and it is not immediately apparent which treatment is correct. The problem for Congress and the courts has been distinguishing redemptions that should be treated as sales or exchanges from those that should be treated as dividends. Under current law, a redemption qualifies for sale or exchange treatment only if it satisfies at least one of the following conditions:

- The redemption is substantially disproportionate.
- The redemption is a complete termination of the shareholder's interest.
- The redemption is not essentially equivalent to a dividend.
- The redemption is a partial liquidation of the distributing corporation in redemption of part or all of a noncorporate shareholder's stock.
- The redemption is made to pay death taxes.

If a redemption qualifies as a sale or exchange, the shareholder is treated as though he or she sold the stock to an outside party. Gain or loss is equal to the FMV of the property received less the shareholder's adjusted basis for the stock surrendered. The gain or loss is capital gain or loss if the stock is a capital asset. The shareholder's basis for any property

---

[25] The stock redemption discussion is for C corporation stock. Different rules apply if an S corporation redeems its stock.

received is its FMV. The holding period for the property begins on the day following the exchange date.

A redemption distribution that does not satisfy any of the five conditions necessary for sale or exchange treatment is treated by the shareholder as a property distribution under Sec. 301. Accordingly, the entire amount of the distribution is a dividend to the extent of the distributing corporation's E&P.[26] The shareholder's surrender of stock is ignored in determining the amount of the dividend. The basis of the surrendered stock is added to the basis of any remaining shares owned by the shareholder. If all the shareholder's stock has been redeemed, the basis of the redeemed shares is added to the basis of shares owned by those individuals whose ownership is attributed to the shareholder under the constructive stock ownership rules described below.[27]

EXAMPLE C4-26 ▶ Amy and Rose each own 50 of the 100 outstanding shares of York stock. York Corporation has $100,000 of E&P. On May 10, York redeems 20 of Amy's shares with property worth $25,000. Amy's adjusted basis for those shares is $20,000. If the redemption distribution satisfies one of the conditions necessary for sale treatment, Amy has $5,000 ($25,000 − $20,000) of capital gain. Her basis for the property received is $25,000, its FMV. Its holding period begins on May 11. If the redemption does not satisfy any of the conditions necessary for sale treatment, the redemption distribution follows the same rules as any other property distribution. Amy reports a $25,000 dividend. Her $20,000 basis for the surrendered stock is added to her basis for her remaining 30 shares of York stock. ◀

SELF-STUDY QUESTION

Why does it matter if a redemption is treated as a dividend or a sale?

ANSWER

One major difference is that the basis of the redeemed stock reduces the gain if the tax treatment is a sale. If the tax treatment is a dividend, no such reduction occurs. Capital gains also can be offset by capital losses from other transactions. In addition, the maximum tax rate on an individual taxpayer's long-term capital gains is significantly lower than the maximum rate applying to ordinary income.

Structuring a stock redemption as a sale or exchange provides several advantages. First, individuals pay a maximum tax rate of 20% on long-term capital gains (18% for capital assets acquired in 2001 or later and held more than five years). Second, capital gains may be offset by capital losses. Third, in a sale or exchange, the basis of the shares redeemed reduces the amount of gain recognized. If a redemption is treated as a dividend, the basis of the shares redeemed does not reduce the dividend income recognized. However, because the basis shifts to the shareholder's remaining stock, it reduces the gain (or increases the loss) recognized on a later sale or exchange of the distributing corporation stock held by the shareholder following the redemption.

Topic Review C4-3 summarizes the tax consequences of stock redemptions to both the shareholders and the distributing corporation.

ATTRIBUTION RULES

Three of the five tests used to determine whether a redemption distribution should be treated as a dividend depend on the shareholder's stock ownership before and after the redemption. The tests determine whether the shareholder's ownership of the corporation has been substantially reduced.

In general, if the shareholder's ownership is substantially reduced, the redemption is treated as a sale. If the ownership interest remains substantially the same or increases, the redemption is treated as a nonliquidating distribution.

In determining stock ownership for this purpose, the constructive ownership or attribution rules of Sec. 318 must be taken into account.[28] These rules provide that a shareholder is considered to own not only the shares he or she owns directly but also shares owned by his or her spouse, other family members, and related entities. Furthermore, entities such as corporations, partnerships, trusts, and estates are considered to own shares owned by their shareholders, partners, and beneficiaries.

The attribution rules prevent shareholders from either taking advantage of favorable tax rules or avoiding unfavorable rules by having family members or related entities own stock that the shareholder is not permitted to own. All stock ownership tests would be subject to potential abuse if only direct ownership of stock were considered.

Section 318(a) prescribes four types of attribution rules: family attribution, attribution from entities, attribution to entities, and option attribution. These rules are discussed below.

[26] Sec. 302(d).
[27] Reg. Sec. 1.302-2(c).
[28] Sec. 302(c).

Topic Review C4-3

Tax Consequences of Stock Redemptions

Shareholders:

General Rule: The amount received by the shareholder in exchange for his or her stock is treated as a dividend (but not in excess of the distributing corporation's E&P). The basis of the surrendered stock is added to the basis of the shareholder's remaining stock.

Sale or Exchange Exception: The amount received by the shareholder is offset by the adjusted basis of the shares surrendered. The difference generally is a capital gain or loss. No basis adjustment occurs.

Distributing Corporation:

Gain/Loss Recognition: The corporation recognizes gain (but not loss) as though it had sold the distributed property for its FMV immediately before the redemption.

Earnings and Profits Adjustment: E&P is reduced for redemptions treated as a dividend in the same manner as for an ordinary distribution (e.g., the amount of money distributed). E&P is reduced for redemptions treated as an exchange by the portion of the current and accumulated E&P attributable to the redeemed stock. The remainder of the distribution reduces the corporation's paid-in capital.

ADDITIONAL COMMENT

The family attribution rules of Sec. 318 are not as inclusive as the family attribution rules of Sec. 267 (covered in Chapter C3). For example, siblings and grandparents are not considered family members by Sec. 318 but are included under Sec. 267.

FAMILY ATTRIBUTION. An individual is considered to own all stock owned by or for a spouse, children, grandchildren, and parents. The individual is not considered to own stock owned by brothers, sisters, or grandparents.

Stock once attributed to an individual is not further reattributed from that individual to another individual under the same rules. Thus, stock attributed to one family member under the family attribution rules cannot be reattributed from that family member to a second family member. However, stock once attributed to an individual under an attribution rule may be reattributed from that individual to another individual under a different attribution rule. For example, stock attributed by the corporate attribution rule from a corporation to its shareholder may be reattributed from the shareholder to the shareholder's spouse under the family attribution rules.

EXAMPLE C4-27 ▶ Harry; his wife, Wilma; their son, Steve; and Harry's father, Frank, each own 25 of the 100 outstanding shares of Strong Corporation stock. Harry is considered to own all 100 Strong shares (25 directly plus the shares owned by Wilma, Steve, and Frank). Wilma is considered to own 75 shares (25 directly plus the 50 shares owned by Harry and Steve). Frank's shares are not attributed to Wilma, nor are his shares that are attributed to Harry reattributed to Wilma. Steve is considered to own 75 shares (25 directly plus the 50 shares owned by his parents Harry and Wilma). Steve is not considered to own the shares owned by his grandfather (Frank), nor are the shares owned by Frank attributed to Harry and then reattributed to Steve. Frank is considered to own 75 shares (25 directly plus the shares owned by Harry and Steve (his grandson)). The shares owned by Wilma that are attributed to Harry are not reattributed to Frank.

The diagram below illustrates the stock ownership of the four shareholders. Constructive ownership is shown by the lines. The arrows indicate the direction(s) in which stock attribution occurs.

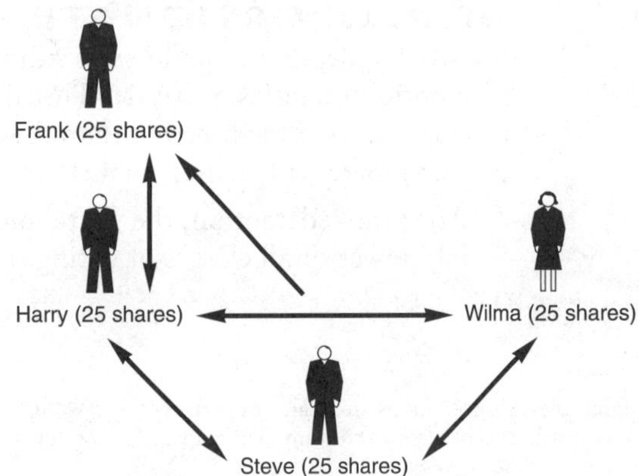

The table below shows each shareholder's direct and constructive stock ownership.

		Shares Owned via Constructive Ownership From:				
Shareholder	*Direct Ownership*	*Spouse*	*Child*	*Grandchild*	*Parent(s)*	*Total*
Frank	25		25	25		75
Harry	25	25	25		25	100
Wilma	25	25	25			75
Steve	25				50	75
	100					

◀

ATTRIBUTION FROM ENTITIES. Stock owned by or for a partnership is considered to be owned proportionately by the partners, and stock owned by or for an estate is considered to be owned proportionately by the beneficiaries. Stock owned by or for a trust is considered to be owned by the beneficiaries in proportion to their actuarial interests. Stock owned by or for a C corporation is considered to be owned proportionately only by shareholders owning (directly or indirectly) 50% or more in value of the corporation's stock.[29]

EXAMPLE C4-28 ▶ Bill, who is married, has a 50% interest in a partnership. The partnership owns 40 of the 100 outstanding shares of Yellow Corporation stock, and Bill owns the remaining 60 shares. Under the attribution rules, however, Bill is considered to own 80 shares, 60 directly and 20 (0.50×40 shares) indirectly. In addition, the stock attributed to Bill under the partnership attribution rules is reattributed to Bill's spouse under the family attribution rules. ◀

ATTRIBUTION TO ENTITIES. All stock owned by or for a partner is considered to be owned by the partnership. All stock owned by or for a beneficiary of an estate or a trust is considered to be owned by the estate or trust. All stock owned by or for a shareholder who owns (directly or indirectly) 50% or more in value of a C corporation's stock is considered to be owned by the corporation.

Stock attributed to a partnership, estate, trust, or corporation from a partner, beneficiary, or shareholder is not reattributed to another partner, beneficiary, or shareholder.

EXAMPLE C4-29 ▶ Assume the same facts as in Example C4-28. The partnership in which Bill is a partner is considered to own all 100 shares of Yellow stock (40 directly and 60 owned by Bill). The stock owned by Bill and attributed to the partnership cannot be reattributed from the partnership to another of Bill's partners. ◀

OPTION ATTRIBUTION. A person who has an option to purchase stock is considered to own the stock.

EXAMPLE C4-30 ▶ John owns 25 of the 100 outstanding shares of Yard Corporation stock. He has an option to acquire an additional 50 shares. John is considered to own 75 Yard shares (25 directly plus the 50 shares he has an option to buy). ◀

SUBSTANTIALLY DISPROPORTIONATE REDEMPTIONS

If a stock redemption qualifies as substantially disproportionate under Sec. 302(b)(2), the redemption qualifies as a sale. This IRC provision, therefore, provides a safe haven for capital gain treatment rather than dividend treatment. A redemption is substantially disproportionate with respect to a shareholder if all the following conditions hold true:

- After the redemption, the shareholder owns less than 50% of the total combined voting power of all classes of voting stock.

[29] For purposes of the attribution rules, S corporations are treated as partnerships, not as corporations. Thus, attribution occurs to and from shareholders owning less than 50% of the S corporation stock. All corporations in the examples are C corporations unless otherwise stated.

- After the redemption, the shareholder owns less than 80% of his or her percentage ownership of voting stock before the redemption.
- After the redemption, the shareholder owns less than 80% of his or her percentage ownership of common stock (whether voting or nonvoting) before the redemption.

TAX STRATEGY TIP
If possible, taxpayers should structure a redemption to meet the substantially disproportionate test rather than the subjective "not equivalent to a dividend" test (discussed on page C4-23), thereby obtaining certainty of results rather than uncertainty.

These tests apply mechanically to each shareholder individually. The 50% test prevents shareholders from qualifying for capital gain treatment if they own a controlling interest in the distributing corporation after the redemption. The 80% tests indicate the degree of change in the shareholder's interest in the corporation that is required to be substantially disproportionate. A redemption may be substantially disproportionate with respect to one shareholder but not disproportionate with respect to another. If only one class of stock is outstanding, the second and third requirements are the same.

EXAMPLE C4-31 ▶ Long Corporation has 400 shares of common stock outstanding, of which Ann, Bob, Carl, and Dana (all unrelated) each own 100 shares. Long redeems 55 shares from Ann, 25 shares from Bob, and 20 shares from Carl.

ADDITIONAL COMMENT
In calculating the percentage of stock owned *after* a redemption note that the denominator used is the number of shares outstanding *after* the redemption.

	Before Redemption			*After Redemption*	
Shareholder	*No. of Shares Owned*	*Percentage of Ownership*	*Shares Redeemed*	*No. of Shares Owned*	*Percentage of Ownership*
	(1)	(1) ÷ 400	(2)	(1) − (2)	[(1) − (2)] ÷ 300
Ann	100	25%	55	45	15.00%
Bob	100	25%	25	75	25.00%
Carl	100	25%	20	80	26.67%
Dana	100	25%	—	100	33.33%
Total	400	100%	100	300	100.00%

The redemption is substantially disproportionate with respect to Ann because, after the redemption, she owns less than 50% of Long's stock, and her stock ownership percentage (15%) is less than 80% of her stock ownership percentage before the redemption (0.80 × 25% = 20%). The redemption is not substantially disproportionate with respect to Bob because he does not have the necessary reduction in his stock ownership percentage. Bob owns the same percentage of stock (25%) after the redemption as he did before the redemption (25%). The redemption is not substantially disproportionate for Carl either, because his stock ownership percentage increases from 25% to 26.67%. ◀

The constructive ownership rules of Sec. 318(a) apply in determining whether the shareholder has met the three requirements for a substantially disproportionate redemption.[30]

EXAMPLE C4-32 ▶ Assume the same facts as in Example C4-31 except that Ann and Bob are mother and son. In this case, the redemption is not substantially disproportionate for either Ann or Bob. Ann and Bob are each considered to own 200 shares, or 50%, of the Long stock before the redemption, and each is considered to own 120 shares, or 40%, after the redemption. Although the 50% test is met, neither Ann nor Bob satisfies the requirement that after the redemption the shareholder must own *less* than 80% of the percentage of stock owned before the redemption. After the redemption each owns *exactly* 80% of the percentage owned before the redemption (0.80 × 50% = 40%). ◀

COMPLETE TERMINATION OF THE SHAREHOLDER'S INTEREST

If a stock redemption qualifies as a complete termination of the shareholder's interest in the corporation under Sec. 302(b)(3), the redemption qualifies as a sale. At first glance, this rule does not offer any additional route to sale treatment for the shareholder. If a corporation redeems all of a shareholder's stock, the requirements for a substantially disproportionate redemption under Sec. 302(b)(2) would seem to have been satisfied. However, the complete termination rule extends sale treatment to two redemptions not covered by the substantially disproportionate redemption rules of Sec. 302(b)(2):

[30] Reg. Sec. 1.302-3(a).

- If a shareholder's interest in a corporation consists of nonvoting stock, a redemption of all the stock could not qualify as substantially disproportionate under Sec. 302(b)(2) because no reduction of voting power occurs. However, it does qualify for sale treatment as a complete termination of the shareholder's interest under Sec. 302(b)(3).
- If a shareholder owns some voting stock and his or her entire interest in the corporation is completely terminated by a redemption, the family attribution rules of Sec. 318(a)(1) may be waived, and the redemption can qualify for sale treatment even if other family members continue to own some or all of the corporation's stock.[31]

To have the family attribution rules waived, all of the following requirements must be met:

- The shareholder must not retain any interest in the corporation after the redemption except as a creditor. This restriction includes any interest as an officer, director, or employee.
- The shareholder must not acquire any such interest (other than by bequest or inheritance) for at least ten years from the date of the redemption.
- The shareholder must file a written agreement with the IRS that he or she will notify the IRS upon acquiring any prohibited interest.

The written agreement allows the IRS to assess additional taxes for the year of the distribution if the prohibited interest is acquired, even if the basic three-year statute of limitations has run.

EXAMPLE C4-33 ▶ Father and Son each own 50 of the 100 outstanding shares of Short Corporation stock. Short Corporation redeems all of Father's shares. Under the family attribution rules, Father is considered to own 100% of the Short stock both before and after the redemption. Thus, the redemption is not substantially disproportionate. However, if Father files the necessary agreement not to retain or acquire any interest in Short Corporation for ten years (except as a creditor or an interest acquired by bequest or inheritance), the family attribution rules are waived, and the redemption is treated as a stock sale. It qualifies as a complete termination of Father's interest in Short Corporation. ◀

Waiver of the family attribution rules is not permitted in the following two situations involving related parties:

- Part or all of the stock redeemed was acquired, directly or indirectly, within the ten-year period ending on the date of the distribution by the distributee from a person whose stock ownership would be attributable (at the time of the distribution) to the distributee under Sec. 318.
- Any person owns (at the time of the distribution) stock of the redeeming corporation the ownership of which is attributable to the distributee under Sec. 318, and such person acquired any stock in the redeeming corporation, directly or indirectly, from the distributee within the ten-year period ending on the distribution date.

The first situation prevents an individual from transferring stock to a related party (e.g., family member or controlled entity) and then having the related party use the complete termination exception to recognize a capital gain when the transferred stock is redeemed. The second situation prevents an individual from transferring a portion of his or her stock to a related party and then using the complete termination exception to recognize a capital gain when the remaining stock is redeemed. These prohibitions against waiving the family attribution rules do not apply if the transfer took place more than ten years before the redemption or if the distributee can show that the acquisition or disposition of the stock of the redeeming corporation did not have as one of its purposes the avoidance of federal income taxes. The family attribution rules also can be waived in the second situation above if the stock acquired by the related party from the distributee also is redeemed in the same transaction.

[31] The waiver of family attribution rules appears in Sec. 302(c)(2).

Note that only the family attribution rules can be waived. However, entities are permitted to have the family attribution rules waived if both the entity and the individual whose stock is attributed to the entity agree not to have any prohibited interest in the corporation for at least ten years.

EXAMPLE C4-34 ▶ The A Trust, which was created by Andrew, owns 30% of Willow Corporation stock. Andrew's wife, Wanda, is the sole beneficiary of the trust. Their son, Steve, owns the remaining 70% of the Willow stock. Willow Corporation redeems all of its stock owned by the A Trust. The redemption is not treated as a sale because the trust is deemed to own all the stock owned by its beneficiary (Wanda), and Wanda is deemed to own all the stock owned by her son (Steve). However, the family attribution rules can be waived if A Trust and Wanda both agree not to have any interest in the corporation for ten years. The redemption then will be treated as a complete termination of the trust's interest in Willow Corporation and eligible for sale treatment. ◀

REDEMPTIONS NOT ESSENTIALLY EQUIVALENT TO A DIVIDEND

KEY POINT

Section 302(b)(1) has generally been interpreted to require that a shareholder incur a "meaningful reduction" of its stock interest. What constitutes a "meaningful reduction" is the subject of controversy.

Section 302(b)(1) provides that a redemption of stock is treated as a sale if the redemption is not essentially equivalent to a dividend. The tax law provides no mechanical test to determine when a redemption is not essentially equivalent to a dividend. Instead, the question depends on the facts and circumstances of each case.[32] Therefore, Sec. 302(b)(1) does not provide the safe harbor afforded by the rules for substantially disproportionate redemptions or redemptions that are a complete termination of a shareholder's interest. This exception prevents the rules on redemptions from being too restrictive, especially in the case of redemptions of preferred stock.

The Supreme Court's decision in *Maclin P. Davis* helped to define some of the criteria for determining when a redemption is not essentially equivalent to a dividend.[33] The Supreme Court held that (1) a business purpose is irrelevant in determining whether a redemption is essentially equivalent to a dividend, (2) the Sec. 318 attribution rules must be used to determine dividend equivalency, and (3) a redemption of part of a sole shareholder's stock is always essentially equivalent to a dividend. The court said that there had to be a "meaningful reduction" in the shareholder's proportionate interest in the corporation after taking into account the constructive ownership rules of Sec. 318(a) for Sec. 302(b)(1) to apply. However, the definition of "a meaningful reduction in interest" remains unclear.

Because of the uncertainty involved in determining when Sec. 302(b)(1) applies, it generally is applied only to a redemption of nonvoting preferred stock when the shareholder does not own any common stock[34] or to redemptions resulting in a substantial reduction in the shareholder's right to vote and exercise control over the corporation, right to participate in earnings, and right to share in net assets on liquidation. Generally, the IRS allows sale treatment if a controlling shareholder reduces his or her interest to a noncontrolling position[35] or a noncontrolling shareholder reduces his or her minority interest.[36] A shareholder does not qualify for sale treatment if he or she has control both before and after the redemption,[37] or if he or she assumes a controlling position.

EXAMPLE C4-35 ▶ Four unrelated individuals own all of Thyme Corporation's single class of stock in the following manner: Alan, 27%; Betty, 24.33%; Clem, 24.33%, and David, 24.33%. Thyme redeems some of Alan's stock holdings, resulting in Alan's interest being reduced to 22.27%. Betty, Clem, and David own equally the remaining 77.73% of the Thyme stock. The redemption of Alan's stock does not qualify as substantially disproportionate because Alan's stock interest is not reduced below 21.6% (0.80 × 27% = 21.6%). Nor will the redemption qualify as a complete termina-

---

[32] Reg. Sec. 1.302-2(b).

[33] *U.S. v. Maclin P. Davis,* 25 AFTR 2d 70-827, 70-1 USTC ¶9289 (USSC, 1970).

[34] Reg. Sec. 1.302-2(a).

[35] A reduction in stock ownership from 57% to 50% where the shareholder no longer had control was considered a meaningful reduction in interest in Rev. Rul. 75-502, 1975-2 C.B. 111.

[36] A reduction in stock ownership from 27% to 22% was considered a meaningful reduction in interest in Rev. Rul. 76-364, 1976-2 C.B. 91.

[37] See *Jack Paparo,* 71 T.C. 692 (1979), where reductions in stock ownership from 100% to 81.17% and from 100% to 74.15% were not considered meaningful reductions in interest.

tion of Alan's interest. The IRS has indicated in Rev. Rul. 76-364 that the redemption of Alan's stock will be treated as a sale transaction under Sec. 302(b)(1) because the transaction results in a meaningful reduction of Alan's noncontrolling interest in Thyme Corporation. ◀

PARTIAL LIQUIDATIONS

Under Sec. 302(b)(4), a redemption is treated as a sale if the distribution qualifies as a partial liquidation and is made to a noncorporate shareholder. A **partial liquidation** occurs when a corporation discontinues one line of business, distributes the assets related to that business to its shareholders, and continues in at least one other line of business.[38] A distribution also qualifies as a partial liquidation if the distribution is not essentially equivalent to a dividend. In either case, the distribution must be made within the tax year in which a plan of partial liquidation has been adopted or within the succeeding tax year.

DETERMINATION MADE AT THE CORPORATE LEVEL. For purposes of the partial liquidation definition, whether a distribution is not essentially equivalent to a dividend is determined at the corporate level.[39] The distribution must be the result of a bona fide contraction of the corporate business. The government provides guidance as to what constitutes a corporate contraction in relevant Treasury Regulations and revenue rulings. Some examples of genuine corporate contractions include

- The distribution of insurance proceeds obtained as a result of a fire that destroys part of a business.[40]
- Termination of a contract representing 95% of the gross income of a domestic corporation.[41]
- Change in a corporation's business from a full-line department store to a discount apparel store resulting in the elimination of certain departments and most forms of credit and a reduction in inventory, floor space, employees, and so on.[42]

SAFE HARBOR RULE. Under Sec. 302(e)(2), a distribution satisfies the not essentially equivalent to a dividend requirement and qualifies as a partial liquidation if

- The distribution is attributable to the distributing corporation's ceasing to conduct a qualified trade or business, or consists of the assets of a qualified trade or business; and
- Immediately after the distribution, the distributing corporation is engaged in the active conduct of at least one qualified trade or business.

A qualified trade or business is any trade or business that

- Has been actively conducted throughout the five-year period ending on the date of the redemption; and
- Was not acquired by the corporation within such five-year period in a partially or wholly taxable transaction.

The definition of an active trade or business is the same as that used for Sec. 355 (corporate division) purposes and is described in Chapter C7.

EXAMPLE C4-36 ▶ Sage Corporation has engaged in the manufacture of hats and gloves for the past five years. In the current year, Sage discontinues the manufacture of hats, sells all of its hat-making machinery, and distributes the proceeds to its shareholders in redemption of part of their stock. The corporation continues to manufacture gloves. The distribution constitutes a partial liquidation of Sage. ◀

EFFECT OF A PARTIAL LIQUIDATION ON THE SHAREHOLDERS. If a distribution qualifies as a partial liquidation, a noncorporate shareholder treats the redemption of his or her stock as a sale whether or not the distribution is pro rata. However, a corporate

---

[38] A partial liquidation also can occur when a corporation sells one line of business, distributes the sales proceeds (after paying corporate income taxes on the sale), and continues in at least one other line of business. See Rev. Rul. 79-275, 1979-2 C.B. 137.

[39] Sec. 302(e)(1)(A).

[40] Reg. Sec. 1.346-1.

[41] Rev. Rul. 75-3, 1975-1 C.B. 108.

[42] Rev. Rul. 74-296, 1974-1 C.B. 80.

shareholder treats the redemption distribution as a dividend unless the shareholder qualifies under one of the other tests for sale treatment (i.e., Secs. 302(b)(1)-(3) or 303). In determining whether stock is held by a corporate or noncorporate shareholder, stock held by a partnership, trust, or estate is considered to be held proportionately by its partners or beneficiaries. Dividend treatment may be more advantageous than sale treatment for a corporate shareholder because a corporation is eligible for a 70%, 80%, or 100% dividends-received deduction.

EXAMPLE C4-37 ▶ Assume the same facts as in Example C4-36 except Sage Corporation is owned by Ted and by Jolly Corporation. Each shareholder owns 50 shares of Sage stock with a $10,000 basis. Sage has $100,000 of current and accumulated E&P. Sage distributes $18,000 to each shareholder in redemption of ten shares of Sage stock worth $18,000. Because the redemption qualifies as a partial liquidation, Ted treats the transaction as a sale. He has a $16,000 ($18,000 − $2,000) capital gain. Jolly Corporation cannot treat the transaction as a sale. Therefore, Jolly must report $18,000 of dividend income. Jolly is eligible for a $14,400 (0.80 × $18,000) dividends-received deduction. Jolly's $2,000 basis in the redeemed stock is added to its basis in its remaining stock. Therefore, Jolly has a $10,000 basis in its 40 remaining Sage shares. ◀

STOP & THINK

Question: Why is a distribution in partial liquidation of a corporation treated as a sale by its noncorporate shareholders and as a dividend by its corporate shareholders?

Solution: Distributions in complete liquidation of a corporation are treated by all shareholders (corporate and noncorporate shareholders alike) as though the shareholders had sold their stock for the amount received (see Chapter C6). In a partial liquidation, a significant portion of the corporation's business is discontinued. Therefore, the shareholder is treated as though he or she sold a portion of his or her stock. On the other hand, even though a partial liquidation has occurred, corporate shareholders are still allowed to treat the distribution as a dividend because it is more advantageous for them. They can receive a dividends-received deduction and, therefore, pay less tax than they would if the transaction were treated as a sale. In other words, both corporate and noncorporate shareholders participating in a partial liquidation can receive the tax treatment that generally is most favorable to them.

TAX STRATEGY TIP

An estate with liquidity problems owing to large holdings of a closely held business also may want to consider installment payment of the estate tax under Sec. 6166. See Chapter C13 for further details.

REDEMPTIONS TO PAY DEATH TAXES

If corporate stock represents a substantial portion of a decedent's gross estate, a redemption of the stock from the estate or its beneficiaries may be eligible for sale treatment under Sec. 303. This IRC section helps shareholders who inherit stock in a closely held corporation and who must sell some of their stock to pay estate taxes, inheritance taxes, and funeral and administrative expenses. If the stock is not readily marketable, a stock redemption may be the only way to provide the estate and beneficiaries with sufficient liquidity to meet their cash needs. In most cases, attribution rules would prevent such a redemption from qualifying as substantially disproportionate or as a complete termination of the shareholder's interest. The redemption then would be treated as a dividend. However, attribution rules do not apply to the portion of a stock redemption that qualifies under Sec. 303.

Section 303 provides that a redemption of stock that was included in a decedent's gross estate is treated as a sale of stock by the shareholder (either the estate or the beneficiary of the estate) if the following conditions are met:

1. The value of the redeeming corporation's stock included in the decedent's gross estate is more than 35% of the adjusted gross estate. The adjusted gross estate is the total gross estate (i.e., the FMV of all property owned by the decedent on the date of death) less allowable deductions for funeral and administrative expenses, claims against the estate, debts, and casualty and other losses.

EXAMPLE C4-38 ▶ A decedent's gross estate is valued at $2.9 million. It includes Pepper Corporation stock worth $1.2 million and $1.7 million in cash. Funeral expenses, debts, and other administrative expenses allowable as estate tax deductions amount to $900,000, so that the decedent's adjusted gross estate is $2 million ($2,900,000 − $900,000). Because the value of the Pepper stock included in the gross estate is more than 35% of the adjusted gross estate [$1.2 million is more than $700,000 (0.35 × $2,000,000)], a redemption of some of Pepper's stock can qualify as a stock sale under Sec. 303. ◀

2. The maximum amount of the redemption distribution that can qualify for sale treatment under Sec. 303 is the sum of all federal and state estate and inheritance taxes, plus any interest due on those taxes, and all funeral and administrative expenses allowable as deductions on the federal estate tax return. The redemption must be of stock held by the estate or by heirs who are liable for the estate taxes and other administrative expenses.

3. Section 303 applies to a redemption distribution only to the extent the recipient shareholder's interest in the estate is reduced by the payment of death taxes and funeral and administration expenses. The maximum distribution to any shareholder that is eligible for sale treatment under Sec. 303 is the amount of estate taxes and expenses the shareholder is obligated to bear.

EXAMPLE C4-39 ▶ Assume the same facts as in Example C4-38 except that all the stock is bequeathed to the decedent's son, Sam. The remainder of the estate is bequeathed to the decedent's wife, Wilma, and she is liable for all taxes and expenses. In such case, Sec. 303 could not be used by Sam. He is not liable for any of the estate taxes or administrative expenses. If instead $800,000 is bequeathed to Wilma and the remainder of the estate to Sam, Sam would be liable for all estate taxes and administrative expenses. He could use Sec. 303 to receive sale treatment on a redemption of enough of his stock to pay the estate taxes and administrative expenses. ◀

4. Section 303 applies only to distributions made within certain time limits.

a. In general, the redemption must take place not later than 90 days after the expiration of the period for assessment of the federal estate tax. Because the statute of limitations for the federal estate tax expires three years after the estate tax return is due and the return is due nine months after the date of death, the redemption generally must take place within four years after the date of death.

b. If a petition for redetermination of an estate tax deficiency is filed with the Tax Court, the distribution period is extended to 60 days after the Tax Court's decision becomes final.

c. If the taxpayer made a valid election under Sec. 6166 to defer payment of federal estate taxes under an installment plan, the distribution period is extended to the time the installment payments are due.

5. The stock of two or more corporations may be aggregated to satisfy the 35% requirement provided that 20% or more of the value of each corporation's outstanding stock is included in the gross estate.

EXAMPLE C4-40 ▶ The gross estate of a decedent is valued at $2.9 million. It includes 80% of the stock of Curry Corporation, valued at $400,000, and 90% of the stock of Brodie Corporation, valued at $450,000. Allowable estate tax deductions for administrative expenses and debts amount to $900,000, so the decedent's adjusted gross estate is $2 million. Although neither the Curry stock nor the Brodie stock has a value greater than 35% of the $2 million adjusted gross estate, the value of the stock of both corporations taken together is greater than 35% of the adjusted gross estate [$850,000 ($400,000 + $450,000) is greater than $700,000 (0.35 × $2,000,000)]. Therefore, a redemption of sufficient Curry stock and/or Brodie stock to pay estate taxes and funeral and administrative expenses is eligible for sale treatment under Sec. 303. ◀

Although the basic purpose of Sec. 303 is to provide liquidity for the payment of estate taxes when a major portion of the estate consists of stock in a closely held corporation, a redemption can qualify under Sec. 303 even when the estate has sufficient liquid assets to pay estate taxes and other expenses. The redemption proceeds do not have to be used for this purpose.

The advantage of qualifying a redemption under Sec. 303 is that the redeeming shareholder usually has little or no capital gain to report because his or her basis in the redeemed stock is the stock's FMV on the decedent's date of death (or an alternate valuation date, if applicable). On the other hand, if the redemption does *not* qualify as a sale, the redeeming shareholder may have dividend income equal to the entire distribution from the redeeming corporation.

EXAMPLE C4-41 ▶ Chili Corporation redeems 100 shares of its stock for $105,000 from Art, who inherited the stock from his father, Fred. The stock's FMV on Fred's date of death was $100,000. Chili Corporation has an E&P balance of $500,000. If the redemption qualifies as a sale under Sec. 303, Art recognizes a $5,000 ($105,000 − $100,000) capital gain. However, if the redemption does not qualify as a sale under Sec. 303 or one of the other sale treatment exceptions, Art has $105,000 of dividend income. ◀

SELF-STUDY QUESTION

How much gain is the redeeming shareholder likely to recognize in a qualifying Sec. 303 redemption?

ANSWER

Probably little or none. The basis in the redeemed stock equals its FMV at the decedent's date of death (or an alternate valuation date). The recognized gain generally is only the post-death appreciation.

Thus, Sec. 303 can make a large difference in the amount of income a redeeming shareholder must report as well as the character of that income.

EFFECT OF REDEMPTIONS ON THE DISTRIBUTING CORPORATION

As in the case of property distributions that are not in redemption of a shareholder's stock, two questions must be answered with respect to a corporation that distributes property in redemption of its stock:

- What amount and character of gain or loss must the distributing corporation recognize on the distribution?
- What effect does the distribution have on the corporation's E&P?

Each of these questions is addressed below.

CORPORATE GAIN OR LOSS ON PROPERTY DISTRIBUTIONS. The rules for the recognition of gain or loss by a corporation that distributes property in redemption of its stock are the same as the rules for property distributions that are not in redemption of the corporation's stock. Under Sec. 311,

- The corporation recognizes gain when it distributes appreciated property in redemption of its stock. The character of the gain depends on the character of the distributed property in the corporation's hands.
- The corporation recognizes no loss when it distributes property that has declined in value.

EFFECT OF REDEMPTIONS ON E&P. A stock redemption affects a corporation's E&P accounts in two ways. First, if the corporation distributes appreciated property, the gain is included in the corporation's gross income, and the excess of FMV over the property's E&P adjusted basis increases the corporation's E&P account. Next, the corporation's E&P balance must be reduced because of the distribution. The amount of the reduction depends on whether the redemption distribution is treated as a sale or as a dividend by the shareholder whose stock is redeemed.

If the shareholder treats the redemption as a dividend, the corporation must reduce its E&P by the amount of money, the principal amount of any obligations, and the greater of the adjusted basis or FMV of any other property distributed, the same as it does for a property distribution that is not a redemption distribution.

If the redemption qualifies for sale treatment, E&P is reduced by the portion of the current and accumulated E&P attributable to the redeemed stock. In other words, E&P is reduced by a percentage equal to the percentage of the stock redeemed, but not by more than the actual redemption distribution amount. The remainder of the distribution reduces the corporation's paid-in capital.[43] An ordinary dividend distribution has first claim to current E&P ahead of any stock redemptions. No such priority exists for accumulated E&P. Both ordinary dividend distributions and stock redemptions reduce accumulated E&P in chronological order.

[43] Sec. 312(n)(7).

EXAMPLE C4-42 ▶ Apex Corporation has 100 shares of stock outstanding, 30 of which are owned by Mona. Apex Corporation redeems all 30 of Mona's shares on December 31 for $36,000 in a redemption qualifying as a sale under Sec. 302(b)(3). At the time of the redemption, Apex has $60,000 in paid-in capital and $40,000 of E&P. Because 30% of the outstanding stock was redeemed, the distribution reduces Apex's E&P by $12,000 (0.30 × $40,000). The remaining $24,000 ($36,000 – $12,000) of the distribution reduces the paid-in capital amount to $36,000 ($60,000 – $24,000).[44] ◀

PREFERRED STOCK BAILOUTS

OBJECTIVE 6

Explain the tax treatment for preferred stock bailouts

ADDITIONAL COMMENT

When the term *bailout* is used in the corporate context, this generally refers to some scheme that allows a corporation to make a dividend distribution, but for tax purposes the transaction is treated as a sale of a capital asset.

The stock redemption rules permit sale treatment for stock redemptions under certain specific circumstances and require dividend treatment in all other situations. In most cases, taxpayers prefer sale treatment. First, sale treatment allows taxpayers to deduct their basis in the stock redeemed. Second, the gain on the stock sale generally is long-term capital gain, which currently is taxed at a maximum rate of 20%, or may be offset by the taxpayer's capital losses and not taxed at all. Consequently, taxpayers have devised methods to obtain sale rather than dividend treatment.

One such method, devised by taxpayers before the enactment of the Internal Revenue Code of 1954, is known as the **preferred stock bailout**. In general, the preferred stock bailout scenario operated as follows:

1. A tax-free stock dividend of nonvoting preferred stock was issued with respect to a corporation's common stock. Under the rules for nontaxable stock dividends, a portion of the common stock's basis is allocated to the preferred stock. Its holding period includes the holding period for the common stock.

2. The preferred stock was sold to an unrelated third party at its FMV. The sale resulted in a capital gain equal to the difference between the preferred stock's sale price and its allocated basis.

3. The corporation redeemed the preferred stock from the third-party purchaser (at a small premium to reward the third party for his or her cooperation in the scheme).

As a result, the shareholder received the corporation's earnings as a long-term capital gain without changing his or her equity position in the company.

To prevent this tax-avoidance possibility, Congress enacted Sec. 306. Section 306 operates by "tainting" certain stock (usually preferred stock) when it is distributed. The tainted stock is not taxed at the time of its distribution, but a subsequent sale or redemption of the stock generally results in the recognition of ordinary or dividend income rather than capital gain. Thus, Sec. 306 prevents taxpayers from using a preferred stock bailout to convert dividend income into capital gain.

SEC. 306 STOCK DEFINED

Section 306 stock is defined as follows:[45]

1. Stock (other than common stock issued with respect to common stock) received as a nontaxable stock dividend
2. Stock (other than common stock) received in a tax-free corporate reorganization or corporate division if the effect of the transaction was substantially the same as the receipt of a stock dividend, or if the stock was received in exchange for Sec. 306 stock
3. Stock that has a basis determined by reference to the basis of Sec. 306 stock (i.e., a substituted or transferred basis)
4. Stock (other than common stock) acquired in an exchange to which Sec. 351 applies if the receipt of money (in lieu of the stock) would have been treated as a dividend

[44] Distributions made during the year require a different calculation, which is beyond the scope of this text.

[45] Sec. 306(c).

Preferred stock issued by a corporation having no current or accumulated E&P in the year the stock is issued cannot be Sec. 306 stock. Also, inherited stock is not Sec. 306 stock because the basis of such stock is its FMV on the date of death (or alternate valuation date) and, therefore, is not determined by reference to the decedent's basis.[46]

TYPICAL MISCONCEPTION

Although the amount of ordinary income recognized in a sale of Sec. 306 stock is measured by the E&P existing in the year the Sec. 306 stock was distributed, the E&P of the distributing corporation is not reduced by the amount of Sec. 306 ordinary income.

DISPOSITIONS OF SEC. 306 STOCK

If a shareholder sells or otherwise disposes of Sec. 306 stock (except in a redemption), the amount realized is treated as ordinary income to the extent the shareholder would have had a dividend at the time of the distribution if money equal to the FMV of the stock were distributed instead of the stock itself. The shareholder's ordinary income is measured by reference to the corporation's E&P in the year the Sec. 306 stock was distributed. Any additional amount received for the Sec. 306 stock generally constitutes a return of capital. If the additional amount exceeds the shareholder's basis in the Sec. 306 stock, the excess is a capital gain. If the additional amount is less than the shareholder's basis, the unrecovered basis is added back to the shareholder's basis in his or her common stock. It is not recognized as a loss.

EXAMPLE C4-43 ▶ Carlos owns all 100 outstanding shares of Adobe Corporation's stock. His basis in those shares is $100,000. Adobe Corporation, which has $150,000 of E&P, distributes 50 shares of nonvoting preferred stock to Carlos as a nontaxable stock dividend. The preferred stock has a $50,000 FMV on the distribution date, and the common stock has a $200,000 FMV. Carlos must allocate his $100,000 basis for the common stock to the common and preferred stock according to relative FMVs as follows:

	FMV	*Basis*
Common stock	$200,000	$ 80,000[a]
Preferred stock	50,000	20,000[b]
Total	$250,000	$100,000

[a] $\frac{\$200,000}{\$250,000} \times \$100,000$ [b] $\frac{\$50,000}{\$250,000} \times \$100,000$

Carlos subsequently sells the preferred stock to Dillon for $50,000. The $50,000 is all ordinary income because Adobe Corporation's E&P in the year it issued the preferred stock dividend exceeded the FMV of the preferred stock. Carlos's $20,000 basis in the preferred stock is added back to his basis in his common stock so that his basis in his common stock is restored to $100,000. If instead Carlos sells the preferred stock for $100,000, he has $50,000 of ordinary income, $20,000 return of capital, and $30,000 of capital gain computed as follows:

Sales price	$100,000
Minus: Ordinary income[a]	(50,000)
Remaining sales proceeds	$ 50,000
Minus: Return of capital[b]	(20,000)
Capital gain[c]	$ 30,000

[a] Smaller of E&P in year stock was issued or stock's FMV on the distribution date.
[b] Smaller of remaining sales proceeds or adjusted basis of stock.
[c] Sales proceeds received in excess of adjusted basis of stock. ◀

KEY POINT

The amount realized in a redemption of Sec. 306 stock is a dividend to the extent of E&P existing in the year of redemption. Unlike a sale of Sec. 306 stock, E&P is reduced as a result of a redemption.

REDEMPTIONS OF SEC. 306 STOCK

If the issuing corporation redeems Sec. 306 stock, the shareholder's total amount realized is a distribution to which the Sec. 301 distribution rules apply. It is, therefore, a dividend to the extent of the redeeming corporation's E&P *in the year of the redemption.* Amounts received in excess of the corporation's E&P are treated as a recovery of the shareholder's basis in his or her Sec. 306 stock, and then as a capital gain once the basis has been recovered. If the shareholder's basis in the redeemed stock is not recovered, the unrecovered basis is added to the basis of the shareholder's common stock.

[46] Reg. Sec. 1.306-3(e).

EXAMPLE C4-44 ▶ Don owns all 100 shares of Brigham Corporation's common stock and has a $300,000 adjusted basis in the stock. On January 1, 1997, Brigham issued 50 shares of preferred stock to Don. The preferred stock and common stock had $100,000 and $400,000 FMVs, respectively, on the distribution date. Brigham's current and accumulated E&P for 1997 was $200,000. Don's allocated basis in the preferred stock was $60,000 {[$100,000 ÷ ($100,000 + $400,000)] × $300,000}. The basis of Don's common stock was reduced to $240,000 ($300,000 − $60,000) as a result of the basis allocation. On January 2, 2001, Brigham redeems the preferred shares for $250,000. In the year of the redemption, Brigham's current and accumulated E&P is $400,000. Don has dividend income of $250,000 (because Brigham's E&P is at least $250,000 in the year of the redemption). If Brigham's E&P is instead $200,000 in the year of the redemption, Don has $200,000 of dividend income and a $50,000 tax-free return of capital. Because Don's basis in his preferred stock is $60,000, the $10,000 unrecovered basis is added to his basis in the common stock, increasing it to $250,000 ($240,000 + $10,000). ◀

EXCEPTIONS TO SEC. 306 TREATMENT

Section 306 does not apply in the following situations.

- A shareholder sells all of his or her common and preferred stock in a corporation, thereby completely terminating his or her interest in the corporation. Section 306 does not apply even if some of the stock sold is Sec. 306 stock.
- The corporation redeems all the shareholder's common and preferred stock, completely terminating the shareholder's interest in the corporation.
- The corporation redeems an individual shareholder's stock in a partial liquidation qualifying under Sec. 302(b)(4).
- A shareholder disposes of Sec. 306 stock in a way in which gain or loss is not recognized (e.g., a gift of Sec. 306 stock). Although the donor recognizes no income when he or she disposes of Sec. 306 stock by gift, the stock retains its taint and remains Sec. 306 stock in the donee's hands. The taint disappears, however, from stock received from a decedent.
- Section 306 does not apply if it is demonstrated to the IRS's satisfaction that the distribution and subsequent disposition of Sec. 306 stock did not have tax avoidance as one of its principal purposes.

STOCK REDEMPTIONS BY RELATED CORPORATIONS

OBJECTIVE 7

Determine when Sec. 304 applies to a stock sale and its tax consequences

If a shareholder sells stock in one corporation (the issuing corporation) to a second corporation (the acquiring corporation), the sale usually results in the recognition of a capital gain or loss by the shareholder. However, if the shareholder controls both corporations the net result may be more similar to a dividend than to a sale.

To prevent shareholders from using two commonly controlled corporations to bail out the E&P of a corporation at capital gains rates, Sec. 304 requires that a sale of stock of one controlled corporation to a second controlled corporation be treated as a stock redemption. If the redemption meets the qualifications for a sale (e.g., if the redemption is substantially disproportionate), the transaction is treated as a sale. Otherwise, the redemption is treated as a dividend, assuming sufficient E&P.

ADDITIONAL COMMENT

The definition of brother-sister corporations for Sec. 304 differs from the definition for controlled groups discussed in Chapter C3.

Section 304 applies to two types of sales. The first is a sale of stock involving two brother-sister corporations. The second is a sale of a parent corporation's stock to one of its subsidiary corporations. The following sections define brother-sister groups and parent-subsidiary groups and explain how Sec. 304 applies to each group.

BROTHER-SISTER CORPORATIONS

Two corporations are called brother-sister corporations when one or more shareholders control each of the corporations and a parent-subsidiary relationship is not present. Control means ownership of at least 50% of the voting power or 50% of the total value of all the corporation's stock. The shareholder(s) who have such ownership are called controlling shareholders. If a controlling shareholder (or shareholders) transfers stock in one corporation to the other corporation in exchange for property, the exchange is recast as a redemption.

To determine whether the redemption is a sale or a dividend, reference is made to the shareholder's stock ownership in the issuing corporation. For purposes of making this test under Sec. 302(b), the attribution rules of Sec. 318(a) apply.[47]

REDEMPTION TREATED AS A DISTRIBUTION. If the redemption does not qualify as a sale, it is treated as a dividend made first by the acquiring corporation to the extent of its E&P, and then by the issuing corporation to the extent of its E&P. The shareholder's basis in the issuing corporation's stock sold is added to his or her basis for the acquiring corporation's stock. The acquiring corporation takes the same basis in the issuing corporation's shares that the shareholder had.

EXAMPLE C4-45 ▶ Bert owns 60 of the 100 outstanding shares of Frog Corporation stock and 60 of the 100 outstanding shares of Tree Corporation stock. Frog and Tree Corporations have $50,000 and $20,000 of E&P, respectively. Bert sells 20 shares of Frog stock (for which his adjusted basis is $10,000) to Tree Corporation for $20,000. Section 304 applies because Frog and Tree are both controlled by Bert (because of his ownership of at least 50% of each corporation's stock). The transaction is recast as a redemption. To determine whether the transaction qualifies as a sale, reference is made to Bert's ownership of Frog stock. Before the redemption, Bert owned 60% of the Frog stock. After the redemption, Bert owns 52% of the Frog stock (40 shares directly and 12 [0.60 × 20] shares indirectly through Tree). The redemption is treated as a Sec. 301 distribution because it satisfies none of the tests for sale treatment. The entire distribution is a dividend because it does not exceed the $70,000 total of Frog and Tree Corporations' E&P. All $20,000 of the distribution is from Tree's E&P. Tree's basis in the Frog stock is $10,000, the same as Bert's basis in the Frog stock. Bert's basis in his Tree stock is increased by $10,000, his basis in the Frog stock that he is deemed to have contributed to Tree Corporation. ◀

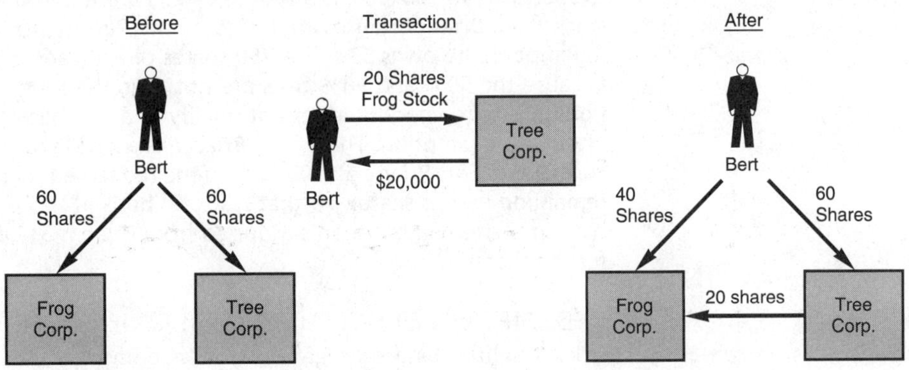

Bert's Ownership of Frog Corporation Stock:
Before: 60 shares (60%) directly
After: 52 shares [40 shares directly + 12 shares (60% x 20 shares) indirectly]

FIGURE C4-1 ▶ ILLUSTRATION OF BROTHER-SISTER REDEMPTION (EXAMPLE C4-45)

REDEMPTION TREATED AS A SALE. If the redemption qualifies as a sale, the shareholder's recognized gain or loss is the difference between the amount received from the acquiring corporation and the shareholder's basis in the surrendered shares. The acquiring corporation is treated as having purchased the issuing corporation's shares and takes a cost basis for such shares.

[47] The attribution rules of Sec. 318(a) are modified for Sec. 304 purposes so that a shareholder is considered to own a proportionate amount of stock owned by any corporation of which he or she owns 5% or more (instead of 50% or more) of the value of the stock.

EXAMPLE C4-46 ▶ Assume the same facts as in Example C4-45 except that Bert sells 40 shares of Frog stock (for which his adjusted basis is $20,000) to Tree Corporation for $40,000. After the redemption, Bert owns 44 shares of Frog stock (20 shares directly and 24 [0.60 × 40] shares indirectly through Tree). Therefore, he meets both the 50% and the 80% tests for a substantially disproportionate redemption, and he treats the redemption as a sale. He has a $20,000 ($40,000 received from Tree − $20,000 adjusted basis in the Frog shares) capital gain. Tree's basis in the Frog shares acquired from Bert is its $40,000 purchase price. ◀

ADDITIONAL COMMENT

The definition of a parent-subsidiary relationship for Sec. 304 differs from the definition for controlled groups or affiliated corporations discussed in Chapter C3.

PARENT-SUBSIDIARY CORPORATIONS

If a shareholder sells stock in a parent corporation to a subsidiary of the parent corporation, the exchange is treated as a distribution in redemption of part or all of the shareholder's stock in the parent corporation. For this purpose, a parent-subsidiary relationship exists if one corporation owns at least 50% of the voting power or 50% of the total value of all stock in the subsidiary.

To determine whether the redemption is a sale or a dividend, reference is made to the shareholder's ownership of the parent corporation stock before and after the redemption. The constructive ownership rules of Sec. 318 apply in making this determination.

REDEMPTION TREATED AS A DIVIDEND. If the redemption does not qualify as a sale, the distribution is treated as a dividend from the subsidiary corporation to the extent of its E&P and then from the parent corporation to the extent of its E&P. The effect of this rule is to make the E&P of both corporations available in determining the portion of the distribution that is a dividend. The shareholder's basis in his or her remaining parent corporation stock is increased by his or her basis in the stock transferred to the subsidiary. The subsidiary's basis in the parent corporation stock is the amount it paid for the stock.[48]

EXAMPLE C4-47 ▶ Brian owns 60 of the 100 shares of Parent Corporation stock and has a $15,000 basis in his shares. Parent Corporation owns 60 of the 100 shares of Subsidiary stock. Parent and Subsidiary Corporations have $10,000 and $30,000 of E&P, respectively. Brian sells ten of his Parent shares to Subsidiary for $12,000. (See Figure C4-2.) Parent Corporation is deemed to have redeemed its stock from Brian. Brian owned 60% of the Parent stock before the redemption. After the redemption, he owns 53 shares (50 shares directly and 3 [0.60 × 0.50 × 10] shares indirectly). Because the 50% and 80% tests are not met, the redemption is not substantially disproportionate. The redemption does not qualify as a sale because Brian remains in control of Parent after the redemption. Therefore, Brian has a dividend. The $12,000 distribution comes from Subsidiary's E&P. Brian's $2,500 basis in the redeemed shares is added to his $12,500 basis in his remaining Parent shares, so that his total basis in those shares remains $15,000. Subsidiary's basis in the ten Parent shares acquired from Brian is $12,000, the amount that Subsidiary paid for the shares. ◀

REDEMPTION TREATED AS A SALE. If the redemption of the parent corporation's stock qualifies as a sale, gain or loss is computed in the usual fashion. The basis of the stock transferred to the subsidiary is subtracted from the amount received in the distribution to determine the shareholder's recognized gain.

EXAMPLE C4-48 ▶ Assume the same facts as in Example C4-47 except that Brian sells 40 shares of Parent stock to Subsidiary Corporation for $48,000. Because Brian owns 60% of the Parent stock before the redemption and he owns 24.8% (20 shares directly and 4.8 [0.60 × 0.20 × 40] shares indirectly after the redemption), the redemption meets the 50% and 80% tests for a substantially disproportionate redemption. In this case, Brian has a $38,000 ($48,000 − $10,000 adjusted basis in the 40 shares sold) capital gain. Brian's adjusted basis for his remaining 20 shares of Parent stock is $5,000. Subsidiary Corporation's basis for the 40 Parent shares purchased from Brian is $48,000, the amount that Subsidiary paid for the shares. ◀

Topic Review C4-4 summarizes the methods by which a redemption transaction can be characterized as a sale or exchange as well as the special stock redemption rules.

[48] Rev. Rul. 80-189, 1980-2 C.B. 106.

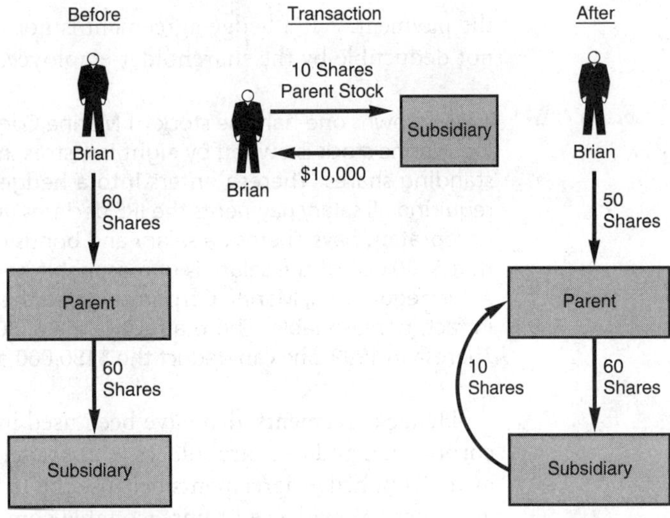

FIGURE C4-2 ▶ ILLUSTRATION OF PARENT-SUBSIDIARY REDEMPTION (EXAMPLE C4-47)

Topic Review C4-4

Alternative Treatments of Stock Redemptions

General Rule: A distribution in redemption of stock is a dividend (Secs. 302(d) and 301).
Exception: Redemptions Treated as Sales or Exchanges

1. Redemptions that are not essentially equivalent to a dividend (Sec. 302(b)(1))
2. Substantially disproportionate redemptions (Sec. 302(b)(2))
3. Complete terminations of a shareholder's interest (Sec. 302(b)(3))
4. Partial liquidation of a corporation in redemption of a noncorporate shareholder's stock (Sec. 302(b)(4))
5. Redemption to pay death taxes (Sec. 303)

Special Redemption Rules

1. Redemptions of Sec. 306 stock generally are treated as dividends to the shareholder (Sec. 306).
2. A sale of stock in one controlled corporation to another controlled corporation is treated as a redemption (Sec. 304).

TAX PLANNING CONSIDERATIONS

AVOIDING UNREASONABLE COMPENSATION

The advantage of using salary and fringe benefit payments to permit a shareholder of a closely held corporation to withdraw funds from the corporation and still be taxed at a single level was discussed in Chapter C3. If a corporation pays too large a salary to a shareholder-employee, some of the salary may be reclassified as a dividend. In such case, double taxation results.

Corporations can avoid the double taxation problem associated with a constructive dividend by entering into a **hedge agreement** with a shareholder-employee, which obligates the shareholder to repay any portion of salary the IRS disallows as a deduction. The shareholder-employee deducts the amount of the repayment under Sec. 162 in the year he or she makes the repayment, provided a legal obligation exists under state law to make the payment.[49] If a hedge agreement is not in effect, voluntary repayment of the salary is not deductible by the shareholder-employee.[50]

EXAMPLE C4-49 ▶ Theresa owns one-half the stock of Marine Corporation and serves as its president. The remaining Marine stock is owned by eight investors, none of whom owns more than 10% of the outstanding shares. Theresa enters into a hedge agreement with Marine Corporation in 1997 requiring all salary payments the IRS declares unreasonable compensation to be repaid. Marine Corporation pays Theresa a salary and bonus of $750,000 in 1999. The IRS subsequently holds that $300,000 of the salary is unreasonable compensation and should be taxed as a dividend. After negotiation, Marine Corporation and the IRS agree that $180,000 of the compensation is, in fact, unreasonable. Theresa repays the $180,000 in 2002. The entire $750,000 is taxable to Theresa in 1999. She can deduct the $180,000 as a trade or business expense in 2002. ◀

Hedge agreements also have been used in connection with other payments involving a corporation and its shareholders (e.g., travel and entertainment expenses). Some firms shy away from hedge agreements because the IRS is likely to consider the existence of such an agreement as evidence of unreasonable compensation.

BOOTSTRAP ACQUISITIONS

A prospective purchaser who wants to acquire the stock of a corporation may not have sufficient cash to make the purchase. Instead, corporate funds may be used to facilitate the purchase by having the corporation's shareholder sell part of his or her stock to the purchaser and having the corporation redeem the remainder of the selling shareholder's stock. Such an arrangement is called a **bootstrap acquisition.**

EXAMPLE C4-50 ▶ Ted owns all 100 shares of Dragon Corporation stock. The stock has a $100,000 FMV. Vickie wants to purchase the stock from Ted but has only $60,000. Dragon Corporation has a large cash balance, which it does not need for its operations. Ted sells Vickie 60 shares of Dragon stock for $60,000 and then causes Dragon Corporation to redeem his remaining shares for $40,000. The redemption qualifies as a complete termination of interest for Ted under Sec. 302(b)(3) and, therefore, is eligible for capital gain treatment. ◀

Court cases have established that redemptions qualify for exchange treatment as long as the sale and redemption are part of an integrated plan to terminate the seller's entire interest. It does not matter whether the redemption precedes the sale.[51] In such situations, however, the purchaser must be careful to avoid having dividend income. For example, a purchaser who contracts to acquire all the stock of a corporation on the installment plan and then uses corporate funds to pay the installment obligations will have dividend income. The use of corporate funds constitutes a constructive dividend to the purchaser when the corporation discharges a purchaser's legal obligation. Even if the corporation uses its own funds to redeem the seller's shares, a purchaser who was legally obligated to purchase the shares is considered to have received a constructive dividend.[52]

EXAMPLE C4-51 ▶ Assume the same facts as in Example C4-50 except that, after Vickie purchases the 60 shares from Ted, she is legally obligated to purchase the remaining 40 shares from Ted. After entering into the contract, Vickie causes Dragon Corporation to redeem Ted's 40 shares. Because Dragon Corporation has paid Vickie's legal obligation, a constructive dividend to Vickie of $40,000 results. No constructive dividend would result from the redemption if Vickie were legally obligated to purchase only 60 shares from Ted. ◀

Rev. Rul. 69-608 contains guidelines for the buyer of stock in a bootstrap redemption transaction to avoid the constructive dividend situation.[53] The guiding principle is that the buyer does not have a constructive dividend when the corporation redeems some of

---

[49] Rev. Rul. 69-115, 1969-1 C.B. 50, and *Vincent E. Oswald*, 49 T.C. 645 (1968), *acq*. 1968-2 C.B. 2.

[50] *Ernest H. Berger*, 37 T.C. 1026 (1962), and *John G. Pahl*, 67 T.C. 286 (1976).

[51] See, for example, *U.S. v. Gerald Carey*, 7 AFTR 2d 1301, 61-1 USTC ¶9428 (8th Cir., 1961).

[52] *H. F. Wall v. U.S.*, 36 AFTR 423, 47-2 USTC ¶9395 (4th Cir., 1947).

[53] Rev. Rul. 69-608, 1969-2 C.B. 42.

WHAT WOULD YOU DO IN THIS SITUATION?

One of the most cherished traditions found in the organizational structure of many professional firms is the year-end bonus. Professionals engaged in the healing arts, law, business services, and accounting often have used the bonus pay structure to clear the books at the end of the year. In the traditional partnership format, these payments have been characterized as distributive shares or some similar form of compensation. As such, these payments are taxed only once as income paid to the professional for services rendered net of any appropriate accounting adjustments.

With the advent of the professional corporation, an entity format designed to limit personal liability exposure, many professionals have opted to do business as shareholders in C corporations. The continued use of the year-end bonus pay structure in the professional corporation context has come under greater IRS scrutiny. The position taken by the IRS is clear. If the payments made to the shareholder-professional are in exchange for his or her services rendered to the firm, the corporation may deduct them as salaries (assuming they are reasonable). However, if they are deemed to be a payout of owners' profits, the corporation cannot deduct the bonus payments. Therefore, the corporation's taxable income is increased by the amount of the disallowed payments. The shareholder who received the bonus, must treat the payment as dividend income rather than salary. However, treating the bonus payments as dividends rather than salary generally makes no difference to the shareholder. The negative consequences are only to the corporation, which may not deduct the dividend payments.

This issue is illustrated by a case decided by the Second Circuit Court of Appeals, *Rapco, Inc. v. CIR*, 77 AFTR 2d 2405, 96-1 USTC ¶50,297 (CA-2, 1996). *Rapco* is just one of a long line of cases dealing with this issue. In *Rapco*, the Second Circuit agreed with the Tax Court and denied a deduction for bonus payments to the president of the company, even though he played a significant role in the company's rapid growth and had guaranteed large loans to Rapco. Reasons for this decision were: Rapco's compensation scheme was "bonus-heavy and salary light," suggesting dividend avoidance; Rapco had ignored its own bonus structure contained in its preincorporation minutes; it had a history of never paying dividends; the shareholder who decided his own salary owned 95% of the corporation's stock; and Rapco's own expert testified that $400,000 to $500,000 was fair compensation for the president's services (the IRS allowed a salary of $405,000).

Assuming your CPA firm is acting as a tax advisor to several similarly situated professional C corporations, what advice would you give that is in compliance with all the rules and regulations of the Internal Revenue Code and the AICPA's *Statements on Standards for Tax Services?*

the seller's shares, as long as the buyer does not have a primary and unconditional obligation to purchase the stock, and as long as the corporation pays no more than the FMV for the redeemed stock. A stock purchaser who has an option—not a legal obligation—to purchase the seller's remaining stock, and who assigns the option to the corporation, is not stuck with a constructive dividend.[54]

TIMING OF DISTRIBUTIONS

Dividends can be paid only out of a corporation's E&P. Therefore, if distributions can be timed to be made when the corporation has little or no E&P, the distributions are treated as a return of capital rather than as a dividend.

If a corporation has a current E&P deficit, the deficit reduces accumulated E&P evenly throughout the year unless the corporation can demonstrate that the deficits arose at particular dates. Thus, if the corporation makes a distribution in a year having a deficit in current E&P, but some accumulated E&P exists at the beginning of the year, the timing of the distribution may determine whether it is a dividend or a return of capital.

EXAMPLE C4-52 ▶ Major Corporation has a $30,000 accumulated E&P balance at the beginning of the year and incurs a $50,000 deficit during the year. Because of its poor operating performance, Major Corporation pays only two of its usual $5,000 quarterly dividend payments to its sole share-

[54] *Joseph R. Holsey v. CIR*, 2 AFTR 2d 5660, 58-2 USTC ¶9816 (3rd Cir., 1958).

holder: those ordinarily paid on March 31 and June 30. The source of the distributions is determined as follows:

E&P balance, January 1	$30,000
Minus: Reduction for first quarter loss	(12,500)
Reduction for March 31 distribution	(5,000)
E&P balance, April 1	$12,500
Minus: Reduction for second quarter loss	(12,500)
E&P balance, June 30	$ -0-

The first and second quarter losses each are $12,500 [($50,000) × 0.25 = ($12,500)].

The operating loss reduces the accumulated E&P balance evenly throughout the year. All of the March 31 distribution is taxable because the corporation has not incurred sufficient losses to offset the accumulated E&P amounts at the beginning of the year. The second quarter loss makes the June 30 distribution and any other distributions made before the end of the year tax-free returns of the shareholder's capital investment (assuming that the shareholder's basis in his or her stock exceeds the distribution amount). Delaying all the distributions until late in the year could have made any cash payments to the shareholder tax-free. ◀

The timing of a distribution also can be of critical importance in determining its tax treatment if the distributing corporation has an accumulated E&P deficit and is accruing a positive current E&P balance.

EXAMPLE C4-53 ▶ Yankee Corporation has an accumulated E&P deficit of $250,000 at the beginning of 2001. During 2001 and 2002, Yankee Corporation reports the following current E&P balances and makes the following distributions to Joe, its sole shareholder:

Year	*Current E&P*	*Distributions*	*Distribution Date*
2001	$100,000	$75,000	December 31
2002	-0-	-0-	None

The $75,000 distribution made in 2001 is taxable as a dividend. The $25,000 of current E&P that is not distributed reduces Yankee's accumulated E&P deficit to $225,000. Had Yankee delayed making the $75,000 distribution until January 1, 2002 or later in 2002, the distribution would have been tax-free to the shareholder as a return of Joe's investment in Yankee Corporation. ◀

COMPLIANCE AND PROCEDURAL CONSIDERATIONS

CORPORATE REPORTING OF NONDIVIDEND DISTRIBUTIONS

ADDITIONAL COMMENT

Information on basis adjustments for tax-free dividends, stock splits, stock dividends, etc. for individual firms can be found in special tax services. For example, CCH's *Capital Changes Reports* provides histories of these types of events for over 60,000 companies.

A corporation that makes a nondividend distribution to its shareholders must file Form 5452 (Corporate Report of Nondividend Distributions) and supporting computations with its income tax return. Form 5452 reports the E&P of the distributing corporation so that the IRS can determine whether the distributions are indeed nontaxable to shareholders. Specifically, the form requires the following information: the corporation's current and accumulated E&P, amounts paid to shareholders during the tax year, the percentage of each payment that is taxable and nontaxable, and a detailed computation of the corporation's E&P from the date of incorporation.

AGREEMENT TO TERMINATE INTEREST UNDER SEC. 302(b)(3)

If a shareholder's interest in a corporation is completely terminated by a redemption, the family attribution rules of Sec. 318(a)(1) may be waived. To have the rules waived, the shareholder must file a written agreement with the Treasury Department that he or she

KEY POINT

The statute of limitation extends to one year beyond the date a shareholder notifies the IRS that a forbidden interest has been acquired. Otherwise, it would be almost impossible for the IRS to administer this provision.

will notify the IRS upon acquiring any prohibited interest within the ten-year period following the redemption. A copy of this agreement (which should be in the form of a statement in duplicate signed by the distributee) must be attached to the first return filed by the shareholder for the tax year in which the redemption occurs. If the agreement is not filed on time, the District Director of the IRS is permitted to grant an extension. Regulation Sec. 1.302-4(a) provides that an extension will be granted only if there is reasonable cause for failure to file the agreement on time and if the request for such an extension is filed within such time as the District Director considers reasonable in the circumstances.

Treasury Regulations do not indicate what constitutes a reasonable cause for failure to file or what constitutes a reasonable extension of time. In *Edward J. Fehrs* the Court of Claims held that late filing of a ten-year agreement is permissible where a taxpayer could not reasonably have expected a filing would be necessary, where the taxpayer files the agreement promptly after he or she has noticed that it is required, and where the agreement is filed before the issues in question are presented for trial.[55] However, in *Robin Haft Trust,* an agreement was filed *after* an adverse court ruling. In an appeal for a rehearing, the judge ruled that the filing of the agreement after the case came to trial was too late and denied the appeal for a rehearing.[56]

If the shareholder *does* acquire a forbidden interest in the corporation within the ten-year period following the redemption, additional taxes may be due. Such an acquisition ordinarily results in the redemption being treated as a dividend distribution rather than a sale. The limitation period for assessing additional taxes extends to one year following the date the shareholder files notice of the acquisition of the forbidden interest with the IRS.[57]

PROBLEM MATERIALS

DISCUSSION QUESTIONS

C4-1 Explain how a corporation computes its current E&P and its accumulated E&P.

C4-2 Why is it necessary to distinguish between current and accumulated E&P?

C4-3 Describe the effect of a $100,000 cash distribution paid on January 1 to the sole shareholder of a calendar year corporation whose stock basis is $25,000 when the corporation has
a. $100,000 of current E&P and $100,000 of accumulated E&P
b. $50,000 of accumulated E&P deficit and $60,000 of current E&P
c. $60,000 of accumulated E&P deficit and $60,000 of current E&P deficit
d. $80,000 of current E&P deficit and $100,000 of accumulated E&P

Answer Parts a through d again, assuming instead that the corporation makes the distribution on October 1.

C4-4 Pecan Corporation distributes land to a noncorporate shareholder. Explain how the following items are computed:
a. The amount of the distribution
b. The amount of the dividend
c. The basis of the land to the shareholder
d. When the holding period for the land begins

How would your answers change if the distribution were made to a corporate shareholder?

C4-5 What effect do the following transactions have on the calculation of Young Corporation's current E&P? Assume that the starting point for the calculation is Young Corporation's taxable income for the current year.
a. The corporation earns tax-exempt interest income of $10,000.
b. Taxable income includes a $10,000 dividend received and is reduced by a $7,000 dividends-received deduction.
c. A $5,000 capital loss carryover from the preceding tax year offsets $5,000 of capital gains.
d. Federal income taxes of $25,280 were accrued.

C4-6 Badger Corporation was incorporated in the current year. It reports an $8,000 NOL on its initial tax return. Badger distributed $2,500 to its shareholders. Is it possible for this distribution to be taxed as a dividend to Badger's shareholders? Explain.

---

[55] *Edward J. Fehrs v. U.S.*, 40 AFTR 2d 77-5040, 77-1 USTC ¶9423 (Ct. Cl., 1977).

[56] *Robin Haft Trust*, 62 T.C. 145 (1974).

[57] Sec. 302(c)(2)(A).

C4-7 Does it matter when during the tax year a corporation makes a distribution as to whether it is taxed as a dividend or as a return of capital? Explain.

C4-8 Hickory Corporation owns a building with a $160,000 adjusted basis and a $120,000 FMV. Hickory's E&P is $200,000. Should the corporation sell the property and distribute the sale proceeds to its shareholders or distribute the property to its shareholders and let them sell the property? Why?

C4-9 Walnut Corporation owns a building with a $120,000 adjusted basis and a $160,000 FMV. Walnut's E&P is $200,000. Should the corporation sell the property and distribute the sale proceeds to its shareholders or distribute the property to its shareholders and let them sell the property? Why?

C4-10 What is a constructive dividend? Under what circumstances are constructive dividends most likely to arise?

C4-11 Why are stock dividends generally nontaxable? Under what circumstances are stock dividends taxable?

C4-12 How is a distribution of stock rights treated by a shareholder for tax purposes? By the distributing corporation?

C4-13 What is a stock redemption? What are some reasons for making a stock redemption? Why are some redemptions treated as sales and others as dividends?

C4-14 Field Corporation redeems 100 shares of its stock from Andrew for $10,000. Andrew's basis in those shares is $8,000. Explain the possible tax treatments of the $10,000 received by Andrew.

C4-15 What conditions are necessary for a redemption to be treated as a sale by the redeeming shareholder?

C4-16 Explain the purpose of the attribution rules in determining stock ownership in a redemption. Describe the four types of attribution rules that apply to redemptions.

C4-17 Abel, the sole shareholder of Ace Corporation, has an opporunity to purchase the assets of a sole proprietorship for $50,000 in cash. Ace Corporation has a substantial E&P balance. Abel does not have sufficient cash to personally make the purchase. If Abel obtains the needed $50,000 from Ace Corporation via a nonliquidating distribution, Abel will have to recognize dividend income. Alternatively, would Ace's purchase of the assets of the sole proprietorship followed by their distribution to Abel in redemption of part of his stock holdings constitute a partial liquidation? Explain.

C4-18 Why does a redemption that qualifies as an exchange under Sec. 303 usually result in little or no gain or loss being recognized by the shareholder?

C4-19 Under what circumstances does a corporation recognize gain or loss when it distributes noncash property in redemption of its stock? What effect does a redemption distribution have on the distributing corporation's E&P?

C4-20 What is a preferred stock bailout? How does Sec. 306 operate to prevent a shareholder from realizing the planned advantages of a preferred stock bailout?

C4-21 Bill owns all 100 of the outstanding shares of Plum Corporation stock and 80 of the 100 outstanding shares of Cherry Corporation stock. He sells 20 Plum shares to Cherry Corporation for $80,000. Explain why this transaction is treated as a stock redemption and how the tax consequences of the transaction are determined.

C4-22 Explain the tax consequences to both the corporation and a shareholder-employee of an IRS determination that a portion of the compensation paid in a prior tax year exceeds the reasonable compensation limit. What steps can the corporation and the shareholder-employee take to avoid the double taxation usually associated with such a determination?

C4-23 What is a bootstrap acquisition? What are the tax consequences of such a transaction?

ISSUE IDENTIFICATION QUESTIONS

C4-24 Marsha receives a $10,000 cash distribution from Dye Corporation in April of the current year. Dye has $4,000 of accumulated E&P at the beginning of the year and $8,000 of current E&P. Dye also distributed $10,000 in cash to Barbara, who purchased all 200 shares of Dye stock from Marsha in June of the current year. What tax issues should be considered with respect to the distributions paid to Marsha and Barbara?

C4-25 Neil purchased land from Spring Harbor Corporation, his 100%-owned corporation, for $275,000. The corporation purchased the land three years ago for $300,000. Similar tracts of land located nearby have sold for $400,000 in recent months. What tax issues should be considered with respect to the corporation's sale of the land?

C4-26 Price Corporation has 100 shares of common stock outstanding. Price repurchased all of Penny's 30 shares for $35,000 cash during the current year. Penny received the shares as a gift from her mother three years ago. They have a basis to her of $16,000. Price

Corporation has $100,000 in current and accumulated E&P. Penny's mother owns 40 of the remaining shares; unrelated individuals own the other 30 shares. What tax issues should be considered with respect to the corporation's purchase of Penny's shares?

C4-27 George owns all 100 shares of Gumby's Pizza Corporation. The shares are worth $200,000, but George's basis is only $70,000. Mary and George have reached a tentative agreement for George to sell all his shares to Mary. However, Mary is unwilling to pay more than $150,000 for the stock because the corporation currently has excess cash balances. They have agreed that George can withdraw $50,000 in cash from Gumby's before the stock sale. What tax issues should be considered with respect to George and Mary's agreement?

PROBLEMS

C4-28 *Current E&P Calculation.* Beach Corporation reports the following results in the current year using the accrual method of accounting:

Income:	
Gross profit from manufacturing operations	$250,000
Dividends received from 25%-owned domestic corporation	20,000
Interest income: Corporate bonds	10,000
Municipal bonds	12,000
Proceeds from life insurance policy on key employee	100,000
Section 1231 gain on sale of land	8,000
Expenses:	
Administrative expenses	110,000
Bad debt expense	5,000
Depreciation:	
Financial accounting	68,000
Taxable income	86,000
Alternative depreciation system (Sec. 168(g))	42,000
NOL carryover	40,000
Charitable contributions: Current year	8,000
Carryover from last year	3,500
Capital loss on sale of stock	1,200
Penalty on late payment of federal taxes	450

a. What is Beach Corporation's taxable income?
b. What is Beach Corporation's current E&P?

C4-29 *Current E&P Computation.* Water Corporation reports $500,000 of taxable income for the current year. The following additional information is available:

- Water Corporation reported an $80,000 long-term capital loss for the current year. It reported no capital gains this year.
- Taxable income included $80,000 of dividends from a 10%-owned domestic corporation.
- Water Corporation paid fines and penalties of $6,000 that were not deducted in computing taxable income.
- Water Corporation deducted a $30,000 NOL carryover from a prior tax year in computing this year's taxable income.
- Taxable income includes a deduction for $40,000 of depreciation that exceeds the depreciation allowed for E&P purposes.

Assume a 34% corporate tax rate. What is Water Corporation's current E&P for this year?

C4-30 *Calculating Accumulated E&P.* Peach Corporation was formed in 1999. Its current E&P (or current E&P deficit) and distributions for the period 1999–2002 are as follows:

Year	*Current E&P (Deficit)*	*Distributions*
1999	$ (8,000)	$2,000
2000	(12,000)	–0–
2001	10,000	5,000
2002	14,000	6,000

What is Apple's accumulated E&P at the beginning of 2000, 2001, 2002, and 2003?

C4-31 *Consequences of a Single Cash Distribution.* Clover Corporation is a calendar year taxpayer. Connie owns all of its stock. Her basis for the stock is $10,000. On April 1 of the current year (not a leap year) Clover Corporation distributes $52,000 to Connie. Determine the tax consequences of the cash distribution to Connie in each of the following independent situations:

a. Current E&P $15,000; accumulated E&P $25,000.
b. Current E&P $30,000; accumulated E&P ($20,000).
c. Current E&P ($73,000); accumulated E&P $50,000.
d. Current E&P ($20,000); accumulated E&P ($15,000).

C4-32 *Consequences of a Single Cash Distribution.* Pink Corporation is a calendar year taxpayer. Pete owns one third of the stock (100 shares). His basis for his stock is $25,000. Cheryl owns two-thirds of the stock (200 shares). Her basis for her stock is $40,000. On June 10 of the current year, Pink Corporation distributes $120,000, $40,000 to Pete and $80,000 to Cheryl. Determine the tax consequences of the cash distributions to Pete and Cheryl in each of the following independent situations:

a. Current E&P $60,000; accumulated E&P $100,000.
b. Current E&P $36,000; accumulated E&P $30,000.

C4-33 *Consequences of Multiple Cash Distributions.* At the beginning of the current year (not a leap year), Charles owns all of Pearl Corporation's outstanding stock. His basis in the stock is $80,000. On July 1, he sells all his stock to Donald for $125,000. During the current year, Pearl Corporation, a calendar year taxpayer, makes two cash distributions: $60,000 on March 1 to Charles and $90,000 on September 1 to Donald. How are these distributions treated in the following independent situations? What are the amount and character of Charles' gain on his sale of stock to Donald? What is Donald's basis in his Pearl stock at the end of the year?

a. Current E&P $40,000; accumulated E&P $30,000.
b. Current E&P $100,000; accumulated E&P ($50,000).
c. Current E&P ($36,500); accumulated E&P $120,000.

C4-34 *Distribution of Appreciated Property.* In the current year, Sedgwick Corporation has $100,000 of current and accumulated E&P. On March 3, Sedgwick Corporation distributes to Dina, a shareholder, a parcel of land (a capital asset) having a $56,000 FMV. The land has a $40,000 adjusted basis (for both tax and E&P purposes) to Sedgwick Corporation and is subject to an $8,000 mortgage, which Dina assumes. Assume a 34% marginal corporate tax rate.

a. What are the amount and character of the income Dina recognizes as a result of the distribution?
b. What is Dina's basis for the land?
c. What are the amount and character of Sedgwick Corporation's gain or loss as a result of the distribution?
d. What effect does the distribution have on Sedgwick Corporation's E&P?

C4-35 *Distribution of Property Subject to a Liability.* On May 10 of the current year, Stowe Corporation distributes to Arlene, a shareholder, $20,000 in cash and land (a capital asset) having a $50,000 FMV. The land has a $15,000 adjusted basis (for both tax and E&P purposes) and is subject to a $60,000 mortgage, which Arlene assumes. Assume Stowe Corporation has an E&P balance exceeding the amount distributed and a 34% marginal corporate tax rate.

a. What are the amount and character of the income Arlene recognizes as a result of the distribution?
b. What is Arlene's basis for the land?
c. What are the amount and character of Stowe Corporation's gain or loss as a result of the distribution?

C4-36 *Distribution of Depreciable Property.* On May 15 of the current year, Quick Corporation distributes to Calvin, a shareholder, a building used in its business having a $250,000 FMV. The building originally cost $180,000. Quick claimed $30,000 of straight-line depreciation, so that the adjusted basis on the date of distribution for taxable income purposes is $150,000. Assume the adjusted basis for E&P purposes is $160,000. The building is subject to an $80,000 mortgage, which Calvin assumes. Assume Quick Corporation has an E&P balance exceeding the amount distributed and a 34% marginal corporate tax rate.

a. What are the amount and character of the income Calvin recognizes as a result of the distribution?

b. What is Calvin's basis for the building?
c. What are the amount and character of Quick Corporation's gain or loss as a result of the distribution?
d. What effect does the distribution have on Quick Corporation's E&P?

C4-37 ***Distribution of Various Types of Property.*** During the current year, Zeta Corporation distributes the items listed below to its sole shareholder, Susan. For each item listed below, determine the gross income recognized by Susan, her basis in the item, the amount of gain or loss recognized by Zeta Corporation, and the effect of the distribution on Zeta Corporation's E&P. Assume that Zeta Corporation has an E&P balance exceeding the amount distributed and a 34% marginal corporate tax rate. Unless stated otherwise, tax and E&P adjusted bases are the same.
a. A parcel of land used in Zeta Corporation's business that has a $200,000 FMV and a $125,000 adjusted basis.
b. Assume the same facts as Part a except that the land is subject to a $140,000 mortgage.
c. FIFO inventory having a $25,000 FMV and an $18,000 adjusted basis.
d. A building used in Zeta's business having an original cost of $225,000, a $450,000 FMV, and a $150,000 adjusted basis for taxable income purposes. Zeta has claimed $75,000 of depreciation for taxable income purposes using the straight-line method. Depreciation for E&P purposes is $60,000.
e. An automobile used in Zeta's business having an original cost of $12,000, an $8,000 FMV, and a $5,760 adjusted basis, on which Zeta has claimed $6,240 of MACRS depreciation for taxable income purposes. For E&P purposes, depreciation was $5,200.
f. Installment obligations having a $35,000 face amount (and FMV) and a $24,500 adjusted basis. The obligations were created when Zeta sold a Sec. 1231 asset.

C4-38 ***Disguised Dividends.*** King Corporation is a very profitable manufacturing corporation with $800,000 of E&P. It is owned equally by Harry and Wilma, who are husband and wife. Both individuals are actively involved in the business. Determine the tax consequences of the following independent events:
a. In reviewing a prior year King Corporation tax return, the IRS determines that the $500,000 of salary and bonuses paid to Wilma is unreasonable compensation. Reasonable compensation would be $280,000.
b. King has loaned Harry $400,000 over the past three years. None of the money has been repaid. Harry does not pay any interest on the loans.
c. King sells a building to Wilma for $150,000 in cash. The property has an adjusted basis of $90,000 and is subject to a $60,000 mortgage, which Wilma assumes. The FMV of the building is $350,000.
d. Harry leases a warehouse to King for $50,000 per year. According to an IRS auditor, similar warehouses can be leased for $35,000 per year.
e. Wilma sells some land to King for $250,000 on which King intends to build a factory. According to a recent appraisal, the FMV of the land is $185,000.
f. The corporation owns an airplane that it uses to fly executives to business sites and business meetings. When the airplane is not being used for business, Harry and Wilma use it to fly to their ranch in Texas for short vacations. The approximate cost of their trips to the ranch in the current year is $8,000.

C4-39 ***Unreasonable Compensation.*** Forward Corporation is owned by a group of 15 shareholders. During the current year, Forward Corporation pays $450,000 in salary and bonuses to Alvin, its president and controlling shareholder. The IRS audits Forward's tax return and determines that reasonable compensation for Alvin would be $250,000. Forward Corporation agrees to the adjustment.
a. What effect does the disallowance of part of the deduction for Alvin's salary and bonuses have on Forward Corporation and Alvin?
b. What tax savings could have been obtained by Forward Corporation and Alvin if an agreement had been in effect that required Alvin to repay Forward Corporation any amounts determined by the IRS to be unreasonable compensation?

C4-40 ***Stock Dividend Distribution.*** Wilton Corporation has a single class of common stock outstanding. Robert owns 100 shares, which he purchased in 1996 for $100,000. In 2002, when the stock is worth $1,200 per share, Wilton Corporation declares a 10% stock dividend payable in common stock. Robert receives ten additional shares on December 10, 2002. On January 30, 2003, he sells five of the new shares for $7,000.
a. How much income must Robert recognize when he receives the stock dividend?

b. How much gain or loss must Robert recognize when he sells the common stock?
c. What is Robert's basis in his remaining common stock? When does his holding period in the new common stock begin?

C4-41 ***Stock Dividend Distribution.*** Moss Corporation has a single class of common stock outstanding. Tillie owns 1,000 shares, which she purchased in 1998 for $100,000. Moss Corporation declares a stock dividend payable in 8% preferred stock having a $100 par value. Each shareholder receives one share of preferred stock for each ten shares of common stock held. On the distribution date—November 10, 2001—the common stock was worth $180 per share, and the preferred stock was worth $100 per share. On April 1, 2002, Tillie sells half of her preferred stock for $5,000.

a. How much income must Tillie recognize when she receives the stock dividend?
b. How much gain or loss must Tillie recognize when she sells the preferred stock? (Ignore the implications of Sec. 306.)
c. What is Tillie's basis in her remaining common and preferred stock? When does her holding period for the preferred stock begin?

C4-42 ***Stock Rights Distribution.*** Trusty Corporation has a single class of stock outstanding. Jim owns 200 shares of the common stock, which he purchased for $50 per share two years ago. On April 10 of the current year, Trusty Corporation distributes to its shareholders one right to purchase a share of common stock at $60 per share for each share of common stock held. At the time of the distribution, the common stock is worth $75 per share, and the rights are worth $15 per right. On September 10, Jim sells 100 rights for $2,000 and exercises the remaining 100 rights. He sells 60 of the shares acquired with the rights for $80 each on November 10.

a. What are the amount and character of income Jim recognizes when he receives the rights?
b. What are the amount and character of gain or loss Jim recognizes when he sells the rights?
c. What are the amount and character of gain or loss Jim recognizes when he exercises the rights?
d. What are the amount and character of gain or loss Jim recognizes when he sells the new common stock?
e. What basis does Jim have in his remaining shares?

C4-43 ***Attribution Rules.*** George owns 100 shares of Polar Corporation's 1,000 shares of outstanding common stock. Under the family attribution rules of Sec. 318, to which of the following individuals will George's stock be attributed?

a. George's wife
b. George's father
c. George's brother
d. George's mother-in-law
e. George's daughter
f. George's son-in law
g. George's grandfather
h. George's grandson
i. George's mother's brother (his uncle)

C4-44 ***Attribution Rules.*** Moose Corporation has 400 shares of stock outstanding owned as follows:

Name	*Shares*
Lara (an individual)	60
LMN Partnership (Lara is a 20% partner)	50
LST Partnership (Lara is a 70% partner)	100
Lemon Corporation (Lara is a 30% shareholder)	100
Lime Corporation (Lara is a 60% shareholder)	90
Total	400

How many shares is Lara deemed to own under the Sec. 318 attribution rules?

C4-45 ***Redemption from a Sole Shareholder.*** Paul owns all 100 shares of Presto Corporation's stock. His basis in the stock is $10,000. Presto Corporation has $100,000 of E&P. Presto Corporation redeems 25 of Paul's shares for $30,000. What are the tax consequences of the redemption to Paul and to Presto Corporation?

C4-46 *Multiple Redemptions.* Benton Corporation has 400 shares of stock outstanding owned by four unrelated shareholders. Benton redeems 100 shares from the shareholders as shown below for $500 per share. Each shareholder has a $230 per share basis for his or her stock. Benton Corporation's current and accumulated E&P at the end of the tax year is $150,000.

Shareholder	*Shares Held Before the Redemption*	*Shares Redeemed*
Ethel	200	40
Fran	100	30
Georgia	50	30
Henry	50	–0–
Total	400	100

a. What are the tax consequences (e.g., amount and character of income, gain, or loss recognized and basis of remaining shares) of the redemptions to Ethel, Fran, and Georgia?
b. How does your answer to Part a change if Ethel is Georgia's mother?

C4-47 *Partial Liquidation.* Unrelated individuals Amy, Beth, and Carla, and Delta Corporation each own 25 of the 100 outstanding shares of Axle Corporation's stock. Axle distributes $20,000 to each shareholder in exchange for five shares of Axle stock in a transaction that qualifies as a partial liquidation. Each share redeemed has a $1,000 basis to the shareholder and a $4,000 FMV. How does each shareholder treat the distribution?

C4-48 *Redemption to Pay Death Taxes.* John died on March 3. His gross estate of $2.5 million includes First Corporation stock (400 of the 1,000 outstanding shares) worth $1.5 million. John's wife, Myra, owns the remaining 600 shares. Funeral and administrative expenses deductible under Secs. 2053 and 2054 amount to $250,000. John, Jr. is the sole beneficiary of John's estate. Estate taxes amount to $350,000.
a. Does a redemption of First stock from John's estate, John. Jr., or John's wife qualify for sale treatment under Sec. 303?
b. On September 10, First Corporation redeems 200 shares of its stock from John's estate for $800,000. How does the estate treat this redemption?

C4-49 *Effect of Redemption on E&P.* White Corporation has 100 shares of stock outstanding. Ann owns 40 of these shares, and unrelated shareholders own the remaining 60 shares. White Corporation redeems 30 of Ann's shares for $30,000. In the year of the redemption, White Corporation has $30,000 of paid-in capital and $80,000 of E&P.
a. How does the redemption affect White Corporation's E&P balance if the redemption qualifies for sale treatment?
b. How does the redemption affect White Corporation's E&P balance if the redemption does *not* qualify for sale treatment?

C4-50 *Various Redemption Issues.* Alan, Barbara, and Dave are unrelated. Each has owned 100 shares of Time Corporation stock for five years and each has a $60,000 basis in those 100 shares. Time's E&P is $240,000. Time redeems all 100 of Alan's shares for $100,000, their FMV.
a. What are the amount and character of Alan's recognized gain or loss? What basis do Barbara and Dave have in their remaining shares? What effect does the redemption have on Time's E&P?
b. Assuming that Alan is Barbara's son, answer the questions in Part a again.
c. Assume the same facts as in Part b except that Alan signs an agreement under Sec. 302(c)(2)(A) to waive the family attribution rules. Answer the questions in Part a again.

C4-51 *Various Redemption Issues.* Andrew, Bea, Carl, and Carl, Jr. (Carl's son), and Tetra Corporation own all of the single class of Excel Corporation stock as follows:

Shareholder	*Shares Held*	*Adjusted Basis*
Andrew	20	$3,000
Bea	30	6,000
Carl	25	4,000
Carl, Jr.	15	3,000
Tetra Corporation	10	2,000
Total	100	

Andrew, Bea, and Carl are unrelated. Bea owns 75% of the Tetra stock, and Andrew owns the remaining 25% of the Tetra stock. Excel Corporation's E&P is $100,000. Determine the tax consequences to the shareholders and Excel Corporation of the following independent redemptions:

a. Excel Corporation redeems 25 of Bea's shares for $30,000.
b. Excel Corporation redeems 10 of Bea's shares for $12,000.
c. Excel Corporation redeems all of Carl's shares for $30,000.
d. Assume the same facts as in Part c except the stock is redeemed from Carl's estate to pay death taxes. The entire redemption qualifies under Sec. 303. The stock has a $28,000 FMV on Carl's date of death. The alternate valuation date is not elected.
e. Excel Corporation redeems all of Andrew's shares for land having a $6,000 basis for taxable income and E&P purposes to Excel Corporation and a $24,000 FMV. Assume a 34% marginal corporate tax rate.
f. Assume that Carl owns 25 shares of Excel Corporation stock and that Carl, Jr. owns the remaining 75 shares. Determine the tax consequences to Carl and Excel Corporation if Excel redeems all 25 of Carl's shares for $30,000.

C4-52 *Comparison of Dividends and Redemptions.* Bailey is one of four equal unrelated shareholders of Checker Corporation. Bailey has held the stock for four years and has a basis in her stock of $40,000. Checker Corporation has $280,000 of current and accumulated E&P. Checker Corporation distributes $100,000 to Bailey.

a. What are the tax consequences to Checker Corporation and to Bailey assuming Bailey is an individual and the distribution is a dividend
b. What are the tax consequences in Part a if Bailey is a corporation?
c. What are the tax consequences to Checker Corporation and to Bailey (an individual) assuming Bailey surrenders all her stock in a redemption qualifying for sale treatment?
d. What are the tax consequences in Part c if Bailey is a corporation?
e. Which treatment would Bailey prefer if Bailey is an individual? Which treatment would Bailey Corporation prefer?

C4-53 *Preferred Stock Bailout.* In each of the following situations, does Sec. 306 apply? If so, what is its effect?

a. Beth sells her Sec. 306 stock to Marvin in a year when the issuing corporation has no E&P.
b. Zero Corporation redeems Sec. 306 stock from Jim in a year in which it has no E&P.
c. Zero Corporation redeems Sec. 306 stock from Ruth in a year in which it has a large E&P balance.
d. Joan gives 100 shares of Sec. 306 stock to her nephew, Barry.
e. Ed completely terminates his interest in Zero Corporation by having Zero redeem all his common stock and preferred stock (the Sec. 306 stock in question).
f. Carl inherits 100 shares of Sec. 306 stock from his uncle Ted.

C4-54 *Preferred Stock Bailout.* Fran owns all 100 shares of Star Corporation stock for which her adjusted basis is $60,000. On December 1, 2000, Star Corporation distributes 50 shares of preferred stock to Fran as a nontaxable stock dividend. In the year of the distribution, Star Corporation's total E&P is $100,000, the preferred shares are worth $150,000, and the common shares are worth $300,000.

a. What are the tax consequences to Fran and to Star Corporation if Fran sells her preferred stock to Ken for $200,000 on January 10, 2001? In 2001, Star Corporation's current E&P is $75,000 (in addition to the $100,000 from the prior year).
b. How would your answer to Part a change if Fran sells her preferred stock to Ken for $110,000 instead of $200,000?
c. How would your answer to Part a change if Star Corporation redeems Fran's preferred stock for $200,000 on January 10, 2001?

C4-55 *Brother-Sister Redemptions.* Bob owns 60 of the 100 outstanding shares of Dazzle Corporation's stock and 80 of the 100 outstanding shares of Razzle Corporation's stock. Bob's basis in his Dazzle shares is $12,000, and his basis in his Razzle shares is $8,000. Bob sells 30 of his Dazzle shares to Razzle Corporation for $50,000. At the end of the year of the sale, Dazzle and Razzle Corporations have E&P of $25,000 and $40,000, respectively.

a. What are the amount and character of Bob's gain or loss on the sale?
b. What is Bob's basis in his remaining shares of the Dazzle and Razzle stock?

c. How does the sale affect the E&P of Dazzle and Razzle Corporations?
d. What basis does Razzle Corporation take in the Dazzle shares it purchases?
e. How would your answer to Part a change if Bob owns only 50 of the 100 outstanding shares of Razzle stock?

C4-56 ***Parent-Subsidiary Redemptions.*** Jane owns 150 of the 200 outstanding shares of Parent Corporation's stock. Parent owns 160 of the 200 outstanding shares of Subsidiary Corporation's stock. Jane sells 50 shares of her Parent stock to Subsidiary for $40,000. Jane's basis in her Parent shares is $15,000 ($100 per share). Subsidiary Corporation and Parent Corporation have E&P of $60,000 and $25,000, respectively, at the end of the year in which the redemption occurs.
a. What are the amount and character of Jane's gain or loss on the sale?
b. What is Jane's basis in her remaining shares of Parent stock?
c. How does the sale affect the E&P of Parent and Subsidiary Corporations?
d. What basis does Subsidiary Corporation take in the Parent shares it purchases?
e. How would your answer to Part a change if Jane instead sells 100 of her Parent shares to Subsidiary Corporation for $80,000?

C4-57 ***Bootstrap Acquisition.*** Jana owns all 100 shares of Stone Corporation stock. Her basis for the stock is $400,000. The corporation's stock has a $1 million FMV. Its E&P balance is $600,000. Michael wants to purchase the Stone stock, but he does not want all the company's assets. He wants the corporation's non-cash assets valued at $750,000. Michael is willing to pay $750,000 for these assets.
a. What are the tax consequences to Jana, Michael, and Stone Corporation if Michael purchases 75 shares of Stone stock for $750,000 and Stone redeems Jana's remaining 25 shares for $250,000 cash?
b. How would your answer to Part a change (if at all) should Stone first redeem 25 shares of Jana's stock for $250,000 and then Michael purchase the remaining 75 shares from Jana for $750,000?

COMPREHENSIVE PROBLEM

C4-58 Brian formed Sigma Corporation several years ago. Sigma uses the accrual method of accounting. In 2002, the corporation incurred the following transactions:

Operating gross profit	$290,000
Long-term capital gain	20,000
Tax-exempt interest received	7,000
Salary paid to Brian	80,000
Payroll tax on Brian's salary (Sigma's share)	6,000
Depreciation	25,000 ($21,000 for E&P purposes)
Other operation expenses	89,000
Dividend distribution to Brian	60,000

In addition to being the 100% owner of Sigma's stock, Brian manages the business and receives the $80,000 salary listed above. This salary is an ordinary and necessary business expense of the corporation and is reasonable in amount. Assume the payroll tax on Brian's $80,000 salary is $12,000, $6,000 of which Sigma pays and deducts, and the other $6,000 of which Brian pays via a reduction of his paycheck. Brian is single with no dependents, and he claims the standard deduction.
a. Compute Sigma's and Brian's taxable income and total tax liability for 2002, and add their tax liabilities together for the combined tax liability. Also, calculate the corporation's current E&P after the dividend distribution.
b. Assume instead that Brian formed the Sigma business as a sole proprietorship. In the current year, the business has the same operating results as above, and Brian withdraws $140,000 in lieu of the salary and dividend. Assume Brian's self-employment tax is $15,000. Compute Brian's total tax liability for 2002.
c. Assume a C corporation such as the one in Part a distributes all of its after-tax earnings. Compare the tax treatment of long-term capital gains, tax-exempt interest, and operating profits in the C corporation situation to the tax treatment of these items if the taxpayer operates his or her business as a sole proprietorship.

TAX STRATEGY PROBLEM

C4-59 John owns all 100 shares of Jamaica Corporation. The corporation has $100,000 of current E&P. John would like a distribution from the corporation worth $50,000. Jamaica has the following assets that it could distribute to John. What are the tax consequences of each of the following alternatives. Assume Jamaica has a 34% marginal tax rate and that its basis for E&P and for tax purposes are the same.

a. $50,000 cash.
b. 100 shares of XYZ stock purchased two years ago for $10,000 and now worth $50,000.
c. 100 shares of ABC stock purchased one year ago for $72,000 and now worth $50,000.
d. Equipment purchased four years ago for $120,000 that now has a tax adjusted basis of $22,000 and an E&P adjusted basis of $40,000. John would assume a liability on the equipment of $31,000. The equipment is now worth $81,000.
e. An installment obligation with a face value of $50,000 and a basis of $32,000. Jamaica Corporation acquired this obligation when it sold some land held as an investment three years ago.
f. Would it make any difference in Parts a-e if Jamaica Corporation redeems 50 of John's shares for each of the properties listed?
g. Which distribution would you recommend? Which distribution(s) should be avoided?

CASE STUDY PROBLEMS

C4-60 Amy, Beth, and Meg each own 100 of the 300 outstanding shares of Theta Corporation stock. Amy wants to sell her shares, which have a $40,000 basis and a $100,000 FMV. Either Beth and/or Meg can purchase her shares (50 shares each if both purchase) or Theta can redeem all of Amy's shares. Theta Corporation has a $150,000 E&P balance.

Required: Write a memorandum to the three sisters, who are active in managing Theta, comparing the tax consequences of the two options.

C4-61 Maria Garcia is a CPA whose firm has for many years prepared the tax returns for Stanley Corporation. A review of Stanley's last three tax returns by a new staff accountant, who has been assigned to the client for the first time, reveals that the corporation may be paying constructive dividends to one of its key officers in the form of excessive compensation. The staff accountant feels that the firm should inform the IRS and/or report the excess amount as nondeductible dividends. The facts are sufficiently gray, i.e., reasonable support exists for the assertion that the compensation paid in the current year and prior years is reasonable in amount.

Required: Discuss Maria's role as an advocate for Stanley Corporation, and discuss the possible consequences of a subsequent audit.

TAX RESEARCH PROBLEMS

C4-62 Hatch Corporation, a manufacturing business, was owned by Mike and his son, Steve. Hatch Corporation redeems all of Mike's stock in a transaction qualifying as a complete termination of Mike's interest in Hatch Corporation. To qualify, Mike must file an agreement not to acquire any interest in Hatch Corporation for ten years. After the redemption, Mike starts a new career as owner of a counseling firm for employees who are about to retire. Two years later, Steve wants to use Mike's firm to counsel some of his employees who are close to retirement. Mike's company charges a fixed fee for each employee counseled, and Hatch Corporation is to pay the same amount as all of Mike's other customers. Prepare a memorandum for your tax manager explaining whether Mike's counseling arrangement with Hatch Corporation violates Mike's agreement not to acquire any interest in Hatch Corporation. Your manager has suggested that, at a minimum, you consult the following resources:

- IRC Sec. 302(c)(2)
- Reg. Sec. 1.302-4
- Rev. Rul. 70-104, 1970-1 C.B. 66
- *Est. of Milton S. Lennard*, 61 T.C. 554, *nonacq.* 1978-2 C.B. 3

C4-63 When the IRS audited Winter Corporation's 1999 tax return, the IRS disallowed $10,000 of travel and entertainment expenses incurred by Charles, an officer-shareholder, because of inadequate documentation. The IRS asserts that the $10,000 expenditure was a constructive dividend to Charles. Charles asserts that the expense was a business expense and that he derived no personal benefit from the expenditure and therefore should not be charged with any dividend income. Prepare a memorandum for your tax manager explaining whether the IRS's assertion or Charles's assertion is correct. Your manager has suggested that, at a minimum, you consult the following resources:

- IRC Secs. 162 and 274
- Reg. Secs. 1.274-1 and -2

C4-64 Scott and Lynn Brown each own 50% of Benson Corporation's stock. During the current year, Benson Corporation made the following distribution to the shareholders:

Shareholder	*Property Distributed*	*Adjusted Basis to Corporation*	*Property's FMV*
Scott Brown	Land parcel A	$ 40,000	$75,000
Lynn Brown	Land parcel B	120,000	75,000

The corporation had E&P of $250,000 immediately preceding the distribution. Prepare a memorandum for your tax manager explaining how Benson Corporation should report these transactions for tax and financial accounting purposes. How will the two shareholders report the distributions? Assume Benson Corporation's marginal tax rate is 34%. Your manager has suggested that, at a minimum, you should consult the following resources:

- IRC Sec 301
- IRC Sec. 311
- IRC Sec. 312
- *Accounting Principles Board Opinion No. 29*

C4-65 Sara owns 60% of Mayfield Corporation's single class of stock. Mayfield Corporation is a calendar year domestic corporation that uses the accrual method of accounting. A group of five family members and three key employees own the remaining 40% of Mayfield Corporation stock. Sara uses the cash method of accounting. She is an officer and a member of the board of directors of Mayfield Corporation. During the period 1999-2001, Sara draws the following amounts as salary and tax-free fringe benefits from Mayfield Corporation: 1999, $160,000; 2000, $240,000; and 2001, $290,000. The amounts are earned evenly throughout the tax years in question. A revenue agent, upon auditing Mayfield's tax returns for 1999-2001, determines in 2002 that reasonable compensation for Sara's services for the three years in question is $110,000, $165,000, and $175,000, respectively. The bylaws of Mayfield Corporation were amended on December 15, 2000, to provide that

> Any payments made to an officer of the corporation, including salary, commissions, bonuses, or other forms of compensation, interest, rent, or travel and entertainment expense that is incurred, and which shall be disallowed in whole or in part as a deductible expense by the Internal Revenue Service, shall be reimbursed by such officer to the corporation to the full extent of such disallowance.

Following the disallowance of the salary expense, the board of directors meets and requests payment of the aforementioned amounts from Sara. Because of the large amount of money involved, the board of directors approves an installment plan whereby the $240,000 would be repaid in five annual installments of $48,000 each over the period 2003-2007. No interest will be required to be paid on the unpaid balance of $240,000. Prepare a memorandum for your tax manager explaining what salary and fringe benefits are taxable to Sara in the period 1999-2001, and what repayments are deductible by Sara during the period 2003-2007.

C4-66 John and Jean own 80% and 20% of Plum Corporation, respectively. Thanks to their hard work, Plum Corporation is a successful computer company. In 1998, Plum's earnings were minimal, but by 2002, Plum grossed $10 million. Plum paid John and Jean a salary that was determined as follows: John received a bonus of 76% of net profits and Jean received a bonus of 19% of net profits at the end of each year. Plum never paid any dividends. Can Plum deduct any or all of the "salaries" paid to John and Jean?

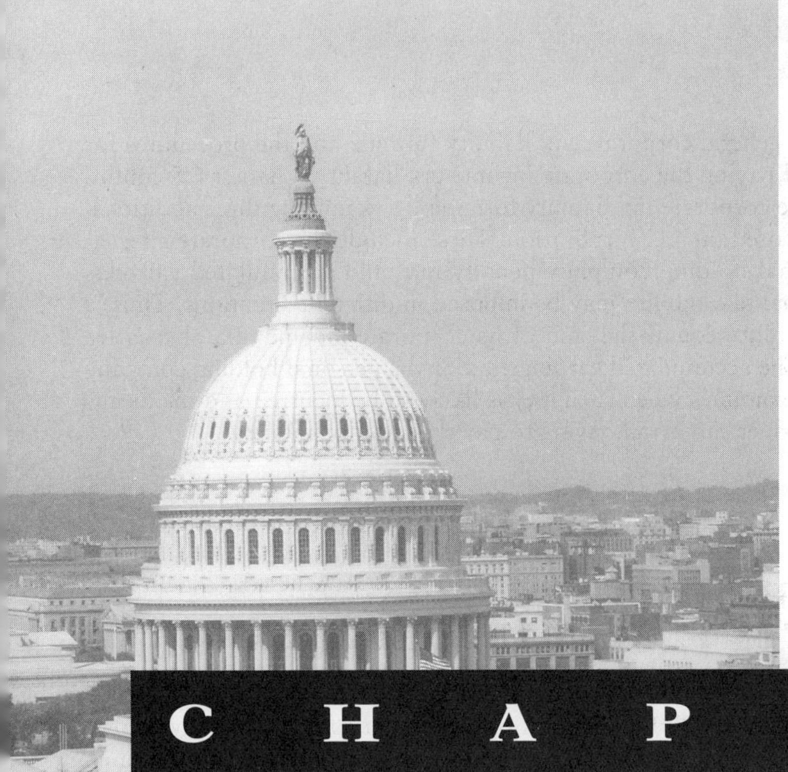

5

CHAPTER

OTHER CORPORATE TAX LEVIES

LEARNING OBJECTIVES

After studying this chapter, you should be able to

1. Calculate the amount of the corporation's alternative minimum tax liability (if any)
2. Determine whether a corporation is a personal holding company (PHC)
3. Calculate the amount of the corporation's PHC tax liability
4. Evaluate whether a corporation has an accumulated earnings tax problem
5. Calculate the amount of the corporation's accumulated earnings tax liability
6. Explain how a corporation can avoid being subject to the personal holding company tax
7. Explain how a corporation can avoid being subject to the accumulated earnings tax

CHAPTER OUTLINE

The Corporate Alternative Minimum Tax...5-2
Personal Holding Company Tax...5-15
Accumulated Earnings Tax...5-24
Tax Planning Considerations...5-35
Compliance and Procedural Considerations...5-37

Chapter C3 examined the general corporate tax liability formula and the procedures for calculating, reporting, and paying the corporate income tax liability. Chapter C5 continues this examination of the corporate tax liability formula by examining three additional tax levies that may be imposed on a C corporation. These include the corporate alternative minimum tax, personal holding company penalty tax, and accumulated earnings penalty tax. Each additional tax liability may be imposed in different situations. Thus, a corporation's total tax liability equals the sum of its corporate income tax, alternative minimum tax, and either the accumulated earnings tax or the personal holding company tax (if any). This chapter examines when each levy is likely to be incurred and the means by which a corporate taxpayer can avoid having to pay the additional taxes.

THE CORPORATE ALTERNATIVE MINIMUM TAX

OBJECTIVE 1

Calculate the amount of the corporation's alternative minimum tax liability (if any)

THE GENERAL FORMULA

The **alternative minimum tax (AMT)** for corporations is similar to that for individuals.[1] The objective of the tax is to ensure that every corporation with substantial economic income pays a corporate tax liability despite its use of exclusions, deductions, and credits in determining its income tax liability.

The starting point for computing a corporation's AMT is its taxable income. Taxable income is increased by tax preference items, modified by adjustments, and reduced by a statutory exemption amount. The resulting tax base is multiplied by 20% to yield the **tentative minimum tax (TMT)**. If the TMT exceeds the corporation's regular (income) tax, the excess is the corporation's AMT liability. If the TMT does not exceed the corporation's regular tax, no AMT liability is owed. The computation of a corporation's AMT is outlined in Table C5-1.

ADDITIONAL COMMENT

The corporate AMT produces little tax revenue. In 1998, AMT collections were $3.32 billion compared to $228.1 billion for the corporate income tax.

For tax years beginning after 1997, the AMT does not apply to a small business corporation. A small business corporation is an entity whose average gross receipts are $7.5 million or less for all three-year periods ending before the year for which the corporation claims the exemption.[2] This moving average gross receipts calculation, however, includes only tax years beginning after December 31, 1993 and is reduced to $5 million for the corporation's first three-year period (or portion thereof) that begins after 1993. Thus, to determine whether the AMT exemption applies in 1998, a corporation in existence on January 1, 1994 applies a $5 million ceiling for the three-year period including 1994-1996 and a $7.5 million ceiling for the three-year period including 1995-1997. If the corporation does not qualify for the exemption in 1998, it cannot qualify for a later year.

REAL WORLD EXAMPLE

The small corporation AMT exemption will exempt 95% of incorporated businesses from the AMT. The expected tax savings are $762 million over the period 1998-2007.

EXAMPLE C5-1 ▶ Ramirez Corporation had gross receipts as shown below:

Year	*Gross Receipts*
1994	$3,000,000
1995	4,000,000
1996	5,000,000
1997	6,000,000
1998	7,000,000
1999	8,000,000
2000	9,000,000
2001	4,000,000

[1] S corporations are not subject to the corporate AMT. These entities pass their tax adjustments and preferences through to their shareholders.

[2] Sec. 55(e). The exemption also applies to a noncorporate entity that elects to be taxed as a C corporation under the check-the-box regulations. Gross receipts are calculated using the entity's tax year.

▼ **TABLE C5-1**
Determination of the Corporate Alternative Minimum Tax Liability

Taxable income or loss before NOL deduction
Plus: Tax preference items
Plus or minus: Adjustments to taxable income other than the ACE adjustment and the alternative tax NOL deduction

Preadjustment AMTI
Plus or minus: 75% of the difference between pre-adjustment AMTI and adjusted current earnings (ACE)
Minus: Alternative tax NOL deduction

Alternative minimum taxable income (AMTI)
Minus: Statutory exemption

Tax base
Times: 0.20 tax rate

Tentative minimum tax before credits
Minus: AMT foreign tax credit (AMT FTC)

Tentative minimum tax (TMT)
Minus: Regular (income) tax

Alternative minimum tax (if any) owed (AMT)

REAL WORLD EXAMPLE

The AMT is not a popular tax because it is complex and is imposed in addition to the income tax. A 1995 Mobil Oil advertisement concluded that repealing the AMT would reduce the cost of capital by 3%, which would trigger more investment, faster productivity growth, higher gross domestic product, and increased employment.

Average gross receipts are as follows:

1994–1996: $4,000,000 = [($3,000,000 + $4,000,000 + $5,000,000) ÷ 3]
1995–1997: $5,000,000 = [($4,000,000 + $5,000,000 + $6,000,000) ÷ 3]
1996–1998: $6,000,000 = [($5,000,000 + $6,000,000 + $7,000,000) ÷ 3]
1997–1999: $7,000,000 = [($6,000,000 + $7,000,000 + $8,000,000) ÷ 3]
1998–2000: $8,000,000 = [($7,000,000 + $8,000,000 + $9,000,000) ÷ 3]
1999–2001: $7,000,000 = [($8,000,000 + $9,000,000 + $4,000,000) ÷ 3]

Ramirez Corporation qualifies as a small corporation in 1998 because its average gross receipts for 1994–1996 do not exceed $5 million and because its average gross receipts for 1995–1997 do not exceed $7.5 million. Since Ramirez qualified for the exemption in 1998, it also qualifies for 1999 and 2000 because its average gross receipts for 1996–1998 and 1997–1999 do not exceed $7.5 million. In 2001, however, Ramirez Corporation loses its AMT exemption because average gross receipts for 1998–2000 exceed $7.5 million. Ramirez Corporation is unable to reacquire its exemption in later years even if its average gross receipts for a three-year period drop below $7.5 million, as it does for 1999–2001. ◀

Section 55(e), which allows the small corporation AMT exemption, refers to Sec. 448(c) for the following special operating rules for applying the average gross receipts calculation:

- Gross receipts for any short tax year (for example, an initial year) must be annualized.
- A corporation not in existence for an entire three-year period determines average gross receipts for the period it was in existence.
- A corporation related to one or more other corporations (for example, a controlled group) must be aggregated with these other corporations.
- A successor corporation must refer to its predecessor (for example, a newly created subsidiary's gross receipts would include those of its parent corporation).

A corporation created after 1997 is exempt from the corporate AMT for its initial tax year regardless of its gross receipts for that year unless the corporation is aggregated with one or more other corporations or is considered to be a successor to another corporation. To qualify for the second year, the corporation's gross receipts for the first year must be less than $5 million. To qualify for the third year, the corporation's average gross receipts for the first two years must be less than $7.5 million. To qualify for the fourth year, the corporation's average gross receipts for the first three years must be less than $7.5 million.

EXAMPLE C5-2 ▶ Rubio Corporation, a calendar year corporation formed on January 1, 1998, has gross receipts as follows:

Year	*Gross Receipts*
1998	$3,000,000
1999	4,000,000
2000	5,000,000
2001	8,000,000
2002	9,000,000

Rubio Corporation is not related to a predecessor corporation under Sec. 448(c)(2). In 1998, Rubio is automatically exempt from the corporate AMT under the small corporation rules without considering its gross receipts. Rubio is exempt from the corporate AMT in 1999 because the gross receipts for its first tax year (1998) do not exceed $5 million.

Rubio needs to calculate its average gross receipts in subsequent tax years to see whether the small business exemption remains available. Rubio Corporation's average gross receipts calculations for subsequent tax years are as follows:

1998–1999: $3,500,000 = [($3,000,000 + $4,000,000) ÷ 2]
1998–2000: $4,000,000 = [($3,000,000 + $4,000,000 + $5,000,000) ÷ 3]
1999–2001: $5,666,667 = [($4,000,000 + $5,000,000 + $8,000,000) ÷ 3]
2000–2002: $7,333,333 = [($5,000,000 + $8,000,000 + $9,000,000) ÷ 3]

Rubio Corporation maintains its exemption in 2000 because its average gross receipts for 1998-1999 do not exceed $7.5 million. Similarly in 2001 through 2003, Rubio Corporation continues to qualify because its average gross receipts for the preceding three-year periods (1998–2000, 1999–2001, and 2000–2002, respectively) do not exceed $7.5 million. The consistent increase in gross receipts, however, makes it unlikely that Rubio Corporation will retain its election after 2003. ◀

Note that the averaging test is based on gross receipts, not gross income or taxable income. Gross receipts does not include any reduction for the corporation's cost of goods sold but does include all the corporation's services income, investment income, and gains and losses (net of the property's adjusted basis). Thus, a corporation with high gross receipts and high expenses could be subject to the AMT even though it might have low taxable income.

Firms not eligible for the small corporation AMT exemption because their gross receipts exceed the $5 or $7.5 million threshold still can take advantage of the $40,000 statutory exemption available under Sec. 55(d)(2). This exemption is described in the Definitions section below.

A corporation that loses its small corporation status because of exceeding the average gross receipts ceiling becomes liable for the AMT. The AMT liability for a corporation losing its exemption includes only preference items and adjustments involving transactions and investments occurring after the corporation loses its small corporation status. The modifications required in making the AMTI calculation and special AMT credit calculation for corporations having lost their small corporation status is beyond the scope of this book.

ADDITIONAL COMMENT

The AMT results in an acceleration of the income recognition process as compared to the income tax. This acceleration is accomplished by adding back tax preference items and making other adjustments to taxable income in arriving at AMTI. Even though the AMT rate (20%) is lower than the top corporate income tax rate (35%), the AMT system results in a higher tax liability for some corporations because the tax base under the AMT is larger than the tax base for income tax purposes.

DEFINITIONS

This section defines the terms used in the AMT[3] computation.

ALTERNATIVE MINIMUM TAXABLE INCOME (AMTI). **Alternative minimum taxable income** is the corporation's taxable income (1) increased by tax preference items, (2) adjusted (either up or down) for income, gain, deduction, and loss items that have to be recomputed under the AMT, (3) increased or decreased for 75% of the difference between pre-adjustment AMTI and adjusted current earnings (ACE), and (4) reduced by the alternative tax NOL deduction.

[3] Sec. 55.

STATUTORY EXEMPTION AMOUNT. AMTI is reduced by a statutory exemption to arrive at the AMT tax base. The exemption amount is $40,000, but it is reduced by 25% of the amount by which AMTI exceeds $150,000. The statutory exemption is phased out when AMTI equals $310,000.

EXAMPLE C5-3 ▶ Yellow Corporation's AMTI is $200,000. Its exemption amount is $27,500 {$40,000 − [0.25 × ($200,000 − $150,000)]}.[4] ◀

TENTATIVE MINIMUM TAX (TMT). The tentative minimum tax is calculated by multiplying 20% times the corporation's AMTI less a statutory exemption amount, and deducting foreign tax credits allowable under the AMT (AMT FTCs).[5]

REGULAR TAX. A corporation's **regular tax** is its tax liability for income tax purposes, as defined in Sec. 26(b), reduced by foreign tax credits and possession tax credits allowable for income tax purposes under Sec. 27 but before other tax credits.

ALTERNATIVE MINIMUM TAX. The AMT equals the amount by which a corporation's TMT exceeds its regular tax for the year.

The following example illustrates the AMT computation.

EXAMPLE C5-4 ▶ Badger Corporation has $400,000 of taxable income. It also has $350,000 of tax preferences and $250,000 of positive adjustments for AMT purposes. It has no tax credits available. Badger's regular tax liability is $136,000 (0.34 × $400,000). Badger's AMTI is $1 million ($400,000 taxable income + $250,000 adjustments + $350,000 tax preferences). Its statutory exemption is zero because AMTI exceeds $310,000. Therefore, its AMT tax base (i.e., AMTI minus statutory exemption) also is $1 million. Its TMT is $200,000 (0.20 × $1,000,000). Badger's AMT liability is $64,000 ($200,000 − $136,000). Thus, Badger must pay a total federal tax liability of $200,000 ($136,000 + $64,000). ◀

STOP & THINK

Question: Badger Corporation in our preceding example pays both the federal income tax and the AMT. How can this be possible if the top federal income tax rate for corporations with less than $10 million of taxable income is 34% and the AMT rate is a constant 20%?

Solution: It is possible because different tax bases are used for the two tax levies. The income tax is based on taxable income. The AMT is based on alternative minimum taxable income less a statutory exemption. A corporation owes the AMT when its TMT exceeds its regular (income) tax. The situation where a corporation owes the AMT can be expressed as follows:

$$[\text{Taxable Income (TI)} + \text{Preferences (P)} + \text{Adjustments (A)}] \times 0.20 > \text{TI} \times 0.34$$

Multiplying the terms on the two sides of the inequality and simplifying the terms produces the following relationship:

$$.20\ (P + A) > 0.14\ TI$$

$$(P + A) > 0.70\ TI$$

In Example C5-4, where Badger Corporation incurred the AMT, the preferences and adjustments were $350,000 and $250,000, respectively, or $600,000 in total. Seventy percent of taxable income is $280,000 (0.70 × $400,000). The general relationship between (P + A) and TI holds in our example.[a]

[a] The relationship between (P + A) and TI may be different if the corporation is subject to a marginal income tax rate lower (e.g., 15% or 25%) or higher (e.g., 35%, 38%, or 39%) than the 34% marginal income tax rate used above.

---

[4] Assume that all corporations in the examples are C corporations that do not qualify as small corporations for AMT purposes.

[5] Sec. 55(b).

TYPICAL MISCONCEPTION

One distinction between tax preference items and adjustments is that tax preference items always increase AMTI, whereas an adjustment can increase or decrease AMTI.

TAX PREFERENCE ITEMS

Common **tax preference items** that must be added to a corporation's taxable income to compute its AMTI include[6]

- The excess of the depletion deduction allowable for the tax year over the adjusted basis of the depletable property at the end of the tax year (excluding the current year's depletion deduction).[7]

EXAMPLE C5-5 ▶ Duffy Corporation mines iron ore in the upper peninsula of Michigan. The adjusted basis for one of its properties has been fully recovered by depletion in previous years. Current year gross income and taxable income earned from the sale of ore taken from this property are $125,000, and $45,000, respectively. The iron ore depletion percentage is 15%. Percentage depletion is $18,750 ($125,000 × 0.15) because it is less than the 50% of taxable income ceiling ($22,500 = $45,000 × 0.50). All the percentage depletion is deductible when determining taxable income. Because the property's basis already has been reduced to zero, all the percentage depletion is a tax preference item. The effect of the preference item is to reduce the depletion deduction to zero when determining AMTI. ◀

- The amount by which excess intangible drilling and development costs (IDCs) incurred in connection with oil, gas, and geothermal wells exceeds 65% of the net income from such property.[8]
- Tax-exempt interest on certain private activity bonds issued after August 8, 1986. Although the interest on private activity bonds is tax-exempt for regular tax purposes it can increase the corporation's federal tax liability by being included as a preference item in determining AMTI and the AMT.[9]

EXAMPLE C5-6 ▶ Salek Corporation reports the following interest income for the current year:

Source	*Amount*
IBM corporate bonds	$25,000
Wayne County school district bonds	30,000
City of Detroit bonds	15,000

The City of Detroit bonds were issued several years ago to finance a parking garage, where 35% of the space is leased to a nonexempt corporation for its exclusive use. The bonds are considered private activity bonds. The Wayne County bonds were issued to renovate existing school facilities. Only the interest from the IBM bonds is taxable for income tax purposes. Only the interest from the City of Detroit bonds is a tax preference item when computing AMTI because the school district bonds were not used for a private activity. ◀

ADDITIONAL COMMENT

Each year, the amount of real property tax preference due to accelerated depreciation declines as the property ages. For most pre-1987 properties, this amount is now zero.

- The excess of accelerated depreciation claimed on real property for the tax year over a hypothetical straight-line depreciation allowance based on the property's useful life or a special ACRS recovery period. This preference item applies only to real property placed in service before 1987.
- 42% of the gain excluded from gross income by Sec. 1202(a) on the sale of small business corporation stock.

---

[6] Sec. 57(a).

[7] The percentage depletion preference is repealed for oil and gas depletion claimed by independent producers and royalty owners for 1993 and later tax years. The oil and gas percentage depletion preference applies almost exclusively to integrated oil companies.

[8] The oil and gas excess IDC preference was repealed for independent producers for 1993 and later years but continues to apply to integrated oil companies. Excess IDCs are the amount by which IDCs arising in the tax year exceed the deduction that would have been allowable if the IDCs had been capitalized and amortized using the straight-line method over a ten-year period.

[9] A private activity bond is part of a bond issue where the proceeds are used for activities unrelated to a governmental use. One example would be the use of the proceeds in a trade or business of a person other than a State or local government (for example, bonds used to construct a sports facility used by professional football and other sports teams for their at-home games).

ADJUSTMENTS TO TAXABLE INCOME

While tax preferences always *increase* taxable income, adjustments require a recomputation of certain income, gain, loss, and deduction items and may either *increase* or *decrease* taxable income. Common adjustments that must be made to taxable income to obtain AMTI are presented below.[10]

DEPRECIATION. Different depreciation rules are used when computing taxable income and AMTI.

- Depreciation on real property placed in service after 1986 and before 1999. For AMT purposes, the taxpayer must use the alternative depreciation system under Sec. 168(g). Annually, taxable income is increased by the excess of regular tax depreciation over AMT depreciation and is decreased by the excess of AMT depreciation over regular tax depreciation. See depreciation Tables 7–9 in Appendix C for regular tax depreciation calculations and Table 12 for AMT depreciation calculations.
- Depreciation on real property placed in service after 1998. Regular tax and AMT depreciation is the same. Thus, no adjustments are required for this property.
- Depreciation on personal property placed in service after 1986 and before 1999. For AMT purposes, the taxpayer must use the alternative depreciation system under Sec. 168(g). While regular tax depreciation ordinarily entails a 200% declining balance method (with a switch to straight-line) over the property's general depreciation recovery period, AMT depreciation requires a 150% declining balance method (with a switch to straight-line) over the property's class life, determined under Sec. 168(g)(3) and related IRS pronouncements. If an item of personal property has no specified class life under these authorities, its class life is deemed to be 12 years. If the taxpayer elected the straight-line method or the alternative depreciation system for regular tax purposes, no AMT adjustments are required. For property using the half-year convention, see depreciation Table 1 in Appendix C for regular tax calculations and depreciation Table 10 for AMT calculations.
- Depreciation on personal property placed in service after 1998. For AMT purposes, the taxpayer must use the 150% declining balance method (with a switch to straight-line) over the property's general depreciation recovery period. Thus, the taxpayer uses the same recovery period for both regular tax and AMT purposes, but uses the 200% declining balance method for regular tax depreciation and the 150% declining balance method for AMT depreciation. If the taxpayer elects the straight-line method or 150% declining balance method for regular tax purposes, no AMT adjustments are required. For property using the half-year convention, see depreciation Table 1 in Appendix C for regular tax calculations and depreciation Table 10 for AMT calculations.

EXAMPLE C5-7 ▶ Early in 1998, Bulldog Corporation places into service office furniture property costing $3,000 having a ten-year class life. The corporation does not elect Sec. 179 expensing for this property. The property's regular tax recovery period is seven years under MACRS. The property's alternative MACRS ten-year recovery period is used when computing AMTI depreciation. Regular tax depreciation is $429 [$3,000 × 0.1429 (Table 1, Appendix C)] in the first year with the half-year convention. AMTI depreciation is $225 [$3,000 × 0.075 (Table 10, Appendix C)] in the first year. The smaller AMTI depreciation results in a $204 ($429 − $225) positive adjustment to taxable income. In 2005, the regular tax depreciation will be $134 while the AMTI depreciation remains at $262. Thus, a negative $128 ($134 − $262) adjustment will result. ◀

EXAMPLE C5-8 ▶ If instead the office furniture in Example C5-7 were placed in service in 1999 or a later year, the 150% declining balance method and a seven-year recovery period would be used to calculate the AMTI depreciation. The AMTI depreciation would be $321 [$3,000 × 0.1071 (Table 10, Appendix C, seven-year recovery period)] instead of the $225 amount originally calculated

---

[10] Sec. 56(a).

using the ten-year recovery period. The AMTI depreciation adjustment would be $108 ($429 – $321). The special 150% declining balance depreciation election for regular tax purposes would eliminate the difference between the two depreciation amounts. ◀

BASIS CALCULATIONS. Separate gain or loss calculations are made for regular tax and AMT purposes when a disposition of real or personal property occurs. A depreciable property's basis for regular tax purposes is adjusted downward by the regular tax depreciation allowance. A depreciable property's basis for AMT purposes is adjusted downward by the AMT depreciation allowance. Therefore, an asset may have different bases for regular tax and AMT purposes. An adjustment is made for the difference between the amount of gain or loss recognized for taxable income purposes and the gain or loss recognized for AMTI purposes. The adjustment process is illustrated in the following example.

EXAMPLE C5-9 ▶ Assume the same facts as in Example C5-7 except that on April 1 of the fourth year Bulldog Corporation sells the property for $2,000. The depreciation allowances claimed for regular tax and AMT purposes, adjusted basis for the property at the beginning of the year for each tax calculation, and the positive or negative adjustment to taxable income in arriving at AMTI for each of the four years are presented below.

	Regular Tax			**AMT**			
Year	*1/1 Adj. Basis(1)*	*Depr.(2)*	*12/31 Adj. Basis(3)*[a]	*1/1 Adj. Basis(4)*	*Depr.(5)*	*12/31 Adj. Basis(6)*[b]	*Taxable Income Adjustment(7)*[c]
1	$3,000	$ 429	$2,571	$3,000	$ 225	$2,775	$204
2	2,571	735	1,836	2,775	416	2,359	319
3	1,836	525	1,311	2,359	354	2,005	171
4	1,311	187	1,124	2,005	151	1,854	36
		$1,876			$1,146		$730

[a] (3) = (1) – (2) Adjusted basis for sale date is reduced for the depreciation claimed in year 4.
[b] (6) = (4) – (5) Six months of depreciation is claimed in years 1 and 4.
[c] (7) = (2) – (5)

Bulldog recognizes an $876 ($2,000 proceeds – $1,124 adjusted basis) gain in Year 4 for regular tax purposes and a $146 ($2,000 proceeds – $1,854 adjusted basis) gain for AMT purposes. This necessitates a $730 negative adjustment to taxable income when computing AMTI to take into account the different depreciation allowances claimed in the four years. The basis adjustment amount is the net of the aggregate positive and negative depreciation adjustments for the four years. ◀

INSTALLMENT SALES. The installment method can be used to report sales of noninventory property when calculating taxable income and AMTI.

LONG-TERM CONTRACTS ENTERED INTO AFTER MARCH 1, 1986. These contracts must be accounted for using the percentage of completion method. Corporations using the percentage of completion-capitalized cost or cash methods of accounting for regular tax purposes must make adjustments when determining AMTI.

LOSS LIMITATIONS. Closely held corporations and personal service corporations must refigure losses coming under the at-risk and passive activity limitation rules, taking into account the corporation's AMTI adjustments and tax preference items.

NOL DEDUCTIONS. The regular tax NOL deduction is replaced with the alternative tax NOL deduction. To compute the alternative tax NOL deduction, the regular tax NOL deduction is adjusted in the same way that taxable income is adjusted in arriving at AMTI. The regular tax NOL is reduced by adding back any tax preference items and any losses disallowed under the passive activity limitation and at-risk rules. Adjustments may either increase or decrease the regular tax NOL in arriving at the alternative tax NOL. Generally, the alternative tax NOL is a different amount from the regular tax NOL because of these adjustments. The resulting alternative tax NOL carries back two years and forward 20 years.[11] The alternative tax NOL deduction cannot exceed 90% of AMTI before the alternative tax NOL deduction.

The following example illustrates the computation of preadjustment AMTI (see Table C5-1). Preadjustment AMTI will become a component of the ACE and AMTI calculations presented later.

EXAMPLE C5-10 ▶ Marion Corporation engages in copper mining activities. In the current year, it reports taxable income of $300,000, which includes deductions of $70,000 for percentage depletion and $80,000 for MACRS depreciation. Of the percentage depletion claimed, $30,000 exceeded the adjusted basis of the depletable property. The hypothetical AMT depreciation deduction under the alternative depreciation system would have been only $55,000. Pre-adjustment AMTI is determined as follows:

Taxable income		$300,000
Plus:	Percentage depletion claimed in excess of basis	30,000
	MACRS depreciation claimed	80,000
Minus:	AMTI depreciation	(55,000)
Pre-adjustment AMTI		$355,000

The depreciation adjustment results in an increase in AMTI of $25,000 ($80,000 − $55,000). ◀

ADJUSTED CURRENT EARNINGS (ACE) ADJUSTMENT

HISTORICAL NOTE

The ACE adjustment is a complex computation. It was added in an attempt to further adjust the AMT tax base towards the corporation's economic income. However, the ACE adjustment, as initially enacted by the Tax Reform Act of 1986, would have been much more complicated. The single most important simplification is that the ACE depreciation does not include the present value depreciation computations required by the 1986 Act.

For 1990 and later tax years, a corporation makes a positive adjustment equal to 75% of the excess of its ACE over its AMTI (before this adjustment and the alternative tax NOL deduction).[12] ACE is a concept based on the earnings and profits (E&P) definition that has been used for years to determine whether a corporate distribution is a dividend or a return of capital (see Chapter C4). ACE equals preadjustment AMTI for the tax year plus or minus a series of special adjustments described below. However, ACE is not the same as E&P even though many items are treated in the same manner for both purposes. The ACE adjustment is not required of S corporations since the AMT tax preferences and adjustments flow through to their noncorporate shareholders.[13] A $1 positive ACE adjustment results in a 15% (0.20 statutory rate × 0.75 inclusion ratio) effective tax rate being incurred if the corporation's TMT (before the ACE adjustment) exceeds its regular tax amount.

A negative adjustment also is permitted equal to 75% of the excess of the corporation's preadjustment AMTI over its ACE. The negative adjustment, however, cannot exceed the cumulative net amount of the corporation's positive and negative ACE adjustments in all post-1989 tax years.[14] Any excess of preadjustment AMTI over ACE not allowed as a negative adjustment because of the limitation cannot be carried over to a later year to reduce a required positive ACE adjustment.

EXAMPLE C5-11 ▶ Bravo Corporation, which was organized in 2000, reports the following ACE and preadjustment AMTI amounts for 2000–2002.

	2000	*2001*	*2002*
ACE	$2,000	$1,500	$1,000
Preadjustment AMTI	1,500	1,500	1,500

A $375 [($2,000 − $1,500) × 0.75] positive ACE adjustment is made in 2000. No ACE adjustment is made in 2001 because ACE and preadjustment AMTI are equal. A $375 [($1,000 − $1,500) × 0.75] negative ACE adjustment is made in 2002. ◀

---

[11] NOLs incurred in tax years beginning on or before August 6, 1997 carry back three years and forward 15 years.

[12] This amount is known as **preadjustment AMTI**.

[13] Sec. 56(g)(6).

[14] Sec. 56(g)(2).

EXAMPLE C5-12 ▶ Assume the same facts as in Example C5-11 except the preadjustment AMTI amount in 2002 is $2,000. The tentative negative ACE adjustment is $750 [($1,000 − $2,000) × 0.75]. Only a $375 negative ACE adjustment can be made because the negative ACE adjustment may not exceed the $375 ($375 + $0) total cumulative net positive ACE adjustments made in prior years. ◀

TYPICAL MISCONCEPTION

Interest on certain state and local government obligations has traditionally not been subject to the federal income tax. However, to the extent that a corporation's tax-exempt income is not already included in AMTI as a preference item (e.g., interest income on private activity bonds), 75% of such income is subjected to the AMT through the ACE adjustment. If the corporation's TMT exceeds its regular tax before the ACE adjustment is made, a 15% effective tax rate is incurred on the bond interest income. State and local governments have expressed concern over this aspect of the ACE adjustment, which they view as an impediment to their ability to raise capital.

Four general rules provide a framework for the ACE calculation:

- Any amount that is permanently excluded from gross income when computing AMTI, but which is taken into account in determining E&P, is included in gross income for ACE purposes (e.g., interest on tax-exempt bonds other than private activity bonds, and the proceeds of life insurance contracts). The adjustment is reduced by any deduction that would have been allowable in computing AMTI had the excluded income amount been included in gross income for AMTI purposes. No adjustment is made for any timing differences. Thus, any item that is, has been, or will be included in preadjustment AMTI will not be included in this category of ACE adjustment.
- A deduction cannot be claimed when computing ACE for any expense, loss, or other deduction not deductible in the tax year when computing E&P even if such item already has been deducted in determining preadjustment AMTI. These deduction items are a positive adjustment to ACE to the extent they already have been deducted in determining pre-adjustment AMTI.[15] Special rules apply for the dividends-received deduction. The 80% and 100% dividends-received deductions are claimed for ACE purposes although they cannot be deducted when computing E&P. The 70% dividends-received deduction, however, is not claimed for either ACE or E&P purposes.
- Income items included in preadjustment AMTI are included in ACE even if the item is not included in E&P.
- Items not deductible in determining preadjustment AMTI are not deducted when computing ACE even if the item is deductible in arriving at E&P. Examples include federal income taxes and capital losses exceeding capital gains.[16]

In addition to the four general rules, a series of specific adjustments mandated by Sec. 56(g) must be made to AMTI to arrive at ACE. The more common adjustments are presented below. As with the general AMT adjustments presented above, these items require a recomputation of certain income, gain, loss, and deduction items and may either increase or decrease AMTI. Unless otherwise indicated, these changes are effective for tax years beginning after 1989.

ADDITIONAL COMMENT

The ACE depreciation adjustment was the single largest ACE adjustment for tax years 1990–1993. Elimination of the need to make such an adjustment for property placed in service in 1994 and later tax years reduces both the taxpayer's expense incurred in calculating the adjustment and the government's revenues from the AMT.

- Depreciation on property placed in service in a tax year beginning after 1989 and before January 1, 1994 is determined using the alternative depreciation system. All property is depreciated using the straight-line method with the appropriate recovery period and averaging convention described under the alternative depreciation system rules.[17] Elimination of the ACE depreciation adjustment for property placed in service after December 31, 1993 does not keep a corporation from having to make the adjustment for property placed in service before 1994. Special transitional rules apply to property placed in service before 1990. These rules are found in Sec. 56(g)(4)(A).
- An asset's adjusted basis is determined by using the depreciation, depletion, or amortization rules appropriate for the ACE calculation. As a result, a basis adjustment similar to that described above for the AMTI calculation may be required when an asset is sold, exchanged, or otherwise disposed of.[18]
- When calculating ACE, the gain realized on an installment sale of noninventory property is fully recognized in the year of sale.[19]
- Organizational expenditures otherwise amortizable under Sec. 248 are not amortized for ACE purposes if incurred after December 31, 1989.[20]

15 Secs. 56(g)(4)(C)(i) and (ii). A partial list of items falling into this category is presented in Reg. Sec. 1.56(g)-1(d)(3) and (4).
16 Reg. Sec. 1.56(g)-1(e).
17 Sec. 56(g)(4)(A).
18 Sec. 56(g)(4)(I).
19 Sec. 56(g)(4)(D)(iv).
20 Sec. 56(g)(4)(D)(ii).

ADDITIONAL COMMENT

Even if a corporation is not currently subject to the AMT, both the AMT and ACE depreciation (pre-1994 assets only) amounts should be calculated annually. A less efficient and more costly approach is to wait until the AMT applies and then try to compute the appropriate depreciation numbers for past years.

- The increase or decrease in the LIFO recapture amount that takes place during the year increases or decreases ACE. The LIFO recapture amount is the amount by which the inventory amount under the first-in, first-out (FIFO) inventory method exceeds the inventory amount under the last-in, first-out (LIFO) method.[21] This adjustment converts a corporation from the LIFO method to the FIFO method for ACE purposes.
- Depletion with respect to any property placed in service after 1989 is determined by using the cost depletion method.[22] Intangible drilling costs must be amortized over 60 months beginning with the month in which they are paid or incurred.
- Charitable contribution and percentage depletion deduction limits must be recalculated to take into account AMT adjustment and preference items.[23] Taxpayers also must maintain separate carryovers for regular tax and AMT purposes. Corporations must determine separate charitable contribution limitations and carryovers for AMTI and ACE purposes. For many corporations, the AMTI and ACE charitable contribution limits will be larger than the regular tax limit because the ACE and AMT adjusted taxable income counterparts are usually larger.

Topic Review C5-1 summarizes the ACE calculation.

STOP & THINK *Question:* Flair Corporation was considering making an investment in debt obligations issued by a state or local government. Flair's Chief Financial Officer (CFO) knew that the interest earned on these obligations was exempt from the federal income tax. In addition, the state in which Flair operates exempts interest income earned from state and local bonds issued within the state from the state income tax. The CFO was surprised to find out over a round of golf that the so-called tax-exempt interest income could be taxed at

Topic Review C5-1

Summary of Common Alternative Minimum Tax Adjustments

Income/Expense Item	Most Common Adjustment to:[a] Taxable Income to Arrive at AMTI	Preadjustment AMTI to Arrive at ACE
Tax-exempt bond interest:		
Private activity bonds	Increase	None
Other bonds	None	Increase
Life insurance proceeds	None	Increase
Deferred gain on nondealer installment sales	None	Increase
LIFO inventory adjustment	None	Increase
"Basis adjustment" on asset sale	Decrease	Decrease
Depreciation	Increase	Increase
Excess charitable contributions	Decrease	Decrease
Excess capital losses	None	None
Dividends-received deduction:		
80% and 100% DRD	None	None
70% DRD	None	Increase
Organizational expenditure amortization	None	Increase
Federal income taxes	None	None
Penalties and fines	None	None
Disallowed travel and entertainment expenses and club dues	None	None

[a] Adjustments such as depreciation may increase or decrease taxable income to arrive at AMTI and ACE.

---

[21] Secs. 56(g)(4)(D)(iii) and 312(n)(4).

[22] Sec. 56(g)(4)(G).

[23] Ltr. Rul. 9320003 (February 1, 1993). Because the IRS treats the AMT as a parallel taxing system independent of the regular tax, the need to recalculate a limit apparently applies to any deduction restricted to a certain fraction of the firm's taxable income.

up to a 20% rate by the federal government if earned by a corporation. She called her CPA to find out more about this problem. What did the CPA say?

Solution: If the debt obligation is a private activity bond issued after 1986, the interest income is a tax preference item. One would expect the $1 of interest income to increase the AMT tax base by $1 and the AMT by $0.20. However, under the corporate alternative minimum tax, $1 of interest income that is a tax preference item can produce one of the following scenarios:

Tenative Minimum Tax		
Excluding Tax-Exempt Interest Income	*Including Tax-Exempt Interest Income*	*Additional Tax on $1 of Tax-Exempt Interest Income*
TMT > regular tax	TMT > regular tax	$0.20
TMT < regular tax	TMT < regular tax	$0.00
TMT < regular tax	TMT > regular tax	$0.00 to $0.20

If the interest income is not a tax preference item, only 75% of the income is included in the ACE adjustment. The $0.20 additional tax ceiling on $1 of interest from private activity obligations is reduced to $0.15 (0.75 × $0.20) for tax-exempt interest income earned from debt obligations other than private activity obligations.

COMPREHENSIVE EXAMPLE. Glidden Corporation is not eligible for the small corporation AMT exemption. Using the accrual method, Glidden reports the following taxable income and tax liability information for 2001:

Gross profit from sales	$300,000
Dividends: From 20%-owned corporation	10,000
From 10%-owned corporation	20,000
Gain on sale of depreciable property	12,778
Gain on installment sale of land	25,000
Gross income	$367,778
Operating expenses	(175,000)
Depreciation	(40,000)
Amortization of organizational expenditures	(2,500)
Dividends-received deduction	(22,000)
Total deductions	($239,500)
Taxable income	$128,278
Income (regular) tax liability	$ 33,278

The following additional information is available:

- The corporation earned tax-exempt bond interest of $15,000. The income is not from private activity bonds.
- The corporation received life insurance proceeds of $100,000 on the death of an executive.
- The corporation sold the land on January 30 of the current year for a total gain of $77,000, of which it reported $25,000 for regular tax purposes this year under the installment method. Glidden is not a dealer, and it pays no interest charge on the taxes owed on the deferred gain.
- The gain reported for AMTI and ACE purposes on the depreciable property sale is $5,860.
- Depreciation for AMTI and ACE purposes is $32,500. All of Glidden Corporation's depreciable assets were placed in service in 1996 or later years. Some of the assets were used in a predecessor proprietorship incorporated in 1998.
- The corporation incurred organizational expenditures in 1998, which are being amortized over a 60-month period for regular tax purposes.

Preadjustment AMTI is calculated as follows:

Taxable income	$128,278
Plus: Depreciation adjustment	7,500[a]
Minus: Basis adjustment on machine sale	(6,918)[b]
Preadjustment AMTI	$128,860

[a] $40,000 − $32,500 = $7,500.
[b] $12,778 − $5,860 = $6,918.

AMTI depreciation is smaller than taxable income depreciation because different depreciation calculations are employed. The gain on the depreciable property sale is smaller for preadjustment AMTI and ACE purposes (than for taxable income purposes) because smaller total depreciation was claimed before the sale under the alternative depreciation system. No adjustment is made for the $52,000 gain deferred on the installment sale because the installment method can be used to report sales of noninventory property when calculating both taxable income and AMTI.

Adjusted current earnings (ACE) is calculated as follows:

Preadjustment AMTI	$128,860
Plus: Tax-exempt bond interest	15,000
Life insurance proceeds	100,000
Deferred gain on land sale	52,000
Organizational expenditures adjustment	2,500
Dividends-received deduction adjustment	14,000
Adjusted current earnings	$312,360

The life insurance policy proceeds and the tax-exempt bond interest are inclusions only for ACE. Part of the gain on the land sale is included in taxable income and preadjustment AMTI under the installment method. The entire gain is reported for ACE purposes in the year of sale because the installment method is not permitted for ACE purposes for dealers or nondealers except where interest is charged for the tax deferral privilege. No deduction is allowed for ACE purposes for either the amortization of the organizational expenditures or the 70% deduction otherwise allowed for dividends received from a 10%-owned corporation.

The AMT liability is calculated as follows:

Preadjustment AMTI		$128,860
Plus: ACE	$312,360	
Minus: Preadjustment AMTI	(128,860)	
Difference	$183,500	
Times: 75% inclusion ratio	× 0.75	137,625
Alternative minimum taxable income		$266,485
Minus: Statutory exemption		(10,879)[a]
AMT tax base		$255,606
Times: 20% tax rate		× 0.20
Tentative minimum tax		$ 51,121
Minus: Regular tax		(33,278)
Alternative minimum tax		$ 17,843

[a] $40,000 − [0.25 × ($266,485 − $150,000)] = $10,879.

A reduced statutory exemption is available because of the phase-out that occurs when AMTI exceeds $150,000. The AMT liability is the excess of the tentative minimum tax over the regular tax. A completed Form 4626 for this comprehensive example appears in Appendix B.

MINIMUM TAX CREDIT

The AMT simply accelerates the payment of a corporation's income taxes. When a corporation pays an AMT liability it may be eligible for a **minimum tax credit** that can offset its future regular tax liabilities. The minimum tax credit prevents the same item from being taxed twice: once as part of the AMT liability and a second time as part of the regular tax liability.

The entire corporate AMT liability may be claimed as a credit. This includes the portion of the AMT liability due to deferral adjustments and preference items that represent timing differences that will reverse in another tax year as well as the portion of the AMT liability due to permanent adjustments and preference items that never will reverse.[24]

The minimum tax credit that a corporation can use in a tax year equals the total of the net minimum taxes paid in all prior post-1986 tax years minus the amount claimed as a minimum tax credit in those years. Use of available minimum tax credits in the current year is limited to the excess of the corporation's regular tax amount (minus all credits other than refundable credits) over its tentative minimum tax.

EXAMPLE C5-13 ▶ In the current year, Seminole Corporation has $400,000 of taxable income plus $250,000 of positive adjustments plus $350,000 of tax preference items. Its regular tax liability is $136,000 (0.34 × $400,000). Its AMT liability is $64,000 [(0.20 × $1,000,000) − $136,000]. Seminole's minimum tax credit is the entire amount of its AMT liability, or $64,000. ◀

ADDITIONAL COMMENT

Use of the AMT credit is limited. Corporate AMT collections for 1997 were $3.9 billion. The AMT credit claimed in 1998 was $3.43 billion. The reason for the difference is that some corporations elect to use other credits that have a limited life, or some corporations end up owing the AMT in consecutive years.

The minimum tax credit carries forward indefinitely and offsets regular tax liabilities in future years, but only to the extent the regular tax exceeds the corporation's TMT in the carryforward year. The minimum tax credit cannot be carried back to an earlier tax year.

TAX CREDITS AND THE AMT

As illustrated in Table C3-2, a corporation is allowed to reduce its regular tax liability by any available tax credits. Special rules restrict the use of tax credits against the corporate AMT. These rules are explained below.

ADDITIONAL COMMENT

Because the general business credit limitation is tied to the TMT, *every* corporation with excess general business credits will have to compute its TMT even though the corporation may not have an AMT liability.

KEY POINT

Because the purpose of the AMT is to ensure that all profitable corporations pay tax, the use of tax credits also is limited. For example, the general business credit cannot reduce the regular tax below the TMT.

AMT AND THE GENERAL BUSINESS CREDIT. Several limitations apply to the general business credit that prevent it from offsetting all of a corporation's regular tax and certain other taxes. The general business credit may not be used to offset the alternative minimum tax, the accumulated earnings tax, or the personal holding company (PHC) tax.

The following rule prevents the general business credit from offsetting all of a corporation's tax, and it also prevents the credit from offsetting any of the corporation's AMT. Under Sec. 38(c), the general business credit for a tax year is limited to the excess (if any) of the corporation's net income tax (reduced by certain other credits) over the greater of its tentative minimum tax or 25% of its net regular tax liability in excess of $25,000.

A corporation's net income tax is the sum of its regular tax and AMT liabilities reduced by the foreign tax credit, possessions tax credit, and Puerto Rico economic activity credit. Any general business credits that cannot be used in the current year because of credit limitations carry back one year and forward 20 years.[25]

The result of this limitation is that the general business credit can offset only the portion of the regular tax that exceeds the TMT, not all of a corporation's regular tax.

EXAMPLE C5-14 ▶ In the current year, Scientific Corporation's net regular tax liability before credits is $125,000. Its TMT is $50,000. Scientific's only available credit for the year is a general business credit of $140,000. Scientific's net income tax is $125,000 because its net regular tax liability ($125,000) is greater than its TMT ($50,000). As computed below, Scientific's general business credit is limited to the smaller of its $75,000 credit limitation or the $140,000 credit earned.

Net income tax		$125,000
Minus: Greater of:		
(1) 25% of net regular tax liability (reduced by other credits) exceeding $25,000 [0.25 × ($125,000 − $25,000)]	$25,000	
OR		

[24] Sec. 53. Most AMT adjustments and preference items result in a deferral of the regular tax liability rather than a permanent reduction. The two permanent preferences are percentage depletion and tax-exempt private activity bond interest. Examples of permanent ACE adjustments include life insurance proceeds and tax-exempt bond interest from bonds other than private activity bonds.

[25] Sec. 38(c)(2). Special rules apply to the empowerment zone employment credit, which can offset up to 25% of a taxpayer's AMT liability.

(2) Tentative minimum tax	$50,000	(50,000)
General business credit limitation		$ 75,000

Scientific has an income tax liability of $50,000 ($125,000 – $75,000 credit) and no AMT liability. Its general business credit carryback or carryover is $65,000 ($140,000 – $75,000), which can be carried back one year and forward 20 years. ◀

The AMT credit for small corporations is limited by the amount the corporation's regular tax liability (reduced by other credits) exceeds 25 percent times the excess (if any) of (a) the corporation's regular tax (reduced by other credits) minus (b) $25,000.[26]

AMT AND THE FOREIGN TAX CREDIT. For purposes of computing the AMT, foreign tax credits (AMT FTCs) are limited to the excess of the TMT over 10% of the TMT excluding the alternative tax NOL deduction. Credits that cannot be used in the current year carry back two years and forward five years to offset the TMT in those years.[27] A simplified AMT foreign tax credit limitation election is available in Sec. 59(a) that calculates the limit using the ratio of foreign source taxable income to worldwide AMTI.

Topic Review C5-2 presents an overview of the alternative minimum tax.

PERSONAL HOLDING COMPANY TAX

HISTORICAL NOTE

Congress enacted the PHC penalty tax in 1934 to target the so-called incorporated pocketbook. At one time, the top marginal corporate tax rate was 39 percentage points (52% vs. 91%) below that for individuals. In 2002, this differential is only 3.6 percentage points. However, the availability of 15% and 25% marginal corporate tax rates and/or a dividends-received deduction may produce substantially lower effective corporate tax rates for certain types of income, which necessitates retention of the PHC tax.

A corporation that satisfies both a stock ownership test and a passive income test is classified as a **personal holding company** (PHC) for the tax year. Congress enacted the **PHC penalty tax** to prevent taxpayers from using closely held corporations to shelter passive income from the higher individual tax rates. This penalty tax is levied at a 38.6% tax rate (in 2002) on the PHC's undistributed personal holding company income (UPHCI). A corporation subject to the PHC tax pays this tax in addition to the corporate regular tax and the corporate alternative minimum tax. Corporations, however, can avoid the PHC tax by failing either the stock ownership or passive income test or by reducing UPHCI to zero by making dividend distributions.

The PHC tax took on added importance following the Omnibus Budget Reconciliation Act of 1993 which increased the top marginal tax rate for individuals to 39.6%. Since 1993, the top marginal tax rate for individuals has been higher than the

Topic Review C5-2

Alternative Minimum Tax (AMT)

1. The AMT is levied in addition to the regular (income) tax.
2. Special AMT exemptions are available for small corporations having gross receipts (generally $7.5 million or less) and for corporations of any size having low levels of alternative minimum taxable income (AMTI) (generally less than $310,000).
3. The starting point for the AMT calculation is taxable income before NOLs. Taxable income is increased by tax preference items and increased or decreased by adjustments to arrive at AMTI.
4. AMTI is reduced by a $40,000 statutory exemption. The statutory exemption is phased-out between $150,000 and $310,000 of AMTI to arrive at the AMT tax base.
5. A 20% tax rate applies to the tax base to arrive at the tentative minimum tax.
6. The tentative minimum tax amount is reduced by the AMT foreign tax credit. Other tax credits, such as the general business credit, do not reduce the tentative minimum tax.
7. The excess of a corporation's tentative minimum tax over its regular tax may be claimed as a minimum tax credit. This credit carries over to a later year to offset the excess of the regular tax over the tentative minimum tax.
8. The AMT liability, as well as the regular tax liability, are subject to the estimated tax requirements.

[26] Sec. 55(e)(5).

[27] Sec. 59(a)(2).

34% or 35% C corporation tax rate that applies to most corporations. The 1993 Act reversed a situation where the top marginal tax rate for individuals was below the top marginal tax rate for corporations. The current rate advantage for corporations provides a situation where individuals may find a substantial tax savings by having their investment assets held by a corporate entity. The tax savings for noncorporate taxpayers will be reduced when the top individual tax rate decreases from 38.6% in 2002 to 35% in 2006 and thereafter. At that time, the 35% top individual tax rate will be the same as the top C corporation tax rate. This portion of the chapter emphasizes determining whether a corporation is a PHC and finding ways to avoid the PHC tax.

ADDITIONAL COMMENT

The Congressional intent behind enacting the personal holding company and accumulated earnings penalty taxes was not to produce large amounts of tax revenues (e.g., only $12.7 million in PHC taxes for 1998). However, the presence of these taxes in the IRS's arsenal prevents substantial revenue losses from certain tax-motivated transactions involving closely held corporations.

PERSONAL HOLDING COMPANY DEFINED

A personal holding company is any corporation that (1) has five or fewer individual shareholders who own more than 50% of the corporation's outstanding stock at any time during the last half of its tax year and (2) has personal holding company income that is at least 60% of its adjusted ordinary gross income for the tax year.[28]

Corporations that retain special tax status generally are excluded from the PHC definition. Among those excluded are S corporations and tax-exempt organizations.

OBJECTIVE 2

Determine whether a corporation is a personal holding company (PHC)

STOCK OWNERSHIP REQUIREMENT

Section 542(a)(2) provides that a corporation satisfies the PHC stock ownership requirement if more than 50% of the value of its outstanding stock is directly or indirectly owned by five or fewer individuals at any time during the last half of its tax year.[29] Any corporation having fewer than ten individual shareholders at any time during the last half of its tax year, which is not an excluded corporation, will meet the stock ownership requirement.[30]

For purposes of determining whether the 50% requirement is met, stock owned directly or indirectly by or for an individual shareholder is considered to be owned by the individual. The Sec. 544 stock attribution rules are used for this purpose. These rules provide that

- Stock owned by a family member is considered to be owned by the other members of his or her family. Family members include brothers and sisters, spouse, ancestors, and lineal descendants.
- Stock owned directly or indirectly by or for a corporation, partnership, estate, or trust is considered to be owned proportionately by its shareholders, partners, or beneficiaries.
- A person who holds an option to acquire stock is considered to own such stock without regard to whether the individual intends to exercise the option.
- Stock owned by a partner is considered to be owned by his or her partners.
- The family, partnership, and option rules can be used only to make a corporation a PHC. They cannot be used to prevent a corporation from acquiring PHC status.[31]

TYPICAL MISCONCEPTION

The PHC penalty tax applies to any corporation that meets the definition of a personal holding company. No improper intent is necessary. Thus, the PHC tax truly fits into the category of "a trap for the unwary."

PASSIVE INCOME REQUIREMENT

A corporation whose shareholders satisfy the stock ownership requirement is not a PHC unless it also earns predominantly passive income. The passive income requirement is met if at least 60% of the corporation's **adjusted ordinary gross income (AOGI)** for the tax year is personal holding company income (PHCI). The following text defines the terms AOGI and PHCI and outlines ways in which a corporation can take steps to avoid satisfying the passive income requirements.

KEY POINT

A corporation must satisfy two tests to be considered a PHC: a stock ownership test and a passive income test. Because most closely held corporations satisfy the stock ownership test, PHC status usually is determined by the passive income test.

ADJUSTED ORDINARY GROSS INCOME DEFINED. The first step toward determining AOGI requires calculating the corporation's gross income (see Figure C5-1). Gross income is determined using the same accounting methods used to compute taxable

[28] Sec. 542(a).

[29] The PHC stock ownership test also is used to determine whether a closely held C corporation is subject to the at-risk rules (Sec. 465) or the passive activity loss and credit limitation rules (Sec. 469). Thus, a closely held corporation that is not a PHC may be subject to other special rules because of satisfying the PHC stock ownership requirement.

[30] This rule may not hold if entities own stock that might be attributed to the individual owners.

[31] Sec. 544(a)(4)(A).

▼ **FIGURE C5-1**

Determining Adjusted Ordinary Gross Income

Gross income (GI) reported for taxable income and PHC purposes
Minus: Gross gains from the sale of capital assets
Gross gains from the sale of Sec. 1231 property

Ordinary gross income (OGI)
Minus: Certain expenses incurred in connection with gross income from rents; mineral, oil, and gas royalties; and working interests in oil or gas wells
Interest received on certain U.S. obligations held for sale to customers by dealers
Interest received due to condemnation awards, judgments, or tax refunds
Rents from tangible personal property manufactured or produced by the corporation, provided it has engaged in substantial manufacturing or production of the same type of personal property in the current tax year

Adjusted ordinary gross income (AOGI)

income. Any income item excluded in determining taxable income also is excluded in determining AOGI. Gross receipts from sales transactions are reduced by the corporation's cost of goods sold.

The next step in determining AOGI requires calculating the corporation's **ordinary gross income (OGI)**. To do this, the corporation's gross income is reduced by the amount of its capital gains and Sec. 1231 gains.[32] The exclusion of capital gains and Sec. 1231 gains from OGI (and, later, from AOGI) means that these items are neutral factors in determining whether a corporation is a PHC; that is, the realization and recognition of a large Sec. 1231 gain or capital gain cannot cause a corporation to be a PHC.

Next, OGI is reduced for certain expenses. These expenses relate to the production of rental income; mineral, oil, and gas (M, O, & G) royalties; and income from working interests in oil or gas wells.[33] The rental income adjustment is described below.

Reduction by Rental Income Expenses. Gross income from rents is reduced by the deductions claimed for depreciation or amortization, property taxes, interest, and rents. This net amount is known as the **adjusted income from rents (AIR)**.[34] No other Sec. 162 expenses incurred in the production of rental income reduce OGI. The expense adjustment cannot exceed the total gross rental income.

EXAMPLE C5-15 ▶ Ingrid owns all of Keno Corporation's single class of stock. Both Ingrid and Keno Corporation use the calendar year as their tax years. Keno Corporation reports the following results for the current year:

Rental income	$100,000
Depreciation	15,000
Interest expense	9,000
Real estate taxes	4,000
Maintenance expenses	8,000
Administrative expenses	12,000

Keno Corporation's AIR is $72,000 [$100,000 − ($15,000 + $9,000 + $4,000)]. The maintenance and administrative expenses are deductible in determining taxable income and, consequently, UPHCI, but do not reduce the AIR amount. ◀

PERSONAL HOLDING COMPANY INCOME DEFINED. **Personal holding company income** includes dividends, interest, annuities, adjusted income from rents, royalties, produced film rents, income from personal service contracts involving a 25% or more share-

[32] Sec. 543(b)(1).
[33] Sec. 543(b)(2).
[34] Sec. 543(b)(3).

ADDITIONAL COMMENT

Income not included in AOGI cannot be PHCI. In calculating the 60% passive income test, PHCI is the numerator and AOGI is the denominator. Because the passive income test is purely objective, both the numerator and denominator can be manipulated. When the ratio is close to 60%, one planning opportunity is to accelerate the recognition of income that is AOGI but not PHCI.

HISTORICAL NOTE

The exception for royalties on computer software was added by the Tax Reform Act of 1986. Without this exception, many computer software companies would almost certainly be classified as PHCs.

TAX STRATEGY TIP

Taxpayers who have a PHC problem should carefully monitor the PHC exclusion requirements to avoid having to pay the tax or having to make a deficiency dividend payment.

holder, rental income for corporate property used by a 25% or more shareholder, and distributions from estates or trusts.

PHCI is determined according to the following general rules:

- *Dividends:* Includes only distributions made out of E&P. Any amounts that are tax exempt (e.g., return of capital distributions) or eligible for capital gain treatment (e.g., liquidating distributions) are excluded from PHCI.[35]
- *Interest income:* Includes interest included in gross income. Any interest excluded from gross income is excluded from PHCI.[36]
- *Annuity proceeds:* Includes only annuities included in gross income. Any annuity amount excluded from gross income (for example, as a return of capital) is excluded from PHCI.[37]
- *Royalty income:* Includes amounts received for the use of intangible property (e.g., patents, copyrights, and trademarks). Special rules apply to copyright royalties, mineral, oil, and gas royalties, active business computer software royalties, and produced film rents. Each of these four special types of royalty income constitutes a separate PHCI category that may be excluded under one of the exceptions described below and shown in Table C5-2.[38]
- *Distributions from an estate or trust:* Included in PHCI.[39]

Special exclusions apply that could result in the exclusion of rents; mineral, oil, and gas royalties; copyright royalties; produced film rents; rental income from the use of property by a 25% or more shareholder; and active business computer software royalties from PHCI. These exclusions, which are summarized in Table C5-2, reduce the probability that a corporation will be a PHC. The two most commonly encountered exclusions, the ones for rental income and personal service contract income, are explained on the next two pages.

▼ TABLE C5-2
Tests to Determine Exclusions From Personal Holding Company Income

PHCI Category	A PHCI Category is Excluded If: Income in the Category Is:	Other PHCI Is:	Business Expenses Are:
Rents	≥50% of AOGI[a]	≤10% of OGI (unless reduced by distributions)	—
Mineral, oil, and gas royalties	≥50% of AOGI[a]	≤10% of OGI	≥15% of AOGI
Copyright royalties	≥50% of OGI	≤10% of OGI	≥25% of OGI
Produced film rents	≥50% of OGI	—	—
Compensation for use of property by a shareholder owning at least 25% of the outstanding stock	—	≤10% of OGI	—
Active business computer software royalties	≥50% of OGI	≤10% of OGI (unless reduced by distributions)	≥25% of OGI[b]
Personal services contract income	—[c]	—	—

[a] Measured in terms of adjusted income from rents or mineral, oil, and gas royalties, respectively.
[b] The deduction test can be applied to either the single tax year in question or the five-year period ending with the tax year in question.
[c] Personal services income is excluded from PHCI if the corporation has the right to designate the person who is to perform the services or the person performing the services owns less than 25% of the corporation's outstanding stock.

[35] Reg. Sec. 1.543-1(b)(1).
[36] Reg. Sec. 1.543-1(b)(2).
[37] Reg. Sec. 1.543-1(b)(4).
[38] Reg. Sec. 1.543-1(b)(3). Royalties include mineral, oil, and gas royalties, working interests in oil or gas wells, computer software royalties, copyright royalties, and all other royalties.
[39] Sec. 543(a)(8).

SELF-STUDY QUESTION

What is the effect of the two-pronged test that allows the exclusion from PHCI of certain AIR?

ANSWER

This two-pronged test makes it difficult to use rents to shelter other passive income. For example, the 50% test would require at least $100 of AIR to shelter $100 of interest income. The 10% test is even more restrictive. To satisfy this test, it would be necessary to generate $900 of OGI (AIR and other items) to shelter the same $100 of interest income.

Exclusion for Rents. Adjusted income from rents (AIR) is included in PHCI unless the special exception applies for corporations earning predominantly rental income. PHCI does not include rents if (1) AIR is at least 50% of AOGI and (2) the dividends-paid deduction equals or exceeds the amount by which nonrental PHCI exceeds 10% of OGI.[40] The special exception permits corporations earning predominantly rental income and having very little nonrental PHCI to avoid PHC status. The dividends-paid deduction is available for dividends paid during the tax year, dividends paid within 2½ months of the end of the tax year for which a special throwback election is made to treat the distribution as having been paid on the last day of the preceding tax year, and consent dividends (see page C5-22). Nonrental PHCI includes all PHCI (determined without regard to the exclusions for copyright royalties and mineral, oil, and gas royalties) *other than* adjusted income from rents and rental income earned from leasing property to a shareholder owning 25% or more of the stock.

EXAMPLE C5-16 ▶ Kwame owns all of Texas Corporation's single class of stock. Both Kwame and Texas use the calendar year as their tax years. Texas reports the following results for the current year:

Rental income	$100,000
Operating profit from sales	40,000
Dividend income	15,000
Interest income from corporate bonds	10,000
Rental expenses:	
Depreciation	15,000
Interest	9,000
Real estate taxes	4,000
Other expenses	20,000

Texas pays no dividends during the current year or during the 2½ month throwback period following year-end. Because one shareholder owns all the Texas stock, Texas satisfies the stock ownership requirement. Texas's AOGI is calculated as follows:

Rental income		$100,000
Operating profit from sales		40,000
Dividends		15,000
Interest		10,000
Gross income and OGI		$165,000
Minus: Depreciation	$15,000	
Interest	9,000	
Real estate taxes	4,000	(28,000)
AOGI		$137,000

The two AIR tests are performed as follows:

Test 1: Rental income	$100,000
Minus: Depreciation	(15,000)
Interest	(9,000)
Real estate taxes	(4,000)
AIR	$ 72,000
50% of AOGI (0.50 × $137,000 AOGI) [Test satisfied]	$ 68,500
Test 2: Dividends	$ 15,000
Interest	10,000
Nonrental income	$ 25,000
Minus: 10% of OGI (0.10 × $165,000)	(16,500)
Minimum amount of distributions	$8,500
Actual dividends paid [Test not satisfied]	$ -0-

[40] Sec. 543(a)(2). The AIR term excludes rental income earned from leasing property to a shareholder owning 25% or more of the stock, which is included in PHCI under its own separate category.

AIR exceeds the 50% threshold, so Test 1 is satisfied. Because no dividends were paid, the nonrental income ceiling is exceeded and Test 2 is failed. AIR is included in PHCI since only one of the two tests was satisfied. The 60% PHC income test is performed as follows:

AIR	$ 72,000
Dividends	15,000
Interest	10,000
PHCI	$ 97,000
AOGI	$137,000
Times: AOGI threshold	× 0.60
AOGI ceiling [Test satisfied]	$ 82,200

Texas is a PHC because PHCI exceeds 60% of AOGI.

Texas could avoid PHC status by paying a sufficient amount of cash dividends during the current year or a consent dividend following year-end for the AIR exclusion to be satisfied. The necessary amount of dividend payments is the amount by which nonrental PHCI ($25,000) exceeds 10% of OGI ($16,500), or $8,500. An $8,500 cash dividend paid during the current year or a consent dividend paid after the year-end would permit Texas to exclude the $72,000 of AIR from PHCI. PHCI then would be $25,000 ($15,000 + $10,000), which is less than 60% of AOGI ($82,200). (Consent dividends are described on page C5-22.) ◀

ADDITIONAL COMMENT

Congress enacted the provision for personal service contracts to prevent entertainers, athletes, and other highly compensated professionals from incorporating their activities and, after taking a below-normal salary, having the rest of the income taxed at the corporate rates. Even if it is apparent that a 25%-shareholder will perform the services, as long as no one other than the corporation has the right to designate who performs the services, the income is not PHCI. Thus, the careful drafting of contracts is important in this area.

Exclusion for Personal Service Contracts. Income earned from contracts under which the corporation is to perform personal services and income earned from the sale of such contracts is included in PHCI if the following two conditions are met:

- (a) Some person other than the corporation has the right to designate (by name or by description) the individual who is to perform the services or (b) the individual who is to perform the services is designated (by name or by description) in the contract.
- 25% or more of the value of the corporation's outstanding stock is directly or indirectly owned by the person who has performed, is to perform, or is designated as the person to perform the services.[41]

The 25% or more requirement needs to be satisfied only at some point during the tax year and is determined by using the Sec. 544 constructive stock ownership rules. Congress enacted this provision to prevent professionals, entertainers, and sports figures from incorporating their activities, paying themselves a below-normal salary, and sheltering at the lower corporate tax rates the difference between their actual earnings and their below-normal salary.

EXAMPLE C5-17 ▶

Dr. Kellner owns all the stock of a professional corporation that provides medical services. The professional corporation has an employment contract with Dr. Kellner that specifies the terms of his employment and his salary. Dr. Kellner is the only doctor under contract with the professional corporation. The corporation provides office space for Dr. Kellner and employs the necessary office staff to enable Dr. Kellner to perform the medical services. The income earned by Dr. Kellner does not constitute PHCI because (1) the normal patient–physician relationship generally does not involve a contract that includes a designation of the doctor who will perform the services, nor will the patient generally be permitted to designate the doctor who will perform the services, and (2) the professional corporation will be able to substitute a qualified replacement when Dr. Kellner is not on duty (for example, when he is on vacation or not on call).[42]

The compensation received by the corporation for Dr. Kellner's services would constitute PHCI if the contract with the patient specified that only Dr. Kellner would provide the services or if the services provided by Dr. Kellner were so unique that only he could provide them. Any portion of the corporation's income from the personal service contract attributable to "important and essential" services provided by persons other than Dr. Kellner is not included in PHCI.[43] ◀

---

[41] Sec. 543(a)(7).

[42] Rev. Rul. 75-67, 1975-1 C.B. 169. See also Rev. Ruls. 75-249, 1975-1 C.B. 171 (relating to a composer), and 75-250, 1975-1 C.B. 172 (relating to an accountant).

[43] Reg. Sec. 1.543-1(b)(8)(ii).

OBJECTIVE 3

Calculate the amount of the corporation's PHC tax liability

KEY POINT

The PHC penalty tax is assessed at a 38.6% rate in 2002. This tax is in addition to the corporate income tax. Thus, the existence of both taxes eliminates any advantage obtained by interposing a corporation between the taxpayer and his or her income-producing assets.

DETERMINING THE PHC PENALTY TAX

Determination of the PHC penalty tax is illustrated in Figure C5-2. First, the amount of undistributed personal holding company income (UPHCI) must be determined. Then the 38.6% PHC tax rate (in 2002) is applied to the UPHCI. If the corporation owes the PHC tax, it can avoid paying the tax if it makes a timely consent or deficiency dividend distribution.

CALCULATING UPHCI. The starting point for the UPHCI calculation is the corporation's taxable income. A series of adjustments must be made to taxable income to arrive at UPHCI. The most important of these adjustments are described below.

Positive Adjustments to Taxable Income. A PHC may not claim a dividends-received deduction. Thus, its taxable income must be increased by the amount of any dividends-received deductions claimed.[44] Rental expenses that exceed rental income also are added back to taxable income in arriving at UPHCI.

Because PHCs are restricted to deducting only the NOL for the immediately preceding tax year, two compensating adjustments must be made for NOLs. First, the amount of the NOL deduction claimed in determining taxable income must be added back to taxable income. Second, the entire amount of the corporation's NOL (computed without regard to the dividends-received deduction) for the immediately preceding tax year is deducted as a negative adjustment.[45]

Negative Adjustments to Taxable Income. Charitable contributions are deductible up to the 20% and 50% of adjusted gross income limitations for individuals. Thus, two adjustments may be required: (1) the deduction of charitable contributions exceeding the 10% corporate limitation (but not exceeding the individual limitations) and (2) the addition of charitable contribution carryovers deducted for regular tax purposes in the current year, but deducted for PHC tax purposes in an earlier year.[46]

Income taxes (i.e., federal income taxes, the corporate AMT, foreign income taxes, and U.S. possessions' income taxes) accrued by the corporation reduce UPHCI.[47]

▼ **FIGURE C5-2**
Determination of the Personal Holding Company Tax

Taxable income
Plus: Positive adjustments
1. Dividends-received deduction claimed
2. NOL deduction claimed
3. Excess charitable contributions carried over from a preceding tax year and deducted in determining taxable income
4. Net loss attributable to the operation or maintenance of property leased by the corporation
5. Rental expenses in excess of rental income

Minus: Negative adjustments
1. Accrued U.S. and foreign income taxes
2. Charitable contributions in excess of the 10% corporate limitation
3. NOL (computed without regard to the dividends-received deduction) incurred in the immediately preceding tax year
4. Net capital gain minus the amount of any income taxes attributed to it

Minus: Dividends-paid deduction claimed

Undistributed personal holding company income (UPHCI)
Times: 0.396

Personal holding company tax

[44] Sec. 545(b)(3).
[45] Sec. 545(b)(4) and Rev. Rul. 79-59, 1979-1 C.B. 209.
[46] Sec. 545(b)(2).
[47] Sec. 545(b)(1).

KEY POINT

The negative adjustments made to taxable income in arriving at UPHCI (e.g., federal income taxes) represent items that do not reduce taxable income but reduce the earnings available for distribution to the shareholders. In contrast, positive adjustments made to taxable income (e.g., the dividends-received deduction) are not allowed in arriving at UPHCI because they do not represent a reduction in earnings available for distribution to the shareholders.

A PHC is permitted a deduction for the amount of its net capital gain (i.e., net long-term capital gain over net short-term capital loss) minus the amount of income taxes attributable to the net capital gain.[48] The federal income taxes attributable to the net capital gain equal the taxes imposed on the corporation's taxable income minus the taxes imposed on the corporation's taxable income as computed by excluding the net capital gain. The tax offset prevents a double benefit for the federal income taxes, which are deductible in determining UPHCI.

The capital gains adjustment made when determining AOGI prevents a large capital gain from causing a corporation to be classified as a PHC. Even if the corporation is a PHC, the capital gains adjustment made in determining UPHCI prevents the corporation from paying the PHC tax on the amount of its long-term (but not its short-term) capital gains.

AVOIDING THE PHC DESIGNATION AND TAX LIABILITY BY MAKING DIVIDEND DISTRIBUTIONS

ADDITIONAL COMMENT

The intent of the PHC rules is not to collect taxes from a corporation. Instead, the rules are meant to compel the distribution of income by a closely held corporation so that such income will be taxed at the shareholders' individual tax rates. This purpose is evidenced by the flexibility of the dividends-paid deduction.

The PHC can claim a **dividends-paid deduction** for distributions made during the current year if they are made out of the corporation's current or accumulated E&P.[49] A dividends-paid deduction is not available for **preferential dividends**. A dividend payment is preferential when (1) the amount distributed to a shareholder exceeds his or her ratable share of the distribution as determined by the number of shares of stock owned or (2) the amount received by a class of stock is more or less than its rightful amount.[50] In either case, the entire distribution (and not just any excess distributions) is a preferential dividend.

Throwback dividends are distributions paid in the first 2½ months after the close of the tax year. A dividend distribution made in the first 2½ months of the next tax year is treated as a throwback distribution of the preceding tax year for PHC tax purposes only if the PHC makes the appropriate election.[51] Otherwise, the dividends-paid deduction is claimed in the tax year in which the PHC makes the distribution. Throwback dividends made by a PHC are limited to the lesser of the PHC's UPHCI or 20% of the amount of any dividends (other than consent dividends) paid during the tax year. Thus, a PHC that fails to make any dividend distributions during its tax year is prevented from paying a throwback dividend.

TAX STRATEGY TIP

If the corporation does not have the cash to pay a throwback dividend, it should consider a consent dividend. Moreover, the consent dividend is not subject to the 20% limitation on throwback dividends and may be made up to the extended due date for the corporation's tax return.

Consent dividends are hypothetical dividends deemed paid to shareholders on the last day of the corporation's tax year. Consent dividends permit a corporation to reduce its PHC tax liability when it is prevented from making an actual dividend distribution because of a lack of available money, a restrictive loan covenant, and so on. Any shareholder who owns stock on the last day of the corporation's tax year can make a consent dividend election.[52] For tax purposes, the election results in a hypothetical money dividend being paid on the last day of the PHC's tax year for which the dividends-paid deduction is claimed. The shareholder treats the consent dividend as being received on the distribution date and immediately contributed by the shareholder to the distributing corporation's capital account. The contribution increases the basis for the shareholder's stock investment. The shareholder can make the consent dividend election through the due date for the corporation's income tax return (including any permitted extensions).

Dividend Carryovers. Dividends paid in the preceding two tax years can be used as a dividend carryover to reduce the amount of the current year's PHC tax liability.[53] Section 564 permits a PHC to deduct the amount by which its dividend distributions that were eligible for a dividends-paid deduction in each of the two preceding tax years exceed the corporation's UPHCI for such a year.

Liquidating Dividends. A dividends-paid deduction is available for liquidating distributions made by a PHC within 24 months of adopting a plan of liquidation.[54]

---

[48] Sec. 545(b)(5).

[49] Secs. 561(a) and 562(a).

[50] Sec. 562(c).

[51] Sec. 563(b).

[52] Sec. 565.

[53] Sec. 561(a)(3).

[54] Sec. 562(b).

TAX STRATEGY TIP

A deficiency dividend can be beneficial if a corporation fails to eliminate its UPHCI, either under the erroneous assumption that it was not a PHC or due to a miscalculation of its UPHCI. If certain requirements are satisfied, a deficiency dividend can be distributed and designated as a retroactive dividend deductible against UPHCI earned in a previous year.

Deficiency Dividends. A corporation that is determined to owe the PHC penalty tax can avoid paying the tax by electing to pay a **deficiency dividend** under Sec. 547. The deficiency dividend procedures substitute an income tax levy on the dividend payment at the shareholder level for the payment of the PHC tax. The distributing corporation's shareholders include the deficiency dividend in their gross income for the tax year in which it is received, not the tax year for which the PHC claims a dividends-paid deduction. Payment of a deficiency dividend does not relieve the PHC from any interest and penalties owed with respect to the PHC tax.

The following requirements must be satisfied to claim a dividends-paid deduction for a deficiency dividend:

- A determination (e.g., judicial decision or agreement entered into by the taxpayer with the IRS) must be made that establishes the amount of the PHC tax liability.
- A dividend must be paid within 90 days after establishing the PHC tax liability.
- A claim for a dividends-paid deduction based on the payment of the deficiency dividend must be filed within 120 days of the determination date.[55]

EXAMPLE C5-18 ▶ Boston Corporation files its current year tax return reporting as a capital gain a $200,000 distribution received pursuant to a stock redemption. Upon an IRS audit of Boston's return, both parties agree that the capital gain classification is erroneous and that dividend treatment for the redemption is indeed correct. This change causes Boston to be classified as a PHC. The liability for the payment of the PHC tax is eliminated if Boston pays a deficiency dividend within 90 days after signing the agreement with the IRS establishing the existence of the PHC tax liability and Boston files a timely claim. ◀

PHC TAX CALCULATION

The following example illustrates the calculation of the PHC's UPHCI and the determination of the PHC's income tax and penalty tax liabilities.

EXAMPLE C5-19 ▶ Marlo Corporation is classified as a PHC for the current year, reporting $227,000 of taxable income on its federal income tax return:

Operating profit	$100,000
Long-term capital gain	60,000
Short-term capital gain	30,000
Dividends (20%-owned corporation)	200,000
Interest	100,000
Gross income	$490,000
Salaries	(40,000)
General and administrative expenses	(20,000)
Charitable contributions	(43,000)[a]
Dividends-received deduction	(160,000)
Taxable income	$227,000

[a] $43,000 = 0.10 × ($490,000 − $40,000 − $20,000).

Federal income taxes (using 2002 rates and ignoring any alternative minimum tax liability) accrued by Marlo are $71,780 [$22,250 + (0.39 × $127,000)]. Actual charitable contributions made by Marlo are $60,000 in the current year. Marlo paid $50,000 in dividends in August.

Calculation of Marlo's PHC tax liability is as follows:

Taxable income			$227,000
Plus:	Dividends-received deduction		160,000
Minus:	Excess charitable contributions		(17,000)[b]
	Federal income taxes		(71,780)
	Dividends-paid deduction		(50,000)
	Long-term capital gain	$60,000	
	Minus: Federal income taxes	(23,400)[c]	
	LTCG adjustment		(36,600)

[55] Secs. 547(c) through (e).

Undistributed personal holding company income	\$211,620
Times: Tax rate	× 0.386
Personal holding company tax	\$ 81,685

[b] \$60,000 total contributions − \$43,000 limitation = \$17,000 excess contributions.
[c] Because Marlo is in the 39% tax bracket with and without the LTCG, it can calculate the applicable federal income tax as 0.39 × \$60,000 = \$23,400.

Marlo's total federal tax liability is \$153,465 (\$71,780 + \$81,685). Payment of the PHC tax (\$83,802) can be avoided by paying a timely deficiency dividend in the amount of \$211,620, which is the amount of UPHCI in 2002. ◀

Topic Review C5-3 presents an overview of the personal holding company penalty tax.

Topic Review C5-3

Personal Holding Company (PHC) Tax

1. The PHC tax applies only to corporations qualifying as PHCs. A PHC has (1) five or fewer individual shareholders owning more than 50% in value of the corporation's stock at any time during the last half of the tax year and (2) PHCI that is at least 60% of its adjusted ordinary gross income for the tax year.
2. Two special exemptions exist for the PHC test. First, certain special corporate forms are excluded from the penalty tax (e.g., S corporations). Second, certain income forms (e.g., rents and active business computer software royalties) are excluded if the percentage of income, maximum level of other PHC income, and minimum level of business expense requirements are met. Table C5-2 summarizes the excludable income forms and their requirements.
3. The PHC tax equals 38.6% (in 2002) times UPHCI. UPHCI equals taxable income plus certain positive adjustments (e.g., dividends-received deduction) and minus certain negative adjustments (e.g., federal income taxes, excess charitable contributions, and net capital gain reduced by federal income taxes attributable to the gain).
4. UPHCI can be reduced by a dividends-paid deduction claimed for cash and property dividends paid during the tax year and consent and throwback dividends distributed after year-end.
5. A PHC tax liability (but not interest and penalties) can be eliminated by the payment of a deficiency dividend. This distribution substitutes an income tax levy at the shareholder level for the corporate-level PHC tax.

ACCUMULATED EARNINGS TAX

ADDITIONAL COMMENT

The accumulated earnings tax is a penalty tax imposed on corporations that accumulate unreasonable amounts of earnings for the purpose of avoiding shareholder taxes. With corporate tax rates lower than individual rates, tax incentives exist for accumulating earnings inside a corporation. These opportunities should lead to the IRS applying the accumulated earnings tax.

Corporations not subject to the personal holding company tax may be subject to the accumulated earnings tax. The **accumulated earnings tax** attempts "to compel the company to distribute any profits not needed for the conduct of its business so that, when so distributed, individual stockholders will become liable" for taxes on the dividends received.[56] Unlike its name, the tax is not levied on the corporation's total accumulated earnings balance but only on its current year addition to the balance. In other words, the tax is levied on accumulated earnings earned currently that are not needed for a reasonable business purpose (for example, earnings invested in portfolio investments to avoid having to pay taxes at the shareholder level when distributed).

CORPORATIONS SUBJECT TO THE PENALTY TAX

Section 532(a) states that the accumulated earnings tax applies "to every corporation . . . formed or availed of for the purpose of avoiding the income tax with respect to its shareholders . . . by permitting earnings and profits to accumulate instead of being divided or distributed." Three special corporate forms are excluded from the accumulated earnings tax:

[56] *Helvering v. Chicago Stock Yards Co.*, 30 AFTR 1091, 43-1 USTC ¶9379 (USSC, 1943).

WHAT WOULD YOU DO IN THIS SITUATION?

Taylor Corporation formed in 2001 with its shareholders initially contributing $1 million of capital on July 1 of that year. However, because of delays in obtaining needed equipment to begin manufacturing operations, the corporation did not begin business until January 2002. During the last six months of 2001, the corporation earned $50,000 of taxable interest income and incurred $20,000 of deductible expenses. A second-year accountant in a small accounting firm was assigned to complete the Taylor corporate tax return. All of his previous tax return assignments were individual tax returns. The senior accountant who made the assignment told the second-year staff accountant that the return "would be simple and that all you need to do is input the interest income and expense information into the Form 1120 software." Because of the rush to finish and deliver the return to the taxpayer by March 15, no one in the office noticed during the review process that the corporation might be a personal holding company (PHC). The corporation filed the return on March 15 without paying any PHC tax. Another Taylor Corporation matter came up in August 2002 and was assigned to you. When you examined the return with respect to the new issue, you identified the potential PHC problem. Does Taylor have a PHC tax problem? If so, what can Taylor and/or you now do regarding the PHC problem?

- ▶ Personal holding companies
- ▶ Corporations exempt from tax under Secs. 501-504
- ▶ S corporations[57]

Theoretically, the accumulated earnings tax applies to both large and small corporations.[58] In practice, however, the accumulated earnings tax only applies to closely held corporations where management can use the corporate dividend policy to reduce the tax liability of the shareholder group.

OBJECTIVE 4

Evaluate whether a corporation has an accumulated earnings tax problem

PROVING A TAX-AVOIDANCE PURPOSE

Section 533(a) provides that the accumulation of E&P by a corporation beyond the reasonable needs of the business indicates a tax-avoidance purpose unless the corporation can prove that the earnings are not being accumulated merely to avoid taxes. In limited circumstances, this burden of proof may be shifted to the IRS under the rules outlined in Sec. 534.

The existence of a tax-avoidance purpose is based on the facts and circumstances of each situation. Under Reg. Sec. 1.533-1(a)(2), the following circumstances indicate a tax-avoidance purpose:

- ▶ Dealings between the corporation and its shareholders (e.g., loans made by the corporation to its shareholders or funds expended by the corporation for the shareholders' benefit).
- ▶ Investments made by the corporation of undistributed earnings in assets having no reasonable connection to the corporation's business.
- ▶ The extent to which the corporation has distributed its E&P (e.g., a low dividend payout rate, low salaries, and a large earnings accumulation may indicate a tax-avoidance purpose).

TAX STRATEGY TIP

If the IRS determines that the accumulation of earnings is unreasonable, the presumption is that the IRS determination is correct. To rebut this presumption, the taxpayer must show that the IRS's determination is improper by a preponderance of the evidence. Thus, periodic updating of the plans to use corporate earnings should be undertaken to reduce accumulated earnings tax problems.

Holding or investment companies are held to a different standard than are operating companies. Section 533(b) provides that the fact that a corporation is a holding or investment company is prima facie evidence of the requisite tax-avoidance purpose.[59] Holding companies, like operating companies, can rebut this presumption by showing that it was neither formed nor availed of for the purpose of avoiding shareholder income taxes.

---

[57] Secs. 532(b) and 1363(a).

[58] Sec. 532(c). See, however, *Technalysis Corporation v. CIR* [101 T.C. 397 (1993)] where the Tax Court held that the accumulated earnings tax can apply to a publicly held corporation regardless of the concentration of ownership or whether the shareholders are actively involved in the operation of the corporation.

[59] Regulation Sec. 1.533-1(c) defines a holding or investment company as "a corporation having no activities except holding property and collecting income therefrom or investing therein."

The presence or absence of a tax-avoidance purpose may be only one of several motives for the corporation's accumulation of corporate earnings. In *U.S. v. The Donruss Company*, the Supreme Court held that tax avoidance does not have to be the dominant motive for the accumulation of earnings for the accumulated earnings tax to be imposed. According to the court, the corporation must know about the tax consequences of accumulating corporate earnings for a tax avoidance purpose to be present.[60] Such knowledge need not be the dominant motive or purpose for the accumulation of the earnings.

EVIDENCE CONCERNING THE REASONABLENESS OF AN EARNINGS ACCUMULATION

The courts have not held a single factor to be indicative of an unreasonable amount of accumulated earnings. Instead, some factors have been found to exhibit evidence of a tax-avoidance motive. Other factors have gained acceptance from the IRS and the courts as reasonable needs of the business for an accumulation of earnings and profits.

TYPICAL MISCONCEPTION

The IRC refers to the existence of a tax-avoidance purpose, which would appear to be a subjective test. However, the existence of the tax-avoidance purpose really hinges on the objective determination of whether a corporation has accumulated earnings beyond the reasonable needs of the business.

EVIDENCE OF A TAX-AVOIDANCE MOTIVE. A corporation that wants to avoid accumulated earnings tax problems should act defensively. Exposure to the accumulated earnings tax can be minimized by limiting the presence of the following factors:

- Loans to shareholders
- Expenditure of corporate funds for the personal benefit of the shareholders
- Loans having no reasonable relation to the conduct of business (e.g., loans made to relatives or friends of shareholders)
- Loans to a corporation controlled by the same shareholders that control the corporation making the loans
- Investments in property or securities unrelated to the activities of the corporation
- Protection against unrealistic hazards[61]

Loans to shareholders or the expenditure of corporate funds for the personal benefit of shareholders act as substitutes for dividend payments to the shareholders. Similarly, corporate loans made to relatives or friends of shareholders are substitutes for paying dividends to shareholders, who then make personal loans to their friends and relatives. All three actions may indicate an unreasonable accumulation of corporate earnings, which instead should be distributed as dividends.

Loans or corporate expenditures made for the benefit of a corporation controlled by the shareholder (or the shareholder group) who controls the payor corporation may be considered to have a tax-avoidance purpose. The corporation instead could make a dividend payment to the shareholder who paid the income taxes on the dividend and then have the shareholder make a capital contribution of the funds to the related corporation.

Other factors not mentioned in Treasury Regulations that are indicative of a tax-avoidance motive include corporations run as holding or investment companies that have a poor dividend payment record.

STOP & THINK

Question: An IRS auditor is examining Baylor Corporation's 1999 C corporation tax return in the year 2002. What information would the auditor use from the tax return to see whether a potential excess earnings accumulation existed that might trigger the imposition of the accumulated earnings tax?

Solution: The auditor would look first at the beginning and year-end balance sheets (Schedule L, Page 4 of Form 1120) to see the retained earnings balances. Next the auditor would review Schedule M-2 (Analysis of Unappropriated Retained Earnings per Books) to see the current year's earnings, the amount of earnings distributed as dividends, and any appropriations of retained earnings that might have occurred during the year. Next,

[60] *U.S. v. The Donruss Company*, 23 AFTR 2d 69-418, 69-1 USTC ¶9167 (USSC, 1969).

[61] Reg. Sec. 1.537-2(c).

the auditor would return to the beginning and year-end balance sheets looking for transactions evidencing a tax-avoidance motive. These transactions might include loans to stockholders (Schedule L, Line 7), loans to persons other than stockholders (Schedule L, Line 6), and portfolio investments (Schedule L, Lines 4, 5, 6, and 9). Information about expenditures of corporate funds made for the personal benefit of shareholders might be found in the noncurrent asset section of the balance sheets (e.g., corporate ownership of a boat, airplane, or second home of a major stockholder).

KEY POINT

In determining whether an accumulation of earnings is reasonable, Treasury Regulations specify the adoption of a "prudent businessman" standard. In applying this standard, the courts are reluctant to substitute their judgment for that of corporate management unless the facts and circumstances clearly suggest that the accumulation of earnings are not for reasonable business needs.

EVIDENCE OF REASONABLE BUSINESS NEEDS. Section 537 defines **reasonable business needs** as

- Reasonably anticipated needs of the business
- Section 303 (death tax) redemption needs
- Excess business holdings redemption needs
- Product liability loss reserves

Regulation Sec. 1.537-1(a) elaborates on this standard by indicating

> An accumulation of the earnings and profits . . . is in excess of reasonable needs of the business if it exceeds the amount that a prudent businessman would consider appropriate for the present business purposes and for the reasonably anticipated future needs of the business. The need to retain earnings and profits must be directly connected with the needs of the corporation itself and must be for bona fide business purposes.

Specific, Definite, and Feasible Plans. A corporation can justify an accumulation of earnings as being for reasonably anticipated future needs only if facts and circumstances indicate that the future needs of the business require such an accumulation. The corporation usually must have specific, definite, and feasible plans for the use of such accumulations.

No Specific Time Limitations. The earnings accumulation need not be used within a short period of time after the close of the tax year, but the plans must provide that the accumulation will be used within a reasonable period of time after the close of the tax year, based on all the facts and circumstances associated with the future needs of the business.

Impact of Subsequent Events. Determination of the reasonably anticipated needs of the business is based on the facts and circumstances that exist at the end of the tax year. Regulation Sec. 1.537-1(b)(2) indicates that subsequent events cannot be used to show that an earnings accumulation is unreasonable if all the elements of reasonable anticipation are present at the close of the tax year. However, subsequent events can be used to determine whether the taxpayer actually intended to consummate the plans for which the earnings are accumulated.

A number of reasons are mentioned in the Treasury Regulations, or have been accepted by the courts, as representing reasonable needs of the business for accumulating earnings.

- Expansion of a business or replacement of plant
- Acquisition of a business enterprise
- Debt retirement
- Working capital
- Loans to suppliers or customers
- Product liability losses
- Stock redemptions
- Business contingencies

Some of the important reasons are now examined.

Expansion of a Business or Replacement of Plant. The IRS and the courts have always accepted the expansion of a corporation's present business facilities or the replacement of existing plant and equipment as reasonable needs of a business. Taxpayers have encountered problems only when the plans are undocumented, indefinite, vague, or infeasible.[62] Although the plans need not be reduced to writing, it is probably best to provide sufficient written documentation.

Acquisition of a Business Enterprise. The acquisition of a business enterprise can involve either the same business or expansion into a new business. It can involve the purchase of either the stock or the assets of the new business. Taxpayers should be careful to acquire a sufficient interest in the new business so that it will not be considered a passive investment.

Working Capital: The Bardahl Formula. Working capital generally is defined as the excess of current assets over current liabilities.The *Bardahl* formula attempts to measure the amount of working capital necessary for an operating cycle. The operating cycle usually includes the period of time needed for acquisition of the inventory, sale of the inventory, and collection of the resulting accounts receivable. Thus, the amount of earnings accumulated to cover one full operating cycle is considered a reasonable business need.

Providing for the needed amount of working capital is considered a reasonable need of a business. The needs of a manufacturing business for working capital differ from those of a service business. At one time, the courts used certain rules of thumb (e.g., a current ratio of 2 to 1 or 3 to 1 or the accumulation of funds to cover a single year's operating expenses) to determine an adequate amount of working capital. However, in the first of two *Bardahl* cases, the Tax Court established a mathematical formula for determining an operating cycle. This formula is now used to ascertain the appropriate amount of working capital in many situations.

For purposes of a manufacturing business, an operating cycle is defined as the "period of time required to convert cash into raw materials, raw materials into an inventory of marketable Bardahl products, the inventory into sales and accounts receivable, and the period of time to collect its outstanding accounts."[63]

In the second *Bardahl* case, the Tax Court determined that amounts advanced to a corporation by its suppliers in the form of short-term credit (e.g., trade payables) reduce the required amount of working capital.[64] The ***Bardahl* formula** for determining the required amount of working capital is as follows:

$$\begin{matrix}\text{Average} \\ \text{operating} \\ \text{cycle}\end{matrix} = \begin{matrix}\text{Inventory} \\ \text{period}\end{matrix} + \begin{matrix}\text{Accounts} \\ \text{receivable} \\ \text{period}\end{matrix} - \begin{matrix}\text{Credit} \\ \text{period}\end{matrix}$$

The *inventory period* in the formula is the time (as a percentage of a year) from the acquisition of the raw materials inventory to the sale of the finished goods inventory. The *accounts receivable period* is the time (as a percentage of a year) from the sale date to the collection of the accounts receivable. The *credit period* is the time (as a percentage of a year) from when the corporation incurs an expense or purchases inventory to when it pays the liability.

The average operating cycle can be expressed with the following equation:

[62] See, for example, *Myron's Enterprises v. U.S.*, 39 AFTR 2d 77-693, 77-1 USTC ¶9253 (9th Cir., 1977) and *Atlas Tool Co., Inc. v. CIR*, 45 AFTR 2d 80-645, 80-1 USTC ¶9177 (3rd Cir., 1980).

[63] *Bardahl Manufacturing Corp.*, 1965 PH T.C. Memo ¶65,200, 24 TCM 1030, at 1044.

[64] *Bardahl International Corp.*, 1966 PH T.C. Memo ¶66,182, 25 TCM 935.

$$\left[\frac{\text{Inventory amount}}{\text{Annual cost of goods sold}} + \frac{\text{Accounts receivable amount}}{\text{Annual sales}} - \frac{\text{Accounts payable amount}}{\text{Annual operating expenses and purchases (less noncash expenses)}}\right] \times 100$$

$$= \text{Average operating cycle (as a percentage of a year)}$$

The average operating cycle and the cash needs of the business for the year are combined to determine the working capital requirements, as follows:

$$\text{Average operating cycle (as a percentage of a year)} \times \left[\text{Cost of goods sold} + \text{Operating expenses}\right] = \text{Working capital requirements}$$

The cost of goods sold is determined on a full-cost basis (i.e., including both direct and indirect expenses). Operating expenses exclude noncash expenses such as depreciation, amortization, and depletion, as well as capital expenditures and charitable contributions. The Tax Court has allowed federal income taxes (e.g., quarterly estimated tax payments) to be included as operating expenses as well as permitting an adjustment to the operating cycle calculation for an inflation factor.[65]

The working capital requirements for one operating cycle of the business are compared with the actual working capital available at year-end. If the working capital requirements exceed the corporation's actual working capital, this need for additional working capital can be used, along with any specific needs of the business, to justify accumulating a portion of the corporation's earnings. If the working capital requirements are less than the corporation's actual working capital, the excess working capital generally is treated as an unreasonable accumulation and available for distribution to the shareholders unless some other justification for its accumulation can be determined (e.g., plant replacement).

TYPICAL MISCONCEPTION

No exact method exists for determining the working capital needs of a corporation. The *Bardahl* formula is merely a rule of thumb adopted by the Tax Court. Even the correct measurement of the components (peak cycle approach versus the average cycle approach) of the *Bardahl* formula is subject to dispute among the courts.

The *Bardahl* formula may provide a false sense of mathematical exactness in calculating working capital because the IRS and the courts have interpreted it differently. Some courts have used the peak month inventory, accounts receivable, and trade payables turnover amounts (instead of an annual average) to determine the length of an operating cycle.[66] The peak month method generally lengthens the corporation's operating cycle. Use of these two different methods can lead to very different estimates of working capital needs. As a result, significant disputes have arisen between the IRS and taxpayers over what constitutes an appropriate working capital amount.

EXAMPLE C5-20 ▶

Austin Corporation's managers believe that Austin may have an accumulated earnings tax problem and ask that its working capital requirements on December 31 of the current year be determined using the *Bardahl* formula. The following information is available from Austin's records for the current year.

Cost of goods sold	$2,700,000
Average inventory	675,000
Purchases	3,000,000
Sales (all on account)	6,000,000
Average accounts receivable	750,000
Operating expenses (including depreciation and other noncash expenditures)	875,000
Depreciation and other noncash expenditures	75,000
Average trade payables	350,000
Federal income taxes	100,000
Working capital on December 31	825,000

Calculation of the operating cycle using the annual average method takes place as follows:

[65] *Doug-Long, Inc.*, 72 T.C. 158 (1979).

[66] *State Office Supply, Inc.*, 1982 PH T.C. Memo ¶82,292, 43 TCM 1481.

$$\text{Inventory turnover} = (\$675{,}000 \div \$2{,}700{,}000) \times 365 = 91.25 \text{ days}$$
$$\text{Receivables turnover} = (\$750{,}000 \div \$6{,}000{,}000) \times 365 = 45.625 \text{ days}$$
$$\text{Payables turnover} = \frac{\$350{,}000}{\$3{,}000{,}000 + \$800{,}000} \times 365 = 33.62 \text{ days}$$
$$\text{Operating cycle} = \frac{91.25 + 45.625 - 33.62}{365} \times 100 = 28.3\% \text{ of a year}$$

Using the operating cycle determined above, an estimate of the working capital requirement can be calculated as follows:

$$\text{Annual operating expenses} = \$2{,}700{,}000 + \$875{,}000 - \$75{,}000 + \$100{,}000 = \$3{,}600{,}000$$
$$\text{Working capital requirement} = \$3{,}600{,}000 \times 0.283 = \$1{,}018{,}800^{a}$$

[a] Removal of the estimated federal income tax payments from the annual operating expenses would reduce the calculated working capital requirement.

The calculated working capital amount of $1,018,800 is $193,800 more than the $825,000 of actual working capital available on December 31. This calculation apparently permits Austin to justify retaining additional current year earnings by needing to expand its working capital. ◀

The *Bardahl* formula also is used to estimate the working capital needs of service companies. A different calculation is used because service companies do not have the same inventory needs. For service companies, one looks primarily to the company's need to finance its accounts receivables. Because the maintenance of an adequate labor supply is important, service companies also need to maintain adequate working capital to retain key personnel when a below-normal level of business is expected. Therefore, some amount may be added to the basic working capital needs to cover the cost of retaining this part of the labor force for a period of time.[67]

REAL-WORLD EXAMPLE

Apparently, an accumulation of funds to redeem stock where a buy–sell agreement exists is not an acceptable business need. Even though a 50% shareholder was killed in a plane crash shortly after the year-end, the Tax Court refused to recognize the validity of an accumulation to redeem such shareholder's stock (*Technalysis Corp.*, 101 T.C. 397 (1993).

Stock Redemptions. Section 537(a) permits corporations to accumulate earnings for two types of stock redemptions: Sec. 303 (death tax) redemptions and excess business holdings redemptions. In the first situation, earnings can be accumulated after the death of the shareholder to redeem stock from the shareholder's estate or a beneficiary of the estate. These earnings cannot exceed the amount that can be redeemed under the Sec. 303 rules. In the second situation, a corporation can accumulate earnings to redeem stock held by a private foundation in excess of the business holdings limit of Sec. 4943.

WHAT WOULD YOU DO IN THIS SITUATION?

Magnum Corporation, your client, has manufactured handguns and rifles for a number of years. Due to competition from foreign manufacturers, demand for U.S. produced guns has declined in recent years. Magnum's total operating assets at the end of its most recent fiscal year were $10 million at historical cost. Total gross operating revenues were $18 million. Over the years, the company accumulated $2.5 million of earnings that Magnum's CEO (Allen Blay) invested in a stock and bond portfolio. The portfolio consists primarily of growth stocks and some debt instruments with very little money invested in internet stocks. Along with his other duties as CEO, Allen manages the investment portfolio. With the recent strong performance of the stock market, Magnum's investment portfolio has done well and has increased in value to more than $12 million. The portfolio took only a small "hit" in Fall 2001. The dividend and interest income received from the portfolio is only a small portion of Magnum's gross income. During a meeting with the client, Allen brings this investment and its performance to your attention. Does Magnum have an accumulated earnings tax problem? What action(s) do you recommend it take?

[67] See, for example, *Simons-Eastern Co. v. U.S.*, 31 AFTR 2d 73-640, 73-1 USTC ¶9279 (D.C. GA, 1972).

Business Contingencies. The courts have permitted corporations to accumulate earnings for a number of business contingencies that were not specifically sanctioned in the Sec. 537 Treasury Regulations. Among the events recognized by the IRS audit guidelines and the courts as business contingencies for which earnings can properly be accumulated are actual or potential litigation, a decline in business activities following the loss of a major customer, a reserve for self-insurance against a particular loss, a threatened strike, and an employee retirement plan.

OBJECTIVE 5

Calculate the amount of the corporation's accumulated earnings tax liability

DETERMINING THE ACCUMULATED EARNINGS TAX LIABILITY

Determination of the accumulated earnings tax liability is illustrated in Figure C5-3. The accumulated earnings tax is levied at a 38.6% rate (in 2002). As with the PHC penalty tax, a corporation can reduce its tax base by making dividend distributions. However, corporations generally do not avail themselves of this tax planning strategy because they often pay only a nominal dividend or no dividend and because the accumulated earnings tax issue usually is not raised by the IRS auditors until one or more years after the corporation files its tax return. Unlike the PHC penalty tax, once the IRS or the courts have determined that the corporation owes the accumulated earnings tax, its payment cannot be avoided by paying deficiency dividends.

ADDITIONAL COMMENT

Accumulated taxable income should not be confused with current E&P. In fact, the accumulated earnings tax has been assessed in years where no increase in the corporation's E&P occurred.

ACCUMULATED TAXABLE INCOME. The starting point for the **accumulated taxable income** calculation is the corporation's taxable income. A series of positive and negative adjustments to taxable income are needed to arrive at the accumulated taxable income.

ADDITIONAL COMMENT

The accumulated earnings tax adjustments derive an amount that more closely corresponds to the corporation's economic income and thus better measures the dividend-paying capability of the corporation than does taxable income.

Positive Adjustments to Taxable Income. As with the PHC penalty tax, a corporation is prohibited from claiming a dividends-received deduction. Thus, taxable income must be increased by the amount of the dividends-received deduction claimed when determining the regular tax liability.[68]

The amount of any NOL deduction claimed when determining taxable income also must be added back to determine accumulated taxable income. Unlike with the PHC tax, no special deduction is provided for an NOL incurred in the immediately preceding year.

▼ FIGURE C5-3
Determining the Accumulated Earnings Tax Liability

Taxable income
Plus: Positive adjustments
1. Dividends-received deduction claimed
2. NOL deduction claimed
3. Excess charitable contributions carried over from a preceding tax year and deducted in determining taxable income
4. Capital loss carryover deduction

Minus: Negative adjustments
1. Accrued U.S. and foreign income taxes
2. Charitable contributions made in excess of the 10% corporate limitation
3. Net capital losses (if capital losses for the year exceed capital gains)
4. Net capital gain minus the amount of any income taxes attributed to it

Minus: Dividends-paid deduction claimed
Minus: Accumulated earnings credit

Accumulated taxable income
Times: 0.386 (in 2002)

Accumulated earnings tax

[68] Sec. 535(b).

Negative Adjustments to Taxable Income. Charitable contributions are deductible without regard to either the 10% corporate limitation or the individual charitable contribution limitations. The same adjustments required for PHC tax purposes are required here.

U.S. and foreign income taxes accrued by the corporation reduce accumulated taxable income whether the corporation uses the accrual or cash method of accounting.

A corporation is permitted a deduction for the amount of its net capital gain, minus the income taxes attributable to the net capital gain. The capital gains adjustment prevents a corporation having large capital gains from paying the accumulated earnings tax on the portion of the gains retained in the business. Net capital losses (the excess of capital losses for the year over capital gains) also are a negative adjustment to taxable income.

Dividends-Paid Deduction. The dividends-paid deduction is available for four types of dividends:

- Dividends paid during the tax year
- Throwback dividends
- Consent dividends
- Liquidating distributions

With some minor exceptions, the rules for the dividends-paid deduction are the same as for the PHC tax. Nonliquidating distributions paid during the tax year are eligible for the dividends-paid deduction only if paid from the corporation's E&P. A dividends-paid deduction is not available for preferential dividends.[69]

Throwback dividends are distributions made out of E&P in the first 2½ months following the close of the tax year. The accumulated earnings tax rules mandate that any distribution made in the first 2½ months following the close of the tax year must be treated as if paid on the last day of the preceding tax year without regard to the amount of actual dividends paid during the preceding tax year.[70] Because the accumulated earnings tax issue usually is not raised until the IRS audits the corporation's tax return, throwback dividends and consent dividends have limited value in avoiding the accumulated earnings tax.

Liquidating distributions made by corporations are eligible for the dividends-paid deduction. Eligible distributions include those made in connection with a complete liquidation, a partial liquidation, or a stock redemption.[71]

ADDITIONAL COMMENT

The minimum accumulated earnings credit is $250,000 ($150,000 for certain personal service corporations) reduced by the accumulated E&P at the close of the preceding year. In many situations, however, corporations that have been in existence for some time have accumulated E&P exceeding $250,000. Thus, the minimum credit is often of little practical significance.

Accumulated Earnings Credit. The accumulated earnings credit permits every corporation to accumulate with impunity E&P either up to a minimum ($250,000 for most C corporations) threshold level (so as to eliminate the need to worry about the accumulated earnings tax until the threshold has been reached), or up to the level of its earnings accumulated for the reasonable needs of the business. Unlike other credits, the **accumulated earnings credit** does not offset the accumulated earnings tax liability on a dollar-for-dollar basis. Instead, it serves to reduce accumulated taxable income. Different rules for the accumulated earnings credit exist for operating companies, service companies, and holding or investment companies.[72]

- Operating companies can claim a credit equal to the greater of (1) $250,000 minus the accumulated E&P at the end of the preceding tax year[73] or (2) the current E&P retained to meet the reasonable needs of the business.
- The accumulated E&P balance used in (1) above to compute the accumulated earnings credit is reduced by the amount of any throwback distributions paid during the current year treated as having been paid out of the preceding year's E&P.
- Current E&P is reduced by any dividends-paid deduction claimed. Any net capital gains (reduced by federal taxes attributable to the gain) reduce the current E&P retained for business needs.

TYPICAL MISCONCEPTION

The maximum accumulated earnings credit is the amount of current E&P retained to meet the reasonable needs of the business minus an adjustment for net capital gains. This amount does not include the entire accumulation needed for business needs but only the accumulation in the current tax year. Thus, to calculate the maximum credit, it is necessary to determine how much of the prior accumulations are retained for reasonable business needs.

---

69 Sec. 562(c). See page C5-22 for a more detailed discussion.

70 Sec. 563(a). Personal holding companies, on the other hand, must elect throwback treatment for dividends paid in the 2½ month period following the end of the tax year.

71 Sec. 562(b)(1)(B).

72 Sec. 535(c).

73 Section 1561(a)(2) limits controlled groups to a single statutory exemption.

- Special rules apply to personal service companies providing their principal services in the fields of health, law, engineering, architecture, accounting, actuarial science, performing arts, and consulting. The basic calculation described above still applies, but the $250,000 minimum credit is reduced to $150,000 for these companies.
- Holding and investment companies can claim a credit equal to $250,000 minus the accumulated E&P at the end of the preceding tax year. An increased credit is not available to a holding or investment company based on the reasonable needs of the business.

EXAMPLE C5-21 ▶ Midway Corporation, a C corporation that is not a personal service or investment company, reports accumulated E&P, current E&P, and current E&P retained for business needs as shown in the table below. Its lifetime minimum credit is $250,000. The corporation paid no dividends during the current year.

Tax Characteristics	*Situation Number* One	Two
1. Accumulated E&P from prior years	$ 75,000	$ 75,000
2. Lifetime minimum credit	250,000	250,000
2a. Current year minimum credit (2a = 2 − 1)	175,000	175,000
3. Current E&P	400,000	400,000
3a. Current E&P retained for business needs	300,000	50,000
3b. Current E&P in excess of business needs (3b = 3 − 3a)	100,000	350,000
4. Accumulated earnings credit (Greater of 2a or 3a)	300,000	175,000

In both situations, $175,000 of the lifetime minimum credit remains. In Situation One, the $175,000 lifetime credit that remains is less than the $300,000 of E&P retained for business needs, so the accumulated earnings credit is the $300,000 business needs amount. In Situation Two, the $175,000 lifetime minimum credit that remains is greater than the $50,000 of E&P retained for business needs, so the accumulated earnings credit is the $175,000 remaining lifetime minimum credit. In both situations, no lifetime minimum credit remains to be used in future years. All future accumulated earnings credits are based on E&P retained for business needs. ◀

ACCUMULATED EARNINGS TAX CALCULATION

The following example illustrates the calculation of accumulated taxable income and the determination of the accumulated earnings tax liability.

EXAMPLE C5-22 ▶ Pasadena Corporation is a closely held family corporation that has conducted a highly successful manufacturing operation for a number of years. On January 1 of the current year, Pasadena Corporation has a $750,000 accumulated E&P balance. The following information pertains to the current year's operations:

Operating profit	$650,000
Long-term capital gain	30,000
Dividends (20%-owned corporation)	150,000
Interest	70,000
Gross income	$900,000
Dividends-received deduction	(120,000)
Salaries	(100,000)
General and administrative expenses	(200,000)
Charitable contributions	(60,000)[a]
Taxable income	$420,000

[a] $60,000 = 0.10 × [$900,000 − ($100,000 + $200,000)].

Federal income taxes (using 2002 rates and assuming no alternative minimum tax liability) accrued by Pasadena Corporation are $142,800. Actual charitable contributions are $70,000.

The corporation paid cash dividends of $20,000 on June 30. Pasadena's current E&P retained for the reasonable needs of the business (after reduction for the dividends-paid deduction) is $160,000.

If an IRS agent challenges Pasadena in a later year on the accumulated earnings tax issue, and the facts as noted above are held to be correct, the accumulated earnings tax liability would be calculated as follows:

Taxable income		$420,000
Plus: Dividends-received deduction		120,000
Minus: Excess charitable contributions		(10,000)[a]
Federal income taxes		(142,800)
Long-term capital gain	$ 30,000	
Minus: Federal income taxes	(10,200)[b]	(19,800)
Dividends-paid deduction		(20,000)
Accumulated earnings credit:		
Increase in current year reasonable needs	$160,000	
Minus: Long-term capital gain (net of taxes)	(19,800)	(140,200)
Accumulated taxable income		$207,200
Times: Tax rate		× 0.386
Accumulated earnings tax liability		$ 79,979

[a] $70,000 total contributions − $60,000 limitation = $10,000 excess contributions.
[b] $10,200 = $30,000 × 0.34

Assuming the corporation owes no AMT liability, Pasadena's total federal tax liability for the current year is $222,779 ($142,800 + $79,979). ◀

Topic Review C5-4 presents an overview of the accumulated earnings penalty tax.

Topic Review C5-4

Accumulated Earnings Tax

1. The accumulated earnings tax applies to all corporations except ones specially excluded (e.g., S corporations). In practice, the accumulated earnings tax applies only to closely held corporations.
2. Transactions that provide evidence of a tax avoidance motive generally lead IRS auditors to conclude that an accumulated earnings tax problem exists. These transactions include loans made by the corporation to its shareholders, expenditures of corporate funds for the personal benefit of the shareholders, and investments in property or securities unrelated to the corporation's activities.
3. Earnings accumulated for the reasonable needs of the business are exempt from the accumulated earnings tax. Business needs for retention of earnings include acquisition of a business enterprise, debt retirement, and working capital. A $250,000 lifetime minimum credit is available. This amount is reduced to $150,000 for certain personal service corporations.
4. The accumulated earnings tax equals 38.6% (in 2002) of accumulated taxable income. Accumulated taxable income equals taxable income plus certain positive adjustments (e.g., dividends-received deduction) and minus certain negative adjustments (e.g., federal income taxes, excess charitable contributions, and net capital gain adjustment). A deduction for the accumulated earnings credit also is available equal to the greater of the unused lifetime earnings exemption or the earnings accumulated during the year for the reasonable needs of the business.
5. Accumulated taxable income can be reduced by a dividends-paid deduction for cash and property dividends paid during the year and consent and throwback dividends paid after the year-end. The deficiency dividend opportunity available to PHCs is not available for accumulated earnings tax purposes.

TAX PLANNING CONSIDERATIONS

This section examines three areas of tax planning: making special accounting method elections for AMT purposes, avoiding the personal holding company (PHC) tax, and avoiding the accumulated earnings tax.

SPECIAL AMT ELECTIONS

ADDITIONAL COMMENT

Not only can these special AMT elections reduce a taxpayer's AMT liability, but these elections also should reduce compliance costs by eliminating the need to keep an additional set of depreciation or amortization records.

Two special elections are available under the AMT rules that permit taxpayers to defer the claiming of certain deductions for income tax purposes. The deferral of these deductions will increase the taxpayer's regular tax liability but can provide an overall savings by reducing the taxpayer's AMT liability.

Section 59(e) permits an extended writeoff period to apply to certain expenditures that otherwise would be tax preference items or adjustments. If the corporation elects the extended writeoff period, Section 59(e)(6) exempts each expenditure from being a tax preference item under Sec. 57, or prevents an adjustment from having to be made for the expenditure under Sec. 56. The expenditures for which the special election can be made and the extended writeoff periods that apply are as follows:

IRC Section	*Type of Expenditure*	*Writeoff Period*
173	Circulation	3 yrs.
174	Research and experimental	10 yrs.
263	Intangible drilling and development	5 yrs.
616	Mining and natural resource development	10 yrs.
617	Mining exploration	10 yrs.

The corporation can make the special election with respect to any portion of a qualified expenditure and can revoke it only with IRS consent.[74]

The second election permits taxpayers to elect to use the depreciation method generally required for AMT purposes—the 150% declining balance method for personal property—in computing their regular tax liability. Such an election permits the taxpayer to change the depreciation method for personal property placed in service after 1998 from the 200% declining balance method to the 150% declining balance method. The election is not relevant for nonresidential real property or residential rental property because, for such property placed in service after 1998, AMT depreciation is the same as regular tax depreciation. By making this election, the taxpayer reduces or eliminates the amount of annual AMT depreciation adjustments and basis adjustments. The taxpayer may make this election with respect to one or more classes of property for any tax year and, once made with respect to a class of property, it applies to all property in such class placed in service during the tax year. The taxpayer must make the election by the due date for its return (including any permissible extensions).[75]

ELIMINATING THE ACE ADJUSTMENT

C corporations must increase their AMTI by the amount of the ACE adjustment. This adjustment can be significant for some C corporations. If the C corporation is closely held, it can elect to be taxed as an S corporation and the ACE adjustment can be avoided.[76] S corporations are not subject to the corporate AMT. These entities pass their adjustments and preferences through to their shareholders.

74 Secs. 59(e)(4)(A) and (B).
75 Secs. 168(b)(2) and (5).
76 Sec. 56(g)(6).

OBJECTIVE 6

Explain how a corporation can avoid being subject to the personal holding company tax

AVOIDING THE PERSONAL HOLDING COMPANY TAX

Five types of tax planning can be used to avoid the PHC tax, as discussed in the following sections.

MAKING CHANGES IN THE CORPORATION'S STOCK OWNERSHIP. Additional stock can be sold to unrelated parties to avoid having five or fewer shareholders owning more than 50% (in value) of the stock at any time during the last half of the tax year. Sales of either common or preferred stock can be made. The sale of nonvoting preferred stock to unrelated parties permits the corporation's stock ownership to be spread among a larger number of individuals without diluting the voting power of the current shareholder group.

CHANGING THE AMOUNT AND TYPE OF INCOME EARNED BY THE CORPORATION. Several tax planning options are available to change the amount and type of corporate income. These include

- Adding additional "operating" activities to the corporation's line of business. Passive income will become a smaller portion of the corporation's total income.
- Converting taxable interest or dividend income earned on an investment portfolio into nontaxable interest income or long-term capital gains. Nontaxable interest income and long-term capital gains are not included in the PHCI definition and, therefore, cannot cause a corporation to be a PHC.
- Adding additional passive income of a type that either is eligible to be excluded from PHCI or reduces the amount of other PHCI earned. For example, a corporation might increase the proportion of its income earned from rents to exceed the 50% of AOGI requirement to exclude adjusted income from rents from PHCI.

KEY POINT

One of the easiest methods of avoiding the PHC penalty tax is through a dividend distribution. If a corporation lacks the funds to pay a dividend, a consent dividend (which is a hypothetical dividend) may be useful. In addition, throwback, consent, and deficiency dividends can be declared after year-end to help in after-the-fact tax planning.

MAKING DIVIDEND DISTRIBUTIONS. Dividends reduce the tax base used to levy the PHC tax. The inclusion in PHCI of certain income forms (e.g., adjusted income from rents) can be avoided by paying enough dividends to reduce the amount of other PHCI to 10% of OGI or less. Some of these dividends (e.g., throwback dividends, consent dividends, and deficiency dividends) can be paid after year-end to engage in last-minute tax planning.

MAKING AN S ELECTION. An S election prevents the imposition of the PHC tax because S corporations are exempt from the penalty tax. Such an election is less attractive than in the past because the top individual tax rates are now above the corporate tax rates, but the election may be used to avoid double taxation of corporate earnings distributed as dividends (see Chapter C11).

LIQUIDATING THE CORPORATION. A PHC could be liquidated and have the assets held by the shareholders instead. Liquidating distributions made by a PHC are eligible for the dividends-paid deduction when made out of the PHC's E&P and can reduce the UPHCI amount. This alternative may be unattractive because the top individual tax rates are now above the corporate tax rates, but it may avoid double taxation of corporate earnings distributed as dividends.

OBJECTIVE 7

Explain how a corporation can avoid being subject to the accumulated earnings tax

AVOIDING THE ACCUMULATED EARNINGS TAX

The primary defense against an IRS position that the corporation has accumulated an unreasonable amount of earnings is to document that the earnings accumulations are necessary to meet the future capital needs of the business. The existence of these business plans must be documented each year. The plans, which should be as specific as possible, should be revised periodically. Completed projects should be documented. Abandoned projects should be eliminated from the plan. A tentative timetable for the current set of projects is a positive factor for the corporation should an IRS challenge be encountered. Such plans might be incorporated into the minutes of one or more board of directors meetings.

Transactions that indicate an unreasonable earnings accumulation (e.g., loans to shareholders or large investment portfolios) should be avoided. The business purpose for engaging in any transaction that appears to indicate an unreasonable earnings accumulation should be thoroughly documented.

Corporations that have a potential accumulated earnings tax problem should consider making an S election. S corporations can avoid accumulated earnings tax problems only on a prospective basis. Thus, an S election does not eliminate the possibility that the penalty tax might be imposed for a tax year prior to the initial S election year in which the IRS determines that an unreasonable earnings accumulation exists.

COMPLIANCE AND PROCEDURAL CONSIDERATIONS

ALTERNATIVE MINIMUM TAX

The corporate AMT liability is reported on Form 4626 (Alternative Minimum Tax—Corporations). A completed Form 4626 is included in Appendix B that uses the facts in the comprehensive example on pages C5-12 and C5-13.

Chapter C3 discussed the corporate estimated tax payment requirements. Section 6655(g) includes the corporate AMT liability as part of the required annual payment. Therefore, corporations must estimate their AMT liability properly when making their quarterly payments or possibly be subject to the underpayment penalties described in Sec. 6655.

PERSONAL HOLDING COMPANY TAX

ETHICAL POINT

A tax practitioner has a responsibility to advise his or her client early in the year about potential PHC problems and steps that can be taken to avoid the penalty tax. Because the PHC tax is self-assessed, a Schedule PH must be filed with the Form 1120 even if the corpoation owes no PHC tax.

FILING REQUIREMENTS FOR TAX RETURNS. A PHC must file a corporate income tax return (Form 1120). Schedule PH must accompany the return. Schedule PH includes the steps necessary to determine whether the corporation is a PHC and to calculate the UPHCI and PHC tax amounts. Regulation Sec. 301.6501(f)-1 extends the statute of limitations for the PHC penalty tax from three to six years if a PHC fails to file the Schedule PH, even if the corporation owes no additional tax.

PAYMENT OF THE TAX, INTEREST, AND PENALTIES. Corporations ordinarily pay the PHC tax when they file their Form 1120 and Schedule PH or when the IRS or the courts determine that the corporation owes the tax. The penalty tax is not part of the corporation's required estimated tax payments. Corporations that pay the PHC penalty tax after the due date for filing their return (without regard to any extensions) generally will also owe interest and penalties on the unpaid PHC tax from the date the return is originally due (without regard to any extensions) until the tax is paid.[77]

ETHICAL POINT

A tax practitioner has a responsibility to advise his or her client during the year about potential accumulated earnings tax problems and steps to be taken to avoid the penalty tax. Because the accumulated earnings tax is not self-assessed, there is no requirement that the CPA or the client notify the IRS of any potential accumulated earnings tax problem.

ACCUMULATED EARNINGS TAX

No formal schedule or return is required of a corporation that owes the accumulated earnings tax. Because of the subjective nature of this tax, a firm generally will not pay the penalty tax until some time after the IRS has audited its income tax return. Because the corporation does not pay the tax when it files the return, Sec. 6601(b) requires interest to be charged on the accumulated earnings tax from the date the return is originally due (without regard to any extensions) until the date the tax payment is received.[78] The penalty for negligent underpayment of taxes imposed by Sec. 6653 may be assessed in accumulated earnings tax situations.[79]

---

[77] *Hart Metal Products Corp. v. U.S.*, 38 AFTR 2d 76-6118, 76-2 USTC ¶9781 (Ct. Cls., 1976).

[78] Rev. Rul. 87-54, 1987-1 C.B. 349.

[79] Rev. Rul. 75-330, 1975-2 C.B. 496.

PROBLEM MATERIALS

DISCUSSION QUESTIONS

C5-1 Explain the legislative intent behind enacting the alternative minimum tax (AMT):

C5-2 Define the following terms connected with the AMT:
a. Tax preference item
b. Adjustment item
c. Alternative minimum taxable income
d. Statutory exemption amount
e. Tentative minimum tax
f. Minimum tax credit

C5-3 What special rules (if any) apply to the calculation of the AMT liability for the following corporate forms:
a. Small corporations
b. Closely-held corporations
c. S corporations

C5-4 Agnew Corporation operates a small manufacturing business. During the fourth tax year (2002), the company reported gross income of $1 million. The gross income originated from sales of small toys that Agnew manufactured and sold for $4.5 million. Agnew's cost of goods sold was $3.5 million. Taxable income was $125,000. The corporation's owner estimates that future sales will grow at 25% per year. Agnew Corporation is not related to any other C corporations. Does Agnew's CPA need to calculate the corporation's alternative minimum tax in the initial year? In any of the next five years? Explain.

C5-5 Seminole Corporation began conducting business in the current year. Its gross receipts for the first year are less than $1 million. Austin and Frank each own 50% of Seminole's stock. The same two individuals also own equally three other corporations that have had gross receipts totaling $10 million or more in the current year and in the three preceding years. Explain to your clients whether Seminole and its sister corporations will be exempt from the corporate AMT in the current year.

C5-6 Dunn Corporation's taxable income is less than $40,000. The corporation is not eligible for the small corporation exemption. The CPA preparing the corporate tax return does not calculate the AMT liability because he knows that taxable income is less than the AMT statutory exemption. Is he correct in his action? Explain.

C5-7 Determine whether the following statements are true or false for the corporate AMT. If false, explain why the statement is false.
a. Tax preference items may either increase or decrease AMTI.
b. The same NOL carryover amount is used for regular tax and AMTI purposes.
c. The minimum tax credit is the entire amount by which the tentative minimum tax exceeds the regular tax.
d. A corporate taxpayer's general business credit can offset not only its regular tax liability but also its AMT liability.
e. The ACE adjustment can increase or decrease preadjustment AMTI.
f. The corporate AMT is levied on and paid by both C corporations and S corporations.
g. The minimum tax credit can be carried back and forward.

C5-8 Identify the following items as adjustments to taxable income (A), a tax preference item (P), or none of the above (N):
a. Percentage depletion claimed in excess of a property's adjusted basis at the end of the tax year.
b. MACRS depreciation claimed on tangible personal property placed in service after 1986 and before 1999 in excess of the depreciation claimed under the alternative depreciation system.
c. Difference between gain reported on the sale of the asset in Part b when determining taxable income and alternative minimum taxable income.
d. Accelerated cost recovery deduction claimed on real estate placed in service before 1987 in excess of a hypothetical straight-line depreciation allowance.
e. Tax-exempt interest on State of Michigan private activity bonds.
f. Tax-exempt interest on State of Michigan general revenue bonds.
g. 75% of the excess of adjusted current earnings (ACE) over preadjustment AMTI.

C5-9 What adjustment must be made if ACE exceeds preadjustment AMTI? Is less than preadjustment AMTI? What restrictions are placed on negative ACE adjustments?

C5-10 Florida Corporation encounters a problem with the AMT for the first time in the current year. The problem is due to a $2 million gain on a nondealer installment sale being reported over ten years for financial accounting and taxable income purposes and is fully included in the current year ACE. Explain the ACE adjustment to Florida Corporation's president, how the adjustment is similar to and different from the E&P concept with which he is familiar, and whether the adjustment will turn around in future years.

C5-11 Some tax authorities say a positive ACE adjustment can produce three different effective tax rates depending on the corporation's tax situation: (1) a 0% effective tax rate, (2) a 15% effective tax rate, or (3) between a 0% and 15% effective tax rate. Explain what the tax authorities are talking about.

C5-12 Indicate whether the following items are included in taxable income, preadjustment AMTI, and ACE.

a. Tax-exempt interest on private activity bonds
b. Proceeds of a life insurance policy on a corporate officer that has no cash surrender value
c. Gain on current year sale of Sec. 1231 property that a nondealer reports using the installment method of accounting.
d. Intangible drilling costs incurred and deducted in the current year
e. Amortization of organizational expenditures incurred last year
f. Dividends-received deduction claimed with respect to a dividend received from a 10%-owned domestic corporation.

C5-13 Describe the taxable income, AMTI, and ACE depreciation rules that apply for the following types of property acquired in 2000 and later tax years.

a. Section 1250 property—a factory building.
b. Section 1245 property—a drill press.

C5-14 Burbank Corporation incurs an AMT liability for the first time in the current year. The liability is due entirely to an ACE adjustment resulting from the receipt of $4 million of life insurance proceeds paid on the death of the firm's Chief Executive Officer in a plane crash. The policy had no cash surrender value. Explain to Burbank's director of taxes whether it is possible to reduce future regular tax liabilities by the AMT liability paid in the current year.

C5-15 The personal holding company tax and the accumulated earnings tax both represent attempts to prevent the corporate entity from being used to avoid taxation. Explain the congressional intent behind these two tax levies.

C5-16 Which of the following special corporate forms are exempt from the PHC tax? The accumulated earnings tax?

a. Closely held corporations
b. S corporations
c. Professional corporations
d. Tax-exempt organizations
e. Publicly held corporations
f. Corporations filing a consolidated tax return
g. Limited liability company

C5-17 Carolina Corporation has always earned 30% to 40% of its gross income from passive sources due to the outstanding performance of its investments. For a number of years, the corporation has held a block of stock in a corporation that was recently acquired in a takeover. A substantial long-term capital gain has been recognized that will increase this year's investment income to 70% of gross income. Explain to the Carolina's president why she should or should not be worried about the personal holding company penalty tax in the current year.

C5-18 Which of the following types of income are included in the definition of personal holding company income (PHCI) when received by a corporation? Indicate whether any special circumstances would exclude a type of income that is generally included in PHCI.

a. Dividends
b. Interest from a corporate bond
c. Interest from a general revenue bond issued by a state government
d. Rental income from a warehouse leased to a third party
e. Rental income from a warehouse leased to the corporation's sole shareholder
f. Royalty income from a book whose copyright is owned by the corporation
g. Royalty income from a computer software copyright developed by the corporation and leased to a software marketing firm
h. Accounting fees earned by a professional corporation that has three equal shareholders and offers public accounting services to a variety of clients
i. Long-term capital gain earned on the sale of a stock investment

C5-19 Which of the following dividend payments are eligible for a dividends-paid deduction when computing the PHC tax? The accumulated earnings tax?

a. Cash dividend paid on common stock during the tax year
b. Annual cash dividend paid on preferred stock where no dividend is paid to the common stock shareholders
c. Dividend payable in the stock of an unrelated corporation
d. Stock dividend payable in the single class of stock of the distributing corporation
e. Cash dividend paid two months after the close of the tax year

C5-20 Define the term *consent dividend*. How can a consent dividend be used to avoid the personal holding company and accumulated earnings penalty taxes? In each case, what requirements must be satisfied by the distributing corporation and/or its shareholders before a consent dividend is eligible for a dividends-paid deduction? What are the tax consequences of a consent dividend to the shareholders and the distributing corporation?

C5-21 Explain the advantages of paying a deficiency dividend. What requirements must be satisfied by the PHC and its shareholders before a deficiency dividend can be used to reduce or eliminate the PHC tax liability? Can a deficiency dividend eliminate the interest and penalties imposed in addition to the PHC penalty tax?

C5-22 Determine whether the following statements about the PHC tax are true or false:
- **a.** A corporation may not owe any PHC tax liability for a tax year even though it is classified as a PHC.
- **b.** A sale of a large tract of land held for investment purposes can cause a manufacturing corporation to be classified as a PHC.
- **c.** Federal income taxes (including the alternative minimum tax) accrued by the PHC reduce the UPHCI amount for the tax year.
- **d.** Consent dividends can be paid any time from the first day of the tax year through the due date for the corporation's income tax return (including any permitted extensions) and reduce the UPHCI amount.
- **e.** The payment of a deficiency dividend permits a PHC to eliminate its PHC tax liability as well as any interest and penalties imposed in addition to the liability.
- **f.** A corporation classified as a PHC for a tax year also can be liable for the accumulated earnings tax for that year.
- **g.** A PHC can be subject to the alternative minimum tax.

C5-23 Explain the implication of the following statement: Like many dogs, the threat (bark) of the personal holding company tax is much worse than the actual penalties that are assessed (bite).

C5-24 Explain the following statement: Although the accumulated earnings tax can be imposed on both publicly held and closely held corporations, it is likely to be imposed only on closely held corporations.

C5-25 The accumulated earnings tax is imposed only when the corporation is "formed or availed of for the purpose of avoiding the income tax." Does tax avoidance have to occur at the corporate or the shareholder level for the penalty tax to be imposed? Does tax avoidance have to be the sole motivation for the earnings accumulation before the penalty tax is imposed?

C5-26 How is it possible for a newly formed corporation in its first year of operation to be subject to the personal holding company tax but exempt from the alternative minimum tax and the accumulated earnings tax?

C5-27 Gamma Corporation has substantial cash flows from its manufacturing activities. Only a moderate need exists to reinvest its earnings in replacement of existing facilities or expansion. In recent years, a large investment portfolio has been accumulated because management has been unwilling to pay dividends due to the possibility of double taxation of the corporate profits. The corporation is in no danger of being classified as a PHC but is concerned about its exposure to the accumulated earnings tax. Explain to Gamma's president what actions can be taken to avoid the possibility of having an accumulated earnings tax penalty imposed in the current year? In future tax years?

C5-28 Explain the operation of the *Bardahl* formula. Why have some tax authorities said that this formula implies a greater amount of mathematical accuracy than actually may be present when determining working capital needs? Does the *Bardahl* formula apply to service companies?

C5-29 Different rules apply to operating companies, holding and investment companies, and service companies when determining the accumulated earnings credit. Explain these differences.

C5-30 Determine whether the following statements about the accumulated earnings tax are true or false:
- **a.** Before the IRS can impose the accumulated earnings tax, it only needs to show that tax avoidance was one of the motives for the corporation's unreasonable accumulation of earnings.
- **b.** Long-term capital gains are included in the tax base for the accumulated earnings tax.
- **c.** Each corporation that is a member of a controlled group can claim a separate $150,000 or $250,000 accumulated earnings credit.
- **d.** A dividends-paid deduction can be claimed for both cash and property distributions (other than nontaxable stock dividends) paid by a corporation.
- **e.** The accumulated earnings tax liability cannot be eliminated by paying a deficiency dividend.
- **f.** Interest and penalties on the accumulated earnings tax deficiency are imposed only from the date the IRS or the courts determine that the liability is owed.
- **g.** The accumulated earnings tax is reported on Form 1120-AET that is filed with the corporate tax return.

C5-31 For each of the following statements, indicate whether the statement is correct for the PHC tax only (P), the accumulated earnings tax only (A), both penalty taxes (B), or neither penalty tax (N).
- **a.** The penalty tax is imposed only if the corporation satisfies certain stock ownership and income requirements.
- **b.** The penalty tax applies to both closely held and publicly held corporations.
- **c.** The penalty tax is subjective in nature.
- **d.** Long-term capital gains are a neutral factor in determining the amount of the penalty tax levy.
- **e.** Tax-exempt interest income is excluded in determining the tax base used to levy the penalty tax.
- **f.** A credit is available that reduces the penalty tax liability on a dollar-for-dollar basis.
- **g.** Throwback dividends are permitted to be paid without limit.
- **h.** Consent dividends are eligible for a dividends-paid deduction.
- **i.** Throwback and consent dividends are effective tools for reducing or eliminating the penalty tax liability.
- **j.** The penalty tax can be avoided by making a deficiency dividend distribution.
- **k.** The penalty tax applies to S corporations.

ISSUE IDENTIFICATION QUESTIONS

C5-32 Bird Corporation purchases a new precision casting machine for its manufacturing facility costing $1 million. Installation costs are $75,000. The machine is placed in service in June 2002. The old casting machine, which was placed in service in 1993, was sold to an unrelated party at a $125,000 financial accounting profit. What asset disposition and capital recovery issues do you, as Bird's director of federal taxes, need to address when removing the old machine from, and placing the new machine on, the financial accounting and tax books and in calculating the 2002 tax depreciation?

C5-33 Parrish Corporation is a closely held C corporation with all the stock owned by Robert and Kim Parrish. The corporation, in its second month of operation in its initial tax year, anticipates earning $200,000 of gross income in the current year. Gross income is expected to be approximately 40% dividends, 30% corporate bond interest, and 30% net real estate rentals (after interest, property taxes, and depreciation). Administrative expenses are expected to be $10,000. What special problems does the large amount of passive income that Parrish Corporation expects to earn present to you as their CPA?

C5-34 McHale Corporation is a C corporation owned by eight individuals. Three shareholders own 51% of the stock and make up the board of directors. The corporation has a successful automobile repair parts manufacturing business. It has accumulated $2 million of E&P and expects to accumulate another $300,000 of E&P annually. Annual dividend payments are $30,000. Because Americans own their vehicles longer than they did 20 years ago, demand for McHale's repair parts has been strong for the past five years. However, little expansion or replacement of the current plant is projected for three to five years. Management has invested $200,000 annually in growth stocks. Its current investment portfolio is $1.2 million, which is held primarily as protection against a business downturn. Loans to shareholder-employees currently are $400,000. As McHale's tax return preparer, what tax issues should you have your client consider?

PROBLEMS

C5-35 ***Small Corporation AMT Exemption.*** Willis Corporation reports the following gross receipts for its initial years of operation.

Year	*Gross Receipts*
2002	$ 2,500,000
2003	5,000,000
2004	6,000,000
2005	9,000,000
2006	10,000,000
2007	12,000,000

Willis Corporation is not related to any other corporations for purposes of applying the gross receipts test, nor is it a successor to another corporation. Year 2002 gross receipts have been annualized. Is Willis Corporation exempt from the corporate alternative minimum tax if it was formed in 2002? Explain.

C5-36 ***Alternative Minimum Tax Calculation.*** Whitaker Corporation reports taxable income of $700,000 for the current year. It had positive AMTI adjustments of $600,000 and tax preference items of $300,000. Whitaker is not eligible for the small corporation exemption.

a. What is Whitaker's AMTI?
b. What is Whitaker's tentative minimum tax?
c. What is Whitaker's regular tax liability?
d. What is Whitaker's AMT liability?
e. What is Whitaker's minimum tax credit?

C5-37 ***Depreciation Calculations.*** Water Corporation placed a machine costing $10,000 in service on June 1, 1996. The machine is seven-year property under the MACRS rules. The machine has a 12-year class life. Using the half-year convention, calculate the annual depreciation deductions for purposes of determining

a. Taxable income
b. Alternative minimum taxable income
c. Are separate depreciation calculations necessary to calculate adjusted current earnings?

How would your answers to Parts a–c change if the machine were instead purchased and placed in service on June 1, 1999?

C5-38 ***Basis Adjustment.*** Assume the same basic facts as in Problem C5-37. Water Corporation sells the machine for $5,000 on August 31, 2002.

a. What gain does Water report for purposes of determining taxable income, AMTI, and adjusted current earnings?
b. If you were using taxable income as the starting point for calculating AMTI, what type of adjustment is needed to properly report the transaction for AMTI purposes?

C5-39 ***ACE Adjustment.*** Calculate the ACE adjustment for Towne Corporation for each year since its incorporation in 1998.

	1998	*1999*	*2000*	*2001*	*2002*
ACE	$500	$500	$500	$500	$(500)
Preadjustment AMTI	(100)	600	900	–0–	(300)
ACE adjustment	?	?	?	?	?

C5-40 ***Regular Tax and AMT Calculations.*** Bronze Corporation, an accrual method of accounting taxpayer, reports the following information about its year 2002 operations:

Taxable income from recurring operations	$278,000
Other income and expense items not included in $278,000 figure:	
Dividend from 10%-owned corporation	40,000
Life insurance proceeds received on the death of a corporate officer	500,000
Tax-exempt bond interest (not from private activity bonds)	50,000
Installment sale of land (a capital asset) in June:	
Total realized gain	400,000
Portion of gain reported on installment collections in 2002	32,000
Depreciation:	
For regular tax purposes	120,000
For AMTI purposes	85,000
For ACE purposes	60,000
Sec. 1245 property sold in current year:	
Recognized gain for regular tax purposes	30,000
Basis for regular tax purposes	54,000
Basis for AMTI purposes	60,000
Basis for ACE purposes	64,000

Bronze is not eligible for the small corporation exemption.

a. What is Bronze Corporation's ACE adjustment?
b. What is Bronze Corporation's AMTI?
c. What is Bronze Corporation's AMT liability?
d. What is Bronze Corporation's available minimum tax credit (if any)?
e. In what years can the minimum tax credit be used?
f. Does Bronze Corporation have to include its projected minimum tax liability in its 2002 estimated tax calculation?
g. Does Bronze Corporation have to includes its minimum tax liability in the determination of its tax underpayment penalty (if any) for 2002?

C5-41 ***Regular Tax and AMT Calculations.*** Campbell Corporation has taxable income of $210,000 for 2002. Campbell is not eligible for the small corporation exemption. The following items were taken into consideration in arriving at this number.

1. Equipment acquired in 1997–2002 was depreciated using the MACRS rules. MACRS depreciation on this equipment for 2002 was $100,000. Depreciation for AMT purposes is $75,000.
2. Campbell recognizes Sec. 1245 gain of $12,000 for income tax purposes on the sale of an asset. The asset's income tax basis is $9,000 less than its AMT basis.
3. Campbell's adjusted current earnings for 2002 are $480,000.

a. What is Campbell Corporation's AMTI?
b. What is Campbell Corporation's AMT liability?
c. What is the amount (if any) of Campbell Corporation's minimum tax credit? To what years can it be carried?
d. Does Campbell Company have to include its projected minimum tax liability in its 2002 estimated tax calculation?
e. Does Campbell Company have to include its minimum tax liability in the determination of its tax underpayment penalty (if any) for 2002?

C5-42 ***Regular Tax and AMT Calculations.*** Sheldon Corporation has taxable income of $100,000 for its second tax year (2002). Its regular tax liability is $22,250. The following items were taken into consideration in arriving at this number.

- Equipment is depreciated using the MACRS rules. The MACRS depreciation claimed was $90,000. Depreciation for AMT purposes is calculated as $60,000 for 2002.
- The corporation includes a $12,000 gain in taxable income on the sale of equipment. The asset's income tax basis at the time of sale is $9,000 less than its AMT basis.
- Sheldon Corporation's adjusted current earnings are $310,000.

No NOL, capital loss, tax credit, or negative ACE carryovers from the first year of operations are available to be used in the second year.

a. What is Sheldon Corporation's AMT liability?

b. Is any minimum tax credit carryback or carryover available to prior or future tax years? If so, to what years may the minimum tax credit be carried?

C5-43 ***Regular Tax and AMT Calculations.*** Subach Corporation, organized in 1995, reports the following results for the year 2002:

Taxable income	$600,000
Preadjustment AMTI	630,000
Adjusted current earnings excluding the following transactions:	900,000
• Tax-exempt interest income (not from a private activity bond)	100,000
• Gain on installment sale of a capital asset made in the current year. No collections were made in the sale year.	150,000
• Life insurance proceeds received on death of corporate executive	600,000
• Amortization of organizational expenditures	5,000

Subach Corporation uses the accrual method of accounting. The only adjustment made to taxable income to arrive at preadjustment AMTI is a $30,000 positive adjustment for the different depreciation method used in calculating AMTI. Taxable income, preadjustment AMTI, and the beginning ACE amounts all include an $80,000 dividends-received deduction claimed with respect to a dividend received from a 25%-owned corporation. No NOL, capital loss, tax credit, or negative ACE adjustment carryovers from prior years are available in the current year. What is Subach Corporation's current year federal tax liability?

C5-44 ***AMTI Calculation.*** Alabama Corporation conducts copper mining activities. During the current year, it reported taxable income of $400,000, which included a $100,000 deduction for percentage depletion. The depletable property's adjusted basis at year-end (before reduction for the current year's depletion) was $40,000. Cost depletion, had it been taken, would have been $30,000. Depreciation on post-1986 property acquisitions under the MACRS rules was $140,000. Under the alternative depreciation system, only $90,000 could have been claimed for AMTI purposes. Alabama Corporation sold an asset for a $12,000 gain that was included in taxable income. The asset's adjusted basis was $10,000 higher for AMT purposes than it was for regular tax purposes. Alabama Corporation's adjusted current earnings are $800,000. Alabama is not eligible for the small corporation exemption.

a. What is Alabama Corporation's AMTI?

b. What is Alabama Corporation's AMT liability?

c. What is the amount (if any) of Alabama Corporation's minimum tax credit? To what years can it be carried?

C5-45 ***Regular Tax and AMT Calculations.*** What is Middle Corporation's regular tax liability, AMT liability, and minimum tax credit (if any) in the following three independent situations? Assume that Middle Corporation has made $120,000 of positive ACE adjustments in prior years. Middle Corporation is not eligible for the small corporation exemption.

		Situation	
	No. 1	*No. 2*	*No. 3*
Taxable income	$200,000	$ 50,000	$300,000
Tax preference items and positive AMTI adjustments (other than the ACE adjustment)	100,000	25,000	160,000
Adjusted current earnings	500,000	150,000	400,000

C5-46 ***Regular Tax and AMT Calculations.*** Delta Corporation reports taxable income of $2 million, tax preference items of $100,000, and net positive AMTI adjustments of $600,000 before the ACE adjustment. Its adjusted current earnings are $4 million. Delta Corporation is not eligible for the small corporation exception.

a. What is Delta Corporation's regular tax liability?
b. What is Delta Corporation's AMT liability?
c. What is the amount (if any) of Delta Corporation's minimum tax credit? To what years can it be carried?

C5-47 ***Minimum Tax Credit.*** Jones Corporation has $600,000 of taxable income plus $400,000 of positive AMTI adjustments and $200,000 of tax preference items. Jones Corporation is not eligible for the small corporation exemption.

a. What is Jones Corporation's regular tax liability and AMT liability?
b. What is Jones Corporation's minimum tax credit (if any)? To what years can it be carried back or carried over?

C5-48 ***Minimum Tax Credit.*** Gulf Corporation reports the following tax amounts for the period 2000–2002:

Tax Amounts	*2000*	*2001*	*2002*
Regular tax	$75,000	$100,000	$210,000
Tentative minimum tax	40,000	150,000	170,000

In what years does a minimum tax credit originate? To what years can the credit be carried? Do any credit carryovers remain to 2003?

C5-49 ***Minimum Tax Analysis.*** Duncan Manufacturing Corporation, an accrual method of accounting taxpayer, sold a parcel of land on July 1, 2002. Duncan had planned to use the land to expand its manufacturing facilities. The land (a Sec. 1231 asset) had a $3 million market value and a $1.2 million adjusted basis. As part of the sale, Duncan received a $300,000 cash down payment on July 1, 2002. The purchaser will pay annual payments of $540,000 [0.20 × ($3,000,000 – $300,000)] over the next five years on July 1 of each year. Duncan charges an appropriate interest rate on the unpaid balance. The CEO has asked you to prepare a year-by-year analysis of the impact of this land sale on the firm's tax position. The interest income earned on the sale can be ignored for purposes of your calculation. What are the expected effects on a year-by-year basis of the installment sale on the corporation's income tax and AMT? Assume that Duncan is not a small corporation for AMT purposes, and assume a 34% regular tax rate.

C5-50 ***General Business Credit.*** Edge Corporation's regular tax before credits is $180,000 in the current year. Its tentative minimum tax is $100,000. The only credit Edge Corporation earns in the current year is a $200,000 general business credit relating to research expenditures.

a. What amount of this credit may Edge Corporation use to reduce its current year liability?
b. What carryovers and carrybacks are available, and to what years may they be carried?

C5-51 ***Estimated Tax Requirement.*** Ajax Corporation anticipates owing a $120,000 regular tax liability and a $60,000 AMT liability for the current year. Last year, it owed a $200,000 regular tax liability and no AMT liability. What is its minimum estimated tax payment for the current year?

C5-52 ***Estimated Tax Payments.*** Dallas Corporation reports the following information with respect to its 2001 and 2002 tax liabilities:

Type of Liability	*2001*	*2002*
Regular tax	$100,000	$120,000
AMT	–0–	25,000

Both tax years cover 12-month periods. Dallas Corporation is not a large corporation, and it made $23,000 of estimated tax payments for each quarter of 2002.

a. What is the amount of tax owed when Dallas files its 2002 tax return?
b. Is Dallas potentially liable for any estimated tax underpayment penalties? If so, how much is underpaid for each quarter?

C5-53 ***PHC Definition.*** In which of the following situations is Small Corporation a PHC? Assume that personal holding company income constitutes more than 60% of Small's adjusted ordinary gross income.

a. Art owns all of Parent Corporation's stock. Parent Corporation owns all the Small stock. Parent and Small Corporations file separate tax returns.

b. Art owns one-third of the Small stock. The PRS Partnership, of which Phil, Robert, and Sue each have a one-third interest in both capital and profits, also owns one-third of the Small stock. The remaining Small stock is owned by 50 individuals unrelated to Art, Phil, Robert, and Sue.

c. Art and his wife, Becky, each own 20% of the Small stock. The remaining Small stock is owned by the Whitaker Family Trust. Becky and her three sisters each have a one-fourth beneficial interest in the trust.

C5-54 ***Personal Holding Company Status.*** For each of the four independent situations listed below, determine whether the corporation is a personal holding company or not. Assume the corporation's outstanding stock is owned equally by three shareholders.

Type of Income Earned	*Situation 1*	*Situation 2*	*Situation 3*	*Situation 4*
Gross profit from sales	$40,000	$ 80,000	$40,000	$ 60,000
Capital gains	–0–	10,000	5,000	10,000
Interest	15,000	15,000	10,000	20,000
Dividends	10,000	10,000	2,000	–0–
Rentals	80,000	150,000	–0–	–0–
Copyright royalties	–0–	5,000	80,000	–0–
Personal service income	–0–	–0–	–0–	100,000
Rent-related expenses	20,000	30,000	–0–	–0–
Copyright-related expenses	–0–	–0–	25,000	–0–
Dividends paid	8,000	10,000	5,000	10,000

C5-55 ***PHC Tax Liability.*** Moore Corporation is a PHC for the current year. Moore reported the following results for the current year:

Taxable income	$200,000
Dividend received by Moore from a 25%-owned domestic corporation	50,000
Dividends paid by Moore during the current year	75,000

a. What is Moore's federal income tax liability (ignoring any AMT implications)?

b. What is Moore's PHC tax liability?

c. What actions can Moore take to eliminate its PHC tax liability after the year-end and before it files its tax return? After it files its tax return?

C5-56 ***PHC Tax Liability.*** Kennedy Corporation is a PHC for the current year. It reported the following results for the current year:

Taxable income	$400,000
Federal income taxes	136,000
Dividends paid to Marlene, Kennedy's sole shareholder, during the current year	75,000

The following information is available about the federal income tax calculation:

- The corporation received $100,000 of dividends from a 25%-owned domestic corporation.
- The corporation received $30,000 of tax-exempt interest income.
- The corporation recognized a $175,000 Sec. 1231 gain on the sale of land.

a. What is Kennedy Corporation's PHC tax liability?

b. What can be done after the year-end and before Kennedy files the tax return to eliminate the PHC tax liability? After Kennedy files the tax return?

C5-57 ***Personal Holding Company Tax Liability.*** Alpha Corporation is equally owned by two individuals, Alice and Barry. For 2002, the corporation reports the following income and expense items:

Rental income		$ 750,000
Dividend income from less than 20%-owned corporations		200,000
Tax-exempt interest income		40,000
Gross margin on sale of merchandise		50,000
Long-term capital gain from the sale of stocks		200,000
Total income		$1,240,000
Minus: Rental income related expenses:		
Interest expense	$140,000	
Depreciation expense	150,000	

Property taxes	175,000	
Other Sec. 162 expenses	165,000	(630,000)
Minus: Administrative expenses		(90,000)
Pre-tax profit		$ 520,000

During 2002, Alpha Corporation paid $30,000 in dividends to its shareholders.

a. Is Alpha characterized as a personal holding company?
b. What is Alpha's corporate income tax liability?
c. What is Alpha's personal holding company tax liability?

C5-58 *Unreasonable Accumulation of Earnings.* For each of the following independent situations, indicate why the IRS might find that an unreasonable accumulation of earnings by Adobe Corporation may exist. Provide one or more arguments the corporation might offer to show that no unreasonable accumulation exists. Assume that Tess owns all the Adobe stock.

a. Adobe Corporation established a sinking fund ten years ago to retire its ten-year notes. Amounts have been added to the fund annually. Six months ago, the corporation decided to refinance the notes when they come due with a new series of notes that have been sold to an insurance company. The amounts in the sinking fund remain invested in stocks and bonds. A general plan exists to use the amounts currently invested in stocks and bonds to purchase operating assets. No definite plans have been established by year-end.
b. Adobe Corporation regularly lends money to Tess at a rate slightly below the rate charged by a commercial bank. Tess has repaid about 20% of these loans. The current balance on the loans is $500,000, which approximates one year's net income for Adobe Corporation.
c. Adobe Corporation has made substantial investments in stocks and bonds. The current market value of its investments is $2 million. The investment portfolio constitutes approximately one-half of Adobe Corporation's assets.
d. Tess owns three corporations other than Adobe Corporation, which, together with Adobe Corporation, form a brother-sister controlled group. Adobe Corporation regularly lends money to Tess's three other corporations. The current loans amount to $500,000. The interest rate charged approximates the commercial interest rate for similar loans.

C5-59 *Bardahl Formula.* Lion Corporation is concerned about a possible accumulated earnings tax problem. It accumulates E&P to maintain the working capital necessary to conduct its manufacturing activities. The following information about Lion Corporation's financial position is taken from its current year balance sheets.

Account	*Beginning Balance*	*Ending Balance*	*Peak Balance for the Year*
Accounts receivable	$300,000	$400,000	$400,000
Inventory	240,000	300,000	375,000
Accounts payable	150,000	200,000	220,000

The following information about operations appears in Lion Corporation's current year income statement:

Sales	$3,200,000
Cost of goods sold	1,500,000
Purchases	1,200,000
Operating expenses (other than cost of goods sold)	1,000,000

Included in operating expenses are depreciation of $150,000 and federal income taxes of $100,000.

a. What is Lion's operating cycle in days? As a decimal percentage?
b. What is Lion's working capital needs as determined with the *Bardahl* formula?
c. What steps must Lion take to justify a larger accumulation than is indicated by the *Bardahl* formula?

C5-60 *Accumulated Earnings Credit.* For each of the following independent situations, calculate the amount of the available accumulated earnings credit. Assume the corporation in question is a manufacturing company that uses a calendar year as its tax year unless otherwise stated. Also assume that it has no current year capital gains.

a. Frank Corporation, a manufacturer of plastic toys, started business last year and reported E&P of $50,000 in that year. In the current year, the corporation reported E&P of $150,000 and paid no dividends. Of the $150,000 current E&P, the corporation retains $130,000 to meet its business needs.
b. How would your answer to Part a change if Frank Corporation were a service company that provides accounting services?

c. Hall Corporation's accumulated E&P balance at January 1 of the current year is $200,000. During the current year, Hall reports $100,000 of current E&P, all of which is retained to meet the reasonable needs of the business. Hall paid no dividends in the current year.

C5-61 *Accumulated Earnings Tax Liability.* Twentieth Century Cleaning Services, Inc. provides cleaning services in Atlanta, Georgia. It is neither a member of a controlled group nor an affiliated group. During 2002, Twentieth Century reports the following results:

Taxable income	$500,000
Federal income taxes (at 34%)	170,000
Dividends paid in August 2002	75,000

Included in the determination of taxable income shown above are the following items that may require special treatment:

Long-term capital gains	$ 30,000
Short-term capital gains	10,000
Dividends from 18%-owned domestic corporation	100,000
Excess charitable contributions from 2001 that are deductible in 2002	25,000

Twentieth Century's accumulated E&P balance and its reasonable business needs on January 1, 2002 were $125,000. The firm can justify the retention of $90,000 of current E&P to meet its reasonable business needs.

a. What is Twentieth Century's accumulated taxable income?
b. What is Twentieth Century's accumulated earnings tax liability?

C5-62 *Accumulated Earnings Tax Liability.* Howard Corporation conducts manufacturing activities and has a substantial need to accumulate earnings. Its January 1, 2002 E&P balance is $600,000. The following operating results are presented for 2002:

Taxable income		$600,000
Federal income taxes		204,000
Dividends paid:	July 15, 2002	50,000
	February 10, 2003	100,000

Other information about Howard's operations for 2002 is as follows:

NOL carryover from 2001 deducted in 2002	$100,000
Net capital gain	80,000
Dividends received from 10%-owned domestic corporation	75,000

Current year E&P is $400,000 before dividend payments. Howard can justify the retention of $120,000 of current E&P to meet the reasonable needs of the business.

a. What is Howard's accumulated taxable income?
b. What is Howard's accumulated earnings tax liability?

COMPREHENSIVE PROBLEM

C5-63 Random Corporation is owned equally by two individual shareholders. During the current year, Random reports the following results:

Income:	Rentals	$200,000
	Dividend (from a 25%-owned domestic corporation)	30,000
	Interest	15,000
	Short-term capital gains	3,000
	Long-term capital gains	17,000
Expenses related to rental income:		
	Interest	30,000
	Depreciation	32,000
	Property taxes	11,000
	Other Sec. 162 expenses	50,000
General and administrative expenses		10,000
Dividend paid on June 30		15,000

a. What is Random's gross income?
b. What is Random's ordinary gross income?
c. What is Random's adjusted income from rents?
d. What is Random's adjusted ordinary gross income?

e. What is Random's personal holding company income?
f. Is Random Corporation a PHC?
g. What is Random's taxable income and regular tax?
h. What is Random's undistributed PHC income (UPHCI) and PHC tax?
i. What action can Random take before year-end to avoid paying any PHC tax? Alternatively, what can be done after year-end but before the corporation files its income tax return? If the corporation takes no action before or after filing its income tax return, what remedy does it have after it files its tax return?
j. Assume that Random's income and expense items will be similar in future years unless management changes Random's asset mix. What changes can management make to Random's asset mix to reduce the corporation's PHC exposure in future years?
k. If Random Corporation is a personal holding company, can it also be subject to the accumulated earnings tax at the same time?

TAX STRATEGY PROBLEMS

C5-64 Galadriel and John, a married couple with no children, own all the stock of Marietta Horse Supplies. The couple's C corporation has been in business for ten years. The business has been successful, permitting both owners to withdraw from the business a reasonable salary. Although the salaries permit the couple to have life's necessities, a review of industry statistics shows that the salary each owner is drawing is about one-half or two-thirds of salaries being paid by similar-sized horse supply businesses. The reason for drawing the low salaries is that, for a number of years, the owners had felt continual pressure to retain as much money in the business as possible to have sufficient working capital to finance inventories and other current business needs. In the past two years, the firm has developed lines of credit with two local banks that have reduced much of the pressure for internally financing the activities. However, the couple has never had time to revisit the amount they were being paid. Recently, the couple received a visit from an Internal Revenue Service agent about some items included in a previously filed tax return. The agent reviewed all three open years and proposed a settlement for the items in question. While in the office, the IRS agent indicated to you as the couple's CPA that, in her opinion, the company had unreasonably accumulated earnings and that she would be devoting time to that issue in the future before closing the audit. What advice can you provide the couple about the salaries they are drawing and the possibility of an accumulated earnings tax problem?

C5-65 Steve and Andrew write the music and lyrics for popular songs. In 1999, Steve and Andrew organized S&A Music Corporation with each brother owning one-half of the stock. The two brothers supplied the initial capital for the business. Through the end of 2001, the brothers have contributed a total of $250,000 in capital to the business. The songs that Steve and Andrew write and promote have proven successful. Annually, the firm earns $300,000 of royalties from the copyrights owned by their firm. Steven and Andrew selected the corporate form with the aid of their aunt who operates a local bookkeeping service. The corporation has made no S election. Thus, the corporation's first three tax returns have been filed with the entity being taxed as a C corporation. The brothers decide that, with the success of the new business, perhaps they should consider moving their accounting services to an accounting firm that specializes in providing tax advice for small- or medium-sized businesses. As a staff member of this accounting firm, what advice can you provide the brothers about possible tax problems and potential tax strategies?

TAX FORM/RETURN PREPARATION PROBLEM

C5-66 King Corporation, I.D. No. 38-1534789, an accrual method of accounting taxpayer, reports the following results for 2001:

Taxable income	$ 800,000
Regular tax liability (before credits)	272,000
Accelerated depreciation on real property placed in service in 1986	40,000
Depreciation adjustment for personal property placed in service after 1986	147,000
Personal property acquired in 1994 sold this year:	
Acquisition cost	50,000
Regular tax depreciation	38,845
AMT depreciation	26,845
Increase in LIFO recapture amount	75,000

Tax-exempt interest income:	
Private activity bonds	15,000
Other bonds	5,000
Adjusted current earnings	1,700,000
General business credit (targeted jobs credit)	10,000
Dividends paid	120,000

King Corporation is not eligible for the small corporation exemption. Taxable income includes $95,000 of Sec. 1231 gain from a payment received in 2001 pertaining to an installment sale of land that King made in 2000. King realized a $950,000 gain on the sale in 2000 and is recognizing gain over a ten-year period as the purchaser makes equal annual payments. King reported the transaction properly in 2000. Prepare Form 4626 for King Corporation to report its AMT liability (if any) for 2001.

CASE STUDY PROBLEMS

C5-67 Eagle Corporation is a family corporation created by Edward Eagle, Sr. ten years ago. Edward Eagle, Sr. dies, and the Eagle stock passed to his children and grandchildren. The corporation is primarily an investment company with its assets consisting of rental property, highly appreciated stocks, and corporate bonds. The tax advisor who regularly handles Eagle Corporation's tax matters made the following profit projection for the current year:

Rentals	$260,000
Dividend income (from a 40%-owned domestic corporation)	90,000
Interest income	20,000
Gross income	$370,000
Rental expenses:	
Depreciation expense	$ 70,000
Interest expense	100,000
Property taxes	10,000
Other Sec. 162 expenses	20,000
General and administrative expenses	15,000
Total expenses	$215,000
Net profit	$155,000

Eagle has paid dividends of $40,000 in each of the past three years. The stock investment has appreciated substantially in value in the past six months. As a result, dividend income is expected to increase from last year's $10,000 amount to $80,000 this year. Assume that Eagle Corporation has not been a PHC in prior years.

Required: Prepare a memorandum to Edward Eagle, Jr. regarding the possible PHC problem. As part of your discussion, make sure you discuss the following two questions.

a. Is Eagle Corporation projected to be a PHC for the current year?

b. If Eagle Corporation is projected to be a PHC for the current year, what actions (if any) should be taken before year-end to eliminate the PHC problem? After year-end?

C5-68 Goss Corporation is a leading manufacturer of hangers for the laundry and dry cleaning industry. The family-owned business has prospered for many years and has approximately $100 million of sales and $8 million in after-tax profits. Your accounting firm has done the audit and tax work for Goss Corporation and its executives since the company was created in 1948. Little technological change has occurred in the manufacturing of hangers and much of the equipment currently being used dates from the 1950s and 1960s. The advent of plastic hangers and improved fabrics has kept the overall market size constant, and the corporation plans no major plant expansions or additions. Salaries paid to corporate executives, most of whom are family members, are above the national averages for similar positions. Dividend payments in recent years have not exceeded 10% of the after-tax profits. You are a recently hired tax manager who has been assigned on December 1, 2002 to oversee the preparation of the 2002 Goss Corporation tax return. Shortly after being assigned to the project you review the 1999–2001 Goss tax returns. You note from Schedule L (the balance sheet) that the corporation has made about $1.5 million in loans to three executives and regularly increased the size of its stock portfolio between 1999 and 2001. These signals lead you to believe that an accumulated earnings tax problem may exist in the current year (2002) as well as for a number of prior years.

Required:

a. What is your responsibility to make the partner in charge of the Goss account or the client aware of the potential accumulated earnings tax problem?

b. Should you advise the IRS of the potential problem with prior year returns? Should you disclose the potential problem on the current year return?

c. Prepare a list of actions that can be taken to reduce or eliminate the client's exposure to the accumulated earnings tax problem.

TAX RESEARCH PROBLEMS

C5-69 Brown Corporation purchased two assets in January 1999, its initial year of operation. The first asset, a commercial factory building, cost $200,000 with $40,000 of the acquisition price being allocated to the land. The second, a machine that is a seven-year MACRS property, cost $80,000. The class life for the machine under the Asset Depreciation Range system is ten years. Brown sold both assets in March 2002 in connection with a relocation of its manufacturing activities. The sale price for the factory building was $225,000, with $45,000 of the sale price being allocated to the land. The sale price for the machine was $70,000. Brown claimed the maximum amount of depreciation on each asset for regular tax purposes. Assume the half-year convention was used with respect to the machine and the mid-month convention with respect to the building. What are the amount and character of the gains reported by Brown Corporation for regular tax and alternative minimum tax purposes?

C5-70 Camp Corporation is owned by Hal and Ruthie, who have owned their stock since the corporation was formed in 1988. The corporation has filed each of its prior tax returns using the calendar year as its tax year and the accrual method of accounting. In 2001, Camp Corporation borrowed $4 million from a local bank. The loan is secured by a lien against some of its machinery. Camp Corporation loaned 90% of the borrowings to Vickers Corporation at the same annual rate at which the borrowing took place. Vickers Corporation also is owned equally by Hal and Ruthie. Vickers Corporation sells parts to the automobile industry that are manufactured by Camp Corporation and other unrelated manufacturers. Camp Corporation experienced a downturn due to a slowdown in the automobile industry, and the gross margin from its sales activities declined from $1 million in 2001 to $200,000 in 2002. Interest income accrued by Camp on the loan to Vickers Corporation is $432,000 in 2002. Other passive income earned by Camp Corporation is $40,000. Camp Corporation's accountant believes that the corporation is not a personal holding company because the interest income Camp Corporation earns can be netted against the $432,000 interest expense paid to the bank for the amounts lent to Vickers Corporation. Is he correct in his assumption?

A partial list of research sources is

- IRC Secs. 542(a) and 543(a)(1)
- Reg. Sec. 1.543-1(b)(2)
- *Bell Realty Trust*, 65 T.C. 766 (1976)
- *Blair Holding Co., Inc.*, 1980 PH T.C. Memo ¶80,079, 39 TCM 1255

C5-71 William Queen owns all the stock of Able and Baker Corporations. Able Corporation has been quite successful and has excess working capital of $3 million. Baker Corporation is still in its developmental stages and has had tremendous needs for capital. To help provide for Baker Corporation's capital needs, William Queen has had Able Corporation lend Baker Corporation $2 million during 2000 and 2001. These loans are secured by Baker Corporation notes but not by any Baker Corporation property. Able Corporation has charged Baker Corporation interest at a rate similar to that charged by a commercial lender. Upon reviewing Able Corporation's books in 2002 as part of an audit of its 2000 income tax return, an IRS agent indicates that Able Corporation has an accumulated earnings tax problem because of its accumulation of excess working capital and its loans to Baker Corporation. Later this week, you are to meet with the agent for a third time. Prior to this meeting you need to research whether loans to a related corporation to provide needed working capital are a reasonable need of the business for retaining its earnings. At a meeting to discuss this problem, Queen Corporation's CFO, Bill, asks whether filing a consolidated tax return would eliminate this potential problem.

A partial list of research sources is

- IRC Secs. 532 and 537
- Reg. Secs. 1.537-2(c) and -3(b) and 1.1502-43
- *Latchis Theatres of Keene, Inc. v. CIR*, 45 AFTR 1836, 54-2 USTC ¶9544 (1st Cir., 1954)
- *Bremerton Sun Publishing Co.*, 44 T.C. 566 (1965)

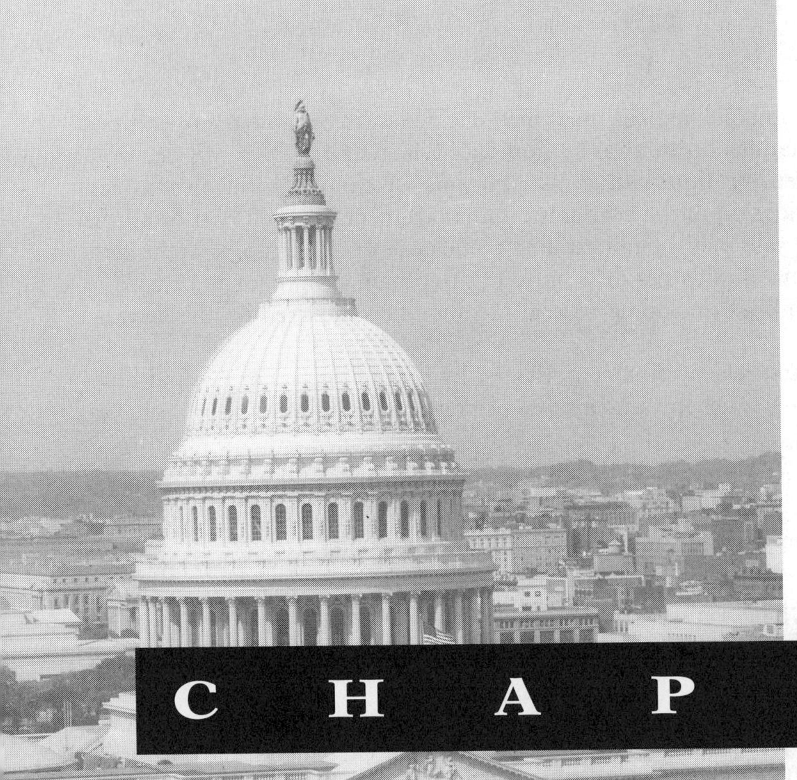

6

CHAPTER

CORPORATE LIQUIDATING DISTRIBUTIONS

LEARNING OBJECTIVES

After studying this chapter, you should be able to

1. Understand the difference between a complete liquidation and a dissolution
2. Apply the general shareholder gain and loss recognition rules for a corporate liquidation
3. Determine when the liquidating corporation recognizes gains and losses on making a liquidating distribution
4. Determine when the Sec. 332 and Sec. 337 nonrecognition rules apply to the liquidation of a subsidiary corporation
5. Determine the effect of a liquidation on the liquidating corporation's tax attributes
6. Understand the different tax treatments for open and closed liquidation transactions
7. Determine when a liquidating corporation recognizes gains and losses on the retirement of debt

As part of the corporate life cycle, management may decide to discontinue the operations of a profitable or unprofitable corporation by liquidating it. As a result of this decision, the shareholders may receive liquidating distributions of the corporation's assets. Preceding the formal liquidation of the corporation, management may sell part or all the corporation's assets. The sale may be undertaken to dispose of assets the shareholders may not want to receive in a liquidating distribution or to obtain cash that can be used to pay the corporation's liabilities (including federal income taxes incurred on the liquidation).

Ordinarily the liquidation transaction is motivated by a combination of tax and business reasons. However, sometimes it is undertaken principally for tax reasons.

- If the corporation is liquidated and its shareholders hold the assets in an unincorporated form (e.g., sole proprietorship or partnership), the marginal tax rate may be reduced from the 35% corporate rate to a lower 10%, 15%, 27%, or 30% individual rate (in 2002). For example, even low amounts of taxable income are taxed at 35% in a personal service corporation.
- If the assets are producing losses, it may be advantageous for the shareholders to hold the assets in an unincorporated form and deduct the losses on their personal tax returns.
- Corporate earnings are taxed once under the corporate income tax rules and a second time when distributed as dividends or realized by selling or exchanging the corporate stock. Liquidation of the corporation permits the assets to be held in an unincorporated form, thereby avoiding double taxation of subsequent earnings.

Liquidating a corporation carries a tax cost, however. The liquidating corporation is taxed as though it sold its assets, and the shareholders receiving liquidating distributions are taxed as though they sold their stock. A C corporation cannot simply elect to be treated as a flow-through entity under the "check-the-box" regulations (see Chapter C2). Thus, the only route to converting a C corporation into a sole proprietorship, partnership, limited liability company, or limited liability partnership is via a taxable corporate liquidation followed by formation of the desired entity. Alternatively, a C corporation could obtain flow-through status without liquidating if it elects S corporation status. Even with this approach, the S corporation faces potential taxation on its built-in gains (see Chapter C11).

This chapter explains the tax consequences of corporate liquidations to both the liquidating corporation and its shareholders. In so doing, the chapter presents two sets of liquidation rules. The general liquidation rules apply to liquidations of corporations not controlled by a parent corporation. Special rules apply to the liquidation of a controlled subsidiary.

CHAPTER OUTLINE

Overview of Corporate Liquidations...6-2
General Liquidation Rules...6-5
Liquidation of a Controlled Subsidiary Corporation...6-10
Special Shareholder Reporting Issues...6-14
Special Corporate Reporting Issues...6-16
Recognition of Gain or Loss When Property Is Distributed in Retirement of Debt...6-17
Tax Planning Considerations...6-18
Compliance and Procedural Considerations...6-20

ADDITIONAL COMMENT

Usually no tax cost is involved in forming a corporation. However, as this chapter will illustrate, the tax costs of liquidating a corporation may be substantial. The tax consequences of liquidating a corporation should be a consideration in the initial decision to use the corporate form to conduct a business.

OVERVIEW OF CORPORATE LIQUIDATIONS

This chapter initially presents an overview of the tax and nontax consequences of a corporate liquidation to both the shareholders and the distributing corporation.

THE SHAREHOLDER

Three questions must be answered to determine the tax consequences of the liquidation transaction to each of the liquidating corporation's shareholders:

- What are the amount and character of the shareholder's recognized gain or loss?
- What is the shareholder's adjusted basis of each property received?
- When does the holding period begin for each property received by the shareholder?

When a corporation liquidates under the general rules, a shareholder treats the liquidating distribution as an amount received in exchange for his or her stock. The shareholder recognizes a capital gain or loss equal to the excess of any money received plus the FMV of any nonmoney property received over the adjusted basis of his or her stock. The basis of each property received is stepped-up or stepped-down to the property's FMV on the liquidation date. The holding period for the asset begins the day after the liquidation date.

If a parent corporation liquidates a controlled subsidiary under special rules, however, the parent corporation (shareholder) recognizes no gain or loss. In addition, the bases and holding periods of the subsidiary's assets carry over to the parent.

THE CORPORATION

Two questions must be answered to determine the tax consequences of the liquidation transaction for the liquiding corporation:

- ▶ What are the amount and character of the corporation's recognized gain or loss?
- ▶ What happens to the corporation's tax attributes upon liquidation?

ADDITIONAL COMMENT

In a complete liquidation other than a liquidation of a controlled subsidiary, taxation can occur at both the shareholder and corporate levels. Assuming a 34% corporate tax rate and a 20% capital gains rate at the shareholder level, the effective tax cost of a complete liquidation is approximately 47.2% {34% + [(1 − 0.34) × 20%]}. Clearly, a decision to liquidate should be carefully considered.

When a liquidation occurs under the general rules, the liquidating corporation recognizes gain or loss on the distribution of property to its shareholders. The recognized gain or loss is the same as what the corporation would recognize had it sold the distributed property to its shareholders. Some restrictions (discussed later in the chapter) limit loss recognition in certain, potentially abusive situations. Also, tax attributions, such as net operating loss (NOL) carryovers and earnings and profits, disappear when the corporation liquidates under the general rules. Thus, these attributes are lost upon liquidation.

If the liquidating corporation is an 80%-controlled subsidiary of the parent corporation, the liquidating corporation recognizes no gain or loss under special rules. In this case, the subsidiary's tax attributes carry over to the parent corporation.

EXAMPLE C6-1 ▶ Randy Jones owns Able Corporation, a C corporation. Randy's basis for his Able stock is $100,000. The corporation's assets are summarized below:

Assets	*Adjusted Basis*	*Fair Market Value*
Cash	$ 50,000	$ 50,000
General Cable stock	75,000	125,000
Machinery	115,000	200,000
Total	$240,000	$375,000

Able Corporation owes $60,000 to its creditors. In step 1, Able sells its machinery to an unrelated purchaser for $200,000 cash. The machinery originally cost $250,000, and Able has claimed $135,000 of depreciation on the machinery. Able recognizes a total gain on the machinery sale of $85,000 ($200,000 − $115,000). In step 2, Able uses $60,000 in cash to pay its creditors. In step 3, Able distributes the General Cable stock, a capital asset, to Randy Jones. Able recognizes a $50,000 ($125,000 − $75,000) capital gain on the distribution. Assuming a 34% marginal tax rate, Able must pay $45,900 [($85,000 + $50,000) × 0.34] in federal income taxes on the distribution of the General Cable stock and the sale of the machinery. The tax payment reduces Able's remaining assets to $144,100 in cash [($50,000 + $200,000) − $60,000 paid to creditors − $45,900 paid in federal income taxes]. Randy Jones recognizes a $169,100 ($144,100 cash + $125,000 securities − $100,000 basis for stock) long-term capital gain on the liquidating distribution. The same federal income taxes would have occurred had Able sold both the stock and machinery to unrelated purchasers, or had Able distributed both the stock and machinery to Randy Jones since each of Able's noncash assets have FMVs exceeding their adjusted bases.[1] (See Figure C6-1 for an illustration of the corporate liquidation.) ◀

OBJECTIVE 1

Understand the difference between a complete liquidation and a dissolution

DEFINITION OF A COMPLETE LIQUIDATION

The term *complete liquidation* is not defined in the IRC, but Reg. Sec. 1.332-2(c) indicates that distributions made by a liquidating corporation must either completely cancel or redeem all its stock in accordance with a plan of liquidation or be one of a series of distributions that completely cancels or redeems all its stock in accordance with a plan of liquidation (see page C6-21 for a discussion of plans of liquidation). When more than one distribution occurs, the corporation must be in a liquidation status when the first liqui-

[1] The corporation's recognized gains and losses might be different if one or more of the properties had declined in value. The loss might be disallowed if the property were distributed to Randy Jones, where it would be recognized if the property had been sold to an unrelated purchaser.

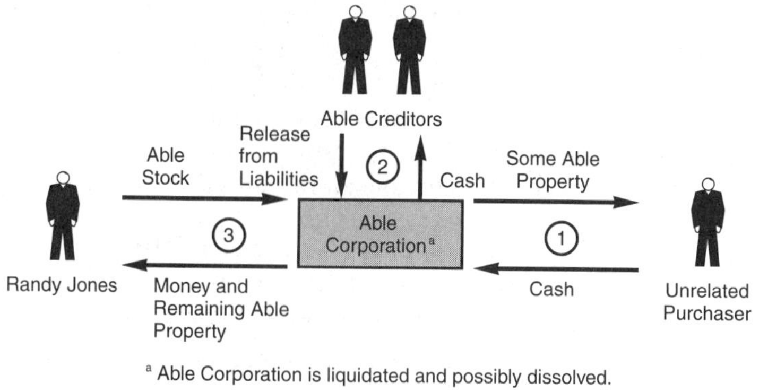

FIGURE C6-1 ▶ ILLUSTRATION OF CORPORATE LIQUIDATION (EXAMPLE C6-1)

dating distribution is made under the plan, and such status must continue until the liquidation is completed. A distribution made before the corporation adopts a plan of liquidation is taxed as a dividend distribution or stock redemption.

Liquidation status exists when the corporation ceases to be a going concern and its activities are for the purpose of winding up its affairs, paying its debts, and distributing any remaining property to its shareholders. A liquidation is completed when the liquidating corporation has divested itself of substantially all property. Retention of a nominal amount of assets (e.g., to retain the corporation's name) does not prevent a liquidation from occurring under the tax rules.

The liquidation of a corporation does not mean the corporation has undergone dissolution. **Dissolution** is a legal term that implies the corporation has surrendered the charter it received from the state. A corporation may complete its liquidation before surrendering its charter to the state and undergoing dissolution. Dissolution may never occur if the corporation retains its charter to protect the corporate name from being acquired by another party.

EXAMPLE C6-2 ▶ Thomas Corporation adopts a plan of liquidation in December of the current year. The corporation distributes all but a nominal amount of its assets to its shareholders in January of the next year. The nominal assets retained are the minimum amount needed to preserve the corporation's existence under state law and to prevent others from acquiring its name. The retention of a nominal amount of assets does not prevent Thomas Corporation from having been liquidated for tax purposes. ◀

STOP & THINK

Question: Peter Jenkins, age 58, is considering forming a new business entity to operate the rental real estate activities that he and his wife have owned personally for a number of years. He has heard about corporations and limited liability companies from reading various real estate journals. Because of their level of personal wealth and the liability protection afforded by the corporate form of doing business, Peter wants to use a corporation to own and operate their real estate. The assets Peter and his wife plan to transfer to the corporation have a $600,000 FMV and a $420,000 adjusted basis. As Peter's CPA, why should you consider the tax cost of liquidating the corporation as part of the overall analysis of the business entity selection decision?

Solution: A transfer of real estate by Peter and his wife to a corporation is tax-free. A subsequent liquidation of the corporation is not tax-free because both the corporation and the shareholder may recognize gain or loss. Peter and his wife have $180,000 ($600,000 – $420,000) of appreciation on their real estate. Even if no change in value occurs, liquidation of the real estate corporation at a later date will cause $180,000 to be taxed twice, once at the corporate level and again at the shareholder level. On the other hand, creation and liquidation of a limited liability company are not a taxable events to the entity or its owners. Thus, the difference in liquidation treatment at a future date is one of many differences that must be considered when forming an entity. More information on liquidating a limited liability company can be found in Chapter C10.

GENERAL LIQUIDATION RULES

This chapter section presents the general liquidation rules. These rules are considered in two parts—the effects of liquidating on the shareholders and the effects of liquidating on the corporation.

OBJECTIVE 2

Apply the general shareholder gain and loss recognition rules for a corporate liquidation

EFFECTS OF LIQUIDATING ON THE SHAREHOLDERS

Three aspects of the general liquidation rules are discussed below: amount and timing of gain or loss recognition, character of the recognized gain or loss, and basis of property received in the liquidation. Table C6-1 summarizes the liquidation rules applying to shareholders under both the general liquidation rules and controlled subsidiary corporation exception.

AMOUNT OF RECOGNIZED GAIN OR LOSS. Section 331(a) requires that liquidating distributions received by a shareholder be treated as full payment in exchange for their stock. The shareholder's recognized gain or loss equals the difference between the amount realized (the FMV of the assets received from the corporation plus any money) and his or her basis in the stock. If a shareholder assumes or acquires liabilities of the liquidating corporation, the amount of these liabilities reduces the shareholder's amount realized.

EXAMPLE C6-3 ▶ Red Corporation liquidates, with Joseph receiving $10,000 in cash plus other property having a $12,000 FMV. Joseph's basis in his Red stock is $16,000. Joseph's amount realized is $22,000 ($12,000 + $10,000). Therefore, he must recognize a $6,000 ($22,000 − $16,000) gain on the liquidation. ◀

EXAMPLE C6-4 ▶ Assume the same facts as in Example C6-3, except that Joseph also assumes a $2,000 mortgage attaching to the other property. Joseph's amount realized is reduced by the $2,000 liability assumed and is $20,000 ($22,000 − $2,000). His recognized gain on the liquidation is $4,000 ($20,000 − $16,000). ◀

▼ **TABLE C6-1**
Tax Consequences of a Liquidation to the Shareholders

	Amount of Gain or Loss Recognized	Character of Gain or Loss Recognized	Adjusted Basis of Property Received	Holding Period of Property Received
General rule	Shareholders recognize gain or loss (money + FMV of nonmoney property received − adjusted basis of stock) upon liquidation (Sec. 331).	Long-term or short-term capital gain or loss (Sec. 1222). Ordinary loss treatment available (Sec. 1244).	FMV of the property (Sec. 334(a)).	Begins on the day after the liquidation date (Sec. 1223(1)).
Controlled subsidiary corporation rule	Parent corporation recognizes no gain or loss when an 80% controlled subsidiary corporation is liquidated into the parent corporation (Sec. 332).[a]	Not applicable.[a]	Carryover basis for property received from subsidiary corporation (Sec. 334(b)).[a]	Includes subsidiary corporation's holding period for the assets (Sec. 1223(2)).[a]

[a] Minority shareholders use the general rule.

Impact of Accounting Method. Shareholders who use the accrual method of accounting recognize gain or loss when all events have occurred that fix the amount of the liquidating distribution and when the shareholders are entitled to receive the distribution upon surrender of their shares. Shareholders who use the cash method of accounting report the gain or loss when they have actual or constructive receipt of the liquidating distribution(s).[2]

SELF-STUDY QUESTION

How is the gain/loss calculated if a shareholder has acquired stock at different times and at varying prices?

ANSWER

A shareholder who has purchased blocks of stock at different times and at varying prices must calculate the gain/loss on each block separately. Calculating the gain/loss separately on each block may result in (1) both gains and losses existing in the same liquidating distribution and (2) the character of the various gains/losses being different.

When Stock Is Acquired. A shareholder may have acquired his or her stock at different times or for different per-share amounts. In this case, the shareholder must compute the gain or loss separately for each share or block of stock owned.[3]

CHARACTER OF THE RECOGNIZED GAIN OR LOSS. Generally, the liquidating corporation's stock is a capital asset in the shareholder's hands. The gain or loss recognized, therefore, is a capital gain or loss for most shareholders. Two exceptions to these rules are indicated below.

- Loss recognized by an individual shareholder on Sec. 1244 stock is an ordinary loss (see Chapter C2).
- Loss recognized by a corporate shareholder on the worthlessness of the controlled subsidiary's stock is an ordinary loss under Sec. 165(g)(3) (see Chapter C2).

BASIS OF PROPERTY RECEIVED IN THE LIQUIDATION. Section 334(a) provides that the shareholder's basis of property received under the general liquidation rules is its FMV on the distribution date. The holding period for the property starts on the day after the distribution date.

OBJECTIVE 3

Determine when the liquidating corporation recognizes gains and losses on making a liquidating distribution

EFFECTS OF LIQUIDATING ON THE LIQUIDATING CORPORATION

Two aspects of the general liquidation rules are discussed below: (1) the recognition of gain or loss by the liquidating corporation when it distributes property in redemption of its stock and (2) the special valuation rules used when the liabilities assumed or acquired by the shareholder exceed the property's adjusted basis in the liquidating corporation's hands. Table C6-2 summarizes rules applying to the liquidating corporation.

RECOGNITION OF GAIN OR LOSS WHEN CORPORATION DISTRIBUTES PROPERTY IN REDEMPTION OF STOCK Section 336(a) provides that the liquidating corporation must recognize gain or loss when it distributes property in a complete liquidation. The amount and character of the gain or loss are determined as if the corporation sold the property to the shareholder at its FMV.

EXAMPLE C6-5 ▶ Under West Corporation's plan of liquidation, the corporation distributes land to one of its shareholders, Arnie. The land, which is used in West's trade or business, has a $40,000 adjusted basis and a $120,000 FMV on the distribution date. West recognizes an $80,000 Sec. 1231 gain ($120,000 − $40,000) when it makes the liquidating distribution. Arnie recognizes a capital gain to the extent the land's FMV exceeds his basis in the West stock. Arnie's basis for the land is its $120,000 FMV. A nonliquidating distribution would have produced similar results except the entire FMV would have been an ordinary dividend instead of a capital gain. Thus, both liquidating and nonliquidating distributions produce double taxation. ◀

With limited exceptions, the liquidating corporation can recognize a loss when it distributes property that has declined in value to its shareholders. This rule eliminates the need for a liquidating corporation to sell property that has declined in value to recognize its losses.

EXAMPLE C6-6 ▶ Assume the same facts as in Example C6-5 except the land's FMV is instead $10,000. West is permitted to recognize a $30,000 Sec. 1231 loss ($10,000 − $40,000 adjusted basis) when it distributes the land to Arnie. Arnie's basis for the land is $10,000. ◀

---

[2] Rev. Rul. 80-177, 1980-2 C.B. 109.

[3] Reg. Sec. 1.331-1(e).

▼ TABLE C6-2
Tax Consequences of a Liquidation to the Liquidating Corporation

	Amount and Character of Gain, Loss, or Income Recognized	Treatment of the Liquidating Corporation's Tax Attributes
General rule	The liquidating corporation recognizes gain or loss when it distributes property as part of a complete liquidation (Sec. 336(a)).	Tax attributes disappear when the liquidation is completed.
Controlled subsidiary corporation rules	1. The liquidating subsidiary corporation recognizes no gain or loss upon a distribution of property to its parent corporation when the Sec. 332 nonrecognition rules apply to the parent corporation (Sec. 337(a)). 2. The liquidating subsidiary corporation recognizes no loss upon a distribution of property to minority shareholders when the Sec. 332 nonrecognition rules apply to the parent corporation (Sec. 336(d)(3)). It does recognize gains, however.	Tax attributes of a subsidiary corporation carry over to the parent corporation when the Sec. 332 rules apply (Sec. 381(a)).
Related party rule	The liquidating subsidiary corporation recognizes no loss upon a distribution of property to a related person, unless such property is distributed ratably to all shareholders *and* the property was not acquired by the liquidating corporation in a Sec. 351 transaction or as a capital contribution during the five years preceding the distribution (Sec. 336(d)(1)).	
Tax avoidance rule	The liquidating subsidiary corporation recognizes no loss when a sale, exchange, or distribution of property occurs and such property was acquired by the liquidating corporation in a Sec. 351 transaction or as a capital contribution having as a principal purpose the recognition of loss (Sec. 336(d)(2)).	

The Sec. 336 rules apply only to property distributed in exchange for the liquidating corporation's stock as part of a complete liquidation. These rules do not apply to distributions of appreciated property as part of a partial liquidation, or when a debt of the liquidating corporation is retired in exchange for appreciated property.

TAX STRATEGY TIP

If possible, a corporation should avoid distributing property subject to a mortgage that exceeds the property's FMV. Such distributions cause excessive corporate gain recognition and uncertainty of results at the shareholder level.

LIABILITIES ASSUMED OR ACQUIRED BY THE SHAREHOLDERS. For purposes of determining the amount of gain or loss recognized under Sec. 336, property distributed by the liquidating corporation is treated as having been sold to the distributee for its FMV on the distribution date. Section 336(b) contains a special restriction on valuing a liquidating property distribution when the shareholders assume or acquire liabilities. According to this rule, the FMV of the distributed property cannot be less than the amount of the liability assumed or acquired. Section 336(b) was enacted because the corporation has an economic gain or benefit equal to the amount of the liability the shareholder assumes or acquires (and not just the lower FMV of the property distributed) as part of the liquidation. Treatment at the shareholder level is not completely clear. Section 336(b) specifically states that this liability rule applies only for determining the corporation's gain or loss. Thus, it does not seem to extend to Sec. 334(a), which requires the shareholder to take a FMV basis in the distributed property. Some commentators have suggested that the strict statutory interpretation of giving the shareholders the actual FMV basis, rather than the greater liability basis, produces an illogical result.[4] Also, given that the liability exceeds the distributed property's FMV, the shareholder's amount realized should be zero, resulting in a capital loss equal to the shareholder's stock basis.

[4] For a detailed discussion, see B.C. Randall and D.N. Stewart, "Corporate Distributions: Handling Liabilities in Excess of the Fair Market Value of Property Remains Unresolved," *The Journal of Corporate Taxation*, Spring 1992, pp. 55-64.

EXAMPLE C6-7 ▶ Jersey Corporation owns an apartment complex costing $3 million that has been depreciated so that its adjusted basis is $2.4 million. The property is secured by a $2.7 million mortgage. A plan of liquidation is adopted, and Jersey distributes the property and the mortgage to Rex, Jersey's sole shareholder, at a time when the property's FMV is $2.2 million. Rex's stock basis is $500,000. Jersey must recognize a $300,000 gain ($2,700,000 − $2,400,000) on distributing the property because its FMV cannot be less than the $2.7 million mortgage. The shareholder recognizes a $500,000 capital loss on the corporate stock and takes either a $2.2 million or $2.7 million basis in the property, depending on which interpretation applies. ◀

EXCEPTIONS TO THE GENERAL GAIN OR LOSS RECOGNITION RULE. The IRC provides four exceptions to the general recognition rule of Sec. 336(a). Two of these exceptions apply to liquidations of controlled subsidiary corporations and are covered later. The other two exceptions prevent certain abusive practices (e.g., the manufacturing of losses) from being accomplished and are examined below.

ADDITIONAL COMMENT

The disqualified property rule prohibits a shareholder from infusing loss property into the liquidating corporation and generating losses at both the corporate and shareholder levels by liquidating the corporation.

Distributions to Related Persons. Section 336(d)(1)(A) prevents loss recognition in connection with property distributions to a related person if the distribution of loss property is other than pro rata to all shareholders based on their stock ownership or if the distributed property is disqualified property. Section 267(b) defines a related person as including, for example, an individual and a corporation whose stock is more than 50% owned (in terms of value) by such individual, as well as two corporations that are members of the same controlled group. Section 336(d)(1)(B) defines disqualified property as (1) any property acquired by the liquidating corporation in a transaction to which Sec. 351 applies, or as a contribution to capital, during the five-year period ending on the distribution date or (2) any property having an adjusted basis that carries over from disqualified property.

EXAMPLE C6-8 ▶ Mesa Corporation is 60% owned by Lei and 40% owned by Betty. Mesa adopts a plan of liquidation. Pursuant to the plan, Mesa distributes Beta stock purchased three years ago to Lei. The Beta stock, which is not disqualified property, has a $40,000 FMV and a $100,000 adjusted basis. Betty receives only cash in the liquidation. The non–pro rata distribution of the Beta stock (the loss property), however, prevents Mesa from claiming a $60,000 capital loss when it makes the distribution. If Mesa instead distributes the Beta stock 60% to Lei and 40% to Betty, Mesa deducts the entire capital loss, assuming Mesa has offsetting capital gains. ◀

EXAMPLE C6-9 ▶ Assume the same facts as in Example C6-8 except Mesa acquired the Beta stock three years ago as a capital contribution from Lei and now distributes it to Lei. The Beta stock is now disqualified property. The $40,000 realized loss is disallowed because Lei is a related party under Sec. 267(b). If the property is instead distributed 60% to Lei and 40% to Betty, Mesa still is prohibited from deducting the portion of the $60,000 capital loss attributable to the stock distributed to the related party even though it is distributed ratably to Lei and Betty. Mesa can deduct only the $24,000 ($60,000 × 0.40) capital loss attributable to the Beta stock distributed to Betty because she is not a related party. Alternatively, a sale of the disqualified property to an unrelated purchaser permits Mesa to recognize the entire $60,000 loss, again assuming offsetting capital gains exist. ◀

Sales Having a Tax-Avoidance Purpose. Section 336(d)(2) restricts loss recognition with respect to the sale, exchange, or distribution of property acquired in a Sec. 351 transaction, or as a contribution to capital, where the liquidating corporation acquired the property as part of a plan having the principal purpose of loss recognition by the corporation in connection with its liquidation. This loss limitation prevents a shareholder from transferring loss property into a corporation to reduce or eliminate the gain the liquidating corporation otherwise would have recognized from the distribution of other appreciated property.

TAX STRATEGY TIP

To avoid loss disallowance, a corporation should delay adopting plan of liquidation until two years after receiving loss property in a Sec. 351 transaction.

Property acquired by the liquidating corporation in any Sec. 351 transaction or as a contribution to capital within two years of the date on which a plan of complete liquidation is adopted are treated as part of a plan having a tax-avoidance purpose unless exempted by forthcoming regulations.[5] Treasury Regulations, when issued, should not

[5] H. Rept. No. 99-841, 99th Cong., 2d Sess., p. II-201 (1986). The Conference Committee Report for the 1986 Tax Act indicates that property transactions occurring more than two years in advance of the adoption of the plan of liquidation will be disregarded unless no clear and substantial relationship exists between the contributed property and the conduct of the corporation's current or future business enterprises.

prevent corporations from deducting losses associated with dispositions of assets that are contributed to the corporation and used in a trade or business (or a line of business), or dispositions occurring during the first two years of a corporation's existence.[6]

The basis of the contributed property for loss purposes equals its adjusted basis on the liquidating corporation's books reduced (but not below zero) by the excess (if any) of the property's adjusted basis over its FMV immediately after its acquisition. No adjustment occurs to the contributed property's adjusted basis when determining the corporation's recognized gain.

EXAMPLE C6-10 ▶ Terry makes a capital contribution of a widget maker having a $1,000 adjusted basis and a $100 FMV to Pirate Corporation in exchange for additional stock on January 10, 2001. On April 1, 2002, Pirate adopts a plan of liquidation. During the time period between January 10, 2001 and the date the plan of liquidation is adopted, the widget maker is not used in Pirate's trade or business. Liquidation occurs on July 1, 2002, and Pirate distributes the widget maker and a second property that has a $2,500 FMV and a $900 adjusted basis. Because the widget maker is contributed to Pirate after April 1, 2000 (two years before Pirate adopted its plan of liquidation) and the widget maker is not used in Pirate's trade or business, its acquisition and distribution are presumed to be motivated by a desire to recognize the $900 loss. Unless Pirate can prove otherwise, Sec. 336(d)(2) will apply to the distribution of the widget maker. Pirate's basis for determining its loss will be $100 [$1,000 – ($1,000 – $100)]. Thus, Pirate cannot claim a loss on distributing the widget maker. Pirate is prevented from offsetting the $1,600 ($2,500 – $900) gain recognized on distributing the second property by the $900 loss realized on distributing the widget maker. ◀

The basis adjustment also affects sales, exchanges, or distributions of property made before the adoption of the plan of liquidation or in connection with the liquidation. Thus, losses claimed in a tax return filed before the adoption of the plan of liquidation may be restricted by Sec. 336(d)(2). The liquidating corporation may recapture these losses in the tax return for the tax year in which the plan of liquidation is adopted, or it can file an amended tax return for the tax year in which it originally claimed the loss.

EXAMPLE C6-11 ▶ Assume the same facts as in Example C6-10 except that Pirate sells the widget maker for $200 on July 10, 2001. Pirate reports an $800 loss ($200 – $1,000) on its 2001 tax return. The adoption of the plan of liquidation on July 1, 2002, causes the loss on the sale of the widget maker to be covered by the Sec. 336(d)(2) rules. Pirate can file an amended 2001 tax return showing the $800 loss being disallowed, or it can file its 2002 tax return reporting $800 of income under the loss recapture rules.[7] ◀

Topic Review C6-1 summarizes the general corporate liquidation rules.

Topic Review C6-1

Tax Consequences of a Corporate Liquidation

General Corporate Liquidation Rules

1. The shareholder's recognized gain or loss equals the amount of cash plus the FMV of the other property received minus the adjusted basis of the stock redeemed. Corporate liabilities assumed or acquired by the shareholder reduce the amount realized.
2. The gain or loss is capital if the stock investment is a capital asset. If the shareholder recognizes a loss on the liquidation, Sec. 1244 permits ordinary loss treatment (within limits) for qualifying individual shareholders.
3. The adjusted basis of the property received is its FMV on the distribution date.
4. The shareholder's holding period for the property begins on the day after the distribution date.
5. With certain limited exceptions, the distributing corporation recognizes gain or loss when making the distribution. The amount and character of the gain or loss are determined as if the corporation sold the property for its FMV immediately before the distribution. Special rules apply when the shareholders assume or acquire corporate liabilities and the amount of such liabilities exceeds the property's FMV.
6. The liquidated corporation's tax attributes disappear upon liquidation.

---

[6] Ibid.

[7] The property has a $1,000 basis when determining Pirate's gain on the sale and a $100 ($1,000 – $900) basis when determining its loss on the sale. Therefore, Pirate recognizes no gain or loss because the $200 sale price lies between the gain and loss basis amounts.

LIQUIDATION OF A CONTROLLED SUBSIDIARY CORPORATION

OBJECTIVE 4

Determine when the Sec. 332 and Sec. 337 nonrecognition rules apply to the liquidation of a subsidiary corporation

The following discussion of the controlled subsidiary exception is divided into three parts—the requirements for using the exception, the effects of liquidating on the parent corporation, and the effects of liquidating on the subsidiary corporation.

Section 332(a) provides that the parent corporation recognizes no gain or loss when a controlled subsidiary corporation is liquidated into its parent corporation. This liquidation rule permits a corporation to modify its corporate structure without incurring any adverse tax consequences. Section 332 applies only to the parent corporation. Other shareholders owning a minority interest are taxed under the general liquidation rules of Sec. 331. When Sec. 332 applies to the parent corporation, Sec. 337 permits the liquidating corporation to recognize no gains or losses on the assets distributed to the parent corporation. The liquidating corporation recognizes gains (but not losses) on distributions made to shareholders holding a minority interest. The nonrecognition of gain or loss rule is logical for the distribution to the parent corporation because the assets remain within the corporate group following the distribution. Thus, the subsidiary corporation can be liquidated and operated as a division of its parent corporation without gain or loss recognition.

EXAMPLE C6-12 ▶ Parent Corporation owns all of Subsidiary Corporation's stock. Subsidiary Corporation's assets have a $1 million FMV and a $400,000 adjusted basis. Parent Corporation's basis for its Subsidiary stock is $250,000. The liquidation of Subsidiary results in a $600,000 ($1,000,000 − $400,000) realized gain for Subsidiary on the distribution of its assets, none of which is recognized. Parent Corporation has a $750,000 ($1,000,000 − $250,000) realized gain on surrendering its Subsidiary stock, none of which is recognized. If Secs. 332 and 337 were not available, both Subsidiary and Parent would recognize their realized gains. In this case, Parent's gain would be reduced by the taxes paid by Subsidiary on its gain because Subsidiary's taxes reduce the amount available for distribution to Parent. ◀

REQUIREMENTS

All the following requirements must be met for a liquidation to qualify for the Sec. 332 nonrecognition rules:

TAX STRATEGY TIP

A parent corporation that does not own the requisite 80% should consider purchasing additional subsidiary stock from minority shareholders or consider having the subsidiary redeem shares from its minority shareholders. In either case, the strategy to attain 80% ownership must be applied before the corporations adopt a plan of liquidation. See Tax Planning Considerations for further details.

- The parent corporation must own at least 80% of the total combined voting power of all classes of stock entitled to vote and 80% of the total value of all classes of stock (other than certain nonvoting preferred stock issues) from the date on which the plan of liquidation is adopted until receipt of the subsidiary corporation's property.[8]
- The property distribution must be in complete cancellation or redemption of all the subsidiary corporation's stock.
- Distribution of the property must occur within a single tax year or be one of a series of distributions completed within three years of the close of the tax year during which the first of the series of liquidating distributions is made.

If all these requirements are met, the Sec. 332 nonrecognition rules are mandatory. If one or more of the conditions listed above are not met, the parent corporation is taxed under the previously discussed general liquidation rules.

STOCK OWNERSHIP. For Sec. 332 to apply, the parent corporation must own the requisite amount of voting and nonvoting stock. In applying this requirement, the Sec. 318 attribution rules for stock ownership are not applied (see Chapter C4).[9] The requisite

---

[8] The stock definition used for Sec. 332 purposes excludes any stock that is not entitled to vote, is limited and preferred as to dividends and does not participate in corporate growth to any significant extent, has redemption and liquidation rights that do not exceed its issue price (except for a reasonable redemption or liquidation premium), and is not convertible into another class of stock.

[9] Sec. 332(b)(1).

TYPICAL MISCONCEPTION

The 80% stock ownership requirement of Sec. 332 is not the same stock ownership requirement for corporate formations in Chapter C2. Instead, the Sec. 332 ownership requirement is the same one used for affiliated groups filing consolidated tax returns.

80% ownership of voting and nonvoting stock must be owned from the date on which the plan of liquidation is adopted until the liquidation is completed. Failure to satisfy this requirement denies the transaction the benefits of Secs. 332 and 337. (See page C6-19 for further discussion of the stock ownership question.)

CANCELLATION OF THE STOCK. The subsidiary corporation must distribute its property in complete cancellation or redemption of all its stock in accordance with a plan of liquidation. When more than one liquidating distribution occurs, the subsidiary corporation must have adopted a plan of liquidation and be in a status of liquidation when it makes the first distribution. This status must continue until the liquidation is completed. Regulation Sec. 1.332-2(c) indicates that a liquidation is completed when the liquidating corporation has divested itself of all its property. The liquidating corporation, however, may retain a nominal amount of property to permit retention or sale of the corporate name.

TIMING OF THE DISTRIBUTIONS. The distribution of all the subsidiary corporation's assets within one tax year of the liquidating corporation in complete cancellation or redemption of all its stock is considered a complete liquidation.[10] Although a formal plan of liquidation can be adopted, the shareholders' adoption of a resolution authorizing the distribution of the corporation's assets in complete cancellation or redemption of its stock is considered to be the adoption of a plan of liquidation when the distribution occurs within a single tax year. The tax year in which the liquidating distribution occurs does not have to be the same as the one in which the plan of liquidation is adopted.[11]

The subsidiary corporation can carry out the plan of liquidation by making a series of distributions that extend over a period of more than one tax year to cancel or redeem its stock. A formal plan of liquidation must be adopted when the liquidating distributions extend beyond a single tax year of the liquidating corporation. The liquidating distributions must include all the corporation's property and must be completed within three years of the close of the tax year during which the first distribution is made under the plan.[12]

EFFECTS OF LIQUIDATING ON THE SHAREHOLDERS

RECOGNITION OF GAIN OR LOSS.

SELF-STUDY QUESTION

What are the tax consequences if the liquidating subsidiary is insolvent?

ANSWER

The parent generally is entitled to an ordinary loss deduction under Sec. 165(g)(3) when it fails to receive any liquidation proceeds because the subsidiary is insolvent.

Parent Corporation. The Sec. 332(a) nonrecognition rules apply only to a parent corporation that receives a liquidating distribution from a solvent subsidiary. Section 332(a) does not apply to a parent corporation that receives a liquidating distribution from an insolvent subsidiary, to minority shareholders who receive liquidating distributions, or to a parent corporation that receives a payment to satisfy the subsidiary's indebtedness to the parent. All of these exceptions are discussed below.

Section 332 does not apply if the subsidiary corporation is insolvent at the time of the liquidation because the parent corporation does not receive the distributions in exchange for its stock investment. An insolvent subsidiary is one whose liabilities exceed the FMV of its assets. Regulation Sec. 1.332-2(b) requires the parent corporation to receive at least partial payment for the stock it owns in the subsidiary corporation to qualify for nonrecognition under Sec. 332. If the subsidiary is insolvent, however, the special worthless security rules of Sec. 165(g)(3) for affiliated corporations and the bad debt rules of Sec. 166 permit the parent corporation to recognize an ordinary loss with respect to its investment in the subsidiary's stock or debt obligations (see Chapter C2).

EXAMPLE C6-13 ▶ Parent Corporation owns all of Subsidiary Corporation's stock. Parent established Subsidiary to produce and market a product that proved unsuccessful. Parent Corporation has a $1.5 million basis in its Subsidiary stock. In addition, it made a $1 million advance to Subsidiary that is not secured by a note. Under a plan of liquidation, Subsidiary distributes all of its assets, having a

---

[10] Sec. 332(b)(2) and Reg. Sec. 1.332-3.

[11] Rev. Rul. 76-317, 1976-2 C.B. 98.

[12] Sec. 332(b)(3) and Reg. Sec. 1.332-4.

TYPICAL MISCONCEPTION

Section 332 applies only to the parent corporation. If a minority interest exists, the general liquidation rules of Sec. 331 apply to the minority shareholders.

$750,000 FMV, to Parent in partial satisfaction of the advance after having paid all third-party creditors. No assets remain to pay the remainder of the advance or to redeem the outstanding stock. Because Subsidiary is insolvent immediately before the liquidating distribution, none of its assets are distributed in redemption of the Subsidiary stock. Therefore, the liquidation cannot qualify under the Sec. 332 rules. Parent Corporation, therefore, claims a $250,000 business bad debt with respect to the unpaid portion of the advance and a $1.5 million ordinary loss for its stock investment. ◀

STOP & THINK

Question: In Example C6-13, assume Subsidiary Corporation had a $3 million net operating loss (NOL) carryover, which would disappear upon liquidation because Sec. 332 did not apply. To prevent this disappearance, Parent Corporation proposes to cancel the $1 million advance as a contribution to Subsidiary's capital. Thus, Parent would have a $2.5 million basis in its Subsidiary stock prior to the liquidation and no advances receivable. Now when Parent liquidates Subsidiary, all of Subsidiary's assets redeem its outstanding stock, and the transaction seems to qualify for Sec. 332 treatment. Under these circumstances, the $3 million NOL would carry over to Parent under Sec. 381, giving Parent $3 million worth of NOL deductions rather than $1.75 million worth of bad debt and worthless stock deductions under the original transaction. Do you think the IRS would condone this proposed transaction?

Solution: No. In Rev. Rul. 68-602, 1968-2 C.B. 135, the IRS held under similar circumstances that, because the cancellation "was an integral part of the liquidation and had no independent significance other than to secure the tax benefits of [Subsidiary's] net operating loss carryover, such step will be considered transitory and, therefore, disregarded." Thus, if Parent proceeded with the proposed transaction, the IRS would ignore it and treat the liquidation the same as originally done in Example C6-13.

Minority Shareholders. Liquidating distributions made to minority shareholders are taxed under the Sec. 331 general liquidation rules. These rules require the minority shareholders to recognize gain or loss—which generally is capital—upon the redemption of their stock in the subsidiary corporation.

EXAMPLE C6-14 ▶ Parent Corporation and Jane own 80% and 20%, respectively, of Subsidiary Corporation's single class of stock. Parent Corporation and Jane have adjusted bases of $100,000 and $15,000, respectively, for their stock interests. Subsidiary Corporation adopts a plan of liquidation on May 30 and makes liquidating distributions of two parcels of land having $250,000 and $62,500 FMVs to Parent Corporation and Jane, respectively, on November 1 in exchange for their stock. Parent Corporation does not recognize its $150,000 ($250,000 − $100,000) gain because of Sec. 332. Jane recognizes a $47,500 ($62,500 − $15,000) capital gain under Sec. 331. ◀

SELF-STUDY QUESTION

What bases do both the parent and minority shareholders take in the assets received in a Sec. 332 liquidation?

ANSWER

Because the parent corporation recognizes no gain or loss in the transaction, the parent corporation takes a carryover basis in its assets. However, because the minority shareholders are involved in a taxable exchange, the minority shareholders take a FMV basis in their assets.

BASIS OF PROPERTY RECEIVED. Under, Sec. 334(b)(1), the parent corporation's basis for property received in the liquidating distribution is the same as the subsidiary corporation's basis prior to the distribution. This carryover basis rule reflects the principle that the liquidating corporation recognizes no gain or loss when it distributes the property and that the property's tax attributes (e.g., the depreciation recapture potential) carry over from the subsidiary corporation to the parent corporation. The parent corporation's basis for its stock investment in the subsidiary corporation is ignored in determining the basis for the distributed property and disappears once the parent surrenders its stock in the subsidiary. Property received by minority shareholders takes a basis equal to its FMV.

EXAMPLE C6-15 ▶ Assume the same facts as in Example C6-14 and that the two parcels of land received by Parent Corporation and Jane have adjusted bases of $175,000 and $40,000, respectively, in the hands of the subsidiary. Parent Corporation takes a $175,000 carryover basis for its land. Jane takes a stepped-up $62,500 FMV basis for her land. ◀

STOP & THINK

Question: Why should a corporation that is 100%-owned by another corporation be treated differently when it liquidates than a corporation that is 100%-owned by an individual?

Solution: A corporation that is 100%-owned by another corporation can file a consolidated tax return (see Chapters C3 and C8). As a result, the parent and its subsidiary corporations are treated as a single entity. This result is the same as if the subsidiary were one of a number of divisions of a single corporation. An extension of the single-entity concept is that a subsidiary corporation can be liquidated tax-free into its parent corporation. An individual and his or her corporation are treated as two separate tax entities when calculating their annual tax liabilities. As separate entities, nonliquidating distributions (e.g., ordinary distributions and stock redemptions) from the corporation to its shareholder(s) are taxable. The same principle applies to liquidating distributions.

EFFECTS OF LIQUIDATING ON THE SUBSIDIARY CORPORATION

RECOGNITION OF GAIN OR LOSS. Section 337(a) provides that the liquidating corporation recognizes no gain or loss on the distribution of property to the 80% distributee in a complete liquidation to which Sec. 332 applies.[13] Section 337(c) defines the term *80% distributee* as a corporation that meets the 80% stock ownership requirement specified in Sec. 332 (see pages C6-10 and C6-11).

EXAMPLE C6-16 ▶ Parent Corporation owns all the stock of Subsidiary Corporation. Pursuant to a plan of complete liquidation, Subsidiary distributes land having a $200,000 FMV and a $60,000 basis to Parent. Subsidiary recognizes no gain with respect to the distribution. Parent takes a $60,000 basis for the land. ◀

TAX STRATEGY TIP

A corporation that sells, exchanges, or distributes the stock of a subsidiary may elect to treat the sale of the stock as a sale of the subsidiary's assets. This election could prove beneficial when a sale of the subsidiary stock occurs and the assets of the subsidiary corporation are substantially less appreciated than the subsidiary stock itself.

The depreciation recapture provisions in Secs. 1245, 1250, and 291 do not override the Sec. 337(a) nonrecognition rule if a controlled subsidiary corporation is liquidated into its parent corporation. Instead, the parent corporation assumes the depreciation recapture potential associated with the distributed property, and recapture occurs when the parent corporation sells or exchanges the property.[14]

The Sec. 337(a) nonrecognition rule applies only to distributions to the parent corporation. Liquidating distributions to minority shareholders are not eligible for nonrecognition under Sec. 337(a). Consequently, the liquidating corporation must recognize gain under Sec. 336(a) when it distributes appreciated property to the minority shareholders. Section 336(d)(3), however, prevents the subsidiary corporation from recognizing loss on distributions made to minority shareholders. Thus, liquidating distributions made to minority shareholders are treated the same way as nonliquidating distributions.

EXAMPLE C6-17 ▶ Assume the same facts as in Example C6-16 except that Parent Corporation owns 80% of the Subsidiary stock, Chuck owns the remaining 20% of such stock, and Subsidiary distributes two parcels of land to Parent and Chuck. The parcels have FMVs of $160,000 and $40,000, and adjusted bases of $50,000 and $10,000, respectively. Subsidiary does not recognize the $110,000 ($160,000 − $50,000) gain realized on the distribution to Parent. However, Subsidiary does recognize the $30,000 ($40,000 − $10,000) gain realized on the distribution to Chuck because the Sec. 337(a) nonrecognition rule applies only to distributions to the 80% distributee. Assume that the land distributed to Chuck instead has a $40,000 FMV and a $50,000 adjusted basis. Subsidiary can deduct none of the $10,000 loss because it distributed the land to a minority shareholder. ◀

OBJECTIVE 5

Determine the effect of a liquidation on the liquidating corporation's tax attributes

TAX ATTRIBUTE CARRYOVERS. The **tax attributes** of the liquidating corporation disappear when the liquidation is completed under the general rules. They carry over, however, in the case of a controlled subsidiary corporation liquidated into its parent corporation under Sec. 332.[15] The following items are included among the carried-over attributes:

---

[13] Section 336(e) permits a corporation to sell, exchange, or distribute the stock of a subsidiary corporation and to elect to treat such a transaction as a disposition of all the subsidiary corporation's assets. No gain or loss is recognized on the sale, exchange, or distribution of the stock. The economic consequences of making this election for a stock sale are essentially the same as if the parent corporation instead liquidates the subsidiary in a transaction to which Sec. 332 applies and then immediately sells the properties to the purchaser.

[14] Secs. 1245(b)(3) and 1250(d)(3).

[15] Sec. 381(a).

- NOL carryovers
- Earnings and profits
- Capital loss carryovers
- General business and other tax credit carryovers

The carryover amount is determined as of the close of the day on which the distribution of all the subsidiary corporation's property is completed. Further discussion of these rules is contained in Chapter C7.

Topic Review C6-2 summarizes the special rules applicable to the liquidation of a controlled subsidiary corporation.

SPECIAL SHAREHOLDER REPORTING ISSUES

Four special shareholder reporting rules apply to liquidation transactions described below. These rules add different degrees of complexity to the general liquidation rules outlined above.

PARTIALLY LIQUIDATING DISTRIBUTIONS

Liquidating distributions often are received in the form of a series of partially liquidating distributions. Section 346(a) indicates that a series of partially liquidating distributions received in complete liquidation of the corporation are taxed under the Sec. 331 liquidation rules instead of under the Sec. 302 rules applying to redemptions in partial liquidation. The IRS permits the shareholder's basis to be recovered first and requires the recognition of gain once the shareholder fully recovers the basis of a particular share or block of stock. A loss cannot be recognized with respect to a share or block of stock until the shareholder receives the final liquidating distribution, or until it becomes clear that no more liquidating distributions will occur.[16]

EXAMPLE C6-18 ▶ Diane owns 1,000 shares of Adobe Corporation stock purchased for $40,000 in 1997. Diane receives the following liquidating distributions: July 23, 2000, $25,000; March 12, 2001, $17,000; and April 5, 2002, $10,000. Diane recognizes no gain in 2000 because her $40,000 basis is not fully recovered by year-end. The $15,000 ($40,000 − $25,000) unrecovered basis that exists after

Topic Review C6-2

Tax Consequences of a Corporate Liquidation

Tax Consequences of Liquidating a Controlled Subsidiary Corporation

1. Specific requirements must be met with respect to (a) stock ownership, (b) distribution of the property in complete cancellation or redemption of all the subsidiary's stock, and (c) distribution of all property within a single tax year or a three-year period. To satisfy the stock ownership requirement, the parent corporation must own at least 80% of the total voting power of all voting stock and at least 80% of the total value of all stock.
2. The parent corporation recognizes no gain or loss when it receives distributed property from the liquidating subsidiary. Section 332 does not apply to liquidations of insolvent subsidiaries and distributions to minority shareholders.
3. The basis of the distributed property carries over to the parent corporation from the subsidiary corporation.
4. The parent corporation's holding period for the assets includes the subsidiary corporation's holding period.
5. The subsidiary corporation recognizes no gain or loss when making a distribution to an 80% distributee (parent). The liquidating subsidiary recognizes gain (but not loss) on distributions to minority shareholders. Also, the liquidating subsidiary recognizes no gain when it distributes appreciated property to satisfy certain subsidiary debts owed to the parent corporation.
6. The subsidiary corporation's tax attributes carry over to the parent corporation as part of the liquidation.

---

[16] Rev. Ruls. 68-348, 1968-2 C.B. 141, 79-10, 1979-1 C.B. 140, and 85-48, 1985-1 C.B. 126.

the first distribution is less than the $17,000 liquidating distribution received on March 12, 2001, so Diane recognizes a $2,000 gain at this time. She recognizes an additional $10,000 gain in 2002 when she receives the final liquidating distribution. ◀

EXAMPLE C6-19 ▶ Assume the same facts as in Example C6-18 except that Diane paid $60,000 for her Adobe stock. The receipt of each of the liquidating distributions is tax-free because Diane's $60,000 basis exceeds the $52,000 ($25,000 + $17,000 + $10,000) total of the distributions. Diane recognizes an $8,000 ($52,000 − $60,000) loss in 2002 when she receives the final liquidating distribution. ◀

SELF-STUDY QUESTION

If a cash method shareholder is subsequently obligated to pay a contingent liability of the liquidated corporation, what are the tax consequences of such a payment?

ANSWER

First, the prior tax year return is not amended. The additional payment results in a loss recognized in the year of payment. The character of the loss depends on the nature of the gain or loss recognized by the shareholder in the year of liquidation.

SUBSEQUENT ASSESSMENTS AGAINST THE SHAREHOLDERS

At some date after the liquidation, the shareholders may be required to pay a contingent liability of the corporation or a liability that is not anticipated at the time of the liquidating distribution (e.g., an income tax deficiency determined after the liquidation is completed or a judgment that is contingent at the time the final liquidating distribution is made). The additional payment does not affect the reporting of the initial liquidating transaction. The tax treatment for the additional payment depends on the nature of the gain or loss originally reported by the shareholder and not on the type of loss or deduction the liquidating corporation would have reported had it paid the liability.[17] If the liquidation results in a recognized capital gain or loss, a cash method of accounting shareholder treats the additional payment as a capital loss in the year of payment (i.e., an amended tax return is not filed for the year in which the shareholder originally reported the gain or loss from the liquidation). An accrual method of accounting shareholder recognizes the capital loss when he or she incurs the liability.

EXAMPLE C6-20 ▶ Coastal Corporation was liquidated three years ago with Tammy, a cash method of accounting taxpayer, reporting a $30,000 long-term capital gain on the exchange of her Coastal stock. In the current year, Tammy pays $5,000 as her part of the settlement of a lawsuit against Coastal. All shareholders pay an additional amount because the settlement exceeds the amount of funds that Coastal placed into an escrow account as a result of the litigation. The amount placed into the escrow account was not included in the amount Tammy realized from the liquidating distribution three years ago. Since Tammy had not been taxed on the cash placed in the escrow account, she cannot deduct the amount of the payment made from the escrow account in the current year. The $5,000 paid from Tammy's personal funds is treated in the current year as a long-term capital loss. ◀

OBJECTIVE 6

Understand the different tax treatments for open and closed liquidation transactions

OPEN VERSUS CLOSED TRANSACTIONS

Sometimes the value of property received in a corporate liquidation cannot be determined by the usual valuation techniques. Property that can be valued only on the basis of uncertain future payments falls into this category. In such a case, the shareholders may attempt to rely on the **open transaction doctrine** of *Burnet v. Logan* and treat the liquidation as an open transaction.[18] Under this doctrine, the shareholder's gain or loss from the liquidation is not determined until the assets that cannot be valued are subsequently sold, collected, or able to be valued. Any assets that cannot be valued are assigned a zero value. The IRS's position is that the FMV of almost any asset should be ascertainable. Thus, the IRS assumes that the open transaction method should be used only in extraordinary circumstances. For example, an open transaction cannot be used merely because a market valuation for an investment in a closely held corporation is not readily available through market quotations for the stock.

ETHICAL POINT

A tax practitioner needs to be careful that appropriate appraisals are obtained to support the values assigned to property when liquidating distributions are being made to shareholders. A 20% substantial underpayment penalty may be imposed on corporations and shareholders that substantially understate their income tax liabilities.

INSTALLMENT OBLIGATIONS RECEIVED BY A SHAREHOLDER

Shareholders who receive an installment obligation as part of their liquidating distribution ordinarily report the FMV of their obligation as part of the consideration received to calculate the amount of the recognized gain or loss. Shareholders who receive an installment obligation that was acquired by the liquidating corporation in connection with the

[17] *F. Donald Arrowsmith v. CIR*, 42 AFTR 649, 52-2 USTC ¶9527 (USSC, 1952).

[18] *Burnet v. Edith A. Logan*, 9 AFTR 1453, 2 USTC ¶736 (USSC, 1931).

sale or exchange of its property are eligible for special treatment in reporting their gain on the liquidating transaction if the sale or exchange takes place during the 12-month period beginning on the date a plan of complete liquidation is adopted and the liquidation is completed during such 12-month period. These shareholders may report their gain as they receive the installment payments.[19]

SPECIAL CORPORATE REPORTING ISSUES

EXPENSES OF THE LIQUIDATION

The corporation can deduct the expenses incurred in connection with the liquidation transaction. These expenses include attorneys' and accountants' fees, costs incurred in drafting the plan of liquidation and obtaining shareholder approval, and so on.[20] Such amounts ordinarily are deductible in the liquidating corporation's final tax return.

Expenses associated with selling the corporation's property are treated as an offset against the sales proceeds. When a corporation sells an asset pursuant to its liquidation, the selling expenses reduce the amount of gain or increase the amount of loss reported by the corporation.[21]

EXAMPLE C6-21 ▶ Madison Corporation adopts a plan of liquidation on July 15 and shortly thereafter sells a parcel of land on which it realizes a $60,000 gain (excluding the effects of a $6,000 sales commission). Madison pays its legal counsel $1,500 to draft the plan of liquidation. Madison distributes all of its remaining properties to its shareholders on December 15. The $1,500 paid to legal counsel is deductible as a liquidation expense in Madison's current year income tax return. The sales commission reduces the $60,000 gain realized on the land sale, so that Madison's recognized gain is $54,000 ($60,000 − $6,000). ◀

Any amounts of capitalized expenditures that are unamortized at the time of liquidation should be deducted if they have no further value to the corporation (e.g., unamortized organizational costs).[22] Capitalized expenditures that have value must be allocated to the shareholders receiving the benefit of such an outlay (e.g., prepaid insurance and prepaid rent).[23] Expenses related to issuing the corporation's stock are nondeductible, even at the time of liquidation, because they are treated as a reduction in paid-in capital. Unamortized bond premiums are deductible, however, at the time that the corporation retires the bonds.

TAX STRATEGY TIP

If a liquidating corporation creates an NOL in the year of liquidation or already has NOL carryovers, these losses may disappear with the liquidated corporation. If the liquidation is a Sec. 332 liquidation, the parent corporation acquires the NOL. If the liquidation is taxed under Sec. 331, the liquidating corporation may want to consider an S election for the liquidation year so any NOLs created in that year can flow through to the shareholders.

TREATMENT OF NET OPERATING LOSSES

If the liquidating corporation reports little or no income in its final income tax return, the corporation may create an NOL when it deducts its liquidating expenses and any remaining capitalized expenditures. The NOL is carried back to reduce corporate taxes paid in prior years. The resultant federal income tax refund increases (decreases) the gain (loss) previously reported by the shareholder. Alternatively, the shareholders might consider having the corporation make an S election for the liquidation year and have the flow-through loss reported on the shareholders' tax returns. (See Chapter C11 for the tax treatment of S corporations.)

The need for a liquidating corporation to recognize gains when distributing appreciated property can be partially or fully offset by expenses incurred in carrying out the

---

[19] Sec. 453(h)(1)(A). A tax deferral is available only with respect to the gain realized by the shareholder. The liquidating corporation must recognize the deferred gain when it distributes the installment obligation to the shareholder as if it had sold the obligation immediately before the distribution.

[20] *Pridemark, Inc. v. CIR*, 15 AFTR 2d 853, 65-1 USTC ¶9388 (4th Cir., 1965).

[21] See, for example, *J. T. Stewart III Trust*, 63 T.C. 682 (1975), *acq.* 1977-1 C.B. 1.

[22] Reg. Sec. 1.248-1(b)(3).

[23] *Koppers Co., Inc. v. U.S.*, 5 AFTR 2d 1597, 60-2 USTC ¶9505 (Ct. Cls., 1960).

liquidation or by any available NOL carryovers. Losses recognized by the liquidating corporation when distributing property that has declined in value can be used to offset operating profits or capital gains earned in the liquidation year. Should such losses produce an NOL or net capital loss, the losses may be carried back to provide a refund of taxes paid in a prior year, or they may be passed through to the corporation's shareholders if the corporation makes an S corporation election for the tax year.

RECOGNITION OF GAIN OR LOSS WHEN PROPERTY IS DISTRIBUTED IN RETIREMENT OF DEBT

OBJECTIVE 7

Determine when a liquidating corporation recognizes gains and losses on the retirement of debt

GENERAL RULE

A shareholder recognizes no gain or loss when the liquidating corporation pays off an unsecured debt obligation it owes to the shareholder. However, when the corporation retires a security at an amount different from the shareholder's adjusted basis for the obligation, the shareholder recognizes gain or loss for the difference. These same rules apply whether the debtor corporation pays or retires the debt as part of its operations or as part of its liquidation. The debtor corporation recognizes no gain or loss when it uses cash to satisfy its debt obligations. However, the debtor corporation recognizes gain when it uses appreciated noncash property to satisfy its debt obligations. Similarly, a debtor corporation recognizes a loss when it uses noncash property that has declined in value to satisfy its debt obligations.

SATISFACTION OF THE SUBSIDIARY'S DEBT OBLIGATIONS

The Sec. 332(a) nonrecognition rules apply only to amounts received by the parent corporation in its role as a shareholder. The parent corporation, however, does recognize gain or loss upon receipt of property in payment of a subsidiary corporation indebtedness if the payment differs from the parent's basis in the debt.[24]

As mentioned above, the use of property to satisfy an indebtedness generally results in the debtor recognizing gain or loss at the time it transfers the property.[25] Section 337(b), however, prevents a subsidiary corporation in the midst of a complete liquidation from recognizing gain or loss when it transfers noncash property to its parent corporation in satisfaction of an indebtedness. The IRC provides this exception because the property remains within the economic unit of the parent-subsidiary group.

Section 337(b) applies only to the subsidiary's indebtedness owed to the parent corporation on the date the plan of liquidation is adopted and that is satisfied by the transfer of property pursuant to a complete liquidation of the subsidiary corporation. It does not apply to liabilities owed to other shareholders or third-party creditors, or to liabilities incurred after the plan of liquidation is adopted. In addition, if the subsidiary corporation satisfies the indebtedness for less than its face amount, it may have to recognize income from the discharge of an indebtedness.

EXAMPLE C6-22 ▶ Parent Corporation owns all of Subsidiary Corporation's single class of stock. At the time of its acquisition of the Subsidiary stock, Parent purchased $1 million of Subsidiary bonds at their face amount. Subsidiary adopts a plan of liquidation. Subsequently, Subsidiary distributes property having a $1 million FMV and a $400,000 adjusted basis to Parent in cancellation of the bonds. Subsidiary also distributes its remaining property to Parent in exchange for all of its outstanding stock. Subsidiary recognizes no gain on the transfer of the property in cancellation of its bonds. Parent recognizes no gain when the liability is satisfied because the property's FMV equals the adjusted basis of the bonds. Section 334(b)(1) provides that Parent takes a $400,000 carryover basis for the noncash property it receives in cancellation of the bonds. ◀

[24] Sec. 1001(c).

[25] Ibid.

WHAT WOULD YOU DO IN THIS SITUATION?

Andrea has operated her trendy, upscale clothing store as a C corporation for a number of years. Annually, the corporation earns $200,000 in pretax profits. Andrea's stock is worth about $800,000. Her stock basis is $125,000. One of her good friends, Jenna, has opened a clothing store as a limited liability company and has been telling Andrea about the advantage of not having to pay the corporate income tax. While reading *The Wall Street Journal* weekly tax column, Andrea sees an article about the check-the-box regulations that permit corporations to elect to be taxed as partnerships and limited liability companies. She calls and tells you that she wants you to file the necessary paperwork with the IRS to make the change from being taxed as a C corporation to being taxed as a flow-through entity. What advice should you provide Andrea in this situation?

TAX PLANNING CONSIDERATIONS

TAX STRATEGY TIP

Timing the distribution of loss property so that the losses may be used to offset high-bracket taxable income at the corporate level makes good tax sense if the general liquidation rules are applicable. However, this planning possibility would not exist in a Sec. 332 parent-subsidiary liquidation because the liquidating subsidiary does not recognize losses.

TIMING THE LIQUIDATION TRANSACTION

Sometimes corporations adopt a plan of liquidation in one year but do not complete the liquidation until a subsequent year. Corporations planning to distribute properties that have both increased in value and decreased in value may find it advantageous to sell or distribute property that has declined in value in a tax year in which they also conducted business activities. As such, the loss recognized when making the liquidating distribution can offset profits that are taxed at higher rates. Deferring the sale or distribution of property that has appreciated in value may delay the recognition of gain for one tax year and also place the gain in a year in which the marginal tax rate is lower.

EXAMPLE C6-23 ▶ Miami Corporation adopts a plan of liquidation in November of the current year, a tax year in which it earns $150,000 in operating profits. Miami discontinues its operating activities before the end of the current year. Pursuant to the liquidation, it distributes assets, producing $40,000 of recognized ordinary losses. In January of next year, Miami distributes assets that have appreciated in value, producing $40,000 of recognized ordinary income. Distributing the loss property in the current year results in a $15,600 tax savings ($40,000 × 39%). Only $6,000 ($40,000 × 0.15) in taxes result from distributing the appreciated property next year. The rate differential provides a $9,600 ($15,600 − $6,000) net savings to Miami. ◀

Timing the liquidating distributions should not proceed without the planner also considering the tax position of the various shareholders. Taxpayers should be careful about timing the liquidating distributions to avoid creating a short-term capital gain taxed at ordinary rates rather than long-term capital gains taxed at 20% or 10% (18% or 8% for property acquired in or after 2001 and held for more than five years). If the liquidation results in a recognized loss, shareholders should take advantage of the opportunity to offset the loss against capital gains plus $3,000 of ordinary income, as well as attempt to increase the portion of the loss eligible for ordinary loss treatment under Sec. 1244 (See next section).

RECOGNITION OF ORDINARY LOSSES WHEN A LIQUIDATION OCCURS

Shareholders sometimes recognize losses when a liquidation occurs. Individual shareholders should be aware that, because a complete liquidation is treated as an exchange transaction, Sec. 1244 ordinary loss treatment is available when a small business corporation liquidates. This treatment permits the shareholder to claim $50,000 of ordinary loss when he or she surrenders the stock ($100,000 if the taxpayer is married and files a joint return).

Ordinary loss treatment also is available for a domestic corporation that owns stock or debt securities in a subsidiary corporation. Because the rules in Sec. 332 regarding nonrecognition of gain or loss do not apply when a subsidiary corporation is insolvent (see pages C6-11 and C6-12), the parent corporation can recognize a loss when the subsidiary corporation's stocks and debt securities are determined to be worthless. This loss is an ordinary loss (instead of a capital loss) if the domestic corporation owns at least 80% of the voting stock and 80% of each class of nonvoting stock and more than 90% of the liquidating corporation's gross income for all tax years has been other than passive income.[26]

OBTAINING 80% OWNERSHIP TO ACHIEVE SEC. 332 BENEFITS

The 80% stock ownership requirement provides tax planning opportunities when a subsidiary corporation liquidates. A parent corporation seeking nonrecognition under Sec. 332 may acquire additional shares of the subsidiary corporation's stock *before* the adoption of the plan of liquidation. This acquisition helps the parent corporation meet the 80% minimum and avoids gain recognition on the liquidation. If the parent corporation purchases these additional shares of stock from other shareholders to satisfy the 80% minimum *after* adopting the plan of liquidation, Sec. 332 will not apply.[27]

EXAMPLE C6-24 ▶ Parent Corporation owns 75% of Subsidiary Corporation's single class of stock. On March 12, Parent Corporation purchases for cash the remaining 25% of the Subsidiary stock from three individual shareholders pursuant to a tender offer. Subsidiary's shareholders approve a plan of liquidation on October 1. Subsidiary Corporation distributes its assets to Parent Corporation on December 1 in exchange for all of Subsidiary's outstanding stock. Parent Corporation recognizes no gain or loss on the redemption of its Subsidiary stock in the liquidation because all the Sec. 332 requirements have been satisfied prior to the adoption of the plan of liquidation. ◀

Alternatively, the parent corporation might cause the subsidiary corporation to redeem some of its shares held by minority shareholders before the plan of liquidation is adopted. The IRS originally held that the intention to liquidate is present once the subsidiary corporation agrees to redeem the shares of the minority shareholders. Thus, redemption of a 25% minority interest did not permit Sec. 332 to be used even though the parent corporation owned 100% of the outstanding stock after the redemption.[28]

In *George L. Riggs, Inc.*, however, the Tax Court held that a parent corporation's tender offer to minority shareholders and the calling of the subsidiary's preferred stock do not invalidate the Sec. 332 liquidation because "the formation of a conditional intention to liquidate in the future is not the adoption of a plan of liquidation."[29] The IRS has acquiesced to the *Riggs* decision.

Thus, careful planning can help both the parent corporation and subsidiary corporation avoid gain recognition under Secs. 332 and 337. Nonrecognition, however, does not extend to minority shareholders as discussed earlier.

EXAMPLE C6-25 ▶ Parent Corporation owns 80% of Subsidiary Corporation's stock. Anthony owns the remaining 20% of the Subsidiary stock. Parent and Anthony have adjusted bases of $200,000 and $60,000, respectively, for their Subsidiary stock. Subsidiary distributes land having a $250,000 adjusted basis and a $400,000 FMV to Parent and $100,000 in cash to Anthony. Subsidiary recognizes no gain or loss on the distribution of the land or the cash. Parent recognizes no gain on the liquidation and takes a $250,000 basis for the land. Anthony recognizes a $40,000 ($100,000 − $60,000) capital gain on the receipt of the money. Alternatively, distribution of the land and cash ratably to Parent and Anthony would require Subsidiary to recognize as gain the appreciation on the portion of land distributed to Anthony. ◀

AVOIDING SEC. 332 TO RECOGNIZE LOSSES

A parent corporation may want to avoid the Sec. 332 nonrecognition rules to recognize a loss when a solvent subsidiary corporation liquidates. Because the stock ownership requirement must be met during the entire liquidation process, the parent corporation

---

26 Sec. 165(g)(3).

27 Rev. Rul. 75-521, 1975-2 C.B. 120.

28 Rev. Rul. 70-106, 1970-1 C.B. 70.

29 *George L. Riggs, Inc.*, 64 T.C. 474 (1975), *acq.* 1976-2 C.B. 2.

ADDITIONAL COMMENT

The parent corporation, however, would not acquire the subsidiary's tax attributes if a taxable liquidation takes place.

apparently can sell some of its stock in the subsidiary corporation to reduce its stock ownership below the 80% level at any time during the liquidation process and be able to recognize the loss.[30] Such a sale permits the parent corporation to recognize a capital loss when it surrenders its stock interest in the subsidiary corporation. The parent corporation may desire this capital loss if it has offsetting capital gains.

The sale of a portion of the subsidiary's stock after the plan of liquidation is adopted prevents Sec. 332 from applying to the parent corporation. The Sec. 337 rules, which prevent the subsidiary corporation from recognizing gain or loss when making a liquidating distribution to an 80% distributee, also do not apply because nonrecognition is contingent on Sec. 332 applying to the distributee. Thus, the subsidiary corporation also can recognize a loss when it distributes property that has declined in value.

COMPLIANCE AND PROCEDURAL CONSIDERATIONS

GENERAL LIQUIDATION PROCEDURES

Section 6043(a) requires a corporation to file Form 966 (Information Return under Sec. 6043) within 30 days after the adoption of any resolution or plan calling for the liquidation or dissolution of the corporation. This form is filed with the District Director of the IRS for the district in which the liquidating corporation files its income tax return. Any amendment or supplement to the resolution or plan must be filed on an additional Form 966 within 30 days of making the amendment or supplement. The liquidating corporation must file Form 966 whether the shareholders' realized gain is recognized or not. The information included with Form 966 is described in Reg. Sec. 1.6043-1(b).

Regulation Sec. 1.6043-2(a) requires every corporation that makes a distribution of $600 or more during a calendar year to any shareholder in liquidation of part or all of its capital stock to file Form 1099-DIV (U.S. Information Return for Recipients of Dividends and Distributions). A separate Form 1099-DIV is required for each shareholder. The information that must be included with the Form 1099-DIV is described in Reg. Secs. 1.6043-2(a) and (b).

A corporation that exists for part of a year is required by Reg. Sec. 1.6012-2(a)(2) to file a corporate tax return for the portion of the tax year that it existed. A corporation that ceases business and dissolves, while retaining no assets, is not considered to be in existence for federal tax purposes even though under state law it may be considered for certain purposes to be continuing its affairs (e.g., for purposes of suing or being sued).

ADDITIONAL COMMENT

As evidenced in this chapter, the compliance and procedural requirements of complete liquidations are formidable. Any taxpayer contemplating either of these types of corporate transactions should consult competent tax and legal advisors to ensure that the technical requirements of the proposed transaction are satisfied.

SECTION 332 LIQUIDATIONS

Regulation Sec. 1.332-6 requires every corporation receiving distributions in a complete liquidation that comes within the purview of the Sec. 332 nonrecognition rules to maintain permanent records. A complete statement of all facts pertinent to the nonrecognition of gain or loss must be included in the corporate distributee's return for the tax year in which it receives a liquidating distribution. This statement includes the following: a certified copy of the plan of liquidation, a list of all property received upon the distribution, a statement of any indebtedness of the liquidating corporation to the recipient corporation, and a statement of stock ownership.

A special waiver of the general three-year statute of limitations is required when the liquidation covers more than one tax year.[31] The distributee corporation must file a waiver of the statute of limitations on assessment for each of its tax years that falls partially or wholly within the liquidation period. This waiver is filed at the time the distributee corporation files its income tax return. This waiver must extend the assessment period to a date not earlier than one year after the last date of the period for assessment of such taxes for the last tax year in which the liquidation may be completed under Sec. 332.

---

[30] *CIR v. Day & Zimmerman, Inc.*, 34 AFTR 343, 45-2 USTC ¶9403 (3rd Cir., 1945).

[31] Reg. Sec. 1.332-4(a)(2).

PLAN OF LIQUIDATION

A **plan of liquidation** is a written document detailing the steps to be undertaken while carrying out the complete liquidation of the corporation. The adoption date of a plan of complete liquidation ordinarily is the date on which the shareholders adopt a resolution authorizing the distribution of all the corporation's assets (other than assets retained to meet creditor claims) in redemption of all its stock.[32] Although it is generally a written document, the IRS and the courts have accepted informal shareholder agreements and resolutions as equivalent to the adoption of a formal plan of liquidation.[33]

Although a formal plan of liquidation is not required, it may assist the corporation in determining when it enters a liquidation status and, therefore, when distributions to the shareholders qualify for exchange treatment under Sec. 331 (instead of possibly being treated as a dividend under Sec. 301). The adoption of a formal plan of liquidation can provide the liquidating corporation or its shareholders additional benefits under the tax laws. For example, the adoption of a plan of liquidation permits a parent corporation to have a three-year time period (instead of one tax year) to carry out the complete liquidation of a subsidiary corporation.

PROBLEM MATERIALS

DISCUSSION QUESTIONS

C6-1 What is a complete liquidation? A partial liquidation? Explain the difference in the tax treatment accorded these two different events.

C6-2 Summitt Corporation has manufactured and distributed basketball equipment for 20 years. Its owners would like to avoid the corporate income tax and are considering becoming a limited liability company (LLC). What tax savings may result from electing to be taxed as an LLC? What federal tax costs will be incurred to make the change from a C corporation to an LLC? Would the same transaction costs be incurred if instead the corporation made an S election? Would the transaction costs be incurred had LLC status been adopted when the entity was initially organized?

C6-3 Explain why tax advisors caution people who are starting a new business that the tax costs of incorporating a business may be low while the tax costs of liquidating a business may be high.

C6-4 Explain the following statement: A corporation may be liquidated for tax purposes even though dissolution has not occurred under state corporation law.

C6-5 Compare the tax consequences to the shareholder and the distributing corporation of the following three kinds of corporate distributions: ordinary dividends, stock redemptions, and complete liquidations.

C6-6 What event or occurrence determines when a cash or accrual method of accounting taxpayer reports a liquidating distribution?

C6-7 Explain why a shareholder receiving a liquidating distribution would prefer to receive either capital gain treatment or ordinary loss treatment.

C6-8 A liquidating corporation could either (1) sell its assets and then distribute remaining cash to its shareholders or (2) distribute its assets directly to the shareholders who then sell the distributed assets. Do the tax consequences of these alternatives differ?

C6-9 Explain the circumstances in which a liquidating corporation does not recognize gain and/or loss when making a liquidating distribution.

C6-10 Kelly Corporation makes a liquidating distribution. Among other property, it distributes land subject to a mortgage. The mortgage amount exceeds both the adjusted basis and FMV for the land. Explain to Kelly Corporation's president how the amount of its recognized gain or loss on the distribution and the shareholder's basis for the land are determined.

C6-11 Explain the congressional intent behind the enactment of the Sec. 332 rules regarding the liquidation of a subsidiary corporation.

C6-12 Compare the general liquidation rules with the Sec. 332 rules for liquidation of a subsidiary corporation with respect to the following items:

---

[32] Reg. Sec. 1.337-2(b).

[33] Rev. Rul. 65-235, 1965-2 C.B. 88, and *Badias & Seijas, Inc.*, 1977 PH T.C. Memo ¶77,118, 36 TCM 518.

a. Recognition of gain or loss by the distributee corporation
b. Recognition of gain or loss by the liquidating corporation
c. Basis of assets in the distributee corporation's hands
d. Treatment of the liquidating corporation's tax attributes

C6-13 What requirements must be satisfied for the Sec. 332 rules to apply to a corporate shareholder?

C6-14 Parent Corporation owns 80% of the stock of an insolvent subsidiary corporation. Tracy owns the remaining 20% of the stock. The courts determine Subsidiary Corporation to be bankrupt. The shareholders receive nothing for their investment. How do they report their losses for tax purposes?

C6-15 Parent Corporation owns all the stock of Subsidiary Corporation and a substantial amount of Subsidiary Corporation bonds. Subsidiary Corporation proposes to transfer appreciated property to Parent Corporation in redemption of its bonds pursuant to the liquidation of Subsidiary Corporation. Explain the tax consequences of the redemption of the stock and bonds to Parent and Subsidiary Corporations.

C6-16 Explain the differences in the tax rules applying to distributions made to the parent corporation and a minority shareholder when a controlled subsidiary corporation liquidates.

C6-17 Parent Corporation owns 80% of Subsidiary Corporation's stock. Sally owns the remaining 20% of the Subsidiary stock. Subsidiary plans to distribute cash and appreciated property pursuant to its liquidation. It has more than enough cash to redeem all of Sally's stock. What strategy for distributing the cash and appreciated property would minimize the gain recognized by Subsidiary Corporation on the distribution? Does the substitution of appreciated property for cash change the tax consequences of the liquidating distribution for Sally?

C6-18 Parent Corporation owns 70% of Subsidiary Corporation's stock. The FMV of Subsidiary's assets is significantly greater than their basis to Subsidiary. The FMV of Parent's interest in the assets also substantially exceeds Parent's basis for the Subsidiary stock. Also, Parent's basis in its Subsidiary stock exceeds Subsidiary's basis in its assets. On January 30, Parent acquired an additional 15% of Subsidiary stock from one of Subsidiary's shareholders who owns none of the Parent stock. Subsidiary Corporation adopts a plan of liquidation on March 12. The liquidation is completed before year-end. What advantages accrue to Parent Corporation with respect to the liquidation by acquiring the additional Subsidiary stock?

C6-19 Texas Corporation liquidates through a series of distributions to its shareholders after a plan of liquidation has been adopted. How are these distributions taxed?

C6-20 Hill Corporation's shareholders are called on to pay an assessment that was levied against them as a result of a liability not anticipated at the time of liquidation. When will the deduction for the additional payment be claimed, assuming all shareholders use the cash method of accounting? What factors determine the character of the deduction claimed?

C6-21 Able Corporation adopts a plan of liquidation. Under the plan, Robert, who owns 60% of the Able stock, is to receive 2,000 acres of land in an area where a number of producing oil wells have been drilled. No wells have been drilled on Able's land. Discussions with two appraisers have produced widely differing market values for the land, both of which are above Able's basis for the land and Robert's basis for the Able stock. Explain the alternatives available to Able Corporation and Robert for reporting the liquidating distribution.

C6-22 Explain the IRS's position regarding whether a liquidation transaction will be considered open or closed.

C6-23 For a corporation that intends to liquidate, explain the tax advantages to the shareholders of having the corporation (1) adopt a plan of liquidation, (2) sell its assets in an installment sale, and then (3) distribute the installment obligations to its shareholders.

C6-24 Cable Corporation is 60% owned by Anna and 40% owned by Jim, who are unrelated. It has noncash assets, which it sells to an unrelated purchaser for $100,000 in cash and $900,000 in installment obligations due 50% in the current year and 50% in the following year. Cable's remaining cash, after payment of the federal income taxes on the sale and other corporate obligations, will be distributed to Jim and Anna along with the installment obligations. Explain to the two shareholders the alternatives for reporting the gain realized on their receipt of the installment obligations.

C6-25 Describe the tax treatment accorded the following expenses associated with a liquidation:
a. Commissions paid on the sale of the liquidating corporation's assets
b. Accounting fees paid to prepare the corporation's final income tax return
c. Unamortized organizational expenditures
d. Prepaid rent for office space occupied by one of the shareholders following the liquidation. Assume the prepaid rent was deducted in the preceding year's corporate tax return.

C6-26 Yong owns 70% of Andover Corporation stock. At the beginning of the current year, the corporation has $400,000 of NOLs. Yong plans to liquidate the corporation and have it distribute assets having a $600,000 FMV and a $350,000 adjusted basis to its shareholders. Explain to Yong the tax consequences of the liquidation to Andover Corporation.

C6-27 Nils Corporation, a calendar year taxpayer, adopts a plan of liquidation on April 1 of the current year. The final liquidating distribution occurs on January 5 of next year. Must Nils Corporation file a tax return for the current year? For next year?

C6-28 What is a plan of liquidation? Why is it advisable for a corporation to adopt a formal plan of liquidation?

C6-29 Indicate whether each of the following statements about a liquidation is true or false. If the statement is false, explain why.

a. Liabilities assumed by a shareholder when a corporation liquidates reduce the amount realized by the shareholder on the surrender of his or her stock.
b. The loss recognized by a shareholder on a liquidation generally is characterized as an ordinary loss.
c. A shareholder's basis for property received in a liquidation is the same as the property's basis in the liquidating corporation's hands.
d. The holding period for property received in a liquidation includes the period of time it is held by the liquidating corporation.
e. The tax attributes of a liquidating corporation are assumed ratably by its shareholders.
f. A parent corporation can elect to recognize gain or loss when it liquidates a controlled subsidiary corporation.
g. A liquidating subsidiary recognizes no gain or loss when it distributes its property to its parent corporation.
h. A parent corporation's basis for the assets received in a liquidation where gain is not recognized remains the same as it was to the liquidating subsidiary corporation.

ISSUE IDENTIFICATION QUESTIONS

C6-30 Cable Corporation, which operates a fleet of motorized trolley cars in a resort city, is undergoing a complete liquidation. John, who owns 80% of the Cable stock, plans to continue the business in another city, and will receive the cable cars, two support vehicles, the repair parts inventory, and other tools and equipment. Peter, who owns the remaining 20% of the Cable stock, will receive a cash distribution. The corporation will incur $15,000 of liquidation expenses to break its lease on its office and garage space and cancel other contracts. What tax issues should Cable, John, and Peter consider with respect to the liquidation?

C6-31 Parent Corporation, which operates an electric utility, created a 100%-owned corporation, Subsidiary, that built and managed an office building. Assume the two corporations have filed separate tax returns for a number of years. The utility occupied two floors of the office building, and Subsidiary offered the other ten floors for lease. Only 25% of the total rental space was leased because of the high crime rate in the area surrounding the building. Rental income was insufficient to cover the mortgage payments, and Subsidiary filed for bankruptcy because of the poor prospects. Subsidiary's assets were taken over by the mortgage lender. Parent lost its entire $500,000 investment. Another $100,000 of debts remained unpaid for the general creditors, which included a $35,000 account payable to Parent, at the time Subsidiary was liquidated. What tax issues should Parent and Subsidiary consider with respect to the bankruptcy and liquidation of Subsidiary?

C6-32 Alpha Corporation is a holding company owned equally by Harry and Rita. They acquired the Alpha stock many years ago when the corporation was formed. Alpha has its money invested almost entirely in stocks, bonds, rental real estate, and land. Market quotations are available for all of its stock and bond investments except for 10,000 shares of Mayfair Manufacturing Corporation stock. Mayfair is privately held with 40 individuals owning all 100,000 outstanding shares. Last year, Mayfair reported slightly more than $3 million in net income. In a discussion with Harry and Rita, you find that they plan to liquidate Alpha Corporation in the next six months to avoid the personal holding company tax. What tax issues should Harry and Rita consider with respect to this pending liquidation?

PROBLEMS

C6-33 ***Shareholder Gain or Loss Calculation.*** For seven years, Monaco Corporation has been owned entirely by Stacy and Monique, who are husband and wife. Stacy and Monique have a $165,000 basis in their jointly owned Monaco stock. The Monaco stock is Sec. 1244 stock. They receive the following assets in liquidation of their corporation: accounts receivable, $25,000 FMV; a car, $16,000 FMV; office furniture, $6,000 FMV; and $5,000 cash.

a. What are the amount and character of their gain or loss?
b. How would your answer change if the accounts receivable instead had a $140,000 FMV?
c. What is the Monacos' basis for each property received in the liquidation in Parts a and b?

C6-34 *Shareholder Gain or Loss Calculation.* For three years, Diamond Corporation has been owned equally by Arlene and Billy. Arlene and Billy have $40,000 and $20,000 adjusted bases, respectively, in their Diamond stock. Arlene receives a $30,000 cash liquidating distribution in exchange for her Diamond stock. Billy receives as a liquidating distribution a parcel of land having a $70,000 FMV and subject to a $45,000 mortgage, which he assumes, and $5,000 of cash in exchange for his Diamond stock.
a. What are the amount and character of each shareholder's gain or loss?
b. What is each shareholder's basis for the property received in the liquidation?

C6-35 *Timing of Gain/Loss Recognition.* Peter owns 25% of Crosstown Corporation stock in which he has a $200,000 adjusted basis. In each of the following situations, what amount of gain/loss will Peter report in the current year? In the next year?
a. Peter is a cash method of accounting taxpayer. Crosstown determines on December 24 of the current year that it will make a $260,000 liquidating distribution to Peter. Crosstown pays the liquidating distribution on January 3 of the next year.
b. Assume the same facts as in Part a except that Peter is an accrual method of accounting taxpayer.

C6-36 *Corporate Formation/Corporate Liquidation.* Ken Wallace contributed assets with a $100 adjusted basis and a $400 FMV to Ace Corporation in exchange for all of its single class of stock. The corporation conducted operations for five years and was liquidated. Ken Wallace received a liquidating distribution of $500 cash (less federal income taxes owed on the liquidation by the corporation) and the assets that he had contributed, which now have a $100 adjusted basis and a $500 FMV. Assume a 34% corporate tax rate.
a. What are the tax consequences of the corporate formation transaction?
b. What are the tax consequences of the corporate liquidation transaction?
c. Would your answers to Parts a and b remain the same if instead the assets had been contributed by Wallace Corporation to Ace Corporation? If not, explain how your answer(s) would change?

C6-37 *Gain or Loss on Making a Liquidating Distribution.* What are the amount and character of the gain or loss recognized by the distributing corporation when making liquidating distributions in the following situations? What is the shareholder's basis for the property received? In any situation where a loss is disallowed, indicate what changes would be necessary to improve the tax consequences of the transaction.
a. Best Corporation distributes land having a $200,000 FMV and a $90,000 adjusted basis to Tanya, its sole shareholder. The land, a capital asset, is subject to a $40,000 mortgage, which Tanya assumes.
b. Wilkins Corporation distributes depreciable property to its two equal shareholders. Robert receives a milling machine having a $50,000 adjusted basis and a $75,000 FMV. The corporation claimed $30,000 depreciation on the machine. The corporation purchased the milling machine from an unrelated seller four years ago. Sharon receives an automobile that originally cost $40,000 two years earlier and has a $26,000 FMV. The corporation claimed $25,000 depreciation on the automobile.
c. Jordan Corporation distributes marketable securities having a $100,000 FMV and a $175,000 adjusted basis to Brad, a 66.67% shareholder. Jordan purchased the marketable securities three years ago. Jordan distributes $50,000 cash to Ann, a 33.33% shareholder.
d. Assume the same facts as in Part c except the securities and cash are instead each distributed two-thirds to Brad and one-third to Ann.

C6-38 *Gain or Loss Recognition by a Distributing Corporation.* Melon Corporation, which is owned equally by four individual shareholders, adopts a plan of liquidation for distributing the following property:

- Land (a capital asset) having a $30,000 FMV and a $12,000 adjusted basis.
- Depreciable personal property having a $15,000 FMV and a $9,000 adjusted basis. Melon has claimed depreciation of $10,000 on the property during the three years since its acquisition.

- Installment obligations having a $30,000 FMV and face amount and a $21,000 adjusted basis, acquired when Melon sold a Sec. 1231 property.
- Supplies that cost $6,000 and were expensed in the preceding tax year. The supplies have a $7,500 FMV.
- Marketable securities having a $15,000 FMV and an $18,000 adjusted basis. Melon purchased the marketable securities from a broker 12 months ago.

a. Which property, when distributed by Melon Corporation to one of its shareholders, will require the distributing corporation to recognize gain or loss?
b. How will your answer to Part a change if the distribution instead is made to Melon's parent corporation as part of a complete liquidation meeting the Sec. 332 requirements?
c. How will your answer to Part b change if the distribution instead is made to a minority shareholder?

C6-39 ***Distribution of Property Subject to a Mortgage.*** Titan Corporation adopts a plan of liquidation. It distributes an apartment building having a $3 million FMV and a $1.8 million adjusted basis, and land having a $1 million FMV and a $600,000 adjusted basis, to MNO Partnership in exchange for all the outstanding Titan stock. MNO Partnership has an $800,000 basis in its Titan stock. Titan has claimed $600,000 of MACRS depreciation on the building. MNO Partnership agrees to assume the $3 million mortgage on the land and building. All of Titan's assets other than the building and land are used to pay its federal income tax liability.

a. What are the amount and character of Titan's recognized gain or loss on the distribution?
b. What are the amount and character of MNO Partnership's gain or loss on the liquidation? What is its basis for the land and building?
c. How would your answer to Parts a and b change if the mortgage instead was $4.5 million?

C6-40 ***Sale of Loss Property by a Liquidating Corporation.*** In March 2001, Mike contributed land having a $75,000 adjusted basis and a $50,000 FMV to Kansas Corporation in exchange for additional Kansas stock. The land is used as a parking lot by Kansas's employees until the corporation sells it in March 2002 for $45,000. One month after the sale, in April 2002, Kansas Corporation adopts a plan of liquidation.

a. What is Kansas's recognized gain or loss on the land sale?
b. How would your answer to Part a change if the land were not used in Kansas's trade or business?
c. How would you answer to Part b change if Mike contributed the land in March 2000 instead of March 2001?
d. How would your answer to Part b change if the corporation sold the land (contributed in March 2001) for $80,000 instead of $45,000?

C6-41 ***Tax Consequences of a Corporate Liquidation.*** Marsha owns 100% of the common stock of Gamma Corporation, an accrual-basis, calendar-year corporation. Marsha formed the corporation six years ago by transferring $250,000 of cash in exchange for the Gamma stock. Thus, she has held the stock for six years and has a $250,000 adjusted basis in the stock. Gamma Corporation's balance sheet at January 1 of the current year is as follows:

Assets	*Basis*	*FMV*
Cash	$ 400,000	$ 400,000
Marketable securities	50,000	125,000
Inventory	300,000	350,000
Equipment	200,000	275,000
Building	500,000	750,000
Total	$1,450,000	$1,900,000

Liabilities and Equity		
Accounts payable	$ 175,000	$ 175,000
Common stock	250,000	1,725,000
Retained earnings (and E&P)	1,025,000	—
Total	$1,450,000	$1,900,000

Gamma has held the marketable securities for two years. In addition, Gamma has claimed $60,000 of MACRS depreciation on the machinery and $90,000 of straight-line depreciation on the building. On January 2 of the current year, Gamma Corporation liquidates and distributes all property to Marsha except that Gamma Corporation retains cash to pay the accounts payable and any resulting tax liability of Gamma Corporation. Assume that Gamma Corporation has no other taxable income or loss. Determine the tax consequences to Gamma Corporation and Marsha.

C6-42 ***Sale of Assets Followed by a Corporation Liquidation.*** Assume the same facts as in Problem C6-41 except, on January 2 of the current year, Gamma Corporation sells all property other than cash to Acquiring Corporation for FMV. Gamma Corporation pays off the accounts payable and retains cash to pay any resulting tax liability of Gamma Corporation. Gamma Corporation then liquidates and distributes all remaining cash to Marsha. Assume that Gamma Corporation has no other taxable income. Determine the tax consequence to Gamma Corporation, Acquiring Corporation, and Marsha. How do these results compare to those in Problem C6-41?

C6-43 ***Tax Consequences of a Corporate Liquidation.*** Pamela owns all the Sigma Corporation stock. She purchased her stock ten years ago, and her current basis for the stock is $300,000. On June 10, Pamela decided to liquidate Sigma. Sigma's balance sheet prior to the sale of the assets, payment of the liquidation expenses, and payment of federal income taxes is as follows:

Assets	*Basis*	*FMV*
Cash	$240,000	$ 240,000
Marketable securities	90,000	80,000
Equipment	150,000	200,000
Land	320,000	680,000
Total	$800,000	$1,200,000
Equity		
Common stock	$300,000	$1,200,000
Retained earnings (and E&P)	500,000	—
Total	$800,000	$1,200,000

- The corporation has claimed depreciation of $150,000 on the equipment.
- The corporation received the marketable securities as a capital contribution from Pamela three years earlier at a time when their adjusted basis was $90,000 and their FMV was $70,000.
- Sigma incurred $20,000 in liquidation expenses in its final tax year.

a. What are the tax consequences of the liquidation to Pamela and Sigma Corporation? Assume a 34% corporate tax rate.

b. How would your answer change if Pamela contributed the marketable securities six years ago?

C6-44 ***Liquidation of a Subsidiary Corporation.*** Parent Corporation owns all the stock of Subsidiary Corporation. The adjusted basis of its stock investment is $175,000. A plan of liquidation is adopted, and Subsidiary distributes to Parent assets having a $400,000 FMV and a $300,000 adjusted basis (to Subsidiary), and liabilities in the amount of $60,000. Subsidiary has a $150,000 E&P balance.

a. What are the amount and character of Subsidiary Corporation's recognized gain or loss on the distribution?

b. What are the amount and character of Parent Corporation's recognized gain or loss on the redemption of the Subsidiary stock?

c. What basis does Parent Corporation take in the assets?

d. What happens to Parent Corporation's basis in the Subsidiary stock and to Subsidiary's tax attributes?

C6-45 ***Liquidation of a Subsidiary Corporation.*** Parent Corporation owns all of Subsidiary Corporation's single class of stock. Its adjusted basis for the stock is $175,000. After adopting a plan of liquidation, Subsidiary Corporation distributes the following property to Parent Corporation: money, $20,000; LIFO inventory, $200,000 FMV; and equipment, $150,000 FMV. The inventory has a $125,000 adjusted basis. The equipment originally cost $280,000. Subsidiary has claimed depreciation of $160,000 on the equipment. Subsidiary Corporation has a $150,000 E&P balance and a $40,000 NOL carryover on the liquidation date.

a. What are the amount and character of Subsidiary Corporation's recognized gain or loss when it makes the liquidating distributions?
b. What are the amount and character of Parent Corporation's recognized gain or loss on its surrender of the Subsidiary stock?
c. What is Parent Corporation's basis in each nonmoney property?
d. What happens to Subsidiary's E&P balance and NOL carryover following the liquidation?
e. What happens to Parent's $175,000 basis in the Subsidiary stock?

C6-46 ***Liquidation of a Subsidiary Corporation.*** Parent Corporation owns all of Subsidiary Corporation's single class of stock and $2 million of Subsidiary Corporation debentures. Parent purchased the debentures in small blocks from various unrelated parties at a $100,000 discount from their face amount. The Subsidiary stock has a $1.3 million basis on Parent's books. Subsidiary Corporation adopts a plan of liquidation whereby it distributes property having a $4 million FMV and a $2.4 million adjusted basis in redemption of the Subsidiary stock. The debentures are redeemed for Subsidiary Corporation property having a $2 million FMV and a $2.2 million adjusted basis.

a. What income or gain does Subsidiary Corporation recognize as a result of making the liquidating distributions?
b. What gain or loss does Parent Corporation recognize on the redemption of the Subsidiary stock? The Subsidiary debentures?
c. What is Parent Corporation's basis for the property received from Subsidiary Corporation?

C6-47 ***Liquidation of an Insolvent Subsidiary.*** Sub Corporation is a wholly-owned subsidiary of Par Corporation. The two corporations have the following balance sheets:

Assets	*Par*	*Sub*
General assets	$1,500,000	$ 750,000
Investment in Sub Corporation stock	200,000	—
Note receivable from Sub Corporation	1,000,000	—
Total	$2,700,000	$ 750,000
Liabilities & Equity		
General liabilities	$1,500,000	$ 150,000
Note payable to Par Corporation	—	1,000,000
Common Stock	300,000	200,000
Retained earnings (deficit)	900,000	(600,000)
Total	$2,700,000	$ 750,000

Other Facts:

- Par Corporation's basis in its Sub Corporation stock is $200,000, which corresponds to the $200,000 common stock on Sub Corporation's balance sheet.
- The $1 million note payable on Sub Corporation's balance sheet is payable to Par Corporation and corresponds to the note receivable on Par Corporation's balance sheet.
- The corporations do not file consolidated tax returns.
- Sub Corporation has $600,000 of net operating loss (NOL) carryovers.
- The FMV and adjusted basis of Sub Corporation's assets are the same amount.
- Just prior to the liquidation, Sub Corporation uses $150,000 of its assets to pay off its general liabilities.
- Sub Corporation transfers all its assets and liabilities to Par Corporation upon a complete liquidation.

Determine the tax consequences to Par Corporation and Sub Corporation upon Sub Corporation's liquidation.

C6-48 ***Liquidation of a Subsidiary Corporation.*** Majority Corporation owns 90% of Subsidiary Corporation's stock and has a $45,000 basis in that stock. Mindy owns the other 10% and has a $5,000 basis in her stock. Subsidiary Corporation holds $20,000 cash and other assets having a $110,000 FMV and a $40,000 adjusted basis. Pursuant to a plan of liquidation, Subsidiary Corporation (1) distributes to Mindy assets having an $11,000 FMV and a $4,000 adjusted basis prior to the liquidation, (2) distributes to Majority Corporation, assets having a $99,000 FMV and a $36,000 adjusted basis prior to the liquidation, and (3) distributes ratably to the two shareholders any cash remaining after taxes. Assume a 34% corporate tax rate and a 20% capital gains tax rate.

a. What are the tax consequences of the liquidation to Majority Corporation, Subsidiary Corporation, and Mindy?

b. Can you recommend a different distribution of assets that will produce better tax results than in Part a?

C6-49 *Tax Consequences of a Corporate Liquidation.* Gabriel Corporation is owned 90% by Zeier Corporation and 10% by Ray Goff, a Gabriel employee. A preliquidation balance sheet for the corporation is presented below:

Assets	*Basis*	*FMV*
Cash	$ 100,000	$ 100,000
Inventory	420,000	700,000
Equipment	80,000	100,000
Land	400,000	300,000
Total	$1,000,000	$1,200,000

Equity		
Accounts payable	$ 100,000	$ 100,000
Bonds payable	500,000	500,000
Common stock	100,000	600,000
Retained earnings (and E&P)	300,000	—
Total	$1,000,000	$1,200,000

Gabriel has claimed $150,000 of MACRS depreciation on the equipment. Gabriel purchased the land three years ago as a potential plant site. Plans to build the plant never were consummated, and Gabriel has held the land since then as an investment. Zeier Corporation and Ray Goff have $90,000 and $10,000 bases, respectively, in their Gabriel stock. Both shareholders have held their stock since the corporation's inception ten years ago. Zeier purchased the bonds from an insurance company two years ago for $20,000 above their face amount. Gabriel Corporation adopts a plan of liquidation. Gabriel transfers $500,000 of inventory to Zeier to retire the bonds. The shareholders receive their share of Gabriel's remaining assets and assume their share of Gabriel's liabilities (other than federal income taxes). Gabriel pays federal income taxes owed on the liquidation. Assume a 34% corporate tax rate. What are the tax consequences of the liquidation to Ray Goff, Zeier Corporation, and Gabriel Corporation?

C6-50 *Tax Consequences of a Corporate Liquidation.* Art owns 80% of Pueblo Corporation stock, and Peggy owns the remaining 20%. Art and Peggy have $320,000 and $80,000 adjusted bases, respectively, for their Pueblo stock. Pueblo Corporation owns the following assets: money, $25,000; inventory, $150,000 FMV and $100,000 adjusted basis; marketable securities, $100,000 FMV and $125,000 adjusted basis; and equipment, $325,000 FMV and $185,000 adjusted basis. Pueblo purchased the equipment four years ago and subsequently claimed $215,000 of MACRS depreciation. The securities are not disqualified property. On July 1 of the current year, Pueblo Corporation adopts a plan of liquidation at a time when it has $250,000 of E&P and no liabilities. Pueblo distributes the equipment, $50,000 of inventory, the marketable securities, and $5,000 of money to Art before year-end as a liquidating distribution. Pueblo also distributes $20,000 of money and $100,000 of inventory to Peggy before year-end as a liquidating distribution.

a. What are the gain and loss tax consequences of the liquidation to Pueblo Corporation and to Art and Peggy?

b. Can you offer any suggestions to Pueblo Corporation's management that could improve the tax consequences of the liquidation? Explain.

c. How would your answers to Parts a and b change if Art and Peggy instead were domestic corporations rather than individuals?

C6-51 *Tax Attribute Carryovers.* Bell Corporation is owned by George, who has a $400,000 basis in his Bell stock. Bell Corporation's operations have been unprofitable in recent years, and it has incurred small NOLs. Its operating assets currently have a $300,000 FMV and a $500,000 adjusted basis. George is approached by Time Corporation, which wants to purchase Bell's assets for $300,000. Bell expects to have approximately $200,000 in money after the payment of its liabilities.

a. What are the tax consequences of the transaction if Bell adopts a plan of liquidation, sells the assets, and distributes the money in redemption of the Bell stock within a 12-month period?

b. What advantages (if any) would accrue to Bell Corporation and George if the corporation remains in existence and uses the $200,000 of money that remains after payment of the liabilities to conduct a new trade or business?

C6-52 *Series of Liquidating Distributions.* Union Corporation is owned equally by Ron and Steve. Ron and Steve purchased their stock several years ago and have adjusted bases for their Union stock of $15,000 and $27,500, respectively. Each shareholder receives two liquidating distributions. The first liquidating distribution, made in the current year, results in each shareholder receiving a one-half interest in a parcel of land that has a $40,000 FMV and an $18,000 adjusted basis to Union Corporation. The second liquidating distribution, made in the next year, results in each shareholder receiving $20,000 in money.

a. What are the amount and character of Ron and Steve's recognized gain or loss for the current year? For the next year?

b. What is the basis of the land in Ron and Steve's hands?

c. How would your answers to Parts a and b change if the land has a $12,000 FMV instead of a $40,000 FMV?

C6-53 *Subsequent Assessment on the Shareholders.* Meridian Corporation originally was owned equally by five individual shareholders. Four years ago, Meridian Corporation adopted a plan of liquidation, and each shareholder received a liquidating distribution. Tina, a cash method of accounting taxpayer, reported a $30,000 long-term capital gain in the prior liquidation year on the redemption of her stock. Pending the outcome of a lawsuit in which Meridian Corporation is one of the defendents, $5,000 of Tina's liquidating distribution was held back and placed in escrow. Settlement of the lawsuit in the current year requires that the escrowed funds plus the interest earned on these funds be paid out to the plaintiff and that each shareholder pay an additional $2,500. Tina pays the amount due in the next year. How does Tina report the settlement of the lawsuit and the payment of the additional amount?

COMPREHENSIVE PROBLEM

C6-54 The following facts pertain to Lifecycle Corporation:

- Able owns a parcel of land (Land A) having a $30,000 FMV and $16,000 adjusted basis. Baker owns an adjacent parcel of land (Land B) having a $20,000 FMV and $22,000 adjusted basis. On January 2, 2002, Able and Baker contribute their parcels of land to newly formed Lifecycle Corporation in exchange for 60% of the corporation's stock for Able and 40% of the corporation's stock for Baker. The corporation elects a calendar tax year and the accrual method of accounting.
- On January 2, 2002, the corporation borrows $2 million and uses the loan proceeds to build a factory ($1 million), purchase equipment ($500,000), produce inventory ($450,000), pay other operating expenses ($30,000), and retain working cash ($20,000). Assume the corporation sells all inventory produced and collects on all sales immediately so that, at the end of any year, the corporation has no accounts receivable or inventory balances.
- Operating results for 2002 are as follows:

Sales	$964,000	
Cost of goods sold	450,000	
Interest paid on loan	140,000	
Depreciation:		
Equipment	70,000	($25,000 for E&P)
Building	24,000	($24,000 for E&P)
Operating expenses	30,000	

- In 2003, Lifecycle Corporation invests $10,000 of excess cash in Macro Corporation stock (less than 20% owned) and $20,000 in tax-exempt bonds. In addition, the corporation pays Able a $12,000 salary and distributes an additional $42,000 to Able and $28,000 to Baker. Results for 2003 are as follows:

Sales	$990,000	
Cost of goods sold	500,000	
Interest paid on loan	130,000	
Depreciation:		
Equipment	125,000	($50,000 for E&P)
Building	25,000	($25,000 for E&P)
Operating expenses	40,000	
Salary paid to Able	12,000	
Dividend received on Macro Corporation stock	2,000	
Short-term capital gain on sale of portion of Macro Corporation stock holdings ($4,000 – $3,000)	1,000	
Tax-exempt interest received	1,500	
Charitable contributions	500	

- In 2004, the corporation did not pay a salary to Able and made no distributions to the shareholders. Results for 2004 are as follows:

Sales	$500,000	
Cost of goods sold	280,000	
Interest paid on loan	125,000	
Depreciation:		
Equipment	90,000	($50,000 for E&P)
Building	25,000	($25,000 for E&P)
Operating expenses	60,000	
Long-term capital gain on sale of remaining Macro Corporation stock ($9,000 – $7,000)	2,000	
Long-term capital gain on sale of tax-exempt bond ($21,000 – $20,000)	1,000	

- On January 2, 2005, the corporation receives a refund for the 2004 NOL carried back to 2002. In addition, the corporation sells its assets, pays taxes on the gain, and pays off the $2 million debt.

	Sales Price	*Tax Adj. Basis**	*E&P Adj. Basis*
Equipment	$ 250,000	$ 215,000	$ 375,000
Building	986,000	926,000	926,000
Land A	80,000	16,000	16,000
Land B	50,000	22,000	22,000
Total	$1,366,000	$1,179,000	$1,339,000

*Note: Technically, the equipment should be depreciated for ½ year in the year of disposition, and the building should be depreciated for ½ month (because of the January disposition). However, for simplicity, the above calculations ignore depreciation deductions in the disposition year, which creates an offsetting overstatement of adjusted basis.

Immediately after these transactions, the corporation makes a liquidating distribution of the remaining cash to Able and Baker. The remaining cash is $337,800, which the corporation distributes in proportion to the shareholders' ownership (60% and 40%).

Required:

a. Determine the tax consequences of the corporate formation to Able, Baker, and Lifecycle Corporation.

b. For 2001-2003, prepare schedules showing corporate taxable income, taxes, and E&P activity.

c. For 2004, prepare a schedule showing the results of this year's transactions on Lifecycle Corporation, Able, and Baker.

TAX STRATEGY PROBLEM

C6-55 One way to compare the accumulation of income by alternative business entity forms is to use mathematical models. The following models express the investment after-tax accumulation calculation for a particular entity form:

Flow-through entities and sole proprietorships: Contribution $\times$ $[1 + R(1 - t_p)]^n$
C corporation: Contribution $\times$ $\{[1 + R(1 - t_c)]^n(1 - gt_p) + gt_p\}$

Where: ATA = after-tax accumulation in n years
R = before-tax rate of return for the business entity
t_p = owner's marginal tax rate on ordinary income
t_c = corporation's marginal tax rate
g = portion of capital gain subject to tax
gt_p = owner's tax rate on capital gains
n = number of periods

In the C corporation model, the corporation operates for n years, paying taxes currently and distributing no dividends. At the end of its existence, the corporation liquidates, causing the shareholder to recognize a capital gain. In the flow-through model, the entity or sole proprietorship distributes just enough cash for the owner or owners to pay individual taxes, and the entity reinvests the remaining after-tax earnings in the business. (See Chapter I18 of the *Individuals* volume for a detailed explanation of these models.)

Now consider the following facts. Twelve years ago, your client formed a C corporation with a \$100,000 investment (contribution). The corporation's before-tax rate of return (R) has been and will continue to be 10%. The corporate tax rate (t_c) has been and will continue to be 35%. The corporation pays no dividends and reinvests all after-tax earnings in its business. Thus, the corporation's value grows at its after-tax rate of return. Your client's marginal ordinary tax rate (t_p) has been 40%, and her capital gains rate (gt_p) has been 20%. Your client expects her ordinary tax rate to drop to 25% at the beginning of this year and stay at that level indefinitely. Her capital gains tax rate will remain at 20%. Assume the corporate stock does not qualify for the Sec. 1202 exclusion.

Your client wants you to consider two alternatives:

(1) Continue the business in C corporation form for the next 20 years and liquidate at that time (32 years in total).

(2) Liquidate the C corporation at the beginning of this year, invest the after-tax proceeds in a sole proprietorship, and operate as a sole proprietorship for the next 20 years.

The sole proprietorship's before-tax rate of return (R) also will be 10% for the next 20 years. Earnings from the sole proprietorship will be taxed currently at your client's ordinary tax rate, and your client will withdraw just enough earnings from the business to pay her taxes on the business's income. The remaining after-tax earnings will remain in the business until the end of the investment horizon (20 years from now).

Required: Show the results of each alternative along with supporting models and calculations. Ignore self employment taxes. Which alternative should your client adopt?

CASE STUDY PROBLEMS

C6-56 Paul, a long-time client of yours, has operated an automobile repair shop (as a C corporation) for most of his life. The shop has been fairly successful in recent years. His children are not interested in continuing the business. Paul is age 62 and has accumulated approximately \$500,000 in assets outside of his business, most of which are in his personal residence and retirement plan. A recent balance sheet for the business shows the following:

Assets	*Adjusted Basis*	*FMV*	*Liabilities & Equity*	*Amount*
Cash	\$ 25,000	\$ 25,000	Accounts payable	\$ 30,000
Inventory	60,000	75,000	Mortgage payable	70,000
Equipment	200,000	350,000	Paid-in capital	120,000
Building	100,000	160,000	Retain earnings	205,000
Land	40,000	60,000		
Goodwill	-0-	100,000		
Total	\$425,000	\$770,000	Total	\$425,000

The inventory is accounted for using the first-in, first-out inventory method. The corporation has claimed depreciation of \$250,000 on the equipment. The corporation acquired the building 11 years ago and has claimed \$25,000 of depreciation under the MACRS rules. The goodwill is an estimate that Paul feels reflects the value of his business over and above the other tangible assets.

Paul has received an offer of $775,000 from a competing automobile repair company for the noncash assets of his business, which will be used to establish a second location for the competing company. The corporation will sell the assets within 60 days and distribute remaining cash to Paul in liquidation of the corporation. The purchaser has obtained the necessary bank financing to make the acquisition. Paul's basis in his stock is $300,000.

Required: Prepare a memorandum for Paul outlining the tax consequences of the sale transaction and liquidation of the corporation.

C6-57 Your accounting firm has done the audit and tax work for the Peerless family and their business entities for 20 years. Approximately 25% of your accounting and tax practice billings come from Peerless family work. Peerless Real Estate Corporation owns land and a building (an ACRS property) having a $4.5 million FMV and a $1.0 million adjusted basis. The corporation owes a $1.3 million mortgage balance on the building. The corporation used substantial leverage to acquire the building so Myron Peerless and his brother Mark Peerless, who are equal shareholders in Peerless Real Estate, each have only $200,000 adjusted bases in their stock. Cash flows are good from the building, and only a small portion of the annual profits is needed for reinvestment in the building. Myron and Mark have decided to liquidate the corporation so as to avoid the federal and state corporate income taxes and continue to operate the business as a partnership. They want the MM Partnership, which has Mark and Myron equally sharing profits, losses, and liabilities, to purchase the building from the corporation for $400,000 cash plus their assumption of the $1.3 million mortgage. Mark knows a real estate appraiser who will provide a $1.7 million appraisal for the right price. Current corporate cash balances are sufficient to pay any federal and state income taxes owed on the sale of the building. Mark and Myron each would receive $200,000 from the corporation in cancellation of their stock.

Required: Prepare notes on the points you will want to cover with Myron and Mark Peerless about the corporate liquidation and the Peerless' desire to avoid federal and state corporate income taxes at your meeting tomorrow.

TAX RESEARCH PROBLEMS

C6-58 Parent Corporation owns 85% of the common stock and 100% of the preferred stock of Subsidiary Corporation. The common stock and preferred stock have adjusted bases of $500,000 and $200,000, respectively, to Parent. Subsidiary Corporation adopts a plan of liquidation on July 3 of the current year, when its assets have a $1 million FMV. Liabilities on that date amount to $850,000. On November 9, Subsidiary Corporation pays off its creditors and distributes $150,000 to Parent Corporation with respect to its preferred stock. No cash is left to be paid to Parent with respect to the remaining $50,000 of its liquidation preference for the preferred stock, or with respect to any of the common stock. In each of Subsidiary Corporation's tax years, less than 10% of its gross income has been passive income. What are the amount and character of Parent's loss on the preferred stock? The common stock?

A partial list of research sources is

- IRC Secs. 165(g)(3) and 332(a)
- Reg. Sec. 1.332-2(b)
- *Spaulding Bakeries, Inc.*, 27 T.C. 684 (1957)
- *H. K. Porter Co., Inc.*, 87 T.C. 689 (1986)

C6-59 Parent Corporation has owned 60% of Subsidiary Corporation's single class of stock for a number of years. Tyrone owns the remaining 40% of the Subsidiary stock. On August 10 of the current year, Parent Corporation purchases Tyrone's Subsidiary Corporation stock for cash. On September 15, Subsidiary Corporation adopts a plan of liquidation. Subsidiary Corporation makes a single liquidating distribution on October 1. The activities of Subsidiary Corporation are continued as a separate division of Parent Corporation. Does the liquidation of Subsidiary Corporation qualify for nonrecognition treatment under Secs. 332 and 337? Must Parent Corporation assume the Subsidiary Corporation's E&P balance?

A partial list of research sources is

- IRC Secs. 332(b) and 381
- Reg. Sec. 1.332-2(a)

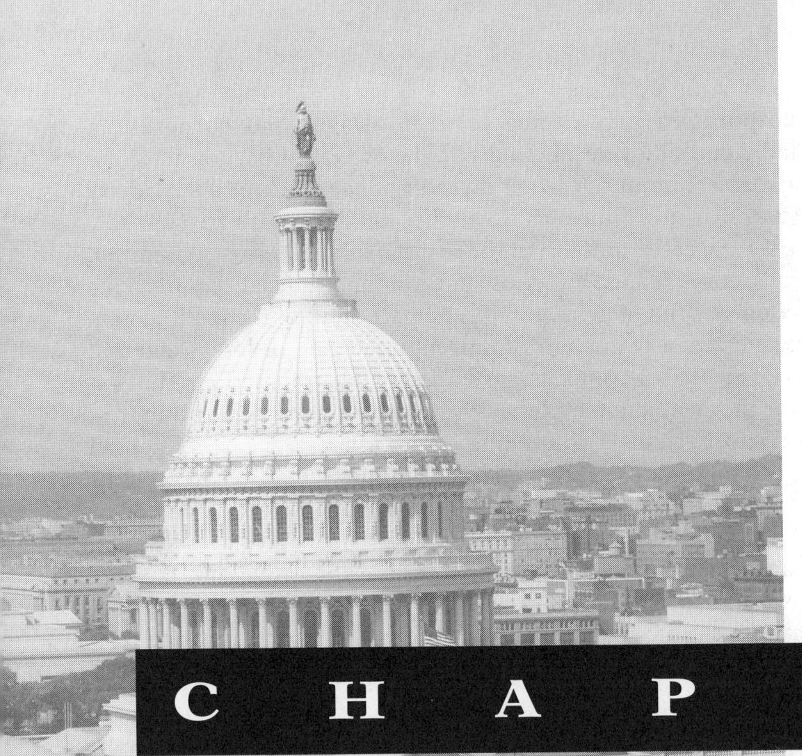

7

C H A P T E R

CORPORATE ACQUISITIONS AND REORGANIZATIONS

LEARNING OBJECTIVES

After studying this chapter, you should be able to

1. Explain the types of taxable acquisition transactions.
2. Explain the differences between taxable and tax-free acquisition transactions.
3. Explain the types of tax-free reorganizations and their requirements.
4. Determine the tax consequences of a tax-free reorganization to the target corporation.
5. Determine the tax consequences of a tax-free reorganization to the acquiring corporation.
6. Determine the tax consequences of a tax-free reorganization to the target corporation's shareholders and security holders.
7. Explain how judicial doctrines can restrict a taxpayer's ability to use corporate reorganizations.
8. Determine which reorganization forms permit the carryover of tax attributes.
9. Explain how NOL carryovers are restricted following an acquisition.

CHAPTER OUTLINE

Taxable Acquisition Transactions...7-2
Comparison of Taxable and Tax-free Acquisitions...7-11
Types of Reorganizations...7-15
Tax Consequences of Reorganizations...7-16
Acquisitive Reorganizations...7-21
Divisive Reorganizations...7-35
Other Reorganization Transactions...7-41
Judicial Restrictions on the Use of Corporate Reorganizations...7-43
Tax Attributes...7-46
Tax Planning Considerations...7-49
Compliance and Procedural Considerations...7-51

The management of a corporation may decide to acquire a second corporation. Alternatively, these same individuals may decide to divest themselves of part or all of the corporate assets, such as the assets of an operating division or the stock of a subsidiary corporation. These acquisitions or divestitures can be either taxable or tax-free transactions. In a taxable transaction, the entire amount of the realized gain or loss is recognized. To qualify as a tax-free transaction, a specific set of statutory and judicial requirements must be met. If the transaction satisfies these requirements, part or all of the realized gain or loss generally goes unrecognized. The amount of unrecognized gain or loss is deferred until the assets or stock involved are sold or exchanged in a taxable transaction. The tax-free reorganization rules are another example of the wherewithal to pay concept; that is, no tax is imposed if the taxpayer retains a continuing equity interest. A tax is imposed only when property other than stock or securities (e.g., money) has been received.[1] Taxpayers, on the other hand, are likely to use a taxable transaction (instead of a tax-free transaction) to avoid having to defer recognition of a loss on an asset or stock disposition.

This chapter presents an overview of the tax consequences of taxable and tax-free acquisitions and divestitures. It also examines the statutory provisions and judicial doctrines that apply to determine the tax consequences for the tax-free acquisition and divestiture transactions.

TAXABLE ACQUISITION TRANSACTIONS

OBJECTIVE 1

Explain the types of taxable acquisition transactions

Taxable acquisition transactions can be divided into two major categories:

- Purchase of a target corporation's assets
- Purchase of a target corporation's stock

Acquiring corporations have two primary ways to acquire the assets of a **target corporation.**[2] The acquiring corporation can acquire the needed assets directly from the target corporation. Alternatively, the acquiring corporation can acquire an indirect interest in the assets by purchasing a controlling (more than 50%) interest in the target corporation's stock. Three options exist once the stock interest is acquired.

- The acquiring corporation and its new subsidiary corporation can exist as separate entities.
- The acquiring corporation can liquidate its new subsidiary corporation in a tax-free liquidation. Following the liquidation, the parent corporation retains a direct interest in the assets.
- The acquiring corporation's management can make a Sec. 338 election on behalf of the subsidiary corporation. A Sec. 338 election permits the adjusted basis of the subsidiary corporation's assets to be stepped-up to the price that the acquiring corporation paid for the subsidiary corporation's stock plus the amount of any subsidiary corporation's liabilities.

The four asset and stock acquisition alternatives are examined below. Table C7-1 summarizes the tax consequences of these alternatives.

ASSET ACQUISITIONS

The asset acquisition is not a difficult transaction for the acquiring and target corporations to accomplish. The selling corporation reports the sale transaction by determining the gain or loss recognized on the sale of each individual asset. Sales of depreciable assets (e.g., Sec. 1245 and 1250 property) result in previously claimed depreciation being recaptured.

---

[1] The tax deferral can be permanent if the stocks and securities are held until death. At death, the carryover or substituted basis is stepped-up to its fair market value (FMV) without incurring any income tax liability.

[2] The terms *target* and *acquired corporation* are used interchangeably here.

▼ **TABLE C7-1**
Comparison of Taxable Acquisition Alternatives

		Taxable Stock Acquisition with:		
	Taxable Asset Acquisition	**No Liquidation of Target**	**Tax-Free Liquidation of Target**	**Sec. 338 Election for Target**
Acquiring corporation's basis for stock	N/A	Cost basis	Cost basis	Cost basis
Parent-subsidiary relationship created	No	Yes	Yes, until liquidation occurs	Yes
Consolidated tax return election available	No	Yes	Yes, until liquidation occurs	Yes
Gain/loss recognized by target corporation on asset sale	Yes	No	No	Yes, on deemed sale of assets from old target corporation to new target corporation.
Gain/loss recognized by target corporation when making liquidating distribution	Yes, if target elects to liquidate before or after the asset sale.	N/A	No	No
Gain recognized by acquiring corporation when receiving liquidating distribution	N/A	N/A	No	No
Acquiring corporation's basis for assets acquired	Cost basis on acquiring corporation's books	No change in basis of assets on target corporation's books	Carryover from target corporation's books	Cost basis of target stock acquired plus amount of target's liabilities
Transfer of tax attributes to acquiring corporation	Remain with target corporation	Remain with target corporation	Carryover to acquiring corporation	Disappear with deemed sale of assets by old target corporation

N/A = Not applicable.

TAX STRATEGY TIP

Three types of state taxes may arise in an *asset* sale—transfer taxes, real property gains taxes, and sales taxes (some state sales tax laws allow certain bulk-sale exceptions). These taxes need to be taken into account by both the buyer and seller when drafting the sales agreement. When a *stock* sale occurs, these taxes can be avoided because the assets remain inside the same entity before and after the stock sale.

The purchaser's bases for the acquired assets are their acquisition cost.[3] The purchaser can claim depreciation based on the property's total acquisition cost.

A taxable asset acquisition offers the purchaser two major advantages. First, a significant portion of the acquisition can be debt-financed, whereas the tax-free reorganization requirements either restrict or prohibit the use of debt. The interest expense incurred with respect to the debt is deductible for tax purposes. Second, only assets and liabilities designated in the purchase-sale agreement are acquired. The purchaser need not acquire all or substantially all the target corporation's assets, as is the case when the target corporation's stock is acquired in either a taxable transaction or a tax-free reorganization or when an asset-for-stock tax-free reorganization takes place. Similarly, the purchaser assumes only liabilities specified in the purchase-sale agreement. Contingent or unknown liabilities remain the responsibility of the seller.

The target corporation (i.e., acquired corporation) may be liquidated after the asset sale takes place. The target corporation recognizes gain or loss with respect to the assets sold. Any property retained by the target corporation is distributed to the shareholders as part of the liquidation. The liquidating corporation recognizes gain or loss at the time of the distribution as if such property were instead sold. The target corporation's shareholders report their gain or loss on the liquidation as capital gain or loss (see Chapter C6).

[3] Sec. 1012.

EXAMPLE C7-1 ▶ Target Corporation is owned by Ann, Bob, and Cathy. Each individual has a $20,000 basis for his or her stock acquired six years ago. Acquiring Corporation purchases Target's noncash assets for $100,000 of cash and $300,000 of Acquiring debt obligations. Target retains its $50,000 of cash. On the sale date, Target's noncash assets have a $280,000 adjusted basis and a $400,000 FMV. Its liabilities are $100,000 on the sale date. Target must recognize a $120,000 gain [($100,000 + $300,000) − $280,000]. The character of the gains and losses recognized depends on the individual properties sold. Assuming a 34% corporate tax rate, Target's tax liability on the sale is $40,800 ($120,000 × 0.34). Acquiring takes a $400,000 basis for the noncash assets acquired. After Target pays its income tax and other liabilities, Ann, Bob, and Cathy each receive a liquidating distribution on which they report a capital gain. ◀

Sometimes Target Corporation will be liquidated before the shareholders sell the assets of the business. The tax consequences of the liquidation are described in Chapter C6. In general, the total tax liability for the corporation and shareholders will be the same whether the liquidation precedes or follows the asset sale.

STOCK ACQUISITIONS

KEY POINT

In a stock acquisition, only the shareholders of Target recognize gain. In an asset acquisition, both Target and Target's shareholders may recognize gain.

STOCK ACQUISITION WITH NO LIQUIDATION. The stock acquisition is the simplest of the acquisition transactions. The gain recognized on the sale receives capital gain treatment if the stock is a capital asset in the seller's hands. If part or all of the consideration is deferred to a later tax year, the seller's gain can be reported using the installment method of accounting.[4] If part of the total consideration received by the seller of the stock represents an agreement with the purchaser not to compete for a specified time period, the consideration received for the agreement is taxed as ordinary income.[5]

The purchaser's basis for the stock is its acquisition cost.[6] The target corporation's basis for its assets does not change as a result of the stock sale. Any payment for the stock that exceeds the book value of the net assets of the acquired company cannot be reflected in a stepped-up basis for the assets. Any potential for depreciation recapture that exists on the transaction date stays with the target corporation's assets and, therefore, is assumed by the purchaser. If the target corporation has loss or credit carryovers, these carryovers can be subject to special limitations in the post-acquisition tax years (see page C7-47).

ADDITIONAL COMMENT

A shareholder's basis in stock sometimes is referred to as "outside basis" as opposed to "inside basis," which is the corporation's basis in its assets

Stock sales have proven to be popular with sellers because they may be less costly than an asset sale since only a single level of taxation is encountered. No adjustment occurs to the basis of the target corporation's assets following a stock sale even though the basis of the stock acquired may be substantially higher than the total tax basis the target corporation retains in its assets. Thus, one of the tax advantages of actually purchasing the assets of the target corporation—the higher basis for the properties for tax purposes—is not available when a stock purchase occurs unless the purchasing corporation makes a Sec. 338 deemed sale election (discussed later in this chapter).

EXAMPLE C7-2 ▶ Assume the same facts as in Example C7-1 except that Acquiring extends a tender offer whereby it will purchase the Target stock at $50 per share. Ann, Bob, and Cathy tender their 7,000 Target shares in response to Acquiring's offer. Acquiring's $350,000 (7,000 shares × $50/share) purchase price equals Target's net asset amount ($450,000 − $100,000 liabilities). Ann, Bob, and Cathy each report a long-term capital gain on the disposition of their stock. Target becomes a wholly-owned subsidiary of Acquiring and, in the absence of a Sec. 338 election, does not adjust the basis of its assets as a result of the sale. ◀

KEY POINT

In Example C7-2, the built-in gain in Target's assets is not recognized in a stock acquisition. Likewise, Target's assets are not stepped-up in basis even though Acquiring pays their full $350,000 FMV for the Target stock.

If the purchasing corporation is already part of an affiliated group that files a consolidated tax return, the subsidiary corporation must join in the consolidated return election if at least 80% of the subsidiary's stock is owned and the subsidiary is an includible cor-

---

[4] Sec. 453(a). Legislation enacted in December 1999 prevented accrual method of accounting taxpayers from using the installment method to defer gains realized on the sale of an asset or business. The restriction largely prevented small businesses or their owners from using an installment sale to defer gain when selling their assets or stock. In December 2000, however, Congress repealed the prohibition against letting an accrual method of accounting taxpayer use the installment method. The repeal removes the December 1999 legislation from the IRC as if it were never enacted.

[5] The purchaser can amortize over a 15-year period any amounts paid to the seller with respect to the agreement not to compete (Sec. 197).

[6] Sec. 1012.

poration (see Chapter C8). Otherwise, the parent and subsidiary corporations can elect to make an initial consolidated return election.

TYPICAL MISCONCEPTION

Taxpayers often do not understand that the parent's basis in its subsidiary's stock disappears in a Sec. 332 liquidation. Instead, the subsidiary's bases in the liquidated assets carry over to the parent.

STOCK ACQUISITION FOLLOWED BY A LIQUIDATION. The stock acquisition described in the preceding section can be followed by a liquidation of the acquired (subsidiary) corporation into its acquiring (parent) corporation. If the parent corporation owns at least 80% of the subsidiary corporation's stock, the liquidation is tax-free under the Sec. 332 and 337 rules outlined in Chapter C6.[7] The basis of the subsidiary corporation's assets carries over to the parent corporation. If the parent corporation paid a premium for the assets (i.e., an amount exceeding the total of the assets' adjusted bases), this premium is lost when the liquidation occurs because the parent corporation's basis for the stock disappears when the tax-free liquidation occurs. The disappearing basis "loss" cannot be deducted and provides no tax benefit. If the parent corporation paid less than the total of the assets' adjusted bases, the parent corporation retains this "excess" basis amount as part of the assets' carryover basis, which can provide additional tax benefits.

EXAMPLE C7-3 ▶ Assume the same facts as in Example C7-2 except that Acquiring and Target Corporations continue to file separate tax returns following the stock acquisition, and Target is liquidated into Acquiring shortly after the acquisition. Target Corporation's assets have the following adjusted bases and FMVs immediately before the sale:

Assets	*Adjusted Basis*	*FMV*
Cash	$ 50,000	$ 50,000
Marketable securities	49,000	55,000
Accounts receivable	60,000	60,000
Inventory	60,000	90,000
Building	27,000	44,000
Land	10,000	26,000
Machinery and equipment[a]	74,000	125,000
Total	$330,000	$450,000

[a]The machinery and equipment are Sec. 1245 property. Recapture potential on the machinery and equipment is $107,000.

Target and Acquiring Corporations recognize no gains or losses on the liquidation. Acquiring assumes Target's $100,000 in liabilities and takes a $330,000 basis for the assets acquired from Target, with each of the individual basis amounts carrying over. In addition, Acquiring assumes all of Target's tax attributes, including any NOL carryovers, E&P, and the $107,000 depreciation recapture potential on the machinery and equipment. ◀

ADDITIONAL COMMENT

A Sec. 338 election triggers immediate taxation to the target corporation. Therefore, in most situations it makes little sense to pay an immediate tax to obtain a step-up in basis when such additional basis can be recovered only in future years. The election can be beneficial, however, if the target corporation has enough NOLs to offset most or all of the gain recognized on the deemed asset sale.

SECTION 338 DEEMED SALE ELECTION. In *Kimbell-Diamond Milling Co.*,[8] the courts held that the purchase of a target corporation's stock followed by a prompt liquidation that occurs to obtain the target corporation's assets is treated as a single transaction. The acquiring corporation was permitted to use its acquisition price for the stock to determine the basis for the acquired assets. Congress codified this decision in 1954 by requiring that the purchase and liquidation of a subsidiary corporation be treated as an asset purchase when the controlling interest in the subsidiary's stock was acquired within a 12-month period and the subsidiary corporation was completely liquidated within two years of the date on which acquisition of the controlling stock interest was completed. These rules created a number of uncertainties for taxpayers and were difficult for the IRS to administer. In 1982, Congress enacted Sec. 338, which permits the acquiring corporation to adjust the basis of the target corporation's assets through a **deemed sale election.**

The Sec. 338 deemed sale election operates in two steps. First the target corporation's shareholders sell their stock to the acquiring corporation. Then the acquiring corporation makes a Sec. 338 deemed sale election with respect to the acquisition of the target corporation's stock. This election results in a hypothetical sale of the "old" target corporation's assets to a "new" target corporation for their **aggregate deemed sale price (ADSP)** in a

[7] The liquidation may be taxable for any minority shareholders and to the subsidiary corporation on distributions made to the minority shareholders.

[8] *Kimbell-Diamond Milling Co. v. CIR,* 40 AFTR 328, 51-1 USTC ¶9201 (5th Cir., 1951).

PRACTICAL APPLICATION

The purchasing corporation most likely would not make a Sec. 338 election if it resulted in the target corporation's asset tax bases being stepped-down.

transaction that requires the seller ("old" target) to recognize all gains and losses. The "old" target corporation goes out of existence for tax purposes only.[9] The "new" target corporation is treated as a new entity for tax purposes (i.e., it makes new accounting method and tax year elections). The bases of the old target corporation's assets are stepped-up or stepped-down to the amount paid by the acquiring corporation for the target corporation's stock plus the amount of the target corporation's liabilities (including any federal income taxes owed on the hypothetical sale). Corporate purchasers generally are less enthusiastic about Sec. 338[10] treatment because the target corporation usually incurs a significant tax cost on the hypothetical sale in the year the purchasing corporation makes the Sec. 338 election.

Eligible Stock Acquisitions. In this type of election, Sec. 338 requires the acquiring corporation to make a qualified stock purchase (i.e., to purchase 80% or more of the target corporation's voting stock and 80% or more of the total value of all classes of stock [except certain nonvoting preferred stock issues] during a 12-month (or shorter) acquisition period).[11] The acquisition period must be a continuous period beginning on the date on which the acquiring corporation first purchases stock in the target corporation that counts toward a qualified stock purchase and ending on the date the qualified stock purchase occurs. If the acquiring corporation does not acquire the necessary 80% minimum within a continuous 12-month period, it cannot make the Sec. 338 election.

EXAMPLE C7-4 ▶ Missouri Corporation purchases a 25% block of Target Corporation's single class of stock on each of four dates: April 1, 2001; July 1, 2001; December 1, 2001; and February 1, 2002. Because Missouri acquires at least 80% of Target's stock within a 12-month period (April 1, 2001 through February 1, 2002), Missouri Corporation can elect to treat the transaction under the Sec. 338 deemed sale rules. ◀

EXAMPLE C7-5 ▶ Assume the same facts as in Example C7-4 except that Missouri Corporation instead makes the final 25% purchase on May 15, 2002. In this case, Missouri acquires only 75% of the Target stock in any 12-month period. Two possible 12-month periods are involved—April 1, 2001 through March 31, 2002, and May 16, 2001 through May 15, 2002. The 80% stock ownership minimum is not met in either period. A Sec. 338 election is unavailable to Missouri Corporation. ◀

Stock acquisitions not treated as purchases for the purpose of meeting the 80% requirement include the following:

- Stock whose adjusted basis is determined in whole or in part by its basis in the hands of the person from whom it was acquired (e.g., stock acquired as a capital contribution)
- Stock whose basis is determined under Sec. 1014(a) (i.e., FMV on the date of death or an alternative valuation date when stock is acquired from a decedent)
- Stock acquired in a tax-free transaction where nonrecognition of gain or loss is permitted by Sec. 351, 354, 355, or 356 (e.g., corporate formations, corporate divisions, or tax-free reorganizations)
- Stock acquired from a related party where stock ownership would be attributed to the purchaser under the attribution rules in Secs. 318(a)(1) through (3)

The Election. A Sec. 338 election must be made not later than the fifteenth day of the ninth month beginning after the month in which the acquisition date occurs. The acquisi-

---

[9] The target corporation's legal existence does not change under the state corporation laws. For federal income tax purposes, the target corporation (commonly referred to as "old" target) goes out of existence. A "new" target corporation is created. This new corporation acquires for tax purposes all the assets of the "old" corporation.

[10] An alternative form of Sec. 338 election is permitted under Sec. 338(h)(10) for members of an affiliated group. This election generally is used by affiliated groups that file consolidated tax returns. The Sec. 338(h)(10) election permits the target corporation (e.g., a subsidiary) to recognize gain or loss as if it had sold its assets in a single transaction. The corporation selling the stock (e.g., a parent corporation) does not recognize gain on the stock sale thereby resulting in a single level of taxation. This special form of Sec. 338 election has become popular in recent years.

[11] The basic Sec. 332 liquidation of a controlled subsidiary corporation stock definition outlined in Chapter C6 also is used for Sec. 338 purposes.

tion date is the first date during the 12-month acquisition period on which the 80% stock ownership requirement is met.[12]

EXAMPLE C7-6 ▶ Arizona Corporation purchases 40% of Target Corporation's single class of stock on April 1, 2002. It purchases an additional 50% of Target's stock on October 20, 2002. The acquisition date is October 20, 2002. Arizona must make the Sec. 338 election on or before July 15, 2003. ◀

Deemed Sale Transaction. When the acquiring corporation makes a Sec. 338 election, the target corporation is treated as having sold all of its assets at their aggregate deemed sale price (ADSP) in a single transaction at the close of the acquisition date. The asset sale is a taxable transaction with gain or loss recognized by the target corporation.

The aggregate deemed sale price is the price at which the old target corporation is deemed to have sold all of its assets in the Sec. 338 deemed sale. Calculation of the ADSP is illustrated by the following equation:[13]

$$\text{ADSP} = \frac{G + L - (T_R \times B)}{(1 - T_R)}$$

Where: G = Acquiring's grossed-up basis in the target corporation's recently purchased stock;
L = Target's liabilities other than its tax liability for the deemed sale gain determined by reference to the ADSP;
T_R = the applicable federal income tax rate; and
B = the adjusted basis of the asset(s) deemed sold.

EXAMPLE C7-7 ▶ Assume the same facts as in Examples C7-2 and C7-3 except that Acquiring Corporation makes a timely Sec. 338 election. Also assume that Target's marginal tax rate is 34%. The aggregate deemed sale price at which old Target is deemed to have sold its assets is determined as follows:

$$\text{ADSP} = \frac{G + L - (T_R \times B)}{(1 - T_R)}$$

$$\text{ADSP} = \frac{\$350{,}000 + \$100{,}000 - (0.34 \times \$330{,}000)}{(1 - 0.34)}$$

$$0.66\ \text{ADSP} = \$337{,}800$$

$$\text{ADSP} = \$511{,}818$$

Thus, Target will recognize a gain of $181,818 ($511,818 – $330,000) and pay taxes of $61,818 (0.34 × $181,818) on the gain. ◀

TAX STRATEGY TIP
Many taxpayers avoid Sec. 338 because it requires an advance payment of taxes to achieve a step-up in basis of target corporation's assets. A Sec. 338 election becomes more viable, however, when the target corporation has NOLs that can offset its gain on the deemed sale of its assets, thereby reducing the cost of making the election.

Because the Sec. 338 election was originally designed for transactions in which the acquisition price of the target corporation's stock exceeded the adjusted basis of the target corporation's assets, the amount of gain recognized by the target in many of these transactions may be substantial. The size of this tax cost may result in companies forgoing the Sec. 338 election when target corporation stock is purchased or lowering the price they are willing to pay for the target corporation's stock if they intend to make a Sec. 338 election. Alternatively, the company may acquire the assets in a tax-free reorganization that is not eligible for a Sec. 338 election but permits the acquiring corporation to use its stock (instead of cash) to make the acquisition. The tax-free transaction, however, requires that the target corporation's basis for the assets carries over to the acquiring corporation. Tax-free acquisitions are explained later in this chapter. Example C7-7 presents an illustration of the deemed sale transaction under Sec. 338.

---

12 Secs. 338(g) and 338(h)(2).

13 This equation is derived as follows:

$$\text{ADSP} = G + L + [T_R \times (\text{ADSP} - B)]$$
$$\text{ADSP} = G + L + (T_R \times \text{ADSP}) - (T_R \times B)$$
$$\text{ADSP} - (T_R \times \text{ADSP}) = G + L - (T_R \times B)$$
$$\text{ADSP} \times (1 - T_R) = G + L - (T_R \times B)$$
$$\text{ADSP} = \frac{G + L - (T_R \times B)}{(1 - T_R)}$$

Tax Basis of the Assets After the Deemed Sale. Similarly to the ADSP, the tax basis for the assets to the new target corporation is based on the amount paid by the acquiring corporation for the target corporation's stock. This amount is called the **adjusted grossed-up basis** for the target corporation's stock. The adjusted grossed-up basis amount equals the sum of

- The purchasing corporation's grossed-up basis in recently purchased target corporation stock;
- The purchasing corporation's basis in nonrecently purchased target corporation stock;
- The liabilities of the new target corporation; and
- Other relevant items.[14]

The adjusted grossed-up basis is determined at the beginning of the day following the acquisition date. Example C7-10 illustrates the calculation of the adjusted grossed-up basis.

The target corporation stock owned by the acquiring corporation is divided into two categories: recently purchased stock and nonrecently purchased stock. This division is necessary because only the recently purchased stock is treated as a deemed purchase of the target corporation's assets. Recently purchased stock includes any target corporation stock held on the acquisition date that the acquiring corporation purchased during the 12-month (or shorter) acquisition period. Nonrecently purchased stock includes all other target corporation stock acquired before the acquisition period and held by the acquiring corporation on the acquisition date.[15] The basis of the purchasing corporation's stock interest equals the grossed-up basis of the recently purchased stock plus the basis of the nonrecently purchased stock.

EXAMPLE C7-8 ▶ Apple Corporation purchases all of Target Corporation's single class of stock on July 23 of the current year. All the Target stock is considered to be recently purchased stock because it is purchased in a single transaction. The acquisition date is July 23 of the current year. ◀

EXAMPLE C7-9 ▶ Assume the same facts as in Example C7-8 except that Apple Corporation already owns 10% of the Target stock (purchased five years ago) and purchases only the remaining 90% of the Target stock. The original block of Target stock is nonrecently purchased stock because it was acquired more than 12 months before the acquisition date (July 23 of the current year). ◀

When the acquiring corporation does not own all the target corporation's stock, the basis of the acquiring corporation's recently purchased stock must be increased or grossed-up to a hypothetical value that reflects ownership of all the target corporation's stock.[16]

The basis of the stock is increased by the face amount of any target corporation liabilities outstanding at the beginning of business on the day following the acquisition date plus any tax liability resulting from gain recognized on the deemed sale.[17] This liability adjustment reflects the fact that, if the acquisition had truly been an asset purchase, the assumption of the liabilities would have been reflected in the total purchase price.

Allocation of Basis to Individual Assets. The adjusted grossed-up basis of the stock is allocated among seven classes of assets by using the residual method.[18] The residual method requires that the adjusted grossed-up basis be allocated to the corporation's tangible and intangible property (other than goodwill and going concern value) on a priority

---

[14] Secs. 338(b)(1) and (2). The IRS has indicated that other relevant items include only items that arise from adjustment events that occur after the close of the new target's first tax year and items discovered as a result of an IRS examination of a tax return (e.g., the payment of contingent amounts for recently or nonrecently purchased stock).

[15] Sec. 338(b)(6). A special gain recognition election is available to adjust the basis of nonrecently purchased stock. This election, which is found in Sec. 338(b)(3), is beyond the scope of this text.

[16] Sec. 338(b)(4). The gross-up operation involves taking the purchasing corporation's basis for the recently purchased target stock and dividing it by the percentage (by value) of recently purchased target stock owned (expressed as a decimal).

[17] Sec. 338(b)(2) and Reg. Secs. 1.338(b)-1(f)(1) and (2).

[18] Reg. Sec. 1.338-6(a).

PRACTICAL APPLICATION

Because goodwill now can be amortized, the fact that the residual purchase price is allocated to goodwill may be a desirable tax result. Goodwill was not amortized under pre-Sec. 197 law because it had an indefinite life. On the negative side, however, the required 15-year amortization period under Sec. 197 is longer than the time period used by many taxpayers under pre-Sec. 197 law to amortize intangible assets that had a shorter determinable life.

basis. Any amount not allocated to specific tangible and intangible property is allocated to the target corporation's goodwill and going concern value.

The seven classes of assets used in allocating the basis are

- Class I: cash and general deposit accounts including demand deposits and similar accounts in banks, savings and loan associations, etc.
- Class II: actively traded personal property (as defined in Sec. 1092(d)(1)), such as stock that is part of a straddle, U.S. government securities, and publicly traded securities.
- Class III: accounts receivable, mortgages, and credit card receivables from customers that arise in the ordinary course of business.
- Class IV: Inventory or other property held primarily for sale to customers in the ordinary course of the taxpayer's trade or business.
- Class V: all assets other than Class I, II, III, IV, VI, and VII assets. Included here would be tangible and intangible property without regard to whether they are depreciable, depletable, or amortizable.
- Class VI: All amortizable Sec. 197 assets except those in the nature of goodwill and going concern value.
- Class VII: Sec. 197 intangible assets in the nature of goodwill and going concern value.[19]

ADDITIONAL COMMENT

The residual method ensures that any premium paid for the target stock is reflected in goodwill. Because the residual method is the only acceptable allocation method, the only uncertainty that remains is to determine the FMVs of the assets listed in Classes II through VII.

Class VI and VII intangible assets acquired after August 6, 1993 are amortizable over a 15-year period if they are used in the active conduct of a trade or business. Among the assets included are goodwill, going concern value, and covenants not to compete.

The adjusted grossed-up basis is first allocated to the individual Class I assets based on their actual dollar amounts.[20] Any amount remaining after the allocation to the Class I assets is assigned to the Class II assets (but not in excess of their gross FMV). A similar allocation process is used for the Class III through VII assets. The total basis amounts allocated to the Class II through VII asset categories are allocated to individual assets within the class based on relative gross FMVs. When making the intraclass allocations, the allocation is based on the asset's total gross FMV, not its net FMV (gross FMV minus specific liens attaching to the property).

EXAMPLE C7-10 ▶ Assume the same facts as in Example C7-7, with assets classified as follows:

Asset Class	*Assets*	*FMV*
I	Cash	$ 50,000
II	Marketable securities	55,000
III	Accounts receivable	60,000
IV	Inventory	90,000
V	Building	44,000
V	Land	26,000
V	Machinery and equipment	125,000
	Total	$450,000

The adjusted grossed-up basis for Acquiring Corporation's interest in Target stock is:

Recently purchased stock	$350,000
Plus: Target corporation's nontax liabilities	100,000
Target corporation's tax liability [($511,818 − $330,000) × 0.34]	61,818
Adjusted grossed-up basis	$511,818

[19] Reg. Sec. 1.338(b)-6(b). The seven-category classification system applies for asset acquisitions taking place after January 5, 2000. Five-and six-category classification systems have applied to asset acquisitions taking place on or before January 5, 2000.

[20] Ibid.

ADDITIONAL COMMENT

Occasionally, a firm will purchase Target Corporation's stock for a price below the total FMV of its tangible assets. In such a case, the adjusted grossed-up basis to be allocated to the Class I through V assets is less than their total FMV. Class I through IV assets will receive a basis equal to their individual FMVs. Any basis remaining after making the allocation to the Class IV assets is allocated to the Class V assets using their relative FMVs.

The adjusted grossed-up basis is allocated to Target Corporation's seven asset classes as follows:

Step 1: Allocate $50,000 to the cash (Class I asset).

Step 2: Allocate $55,000 to the marketable securities (Class II asset).

Step 3: Allocate $60,000 to accounts receivable (Class III asset).

Step 4: Allocate $90,000 to inventory (Class IV asset).

Step 5: Allocate $195,000 to the building, land, and machinery and equipment (Class V assets). Because the total basis that remains after the allocation in Step 4 ($256,818) exceeds the FMV of the Class V assets ($195,000), each asset will take a basis equal to its FMV.

Step 6: No allocation to Class VI assets.

Step 7: Allocate $61,818 [$511,818 − ($50,000 + $55,000 + $60,000 + $90,000 + $195,000)] to goodwill (Class VII asset). This amount is amortizable under Sec. 197. ◀

STOP & THINK

Question: Target Corporation in Example C7-10 is thinking about changing from the FIFO to the LIFO inventory method once the Sec. 338 adjustments have been made. How and when will the $30,000 ($90,000 FMV − $60,000 adjusted basis) step-up made to the inventory's basis be recovered if Target Corporation makes the LIFO election?

Solution: The basis step-up is recovered only if Target sells the LIFO inventory layers in existence on the acquisition date. In general, such sales do not occur unless inventory levels are reduced below the amount held on the acquisition date. If Target retains the FIFO inventory method, the step-up in the inventory's basis will be included in cost of goods sold in the first post-election tax year. Other reasons for possibly not making the Sec. 338 election are the lengthy capital recovery periods for the building and goodwill adjustments, and the fact that an adjustment made to the basis of the land is neither depreciable or amortizable.

SELF-STUDY QUESTION

What are some of the tax consequences of a Sec. 338 election?

ANSWER

The effects of a Sec. 338 election include termination of the "old" target corporation, creation of a "new" target corporation with the option of a new tax year and different accounting methods, new depreciation elections without regard to anti-churning rules, and elimination of tax attributes of the old target (i.e., NOL carryforwards).

Tax Accounting Elections for the New Corporation. The "new" target corporation files a tax return separate from that of the acquiring corporation (unless the group files a consolidated return) because it is a separate legal entity. In many respects, the "new" target corporation is treated as a new entity. For example, the target corporation may adopt, without obtaining prior approval from the IRS, any tax year that meets the requirements of Sec. 441 and any accounting method that meets the requirements of Sec. 446.

The new target corporation can claim depreciation deductions under the MACRS rules without regard to the elections made by the old target corporation and without regard to the anti-churning rules.[21] The holding period for the new target corporation's assets begins on the day after the acquisition date.

The new target corporation is not a continuation of the old target corporation for purposes of the tax attribute carryover rules.[22] As a result, tax attribute carryovers that exist on the acquisition date are permanently lost when the purchasing corporation makes a Sec. 338 deemed sale election. Gain recognized on the deemed sale transaction can reduce the amount of any target corporation loss and credit carryovers that otherwise might be lost. Thus, if Target in Examples C7-7 and C7-10 had a $200,000 NOL on the acquisition date, the Sec. 338 step-up in basis could take place tax-free. Only a small portion of Target's $200,000 NOL would be lost. The acquiring corporation must carefully consider the relative benefit of obtaining a step-up in basis for the individual assets versus the value of the available tax attributes (e.g., NOL carryovers).

Topic Review C7-1 summarizes the requirements for, and tax consequences of, having made a Sec. 338 deemed liquidation election.

[21] Reg. Sec. 1.338-2(d)(1)(i).

[22] Sec. 381(a)(1).

Topic Review C7-1

Section 338 Deemed Liquidation

Election Requirements

1. The acquiring corporation must have made a qualified stock purchase (i.e., a purchase of 80% or more of the target corporation's voting stock and 80% or more of the total value of all stock within a 12-month period). Certain nonvoting preferred stock issues are excluded from the 80% requirements.
2. Stock acquisitions involving substituted basis (e.g., tax-free reorganizations, corporate formations, and gifts), transfers at death, or related parties do not count toward the 80% minimum.
3. The election must be made not later than the fifteenth day of the ninth month beginning after the month in which the acquisition date occurs. The acquisition date is the first date on which the 80% stock ownership requirement is met.

Tax Consequences of a Sec. 338 Election

1. The old target corporation is treated as having sold all of its assets to the new target corporation at their aggregate deemed sales price in a single transaction at the close of the acquisition date. The old target corporation recognizes gain or loss on the deemed sale.
2. The new target corporation takes a basis for the assets equal to the acquiring corporation's adjusted grossed-up basis for the target stock, that is, the sum of the acquiring corporation's basis for its stock interest in the target corporation on the day following the acquisition date, the target corporation's liabilities on the day following the acquisition date, and other relevant items (e.g., contingent liabilities that become fixed).
3. The total adjusted grossed-up basis is allocated to the individual assets using the residual method. The residual method allocates the basis first to cash and near-cash items, other tangible and intangible assets, and finally to goodwill and going concern value.
4. The tax attributes of the old target corporation disappear with the Sec. 338 deemed sale.
5. The new target corporation makes new tax year and accounting method elections.

COMPARISON OF TAXABLE AND TAX-FREE ACQUISITIONS

OBJECTIVE 2

Explain the differences between taxable and tax-free acquisition transactions

TAXABLE AND TAX-FREE ASSET ACQUISITIONS

One way to illustrate the difference between taxable and tax-free transactions is to compare the tax consequences. For purposes of our discussion, assume that Acquiring Corporation acquires all the assets and liabilities of Target Corporation and that Target is liquidated immediately following the acquisition. If Acquiring uses cash and debt obligations to make the purchase, the acquisition is taxable. If Acquiring acquires all of Target's assets using primarily its voting stock and limited cash and debt to accomplish the transaction, the acquisition may qualify as a tax-free reorganization.

KEY POINT

Determining whether a transaction is taxable or nontaxable is doubly important to Target because it is involved in two potentially taxable exchanges: the exchange between Target and Acquiring and the exchange between Target and Target's shareholders.

TAX CONSEQUENCES FOR TARGET CORPORATION. Section 1001(c) requires that, with certain exceptions, the entire gain or loss realized on a sale or exchange must be recognized. Thus, Target Corporation recognizes all gains and losses realized on selling its assets.

A tax-free reorganization is one exception to the general rule. Target generally recognizes no gain or loss when it exchanges its assets for Acquiring's stock. It also recognizes no gain or loss when it distributes the Acquiring stock to its shareholders. Target, however, could recognize gain if it receives boot property and does not distribute the boot to its shareholders or if it distributes boot property or retained property whose FMV exceeds its adjusted basis. The term *retained property* refers to property not transferred to Acquiring as part of the acquisition.

SELF-STUDY QUESTION

Why would Acquiring want an acquisition to be tax-free if it gets only a substituted basis rather than a step-up in basis for the acquired assets?

ANSWER

Usually the motivation for an acquisition to be tax-free comes from Target and Target's shareholders. However, two reasons why Acquiring may desire a tax-free acquisition are (1) Acquiring has no cash to acquire the assets, so it must use stock as the consideration for the purchase, and (2) Target may have favorable tax attributes (e.g., a NOL) that Acquiring would like to use.

TAX CONSEQUENCES FOR ACQUIRING CORPORATION. Acquiring Corporation recognizes no gain or loss when it issues stock in exchange for property in either a taxable or tax-free transaction. Assets received in a taxable transaction have their tax basis adjusted upward or downward to their acquisition cost. The holding period for the acquired assets begins on the day after the transaction date. If the assets are acquired in a tax-free reorganization, Acquiring takes a carryover basis that is the same as Target's basis before the transfer. If Target recognizes a gain because it does not distribute boot property to its shareholders, the carryover basis is adjusted upward for this recognized gain. Acquiring's holding period tacks on to Target's holding period.

Because a taxable acquisition is treated as a purchase transaction, all of Target's tax attributes (e.g., an NOL carryover) disappear when it is liquidated. On the other hand, the tax attributes carry over to Acquiring Corporation in a tax-free reorganization.

TAX CONSEQUENCES FOR TARGET CORPORATION'S SHAREHOLDERS. When Target Corporation is liquidated as part of a taxable acquisition, its shareholders recognize gain or loss on the surrender of their stock. The assets received from the Acquiring Corporation take a basis equal to their FMV. A tax-free reorganization requires the shareholder to recognize gain only to the extent he or she receives boot. The gain generally is taxed as a capital gain, although dividend income may be reported in certain situations. The stocks and securities received take a substituted basis that references the basis of the Target stocks and securities surrendered. The basis of any boot property is its FMV.

ACCOUNTING FOR THE ACQUISITION. Not all of the variables used in choosing between taxable or tax-free acquisitions relate to the tax consequences. For many years, a taxable acquisition generally was reported for financial accounting purposes using the purchase method of accounting. On the other hand, a tax-free acquisition generally was reported for financial accounting purposes using the pooling method of accounting. Because of the stringent pooling requirements, some tax-free acquisitions did not qualify for pooling treatment and were required to use the purchase method. In Summer 2001, the Financial Accounting Standards Board (FASB) adopted *Statement of Financial Accounting Standards No. 141* (Business Combinations), which eliminates the pooling method as an acceptable method of reporting a business combination for all combinations initiated after June 30, 2001. Thus, after this effective date, the purchase method of accounting is the only available method to account for acquisitions.

In addition to repealing the pooling method, the FASB enacted *Statement of Financial Accounting Standards No. 142* (Goodwill and Other Intangible Assets), which requires that all goodwill be tested for impairment. Any impairment loss from an indefinite-lived intangible asset must be recognized as part of the income from continuing operations reported in a firm's profit and loss statements. Thus, firms no longer will amortize goodwill over a fixed period, such as 40 years.

The availability of both purchase and pooling accounting, in some cases, produced substantial differences in the financial reporting for prior and future results of the combined activities for two seemingly similar acquisitions. The FASB's elimination of one of the two alternatives should provide users of financial statements with greater comparability among firms.

Topic Review C7-2 compares taxable and tax-free asset acquisition transactions.

COMPARISON OF TAXABLE AND TAX-FREE STOCK ACQUISITIONS

For purposes of our discussion, assume that Acquiring Corporation acquires all of Target Corporation's stock instead of its assets. Target becomes a controlled subsidiary of Acquiring. If Acquiring uses cash, debt obligations, and its stock to make the purchase, the acquisition is taxable. If Acquiring acquires all of Target's stock using solely its voting stock or voting stock of its parent corporation to effect the transaction, the acquisition qualifies as a tax-free reorganization.

TAX CONSEQUENCES FOR TARGET CORPORATION. Target Corporation's basis

Topic Review C7-2

Comparison of Taxable and Tax-Free Asset Acquisitions

Variable	Taxable Acquisition	Tax-Free Reorganization
1. Consideration employed to effect acquisition	Primarily cash and debt instruments; may involve some stock of the acquiring corporation or its parent corporation.	Primarily stock and limited cash or debt of the acquiring corporation or its parent corporation.
2. Target Corporation		
a. Amount of gain or loss	All gains and losses are recognized. Installment method available if payments are deferred.	Generally, no gain or loss recognized. Gain recognized on an asset transfer when the target corporation receives boot property and does not distribute the boot property to its shareholders. Gain also recognized on the distribution of appreciated boot or retained property.
b. Character of gain or loss	Depends on nature of each asset transferred or distributed.	Depends on nature of each asset transferred or distributed.
c. Recapture provisions	Sec. 1245 or 1250 gains are recaptured.	Secs. 1245 or 1250 do not apply unless boot triggers the recognition of gain.
3. Acquiring Corporation		
a. Gain or loss when stock is issued for property	None recognized.	None recognized.
b. Gain or loss when boot is transferred for property	Gain or loss recognized if noncash boot property is transferred to target corporation.	Gain or loss recognized if noncash boot property is transferred to target corporation.
c. Basis of acquired assets	Cost.	Same as target corporation's basis, increased by gain recognized.
d. Holding period of acquired assets	Begins on the day after the transaction date.	Includes holding period of the target corporation.
e. Acquisition of target corporation's tax attributes	No.	Yes.
f. Accounting for the acquisition	Purchase accounting is used exclusively for transactions occurring after June 30, 2001. Goodwill is subject to an impairment test (rather than amortization).	Pooling-of-interests reporting is no longer allowed. Purchase accounting is used exclusively for transactions occurring after June 30, 2001. Goodwill is subject to an impairment test (rather than amortization).
4. Target Corporation's shareholders		
a. Amount of gain or loss	Realized gain or loss is recognized. Installment method available if payments are deferred.	Gain is recognized to the extent of boot received; losses are not recognized.
b. Character of gain or loss	Capital gain or loss; may be Sec. 1244 loss.	Capital gain and/or dividend income in some circumstances.
c. Basis of stock and securities received	Cost; generally FMV of stock, securities, or other property received.	Substituted basis from the stock and securities surrendered; FMV for boot property.
d. Holding period of stock and securities received	Begins on the day after the transaction date.	Includes holding period for the stock and securities surrendered; Day after the transaction date for boot property.

for its assets does not change as a result of either a taxable or tax-free stock transaction (unless Acquiring Corporation makes a Sec. 338 election after a taxable stock purchase). Any depreciation recapture potential existing on the transaction date stays with Target's assets and, therefore, is assumed by the purchaser. If Target has loss or credit carryovers, it retains these carryovers, but they may be subject to special limitations in its post-acquisition tax years.

If Acquiring Corporation is part of an affiliated group that files a consolidated tax return, Target must join in the consolidated return election if at least 80% of its stock is owned and Target is an includible corporation. Otherwise, Acquiring and Target can elect to make an initial consolidated tax return election (see Chapter C8).

TAX CONSEQUENCES FOR ACQUIRING CORPORATION. Acquiring Corporation does not recognize gain or loss when it issues its own stock in exchange for property in either a taxable or tax-free transaction. Acquiring's basis for the stock in a taxable acquisition is its acquisition cost. The taxable stock acquisition may qualify as a purchase for purposes of the Sec. 338 deemed sale election. In a tax-free reorganization, Acquiring's basis for the stock is the same as it was in the hands of Target's shareholders, and a Sec. 338 election is not available. Acquiring Corporation recognizes gain or loss when it exchanges noncash boot property for Target Corporation stock.

TAX STRATEGY TIP

Taxes can be an important variable in determining the acquisition method used to acquire the target corporation's stock or assets. All parties also need to consider the non-tax variables associated with the transaction. For example, a stock-for-stock acquisition may minimize taxes but leave the target corporation's shareholders controlling the acquiring corporation. Facing loss of control, the acquiring corporation's owners may prefer to have the transaction financed with borrowed funds (and make the acquisition taxable to the seller) while retaining control over the acquiring corporation.

TAX CONSEQUENCES FOR TARGET CORPORATION'S SHAREHOLDERS. The gain recognized on a taxable sale transaction is capital gain if the stock is a capital asset in the seller's hands. The seller can report the gain using the installment method of accounting if part or all of the consideration is deferred into a later year and the stock is not traded on an established securities market. Consideration received by the seller that represents compensation for an agreement with the purchaser not to compete for a specified time period is taxable as ordinary income.

Because only voting stock is used in a tax-free stock acquisition, Target's shareholders recognize no gain or loss. The shareholders take a substituted basis for the Acquiring stock that is the same as their basis in the Target stock.

ACCOUNTING FOR THE TRANSACTION. Prior to July 1, 2001, a taxable acquisition of Target Corporation stock was reported for financial accounting purposes using purchase accounting. A tax-free stock-for-stock reorganization ordinarily satisfied the pooling-of-interests method requirements. Because only 50% stock ownership by a parent corporation is needed for a subsidiary's inclusion in a set of consolidated financial statements, some parent-subsidiary relationships may permit consolidation for financial accounting purposes yet not satisfy the 80% minimums needed for consolidation for tax purposes.

Effective July 1, 2001, the Financial Accounting Standards Board (FASB) changed the financial accounting rules for mergers and acquisitions. Companies are no longer permitted to use the pooling-of-interests accounting method for a business combination. While still being permitted to use the purchase method of accounting, a firm is no longer required to amortize goodwill assets over a specific time period, not to exceed 40 years, and annually take a portion of the goodwill amount into the calculation of net income. Although purchased goodwill still remains a separate asset on a corporation's balance sheet, the goodwill is now subject to an annual goodwill impairment test. These changes in the financial reporting for an acquisition transaction will permit two companies to structure an acquisition with no concern about whether the transaction complies with the pooling-of-interests requirement. Prior to the change, many companies structured transactions as poolings of interests to avoid having to report and amortize goodwill.

Topic Review C7-3 compares taxable and tax-free stock acquisitions.

Topic Review C7-3

Comparison of Taxable and Tax-Free Stock Acquisitions

Variable	Taxable Acquisition	Tax-free Reorganization
1. Consideration employed to effect acquisition	Primarily cash and debt instruments; may involve some stock of the acquiring corporation or its parent corporation.	Solely voting stock of the acquiring corporation or its parent corporation.
2. Target Corporation		
a. Parent-subsidiary relationship established	Yes.	Yes.
b. Consolidated tax return election available	Yes.	Yes.
c. Basis for assets	Unchanged by stock acquisition unless a Sec. 338 election is made.	Unchanged by stock acquisition. No Sec. 338 election available.
d. Tax attributes	Retained by Target Corporation.	Retained by Target Corporation.
3. Acquiring Corporation		
a. Basis for stock acquired	Cost basis.	Carryover basis from Target's shareholders.
4. Target Corporation's shareholders		
a. Amount of gain or loss recognized	Realized gain or loss is recognized.	No boot is received; therefore, no gain is recognized.
b. Character of gain or loss	Capital gain or loss; may be Sec. 1244 loss.	Not applicable.
c. Basis of stock, securities, or other property received	Cost; generally FMV of stock, securities, or other property received.	Substituted basis from stock surrendered.
d. Holding period of stock, securities, or other property received	Begins on the day after the transaction date.	Includes holding period for the stock surrendered.

TYPES OF REORGANIZATIONS

OBJECTIVE 3

Explain the types of tax-free reorganizations and their requirements

Section 368(a)(1) authorizes seven types of reorganizations to accommodate the major forms of business acquisitions, divestitures, and restructurings. Generally, tax practitioners refer to the specific type of reorganization by the subparagraph of Sec. 368(a)(1) that contains its definition. For example, a merger transaction is referred to as a *Type A* reorganization because it is defined in Sec. 368(a)(1)(A). The seven types of reorganizations also can be classified according to the nature of the transaction, with the most common forms being acquisitive transactions and divisive transactions. In an **acquisitive reorganization,** the acquiring corporation obtains part or all of a target (or transferor) corporation's assets or stock. Types A, B, C, D, and G reorganizations can be classified as acquisitive transactions. In a **divisive reorganization,** part of a transferor corporation's assets are transferred to a second corporation that is controlled by either the transferor or its shareholders. The controlled (or transferee) corporation's stock or securities received in exchange for the assets are distributed as part of a reorganization plan to the transferor corporation's shareholders. The transferor corporation can either remain in existence or be liquidated. If the transferor corporation remains in existence, its assets end up being divided between at least two corporations. Type D and G reorganizations can be either acquisitive or divisive transactions.

TYPICAL MISCONCEPTION

For an acquisition to qualify for tax-free treatment, the transaction must be a reorganization. The term *reorganization* includes only transactions specifically enumerated in Sec. 368. Other transactions that may constitute reorganizations in a more general context are not considered tax-free reorganizations.

REFERENCE POINT

A summary of the acquisitive reorganizations is presented below:

Type	*Description*
A	Merger or consolidation
B	Stock-for-stock
C	Asset-for-stock
D	Asset-for-stock
G	Bankruptcy

Two reorganization forms are neither acquisitive or divisive. Type E and F reorganizations involve a single corporation that does *not* acquire additional assets and does *not* transfer a portion of its assets to a transferee corporation. The Type E reorganization—a recapitalization—involves changes to a corporation's capital structure. Type F reorganizations—a change in identity, legal form, or state of incorporation—may involve the transfer of the assets of an existing corporation to a new corporation, but the shareholders of the transferor corporation generally retain the same equity interest in the transferee corporation.

Not all reorganization transactions fit neatly into one of the seven classifications. In fact, some reorganizations may satisfy the requirements for two or more of the classifications. If this situation occurs, the IRC or the IRS generally determines which reorganization rules prevail. In other transactions, a reorganization may satisfy the literal requirements of one of the classifications, but for other reasons the IRS and courts may find that an entirely different tax treatment results (e.g., if the transaction lacks a business purpose, it may be a taxable transaction). Further discussion of these problems is presented in the next section.

TAX CONSEQUENCES OF REORGANIZATIONS

OBJECTIVE 4

Determine the tax consequences of a tax-free reorganization to the target corporation

This portion of the chapter examines the tax consequences of a tax-free reorganization to the target (or transferor) corporation, the acquiring (or transferee) corporation, and the shareholders and security holders.[23]

TARGET OR TRANSFEROR CORPORATION

TYPICAL MISCONCEPTION

One perplexing aspect of the tax-free reorganization provisions is the overlap between the different statutory reorganizations. One transaction often can qualify as more than one type of tax-free reorganization.

RECOGNITION OF GAIN OR LOSS ON ASSET TRANSFER. Under Sec. 361(a), the target corporation recognizes no gain or loss on any exchange of property that occurs as part of a tax-free reorganization when it receives only stock of another corporation that is a party to the reorganization.[24] In addition, the target corporation recognizes no gain under Sec. 361(b) if it also receives money or nonmoney boot property as part of the reorganization and it distributes such property to its shareholders or creditors. Nevertheless, the target corporation must recognize gain equal to the lesser of the realized gain or the amount of money plus the FMV of any boot property (other than money) received in the exchange that is not distributed. However, because most acquisitive and divisive reorganizations require the target corporation to be liquidated or distribute all its assets, boot generally is not retained and thus the target corporation recognizes no gain on the exchange with the acquiring corporation. (Note: the target corporation can recognize gain on the distribution of appreciated property to its shareholders as discussed below.)

EXAMPLE C7-11 ▶ Target Corporation transfers assets having a $175,000 adjusted basis to Acquiring Corporation in exchange for $400,000 of Acquiring common stock as part of a tax-free reorganization. Target realizes a $225,000 gain ($400,000 amount realized − $175,000 adjusted basis) on the asset transfer. Because Target received no boot, it recognizes none of the gain. If Target instead receives $350,000 of Acquiring common stock and $50,000 of money, Target recognizes no gain if it distributes the boot property to its shareholders. ◀

---

[23] The corporation that transfers its assets as part of a reorganization is referred to as either a **target** or **transferor corporation**. The term *target corporation* generally is used with an acquisitive reorganization where substantially all of a corporation's assets are acquired by the acquiring corporation. The term *transferor corporation* is used with divisive and other reorganizations where only part of a corporation's assets are transferred to a transferee corporation and the transferor corporation may remain in existence. Tax law provisions generally are applied the same to target or transferor corporations and acquiring or transferee corporations, so only a single reference to the target or acquiring corporation is provided in connection with an explanation.

[24] Section 361(a) permits securities (e.g., long-term debt obligations) to be received tax-free when the same face amount of securities, or a larger amount, is surrendered by the target corporation. Generally, a securities exchange does not occur in an acquisitive reorganization, so all debt obligations received by the target corporation are boot property.

TYPICAL MISCONCEPTION

Often, taxpayers do not realize that Sec. 361 applies to two exchanges. Section 361(a) applies to the exchange between Acquiring and Target (which already has been discussed). Section 361(c) deals with the exchange between Target and Target's shareholders. Therefore, Target is the only party to the reorganization that may recognize two separate gains.

SELF-STUDY QUESTION

How can Target distribute appreciated boot property to its shareholders if Target receives a FMV basis in all such property received from Acquiring?

ANSWER

If the property appreciates in the hands of Target before it is distributed, gain will result. In addition, Target may retain some of its own assets and distribute these assets to its shareholders. Consistent with Secs. 311(b) and 336(a), distributing appreciated property causes gain recognition by Target.

DEPRECIATION RECAPTURE. The depreciation recapture rules of Secs. 1245 and 1250 do not override the nonrecognition of gain or loss rules of Sec. 361.[25] The recapture potential that accrues before the asset transfer carries over to the acquiring corporation and is recognized when the acquiring corporation sells or exchanges the assets in a taxable transaction.

ASSUMPTION OF LIABILITIES. Neither the acquiring corporation's assumption of the target corporation's liabilities nor the acquisition of the target corporation's property subject to a liability will trigger the recognition of gain on the asset transfer. Section 357(c), however, requires the target corporation to recognize gain if the sum of the liabilities assumed or acquired exceeds the total adjusted bases of the property transferred *and* the tax-free reorganization is either an acquisitive or a divisive Type D reorganization. An additional explanation of the Sec. 357(c) rules is presented in connection with the discussion of the acquisitive Type D reorganization.

RECOGNITION OF GAIN OR LOSS ON DISTRIBUTION OF STOCK AND SECURITIES. The target corporation recognizes no gain or loss when it distributes either (1) its stock, stock rights, or obligations or (2) any stock, stock rights, and obligations of a party to a reorganization received in the reorganization to its shareholders or creditors as part of the plan of reorganization (see page C7-51 for an explanation of a plan of reorganization).[26] Distributions of nonmoney boot property (including property retained by the target corporation) made pursuant to the reorganization plan requires the recognition of gain (but not loss) in the same manner as if the target corporation sold such property at its FMV.[27] Normally the gain recognized when boot property is distributed is small because of the short amount of time that passes between when it is received from the acquiring corporation (and takes a basis equal to its FMV) and when it is distributed to a shareholder.

EXAMPLE C7-12 ▶ Target Corporation transfers all of its assets and liabilities to Acquiring Corporation as part of its being merged into Acquiring (a Type A reorganization). To effect the merger, Acquiring transfers $300,000 of its common stock and $100,000 of money to Target in exchange for Target's assets. Target's basis for the assets is $250,000. Target realizes a $150,000 gain on the asset transfer [($300,000 + $100,000) − $250,000]. Target recognizes none of this gain, even though boot is received, because Target must be liquidated as part of the merger transaction. Target's distribution of the Acquiring stock to its shareholders as part of the reorganization does not trigger the recognition of any gain by Target. Gain may be recognized by Target shareholders who receive money. ◀

OBJECTIVE 5

Determine the tax consequences of a tax-free reorganization to the acquiring corporation

ACQUIRING OR TRANSFEREE CORPORATION

AMOUNT OF GAIN OR LOSS RECOGNIZED. Under Sec. 1032, the acquiring corporation recognizes no gain or loss when it receives money or other property in exchange for its stock as part of a tax-free reorganization. Similarly, a corporation recognizes no gain or loss when it receives money or other property in exchange for its securities as part of a tax-free reorganization. The acquiring corporation, however, will recognize gain or loss under Sec. 1001 if it transfers noncash boot property to the target corporation or its shareholders.[28]

SELF-STUDY QUESTION

Because Acquiring is merely purchasing assets, can Acquiring ever recognize gain or loss on the transaction?

BASIS OF ACQUIRED PROPERTY. Section 362(b) requires property acquired in a tax-free reorganization to take a carryover basis from the target corporation, increased by the amount of gain recognized by the target corporation on the exchange. However, because the target corporation generally recognizes no gain on the asset transfer, no step-up in basis occurs.

[25] Secs. 1245(b)(3) and 1250(d)(3). Similar provisions are found as part of the other recapture rules.

[26] Secs. 361(c)(1)–(c)(3).

[27] Sec. 361(c).

[28] Rev. Rul. 72-327, 1972-2 C.B. 197.

EXAMPLE C7-13 ▶ Assume the same facts as in Example C7-12. Acquiring's basis for the acquired property is the same as Target Corporation's basis, or $250,000. ◀

ANSWER

Yes. If Acquiring uses nonmoney boot property, Acquiring will recognize gain or loss to the extent of the built-in gain or loss in such property (Sec. 1001(a)).

HOLDING PERIOD OF ACQUIRED PROPERTY. The acquiring corporation's holding period for the acquired property includes the target corporation's holding period for the property.[29]

OBJECTIVE 6

Determine the tax consequences of a tax-free reorganization to the target corporation's shareholders and security holders

SHAREHOLDERS AND SECURITY HOLDERS

AMOUNT OF GAIN OR LOSS RECOGNIZED. Under Sec. 354(a), shareholders recognize no gain or loss if stock or securities in a corporation that is a party to a reorganization are, in pursuance of a plan of reorganization, exchanged solely for stock or securities in the same corporation, or for stock or securities of another corporation that is a party to the reorganization. The receipt of property other than stock or securities (nonqualifying property) does not automatically disqualify the transaction from tax-free treatment. Section 356(a), however, requires that the shareholder or security holder recognize gain to the extent of the lesser of the realized gain or the amount of money received plus the FMV of any other property received. Thus, shareholders recognize gain to the extent they receive nonqualifying property that does not represent a continuation of the former equity interest.

EXAMPLE C7-14 ▶ Brian exchanges 1,000 shares of Target Corporation stock having a $13,000 basis for Acquiring Corporation stock having a $28,000 FMV as part of a tax-free reorganization. Brian's realized gain is $15,000 ($28,000 – $13,000), none of which is recognized. If Brian had instead received $25,000 of Acquiring stock and $3,000 of cash, his realized gain would remain $15,000, but Brian would now recognize a $3,000 gain. ◀

ADDITIONAL COMMENT

Acquiring may increase its basis in the assets received only by the gain recognized by Target on its exchange with Acquiring. Any gain recognized by Target on its distribution of stock or other property to Target's shareholders does not increase the basis of any assets.

With some limitations, the general rule of Sec. 354(a) permits a tax-free exchange of stocks and securities. Nontraditional preferred stock (for example, preferred stock that must be redeemed or purchased by the issuer) also may be considered boot property. The receipt of securities is completely tax-free only if the principal amount of the securities surrendered equals or exceeds the principal amount of the securities received. If the principal amount of securities received exceeds the principal amount of securities surrendered, the FMV of the "excess" principal amount of the securities received constitutes boot.[30] If no securities are surrendered, the FMV of the entire principal amount of securities received constitutes boot.

EXAMPLE C7-15 ▶ Assume the same facts as in Example C7-14 except that Brian instead receives Acquiring Corporation securities having a $3,000 principal amount and a $2,850 FMV. Brian's realized gain is $14,850 [($25,000 + $2,850) – $13,000], of which $2,850 is recognized. The result would be much the same if Brian had received $3,000 in Acquiring securities and surrendered $2,000 of Target securities. Then the FMV of the $1,000 "excess" principal amount, or $950 [$1,000 × ($2,850 FMV/$3,000 principal)], is treated as boot. ◀

SELF-STUDY QUESTION

In addition to receiving stock in Acquiring, shareholder Sue receives securities with a FMV of $120,000 and a principal amount of $100,000. In the exchange, Sue surrenders securities of Target with a FMV and principal amount of $80,000. Is Sue treated as having received any boot?

ANSWER

Yes. $100,000 – $80,000 = $20,000 of excess principal amount received. The boot received is $24,000. This amount represents the FMV of the excess principal amount [($20,000/$100,000) × $120,000].

CHARACTER OF THE RECOGNIZED GAIN. Section 356(a)(2) requires that the recognized gain be characterized as dividend income if the receipt of the boot property has the same effect as the distribution of a dividend. The dividend income recognized equals the lesser of the shareholder's recognized gain or the shareholder's ratable share of the transferor or target corporation's current and accumulated earnings and profits (E&P). Any additional gain that must be recognized generally is reported as a capital gain.

The Sec. 302(b) stock redemption rules are used to test whether the exchange has the effect of a dividend distribution.[31] (See Chapter C4 for a review of the Sec. 302(b) rules.) Tax-free reorganizations generally do not involve actual redemptions of the stock of the target corporation's shareholders. Instead, the Supreme Court in its *Donald E. Clark* deci-

[29] Sec. 1223(1).

[30] Secs. 354(a)(2) and 356(d)(2)(B). The FMV of the debt obligations surrendered is irrelevant when determining the amount of the recognized gain.

[31] *CIR v. Donald E. Clark*, 63 AFTR 2d 89-1437, 89-1 USTC ¶9230 (USSC, 1989). The IRS has agreed to follow the *Clark* decision in Rev. Rul. 93-61, 1993-2 C.B. 118.

sion held that a shareholder is treated as having exchanged his or her target corporation stock in a tax-free reorganization solely for stock in the acquiring corporation. After having received the acquiring corporation's stock, a hypothetical redemption (but no actual stock redemption) of a portion of the acquiring corporation's stock occurs. Capital gain treatment results when the boot received causes the hypothetical redemption to qualify for exchange treatment under Sec. 302(b).

Application of the dividend equivalency test used when boot is received in a tax-free reorganization is illustrated in the following example.

EXAMPLE C7-16 ▶ Betty owns all 60 of the outstanding shares of Fisher Corporation stock. Fisher Corporation is merged with Gulf Corporation in a tax-free reorganization, with Betty receiving 35 shares of Gulf stock worth $350,000 and $250,000 in money. Four other individuals own the remaining 100 shares of Gulf stock. Betty's Fisher stock has a $200,000 basis. Fisher and Gulf Corporations have E&P balances of $300,000 and $500,000, respectively. Betty's realized gain is $400,000 [($350,000 stock + $250,000 money) − $200,000 adjusted basis], of which $250,000 must be recognized because the money is treated as boot property.

The Fisher stock initially is treated as having been exchanged for only Gulf stock. Because the Fisher stock is worth $600,000 and the Gulf stock is worth $10,000 per share ($350,000 ÷ 35), Betty is initially treated as owning 60 of the 160 (100 + 60) shares of Gulf stock supposedly outstanding immediately after the stock-for-stock swap. The $250,000 in money Betty receives is treated as having been exchanged for 25 ($250,000 ÷ $10,000 per share) of the 60 shares of Gulf stock that would have been received in an all-stock transaction. Because Betty owns 37.5% (60 shares ÷ 160 shares) of the Gulf stock before the hypothetical redemption and 25.93% (35 shares ÷ 135 shares) after the hypothetical redemption, the $250,000 gain is characterized as capital gain under the Sec. 302(b)(2) substantially disproportionate redemption rules (i.e., 25.93% is less than 80% × 37.5% = 30%). ◀

TYPICAL MISCONCEPTION

Before the *Clark* decision, the IRS looked to Target's E&P to measure the amount of dividend income. The IRS thus far has declined to rule whether it has changed this position with respect to the E&P "pool" used to determine the amount of dividend income now that *Clark* treats the receipt of boot as a redemption between Target's shareholder and Acquiring Corporation.

The Sec. 302(b) test would be applied in the same manner if securities were received in the reorganization. In such a case, the boot portion of the transaction would equal the FMV of the "excess" principal amount received by the shareholder or security holder.

Whether capital gain treatment is available for boot received in a reorganization depends on the relative sizes of the target and acquiring corporations. If the acquiring corporation is larger than the target corporation, the Sec. 302(b)(2) (substantially disproportionate redemption) or Sec. 302(b)(1) (not essentially equivalent to a dividend) rules generally will provide for capital gain treatment. (See Chapter C4 for an explanation of these rules.) If the acquiring corporation is smaller than the target corporation, the target corporation's shareholder possibly may be considered as having received dividend income or a combination of dividend income and capital gain (e.g., if the boot received exceeds the shareholder's ratable share of E&P).

Capital gain treatment may be preferred by individual shareholders for the recognized gain because a 20% or lower tax rate can apply to many long-term capital gains, which is substantially less than the 38.6% maximum rate applicable to ordinary income (in 2002). Dividend income treatment may be preferred by corporate shareholders because they can claim a 70%, 80%, or 100% dividends-received deduction to reduce their tax burden. In addition, capital gains recognized in the reorganization can offset capital losses recognized by corporate and noncorporate shareholders in other transactions. Finally, Sec. 453(f)(6)(C) permits a corporate or noncorporate shareholder involved in a tax-free reorganization to use the installment method of accounting to defer the reporting of the gain recognized when securities are received, provided such gain is not characterized as a dividend.[32]

STOP & THINK

Question: The character of the shareholder's recognized gain is determined by applying the Sec. 302(b) stock redemption rules. Why are the relative sizes of the acquiring and target corporations important when determining the character of the gain recognized in a tax-free reorganization?

[32] *King Enterprises, Inc. v. U.S.*, 24 AFTR 2d 69-5866, 69-2 USTC ¶9720 (Ct. Cls., 1969).

Solution: A shareholder receives capital gain treatment for his or her recognized gain when the hypothetical redemption qualifies for exchange treatment under the Sec. 302(b) rules. If the target corporation is smaller than the acquiring corporation, the receipt of boot almost always should qualify under one of the capital gains exceptions since no shareholder(s) will generally own more than 50% of the acquiring corporation's stock before and after the hypothetical redemption. If the boot is distributed proportionate to the stock ownership, the target corporation's shareholder(s) should see a reduction in his or her pre-and post-redemption interests. However, if the target corporation is larger than the acquiring corporation, a shareholder(s) possibly may own more than 50% of the acquiring corporation's stock, thereby causing the boot to be characterized as a dividend. Classification of the boot as a dividend prevents the preferential capital gains rules from applying to an individual shareholder.

KEY POINT

When a reorganization is tax-free, shareholders defer recognition of their realized gain or loss. Consequently, they take a substituted basis in the new nonrecognition property received (i.e., any deferred gain or loss is reflected in the basis of the nonrecognition property received).

BASIS OF STOCKS AND SECURITIES RECEIVED. The basis of the stocks and securities (nonrecognition property) received by the target corporation's shareholders and security holders is determined according to the Sec. 358 rules introduced in Chapter C2. The basis of nonrecognition property is determined as follows:

Adjusted basis of the stocks and securities exchanged
Plus: Any gain recognized on the exchange
Minus: Money received in the exchange
FMV of any property (other than money) received in the exchange
Basis of the nonrecognition property received

If the shareholder or security holder receives no boot, the stocks and securities will take a substituted basis from the stocks and securities exchanged. If a gain must be recognized, the basis of the stocks and securities exchanged is increased by the amount of such gain and then reduced by the amount of money plus the FMV of any other boot property received in the reorganization. The basis of any other boot property received is its FMV.

EXAMPLE C7-17 ▶ Ken owns Target Corporation stock having a $10,000 adjusted basis. As part of a tax-free reorganization involving Target and Acquiring Corporations, Ken exchanges his Target stock for $12,000 of Acquiring stock and $4,000 of Acquiring securities. Ken realizes a $6,000 gain [($12,000 + $4,000) − $10,000], of which $4,000 must be recognized because he received securities worth $4,000 but surrendered no securities. The basis of the Acquiring securities that Ken received is $4,000. Ken's basis for the Acquiring stock is $10,000 ($10,000 basis of Target stock + $4,000 gain recognized − $4,000 FMV of Acquiring securities). ◀

When the target corporation's shareholders own a single class of stock (or a single class of securities) and end up owning two or more classes of stock or securities as a result of a tax-free reorganization, the total basis for the nonrecognition property determined above must be allocated between the stocks and/or the securities owned in proportion to the relative FMVs of the classes.[33]

HOLDING PERIOD. The holding period of the stocks and securities that are nonrecognition property includes the holding period for the stocks and securities surrendered. The holding period for boot property begins on the day after the exchange date.[34]

Topic Review C7-4 summarizes the tax consequences of a tax-free reorganization to the target corporation, the acquiring corporation, and the target corporation's shareholders and security holders.

[33] Reg. Sec. 1.358-2(a)(2)-(4).
[34] Sec. 1223(1).

Topic Review C7-4

Tax Consequences of a Tax-Free Reorganization

TARGET CORPORATION

1. The target corporation recognizes no gain or loss on the asset transfer except to the extent that it receives and retains money or other boot property (Secs. 361(a)–(b)). Generally, boot is not retained because the target corporation usually is liquidated or required to distribute all its assets.
2. The character of any gain or loss recognized depends on the nature of the assets transferred.
3. The acquiring corporation's assumption or acquisition of target corporation liabilities does not trigger recognition of gain on the asset transfer except to the extent Sec. 357(c) applies to "excess" liability situations involving Type D reorganizations (Sec. 357(a)).
4. The target corporation recognizes no gain or loss when it distributes qualified property (i.e., stock and securities) to its shareholders and security holders. The target corporation recognizes gain (but not loss) when it distributes noncash boot property or retained assets to shareholders or security holders (Sec. 361(c)).

ACQUIRING CORPORATION

1. The acquiring corporation recognizes no gain or loss when it receives money or other boot property in exchange for its stock or debt obligations (Sec. 1032).
2. The acquiring corporation, however, does recognize gain or loss when it transfers noncash boot property to the target corporation or its shareholders (Sec. 1001).
3. The basis of the acquired property equals its basis in the transferor's hands increased by any gain recognized by the transferor (Sec. 362(b)).
4. The acquiring corporation's holding period for the acquired property includes the transferor's holding period (Sec. 1223(1)).

SHAREHOLDERS AND SECURITY HOLDERS

1. No gain or loss is recognized if only stock is received (Sec. 354(a)). Gain (but not loss) is recognized when money, excess securities, or other boot property is received. The amount of the recognized gain equals the lesser of the realized gain or the amount of money plus the FMV of any other boot property received (Sec. 356(b)).
2. The character of the gain recognized is determined by applying the Sec. 302(b) rules to the acquiring corporation. Dividend income cannot exceed the shareholder's ratable share of the transferor or target corporation's E&P (Sec. 356(a)(2)).
3. The total basis of the stocks and securities received equals the adjusted basis of the stocks and securities exchanged plus any gain recognized by the shareholders and security holders on the exchange minus the sum of the money and the FMV of other boot property received. This basis is allocated to the stocks and securities received based on their relative FMVs. The basis of boot property is its FMV (Sec. 358(a)).
4. The holding period of stocks and securities received includes the holding period of the stocks and securities surrendered. The holding period for boot property received begins on the day after the exchange date (Sec. 1223(1)).

ACQUISITIVE REORGANIZATIONS

This portion of the chapter is devoted to the Types A, B, C, D, and G acquisitive reorganizations. Each of these types of reorganizations is explained below. Topic Review C7-5 summarizes the requirements for acquisitive reorganizations.

TYPE A REORGANIZATION

The IRC permits four kinds of **Type A reorganizations:** mergers, consolidations, triangular mergers, and reverse triangular mergers. Each of these transactions is described below.

Topic Review C7-5

Summary of Major Acquisitive Reorganizations

Type of Reorganization	Target (T) Corporation Property Acquired	Consideration That Can Be Used	What Happens to the Target (T) Corporation?	Shareholders' Recognized Gain	Other Requirements
A—Merger or consolidation	Assets and liabilities of T Corporation.[a]	Voting and nonvoting stock, securities, and other property of A Corporation[b]	T Corporation liquidates as part of the merger.	Lesser of realized gain or boot received	For advance ruling purposes, at least 50% of the consideration employed must be A stock (continuity of interest requirement)
B—Stock for stock	At least 80% of the voting and 80% of the nonvoting T stock.	Voting stock of A Corporation	Remains in existence as a subsidiary of A Corporation.	None	Boot can cause the transaction to be taxable.
C—Assets for stock	Substantially all the assets of T Corporation (and possibly some or all of its liabilities).	Stock, securities, and other property of A Corporation, provided at least 80% of the assets are acquired for voting stock	Stock, securities, and boot received in the reorganization and all of T's remaining properties must be distributed; as a practical matter, T usually is liquidated.	Lesser of realized gain or boot received	For advance ruling purposes, "substantially all" is 70% of the gross assets and 90% of the net assets of T Corporation.
D—Acquisitive	Substantially all the assets of T Corporation (and possibly some or all of its liabilities) are acquired by a "controlled". transferee corporation (A Corporation[b]).	Stock, securities, and other property of A Corporation	Stocks, securities, and boot received in the reorganization and all of T's remaining property must be distributed; as a practical matter, T usually is liquidated.	Lesser of realized gain or boot received	"Substantially all" is defined as it was for a Type C reorganization; the continuity of interest requirement also applies here for advance ruling purposes; control is defined as 50% of the voting power or 50% of the value of A's stock.

[a] T Corporation is the target or transferor corporation.
[b] A Corporation is the acquiring or controlled transferee corporation. In a Type D reorganization, Acquiring is 50% or more controlled by Target's shareholders.

KEY POINT

The Type A reorganization is unique in comparison to the other statutory reorganizations because state law, rather than federal law, is an important factor in determining whether a transaction qualifies as a tax-free merger.

MERGER OR CONSOLIDATION. A Type A reorganization is a **merger** or a **consolidation** that satisfies the corporation laws of the United States, a state, or the District of Columbia.[35] State law authorizes several different forms of mergers. Two common forms are discussed below. Other permitted forms, such as triangular mergers and reverse triangular mergers, are discussed later in this chapter. The first form involves the acquiring corporation transferring its stock, securities, and other consideration (boot) to the target corporation in exchange for its assets and liabilities. The acquiring corporation stock, securities, and other consideration received by the target corporation are distributed to its shareholders and security holders in exchange for their target corporation stock and securities. The target corporation then goes out of existence. Figure C7-1 illustrates this type of merger. The second type of merger involves the acquiring corporation exchanging its stock, securities, and other consideration directly for the stock and securities held by the target corporation's shareholders and security holders. The acquiring corporation then liquidates the target corporation and acquires its assets and liabilities.

A consolidation involves two or more corporations having their assets acquired by a new corporation. The stock, securities, and other consideration transferred by the acquiring corporation is distributed by each target corporation to its shareholders and security holders pursuant to its liquidation in exchange for its own stock and securities. Figure C7-2 illustrates this type of consolidation. As with a merger, an alternative form of consolidation is where the acquiring corporation transfers its stock, securities, and other consideration directly to the target corporations' shareholders and security holders in exchange for their stock and securities. In this case, each target corporation then liquidates, with the acquiring corporation receiving its assets and liabilities.

KEY POINT

The Type A reorganization is the most flexible reorganization with respect to the type of consideration that must be used. The only requirement that must be satisfied is the continuity of interest test, which is discussed later in the chapter.

Requirements for Mergers and Consolidations. The Type A reorganization provides the acquiring corporation with the greatest flexibility in selecting the consideration to be used to effect the reorganization. Section 368 places no restrictions on the types of con-

ADDITIONAL COMMENT

The actual exchange of Acquiring stock for Target stock may be different from the illustrations provided in this chapter. These illustrations represent how the IRC construes the steps in each of the reorganizations. As a practical matter, the exchange of stock between Acquiring and Target usually is performed by an independent stock transfer agent rather than flowing from Acquiring to Target and finally to Target's shareholders.

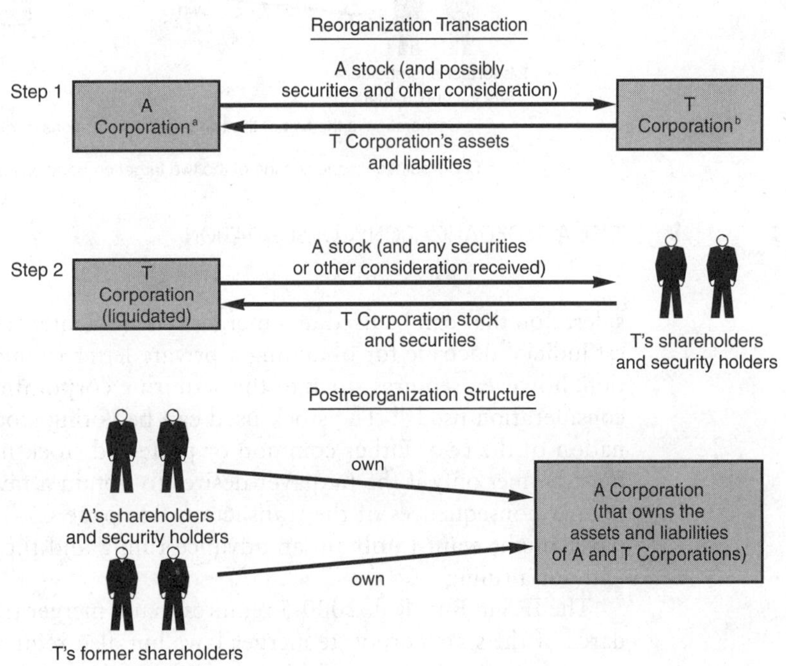

[a] Unless otherwise indicated in this chapter, A Corporation designates the acquiring or transferee corporation.

[b] Unless otherwise indicated in this chapter, T Corporation designates the target or transferor corporation.

FIGURE C7-1  TYPE A REORGANIZATION—MERGER

[35] Sec. 368(a)(1)(A) and Reg. Sec. 1.368-2(b)(1).

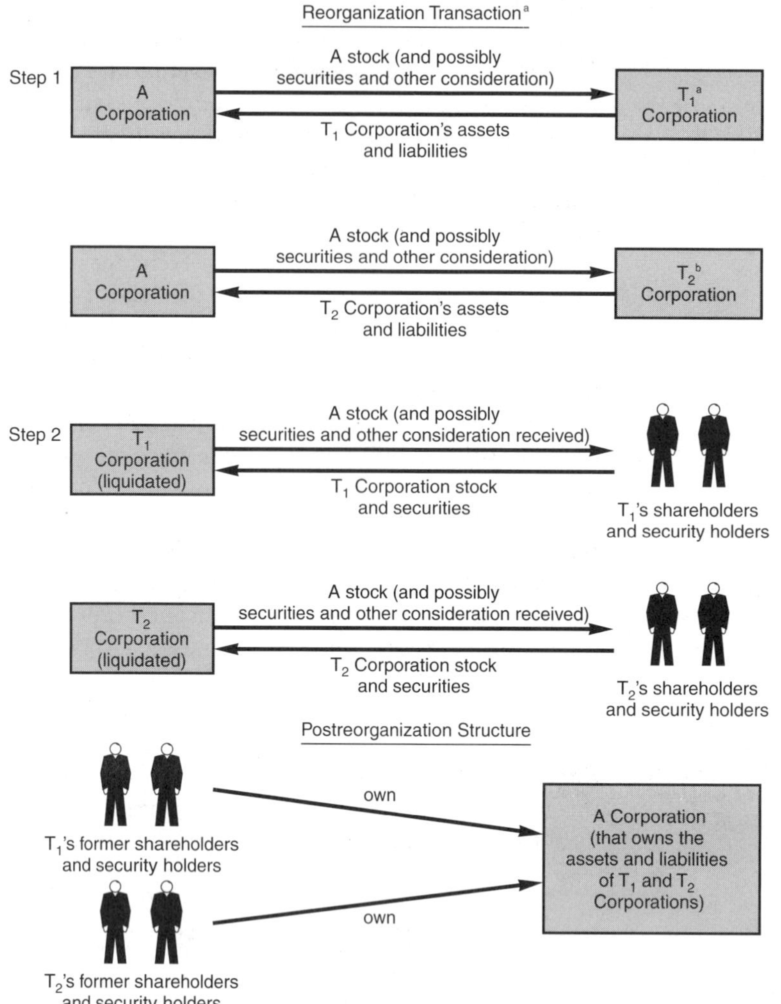

FIGURE C7-2 ▶ TYPE A REORGANIZATION: CONSOLIDATION

sideration that can be used in a merger. The IRS interpretation of the continuity of interest judicial doctrine for obtaining a private letter ruling involving a tax-free reorganization, however, requires stock of the acquiring corporation to be at least 50% of the total consideration used.[36] The stock used can be voting stock, nonvoting stock, or a combination of the two. Either common or preferred stock may be used. The 50% minimum must be met only if the taxpayer desires to obtain a favorable advance ruling regarding the tax consequences of the transaction (see page C7-51 for a discussion of why a taxpayer might want to obtain an advance ruling and the tax consequences of proceeding without a ruling).

The IRS in Rev. Rul. 2000-5 requires that a merger transaction meet not only the standards of the state corporate merger laws but also requires that the target corporation go out of existence.[37] An acquisition transaction does not qualify as a Type A asset-for-stock "merger" reorganization if the target corporation retains the remainder of its assets not acquired by the acquiring corporation and the target corporation's shareholders retain their remaining target stock not acquired by the acquiring corporation. Revenue Ruling 2000-5 also hold that, if a target merges under state law into two or more acquiring cor-

[36] Rev. Proc. 77-37, 1977-2 C.B. 568, Sec. 3.02.

[37] Rev. Rul. 2000-5, 2000-1 C.B. 436.

porations and the target does not go out existence, the transaction does not qualify as a Type A reorganization.

ADDITIONAL COMMENT

Shareholder approval is time consuming, expensive, and not always possible to obtain.

Because a merger or consolidation must comply with state or federal corporation laws, transactions that qualify as mergers or consolidations, and the procedures that must be followed to effect them, vary according to the law of the states in which the acquiring and target corporations are incorporated. Generally, these laws require a favorable vote by a majority of the shareholders of the two corporations involved in the merger. State law dictates the procedures that must be followed. Where the stock of one or both of the companies is publicly traded, the need to hold a shareholder's meeting, solicit proxies, and obtain the necessary approval may make the procedure both costly and time-consuming.

The rights of any dissenting shareholders also are dictated by the state law. These shareholders may have the right under state law to dissent and have their shares independently valued and purchased for cash. A substantial number of dissenting shareholders may necessitate a large cash outlay to purge their interests and may make the continuity-of-interest doctrine difficult to achieve.

A transaction that fails to satisfy the state corporation laws does not qualify as a merger or consolidation.[38] Generally, this failure causes the acquisition to be a taxable transaction.

Advantages and Disadvantages of a Merger Transaction. A number of advantages and disadvantages exist with a merger transaction.

Advantages:

- A merger allows greater flexibility than other types of reorganizations because the consideration need not be solely voting stock, as in the case of some other reorganization forms. Money, securities, assumption of the target corporation's liabilities, and other property can be 50% or more of the total consideration used.[39]
- Substantially all the assets of the target corporation need not be acquired, as in the case of a Type C reorganization. Thus, dispositions of unwanted assets by the target corporation generally do not prevent a merger from being a tax-free reorganization.

Disadvantages:

- Compliance with state corporation laws is required. In most states, the shareholders of both the acquiring and target corporations have to approve the plan. Such approvals can take time and can be costly if one or both of the corporations is publicly traded. Dissenting shareholders of both corporations also have the right under state law to have their shares independently appraised and purchased for cash, which may require a substantial cash outlay.
- All liabilities of the target corporation must be assumed, including unknown and contingent liabilities.
- A merger requires the transfer of real estate titles, leases, and contracts. The target corporation may have contracts, rights, or other privileges that are nontransferable and may necessitate use of a reverse triangular merger or other reorganization forms discussed below.

Tax Consequences of a Merger Transaction. The following example illustrates the tax consequences of a merger transaction.

EXAMPLE C7-18 ▶ Acquiring Corporation acquires all of Target Corporation's assets in a merger transaction that qualifies as a Type A reorganization. Target transfers assets having a FMV and an adjusted basis of $2 million and $1.3 million, respectively, and $400,000 in liabilities to Acquiring in exchange for $1 million of Acquiring's common stock and $600,000 of cash. At the time of the transfer, Acquiring's E&P balance is $1 million, and Target's E&P is $750,000. Target distributes the Acquiring stock and cash to its sole shareholder, Millie, in exchange for all of her Target stock,

[38] *Edward H. Russell v. CIR*, 15 AFTR 2d 1107, 65-2 USTC ¶9448 (5th Cir., 1965).

[39] The advance ruling requirements generally limit nonstock consideration to 50% of the total consideration. In limited circumstances, the courts have permitted the 50% ceiling to be exceeded.

which has a $175,000 basis. If Millie had received only Acquiring stock in the reorganization, she would have held 6.25% of the Acquiring stock (100,000 out of 1.6 million shares) immediately after the reorganization.

Target realizes a $700,000 gain [($1,000,000 stock + $600,000 cash + $400,000 liabilities) − $1,300,000 adjusted basis] on the asset transfer. Target recognizes none of this gain. Acquiring takes a $1.3 million carryover basis for the assets it receives. Target recognizes no gain when it distributes the stock and cash to Millie. Millie realizes a $1,425,000 gain on the liquidation of Target [($1,000,000 stock + $600,000 cash) − $175,000 adjusted basis], of which $600,000 must be recognized because of the cash received. Each share of Acquiring stock is worth $16 ($1,600,000 total consideration ÷ 100,000 shares that would be held if all stock were received). The hypothetical redemption of Millie's Acquiring stock required under the *Clark* case and Rev. Rul. 93-61 (see pages C7-18 and C7-19) qualifies as an exchange under Sec. 302(b)(2) because the redemption of 37,500 ($600,000 cash ÷ $16) shares of Acquiring stock deemed to have been redeemed reduces Millie's interest from 6.25% (100,000 shares ÷ 1,600,000 shares) to 4.00% (62,500 shares ÷ 1,562,500 shares). Millie's basis for her Acquiring stock is $175,000 ($175,000 basis of Target stock + $600,000 gain recognized − $600,000 cash received). In addition, Millie's holding period for the Acquiring stock includes her holding period for the Target stock. ◀

DROP-DOWN TYPE A REORGANIZATION. The tax-free reorganization rules permit the acquiring corporation to transfer (drop-down) part or all of the assets and liabilities acquired in the merger or consolidation to a controlled subsidiary corporation.[40] The asset transfer does not affect the tax-free nature of the transaction. Neither the parent nor subsidiary corporation recognize gain or loss on the transfer. The subsidiary corporation takes a carryover basis from its parent corporation in the assets.

HISTORICAL NOTE

Although most state laws allow triangular mergers, the IRS initially ruled that the parent corporation was not a party to the reorganization. This position caused the transaction to be taxable. In response to this IRS position, Congress added in 1968 and 1971 the forward and reverse triangular mergers to Sec. 368's list of tax-free reorganizations.

TRIANGULAR MERGERS. **Triangular mergers** are authorized by Sec. 368(a)(2)(D). They are similar to the conventional Type A merger (previously discussed) except that the parent corporation uses a controlled subsidiary corporation to serve as the acquiring corporation. The target corporation is then merged into the subsidiary corporation using one of the two alternative merger forms described earlier (see Figure C7-3).

Triangular mergers must satisfy the same state law requirements as basic merger transactions. In addition, the stock used to carry out the reorganization is limited to that of the parent corporation. However, the subsidiary corporation's cash and securities can be used as part of the transaction, and the subsidiary corporation can assume the target corporation's liabilities.

The "Substantially All" Requirement. The subsidiary corporation must acquire substantially all the target corporation's assets as part of the plan of reorganization. For advance ruling purposes, the IRS has defined *substantially all* to be at least 70% of the FMV of the target corporation's gross assets and 90% of the FMV of its net assets.[41]

EXAMPLE C7-19 ▶ Acquiring Corporation plans to acquire Target Corporation's assets by using a triangular merger involving its subsidiary Acquiring-Sub Corporation. Target Corporation has $2.5 million (FMV) in assets and $1 million in liabilities. To satisfy the IRS's advance ruling policy, Acquiring must acquire at least 70% of Target's gross assets ($1,750,000 = $2,500,000 FMV of assets × 0.70) and 90% of its net assets [$1,350,000 = ($2,500,000 FMV of assets − $1,000,000 liabilities) × 0.90], or $1.75 million in assets. Target can sell or otherwise dispose of the remaining assets. ◀

Advantages of a Triangular Merger. The tax treatment accorded a triangular merger is the same as for the conventional Type A merger transaction. The triangular merger provides three additional advantages (over the conventional Type A merger):

- The target corporation's assets and liabilities become the property of the subsidiary corporation. Thus, the parent corporation generally cannot be held liable for any liabilities that are not known to the acquiring corporation at the time of the transfer or

[40] Sec. 368(a)(2)(C). As defined in Sec. 368(c), *control* requires the parent corporation to own at least 80% of the voting power and 80% of each class of nonvoting stock. The ability to "drop down" the assets acquired to a subsidiary corporation without recognizing any gain also applies to Type B, C, and G reorganizations.

[41] Rev. Proc. 77-37, 1977-2 C.B. 568, Sec. 3.01.

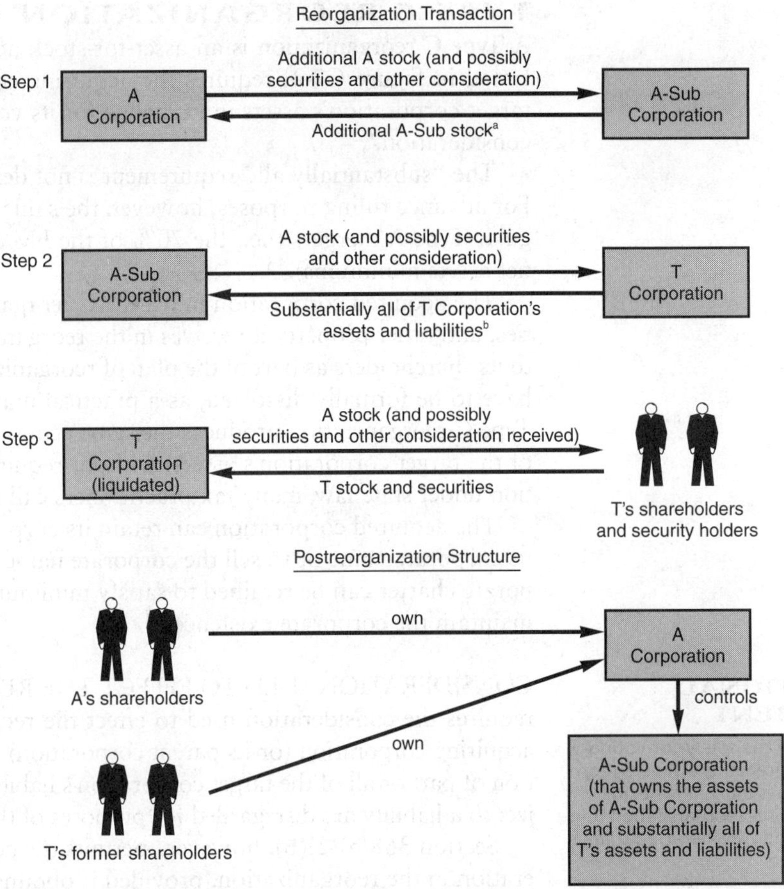

FIGURE C7-3 ▶ TRIANGULAR TYPE A REORGANIZATION

PRACTICAL APPLICATION

The triangular merger is a very popular type of acquisition because the consideration that must be used is still very flexible and yet the parent corporation does not have to assume the known or unknown liabilities of Target. Rather, the controlled subsidiary assumes these liabilities.

for any contingent liabilities. Creditor claims against the parent corporation's assets are thus minimized.

- Shareholder approval on behalf of the acquiring subsidiary corporation comes from its parent corporation. Thus, if the parent corporation's stock is widely held, the cost of obtaining approval of the shareholders may be reduced.
- The target corporation's shareholders may prefer to receive parent corporation stock because of its increased marketability. By receiving marketable stock, the target corporation's shareholders can sell off a portion of the parent corporation stock over an extended period of time and recognize the gain as if they were using the installment method of accounting.

ADDITIONAL COMMENT

In addition to the Type B reorganization, which will be discussed later, the reverse triangular merger is an acquisitive reorganization that keeps Target in existence. It is a popular reorganization form because, unlike the Type B reorganization, the acquiring corporation can use a limited amount of boot.

REVERSE TRIANGULAR MERGERS. **Reverse triangular mergers** are similar to the triangular merger illustrated in Figure C7-3 except the subsidiary corporation (A-Sub Corporation) merges into the target corporation (T Corporation), and the target corporation stays alive as a subsidiary of the parent corporation (A Corporation). This type of transaction permits the target corporation to continue its corporate existence. This action may be desirable from a business standpoint (e.g., to maintain a special authorization or a special license owned by the target corporation). Technical details of this type of acquisition are beyond the scope of this text.

TYPE C REORGANIZATION

A **Type C reorganization** is an asset-for-stock acquisition. This type of transaction, illustrated in Figure C7-4, requires the acquiring corporation to obtain substantially all the target corporation's assets in exchange for its voting stock and a limited amount of other consideration.[42]

The "substantially all" requirement is not defined in the IRC or Treasury Regulations. For advance ruling purposes, however, the same standard holds here that applies to triangular Type A mergers (i.e., the 70% of the FMV of gross assets and 90% of the FMV of net assets minimums).[43]

The acquired corporation in a Type C reorganization must distribute the stock, securities, and other property it receives in the reorganization, plus any other property it retains, to its shareholders as part of the plan of reorganization. Although the corporation does not have to be formally dissolved, as a practical matter it usually is liquidated.[44] Because the Type C reorganization produces the same economic result as a merger (i.e., the acquisition of the target corporation's assets) without requiring the dissolution of the target corporation under state law, many tax practitioners call it a practical merger transaction.

The acquired corporation can retain its corporate charter to prevent others from using its corporate name or to sell the corporate name to a purchaser. Assets other than the corporate charter can be retained to satisfy minimum capital requirements under state law to maintain the corporate existence.[45]

ADDITIONAL COMMENT

Because of the solely-for-voting-stock requirement, a Type C reorganization is much less flexible than a Type A reorganization in terms of the consideration that can be used.

CONSIDERATION USED TO EFFECT THE REORGANIZATION. Section 368(a)(1)(C) requires the consideration used to effect the reorganization be solely voting stock of the acquiring corporation (or its parent corporation). Both the acquiring corporation's assumption of part or all of the target corporation's liabilities and the acquisition of a property subject to a liability are disregarded for purposes of the solely-for-voting-stock requirement.

Section 368(a)(2)(B), however, permits the acquiring corporation to use other consideration in the reorganization, provided it obtains at least 80% of the target corporation's property solely for its voting stock. This rule permits the acquiring corporation to use

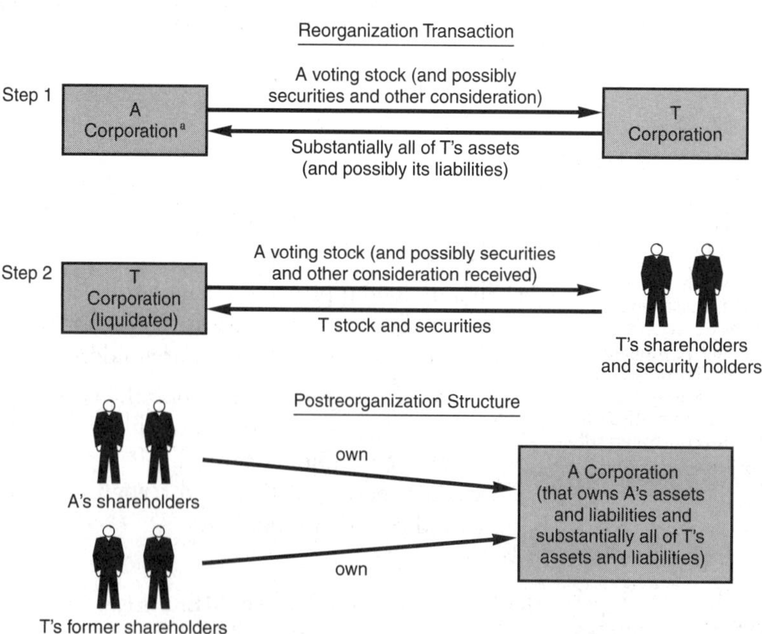

FIGURE C7-4 ▶ TYPE C (ASSET-FOR-STOCK) REORGANIZATION

[42] Sec. 368(a)(1)(C).
[43] Rev. Proc. 77-37, 1977-2 C.B. 568, Sec. 3.01.
[44] Sec. 368(a)(2)(G).
[45] Rev. Proc. 89-50, 1989-1 C.B.631.

money, securities, nonvoting stock, or other property to acquire up to 20% of the target corporation's property. Liabilities assumed or acquired reduce the amount of money that can be used in the reorganization on a dollar-for-dollar basis. If the liabilities assumed or acquired exceed 20% of the FMV of the target corporation's assets, the transaction can take place as a Type C reorganization only if the acquiring corporation uses no money, securities, nonvoting stock, or other property.

EXAMPLE C7-20 ▶ Acquiring Corporation wants to acquire all of Target Corporation's assets and liabilities as part of a Type C reorganization. The following table illustrates the application of the solely-for-voting-stock requirement for four different situations:

	Situation 1	*Situation 2*	*Situation 3*	*Situation 4*
FMV of Target's assets	$200,000	$200,000	$200,000	$200,000
Target's liabilities assumed by Acquiring	–0–	30,000	100,000	100,000
Consideration given by Acquiring:				
FMV of Acquiring voting stock	160,000	160,000	100,000	99,900
Money	40,000	10,000	–0–	100

In Situation 1, the FMV of the Acquiring stock equals 80% of the total assets, so the transaction is a Type C reorganization. The liabilities assumed in Situation 2 reduce the money that Acquiring can pay, but the transaction is still a Type C reorganization because the money and liabilities, in total, do not exceed 20% of the FMV of Target's total assets. In Situation 3, the high percentage of liabilities does not prevent the transaction from being a Type C reorganization because Acquiring used no money to effect the reorganization.[46] In Situation 4, the transaction is disqualified from being a Type C reorganization because some money is used along with the Acquiring stock, and the total money given by Acquiring plus liabilities assumed by Acquiring exceed 20% of the total FMV of Target's assets. ◀

ADDITIONAL COMMENT

Target's liabilities assumed by Acquiring are not a problem unless Target receives boot as part of the consideration. In this case, when applying the 20% boot relaxation rule, liabilities are treated as money. Situation 4 in Example C7-20 illustrates that, if Target has liabilities exceeding 20% of the FMV of its assets, the boot relaxation rule is of no benefit.

ADVANTAGES AND DISADVANTAGES OF A TYPE C REORGANIZATION. A number of advantages and disadvantages exist when comparing a Type C reorganization and a merger.

- The acquiring corporation acquires only the assets specified in the acquisition agreement in a Type C reorganization. However, it needs to acquire substantially all the target corporation's assets. The target corporation might sell, dispose of, or retain assets the acquiring corporation does not want. These unwanted assets are not counted as acquired in testing whether the transaction satisfies the "substantially all" requirement. Thus, a disposition of a substantial amount of assets shortly before an asset-for-stock acquisition may prevent the transaction from being a Type C reorganization. On the other hand, the "substantially all" requirement does not apply to a merger, and dispositions of unwanted assets generally will not prevent an acquisition from being a merger.
- In a Type C reorganization, the acquiring corporation acquires only the liabilities specified in the acquisition agreement. Unknown and contingent liabilities are not acquired, as they are in a merger.
- In a Type C reorganization, shareholders of the acquiring corporation generally do not have to approve the acquisition, thereby reducing the cost to accomplish the transaction. In a merger transaction, the acquiring and target corporations' shareholders must approve the transaction.
- For many target corporations, the liabilities acquired or assumed are so large (i.e., exceeding 20% of total consideration) as to prevent the acquiring corporation in a Type C reorganization from using any consideration other than voting stock. Merger transactions permit 50% nonstock consideration to be used and do not require the stock to have voting rights.

SELF-STUDY QUESTION

Must Acquiring assume all liabilities of Target in a Type C reorganization?

ANSWER

No. Acquiring may leave Target's liabilities in Target. These liabilities would then have to be satisfied with assets retained by Target or with assets acquired by Target in the reorganization.

[46] The IRS may attempt to treat a transaction as a purchase under the continuity of proprietary interest doctrine (see page C7-43) when the amount of liabilities assumed or acquired is high relative to the total FMV of the assets acquired.

- Dissenting shareholders of the target corporation in both transactions may have the right under state law to have their shares independently appraised and purchased for cash.

TAX CONSEQUENCES OF A TYPE C REORGANIZATION. The tax consequences of a Type C reorganization are illustrated by the following example.

EXAMPLE C7-21 ▶ Acquiring Corporation acquires all Target Corporation's assets and liabilities in exchange for \$1.2 million of Acquiring voting stock. Target distributes the Acquiring stock to its sole shareholder, Andrew, in exchange for all his Target stock. Target's assets have a \$1.4 million FMV and a \$600,000 adjusted basis. Acquiring assumes liabilities of \$200,000. Target has a \$500,000 E&P balance. Andrew's basis for his Target stock is \$400,000. Target realizes an \$800,000 gain [(\$1,200,000 + \$200,000) − \$600,000], none of which must be recognized. Acquiring recognizes no gain when it exchanges its stock for the assets and, it takes a \$600,000 basis in the acquired assets. Andrew realizes an \$800,000 (\$1,200,000 − \$400,000) gain on the surrender of his shares when Target liquidates, none of which must be recognized. Andrew's basis for the Acquiring stock is \$400,000. Andrew's holding period for the Acquiring stock includes the time he held the Target stock. Acquiring assumes all of Target's tax attributes, including the \$500,000 E&P balance. ◀

TYPICAL MISCONCEPTION

As with a Type A reorganization, a Type C reorganization can be structured as a triangular acquisition. Although this ability provides greater flexibility in tax planning, it makes the area more confusing because of the substantial overlap between the different types of reorganizations.

DROP-DOWN AND TRIANGULAR TYPE C REORGANIZATIONS. Section 368(a)(2)(C) permits the acquiring corporation in a Type C reorganization to transfer part or all of the assets and liabilities acquired in the reorganization to a controlled subsidiary corporation without destroying the tax-free nature of the transaction. Section 368(a)(1)(C) permits a triangular Type C reorganization to be used whereby a subsidiary corporation uses voting stock of the parent corporation to acquire substantially all the target corporation's assets. The triangular Type C reorganization requirements are the same as for the basic Type C reorganization except that the voting stock used to acquire the assets must consist solely of the stock of the acquiring corporation's parent corporation. However, the subsidiary corporation can provide additional consideration in the form of securities, money, or other property.

KEY POINT

When a Type D reorganization is used as an acquisitive reorganization, it generally involves commonly controlled corporations. However, its most common usage is as part of a divisive reorganization under Sec. 355 (discussed later in this chapter).

TYPE D REORGANIZATION

Type D reorganizations can be either acquisitive or divisive. (Divisive Type D reorganizations are discussed on pages C7-35 through C7-41.) An acquisitive Type D reorganization involves the transfer by a target (transferor) corporation of substantially all of its assets to an acquiring (transferee) corporation in exchange for such corporation's stock and securities (and possibly other consideration) pursuant to a plan of reorganization. The exchange must be followed by a distribution to the transferor's shareholders and security holders of the stock, securities, and other consideration received in the reorganization, plus any other property retained by the transferor corporation, pursuant to a complete liquidation of the transferor corporation.[47] (See Figure C7-5 for an illustration of an acquisitive Type D reorganization.)

The "substantially all" requirement is based on the facts and circumstances of the situation. For advance ruling purposes, however, the 70% of the FMV of gross assets and 90% of the FMV of net assets standard used in the triangular Type A and Type C reorganizations also applies here.[48]

ADDITIONAL COMMENT

The 50% control requirement makes the Type D reorganization a useful tool for the IRS to recast certain tax avoidance transactions.

CONTROL REQUIREMENTS. The transferor (target) corporation or one or more of its shareholders must control the transferee (acquiring) corporation immediately after the asset transfer. For this purpose, Sec. 368(a)(2)(H) defines control as either 50% or more of the total combined voting power of all classes of voting stock, or 50% or more of the total value of all classes of stock.

One example of an acquisitive Type D reorganization is when an acquiring corporation acquires all the assets of a larger corporation (target corporation), and the target cor-

[47] Secs. 368(a)(1)(D) and 354(b)(1).

[48] Rev. Proc. 77-37, 1977-2 C.B. 568, Sec. 3.01.

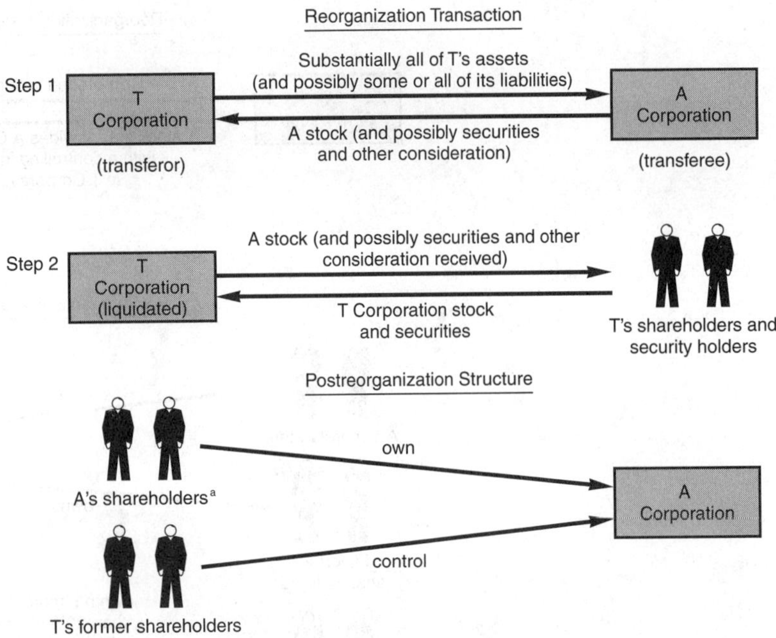

FIGURE C7-5 ▶ ACQUISITIVE TYPE D REORGANIZATION

poration's shareholders end up controlling the acquiring corporation after the reorganization. Type C reorganizations (where the target does not control the acquiring corporation) and Type A reorganizations (where the transaction satisfies the state law merger requirements) are more common than the acquisitive Type D reorganization.

The Sec. 368(a)(1)(D) rules do not limit the consideration that may be exchanged in the transaction. The IRS and the courts, however, require that the transferor corporation's shareholders maintain a continuing equity interest in the transferee corporation. For advance ruling purposes, the IRS requires that the transferor corporation's shareholders receive transferee corporation stock equal to at least 50% of the value of the transferor corporation's outstanding stock to satisfy this requirement.[49]

TAX CONSEQUENCES OF A TYPE D REORGANIZATION. The Type C and acquisitive Type D reorganization requirements and tax consequences are quite similar. If the reorganization satisfies both the Type C and Type D reorganization requirements, Sec. 368(a)(2)(A) requires that the transaction be treated as a Type D reorganization. The basic tax consequences of a Type D reorganization for the target corporation, the acquiring corporation, and the target corporation's shareholders are the same as for a Type C reorganization except in the application of the Sec. 357(c) "excess" liability rule. Section 357(c) requires the transferor (target) corporation in a Type D reorganization to recognize gain equal to the amount by which the liabilities assumed or acquired by the transferee (acquiring) corporation exceed the total adjusted basis of the transferor corporation's assets transferred. Such gain does not have to be recognized if the asset acquisition qualifies only as a Type C reorganization (e.g., when the target corporation does not control the acquiring corporation).

ADDITIONAL COMMENT

If Acquiring wants Target to remain in existence, the two choices in Sec. 368 that can accomplish this objective are a Type B reorganization or a reverse triangular merger.

TYPE B REORGANIZATION

A **Type B reorganization** is the simplest form of acquisitive reorganization. In this type of reorganization, two things happen: the target corporation's shareholders exchange their stock for the acquiring corporation's voting stock, and the target corporation remains in existence as the acquiring corporation's subsidiary (see Figure C7-6).

[49] Rev. Proc. 77-37, 1977-2 C.B. 568, Sec. 3.02.

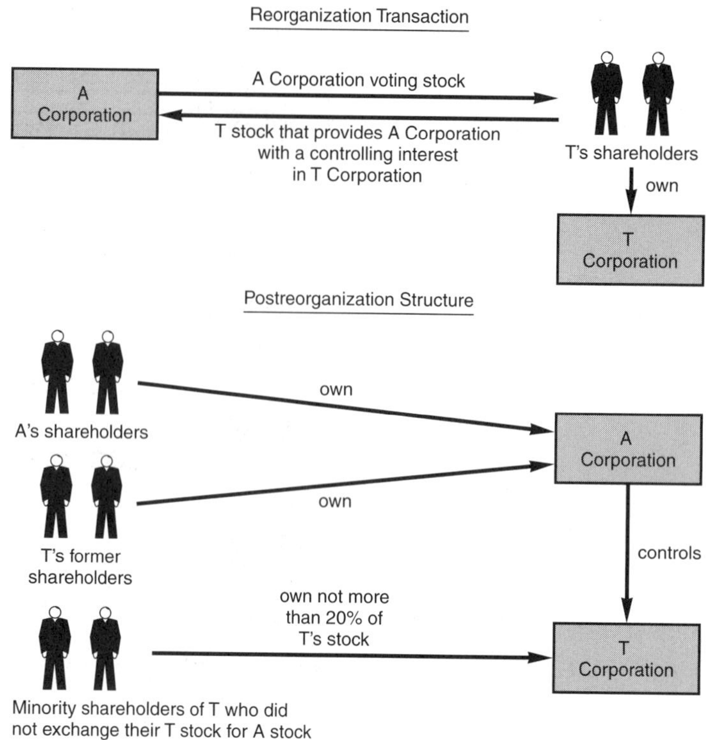

FIGURE C7-6 ▶ TYPE B (STOCK-FOR-STOCK) REORGANIZATION

The Type B reorganization generally is accomplished independent of the target corporation. The basis of the target corporation's assets (inside basis) and the amount of its tax attributes generally remain unchanged by the reorganization. After the reorganization, the target corporation and the parent corporation may elect to file a consolidated tax return. If the target corporation is liquidated into the parent corporation shortly after the stock-for-stock exchange occurs, the IRS may attempt to collapse the two parts of the transaction into a single transaction and treat it as a Type C asset-for-stock reorganization.[50]

KEY POINT

The IRC allows no relaxation of the solely-for-voting-stock requirement for the Type B reorganization. Thus, the Type B reorganization has the least flexible consideration requirement of any of the reorganizations.

SOLELY-FOR-VOTING-STOCK REQUIREMENT. Section 368(a)(1)(B) requires the acquiring corporation to acquire the target corporation's stock in exchange solely for the acquiring corporation's voting stock. The acquiring corporation must own sufficient stock to be in control of the target corporation immediately after the exchange.

The solely-for-voting-stock requirement generally precludes the use of other property to effect the transaction. However, the voting stock used can be either common or preferred stock. If the acquiring corporation uses consideration other than voting stock to effect the reorganization (e.g., nonvoting preferred stock), the transaction does not qualify as a Type B reorganization, and the transaction is taxable to the target corporation's shareholders (see pages C7-49 and C7-50).

SELF-STUDY QUESTION

Is there any way to take care of dissenters in a Type B reorganization?

ANSWER

Yes. Even though Acquiring cannot use any boot to acquire Target's stock, Target can redeem out the dissenters before the reorganization. Also, Target's nondissenting shareholders could buy out the dissenters' stock.

In a Type B reorganization, debt obligations of the acquiring corporation can be exchanged for debt obligations of the target corporation held by the target corporation's shareholders without any gain or loss being recognized when the face amount of the two debt obligations are the same.[51]

Exceptions. The acquiring corporation can use cash in limited circumstances without violating the solely-for-voting-stock requirement. For example:

[50] Rev. Rul. 67-274, 1967-2 C.B. 141. If the transaction is "collapsed" into a Type C reorganization, the Type C reorganization requirements (and not the Type B) must be satisfied.

[51] Rev. Rul. 98-10, 1998-1 C.B. 643.

- The target corporation's shareholders can receive cash in exchange for their right to receive a fractional share of the acquiring corporation's stock.[52]
- Reorganization expenses of the target corporation (such as legal expenses, accounting fees, and administrative costs) can be paid by the acquiring corporation without violating the solely-for-voting-stock requirement.[53]

ADDITIONAL COMMENT

"Creeping acquisitions" are allowed in a Type B reorganization because the requirement is merely that 80% must be owned after the transaction. Transactions within 12 months generally are considered related transactions. This aggregation rule can be either an advantage or a disadvantage depending on what consideration was used in the various steps of the acquisition.

Control. For Type B reorganizations, Sec. 368(c) defines control as 80% of the total combined voting power of all classes of voting stock and 80% of each class of nonvoting stock. Because the acquiring corporation does not have to acquire all the target corporation's stock, a minority interest of up to 20% may be present. Minority shareholders can have their shares independently valued and acquired for cash under state law without destroying the tax-free nature of the transaction. For example, the target corporation can use its cash to redeem the stock of the minority shareholders before or after the reorganization. On the other hand, a cash acquisition by the acquiring corporation of the shares of a group of dissenting minority shareholders either before or as part of the reorganization prevents the transaction from being tax-free.[54]

Timing of the Transaction. Some Type B reorganizations are accomplished simply by exchanging stock of the acquiring corporation for 100% of the target corporation's shares in a single transaction. In other cases, the reorganization is accomplished in a series of transactions taking place over an extended period of time. Regulation Sec. 1.368-2(c) states that a cash purchase of stock may be disregarded for purposes of the solely-for-voting-stock requirement if it was independent of the stock-for-stock exchange. Stock acquisitions made over a relatively short period of time—12 months or less—are, according to this regulation, to be aggregated for purposes of applying the solely-for-voting-stock requirement.

EXAMPLE C7-22 ▶ Acquiring Corporation acquires 12% of Target Corporation's single class of stock for cash in July 2002. Acquiring acquires the remaining 88% in January 2003 in a stock-for-stock exchange. The cash and stock-for-stock acquisitions probably will be aggregated by the IRS because they occur within a 12-month period. Even though Acquiring obtains 80% control in a single stock-for-stock transaction, the transaction does not meet the Type B reorganization requirements because the solely-for-voting-stock requirement is not met if the two transactions are aggregated. The transaction could qualify as a Type B reorganization if Acquiring unconditionally sold its 12% interest in the Target stock and then acquired the necessary 80% interest in a single stock-for-stock exchange, or if Acquiring delayed the stock-for-stock exchange until some time after July 2003, when it probably would be considered a separate transaction.[55] ◀

EXAMPLE C7-23 ▶ Acquiring Corporation acquires 85% of Target Corporation's single class of stock in April 1996 in a transaction that qualifies as a Type B reorganization. Acquiring acquires the remaining 15% of Target's stock in December 2002 in a stock-for-stock exchange. Even though Acquiring already controls Target, the second acquisition is treated as a Type B reorganization. ◀

TAX CONSEQUENCES OF A TYPE B REORGANIZATION. The tax consequences of a Type B reorganization are straightforward.

- The target corporation's shareholders recognize no gain or loss on the exchange unless their fractional shares of stock are acquired for cash or the target corporation redeems some of their stock.
- The target corporation's shareholders take a substituted basis for their new acquiring corporation stock from the basis of their target corporation stock surrendered. The holding period for the acquiring corporation stock includes their holding period for the target corporation stock surrendered.
- The acquiring corporation recognizes no gain or loss when it issues its voting stock for the target corporation's stock.

---

[52] Rev. Rul. 66-365, 1966-2 C.B. 116.
[53] Rev. Rul. 73-54, 1973-1 C.B. 187.
[54] Rev. Rul. 68-285, 1968-1 C.B. 147.
[55] See, for example, *Eldon S. Chapman et al. v. CIR*, 45 AFTR 2d 80-1290, 80-1 USTC ¶9330 (1st Cir., 1980).

WHAT WOULD YOU DO IN THIS SITUATION?

Tobin Rote, a wealthy investor, owns all of the single class of stock of Detroit Corporation, a calendar year taxpayer. Mr. Rote has wanted to acquire Cleveland Corporation, which produces metal and plastic parts for the automobile industry. Detroit Corporation purchases for cash 4.9% of the Cleveland voting stock on August 1, 2002. The Cleveland stock trades on the New York Stock Exchange. The acquisition provides Tobin Rote, as a Cleveland shareholder, access to its books and records. The 4.9% ownership position, however, is below the 5% threshold at which Detroit must file with the SEC a Tender Offer Statement (Schedule 14-D) regarding its stock position. Based on an analysis of Cleveland's books and records made shortly after becoming a shareholder, Tobin Rote wants to make a tender offer sometime in the next two months whereby part or all of the remaining Cleveland voting and nonvoting stock would be acquired in exchange for Detroit stock. He comes to you for advice concerning the tender offer, which he wants to complete by December 31, 2002. No shares would be acquired unless sufficient shares were tendered to provide Detroit Corporation with 80% of the voting stock and 80% of all other classes of stock. Mr Rote wants to use the pooling method to report the transaction for book purposes. As Mr. Rote's CPA, you know that he has used this method to report a number of previous acquisitions. Mr. Rote explains to you that he hopes to continue to avoid having to place the goodwill that results from a cash purchase of a target corporation's stock on Cleveland's financial statements because the amortization drives down corporate earnings per share. As Mr. Rote's CPA, you have guided him through a number of acquisitions where he has used the pooling method. You know that the FASB recently issued two pronouncements that apply to Mr. Rote's situation. What information do you need to provide Mr. Rote about these changes? What advantages can you see in the new pronouncements that may make Mr. Rote happier about the effect that these pronouncements will have on his business?

- The acquiring corporation's basis for the target corporation's stock is the same as it was in the hands of the target corporation's shareholders.

EXAMPLE C7-24 ▶ Target Corporation's single class of stock is owned entirely by Mark, who has a $400,000 basis for his stock. Mark exchanges his Target stock for $700,000 of Acquiring Corporation's voting stock. Mark realizes a $300,000 gain ($700,000 − $400,000), none of which is recognized. Mark's basis for the Acquiring stock is $400,000. Acquiring Corporation recognizes no gain or loss when it issues its stock to Mark and takes a $400,000 basis for the acquired Target stock. ◀

STOP & THINK

Question: Assume that Acquiring and Target Corporations are both publicly traded corporations with each corporation having several thousand shareholders. Acquiring Corporation acquires Target Corporation stock in a Type B reorganization. What problems can accrue in attempting to determine Acquiring Corporation's basis for the Target Corporation stock acquired in this transaction?

Solution: Under Sec. 358(a), Acquiring's basis for the Target stock acquired is the same as it was in the hands of Target's shareholders. Many shareholders may not know their historical cost basis for stock purchased a number of years ago. The basis for these shares may have changed due to stock dividends, stock splits, or nontaxable "dividend" distributions. This lack of information about events occurring between the acquisition and sale dates for a large number of individuals may make it difficult to accurately determine Acquiring's basis for the Target stock acquired. The IRS permits sampling to be used to extrapolate a total basis from the stock holdings of a small number of Target shareholders.

ADVANTAGES OF A TYPE B REORGANIZATION. The Type B reorganization has a number of advantages. First, as explained earlier, it usually can be accomplished quite simply and without formal shareholder approval. The acquiring corporation can acquire the necessary shares with a tender offer made directly to the target corporation's shareholders even if the target corporation's management does not approve of the transaction. Second, the target corporation remains in existence, and its assets, liabilities, and tax attributes do not transfer to the acquiring corporation. Nevertheless, use of its NOLs may be limited under Sec. 382

(see pages C7-47 through C7-49).[56] Third, the corporate name, goodwill, licenses, and rights of the target company can continue on after the acquisition. Fourth, the acquiring corporation does not directly acquire the target corporation's liabilities, as is the case of some other reorganizations. Finally, the acquiring and target corporations can report the results for the post-acquisition time period by filing a consolidated tax return (see Chapter C8).

DISADVANTAGES OF A TYPE B REORGANIZATION. Offsetting the advantages noted above are a number of disadvantages. First, the sole consideration that may be used to effect the transaction is voting stock. The issuing of the additional voting stock can dilute the voting power of the acquiring corporation's shareholders and restrict their flexibility to structure the transaction to retain control of the acquiring corporation. Second, at least 80% of the target corporation's stock must be acquired even though effective control of the acquired company might be obtained with ownership of less than 80%. Third, the acquisition of less than 100% of the target corporation's stock may lead to a vocal group of dissenting minority shareholders. These shareholders have the right under state law to have their shares appraised and purchased for cash. Fourth, the bases of the target corporation's stock (outside basis) and assets (inside basis) are not stepped-up to their FMVs when the change in ownership occurs, as would be the case in a taxable asset acquisition.

DROP-DOWN AND TRIANGULAR TYPE B REORGANIZATIONS. As with the Type A and C reorganizations, a triangular Type B reorganization, or a drop-down of the target corporation's stock into a subsidiary corporation before accomplishing the stock-for-stock exchange, can be accomplished tax-free. In a triangular reorganization, the stock of the acquiring corporation's parent corporation is exchanged for a controlling stock interest in the target corporation. As in the basic Type B reorganization, the target corporation remains in existence as a subsidiary of the acquiring (subsidiary) corporation.

HISTORICAL NOTE

The Type G reorganization is the newest of the Sec. 368 reorganizations. Previously, reorganizations used in restructuring corporations involved in bankruptcy proceedings had their own statutory provisions. As part of the Bankruptcy Tax Act of 1980, the old provisions were repealed and the Type G reorganization was enacted. This change was made to allow more flexibility in restructuring bankrupt corporations.

TYPE G REORGANIZATION

Section 368(a)(1)(G) defines a **Type G reorganization** as "a transfer by a corporation of part or all of its assets to another corporation in a title 11 [bankruptcy] or similar case, but only if, in pursuance of the plan, stock or securities of the corporation to which the assets are transferred are distributed in a transaction that qualifies under sections 354, 355, or 356." Use of a Type G reorganization is quite limited because the reorganization must take place according to a court-approved plan in a bankruptcy, receivership, or other similar situation.

In an acquisitive Type G reorganization, the financially troubled corporation might transfer substantially all of its assets to an acquiring corporation according to a court-approved plan (e.g., a bankruptcy reorganization plan) and then distribute all the stock, securities, and other property received in the exchange, plus any property it had retained, to its shareholders and creditors in exchange for their stock and debt interests.

DIVISIVE REORGANIZATIONS

A divisive reorganization involves the transfer of *part* of a transferor corporation's assets to a controlled corporation in exchange for its stock and securities (and possibly some boot property).[57] The stock and securities (and possibly some boot property) are then distributed to the transferor's shareholders. The primary divisive reorganization comes under the Type D reorganization rules, although a divisive reorganization involving a financially troubled corporation could be a Type G reorganization. Topic Review C7-6 summarizes the requirements for the divisive and other reorganizations.

---

[56] A Type B reorganization can result in an ownership change that restricts the ability of the target corporation's NOL carryovers to be used under Sec. 382 but does not, in total, diminish the amount of its carryovers (see page C7-47).

[57] In a divisive Type D reorganization, control is defined by Sec. 368(c) because Sec. 355 (not Sec. 354) governs the distribution. Section 368(c) requires ownership of at least 80% of the voting and nonvoting stock to constitute control. An acquisitive Type D reorganization, on the other hand, requires only 50% of the voting and nonvoting stock to be owned to constitute control (see page C7-30).

Topic Review C7-6

Summary of Divisive and Other Reorganizations

Type of Reorganization	Distributing (D) or Transferor (T) Corporation Property Acquired	Consideration That Can Be Used	What Happens to the Distributing (D) or Transferor (T) Corporation?	Shareholders' Recognized Gain	Other Requirements
D—Divisive	Part or all of D[a] Corporation's assets (and possibly some or all of its liabilities) are transferred to a "controlled" corporation (C[b] Corporation).	Stock, securities, and other property of C Corporation	Stock, securities, and boot received in the reorganization must be distributed; D Corporation may be liquidated but can remain in existence.	Lesser of realized gain or boot received	Transactions can take three forms—spinoff, split-off, or split-up. Control is defined at the 80% level under Sec. 368(c).
E—Recapitalization	No increase or decrease in assets occurs. A change to the capital structure of T[c] Corporation takes place.	Stock, securities, and other property of T Corporation	T Corporation remains in existence.	Lesser of realized gain or boot received	May involve stock-for-stock, bond-for-bond, or bond-for-stock exchanges.
F—Change in form, identity, or place of organization	Assets or stock of old T Corporation are transferred to new T Corporation.	Stock, securities, and other property of new T Corporation	Old T Corporation is liquidated.	Lesser of realized gain or boot received	Must involve only a single operating company.
G—Acquisitive or divisive	Part or all of T Corporation's assets (and possibly some or all of its liabilities) are transferred to A Corporation[d] in a bankruptcy case.	Stock, securities, and other property of A Corporation	T Corporation may be liquidated or divided but can remain in existence.	Lesser of realized gain or boot received	Stock and securities of A Corporation received by T Corporation must be distributed to its shareholders, security holders, or creditors.

[a] D Corporation refers to the distributing corporation.
[b] C Corporation refers to the controlled corporation.
[c] T Corporation refers to the transferor corporation.
[d] A Corporation refers to the transferee or acquiring corporation.

DIVISIVE TYPE D REORGANIZATION

The Type D reorganization must take place as part of a plan of reorganization and satisfy the requirements of Secs. 368(a)(1)(D) and 355, which are explained below.[58] The Type D divisive reorganizations can take three forms: spinoffs, split-offs, and split-ups (see Figure C7-7).

A distribution of a controlled corporation's stock can be tax-free under Sec. 355 even if the distributing corporation transfers no assets to the controlled corporation. For a transaction to constitute one of the three divisive Type D reorganization forms, however, both the asset transfer and the Sec. 355 distribution must take place as part of a single transaction governed by a plan of reorganization. Both divisive reorganizations and tax-free distributions of the stock of an existing controlled subsidiary are examined in this section.

TYPICAL MISCONCEPTION

The existence of a corporate business purpose is necessary before the stock of a controlled subsidiary can be distributed to the shareholders of the distributing corporation. This requirement is much more difficult to satisfy in a Sec. 355 distribution than it is in an acquisitive reorganization.

A divisive Type D reorganization can be used to accomplish various types of business adjustments, including

- Dividing a business into two corporations to separate a high-risk business from a low-risk business
- Dividing a single business between two shareholders that have major disagreements
- Dividing a corporation's business activities according to its separate functions or the geographical areas in which it operates
- Dividing a business because of antitrust law violations

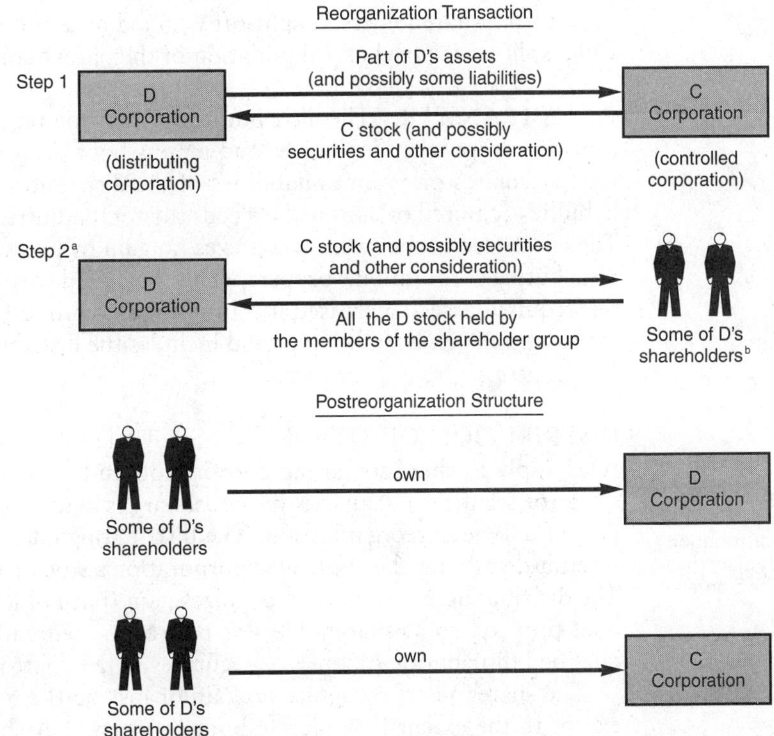

[a] Step 1 remains the same for the spinoff transaction. In a spinoff transaction, D's shareholders surrender no D stock. In a split-up transaction, Step 1 involves D Corporation's assets and liabilities being transferred to two controlled corporations. Step 2 involves the distribution of the stock of the two controlled corporations pursuant to the liquidation of D Corporation.

[b] This distribution also could occur on a pro rata basis to all D's shareholders, in which case the shareholders surrender only a portion of their D shares.

FIGURE C7-7 ▶ DIVISIVE TYPE D REORGANIZATION (SPLIT-OFF FORM)

[58] The requirements of the divisive Type D reorganization may be contrasted with the acquisitive Type D reorganization (previously discussed), where substantially all the transferor's assets must be transferred to a controlled corporation.

FORMS OF DIVISIVE TYPE D REORGANIZATIONS. Three types of divisive transactions are tax-free if the Sec. 368(a)(1)(D) requirements are met:

- **Split-off**—the distributing corporation transfers part of its assets to a controlled corporation in exchange for stock and possibly securities, money, or other boot property. The distributing corporation then distributes the stock of the subsidiary to part or all of its shareholders, receiving some of its stock in exchange. Such a transaction may occur because of a management dispute between two dissenting shareholder groups whereby the parent corporation redeems all the stock of one of the groups (see Figure C7-7).
- **Spinoff**—the distributing corporation transfers part of its assets to a controlled corporation in exchange for stock and possibly securities, money, or other boot property. The distributing corporation then distributes the stock of the subsidiary ratably to all of its shareholders, receiving nothing in exchange. Such a transaction may occur because of a desire to reduce the risk inherent in having two operating divisions (e.g., steel and glass manufacturing) within a single corporation.
- **Split-up**—the distributing corporation transfers all of its assets to two controlled corporations in exchange for stock and possibly securities, money, or other boot property. The distributing corporation then distributes the stock of the two subsidiaries to all of its shareholders, receiving in exchange all of its outstanding stock. Such a transaction may occur because of a desire to have two operating divisions transferred to new corporations, which will continue in existence as brother-sister corporations while the old corporation is liquidated.

If the Sec. 355 requirements described below are *not* met, a spinoff is taxed as a dividend to the shareholders, a split-off is taxed as a stock redemption to the shareholders, and a split-up is taxed as a liquidation of the parent corporation to the shareholders.

ASSET TRANSFER. The distributing corporation recognizes no gain or loss on the asset transfer except when it receives and retains boot property or when the controlled corporation acquires or assumes liabilities of the distributing corporation and the total of the liabilities acquired or assumed exceeds the total adjusted bases of the assets transferred.[59] The controlled corporation recognizes no gain or loss when it exchanges its stock for the distributing corporation's property. The controlled corporation takes a carryover basis for the acquired assets, increased for any gain recognized by the distributing corporation on the asset transfer. Its holding period includes the distributing corporation's holding period for the assets.

TYPICAL MISCONCEPTION

Section 355 can apply to a distribution of stock of an existing subsidiary as well as the distribution of stock of a new subsidiary that is created as part of the transaction.

DISTRIBUTION OF STOCK AND SECURITIES. The same gain or loss recognition rules apply to the distributing corporation and its shareholders when a distribution of stock (or securities) of an existing subsidiary is made under Sec. 355 or when it is made as part of a Type D reorganization. The distributing corporation recognizes no gain or loss when it distributes the controlled corporation's stock (or securities) to its shareholders.[60] The distributing corporation recognizes gain (but not loss) when it distributes nonmoney boot property to its shareholders as part of the reorganization and when it makes a disqualified distribution of stock or securities in the controlled corporation.

The shareholders recognize no gain or loss on the receipt of the stock (and securities) except to the extent they receive boot property.[61] A shareholder's basis in the stock (or securities) held after the distribution equals his or her basis in the stock (or securities) held before the distribution, increased by any gain recognized and decreased by the sum of

---

[59] Secs. 361(a) and 357(c)(1)(B).

[60] Sec. 361(c)(1). Two special rules may require the distributing corporation to recognize gain when it distributes stocks and securities. A disqualifying distribution occurs if, immediately after the distribution, any person holds a 50% disqualified stock interest in either the distributing corporation or the controlled corporation. Disqualified stock generally is defined as any stock in the distributing or a controlled corporation purchased within the five-year period ending on the distribution date. The disqualifying distribution rules prevent a divisive transaction from following a stock purchase to accomplish the disposition of a significant part of the historic shareholders' interests in one or more of the divided corporations. A second set of rules, the anti-Morris Trust rules, also requires the distributing corporation to recognize gain when a distribution of stock or securities is made and is preceded or followed by a disposition of the stock or securities.

[61] Sec. 355(a). As with an acquisitive reorganization, Sec. 361(a) permits securities (e.g., long-term debt obligations) to be received tax-free in a divisive transaction when the shareholders surrender the same face amount of securities, or a larger amount. Excess securities received are boot property.

money received and the FMV of any other boot property received. If more than one class of stock or securities is held before or after the distribution, the total basis for the nonrecognition property is allocated to each class based on their relative FMVs. The basis for any boot property (other than money) is its FMV. The holding period for the stock and nonboot securities received includes the holding period of the stock and securities surrendered. The holding period for boot property begins on the day after the distribution date.

EXAMPLE C7-25 ▶ Distributing Corporation transfers assets having a $600,000 FMV and a $350,000 adjusted basis to Controlled Corporation in exchange for all of Controlled's single class of stock. Distributing has been owned equally by Ruth and Pat for ten years. Ruth and Pat are no longer able to agree on the management of Distributing and have agreed to a division of the assets in exchange for Pat surrendering her Distributing shares. Pat's basis for her Distributing shares is $400,000. Distributing realizes a $250,000 gain ($600,000 – $350,000) on the asset transfer, none of which is recognized. Distributing also recognizes no gain on the distribution of the Controlled shares to Pat. Pat realizes a $200,000 ($600,000 – $400,000) gain on surrendering her Distributing shares, none of which is recognized. Her basis in the Controlled stock is $400,000. The holding period for the Controlled shares includes Pat's holding period for the Distributing shares. Controlled recognizes no gain when it issues its stock for Distributing's assets and takes a $350,000 basis in the acquired assets. ◀

SELF-STUDY QUESTION

Does the receipt of boot make the entire Sec. 355 transaction taxable to the shareholders?

ANSWER

No. The shareholders may have a partial recognition of gain. The amount and type of gain depends on whether the shareholders surrender stock of the distributing corporation in the transaction.

TYPICAL MISCONCEPTION

In a spinoff, the FMV of the boot received is treated as a Sec. 301 distribution to the shareholder. In a split-off or split-up, the shareholders recognize gain to the extent of the lesser of boot received or the gain realized. This gain may be a dividend or capital gain under Sec. 302.

Under Sec. 355, boot may consist of money, short-term debt, any property other than the stock or securities of a controlled corporation, any stock of the controlled corporation purchased within the previous five years in a taxable transaction, securities of the controlled corporation to the extent the principal amount of the securities received exceeds the principal amount of the securities surrendered by the shareholder, and stock or securities attributable to accrued interest.[62] When the shareholder receives boot, the amount and character of the income or gain recognized depend on whether he or she surrendered stock and securities in the distributing corporation (i.e., a split-off or split-up) or did not surrender any stock or securities (i.e., a spinoff).

When the shareholder receives boot in a spinoff, the FMV of the boot is a dividend to the extent of the shareholder's ratable share of the distributing corporation's E&P. Any securities the shareholders receive in a spinoff are boot because the shareholders do not surrender any securities in a spinoff transaction. Thus, the FMV of the securities is a dividend to the extent of the shareholder's ratable share of the distributing corporation's E&P.

In a split-off or a split-up, in addition to the exchange of stock, a shareholder may receive some boot property. If the shareholder realizes a loss on the exchange, the loss is not recognized, whether boot is received or not.[63] If the shareholder realizes a gain on the exchange, he or she recognizes the gain to the extent of the FMV of any boot received.

If the exchange has the effect of a dividend under the Sec. 302 stock redemption rules, the recognized gain is treated as a dividend up to the amount of the shareholder's ratable share of the distributing corporation's E&P.[64] Otherwise it is a capital gain. The Sec. 302 rules are applied by treating the shareholder as though he or she continued to own stock in the distributing corporation and surrendered only the portion of his or her shares equal in value to the amount of boot received. This hypothetical redemption is then tested under the Sec. 302(b) rules to see whether it receives exchange or dividend treatment.[65]

EXAMPLE C7-26 ▶ Distributing Corporation owns assets with a $60,000 FMV plus all the outstanding shares of Controlled Corporation, which was created by an asset transfer made by Distributing. The Controlled stock is worth $40,000. Distributing's E&P balance is $35,000. Distributing is owned by Carl and Diane, each of whom owns 100 shares of Distributing stock. Distributing distributes all the Controlled stock to Carl in exchange for Carl's 100 shares of Distributing stock in a transaction that qualifies as a split-off under Secs. 368(a)(1)(D) and 355, except that Carl also receives $10,000 in cash. Carl's basis in the Distributing shares he surrenders is $22,000. Carl has a $28,000 realized gain, determined as follows:

---

62 Secs. 355(a)(3) and 356(b).

63 Sec. 356(c).

64 Sec. 356(a)(2).

65 Rev. Rul. 93-62, 1993-2 C.B. 118.

FMV of Controlled stock	$40,000
Plus: Cash received	10,000
Amount realized	$50,000
Minus: Basis of Distributing stock	(22,000)
Realized gain	$28,000

Carl must recognize $10,000 of this gain (i.e., the lesser of the $28,000 realized gain or the $10,000 boot received). If Carl surrenders Distributing stock solely for the $10,000 boot, he would be surrendering 20 Distributing shares worth $10,000 ($10,000 boot ÷ $500 FMV for each share of Distributing stock). Before this hypothetical redemption, he owns 50% of the outstanding Distributing shares (100 ÷ 200), and afterward he owns 44% (80 ÷ 180). Thus, the hypothetical redemption is not substantially disproportionate under Sec. 302(b)(2) because the 44% post-redemption stock ownership exceeds 80% of the pre-redemption stock ownership (50% × 0.80 = 40%). If the exchange can meet one of the other tests for sale treatment (e.g., not essentially equivalent to a dividend), the $10,000 is a capital gain. Otherwise it is a dividend. ◀

TYPICAL MISCONCEPTION

Unlike Sec. 351, securities (long-term debt) can be exchanged in a Sec. 355 transaction without the recognition of gain as long as the principal amount surrendered is equal to or greater than the principal amount received.

In a split-off or a split-up, a shareholder may receive securities of the controlled corporation tax-free but only if the shareholder surrenders securities in the distributing corporation with an equal or larger principal amount. To the extent the principal amount of the securities received by a shareholder exceeds the principal amount of the securities surrendered by that shareholder, the FMV of the excess principal amount is boot.

THE SEC. 355 REQUIREMENTS. The Sec. 355 requirements must be met for the distribution of a subsidiary's stock as part of a Type D reorganization or as an independent divisive transaction to be tax-free.

Under Sec. 355, a distributing corporation's distribution of a controlled corporation's stock is tax-free to the shareholders if the following six requirements are met:[66]

ADDITIONAL COMMENT

The control requirement for Sec. 355 is the same control requirement previously discussed relating to the formation of a corporation under Sec. 351 (Chapter C2).

- The property distributed must consist solely of stock or securities of a corporation controlled by the distributing corporation immediately before the distribution. The distributing corporation must own and distribute stock possessing at least 80% of the total combined voting power of all classes of stock entitled to vote and at least 80% of the total number of shares of all other classes of stock.[67]
- The distribution must not have been used principally as a device to distribute the E&P of the distributing corporation, the controlled corporation, or both. Whether a transaction has been used as a device to distribute the E&P of the distributing corporation, the controlled corporation, or both is a matter of the facts and circumstances in each case. A sale or exchange of stock of the distributing or controlled corporation after the distribution is evidence that the distribution was used as such a device, especially if the sale was prearranged.[68]

TYPICAL MISCONCEPTION

The active trade or business requirement has two parts: a pre-distribution five-year history and both the distributing and controlled corporations must be actively engaged in a trade or business immediately after the distribution.

- Immediately after the distribution, the distributing corporation and the controlled corporation each must be engaged in the active conduct of a trade or business that also was actively conducted for at least five years before the distribution. The main reason for this requirement is to prevent a corporation from spinning off a newly formed subsidiary whose only assets are unneeded cash and other liquid assets. The shareholders could then sell or liquidate the subsidiary and obtain the liquid assets in an exchange transaction rather than as a dividend.[69]
- The distributing corporation must distribute either all the stock and securities in the controlled corporation held by it immediately before the distribution or an amount of stock in the controlled corporation constituting control. The distributing corporation

[66] Sec. 355(a) and Reg. Secs. 1.355-2(b) and (c). Rev. Proc. 96-30, 1996-1 C.B. 696, is a checklist questionnaire of the information that must be included in a ruling request coming under Sec. 355. Appendix A of this revenue procedure contains guidelines regarding the business purpose requirement for Sec. 355 transactions including information submission requirements for nine specific situations where rulings may or may not be granted.

[67] Sec. 368(c).

[68] Reg. Sec. 1.355-2(d).

[69] Sec. 355(b)(2). A corporation is engaged in the active conduct of a trade or business if it actively conducts all activities needed for generating a profit and these activities encompass all steps in the process of earning income. Specifically excluded are passive investment activities such as holding stock, securities, and land.

is allowed to retain some stock if it can establish to the IRS's satisfaction that it was not retained as part of a tax-avoidance plan.

- The distribution must have a substantial corporate business purpose. Qualifying distributions include those made to comply with antitrust litigation and those made to separate businesses where the shareholders have major disagreements.[70]
- The shareholders who directly or indirectly owned the controlled corporation(s) before the distribution must maintain a continuing equity interest in one or more of the corporations following the division. A substantial number of the shareholders who owned the distributing corporation's stock before the division must maintain a continuing equity interest in the distributing and/or controlled corporations following the division.[71] The distribution of stock and securities need not be pro rata. Disproportionate distributions may be used to eliminate the stock ownership of a dissenting shareholder group. In a split-off transaction, some shareholders may exchange all their distributing corporation stock for all the controlled corporation's stock.

TYPE G DIVISIVE REORGANIZATION

The divisive Type G reorganization involves the transfer of *part* of the assets of a corporation to a second corporation according to a court-approved plan. The transferor corporation then distributes the transferee corporation's stock and securities to its shareholders, security holders, and creditors. The transferor corporation may continue in business separate from the transferee corporation after its operations have been restructured. Alternatively, the transferor corporation may be liquidated by the courts as part of the bankruptcy proceedings.

OTHER REORGANIZATION TRANSACTIONS

Two types of transactions do not fit into the acquisitive or divisive reorganization categories. These are Type E reorganizations, which are recapitalizations, and Type F reorganizations, which are changes in identity, form, or state of incorporation. Topic Review C7-6 presented earlier summarizes the requirements for the Type E and Type F reorganizations.

TYPE E REORGANIZATION

KEY POINT

A Type E reorganization is neither acquisitive nor divisive in nature. Instead, it simply allows a single corporation to restructure its capital without creating a taxable exchange between the corporation and its shareholders or creditors.

Section 368(a)(1)(E) defines a **Type E reorganization** quite simply as a "recapitalization." A 1942 Supreme Court decision defined a **recapitalization** as "the reshuffling of the corporate structure within the framework of an existing corporation."[72] A recapitalization needs to have a bona fide business purpose. One reason for engaging in a recapitalization might be to issue additional common or preferred stock that will be exchanged for outstanding bonds to reduce the corporation's interest payments and its debt to equity ratio. Alternatively, a family corporation might issue preferred stock in exchange for part or all of the common stock held by an elderly, controlling shareholder to permit that shareholder to turn over active management of the corporation to his or her children and to engage in estate planning (see page C7-42).

Three types of adjustments to the corporate capital structure can qualify as a Type E reorganization. These are a stock-for-stock exchange, a bond-for-stock exchange, and a bond-for-bond exchange.[73] Normally, these exchanges do not result in an increase or decrease in the corporation's assets except to the extent the shareholders receive a distribution of money or other property as part of the transaction.

---

70 Reg. Sec. 1.355-2(b)(5), Exs. (1) and (2).

71 Reg. Sec. 1.355-2(c).

72 *Helvering v. Southwest Consolidated Corp.*, 28 AFTR 573, 42-1 USTC ¶9248 (USSC, 1942).

73 An exchange of stock for bonds has been held in *J. Robert Bazely v. CIR* (35 AFTR 1190, 47-2 USTC ¶9288 [USSC, 1947]) not to be a recapitalization. Even if it were a recapitalization, it generally would be taxable because receipt of the entire principal amount of the bonds represents boot under Sec. 356. The IRS has held that, if no stock is held after the exchange, the Sec. 302 stock redemption rules apply to the transaction, thereby resulting in sale or exchange treatment (Rev. Rul. 77-415, 1977-2 C.B. 311).

STOCK-FOR-STOCK EXCHANGE. An exchange of common stock for common stock or preferred stock for preferred stock within a single corporation can qualify as a recapitalization if it is made pursuant to a plan of reorganization. Section 1036 also permits the same types of exchanges to take place outside of the reorganization rules. In either case, shareholders recognize no gain or loss and take a substituted basis in the shares received that references the basis in the shares surrendered.

EXAMPLE C7-27 ▶ The shareholders of Pilot Corporation exchange all of their nonvoting Class B common stock for additional shares of Pilot's Class A common stock. The Class A stock retains voting rights. The exchange is tax-free under Sec. 1036 even if no plan of reorganization has been created. An exchange of some of Pilot's Class A preferred stock for Class B preferred stock also would be tax-free under Sec. 1036. ◀

Section 1036 does not apply to an exchange of common stock for preferred stock, or preferred stock for common stock, within the same corporation, or an exchange of stock involving two corporations. However, the recapitalization rules apply to an exchange of two different classes of stock (e.g., common for preferred) in the same corporation if the exchange is made as part of a plan of reorganization. The exchange is tax-free for the shareholders under the Sec. 354(a) nonrecognition rules except to the extent they receive boot property. If the FMV of the stock received differs from that of the stock surrendered, the difference may be a gift, a contribution to capital, compensation for services, a dividend, or a payment made to satisfy a debt obligation, depending on the facts and circumstances of the situation.[74] The tax consequences of that portion of the exchange will fall outside the reorganization rules.

EXAMPLE C7-28 ▶ John owns 60% of Boise Corporation's common stock and all of its preferred stock. The remainder of Boise's common stock is held by 80 unrelated individuals. John's basis for his preferred stock is $300,000. John exchanges his preferred stock for $400,000 of additional common stock and $100,000 in money. The preferred stock is valued at $500,000. John realizes a $200,000 [($400,000 + $100,000) − $300,000] gain on the exchange. John must recognize $100,000 of the gain as dividend income (assuming Boise has sufficient E&P) because none of the Sec. 302(b) exceptions that permit capital gain treatment apply. John's basis for the additional common stock is $300,000 ($300,000 + $100,000 gain − $100,000 money). ◀

A recapitalization often is used as an estate planning device whereby a parent's controlling interest in a corporation's common stock is exchanged for both common stock and preferred stock. The common stock often is gifted to a child who, following the recapitalization, will own a controlling interest in the common stock and manage the company. The parent will receive annual income from the preferred stock's cash dividends. The preferred stock's value will not increase over time, thereby freezing the value of the parent's estate and reducing his or her estate tax liability. The capital appreciation will accrue to the child who owns the common stock.

Substantial income tax and estate and gift tax planning opportunities existed at one time when recapitalizing a closely held corporation. To prevent abuses in this area, Congress added Secs. 2701-2704, which provide detailed procedures for more accurately valuing, for transfer tax purposes, interests that are transferred and retained in corporations and partnerships. Additional coverage of this topic is presented in the gift tax chapter.

BOND-FOR-STOCK EXCHANGE. A bond-for-stock exchange is tax-free to the shareholder except to the extent the shareholder receives a portion of the stock in satisfaction of the corporation's liability for accrued interest on the bonds.[75] Stock received in settlement of the interest owed is ordinary income.

BOND-FOR-BOND EXCHANGE. These exchanges are tax-free only when the principal amount of the bonds received does not exceed the principal amount of the bonds sur-

[74] Rev. Ruls. 74-269, 1974-2 C.B. 87 and 83-120, 1983-2 C.B. 170.

[75] Sec. 354(a)(2)(B).

rendered. If the principal amount of the bonds received exceeds the principal amount of the bonds surrendered, the FMV of the "excess" principal amount received is taxed to the bondholder as boot. (See page C7-18 for a discussion of the boot rules.)

TYPE F REORGANIZATION

HISTORICAL NOTE

Congress changed the IRC in 1982 to limit a Type F reorganization to one corporation. Since that time, the importance of a Type F reorganization has greatly diminished.

Section 368(a)(1)(F) defines a **Type F reorganization** as a "mere change in identity, form, or place of organization of one corporation, however effected." Traditionally, Type F reorganizations are used to change either the state in which the business is incorporated or the name of a corporation, without requiring the old corporation or its shareholders to recognize any gain or loss. In a Type F reorganization, the assets and liabilities of the old corporation become the property of the new corporation. Thus, the shareholders and creditors of the old corporation exchange their stock and debt interests for similar interests in the new corporation.

EXAMPLE C7-29 ▶ Rider Corporation is incorporated in the State of Illinois. Its management decides to change its state of incorporation to Delaware because of the favorable securities and corporation laws in Delaware. Old Rider Corporation exchanges its assets for all the stock of new Rider Corporation. The shareholders of old Rider then exchange their stock for new Rider stock. Old Rider Corporation goes out of existence. Neither the shareholders nor the two corporations involved in the reorganization recognize any gain on the transaction. Each shareholder takes a substituted basis for the new Rider stock that references their basis in the old Rider stock. Their holding period for the new Rider stock includes their holding period for the old Rider stock. New Rider Corporation's assets have the same basis they had on old Rider Corporation's books. New Rider Corporation also acquires old Rider Corporation's tax attributes. Although this example refers to two corporations, these two corporations are the same entity that has changed its legal state of incorporation. ◀

The reorganization illustrated in Example C7-29 also could take place if old Rider Corporation's shareholders exchange their stock for new Rider stock. Old Rider Corporation would then be liquidated into new Rider Corporation. The tax consequences are the same for both transaction forms.

JUDICIAL RESTRICTIONS ON THE USE OF CORPORATE REORGANIZATIONS

OBJECTIVE 7

Explain how judicial doctrines can restrict a taxpayer's ability to use corporate reorganizations

The Supreme Court holds that literal compliance with the statutory requirements for a reorganization transaction is not enough for a transaction to receive tax-free treatment.[76] As a result, the courts have placed four primary restrictions on reorganization transactions:

- ▶ Continuity of the investor's proprietary interest
- ▶ Continuity of the business enterprise
- ▶ A business purpose for the transaction
- ▶ The step transaction doctrine, which collapses a series of related transactions into a single transaction reflecting their economic substance

All four requirements relate to the overall doctrine of substance over form and are explained below.

TYPICAL MISCONCEPTION

The continuity-of-interest requirement has nothing to do with the relative sizes of Acquiring and Target. Target's shareholders may end up with a minimal amount of the total outstanding stock of Acquiring, and yet the merger will be a valid reorganization as long as 50% of the consideration received by Target's shareholders is an equity interest in Acquiring.

CONTINUITY OF PROPRIETARY INTEREST

The requirement for the continuity of the investor's proprietary interest is based on the principle that the tax deferral associated with a reorganization is available because the shareholder has changed his or her investment from one form to another rather than liq-

[76] *Evelyn F. Gregory v. Helvering*, 14 AFTR 1191, 35-1 USTC ¶9043 (USSC, 1935).

uidating it. According to Reg. Sec. 1.368-1(b), this test is met by continuity of the business enterprise under a modified corporate form and continuity of interest on the part of the shareholders who, directly or indirectly, own the enterprise before its reorganization. In a series of decisions, the courts have held that the continuing proprietary interest must be a common or preferred stock interest.[77] Thus, a transaction that involves the target corporation or its shareholders receiving only cash or short-term debt obligations does not qualify as a tax-free reorganization.

SELF-STUDY QUESTION

For which reorganizations is the continuity-of-interest requirement most important?

ANSWER

The only limitation on consideration used for both regular and triangular mergers is the continuity-of-interest requirement. The other reorganizations, including reverse triangular mergers, have statutory requirements more restrictive than the continuity-of-interest doctrine.

The IRC does not specify how much stock constitutes the required proprietary interest. For advance ruling purposes, however, the IRS requires the former shareholders of the target corporation to receive at least 50% of their total consideration in the form of acquiring corporation stock. The 50% rule applies only for advance ruling purposes, and the courts have accepted lesser percentages.[78] Despite the existence of judicial support, few taxpayers are willing to proceed with a reorganization without the receipt of an advance ruling because of the risk associated with a possible disallowance of the tax-free status and the large dollar amounts involved. Thus, the IRS exercises substantial power through its ruling position in the reorganization area.

EXAMPLE C7-30 ▶ Target Corporation transfers all of its assets to Acquiring Corporation in a Type C reorganization in exchange for $200,000 of Acquiring stock and the assumption of $800,000 of Target liabilities. Target distributes the Acquiring stock to its sole shareholder, Nancy, in exchange for all of her Target stock. Even though the transaction meets the statutory requirements for a Type C reorganization, the IRS most likely will hold that the transaction is not a reorganization because the continuity-of-proprietary-interest requirement is not met (i.e., only 20% of the total consideration received by Target represents an equity interest in Acquiring). ◀

CONTINUITY OF BUSINESS ENTERPRISE

The requirement for continuity of the business enterprise necessitates that the acquiring corporation either continue the target corporation's historic business or use a significant portion of the target corporation's historic business assets in a new business.[79] This restriction limits tax-free reorganizations to transactions involving *continuing interests* in the target corporation's business or property under a modified corporate form. The **continuity-of-interest doctrine**, however, does not require that the target corporation's historic business be continued.

SELF-STUDY QUESTION

Does Acquiring have to continue its own historic business?

ANSWER

No. The IRS has specifically ruled that the continuity-of-business-enterprise test requires only that the historic business of Target be continued (Rev. Rul. 81-25, 1981-1 C.B. 132).

Whether the requirements for continuity of the business enterprise are satisfied depends on the facts and circumstances of the particular situation. The historic business requirement can be satisfied if the acquiring corporation continues one or more of the target corporation's significant lines of business.

EXAMPLE C7-31 ▶ Target Corporation is merged into Acquiring Corporation. Immediately before the merger, Target manufactures resins and chemicals and distributes chemicals for use in making other products. All three lines of business are approximately the same size. Two months after the merger, Acquiring sells the resin manufacturing and chemicals distribution activities to an unrelated party for cash. The transaction satisfies the requirement for the continuity of the business enterprise because Acquiring continues at least one of Target's three significant lines of business.[80] ◀

The asset continuity requirement is satisfied if the acquiring corporation uses in its business a significant portion of the assets that were used in the target corporation's historic business. The significance of the assets used is based on the relative importance of the assets to the operation of the historic business of the target corporation.

EXAMPLE C7-32 ▶ Acquiring and Target Corporations are both computer manufacturers. Target is merged into Acquiring. Acquiring terminates Target's manufacturing activities and maintains Target's equipment as a backup source of supply for its components. Acquiring satisfies the continuity-

[77] See, for example, *V. L. LeTulle v. Scofield*, 23 AFTR 789, 40-1 USTC ¶9150 (USSC, 1940).
[78] Rev. Proc. 77-37, 1977-2 C.B. 568, Sec. 3.02. See also *John A. Nelson Co. v. Helvering*, 16 AFTR 1262, 36-1 USTC ¶9019 (USSC, 1935), where the Supreme Court permitted a tax-free reorganization to take place where the stock exchanged constituted only 38% of the total consideration.
[79] Reg. Sec. 1.368-1(d)(1).
[80] Reg. Secs. 1.368-1(d)(3) and -1(d)(5), Ex. (1).

ADDITIONAL COMMENT

Because Target and its shareholders have the most to lose, they should protect themselves by stipulating that Acquiring retain the historic assets. If not, Acquiring can unilaterally dispose of the historic assets and bust the tax-free reorganization.

of-business-enterprise requirement by continuing to use Target's historic business assets. If Acquiring had instead sold Target's assets for cash and invested the proceeds in an investment portfolio, the continuity-of-business-enterprise requirement would not be met. Acquiring need not continue Target's business to satisfy the continuity-of-business-enterprise requirement.[81] ◀

Acquiring does not have to directly hold Target's business assets or continue Target's line of business. The assets (business activities) can be owned (conducted) by an 80%-or-more-owned subsidiary corporation that is included in a chain of corporations that includes Acquiring. In some cases, the acquired assets can be owned by (or business conducted by) a partnership or LLC owned in full or in part by Acquiring or one of its subsidiaries.

BUSINESS PURPOSE REQUIREMENT

A transaction must serve a bona fide **business purpose** to qualify as a reorganization.[82] Regulation Sec. 1.368-1(c) states that a transaction that takes "the form of a corporate reorganization as a disguise for concealing its real character, and the object and accomplishment of which is the consummation of a preconceived plan having no business or corporate purpose, is not a plan of reorganization."

EXAMPLE C7-33 ▶

KEY POINT

Business purpose is much more difficult to establish in divisive (Sec. 355) transactions than it is in acquisitive (Sec. 354) transactions.

Distributing Corporation transfers some highly appreciated stock from its investment portfolio to newly created Controlled Corporation in exchange for all of its stock. The Controlled stock is distributed to Distributing's sole shareholder, Kathy, in exchange for part of her Distributing stock. Shortly after the stock transfer, Controlled is liquidated, with Kathy receiving the appreciated stock. Treating the liquidation of Controlled as a separate event, Kathy recognizes a capital gain on the liquidation, which she uses to offset capital loss carryovers from other tax years, and is able to step-up the basis of the appreciated stock to its FMV without incurring a tax liability. Even though the stock transfer to Controlled fits within a literal reading of the Sec. 368(a)(1)(D) definition of a divisive Type D reorganization, the IRS probably will state that the Sec. 355 trade or business requirement has not been met and also will rely on *Gregory v. Helvering,* to hold that the series of transactions serves no business purpose. As a result, Kathy's receipt of the appreciated stock from Controlled is a dividend. ◀

STEP TRANSACTION DOCTRINE

The **step transaction doctrine** may be used by the IRS to collapse a multistep reorganization into a single taxable transaction. Alternatively, the IRS may attempt to take a series of steps, which the taxpayer calls independent events, and collapse them into a single tax-free reorganization transaction. Both of these IRS actions prevent the taxpayer from arranging a series of business transactions to obtain a tax result not available if only a single transaction is used.

EXAMPLE C7-34 ▶

Jody transfers business property from his sole proprietorship to his wholly owned Target Corporation. Three days after the incorporation, Target Corporation transfers all of its assets to Acquiring Corporation in a Type C reorganization in which the Acquiring stock is distributed to Jody upon Target Corporation's liquidation. After the liquidation, Jody owns 15% of the Acquiring stock. The IRS probably will attempt to collapse the two transactions (the Sec. 351 asset transfer to Target Corporation and the Type C asset-for-stock reorganization) into a single transaction: an asset transfer by Jody to Acquiring Corporation. Under the IRS's position, the Sec. 351 rules do not apply because Jody does not own at least 80% of the Acquiring stock immediately after the transfer. Because Jody owns only 15% of Acquiring's stock, Jody must recognize gain or loss on the transfer of assets from his sole proprietorship to Acquiring Corporation.[83] ◀

---

[81] Reg. Secs. 1.368-1(d)(4) and -1(d)(5), Ex. (2).

[82] *Evelyn F. Gregory v. Helvering,* 14 AFTR 1191, 35-1 USTC ¶9043 (USSC, 1935). Other Sec. 355 requirements probably were failed in this case, such as being a device for the distribution of E&P.

[83] Rev. Rul. 70-140, 1970-1 C.B. 73.

TAX ATTRIBUTES

Section 381(a) requires the target or transferor corporation's tax attributes (e.g., loss or tax credit carryovers) to be assumed by the acquiring or transferee corporation in certain types of reorganizations. Sections 269, 382, 383, and 384 restrict the taxpayer's ability to use certain corporate tax attributes (e.g., NOL carryovers) obtained through the acquisition of the loss corporation's stock or assets.

OBJECTIVE 8

Determine which reorganization forms permit the carryover of tax attributes

ASSUMPTION OF TAX ATTRIBUTES

In the Type A, C, acquisitive D, F, and acquisitive G reorganizations, the acquiring corporation obtains both the target corporation's tax attributes and assets. The tax attributes do not change hands in either the Type B or Type E reorganization because no transfer of assets from one corporation to another occurs. Even though a division of assets occurs between a transferor corporation and a controlled corporation in the divisive Type D and G reorganizations, the only tax attribute allocated between the two entities is the transferor corporation's E&P.[84]

KEY POINT

An often-cited advantage to a tax-free asset reorganization over a taxable acquisition is that the tax attributes (e.g., NOLs and net capital losses) carry over to the acquiring corporation.

Some of the tax attributes carried over under Sec. 381(c) include

- Net operating losses
- Capital losses
- Earnings and profits (E&P)
- General business credits
- Inventory methods

KEY POINT

The thrust of Sec. 381, as it relates to NOLs, is to allow Target's NOL carryforwards to offset only the post-acquisition income of the acquiring corporation.

The acquired corporation's NOL carryover is determined as of the transaction's acquisition date and carries over to tax years ending after such date. Generally, the acquisition date for a tax-free reorganization is the date on which the transferor or target corporation transfers the assets. When loss carryovers from more than one tax year are present, the loss from the earliest ending tax year is used first. NOLs from the time period following the acquisition date cannot be carried back by the acquiring corporation to offset profits earned by the target corporation in its tax years preceding the acquisition date.[85]

EXAMPLE C7-35 ▶ Target Corporation is merged into Acquiring Corporation at the close of business on June 30, 2002. Both corporations use the calendar year as their tax year. At the beginning of 2002, Target reports a $200,000 NOL carryover from 2001. Target must file a final tax return for the period January 1, 2002 through June 30, 2002. Target reports $60,000 of taxable income (before any NOL deductions) in its tax return for the short period. Target's taxable income for the January 1 through June 30, 2002 period reduces its NOL carryover to $140,000 ($200,000 − $60,000). Acquiring assumes this carryover. ◀

Section 381(c) restricts the acquiring corporation's use of the NOL carryover in its first tax year that ends after the acquisition date. The NOL deduction is limited to the portion of the acquiring corporation's taxable income allocable on a daily basis to the post-acquisition period.

EXAMPLE C7-36 ▶ Assume the same facts as in Example C7-35 except that it is now known that Acquiring's taxable income is $146,000 in 2002. Acquiring can use Target's NOL carryover to offset its taxable income attributable to the 184 days in the July 1 through December 31, 2002 post-acquisition period, or $73,600 [(184 ÷ 365) × $146,000]. The remaining NOL carryover of $66,400 ($140,000 − $73,600) carries forward to offset Acquiring's taxable income in 2003. Both the pre- and post-acquisition portions of 2002 count as full tax years for loss carryover purposes. ◀

[84] Reg. Sec. 1.312-10.

[85] Special rules apply to Type F reorganizations. Because only a change in form or identity involving a single corporation occurs in such a transaction, NOLs incurred following the acquisition date can be carried back in an F reorganization to offset profits earned in pre-acquisition tax years.

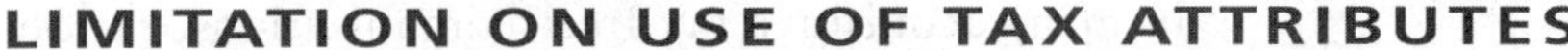

OBJECTIVE 9

Explain how NOL carryovers are restricted following an acquisition

LIMITATION ON USE OF TAX ATTRIBUTES

Sections 382 and 269 prevent taxpayers from purchasing the assets or stock of a corporation having loss carryovers (known as the **loss corporation**) primarily to acquire the corporation's tax attributes. Similarly, Secs. 382 and 269 prevent a corporation having loss carryovers (also known as a loss corporation) from acquiring the assets or stock of a profitable corporation primarily to enable the loss corporation to use its carryovers. Section 383 provides similar restrictions for acquisitions intended to facilitate the use of capital loss and tax credit carryovers. Section 384 additionally restricts the use of pre-acquisition losses to offset built-in gains.

SECTION 382. Section 382 restricts the use of NOLs in purchase transactions and tax-free reorganizations when a substantial change in the stock ownership of the loss corporation occurs.

TYPICAL MISCONCEPTION

To create an ownership change, the 5% shareholders must increase their stock ownership by more than 50 *percentage points.* Thus, if shareholder A increases her stock ownership from 10% to 20%, this alone is not an ownership change even though it represents a 100% increase in A's ownership.

Stock Ownership Change. The requisite stock ownership change has taken place when

- Any shift in the stock ownership involving any person(s) owning 5% or more of a corporation's stock occurs or a tax-free reorganization (other than a divisive Type D or G reorganization or a Type F reorganization) has taken place *and*
- The percentage of stock of the new loss corporation owned by one or more 5% shareholders has increased by more than 50 percentage points over the *lowest* percentage of stock in the old loss corporation owned by such shareholder(s) at *any* time during the preceding three-year (or shorter) "testing" period.[86]

The 5% shareholder test is based on the value of the loss corporation's stock. Nonvoting preferred stock is excluded from the calculation.

An **old loss corporation** is any corporation entitled to use an NOL carryover or has an NOL for the tax year in which the ownership change occurs, and undergoes the requisite stock ownership change. A **new loss corporation** is any corporation entitled to use an NOL carryover after the stock ownership change.[87] The old and new loss corporations are the same for most taxable acquisitions (e.g., the purchase of a loss corporation's stock by a new shareholder group). The old and new loss corporations differ, however, in many acquisitive reorganizations (e.g., a merger transaction where an unprofitable target [old loss] corporation is merged into the acquiring [new loss] corporation).

KEY POINT

One of the burdensome aspects of Sec. 382 is that each time the stock ownership of a 5% shareholder changes, all 5% shareholders must be tested at that date to see whether an ownership change has occurred.

Ownership changes are tested any time a stock transaction occurs affecting the stock owned by a person who owns 5% or more of the stock either before or after the change. Such change may occur because of a stock transaction involving a 5% shareholder or involving a person who does not own a 5% interest in the loss corporation that affects the size of the stock interest owned by a 5% shareholder (i.e., a stock redemption). When applying the 5% rule, all shareholders who own less than 5% of the loss corporation's stock are considered to be a single shareholder.

EXAMPLE C7-37 ▶ Spencer Corporation is a publicly traded corporation with no single individual owning more than 5% of its outstanding stock. Spencer has incurred a series of NOLs in recent years, substantial amounts of which are available as carryovers. On July 3, Barry acquires 80% of Spencer's single class of stock in a cash purchase. Barry had not owned any of the Spencer stock before making the acquisition. Spencer Corporation has experienced a stock ownership change because it now has a 5% shareholder (Barry), who owns 80 percentage points more stock than he owned at any time during the testing period (Barry owned 0% during the three-year testing period) because of a purchase transaction. Because Spencer Corporation both incurred the losses prior to the ownership change, and can use the NOLs after the change, it is both the old and new loss corporation. Spencer Corporation's NOLs are subject to the Sec. 382 limitations. ◀

[86] Sec. 382(g). Special rules permit the use of a testing period of less than three years for applying the 50-percentage-point ownership change rule. One such situation is when a recent change in the stock ownership has occurred involving a 5% shareholder. In such case, the testing period goes back only to the date of the earlier ownership change.

[87] Secs. 382(k)(1)–(3).

In many acquisitive tax-free reorganizations, the Sec. 382 stock ownership test is applied against the old loss (or target) corporation and then against the new loss (or acquiring) corporation.

EXAMPLE C7-38 ▶ Target Corporation has a single class of stock outstanding. None of its 300 shareholders owns more than 5% of the outstanding stock. Target has incurred substantial NOLs in recent years. Pursuant to a merger agreement, Target Corporation is merged into Jackson Corporation. Jackson also has a single class of stock outstanding, and none of its 500 shareholders owns more than 5% of its outstanding stock. None of Target's shareholders owned any of the Jackson stock before the merger. After the merger, Target's shareholders own 40% of the Jackson stock. All of Jackson's shareholders are aggregated when applying the Sec. 382 stock ownership test. The Sec. 382 rules limit the use of Target's NOL carryovers because Jackson's shareholders owned none of the old loss corporation (Target) stock before the reorganization and owned 60% of the new loss corporation (Jackson) stock immediately after the reorganization. ◀

Divisive Type D and G reorganizations or Type F reorganizations may be subject to the Sec. 382 limitations if the transaction results in a more-than-50-percentage-point shift in stock ownership for the transferor corporation.

TYPICAL MISCONCEPTION

Section 382 does not disallow NOLs. Section 382 merely limits the amount of NOL carryovers the new loss corporation can use on an annual basis.

Loss Limitation. The Sec. 382 loss limitation for any tax year ending after the stock ownership change equals the value of the old loss corporation's stock (including nonvoting preferred stock) immediately before the ownership change multiplied by the long-term tax-exempt federal rate.[88] The long-term tax-exempt federal rate is determined by the IRS and is the highest of the adjusted federal long-term tax-exempt rates in effect for any month in the three-calendar-month period ending with the month in which the stock ownership change occurs.[89]

ADDITIONAL COMMENT

The reason the new loss corporation's use of the old loss corporation's NOLs is limited annually to the FMV of the old loss corporation multiplied by the long-term tax-exempt federal rate is that this limitation is supposed to approximate the rate at which the old loss corporation could have used the NOLs. Thus, the underlying theory of Sec. 382 is one of neutrality.

A new loss corporation can claim its current-year deductions. Then any NOLs from the old loss corporation (pre-change tax years) can be deducted. If the NOL carryovers from the old loss corporation exceed the Sec. 382 loss limitation, the unused carryovers are deferred until the following year, provided the end of the 20-year NOL carryforward period has not been reached. If the Sec. 382 loss limitation exceeds the new loss corporation's taxable income for the current year, the unused loss limitation carries forward and increases the Sec. 382 loss limitation for the next year.[90] Finally, any of its NOL and other deduction carryovers from post-change taxable years can be deducted. A new loss corporation that does not continue the business enterprise of the old loss corporation at all times during the two-year period beginning on the stock ownership change date must use a zero Sec. 382 limitation for any post-change year. This zero limitation, in effect, disallows the use of the NOL carryovers.[91]

EXAMPLE C7-39 ▶ Peter purchased all the Taylor Corporation stock (the old and new loss corporation) from Karl at the close of business on December 31, 2001. Taylor is engaged in the manufacture of brooms and has a $1 million NOL carryover from 2001. Taylor continues to manufacture brooms after Peter's acquisition of a controlling interest and earns $300,000 of taxable income for 2002. The value of the Taylor stock immediately before the acquisition is $3.5 million. The applicable long-term tax-exempt federal rate is 5%. The requisite stock ownership change has taken place because Peter has increased his ownership from zero during the testing period to 100% immediately after the acquisition. The Sec. 382 loss limitation for 2002 is $175,000 ($3,500,000 × 0.05). Taylor can claim a $175,000 NOL deduction in 2002, thereby reducing its taxable income to $125,000. The remaining $825,000 ($1,000,000 − $175,000) of NOL carries over to 2003 and later years. ◀

KEY POINT

If the old loss corporation is a very large corporation relative to its NOL carryovers, Sec. 382 will not be a real obstacle in the use of the NOLs by the new loss corporation. Only when the old loss corporation has a small FMV relative to its NOL carryovers does Sec. 382 represent a major obstacle.

Special rules apply to the loss corporation for the year in which the stock ownership change occurs. Taxable income earned before the change is not subject to the Sec. 382 limitation. Taxable income earned after the change, however, is subject to the limitation.

[88] Sec. 382(b)(1).

[89] Sec. 382(f). The long-term tax-exempt federal rate for December 2001 is 4.65% (Rev. Rul. 2001-58, I.R.B. 2001-50, 570). The highest long-term tax-exempt federal rate for December 2001 and the two preceding months is 4.74%.

[90] Sec. 382(b)(2).

[91] Sec. 382(c). Failure to continue the old loss corporation's business enterprise also may cause a corporate reorganization to lose its tax-free status.

ADDITIONAL COMMENT

Although the legislative intent of Sec. 382 has not been seriously opposed, the complexity of the statute with its accompanying Treasury Regulations is of concern to many tax practitioners.

Allocation of income earned during the tax year to the time periods before and after the ownership change is based on the number of days in each of the two time periods similar to the procedures illustrated earlier for tax attributes under Sec. 381.

Old loss corporation NOLs incurred before the date of the stock ownership change are limited by Sec. 382. These include NOLs incurred in tax years ending before the date of change plus the portion of the NOL for the tax year that includes the date of change considered to have been incurred before the change. Allocation of an NOL for the tax year that includes the date of change is based on the number of days before and after the change.[92]

SECTION 383. Section 383 restricts the use of tax credit and capital loss carryovers when stock ownership changes occur that come under the purview of Sec. 382. The same restrictions that apply to NOLs apply to the general business credit, the minimum tax credit, and the foreign tax credit.

SECTION 384. Section 384 prevents pre-acquisition losses of either the acquiring or target corporation (the loss corporation) from offsetting built-in gains recognized during the five-year post-acquisition recognition period by another corporation (the gain corporation). Such gains can offset pre-acquisition losses of the gain corporation. This limitation applies if a corporation acquires either a controlling stock interest or the assets of another corporation and either corporation is a gain corporation.

ADDITIONAL COMMENT

Section 269 represents the IRS's oldest and broadest weapon in dealing with trafficking in NOLs. However, because of the subjectivity of the statute, Secs. 382, 383, and 384 have turned out to be the IRS's main statutory weapons in this area.

SECTION 269. Section 269 applies to transactions where control of a corporation is obtained, and the principal purpose of the acquisition is "the evasion or avoidance of federal income tax by securing the benefit of a deduction" or credit that otherwise would not be available. Control is defined as 50% of the voting power or 50% of the value of the outstanding stock. The IRS can use this provision to disallow a loss or credit carryover in situations where Sec. 382 does not apply. The IRS's primary problem in applying these rules is showing that the requisite principal purpose is present.

TAX PLANNING CONSIDERATIONS

WHY USE A REORGANIZATION INSTEAD OF A TAXABLE TRANSACTION?

ETHICAL POINT

The choice between making an acquisition a taxable or tax-free transaction involves a large number of considerations for both the buyer and the seller. All parties must examine the tax, financial, and legal considerations with the assistance of their own experts. Because what may be good for the buyer may not be good for the seller in an acquisition, it probably is not a good idea for both parties to save money by using the same experts.

The choice between a taxable and tax-free transaction can be a difficult one. The advantages and disadvantages of the tax-free reorganization are important considerations for the buyer and seller. Depending on their relative importance to each party, they may serve as points for negotiation and compromise when attempting to structure the transaction.

From the point of view of the target corporation's shareholders, a number of considerations must be evaluated. First, a tax-free reorganization permits a complete deferral of tax to the shareholders unless they receive boot. This tax deferral may permit a shareholder to retain a higher percentage of his or her capital investment than would be possible if a taxable acquisition had been used. A second factor is that a taxable transaction permits the shareholders of the target corporation to convert their former equity interests into liquid assets (e.g., when they receive cash or property other than stock or securities of the acquiring corporation). These funds can be invested in whatever manner the shareholder chooses.

In a reorganization, the shareholder must obtain a proprietary interest in the acquiring corporation. Future success by the acquiring corporation is likely to enhance the value of this interest. Conversely, if the acquiring corporation encounters financial prob-

[92] Sec. 382(b)(3).

SELF-STUDY QUESTION

Is a tax-free reorganization always preferable to a taxable acquisition?

ANSWER

No. The determination of what form an acquisition should take involves resolving of a myriad of issues relating to the parties involved in the reorganization. A number of these issues are discussed in this section.

lems, the value of the shareholder's investment may diminish. Third, losses realized as part of a tax-free reorganization cannot be recognized. A taxable transaction permits an immediate recognition of the loss. Fourth, gains recognized as part of a tax-free reorganization are taxed as dividend income if the boot distribution is equivalent to a dividend. Taxable transactions generally result in the shareholder recognizing only capital gains. This difference is important with the top ordinary income rate at 38.6% (in 2002). Finally, a taxable transaction permits the shareholder to step-up the basis of the stock and securities received to their FMV. A tax-free transaction, however, requires a substituted basis to be used.

From the transferor corporation's point of view, a tax-free reorganization permits the assets to be exchanged with no gain being recognized. In addition, the depreciation recapture rules do not apply to a reorganization. In each case, the recapture burden shifts to the purchasing party.

From the acquiring corporation's point of view, a tax-free reorganization permits an acquisition to take place without the use of substantial amounts of cash or securities. Because the target corporation's shareholders do not have to recognize any gain unless they receive boot, they may be willing to accept a lower sales price than would be required if a taxable acquisition occurs. The acquiror must use the same basis for property acquired in a tax-free reorganization that the assets had on the transferor's books. This inability to step-up the basis of the assets to their cost or FMV reduces the attractiveness of a tax-free reorganization. This inability, in turn, may lower the price the acquiror is willing to offer.

TYPICAL MISCONCEPTION

When a plan for an acquisition is developed, the tax consequences are only one of many considerations that must be addressed. Often, the form of the final acquisition plan will not be optimal from a tax perspective because other factors were deemed more important.

The cost of using a taxable asset or stock acquisition transaction was increased dramatically by the Tax Reform Act of 1986. Before the 1986 Tax Act, a corporation that sold its assets could avoid recognizing its gains on the transaction by liquidating within 12 months of adopting its plan of liquidation. Similarly, a corporation that purchased the stock of a target corporation and caused the target corporation to make a Sec. 338 election did not incur any tax costs on the deemed sale transaction. Today, a target corporation that makes a sale of its assets ends up recognizing all of its gains and losses in a taxable transaction. These additional tax costs make the tax exemption available for the target corporation in a tax-free reorganization even more attractive.

A tax-free reorganization permits the acquiror to obtain the benefits of NOL, tax credit, and other carryovers from the target corporation (subject to possible limitations). Such tax attributes do not carry over to the buyer in a taxable transaction, but they can be used to reduce the seller's tax cost for the sale.

AVOIDING THE REORGANIZATION PROVISIONS

TYPICAL MISCONCEPTION

The tax-free reorganization provisions are not elective. If a transaction qualifies as a Sec. 368 reorganization, it must be treated as such. It is usually not difficult to bust a tax-free reorganization if the desire is for a taxable acquisition.

An acquisition can be changed from a tax-free reorganization to a taxable transaction if the restrictions on the use of consideration for the particular type of reorganization are not met. This change can be advantageous for the taxpayers involved. For example, the Type B reorganization rules can be avoided if the acquiring corporation makes a tender offer to the target corporation's shareholders involving an exchange of both acquiring corporation stock and cash for the target corporation's stock. Because this transaction does not meet the solely-for-voting-stock requirement, it is considered a taxable transaction for the shareholders. It also is considered to be a purchase of the target corporation's stock, thereby permitting the acquiring corporation to make a Sec. 338 election and step-up the basis of the target corporation's assets to the price paid for the stock.

EXAMPLE C7-40 ▶ Acquiring Corporation offers to exchange one share of its common stock (valued at $40) plus $20 cash for each share of Target Corporation's single class of common stock. All of Target's shareholders agree to the proposal and exchange a total of 2,000 shares of Target stock for 2,000 shares of Acquiring common stock and $40,000 cash. At the time of the acquisition, Target's assets have a $35,000 adjusted basis and a $110,000 FMV. Target recognizes no gain or loss with respect to the exchange. The basis of its assets remains at $35,000 unless Acquiring makes a Sec. 338 election. Target's shareholders must recognize gain or loss on the exchange of their Target stock whether or not Acquiring makes a Sec. 338 election. ◀

COMPLIANCE AND PROCEDURAL CONSIDERATIONS

SECTION 338 ELECTION

The acquiring corporation makes the election under Sec. 338 on Form 8023 (Election under Sec. 338(g)). This election is made by the fifteenth day of the ninth month beginning after the month in which the acquisition date occurs. The information about the acquiring corporation, the target corporation, and the election filed with Form 8023 is contained in Reg. Sec. 1.338-1(d).

PLAN OF REORGANIZATION

One requirement for nonrecognition of gain by a transferor corporation on an asset transfer (Sec. 361) or by a shareholder on a stock transfer (Sec. 354) is that there be a plan of reorganization. A written plan is not needed, but it is safest for all parties involved in the reorganization when the plan is reduced to writing either as a communication to the shareholders, as part of the corporate records, or as part of a written agreement between the parties. The transaction generally is a taxable event if a plan of reorganization does not exist or if a transfer or distribution is not part of the plan.[93] A **plan of reorganization** is defined as a consummated transaction specifically defined as a reorganization. Nonrecognition of gain or loss is limited to exchanges or distributions that are a direct part of a reorganization and undertaken for reasons germane to the continuance of the business of a corporation that is a party to a reorganization.[94]

PARTY TO A REORGANIZATION

Sections 354 and 361 require that a shareholder or a transferor be a party to a reorganization to have the asset or stock transfer be tax-free. Section 368(b) defines a **party to a reorganization** as "including any corporation resulting from a reorganization, and both corporations involved in a reorganization where one corporation acquires the stock or assets of a second corporation." In the case of a triangular reorganization, the corporation controlling the acquiring corporation and whose stock is used to effect the reorganization also is a party to a reorganization.

RULING REQUESTS

Before proceeding with a taxable or tax-free acquisition or disposition, many taxpayers request an advance ruling from the IRS on the tax consequences of the transaction. Advance rulings generally are requested because of the complexity of the tax law in the reorganization area and because these transactions involve dollar amounts that are quite large. A subsequent redetermination by the IRS or the courts that a completed reorganization is taxable might have substantial adverse tax consequences to the parties involved in the transaction. The IRS will issue an advance ruling only for reorganizations that conform with the guidelines set out in Rev. Proc. 77-37 and other IRS promulgations.[95] However, these guidelines do not have the force of law and, in many cases, may be stricter than the court precedents (see Chapter C15).

---

93 *A. T. Evans*, 30 B.T.A. 746 (1934), *acq.* XIII-2 C.B. 7; and *William Hewitt*, 19 B.T.A. 771 (1930).

94 Reg. Sec. 1.368-2(g).

95 1977-2 C.B. 568. In Rev. Proc. 2002-3, I.R.B. 2002-1, the IRS has stated that it will not issue advance rulings for reorganizations if the consequences are adequately addressed in the IRC, Treasury Regulations, Supreme Court decisions, tax treaties, revenue rulings, revenue procedures, notices, or other IRS pronouncements. The IRS, however, will rule on reorganizations if the consequences are not adequately addressed by these authorities.

PROBLEM MATERIALS

DISCUSSION QUESTIONS

C7-1 Debate the following statements: All acquisition transactions should be taxable events. No acquisitions should be permitted to be tax-free reorganizations. Required: Present the arguments for and against such a tax policy change.

C7-2 What tax advantages exist for the buyer when he or she acquires the assets of a corporation in a taxable transaction? For the seller when he or she exchanges stock in a taxable transaction?

C7-3 What tax and nontax advantages and disadvantages accrue when an acquiring corporation purchases all of the target corporation's stock for cash and subsequently liquidates the target corporation?

C7-4 Why might a parent corporation make a Sec. 338 election after acquiring a target corporation's stock? When would such an election not be advisable?

C7-5 Explain the following items related to a Sec. 338 election:
a. The rule used to determine the time period within which the Sec. 338 stock purchase(s) can be made
b. The types of stock acquisition transactions that are not counted when determining whether a qualified stock purchase has been made
c. The method for determining the sale price for the target corporation's assets
d. The method for determining the total basis for the target corporation's assets
e. The effect of the deemed sale on the target corporation's tax attributes.
f. The date by which the Sec. 338 election must be made.

C7-6 a. Holt Corporation acquires all the stock of Star Corporation and makes a timely Sec. 338 election. The adjusted grossed-up basis of the Star stock is $2.5 million. Tangible assets on Star's balance sheet have a $1.8 million FMV. Explain to Holt's president how the new bases for Star's individual assets are determined.
b. How would your answer change if the adjusted grossed-up basis were instead $1.4 million?

C7-7 Compare the tax consequences arising from a taxable asset acquisition transaction and an asset-for-stock tax-free reorganization, giving consideration to the following points:
a. Consideration used to effect the transaction
b. Recognition of gain or loss by the target corporation on the asset transfer
c. Basis of property to the acquiring corporation
d. Recognition of gain or loss when the target corporation is liquidated
e. Use and/or carryover of the target corporation's tax attributes

C7-8 Which of the following events that occur as part of an acquisitive tax-free reorganization require the target corporation to recognize gain? Assume in all cases that the target corporation is liquidated as part of the reorganization.
a. Transfer of appreciated target corporation assets in exchange for stock and short-term notes
b. Transfer of appreciated target corporation assets in exchange for stock and the assumption of the target corporation's liabilities
c. Assume the same facts as in Part b except the amount of liabilities assumed by the acquiring corporation exceeds the adjusted basis of the target corporation's assets transferred.
d. Transfer of appreciated target corporation assets in exchange for stock and money. Target distributes the money to its shareholders.
e. Transfer of appreciated target corporation assets in exchange for stock and money. Target uses the money to pay off its liabilities.

C7-9 Explain the boot rule as it applies to the shareholders in a tax-free reorganization. How is the character of a shareholder's recognized gain determined in a tax-free reorganization?

C7-10 Evaluate the following statement: Individual shareholders who must recognize gain as the result of receiving boot in a corporate reorganization generally prefer to report capital gain income, whereas corporate shareholders generally prefer to report dividend income.

C7-11 How is the basis for nonboot stocks and securities received by a shareholder determined? How is the basis determined for boot property?

C7-12 Which tax-free reorganization(s) are acquisitive transactions? Divisive transactions? Which tax-free reorganization(s) are neither acquisitive nor divisive? Which tax-free reorganization(s) can be either acquisitive or divisive?

C7-13 Compare the type of consideration that can be used to effect Type A, B, and C reorganizations.

C7-14 How does the IRS interpret the continuity-of-interest doctrine for a Type A merger transaction?

C7-15 How does the IRS interpret the continuity of business enterprise requirement for a Type A merger transaction?

C7-16 What are the advantages of using a Type C asset-for-stock reorganization instead of a Type A merger transaction? The disadvantages?

C7-17 How does the IRS interpret the "substantially all" the assets requirement for a Type C reorganization?

C7-18 Explain why an acquiring corporation might be prohibited from using cash as part of the consideration given to accomplish a Type C reorganization.

C7-19 Some transactions may be characterized as either a Type C or a Type D reorganization. Which reorganization provision controls in the case of an overlap?

C7-20 What is the difference between an acquisitive Type C reorganization and an acquisitive Type D reorganization?

C7-21 Explain the circumstances in which money and other property can be used in a Type B reorganization.

C7-22 Acquiring Corporation has purchased for cash a 5% interest in Target Corporation's stock. After examining Target Corporation's books, Acquiring Corporation's management wants to make a tender offer to acquire the remaining Target stock in exchange for Acquiring voting stock. Can this tender offer be accomplished as a Type B reorganization? What problems may be encountered in structuring the acquisition as a tax-free reorganization?

C7-23 Acquiring Corporation wants to exchange its voting common stock for all of Target Corporation's single class of stock in a tender offer. Only 85% of Target Corporation's shareholders agree to tender their shares. Assuming the reorganization is accomplished, what options exist for Acquiring to acquire the remaining shares as part of the reorganization? At a later date?

C7-24 Compare and contrast the requirements for, and the tax treatment of, the spinoff, split-off, and split-up forms of the divisive Type D reorganization.

C7-25 Stock of a controlled subsidiary corporation can be distributed tax-free to the distributing corporation's shareholders under Sec. 355. Explain the difference between such a distribution and a divisive Type D reorganization.

C7-26 When is the distribution of a controlled corporation's stock or securities tax-free to the distributing corporation's shareholders? What events trigger the recognition of gain or loss by the shareholders?

C7-27 When does the distributing corporation recognize gain or loss on the distribution of stock or securities of a controlled corporation to its shareholders?

C7-28 What is a recapitalization?

C7-29 How can a recapitalization type of reorganization be used to transfer voting control within a family corporation from a senior generation to a junior generation without incurring income taxes?

C7-30 Explain why a transaction might satisfy a literal interpretation of the Sec. 368 requirements for a tax-free reorganization, yet fail to be treated as a reorganization.

C7-31 Which types of tax-free reorganizations (acquisitive, divisive, and other) permit the carryover of tax attributes from a target or transferor corporation to an acquiring or transferee corporation?

C7-32 What restrictions are placed on the acquisition of a loss corporation's tax attributes?

C7-33 Explain why Sec. 382 will not be an obstacle to the use of NOL carryovers following a purchase transaction taking place if the value of the old loss corporation is large relative to its NOL carryovers.

C7-34 What is a plan of reorganization?

C7-35 Why is it generally advantageous for a taxpayer to secure an advance ruling regarding a reorganization transaction?

ISSUE IDENTIFICATION QUESTIONS

C7-36 Rodger Powell owns all the stock of Fireside Bar and Grill Corporation in Pittsburgh. Rodger would like to sell his business and retire to sunny Florida now that he has turned 65. Karin, a long-time bartender at Fireside, offers to purchase all the business's noncash assets in exchange for a 25% down payment, with the remaining 75% being paid in five equal annual installments. Interest will be charged at a 10% rate on the unpaid installments. Rodger plans to liquidate the corporation that has operated the Bar and Grill and have Fireside Bar and Grill distribute the installment notes and any remaining assets. What tax issues should Fireside Bar and Grill, Rodger, and Karin consider with respect to the purchase transaction?

C7-37 In Fall 1999, Ford Motor Company's board of directors announced the $25.8 billion spinoff of its 80.7% interest in the Associates First Capital Corporation finance unit to the Ford shareholders. Ford said that it would distribute about $22.7 billion in Associates shares to its holders of Ford common and Class B stock, and $3.1 billion in cash to shareholders who hold Ford stock in U.S. employee savings accounts. According to market observers who track Ford operations, the spinoff is one of several moves Ford has taken to increase shareholder value by selling off nonautomotive assets, moves that included the initial public offering in April 1999 of Hertz Corporation. Ford said that it will take a one-time, noncash, nontaxable gain of about $16.5 billion in the first quarter as a result of the spinoff. What tax issues should the parties to the divisive transaction consider?

C7-38 Adolph Coors Co. transferred part of its assets to ACX Technologies Corporation in exchange for all of ACX's stock. The assets transfered included its aluminum unit, which makes aluminum sheet; its paper packaging unit, which makes consumer-products packaging; and its ceramic unit, which makes high-technology ceramics used in computer boards and automotive parts. The ACX Technologies stock received for the assets was distributed to the Coors shareholders. What tax issues should the parties to the divisive reorganization consider?

C7-39 An excerpt from the Alza Corporation annual report provided the following information. On March 27, 2001, Johnson & Johnson announced that it had entered into a merger agreement with Alza Corporation, a research-based pharmaceutical company and a leader in drug delivery technologies. Alza Corporation shareholders are to receive a fixed exchange ratio of 0.49 shares of Johnson & Johnson common stock for each share of Alza stock in a tax-free reorganization. Alza had approximately 295 million shares outstanding at the time of the announcement. The boards of directors of both companies approved the merger. Johnson & Johnson indicated that it intends to account for the transaction as a pooling of interests. What tax issues would be important to the two companies and to the two shareholder groups? Would the financial reporting change if the merger transaction had taken place in calendar year 2002? Explain.

PROBLEMS

C7-40 ***Qualified Stock Purchase.*** Acquiring Corporation purchased 20% of Target Corporation's stock on each of the following dates: January 2, 2002, April 1, 2002, June 1, 2002, October 1, 2002, and December 31, 2002.

a. Has a qualified stock purchase occurred? When must Acquiring make an election to have the stock purchase treated as an asset acquisition under Sec. 338?

b. How would your answer to Part a change if the purchase dates instead were January 1, 2002, April 1, 2002, September 2, 2002, January 3, 2003, and April 15, 2003?

c. If either Part a or b fails to be a qualified stock purchase, what is the latest date on which Acquiring Corporation can make the final stock purchase needed to qualify for a Sec. 338 election?

C7-41 ***Sec. 338 Election.*** Acquiring Corporation acquires 20% of the Target Corporation stock from Milt on August 10, 2002. Acquiring Corporation acquires an additional 30% of the stock from Nick on November 15, 2002. Acquiring Corporation acquires the remaining 50% of the Target stock from Phil on April 10, 2003. The total price paid for the stock is \$1.9 million. Target Corporation's balance sheet on April 10, 2003 shows assets with a \$2.5 million FMV, a \$1.8 million adjusted basis, and \$500,000 in liabilities.

a. What is the acquisition date for the Target stock for Sec. 338 purposes? By what date must Acquiring make the Sec. 338 election?

b. If Acquiring makes a Sec. 338 election, what is the aggregate deemed sale price for the assets?

c. What is the total basis of the assets following the deemed sale, assuming a 34% corporate tax rate?

d. How does the tax liability attributable to the deemed sale affect the price Acquiring Corporation should be willing to pay for the Target stock?

e. What happens to Target's tax attributes following the deemed sale?

C7-42 ***Sec. 338 Election.*** Gator Corporation is considering the acquisition of Bulldog Corporation's stock in exchange for cash. Two options are being considered: (1) Gator acquires the assets from Bulldog for \$1.4 million or (2) Gator acquires the Bulldog stock for \$1 million and makes a Sec. 338 election shortly after the stock acquisition. Bulldog has no NOL or capital loss carryovers. Bulldog's balance sheet is presented below.

Assets	*Adjusted Basis*	*FMV*	*Liabilities and Equity*	*Amount*
Cash	\$100,000	\$ 100,000	Short-term debt	\$ 200,000
Marketable securities	140,000	200,000	Long-term debt	200,000
Accounts receivable	100,000	100,000	Paid-in capital	300,000
Inventory (FIFO)	100,000	150,000	Retained earnings	700,000
Plant and equipment	200,000	500,000		
Intangibles	–0–	350,000		
Total	\$640,000	\$1,400,000	Total	\$1,400,000

a. What advantages would accrue to Gator Corporation if it acquires the assets directly? What disadvantages would accrue to Bulldog Corporation if it sells the assets and then liquidates?
b. What advantages would accrue to Gator Corporation if it acquires the Bulldog stock for cash and subsequently makes a Sec. 338 election? What advantage would accrue to Bulldog Corporation if its shareholders sell the Bulldog stock?
c. How would your analysis change if Bulldog had incurred $250,000 of NOLs in the current year that it cannot carry back in full due to low taxable income being reported in the preceding two years?

C7-43 ***Sec. 338 Basis Allocation.*** Apache Corporation purchases all of Target Corporation's stock for $300,000 cash. Apache makes a timely Sec. 338 election. Target's balance sheet at the close of business on the acquisition date is as follows:

Assets	*Adjusted Basis*	*FMV*	*Liabilities and Equity*	*Amount*
Cash	$ 50,000	$ 50,000	Accounts payable	$ 40,000
Marketable securities	18,000	38,000	Note to bank	60,000
Accounts receivable	66,000	65,000	Owner's equity	300,000
Inventory (FIFO)	21,000	43,000		
Equipment[a]	95,000	144,000		
Land	6,000	12,000		
Building[b]	24,000	48,000		
Total	$280,000	$400,000	Total	$400,000

[a] The equipment cost $200,000 when purchased.
[b] The building is a MACRS property on which Target has claimed $10,000 of depreciation.

a. What is the aggregate deemed sale price for Target's assets (assume a 34% corporate tax rate)?
b. What amount and character of gain or loss must Target Corporation recognize on the deemed sale?
c. What is the adjusted grossed-up basis for the Target stock? What basis is allocated to each of the individual properties?

C7-44 ***Amount of Corporate Gain or Loss.*** Thomas Corporation transfers all of its assets and $100,000 of its liabilities in exchange for Andrews Corporation voting common stock, having a $600,000 FMV, as part of a merger transaction in which Thomas is liquidated. Thomas Corporation's basis for its assets is $475,000.
a. What is the amount of Thomas's recognized gain or loss on the asset transfer?
b. What is Andrews's basis for the assets received?
c. What is the amount of Thomas's recognized gain or loss when it distributes the stock to its shareholders?
d. How would your answers to Parts a-c change if Thomas's basis for the assets instead had been $750,000?
e. How would your answers to Parts a-c change if Andrews Corporation instead had exchanged $600,000 cash for Thomas Corporation's assets and Thomas was subsequently liquidated. Assume a 34% corporate tax rate.

C7-45 ***Amount of Shareholder Gain or Loss.*** Silvia exchanges all of her Talbot Corporation stock for $300,000 of Anderson Corporation voting common stock pursuant to Talbot's merger into Anderson Corporation. Immediately after the stock-for-stock exchange Silvia owns 25% of Anderson's 2,000 outstanding shares of stock. Silvia's adjusted basis in the Talbot stock is $175,000 before the merger.
a. What are the amount and character of Silvia's recognized gain or loss?
b. What is Silvia's basis for the Anderson stock?
c. How would your answers to Parts a and b change if Silvia instead received Anderson common stock worth $250,000 and $50,000 cash?

C7-46 ***Amount and Character of Shareholder Gain or Loss.*** Yong owns 100% of Target Corporation's stock having a $600,000 adjusted basis. As part of the merger of Target Corporation into Allied Corporation, Yong exchanges his Target stock for Allied Corporation common stock having a $3 million FMV and $750,000 in cash. Yong retains a 60% interest in Allied Corporation's 100,000 shares of outstanding stock immediately after the merger.
a. What are the amount and character of Yong's recognized gain?

b. What is Yong's basis in the Allied stock?
c. How would your answer to Parts a and b change if Yong's 60,000 Allied shares were instead one-third of Allied's outstanding shares?

C7-47 *Amount and Character of Shareholder Gain or Loss.* Archer Corporation exchanges $375,000 of its nonvoting preferred stock for all of Town Corporation's assets pursuant to Town's merger into Archer Corporation. The assets have an adjusted basis of $225,000. Town Corporation's sole shareholder, Lois, exchanges her Town common stock having an adjusted basis of $200,000 for the preferred stock. Lois owns none of Archer's voting stock and owns only 4% (by value) of the Archer stock immediately after the reorganization.
a. What is the amount of Town Corporation's recognized gain or loss on the asset transfer? On the distribution of the stock to Lois?
b. What is Archer Corporation's basis for the assets received?
c. What are the amount and character of Lois's recognized gain or loss?
d. What is Lois's basis for the Archer stock? Her holding period?

C7-48 *Characterization of the Shareholder's Gain or Loss.* Turbo Corporation has one million shares of common stock and 200,000 shares of nonvoting preferred stock outstanding. Pursuant to a merger agreement, Ace Corporation exchanges its common stock worth $15 million for the Turbo common stock and pays $10 million in cash for the Turbo preferred stock. Some shareholders of Turbo Corporation received only Ace common stock for their common stock, some shareholders received only cash for their preferred stock, and some shareholders received both cash and Ace common stock for their Turbo preferred and common stock, respectively. Shareholders owning approximately 10% of the Turbo common stock also owned Turbo preferred stock. The total cash received by these shareholders amounted to $1.5 million. The Turbo Corporation common stockholders end up owning 15% of the Ace stock. What is the tax treatment of the common stock and cash received by each of the three groups of Turbo Corporation shareholders? Assume that, in the group of Turbo shareholders, some shareholders realize a gain while other shareholders realize a loss.

C7-49 *Requirements for a Type A Reorganization.* Anchor Corporation is planning to acquire all the assets of Tower Corporation in a merger transaction. Tower's assets have a $5 million FMV and a $2.2 million adjusted basis. Which of the following transactions qualify as a Type A reorganization assuming Tower Corporation is liquidated?
a. The assets are exchanged for $5 million of Anchor common stock.
b. The assets are exchanged for $5 million of Anchor nonvoting preferred stock.
c. The assets are exchanged for $5 million of Anchor securities.
d. The assets are exchanged for $3.5 million of Anchor nonvoting preferred stock and $1.5 million in cash.
e. The assets are exchanged for $3 million of Anchor common stock and Anchor's assumption of $2 million of Tower liabilities.
f. The assets are exchanged for $5 million in cash provided by Anchor Corporation. An "all cash" merger is permitted under state law.

C7-50 *Tax Consequences of a Merger.* Armor Corporation exchanges $1 million of its common stock and $250,000 of Armor bonds for all of Trail Corporation's outstanding stock. Trail Corporation is then merged into Armor Corporation, with Armor receiving assets having a $1.25 million FMV and an $875,000 adjusted basis. As part of the merger, Antonello exchanges his 15% interest (3,000 shares) in Trail Corporation's single class of stock, having an adjusted basis of $80,000, for $150,000 in Armor stock and $37,500 in Armor bonds. Following the reorganization, Antonello owns 6% (1,000 shares) of Armor's stock. Armor Corporation's E&P balance is $300,000.
a. What is the amount of Trail Corporation's recognized gain or loss on the asset transfer?
b. What is Armor Corporation's basis for the assets received in the exchange?
c. What are the amount and character of Antonello's recognized gain or loss?
d. What is Antonello's basis for the Armor stock? For the Armor bonds?

C7-51 *Requirements for a Type C Reorganization.* Arnold Corporation is planning to acquire all the assets of Turner Corporation in an asset-for-stock (Type C) tax-free reorganization. Turner's assets have a $600,000 adjusted basis and a $1 million FMV. Which of the following transactions qualify as a Type C reorganization (assuming Turner is liquidated as part of the reorganization)?
a. The assets are exchanged for $800,000 of Arnold voting common stock and $200,000 of cash.

b. The assets are exchanged for $800,000 of Arnold voting common stock and $200,000 of Arnold bonds.
c. The assets are exchanged for $1 million of Arnold nonvoting preferred stock.
d. The assets are exchanged for $700,000 of Arnold voting common stock and Arnold's assumption of $300,000 of Turner's liabilities.
e. The assets are exchanged for $700,000 of Arnold voting common stock, Arnold's assumption of $200,000 of Turner's liabilities, and $100,000 in cash.

C7-52 *Tax Consequences of a Type C Reorganization.* Ash Corporation exchanges $250,000 of its voting common stock and $50,000 of its bonds for all of Texas Corporation's assets as part of a Type C tax-free reorganization. Texas Corporation is liquidated, with each of its two shareholders receiving equal amounts of the Ash Corporation stock and bonds. Barbara has a $50,000 basis in her stock, and George has a $200,000 basis in his stock. George and Barbara, who are unrelated, each own 8% of Ash's stock (5,000 shares) immediately after the reorganization. At the time of the reorganization, Texas Corporation's E&P balance is $75,000 and its assets have an adjusted basis of $225,000.
a. What is the amount of Texas Corporation's recognized gain or loss on the asset transfer? On the distribution of the stock and bonds?
b. What is Ash Corporation's basis in the assets it acquired?
c. What are the amount and character of each shareholder's recognized gain or loss?
d. What is the basis of each shareholder's Ash stock? Ash bonds?

C7-53 *Tax Consequences of a Type C Reorganization.* Tulsa Corporation exchanges assets having a $300,000 FMV and a $175,000 adjusted basis for $250,000 of Akron Corporation voting common stock and Akron's assumption of $50,000 of Tulsa's liabilities as part of a Type C tax-free reorganization. Tulsa is liquidated, with its sole shareholder, Michelle, receiving the Akron stock in exchange for her Tulsa stock having an adjusted basis of $100,000. Michelle owns 12% (2,500 shares) of Akron's stock immediately after the reorganization.
a. What is the amount of Tulsa's recognized gain or loss on the asset transfer? On the distribution of the stock?
b. What is Akron's basis for the assets it receives?
c. What effect would the transfer of Tulsa's assets to Subsidiary Corporation (a subsidiary controlled by Akron Corporation) have on the reorganization?
d. What are the amount and character of Michelle's recognized gain or loss?
e. What is Michelle's basis and holding period for her Akron stock?
f. What are the tax consequences of the transaction if Akron shares are first transferred to Akron-Sub Corporation who then carries out the acquisition of Tulsa Corporation's assets?

C7-54 *Requirements for a Type B Reorganization.* Allen Corporation is planning to acquire all the stock of Taylor Corporation in a stock-for-stock (Type B) tax-free reorganization. Which of the following transactions will qualify as a Type B reorganization?
a. All of Taylor's common stock is exchanged for $1 million of Allen voting preferred stock.
b. All of Taylor's common stock is exchanged for $1 million of Allen voting common stock, and $500,000 face amount of Taylor bonds are exchanged for $500,000 face amount of Allen bonds. Both bonds are trading at their par values.
c. All of Taylor's stock is exchanged for $750,000 of Allen voting common stock and $250,000 of Allen bonds.
d. All of Taylor's stock is exchanged for $1 million of Allen voting common stock, and the shareholders of Taylor end up owning less than 1% of Allen's stock.
e. Ninety percent of Taylor's stock is exchanged for $900,000 of Allen voting common stock. One shareholder who owns 10% of the Taylor stock exercises his right under state law to have his shares independently appraised and redeemed for cash by Taylor Corporation. He receives $100,000.
f. Assume the same facts as in Part d except the Allen stock is contributed to Allen-Sub Corporation. The Allen stock is exchanged by Allen-Sub for all the Taylor stock.

C7-55 *Tax Consequences of a Type B Reorganization.* Trent Corporation's single class of stock is owned equally by Juan and Miguel, who are unrelated. Juan has a $125,000 basis for his 1,000 shares of Trent stock, and Miguel has a $300,000 basis for his Trent stock. Adams Corporation exchanges 2,500 shares of its voting common stock having a $100 per share FMV for each shareholder's Trent stock in a single transaction. Immediately after the reorganization, each shareholder owns 15% of the Adams stock.

a. What are the amount and character of each shareholder's recognized gain or loss?
b. What is each shareholder's basis for his Adams stock?
c. What is Adams Corporation's basis for the Trent stock?
d. How would your answers to Parts a–c change if Adams Corporation instead exchanged 2,000 shares of Adams common stock and $50,000 in cash for each shareholder's Trent stock?

C7-56 *Tax Consequences of a Type B Reorganization.* Austin Corporation exchanges $1.5 million of its voting common stock for all of Travis Corporation's single class of stock. Ingrid, who owns all the Travis stock, has a basis of $375,000 in her stock. Ingrid owns 25% of the 15,000 outstanding shares of Austin stock immediately after the reorganization.
a. What are the amount and character of Ingrid's recognized gain or loss?
b. What is Ingrid's basis for her Austin stock?
c. What is Austin Corporation's basis for the Travis stock?
d. What are the tax consequences for all parties to the acquisition if Austin Corporation subsequently liquidates Travis Corporation as part of the plan of reorganization?
e. As part of the reorganization, Austin Corporation exchanges $1 million of its 7% bonds for $1 million Travis Corporation 7% bonds held equally by ten private investors.

C7-57 *Tax Consequences of a Type B Reorganization.* Ashton Corporation purchases 10% of the Todd Corporation stock from Cathy for $250,000 in cash on January 30, 2001. Andrea and Bill each exchange one-half of the remaining 90% of the Todd stock for $1.2 million of Ashton voting common stock on May 30, 2002. Andrea and Bill each have a $200,000 basis for their Todd stock. Andrea and Bill each own 15% of the Ashton stock (12,000 shares) immediately after the reorganization.
a. What are the amount and character of each shareholder's recognized gain or loss?
b. What is each shareholder's basis for his or her Ashton stock?
c. What is Ashton Corporation's basis for the Todd stock?
d. How would your answer to Parts a-c change if Ashton Corporation instead had acquired the remaining Todd stock on May 30, 2001?
e. What effect would the stock acquisition have on the adjusted bases of individual assets and the tax attributes of Todd Corporation?
f. Can the Ashton-Todd corporate group file a consolidated tax return?

C7-58 *Tax Consequences of a Divisive Type D Reorganization.* Road Corporation is owned equally by four shareholders. It conducts activities in two operating divisions: the road construction division and meat packing division. To separate the two activities into separate corporations, Road Corporation transferred the assets and liabilities of the meat packing division (60% of Road's total net assets) to Food Corporation in exchange for all of Food's single class of stock. The assets of the meat packing division have a $2.75 million FMV and a $1.1 million adjusted basis. A total of $500,000 of liabilities are transferred to Food Corporation. The $2.25 million of Food stock (90,000 shares) is distributed ratably to each of the four shareholders.
a. What is the amount of Road Corporation's recognized gain or loss on the asset transfer? On the distribution of the Food stock?
b. What are the amount and character of each shareholder's recognized gain or loss on the distribution? (Assume each shareholder's basis in their Road stock is $200,000.)
c. What is the basis of each shareholder's Road and Food stock after the reorganization? (Assume the Road stock is worth $1.5 million immediately after the distribution.)

C7-59 *Tax Consequences of a Divisive Type D Reorganization.* Light Corporation is owned equally by two individual shareholders, Bev and Tarek. The shareholders no longer agree on matters concerning Light's operations. Tarek agrees to a plan whereby $500,000 of Light's assets (having an adjusted basis of $350,000) and $100,000 of Light's liabilities are transferred to Dark Corporation in exchange for all of its single class of stock (5,000 shares). Tarek will exchange all of his Light common stock, having a $150,000 adjusted basis, for the $400,000 of Dark stock. Bev will continue to operate Light Corporation.
a. What is the amount of Light Corporation's recognized gain or loss on the asset transfer? On the distribution of the Dark stock?
b. What are the amount and character of Tarek's recognized gain or loss?
c. What is Tarek's basis for his Dark stock?
d. What tax attributes of Light will be allocated to Dark?

C7-60 ***Distribution of Stock: Spinoff.*** Parent Corporation has been in the business of manufacturing and selling trucks for the past eight years. Its subsidiary, Diesel Corporation, has been in the business of manufacturing and selling diesel engines for the past seven years. Parent acquired control of Diesel Corporation six years ago when it purchased 100% of its single class of stock from Large Corporation. A federal court has ordered Parent to divest itself of Diesel Corporation as the result of an antitrust judgment. Consequently, Parent distributes all of its Diesel Corporation stock to its shareholders. Alan owns less than 1% of Parent's outstanding stock having a $40,000 basis. He receives 25 shares of Diesel stock having a $25,000 FMV as a result of Parent's distribution. No cash or other assets are distributed by Parent. Parent's E&P at the end of the year in which the spinoff occurs is $2.5 million. The Parent stock held by Alan has a $75,000 FMV immediately after the distribution.

a. What are the amount and character of the gain, loss, or income Alan must recognize as a result of Parent's distributing the Diesel stock?
b. What basis does Alan take for the Diesel stock he receives?
c. When does Alan's holding period for the Diesel stock begin?
d. What amount and character of gain or loss does Parent recognize on making the distribution?
e. How would your answer to Part a change if Parent had been in the truck business for only three years before making the distribution and that it had acquired the Diesel stock in a taxable transaction only two years ago?

C7-61 ***Distribution of Stock: Split-Off.*** Parent Corporation has owned all 100 shares of the Subsidiary Corporation common stock since 1992. Parent Corporation has been in the business of manufacturing and selling light fixtures, and Subsidiary Corporation has been in the business of manufacturing and selling light bulbs. Amy and Bill are the two equal shareholders of the Parent stock and have owned their stock since 1992. Amy's basis in her 50 shares of Parent stock is $80,000, and Bill's basis in his 50 shares of Parent stock is $60,000. On April 10, 2002, Parent distributes all 100 shares of Subsidiary stock to Bill in exchange for all of his Parent stock (which is cancelled). The distribution has an acceptable business purpose. The Subsidiary stock had a $30,000 basis to Parent on the distribution date. At the end of 2002, Parent has $150,000 of E&P. Immediately after the distribution, the FMVs of the Parent and Subsidiary stocks are $3,000 and $1,000 per share, respectively.

a. What are the amount and character of the gain, loss, or income Bill must recognize as a result of Parent's distributing the Subsidiary stock?
b. What basis does Bill take in the Subsidiary stock?
c. When does Bill's holding period for the Subsidiary stock begin?
d. Assume instead that Andrew formed Subsidiary Corporation in 1997 to manufacture and sell lightbulbs. Andrew sold the Subsidiary stock to Parent for cash in 2001. How would your answer to Parts a-c change?

C7-62 ***Distribution of Stock and Securities: Split-Off.*** Ruby Corporation has 100 shares of common stock outstanding. Fred, a shareholder of Ruby Corporation, exchanges his 25% interest in the Ruby stock for Garnet Corporation stock and securities. Ruby purchased 80% of the Garnet stock ten years ago for $25,000. At the time of the exchange, Fred has a $50,000 basis in his Ruby stock, and the stock has an $80,000 FMV. Fred receives Garnet stock that has a $60,000 FMV and Garnet securities that have a $20,000 FMV. Ruby has $50,000 of E&P. Assume that all the requirements of Sec. 355 are met except for the receipt of boot.

a. What are the amount and character of Fred's recognized gain or loss on the exchange?
b. What is Fred's basis for the Garnet stock and the Garnet securities?
c. What are the amount and character of Ruby Corporation's recognized gain or loss on the distribution?
d. When does Fred's holding period begin for the Garnet stock and the Garnet securities?
e. How would your answer to Part a change if the exchange did not meet the requirements of Sec. 355 or Sec. 356?

C7-63 ***Requirements for a Type E Reorganization.*** Master Corporation plans to undertake a recapitalization. Explain the tax consequences of each of the following independent transactions:

a. Holders of Class A nonvoting preferred stock will exchange their stock for newly issued common stock. Master paid $300,000 of cash dividends in the current year and each prior year on the preferred stock.

b. Holders of Master Corporation bonds in the amount of $3 million will exchange their bonds for a similar dollar amount of preferred stock. In addition, $180,000 of unpaid interest will be paid by issuing additional Master preferred stock to the former bondholders.

c. Master Corporation 12% bonds in the amount of $3 million are called and exchanged by their holders before their maturity date for a similar dollar amount of Master Corporation 8% bonds because of a decline in the prevailing market rate of interest. In addition, $180,000 of unpaid interest will be paid in cash.

C7-64 *Tax Consequences of a Type E Reorganization.* Milan Corporation is owned by four shareholders. Andy and Bob each own 40% of the outstanding common and preferred stock. Chris and Doug each own 10% of the outstanding common and preferred stock. The shareholders want to retire the preferred stock that was issued five years ago when the corporation was in the midst of a major expansion. Retirement of the preferred stock will eliminate the need to pay annual dividends on the preferred stock. Explain the tax consequences of the following two alternatives to the shareholders:

- Milan redeems the $100 par preferred stock for its $120 call price. Each shareholder purchased his preferred stock at its par value five years ago.
- The shareholders exchange each share of the $100 par value preferred stock for $120 of additional common stock.

What nontax advantages might exist for selecting one alternative over the other?

C7-65 *Reorganization Requirements.* Discuss the tax consequences of the following corporate reorganizations to the parties to the reorganization:

a. Adobe Corporation and Tyler Corporation are merged under the laws of the State of Florida. The shareholders of Tyler Corporation receive $300,000 of Adobe common stock and $700,000 of Adobe securities for their Tyler stock.

b. Alabama Corporation exchanges $1 million of its voting common stock for all the noncash assets of Texas Corporation. The transaction meets all the requirements for a Type C reorganization. Texas Corporation is divided into two operating divisions: meat packing and meat distribution. Alabama Corporation retains the meat packing division's assets and continues to conduct its activities but sells the assets of the meat distribution division. The meat distribution division's assets constitute 40% of Texas Corporation's noncash assets.

c. Parent Corporation transfers $500,000 of investment securities to Subsidiary Corporation in exchange for all of its single class of stock. The Subsidiary stock is exchanged for one-third of the stock held by each of Parent Corporation's shareholders. Six months after the reorganization, the investment securities are distributed to Subsidiary Corporation's shareholders pursuant to the liquidation of Subsidiary.

C7-66 *Determining the Type of Reorganization Transaction.* For each of the following transactions, indicate its reorganization designation (e.g., Type A, Type B, etc.). Assume all common stock is voting stock.

a. Anderson and Brown Corporations exchange their assets for all of the single class of stock of newly created Computer Corporation. Following the exchange, Anderson and Brown Corporations are liquidated. The transaction satisfies the State of Michigan corporation law requirements.

b. Price Corporation (incorporated in the State of Texas) exchanges all of its assets for all the single class of stock of Price Corporation (incorporated in the State of Delaware). Following the exchange, Price Corporation (Texas) is liquidated.

c. All of Gates Corporation's noncumulative, 10% preferred stock is exchanged for Gates Corporation common stock.

d. Hobbs Corporation exchanges its common stock for 90% of the outstanding common stock and 80% of the outstanding nonvoting preferred stock of Calvin Corporation. The remaining Calvin stock is held by about 30 individual investors.

e. Scale Corporation transfers the assets of its two operating divisions to Major and Minor Corporations in exchange for all of each corporation's single class of stock. The Major and Minor stocks are distributed pursuant to the liquidation of Scale.

f. Tobias Corporation has $3 million of assets and $1 million of liabilities. Andrew Corporation exchanges $2 million of its voting common stock for all of Tobias Corporation's assets and liabilities. Tobias Corporation is liquidated, and its shareholders end up owning 11% of the Andrew stock following the transaction.

C7-67 *Tax Attribute Carryovers.* Alaska Corporation exchanges $2 million of its voting common stock for all the noncash assets of Tennessee Corporation at the close of business on

May 31, 2002. Tennessee Corporation uses its cash to pay off its liabilities and then liquidates. Tennessee and Alaska Corporations report the following taxable income amounts:

Tax Year Ending	*Alaska Corp.*	*Tennessee Corp.*
December 31, 1999	($100,000)	($95,000)
December 31, 2000	60,000	20,000
December 31, 2001	70,000	(90,000)
May 31, 2002	XXX	(40,000)
December 31, 2002	73,000	XXX

a. What tax returns must Alaska and Tennessee file for 2002?
b. What amount of the NOL carryover does Alaska acquire?
c. Ignoring any implications of Sec. 382, what amount of Tennessee Corporation's NOL can Alaska Corporation use in 2002?

C7-68 ***Sec. 382 Limitation: Purchase Transaction.*** Murray Corporation's stock is owned by about 1,000 shareholders, none of whom own more than 1% of the stock. Pursuant to a tender offer, Said purchases all the Murray stock for $7.5 million cash at the close of business on December 31, 2001. Before the acquisition, Said owned no Murray stock. Murray Corporation had incurred substantial NOLs, which at the end of 2000 totaled $1 million. Murray Corporation's taxable income is expected to be $200,000 and $600,000, respectively, for 2002 and 2003. Assuming the long-term tax-exempt federal rate is 5% and Murray Corporation continues in the same trade or business, what amount of NOLs can Murray Corporation use in 2002 and/or 2003? What amount of NOLs and Sec. 382 limitation carryover to 2004?

C7-69 ***Sec. 382 Limitation: Tax-Free Reorganization.*** Albert Corporation is a profitable publicly traded corporation. None of its shareholders owns more than 1% of its stock. On December 31, 2001, Albert Corporation exchanges $8 million of its stock for all the stock of Turner Corporation as part of a merger transaction. Turner Corporation is owned by Tara, who receives 15% of the Albert stock as part of the reorganization. Tara owned none of the Albert stock before the merger. Turner Corporation accumulated $2.5 million in NOL carryovers before being merged into Albert. Albert expects to earn $1 million and $1.5 million in taxable income during 2002 and 2003, respectively. Assuming the long-term tax-exempt federal rate is 5%, what amount of NOLs can Albert Corporation use in 2002 and 2003?

COMPREHENSIVE PROBLEM

C7-70 Sid Kess, a long-time tax client of yours, has decided to acquire the snow blower manufacturing firm owned by Richard Smith, one of his closest friends. Richard has a $200,000 adjusted basis for his Richard Smith Snow Blowers (RSSB) stock. Sid Kess Enterprises (SKE), a C corporation 100%-owned by Sid Kess, will make the acquisition. RSSB operates as a C corporation and reports the following assets and liabilities as of November 1 of the current year.

Asset	*Adj. Basis*	*FMV*
Cash	$ 250,000	$ 250,000
Inventory (LIFO)	470,000	600,000
Equipment	150,000	250,000
Building	100,000	320,000
Land	80,000	120,000
Goodwill	–0–	200,000
Total	$1,050,000	$1,740,000

Equities	*Amount*
Accounts payable	$ 60,000
Mortgage payable	120,000
Paid-in capital	220,000
Retained earnings	650,000
Total	$1,050,000

RSSB has claimed depreciation of $200,000 and $80,000 on the equipment and building, respectively, and has claimed no amortization on the goodwill. Retained earnings approximate RSSB's E&P. No NOL, capital loss, or credit carryovers exist at the time of the acquisition. What are the tax consequences of each alternative acquisition methods to SKE and RSSB corporations? Assume a 34% corporate tax rate.

a. SKE acquires all the single class of RSSB stock for $1.56 million in cash. RSSB is not liquidated.
b. SKE acquires all the assets of RSSB for $1.74 million in cash. RSSB is liquidated.
c. SKE acquires all the RSSB stock for $1.56 million in cash. RSSB is liquidated into SKE shortly after the acquisition.
d. SKE acquires all the RSSB stock for $1.56 million in cash. SKE makes a timely Sec. 338 election. RSSB's tax rate is 34%.
e. SKE exchanges $1.49 million of its common stock for all of RSSB's noncash assets ($1,490,000 = $1,740,000 total assets − $250,000 cash). SKE has 10,000 shares of stock with a $3 million FMV outstanding before the acquisition. RSSB is liquidated as part of the transaction. RSSB uses part of the cash that has been retained to pay off the corporation's liabilities. The remaining cash is distributed with the SKE stock in liquidation of RSSB.
f. SKE exchanges $1.56 million of its common stock for all of Richard Smith's RSSB stock. Assume that RSSB is not liquidated. Each share of SKE stock has a $300 FMV.
g. Assume the same facts as in Part d except that SKE transfers $1.56 million of its common stock to SKE-Sub. SKE-Sub serves as the acquiring corporation for the transaction and uses $1.56 million of the SKE stock to acquire RSSB's stock.
h. Assume the same facts as in Part e except that SKE transfers $1.49 million of its common stock to SKE-Sub. SKE-Sub serves as the acquiring corporation for the transaction and uses $1.49 million of the SKE stock to acquire RSSB's noncash assets.

TAX STRATEGY PROBLEMS

C7-71 Angel Macias is considering the possibility of selling his business. The business (Target Corporation) has the following assets and liabilities:

Assets	*Adjusted Basis*	*FMV*
Cash	$ 400,000	$ 400,000
Securities	400,000	300,000
Inventory (LIFO)	100,000	200,000
Equipment	200,000	400,000
Building (no Sec. 1250 recapture)	50,000	300,000
Goodwill	–0–	200,000
Total	$1,150,000	$1,800,000

Target Corporation owes $200,000 of accounts payable and $400,000 in bank loans. No NOL carryovers or carrybacks are available. Bill Jones and Sam Smith, each of whom have a net worth exceeding $1 million, are interested in purchasing the business using their S&J Corporation as the vehicle for making the purchase. Target's management and its owners are interested in selling the business. Assume that both entities are C corporations and that the C corporations are taxed at a flat 34% rate. The individual owners are taxed at a 39% tax rate on their ordinary income and a 20% rate on their capital gains. What advice would you give Bill and Sam about acquiring the assets directly from Target, or indirectly by purchasing Target's stock from its shareholders and then liquidating Target Corporation into S&J Corporation? Bill and Sam also have expressed a concern about possible differences in the financial reporting of a tax-free versus a taxable acquisition.

C7-72 Adam Smith owns 100% of Alpha Corporation's single class of stock, and Alpha Corporation owns 100% of Beta Corporation's single class of stock. Alpha and Beta Corporations have filed separate tax returns for a number of years. Neither corporation has any NOL carryovers. Although Alpha and Beta both have been profitable in recent years, Beta Corporation needs an infusion of additional capital from outside investors. The corporations have received a proposal from an investor, Dominique, to invest $2 million in Beta Corporation to enable Beta to expand its operations and to eliminate a current working capital shortage that cannot be solved without additional funds. Dominique has imposed one constraint on his capital contribution—that Alpha and Beta become two free-standing entities. Alpha would continue to be completely owned by Adam Smith, but Beta would be owned by the two individuals, Adam and Dominique, with each owning 50% of Beta's stock. What strategies can you offer for separating the two companies?

CASE STUDY PROBLEMS

TAX & FINANCIAL ACCOUNTING

C7-73 *Comparative Acquisition Forms.* Bailey Corporation owns a number of automotive parts shops. Bill Smith owns an automotive parts shop that has been in existence for 40 years and has competed with one of Bailey's locations. Bill is thinking about retirement and would like to sell his business. He has his CPA prepare a balance sheet, which he takes to John Bailey, president of Bailey Corporation, who has been a long-time friend.

Assets	*Adjusted Basis*	*FMV*
Cash	$ 250,000	$ 250,000
Accounts receivable	75,000	70,000
Inventories (LIFO)	600,000	1,750,000
Equipment	200,000	250,000
Building	30,000	285,000
Land	30,000	115,000
Total	$1,185,000	$2,720,000

Should Bailey Corporation make the acquisition, it intends to operate the automotive parts shop using its own tradename in the location Bill has used for 40 years. The president has asked you to prepare a summary of the tax consequences of the following three transactions: (1) a purchase of the noncash assets using cash, (2) the purchase of the stock of Bill's corporation using cash and Bailey Corporation notes, and (3) an asset-for-stock tax-free reorganization using solely Bailey stock. Upon interviewing Bill, you obtain the following additional information: Bill's business is operated as a C corporation, with a $160,000 adjusted basis for his stock. Accounts payable of $200,000 are outstanding. The corporation has depreciated the building using the straight-line method and has claimed $100,000 in depreciation. The equipment is Sec. 1245 property for which the corporation has claimed $150,000 in depreciation. The after-tax profits for each of the last three years have exceeded $300,000, and Bill suspects that some goodwill value exists that is not shown on the balance sheet. No NOL carryovers are available from prior years.

Required: Prepare a memorandum that outlines the tax consequences of each of the three alternative acquisition transactions assuming that the anticipated cash purchase price is $2.55 million for the noncash assets and $2.6 million for the stock and that the transaction takes place in 2002. How would the acquiring corporation report each of the three alternatives for financial reporting purposes under GAAP?

C7-74 The following advertisement appeared in *The Wall Street Journal.*

$12 MILLION CASH WITH
ADDITIONAL CASH AVAILABLE
$89 MM TAX LOSS GOOD THROUGH 2015
TIGERA GROUP, INC.
NASDAQ listed w/300 shareholders
WANTS TO ACQUIRE COMPANY
w/NBT Audited Earnings of $3MM to $7MM
Exceptional Opportunity and Participation for Sellers and
Existing Management. Contact: Albert M. Zlotnick or Ross P.
Lederer, Tel: (000)-000-0000 and Fax: (000)-000-0000.

Required: Prepare a memorandum explaining the tax advantages that would accrue to the Tigera Group if it acquired the stock or the assets of a profitable corporation in a tax-free reorganization or a taxable transaction. Would the advantages be the same if a profitable corporation acquired Tigera? In addition, explain any tax law provisions that might restrict the use of these loss carryovers.

TAX RESEARCH PROBLEMS

C7-75 Austin Corporation acquires 8% of Travis Corporation's single class of stock for cash on January 10, 2002. On August 25, 2002, Austin Corporation makes a tender offer to exchange Austin common stock for the remaining Travis stock. Travis Corporation shareholders tender an additional 85% of the outstanding Travis stock. The exchange is completed on September 25, 2002. Austin Corporation ends up owning slightly more than 93% of the Travis stock. Your tax manager has asked you to draft a memorandum explaining whether one or both of the two acquisition transactions qualify as a tax-free reorganization? If part or all of either transaction is taxable to Travis Corporation's shareholders, offer any suggestions for restructuring the acquisitions to improve the tax consequences of the transaction assuming that Austin Corporation does not desire to make a Sec. 338 election.

At a minimum you should consider:

- IRC Sec. 368(a)(1)(B)
- Reg. Sec. 1.368-2(c)
- *Eldon S. Chapman, et al. v. CIR*, 45 AFTR 2d 80-1290, 80-1 USTC ¶9330 (1st Cir., 1980)
- *Arden S. Heverly, et al. v. CIR*, 45 AFTR 2d 80-1122, 80-1 USTC ¶9322 (3rd Cir., 1980)

C7-76 Diversified Corporation is a successful bank with ten branches. Al, Bob, and Cathy created Diversified Corporation six years ago and own all the Diversified stock. Diversified has constructed a new building in downtown Metropolis that houses a banking facility on the first floor, offices for its employees on the second and third floors, and office space to be leased out to third parties on the fourth through twelfth floors. Since the building was completed six months ago, approximately 20% of the floor space on the upper floors has been occupied. Pursuant to a plan of reorganization, Diversified proposes to transfer the building to Metropolis Real Estate (MRE) Corporation in exchange for all the MRE common stock. The building will be the only property owned by MRE following the reorganization. Diversified owns no other real estate because it currently leases the locations for its ten retail banking branches. Diversified will distribute the MRE common stock ratably to Al, Bob, and Cathy, who will end up holding all the Diversified and MRE common stocks. Your tax manager has asked you to draft a memorandum explaining whether or not the proposed transaction will satisfy the requirements for a tax-free reorganization?

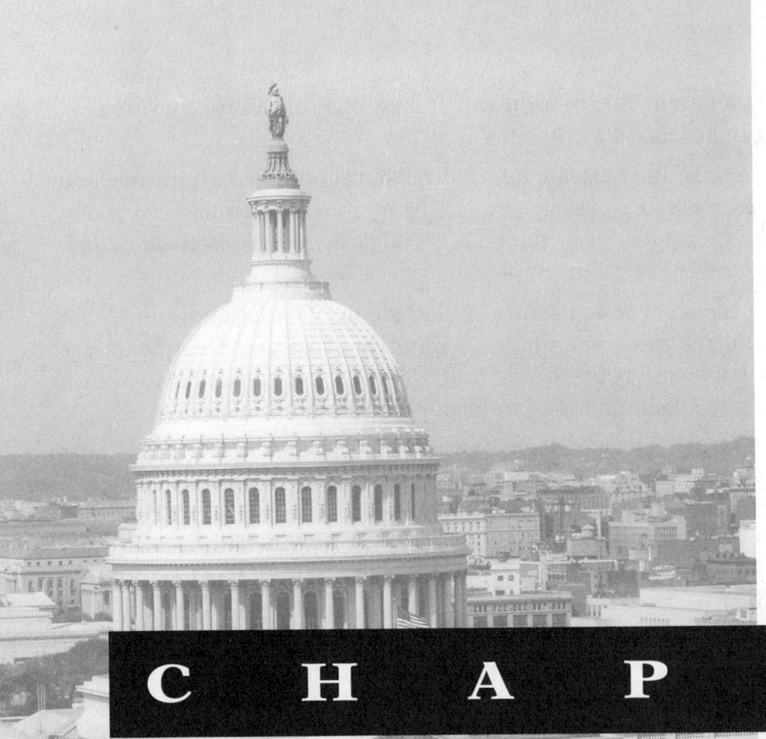

8

CHAPTER

CONSOLIDATED TAX RETURNS

LEARNING OBJECTIVES

After studying this chapter, you should be able to

1. Determine whether a group of corporations is an affiliated group
2. Explain the advantages and disadvantages of filing a consolidated tax return
3. Calculate consolidated taxable income for an affiliated group
4. Calculate the consolidated regular tax liability for an affiliated group
5. Calculate the consolidated AMT liability for an affiliated group
6. Determine whether a transaction is an intercompany transaction
7. Explain the reporting of an intercompany transaction
8. Calculate an affiliated group's consolidated NOL
9. Calculate the carryback or carryover of a consolidated NOL
10. Determine how the special loss limitations restrict the use of separate and consolidated NOL carrybacks and carryovers
11. Explain the procedures for making an initial consolidated return election

CHAPTER OUTLINE

Source of the Consolidated Tax Return Rules...8-2
Definition of an Affiliated Group...8-2
Should a Consolidated Return Be Filed?...8-4
Consolidated Taxable Income...8-5
Computation of the Affiliated Group's Tax Liability...8-9
Intercompany Transactions...8-11
Dividends Received by Group Members...8-21
Consolidated Charitable Contributions Deduction...8-22
Net Operating Losses (NOLs)...8-23
Consolidated Capital Gains and Losses...8-32
Stock Basis Adjustments...8-33
Tax Planning Considerations...8-35
Compliance and Procedural Considerations...8-36

Affiliated corporations (i.e., a parent corporation and at least one subsidiary corporation) have two options for filing their federal income tax returns:

- Each member of the group can file separate tax returns that report its own income and expenses. No special treatment is generally provided for transactions between group members.[1] However, the group can elect to claim a 100% dividends-received deduction for intragroup dividends.
- The affiliated group can file a single tax return, called a consolidated tax return, that reports the results for all its group members. A number of special treatments are applied to transactions between group members (e.g., deferring gains and losses on intercompany transactions and eliminating intragroup dividends).

Some consolidated tax returns include as few as two corporations. Other consolidated tax returns include hundreds of corporations. The importance of the consolidated return election to the U.S. corporate taxing system is illustrated for 1998, when 60,812 consolidated tax returns were filed. These consolidated tax returns represented only 2.69% of the 2.26 million C corporation federal income tax returns. However, consolidated tax returns are being filed by most of the nation's largest corporate groups. For the ten years, affiliated groups filing on a consolidated basis reported 90% of total taxable income for all C corporations and paid more than 80% of the income taxes paid by all C corporations even though they made up less than 3% of all C corporation tax returns that were filed.[2]

This chapter considers the advantages and disadvantages of filing a consolidated tax return. It also examines the basic requirements for computing the consolidated tax liability.

SOURCE OF THE CONSOLIDATED TAX RETURN RULES

ADDITIONAL COMMENT

Filing a consolidated tax return does not affect the reporting of other taxes such as payroll, sales, or property taxes. Also, some states do not allow the filing of consolidated tax returns for state income tax purposes.

REAL WORLD EXAMPLE

Mobil Oil's 1996 federal income tax return was 6,300 pages long and weighed 76 pounds. Work papers for the return constitute 146,000 documents. The return took 57 person years to prepare at a cost of $10 million. In addition, $5 million of expenses are incurred annually in connection with the IRS's audit of the Mobil return.

Sections 1501-1504 are the primary statutory provisions governing the filing of a consolidated tax return. These four sections are very general and primarily define the composition of the affiliated groups eligible to elect to file a consolidated tax return. This topic is quite complex. The Treasury Department was given the responsibility of drafting the Treasury Regulations needed to determine (1) the consolidated tax liability and (2) the filing requirements for a consolidated tax return. Because it is unusual for the Treasury Department to have the authority to draft both statutory and interpretive regulations for a particular topical area, Sec. 1501 requires that all affiliated groups filing a consolidated tax return must consent to all the consolidated tax return regulations in effect when the return is filed. The purpose of Sec. 1501 is to reduce or avoid conflicts in applying the statutory and interpretive regulations. The consolidated return regulations have the same authority as the Internal Revenue Code because of the consent requirement and the fact that they are legislative in nature.

DEFINITION OF AN AFFILIATED GROUP

OBJECTIVE 1

Determine whether a group of corporations is an affiliated group

REQUIREMENTS

STOCK OWNERSHIP REQUIREMENT. Only an affiliated group of corporations can elect to file a consolidated return. Section 1504(a) outlines the stock ownership requirements that must be satisfied, as follows:

---

[1] Some special treatments apply to related corporations filing separate returns under the controlled group rules. These include but are not limited to matching of income and deductions, Sec. 267(a)(1); deferral of loss on intragroup sales, Sec. 267(f)(2); and ordinary income recognition on intragroup sales of depreciable property, Sec. 1239.

[2] IRS web site: *www.irs.gov*.

- A parent corporation must directly own stock[3] having at least 80% of the total voting power of all classes of stock entitled to vote and at least 80% of the total value of all outstanding stock in at least one includible corporation.
- For *each* other corporation eligible to be included in the affiliated group, stock having at least 80% of the total voting power of all classes of stock entitled to vote and at least 80% of the total value of all outstanding stock must be owned directly by the parent corporation and the other group members.

EXAMPLE C8-1 ▶ P Corporation owns 90% of S_1 Corporation's single class of stock and 30% of S_2 Corporation's single class of stock.[4] S_1 Corporation owns 50% of S_2's stock. The remainder of S_1 and S_2's stock is owned by 100 individual shareholders. P, S_1, and S_2 Corporations form the P-S_1-S_2 affiliated group because P owns more than the 80% of the S_1 stock needed to satisfy the direct ownership requirement and P and S_1 together own 80% (50% + 30%) of S_2's stock. The P-S_1-S_2 group can elect to file a consolidated tax return with P as the common parent corporation. ◀

EXAMPLE C8-2 ▶ Ted owns all of the stock of Alpha and Beta Corporations. Alpha and Beta Corporations do not constitute an affiliated group, even though each corporation is directly owned by the same individual shareholder. Because a parent-subsidiary relationship is not present, they are ineligible to make a consolidated return election (see below). ◀

SELF-STUDY QUESTION

What issues determine whether an affiliated group exists?

ANSWER

In determining whether an affiliated group exists, three questions must be addressed. Does a corporation (common parent) own directly 80% or more of at least one includible corporation? What are the includible corporations? What chains of includible corporations are connected by at least 80% ownership?

PRACTICAL APPLICATION

Because of the different stock ownership rules, the corporations included in a consolidated group for financial reporting purposes may be quite different from the includible corporations for federal income tax purposes.

INCLUDIBLE CORPORATION REQUIREMENT. As few as two corporations may satisfy the affiliated group definition. In many of the nation's largest affiliated groups, however, the number of related corporations runs into the hundreds. Some of these corporate groups may have a number of subsidiary corporations that are not able to participate in the consolidated tax return election because they are not includible corporations under Sec. 1504(b). Because they are not includible corporations, their stock ownership cannot be counted toward satisfying the 80% stock ownership minimums, nor can their operating results be reported as part of the consolidated tax return. In general, each excluded corporation must file its own separate corporate tax return.

The following special tax status corporations are not includible corporations:

- Corporations exempt from tax under Sec. 501[5]
- Insurance companies subject to tax under Sec. 801[6]
- Foreign corporations
- Corporations claiming the Puerto Rico and U.S. possessions tax credit
- Regulated investment companies
- Real estate investment trusts
- Domestic international sales corporations
- S corporations

If both the stock ownership and includible corporation requirements are satisfied, the subsidiary corporation must be included in the consolidated return election made by a parent corporation.

EXAMPLE C8-3 ▶ P Corporation owns all the single class of stock of S_1 and S_2 Corporations. S_1 Corporation owns all of S_3 Corporation's stock. S_2 Corporation owns all of S_4 Corporation's stock. P, S_1, and S_3 are domestic corporations. S_2 and S_4 are foreign corporations. P, S_1, and S_3 Corporations constitute the P-S_1-S_3 affiliated group with P as the common parent corporation. S_2 and S_4 are not members of the affiliated group because as foreign corporations they are not includible corporations. ◀

ADDITIONAL COMMENT

Even if S_4 were an includible corporation, S_4 would not be part of the P-S_1-S_3 affiliated group. The chain is broken because S_2 is not an includible corporation.

[3] The term *stock* does not include nonvoting preferred stock that is limited and preferred as to its dividends (and does not participate in corporate growth to any significant extent), has redemption or liquidation rights limited to its issue price (plus a reasonable redemption or liquidation premium), and is not convertible into another class of stock (Sec. 1504(a)(4)).

[4] All corporations referred to in the examples are includible domestic corporations unless otherwise indicated. See definition of *includible corporation* later in this chapter.

[5] Two tax-exempt organizations can file a consolidated return if one is a Sec. 501(c)(2) "feeder" corporation that holds title to property, collects the income from the property, and remits such income to the second tax-exempt organization.

[6] Two or more Sec. 801 domestic life insurance companies may join together to form an affiliated group. If an affiliated group contains one or more Sec. 801 domestic life insurance companies, Sec. 1504(c)(2)(A) permits the parent corporation to elect to treat all such companies that have met the affiliated group stock ownership test for the five immediately preceding tax years as includible corporations.

REAL WORLD EXAMPLE

The check-the-box regulations permit partnerships and LLCs to elect C corporation tax treatment. If the election is made, an LLC or partnership can be a member of an affiliated group filing a consolidated tax return.

Under the check-the-box regulations, noncorporate entities can elect to be taxed as a C corporation. Partnerships and LLCs that elect to be taxed as a C corporation under the check-the-box regulations and that meet all the requirements for inclusion in an affiliated group come under the consolidated return rules of Secs. 1501-1504. Partnerships and LLCs that are wholly- or partially-owned by a member of an affiliated group are not considered members of the affiliated group unless the election is made to have the entity taxed as a C corporation. Partnerships and LLCs for which such an election is made are taxed like a corporate group member. Each group member investing in a partnership or LLC for which no C corporation election is made reports its ratable share of the income/loss earned by the conduit entity in its separate tax return. Such income/loss becomes part of the consolidated tax return of the affiliated group. Partnerships and LLCs for which no C corporation election is made are not subject to the various special consolidated tax return rules, such as those applying to intercompany sales.

TYPICAL MISCONCEPTION

The terms *affiliated group, consolidated group,* and *controlled group* are sometimes used interchangeably. However, these terms have very different definitions and purposes.

COMPARISON WITH CONTROLLED GROUP DEFINITIONS

Three types of controlled groups—brother-sister groups, parent-subsidiary groups, and combined groups—were defined in Chapter C3. As illustrated in Example C8-2, the brother-sister category of controlled groups cannot elect to file a consolidated tax return because they do not satisfy the direct stock ownership requirement. However, most parent-subsidiary controlled groups and the parent-subsidiary portion of a combined controlled group can elect to file a consolidated tax return.

TAX STRATEGY TIP

A brother-sister controlled group cannot file a consolidated tax return. To convert a brother-sister group into a parent-subsidiary affiliated group, the owner(s) of one corporation should make a capital contribution of 80% or more of the corporation's stock to the other group member in a tax-free transaction meeting the Sec. 351 requirements. The two corporations, being in a parent-subsidiary relationship, then can make the initial consolidated return election and begin filing on a consolidated basis.

Only affiliated groups can elect to file consolidated tax returns. Four differences between the definitions of Sec. 1504 (affiliated group) and Sec. 1563 (parent-subsidiary controlled group) do exist. These differences include:

- A parent corporation must own 80% of total voting power *and* total value (instead of voting power **or** value) of a subsidiary's stock to include the subsidiary in the affiliated group.
- The stock attribution rules are not used in determining the inclusion of a subsidiary in an affiliated group but are used in determining the existence of a controlled group.
- The types of corporations excluded from an affiliated group are different from those that are excluded from a controlled group.
- The affiliated group definition is tested on each day of the tax year (instead of only on December 31).

These differences can cause some members of a controlled group to be excluded from the affiliated group.

SHOULD A CONSOLIDATED RETURN BE FILED?

OBJECTIVE 2

Explain the advantages and disadvantages of filing a consolidated tax return

ADVANTAGES OF FILING A CONSOLIDATED TAX RETURN

Filing a consolidated tax return offers a number of advantages and disadvantages, some of the more important of which are discussed below. Some of the advantages that may be gained by filing a consolidated tax return include the following:

- The separate return losses of one affiliated group member may be offset against the taxable income of other group members in the current tax year. Such losses provide an immediate tax benefit by reducing the tax due on the other group member's income or eliminating the need to carry a loss to a subsequent tax year.
- Capital losses of one group member may be offset against the capital gains of other group members in the current tax year. Again, this offset avoids carrying these losses to a subsequent tax year.

KEY POINT

The elimination of intercompany dividends is an advantage of filing consolidated tax returns. However, even if a consolidated tax return is not filed, the owning member should be eligible for a 100% dividends-received deduction.

- Dividends paid from one group member to a second group member are "eliminated" in the consolidated tax return.
- The various credit and deduction limitations are computed on a consolidated basis. This treatment permits group members to use "excess" credits or "excess" deductions in the current tax year and avoid carrying them to a subsequent tax year.
- Gains on intercompany transactions are deferred until a subsequent event occurs that causes the profit or gain to be included in the consolidated return.
- Calculation of the alternative minimum tax (AMT) takes place on a consolidated basis (rather than for each group member) and may reduce the negative effects of tax preference items and adjustments. This treatment may eliminate the need for the affiliated group as a whole to pay an AMT liability. On the other hand, the affiliated group is limited to a single AMT exemption.

DISADVANTAGES OF FILING A CONSOLIDATED TAX RETURN

TYPICAL MISCONCEPTION

One disadvantage of filing a consolidated tax return that should be apparent after going through this chapter is the added recordkeeping costs necessary to file a consolidated tax return.

Some disadvantages of filing a consolidated tax return include the following:

- A consolidated return election is binding on all subsequent tax years unless the IRS grants the group permission to discontinue filing a consolidated return or the affiliated group is terminated.
- All group members must use the same taxable year.
- Gains, losses, and deductions on intercompany transactions are deferred until a subsequent event occurs that causes the gain, loss, or deduction to be included in the consolidated tax return.[7]
- Operating losses and capital losses of group members may reduce or eliminate the ability of profitable group members to take advantage of credits or deductions by lowering the applicable credit or deduction limitation for the affiliated group.
- Additional administrative costs may be incurred in maintaining the necessary records to account for deferred intercompany transactions and the special loss limitations, although some savings may occur by filing a single return and filing all tax returns at the same time.

No general rule can be applied to determine whether an affiliated group should elect to file a consolidated tax return. Each group should examine the long- and short-term advantages and disadvantages of filing a consolidated tax return before making a decision.

CONSOLIDATED TAXABLE INCOME

OBJECTIVE 3

Calculate consolidated taxable income for an affiliated group

The heart of the computation of the consolidated federal income tax liability is the calculation of **consolidated taxable income**. The calculation of consolidated taxable income is divided into the following five steps. An overview of the five-step consolidated taxable income calculation is presented in Table C8-1.

STEP 1. The starting point is the determination of each member's taxable income. The amount of a group member's taxable income is determined as if the group member were filing a separate tax return.

---

[7] The deferral of losses and deductions in a consolidated return is less of a disadvantage now that related-party loss and deduction rules also apply to controlled groups in Sec. 267.

TYPICAL MISCONCEPTION

This table illustrates that the filing of a consolidated tax return instead of separate tax returns is clearly not easier from a compliance point of view.

▼ **TABLE C8-1**

Consolidated Taxable Income Calculation

Step 1: Compute each group member's taxable income (or loss) based on the member's own accounting methods as if the corporation were filing its own separate tax return.

Step 2: Adjust each group member's taxable income as follows:
1. Gains and losses on certain intercompany transactions are deferred. If a restoration event occurs during the year, previously deferred gains and losses are included in the calculation.
2. An inventory adjustment may be required.
3. Dividends received by a group member from another group member are excluded from the recipient's gross income.
4. An adjustment for an excess loss (negative investment basis) account of an affiliate may be required.
5. Built-in deductions may be deferred.

Step 3: The following gains, losses, and deductions are removed from each member's taxable income because they must be computed on a consolidated basis:
1. Net operating loss (NOL) deductions
2. Capital gains and losses
3. Section 1231 gains and losses (including net casualty gain)
4. Charitable contribution deductions
5. Dividends-received deductions
6. Percentage depletion deductions

The result of making the adjustments to a member's taxable income in Steps 2 and 3 is the member's separate taxable income.

Step 4: Combine the members' separate taxable income amounts. This amount is called the group's combined taxable income.

Step 5: Adjust the group's combined taxable income for the following items that are reported on a consolidated basis:
1. Deduct the consolidated Sec. 1231 net loss.
2. Deduct the consolidated net casualty loss.
3. Add the consolidated capital gain net income (taking into account capital loss carrybacks and carryovers and Sec. 1231 gains).
4. Deduct the consolidated charitable contribution deduction.
5. Deduct the consolidated percentage depletion deduction.
6. Deduct the consolidated NOL deduction (taking into account any allowable NOL carryovers and carrybacks).
7. Deduct the consolidated dividends-received deductions.

Consolidated taxable income (or consolidated NOL)

STEP 2. Once each group member's taxable income has been determined, a series of adjustments (e.g., deferral of gain on certain intercompany transactions) must be made to take into account the special treatment that certain transactions receive in consolidated returns.

STEP 3. Any income, loss, or deduction items that must be reported on a consolidated basis are removed from the taxable income calculation. The resulting amount is the group member's **separate taxable income.**

STEP 4. The separate taxable income amounts of the individual group members are aggregated into a **combined taxable income** amount.

STEP 5. Each of the tax attributes stated on a consolidated basis (which were removed in Step 3) are added to or subtracted from the combined taxable income amount. The resulting amount is the affiliated group's consolidated taxable income.[8]

[8] Reg. Sec. 1.1502-12.

Consolidated taxable income is subject to the corporate tax rates of Sec. 11 to determine the consolidated regular tax liability. This amount may be increased if the affiliated group is found to owe an additional amount under the corporate AMT, one of the other special tax levies, or as the result of recapturing previously claimed tax credits. Any tax credits and estimated tax payments are subtracted from the regular tax liability to determine the taxes owed when the return is filed. A sample consolidated tax return worksheet is included in Appendix B, which illustrates the consolidated taxable income calculation.

INCOME INCLUDED IN THE CONSOLIDATED TAX RETURN

KEY POINT

Two basic rules exist for determining what income must be included in a consolidated tax return: common parent's income for the entire tax year and a subsidiary's income only for the time period the subsidiary is a member of the consolidated group.

A consolidated tax return includes the parent corporation's income for its entire tax year, except for any portion of the year that it was a member of another affiliated group that filed a consolidated tax return. A subsidiary corporation's income is included in the consolidated tax return only for the portion of the affiliated group's tax year for which it was a group member. When a corporation is a member of an affiliated group for only a portion of its tax year, the member's income for the remainder of its tax year is included in a separate tax return or the consolidated tax return of another affiliated group.[9]

A corporation that becomes or ceases to be a group member during a consolidated return year[10] changes its status at the end of the day on which such change occurs (i.e., the change date). Its tax year ends for federal income tax purposes at the end of the change date. Transactions that occur on the change date that are allocable to the portion of the day after the event resulting in the change (e.g., a stock sale or merger) are accounted for by the group member (and all related parties) as having occurred on the next day.[11]

EXAMPLE C8-4 ▶ P and S Corporations file separate tax returns for calendar year 2001. At the close of business on April 30, 2002, P Corporation acquires all of S Corporation's stock. If the P-S affiliated group files a consolidated tax return for 2002, P's income is included in the consolidated tax return for all of 2002, and S's income is included only for the period May 1 through December 31, 2002. S Corporation must file a separate tax return to report its income for the pre-affiliation period January 1 through April 30, 2002. ◀

WHAT WOULD YOU DO IN THIS SITUATION?

The P-S-T affiliated group has filed consolidated tax returns using the calendar year as its tax year for many years. On October 1, P Corporation created a new subsidiary, X Corporation, with a $5,000 initial capital contribution, and X Corporation issued its stock to P Corporation. A bank account was opened when X Corporation was created. A federal tax identification number was also applied for and obtained. X did not conduct any business activities before year-end. Its only income was $125 in interest earned on the initial capital contribution. Due to a lack of communication or an oversight, P's tax department did not include X Corporation in the affiliated group's consolidated tax return.

Your CPA firm has provided federal tax advice to P Corporation for a number of years, but your client's tax department has handled the federal tax return filings. Most of your work for P Corporation has been in the state and local taxation area and on special federal tax assignments. You were aware of the affiliated group's future business plans for creating X Corporation. Will the oversight with respect to X Corporation disqualify the affiliated group from filing a consolidated tax return for the current year and all future years? Can you avoid having to file a federal tax return for X Corporation because of the small amount of income the corporation earned? Does the failure to include X Corporation in this year's consolidated tax return prevent it from being included in future years? What advice can you give your client about needing to include X Corporation in the consolidated tax return?

---

[9] Reg. Sec. 1.1502-76(b)(1)(i).

[10] **A consolidated return year** is defined by Reg. Sec. 1.1502-1(d) as a tax year for which a consolidated return is filed or is required to be filed by the affiliated group. A **separate return year** is defined by Reg. Sec. 1.1502-1(e) as a tax year for which a corporation files a separate return or joins in the filing of a consolidated tax return with a different affiliated group.

[11] Reg. Sec. 1.1502-76(b)(1)(ii).

Tax returns for the years that end and begin with a corporation becoming or ceasing to be a member of an affiliated group are separate return years. The separate returns, in general, are short period returns (i.e., for applying the MACRS rules) but do not require annualization of the tax liability or estimated tax calculations when a corporation joins an affiliated group. The short period return is a full tax year for purposes of NOL and other carryovers. Allocation of income between the consolidated tax return and a member's separate return year takes place according to the accounting methods used by the individual corporation. If this allocation cannot be readily determined, allocation of items included in each tax return (other than ones considered below to be extraordinary) can be based on the relative number of days of the original tax year included in each tax year. A ratable allocation of income, expense, gain, loss, and credit items between periods is permitted if the new or departing group member is not required to change its annual accounting period or accounting method as a result of its change in status, and an irrevocable election is made by the group member and the parent corporation of the affected group. Extraordinary items are allocated to the day they are reported using the group member's accounting methods. Extraordinary items include but are not limited to gains or losses arising from the disposition or abandonment of capital assets, Sec. 1231 property, or inventory; NOL carrybacks or carryovers; settlements of a tort or third-party liability; and compensation-related deductions arising from the group member's change in status (e.g., bonuses, severance pay, and option cancellation payments).[12]

AFFILIATED GROUP ELECTIONS

TAX YEARS. An affiliated group's consolidated tax return must be filed using the parent corporation's tax year. Beginning with the initial consolidated return year for which it is includible in the consolidated tax return, each subsidiary corporation must adopt the parent corporation's tax year. The requirement for a common tax year applies to affiliated group members both when an initial consolidated tax return is being filed and when the stock of a new member is acquired.[13]

EXAMPLE C8-5 ▶ P and S Corporations file separate tax returns for 2001. P Corporation uses a calendar year as its tax year. S Corporation uses a fiscal year ending June 30 as its tax year. At the close of business on April 30, 2002, P Corporation acquires all of S Corporation's stock. If the P-S affiliated group files a consolidated tax return for 2002, S must change its tax year so that it ends on December 31. S must file a short-period tax return for the period July 1, 2001 through April 30, 2002. P's income for all of 2002 and S's income for the period May 1, 2002 through December 31, 2002 are included in the initial consolidated tax return. ◀

SELF-STUDY QUESTION

When a subsidiary leaves an affiliated group that has filed consolidated tax returns, may it select any year-end it wishes?

ANSWER

Without permission from the IRS to do otherwise, a subsidiary must retain the group's year-end (if filing a separate tax return) or adopt the year-end of the acquiring consolidated group, if applicable.

METHODS OF ACCOUNTING. Unless the IRS grants permission for a change in accounting method, the accounting methods used by each group member are determined by using the same rules as if the member were filing a separate tax return.[14] This requirement applies when a consolidated tax return election is made or a new corporation joins an existing affiliated group. Thus, one group member may use the cash method of accounting and another group member may use the accrual method of accounting during a consolidated return year. The possibility of finding a mixture of cash and accrual method corporations in an affiliated group is limited because of the Sec. 448 restrictions on the use of the cash method of accounting by C corporations described in Chapter C3.

KEY POINT

Even though members of a consolidated group must use the same year-end, members are not required to use the same accounting methods. It is common to find different inventory methods (e.g., LIFO and FIFO) within the same affiliated group.

TERMINATION OF THE AFFILIATED GROUP

An affiliated group that elects to file a consolidated tax return must continue to file on a consolidated basis as long as the affiliated group exists unless the IRS grants permission for it to do otherwise. An affiliated group exists as long as the parent corporation and at least one subsidiary corporation remain affiliated. It does not matter whether the parent corporation owns the *same* subsidiary throughout the entire tax year or even whether the continuing subsidiary exists at the beginning of the year.

[12] Reg. Sec. 1.1502-76(b)(2)

[13] Reg. Sec. 1.1502-76(a).

[14] Reg. Sec. 1.1502-17(a).

EXAMPLE C8-6 ▶ P and S_1 Corporations have filed a consolidated tax return for several calendar years. At the close of business on August 31, 2002, P purchases all of S_2 Corporation's stock. S_2 Corporation uses the calendar year as its tax year. At the close of business on September 30, 2002, P sells its entire holding of S_1 stock. The affiliated group, with P as the parent corporation, must file a consolidated tax return for 2002 because P remained the parent corporation of at least one subsidiary corporation (first S_1, later S_2) at all times during the year.

If the order of the purchase and sale transactions were reversed, the affiliated group would have been terminated following the sale of the S_1 stock (on August 31, 2002). A new affiliated group would have been created with the purchase of the S_2 stock (on October 1, 2002). The creation of the new affiliated group would require a new consolidated return election. If such an election were made, the consolidated return for the P-S_2 affiliated group would contain the income of P and S_2 Corporations from October 1, 2002 through December 31, 2002. The original P-S_1 affiliated group must file a consolidated tax return including their operating results from January 1, 2002 through September 30, 2002. ◀

EXAMPLE C8-7 ▶ P and S Corporations have filed a consolidated tax return for several calendar years. At the close of business on August 31, 2002, P Corporation sells its entire holding of S stock to Artie. P's income is included in the 2002 consolidated tax return for the entire calendar year. S's income is included only for the period January 1 through August 31, 2002. S also must file a separate tax return to report its income for the period September 1 through December 31, 2002. ◀

ADDITIONAL COMMENT

Permission to discontinue the filing of consolidated tax returns is seldom granted by the IRS when the request relates to a change in the tax situation of the affiliated group that is not related to a law change.

GOOD CAUSE REQUEST TO DISCONTINUE STATUS. Permission to discontinue filing a consolidated tax return sometimes is granted by the IRS in response to a "good cause" request initiated by the taxpayer. A good cause reason for discontinuing the consolidated tax return election includes a substantial adverse effect on the consolidated tax liability for the tax year (relative to what the aggregate tax liability would be if the group members filed separate tax returns) originating from amendments to the IRC or Treasury Regulations having effective dates in the tax year in question.[15]

SELF-STUDY QUESTION

In the second half of Example C8-6, the order of the transactions is reversed. In this case, what tax returns are required, and what income is included in these returns?

ANSWER

(1) Final P-S_1 consolidated return that includes P's income from 1/1 to 9/30 and S_1's income from 1/1 to 8/31. (2) New P-S_2 consolidated return with P and S_2's income from 10/1–12/31. (3) Short-period separate return for S_1 from 9/1–12/31. (4) Short-period separate return for S_2 from 1/1–9/30.

EFFECTS ON FORMER MEMBERS. The termination of an affiliated group affects its former members in several ways, two of which are examined in subsequent sections of this chapter.

- ▶ Any gains and losses that have been deferred on intercompany transactions (e.g., intercompany profits on sales of inventory between group members) may have to be recognized.
- ▶ Consolidated tax attributes (such as NOL, capital loss, tax credit, and charitable contribution carryovers) must be allocated among the former group members.

In addition, disaffiliation of a corporation from an affiliated group prevents the corporation from being included in a consolidated return with the same affiliated group until five years after the beginning of its first tax year in which it ceased to be a group member. The IRS can waive the five-year requirement and permit the departing group member to join in a consolidated return at an earlier date.

COMPUTATION OF THE AFFILIATED GROUP'S TAX LIABILITY

OBJECTIVE 4

Calculate the consolidated regular tax liability for an affiliated group

REGULAR TAX LIABILITY

The affiliated group determines its consolidated regular income tax liability by applying the corporate tax rates found in Sec. 11 to the group's consolidated taxable income. Thus, the aggregate group obtains the benefit of the 15% tax rate for the first $50,000 of con-

[15] An example of such an exemption is Rev. Proc. 95-39, 1995-2 C.B. 399, where the IRS determined that changes to its rules regarding intercompany transactions may have adverse effects on the filing of consolidated tax returns. It granted all affiliated groups blanket permission to discontinue filing consolidated returns for its first tax year beginning after July 12, 1995, provided the election was made before June 30, 1996.

solidated taxable income and the 25% tax rate for the next $25,000 of consolidated taxable income. If consolidated taxable income exceeds $100,000, however, the 5% surtax applies until consolidated taxable income reaches $335,000, at which point the benefits of the 15% and 25% tax brackets are completely recaptured.[16]

The result for consolidated tax returns has some similarities to the total tax liability for a controlled group (see Chapter C3). Section 1561 limits a controlled group of corporations to an aggregate of $50,000 for which the 15% tax rate applies and an aggregate of $25,000 for which the 25% tax rate applies. In the controlled group situation, however, each corporation computes its separate tax liability with the benefits of the reduced rates allocated among the members of the group.

OBJECTIVE 5

Calculate the consolidated AMT liability for an affiliated group

KEY POINT

Determining the alternative minimum tax for corporations is discussed in Chapter C5. Determining the alternative minimum tax for a consolidated group merely adds to the complexity of this already difficult computation.

CORPORATE ALTERNATIVE MINIMUM TAX LIABILITY

The corporate alternative minimum tax (AMT) liability is determined on a consolidated basis for all group members. The consolidated AMT is determined under an approach that generally parallels the determination of the group's consolidated taxable income. The starting point for the calculation is consolidated taxable income. The AMT procedures and definitions of Secs. 55-59 apply in determining consolidated AMT. Consolidated alternative minimum taxable income (AMTI) is computed using the rules of Prop. Reg. Sec. 1.1502-55(b). These Treasury Regulations require the deferral and restoration of AMT items. Consolidated AMTI equals consolidated preadjustment AMTI plus or minus 75% of the difference between consolidated adjusted current earnings (ACE) and consolidated preadjustment AMTI and decreased by the consolidated alternative tax NOL.[17] The negative ACE adjustment limitation is determined on a consolidated basis and requires the tracking of separate return and consolidated return positive and negative ACE adjustments.

The consolidated AMT is the excess of the consolidated tentative minimum tax (TMT) over the consolidated regular tax liability for the tax year. The consolidated TMT amount is determined by first computing 20% of the excess of consolidated AMTI over a consolidated statutory exemption amount. This amount is reduced by the consolidated AMT foreign tax credit amount to arrive at the consolidated TMT. Any excess of the consolidated TMT over the consolidated regular tax must be paid by the affiliated group and is available as a minimum tax credit.

A group's consolidated minimum tax credit (MTC) equals the sum of the consolidated return year MTCs and any prior separate return year MTCs. Use of the consolidated minimum tax credit is limited to the excess (if any) of the modified consolidated regular tax over the consolidated TMT for the year. Modified consolidated regular tax equals the consolidated regular tax amount reduced by any credits allowable for the AMT (other than the MTC).[18]

Affiliated groups of corporations filing a consolidated tax return, like corporations filing separate tax returns, are eligible for the small corporation exemption from the corporate alternative minimum tax. The $5 million and $7.5 million gross receipts ceilings on the small corporation AMT exemption apply to the entire group that includes the affiliated group's members.

CONSOLIDATED TAX CREDITS

The affiliated group can claim all tax credits available to corporate taxpayers. The discussion that follows examines the two major credits claimed by most affiliated groups—the general business credit and the foreign tax credit.

GENERAL BUSINESS CREDIT. The affiliated group's general business credit is determined on a consolidated basis, with all of the group members' separate component credit amounts being combined into a single amount for the affiliated group. For these credits,

[16] A similar recapture of the tax savings produced by the 34% corporate tax rate is applicable to the next $9,925,000 of taxable income and also may apply when taxable income is between $15 and $18.333 million (see Chapter C3).

[17] Prop. Reg. Secs. 1.1502-55(b)(1) and (f).

[18] Prop. Reg. Sec. 1.1502-55(h).

an affiliated group is limited to the excess of the affiliated group's net income tax over the greater of (1) the affiliated group's tentative minimum tax for the year or (2) 25% of the affiliated group's net regular tax liability for the year exceeding $25,000.[19] Any unused general business tax credits may be carried back one year and forward 20 years under Sec. 39(a) for tax years beginning after August 6, 1997. (See Chapter C3 for more detailed coverage of the tax credit limitation.)

A profitable group member may find that use of the consolidated tax liability as the basis for the general business credit limitation may result in a reduced credit amount because the losses of other group members are used to offset its separate taxable income. An unprofitable member, however, may find its general business credit limitation increased by the separate taxable income of another member, so that credits that otherwise would have been carried back or forward if separate returns were filed may be used currently by the group.

EXAMPLE C8-8 ▶ The P-S affiliated group files a consolidated tax return for the current year. P and S Corporations contribute separate taxable income (or loss) amounts of $300,000 and ($100,000), respectively, to the group's $200,000 consolidated taxable income. P and S can tentatively claim a $40,000 research credit and a $10,000 targeted jobs credit, or a tentative $50,000 consolidated general business credit. The P-S group's regular tax liability is $61,250. The P-S group's tentative minimum tax liability (assuming no differences between AMTI and taxable income other than the statutory exemption) is $34,500.[20] The group's general business credit limitation is calculated as follows:

Regular tax		$61,250
Plus: Alternative minimum tax		-0-
Net income tax		$61,250
Minus: Greater of:		
(1) 25% of group's net regular tax liability exceeding $25,000 [0.25 × ($61,250 − $25,000)]	$ 9,062	
(2) Group's tentative minimum tax for the year	34,500	(34,500)
General business credit limitation		$26,750

The $23,250 ($50,000 tentative credit − $26,750 credit limitation) of unused general business credits can be carried back one year and forward 20 years. ◀

FOREIGN TAX CREDIT. An affiliated group's foreign tax credit for a consolidated return year is determined on a consolidated basis. The parent corporation makes the election to claim either a deduction or a credit for the group's foreign taxes. If the credit is chosen, the affiliated group's foreign tax credit limitation is computed by taking into account the group's income from U.S. and foreign sources, the consolidated taxable income, and the consolidated regular and alternative minimum tax amounts in the manner described in Chapter C16.

INTERCOMPANY TRANSACTIONS

OBJECTIVE 6

Determine whether a transaction is an intercompany transaction

An **intercompany transaction** is defined as a transaction between corporations that are members of the same affiliated group immediately after the transaction.[21] Intercompany transactions include:

- Sales, exchanges, contributions, or other transfers of property from one group member to a second group member whether or not the gain or loss is recognized.

---

[19] Sec. 38(c).

[20] $200,000 AMTI − {$40,000 statutory exemption − [0.25 × ($200,000 AMTI − $150,000 threshold)]} × 0.20 = $34,500.

[21] Reg. Sec. 1.1502-13(b)(1)(i).

ADDITIONAL COMMENT

The rules that apply to intercompany transactions are an excellent example of the additional recordkeeping necessary to file consolidated tax returns.

- The performance of services by one group member for a second group member, and the second member's payment or accrual of its expenditure.
- The licensing of technology, renting of property, or lending of money by one group member, and the second member's payment or accrual of its expenditure.
- Payment of a dividend distribution by a subsidiary corporation to its parent corporation in connection with the parent's investment in the subsidiary's stock.

For purposes of our discussion, we will divide our coverage into two categories (1) property acquired in intercompany transactions, and (2) **other intercompany transactions.**

OBJECTIVE 7

Explain the reporting of an intercompany transaction

PROPERTY TRANSACTIONS

GENERAL RULE. Gains and losses on intercompany transactions receive special treatment under the consolidated return Treasury Regulations. In general, gains and losses on intercompany transactions involving the sale or exchange of property between two group members (also known as an intercompany item) are recognized in calculating the group member's separate taxable income. Exceptions to this general rule include intercompany transactions that qualify for nonrecognition treatment under Secs. 351 (corporate formation transaction) and 1031 (like-kind exchange). The recognized gain/loss is deferred under the consolidated tax return regulations and therefore not included in determining consolidated taxable income until a subsequent event occurs that requires the recognition of income, gain, deduction or loss (also known as a corresponding item) by the buyer (see Step 2 in Table C8-1). Events that can trigger the recognition of an intercompany item include:

- The claiming of a depletion, depreciation, or amortization deduction with respect to a property acquired in an intercompany transaction.
- Amortization of services, or any other nonproperty asset, acquired by a group member in an intercompany transaction that has previously been capitalized.
- The disposition outside the affiliated group of a property acquired in an intercompany transaction.
- The departure from an affiliated group of the group member that either sells or owns a property that is acquired in an intercompany transaction.
- The first day of a separate return year for the parent corporation.

TAX STRATEGY TIP

An affiliated corporation should consider a loss recognition transaction to a party outside the group in lieu of a deferred recognition intercompany transaction. For example, P Corporation has a machine that it intends to sell to its wholly owned subsidiary, S Corporation. The machine has a $15,000 adjusted basis and a $9,000 FMV. An intercompany sale of the machine from P to S results in a $6,000 ($9,000 – $15,000) Sec. 1231 loss that is deferred until a restoration event occurs. A sale of the same property to an entity that is not part of the affiliated group permits P Corporation to deduct the $6,000 loss immediately. Thus, P should consider recognizing the loss to reduce its income taxes and using the tax savings to help S reduce the cost of making an investment in a new machine.

In general, buyers and sellers engaging in an intercompany transaction are treated as separate entities.[22] A sale of property by one group member to a second group member is reported on the selling and buying corporations' books using the same basic rules that would apply if the sale involved two unrelated parties. Of course, different rules would be used if the property were acquired in a like-kind exchange, or corporate formation transaction where part or all of the realized gain or loss is not recognized. The basic rules for reporting an intercompany property transaction are presented below.

SELF-STUDY QUESTION

What is the basis of property purchased by the buying member in an intercompany transaction?

ANSWER

The purchasing member takes a cost basis in any assets purchased in an intercompany transaction.

AMOUNT AND CHARACTER OF THE INTERCOMPANY GAIN OR LOSS. At the time of the transaction, the amount and character of the intercompany gain or loss are determined as if the transaction had occurred in a separate return year.

BASIS AND HOLDING PERIOD. The basis and holding period for a property acquired in a intercompany transaction are determined as if the acquisition occurred in a separate return year. Thus, the adjusted basis for an asset is the property's acquisition cost if the property is purchased by the buying member for cash, or cash and a debt obligation, from the selling member. The holding period for such property begins on the day after the acquisition date.

[22] Reg. Sec. 1.1502-13(a)(2).

EXAMPLE C8-9 ▶ S (Seller) and B (Buyer) Corporations have filed consolidated tax returns for several years, with S being the common parent of the affiliated group.[23] S and B Corporations both use the accrual method of accounting. S acquired a block of marketable securities in 1992, which have been held as a capital asset since that date. The adjusted basis for the securities is $120,000. S sells the marketable securities to B for $200,000 cash on August 8, 2002. This gain is determined on a separate entity basis and is reported in S's separate tax return calculation. S's deferred intercompany capital gain is $80,000 ($200,000 – $120,000). The $80,000 deferred gain is not reported in the 2002 consolidated tax return. An adjustment is made to remove it from consolidated taxable income (as illustrated in Step 2 of Table C8-1). B's basis for the securities is $200,000. Its holding period for determining the character of the gain or loss on a subsequent sale of the securities begins with August 9, 2002. No gain is recognized by S until one of the events described above that produces a corresponding item for B occurs. At that time, part or all of the deferred gain will be included in the consolidated return (but not S's separate tax return calculation). ◀

A sample completed consolidated tax return (Form 1120) and worksheet appears in Appendix B. The worksheet shows the reporting of an intercompany sale of inventory (see worksheet footnote 1) followed by the sale of the inventory outside the affiliated group. The use of the worksheet to report intercompany transactions will be further developed within the examples that follow.

The intercompany transaction rules are based on two concepts—intercompany items and corresponding items. **Intercompany items** are the Seller's income, gain, deduction, or loss from an intercompany transaction.[24] **Corresponding items** are the Buyer's income, gain, deduction, or loss from an intercompany transaction, or from property acquired in an intercompany transaction.[25]

MATCHING AND ACCELERATION RULES. Two principles are used to implement the single entity approach to reporting intercompany transactions. They are the matching rule and the acceleration rule. The matching rule generally treats the Seller and Buyer as divisions of a single corporation for purposes taking into account the intercompany items. In general, a transfer of an asset between two divisions is not considered a taxable event. A taxable event can occur when, for example, a division sells an asset to a third party. The acceleration rule provides a series of exceptions to the general rule for taking items into account if the treatment of the Seller and Buyer as divisions within a single entity cannot be achieved (e.g., if either S or B leaves the group and becomes a nonmember).

The intercompany transaction rules override the basic accounting method elections used by the seller. Assume that S's sale to B in Example C8-9 was instead made for a series of notes payable in equal amounts over a five-year period. Normally, the Sec. 453 installment sale rules would require the $80,000 gain to be reported as the collections were made over the five-year period. Instead, the $80,000 gain is an intercompany item which, in general, is not reported until a corresponding item is reported by the Buyer.[26]

INTERCOMPANY ITEM AMOUNT. When determining the intercompany item amount, all the Seller's direct and indirect costs related to the sale or the providing of services are included. As a result, the Uniform Capitalization rules of Sec. 263A apply in determining (1) the basis of inventory sold, (2) an employee's wages and other related costs included in determining the intercompany item when services are performed, and (3) depreciation and other direct expenses included in determining the intercompany item when property is rented.[27]

CORRESPONDING ITEM AMOUNT. Corresponding items are the Buyer's income, gain, deduction, and loss from an intercompany transaction, or from property acquired in an intercompany transaction.[28] Three corresponding items are illustrated in the text that follows:

---

[23] S and B Corporations are used for the two members of the consolidated group, instead of our usual P and S Corporations, to make it easier to remember which group member is the seller (S) and which group member is the buyer (B).

[24] Reg. Sec. 1.1502-13(b)(2)(i).

[25] Reg. Sec. 1.1502-13(b)(3)(i).

[26] Reg. Sec. 1.1502-13(a)(3)(i).

[27] Reg. Sec. 1.1502-13(b)(2)(ii).

[28] Reg. Sec. 1.1502-13(b)(3)(i).

- When a Buyer acquires property from a Seller and sells it to a nonmember of the affiliated group, the Buyer's gain or loss from the sale to the nonmember is a corresponding gain or loss.
- When a Buyer acquires property from a Seller and makes an installment sale of the property to a nonmember of the affiliated group, the Buyer's gain from the installment sale is a corresponding gain or loss.
- When a Buyer acquires depreciable property from a Seller, the Buyer's depreciation deductions are corresponding deductions.

Buyer's corresponding items also include disallowed losses and expenses or excluded income. Examples of such items include tax-exempt income, expenses related to the production of tax-exempt income and disallowed under Sec. 265, and losses disallowed on the distribution of appreciated property as a dividend under Sec. 311(a).[29]

In Example C8-10 below, the corresponding item is B's $50,000 gain reported on its sale of the securities. The Buyer (B) reports its corresponding item using its regular accounting method. The Seller (S) reports its intercompany item (i.e., the deferred gain) at the same time. In our example, Treasury Regulations have matched the intercompany item and the corresponding item to affect consolidated taxable income simultaneously as if the two corporations were divisions of one corporation. Although the regulations contain an acceleration rule, which requires the intercompany item and the corresponding item to be taken into account when matching can no longer produce a single entity effect, this exception to the matching rule is not needed since the Seller and Buyer remained members of the affiliated group at the time of the Buyer's sale to the unrelated party.

The Seller and Buyer report their individual parts of an intercompany transaction as if they were separate entities when calculating their separate return taxable income. For this purpose, the Seller and Buyer are treated as engaging in their actual transaction and owning any actual property involved in the transaction. The intercompany transaction rules require a recomputation of the affiliated group's gain or loss at the time a corresponding item is reported. When making the recomputation of the affiliated group's gain or loss, the Buyer takes the Seller's basis for the securities instead of the step-up in basis that normally occurs with cash sales between two related or unrelated corporations.[30]

REPORTING SELECTED INTERCOMPANY TRANSACTIONS. The reporting of the intercompany securities transaction originally illustrated in Example C8-9 is presented below in four different situations.

EXAMPLE C8-10 ▶ **Buyer sells securities to a third party at a profit.** Assume the same facts as in Example C8-9 except B sells the securities to a third party for $250,000 in 2005. If S and B are divisions of a single corporation and the sale was a transfer between the divisions, B would assume S's $120,000 basis for the securities, and the affiliated group will report a $130,000 ($250,000 proceeds − $120,000 basis) recomputed capital gain in 2005. B reports $50,000 of this gain. B's $50,000 gain is reported in its separate taxable income calculation. Since the affiliated group reported none of the $80,000 deferred gain in prior years, all the $80,000 ($130,000 − $50,000) difference between the affiliated group's total gain and B's separate taxable income gain is reported as an adjustment on the consolidated return worksheet (as illustrated in Step 2 of Table C8-1). ◀

The reporting of the two sales made by S and B in Examples C8-9 and C8-10 can be presented in the worksheet format used in the completed consolidated tax return contained in Appendix B (see worksheet below). Each transaction is initially reported in the selling (S) corporation's separate tax return column. The adjustment for the deferred gain on S's sale of the securities to B in Example C8-9 appears as a negative entry in the adjustments and eliminations column of the worksheet. The adjustment removes the $80,000 profit earned on the intercompany sale from the consolidated tax return. The adjustment for the restoration of the deferred gain when B sells the securities outside the affiliated group in Example C8-10 is reported as a positive entry in the adjustments and elimina-

[29] Reg. Sec. 1.1502-13(b)(3)(ii).

[30] Reg. Sec. 1.1502-13(c)(3).

tions column of the worksheet. The adjustment increases the profit resulting from B's sale of the securities to a third party included in the consolidated tax return from $50,000 to $130,000.

Transaction	*Consolidated Taxable Income*	*Adjustments & Eliminations*	*S Corporation's Tax Return*	*B Corporation's Tax Return*
S's sale to B in 2002	$ –0–	($80,000)	$80,000	
B's sale to a third party in 2005	130,000	80,000		$50,000
Total	$130,000	$ –0–	$80,000	$50,000

EXAMPLE C8-11 ▶ **Buyer sells securities to a third party at a loss.**[31] Assume the same facts as in Example C8-9 except the securities were instead sold by B to a third party for $190,000. The recomputed gain is $70,000 ($190,000 – $120,000). B reports a $10,000 ($190,000 – $200,000 adjusted basis) capital loss in 2005. B's $10,000 capital loss is reported in its separate taxable income calculation. Since the affiliated group reported none of the $80,000 deferred gain in prior years, all of the $80,000 ($70,000 + $10,000) difference between the affiliated group's total gain and B's separate taxable income loss is reported as an adjustment on the consolidated return worksheet. ◀

The separate return reporting of the transaction by S is the same as in Examples C8-9 and C8-10. The $50,000 capital gain that B reported when it sold the securities to a third party in Example C8-9 becomes a $10,000 capital loss because the sales price was reduced from $250,000 to $190,000. Restoration of S's $80,000 deferred gain causes the $10,000 separate return capital loss reported by B to become a $70,000 consolidated capital gain in 2005. The worksheet is as follows:

Transaction	*Consolidated Taxable Income*	*Adjustments & Eliminations*	*S Corporation's Tax Return*	*B Corporation's Tax Return*
S's sale to B in 2002	$ –0–	($80,000)	$80,000	
B's sale to a third party in 2005	70,000	80,000		($10,000)
Total	$70,000	$ –0–	$80,000	($10,000)

EXAMPLE C8-12 ▶ **Buyer sells inventory to a third party at a profit.** Assume the same facts as in Example C8-9 except the securities were instead inventory in B's hands prior to their sale for $250,000. Although S held the securities as a capital asset, the character of the reported gain is based on the character of the asset at the time it was sold by B. Both B's $80,000 gain and S's $50,000 gain are ordinary income. The consolidated return worksheet is the same as for Example C8-10 except the income character changes. ◀

EXAMPLE C8-13 ▶ Assume the same facts as in Example C8-9 except that B's $250,000 sale proceeds are from the sale of a noninventory item and are to be collected in two equal, annual installments starting in 2005. Interest at a rate acceptable to the IRS is charged on the unpaid balance. The recomputed gain and the individual group member's gains are the same as in Example C8-10. After selling the securities, B reports the transaction in its separate taxable income using the installment sale provisions of Sec. 453 applicable to nondealers. Likewise, the affiliated group does not report the entire amount of the deferred gain in 2005. Instead, the affiliated group reports the deferred gain as B collects the amounts due under the installment contract.

TYPICAL MISCONCEPTION

Even though the restoration event illustrated in Example C8-13 is based on the receipt of installment obligations, remember that intercompany sales cannot be reported by the selling group member on the installment method.

The following formula is used to determine the affiliated group's reported gain:

---

[31] Section 267(f)(2) requires a realized loss to be deferred when a sale of property occurs between members of a controlled group. Regulation Sec. 1.267(f)-1 provides special rules for property sales involving members of a controlled group that parallel the intercompany transaction rules for consolidated groups. These rules apply to the members of an affiliated group who sells property to a member of its controlled group that is unable to join in the consolidated return election. A discussion of these rules is beyond the scope of this introductory text.

$$\frac{\text{Amount of the installment payment received}}{\text{Total contract price}} \times \text{Deferred intercompany gain} = \text{Affiliated group's restored gain or loss}$$

The affiliated group reports $40,000 of the deferred gain [($125,000 ÷ $250,000) × $80,000] in each 2005 and 2006 as an adjustment to determine consolidated taxable income. B reports its $50,000 gain in two installments of $25,000 each ($50,000 ÷ 2) in 2005 and 2006 plus reporting any interest income earned on the unpaid balance. ◀

S's separate return reporting of the transaction in 2002 is the same as in Examples C8-9 through C8-11. S Corporation reports its $80,000 gain in its 2002 separate tax return. A negative $80,000 adjustment is made when preparing the 2002 consolidated tax return thereby resulting in no gain being included in consolidated taxable income. The $50,000 capital gain that B reported when it sold the securities to a third party in Example C8-9 is reported in its separate tax returns when the obligations are collected in 2005 and 2006. In summary, $25,000 of gain is recognized each year, $40,000 of the deferred gain is restored as a positive adjustment in preparing the 2005 and 2006 consolidated tax returns, and $65,000 of gain is included in consolidated taxable income in each 2005 and 2006.

Transaction	*Consolidated Taxable Income*	*Adjustments & Eliminations*	*S Corporation's Tax Return*	*B Corporation's Tax Return*
S's sale to B in 2002	$ –0–	($80,000)	$80,000	
B's sale to third party in 2005	–0–			$ –0–
B's collection of installment receivable in 2005	65,000	40,000		25,000
B's collection of installment receivable in 2006	65,000	40,000		25,000
Total	$130,000	$ –0–	$80,000	$50,000

DEPRECIATION OF RECOVERY PROPERTY BY THE BUYER. Recovery property sold between two group members in an intercompany transaction results in a continuation of the selling group member's recovery period and recovery method under the Sec. 168(i)(7) anti-churning rules to the extent the purchasing group member's basis equals or is less than the selling group member's adjusted basis. To the extent that the purchasing group member's basis exceeds the selling group member's basis, the excess is treated under Reg. Sec. 1.1502-13(c)(7) as a separate property acquired from an unrelated party. The purchasing party depreciates the step-up in basis as a new property and uses the appropriate MACRS depreciation method and recovery period. The purchaser's depreciation for the carryover portion of the basis is the same each year as the seller's depreciation would have been had the seller not sold the property. The amount of the intercompany gain attributable to the sale that the seller must report in any year (that is, the amount of the increased depreciation deduction to the group) is the amount of the depreciation deduction attributable to the purchaser's step-up in basis. This scenario is illustrated in the following example.

EXAMPLE C8-14 ▶ S and B Corporations form the S-B affiliated group. On July 1, 2000, S pays $10,000 to a nonmember of the group for machinery that under the MACRS rules is five-year property. S claims the following depreciation deductions:

Year	*Deduction*
2000	$2,000 ($10,000 × 0.20)
2001	$3,200 ($10,000 × 0.32)

On January 3, 2002, S sells the machinery to B for $9,000. All the depreciation for 2002 is allocated to B. Under the MACRS rules, the purchaser is allocated the depreciation for the month of transfer when depreciable property is transferred between related parties.[32] S's $4,200 Sec. 1245 gain ($9,000 proceeds − $4,800 adjusted basis) is deferred until B depreciates the asset.

KEY POINT

Depending on when an asset is placed in service and then sold in a deferred intercompany transaction, an asset can be divided into two pieces for depreciation purposes. These situations are covered by special anti-churning rules.

B is treated as continuing the MACRS depreciation on the $4,800 portion of the acquisition price that equals the carryover portion of S's adjusted basis for the machinery. The MACRS provisions also would apply to the $4,200 portion of the acquisition price that represents a step-up in basis (or gain portion of the basis) on B's books. B recovers the asset's $4,200 step-up in basis over five years under the MACRS rules. The amount of the capital recovery deductions claimed by B in its separate taxable income calculation and the intercompany gain or loss reported by the affiliated group as an adjustment to determine consolidated taxable income during B's holding period for the asset are as follows:[33]

ADDITIONAL COMMENT

The result of the depreciation restoration event is to synchronize the additional depreciation deductions with the restoration of the intercompany gain. Notice that the net depreciation reported in the 2004 consolidated return of $1,152 ($1,152 + $806 − $806 restored gain) is the same amount that would have been reported had S never transferred the property.

		Depreciation on			
Year		*Carryover Basis*	*Step-Up in Basis*	*Total Depreciation*	*Restoration of Deferred Gain*
2002	$10,000 × 0.1920	$1,920		$1,920	
	$ 4,200 × 0.2000		$ 840	840	$ 840
				$2,760	
2003	$10,000 × 0.1152	1,152		$1,152	
	$ 4,200 × 0.3200		1,344	1,344	1,344
				$2,496	
2004	$10,000 × 0.1152	1,152		$1,152	
	$ 4,200 × 0.1920		806	806	806
				$1,958	
2005	$10,000 × 0.0576	576		$ 576	
	$ 4,200 × 0.1152		484	484	484
				$1,060	
2006	$ 4,200 × 0.1152		484	484	484
2007	$ 4,200 × 0.0576		242	242	242
Total depreciation and restoration		$4,800	$4,200	$9,000	$4,200

The reporting of the sale of the machine by S to B and the depreciation of the machine by B in 2002 is illustrated in a worksheet similar to that used for the securities sales above. No net gain is reported on the sale of the machine in 2002. The affiliated group reports net depreciation of $1,920 ($2,760 depreciation − $840 restored gain) on the machine in 2002.

Transaction Title	*Consolidated Taxable Income*	*Adjustments & Eliminations*	*S Corporation's Tax Return*	*B Corporation's Tax Return*
Sale of the machine by S to B in 2002	$ -0-	($4,200)	$4,200	
Depreciation of the machine by B in 2002	(1,920)	840		($2,760)
Total	($1,920)	($3,360)	$4,200	($2,760)

PRACTICE NOTE

Some firms that make infrequent intercompany sales will follow the practice of making the sale at the asset's tax book value to avoid having to defer and restore a gain or loss.

S recognizes the $4,200 intercompany gain as ordinary income under Sec. 1245. A sample consolidated tax return is included in Appendix B, which includes the restoration of an intercompany gain via depreciation. ◀

32 Prop. Reg. Secs. 1.168-5(b)(4)(i) and 1.168-5(b)(2)(i)(B).

33 Intercompany sales of property that will be depreciated in the purchasing group member's hands generally result in the recognition of ordinary income under Sec. 1239 because the selling and purchasing group members are usually also members of a controlled group and, therefore, are related parties under Sec. 1239(b).

DEPARTING GROUP MEMBER. The Seller's intercompany items and Buyer's corresponding items are taken into account under the acceleration rule when they no longer can be taken into account to produce the effect of treating the two entities as divisions of a single corporation.

If the Seller leaves the affiliated group and the intercompany item originated from a sale, exchange, or distribution, the acceleration rule treats the item as having been sold by the Buyer for a cash payment equal to the Buyer's adjusted basis in the property.

EXAMPLE C8-15 ▶ Assume the same facts as in Example C8-9 except that S's stock is sold by its parent corporation on the last day of 2005, and S immediately leaves the affiliated group. B continues to be owned by its parent corporation (and S's former parent corporation). No portion of S's intercompany item has been reported in 2002-2005 prior to S's leaving the affiliated group. The affiliated group must report the $80,000 ($200,000 deemed sale price − $120,000 S's adjusted basis) intercompany gain immediately before S becomes a nonmember. B continues to report its corresponding items using its regular accounting methods. Thus, it does not recognize any gain until it sells the securities. ◀

If the S and B stock had been sold together by their parent company, the two corporations would continue to be treated as divisions of a single corporation for as long as S and B continued to file a consolidated tax return. Therefore, a deemed sale of the securities would not occur, and none of S's intercompany profit would be reported.

OTHER INTERCOMPANY TRANSACTIONS

SELF-STUDY QUESTION

Why are the other intercompany transactions not given any special treatment?

ANSWER

Because both sides of the transaction are reported in the same consolidated return, they simply net each other out. If, due to accounting method differences, the items would be reported in different tax periods, both the income and deduction must be reported in the later of the two tax years.

Any income, gain, deduction, or loss realized or incurred on other intercompany transactions is included in the income and expense classifications for the tax year in which the transaction is ordinarily reported. Both parties report their sides of the transaction in determining separate taxable income.[34] When both parties use the same accounting method, these amounts net to zero because the income and expense are included in consolidated taxable income.

Section 267(a)(2) imposes a special rule on related party transactions requiring the matching of the recognition of the payer's deduction item and the payee's income item. Thus, when two group members would ordinarily report the income and deduction items in different consolidated return years under their regular accounting methods, the payer must defer the reporting of the deduction until the tax year in which the payee member reports the income.

Section 267(b)(3) includes two corporations that are members of the same controlled group as related parties. This definition includes most members of affiliated groups, whether separate returns or consolidated returns are filed. It also may include certain corporations that are not included in the affiliated group because they are not includible corporations (for example, brother-sister corporations included in a combined controlled group).

Regulation Sec. 1.1502-2(b)(1) requires the two group members to match the income and expense items as if they were incurred by two divisions of a single corporation. As two divisions, S and B would report a recomputed expense amount of zero (i.e., the income of one division would exactly offset the expense of the other division, so that neither income or loss would be reported to external parties). Because S's intercompany items are recognized when B's corresponding item is incurred, amounts earned by S from an intercompany transaction can be included in the consolidated tax return before they are taken into account under its separate entity method of accounting.

EXAMPLE C8-16 ▶ S and B Corporations have filed calendar year consolidated tax returns for several years. S and B Corporations use the accrual method of accounting. S lends B $100,000 on March 1, 2002; this debt and the related interest are unpaid at the end of 2002. Interest is charged by S at an

[34] Reg. Sec. 1.1502-13(b)(1) and (2). This procedure may be contrasted with financial accounting, in which both sides of the transaction are eliminated in preparing the consolidated financial statements.

annual rate of 12%. The $10,000 interest charge owed at year-end is paid by B on March 1, 2003. S accrues $10,000 of interest income in 2002, and B accrues $10,000 of interest expense in 2002. S and B Corporations report the interest income and expense in a worksheet format similar to that used for the earlier intercompany sales. No net income or loss is reported in the consolidated tax return as a result of the loan being made by S in 2002.

Transaction	*Consolidated Taxable Income*	*Adjustments & Eliminations*	*S Corporation's Tax Return*	*B Corporation's Tax Return*
Accrual of interest expense by B in 2002	($10,000)			($10,000)
Accrual of interest income by S in 2002	10,000		$10,000	
Total	$ -0-		$10,000	($10,000)

◀

EXAMPLE C8-17 ▶ Assume the same facts as in Example C8-16 except that S Corporation is a cash method of accounting taxpayer. Ordinarily, S, a cash method corporation, would report no interest income and B, an accrual method corporation, would report $10,000 of interest expense in the computation of their separate taxable incomes for 2002's consolidated tax return. Because B has reported $10,000 of interest expense in its separate return and the recomputed expense amount is zero, an adjustment must be made to report $10,000 of interest income in the 2002 consolidated tax return even though S has yet to receive a payment from B. After the adjustment, the income and expense items are matched within the 2002 consolidated tax return, and no "net" interest income or expense is reported. ◀

In 2002, B normally would report its $10,000 of interest expense related to the loan using its overall accrual method of accounting. The consolidated tax return Treasury Regulations require B to defer the $10,000 of interest income from 2002 to 2003. At this time, S will report $10,000 of interest income from the loan and B likewise will report its $10,000 interest expense. The consolidated return regulations require B to defer the reporting of its tax deduction until the point in time when B reports its interest income. The consolidated return worksheet is as follows:

Transaction	*Consolidated Taxable Income*	*Adjustments & Eliminations*	*S Corporation's Tax Return*	*B Corporation's Tax Return*
Interest expense reported by B in 2002	$ -0-			$ -0-
Interest income reported by S in 2002	-0-		$ -0-	
Interest income reported by S in 2003	10,000		10,000	
Interest expense reported by S in 2003	(10,000)			(10,000)
Total	$ -0-		$10,000	($10,000)

At the end of the two years, $10,000 of income is reported in S's separate tax return, $10,000 of expense is reported in B's tax return. These two amounts net to the same zero amount reported in Example C8-16 when both taxpayers were accrual method corporations.

A Seller's profit or loss from the sale of the capitalized services to another group member is an intercompany item. When a Buyer capitalizes the acquisition cost of the services, the Buyer's amortization deduction becomes the corresponding item. Thus, Buyer's capitalization of the purchase under its separate method of accounting permits the Seller to spread the recognition of its profit, which otherwise would be recognized under its separate method of accounting, over the amortization time period.

EXAMPLE C8-18 ▶ S and B Corporations have filed consolidated tax returns for a number of years. S Corporation, an accrual method of accounting taxpayer, drills wells. B Corporation, operates a farm, and uses the cash method of accounting. S drills a well in 2002 for B for $10,000, which creates a $2,000 profit. B pays S the cost of the well, capitalizes the well cost, and begins to amortize it over a five-year period. Under the accrual method of accounting, S would report its income and expenses when the drilling occurred. Because it is an intercompany transaction, S reports its profit over the five-year amortization period used by B.

Transaction	*Consolidated Taxable Income*	*Adjustments & Eliminations*	*S Corporation's Tax Return*	*B Corporation's Tax Return*
Amortization of well-drilling cost by B in 2002	($2,000)			($2,000)
Accrual of well-drilling income by S in 2002	2,000	($8,000)	$10,000	
Total	$ -0-	($8,000)	$10,000	($2,000) ◀

Topic Review C8-1 summarizes the intercompany transaction rules.

Topic Review C8-1

Reporting Intercompany Transactions

INTERCOMPANY TRANSACTIONS

1. Intercompany transaction definition: a transaction taking place during a consolidated return year between corporations that are members of the same affiliated group immediately after the transaction.
2. There are two types of intercompany transactions: property transactions and other intercompany transactions.
   a. Property transactions—the intercompany item (gain or loss) is deferred until a corresponding event occurs.
   b. Other transactions—the intercompany item (income or expense item) is reported in the year in which the corresponding event occurs.
3. The selling and buying members of the affiliated group generally are treated as separate entities when reporting the intercompany transaction.
   a. **Exception:** the selling and buying members are treated as two divisions of the same entity when determining the recomputed corresponding gain, income, loss, or deduction item.
4. The reporting of intercompany transactions are based on two concepts.
   a. **Intercompany items** are the Seller's income, gain, deduction, or loss from an intercompany transaction.
   b. **Corresponding items** are the Buyer's income, gain, deduction or loss from an intercompany transaction, or from property acquired in an intercompany transaction.
5. The following are some of the corresponding items that can trigger the recognition of an intercompany item (e.g., gain, loss, income, or deduction amount).
   a. Property is sold by the Buyer to a nonmember of the group.
   b. Property acquired by the Buyer is depreciated, depleted, or amortized.
   c. The corporation that sold a property or owns a property leaves the affiliated group.
   d. The affiliated group discontinues filing a consolidated tax return and begins filing separate tax returns.

DIVIDENDS RECEIVED BY GROUP MEMBERS

SELF-STUDY QUESTION

Are dividends received from members of the same affiliated group entitled to a dividends-received deduction?

ANSWER

Not if the affiliated group is filing a consolidated tax return because intercompany dividends are excluded; hence, no dividends-received deduction is necessary.

TYPICAL MISCONCEPTION

One difference between consolidated tax returns and separate tax returns is that, in a consolidated setting, intercompany distributions exceeding both E&P and basis in the shareholder member's stock investment do not create a capital gain but rather create an excess loss account (i.e., a negative basis account for the distributee's investment in the distributing corporation).

REAL WORLD EXAMPLE

When each corporation within an affiliated group prepares its own separate tax return, dividends received from related corporations may be included in gross income. In such a situation, a worksheet adjustment is then needed during the consolidation process to remove the dividend from consolidated taxable income.

Dividends received by group members are treated differently depending on whether they come from corporations within the affiliated group or from firms outside it. In determining consolidated taxable income, the dividends received from other group members are excluded, while those received from nonmembers of the group are eligible for a 70%, 80%, or 100% dividends-received deduction.

EXCLUSION PROCEDURE

A dividend distribution from one group member (the distributing member) to a second group member (the distributee member) during a consolidated return year is an intercompany transaction. An intercompany distribution is not included in the gross income of the distributee member. The exclusion applies only to distributions that otherwise would be taxable if paid to a non-affiliated corporation and which produce a corresponding negative adjustment to the basis of the distributing member's stock.[35] Such an adjustment is illustrated in Step 2 of Table C8-1.

Within an affiliated group, nondividend distributions (e.g., a distribution made when there is no earnings and profits balance) reduce the distributee member's basis in the distributing member's stock.[36] If the amount of the distribution exceeds the distributee's adjusted basis in the stock, the excess either creates a new, or increases an existing, **excess loss account** (i.e., a negative investment account). However, the distributee does not recognize any gain from the portion of the distribution that exceeds its basis in the distributing member's stock (as it would with nonaffiliated corporations).[37] The creation of an excess loss account is discussed in the basis adjustment section of this chapter.

The amount of any distribution received by one group member from another equals the money distributed plus the sum of the adjusted basis of any property distributed and the gain recognized by the distributing member. Because under Sec. 311(b) gain is recognized on most distributions of appreciated property, the gain recognized plus the adjusted basis of the distributed property generally will equal its FMV where a distribution of appreciated property takes place between group members. Gain recognized by the distributing member under Sec. 311(b) due to the distribution of property to another group member is treated as an intercompany item. The deferred gain is included in consolidated taxable income by the distributing member when a corresponding item is reported by the distributee (e.g., the distributee member begins to depreciate the property).[38]

CONSOLIDATED DIVIDENDS-RECEIVED DEDUCTION

The basic dividends-received deduction rules, as set forth in Chapter C3, apply to the calculation of the consolidated dividends-received deduction. The dividends-received deduction for dividends received from nonmembers is computed on a consolidated basis. It is not applied to the separate taxable income of each group member. The consolidated dividends-received deduction equals the sum of 70% of dividends received from unaffiliated domestic corporations in which a less than 20% interest is held, 80% of dividends received from unaffiliated domestic corporations in which a 20% or more interest is held, and 100% of dividends received from an 80% or more owned domestic corporation that is not included in the consolidated return election (e.g., a 100%-owned life insurance company prohibited from being part of a consolidated tax return). The 70% and 80% dividends-received deductions are separately limited by consolidated taxable income. The 80% dividends-received deduction limitation is calculated first, and the deduction cannot exceed 80% of consolidated taxable income excluding the consolidated dividends-

[35] Reg. Sec. 1.1502-13(f)(2).

[36] Reg. Sec. 1.1502-13(f)(7).

[37] Reg. Sec. 1.1502-14(a)(2). The amount of the excess loss account's negative balance is reported as either ordinary income or capital gain when a disposition of the subsidiary corporation's stock occurs.

[38] Reg. Secs. 1.1502-13(f).

received deduction, any consolidated NOL, or capital loss carryback. The 70% dividends-received deduction limitation is then calculated and the deduction cannot exceed 70% of consolidated taxable income reduced by the amount of the dividends eligible for the 80% dividends-received deduction and excluding the consolidated dividends-received deduction, any consolidated NOL, or capital loss carryback. The limitations do not apply if the full amount of the deduction creates or increases a consolidated NOL.[39]

EXAMPLE C8-19 ▶ P, S_1, and S_2 Corporations create the P-S_1-S_2 affiliated group. Consolidated taxable income (without considering any dividends-received exclusions or deductions, NOLs, and capital losses) is $200,000. The following dividend income is received by the group members from unaffiliated corporations that are less than 20%-owned: P, $6,000; S_1, $10,000; and S_2, $34,000. In addition, P receives a $40,000 dividend from S_1, and S_1 receives a $60,000 dividend from a 100%-owned life insurance company that cannot join in the consolidated return election at the present time. S_1's distribution reduces P's basis for its investment in S_1.

- The $40,000 dividend that P receives from S_1 is excluded from P's gross income since it results in a basis reduction for P's investment in S_1.
- S_1's $60,000 dividend from the 100%-owned life insurance company is eligible for a 100% dividends-received deduction. This $60,000 deduction is not subject to any limitation and reduces consolidated taxable income before applying the 70% limitation.
- The 70% dividends-received deductions included in the separate taxable income calculations are P, $4,200 (0.70 × $6,000); S_1, $7,000 (0.70 × $10,000); and S_2, $23,800 (0.70 × $34,000), or a total $35,000 reduction in consolidated taxable income. The 70% dividends-received deduction ($35,000) is not restricted by the dividends-received deduction limitation [($200,000 consolidated taxable income given in the facts − $60,000 dividends-received deduction) × 0.70 = $98,000].

The consolidated dividends-received deduction is $95,000 ($35,000 + $60,000). ◀

SELF-STUDY QUESTION

What is the dividends-received deduction in Example C8-19 if the group has consolidated taxable income before special deductions of (a) $95,000? (b) $94,999?

ANSWER

(a) $84,500 [$60,000 + (0.70 × $35,000)] due to the consolidated taxable income limitation.
(b) All $95,000 ($60,000 + $35,000) is allowed because the full dividends-received deduction creates an NOL. Should a $1 difference in consolidated taxable income make a $10,500 difference in the dividends-received deduction?

STOP & THINK *Question:* Alpha Corporation has owned the stock of a subsidiary for a number of years. Peter Gray, the CPA, who has prepared both corporations' tax returns since their creation has been trying to sell Alpha's Director of Federal Taxes on beginning to file a consolidated tax return based on the tax exemption for intragroup dividends. Is he right or wrong in his approach?

Solution: He is wrong. If the two companies file separate tax returns, a 100% dividends-received deduction is available for intragroup dividends. If a consolidated return were filed, the dividend can be excluded from Alpha's gross income. Typically, these two alternatives provide the same outcome. A difference between these two alternatives may be found when preparing state tax returns (see page C8-35). Peter should be concentrating on advantages such as offsetting profits and losses between the two companies should one company incur a loss, deferring intercompany profits, etc. (see pages C8-4 and C8-5).

CONSOLIDATED CHARITABLE CONTRIBUTIONS DEDUCTION

The basic charitable contributions deduction rules, as set forth in Chapter C3, apply to the calculation of the consolidated charitable contribution deduction. The affiliated group's charitable contributions deduction is computed on a consolidated basis. The consolidated charitable contributions deduction equals the sum of the charitable contributions deductions of the individual group members for the consolidated return year (computed without regard to any individual group member's limitation) plus any charitable contribution carryovers from earlier consolidated or separate return years. The charitable contributions deduction is limited to 10% of adjusted consolidated taxable income.

KEY POINT

Determining the charitable contribution deduction on a consolidated basis rather than for each corporation separately may or may not be beneficial. The outcome depends on the actual numbers in each individual situation.

[39] Reg. Sec. 1.1502-26(a)(1).

Adjusted consolidated taxable income is computed without regard to the consolidated dividends-received deduction, any consolidated NOL or capital loss carrybacks, and the consolidated charitable contributions deduction. Any charitable contributions made by the group that exceeds the 10% limitation carry over to the five succeeding tax years.[40] Any unused contributions remaining at the end of the carryover period are lost.

EXAMPLE C8-20 ▶ P, S_1, and S_2 Corporations form the P-S_1-S_2 affiliated group. The group members report the following charitable contributions and adjusted consolidated taxable income for 2002:

Group Member	*Charitable Contributions*	*Adjusted Consolidated Taxable Income*
P	$12,500	$150,000
S_1	5,000	(40,000)
S_2	2,000	10,000
Total	$19,500	$120,000

The P-S_1-S_2 affiliated group's charitable contributions deduction is the lesser of its actual charitable contributions ($19,500) or 10% of its adjusted consolidated taxable income ($12,000). The $7,500 ($19,500 − $12,000) of excess charitable contributions carry over to tax years 2003 through 2007. ◀

A member leaving the affiliated group takes with it any excess contributions arising in a prior separate return year plus its allocable share of any excess consolidated charitable contributions for a consolidated return year. The excess consolidated charitable contributions are allocated to each group member based on the relative amount of their contributions (when compared to the total contributions of all group members) for the consolidated return year.

NET OPERATING LOSSES (NOLs)

OBJECTIVE 8

Calculate an affiliated group's consolidated NOL

One advantage of filing a consolidated tax return is the ability of an affiliated group to offset one member's current NOLs against the taxable income of other group members. If these losses cause the affiliated group to report a consolidated NOL, the NOL may be carried back or carried forward to other consolidated return years of the affiliated group. In some cases, part or all of the consolidated NOL can be carried back or carried over to separate return years of the individual group members. NOLs of group members arising in separate return years also may be carried back or carried over to consolidated return years, subject to the separate return limitation year (SRLY) limit. In addition, NOLs, capital losses, and excess credits of a loss corporation that is a member of an affiliated group can be subject to the consolidated Sec. 382-384 limitations. The rules that apply to carrybacks and carryovers are examined below.

CURRENT YEAR NOLs

KEY POINT

Generally, the most significant benefit to filing consolidated tax returns is the ability to offset losses of one member against the income of other members.

Each member's separate taxable income is combined to determine combined taxable income before any adjustment is made for NOL carryovers (see Table C8-1).[41] The combining process allows the losses of one group member to offset the taxable income of other group members. A group member cannot elect separately to carry back its own losses from a consolidated return year to one of its earlier profitable separate return years. Only the consolidated group's NOL (if any) may be carried back or over.

[40] Reg. Sec. 1.1502-24(a).

[41] Reg. Sec. 1.1502-12(h).

EXAMPLE C8-21 ▶ P and S Corporations form the P-S affiliated group. During 2001, the initial year of operation, P and S file calendar year separate tax returns. Beginning in 2002, the P-S group elects to file a consolidated tax return. P and S report the following results for 2001 and 2002:

Group Member	Taxable Income 2001	Taxable Income 2002
P	($15,000)	$40,000
S	250,000	(27,000)
Consolidated taxable income	N/A	$13,000

N/A = Not applicable

P's 2001 NOL may not be used to offset S's 2001 profits because separate returns were filed. This NOL carryover may be used only to reduce the $13,000 of 2002 consolidated taxable income reported after S's 2002 loss is offset against P's 2002 separate taxable income. Because S's 2002 loss must be offset against P's 2002 taxable income, S cannot carry its 2002 NOL back against its 2001 taxable income to increase the value of the tax savings obtained from the loss. The remaining NOL carryover of $2,000 ($15,000 loss from 2001 − $13,000 2002 consolidated taxable income) carries over to 2003. ◀

OBJECTIVE 9

Calculate the carryback or carryover of a consolidated NOL

CARRYBACKS AND CARRYFORWARDS OF CONSOLIDATED NOLs

The consolidated NOL rules are similar to the NOL rules applying to a corporation filing a separate tax return. A consolidated NOL is determined after the following computation:[42]

Separate taxable income of each group member (from Table C8-1)
Plus: Consolidated capital gain net income
Minus: Consolidated Sec. 1231 net loss
Consolidated charitable contributions deduction
Consolidated dividends-received deduction

Consolidated NOL

A consolidated NOL incurred in a tax year beginning after August 5, 1997 may be carried back to the two preceding consolidated return years or carried over to the 20 succeeding consolidated return years. The parent corporation also may elect for the affiliated group to relinquish the entire carryback period for a consolidated NOL and use it only as a carryforward to succeeding years.[43] (See Chapter C3 for a discussion of the reasons for making this election and how this election is made.)

TYPICAL MISCONCEPTION

A consolidated NOL incurred in 1998 and later years may be carried back two years and carried forward 20 years. This procedure is not complicated unless the members of the group change before the loss is fully used.

A carryback or carryforward of the consolidated NOL to a tax year in which the members of the affiliated group have not changed poses no real problem. The amount of the consolidated NOL absorbed in a given tax year is determined according to the basic Sec. 172 rules for NOLs outlined in Chapter C3.

Determining the amount of the consolidated NOL that may be absorbed in a tax year is more difficult when the group members are not the same in the carryback or carryforward year. In such a case, the consolidated NOL is apportioned to each corporation that was both a member of the affiliated group and incurred a separate NOL during the loss year. When a loss corporation is not also a group member in the carryback or carryforward year, the rules relating to carrybacks and carryforwards to separate return years (discussed below) must be applied.

CARRYBACK OF CONSOLIDATED NOL TO SEPARATE RETURN YEAR

GENERAL RULE. A consolidated NOL may be carried back and absorbed against a member's taxable income from the preceding two separate return years. To effect a carryback, part or all of the consolidated NOL must be apportioned to the member. To the extent

[42] Reg. Sec. 1.1502-21(e). NOLs incurred in tax years beginning on or before August 5, 1997 are carried back three years and forward 15 years.

[43] Reg. Sec. 1.1502-21(b)(3)(i).

a member uses its allocable share of the consolidated NOL, such an amount is not available to the remaining members as a carryback or carryforward to a consolidated return year. The consolidated NOL is apportioned to a loss member in the following manner:[44]

$$\frac{\text{Separate NOL of the individual member}}{\text{Sum of the separate NOLs incurred by all members having such losses}} \times \text{Consolidated NOL} = \text{Portion of consolidated NOL attributable to member}$$

EXAMPLE C8-22 ▶ P and S Corporations form the P-S affiliated group. The P-S group files separate tax returns in 2000 and 2001. S reports taxable income of $275,000 in 2000. The group elects to file a consolidated tax return for 2002. The P-S group reports a $150,000 consolidated NOL for 2002, all of which is attributable to S. S carries the $150,000 NOL back to 2000 and uses the loss to partially offset the taxable income it reported in 2000. The loss is used up in 2000 and therefore cannot be used by S in 2001 or by the P-S group in any subsequent consolidated return year. Alternatively, an election by P to forgo the carryback permits the loss to be used in 2003 and any subsequent consolidated return year. ◀

KEY POINT

In Example C8-22, because P-S did not file a consolidated tax return in 2000, P must either forgo the two-year carryback or allow all the consolidated NOL to be carried back to S's 2000 separate tax return year.

SPECIAL CARRYBACK RULE FOR NEW MEMBERS. When the consolidated NOL is apportioned to a member, it normally is carried back to the two immediately preceding consolidated return years or the loss corporation's separate return years. A special rule permits an affiliated group member to carry an NOL back two years to a separate return year of its common parent corporation or a consolidated return year of the affiliated group if

- ▶ The member corporation with the loss carryback did not exist in the carryback year, and
- ▶ The loss corporation has been a member of the affiliated group continually since its organization.

If these two requirements are met, the portion of the consolidated NOL attributable to the loss member is carried back to the two preceding consolidated return years of the affiliated group (or separate return year of the common parent corporation) only if the common parent was not a member of a different consolidated group or affiliated group filing separate returns for the year to which the loss is carried or a subsequent year in the carryback period.[45]

EXAMPLE C8-23 ▶ P, S_1, and S_2 Corporations form the P-S_1-S_2 affiliated group. P and S_1 are affiliated for 2000 and 2001 and file consolidated tax returns. P acquires all of S_2 Corporation's stock on January 1, 2002, the date on which S_2 is created by P. P, S_1, and S_2 report the following results (excluding NOL deductions) for 2000 through 2002:

Group Member	*Taxable Income 2000*	*2001*	*2002*
P	$12,000	$10,000	$16,000
S_1	8,000	7,000	4,000
S_2	XXX	XXX	(30,000)
Consolidated taxable income	$20,000	$17,000	($10,000)

All the 2002 consolidated NOL is attributable to S_2. As illustrated, S_2's separate NOL of $30,000 is first used to offset P and S_1's taxable income in 2002 leaving only a $10,000 consoli-

SELF-STUDY QUESTION

What is the reason for allowing S_2's portion of the consolidated NOL to be carried back to 2000 and 2001?

ANSWER

Because the assets that make up S_2 Corporation in 2002 were really P's assets in 2000 and 2001, it only makes sense to allow the NOLs to be carried back against whatever tax return P filed in 2000 and 2001.

---

[44] Reg. Sec. 1.1502-21(b)(2)(iv). The member's separate NOL is determined in a manner similar to the calculation of separate taxable income except for a series of adjustments to account for the member's share of the consolidated charitable contributions and dividends-received deductions, the member's capital gain net income, and the member's net capital loss or Sec. 1231 net loss minus any portion of the consolidated amounts attributable to the member that were absorbed currently.

[45] Reg. Sec. 1.1502-21(b)(2)(ii)(B). A consolidated group is an affiliated group that has elected to file a consolidated tax return.

dated NOL. Two options are available with respect to the consolidated NOL: the NOL may be carried over to subsequent tax years, or the NOL may be carried back to 2000 and 2001. If the first alternative is selected, the NOL offsets consolidated taxable income reported in 2003 and up to 19 subsequent tax years. If the second alternative is selected, the $10,000 NOL is carried back to offset part of the 2000 consolidated taxable income. This result is possible because S_2 did not exist at the end of 2001 and because it joined the affiliated group immediately after it was created on January 1, 2002 and has been a group member continually since its organization. ◀

If the loss corporation is not a member of the affiliated group immediately after its organization, that member's portion of the consolidated NOL is carried back only to its prior separate return years.

EXAMPLE C8-24 ▶

SELF-STUDY QUESTION

Is there any reason for P to elect not to carry back the NOL to S_2's separate tax return years?

ANSWER

Probably not. But if S_2 has minority shareholders, because the refund is issued to S_2, the minority stock interest will share in the increase in FMV of S_2's stock. Don't overlook minority shareholders!

Assume the same facts as in Example C8-23 except S_2 Corporation files a separate tax return for 2001 prior to its stock being acquired by P on January 1, 2002. P, S_1, and S_2 report the following results (excluding NOL deductions) for 2000 through 2002:

Group Member	Taxable Income 2000	2001	2002
P	$12,000	$10,000	$16,000
S_1	8,000	7,000	4,000
S_2	XXX	8,000	(30,000)
Consolidated taxable income	$20,000	$17,000[a]	($10,000)

[a] Including only the results of P and S_1.

All the 2002 consolidated NOL can be carried back by S_2 to 2001. The $10,000 NOL offsets all of S_2's 2001 separate return taxable income of $8,000. The remaining loss carryback of $2,000 cannot be used to reduce the taxable income reported in 2000 or 2001 by P and S_1. It can be carried forward to offset the affiliated group's 2003 and later taxable income. Alternatively, the P-S_1-S_2 affiliated group could elect to carry the entire loss forward to offset 2003 and later years taxable income (see Chapter C3's discussion regarding why such an election might be advisable). ◀

CARRYFORWARD OF CONSOLIDATED NOL TO SEPARATE RETURN YEAR

If a corporation ceases to be a member of the affiliated group during the current year, the portion of the consolidated NOL allocable to the departing member becomes the member's separate carryforward. However, the allocation of the NOL to the departing group member cannot be made until the available carryover is absorbed in the current consolidated return year. This requirement exists even when all of the carryover is attributable to the departing member. The departing member's share of the NOL carryforward then may be used in its first separate return year.[46]

EXAMPLE C8-25 ▶

P, S_1, and S_2 Corporations form the P-S_1-S_2 affiliated group, with P owning all the S_1 and S_2 stock. The group files consolidated tax returns for several years. At the close of business on September 30, 2002, P sells its investment in S_1. S_1 must file a separate tax return covering the period October 1, 2002 through December 31, 2002. During pre-2002 tax years, P, S_1, and S_2 incur substantial NOLs. At the beginning of 2002, a consolidated NOL carryforward of $100,000 is still available. Two-thirds of this loss is allocable to S_1; the remainder is allocable to S_2. The affiliated group reports the following results (excluding NOL deductions) for 2002:

TYPICAL MISCONCEPTION

In Example C8-25, it is important to understand that the group is entitled to use the consolidated NOL before S_1 determines its NOL carryforward. This can have an impact on negotiating an equitable purchase price for S_1.

Group Member		Taxable Income
P		$20,000
S_1:	January 1 through September 30	30,000
	October 1 through December 31	15,000
S_2		10,000
Total		$75,000

The consolidated NOL carryforward of $100,000 offsets the $60,000 ($20,000 + $30,000 + $10,000) of taxable income reported by P, S_1, and S_2 in their 2002 consolidated tax return. This

[46] Reg. Sec. 1.1502-21(b)(2)(ii)(A).

leaves $40,000 of carryforward to be allocated between S_1 and S_2. S_1 receives $26,667 (0.667 × $40,000), and S_2 receives $13,333 (0.333 × $40,000) of the carryforward. Of S_1's carryforward, $15,000 can be used in its separate tax return for the period ending December 31, 2002. The remainder is carried over to S_1's 2003 separate tax return. The affiliated group can carry forward S_2's $13,333 allocable share of the NOL to 2003 and subsequent years. ◀

OBJECTIVE 10

Determine how the special loss limitations restrict the use of separate and consolidated NOL carrybacks and carryovers

SPECIAL LOSS LIMITATIONS

Two special loss limitations, the **separate return limitation year (SRLY) rules** and the **Sec. 382 loss limitation rules**, are imposed on affiliated groups. The SRLY rules limit the separate return NOL amount that can be deducted as a NOL carryback or carryover by an affiliated group to a member's contribution to consolidated taxable income.[47] This treatment prevents the affiliated group from offsetting its current taxable income by purchasing loss corporations solely to use their NOLs. The Sec. 382 loss limitation rules, which were explained in Chapter C7 on a separate return basis, also apply to affiliated groups filing consolidated returns. The special Sec. 382 consolidated return rules restrict an affiliated group from using NOLs following an ownership change that results from a purchase transaction or a tax-free reorganization. Each set of rules is explained below.

KEY POINT

The SRLY rules are used to limit a group from acquiring already existing losses and offsetting those losses against the group's income.

SEPARATE RETURN LIMITATION YEAR RULES. A member incurring an NOL in a separate return year (that is available as a carryback or a carryforward to a consolidated return year) is subject to a limit on the use of the NOL when the loss year is designated a separate return limitation year. A **separate return limitation year** is defined as any separate return year, except

- A separate return year of the group member designated as the parent corporation for the consolidated return year to which the tax attribute (e.g., NOL) is carried, or
- A separate return year of any corporation that was a group member for every day of the loss year (i.e., a consolidated return was not elected or the corporation was not eligible to participate in the filing of a consolidated return in the loss year).

ADDITIONAL COMMENT

These two exceptions to the SRLY rules exist because in both cases the group has not acquired already existing NOLs.

NOL Carryforwards. An NOL incurred in an SRLY may be used as a carryforward in a consolidated return year equal to the lesser of (1) the aggregate of the consolidated taxable income amounts for all consolidated return years of the group determined by taking into account only the loss member's items of income, gain, deduction, and loss minus any NOL carryovers previously absorbed, (2) consolidated taxable income, or (3) the amount of the NOL carryforward.[48] A SRLY carryover cannot be used when a member's cumulative contribution is less than zero. Any NOL carryovers or carrybacks that cannot be used currently because of the member's contribution to consolidated taxable income or the group's current year consolidated taxable income must be carried over to subsequent tax years.

EXAMPLE C8-26 ▶ P and S Corporations form the P-S affiliated group. P acquires the S stock shortly after its creation in mid-2002.[49] P and S file separate tax returns for 2002 and begin filing a consolidated tax return in 2003. The group reports the following results (excluding NOL deductions) for 2002 through 2006:

Group Member	Taxable Income 2002	2003	2004	2005	2006
P	($ 9,000)	$17,000	$ 6,000	($6,000)	$ 2,000
S	(20,000)	(2,000)	5,000	5,000	16,000
Consolidated taxable income	$ XXX	$15,000	$11,000	($1,000)	$18,000

SELF-STUDY QUESTION

What is the consequence of having losses subject to the SRLY limitations?

ANSWER

The effect of having a loss tainted as a SRLY loss is that it can be used only to offset taxable income of the subsidiary member (or possibly loss subgroup) that created the NOL.

[47] The SRLY rules do not apply to the foreign tax credit, the general business credit, the minimum tax credit, and overall foreign losses for corporations joining the affiliated group.

[48] Reg. Sec. 1.1502-21(b)(1). Any unused NOLs that are carried to the consolidated return year from tax years ending before the separate return limitation year reduce the SRLY limitation on a first-in, first-out (FIFO) basis. Tax years ending on the same date reduce the SRLY limitations on a pro rata basis. A loss member's contribution to CTI is determined on a "with" and "without" basis. The difference between CTI "with" the loss member and "without" the loss member is the loss member's contribution to CTI.

[49] P's acquisition of the S stock can trigger both the SRLY rules and the Sec. 382 rules. The overlap rules have not yet been discussed. To simplify the example, assume that the Sec. 382 limitation does not apply.

Under the SRLY rules, the separate NOLs are used as follows:

- P's 2002 loss is offset against the group's $15,000 of 2003 consolidated taxable income (CTI). None of S's 2002 loss can be used because it incurred a separate NOL in 2003, which already has been offset against P's $17,000 profit. The group's 2003 CTI is reduced to $6,000 ($15,000 − $9,000).
- $3,000 of S's 2002 loss is offset against 2004 CTI: the smaller of S's $3,000 cumulative contribution to CTI [($2,000) + $5,000], its $20,000 NOL carryover, or the $11,000 of CTI. The $3,000 of NOL used reduces S's NOL carryover to $17,000.
- None of S's 2002 loss can be used in 2005 because the group reported a consolidated NOL. Assuming the 2005 NOL is carried back, 2003's CTI is reduced from $6,000 to $5,000 ($15,000 − $9,000 carryover from 2002 − $1,000 carryback from 2005).
- $17,000 of S's 2002 loss is offset against 2006 CTI, which is the smaller of S's $21,000 cumulative contributions to CTI in 2003–2006 ($24,000 net contributions to CTI in 2003–2006 − $3,000 NOL used in 2004), its $17,000 remaining loss carryover, or the $18,000 of CTI. Consolidated taxable income is reduced to $1,000 ($18,000 − $17,000), and no carryovers remain to 2007. ◀

The SRLY rules generally apply to each individual corporation that has a loss carryover from a separate return limitation year. The SRLY limitation must be determined for a subgroup of two or more corporations within an affiliated group that are continuously affiliated after ceasing to be members of a former affiliated group, that joined the affiliated group at the same time, and where at least one of the corporations carries over losses from the former group to the current group. If the subgroup has remained continuously affiliated up to the beginning of the year to which the loss is carried, the subgroup's loss carryovers can be used to the extent the subgroup contributes to consolidated taxable income.[50]

EXAMPLE C8-27 ▶ P and S Corporations have filed consolidated tax returns together for a number of years. At the close of business on December 31, 2002, A Corporation purchases all of P's stock. The taxable income for P, S, and A Corporations for 2002 and 2003 are as follows:

	Taxable Income	
Group Member	*2002*	*2003*
A	xxx	$120
P	$100	40
S	(250)	30
CTI	($150)	$190

P and S are a subgroup when calculating the use of the SRLY losses in 2003. Their $150 NOL can be used to the extent of the smaller of their contribution to CTI ($70 = $40 + $30), the NOL carryover ($150), or CTI ($190), or $70. The remaining $80 NOL ($150 − $70) is carried over to 2004, and the subgroup rules are applied again. ◀

KEY POINT

The SRLY rules apply to both carryforwards and carrybacks. Remember that SRLYs stem from either a year in which a member files a separate return or a year in which a member joins in the filing of a consolidated return with a different affiliated group.

NOL Carrybacks. The SRLY rules also apply to NOL carrybacks from a separate return limitation year to a consolidated return year. For example, assume that S Corporation in Example C8-26 leaves the P-S group at the end of 2004. Any NOL that S incurs in a subsequent separate return year (2005) that is carried back to the 2003 consolidated return year is subject to the SRLY rules. Its use is restricted under the SRLY rules to S's contribution to consolidated taxable income for all consolidated return years. However, S has not provided a contribution to consolidated taxable income in those years and would be prevented from using the carryback in those earlier years.

The use of built-in deductions also is limited by the SRLY rules. A **built-in deduction** is a deduction that accrues in a separate return year but is recognized for tax purposes in a consolidated return year. One example of such a deduction is the depreciation connected with a subsidiary corporation's asset that declines in value between the time it was

[50] Reg. Sec. 1.1502-21(c)(2)(i). This rule holds only if the losses were non-SRLY losses to the former affiliated group.

ADDITIONAL COMMENT

The built-in deduction rules eliminate the ability to circumvent the SRLY rules by acquiring a corporation with losses that have economically accrued and having these losses recognized after the subsidiary is a member of the group.

acquired in a separate return year and the beginning of the initial consolidated return year. Built-in deductions also can result from the sale of a capital or noncapital asset at a loss in a consolidated return year when the decline in value takes place in a prior separate return year. For example, S purchases inventory in a separate return year for $60,000. The inventory declines to a $45,000 FMV before the time P purchases the S stock and the two corporations start filing on a consolidated basis. The $15,000 ($60,000 − $45,000) built-in deduction can be deducted by S when it sells the inventory only if its SRLY limitation equals or exceeds the built-in deduction amount.[51]

SECTION 382 LOSS LIMITATION. Section 382 prevents the purchase of assets or stock of a corporation having loss carryovers (known as the loss corporation) where a substantial portion of the purchase price is related to the acquisition of the corporation's tax attributes.[52] Trafficking in NOLs and other tax attributes is prevented by applying the Sec. 382 loss limitation to any tax year ending after the ownership change. The 50 percentage point minimum stock ownership change needed to trigger the Sec. 382 rules can occur in acquisitive transactions involving a single corporation or a group of corporations that file separate or consolidated returns. (See Chapter C7 for a discussion of Sec. 382.)

The consolidated Sec. 382 rules generally provide that the ownership change and Sec. 382 limitation are determined with respect to the entire affiliated group (or a subgroup of affiliated corporations) and not for individual entities.[53] Following an ownership change for a loss group, the consolidated taxable income for a post-change tax year that may be offset by a pre-change NOL cannot exceed the consolidated Sec. 382 limitation. If the post-change tax year includes the ownership change date, the Sec. 382 limitation applies to the consolidated taxable income that is earned in the portion of the tax year following the ownership change date.

ADDITIONAL COMMENT

Section 382 adopts a single-entity approach in determining ownership changes and Sec. 382 limitations. This means that the members of a consolidated group are treated like divisions of a single taxpayer.

A loss group is an affiliated group entitled to use an NOL carryover (other than a SRLY carryover) to the tax year in which the ownership change occurs, or has a consolidated NOL for the tax year in which the ownership change occurs.[54] An affiliated group can have two forms of ownership changes: a parent ownership change and a subgroup ownership change. A parent ownership change occurs when (1) the loss group's common parent corporation (a) has a shift in stock ownership involving a 5% or more shareholder or (b) is involved in a tax-free reorganization, and (2) the percentage of stock of the new loss corporation owned by one or more 5% shareholders has increased by more than 50 percentage points over the lowest percentage of stock owned in the old loss corporation by such shareholders during the preceding three-year (or shorter) testing period.[55] A parent ownership change is illustrated in the following example.

EXAMPLE C8-28 ▶ Dwayne owns all of P Corporation's stock. P owns 80% of the S Corporation stock. The remaining 20% of the S stock is owned by Mitzi. For 2002, the P-S group has a consolidated NOL that can be carried over to 2003. The P-S affiliated group is a loss group. On December 31, 2002, Dwayne sells 51% of the P stock to Carter, who has owned no P stock previously. The Sec. 382 stock ownership requirements are applied to P to determine whether an ownership change has occurred. The 51 percentage point increase in Carter's stock ownership is an ownership change that causes the Sec. 382 loss limitation to apply to the carryover of the 2002 NOL to 2003. If Carter had instead acquired only 49% of the P stock, the requisite ownership change would not have occurred, and the Sec. 382 limit would not apply. ◀

The preceding example applied the ownership change rules to a parent corporation. An ownership change also can occur with respect to a loss subgroup. A loss subgroup generally consists of two or more corporations that are continuously affiliated after leaving one affiliated group when at least one of the corporations brings with it NOLs from the old group to the new group.[56] The loss subgroup can have an ownership change if, for

[51] Reg. Sec. 1.1502-15(a).

[52] The Sec. 382 limitation rules apply to the tax attributes limited by Secs. 382-384 (e.g., NOLs, capital losses, foreign tax credits, general business credits, minimum tax credit, built-in gains, and built-in losses).

[53] Reg. Sec. 1.1502-91(a)(1).

[54] Reg. Sec. 1.1502-91(c).

[55] Reg. Sec. 1.1502-92(b)(1)(i).

[56] Reg. Sec. 1.1502-92(b)(1)(ii).

example, the common parent of the loss subgroup has an ownership change (e.g., when an acquisition of subsidiaries from another affiliated group occurs). The 50 percentage point ownership change test is applied to the common parent of the loss subgroup. Further discussion of this type of ownership change is beyond the scope of an introductory text.

The consolidated Sec. 382 limitation (or subgroup limitation) for any post-change tax year equals the value of the loss group (or subgroup) times the highest adjusted federal long-term tax-exempt rate that applies with respect to the three-month period ending in the month of the ownership change. The value of the loss group is the value of the common and preferred stock of each member, other than stock owned by other group members, immediately before the ownership change.

EXAMPLE C8-29 ▶ Assume the same basic facts as in Example C8-28. In addition, the value of the P stock is $1 million and the value of the S stock is $750,000. The value of the P-S affiliated group when applying the Sec. 382 limitation is $1.15 million [$1,000,000 value of P stock + (0.20 × $750,000 value of S stock owned by Mitzi)]. The $1.15 million value is multiplied by the appropriate federal long-term tax-exempt rate to determine the maximum amount of the 2002 consolidated NOL that can be used in 2003.[57] ◀

ADDITIONAL COMMENT

In Example C8-29, if S leaves the group, the loss that is attributable to S will be subject to whatever amount of the Sec. 382 limitation P apportions to S. S's Sec. 382 limitation is zero if P chooses not to apportion any of the group's Sec. 382 limitation to S.

Two special Sec. 382 rules that apply to affiliated groups deserve brief recognition here.

- If the Sec. 382 limitation for a post-change tax year exceeds the consolidated taxable income that may be offset by a pre-change NOL, the excess limitation amount carries forward to the next tax year to increase that year's Sec. 382 limitation.[58]
- A loss group (or loss subgroup) is treated as a single entity for purposes of determining whether it satisfies the Sec. 382 continuity of enterprise requirement. The group's Sec. 382 limitation is zero should the loss group not meet the continuity of enterprise requirement at any time in its first two years.[59]
- When an affiliated group terminates or a member leaves the affiliated group, the Sec. 382 limitation is apportioned to the individual group members.[60] Failure to allocate any of the Sec. 382 limitation to a departing group member prevents the member from using any of its NOLs in post-departure tax years.

EXAMPLE C8-30 ▶ In the P-S-T affiliated group, P owns 100% of the S stock, and S owns 100% of the T stock. The group has an annual Sec. 382 limit of $100, and 30% of the group's losses are allocable to T. When S sells the T stock to individual A, T receives its allocable share of the consolidated NOL. If T is allocated none of the affiliated group's Sec. 382 loss limitation, T's separate Sec. 382 limitation is set to zero. Consequently, T can use none of its allocable loss carryover. ◀

SRLY-SEC. 382 OVERLAP. An overlap problem exists because transactions that qualify under the SRLY rules (for example, the purchase by an acquiring corporation of 100% of the stock of a target corporation having a NOL) also may qualify under the Sec. 382 loss limitation rules. Under previous law, both the SRLY rules and Sec. 382 rules could apply to a single transaction involving members of an affiliated group. This overlap caused difficulty in complying with the consolidated tax return rules. The Treasury Department and the IRS considered a number of alternatives including applying both sets of rules, applying one set of rules but not the other, and creating a new version of the SRLY rules using the loss limitation structure found in Sec. 382.

---

[57] A daily allocation of the loss is not needed since the acquisition occurred on the last day of the loss corporation's tax year.
[58] Reg. Sec. 1.1502-93(a).
[59] Reg. Sec. 1.1502-93(d).
[60] Reg. Sec. 1.1502-95(b).

The final Treasury Regulations apply a compromise to situations involving the NOL overlap. The new regulations eliminate the application of the SRLY rules in this situation. To qualify for the overlap rule, a corporation must become a member of an affiliated group filing a consolidated tax return within six months of the date of an ownership change that creates a Sec. 382 limitation. If the Sec. 382 event precedes the SRLY event by six months or less, the overlap rule applies beginning with the tax year that includes the SRLY event. If the SRLY event precedes the Sec. 382 event by six months or less, the overlap rule applies for the first tax year beginning after the Sec. 382 event (and the SRLY rules apply for the interim period).

EXAMPLE C8-31 ▶ The P-S affiliated group has filed consolidated tax returns for a number of years. The P-S group has a $200 consolidated NOL, of which $100 is allocable to each corporation. The A-B affiliated group also has filed consolidated returns for a number of years. The A-B group acquires the P-S affiliated group in a taxable transaction. The P-S affiliated group is a SRLY subgroup and a Sec. 382 subgroup. The overlap rule eliminates the application of the SRLY rules in the surviving A-B-P-S affiliated group for the $200 consolidated NOL it acquired from the P-S group. The Sec. 382 rules, however, still apply. ◀

The overlap rule does not apply if all the corporations included in a Sec. 382 loss subgroup are not included in a SRLY subgroup. A similar set of overlap rules applies to built-in losses.

Topic Review C8-2 summarizes the rules applying to carrybacks and carryovers of consolidated return and separate return NOLs.

Topic Review C8-2

Rules Governing Affiliated Group NOL Carrybacks and Carryovers

Loss Year	Carryover/ Carryback Year	Rule and Special Limitations
CRY[a]	CRY	1. Consolidated NOLs are carried back two years and forward 20 years. Election to forgo the carryback period is made by the parent corporation. No special problems are encountered if the group members are the same in the loss year and carryback or carryover year. 2. Section 382 limitation can apply to the loss carryover if an ownership change has occurred.
CRY	SRY[b]	1. Carryback to a member's prior separate return year is possible only if part or all of the NOL is apportioned to the member. Offspring rule permits carryback of an offspring member's allocable share of the consolidated NOL to a separate return year of the parent corporation or consolidated return year of the affiliated group. 2. The departing member is allocated part of the consolidated NOL carryover. The consolidated NOL is used first in the consolidated return year in which the departing member leaves the group before an allocation is made. The allocated share of the loss is then used in the departing member's first separate return year. The departing member may be allocated a portion of the Sec. 382 loss limitation by the parent corporation.
SRY	CRY	1. A separate return year NOL can be carried over and used in a consolidated return year. SRLY rules will apply to NOLs other than those of a corporation that is the parent corporation in the carryover year or that is a group member on each day of the loss year. 2. Carryback of a loss of a departed group member to a consolidated return year is a SRLY loss.

[a]Consolidated return year.
[b]Separate return year.

CONSOLIDATED CAPITAL GAINS AND LOSSES

In the previous discussion of separate taxable income (see page C8-5), all capital gains and losses, Sec. 1231 gains and losses, and casualty and theft gains and losses were excluded. These three types of gains and losses are reported by the affiliated group on a consolidated basis. For a consolidated return year, the affiliated group's consolidated net capital gain or loss is composed of

- The aggregate amount of the capital gains and losses of the group members (without regard to any Sec. 1231 transactions or net capital loss carryovers or carrybacks)
- The net Sec. 1231 gain
- The net capital loss carryovers or carrybacks to the year[61]

Any capital gain net income that is part of consolidated taxable income is taxed at the regular corporate tax rates. Any consolidated net capital loss carries back three years or forward five years as a short-term capital loss.

ADDITIONAL COMMENT

Netting Sec. 1231 gains/losses on a consolidated basis rather than on a separate corporation basis can dramatically alter the amount of ordinary versus capital gain income.

SECTION 1231 GAINS AND LOSSES

A group member's Sec. 1231 gains and losses exclude any such amounts deferred when an intercompany transaction occurs. These intercompany gains and losses are reported when a corresponding item triggers the recognition of the intercompany item. The consolidated Sec. 1231 net gain or loss for the tax year is determined by taking into account the aggregate gains and losses of the group members' Sec. 1231 results. If the group's total Sec. 1231 gains (including net gain from casualty and theft occurrences involving Sec. 1231 property and certain capital assets) exceed similar losses, the net gain from these transactions is the consolidated net Sec. 1231 gain and is eligible for long-term capital gain treatment unless recaptured as ordinary income because of prior net Sec. 1231 losses. If the group reports a net loss either from Sec. 1231 transactions or from its casualty and theft occurrences, the net Sec. 1231 loss is treated as an ordinary loss and is deductible in determining consolidated taxable income.

SELF-STUDY QUESTION

How do intercompany transactions affect the calculation of capital gains/losses?

ANSWER

Deferred intercompany gains/losses are included in the netting of capital gains/losses only when a corresponding item triggers the recognition of the intercompany item.

CAPITAL GAINS AND LOSSES

DETERMINING THE AMOUNT OF GAIN OR LOSS. The amount of any group member's capital gains and losses excludes any such gains deferred when an intercompany transaction occurs. These intercompany gains and losses are reported when a corresponding item triggers the recognition of the intercompany item. Once the recognized gains and losses of each group member are determined, each member's short- and long-term transactions (including any consolidated Sec. 1231 net gain not treated as ordinary income) are combined into separate net gain or net loss positions. The sum of these separate positions then determines the amount of the affiliated group's aggregate short- or long-term capital gain or loss. These aggregate amounts are combined to determine the group's consolidated capital gain net income.

CARRYBACKS AND CARRYFORWARDS. The treatment of consolidated capital loss carrybacks and carryovers is similar to NOLs. The losses that carry back or forward to other consolidated return years are treated as short-term capital losses and serve as a component of the consolidated capital gain or loss position.

The capital loss carrybacks or carryovers that can be used in a consolidated return year equal the sum of the affiliated group's unused consolidated capital loss carrybacks or carryovers and any unused capital loss carrybacks or carryovers of individual group members arising in separate return years. These capital loss carrybacks and carryovers are absorbed according to the same rules described above for NOLs (see pages C8-23 through C8-31).[62]

[61] Reg. Sec. 1.1502-22(a)(1).

[62] Reg. Sec. 1.1502-22(b).

EXAMPLE C8-32 ▶ P, S_1, and S_2 Corporations form the P-S_1-S_2 affiliated group. This group has filed consolidated tax returns for several years. During the current year, the affiliated group reports $100,000 of ordinary income, and the following property transaction results:

Group Member	Capital Gains and Losses: Short-Term	Capital Gains and Losses: Long-Term	Sec. 1231 Gains and Losses
P	$2,000	($1,000)	($2,500)
S_1	(1,000)	7,000	2,000
S_2	(2,000)	3,000	2,000
Total	($1,000)	$9,000	$1,500

In addition, the group carries over a consolidated capital loss of $3,000 from the preceding year. No net Sec. 1231 losses have been recognized in prior years. The P-S_1-S_2 affiliated group's $1,500 consolidated net Sec. 1231 gain is combined with the $8,000 aggregate amount of capital gains and losses ($9,000 − $1,000) and the $3,000 consolidated net capital loss carryover to obtain the current year consolidated capital gain net income of $6,500 ($1,500 + $8,000 − $3,000). This entire amount is taxed at the regular corporate tax rates. ◀

Carryback of a Consolidated Net Capital Loss. A carryback of a member's apportionment of a consolidated capital loss to one of its preceding separate return years is required when capital gains are available in the carryback year against which the loss may be offset. Apportionment of the consolidated capital loss to the loss members occurs in a manner similar to that described for NOLs.

TYPICAL MISCONCEPTION

The allocation of net capital losses to the individual group members is based in part on each member's Sec. 1231 losses. Thus, it is possible for a member with only a Sec. 1231 loss to share in the net capital loss carryforward or carryback.

SRLY Limitation. Carryovers or carrybacks of capital losses from a separate return limitation year invoke the SRLY rules. The amount of the loss carryback or carryover from a separate return limitation year that may be used in a consolidated return year equals the lesser of the loss member's contribution to the consolidated capital gain net income or consolidated capital gain net income.[63]

Sec. 382 Limitation. The Sec. 382 loss limitation rules apply to consolidated and separate return capital loss carryovers as well as consolidated and separate return NOLs. Under Sec. 383, capital losses are subject to the general Sec. 382 limitation described earlier.

ADDITIONAL COMMENT

The IRC provides that no election is available to forgo the three-year carryback for a net capital loss. This can complicate matters when the three prior years include separate tax return years of the members of the group.

Taxable Income Limitation. In addition to the special capital loss limitations outlined above, Sec. 1212(a)(1)(A)(ii) contains a general limitation that prevents a capital loss from being carried back or over and creating or increasing the NOL for the tax year to which it is carried. Therefore, use of a capital loss also is limited to the group's consolidated taxable income.

Departing Group Members' Losses. A member leaving the affiliated group may take with it an apportionment of any consolidated capital loss carryover and any of its unused capital loss carryovers that originated in a separate return year. These losses are used in subsequent years until they expire. Apportionment of the consolidated capital loss to the departing group member occurs in a manner similar to that described above for NOLs.

STOCK BASIS ADJUSTMENTS

KEY POINT

Positive stock basis adjustments will reduce the amount of gain reported when a sale of the stock of an affiliated group member occurs.

The basis for an investment in a subsidiary corporation is adjusted annually for its profits and losses as well as for distributions made to higher-tier subsidiaries or to its parent corporation. These rules parallel those used by S corporations and partnerships. If the stock of a profitable subsidiary is sold, a "net" positive basis adjustment produces a smaller capital gain than the gain that would otherwise have been recognized if separate tax

[63] As with a NOL, the SRLY rules can apply a single-year or multiple-year contribution comparison.

returns were filed. The basis adjustment prevents the income earned by the subsidiary during the affiliation from being taxed a second time when the parent corporation disposes of the subsidiary's stock.

The starting point for the calculation is the original basis of the parent corporation's investment in the subsidiary, which depends on the acquisition method used to acquire the stock (e.g., purchase, tax-free corporate formation, or tax-free reorganization). The following basis adjustments must be made to the original basis:

- Basis is increased for the subsidiary's income and gain items and decreased for the subsidiary's deduction and loss items that are taken into account in determining consolidated taxable income. The adjustment includes net operating losses but excludes deferred gains and losses, and unused capital losses.
- Basis is increased for income that is permanently excluded from taxation (e.g., tax-exempt bond interest and federal income tax refunds).
- Basis is increased for distributions received from lower-tier group members.
- Basis in increased for a deduction that does not represent a recovery of basis or an expenditure of money (for example, a dividends-received deduction).
- Basis is decreased for NOLs used in the current year against other group members' taxable income or carried back and used in an earlier year. NOL carryovers and other suspended losses reduce basis in the year they are used. Expiring NOLs and capital losses reduce basis in the year they expire.
- Basis is decreased for noncapital expenses that are not deductible (e.g., federal income taxes, the 50% of meals and entertainment expenses that are nondeductible, expenses related to tax-exempt income, and losses disallowed under Sec. 267).
- The stock basis for an investment in a lower-tier corporation incurring a pre-acquisition separate return NOL or capital loss is reduced when the loss is used in the current year to offset income or gains reported by other group members. If the pre-acquisition loss expires unused, the unused loss reduces the basis of the stock investment unless the use of part or all of such losses is waived.
- Basis is decreased for all distributions without regard to the E&P balance, or whether such amounts accumulated in pre- or post-affiliation years.
- If the negative basis adjustments for losses and distributions, etc. are sufficiently large, the basis of the subsidiary's stock is reduced to zero. Additional basis reductions that occur create an excess loss account. No recognition of income or gain is triggered by the creation of this "negative basis account." Subsequent profits or additional capital contributions may reduce or eliminate the excess loss account and, if large enough, can produce a positive basis.

EXAMPLE C8-33 ▶ Parent Corporation purchased all of Subsidiary's stock on January 1, 2001 for $1 million. An election was made for Parent and Subsidiary to begin filing a consolidated tax return in 2001. Subsidiary reported taxable income of $300,000, tax-exempt bond interest of $25,000, and a $5,000 nondeductible capital loss in 2001. On January 1, 2002, Parent sells Subsidiary's stock for $1.4 million. The portion of the consolidated tax liability allocable to Subsidiary is $102,000 ($300,000 × 0.34). Parent recognizes a $177,000 [$1,400,000 − ($1,000,000 + $300,000 + $25,000 − $102,000)] capital gain on the sale. This gain is $223,000 ($400,000 gain if no consolidated return election − $177,000 gain with a consolidated return election) smaller than the gain reported had Parent and Subsidiary not elected to file a consolidated return.[64] ◀

EXAMPLE C8-34 ▶ Parent Corporation purchased all of Subsidiary Corporation's stock on January 1, 2001 for $1 million. During 2001, Subsidiary reported a $750,000 NOL and made a $300,000 distribution to Parent. The $750,000 NOL offsets part of Parent's $2.5 million of taxable income. The basis of

[64] Separate basis calculations are required for regular tax and AMT purposes. The AMT basis calculations parallel those made for regular tax purposes but use the appropriate numbers from the AMT calculation. Because of the possible differences in these two amounts, the sale of a stock investment may result in different gain or loss amounts for regular tax and AMT purposes.

the Subsidiary stock is first reduced to zero ($1,000,000 − $750,000 loss − $250,000 distribution). The remaining $50,000 of distribution creates an excess loss account. No gain is recognized by the creation of this "negative basis" account. The excess loss account will be reduced or eliminated in 2002 by subsequent profits or capital contributions, or increased by additional losses and distributions. ◀

TAX PLANNING CONSIDERATIONS

100% DIVIDENDS-RECEIVED DEDUCTION ELECTION

Intercompany dividends are excluded when a consolidated tax return is filed. The 100% dividends-received deduction election (as discussed in Chapter C4) may be used by the affiliated group to exempt from taxation any dividends received from corporations not eligible to be included in the consolidated return (e.g., a 100%-owned life insurance company).

If a state does not permit the filing of a consolidated tax return for state income tax purposes,[65] it may be necessary for an affiliated group to elect the 100% dividends-received deduction for both state and federal tax purposes. In such a case, the state requires the filing of separate tax returns by each member of the affiliated group. Generally, the state also permits the claiming of any dividends-received deduction elected for federal income tax purposes. When a consolidated tax return is not filed for state income tax purposes, no exclusion of the dividends is possible, and the 100% dividends-received deduction (which was elected but not used on the federal tax return) is substituted on the state income tax return.

ESTIMATED TAX PAYMENTS

Once consolidated tax returns have been filed for two consecutive years, the affiliated group must pay estimated taxes on a consolidated basis.[66] The affiliated group is treated as a single corporation for this purpose. Thus, the estimated tax payments and any underpayment exceptions or penalties are based on the affiliated group's income for the current year and the immediately preceding tax year without regard to the number of corporations that comprise the affiliated group. This treatment can be advantageous if new, profitable corporations are added to the affiliated group.

EXAMPLE C8-35 ▶ The P-S_1 affiliated group files consolidated tax returns for several years. During 2001, the P-S_1 group reports a $100,000 consolidated tax liability. The P-S_1 affiliated group acquires all of S_2 Corporation's stock during 2002. S_2 is very profitable and causes the P-S_1-S_2 group to report a $300,000 consolidated tax liability in 2002. Assuming the P-S_1-S_2 group does not come under the large corporation rules outlined below, its 2002 estimated tax payments can be based on the P-S_1 group's $100,000 consolidated tax liability for the prior tax year. No underpayment penalties are imposed provided the P-S_1-S_2 group makes $25,000 ($100,000 ÷ 4) estimated tax payments by the fifteenth day of the fourth, sixth, ninth, and twelfth months of the tax year, because the prior year's tax liability exception to the underpayment rules is satisfied. The balance of the consolidated tax liability must be paid by the due date for the consolidated tax return (without regard to any extensions) to avoid penalty. ◀

UNDERPAYMENT RULES. Affiliated groups also are subject to the special underpayment rules of Sec. 6655(d)(2) for large corporations (that is, corporations having taxable income of at least $1 million in any one of the three immediately preceding tax years). An affiliated group is considered one corporation when applying the large corporation rules. Only the actual members of the affiliated group for the three preceding tax years are used in applying the $1 million threshold. New members entering the group are ignored for the three-preceding-years test.[67]

[65] Rev. Rul. 73-484, 1973-2 C.B. 78.

[66] Reg. Sec. 1.1502-5(a).

[67] Proposed Reg. Sec. 1.6655-4(e)(3) requires the $1 million threshold to be applied to all members of the controlled group.

CONSOLIDATED OR SEPARATE BASIS. For the first two years for which a group files consolidated tax returns, the affiliated group may elect to make estimated tax payments on either a consolidated or separate basis. Starting in the third year, however, the affiliated group must make consolidated estimated tax payments. It must continue to do so until separate tax returns are again filed. During the first two tax years for which the election is in effect, the affiliated group sometimes can reduce its quarterly payments by making separate estimated tax payments in the first year and consolidated estimated tax payments in the second year or vice versa. Application of the exceptions to the penalty for underpayment of estimated taxes depends on whether estimated taxes are paid on a separate or consolidated basis. Different exceptions (e.g., prior year's liability or annualization of current year's income) to the underpayment rules should be used by the individual group members if it will reduce the amount of the required estimated tax payments. Determination of the actual separate or consolidated limitations, however, is beyond the scope of this book.

ADDITIONAL COMMENT

The final estimated tax payment for a member joining a consolidated group is due the fifteenth day of the last month of the short taxable year. If a member is acquired after the fifteenth, the final estimated tax payment is already overdue.

SHORT-PERIOD RETURN. If a corporation joins an affiliated group after the beginning of its tax year, a short-period return covering the pre-affiliation time period generally must be filed. The payment rules covering the short-period return are found in Reg. Sec. 1.6655-3. If a corporation leaves an affiliated group, it must make the necessary estimated tax payments required of a corporation filing a separate tax return for the post-affiliation, short-period tax year, unless it joins in the filing of a consolidated tax return with another affiliated group. No estimated tax payment is required for a short tax year that is less than four months.

COMPLIANCE AND PROCEDURAL CONSIDERATIONS

OBJECTIVE 11

Explain the procedures for making an initial consolidated return election

THE BASIC ELECTION AND RETURN

An affiliated group makes an election to use the consolidated method for filing its tax return by filing a consolidated tax return (Form 1120) that includes the income, expenses, etc. of all its members. The election must be made no later than the due date for the common parent corporation's tax return including any permitted extensions.[68] An affiliated group can change from a consolidated tax return to separate tax returns,[69] or from separate tax returns to a consolidated tax return, at any time on or before the last day for filing the consolidated tax return. Once that day has passed, no change can be made.

A sample Form 1120 is presented in Appendix B for reporting the current year's results for the Alpha affiliated group described in Example C8-36. The Form 1120 involves the five intercompany transactions mentioned in the example, and a worksheet that summarizes the income and expense items for the five companies illustrates the reporting of the intercompany transactions and presents the details of the consolidated taxable income calculation.

EXAMPLE C8-36 ▶ Alpha Manufacturing Corporation owns 100% of the stock of Beta, Charlie, Delta, and Echo corporations. The affiliated group has filed consolidated returns for a number of years using the calendar year as their tax year. The components of the separate taxable income amounts of the five corporations are reported on the supporting schedule of the group's consolidated tax return contained in Appendix B. This return illustrates four common transactions involving members of an affiliated group. These are

- ▶ The sale of inventory from Alpha to Beta, which increases Alpha's deferred intercompany profit amount. Beta sells additional inventory to outsiders.

[68] Reg. Sec. 1.1502-75(a)(1).

[69] Such a change can take place only for the initial consolidated return year or for a tax year for which the IRS has granted permission to discontinue the consolidated return election.

- Intragroup dividends paid from Beta and Echo to Alpha
- Payment of interest from Delta to Alpha
- The sale of a truck from Alpha to Beta
- Beta's depreciation of the truck acquired in the intercompany transaction ◀

ADDITIONAL COMMENT

If a group is considering making a consolidated return election, a properly executed Form 1122 should be obtained before any corporation is sold during the election year. After the sale, the consent form may be difficult to obtain.

Students should review this sample return to see how the transactions are reported and how the numbers from the consolidated taxable income schedule are reported in the affiliated group's Form 1120.

In addition to filing the necessary Form 1120 reflecting the consolidated results of operations, each corporation that is a member of the affiliated group during the initial consolidated return year must consent to the election. The parent corporation's consent is evidenced by its filing the consolidated tax return (Form 1120). Subsidiary corporations consent to the election by filing a Form 1122 (Authorization and Consent of Subsidiary to be Included in a Consolidated Income Tax Return) and submitting it as a part of the initial consolidated tax return. Only newly acquired subsidiary corporations file Form 1122 with subsequent consolidated tax returns.

Each consolidated tax return also must include an Affiliations Schedule (Form 851). This form includes the name, address, and identification number of the corporations included in the affiliated group, the corporation's tax prepayments, the stock holdings at the beginning of the tax year, and all stock ownership changes occurring during the tax year.

Affiliated groups commonly use two types of consolidated tax return formats. One type is a schedular format where the affiliated group files a single tax return with separate spreadsheets showing the calculation of consolidated taxable income and any supporting data. (This format is used in the sample consolidated tax return included in Appendix B.) A second type is a "pancake" format where individual Form 1120s report the activity of each group member. In addition, a separate Form 1120 for an "eliminations" company reports all the adjustments and eliminations needed to go from the various separate tax returns to a single consolidated return, and a final Form 1120 reports the affiliated group's combined results. The pancake format tends to be used by affiliated groups comprised of large sized firms.

The due date for the consolidated tax return is 2½ months after the end of the affiliated group's tax year. A six-month extension for filing the consolidated tax return is permitted if the parent corporation files Form 7004 and pays the estimated balance of the consolidated tax liability. The due date for the tax return of a subsidiary corporation that is not included in the consolidated return depends on whether the affiliated group's consolidated tax return has been filed by the due date for the subsidiary corporation's tax return. These rules are beyond the scope of this introductory text but can be reviewed in Reg. Sec. 1.1502-76(c).

PARENT CORPORATION AS AGENT FOR THE AFFILIATED GROUP

The parent corporation acts as agent for each subsidiary corporation and for the affiliated group. As agent for each subsidiary, the parent corporation is authorized to act in its own name in all matters relating to the affiliated group's tax liability for the consolidated return year.[70]

No subsidiary corporation can act in its own behalf with respect to a consolidated return year except to the extent that the parent corporation is prohibited from acting in its behalf. Thus, a subsidiary corporation is prevented from making or changing any election used in computing separate taxable income, carrying on correspondence with the IRS regarding the determination of a tax liability, filing any requests for extensions of time in which to file a tax return, filing a claim for a refund or credit relating to a consolidated return year, or electing to deduct or credit foreign tax payments.

[70] Reg. Sec. 1.1502-77(a).

ADDITIONAL COMMENT

Each member corporation is severally liable for the entire tax liability of the affiliated group. Anyone purchasing a corporation out of an affiliated group should consider this factor when negotiating the purchase price of the target corporation.

LIABILITY FOR TAXES DUE

The parent corporation and every other corporation that was a group member for any part of the consolidated return year are severally liable for that year's consolidated taxes.[71] Thus, the entire consolidated tax liability may be collected from one group member if, for example, the other group members are unable to pay their allocable portion. The IRS can ignore attempts made by the group members to limit their share of the liability by entering into agreements with one another or with third parties. Thus, the potential consolidated tax liability and any deficiencies could accrue to a corporation that is a member of an affiliated group for even a few days during a tax year.

An exception to this several liability principle occurs when a subsidiary corporation ceases to be a group member as a result of its stock being sold or exchanged before a deficiency is assessed against the affiliated group. Thus, the IRS can opt to assess a former subsidiary corporation for only its allocable portion of the total deficiency if it believes that the assessment and collection of the balance of the deficiency from the other group members will not be jeopardized.

PROBLEM MATERIALS

DISCUSSION QUESTIONS

C8-1 What minimum level of stock ownership is required for a corporation to be included in an affiliated group?

C8-2 Which of the following equity items are considered to be stock for purposes of the stock ownership portion of the affiliated group definition?
a. Common stock
b. A second class of common stock
c. Nonvoting preferred stock
d. Voting preferred stock
e. Nonvoting preferred stock convertible into common stock

C8-3 Which of the following entities are includible in an affiliated group?
a. C corporation
b. S corporation
c. Foreign corporation
d. Real estate investment trust
e. Regulated investment company
f. Life insurance company taxed under Sec. 801
g. Limited liability company.

C8-4 Explain the difference between the stock ownership requirements for having a group of companies that can consolidate their financial reporting activities and an affiliated group and a controlled group as used within the tax law.

C8-5 P Corporation is 100% owned by Peter McKay. P Corporation owns 100% of S Corporation and 49% of T Corporation. S Corporation owns the remaining 51% of T Corporation. S Corporation also owns 100% of PeterM, a limited liability company (LLC). The LLC has elected to be taxed as a C corporation. Peter McKay also owns 100% of Z corporation's stock. All are U.S. entities. Which entities are included in an affiliated group? In a controlled group?

C8-6 P, S_1, S_2, and S_3 Corporations form a controlled group of corporations. Because S_3 Corporation is a nonincludible insurance corporation, only P, S_1, and S_2 Corporations are permitted to file their income tax returns on a consolidated basis. Explain to P Corporation's president the alternatives available for allocating the tax savings from the 15%, 25%, and 34% tax rates to the members of the controlled group.

C8-7 P Corporation has two subsidiaries, S_1 and S_2, both of which are 100%-owned. All three corporations are currently filing separate tax returns. P and S_1 have been profitable. S_2 is a start-up company that has reported losses for its first two years of existence. S_2 eventually will be selling cosmetics to S_1 for distribution to retailers. Explain to P Corporation's president the advantages (and disadvantages) of the three corporations filing a consolidated tax return.

C8-8 Briefly explain how consolidated taxable income is calculated starting with the financial accounting (book) income information for each individual group member. Explain how the consolidated taxable income calculation is different from the taxable income calculation for a corporation filing a separate tax return.

---

[71] Reg. Sec. 1.1502-6(a)

C8-9 Determine whether each of the following statements is true or false:

a. One member of an affiliated group may elect to use the accrual method of accounting even though another group member uses the cash receipts and disbursements method of accounting.

b. A corporation that uses the calendar year as its tax year acquires all the stock of another corporation that has for years used a fiscal year as its tax year. They both may continue to use their previous separate return tax years when filing their initial consolidated tax return.

c. T Corporation, a calendar year taxpayer, becomes a member of the P-S affiliated group at the close of business on February 28 of a non-leap year. The P-S group has filed consolidated tax returns using the calendar year for a number of years. The P-S-T affiliated group's consolidated tax return includes 306/365ths of T's separate taxable income for the year.

C8-10 What events permit an affiliated group to terminate its consolidated tax return election? If a corporation leaves an affiliated group, how long must the corporation be disaffiliated before it can again be included in the consolidated tax return?

C8-11 The P-S_1-S_2 affiliated group has filed consolidated tax returns using a calendar year for a number of years. At the close of business on July 15, P Corporation sells all its S_1 Corporation stock to Mickey. P Corporation retains its investment in S_2 Corporation. Explain what tax returns are required of the three corporations for the current year. What effect does the sale have on the P-S_1-S_2 group's prior year intercompany items and its charitable contributions carryover that is unused in the current year consolidated tax return?

C8-12 Assume the same facts as in Question C8-11 except that the original affiliated group was just P and S_1 Corporations and that the S_1 stock was sold to Mickey at the close of business on July 15. What affect does the sale have on the P-S_1 group's prior year intercompany items and its charitable contributions carryover that is unused in the final consolidated tax return?

C8-13 Determine whether the following statements regarding the alternative minimum tax are true or false:

a. An affiliated group calculates its alternative minimum tax liability on a separate company basis.

b. The affiliated group is eligible for an exemption from the AMT if its average consolidated gross receipts are less than $5 million in its first three-year period and less than $7.5 million in subsequent three-year periods.

c. Each member of an affiliated group receives a separate $40,000 statutory exemption.

d. An affiliated group must make an adjustment for 75% of the difference between its consolidated ACE and its consolidated pre-adjustment AMTI.

C8-14 Define the following terms:

a. Intercompany transaction
b. Intercompany item
c. Corresponding item
d. Matching rule
e. Acceleration rule

C8-15 Explain how the rules governing depreciation recapture, basis, and depreciation operate when a seven-year recovery class property under the MACRS rules is sold at a profit by one group member to a second group member after the property has been held for three years. The purchasing group member will depreciate the property using the MACRS rules over a seven-year recovery period.

C8-16 Compare and contrast the reporting of interest income and interest expense by P and S Corporations for financial accounting and consolidated tax return purposes when P Corporation lends money to S Corporation on August 1 for a three-year period. Both corporations use the calendar year as their tax year, and interest is paid on July 31 each year. First, assume both corporations use the accrual method of accounting. Then assume that P and S Corporations use the cash and accrual methods of accounting, respectively.

C8-17 P and S_1 Corporations constitute the P-S_1 affiliated group on January 1. S_1 Corporation acquires all the stock of S_2 Corporation at the close of business on April 1. Which of the following transactions are intercompany transactions?

a. P Corporation sells inventory to S_1 Corporation throughout the current year.

b. S_2 Corporation sells land (a capital asset) to P Corporation on March 15.

c. S_1 Corporation sells machinery (Sec. 1245 property) to S_2 Corporation on September 1.

d. P Corporation sells inventory to the PS_1 Partnership, which is owned equally by P and S_1 Corporations, on July 23.

C8-18 P, S_1, and S_2 Corporations constitute the P-S_1-S_2 affiliated group. The affiliated group members use the accrual method of accounting and the calendar year as their tax year. Determine whether each of the following transactions that take place during the current year are intercompany transactions. For each item, indicate the intercompany item and corresponding item.

a. P Corporation lends S_1 Corporation money, and P charges interest at a 10% annual rate. The money and interest remains unpaid at the end of the tax year.

b. S_1 Corporation sells inventory to P Corporation. At year end, P Corporation holds the entire inventory purchased from S_1 Corporation.

c. P Corporation sells land (Sec. 1231 property) to S_2 Corporation. S_2 Corporation holds the land (Sec. 1231 property) at year-end.

d. S_2 Corporation pays a cash dividend to P Corporation.

e. S_1 Corporation provides engineering services that are capitalized as part of the cost of S_2's new factory building.

C8-19 Indicate for each of the following dividend payments the tax treatment available in computing consolidated taxable income:

a. Dividend received from a C corporation that is 10%-owned by the parent corporation.

b. Dividend received from a C corporation that is 100%-owned by the parent corporation and included in the consolidated tax return election.

c. Dividend received from a foreign corporation that is 50%-owned by the parent corporation. The foreign corporation earns no U.S. source income.

d. Dividend received from an unconsolidated life insurance corporation that is 100%-owned by the parent corporation.

C8-20 Explain the circumstances in which a consolidated NOL can be carried back to a preceding separate return year.

C8-21 What advantages can accrue to an affiliated group or an individual group member by electing to forgo the carryback of an NOL incurred in a consolidated return year? A separate return year? Who makes the election to forgo each of the carrybacks?

C8-22 Define the term SRLY and explain its significance and application to an affiliated group filing a consolidated tax return.

C8-23 What is a Sec. 382 ownership change? What is the Sec. 382 loss limitation? Explain their significance and application to an affiliated group filing a consolidated tax return.

C8-24 P Corporation purchases 100% of the stock of S Corporation on January 1. S Corporation is P Corporation's only subsidiary. Explain to the president of P Corporation what basis adjustment must be made at year-end for its $2 million investment in S Corporation when S earns $350,000 of taxable income and $30,000 of tax-exempt interest income, while it distributes a $150,000 dividend to its parent corporation. Each company paid its own tax liability. Assume a 34% corporate tax rate.

C8-25 Explain why an affiliated group filing a consolidated tax return might make a federal tax election to claim a 100% dividends-received deduction for a tax year even though all dividends received during that year are received from corporations that are 100%-owned by the parent company.

C8-26 During what time period can an affiliated group elect to file a consolidated tax return? How is the election made? During what time period is the election to disaffiliate made?

C8-27 Indicate for which of the following tax-related matters the parent corporation can act as the affiliated group's agent:

a. Making an initial consent for a subsidiary corporation to participate in a consolidated return election

b. Changing an accounting method election for a subsidiary corporation

c. Carrying on correspondence with the IRS during an audit regarding a transaction entered into by a subsidiary corporation that affects the group's determination of consolidated taxable income

d. Requesting an extension of time within which to file a consolidated tax return

C8-28 You are the managing partner of a local CPA firm. The President of your largest client, a medium-size manufacturing firm, advises you that the firm is about to acquire its largest supplier. Both firms have been profitable for the past ten years and have filed separate tax returns. The President wants to know what tax return filing options are available for the two companies. What additional information do you need to make an informed decision? What factors do you think are most important in the firm's decision?

ISSUE IDENTIFICATION QUESTIONS

C8-29 Mark owns all the stock of Red and Green Corporations. Red Corporation has been reporting $150,000 in taxable income for each of the past five years. Green Corporation annually has been reporting $30,000 NOLs, which have accumulated to $150,000. Approximately one-third of Red's profits come from sales to Green. Intercompany sales between Red and Green have increased during each of the last five years. What tax issues should Mark consider with respect to his investments in Red and Green Corporations?

C8-30 Alpha and Baker Corporations, two accrual method of accounting corporations that use the calendar year as their tax year, have filed consolidated tax returns for a number of years. Baker Corporation, a 100%-owned subsidiary of Alpha, is transferring a patent, equipment, and working capital to newly created Charles Corporation in exchange for 100% of its stock. In 2002, the corporation will begin to produce parts for the automotive industry. Charles Corporation expects to incur organizational expenditures of $10,000 and start-up expenditures of $60,000. What tax issues should Charles Corporation consider with respect to the selection of its overall accounting method, inventory method, and tax year, and the proper reporting of its organizational and start-up expenditures?

C8-31 Crimson Tide Corporation is the parent corporation of a 14-member affiliated group that has filed consolidated tax returns for a number of years. Last year, the group sold all the stock of Tiger Corporation to Mark Jones. This year, Tiger Corporation reported a $300,000 NOL. Tiger's taxable income while a group member averaged $200,000 annually for the past five years but is expected to be only $50,000 next year due to start-up costs that will be incurred with the introduction of a new product line. Profits are expected to increase in each succeeding year. What issues should Crimson Tide have considered when trying to value Tiger's NOL prior to its sale? What tax issues should Tiger now consider when deciding how to use its NOL?

PROBLEMS

C8-32 ***Affiliated Group Definition.*** Which of the following independent situations result in an affiliated group being created? In each case, indicate the corporations that are eligible to be included in the consolidated tax return election. All corporations are domestic corporations unless otherwise indicated.

a. Zeke, an individual, owns all the stock of A and B Corporations.

b. Kelly, an individual, owns all the stock of P and W Corporations. P Corporation owns all of the stock of both S_1 and S_2 Corporations.

c. P Corporation owns all the stock of S_1 and S_2 Corporations. S_1 Corporation owns 40% of the stock of S_3 Corporation. P Corporation owns the remaining S_3 stock. S_2 Corporation is a foreign corporation.

C8-33 ***Affiliated Group Definition.*** Jane owns all the stock of P Corporation. P Corporation owns all of S Corporation's stock. S Corporation owns all the stock of F Corporation. P Corporation also owns all of T Corporation's stock and 70% of U Corporation's stock. T Corporation owns the remaining 30% of U Corporation's stock and 80% of V Corporation's stock. F Corporation is a French corporation. All other corporations are domestic corporations. V Corporation is an insurance company taxed under Sec. 801 that has been 80%-owned by T for the past five tax years. All undisclosed minority interests are held by unrelated individuals. S Corporation owns 80% of an LLC. Jane's brother Bob owns the remaining 20% of the LLC. The LLC produces parts that it sells to S. The LLC is classified as a partnership under the check-the-box regulations. Which of the entities can join in a consolidated tax return election?

C8-34 ***Stock Ownership Requirement.*** P Corporation is the parent corporation of the P-S_1-S_2 affiliated group. P Corporation is conducting negotiations to purchase the stock of T Corporation. The management of P would like to include T in the affiliated group's consolidated tax return. T Corporation's outstanding shares are as listed.

Type of Stock	*Shares Outstanding*	*Par Value*	*Market Value*
Common stock (1 vote per share)	50,000	$ 1	$30
Voting preferred stock (4 votes per share)	5,000	100	95
Nonvoting preferred stock	20,000	100	90

Determine a plan that permits P to acquire enough stock to include T in the affiliated group.

C8-35 ***Consolidated Return Election.*** P and S Corporations have been in existence for a number of years. P uses the calendar year as its tax year. S Corporation uses a fiscal year ending June 30 as its tax year. Both corporations are involved in manufacturing electronic circuitry and use the FIFO method of accounting for their inventories. At the close of business on September 30, 2002, P acquires all the S stock and elects to file a consolidated tax return for 2002.

a. What tax year must be used in filing the consolidated tax return?

b. What overall accounting method(s) can P and S Corporations elect?

c. What is the last date on which the election to file a consolidated tax return can be made?

d. What income of P and S is included in the consolidated tax return? In a separate return?

C8-36 ***Consolidated Return Election.*** The P-S_1 affiliated group has filed consolidated tax returns for several years. All P-S_1 returns have been filed using the calendar year as the tax year. At the close of business on August 8, 2002, P Corporation purchases all the stock of S_2 Corporation. S_2 has been filing its separate tax returns using a fiscal year ending September 30. At the close of business on November 9, 2002, P Corporation sells all its S_1 stock.

a. What tax year must S_2 Corporation use after joining the affiliated group?
b. What tax returns are required of S_2 Corporation to report its results from October 1, 2001 through December 31, 2002?
c. What tax year must S_1 Corporation use after leaving the affiliated group?
d. What action is needed (if any) should S_1 desire to change to a fiscal year filing basis?

C8-37 *Income Included in Consolidated Return.* P and S_1 Corporations form the P-S_1 affiliated group, which has filed consolidated tax returns on a calendar year basis for a number of years. At the close of business on February 25 of the current year, P Corporation sells all the stock of S_1 Corporation. P Corporation acquires all the stock of S_2 Corporation at the close of business for both firms on September 25. S_2 Corporation has always used the calendar year as its tax year. The new P-S_2 affiliated group elects to file a consolidated tax return for this year. What tax returns are required of P, S_1, and S_2 Corporations with respect to reporting the current year's income?

C8-38 *Alternative Minimum Tax.* P and S Corporations are members of the P-S affiliated group, which has filed consolidated tax returns for a number of years. Consolidated adjusted current earnings is $700,000. Consolidated preadjustment alternative minimum taxable income is $400,000. Consolidated taxable income is $325,000. The consolidated general business credit amount (computed without regard to the overall limitation) is $10,000. Assume P and S are not eligible for the small corporation AMT exemption that is based on gross receipts. What is the P-S group's federal tax liability? Are any carryovers created to subsequent tax years?

C8-39 *Intercompany Transactions.* P, S_1, and S_2 Corporations form the P-S_1-S_2 affiliated group, with P Corporation owning all the stock of S_1 and S_2 Corporations. The P-S_1-S_2 group has filed consolidated tax returns for several years. In 2002, S_1 sells land it has held for a possible expansion to S_2 for $300,000. The land originally cost S_1 $120,000 in 1997. S_2 constructs a new plant facility on the land. The land and the plant facility are sold to a third party in 2003 with $400,000 of the sales price attributable to the land.
a. What are the amount and character of S_1's recognized gain or loss? In what year(s) is the gain or loss included in S_1's separate taxable income? In what year(s) is the gain or loss included in consolidated taxable income?
b. What are the amount and character of S_2's recognized gain or loss? In what year(s) is the gain or loss included in S_2's separate taxable income? In what year(s) is the gain or loss included in consolidated taxable income?
c. How would your answer to Part b change if the portion of the sales price attributable to the land was instead $250,000?

C8-40 *Intercompany Transactions.* P and S Corporations form the P-S affiliated group. The P-S group has filed consolidated tax returns for several years. S acquires some land from P Corporation in 2002 for $60,000. P acquired the land in 1991 as an investment at a cost of $20,000. S uses the land for four years as additional parking space for its employees. No improvements are made to the land. The land is sold by S to an unrelated party in 2006 for $180,000. Terms of the sale require a 20% down payment in the year of sale and four equal installments to be paid annually in years 2007 through 2010. Interest is charged at a rate acceptable to the IRS. Assume all payments are made in a timely fashion.
a. What are the amount and character of P's recognized gain or loss? In what year(s) is the gain or loss included in P's separate taxable income? In what year(s) is it included in consolidated taxable income?
b. What are the amount and character of S's recognized gain or loss? In what year(s) is the gain or loss included in S's separate taxable income? In what year(s) is it included in consolidated taxable income?

C8-41 *Intercompany Transactions.* P and S Corporations form the P-S affiliated group, which has filed consolidated tax returns for several years. On June 10, 2000, P purchases a new machine (five-year MACRS property) for $20,000 cash. No special expensing elections under Sec. 179 were made. On April 4, 2002, P sells the machine to S for $15,000 cash. S uses the property for two years before selling it to an unrelated party on March 10, 2004, for $12,000.
a. What are the amount and character of P's recognized gain or loss? In what year(s) is the gain or loss included in P's separate taxable income? In what year(s) is the gain or loss included in consolidated taxable income?
b. What is S's basis for the equipment?

c. What depreciation method should S use for the equipment?
d. What are the amount and character of S's recognized gain or loss? In what year(s) is the gain included in S's separate taxable income? In what year(s) is the gain or loss included in consolidated taxable income?

C8-42 *Intercompany Transactions.* P and S Corporations form the P-S affiliated group, which has filed consolidated tax returns for a number of years. On January 1, 1999 P Corporation purchased a new machine (seven-year MACRS property) for $50,000. $10,000 of the acquisition cost was expensed under Sec. 179. At the close of business on June 30, 2002, P sells the machine to S for $35,000. The machine is still classified as seven-year MACRS property in S's hands. S holds the asset until March 15, 2005, when it is sold to an unrelated party for $20,000.

a. What are the amount and character of P's recognized gain or loss? In what year(s) is the gain or loss included in P's separate taxable income? In what year(s) is it included in consolidated taxable income?
b. What are the amount and character of S's recognized gain or loss? In what year(s) is the gain or loss included in S's separate taxable income? In what year(s) is it included in consolidated taxable income?

C8-43 *Intercompany Transactions.* P and S Corporations form the P-S affiliated group, which has filed consolidated tax returns for a number of years. During 2002, P Corporation began selling inventory items to S Corporation. P and S use the first-in, first-out inventory method. The intercompany profit on P's sales to S was $125,000 in 2002. Goods remaining in S's inventory at the end of 2002 accounted for $35,000 of the intercompany profit. During 2003, all of S's beginning inventory of goods acquired from P in 2002 was sold to unrelated parties and the intercompany profit on P's current sales of inventory to S amounted to $240,000. Goods remaining in S's inventory at the end of 2003 accounted for $60,000 of the intercompany profit. Taxable income for the P-S affiliated group (excluding the deferral and restoration of profits on intercompany inventory sales) is $100,000 in each year. What is consolidated taxable income for 2002 and 2003 for the P-S group?

C8-44 *Intercompany Transactions.* P and S Corporations form the P-S affiliated group. P has owned all the S Corporation stock since 1996. The affiliated group has filed consolidated tax returns since 1996. No intragroup inventory sales occurred before 2002. During 2002, P sells S 100,000 widgets, earning $5 per unit profit on the sale. S uses the FIFO method to account for its inventories. On January 1, 2003, 25,000 widgets remain in S's inventory. During 2003, S sells the beginning widget inventory and purchases 175,000 additional widgets. P earns a $6 per unit profit on the sale. S retains 40,000 of these units in its 2003 ending inventory. No additional widgets are purchased in 2004. All widgets in beginning inventory are sold by S during 2004.

a. What intercompany profit amounts are deferred in 2002? In 2003? In 2004?
b. How would your answer to Part a change if the LIFO inventory method were instead used? (Assume the 2003 year-end LIFO inventory includes 25,000 units acquired in 2002 and 15,000 units acquired in 2003.)

C8-45 *Intercompany Transactions.* P Corporation has owned all of the stock of S Corporation since 1997. The P-S affiliated group begins filing a consolidated tax return in 2001 using the calendar year as its tax year. Both corporations use the accrual method of accounting. On July 1, 2002, P lends S $250,000 on a one-year note. Interest is charged at a 12% simple rate. The loan and interest are paid on June 30, 2003.

a. When does P report its interest income in its separate tax return? When does S report its interest expense in its separate tax return?
b. How would your answer to Part a change if P instead used the cash method of accounting?

C8-46 *Intercompany Transactions.* P and S Corporations form the P-S affiliated group. S Corporation owns 80% of an LLC that is engaged in a manufacturing business. Peter Hart owns the remaining 20% of the LLC. The LLC has not elected under the check-the-box regulations to be taxed as a corporation. S Corporation sells inventory costing $125,000 to the LLC for $250,000. How does S Corporation report the profit on the sale?

C8-47 *Dividends-Received Deduction.* P, S and T Corporations form the P-S-T affiliated group. The P-S-T group has filed consolidated tax returns for several years. P, S and T report separate taxable income amounts (excluding any dividend payments, eliminations, and dividends-received deductions) of $200,000, ($70,000), and $175,000, respectively, for the current year. Cash dividend payments received by P and S this year are as follows:

Shareholder Corporation	*Distributing Corporation*	*Amount*
P	T	$125,000
P	100%-owned nonconsolidated domestic life insurance company	15,000
S	20%-owned domestic corporation	40,000
P	51%-owned nonconsolidated foreign corporation	10,000

a. What is the amount of the gross income reported in the P and S separate tax returns as a result of the four distributions?

b. What is the amount of the consolidated dividends-received deduction?

c. Why might P elect to claim a 100% dividends-received deduction for the dividend received from T for federal income tax purposes, even though a consolidated tax return is being filed?

C8-48 ***Charitable Contribution Deduction.*** P and S Corporations form the P-S affiliated group. This group has filed consolidated tax returns for several years. The group reports consolidated taxable income (excluding charitable contributions) for the current year of $60,000. Included in this amount are a consolidated dividends-received deduction of $8,000 and an NOL deduction of $25,000 that represents a carryover of last year's consolidated NOL. P and S Corporations make cash contributions to public charities of $18,000 and $10,000, respectively, during this year.

a. What is the P-S group's consolidated taxable income?

b. What is the amount of the charitable contributions carryover?

C8-49 ***NOL Carrybacks and Carryovers.*** P and S Corporations form the P-S affiliated group, which files consolidated tax returns for the period 2001 through 2004. The affiliated group reports the following results for this period:

	Taxable Income			
Group Member	*2001*	*2002*	*2003*	*2004*
P	$10,000	($6,000)	$20,000	$15,000
S	2,000	2,000	(30,000)	10,000
Consolidated taxable income (excluding NOL deduction)	$12,000	($4,000)	($10,000)	$25,000

No elections were made to forgo the NOL carrybacks.

a. What portion of the 2002 and 2003 consolidated NOLs can be carried back to 2001? Forward to 2004?

b. Who files for the tax refund when the 2002 and 2003 NOLs are carried back?

C8-50 ***NOL Carryover.*** P, S_1, and S_2 Corporations form the P-S_1-S_2 affiliated group, which has filed consolidated tax returns since the creation of all three corporations in 2001. At the close of business on July 10, 2003, P Corporation sells its entire interest in S_2 Corporation. The affiliated group remains in existence after the sale because P Corporation still owns all the S_1 stock. The P-S_1-S_2 group reports the following results for 2001 through 2003:

	Taxable Income		
Group Member	*2001*	*2002*	*2003*
P	$ 8,000	($12,000)	$16,000
S_1	9,000	(24,000)	(4,000)
S_2	10,000	(36,000)	6,000[a]
S_2 (7/11–12/31)			8,000[b]
Consolidated taxable income (excluding NOL deduction)	$27,000	($72,000)	$18,000

[a] Taxable income earned from January 1, 2003 through July 10, 2003.

[b] Taxable income from July 11, 2003 through December 31, 2003 is included in S_2's separate tax return.

What amount of 2002's consolidated NOL can the P-S_1 affiliated group carry over to 2003 and 2004? What amount can S_2 carry over to 2003 and 2004? When does the carryover expire?

C8-51 ***NOL Carryovers and Carrybacks.*** P Corporation acquires S Corporation on January 1, 2003. Each company filed separate calendar year tax returns for 2002. P and S report the following results for 2002 and 2003:

Group Member	*2002*	*2003*
P	$40,000	($30,000)
S	(30,000)	20,000
Taxable income	N/A	($10,000)

N/A = Not applicable

a. What are the 2003 tax consequences assuming a consolidated tax return is filed? What are the tax consequences if separate tax returns had instead been filed? (Ignore the Sec. 382 loss limitation that might apply to the acquisition of S.)

b. Assume P and S report the following taxable income in 2004 before any NOL carryover: P, $21,000; S, $6,000. What is the consolidated taxable income assuming a consolidated return was filed in 2003?

C8-52 ***Special NOL Limitation.*** P, S_1, and S_2 Corporations form the P-S_1-S_2 affiliated group. P Corporation was created by Bart on January 1, 2002. P purchased all the S_1 and S_2 Corporation stock on September 1, 2002, after both corporations were in operation for about six months. All three corporations filed separate tax returns in 2002. The P-S_1-S_2 affiliated group elected to file a consolidated tax return starting in 2003. The P-S_1-S_2 group, which is still owned by Bart, reports the following results for 2002 through 2004:

		Taxable Income	
Group Member	*2002*	*2003*	*2004*
P	($8,000)	$50,000	$10,000
S_1	(24,000)	20,000	(18,000)
S_2	(16,000)	(10,000)	15,000
Consolidated taxable income (excluding NOL deduction)	XXX	$60,000	$7,000

a. What loss carryovers are available to be used in 2003, 2004, and 2005? (Ignore the Sec. 382 loss limitation that might apply to the acquisitions of S_1 and S_2.)

b. How would your answer to Part a change if Bart instead created P, S_1, and S_2 Corporations as an affiliated group on January 1, 2002?

C8-53 ***Sec. 382 Loss Limitation.*** Mack owns all of the stock of P Corporation. P Corporation owns all the stock of S_1 and S_2 Corporations. At the close of business on December 31, 2001, Mack sells his P Corporation stock to Jack for $9 million. The P-$S_1$-$S_2$ affiliated group has a consolidated NOL carryover to 2002 of $1.5 million at the end of 2001.

a. Has a Sec. 382 ownership change occurred? Explain.

b. What is the P-S_1-S_2 affiliated group's consolidated Sec. 382 limitation for 2002 if the federal long-term tax-exempt rate is 5%? (Ignore the SRLY loss limitation that might apply to Jack's acquisition of the P Corporation stock.)

c. How much of the consolidated NOL carryover can be used in 2002 if the affiliated group's taxable income is $750,000? In 2003 if the affiliated group's consolidated taxable income is $200,000?

C8-54 ***Consolidated Taxable Income.*** P and S Corporations have filed consolidated tax returns for a number of years. P is an accrual method of accounting taxpayer, and S is a cash method of accounting taxpayer. P and S report separate return taxable income (before NOL and special deductions) for the current year of $100,000 and $150,000, respectively. These numbers include the following current year transactions or events accounted for appropriately on a separate return basis.

- P sold land held for investment purposes to S at a $25,000 profit three years ago. S sold the land (a Sec. 1231 asset) to an unrelated corporation this year for a $12,000 gain. The current year's gain is included in S's separate taxable income.
- P's separate taxable income includes a $15,000 dividend received from S Corporation.

- P sold inventory to S last year for which the deferred intercompany profit at the beginning of this year was $50,000. All this inventory was sold outside the affiliated group this year. Additional inventory was sold by P to S this year. Some of this inventory remained unsold at year-end. The intercompany profit on the unsold inventory included in P's separate taxable income is $80,000.
- The P-S group has a $20,000 NOL carryover available from last year.
- S receives a $10,000 dividend from an unrelated corporation. A $7,000 dividends-received deduction was claimed when determining S's separate return taxable income.
- P and S made charitable contributions of $16,000 and $12,000, respectively, this year that are included in the separate taxable income calculations.
- P lent S $150,000 early in the current year. S repaid the loan before year-end. In addition, S paid P $6,000 of interest at the time of the repayment for the use of the borrowed money.

a. What is consolidated taxable income for the P-S affiliated group for the current year?
b. What is the consolidated tax liability?

COMPREHENSIVE PROBLEM

C8-55 Using the facts from Problem C8-57 below calculate the separate return tax liabilities of P and S Corporations. How much larger (or smaller) will the total of the two separate return tax liabilities be than the affiliated group's consolidated return tax liability? What taxes are due (or refund available) if Flying Gator made $125,000 of estimated tax payments and T Corporation made $25,000 of estimated tax payments?

TAX STRATEGY PROBLEM

C8-56 Sandra and John, who are unrelated, own all of Alpha and Beta Corporations. John owns 60% of Alpha's stock and 40% of Beta's stock. Sandra owns 40% of Alpha's stock and 60% of Beta's stock. For five years, Alpha has conducted manufacturing activities and sold machine parts primarily in the eastern United States. Alpha has reported $75,000 of operating profits in each of the last two years. Alpha's operating profits are expected to grow to $150,000 during the next five years. Alpha still has $100,000 of NOLs that need to be used before it starts paying federal income taxes. Alpha sells 25% of its product to Beta. Beta has been working to establish a market niche for reselling Alpha products in the southwestern United States. In the start-up phase of establishing the market, Beta incurred $200,000 of NOLs. Under the sales arrangement with Alpha, probably the best that Beta can hope to achieve in the short-run is reach a break-even point.

Required: What suggestions can you offer Sandra and John about the short-term possibility of using Alpha and Beta's NOLs against the profits that Alpha expects to earn and about minimizing their overall tax liabilities if both businesses become profitable? Sandra has specifically asked about merging the two companies into a single entity so the losses of one entity can offset the profits of the other and delay the need to pay income taxes to the federal government. Sandra indicates that the two companies were created for non-tax reasons. The operating situation has changed and, according to Sandra, now may be the time to combine the entities into one. However, John is not sure that bringing the two businesses together is a good idea.

TAX FORM/RETURN PREPARATION PROBLEM

C8-57 The Flying Gator Corporation and its 100%-owned subsidiary, T Corporation, have filed consolidated tax returns for a number of years. Both corporations use the hybrid method of accounting. During the current year, they report the operating results as listed in Table C8-2. Note the following additional information:

- Flying Gator and T Corporations are the only members of their controlled group.
- Flying Gator's address is 2101 W. University Ave., Gainesburg, FL 32611. Its employer identification number is 38-2345678. Flying Gator was incorporated on June 11, 1990. Its total assets are $430,000. Flying Gator made estimated tax payments of $150,000 for the affiliated group in the current year. Stephen Marks is Flying Gator's president.
- A $30,000 NOL carryover from the immediately preceding year is available. P Corporation incurred the NOL last year.

- Flying Gator uses the last-in, first-out (LIFO) inventory method. T began selling inventory to Flying Gator in the preceding year, which resulted in a $40,000 year-end deferred intercompany profit. An additional LIFO inventory layer was created by T's sales to Flying Gator during the current year that remained unsold at year-end. The intercompany profit on the additional inventory is $45,000. None of the original LIFO layer was sold during the current year.
- All of Flying Gator's dividends are received from T. T's dividends are received from a 25%-owned domestic corporation. All distributions are from E&P.
- Flying Gator received its interest income from T. The interest is paid on March 31 of the current year on a loan that was outstanding from October 1 of the preceding year through March 31 of the current year. No interest income was accrued at the end of the preceding tax year. T paid $5,000 of its interest expense to a third party.
- Officer's salaries are $80,000 for Flying Gator and $65,000 for T Corporation These amounts are included in salaries and wages in Table C8-2.
- Flying Gator's capital losses include a $10,000 long-term loss on a sale of land to T in the current year. T held the land at year-end.
- There are no non-recaptured net Sec. 1231 losses from prior tax years.
- T's Sec. 1245 gains include $20,000 recognized on the sale of equipment to Flying Gator at the close of business on September 30 in the current year. The asset cost $100,000 and had been depreciated for two years by T as five-year property under the MACRS rules. T claimed nine months of depreciation in the current (second) year. Flying Gator began depreciating the property in the current year by using the MACRS rules and a five-year recovery period. Flying Gator claimed three months of depreciation on the property in the current year.

Determine the affiliated group's current year consolidated tax liability. Prepare the front page of the affiliated group's current year corporate income tax return (Form 1120). Hint: Prepare a spreadsheet similar to the one included in Appendix B to arrive at consolidated taxable income.

▼ TABLE C8-2

Flying Gator Corporation's Current Year Operating Results (Problem C8-57)

Income or Deductions	Flying Gator	T	Total
Gross receipts	$2,500,000	$1,250,000	$3,750,000
Cost of goods sold	(1,500,000)	(700,000)	(2,200,000)
Gross profit	$1,000,000	$ 550,000	$1,550,000
Dividends	100,000	50,000	150,000
Interest	15,000		15,000
Sec. 1231 gain		20,000	20,000
Sec. 1245 gain		25,000	25,000
Long-term capital gain (loss)	(5,000)	6,000	1,000
Short-term capital gain (loss)		(3,000)	(3,000)
Total income	$1,110,000	$ 648,000	$1,758,000
Salaries and wages	175,000	200,000	375,000
Repairs	25,000	40,000	65,000
Bad debts	10,000	5,000	15,000
Taxes	18,000	24,000	42,000
Interest	30,000	20,000	50,000
Charitable contributions	22,000	48,000	70,000
Depreciation (other than that included in cost of goods sold)	85,000	40,000	125,000
Other expenses	160,000	260,000	420,000
Total deductions	$ 525,000	$ 637,000	$1,162,000
Separate return taxable income (before NOL and special deductions)	$ 585,000	$ 11,000	$ 596,000

CASE STUDY PROBLEMS

C8-58 P Corporation operates six fast-food restaurants in a metropolitan area. The restaurants have been a huge success in their first three years of operation and P's annual taxable income exceeds $600,000. The real estate associated with the six restaurants is owned by J Corporation. P Corporation leases its restaurant locations from J Corporation. J Corporation is reporting large interest and MACRS depreciation deductions because of a highly leveraged operation. As a result, J Corporation has reported NOLs in its first three years of operation. Both P and J Corporations file separate tax returns.

Both corporations are owned by Carol, who is in her late 20s. Carol sees the idea for the restaurant chain starting to really develop and expects to add six more locations in each of the next two years. You and Carol have been friends for a number of years. Because of the rapid expansion that is planned, she feels that she has outgrown her father's accountant and needs to have new ideas to help her save tax dollars so that she can reinvest more money in the business.

Required: The tax partner that you have been assigned to requests that you prepare a memorandum outlining your thoughts about Carol's tax problems and the suggested solutions to those problems in preparation for his meeting next week with Carol.

TAX RESEARCH PROBLEMS

C8-59 Angela owns all the stock of A, B, and P Corporations. P Corporation has owned all the stock of S_1 Corporation for six years. The P-S_1 affiliated group has filed a consolidated tax return in each of these six years using the calendar year as its tax year. On July 10 of the current year, Angela sells her entire stock investment in A Corporation, which uses the calendar year as its tax year. No change takes place in Angela's ownership of B stock during the tax year. At the close of business on November 25 of this year, S_1 Corporation purchases 90% of the common stock and 80% of the nonconvertible, nonvoting preferred stock (measured by value) of S_2 Corporation. A, P, S_1, and S_2 Corporations are domestic corporations that do not retain any special filing status. Which corporations are included in the affiliated group? In the controlled group? What income is included in the various tax returns? How is the allocation of the income between tax years made if the books are not closed on the sale or acquisition dates? If no special allocations are made, what portion of the reduced tax rate benefits of Sec. 11(b) can be claimed in the current year by the affiliated group? In future years?

TAX & FINANCIAL ACCOUNTING

C8-60 P Corporation owns 100% of S Corporation's single class of stock. The two corporations prepare consolidated financial statements and file consolidated tax returns on a calendar year basis. Both corporations use the accrual method of accounting. During 2002, the affiliated group reports the following two intercompany transactions.

- P sold a machine to S for $22,000 cash at the close of business on June 30, 2002. The machine was acquired on July 1, 2000 for $24,000. The machine was depreciated over ten years using the straight-line method for financial accounting purposes. The machine was depreciated for tax purposes as five-year property under the MACRS rules.
- S loaned P $100,000 on January 1, 2002. The interest rate is 12%. The first six months of interest (but none of the principal) has been paid by year-end.
- P and S contributed $50,000 and $25,000, respectively, to charitable organizations during 2002. All contributions were made in cash. The contributions were expensed for financial accounting purposes and deducted in arriving at each firm's separate taxable income amount. The consolidated charitable contribution limitation is $40,000.

Explain how the three events are reported for financial accounting and tax purposes.

C8-61 P, S, and T Corporations have filed a consolidated tax return for a number of years using the calendar year as its tax year. Current plans call for P Corporation to purchase all of X Corporation's stock at the close of business on June 30 of the current year from three individuals. X Corporation was created seven years ago and always has been an S corporation using the calendar year as its tax year. The chief financial officer of P Corporation comes to your office and makes a number of inquiries about the tax consequences of the acquisition including: Can X Corporation retain its S election? If so, does it file a federal income tax return separate from the affiliated group? Does X Corporation have to be included in the P-S-T group's consolidated tax return? Assuming the acquisition takes place as planned, what tax returns are required of the affiliated group and X Corporation? What income is included in the pre-affiliation tax return of X Corporation (if required) and the affiliated group's consolidated tax return? Prepare a brief memo for the chief financial officer outlining the answers to these questions and any other questions you feel are relevant.

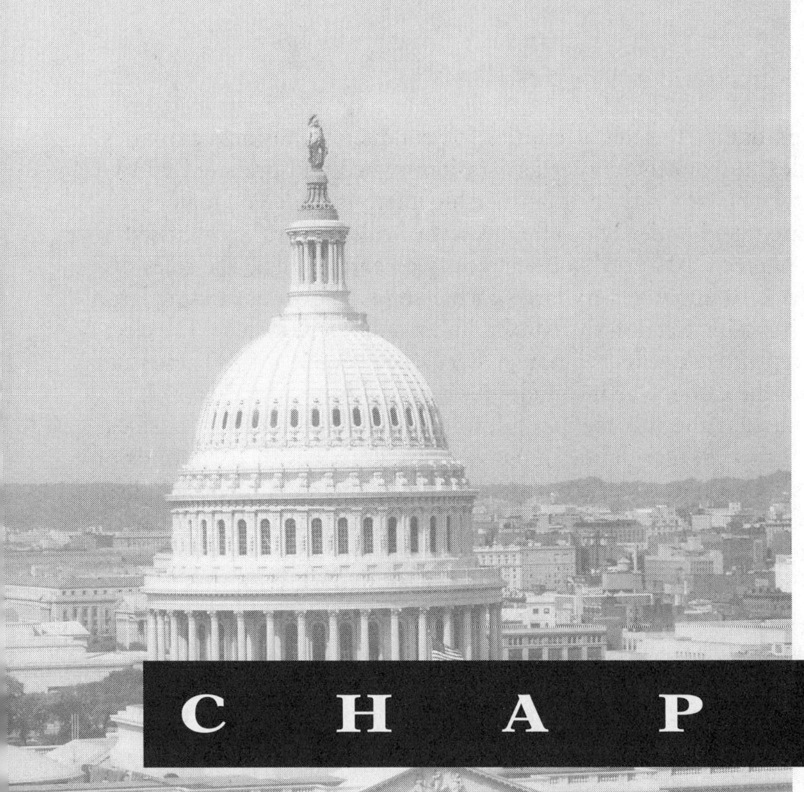

9

CHAPTER

PARTNERSHIP FORMATION AND OPERATION

LEARNING OBJECTIVES

After studying this chapter, you should be able to

1. Differentiate between general and limited partnerships
2. Explain the tax results of a contribution of property or services in exchange for a partnership interest
3. Determine the permitted tax years for a partnership
4. Differentiate between items that must be separately stated and those that are included in ordinary income or loss for partnerships that are not electing large partnerships
5. Calculate a partner's distributive share of partnership income, gain, loss, deduction, or credit items
6. Explain the requirements for a special partnership allocation
7. Calculate a partner's basis in a partnership interest
8. Determine the limitations on a partner's deduction of partnership losses
9. Determine the tax consequences of a guaranteed payment
10. Explain the requirements for recognizing the holder of a partnership interest as a partner in a family partnership
11. Determine the allocation of partnership income between a donor and a donee of a partnership interest
12. Determine the requirements for filing a partnership tax return

CHAPTER OUTLINE

Definition of a Partnership...9-2
Overview of Taxation of Partnership Income...9-4
Tax Implications of Formation of a Partnership...9-5
Partnership Elections...9-12
Partnership Reporting of Income...9-16
Partner Reporting of Income...9-17
Basis for Partnership Interest...9-21
Special Loss Limitations...9-24
Transactions Between a Partner and the Partnership...9-26
Family Partnerships...9-29
Tax Planning Considerations...9-30
Compliance and Procedural Considerations...9-31

Partnerships have long been one of the major entities for conducting business activities. Partnerships vary in complexity from the corner gas station owned and operated by two brothers to syndicated tax partnerships with their partnership interests traded on major security markets. Partnerships are taxed under two different sets of rules: the rules discussed in Chapter C9 and most of Chapter C10 apply to the majority of partnerships; the rules discussed at the end of Chapter C10 apply to very large partnerships (known as electing large partnerships), which make a specific election to be taxed under a different system. The electing large partnership rules apply to tax years beginning after December 31, 1997. These rules are found in Subchapter K of the Code, which includes the material from Secs. 701-777.

Chapters C9 and C10 discuss the income tax rules applying to partnership business operations. The first part of this chapter defines a partnership, describes the two kinds of partnerships, and discusses the formation of a partnership. The remainder of this chapter deals with the ongoing operations of a partnership, such as the annual taxation of partnership earnings, transactions between partners and the partnership, and a partner's basis in a partnership interest. This chapter also considers procedural matters, such as reporting the annual partnership income and IRS audit procedures for partnerships and their partners. Chapter C10 continues by discussing distributions to the partners and the tax implications of the numerous transactions that can be used to terminate a partner's interest in a partnership. Chapter C10 also discusses the unique problems of limited partnerships and the taxation of publicly traded partnerships and electing large partnerships.

DEFINITION OF A PARTNERSHIP

ADDITIONAL COMMENT

Even though the formation of a partnership requires no legal documentation, to prevent subsequent disagreements and arguments, a formal written partnership agreement is recommended.

For tax purposes, the definition of a partnership includes "a syndicate, group, pool, joint venture, or other unincorporated organization" that carries on a business or financial operation or venture. However, a trust, estate, or corporation cannot be taxed as a partnership. Unlike a corporation, which can exist only after incorporation documents are finalized, formation of a partnership requires no legal documentation. If two people (or business entities) work together to carry on any business or financial operation with the intention of making a profit and sharing that profit as co-owners, a partnership exists for federal income tax purposes.[1]

The IRC and Treasury Regulations define a **partner** only as a member of a partnership. It is clear from years of case law and common business practice that a partner can be an individual, trust, estate, or corporation. The only restriction on the number of partners is that a partnership must have at least two partners, but a large syndicated partnership may have hundreds or even thousands of partners.

GENERAL AND LIMITED PARTNERSHIPS

OBJECTIVE 1

Differentiate between general and limited partnerships

Each state has laws governing the rights and restrictions of partnerships. Almost all state statutes are modeled on the Uniform Partnership Act (UPA) or the Uniform Limited Partnership Act (ULPA) and thus have strong similarities to each other. A partnership can take two legal forms: a general partnership or a limited partnership. The differences between the two forms are substantial and extend to the partners' legal rights and liabilities as well as the tax consequences of operations to the partners. Because these differences are so important, we examine the two partnership forms before proceeding with further discussion of the partnership tax rules.

KEY POINT

When deciding on the form in which to conduct a business, probably the strongest argument against a general partnership is that each partner has unlimited liability for partnership debts.

GENERAL PARTNERSHIPS. A **general partnership** exists any time two or more partners join together and do not specifically provide that one or more of the partners is a limited partner (as defined below). In a general partnership, each partner has the right to par-

[1] Section 761(a) allows an election to avoid the Subchapter K rules for a very limited group of business owners.

ticipate in the management of the partnership. However, the general partnership form is flexible enough to allow the business affairs of the general partnership to be managed by a single partner chosen by the general partners.

While only one (or a few) of the general partners may exercise management duties, each **general partner** has the ability to make commitments for the partnership.[2] In a general partnership, each partner has unlimited liability for all partnership debts. If the partnership fails to pay its debts, each partner may have to pay far more than the amount he or she has invested in the venture. Thus, each partner faces the risk of losing personal assets if the partnership incurs business losses. This fact is the single biggest drawback to the general partnership form of doing business.

REAL-WORLD EXAMPLE

For 1998, 1.76 million partnership returns were filed. Of these, 945,000 were general partnerships, 343,000 were limited partnerships and 470,000 were limited liability companies. The average general partnership had 3.9 partners, the average limited partnership had 27.2 partners, and the average limited liability company had 4.0 members.

LIMITED PARTNERSHIPS. A **limited partnership** has two classes of partners. It must have at least one general partner, who essentially has the same rights and liabilities as any general partner in a general partnership,[3] and at least one **limited partner**. Even if a partnership becomes bankrupt, a limited partner can lose no more than his or her original investment plus any additional amount he or she has committed to contribute. However, a limited partner has no right to be active in the partnership's management.[4]

Even with this rudimentary explanation of the rights of general and limited partners, it should be apparent that a general partnership is an unwieldy form for operating a business with a large number of owners. A limited partnership having one (or a small number of) general partners, however, can be useful for a business operation that needs to attract a large amount of capital. In fact, one common form for a tax shelter investment is a limited partnership having a corporation with a small amount of capital as its sole general partner. Such an arrangement allows the tax advantages of the partnership form (detailed in the remainder of this chapter and in the next chapter) while retaining the limited liability feature for virtually every investor.

Many of these limited partnerships are so large and widely held that in many ways they appear more like corporations than partnerships. As discussed in Chapter C10, the tax laws provide that publicly traded partnerships may be reclassified for tax purposes as corporations.

REAL-WORLD EXAMPLE

The number of limited liability companies has increased from 50,000 in 1994 to 470,000 in 1998.

LIMITED LIABILITY COMPANIES (LLCs). With the advent of LLCs, businesses have the opportunity to be taxed as a partnership while having limited liability protection for every owner. State law provides this limited liability. Unique tax rules for LLCs have not been developed. Instead, the check-the-box regulations (discussed in Chapter C2) permit each LLC to choose whether to be taxed as a partnership or as a corporation. If an LLC is considered a partnership for tax purposes, the same tax rules apply to the LLC that apply to a traditional partnership. Chapter C10 further discusses the taxation of LLCs.

TAX STRATEGY TIP

A business that expects losses in its early years may wish to form an LLC initially so that losses pass through to the owners. Later, if the business expects to grow, it can consider incorporating as a C corporation and retaining its earnings to fund this expansion.

LIMITED LIABILITY PARTNERSHIPS (LLPs). Initially, professional organizations in certain fields (e.g., public accounting and law) were not permitted to operate as LLCs and therefore remained general partnerships. Subsequently, many states have added LLPs to the list of permissible business forms. The primary difference between a general partnership and an LLP is that, in an LLP, a partner is not liable for damages resulting from failures in the work of other partners or of people supervised by other partners. An LLP can be taxed under the check-the-box regulations as a partnership or as a corporation. Like an LLC, the default tax classification of an LLP is a partnership. The same tax rules apply to an LLP that apply to a traditional partnership. Chapter C10 further discusses the taxation of LLPs.

ELECTING LARGE PARTNERSHIPS. Partnerships that qualify as "large partnerships" may elect to be taxed under a simplified reporting arrangement. To qualify as a large partnership, the partnership must not be a service partnership and must not be engaged in

[2] Uniform Partnership Act.

[3] Uniform Limited Partnership Act.

[4] Under Sec. 9 of the Uniform Limited Partnership Act only general partners are empowered to manage the partnership's business.

commodity trading. Further, to qualify to make this election, the partnership must have at least 100 partners (excluding those partners who do provide substantial services in connection with the partnership's business activities) throughout the tax year. Once the partnership makes the election, it reports its income under a simplified reporting scheme, is subject to different rules about when the partnership terminates, and is subject to a different system of audits. The election is irrevocable without IRS permission. Chapter C10 presents details about the taxation of electing large partnerships.

OVERVIEW OF TAXATION OF PARTNERSHIP INCOME

REAL-WORLD EXAMPLE

In 1998, 56.8% of all partnerships were in finance, insurance, and real estate industries, and 17.4% were in service industries.

This overview gives a broad perspective of the taxation of partnership income other than income earned by electing large partnerships. (Appendix F compares the tax characteristics of a partnership, a C corporation, and an S corporation.) More detailed descriptions follow the overview. Chapter C10 presents details about the taxation of electing large partnerships.

PARTNERSHIP PROFITS AND LOSSES

A partnership is not a taxpaying entity, and income earned by a partnership is not subject to two layers of federal income taxes. Instead, each partner reports a share of the partnership's income, gain, loss, deduction, and credit items as a part of his or her income tax return. The partnership, however, must file Form 1065 (U.S. Partnership Return of Income), an information return that provides the IRS with information about partnership earnings as well as how the earnings are allocated among the partners. The partnership must elect a tax year and accounting methods to calculate its earnings. (Appendix B includes a completed partnership tax return that shows a Form 1065 and Schedule K-1 for a partner along with a set of supporting facts.)

ADDITIONAL COMMENT

Because most partnerships use the calendar year as their tax year, the K-1s are not due until April 15. Because a calendar year corporate partner's return is due on March 15 and an individual partner's return is due on April 15, partners often must request extensions for filing their returns. An electing large partnership must provide K-1s by March 15 following the close of the partnership tax year.

Each partner receives a Schedule K-1 from the partnership, which informs the partner of the amount and character of his or her share of partnership income. The partner then combines his or her partnership earnings and losses with all other items of income or loss to be reported for the tax year, computes the amount of taxable income, and calculates the tax bill. Partnership income is taxed at the applicable tax rate for its partners, which can range from 15% to 38.6% (in 2002) for partners who are individuals, trusts, or estates. Corporate partners pay tax on partnership income at rates ranging from 15% to 39%.

One of the major advantages of the partnership form of doing business is that partnership losses are allocated among the partners. If the loss limitation rules (explained later in this chapter) do not apply, these losses are combined with the partners' other income, and the result is an immediate tax savings for the partners. The immediate tax saving available to the partner contrasts sharply with the net operating loss (NOL) carrybacks or carryforwards that result from a C corporation's tax loss.

SELF-STUDY QUESTION

Why does a partner need to know his or her basis in his or her partnership interest?

ANSWER

Three important reasons are (1) to determine the gain/loss on a sale of the partnership interest, (2) to determine the amount of partnership losses a partner can deduct, and (3) to determine the amount of distributions that are tax-free to the partner.

THE PARTNER'S BASIS

A partner's basis in his or her partnership interest is a crucial element in partnership taxation. When a partner makes a contribution to a partnership or purchases a partnership interest, he or she establishes a beginning basis. Because the partners are personally liable for partnership debts, a partner's basis in his or her partnership interest is increased by his or her share of any partnership liabilities. Accordingly, the partner's basis fluctuates as the partnership borrows and repays loans or increases and decreases its accounts payable. In addition, a partner's basis in his or her partnership interest is increased by the partner's share of partnership income and decreased by his or her share of partnership losses. Because a partner's basis in his or her partnership interest can never be negative, the basis serves as one limit on the amount of deductible partnership losses. (See the discussion on pages C9-24 through C9-26 about the various loss limitations.)

EXAMPLE C9-1 ▶ Tom purchases a 20% interest in the XY Partnership for $8,000 on January 1, 2002, and begins to materially participate in the partnership's business. The XY Partnership uses the calendar year as its tax year. At the time of the purchase, the XY Partnership has $2,000 in liabilities, and Tom's share is 20%. Tom's basis in his partnership interest on January 1 is $8,400 [$8,000 + (0.20 × $2,000)]. ◀

EXAMPLE C9-2 ▶ Assume the same facts as in Example C9-1 except the XY Partnership incurs $10,000 in losses, and its liabilities increase by $4,000 during 2002. What is Tom's basis on December 31?

January 1 basis	$8,400
Plus: Share of liability increase ($4,000 × 0.20)	800
Minus: Share of partnership losses ($10,000 × 0.20)	(2,000)
December 31 basis	$7,200 ◀

EXAMPLE C9-3 ▶ Assume the same facts as in Example C9-2 except the XY Partnership incurs $60,000 in losses, and its liabilities increase by $10,000 during 2003. Tom's share of the losses is $12,000 ($60,000 × 0.20). What is the maximum amount that he can deduct?

January 1 basis	$7,200
Plus: Share of liability increase	2,000
December 31 basis before losses	$9,200
Minus: Maximum loss to be deducted	(9,200)
December 31 basis	$ -0-

Tom's remaining $2,800 in losses carry over to a later year and are deducted when he has sufficient basis in his partnership interest. ◀

TYPICAL MISCONCEPTION

Many taxpayers think that partners pay taxes when they receive distributions from the partnership. However, distributions generally are tax-free because they are merely the receipt of earnings that already have been taxed to the partners.

PARTNERSHIP DISTRIBUTIONS

When a partnership makes a current distribution, the distribution generally is tax-free to the partners because it represents the receipt of earnings that already have been taxed to the partners. Distributions reduce the partner's basis in his or her partnership interest. If a cash distribution is so large that it exceeds a partner's basis in his or her partnership interest, the partner recognizes gain equal to the amount of the excess. When the partnership goes out of business or when a partner withdraws from the partnership, the partnership makes liquidating distributions to the partner. Like current distributions, these distributions generally cause the partner to recognize gain only if the cash received exceeds the partner's basis in his or her partnership interest. A partner may recognize a loss if he or she receives only cash, inventory, and unrealized receivables in complete liquidation of his or her partnership interest. (Distributions are discussed in Chapter C10.)

TAX IMPLICATIONS OF FORMATION OF A PARTNERSHIP

When two or more individuals or entities decide to operate an unincorporated business together, they form a partnership. The following sections examine the tax implications of property contributions, service contributions, and organization and syndication expenditures.

OBJECTIVE 2

Explain the tax results of a contribution of property or services in exchange for a partnership interest

CONTRIBUTION OF PROPERTY

NONRECOGNITION OF GAIN OR LOSS. Section 721 governs the formation of a partnership. In most cases, the IRC provides that a partner who contributes property in exchange for a partnership interest recognizes no gain or loss on the transaction. Likewise, the partnership recognizes no gain or loss on the contribution of property. The partner's basis for his or her partnership interest and the partnership's basis for the property both reference the property's basis in the transferor partner's hands.[5]

Nonrecognition treatment is limited to transactions in which a partner receives a partnership interest in exchange for a contribution of property. As in the corporate formation area, the term *property* includes cash, tangible property (e.g., buildings and land), and intangible property (e.g., franchise rights, trademarks, and leases).[6] Services are specifically excluded from the definition of property, so a contribution of services for a partnership interest is not a tax-free transaction.

ADDITIONAL COMMENT

For contributions to a corporation to be nontaxable, the contributing shareholders must control (own at least 80%) the corporation immediately after the transaction. No such control requirement exists for contributions to a partnership to be nontaxable.

RECOGNITION OF GAIN OR LOSS. The general rule of Sec. 721(a) provides that neither the partnership nor any partner recognizes gain or loss when partners contribute property in exchange for a partnership interest. Three exceptions to this general rule may require a partner to recognize a gain upon the contribution of property to a partnership in exchange for a partnership interest:

- Contribution of property to a partnership that would be treated as an investment company if it were incorporated
- Contribution of property followed by a distribution in an arrangement that may be considered a sale rather than a contribution
- Contribution of property to a partnership along with the partnership's assumption of liabilities previously owed by the partner

The investment company exception of Sec. 721(b) requires recognition of gain only if the exchange results in diversification of the transferor's property interest.[7] If the contribution of property is to an investment partnership, the contributing partner must recognize any gain (but not loss) realized on the property transfer as if the stocks or securities were sold.

Sections 707(a)(2)(A) and (B) set out the second exception, which holds that a property contribution followed by a distribution (or an allocation of income or gain) may be treated as a sale of property by the partner to the partnership rather than as a contribution made by the partner to the partnership. For example, Treasury Regulations may require sale treatment (and the recognition of gain or loss) if the distribution would not have occurred except for the contribution.

EXAMPLE C9-4 ▶ In return for a 40% interest in the CD Partnership, Cara contributed land with a $100,000 fair market value (FMV). The partners agreed that the partnership would distribute $100,000 in cash to Cara immediately after the contribution. Because the cash distribution would not have happened had Cara not first contributed the land and become a partner, the transaction is likely to be treated as a sale of the land by Cara to the partnership. ◀

If the distribution does not occur simultaneously with the contribution, the transaction is treated as a sale if the later distribution is not dependent on the normal business risk of the enterprise.

EXAMPLE C9-5 ▶ Elena received a 30% interest in the DEF Partnership in return for her contribution of land having a $60,000 FMV. The partnership waits six months and then distributes $60,000 in cash to Elena. If the $60,000 distribution was not contingent on the partnership's earnings or ability to borrow funds or other normal risks of doing business, the distribution and contribution will be treated as a sale of land by Elena to the partnership. ◀

EFFECTS OF LIABILITIES. The third condition that may cause a partner to recognize gain (but not loss) on the formation of a partnership is the contribution of property to a partnership along with the partnership's assumption of liabilities previously owed by the

---

[5] Secs. 722 and 723.

[6] For an excellent discussion of the definition of the term *property*, see footnote 6 of *D.N. Stafford v. U.S.*, 45 AFTR 2d 80-785, 80-1 USTC ¶9218 (5th Cir., 1980).

[7] Reg. Sec. 1.351-1(c)(1). This investment is taxed only when immediately after the exchange more than 80% of the value of the partnership's assets (excluding cash and nonconvertible debt obligations) is held for investment or is readily marketable stocks, securities, or interests in regulated investment companies or real estate investment trusts.

KEY POINT

A partner's relief of debt is treated as if the partner receives a cash distribution. A partner's assumption of debt is treated as if the partner makes a cash contribution. These two simple rules are critical to understanding transactions such as formations of partnerships, distributions from partnerships, and sales or liquidations of partnership interests.

partner. Because each partner is liable for his or her share of partnership liabilities, increases and decreases in the partnership liabilities are reflected in each partner's basis. Specifically, Sec. 752 provides that two effects result from a partner's contribution of property to a partnership if the partnership also assumes the partner's liabilities.

- Each partner's basis is increased by his or her share of the partnership's liabilities as if he or she had contributed cash to the partnership in the amount of his or her share of partnership liabilities.
- The partner whose personal liabilities are assumed by the partnership has a reduction in the basis of his or her partnership interest as if the partnership distributed cash to him or her in the amount of the assumed liability. A cash distribution first reduces the partner's basis in the partnership interest. If the cash distribution exceeds the partner's predistribution basis in the partnership interest, the partner recognizes gain.

The net effect of these two basis adjustments, however, is seldom large enough to cause a transferor partner to recognize gain when he or she contributes property to the partnership. The transferor partner is deemed first to have made a contribution of property plus a contribution of cash equal to the partner's share of any partnership liabilities existing prior to his or her entrance into the partnership (or contributed by other partners concurrently with this transaction). The partner then is deemed to have received a cash distribution equal to the total amount of his or her own liability assumed by the *other* partners. (No basis adjustment is required for the portion of the liability transferred to the partnership by the transferor that he or she will retain as a partner.) The following examples help clarify the necessary basis adjustments.

EXAMPLE C9-6 ▶

In return for a 20% partnership interest, Mary contributes land having a $60,000 FMV and a $30,000 basis to the XY Partnership. The partnership assumes Mary's $15,000 liability arising from her purchase of the land, and Mary has a 20% share of partnership liabilities. The XY Partnership has $4,000 in liabilities immediately before her contribution. What is Mary's basis in her partnership interest?

Basis of contributed property		$30,000
Plus:	Mary's share of existing partnership liabilities ($4,000 × 0.20)	800
Minus:	Mary's liabilities assumed by the other partners ($15,000 × 0.80)	(12,000)
Mary's basis in her partnership interest		$18,800

Mary recognizes no gain on the partnership's assumption of her liability because the deemed cash distribution from the assumption of her $12,000 in liabilities by the partnership does not exceed her $30,800 basis in the partnership interest immediately preceding the fictional distribution. ◀

ADDITIONAL COMMENT

In Example C9-6, the $12,000 reduction in basis also can be viewed as the net of $3,000, which is Mary's 20% share of the $15,000 increase in partnership liabilities, and $15,000, which is Mary's liability assumed by the partnership.

EXAMPLE C9-7 ▶

Assume the same facts as in Example C9-6 except the amount of the liability assumed by the XY Partnership is $50,000. Mary's basis in her partnership interest is calculated as follows:

Basis of contributed property		$30,000
Plus:	Mary's share of existing partnership liabilities ($4,000 × 0.20)	800
Predistribution basis		$30,800
Minus:	Mary's liabilities assumed by the other partners ($50,000 × 0.80)	(40,000)
Basis in partnership interest (cannot be negative)		$ –0–

The cash deemed distributed in excess of Mary's predistribution basis causes her to recognize a $9,200 ($40,000 − $30,800) gain. Mary reduces her basis to zero by the distribution because a partner's basis in the partnership interest can never be less than zero. ◀

ADDITIONAL COMMENT

In contrast to partnership formations, had Example C9-7 involved a formation of the XY Corporation, Mary would have recognized a $20,000 Sec. 357(c) gain.

STOP & THINK

Question: Assume the land Mary contributed in Example C9-6 has a $60,000 FMV and an $85,000 adjusted basis. Should Mary contribute it to the partnership?

Solution: If Mary contributes the land, she cannot recognize her $25,000 ($60,000 FMV − $85,000 adjusted basis) loss until the partnership disposes of the property. Accordingly, Mary might prefer to sell the property and recognize her loss now. If the partnership can afford the $60,000 price and needs this property, Mary could sell the land to the partnership, recognize her loss on the sale, and then contribute the cash she receives from the partnership in exchange for her partnership interest. If the partnership does not need the property, Mary could sell the land to a third party, recognize her loss, and contribute the sales proceeds to the partnership in exchange for her partnership interest. However, a problem arises if the partnership needs this property and cannot afford to buy it from Mary. In that case, contributing the property to the partnership may be the best alternative despite the less-than-optimal tax results.

TYPICAL MISCONCEPTION

Example C9-7 illustrates another difference between partnership and corporate formations. In the example, XY Partnership does not increase its basis in the property for the gain recognized by Mary, but if XY were a corporation, XY would increase its basis in the property by Mary's recognized gain.

Because the partnership's assumption of a partner's liabilities is treated as a cash distribution, the character of any gain recognized by the partner is controlled by the partnership distribution rules. Cash distributions exceeding predistribution basis always result in gain recognition, and that gain is deemed to be gain from the sale of the partnership interest.[8] Because a partnership interest is usually a capital asset, any gain arising from assumption of a partner's liabilities normally is a capital gain.

PARTNER'S BASIS IN THE PARTNERSHIP INTEREST (COMMONLY CALLED THE OUTSIDE BASIS). In general, the transferor partner's beginning basis in the partnership interest equals the sum of money contributed plus his or her basis in contributed property. If the partner recognizes any gain on the contribution because the partnership is an investment company, the amount of recognized gain increases his or her basis in the partnership interest.[9] Beginning basis is adjusted to reflect liability share. Any gain recognized because of the effects of liabilities on the partner's basis does not increase the basis for the partnership interest because in this situation the basis is zero.

It should be noted that valuable property having little or no basis may be contributed. For example, accounts receivable or notes receivable of a partner using the cash method of accounting can be a valued contribution to a partnership, but if the receivables' bases are zero, the beginning basis of the partnership interest also is zero.

TYPICAL MISCONCEPTION

If a partner contributes both ordinary income property and capital gain property to a partnership, the partner apparently has two different holding periods for his or her partnership interest. Once the partner has held this interest more than 12 months, this difference becomes a moot point.

HOLDING PERIOD FOR PARTNERSHIP INTEREST. The holding period for the partnership interest includes the transferor's holding period for the contributed property if that property is a capital asset or a Sec. 1231 asset in the transferor's hands.[10] If the contributed property is an ordinary income asset (e.g., inventory) to the partner, the holding period for the partnership interest begins the day after the date of the contribution.[11]

EXAMPLE C9-8 ▶ On April 1, Sue contributes a building (a Sec. 1231 asset) to the ST Partnership in exchange for a 20% interest. Sue purchased the building three years ago. Her holding period for her partnership interest includes her holding period for the contributed building. ◀

EXAMPLE C9-9 ▶ On April 1, Ted contributes inventory to the ST Partnership in exchange for a 20% interest. No matter when Ted acquired the inventory, his holding period for his partnership interest begins on April 2, the day after the date of his contribution. ◀

PARTNERSHIP'S BASIS IN PROPERTY. Under Sec. 723, the partnership's basis for contributed property is the same as the property's basis in the hands of the contributing partner. If, however, the contributing partner recognizes gain because the partnership is an investment company, such gain increases the partnership's basis in the contributed property. Gain recognized by the contributing partner because of the assumption of a partner's liability does not increase the partnership's basis in the property.[12]

Not only does the property's basis carry over to the partnership from the contributing partner, but for some property the character of gain or loss on a subsequent disposition of the property by the partnership also references the character of the property in the contributing partner's hands. Section 724 prevents the transformation of ordinary income into capital gains (or capital losses into ordinary losses) when a partner contributes prop-

---

[8] Sec. 731(a).
[9] Sec. 722.
[10] Sec. 1223(1).
[11] Reg. Sec. 1.1223-1(a).
[12] Rev. Rul. 84-15, 1984-1 C.B. 158.

erty to a partnership. Properties that were (1) unrealized receivables, inventory, or capital loss property in the hands of the contributing partner and (2) contributed to a partnership after March 31, 1984 retain their character for some subsequent partnership dispositions.[13]

Unrealized Receivables. The concept of unrealized receivables plays a key role for tax purposes in many different partnership transactions. An **unrealized receivable** is any right to payment for goods or services that has not been included in income because of the accounting method being used.[14] The most common examples of unrealized receivables are the accounts receivable of a cash method of accounting taxpayer.

If property is an unrealized receivable in the hands of the contributing partner, any gain or loss recognized on the partnership's later disposition of the property is treated as ordinary income or loss. Ordinary income or loss treatment is mandated without regard to the period of time the partnership holds the property before disposition or the character of the property in the partnership's hands.

Inventory. If property was inventory in the hands of the contributing partner, its character cannot be changed for five years. Any gain or loss recognized by the partnership on the disposition of such property during the five-year period beginning on the date of contribution is ordinary gain or loss. Ordinary gain or loss treatment is mandated even if the asset is a capital asset or Sec. 1231 asset in the partnership's hands.

EXAMPLE C9-10 ▶ On June 1, Jose, a real estate developer, contributes ten acres of land in an industrial park he developed to the Hi-Tech Partnership in exchange for a 30% interest in the partnership. Although Jose was holding the acreage in inventory, the land serves as the site for Hi-Tech's new research facility. Four years later Hi-Tech sells its research facility and the land. Gain on the sale of the land, which usually would be taxed as Sec. 1231 gain, is reported as ordinary income under Sec. 724. ◀

ADDITIONAL COMMENT

Congress enacted Sec. 724 to eliminate the ability to transform the character of gain/loss on property by contributing the property to a partnership and having the partnership subsequently sell it.

Capital Loss Property. The final type of property whose character is fixed at the time of the contribution is property that would generate a capital loss if it were sold by the contributing partner rather than contributed to the partnership. A loss recognized by the partnership on the disposition of the property within five years of the date it is contributed to the partnership is a capital loss. However, the amount of loss characterized as capital may not exceed the capital loss the contributing partner would have recognized had the partner sold the property on the contribution date. The character of any loss that exceeds the difference between the property's FMV and its adjusted basis on the contribution date is determined by the property's character in the hands of the partnership.

EXAMPLE C9-11 ▶ Pam holds investment land that she purchased for $50,000 in 1997. The FMV of the land was only $40,000 in 2000 when she contributed it to the PK Partnership, which is in the business of developing and selling lots. PK develops the contributed land and sells it in 2002 for $28,000, or at a $22,000 loss. The $10,000 loss that accrued while Pam held the land as a capital asset retains its character as a capital loss. The remaining $12,000 of loss that accrues while the land is part of the partnership's inventory is an ordinary loss. ◀

PARTNERSHIP'S HOLDING PERIOD. Under Sec. 1223(2), the partnership's holding period for its contributed assets includes the holding period of the contributing partner. This rule applies without regard to the character of the property in the contributing partner's hands or the partnership's hands.

SECTION 1245 AND 1250 RECAPTURE RULES. Although the Sec. 1245 and Sec. 1250 depreciation recapture rules override most other gain nonrecognition provisions in

[13] Sec. 724. The determination of whether property is an unrealized receivable, inventory, or a capital loss property in the contributing partner's hands occurs immediately before the contribution.

[14] Section 724(d)(1) references the unrealized receivables definition found in Sec. 751(c). For distributions and sale transactions, the unrealized receivables definition is broadened to include certain recapture items; this difference is discussed more fully in Chapter C10.

the IRC, the partner incurs no depreciation recapture unless he or she recognizes gain upon contributing property in exchange for a partnership interest.[15] Instead, both the adjusted basis and depreciation recapture potential carry over to the partnership. If the partnership later sells the property at a gain, the Sec. 1245 and 1250 provisions affect the character of the gain.

CONTRIBUTION OF PROPERTY AFTER FORMATION. Any time a partner contributes property in exchange for a partnership interest, the rules outlined above apply whether the contribution occurs during the formation of the partnership or at a later date. This treatment contrasts sharply with corporate contributions, where a tax-free contribution after formation is rare because of the 80% control requirement. Most contributions of property in exchange for a partnership interest are tax-free even if they occur years after the partnership was formed.

CONTRIBUTION OF SERVICES

A partner who receives a partnership interest in exchange for services has been compensated as surely as if he or she receives cash and thus must recognize ordinary income. The amount and timing of the income to be recognized are determined under Sec. 83. Consequently, receipt of an unrestricted interest in a partnership requires the service partner to immediately recognize income equal to the FMV of the partnership interest less any cash or property contributed by the partner. Generally, the service partner recognizes no income upon receiving a restricted interest in a partnership until the restriction lapses or the interest can be freely transferred.

SELF-STUDY QUESTION

Does the contribution of services to a partnership in exchange for an unrestricted partnership interest qualify for Sec. 721 nontaxable treatment?

ANSWER

No. The service partner recognizes income to the extent of the FMV of the partnership interest received less any cash or other property contributed by the partner.

Although a partnership interest seems to be a unified interest, it really is made up of two components: a capital interest and a profits interest. A partner may receive both components or only a profits interest in exchange for his or her services. (It is rare to have a capital interest without a profits interest.) Treasury Regulations indicate that a **capital interest** can be valued by determining the amount the partner would receive if the partnership liquidated on the day the partner receives the partnership interest.[16] If the partner would receive proceeds from the sale of the partnership's assets or receive the assets themselves, he or she is considered to own a capital interest. Alternatively, if the partner's only interest is in the future earnings of the partnership (with no interest in the current partnership assets), the partner owns a **profits interest** (but not a capital interest).

It has long been settled that receipt of a capital interest in a partnership in exchange for services is taxable under the rules outlined above. A profits interest is no more than a right to future income that will be taxed to the partner when it is earned. To the extent the profits interest itself has a value, it is reasonable to expect that the value be taxed when the partner receives the profits interest, as any other property received for services would be taxed.

EXAMPLE C9-12 ▶ Carl arranges favorable financing for the purchase of an office building and receives a 30% profits interest in a partnership formed to own and operate the building. Less than three weeks later, Carl sells his profits interest to his partner for $40,000. Carl must recognize $40,000 as ordinary income from the receipt of a partnership profits interest in exchange for services. ◀

The facts in Example C9-12 approximate those of *Sol Diamond,* a landmark partnership taxation case, which was the first case to tax the partner upon receipt of a profits interest.[17] The Tax Court pointed out that Sec. 61 included all compensation for services, and no other provision contained in the IRC or Treasury Regulations removed this transaction from taxation. The Seventh Circuit Court of Appeals seemed to limit the inclusion of a profits interest to situations in which the market value of the profits interest could be

---

[15] Secs. 1245(b)(3) and 1250(d)(3). Property acquired as a capital contribution where gain is not recognized under Sec. 721 is subject to the MACRS anti-churning rules of Sec. 168(i)(7)(A). In general, the anti-churning rules require the partnership to use the same depreciation method as the partner who contributed the property. See Chapter C2 for a discussion of these rules in connection with a corporate formation transaction.

[16] Reg. Sec. 1.704-1(e)(1)(v). The capital interest definition that is referenced relates to family partnerships. There is no reason to believe that such definition differs from the one used for this purpose.

[17] 33 AFTR 2d 74-852, 74-1 USTC ¶9306 (7th Cir., 1974), *aff'g.* 56 T.C. 530 (1971).

determined. Much of the uncertainty in this area of tax law was resolved when the IRS issued Rev. Proc. 93-27, which provides that the IRS generally will not tax a profits interest received for services. Such a profits interest will be taxed upon receipt only in three specified instances in which a FMV is readily ascertainable.[18] In the general case, an income tax is not levied on the profits interest separately, but all partnership profits that accrue to the partner are taxed under the normal rules of partnership taxation.

CONSEQUENCES TO THE PARTNERSHIP. Normally, payments made by the partnership for services are either deductible as an expense or capitalized. This result is unchanged when the partnership pays for services with an interest in the partnership. The timing of the partnership's deduction for the expense generally matches the timing for the partner to include the value of his or her partnership interest in income.[19]

Allocating The Expense Deduction. The expense deduction or the amortization of the capital expenditure is allocated among the partners other than the service partner. This allocation occurs because these partners make the outlay by relinquishing part of their interest in the partnership.

EXAMPLE C9-13 ▶ In June of the current year Jay, a lawyer, receives a 1% capital and profits interest (valued at $4,000) in the JLK Partnership in return for providing legal services to JLK's employees during the first five months of the current year. The legal services were a fringe benefit for JLK's employees and were deductible by JLK. Jay must include $4,000 in his current year gross income, and JLK can deduct the expense in the current year. JLK allocates the $4,000 expense to all partners other than Jay. ◀

If the service performed is of a nature that should be capitalized, the partnership capitalizes the amount and amortizes it as appropriate. The asset's basis is increased at the same time and in the same amount as the partner's gross income inclusion.[20]

EXAMPLE C9-14 ▶ In June of the current year, Rob, an architect, receives a 10% capital and profits interest in the KLB Partnership for his services in designing a new building to house the partnership's operations. The June value of the partnership interest is $24,000. Rob must recognize $24,000 of ordinary income in the current year as a result of receiving the partnership interest. The KLB Partnership must capitalize the $24,000 as part of the building's cost and depreciate that amount (along with the building's other costs) over its recovery period. ◀

The timing of the partner's recognition of income is not changed in the preceding two examples by the fact that the partnership could deduct one payment but had to capitalize the other.

Partnership Gain Or Loss. The partnership, in effect, pays for services by transferring an interest in partnership property. Generally, when a debtor uses property to pay a debt, the debtor must recognize gain or loss equal to the difference between the property's FMV and adjusted basis. Likewise, the partnership must recognize the gain or loss existing in the proportionate share of its assets deemed to be transferred to the service partner.[21] Furthermore, because the partnership must recognize gain or loss, the partnership's bases in its assets are adjusted.

EXAMPLE C9-15 ▶ On January 1 of the current year, Maria is admitted as a 25% partner in the XYZ Partnership in exchange for services valued at $16,500. The partnership has no liabilities at the time but has assets with a basis of $50,000 and FMV of $66,000. The transaction is taxed as if Maria received an undivided one-fourth interest in each asset. She is taxed on the $16,500 FMV of the assets

[18] 1993-2 C.B. 343. The three exceptions involve receipt of a profits interest having a substantially certain and predictable income stream, the partner disposes of the profits interest within two years of receipt, or the profits interest is a limited interest in a publicly traded partnership.

[19] Reg. Sec. 1.83-6(a)(1).

[20] Reg. Sec. 1.83-6(a)(4).

[21] Reg. Sec. 1.83-6(b).

and takes a $16,500 basis in the partnership interest. The partnership must recognize $4,000 of gain [0.25 × ($66,000 FMV − $50,000 adjusted basis)] on the assets deemed paid to Maria. The partnership calculates gain or loss for each asset XYZ holds, and the character of each asset determines the character of the gain or loss recognized. The partnership's original basis in its assets ($50,000) is increased by the $4,000 recognized gain. ◀

SELF-STUDY QUESTION

What is the importance of the distinction between organizational expenditures and syndication expenditures?

ANSWER

Organizational expenditures can be amortized over a period of not less than 60 months, but syndication expenditures are *not* deductible or amortizable.

ORGANIZATIONAL AND SYNDICATION EXPENDITURES

The costs of organizing a partnership are treated as capital expenditures. The capitalized amount can be amortized on a straight-line basis and deducted over a period of not less than 60 months beginning with the month in which the partnership begins business.[22] To amortize the organizational expenditures, the partnership must make an election that is included with the partnership tax return for the period including the month in which it begins business.

Organizational expenditures that can be capitalized and amortized must meet the same requirements as the costs incurred by a corporation making the Sec. 248 election to amortize organizational expenditures (see Chapter C3). The organizational expenditures must be incident to the creation of the partnership, chargeable to a capital account, and of a character that would be amortizable over the life of the partnership if the partnership had a limited life. Eligible expenditures include legal fees for negotiating and preparing partnership agreements, accounting fees for establishing the initial accounting system, and filing fees. Syndication expenditures for the issuing and marketing of interests in the partnership are not organizational expenditures and cannot be included in this election.[23] The partnership deducts unamortized organizational expenditures when it is terminated or liquidated.

Topic Review C9-1 summarizes the tax consequences of forming a partnership.

PARTNERSHIP ELECTIONS

OBJECTIVE 3

Determine the permitted tax years for a partnership

Once formed, the partnership must make a number of elections. For example, partnerships must select a tax year and elect accounting methods for all but a few items affecting the computation of partnership taxable income or loss.

PARTNERSHIP TAX YEAR

The partnership's selection of a tax year is critical because it determines when each partner reports his or her share of partnership income or loss. Under Sec. 706(a), each partner's tax return includes his or her share of partnership income, gain, loss, deduction, or credit items for any taxable year of the partnership ending within or with the partner's taxable year.

EXAMPLE C9-16 ▶ Vicki is a member of a partnership having a November 30 year-end. In her tax return for calendar year 2002, she must include her share of partnership items from the partnership tax year that ends November 30, 2002. Results of partnership operations in December 2002 are reported along with all other partnership items from the partnership year that ends on November 30, 2003 in Vicki's 2003 tax return. She receives, in essence, a one-year deferral of the taxes due on December's partnership income. ◀

SECTION 706 RESTRICTIONS. Because the choice of a tax year for a partnership can provide a substantial opportunity for tax deferral, Congress enacted Sec. 706 to restrict the available choices for a partnership's tax year. The partnership must use the same tax year as the one or more **majority partners** who have an aggregate interest in partnership profits and capital exceeding 50%. This rule must be used only if these majority partners have a common tax year and have had this tax year for the shorter of the three preceding

[22] Sec. 709(b).

[23] Reg. Sec. 1.709-2(a).

Topic Review C9-1

Formation of a Partnership

	Contribution to a Partnership	
	Property	**Services**
Recognition of gain, loss, or income by partner	Tax-free unless (1) liabilities assumed by the partnership exceed partner's predistribution basis in partnership interest (gain recognized is amount by which liabilities assumed by partnership exceed tentative basis), (2) the partnership formed is an investment partnership (gain recognized is excess of FMV of partnership interest over basis of assets contributed), or (3) a contribution is followed by a distribution that is treated as a sale (gain or loss recognized on sale transaction).	Taxable to partner equal to FMV of partnership interest received.
Basis of partnership interest	Substituted basis from property contributed plus share of partnership liabilities assumed minus the partner's liabilities assumed by the partnership. Gain recognized because of the investment company rules increases the basis of the partnership interest.	Amount of income recognized plus share of partnership liabilities assumed by the partner minus partner's liabilities assumed by the partnership.
Gain or loss recognized by the partnership	No gain or loss recognized by the partnership.	1. Deduction or capitalized expense is created depending on the type of service rendered. 2. Gain or loss recognized equals difference between FMV of portion of assets used to pay service partner and the basis of such portion of the assets.
Basis of assets to the partnership	Carryover basis is increased by gain recognized by the partner only if gain results from the formation of an investment partnership. No basis adjustment occurs when assumption of partner's liabilities results in gain recognition. In a sale transaction, assets take a cost basis.	Increased or decreased to reflect the FMV of the assets paid to the service partner.

years or the partnership's period of existence. If the tax year of the partner(s) owning a majority interest cannot be used, the partnership must use the tax year of all its principal partners (or the tax year to which all of its principal partners are concurrently changing). A **principal partner** is defined as one who owns a 5% or more interest in capital or profits.[24] If the principal partners do not have a common tax year, the partnership must use the tax year that allows the least aggregate deferral. The least aggregate deferral test provided in Treasury Regulations[25] requires that, for each possible tax year-end, each partner's ownership percentage be multiplied by the number of months the partner would defer income (number of months from partnership year-end to partner year-end). The number arrived at for each partner is totaled across all partners. The same procedure is followed for each alternative tax year, and the partnership must use the tax year that produces the smallest total.

EXAMPLE C9-17 ▶ Jane, Kerry Corporation, and Bob form the JKB Partnership. The three partners use tax years ending on December 31, June 30, and September 30, respectively. Jane, Kerry Corporation, and Bob own 40%, 40%, and 20%, respectively, of the partnership. Neither the majority partner rule nor the principal partner rule can be applied to determine JKB's tax year because each partner has a different year-end. To determine the least aggregate deferral, all three possible year-ends must be analyzed as follows:

[24] Sec. 706(b)(3).

[25] Temp. Reg. Sec. 1.706-1T.

WHAT WOULD YOU DO IN THIS SITUATION?

Bob Krause, and his large family corporation, have been longtime clients of your accounting firm. During the current year, Bob and his adult son, Tom, formed the BT Partnership to develop and sell vacation homes on the Suwanee River. Bob contributed a 1,000-acre tract of land in exchange for a 50% interest in BT Partnership's profits and losses. The land had a $300,000 FMV and a $30,000 adjusted basis. Tom contributed $150,000 in cash for the remaining 50% interest in the partnership. Two months after being formed, BT Partnership used the land as security for a $200,000 loan from a local bank. Of the $200,000 loan proceeds, the partnership used $50,000 to subdivide and plot the land. The partnership then distributed the other $150,000 of the loan proceeds to Bob. Bob plans not to report these transactions since property contributions in exchange for a partnership interest and distributions of money by a partnership that do not exceed the partner's basis are tax-free transactions. What would you advise your client to do in this situation?

			Possible Tax Year-Ends					
			6/30		*9/30*		*12/31*	
Partner	*Partnership Interest*	*Partner Tax Year*	*Months Deferred*[a]	*Total*[b]	*Months Deferred*	*Total*	*Months Deferred*	*Total*
Jane	40%	12/31	6	2.4	3	1.2	0	0
Kerry	40%	6/30	0	0	9	3.6	6	2.4
Bob	20%	9/30	3	0.6	0	0	9	1.8
				3.0		4.8		4.2

[a] Months from possible partnership tax year-end to partner tax year-end.
[b] Partnership interest × months deferred = Total.

The partnership must use a June 30 year-end because, with a total score of 3.0, that tax year-end produces the least aggregate deferral. ◀

If the partnership has a business purpose for using some tax year other than the year prescribed by these rules, the IRS may approve use of another tax year. Revenue Procedure 74-33[26] states that an acceptable business purpose for using a different tax year is to end the partnership's tax year at the end of the partnership's natural business year. This revenue procedure explains that a business having a peak period and a nonpeak period completes its natural business year at the end of its peak season (or shortly thereafter). For example, a ski lodge has a natural business year that ends in early spring. Partnerships that do not have a peak period cannot use the natural business year exception.

EXAMPLE C9-18 ▶ Amy, Brad, and Chris are equal partners in the ABC Partnership. Each partner uses a December 31 tax year-end. ABC earns 30% of its gross receipts in July and August each year and has experienced this pattern of earnings for more than three years. This is the peak season for their business each year. The IRS probably would grant approval for the partnership to use an August 31 tax year-end. ◀

KEY POINT

Because of the Sec. 706 requirements, most partnerships are required to adopt a calendar year. As a compromise, a Sec. 444 election permits a fiscal tax year as long as no more than a three-month deferral exists and as long as the deferral is not increased from any deferral already approved.

Section 444 provides an *election* that permits a partnership to use a year-end that results in a deferral of the lesser of the current deferral period or three months. The deferral period is the time from the beginning of the partnership's fiscal year to the close of the first required tax year ending within such year (i.e., usually December 31). The Sec. 444

[26] 1974-2 C.B. 489. The IRS in Rev. Rul. 87-57, 1987-2 C.B. 224, has provided a series of situations illustrating the business purpose requirement. In addition, Rev. Proc. 87-32, 1987-2 C.B. 396, provides expeditious IRS approval if the natural business year satisfies a 25% test. This test requires that 25% of the partnership's gross receipts be earned in the last two months of the requested year and in the last two months of the two preceding similar 12-month periods.

election is available to both new partnerships making an initial tax year election or existing partnerships that are changing tax years. A partnership that satisfies the Sec. 706 requirements described above or has established a business purpose for its choice of a year-end (i.e., natural business year) does not need a Sec. 444 election.

STOP & THINK *Question:* Suppose the ABC Partnership has had a December 31 year-end for many years. All its partners are individuals with calendar tax year-ends. Using Sec. 444, what tax year-ends are available for ABC?

Solution: Only December 31 can be used for a tax year-end for ABC even with Sec. 444. Section 444 allows a minimum deferral of the shorter of three months or the existing deferral. Because the existing deferral is zero months (the required tax year-end and the existing tax year-end are both December 31), no deferral is allowed under Sec. 444. The section allows a deferral only for new partnerships or for partnerships that already have a deferral.

HISTORICAL NOTE

Congress enacted Sec. 444, in part, as a concession to tax return preparers who already have the majority of their clients with calendar year-ends.

A partnership that makes a Sec. 444 election must make a required payment under Sec. 7519 (see the Compliance and Procedural Considerations section of this chapter for a discussion of the Sec. 444 election and Sec. 7519 required payment). The required payment has the effect of assessing a tax on the partnership's deferred income at the highest individual marginal tax rate plus one percentage point.

Topic Review C9-2 summarizes the allowable partnership tax year elections.

OTHER PARTNERSHIP ELECTIONS

With the exception of three specific elections reserved to the partners, Sec. 703(b) requires that the partnership make all elections that can affect the computation of taxable income derived from the partnership.[27] The three elections reserved to the individual partners relate to income from the discharge of indebtedness, deduction and recapture of certain mining exploration expenditures, and the choice between deducting or crediting foreign income taxes. Other than these elections, the partnership makes all elections at the entity level. Accordingly, the partnership elects its overall accounting method, which can differ from the methods used by its partners. The partnership also elects its inventory and depreciation methods.

Topic Review C9-2

Allowable Tax Year For a Partnership

Section 706 requires that a partnership select the highest ranked tax year-end from the ranking that follows:

1. The tax year-end used by the partners who own a majority of the partnership capital and profits.
2. The tax year-end used by all principal partners (i.e., a partner who owns at least 5% of the partnership capital or profits).
3. The tax year-end determined by the least aggregate deferral test.

The IRS may grant permission for the partnership to use a fiscal year-end if the partnership has a natural business year. If the partnership does not have a natural business year, it must either

- Use the tax year-end required by Sec. 706 or
- Elect a fiscal year-end under Sec. 444 and make a required payment that approximates the tax due on the deferred income.

[27] The partnership does not include depletion from oil or gas wells in its computation of income (Sec. 703(a)(2)(F)). Instead each partner elects cost or percentage depletion (Sec. 613A(c)(7)(D)).

PARTNERSHIP REPORTING OF INCOME

OBJECTIVE 4

Differentiate between items that must be separately stated and those that are included in ordinary income or loss for partnerships that are not electing large partnerships

PARTNERSHIP TAXABLE INCOME

Although the partnership is not a taxable entity, the IRC requires that the partnership calculate **partnership taxable income** for various computational reasons, such as adjusting the partners' basis in their partnership interests. Partnership taxable income for partnerships that are not electing large partnerships is calculated in much the same way as the taxable income of individuals, with a few differences mandated by the IRC. First, taxable income is divided into separately stated items and ordinary income or loss. Section 703(a) specifies a list of deductions available to individuals but that cannot be claimed by a partnership. The forbidden deductions include income taxes paid or accrued to a foreign country or U.S. possession, charitable contributions, oil and gas depletion, and net operating loss (NOL) carrybacks or carryovers. The first three items must be separately stated and may or may not be deductible by the partner. Because all losses are allocated to the partners for deduction on their tax returns, the partnership itself never has an NOL carryover or carryback. Instead, a partner may have an NOL if his or her deductible share of partnership losses exceeds his or her other business income. These NOLs are used at the partner level without any further regard for the partnership entity.

SEPARATELY STATED ITEMS

Each partner must report his or her distributive share of partnership income. However, Sec. 702 establishes a list of items that must be separately stated at the partnership level so that their character can remain intact at the partner reporting level. Section 702(a) lists the following items that must be separately stated:

- Net short-term capital gains and losses
- Net long-term capital gains and losses
- Sec. 1231 gains and losses
- Charitable contributions
- Dividends eligible for a dividends-received deduction
- Taxes paid or accrued to a foreign country or to a U.S. possession
- Any other item provided by Treasury Regulations

Regulation Sec. 1.702-1(a)(8) adds several other items to this list, including:

- Tax-exempt or partially tax-exempt interest
- Any items subject to special allocations (discussed below)

As a general rule, an item must be separately stated if the income tax liability of any partner that would result from treating the item separately is different from the liability that would result if that item were included in partnership ordinary income.[28]

EXAMPLE C9-19 ▶ Amy and Big Corporation are equal partners in the AB Partnership, which purchases new equipment during the current year at a total cost of $100,000. In 2002, AB elects to expense $24,000 under Sec. 179. Big Corporation already has expensed $9,000 under Sec. 179 this year. The Sec. 179 expense must be separately stated because Big Corporation is subject to a separate $24,000 limit of its own. ◀

Once the partnership separately states each item and allocates a distributive share to each partner, the partners report the separately stated items on their tax returns as if the partnership entity did not exist. A partner's share of partnership net long-term capital

[28] Reg. Sec. 1.702-1(a)(8)(ii).

ADDITIONAL COMMENT

The pass-through aspect of partnerships reflects the aggregate theory of partnerships, which holds that the partnership is merely an aggregate of its partners. In other ways, however, partnerships conform to the entity theory, for example, they report income and make elections at the entity level.

TYPICAL MISCONCEPTION

Partnership ordinary income/loss is the sum of all taxable income/loss items not separately stated. This amount is reported as a residual number on line 22 of Form 1065. Partnership taxable income includes both the taxable separately stated items and the partnership ordinary income/loss. Students should not use these two terms interchangeably.

gains or losses is combined with the partner's personal long-term capital gains and losses to calculate the partner's net long-term capital gain or loss. Likewise, a partner's share of partnership charitable contributions is combined with the partner's own charitable contributions with the total subject to the partner's charitable contribution limitations. In summary, Sec. 702(b) requires that the character of each separately stated item be determined at the partnership level. The amount then passes through to the partners and is reported in each partner's return as if the partner directly realized the amount.

PARTNERSHIP ORDINARY INCOME

All taxable items of income, gain, loss, or deduction that do not have to be separately stated are combined into a total called **partnership ordinary income** or **loss.** This ordinary income amount sometimes is incorrectly referred to as partnership taxable income. Partnership taxable income is the sum of all taxable items among the separately stated items plus the partnership ordinary income or loss. Therefore, partnership taxable income often is substantially greater than partnership ordinary income.

Included in the partnership's ordinary income are items such as gross profit on sales, administrative expenses, and employee salaries. Such items are always ordinary income or expenses not subject to special limitations. Partnership ordinary income also includes Sec. 1245 depreciation recapture because such ordinary income is not eligible for preferential treatment.

The partnership allocates a share of partnership ordinary income or loss to each partner. Such an allocation is reported on Schedules K and K-1 of the partnership's Form 1065 (see the completed partnership tax return in Appendix B). An individual partner reports his or her distributive share of ordinary income, or the deductible portion of his or her distributive share of ordinary loss, on Schedule E of Form 1040. Schedule E includes rental and royalty income and income or losses from estates, trusts, S corporations, and partnerships. A corporate partner reports partnership ordinary income or loss in the Other Income category of Form 1120.

PARTNER REPORTING OF INCOME

OBJECTIVE 5

Calculate a partner's distributive share of partnership income, gain, loss, deduction, or credit items

PARTNER'S DISTRIBUTIVE SHARE

Once the partnership determines separately stated income, gain, loss, deduction, or credit items, and partnership ordinary income or loss, the partnership must allocate the totals among the partners. Each partner must report and pay taxes on his or her distributive share. Under Sec. 704(b), the partner's distributive share normally is determined by the terms of the partnership agreement or, if the partnership agreement is silent, by the partner's overall interest in the partnership as determined by taking into account all facts and circumstances.

Note that the term **distributive share** is misleading because it has nothing to do with the amount actually distributed to a partner. A partner's distributive share is the portion of partnership taxable and nontaxable income that the partner has agreed to report for tax purposes. Actual distributions in a given year may be more or less than the partner's distributive share.

PARTNERSHIP AGREEMENT. The **partnership agreement** may describe a partner's distributive share by indicating the partner's profits and loss interest, or it may indicate separate profits and loss interests. For example, the partnership agreement may state that a partner has a 10% interest in both partnership profits and losses or a partner has only a 10% interest in partnership profits (i.e., profits interest) but has a 30% interest in partnership losses (i.e., loss interest).

If the partnership agreement states only one interest percentage, it is used to allocate both partnership profit and loss. If the partnership agreement states profit and loss percentages separately, the partnership's taxable income for the year is first totaled to determine whether a net profit or net loss has occurred. Then the appropriate percentage (either profit or loss) applies to each class of income for the year.[29]

EXAMPLE C9-20 ▶ The ABC Partnership reports the following income and loss items for the current year:

Net long-term capital loss	$100,000
Net Sec. 1231 gain	90,000
Ordinary income	220,000

Carmelia has a 20% profits interest and a 30% loss interest in the ABC Partnership. Because the partnership earns a $210,000 ($90,000 + $220,000 − $100,000) net profit, Carmelia's distributive share is calculated using her 20% profits interest and is reported as follows:

Net long-term capital loss	$ 20,000
Net Sec. 1231 gain	18,000
Ordinary income	44,000

Her loss percentage is used only in years in which the partnership has a net loss. ◀

VARYING INTEREST RULE. If a partner's ownership interest changes during the partnership tax year, the income or loss allocation takes into account the partner's varying interest.[30] This varying interest rule applies for changes occurring to a partner's interest as a result of buying an additional interest in the partnership, selling part (but not all) of a partnership interest, or giving or being given a partnership interest, or the admission of a new partner. The partner's ownership interest generally applies to the income earned on a pro rata basis.

EXAMPLE C9-21 ▶ Maria owns 20% of the XYZ Partnership from January 1 through June 30 of the current year (not a leap year). On July 1 she buys an additional 10% interest in the partnership. During this year, XYZ Partnership has ordinary income of $120,000, which it earned evenly throughout the year. Maria's $30,049 ($11,901 + $18,148) distributive share of income is calculated as follows:

Pre-July 1: $\$120{,}000 \times \frac{181 \text{ days}}{365 \text{ days}} \times 0.20 = \$11{,}901$

Post-June 30: $\$120{,}000 \times \frac{184 \text{ days}}{365 \text{ days}} \times 0.30 = \$18{,}148$

Similar calculations would be made if the XYZ Partnership reported separately stated items such as capital gains and losses. ◀

SPECIAL ALLOCATIONS

OBJECTIVE 6

Explain the requirements for a special partnership allocation

Special allocations are unique to partnerships and allow tremendous flexibility in sharing specific items of income and loss among the partners. Special allocations can provide a specified partner with more or less of an item of income, gain, loss, or deduction than would be available using the partner's regular distributive share. Special allocations fall into two categories. First, Sec. 704 requires certain special allocations with respect to contributed property. Second, other special allocations are allowed as long as they meet the tests laid out in Treasury Regulations for having substantial economic effect. If the special allocation fails the substantial economic effect test, it is disregarded, and the income, gain, loss, or deduction is allocated according to the partner's interest in the partnership as expressed in the actual operations and activities.

BOOK-TO-TAX ACCOUNTING COMPARISON

For tax purposes, the partnership takes a carryover basis in contributed property. For book purposes, however, the partnership records the contributed property at its FMV.

ALLOCATIONS RELATED TO CONTRIBUTED PROPERTY. As previously discussed, when a partner contributes property to a partnership, the property takes a carryover basis that references the contributing partner's basis. With no special allocations, this carryover basis rule would require the partnership (and each partner) to accept the tax burden of any gain or loss that accrued to the property before its contribution.

---

[29] This rule is derived from the House and Senate reports on the original Sec. 704(b) provisions. The two reports are identical and read, "The income ratio shall be applicable if the partnership has taxable income . . . and the loss ratio shall be applicable [if] the partnership has a loss." H. Rept. No. 1337, 83d Cong., 2d Sess., p. A223 (1954); S. Rept. No. 1622, 83d Cong., 2d Sess., p. 379 (1954).

[30] Sec. 706(d)(1).

EXAMPLE C9-22 ▶ In the current year, Elizabeth contributes land having a $4,000 basis and a $10,000 FMV to the DEF Partnership. Assuming the property continues to increase in value, or at least does not decline in value, DEF's gain on the ultimate sale of this property is $6,000 greater than the gain that accrues while the partnership owns the property. Without a special allocation, this $6,000 precontribution gain would be allocated among all partners. ◀

Section 704(c), however, requires precontribution gains or losses to be allocated to the contributing partner for any property contributed to a partnership after March 31, 1984. Thus, the precontribution gain of $6,000 in Example C9-22 would be allocated to Elizabeth. In addition, income and deductions reported with respect to contributed property must be allocated to take into account the difference between the property's basis and FMV at the time of contribution. The allocation of depreciation is a common example of the special deduction allocation related to contributed property that is necessary under these rules.

EXAMPLE C9-23 ▶ Kay and Sam form an equal partnership when Sam contributes cash of $10,000 and Kay contributes land having a $6,000 basis and a $10,000 FMV. If the partnership sells the land two years later for $12,000, the $4,000 precontribution gain ($10,000 FMV − $6,000 basis) is allocated only to Kay. The $2,000 gain that accrued while the partnership held the land ($12,000 sales price − $10,000 FMV at contribution) is allocated to Kay and Sam equally. Kay reports a total gain of $5,000 ($4,000 + $1,000), and Sam reports a $1,000 gain on the sale of the land. ◀

SUBSTANTIAL ECONOMIC EFFECT. Special allocations not related to contributed property must meet several specific criteria established by Treasury Regulations. These criteria ensure that the allocations affect the partner's economic consequences and not just their tax consequences.

EXAMPLE C9-24 ▶ The AB Partnership earns $10,000 in tax-exempt interest income and $10,000 in taxable interest income each year. Andy and Becky each have 50% capital and profit interests in the partnership. An allocation of the tax-exempt interest income to Andy, a 38.6% tax bracket partner, and the taxable interest income to Becky, a 15% tax bracket partner, does not have substantial economic effect. ◀

The allocation described in Example C9-24 affects only the tax consequences to the partners because a 50% distributive share would not really change the partner's economic position separate from the tax consequences.

BOOK-TO-TAX ACCOUNTING COMPARISON

The capital accounts for meeting the substantial economic effect requirements are maintained using book value accounting rather than tax accounting.

To separate transactions only affecting taxes from those affecting the partner's economic position, Treasury Regulations look at whether the allocation has an economic effect and whether the economic effect is substantial. Under the Sec. 704 regulations, the allocation has economic effect if it meets all three of the following conditions:

- ▶ The allocation results in the appropriate increase or decrease in the partner's capital account.
- ▶ The proceeds of any liquidation occurring at any time in the partnership's life cycle are distributed in accordance with positive capital account balances.
- ▶ Partners must make up negative balances in their capital accounts upon the liquidation of the partnership, and these contributions are used to pay partnership debts or are allocated to partners having positive capital account balances.[31]

EXAMPLE C9-25 ▶ Arnie and Bonnie each contribute $100,000 to form the AB Partnership on January 1, 2002. The partnership uses these contributions plus a $1.8 million mortgage to purchase a $2 million office building. To simplify the calculations, assume the partnership depreciates the building using the straight-line method over a 40-year life and that in each year income and expenses are equal before considering depreciation. AB makes a special allocation of depreciation to Arnie. The allocation reduces Arnie's capital account, and the partnership makes any liquidating distributions in accordance with the capital account balances. Allocations through 2004 are as follows:

[31] Reg. Sec. 1.704-1(b)(2)(ii). Treasury Regulations provide other alternatives for meeting this portion of the requirements.

	Capital Account Balance	
	Arnie	Bonnie
January 1, 2002 balance	$100,000	$100,000
2002 loss	(50,000)	–0–
2003 loss	(50,000)	–0–
2004 loss	(50,000)	–0–
December 31, 2004 balance	($ 50,000)	$100,000

If we assume that the property has declined in value in an amount equal to the depreciation claimed and that the partnership is now liquidated, the need for the requirement to restore negative capital account balances becomes apparent.

Sales price of property on December 31, 2004	$1,850,000
Minus: Mortgage principal	(1,800,000)
Partnership cash to be distributed to partners	$ 50,000

If Arnie does not have to restore his negative capital account balance, Bonnie can receive only $50,000 in cash even though her capital account balance is $100,000. In effect, Bonnie has borne the economic burden of the 2004 depreciation. Without a requirement to restore the negative capital account balance, the special allocation to Arnie would be ignored for 2004, and Bonnie would receive the depreciation deduction. However, if Arnie must restore any negative capital account balance, he will contribute $50,000 when the partnership liquidates at the end of 2004, and Bonnie will receive her full $100,000 capital account balance. The 2004 special allocation to Arnie will then have economic effect. Note that Arnie's allocation for 2002 and 2003 is acceptable even without an agreement to restore negative capital account balances. This result occurs in each of these two years because Arnie has sufficient capital to absorb the economic loss if the property declines in value in an amount equal to the depreciation allocated to him.[32] ◀

ADDITIONAL COMMENT

The substantial economic effect rules ensure that cash flows ultimately conform to allocations and that allocations do not allow for abusive shifting of tax benefits among partners.

The second requirement for a special allocation to be accepted under Treasury Regulations is that the economic effect must be substantial, which requires that a reasonable possibility exists that the allocation will substantially affect the dollar amounts to be received by the partners independent of tax consequences.[33] For example, the allocation in Example C9-24 does not have a substantial effect. It also is highly unlikely that any special allocation of a tax credit can pass this test.

STOP & THINK

Question: The special allocation rules require that a partner who receives a special allocation of loss or expense receive less cash or property when the partnership liquidates. As we will see later in this chapter, losses reduce the partner's basis in the partnership interest, so a sale or liquidation of the partnership interest will cause the partner to recognize a larger gain (or a smaller loss) than would have resulted without this loss allocation. Because the basis is reduced, the partner also is more likely to recognize taxable gain on a distribution from the partnership. With these negative consequences, why would anyone want to be given a special allocation of partnership loss or expense?

Solution: The answer is a matter of timing. The specially allocated loss reduces taxable income now and saves more taxes now for the partner than would a "normal" loss allocation. The negative consequences occur when the partner incurs a larger gain (or smaller loss) upon a future sale or liquidation of his or her partnership interest. The special allocation scenario may have a greater after-tax present value to the partner than would the after-tax present value of receiving a normal share of losses and an increased liquidating distribution.

[32] Such allocations do not literally meet the three requirements outlined above for special allocations. However, allocations that meet the alternate standard—having sufficient capital to absorb the economic loss—are considered to be made in accordance with the partner's interest in the partnership and will be allowed.

[33] Reg. Sec. 1.704-1(b)(2)(iii)(A). It should be noted that the substantial economic effect regulations go far beyond the rules covered in this text.

BASIS FOR PARTNERSHIP INTEREST

OBJECTIVE 7

Calculate a partner's basis in a partnership interest

The calculation of a partner's beginning basis in a partnership interest depends on the method used to acquire the interest, with different valuation techniques for a purchased interest, a gifted interest, and an inherited interest. The results of the partnership's operations and liabilities both cause adjustments to the beginning amount. Additional contributions to the partnership and distributions from the partnership further alter the partner's basis.

ADDITIONAL COMMENT

A partner's basis in a partnership interest commonly is referred to as "outside basis" as opposed to "inside basis," which is the partnership's basis in its assets.

BEGINNING BASIS

A partner's beginning basis for a partnership interest received for a contribution of property or services has been discussed. However, a partner also can acquire a partnership interest by methods other than contributing property or services to the partnership. If the partnership interest is purchased from an existing partner, the new partner's basis is simply the price paid for the partnership interest, including assumption of partnership liabilities. If the partnership interest is inherited, the heir's basis is the FMV of the partnership interest on the decedent's date of death or, if elected by the executor, the alternate valuation date but not less than liabilities assumed. If a partnership interest is received as a gift, the donee's basis generally equals the donor's basis (including the donor's ratable share of partnership liabilities) plus the portion of any gift tax paid by the donor that relates to appreciation attaching to the gift property. In summary, the beginning basis for a partnership interest is calculated following the usual rules for the method of acquisition.

EFFECTS OF LIABILITIES

The effect of partnership liabilities on the basis of a partnership interest was briefly discussed in connection with the contribution of property subject to a liability. However, a more complete explanation is necessary to fully understand the pervasive impact of liabilities on partnership taxation.

SELF-STUDY QUESTION

What are some of the common methods of acquiring a partnership interest, and what is the beginning basis?

ANSWER

1. Purchase—cost basis
2. Inherit—FMV
3. Gift—usually donor's basis with a possible gift tax adjustment

INCREASES AND DECREASES IN LIABILITIES. Two changes in a partner's liabilities are considered contributions of cash by the partner to the partnership. The first is an increase in the partner's share of partnership liabilities. This increase can arise from either an increase in the partner's profit or loss interests or from an increase in total partnership liabilities. Accordingly, if a partnership incurs a large debt, the partners' bases in their partnership interests increase. The second way to increase a partner's basis is to have the partner assume partnership liabilities in an individual capacity.[34]

Conversely, two liability changes are treated as distributions of cash from the partnership to the partner. These changes are a decrease in a partner's share of partnership liabilities and a decrease in the partner's individual liabilities caused by the partnership's assumption of the partner's liability.[35] Often, both an increase and a decrease in a partner's basis for his or her interest can result from a single transaction. The steps used to calculate the partner's basis in his or her partnership interest are illustrated by the framework below.

	Partner's basis before liabilities
Plus:	Increases in share of partnership liabilities
Minus:	Decreases in share of partnership liabilities
Plus:	Partnership liabilities assumed by this partner
Minus:	This partner's liabilities assumed by the partnership
	Partner's basis in the partnership interest

[34] Sec. 752(a).

[35] Sec. 752(b).

EXAMPLE C9-26 ▶ Juan, a 40% partner in the ABC Partnership, has a $30,000 basis in his partnership interest before receiving a partnership distribution of land. As part of the transaction, Juan agrees to assume a $10,000 mortgage on the land. First, Juan's basis in his partnership interest will decrease by $4,000 for the decline in Juan's share of partnership liabilities resulting from the partnership no longer owing the $10,000 mortgage. Second, his basis in the partnership interest will increase by $10,000, which is the partnership liability he assumes in his individual capacity. The net change in basis in his partnership resulting from the liabilities is $6,000 (−$4,000 + $10,000). His basis in his partnership interest also must be adjusted for the land distribution he receives. Distributions will be discussed further in Chapter C10. ◀

A PARTNER'S SHARE OF LIABILITIES. Once the general impact of liabilities as increases and decreases in a partner's basis for his or her partnership interest is understood, the specific amount of the partner's share of the partnership's liabilities must be determined. In all examples until now, we have considered only general partners who have the same interest in profits and losses. Partnerships, however, commonly have one or more limited partners, and thus partners can have differing profit and loss ratios. Treasury Regulations provide guidelines for allocating partnership liabilities to the individual partners.

ADDITIONAL COMMENT

That a partner gets basis for his or her share of recourse debt is not controversial. That a partner gets basis for debt on which the partner is not personally liable seems questionable, yet other rules limit the benefit of the basis created by the nonrecourse debt.

Recourse And Nonrecourse Loans. A **recourse loan** is the usual kind of loan for which the borrower remains liable until the loan is paid. If the recourse loan is secured and the borrower fails to make payments as scheduled, the lender can sell the property used as security. If the sales proceeds are insufficient to repay a recourse loan, the borrower must make up the difference. Under Treasury Regulations, a recourse loan is one for which any partner or a related party will stand an economic loss if the partnership cannot pay the debt.[36] A **nonrecourse loan** is one in which the lender may sell the security if the loan is not paid, but no partner is liable for any deficiency. In short, the lender has no recourse against the borrower for additional amounts. Nonrecourse debts most commonly occur in connection with the financing of real property that is expected to substantially increase in value over the life of the loan.

TYPICAL MISCONCEPTION

Nonrecourse debt is allocated among all partners primarily according to their profit ratios. Recourse debt, on the other hand, is allocated to the limited partners to the extent they bear an economic risk of loss, but generally a limited partner's economic risk of loss is not greater than any additional amounts those partners have pledged to contribute. The remaining recourse debt is allocated among the general partners according to their economic risk of loss.

General And Limited Partners. A limited partner normally is not liable to pay partnership debts beyond the original contribution (which already is reflected in basis) and any additional amount the partner has pledged to contribute.[37] Therefore, recourse debt increases a limited partner's basis only to the extent the partner has a risk of economic loss. Nonrecourse debts increase a limited partner's basis based primarily on the profit ratio.[38]

A general partner's share of nonrecourse liabilities also is determined primarily by his or her profit ratio. Because limited partners seldom receive an allocated share of the recourse liabilities, the general partners share all recourse liabilities beyond any amounts the limited partners can claim according to their economic loss potential.

The Sec. 752 Treasury Regulations require that recourse liabilities be allocated to the partner who will bear the economic loss if the partnership cannot pay the debt. The regulations provide a complex procedure using a hypothetical liquidation to determine who would bear the loss. In this text, we assume that the hypothetical liquidation analysis has been completed and that the appropriate shares of economic loss as determined by the hypothetical liquidation procedure are stated as part of the problem or example information.

EXAMPLE C9-27 ▶ The ABC Partnership has one general partner (Anna) and a limited partner (Clay) with the following partnership interests:

---

36 Reg. Sec. 1.752-1(a).

37 This rule may be modified by the limited partner agreeing to assume some of the risk of economic loss despite his or her limited partner status. For example, a limited partner may guarantee the debt or may agree to reimburse the general partner some amount if the general partner has to pay the debt. These arrangements mean that the limited partner shares the risk of loss.

38 Some nonrecourse debt allocations involve two steps before an allocation according to profits interests. These two steps of the allocation process are beyond the scope of this explanation.

	Anna (General)	Clay (Limited)
Loss interest	80%	20%
Profits interest	60%	40%
Basis before liabilities	$100,000	$100,000

Clay has an obligation to make an additional $5,000 contribution. He has made no other agreements or guarantees. The partnership has two liabilities at year-end: a $300,000 nonrecourse debt and a $400,000 debt with recourse to the partnership. Clay has a risk of economic loss only to the extent that he has agreed to make additional contributions. The partners' year-end bases are calculated as follows:

	Anna (General)	Clay (Limited)
Year-end basis (excluding liabilities)	$100,000	$100,000
Share of:		
Recourse debt	395,000	5,000
Nonrecourse debt	180,000[a]	120,000[b]
Year-end basis	$675,000	$225,000

[a] 60% × $300,000 = $180,000
[b] 40% × $300,000 = $120,000

EFFECTS OF OPERATIONS

A partner's basis is a summary of his or her contributions and the partnership's liabilities, earnings, losses, and distributions. Basis prevents a second tax levy on a distribution of income that was taxed previously as a partner's distributive share. Section 705 mandates a basis increase for additional contributions made by the partner to the partnership plus the partner's distributive share for the current and prior tax years of the following items:

- Partnership taxable income (both separately stated items and partnership ordinary income)
- Tax-exempt income of the partnership

BOOK-TO-TAX ACCOUNTING COMPARISON

Although a partner's basis in the partnership cannot go below zero, a partner's book capital account (equity) may be negative.

Basis is decreased (but not below zero) by distributions from the partnership to the partner plus the partner's distributive share for the current and prior tax years of the following items:

- Partnership losses (both separately stated items and partnership ordinary loss)
- Expenditures that are not deductible for tax purposes and that are not capital expenditures

The positive basis adjustment for tax-exempt income and the negative basis adjustment for nondeductible expenses preserve that tax treatment for the partner. If these adjustments were not made, tax-exempt income would be taxable to the partner upon a subsequent distribution or upon the sale or other disposition of the partnership interest.

EXAMPLE C9-28 ▶ **LMN Partnership has only one asset—a $100,000 municipal bond. Marta has a $20,000 basis in her 20% partnership interest. In the current year, the partnership collects $4,000 tax-exempt interest from the bond. Marta's basis at year-end is:**

Beginning basis	$20,000
Share of tax-exempt income	800
Basis at year end	$20,800

On the first day of the next year, the partnership sells the bond for $100,000 cash. At this point, the partnership has $104,000 in cash and no other assets. The partnership liquidates and distributes her 20% share of the cash ($20,800) to Marta. Marta has no gain or loss because her $20,800 basis exactly equals her distribution. If the tax-exempt income had not increased her basis, she would have recognized an $800 gain on the distribution ($20,800 cash distribution − $20,000 basis if no increase were made for the tax-exempt income.) Her basis must be increased by tax-exempt income to prevent a taxable gain upon its distribution. ◀

OBJECTIVE 8

Determine the limitations on a partner's deduction of partnership losses

LOSS LIMITS. Each partner is allocated his or her distributive share of ordinary income or loss and separately stated income, gain, loss, or deduction items each year. The partner always reports income and gain items in his or her current tax year, and these items increase the partner's basis in the partnership interest. However, the partner may not be able to use his or her full distributive share of losses because Sec. 704(d) allows losses to be deducted only up to the amount of the partner's basis in the partnership interest before the loss. All positive basis adjustments for the year and all reductions for actual or deemed distributions must be made before determining the amount of the deductible loss.[39]

EXAMPLE C9-29 ▶ On January 1 of the current year, Miguel has a $32,000 basis for his general interest in the MT Partnership. He materially participates in the partnership's business activities. On December 1, Miguel receives a $1,000 cash distribution. His distributive share of MT's current items are a $4,000 net long-term capital gain and a $43,000 ordinary loss. Miguel's deductible loss is calculated as follows:

January 1 basis	$32,000
Plus: Long-term capital gain	4,000
Minus: Distribution	(1,000)
Limit for loss deduction	$35,000

Miguel can deduct $35,000 of the ordinary loss in the current year, which reduces his basis to zero. He cannot deduct the remaining $8,000 of ordinary loss currently but can deduct it in the following year if he has sufficient basis in his partnership interest. ◀

SELF-STUDY QUESTION

What happens to losses that are disallowed due to lack of basis in a partnership interest?

ANSWER

The losses are suspended until that partner obtains additional basis.

Any distributive share of loss that cannot be deducted because of the basis limit is simply noted in the partner's financial records. It is not reported on the partner's tax return, nor does it reduce the partner's basis. However, the losses carry forward until the partner again has positive basis from capital contributions, additional partnership borrowings, or partnership earnings.[40]

EXAMPLE C9-30 ▶ Assume the same facts as in Example C9-29. Miguel makes no additional contributions in the following year, and the MT Partnership's liabilities remain unchanged. Miguel's distributive share of MT's partnership items in the following year is $2,500 of net short-term capital gain and $14,000 of ordinary income. These items restore his basis to $16,500 (0 + $2,500 + $14,000), and he can deduct the $8,000 loss carryover. After taking these transactions into account, Miguel's basis is $8,500 ($16,500 − $8,000). ◀

Topic Review C9-3 summarizes the rules for determining the initial basis for a partnership interest and the annual basis adjustments required to determine the adjusted basis of a partnership interest.

SPECIAL LOSS LIMITATIONS

Three sets of rules limit the loss from a partnership interest that a partner may deduct. The Sec. 704(d) rules explained above limit losses to the partner's basis in the partnership interest. Two other rules establish more stringent limits. The at-risk rules limit losses to an amount called *at-risk basis*. The passive activity loss or credit limitation rules disallow most net passive activity losses.

AT-RISK LOSS LIMITATION

The Sec. 704(d) loss limitation rules were the only loss limits for many years. However, Congress became increasingly uncomfortable with allowing partners to increase their basis by a portion of the partnership's nonrecourse liabilities and then offset this basis with partnership losses. Accordingly, Congress established the **at-risk rules**, which limit loss deductions to the partner's at-risk basis. The **at-risk basis** is essentially the same amount as the regular partnership basis with the exception that liabilities increase the at-risk basis only if the partner is at risk for such an amount. The at-risk rules apply to individuals and closely held C corporations. Partners that are widely held C corporations are not subject to these rules.

[39] Reg. Sec. 1.704-1(d)(2).

[40] Reg. Sec. 1.704-1(d)(1).

Topic Review C9-3

Basis of a Partnership Interest

Method of Acquisition	Beginning Basis Is
Property contributed	Substituted basis from property contributed plus gain recognized for contributions to an investment partnership
Services contributed	Amount of income recognized for services rendered (plus any additional amount contributed)
Purchase	Cost
Gift	Donor's basis plus gift tax on appreciation
Inheritance	Fair market value at date of death or alternative valuation date
Liability Impact on Basis	
Increase basis for	Increases in the partner's share of partnership liabilities Liabilities of the partnership assumed by the partner in his or her individual capacity
Decrease basis for	Decreases in the partner's share of partnership liabilities Liabilities of the partner assumed by the partnership
Operations Impact on Basis	
Increase basis for	Partner's share of ordinary income and separately stated income and gain items (including tax-exempt items) Additional contributions to the partnership Precontribution gain recognized.
Decrease basis for	Distributions from the partnership to the partner Partner's share of ordinary loss and separately stated loss and deduction items (including items that are not deductible for tax purposes and are not capital expenditures) Precontribution loss recognized

Although much of the complexity of the *at-risk* term is beyond the scope of this text, a simplified working definition is possible: A partner is at risk for an amount if he or she would lose that amount should the partnership suddenly become worthless. Because a partner would not have to pay a partnership's nonrecourse liabilities even if the partnership became worthless, the usual nonrecourse liabilities cannot be included in any partner's at-risk basis. Under the at-risk rules, the loss that a partner can deduct may be substantially less than the amount deductible under the Sec. 704(d) rules.[41]

EXAMPLE C9-31 ▶ Keesha is a limited partner in the KM Manufacturing Partnership. At the end of the partnership's tax year, her basis in the partnership interest is $30,000 ($10,000 investment plus a $20,000 share of nonrecourse financing). Keesha's distributive share of partnership losses for the tax year is $18,000. Although she has sufficient basis in the partnership interest, the at-risk rules limit her deduction to $10,000 because she is not at risk for the nonrecourse financing. ◀

TYPICAL MISCONCEPTION

The at-risk rules severely limit the use of nonrecourse debt to obtain loss deductions except for certain qualified real estate financing, yet this real estate exception is more apparent than real because of the final set of rules that must be satisfied: the passive activity limitations.

The IRC allows one significant exception to the application of the at-risk rules. At-risk rules do not apply to nonrecourse debt if it is qualified real estate financing. The partner is at risk for his or her share of nonrecourse real estate financing if all of the following requirements are met:

- The financing is secured by real estate used in the partnership's real estate activity.
- The debt is not convertible to any kind of equity interest in the partnership.
- The financing is from a qualified person or from any federal, state, or local government, or is guaranteed by any federal, state, or local government.[42] A qualified person is an unrelated party who is in the trade or business of lending money (e.g., bank, financial institution, or mortgage broker).

---

[41] Sec. 465(a).

[42] Sec. 465(b)(6).

PASSIVE ACTIVITY LIMITATIONS

The 1986 Tax Reform Act added still a third set of limits to the loss that a partner may deduct: the passive activity loss and credit limitations.

Under the passive activity limitation rules of Sec. 469, all income is divided into three categories: amounts derived from passive activities; active income such as salary, bonuses, and income from businesses in which the taxpayer materially participates; and portfolio income such as dividends and interest. Generally, losses of an individual partner from a passive activity cannot be used to offset either active income or portfolio income. However, passive losses carry over to future years. These passive losses are allowed in full when a taxpayer disposes of the entire interest in the passive activity. Passive losses generated by a passive rental activity in which an individual partner is an active participant can be deducted up to a maximum of $25,000 per year. This deduction is phased out by 50% of the amount of the partner's adjusted gross income (AGI) that exceeds $100,000, so that no deduction is allowed if the partner has AGI of $150,000 or more. (The phase-out begins at $200,000 for low-income housing or rehabilitation credits.) Losses disallowed under the phase-out are deductible to the extent of passive income.

TAX STRATEGY TIP

If a partner is unable to use all of his or her share of partnership losses due to a lack of basis, contributions to capital or increasing partnership liabilities may provide the additional needed tax basis. If the passive activity limitation rules are the reason the partnership losses cannot be used, the possibility of investing in passive activities that generate passive income may be the best planning alternative. See Tax Planning Considerations for further discussion.

A passive activity is any trade or business in which the taxpayer does not materially participate. A taxpayer who owns a limited partnership interest in any activity generally fails the material participation test. Accordingly, losses from most limited partnership interests can be used only to offset income from passive activities even if the limited partner has sufficient Sec. 704(d) and at-risk basis.[43]

Although passive activity limitations may greatly affect the taxable income or loss reported by a partner, they have no unusual effect on basis. Basis is reduced (but not below zero) by the partner's distributive share of losses whether or not the losses are limited under the passive loss rules.[44] When the suspended passive losses later become deductible, the partner's basis in the partnership interest is not affected.

EXAMPLE C9-32 ▶ Chris purchases a 20% capital and profits interest in the CJ Partnership in the current year, but he does not participate in CJ's business. Chris owns no other passive investments. His Sec. 704(d) basis in CJ is $80,000, and his at-risk basis is $70,000. Chris's distributive share of the CJ Partnership's loss for the current year is $60,000. Chris's Sec. 704(d) basis is $20,000 ($80,000 − $60,000) and his at-risk basis is $10,000 ($70,000 − $60,000) after the results of this year's operations are taken into account. However, Chris cannot deduct any of the CJ loss in the current year because it is a passive activity loss. The $60,000 loss, however, can be used in a subsequent year if the partner generates passive income. Because the $60,000 loss already has reduced basis for purposes of both Sec. 704(d) and the at-risk rules, the disallowed loss need not be tested against those rules a second time. ◀

TRANSACTIONS BETWEEN A PARTNER AND THE PARTNERSHIP

The partner and the partnership are treated as separate entities for many transactions. Section 707(b) restricts the use of sales of property between the partner and partnership by disallowing certain losses and converting certain capital gains into ordinary income. Section 707(c) permits a partnership to make guaranteed payments for capital and services to a partner that are separate from the partner's distributive share. Each of these rules is explored below.

SALES OF PROPERTY

LOSS SALES. Without restrictions to prevent it, a controlling partner could sell property to the partnership to recognize a loss for tax purposes while retaining a substantial interest in the property through ownership of a partnership interest. Congress closed the door to such loss recognition with the Sec. 707(b) rules.

---

[43] Sec. 469(h)(2).

[44] S. Rept. No. 99-313, 99th Cong., 2d Sess., p. 723, footnote 4 (1986).

KEY POINT

The IRC disallows losses on sales between persons and certain related partnerships, similar to the related party rules of Sec. 267. The concern is that tax losses can be artificially recognized without the property being disposed of outside the economic group.

The rules for partnership loss transactions are quite similar to the Sec. 267 related party rules discussed in Chapter C3. Under Sec. 707(b)(1), no loss can be deducted on the sale or exchange of property between a partnership and a person who directly or indirectly owns more than 50% of the partnership's capital or profits interests. (Indirect ownership includes ownership by related parties such as members of the partner's family.[45]) Similarly, losses are disallowed on sales or exchanges of property between two partnerships in which the same persons own, directly or indirectly, more than 50% of the capital or profits interests. If the seller is disallowed a loss under Sec. 707(b)(1), the purchaser can reduce any subsequent gain realized on a sale of the property by the previously disallowed loss.

EXAMPLE C9-33 ▶ Jamail, Kareem, and Takedra own equal interests in the JKT Partnership. Kareem and Takedra are siblings but Jamail is unrelated to the others. For purposes of Sec. 707, Kareem owns 66.66% of the partnership (33.33% directly and 33.33% indirectly from Takedra). Likewise, Takedra also owns 66.66%, but Jamail has only a direct ownership interest of 33.33%. ◀

EXAMPLE C9-34 ▶ Pat sold land having a $45,000 basis to the PTA Partnership for $35,000, its FMV. If Pat has a 60% capital and profits interest in the partnership, Pat realizes but cannot recognize a $10,000 loss on the sale. If Pat owns only a 49% interest, directly and indirectly, he can recognize the loss. ◀

EXAMPLE C9-35 ▶ Assume the same facts as in Example C9-34 except the partnership later sells the land for $47,000. The partnership's realized gain is $12,000 ($47,000 − $35,000 basis). If Pat has a 60% capital and profits interest, his previously disallowed loss of $10,000 reduces the partnership's recognized gain to $2,000. This $2,000 gain is then allocated to the partners according to the partnership agreement. ◀

GAIN SALES. When gain is recognized on the sale of a capital asset between a partnership and a related partner, Sec. 707(b)(2) requires that the gain be ordinary (and not capital gain) if the property will not be a capital asset to its new owner. Sales or exchanges resulting in the application of Sec. 707(b)(2) include transfers between (1) a partnership and a person who owns, directly or indirectly, more than 50% of the partnership's capital or profits interests, or (2) two partnerships in which the same persons own, directly or indirectly, more than 50% of the capital or profits interests.[46] This provision prevents related parties from increasing the depreciable basis of assets (and thereby reducing future ordinary income) at the cost of recognizing only a current capital gain.

EXAMPLE C9-36 ▶ Sharon and Tony have the following capital and profits interests in two partnerships:

Partner	*ST Partnership (%)*	*QRS Partnership (%)*
Sharon	42	58
Tony	42	30
Other unrelated partners	16	12
Total	100	100

The ST Partnership sells land having a $150,000 basis to the QRS Partnership for $180,000. The land was a capital asset for the ST Partnership, but QRS intends to subdivide and sell the land. Because the land is ordinary income property to the QRS Partnership and because Sharon and Tony control both partnerships, the ST Partnership must recognize $30,000 of ordinary income on the land sale. ◀

GUARANTEED PAYMENTS

A corporate shareholder can be an employee of the corporation. However, a partner generally is not an employee of the partnership, and most fringe benefits are disallowed for a partner who is employed by his or her partnership.[47]

---

[45] For purposes of Sec. 707, related parties include an individual and members of his or her family (spouse, brothers, sisters, lineal descendants, and ancestors), an individual and a more-than-50%-owned corporation, and two corporations that are members of the same controlled group.

[46] Sec. 707(b)(2).

[47] Rev. Rul. 91-26, 1991-1 C.B. 184, holds that accident and health insurance premiums paid for a partner by the partnership are guaranteed payments.

OBJECTIVE 9

Determine the tax consequences of a guaranteed payment

It is reasonable that a partner who provides services to the partnership in an ongoing relationship might be compensated like any other employee. Section 707(c) provides for just this kind of payment and labels it a **guaranteed payment.** The term *guaranteed payment* also includes certain payments made to a partner for the use of invested capital. These payments are similar to interest. Both types of guaranteed payments must be determined without regard to the partnership's income.[48] Conceptually, this requirement separates guaranteed payments from distributive shares. As indicated below, however, such a distinction may not be so clear in practice.

TYPICAL MISCONCEPTION

If a partner, acting in his or her capacity as a partner, receives payments from the partnership determined without regard to the partnership's income, the partner has received a guaranteed payment. If the partner is acting as a nonpartner, the partner is treated as any other outside contractor.

DETERMINING THE GUARANTEED PAYMENT. Sometimes the determination of the guaranteed payment is quite simple. For example, some guaranteed payments are expressed as specific amounts (e.g., $20,000 per year), with the partner also receiving his or her normal distributive share. Other times, the guaranteed payment is expressed as a **guaranteed minimum.** However, these guaranteed minimum arrangements make it difficult to distinguish the partner's distributive share and guaranteed payments because no guaranteed payment occurs under this arrangement unless the partner's distributive share is less than his or her guaranteed minimum. If the distributive share is less than the guaranteed minimum, the guaranteed payment is the difference between the distributive share and the guaranteed minimum.

EXAMPLE C9-37 ▶ Tina manages the real estate owned by the TAV Partnership, in which she also is a partner. She receives 30% of all partnership income before guaranteed payments, but no less than $60,000 per year. In the current year, the TAV Partnership reports $300,000 in ordinary income. Tina's 30% distributive share is $90,000 (0.30 × $300,000), which exceeds her $60,000 guaranteed minimum. Therefore, she has no guaranteed payment. ◀

EXAMPLE C9-38 ▶ Assume the same facts as in Example C9-37 except the TAV Partnership reports $150,000 of ordinary income. Tina has a guaranteed payment of $15,000, which represents the difference between her $45,000 distributive share (0.30 × $150,000) and her $60,000 guaranteed minimum.[49] ◀

TAX IMPACT OF GUARANTEED PAYMENTS. Like salary or interest income, guaranteed payments are ordinary income to the recipient. The guaranteed payment must be included in income for the recipient partner's tax year during which the partnership year ends and the partnership deducts or capitalizes the payments.[50]

EXAMPLE C9-39 ▶ In January 2003, a calendar year taxpayer, Will, receives a $10,000 guaranteed payment from the WRS Partnership, which uses the accrual method of accounting. WRS accrues and deducts the payment during its tax year ending November 30, 2002. Will must report his guaranteed payment in his 2002 tax return because that return includes the 2002 partnership income that reflects the impact of the guaranteed payment. ◀

For the partnership, the guaranteed payment is treated as if it is made to an outsider. If the payment is for a service that is a capital expenditure (e.g., architectural services for designing a building for the partnership), the guaranteed payment must be capitalized and, if allowable, amortized. If the payment is for services deductible under Sec. 162, the partnership deducts the payment from ordinary income. Thus, deductible guaranteed payments offset the partnership's ordinary income but never its capital gains. If the guaranteed payment exceeds the partnership's ordinary income, the payment creates an ordinary loss that is allocated among the partners.[51]

EXAMPLE C9-40 ▶ Theresa is a partner in the STU Partnership. She is to receive a guaranteed payment for deductible services of $60,000 and 30% of partnership income computed after deducting the guaranteed payment. The partnership reports $40,000 of ordinary income and a $120,000 long-term capital gain before deducting the guaranteed payment. Theresa's income from the partnership is determined as follows:

---

[48] Sec. 707(c).
[49] Reg. Sec. 1.707-1(c), Exs. (1) and (2).
[50] Reg. Secs. 1.707-1(c) and 1.706-1(a).
[51] Reg. Sec. 1.707-1(c), Ex. (4).

	STU Partnership	Theresa's Share: Ratable Share	Theresa's Share: Amount
Ordinary income (before guaranteed payment)	$ 40,000		
Minus: Guaranteed payment	(60,000)	100%	$60,000
Ordinary loss	($ 20,000)	30%	(6,000)
Long-term capital gain	$120,000	30%	36,000 ◀

FAMILY PARTNERSHIPS

OBJECTIVE 10

Explain the requirements for recognizing the holder of a partnership interest as a partner in a family partnership

CAPITAL OWNERSHIP

Because each partner reports and pays taxes on a distributive share of partnership income, a family partnership is an excellent way to spread income among family members and minimize the family's tax bill. However, to accomplish this tax minimization goal, the IRS must accept the family members as real partners. The question of whether someone is a partner in a family partnership is often litigated, but safe-harbor rules under Sec. 704(e) provide a clear answer if three tests are met: the partnership interest must be a capital interest, capital must be a material income-producing factor in the partnership's business activity, and the family member must be the true owner of the interest.

A capital interest gives the partner the right to receive assets if the partnership liquidates immediately upon the partner's acquisition of the interest. Capital is a material income-producing factor if the partnership derives substantial portions of gross income from the use of capital. For example, capital is a material income-producing factor if the business has substantial inventory or significant investment in plant or equipment. Capital is seldom considered a material income-producing factor in a service business.[52]

TAX STRATEGY TIP

In certain situations, family partnerships provide an excellent tax-planning tool, but the family members must be real partners. The rules that determine who is a real partner in a family partnership are guided by the assignment-of-income principle.

The remaining question is whether the family member is the true owner of the interest. Ownership is seldom questioned if one family member purchases the interest at a market price from another family member. However, when one family member gifts the interest to another, the major question is whether the donor retains so much control over the partnership interest that the donor is still the owner of the interest. If the donor still controls the interest, the donor is taxed on the distributive share.

DONOR RETAINED CONTROL. No mechanical test exists to determine whether the donor has retained too much control, but several factors may indicate a problem:[53]

- Retention of control over distributions of income can be a problem unless the retention occurs with the agreement of all partners or the retention is for the reasonable needs of the business.
- Retention of control over assets that are essential to the partnership's business can indicate too much control by the donor.
- Limitation of the donee partner's right to sell or liquidate his or her interest may indicate that the donor has not relinquished full control over the interest.
- Retention of management control that is inconsistent with normal partnership arrangements can be another sign that the donor retains control. This situation is not considered a fatal problem unless it occurs in conjunction with a significant limit on the donee's ability to sell or liquidate his or her interest.

If the donor has not directly or indirectly retained too much control, the donee is a full partner. As a partner, the donee must report his or her distributive share of income.

---

[52] Reg. Sec. 1.704-1(e)(1)(iv).

[53] Reg. Sec. 1.704-1(e)(2)(ii).

KEY POINT

A valid family partnership is a useful method for allocating income among family members. However, the distributive share of income from a partnership interest to a partner under age 14 is subject to the "kiddie tax."

MINOR DONEES. When income splitting is the goal of a family, the appropriate donee for the partnership interest is often a minor. With the problem of donor-retained controls in mind, gifts to minors should be made with great attention to detail. Further, net unearned income of a child under age 14 is taxed to the child at the parents' marginal tax rate. This provision removes much of the incentive to transfer family partnership interests to young children, but gifting partnership interests to minors age 14 or older still can reap significant tax advantages.

DONOR-DONEE ALLOCATIONS OF INCOME

OBJECTIVE 11

Determine the allocation of partnership income between a donor and a donee of a partnership interest

Partnership income must be properly allocated between a donor and a donee to be accepted by the IRS. Note that only the allocation between the donor and donee is questioned, with no impact on the distributive shares of any other partners.

Two requirements apply to donor-donee allocations. First, the donor must be allocated reasonable compensation for services rendered to the partnership. Then, after reasonable compensation is allocated to the donor, any remaining partnership income must be allocated based on relative capital interests.[54] This allocation scheme apparently overrides the partnership's ability to make special allocations of income.

EXAMPLE C9-41 ▶

ETHICAL POINT

CPAs have a responsibility to review an entity's conduct of its activities to be sure it is operating as a partnership. If a donee receives a partnership interest as a gift and the donee is not the true owner of the interest (e.g., the donor retains too much control over the donee's interest), the partnership return must be filed without a distributive share of income or loss being allocated to the donee.

Andrew, a 40% partner in the ABC Partnership, gives one-half of his interest to his brother, John. During the current year, Andrew performs services for the partnership for which reasonable compensation is $65,000 but for which he accepts no pay. Andrew and John are each credited with a $100,000 distributive share, all of which is ordinary income. Reallocation between Andrew and John is necessary to reflect the value of Andrew's services.

Total distributive shares for the brothers	$200,000
Minus: Reasonable compensation for Andrew	(65,000)
Income to allocate	$135,000

John's distributive share: $\frac{20\%}{40\%} \times \$135,000 = \$67,500$

Andrew's distributive share: $\left(\frac{20\%}{40\%} \times \$135,000\right) + \$65,000 = \$132,500$ ◀

TAX PLANNING CONSIDERATIONS

TIMING OF LOSS RECOGNITION

The loss limitation rules provide a unique opportunity for tax planning. For example, if a partner knows that his or her distributive share of active losses from a partnership for a tax year will exceed the Sec. 704 basis limitation for deducting losses, he or she should carefully examine the tax situation for the current and upcoming tax years. Substantial current personal income may make immediate use of the loss desirable. Current income may be taxed at a higher marginal tax rate than will future income because of, for example, an extraordinarily good current year, an expected retirement, or a decrease in future years' tax rates. If the partner chooses to use the loss in the current year, he or she can make additional contributions just before year-end (perhaps even from funds the partner borrows, as long as the additional benefit exceeds the cost of the funds). Alternatively, one partner may convince the other partners to have the partnership incur additional liabilities so that each partner's basis increases. This last strategy should be exercised with caution unless a business reason (rather than solely a tax reason) exists for the borrowing.

[54] Sec. 704(e)(2).

EXAMPLE C9-42 ▶ Ted, a 60% general partner in the ST Partnership, expects to be allocated partnership losses of $120,000 for the current year from a partnership in which he materially participates but where his partnership basis is only $90,000. Because he has a marginal tax rate of 38.6% for the current year (and anticipates only a 27% marginal tax rate for next year), Ted wants to use the ST Partnership losses to offset his current year income. He could make a capital contribution to raise his basis by $30,000. Alternatively, he could get the partnership to incur $50,000 in additional liabilities, which would increase his basis by his $30,000 ($50,000 × 0.60) share of the liability. The partnership's $50,000 borrowing must serve a business purpose for the ST Partnership. ◀

Alternatively, a partner may prefer to delay the deduction of partnership losses that exceed the current year's loss limitation. If the partner has little current year income and expects substantial income in the following year. If the partner has loss, deduction, or credit carryovers that expire in the current year, a deferral of the distributive share of partnership losses to the following year may be desirable. If the partner opts to deduct the loss in a later year, he or she needs only to leave things alone so that the distributive share of losses exceeds the loss limitation for the current year.

COMPLIANCE AND PROCEDURAL CONSIDERATIONS

OBJECTIVE 12

Determine the requirements for filing a partnership tax return

REPORTING TO THE IRS AND THE PARTNERS

FORMS. If the partnership is not an electing large partnership, the partnership must file a Form 1065 with the IRS by the fifteenth day of the fourth month after the end of the partnership tax year. (See Appendix B for a completed Form 1065.) The IRS can allow reasonable extensions of time of up to six months, although initial extensions usually are limited to 60 days. Penalties are imposed for failure to file a timely or complete partnership return. Because the partnership is only a conduit, Form 1065 is an information return and is not accompanied by any tax payment.[55] Included on the front page of Form 1065 are all the ordinary items of income, gain, loss and deduction that are not separately stated. Schedule K of Form 1065 reports both a summary of the ordinary income items and the partnership total of the separately stated items. Schedule K-1, which must be prepared for each partner, reflects that partner's distributive share of partnership income including his or her special allocations. The partner's Schedule K-1 is notification of his or her share of partnership items for use in calculating income taxes and self-employment taxes.

HISTORICAL NOTE

Turn to the partnership Schedule K in Appendix B of this book. The large number of items that now have to be separately stated illustrates how certain tax laws, such as the passive activity limitation rules and the investment interest limitation rules, have complicated the preparation of Form 1065.

SECTION 444 ELECTION AND REQUIRED PAYMENTS. A partnership can elect to use a tax year other than a required year by filing an election under Sec. 444. This election is made by filing Form 8716 (Election to Have a Tax Year Other Than a Required Tax Year) by the earlier of the fifteenth day of the fifth month following the month that includes the first day of the tax year for which the election is effective or the due date (without regard to extension) of the income tax return resulting from the Sec. 444 election. In addition, a copy of Form 8716 must be attached to the partnership's Form 1065 for the first tax year for which the Sec. 444 election is made.

A partnership making a Sec. 444 election must make a required payment annually under Sec. 7519. The required payment has the effect of remitting a deposit equal to the tax (at the highest individual tax rate plus one percentage point) on the partnership's deferred income.

---

[55] Reg. Sec. 301.6031-1(e)(2). Although the partnership pays no income tax, it still must pay the employer's share of social security taxes and any unemployment taxes as well as withhold income taxes from its employees' salaries. In addition, some publicly traded partnerships may pay a tax as explained in Chapter C10.

A partnership can obtain a refund if past payments exceed the tentative payment due on the deferred income for the current year. Similar refunds are available if the partnership terminates a Sec. 444 election or liquidates. The required payments are not deductible by the partnership and are not passed through to a partner. The required payments are in the nature of a refundable deposit.

The Sec. 7519 required payment is due on or before May 15 of the calendar year following the calendar year in which the election year begins. The partnership remits the required payment with Form 8752 (Required Payment or Refund Under Section 7519) along with a computational worksheet, which is illustrated in the instructions to Form 1065. Refunds of excess required payments also are obtained by filing Form 8752.

ESTIMATED TAXES. If the partnership is not an electing large partnership, it pays no income taxes and makes no estimated tax payments. However, the partners must make estimated tax payments based on their separate tax positions including their distributive shares of partnership income or loss for the current year. It should be emphasized that the partners are not making separate estimated tax payments for their partnership income but rather are including the effects of the partnership's results in the calculation of their normal estimated tax payments.

SELF-EMPLOYMENT INCOME. Every partnership must report the net earnings (or loss) for the partnership that constitute self-employment income to the partners. The instructions to Form 1065 contain a worksheet to make such a calculation. The partnership's self-employment income includes both guaranteed payments, partnership ordinary income and loss, and separately stated items, but generally excludes capital gains and losses, Sec. 1231 gains and losses, interest, dividends, and rentals. The distributive share of self-employment income for each partner is shown on a Schedule K-1 and is included with other self-employment income in determining a partner's self-employment tax liability (Schedule SE, Form 1040). The distributive share of partnership income allocable to a limited partner is not self-employment income.

EXAMPLE C9-43 ▶ Adam is a general partner in the AB Partnership. His distributive share of partnership income and his guaranteed payment for the year are as follows:

Ordinary income	$15,000
Short-term capital gain	9,000
Guaranteed payment	18,000

Adam's self-employment income is $33,000 ($15,000 + $18,000). ◀

EXAMPLE C9-44 ▶ Assume the same facts as in Example C9-43 except that Adam is a limited partner. His self-employment income includes only the $18,000 guaranteed payment. ◀

IRS AUDIT PROCEDURES

Any questions arising during an IRS audit about a partnership item must be determined at the partnership level (instead of at the partner level).[56] Section 6231(a)(3) defines **partnership items** as virtually all items reported by the partnership for the tax year including tax preference items, credit recapture items, guaranteed payments, and the at-risk amount. In fact, almost every item that can appear on the partnership return is treated as a partnership item. Each partner must either report partnership items in a manner consistent with the Schedule K-1 received from the partnership or notify the IRS of the inconsistent treatment.[57]

The IRS can bring a single proceeding at the partnership level to determine the characterization or tax impact of any partnership item. All partners have the right to participate in the administrative proceedings, and the IRS must offer a consistent settlement to all partners.

---

[56] Sec. 6221.

[57] Sec. 6222.

KEY POINT

To alleviate the administrative nightmare of having to audit each partner of a partnership, Congress has authorized the IRS to conduct audits of partnerships in a unified proceeding at the partnership level. This process is more efficient and should provide greater consistency in the treatment of the individual partners than did the previous system.

A **tax matters partner** generally is assigned to facilitate communication between the IRS and the partners of a large partnership and to serve as the primary representative of the partnership.[58] The tax matters partner is a partner designated by the partnership or, if no one is so designated, the general partner having the largest profits interest at the close of the partnership's tax year.

These audit procedures, however, do not apply to small partnerships. For this purpose, a small partnership is defined as one having no more than ten partners who must be natural persons (but excluding nonresident aliens), C corporations, or estates. In counting partners, a husband and wife (or their estates) count as a single partner. Further, the IRS has announced that a partnership can be excluded from the audit procedures only if it can be established that all partners fully reported their shares of partnership items on timely filed tax returns.[59]

PROBLEM MATERIALS

DISCUSSION QUESTIONS

C9-1 Yong and Li plan to begin a business that will grow plants for sale to retail nurseries. They expect to have substantial losses for the first three years of operations while they develop their plants and their sales operations. Both Yong and Li have substantial interest income, and both expect to work full-time in this new business. List three advantages for operating this business as a partnership instead of a C corporation.

C9-2 Bob and Carol want to open a bed and breakfast inn as soon as they buy and renovate a turn-of-the-century home. What would be the major disadvantage of using a general partnership rather than a corporation for this business?

C9-3 Sam wants to help his brother, Lou, start a new business. Lou is a capable auto mechanic but has little business sense, so he needs Sam to help him make business decisions. Should this partnership be arranged as a general partnership or a limited partnership? Why?

C9-4 Doug contributes services but no property to the CD Partnership upon its formation. What are the tax implications of his receiving only a profits interest versus his receiving a capital and profits interest?

C9-5 An existing partner wants to contribute property having a basis less than its FMV for an additional interest in a partnership.

a. Should he contribute the property to the partnership?
b. What are his other options?
c. Explain the tax implications for the partner of these other options.

C9-6 Jane contributes valuable property to a partnership in exchange for a general partnership interest. The partnership also assumes the recourse mortgage Jane incurred when she purchased the property two years ago.

a. How will the liability affect the amount of gain that Jane must recognize?
b. How will it affect her basis in the partnership interest?

C9-7 Which of the following items can be amortized as part of a partnership's organizational expenditures?

a. Legal fees for drawing up the partnership agreement
b. Accounting fees for establishing an accounting system
c. Fees for securing an initial working capital loan
d. Filing fees required under state law in initial year to conduct business in the state
e. Accounting fees for preparation of initial short-period tax return
f. Transportation costs for acquiring machinery essential to the partnership's business
g. Syndication expenses

C9-8 The BW Partnership reported the following current year earnings: $30,000 interest from tax-exempt bonds, $50,000 long-term capital gain, and $100,000 net income from operations. Bob saw these numbers and told his partner, Wendy, that the partnership had $100,000 of taxable income. Is he correct? Explain your answer.

C9-9 How will a partner's distributive share be determined if the partner sells one-half of his or her

[58] Sec. 6231(a)(7).

[59] Rev. Proc. 84-35, 1984-1 C.B. 509.

beginning-of-the-year partnership interest at the beginning of the tenth month of the partnership's tax year?

C9-10 Can a recourse debt of a partnership increase the basis of a limited partner's partnership interest? Explain.

C9-11 The ABC Partnership has a nonrecourse liability that it incurred by borrowing from an unrelated bank. It is secured by an apartment building owned and managed by the partnership. The liability is not convertible into an equity interest. How does this liability affect the at-risk basis of general partner Anna and limited partner Bob?

C9-12 Is the Sec. 704(d) loss limitation rule more or less restrictive than the at-risk rules? Explain.

C9-13 Jeff, a 10% limited partner in the recently formed JRS Partnership, expects to have losses from the partnership for several more years. He is considering purchasing an interest in a profitable general partnership in which he will materially participate. Will the purchase allow him to use his losses from the JRS Partnership?

C9-14 Helen, a 55% partner in the ABC Partnership, owns land (a capital asset) having a $20,000 basis and a $25,000 FMV. She plans to transfer the land to the ABC Partnership, which will subdivide the land and sell the lots. Discuss whether Helen should sell or contribute the land to the partnership.

C9-15 What is the difference between a guaranteed payment that is a guaranteed amount and one that is a guaranteed minimum?

C9-16 The TUV Partnership is considering two compensation schemes for Tracy, the partner who runs the business on a daily basis. Tracy can be given a $10,000 guaranteed payment, or she can be given a comparably larger distributive share (and distribution) so that she receives about $10,000 more each year. From the standpoint of when the income must be reported in Tracy's tax return, are these two compensation alternatives the same?

C9-17 Roy's father gives him a capital interest in Family Partnership. Discuss whether the Sec. 704(e) family partnership rules apply to this interest.

C9-18 Andrew gives his brother Steve a 20% interest in the AS Partnership, and he retains a 30% interest. Andrew works for the partnership but is not paid. How will this arrangement affect the income from the AS Partnership reported by Andrew and Steve?

ISSUE IDENTIFICATION QUESTIONS

C9-19 Bob and Kate form the BK Partnership, a general partnership, as equal partners. Bob contributes an office building with a $130,000 FMV and a $95,000 adjusted basis to the partnership along with a $60,000 mortgage, which the partnership assumes. Kate contributes the land on which the building sits with a $50,000 FMV and a $75,000 adjusted basis. Kate will manage the partnership for the first five years of operations but will not receive a guaranteed payment for her work in the first year of partnership operations. Starting with the second year of partnership operations, Kate will receive a $10,000 guaranteed payment for each year she manages the partnership. What tax issues should Bob, Kate, and the BK Partnership consider with respect to the formation and operation of the partnership?

C9-20 Suzanne and Laura form a partnership to market local crafts. In April, the two women spent $400 searching for a retail outlet, $1,200 to have a partnership agreement drawn up, and $300 to have an accounting system established. During April, they signed contracts with a number of local crafters to feature their products in the retail outlet. The outlet was fitted and merchandise organized during May. In June, the store opened and sold its first crafts. The partnership paid $100 to an accountant to prepare an income statement for the month of June. What tax issues should the partnership consider with regard to beginning this business?

C9-21 Cara, a CPA, established an accounting system for the ABC Partnership and, in return for her services, received a 10% profits interest (but no capital interest) in the partnership. Her usual fee for the services would be approximately $6,000. No sales of profits interests in the ABC Partnership occurred during the current year. What tax issues should Cara and the ABC Partnership consider with respect to the payment made for the services?

C9-22 George, a limited partner in the EFG Partnership, has a 20% interest in partnership capital, profits, and losses. His basis in the partnership interest is $15,000 before accounting for events of the current year. In December of the current year, the EFG Partnership repaid a $100,000 nonrecourse liability. The partnership earned $20,000 of ordinary income this year. What tax issues should George consider with respect to reporting the results of this year's activities for the EFG Partnership on his personal return?

C9-23 Katie works 40 hours a week as a clerk in the mall and earns $20,000. In addition, she works five hours each week in the JKL Partnership's office. Katie, a 10% limited partner in the JKL Partnership, has been allocated a $2,100 loss from the partnership for the current year. The basis for her interest in JKL before accounting for current operations is $5,000. What tax issues should Katie consider with respect to her interest in, and employment by, the JKL Partnership?

C9-24 Daniel has no family to inherit his 80% capital and profits interest in the CD Partnership. To ensure the continuation of the business, he gives a 20% capital and profits interest in the partnership to David, his best friend's son, on the condition that David work in the partnership for at least five years. David receives guaranteed payments for his work. Daniel takes no salary from the partnership, but he devotes all his time to the business operations of the partnership. What tax issues should Daniel and David consider with respect to the gift of the partnership interest and Daniel's employment arrangement with the partnership?

PROBLEMS

C9-25 ***Formation of a Partnership.*** Suzanne and Bob form the SB General Partnership as equal partners. They make the following contributions:

Individual	*Asset*	*Basis to Partner*	*FMV*
Suzanne	Cash	$45,000	$ 45,000
	Inventory (securities)	14,000	15,000
Bob	Land	45,000	40,000
	Building	50,000	100,000

The SB Partnership assumes the $80,000 recourse mortgage on the building that Bob contributes, and the partners share the economic risk of loss on the mortgage equally. Bob has claimed $40,000 in straight-line depreciation under the MACRS rules on the building. Suzanne is a stockbroker and contributed securities from her inventory. The partnership will hold them as an investment.

a. What amount and character of gain or loss must each partner recognize on the formation of the partnership?
b. What is each partner's basis in his or her partnership interest?
c. What is the partnership's basis in each asset?
d. What is the partnership's initial book value of each asset?
e. The partnership holds the securities for two years and then sells them for $20,000. What amount and character of gain must the partnership and each partner report?

C9-26 ***Formation of a Partnership.*** On May 31, six brothers decided to form the Grimm Brothers Partnership to publish and print children's stories. The contributions of the brothers and their partnership interests are listed below. They share the economic risk of loss from liabilities according to their partnership interests.

Individual	*Asset*	*Basis to Partner*	*FMV*	*Partnership Interest*
Al	Cash	$15,000	$ 15,000	15%
Bob	Accounts receivable	–0–	20,000	20%
Clay	Office equipment	13,000	15,000	15%
Dave	Land	50,000	15,000	15%
Ed	Building	15,000	150,000	20%
Fred	Services	?	15,000	15%

Other information about the contributions may be of interest, as follows:

- Bob contributes accounts receivable from his proprietorship, which uses the cash method of accounting.
- Clay uses the office equipment in a small business he owns. When he joins the partnership, he sells the remaining business assets to an outsider. He has claimed $8,000 of MACRS depreciation on the office equipment.
- The partnership assumes a $130,000 mortgage on the building Ed contributes. Ed claimed $100,000 of straight-line MACRS depreciation on the commercial property.

- Fred, an attorney, drew up all the partnership agreements and filed the necessary paperwork. He receives a full 15% capital and profits interest for his services.

a. How much gain, loss, or income must each partner recognize as a result of the formation?
b. How much gain, loss, or income must the partnership recognize as a result of the formation?
c. What is each partner's basis in his partnership interest?
d. What is the partnership's basis in its assets?
e. What is the partnership's initial book value of each asset?
f. What effects do the depreciation recapture provisions have on the property contributions?
g. How would your answer to Part a change if Fred received only a profits interest?
h. What are the tax consequences to the partners and the partnership when the partnership sells for $9,000 the land contributed by Dave? Prior to the sale, the partnership held the land as an investment for two years.

C9-27 *Formation of a Partnership.* On January 1, Julie, Kay, and Susan form a partnership. The contributions of the three individuals are listed below. Julie received a 30% partnership interest, Kay received a 60% partnership interest, Susan received a 10% partnership interest. They share the economic risk of loss from recourse liabilities according to their partnership interests.

Individual	*Asset*	*Basis to Partner*	*FMV*
Julie	Accounts receivable	$ -0-	$ 60,000
Kay	Land	30,000	58,000
	Building	45,000	116,000
Susan	Services	?	20,000

Kay has claimed $15,000 of straight-line MACRS depreciation on the building. The land and building are subject to a $54,000 mortgage, of which $18,000 is allocable to the land and $36,000 is allocable to the building. The partnership assumes the mortgage. Susan is an attorney, and the services she contributes are the drawing-up of all partnership agreements.

a. What amount and character of gain, loss, or income must each partner recognize on the formation of the partnership?
b. What is each partner's basis in her partnership interest?
c. What is the partnership's basis in each of its assets?
d. What is the partnership's initial book value of each asset?
e. To raise some immediate cash after the formation, the partnership decides to sell the land and building to a third party and lease it back. The buyer pays $40,000 cash for the land and $80,000 cash for the building in addition to assuming the $54,000 mortgage. Assume the partnership claim no additional depreciation on the building before the sale. What is each partner's distributive share of the gains, and what is the character of the gains?

C9-28 *Contribution of Services.* Sean is admitted to the XYZ Partnership in December of the current year in return for his services managing the partnership's business during the year. The partnership reports ordinary income of $100,000 for the current year without considering this transaction.

a. What are the tax consequences to Sean and the XYZ Partnership if Sean receives a 20% capital and profits interest in the partnership with a $75,000 FMV?
b. What are the tax consequences to Sean and the XYZ Partnership if Sean receives only a 20% profits interest with no determinable FMV?

C9-29 *Contribution of Services and Property.* Marjorie works for a large firm whose business is to find suitable real estate, establish a limited partnership to purchase the property, and then sell the limited partnership interests. In the current year, Marjorie received a 5% limited partnership interest in the Eldorado Limited Partnership. Marjorie received this interest partially in payment for her services in selling partnership interests to others, but she also was required to contribute $5,000 in cash to the partnership. Similar limited partnership interests sold for $20,000 at approximately the same time that Marjorie received her interest. What are the tax consequences for Marjorie and the Eldorado Limited Partnership of Marjorie's receipt of the partnership interest?

C9-30 ***Partnership Tax Year.*** The BCD Partnership is being formed by three equal partners, Beth, Cindy, and Delux Corporation. The partners' tax year-ends are June 30 for Beth, September 30 for Cindy, and October 31 for Delux. The BCD Partnership's natural business year ends on January 31.

a. What tax year(s) can the partnership elect without IRS permission?
b. What tax year(s) can the partnership elect with IRS permission?
c. How would your answers to Parts a and b change if Beth, Cindy, and Delux own 4%, 4%, and 92%, respectively, of the partnership?

C9-31 ***Partnership Tax Year.*** The BCD Partnership is formed in April of the current year. The three equal partners, Boris, Carlos, and Damien have had tax years ending on December 31, August 30, and December 31, respectively, for the last five years. The BCD Partnership has no natural business year.

a. What tax year is required for the BCD Partnership under Sec. 706?
b. Can the BCD Partnership make a Sec. 444 election? If so, what are the alternative tax years BCD could select?

C9-32 ***Partnership Income and Basis Adjustments.*** Mark and Pamela are equal partners in MP Partnership. The partnership, Mark, and Pamela are calendar year taxpayers. The partnership incurred the following items in the current year:

Sales	$450,000
Cost of goods sold	210,000
Dividends on corporate investments	15,000
Tax-exempt interest income	4,000
Section 1245 gain (recapture) on equipment sale	33,000
Section 1231 gain on equipment sale	18,000
Long-term capital gain on stock sale	12,000
Long-term capital loss on stock sale	10,000
Short-term capital loss on stock sale	9,000
Depreciation	27,000
Guaranteed payment to Pamela	30,000
Meals and entertainment expenses	11,600
Interest expense on loans allocable to:	
Business debt	42,000
Stock investments	9,200
Tax-exempt bonds	2,800
Principal payment on business loan	14,000
Charitable contributions	5,000
Distributions to partners ($30,000 each)	60,000

a. Compute the partnership's ordinary income and separately stated items.
b. Show Mark's and Pamela's shares of the items in Part a.
c. Compute Mark's and Pamela's ending basis in their partnership interests assuming their beginning balances are $150,000 each.

C9-33 ***Financial Accounting and Partnership Income.*** Jim, Liz, and Ken are equal partners in the JLK Partnership, which uses the accrual method of accounting. All three materially participate in the business. JLK reports financial accounting income of $186,000 for the current year. The partnership used the following information to determine financial accounting income.

Operating profit (excluding the items listed below)	$ 94,000
Rental income	30,000
Interest income:	
Municipal bonds (tax-exempt)	15,000
Corporate bonds	3,000
Dividend income (all from less-than-20%-owned domestic corporations)	20,000
Gains and losses on property sales:	
Gain on sale of land held as an investment (contributed by Jim six years ago when its basis was $9,000 and its FMV was $15,000)	60,000
Long-term capital gains	10,000
Short-term capital losses	7,000
Sec. 1231 gain	9,000
Sec. 1250 gain	44,000

Depreciation:	
Rental real estate	12,000
Machinery and equipment	27,000
Interest expense related to:	
Mortgages on rental property	18,000
Loans to acquire municipal bonds	5,000
Guaranteed payments to Jim	30,000
Low-income housing expenditures qualifying for credit	21,000

The following additional information is available about the current year's activities.

- The partnership received a $1,000 prepayment of rent for next year but has not recorded it as income for financial accounting purposes.
- The partnership recorded the land for financial accounting purposes at $15,000.
- MACRS depreciation on the rental real estate and machinery and equipment were $12,000 and $29,000, respectively, in the current year.
- MACRS depreciation for the rental real estate includes depreciation on the low-income housing expenditures.

a. What is JLK's financial accounting income?
b. What is JLK's partnership taxable income? (See Appendix B for an example of a financial accounting-to-tax reconciliation.)
c. What are JLK's separately stated items?
d. What is JLK's ordinary income (loss)?

C9-34 ***Partner's Distributive Shares.*** On January of the current year, Becky (20%), Chuck (30%), and Dawn (50%) are partners in the BCD Partnership. During the current year, BCD reports the following results. All items occur evenly throughout the year unless otherwise indicated.

Ordinary income	$120,000
Long-term capital gain (recognized September 1)	18,000
Short-term capital loss (recognized March 2)	6,000
Charitable contribution (made October 1)	20,000

a. What are the distributive shares for each partner, assuming they all continue to hold their interests at the end of the year?
b. Assume that Becky purchases a 5% partnership interest from Chuck on July 1 so that Becky and Chuck each own 25% from that date through the end of the year. What are Becky and Chuck's distributive shares for the current year?

C9-35 ***Partner's Distributive Share.*** On January 1, Amy (25%), Brad (35%), and Craig (40%) are partners in the ABC Partnership. During the year, the partnership earned the following amounts. Assume items occurred evenly throughout the year, and the year is not a leap year.

Ordinary loss	$120,000
Long-term capital gain	190,000
Sec. 1231 gains	40,000
Short-term capital losses	30,000

a. What is each partner's distributive share of partnership income assuming no change in ownership occurs during the year?
b. Assume that on July 1 Craig sold one-half of his partnership interest to Brad. What are the distributive shares of Brad and Craig?

C9-36 ***Allocation of Precontribution Gain.*** Last year, Patty contributed land with a $4,000 basis and a $10,000 FMV in exchange for a 40% profits, loss, and capital interest in the PD Partnership. Dave contributed land with an $8,000 basis and a $15,000 FMV for the remaining 60% interest in the partnership. During the current year, PD Partnership reported $8,000 of ordinary income and $10,000 of long-term capital gain from the sale of the land Patty contributed. What income or gain must Patty and Dave report from the PD Partnership in the current year?

C9-37 ***Special Allocations.*** Clark sold securities for a $40,000 capital loss during the current year, but he has no personal capital gains to recognize. The C&L General Partnership, in which Clark has a 50% capital, profits, and loss interest, reported a $60,000 capital gain this year. In addition, the partnership earned $140,000 of ordinary income. Clark's only partner, Lois, agrees to divide the year's income as follows:

Type of Income	*Total*	*Clark*	*Lois*
Capital gain	$ 60,000	$50,000	$10,000
Ordinary income	140,000	50,000	90,000

Both partners and the partnership use a calendar year-end.

a. Have the partners made a special allocation of income that has substantial economic effect?

b. What amount and character of income must each partner report on his or her tax return?

C9-38 ***Special Allocations.*** Diane and Ed have equal capital and profits interests in the DE Partnership, and they share the economic risk of loss from recourse liabilities according to their partnership interests. In addition, Diane has a special allocation of all depreciation on buildings owned by the partnership. The buildings are financed with recourse liabilities. The depreciation reduces Diane's capital account, and liquidation is in accordance with the capital account balances. Depreciation for the DE Partnership is $50,000 annually. Diane and Ed each have $50,000 capital account balances on January 1, 2002. Will the special allocation be acceptable for 2002, 2003, and 2004 in the following independent situations?

a. The partners have no obligation to repay negative capital account balances, and the partnership's operations (other than depreciation) each year have no net effect on the capital accounts.

b. The partners have an obligation to repay negative capital account balances.

c. The partners have no obligation to repay negative capital account balances. The partnership operates at its break-even point (excluding any depreciation claimed) and borrows $200,000 on a full recourse basis on December 31, 2003.

C9-39 ***Basis in Partnership Interest.*** What is Kelly's basis for her partnership interest in each of the following independent situations? The partners share the economic risk of loss from recourse liabilities according to their partnership interests.

a. Kelly receives her 20% partnership interest for a contribution of property having a $14,000 basis and a $17,000 FMV. The partnership assumes her $10,000 recourse liability but has no other debts.

b. Kelly receives her 20% partnership interest as a gift from a friend. The friend's basis (without considering partnership liabilities) is $34,000. The FMV of the interest at the time of the gift is $36,000. The partnership has liabilities of $100,000 when Kelly receives her interest. No gift tax was paid with respect to the transfer.

c. Kelly inherits her 20% interest from her mother. Her mother's basis was $140,000. The FMV of the interest is $120,000 on the date of death and $160,000 on the alternate valuation date. The executor chooses the date of death for valuing the estate. The partnership has no liabilities.

C9-40 ***Basis in Partnership Interest.*** Yong received a 40% general partnership interest in the XYZ Partnership in each of the independent situations below. In each situation, assume the general partners have agreed that their economic risk of loss related to recourse liabilities will be shared according to their loss interests. What is Yong's basis in his partnership interest?

a. Yong designs the building the partnership will use for its offices. Yong normally would charge a $20,000 fee for a similar building design. Based on the other partner's contributions, the 40% interest has a FMV of $25,000. The partnership has no liabilities.

b. Yong contributes land with a $6,000 basis and an $18,000 FMV, a car (which he has used in his business since he purchased it) with a $15,000 adjusted basis and a $6,000 FMV, and $2,000 cash. The partnership has recourse liabilities of $100,000.

C9-41 ***Basis in Partnership Interest.*** Tina purchases an interest in the TP Partnership on January 1 of the current year for $50,000. The partnership uses the calendar year as its tax year and has $200,000 in recourse liabilities when Tina acquires her interest. The partners share economic risk of loss associated with recourse debt according to their loss percentage. Her distributive share of partnership items for the year is as follows:

Ordinary income (excluding items listed below)	$30,000
Long-term capital gains	10,000
Municipal bond interest income	8,000
Charitable contributions	1,000
Interest expense related to municipal bond investment	2,000

TP reports the following liabilities on December 31:

Recourse debt	$100,000
Nonrecourse debt (not qualified real estate financing)	80,000

a. What is Tina's basis on December 31 if she has a 40% interest in profits and losses? TP is a general partnership. Tina has not guaranteed partnership debt, nor has she made any other special agreements about partnership debt.
b. How would your answer to Part a change if Tina instead had a 40% interest in profits and a 30% interest in losses? Assume TP is a general partnership, and all other agreements continue in place.
c. How would your answer to Part a change if Tina were instead a limited partner having a 40% interest in profits and 30% interest in losses? The partnership agreement contains no guarantees or other special arrangements.

C9-42 *At-Risk Loss Limitation.* The KC Partnership is a general partnership that manufactures widgets. The partnership uses a calendar year as its tax year and has two equal partners, Kerry and City Corporation, a widely held corporation. On January 1 of the current year, Kerry and City Corporation each has a $200,000 basis in the partnership interest. Operations during the year produce the following results:

Ordinary loss	$900,000
Long-term capital loss	100,000
Short-term capital gain	300,000

The only change in KC's liabilities during the year is KC's first borrowing, a $100,000 nonrecourse loan (not qualified real estate financing) that remains outstanding at year-end.
a. What is each partner's deductible loss from the partnership's activities before any passive loss limitation?
b. What is each partner's basis in the partnership interest after the year's operations?
c. How would your answers to Parts a and b change if the KC Partnership's business were totally in real estate but not a rental activity? Assume the loan is qualified real estate financing.

C9-43 *At-Risk Loss Limitation.* Mary and Gary are partners in the MG Partnership. Mary owns a 40% capital, profits, and loss interest; Gary owns the remaining interest. Both materially participate in partnership activities. At the beginning of the current year, MG's only liabilities are $30,000 in accounts payable, which remain outstanding at year-end. In November, MG borrows $100,000 on a nonrecourse basis from First Bank. The loan is secured by property with a $200,000 FMV. These are MG's only liabilities at year-end. Basis for the partnership interests at the beginning of the year is $40,000 for Mary and $60,000 for Gary before considering the impact of liabilities and operations. MG has a $200,000 ordinary loss during the current year. How much loss can Mary recognize? Gary?

C9-44 *Passive Loss Limitation.* Eve and Tom own 40% and 60%, respectively, of the ET Partnership, which manufactures clocks. The partnership is a limited partnership, and Eve is the only general partner. She works full-time in the business. Tom essentially is an investor in the firm and works full-time at another job. Tom has no other income except his salary from his full-time employer. During the current year, the partnership reports the following income, gain, and losses:

Ordinary loss	$140,000
Long.-term capital gain	20,000

Before including the current year's income, gains, and losses, Eve and Tom had $46,000 and $75,000 bases for their partnership interests, respectively. The partnership has no nonrecourse liabilities. Tom has no further obligation to make any additional investment in the partnership.
a. What income, gain, or loss should each partner report on his or her individual tax return?
b. If the partnership borrowed an additional $100,000 of recourse liabilities, how would your answer to Part a change?

C9-45 *Passive Loss Limitation.* Kate, Chad, and Stan are partners in the KCS Partnership, which operates a manufacturing business. The partnership was formed ten years ago with Kate and Chad each as general partners having a 40% capital and profits interest. Kate materially participates; Chad does not. Stan has a 20% interest as a limited partner. At the end of the current year, the following information was available:

	Kate	*Chad*	*Stan*
Basis in partnership (immediately before year-end)	$100,000	$100,000	$50,000
Distributive share of:			
Nonrecourse liability (already included in basis and not qualified real estate financing)	50,000	50,000	25,000
Operating losses	(80,000)	(80,000)	(40,000)
Capital gains	20,000	20,000	10,000

a. How much operating loss can each partner deduct in the current year?
b. How much loss could each partner deduct if the KCS Partnership were engaged in rental activities? Assume Kate and Chad both actively participate, but Stan does not.

C9-46 ***At-Risk and Passive Loss Limitations.*** At the beginning of year 1, Ed and Fran each contributed $1,000 cash to EF Partnership as equal partners. The partnership immediately borrowed $98,000 on a nonrecourse basis and used the contributed cash and loan proceeds to purchase equipment costing $100,000. The partnership leases out the equipment on a five-year lease for $10,000 per year. Over the five-year period, the partnership makes the following principal and interest payments on the loan:

Year	*Principal*	*Interest*
1	$3,000	$7,000
2	3,500	6,500
3	3,500	6,500
4	4,000	6,000
5	4,000	6,000

Assume the partnership depreciates the equipment according to the following schedule (including Sec. 179 expensing in year 1; numbers are adjusted and rounded for simplicity):

Year	*Depreciation*
1	$40,000
2	25,000
3	15,000
4	8,000
5	8,000
6	4,000

At the beginning of year 6, the partnership sells the equipment for $82,000. The partnership claims the last $4,000 of depreciation at the beginning of year 6 as an expense, so the equipment has a zero basis when sold. At the beginning of year 6, the partnership also pays off the $80,000 loan balance and distributes any remaining cash to Ed and Fran. Assume that each partner has a 40% ordinary tax rate and a 20% capital gains tax rate.
a. Determine the partnership's gain (loss) for each of the five years and the beginning of the sixth year.
b. Assume that depreciation recapture applies but that the at-risk and passive activity loss rules do not apply. Using the results from Part a and a 7% discount rate, determine the present value of tax savings for both partners combined over the five-year period including the beginning of the sixth year. Why do these tax savings occur?
c. Now assume the at-risk and passive activity loss rules do apply. Determine what the partners recognize over the five-year period including the beginning of the sixth year. Do the partners have any tax savings in this situation? Why or why not?
d. Provide a schedule analyzing each partner's outside basis over the five-year period including the sixth year.

C9-47 ***Related Party Transactions.*** Susan, Steve, and Sandy own 15%, 35%, and 50%, respectively, in the SSS Partnership. Susan sells securities for their $40,000 FMV to the partnership. What are the tax implications of the following independent situations?
a. Susan's basis in the securities is $60,000. The three partners are siblings.
b. Susan's basis in the securities is $50,000. Susan is unrelated to the other partners.
c. Susan's basis in the securities is $30,000. Susan and Sandy are sisters. The partnership will hold the securities as an investment.

d. What are the tax consequences in Part a if the partnership subsequently sells the securities to an unrelated third party for $70,000? For $55,000? For $35,000?

C9-48 *Related Party Transactions.* Kara owns 35% of the KLM Partnership and 45% of the KTV Partnership. Lynn owns 20% of KLM and 3% of KTV. Maura, Kara's daughter, owns 15% of KTV. No other partners own an interest in both partnerships or are related to other partners. The KTV Partnership sells to the KLM Partnership 1,000 shares of stock, which KTV has held for investment purposes, for its $50,000 FMV. What are the tax consequences of the sale in each of the following independent situations?

a. KTV's basis for the stock is $80,000.
b. KTV's basis for the stock is $23,000 and KLM holds the stock as an investment.
c. KTV's basis for the stock is $35,000 and KLM holds the stock as inventory.
d. What are the tax consequences in Part a if the KLM Partnership subsequently sells the stock to an unrelated third party for $130,000? For $105,000? For $70,000?

C9-49 *Guaranteed Payments.* Scott and Dave each invested $100,000 cash when they formed the SD Partnership and became equal partners. They agreed that the partnership would pay each partner a 5% guaranteed payment on his $100,000 capital account. Before the two guaranteed payments, current year results were $23,000 of ordinary income and $14,000 of long-term capital gain. What amount and character of income will Scott and Dave report for the current year from their partnership?

C9-50 *Guaranteed Payments.* Allen and Bob are equal partners in the AB Partnership. Bob manages the business and receives a guaranteed payment. What amount and character of income will Allen and Bob report in each of the following independent situations?

a. The AB Partnership earns $160,000 of ordinary income before considering Bob's guaranteed payment. Bob is guaranteed a $90,000 payment plus 50% of all income remaining after the guaranteed payment.
b. Assume the same facts as Part a except Bob's distributive share is 50% with a guaranteed minimum of $90,000.
c. The AB Partnership earns a $140,000 long-term capital gain and no ordinary income. Bob is guaranteed $80,000 plus 50% of all amounts remaining after the guaranteed payment.

C9-51 *Guaranteed Payments.* Pam and Susan own the PS Partnership. Pam takes care of daily operations and receives a guaranteed payment for her efforts. What amount and character of income will each partner report in each of the following independent situations?

a. The PS Partnership reports a $10,000 long-term capital gain and no ordinary income. Pam receives a $40,000 guaranteed payment plus a 30% distributive share of all partnership income after deducting the guaranteed payment.
b. The PS Partnership reports $80,000 of ordinary income and a $60,000 Sec. 1231 gain. Pam receives a $35,000 guaranteed payment plus a 20% distributive share of all partnership income after deducting the guaranteed payment.
c. The PS Partnership reports $120,000 of ordinary income. Pam receives 40% of partnership income but no less than $60,000.

C9-52 *Family Partnership.* Dad gives Son a 20% capital and profits interest in the Family Partnership. Dad holds a 70% interest, and Fred, an unrelated individual, holds a 10% interest. Dad and Fred work in the partnership, but Son does not. Dad and Fred receive reasonable compensation for their work. The partnership earns $100,000 ordinary income, and the partners agree to divide this amount based on their relative ownership interests. Fred does not know that Son has a partnership interest. What income must Father, Son, and Fred report if Family Partnership is a manufacturing firm with substantial inventories?

C9-53 *Family Partnership.* Steve wishes to pass his business on to his children, Tracy and Vicki, and gives each daughter a 20% partnership interest to begin getting them involved. Steve retains the remaining 60% interest. Neither daughter is employed by the partnership, which buys and manages real estate. Steve draws only a $40,000 guaranteed payment for his work for the partnership. Reasonable compensation for his services would be $70,000. The partnership reports ordinary income of $120,000 after deducting the guaranteed payment. Distributive shares for the three partners are tentatively reported as: Steve, $72,000; Tracy, $24,000; and Vicki, $24,000. What is the proper distributive share of income for each partner?

COMPREHENSIVE PROBLEMS

C9-54 Rick has a $50,000 basis in the RKS General Partnership on January 1 of the current year, and he owns no other investments. He has a 20% capital interest, a 30% profits interest, and a 40% loss interest in the partnership. Rick does not work in the partnership. The partnership's only liability is a $100,000 nonrecourse debt borrowed several years ago, which remains outstanding at year-end. Rick's share of the liability is based on his profits interest and is included in his $50,000 partnership basis. Rick and the partnership each report on a calendar year basis. Income for the entire partnership during the current year is:

Ordinary loss	$440,000
Long-term capital gain	100,000
Sec. 1231 gain	150,000

a. What is Rick's distributive share of income, gain, and loss for the current year?
b. What partnership income, gain, and loss should Rick report on his tax return for the current year?
c. What is Rick's basis in his partnership interest on the first day of next year?

C9-55 Charles and Mary formed CM Partnership on January 1 of the current year. Charles contributed Inventory A with a $100,000 FMV and a $70,000 adjusted basis for a 40% interest, and Mary contributed $150,000 cash for a 60% interest. The partnership operates on a calendar year. The partnership used the cash to purchase equipment for $50,000, Inventory B for $80,000, and stock in ST Corporation for $5,000. The partnership used the remaining $15,000 for operating expenses and borrowed another $5,000 for operating expenses. During the year, the partnership sold one-half of Inventory A for $60,000 (tax basis, $35,000), one-half of Inventory B for $58,000 (tax basis, $40,000), and the ST stock for $6,000. The partnership claimed $7,000 of depreciation on the equipment for both tax and book purposes. Thus, for the year, the partnership incurred the following items:

Sales—Inventory A	$60,000
Sales—Inventory B	58,000
COGS—Inventory A	35,000
COGS—Inventory B	40,000
Operating expenses	20,000
Depreciation	7,000
Short-term capital gain	1,000
Interest on business loan	500

On December 30 of the current year, the partnership made a $1,000 principal payment on the loan and distributed $2,000 cash to Charles and $3,000 cash to Mary.

a. Determine partnership ordinary income for the year and each partner's distributive share.
b. Determine the separately stated items and each partner's distributive share.
c. Determine each partner's basis in the partnership at the end of the current year.
d. Determine each partner's book capital account at the end of the current year.
e. Provide an analysis of the ending cash balance.
f. Provide beginning and ending balance sheets using tax numbers.
g. Provide beginning and ending balance sheets using book values.

TAX STRATEGY PROBLEM

C9-56 Sarah and Rex formed SR Entity on December 30 of last year. The entity operates on a calendar tax year. Each individual contributed $800,000 cash in exchange for a 50% ownership interest in the entity (common stock if a corporation; partnership interest if a partnership). In addition, the entity borrowed $400,000 from the bank. The entity operates on a calendar year. On December 30 of last year, the entity used the $2 million cash (contributions and loan) to purchase assets as indicated in the following balance sheet as of December 30 of last year:

Cash	$ 100,000
Inventory	1,770,000
Investment in tax-exempt bonds	50,000
Investment in corporate stock (less than 20%-owned)	80,000
Total	$2,000,000
Liability	$ 400,000
Equity*	1,600,000
Total	$2,000,000

*If a partnership, each partner's beginning capital account is $800,000.

The balance sheet did not change between December 30 of last year and the beginning of the current year. Thus, the above balance sheet also represents the balance sheet at January 1 of the current year.

The following data apply to the entity for the current year:

Sales	$3,000,000
Purchase of additional inventory	2,100,000
Ending inventory at December 31 of the current year	1,650,000
Gain on sale of corporate stock on December 31 of the current year	20,000
Dividends received on stock prior to its sale	4,000
Tax-exempt interest received	2,200
Operating expenses	500,000
Interest paid on loan (no principal paid)*	30,000
Distribution on December 31 of the current year:	
Sarah	50,000
Rex	50,000

*Of the $30,000 interest expense, $1,000 is allocable to the tax-exempt interest income, and $1,500 is allocable to investment income. The rest is business interest expense.

Sarah and Rex actively manage the entity's business. At the individual level, Sarah and Rex are each single with no dependents. Each individual claims a standard deduction and one personal exemption (if applicable). Neither individual has income from sources other than listed above.

a. First, assume the entity is a regular C corporation and the distributions are dividends to Sarah and Rex. For the current year, determine the following:
   (1) The corporation's taxable income and tax liability.
   (2) Sarah's and Rex's individual AGI, taxable income, and tax liability.
   (3) The total tax liability for the corporation and its owners.
b. Next, assume the entity is a partnership. For the current year, determine the following:
   (1) Partnership ordinary income and each partner's share of partnership ordinary income.
   (2) Partnership separately stated items and each partner's share of each item.
   (3) Sarah's and Rex's AGI, taxable income, and total tax liability. Assume each partner will incur a $14,000 self-employment tax.
   (4) Each partner's basis in the partnership (outside basis) at the end of the current year.
c. Based on your analysis for the current year, which entity is better from an overall tax perspective? What are the shortcomings of examining only one year?
d. Concerning the $50,000 distribution to each individual. Given the corporate form, explain how the corporation can restructure these payments to reduce the overall tax liability.

TAX FORM/RETURN PREPARATION PROBLEM

C9-57 The Dapper-Dons Partnership (employer identification no. 89-3456798) was formed ten years ago as a general partnership to custom tailor men's clothing. Dapper-Dons is located at 123 Flamingo Drive in Miami, Florida 33131. Bob Dapper (Social Security No. 654-32-1098) manages the business and has a 40% capital and profits interest. His address is 709 Brumby Way, Miami, Florida 33131. Jeremy Dons (Social Security No. 354-12-6531) owns the remaining 60% interest but is not active in the business. His address is 807 9th Avenue, North Miami, Florida 33134. The partnership values its inventory using the cost method and did not change the method used during the current year. The partnership uses the accrual method of accounting. Because of its simplicity, the partnership is not subject to the partnership audit procedures. The partnership has no foreign partners, no foreign transactions, no interests in foreign trusts, and no foreign financial accounts. This partnership is neither a tax shelter nor a publicly traded partnership. No changes in ownership of partnership interests occurred during the current year. The partnership made cash distributions of $155,050 and $232,576 to Dapper and Dons, respectively, on December 30 of the current year. It made no other property distributions. Financial statements for the current year are presented in Tables C9-1 and C9-2.

Prepare a current year partnership tax return for Dapper-Dons Partnership.

CASE STUDY PROBLEMS

C9-58 Abe and Brenda formed the AB Partnership ten years ago and have been very successful with the business. However, in the current year, economic conditions caused them to lose significant amounts, but they expect the economy and their business to return to profitable operations by next year or the year after. Abe manages the partnership business and works in it full-time. Brenda has a full-time job as an accountant for a $39,000 annual salary, but she also works in the partnership occasionally. She estimates that she spent about 120 hours working in the partnership this year. Abe has a 40% profits interest, a 50% loss interest, and a basis in his partnership interest on December 31 (before considering this year's operations or outstanding liabilities) of $65,000. Brenda has a 60% profits interest, a 50% loss interest, and a basis of $80,000 on December 31 (before considering this year's operations or outstanding liabilities). The only liability outstanding on December 31 is a recourse debt of $40,000. Neither Abe nor Brenda currently has other investments. The AB Partnership incurs the following amounts during the year.

Ordinary loss	$100,000
Sec. 1231 gain	10,000
Tax-exempt municipal bond income	14,000
Long-term capital loss	14,000
Short-term capital loss	136,000

Early next year, the AB Partnership is considering borrowing $100,000 from a local bank to be secured by a mortgage on a building owned by the partnership with $150,000 FMV.

Required: Prepare a presentation to be made to Abe and Brenda discussing this matter. Points that should be discussed include: What amounts should Abe and Brenda report on their income tax return for the current year from the AB Partnership? What are their bases in their partnership interests after taking all transactions into effect? What happens to any losses they cannot deduct in the current year? What planning opportunities are presented by the need to borrow money early next year? What planning ideas would you suggest for Brenda?

C9-59 On the advice of his attorney, Dr. Andres, a local pediatrician, contributed several office buildings, which he had previously owned as sole proprietor, to a new Andres Partnership in which he became a one-third general partner. He gave the remaining limited partnership interests to his two sons, Miguel and Esteban. Last year, when the partnership was formed, the boys were 14 and 16. The real estate is well-managed and extremely profitable. Dr. Andres regularly consults with a full-time hired manager about the business, but neither of his sons has any dealings with the partnership. Under the terms of the partnership agreement, the boys can sell their partnership interest to no one but their father. Distributions from the partnership have been large, and Dr. Andres has insisted that the boys put all their distributions into savings accounts to pay for their college education.

Last year's return (the partnership's first) was filed by Mr. Jones, a partner in the local CPA firm of Wise and Johnson. Mr. Jones, who was Dr. Andres's accountant for a decade, retired last summer. Dr. Andres's business is extremely profitable and is an important part of the client base of this small-town CPA firm. Ms. Watson, the young partner who has taken over Dr. Andres's account, asked John, a second-year staff accountant, to prepare the current year's partnership return.

John has done considerable research and is positive that the Andres Partnership does not qualify as a partnership at all because the father has retained too much control over the sons' interests. John has briefly talked to Mr. Jones about his concerns. Mr. Jones said he was really rushed in the prior year when he filed the partnership return and admitted he never looked into the question of whether the arrangement met the requirements for being taxed as a partnership. After hearing more of the details, Mr. Jones stated that John

▼ **TABLE C9-1**

Dapper-Dons Partnership Income Statement for the 12 Months Ending December 31 of the Current Year (Problem C9-57)

Sales		$2,350,000
Returns and allowances		(20,000)
		$2,330,000
Beginning inventory (FIFO method)	$ 200,050	
Purchases	624,000	
Labor	600,000	
Supplies	42,000	
Other costs[a]	12,000	
Goods available for sale	$1,478,050	
Ending inventory[b]	(146,000)	(1,332,050)
Gross profit		$ 997,950
Salaries for employees other than partners	$51,000	
Guaranteed payment for Dapper	85,000	
Utilities expense	46,428	
Depreciation (MACRS depreciation is $74,311)[c]	49,782	
Automobile expense	12,085	
Office supplies expense	4,420	
Advertising expense	85,000	
Bad debt expense	2,100	
Interest expense (all trade- or business-related)	45,000	
Rent expense	7,400	
Travel expense (meals cost $4,050 of this amount)	11,020	
Repairs and maintenance expense	68,300	
Accounting and legal expense	3,600	
Charitable contributions[d]	16,400	
Payroll taxes	5,180	
Other taxes (all trade- or business-related)	1,400	
Total expenses		494,115
Operating profit		$ 503,835
Other income and losses:		
Gain on sale of AB stock[e]	$ 18,000	
Loss on sale of CD stock[f]	(26,075)	
Sec. 1231 gain on sale of land[g]	5,050	
Interest on U.S. treasury bills for entire year ($80,000 face amount)	9,000	
Dividends from 15%-owned domestic corporation	11,000	16,975
Net income		$ 520,810

[a] Additional Sec. 263A costs of $7,000 for the current year are included in other costs.
[b] Ending inventory includes the appropriate Sec. 263A costs, and no further adjustment is needed to properly state cost of sales and inventories for tax purposes.
[c] The tax depreciation includes depreciation adjustments of $8,000 and $2,000 on personal property and real property, respectively, placed in service after 1986. Dapper-Dons acquired and placed in service $40,000 of rehabilitation expenditures for a certified historical property this year. The appropriate MACRS depreciation on the rehabilitation expenditures already is included in the MACRS depreciation total.
[d] The partnership made all contributions in cash to qualifying charities.
[e] The partnership purchased the AB stock as an investment two years ago on December 1 for $40,000 and sold it on June 14 of the current year for $58,000.
[f] The partnership purchased the CD stock as an investment on February 15 of the current year for $100,000 and sold it on August 1 for $73,925.
[g] The partnership use the land as a parking lot for the business. The partnership purchased the land four years ago for $30,000 and sold it on August 15 of the current year for $35,050.

▼ **TABLE C9-2**
Dapper-Dons Partnership Balance Sheet for January 1 and December 31 of the Current Year (Problem C9-57)

	Balance January 1	Balance December 31
Assets:		
Cash	$ 10,000	$ 40,000
Accounts receivable	72,600	150,100
Inventories	200,050	146,000
Marketable securities[a]	220,000	260,000
Building and equipment	374,600	465,000
Minus: Accumulated depreciation	(160,484)	(173,100)
Land	185,000	240,000
Total assets	$901,766	$1,128,000
Liabilities and equities:		
Accounts payable	$ 35,000	$ 46,000
Accrued salaries payable	14,000	18,000
Payroll taxes payable	3,416	7,106
Sales taxes payable	5,200	6,560
Mortgage and notes payable (current maturities)	44,000	52,000
Long-term debt	210,000	275,000
Capital:		
Dapper	236,060	289,334
Dons	354,090	434,000
Total liabilities and equities	$901,766	$1,128,000

[a] Short-term investment.

was probably correct in his conclusion. Dr. Andres's tax bill will be significantly larger if he has to pay tax on all the partnership's income. When John approached Ms. Watson with his conclusions, her response was, "Oh, no! Dr. Andres already is unhappy because Mr. Jones is no longer preparing his returns. He'll really be unhappy if we give him a big tax increase too." She paused thoughtfully, and then went on. "My first thought is just to leave well enough alone and file the partnership return. Are you positive, John, that this won't qualify as a partnership? Think about it, and let me know tomorrow."

Required: Prepare a list of points you want to go over with the tax partner that would support finding that the business activity is a partnership. Prepare a second list of points that would support finding that the business activity is not a partnership.

Optional: Act out the final meeting between John and Ms. Watson.

TAX RESEARCH PROBLEMS

C9-60 Caitlin and Will formed the C & W Partnership on January 5 of the current year. Caitlin contributed cash of $150,000, and Will contributed office furniture with a FMV of $21,000. He bought the furniture for $20,000 on January 1 last year and has depreciated it using MACRS depreciation. Will did not claim a Sec. 179 expense deduction when he bought the furniture. He also contributed an office building and land with a combined FMV of $129,000. The land's FMV is $9,000. Will bought the land in 1995 for $8,000 and had the building constructed for $100,000. The building was placed in service in June 1997.

Required: Your tax manager has asked you to prepare a schedule for the file indicating the basis of property at the time of contribution that Will contributed, the depreciation for each piece of property that the partnership can claim, and the allocation of the depreciation to the two partners. Also indicate the amount and type of any recapture to which the contributed property may be subject at the time of the contribution and at a later time when the partnership sells the property. Your tax manager knows that, under Reg. Sec.

1.704-3, several alternatives exist for allocating depreciation relating to contributed property. He remembers that the Treasury Regulations describe a traditional method and a couple of others, but he's not sure what method applies in this situation. He wants you to check the alternatives and indicate which method should be used. Be certain to clearly label your schedule so that anyone who looks at the file later can determine where your numbers came from and the authority for your calculations. The manager has asked you to consult, at a minimum, Secs. 168, 704, 1231, 1245, and 1250 and the related Treasury Regulations as well as Rev. Proc. 87-57. Consult other tax authorities if you do not obtain a complete answer from these sources.

C9-61 Your clients, Lisa and Matthew, plan to form Lima General Partnership. Lisa will contribute $50,000 cash to Lima for a 50% interest in capital and profits. Matthew will contribute land having a $35,000 adjusted basis and a $50,000 FMV to Lima for the remaining 50% interest in capital and profits. Lima will borrow additional funds of $100,000 from a bank on a recourse basis and then will subdivide and sell the land. Prepare a draft memorandum for your tax manager's signature outlining the tax treatment for the partnership formation transaction. As part of your memorandum, compare the reporting of this transaction on the tax and financial accounting books. References:

- IRC Sec. 721
- APB, *Opinions of the Accounting Principles Board No. 29* [Accounting for Nonmonetary Transactions]

C9-62 Almost two years ago, the DEF Partnership was formed when Demetrius, Ebony, and Farouk each contributed $100,000 in cash. They are equal general partners in the real estate partnership, which has a December 31 year-end. The partnership uses the accrual method of accounting for financial accounting purposes but uses the cash method of accounting for tax purposes. The first year of operations resulted in a $50,000 loss. Because the real estate market plummeted, the second year of operations will result in an even larger ordinary loss. On November 30, calculations reveal that the year's loss is likely to be $100,000 for financial accounting purposes. Financial accounting results for the year are as follows:

	Quarter			
	First	*Second*	*Third*	*Fourth**
Revenue	$40,000	$60,000	$80,000	$100,000
Maintenance expense	(30,000)	(58,000)	(70,000)	(85,000)
Interest expense	(10,000)	(30,000)	(35,000)	(50,000)
Utilities expense	(3,000)	(3,000)	(3,000)	(3,000)
Projected loss	($ 3,000)	($31,000)	($28,000)	($38,000)

* Fourth quarter results are the sum of actual October and November results along with estimates for December results. December estimates are revenue, $33,000; maintenance, $60,000; interest, $20,000; and utilities, $1,000.

Cash has been short throughout the second year of operations, so more than $65,000 of expenses for second year operations have resulted in bills that are currently due or overdue. The unpaid bills are for July 1 through November 30 interest on a loan from the bank. In addition, all but essential maintenance has been postponed during the fourth quarter so that most of the fourth quarter maintenance is scheduled to be completed during December.

The DEF partners wants to attract a new partner to obtain additional capital. Raj is interested in investing $100,000 as a limited partner in the DEF Partnership if a good deal can be arranged. Raj would have a 25% profits and loss interest in the partnership but would expect something extra for the current year. In the current tax year, Raj has passive income of more than $200,000 from other sources, so he would like to have large passive losses allocated to him from DEF.

Required: Your tax partner has asked you to prepare a memorandum suggesting a plan to maximize the amount of current year loss that can be allocated to Raj. Assume none of the partners performs more than one-half of his or her personal service time in connection with real estate trades or businesses in which he or she materially participates. She reminded you to consider the varying interest rules for allocating losses to new partners found in Sec. 706 and to look into the possibilities of somehow capitalizing on the cash method of accounting or of using a special allocation. She wants you to be sure to check all the relevant case law for the plan you suggest.

10

C H A P T E R

SPECIAL PARTNERSHIP ISSUES

LEARNING OBJECTIVES

After studying this chapter, you should be able to

1. Determine the amount and character of the gain or loss recognized by a partner from a nonliquidating partnership distribution
2. Determine the basis of assets received by a partner from a nonliquidating partnership distribution
3. Identify the partnership's Sec. 751 assets
4. Determine the tax implications of a cash distribution when the partnership has Sec. 751 assets
5. Determine the amount and character of the gain or loss recognized by a partner from a liquidating partnership distribution
6. Determine the basis of assets received in a liquidating distribution
7. Determine the amount and character of the gain or loss recognized when a partner retires from the partnership or dies
8. Determine whether a partnership has terminated for tax purposes
9. Understand the effect of optional basis adjustments
10. Determine the appropriate reporting for the income of an electing large partnership

CHAPTER OUTLINE

Nonliquidating Distributions...10-2
Nonliquidating Distributions with Sec. 751...10-7
Terminating an Interest in a Partnership...10-11
Optional Basis Adjustments...10-26
Special Forms of Partnerships...10-28
Tax Planning Considerations...10-33

Chapter C10 continues the discussion of partnership taxation. The chapter first explains simple nonliquidating distributions and then discusses more complex nonliquidating and liquidating distributions. The chapter also explains methods of disposing of a partnership interest, including sales of the partnership interest and the retirement or death of a partner as well as transactions that terminate the entire partnership.

The final topic in this chapter is an examination of special partnership forms. These forms include publicly traded partnerships, limited liability companies, limited liability partnerships, and electing large partnerships.

NONLIQUIDATING DISTRIBUTIONS

Distributions from a partnership fall into two categories: liquidating distributions and nonliquidating (or current) distributions. A **liquidating distribution** is a single distribution, or one of a planned series of distributions, that terminates a partner's entire interest in the partnership. All other distributions, including those that substantially reduce a partner's interest in the partnership, are governed by the **nonliquidating (current) distribution** rules.

Although the tax consequences of the two types of distributions are similar in many respects, they are sufficiently different to require separate study. First, simple current distributions are discussed. Then complex current distributions involving Sec. 751 property (explained later in this chapter) and liquidating distributions are covered.

OBJECTIVE 1

Determine the amount and character of the gain or loss recognized by a partner from a nonliquidating partnership distribution

RECOGNITION OF GAIN

A current distribution that does not bring Sec. 751 into play cannot result in the recognition of a loss by either the partner who receives the distribution or the partnership. Moreover, the partnership usually recognizes no gain on a current distribution (except for Sec. 751 property). Under Sec. 731, partners who receive distributions recognize a gain if they receive money distributions that exceed their basis in the partnership. For distribution purposes, money includes cash, deemed cash from reductions in a partner's share of liabilities, and the fair market value (FMV) of marketable securities.

EXAMPLE C10-1 ▶

Melissa is a 30% partner in the ABC Real Estate Partnership until Josh is admitted as a partner in exchange for a cash contribution. After Josh's admission, Melissa holds a 20% interest. Because of large loss deductions, Melissa's basis (before Josh's admission) is $20,000 including her 30% interest in the partnership liabilities of $250,000. She is deemed to receive a cash distribution equal to the $25,000 [(30% − 20%) × $250,000] reduction in her share of partnership liabilities. Because the cash distribution exceeds her basis, Melissa must recognize a $5,000 ($25,000 distribution − $20,000 basis) gain. ◀

KEY POINT

Remember that reductions in a partner's share of liabilities are treated as cash distributions.

SELF-STUDY QUESTION

Can gain or loss be recognized in a current distribution?

ANSWER

Current distributions with no Sec. 751 implications do not create losses to either the partner or partnership. Ignoring Sec. 751, the partnership recognizes no gains. However, a partner recognizes a gain if the partner receives a money distribution exceeding his or her basis in his or her partnership interest. A distribution also may trigger recognition of precontribution gain or loss for a partner.

Precontribution Gain Recognition. Although a current distribution causes gain recognition only if money distributions exceed a partner's basis, the distribution also may trigger recognition of previously unrecognized precontribution gain or loss. A precontribution gain or loss is the difference between the FMV and adjusted basis of property when contributed to the partnership. Two different events may trigger recognition of precontribution gain or loss.

First, if property is contributed to a partnership with a deferred precontribution gain or loss, the contributing partner must recognize the precontribution gain or loss when the partnership distributes the property to any other partner within seven years of the contribution. The amount of precontribution gain or loss recognized by the contributing partner equals the amount of precontribution gain or loss remaining that would have been allocated to the contributing partner had the property instead been sold for its FMV on the distribution date. The partnership's basis in the property immediately before the distribution and the contributing partner's basis in his or her partnership interest are both increased for any gain recognized or decreased for any loss recognized.[1]

EXAMPLE C10-2 ▶ Several years ago, Michael contributed land with a $3,000 basis and a $7,000 FMV to the AB Partnership. In the current year, the partnership distributed the land to Stephen, another partner in the partnership. At the time of the distribution, the land had a $9,000 FMV. Stephen recognizes no gain on the distribution. Michael must recognize his $4,000 precontribution gain when the partnership distributes the property to Stephen. Michael increases the basis in his partnership interest by $4,000, and the partnership's basis in the land immediately before the distribution is increased by $4,000. This increase in the partnership's basis for the land also increases the land's basis to the distributee partner (Stephen). ◀

KEY POINT

Note the differences in the two distributions that cause a contributing partner to recognize remaining precontribution gains. In the first distribution, the *contributed property* is distributed to *another partner.* In the second distribution, *property other than the contributed property* is distributed to the *contributing partner.*

Second, under Sec. 737, property distributions to a partner may cause the partner to recognize his or her remaining precontribution gain if the FMV of the distributed property exceeds the partner's basis in his or her partnership interest before the distribution. The gain recognized under Sec. 737 is the lesser of the remaining precontribution net gain or the excess of the FMV of the distributed property over the adjusted basis of the partnership interest immediately before the property distribution (but after reduction for any money distributed at the same time).[2] The remaining precontribution gain is the net of all precontribution gains and losses for property contributed to the partnership in the seven years immediately preceding the distribution to the extent that such precontribution gains and losses have not already been recognized. The character of the recognized gain is determined by referencing the type of property that had precontribution gains or losses. The gain recognized under Sec. 737 is in addition to any gain recognized on the same distribution under Sec. 731.

EXAMPLE C10-3 ▶ Several years ago, Sergio contributed land, a capital asset, with a $20,000 FMV and a $15,000 basis to the STU Partnership in exchange for a 30% general interest in the partnership. The partnership still holds the land on January 31 of the current year, and none of the $5,000 precontribution gain has been recognized. On January 31 of the current year, Sergio has a $40,000 basis in his partnership interest when he receives an $8,000 cash distribution plus property purchased by the partnership with a $45,000 FMV and a $30,000 basis. Under the Sec. 731 distribution rules Sergio recognizes no gain because the cash distribution ($8,000) does not exceed Sergio's predistribution basis in his partnership interest ($40,000). However, Sec. 737 mandates that he must recognize gain equal to the lesser of the $5,000 remaining precontribution gain or the $13,000 difference between the FMV of the property distributed ($45,000) and the basis of the partnership interest after the cash distribution but before any property distributions ($32,000 = $40,000 adjusted basis − $8,000 cash distributed). Thus, Sergio recognizes a $5,000 capital gain. ◀

EXAMPLE C10-4 ▶ Assume the same facts as in Example C10-3 except the distribution was $20,000 in cash and $23,000 (FMV) in marketable securities plus the property. Sergio recognizes a $3,000 gain under Sec. 731 because he received a money distribution exceeding his basis in the partnership interest ($43,000 money distribution − $40,000 adjusted basis before distributions). Under Sec. 737 he also must recognize gain equal to the lesser of the remaining precontribution gain ($5,000) or the excess of the FMV of the property distributed ($45,000) over the zero basis of the partnership interest after money distributions but before property distributions ($0 = $40,000 adjusted basis − $43,000 money distributed). Sergio, therefore, recognizes both a $5,000 capital gain under Sec. 737 and a $3,000 capital gain under Sec. 731. ◀

If a partner recognizes gain under Sec. 737, the partner's basis in his or her partnership interest is increased by the gain recognized (illustrated in the next section). Further, the partnership's basis in the property that was the source of the precontribution gain also is increased by the recognized gain.

---

[1] Sec. 704(c). See Chapter C9 for a discussion of precontribution gains and losses.

[2] Section 737 does not apply if the property distributed was contributed by this same partner. Only the provisions of Sec. 731 would be considered in such a situation.

EXAMPLE C10-5 ▶ Assume the same facts as in Example C10-3. At the time Sergio contributed the land, the partnership assumed Sergio's $15,000 basis in the land. Now, the partnership's basis in the land increases to $20,000 by Sergio's $5,000 Sec. 737 gain. ◀

OBJECTIVE 2

Determine the basis of assets received by a partner from a nonliquidating partnership distribution

BASIS EFFECTS OF DISTRIBUTIONS

In general, the partner's basis for property distributed by the partnership carries over from the partnership. The partner's basis in the partnership interest is reduced by the amount of money received and by the partner's basis in the distributed property.

EXAMPLE C10-6 ▶ Jack has a $35,000 basis for his interest in the MLV Partnership before receiving a current distribution consisting of $7,000 in money, accounts receivable having a zero basis to the partnership, and land having an $18,000 basis to the partnership. Jack takes a carryover basis in the land and receivables. Following the distribution, his basis in the partnership interest is calculated as follows:

Predistribution basis in partnership interest	$35,000
Minus: Money received	(7,000)
Carryover basis in receivables	(–0–)
Carryover basis in land	(18,000)
Postdistribution basis in partnership interest	$10,000

◀

The total bases of all distributed property in the partner's hands is limited to the partner's predistribution basis in his or her partnership interest plus any gain recognized on the distribution under Sec. 737.[3] If the partner's predistribution basis plus Sec. 737 gain is less than the sum of the money received plus the carryover basis of any nonmoney property received, the order in which the basis is allocated is crucial. First, cash and deemed cash distributions reduce the partner's basis in his or her partnership interest. Next, the remaining basis is allocated to provide a carryover of the partnership's basis for receivables and inventory. If the partner's predistribution basis is not large enough to allow a carryover of the partnership's basis for these two property categories, the partner's remaining basis is allocated among the receivables and inventory items based on both the partnership's basis in the assets and their FMV.[4] First, each asset is given its basis to the partnership, then the difference between the carryover basis from the partnership and the partner's basis in the partnership interest is cal-

WHAT WOULD YOU DO IN THIS SITUATION?

You have done the personal and business tax work for Betty and Thelma for a number of years. Betty and Thelma are partners in a retail shop. In addition, the two have decided they want to exchange some property that is not associated with their partnership. Betty wants to exchange undeveloped land she personally holds as an investment, having a $40,000 FMV and a $10,000 adjusted basis, for machinery and office equipment that Thelma owns but no longer uses. Thelma's machinery and office equipment in total have a $40,000 FMV and a $28,000 adjusted basis. At a golf outing, a friend told Betty that several years ago he and an associate did a similar swap tax-free by contributing both pieces of property to be exchanged to a partnership, having the partnership hold the property for a few months, and then having the partnership distribute the property to the partner who wanted to receive it. The friend said the arrangement was tax-free because the initial transfer qualified as a tax-free contribution of property to the partnership in exchange for a partnership interest, and the distribution was tax-free because it was simply a pro rata property distribution made by the partnership. Thelma and Betty have come to you asking that you structure their exchange using their retail shop partnership so that the transfer will be tax-free also. How should you respond to their request?

[3] Secs. 732(a)(2) and 737(c). Marketable securities have a basis equal to their Sec. 732 basis plus any gain recognized under Sec. 731(c).

[4] Sec. 732(c).

culated. A decrease must be allocated if the partner's basis in the partnership interest (after any money distribution) is less than the carryover basis from the partnership. The decrease is first allocated to any asset that has declined in value in an amount equal to the smaller of the decline in value for the asset or the asset's share of the decrease. If the decrease is not fully used at this point in the calculation, the remaining decrease is allocated to the assets based on their relative adjusted bases at this point in the calculation.

KEY POINT

If different types of property are distributed, the partnership distribution rules assume that the property is distributed in the following order: (1) cash, (2) receivables and inventory, and (3) other property. This ordering can affect both the recognition of gain to the partner and the basis the partner takes in the distributed property.

EXAMPLE C10-7 ▶ Tracy has a $15,000 basis in her interest in the TP Partnership and no remaining precontribution gain immediately before receiving a current distribution that consists of $6,000 in money, power tools held as inventory with a $4,000 basis to the partnership and FMV of $3,500, and steel rod held as inventory with an $8,000 basis to the partnership and FMV of $9,200. The basis of the distributed property in Tracy's hands is determined as follows:

Predistribution basis in partnership interest	$15,000
Minus: Money received	(6,000)
Plus: Sec. 737 gain	–0–
Basis to be allocated	$ 9,000

The calculation of bases for the steel rod and power tools is as follows:

	Steel Rods	*Power Tools*	*Total*
FMV of asset	$9,200	$3,500	$12,700
Minus: Partnership's basis for asset	(8,000)	(4,000)	(12,000)
Difference	$1,200	($ 500)	$ 700
Step 1: Give each asset the partnership's basis for the asset	$8,000	$4,000	$12,000
Minus: Tracy's basis to be allocated			(9,000)
Decrease to allocate			$ 3,000
Step 2: Asset basis after Step 1	$8,000	$4,000	$12,000
Allocate the decrease first to assets that have declined in value	–0–	(500)	(500)
Adjusted bases at this point in the calculation	$8,000	$3,500	$11,500
Step 3: Allocate $2,500 remaining decrease based on relative adjusted bases at this point in the calculation	(1,739)[a]	(761)[b]	(2,500)
Tracy's bases in the assets	$6,261	$2,739	$ 9,000

[a]$8,000 ÷ ($8,000 + $3,500) × $2,500 = $1,739
[b]$3,500 ÷ ($8,000 + $3,500) × $2,500 = $ 761

This process results in Tracy's total basis in the two assets she receives being exactly equal to the $9,000 amount to be allocated. Moreover, Tracy's basis in her partnership interest is zero after the property distributions. ◀

EXAMPLE C10-8 ▶ Assume the same facts as in Example C10-7 except Tracy must recognize $1,000 of remaining precontribution gain under Sec. 737 as a result of the distribution. The basis of the distributed property in Tracy's hands is determined as follows:

Predistribution basis in partnership interest	$15,000
Minus: Money received	(6,000)
Plus: Sec. 737 gain	1,000
Amount to be allocated	$10,000

The calculation of the basis for the steel rods and power tools are as follows:

	Steel Rods	*Power Tools*	*Total*
FMV of asset	$9,200	$3,500	$12,700
Minus: Partnership's basis for asset	(8,000)	(4,000)	(12,000)
Difference	$1,200	($ 500)	$ 700

Step 1: Give each asset the partnership's basis for the asset	$8,000	$4,000	$12,000
Minus: Tracy's basis to be allocated			(10,000)
Decrease to allocate			$ 2,000
Step 2: Adjusted basis after Step 1	$8,000	$4,000	$12,000
Allocate the decrease first to assets that have declined in value	-0-	(500)	(500)
Adjusted basis at this point in the calculation	$8,000	$3,500	$11,500
Step 3: Allocate $1,500 remaining decrease based on relative adjusted bases at this point in the calculation	(1,043)[a]	(457)[b]	(1,500)
Tracy's bases in the assets	$6,957	$3,043	$10,000

[a]$8,000 ÷ ($8,000 + $3,500) × $1,500 = $1,043
[b]$3,500 ÷ ($8,000 + $3,500) × $1,500 = $ 457

Again, Tracy's basis in her partnership interest is zero after the distributions. ◀

If a partner's predistribution basis plus Sec. 737 gain recognized exceeds the sum of his or her money distribution plus the carryover basis for any receivables and inventory, a carryover basis is allocated to the other property received. If the partner has an insufficient basis for the partnership interest to provide a carryover basis for all the distributed property, the remaining basis for the partnership interest is allocated to the other property first to any decrease in FMV below basis and then based on the relative bases of such property in the partnership's hands just as was calculated above.

EXAMPLE C10-9 ▶ John has a $15,000 basis for his partnership interest and no remaining precontribution gain before receiving the following property as a current distribution:

Property	*Basis to the Partnership*	*FMV*
Money	$ 5,000	$5,000
Inventory	4,000	4,500
Land parcel 1	4,500	6,000
Land parcel 2	3,000	4,000

John's basis in his distributed property is calculated as follows:

Predistribution basis	$15,000
Minus: Money received	(5,000)
Plus: Sec. 737 gain	-0-
Basis for nonmoney property	$10,000
Minus: Carryover basis for inventory	(4,000)
Remaining basis to be allocated	$ 6,000

The calculation of the basis for the two parcels of land is as follows:

	Parcel One	*Parcel Two*	*Total*
FMV of asset	$6,000	$4,000	$10,000
Minus: Partnership's basis for asset	(4,500)	(3,000)	(7,500)
Difference	$1,500	$1,000	$ 2,500
Step 1: Give each asset the partnership's basis for the asset	$4,500	$3,000	$ 7,500
Minus: John's basis to be allocated			(6,000)
Decrease to allocate			$ 1,500
Step 2: Adjusted basis after Step 1	$4,500	$3,000	$ 7,500
Allocate the decrease first to assets that have declined in value	-0-	-0-	-0-
Adjusted basis at this point in the calculation	$4,500	$3,000	$ 7,500

SELF-STUDY QUESTION

Assume the same facts as in Example C10-9 except that the basis in the two parcels of land is only $4,000 in total. What are the tax consequences of the distribution?

ANSWER

Example C10-9 is a good illustration of the three types of property that can be included in a partnership distribution. If the basis in the two parcels of land were only $4,000 in total, the partner would take a $4,000 carryover basis in the land and retain a $2,000 basis in his partnership interest.

Step 3: Allocate $1,500 remaining decrease based on relative adjusted bases at this point in the calculation	(900)[a]	(600)[b]	(1,500)
John's bases in the assets	$3,600	$2,400	$ 6,000

[a]$4,500 ÷ ($4,500 + $3,000) × $1,500 = $900
[b]$3,000 ÷ ($4,500 + $3,000) × $1,500 = $600

John's basis in his partnership interest is zero after the distribution because all of its basis is allocated to the money and other property received. ◀

TYPICAL MISCONCEPTION

The partner's basis in his or her partnership interest cannot be less than zero. However, a partner's capital account can be less than zero. One must distinguish between references to a partner's basis in his or her partnership interest (his outside basis) and the balance in a partner's capital account.

Two other points should be noted. First, even when a partner's basis in the partnership interest is reduced to zero by a current distribution, he or she retains an interest in the partnership. If the partner has no remaining interest in the partnership (as opposed to a zero basis), the distribution would have been a liquidating distribution. Second, the distributee's basis in property distributed as a current distribution is always equal to or less than the carryover basis. Basis for distributed property cannot be increased above the carryover basis amount when it is received as a nonliquidating distribution.

HOLDING PERIOD AND CHARACTER OF DISTRIBUTED PROPERTY

The partner's holding period for property distributed as a current distribution includes the partnership's holding period for such property.[5] The length of time the partner owns the partnership interest is irrelevant when determining the holding period for the distributed property. Thus, if a new partner receives a distribution of property that the partnership held for two years before he or she became a partner, the new partner's holding period for the distributed property is deemed to begin when the partnership purchased the property (i.e., two years ago) rather than on the more recent date when the partner purchases the partnership interest.

KEY POINT

Consistent with the discussion in Chapter C9, certain rules ensure that neither contributions to nor distributions from a partnership can be used to alter the character of certain gains and losses on property held by the partnership or by the individual partners.

A series of rules regulate the character of the gain or loss recognized when certain property distributed to a partner is subsequently sold or exchanged. These rules are similar to provisions regulating the character of gain or loss on contributed property.

If property that is an unrealized receivable in the partnership's hands is distributed, the income or loss recognized on a subsequent sale of that property by the distributee partner is ordinary income or loss. This ordinary income or loss treatment occurs without regard to the character of the property in the distributee partner's hands or the length of time the partner holds the property before its disposition.[6]

If property that is inventory in the hands of the partnership is distributed, the income or loss recognized on a subsequent sale by the distributee partner occurring within five years of the distribution date is ordinary income or loss.[7] The inventory rule mandates the ordinary income or loss result only for the five-year period beginning on the distribution date. After five years, the character of the gain or loss recognized on the sale of such property is determined by its character in the hands of the distributee partner.

NONLIQUIDATING DISTRIBUTIONS WITH SEC. 751

OBJECTIVE 3

Identify the partnership's Sec. 751 assets

So far, the discussion of current distributions has ignored the existence of the Sec. 751 property rules. Now, we must expand our discussion to include them.

SECTION 751 ASSETS DEFINED

Sec. 751 assets include unrealized receivables and inventory. These two categories encompass all property that is likely to produce ordinary income when sold or collected. Each of these categories must be carefully defined before further discussion of Sec. 751.

[5] Sec. 735(b).
[6] Sec. 735(a)(1).
[7] Sec. 735(a)(2).

KEY POINT

Section 751 property represents property in a partnership that is likely to produce ordinary income or loss. The application of Sec. 751 in conjunction with partnership distributions or sales of a partnership interest is of concern to individual partners because the rules may trigger ordinary income recognition rather than capital gains.

UNREALIZED RECEIVABLES. *Unrealized receivables* includes a much broader spectrum of property than the name implies. Unrealized receivables are certain rights to payments to be received by a partnership to the extent they are not already included in income under the partnership's accounting methods. They include rights to payments for services performed or to be performed as well as rights to payment for goods delivered or to be delivered (other than capital assets). A common example of unrealized receivables is the accounts receivable of a cash method of accounting partnership.

In addition to rights to receive payments for goods and services, the term *unrealized receivables* includes most potential ordinary income recapture items. A primary example of this type of unrealized receivable is the potential Sec. 1245 or 1250 recapture on the partnership's depreciable property, which is the amount of depreciation that would be recaptured as ordinary income under Sec. 1245 or 1250 if the partnership sold property at its FMV.[8]

EXAMPLE C10-10 ▶ The LK Partnership has two assets: $10,000 cash and a machine having a $14,000 basis and a $20,000 FMV. The partnership has claimed depreciation of $8,000 on the machine since its purchase. If the partnership sells the machine for its FMV, all $6,000 of the gain would be recaptured under Sec. 1245. Therefore, the LK Partnership has a $6,000 unrealized receivable item. ◀

SELF-STUDY QUESTION

What is included in the definition of unrealized receivables?

ANSWER

Unrealized receivables include not only the obvious cash method accounts receivable that have yet to be recognized but also most of the potential ordinary income recapture provisions. Therefore, the term *unrealized receivables* is broader than it may appear.

The definition of unrealized receivables is not limited to Sec. 1245 and 1250 depreciation recapture. Among the other recapture provisions creating unrealized receivables are Sec. 617(d) (mining property), Sec. 1252 (farmland), and Sec. 1254 (oil, gas, and geothermal property). Assets covered by Sec. 1278 (market discount bonds) and Sec. 1283 (short-term obligations) generate unrealized receivables to the extent the taxpayer would recognize ordinary income if the asset were sold. This type of unrealized receivable is deemed to have a zero basis.

INVENTORY. *Inventory* is equally surprising in its breadth. Inventory for purposes of Sec. 751 includes three major types of property:

- Items held for sale in the normal course of partnership business
- Any other property that, if sold by the partnership, would not be considered a capital asset or Sec. 1231 property
- Any other property held by the partnership that, if held by the selling or distributee partner, would be property of the two types listed above[9]

In short, cash, capital assets, and Sec. 1231 assets are the only properties that are not inventory.

TYPICAL MISCONCEPTION

The definition of inventory is broadly construed by Sec. 751. In fact, for purposes of determining whether inventory is substantially appreciated, even unrealized receivables are treated as inventory items.

For purposes of calculating the impact of Sec. 751 on distributions (but not sales), inventory is considered a Sec. 751 asset only if the inventory is **substantially appreciated.** The test to determine whether inventory is substantially appreciated (and therefore taxed under Sec. 751) is purely mechanical. Inventory is substantially appreciated if its FMV exceeds 120% of its adjusted basis to the partnership. For purposes of testing whether the inventory is substantially appreciated (but *only* for that purpose), inventory also includes unrealized receivables. The inclusion of unrealized receivables in the definition of inventory increases the likelihood that the inventory will be substantially appreciated.

EXAMPLE C10-11 ▶ The ABC Partnership owns the following assets on December 31:

Assets	*Basis*	*FMV*
Cash	$10,000	$ 10,000
Unrealized receivables	–0–	40,000
Inventory	30,000	34,000
Land (Sec. 1231 property)	40,000	70,000
Total	$80,000	$154,000

[8] Sec. 751(c). Unrealized receivables may have basis if costs or expenses have been incurred but not taken into account under the partnership's method of accounting (e.g., the basis of property sold in a nondealer installment sale).

[9] Sec. 751(d)(2).

For purposes of the substantially appreciated inventory test, both ABC's unrealized receivables and inventory are included. The inventory's $74,000 FMV exceeds 120% of its adjusted basis [($30,000 + 0) × 1.20 = $36,000]. Therefore, the ABC Partnership has substantially appreciated inventory. ◀

OBJECTIVE 4

Determine the tax implications of a cash distribution when the partnership has Sec. 751 assets

EXCHANGE OF SEC. 751 ASSETS AND OTHER PROPERTY

A current distribution receives treatment under Sec. 751 only if the partnership has Sec. 751 assets and an exchange of Sec. 751 property for non-Sec. 751 property occurs. Accordingly, if a partnership does not have *both* Sec. 751 property and other property, the rules discussed above for simple current distributions control the taxation of the distribution. Similarly, a distribution that is proportionate to all partners or (1) consists of only the partner's share of either Sec. 751 property or non-Sec. 751 property and (2) does not reduce the partner's interest in other property is not affected by the Sec. 751 rules.

However, any portion of the distribution that represents an exchange of Sec. 751 property for non-Sec. 751 property must be isolated and is not treated as a distribution at all. Instead, it is treated as a sale between the partnership and the partner, and any gain or loss realized on the sale transaction is fully recognized.[10] The character of the recognized gain or loss is determined by the character of the property deemed sold. For the party deemed the seller of the Sec. 751 assets, the gain or loss is ordinary income or loss.

TYPICAL MISCONCEPTION

Even if a partnership has Sec. 751 property, Sec. 751 is not applicable as long as a partner's interest in the ordinary-income type assets is not altered. However, if a distribution of the partnership assets is disproportionate, Sec. 751 treats that portion of the distribution as a deemed sale between the partnership and the distributee partner, with the corresponding income/loss being recognized.

Analyzing the transaction to determine what property was involved in the Sec. 751 transaction is best accomplished by using an orderly, step-by-step approach.

STEP 1: DIVIDE THE ASSETS INTO SEC. 751 ASSETS AND NON-SEC. 751 ASSETS. Inventory must be tested at this time to see whether it is substantially appreciated to know whether it is a Sec. 751 asset for distribution purposes.

STEP 2: DEVELOP A SCHEDULE, SUCH AS THE ONE IN TABLE C10-1, TO DETERMINE WHETHER THE PARTNER EXCHANGED SEC. 751 ASSETS FOR NON-SEC. 751 ASSETS OR VICE VERSA. This schedule must be based on the FMV of all the partnership's assets. To make the determination, it is necessary to compare the partner's interest in the partnership's assets before the distribution with his or her interest in the assets after the distribution. This part of our analysis assumes a fictional nontaxable pro rata distribution equal to the partner's decreased interest in the assets. We can see whether the partner exchanged Sec. 751 assets for non-Sec. 751 assets by comparing the fictional distribution with the actual distribution. Thus, in Table C10-1,

KEY POINT

Steps 2 and 3 try to identify whether a disproportionate distribution of Sec. 751 assets has taken place. In Table C10-1, if the column 5 total for Sec. 751 assets is zero, Sec. 751 is not applicable. But as the table illustrates, Anne received $10,000 more than her share of the partnership cash without receiving any of her $10,000 share of Sec. 751 assets.

- Column 1 represents the partner's interest (valued at FMV) in each asset before the distribution.
- Column 2 represents the partner's interest (valued at FMV) in each asset after the distribution.
- Column 3 shows the amount of a fictional proportionate distribution that would have occurred had the partner's ownership interest been reduced by the partner taking a pro rata share of each asset. (As such, the proportionate distribution would be nontaxable.)
- Column 4 shows the amounts actually distributed.
- Column 5 shows the difference between the fictional and actual distributions. This column contains the information that must be analyzed to see whether a Sec. 751 exchange has occurred.

STEP 3: ANALYZE COLUMN 5 TO DETERMINE WHETHER SEC. 751 ASSETS WERE EXCHANGED FOR NON-SEC. 751 ASSETS. If the column 5 total for the Sec. 751 assets section of Table C10-1 is zero, no Sec. 751 exchange has occurred. The partner simply received an additional amount of one type of Sec. 751 asset in exchange for relinquishing an interest in some other type of Sec. 751 asset. For example, no Sec. 751 exchange has occurred if a partner exchanged an interest in substantially appreciated inventory for an interest in unrealized receivables. However, if the column 5 total for the

---

10 Sec. 751(b).

▼ **TABLE C10-1**

Analysis of Sec. 751 Nonliquidating Distribution (Example C10-12)

	Beginning Partnership Amount[a]	(1) Anne's Interest Before Distribution[a] (1/3)	(2) Anne's Interest After Distribution[a] (1/5)	(3) Fictional Proportionate Distribution (3) = (1) – (2)[a]	(4) Actual Distribution[a]	(5) Difference[b] (5) = (4) – (3)
Sec. 751 assets:						
Unrealized receivables	$15,000	$ 5,000	$ 3,000	$ 2,000	$ –0–	$ (2,000)
Inventory	60,000	20,000	12,000	8,000	–0–	(8,000)
Total Sec. 751 assets	$75,000	$25,000	$15,000	$10,000	$ –0–	($ 10,000)
Non-Sec. 751 assets:						
Cash	$75,000	$25,000	$10,000[c]	$15,000	$25,000	$ 10,000
Total non-Sec. 751 assets	$75,000	$25,000	$10,000	$15,000	$25,000	$ 10,000

[a] Valued at fair market value.
[b] A negative amount means that Anne gave up her interest in a particular property. A positive amount means that she received more than her proportionate interest.
[c] One-fifth interest in remaining cash of $50,000.

Sec. 751 assets is an amount other than zero, a Sec. 751 exchange has occurred. One (or more) Sec. 751 properties has been exchanged for one (or more) non-Sec. 751 properties.

EXAMPLE C10-12 ▶ On January 1, the ABC Partnership holds the assets listed below before making a $25,000 cash distribution to Anne that reduces her interest in the partnership from one-third to one-fifth.

Assets	*Basis*	*FMV*
Cash	$ 75,000	$ 75,000
Unrealized receivables	–0–	15,000
Inventory	30,000	60,000
Total	$105,000	$150,000

ABC owes no liabilities on January 1. Before the distribution, Anne has a $35,000 basis in her partnership interest. The following steps are needed to determine the tax effects of the distribution:

STEP 1. Determine ABC's Sec. 751 and non-Sec. 751 assets. ABC's Sec. 751 assets include the unrealized receivables and the substantially appreciated inventory. The cash is ABC's only non-Sec. 751 property.

STEP 2. Complete the table used to analyze the Sec. 751 distribution (see Table C10-1).

STEP 3. Analyze column 5 of Table C10-1 to see whether a Sec. 751 exchange has occurred. Because Anne's Sec. 751 asset total declined by $10,000, we know she gave up $10,000 of her proportionate interest in ABC's Sec. 751 assets in exchange for cash. ◀

ADDITIONAL COMMENT

Step 4 is crucial if a student is to understand the deemed sale that Sec. 751 creates. In Example C10-13, Anne is treated as if she had exchanged her $10,000 interest in the unrealized receivables and inventory for $10,000 of cash. Thus, Anne has a taxable gain/loss on the deemed sale. To determine Anne's gain/loss on the deemed sale, the adjusted basis of the unrealized receivables and inventory equals whatever her basis would have been if those assets actually had been distributed to her.

STEP 4: DETERMINE THE GAIN OR LOSS ON THE SEC. 751 DEEMED SALE. We must assume that the exchange occurring in step 3 above was actually a sale of the exchanged property between the partnership and the partner. This step follows logically from the fact that the partner "bargained" to receive the amounts actually distributed rather than a proportionate distribution. She sold her interest in some assets to receive more than her proportionate interest in other assets. This sale is analyzed exactly the same way any other sale is analyzed. The gain (or loss) equals the difference between the FMV of the property received and the adjusted basis of the property given up. Note that up to this point we have been dealing only in terms of the FMV, so the adjusted basis of property given up must be determined as if that fictional distribution actually had been received.

EXAMPLE C10-13 ▶ Assume the same facts as in Example C10-12. The Sec. 751 sale portion of the distribution is analyzed as Anne receiving $10,000 more cash than her proportionate share and giving up a $2,000 (FMV) interest in the unrealized receivables and an $8,000 (FMV) interest in the inventory. By examining the balance sheet, we can see that the partnership's bases for the unrealized receivables and inventory are $0 and $4,000 [$8,000 × ($30,000 ÷ $60,000)]. If Anne received these properties in a current distribution, her basis would be the same as the property's basis in the partnership's hands, or $0 and $4,000, respectively. Therefore, Anne's deemed sale of the Sec. 751 assets is analyzed as follows:

Amount realized (cash)	$10,000
Minus: Adjusted basis of property sold	(4,000)
Realized and recognized gain	$ 6,000

The character of the recognized gain depends on the character of the property sold (in this case, the unrealized receivables and inventory). Therefore, Anne's $6,000 gain is ordinary income. ◀

STEP 5: DETERMINE THE IMPACT OF THE CURRENT DISTRIBUTION. The last step in analyzing the distribution's effect on the partner is to determine the impact of the portion of the distribution that is not a Sec. 751 exchange. This distribution is treated exactly like any other nonliquidating distribution.

EXAMPLE C10-14 ▶ Assume the same facts as in Examples C10-12 and C10-13. Examining the distribution, we see in column 4 of Table C10-1 that, as part of the Sec. 751 exchange, Anne received only $10,000 of the $25,000 cash actually distributed. The remaining $15,000 distributed represents a current distribution. Under Sec. 731(a)(1), a partner recognizes gain on a current distribution only if the money distributed exceeds his or her basis in the partnership interest. Anne recognizes no gain because she has a $16,000 basis in the partnership interest immediately after the current distribution. This basis is calculated as follows:

Predistribution basis for partnership interest	$35,000
Minus: Basis of property deemed distributed in Sec. 751 exchange ($0 unrealized receivables + $4,000 inventory)	(4,000)
Basis before current distribution	$31,000
Minus: Money distributed	(15,000)
Postdistribution basis of partnership interest	$16,000

After the entire distribution is complete, Anne owns a one-fifth partnership interest with a basis of $16,000 and has $25,000 in cash. In addition, she has recognized $6,000 in ordinary income. ◀

STOP & THINK *Question:* Do most current distributions made by a partnership require a Sec. 751 calculation?

Solution: No. Many current distributions are made pro rata to all partners, so Sec. 751 is not involved. Even if the distribution is not pro rata, the distribution often does not create an exchange of an interest in Sec. 751 assets for an interest in other assets. This exchange happens only when (1) the partner is reducing his or her overall interest in the partnership, (e.g., from a 15% to a 5% general partner) or (2) an explicit agreement provides that the distribution results in a partner giving up all or part of his or her interest in some asset(s) maintained by the partnership. Most current distributions do not involve Sec. 751.

TERMINATING AN INTEREST IN A PARTNERSHIP

There are numerous ways to terminate or dispose of an interest in a partnership. The two most common are receiving a liquidating distribution and selling the interest. Other possibilities include giving the interest away, exchanging the interest for corporate stock, and transferring the interest at death. This part of the chapter considers each of these methods.

OBJECTIVE 5

Determine the amount and character of the gain or loss recognized by a partner from a liquidating partnership distribution

LIQUIDATING DISTRIBUTIONS

A liquidating distribution is defined as a distribution, or one of a series of distributions, that terminates a partner's interest in the partnership.[11] If the partner's interest is drastically reduced but not terminated, the distribution is treated as a current distribution. A liquidating distribution can occur when only one member of a partnership terminates his or her interest, several partners terminate their interests but the partnership continues, or the entire partnership terminates and each partner receives a liquidating distribution. Rules for taxation of a liquidating distribution are the same whether one partner terminates his or her interest or the entire partnership liquidates.

GAIN OR LOSS RECOGNITION BY THE PARTNER. The rule for recognizing gain on a liquidating distribution is exactly the same rule used for a current distribution. A partner recognizes gain only if the money distributed (including money deemed distributed to the partner from a liability reduction or the FMV of marketable securities that are treated as money) exceeds the partner's predistribution basis in his or her partnership interest.[12]

Although a partner can never recognize a loss from a current distribution, he or she can recognize a loss from a liquidating distribution. A partner recognizes a loss only if the liquidating distribution consists of money (including money deemed distributed), unrealized receivables, and inventory, but no other property.[13] The amount of the loss is the difference between the partner's basis in the partnership interest before the distribution and the sum of money plus the bases of the receivables and inventory (to the partnership immediately before the distribution) that are received.

EXAMPLE C10-15 ▶ Maria's interest in the ABC Partnership is terminated when her basis in the partnership is $35,000. She receives a liquidating distribution of $10,000 cash and inventory with a $12,000 basis to the partnership. Her recognized loss is $13,000 [$35,000 − ($10,000 + $12,000)]. The inventory has a $12,000 basis to Maria. ◀

OBJECTIVE 6

Determine the basis of assets received in a liquidating distribution

BASIS IN ASSETS RECEIVED. The basis of an asset received by the partner from a liquidating distribution is determined using rules similar to those used to determine the basis of an asset received in a current distribution. For both kinds of distributions, the basis in unrealized receivables and inventory is generally the same as the property's basis in the partnership's hands. Under no condition is the basis of these two types of assets increased. Occasionally, however, the partner's basis in his or her partnership interest is so small that after making the necessary reduction for money (and deemed money) distributions, the basis in the partnership interest is smaller than the partnership's bases for the unrealized receivables and inventory distributed. In such cases, the remaining basis in the partnership interest must be allocated among the unrealized receivables and inventory items based first on their decline in value and then on their relative bases as adjusted to reflect the decline in value.[14] As a result, the bases for the unrealized receivables and inventory are reduced, and the amount of ordinary income to be recognized on their ultimate sale, exchange, or collection is increased.

TYPICAL MISCONCEPTION

The basis to a partner of distributed unrealized receivables or inventory can never be greater than the partnership's basis in those assets. Also, if the partner's basis in his or her partnership interest is not sufficient, the partner's basis in the distributed unrealized receivables and inventory is less than the partnership's basis in those assets.

Remember that a liquidating distribution of cash, unrealized receivables, and inventory with a total basis to the partnership that is less than the partner's basis in his or her partnership interest results in the recognition of a loss. However, the partner recognizes no loss if the distribution includes any property other than cash, unrealized receivables, and inventory. Instead, all the remaining basis in the partnership interest must be allocated to the other property received regardless of that property's basis to the partnership or its FMV. Application of this rule can create strange results.

EXAMPLE C10-16 ▶ Assume the same facts as in Example C10-15 except Maria's distribution also includes an office typewriter having a $50 basis to the partnership and a $100 FMV. The allocation of basis proceeds as follows:

---

[11] Sec. 761(d).
[12] Sec. 731(a)(1).
[13] Sec. 731(a)(2).
[14] Sec. 732(c).

Predistribution basis for partnership interest	$35,000
Minus: Money received	(10,000)
Basis after money distribution	$25,000
Minus: Basis of inventory to partnership	(12,000)
Remaining basis of partnership interest	$13,000

The entire $13,000 remaining basis of the partnership interest is allocated to the typewriter. ◀

TAX STRATEGY TIP

The partnership in Example C10-16 should avoid distributing low basis property along with cash, unrealized receivables, and inventory so that the partner can obtain an immediate loss deduction.

The basis allocation procedure illustrated in Example C10-16 delays the loss recognition until the typewriter is either depreciated or sold. However, the allocation procedure also may change the character of the loss because Maria would recognize a capital loss when she receives the liquidating distribution in Example C10-15. In Example C10-16, the character of Maria's loss is determined by the character of the typewriter in her hands (or in some cases by a series of specific rules that are discussed below). Worst of all, if she converts the typewriter into personal-use property, the loss on its sale or exchange is nondeductible.

If two or more assets other than unrealized receivables or inventory are distributed together, the remaining basis in the partnership interest is allocated among them based on both their relative FMVs and bases in the partnership's hands. Such an allocation process can lead to either a decrease or increase in the total basis of these assets. This potential for increasing the assets' bases is unique to liquidating distributions.

The allocation that results in a decrease in the basis of a distributed asset is identical to the allocation process described for current distributions. However, if the amount to be allocated is greater than the carryover bases of the distributed assets, the basis is first allocated among the distributed assets in an amount equal to their carryover basis from the partnership. Then allocations are made based on relative appreciation of the assets up to the amount of appreciation, and further allocations are made to the assets based on their relative FMVs.

EXAMPLE C10-17 ▶

Before receiving a liquidating distribution, Craig's basis in his interest in the BCD Partnership is $60,000. The distribution consists of $10,000 in cash, inventory having a $2,000 basis to the partnership and a $4,000 FMV, and two parcels of undeveloped land (not held as inventory) having bases of $6,000 and $18,000 to the partnership and having FMVs of $10,000 and $24,000, respectively. Assume that Sec. 751 does not apply. His bases in the assets received are calculated as follows:

Predistribution basis for partnership interest	$60,000
Minus: Money received	(10,000)
Basis of inventory to the partnership	(2,000)
Basis allocated to two parcels of land	$48,000

The calculation of the basis for the two parcels of land are as follows:

		Parcel One	*Parcel Two*	*Total*
	FMV of asset	$10,000	$24,000	$34,000
	Minus: Partnership's basis for asset	(6,000)	(18,000)	(24,000)
	Difference	$ 4,000	$ 6,000	$10,000
Step 1:	Give each asset the partnership's basis for the asset	$ 6,000	$18,000	$24,000
	Minus: Craig's basis to be allocated			(48,000)
	Increase to allocate			$24,000
Step 2:	Adjusted basis after Step 1	$ 6,000	$18,000	$24,000
	Allocate the increase first to assets that have increased in value	4,000	6,000	10,000
	Adjusted basis at this point in the calculation	$10,000	$24,000	$34,000

Step 3: Allocate $14,000 remaining increase based on relative FMVs	4,118[a]	9,882[b]	14,000
Craig's bases in the assets	$14,118	$33,882	$48,000

[a]$10,000 ÷ ($10,000 + $24,000) × $14,000 = $4,118
[b]$24,000 ÷ ($10,000 + $24,000) × $14,000 = $9,882 ◀

KEY POINT

If the partner recognizes neither gain nor loss in a liquidating distribution, the partner's total basis in the distributed assets always equals the partner's former basis in his or her partnership interest.

In a liquidating distribution, the amount of money received plus the total basis of the nonmoney property received in the hands of the distributee partner normally equals the partner's predistribution basis in the partnership interest. The only two exceptions to this rule occur when the money received exceeds the partner's basis in his or her partnership interest, causing the partner to recognize a gain, or when money, unrealized receivables, and inventory are the only assets distributed and the partner recognizes a loss. In all other liquidating distributions, the distributee partner recognizes no gain or loss. Instead, that partner's predistribution basis in his or her partnership interest is transferred to the cash and other property received.

Holding Period in Distributed Assets. The distributee partner's holding period for any assets received in a liquidating distribution includes the partnership's holding period for such property.[15] If the partnership received the property as a contribution from a partner, the partnership's holding period also may include the period of time the contributing partner held the property prior to making the contribution (see Chapter C9). Note that the distributee partner's holding period for his or her partnership interest is irrelevant in determining the holding period of the assets received.

EXAMPLE C10-18 ▶ George purchases an interest in the DEF Partnership on June 1, 2002, but he cannot get along with the other partners. Therefore, on July 1, 2002, he receives a liquidating distribution that terminates his interest in the partnership. George's distribution includes land that the partnership has owned since August 1, 1996. George's holding period for the land begins on August 1, 1996, even though his holding period for the partnership interest begins much later. ◀

The character of the gain or loss recognized on a subsequent sale of distributed property is determined using the same rules as for a current distribution.

KEY POINT

The main difference in how the mechanics of the Sec. 751 rules are applied to current versus liquidating distributions is that after a liquidating distribution, the partner always has a zero interest in the partnership assets because he or she is no longer a partner in the partnership.

EFFECTS OF SEC. 751. Section 751 has essentially the same impact on both liquidating and current distributions. To the extent the partner's interest in Sec. 751 assets is exchanged for other assets (or vice versa), that portion of the transaction is removed from the distribution rules. Instead, this portion of the transaction is treated as a sale occurring between the partnership and the partner. There is one notable difference between liquidating distributions and current distributions having Sec. 751 implications: the postdistribution interest in partnership assets is zero for the liquidating distribution because it terminates the partner's interest in the partnership.

EXAMPLE C10-19 ▶ The ABC Partnership holds the assets listed below on December 31 before making a $50,000 cash distribution that reduces Al's one-third interest in the partnership to zero.

Assets	*Basis*	*FMV*
Cash	$75,000	$ 75,000
Unrealized receivables	–0–	15,000
Inventory	15,000	60,000
Total	$90,000	$150,000

The partnership has no liabilities, and Al's predistribution basis in his partnership interest is $30,000. The following steps are needed to determine the tax effects of the liquidating distribution:

[15] Sec. 735(b).

STEP 1. Determine ABC's Sec. 751 and non-Sec. 751 assets. The Sec. 751 assets include the unrealized receivables and the substantially appreciated inventory. The cash is ABC's only non-Sec. 751 asset.

STEP 2. Complete the table used to analyze the Sec. 751 distributions (see Table C10-2).

STEP 3. Analyze column 5 of Table C10-2 to see whether a Sec. 751 exchange has occurred. Table C10-2 shows that Al exchanges $5,000 of unrealized receivables and $20,000 of inventory for $25,000 cash.

SELF-STUDY QUESTION

What is the deemed Sec. 751 exchange shown in Table C10-2?

ANSWER

Column 5 shows that Al received $25,000 of excess cash in lieu of $25,000 of Sec. 751 assets. Thus, the Sec. 751 exchange is a deemed sale by Al of $25,000 of unrealized receivables and inventory to the partnership in exchange for $25,000 of cash. With a table similar to Table C10-2, the Sec. 751 computations are much easier to understand.

STEP 4. Determine the gain or loss on the Sec. 751 deemed sale. Al is deemed to have sold unrealized receivables and inventory for cash. Assume Al first got the receivables and inventory in a current distribution. He obtains the partnership's bases for the assets of $0 and $5,000, respectively. The subsequent deemed sale results in Al recognizing a $20,000 gain.

Amount realized (cash)	$25,000
Minus: Adjusted basis of property sold	(5,000)
Realized and recognized gain	$20,000

Al's gain is ordinary income because it results from his deemed sale of receivables and inventory to the partnership.

STEP 5. Determine the impact of the non-Sec. 751 portion of the distribution. The liquidating distribution is only the $25,000 cash he receives that was *not* a part of the Sec. 751 transaction. To determine its impact, we first must find Al's basis in his partnership interest after the Sec. 751 transaction but before the $25,000 liquidating distribution.

Predistribution basis in the partnership interest	$30,000
Minus: Basis of receivables and inventory deemed distributed in Sec. 751 exchange	(5,000)
Basis before money distribution	$25,000
Minus: Money distribution	(25,000)
Gain recognized on liquidating distribution	$ -0-

Al recognizes no further gain or loss from the liquidating distribution portion of the transaction. ◀

▼ **TABLE C10-2**

Analysis of Sec. 751 Liquidating Distribution (Example C10-19)

	Beginning Partnership Amount[a]	(1) Al's Interest Before Distribution[a] (1/3)	(2) Al's Interest After Distribution[a] (-0-)	(3) Fictional Proportionate Distribution[a] (3) = (1) − (2)	(4) Actual Distribution[a]	(5) Difference[b] (5) = (4) − (3)
Sec. 751 Assets:						
Unrealized receivables	$15,000	$ 5,000	$ -0-	$ 5,000	$ -0-	$ (5,000)
Inventory	60,000	20,000	-0-	20,000	-0-	(20,000)
Total Sec. 751 Assets	$75,000	$25,000	$ -0-	$25,000	$ -0-	($ 25,000)
Non-Sec. 751 Assets:						
Cash	$75,000	$25,000	$ -0-	$25,000	$50,000	$ 25,000
Total Non-Sec. 751 Assets	$75,000	$25,000	$ -0-	$25,000	$50,000	$ 25,000

[a] Valued at fair market value.
[b] A negative amount means that Al gave up his interest in a particular property. A positive amount means that Al received more than his proportionate interest.

SELF-STUDY QUESTION

What is the character of gain/loss on the sale of a partnership interest?

ANSWER

Because a partnership interest is generally a capital asset, the sale of a partnership interest results in a capital gain or loss being recognized. However, if a partnership has Sec. 751 assets, the partner is deemed to sell his or her share of Sec. 751 assets directly with a corresponding ordinary gain or loss being recognized.

EFFECTS OF DISTRIBUTION ON THE PARTNERSHIP. A partnership recognizes no gain or loss on liquidating distributions made to its partners.[16] If a Sec. 751 deemed sale occurs, however, the partnership may be required to recognize gain or loss on assets deemed sold to its partner. A liquidating distribution normally does not itself terminate the partnership. The partnership terminates if none of the remaining partners continue to operate the business of the partnership in a partnership form.

Topic Review C10-1 summarizes the tax consequences of current and liquidating distributions.

SALE OF A PARTNERSHIP INTEREST

Absence any contrary rules, a partner's sale or exchange of a partnership interest would generate a capital gain or loss under Sec. 741 because a partnership interest is usually a capital asset. Section 751, however, modifies this result by requiring the partner to recognize ordinary income or loss on the sale or exchange of a partnership interest to the extent the consideration received is attributable to the partner's share of unrealized receivables and inventory items. The sale of a partnership interest also may have two other effects: the purchaser acquires the partner's share of the partnership's liabilities, and the partnership may be terminated. Each of these situations related to the sale of a partnership interest is examined below.

Topic Review C10-1

Current and Liquidating Distributions

TAX CONSEQUENCES	CURRENT DISTRIBUTIONS	LIQUIDATING DISTRIBUTIONS
Impact on Partner:		
Money (or deemed money from liability changes or marketable securities) distributed	Gain recognized only if money distributed exceeds basis in partnership interest before distribution.	Gain recognized only if money distributed exceeds basis in partnership interest before distribution.
Unrealized receivables and/or inventory distributed	Carryover basis (limited to basis in partnership interest before distribution reduced by money distributed).	Carryover basis (limited to basis in partnership interest before distribution reduced by money distributed).
	No gain or loss recognized.[a]	Loss recognized if money, inventory and receivables are distributed with basis less than basis in partnership interest before distribution and no other property is distributed.[a]
Other property distributed	Carryover basis (limited to basis in partnership interest before distribution reduced by money and carryover basis in inventory and receivables).	Basis equal to basis in partnership interest before distribution reduced by money and carryover basis in inventory and receivables.
	No gain or loss recognized.[a]	No gain or loss recognized.[a]
Impact on Partnership:		
General rule	No gain or loss recognized.	No gain or loss recognized.
Other Tax Consequences:	If a Sec. 751 deemed sale or exchange occurs, the partner and/or the partnership may recognize gain or loss on the deemed sale.	If a Sec. 751 deemed sale or exchange occurs, the partner and/or the partnership may recognize gain or loss on the deemed sale.

[a] Precontribution gain (but not loss) may be recognized under Sec. 737 if a precontribution net gain remains and the FMV of the property distributed exceeds the adjusted basis of the partnership interest immediately before the property distribution (but after any money distribution). The contributing partner also may recognize precontribution gain or loss if the partnership distributes the contributed property to another partner within seven years of the contribution (Sec. 704(c)).

[16] Sec. 731(b).

SECTION 751 PROPERTY. The definition of Sec. 751 property is slightly different for sales or exchanges than for distributions because inventory does not have to be substantially appreciated to be included as Sec. 751 property. Thus, all inventory and all unrealized receivables are Sec. 751 assets in a sale or exchange situation.[17]

Treasury Regulations under Sec. 751 take a hypothetical asset sale approach to determining the amount of ordinary income or loss the partner recognizes on the sale or exchange of a partnership interest.[18] Under the regulations, the partnership is deemed to sell all its assets for their FMV immediately before the partner sells his or her interest in the partnership. The partner then is allocated his or her share of ordinary gain or loss attributable to the Sec. 751 assets. With this approach, the results of the sale or exchange can be determined using the following three steps:

STEP 1. Determine the total gain or loss on the sale or exchange of the partnership interest.

STEP 2. Determine the ordinary gain or loss component and the Sec. 1250 gain component, if applicable, using the hypothetical asset sale approach.[19]

STEP 3. Determine the capital gain component by calculating the residual gain or loss after assigning the ordinary gain or loss and the Sec. 1250 gain components.

EXAMPLE C10-20 ▶ Troy sells his one-fourth interest in the TV Partnership to Steve for $50,000 cash when the partnership's assets are as follows:

Assets	*Basis*	*FMV*
Cash	$ 20,000	$ 20,000
Unrealized receivables	-0-	24,000
Inventory	20,000	68,000
Building	40,000	56,000
Land	40,000	32,000
Total	$120,000	$200,000

The partnership has no liabilities on the sale date and has claimed $19,000 of straight-line depreciation on the building. Troy's basis in his partnership interest is $30,000 on such date. Both the receivables and inventory are Sec. 751 assets, and the building is Sec. 1250 property. Application of step 1 yields the following gain on Troy's sale of his partnership interest:

Amount realized on sale	$50,000
Minus: Adjusted basis of partnership interest	(30,000)
Total gain realized	$20,000

Application of step 2 yields the following allocation to Sec. 751 and Sec. 1250 property:

Deemed Sale of Assets	*Partnership Gain (Loss)*	*Troy's Share (25%)*
Unrealized receivables	$24,000	$ 6,000
Inventory	48,000	12,000
Building	16,000	4,000
Land	(8,000)	(2,000)

Thus, on the sale of his partnership interest, Troy recognizes ordinary income of $18,000 ($6,000 + $12,000). Because the $19,000 of depreciation exceeds the hypothetical gain on the building, the entire $16,000 gain is Sec. 1250 gain, $4,000 of which is Troy's share.

Application of step 3 yields the following residual allocation to capital gain or loss:

Total gain realized	$20,000
Minus: Allocation to ordinary income and Sec. 1250 gain	(22,000)
Capital loss recognized	($ 2,000)

[17] Regulation Sec. 1.751-1(a)(1) is outdated to some extent and still speaks in terms of substantially appreciated inventory. However, Sec. 751(a) in the IRC, which deals with the sale or exchange of a partnership interest, includes all inventory items, not just those that are substantially appreciated.

[18] Reg. Sec. 1.751-1(a)(2). This hypothetical sale approach allows for easy incorporation of special allocations under Sec. 704 into the Sec. 751 calculation.

[19] The Sec. 1250 gain is the lesser of the hypothetical gain on Sec. 1250 property (e.g., buildings) or the amount of depreciation claimed on the Sec. 1250 property (assuming straight-line depreciation). This gain applies to noncorporate taxpayers and is subject to the 25% capital gains tax rate. A similar rule applies to a collectibles gain subject to the 28% capital gains tax rate. See Reg. Sec. 1.1(h)-1.

In summary, on the sale of his partnership interest, Troy recognizes $18,000 of ordinary income, $4,000 of Sec. 1250 gain, and a $2,000 capital loss. Without Sec. 751, these three components would have been netted together as a $20,000 capital gain. ◀

STOP & THINK *Question:* Bill owns 20% of Kraco and plans to sell his ownership interest for a $40,000 gain. Kraco has both unrealized receivables and inventory. If Kraco is a corporation, Bill will report a $40,000 capital gain. If Kraco is a partnership, part of the $40,000 gain (the gain on his 20% share of the Sec. 751 assets) will be ordinary income, and the remainder will be capital gain. Why did Congress decide to tax the gain on the sale of corporate stock differently from the gain on the sale of a partnership interest?

Solution: The corporation itself will pay tax on the ordinary income realized when it collects unrealized receivables or sells inventory, and the corporation's tax is unaffected by the identity of the shareholder. Under no conditions will the shareholder have to report any of the corporation's ordinary income. Accordingly, the sale of the corporate stock does not provide an opportunity to avoid ordinary income for the owner, nor can the owner convert ordinary income into capital gain by selling the corporate stock.[20]

Because the ordinary income earned by the partnership is reported by and taxed to the partners, a sale of a partnership interest that produces only capital gains would represent an opportunity for a partner to avoid recognizing ordinary income and recognize capital gains instead. Imagine, for example, that Kraco is a cash basis service business whose only asset is a large account receivable where all work has been completed. If Bill stays in the partnership, he will recognize ordinary income when the partnership collects the receivable. If he were allowed to sell his partnership interest in this setting for a capital gain, he would be able to convert his ordinary income into capital gain. However, Sec. 751 prevents this conversion from happening by requiring him to recognize ordinary income on the sale of the partnership interest to the extent the sales proceeds are payments for Sec. 751 assets.

ADDITIONAL COMMENT

Section 751 treatment is another application of the aggregate theory of partnership taxation as opposed to the entity theory.

LIABILITIES. When a partnership has liabilities, each partner's distributive share of any liabilities is always part of the basis for the partnership interest. When the partnership interest is sold, the partner is relieved of the liabilities. Accordingly, the amount realized on the sale of a partnership interest is made up of money plus the FMV of nonmoney property received plus the seller's share of partnership liabilities assumed or acquired by the purchaser.

EXAMPLE C10-21 ▶ Andrew is a 30% partner in the ABC Partnership when he sells his entire interest to Miguel for $40,000 cash. At the time of the sale, Andrew's basis is $27,000 (which includes his $7,000 share of partnership liabilities). The partnership has no Sec. 751 assets. Andrew's $20,000 gain on the sale is calculated as follows:

Amount realized:		
Cash	$40,000	
Liabilities assumed by purchaser	7,000	$47,000
Minus: Adjusted basis		(27,000)
Gain recognized on sale		$20,000

◀

IMPACT ON THE PARTNERSHIP. When one partner sells his or her partnership interest, the sale usually has no more impact on the partnership than the sale of corporate stock by one shareholder has on the corporation. Only the partner and the purchaser of the interest are affected. However, the partnership itself is affected if the partnership interest sold is sufficiently large that, under Sec. 708, its sale terminates the partnership for tax purposes. This effect is discussed later in this chapter.

[20] An exception exists for a so-called collapsible corporation, the discussion of which is beyond the scope of this text.

OBJECTIVE 7

Determine the amount and character of the gain or loss recognized when a partner retires from a partnership or dies

RETIREMENT OR DEATH OF A PARTNER

If a partner dies or retires from a partnership, that partner's interest can be sold either to an outsider or to one or more existing partners.[21] The results of such a sale are outlined above. Often, however, a partner or a deceased partner's successor-in-interest departs from the partnership in return for payments made by the partnership itself. When the partnership buys out the partner's interest, the analysis of the tax results focuses on two types of payments: payments made in exchange for the partner's interest in partnership property and other payments.

PAYMENTS FOR PARTNERSHIP PROPERTY. Generally, the IRS accepts the valuation placed on the retiring partner's interest in the partnership property by the partners in an arm's-length transaction. Payments made for the property interest are taxed under the liquidating distribution rules. Like any liquidating distribution made to a partner, payments made to a retiring partner or a deceased partner's successor-in-interest[22] in exchange for his or her property interest are not deductible by the partnership.[23]

If the retiring or deceased partner was a general partner and the partnership is a service partnership (i.e., capital is not a material income producing factor), payments made to a general partner for unrealized receivables and goodwill (when the partnership agreement does not provide for a goodwill payment on retirement or death) are not considered payments for property. Instead, any such payments are treated as other payments. The other payment treatment permits the partnership to deduct the amounts paid to the retiring or deceased partner or to reduce the distributive share allocable to the other partners.

TYPICAL MISCONCEPTION

The significance of the two different kinds of payments is not readily apparent to some taxpayers. The payments for partnership property are not deductible by the partnership and often are not income to the retiring partner. However, payments considered in the second category are deductible by the partnership (or they reduce the distributive shares that other partners must recognize) and usually are income to the retiring partner.

OTHER PAYMENTS. Payments made to a retiring partner or to a deceased partner's successor-in-interest that exceed the value of that partner's share of partnership property have a very different tax result for both the retiring partner and for the partnership. A few payments that do represent payments for property (e.g., payments to a general partner retiring from a service partnership for his or her interest in unrealized receivables and for his or her interest in partnership goodwill) also are taxed under these rules.

Under these rules, a payment is taxed as either a distributive share or a guaranteed payment. If the excess payment is a function of partnership income (e.g., 10% of the partnership's net income), the income is considered a distributive share of partnership income.[24] Accordingly, the character of the income flows through to the partner, and each of the remaining partners is taxed on a smaller amount of partnership income. The income must be reported in the partner's tax year that includes the partnership year-end from which the distributive share arises, regardless of when the partner actually receives the distribution.

If the amount of the excess payment is determined without regard to the partnership income, the payment is treated as a guaranteed payment.[25] If the payment is a guaranteed payment, the retiring partner recognizes ordinary income, and the partnership generally has an ordinary deduction. Like all guaranteed payments, the income is includible in the recipient's income for his or her tax year within which ends the partnership tax year in which the partnership claims its deduction (see Chapter C9).

TYPICAL MISCONCEPTION

The main difference between a payment being taxed as a distributive share or as a guaranteed payment is the character of the income recognized by the recipient partner. If the payment is taxed as a distributive share, the character of the income is determined by the type of income earned by the partnership. In contrast, the payment is always ordinary income if it is treated as a guaranteed payment.

EXAMPLE C10-22 ▶ When Sam retires from the STU Partnership, he receives a cash payment of $30,000. At the time of his retirement, his basis for his one-fourth limited partnership interest is $25,000. The partnership has no liabilities and the following assets:

[21] Note that retirement from the partnership in this context has nothing to do with reaching a specific age and leaving the employ of the partnership but instead refers to the partner's withdrawal at any age from a continuing partnership.

[22] A deceased partner's successor-in-interest is the party that succeeds to the rights of the deceased partner's partnership interest (e.g., the decedent's estate or an heir or legatee of the deceased partner). A deceased partner's successor-in-interest is treated as a partner by the tax laws until his or her interest in the partnership has been completely liquidated.

[23] Sec. 736(b).

[24] Sec. 736(a)(1).

[25] Sec. 736(a)(2).

Assets	*Basis*	*FMV*	*Sam's 1/4 FMV*
Cash	$ 40,000	$ 40,000	$10,000
Marketable securities	25,000	32,000	8,000
Land	35,000	48,000	12,000
Total	$100,000	$120,000	$30,000

In the absence of a valuation agreement, the partnership presumably pays Sam a ratable share of the FMV of each asset (and he receives no payment for any partnership goodwill). The $30,000 amount paid to Sam equals the FMV of his one-fourth interest in the partnership assets. The $30,000 Sam receives in exchange for his interest in partnership property is analyzed as a liquidating distribution in the following manner:

Cash distribution received	$30,000
Minus: Basis in partnership interest	(25,000)
Gain recognized on liquidating distribution	$ 5,000

Because the partnership holds no Sec. 751 assets, the entire gain is a capital gain. The partnership gets no deduction for the distribution. ◀

EXAMPLE C10-23 ▶ Assume the same facts as in Example C10-22 except Sam receives $34,000 instead of $30,000. This amount represents payment for Sam's one-fourth interest in partnership assets plus an excess payment of $4,000. Accordingly, this excess payment must be either a distributive share or a guaranteed payment. Because the $4,000 payment is not contingent on partnership earnings, it is taxed as a guaranteed payment. The partnership deducts the $4,000 payment, and Sam recognizes $4,000 of ordinary income.

In summary, Sam receives $34,000 as a payment on his retirement from the STU Partnership, $4,000 of which is considered a guaranteed payment taxed as ordinary income to Sam and deductible by the partnership. The remaining $30,000 Sam receives is in exchange for his interest in partnership property. Because the $30,000 cash payment exceeds his $25,000 basis in his partnership interest, he recognizes a $5,000 gain on the liquidating distribution. The partnership gets no deduction for the $30,000, which is considered a distribution. ◀

If the partnership has Sec. 751 assets, the calculations for a retiring partner are slightly more difficult. First, payments for substantially appreciated inventory and unrealized receivables are payments for property and must be analyzed using the liquidating distribution rules along with Sec. 751. The remainder of the transaction is analyzed as indicated above. (For partnership retirements only, unrealized receivables do not include recapture items.)

A retiring partner who receives payments from the partnership is considered to be a partner in that partnership for tax purposes until he or she receives the last payment. Likewise, a deceased partner's successor-in-interest is a member of the partnership until receiving the last payment.[26]

EXCHANGE OF A PARTNERSHIP INTEREST

EXCHANGE FOR ANOTHER PARTNERSHIP INTEREST. A partner also may terminate a partnership interest by exchanging it for either an interest in another partnership or a different interest in the same partnership. Exchanges involving interests in different partnerships do not qualify for like-kind exchange treatment.[27] Nevertheless, the IRS allows exchanges of interests within a single partnership.[28]

EXAMPLE C10-24 ▶ Pam and Dean are equal partners in the PD General Partnership, which owns and operates a farm. The two partners agree to convert PD into a limited partnership with Pam becoming a limited partner and Dean having both a general and a limited partnership interest in PD. Even though the partners exchange a general partnership interest for a limited partnership interest (plus an exchange of a general partnership interest for a general partnership interest for Dean), they recognize no gain or loss on the exchange. If, however, a partner's interest in the partner-

[26] Reg. Sec. 1.736-1(a)(1)(ii).
[27] Sec. 1031(a)(2)(D).
[28] Rev. Rul. 84-52, 1984-1 C.B. 157.

ship's liabilities is changed, that partner's basis must be adjusted. If liabilities are reduced and a deemed distribution exceeding the basis for the partnership interest occurs, the partner must recognize gain on the excess. ◀

EXCHANGE FOR CORPORATE STOCK. A partnership interest may be exchanged for corporate stock in a transaction that qualifies under the Sec. 351 nonrecognition rules (see Chapter C2). For Sec. 351 purposes, a partnership interest is property. If the other Sec. 351 requirements are met, a single partner's partnership interest can be transferred for stock in a new or an existing corporation in a nontaxable exchange. This exchange is taxed to the partner as if he or she had exchanged any other property under the Sec. 351 rules. The basis in the corporate stock is determined by the partner's basis in the partnership interest. The holding period for the stock received in the exchange includes the holding period for the partnership interest. As a result of the exchange, one of the corporation's assets is an interest in a partnership, and the corporation (not the transferor) is now the partner of record. Thus, the corporation must report its distributive share of partnership income along with its other earnings.

INCORPORATION. When limited liability is important, the entire partnership may choose to incorporate. Normally such an incorporation can be structured to fall within the Sec. 351 provisions and can be partially or totally tax exempt. When a partnership chooses to incorporate, three possible alternatives are available:

- The partnership contributes its assets and liabilities to the corporation in exchange for the corporation's stock. The stock is then distributed to the partners in a liquidating distribution of the partnership.
- The partnership liquidates by distributing its assets to the partners. The partners then contribute the property to the new corporation in exchange for its stock.
- The partners contribute their partnership interests directly to the new corporation in exchange for its stock. The partnership is liquidated, with the corporation receiving all the partnership's assets and liabilities.

The tax implications of the incorporation and the impact of partnership liabilities, gain to be recognized, basis in the corporate assets, and the new shareholders' bases in their stock and securities may be different depending on the form chosen for the transaction.[29]

FORMATION OF AN LLC OR LLP. A second option for obtaining limited liability protection for all owners is for the partnership to become an LLC. Under the check-the-box regulations, an LLC with more than one member is treated as a partnership unless it elects to be taxed as a corporation (see Chapter C2). If the LLC elects to be taxed as a C or an S corporation, the transfer of the property to the LLC falls under the incorporation rules discussed above. If the LLC is treated as a partnership, Rev. Rul. 95-37[30] specifies that the transfer will be viewed as a partnership-to-partnership transfer. The property transfer does not cause the partners to recognize gain or loss nor does the transfer terminate the tax year for the partnership or any partner. The basis for the partners' interest in the partnership will be changed only if the liability shares for the partners change.

If a partnership chooses LLP status to reduce some of the liability risks facing the partners, the change from partnership to LLP status also is taxed under the partnership-to-partnership transfer rules described above. The transfer does not cause the partners to recognize gain or loss nor does the property transfer terminate the tax year for the partnership or any partner. Basis for the partners' interest in the partnership will be changed only if the liability shares for the partners change.[31]

Topic Review C10-2 summarizes the tax consequences of a number of alternative methods for terminating an investment in a partnership.

---

[29] Rev. Rul. 84-111, 1984-2 C.B. 88. In addition, Reg. Secs. 301.7701-1, 2, and 3 describe the tax consequences of a partnership electing to be taxed as a corporation under the check-the-box regulations.

[30] 1995-1 C.B. 130.

[31] Ibid.

Topic Review C10-2

Terminating an Investment in a Partnership

Method	Tax Consequences to Partner
Death or retirement:	
Amounts paid for property[a]	Liquidating distribution tax consequences apply to the amount paid.
Amounts paid in excess of property values:	
Amounts not determined by reference to partnership income	Ordinary income.
Amounts determined by reference to partnership income	Distributive share of partnership income.
Sale of partnership interest to outsider	Capital gain (loss) except for ordinary income (loss) reported on Sec. 751 assets.
Exchange for partnership interest:	
In same partnership	No tax consequences
In different partnership	Capital gain (loss) except for ordinary income (loss) on Sec. 751 assets.
Exchange for corporate stock	No gain or loss generally recognized if it qualifies for Sec. 351 tax-free treatment. Capital gain (loss) except for ordinary income (loss) on Sec. 751 assets if the exchange does not qualify for Sec. 351 treatment.
Incorporation of partnership	Tax consequences depend on form of transaction used for incorporation.
Formation of LLC or LLP	No tax consequences except for distributions or contributions deemed to occur if liability shares change.

[a]Only for a general partner departing from a service partnership, property excludes unrealized receivables and goodwill if it is not mentioned in the partnership agreement.

INCOME RECOGNITION AND TRANSFERS OF A PARTNERSHIP INTEREST

The partnership tax year closes with respect to any partner who sells or exchanges his or her entire interest in a partnership or any partner whose interest in the partnership is liquidated. The partnership tax year closes on the sale or exchange date or the date of final payment on a liquidation. As a result, that partner's share of all items earned by the partnership must be reported in the partner's tax year that includes the transaction date.[32]

A partner's tax year also closes on the date of death. The partner's final return will include all partnership income up to the date of death.

TERMINATION OF A PARTNERSHIP

OBJECTIVE 8

Determine whether a partnership has terminated for tax purposes

EVENTS CAUSING A TERMINATION TO OCCUR. Because of the complex relationships among partners and their liability for partnership debts, state partnership laws provide for the termination of a partnership under a wide variety of conditions. Section 708(b), however, avoids the tax complexity created by the wide variety of state laws and the numerous termination conditions. That IRC section provides that a partnership terminates for tax purposes only if

- No part of any business, financial operation, or venture of the partnership continues to be carried on by any of its partners in a partnership or
- Within a 12-month period a sale or exchange of at least 50% of the total interest in partnership capital and profits occurs.

[32] Sec. 706(c)(2).

TYPICAL MISCONCEPTION

Taxpayers often do not understand the difference between a partnership tax year closing for a specific partner versus a partnership tax year closing for all partners due to a termination of the partnership itself. The tax consequences of these two events are drastically different.

NO BUSINESS OPERATED AS A PARTNERSHIP. If no partner continues to operate any business of the partnership through the same or another partnership, the original partnership terminates. To avoid termination, the partnership must maintain both partners and business activity. For example, if one partner retires from a two-person partnership and the second partner continues the business alone, the partnership terminates. However, if one partner in a two-member partnership dies, the partnership does not terminate as long as the deceased's estate or successor-in-interest continues to share in the profits and losses of the partnership business.[33]

Likewise, a partnership terminates if it ceases to carry on any business or financial venture. The courts, however, have allowed a partnership to continue under this rule even though the partnership sold all its assets and retained only a few installment notes.[34] Despite the courts' flexibility in these circumstances, it is wiser to maintain more than a nominal level of assets if continuation of the partnership is desired.

KEY POINT

For the 50% rule to terminate a partnership, a *sale* or *exchange* of 50% or more of the capital *and* profits interests must occur. Sales or exchanges occurring within a 12-month period are aggregated; however, if the same interest is sold twice within 12 months, it is only counted once.

SALE OR EXCHANGE OF AT LEAST A 50% INTEREST. The second condition that leads to the termination of a partnership is the sale or exchange of at least a 50% interest in both partnership capital and profits within a 12-month period.[35] The relevant 12-month period is determined without reference to the tax year of either the partnership or any partner but rather is any 12 consecutive months. To cause termination, the partnership interest must be transferred by sale or exchange. Transactions or occurrences that do not constitute a sale or exchange (e.g., the gifting of a partnership interest or the transferring of a partnership interest at death) cannot cause a partnership to terminate as long as partners continue the partnership business. Likewise, as long as at least two partners remain, the removal of a partner who owns more than 50% of the total partnership capital and profits interests can be accomplished without terminating the partnership by making a liquidating distribution.[36]

Measuring the portion of the total partnership capital and profits interest transferred often presents difficulties. Multiple exchanges of the same partnership interest are counted only once for purposes of determining whether the 50% maximum is exceeded. When several different small interests are transferred within a 12-month period, the partnership's termination occurs on the date of the transfer that first crosses the 50% threshold.[37]

EXAMPLE C10-25 ▶ On August 1, 2002, Miguel sells his 30% capital and profits interest in the LMN Partnership to Steve. On June 1, 2003, Steve sells the 30% interest acquired from Miguel to Andrew. For purposes of Sec. 708, the two sales are considered to be the transfer of a single partnership interest. Thus, the LMN Partnership does not terminate unless other sales of partnership interests occur totaling at least 20% of LMN's capital and profits interests during any 12-month period that includes either August 1, 2002, or June 1, 2003. ◀

EXAMPLE C10-26 ▶ On July 15, 2002, Kelly sells Carlos a 37% capital and profits interest in the KRS Partnership. On November 14, 2002, Rick sells Diana a 10% capital and profits interest in the KRS Partnership. On January 18, 2003, Sherrie sells Evan a 5% capital and profits interest in the KRS Partnership. The KRS Partnership terminates on January 18, 2003 because the cumulative interest sold within the 12-month period that includes January 18, 2003, first exceeds 50% on that date. ◀

EFFECTS OF TERMINATION.

Importance of Timing. When a partnership terminates, its tax year closes, requiring the partners to include their share of partnership earnings for the short-period partnership tax year in their tax returns. If the termination is not properly timed, partnership income for a regular 12-month tax year already may be included in the same return that must include the short tax year, resulting in more than 12 months of partnership income or loss being reported in some partners' tax returns. As partners and partnerships are increasingly forced to adopt the same tax year, this problem will lessen.

---

[33] Reg. Sec. 1.708-1(b)(1)(i)(A).

[34] For example, see *Max R. Ginsburg v. U.S.*, 21 AFTR 2d 1489, 68-1 USTC ¶9429 (Ct. Cls., 1968).

[35] Under Sec. 774(c), an electing large partnership does *not* terminate solely because 50% or more of its interests are sold within a 12-month period.

[36] Reg. Sec. 1.708-1(b)(1)(ii).

[37] Ibid.

EXAMPLE C10-27 ▶ Joy is a calendar year taxpayer who owns a 40% capital and profits interest in the ATV Partnership. ATV has a natural business year-end of March 31 and with IRS permission uses that date as its tax year-end. For the partnership tax year ending March 31, 2002, Joy has an $80,000 distributive share of ordinary income. Pat, who owns the remaining 60% capital and profits interests, sells his interest to Collin on November 30, 2002. Because more than 50% of the capital and profits interests have changed hands, the ATV Partnership terminates on November 30, 2002, and the partnership's tax year ends on that date.

Joy's tax return for the tax year ending December 31, 2002, must include the $80,000 distributive share from the partnership tax year for the period April 1, 2001 through March 31, 2002 and the distributive share of partnership income for the short tax year including the period April 1, 2002 through November 30, 2002. ◀

Liquidating Distributions and Contributions. When a termination occurs for tax purposes, the partnership is deemed to have made a pro rata liquidating distribution to all partners. Accordingly, the partners must recognize gain or loss under the liquidating distribution rules. An actual liquidating distribution may occur if the termination occurs because of the cessation of business. However, if the termination occurs because of a 50% or greater change in ownership of the capital and profits interests, an actual distribution usually does not occur. In this case, the new group of partners continue the business, and Treasury Regulations provide for the termination of the old partnership and the formation of a new partnership. Specifically, the old partnership is deemed to contribute all of its property and liabilities to a new partnership in exchange for the interests in the new partnership. The old partnership then is deemed to liquidate by distributing its only remaining asset (the interests in the new partnership) to its partners.[38]

EXAMPLE C10-28 ▶ The AB Partnership terminates for tax purposes on July 15 when Anna sells her 60% capital and profits interest to Diane for $123,000. The partnership has no liabilities, and its assets at the time of termination are as follows:

Assets	*Basis*	*FMV*
Cash	$ 20,000	$ 20,000
Receivables	30,000	32,000
Inventory	22,000	28,000
Building	90,000	95,000
Land	40,000	30,000
Total	$202,000	$205,000

Beth, a 40% partner in the AB Partnership, has an $80,800 basis in her partnership interest at the time of the termination. She has held her AB Partnership interest for three years at the time of the termination.

The old AB Partnership is deemed to transfer all its assets to a new partnership (NewAB) on July 15 in exchange for all the interests in NewAB. The old partnership then is deemed to transfer all the NewAB interests to the partners of the old partnership (Diane and Beth). At this point, the old AB Partnership ceases to exist because it no longer has partners, nor does it carry on any business.

The basis and holding period of the assets held by NewAB are identical to the basis and holding period of the old AB Partnership assets.[39] The basis of Beth's interest in NewAB is identical to her basis in her interest in the AB Partnership ($80,800).[40] Her holding period for the NewAB partnership interest begins when she acquired the old AB Partnership interest. Diane's basis in her partnership interest is its $123,000 cost, and her holding period begins when she purchases the interest. ◀

Changes in Accounting Methods. The termination ends all partnership elections. Thus, all partnership elections concerning its tax year and accounting methods must be made in the new partnership's first tax year.

---

[38] Reg. Sec. 1.708-1(b)(1)(iv). These rules apply to terminations occurring on or after May 9, 1997.

[39] Secs. 723 and 1223(2).

[40] Sec. 722.

KEY POINT

The principal concern when two or more partnerships are combined is which partnership's tax year, accounting methods, and elections will survive the merger. This determination is made by examining the capital and profits interests of the partners of the old partnerships.

MERGERS AND CONSOLIDATIONS

When two or more partnerships join together to form a new partnership, it is necessary to know which, if any, of the old partnerships are continued and which are terminated. An old partnership whose partner(s) own more than 50% of the profits and capital interests of the new partnership is considered to be continued as the new partnership.[41] Accordingly, the new partnership must continue with the tax year and accounting methods and elections of the old partnership that is considered to continue. All the other old partnerships are considered to have been terminated.

EXAMPLE C10-29 ▶ The AB and CD Partnerships are merged to form the ABCD Partnership. April and Ben each own 30% of ABCD, and Carole and David each own 20% of ABCD. The ABCD Partnership is considered a continuation of the AB Partnership because April and Ben, the former partners of AB, own 60% of ABCD. ABCD is bound by the tax year, accounting method, and other elections made by AB. CD, formerly owned by Carole and David, is considered to terminate on the merger date. ◀

In some combinations, the partners of two or more of the old partnerships might hold the requisite profits and capital interest in the new partnership. When two or more old partnerships satisfy this requirement, the old partnership credited with contributing the greatest dollar value of assets to the new partnership is considered the continuing partnership, and all other partnerships are terminated. Sometimes, none of the old partnerships account for more than 50% of the capital and profits of the new partnership. In that case, all the old partnerships terminate, and the merged partnership is a new entity that can make its own tax year and accounting method elections.

EXAMPLE C10-30 ▶ Three partnerships merge to form the ABCD Partnership. The AB Partnership (owned by Andy and Bill) contributes assets valued at $140,000 to ABCD. BC (owned by Bill and Cathy) and CD (owned by Cathy and Drew) Partnerships contribute assets valued at $180,000 and $120,000, respectively. The capital and profits interests of the partners in the new partnership are Andy, 20%; Bill, 35%; Cathy, 19%; and Drew, 26%. Both the AB and BC Partnerships had partners who now own more than 50% of the new partnership (Andy and Bill own 55%, and Bill and Cathy own 54%). The BC Partnership contributed more assets ($180,000) to the new partnership than did the AB Partnership ($140,000). Therefore, the ABCD Partnership is a continuation of the BC Partnership. Both the AB and CD Partnerships terminate on the merger date. ◀

KEY POINT

The principal concern of a partnership division is to determine which of the new partnerships is the continuation of the prior partnership.

DIVISION OF A PARTNERSHIP

When a partnership divides into two or more new partnerships, all the new partnerships whose partners own collectively more than 50% of the profits and capital interests in the old partnerships are considered a continuation of the old partnership.[42] All partnerships that are continuations of the old partnership are bound by the old partnership's tax year and accounting method elections. Any other partnership created by the division is considered a new partnership eligible to make its own tax year and accounting method elections. If no new partnership meets the criteria for continuation of the divided partnership, the divided partnership terminates on the division date. The interest of any partner of the divided partnership who does not own an interest in a continuing partnership is considered to be liquidated on the division date.

EXAMPLE C10-31 ▶ The RSTV Partnership is in the real estate and insurance business. Randy owns a 40% interest and Sam, Tomas, and Vicki each own 20% of RSTV. The partners agree to split the partnership, with the RS Partnership receiving the real estate operations and the TV Partnership receiving the insurance business. Because Randy and Sam own more than 50% of the RSTV Partnership (40% + 20% = 60%), the RS Partnership is a continuation of the RSTV Partnership and must report its results using the same tax year and accounting method elections that RSTV used. Tomas and Vicki are considered to have terminated their interests in RSTV and to have received a liquidating distribution of the insurance business property. The TV Partnership makes its tax year and accounting method elections following the rules for a new partnership. ◀

---

[41] Sec. 708(b)(2)(A).

[42] Sec. 708(b)(2)(B).

OPTIONAL BASIS ADJUSTMENTS

OBJECTIVE 9

Understand the effect of optional basis adjustments

In general, a partnership makes no adjustment to the basis of its property when a partner sells or exchanges his or her interest in the partnership, when a partner's interest transfers upon the partner's death, or when the partnership makes a property distribution to a partner. A partnership, however, may adjust basis of its assets if the partnership makes an **optional basis adjustment** election under Sec. 754. The following paragraphs compare the consequences of having no election to having such an election. The discussion focuses primarily on sale transactions but also briefly mentions distributions. Once made, the Sec. 754 election applies to all subsequent transfers of partnership interests (e.g., sales, exchanges, and transfers upon death) and all subsequent distributions.

OPTIONAL ADJUSTMENT ON TRANSFERS

If a new incoming partner purchases his or her partnership interest from an existing partner, the new partner's basis in the partnership interest equals the purchase price plus the new partner's share of partnership liabilities. The new partner's basis in the partnership is likely to be different from his or her share of basis of the underlying assets in the partnership. This difference could lead to inequitable results as demonstrated by the following example.

EXAMPLE C10-32 ▶ Amy, Bill, and Corey each own a one-third interest in ABC partnership, which has the following simple balance sheet:

	Basis	*FMV*
Assets:		
Cash	$30,000	$ 30,000
Inventory	60,000	90,000
Total	$90,000	$120,000
Liabilities and capital:		
Liabilities	$15,000	$ 15,000
Capital—Amy	25,000	35,000
—Bill	25,000	35,000
—Corey	25,000	35,000
Total	$90,000	$120,000

Eric purchases Amy's one-third interest for $35,000 cash and assumes her $5,000 share of partnerships liabilities. Eric pays this amount because one-third the FMV of the underlying partnership assets is $40,000 (1/3 × $120,000). In addition, the cash paid plus Eric's share of partnership liabilities gives him a $40,000 basis in his new partnership interest. Amy's basis at the time of sale is $30,000. Therefore, Amy recognizes a $10,000 gain ($40,000 amount realized − $30,000 basis). Amy's $10,000 gain also reflects her share of the difference between the inventory's FMV and basis at the partnership level. Thus, her gain will be ordinary income under Sec. 751.

Now suppose the partnership later sells the inventory for $90,000. The partnership recognizes $30,000 of ordinary income. Therefore, each partner, Bill, Corey, and Eric, recognizes a $10,000 distributive share of ordinary income from that sale, and each partner increases the basis of his partnership interests by the same amount. Accordingly, Eric increases his basis in the partnership from $40,000 to $50,000. In this situation, Eric appears to be taxed on the same gain as was Amy even though he paid a FMV price for his partnership interest (and the underlying partnership assets).

However, this result primarily is an issue of timing and possibly character of income and loss. For example, suppose further that, sometime after selling the inventory, the partnership distributes the $120,000 cash to the partners in liquidation. Eric would receive $40,000 and recognize a $10,000 ($40,000 distribution − $50,000 basis) capital loss.

In short, with no optional basis adjustment election in effect, Eric recognizes $10,000 of ordinary income when the partnership sells the inventory and a $10,000 capital loss when the partnership liquidates. This timing difference could be substantial if the partnership remains in existence for a long time. Also, the capital loss may offset only capital gains and up to $3,000 of ordinary income in the partner's personal tax return. ◀

ADDITIONAL COMMENT

The situation of a new partner purchasing an interest in a partnership is a good example of where a partner's outside basis can differ significantly from his or her share of the partnership's inside basis. The Sec. 754 election mitigates this difference.

AMOUNT OF THE ADJUSTMENT. An incoming partner might view the situation in Example C10-32 as unacceptable and wish the partnership to make a Sec. 754 election. If the partnership makes such an election or has a Sec. 754 election already in effect, Sec. 743 mandates a special basis adjustment equal to the difference between the transferee (purchasing) partner's basis in the partnership interest and the transferee partner's share of basis of partnership assets. This basis adjustment, arising from a transfer, belongs only to the transferee partner (and not to the other partners), and it eliminates the inequities noted in Example C10-32.

EXAMPLE C10-33 ▶ Assume the same facts as in Example C10-32 except the partnership makes a Sec. 754 election. Eric's optional basis adjustment is calculated as follows:

Cash purchase price	$35,000
Share of partnership liabilities	5,000
Initial basis in partnership	$40,000
Minus: Eric's share of partnership's basis in assets (1/3 × $90,000)[43]	(30,000)
Optional basis adjustment	$10,000

Now when the partnership sells the inventory, Eric has an additional $10,000 basis in his share of the inventory that offsets the $10,000 income he otherwise would recognize. The other partners, however, still recognize their $10,000 distributive shares of income. Because Eric did not recognize any income, he does not increase his partnership basis. Suppose the partnership liquidates sometime after selling the inventory. Again, Eric receives a $40,000 distribution, but he recognizes no capital gain or loss ($40,000 distribution − $40,000 basis). Thus, the optional basis adjustment eliminated both the timing and character differences that occurred in Example C10-32. ◀

OTHER ISSUES. Examples C10-32 and C10-33 assume inventory is the only asset other than cash. If the asset instead had been depreciable property, the optional basis adjustment would give the transferee partner additional depreciation deductions. Also, if a partnership has more than one asset other than cash, the optional basis adjustment must be allocated to the assets under special rules found in Sec. 755 and related Treasury Regulations. These allocation rules are beyond the scope of this text.

OPTIONAL ADJUSTMENT ON DISTRIBUTIONS

As mentioned earlier, if a partnership distributes property to a partner, the partnership makes no adjustment to the basis of its remaining property unless an optional basis adjustment election is in place. On the other hand, if the partnership has made a Sec. 754 election, the partnership makes the following adjustments upon the distribution to a partner:

- Increases the basis of *partnership* property by:
  1. Any gain recognized by the distributee partner on the distribution (e.g., cash distribution exceeding the partner's basis in his or her partnership interest)
  2. The amount by which the distributee partner decreases the basis of property received in a property distribution from the basis of the property in the partnership's hands
- Decreases the basis of *partnership* property by:
  1. Any loss recognized by the distributee partner on a liquidating distribution
  2. The amount by which the distributee partner increases the basis of property received in a property distribution from the basis of the property in the partnership's hands

43 In some cases, the calculation of the transferee's share of the partnership's basis in assets can be more complicated than shown in this example. See Reg. Sec. 1.743-1(d).

Unlike the optional basis adjustments arising from a transfer of partnership interest, the basis adjustments arising from a distribution belong to the partnership as a whole. These adjustments eliminate many (but not all) basis and timing disparities resulting from distributions.

A partnership should take care in making a Sec. 754 election because, once made, the election affects many transactions in complicated ways. Moreover, the election can cause downward as well as upward adjustments. Finally, the election has long-range implications because it can be revoked only with IRS approval. The IRS will not grant such approval if the primary purpose of the revocation is to avoid reducing the basis of partnership assets.

SPECIAL FORMS OF PARTNERSHIPS

Here, we examine a series of special partnership forms, including tax shelters organized as limited partnerships, publicly traded partnerships, limited liability companies, limited liability partnerships, and electing large partnerships.

TAX SHELTERS AND LIMITED PARTNERSHIPS

ADDITIONAL COMMENT

The passive activity loss limitations eliminate the deferral benefit of tax shelters.

Tax shelters at their best are good investments that reduce the amount of an investor's tax bill. Traditionally, shelter benefits arise from leverage, income deferral, and tax credits.

Before the Tax Reform Act of 1986, limited partnerships were the primary vehicle for tax shelter investments. However, the Tax Reform Act of 1986 greatly reduced the benefits of limited partnerships as tax shelters by invoking the passive activity loss limitations for activity conducted in a limited partnership form. The limited partnership, however, still allows an investor to limit liability while receiving the benefits of the shelter's tax attributes to save taxes on other passive income. Since the Tax Reform Act of 1986, limited partnerships that generate passive income rather than losses have become popular investments for investors who already hold loss-generating limited partnership interests.

PUBLICLY TRADED PARTNERSHIPS

The Revenue Act of 1987 moved to restrict still further the benefits of tax shelter ownership by changing the taxation of **publicly traded partnerships** (PTPs). A PTP is a partnership whose interests are traded either on an established securities exchange or in a secondary market or the equivalent thereof. A partnership that meets the requirements is taxed as a C corporation under Sec. 7704.

Two exceptions apply to partnerships that otherwise would be classified as PTPs:

- Partnerships that have 90% or more of their gross income being "qualifying income" continue to be taxed under the partnership rules.
- Partnerships that were in existence on December 17, 1987 and have not added a substantial new line of business since that date are grandfathered. In general, application of the PTP rules for these partnerships was delayed until tax years beginning after December 31, 1997.

REAL-WORLD EXAMPLE

The Chicago Board of Partnerships acts as a secondary market for limited partnership interests. Trades can range from a few thousand dollars to millions of dollars. This market increases the liquidity of limited partnership investments. Some partnerships are publicly traded on the major stock exchanges.

The Taxpayer Relief Act of 1997 added an election that allows the grandfathered partnerships to continue to be taxed as partnerships after the original ten-year window and until the election is revoked. To elect to continue to be taxed as a partnership, the publicly traded partnership (which must have been taxed as a partnership under the grandfather provision) must agree to pay a 3.5% annual tax on gross income from the active conduct of any trade or business.[44] The election may be revoked by the partnership, but once revoked, it cannot be reinstated.

For the 90% of gross income test, qualifying income is defined in Sec. 7704(d) as including certain interest, dividends, real property rents (but not personal property rents), income and gains from the sale or disposition of a capital asset or Sec. 1231(b) trade or

[44] Sec. 7704(g)(3).

business property held for the production of passive income, and gain from the sale or disposition of real property. It also includes gains from certain commodity trading and natural resource activities. Any PTP not taxed as a corporation because of this 90% exception is subject to separate and more restrictive Sec. 469 passive loss rules than are partnerships that are not publicly traded.

If a partnership is first classified as a PTP taxed as a corporation during a tax year, the PTP incurs a deemed contribution of all partnership assets and all partnership liabilities to a corporation in exchange for all the corporation's stock. The stock is then deemed distributed to the partners in complete liquidation of the partnership. This transaction is taxed exactly as if it had physically occurred.

LIMITED LIABILITY COMPANIES

In recent years, the limited liability company (LLC) has emerged as a popular form of business entity in the United States. The LLC combines the legal and tax benefits of partnerships and S corporations. Currently, all 50 states have adopted LLC laws. The LLC business form combines the advantage of limited liability for all its owners with the ability of achieving the conduit treatment and the flexibility of being taxed as a partnership.

In the past, whether an LLC was characterized as a corporation or a partnership for federal tax purposes depended on the number of corporate characteristics that were present, such as limited liability, free transferability of interests, centralized management, and continuity of life. The process of determining tax treatment was complex and time consuming. However, in December 1996, the Treasury Department issued regulations that allow entities (other than corporations and trusts) to choose whether to be taxed as a partnership or as an association. (An association is an unincorporated entity taxed as a corporation.) According to these check-the-box regulations, an LLC with two or more members can choose either partnership or association tax treatment. With a written and properly filed election, any LLC can choose to be taxed as an association. If the LLC makes no such election, an LLC with two or more members is treated as a partnership for tax purposes, while a single member LLC is treated as a sole proprietorship.

TAX STRATEGY TIP

The list of advantages of an LLC over an S corporation is substantial and suggests that an LLC should always be seriously considered as an option for a pass-through entity. However, one current, important advantage of an S corporation is that the shareholders are not subject to self-employment taxes on their share of the entity's earnings.

As already mentioned, an LLC with two or more members that does not elect association status is a partnership for tax purposes and is subject to all the rules applicable to other partnerships. Thus, the formation of the LLC; income, gain, loss, and deductions that flow through to the LLC members; current and liquidating distributions; and sale, gift, or exchange of an interest in the LLC are all taxed under the partnership rules. An LLC treated as a partnership is subject to the Sec. 704 rules for special allocations and allocations of precontribution gain or loss, to the Sec. 736 rules for retirement distributions, and to the Sec. 751 rules.

Using the LLC form for a business with publicly traded ownership interests is likely to result in taxation as a corporation. Even if the LLC does not elect association status, the public trading of the ownership interest brings the LLC under the publicly traded partnership rules. As discussed above, these rules result in the business being taxed as a corporation unless 90% or more of the income is qualifying income or unless the LLC is covered under the grandfather rules. However, given the recency of LLCs as a form for conducting business, the grandfather provisions are unlikely to apply.

If an LLC is treated as a partnership, it offers greater flexibility than does an S corporation in that there is no limit on the number of shareholders, the number of classes of stock, or the types of investments in related entities that the LLC can make. Unlike S corporations, LLCs can use the special allocation rules of Sec. 704 to allocate income, gain, loss or deductions to their members. Each member's basis in the LLC interest includes that member's share of the organization's debts (and not just shareholder debt as with an S corporation).

REAL WORLD EXAMPLE

All the Big 5 accounting firms and a number of other national accounting firms have become LLPs. Many local and regional professional accounting and law firms also have changed to LLPs.

LIMITED LIABILITY PARTNERSHIPS

Many states have added limited liability partnerships (LLPs) to the list of business forms that can be formed. Under the current state laws, the primary difference between a general partnership and an LLP is that in a limited liability partnership, a partner is not liable for damages resulting from failures in the work of other partners or of people supervised by other partners. For example, assume that a limited liability accounting partnership is assessed damages in a lawsuit that resulted from an audit partner in New York being negligent in an audit. The tax partner for the same firm, who is based in San Diego and who had no involvement with the audit or the auditor, should not be liable to pay damages resulting from the suit.

Like a general or limited partnership, this business form is a partnership for tax purposes. All the partnership tax rules and regulations apply to this business form just as they do to any other partnership.

STOP & THINK

Question: What changes do you expect the check-the-box regulations to bring about for new businesses making their initial choice of entity decision? What changes do you expect these regulations to have on existing corporations?

Solution: Consider the options facing a new business. The business can be formed as a C corporation, which provides limited liability protection to owners but subjects the corporate income to double taxation. A business formed as a C corporation can make an S election for tax purposes, which keeps the limited liability protection for the owners and eliminates the double taxation by taxing all income directly to the owners. However, as you will see in Chapter C11, numerous restrictions prevent many corporations from electing S status. In addition, all income and loss of an S corporation must be allocated among the shareholders on a pro rata basis. A partnership offers the most flexible tax treatment with no double taxation of income, but the traditional partnership must have at least one general partner whose liability for partnership debts is not limited. An LLC, which is treated as a partnership, provides limited liability protection to its owners while avoiding both the double taxation of income found in a regular C corporation as well as the restrictions placed on S corporations. Because an LLC is treated as a partnership, the income and loss shares reported by each partner is flexible, and the partner's basis for his partnership interest includes his or her share of the LLC's liabilities. In some senses, the LLC has the best attributes of both the corporation and the partnership.

These are strong reasons why a new entity would choose to form as an LLC and elect to be treated as a partnership. However, because the LLC is a new business form, statutes, case law, and regulations are still being developed, and thus many areas of uncertainty remain to be resolved over time.

The check-the-box regulations are likely to be of much less interest to existing C corporations and S corporations because an existing corporation must liquidate (with all the tax consequences of a liquidation, as described in Chapter C6) before it can form as an LLC. Potentially, the change in entity form has a very high tax cost for an existing corporation.

OBJECTIVE 10

Determine the appropriate reporting for the income of an electing large partnership

ELECTING LARGE PARTNERSHIPS

The Taxpayer Relief Act of 1997 added a significant new election to the partnership arena. Partnerships that qualify as "large partnerships" may elect to be taxed under a simplified reporting arrangement.[45] Four qualifications must be met for a partnership to be taxed as an electing large partnership. The partnership

- Must not be a service partnership
- Must not be engaged in commodity trading
- Must have at least 100 partners, and
- Must file an election to be taxed as an electing large partnership.

Section 775 defines a service partnership as one in which substantially all the partners perform substantial services in connection with the partnership's activities or the partners are retired but in the past performed substantial services in connection with the partnership's activities. One example of a partnership that could not make this election is a partnership that provides accounting services. An electing large partnership also cannot be engaged in commodity trading. Further, to qualify to make this election, the partnership must have at least 100 partners (excluding those partners who do provide substantial services in connection with the partnership's business activities) throughout the tax year.

---

[45] Sec. 775.

Once the election is made, the partnership reports its income under a simplified reporting scheme, is subject to different rules about when the partnership terminates, and is subject to a different system of audits. The election is irrevocable without IRS permission.

ELECTING LARGE PARTNERSHIP TAXABLE INCOME. Much like other partnerships, the calculation of electing large partnership taxable income includes separately stated income and other income. However, the items that must be separately stated are very different for the electing large partnership. Likewise, the items included in other income differ significantly. The main reason that electing large partnerships were added to the IRC was to provide a form of flow-through entity that does not require so much separate reporting to each partner of many different income, loss, and deduction items. Simpler reporting from the partnership to the partners was the goal, so it should be no surprise that fewer items are separately stated and that many more items are combined at the partnership level.

Like a regular partnership, calculation of the taxable income of an electing large partnership is similar to the calculation for an individual. For an electing large partnership (just like for other partnerships), the deductions for personal exemptions and net operating losses are disallowed as well as most additional itemized deductions, such as medical expenses and alimony. However, calculation of the items that would qualify as miscellaneous itemized deductions for an individual differs from the calculation for either individuals or other partnerships. For an electing large partnership, miscellaneous itemized deductions are combined at the partnership level and subject to a 70% deduction at the partnership level. After the 70% deduction, the remaining miscellaneous itemized deductions are combined with other income and passed through to the partners. Because they are combined with other income at the partnership level, they are not subject to the 2% nondeductible floor at the individual partner level.[46]

Instead of flowing through as a separately stated item as they do with a regular partnership, charitable contributions made by an electing large partnership are subject to the 10% of taxable income limit similar to the limit that normally applies to corporations. Once the limit is applied, the partnership deducts allowable charitable contribution from its ordinary income, and the partners do not report the charitable contributions as a separate item.[47]

For a regular partnership, the first-year expensing deduction allowed under Sec. 179 is both limited at the partnership level and is separately stated and limited at the partner level. For an electing large partnership, the only limit is at the partnership level. The allowable deduction is calculated at the partnership level, and the deduction amount offsets the partnership's ordinary income. For an electing large partnership, the Sec. 179 deduction is not separately stated and the impact of the Sec. 179 deduction is buried in the ordinary income amount reported by the partnership to the partners.

SEPARATELY STATED LARGE PARTNERSHIP ITEMS. An electing large partnership nevertheless is a pass-through entity so some items still must be separately stated at the partnership level, and these items maintain their character when reported on the partners' tax returns. Section 772 lists the following items the electing large partnership must report separately:

- Taxable income or loss from passive loss limitation activities
- Taxable income or loss from other partnership activities
- Net capital gain or loss from passive loss limitation activities
- Net capital gain or loss from other partnership activities
- Tax-exempt interest
- Applicable net alternative minimum tax adjustment separately computed for passive loss limitation activities and other activities
- General credits

[46] Sec. 773(b).

[47] Sec. 773(b)(2).

- Low income housing credit
- Rehabilitation credit
- Foreign income taxes
- Credit for producing fuel from a nonconventional source
- Any other item the IRS determines should be separately stated

The differences between the treatments for other partnerships and for electing large partnerships is significant. The most interesting aspect of this list is what items are combined for reporting by an electing large partnership. For example, Sec. 1231 gains and losses are netted at the partnership level, net 1231 losses are included in ordinary income or loss, and net 1231 gains are reported with capital gains and losses. The capital gains and losses also are combined at the partnership level with only a single, net number reported to the partners. The capital gain or loss is treated as long-term at the partner level. However, if the net is a short-term capital gain, that gain is treated as ordinary income and combined at the partnership level with other ordinary income amounts. All the partnership's credits are combined at the partnership level with the exceptions of the low income housing credit and the rehabilitation credit.

Both ordinary income and capital gains attributed to passive loss activities are reported separately from the results of other partnership activities. In addition, the taxable income or loss from activities other than passive activities generally are treated as items of income or expense with respect to property held for investment rather than as active trade or business income.

For the electing large partnership, all limits, such as the charitable contributions limit and the Sec. 179 expensing deduction limit, are applied at the partnership level rather than at the individual partner level with three exceptions. The three limits applied at the partner level are the Sec. 68 limit on itemized deductions, the limit on at risk losses, and the limit on passive activity losses.[48] For the limitation to be applied at the partner level, these items must be separately stated.

For separately stated items, the character of amounts flowing through the partnership retain their character when reported on the partners' tax returns. However, because many more items are combined at the partnership level and not separately stated, the character of many fewer kinds of income is retained to flow through with the electing large partnership form.

EXAMPLE C10-34 ▶ The ABC Partnership is an electing large partnership that reports the following transactions for the current year: ABC has no passive activities.

Net long-term capital loss	$100,000
Sec. 1231 gain	120,000
Ordinary income	40,000
Charitable contributions	30,000
Tax-exempt income	4,000

ABC will report these earnings to its partners as follows:

Long-term capital gain	$20,000
Ordinary income	34,000
Tax-exempt income	4,000

Because the partnership has a net Sec. 1231 gain, it is treated as a long-term capital gain ($120,000) and combined at the partnership level with the long-term capital loss ($100,000) to result in a net long-term capital gain of $20,000. At the partnership level, the charitable contribution deduction is limited to 10% of taxable income, or $6,000 [0.10 × ($20,000 capital gain + $40,000 ordinary income)] and is subtracted from ordinary income of $40,000 before ordinary income is reported to the partners. The character of the long-term capital gain, tax-exempt income, and ordinary income pass through to the partner. ◀

---

[48] Sec. 773(a)

REPORTING REQUIREMENT. An electing large partnership must provide a Schedule K-1 to each of its partners on or before March 15 following the close of the partnership tax year without regard to when the partnership tax return is due.[49] Partnerships that are not electing large partnerships are only required to provide the information return by the due date of the partnership tax return—which, for a calendar year partnership, is April 15. The IRS expects that the March 15 provision will reduce the number of partners who must file an extension of their individual tax returns because they do not receive the Schedule K-1 from a regular partnership early enough to file a timely individual return.

TERMINATION OF THE PARTNERSHIP. Because electing large partnerships are quite large and often may be widely traded, Congress decided to change the conditions under which these partnership will be considered to terminate. An electing large partnership terminates only if its partners cease to conduct any business, financial operation, or venture in a partnership form. Unlike other partnerships, an electing large partnership will not terminate because of the sale or exchange of partnership interests involving at least a 50% interest in partnership capital or profits during a 12-month period.[50]

ELECTING LARGE PARTNERSHIP AUDITS. An electing large partnership is not subject to the partnership audit rules but is subject to a much more restrictive set of partnership audit procedures.[51] First, all electing large partnership partners must report all items of partnership income, gain, loss, or deduction in the way the partnership reports the item. Deviations from that partnership reporting will be "corrected" by the IRS just as a math mistake is corrected.[52]

Once all partners are required to use identical reporting for partnership items, it becomes somewhat easier to audit partnership results only at the partnership level. Notice of audit proceedings, determination of errors, settlement offers, appeals proceedings, and court cases are all handled at the partnership level, but no individual partner can request separate treatment or refuse to participate in the partnership level result. In general, any adjustments determined at the partnership level by an audit agreement or court decision will be considered to be income or deduction that occurs in the year of the agreement or decision.[53] Accordingly, any effect on partners is felt by the partners who own interests in the year of the agreement or decision and not by the partners who originally reported the contested transaction results.

TAX PLANNING CONSIDERATIONS

LIQUIDATING DISTRIBUTION OR SALE TO PARTNERS

An unusual tax planning opportunity exists when one partner withdraws from a partnership and the remaining partners proportionately increase their ownership of the partnership. The partners can structure the ownership change as either a liquidating distribution made by the partnership or as a sale of the partnership interest to the remaining partners. In fact, the substance of the two transactions is the same, only the form is different. However, this difference in form can make a substantial difference in the tax consequences in a number of areas.

- If the transferor partner receives payment for his or her interest in the partnership's Sec. 751 assets, he or she must recognize ordinary income no matter how the transaction is structured. The partnership's basis in Sec. 751 assets is increased in the case of

[49] Sec. 6031.
[50] Sec. 774(c).
[51] Sec. 6240.
[52] Sec. 6241.
[53] Sec. 6242.

a liquidating distribution. When a sale transaction takes place, the partnership's basis in Sec. 751 assets is increased only if the partnership has an optional basis adjustment election in effect.

- If the partnership has an optional basis adjustment election in effect, the allocation of the adjustment to the individual partnership assets can be different depending on whether the transaction is structured as a sale or as a liquidating distribution.
- If the interest being transferred exceeds 50% of the profits and capital interests, a sale to the remaining partners terminates the partnership. A liquidating distribution does not cause a termination to occur.

Because the tax implications of the sale transaction and liquidating distribution alternatives are both numerous and complex, the partners should make their choice only after careful consideration. See the Tax Strategy Problem below.

PROBLEM MATERIALS

DISCUSSION QUESTIONS

C10-1 Javier is retiring from the JKL Partnership. In January of the current year, he has a $100,000 basis in his partnership interest when he receives a $10,000 cash distribution. The partnership plans to distribute $10,000 each month this year, and Javier will cease to be a partner after the December payment. Is the January payment to Javier a current distribution or a liquidating distribution?

C10-2 Lia has a $40,000 basis in her partnership interest just before receiving a parcel of land as a nonliquidating (current) distribution. The partnership purchased the land, and Lia has no precontribution gain. Under what conditions will Lia's basis in the land be $40,000? Under what conditions will Lia's basis in the land be a carryover basis from the partnership's basis in the land?

C10-3 Mariel has a $60,000 basis in her partnership interest just before receiving a parcel of land as a liquidating distribution. She has no remaining precontribution gain and will receive no other distributions. Under what conditions will Mariel's basis in the land be $60,000?

C10-4 Cindy has a $4,000 basis in her partnership interest before receiving a nonliquidating (current) distribution of property having a $4,500 basis and a $6,000 FMV from the CDE Partnership. Cindy has a choice of receiving either inventory or a capital asset. She will hold the distributed property as an investment for no more than two years before she sells it. What tax difference (if any) will occur as a result of Cindy's selection of one property or the other to be distributed by the partnership?

C10-5 The AB Partnership purchases plastic components and assembles children's toys. The assembly operation requires a number of special machines that are housed in a building the partnership owns. The toys are sold on account to a number of retail establishments. The partnership uses the accrual method of accounting. Identify any items you think might be classified as unrealized receivables.

C10-6 Which of the following items are considered to be inventory for purposes of Sec. 751?

a. Supplies
b. Inventory
c. Notes receivable
d. Land held for investment purposes
e. Lots held for resale

C10-7 Explain the conditions under which Sec. 751 has an impact on nonliquidating (current) distributions.

C10-8 What conditions are required for a partner to recognize a loss upon receipt of a distribution from a partnership?

C10-9 Can the basis of unrealized receivables and inventory received in a liquidating distribution be greater to the partner than to the partnership? Can the basis of unrealized receivables and inventory received in a distribution be smaller to the partner than to the partnership? Explain.

C10-10 Can a partner recognize both a gain and a loss on the sale of a partnership interest? If so, under what conditions?

C10-11 Tyra has a zero basis in her partnership interest and a share in partnership liabilities, which are quite large. Explain how these facts will affect the taxation of her departure from the partnership using the following methods of terminating her interest in the partnership.

a. A liquidating distribution of property
b. A sale of the partnership interest to a current partner for cash

C10-12 Tom is a 55% general partner in the RST Partnership. Tom wants to retire, and the other two partners, Stacy and Rich, want to continue the partnership business. They agree that the partnership will liquidate Tom's interest in the partnership by paying him 20% of partnership profits for each of the next ten years. Explain why Sec. 736 does (or does not) apply to the partnership's payments to Tom.

C10-13 Lucia has a $20,000 basis in her limited partnership interest before her retirement from the partnership. Her share of partnership assets have a $23,000 FMV, and the partnership has no Sec. 751 assets. In addition to being paid cash for her full share of partnership assets, Lucia will receive a share of partnership income for the next three years. Explain Lucia's tax treatment for the payments she receives.

C10-14 What are the advantages and disadvantages to the partnership and its partners when a partnership termination is caused by a sale of more than a 50% capital and profits interest?

C10-15 What is a publicly traded partnership? Are all publicly traded partnerships taxed as corporations?

C10-16 What are the advantages of a firm being formed as a limited liability company (LLC) instead of as a limited partnership?

C10-17 What is an electing large partnership? What are the advantages to the partnership of electing to be taxed under the electing large partnership rules?

ISSUE IDENTIFICATION QUESTIONS

C10-18 When Kayla's basis in her interest in the JKL Partnership is $30,000, she receives a current distribution of office equipment. The equipment has an FMV of $40,000 and basis of $35,000. Kayla will not use the office equipment in a business activity. What tax issues should Kayla consider with respect to the distribution?

C10-19 Joel receives a $40,000 cash distribution from the JM Partnership, which reduces his partnership interest from one-third to one-fourth. The JM Partnership is a general partnership that uses the cash method of accounting and has substantial liabilities. JM's inventory has appreciated substantially since it was purchased. What issues should Joel consider with regard to the distribution?

C10-20 Scott sells his one-third partnership interest to Sally for $40,000 when his basis in the partnership interest is $35,000. On the date of sale, the partnership has no liabilities and the following assets:

Assets	*Basis*	*FMV*
Cash	$30,000	$30,000
Inventory	12,000	21,000
Building	53,000	59,000
Land	10,000	10,000

The building is depreciated on a straight-line basis. What tax issues should Scott and Sally consider with respect to the sale transaction?

C10-21 David owns a 60% interest in the DDD Partnership, a general partnership, which he sells to the two remaining partners—Drew and Dana. The three partners have agreed that David will receive $150,000 in cash from the sale. David's basis in the partnership interest before the sale is $120,000, which includes his $30,000 share of partnership recourse liabilities. The partnership has assets with a $300,000 FMV and a $200,000 adjusted basis. What issues should David, Drew, and Dana consider before this sale takes place?

C10-22 Andrew and Beth are equal partners in the AB Partnership. On December 30 of the current year, the AB Partnership agrees to liquidate Andrew's partnership interest for a cash payment on December 30 of each of the next five years. What tax issues should Andrew and Beth consider with respect to the liquidation of Andrew's partnership interest?

C10-23 Alex owns 60% of the Hot Wheels LLC that is treated as a partnership. He plans to give 15% of the LLC (one-fourth of his interest) to his daughter Haley for her high school graduation. He plans to put her interest in a trust, and he will serve as the trustee until Haley is 21. The trust will receive any distributions from the LLC, but Haley is unlikely to be given any of the cash until she is age 21. Alex's 60% interest has a $120,000 FMV and an $80,000 adjusted basis including his $48,000 share of the LLC's liabilities. Alex works full time for the LLC for a small salary and his share of LLC income. Alex also has a special allocation of income from rental property he manages for the LLC. What issues should Alex consider before he completes the gift?

C10-24 Krypton Company recently has been formed as a limited liability company (LLC). Krypton Company is owned equally by three individuals—Jeff, Susan, and Richard—all of whom have substantial income from other sources. Krypton is a manufacturing firm and expects to earn approximately $130,000 of ordinary income and $30,000 of long term capital gain each year for the next several years. Jeff will be a full time manager and will receive a salary of $60,000 each year. What tax issues should the owners consider regarding the LLC's initial year of operations?

C10-25 XYZ Limited Partnership has more than 300 partners and is publicly traded. XYZ was grandfathered under the 1987 Tax Act and has consistently been treated as a partnership. In the current year, XYZ will continue to be very profitable and will continue to pay out about 30% of its income to its owners each year. The managing partners of XYZ want to consider the firm's options for taxation in the current and later years.

PROBLEMS

C10-26 *Current Distributions.* Lisa has a $25,000 basis in her partnership interest before receiving a current distribution of $4,000 cash and land with a $30,000 FMV and a $14,000 basis to the partnership. Assume that any distribution involving Sec. 751 property is pro rata and that any precontribution gains have been recognized before the distribution.

a. Determine Lisa's recognized gain or loss, Lisa's basis in distributed property, and Lisa's ending basis in her partnership interest.
b. How does your answer to Part a change if the partnership's basis in the land is $27,000 instead of $14,000?
c. How does your answer to Part a change if Lisa receives $28,000 cash instead of $4,000 (along with the land)?
d. How does your answer to Part a change if, in addition to the cash and land, Lisa receives inventory with a $25,000 FMV and a $10,000 basis and receivables with a $3,000 FMV and a zero basis?
e. Suppose instead that Lisa receives the distribution in Part a from a C corporation instead of a partnership. The corporation has $100,000 of E&P before the distribution, and Lisa's stock basis before the distribution is $25,000. What are the tax consequences to Lisa and the C corporation?
f. Note: This part can be answered only after the student studies Chapter C11 but is placed here to allow comparison with Parts a and e. Suppose instead that Lisa receives the distribution in Part a from an S corporation instead of a partnership. Lisa is a 50% owner in the corporation, and her stock basis before the distribution is $25,000. What are the tax consequences to Lisa and the S corporation?

C10-27 *Current Distributions.* Complete the chart for each of the following independent distributions. Assume all distributions are nonliquidating and pro rata to the partners, and no contributed property was distributed. All precontribution gain has been recognized before these distributions.

Partner's Basis and Gain/Loss	*Property Distributed*	*Property's Basis to Partnership*	*Property's FMV*	*Property's Basis to Partner*	
a. Basis:					
Predistribution	$20,000	Cash	$ 6,000	$ 6,000	
Postdistribution	$_____	Land	4,000	15,000	$_____
Gain or loss	$_____	Machinery	3,000	2,000	$_____
b. Basis:					
Predistribution	$20,000	Land	$ 6,000	$ 4,000	$_____
Postdistribution	$_____	Inventory	7,000	7,500	$_____
Gain or loss	$_____	Cash	3,000	3,000	
c. Basis					
Predistribution	$26,000	Cash	$35,000	$35,000	
Postdistribution	$_____	Land—Parcel 1	6,000	10,000	$_____
Gain or loss	$_____	Land—Parcel 2	18,000	18,000	$_____

d. Basis:

Predistribution	$28,000	Land—Parcel 1	$ 4,000	$ 6,000	$_____
Postdistribution	$_____	Land—Parcel 2	6,000	10,000	$_____
Gain or loss	$_____	Land—Parcel 3	4,000	10,000	$_____

C10-28 ***Current Distribution with Precontribution Gain.*** Three years ago, Mario joined the MN Partnership by contributing land with a $10,000 basis and an $18,000 FMV. On January 15 of the current year, Mario has a basis in his partnership interest of $20,000, and none of his precontribution gain has been recognized. On January 15, Mario receives a current distribution of a property other than the contributed land with a $15,000 basis and a $23,000 FMV.

a. Does Mario recognize any gain or loss on the distribution?
b. What is Mario's basis in his partnership interest after the distribution?
c. What is the partnership's basis in the land Mario contributed after Mario receives this distribution?

C10-29 ***Current Distribution of Contributed Property.*** Andrew contributed investment land having an $18,000 basis and a $22,000 FMV along with $4,000 in money to the ABC Partnership when it was formed. Two years later, the partnership distributed the investment land Andrew had contributed to Bob, another partner. At the time of the distribution, the land had a $21,000 FMV, and Andrew and Bob's bases in their partnership interests were $21,000 and $30,000, respectively.

a. What gain or loss must be recognized on the distribution, and who must recognize it?
b. What are the bases for Andrew and Bob's interests in the partnership after the distribution?
c. What is Bob's basis in the distributed land?

C10-30 ***Current Distribution of Contributed Property.*** The ABC Partnership made the following current distributions in the current year. The dollar amounts listed are the amounts before considering any implications of the distribution.

	Property Received			
Partner	*Type of Property*	*Basis*	*FMV*	*Partner's Basis in Partnership Interest*
Alonzo	Land	$ 4,000	$10,000	$19,000
Beth	Inventory	1,000	10,000	15,000
Cathy	Money	10,000	10,000	18,000

The land Alonzo received had been contributed by Beth two years ago when its basis was $4,000 and its FMV was $8,000. The inventory Beth received had been contributed by Cathy two years ago when its basis was $1,000 and its FMV was $4,000. For each independent situation, what gain or loss must be recognized? What is the basis of the distributed property after the distribution? What are the bases of the partnership interests after the distribution? Assume the distribution has no Sec. 751 implications.

C10-31 ***Current Distribution with Sec. 751.*** The KLM Partnership owns the following assets on March 1 of the current year:

Assets	*Partnership's Basis*	*FMV*
Cash	$ 30,000	$ 30,000
Receivables	–0–	16,000
Inventory	50,000	52,000
Supplies	6,000	6,500
Equipment[a]	9,000	10,500
Land (investment)	40,000	65,000
Total	$135,000	$180,000

[a] The partnership has claimed depreciation of $4,000 on the equipment.

a. Which partnership items are unrealized receivables?
b. Is the partnership's inventory substantially appreciated?
c. Assume the KLM Partnership has no liabilities and that Kay's basis for her partnership interest is $33,750. On March 1 of the current year, Kay receives a $20,000 current distribution in cash, which reduces her partnership interest from one-third to one-fourth. What are the tax results of the distribution (i.e., the amount and character of any gain, loss, or income recognized and Kay's basis in her partnership interest)?

C10-32 ***Current Distribution with Sec. 751.*** The JKLM Partnership owns the following assets on October 1 of the current year:

Assets	*Partnership's Basis*	*FMV*
Cash	$ 48,000	$ 48,000
Receivables	12,000	12,000
Inventory	21,000	24,000
Machinery[a]	190,000	240,000
Land	36,500	76,000
Total	$307,500	$400,000

[a] Sale of the machinery for its FMV would result in $50,000 of Sec. 1245 depreciation recapture. Thus, the machinery's FMV and original cost are the same numerical value, $240,000.

a. Which partnership items are unrealized receivables?
b. Is the partnership's inventory substantially appreciated?
c. Assume the JKLM Partnership has no liabilities and Jack's basis in his partnership interest is $76,875. On October 1 of the current year, Jack receives a $25,000 current distribution in cash, which reduces his partnership interest from one-fourth to one-fifth. What are the tax results of the distribution (i.e., the amount and character of any gain, loss, or income recognized and Jack's basis in his partnership interest)?

C10-33 ***Current Distribution with Sec. 751.*** The PQRS Partnership owns the following assets on December 30 of the current year:

Assets	*Partnership's Basis*	*FMV*
Cash	$ 20,000	$ 20,000
Receivables	–0–	40,000
Inventory	80,000	100,000
Total	$100,000	$160,000

The partnership has no liabilities, and each partner's basis in his or her partnership interest is $25,000. On December 30 of the current year, Paula receives a current distribution of inventory having a $10,000 FMV, which reduces her partnership interest from one-fourth to one-fifth. What are the tax consequences of the distribution to the partnership, Paula, and the other partners?

C10-34 ***Liquidating Distributions.*** Assume the same four independent distributions as in Problem C10-27. Fill in the blanks in that problem assuming the only change in the facts is that the distributions are now liquidating distributions instead of nonliquidating distributions.

C10-35 ***Liquidating Distribution.*** Marinda is a one-third partner in the MWH Partnership before she receives $100,000 cash as a liquidating distribution. Immediately before Marinda receives the distribution, the partnership has the following assets:

Assets	*Partnership's Basis*	*FMV*
Cash	$100,000	$100,000
Marketable securities	50,000	90,000
Investment land	90,000	140,000
Total	$240,000	$330,000

At the time of the distribution, the partnership has $30,000 of outstanding liabilities, which the three partners share equally. Marinda's basis in her partnership interest before the distribution was $80,000, which, as always, includes her share of liabilities. What are the amount and character of the gain or loss recognized by Marinda and the MWH Partnership on the liquidating distribution?

C10-36 ***Liquidating Distributions.*** The AB Partnership pays its only liability (a $100,000 mortgage) on April 1 of the current year and terminates that same day. Alison and Bob were equal partners in the partnership but have partnership bases immediately preceding these transactions of $110,000 and $180,000, respectively. As always, each partner's basis includes his or her share of liabilities. The two partners receive identical distributions with each receiving the following assets:

Assets	*Partnership's Basis*	*FMV*
Cash	$ 20,000	$ 20,000
Inventory	33,000	35,000
Receivables	10,000	8,000
Building	40,000	60,000
Land	15,000	10,000
Total	$118,000	$133,000

The building has no depreciation recapture potential. What are the tax implications to Alison, Bob, and the AB Partnership of the April 1 transactions (i.e., basis of assets to Alison and Bob, amount and character of gain or loss recognized, etc.)?

C10-37 ***Liquidating Distribution.*** The LQD Partnership distributes the following property to Larry in a distribution that liquidates Larry's interest in the partnership. Larry's basis in his partnership interest before the distribution is $40,000. The adjusted bases and FMVs of the distributed property to the partnership before the distribution are as follows:

	Partnership's Basis	*FMV*
Cash	$ 2,500	$ 2,500
Inventory	8,000	9,000
Capital asset 1	10,000	15,000
Capital asset 2	15,000	17,500
Total	$35,500	$44,000

a. Determine Larry's basis in each distributed asset.
b. Same as Part a except Larry's partnership basis before the distribution is $46,500.
c. Same as Part b except the basis of capital asset 2 is $20,000 instead of $15,000.

C10-38 ***Sale of a Partnership Interest.*** Pat, Kelly, and Yvette are equal partners in the PKY Partnership before Kelly sells her partnership interest. On January 1 of the current year, Kelly's basis in her partnership interest, including her share of liabilities, was $35,000. During January, the calendar year partnership earned $15,000 ordinary income and $6,000 of tax-exempt income. The partnership has a $60,000 recourse liability on January 1, and this amount remains constant throughout the tax year. Kelly's share of that liability is $20,000. The partnership has no other liabilities. Kelly sells her interest on February 1 to Margaret for a cash payment of $45,000. On the sale date the partnership had the following assets:

Assets	*Partnership's Basis*	*FMV*
Cash	$ 20,000	$ 20,000
Inventory	60,000	120,000
Building	36,000	40,000
Land	10,000	15,000
Total	$126,000	$195,000

The partnership has claimed $5,000 of depreciation on the building using the straight-line method.
a. What is Kelly's basis in her partnership interest on February 1 just before the sale?
b. What are the amount and character of Kelly's gain or loss on the sale?
c. What is Margaret's basis in her partnership interest?
d. What is the partnership's basis in its assets after the sale?

C10-39 ***Sale of Partnership Interest and Termination.*** Clay owned 60% of the CAP Partnership and sold one-half of his interest (30%) to Steve for $75,000 cash. Before the sale, Clay's basis in his entire partnership interest was $168,000 including his $30,000 share of partnership liabilities and his share of income up to the sale date. Partnership assets on the sale date were

Assets	*Partnership's Basis*	*FMV*
Cash	$ 50,000	$ 50,000
Inventory	30,000	60,000
Land	200,000	190,000
Total	$280,000	$300,000

a. What are the amount and character of Clay's recognized gain or loss on the sale? What is his remaining basis in his partnership interest?
b. What is Steve's basis in his partnership interest?
c. How will the partnership's basis in its assets be affected?
d. How would your answers to Parts a and c change if Clay sold his entire interest to Steve for $150,000 cash?

C10-40 *Sale of a Partnership Interest.* Alice, Bob, and Charles are one-third partners in the ABC Partnership. The partners originally formed the partnership with cash contributions, so no partner has precontribution gains or losses. Prior to Alice's sale of her partnership interest, the partnership has the following balance sheet:

Assets	*Partnership's Basis*	*FMV*
Cash	$ 12,000	$ 12,000
Receivable	–0–	21,000
Inventory	57,000	72,000
Machinery[a]	90,000	132,000
Building[b]	120,000	165,000
Land	36,000	30,000
Investments[c]	15,000	48,000
Total	$330,000	$480,000
Liabilities and capital		
Liabilities	$105,000	$105,000
Partners' capital:		
Alice	75,000	125,000
Bob	75,000	125,000
Charles	75,000	125,000
Total	$330,000	$480,000

[a]The machinery cost $126,000, and the partnership has claimed $36,000 of depreciation.
[b]The building cost $150,000, and the partnership has claimed $30,000 of straight-line depreciation.
[c]The partnership has held the investments for more than one year.

Alice has a $110,000 basis in her partnership interest including her share of partnership liabilities, and she sells her partnership interest to Darla for $125,000 cash.
a. What are the amount and character of Alice's recognized gain or loss on the sale?
b. What is Darla's basis in her partnership interest?

C10-41 *Retirement of a Partner.* Suzanne retires from the BRS Partnership when the basis of her one-third interest is $105,000, which, as always, includes her share of liabilities. At the time of her retirement, the partnership had the following assets:

Assets	*Partnership's Basis*	*FMV*
Cash	$145,000	$145,000
Receivables	40,000	40,000
Land	130,000	220,000
Total	$315,000	$405,000

The partnership has $60,000 of liabilities when Suzanne retires. The partnership will pay Suzanne cash of $130,000 to retire her partnership interest.
a. What are the amount and character of the gain or loss Suzanne must recognize?
b. What is the impact of the retirement on the partnership and the remaining partners?

C10-42 *Retirement of a Partner.* Brian owns 40% of the ABC Partnership before his retirement on April 15 of the current year. On that date, his basis in the partnership interest was $40,000 including his share of liabilities. The partnership's balance sheet on that date is as follows:

	Partnership's Basis	FMV
Assets:		
Cash	$ 60,000	$ 60,000
Receivables	24,000	24,000
Land	16,000	40,000
Total	$100,000	$124,000
Liabilities and capital:		
Liabilities	$ 20,000	$ 20,000
Capital—Abner	16,000	20,800
—Brian	32,000	41,600
—Charles	32,000	41,600
Total	$100,000	$124,000

What are the amount and character of the gain or loss that Brian and the ABC Partnership must recognize for the following independent retirement payments?

a. Brian receives $41,600 cash on April 15.

b. Brian receives $50,000 cash on April 15.

C10-43 ***Retirement of a Partner.*** Kim retires from the KLM Partnership on January 1 of the current year. At that time, her basis in the partnership is $75,000, which, as always, includes her share of liabilities. The partnership reports the following balance sheet:

	Partnership's Basis	FMV
Assets:		
Cash	$100,000	$100,000
Receivables	30,000	30,000
Inventory	40,000	40,000
Land	55,000	100,000
Total	$225,000	$270,000
Liabilities and capital:		
Liabilities	$ 75,000	$ 75,000
Capital—Kim	50,000	65,000
—Larry	50,000	65,000
—Michael	50,000	65,000
Total	$225,000	$270,000

Explain the tax consequences (i.e., amount and character of gain or loss recognized and Kim's basis for any assets received) of the partnership making the retirement payments described in the following independent situations. Kim's share of liabilities is $25,000.

a. Kim receives $65,000 cash on January 1.

b. Kim receives $75,000 cash on January 1.

C10-44 ***Death of a Partner.*** When Jerry died on April 16 of the current year, he owned a 40% interest in the JM Partnership, and Michael owns the remaining 60% interest. All his assets are held in his estate for a two-year period while the estate is being settled. Jerry's estate is his successor-in-interest for the partnership interest. Under a formula contained in the partnership agreement, the partnership must pay Jerry's successor-in-interest $40,000 cash shortly after his death plus $90,000 for each of the two years immediately following a partner's death. The partnership agreement provides that all payments to a retiring partner will first be payments for the partner's share of assets, and then any additional payments will be Sec. 736(a) payments. When Jerry died, the partnership had the following assets:

Assets	Partnership's Basis	FMV
Cash	$100,000	$100,000
Land	200,000	300,000
Total	$300,000	$400,000

Jerry's basis for the partnership interest on the date of his death was $120,000 including his $30,000 share of partnership liabilities.

a. How will the payments be taxed to Jerry's successor-in-interest?
b. What are the tax implications of the payments for the partnership?

C10-45 *Death of a Partner.* Bruce died on June 1 of the current year. On the date of his death, he held a one-third interest in the ABC Partnership, which had a $100,000 basis including his share of liabilities. Under the partnership agreement, Bruce's successor-in-interest, his wife, is to receive the following amounts from the partnership: $130,000 cash, the partnership's assumption of Bruce's $20,000 share of partnership liabilities, plus 10% of partnership net income for the next three years. The partnership's assets immediately before Bruce's death are as follows:

Assets	*Partnership's Basis*	*FMV*
Cash	$100,000	$100,000
Receivables	90,000	90,000
Inventory	40,000	40,000
Land	70,000	220,000
Total	$300,000	$450,000

a. What are the amount and character of the gain or loss that Bruce's wife must recognize when she receives the first year's payment?
b. What is the character of the gain recognized from the partnership interest when she receives the payments in each of the following three years?
c. When does Bruce's successor-in-interest cease to be a member of the partnership?

C10-46 *Liquidation or Sale of a Partnership Interest.* John has a 60% capital and profits interest in the JAS Partnership with a basis of $331,200, which includes his share of liabilities, when he decides to retire. Andrew and Stephen want to continue the partnership's business. On the date John retires, the partnership's balance sheet is as follows:

	Partnership's Basis	*FMV*
Assets:		
Cash	$160,000	$160,000
Receivables	96,000	96,000
Building[a]	200,000	300,000
Land	96,000	180,000
Total	$552,000	$736,000
Liabilities and capital:		
Liabilities	$120,000	$120,000
Capital—John	259,200	369,600
—Andrew	86,400	123,200
—Stephen	86,400	123,200
Total	$552,000	$736,000

[a] The partnership has claimed $60,000 of straight-line depreciation on the building.

a. What are the tax implications for John, Andrew, Stephen, and the JAS Partnership if Andrew and Stephen each purchase one-half of John's partnership interest for a cash price of $184,800 each? (Include in your answer the amount and character of the recognized gain or loss, basis of the partnership assets, and any other relevant tax implications.)
b. What are the tax implications for John, Andrew, Stephen, and the JAS Partnership if the partnership pays John a liquidating distribution equal to 60% of each partnership asset?

C10-47 *Liquidation or Sale of a Partnership Interest.* Amy retires from the AJS Partnership on January 1 of the current year. Her basis in her partnership interest is $120,000 including her share of liabilities. Amy receives $160,000 in cash from the partnership for her interest. On that date, the partnership balance sheet is as follows:

	Partnership's Basis	*FMV*
Assets:		
Cash	$180,000	$180,000
Receivables	60,000	60,000
Land	120,000	300,000
Total	$360,000	$540,000
Liabilities and capital:		
Liabilities	$ 60,000	$ 60,000
Capital—Amy	100,000	160,000
—Joan	100,000	160,000
—Stephanie	100,000	160,000
Total	$360,000	$540,000

a. What are the amount and character of Amy's recognized gain or loss?
b. How would your answers to Part a change if Joan and Stephanie each purchased one-half of Amy's partnership interest for $80,000 cash instead of having the partnership distribute the $160,000 in cash to Amy?

C10-48 ***Exchange of Partnership Interests.*** Josh holds a general partnership interest in the JLK Partnership having a $40,000 basis and a $60,000 FMV. The JLK Partnership is a limited partnership that engages in real estate activities. Diana has an interest in the CDE Partnership having a $20,000 basis and a $60,000 FMV. The CDE Partnership is a general partnership that also engages in real estate activities. Neither partnership has any Sec. 751 assets or any liabilities.
a. What are the tax implications if Josh and Diana simply exchange their partnership interests?
b. What are the tax implications if instead Diana exchanges her general partnership interest in the CDE Partnership for a limited partnership interest in the same partnership (and Josh retains his general partnership interest in the JLK Partnership)?

C10-49 ***Termination of a Partnership.*** Wendy, Xenia, and Yancy own 40%, 8%, and 52%, respectively, of the WXY Partnership. For each of the following independent situations occurring in the current year, determine whether the WXY Partnership terminates and, if so, the date on which the termination occurs.
a. Wendy sells her entire interest to Alan on June 1. Alan sells one-half of the interest to Beth on November 15.
b. Yancy receives a series of liquidating distributions totaling $100,000. He receives four equal annual payments on January 1 of the current year and the three subsequent years.
c. Wendy and Xenia each receive a liquidating distribution on September 14.
d. Yancy sells his interest to Karen on June 1 for $10,000 cash and a $90,000 installment note. The note will be paid in monthly installments of $10,000 principal plus interest (at a rate acceptable to the IRS) beginning on July 1.
e. The WXY and ABC Partnerships combine their businesses on December 30. Ownership of the new, combined partnership is as follows: Wendy, 20%; Xenia, 4%; Yancy, 26.5%; Albert, 20%; Beth, 19.5%; and Carl, 10%.
f. On January 1, the WXY Partnership divides its business into two new businesses. The WX Partnership is owned equally by Wendy and Xenia. Yancy continues his share of the business as a sole proprietorship.

C10-50 ***Termination of a Partnership.*** For each of the following independent situations, determine which partnership(s) (if any) terminate and which partnership(s) (if any) continue.
a. The KLMN Partnership is created when the KL Partnership merges with the MN Partnership. The ownership of the new partnership is held 25% by Katie, 30% by Laura, 25% by Michael, and 20% by Neal.
b. The ABC Partnership, with $150,000 in assets, is owned equally by Amy, Beth, and Chuck. The CD Partnership, with $100,000 in assets, is owned equally by Chuck and Drew. The two partnerships merge and the resulting ABCD Partnership is owned as follows: Amy, 20%; Beth, 20%; Chuck, 40%; and Drew, 20%.
c. The WXYZ Partnership results when the WX and YZ Partnerships merge. Ownership of WXYZ is held equally by the four partners. WX contributes $140,000 in assets, and YZ contributes $160,000 in assets to the new partnership.

d. The DEFG Partnership is owned 20% by Dawn, 40% by Eve, 30% by Frank, and 10% by Greg. Two new partnerships are formed by the division of DEFG. The two new partnerships, the DE and FG Partnerships, are owned in proportion to their relative interests in the DEFG Partnership by the individuals for whom they are named.

e. The HIJK Partnership is owned equally by its four partners, Hal, Isaac, Juan, and Kwangho, before its division. Two new partnerships, the HI and JK Partnerships, are formed out of the division with the new partnerships owned equally by the partners for whom they are named.

C10-51 *Disposal of a Tax Shelter.* Maria purchased an interest in a real estate tax shelter many years ago and deducted losses from its operation for several years. The real property owned by the tax shelter when Maria made her investment has been fully depreciated on a straight-line basis. Her basis in her limited partnership interest is zero, but her share of partnership liabilities is $100,000. Explain the tax results if Maria sells her partnership interest for $5 cash.

C10-52 *Optional Basis Adjustment.* Patty pays $100,000 cash for Stan's one-third interest in the STU Partnership. The partnership has a 754 election in effect. Just before the sale of Stan's interest, STU's balance sheet appears as follows:

	Partnership's Basis	*FMV*
Assets:		
Cash	$ 80,000	$ 80,000
Land	160,000	220,000
Total	$240,000	$300,000
Partner's capital		
Stan	$ 80,000	$100,000
Traffic Corporation	80,000	100,000
Union Corporation	80,000	100,000
Total	$240,000	$300,000

a. What is Patty's total optional basis adjustment?

b. If STU Partnership sells the land for its $220,000 FMV immediately after Patty purchases her interest, how much gain or loss will the partnership recognize?

c. How much gain will Patty report as a result of the sale?

C10-53 *Taxation of LLC Income.* ABC Company, a limited liability company (LLC) organized in the state of Florida, reports using a calendar tax year-end. The LLC chooses to be taxed as a partnership. Alex, Bob, and Carrie (all calendar year taxpayers) own ABC equally, and each has a basis of $40,000 in his or her ABC interest on the first day of the current tax year. ABC has the following results for the current year's operation:

Operating income	$30,000
Short-term capital gain	12,000
Long-term capital loss	6,000

Each owner received a $12,000 cash distribution during the current year.

a. What are the amount and character of the income, gain, and loss Alex must report on his tax return as a result of ABC's operations?

b. What is Alex's basis in his ownership interest in ABC after the current year's operations?

C10-54 *Electing Large Partnership.* Austin & Becker is an electing large partnership. During the current year, the partnership has the following income, loss, and deduction items:

Ordinary income	$5,200,000
Rental loss	(2,000,000)
Long-term capital loss from investments	(437,100)
Short-term capital gain from investments	827,400
Charitable contributions	164,000

a. What ordinary income will Austin & Becker report?

b. What are the separately stated items for Austin & Becker?

C10-55 *Electing Large Partnership.* Happy Times Film Distributions is an electing large partnership. During the current year, the partnership has the following income, loss, and deduction items:

Ordinary income	$ 700,000
Passive income	3,000,000
Sec. 1231 gains	27,000
Sec. 1231 losses	(134,800)
Long-term capital gains from investments	437,600
General business tax credits	43,000

a. What ordinary income will Happy Times report?
b. What are the separately stated items reported by Happy Times?

COMPREHENSIVE PROBLEMS

C10-56 Refer to the facts in Comprehensive Problem C6-54. Now assume the entity is a partnership named Lifecycle Partnership. Additional facts are as follows:

- Except for precontribution gains and losses, the partners agree to share profits and losses in a 60% (Able)—40% (Baker) ratio.
- The partners actively and materially participate in the partnership's business. Thus, the partnership is not a passive activity.
- Partnership debt is recourse debt.
- The salary to Able is a guaranteed payment.
- The refund for the NOL is not relevant to the partnership, nor are the E&P numbers.
- In addition to the numbers provided for the assets on January 2, 2005, the following partnership book values apply:

Equipment	$ 215,000
Building	926,000
Land A	30,000
Land B	20,000
Total	$1,191,000

- On January 2, 2005, the partnership sells its assets and pays off the $2 million debt. The partnership then makes liquidating distributions of the remaining cash to Able and Baker in accordance with their book capital account balances.

Required:

a. Determine the tax consequences of the partnership formation to Able, Baker, and Lifecycle Partnership.
b. For 2002-2004, prepare a schedule showing:
   (1) Partnership ordinary income and other separately stated items
   (2) Able's and Baker's book capital accounts at the end of 2002, 2003, and 2004
   (3) Able's and Baker's bases in their partnership interests at the end of 2002, 2003, and 2004
c. For 2005, determine:
   (1) The results of the asset sales
   (2) Able's and Baker's book capital accounts after the asset sales but before the final liquidating distribution
   (3) Able's and Baker's bases in their partnership interests after the asset sales but before the final liquidating distribution
   (4) The results of the liquidating distributions

C10-57 Anne decides to leave the ABC Partnership after owning the interest for many years. She owns a 52% capital, profits, and loss interest in the general partnership (which is not a service partnership). Anne's basis in her partnership interest is $120,000 just before she leaves the partnership. The partnership agreement does not mention payments to partners who leave the partnership. The partnership has not made an optional basis adjustment election (Sec. 754). All partnership liabilities are recourse liabilities, and Anne's share is equal to her loss interest. When Anne leaves the partnership, the assets and liabilities for the partnership are as follows:

	Partnership's Basis	*FMV*
Assets:		
Cash	$240,000	$240,000
Receivables	–0–	64,000
Inventory	24,000	24,000
Land	60,000	100,000
Total	$324,000	$428,000
Liabilities	$ 60,000	$ 60,000

Analyze the following two alternatives, and answer the associated questions for each alternative.

a. Anne could receive a cash payment of $220,000 from the partnership to terminate her interest in the partnership. Does Anne or the partnership have any income, deduction, gain, or loss? Determine both the amount and character of any items.

b. Carrie already owns a 30% general interest in the ABC partnership prior to Anne's departure. Carrie is willing to buy Anne's partnership interest for a cash payment of $220,000. What income, gain, loss, or deduction will Anne recognize on the sale? What are the tax implications for the partnership if Carrie buys Anne's interest?

TAX STRATEGY PROBLEM

C10-58 Consider the following balance sheet for DEF Partnership:

	Partnership's Basis	*FMV*
Assets:		
Cash	$60,000	$ 60,000
Receivables	–0–	60,000
Land A	10,000	20,000
Land B	10,000	20,000
Land C	10,000	20,000
Total	$90,000	$180,000
Partners' capital:		
Daniel	$30,000	$ 60,000
Edward	30,000	60,000
Frances	30,000	60,000
Total	$90,000	$180,000

Note: Land A, B, and C are Sec. 1231 property, and each partner's outside basis is $30,000.

Suppose Daniel wishes to exit the partnership completely. After discussions with Edward and Frances, the partners agree to let Daniel choose one of three options:

1. Daniel takes a liquidating distribution of $60,000 cash.
2. Daniel takes a pro rata liquidating distribution of $20,000 cash, $20,000 receivables, and Land A (FMV $20,000).
3. Daniel sells his entire partnership interest to Doris for $60,000 cash.

Required:

a. Determine the tax consequences to Daniel of each option including gains (losses) realized, recognized, and deferred; character of gains (losses); and bases of assets.

b. Discuss the relative merits of each option to Daniel, that is, what are the advantages and disadvantages of each option? What factors could sway your recommendation one way or the other?

Note: See Case Study Problem C10-59 for another situation involving various exit strategies.

CASE STUDY PROBLEMS

C10-59 Mark Green and his brother Michael purchased land in Orlando, Florida many years ago. At that time, they began their investing as Green Brothers Partnership with capital they obtained from placing second mortgages on their homes. Their investments have flourished both because of the prosperity and growth of the area and because they have shown an ability to select prime real estate for others to develop. Over the years, they have acquired a great amount of land and have sold some to developers.

Their current tax year has just closed, and the partnership has the following balance sheet:

	Partnership's Basis	*FMV*
Assets:		
Cash	$200,000	$ 200,000
Accounts receivable	90,000	90,000
Land held for investment	310,000	1,010,000
Total	$600,000	$1,300,000
Liabilities and capital:		
Mortgages	$400,000	$ 400,000
Capital—Mark	100,000	450,000
—Michael	100,000	450,000
Total	$600,000	$1,300,000

Mark and Michael each have a basis in their partnership interest of $300,000 including their share of liabilities. They share the economic risk of loss from the liabilities equally. Last spring, Mark had a serious heart attack. On his doctor's advice, Mark wants to retire from all business activity and terminate his interest in the partnership. He is interested in receiving some cash now but is not averse to receiving part of his payment over time.

You have been asked to provide the brothers with information on how to terminate Mark's interest in the partnership. Several possibilities have occurred to Mark and Michael, and they want your advice as to which is best for Mark from a tax standpoint. Michael understands that the resulting choice may not be the best option for him. The possibilities they have considered include the following:

- Michael has substantial amounts of personal cash and could purchase Mark's interest directly. However, the brothers think that option probably would take almost all the cash Michael could raise, and they are concerned about any future cash needs Michael might have. They would prefer to have Mark receive $120,000 now plus $110,000 per year for each of the next three years. Mark also would receive interest at a market rate on the outstanding debt. This alternative would qualify for installment reporting. However, the installment sale rules for related parties would apply.
- The partnership could retire Mark's interest. They have considered the option of paying Mark $150,000 now plus 50% of partnership profits for the next three years. Alternatively, they could arrange for Mark to have a $150,000 payment now and a guaranteed payment of $100,000 per year for the next three years. They expect that the dollar amounts to be received by Mark would be approximately the same for the next three years under these two options. Mark also would receive interest at a market rate on any deferred payments.
- John Watson, a long-time friend of the family, has expressed an interest in buying Mark's interest for $450,000 cash immediately. Michael and John are comfortable that they could work well together.

Mark has substantial amounts of money in savings accounts and in stocks and bonds that have a ready market. He has invested in no other business directly. Assume that Mark's ordinary tax rate is 38% and that his capital gains tax rate is 20%.

Required: Prepare a memorandum summarizing the advice you would give the two brothers on the options that they have considered.

C10-60 Two years ago, Miguel's long-time friend and attorney introduced him to Mr. Azul, a successful businessman who had just purchased some local land. Mr. Azul was planning to purchase a cattle feeding operation and sell limited partnership interests in the business. To sell the interests, he needed an accountant to prepare an opinion about the tax attributes of the operation for use in the prospectus. He told Miguel that he intended to use the same accountant to do all future partnership tax work. Even though he had previously used an accountant from his home state of New York, Mr. Azul said he wanted someone near the cattle feeding operation as the partnership's accountant.

Although Miguel had done previous work with local ranchers, he had no experience with a cattle feeding operation of the scope that Mr. Azul planned. He spent a little time studying the operations and was impressed with Mr. Azul's expertise in lining up interested investors and getting the operation organized. Although the tax advantages discussed in the prospectus looked generous to Miguel, Mr. Azul assured him that they were fairly usual for the industry. Miguel's opinion letter was included in the prospectus, and the limited partnership interests sold quickly.

At the end of the first year of operations, Miguel received the information for preparing the partnership's tax return and filed the return without question. The asset values looked a little high based on local land and cattle values, but Miguel figured that Mr. Azul knew what he was doing. During the second year of operations, local gossip is spreading that the cattle feeding operations are about to fold. However, when Miguel gets information to use in preparing the second year's tax return, the numbers look great and the investors will receive substantial tax benefits. Miguel's curiosity is aroused, so he begins to investigate both Mr. Azul and the cattle feeding operation. Miguel soon realizes that values for the partnership assets were grossly overstated and that Mr. Azul has falsified much of the information he has given Miguel. Miguel believes that the IRS is very likely to start to investigate it. Further, he is concerned that the IRS may try to find him liable under Sec. 6694 for willful negligence if they start investigating the tax shelter.

Required: What should Miguel do now?

TAX RESEARCH PROBLEMS

TAX & FINANCIAL ACCOUNTING

C10-61 Arnie, Becky, and Clay are equal partners in the ABC General Partnership. The three individuals have tax bases in their partnership interests of $80,000, $120,000, and $160,000, respectively, and their financial accounting capital accounts are equal. For business reasons, the partnership needs to be changed into the ABC Corporation, and all three owners agree to the change. The partnership is expected to have the following assets on the date that the change is to occur:

Assets	*Partnership's Tax Basis*	*FMV*	*Partnership's Fin. Acctg. Book Value*
Cash	$ 50,000	$ 50,000	$ 50,000
Accounts receivable	60,000	55,000	55,000
Inventory	150,000	200,000	150,000
Land	200,000	295,000	235,000
Total	$460,000	$600,000	$490,000

Liabilities of $100,000 are currently outstanding and will be owed on the exchange date. Liabilities are shared equally and, as always, are already included in the bases of the partnership interest. The structure being considered for making the change is as follows:

- ABC Partnership transfers all its assets and liabilities to the new ABC Corporation in exchange for all the corporation's stock.
- ABC Partnership then liquidates by distributing the ABC stock to Arnie, Becky, and Clay.

Required: The tax manager you work for has asked you to determine the tax and financial accounting consequences. Describe the financial and tax treatments in a short memorandum to the partnership. Be sure to mention any relevant IRC sections, Treasury Regulations, revenue rulings, and APB or FASB opinions.

C10-62 Della retires from the BCD General Partnership when her basis in her partnership interest is $60,000 including her $10,000 share of liabilities. The partnership is in the business of providing house cleaning services for local residences. At the date of Della's retirement, the partnership's balance sheet is as follows:

	Partnership's Basis	*FMV*
Assets:		
Cash	$ 50,000	$ 50,000
Receivables	–0–	30,000
Equipment[a]	40,000	50,000
Building[b]	90,000	100,000
Land	30,000	40,000
Total	$210,000	$270,000

Liabilities and capital:		
Liabilities	$ 30,000	$ 30,000
Capital—Bruce	60,000	80,000
—Celia	60,000	80,000
—Della	60,000	80,000
Total	$210,000	$270,000

[a] If the equipment were sold for $50,000, the entire gain would be recaptured as Sec. 1245 ordinary income.
[b] The building has been depreciated using the straight-line method.

Della will receive payments of $20,000 cash plus 5% of partnership ordinary income for each of the next five years. The partnership agreement specifies that goodwill will be paid for when a partner retires. Bruce, Celia, and Della agree that the partnership has $21,000 in goodwill when Della retires and that she will be paid for her one-third share.

Required: A tax manager in your firm has asked you to determine the amount and character of the income Della must report for each of the next five years. In addition, he wants you to research the tax consequences of the retirement on the partnership for the next five years. (Assume the partnership earns $100,000 of ordinary income each year for the next five years.) Prepare an oral presentation to be made to Della explaining the tax consequences of the payments she will receive.

C10-63 Pedro owns a 60% interest in the PD General Partnership having a $40,000 basis and $200,000 FMV. His share of partnership liabilities is $100,000. Because he is nearing retirement age, he has decided to give away his partnership interest on June 15 of the current year. The partnership's tax year ends on December 31. Pedro's tax year ends on June 30. He intends to give a 30% interest to his son, Juan, and the remaining 30% interest to the American Red Cross.

Required: A tax manager in your firm has asked you to prepare a letter to Pedro explaining fully the tax consequences of this gift to him, the partnership, and the donees. She reminds you to be sure to include information about the allocation of the current year's partnership income.

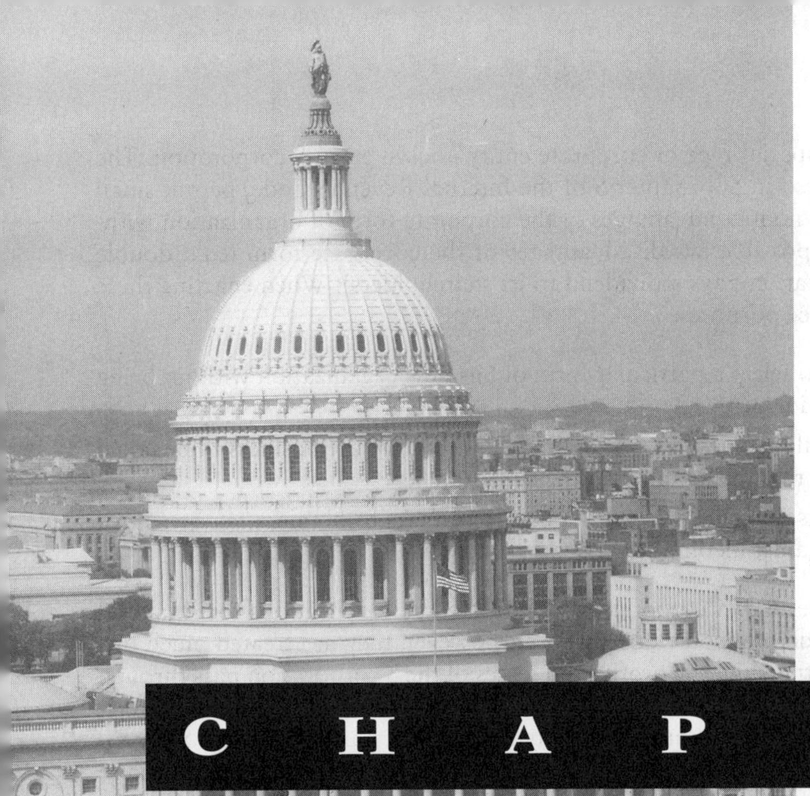

11

CHAPTER

S CORPORATIONS

LEARNING OBJECTIVES

After studying this chapter, you should be able to

1. Explain the requirements for being taxed under Subchapter S
2. Explain the procedures for electing to be taxed under Subchapter S
3. Identify the events that will terminate an S election
4. Determine the permitted tax years for an S corporation
5. Calculate ordinary income or loss
6. Calculate the amount of any special S corporation taxes
7. Calculate a shareholder's allocable share of ordinary income or loss and separately stated items
8. Determine the limitations on a shareholder's deduction of S corporation losses
9. Calculate a shareholder's basis in his or her S corporation's stock and debt
10. Determine the taxability of an S corporation's distributions to its shareholders
11. Explain the procedures for filing an S corporation tax return
12. Determine the estimated tax payments required of an S corporation and its shareholders

CHAPTER OUTLINE

Should an S Election Be Made?...11-3
S Corporation Requirements...11-4
Election of S Corporation Status...11-7
S Corporation Operations...11-13
Taxation of the Shareholder...11-19
Basis Adjustments...11-24
S Corporation Distributions...11-27
Other Rules...11-32
Tax Planning Considerations...11-34
Compliance and Procedural Considerations...11-37

This chapter discusses a special type of corporate entity known as an S corporation. The S corporation rules, located in Subchapter S of the Internal Revenue Code, permit small corporations to enjoy the nontax advantages of the corporate form of organization without being subject to the possible tax disadvantages of the corporate form (e.g., double taxation when the corporation pays a dividend to its shareholders). When enacting these rules, Congress stated three purposes:

- To permit businesses to select a particular form of business organization without being influenced by tax considerations
- To provide aid for small businesses by allowing the income of the business to be taxed to shareholders rather than being taxed at the corporate level
- To permit corporations realizing losses for a period of years to obtain a tax benefit of offsetting the losses against income at the shareholder level[1]

As discussed in Chapter C2, S corporations are treated as corporations for legal and business purposes. For federal income tax purposes, however, they are treated much like partnerships.[2] As in a partnership, the profits and losses of the S corporation pass through to the owners, and the S corporation can make tax-free distributions of earnings previously taxed to its shareholders. Although generally taxed like a partnership, the S corporation still follows many of the basic Subchapter C tax provisions (e.g., S corporations use the corporate tax rules regarding liquidations and tax-free reorganizations instead of the partnership rules). A tabular comparison of the S corporation, partnership, and C corporation rules appears in Appendix F.

REAL-WORLD EXAMPLE

The 1986 Tax Act reduced the top individual tax rate below the top corporate tax rate for the first time in the history of the modern income tax. S corporation filings rose from 826,000 in 1986 to 3.0 million in 2000. The upward trend has continued through 2000 even though the top individual tax rate increased to 39.6% after 1993. Under the 2001 Act, the top individual rate is 38.6% in 2002 and is scheduled to decrease to 35% by 2006.

Recent changes have caused many businesses to reexamine the implications of an S election. First, the restrictive nature of the S corporation requirements has caused many new businesses that were potential S corporations to look at alternative business forms. All 50 states have adopted limited liability company (LLC) legislation. LLCs offer many of the same tax advantages of S corporations because they are treated as partnerships. LLCs, however, are not subject to the same requirements that must be satisfied by an S corporation and its shareholder(s) to make and retain an S election. Partially because of the S corporation restrictions, some new businesses have organized as LLCs to take advantage of the greater operational flexibility the LLC form provides the entity and its owners, as well as its liability protection. A number of small businesses, however, elected to be S corporations because of the greater certainty available within the legal system for corporate entities.

For many existing C corporations, the cost of liquidating the corporate entity and creating an LLC is a prohibitively expensive way to avoid the corporate level income tax (see Chapter C6). However, many of these C corporations have taken the next best alternative, that is, making an S election.

REAL-WORLD EXAMPLE

It is unlikely that large numbers of LLCs, partnerships, or proprietorships will elect to be taxed as an S corporation under the check-the-box regulations. It is more likely that an S election might be made following a conversion of one of these three entity forms into a corporation under state law.

The 1993 Tax Act's increase in the top individual tax rates above the top corporate tax rate caused some S corporations to terminate their S election to take advantage of the lower C corporation rates. Despite the tax cost for high-income taxpayers, the S election still remains a popular business form. Tax legislation in 1996 introduced about 20 changes to the S corporation rules. Some of these changes increased the S corporation's popularity (e.g., the 35 shareholder limit was increased to 75, and the prohibitions against certain entities and trusts becoming S corporation shareholders were lessened). These changes reduced some of the differences between S corporations and LLCs and brought out renewed interest in S corporations and their shareholders.

This chapter examines the requirements for making an S election and the tax rules that apply to S corporations and their shareholders.

---

[1] S. Rept. No. 1983, 85th Cong., 2d Sess., p. 87 (1958).

[2] Some states do not recognize an S corporation as a conduit for state income tax purposes. Instead, they are taxed under the state income tax laws in the same manner as a C corporation.

SHOULD AN S ELECTION BE MADE?

ADVANTAGES OF S CORPORATION TREATMENT

A number of advantages are available to a corporation that makes an S election.

- The corporation's income is exempt from the corporate income tax. An S corporation's income is taxed only to its shareholders, whose tax bracket may be lower than a C corporation's tax bracket.
- The corporation's losses pass through to its shareholders and can be used to reduce the taxes owed on other types of income. This feature can be especially important for new businesses. The corporation can make an S election, pass through the start-up losses to the owners, and terminate the election once a C corporation becomes advantageous.
- Undistributed income taxed to the shareholder is not taxed again when subsequently distributed unless the distribution exceeds the shareholder's basis for his or her stock.
- Capital gains and tax-exempt income are separately stated and retain their character when passed through to the shareholders. Such amounts become commingled with other earnings and are taxed as dividends when distributed by a C corporation.
- Deductions, losses, and tax credits are separately stated and retain their character when passed through to the shareholders. These amounts may be subject to the various limitations at the shareholder level. This treatment can permit the shareholder to claim a tax benefit when it otherwise would be denied to the corporation (e.g., a shareholder can claim the general business credit benefit even though the S corporation reports a substantial loss for the year).
- Splitting the S corporation's income between family members is possible. However, income splitting is restricted by the requirement that reasonable compensation be provided to family members who provide capital and services to the S corporation.
- An S corporation's earnings that flow through to the individual shareholders are not subject to the self-employment tax. In contrast, a partnership must determine what portion of each general partner's net earnings constitutes self-employment income.

DISADVANTAGES OF S CORPORATION TREATMENT

A number of tax disadvantages also exist for a corporation that makes an S election.

- A C corporation is treated as a separate tax entity from its shareholders, thereby permitting its first $50,000 of income to be taxed at a 15% marginal rate instead of the shareholder's marginal rate. In addition, the corporate rates generally are lower than the individual rates and may reduce the total tax burden if the corporation retains the earnings in its business.
- The S corporation's earnings are taxed to the shareholders even though they are not distributed. This treatment may require the corporation to make distributions or salary payments so the shareholder can pay taxes owed on the S corporation's earnings.
- S corporations are subject to an excess net passive income tax and a built-in gains tax. Partnerships are not subject to either of these taxes.
- Dividends received by the S corporation are not eligible for the dividends-received deduction, as is the case for a C corporation.
- Allocation of ordinary income or loss and the separately stated items is based on the stock owned on each day of the tax year. Special allocations of particular items are not permitted, as they are in a partnership.
- The loss limitation for an S corporation shareholder is smaller than for a partner in a partnership because of the treatment of liabilities. Shareholders can increase their loss limitations by the basis of any debt they loan to the S corporation. Partners, on the

KEY POINT

The structure of an S corporation can create a real hardship for a shareholder if large amounts of income flow through without any compensation payments or distributions of cash to help pay the tax on the income.

other hand, can increase their loss limitation by their ratable share of all partnership liabilities.

- S corporations and their shareholders are subject to the at-risk, passive activity limitation, and hobby loss rules. C corporations generally are not subject to these rules.
- An S corporation is restricted in the type and number of shareholders it can have and the capital structure it can use. Partnerships and C corporations are not so restricted.
- S corporations must use a calendar year as their tax year unless they can establish a business purpose for a fiscal year or unless they make a special election to use an otherwise nonpermitted tax year. Similar restrictions also apply to partnerships.

Once the owners decide to incorporate, no general rule determines whether the corporation should make an S election. Before making a decision, management and the shareholders should examine the long- and short-run tax and non-tax advantages and disadvantages of filing as a C corporation versus filing as an S corporation. Unlike a consolidated return election, the S election can be revoked or terminated at any time with minimal effort.

S CORPORATION REQUIREMENTS

OBJECTIVE 1

Explain the requirements for being taxed under Subchapter S

The S corporation requirements are divided into two categories: shareholder-related and corporation-related requirements. A corporation that satisfies all the requirements is known as a small business corporation. Only small business corporations can make an S election. Each set of requirements is outlined below.

SHAREHOLDER-RELATED REQUIREMENTS

Three shareholder-related requirements must be satisfied on each day of the tax year.[3]

- The corporation must not have more than 75 shareholders.
- All shareholders must be individuals, estates, certain tax-exempt organizations, or certain kinds of trusts.
- None of the individual shareholders can be classified as a nonresident **alien.**

ADDITIONAL COMMENT

The Sec. 1244 stock rules (Chapter C2) and the S corporation rules both use the term *small business corporations.* The definitions have different requirements, although most S corporation stock can qualify as Sec. 1244 stock.

75-SHAREHOLDER RULE. Section 1361(c)(1) treats a husband and wife (and their estates) as a single shareholder for purposes of applying the 75-shareholder limit. When two unmarried individuals own stock jointly (e.g., as tenants in common or as joint tenants), each owner is considered a separate shareholder.

REAL-WORLD EXAMPLE

In 1998, 84.3% of all S corporations had one or two owners. Only 0.75% of the 2.59 million S corporations that filed in 1998 had more than ten owners.

ELIGIBLE SHAREHOLDERS. Corporations and partnerships cannot own S corporation stock. This restriction prevents a corporation or a partnership having a large number of owners from avoiding the 75-shareholder limitation by purchasing S corporation stock and being treated as a single shareholder. Organizations exempt from the federal income tax under Sec. 501(a) (e.g., a tax-exempt public charity or private foundation) can hold S corporation stock starting in 1998. These organizations count as one shareholder when calculating the 75-shareholder limit.

Seven types of trusts can own S corporation stock: grantor trusts, voting trusts,[4] testamentary trusts, **qualified Subchapter S trusts (QSSTs),**[5] qualified retirement plan trusts,

---

[3] Secs. 1361(b)(1)(A)–(C).

[4] A **voting trust** is an arrangement whereby the stock owned by a number of shareholders is placed under the control of a trustee, who exercises the voting rights possessed by the stock. One reason for creating a voting trust is to increase the voting power of a group of minority shareholders in the selection of corporate directors or the establishment of corporate policies.

[5] A QSST is a domestic trust that owns stock in one or more S corporations and distributes (or is required to distribute) all its income to its sole income beneficiary. The income beneficiary must make an irrevocable election to have the QSST rules of Sec. 1361(d) apply. The beneficiary is treated as the owner (and, therefore, the shareholder) of the portion of the trust consisting of the S corporation stock. A separate election is made for each S corporation's stock owned by the trust.

small business trusts, and beneficiary-controlled trusts (i.e., trusts that distribute all their income to a single income beneficiary who is treated as the owner of the trust). Grantor trusts, QSSTs, and beneficiary-controlled trusts can own S corporation stock only if the grantor or the beneficiary is a qualified shareholder. Each beneficiary of a voting trust also must be an eligible shareholder. A qualified retirement plan trust is one formed as part of a qualified stock bonus, pension, or profit sharing plan or employee stock ownership plan (ESOP) that is exempt from the federal income tax under Sec. 501(a).

ETHICAL POINT

Tax professionals must assist their clients in monitoring that the S corporation requirements are met on each day of the tax year. Failing to meet one of the requirements for even one day terminates the election. Ignoring the fact that a terminating event has occurred until it is discovered in an IRS audit probably will cause the corporation to be taxed as a C corporation and prevent it from having the termination treated as being inadvertent.

Small business trusts can own S corporation stock starting in 1997. These trusts can be complex trusts and primarily are used as estate planning devices. No interest in a small business trust can be acquired in a "purchase" transaction, that is, a transaction where the holder's interest takes a cost basis under Sec. 1012. Interests in small business trusts generally are acquired as a result of a gift or bequest. All current beneficiaries of a small business trust must be individuals, estates, or charitable organizations. Current beneficiaries are parties that can receive an income distribution for the period in question. Each beneficiary is counted for purposes of the 75-shareholder limit. QSSTs and tax-exempt trusts are ineligible to elect to be a small business trust. The trustee must make an election to obtain small business trust status.

A testamentary trust (i.e., a trust created under the terms of a will) that receives S corporation stock can hold the stock and continue to be an eligible shareholder for a two-year period, beginning on the date the stock transfers to the trust. A grantor trust that held S corporation stock immediately before the death of the deemed owner, and which continues in existence after the death of the deemed owner, can continue to hold the stock and be an eligible shareholder for the two-year period beginning on the date of the deemed owner's death. Charitable remainder unitrusts and charitable remainder annuity trusts do not qualify as small business trusts.

EXAMPLE C11-1 ▶ Joan, a U.S. citizen, owns 25% of Waldo Corporation's stock. Waldo is an electing S corporation. At the time of her death in the current year, the Waldo stock passes to Joan's estate. The estate is a qualifying shareholder, and the transfer does not affect the S election. If the stock subsequently transfers to a trust provided for in Joan's will, the testamentary trust can hold the Waldo stock for a two-year period before the election terminates. ◀

The trust in Example C11-1 can hold the S corporation stock for an indefinite period of time only if the trust's income beneficiary makes an election to have it treated as a QSST or small business trust. Otherwise, the S election will be terminated at the end of the two-year period.

ALIEN INDIVIDUALS. Individuals who are not U.S. citizens (i.e., alien individuals) can own S corporation stock only if they are U.S. residents or are married to a U.S. citizen or resident alien and make an election to be taxed as a resident alien. The S election terminates if an alien individual purchases S corporation stock and does not reside in the United States or has not made the appropriate election.

CORPORATION-RELATED REQUIREMENTS

Three corporation-related requirements must be satisfied on each day of the tax year:

- The corporation must be a domestic corporation.
- The corporation must not be an "ineligible" corporation.
- The corporation must have only one class of stock.[6]

The first requirement precludes a foreign corporation from making an S election.

A corporation may be an ineligible corporation and thereby violate the second requirement in one of two ways:

- Corporations that maintain a special federal income tax status are not eligible to make an S election. For example, financial institutions (e.g., banks) that use the reserve method to account for bad debts and insurance companies are not eligible.

---

[6] Sec. 1361(b)(1).

- Corporations that have elected the special Puerto Rico and U.S. possessions tax credit (Sec. 936) or the special Domestic International Sales Corporation tax exemption are ineligible to make the S election.

REAL-WORLD EXAMPLE

The 1996 Act changes to the S corporation stock ownership rules and the approval of the check-the-box regulations permit great flexibility in creating groups of entities that fit the business needs of their owners.

S corporations can own the stock of a C corporation or an S corporation without any limitation on the percentage of voting power or value held. However, as mentioned earlier, a C corporation cannot own the stock of an S corporation. An S corporation that owns the stock of a C corporation cannot participate in the filing of a consolidated tax return. An S corporation also can own the stock of a **Qualified Subchapter S Subsidiary** (QSSS). A QSSS is a domestic corporation that qualifies as an S corporation, is 100% owned by an S corporation, and for which the parent S corporation elects to treat the subsidiary as a QSSS. The assets, liabilities, income, deductions, losses, etc. of the QSSS are treated as those of its S corporation parent and reported on the parent's tax return.[7]

A corporation that has two classes of stock issued and outstanding has violated the third requirement and cannot be an S corporation. The single class of stock determination is more difficult than it appears at first glance because of the many different financial arrangements that are possible between an S corporation and its shareholders. A corporation is treated as having only one class of stock if all of its outstanding shares of stock possess identical rights to distribution and liquidation proceeds and the corporation has not issued any instrument or obligation, or entered into any arrangement, that is treated as a second class of stock.[8] A second class of stock is not created if the only difference between the two classes of stock relates to voting rights.[9]

EXAMPLE C11-2 ▶ Kelly Corporation has two classes of common stock outstanding. The Class A and Class B common stock give the shareholders identical rights and interests in the profits and assets of the corporation. Class A stock has one vote per share. Class B stock is nonvoting. Kelly Corporation is treated as having only one class of stock outstanding and can make an S election. ◀

GENERAL RULES. The determination of whether all outstanding shares of stock confer identical rights to distribution and liquidation proceeds is based on the corporate charter, articles of incorporation, bylaws, applicable state law, and binding agreements relating to distribution and liquidation proceeds (i.e., the governing agreements).[10] Treasury Regulations permit certain types of state laws, agreements, distributions, etc., to be disregarded in determining whether all of a corporation's outstanding shares confer identical rights to distribution and liquidation proceeds. These include

- Agreements to purchase stock at the time of death, divorce, disability, or termination of employment
- Distributions made on the basis of the shareholder's varying stock interests during the year
- Distributions that differ in timing (e.g., one shareholder receives a distribution in the current year and a second shareholder receives a similar dollar amount distribution shortly after the beginning of the next tax year)

Agreements to increase cash or property distributions to shareholders who bear heavier state income tax burdens so as to provide equal after-tax distributions provide unequal distribution and liquidation rights. The unequal distributions probably will cause a second class of stock to be created. However, state laws that require a corporation to pay or withhold state income taxes on behalf of some or all of a corporation's shareholders are disregarded.

DEBT INSTRUMENTS. Debt instruments, corporate obligations, and deferred compensation arrangements, in general, are not treated as a second class of stock.[11] A number of

---

[7] Sec. 1361(c)(2)(3).
[8] Reg. Sec. 1.1361-1(l).
[9] Sec. 1361(c)(4).
[10] Reg. Sec. 1.1361-1(l)(2).
[11] Reg. Sec. 1.1361-1(l)(4)(i). An exception applies to debt instruments, corporate obligations, and deferred compensation arrangements that are treated as stock under the general principles of the federal tax law where the principal purpose for the debt instrument, etc., is to circumvent the distribution or liquidation proceeds rights provided for by the outstanding stock or to circumvent the 75-shareholder limit.

safe harbors exist for characterizing corporate obligations as debt (and not as a second class of stock):

- Unwritten advances from a shareholder that do not exceed $10,000 during the tax year, are treated as debt by the two parties, and are expected to be repaid within a reasonable time
- Obligations that are considered equity under the general tax laws, but are owned solely by the shareholders in the same proportion as the corporations's outstanding stock

KEY POINT

If debt instruments satisfy the safe harbor rules, such instruments cannot be construed as equity. However, such debt must have been issued in an S corporation tax year.

Section 1361(c)(5) provides a safe harbor for straight debt instruments so that the debt is not treated as a second class of stock. For debt to qualify under the safe harbor, it must meet the following requirements if issued while an S election is in effect:

- The debt must represent an unconditional promise to pay a certain sum of money on a specified date or on demand.
- The interest rate and interest payment dates must not be contingent on profits, the borrower's discretion, or similar factors.[12]
- The debt must not be convertible directly or indirectly into stock.
- The creditor must be an individual, estate, or trust eligible to be an S corporation shareholder, or a nonindividual creditor actively and regularly engaged in the business of lending money.[13]

The safe harbor rules can apply to debt even if the debt otherwise would be considered a second class of stock under case law or other IRC provisions. An obligation that originally qualifies as straight debt may no longer qualify if it is materially modified so that it no longer satisfies the safe harbor or is transferred to a third party who is not an eligible shareholder.[14]

ELECTION OF S CORPORATION STATUS

OBJECTIVE 2

Explain the procedures for electing to be taxed under Subchapter S

The S election exempts a corporation from all taxes imposed by Chapter 1 of the Internal Revenue Code (Secs. 1-1399) except for the following:

- Sec. 1374 built-in gains tax
- Sec. 1375 excess net passive income tax
- Sec. 1363(d) LIFO recapture tax
- Recapture of previously claimed investment tax credits

This rule exempts the S corporation from the regular income tax, accumulated earnings tax, the personal holding company tax, and the corporate alternative minimum tax for the tax year in which the election is first effective and all subsequent tax years the election remains in effect.

The S election affects the shareholders in three ways:

- The shareholders must report their pro rata share of the S corporation's ordinary income or loss as well as any separately stated items.
- Distributions made to the shareholders come under special rules that generally treat most distributions as a tax-free recovery of the shareholders' stock investments.
- The shareholders' bases in their stock are adjusted for the shareholders' ratable share of ordinary income or loss and any separately stated items.

---

[12] That the interest rate depends on the prime rate or a similar factor not related to the debtor corporation will not disqualify the instrument from coming under the safe harbor rules. If the interest being paid is unreasonably high, an appropriate portion may be treated as a payment of something other than interest.

[13] Sec. 1361(c)(5).

[14] Reg. Sec. 1.1361-1(l)(5)(ii) and (iii).

MAKING THE ELECTION

Only small business corporations can make the S election.[15] For a small business corporation to make a valid S election, the corporation must file a timely election (Form 2553), and all the corporation's shareholders must consent to the election. Existing corporations can make a timely S election at any time during the tax year preceding the year for which the election is to be effective or on or before the fifteenth day of the third month of the year for which the election is to be effective.

For a new corporation, the S election can be made at any time on or before the fifteenth day of the third month of its initial tax year. A new corporation's initial tax year begins with the first day on which the corporation has shareholders, acquires assets, or begins business.

If the S election is made during the first 2½ months of the tax year for which it is first to be effective, the corporation also must meet all the small business corporation requirements on each day of the tax year that precedes the election date and on the election date. If the corporation fails to meet one of the requirements on any day that precedes the election date, the election becomes effective in the S corporation's next tax year.

The tax law, however, provides some relief for improper elections. First, if the corporation misses the deadline for making the S corporation election, the IRS can treat the election as timely made if the IRS determines that the corporation had reasonable cause for making the late election. Second, if the election was ineffective because the corporation inadvertently failed to qualify as a small business corporation or because it inadvertently failed to obtain shareholder consents (see below), the IRS nevertheless can honor the election if the corporation and shareholders take steps to correct the deficiency within a reasonable period of time.[16]

EXAMPLE C11-3 ▶ Wilco Corporation, a calendar year taxpayer, has been in existence for several years. Wilco wants to be treated as an S corporation for 2003 and subsequent years. The corporation can make the election any time during 2002 or between January 1 and March 17, 2003 (March 15 falls on a Saturday). If the corporation makes the election after March 17, 2003, it becomes effective in 2004. However, if Wilco Corporation can show reasonable cause for making the late election, the IRS may allow the election to be effective for 2003. ◀

SELF-STUDY QUESTION

Would the answer to Example C11-3 change if Wilco is a member of an affiliated group through January 15, 2003?

ANSWER

Yes. Because Wilco is an ineligible corporation for a portion of the 2½-month period of 2003, an S election would not be effective until January 1, 2004.

CONSENT OF SHAREHOLDERS. Each person who is a shareholder on the election date must consent to the election. The consent is binding on the current tax year and all future tax years. No additional consents are required of shareholders who acquire the stock between the election date and its effective date or at any subsequent date.

Section 1362(b)(2) imposes a special rule on the shareholders when the corporation makes an election after the beginning of the tax year for which it is to be effective. Each shareholder who owned stock at any time during the portion of the year that precedes the time the election is made, and who is not a shareholder at the time the election is made, also must consent to the election.

EXAMPLE C11-4 ▶ Sara and Harry own all of Kraft Corporation's stock. Sara sells all her Kraft stock to Lisa on February 10. The next day Kraft makes an S election. For the election to apply in the current year, Sara, Harry, and Lisa must consent to the election. If Sara refuses to consent to the election, the election will not begin until next year. ◀

Each tenant (whether or not husband and wife) must consent to the S election if the shareholders own the stock as tenants in common, joint tenants, or tenants in the entirety. If the shareholders own the S corporation stock as community property, each person hav-

---

15 Election rules are in Sec. 1362.

16 The IRS spells out procedures for relief in Rev. Proc. 98-55, 1998-2 C.B. 643.

ing a community property interest must consent to the election. If the shareholder is a minor, either the minor or the minor's legal representative (e.g., a natural parent or legal guardian) can make the consent.

Topic Review C11-1 summarizes the S corporation requirements and procedures for making the S election.

OBJECTIVE 3

Identify the events that will terminate the S election

TERMINATION OF THE ELECTION

Once made, the S election remains in effect until the corporation either revokes the election or terminates the election because it ceases to meet the small business corporation requirements. Each action is examined below.[17] The requirements for making a new S election following a termination also are discussed.

REVOCATION OF THE ELECTION. A corporation can revoke its S election in any tax year as long as it meets the requirements regarding shareholder consent and timeliness. Shareholders owning more than one-half the corporation's stock (including nonvoting stock) on the day the corporation makes the revocation must consent to the revocation. A revocation made on or before the fifteenth day of the third month of the tax year is effective on the first day of the S corporation's tax year. A revocation made after the first 2½ months of the tax year is effective on the first day of the next tax year. An exception permits the S corporation to select a prospective date for the revocation to be effective. The prospective date can be the date the corporation makes the revocation or any subsequent date.

EXAMPLE C11-5 ▶ Adobe Corporation, a calendar year taxpayer, has been an S corporation for several years. However, the corporation has become quite profitable, and management feels that it would be advantageous to make a public stock offering to obtain additional capital during 2003. Adobe can revoke its S election any time before March 18, 2003, making the revocation effective on January 1, 2003. If the corporation makes the revocation election after March 17, 2003, it does not take effect until January 1, 2004. In either case, the corporation may specify a prospective 2003 revocation date as long as the date specified is on or after the date it makes the revocation. ◀

TAX STRATEGY TIP

When it is difficult to obtain the majority shareholder vote necessary for revocation, consideration should be given to purposely triggering a termination event.

TERMINATION OF THE ELECTION. The S election terminates if the corporation fails one or more of the small business corporation requirements on any day after the first day the election is effective. The termination generally occurs on the day of the terminating event. Events that can terminate the election include

- ▶ Exceeding the 75-shareholder limit
- ▶ Having an ineligible shareholder own some of the stock
- ▶ Creating a second class of stock
- ▶ Attaining a prohibited tax status
- ▶ Selecting an improper tax year
- ▶ Failing the passive investment income test for three consecutive years

The passive investment income test applies annually. It terminates the S election if more than 25% of the corporation's gross receipts are passive investment income for each of three consecutive tax years *and* the corporation has Subchapter C earnings and profits (E&P) at the end of each of the three consecutive tax years. If the corporation meets these conditions for three consecutive tax years, the election terminates on the first day of the next (fourth) tax year.

Passive investment income includes royalties, rents,[18] dividends, interest, annuities, and gains from the sale or exchange of stocks and securities. Regulation Sec. 1.1362-2(c)(5) holds that passive investment income excludes income derived from the active con-

[17] Termination and revocation rules are in Sec. 1362.

[18] Regulation Sec. 1.1362-2(c)(5)(ii)(B)(2) excludes from rents payments received for the use or occupancy of property if the corporation provides significant services or incurs substantial costs in the rental business. See page C11-36 for additional explanations of the significant services and substantial costs definitions.

Topic Review C11-1

S Corporation Requirements and Election Procedures

Requirements

Shareholder-related:

1. The corporation may have no more than 75 shareholders. Husbands and wives and their estates count as one shareholder.
2. All shareholders must be individuals, estates, certain kinds of trusts, or certain kinds of tax-exempt organizations. Eligible trusts include grantor trusts, voting trusts, testamentary trusts, beneficiary-controlled trusts, qualified Subchapter S trusts, qualified retirement plan trusts, and small business trusts.
3. All the individual shareholders must be U.S. citizens or resident aliens.

Corporation-related:

1. The corporation must be a domestic corporation or an unincorporated entity that makes an election to be taxed as a domestic corporation.
2. The corporation must not be an ineligible corporation (e.g., an ineligible bank or other financial institution, an insurance company, or a foreign corporation).
3. The corporation must have only one class of stock issued and outstanding. Differences in voting rights are ignored.

Making the Election

1. The corporation can make the S election any time during the tax year preceding the year for which the election is effective or on or before the fifteenth day of the third month of the tax year for which the election is effective. Late elections are effective with the next tax year unless the corporation obtains IRS relief for reasonable cause.
2. Each shareholder who owns stock on the date the corporation makes the election must consent to the election. If the corporation makes the election after the beginning of the tax year, each person who was a shareholder during the portion of the tax year preceding the election also must consent to the election.

duct of a trade or business. Subchapter C E&P includes only earnings that accrued in tax years in which an S election was not in effect (i.e., the corporation was taxed under the C corporation rules).

EXAMPLE C11-6 ▶ Silver Corporation is created in the current year and promptly makes an S election. Silver can earn an unlimited amount of passive income during a tax year without any fear of losing its S corporation status or being subject to the Sec. 1375 tax on excess net passive income because it has never been a C corporation and thus has no Subchapter C E&P. (See pages C11-15 and C11-16 for a discussion of this tax.) ◀

HISTORICAL NOTE

Previously, a termination was deemed to be effective on the first day of the tax year in which the terminating event occurred. To stop potential abuse, the rule was changed so that an S election terminates on the day of the terminating event.

ALLOCATION OF INCOME. If a terminating event occurs at some time other than on the first day of the tax year, an S termination year is created. The **S termination year** is divided into an S short year and C short year. The **S short year** begins on the first day of the tax year and ends on the day preceding the day on which the termination is effective. The **C short year** begins on the day on which the termination is effective and continues through the last day of the corporation's tax year.

EXAMPLE C11-7 ▶ Dixon Corporation has been an S corporation for several years. Paula and Frank each own one-half of Dixon's stock. Paula sells one-half of her Dixon stock to Eagle Corporation on July 1. The sale terminates the S election on July 1 because Eagle Corporation is an ineligible shareholder. Assuming that Dixon is a calendar year taxpayer, the S short year includes the period January 1 through June 30. The C short year includes the period July 1 through December 31. ◀

The S corporation's shareholders report the S short year income according to the normal reporting rules described below. The C corporation reports the income earned during the

TAX STRATEGY TIP

Income/loss can be allocated in the termination year under either of two methods. Careful consideration should be given to the possible tax advantages of a daily allocation versus an actual closing of the books. See Tax Planning Considerations for further details.

ADDITIONAL COMMENT

To use an actual closing of the books to allocate the income/loss of Dixon in Example C11-7, Eagle Corporation must consent. Due to the consequences of such an election, the method of allocation should be considered in negotiating the Dixon stock sale.

C short year. The C short year income tax liability is calculated on an annualized basis (see Chapter C3). The S short year and C short year returns are due on the due date for the corporation's tax return for the tax year had the termination not occurred (including any extensions).

Two rules can be used to allocate the termination year's income between the S short year and the C short year. The general rule of Sec. 1362(e)(2) allocates the ordinary income or loss and the separately stated items between the S short year and C short year based on the number of days in each year. A special election under Sec. 1362(e)(3) permits the allocation to be made according to the corporation's normal tax accounting rules. The special allocation can be used only if all persons who were shareholders at any time during the S short year and all persons who are shareholders on the first day of the C short year consent to the election. A daily allocation cannot be used when an S termination year occurs and, during such year, sales or exchanges of 50 percent or more of the corporation's outstanding stock occur. In such a case, the corporation's normal accounting rules must be used to make the allocation.

INADVERTENT TERMINATION. Special rules permit the S election to continue if an inadvertent termination occurs by ceasing to be a small business corporation or by failing the passive investment income test for three consecutive years. If such a termination occurs, the S corporation or its shareholders must take the necessary steps, within a reasonable time period after discovering the event creating the termination, to restore its small business corporation status. If the IRS determines that the termination was inadvertent, the corporation and all persons owning stock during the termination period must agree to make the adjustments necessary to report the income for this period as if the S election had been in effect continuously.[19]

EXAMPLE C11-8 ▶ Frye Corporation was created in 1999 and operated as a C corporation during that year. Frye made an S election in 2000. During 1999, the corporation incorrectly computed its E&P and believed that no Subchapter C E&P existed for its only pre–S corporation tax year. From 2000 through 2002, Frye earns large amounts of passive income but does not pay the Sec. 1375 excess net passive income tax or worry about termination of its election because it thinks it has no accumulated E&P from 1999. Upon auditing Frye's tax returns, the IRS finds that Subchapter C E&P, in fact, did exist from 1999 and terminates the S election effective on January 1, 2003. If the corporation distributes the E&P and the shareholders report the dividend income, the IRS probably will treat the occurrence as an inadvertent termination and not revoke the election. ◀

OTHER IRS WAIVERS. The IRS not only can waive a termination it deems to be inadvertent, it also can validate certain invalid elections. Validation of an invalid election can occur when the election failed to meet the basic S corporation requirements of Sec. 1361 or failed to provide the necessary shareholder consents. The IRS also can exercise this authority in situations where a corporation never filed an election. In addition, the IRS can treat a late-filed S election as being timely filed if the IRS determines that reasonable cause existed for failing to make a timely election.[20] To obtain relief for a late election, the corporation must have the IRS issue a private letter ruling. Committee reports to the 1996 tax legislation enacting these rules indicate that Congress intended for the IRS to be reasonable in exercising this authority and apply standards similar to those applied to inadvertent terminations and other late or invalid elections.

NEW ELECTION FOLLOWING A TERMINATION. A corporation that terminates its S election must wait five tax years before making a new election.[21] This delay applies

[19] Regulation Sec. 1.1362-4(b) holds that a termination will be inadvertent if the terminating event was not reasonably within the control of the corporation and was not part of a plan to terminate the election or if it took place without the corporation's knowledge and reasonable safeguards were in place to prevent the event from occurring.

[20] See Rev. Procs. 97-48, 1997-2 C.B. 521, and 98-55, 1998-2 C.B. 643, for additional guidance on this issue and a special transition rule.

[21] *Termination* includes both revocation of the S election and loss of the election because one or more of the small business corporation requirements were not met.

unless the IRS consents to an earlier reelection. Regulation Sec. 1.1362-5(a) indicates that permission for an early reelection can occur (1) when more than 50% of the corporation's stock is owned by persons who did not own stock on the date of termination or (2) when the event causing the termination was not reasonably within the control of the corporation or the shareholders having a substantial interest in the corporation *and* was not part of a plan to terminate the election involving the corporation or such shareholders.

EXAMPLE C11-9 ▶ Terri owns Victor Corporation, a calendar year taxpayer, which has been an S corporation for ten years. In January 2001, Terri sells all the Victor stock to Michelle. Payments for the stock are to be made over a five-year period. In March 2003, Michelle fails to make the necessary payments and Terri repossesses the stock. During the time Michelle holds the stock, Victor Corporation revokes its S election. Victor Corporation should be able to immediately apply for reelection of S status because a more than 50% ownership change has occurred since the date of termination. ◀

AVOIDING THE TERMINATION OF AN S ELECTION. Termination of an S election generally results in substantial negative tax consequences in the form of increased corporate or shareholder taxes. The S corporation's owners, management, and tax advisor need to understand the various events that can cause the termination of the S election. Some of the steps that can be taken to prevent an untimely termination include the following:

- Monitor all transfers of S corporation stock. Make certain that the purchaser or transferee of the stock is not an ineligible shareholder (e.g., corporation, partnership, or nonresident alien) or that the total number of shareholders does not exceed 75 (e.g., a seventy-sixth shareholder resulting from creation of a joint interest).
- Establish procedures for the S corporation to purchase the stock of deceased shareholders to avoid the stock being acquired by a trust that is ineligible to be a shareholder.
- Establish restrictions on the transferability of the S corporation stock by having the shareholders enter into a stock purchase agreement. Such an agreement could provide that the stock cannot be transferred without the prior consent of all other shareholders and, if the necessary consent cannot be obtained, the stock will be repurchased by the corporation at a specified price (e.g., at book value).
- Monitor the passive income earned by an S corporation that previously had been a C corporation for one or more years. Make certain the passive income requirement is not failed for three consecutive years by taking action to reduce the level of passive income or to distribute the Subchapter C E&P.

WHAT WOULD YOU DO IN THIS SITUATION?

Harry Baker formed Xeno Corporation on January 4, 2000. The corporation filed a valid S corporation election on January 17, 2000 to be effect for 2000. Harry, the corporation's sole shareholder, consented to the election. The corporation had business ties to Mexico, and to strengthen these ties, Harry sold 25% of his Xeno shares to Pedro Gonzales on February 12, 2001. Pedro is one of Harry's business associates and is a citizen and resident of Mexico. Harry continued to operate Xeno as an S corporation throughout 2001. On March 3, 2002, Harry read an article on S corporations that made him aware that, by selling stock to an ineligible shareholder, he may have jeopardized the corporation's S election. Thus, Harry immediately contacted Pedro and persuaded Pedro to sell his Xeno shares back to him (Harry). Harry hires you as his tax advisor on December 16, 2002, at which time you learn about the sale and repurchase of the Xeno shares. However, Harry tells you not to worry because, by buying back the shares, he already has rectified the situation, and thus the IRS need not be told about the transfers. How do you advise Harry on this matter?

S CORPORATION OPERATIONS

S corporations make the same accounting period and accounting method elections that a C corporation makes. Each year, the S corporation must compute and report to the IRS and to its shareholders its ordinary income or loss and its separately stated items. The special S corporation rules are explained below.

OBJECTIVE 4

Determine the permitted tax years for an S corporation

TAXABLE YEAR

Section 1378(a) requires that the S corporation's taxable year be a permitted year. A permitted year is defined as

- A taxable year ending on December 31 (including a 52–53 week year)
- Any fiscal year for which the corporation establishes a business purpose[22]

Section 1378(b) specifically notes that income deferral for the shareholders is not a necessary business purpose. An S corporation that adopts a fiscal year coinciding with its natural business year has satisfied the business purpose requirement. The natural business year for an S corporation depends on the type of business conducted. When a trade or business has nonpeak and peak periods of business, the natural business year is considered to end at, or soon after, the close of the peak business period. A business whose income is steady from month to month, year-round, does not have a natural business year.[23]

EXAMPLE C11-10 ▶ Sable Corporation, an electing S corporation, operates a ski resort and reports $1 million of gross receipts for each of its last three tax years. If at least $250,000 (25% of gross receipts) of the receipts are included in the months of February and March for each of the three consecutive years, Sable can adopt, or change to, or continue to use a natural business year ending March 31.[24] ◀

An S corporation's adoption of, or a change to, a fiscal year that is an ownership tax year also is permitted. An ownership tax year is the same tax year used by shareholders owning more than 50% of the corporation's outstanding stock. The 50% requirement must be met on the first day of the tax year to which the change relates. Failure to meet the 50% ownership requirement on the first day of any later tax year requires a change to a calendar year or other approved fiscal year. S corporations also can adopt or change to a fiscal year for which IRS approval is obtained based on the facts and circumstances of the situation.[25]

ADDITIONAL COMMENT

The requirement that all S corporations adopt calendar years (with March 15 return due dates) caused a hardship for tax return preparers. Section 444 is a compromise provision that allows a fiscal year for filing purposes, but it mandates a special payment of the deferred taxes.

Section 444 permits an S corporation to elect a fiscal year other than a permitted year. The fiscal year elected under Sec. 444 must have a deferral period of three months or less (e.g., a September 30 or later fiscal year-end for an S corporation otherwise required to use a calendar year). An S corporation that is changing its tax year can elect to use a new fiscal year under Sec. 444 only if the deferral period is no longer than the shorter of three months or the deferral period of the tax year that is being changed.[26] A Sec. 444 election is not required of an S corporation that satisfies the business purpose exception.

S corporations that elect a fiscal year under Sec. 444 must make the necessary required payments under Sec. 7519, which approximate the deferral benefit of the fiscal year. Revocation or termination of the S election also terminates the Sec. 444 election unless the corporation becomes a personal service corporation. Termination of the Sec. 444 election permits the S corporation to obtain a refund of prior Sec. 7519 payments.

Topic Review C11-2 summarizes the alternative tax years available to an S corporation.

[22] Some S corporations use a "grandfathered" fiscal year, which is a fiscal year for which IRS approval was obtained after June 30, 1974. Excluded are fiscal years that result in an income deferral of three months or less.

[23] Rev. Procs. 74-33, 1974-2 C.B. 489, and 87-32, 1987-2 C.B. 396.

[24] See Rev. Proc. 87-32, 1987-2 C.B. 396 for an explanation of the 25% test.

[25] Regulation Sec. 18.1378-1 and Rev. Proc. 87-32, 1987-2 C.B. 396, explain the procedures for an S corporation adopting a fiscal year or changing the tax year of a new or existing S corporation. Rev. Rul. 87-57, 1987-2 C.B. 224, examines eight situations concerning whether the tax year is a permitted year.

[26] Special Sec. 444 transitional rules for 1986 permitted many S corporations to retain a previously adopted fiscal year (e.g., January 31) even though the deferral period is longer than three months.

Topic Review C11-2

Alternative S Corporation Tax Years

TAX YEAR	REQUIREMENTS
Calendar year (including certain 52–53 week years)	The permitted tax year that is required unless one of the other exceptions applies.
Permitted fiscal year:	IRS approval will be granted if:
a. Ownership year	The tax year requested is the same as that used by shareholders owing more than 50% of the corporation's outstanding stock. This test must be met on the first day of the year for which approval is requested as well as for each succeeding year.
b. Natural business year	25% or more of the gross receipts for each of the three most recent 12-month periods are in the last two months of the requested tax year.
c. Facts and circumstances year	A business purpose (other than an ownership year or natural business year) is established using the facts and circumstances of the situation.
Nonpermitted fiscal year	A Sec. 444 election permits the S corporation to use an otherwise nonpermitted tax year if the deferral period is three months or less and the corporation makes the necessary required payments.

ACCOUNTING METHOD ELECTIONS

The accounting method elections used to compute ordinary income or loss and the separately stated items are made by the S corporation rather than the individual shareholders. As with a partnership, the S corporation makes these elections independent of the accounting method elections made by its shareholders. Three elections generally reserved for the S corporation's shareholders are as follows:

- Sections 108(b)(5) or (c)(3) relating to income from the discharge of indebtedness
- Section 617 election relating to deduction and recapture of mining exploration expenditures
- Section 901 election to take a credit for foreign income taxes[27]

OBJECTIVE 5

Calculate ordinary income or loss

ORDINARY INCOME OR LOSS AND SEPARATELY STATED ITEMS

S corporations do not compute taxable income in the same manner as do C corporations. Instead, they are treated much like partnerships and thus report both an ordinary income or loss amount and a series of separately stated items. Ordinary income or loss is the net of income and deductions other than the separately stated items described in the next paragraph.

KEY POINT

S corporations are most like partnerships in their method of reporting income/losses. Both are flowthrough entities that provide K-1s to their owners with their respective shares of income/loss items.

The S corporation's separately stated items are the same ones that apply in partnership taxation under Sec. 702(a).[28] The items required to be separately stated by Sec. 702(a) include

- Net short-term capital gains and losses
- Net long-term capital gains and losses
- Sec. 1231 gains and losses
- Charitable contributions
- Dividends eligible for a dividends-received deduction[29]
- Taxes paid to a foreign country or to a U.S. possession
- Any other item provided by Treasury Regulations

---

[27] Secs. 1363(c).

[28] Sec. 1366(a).

[29] Partnerships are permitted to have C corporations as owners of partnership interests. Such is not the case with an S corporation who cannot have a corporate shareholder.

Regulation Sec. 1.702-1(a)(8) adds for partnerships several other items to the list. The same additions from the Treasury Regulations apply to S corporations and include the following:

- Tax-exempt or partially tax-exempt interest
- Soil and water conservation expenditures
- Intangible drilling and development costs
- Certain mining exploration expenditures

Additional separately stated items not mentioned in Sec. 702 or its regulations include

- Passive income and loss
- Portfolio income (e.g., dividends and interest)

For a more complete list of the separately stated items see the Form 1120S Schedule K included in Appendix B.

Section 1366(b) requires that the character of any separately stated item be determined as if the item were (1) realized directly by the shareholder from the same source from which it was realized by the corporation or (2) incurred by the shareholder in the same manner as it was incurred by the corporation. Thus, the character of an income, gain, deduction, loss, or credit item does not change merely because the item passes through to the shareholders.

DEDUCTIONS THAT CANNOT BE CLAIMED. S corporations also have several deductions that it cannot claim, including

- The 70%, 80%, or 100% dividends-received deduction (because dividends pass through to the S corporation's shareholders)
- The same deductions disallowed to a partnership under Sec. 703(a)(2) (e.g., personal and dependency exemptions, additional itemized deductions for individuals, taxes paid or accrued to a foreign country or to a U.S. possession, charitable contributions, oil and gas depletion, and NOL carrybacks and carryforwards).[30]

SIMILARITY TO C CORPORATION TREATMENT. S corporations are treated as corporations for certain tax matters. For example, an S corporation can elect to amortize its organizational expenditures under Sec. 248. Also, the 20% reduction in certain tax preference benefits under Sec. 291 applies to an S corporation if the corporation was a C corporation in any of its three preceding tax years.[31]

SELF-STUDY QUESTION

Because S corporations are conduits, can NOL carryforwards from a C corporation tax year flow through to the S corporation's shareholders?

ANSWER

No. C corporation NOLs are not a good reason to make an S election because the NOLs cannot be carried to an S corporation tax year and passed through to the shareholder.

CARRYFORWARDS AND CARRYBACKS WHEN STATUS CHANGES. Some S corporations may operate as C corporations during a period of years that either precede the making of an S election or follow the termination of an S election. No carryforwards or carrybacks that originate in a C corporation tax year can be carried to an S corporation tax year other than carryforwards that can be used to offset the built-in gains tax (see page C11-16). Similarly, no carryforwards or carrybacks created in an S corporation tax year can be taken to a C corporation tax year.[32] Losses from an S corporation tax year pass through to the shareholder and, if greater than the shareholder's income for the year, can create an NOL carryforward or carryback for the shareholder.

OBJECTIVE 6

Calculate the amount of any special S corporation taxes

SPECIAL S CORPORATION TAXES

The S corporation is subject to three special taxes: the excess net passive income tax, the built-in gains tax, and the LIFO recapture tax. Each of these taxes is explained below.

EXCESS NET PASSIVE INCOME TAX. The **excess net passive income (or Sec. 1375) tax** applies when an S corporation has passive investment income for the tax year that

[30] Sec. 1363(b)(2).

[31] Secs. 1363(b)(3) and (4).

[32] Sec. 1371(b).

KEY POINT

The excess net passive income tax is of concern to a former C corporation that has accumulated E&P. A corporation that always has been an S corporation will not have a passive income problem.

exceeds 25% of its gross receipts and, at the close of the tax year, the S corporation has Subchapter C E&P. The excess net passive income tax equals the S corporation's excess net passive income times the highest corporate tax rate (35% in 2002).[33]

The **excess net passive income** is determined as follows:

$$\text{Excess net passive income} = \text{Net passive income} \times \frac{\text{Passive investment income} - 25\% \text{ of gross receipts}}{\text{Passive investment income}}$$

The excess net passive income is limited to the corporation's taxable income, which is defined as a C corporation's taxable income except with no reduction for the NOL deduction or the dividends-received deduction. Net passive income equals passive investment income minus any deductions directly related to its production.[34]

Regulation Sec. 1.1362-2(c)(5) holds that passive investment income excludes income derived from the active conduct of a trade or business.

EXAMPLE C11-11 ▶ Paoli Corporation, an S corporation, reports the following results for 2002:

Service (nonpassive) income	$35,000
Dividend income	37,000
Interest income	28,000
Passive income-related expenses	10,000
Other expenses	25,000

TAX STRATEGY TIP

A former C corporation can avoid the Sec. 1375 tax (and the possibility of having its S election terminated) by electing to distribute its Subchapter C E&P. See Tax Planning Considerations for further details.

At the end of this year, Paoli's E&P from its prior C corporation tax years amounts to $60,000. Paoli's excess net passive income is determined as follows:

$$\$33{,}846 = (\$65{,}000 - \$10{,}000) \times \frac{\$65{,}000 - (0.25 \times \$100{,}000)}{\$65{,}000}$$

The excess net passive income tax is $11,846 ($33,846 × 0.35). The special tax reduces (on a pro rata basis) the dividend income and interest income items that pass through to the shareholders. The S election is not terminated at the end of 2002 unless Paoli also was subject to the tax in 2000 and 2001. ◀

BUILT-IN GAINS TAX. A second corporate level tax may apply to gains recognized by an S corporation that formerly was a C corporation. This tax, called the **built-in gains (or Sec. 1374) tax,** is imposed on any income or gain that would have been included in gross income while a C corporation if the corporation had used the accrual method of accounting (known as a **built-in gain**) and that is reported during the ten-year period beginning on the date the S election took effect (known as the recognition period). Built-in losses reduce the amount of recognized built-in gains in determining the built-in gains tax liability. **Built-in losses** are any deductions or losses that would have been deductible while a C corporation if the corporation had used the accrual method of accounting and that are reported during the ten-year period beginning on the date the S election took effect.

REAL WORLD EXAMPLE

The special S corporation taxes account for only a small amount of federal revenues. In 1998, collections on the built-in gains and excess net passive income taxes were $393.3 and $17.5 million, respectively. In contrast, total C corporation tax revenues collected in 1998 were $213.3 billion.

Congress enacted this tax to prevent taxpayers from avoiding the corporate level tax on liquidating distributions by making an S election before liquidating the corporation or selling its assets. However, the tax ramifications of the built-in gains tax extend beyond corporations that are in the process of liquidating. The built-in gains tax applies to S corporation tax years beginning after December 31, 1986 where the S corporation was formerly a C corporation and the current S election was made after December 31, 1986.

EXAMPLE C11-12 ▶ Tatum Corporation, a calendar year taxpayer, was incorporated in 1986 and operated as a C corporation through the end of 2001. On February 4, 2002, Tatum Corporation filed an S election that was effective for 2002 and later tax years. Because Tatum filed its S election after December 31, 1986, it is subject to the built-in gains tax for ten years starting with January 1, 2002. ◀

---

[33] *Passive investment income* and *Subchapter C E&P* have the same definition here as when they were defined on pages C11-9 and C11-10.

[34] Regulation Sec. 1.1375-1(f), Ex. (2) indicates that passive income subject to the Sec. 1375 tax includes municipal bond interest that otherwise is exempt from the federal income tax.

The Sec. 1374 tax is determined by using the following four-step calculation:

STEP 1: Determine the corporation's net recognized built-in gain for the tax year.

STEP 2: Reduce the net recognized built-in gain from Step 1 (but not below zero) by any NOL or capital loss carryovers from any prior C corporation tax years.

STEP 3: Compute a tentative tax by multiplying the amount determined in Step 2 by the highest corporate tax rate (35% in 2002).

STEP 4: Reduce the tax determined in Step 3 (but not below zero) by the amount of the general business credit and minimum tax credit carryovers from any prior C corporation tax years and the nonhighway use of gasoline and other fuels credit.

TAX STRATEGY TIP

An S corporation with NOL, capital loss, general business credit, and minimum tax credit carryovers can use these carryovers to reduce the effect of the built-in gains tax. Both NOL and capital loss carryforwards reduce the amount of recognized built-in gain taxed under Sec. 1374. The general business and minimum tax credit carryforwards reduce the actual built-in gains tax.

A recognized built-in gain or loss is any gain or loss recognized on an asset disposition during the ten-year recognition period unless the S corporation can establish that it did not hold the asset on the first day of the first tax year to which the S election applies. A recognized built-in gain cannot exceed the excess of a property's FMV over its adjusted basis on the first day of the ten-year recognition period. Dispositions include sales or exchanges and other events, including the collection of accounts receivable by a cash method of accounting taxpayer, collection of an installment sale obligation, and the completion of a long-term contract by a taxpayer using the completed contract method.[35]

Built-in losses include not only losses originating from a disposition of property, but also any deductions claimed during the ten-year recognition period that are attributable to periods before the first S corporation tax year. A recognized built-in loss cannot exceed the excess of a property's adjusted basis over its FMV on the first day of the ten-year recognition period. Built-in losses, however, do not include any loss, deduction, or carryforward originating from the disposition of an asset acquired before or during the recognition period where the principal purpose of such acquisition was avoiding the Sec. 1374 tax.

PRACTICAL APPLICATION

The application of the Sec. 1374 tax requires detailed records, which enable the taxpayer to track the built-in gain assets and determine when these gains are recognized.

The net recognized built-in gain for a tax year is limited to the smaller of:

- The excess of (1) the net unrealized built-in gain (i.e., excess of the FMV of the S corporation's assets at the beginning of its first tax year for which the S election is in effect over their total adjusted basis on such date) over (2) the total net recognized built-in gain for prior tax years beginning in the ten-year recognition period.[36]
- The S corporation's taxable income as if it were a C corporation but with no dividends-received deduction or NOL deduction allowed.

If the net of the recognized built-in gains and losses exceeds the corporation's taxable income and the corporation made the S election after March 30, 1988, the excess built-in gain amount is carried over to the next tax year, where it may be subject to the Sec. 1374 built-in gains tax. The built-in gain carryover consists of a ratable share of each of the income categories (e.g., ordinary income, capital gains) making up the net recognized built-in gain amount for the tax year.

The built-in gains tax passes through to the shareholders as if it were a loss. The loss must be allocated proportionately among the recognized built-in gains that resulted in the tax being imposed.

EXAMPLE C11-13 ▶ Assume the same facts as in Example C11-12 except that Tatum Corporation uses the accrual method of accounting and owns the following assets on January 1, 2002:

[35] Income and gains potentially can be taxed under both the excess net passive income (Sec. 1375) and built-in gains (Sec. 1374) taxes. Any such income or gain is fully taxed under the Sec. 1374 rules. The portion of the income or gain taxed under the Sec. 1374 tax is exempt from the Sec. 1375 tax.

[36] The recognition period can be extended beyond ten years if property having a carryover basis is acquired in a tax-free transaction (e.g., a tax-free reorganization) from a C corporation. For such property, the ten-year recognition period begins on the date the S corporation acquired the property.

ETHICAL POINT

A C corporation that has substantially appreciated assets and wants to make an S election should obtain an appraisal of its assets on or about the first day of the S election period. The S corporation's tax accountant must make sure the appraiser does not assign an artificially low value to these assets to minimize the potential built-in gains tax burden.

Assets	*Adjusted Basis*	*FMV*
Cash	$10,000	$10,000
Marketable securities	39,000	45,000
Accounts receivable	60,000	60,000
Inventory (FIFO)	60,000	75,000
Building	27,000	44,000
Land	10,000	26,000
Machinery and equipment[a]	74,000	140,000
Total	$280,000	$400,000

[a] $50,000 of the gain is subject to recapture under Sec. 1245.

During 2002, Tatum collects $58,000 of accounts receivable and declares $2,000 uncollectible. It sells the FIFO inventory at a $25,000 profit in the first quarter of 2002, replacing the sold inventory with new inventory. It also sells two machines during 2002. One machine, having an $18,000 FMV and an $11,000 adjusted basis on January 1, was sold for an $8,000 gain (Sec. 1245 income) on September 2. A second machine, having a $15,000 FMV and a $19,000 adjusted basis on January 1, was sold for a $7,000 loss on March 15.

- ▶ Tatum recognizes no built-in gain or loss on collecting the receivables because it is an accrual method taxpayer. The $2,000 uncollectible debt is not a built-in loss because the loss arose after January 1. It is deductible as part of the ordinary income/loss calculation.
- ▶ Of the $25,000 inventory profit, $15,000 ($75,000 – $60,000) is a built-in gain taxed under Sec. 1374. The entire $25,000 profit is included in ordinary income/loss.
- ▶ The corporation recognizes a $7,000 built-in gain ($18,000 – $11,000) and a $4,000 ($15,000 – $19,000) built-in loss on the sale of the two machines. An $8,000 Sec. 1245 gain is included in ordinary income/loss, and a $7,000 Sec. 1231 loss passes through separately to the shareholders.

In total, an $18,000 ($15,000 + $7,000 – $4,000) net recognized built-in gain is taxed under Sec. 1374, subject to the taxable income ceiling. Assuming C corporation taxable income (with no NOL deduction or dividends-received deduction) is at least $18,000, the built-in gains tax is $6,300 ($18,000 × 0.35). The entire tax amount reduces the ordinary income from the inventory and machinery sales. ◀

LIFO RECAPTURE TAX. If a C corporation using the LIFO inventory method makes an S election, Sec. 1363(d)(3) requires the corporation to include its LIFO recapture amount in gross income for its last C corporation tax year. The LIFO recapture amount is the excess of the inventory's basis for tax purposes under the FIFO method over its basis under the LIFO method at the close of the final C corporation tax year. Any tax increase incurred in the final C corporation tax year is payable in four annual installments, on or before the due date for the final C corporation tax return and on or before the due date for the first three S corporation tax returns. The S corporation's inventory basis is increased by the LIFO recapture amount included in gross income.

EXAMPLE C11-14 ▶ Taylor Corporation, a calendar year C corporation since its inception in 1986, makes an S election on December 24, 2001, effective for its 2002 tax year. Taylor has used the LIFO inventory method for a number of years. Its LIFO inventory has a $400,000 adjusted basis, a $650,000 FIFO inventory value, and an $800,000 FMV. Taylor's LIFO recapture amount is $250,000 ($650,000 – $400,000). Taylor includes this amount in gross income reported on its 2001 corporate tax return. Assuming a 34% corporate tax, Taylor's increased tax liability is $85,000 (0.34 × $250,000), of which $21,250 (0.25 × $85,000) is due with Taylor's 2001 C corporation tax return. An additional $21,250 is due with the 2002 through 2004 S corporation tax returns. Taylor increases the basis of its inventory by the $250,000 LIFO recapture amount. ◀

STOP & THINK

Question: Former C corporations that are now treated as S corporations are subject to three corporate level taxes—the **LIFO recapture tax**, the built-in gains tax, and the excess net passive income tax. What are the reasons behind enacting these three taxes?

Solution: In 1986, Congress debated making the conversion of a C corporation into an S corporation a taxable event subject to the corporate liquidation rules. All gains and losses would have been recognized by the corporation at the time of conversion. As a compromise, only LIFO users are subject to an "automatic" tax when conversion occurs, and this tax is imposed only on the LIFO recapture amount and not all inventory appreciation. The built-in gains tax is imposed only when the corporation sells or exchanges assets during its first ten years under the S election. Assets not sold or exchanged during this time period escape the tax. The excess net passive income tax is imposed to encourage S corporations to distribute their accumulated E&P. No tax is imposed if passive income is kept below the 25% of gross receipts threshold. Thus, former C corporations and their shareholders generally are better off under the current system than if corporate liquidation treatment were mandated.

TAXATION OF THE SHAREHOLDER

INCOME ALLOCATION PROCEDURES

OBJECTIVE 7

Calculate a shareholder's allocable share of ordinary income or loss and separately stated items

An S corporation's shareholders must report their pro rata share of the ordinary income or loss and separately stated items for the S corporation's tax year that ends with or within the shareholder's tax year.[37] Each shareholder's pro rata share of the aforementioned items is determined by

1. Allocating an equal portion of the item to each day in the tax year (by dividing the amount of the item by the number of days in the S corporation's tax year)
2. Allocating an equal portion of the daily amount for the item to each share of stock that is outstanding on each day (by dividing the daily amount for the item by the number of shares of stock outstanding on a particular day)
3. Totaling the daily allocations for each share of stock
4. Totaling the amounts allocated for each share of stock held by the shareholder

TYPICAL MISCONCEPTION

An S corporation's income/loss is allocated basically the same as a partnership's except that a partnership may have the added flexibility of making certain special allocations under Sec. 704(b).

These allocation rules are known as the "per day/per share" method. Special allocations (such as those possible under the partnership tax rules) of the ordinary income or loss and separately stated items are not permitted.

If a sale of the S corporation stock occurs during the year, the transferor reports the earnings allocated to the transferred shares through the day of the transfer.[38] The transferee reports his or her share of the earnings from the day after the transfer date through the end of the tax year.

EXAMPLE C11-15 ▶ Fox Corporation, an electing S corporation, is owned equally by Arnie and Bonnie during all of 2002. During this year, Fox reports ordinary income of $146,000 and a long-term capital gain of $36,500. Arnie and Bonnie each report $73,000 (0.50 × $146,000) of ordinary income and $18,250 (0.50 × $36,500) of long-term capital gain. ◀

EXAMPLE C11-16 ▶ Assume the same facts as in Example C11-15, except that Bonnie sells one-half of her shares to Clay on March 31, 2002 (the 90st day of Fox's tax year). Arnie reports the same ordinary income and long-term capital gain from his investment. Bonnie and Clay report ordinary income and long-term capital gain as follows:

---

[37] Sec. 1366(a). If the shareholder dies during the S corporation's tax year, the income earned during the portion of the tax year preceding death is reported on the shareholder's tax return. The income for the period of time that the estate holds the S corporation stock is reported on the estate's fiduciary tax return.

[38] Reg. Sec. 1.1377-1(a)(2)(ii). Also see examples under Reg. Sec. 1.1377-1(c).

Ordinary Income

Bonnie: $\left(\$146{,}000 \times \frac{1}{2} \times \frac{90}{365}\right) + \left(\$146{,}000 \times \frac{1}{4} \times \frac{275}{365}\right) = \$45{,}500$

Clay: $\$146{,}000 \times \frac{1}{4} \times \frac{275}{365} = 27{,}500$

Total $73,000

Long-Term Capital Gain

Bonnie: $\left(\$36{,}500 \times \frac{1}{2} \times \frac{90}{365}\right) + \left(\$36{,}500 \times \frac{1}{4} \times \frac{275}{365}\right) = \$11{,}375$

Clay: $\$36{,}500 \times \frac{1}{4} \times \frac{275}{365} = 6{,}875$

Total $18,250 ◀

KEY POINT

Shareholders of an S corporation need to be aware that when they dispose of their stock, they have the option of having income/loss determined by an actual closing of the books rather than an allocation on a daily basis.

A special election is available for allocating the ordinary income or loss and separately stated items when the shareholder's interest in the S corporation terminates during the tax year, or when the interest is substantially reduced even if not completely terminated. Under this election, the income is allocated according to the accounting methods used by the S corporation (instead of on a daily basis). The election divides the S corporation's tax year into two parts ending on

- The day the shareholder's interest in the corporation terminates
- The last day of the S corporation's tax year

This election can be made only if all affected shareholders agree to the election.[39] An affected shareholder includes the shareholder whose interest terminated and all shareholders to whom the transferor transferred S corporation shares during the year. This election is explored in greater detail in the Tax Planning Considerations section of this chapter.

OBJECTIVE 8

Determine the limitations on a shareholder's deduction of S corporation losses

LOSS AND DEDUCTION PASS-THROUGH TO SHAREHOLDERS

The S corporation's ordinary loss and separately stated loss and deduction items pass through to the shareholders at the end of the corporation's tax year. These items are reported in the shareholder's tax year in which the S corporation's tax year ends.

ALLOCATION OF THE LOSS. Using the rules outlined above, allocation of the loss also occurs on a daily basis. Thus, shareholders receive an allocation of the ordinary loss and separately stated items even if they own the stock for only a portion of the year. If the ordinary loss and other separately stated loss and deduction pass-throughs exceed the shareholder's income, the excess may create an NOL for the shareholder and result in a carryback or carryover to the shareholder's other tax years.

EXAMPLE C11-17 ▶ Kauai Corporation, an electing S corporation, reports a $73,200 ordinary loss during 2002. At the beginning of 2002, Elvis and Frank own equally all of Kauai's stock. On June 30, 2002 (the 181st day of Kauai's tax year), Frank gives one-fourth of his stock to his son George. Elvis is allocated $36,500 ($73,000 × 0.50) of ordinary loss. Frank and George are allocated ordinary losses as follows:

Frank: $\left(\$73{,}000 \times \frac{1}{2} \times \frac{181}{365}\right) + \left(\$73{,}000 \times \frac{3}{8} \times \frac{184}{365}\right) = \$31{,}900$

George: $\$73{,}000 \times \frac{1}{8} \times \frac{184}{365} = 4{,}600$

Total $36,500

[39] Sec. 1377(a)(2).

All three shareholders can deduct these losses on their individual tax returns subject to the loss limitations described below. ◀

SHAREHOLDER LOSS LIMITATIONS. Each shareholder's deduction for his or her share of the ordinary loss and the separately stated loss and deduction items is limited to the sum of the adjusted basis for his or her S corporation stock plus the adjusted basis of any indebtedness owed *directly* by the S corporation to the shareholder. Thus, a shareholder must account for stock basis and debt basis. Unlike the partnership taxation rules, however, a shareholder cannot increase his or her stock basis by a ratable share of the *general* S corporation liabilities.[40]

In determining the stock basis limitation for losses, the shareholder makes the following positive and negative adjustments:[41]

- Increase stock basis for any capital contributions during the year
- Increase stock basis for ordinary income and separately stated income or gain items
- Decrease stock basis for distributions not included in the shareholder's income
- Decrease stock basis for nondeductible, noncapital expenditures (unless the shareholder elects to determine the loss limitation without this decrease)

REAL WORLD EXAMPLE

A recent U.S. Supreme Court case held that discharge of indebtedness income excluded from gross income under Sec. 108 nevertheless is a pass-through item that increases the shareholders' stock bases, thereby allowing loss pass-through items to be deducted by the shareholders. *Gitlitz el at. v. Comm.* 87 AFTR 2d 2001-417, 2001-1 USTC ¶50,147 (USSC, 2001). Pending legislation, if enacted, would not allow a stock basis increase.

Sequencing the basis reduction for distributions ahead of losses means that distributions reduce the deductibility of S corporation loss and deduction pass-throughs, but losses do not affect the treatment of S corporation distributions.

Many S corporations are nothing more than incorporated forms of sole proprietorships or partnerships. As a result, banks and other lending institutions often require one or more of the shareholders to personally guarantee any loans made to the S corporation. In general, the IRS and the courts have held that this form of indirect borrowing by the S corporation does not create a corporate indebtedness to the shareholder. As a result, the shareholder's loss limitation is not increased as a result of his or her acting as a guarantor until the shareholder makes a payment of part or all of the corporation's liability or the shareholder executes a note at the bank in full satisfaction of the corporation's liability. Such action by the shareholder converts the guarantee into an indebtedness of the corporation to the shareholder, which increases the shareholder's debt basis and loss limitation.[42]

TAX STRATEGY TIP

Rather than having the corporation borrow money, an S corporation shareholder might consider borrowing money directly from the bank and then lending the loan proceeds to the corporation with the corporation guaranteeing the bank loan. In this way, the shareholder will obtain debt basis.

The adjusted basis of the S corporation stock and debt generally is determined as of the last day of the S corporation's tax year. If the shareholder disposes of the S corporation stock before that date, the adjusted basis of the stock and debt is instead determined immediately prior to the disposition.

EXAMPLE C11-18 ▶ Pat and Bill equally own Tillis Corporation, an electing S corporation. During the current year, Tillis reports an ordinary loss of $100,000. Tillis's liabilities at the end of the current year include $110,000 of accounts payable, $150,000 of mortgage payable, and a $20,000 note owed to Bill. Pat and Bill each had a $40,000 adjusted basis for their Tillis stock on January 1. The ordinary loss is allocated equally to Pat and Bill. Pat's $50,000 loss allocation is only partially deductible this year (i.e., up to $40,000) because the loss exceeds his $40,000 basis for the Tillis stock. Bill's $50,000 loss allocation is fully deductible this year because his loss limitation is $60,000 ($40,000 + $20,000). ◀

The loss and deduction pass-through is allocated to each share of stock. If the pass-through for an individual share of stock exceeds that share's basis, the excess amount is allocated proportionately (by relative basis) to all the shareholder's remaining shares having basis. Once the losses and deductions have reduced the basis of all shares of stock to zero, they are applied against the basis of any debt owed by the S corporation to the shareholder.

[40] Sec. 1366(d)(1). Amounts owed by an S corporation to a conduit entity that has the shareholder as an owner or beneficiary will not increase the shareholder's loss limitation.

[41] Sec. 1366(d) and Reg. Sec. 1.1366-2(a)(3). Special basis adjustment rules apply to oil and gas depletion.

[42] Rev. Ruls. 70-50, 1970-1 C.B. 178; 71-288, 1971-2 C.B. 319; and 75-144, 1975-1 C.B. 277. See also *Estate of Daniel Leavitt v. CIR*, 63 AFTR 2d 89-1437, 89-1 USTC ¶9332 (4th Cir., 1989) among a series of decisions that uphold the IRS's position. However, see *Edward M. Selfe v. U.S.*, 57 AFTR 2d 86-464, 86-1 USTC ¶9115 (11th Cir., 1986) for a transaction where a guarantee was held to increase the shareholder's loss limitation because the transaction was structured so the bank looked primarily to the shareholder instead of the corporation for repayment.

TYPICAL MISCONCEPTION

If a shareholder sells his S corporation stock still having unused losses due to lack of stock basis, these losses do not transfer to the new shareholder. Instead, the unused losses lapse when shareholder sells the stock.

Any loss or deduction pass-through not currently deductible is suspended until the shareholder has a basis in his stock or in an amount owed to him or her by the S corporation (debt basis). The carryover period for the loss or deduction item is unlimited.[43] The additional adjusted basis amount can originate from a number of sources, including subsequent profits earned by the S corporation, additional capital contributions or loans made by the shareholder to the corporation, or purchases of additional stock from other shareholders.

EXAMPLE C11-19 ▶ Assume the same facts as in Example C11-18 except that Tillis Corporation reports ordinary income of $20,000 in the next year. Pat and Bill are each allocated $10,000 of ordinary income. This income provides Pat with the necessary $10,000 stock basis to deduct the $10,000 loss carryover. ◀

SPECIAL SHAREHOLDER LOSS AND DEDUCTION LIMITATIONS. The S corporation's shareholders are subject to three special loss and deduction limitations. These limitations may prevent the S corporation's shareholder from using losses or deductions even though the general loss limitation described above does not otherwise apply. Application of the special loss limitations occurs as follows:

KEY POINT

An oft-quoted advantage of an S election is that losses flow through to the shareholders. This advantage is significantly limited by the at-risk and passive activity rules.

- *At-Risk Rules:* The Sec. 465 at-risk rules apply at the shareholder level. The loss from a particular S corporation activity is deductible only to the extent of the aggregate amount for which the shareholder is at risk in the activity at the close of the S corporation's tax year.
- *Passive Activity Limitation Rules:* Losses and credits from a passive activity can be applied against income from that passive activity or other passive activities earned in the same or a subsequent tax year. An S corporation shareholder must personally meet the material participation standard for an activity to avoid the passive activity limitation. Material participation by the S corporation in an activity does not permit a passive investor to deduct the portion of the S corporation's loss against his or her salary and other "active" income.
- *Hobby Loss Rules:* Losses incurred by an S corporation are subject to the Sec. 183 hobby loss rules. Deductions incurred by the S corporation are limited to the activity's gross income unless the taxpayer can establish that the activity is engaged in for profit.

In addition, various separately stated loss and deduction items are subject to shareholder limitations (e.g., charitable contributions, long-term capital losses, and investment interest expense), but they are not subject to corporate limitations. Some separately stated items are subject to corporate limitations but not shareholder limitations (e.g., the 50% nondeductible portion of travel and entertainment expenses).

SELF-STUDY QUESTION

If losses are suspended due to the lack of basis in S corporation stock, do the losses expire when the S election terminates?

ANSWER

No. These loss carryovers may be deducted in the post-termination transition period (usually one year) if the shareholder creates additional stock basis in that period of time.

POST-TERMINATION LOSS CARRYOVERS. Loss and deduction carryovers incurred in S corporation tax years can be carried over even though the S election has been terminated. Shareholders can deduct these carryovers only in the **post-termination transition period.**[44] The length of the post-termination transition period depends on the event causing the termination of the S election. In general, the period begins on the day after the last day of the corporation's final S corporation tax year and ends on the later of one year after the last day or the due date for the final S corporation tax return (including any extensions).

If the S election terminates for a prior tax year as a result of a determination, the period runs for 120 days beginning on the determination date. Section 1377(b)(2) defines a determination as a court decision that becomes final; a closing agreement entered into; an audit determination that adjusts any Subchapter S item of income, loss, or deduction claimed by a former S corporation; a final disposition of a refund claim by the IRS; or an agreement between the corporation and the IRS that the corporation failed to qualify as an S corporation.

---

[43] Sec. 1366(d)(2). If more than one type of loss or deduction item passes through to the shareholder, the carryover amount is allocated to each of the pass-through items based on their relative amounts.

[44] Sec. 1366(d)(3). The loss carryovers that carry over include those disallowed by the at risk rules.

The loss and deduction carryovers can be deducted only up to the adjusted basis of the shareholder's stock at the end of the post-termination transition period.[45] Losses that cannot be deducted because of the basis limitation are lost forever. Deducted losses reduce the shareholder's stock basis.

EXAMPLE C11-20 ▶ Pearson Corporation has been a calendar year S corporation for several years. Helen's stock basis is $45,000. On July 1, 2002, its S election terminates when an ineligible shareholder acquires part of its stock. For the period ended June 30, 2002, Helen is allocated $60,000 of Pearson's ordinary loss. Helen can deduct only $45,000 of this loss because of her Pearson stock basis, which is reduced to zero by the loss. The $15,000 unused loss carries over to the post-termination transition period, which ends on June 30, 2003 (assuming Pearson does not extend the March 17, 2003 due date for the S short year tax return). Helen must have an adjusted basis for the Pearson stock of at least $15,000 at the close of business on June 30, 2003, to use the loss. Helen should consider making additional capital contributions of at least $15,000 between July 1, 2002 and June 30, 2003 to use the loss. ◀

Topic Review C11-3 summarizes the rules governing deductibility of S corporation losses and deductions that pass through to the shareholders.

FAMILY S CORPORATIONS

Family S corporations have been an important tax planning device. This type of tax planning quite often involves a high-tax-bracket taxpayer gifting stock to a minor child who generally has little other income. The transfer results in income splitting among family members.

The IRS has the power to ignore such transfers when they appear to be primarily tax motivated. Regulation Sec. 1.1373-1(a)(2) indicates that "a donee or purchaser of stock in the corporation is not considered a shareholder unless such stock is acquired in a bona fide transaction and the donee or purchaser is the real owner of the stock." The IRS has enjoyed success in litigating cases dealing with intrafamily transfers of S corporation stock when the transferor (usually a parent) retains the economic benefits and control over the stock transferred to the transferee (usually a child).[46] The IRS has enjoyed less success when one family member purchases the stock from another family member at its market value.

ADDITIONAL COMMENT

The advantages of family S corporations have been somewhat curtailed. For example, income from stock of an S corporation gifted to a child under age 14 is subject to the "kiddie tax," where unearned income exceeding $1,500 (in 2002) is taxed at the parents' marginal tax rate.

The IRS also has the statutory authority under Sec. 1366(e) to adjust the income, loss, deduction, or credit items allocated to a family member to reflect the value of services rendered or capital provided to the corporation. Section 1366(e) defines family as including spouse, ancestors, lineal descendants, and trusts created for such individuals. This provision permits the reallocation of income to provide for full compensation of a shareholder or nonshareholder for services and capital provided to the corporation. It also reduces the residual income reported by the S corporation and allocated to the shareholders according to their stock ownership. Such a reallocation prevents not only the shifting of income from the family member providing the services or capital to other family members, but also the avoidance of employment taxes. Alternatively, the IRS can determine that too much compensation is paid to a shareholder and reduce that shareholder's salary and increase the residual income allocated based on stock ownership.

EXAMPLE C11-21 ▶ Harvey Corporation, an electing S corporation, reports ordinary income of $200,000 after it claims a $20,000 deduction for Sid Harvey's salary. Sid and his three children own the Harvey stock equally. None of Sid's three children is employed by Harvey Corporation. The IRS subsequently determines that reasonable compensation for Sid is $80,000. This adjustment increases Sid's salary income and Harvey Corporation's compensation deduction by $60,000 ($80,000 − $20,000) and reduces Harvey Corporation's ordinary income to $140,000 ($200,000 − $60,000). Each shareholder's ratable share of ordinary income is reduced from $50,000 ($200,000 ÷ 4) to $35,000 ($140,000 ÷ 4). Alternatively, if the IRS can prove that the stock transfer to the three children is not a bona fide transfer, all $220,000 of Harvey Corporation's income is taxed to Sid—$80,000 as salary and $140,000 as an allocation of ordinary income. ◀

---

[45] Sec. 1366(d)(3)(B).

[46] See, for example, *Gino A. Speca v. CIR*, 47 AFTR 2d 81-468, 80-2 USTC ¶9692 (7th Cir., 1980) and *Henry D. Duarte*, 44 T.C. 193 (1965), where the IRS's position prevailed. See also *Gavin S. Millar*, 1975 PH T.C. Memo ¶75,113, 34 TCM 554, and *Donald O. Kirkpatrick*, 1977 PH T.C. Memo ¶77,281, 36 TCM 1122, where the taxpayers prevailed.

Topic Review C11-3

Deductibility of S Corporation Losses and Deductions

Allocation Process

1. Losses and deductions are allocated based on the number of shares of stock owned by each shareholder on each day of the tax year. Special allocations of losses and deductions are not permitted.
2. Termination of the S election requires the tax year to be divided into two parts. The corporation can elect (with the shareholders' consent) to allocate the loss or deduction according to the accounting methods used by the corporation. This election also is available when a shareholder's interest in the S corporation terminates.

Loss Limitations

1. Losses and deductions pass through on a per-share basis and are limited to the shareholder's basis in the stock and to the shareholder's debt basis. Once the basis for all the shareholder's stock is reduced to zero, the losses reduce the basis of any S corporation indebtedness to the shareholder.
2. Losses and deductions that are not deducted carry over to a tax year in which the shareholder again has stock or debt basis. The time period for the carryover is unlimited.
3. S corporation shareholders are subject to three special loss limitations:
   - At-risk rules
   - Passive activity limitations
   - Hobby loss rules

   Some separately stated loss and deduction items also are subject to shareholder limitations (e.g., investment interest expense). Other separately stated items are subject to corporate limitations but not shareholder limitations (e.g., the 50% nondeductible portion of travel and entertainment expenses).

Basis Adjustments

OBJECTIVE 9

Calculate a shareholder's basis in his or her S corporation's stock and debt

Adjustments must be made annually to the shareholder's S corporation stock basis. In addition, if the S corporation is indebted to the shareholder, he or she may have to adjust the debt basis downward for loss or deduction pass-throughs and upward to reflect restoration of the basis when the corporation earns subsequent profits. Each of these adjustments is described below.

SELF-STUDY QUESTION

Why is the determination of stock basis in an S corporation important?

ANSWER

To determine gain/loss on the sale of the stock, to determine the amount of losses that can be deducted, and to determine the amount of distributions to shareholders that are tax-free.

BASIS ADJUSTMENTS TO S CORPORATION STOCK

Basis adjustments to the shareholder's stock are made in the following order:[47]

Initial investment (or basis at beginning of tax year)	
Plus:	Additional capital contributions made during the year
	Allocable share of ordinary income
	Allocable share of separately stated income and gain items
Minus:	Distributions excluded from the shareholder's gross income
	Allocable share of any expense not deductible in determining ordinary income (loss) and not chargeable to the capital account
	Allocable share of ordinary loss
	Allocable share of separately stated loss and deduction items
Adjusted basis for stock (but not less than zero)	

A shareholder's initial basis for S corporation stock depends on how he or she acquires it. Stock purchased from the corporation or another shareholder takes a cost basis. Stock received as part of a corporate formation transaction takes a substituted basis from the assets transferred. Stock acquired by gift takes the donor's basis (adjusted for gift taxes paid) or FMV (if lower). Stock acquired at death takes its FMV on the decedent's date of death or the alternate valuation date (if elected). The basis of S corporation stock inher-

[47] Sec. 1367(a) and Reg. Sec. 1.1367-1(f).

ited from a deceased shareholder is its FMV minus any corporate income that would have been income in respect of a decedent (see Chapter C14) if the income had been acquired from the decedent. No basis adjustment occurs when the corporation makes the initial S election.

The basis adjustments to the S corporation stock parallel those made to a partnership interest. The ordinary income and separately stated income and gain items increase the shareholder's basis whether they are taxable or tax-exempt, or receive preferential tax treatment.

EXAMPLE C11-22 ▶ Cathy owns Marlo Corporation, an electing S corporation. At the beginning of the current year, Cathy's adjusted basis for her Marlo stock is $105,000. Marlo reports the following operating results this year:

Ordinary income	$70,000
Municipal bond interest income	15,000
Dividends from domestic corporations	6,000
Long-term capital gain	8,000
Short-term capital loss	17,000

Cathy's adjusted basis for the Marlo stock at the end of the year is $187,000 ($105,000 + $70,000 + $15,000 + $6,000 + $8,000 − $17,000). ◀

The basis adjustment is made at the end of the S corporation's tax year, when the results for the entire period are known. Because the profits and losses are allocated ratably on a daily basis to all shares held on each day of the tax year, a shareholder's gain or loss realized on the sale of S corporation stock during the tax year is not determinable until the ordinary income or loss and separately stated items allocable to the shares sold are known. Similarly, when the S corporation stock becomes worthless during a tax year, the shareholder must make the necessary positive and negative basis adjustments before the amount of the worthless security loss can be determined.

EXAMPLE C11-23 ▶ Mike, Carlos, and Juan equally own Diaz Corporation, an electing S corporation. Mike's 100 shares of Diaz stock have a $25,000 adjusted basis at the beginning of 2002. Diaz Corporation reports ordinary income of $36,500 and municipal bond interest income of $14,600 in 2002. On February 14, 2002, (the 45th day of Diaz's tax year), Mike sells all his Diaz stock for $30,000. Assuming the daily method is used to allocate the income items, Mike's basis for the Diaz stock is determined as follows:

$$\$27{,}100 = \$25{,}000 + \left(\$36{,}500 \times \frac{45}{365} \times \frac{1}{3}\right) + \left(\$14{,}600 \times \frac{45}{365} \times \frac{1}{3}\right)$$

Mike reports a $2,900 ($30,000 − $27,100) gain on the sale. ◀

BASIS ADJUSTMENTS TO SHAREHOLDER DEBT

KEY POINT

Losses first reduce the basis in the stock and then any amount of debt owed to the shareholder by the S corporation. Subsequent net increases in basis are added first to the debt and then to the stock.

After the shareholder's basis in the S corporation stock is reduced to zero, the basis of any S corporation indebtedness to the shareholder still outstanding at the end of the S corporation's tax year is reduced (but not below zero) by the remainder of the available loss and deduction items.[48] If a shareholder has more than one loan outstanding at year-end, the basis reduction applies to all the indebtednesses based on the relative adjusted basis for each loan. Ordinary income and separately stated gain or income items allocated to the shareholder in subsequent tax years (net of distributions and losses to the shareholders) first restore the basis of any S corporation indebtedness to the shareholder that is outstanding at the end of its tax year. Once all previous decreases to the debt basis are restored, any additional positive basis adjustments increase the shareholder's stock basis.[49]

[48] No basis reductions are made to debt repaid before the end of the tax year. Regulation Sec. 1.1367-2(d)(1) holds that restoration occurs immediately before any shareholder indebtednesses are repaid or disposed of during the tax year.

[49] Sec. 1367(b)(2)(B).

Repayment of a shareholder indebtedness results in gain recognition to the shareholder if the payment amount exceeds the debt's adjusted basis. If the indebtedness is secured by a note, the difference is a capital gain. If the indebtedness is not secured by a note or other evidence of the indebtedness, the repayment is ordinary income.[50]

EXAMPLE C11-24 ▶ At the beginning of 2001, Betty owns one-half the stock of Trailer Corporation, an electing S corporation. Betty's basis for the Trailer stock is $40,000. Trailer Corporation owes Betty $20,000 on January 1, 2001. During 2001 and 2002, Trailer reports an ordinary loss of $100,000 and ordinary income of $10,000, respectively. Betty's $50,000 loss pass-through from 2001 first reduces the basis of her Trailer stock from $40,000 to zero. Next, the $10,000 remainder of the loss pass-through reduces the basis of Trailer's note from $20,000 to $10,000. Betty's $5,000 allocation of 2002's ordinary income increases the basis for the Trailer note from $10,000 to $15,000. If the corporation repays the note before the end of 2002, Betty reports a $5,000 ($20,000 − $15,000) long-term capital gain resulting from the repayment plus any ordinary income or separately stated items resulting from Trailer's 2002 operations. If the debt instead were unsecured (i.e., an advance from the shareholder not secured by a note), the gain would be ordinary income. ◀

STOP & THINK

Question: The text preceding Example C11-24 says that ordinary income and separately stated gain or income items (net of losses and distributions) restore debt basis before increasing stock basis; that is, debt is restored first by any net increase. The following rule also applies: total basis for the loss limitation equals (1) stock basis *after* all current year adjustments other than for losses plus (2) debt basis *before* any current year adjustments.

Consider the following situation: Omega Corporation is an S corporation with one shareholder. At the beginning of last year, the shareholder's stock basis was $15,000, and her debt basis was $20,000. Last year, Omega incurred a $45,000 ordinary loss, $35,000 of which the shareholder could deduct and $10,000 of which carries over. The loss affected basis as follows:

	Stock Basis	*Debt Basis*
Basis at beginning of last year	$15,000	$20,000
Ordinary loss last year ($45,000)	(15,000)	(20,000)
Basis at beginning of current year	$ –0–	$ –0–

In the current year, Omega earns $18,000 of ordinary income. What does the shareholder recognize in the current year, and what is the effect on her stock and debt bases? Why is the net increase rule for debt basis restoration beneficial to the shareholder?

Solution: The shareholder recognizes $18,000 of ordinary income and deducts the entire $10,000 loss carryover. Current year basis adjustments are as follows:

	Stock Basis	*Debt Basis*
Balance at beginning of current year	$ –0–	$ –0–
Ordinary income	10,000	8,000
Loss carryover allowed	(10,000)	–0–
Basis at end of current year	$ –0–	$8,000

The net increase approach benefits the shareholder because it allows her to deduct the $10,000 loss carryover in the current year rather than next year. The net increase for debt restoration is $8,000 ($18,000 − $10,000), which leaves $10,000 of the $18,000 ordinary income to increase stock basis. This net increase approach to debt restoration allows a stock basis increase sufficient to use the loss carryover. Alternatively, if debt were restored by ordinary income without netting, the debt basis would increase by the entire $18,000, leaving no positive adjustment to the stock basis. This increase to debt basis would not help the shareholder in the current year because debt basis for the loss limita-

[50] Rev. Ruls. 64-162, 1964-1 (Part I) C.B. 304 and 68-537, 1968-2 C.B. 372.

tion is the balance before any current year adjustments. Under this hypothetical alternative approach, the shareholder could deduct the loss next year because next year's beginning debt basis would be $18,000. However, the net increase approach is better than the alternative because it allows the shareholder to deduct the loss in the current year.

S CORPORATION DISTRIBUTIONS

OBJECTIVE 10

Determine the taxability of an S corporation's distributions to its shareholders

Two sets of rules apply to S corporation distributions. One applies to S corporations having accumulated E&P. Accumulated E&P may exist if an S corporation was a C corporation in a pre–S election tax year. Another set of distribution rules applies to S corporations that do not have E&P (e.g., a corporation formed after 1982 that makes a timely S election in its initial tax year). These rules are explained below.

CORPORATIONS HAVING NO EARNINGS AND PROFITS

For S corporations with no accumulated E&P, a two-tier rule applies. Distributions are initially tax-free and reduce the shareholder's adjusted basis in the stock (but not below zero). If the distribution exceeds the shareholder's stock basis, the "excess" is treated as a gain from the sale or exchange of the stock. The stock basis for determining excess distributions is that after positive adjustments for ordinary income and separately stated income and gain items but before negative adjustments.[51]

EXAMPLE C11-25 ▶ Sandy owns 100% of Liberty Corporation, an electing S corporation. At the beginning of the current year, Sandy's adjusted basis in her Liberty stock (a capital asset) is $20,000. Liberty reports ordinary income of $30,000 and a long-term capital loss of $7,000 this year. Liberty makes a $35,000 cash distribution to Sandy on June 15. Sandy's basis for the stock must be adjusted for the ordinary income before determining the taxability of the distribution. Because Sandy's $50,000 ($20,000 + $30,000) adjusted basis for the stock exceeds the $35,000 distribution amount, she excludes the entire distribution from her gross income. The distribution reduces the stock's basis to $15,000 ($50,000 − $35,000). Because Sandy still has sufficient stock basis, she can deduct the $7,000 capital loss, which reduces her stock basis to $8,000.

If Liberty instead reports only $5,000 of ordinary income and a $7,000 capital loss, $10,000 of the distribution is taxable. The ordinary income increases the stock's basis to $25,000 ($20,000 + $5,000). Because the distribution exceeds the stock's adjusted basis by $10,000 ($35,000 − $25,000), the excess distribution is taxable to Sandy as a capital gain. The distribution not included in Sandy's income ($25,000) reduces her stock basis to zero at year-end. Because the stock basis after the distribution is zero, Sandy cannot deduct the $7,000 capital loss in the current year. She must wait until she regains a positive stock basis (or obtains debt basis). ◀

SELF-STUDY QUESTION

Can distributions that exceed stock basis be tax-free to the extent of shareholder loans?

ANSWER

No. Although the amount of deductible losses can be increased by the amount of shareholder loans, tax-free distributions are strictly limited to stock basis. Also, distributions never reduce debt basis.

If an S corporation makes a distribution to its shareholders, the S corporation must recognize gain when it distributes appreciated property.[52] The corporation recognizes no loss, however, when it distributes property that has declined in value. The gain recognized on the distribution may be taxed at the corporate level as part of the S corporation's built-in gains or the excess net passive income tax. The gain also becomes part of the S corporation's ordinary income or loss, or is passed through as a separately stated item, depending on the type of property distributed and the character of the gain recognized. After this recognition occurs, the property can be distributed without further taxation provided the sum of the money plus the FMV of the nonmoney property distributed does not exceed the shareholder's stock basis. The shareholder's stock basis is reduced by the distribution amount.

[51] Secs. 1368(b)and (d).

[52] Sec. 311(b).

EXAMPLE C11-26 ▶ Tad owns 100% of Echo Corporation, which always has been an S corporation. Tad's adjusted basis in the Echo stock at the beginning of the current year is $50,000. Echo reports $30,000 of ordinary income for this year (exclusive of the effects of a property distribution made to Tad). On December 1, Echo distributes some Cable Corporation stock to Tad. The stock, which cost $40,000 and has a $100,000 FMV, was held as an investment for three years. Echo reports $60,000 ($100,000 − $40,000) of capital gain from distributing the stock. Tad reports $30,000 of ordinary income and $60,000 of long-term capital gain from Echo's current year activities. Tad's adjusted basis for his Echo stock increases to $140,000 ($50,000 + $30,000 + $60,000). The distribution is free of further taxation because the $140,000 basis for the Echo stock exceeds the $100,000 distribution amount. The basis of the Echo stock is $40,000 ($140,000 − $100,000) at year-end. The Cable stock has a $100,000 FMV basis in Tad's hands. ◀

ADDITIONAL COMMENT

The distribution of appreciated stock in Example C11-26 produced income to Echo, which passed through to Tad. A similar distribution by a C corporation would result in a double tax by causing income recognition to both Echo and Tad.

CORPORATIONS HAVING ACCUMULATED EARNINGS AND PROFITS

PRIOR RULES. Under pre-1983 rules, a corporation's undistributed taxable income was taxed to its shareholders as a deemed distribution at year-end. This income accumulated in a **previously taxed income (PTI)** account, which can be a source of S corporation distributions. For simplicity in this text, however, the following discussion assumes that S corporation status occurs after 1982 and thus ignores the implications of PTI.

KEY POINT

The AAA represents the cumulative income/loss recognized in post-1982 S corporation years. To the extent that the AAA is positive and sufficient basis exists in the stock, distributions from an S corporation are tax-free and reduce stock basis.

CURRENT RULES. Under current (post-1982) rules, some S corporations have a post-1982 accumulated E&P balance, earned while a C corporation. Part or all of a distribution may be treated as made from this balance. The current rules, however, also require S corporations that have accumulated E&P balances to maintain an **accumulated adjustments account (AAA)** from which they make most of their distributions. The existence of accumulated E&P and AAA balances makes the tax treatment of cash and property distributions somewhat more complicated than do the rules explained in the preceding section.

MONEY DISTRIBUTIONS. For corporations making a post-1982 S election and having an accumulated E&P balance, money distributions come from the two tiers of earnings illustrated in Table C11-1. The corporation makes distributions from the first tier until it is exhausted. The corporation then makes distributions from the second tier until that tier is used up. Amounts distributed after the two tiers of earnings are exhausted reduce the shareholder's remaining basis in his or her S corporation stock. Any additional amounts distributed once the stock basis has been reduced to zero are taxed to the shareholder as a capital gain. These tiers usually are maintained as a working paper accounts and not as general ledger accounts.

▼ TABLE C11-1
Source of Distributions Made by S Corporations Having Accumulated Earnings and Profits

		Types of Distributions Coming from Tier		
Tier	Classification	Money Distributions?	Property (Nonmoney) Distributions?	Taxable or Tax-Free Distributions?
1	Accumulated adjustments account	Yes	Yes	Tax-free[a]
2	Accumulated E&P	Yes	Yes	Taxable
3	Basis of S corporation stock	Yes	Yes	Tax-free[a]
4	Excess over stock basis	Yes	Yes	Taxable

[a] These distributions reduce the basis of the S corporation stock. Although generally tax-free, gain can be recognized if the amount of money plus the FMV of the nonmoney property distributed exceeds the shareholder's adjusted basis in the S corporation stock as indicated in Tier 4.

The AAA is the cumulative total of the ordinary income or loss and separately stated items accumulated for the S period but excluding tax-exempt income and expenses related to its production. The S period is the most recent continuous period during which the corporation has been an S corporation. No tax years beginning before January 1, 1983 are included in this period.[53]

The year-end AAA balance is determined as follows:

AAA balance at the beginning of the year
Plus: Ordinary income
Separately stated income and gain items (except for tax-exempt income)
Minus: Distributions made from AAA (see first bullet item below)
Expenses not deductible in determining ordinary income (loss) and not chargeable to the capital account
Ordinary loss
Separately stated loss and deduction items (except for expenses or losses related to the production of tax-exempt income)

AAA balance at the end of the year

Four differences exist between the positive and negative adjustments required for the AAA and the basis calculation for the S corporation stock:

- Distributions not included in gross income reduce stock basis *before* other negative adjustments. Distributions reduce the AAA *after* other negative adjustments unless the other negative adjustments, when netted against positive adjustments, produce a "net negative adjustment." In this case, positive adjustments increase the AAA and negative adjustments other than distributions reduce the AAA to the extent of the positive adjustments. Then, distributions reduce the AAA before the net negative adjustment, and the net negative adjustment reduces the AAA after the distribution.[54]
- Tax-exempt income does not increase the AAA but increases the basis of the S corporation stock.
- Nondeductible expenses that reduce the basis of the S corporation stock also reduce the AAA except for expenses related to the production of tax-exempt income and federal income taxes related to a C corporation tax year.
- The AAA balance can be negative (e.g., when the cumulative losses exceed the cumulative profits), but the shareholder's basis in the S corporation stock cannot be less than zero.

TYPICAL MISCONCEPTION

Even though the basis of S corporation stock cannot be less than zero, the AAA can be negative if cumulative losses exceed cumulative profits.

Allocation of the AAA balance to individual distributions occurs at year-end after taking into account current year income and loss items. In general, the AAA amount is allocated ratably to individual distributions within a tax year (other than distributions coming from E&P) based on the amount of money or FMV of nonmoney property distributed.

Corporations also maintain an Other Adjustments Account (OAA) if they have accumulated E&P at year-end. This account is increased for tax-exempt income earned and decreased by the expenses incurred in earning the tax-exempt income, distributions out of the OAA, and federal taxes paid by the S corporation that are attributable to C corporation tax years. The effect of creating a separate account for tax-exempt income earned by companies having accumulated E&P is that the AAA is determined by taking into account only the taxable portion of the S corporation's income and any expenses and losses other than those related to the production of the tax-exempt income. Although the OAA balance is reported on page 4 of the Form 1120S, it is not an accumulated earnings account. Municipal bond interest and other forms of tax-exempt income (net of related deduc-

---

[53] Sec. 1368(e). An S corporation without accumulated E&P need not maintain the AAA to determine the tax effect of its distributions. If an S corporation having no E&P subsequently acquires E&P in a transaction where it assumes tax attributes under Sec. 381(a) (e.g., a merger), the corporation must calculate its AAA at the merger date to determine the tax effects of post-merger distributions. To accomplish this calculation, a firm may need to make calculations back to the original S election date. To reduce this hardship, the IRS, in the Form 1120S instructions, recommends that all S corporations maintain AAA information.

[54] Reg. Secs. 1.1367-1(f) and 1.1368-2(a)(5). This ordering for AAA preserves tax-free treatment for S corporation earnings from prior years distributed in the loss year.

tions) become part of the stock basis and thus are placed behind accumulated E&P when determining the distribution order. A corporation having an accumulated E&P balance might consider having the tax-exempt income-producing property owned at the shareholder level rather than at the corporate level.

EXAMPLE C11-27 ▶ Omega Corporation is an electing S corporation with one shareholder, George. George's stock basis at the beginning of the current year is $22,000. Omega has the following results for the current year:

Ordinary loss	$10,000
Dividend income	2,000

In addition, at the beginning of the current year, the corporation has a $12,000 AAA balance and a $4,000 accumulated E&P balance. In December of the current year, Omega distributes $7,500 cash to George. Because the ordinary loss and dividend income produce an $8,000 ($2,000 − $10,000) net negative adjustment, the predistribution AAA remains at $12,000 while the $2,000 dividend increases predistribution stock basis. Accordingly, the predistribution balances are as follows:

	Stock Basis	*AAA*	*E&P*
Beginning balances	$22,000	$12,000	$4,000
Dividend income	2,000	2,000	
Partial ordinary loss		(2,000)	
Predistribution balance	$24,000	$12,000	$4,000

Given these predistribution balances, the distribution has the following effects:

	Stock Basis	*AAA*	*E&P*
Predistribution balance	$24,000	$12,000	$4,000
AAA distribution	(7,500)	(7,500)	
Ordinary loss	(10,000)		
Net negative adjustment		(8,000)	
Ending balance	$ 6,500	($3,500)	$4,000

Because the net negative adjustment to the AAA occurs after the distribution, the entire distribution comes out of the AAA, and none comes out of accumulated E&P. Also, the distribution does not exceed the predistribution stock basis. Thus, the entire distribution is tax free. ◀

EXAMPLE C11-28 ▶ Smith Corporation, an electing S corporation, reports the following results during the current year:

Ordinary income	$30,000
Long-term capital gain	15,000
Municipal bond interest income	5,000
Dividend from domestic corporation	3,000
Charitable contribution	8,000

Smith's sole shareholder, Silvia, has a $60,000 stock basis on January 1. On January 1, Smith has a $40,000 AAA balance, a $27,000 accumulated E&P balance, and a zero OAA balance. Smith makes $50,000 cash distributions to Silvia, its sole shareholder, on June 1 and December 1. The stock basis, AAA, OAA, and accumulated E&P activity for the year (before any distributions) is summarized as follows:

	Stock Basis	*AAA*	*E&P*	*OAA*
Beginning balance	$ 60,000	$40,000	$27,000	$ -0-
Ordinary income	30,000	30,000		
Long-term capital gain	15,000	15,000		
Municipal bond interest	5,000			5,000
Dividend income	3,000	3,000		
Charitable contribution		(8,000)		
Predistribution balance	$113,000	$80,000	$27,000	$5,000

TYPICAL MISCONCEPTION

If shareholders sell their S corporation stock, the AAA account remains with the S corporation. But if an S election terminates, other than for the post-termination transition period, the AAA disappears.

The $80,000 AAA balance is allocated ratably to each of the distributions. The AAA allocation occurs as follows:

$$\$40{,}000 = \$50{,}000 \times \frac{\$80{,}000}{\$50{,}000 + \$50{,}000}$$

The charitable contribution does not reduce the predistribution stock basis but does reduce the predistribution AAA because the reduction does not produce a net negative adjustment. Accordingly, $40,000 of each distribution comes out of AAA. This portion of the distribution is tax-free because the AAA distributions in total are less than the stock's $113,000 predistribution basis. The remaining $10,000 ($50,000 – $40,000) of each distribution comes out of accumulated E&P and is taxable as dividend income. Accumulated E&P is reduced to $7,000 ($27,000 – $20,000) at year-end. The OAA balance reported on Form 1120S is not affected by the distribution because the accumulated E&P has not been exhausted. The stock's basis is $25,000 ($113,000 – $80,000 – $8,000) at year-end because a dividend distribution from accumulated E&P does not reduce its basis, but the charitable contribution does. After adjustment for the distribution, the AAA is zero. The effects of the distribution are summarized below:

	Stock Basis	*AAA*	*E&P*	*OAA*
Predistribution balance	$113,000	$80,000	$27,000	$5,000
AAA distribution	(80,000)	(80,000)		
E&P distribution			(20,000)	
Charitable contribution	(8,000)			
Ending balance	$ 25,000	$ -0-	$ 7,000	$5,000

◀

PROPERTY DISTRIBUTIONS. Property distributions (other than money) made by an S corporation having accumulated E&P require the recognition of gain according to the general rules outlined on pages C11-27 and C11-28. The FMV of the nonmoney property distributed reduces AAA.

TAX STRATEGY TIP

If a shareholder has NOL carryforwards that are about to expire, the election to treat distributions as dividend income to the extent of E&P (as opposed to AAA distributions) may make sense.

DISTRIBUTION ORDERING ELECTIONS. An S corporation can elect to change the distribution order of E&P and the AAA. Specifically, the S corporation can elect to skip over the AAA in determining the source of a cash or property distribution, in which case distributions will come from accumulated E&P and then AAA. This election permits the S corporation to distribute Subchapter C E&P so as to avoid the excess net passive income tax and termination of the S election. The Tax Planning Considerations section of this chapter contains further discussion of this election.

POST-TERMINATION TRANSITION PERIOD. Distributions of money made during the S corporation's post-termination transition period can be made tax-free to those shareholders who owned S corporation stock at the time of the termination. These distributions come first from the former S corporation's AAA balance and then from current and accumulated E&P. The amounts from the AAA are tax-free and reduce the shareholder's stock basis.[55] The AAA balance disappears when the post-termination period ends. Even though the profits earned during the S election period no longer can be distributed tax-free from the AAA after the post-termination period ends, they still can be distributed tax-free to the extent of the shareholder's stock basis once the corporation distributes its current and accumulated E&P. Any distributions made from current or accumulated E&P and nonmoney distributions made during the post-termination transition period are taxable.

Topic Review C11-4 summarizes the taxation of S corporation income and gains that pass through to the shareholders and the treatment of S corporation distributions.

[55] Sec. 1371(e).

Topic Review C11-4

Taxation of S Corporation Income and Distributions

Taxation of Income to the Corporation

1. Unlike with a partnership, special entity level taxes are imposed on an S corporation.
   a. Built-in gains tax: applicable to the net recognized built-in gain of an S corporation that has a history as a C corporation and that made its S election after December 31, 1986.
   b. Excess net passive income tax: applicable to S corporations that have Subchapter C E&P at the close of the tax year and that earn passive investment income exceeding 25% of gross receipts during the tax year.
   c. LIFO recapture tax: imposed when a C corporation that uses the LIFO inventory method in its final C corporation tax year makes an S election.

Allocation of Income to the Shareholders

1. Income and gains are allocated based on the number of shares of stock owned by each shareholder on each day of the tax year.
2. Termination of the S election or termination of the shareholder's interest in the S corporation during the tax year requires the tax year to be divided into two parts. An election can be made to allocate the income or gain according to the general rule in (1) or the accounting methods used by the corporation.

Shareholder Distributions

1. Income and gain allocated to the shareholder increase the basis of the S corporation stock. For any S corporation that does not have an E&P balance, the amount of money plus the FMV of any nonmoney property distributed is tax-free provided it does not exceed the shareholder's basis in the S corporation stock, determined before negative adjustments. The corporation recognizes gain (but not loss) when it distributes nonmoney property. The gain passes through to the shareholders.
2. If the S corporation made the S election after 1982 and has accumulated E&P, two earnings tiers must be maintained: the AAA and accumulated E&P. Distributions come from each tier in succeeding order until the tier is exhausted. Only distributions out of accumulated E&P are taxable to the shareholder unless the stock basis is reduced to zero, in which case the shareholder recognizes capital gain on the excess distribution.

STOP & THINK

Question: Special earnings tracking rules apply to S corporations that formerly were C corporations. Why do we need to have these special rules, which add to the complexity of the distribution topic?

Solution: Former C corporations that were profitable usually have an accumulated E&P balance when they become an S corporation. These earnings have never been taxed as a dividend to the corporation's shareholders. If separate tracking of the S corporation earnings (AAA) and C corporation earnings (accumulated E&P) did not occur, it would be impossible to determine which cash and property distributions came from S corporation earnings and which ones came from C corporation earnings, thereby frustrating the government's ability to collect taxes on distributed E&P.

OTHER RULES

In addition to the differences discussed above, S corporations are treated differently than C corporations in a number of other ways. Some of these differences are examined below. They include tax preference items and other alternative minimum tax (AMT) adjustments, expenses owed by the S corporation to a shareholder, related party sales and exchanges, and fringe benefits paid by the S corporation to a shareholder-employee.

TAX PREFERENCE ITEMS AND OTHER AMT ADJUSTMENTS

The S corporation is not subject to the corporate AMT. Instead, the S corporation computes and passes through tax preference items contained in Sec. 57(a) to its shareholders.

The shareholders then include these tax preference items in their individual AMT calculations. Allocation of the tax preference items occurs on a daily basis unless the corporation makes one of the two special elections to allocate the items based on the corporation's tax accounting methods.

Section 56(a) prescribes a number of adjustments to the tax reporting of certain transactions and occurrences for AMT purposes from that used for income tax purposes. As with tax preference items, the amount of these special AMT adjustments pass through to the S corporation's shareholders to be included in their individual AMT calculations.

S corporations do not have to make an adjustment for the difference between adjusted current earnings and preadjustment alternative minimum taxable income that is made by a C corporation in calculating its AMT liability. For certain corporations, this difference may make an S election attractive.[56]

TRANSACTIONS INVOLVING SHAREHOLDERS AND OTHER RELATED PARTIES

The Sec. 267(a)(2) related party transaction rules deny a payor a deduction for an expense paid to a related payee when a mismatching of the expense and income items occurs as a result of differences in accounting methods. A number of related party situations directly involve S corporations. Some of these transactions involve two S corporations or an S corporation and a C corporation where more than 50% of the value of each corporation's stock is directly or indirectly owned by the same persons. Section 267(a)(2), for example, prevents an S corporation using the accrual method of accounting from currently deducting a year-end expense accrued for an item owed to a second S corporation that uses the cash method of accounting when the same shareholders own both corporations. The first S corporation can deduct the expense on the day the second S corporation includes the income in its gross income.

The S corporation is a pass-through entity and is subject to Sec. 267(e), which extends the Sec. 267(a)(2) related party transaction rules described above to any payment made by the S corporation to *any* person who directly or indirectly owns S corporation stock. This rule prevents the S corporation from deducting a payment to be made to one of its shareholders or to someone who indirectly owns such stock until the payee reports the income. Payments made to the S corporation by a person who directly or indirectly owns S corporation stock are similarly restricted.

EXAMPLE C11-29 ▶ Vassar Corporation, an electing S corporation, uses the accrual method of accounting. On September 1, 2002, Vassar borrows $50,000 from Joan, who owns 10% of the Vassar stock. Joan charges interest at a 12% annual rate. Joan uses the cash method of accounting. At year-end, Vassar accrues $1,500 of interest expense on the loan. The corporation pays six months of interest (including the $1,500 of accrued interest) to Joan on April 1, 2003. Vassar cannot deduct the 2002 interest accrual when determining its ordinary income or loss until it is paid in 2003. ◀

Section 267(a)(1) denies a deduction for losses incurred on the sale or exchange of property directly or indirectly between related parties. The same definition of a related party is used for this purpose as is used in applying Sec. 267(a)(2) to expense transactions involving an S corporation. Any loss disallowed to the seller on the related party sale or exchange can be used to offset gains realized by the purchaser on a subsequent sale or exchange.

FRINGE BENEFITS PAID TO A SHAREHOLDER-EMPLOYEE

The S corporation is not treated as a corporate taxpayer with respect to many fringe benefits paid to any 2% shareholder.[57] Instead, the S corporation is treated the same as a partnership, and the 2% shareholder is treated as a partner of such partnership.[58]

---

[56] Sec. 56(g)(6).

[57] Section 1372(b) defines a 2% shareholder as any person who directly or indirectly owns on any day of the S corporation's tax year more than 2% of its outstanding stock or stock possessing more than 2% of its voting power. The Sec. 318 stock attribution rules are used to determine whether the 2% threshold has been exceeded.

[58] Sec. 1372(a).

TYPICAL MISCONCEPTION

Most fringe benefits provided by a C corporation are deductible to the corporation and nontaxable to the employee. However, fringe benefits paid to a more-than-2% shareholder-employee of an S corporation are in many cases nondeductible unless taxable to the shareholder-employee as compensation.

Because of this restriction, many fringe benefits paid to a 2% shareholder-employee of an S corporation are taxable as compensation to the shareholder and deductible by the corporation if the benefit is not excludible from the shareholder's the gross income. Shareholders owning 2% or less of the S corporation stock are treated as ordinary employees.

The special fringe benefit rules apply only to statutory fringe benefits. They do not apply to stock options, qualified retirement plans, and nonqualified deferred compensation. The fringe benefits limited by the more-than-2%-shareholder rule include group term life insurance premiums (Sec. 79), accident and health benefit plan insurance premiums and payments (Secs. 105 and 106), meals and lodging furnished by the employer (Sec. 119), cafeteria plan benefits (Sec. 125), and employer-provided parking (Sec. 132). Fringe benefits that may be excluded by more-than-2%-shareholders include compensation for injuries and sickness (Sec. 104); educational assistance program benefits (Sec. 127); dependent care assistance program benefits (Sec. 129); and no-additional-cost benefits, qualified employee discounts, working condition fringe benefits, de minimis fringe benefits, and on-premises athletic facilities (Sec. 132). For purposes of the Sec. 162(l) above-the-line deduction for self-employed taxpayer's health insurance premiums, a more-than-2%-shareholder is deemed to be self-employed.

EXAMPLE C11-30 ▶ Billy and his wife Cathy equally own Edison Corporation, an electing S corporation. Edison employs Billy and ten other individuals. All employees receive group term life insurance benefits based on their annual salaries. All employees except Billy can qualify for the Sec. 79 group term life insurance premium exclusion. Billy is treated as a partner and, therefore, does not qualify as an employee. Billy's premiums are treated as compensation and taxable to Billy. Edison can deduct the premiums paid to all its employees, including Billy. Since Billy is treated as self-employed under the 2% shareholder rules, he can deduct a portion of the premiums paid on the health insurance as a "for" AGI deduction under the Sec.162(l) rules applicable to health insurance payments made by all self-employed individuals. ◀

TAX PLANNING CONSIDERATIONS

ELECTION TO ALLOCATE INCOME BASED ON THE S CORPORATION'S ACCOUNTING METHODS

As a general rule, the S corporation's ordinary income or loss and separately stated items are allocated based on the amount of stock owned by each shareholder on each day of the S corporation's tax year. A special election is available to allocate the income based on the S corporation's accounting methods when the S election terminates or when a shareholder terminates or substantially reduces his or her entire interest in the S corporation.[59] The use of the S corporation's tax accounting method to allocate the year's profit or loss can permit income shifting among shareholders.

EXAMPLE C11-31 ▶ At the beginning of 2002, Rod and Dana equally own Apex Corporation, an electing S corporation. During 2002, Apex reports ordinary income of $146,000. On March 31, 2002 (the 90th day of Apex's tax year), Dana sells all his Apex stock to Randy. Apex Corporation earns $125,000 of its ordinary income after March 31, 2002. Rod is allocated $73,000 ($146,000 × 0.50) of ordinary income. His income allocation is the same whether the daily allocation method or the special allocation election is used. In total, Dana and Randy are allocated $73,000 of ordinary income. Dana and Randy can allocate the ordinary income amount in the following ways:

---

[59] The shareholder, however, still can be a creditor, director, or employee of the corporation. Sections 1362(e) and 1377(a) prevent the daily allocation method from applying to any items resulting from a sale or exchange of 50% or more of the S corporation's stock during an S termination year.

	Daily Allocation	Special Election
Dana:	$\$146{,}000 \times \frac{1}{2} \times \frac{90}{365} = \$18{,}000$	$(\$146{,}000 - \$125{,}000) \times \frac{1}{2} = \$10{,}500$
Randy:	$\$146{,}000 \times \frac{1}{2} \times \frac{275}{365} = \$55{,}000$	$\$125{,}000 \times \frac{1}{2} = \$62{,}500$

The shifting of the $7,500 ($18,000–$10,500) in income from Dana to Randy under the special election also will reduce Dana's adjusted basis for his Apex stock when determining his gain or loss on the sale. The $7,500 difference between the income allocations under the two methods may be a point for negotiation between Dana and Randy, particularly if their marginal tax rates are different. ◀

By electing to use the S corporation's tax accounting method to allocate profits or losses between the C short year and S short year in the year in which the S corporation election terminates, losses can be shifted into an S short year where the shareholders obtain an immediate benefit at a marginal tax rate of up to 38.6% (in 2002), or profits can be shifted into a C short year to take advantage of the 15% and 25% marginal corporate tax rates. One such scenario is illustrated below.

EXAMPLE C11-32 ▶ Choe Corporation has been an S corporation for several years using a calendar year as its tax year. Its S election terminates on July 1. The S short year includes January 1 through June 30 and the C short year includes July 1 through December 31. Total ordinary income this year is $10,000. If the books are closed on June 30, $40,000 of ordinary loss is allocable to the S short year and $50,000 of ordinary income is allocable to the C short year. Assuming each month has 30 days, the following income allocations are possible:

Period	Daily Allocation	Closing of Books
S short year	$ 5,000	($40,000)
C short year	5,000	50,000
Total	$10,000	$10,000

By closing the books, the $40,000 S short year loss passes through to the shareholders, and the $50,000 C short year income is taxed to the C corporation. With the daily allocation, one-half the income is taxed to the shareholders, and the other half is taxed to the C corporation.[60] Whether the special election is beneficial can be determined only by calculating the shareholder and corporate tax liabilities under each alternative. ◀

INCREASING THE BENEFITS FROM S CORPORATION LOSSES

At the shareholder level, the deduction for S corporation pass-through losses is limited to the S corporation stock basis plus the basis of any debt owed by the S corporation to the shareholder. Pass-through losses that exceed this limitation carry over to a subsequent tax year when the shareholder again has stock or debt basis. If the shareholder expects his or her marginal tax rate to be the same or lower in a future tax year when the loss carryover can be used, the shareholder should consider either increasing his or her stock basis or loaning additional funds to the corporation before the end of the current tax year. Conversely, if the loans are never expected to be repaid, he or she should not lend the S corporation additional amounts just to secure an additional tax deduction, which is worth at most 38.6 cents (at 2002 rates) for each dollar loaned. If the shareholder expects his or her marginal tax rate to be higher in future tax years, the shareholder should consider deferring additional capital contributions or loans until after the end of the current tax year.

[60] Section 1362(e)(5)(A) requires calculation of the tax liability for the C short year to be based on the annualized income of the former S corporation (see Chapter C3 for a discussion of annualization).

EXAMPLE C11-33 ▶ Nancy owns 100% of Bailey Corporation, an electing S corporation. Bailey Corporation expects large losses in 2002 that will result in a $100,000 ordinary loss. Nancy's Bailey stock basis (before adjustment for the current loss) is $35,000. Bailey also owes Nancy $25,000. Nancy's 2002 marginal tax rate is 38.6%. Nancy expects her marginal tax rate to decline to 15% in 2003. Nancy should consider making $40,000 [$100,000 loss − ($35,000 stock basis + $25,000 debt basis)] of additional capital contributions or loans before the end of 2002 to obtain an additional $9,440 [(0.386 − 0.15) × $40,000] of tax benefits from deducting the anticipated loss carryover in the current year. If Nancy instead expects her 2002 and 2003 marginal tax rates to be 15% and 38.6%, respectively, the $9,440 tax benefit (less the time value of money for one year) can be obtained by having Nancy defer her capital contributions or loans until 2003. Alternatively, Nancy could use the loss carryover to offset profits reported in 2003. These profits would restore part or all of the debt basis (and possibly increase the stock basis). The basis then would be partially or fully offset by the $40,000 loss carryover. ◀

KEY POINT

If an S corporation shareholder has losses that have been suspended due to lack of basis, either contributions to capital or bona fide loans to the corporation will create the necessary basis to use the losses.

The S corporation loss carryover is available only to the shareholder who held the stock when the loss occurred. A shareholder should consider increasing the stock basis to take advantage of the carryover before selling the stock. The purchasing shareholder does not acquire the carryover.

PASSIVE INCOME REQUIREMENTS

The S corporation can earn an unlimited amount of passive income each year without incurring any penalty provided it does not have any E&P accumulated in a C corporation tax year (known as Subchapter C E&P) at the end of its tax year. Thus, a corporation can make an S election to avoid the personal holding company penalty tax.

Potentially, S corporations that have operated as C corporations and have accumulated Subchapter C E&P are liable for the excess net passive income tax. In addition, their S election may terminate if the passive investment income exceeds 25% of gross receipts for three consecutive tax years. The S corporation can avoid both of these possible problems by making a special election under Sec. 1368(e)(3) to distribute its entire Subchapter C E&P balance to its shareholders. A corporation that makes the election to distribute Subchapter C E&P before its accumulated adjustments account (AAA) can make a second special election to treat part or all of this "distribution" as a deemed dividend, which is deemed distributed to the shareholders and immediately contributed by the shareholders to the corporation on the last day of the corporation's tax year.[61] Such an election requires no cash outlay. The distribution results in a tax cost for the shareholders, who pay tax on the resulting dividend income. To the shareholders, the cost of the election can be small if the accumulated E&P balance is insignificant or if the shareholder has a current year NOL (excluding the distribution) or an NOL carryover. The ultimate long-run benefit, however, may be great because it permits the S corporation to earn an unlimited amount of passive investment income free from corporate taxes in subsequent tax years.

EXAMPLE C11-34 ▶ Hawaii Corporation incorporated in 1989. It operated for a number of years as a C corporation, during which time it accumulated $30,000 of E&P. Most of Hawaii's gross income now comes from rentals and interest, constituting passive investment income. Hawaii makes an S election starting in 2002. The excess net passive income tax will apply in 2002 if Hawaii's rentals and interest exceed 25% of its gross receipts for the year unless the corporation makes an election to distribute the accumulated E&P and then distributes the earnings by the end of its first tax year as an S corporation. ◀

S corporations that earn rental income also can avoid the passive income tax and the possibility of having its election terminated if the corporation renders significant services to the occupant of the space or if the corporation incurs significant costs in the rental business.[62] Whether significant services are performed or substantial costs are incurred in

[61] Reg. Sec. 1.1368-1(f)(3).

[62] According to Reg. Sec. 1.1362-2(c)(5)(ii)(B)(3), however, significant services are not rendered and substantial costs are not incurred in connection with net leases.

the rental business is determined based on all the facts and circumstances including, but not limited to, the number of persons employed to provide the services and the types and amounts of costs and expenses incurred (other than depreciation).

EXAMPLE C11-35 ▶ Assume the same facts as in Example C11-34 except that Hawaii Corporation provides significant services to its tenants in connection with its rental activities. Because the services are significant, Hawaii Corporation has a passive income problem only if its interest income exceeds 25% of its gross receipts. If the 25% threshold is not exceeded, Hawaii can avoid having to distribute its Subchapter C E&P in 2002. ◀

S corporations that experience a passive income problem in two consecutive tax years should carefully monitor their passive income in the next year. If they see that their passive income for the third year will exceed the 25% threshold, they should make certain that they elect to distribute their accumulated Subchapter C E&P before year-end. This strategy not only will prevent loss of the S election but also will avoid having to pay the Sec. 1375 tax.

COMPLIANCE AND PROCEDURAL CONSIDERATIONS

MAKING THE ELECTION

A corporation makes the S election by filing Form 2553 (Election by Small Business Corporation to Tax Corporation Income Directly to Shareholders). The election form can be signed by any person authorized to sign the S corporation's tax return under Sec. 6037. Form 2553 is filed with the IRS Service Center designated in the instructions. The IRS can treat a late election as timely made if the corporation can show reasonable cause.[63]

Shareholder consents to the S election can be made either on Form 2553 or on a separate consent statement signed by the shareholder and attached to the corporation's election form. Regulation Sec. 1.1362-6(b) outlines other information that must be provided with a separate consent. The IRS can grant extensions of time for filing shareholder consents to the S election.[64]

A corporation makes a Sec. 444 election to use a fiscal year on Form 8716, which the corporation must file by the earlier of (1) the fifteenth day of the fifth month following the month that includes the first day of the tax year for which the election will first be effective or (2) the due date for the income tax return resulting from the election.[65] A copy of Form 8716 must be attached to Form 1120S for the first tax year for which the Sec. 444 election is effective. A corporation desiring to make a Sec. 444 election also must state its intention in a statement attached to its S election form (Form 2553).[66]

OBJECTIVE 11

Explain the procedures for filing an S corporation tax return

FILING THE CORPORATE TAX RETURN

All S corporations, whether or not they owe taxes under Secs. 1374 or 1375, must file a tax return if they exist for part or all of the tax year. An S corporation must file its corporate tax return not later than the fifteenth day of the third month following the end of the tax year.[67] The S corporation reports its results on Form 1120S (U.S. Income Tax Return for an S Corporation). A completed S corporation tax return and the facts supporting the return are illustrated in Appendix B. An S corporation is allowed an automatic six-month extension of time for filing its tax return by filing Form 7004 (Application for Automatic Extension of Time to File U.S. Corporation Income Tax Return), also illustrated in Appendix B.[68]

[63] Sec. 1362(b)(5).
[64] Reg. Sec. 1.1362-6(b)(3)(iii).
[65] Temp. Reg. Sec. 1.444-3T(b)(1).
[66] Temp. Reg. Sec. 1.444-3T(b)(3).
[67] Sec. 6072(b).
[68] Reg. Sec. 1.6081-3.

EXAMPLE C11-36 ▶ Simpson Corporation, an S corporation, uses the calendar year as its tax year. Its tax return generally is due on March 15. An automatic extension of six months is permitted for the return, thereby extending its due date until September 15. ◀

KEY POINT

An S corporation must file Form 1120S, which is basically an informational return. The shareholders each receive a K-1 with their share of the income/loss/credit items for the year.

All S corporations that file a tax return must furnish each person who is a shareholder at any time during the tax year with pertinent information from the tax return, usually via Form 1120S, Schedule K-1. The Schedule K-1 must be made available to the shareholder not later than the day on which it is filed.[69] The S corporation's pass-through ordinary income or loss and certain passive income or loss items are reported on an individual shareholder's Form 1040, Schedule E. Most separately stated items are reported on other supporting schedules to Form 1040, as illustrated on the Form 1120S, Schedule K-1 presented in Appendix B.

An S corporation is subject to the same basic three-year statute of limitations that applies to other taxpayers. This three-year period applies for purposes of determining the time period during which

- ▶ The corporation remains liable for assessments of the excess net passive income tax and the built-in gains tax
- ▶ The IRS can question the correctness of an S election made for a particular tax year[70]

The limitation period for assessing the income tax liability of an S corporation shareholder (e.g., for an erroneous S corporation loss deduction claimed), however, runs from the date on which the shareholder's return is filed and not from the date the S corporation's tax return is filed.[71]

Determination of the Sec. 7519 required payment is made on a computation worksheet provided in the instructions for the Form 1120S. The corporation need not make a required payment if the total of such payments for the current year and all preceding years is $500 or less. Amounts less than the $500 threshold carry over to succeeding years. The required payment is due on or before May 15 regardless of the fiscal year used. The required payment and the computation worksheet must accompany a Form 8752, which also is used to secure a refund of prior Sec. 7519 payments.[72]

OBJECTIVE 12

Determine the estimated tax payments required of an S corporation and its shareholders

ESTIMATED TAX PAYMENTS

S corporations must make estimated tax payments if their estimated tax liability is reasonably expected to be $500 or more.[73] Estimated tax payments are required for the corporate liability attributable to the built-in gains tax (Sec. 1374) and the excess net passive income tax (Sec. 1375). In addition, the S corporation's shareholders must include their income, gain, loss, deduction, and credit pass-throughs in their own estimated tax calculations.

SELF-STUDY QUESTION

Is an S corporation required to make estimated tax payments?

ANSWER

Yes. An S corporation is required to pay estimated taxes if the corporation is subject to built-in gains or excess net passive income taxes. Also, shareholders are required to include their S corporation income/loss and credit pass-throughs in determining their estimated tax payments.

The corporate estimated tax payment requirements described for a C corporation in Chapter C3 also apply to an S corporation's tax liabilities. The required quarterly installment is 25% of the lesser of (1) 100% of the tax shown on the return for the tax year and (2) the sum of 100% of the built-in gains tax shown on the return for the tax year plus 100% of the excess net passive income tax shown on the return for the preceding tax year.

An S corporation cannot use the prior year tax liability exception when determining the required payment to be made with respect to the built-in gains tax. This exception is available with respect to the excess net passive income tax portion of the required payment without regard to whether the corporation owed any tax in the prior year. All corporations can use the prior year tax liability exception for the excess net passive income tax whether or not they are "large" corporations under Sec. 6655(d)(2). The annualization election of Sec. 6655(e) also is available when determining the quarterly estimated tax payment amounts. An S corporation's failure to make timely estimated tax payments, or a timely final payment when it files the tax return, will cause it to be subject to interest and penalties like other taxpayers.

---

[69] Sec. 6037(b).

[70] Sec. 6233.

[71] *Sheldon B. Bufferd v. CIR*, 71 AFTR 2d 93-573, 93-1 USTC ¶50,038 (USSC, 1993).

[72] Temp. Reg. Sec. 1.7519-2T.

[73] Estimate tax rules appear in Sec. 6655.

The S corporation's shareholders must include their ratable share of ordinary income or loss and separately stated items in determining their estimated tax liability. Such amounts are treated as having been received concurrently by the shareholders throughout the S corporation's tax year. Thus, ordinary income or loss and separately stated items for an S corporation tax year that ends with or within the shareholder's tax year are included in the estimated tax calculation to the extent they are attributable to months in the S corporation tax year that precede the month in which the installment is due.

CONSISTENCY RULES

ADDITIONAL COMMENT

If the IRS is conducting an audit of an S corporation, the audit is conducted in a unified proceeding at the corporate level rather than in separate audits of each S corporation shareholder.

Section 6037(c) requires an S corporation shareholder to report on his or her return a Subchapter S item in a manner consistent with the treatment accorded the item on the S corporation's return. A Subchapter S item is any item (e.g., income, gain, deduction, loss, credit, accounting method, or tax year) of an S corporation where the reporting of the item is more appropriately determined at the corporation level than at the shareholder level. A shareholder must notify the IRS of any inconsistency when the corporation has filed a return but the shareholder's treatment on his return is (or may be) inconsistent with the treatment of the item on the corporation return. Failure to do so may result in the imposition of a negligence penalty under Sec. 6662. Any adjustment required to produce consistency with the corporate return is treated as a mathematical or clerical error for penalty calculation purposes. A similar notification also is required when the corporation has not filed a return. If a shareholder receives incorrect information from the S corporation regarding a Subchapter S item, the shareholder's consistent reporting of the item consistently with the information provided by the corporation generally will eliminate the imposition of any penalty.

SAMPLE S CORPORATION TAX RETURN

A sample S corporation Form 1120S and supporting Schedule K-1 appear in Appendix B, along with the facts supporting the return. Two differences should be noted between the S corporation tax return and a partnership tax return. First, the S corporation tax return provides for the determination of a corporate tax liability and the payment of the special taxes that can be levied on the S corporation. No such items are shown on the partnership return. Second, the S corporation return does not require a reconciliation of the shareholders' basis adjustments as occurs on a partnership tax return. Schedule M-1 and M-2 reconciliations similar to those required of a C corporation are required of an S corporation. The Schedule M-1 requires a reconciliation of book income with the income or loss reported on line 23 of Schedule K, which includes not only the ordinary income (loss) amount but also separately stated income and deduction items. The Schedule M-2 requires a reconciliation of the AAA, OAA, and PTI accounts. (The PTI account pertains to pre-1983 S corporations.) The AAA reconciliation is required only of S corporations that have an accumulated E&P balance, although the IRS recommends that the AAA be maintained by all S corporations. The OAA balance is calculated and reported only by corporations that have an accumulated E&P balance at year-end. The account is adjusted for tax-exempt income and the related nondeductible expenses for the year.

PROBLEM MATERIALS

DISCUSSION QUESTIONS

C11-1 List five advantages and five disadvantages of making an S election. Briefly explain each item.

C11-2 Julio, age 50, is a U.S. citizen who has a 30% marginal tax rate. He has operated the A&B Automotive Parts Company for a number of years as a C corporation. Last year, A&B reported $200,000 of pre-tax profits, from which it paid $50,000 in salary and $25,000 in dividends to Julio. The corporation expects this year's pre-tax profits to be $300,000. To date, the corporation has created no fringe benefits or pension plans for Julio. Julio asks you to explain whether an S corporation election would reduce his taxes. How do you respond to Julio's inquiry?

C11-3 Celia, age 30, is leaving a major systems development firm to establish her own firm. She will design computer-based systems for small- and medium-sized businesses. Celia will invest $100,000 in the business. She hopes to operate near her breakeven point during her first year, although a small loss is possible. Profits will build up slowly over the next four years until she is earning $150,000 a year in her fifth year. Celia has heard some of the tax people who worked for her former employer talk about S corporations. She comes to you to ask whether the S corporation form would be advisable for her new business. How do you respond to Celia's inquiry?

C11-4 Lance and Rodney are contemplating starting a new business to manufacture computer software games. They expect to encounter losses in the initial years. Lance's CPA has talked to them about using an S corporation. Rodney, while reading a business publication, encounters a discussion on limited liability companies (LLCs). The article talks about the advantages of using an LLC instead of an S corporation. How would you respond to their inquiry?

C11-5 Which of the following classifications make a shareholder ineligible to own the stock of an S corporation?
a. U.S. citizen
b. Domestic corporation
c. Partnership where all the partners are U.S. citizens
d. Estate of a deceased U.S. citizen
e. Grantor trust created by a U.S. citizen
f. Nonresident alien individual

C11-6 Which of the following taxes do not apply to an S corporation?
a. Regular (income) tax
b. Accumulated earnings tax
c. Corporate alternative minimum tax
d. Built-in gains tax
e. Personal holding company tax
f. Excess net passive income tax
g. LIFO recapture tax

C11-7 Which of the following events will cause an S election to terminate?
a. The S corporation earning 100% of its gross receipts in its first tax year from passive sources
b. The S corporation issuing nonvoting stock that has a dividend preference
c. The S corporation purchasing 100% of the single class of stock of a second domestic corporation that has conducted business activities for four years
d. An individual shareholder donating 100 shares of S corporation stock to a charity that is exempt from tax under Sec. 501(c)(3)
e. The S corporation earning tax-exempt interest income

C11-8 What is an inadvertent termination? What actions must the S corporation and its shareholders take to correct an inadvertent termination?

C11-9 After an S corporation revokes its S election, how long must the corporation wait to make a new election? What circumstances permit an early reelection?

C11-10 What tax years can be adopted by a newly created corporation that makes an S election for its first tax year? If a fiscal year is permitted, does it require IRS approval?

C11-11 At the time Cable Corporation makes its S election, it elects to use a fiscal year based on a Sec. 444 election. What other requirement(s) must be satisfied for Cable Corporation to continue to use its fiscal year election for future tax years?

C11-12 What are Subchapter C earnings and profits? How does the existence of such earnings affect the S corporation's ability to earn passive income?

C11-13 Explain the procedures for allocating an S corporation's ordinary income or loss to each of the shareholders. What special allocation elections are available?

C11-14 What limitations apply to the amount of loss pass-through an S corporation shareholder can deduct? What happens to any losses exceeding this limitation?

C11-15 What actions can an S corporation shareholder take before year-end to increase the amount of the S corporation's losses he or she can deduct in the year they are incurred?

C11-16 What is a post-termination transition period? What loss carryovers can an S corporation shareholder deduct during this period?

C11-17 Explain the positive and negative adjustments to the basis of an S corporation shareholder's stock investment and the basis of an S corporation debt owed to the shareholder.

C11-18 Explain the differences between the tax treatment accorded nonliquidating property distributions made by S corporations and partnerships.

C11-19 What nonliquidating distributions made by an S corporation are taxable to its shareholders? Tax-free to its shareholders?

C11-20 What is an accumulated adjustments account (AAA)? What income, gain, loss, and deduction items *do not* affect this account assuming the S corporation has an accumulated E&P balance?

C11-21 Explain the differences between the way the following items are reported by a C corporation and an S corporation:
a. Ordinary income or loss
b. Capital gains and losses
c. Tax-exempt interest income
d. Charitable contributions

e. Nonliquidating property distributions
f. Fringe benefits paid to a shareholder-employee

C11-22 When is the S corporation's tax return due? What extensions are available for filing the return?

C11-23 What S corporation taxes must be prepaid by having the corporation make quarterly estimated tax payments? Can a shareholder owning S corporation stock use the corporation's estimated tax payments to reduce the amount of his or her individual estimated tax payments? Explain.

C11-24 Review the completed C corporation, partnership, and S corporation tax returns presented in Appendix B. List three major tax reporting similarities and three major tax reporting differences in either content or format among the three tax returns.

ISSUE IDENTIFICATION QUESTIONS

C11-25 J & P Corporation is to be owned equally by Jennelle and Paula. The corporation will be formed by exchanging the assets and liabilities of the J & P Manufacturing Partnership for all the corporation's stock on September 1 of the current year. Both shareholders use the calendar year as their tax year and desire to make an S election. What tax issues should Jennelle and Paula consider with respect to the incorporation?

C11-26 Williams Corporation has operated as a C corporation for the last seven years. The corporation has assets with a $450,000 adjusted basis and an $800,000 FMV. Liabilities amount to $100,000. All the Williams Corporation stock is owned by Dan Williams, who uses a calendar year as his tax year. The corporation uses the accrual method of accounting and a June 30 year-end. Dan's CPA has told him to convert the corporation to S corporation status to reduce his total corporate/personal federal income tax liability. Dan would like to complete the conversion on the last day of the corporation's tax year. What tax issues should Dan and his CPA consider with respect to the S election?

C11-27 Peter owns 50% of Air South Corporation, an air charter service. His S corporation stock basis at beginning of the year is $100,000. Air South has not done well this year and will report an ordinary loss of $375,000. Peter's marginal tax rate for the current year is 35%. What tax issues should Peter consider with respect to the loss?

C11-28 Glacier Smokeries has been an S corporation since its inception six years ago. On January 1 of the current year, the corporation's two equal shareholders, Adam and Rodney, had adjusted bases of $175,000 and $225,000, respectively, for their S corporation's stock. The shareholders plan to have the corporation distribute land with a $75,000 adjusted basis and a $300,000 FMV in the current year. Ordinary income is expected to be $125,000 in the current year. What tax issues should Adam and Rodney consider with respect to the distribution?

PROBLEMS

C11-29 *Comparison of Entity Forms.* King Corporation is 100%-owned by Ken Munro, a single taxpayer. During 2002, King reports $100,000 of taxable income. Ken Munro reports no income other than that earned from King, and Ken claims the standard deduction.

a. What is King Corporation's income tax liability assuming Ken withdraws none of the earnings from the C corporation? What is Ken's income tax liability? What is the total tax liability for the corporation and its shareholder?
b. Assume that King Corporation instead distributes 100% of its after-tax earnings to Ken as a dividend in the current year. What is the total income tax liability for the C corporation and its shareholder?
c. How would your answer to Part a change if Ken withdrew $50,000 from the business in salary? Must any taxes other than corporate and individual income taxes be considered now that the corporation pays a salary?
d. How would your answers to Parts a–c change if King Corporation were instead an S corporation?

C11-30 *Making the Election.* Voyles Corporation, a calendar year taxpayer formed five years ago, desires to make an S election beginning in 2002. Sue and Andrea each own one-half of the Voyles stock.

a. How does Voyles Corporation make the S election?
b. When can Voyles Corporation file its election form?
c. If the election in Part b is not filed in a timely manner, when will it first take effect?

C11-31 *Termination of the Election.* Orlando Corporation, a calendar year taxpayer, has been an S corporation for several years. On July 10, 2002, Orlando Corporation authorizes a second class of nonvoting preferred stock that pays a 10% annual dividend. The corporation issues the stock to Sid on September 15, 2002 to raise additional equity capital. Sid owns no other Orlando stock.

a. Does Orlando Corporation's S election terminate? If so, when is the termination effective?
b. What tax returns must Orlando Corporation file for 2002? When are they due?
c. How would your answer to Parts a and b change if the second class of stock were instead nonvoting Class B common stock?

C11-32 *Revocation of the Election.* Tango Corporation, a calendar year taxpayer, has been an S corporation for several years. Tango's business activities have become very profitable in recent years. On June 15, 2002, its sole shareholder, who is in the 38.6% marginal tax bracket, desires to revoke the S election.

a. How does Tango revoke its S election? When does the revocation take effect?
b. Assume the revocation is effective July 1, 2002. What tax returns are required of Tango for 2002? For 2003? When are these returns due?
c. If the corporation makes a new S election after the revocation, when does it take effect?

C11-33 *Sale of S Corporation Interest.* Peter and his wife, Alice, own all the stock of Galleon Corporation. Galleon Corporation made its S election 12 years ago. Peter and Alice sold one-half their Galleon stock to a partnership owned by Rob and Susan (not husband and wife) at the close of business on December 31, 2002 for a $75,000 profit. What are the tax consequences of the sale transaction for Peter and Alice? For the corporation? As Peter and Alice's CPA, do you have any advice for them if all parties would like the S election to continue?

C11-34 *Selecting a Tax Year.* Indicate in each of the following situations whether the taxpayer can accomplish what is proposed. Provide adequate authority for your answer including any special elections that are needed or requirements that must be satisfied. Assume that all individuals use the calendar year as their tax year unless otherwise indicated.

a. Will and Carol form Classic Corporation. They want the corporation to adopt a fiscal year ending January 31 as its tax year to provide a maximum deferral for their income. The corporation makes an S election for its initial tax year ending January 31, 2003.
b. Mark and Dennis have owned and operated the Plastic Corporation for several years. Plastic Corporation has used a fiscal year ending June 30 since its organization as a C corporation because it conforms to the corporation's natural business year. The corporation makes an S election for its tax year beginning July 1, 2002.

C11-35 *Passive Income Tax.* Oliver organized North Corporation 15 years ago. The corporation made an S election three years ago after it accumulated $60,000 of E&P as a C corporation. None of the accumulated E&P has been distributed as of December 31, 2002. In 2002, North Corporation reports the following results:

Dividends from domestic corporations	$ 60,000
Rental income	100,000
Services income	50,000
Expenses related to rental income	30,000
Expenses related to services income	15,000
Other expenses	5,000

The corporation has not provided significant services nor incurred substantial costs in connection with earning the rental income. The services income are the gross receipts derived from the active conduct of a trade or business.

a. Is North Corporation subject to the excess net passive income tax? If so, what is its tax liability?
b. What is the effect of the excess net passive income tax liability on North's passthroughs of ordinary income and separately stated items?
c. What advice would you give North Corporation regarding its activities?

C11-36 ***Built-in Gains Tax.*** Theta Corporation was created 15 years ago. In its first year, it elected to use the cash method of accounting and adopted a calendar year as its tax year. It made an S election on August 15, 2001 effective for Theta's 2002 tax year. At the beginning of 2002, Theta had assets with a $600,000 FMV and a $180,000 adjusted basis. During 2002, Theta reports taxable income of $400,000.

- Theta collects all accounts receivables outstanding on January 1, 2002 in the amount of $200,000. The receivables had a zero adjusted basis.
- Theta sells an automobile on February 1, 2002 for $3,500. The automobile had a $2,000 adjusted basis and a $3,000 FMV on January 1, 2002. Theta claimed $1,000 of MACRS depreciation on the automobile in 2002.
- Theta sells land (a Sec. 1231 asset) that it held three years in anticipation of building its own office building for a $35,000 gain. The land had a $45,000 FMV and a $25,000 adjusted basis on January 1, 2002.
- Theta paid accounts payable outstanding on January 1, 2002 of $125,000. All the payables are deductible expenses.

What is the amount of Theta's built-in gains tax liability?

C11-37 ***Determination of Pass-Throughs and Stock Basis Adjustments.*** Mike and Nancy are equal shareholders in MN Corporation, an S corporation. The corporation, Mike, and Nancy are calendar year taxpayers. The corporation has been an S corporation during its entire existence and thus has no accumulated E&P. The shareholders have no loans to the corporation. The corporation incurred the following items in the current year:

Sales	$300,000
Cost of goods sold	140,000
Dividends on corporate investments	10,000
Tax-exempt interest income	3,000
Section 1245 gain (recapture) on equipment sale	22,000
Section 1231 gain on equipment sale	12,000
Long-term capital gain on stock sale	8,000
Long-term capital loss on stock sale	7,000
Short-term capital loss on stock sale	6,000
Depreciation	18,000
Salary to Nancy	20,000
Meals and entertainment expenses	7,800
Interest expense on loans allocable to:	
Business debt	32,000
Stock investments	6,400
Tax-exempt bonds	1,800
Principal payment on business loan	9,000
Charitable contributions	2,000
Distributions to shareholders ($15,000 each)	30,000

a. Compute the S corporation's ordinary income and separately stated items.
b. Show Mike's and Nancy's shares of the items in Part a.
c. Compute Mike's and Nancy's ending stock bases assuming their beginning balances are $100,000 each. When making basis adjustments, apply the adjustments in the order outlined on page C11-24 of the text.

C11-38 ***Allocation of Income to Shareholders.*** John owns all the stock of Lucas Corporation, an electing S corporation. John's basis for the 1,000 shares is $130,000. On June 11 of the current year (assume a non-leap year), John gifts 100 shares of stock to his younger brother Michael, who has been working in the business for one year. Lucas Corporation reports $125,000 of ordinary income for the current year. What amount of income is allocated to John? To Michael?

C11-39 ***Sale of S Corporation Interest.*** Al and Ruth each own one-half the stock of Chemical Corporation, an electing S corporation. During the current year (assume a non-leap year), Chemical Corporation earns $15,000 per month of ordinary income. On April 5, Ruth sells her entire stock interest to Patty. The corporation sells a business asset on August 18 and realizes a $75,000 Sec. 1231 gain. What alternatives (if any) exist for allocating Chemical Corporation's current year income?

C11-40 *Allocation of Income to Shareholders.* Toyland Corporation, an electing S corporation, uses the calendar year as its tax year. Bob, Alice, and Carter own 60, 30, and 10 shares, respectively, of the Toyland stock. Carter's basis for his stock is $26,000 on January 1 of the current year (assume a non-leap year). On June 30, Alice gifted one-half of her stock to Mike. On November 30, Carter sold his stock to Mike for $45,000. Toyland reports the following results for the current year:

Ordinary income	$120,000
Long-term capital loss	10,000
Charitable contributions	6,000

a. What amount of income, loss, or deduction do the four shareholders report (assuming no special elections are made)?
b. What gain or loss does Carter recognize when he sells the Toyland stock?

C11-41 *Allocation of Income to Shareholders.* Redfern Corporation, a calendar year taxpayer, has been an S corporation for several years. The Redfern stock is owned equally by Rod and Ken. On July 1 of the current year (assume a non-leap year), Redfern Corporation issues additional common stock to Blackfoot Corporation for cash. Rod, Ken, and Blackfoot Corporation each end up owning one-third of the Redfern stock. Redfern Corporation reports ordinary income of $125,000 and a short-term capital loss of $15,000 in the current year. Eighty percent of the ordinary income and all the capital loss accrue after Blackfoot Corporation purchases its stock. Redfern makes no distributions to its shareholders in the current year. What income and losses do Redfern and Blackfoot Corporations and Rod and Ken report as a result of the current year's activities?

C11-42 *Allocation of Income Between Family Members.* Bright Corporation, an electing S corporation, has been 100% owned by Betty since it was created 12 years ago. The corporation has been quite profitable in recent years, and in the current year (assume a non-leap year) it reports ordinary income of $240,000 after paying Betty a $60,000 salary. On January 1, Betty gifts 15% of the Bright stock to each of her three sons, John, Andrew, and Stephen, in the hope that they will work in the family business. Betty pays gift taxes on the transfers. The sons are ages 16, 9, and 2 at present and are not currently active in the business. Bright distributes $7,500 in cash to each son and $27,500 in cash to Betty in the current year.

a. What income does Betty, John, Andrew, and Stephen report for the current year as a result of Bright's activities assuming the sons are considered bona fide owners of the stock? How will the income be taxed to the children?
b. Assuming the IRS determines a reasonable salary for Betty to be $120,000, how would your answer to Part a change?
c. How would your answer to Part a change if the sons were not considered bona fide owners of the stock?

C11-43 *Use of Losses by Shareholders.* Raider Corporation, an electing S corporation, is owned equally by Monte and Allie. Both individuals actively participate in Raider's business. On January 1, Monte and Allie have adjusted bases for their Raider stock of $80,000 and $90,000, respectively. During the current year, Raider Corporation reports the following results:

Ordinary loss	$175,000
Tax-exempt interest income	20,000
Long-term capital loss	32,000

Raider's balance sheet at year-end shows the following liabilities: accounts payable, $90,000; mortgage payable, $30,000; and note payable to Allie, $10,000.

a. What income and deductions will Monte and Allie report from Raider's current year activities?
b. What basis does Monte have in his stock investment on December 31?
c. What basis does Allie have in her stock investment and note on December 31?
d. What loss carryovers are available for Monte and Allie?
e. Explain how the use of the losses in Part a would change if Raider Corporation were instead a partnership and Monte and Allie were partners who shared profits, losses, and liabilities equally.

C11-44 *Use of Loss Carryovers.* Assume the same facts as in Problem C11-43 except that Raider Corporation reports $75,000 of ordinary income, $20,000 of tax-exempt income, and a $25,000 long-term capital gain in the next year.

a. What income and deductions will Monte and Allie report from next year's activities?
b. What basis does Monte have in his stock investment on December 31 of next year?
c. What basis does Allie have in her stock investment and note on December 31 of next year?
d. What loss carryovers (if any) are available to Monte and Allie?

C11-45 *Use of Losses by Shareholders.* Hammer Corporation, an electing S corporation, is owned by Tommy, who has a $100,000 stock basis on January 1. Tommy actively participates in Hammer's business. The Hammer Corporation operating results were not good in the current year, with an ordinary loss of $175,000 being reported. The size of the loss required Tommy to lend Hammer Corporation $50,000 on August 10 of the current year to provide funds needed for operations. The loan is secured by a Hammer Corporation note. Hammer Corporation rebounds during the next year and reports ordinary income of $60,000. Hammer Corporation repays the $50,000 note on December 15.

a. What amount of Hammer's current year loss can Tommy report on his income tax return?
b. What is Tommy's basis for the Hammer stock and note at the end of the loss year?
c. What income and deductions will Tommy report in the next year from Hammer's activities and the loan repayment?

C11-46 *Allocation of Losses to Shareholders.* Harry and Rita formed Alpha Corporation as an S corporation, with each shareholder contributing $10,000 in exchange for stock. In addition, Rita loaned the corporation $7,000, and the corporation borrowed another $8,000 from the bank. In the current year, the corporation incurred a $26,000 operating loss. In the next year, the corporation will earn $16,000 of operating income.

a. For the current year and next year, determine the pass-through items for each shareholder and each shareholder's stock basis at the end of each year. Also, determine Rita's debt basis at the end of each year.
b. Same as Part a except the corporation also distributes $6,000 cash to each shareholder at the end of next year.
c. Assume Alpha is a partnership instead of an S corporation. For the current year and next year, determine the pass-through items for each partner and each partner's basis in his or her partnership interest at the end of each year.

C11-47 *Post-Termination Loss Use.* Stein Corporation, an electing S corporation, has 400 shares of stock outstanding. The shares are owned equally by Chuck and Linda, both of whom actively participate in Stein's business. Each shareholder contributed $60,000 when Stein was organized on September 10, 2001. Start-up losses during 2001 resulted in Stein reporting a $210,000 ordinary loss. Stein's activities have since become profitable, and the corporation voluntarily revokes the S election on March 1, 2002, with no prospective revocation date being specified. In 2002, Stein reports $360,000 of taxable income ($30,000 per month). Stein makes no distributions to its shareholders in either year.

a. What amount of loss can Chuck and Linda deduct in 2001?
b. What amount of loss do Chuck and Linda carry over to 2002?
c. If Chuck reported only $5,000 of other business income in 2001, what happens to the "excess" deductible S corporation losses?
d. What portion of the loss carryover from Part b can Chuck and Linda deduct in 2002? What happens to any unused portion of the loss?
e. What advice can you offer to Chuck and Linda to enhance their use of the Stein loss?

C11-48 *Use of Losses by Shareholders.* Rocket Corporation, an electing S corporation, is owned by Tina, who has an $80,000 stock basis for her investment on January 1. During the first 11 months of the current year, Rocket Corporation reports an ordinary loss of $100,000. The corporation expects an additional $20,000 loss for December. Tina earns $270,000 of ordinary income from her other activities in the current year. She expects her other income to decline to $140,000 next year and continue at that level in future years. The corporation expects next year's losses to be only $20,000. Rocket Corporation projects a $50,000 profit for the following year and each of the next four years. What advice can you offer Tina about using her Rocket Corporation losses and retaining S corporation status in future years? How would your answer change if Tina expected her income from other activities to be $75,000 in the current year and $270,000 next year.

C11-49 *Stock Basis Adjustment.* For each of the following items, indicate whether the item will increase, decrease, or cause no change in the S corporation's ordinary income (loss), AAA, and in the shareholder's stock basis. The corporation in question was formed four years ago and made its S election two years ago. During the time period it was a C corporation, it accumulated $30,000 of E&P. This amount has not been distributed.

a. Operating profit
b. Dividend income received from domestic corporation
c. Interest income earned on corporate bond held as an investment
d. Life insurance proceeds paid on death of corporate officer
e. Long-term capital gain
f. Sec. 1231 loss
g. Sec. 1245 gain (recapture)
h. Charitable contributions
i. Fines paid for having overweight trucks
j. Depreciation
k. Pension plan contributions for employees
l. Salary paid to owner
m. Premiums paid on life insurance policy in Part d
n. Distribution of money (but not exceeding current year's earnings)

C11-50 *Taxability of Distributions.* Sweets Corporation is organized in January of the current year and immediately elects to be an S corporation. All the Sweets stock is owned by Tammy, who contributes $40,000 in cash to start the business. Sweets' current year results are reported below:

Ordinary income	$36,000
Short-term capital loss	5,000

On July 10, Sweets Corporation makes a $10,000 cash distribution to Tammy.

a. What income is recognized as a result of the distribution?
b. What is Tammy's basis for the Sweets stock on December 31?
c. How would your answers to Parts a and b change if Sweets' distribution were instead $80,000?

C11-51 *Property Distributions.* George and Martha formed Washington Corporation as an S corporation several years ago. George and Martha each have a 50% interest in the corporation. At the beginning of the current year, their stock bases are $45,000 each. In the current year, the corporation earns $40,000 of ordinary income. In addition, the corporation distributes property to George having a $26,000 FMV and a $40,000 adjusted basis and distributes property to Martha having a $26,000 FMV and a $16,000 adjusted basis.

a. Determine what George and Martha recognize in the current year, and determine their ending stock bases. What bases do George and Martha have in the distributed property?
b. What tax planning disadvantages do you see with these property distributions?

C11-52 *Taxability of Distributions.* Curt incorporates Vogel Corporation on January 15 of the current year. Curt makes a $70,000 capital contribution including land having a $12,000 FMV, and Vogel makes a timely S election for this year. Vogel reports $60,000 of ordinary income, $40,000 of Sec. 1231 gain, $5,000 of tax-exempt interest income, and $3,000 of charitable contributions this year. On December 1, Vogel distributes $5,000 cash plus the land contributed by Curt because it no longer is needed in the business. The land, which had a $10,000 basis and a $12,000 FMV when contributed to the corporation in January, has an $18,000 FMV when distributed.

a. What income do Vogel Corporation and Curt report as a result of the distribution?
b. What is Curt's basis for the Vogel stock on December 31?
c. What is Vogel's accumulated adjustments account (AAA) balance on December 31?

C11-53 *Taxability of Distributions.* Stable Corporation was organized 18 years ago by Hal, who has continued to own all its stock. The corporation made an S election one year after its incorporation. At the beginning of 2002, Stable Corporation reports the following earnings accumulations:

Accumulated adjustments account (AAA)	$85,000
Accumulated E&P	22,000

Hal's basis for his Stable stock on January 1, 2002 is $120,000. During 2002, Stable reports the following results from its operations:

Ordinary income	$30,000
Tax-exempt interest income	15,000
Long-term capital loss	20,000

Stable Corporation makes a $65,000 cash distribution to Hal on August 8.

a. What income, gain, or loss is recognized as a result of the distribution?

b. What is Hal's basis for the Stable stock on December 31?

c. What are Stable's AAA, E&P, and OAA balances on December 31?

d. How would your answers to Parts a-c change if Stable instead distributed $117,000?

C11-54 ***Taxability of Distributions.*** Sigma Corporation, an S corporation with one shareholder, incurred the following items 2001 and 2002:

2001	
Tax-exempt income	$ 5,000
Ordinary income	30,000

2002	
Ordinary loss	$(40,000)
Cash distribution	15,000

At the beginning of 2001, the corporation had a AAA balance of zero and accumulated E&P of $6,000. At the beginning of 2001, the shareholder had a $10,000 basis in stock and a $12,000 basis in debt he loaned to the corporation.

a. Determine items reported by the shareholder in 2001 and 2002.

b. Determine the balances in each corporate account and the shareholder's stock and debt bases at the end of each year.

c. Determine the results if the distribution in 2002 is $35,000 instead of $15,000.

d. How does the answer to Part c change if, in 2002, the corporation has an $18,000 long-term capital gain in addition to the $40,000 ordinary loss

C11-55 ***Taxability of Distributions.*** Beta Corporation, an S corporation with one shareholder, incurred the following items:

2001	
Ordinary loss	$(40,000)

2002	
Ordinary income	$27,000
Cash distribution	10,000

2003	
Ordinary income	$22,000
Cash distribution	17,000

At the beginning of 2001, the shareholder's stock basis was $20,000, and her debt basis was $16,000.

a. Assuming the corporation has no accumulated E&P, show items reported by the shareholder in each year, show all basis adjustments to stock and debt, and show the stock and debt bases at the end of each year.

b. Redo Part a for 2002 and 2003 assuming ordinary income in 2002 is $8,000 instead of $27,000.

c. Go back to the original facts and again redo Part a for all years assuming that, at the beginning of 2001, the corporation had a AAA balance of zero and accumulated E&P of $12,000.

COMPREHENSIVE PROBLEMS

C11-56 ***Comparison of Entity Formations.*** Cara, Bob, and Steve want to begin a business on January 1, 2002. The individuals are considering three business forms—C corporation, partnership, and S corporation.

- Cara has investment land with a $36,000 adjusted basis and a $50,000 FMV that she is willing to contribute. The land has a rundown building on it having a $27,000 basis and a $15,000 FMV. Cara has never used the building nor rented it. She would like to get rid of the building. Because she needs cash, Cara will take out a $25,000 mortgage on the property before the formation of the new business and have the new business assume the debt. Cara obtains a 40% interest in the entity.
- Bob will contribute machinery and equipment, which he purchased for his sole proprietorship in January 1997. He paid $100,000 for the equipment and has used the MACRS rules with a half-year convention on this seven-year recovery period property. He did not make a Sec. 179 expensing election for this property. The FMV of the machinery and equipment is $39,000. Bob obtains a 39% interest in the entity.
- Steve will contribute cash of $600 and services worth $20,400 for his interest in the business. The services he will contribute include drawing up the necessary legal documentation for the new business and setting up the initial books. Steve obtains a 21% interest in the entity.

To begin operations, the new business plans to borrow $50,000 on a recourse basis from a local bank. Each owner will guarantee his or her ownership share of the debt.

What are the tax and nontax consequences for the new business and its owners under each alternative? Assume that any corporation will have 200 shares of common stock authorized and issued. For the partnership alternative, each partner receives a capital, profits, and loss interest. How would your answer to the basic facts change if instead Steve contributes $2,600 in cash and $18,400 in services?

C11-57 ***Comparison of Operating Activities.*** RST business entity reported the following items during 2002:

Dividends from 25%-owned domestic corporation	$19,000
State of Florida bond interest	18,000
General Electric Corporation bond interest	29,000
Gain on land contributed by Karen	40,000[a]
Operating profit (excluding depreciation)	120,000
MACRS depreciation	36,000
Section 1245 gain (recapture)	5,000
Section 1231 loss	28,000
Long-term capital losses	4,000
Short-term capital losses	5,000
Charitable contributions	23,000
Investment interest expense (related to General Electric bonds)	16,000
Salary (guaranteed payment)	37,000

[a] Karen held the land as an investment prior to contributing it to RST business entity three years ago in exchange for her ownership interest. When Karen contributed the land, it had a basis of $15,000 and a FMV of $40,000. RST sold the land in the current year for $55,000. RST business entity held the land as an investment. Assume that Sec. 351 applied to any corporate formation transaction.

a. What is the corporate taxable income and income tax liability for 2002 if RST is taxed as a C corporation?
b. What is the ordinary income and separately stated items for 2002 if RST elects to be an S corporation? Assume that RST has never operated as a C corporation.
c. What are the ordinary income and separately stated items if RST is treated as a general partnership?

C11-58 ***Comparison of Nonliquidating Distributions.*** Tampa Corporation was organized 18 years ago and always has been equally owned by Jeff and John. In 2002, Tampa reports ordinary income/taxable income of $40,000. On April 5, Tampa distributes $100,000 cash to Jeff and distributes land with a $100,000 FMV and a $70,000 adjusted basis to John. Tampa had purchased the land as an investment two years ago. What are the tax implications to Tampa, Jeff, and John of the land distribution in each of the four situations that follow?

a. Tampa has been a C corporation since its formation. On January 1, 2002, Jeff's basis in his stock is $50,000, and John's basis is $45,000. Tampa has accumulated E&P of $155,000 on January 1, 2002.

b. Tampa was formed as a C corporation but made an S election three years after its formation. On January 1, 2002, Jeff's basis in his stock is $100,000, and John's basis is $80,000. Tampa had the following earnings balances on January 1, 2002:

Accumulated Adjustments Account	$125,000
Accumulated E&P	30,000

c. Tampa was formed as a partnership and continues to operate in that form. On January 1, 2002, Jeff's basis in his partnership interest is $100,000, and John's basis is $80,000. The partnership has no liabilities and no unrecognized precontribution gains.

d. How would your answers to Parts a–c change if the land held as an investment that was distributed to John had been contributed to Tampa by Jeff two years ago? At the time of Jeff's contribution, the land had a FMV of $95,000 and a $70,000 basis.

TAX STRATEGY PROBLEMS

C11-59 Alice, a single taxpayer, will form Morning Corporation in the current year. Alice plans to acquire all of Morning's common stock for a $100,000 contribution to the corporation. Morning will obtain additional capital by borrowing $75,000 from a local bank. Morning will conduct a variety of service activities with little need to retain its capital in the business. Alice expects start-up losses of $90,000 during Morning's first year of operation. She expects the corporation to earn pre-tax operating profits of $230,000 (before reduction for Alice's salary) starting next year. Alice plans to withdraw $100,000 of Morning's profits as salary. Her other income consists primarily of dividends and interest from other sources, and she expects these amounts to total $100,000 annually. What advice can you provide Alice about the advisability of making an S election in the initial tax year? In the next tax year? In answering these questions, compare the following alternatives: (1) S corporation in both the current year and the next year, (2) S corporation in the current year and C corporation in the next year (i.e., by revoking the S election next year), (3) C corporation in both the current year and the next year, and (4) C corporation in the current year and S corporation in the next year. When analyzing these alternatives, consider the total taxes associated with each alternative, specifically, at the corporate and shareholder levels and across both years. Also, assume the following facts: (1) Alice takes the standard deduction; (2) the current tax rate schedules, standard deduction, and exemption phase out thresholds remain the same for both years; and (3) a 7% discount rate applies for present value calculations. Although this problem asks for only a two-year analysis, discuss some shortcomings of such a short time frame.

C11-60 One way to compare the accumulation of income by alterative business entity forms is to use mathematical models. The following models express the investment after-tax accumulation calculation for a particular entity form:

Flow-through entities (S corporations, partnerships, and LLCs): $ATA = [1 + R(1 - t_p)]^n$

C corporation: $ATA = [1 + R(1 - t_c)]^n(1 - gt_p) + gt_p$

where: ATA = after-tax accumulation in n years

R = before-tax rate of return;

t_p = owner's marginal tax rate on ordinary income

t_c = corporation's marginal tax rate

g = portion of capital gain subject to tax

gt_p = owner's tax rate on capital gains

n = number of periods

For each alternative business form, the owner makes an initial investment of $1. The following operating assumptions apply:

Before-tax rate of return (R) = 0.18.

Marginal tax rate for owner (t_p) = 0.386

Corporate tax rate (t_c) = 0.34

Capital gains rate (gt_p) = 0.20 for regular capital gains; 0.28 × 0.50 = 0.14 for Sec. 1202 gains

Investment horizon (n) = 1, 5, 10, 20, or 30 years

A flow-through entity distributes only enough cash each year for the owners to pay their taxes. The corporation pays no dividends. The shareholders sell their stock at the end of the investment horizon, and their gains are taxed at capital gains rates. (See Chapter I18 of the *Individuals* volume for a detailed explanation of these models.)

Required: What is the after-tax accumulation if each business form is operated for the investment horizon and then sold for the amount of the accumulation? Which entity form is best for each investment horizon? How would your calculations and conclusions change if the C corporation qualified as a small business corporation eligible for the tax benefits contained in Sec. 1202?

TAX FORM/RETURN PREPARATION PROBLEM

C11-61 Bottle-Up, Inc., was organized on January 8, 1992 and made its S election on January 24, 1992. The necessary consents to the election were filed in a timely manner. Its federal tax identification number is 38-1507869. Its address is 1234 Hill Street, Gainesville, FL 32607. Bottle-Up, Inc., uses the calendar year as its tax year, the accrual method of accounting, and the first-in, first-out (FIFO) inventory method. Bottle-Up manufactures ornamental glass bottles. It made no changes to its inventory costing methods this year. It uses the specific identification method for bad debts for book and tax purposes. Herman Hiebert (S.S. No. 123-45-6789) and Melvin Jones (S.S. No. 100-67-2000) own 500 shares each. Both individuals materially participate in Bottle-Up's single activity. Herman Hiebert is the tax matters person. Financial statements for Bottle-Up for the current year are shown in Tables C11-2 through C11-4. Prepare a current year S corporation tax return for Bottle-Up, showing yourself as the paid preparer. Hint: To simplify your work, prepare a worksheet (spreadsheet) to convert your financial accounting numbers to tax accounting numbers. The worksheet should contain two columns (dr. and cr.) for the financial accounting income and expense numbers, two columns (dr. and cr.) for the book-to-tax adjustments, two columns (dr. and cr.) for the tax numbers, one column for the items included in ordinary income/loss, and one column for the separately stated items.

CASE STUDY PROBLEM

C11-62 Debra has operated a family counseling practice for a number of years as a sole proprietor. She owns the condominium office space that she occupies in addition to her professional library and office furniture. She has a limited amount of working capital and little need to accumulate additional business assets. Her total business assets are about $150,000, with an $80,000 mortgage on the office space being her only liability. Typically, she has withdrawn any unneeded assets at the end of the year. Debra has used her personal car for business travel and charged the business for the mileage at the appropriate mileage rate provided by the IRS. Over the last three years, Debra's practice has grown so that she now forecasts $80,000 of income being earned this year. Debra has contributed small amounts to an Individual Retirement Account (IRA) each year, but her contribution has never reached the $2,000 or $3,000 (in 2002) annual limit. Although she has never been sued, Debra recently has become concerned about legal liability. An attorney friend of hers has suggested that she incorporate her business to protect herself against being sued and to save taxes.

Required: You are a good friend of Debra's and a CPA; she asks your opinion on incorporating her business. You are to meet with Debra tomorrow for lunch. Prepare a draft of the points you feel should be discussed over lunch about incorporating the family counseling practice.

TAX RESEARCH PROBLEMS

C11-63 Cato Corporation incorporated on July 1, 1997 in California, with Tim and Elesa, husband and wife, owning all the Cato stock. On August 15, 1997, Cato Corporation made an S election effective for tax year 1997. Tim and Elesa file the necessary consents to the election. On March 10, 2001, Tim and Elesa transferred 15% of the Cato stock to the Reid and Susan Trust, an irrevocable trust created three years earlier for the benefit of their two minor children. In early 2002, Tim and Elesa's tax accountant learns about the transfer and advises the couple that the transfer of the stock to the trust may have terminated Cato's S election. Prepare a memorandum for your tax manager indicating any action Tim and Elesa can take that will permit Cato Corporation to retain its S election? Research sources suggested by the tax manager include Secs. 1361(c)(2), 1362(d)(2), and 1362(f).

▼ **TABLE C11-2**

Bottle-Up, Inc. Income Statement for the Year Ended December 31 of the Current Year (Problem C11-61)

Sales		$2,500,000
Returns and allowances		(15,000)
Net sales		$2,485,000
Beginning inventory	$ 102,000	
Purchases	900,000	
Labor	200,000	
Supplies	80,000	
Utilities	100,000	
Other manufacturing costs	188,000[a]	
Goods available for sale	$1,570,000	
Ending inventory	(96,000)	1,474,000[b]
Gross profit		$1,011,000
Salaries[c]	$ 451,020	
Utilities expense	54,000	
Depreciation (MACRS depreciation is $36,311)	11,782	
Automobile and truck expense	26,000	
Office supplies expense	9,602	
Advertising expense	105,000	
Bad debts expense	620	
Rent expense	30,000	
Interest expense[d]	1,500	
Meals and entertainment expense	21,000	
Selling expenses	100,000	
Repairs and maintenance expense	38,000	
Accounting and legal expense	4,500	
Charitable contributions[e]	9,000	
Insurance expense[f]	24,500	
Hourly employees' fringe benefits	11,000	
Payroll taxes	36,980	
Other taxes	2,500	
Penalties (fines for overweight trucks)	1,000	(938,004)
Operating profit		$ 72,996
Other income and losses:		
Long-term gain on sale of capital assets	$ 48,666	
Sec. 1231 loss	(1,100)	
Interest on U.S. Treasury bills	1,200	
Interest on State of Florida bonds	600	
Dividends from domestic corporations	11,600	
Investment expenses	(600)	60,366
Net income		$ 133,362

[a] Total MACRS depreciation is $74,311. Assume that $38,000 of depreciation has been allocated to cost of sales for both book and tax purposes so that the book and tax inventory and cost of sales amounts are the same. The depreciation adjustment on personal property is $9,000.
[b] The cost of goods sold amount reflects the Uniform Capitalization Rules of Sec. 263A. The appropriate restatements have been made in prior years.
[c] Officer salaries of $120,000 are included in the total.
[d] Investment interest expense is $500. All other interest expense is trade- or business-related. None of the interest expense relates to the production of tax-exempt income.
[e] The corporation made all contributions in cash to qualifying charities.
[f] Includes $3,000 of premiums paid for policies on lives of corporate officers. Bottle-Up is the beneficiary for both policies.

▼ TABLE C11-3
Bottle-Up, Inc. Balance Sheet for January 1 and December 31 of the Current Year (Problem C11-61)

	January 1	December 31
Assets:		
Cash	$ 15,000	$116,948
Accounts receivable	41,500	45,180
Inventories	102,000	96,000
Stocks	103,000	74,000
Treasury bills	15,000	16,000
State of Florida bonds	10,000	10,000
Building and equipment	374,600	375,000
Minus: Accumulated depreciation	(160,484)	(173,100)
Land	160,000	190,000
Total	$660,616	$750,028
Liabilities and equities:		
Accounts payable	$ 36,000	$ 10,000
Accrued salaries payable	12,000	6,000
Payroll taxes payable	3,416	7,106
Sales taxes payable	5,200	6,560
Due to Mr. Hiebert	10,000	5,000
Mortgage and notes payable (current maturities)	44,000	52,000
Long-term debt	210,000	260,000
Capital stock	10,000	10,000
Retained earnings	330,000	393,362
Total	$660,616	$750,028

▼ TABLE C11-4
Bottle-Up, Inc. Statement of Change in Retained Earnings, for the Current Year Ended December 31 (Problem C11-61)

Balance, January 1		$330,000[a]
Plus: Net income	$133,362	
Minus: Dividends	(70,000)	63,362
Balance, December 31		$393,362

[a]The January 1 accumulated adjustments account balance is $274,300.

C11-64 One of your wealthy clients, Cecile, invests $100,000 for sole ownership of an electing S corporation's stock. The corporation is in the process of developing a new food product. Cecile anticipates that the new business will need approximately $200,000 in capital (other than trade payables) during the first two years of its operations before it starts to earn sufficient profits to pay a return on the shareholder's investment. The first $100,000 of this total is to come from Cecile's contributed capital. The remaining $100,000 of funds will come from one of the following three sources:

- Have the corporation borrow the $100,000 from a local bank. Cecile is required to act as a guarantor for the loan.
- Have the corporation borrow $100,000 from the estate of Cecile's late husband. Cecile is the sole beneficiary of the estate.
- Have Cecile lend $100,000 to the corporation from her personal funds.

The S corporation will pay interest at a rate acceptable to the IRS. During the first two years of operations, the corporation anticipates losing $125,000 before it begins to earn a profit. Your tax manager has asked you to evaluate the tax ramifications of each of the three financing alternatives. Prepare a memorandum to the tax manager outlining the information you found in your research.

C11-65 Andy and Karen are 30 year-old engineering school graduates who are starting a new business to manufacture and sell digital circuits. One year ago, they left a large digital circuit manufacturer and obtained a patent on a new circuitry design. They intend to start a business with $500,000 of their own capital and $2 million obtained from 20 other investors. Each outside investor has committed to contribute $100,000. Andy and Karen expect the company to incur organizational and start-up expenditures of $125,000 in its first year.

Andy and Karen already have spent $200,000 to develop their idea. They plan to contribute the patent to the new business as part of their $500,000 commitment. All research and development (R&D) costs have been capitalized. The company expects to incur losses of $500,000 in each of the first two years of operations. The company then expects to breakeven in the third year and be profitable at the end of the fourth year even though the nature of the digital circuit business requires continual R&D activities. If losses exceed expectations, the company will obtain funds from additional investors.

Andy is an absolute genius, who has always succeeded at whatever he has attempted. However, Andy is a bit sloppy with his attention to detail. Karen, on the other hand, is a methodical organizer who intends to oversee the business operations. They feel that they will be a successful team.

Karen is married to a successful author, who earns approximately $500,000 a year from his writing. Andy is single, and his only income will come from the business. Both individuals will devote full time to the business. If needed, Karen has indicated she may be able to contribute more than her original $250,000 commitment, and possibly guarantee some bank loans.

Andy and Karen have approached Stan about helping them promote their business. Stan has connections in the electronics industry and feels that the new circuitry will be quite successful. Stan is willing to work in the business on a full-time basis drawing only a small salary until the business gets on its feet. Unfortunately, Stan does not have any cash to invest in the business at the present time.

Required: Your tax manager has asked you to prepare a presentation to be delivered to Andy and Karen about what entity form you would recommend and any particular tax issues they will face on the formation of the entity. Karen has heard about using a limited liability company from a friend, and she wonders if it would be better than the S corporation that she and Andy have been considering. She recommends that you examine, at a minimum, the following articles:

- Richard M. Lipton, "Choice of Entity: How to Choose, How to Change," *Taxes* (June 1994).
- Kent H. McMahan, "The Limited Liability Company Part One: Fundamentals," *Estate Planning Studies*, April 1995.
- Jerald D. August, "Choice of Entity: A Comparison of S Corporations and LLCs After Reform," *Journal of S Corporation Taxation*, Spring 1998.
- Mary A. McNulty, "Tax Considerations in Choice of Entity Decision," *Business Entities*, September/October 2001.

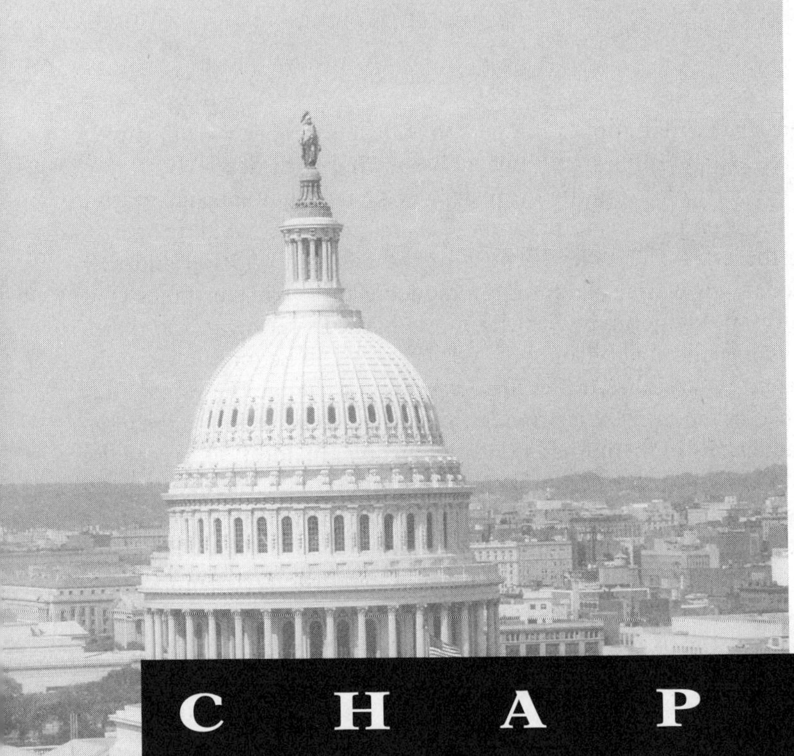

12

CHAPTER

THE GIFT TAX

LEARNING OBJECTIVES

After studying this chapter, you should be able to

1. Understand the concept of a unified transfer tax system
2. Describe the gift tax formula
3. Identify a number of transactions subject to the gift tax
4. Determine whether an annual gift tax exclusion is available
5. Identify deductions available for gift tax purposes
6. Apply the gift-splitting rules
7. Calculate the gift tax liability
8. Understand how basis affects the overall tax consequences
9. Recognize the filing requirements for gift tax returns

CHAPTER OUTLINE

Concept of Transfer Taxes...12-2
The Unified Transfer Tax System...12-3
Gift Tax Formula...12-4
Transfers Subject to the Gift Tax...12-7
Exclusions...12-16
Gift Tax Deductions...12-18
The Gift-Splitting Election...12-22
Computation of the Gift Tax Liability...12-23
Comprehensive Illustration...12-25
Basis Considerations for a Lifetime Giving Plan...12-26
Below-Market Loans: Gift and Income Tax Consequences...12-28
Tax Planning Considerations...12-29
Compliance and Procedural Considerations...12-30

The **gift tax** is a **wealth transfer tax** that applies if a person transfers property while alive. It is similar to the estate tax, which applies to transfers associated with death. Both the gift tax and the estate tax are part of the unified transfer tax system that subjects gratuitous transfers of property between persons to taxation. The vast majority of all property transfers are exempt from these transfer taxes because of the annual exclusion and the various deductions and credits. However, planning for reducing these transfer taxes is a significant matter for wealthy or moderately wealthy individuals. In recent years, there has been considerable discussion about abolishing the estate tax.[1] The Economic Growth and Tax Relief Reconciliation Act of 2001 (the 2001 Act) did not change the estate and gift tax area for 2001, but beginning in 2002 it provides for phased in increases to the unified credit and phased in reductions in the unified tax rate schedule. In addition, it repeals the estate and generation skipping transfer taxes, *but not the gift tax*, effective January 1, 2010. However, if Congress takes no further action, the 2001 Act provides that the rules for gift, estate, and generation skipping taxes will revert on January 1, 2011 to what they were prior to the 2001 Act. Congress adopted this "sunsetting" provision to comply with the Congressional Budget Act of 1974.

This chapter discusses both the structure of the gift tax (including the exclusion, deduction, and credit provisions) and exactly which property transfers fall within its purview. It reviews the income tax basis rules in the context of their implications for selecting properties to transfer by gift instead of at death.

CONCEPT OF TRANSFER TAXES

OBJECTIVE 1

Understand the concept of a unified transfer tax system

The recipient of a gift incurs no income tax liability because Sec. 102 explicitly excludes gifts and inheritances from the recipient's gross income.[2] The gift tax, a type of excise tax, is levied on the donor, the person who transferred the property. The gift tax applies to the act of transferring property to a recipient who pays either no consideration or consideration with a value lower than that of the property received.

HISTORY AND PURPOSE OF TRANSFER TAXES

The United States has had an estate tax since 1916 and a gift tax continuously since 1932. The structure of the gift and estate taxes has remained fairly constant, but details such as the amount of the exclusion and the rate schedules have changed numerous times. The Tax Reform Act of 1976 (the 1976 Act) made a very significant change by enacting a unified rate schedule for gift and estate tax purposes.

The gift tax has had several purposes, one of the most important of which was to raise revenue. However, because of the fairly generous annual exclusion and unified credit legislated by Congress, the gift tax yields only a small fraction of the federal government's total revenues. Only donors making relatively large gifts owe any gift taxes. Another purpose of the gift tax is to serve as a backstop to the estate tax and to prevent individuals from avoiding a significant amount of—or all—estate taxes by disposing of property before death. For example, without the gift tax, persons who know they are terminally ill could dispose of property "on their deathbed" and escape the transfer tax. In addition, the gift tax provides revenue to make up for some of the income tax revenue lost because income produced by the gifted property sometimes is taxed to a person in a lower income tax bracket. Another purpose for levying gift and estate taxes is to redistribute wealth.

ADDITIONAL COMMENT

The IRS estimates that the number of gift tax returns filed will increase from 317,000 for 2000 to 329,000 for 2001.

[1] Proposals to abolish the estate tax received criticism, in part, because in 1998, for example, only 47,500 estates owed any tax, and most of the tax was paid by estates above $5 million. See "House Republicans Shift Their Strategy in Effort to Push Two Popular Tax Cuts," *The Wall Street Journal* (August 22, 2000), p. A20.

[2] The income earned from property received as a gift or an inheritance, however, is not exempt from the income tax.

There is no way to know what the distribution of wealth would have been had Congress not enacted transfer taxes. However, one study estimates that the top 1% of the population held 22.5% of this nation's personal wealth in 1995, about the same percentage as in 1992.[3]

THE UNIFIED TRANSFER TAX SYSTEM

In 1976, Congress greatly revamped the transfer tax system by combining the separate estate and gift tax systems into one unified transfer tax system. Although Chapters C12 and C13 use the terms *gift tax* and *estate tax,* these taxes actually are components of the same unified transfer tax system. The system also includes the generation-skipping transfer tax, a topic discussed in Chapter C13. The unification of the transfer tax system removed the previous law's bias favoring tax treatment of lifetime gifts in comparison with transfers at death. The three most significant elements of the unified system—the unified rate schedule, the inclusion of taxable gifts in the death tax base, and the unified credit—are discussed below.

UNIFIED RATE SCHEDULE

SELF-STUDY QUESTION

Use the rate schedule inside the back cover of this text to determine the amount of gift tax (before credits) on 2002 taxable gifts of $4 million.

ANSWER

The tax is: On the first $2.5 million, $1,025,800; plus 50% of the excess over $2.5 million, or $750,000. Gross tax equals $1,775,800.

ADDITIONAL COMMENT

At the taxpayer's death, the unified tax is computed on the sum of the taxable estate plus the adjusted taxable gifts. The tax on this sum is reduced by the tax that would have been payable (at current rates) on the taxable gifts made after December 31, 1976.

Before the 1976 Act mandated a **unified rate schedule,** effective for gifts made after 1976 and deaths occurring after 1976 and applicable to both lifetime transfers and transfers at death, the gift tax rates were only 75% of the estate tax rates on a transfer of the same size. The rates are progressive and have varied over the years. The 2001 Act reduced the unified transfer tax rates beginning in 2002 by replacing the former top two brackets (on amounts exceeding $2.5 million) with a 50% maximum tax rate. Thus, in 2002 amounts exceeding $2.5 million will be taxed at a 50% maximum rate. In subsequent years, for both estate and gift tax purposes the maximum tax rate will be reduced as follows:

Year	*Maximum Tax Rate*	*For Amounts Exceeding*
2003	49%	$2,000,000
2004	48%	2,000,000
2005	47%	2,000,000
2006	46%	2,000,000
2007	45%	1,500,000
2008	45%	1,500,000
2009	45%	1,500,000

As mentioned earlier, the 2001 Act repeals the estate and generation skipping taxes effective January 1, 2010. At that date, the maximum gift tax rate will decline to 35%. The 35% rate will apply to tax bases exceeding $500,000. Congress retained the gift tax to make up for the loss in income tax revenue that could occur should wealthy individuals shift assets free of gift tax to donees in lower income tax brackets. (See the inside back cover for the unified transfer tax rates).

IMPACT OF TAXABLE GIFTS ON DEATH TAX BASE

Before 1977, a separate system applied to lifetime gifts compared with dispositions at death. By making gifts, an individual could shift the taxation of property from the top of the estate tax rate schedule to the bottom of the gift tax rate schedule. Few taxpayers could take advantage of this shifting, however, because only people with a relatively large amount of property could afford to part with sizable amounts of their assets while alive.

[3] "Tax Report," *The Wall Street Journal* (April 19, 2000), p. A1).

Under today's unified system, taxable gifts affect the size of the tax base at death. Any post-1976 taxable gifts (other than gifts included in the gross estate) are called **adjusted taxable gifts**, and such gifts are included in the donor's death tax base. Although they are valued at their fair market value (FMV) on the date of the gift, the addition of such taxable gifts to the tax base at death can cause the donor-decedent's estate to be taxed at a higher marginal tax rate. However, such gifts are not taxed for a second time upon the donor's death because gift taxes (computed at current rates) on these gifts are subtracted in determining the estate tax liability.

EXAMPLE C12-1 ▶ In 1993, Dan made taxable gifts totaling $500,000. When Dan dies in the current year, the value of the gifted property has tripled. Dan's death tax base includes the $500,000 of post-1976 taxable gifts. They are valued for estate tax purposes at their FMV on the date of the gift; the post-gift appreciation escapes the transfer tax system. Thus, the transfer tax value is fixed or frozen at the date-of-gift value. ◀

Note that unification (including taxable gifts that become part of the tax base at death) extends only to gifts made after 1976. Congress exempted gifts made before 1977 from unification because it did not want to retroactively change the two separate transfer tax systems that previously existed.

UNIFIED CREDIT

The **unified credit** reduces dollar for dollar a certain amount of the tax computed on the taxable gifts or the taxable estate. The amount of the credit varies depending on the year of the transfer. In the gift and estate tax formulas, the full credit is available for lifetime transfers and again in determining the tax payable at death. In concept, however, an individual's estate does not receive the benefit of this unified credit amount at death to the extent the decedent had already used the credit against lifetime transfers (as explained in Chapter C13). The gift tax formula, including the unified credit, is discussed below.

GIFT TAX FORMULA

OBJECTIVE 2

Describe the gift tax formula

The formula described in this section is used to calculate a donor's gift tax liability for the year of the transfer. As with income taxes, gift tax reporting is done on an annual basis. Figure C12-1 illustrates the formula for determining the donor's annual gift tax liability. This formula is discussed in detail later in the chapter.

ADDITIONAL COMMENT

The gift tax applies to cumulative lifetime gifts made since the enactment of the gift tax in 1932. The unified gift and estate tax, enacted in 1976, applies only to cumulative lifetime gifts made after 1976. This means that a taxable gift of $75,000 made in 1970 would not be included in a decedent's unified tax base but would affect the gift tax payable by that person.

DETERMINATION OF GIFTS

The starting point in the process is to determine which, if any, of the taxpayer's transfers constitute gifts. The next section discusses the various types of transfers that the statute views as gifts. All gifts are valued at their FMVs on the date of the gift. Next, the aggregate amount of gifts for the period is determined. The aggregate gifts are then reduced by any exclusions and deductions. Finally, the tax is computed according to the formula illustrated in Figure C12-1.

EXCLUSIONS AND DEDUCTIONS

The maximum amount excludible annually was $10,000 per donee for many years, but the exclusion became indexed beginning with gifts made after 1998. Inflation adjustments are rounded to the next *lowest* multiple of $1,000.[4] Accordingly, the annual exclusion rose to $11,000 in 2002 and will remain at this level until cumulative inflation raises it to $12,000. If the gifts made to a donee are less than the annual exclusion amount, the amount excludible is limited to the amount of the gift made to such donee. A donor may claim exclusions for transfers to an unlimited number of donees.

[4] Sec. 2503(b).

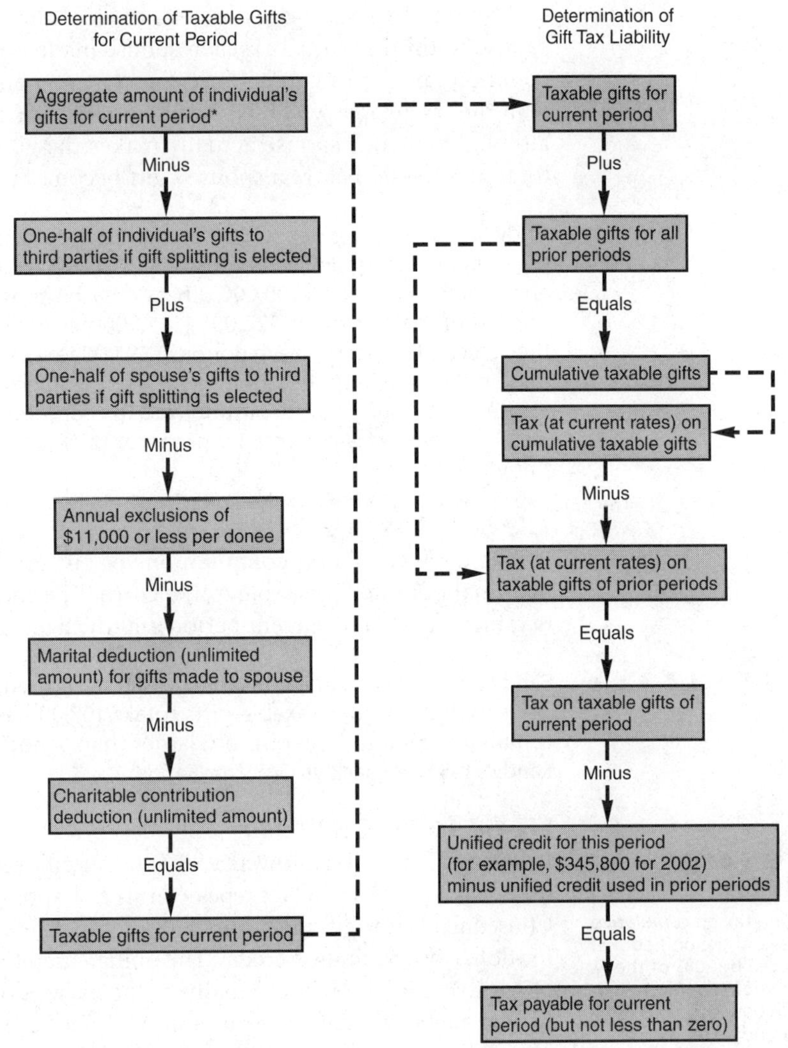
Determination of Taxable Gifts for Current Period
Aggregate amount of individual's gifts for current period*
Minus
One-half of individual's gifts to third parties if gift splitting is elected
Plus
One-half of spouse's gifts to third parties if gift splitting is elected
Minus
Annual exclusions of $11,000 or less per donee
Minus
Marital deduction (unlimited amount) for gifts made to spouse
Minus
Charitable contribution deduction (unlimited amount)
Equals
Taxable gifts for current period
Determination of Gift Tax Liability
Taxable gifts for current period
Plus
Taxable gifts for all prior periods
Equals
Cumulative taxable gifts
Tax (at current rates) on cumulative taxable gifts
Minus
Tax (at current rates) on taxable gifts of prior periods
Equals
Tax on taxable gifts of current period
Minus
Unified credit for this period (for example, $345,800 for 2002) minus unified credit used in prior periods
Equals
Tax payable for current period (but not less than zero)
* Valued at FMV on date of gift.

SELF-STUDY QUESTION

Al and Beth, husband and wife, live in a common law state. Al makes a $620,000 gift to each of two children by a previous spouse. Al and Beth agree to split the gift. Neither Al nor Beth has made taxable gifts in any prior year. Explain Al's and Beth's gift tax liability.

ANSWER

One-half of each gift, a total of $620,000, is reported on each taxpayer's gift tax return. Neither Al nor Beth has any gift tax liability for the current year due to the annual exclusions and the unified credit. Al has effectively used some of Beth's unified credit without Beth ever having ownership or control over Al's property.

FIGURE C12-1 ▶ THE GIFT TAX FORMULA

Two types of deductions reduce the amount of the taxable gifts. Most transfers to one's spouse generate a marital deduction; there is no ceiling on the amount of this deduction. Similarly, most transfers to charitable organizations are cancelled out by the charitable contribution deduction, which also is unlimited.

KEY POINT

The annual exclusion applies to each *donee* per year; therefore, the total amount of tax-free gifts in a given year can be much greater than the annual exclusion amount. Also, gift-splitting can double the tax-free amount per donee.

GIFT-SPLITTING ELECTION

Congress authorized gift-splitting provisions to achieve more comparable tax consequences between taxpayers of community property and noncommunity property (common law) states.[5] Under **community property law**, assets acquired after marriage are community property unless they are acquired by gift or inheritance. Typically, in a **community property state**, a large portion of the spouses' assets is community property, property in which each spouse has a one-half interest. One-half of a community property gift is automatically considered to be given by each spouse. By contrast, in a **common law state**, all assets acquired during the marriage are the property of the acquiring spouse. The other spouse does not automatically acquire an interest in the property. Thus, often only one spouse owns enough assets to dispose of property by gifts.

[5] The eight traditional community property states are Louisiana, Texas, New Mexico, Arizona, California, Washington, Idaho, and Nevada. Wisconsin's marital property law, though not providing for community property, is basically the same as community property.

Section 2513 authorizes spouses to elect gift splitting, which treats gifts made by each spouse to third parties as if each spouse made one-half of the gift. As a result, spouses in common law states can achieve the same benefits that apply automatically for gifts of community property. Thus, both spouses can claim an $11,000 per donee exclusion although only one spouse actually makes the gift, and the spouses can give each donee a total of $22,000 before a spouse's gift becomes taxable.

EXAMPLE C12-2 ▶ Andy and Bonnie, residents of a common law state, are married throughout the current year. In the current year, Andy gives his brother $100,000 cash. Andy and Bonnie may elect gift splitting and thereby treat the $100,000 gift as if each spouse gave $50,000. As a result, the excludible portion of the gift totals $22,000 ($11,000 per donee for each of the two deemed donors). If they elect gift splitting, each donor's $39,000 taxable gift may be taxed at a lower marginal tax rate. In addition, Bonnie can use a unified credit amount that she might not otherwise be able to use. As a result of gift splitting, the tax consequences are the same as if Andy and Bonnie were residents of a community property state and gave $100,000 of community property to Andy's brother. ◀

CUMULATIVE NATURE OF GIFT TAX

Unlike the income tax, computations of gift tax liabilities are cumulative in nature. The marginal tax rate applicable to the current period's taxable gifts is a function of both the taxable gifts for the current period and the aggregate taxable gifts for all earlier periods.

EXAMPLE C12-3 ▶ Sandy and Jack each make taxable gifts in the current year totaling $200,000. However, for previous periods, Sandy's taxable gifts total $100,000 and Jack's total $1.5 million. Because Jack's cumulative total taxable gifts are larger than Sandy's, Jack's current marginal tax rate exceeds Sandy's (45% for Jack vs. 34% for Sandy). ◀

UNIFIED CREDIT

ADDITIONAL COMMENT

The gift tax is a tax on *cumulative* lifetime gifts, and the unified credit is reduced by 20% of the pre-1977 specific exemption used on gifts made between September 9 and December 31, 1976. Thus, taxpayers must keep track of all gifts because all previous taxable gifts are part of the calculation for current gift tax due, and post-1976 taxable gifts affect the estate tax liability. Taxpayers must keep a record of how much of the specific exemption they used between September 9 and December 31, 1976 to determine how much of the unified credit is available to them. Such information appears on the gift tax forms.

Before 1977, the IRC allowed a $30,000 specific exemption deductible by donors whenever they desired. The 1976 Act repealed this exemption and replaced it with the unified credit.[6] Consequently, the gift tax computed for gifts made in 1977 and later years is reduced dollar for dollar by the unified credit. The unified credit allows donors to make a certain amount of taxable gifts (known originally as the **exemption equivalent** and now referred to in the IRC as **applicable exclusion amount**) without needing to pay the gift tax. For 1977 through 1987, the maximum amount of the credit increased progressively until in 1987 it reached $192,800, which was equivalent to a $600,000 exemption from the gift tax. Legislation in 1997 again increased the size of the credit. For 2000 and 2001, the credit was $220,550 (equivalent to a $675,000 exemption). As a result of the 2001 Act, the credit against gift taxes and the gift tax exemption equivalent increase to $345,800 and $1 million, respectively, in 2002 and stay at those levels. On the other hand, the credit for estate tax purposes later increases above $345,800. The unified credit amount for various years appears on the inside back cover.

The amount creditable for a particular year is the credit amount for that year minus the credit that could have been claimed for the taxable gifts made by the individual in earlier years. Recall that no credit was allowed for gifts made before 1977.

EXAMPLE C12-4 ▶ Zheng made her first taxable gift,[7] $500,000 in amount, in 1986. Zheng used the $155,800 unified credit available for 1986 (as shown on the inside back cover) to reduce her $155,800 gift tax liability to zero. Zheng made her next taxable gift in 1994. The taxable amount was $250,000. Zheng's 1994 gift tax liability of $92,500 ($248,300 – $155,800) was reduced by a unified credit of $37,000 ($192,800 – $155,800). The $92,500 represents the tax on the $750,000 of cumulative taxable gifts, which is $248,300, minus the tax on the $500,000 of 1986 taxable gifts, which was $155,800. If she makes taxable gifts in 2002, the maximum credit she can claim against her current tax is $153,000 ($345,800 – $192,800 already used). ◀

After passage of the 1976 Act, prospective donors quickly realized they could make gifts in 1976 and avoid the unification provisions, but Congress adopted a special rule

[6] Sec. 2505.

[7] No credit is used for a gift that is completely nontaxable.

that affects donors who used any portion of their specific exemption between September 9, 1976 and December 31, 1976.[8] The rule reduced the amount of unified credit otherwise available to such donors by 20% of the amount of the specific exemption they claimed between September 9 and December 31, 1976. The maximum reduction in the unified credit as a result of this provision is $6,000 (0.20 × $30,000 maximum specific exemption).

EXAMPLE C12-5 ▶ In November 1976, Maria made a large taxable gift, her first gift, and used her $30,000 specific exemption. As a result, the unified credit that Maria could otherwise claim after 1976 is reduced by $6,000 (0.20 × $30,000). Her 1976 taxable gifts are not includible in her death tax base. ◀

TRANSFERS SUBJECT TO THE GIFT TAX

OBJECTIVE 3

Identify a number of transactions subject to the gift tax

In general, property transferred for less than adequate consideration in money or money's worth is deemed to be a gift in the gift tax context. The gift occurs when the donor gives up control over the transferred property. Congress has legislated several provisions that exempt various property transfers that otherwise might be viewed as gifts from the scope of the gift tax. These exemptions include direct payments of medical expenses and tuition, transfers to political organizations, property settlements in conjunction with a divorce, and qualified disclaimers.

TRANSFERS FOR INADEQUATE CONSIDERATION

As mentioned earlier, the initial step in determining the donor's gift tax liability is deciding which transactions constitute gifts for gift tax purposes. Section 2501(a) states that a gift tax is imposed on "the transfer of property by gift." Thus, if *property* is transferred *by gift,* the transferor potentially incurs a gift tax liability. Perhaps surprisingly, the IRC does not define the term *gift.* Section 2511(a) expands on Sec. 2501(a) by indicating that the tax is applicable "whether the transfer is in trust or otherwise, whether the gift is direct or indirect, and whether the property is real or personal, tangible or intangible."

A transaction is subject to the gift tax even though not entirely gratuitous if "the value of the property transferred by the donor exceeds the value in money or money's worth of the consideration given therefor."[9] In such circumstances, the amount of the gift is the difference between the value of the property the donor gives up and the value of the consideration in money or money's worth received. The following discussion examines in more depth the scope of the rule regarding transfers for less than adequate consideration.

ADDITIONAL COMMENT

At times, a transferor can get caught in the trap of inadvertently making a gift by selling property to a family member for an amount determined in an IRS audit to be less than its fair market value.

BARGAIN SALES. Often, an individual wants to sell an asset to a family member, but the prospective buyer cannot afford to pay the full FMV of the property. If the buyer pays consideration of less than the FMV of the transferred property, the seller makes a gift to the buyer equal to the bargain element of the transaction, which is the excess of the property's FMV over its sales price.

EXAMPLE C12-6 ▶ Martha sells her ranch, having a $1 million FMV, to her son Stan, who can afford to pay only $300,000 of consideration. In the year of the sale, Martha makes a gift to Stan of $700,000, the excess of the ranch's FMV over the consideration received. ◀

TRANSFERS IN NORMAL COURSE OF BUSINESS. Treasury Regulations provide an exception to the general rule that a transfer for inadequate consideration triggers a gift. Specifically, a transaction arising "in the ordinary course of business (a transaction which

---

[8] Sec. 2505(b).

[9] Reg. Sec. 25.2512-8.

is bona fide, at arm's length, and free from any donative intent)" is considered to have been made for adequate consideration.[10] Thus, no gift arises when a buyer acquires property for less than its FMV *if* the acquisition is in the ordinary course of business.

EXAMPLE C12-7 ▶ John, a merchant, has a clearance sale and sells a diamond bracelet valued at $30,000 to Bess who pays $12,000, the clearance sale price. Because the clearance sale arose in the ordinary course of John's business, the bargain element ($18,000) does not constitute a gift to Bess. ◀

STATUTORY EXEMPTIONS FROM THE GIFT TAX

For various reasons, including simplifying the administration of the gift tax, Congress enacted several provisions that exempt certain transactions from the purview of the gift tax. In the absence of these statutory rules, some of these transactions could constitute gifts.

PAYMENT OF MEDICAL EXPENSES OR TUITION. Section 2503(e) states that a qualified transfer is not treated as a transfer of property by gift. The IRC defines *qualified transfer* as an amount paid on behalf of an individual to an educational organization for tuition or to any person who provides medical care as payment for such medical care. Such payments are exempt from gift treatment only if made *directly* to the educational organization or to the person providing the medical care. *Educational organization* has the same definition as for charitable contribution purposes,[11] and *medical care* has the same definition as for medical expense deduction purposes.[12] Note that the rule addresses only tuition, not room, board, and books. Note also that the identity of the person whose expenses are paid is not important. The special exemption applies even if an individual makes payments on behalf of a non-relative.

SELF-STUDY QUESTION

Ben's adult son Clarence, who is not Ben's dependent, needs a liver transplant. Because Clarence cannot afford the surgical procedure, Ben pays the $100,000 medical fee directly to the hospital. Is the payment for Clarence's benefit a taxable gift?

ANSWER

The payment is not a taxable gift because of Sec. 2503(e).

If one taxpayer pays amounts benefitting someone else and the expenditures constitute support that the payor must furnish under state law, such payments are support, not gifts. State law determines the definition of support. Generally, payments of medical expenses for one's minor child would be categorized as support and not a gift, even in the absence of Sec. 2503(e). On the other hand, state law generally does not require parents to pay medical expenses or tuition for an adult child. Thus, the enactment of Sec. 2503(e) removed such payments from the gift tax.

According to the Staff of the Joint Committee on Taxation, special rules concerning tuition and medical expense payments were enacted because

> Congress was concerned that certain payments of tuition made on behalf of children who have attained their majority, and of special medical expenses on behalf of elderly relatives, technically could be considered gifts under prior law. The Congress believed such payments should be exempt from gift taxes.[13]

EXAMPLE C12-8 ▶ Sergio pays $18,000 for his adult grandson's tuition at medical school and $12,000 for the grandson's room and board in the medical school's dormitory. Sergio makes all payments directly to the educational organization. Section 2503(e) exempts the direct payment of the tuition to the medical school from being treated as a gift. Because Sergio is not required under state law to pay room and board for an adult grandson, such payments are not support. Sergio has made a $12,000 gift to the grandson. ◀

EXAMPLE C12-9 ▶ Assume the same facts as in Example C12-8 except that Sergio pays the money to his grandson, who in turn pays the money to the medical school. Sergio has made a $30,000 gift. Because Sergio does not pay the tuition directly to the school, Sergio does not meet all the conditions for exempting the tuition payments from gift tax treatment. ◀

---

[10] Ibid.

[11] Section 170(b)(1)(A)(ii) defines *educational organization* in the context of the charitable contribution deduction.

[12] Section 213(d) defines *medical care* in the context of the medical expense deduction.

[13] U.S., Congress, Staff of the Joint Committee on Taxation, *General Explanation of the Economic Recovery Tax Act of 1981* (Washington, DC: U.S. Government Printing Office, 1981), p. 273.

What would you do in this situation?

You are a CPA and your tax preparation client is a very wealthy elderly woman named Ms. Atsushi Trong. She is a model of the U.S. success story. Having struggled in her native country, she immigrated to the United States as a teenager and studied clothing trends among her peers in both high school and college. She started her own clothing company and over the years has led the way by promoting such trends as miniskirts, bell-bottom pants, the so-called "Mature Elvis" look, and the hip-hop-rap grunge fashion. She has a net worth of over $100 million and no immediate family.

She has decided to plow some of her good fortune back into the educational system, which provided the intellectual foundation for her success. She selected the current class of her old high school, P.S. 101, and in 2002 gave each of 100 graduating students $100,000. This money was to be used to pay tuition costs for four years at her college alma mater. Each of the 100 student donees used the $100,000 to prepay the four-year tuition costs. All these transactions took place during the current tax year.

You have now been asked to report these transactions to the federal government on Ms. Trong's tax returns. What position would you take after considering the requirements of the IRC and Treasury Department Circular 230?

TRANSFERS TO POLITICAL ORGANIZATIONS. Congress adopted a provision specifically exempting transfers to political organizations from being deemed to be a transfer of property by gift.[14] Without this special rule, these transfers generally would be subjected to gift tax treatment.

EXAMPLE C12-10 ▶ Ann transfers $2,000 to a political organization founded to promote Thomas's campaign for governor. Ann's $2,000 transfer does not fall within the statutory definition of a gift. ◀

PROPERTY SETTLEMENTS IN CONJUNCTION WITH DIVORCE. To reduce litigation, Congress enacted special rules addressing property transfers in the context of a divorce. Section 2516 specifies the circumstances in which it automatically exempts property settlements in connection with a divorce from being treated as gifts.

For Sec. 2516 to be applicable, the spouses must adopt a written agreement concerning their marital and property rights and the divorce must occur during a three-year period beginning one year before they make the agreement. No gift arises from any transfer made in accordance with such agreement if a spouse transfers property to settle the other spouse's marital or property rights or to provide reasonable support for the children while they are minors.

EXAMPLE C12-11 ▶ In June 2001, Hal and Wanda signed a property agreement whereby Hal is to transfer $750,000 to Wanda in settlement of her property rights. Hal makes the transfer in May 2002. Hal and Wanda receive a divorce decree in July 2002. Hal is not deemed to have made a gift to Wanda by making the transfer. ◀

QUALIFIED DISCLAIMERS. Sometimes a person named to receive property under a decedent's will prefers not to receive such property and would like to disclaim (not accept) it. Typically, the person is quite ill and/or elderly or very wealthy. State disclaimer statutes allow individuals to say "no thank you" to the property willed to them. State law or another provision in the will addresses how to determine who will receive the property after the original beneficiary (the disclaimant) declines to accept it.

Section 2518(a) states that people making a qualified disclaimer are treated as if the disclaimed property were never transferred to them. Thus, the person making the disclaimer is not deemed to have made a gift to the person who receives the property because of the disclaimer.

A **qualified disclaimer** must meet the following four tests:

---

[14] Sec. 2501(a)(5).

- It is an irrevocable, unqualified, written refusal to accept property.
- The transferor or his or her legal representative receives the refusal no later than nine months after the later of the day the transfer is made or the day the person named to receive the property becomes age 21.
- The disclaiming person has not accepted the property interest or any of its benefits.
- As a result of the disclaimer, the property passes to the decedent's spouse or a person other than the one disclaiming it. In addition, the person disclaiming the property cannot direct who is to receive the property.[15]

EXAMPLE C12-12 ▶ Doug dies on February 1, 2002 and wills 500 acres of land to Joan. If Joan disclaims the property in a manner that meets all four of the tests for a qualified disclaimer, Joan will not be treated as making a gift to the person who receives the property as a result of her disclaimer. ◀

EXAMPLE C12-13 ▶ Assume the same facts as in Example C12-12 except that Joan instead disclaims the property on January 2, 2003. Joan's action arose too late to meet the second qualified disclaimer test above. Thus, Joan makes a gift to the person who receives the property she disclaims. ◀

CESSATION OF DONOR'S DOMINION AND CONTROL

A gift occurs when a transfer becomes complete and is valued as of the date the transfer becomes complete. Thus, the concept of a completed transfer is important in two contexts: determination of whether a gift has arisen and, if so, the amount of its value. According to Treasury Regulations, a gift becomes complete—and is thus deemed made and valued—when the donor "has so parted with dominion and control as to leave in him no power to change its disposition, whether for his own benefit or for the benefit of another."[16] A gift is not necessarily complete just because the transferor is not entitled to any further personal benefits from the property. If the transferor still can influence the benefits others may receive from the transferred property, the transfer is incomplete with respect to the portion of the property over which the transferor retained control.

REVOCABLE TRUSTS. A transferor who conveys property to a revocable trust has made an incomplete transfer because the creator of a revocable trust can change the trust provisions, including the identity of the beneficiaries. Moreover, the creator may demand the return of the trust property. Because the transferor does not give up any control over property conveyed to a revocable trust, the individual does not make a gift upon funding the trust. Once the trustee distributes trust income to a beneficiary, however, the creator of the trust loses control over the distributed funds and then makes a completed gift of the income the trustee pays out.

EXAMPLE C12-14 ▶ On May 1, Ted transfers $500,000 to a revocable trust with First National Bank as trustee. The trustee must pay out all the income to Ed during Ed's lifetime and at Ed's death distribute the property to Ed, Jr. On December 31, the trustee distributes $35,000 of income to Ed. The May 1 transfer is incomplete because Ted may revoke the trust; thus, no gift arises upon the funding of the trust. A $35,000 gift to Ed occurs on December 31 because Ted no longer has control over the distributed income. ◀

EXAMPLE C12-15 ▶ Assume the same facts as in Example C12-14 except that Ted amends the trust instrument on July 7 of the next year to make the trust irrevocable. By this date, the trust property has appreciated to $612,000. Ted makes a completed gift of $612,000 on July 7 of the next year because he gives up his powers over the trust. ◀

KEY POINT

If the donor retains control over any portion of the property, no gift is considered to have been made with respect to the portion of the property the donor still controls.

OTHER RETAINED POWERS. Even transfers to an irrevocable trust can be deemed incomplete with respect to the portion of the trust over which the creator kept control. Treasury Regulations state that if "the donor reserves any power over its [the property's]

[15] Sec. 2518(b).

[16] Reg. Sec. 25.2511-2(b).

disposition, the gift may be wholly incomplete, or may be partially complete and partially incomplete, depending upon all the facts in the particular case."[17] They add that one must examine the terms of the power to determine the scope of the donor's retention of control. The regulations elaborate by indicating that "[a] gift is . . . incomplete if and to the extent that a reserved power gives the donor the power to name new beneficiaries or to change the interests of the beneficiaries."[18]

EXAMPLE C12-16 ▶ On May 3, Art transfers $300,000 of property in trust with a bank as trustee. Art names his friends Bob and/or Sue to receive the trust income for 15 years and Karl to receive the trust property at the end of 15 years. Art reserves the power to determine how the income is to be divided between Bob and Sue each year. Because Art reserves the power over payment of the income for the 15-year period, this portion of the transfer is incomplete on May 3. Actuarial tables discussed in the next section of the chapter address the valuation of the completed gift to Karl. ◀

EXAMPLE C12-17 ▶ Assume the same facts as in Example C12-16 except that on December 31 Art instructs the trustee to distribute the trust's $30,000 of income as follows: $18,000 to Bob and $12,000 to Sue. Once the trustee pays out income, Art loses control over it. Thus, Art makes an $18,000 gift to Bob and a $12,000 gift to Sue on December 31. Each gift qualifies for the annual exclusion. ◀

EXAMPLE C12-18 ▶ Assume the same facts as in Example C12-16 except that on May 3 of the next year, when the trust assets are valued at $360,000, Art relinquishes his powers over payment of income and gives this power to the trustee. Art's transfer of the income interest (with a remaining term of 14 years) becomes complete on May 3 of the next year. The valuation of the gift of a 14-year income interest is determined from actuarial tables in Appendix H. ◀

Topic Review C12-1 summarizes various complete, incomplete, and partially complete transfers.

VALUATION OF GIFTS

ADDITIONAL COMMENT

Because the determination of value is such a subjective issue, a large number of the tax controversies involving gift taxes are nothing more than valuation disagreements.

GENERAL RULES. All gifts are valued at their FMV as of the date of the gift (i.e., the date the transfer becomes complete). Treasury Regulations state that a property's value is "the price at which such property would change hands between a willing buyer and a willing seller, neither being under any compulsion to buy or to sell, and both having reasonable knowledge of relevant facts."[19] According to the regulations, stocks and bonds traded on a stock exchange or over the counter are valued at the mean of the highest and lowest selling price on the date of the gift.[20] In general, the guidelines for valuing properties are the same, regardless of whether the property is conveyed during life or at death.

Topic Review C12-1

Examples of Complete and Incomplete Transfers

1. Complete Transfers, Subject to Gift Tax:
   a. Property transferred outright to donee
   b. Property transferred in trust with donor retaining no powers over the trust
2. Incomplete Transfers, Not Subject to Gift Tax:
   a. Property transferred to a revocable trust
   b. Property transferred to an irrevocable trust for which the donor has discretionary powers over both income and the remainder interest
3. Partially Complete Transfers, Only a Portion Subject to Gift Tax:
   a. Property transferred to an irrevocable trust for which the donor has discretionary powers over income but not the remainder interest[a]

[a]The gift of the remainder interest constitutes a completed transfer.

[17] Ibid.
[18] Reg. Sec. 25.2511-2(c).
[19] Reg. Sec. 25.2512-1.
[20] Reg. Sec. 25.2512-2.

An exception is life insurance policies, which are less valuable while the insured is alive. Valuation of life insurance policies is discussed in a later section of this chapter, as well as in Chapter C13's coverage of the estate tax.

KEY POINT

The value of the life estate plus the value of the remainder interest equals the total FMV of the property.

LIFE ESTATES AND REMAINDER INTERESTS. Often one may transfer less than his or her entire interest in an asset. For example, an individual may transfer property in trust and reserve the right to the trust's income for life and name another individual to receive the property upon the transferor's death. In such a situation, the transferor retains a **life estate** and gives a **remainder interest**. In general, only the remainder interest is subject to the gift tax. An exception applies if the gift is to a family member, as discussed in the estate freeze section below. If the transferor keeps an annuity (a fixed amount) for life and names another person to receive the remainder at the transferor's death, in all situations the gift is of just the remainder interest.

TAX STRATEGY TIP

When gifting a remainder interest, the donor should consider using property that appreciates in value at a greater rate than the Sec. 7520 interest rate.

A grantor also may transfer property in trust with the promise that another person will receive the income for a certain number of years and at the end of that time period the property will revert to the grantor. In this case, the donor retains a reversionary interest, whereas the other party receives a **term certain interest**.[21] Unless the donee is a family member, only the term certain interest is subject to the gift tax. Trusts whereby the grantor retains a reversionary interest have disadvantageous income tax consequences to the grantor if they were created after March 1, 1986. Chapter C14 discusses the income tax treatment of such trusts.

Life estates, annuity interests, remainders, and term certain interests are valued from actuarial tables that incorporate the Sec. 7520 interest rate. In general, these tables must be used regardless of the actual earnings rate of the transferred assets. Excerpts from the tables appear in Appendix H. Table S is used for valuing life estates and remainders and Table B for term certain interests. The factor for a life estate or term certain interest is 1.0 minus the remainder factor. The remainder factor simply represents the present value of the right to receive a property at the end of someone's life (in the case of Table S) or at the end of a specified time (in the case of Table B). The value of the income interest plus the remainder interest is 1.0, the entire value of the property. The factor for an annuity is the life estate or the term factor divided by the Sec. 7520 interest rate. Section 7520 calls for the interest rate to be revised every month to the rate, rounded to the nearest 0.2%, that is 120% of the Federal midterm rate applicable for the month of the transfer.[22] Congress mandated revisions to the tables to reflect mortality experience at least once every ten years, and the Treasury Department issued revised life tables effective for transfers on May 1, 1999 and later.

EXAMPLE C12-19 ▶ Refer to Example C12-16, wherein on May 3 Art transfers $300,000 of property in trust with a bank as trustee. Art names his friends Bob and Sue to receive the trust income for 15 years but reserves the power to determine how the income is to be divided between them each year. However, the trustee must distribute all the income. Art specifies that Karl is to receive the trust property at the end of the fifteenth year. Only the gift of the remainder interest is a completed transfer on May 3. The gift is valued from Table B. If the interest rate is 10%, the amount of the gift is $71,818 (0.239392 × $300,000), the present value of the property to be received at the end of 15 years. ◀

EXAMPLE C12-20 ▶ Assume the same facts as in Example C12-19 except that three years later, when the trust assets are valued at $360,000, Art transfers his power over the payment of trust income to the trustee. The income interest has a remaining term of 12 years. The gift is the present value of the 12-year income interest, which is valued from Table B by subtracting the factor for a remainder interest (0.318631 if the interest rate is 10%) from 1.0. Thus, the amount of the gift is $245,293 [(1.0 − 0.318631) × $360,000]. ◀

EXAMPLE C12-21 ▶ On July 5 of the current year, Don transfers $100,000 of property in trust and names his friends Larry (age 60) to receive all of the income for the rest of Larry's life and Ruth (age 25) to receive

[21] *Term certain interest* means that a particular person has an interest in the property held in trust for a specified time period. The person having such interest does not own or hold title to the property, but has a right to receive the income from such property for a specified time period. At the end of the time period, the property reverts to the grantor (or passes to another person, the remainderman).

[22] The IRS regularly issues revenue rulings with applicable rate information.

the trust assets upon Larry's death. Don names a bank as the trustee. The amount of each donee's gift is determined from Table S. If the interest rate is 10% and Larry is age 60, the value of the remainder interest gift to Ruth, as calculated from the single life remainder factors column of Table S, is $21,196 (0.21196 × $100,000). This amount represents the present value of the property to be received after the death of a person age 60. The remaining portion of the $100,000 of property, $78,804 ($100,000 – $21,196), is the value of the life estate transferred to Larry. The total value of the income plus remainder interests is 1.0. ◀

STOP & THINK *Question:* In which scenario would the amount of the gift be larger: (1) a gift of a remainder interest to a friend if a 68-year-old donor retained the income for life or (2) a gift of a remainder interest to a friend if an 86-year-old donor retained the income for life? Assume that each donor makes the gift on the same day so that the applicable interest rates are the same for each scenario.

Solution: The gift of the remainder interest would be larger if the donor is 86, instead of 68, because the actuarial value of the income interest the donor retains would be smaller if the donor is older. Older donors generally have shorter life expectancies.

ADDITIONAL COMMENT

In estate freeze transfers, Congress has provided rules that generally will increase the amount classified as a gift at the time of the actual transfer.

SPECIAL VALUATION RULES: ESTATE FREEZES. Congress became concerned that individuals were able to shift wealth to other individuals, usually in a younger generation, without paying their "fair share" of the transfer taxes. An approach donors commonly used was to recapitalize a corporation (by exchanging common stock for both common and preferred shares) and then to give the common stock to individuals in the younger generation. This technique was one of a variety of transactions known as estate freezes.

In 1990, Congress decided to address the perceived problem of estate freezes by writing new valuation rules that apply when a gift occurs. The thrust of these rules—current IRC Chapter 14 (Secs. 2701 through 2704)—is to ensure that gifts are not undervalued. A couple of the more common situations governed by the new rules are described below, but the rules are too complicated to warrant a complete discussion. If a parent owns 100% of a corporation's stock and then gives the common stock to his or her children and retains the preferred stock, the value of the right to the preferred dividends is treated as zero unless the stock is cumulative preferred. Unless the donor retains *cumulative* preferred stock, the value assigned to the common stock given away is relatively high. If the donor creates a trust in which he or she retains an interest and in which he or she gives an interest to a family member, the value of the transferor's interest is treated as zero unless the retained interest is an annuity interest (fixed payments) or a unitrust interest (calling for distributions equal to a specified percentage of the current FMV of the trust). Thus, the donor is treated as having kept nothing. The effect of these rules increases the gift amount, compared with the result under prior law, unless the transferor structures the transaction to avoid having a zero value assigned to his or her retained interest.[23]

SELF-STUDY QUESTION

Madge deposits $50,000 in a joint bank account in the name of herself and Susan, her niece. During the current year, the bank credited the account with interest of $4,000. No withdrawals are made during the year. Has Madge made a gift to Susan?

ANSWER

Madge has not made a gift to Susan because Susan has not withdrawn anything from the account. The interest earned by the account is reported by Madge on her personal income tax return because Susan owns none of the money in the account.

GIFT TAX CONSEQUENCES OF CERTAIN TRANSFERS

Some transactions that cause the transferor to make a gift are straightforward. It is easy to see that the disposition is within the scope of the gift tax if, for example, an individual places the title to stock or real estate solely in another person's name and receives less than adequate consideration in return. Treasury Regulations include the following examples of transactions that may be subject to the gift tax: forgiving of a debt; assignment of the benefits of a life insurance policy; transfer of cash; and transfer of federal, state, or municipal bonds.[24] The gratuitous transfer of state and local bonds falls within the scope of the gift tax, even though interest on such bonds is exempt from federal income taxation. The following discussion concerns the gift tax rules for several transfers that are more complicated than, for example, transferring the title to real property or stock to another person.

[23] See Reg. Secs. 25.2701-1 through -6 and 25.2702-1 through -6 for guidance concerning the estate freeze provisions.

[24] Reg. Sec. 25.2511-1(a).

CREATION OF JOINT BANK ACCOUNTS. Parties maintaining a jointly owned bank account face gift tax consequences. Funding a joint bank account is an incomplete transfer because the depositor is free to withdraw the amount deposited into the account. A gift occurs when one party withdraws an amount exceeding the amount he or she deposited.[25] The transfer is complete at that time because the withdrawn money is subject to only the control of the person who made the withdrawal.

EXAMPLE C12-22 ▶ On May 1, Connie deposits $100,000 into a joint bank account in the names of Connie and Ben. Her friend Ben makes no deposits. On December 1, Ben withdraws $20,000 from the joint account and purchases an automobile. No gift arises upon the creation of the bank account. However, on December 1 Connie makes a gift to Ben of $20,000, the excess of Ben's withdrawal over Ben's deposit. ◀

CREATION OF OTHER JOINT TENANCIES. **Joint tenancy** is a popular form of property ownership from a convenience standpoint because, when one joint owner dies, the property is automatically owned by the survivor(s). Each joint tenant is deemed to have an equal interest in the property. A completed gift arises when the transferor titles real estate or other property in the names of himself or herself and another (e.g., a spouse, a sibling, or a child) as joint tenants. The person furnishing the consideration to acquire the property is deemed to have made a gift to the other joint tenant in an amount equal to the value of donee's pro rata interest in the property.[26]

EXAMPLE C12-23 ▶ Kwame purchases land for $250,000 and immediately has it titled in the names of Kwame and Kesha, as joint tenants with right of survivorship. Kwame and Kesha are not husband and wife. Kwame makes a gift to Kesha of $125,000, or one-half the value of the property. ◀

TAX STRATEGY TIP

An owner of a life insurance policy who wishes to gift the ownership to someone else, such as the beneficiary, can use the following strategies to avoid the gift tax:
(1) Before making the gift, borrow enough against the policy to reduce its net value to the amount of the annual exclusion ($11,000 in 2002). The former owner (borrower) then can pay premiums and make loan repayments, not to exceed the annual exclusion in any given year.
(2) Have the insurance company rewrite the policy into separate policies, each having a value that does not exceed the annual exclusion. Then, gift one policy each year for several years.

TRANSFER OF LIFE INSURANCE POLICIES. The mere naming of another as the beneficiary of a life insurance policy is an incomplete transfer because the owner of the policy can change the beneficiary designation at any time. However, if an individual irrevocably assigns all ownership rights in an insurance policy to another party, this event constitutes a gift of the policy to the new owner.[27] Ownership rights include the ability to change the beneficiary, borrow against the policy, and cash the policy in for its cash surrender value.

The payment of a premium on an insurance policy owned by another person is considered a gift to the policy's owner. The amount of the gift is the amount of the premium paid. The tax result is the same as if the donor transferred cash to the policy owner and the owner used the cash to pay the premium.

According to Reg. Sec. 25.2512-6, the value of the gift of a life insurance policy is the amount it would cost to purchase a comparable policy on the date of the gift. The regulations point out, however, that if the policy is several years old, the cost of a comparable policy is not readily ascertainable. In such a situation, the policy is valued at its interpolated terminal reserve (i.e., an amount similar to the policy's cash surrender value) plus the amount of any unexpired premiums. The insurance company will furnish information concerning the interpolated terminal reserve.

EXAMPLE C12-24 ▶ On September 1, Bill transfers his entire ownership rights in a $300,000 life insurance policy on his own life to his sister Susan. The policy's interpolated terminal reserve is $24,000 as of September 1. On July 1, Bill had paid the policy's $4,800 annual premium. Bill makes a gift to Susan on September 1 of $28,000 [$24,000 + (10/12 × $4,800)] because he transferred ownership to Susan. If, however, the policy had been a term insurance policy, which has no interpolated terminal reserve, the gift would have been $4,000 (10/12 × $4,800). ◀

EXAMPLE C12-25 ▶ Assume the same facts as in Example C12-24. On July 1 of the next year, Bill pays the $4,800 annual premium on the policy now owned by Susan. As a result of the premium payment, Bill makes a $4,800 gift to Susan that year, the same result as if he had given her $4,800 of cash to pay the premium. ◀

---

[25] Reg. Sec. 25.2511-1(h)(4).

[26] Reg. Sec. 25.2511-1(h)(5). If the two joint tenants are husband and wife, no taxable gift will arise because of the unlimited marital deduction.

[27] Reg. Sec. 25.2511-1(h)(8).

EXAMPLE C12-26 ▶ Assume the same facts as in Examples C12-24 and C12-25 except that Susan, who now owns the policy, changes the beneficiary of the policy from Frank to John. This event is not a gift because Susan has not given up control; she can change the beneficiary again in the future. ◀

EXERCISE OF A GENERAL POWER OF APPOINTMENT. Section 2514 provides the rules concerning powers of appointment. A **power of appointment** exists when a person transfers property (perhaps in trust) and grants someone else the power to specify who eventually will receive the property. Thus, possession of a power of appointment has some of the same benefits as ownership of the property. Powers can be general or special. *Potential* gift tax consequences are associated with the powerholder's exercise of a **general power of appointment.** A person possesses a general power of appointment if he or she has the power to appoint the property (have the property distributed) to him- or herself, his or her creditors or estate, or the creditors of his or her estate. The words *his or her estate* mean that there are no restrictions concerning to whom the individual may bequeath the property.

A gift occurs when a person exercises a general power of appointment and names some other person to receive the property.[28] The donee is the person named to receive the property. Exercising a general power of appointment in favor of the powerholder is not a gift (i.e., one cannot make a gift to him- or herself).

EXAMPLE C12-27 ▶ In 2002, Tina creates an irrevocable trust and names Van to receive the income for life. In addition, Tina gives Van a general power of appointment exercisable during his life as well as at his death. Tina made a gift to Van at the time she transferred the property to the trust in 2002. In 2003, Van instructs the bank trustee to distribute $50,000 of trust property to Kay. Through the exercise of his general power of appointment in favor of Kay, Van makes a $50,000 gift to Kay in 2003 because he diverted property to her. ◀

NET GIFTS. A **net gift** occurs when an individual makes a gift to a donee who agrees to pay the gift tax as a condition of receiving the gift. The donee's payment of the gift tax is treated as consideration paid to the donor. The amount of the gift is the excess of the FMV of the transferred property over the amount of the gift tax paid by the donee. Because the amount of the gift depends on the amount of gift tax payable, which in turn depends on the amount of the gift, the calculations require the use of simultaneous equations.[29]

The net gift strategy is especially attractive for people who would like to remove a rapidly appreciating asset from their estate but are unable to pay the gift tax because of liquidity problems. However, a net gift has one potential disadvantage: the Supreme Court has ruled that the donor must recognize as a gain the excess of the gift tax payable over his or her adjusted basis in the property.[30] The Court's rationale is that the donee's payment of the donor's gift tax liability constitutes an "amount realized" for purposes of determining the gain or loss realized on a sale, exchange, or other disposition. From a practical standpoint, this decision affects only donors who transfer property so highly appreciated that the property's adjusted basis is less than the gift tax liability.

EXAMPLE C12-28 ▶ Mary transfers land with a $3 million FMV to her son, Sam, who agrees to pay the gift tax liability. Mary's adjusted basis in the land is $15,000. Earlier in the year, she gave him $11,000. The amount of the taxable gift is $3 million, less the gift tax paid by Sam. Simultaneous equations are used to calculate the amount of the gift and the gift tax liability. Mary must recognize gain equal to the excess of the gift tax liability paid by Sam minus Mary's $15,000 basis in the property.

---

[28] In general, the exercise of a special power of appointment is free of gift tax consequences. In the case of special powers of appointment, the holder of the power does not have an unrestricted ability to name the persons to receive the property. For example, he or she may be able to appoint to only his or her descendants.

[29] In Rev. Rul. 75-72 (1975-1 C.B. 310), the IRS explained how to calculate the amount of the net gift and the gift tax. In Ltr. Rul. 7842068 (July 20, 1978), the IRS stated that the donor's available unified credit, not the donee's, is used to calculate the gift tax payable.

[30] *Victor P. Diedrich v. CIR*, 50 AFTR 2d 82-5054, 82-1 USTC ¶9419 (USSC, 1982).

TAX STRATEGY TIP

As a general rule, substantially appreciated property should not be transferred by gift. It should be transferred at death to take advantage of the step-up in basis to the estate tax value (usually FMV at date of death). If Mary in Example C12-28 were elderly, it might be better to transfer an asset other than the land to obtain the basis increase for the land.

Assume that, because of sizable previous taxable gifts, any additional gifts Mary makes will be subject to the 50% gift tax rate. Also, for simplicity ignore any increase in the unified credit. If G represents the amount of the gift and T is the amount of the tax, then

$$G = \$3{,}000{,}000 - T$$
$$T = 0.50G$$

Substituting 0.50G for T in the first equation and solving for G yields G = \$2 million, the amount of the gift. The tax is 50% of this amount, or \$1 million. The calculation increases in difficulty when, because of splitting brackets, more than one gift tax rate applies. Mary's gain equals the \$1 million gift tax paid by Sam minus her \$15,000 basis in the property, or \$985,000. ◀

EXCLUSIONS

OBJECTIVE 4

Determine whether an annual gift tax exclusion is available

In many instances, a portion or all of a transfer by gift is tax-free because of the annual exclusion authorized by Sec. 2503(b). In 1932, the Senate Finance Committee explained the purpose of the **annual exclusion** as follows:

> Such exemption . . . is to obviate the necessity of keeping an account of and reporting numerous small gifts, and . . . to fix the amount sufficiently large to cover in most cases wedding and Christmas gifts and occasional gifts of relatively small amount.[31]

Because of the annual exclusion, most gift transactions result in the donor's making no taxable gift. Consequently, administration of the gift tax provisions is a much simpler task than it otherwise would be.

AMOUNT OF THE EXCLUSION

The amount of this exclusion, which is analogous to an exclusion from gross income for income tax purposes, currently is \$11,000.[32] It is available each year for an unlimited number of donees. For transfers made in trust, each beneficiary is deemed to be a separate donee. Any number of donors may make a gift to the same donee, and each is eligible to claim the exclusion. The only limitations on the annual exclusion are the donor's wealth, generosity, and imagination in identifying donees.

EXAMPLE C12-29 ▶ In 2002, Ann and Bob each give \$11,000 cash to each of Tad and Liz. Ann and Bob again make \$11,000 cash gifts to Tad and Liz in 2003. For both 2002 and 2003, Ann receives \$22,000 of exclusions (\$11,000 for the gift to Tad and \$11,000 for the gift to Liz). The same result applies to Bob. ◀

TAX STRATEGY TIP

Gifts up to the amount of the annual exclusion not only remove the gifted amounts from the donor's estate with no gift taxes but also remove the property's future income from the donor's estate. In addition, the property's income can be shifted to someone whose tax bracket might be lower than the donor's, thereby reducing income taxes.

The annual exclusion is a significant tax planning device that has no estate tax counterpart. So long as a donor's gifts to a particular donee do not exceed the excludable amount, the donor will never make any taxable gifts or have any gift tax liability. Because taxable gifts will be zero, the donor's estate tax base will not include any adjusted taxable gifts. A donor, who each year for the past ten years gave \$10,000 per donee to each of ten donees, removed \$1 million (10 × \$10,000 × 10) from being taxed in his or her estate. The donor accomplishes these transfers without making any taxable gifts or paying any gift tax. If retained, the \$1 million would have been taxed in the donor's estate, at perhaps the top estate tax rate, unless the property was willed to the donor's surviving spouse.

PRESENT INTEREST REQUIREMENT

Although we generally speak of the annual exclusion as if it were available automatically for all gifts, in actuality it is not. A donor receives an exclusion only for gifts that constitute a present interest.

---

[31] S. Rept. No. 665, 72nd Cong., 1st Sess. (1932), reprinted in 1939-1 C.B. (Part 2), pp. 525–526.

[32] On January 1, 1982, the annual exclusion was increased from \$3,000 to \$10,000. The exclusion became indexed after 1998, but inflation adjustments are rounded to the next lowest multiple of \$1,000. In 2002, the exclusion rose to \$11,000.

DEFINITION OF PRESENT INTEREST. A **present interest** is "an unrestricted right to the immediate use, possession, or enjoyment of property or the income from property (such as a life estate or term certain)."[33] Only such interests qualify for the annual exclusion. If only a portion of a transfer constitutes a present interest, the excluded portion of the gift may not exceed the value of the present interest.

DEFINITION OF FUTURE INTEREST. A future interest is the opposite of a present interest. A **future interest** "is a legal term, and includes reversions, remainders, and other interests . . . which are limited to commence in use, possession, or enjoyment at some future date or time."[34] Gifts of future interests are ineligible for the annual exclusion. The following examples help demonstrate the attributes of present and future interests.

EXAMPLE C12-30 ▶ Nancy transfers $500,000 of property to an irrevocable trust with a bank serving as trustee. Nancy names Norm (age 55) to receive all the trust income quarterly for the rest of Norm's life. At Norm's death, the property is to pass to Ellen (age 25) or Ellen's estate. Norm has an unrestricted right to immediate enjoyment of the income. Thus, Norm has a present interest. Ellen, however, has a future interest because Ellen cannot enjoy the property or any of the income until Norm dies. The taxable gift is $489,000 ($500,000 − $11,000). ◀

EXAMPLE C12-31 ▶ Greg transfers $800,000 of property to an irrevocable trust with a bank serving as trustee and instructs the trustee to distribute all the trust income semiannually to Greg's three adult children, Jill, Katy, and Laura. The trustee is to use its discretion in deciding how much to distribute to each beneficiary. Moreover, it is authorized to distribute nothing to a particular beneficiary if it deems such action to be in the beneficiary's best interest. Although all the income must be paid out, the trustee has complete discretion to determine how much to pay to a particular beneficiary. None of the beneficiaries has the assurance that he or she will receive a trust distribution. Thus, no present interests are created, and the annual exclusion does not apply. The taxable gift, therefore, is $800,000. ◀

SPECIAL RULE FOR TRUSTS FOR MINORS. Congress realized that many parents would find it undesirable to require trusts created for minor children to distribute all their income to the young children. Accordingly, Congress enacted Sec. 2503(c), which authorizes special trusts for minors, to address parents' concerns about the distribution of trust income to minors. Section 2503(c) authorizes an annual exclusion for gifts to trusts for beneficiaries under age 21 even though the trusts need not distribute all their income annually. Such trusts, known as **Sec. 2503(c) trusts**, allow donors to claim the annual exclusion if the following two conditions are met:

- ▶ Until the beneficiary becomes age 21, the trustee may pay the income and/or the underlying assets to the beneficiary.
- ▶ Any income and underlying assets not paid to the beneficiary will pass to that beneficiary when he or she reaches age 21. If the beneficiary should die before becoming age 21, the income and underlying assets are payable to either the beneficiary's estate or any person the minor may appoint if the minor possesses a general power of appointment over the property.

ADDITIONAL COMMENT

The donor may serve as trustee of a Sec. 2503(c) trust, but this approach generally is not advisable. If the donor's powers are not sufficiently limited, the trust property will be included in the donor's estate if the donor's death occurs while the trust is in force.

If the trust instrument contains the provisions listed above, no part of the trust is considered to be a gift of a future interest. Therefore, the entire transfer is eligible for the annual exclusion.

As a result of Sec. 2503(c), donors creating trusts for donees under age 21 receive an exclusion even though the trustee has discretion over paying out the trust income. However, the trustee must distribute the assets and accumulated income to the beneficiary at age 21.

CRUMMEY TRUST. The **Crummey trust** is yet another technique that allows the donor to obtain an annual exclusion upon funding a discretionary trust. The trust can terminate at whatever age the donor specifies and can be created for a beneficiary of any age. Thus, the *Crummey* trust is a much more flexible arrangement than the Sec. 2503(c) trust.

---

[33] Reg. Sec. 25.2503-3(b).

[34] Reg. Sec. 25.2503-3(a).

ADDITIONAL COMMENT

The holder of a *Crummey* power must be given notice of a contribution to the trust to which the power relates and must be given a reasonable time period within which to exercise the power. The donor receives the annual exclusion regardless of whether the donee exercises the power.

The *Crummey* trust is named for a Ninth Circuit Court of Appeals decision holding that the trust beneficiaries had a present interest as a result of certain language in the trust instrument.[35] That language, which is referred to interchangeably as a *Crummey* power, *Crummey* demand power, or *Crummey* withdrawal power, entitled each beneficiary to demand a distribution of the lesser of $4,000 or the amount transferred to the trust that year. If such power was not exercised by a specified date, it expired. The reason for the "lesser of" language for the demand power is as follows: The largest present interest the donor needs to create is equal to the annual exclusion amount. In years in which the gift is smaller than the annual exclusion amount, the donor simply needs to be able to exclude the amount of that year's gift. In addition, the donor wants to restrict the amount to which the beneficiary can have access. Today, the maximum amount the beneficiary can withdraw is likely to be set at an amount equal to the annual exclusion for federal gift tax purposes or twice that amount if gift splitting is anticipated.

The court held that the demand power provided each beneficiary with a present interest equal to the maximum amount the beneficiary could require the trustee to pay over to him or her that year. Use of the *Crummey* trust technique entitles the donor to receive the annual exclusion while creating a discretionary trust that terminates at whatever age the donor deems appropriate. The donor thereby avoids the restrictive rules of Sec. 2503(c). Generally, the donor hopes the beneficiary will not exercise the demand right.

EXAMPLE C12-32 ▶ Al funds two $100,000 irrevocable trusts and names First Bank the trustee. The first trust is for the benefit of Kay, his 15-year-old daughter. The trustee has discretion to distribute income and/or principal to Kay until she reaches age 21. If she dies before age 21, the trust assets are payable to whomever she appoints in her will or to her estate if she dies without a will. The second trust is for the benefit of Bob, Al's 25-year-old son. Income and/or principal are payable to Bob in the trustee's discretion until Bob reaches age 35, whereupon Bob will receive the trust assets. Bob may demand by December 31 of each year that the trustee pay him the lesser of $11,000 or the amount transferred to the trust that calendar year. The trust for Kay is a Sec. 2503(c) trust, and the one for Bob is a *Crummey* trust. An annual exclusion is available for each trust. ◀

STOP & THINK

Question: For which of the following gifts would the donor receive an annual exclusion:

- ▶ A gift of a remainder interest in land if the donor retains the income interest for life
- ▶ A gift outright of a life insurance policy that has a cash surrender value
- ▶ A gift to a discretionary trust that is classified as a Sec. 2503(c) trust
- ▶ A gift to a Crummey trust?

Solution: All the transfers except the gift of the remainder interest are eligible for the annual exclusion. Even though the gift to the Sec. 2503(c) trust does not literally involve a gift of a present interest (the right to current income or enjoyment), the IRC explicitly allows this kind of transfer to qualify for the annual exclusion.

GIFT TAX DEDUCTIONS

OBJECTIVE 5

Identify deductions available for gift tax purposes

The formula for determining taxable gifts allows both a marital deduction and a charitable contribution deduction. The **marital deduction** is for transfers to one's spouse. The **charitable contribution deduction** is for gifts to charitable organizations. Section 2524 states that the deductible amount in either case may not exceed the amount of the "includible gift"— that is, the amount of the gift exceeding the annual exclusion. Thus, the taxable amount of the gift is zero, not a negative number, as would be the case if the deduction equaled the total amount of the gift.

[35] *D. Clifford Crummey v. CIR*, 22 AFTR 2d 6023, 68-2 USTC ¶12,541 (9th Cir., 1968).

MARITAL DEDUCTION

ADDITIONAL COMMENT

Congress allowed a marital deduction because a taxpayer who transfers property to his or her spouse has not made a transfer outside the economic (husband/wife) unit. For similar reasons, the interspousal gift has no *income* tax consequences. The donor spouse recognizes no gain or loss, and the donee spouse takes a carryover basis.

Generally, the marital deduction results in tax-free interspousal transfers, but an exception discussed below applies to gifts of certain terminable interests. Congress first enacted the marital deduction in 1948 to provide more uniform treatment of community property and noncommunity property donors. To recap, in community property states, most property acquired after marriage is owned equally by each spouse. In noncommunity property states, however, the spouses' wealth often is divided unequally, and such spouses can equalize each individual's share of the wealth only by engaging in a gift-giving program. As a result of the marital deduction, spouses can shift wealth between themselves completely free of any gift tax consequences.

UNLIMITED AMOUNT. Over the years, the maximum marital deduction has varied, but after 1981 one spouse may deduct up to 100% of the amount of gifts made to the other spouse. The amount of the marital deduction, however, is limited to the amount of the gift that exceeds the annual exclusion.[36] For gifts made after 1981, transfers of community property are eligible for the marital deduction; earlier, such gifts did not qualify for the deduction.

EXAMPLE C12-33 ▶ A wife gives her husband stock valued at $450,000. She excludes $11,000 because of the annual exclusion and claims a $439,000 marital deduction. Thus, no taxable gift arises. ◀

GIFTS OF TERMINABLE INTERESTS: GENERAL RULE.

Nondeductible Terminable Interests. A **terminable interest** is an interest that ends or is terminated when some event occurs (or fails to occur) or a specified amount of time passes. Some, but not all, terminable interests are ineligible for the marital deduction.[37] A marital deduction is denied only when the transfer is of a *nondeductible* terminable interest. A nondeductible terminable interest has one of the following characteristics:

- The donee-spouse's interest ceases at a set time (such as at death) and the property then either passes back to the donor or passes to a third party who does not pay adequate consideration.
- Immediately after making the gift, the donor has the power to name someone else to receive an interest in the property, and the person named may possess the property upon the termination of the donee-spouse's interest.[38]

The next three examples illustrate some of the subtleties of the definition of nondeductible terminable interests. In Example C12-34, a marital deduction is available because the interest transferred is not a nondeductible terminable interest.

EXAMPLE C12-34 ▶ A patent is a terminable interest because the property interest terminates at the end of the patent's legal life. Nevertheless, the patent does not constitute a nondeductible terminable interest. When the patent's legal life expires, a third party will not possess an interest in the patent. Thus, a donor will receive a marital deduction for a patent transferred to a spouse. ◀

In Example C12-35, a marital deduction is denied because the first of the two alternative characteristics of a nondeductible terminable interest exists.

EXAMPLE C12-35 ▶ A donor transfers property in trust and (1) names his wife to receive trust income, at the trustee's discretion, annually for the next 15 years and (2) states that at the end of the 15-year period the trust's assets are to be distributed to their child. The donor has given his wife a nondeductible terminable interest. When the spouse's interest ceases, the property passes to their child, a recipient who did not pay adequate consideration. Thus, the donor receives no marital deduction. ◀

In Example C12-36, a marital deduction is available. In this case, the donee-spouse has a general power of appointment over the trust's assets in addition to having a lifetime income interest. The donee-spouse specifies the persons to eventually receive the property.

[36] Sec. 2524.

[37] Sec. 2523(b).

[38] Ibid.

EXAMPLE C12-36 ▶ The donor gives his wife the right to all the income from a trust annually for life plus a general power of appointment over the trust's assets. He has transferred an interest eligible for the marital deduction. The general power of appointment may be exercisable during life, at death, or at both times. In addition, the donee-spouse is entitled to receive the income annually. ◀

TAX STRATEGY TIP

A general power of appointment can qualify a transfer for the marital deduction. For example, assume that last year Brad transferred property to a trust, income to be distributed annually to his wife Sonia until her death, with a general power of appointment in Sonia over the remainder. The general power of appointment in Sonia allowed the transfer to be eligible for the gift tax marital deduction.

TAX STRATEGY TIP

By using a QTIP, a donor can achieve a marital deduction while exercising some control over the property. For example, assume the same facts as in the previous annotation except that Brad has been married twice. He had two children by his first wife and three children with Sonia. Brad could not be sure his first two children would ever receive anything from the trust because Sonia could exercise her general power of appointment in favor of just their three children (or someone else). If Brad funded a QTIP, the trust instrument could specify that the remainder, on Sonia's death, would go equally to all five children. Brad could thus control the ultimate disposition of the remainder and still receive a marital deduction.

The rationale behind the nondeductible terminable interest rule is that a donor should obtain a marital deduction only if he or she conveys an interest that will have transfer tax significance to the donee-spouse. In other words, when a donee spouse later gives away property that he or she received as a result of an interspousal transfer, a transfer subject to the gift tax occurs. If the donee-spouse retains such property until death, the item is included in the donee-spouse's gross estate.

QTIP PROVISIONS. Beginning in 1982, Congress made a major change to the nondeductible terminable interest rule and allowed transfers of qualified terminable interest property to be eligible for the marital deduction.[39] Such transfers are commonly referred to as *QTIP transfers*. **Qualified terminable interest property** is property

- That is transferred by the donor-spouse,
- In which the donee has a "qualifying income interest for life," and
- For which a special election has been made.

A spouse has the necessary "qualifying income interest for life" if

- The spouse is entitled to all the income from the property annually or more often, and
- No person has a power to appoint any part of the property to any person other than the donee-spouse unless the power cannot be exercised while the spouse is alive.

The QTIP rule enhances the attractiveness of making transfers to one's spouse because a donor can receive a marital deduction—and thereby make a nontaxable transfer—without having to grant the spouse full control over the gifted property. The QTIP rule is especially attractive for a donor who wants to ensure that the children by a previous marriage will receive the property upon the donee-spouse's death.

The donor does not have to claim a marital deduction even though the transfer otherwise qualifies as a QTIP transfer. Claiming the deduction on such transfers is elective.[40] If the donor elects to claim a marital deduction, the donee-spouse must include the QTIP trust property in his or her estate at its value as of the donee-spouse's date of death. Thus, as with other transfers qualifying for the marital deduction, the interspousal transfer is tax-free, and the taxable event is postponed until the donee-spouse transfers the property.

EXAMPLE C12-37 ▶ Jo transfers $1 million of property in trust with a bank acting as trustee. All the trust income is payable to Jo's husband, Ed (age 64), quarterly for the rest of his life. Upon Ed's death, the property will pass to Jo's nieces. This gift is eligible for a marital deduction. If Jo elects to claim the marital deduction, she will receive a $989,000 ($1,000,000 − $11,000) marital deduction. The deduction is limited to the amount of the includible gift, i.e., the gift exceeding the annual exclusion. ◀

Note that Jo's marital deduction in the preceding example is for $989,000 and not for the value of Ed's life estate. If Jo elects to claim the marital deduction, Ed's gross estate will include the value of the entire trust, valued as of the date of Ed's death. The QTIP provision permits Jo to receive a marital deduction while still being able to specify who will receive the property upon her husband's death.

Topic Review C12-2 summarizes the eligibility of a transfer for the marital deduction and the amount of the marital deduction that can be claimed.

---

39 Sec. 2523(f).

40 The donor might decide not to claim the marital deduction if the donee-spouse has substantial assets already or a short life expectancy, especially if the gifted property's value is expected to appreciate at a high annual rate.

Topic Review C12-2

Eligibility for and Amount of the Marital Deduction

Examples of Transfers Eligible for the Marital Deduction

Property transferred to spouse as sole owner

Property transferred in trust with all the income payable to the spouse for life and over which the donee-spouse has a general power of appointment

Property transferred in trust with all the income payable annually or more often to the spouse for life and for which the donor-spouse named the remainderman—marital deduction available if elected under QTIP rule

Examples of Transfers Ineligible for the Marital Deduction

Property transferred in trust with the income payable in the trustee's discretion to the spouse for life, and for which the donor-spouse named the remainderman

Property transferred in trust with all the income payable to the spouse for a specified number of years and for which the donor-spouse named the remainderman

Amount of the Marital Deduction, If Available

The amount of the transfer minus the portion eligible for the annual exclusion

CHARITABLE CONTRIBUTION DEDUCTION

If a donor is not required to file a gift tax return to report noncharitable gifts, that donor does not have to report gifts to charitable organizations on a gift tax return, provided a charitable contribution deduction is available and the charitable organization receives the donor's entire interest in the property. Claiming an income tax deduction for a charitable contribution does not preclude the donor from also obtaining a gift tax deduction. In contrast with the income tax provisions, the gift tax charitable contribution deduction has no percentage limitation. The only ceiling on the deduction is imposed by Sec. 2524, which limits the deduction to the amount of the gift that exceeds the excluded portion.

EXAMPLE C12-38 ▶ Julio gives stock valued at $76,000 to State University. Julio receives an $11,000 annual exclusion and a $65,000 charitable contribution deduction for *gift* tax purposes. However, he need not report the gift on a gift tax return if he does not have to file a return to report gifts to noncharitable donees. On his *income* tax return, he receives a $76,000 charitable contribution deduction, subject to AGI limitations. ◀

TAX STRATEGY TIP

A charitably-minded taxpayer could avoid the gift (and the estate) tax entirely by giving all his or her property to a qualified charitable organization. Actually, in 2002 the taxpayer could give (or will) up to $1 million to noncharitable donees as long as the balance of his or her property was given (or willed) to charity and still pay no gift (or estate) tax.

TRANSFERS ELIGIBLE FOR THE DEDUCTION. To be deductible, the gift must be made to a charitable organization. The rules defining charitable organizations are quite similar for income, gift, and estate tax purposes.[41] According to Sec. 2522, a gift tax deduction is available for contributions to the following:

- The United States or any subordinate level of government within the United States as long as the transfer is solely for public purposes
- A corporation, trust fund, etc., organized exclusively for religious, charitable, scientific, literary, or educational purposes, or to foster amateur sports competition, including the encouragement of art and the prevention of cruelty to children or animals
- A fraternal society or similar organization operating under the lodge system if the gifts are to be used in the United States only for religious, charitable, scientific, literary, or educational purposes
- A war veterans' post or organization organized in the United States or one of its possessions if no part of its net earnings accrues to the benefit of private shareholders or individuals

[41] In contrast to the income tax rules, a charitable contribution deduction is available under the gift tax rules for transfers made to foreign charitable organizations. No deduction is available, however, for gifts made to foreign governments.

SPLIT-INTEREST TRANSFERS. Specialized rules apply when a donor makes a transfer for both private (i.e., an individual) and public (i.e., a charitable organization) purposes. Such arrangements are known as **split-interest transfers.** An example of a split-interest transfer is the gift of a residence to one's sister for life with the remainder interest to a university. If a donor gives a charitable organization a remainder interest, the donor forfeits the charitable contribution deduction unless the remainder interest is in either a personal residence (not necessarily the donor's principal residence), a farm, a charitable remainder annuity trust or unitrust, or a pooled income fund.[42] A split-interest gift of a present interest to a charity qualifies for a charitable contribution deduction only if the charity receives a guaranteed annuity interest or a unitrust interest.

EXAMPLE C12-39 ▶ Al transfers $800,000 of property to a charitable remainder annuity trust. He reserves an annuity of $56,000 per year for his remaining life and specifies that upon his death the trust property will pass to the American Red Cross. Al must report this transaction because the Red Cross did not receive his entire interest in the property. In the same year, Al gives a museum a remainder interest in his antique furniture collection and reserves a life estate for himself.

Each of these is a split-interest transfer. Unfortunately for the donor, only the remainder interest in the charitable remainder annuity trust is eligible for a charitable contribution deduction. Consequently, Al makes a taxable gift equal to the value of the remainder interest in the antique furniture. Even though the furniture is not an income-producing property, the value of the remainder interest is determined from the actuarial tables found in Appendix H.

Assume that Al was age 60 at the time of the gifts and that the appropriate interest rate was 10%. What is the amount of Al's charitable contribution deduction?

Answer: The portion of the annuity trust retained by Al is $441,302 {[(1.0 – 0.21196) ÷ 0.10] × $56,000}. The charitable deduction on the gift tax return is $358,698 ($800,000 – $441,302). The same amount also is allowable—subject to the ceiling rules—as a charitable contribution deduction on Al's income tax return for that year. ◀

SELF-STUDY QUESTION

In Example C12-39, does Al receive an annual exclusion for the gift of the furniture?

ANSWER

No. The remainder interest is a future interest, as is the remainder in the trust.

THE GIFT-SPLITTING ELECTION

OBJECTIVE 6

Apply the gift-splitting rules

The gift-splitting provisions of Sec. 2513 allow spouses to treat a gift actually made by one of them to a third party as if each spouse made one-half of the gift. This election offers several advantages, as follows:

- If only one spouse makes a gift to a particular donee, the election enables a spouse to give $22,000 (instead of $11,000) to the donee before a taxable gift arises.
- If per-donee annual transfers exceed $22,000 and taxable gifts occur, the election may reduce the applicable marginal gift tax rate.
- Each spouse may use a unified credit to reduce the gift tax payable.

TAX STRATEGY TIP

Donors can magnify the benefits of the annual exclusion by using gift splitting techniques.

To take advantage of the gift-splitting election, the spouses must meet the following requirements at the time of the transfer:

- They must be U.S. citizens or residents.
- At the time of the gift(s) for which the spouses make an election, the donor-spouse must be married to the person who consents to gift splitting. In addition, the donor-spouse must not remarry before the end of the year.

The gift-splitting election is effective for all transfers to third parties made during the portion of the year that the spouses were married to each other.

[42] In a **charitable remainder annuity trust**, an individual receives trust distributions for a certain time period or for life. The annual distributions are a uniform percentage (5% or higher) of the value of the trust property, valued on the date of the transfer. For a **charitable remainder unitrust**, the distributions are similar, except that they are a uniform percentage (5% or higher) of the value of the trust property, revalued at least annually. Thus, the annual distributions from a unitrust, but not an annuity trust, vary from one year to the next. Both unitrusts and annuity trusts must meet the requirements that the payout rate does not exceed 50% of the value of the property and the value of the remainder interest is at least 10% of the initial FMV. A **pooled income fund** is similar in concept to a mutual fund. The various individual beneficiaries receive annual distributions of their proportionate shares of the pooled income fund's total income.

ADDITIONAL COMMENT

A wife makes a gift of $40,000 to a child in March and a gift of $60,000 to another child in November of the same year. The gift-splitting election, if made, will apply to both gifts because the election to gift split applies to all gifts made during the year. With gift splitting, her husband will report one-half of each gift on his own gift tax return.

A spouse living in a community property state who makes a gift of separate property (e.g., an asset received by inheritance) may desire to use gift splitting. In this case, the election automatically extends to gifts of community property even though splitting each spouse's gifts of community property has no impact on the amount of adjusted taxable gifts.

Note that gift splitting is an all-or-nothing proposition. Spouses electing it for one gift must elect it for all gifts to third parties for that year. Each year's election stands alone, however, and is not binding on future years.[43] The procedural aspects of the gift-splitting election are discussed in the Compliance and Procedural Considerations section of this chapter.

EXAMPLE C12-40 ▶ Eli marries Joy on April 1 of the current year. They are still married to each other at the end of the year. In March, Eli gave Amy $60,000. In July, Eli gave Barb $48,000, and Joy gave Claire $22,000. If the couple elects gift splitting, the election is effective only for the July gifts. Each spouse is treated as giving $24,000 and $11,000 to Barb and Claire, respectively. Because they may not elect gift splitting for the gift Eli makes before their marriage, Eli is treated as giving $60,000—the amount he actually transfers—to Amy. Under gift splitting, both Eli and Joy exclude $11,000 of gifts to both Barb and Claire, or a total of $44,000. Eli also excludes $11,000 of his gift to Amy. ◀

ADDITIONAL COMMENT

The gift-splitting election is a year-by-year election. For example, a husband and wife could elect to gift split in 1997, 1999, and 2001, but elect not to gift split in 1998, 2000, and 2002.

Upon the death of the actual donor or the spouse who consented to gift splitting, such decedent's estate tax base includes that decedent's post-1976 taxable gifts, known as adjusted taxable gifts. By electing gift splitting, a couple can reduce the amount of the taxable gifts the donor-decedent is deemed to have made. Under gift splitting, the adjusted taxable gifts include only the portions of the gifts that are taxable on the gift tax returns filed by the donor-decedent. Of course, the nondonor-spouse's estate reports his or her post-1976 taxable gifts.

STOP & THINK

Question: Bob made taxable gifts of $4 million in 2000, and Betty, his spouse, has not made any taxable gifts. Betty inherited a large fortune last year and is contemplating gifting $500,000 in 2002 to each of her two children. Bob does not anticipate making any taxable gifts this year. Should they elect gift splitting for Betty's gifts?

Solution: They should not necessarily elect gift splitting because the main advantage of the election will be that the aggregate annual exclusions will be $44,000 instead of $22,000. An adverse effect will be that Bob, who has exhausted his unified credit (except for the increase from $220,550 to $345,800) and is in a higher marginal tax bracket, will be the deemed donor of $478,000 [(0.50 × $1,000,000) − $22,000] of taxable gifts.

COMPUTATION OF THE GIFT TAX LIABILITY

OBJECTIVE 7

Calculate the gift tax liability

EFFECT OF PREVIOUS TAXABLE GIFTS

The gift tax computation involves a cumulative process. All the donor's previous taxable gifts (i.e., those made in 1932 or later years) plus the donor's taxable gifts for the current year affect the marginal tax rate for current taxable gifts. Thus, two donors making the same taxable gifts in the current period may incur different gift tax liabilities because one donor may have made substantially larger taxable gifts in earlier periods than did the other donor. The process outlined below must be used to compute the gross tax levied on the current period's taxable gifts.

43 If the nondonor-spouse has made substantial taxable gifts relative to those made by the donor-spouse, the gift tax liability for the period in question may be lower if the spouses do not elect gift splitting because the nondonor-spouse may have no unified credit left and may have reached the highest marginal transfer tax rate.

1. Determine the gift tax liability (at current rates) on the donor's cumulative taxable gifts (taxable gifts of current period plus aggregate taxable gifts of previous periods).
2. Determine the gift tax liability (at current rates) on the donor's cumulative taxable gifts made through the end of the preceding period.
3. Subtract the gift tax determined in Step 2 from that in Step 1. The difference equals the gross gift tax on the current period's taxable gifts.

This calculation process results in taxing the gifts on a progressive basis over the donor's lifetime.

Note that, although the gift tax rates have varied over the years, the current rate schedules are used in the calculation even when the donor made some or all the gifts when different rates were in effect. This process ensures that current taxable gifts are taxed at the appropriate rate, given the donor's earlier gift history.

EXAMPLE C12-41 ▶ In 1975, Tony made $2 million in taxable gifts. These gifts were the first Tony ever made. The tax imposed under the 1975 rate schedule was $564,900. Tony's next taxable gifts are made in 2002. The taxable amount of these gifts is $400,000. The tax on Tony's 2002 taxable gifts before applying the unified credit is calculated as follows:

Tax at current rates on $2.4 million of cumulative taxable gifts	$976,800
Minus: Tax at current rates on $2 million of prior period taxable gifts	(780,800)
Tax on $400,000 of taxable gifts made in the current period	$196,000 ◀

This cumulative process results in the $400,000 gift in Example C12-41 being taxed at a 49% rate, the marginal gift tax rate applicable to taxable transfers ranging between $2 million and $2.5 million. If the gift tax computations were not cumulative, the tax on the $400,000 of gifts would be determined by using the lowest marginal rates and would have been only $121,800. Because the tax on taxable transfers made in previous periods is determined by reference to the current rate schedule, Tony's actual 1975 gift tax liability, incurred when the gift tax rates were lower, is not relevant to the determination of his current gift tax. As discussed below, the unified credit will reduce the tax liability.

UNIFIED CREDIT AVAILABLE

Congress enacted a unified credit for both gift and estate tax purposes beginning in 1977. The unified credit reduces the amount of the gross gift tax owed on current period gifts. The amount of the credit has increased over the years (see inside back cover). As a result of the 2001 Act, the credit for gift tax purposes will rise to $345,800 in 2002 and remain at that amount even though the credit against estate taxes will increase further through 2009. Donors who have made taxable gifts in the post-1976 period have used some of their credit. The amount of the credit available to those donors for the current year is reduced by the aggregate amount allowable as a credit in all preceding years.

EXAMPLE C12-42 ▶ Hu made her first taxable gift in 1985. The taxable amount of the 1985 gift was $100,000, which resulted in a gross gift tax of $23,800. Hu claimed $23,800 (of the $121,800 credit then available) on her 1985 return to reduce her net gift tax liability to zero. Hu made her next taxable gift in 1994. The taxable amount of the gift was $400,000. The tax on the $400,000 gift equaled (1) the tax on $500,000 of total gifts (at 1994 gift tax rates) of $155,800 minus (2) the tax on $100,000 of previous gifts (at 1994 gift tax rates) of $23,800, or $132,000. The credit amount for 1994 was $192,800. Hu's gift tax was reduced to zero by a credit of $132,000 because for 1994 she had a credit of $169,000 ($192,800 − $23,800) left. If in 2002 Hu makes additional taxable gifts, $190,000 [$345,800 −($23,800 + $132,000)] of unified credit will be available to reduce the gift tax liability in 2002. ◀

STOP & THINK *Question:* You are reviewing a 2002 gift tax return that a co-worker prepared. The tax return reflects current taxable gifts of $250,000 and $625,000 of taxable gifts made in 1992. You note that on the return your colleague (a new staff member) claimed a unified credit of $70,800 and, thus, reported zero gift tax payable. What should you discuss with your colleague?

Solution: You should explain that the 2002 unified credit of $345,800 (which equals the tax on the first $1 million of taxable gifts) is not an annual credit maximum but rather is the credit available during a donor's lifetime. Because in 1992 the donor made $625,000 of taxable gifts, he exhausted his $192,800 unified credit then available. In addition, you should explain the cumulative nature of the gift tax calculations. The tax calculated on the first $250,000 of taxable gifts is $70,800. If the colleague claimed a $70,800 unified credit and showed zero tax payable, he did not calculate the tax on the current taxable gift of $250,000 by performing the cumulative calculations that take into effect the $625,000 of earlier taxable gifts. The tax *before* the credit was calculated incorrectly. The credit available is $153,000 ($345,800 − $192,800), the 2002 credit less the credit already used. The gift tax payable is still zero.

COMPREHENSIVE ILLUSTRATION

The following comprehensive illustration demonstrates the computation of one donor's gift tax liability for the situation where the donors elect gift splitting. It demonstrates the computation of the wife's gift tax liability.

BACKGROUND DATA

Hugh and Wilma Brown are married to each other throughout 2001. Hugh made no taxable gifts in earlier periods. Wilma's previous taxable gifts were $300,000 in 1975 and $200,000 in 1988. In August 2001, Wilma makes the following gratuitous transfers:

- $80,000 in cash to son Billy
- $24,000 in jewelry to daughter Betsy
- $30,000 in medical expense payments to Downtown Infirmary for medical care of grandson Tim
- Remainder interest in vacation cabin to friend Ruth Cain. Wilma (age 60) retains a life estate. The vacation cabin is valued at $100,000.
- $600,000 of stocks to a bank in trust with all of the income payable semiannually to husband Hugh (age 72) for life and remainder payable at Hugh's death to Jeff Bass, Wilma's son by an earlier marriage, or Jeff's estate. Wilma wants to elect the marital deduction.

In 2001, Hugh's only gifts were

- $80,000 of stock to State University
- $600,000 of land to daughter Betsy

Assume the applicable interest rate for valuing life estates and remainders is 10%.

CALCULATION OF TAX LIABILITY

The medical expense payments are exempt from the gift tax under Sec. 2503(e). The Browns need to report the gift to State University even though the university received Hal's entire interest in the property because they must file a gift tax return to report gifts to noncharitable donees. In addition, a charitable contribution deduction is available. The vacation cabin is valued at $100,000, and the remainder interest therein at $21,196 (0.21196 ×$100,000) (see Table S, age 60 in Appendix H) for gift tax purposes. The stock is transferred to a QTIP trust, and the marital deduction election treats the entire interest (not just the life estate) as having been given to Hugh Brown.

Table C12-1 shows the computation of Wilma's gift tax liability for 2001. These same facts are used for the sample United States Gift Tax Return, Form 709, in Appendix B.

▼ **TABLE C12-1**
Comprehensive Gift Tax Illustration

Wilma's actual 2001 gifts:		
Billy, cash		$ 80,000
Betsy, jewelry		24,000
Ruth, remainder interest in vacation cabin (future interest)		21,196
Husband Hugh and son Jeff, transfer to QTIP trust		600,000
Total gifts made by Wilma		$725,196
Minus: One-half of Wilma's gifts made to third parties that are deemed made by Hugh [0.50 × ($725,196 − $600,000)]		(62,598)
Plus: One-half of Hugh's gifts made to third parties (Betsy and State University that are deemed made by Wilma (0.50 × $680,000)		340,000
Minus: Annual exclusions for gifts of present interests ($10,000 each for gifts made to Billy, Betsy, Hugh, and State University)		(40,000)
Minus: Marital deduction ($600,000 − $10,000 exclusion)		(590,000)
Minus: Charitable contribution deduction ($40,000 − $10,000 exclusion)		(30,000)
Taxable gifts for current period		$342,598
Tax on cumulative taxable gifts of $842,598[a]		$284,413
Minus: Tax on previous taxable gifts of $500,000 (current rate schedule)		(155,800)
Tax on taxable gifts of $342,598 for the current period		$128,613
Minus: Unified credit:		
Credit for 2001	$220,550	
Minus: Credit allowable for prior periods	(68,000)[b]	(152,550)[c]
Tax payable for 2001		$ -0-

[a] $300,000 (in 1975) + $200,000 (in 1988) + $342,598 (in 2001).
[b] $0 (for 1975) + $68,000 (for 1988). The $68,000, which is smaller than the maximum credit of $192,800 for1988, is the excess of the $155,800 tax on cumulative taxable gifts less the $87,800 tax on the $300,000 previous taxable gifts.
[c] Actually, for 2001 Wilma uses only $128,613 of her remaining credit. In a later year, she will have available a credit of $149,187 [$345,800 − ($128,613 + $68,000)].

BASIS CONSIDERATIONS FOR A LIFETIME GIVING PLAN

OBJECTIVE 8

Understand how basis affects the overall tax consequences

Prospective donors should consider the tax-saving features of making a series of lifetime gifts (discussed in the Tax Planning Considerations section of this chapter). Lifetime giving plans can remove income from the donor's income tax return and transfer it to the donee's income tax return, where it may be taxed at a lower marginal tax rate. A series of gifts may permit property to be transferred to a donee without incurring a gift tax liability and thus enable the donor to eliminate part or all of his or her estate tax liability. These two advantages must be weighed against the unattractive basis rules (discussed below) applicable for such transfers.

PROPERTY RECEIVED BY GIFT

The carryover basis rules apply to property received by gift. Provided the property's FMV on the date of the gift exceeds its adjusted basis, the donee's basis in such property is the same as the donor's basis. In addition, the donee's basis may be increased by some or all of the gift tax paid by the donor. For pre-1977 gifts, all the gift taxes paid by the donor may be added to the donor's adjusted basis. For post-1976 transfers, however, only the portion of the gift taxes represented by the following fraction may increase the donor's adjusted basis:

SELF-STUDY QUESTION

Barkley purchased land in 1955 for $90,000. In 1974, when the FMV of the land was $300,000, he gave the land to his son Tracy. He paid gift taxes of $23,000 on the gift. What is Tracy's basis in the land? What if the gift had been made in 1984? For simplicity, assume the 1984 tax was $23,000.

ANSWER

If the gift were made in 1974, Tracy's basis is $90,000 plus the $23,000 gift tax, or $113,000. Had Barkley made the gift in 1984, Tracy's basis would be $90,000 plus [($210,000/$290,000) × $23,000], or $106,655.

ADDITIONAL COMMENT

Phil owns investment property worth $350,000 in which his adjusted basis is $500,000. Unless there are reasons why the property should be kept in the family, Phil should sell the property and recognize an income tax loss. If he gifts the property to his child, the loss basis in the child's hands is $350,000 (and the gain basis is $500,000). Thus, if the value does not increase, the income tax loss for the $150,000 decline in market value can never be taken. If Phil dies holding the loss property, his heirs will take the estate tax return value (FMV) as their basis, and the potential income tax loss will not be recognized.

$$\frac{\text{Amount of property's appreciation from acquisition date through date of gift}}{\text{FMV of property on the date of the gift minus exclusions and deductions}}$$

In no event, however, can the gift tax adjustment increase the donee's basis above the property's FMV on the date of the gift.[44]

If the gifted property's FMV on the date of the gift is less than the donor's adjusted basis, the basis rules are more complicated. For purposes of determining gain, the donee's basis is the same as the donor's adjusted basis. For purposes of determining loss, the donee's basis is the property's FMV on the date of the gift. If the donee sells the property for an amount between its FMV as of the date of the gift and the donor's adjusted basis, the donee recognizes no gain or loss. The property's basis cannot be increased by any gift taxes paid if the donor's adjusted basis exceeds the property's FMV as of the date of the gift. In general, prospective donors should dispose of property that has declined in value by selling it instead of gifting it.

PROPERTY RECEIVED AT DEATH

In general, the basis rules that apply to property received as a result of another's death call for a step up or step down to the property's FMV as of the decedent's date of death. The recipient's basis is the same as the amount at which the property is valued on the estate tax return, which is its FMV on either the decedent's date of death or the alternate valuation date. Generally, the alternate valuation date is six months after the date of death. Although these rules are usually thought of as providing for a step-up in basis, if the property has declined in value as of the transferor's death, the basis is stepped-down to its FMV at the date of death or alternate valuation date.

In certain circumstances, no step up in basis occurs for appreciated property transferred at death.[45] This exception applies if both of the following conditions are present:

- The decedent receives the appreciated property as a gift during the one-year period preceding his or her death, and
- The property passes to the donor or to the donor's spouse as a result of the donee-decedent's death.

Before the enactment of this rule, a widely publicized planning technique was the transfer of appreciated property to an ill spouse who, in turn, could will the property back to the donor-spouse, who would receive the property at a stepped-up basis. The interspousal transfers by gift and at death are tax-free because of the unlimited marital deduction for both gift tax and estate tax purposes. Consequently, before the rule change, the property received a step-up in basis at no transfer tax cost.

EXAMPLE C12-43 ▶ In June 2001, Sarah made a gift of property valued at $700,000 to Tom, her husband. Sarah's adjusted basis in the property was $120,000. Tom dies in March 2002. At this time, the property is worth $740,000. If the property passes back to Sarah under Tom's will upon Tom's death, Sarah's basis will be $120,000. However, if the property passes to someone other than Sarah at Tom's death, its basis will be stepped-up to $740,000. If Tom lives for more than one year after receiving the gift, the basis is stepped-up to its FMV as of Tom's date of death regardless of whether the property passes at Tom's death to Sarah or someone else. If Tom (the donee) sold the property a few months before his death in March 2002, Tom's basis would be the same as Sarah's was, or $120,000. ◀

In conjunction with the repeal of the estate tax in 2010, the step-up in basis rule for property received from a decedent will be replaced with a modified carryover basis rule. Under this rule, a person receiving property from a decedent will have a basis equal to the lesser of (1) the decedent's adjusted basis in the property or (2) the property's fair market value at the date of the decedent's death. A special rule, however, will allow a $1.3 million

---

44 See Reg. Sec. 1.1015-5(c) for examples of how to calculate the gift tax that can increase the property's basis.

45 Sec. 1014(e).

basis increase (and an additional $3 million basis increase for property transferred to a surviving spouse) not to exceed the property's fair market value. For example, assume the decedent's entire estate consists of land for which the decedent paid $2 million. He dies in 2010, when the land is worth $12 million and leaves the land to his surviving spouse. Her basis will be $6.3 million ($2,000,000 + $1,300,000 + $3,000,000), compared with $12 million under current law. Some additional special rules will apply to the basis of property received from a decedent but are not detailed in this text.

BELOW-MARKET LOANS: GIFT AND INCOME TAX CONSEQUENCES

GENERAL RULES

Section 7872 provides rules concerning the gift and income tax consequences of below-market loans. In general, it treats the lender as both making a gift to the borrower and receiving interest income. The borrower is treated as paying interest expense.

In the case of a demand loan, the lender is treated as having made a gift in each year in which the loan is outstanding. The amount of the gift equals the forgone interest income for the portion of the year the loan is outstanding. The forgone interest income is calculated by referring to the difference between the interest rate the lender charged and the federal short-term rate of Sec. 1274(d), for the period in question.

For income tax purposes, the forgone interest is treated as being retransferred from the borrower to the lender on the last day of each calendar year in which the loan is outstanding. The amount of the forgone interest is the same as for gift tax purposes and is reported by the lender as income for the year in question. The borrower gets an interest expense deduction for the same amount unless one of the rules limiting the interest deduction applies (e.g., personal interest or investment interest limitations).

EXAMPLE C12-44 ▶ On July 1, Frank lends $500,000 to Susan, who signs an interest-free demand note. The loan is still outstanding on December 31. Assume that 10% is the applicable annual interest rate. Frank is deemed to have made a gift to Susan on December 31 of $25,000 (0.10 × $500,000 × 6⁄12). Frank must report $25,000 of interest income. Susan deducts $25,000 of interest expense provided the deduction is not otherwise limited or disallowed. ◀

DE MINIMIS RULES

Under one of the *de minimis* rules, neither the income nor the gift tax rules apply to any gift loan made directly between individuals for any day on which the aggregate loans outstanding between the borrower and the lender are $10,000 or less. The *de minimis* exception does not apply to any loan directly attributable to the purchase or carrying of income-producing assets.

A second *de minimis* exception potentially permits loans of $100,000 or less to receive more favorable income tax (but not gift tax) treatment by limiting the lender's imputed income to the borrower's net investment income (as defined in Sec. 163(d)(3)) for the year. Moreover, if the borrower's net investment income for the year is $1,000 or less, such amount is treated as being zero.

The *de minimis* provisions do not apply to transactions having tax avoidance as a principal purpose and do not apply to any day on which the total outstanding loans between the borrower and the lender exceed $100,000. For purposes of the $100,000 or $10,000 loan limitations, a husband and wife are treated as one person.

EXAMPLE C12-45 ▶ On August 1, Mike lends $100,000 to Don. No other loans are outstanding between the parties. Avoidance of federal taxes is not a principal purpose of the loan. Don signs an interest-free demand note when 10% is the applicable interest rate. The loan is still outstanding on December 31. Mike is treated as having made a gift to Don on December 31 of $4,167 [$100,000 × 0.10 × 5⁄12]. Mike need not report this gift unless his aggregate gifts to Don this year exceed the gift tax annual exclusion.

The income tax consequences depend on Don's net investment income. If Don's net investment income for the year exceeds $4,167, Mike reports $4,167 of imputed interest income under Sec. 7872. Subject to rules that may disallow some or all of the interest expense deduction, Don deducts the $4,167 interest expense imputed under Sec. 7872. If Don's net investment income is between $1,001 and $4,167, each party reports interest income or expense under Sec. 7872 equal to Don's net investment income. Mike and Don report no interest income or expense under Sec. 7872 if Don's net investment income is $1,000 or less. ◄

TAX PLANNING CONSIDERATIONS

The 1976 Act, which introduced the unification concept, reduced the tax law's bias in favor of lifetime transfers. The 2001 Act, on the other hand, is more favorable toward transfers at death than by gift. Nevertheless, lifetime gifts still provide more advantages than disadvantages. Many factors, including the expected appreciation rate and now the donor's expectations about whether estate tax repeal will actually occur, affect the decision of whether to make gifts. Thus, the optimal result is not always clear. The pros and cons of lifetime gifts from an estate planning perspective are discussed below.

TAX-SAVING FEATURES OF INTER VIVOS GIFTS

USE OF ANNUAL EXCLUSION. The annual exclusion offers donors the opportunity to start making gifts to several donees per year relatively early in their lifetime and keep substantial amounts of property off the transfer tax rolls. The tax-free amount doubles if a husband and wife use the gift-splitting election.

The law provides no estate tax counterpart to the annual gift tax exclusion. Consequently, a terminally ill person whose will includes bequests of approximately $11,000 to each of several individuals would realize substantial transfer tax savings if gifts—instead of bequests—were made to these individuals.

REMOVAL OF POST-GIFT APPRECIATION FROM TAX BASE. Another important advantage of lifetime gifts is that their value is frozen at their date-of-gift value. That is, any post-gift appreciation escapes the transfer tax rolls. Consequently, transfer tax savings are maximized if the donor gives away the assets that appreciate the most.

REMOVAL OF GIFT TAX AMOUNT FROM TRANSFER TAX BASE. With one exception, gift taxes paid by the donor are removed from the transfer tax base. The lone exception applies to gift taxes paid on gifts the donor makes within three years of dying. Under the gross-up rule (discussed in Chapter C13), the donor's gross estate includes gift taxes paid on gifts made within three years of the donor's death.

INCOME SHIFTING. Originally, one of the most favorable consequences of lifetime gifts was income shifting, but the compression of the income tax rate schedules beginning in 1987 has lessened these benefits. The income produced by the gifted property is taxed to the donee, who may have a lower marginal income tax rate than does the donor, and if income tax savings do arise, they accrue each year during the post-gift period. Thus, the income tax savings can be quite sizable over a span of several years. This tax saving aspect of gifts is a major reason Congress retained the gift tax in the 2001 Act.

ADDITIONAL COMMENT

If a terminally ill spouse, Sam, has no property, an election to gift split can effectively use up Sam's unified credit. Another method of using Sam's unified credit is to give Sam property in trust that meets the following requirements: income from the trust must go to Sam for life, remainder is subject to a general power of appointment in Sam, and if the general power of appointment is not exercised during Sam's lifetime (or by will on Sam's death), the remainder must pass to specified beneficiaries other than the donor.

GIFT IN CONTEMPLATION OF DONEE-SPOUSE'S DEATH. At times, a terminally ill spouse may have very few assets. If such a spouse died, a sizable portion of his or her unified credit would be wasted because the decedent's estate would be well below the amount of the exemption equivalent provided by the unified credit. If the healthier spouse is relatively wealthy, he or she could make a gift to the ill spouse to create an estate in an amount equal to the estate tax exemption equivalent. Because of the unlimited marital deduction, the gift would be tax-free. Upon the death of the donee-spouse, no estate tax would be payable because the estate tax liability would not exceed the unified credit. The donee-spouse should not transfer his or her property back to the donor-spouse at death. Otherwise, the donee-spouse's unified credit would be wasted, and the original tax planning would be negated. Moreover, the returned property would be included in the surviving spouse's estate.

A gift of appreciated property in contemplation of the donee-spouse's death provides an additional advantage. If the property does not pass back to the donor-spouse, its basis is increased to its value on the donee's date of death. In the event the property is willed to the donor-spouse, a step-up in basis still occurs if the date of the gift precedes the donee-spouse's date of death by more than one year.

LESSENING STATE TRANSFER TAX COSTS. All states levy a death tax, but only four states currently impose a gift tax.[46] Therefore, in most states the tax cost of lifetime transfers is lower than that for transfers at death.

INCOME TAX SAVINGS FROM CHARITABLE GIFTS. Some individuals are inclined to donate a portion of their property to charitable organizations. Assuming the donation is eligible for a charitable contribution deduction, the transfer tax implications are the same—no taxable transfer—irrespective of whether the transfer occurs *inter vivos* or at death. From an income tax standpoint, however, a lifetime transfer is preferable because only lifetime transfers produce an income tax deduction for charitable contributions.

NEGATIVE ASPECTS OF GIFTS

LOSS OF STEP-UP IN BASIS. Taxpayers deliberating about whether to make gifts or which property to give should keep in mind that the donee receives no step-up in basis for property acquired by gift. From a practical standpoint, sacrifice of the step-up in basis is insignificant if the donee does not plan to sell the property or if the property is not subject to an allowance for depreciation. Also, keep in mind that gain on the sale is likely to be taxed at a 20% rate, and property in the estate may be taxed at a 50% rate.

PREPAYMENT OF ESTATE TAX. A donor who makes taxable gifts that exceed the exemption equivalent must pay a gift tax. Upon such a donor's death, the taxable gift is included in his or her estate tax base as an adjusted taxable gift. Because the gift tax paid during the donor's lifetime reduces the donor's estate tax liability, in a sense, the donor's payment of the gift tax results in prepayment of a portion of the estate tax.

COMPLIANCE AND PROCEDURAL CONSIDERATIONS

OBJECTIVE 9

Recognize the filing requirements for gift tax returns

FILING REQUIREMENTS

Section 6019 specifies the circumstances in which a gift tax return should be filed. In general, the donor will file Form 709 (United States Gift Tax Return). In certain circumstances, however, the donor may file a simpler return, Form 709A (United States Short Form Gift Tax Return). A completed Form 709 appears in Appendix B. The facts used in the preparation of the completed Form 709 are the same as the facts in the comprehensive illustration.

As is the case for income tax returns, a return can be required even though the taxable amount and the tax payable are both zero. A donor must file a gift tax return for any calendar year in which the donor makes gifts other than

- Gifts to the spouse that qualify for the marital deduction
- Gifts that are fully shielded from taxation because they fall within the annual exclusion amount or are exempted from classification as a gift under the exception for educational or medical expenses

[46] The four states that impose a gift tax are Connecticut, Louisiana, North Carolina, and Tennessee. New York repealed its gift tax beginning with 2000. Connecticut is phasing out its gift tax on gifts of $1 million or less during the period 2001–2006.

- Gifts to charitable organizations if the gift is deductible and the organization receives the donor's entire interest in the property

However, if the gift to the spouse is of qualified terminable interest property (QTIP), the gift must be reported on the gift tax return. The marital deduction is not available for these transfers unless the donor makes the necessary election, which is done by claiming a marital deduction on the gift tax return.

United States persons who receive aggregate foreign gifts or bequests exceeding $10,000 (indexed for inflation) a year that they treat as gifts or bequests must report such amounts as prescribed in Treasury Regulations. For 2002, the indexed amount is $11,642.[47]

DUE DATE

All gift tax returns must be filed on a calendar-year basis. Under the general rule, gift tax returns are due no later than April 15 following the close of the year of the gift.[48] An extension of time granted for filing an individual income tax return is deemed to automatically extend the filing date for the individual's gift tax return for that year. At present, such extensions are until August 15.

If the donor dies early in the year in which a gift is made, the due date for the donor's final gift tax return may be earlier than April 15. Because information concerning the decedent's taxable gifts is necessary to complete the estate tax return, the gift tax return for the year of death is due no later than the due date (including extensions) for the donor's estate tax return.[49] Estate tax returns are due nine months after the date of death.

Receipt of an extension for filing a gift tax return does not postpone the due date for payment of the tax. Interest is imposed on any gift tax not paid by April 15. Unlike with the income tax, estimated payments of gift taxes throughout the reporting period are not required.

GIFT-SPLITTING ELECTION

For taxable gifts to be computed under the gift-splitting technique, both spouses must indicate their consent to gift splitting in one of the following ways:[50]

- Each spouse signifies his or her consent on the other spouse's gift tax return.
- Each spouse signifies his or her consent on his or her own gift tax return.
- Both spouses signify their consent on one of the gift tax returns.

Treasury Regulations state that the first approach listed above is the preferred manner for designating consent.

KEY POINT

Similarly to a husband and wife filing a joint income tax return, if gift splitting is elected, the husband and wife have joint and several liability for the entire gift tax liability regardless of who actually made the gifts.

LIABILITY FOR TAX

The donor pays the gift tax,[51] and if the spouses consent to gift splitting, the entire gift tax liability is a joint and several liability of the spouses.[52] Thus, if spouses do not pay the tax voluntarily, the IRS may attempt to collect whatever amount it deems appropriate from either spouse, irrespective of the size of the gift that spouse actually made.

In the rare event that the donor does not pay the gift tax, the donee becomes personally liable for the gift tax.[53] However, a donee's liability is limited to the value of the gift.

DETERMINATION OF VALUE

One of the most difficult problems encountered by donors and their tax advisors is determining the gifted property's FMV. This task is especially difficult if the gifted property is stock in a closely held business, an oil and gas property, or land in an area where few sales occur.

---

47 Sec. 6039F.
48 Sec. 6075(b).
49 The decedent's post-1976 taxable gifts affect the size of his or her estate tax base, as discussed in the next chapter.
50 Reg. Sec. 25.2513-2(a)(1).
51 Sec. 2502(c).
52 Sec. 2513(d).
53 Reg. Sec. 301.6324-1.

ETHICAL POINT

A CPA who advises a client about the tax consequences of making a gift also has a responsibility to make sure the property is correctly valued. Otherwise, if the valuation claimed is too low, the IRS can levy a penalty on the donor. For example, a gift of non-cash property (e.g., land) may require that an appraisal be obtained. Failure to obtain an appraisal, or failure to investigate an appraisal that seems too low, may result in an undervaluation of the gift property, which may lead to the IRS imposing additional gift taxes, interest, and penalties.

If a transaction involves a sale, the IRS can argue that the asset's value exceeds its sales price and, thus, there is a gift to the extent of the bargain element. This problem is especially common with sales to family members. In situations where the donor gives property or sells to a family member property whose value is not readily determinable, it is advisable for the donor to have the property appraised before filing the gift tax return.

PENALTY FOR UNDERVALUATION. Section 6662 imposes a penalty, at one of two rates, on underpayments of gift or estate taxes resulting from too low a valuation of property. The amount on which the penalty is imposed is the underpayment of the transfer tax attributable to the valuation understatement.

No penalty applies if the valuation shown on the return exceeds 50% of the amount determined during an audit or court trial to be the correct value. If the value reported on the return is 50% or less of the correct value, the penalty rate is as shown below.

Ratio of Value Per Return to Correct Value	*Penalty Rate*
More than 25% but 50% or less	20%
25% or less	40%

Section 6662(g)(2) exempts a taxpayer from the penalty if the underpayment is less than $5,000. In addition, the IRS will not levy the penalty if the taxpayer shows good faith and a reasonable cause for the valuation claimed.

EXAMPLE C12-46 ▶ Assume Donna already has used her available unified credit. She gives land to her son and reports its value at $400,000 on her gift tax return. The IRS audits Donna's return, and she agrees that $900,000 was the correct value of the property. Because the value stated on the return is only 44.44% [($400,000 ÷ $900,000) × 100] of the correct value, the IRS levies a 20% penalty on the underpayment attributable to the valuation understatement. If Donna is in the 50% marginal gift tax bracket, the gift tax underpayment is $250,000 [0.50 × ($900,000 – $400,000)]. Thus, the penalty is $50,000 (0.20 × $250,000) unless Donna can demonstrate reasonable cause and good faith for the valuation. ◀

ADDITIONAL COMMENT

Even if a taxpayer questions whether a taxable gift has been made, it is a good idea to file a gift tax return and at least disclose the transaction. The filing of the return, if there is adequate disclosure of the transaction, causes the statute of limitations to begin and limits the time during which the IRS may question the valuation and the amount of the gift, if any.

STATUTE OF LIMITATIONS

In general, the statute of limitations for gift tax purposes is three years after the later of the date the return was filed or the return's due date.[54] The statute of limitations increases from three to six years if the donor omits from the gift tax return gifts whose total value exceeds 25% of the gifts reported on the return. If the donor files no return because, for example, he or she is unaware that he or she made any gifts, the IRS may assess the tax at any time.

The cumulative nature of the gift tax causes the taxable gifts of earlier years to affect the gift tax owed in subsequent periods. Once the statute of limitations has expired for pre-1997 gifts, the IRS cannot argue that taxable gifts of prior periods were undervalued (and thus that the current period's gifts should be taxed at a higher rate than that used by the donor) as long as a gift tax was paid on the earlier gifts. However, for gifts reported after August 5, 1997, this rule applies even if the donor paid no gift tax.[55]

For gifts made in 1997 and later, it is important to adequately disclose potential gifts because the gift status of these transactions is unclear. The statute of limitations will not expire on a transaction unless the donor makes adequate disclosure.[56]

EXAMPLE C12-47 ▶ Andy filed a gift tax return for 2001, reporting taxable gifts of $850,000 made in October 2001. Andy paid gift tax. If Andy adequately disclosed all potential gifts, once the statute of limitations expires for 2001, the IRS cannot contend that, for purposes of calculating the tax on later taxable gifts, the 2001 taxable gifts exceeded $850,000. ◀

[54] Sec. 6501.
[55] Sec. 2504(c).
[56] Sec. 6501(c)(9).

PROBLEM MATERIALS

DISCUSSION QUESTIONS

C12-1 Describe two ways in which the transfer tax (estate and gift tax) system is a unified system.

C12-2 What was the Congressional purpose for enacting the gift-splitting provisions?

C12-3 Determine whether the following statement is true or false: Every donor who makes a taxable gift incurs a gift tax liability. Explain your answer.

C12-4 Under what circumstances must the unified credit that is usually available be reduced (by a maximum amount of $6,000) even though the donor has never claimed any unified credit?

C12-5 Does the exemption from the gift tax for direct payment of medical expenses apply only for payments of relatives' expenses? Explain.

C12-6 Steve is considering the following actions. Explain to him which actions will constitute gifts for gift tax purposes.

a. Transferring all his ownership rights in a life insurance policy to another person
b. Depositing funds into a joint bank account in the names of Steve and another party (who deposits nothing)
c. Paying for land and having it titled in the names of Steve and his son as joint tenants with right of survivorship
d. Paying a hospital for the medical expenses of a neighbor
e. Making a $1 million demand loan to an adult child and charging no interest

C12-7 Dick wants to transfer property with a $400,000 FMV to an irrevocable trust with a bank as the trustee. Dick will name his distant cousin Earl to receive all of the trust income annually for the next 13 years. Then the property will revert to Dick. In the last few years, the income return (yield) on the property has been 4%. Assume this yield is not likely to increase and that the applicable rate from the actuarial tables is 7%.

a. What will be the amount of Dick's gift to Earl?
b. Would you recommend that Dick transfer the property yielding 4% to this type of a trust? Explain. If not, what type of property would you recommend that Dick transfer to the trust?

C12-8 Antonio would like to make a gift of a life insurance policy. Explain to him what action he must take to make a completed gift.

C12-9 When might a potential donor be interested in making a net gift? Explain the potential income tax problem with making a net gift.

C12-10 What is the purpose of the gift tax annual exclusion?

C12-11 A client is under the impression that all gifts are eligible for the gift tax annual exclusion. Is the client correct? Explain.

C12-12 Compare and contrast a Sec. 2503(c) trust and a *Crummey* trust.

C12-13 From a nontax standpoint, would a parent probably prefer to make a transfer to a minor child by using a Sec. 2503(c) trust or a *Crummey* trust?

C12-14 Explain the requirements for classifying a transaction as a transfer of a qualified terminable interest property (QTIP).

C12-15 Why is the qualified terminable interest property (QTIP) transfer an especially attractive arrangement for some donors who make gifts to their spouses?

C12-16 A client is under the impression that a donor cannot incur a gift tax liability if his or her only gifts are gifts to a U.S. charitable organization. What would you say to the client?

C12-17 Describe to a married couple three advantages of making the gift-splitting election.

C12-18 Both Damien and Latoya make taxable gifts of $250,000 in the current year. Will their current year gift tax liabilities necessarily be identical? Explain.

C12-19 A donor made his first taxable gift before 1977 and his second taxable gift in the current year. In the intervening years, the gift tax rates increased. In calculating the tax on taxable gifts of previous periods, which rate schedule is used: the one for the year in which the donor made the earlier gift or the one for the current period?

C12-20 A mother is trying to decide which of the two assets listed below to give to her adult daughter.

Asset	*FMV*	*Adjusted Basis*	*Annual Net Income from the Asset*
Apartment	$2,400,000	$1,500,000	$(10,000)
Stock	2,400,000	2,200,000	240,000

The mother has a higher marginal income tax rate than does her daughter. Describe the pros and cons of giving each of the two properties.

C12-21 Phil and Marcy have been married for a number of years. Marcy is very wealthy, but Phil is not. In fact, Phil has only $10,000 of property. Phil is very ill, and his doctor believes that he probably will die within the next few months. Make one (or more) tax planning suggestions for the couple.

C12-22 Assume the same facts as in Problem C12-21 except that Marcy has decided to give Phil property valued at $990,000. Phil probably will leave the gifted property to their children under his will.

a. What are the gift tax consequences to Marcy and the estate tax consequences to Phil of the transfer (assuming the property does not appreciate before his death)?
b. Assume Marcy is trying to decide whether to give Phil stock with an adjusted basis of $80,000 or land with an adjusted basis of $500,000. Each asset is valued at $990,000. Which asset would you recommend she give and why?

C12-23 Carlos has heard about the unified transfer tax system and does not understand how making gifts can be beneficial. Explain to Carlos how a lifetime gift fixes (freezes) the gifted property's value for transfer tax purposes.

C12-24 Describe for a client five advantages and two disadvantages of disposing of property by gift instead of at death.

C12-25 In general, what is the due date for the gift tax return? What are two exceptions?

C12-26 In 1994, Frank sold real property to Stu, his son, for $400,000. Frank did not file a gift tax return. In 2003, the IRS audits Frank's 2001 income tax return and somehow finds out about the sale. The IRS then contends that the property Frank sold was worth $700,000 in 1994 and that Frank made a $300,000 gift to Stu in 1994.

a. Can the IRS collect the gift tax on the 1994 gift? If not, will the 1994 gift affect the tax due on later gifts that may be made by Frank?
b. Will Frank potentially incur any penalty? Explain.

ISSUE IDENTIFICATION QUESTIONS

C12-27 Kwambe is thinking of making a substantial gift of stock to his fiancée, Maya. The wedding is scheduled for October 1 of the current year. Kwambe already has exhausted his unified credit. He also is considering giving $22,000 cash this year to each of his three children by a previous marriage. What tax issues should Kwambe consider with respect to the gifts he plans to make to Maya and his three children?

C12-28 Janet is considering transferring assets valued at $300,000 to an irrevocable trust (yet to be created) for the benefit of her son, Gordon, age 15, with Farmers Bank as trustee. Her attorney has drafted a trust agreement that provides that Gordon is to receive income in the trustee's discretion for the next 20 years and that at age 35 the trust assets will be distributed equally between Gordon and his sister Joanna. Janet anticipates that her husband will consent to gift splitting. What tax issues should Janet and her husband consider with respect to the trust she is creating?

C12-29 Melvin funds an irrevocable trust with Holcomb Bank as trustee and reserves the right to receive the income for seven years. He provides that at the end of the seventh year the trust assets will pass outright to his adult daughter, Pamela, or to Pamela's estate should Pamela not be alive. Melvin transfers assets valued at $1 million to the trust; the assets at present are producing income of about 4.5% per year. Assume that the Sec. 7520 rate per the actuarial tables for the month of the transfer is 8%. What tax issues should Melvin consider regarding the trust?

PROBLEMS

C12-30 *Calculation of Gift Tax.* In 2002, Latesha makes taxable gifts aggregating $2 million. Her only other taxable gifts amount to $400,000, all of which she made in 1997.

a. What is Latesha's 2002 gift tax liability?
b. What is her 2002 gift tax liability under the assumption that she made the $400,000 of taxable gifts in 1974 instead of 1997?

C12-31 *Calculation of Gift Tax.* Amir made taxable gifts as follows: $500,000 in 1974, $350,000 in 1978, and $400,000 in 2002. What is Amir's gift tax liability for 2002?

C12-32 *Determination of Taxable Gifts.* In the current year, Beth, who is single, sells stock valued at $40,000 to Linda for $18,000. Later that year, Beth gives Linda $12,000 in cash.

a. What is the amount of Beth's taxable gifts?
b. How would your answer to Part a change if Beth instead gave the cash to Patrick?

C12-33 *Determination of Taxable Gifts.* In the current year, Clay gives $31,000 cash to each of his eight grandchildren. His wife makes no gifts during the current year.

a. What are Clay's taxable gifts, assuming Clay and his wife do *not* elect gift splitting?
b. How would your answer to Part a change if the couple elects gift splitting?

C12-34 ***Determination of Taxable Gifts.*** In the current year, Diane gives $50,000 of stock to Mel and $120,000 of bonds to Nan. In the current year, Diane's husband gives $150,000 of land to Opal. Assume the couple elects gift splitting for the current year.

a. What are the couple's taxable gifts?
b. How would your answer to Part a change if Diane gave the $50,000 of stock to Opal (instead of to Mel)?

C12-35 ***Recognition of Transactions Treated as Gifts.*** In 2002, Emily, a widow, engages in the following transactions. Determine the amount of the completed gift, if any, arising from each of the following occurrences.

a. Emily names Lauren the beneficiary of a $100,000 life insurance policy on Emily's life. The beneficiary designation is not irrevocable.
b. Emily deposits $50,000 cash into a checking account in the joint names of herself and Matt, who deposits nothing to the account. Later that year, Matt withdraws $12,000 from the account.
c. Emily pays $22,000 of nephew Noah's medical expenses directly to County Hospital.
d. Emily transfers the title to land valued at $60,000 to Olive.

C12-36 ***Calculation of Gift Tax.*** Assume the same facts as in Problem C12-35. Emily's history of prior gifts is as follows:

Year	*Amount of Taxable Gifts*
1974	$ 500,000
1998	2,000,000

What is the gift tax liability with respect to Emily's 2002 gifts?

C12-37 ***Recognition of Transactions Treated as Gifts.*** In the current year, Marge (age 67) engages in the following transactions. Determine the amount of the completed gift, if any, arising from each of the following events. Assume 10% is the applicable interest rate.

a. Marge transfers $100,000 of property in trust and irrevocably names herself to receive $8,000 per year for life and daughter Joy (age 37) to receive the remainder.
b. Marge pays her grandson's $15,000 tuition to State University.
c. Marge gives the same grandson stock valued at $72,000.
d. Marge deposits $150,000 into a revocable trust. Later in the year, the bank trustee distributes $18,000 of income to the named beneficiary, Gail.

C12-38 ***Recognition of Transactions Treated as Gifts.*** Determine the amount of the completed gift, if any, arising from each of the following occurrences.

a. A parent sells real estate valued at $1.8 million to an adult child, who pays $1 million in consideration.
b. A furniture store holds a clearance sale and sells a customer a $5,000 living room suite for $1,500.
c. During the year, a father purchases food and clothing costing $8,500 for his minor child.
d. A citizen contributes $1,500 cash to a political organization.
e. Zeke lends $600,000 interest free to Henry, who signs a demand note on August 1. Assume 10% is the applicable interest rate and the note remains unpaid at year-end.

C12-39 ***Determination of Unified Credit.*** In March 1976, Sue made a taxable gift of $200,000. In arriving at the amount of her taxable gift, Sue elected to deduct the $30,000 specific exemption formerly available. In 2002, Sue makes her next gift; the taxable amount is $1.5 million.

a. What unified credit can Sue claim on her 2002 return?
b. What unified credit can Sue claim on her 2002 return if she made the 1976 gift in December instead of March?

C12-40 ***Valuation of Gifts.*** On September 1 of the current year, Mario irrevocably transfers a $100,000 whole life insurance policy on his life to Mario, Jr. as owner. On September 1, the policy's interpolated terminal reserve is $30,000. Mario paid the most recent annual premium ($1,800) on June 1. What is the amount of the gift Mario made in the current year?

C12-41 ***Determination of Gift Tax Deductions.*** Tina makes cash gifts of $700,000 to her husband and $100,000 to the City Art Museum. What are the amounts of the deductions available for these gifts when calculating Tina's income tax and gift tax liabilities?

C12-42 *Determination of Annual Exclusion.* For each of the following transactions that happen in the current year, determine the amount of the annual exclusion available. Explain your answer.

a. Tracy creates a trust in the amount of $300,000 for the benefit of her eight-year-old daughter, May. She names a bank as trustee. Before May reaches age 21, the trustee in its discretion is to pay income or corpus (trust assets) to May or for her benefit. When May reaches age 21, she will receive the unexpended portion of the trust income and corpus. If May dies before reaching age 21, the unexpended income and corpus will be paid to her estate or a party (or parties) she appoints under a general power of appointment.

b. Assume the same facts as in Part a except Tracy's daughter is age 28 when Tracy creates the trust and the trust agreement contains age 41 wherever age 21 appears in Part a.

c. Assume the same facts as in Part b except the trust instrument allows May to demand a distribution by December 31 of each year equal to the lesser of the amount of the annual exclusion for federal gift tax purposes or the amount transferred to the trust that year.

C12-43 *Determination of Annual Exclusion.* During 2002, Will gives $40,000 cash to Will, Jr. and a remainder interest in a few acres of land to his friend Suzy. The remainder interest is valued at $32,000. Will and his wife, Helen, elect gift splitting, and during the current year Helen gives Joyce $8,000 of stock. What is the total amount of the annual gift tax exclusions available to Will and Helen?

C12-44 *Availability of Annual Exclusion.* Bonnie, a widow, irrevocably transfers $1 million of property to a trust with a bank named as trustee. For as long as Bonnie's daughter Carol is alive, Carol is to receive all the trust income annually. Upon Carol's death, the property is to be distributed to Carol's children. Carol is age 32 and currently has three children. How many gift tax exclusions does Bonnie receive for the transfer?

C12-45 *Calculation of Gift Tax.* Before last year, neither Hugo nor Wanda, his wife, made any gifts. Last year, Hugo gave $10,000 cash to each of his 30 nieces, nephews, and grandchildren. This year (2002), Wanda gives $32,000 of stock to each of the same people. What is the *minimum* legal gift tax liability (*before* reduction for the unified credit) for each spouse for each year?

C12-46 *Calculation of Marital Deduction.* Hugh makes the gifts listed below to Winnie, his wife, age 37. What is the amount of the marital deduction, if any, attributable to each?

a. Hugh transfers $500,000 to a trust with a bank named as trustee. All the income must be paid to Winnie monthly for life. At Winnie's death, the property passes to Hugh's sisters or their estates.

b. Hugh transfers $300,000 to a trust with a bank named as trustee. Income is payable at the trustee's discretion to Winnie annually until the earlier of her death or her remarriage. When payments to Winnie cease, the trustee must distribute the property to Hugh's children by a previous marriage or to their estates.

C12-47 *Calculation of the Marital Deduction.* In the current year, Louise makes the transfers described below to Lance, her husband, age 47. Assume 7% is the applicable interest rate. What is the amount of her marital deduction, if any, attributable to each transfer?

a. In June, she gives him land valued at $45,000.

b. In October, she gives him a 12-year income interest in a trust with a bank named as trustee. She names their daughter to receive the remainder interest. She funds the irrevocable trust with $400,000 in assets.

C12-48 *Charitable Contribution Deduction.* Tien (age 67) transfers a remainder interest in a vacation cabin (with a total value of $100,000) to a charitable organization and retains a life estate in the cabin for herself.

a. What is the amount of the gift tax charitable contribution deduction, if any, attributable to this transfer? Assume that 10% is the applicable interest rate.

b. How will your answer to Part a change if Tien instead gives a remainder interest in a valuable oil painting (worth $100,000) to the organization?

C12-49 *Calculation of Gift Tax.* In 2002, Homer and his wife, Wilma (residents of a non–community property state) make the gifts listed below. Homer's previous taxable gifts consist of $100,000 made in 1975 and $1.4 million made in 1996. Wilma has made no previous taxable gifts.

Wilma's current year gifts were	
to Art	$400,000
to Bart	6,000
Homer's current year gifts were	
to Linda	$600,000
to a charitable organization	100,000
to Norma (future interest)	200,000

a. What are the gift tax liabilities of Homer and Wilma for 2002 if they elect gift splitting and everyone except Norma receives a present interest?
b. How would the gift tax liabilities for each spouse in Part a change if they do not elect gift splitting?

C12-50 ***Calculation of Gift Tax.*** In 2002, Henry and his wife, Wendy, made the gifts shown below. All gifts are of present interests. What is Wendy's gift tax payable for 2002 if the couple elects gift splitting and Wendy's previous taxable gifts (made in 1995) total $1 million?

Wendy's current gifts were	
to Janet	$80,000
to Cindy	70,000
to Henry	50,000
Henry's current gifts were	
to Janet	30,000

C12-51 ***Basis Rules.*** In June 2001, Karen transfers property with a $75,000 FMV and a $20,000 adjusted basis to Hal, her husband. Hal dies in March 2002; the property has appreciated to $85,000 in value by then.
a. What is the amount of Karen's taxable gift in 2001?
b. What gain would Hal recognize if he sells the property for $95,000 in July 2001?
c. If Hal wills the property to Dot, his daughter, what basis would Dot have?
d. How would your answer to Part c change if Hal instead willed the property to Karen?
e. How would your answer to Part d change if Hal did not die until August 2002?

C12-52 ***Basis Rules.*** Siu is considering giving away stock in Ace Corporation or Gold Corporation. Each has a current FMV of $500,000, and each has the same estimated appreciation rate. Siu's basis in the Ace stock is $100,000, and her basis in the Gold stock is $450,000. Which stock would you suggest that she give away and why, or does it make any difference?

C12-53 ***Below-Market Loans.*** On October 1, Sam lends Tom $10 million. Tom signs an interest-free demand note. The loan is still outstanding on December 31. Explain the income tax and gift tax consequences of the loan to both Sam and Tom. Assume that the federal short-term rate is 9%.

COMPREHENSIVE PROBLEM

C12-54 In 2002, Ginger Graham, age 46 and wife of Greg Graham, engaged in the transactions described below. Determine Ginger's gift tax liability for 2002 if she and Greg elect gift splitting and Greg gave their son Stevie stock valued at $80,000 during 2002. Ginger's grandmother Mamie died November 12, 2001, and Mamie's will bequeathed $250,000 to Ginger. On March 4, 2002, Ginger irrevocably disclaimed the $250,000 in writing, and, as a result, the property passed instead to Ginger's sister Gertie. In 2002, Ginger gave $100,000 cash to her alma mater, State University. In 1994, Ginger had given ownership of a life insurance policy on her own life to her daughter, Denise, and in 2002 Ginger paid the $22,000 annual premium on the policy. In 2001, Ginger deposited $45,000 into a bank account in the name of herself and son Stevie, joint tenants with rights of survivorship. Stevie deposited nothing. Neither party made a withdrawal until 2002, when Stevie withdrew $30,000. In 2002, Ginger created a trust with County Bank as trustee and transferred $300,000 of stock to the irrevocable trust. She named her husband Greg (age 47) to receive all the trust income semi-annually for life and daughter Drucilla to receive the remainder. In 2002, she gave a remainder interest in her beach cottage to the American Red Cross and kept the right to use the cottage for the rest of her life. The fair market value of the cottage was $70,000.

Other information: Ginger's earlier *taxable* gifts are $175,000, all made in 1994. Ginger will make whatever elections are necessary to minimize her current gift tax liability. Assume the Sec. 7520 interest rate is 8%.

TAX STRATEGY PROBLEM

C12-55 Ilene Ishi is planning to fund an irrevocable charitable remainder annuity trust with $100,000 of cash. She will designate her sister, age 60, to receive an annuity of $8,000 per year for 15 years and State University to receive the remainder at the end of the fifteenth year. The valuation of the charitable portion of the transfer, according to Reg. Sec. 25.2522(c)-3(d)(2)(i), is to be determined under Reg. Sec. 1.664-2(c), an income tax regulation. Regulation Sec. 1.664-2(c) provides that, in valuing the remainder interest, the donor may elect to use the Sec. 7520 interest rate for either of the two months preceding the month of the transfer as an alternative to using the rate for the actual month of transfer. Otherwise, the value will be determined by using the Sec. 7520 rate for the month of the transfer. Assume that in the month of the transfer the interest rate was 7% but that in the two preceding months the rate was 7.2%. Should the donor elect to do the computations by using the interest rate for one of the two preceding months? Explain your answer. Note: The 7.2% rate does not appear in the excerpts from the actuarial tables, but the absence of such rate from the tables will not preclude you from answering this question.

TAX FORM/RETURN PREPARATION PROBLEMS

C12-56 Dave and Sara Moore, of 10105 Lake View Lane, Chicago, Illinois 60108, engage in the transactions described below in August 2001. Use this information to prepare a gift tax return (Form 709) for Dave. He and Sara want to use gift splitting. Both are U.S. citizens. His Social Security number is 477-11-1333 and hers is 272-92-4403. For simplicity, assume the rate for the actuarial tables used is 10%. Dave's transactions are summarized below.

	Amount
1. Tuition paid to Harvard University for son-in-law, Jim Smith.	$ 22,000
2. Room and board paid to Harvard University for Jim Smith.	11,000
3. Sports car purchased for Jim Smith.	18,000
4. Premium paid on life insurance policy on Dave's life. Dave transferred the policy to his sister, Amy Lane, as owner in 1994.	11,000
5. Land given to daughter, Glenda Muñoz.	68,000
6. Remainder interest in personal residence given to State University. Dave (age 70) retains a life estate. The total value of the residence is $80,000.	
7. Stocks transferred to an irrevocable trust with First National Bank as trustee. The trust income is payable to Sara (age 60) semiannually for life. The remainder is payable at Sara's death to daughter, Amanda Webb, or her estate.	350,000

Sara gave $42,000 of cash to Dave's sister, Amy Lane. Dave's gift history includes a $600,000 taxable gift made in 1975 and a $400,000 taxable gift made in 1992.

C12-57 Alice Arnold, Social Security number 572-13-4409, a widow, engages in the transactions listed below in 2001. Use this information to prepare a gift tax return (Form 709) for Alice.

	Amount
1. Stock given to daughter, Brenda Bell.	$700,000
2. Cash transferred to son, Al Arnold.	600,000
3. $500,000 interest-free demand loan made to Brenda Bell on July 1. The loan is still outstanding on December 31.	
4. Land given to niece, Lou Lane	100,000

Assume 8% is the applicable interest rate. Alice has made only one previous taxable gift: $300,000 (taxable amount) in 1999. Alice, a U.S. citizen, resides at 105 Peak Rd., Denver, Colorado 80309.

CASE STUDY PROBLEMS

C12-58 Your client, Karen Kross, recently married Larry Kross. She is age 72, quite wealthy, and in reasonably good health. To date, Karen has not made any taxable gifts, but Larry made taxable gifts totaling $700,000 in 1998. Karen is considering giving each of her five college-age grandchildren approximately $22,000 of cash for them to use to pay their college expenses of tuition and room and board for the year. In addition, she is considering giving her three younger grandchildren $3,000 each to use for orthodontic bills. Karen wants to give her daughter property valued at $400,000. She is trying to choose between giving her daughter cash or stock with a basis of $125,000. She would like to give her son $400,000 of property also, but would like for the property to be tied up in a discretionary trust with a bank as trustee for the son for at least 15 years. Karen has been approached by an agricultural museum about making a contribution to it and, as a result, is contemplating deeding her family farm to the museum but retaining a life estate in the farm.

Required: Prepare a memorandum to the tax partner of your firm that discusses the transfer tax and income tax consequences of the proposed transactions described above. Also, make any recommendations that you deem appropriate.

C12-59 Morris Jory, a long-time tax client of the firm you work for, has made substantial gifts during his lifetime. Mr. Jory transferred Jory Corporation stock to several donees in December 2001. Each donee received shares valued at $10,000. Two of the donees were Mr. Jory's adult children, Amanda and Peter. The remaining 12 donees were employees of Jory Corporation who are not related to Mr. Jory. Mr. Jory, a widower, advised the employees that within two weeks of receiving the stock certificates they must endorse such certificates over to Amanda and Peter. Six of the donees were instructed to endorse their certificates to Amanda and six to Peter. During 2001, Mr. Jory also gave $35,000 cash to his favorite grandchild, Robin. Your firm has been engaged to prepare Mr. Jory's 2001 gift tax return. In January 2002, you have a meeting with Mr. Jory. At this meeting, Mr. Jory insists that his 2001 taxable gifts will be only $25,000 ($35,000 to Robin − $10,000 annual exclusion). After your meeting with Mr. Jory, you are uncertain about his position regarding the amount of his 2001 gifts and have scheduled a meeting with your firm's senior tax partner, who has advised Mr. Jory for more than 20 years. In preparation for the meeting, prepare a summary of the tax and ethical considerations (with supporting authority where possible) regarding whether you should prepare a gift tax return that reports the taxable gifts in accordance with Mr. Jory's wishes.

TAX RESEARCH PROBLEMS

C12-60 Karl Kremble funded an irrevocable trust in March 2002 with oil and gas property valued at $400,000. Assume the Sec. 7520 interest rate for the actuarial tables was 7% on the date of funding. Karl named a bank trustee and provided that his distant cousin, Louise Lane, will receive all the trust income annually for the next 34 years. Then the assets will revert (pass back) to Karl or his estate. The trust instrument specifically states that the trust is not to maintain a reserve for depletion (that is, no portion of the royalties received from the oil and gas properties is to be transferred to the trust's principal account to account for the wasting nature of the trust assets). Your manager has requested that you research whether the amount of Karl's gift to Louise may be determined by using the actuarial tables and that you write a memo summarizing your conclusions. Your manager indicated further that your memo should address the amount of the gift Karl is deemed to have made.

C12-61 Sarah Studer, resident of Arkansas, is the daughter of Maude Mason, a widow, who died intestate March 12, 2002. Under Arkansas law, Sarah, Maude's only child, received all of her mother's probate estate, $780,000 in amount. Sarah owes the IRS $820,000 in "back taxes" and interest, and under Sec. 6321 there is a tax lien against all of Sarah's property and rights to property. Sarah has virtually no property and knows that if she accepts the property from her mother's estate she will have to use it to pay her debts to the IRS. It is now November 20, 2002, and Sarah has inquired whether a disclaimer would allow her mother's property to stay within the family unit, given that, if she disclaimed the property, it would pass under state law to her son, Steven Studer, Jr.

Your manager has requested that you write a memorandum in which you address the consequences to Sarah of a disclaimer. Your manager suggested that you consult *Rohn F. Drye, Jr.,* 84 AFTR 2d 99-7160, 99-2 USTC ¶51, 006 (USSC, 1999).

C12-62 George Schwinger is employed by Latitude, Inc., a public firm. In the current year, George received non-qualified stock options that entitle him to purchase 1,000 shares of Latitude common stock for $36 per share. Latitude shares were trading for $36 per share on the date of grant. The terms of the grant provide that George cannot exercise the options unless, and until, he works for Latitude for two more years. At that time, the options will become fully exercisable. The stock options must be exercised by the end of ten years; otherwise, the options will expire. The stock option plan allows options to be transferred by gift to the employee's spouse and/or children.

George seeks your advice about the gift tax consequences of giving the stock options to his adult daughter, Belinda, who has enough cash to exercise the options. He also wants to know how these gift tax consequences compare with the gift tax consequences of giving Belinda the stock in the future, after he has exercised the options. Incidentally, in recent years the fair market value of Latitude stock has increased by about 15% per year. Draft a brief letter to George in which you address his issues.

C12-63 ***Internet Research Problem.*** Your client, Angela Zulch, contributed stock valued at $38,000 to Pacificare, Inc. of Burbank, California. You are unsure whether contributions to this organization are eligible for the charitable contribution deduction for gift and income tax purposes. Use the Internet to research the issue of whether contributions to Pacificare, Inc. of Burbank, California qualify for the charitable contribution deduction for gift and income tax purposes. Start by going to the IRS web page, *http://www.irs.gov*. Then click on the site tree. Under the topical index, select exempt organizations, and on the right side select exempt organizations search. Will she be able to deduct contributions to this organization? Draft a brief letter to your client outlining your findings.

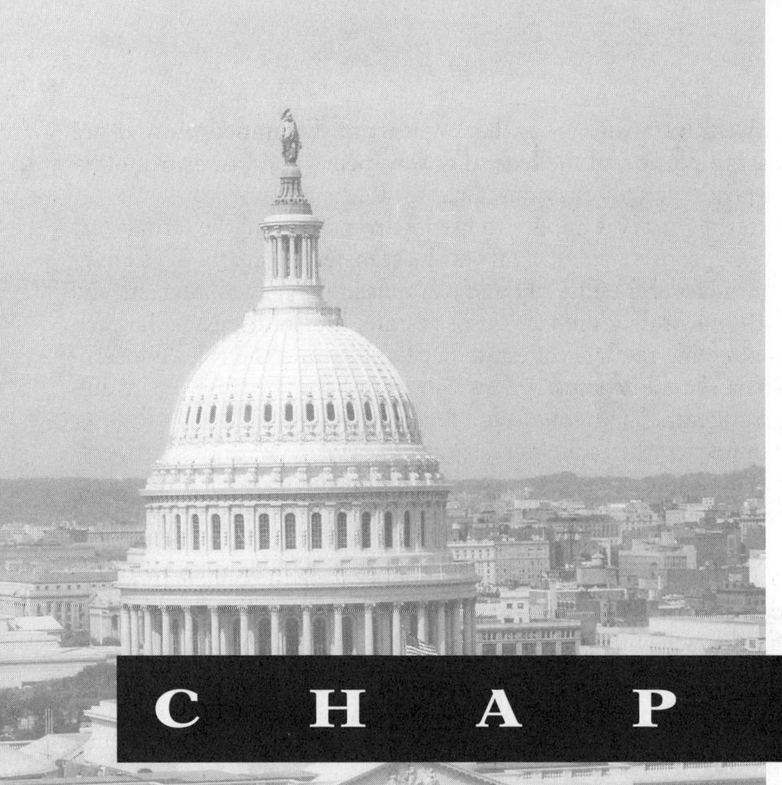

13

CHAPTER

THE ESTATE TAX

LEARNING OBJECTIVES

After studying this chapter, you should be able to

1. Describe the formula for the estate tax
2. Describe the methods for valuing interests
3. Determine which interests are includible in the gross estate
4. Identify deductions available for estate tax purposes
5. Calculate the estate tax liability
6. Identify tax provisions that alleviate liquidity problems
7. Recognize the filing requirements for estate tax returns

CHAPTER OUTLINE

Estate Tax Formula...13-2
The Gross Estate: Valuation...13-6
The Gross Estate: Inclusions...13-8
Deductions...13-18
Computation of Tax Liability...13-23
Comprehensive Illustration...13-25
Liquidity Concerns...13-28
Generation-Skipping Transfer Tax...13-30
Tax Planning Considerations...13-32
Compliance and Procedural Considerations...13-35

Gift taxes and estate taxes, wealth transfer taxes that are part of the unified transfer tax system, account for only a small portion of the federal government's collections from taxation. Their history and purposes were discussed in Chapter C12.

As previously noted, the term *gift taxes* applies to lifetime transfers and the term *estate taxes* applies to dispositions of property resulting from the transferor's death. This chapter discusses the structure of the federal estate tax and examines the types of interests and transactions that cause inclusions in the decedent's gross estate. It also discusses the various deductions and credits affecting the federal estate tax liability and the rules concerning the taxable gifts that affect the estate tax base, an important issue because of the unified nature of the tax levied at death.

It is essential to keep in mind that the estate tax is a *wealth transfer tax,* not a property or an income tax. Understanding that the estate tax is levied on the transfer of property makes it easier to understand the rules for estate taxation, which are part of the unified transfer tax system.

As described in Chapter C12, the Economic Growth and Tax Relief Reconciliation Act of 2001 (the 2001 Act) provides for phased-in increases to the unified credit and phased-in reductions to the unified tax rate schedule beginning with 2002. In addition, it repeals the estate and generation skipping transfer taxes, effective January 1, 2010. However, the 2001 Act further provides that, in the absence of additional congressional action, the rules for gift, estate, and generation skipping taxes will revert on January 1, 2011 to what they were prior to the 2001 Act.

ESTATE TAX FORMULA

OBJECTIVE 1

Describe the formula for the estate tax

The tax base for the federal estate tax is the *total* of the decedent's taxable estate (i.e., the gross estate less the deductions discussed below) and adjusted taxable gifts (post-1976 taxable gifts). After the gross tax liability on the tax base is determined, various credits—including the unified credit—are subtracted to arrive at the net estate tax payable. The estate tax formula appears in Figure C13-1.

GROSS ESTATE

As illustrated in Figure C13-1, calculation of the decedent's estate tax liability begins with determining which items are included in the gross estate. Such items are valued at either the decedent's date of death or the alternate valuation date.[1] As a transfer tax, the estate tax is levied on dispositions that are essentially testamentary in nature. Transactions are viewed as being essentially **testamentary transfers** if the transferor's control or enjoyment of the property in question ceases at death, not before death.[2]

Inclusions in the gross estate extend to a much broader set of properties than merely those to which the decedent holds title at the time of death. Making a lifetime transfer that generates a taxable gift does not guarantee that the donor removes the transferred property from his or her gross estate. Although an individual usually removes property from his or her gross estate by giving it to another before death, the donor's gross estate must include the gifted property if the donor retains either the right to receive the income generated by such property or control over the property for the donor's lifetime.

REAL-WORLD EXAMPLE

In 1995, the top 4,400 wealth holders held total assets worth $6.7 billion in the following proportions:

Personal residences	9.7%
Other real property	16.1
Closely held stock	11.6
Other stock	17.5
Tax exempt bonds	7.0
Various other assets	31.4

EXAMPLE C13-1 ▶ In the current year, Ted transfers stocks to an irrevocable trust with a bank named as trustee. Under the terms of the trust agreement, Ted is to receive the trust income annually for the rest of his life and Ted's cousin Ed (or Ed's estate) is to receive the remainder. For gift tax purposes, Ted has made a taxable gift in the current year of the remainder interest (but not the income interest) in the trust. If, for example, Ted already has used his entire unified credit, he incurs a gift tax liability. When Ted dies, the entire value of the trust is included in Ted's gross estate,

[1] Under Sec. 2032, the alternate valuation date is the earlier of six months after the date of death or the date the property is disposed of.

[2] An example of a transaction that is essentially **testamentary** in nature is a situation where the donor transfers property in trust but reserves a lifetime right to receive the trust income and, thus, continues to enjoy the economic benefits.

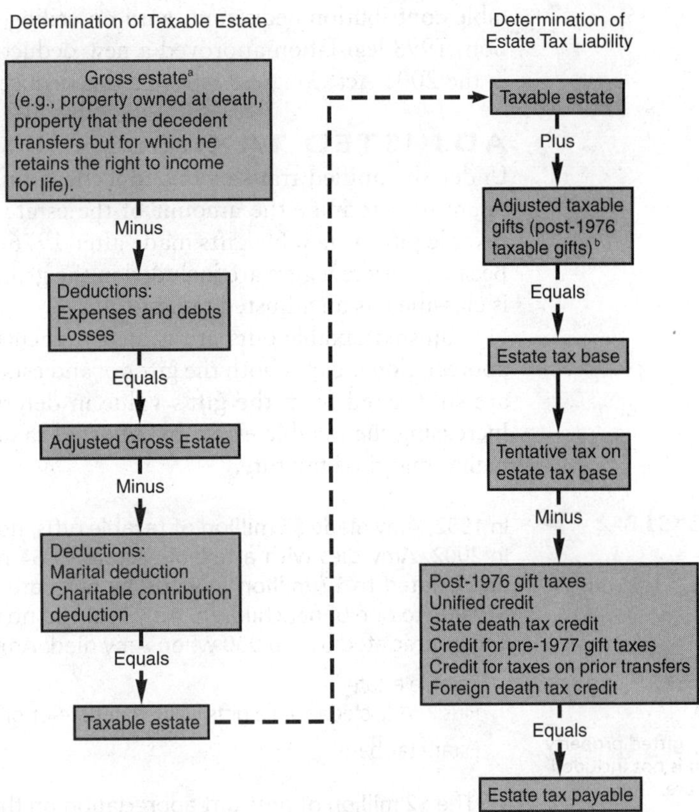

FIGURE C13-1 ▶ ESTATE TAX FORMULA

SELF-STUDY QUESTION

In 1999, Barb transferred $500,000 in trust, income for life to herself, remainder to her daughter. What part, if any, of the value of the trust's assets will be included in Barb's estate?

ANSWER

The value of the entire trust will be included in Barb's estate, because she retained the income from the trust until her death.

ADDITIONAL COMMENT

If a decedent leaves all his or her property to his or her spouse, the decedent wastes his or her unified credit. In addition, the estate of the surviving spouse is increased and may be pushed into higher tax brackets.

even though Ted does not have legal title to the property. Because the shift in the right to the income does not occur until Ted's death, the transfer is testamentary in nature. ◀

The categories of items included in the gross estate and their valuation are examined in detail later in this chapter. Once the components of the gross estate have been determined and valued, the deductions from the gross estate are calculated.

DEDUCTIONS

The IRC authorizes five categories of items that may be deducted in arriving at the amount of the taxable estate:

- Expenses and debts
- Casualty and theft losses
- Transfers to the decedent's spouse
- Transfers to charitable organizations
- Certain family business interests

Deductible expenses include funeral expenses and expenses of administering the decedent's property. As is true for gift tax purposes, there is no ceiling on the marital deduction. Thus, the death of the first spouse is free of estate taxes if the decedent's spouse receives all the decedent's property, or all the property except for an amount equal to the exemption equivalent.[3] Property passing to charitable organizations qualifies, in general, for a chari-

[3] The exemption equivalent ($1 million for 2002), as explained in Chapter C12, is the size of the tax base for which the gift tax or estate tax liability is exactly cancelled by the unified credit of $345,800.

table contribution deduction, with no ceiling on the amount of such deductions. In addition, 1998 legislation approved a new deduction for certain family business interests, but in the 2001 Act Congress repealed this deduction effective after 2003.

ADJUSTED TAXABLE GIFTS AND TAX BASE

Under the unified transfer tax concept, adjusted taxable gifts are added to the taxable estate to determine the amount of the estate tax base. Section 2001(b) defines adjusted taxable gifts as taxable gifts made after 1976 other than gifts included in the gross estate. Because very few gifts are included in the gross estate, almost every post-1976 taxable gift is classified as an adjusted taxable gift.

Adjusted taxable gifts are valued at their date-of-gift values. Therefore, any post-gift appreciation escapes both the gift tax and estate tax. Allowable deductions and exclusions are subtracted from the gift's value in determining the adjusted taxable gifts amount. Increasing the taxable estate by adjusted taxable gifts potentially forces the estate into a higher marginal tax rate.

EXAMPLE C13-2 ▶ In 1982, Amy made $5 million of taxable gifts, none of which were included in her gross estate. In 2002, Amy dies with a taxable estate of $4 million. The property Amy gave away in 1982 appreciated to $7 million in value by her date of death. In 1998, Amy gave stock valued at $10,000 to one of her children. Amy incurred no transfer tax on the 1998 transaction. The stock had appreciated to $70,000 when Amy died. Amy's estate tax base is calculated as follows:

ADDITIONAL COMMENT

Income earned by gifted property is the donee's and is not included in the donor's estate.

Taxable estate	$4,000,000
Plus: Adjusted taxable gifts (valued at date-of-gift values)	5,000,000
Estate tax base	$9,000,000

The $2 million of post-gift appreciation on the property gifted in 1982 escapes transfer taxation. Amy's $9 million tax base includes the gifted property, whose value is "frozen" at its date-of-gift value. The 1998 gift does not affect Amy's estate tax base because the 1998 *taxable* gift was zero. ◀

TENTATIVE TAX ON ESTATE TAX BASE

Once the amount of the tax base has been determined, the next step is to calculate the tax on this base. Section 2001(c) contains the unified tax rates, which are reproduced on the inside back cover. In 2002, the top marginal tax rate of 50% applies to tax bases exceeding $2.5 million. After 2002, the 2001 Act provides that, for both estate and gift tax purposes, the maximum tax rate will be reduced as follows:

Year	*Maximum Tax Rate*	*For Amounts Exceeding*
2003	49%	$2,000,000
2004	48%	2,000,000
2005	47%	2,000,000
2006	46%	2,000,000
2007	45%	1,500,000
2008	45%	1,500,000
2009	45%	1,500,000

EXAMPLE C13-3 ▶ Assume the same facts as in Example C13-2. The gross tax on Amy's $9 million tax base is $4,275,800. The estate is taxed at a 50% marginal tax rate, the highest rate applicable in the year Amy dies. ◀

REDUCTION FOR POST-1976 GIFT TAXES

Adjusted taxable gifts, in effect, are not taxed twice because Sec. 2001(b)(2) allows a reduction to the estate tax for gift taxes imposed on post-1976 taxable gifts. If the rate schedule for the year of death differs from the schedule applicable for the year of the gift, the tax on post-1976 taxable gifts is determined by using the rate schedule in effect for the year of death. This rule works to the disadvantage of decedents who made taxable gifts and paid taxes at a higher rate than the rate in effect on the date of death. This rule ensures that the estate pays a transfer tax at the current marginal tax rate applicable for the decedent's amount of taxable estate and adjusted taxable gifts.

EXAMPLE C13-4 ▶ Assume the same facts as in Examples C13-2 and C13-3. Recall that in 1982 Amy made $5 million of taxable gifts. The tax on $5 million of 1982 taxable gifts was $2,530,800. Amy was entitled to a $62,800 unified credit and paid $2,468,000 of gift taxes. Amy's 1982 gifts were taxed at a 65% marginal rate. For the year of Amy's death (2002), the marginal rate for $5 million of transfers is 50%. Consequently, the reduction for gift taxes on post-1976 taxable gifts is limited to the amount of gift taxes that would be payable if the 2002 rate schedule were in effect in the year of the gift. This amount is calculated as follows:

Tax on $5 million at 2002 rates	$2,275,800
Minus: Unified credit for 1982 (the year of the gift)	(62,800)
Tax that would have been payable on $5 million if 2002 rates were in effect	$2,213,000

Note that the only change to the gift tax computation is that the 2002 transfer tax rates are used. The actual credit applicable for the year of the gift (and not the credit for the year of death) is subtracted. ◀

EXAMPLE C13-5 ▶ From Examples C13-3 and C13-4, Amy's estate tax, before reduction for any credits, is calculated as follows:

Tax on $9 million tax base (Example C13-3)	$4,275,800
Minus: Tax that would have been payable on $5 million of post-1976 taxable gifts, at 2002 rates (Example C13-4)	(2,213,000)
Estate tax, before reduction for credits (discussed below)	$2,062,800 ◀

SELF-STUDY QUESTION

Taxpayer made $3 million of taxable gifts in 1992 and paid gift taxes of $1,098,000 (gross tax of $1,290,800 minus the unified credit of $192,800). Taxpayer died in 2002 with a taxable estate of $100,000. At current rates, the gift taxes payable on $3 million still would be $1,083,000. Determine the amount of her estate tax liability.

ANSWER

The unified transfer tax base is $3.1 million, the sum of the $3 million of 1992 taxable gifts and the $100,000 estate. The current tax on $3.1 million is $1,325,800. The unified credit of $345,800 and the subtraction for gift taxes of $1,083,000 reduce the tax liability to zero.

UNIFIED CREDIT

As shown in the inside back cover, the unified credit of Sec. 2010 has varied over the years since its inception in 1977. The credit enables a certain size tax base, referred to as the exemption equivalent or applicable exclusion amount, to be completely free of transfer taxes. For 2002, the credit is $345,800 (equivalent to a $1 million exemption). The credit and exemption equivalent gradually will increase through 2009 as follows:

Year of Death	*Amount of Credit*	*Exemption Equivalent*
2002	$ 345,800	$1,000,000
2003	345,800	1,000,000
2004	555,800	1,500,000
2005	555,800	1,500,000
2006	780,800	2,000,000
2007	780,800	2,000,000
2008	780,800	2,000,000
2009	1,455,800	3,500,000

The estate tax computation permits an estate to subtract the entire unified credit applicable for the year of death (reduced by any phaseout for certain pre-1977 gifts) regardless of how much unified credit the decedent claimed for gift tax purposes. As a conceptual matter, however, only one unified credit is available. Under the unification concept, the estate tax is computed on a tax base consisting of the taxable estate plus the adjusted taxable gifts. The tentative tax on the tax base is reduced not by the amount of the "gross" tax on the adjusted taxable gifts, but by the "gross" tax on such gifts minus the unified credit. Ignoring changes in the amount of the unified credit, this computation achieves the same result as allowing the unified credit amount to be subtracted only once against all of a person's transfers but allowing a reduction to the estate tax for the gift tax liability *before* reduction for the unified credit.

OTHER CREDITS

In addition to the unified credit—the only credit available for gift tax purposes—the IRC authorizes four credits for estate tax purposes. These additional credits (shown in Figure C13-1) are discussed in more detail on pages C13-24 and C13-25.

THE GROSS ESTATE: VALUATION

OBJECTIVE 2

Describe the methods for valuing interests

TYPICAL MISCONCEPTION

The basis of inherited property is the FMV of the property on the decedent's date of death, which could be higher or lower than the decedent's basis. This change is referred to as a step-up or a step-down in basis. Many taxpayers hear so much about step-up that they forget that a step-down also may occur.

ETHICAL POINT

Valuation of interests in closely held corporations and real estate is an area where a CPA or attorney may need to engage a qualified appraiser. Because appraisals are subjective, two appraisers may arrive at different values. Using the highest appraisal may mean additional estate taxes, but it will provide a greater step-up in basis. Using too low an appraisal may subject the estate to undervaluation penalties (see page C13-36).

DATE-OF-DEATH VALUATION

All property included in the gross estate is valued at either its fair market value (FMV) on the date of death or the alternate valuation date. The valuation date election is an all-or-nothing proposition. Each item included in the gross estate must be valued as of the same date. In other words, the executor (called the personal representative in some states) may not value some items as of the date of death and others as of the alternate valuation date.

Fair market value is defined as "the price at which the property would change hands between a willing buyer and a willing seller, neither being under any compulsion to buy or to sell and both having reasonable knowledge of relevant facts."[4] In general, the FMV of a particular asset on a certain date is the same regardless of whether the property is being valued for gift or estate tax purposes. Life insurance on the life of the transferor is an exception to this rule. Upon the death of the insured, the policy is valued at its face value, whereas it is valued at a lesser amount while the insured is alive. Generally, this lesser amount is either the cost of a comparable contract or the policy's interpolated terminal reserve plus the unexpired portion of the premium.

For certain types of property, Treasury Regulations contain detailed descriptions of the valuation approach. However, the valuation of interests in closely held businesses is described in only very general terms. Judicial decisions and revenue rulings provide additional guidance for valuation of assets. Valuation rules for several interests are discussed below. For purposes of this discussion, it is assumed that date-of-death valuation is elected.

LISTED STOCKS. Stocks traded on a stock exchange are valued at the average of their highest and lowest selling prices on the date of death.[5] If no sales occur on the date of death, but sales do take place within a few days of such date, the estate tax value is a weighted average of the high and low sales prices on the nearest trade dates before and after the date of death. The average is weighted inversely in relation to the number of days separating the sales dates and the date of death.

EXAMPLE C13-6 ▶ Juan, who dies on November 15, owns 100 shares of Jet Corporation stock. Jet stock is traded on the New York Stock Exchange. It trades at a high of \$120 and a low of \$114 on November 15. On Juan's estate tax return, the stock is valued at \$117 per share, the average of \$120 and \$114. The total value of the block of Jet stock is \$11,700 (100 × \$117). ◀

EXAMPLE C13-7 ▶ Susan, who dies on May 7, owns 100 shares of Top Corporation stock. Top stock is traded on the New York Stock Exchange. No sales of Top stock occur on May 7. The sales occurring closest to May 7 take place two business days before May 7 and three business days after May 7. On the earlier date, the stock trades at a high of \$500 and a low of \$490, with an average of \$495. On the later date, the high is \$492 and the low is \$490, for an average of \$491. The date-of-death per-share valuation of the stock is computed under the inverse weighted average approach, as follows:

$$\frac{[3 \times \$495] + [2 \times \$491]}{5} = \$493.40$$

The total value of the block of Top stock is \$49,340 (100 × \$493.40). ◀

In certain circumstances, the decedent may own such a large block of stock that the price at which the stock trades in the market may not represent the FMV per share for the decedent's number of shares. In such circumstances, Treasury Regulations allow a departure from the traditional valuation rule for stocks. These regulations, referred to as the blockage regulations, state that

[4] Reg. Sec. 20.2031-1(b).

[5] Reg. Sec. 20.2031-2(b).

In certain exceptional cases, the size of the block of stock to be valued in relation to the number of shares changing hands in sales may be relevant in determining whether selling prices reflect the fair market value of the block of stock to be valued. If the executor can show that the block of stock to be valued is so large in relation to the actual sales on the existing market that it could not be liquidated in a reasonable time without depressing the market, the price at which the block could be sold as such outside the usual market, as through an underwriter, may be a more accurate indication of value than market quotations.[6]

INTERESTS IN FIRMS WHOSE STOCK IS NOT PUBLICLY TRADED. Often, the decedent owns stock in a firm whose shares are not publicly traded. Treasury Regulations do not specifically address the valuation rules for this type of an interest. However, detailed guidelines about relevant factors, including book value and earning capacity, are found in Rev. Rul. 59-60.[7] If the stock is a minority interest in a closely held firm, the courts often grant a discount for the minority interest.

REAL ESTATE. Perhaps surprisingly, Treasury Regulations do not specifically address the valuation approach for real estate. Thus, the general valuation principles concerning a price that would be acceptable to a willing buyer and a willing seller must be implemented without the benefit of more specific guidance. Appraisal literature discusses three techniques for valuing real property: comparable sales, reproduction cost, and capitalization of earnings.[8] Unfortunately, it may be difficult to locate a comparable real estate sale. The reproduction cost, of course, is not applicable to valuing land. Capitalization of earnings often is used in valuing commercial real property. At times, an appraiser may use all three approaches.

ANNUITIES, INTERESTS FOR LIFE OR A TERM OF YEARS, REVERSIONS, REMAINDERS. Actuarial tables are used to value annuities, interests for life or a term of years, reversions, and remainders included in the gross estate.[9] The same tables apply for both estate and gift tax purposes. (See Chapter C12 for a discussion of the use of these tables.) The following example illustrates a situation when the actuarial tables must be used to value an inclusion in the decedent's estate.

EXAMPLE C13-8 ▶ Tony gives property to a trust with a bank named as trustee and his cousin named to receive all of the trust income for the next 15 years (i.e., a term certain interest). At the end of the fifteenth year, the property reverts to Tony or his estate. Tony dies exactly four years after creating the trust, and the trust property is valued at $100,000 at Tony's death. At Tony's death, the trust has 11 years to continue until the property reverts to Tony's estate. The inclusion in Tony's estate is the value of a reversionary interest following a term certain interest with 11 remaining years. If 10% is the applicable rate, the reversionary interest is valued at $35,049 (0.350494 × $100,000) by using the excerpt from Table B of the actuarial tables included in Appendix H. ◀

ALTERNATE VALUATION DATE

Section 2032 authorizes the executor to elect to value all property included in the gross estate at its FMV on the alternate valuation date. Congress enacted this provision in response to the stock market crash of 1929 to make sure that an entire estate could not be confiscated for taxes because of a sudden, substantial drop in values.

In general, the **alternate valuation date** is six months after the date of death. However, if the property is distributed, sold, exchanged, or otherwise disposed of within six months of the date of death, the alternate valuation date is the date of sale or other disposition.

EXAMPLE C13-9 ▶ Ron dies on March 3. Ron's estate includes two items: stock and land. The estate still owns the stock on September 3, but the executor sold the land on August 20. If Ron's executor elects the alternate valuation date, the stock is valued as of September 3. The land, however, is valued as

---

[6] Reg. Sec. 20.2031-2(e). As examples of cases dealing with the blockage discount, see *Horace Havemeyer v. U.S.*, 33 AFTR 1069, 45-1 USTC ¶10,194 (Ct. Cls., 1945); *Estate of Charles M. Prell*, 48 T.C. 67 (1967); and *Estate of David Smith*, 57 T.C. 650 (1972). The *Smith* case extended the blockage concept to large holdings of works of art.

[7] 1959-1 C.B. 237.

[8] For a discussion of techniques for appraising real estate, see The Appraisal Institute, *The Appraisal of Real Estate*, 11th ed. (Arlington Heights, IL: The Appraisal Institute, 1996).

[9] Section 7520 provides that the interest rate potentially changes every month. Regulation Sec. 20.7520-1(a)(2) provides these tables. An excerpt from these tables is included in Appendix H.

of August 20 because it is disposed of before the end of the six-month period. Of course, the value of land generally would change very little, if any, between August 20 and September 3. ◀

If the executor elects the alternate valuation date, generally any changes in value that occur *solely* because of a "mere lapse of time" must be ignored in determining the property's value.[10] In a limited number of situations, one must concentrate on this rule concerning the mere passage of time. For example, if the executor elects the alternate valuation date to value a patent, he or she must ignore any change in value attributable to the fact that the patent's remaining life is six months shorter on the alternate valuation date than it was on the date of death.

The alternate valuation date election can be made only if it decreases the value of the gross estate *and* the estate tax liability (after reduction for credits).[11] As a result of this provision, electing the alternate valuation date cannot produce a higher step-up in basis. Congress enacted this strict rule because the alternate valuation date formerly offered a substantial tax planning advantage in situations where, because of the unlimited marital deduction, no estate tax was owed. If the property appreciated between the date of death and the alternate valuation date, the recipient could receive an increased basis if the executor elected the alternate valuation date.[12] With the unlimited marital deduction, the estate could achieve an additional step-up in basis without increasing the estate tax liability.

STOP & THINK

Question: Joan died on April 1. Her estate consisted of three assets: an apartment building valued at $1.2 million on April 1, stock valued at $700,000 on April 1, and $400,000 of cash. On October 1, the values were as follows: apartment building—$1.5 million, stock—$100,000, and cash of $400,000. Joan willed all her property to her son, who anticipates owning the property for a long time. Assume the deductions for Joan's estate are negligible. Is there an estate tax benefit in electing the alternate valuation date? Is there an income tax benefit in electing the alternate valuation date?

Solution: An estate tax benefit results from using the alternate valuation date. The estate tax liability would be lower because the taxable estate would be $300,000 smaller if the alternate valuation date value ($2 million minus deductions) were used instead of the date of death value ($2.3 million minus deductions). Some income tax benefit also results from using the alternate valuation date. By using the alternate valuation date value, the tax basis for calculating cost recovery on the apartment building is $300,000 higher, ignoring any allocation of value to the land. However, a related detriment occurs because the basis of the stock is $600,000 less with the alternate valuation date. If it is anticipated that the stock will be sold in the near future, the $600,000 capital loss that would be available by using the date of death value might permit Joan's son to sell a number of highly-appreciated assets and offset a large capital gain with the $600,000 capital loss.

THE GROSS ESTATE: INCLUSIONS

OBJECTIVE 3

Determine which interests are includible in the gross estate

As Figure C13-1 illustrates, the process of calculating the decedent's estate tax liability begins with determining the components of the gross estate. The **gross estate** is analogous to gross income. Once the components of the gross estate have been identified, they must be valued. As previously mentioned, the gross estate encompasses a much wider array of items than merely those to which the decedent held title at death. For example, under certain statutory provisions, referred to as the *transferor sections,* the gross estate includes items previously transferred by the decedent. For decedents other than nonresident aliens,

[10] Reg. Sec. 20.2032-1(f).
[11] Sec. 2032(c).
[12] Sec. 1014(a).

SELF-STUDY QUESTION

Which of the following properties will be included in (1) the probate estate, (2) the gross estate, (3) both the probate and gross estate, or (4) neither estate?

1. Real property held in joint tenancy with the decedent's spouse. (The answer is 2.)
2. Real property held as a tenant in common with the decedent's spouse. (The answer is 3.)
3. A life insurance policy owned by the decedent in which the decedent's spouse is named the beneficiary. (The answer is 2.)
4. A life insurance policy always owned by the decedent's spouse in which the decedent's children are named the beneficiaries. (The answer is 4.)

the fact that property is located in a foreign country does not preclude it from being included in the gross estate. Table C13-1 provides an overview of the inclusions in the gross estate.

COMPARISON OF GROSS ESTATE WITH PROBATE ESTATE

The gross estate is a federal tax law concept, and the probate estate is a state law concept. To oversimplify, the **probate estate** can be defined as encompassing property that passes subject to the will (or under an intestacy statute) and is subject to court administration. Often, a decedent's gross estate is substantially larger than his or her probate estate. For example, suppose that at the time of death, a decedent owns a life insurance policy on his own life with his daughter as the beneficiary. The policy is not a part of the decedent's probate estate because the policy proceeds are payable directly to the daughter, but it is included in the gross estate.

STOP & THINK *Question:* Karl died recently, and Karl's executor has included the following properties in Karl's gross estate: life insurance payable to the beneficiary, Karl's wife; savings account solely in Karl's name; land titled in the names of Karl and his son as joint tenants with right of survivorship; and a trust created under the will of Karl's mother. Karl had an income interest in the trust for his lifetime and complete power to choose the owners of the property on his death. With the exception of the trust assets (willed to his children), Karl's will leaves all his property to his beloved cousin, Karla. Which assets pass under the terms of Karl's will? Which assets will Karla receive?

Solution: This scenario illustrates the difference between the property included in a decedent's gross estate and in the probate estate. Karl's gross estate is larger than his probate estate. Only two assets included in his gross estate—the savings account and the trust property—pass under the terms of Karl's will. Karla will receive only the savings account. The life insurance passes to the named beneficiary, the spouse, and the land passes to the surviving joint tenant, the son.

▼ **TABLE C13-1**
Inclusions in the Gross Estate

IRC Section	Type of Property or Transaction Included
2033	Property in which the decedent had an interest
2035	Gift taxes on property given away within three years of death *plus* certain property (primarily life insurance) given away within three years of death
2036	Property that the decedent transferred during life but in which the decedent retained economic benefits or the power to control enjoyment
2037	Property that the decedent transferred during life but for which the decedent has too large a reversionary interest
2038	Property that the decedent transferred during life but over which the decedent held the power to alter, amend, revoke, or terminate an interest
2039	Annuities
2040	Jointly owned property
2041	Property over which the decedent possessed a general power of appointment
2042	Life insurance on the decedent's life
2044	QTIP trust for which a marital deduction was claimed by the decedent's spouse

PROPERTY IN WHICH THE DECEDENT HAD AN INTEREST

Section 2033, sometimes called the *generic section,* provides that the gross estate includes the value of all property the decedent beneficially owned at the time of death. Its broad language taxes such items as a personal residence, an automobile, stocks, and any other asset titled in the decedent's name. Because the rule refers to beneficial ownership, however, its scope extends beyond assets to which the decedent held title. For example, such items as remainder interests also are included in the gross estate.

EXAMPLE C13-10 ▶ At the time of his death, the following assets are in Raj's name: personal residence, mountain cabin, Zero Corporation stock, checking account, and savings account. Raj beneficially owns each of these items when he dies. Under Sec. 2033, each item is included in Raj's gross estate. ◀

EXAMPLE C13-11 ▶ Ken's will named Ann to receive trust income for life and Raj or Raj's estate to receive the trust remainder upon Ann's death. Raj's gross estate, therefore, includes the value of the remainder interest if Raj predeceases Ann because Raj's will controls the passage of the remainder interest. The transfer is associated with Raj's death, and, hence, is subject to the estate tax. ◀

DOWER OR CURTESY RIGHTS

Certain state laws provide wealth protection to surviving spouses through **dower** or **curtesy** rights.

- ▶ Dower is a widow's interest in her deceased husband's property.
- ▶ Curtesy is a widower's interest in his deceased wife's property.

Dower or curtesy rights entitle the surviving spouse to a certain portion of the decedent spouse's estate, even though the decedent may have willed a smaller portion to the spouse. Because the decedent spouse does not have complete control over the portion of his or her estate that is subject to dower or curtesy rights, some might argue that the portion of the estate that the surviving spouse is entitled to receive is excluded from the gross estate. Thus, Congress made it crystal clear that the decedent's gross estate is not reduced for the value of the property in which the surviving spouse has a dower or curtesy interest or some other statutory interest.[13]

ADDITIONAL COMMENT

Any property that passes outright to the decedent's spouse, due to dower or curtesy rights under state law, is eligible for the marital deduction and will not increase the unified tax base.

EXAMPLE C13-12 ▶ The laws of a certain state provide that widows are entitled to receive one-third of their deceased husband's property. The husband's gross estate does not exclude his widow's dower rights (one-third interest) in his property. ◀

SELF-STUDY QUESTION

When Dorothy died on April 10, she owned Z Corporation bonds, that paid interest on April 1 and October 1, and stock in X and Y Corporations. X Corporation had declared a dividend on March 15 payable to stockholders of record on April 1. Y Corporation had declared a dividend on March 31 payable to stockholders of record on April 15. Dorothy's estate received the interest and dividends on the payment dates. Should any of the interest or dividends be included in Dorothy's gross estate?

ANSWER

The X Corporation dividend must be included because the date of record preceded Dorothy's death. The Y Corporation dividend will not be included because the date of record was after her death. The Z Corporation bond interest that must be included is the interest that accrued between the April 1 payment date and the April 10 date of death.

TRANSFEROR PROVISIONS

Sections 2035 through 2038 are called the *transferor provisions.* They apply if the decedent made a transfer while alive of a type specified in the IRC section in question, *and* the decedent did not receive adequate consideration in money or money's worth for the transferred interest. If one of the transferor provisions applies, the transferred property is included in the gross estate at its date-of-death or alternate valuation date value.

GIFTS MADE WITHIN THREE YEARS OF DEATH. Section 2035(a) specifies the circumstances in which a gift that a decedent makes within three years of death triggers an inclusion in the gross estate. The scope of this provision, which is relatively narrow, encompasses the following two types of transfers made by the donor-decedent within three years before death:

- ▶ A life insurance policy on the decedent's life that would have been taxed under Sec. 2042 (life insurance proceeds received by the executor or for the benefit of the estate) had the policy not been given away, or
- ▶ An interest in property that would have been taxed under Sec. 2036 (transfers with a retained life estate), Sec. 2037 (transfers taking effect at death), or Sec. 2038 (revocable transfers) had it not been transferred.

[13] Sec. 2034.

Of these situations, the most common involves the insured's gifting a life insurance policy on his or her own life and dying within three years of the transfer. With new insurance policies, the potential for an inclusion can be avoided if the decedent never owns the new policy. In other words, instead of the insured purchasing a new policy and then giving it to a transferee as owner, the other party should buy the new policy. A common planning technique involves a transfer of cash by an individual to a trust, and the trust (a life insurance trust) using the cash to purchase an insurance policy on the transferor's life.

EXAMPLE C13-13 ▶ On April 1, 1999, Roy transferred to Sally ownership of a $400,000 life insurance policy on his own life purchased in 1995. Sally is the policy's beneficiary. Roy dies on February 3, 2002. Because Roy dies within three years of giving away the policy, the policy is included in Roy's gross estate. The estate tax value of the policy is its $400,000 face value. If Roy had lived until at least April 2, 2002, the policy transfer would have fallen outside the three-year rule, and the policy would not have been included in Roy's gross estate. ◀

EXAMPLE C13-14 ▶ Roy made a gift of stock to Troy on May 1, 2001. Roy dies on February 3, 2002. The stock was worth $80,000 on the gift date and is worth $125,000 at the time of Roy's death. The gifted property is not included in Roy's gross estate because it is not life insurance on Roy's life, nor is it property that would have been taxed in Roy's estate under Secs. 2036 through 2038 had he kept such property. ◀

GROSS-UP RULE. The donor-decedent's gross estate is increased by any gift tax that he or she, or his or her estate pays on any gift the decedent or his or her spouse makes during the three-year period ending with the decedent's death.[14] This provision, known as the gross-up rule, applies to the gift tax triggered by a gift of any type of property during the three-year look-back period.

The purpose of the gross-up rule is to foreclose the opportunity that existed under pre-1977 law to reduce one's gross estate (and thereby one's taxable estate) by removing the gift tax on "deathbed" gifts from the gross estate. Because the donor's estate received a credit for some or all of the gift tax paid, under the pre-1977 rules, a person on his or her deathbed in effect could prepay a portion of his or her estate tax and at the same time reduce his or her gross estate by the amount of the gift tax.

The gross-up rule, as illustrated in the two examples below, reinstates the estate to the position it would have been in had no gift tax liability been incurred.

EXAMPLE C13-15 ▶ In late 1999, Cheron made a $1 million taxable gift of stock and paid a gift tax of $134,500 ($345,800 gross tax − $211,300 unified credit). Cheron dies in early 2002. Cheron's gross estate does not include the stock, but it does include the $134,500 gift tax paid because she made the gift within three years of her death. ◀

EXAMPLE C13-16 ▶ In late 1999, Hal gave Jody stock having a $2,020,000 FMV, and he and Wanda, his wife, elected gift splitting. Each is deemed to have made a $1 million [($2,020,000 ÷ 2) − $10,000 annual exclusion] taxable gift, and each paid $134,500 ($345,800 gross tax − $211,300 unified credit) of gift tax. Wanda dies in early 2002. Wanda's gross estate includes the $134,500 in gift tax she paid on the portion of her husband's gift that she is deemed to have made within three years of her death. Her cash balance had declined because of paying the gift tax, and the gross-up for the tax replenishes her estate. ◀

SELF-STUDY QUESTION

Refer to Example C13-16. Assume that Hal, the spouse who actually made the gift, paid Wanda's $134,500 gift tax as well as his own $134,500 gift tax. Would Wanda's $134,500 gift tax be included in her gross estate?

ANSWER

No. It would not be included because payment of the tax from Hal's account did not reduce her cash balance and gross estate.

TRANSFERS WITH RETAINED LIFE ESTATE. Section 2036, although titled "Transfers with Retained Life Estate," extends beyond taxing solely lifetime transfers made by the decedent in which he or she retained a life estate (the right to income or use for life). The two primary types of transfers taxed under Sec. 2036 are those for which the decedent

- Kept possession or enjoyment of the property or the right to its income
- Retained the power to designate the person who is to possess or enjoy the property or to receive its income

[14] Sec. 2035(b).

Thus, Sec. 2036 applies when the transferor kept the income or enjoyment *or* the right to control other individuals' income or enjoyment.

The direct or indirect retention of voting rights in stock of a controlled corporation that the decedent transferred also can cause the gifted stock to be included in the transferor's gross estate.[15] A controlled corporation is one in which the decedent owned (directly, indirectly, or constructively), or had the right to vote, stock that possessed at least 20% of the voting power.[16]

The retention of income, control, or voting rights for one of the three retention periods listed below causes the transferred property to be included in the transferor's gross estate. The three periods are

- The transferor's lifetime
- A period that cannot be determined without referring to the transferor's death (e.g., the transferor retained the right to quarterly payments of income, but payments ceased with the last quarterly payment before the transferor's death)
- A period that does not end before the transferor's death

An implied agreement or understanding is sufficient to trigger inclusion. For example, if a mother gives a residence to her daughter and continues to occupy the residence alone and rent free, the residence probably will be included in the mother's gross estate because there was an implied understanding that the mother could occupy the residence for life.

If Sec. 2036 applies to a transfer and if the decedent's retention of enjoyment or control extends to all the transferred property, 100% of the transferred property's value is included in the transferor's gross estate.[17] However, if the transferor keeps the right to only one-third of the income for life and retains no control over the remaining two-thirds, his estate includes just one-third of the property's date-of-death value. The following three examples illustrate some of the transactions that cause Sec. 2036 to apply.

EXAMPLE C13-17 ▶ In 1997, David (age 30) transferred an office building to Ellen but retained the right to collect all the income from the building for life. David dies in 2002. Because David retained the income right for life, the Sec. 2036 inclusion applies. The amount included is 100% of the building's date-of-death value. ◀

EXAMPLE C13-18 ▶ Assume the same facts as in Example C13-17 except that David retains the right to income for only 15 years. David dies five years after the transfer; therefore, David has the right to receive the income for the remaining ten-year period. Because the retention period does not *in fact* end before David's death, his gross estate includes 100% of the property's date-of-death value. ◀

EXAMPLE C13-19 ▶ Tracy creates a trust with a bank as trustee and names Alice, Brad, and Carol to receive the trust income for their joint lives and Dick to receive the remainder upon the death of the first among Alice, Brad, or Carol to die. Tracy reserves the right to designate the portion of the income to be paid to each income beneficiary each year. Only the gift to Dick was a completed transfer and subject to gift taxes. Tracy dies before any of the other parties. Because her control over the flow of income does not end before Tracy's death, the date-of-death value of the trust assets is included in Tracy's estate even though a portion of the transfer was subject to gift taxes. If Tracy had instead "cut the string" and not kept control over the income flow, she could have removed the trust property from her estate. ◀

SELF-STUDY QUESTION

Refer to Example C13-19. Assume the same facts except that the trustee is directed to distribute its annual income equally to Alice, Brad, and Carol for their joint lives. Also assume that Tracy names Dick the remainderman. Will the value of the trust be included in Tracy's gross estate?

ANSWER

No, because Tracy retained no power to control the enjoyment of the property.

REVERSIONARY INTERESTS. If the chance exists that the property will pass back to the transferor under the terms of the transfer, the transferor has a **reversionary interest**. Under Sec. 2037, the transferor's gross estate includes earlier transferred property if the decedent stipulates that another person must survive him or her to own the property and the value of the decedent's reversionary interest exceeds 5% of the value of the transferred property. Actuarial techniques are used to value the reversionary interest.[18] Section 2037 does not apply if the value of the reversionary interest does not exceed the 5% *de minimis* amount.

---

[15] Sec. 2036(b)(1).

[16] Sec. 2036(b)(2).

[17] Reg. Sec. 20.2036-1(a).

[18] The **reversionary interest** is the interest that will return to the transferor. Often, it will return only if certain contingencies occur. The value of Beth's reversionary interest in Example C13-20 is a function of the present value of the interest Beth would receive after the deaths of Tammy and Doug, valued as from actuarial tables (see Appendix H), and coupled with the probability that Tammy and Doug would die before Beth.

EXAMPLE C13-20 ▶ Beth transfers an asset to Tammy for life and then to Doug for life. The asset is to revert to Beth, if Beth is still alive, upon the death of either Tammy or Doug, whoever dies second. If Beth is not alive upon the death of the survivor of Tammy and Doug, the asset is to pass to Don or to a charitable organization if Don is not alive. Thus, Don must live longer than Beth to receive the property. The property is included in Beth's estate if the value of Beth's reversionary interest exceeds 5% of the property's value. The amount included is not the value of Beth's reversionary interest, but rather the date-of-death value of the asset less the value of Tammy's and Doug's intervening life estates. ◀

ADDITIONAL COMMENT

Sections 2036 through 2038 draw back into the gross estate certain previously transferred property and include it in the gross estate at its FMV on the date of the decedent's death. For income tax purposes, if the property has appreciated in value, donees will obtain a stepped-up basis rather than a carryover gift tax basis.

REVOCABLE TRANSFERS. Section 2038 covers the rules for revocable transfers (i.e., revocable trusts). However, this provision also taxes all transfers over which the decedent has, at the time of his or her death, the power to change the enjoyment by altering, amending, revoking, or terminating an interest. Revocable trusts, sometimes called living trusts, are popular arrangements from a non-tax standpoint because assets held by a revocable trust pass outside of probate. Advantages of avoiding probate include lower probate costs and easier administration for real property located in a state that is not the decedent's state of domicile. In addition, unlike a will, a revocable trust is not a matter of public record. Section 2038 can apply even though the decedent does not originally retain powers over the property. The crucial factor is that the transferor possesses the powers at the time of death regardless of whether the transferor retained such powers originally.

The estate must include only the value of the interest that is subject to the decedent's power to change. Sections 2038 and 2036 overlap greatly, and if one amount is taxable under one section and a different amount is taxable under the other section, the gross estate includes the larger amount. Two types of transfers taxed by Sec. 2038 are illustrated in the following examples.

EXAMPLE C13-21 ▶ Joe creates and funds a revocable trust. He names his son to receive the income for life and his grandson to receive the property upon the son's death. Because the trust is revocable, Joe may change the terms of the trust or take back the trust property during his lifetime. Joe's power to revoke the transfer extends to the entire amount of the trust. Thus, Joe's gross estate includes the date-of-death value of the entire trust. ◀

EXAMPLE C13-22 ▶ Vicki creates a trust and names Gina to receive the income for life and Matt to receive the remainder. Vicki, however, retains the right to substitute Liz (for Matt) as remainderman. When Vicki dies, she has the authority to change the enjoyment of the remainder. Thus, the value of the trust's remainder interest is includible in Vicki's estate. ◀

SELF-STUDY QUESTION

Reggie purchased a 15-year term certain annuity. If Reggie dies before the end of the 15-year term of the annuity, his estate will be entitled to the remaining payments. Assume Reggie died after receiving nine of the 15 payments. Will the value of the remaining six payments be included in Reggie's estate?

ANSWER

Yes. Section 2039 requires that the cost of a comparable contract of six payments be included in his gross estate.

ANNUITIES AND OTHER RETIREMENT BENEFITS

Section 2039 explicitly addresses the estate tax treatment of annuities. Even if this section had not been enacted, some annuities probably would have been taxable under the general language of Sec. 2033 because the decedent would have been viewed as having an interest in the property. For an annuity to be included in the gross estate, it must involve payments made under a contract or an agreement. In addition, the decedent must be receiving such payments at the time of his or her death or must have the right to collect such payments alone or with another person. If the annuity simply ceases with the death of the decedent in question, nothing is to be received by another party and nothing is included in the gross estate. For the payments to be included in the decedent's estate, they must be paid for the decedent's life, a period that may not be determined without referring to the decedent's date of death or for a period that does not actually end before the decedent's death.

ANNUITIES NOT RELATED TO EMPLOYMENT. The purchase of an annuity designed to pay benefits to the purchaser and then to a named survivor upon the purchaser's death, or to both parties simultaneously and then to the survivor, is a form of wealth shifting. The other party receives wealth that originates with the purchaser. This type of transfer is different from most other wealth transfers because it involves a series of annuity payments instead of a transfer of a tangible property.

The amount included in the gross estate with respect to annuities or other retirement benefits is a fraction (described below) of the value of the annuity or lump-sum payment to be received by the surviving beneficiary. Annuities are valued at the cost of a comparable contract.[19] To determine the figure to be included in the gross estate, this cost is multiplied by a fraction that represents the portion of the purchase price the decedent has contributed.

EXAMPLE C13-23 ▶

Twelve years ago, Jim purchased a joint and survivor annuity to pay benefits to himself and his son and then to the survivor for life. Jim and his son started collecting payments four years ago. Jim dies in the current year, survived by his son. At the time of Jim's death, the cost of a comparable contract providing the same benefits to the son is $180,000. Because Jim provided all the consideration to purchase the annuity, his gross estate includes 100% of the $180,000 cost of a comparable contract. This annuity arrangement represents a shifting of wealth from Jim to his son upon Jim's death. ◀

SELF-STUDY QUESTION

On his retirement at age 65, Winslow elected to take a joint and survivor annuity from his qualified pension plan. The plan provided Winslow and his wife with a monthly pension of $2,500 until the death of the survivor. Winslow died seven years later. What amount (if any) must be included in Winslow's gross estate if his wife survives?

ANSWER

The gross estate includes the cost of a comparable contract providing $2,500 a month for the rest of the spouse's life. The age of the spouse would affect this amount.

EMPLOYMENT-RELATED RETIREMENT BENEFITS. Recall that, to determine the amount of an annuity includible in the decedent's gross estate, the cost of a comparable contract is multiplied by a fraction representing the portion of the purchase price contributed by the decedent. Section 2039(b) states that contributions from the decedent's employer (or former employer) are treated as contributions made by the decedent, provided such payments are made as a result of the employment relationship. Thus, 100% of the benefits from an employment-related annuity are included in the gross estate.

EXAMPLE C13-24 ▶

Pat was employed by Wheel Corporation at the time of his death. Wheel Corporation maintains a qualified retirement plan to which it makes 60% of the contributions and its employees contribute 40%. Pat's spouse is to receive an annuity valued at $350,000 from the retirement plan. Because the employer's contributions are considered to have been made by the employee, Pat is deemed to have provided all the consideration for the retirement benefits. Consequently, Pat's gross estate includes 100% of the annuity's $350,000 date-of-death value. ◀

JOINTLY OWNED PROPERTY

Section 2040 addresses the estate tax treatment of jointly owned property (i.e., property owned in a joint tenancy with right of survivorship or tenancy by the entirety arrangement).[20] An important characteristic of this form of ownership is that, upon the death of one joint owner, the decedent's interest passes automatically (by right of survivorship) to the surviving joint owner(s). Thus, the property is not part of the probate estate and does not pass under the will. Section 2040 contains two sets of rules, one for property jointly owned by spouses and one for all other jointly owned properties.

OWNERSHIP INVOLVING PERSONS OTHER THAN SPOUSES. When persons other than spouses or persons in addition to spouses own property as joint owners, the amount includible is determined by the consideration-furnished test.[21] Under this test, property is included in a joint owner's gross estate in accordance with the portion of the consideration he or she furnished to acquire the property. Obviously, this portion can range between 0% and 100%.

---

[19] Reg. Sec. 20.2031-8(a).

[20] Both joint tenancies with right of survivorship and tenancies by the entirety have the feature of survivorship. When one joint owner dies, his or her interest passes by right of survivorship to the remaining joint owner(s). Only spouses may use the tenancy by the entirety arrangement, whereas any persons may own as joint tenants with right of survivorship. A joint tenancy with right of survivorship may be severed by the action of any joint owner, whereas a tenancy by the entirety arrangement continues unless severed by the joint action of both joint owners.

The following definitions are from Henry Campbell Black, *Black's Law Dictionary*, Rev. 6th ed., Ed. by Joseph R. Nolan and Jacqueline M. Nolan-Haley (St. Paul, MN: West Publishing Co., 1990), p. 1,465.

Joint tenancy with right of survivorship: The primary incident of joint tenancy is survivorship, by which the entire tenancy on the decease of any joint tenant remains to the survivors, and at length to the last survivor.

Tenancy by the entirety: A tenancy which is created between husband and wife and by which together they hold title to the whole with right of survivorship so that upon death of either, other takes whole to exclusion of deceased heirs. It is essentially a "joint tenancy" modified by the common-law theory that husband and wife are one person, and survivorship is the predominant and distinguishing feature of each. Neither party can alienate or encumber the property without the consent of the other.

[21] Sec. 2040(a).

EXAMPLE C13-25 ▶ Seven years ago, Fred and Jack provided $10,000 and $30,000 of consideration, respectively, to purchase real property titled in the names of Fred and Jack as joint tenants with right of survivorship. Fred dies in the current year and is survived by Jack. The real property is valued at $60,000. Fred's gross estate includes $15,000 (0.25 × $60,000) because Fred furnished 25% of the consideration to acquire the property. If Jack instead predeceases Fred, his estate would include $45,000 (0.75 × $60,000). ◀

ADDITIONAL COMMENT

The tracing rule is easy to understand but difficult to implement. Suppose a joint tenancy between a parent and a child was created in a parcel of real estate 30 years ago when the parent paid for the property. The child died of a heart attack, and the parent is senile. Nothing should be included in the child's gross estate. Unfortunately the burden of proof to keep a portion of the property out of the estate is on the estate, not the IRS.

If part of the consideration furnished by one joint tenant is originally received gratuitously from another joint tenant, the consideration is attributable to the joint tenant who made the gift. If all joint owners acquire their interests by gift, devise, bequest, or inheritance, the decedent joint owner's estate includes his or her proportionate share of the date-of-death value of the jointly owned property.

EXAMPLE C13-26 ▶ Ray gives stock valued at $50,000 to Sandy. Three years later Sandy uses this stock (now valued at $60,000) as partial consideration to acquire real property costing $120,000. Ray furnishes the remaining $60,000 of consideration. The real property is titled in the names of Ray and Sandy as joint tenants with right of survivorship. Because Sandy received the asset that he used for consideration as a gift from Ray (the other joint tenant), Sandy is treated as having furnished no consideration. If Sandy dies before Ray, Sandy's estate will include none of the real property's value. If Ray predeceases Sandy, however, Ray's estate will include the entire date-of-death value. ◀

SELF-STUDY QUESTION

Fred and Myrtle, husband and wife, hold title to their home in joint tenancy with right of survivorship. They have three children. Fred is killed in an airplane crash. What part of the value of the residence will be included in Fred's gross estate? Who will own the residence if Fred wills his property to the children?

OWNERSHIP INVOLVING ONLY SPOUSES. If spouses are the only joint owners, the property is classified as a **qualified joint interest**. Section 2040(b)(1) provides that, in the case of qualified joint interests, the decedent's gross estate includes one-half the value of the qualified joint interest. The 50% inclusion rule applies automatically regardless of the relative amount of consideration provided by either spouse.

EXAMPLE C13-27 ▶ Wilma provides all the consideration to purchase stock costing $80,000. She has the stock registered in her name and her husband's name as joint tenants with right of survivorship. The estate of the first spouse to die, regardless of which spouse it is, will include 50% of the value of the jointly owned stock. Upon the second spouse's death, all the property will be included in the gross estate because it no longer will be jointly owned property. ◀

ANSWER

One-half the value of the residence will be included in Fred's gross estate. Myrtle will own the residence after Fred's death because it passes to her by right of survivorship.

GENERAL POWERS OF APPOINTMENT

Section 2041 requires inclusion in the gross estate of certain property interests that the decedent never owns in a legal sense. Inclusion occurs because the decedent had the power to designate who eventually would own the property. The authority to designate the owner—a significant power—is called a power of appointment. Powers of appointment can be general or special (i.e., more restricted).

Only a general power of appointment results in an addition to the gross estate. If a general power was created before October 22, 1942, however, no inclusion occurs unless the decedent exercised the power. For a post-1942 general power of appointment, inclusion occurs regardless of whether the power is exercised. A general power of appointment exists if the holder can exercise the power in favor of him- or herself, his or her estate or creditors, *or* the creditors of his or her estate. Being exercisable in favor of the decedent's estate means there is no restriction on the powerholder's ability to specify the person(s) to receive the property. The power may be exercisable during the decedent's life, by his or her will, or both.

Sometimes a powerholder can exercise a power for only specified purposes. Appointment powers are governed by an ascertainable standard and are free of estate tax consequences if they may be exercised solely for purposes of the decedent's health, support, maintenance, or education.

EXAMPLE C13-28 ▶ When Kathy died in 1985, her will created a trust from which Doris is to receive the income for life. In addition, Doris is granted the power to designate by will the person or persons to receive the trust's assets. Doris has a testamentary general power of appointment. The trust's assets are included in Doris's gross estate regardless of whether Doris exercises the power. If Kathy had instead died in 1940, Doris would have had a pre-1942 power of appointment. Such powers are taxed only if exercised. ◀

EXAMPLE C13-29 ▶ Assume the same facts as in Example C13-28 except that Kathy's will merely empowers Doris to name which of her descendants would receive the trust assets. Doris now has only a special power of appointment because she does not have the power to leave the property to whomever she desires (e.g., the power to appoint the property to her estate). Because Doris's power of appointment is only a special power, the value of the trust is not included in Doris's gross estate. ◀

TYPICAL MISCONCEPTION

Many taxpayers who own life insurance policies on their own lives believe that their estates will not owe estate taxes on the life insurance proceeds if they name someone other than their estate as the beneficiary. Life insurance will be included in the gross estate of the decedent if, at the time of death, the decedent held *any* (one) of the incidents of ownership in the policy.

LIFE INSURANCE

Section 2042 addresses the estate tax treatment of life insurance policies on the decedent's life. Life insurance policies owned by the decedent on the lives of others are taxed under the general language of Sec. 2033. According to Sec. 2042, a decedent's gross estate includes the value of policies on his or her own life if the proceeds are receivable by the executor or for the benefit of the estate, or if the decedent had any "incidents of ownership" in the policy at the time of death. Treasury Regulations list the following powers as a partial inventory of the incidents of ownership:

- To change the beneficiary
- To surrender or cancel the policy
- To borrow against the policy
- To pledge the policy for a loan
- To revoke an assignment of the policy[22]

Examples in the regulations pertaining to incidents of ownership involve economic rights over the insurance policies. Judicial decisions also have been important in defining what constitutes incidents of ownership. In some jurisdictions, the phrase has been interpreted to be broader than simply relating to economic powers.[23]

If the decedent could have exercised the incidents of ownership only in conjunction with another party, the policy nevertheless is included in the gross estate. Moreover, it is the legal power to exercise ownership rights, not the practical ability to do so, that leads to an inclusion. The Supreme Court in the *Estate of Marshal L. Noel* emphasized the importance of the decedent-insured's legal powers in a situation where the insured was killed in a plane crash and the policies he owned on his life were in the possession of his spouse, who was on the ground. The Court held that the decedent possessed incidents of ownership and thus the policies were includible in his gross estate.[24]

EXAMPLE C13-30 ▶ Tracy purchased an insurance policy on her life in 1986. Later, she transferred all her incidents of ownership in the policy to her daughter. Seven years after the transfer, Tracy dies. Tracy's niece has always been the policy's beneficiary. The policy is not included in Tracy's gross estate because Tracy did not have any incidents of ownership in the policy at the time of her death, nor is her estate the beneficiary. (Also, she did not give the policy away within three years of death.) ◀

EXAMPLE C13-31 ▶ Assume the same facts as in Example C13-30 except that Tracy's estate instead is designated as the policy's beneficiary. Because Tracy's estate is designated as the beneficiary, the policy is included in her gross estate. The policy is valued at its face value. ◀

It is not sufficient to consider only Sec. 2042 in determining whether a life insurance policy on the decedent's life is includible in the gross estate. Recall from the discussion earlier in this chapter that a life insurance policy is includible in a decedent's gross estate if the individual makes a gift of a life insurance policy on his or her own life within three years of dying.[25]

EXAMPLE C13-32 ▶ Two years ago, Peng gave all his incidents of ownership in a life insurance policy on his own life to his son, Phong. The face value of the policy is $400,000. Phong has always been the benefi-

---

[22] Reg. Sec. 20.2042-1(c)(2).

[23] See, for example, *Estate of James H. Lumpkin, Jr. v. CIR*, 31 AFTR 2d 73-1381, 73-1 USTC ¶12,909 (5th Cir., 1973), wherein the court held that the right to choose how the proceeds were to be paid—in a lump sum or in installments—was an incident of ownership.

[24] *CIR v. Estate of Marshal L. Noel*, 15 AFTR 2d 1397, 65-1 USTC ¶12,311 (USSC, 1965).

[25] The gifted insurance policy is included under Sec. 2035(a)(2).

ciary. Peng dies in the current year. Because Peng died within three years of giving Phong the policy, Peng's gross estate includes the policy. The policy is valued at its $400,000 date-of-death value. The potential problem of making a transfer of a life insurance policy within three years of death could have been avoided had Phong been the one who originally owned the policy. In that case, Peng would not have made a transfer and need not have been concerned with the three-year rule. ◀

TAX STRATEGY TIP

An individual may be concerned that his or her estate will not have sufficient cash to pay its estate taxes. The individual could buy life insurance so his or her estate will have sufficient cash. However, if the individual owns the policy or names his or her estate the beneficiary of the policy, the proceeds of the policy will be taxed in the gross estate. In this case, the individual should have his or her children (or an irrevocable life insurance trust) buy the life insurance and name themselves the beneficiaries, even if the individual has to provide the funds for the premiums (by making gifts). If the children are the beneficiaries, they can use the policy proceeds to buy an asset from the estate so the estate can raise cash needed to pay the estate taxes.

CONSIDERATION OFFSET

Property is included in the gross estate at its FMV on the date of death or alternate valuation date. Section 2043 allows an offset against the amount included in the gross estate for consideration received in certain transactions.[26] This offset is allowed only if the decedent received some, but less than adequate, consideration in connection with an earlier transaction. The gross estate is reduced by an offset for the partial consideration received. The offset is for the actual dollars received, not for the pro rata portion of the cost paid by the decedent. This offset, called the consideration offset, serves the same function as a deduction in that it reduces the taxable estate. If the decedent receives consideration equal to the value of the property transferred, the property in question is not included in the gross estate. No offset is permitted if the property is excluded from the decedent's gross estate.

The consideration offset prevents a double counting of property in the decedent's estate. For example, if an individual makes a transfer that is includible in the gross estate and receives partial consideration in return, the consideration received is part of the gross estate unless it has been consumed. Sections 2035 through 2038 also require the transferred property to be included in the gross estate, even though the transferor does not own it at the date of death.

EXAMPLE C13-33 ▶ Two years ago, Steve transferred a $300,000 life insurance policy on his life to Earl. The policy was worth $75,000 at the time of transfer, but Earl paid only $48,000 for the policy. Steve dies in the current year with the $48,000 still in his savings account. Steve's gross estate includes both the amount in the savings account and the $300,000 face value of the insurance policy. Under Sec. 2043, Steve's gross estate is reduced by the $48,000 consideration received on the transfer of the insurance policy. The insurance policy on Steve's life would be excluded from Steve's estate if Steve survived the transfer by more than three years, and no consideration offset would be permitted because the insurance is not included in the gross estate. ◀

RECIPIENT SPOUSE'S INTEREST IN QTIP TRUST

Recall from Chapter C12 that a gift tax marital deduction is available for transferring qualified terminable interest property (QTIP) to one's spouse. A QTIP interest involves a transfer entitling the recipient spouse to all the income for life. The estate tax rules for QTIP interests are explained on pages C13-21 and C13-22. Claiming a marital deduction with respect to QTIP interests is voluntary. If the donor or the executor elects to claim a marital deduction for QTIP interests transferred to the spouse during life or at death, the transferred property generally is included in the recipient spouse's gross estate.[27] A QTIP interest included in the gross estate, like other property included in the gross estate, is valued at its date-of-death or alternate valuation date value.

The gross estate of the surviving spouse excludes the QTIP interest if the transferor spouse does not elect to claim a marital deduction. If the recipient spouse has a life estate, has no general power of appointment, and was not the transferor, no IRC sections other than Sec. 2044 (dealing with QTIPs) include the property in the gross estate.

No inclusion in the gross estate is required for QTIP interests for which a marital deduction is elected if the recipient spouse disposes of all or a portion of his or her income interest during his or her lifetime. Dispositions of all or a portion of a spouse's income interest in a QTIP are treated under Sec. 2519 as a transfer of all interests in the QTIP other than the qualifying income interest. Thus, such dispositions are subject to the gift tax.

---

[26] Section 2043 provides a consideration offset for items included in the gross estate under Secs. 2035 through 2038 and Sec. 2041.

[27] Sec. 2044.

EXAMPLE C13-34 ▶ Henry died five years ago. His will created a $650,000 QTIP trust for his widow, Wendy, age 75. Henry's executor elected to claim a marital deduction for the QTIP trust. Wendy dies in the current year. By then, the assets in the QTIP trust have appreciated to $850,000. Wendy's gross estate includes the QTIP trust, which is valued at $850,000. If Henry's executor had not claimed a marital deduction for the QTIP trust, the value of the trust would be excluded from Wendy's estate. If Henry's executor had made a partial QTIP election for 70% of the trust, only 70% of the $850,000 value would be in Wendy's gross estate. ◀

DEDUCTIONS

OBJECTIVE 4

Identify deductions available for estate tax purposes

As mentioned earlier in this chapter, deductions from the gross estate fall into five categories. Two of these categories (debts and funeral and administration expenses and casualty and theft losses) allow the tax base to reflect the net wealth passed to the decedent's heirs, legatees, or devisees. Two other deduction categories reduce the estate tax base for transfers to the surviving spouse (the marital deduction) or to charitable organizations (the charitable contribution deduction). No deduction is available, however, for the amount of wealth diverted to the government in the form of estate taxes. A special deduction for certain family-owned business interests lessens the estate tax cost for the owner of a family business. The aggregate amount of the five categories of deductions is subtracted from the gross estate amount to determine the taxable estate. Each deduction category is examined below. Table C13-2 provides an overview of the estate tax deductions.

TYPICAL MISCONCEPTION

Most taxpayers are so familiar with the fact that expenses for income tax purposes must be paid or accrued to be deductible, they do not recognize that the expenses of administering an estate can be estimated at the time the estate tax return is filed. Estimation is necessary because the administration of the estate can continue long after the estate tax return is filed.

DEBTS AND FUNERAL AND ADMINISTRATION EXPENSES

Section 2053 authorizes deductions for mortgages and other debts owed by the decedent, as well as for the decedent's funeral and administration expenses. Mortgages and all other debts of the decedent are deductible provided they represent bona fide contracts for an adequate and full consideration in money or money's worth. Even debts relating to an expenditure for which no income tax deduction would be allowable are deductible. Interest, state and local taxes, and trade or business expenses accrued at the date of death are deductible on both the estate tax return (as a debt of the decedent) and on the estate's income tax return (as an expense known as a deduction in respect of a decedent) when they are paid. (See Chapter C14 for a discussion of the income tax implications.)

Examples of administration expenses include executor's commissions, attorneys' fees, court costs, accountants' fees, appraisers' fees, and expenses of preserving and distributing the estate. The executor must decide whether to deduct administration expenses on the estate tax return (Form 706) or the estate's income tax return (Form 1041). Such expenses cannot be deducted twice, although some may be deducted on the estate tax return and others on the estate's income tax return.

▼ TABLE C13-2
Estate Tax Deductions

IRC Section	Type of Deduction
2053	Funeral and administration expenses[a] and debts
2054	Casualty and theft losses[a]
2055	Charitable contributions[b]
2056	Marital deduction[b]
2057	Family business deduction[c]

[a] Deductible on the estate tax return or on the estate's income tax return.
[b] No limit on deductible amount.
[c] Repealed after 2003.

An estate that owes no estate tax (e.g., because of the unlimited marital deduction or the unified credit) should deduct administration expenses on its income tax return because no tax savings will result from a deduction on the estate tax return. If an estate owes estate taxes, its marginal estate tax rate will be at least 41% because the tax base will exceed the $1 million (in 2002) exemption equivalent. In 2002 and 2003, the highest income tax rate for an estate is 38.6%. Thus, for taxable estates exceeding $1 million, administration expenses should be deducted on the estate tax return.

Funeral expenses are deductible only on the estate tax return. The estate may deduct any funeral expenses allowable under local law including "[a] reasonable expenditure for a tombstone, monument, or mausoleum, or for a burial lot, either for the decedent or his family, including a reasonable expenditure for its future care."[28] The transportation costs of the person bringing the body to the burial place also are deductible as funeral expenses.

EXAMPLE C13-35 ▶ At Ed's date of death, Ed owes a $75,000 mortgage on his residence, plus $280 of interest accrued thereon, and $320 of personal expenditures charged to a department store charge card. The estate's administration expenses are estimated to be $32,000. His funeral expenses total $12,000. Under Sec. 2053, Ed's estate can deduct $75,600 ($75,000 + $280 + $320) for debts and $12,000 for funeral expenses. The $32,000 of administration expenses are deductible on the estate tax return, on the estate's income tax return for the year in which they are paid, or some on each return. Ed's estate will get an income tax deduction for the accrued interest whenever it is paid. ◀

TAX STRATEGY TIP

The executor should elect to deduct any casualty or theft loss, when such loss is allowable, from the estate tax return if the taxable estate will exceed $1 million. The highest marginal income tax rate is 38.6% (in 2002), and the marginal estate tax rate is at least 41% when the taxable estate exceeds $1 million.

LOSSES

Section 2054 authorizes a deduction for losses incurred from theft or casualty while the estate is being settled. Just as in the context of the income tax, examples of casualties include fires, storms, and earthquakes. Any insurance compensation received affects the amount of the loss. If the alternate valuation date is elected, the loss may not be used to reduce the alternate value and then used again as a loss deduction. As with administration expenses, the executor must decide whether to deduct the loss on the estate tax return or the estate's income tax return. No double deduction is allowed for these losses, and the nondeductible floor applicable for income tax purposes does not exist for estate tax purposes.

EXAMPLE C13-36 ▶ Sam dies on May 3. One of the items included in Sam's gross estate is a mountain cabin valued at $75,000. The uninsured cabin is totally destroyed in a landslide on August 18. If the date-of-death valuation is chosen, the cabin is included in the gross estate at $75,000. The executor must choose between claiming a Sec. 2054 deduction on the estate tax return or a casualty loss deduction on the estate's income tax return. ◀

EXAMPLE C13-37 ▶ Assume the same facts as in Example C13-36 except that Sam's executor elects the alternate valuation date. The cabin is valued at zero when determining the value of the gross estate. No loss deduction is available for the casualty on the estate tax return. The estate cannot claim an income tax deduction for the casualty loss either because the property's adjusted basis in its hands is zero. ◀

CHARITABLE CONTRIBUTION DEDUCTION

Section 2055 authorizes a deduction for transfers to charitable organizations. The rules concerning eligible donee organizations are the same as for gift tax purposes.

Because the estate tax charitable contribution deduction is unlimited, a decedent could eliminate his or her estate tax liability by willing all his or her property (or all property except for an amount equal to the exemption equivalent) to a charitable organization. Similarly, a decedent could eliminate an estate tax liability by willing an amount equal to the exemption equivalent to the children and the rest of the estate to the surviving spouse and a charitable organization (e.g., in equal shares).[29] People who desire to leave some property to a charity at their death should be encouraged to consider giving the property before death, so they can obtain an income tax deduction for the gift and also reduce their gross estate by the amount of the gift.

---

[28] Reg. Sec. 20.2053-2.

[29] Another way the estate could owe no taxes is if all of the property, or all of the property except for the exemption equivalent, is shielded from taxation by the marital deduction.

COMPUTING THE DEDUCTION. Computation of the estate tax charitable contribution deduction can be somewhat complicated in certain circumstances. Suppose the decedent (a widow) has a $5 million gross estate and no Sec. 2053 or 2054 deductions. The decedent's will specifies that her son is to receive $3 million and a charitable organization is to receive the residue (the rest not explicitly disposed of). Assume that state law specifies that death taxes are payable from the residue. Because $3 million of property passes to the decedent's child, the estate will definitely owe some estate taxes. The charitable organization will receive $2 million, less the estate taxes payable therefrom. The estate tax liability depends on the amount of the charitable contribution deduction, which in turn depends on the amount of the estate tax liability. Simultaneous equations are required to calculate the amount of the charitable contribution deduction.[30]

EXAMPLE C13-38 ▶ Ahmed, a widower, dies with a gross estate of $6 million. Ahmed wills State University $1 million and the residue of his estate to his children. Under state law, death taxes are payable from the residue. Ahmed's estate receives a charitable contribution deduction for $1 million because here the estate taxes are charged against the children's share (the residue). ◀

SPLIT-INTEREST TRANSFERS. If the decedent's will provides for a split-interest transfer (i.e., a transfer of interests to both an individual and a charitable organization), the rules concerning whether a charitable contribution deduction is available are very technical. Basically, the rules are the same as for gift tax purposes.

EXAMPLE C13-39 ▶ Jane dies in the current year with a gross estate of $2.5 million. Under Sec. 2036, Jane's gross estate includes her personal residence, valued at $350,000. She gave City Art Museum a remainder interest in the residence in 1990 but retained the right to live there rent-free for the rest of her life. Upon Jane's death, no other individuals have an interest in the residence. Jane received an income tax deduction in 1990 for the value of the remainder interest and incurred no gift tax liability. Her estate receives a $350,000 charitable contribution deduction.

Her lifetime transfer triggers no added estate tax cost. The residence is included in her gross estate, but the inclusion is a wash because of the estate tax charitable contribution deduction claimed for the value of the residence. ◀

MARITAL DEDUCTION

The fourth category of deductions is the marital deduction for certain property passing to the decedent's surviving spouse.[31] For estates of decedents dying after 1981, the marital deduction is unlimited. Thus, the decedent's estate does not owe any federal estate taxes if all the items includible in the gross estate (or all items except an amount equal to the exemption equivalent) pass to the surviving spouse.[32] If the surviving spouse is not a U.S. citizen, however, a marital deduction is not available unless the decedent's property passes to a special trust called a qualified domestic trust.

TAX STRATEGY TIP

The marital deduction defers the estate tax until the death of the surviving spouse and avoids liquidity problems when the first spouse dies. Moreover, the surviving spouse can reduce the overall estate tax through personal consumption and a lifetime gifting program.

The marital deduction provides equal treatment for decedents of common law and community property states. As mentioned in Chapter C12, marital property is treated differently under each type of state law. In community property states, for example, a large portion of the assets acquired after a couple marries constitutes community property (i.e., property owned equally by each spouse). On the other hand, in common law states, one spouse may own the majority of the assets acquired after marriage. Thus, with no marital deduction, the progressive estate tax rates could cause the combined estate tax liability to be higher for a couple living in a noncommunity property state. Nevertheless, since 1981, a marital deduction has been available even to decedents who own nothing but community property.

Only certain transfers to the surviving spouse are eligible for the marital deduction. The estate does not receive a marital deduction unless the interest conveyed to the surviving spouse will be subject to either the estate tax in the recipient spouse's estate or to the gift

---

[30] The simultaneous equation problem generally does not occur if a charity receives a bequest of a specific dollar amount. See Reg. Sec. 20.2055-3 for a discussion of death taxes payable from charitable transfers.

[31] Sec. 2056.

[32] Some states have not adopted an unlimited marital deduction; therefore, some estates may owe state death taxes even though no federal liability would otherwise exist. Passage of substantial sums to a state as taxes will reduce the amount passing to the spouse as a marital deduction and can cause federal taxes to be owed.

tax if transferred while the surviving spouse is alive. In other words, the surviving spouse generally can escape transfer taxation on the transferred property only by consuming it.

The following three tests must be met before an interest qualifies for the marital deduction:

- The property must be included in the decedent's gross estate.
- The property must pass to the recipient spouse in a qualifying manner.
- The interest conveyed must not be a nondeductible terminable interest.

TEST 1: INCLUSION IN THE GROSS ESTATE. No property passing to the surviving spouse is eligible for the marital deduction unless the property is included in the decedent's gross estate. The reason for this rule is obvious: Assets excluded from the gross estate cannot generate a deduction.

EXAMPLE C13-40 ▶ Gail is insured under a life insurance policy for which her husband, Al, is the beneficiary. Gail's sister always had the incidents of ownership in the policy. Gail held the title to the personal residence in which she and Al lived. She willed the residence to Al, and the residence qualifies for the marital deduction. Even though the insurance proceeds are payable to Al, Gail's estate receives no marital deduction for the insurance. The policy is excluded from Gail's gross estate because she had no incidents of ownership, her estate was not the beneficiary, and the policy was not transferred within three years of her death. ◀

TEST 2: THE PASSING REQUIREMENT. Property is not eligible for the marital deduction unless it passes to the decedent's spouse in a qualifying manner. According to Sec. 2056(c), property is deemed to pass from one spouse to the other if the surviving spouse receives the property because of

- A bequest or devise under the decedent's will
- An inheritance resulting from the decedent dying intestate
- Dower or curtesy rights
- An earlier transfer from the decedent
- Right of survivorship
- An appointment by the decedent under a general power of appointment or in default of appointment
- A designation as the beneficiary of a life insurance policy on the decedent's life

In addition, a surviving spouse's interest in a retirement benefit plan is considered to have passed from the decedent to the survivor to the extent the retirement benefits are included in the gross estate.[33]

TEST 3: THE TERMINABLE INTEREST RULE. The last statutory test requires that the recipient-spouse's interest *not* be classified as a nondeductible terminable interest.[34] A terminable interest is one that ceases with the passage of time or the occurrence of some event. Some terminable interests qualify for the marital deduction, however, because only *nondeductible* terminable interests fail to generate a marital deduction. Nondeductible terminable interests have the following features:

- An interest in the property must pass or have passed from the decedent to a person other than the surviving spouse, and such person must have paid less than adequate consideration in money or money's worth.
- The other person may possess or enjoy any part of the property after the termination of the surviving spouse's interest.

Thus, if the decedent makes a transfer granting the surviving spouse the right to receive all the income annually for life and a general power of appointment over the property, the property is eligible for the marital deduction. As discussed below, as a result of

[33] Reg. Sec. 20.2056(e)-1(a)(6).

[34] Nondeductible terminable interests also are precluded from eligibility for the marital deduction for gift tax purposes.

the QTIP provisions a marital deduction is available for certain transfers that otherwise would be disqualified under the nondeductible terminable interest rule.

EXAMPLE C13-41 ▶ At the time of Louis's death, he wills a copyright with a ten-year remaining life to his wife, Tina, age 42. His will also sets up a trust for the benefit of Tina, whom he entitles to receive all of the income semiannually until the earlier of her remarriage or her death. Upon Tina's remarriage or death, the trust property is to be distributed to the couple's children or their estates. Both the copyright and the trust are terminable interests. The copyright is eligible for the marital deduction because it is not a nondeductible terminable interest; the copyright simply ends at the expiration of its legal life. No person other than Tina receives an interest in the copyright. No marital deduction is available for the trust because it is a nondeductible terminable interest. Upon the termination of Tina's interest, the children will possess the property, and they receive their interests from Louis without paying adequate consideration. ◀

SELF-STUDY QUESTION

A decedent, by will, creates a trust with income to the surviving spouse for 25 years, the remainder to their children. The surviving spouse's life expectancy is 16 years. Does the property qualify for the marital deduction?

ANSWER

The property does not qualify because the surviving spouse's interest terminates at the end of 25 years. The spouse's shorter life expectancy is irrelevant.

QTIP TRANSFERS. Section 2056(b)(7) authorizes a marital deduction for transfers of qualified terminable interest property (called QTIP transfers). The QTIP provisions are somewhat revolutionary compared with earlier law because they allow a marital deduction in situations where the recipient spouse is not entitled to designate which parties eventually receive the property.

Qualified terminable interest property is defined as property that passes from the decedent, in which the surviving spouse has a qualifying income interest for life, and to which an election applies. A spouse has a qualifying income interest for life if the following are true:

- He or she is entitled to all the income from the property, payable at least annually.
- No person has a power to appoint any portion of the property to anyone other than the surviving spouse unless the power cannot be exercised during the spouse's lifetime (e.g., it is exercisable only at or after the death of the surviving spouse).

SELF-STUDY QUESTION

How does the donor spouse or decedent spouse who establishes a QTIP trust control the disposition of the trust corpus?

ANSWER

The donor or decedent spouse states in the trust instrument or in his or her will who will receive the remainder interest on the death of the recipient spouse.

Claiming the marital deduction with respect to QTIP transfers is not mandatory, and partial elections also are allowed. In the event the executor elects to claim a marital deduction for all the QTIP transfer, the marital deduction is for the entire amount of the QTIP transfer. In other words, the deduction is not limited to the value of the surviving spouse's life estate.

If the marital deduction is elected in the first spouse's estate, the property is taxed in the surviving spouse's estate under Sec. 2044 or is subject to the gift tax in such spouse's hands if disposed of during the spouse's lifetime.[35] Thus, as with other interspousal transfers, the QTIP provisions allow a postponement of the taxable event until the second spouse dies or disposes of the interest by gift. If the taxable event is postponed, the property is valued at its FMV as of the date the second spouse transfers the property by gift or at death. See the Tax Planning Considerations section of this chapter for a discussion of planning opportunities (including partial QTIP elections) with the marital deduction.

EXAMPLE C13-42 ▶ Tom died in 1995, survived by his wife, Mary, who lives until the current year. Tom's will called for setting up a $1 million trust from which Mary would receive all the income quarterly for the rest of her life. Upon Mary's death, the property is to be distributed to Tom's children by a previous marriage. At Mary's death, the trust assets are valued at $1.3 million. If Tom's executor elects to claim a marital deduction, Tom's estate receives a $1 million marital deduction. Section 2044 includes $1.3 million in Mary's gross estate. If Tom's executor forgoes electing the marital deduction, Mary's gross estate excludes the value of the trust. The trust assets will be taxed in the estate of one of the spouses. ◀

ADDITIONAL COMMENT

Refer to Example C13-42. The executor may elect QTIP status for less than the entire property in the trust. For example, the executor might elect QTIP treatment for only 60% of the $1 million placed in the trust. If this is done, on Mary's death, 60% of $1.3 million, or $780,000, is included in her gross estate.

DEDUCTION FOR CERTAIN INTERESTS IN FAMILY-OWNED BUSINESSES

In 1998, Congress enacted Sec. 2057 to provide a deduction for certain family-owned businesses. To qualify for this deduction, the estate must meet many requirements, including concentrated ownership and material participation in the business by the decedent or

---

[35] Section 2519 states that, if a recipient spouse disposes of a qualifying income interest for life for which the donor or the executor elected a marital deduction under the QTIP rules, the recipient spouse is treated as having made a gift of everything except the qualifying income interest. Under the generic gift rules of Sec. 2511, the gift of the income interest is treated as a gift.

a family member. In the 2001 Act, Congress repealed this deduction for estates of decedents dying after 2003. Because of the limited applicability and impending repeal, this deduction is not discussed further.

COMPUTATION OF TAX LIABILITY

OBJECTIVE 5

Calculate the estate tax liability

As mentioned earlier, the estate tax base is the aggregate of the decedent's taxable estate and his or her adjusted taxable gifts. Figure C13-1 earlier in this chapter illustrates how these two concepts are combined in the estate tax formula.

TAXABLE ESTATE AND TAX BASE

The gross estate's value is reduced by the deductions to arrive at the amount of the taxable estate. Under the unification provisions effective after 1976, the estate tax base consists of the taxable estate plus the adjusted taxable gifts, defined as *all* taxable gifts made *after 1976 other than* gifts included in the gross estate. The addition of the adjusted taxable gifts to the estate tax base may cause an estate to be taxed at a higher marginal tax rate. If the decedent elects gift splitting (discussed in Chapter 12), the decedent's adjusted taxable gifts equal the amount of the taxable gifts the individual is deemed to have made after applying the gift-splitting provisions. Adjusted taxable gifts can arise from consenting to gift splitting, even though the decedent never actually gives away any property.

Adjusted taxable gifts are valued at date-of-gift values; therefore, any post-gift appreciation is exempt from the transfer taxes. The estate tax computations for decedents who never made gifts exceeding the excludable amount reflect no adjusted taxable gifts.

SELF-STUDY QUESTION

Verda died penniless in 2002. Because of consenting to gift splitting, her taxable gifts made after 1976 were $750,000. She paid $55,500 of gift taxes on these gifts. What is her unified tax base?

ANSWER

Her unified tax base is $750,000, the amount of her lifetime taxable gifts. Note that the gifts are valued at what they were worth on the date of the gift.

TENTATIVE TAX AND REDUCTION FOR POST-1976 GIFT TAXES

The tentative tax is computed on the estate tax base, which is the sum of the taxable estate and the adjusted taxable gifts, if any.[36] The unified transfer tax rates are found in Sec. 2001(c) and are reproduced on the inside back cover. The tentative tax is reduced by the decedent's post-1976 gift taxes. In determining the tax on post-1976 taxable gifts, the effect of gift splitting is taken into consideration. That is, the amount of the post-1976 gift taxes is usually the levy imposed on the taxable gifts the decedent is deemed to have made after applying any gift-splitting election.

If the tax rates change between the time of the gift and the time of death, the subtraction for gift taxes equals the amount of gift taxes that would have been payable on post-1976 gifts had the rate schedule applicable in the year of death been in effect in the year of the gift. The only "as if" computation is for the gross tax amount; the unified credit actually used on the gift tax return is subtracted to determine the amount of gift tax that would have been payable at current rates.

SELF-STUDY QUESTION

Refer to the previous self-study question. What is the amount of the unified tax before credits? After credits?

ANSWER

The unified tax before credits is $248,300. This tax is reduced by the unified credit of $345,800 and by post-1976 gift taxes of $55,500, which leaves zero tax due.

UNIFIED CREDIT

The excess of the tentative tax over the post-1976 gift taxes is reduced by the unified credit of Sec. 2010. The amount of this credit has changed over the years and will increase through 2009; in 2002 it is $345,800 (see inside back cover). With a credit of $345,800, the tax on a $1 million tax base is completely eliminated. The unified credit never generates a refund; the most relief it can provide is to eliminate an estate's federal estate tax liability.

Section 2010(c) provides that the unified credit otherwise available for estate tax purposes must be reduced because of certain pre-1977 gifts. Before 1977, a $30,000 lifetime exemption was available for the gift tax. Donors could claim some or all of this exemption whenever they so desired. For post-1976 years, Congress repealed the exemption and replaced it with the unified credit. If the decedent claimed any portion of the $30,000

---

[36] Sec. 2001(b).

exemption against gifts made after September 8, 1976 and before January 1, 1977, the unified credit is reduced by 20% of the exemption claimed.

EXAMPLE C13-43 ▶ Carl dies in 2002 with a tax base of $2 million. In October 1976, Carl made his first taxable gift. Carl claimed the $30,000 exemption to reduce the amount of his taxable gifts. Thus, Carl's $345,800 unified credit is reduced by $6,000 (0.20 × $30,000). If Carl claimed the exemption by making a gift on or before September 8, 1976, his estate would be entitled to the full $345,800 credit. ◀

OTHER CREDITS

The IRC authorizes four additional credits: a state death tax credit, a gift tax credit on pre-1977 gifts, a credit for another decedent's estate taxes paid on prior transfers, and a credit on foreign death taxes. The last three credits apply less often than do the unified credit and the state death tax credit. These credits, like the unified credit, cannot exceed the amount of the estate tax actually owed.

STATE DEATH TAX CREDIT. All states levy some form of death tax: an inheritance tax, an estate tax, or both. Many states have enacted a simple system whereby the state death tax liability equals the credit for state death taxes allowed on the federal estate tax return.

The maximum credit allowable on the federal return is calculated in accordance with the table contained in Sec. 2011(b), reproduced in Appendix G. As a result of the 2001 Act, the credit for state death taxes will be reduced by multiplying the amount determined from the table by a specified percentage, which is 75% in 2002, 50% in 2003, and 25% in 2004. Beginning in 2005, the credit is replaced with a deduction. Thus, with the demise of the credit, in jurisdictions imposing a state death tax equal to the credit allowed on the federal return for state death taxes, no state death tax will be owed after 2004 *unless* the jurisdictions change their tax rules. To claim the maximum credit, the estate must have paid state death taxes equal to or greater than the maximum credit allowed by Sec. 2011.

The Sec. 2011(b) calculations are based on the size of the decedent's "adjusted taxable estate," which according to Sec. 2011 means the taxable estate reduced by $60,000. Thus, adjusted taxable gifts have no impact on the state death tax credit. Section 2011(f) limits the state death tax credit to the amount of the estate tax (after reduction for the unified credit).

EXAMPLE C13-44 ▶ John dies in 2002 with a taxable estate of $3.6 million and adjusted taxable gifts of $1 million. John's estate pays $250,000 of state death taxes. John's adjusted taxable estate is $3,540,000 ($3,600,000 − $60,000), and the maximum calculated from the Sec. 2011(b) table in Appendix G is $238,800. The estate's maximum credit is $179,100 (0.75 × $238,800). ◀

EXAMPLE C13-45 ▶ Assume the same facts as in Example C13-44 except that John's estate pays state death taxes of $170,000. The credit for state death taxes is limited to the smaller of the maximum state death tax credit under Sec. 2011 ($179,100) or the actual death taxes paid ($170,000), or $170,000. ◀

CREDIT FOR PRE-1977 GIFT TAXES. Section 2012(a) authorizes a credit for gift taxes paid by the decedent on pre-1977 gifts that must be included in the gross estate. Remember that Sec. 2001(b)(2) allows a reduction for gift taxes paid on post-1976 gifts, but the IRC does not refer to this item as a credit. The following transaction involves a situation in which the credit for pre-1977 gift taxes applies.

EXAMPLE C13-46 ▶ In 1975, Yuji created a trust from which he is to receive the income for life and his son, Yuji, Jr., is to receive the remainder. Yuji paid a gift tax on the gift of the remainder. Upon Yuji's death in the current year, the date-of-death value of the trust's assets is included in his estate under Sec. 2036. Yuji's estate receives a credit for some or all of his 1975 gift taxes. ◀

In general, the credit for pre-1977 gift taxes equals the amount of gift taxes paid with respect to transfers included in the gross estate. Because of a ceiling rule, however, the amount of the credit sometimes is lower than the amount of gift taxes paid. A discussion of the credit ceiling computation is beyond the scope of this text.

CREDIT FOR TAX ON PRIOR TRANSFERS. The credit available under Sec. 2013 for the estate taxes paid on prior transfers reduces the cost of having property taxed in more than one estate in quick succession. Without this credit, the overall tax cost could be quite severe if the legatee dies soon after the original decedent. The credit applies if the person who transfers the property (i.e., the transferor-decedent) to the decedent in question (i.e., the transferee-decedent) dies no more than ten years before, or within two years after, the date of the transferee-decedent's death. The potential credit is the smaller of the federal estate tax of the transferor-decedent attributable to the transferred interest or the federal estate tax of the transferee-decedent attributable to the transferred interest.

To determine the final credit, the potential credit is multiplied by a percentage that varies inversely with the period of time separating the two dates of death. If the transferor dies no more than two years before or after the transferee, the credit percentage is 100%. As specified in Sec. 2013(a), the other percentages are as follows:

Number of Years by Which Transferor's Death Precedes the Transferee's Death	*Credit Percentage*
More than 2, but not more than 4	80
More than 4, but not more than 6	60
More than 6, but not more than 8	40
More than 8, but not more than 10	20

The following two examples illustrate situations in which the credit for the taxes paid on prior transfers applies.

EXAMPLE C13-47 ▶ Mary died on March 1, 1997. All of Mary's property passed to Debra, her daughter. Debra dies on June 1, 2002. All of Debra's property passes to her son. Both Mary's and Debra's estates pay federal estate taxes. Debra's estate is entitled to a credit for a percentage of some, or all, of the taxes paid by Mary's estate. Because Mary's death preceded Debra's death by five years and three months, the credit for the tax paid on prior transfers is 60% of the potential credit. ◀

EXAMPLE C13-48 ▶ Ed died on May 7, 2001. One of the items included in Ed's estate is a life insurance policy on Sam's life. Sam had given Ed all his incidents of ownership in this policy on December 13, 2000. Sam dies on June 15, 2002, which is within three years of making a gift of the insurance policy on his own life. The policy is included in Sam's gross estate under Sec. 2035. Because Sam dies within two years of Ed's death, Ed's estate is entitled to a credit for 100% of the potential credit and an amended return must be filed to claim this credit. ◀

SELF-STUDY QUESTION

What is the effect of the maximum credit provision for the foreign death tax credit?

ANSWER

The effect is to tax the property located in the foreign country at the higher of the U.S. estate tax rate or the foreign death tax rate.

FOREIGN DEATH TAX CREDIT. Under Sec. 2014, the estate is entitled to a credit for some or all of the death taxes paid to a foreign country for property located in that foreign country and included in the gross estate. The maximum credit is the smaller of the foreign death tax attributable to the property located in the foreign country that imposed the tax or the federal estate tax attributable to the property located in the foreign country and taxed by such country.

COMPREHENSIVE ILLUSTRATION

The following comprehensive illustration demonstrates the computation of the estate tax liability.

BACKGROUND DATA

Herman Estes dies on October 13, 2001. Herman, an Ohio resident, is survived by his widow, Ann, and three adult children. During his lifetime, Herman made three gifts, as follows:

- In 1974, he gave his son Billy $103,000 cash. Herman claimed the $30,000 exemption (then available) and a $3,000 annual exclusion available then. The taxable gift was $70,000.

- In 1978, he gave his daughter, Dotty, $203,000 cash. He claimed a $3,000 annual exclusion available then and made a $200,000 taxable gift on which he paid a $28,000 gift tax.
- In December 1998, he gave his son, Johnny, land then worth $490,000. Herman claimed a $10,000 annual exclusion and made a $480,000 taxable gift on which he claimed the available unified credit, and he paid a $2,650 gift tax. On October 13, 2001, the land is worth $550,000.

Property discovered after Herman's death appears below. All amounts represent date-of-death values.

- Checking account containing $19,250.
- Savings account containing $75,000.
- Land worth $400,000 held in the names of Herman and Ann, joint tenants with right of survivorship. Herman provided all the consideration to buy the land in January 1993.
- Life insurance policy 123-A with a face value of $200,000. Herman had incidents of ownership; Johnny is the beneficiary.
- A personal residence titled in Herman's name worth $325,000.
- Stock in Ajax Corporation worth $600,000.
- Qualified pension plan to which Herman's employer made 60% of the contributions and Herman made 40%. Ann is to receive a lump-sum distribution of $240,000.
- A trust created under the will of Herman's mother, Amelia, who died in 1986. Herman was entitled to receive all the income quarterly for life. In his will, Herman could appoint the trust assets to such of his descendants as he desired. The trust assets are valued at $375,000.

At his death, Herman owes a $25,200 bank loan, including accrued interest. Balances due on his various charge cards total $6,500. Herman's funeral expenses are $15,000, and his administration expenses are estimated to be $70,000. Assume that the maximum tax savings will occur by deducting the administration expenses on the estate tax return.

Herman's will contains the following provisions:

- "To my wife, Ann, I leave my residence, my savings account, and $10,000 from my checking account."
- "I leave $200,000 of property in trust with First Bank as trustee. My wife, Ann, is to receive all the income from this trust fund quarterly for the rest of her life. Upon Ann's death, the trust property is to be divided equally among our three children."
- "To the American Cancer Society I leave $10,000."
- "I appoint the property in the trust created by my mother, Amelia Estes, to my daughter, Dotty."
- "The residue of my estate is to be divided equally between my sons, Johnny and Billy."

CALCULATION OF TAX LIABILITY

Table C13-3 illustrates the computation of Herman's estate tax liability. These same facts are used for the sample Estate Tax Return (Form 706) included in Appendix B. For illustration purposes, it is assumed that the executor elects to claim the marital deduction on the QTIP trust and that Herman's state death taxes equal the maximum federal credit for state death taxes.

Note that several factors affect the computation set out in Table C13-3:

- Herman had only a special power of appointment over the assets in the trust created by his mother because he could will the property only to his descendants. Therefore, the trust property is not included in his estate.

▼ **TABLE C13-3**
Comprehensive Estate Tax Illustration

Gross estate:	
Checking account (Sec. 2033)	$ 19,250
Savings account (Sec. 2033)	75,000
Land held in joint tenancy with wife (0.50 × $400,000) (Sec. 2040)	200,000
Life insurance (Sec. 2042)	200,000
Personal residence (Sec. 2033)	325,000
Stock (Sec. 2033)	600,000
Qualified pension plan (Sec. 2039)	240,000
Gross-up for gift tax paid on 1998 gift (Sec. 2035)	2,650
Total gross estate	$1,661,900
Minus:	
Debts (Sec. 2053):	
Bank loan, including accrued interest	(25,200)
Charge cards	(6,500)
Funeral expenses (Sec. 2053)	(15,000)
Administration expenses (Sec. 2053)	(70,000)
Marital deduction (Sec. 2056):	
Residence	(325,000)
Checking account	(10,000)
Savings account	(75,000)
QTIP trust	(200,000)
Land	(200,000)
Qualified pension plan	(240,000)
Charitable contribution deduction (Sec. 2055)	(10,000)
Total reductions to gross estate	($1,176,700)
Taxable estate	$ 485,200
Plus adjusted taxable gifts (Sec. 2001(b)):	
1978 taxable gifts	200,000[a]
1998 taxable gifts	480,000[a]
Estate tax base	$1,165,200
Tentative tax on tax base (Sec. 2001)	$ 413,532
Minus:	
Reduction for post-1976 gift taxes (Sec. 2001(b))	(30,650)[b]
Unified credit (Sec. 2010)	(220,550)
State death tax credit (Sec. 2011)	(9,526)[c]
Estate tax payable	$ 152,806

[a] Valued at date-of-gift fair market values.
[b] $28,000 (for 1978) + $2,650 (for 1998) = $30,650.
[c] This figure is calculated based on the table reproduced in Appendix G and a $425,200 adjusted taxable estate.

- Assets that pass to the surviving spouse outside the will, such as by survivorship and by beneficiary designation, can qualify for the marital deduction.
- Adjusted taxable gifts (added to the taxable estate) include only post-1976 taxable gifts.
- The estate tax payable is not reduced by pre-1977 gift taxes unless the gifted property is included in the gross estate.
- Because the highest marginal income tax rate for the estate is less than the 41% marginal estate tax rate and an estate tax liability is owed (even with the available credits), administration expenses should be deducted on the estate tax return.

LIQUIDITY CONCERNS

OBJECTIVE 6

Identify tax provisions that alleviate liquidity problems

Liquidity is one of the major problems facing individuals planning their estates and executors eventually managing the estates. Individuals often use life insurance to help address this problem. In general, the entire amount of the estate tax liability is due nine months after the decedent's death. Certain provisions, however, allow the executor to pay some or all of the estate tax liability at a later date. Deferral of part or all of the estate tax payments and three other provisions aimed at alleviating a liquidity problem are discussed below.

DEFERRAL OF PAYMENT OF ESTATE TAXES

REASONABLE CAUSE. Section 6161(a)(1) authorizes the Secretary of the Treasury to extend the payment date for the estate taxes for a *reasonable period,* defined as a period of not longer than 12 months. Moreover, the Secretary of the Treasury may extend the payment date for a maximum period of ten years if the executor shows reasonable cause for not being able to pay some, or all, of the estate tax liability on the regular date.[37]

Whenever the executor pays a portion of the estate tax after the regular due date, the estate owes interest on the portion of the tax for which it postpones payment. In general, the interest rate, which is governed by Sec. 6621, is the same as that applicable to underpayments. The interest rate on underpayments potentially fluctuates quarterly with changes in the rate paid on short-term U.S. Treasury obligations.[38]

REMAINDER OR REVERSIONARY INTERESTS. If the gross estate includes a relatively large remainder or reversionary interest, liquidity problems could result if the estate has to pay the entire estate tax liability soon after the decedent's death. For example, the estate might include a remainder interest in an asset in which a healthy, 30-year-old person has a life estate. The estate might not gain possession of the assets until many years after the decedent's death. Section 6163 permits the executor to elect to postpone payment of the tax attributable to a remainder or reversionary interest until six months after the other interests terminate, which in the example would be after the person currently age 30 died. In addition, upon being convinced of reasonable cause, the Secretary of the Treasury may grant an additional extension of not more than three years.

TAX STRATEGY TIP

A person who owns a substantial interest in a small business might choose to gift property other than the business interest. He or she may want to retain the business interest in his or her estate so that his or her estate will qualify for the five-year deferral, ten-installment option of Sec. 6166. See Tax Planning Considerations for further details.

INTERESTS IN CLOSELY HELD BUSINESSES. Section 6166 authorizes the executor to pay a portion of the estate tax in as many as ten annual installments in certain situations. Executors may elect to apply Sec. 6166 if

- The gross estate includes an interest in a closely held business, and
- The value of the closely held business exceeds 35% of the value of the adjusted gross estate.

Closely held businesses are defined as proprietorships and partnerships or corporations having no more than 45 owners.[39] If a corporation or partnership has more than 45 owners, it can be classified as closely held if the decedent's gross estate includes 20% or more of the capital interest (in the partnership) or 20% or more of the value of the voting stock (in the corporation).[40]

The adjusted gross estate is defined as the gross estate less *allowable* Sec. 2053 and 2054 deductions. Consequently, in determining whether the estate meets the 35% requirement, all administration expenses and casualty and theft losses are subtracted, regardless of whether the executor elects to deduct them on the estate tax return or the estate's income tax return.

Once the election is chosen, the following restrictions apply:

- The portion of the estate tax that can be paid in installments is the ratio of the value of the closely held business interest to the value of the adjusted gross estate.

---

[37] Sec. 6161(a)(2).
[38] Sec. 6621. The interest rate is discussed in Chapter C15.
[39] Sec. 6166(b)(1).
[40] Ibid.

- The first of the ten allowable installments generally is not due until five years after the due date for the return. (This provision defers the last payment for as many as 15 years.)
- Interest on the tax due is payable annually, even during the first five years.

Some or all of the installment payments may accrue interest at a rate of only 2%. The maximum amount of deferred tax to which the 2% rate applies is (1) the tax on the total of $1 million of value (as indexed) and the exemption equivalent amount less (2) the unified credit. In no event, however, may the amount exceed the tax postponed under Sec. 6166.[41] The $1 million amount is indexed for inflation with inflation adjustments rounded to the next lowest $10,000; for 2002, this amount is $1.1 million. The interest rate on any additional deferred tax is 45% of the rate applicable to underpayments. The downside is the interest paid is not deductible as interest expense on the estate's income tax return or as an administrative expense on the estate tax return.

EXAMPLE C13-49 ▶ Frank dies on March 1, 2002. Frank's gross estate, which includes a proprietorship interest valued at $1 million, is $2.6 million. The executor deducts all $100,000 of the potential Sec. 2053 and 2054 deductions on the estate tax return. Frank has no marital or charitable contribution deductions and makes no taxable gifts. Frank's adjusted gross estate, taxable estate, and tax base are $2.5 million. His estate tax payable is $680,000 ($1,025,800 − $348,800). Frank's closely held business interest makes up 40% ($1,000,000 ÷ $2,500,000) of his adjusted gross estate.

Thus, $272,000 (0.40 × $680,000) may be paid in ten equal annual installments. The first installment payment is due on December 1, 2007. The 2% interest rate potentially applies to $484,000 [$829,800, the tax on $2,100,000 ($1,100,000 + $1,000,000), minus the unified credit of $345,800] of deferred tax liability. However, because this estate's postponed tax is only $272,000, all the interest accrues at the 2% rate. ◀

STOCK REDEMPTIONS TO PAY DEATH TAXES

Sometimes an estate's major asset is stock in a closely held corporation. In this situation, the corporation may have to redeem some of the corporate stock to provide the estate sufficient liquidity to pay death taxes. As discussed in Chapter C4, stock redemptions generally receive sale or exchange treatment only if they meet certain requirements under Sec. 302, such as being substantially disproportionate or involving a complete termination of the shareholder's interest. Without exchange treatment, the redeemed shareholder (e.g., the estate) recognizes a dividend equal to the redemption proceeds rather than a capital gain equal to the difference between the redemption proceeds and the stock's adjusted basis. To alleviate the ordinary income problem upon a shareholder's death, Sec. 303 allows the estate to treat a redemption as an exchange even if it does not satisfy the Sec. 302 requirements. This treatment minimizes any gain recognized because the stock's adjusted basis, which is subtracted from the redemption proceeds, is stepped up to its FMV upon the decedent's death.

To qualify for Sec. 303 treatment, the stock in the corporation redeeming the shares must make up more than 35% of the value of the decedent's gross estate, less any *allowable* Sec. 2053 and 2054 deductions. The maximum amount of redemption proceeds eligible for exchange treatment is the total of the estate's death taxes and funeral and administration expenses, regardless of whether they are deducted on the estate tax return or the estate's income tax return.

SPECIAL USE VALUATION OF FARM REAL PROPERTY

In 1976, Congress became concerned that farms sometimes had to be sold to generate funds to pay estate taxes. This situation was attributable, in part, to the FMV of farm

[41] Sec. 6601(j).

SELF-STUDY QUESTION

Why might an heir to farmland not want an estate to use the special valuation method of Sec. 2032A?

ANSWER

The heir may contemplate selling the land and prefer the higher basis he or she would get if FMV is used rather than the special farmland value, especially if the estate taxes are payable out of the residual estate and the heir does not share in that residual.

land in many areas being relatively high, perhaps because of suburban housing being built nearby. Congress enacted Sec. 2032A, which allows a property used for farming or in a trade or business other than farming to be valued using a formula approach that attempts to value the property at what it is worth for farming purposes. The lowest valuation permitted is $750,000 less than the property's FMV, but the $750,000 is indexed after 1998 with adjustments rounded to the next lowest $10,000. In 2002, the indexed amount is $820,000.

The estate must meet a number of requirements before the executor can elect the special valuation rules.[42] Moreover, if during the ten-year period after the decedent's death the new owner of the property disposes of it or no longer uses it as a farm, in general, an additional tax equal to the estate tax savings that arose from the lower Sec. 2032A valuation is levied.

GENERATION-SKIPPING TRANSFER TAX

The Tax Reform Act of 1976 enacted a third transfer tax—the generation-skipping transfer tax (GSTT)—to fill a void in the gift and estate tax structure. In 1986, Congress repealed the original GSTT retroactive to its original effective date and replaced it with a revised GSTT. The revised GSTT generally applies to *inter vivos* transfers made after September 25, 1985 and transfers at death made after October 22, 1986.

For years, a popular estate planning technique, especially among the very wealthy, involved giving individuals in several generations an interest in the same property. For example, a decedent might set up a testamentary trust creating successive life estates for a child and a grandchild and a remainder interest for a great grandchild. Under this arrangement, an estate tax would be imposed at the death of the person establishing the trust but not again until the great grandchild's death. The GSTT's purpose is to ensure that some form of transfer taxation is imposed one time a generation. It accomplishes its purpose by subjecting transfers that escape gift or estate taxation for one or more generations to the GSTT.

The GSTT is levied at a flat rate, the highest estate tax rate.[43] The tax applies to direct skip gifts and bequests and to taxable terminations of and taxable distributions from generation-skipping transfers. A **generation-skipping transfer** involves a disposition that

- ▶ Provides interests for more than one generation of beneficiaries who are in a younger generation than the transferor, or
- ▶ Provides an interest solely for a person two or more generations younger than the transferor.[44]

The recipient must be a skip person, a person two or more generations younger than the decedent (or the donor). For family members, generation assignments are made according to the family tree. Transfers to skip persons outside of a trust are known as direct skips because they skip one or more generations.

EXAMPLE C13-50 ▶ Tom transfers an asset directly to Tom, III, his grandson. This is a direct skip type of generation-skipping transfer because the transferee (Tom, III) is two generations younger than the transferor (Tom). ◀

The termination of an interest in a generation-skipping arrangement is known as a taxable termination.[45] This event triggers imposition of the GSTT. The tax is levied on the before-tax amount transferred, and the trustee pays the tax.

---

[42] For example, the farm real and personal property must make up at least 50% of the adjusted value of the gross estate, and the farm real property must make up 25% or more of the adjusted value of the gross estate.

[43] Sec. 2641.

[44] Sec. 2611.

[45] Sec. 2612(a).

WHAT WOULD YOU DO IN THIS SITUATION?

You are a CPA specializing in wealth transfer taxation. You have established your practice in Aspen, Colorado because there is a lot of wealth situated in that ski resort. You client is a long-time resident of Aspen, and his health has recently taken a downhill turn. His doctor told him to consider putting his affairs in order because he will probably not ski any moguls for more than six months.

Your client is a merchant who owns a number of assets with FMVs totaling $1.4 million under some estimates. His largest single asset is his Victorian era store building situated in the desirable and exclusive West End of Aspen. Based on comparable fair market sales in the area, your client's building appears to be worth approximately $760,000 in the current real estate market. Because your client is in poor health, he does not use all of the store space and occasionally rents out some space in his building to vendors for selling crafts and gifts. During the ski season, the full price fair market rental value of the space would be over $1,000 per week. Your client's only son has indicated that he is not interested in moving to Aspen. The son is independently wealthy, does not really need to liquidate the building, and plans to continue the rental practices initiated by his father.

You are interested in saving your client some estate taxes. The estate probably will have no deductions. Would you propose to him that this asset be listed in the estate as Special Use Value property pursuant to Sec. 2032A? Would it be ethical to propose a valuation method based on the historical income generated by this property for the estate tax return of your client? Using the historical income stream, the capitalized value would be $350,000. With this value, his estate would be lower by $410,000 and no tax would be owed because of an overall valuation of under $1 million (in 2002) for the entire estate.

EXAMPLE C13-51 ▶ Tom creates a trust with income payable to his son, Tom, Jr., for life and a remainder interest distributable to Tom, III, upon the death of Tom, Jr. (his father). This is a generation-skipping transfer because Tom, Jr., and Tom, III, are one and two generations younger, respectively, than the transferor (Tom). A taxable termination occurs when Tom, Jr. dies. ◀

EXAMPLE C13-52 ▶ The trust in Example C13-51 is worth $2 million when Tom, Jr. dies in 2002. The amount of the taxable termination is $2 million. The tax is $1 million (0.50 × $2,000,000). The trustee pays the tax and distributes the $1 million of remaining assets to the beneficiary. ◀

In the case of a direct skip, the amount subject to the GSTT is the value of the property received by the transferee.[46] The transferor is liable for the tax. If the direct skip occurs *inter vivos*, the GSTT paid by the transferor is treated as an additional transfer subject to the gift tax.[47] As a result, the total transfer tax liability (GSTT plus gift tax) can exceed the value of the property received by the donee.

EXAMPLE C13-53 ▶ Susan gives $1 million to her granddaughter. Susan has used her entire unified credit and is in the 50% marginal gift tax bracket; ignore the annual exclusion. The GSTT is $500,000 (0.50 × $1,000,000). The amount subject to the gift tax is the value of the property transferred ($1 million) plus the GSTT paid ($500,000). Thus, the gift tax is $750,000 (0.50 × $1,500,000). It costs $1,250,000 ($500,000 + $750,000) to shift $1 million of property to the granddaughter. ◀

Every grantor is entitled to a $1 million exemption from the GSTT, but the exemption is indexed for inflation (with adjustments rounded to the next lowest $10,000) beginning for estates of decedents dying after 1998.[48] For 2002, the exemption is $1.1 million. The grantor elects when, and against which transfers, to apply this exemption. Appreciation on the property for which the exemption is elected is also exempt from the GSTT.

---

46 Sec. 2623.

47 Sec. 2515.

48 Sec. 2631(a).

TAX PLANNING CONSIDERATIONS

The effectiveness of many of the pre-1977 transfer tax-saving strategies was diluted by the unification of the transfer tax system in general and by the adoption of a unified rate schedule and the concept of adjusted taxable gifts in particular. To some extent, provisions that allow a higher tax base to be free of estate taxes and permit most interspousal transfers to be devoid of transfer tax consequences counterbalance unification. This section discusses various tax planning considerations that tax advisors should explore to reduce the transfer taxes applicable to a family unit.

USE OF *INTER VIVOS* GIFTS

One of the most significant strategies for reducing transfer taxes is a well-designed, long-term gift program. As long as the gifts to each donee do not exceed the per donee annual exclusion, there will be no additions to the gross estate and no adjusted taxable gifts. A donor may pass thousands of dollars of property to others free of any transfer tax consequences if he or she selects enough donees and makes gifts over a substantial number of years. If taxable gifts do occur, the donor removes the post-gift appreciation from the estate tax base. Moreover, if the donor lives more than three years after the date of the gift, the gift tax paid is removed from the gross estate.

SELF-STUDY QUESTION

What types of property should one consider gifting?

ANSWER

Give property that is expected to appreciate substantially in future years, produces substantial amounts of income, or is a family heirloom that probably will be passed from the donee to the donee's heirs and not sold.

Prospective donors should weigh the opportunities for reducing transfer taxes through the use of lifetime gifts against the income tax disadvantage of foregoing the step up in basis that occurs if the donor retains the property until death. However, unless the donee is the donor's spouse, income taxes on the income produced by the gifted property can be reduced if shifted to a donee in a lower tax bracket.

USE OF EXEMPTION EQUIVALENT

As a result of the exemption equivalent (or applicable exclusion amount), a certain amount of property—$1 million in 2002—may pass to people other than the decedent's spouse without any estate taxes being extracted therefrom. A donor can transfer property to the spouse tax-free without limit. Thus, because the spouse presumably will die before any children or grandchildren (i.e., individuals to whom people often will property), a wealthy person should contemplate leaving at least an amount equal to the exemption equivalent to people other than his or her spouse. (If one leaves this amount of property in trust, the trust is often called a credit shelter or bypass trust.) Otherwise, he or she will waste some or all of the exemption equivalent, and the property will be taxed when the surviving spouse dies.

Making full use of the exemption equivalent enables a husband and wife to transfer to third parties an aggregate of $2 million (using 2002 amounts) without incurring any estate taxes. The strategy of making gifts to an ill spouse, who is not wealthy, to keep the donee-spouse's exemption equivalent from being wasted was discussed earlier (see Chapter C12). Under this technique, the wealthier spouse makes gifts to the other spouse free of gift taxes because of the marital deduction. The recipient spouse then has an estate that can be passed tax-free to children, grandchildren, or other individuals because of the exemption equivalent.

STOP & THINK

Question: Sol made $600,000 in taxable gifts six years before his death but did not have to pay any gift tax. Sol's taxable estate (gross estate minus estate tax deductions) was $1 million. Sol died in 2002, when the gifted property was worth $825,000. Because of the exemption equivalent, is Sol's estate tax payable zero?

Solution: No. In concept, the unified credit of $345,800, which cancels out the tax on the 2002 $1 million exemption equivalent, is available only once. Calculation of Sol's estate tax payable would be as follows:

Taxable estate	$1,000,000
Plus: Adjusted taxable gifts	600,000
Estate tax base	$1,600,000
Tentative tax on estate tax base	$ 600,800
Minus:	
Post-1976 gift tax (on $600,000 gift)	-0-
Unified credit	(345,800)
Estate tax payable	$ 255,000

The $255,000 represents the tax on the incremental $600,000 (the taxable portion of Sol's estate), which, because of the progressive rates, is a higher tax than the tax on the first $1 million, the tax-free amount.

WHAT SIZE MARITAL DEDUCTION IS BEST?

To reiterate, the tax law imposes no ceiling on the amount of property eligible for the marital deduction. Even so, the availability of an unlimited marital deduction does not necessarily mean that a person should use it. From a tax perspective, wealthier people should leave an amount equal to the exemption equivalent to someone other than the spouse. Alternatively, they could leave the spouse an income interest in the exemption equivalent amount of property along with the power to invade such property for reasons of health, support, maintenance, or education. These powers do not cause an inclusion in the gross estate.

In certain circumstances, it may be preferable for an amount exceeding the exemption equivalent to pass directly to third parties. It might be beneficial for the first spouse's estate to pay some estate taxes if the surviving spouse already has substantial property and has a relatively short life expectancy, especially if the decedent spouse's assets are expected to rapidly increase in value.

EXAMPLE C13-54 ▶ Paul dies in 2002 with a $3 million gross estate and no deductions other than the marital deduction. At the time of Paul's death, his wife's life expectancy is two years. The assets she owns in the current year are estimated to be worth $6 million in two years. Paul's property is expected to increase in value by 25% during the two-year period following his death. Paul wills his wife, Jill, $1 million and his children the rest. The estate tax payable for each spouse's estate is as follows:

	Paul		*Jill*
Gross estate	$3,000,000		$7,250,000[a]
Minus: Marital deduction	(1,000,000)		–0–
Taxable estate and tax base	$2,000,000		$7,250,000
Estate tax, after unified credit[b]	$ 435,000		$2,745,000
Combined estate tax	⟶	$3,180,000	⟵

[a]$6,000,000 + (1.25 × $1,000,000) = $7,250,000.
[b]$345,800 in 2002 and $555,800 in 2004. The top rate in 2004 is 48%. ◀

EXAMPLE C13-55 ▶ Assume the same facts as in Example C13-54 except that Paul wills everything except $1 million to Jill. The estate tax payable for each spouse's estate is as follows:

	Paul		*Jill*
Gross estate	$3,000,000		$8,500,000[a]
Minus: Marital deduction	(2,000,000)		–0–
Taxable estate and tax base	$1,000,000		$8,500,000
Estate tax, after unified credit	$ –0–		$3,345,000
Combined estate tax	⟶	$3,345,000	⟵

[a]$6,000,000 + (1.25 × $2,000,000) = $8,500,000. ◀

The combined estate tax liability is $165,000 higher in Example C13-55 than in Example C13-54. However, in Example C13-55, no tax is owed upon the first spouse's death. Because the estate taxes for the second spouse's estate are not payable until a later date, their discounted present value also should be considered. Also note that, if Paul's will had created a trust eligible for QTIP treatment instead of leaving the property to Jill outright, the arrangement would have been more flexible because of the availability of partial QTIP elections.

STOP & THINK

Question: Tarik died recently at age 78. He was survived by his wife, Saliah, and several children and grandchildren. Saliah is 54 and in excellent health. Tarik's adjusted gross estate is $6.2 million, and his will leaves $1 million outright to his children and the rest to a trust for Saliah. The trust is eligible for the QTIP election. An investment advisor believes that the trust assets will likely appreciate annually at the rate of at least 10%. Name two advantages and one disadvantage of electing the marital deduction on the entire trust.

Solution: One advantage is that the tax on the trust will be deferred, perhaps for a long time, given the wife's age and health. Another advantage is that, because no tax is owed at Tarik's death, the trust assets remain intact to appreciate and produce more income for Saliah. That is, there is no current capital drain to pay transfer taxes. A disadvantage is that, because of the anticipated appreciation and the long time before Saliah's estimated death, the amount taxed in Saliah's estate will likely be much greater than the $5,200,000 Tarik willed to Saliah.

USE OF DISCLAIMERS

Because the IRC does not treat a **qualified disclaimer** as a gift, disclaimers can be valuable estate planning tools (see Chapter C12). For example, if a decedent wills all his or her property to the surviving spouse, such spouse could disclaim an amount at least equal in size to the exemption equivalent and thereby enable the decedent's estate to take full advantage of the unified credit. Alternatively, a decedent's children might disclaim some bequests if, as a result of their disclaimer, the property would pass instead to the surviving spouse. This approach might be desirable if the estate otherwise would receive a relatively small marital deduction. Another scenario where a disclaimer could be appropriate is where the disclaimant is elderly and in poor health and wishes to preclude the property from being taxed again relatively soon. (Of course, the credit for tax on prior transfers would provide some relief from double taxation.) Bear in mind, however, that the person making the qualified disclaimer has no input concerning which people receive the disclaimed property.

ROLE OF LIFE INSURANCE

Life insurance is an important asset with respect to estate planning for the following reasons:

- It can help provide the liquidity for paying estate taxes and other costs associated with death.
- It has the potential for large appreciation. If the insured gives away his or her incidents of ownership and survives the gift by more than three years, his or her estate benefits by keeping the appreciation out of the estate.

Assume an individual is contemplating purchasing a new insurance policy on his or her life and transferring it to another individual as a gift. The insured must live for more than three years after making the gift to exclude the face amount of the policy from his or her gross estate. Should the insured die within three years of gifting the policy, the donor's gross estate includes the policy's face amount. If the donee instead purchases the policy, the insured will not make a gift of the policy, and the three-year rule will not be of concern.

QUALIFYING THE ESTATE FOR INSTALLMENT PAYMENTS

It can be quite beneficial for an estate owning an interest in a closely held business to qualify for installment payment of estate taxes under Sec. 6166. In a sense, the estate can bor-

TAX STRATEGY TIP

The payment of estate taxes can be deferred as much as 14 years if the estate's executor makes a timely Sec. 6166 election. The interest charged on the deferred taxes is at a favorable rate.

row a certain amount of dollars from the government at 2% and the rest at a higher, but still favorable, rate.

Judicious selection of the property disposed of by lifetime gifts can raise the odds that the estate will qualify for such treatment. Retaining closely held business interests and gifting other assets will increase the likelihood of the estate's being able to elect the installment payments. However, closely held business interests often have a potential for great appreciation. Consequently, from the standpoint of reducing the size of the estate by freezing values, they are good candidates for gifts.

People cannot make gifts to restructure their estates and thereby qualify for Sec. 6166 if they wait until soon before their death to do so. If the decedent makes gifts within three years of dying, the closely held business interest must make up more than 35% of the adjusted gross estate in both of the following calculations:

1. Calculate the ratio of the closely held business to the actual adjusted gross estate.
2. Redo the calculations after revising the ratio to include (at date-of-death values) any property given away within three years of death.

EXAMPLE C13-56 ▶ Joe dies in 2002. Joe's gross estate includes a closely held business interest valued at $2 million and other property valued at $3.6 million. Joe's allowable Sec. 2053 and 2054 deductions total $100,000. In 2000, partly in hopes of qualifying his estate for Sec. 6166 treatment, Joe made gifts of listed securities of $300,000 (at 2002 valuations) and paid no gift tax on the gifts. The two tests for determining whether Joe's estate is eligible for Sec. 6166 are as follows:

Excluding gifts:	$2,000,000 ÷ $5,500,000 = 36.36%
Including gifts:	$2,000,000 ÷ $5,800,000 = 34.48%

The estate may not elect Sec. 6166 treatment because it meets the more than 35% test in only one of the two computations. ◀

WHERE TO DEDUCT ADMINISTRATION EXPENSES

Another tax planning opportunity concerns the choice of where to deduct administration expenses: on the estate tax return, on the estate's income tax return, or some in each place. The executor should make the decision based on where the deduction will yield the greatest tax savings. Thus, if the marginal estate tax rate exceeds the estate's marginal income tax rate, which it will if the estate tax base exceeds $1 million, the executor should deduct the expenses on the estate tax return. If no estate taxes are owed because of the exemption equivalent or the marital and/or charitable contribution deduction, administration expenses should be deducted on the estate's income tax return.

COMPLIANCE AND PROCEDURAL CONSIDERATIONS

OBJECTIVE 7

Recognize the filing requirements for estate tax returns

FILING REQUIREMENTS

Section 6018 indicates the circumstances in which estate tax returns are necessary. In general, no return is necessary unless the value of the gross estate plus adjusted taxable gifts exceeds the exemption equivalent (also known as the applicable exclusion amount). An exception applies, however, if the decedent made any post-1976 taxable gifts or claimed any portion of the $30,000 specific exemption after September 8, 1976 and before January 1, 1977. In such circumstances, a return must be filed if the value of the gross estate exceeds the amount of the exemption equivalent minus the total of the decedent's adjusted taxable gifts and the amount of the specific exemption claimed against gifts made after September 8, 1976 and before January 1, 1977.

REAL-WORLD EXAMPLE

The IRS expects 139,000 estate tax returns to be filed for 2001.

A completed sample Estate Tax Return (Form 706) appears in Appendix B. The facts on which the preparation of the return is premised are the same as for the comprehensive illustration appearing on pages C13-25 through C13-27.

DUE DATE

Estate tax returns generally must be filed within nine months after the decedent's death.[49] The Secretary of the Treasury is authorized to grant a reasonable extension of time for filing.[50] The maximum extension period is six months. Obtaining an extension does not extend the time for paying the estate tax. Section 6601 imposes interest on any portion of the tax not paid by the due date of the return, determined without regard to the extension period. Thus, to avoid interest, the estate must pay the tax by the original due date.

VALUATION

One of the most difficult tasks of preparing estate tax returns is valuing the items included in the gross estate. Some items (e.g., one-of-a-kind art objects) may truly be unique. For many properties the executor should arrange for appraisals by experts.

If the value of any property reported on the return is 50% or less of the amount determined to be the proper value during an audit or court case, a 20% undervaluation penalty is imposed.[51] The penalty will not be imposed, however, with proof that reasonable cause exists for the valuation claimed and that the claim is made in good faith. The penalty is higher if a gross valuation misstatement occurs; that is, the estate tax valuation is 25% or less than the amount determined to be the proper value.[52] Chapter C12 discusses these penalties in more detail.

ELECTION OF ALTERNATE VALUATION DATE

The executor may value the gross estate on the alternate valuation date instead of on the date of death by making an irrevocable election on the estate tax return. The election does not necessarily have to be made on a timely return, but no election is possible if the return is filed more than a year after the due date (including extensions).

DOCUMENTS TO BE INCLUDED WITH RETURN

The instructions for the Estate Tax Return (Form 706) indicate that the executor must file numerous documents and other papers with the return. Some of the more important items that should accompany the form include

- The death certificate
- A certified copy of the will if the decedent died testate (i.e., died with a valid will)
- A listing of the qualified terminable interest property and its value if the executor wishes to make the QTIP election
- Copies of gift tax returns the decedent filed
- Copies of appraisals for real estate
- A Form 712 (obtained from the insurance companies) for each life insurance policy on the decedent's life
- Copies of written trust and other instruments for lifetime transfers the decedent made
- Certified or verified copies of instruments granting the decedent a power of appointment, even if the power is not a general one
- A certified copy of the order admitting the will to probate if the will makes bequests for which a marital deduction or charitable contribution deduction is claimed

In addition, the executor should submit at the time of filing the return (or as soon thereafter as possible) a certificate from the proper officer of the taxing state that denotes the amount of the state death taxes and the payment date.

[49] Sec. 6075(a).
[50] Sec. 6081(a).
[51] Sec. 6662(g).
[52] Sec. 6662(h).

PROBLEM MATERIALS

DISCUSSION QUESTIONS

C13-1 In general, at what amount are items includible in the gross estate valued? (Answer in words.) Indicate one exception to the general valuation rules and the reason for this exception.

C13-2 A client requests that you explain the valuation rules used for gift tax and estate tax purposes. Explain the similarities and differences of the two sets of rules.

C13-3 Compare the valuation for gift and estate tax purposes of a $150,000 group term life insurance policy on the transferor's life.

C13-4 Explain how shares of stock traded on a stock exchange are valued. What is the blockage rule?

C13-5 Assume that the properties included in Alex's gross estate have appreciated during the six-month period immediately after his death. May Alex's executor elect the alternate valuation date and thereby achieve a larger step-up in basis? Explain.

C13-6 Explain to an executor an advantage and a disadvantage of electing the alternate valuation date.

C13-7 Is land that a decedent transferred to an adult child by gift two years before death included in the decedent's gross estate? In the estate tax base?

C13-8 From a tax standpoint, which of the following alternatives is more favorable for a client?

a. Buying a new insurance policy on his life and soon thereafter giving it to another person
b. Encouraging the other person to buy the policy with funds previously received from the client

Explain your answer.

C13-9 Explain the difference between the estate tax treatment for gift taxes paid on gifts made two years before death and on gifts made ten years before death.

C13-10 A client is considering making a very large gift. She wants to know whether the gross-up rule will apply to the entire amount of gift taxes paid by both her and her spouse if the spouses elect gift splitting and she dies within three years of the gift. Explain.

C13-11 A widow owns a valuable eighteenth-century residence that she would like the state historical society to own someday. Explain to her the estate tax consequences of the following two alternatives:

a. She deeds the state historical society a remainder interest in the residence and reserves the right to live there rent free for the rest of her life.
b. She gifts her entire interest in the house to the society and moves to another home for the rest of her life.

C13-12 Which three retention periods can cause Sec. 2036 (transfers with retained life estate) to apply to a transferor's estate?

C13-13 What characteristics do Secs. 2035 through 2038 have in common?

C13-14 When does the consideration furnished test apply to property that the decedent held as a joint tenant with right of survivorship?

C13-15 In which two circumstances is life insurance on the decedent's life includible in the gross estate under Sec. 2042? If insurance policies on the decedent's life escape being included under Sec. 2042, are they definitely excluded from the gross estate? Explain.

C13-16 Indicate two situations in which property that has previously been subject, at least in part, to gift taxation is nevertheless included in the donor-decedent's gross estate.

C13-17 Art died in the current year. Under Art's will, property is put in trust with a bank as trustee. Art's will names his sister Kay to receive the trust income annually for life and empowers Kay to will the property to whichever of her descendants she so desires. In addition, Kay may require that the trustee make distributions of principal to her for her health or education needs. Kay plans to leave the property by will to two of her five children in equal shares. Kay seeks your advice about whether the trust will be included in her gross estate. Respond to Kay.

C13-18 Determine the accuracy of the following statement: The gross estate includes a general power of appointment possessed by the decedent only if the decedent exercised the power.

C13-19 Carlos died six years ago. His will called for the creation of a trust to be funded with $1 million of property. The bank trustee must distribute all the trust income semiannually to Carlos's widow for the rest of her life. Upon her death, the trust assets are to be distributed to the couple's children. The widow dies in the current year, by which time the trust assets have appreciated to $1.3 million. Are the trust assets included in the widow's gross estate? Explain.

C13-20 List the various categories of estate tax deductions, and compare them with the categories of gift tax deductions. What differences exist?

C13-21 Compare the tax treatment of administration expenses with that of the decedent's debts.

C13-22 Judy dies and is survived by her husband, Jason, who receives the following interests as a result of his wife's death. Does Judy's estate receive a marital deduction for them? Explain.

a. $400,000 of life insurance proceeds; Jason is the beneficiary; Judy held the incidents of ownership.
b. Outright ownership of $700,000 of land held by Judy and Jason as joint tenants. Jason provided all the consideration to purchase the land.

C13-23 Compare the credits available for estate tax purposes with the credits available for gift tax purposes. What differences exist?

C13-24 Explain to a client the tax policy reason for allowing installment payments of the estate taxes attributable to closely held business interests.

C13-25 Assume that Larry is wealthier than Jane, his wife, and that he is likely to die before her. From an overall tax standpoint (considering transfer taxes and income taxes), is it preferable for Larry to transfer property to Jane *inter vivos* or at death, or does it matter? Explain.

C13-26 Bala desires to freeze the value of his estate. Explain which of the following assets you would recommend that Bala transfer during his lifetime (more than one asset may be suggested):

a. Life insurance on his life
b. Cash
c. Corporate bonds (assume interest rates are expected to rise)
d. Stock in a firm with a bright future
e. Land in a boom town

C13-27 Refer to Problem C13-26. Explain the negative tax considerations (if any) with respect to Bala's making gifts of the assets that you recommended.

C13-28 From a tax standpoint, why is it advisable for a wealthy married person to dispose of an amount equal to the exemption equivalent (applicable exclusion amount) to people other than his or her spouse?

C13-29 In general, when is the estate tax due? What are some exceptions?

ISSUE IDENTIFICATION QUESTIONS

C13-30 Henry Arkin (a widower) is quite elderly and is beginning to do some estate planning. His goal is to reduce his transfer taxes. He is considering purchasing land with a high potential for appreciation and owning it with his grandson as joint tenants with rights of survivorship. Henry would provide all of the consideration, estimated to be about $4.5 million. What tax issues should Henry Arkin consider with respect to the purchase of the land?

C13-31 Annie James dies early in 2002. All her property passes subject to her will, which provides that her surviving husband, Dave James, is to receive all the property outright. Her will further states that any property Dave disclaims will pass instead to their children in equal shares. Annie's gross estate is about $5 million, and her Sec. 2053 deductions are very small. Dave, who is in poor health, already owns about $3 million of property. What tax issues should Dave James consider with respect to the property bequested to him by his wife?

C13-32 Assume the same facts as in Problem C13-31 except that Annie's will leaves all her property to a QTIP trust for Dave for life with the remainder to their children. What tax issues should Dave James and the estate's executor consider with respect to the property that passes to the QTIP trust?

C13-33 Jeung Hong, a widower, died in March 2002. His gross estate is $2 million and, at the time of his death, he owed debts of $60,000. His will made a charitable bequest of $300,000 and left the rest of his property to his children. His administrative expenses are estimated to be about $75,000. What tax issues should the estate's CPA consider when preparing Jeung's estate tax return and his estate's income tax return?

PROBLEMS

C13-34 *Valuation.* Sara dies on May 5 of the current year. Her executor elects date-of-death valuation. Sara's gross estate includes the items listed below. What is the estate tax value of each item?

a. 2,000 shares of Highline Corporation stock, traded on a stock exchange on May 5 at a high of 50, a low of 44, and a close of 49.
b. Life insurance policy on the life of Sara having a face value of $800,000. The cost of a comparable policy immediately before Sara's death is $212,240.
c. Life insurance policy on the life of Sara's son having a face value of $50,000. The interpolated terminal reserve immediately before Sara's death is $20,120. Unexpired premiums are $710.

d. Personal residence appraised at a FMV of $250,000 and valued for property tax purposes at $178,000.

C13-35 ***Valuation.*** Mary dies on April 3, 2002. As of this date, Mary's gross estate is valued at $2.8 million. On October 3, Mary's gross estate is valued at $2.5 million. The estate neither distributes nor sells any assets before October 3. Mary's estate has no deductions or adjusted taxable gifts. What is Mary's *lowest* possible estate tax liability? Ignore the state death tax credit.

C13-36 ***Estate Tax Formula.*** Sue dies on May 3, 2002. On March 1, 2001, Sue gave Tom some land valued at $810,000. Sue applied a unified credit of $220,550 against the gift tax due on this transfer. On Sue's date of death the land is valued at $600,000.

a. With respect to this transaction, what amount is included in Sue's gross estate?
b. What is the amount of Sue's adjusted taxable gifts attributable to the 2001 gift?

C13-37 ***Transferor Provisions.*** Val dies on May 13, 2002. On October 3, 2001, she gave a $400,000 life insurance policy on her own life to Ray. Because the value of the policy was relatively low, the transfer did not cause any gift tax to be payable.

a. What amount is included in Val's gross estate as a result of the 2001 gift?
b. What amount is included in Val's gross estate if the property given is land instead of a life insurance policy?
c. Refer to Part a. What amount would be included in Val's gross estate if she instead dies on May 13, 2006?

C13-38 ***Transferor Provisions.*** In 2000, Jody transferred stock having a $1,010,000 FMV to her daughter Joan. Jody paid $125,250 of gift taxes on this transfer. When Jody died in 2002, the stock was valued at $920,000. Jody made no other gifts during her lifetime. With respect to this gift transaction, what amount is included in Jody's gross estate and what amount is reported as adjusted taxable gifts?

C13-39 ***Transferor Provisions.*** In 2000, Curt and Kate elected gift splitting to report $2,020,000 of gifts Curt made. Each paid gift taxes of $125,250 by spending his or her own funds. Kate died in 2002 and was survived by Curt. Her only taxable gift was the one reported for 2000. When Kate died in 2002, the gifted property had appreciated to $2.8 million. With respect to the 2000 gift, what amount is included in Kate's gross estate and what amount is reported as adjusted taxable gifts?

C13-40 ***Transferor Provisions.*** What amount, if any, is included in John's gross estate in each of the following situations:

a. In 1993, John created a revocable trust and funded it with $400,000 of assets. He named a bank as trustee. The trust instrument provides that the income is payable to John annually for life. Upon John's death, the assets are to be divided equally among John's descendants. John dies at the age of 72, and the trust is still revocable. The trust assets are then worth $480,000.
b. In 1994, John transferred title to his personal residence to a charitable organization. The residence was worth $150,000 on the transfer date. John continues to live alone in the residence until his death and pays no rent. At John's death, the residence is worth $230,000.
c. In 1994, John created an irrevocable trust and funded it with $200,000 of assets. John named a bank as trustee. According to the trust agreement, all the trust income is to be paid out annually for 25 years. The trustee, however, is to decide how much income to pay each year to each of the three beneficiaries (John's children). Upon termination of the trust, the assets are to be distributed equally among John's three children (now adults) or their estates. The trust's assets are worth $500,000 when John dies.
d. In 1995, John created an irrevocable trust with a bank named as trustee. He named his grandson Al as the beneficiary for life. Upon Al's death, the property is to be distributed equally among Al's descendants. The trust assets are worth $400,000 when John dies.

C13-41 ***Transferor Provisions.*** Latoya transferred property to an irrevocable trust in 1996 with a bank trustee. Latoya named Al to receive the trust income annually for life and Pat or Pat's estate to receive the remainder upon Al's death. Latoya reserved the power to designate Mike or Mike's estate (instead of Pat or Pat's estate) to receive the remainder. Upon Latoya's death in August 2002, the trust assets are valued at $200,000; Al is age 50; Mike, age 27; and Pat, age 32. Assume a 10% rate for the actuarial tables.

a. How much, if any, is included in Latoya's gross estate?

b. How much would have been included in Latoya's gross estate if she had *not* retained any powers over the trust? (Assume that Latoya survives for more than three years after the transfer.)

C13-42 *Annuities.* Maria dies in the current year, two years after her retirement. At the time of her death at age 67, she is covered by the two annuities listed below.

- An annuity purchased by Maria's father providing benefits to Maria upon her reaching age 65. Upon Maria's death, survivor benefits are payable to her sister. The sister's total benefits are valued at $45,000.
- An annuity purchased by Maria's former employer under a qualified plan to which only the employer contributes. Benefits became payable to Maria upon her retirement. Upon Maria's death a survivor annuity valued at $110,000 is payable to her son.

a. What is the amount of the inclusion in Maria's gross estate with respect to each annuity?
b. How would your answer for the first annuity change if Maria had instead purchased the annuity?
c. How would your answer for the second annuity change if the employer had instead made 70% of the contributions to the qualified plan and Maria had made the remaining 30%?

C13-43 ***Jointly Owned Property.*** In 1994, Art purchased land for $60,000 and immediately titled it in the names of Art and Bart, joint tenants with right of survivorship. Bart paid no consideration. In 2002, Art dies and is survived by Bart, his brother. The land's value has appreciated to $300,000.
a. What is the amount of the inclusion in Art's gross estate?
b. If Bart dies before Art, what amount would be included in Bart's gross estate?
c. Assume that Art dies in 2002 and Bart dies in 2004, when the land is worth $320,000. What amount is included in Bart's gross estate?

C13-44 ***Jointly Owned Property.*** Eight years ago, Fred and Gail, who are not married, pooled their resources and purchased a mountain cabin. Fred provided $30,000 of consideration, and Gail furnished $50,000. Fred dies and is survived by Gail. The property, which they had titled in the names of Fred and Gail, joint tenants with right of survivorship, is valued at $240,000 when Fred dies. What amount is included in Fred's gross estate?

C13-45 ***Jointly Owned Property.*** Mrs. Cobb purchased land costing $80,000 in 1995. She had the land titled in the names of Mr. and Mrs. Cobb, joint tenants with right of survivorship. Mrs. Cobb dies and is survived by Mr. Cobb. At Mrs. Cobb's death, the land's value is $200,000.
a. What amount is included in Mrs. Cobb's gross estate?
b. What is the amount, if any, of the marital deduction that Mrs. Cobb's estate can claim for the land?
c. Assume Mr. Cobb dies after Mrs. Cobb and the land is worth $240,000 at his death. What amount is included in his gross estate?

C13-46 ***Powers of Appointment.*** Tai, who dies in the current year, is the sole income beneficiary for life of each of the trusts described below. For each trust indicate whether and why it is includible in Tai's gross estate.
a. A trust created under the will of Tai's mother, who died in 1986. Upon Tai's death, the trust assets are to pass to those of Tai's descendants whom Tai directs by his will. Should Tai fail to appoint the trust property, the trust assets are to be distributed to the Smithsonian Institution. Tai wills the property to his twin daughters in equal shares.
b. An irrevocable *inter vivos* trust created in 1981 by Tai's father. The trust agreement authorizes Tai to appoint the property to whomever he so desires. The appointment could be made only by his will. Tai appoints the property to an elderly neighbor.
c. An irrevocable trust funded by Tai in 1996. Upon Tai's death, the property is to pass to his children.
d. A trust created under the will of Tai's grandmother, who died in 1941. Her will authorizes Tai to appoint the property by his will to whomever he so desires. In default of appointment, the property is to pass to Tai's descendants in equal shares. Tai's will does not mention this trust.
e. Assume the same facts as in Part b except that Tai's will does not mention the trust property.

C13-47 ***Life Insurance.*** Joy dies on November 5, 2002. Soon after Joy's death, the executor discovers the following insurance policies on Joy's life. Indicate the amount includible in Joy's gross estate for each policy.

Policy Number	*Owner*	*Beneficiary*	*Face Value*
123	Joy	Joy's husband	$400,000
757	Joy's son	Joy's estate	225,000
848	Joy's son	Joy's son	300,000
414	Joy's daughter	Joy's husband	175,000

Joy transferred policies 757 and 848 to her son in 1995. She transferred policy 414 to her daughter in 2001.

C13-48 ***Life Insurance.*** Refer to Problem C13-47. What is the net addition to Joy's *taxable estate* with respect to the insurance policies listed above if all the property passing under Joy's will goes to Joy's son?

C13-49 ***Deductions.*** When Yuji dies in 2002, his gross estate is valued at $5.2 million. He owes debts totaling $800,000. Funeral and administration expenses are estimated at $10,000 and $90,000, respectively. It is estimated that the marginal estate tax rate will exceed his estate's marginal income tax rate. Yuji wills his church $250,000 and his spouse $800,000. What is Yuji's adjusted gross estate? His taxable estate?

C13-50 ***Marital Deduction.*** Assume the same facts as in Problem C13-49 except that Yuji's will also provides for setting up a trust to be funded with $400,000 of property with a bank named as trustee. His wife is to receive all the trust income semiannually for life, and upon her death the trust assets are to be distributed equally among Yuji's children and grandchildren.

a. What is the amount of Yuji's taxable estate? Provide two possible answers.

b. Assume Yuji's widow dies in 2005. With respect to Yuji's former assets, which items will be included in the widow's gross estate? Provide two possible answers, but you need not indicate amounts.

C13-51 ***Marital Deduction.*** Assume the same facts as in Problems C13-49 and C13-50 and that before Yuji's death his wife already owns property valued at $300,000. Assume that each asset owned by each spouse increases 20% in value by 2005 and that Yuji's executor elects to claim the maximum marital deduction possible. Assume there are no state death taxes. From a tax standpoint, was the executor's strategy of electing the marital deduction on the QTIP trust a wise decision? Support your answer with computations.

C13-52 ***Adjusted Taxable Gifts.*** Will, a bachelor, dies in the current year. At the time he dies, his sole asset is cash of $1 million. Assume no debts or funeral and administration expenses. His gift history is as follows:

Date	*Amount of Taxable Gifts*	*FMV of Gift Property at Date of Death*
October 1987	$270,000	$290,000
October 1991	90,000	65,000

a. What is Will's estate tax base?

b. How would your answer to Part a change if Will made the first gift in 1974 (instead of 1987)?

C13-53 ***Estate Tax Base.*** Bess dies in 2002. Her gross estate, which totals $3 million, includes a $100,000 life insurance policy on her life that she gave away in 2001. The taxable gift that arose from giving away the policy was $15,000. In 2000, Bess made a $740,000 taxable gift of stock whose value increased to $790,000 by the time Bess died. Assume her estate tax deductions total $80,000.

a. What is her estate tax base?

b. What unified credit may her estate claim?

C13-54 ***Installment Payments.*** Elaine dies on May 1, 2002. Her gross estate consists of the following items:

Cash	$ 40,000
Stocks traded on a stock exchange	520,000
Personal residence	250,000
25% capital interest in 60-person partnership	610,000

Elaine's Sec. 2053 deductions total $30,000. She has no other deductions.

a. Ignoring the provision allowing a deduction for family owned businesses, what percentage of Elaine's federal estate taxes may be paid in installments under Sec. 6166? When is the first installment payment due?

b. May Elaine's estate elect Sec. 6166 treatment if the stocks are valued at $2,520,000 instead of $520,000?

C13-55 *State Death Tax Credit.* Demetrius dies in 2002 with a taxable estate of $1.54 million, adjusted taxable gifts of $30,000 and a tax base of $1.57 million. His estate pays state death taxes of $82,100. What is the estate's credit for state death taxes?

COMPREHENSIVE PROBLEMS

C13-56 Bonnie dies on June 1, 2002. Bonnie is survived by her husband, Abner, and two sons, Carl and Doug. Bonnie's only lifetime taxable gift was made in October 1999 in the taxable amount of $700,000. She did not elect gift splitting. By the time of her death, the value of the gifted property (stock) has risen to $820,000.

Bonnie's executor discovers the items shown below. Amounts shown are the FMVs of the items as of June 1, 2002.

Cash in checking account in her name	$118,500
Cash in savings account in her name	430,000
Stock in names of Bonnie and Doug, joint tenants with right of survivorship. Bonnie provided all the consideration ($3,000) to purchase the stock.	25,000
Land in names of Bonnie and Abner, joint tenants with right of survivorship. Abner provided all the consideration to purchase the land.	360,000
Personal residence in only Bonnie's name	250,000
Life insurance on Bonnie's life. Bonnie is owner, and Bonnie's estate is beneficiary (face value)	210,000
Trust created under the will of Bonnie's mother (who died in 1984). Bonnie is entitled to all the trust income for life, and she could will the trust property to whomever she desired. She wills it to her sons in equal amounts.	700,000

Bonnie's debts, as of her date of death, are $60,000. Her funeral and administration expenses total $80,000. The executor deducts the administration expenses on the estate tax return.

Bonnie's will includes the following:

"I leave my residence to my husband Abner."

"$250,000 of property is to be transferred to a trust with First Bank named as trustee. All of the income is to be paid to my husband, Abner, semiannually for the rest of his life. Upon his death the property is to be divided equally between my two sons or their estates."

"I leave $47,000 to the American Cancer Society."

Assume the executor elects to claim the maximum marital deduction possible. Compute the following with respect to Bonnie's estate:

a. Gross estate

b. Adjusted gross estate

c. Taxable estate

d. Adjusted taxable gifts

e. Estate tax base

f. Tentative tax on estate tax base

g. Federal estate tax payable (assume her state death taxes are equal to the amount of the maximum credit for state death taxes on the federal return.)

C13-57 Assume the same facts as in Problem C13-56 except the joint tenancy land is held in the names of Bonnie and Doug, joint tenants with right of survivorship. Also assume that Bonnie provided 55% of the consideration to buy the land; Bonnie's executor does not elect to claim the marital deduction on the QTIP trust; and the administration expenses ($65,000) are deducted on the estate's income tax return. (Assume that no taxable gift arose on the purchase of the joint tenancy land.)

TAX STRATEGY PROBLEM

C13-58 Gaylord Gunnison (GG) died January 13, 2002, and his gross estate consisted of three properties—cash, land, and stock in a public company. The amount of cash on the date of his death was $1.9 million, which went into the estate. On January 13, 2002, the land had a fair market value of $1 million, and the stock had a fair market value of $2 million. On July 13, 2002, the fair market values of the land and stock were $1.1 million and $1.6 million, respectively, and the cash remained at $1.9 million. Assume, for simplicity, that the estate has no deductions, GG made no taxable gifts, and no state death tax applies. GG willed all of his property to his daughter, Gilda, who anticipates that the stock will appreciate at the rate of 9% per year before taxes. She anticipates selling the stock on or about July 13, 2008. Assume that the land's fair market value will remain at $1.1 million through 2008.

Considering both income tax and estate tax effects, compare after-tax wealth using the alternate valuation date or the date of death to value the estate. Which date should the executor elect? For simplicity, assume that the cash is not invested. (Incidentally, the factor for the future value, six years hence, at 9% is 1.677.) Prepare a worksheet on which you calculate the amount of after-tax wealth using the two possible valuation dates. Assume the gain will be taxed at a 20% rate in 2008.

TAX FORM/RETURN PREPARATION PROBLEMS

C13-59 Prepare an Estate Tax Return (Form 706) for Judy Griffin (464-55-3434), who died on June 30, 2001. Judy is survived by her husband, Greg, and her daughter, Candy. Judy was a resident of 17 Fiddlers Way, Nashville, Tennessee 37205. She was employed as a corporate executive with Sounds of Country, Inc., a recording company, at the time of her death. The assets discovered at Judy's death are listed below at their date-of-death values.

Savings account in Judy's name	$190,000
Checking account in Judy's name	10,000
Personal residence (having a $200,000 mortgage)	500,000
Household furnishings	75,000
400 shares of stock in Omega Corporation (quotes on June 30, 2001 are high of 70, low of 60, close of 67)	?
Land in New York (inherited from her mother in 1981)	140,000
Porsche purchased by Greg in 1996 as an anniversary gift to Judy	45,000

Other items include the following:

1. Life insurance policy 1: Judy purchased a $200,000 life insurance policy on her life on November 1, 1998 and paid the first annual premium of $2,500. The next day, she transferred the policy to her brother, Todd Williams, who also is the beneficiary. Judy paid the premium on August 1, 1999 and 2000.
2. Life insurance policy 2: A $150,000 whole life policy on Greg's life. Judy purchased the policy in 1994 and has always paid the $1,200 semiannual premium due on March 30 and September 30. Interpolated terminal reserve is $25,000. The beneficiary is Judy or her estate. Judy is the owner of the policy.
3. Employer annuity: Judy's employer established a qualified pension plan in 1982. The employer contributes 60% and the employee pays 40% of the required annual contributions. Judy chose a settlement option that provides for annual payments to Greg until his death. The annuity receivable by Greg is valued at $600,000.

Other information includes the following:

1. In October 1998, Judy transferred to her brother, Todd, $1.52 million of stock that she received as a gift. Judy and Greg elected gift splitting. This was the first taxable gift for each spouse, and they paid their own portion of the gift tax from their own funds. When Judy dies, the stocks have appreciated to $1.6 million.
2. Unpaid bills at death include $2,500 owed on a bank credit card.
3. The cost of Judy's funeral and tombstone totals $25,000.
4. Judy's administration expenses are estimated at $55,000. Her estate's marginal transfer tax rate will be higher than the estate's marginal income tax rate.
5. Judy's will includes the following dispositions of property:
"I leave $60,000 of property in trust with Fourth Bank named as trustee. All income is to be paid semiannually to my husband, Greg, for life or until he remarries, whichever

occurs first. At the termination of Greg's interest, the property will pass to my daughter, Candy, or her estate."

"To my beloved husband, Greg, I leave my Omega stock. The rest of my property I leave to my daughter, Candy, except that I leave $10,000 to the University of Tennessee."

6. Assume the state estate tax payable equals the maximum credit available on the federal return for state death taxes.
7. Make the QTIP election if possible.

C13-60 Prepare an Estate Tax Return (Form 706) for Joe Blough (177-47-3217) of 1412 Robin Lane, Birmingham, Alabama 35208. Joe died on November 12, 2001; he was survived by his wife, Joan, and their daughter, Katy. Joe was a bank vice president. Date-of-death values of the assets discovered at Joe's death are listed below.

Checking and savings accounts in names of Joe and Joan, joint tenants with right of survivorship	$800,000
Second home, in Joe's name	450,000
Life insurance policy on Joe's life; his estate is the beneficiary and Joan is the owner	250,000

Other pertinent information is as follows:

1. In 1988, Joe gave his sister land then valued at $220,000. He and Joan elected gift splitting. This was Joe's first taxable gift. The land was worth $350,000 when Joe died.
2. Joan owns the house that had been the couple's principal residence. Its value is $750,000.
3. Joe willed all his property to their daughter, Katy.
4. For simplicity, assume no administration expenses and that funeral expenses are $11,000.
5. Assume that state death taxes are equal to the federal credit for state death taxes.

CASE STUDY PROBLEMS

C13-61 Your clients, Matt and Mindy Mason, have come to you for estate planning advice. Each is age 66 and in reasonably good health. Mr. and Mrs. Mason have no children by their marriage, but Mrs. Mason has two children (Brett and Becky) by her previous marriage. Mr. and Mrs. Mason, residents of a non-community property state, own the assets with the FMVs listed below:

	Mr. Mason	*Mrs. Mason*
Cash	$1,000,000	$1,500,000
Life insurance on self	1,300,000	–0–
Stocks in public companies	2,000,000	800,000
Residence	–0–	400,000
Stock in solely owned company	125,000	–0–

In addition, Mrs. Mason is the beneficiary of a trust created under her mother's will. Her mother died in 1978. The trust currently is valued at $350,000. Under the trust instrument, Mrs. Mason is entitled to receive all the trust income for life and may specify in her will the person(s) to receive the remainder interest. Mr. Mason's nephew (Norman) is the beneficiary of the insurance policy on Mr. Mason's life.

Fortunately, both Mr. and Mrs. Mason are free of debt.

Mr. Mason's will includes the following provisions at present:

> "I leave all my property to my wife, Mindy Mason, if she survives me. If she does not survive me, I leave all my property to my favorite charitable organization, the Humane Society of Louisville."

Mrs. Mason's will includes the following provisions at present:

> "I leave each of my grandchildren [five people are named] and each of my nieces and nephews [twenty-five people are named] $15,000 each."

"I leave assets equal in amount to the exemption equivalent amount for Federal estate tax purposes to my son and daughter (Brett and Becky) in equal shares."

"I appoint the property of the trust created under my mother's will to my sister, Helen Adams, or her descendants."

"The rest of my estate I leave to a trust with First Bank as trustee. My husband, Matt, is to receive all the trust income annually until the earlier of his death or remarriage. The remainder is to pass in equal shares to my son and daughter, or their descendants. Should my spouse predecease me, the rest of my estate is to be divided equally between my son and daughter, or their descendants."

For simplicity, assume that no funeral or administration expenses are incurred for either spouse and that no death taxes are payable from property eligible for the marital or charitable contribution deductions. Assume also that state death taxes are equal to the credit for state death taxes available on the federal estate tax return. For your projections, assume that the first spouse dies in 2002 and the second dies six years later.

Required:

a. Prepare a memorandum to the tax partner of your firm that shows calculations of the total estate taxes payable by the two estates under the situations listed below. Ignore further appreciation. Assume that:
   1. Matt dies first.
   2. Mindy dies first.
b. Make estate planning recommendations in your memorandum that would reduce the couple's estate tax liability. Assume that Matt will die first.
c. In making your suggestions to the clients, what factors besides tax consequences should you consider?

C13-62 Your client is Jon Jake, the executor of the Estate of Beth Adams. Mrs. Adams died a widow, 11 years after the death of her husband, Sam. Mr. Jake wants assistance in the preparation of the estate tax return for Mrs. Adams, whose estate consists primarily of real estate. Mrs. Adams's estate will be divided among her three adult children except for a small amount of property willed to charity. The real estate has been appraised at $2 million by her son-in-law (who is married to one of Mrs. Adams's three children), an experienced real estate appraiser. You have a number of real estate clients and have considerable familiarity with property values for real estate located in the same general area as the estate's property. Your "gut feeling" is that the appraised values may be somewhat understated. What responsibilities do you have as a tax adviser to make additional inquiries? What information should you give Mr. Jake concerning possible penalties?

TAX RESEARCH PROBLEMS

C13-63 Ted Greene died on July 7, 2002. He was a resident of Vermont. Six years prior to his death he had executed a durable power of attorney whereby he granted his daughter Louisa Greene a durable power of attorney. (A durable power of attorney is effective even after the person granting the power of attorney becomes mentally incompetent.) In the power of attorney, Mr. Greene granted Louisa the power to "sell, purchase, lease, mortgage, and convey any real property owned by me." The document in other places used the word "convey" in a slightly different context. Four years before her father's death, Louisa used the power of attorney to transfer (convey) four acres of land to her child, Zed Bright-Greene; Zed paid no consideration. Ted's executor would like to exclude the four acres of land from Mr. Greene's gross estate under the proposition that the transfer was a valid gift. However, he wonders if Louisa really had the power to make a gift of any of her father's property. Research whether the four acres of land should be included in Mr. Greene's gross estate.

C13-64 Val, a resident of Illinois, died on June 12 of the current year. On May 5, she wrote four checks for $10,000 each, payable to each of her four grandchildren. Val mailed the checks on May 6, and each donee received the check on or before May 9. None of the donees deposited his or her checks until after Val's death. As of Val's date of death, the balance in her checking account was $52,127. This balance includes the $40,000 of outstanding checks issued to her grandchildren. Assume the executor will elect date-of-death valuation.

Your senior requested that you prepare a memorandum concerning whether the checks can be subtracted from the $52,127 account balance in arriving at the cash includible in Val's gross estate. Your senior indicates that you should start with the following authorities:

- IRC Sec. 2031(a)
- Reg. Secs. 20.2031-5 and 25.2511-2(b)

C13-65 Randy died on June 10 of the current year. His will created a trust from which his surviving spouse is entitled to receive all the trust income quarterly for life. However, any income accumulated between the last quarterly payment date and his spouse's date of death is to be paid to the remainderman, Randy, Jr. Prepare a memorandum in which you address whether the trust is eligible for the marital deduction under the QTIP rules.

C13-66 *Internet Research Problem.* You have been asked to make a presentation to a group of laypersons and explain which types of property do not pass under the decedent's will (that is, they pass outside probate). Consult the internet address: *http://www.mtpalermo.com.* This address has a number of estate tax related materials you can use to conduct the research for your presentation. Prepare a presentation explaining several types of property that do not pass under the terms of the will.

C13-67 *Internet Research Problem.* Assume that you want to do some research regarding how property typically passes if the decedent dies intestate (without a will) because you soon will be meeting with a client who is considering moving to one of several other states and who does not currently have a will. The client plans to execute a will soon but makes the inquiry because of his busy schedule and tendency to procrastinate. Consult the internet address: *http://www.suffolklaw.com.* On the left side, select "Publications," then select "Estate Planning," and finally select "What Happens If You Die Intestate." Prepare a brief memo about what you learn.

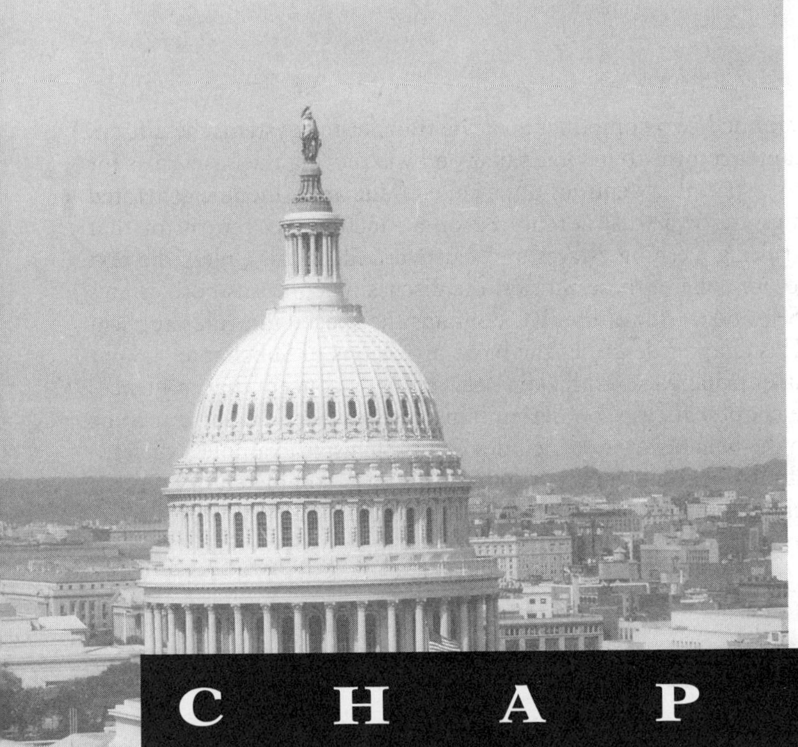

14

CHAPTER

INCOME TAXATION OF TRUSTS AND ESTATES

LEARNING OBJECTIVES

After studying this chapter, you should be able to

1. Understand the basic concepts concerning trusts and estates
2. Distinguish between principal and income
3. Explain how to calculate the tax liability of a trust or an estate
4. Understand the significance of distributable net income
5. Determine the taxable income of a simple trust
6. Determine the taxable income of a complex trust and an estate
7. Recognize the significance of income in respect of a decedent
8. Explain the effect of the grantor trust provisions
9. Recognize the filing requirements for fiduciary returns

CHAPTER OUTLINE

Basic Concepts...14-2
Principles of Fiduciary Accounting...14-4
Formula for Taxable Income and Tax Liability...14-7
Distributable Net Income...14-10
Determining a Simple Trust's Taxable Income...14-13
Comprehensive Illustration: Determining a Simple Trust's Taxable Income...14-17
Determining Taxable Income for Complex Trusts and Estates...14-19
Comprehensive Illustration: Determining a Complex Trust's Taxable Income...14-24
Income in Respect of a Decedent...14-27
Grantor Trust Provisions...14-30
Tax Planning Considerations...14-34
Compliance and Procedural Considerations...14-35

Chapters C12 and C13 examined two components of the transfer tax system: the gift tax and the estate tax. This chapter returns to income taxation by exploring the basic rules for taxing trusts and estates, two special tax entities often called **fiduciaries.** Income generated by property owned by an estate or a **trust** is reported on an income tax return for that entity. In general, the tax rules governing estates and trusts are identical. Unless the text states that a rule applies to only one of these entities, the discussion concerns both estates and trusts. Subchapter J (Secs. 641-692) of the IRC contains the special tax rules applicable to estates and trusts. This chapter describes the basic provisions of Subchapter J.

This chapter also discusses principles of fiduciary accounting, a concept that influences the tax consequences. The chapter focuses on determining the fiduciary's taxable income and the amount taxable to the beneficiaries. It includes comprehensive examples concerning the computations of taxable income, and Appendix B displays completed tax returns (Form 1041) for both a simple and a complex trust. The chapter also explores the circumstances that cause the grantor (transferor) to be taxed on the trust's income.

BASIC CONCEPTS

OBJECTIVE 1

Understand the basic concepts concerning trusts and estates

INCEPTION OF TRUSTS

Often a relatively wealthy person (one concerned with gift and/or estate taxes) will create trusts for tax and/or other reasons (e.g., conserving assets). A person may create a trust at any point in time by transferring property to the trust. A **trustee** (named by the transferor) administers the trust property for the benefit of the beneficiary. The trustee may be either an individual or an institution, such as a bank, and there can be more than one trustee.

If the transfer occurs during the transferor's lifetime, the trust is called an **inter vivos trust**, meaning among the living. The transferor is known as the **grantor** or the **trustor.** A trust created under the direction of a decedent's will is called a **testamentary trust** and contains assets formerly held by the decedent's estate. A trust may continue to exist for whatever time the trust instrument or the will specifies subject to the constraints of the **Rule Against Perpetuities.**[1]

INCEPTION OF ESTATES

ADDITIONAL COMMENT

The IRS reports that 3.4 million fiduciary income tax returns (Forms 1041 and 1041S) were filed in 1999.

Estates originate only upon the death of the person whose assets are being administered. The estate continues in existence until the executor[2] (i.e., the person(s) named in the will to manage the property and distribute the assets) or administrator (where the decedent died without a will) completes his or her duties. An executor's or administrator's duties include collecting the assets, paying the debts and taxes, and distributing the property. The time to perform the duties may vary from a year or two to over a decade, depending on many factors (e.g., whether anyone contests the will).

Because the estate is a separate tax entity, continuing the estate's existence achieves having some income taxed to yet another taxpayer, but the estate's tax rates are very compressed. Nevertheless, the decedent's survivors sometimes can reduce their personal income taxes by preserving the estate's existence as a separate taxpayer. Treasury Regulations provide, however, that if the IRS considers the administration of an estate to have been unreasonably prolonged, it will view the estate as having been terminated for federal tax purposes after the expiration of a reasonable period for performance of the administrative duties.[3] In such a situation, the income is taxed directly to the individuals entitled to receive the estate's assets, and these individuals may have a higher marginal tax rate than does the estate.

[1] The Rule Against Perpetuities addresses how long property may be tied up in trust and is the "principle that no interest in property is good unless it must vest, if at all, not later than 21 years, plus period of gestation, after some life or lives in being at time of creation of interest." Henry Campbell Black, *Black's Law Dictionary*, Rev. 6th ed., Ed. by Joseph R. Nolan and Jacqueline M. Nolan-Haley (St. Paul, MN: West Publishing Co., 1990), p. 1,331. Some state have abolished the Rule Against Perpetuities.

[2] In some states, this individual is called a personal representative.

[3] Reg. Sec. 1.641(b)-3(a).

REASONS FOR CREATING TRUSTS

A myriad of reasons—both tax and nontax—exist for creating trusts. A discussion of some of these reasons follows.

KEY POINT

A trust is a contract between two parties: the grantor and the trustee. The grantor gives the trustee legal title to property, which the trustee holds for the benefit of a third party(ies), the beneficiary(ies). The trustee, acting in a fiduciary capacity, manages the property for the duration of the trust. Beneficiaries of a trust may have an income interest, which means that they receive part or all of the trust's income, or they may have a remainder interest, which means that they will receive the property held by the trust on some specified future date. A beneficiary may hold both an income interest and a remainder interest. The grantor may be a beneficiary and/or the trustee.

TAX SAVING ASPECTS OF TRUSTS. If the trust is irrevocable, meaning the grantor cannot require the trustee to return the assets, one of the primary tax purposes for establishing the trust traditionally was to achieve income splitting. With income splitting, the income from the trust assets is taxed to at least one taxpayer (i.e., the trust or the beneficiary) at a lower marginal tax rate than that of the grantor. Today's compressed fiduciary tax rate schedules, under which the top rate of 38.6% (in 2002) occurs at an income level less than $10,000, often make achieving income tax reduction difficult. Sometimes the trust instrument authorizes the trustee to use his or her discretion in "sprinkling" the income among several beneficiaries or accumulating it within the trust. In such circumstances, the trustee may consider the tax effects of making a distribution of income to one beneficiary rather than to another or retaining income in the trust.

Individuals also have created trusts to minimize their estate taxes. As discussed in Chapter C13, for the transferor to exclude the property conveyed to the trust from the gross estate, the transferor must not retain the right to receive the trust income or the power to control which other people receive the income or have, at the time of death, the power to alter the identity of any people named earlier to receive such assets.[4]

NONTAX ASPECTS OF TRUSTS. Reduction of taxes is not always the foremost reason for establishing trusts. Individuals often use trusts, including Sec. 2503(c) trusts and *Crummey* trusts, when minors are the donees so that a trustee can manage the assets. (See Chapter C12 for a discussion of such trusts.) Even when the donee is an adult, donors sometimes may prefer that the assets be managed by a trustee deemed to have better management skills than the donee. Other donors may want to avoid conveying property directly to a donee if they fear the donee would soon consume most of the assets. In addition, donors sometimes use trusts to protect assets from creditors.

The creation of a **revocable trust** (i.e., one in which the grantor may demand that the assets be returned) does not yield any income or estate tax savings for the grantor. Nevertheless, donors often establish revocable trusts, including ones in which the grantor is also the beneficiary, for nontax purposes such as having the property managed by an individual or an institution with superior management skills. Use of a revocable trust reduces probate costs because assets in a revocable trust avoid probate. Such a strategy is especially important in states in which probate costs are high. In this text, a trust is deemed to be an **irrevocable trust** unless explicitly denoted as being revocable.

BASIC PRINCIPLES OF FIDUCIARY TAXATION

Throughout the rest of this chapter, you should keep several basic principles of **fiduciary taxation** in mind. These features (discussed below) apply to all trusts other than grantor trusts, a type of trust where generally the grantor instead of the trust or the beneficiary pays tax on the income. (See pages C14-30 through C14-33 for a description of the tax treatment of grantor trusts.)

TRUSTS AND ESTATES AS SEPARATE TAXPAYERS. An estate or a trust is a separate taxpaying entity, and if it has any taxable income, it pays an income tax. Such tax is reported on Form 1041. The 2002 tax rates applicable to estates and trusts appear on the inside back cover. These rates, which are indexed annually for inflation, are very compressed in comparison with the rates for individuals. As is true for individuals, an estate's or trust's long-term capital gains are taxed at a top tax rate of 20% if the asset was held for more than one year (18% if acquired after 2000 and held more than five years).

---

[4] Sec. 2036, relating to retention of income or control, and Sec. 2038, relating to the power to alter the identity of beneficiaries.

EXAMPLE C14-1 ▶ For calendar year 2002, a trust reports taxable income of $10,000. Its tax liability is $2,837. An unmarried individual not qualifying as a head of household would owe taxes of $1,200 on $10,000 of taxable income. ◀

NO DOUBLE TAXATION. Unlike the situation for corporations, no double taxation of income earned by an estate or trust (a fiduciary taxpayer) occurs because an estate or trust receives a deduction for the income it distributes to its beneficiaries. The beneficiaries, in turn, report the taxable portion of their receipts as income on their individual returns. Thus, the current income is taxed once, to the fiduciary or to the beneficiary or some to each, depending on whether it is distributed. In total, all the estate or trust's current income is taxed, sometimes some to the fiduciary and the remaining amount to the beneficiary. One of the primary purposes of the Subchapter J rules is to address exactly where the estate or trust's current income is taxed.

EXAMPLE C14-2 ▶ In the current year, the Lopez Trust receives total dividend income of $25,000, $15,000 of which the trustee in its discretion distributes to Lupe. Lupe is taxed on $15,000, the amount of the distribution. The trust is taxed on the income it retains or accumulates, $10,000 in this case, less a $100 personal exemption (discussed on pages C14-9 and C14-10). ◀

CONDUIT APPROACH. A conduit approach governs fiduciary income taxation. Under this approach, the distributed income has the same character in the hands of the beneficiary as it has to the trust. Thus, if the trust distributes tax-free interest income on state and local bonds, such income retains its tax-free character at the beneficiary level.

EXAMPLE C14-3 ▶ In the current year, the Lopez Trust receives $15,000 of dividends and $10,000 of tax-free interest. It distributes all of its receipts to its beneficiary. The beneficiary is deemed to receive $15,000 of dividend income and $10,000 of tax-free interest. ◀

SELF-STUDY QUESTION

King Trust receives interest on a savings account and distributes it to Anne. Because the trust is treated as a conduit, the interest is reported by Anne as taxable interest. Why might this be important?

ANSWER

For purposes of the limitation on the investment interest deduction, the interest from the trust is part of Anne's investment income. For purposes of the passive loss limitations, it is classified as portfolio income.

SIMILARITY TO RULES FOR INDIVIDUALS. Section 641(b) states "[T] he taxable income of an estate or trust shall be computed in the same manner as in the case of an individual, except as otherwise provided in this part." Sections 641–683 appear in this part (Part I) of Subchapter J. Thus, the tax effect for fiduciaries is the same as for individuals if the provisions of Secs. 641–683 do not specify rules that differ from those applicable for individual taxpayers. Sections 641–683 do not provide any special treatment for interest income from state and local bonds or for state and local tax payments. Consequently, an estate or trust receives an exclusion for state and local bond interest and the same deductions as individuals for state and local taxes. On the other hand, Sec. 642(b) specifies the amount of the personal exemption for fiduciaries. Thus, this subsection preempts the Sec. 151 rule concerning the amount of the personal exemption for individuals.

PRINCIPLES OF FIDUCIARY ACCOUNTING

OBJECTIVE 2

Distinguish between principal and income

To better understand the special tax treatment of fiduciary income, especially the determination of to whom the estate or trust's current income is taxed, one needs a general knowledge of the principles of fiduciary accounting. In a sense, fiduciary accounting is similar to fund accounting for government entities. Instead of having separate funds, all receipts and disbursements are classified as either income or principal (corpus).

THE IMPORTANCE OF IDENTIFYING INCOME AND PRINCIPAL

When computing taxable income, we generally are concerned with whether a particular item is included in or deducted from gross income. When answering fiduciary tax questions, however, we also need to consider whether an item is classified as principal (corpus) or income for fiduciary accounting purposes. For example, certain items (e.g., interest on state bonds) may constitute fiduciary accounting gross income but are not included in the gross income calculation for tax purposes. Other items (e.g., capital gains) may be included in gross income but classified as principal for fiduciary accounting purposes.

One of the most difficult aspects of feeling comfortable with the fiduciary taxation rules is appreciating the difference between fiduciary accounting income and income in the general tax sense. To understand and apply the IRC, one has to know in which context the word *income* is used. Section 643(b) provides guidance for this matter. It states, "[F]or purposes of this subpart and subparts B, C and D [Secs. 641–668] , the term 'income' when not preceded by the words 'taxable,' 'distributable net,' 'undistributed net,' or 'gross,' means the amount of income of the estate or trust for the taxable year determined under the terms of the governing instrument and applicable local law." In other words, in most of Subchapter J, the word *income* refers to income in the fiduciary accounting context unless other words modify the word *income*. In this text, the term **net accounting income** is used to refer to the excess of accounting gross income over expenses charged to accounting income.

SELF-STUDY QUESTION

A trust agreement provides that all trust income is to be distributed to Janet until Joe's thirty-fifth birthday, at which time the trust is to terminate and distribute all of its corpus to Joe. Stock is the only property owned by the trust. The stock, purchased for $15,000 by the trust 15 years ago, is worth $100,000. If the trust sells the stock before it terminates, is Janet entitled to the $85,000 profit and Joe to the $15,000 original investment?

ANSWER

This question stresses the importance of differentiating between income and principal. The trustee, in his or her fiduciary capacity, must follow the definitions of income and corpus as stated in the trust agreement, or if not there, under state law. Janet receives nothing if the proceeds are classified as corpus.

The categorization of a receipt or disbursement as principal or income generally affects the amount that can be distributed and the amount taxed to the fiduciary or the beneficiary. For example, if a gain is classified as principal and the trustee can distribute only income, the trust is taxed on the gain. Even though an item constitutes gross income for tax purposes, the trustee cannot distribute it to a beneficiary if it constitutes principal under the fiduciary accounting rules unless the trust instrument authorizes the trustee to distribute principal. If the trust instrument stipulates that the trustee can distribute only income prior to the termination of the trust, the amount of fiduciary accounting income sets the ceiling on the current distribution that the trustee can make to a beneficiary.

EXAMPLE C14-4 ▶ In the current year, the Bell Trust reports net accounting income of $18,000. In addition, it sells stock for a $40,000 capital gain. Under state law, the gain is allocated to principal. The trust instrument (which does not define principal or income) requires the trustee to distribute all the trust's income to Beth annually until she reaches age 45. The trust assets are to be held and paid to Beth on her forty-fifth birthday (five years from now). The trustee must distribute $18,000 to Beth in the current year. The capital gain cannot be distributed currently because it is allocated to principal, and the trustee is not empowered to make distributions of principal. The trust will pay tax on the gain. ◀

EFFECTS OF STATE LAW OR TERMS OF TRUST INSTRUMENT

Recall that, for purposes of Subchapter J, *income* generally refers to income as determined under the governing instrument and applicable local law. Grantors can influence the tax consequences to trusts and their beneficiaries because they can define income and principal in the trust instrument in whatever manner they desire. For example, they can specify that gains are to be included in income. Under state law, the definitions in the trust instrument preempt any definitions contained in state statutes. In the absence of definitions in the trust instrument, the applicable state statute controls for classifying items as principal or income. For purposes of defining principal and income, many states have adopted the *Revised Uniform Principal and Income Act* (enacted in 1962 and hereafter referred to as the Uniform Act of 1962) in its entirety or with minor modifications.[5]

SELF-STUDY QUESTION

Why does the Uniform Act of 1962 allocate to principal part of the royalty from a property such as a gravel pit?

ANSWER

The property is a wasting asset, which means that the removal of the mineral eventually uses up the property. The principal of the trust would be reduced by such removal if some part of the proceeds were not added back into principal, ostensibly to be used to replace whatever was removed.

PRINCIPAL AND INCOME: THE UNIFORM ACT

INCOME RECEIPTS. The Uniform Act of 1962 defines *income* as "the return in money or property derived from the use of principal." It lists income as including the following: rent, interest, corporate distributions of dividends, distributions by a regulated investment company from ordinary income, and the net profits of a business. The rules are more

[5] The *Revised Uniform Principal and Income Act* (1962) is a model set of rules proposed by the National Conference of Commissions on Uniform State Laws. States can voluntarily adopt such provisions verbatim or in amended form.

detailed for receipts from the disposition of natural resources. A portion (27.5%) of the receipts from royalties is added to principal as a depletion allowance. The remainder of the royalties constitutes income.

ADDITIONAL COMMENT

The Commissioners approved and recommended for enactment the *Uniform Principal and Income Act* (1997). It contains a number of changes. To date, few states have adopted it.

PRINCIPAL RECEIPTS. ***Principal*** is defined in the Uniform Act of 1962 as "the property which has been set aside by the owner or the person legally empowered so that it is held in trust eventually to be delivered to the **remainderman** while the return or use of the principal is in the meantime taken or received by or held for accumulation for an **income beneficiary**." Among the categories of receipts included in principal are the following: consideration received on the sale or other transfer of principal or on repayment of a loan, stock dividends, receipts from disposition of corporate securities, and 27.5% of royalties received from natural resources.

EXPENDITURES. The Uniform Act of 1962 provides guidance for expenditures also. Among the important charges that reduce income are the following:

- Ordinary expenses, including regularly recurring property taxes, insurance premiums, interest, and ordinary repairs
- A reasonable allowance for depreciation
- Tax payable by the trustee if it is levied on receipts classified as income

Some of the significant expenditures chargeable to principal are

- Principal payments on an indebtedness
- Extraordinary repairs or expenses incurred in making a capital improvement
- Any tax levied on gain or other receipts allocated to principal even if the tax is described as an income tax

Frequently, the agreement with the trustee specifies the respective portions of the trustee's fee that are chargeable to income and corpus.

EXAMPLE C14-5 ▶

The governing instrument for the Wang Trust does not define income and principal. The state in question has adopted the Uniform Act of 1962. In the current year, the trust reports the following receipts and disbursements:

Dividends	$12,000
Proceeds from sale of stock, including $20,000 of gain	70,000
Trustee's fee, all charged to income	1,000
CPA's fee for preparation of tax return	500

The trust's net accounting income is $10,500 ($12,000 − $1,000 − $500). The gain on the sale of stock and the rest of the sales proceeds constitute corpus. Consequently, if the trustee can distribute nothing but income, the maximum distribution is $10,500. ◀

SELF-STUDY QUESTION

Wilson Trust, which owns a commercial building, is required to distribute all of its income each year. The building is leased to a tenant on a net lease, so the only expense the trust has is depreciation. The rental income is $25,000, and the depreciation is $11,000. If depreciation is chargeable to income, the distribution to the income beneficiary will be $14,000, and the trustee will set aside $11,000 of the income for the remainderman. What is the impact if depreciation is chargeable to principal?

ANSWER

The income distribution will be $25,000. If the trust holds the building to the end of its useful life, the building will theoretically "turn to dust" overnight, and the remainderman would receive nothing (as far as the building is concerned) because the trust had no depreciation reserve.

CATEGORIZATION OF DEPRECIATION

As mentioned above, the Uniform Act of 1962 charges depreciation to income. Depreciation thereby reduces net accounting income and the maximum amount that can be distributed to a beneficiary if the trust instrument does not authorize the distribution of corpus. Many states have departed from the Uniform Act's treatment of depreciation by providing that depreciation is a charge against principal (instead of against income). If depreciation is charged against principal, the maximum amount that can be distributed to the income beneficiaries is not reduced by the depreciation deduction. This result is advantageous to the income beneficiary. (See page C14-9 for a discussion of the tax treatment of depreciation.)

Some trust instruments require the trustee to set aside (and not distribute) a certain amount of income as a depreciation reserve. A statement in the trust instrument concerning the accounting treatment for depreciation overrides a provision of state law.

EXAMPLE C14-6 ▶

Park Trust, whose trust instrument is silent with respect to depreciation, collects rental income of $17,000 and pays property taxes of $1,000. Its depreciation expense is $4,000. Under state law, all depreciation is charged to principal. Therefore, the trust's net accounting income is $16,000 ($17,000 − $1,000). If the trust instrument mandates current distribution of all the income, the beneficiary receives $16,000. If the trust instrument states that depreciation is charged against income, the income distribution is limited to $12,000. ◀

Topic Review C14-1 summarizes the treatment under the Uniform Act of the major receipts and expenditures of fiduciaries.

FORMULA FOR TAXABLE INCOME AND TAX LIABILITY

OBJECTIVE 3

Explain how to calculate the tax liability of a trust or an estate

With three major exceptions, the formula for determining a fiduciary's taxable income and income tax liability is very similar to the formula applicable to individuals. A fiduciary's deductions are not divided between deductions *for* and *from* adjusted gross income (AGI). Instead, a fiduciary's deductions are simply deductible in arriving at taxable income. A fiduciary receives no standard deduction. A type of deduction inapplicable to individuals—the distribution deduction—is available in computing a fiduciary's taxable income. Figure C14-1 illustrates the formula for computing a fiduciary's taxable income and tax liability.

GROSS INCOME

The items included in a trust or estate's gross income are the same as those included in an individual's gross income. However, the categorization of a fiduciary's income is not identical for tax and accounting purposes. For example, a gain usually constitutes principal for accounting purposes, but it is part of gross income for tax purposes.

EXAMPLE C14-7 ▶ In the current year, Duke Trust receives $8,000 interest on corporate bonds, $20,000 interest on state bonds, and a $50,000 capital gain. The trust reports gross income of $58,000 ($8,000 + $50,000). Its accounting income is $28,000 ($8,000 + $20,000) because the gain is part of principal. ◀

DEDUCTIONS FOR EXPENSES

Fiduciaries incur numerous deductible expenses that parallel those of individuals and include interest, taxes (e.g., state and local income taxes and property taxes), fees for investment advice, fees for tax return preparation, expenses associated with producing income, and trade or business expenses. In addition, fiduciaries may deduct the trustee's fee. This fee, which is similar to a property management fee incurred by an individual, is deductible under Sec. 212 as an expense incurred for the management of property held for the production of income.

Topic Review C14-1

Classification of Receipts and Expenditures as Principal or Income Under the Uniform Act of 1962

INCOME ACCOUNT	PRINCIPAL ACCOUNT
Income:	Receipts:
Rent	Consideration (including gains) received upon disposition or property
Interest	Stock dividends
Dividends	27.5% of royalties
Net profits of a business	
72.5% of royalties	
Expenses:	Expenditures:
Ordinary expenses (e.g., property taxes, insurance, interest, and ordinary repairs)	Principal payments on debt
Taxes levied on accounting income	Extraordinary repairs and capital improvements
Depreciation[a]	Taxes levied on gains and other items of principal

[a]Many state laws depart from the Uniform Act and characterize depreciation as a charge to principal.

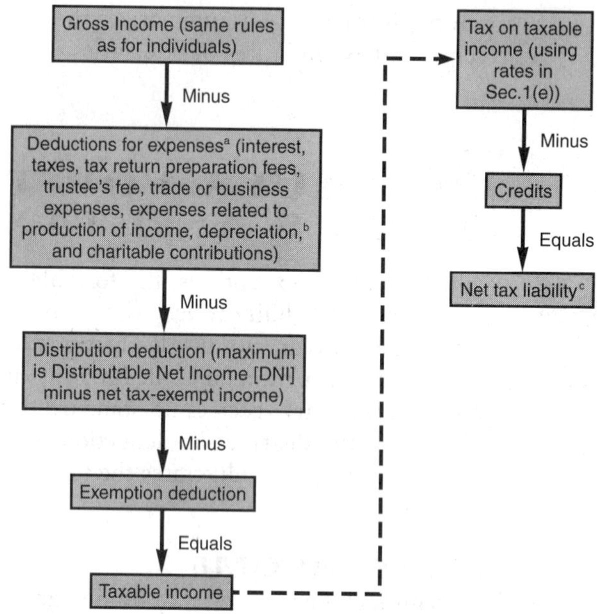

[a]No deduction is available for expenses allocable to tax-exempt income.

[b]When the trust instrument is silent, depreciation is allocated between the fiduciary and the beneficiary according to the portion of income attributable to each.

[c]Trusts and estates also are subject to the alternative minimum tax (AMT). The AMT may be owed by a trust or estate in addition to the income tax levy described in this figure. The AMT is calculated in the same way as for individual taxpayers. Trusts and estates, however, are allowed only a $22,500 statutory exemption. This exemption is phased-out from $75,000 to $165,000 of alternative minimum taxable income.

FIGURE C14-1 ▶ FORMULA FOR DETERMINING THE TAXABLE INCOME AND TAX LIABILITY OF A FIDUCIARY

KEY POINT

Trustees' and executors' fees, as well as tax return preparation fees, are *not* subject to the 2% miscellaneous itemized deduction floor.

Miscellaneous itemized deductions are deductible only to the extent the aggregate amount of such deductions exceeds 2% of the taxpayer's AGI. Although estates and trusts do not literally have AGI, according to Sec. 67(e), a hypothetical AGI amount for an estate or trust is determined in the same fashion as for an individual *except* that expenses paid or incurred in connection with the administration of the estate or trust *that would not have been incurred if the property were not held in such trust or estate,* the personal exemption, and the distribution deduction are treated as deductible for hypothetical AGI. Thus, these deductions are not subject to the 2% floor, and by being subtracted to arrive at hypothetical AGI, they reduce the amount of disallowed miscellaneous deductions. The trustees' or executors' fees and the cost of preparation of a fiduciary return would have been avoided had the trust or estate not existed and therefore are excepted from the 2% floor. In *William J. O'Neill, Jr. Irrevocable Trust*[6] the Sixth Circuit reversed the Tax Court's decision, which had held that amounts paid for investment counsel fees were subject to the floor because they were not unique to the administration of estates and trusts. In *Mellon Bank, N.A.,*[7] the Federal Circuit upheld the decision of the U.S. Court of Federal Claims that fees for investment advice were subject to the 2% floor. The court reasoned that such fees failed the requirement that they would not have been incurred had there been no trust.

An executor can deduct administration expenses on the estate's income tax return if he or she does not deduct such items on the estate tax return. Unlike the situation for individuals, a fiduciary's charitable contribution deduction is not limited. The IRC does not allow a deduction, however, unless the trust instrument authorizes a charitable contribution.[8]

[6] 71 AFTR 2d 93-2052, 93-1 USTC ¶50,332 (6th Cir., 1993), reversing 98 T.C. 227 (1992), nonacq., I.R.B. 1994-38, 4.

[7] 88 AFTR 2d 2001-5800, 2001-2 USTC ¶50,621 (Fed. Cir., 2001).

[8] Sec. 642(c)(1).

A depreciation or depletion deduction is available to an estate or trust only to the extent it is not allowable to beneficiaries under Secs. 167(h) or 611(b).[9] According to Sec. 167(h), the depreciation deduction for trusts is apportioned between the income beneficiaries and the trust pursuant to the terms of the trust instrument. If the instrument is silent, the depreciation is divided between the parties on the basis of the trust income allocable to each. For estates, however, the depreciation always must be apportioned according to the share of the income allocable to each party. The Sec. 611(b) rules for depletion parallel those described above for the allocation of depreciation.

EXAMPLE C14-8 ▶

In the current year, Nunn Trust distributes 20% of its income to Bob and 50% to Clay. It accumulates the remaining 30%. The trust's current year depreciation is $10,000. The trust instrument is silent concerning the depreciation deduction. Under state law, depreciation is charged to principal. Even though net accounting income and the maximum distributable amount are not reduced by the depreciation deduction, Bob receives a $2,000 (0.20 × $10,000) depreciation deduction, and Clay receives a $5,000 (0.50 × $10,000) depreciation deduction. The remaining $3,000 (0.30 × $10,000) of depreciation is deducted in calculating the trust's taxable income. ◀

KEY POINT

If a trust *must* distribute all of its income currently, has no charitable beneficiary, *and* does *not* distribute corpus during the year, it is a simple trust for that year. *Income,* as used here, is accounting net income.

DISTRIBUTION DEDUCTION

SIMPLE TRUSTS. Some trusts must distribute all their income currently and are not empowered to make charitable contributions. Treasury Regulations refer to such trusts as **simple trusts.**[10] According to Sec. 651(a), these trusts receive a distribution deduction for the income required to be distributed currently, that is, 100% of the trust income. No words modify the word *income;* therefore, *income* means accounting income. If the accounting income that must be distributed exceeds the trust's distributable net income (see page C14-10), the distribution deduction may not exceed the distributable net income. As used in this context, distributable net income does not include any tax-free income (net of related deductions) that the trust earned.[11] Whatever amount is deductible at the trust level is taxed to the beneficiaries, and they are taxed on all the income, irrespective of the amount they receive.

COMPLEX TRUSTS. Trusts that are not required to distribute all their income currently are referred to as **complex trusts.**[12] The distribution deduction for complex trusts and all estates is the sum of the income required to be distributed currently and any other amounts (such as discretionary payments) properly paid, credited, or required to be distributed for the year. As is the case for simple trusts, the distribution deduction may not exceed the trust or estate's distributable net income (reduced by its tax-exempt income net of any related deductions).[13] The complex trust or estate's beneficiaries report, in the aggregate, gross income equal to the amount of the distribution deduction.[14]

EXAMPLE C14-9 ▶

Green Trust must distribute 25% of its income annually to Amy. In addition, the trustee in its discretion may distribute additional income to Amy or Brad. In the current year, the trust has accounting net income and distributable net income of $100,000, none from tax-exempt sources. The trust makes a $25,000 mandatory distribution to Amy and $10,000 discretionary distributions each to Amy and Brad. The trust's distribution deduction is $45,000 ($25,000 + $10,000 + $10,000). Amy and Brad report trust income of $35,000 and $10,000, respectively, on their individual returns. ◀

PERSONAL EXEMPTION

One of the differences between the rules for individuals and for fiduciaries is the amount of the personal exemption. Under Sec. 151, individuals are allowed personal exemptions. Section 642(b) authorizes an exemption for fiduciaries that applies in lieu of the amount for individuals. A trust or estate, however, receives no exemption in the year of its termination.

[9] Sec. 642(e).
[10] Reg. Sec. 1.651(a)-1.
[11] Sec. 651(b).
[12] Reg. Sec. 1.661(a)-1.
[13] Secs. 661(a) and (c).
[14] Sec. 662(a).

Estates are entitled to a $600 exemption. The exemption amount for trusts differs, depending on the terms of the trust. If the trust instrument requires that the trustee distribute all the income annually, the trust receives a $300 exemption. Otherwise, $100 is the exemption amount. Some trusts may be required to make current distributions of all their income in certain years, whereas in other years they may be directed to accumulate the income or to make distributions at the trustee's discretion. For such trusts the exemption amount is $300 in some years and $100 in other years.

EXAMPLE C14-10 ▶ Gold Trust is established in 2001 with Jack as the beneficiary. The trust instrument instructs the trustee to make discretionary distributions of income to Jack during the years 2001 through 2005. Beginning in 2006, the trustee is to pay all the trust income to Jack currently. For 2001 through 2005, the trust's exemption is $100. Beginning in 2006, it rises to $300. ◀

Recall that a trust receives a distribution deduction for income currently distributed to its beneficiaries. At first blush, it appears that the distribution deduction balances out the income of trusts that must distribute all their income currently, and such trusts receive no tax benefits from their exemption deduction. True, the exemption produces no tax savings for such trusts if they have no gains credited to principal. Tax savings do result from the personal exemption, however, if the trust has undistributed gains. The exemption reduces the amount of gain otherwise taxed at the trust level.

EXAMPLE C14-11 ▶ Rizzo Trust must distribute all of its income currently. Capital gains are characterized as principal. In the current year, Rizzo Trust has $25,000 of interest income from corporate bonds and a $10,000 capital gain. It has no expenses. It receives a distribution deduction of $25,000 and a $300 personal exemption. Its taxable income is $9,700 ($25,000 + $10,000 − $25,000 − $300). ◀

SELF-STUDY QUESTION

A trust, although not required to do so, distributes all of its income for the year. In the same year, it has a long-term capital gain. The trust agreement allocates the gain to principal. The trust does not distribute corpus, and none of its beneficiaries are charities. Is the trust a simple trust? What is its personal exemption?

ANSWER

It is a complex trust because it is not required to distribute all of its income. The exemption is $100 because distributions are discretionary.

The personal exemption amount for individuals is adjusted annually for changes in the consumer price index, but no comparable provision exists for the personal exemption for fiduciaries. The tax rate schedules for both fiduciaries and individuals are indexed for inflation.

CREDITS

In general, the rules for tax credits for fiduciaries are the same as those for individuals, but a fiduciary generally does not incur expenditures of the type that trigger some of the personal credits, such as the credit for household and dependent care expenses. Trusts and estates are allowed a foreign tax credit determined in the same manner as for individual taxpayers except that the credit is limited to the amount of foreign taxes not allocable to the beneficiaries.[15]

DISTRIBUTABLE NET INCOME

OBJECTIVE 4

Understand the significance of distributable net income

As stated earlier in this chapter, the primary function of Subchapter J is to determine to whom—the fiduciary, the beneficiary, or some to each—the estate or the trust's current income is to be taxed. **Distributable net income (DNI)** plays a key role in determining the amount taxed to each party. In fact, DNI has been called the pie to be cut for tax purposes.[16]

SELF-STUDY QUESTION

What functions does distributable net income (DNI) serve?

SIGNIFICANCE OF DNI

DNI sets the ceiling on the amount of distributions taxed to the beneficiaries. As mentioned earlier, beneficiaries are taxed on the lesser of the amount of the distributions they receive or their share of DNI (reduced by net tax-exempt income).

[15] Sec. 642(a)(1).

[16] M. Carr Ferguson, James L. Freeland, and Richard B. Stephens, *Federal Income Taxation of Estates and Beneficiaries* (Boston, MA: Little, Brown, 1970), p. 1x.

ANSWER

1. It establishes the maximum amount on which the beneficiaries may be taxed.
2. It establishes the maximum amount the trust or estate may deduct as a distribution deduction.
3. It establishes the character of the income or expense in DNI that flows to the beneficiaries (income or expense flows to the beneficiaries in proportion to the part each different type of income or expense bears to DNI).

Just as the total amount taxed to the beneficiaries equals the fiduciary's distribution deduction, DNI represents not only the maximum that can be taxed to the beneficiaries but also the maximum that can be deducted at the fiduciary level. Recall from the preceding section that the distribution deduction is the smaller of the amount distributed or the fiduciary's DNI. The distribution deduction, however, may not include any portion of tax-exempt income (net of any related deductions) deemed to have been distributed.

DNI also determines the character of the beneficiaries' income. Under the conduit approach, each beneficiary's distribution is deemed to consist of various categories of income (net of deductions) in the same proportion as the total of each class of income bears to the total DNI. For example, if 40% of the trust's income consists of dividends, 40% of each beneficiary's distribution is deemed to consist of dividends.

EXAMPLE C14-12 ▶ Sun Trust has $30,000 of DNI for the current year. Its DNI includes $10,000 of rental income and $20,000 of corporate bond interest. The trust instrument requires that each year the trustee distribute 30% of the trust's income to Jose and 70% to Petra. Because the trust has no tax-exempt income and must distribute all of its income, it receives a $30,000 distribution deduction.

Jose reports $9,000 (0.30 × $30,000) of trust income, and Petra reports $21,000 (0.70 × $30,000) of trust income. Because rents make up one-third ($10,000 ÷ $30,000) of DNI, the composition of the income reported by Jose and Petra is one-third rental income and two-thirds corporate bond interest. ◀

DEFINITION OF DNI

Section 643(a) defines *DNI* as the fiduciary's taxable income, adjusted as follows:

- No distribution deduction is subtracted.
- No personal exemption is subtracted.
- Capital gains are not included and capital losses are not subtracted unless such gains and losses are allocated to accounting income instead of to principal.
- Extraordinary dividends and taxable stock dividends are not included if they are allocable to principal.
- An addition is made for tax-exempt interest (minus the expenses allocable thereto).

Because one purpose of DNI is to set a ceiling on the distribution deduction, the distribution deduction is not subtracted from taxable income in determining DNI. If capital gains and extraordinary dividends are allocated to corpus, they are excluded from DNI because they cannot be distributed. Tax-exempt interest is part of accounting income and can be distributed even though it is excluded from gross income. Consequently, DNI includes tax-exempt income (net of the nondeductible expenses allocable to such income). Even though net tax-exempt income is included in DNI, no distribution deduction is available for the portion of the distribution deemed to consist of tax-exempt income.

KEY POINT

A significant difference between net accounting income and DNI is that DNI is reduced by certain expenses charged to principal. These expenses do not decrease net accounting income, nor do they decrease the amount of money that can be distributed.

In general, net accounting income and DNI are the same, with one exception. Any expenses (e.g., trustee's fees) charged to principal reduce DNI even though they do not lessen net accounting income. The trustee's fees (whether charged to income or to principal) are deductible in arriving at taxable income, and to arrive at DNI no further adjustment is made to taxable income for such expenses. Reduction of DNI by the expenses charged to principal provides a tax advantage for the income beneficiary because these fees lessen the amount that is taxable to the beneficiary. However, they do not decrease the money that can be distributed to the beneficiary.

MANNER OF COMPUTING DNI

The amount of taxable income is in large measure a function of the distribution deduction, and the distribution deduction depends on the amount of DNI. The distribution deduction cannot exceed DNI. Thus, the Sec. 643(a) definition of DNI, which involves making adjustments to a fiduciary's taxable income, is not a workable definition from a practical standpoint because the computation is circular. The distribution deduction must be computed to arrive at the amount of income taxable to the fiduciary, and the distribution deduction depends, in part, on the amount of DNI.

However, there are two other practical means of determining DNI. The first approach, as illustrated below, begins with taxable income exclusive of the distribution deduction and makes the adjustments (other than the distribution deduction) to taxable income that the IRC specifies.

EXAMPLE C14-13 ▶ In the current year, Darby Trust reports the following results. The trust must distribute all of its income annually.

	Amounts Allocable to	
	Income	*Principal*
Corporate bond interest	$20,000	
Rental income	30,000	
Gain on sale of investment land		$40,000
Property taxes	5,000	
Trustee's fee charged to corpus		2,000
Distribution to beneficiary	45,000	

The trust's taxable income exclusive of the distribution deduction is computed as follows:

Corporate bond interest	$20,000
Rental income	30,000
Capital gain	40,000
Minus: Property taxes	(5,000)
Trustee's fee	(2,000)
Personal exemption	(300)
Taxable income exclusive of distribution deduction	$82,700

Now that taxable income exclusive of the distribution deduction has been determined, DNI can be computed in the following manner:

Taxable income exclusive of distribution deduction	$82,700
Plus: Personal exemption	300
Minus: Capital gain	(40,000)
DNI	$43,000 ◀

A second method for determining DNI is to calculate the amount of net accounting income and reduce such amount by any expenses charged to corpus. In a few situations, however, DNI is a larger amount than the amount arrived at under this approach, but the discussion of such situations is beyond the scope of this book.

EXAMPLE C14-14 ▶ Assume the same facts as in Example C14-13. The following steps illustrate the second approach to calculating the DNI amount.

Corporate bond interest	$20,000
Rental income	30,000
Minus: Property taxes	(5,000)
Net accounting income	$45,000
Minus: Trustee's fee charged to corpus	(2,000)
DNI	$43,000 ◀

Although the beneficiary receives a cash distribution of $45,000 (net accounting income), he or she reports only $43,000 (DNI) as income. The beneficiary receives $2,000 tax-free. Thus, an income beneficiary benefits from trustee's fees charged to principal by getting to report a smaller amount of gross income than the amount of cash he or she receives. The trust's distribution deduction cannot exceed $43,000 (DNI) even though the amount paid to the beneficiary is higher than this amount.

Topic Review C14-2 summarizes the DNI concept.

STOP & THINK *Question:* Wei is the beneficiary of a two unrelated simple trusts. His marginal tax rate is 27%. From which simple trust would Wei's after-tax cash flow be larger?

- Trust A collects dividend income of $40,000 and pays a trustee's fee of $1,000. The trustee's fee is charged to corpus.
- Trust B collects corporate bond interest of $40,000 and pays a trustee's fee of $800. The trustee's fee is charged to income.

Solution: Wei would receive $40,000 in cash from Trust A but pay federal income taxes on only $39,000, which is the trust's DNI. The trust's distribution is based on net accounting income, which is not reduced by the trustee's fee. Wei's gross income is based on the trust's DNI, which is reduced by the trustee's fee. Wei would receive $39,200 in cash from Trust B. He would pay federal income taxes on the same $39,200 amount, which is the trust's DNI. The trustee's fee paid by Trust B reduces both net accounting income and DNI. Even though the trust's economic income is larger with Trust B, Wei would have a larger amount of after-tax cash flow from Trust A.

DETERMINING A SIMPLE TRUST'S TAXABLE INCOME

OBJECTIVE 5

Determine the taxable income of a simple trust

The term *simple trust* does not appear in the IRC. Treasury Regulations interpreting Secs. 651 and 652—the statutory rules for trusts that distribute current income only—introduce the term *simple trust.* The provisions of Secs. 651 and 652 are applicable only to trusts whose trust agreements require that all income be distributed currently and do not authorize charitable contributions. Moreover, such provisions are inapplicable if the trust makes distributions of principal.

Some trusts may be required to pay out all their income currently in certain years but are permitted to retain a portion of their income in other years. In some of the years in which they must distribute all their income, they also may make mandatory or discretionary distributions of principal. These trusts are simple trusts in some years and complex trusts in others. The amount of the personal exemption, however, turns not on whether the trust is simple or complex but on whether it must pay out all its income currently. Suppose,

Topic Review C14-2

The Distributable Net Income (DNI) Concept

Significance of DNI

DNI, exclusive of net tax-exempt interest included therein, sets the ceiling on:

1. The distribution deduction, and
2. The aggregate amount of gross income reportable by the beneficiaries.

Calculation of DNI

Taxable income, exclusive of distribution deduction[a]	
Plus:	Personal exemption
Minus:	Capital gains (or plus deductible capital losses)
Plus:	Tax-exempt interest (net of allocable expenses)
DNI[b]	

[a] Gross income (dividends, taxable interest, rents, and capital gains) minus deductible expenses and the personal exemption.
[b] In general, DNI is the same amount as net accounting income minus trustee's fees charged to corpus.

▼ **TABLE C14-1**
Trust Classification Rules and the Size of the Exemption

Situation	Classification	Exemption Amount
Required to pay out all of its income, makes no charitable contributions, distributes no principal	Simple	$300
Required to pay out all of its income, makes no charitable contributions, distributes principal	Complex	$300
Required to pay out all of its income, authorized to make charitable contributions, distributes no principal	Complex	$300
Authorized to make discretionary distributions of income, makes no charitable contributions, distributes no principal	Complex	$100
Authorized to make discretionary distributions of income and principal, makes no charitable contributions	Complex	$100

for example, a trust must pay out all of its current income and one-fourth of its principal. Because the trust distributes principal, it is a complex trust. It claims a $300 personal exemption because of the mandate to distribute all of its income. Table C14-1 highlights the trust classification rules and the $300 or $100 exemption dichotomy.

ALLOCATION OF EXPENSES TO TAX-EXEMPT INCOME

Recall that expenses related to producing tax-exempt income are not deductible.[17] Thus, if a trust has income from both taxable and tax-exempt sources and it incurs expenses that are not directly attributable to the production of taxable income, a portion of such expenses may not be deducted. Regulation Secs. 1.652(b)-3 and 1.652(c)-4(e) address the issue of the allocation of deductions. An expense directly attributable to one type of income, such as a repair expense for rental property, is allocated thereto. Expenses not directly related to a particular item of income, such as a trustee's fee for administering the trust's assets, may be allocated to any type of income included in computing DNI, provided a portion of the expense is allocated to nontaxable income. Regulation Sec. 1.652(b)-3 sets forth the following formula for determining the amount of indirect expenses allocable to nontaxable income:

$$\frac{\text{Tax-exempt income (net of expenses directly attributable thereto)}}{\text{Accounting income (net of all direct expenses)}^{18}} \times \text{Expenses not directly attributable to any item of income} = \text{Indirect expenses allocable to nontaxable income}$$

EXAMPLE C14-15 ▶ In the current year, the Mason Trust reports the following results:

Dividends	$16,000
Interest from corporate bonds	6,000
Tax-exempt interest from state bonds	18,000
Capital gain (allocated to corpus)	20,000
Trustee's fee, all allocated to corpus	4,000

[17] Sec. 265(a)(1).

[18] A discrepancy exists in the Treasury Regulations with respect to how to allocate expenses to tax-exempt income. According to Reg. Sec. 1.652(b)-3(b), the denominator is accounting income net of direct expenses. Regulation Sec. 1.652(c)-4(e), however, shows computations where accounting income is not reduced by direct expenses to arrive at the denominator. The text uses the latter approach.

SELF-STUDY QUESTION

A trust can allocate indirect expenses arbitrarily (after the appropriate allocation is made to tax-exempt income). Hill Trust has rental income, taxable interest income, and dividend income this year. To which income would you suggest allocating the trustee's fee?

ANSWER

If possible, the trust should take into consideration the tax status of its beneficiaries. In a situation where the sole beneficiary has nondeductible rental losses of his or her own, it would be beneficial to charge the fee to interest or dividend income, thereby reducing the beneficiaries' portfolio income.

Accounting gross income is \$40,000 (\$16,000 + \$6,000 + \$18,000). The trustee's fee is an indirect expense that must be allocated to the tax-exempt income as follows:

$$\frac{\$18,000}{\$40,000} \times \$4,000 = \$1,800$$

Thus, the Mason Trust cannot deduct \$1,800 of its trustee's fee. The remaining \$2,200 may be allocated to dividends or corporate bond interest in whatever amounts the return preparer desires. ◀

DETERMINATION OF DNI AND THE DISTRIBUTION DEDUCTION

As mentioned above, DNI is defined as taxable income with several adjustments, including a subtraction for capital gains credited to principal. According to the methods described above, a practical technique for determining DNI involves beginning with taxable income exclusive of the distribution deduction. Once DNI has been determined, both the distribution deduction and the trust's taxable income can be calculated.

A simple trust must distribute all of its net accounting income currently. Thus, a simple trust generally receives a distribution deduction equal to the amount of its net accounting income.[19] The following two exceptions modify this general rule:

- The distribution deduction may not exceed DNI. Therefore, if a trust has expenses that are charged to corpus (as in Example C14-13), the distribution deduction is limited to the DNI amount because DNI is smaller than net accounting income.
- Because tax-exempt income is not included in the trust's gross income, no distribution deduction is available for tax-exempt income (net of the expenses allocable thereto) included in DNI.[20]

TAX TREATMENT FOR BENEFICIARY

The aggregate gross income reported by the beneficiaries equals the trust's net accounting income, subject to the constraint that the aggregate of their gross income amount does not exceed the trust's DNI. If DNI is lower than net accounting income and the trust has more than one beneficiary, each beneficiary's share of gross income is the following fraction of total DNI:[21]

$$\frac{\text{Income required to be distributed to such beneficiary}}{\text{Income required to be distributed to } \textit{all} \text{ beneficiaries}}$$

The income received by the beneficiaries retains the character it had at the trust level. Thus, if the trust receives tax-exempt interest, the beneficiaries are deemed to have received tax-exempt interest. Unless the trust instrument specifically allocates particular types of income to certain beneficiaries, the income of each beneficiary is viewed as consisting of the same fraction of each category of income as the total of such category bears to total DNI.

EXAMPLE C14-16 ▶ In the current year, Crane Trust has \$22,000 of tax-exempt interest and \$66,000 of dividends and pays \$8,000 of trustee's fees from corpus. Its DNI is \$80,000: \$20,000 of net tax-exempt interest and \$60,000 of net dividends. The trust instrument requires distribution of one-eighth of the income annually to Matt and the remaining seven-eighths of the income to Pat. The distributions to Matt and Pat are \$11,000 and \$77,000, respectively. The distribution deduction and the aggregate gross income of the beneficiaries are limited to \$60,000 (\$80,000 DNI − \$20,000 net tax-exempt interest). Matt and Pat will report gross income of \$7,500 (0.125 × \$60,000) and \$52,500 (0.875 × \$60,000), respectively. Dividends make up 75% (\$60,000 ÷ \$80,000) of DNI and 100% (\$60,000 ÷ \$60,000) of taxable DNI. Therefore, all of Matt's and Pat's *gross* income is deemed to consist of dividends. Matt and Pat also are viewed as having received \$2,500 (0.125 × \$20,000) and \$17,500 (0.875 × \$20,000), respectively, of tax-exempt interest. ◀

---

[19] Sec. 651(a).

[20] Sec. 651(b).

[21] Sec. 652(a).

Because a simple trust must distribute all of its income currently, trustees cannot defer the taxation of trust income to the beneficiaries by postponing distributions until the beginning of the next year. Beneficiaries of simple trusts are taxed currently on their pro rata share of taxable DNI regardless of the actual amount distributed to them during the year.[22]

SHORT-CUT APPROACH TO PROVING CORRECTNESS OF TAXABLE INCOME

A short-cut approach may be used to verify the correctness of the amount calculated as a simple trust's taxable income. Because a simple trust must distribute all of its income currently, the only item taxable at the trust level should be the amount of gains (net of losses) credited to principal, reduced by the personal exemption. The taxable income calculated under the short-cut approach should equal the taxable income determined under the formula illustrated in Figure C14-1. The steps of the short-cut approach are as follows:

1. Start with the excess of gains over losses credited to principal.
2. Subtract the $300 personal exemption.

EXAMPLE C14-17 ▶ In the current year, West Trust, which must distribute all of its income currently, reports $25,000 of corporate bond interest, a $44,000 long-term capital gain, and a $4,000 long-term capital loss. Under the short-cut approach, its taxable income is calculated as $39,700 [($44,000 − $4,000) − $300 personal exemption]. In the actual calculation of taxable income, the trust also reports $25,000 of gross income from interest and a $25,000 distribution deduction. ◀

EFFECT OF A NET OPERATING LOSS

If a trust incurs a net operating loss (NOL), the loss does not pass through currently to the beneficiaries unless the loss arises in the year the trust terminates, but the trust can carry the NOL back and forward. In determining the amount of the NOL, deductions are not allowed for charitable contributions or the distribution deduction.[23] In the year a trust terminates, any loss that would otherwise qualify for a loss carryover at the trust level passes through to the individual return of the beneficiary(ies) succeeding to the trust's property.[24]

EXAMPLE C14-18 ▶ In 2002, the year it terminates, New Trust incurs a $10,000 NOL. It also has a $40,000 NOL carryover from 2000 and 2001. At termination, New Trust distributes 30% of its assets to Kay and 70% to Liz. Because 2002 is the termination year, Kay may report a $15,000 (0.30 × $50,000) NOL on her 2002 return, and Liz may report a $35,000 (0.70 × $50,000) NOL on her 2002 return. Before 2002, the beneficiaries cannot report any of the trust's NOLs on their returns. ◀

EFFECT OF A NET CAPITAL LOSS

The maximum capital loss that a trust can deduct is the lesser of $3,000 or the excess of its capital losses over capital gains.[25] Because simple trusts must distribute all of their accounting income currently and the distribution deduction reduces their taxable income to zero, they receive no tax benefit from capital losses that exceed capital gains. Nevertheless, the trust's taxable income for the year of the loss is reduced by its net capital loss, up to $3,000. In determining the capital loss carryover, capital losses that produced no tax benefit are available as a carryover to offset capital gains realized by the trust in subsequent years. In addition, if all of the capital loss carryovers have not been absorbed by capital gains before the trust's termination date, the remaining capital loss is passed through in the termination year to the beneficiaries succeeding to the trust's property.[26]

---

[22] Reg. Sec. 1.652(a)-1.

[23] Reg. Sec. 1.642(d)-1(b).

[24] Reg. Sec. 1.642(h)-1. A trust is never categorized as a simple trust in the year it terminates because in its final year it always makes distributions of principal.

[25] Sec. 1211(b).

[26] Reg. Sec. 1.642(h)-1.

EXAMPLE C14-19 ▶ Old Trust, which must distribute all of its income currently, sells two capital assets during its existence. In 2000, it sells an asset at a $20,000 loss. In 2001, it sells an asset for a $6,000 gain. In 2002, it terminates and distributes its assets equally between its two beneficiaries, Joy and Tim. The trust is not a simple trust in 2002 because it distributes principal that year. Because the $20,000 loss provided no benefit on the 2000 return, the carryover to 2001 is $20,000, and $6,000 of it offsets 2001's $6,000 capital gain. The remaining $14,000 carries forward to 2002. Because 2002 is the termination year, a $7,000 (0.50 × $14,000) capital loss passes through to both Joy's and Tim's individual returns for 2002. Joy realizes a $12,000 capital gain by selling assets in 2002. Joy offsets the $7,000 trust loss against her own gain. Tim sells no assets in 2002. Therefore, Tim deducts $3,000 of the loss from the trust against his other income. His remaining $4,000 loss carries over to 2003. ◀

SELF-STUDY QUESTION

Why do Treasury Regulations (see footnotes 25 and 26) allow unused NOLs and capital losses to be used by the remainderman on the termination of a trust?

ANSWER

Losses have depleted the corpus of the trust. Because the remainderman's interest has been depleted by these losses, it is reasonable to allow the trust to pass these losses through to the remainderman at the end of its life.

Topic Review C14-3 describes how to calculate the trust's taxable income.

COMPREHENSIVE ILLUSTRATION: DETERMINING A SIMPLE TRUST'S TAXABLE INCOME

The following comprehensive illustration reviews a number of the points discussed previously. The facts for this illustration are used to complete the Form 1041 for a simple trust that appears in Appendix B.

BACKGROUND DATA

Zeb Brown established the Bob Adams Trust by a gift in 1992. The trust instrument requires that the trustee (First Bank) distribute all of the trust income at least annually to Bob Adams for life. Capital gains are credited to principal. The 2001 results of the trust are as follows:

	Amounts Allocable	
	Income	*Principal*
Dividends	$30,000	
Rental income from land	5,000	
Tax-exempt interest	15,000	
Rental expenses (realtor's commission on rental income)	1,000	
Trustee's fee		$ 1,200
Fee for preparation of tax return	500	
Capital gain on sale of stock[a]		12,000
Distribution of net accounting income to Bob	48,500	
Payments of estimated tax		2,600

[a] The trust sold the stock in October, having acquired it four years earlier.

Topic Review C14-3

Calculation of Trust Taxable Income

Gross income[a]
Minus: Deductions for expenses[a]
Distribution deduction[b]
Personal exemption ($300 or $100)

Taxable income

[a] Rules for calculating these amounts are generally the same as for individual taxpayers.
[b] Deduction cannot exceed the amount of DNI from taxable sources.

TRUSTEE'S FEE

As mentioned earlier, a portion of the trustee's fee is nondeductible because it must be allocated to tax-exempt income. The trust receives \$50,000 (\$30,000 + \$5,000 + \$15,000) of gross accounting income, of which \$15,000 is tax-exempt. Therefore, \$360 [(\$15,000 ÷ \$50,000) × \$1,200] of the trustee's fee is allocated to tax-exempt income and is nondeductible. The entire return preparation fee is deductible because no such fee would have been incurred had the trust's income been entirely from tax-exempt sources.

DISTRIBUTION DEDUCTION AND DNI

One of the key amounts affecting taxable income is the distribution deduction. Taxable income exclusive of the distribution deduction can be the starting point for determining the amount of DNI, a number crucial in quantifying the distribution deduction. The trust's taxable income, exclusive of the distribution deduction, is calculated as follows:

Dividends		\$30,000
Rental income		5,000
Capital gain on sale of stock		12,000
Minus:	Rental expenses	(1,000)
	Deductible portion of trustee's fee	(840)
	Fee for tax return preparation	(500)
	Personal exemption	(300)
Taxable income, exclusive of distribution deduction		\$44,360

DNI now can be calculated by making the adjustments shown below to taxable income, exclusive of the distribution deduction.[27]

Taxable income, exclusive of distribution deduction		\$44,360
Plus:	Personal exemption	300
Minus:	Capital gain on sale of stock	(12,000)
Plus:	Tax-exempt interest, net of \$360 of allocable expenses	14,640
DNI		\$47,300

Recall that the distribution deduction cannot exceed the DNI, as reduced by tax-exempt income (net of any allocable expenses). The distribution deduction may be computed as follows:

Smaller of:	Net accounting income (\$48,500) or DNI (\$47,300)		\$47,300
Minus:	Tax-exempt interest	\$15,000	
	Minus: Allocable expenses	(360)	(14,640)
Distribution deduction			\$32,660

TRUST'S TAXABLE INCOME

Once the amount of the distribution deduction is determined, the trust's taxable income can be calculated as illustrated in Table C14-2.

CATEGORIZING A BENEFICIARY'S INCOME

In addition to the trust's taxable income, the amount of each category of income received by the beneficiary must be determined. Income reported by the beneficiary retains the same character it had at the trust level. Thus, Bob is deemed to have received dividends, rents, and tax-exempt interest. Rental expenses are charged entirely against rental income. The deductible portion of the trustee's fee and the tax return preparation fee can be allocated in full to rents or dividends, or some to each. If they are allocated in full to rental income, the character of Bob's income is determined as follows:

[27] Another way of determining the amount of DNI is to reduce the net accounting income of \$48,500 by the \$1,200 of expenses charged to principal. The resulting amount is \$47,300.

	Dividends	Rents	Tax-Exempt Interest	Total
Accounting income	$30,000	$5,000	$15,000	$50,000
Minus: Expenses:				
Rental expenses		(1,000)		(1,000)
Trustee's fee		(840)	(360)	(1,200)
Tax return preparation fee		(500)		(500)
DNI	$30,000	$2,660	$14,640	$47,300

Bob reports $30,000 of dividend income and $2,660 of rental income on his individual return.

DETERMINING TAXABLE INCOME FOR COMPLEX TRUSTS AND ESTATES

OBJECTIVE 6

Determine the taxable income of a complex trust and an estate

The caption to Subpart C of Part I of Subchapter J (Secs. 661-664) reads "Distribution for Estates and Trusts Accumulating or Distributing Corpus." In general, the rules applicable to estates and these trusts (complex trusts) are the same. The IRC does not contain the term *complex trust,* but according to Treasury Regulations, "A trust to which subpart C is applicable is referred to as a 'complex' trust."[28] Recall from the discussion about simple trusts that a trust that must distribute all of its income currently can be classified as a complex trust for a particular year if it also pays out some principal during the year.

▼ TABLE C14-2

Comprehensive Illustration: Determining a Simple Trust's Taxable Income and Tax Liability

Gross income:	
Dividends	$30,000
Rental income	5,000
Capital gain on sale of stock	12,000[a]
Minus: Expense deductions:	
Rental expenses	(1,000)
Deductible portion of trustee's fee	(840)
Fee for tax return preparation	(500)
Minus: Distribution deduction	(32,660)
Minus: Personal exemption	(300)
Taxable income	$11,700[b]
Tax liability (2001 rates)	$ 2,160[c]
Minus: Estimated tax payments	(2,600)
Tax owed (refunded)	($ 440)

[a] The stock sale took place in October and involved stock purchased four years ago.

[b] The short-cut approach to verifying taxable income is as follows:

Long-term capital gain	$12,000
Minus: Personal exemption	(300)
Taxable income	$11,700

[c] The taxable income consists of a long-term capital gain, which is taxed at a maximum rate of 10% on the first $1,800 and 20% on the rest.

ADDITIONAL COMMENT

The short-cut approach to computing taxable income used in Table C14-2 consists of reducing the income allocated to corpus by the personal exemption.

[28] Reg. Sec. 1.661(a)-1.

Trusts that can accumulate income are categorized as complex trusts, even in years in which they make discretionary distributions of all their income. A trust also is a complex trust if the trust instrument provides for amounts to be paid to, or set aside for, charitable organizations (see Table C14-1).

Many of the rules are the same for simple and complex trusts, but some differences exist. Different rules are used to determine the distribution deduction for the two types of trusts. The rules for determining an estate's distribution deduction are the same as those applicable to complex trusts. The personal exemption, however, is $600 for an estate and $300 or $100 for a complex trust. The $300 amount applies for years in which a trust must pay out all of its income; otherwise, the exemption is $100.

TAX STRATEGY TIP

Trust managers can reduce overall taxes by carefully planning the amount and timing of distributions. See Tax Planning Considerations later in text for details.

DETERMINATION OF DNI AND THE DISTRIBUTION DEDUCTION

Section 661(a) defines the distribution deduction for complex trusts and estates as being the sum of the total current income *required* to be paid out currently plus any other amounts "properly paid or credited or required to be distributed" (i.e., discretionary distributions) to the beneficiary during the year. If the fiduciary has the option of making mandatory distributions from either the income or the principal account, distributions are counted as "current income required to be paid" if paid out of the trust's income account. Just as in the case of simple trusts, the amount of the trust's DNI limits the amount of the distribution deduction.

EXAMPLE C14-20 ▶ In the current year, Able Trust has net accounting income and DNI of $30,000, all from taxable sources. It makes a $15,000 mandatory distribution of income to Kwame and a $4,000 discretionary distribution to Kesha. Its distribution deduction is computed as follows:

Income required to be distributed currently	$15,000
Plus: Other amounts properly paid, etc.	4,000
Tentative distribution deduction	$19,000
DNI	$30,000
Distribution deduction (lesser of tentative distribution deduction or DNI)	$19,000 ◀

As is the case for simple trusts, an additional constraint applies to the amount of the distribution deduction. No distribution deduction is allowed with respect to tax-exempt income (net of allocable expenses).

EXAMPLE C14-21 ▶ Assume the same facts as in Example C14-20 except that net accounting income and DNI consist of $20,000 of corporate bond interest and $10,000 of tax-exempt interest. Because one-third ($10,000 ÷ $30,000) of the DNI is from tax-exempt sources, tax-exempt income is deemed to make up one-third of the distributions. Thus, the distribution deduction is only $12,667 (0.667 × $19,000). ◀

DNI is not reduced by the charitable contribution deduction when determining the maximum distribution deduction for mandatory distributions of income. However, DNI is reduced by the charitable contribution deduction when calculating the deductible discretionary distributions.

EXAMPLE C14-22 ▶ Assume instead that the trust in Example C14-20 has net accounting income and DNI (exclusive of the charitable contribution deduction) of $16,000. The trust makes a $15,000 mandatory distribution to Kwame and a $4,000 mandatory distribution to Kesha. In accordance with its trust instrument, the trust pays $3,000 to a charitable organization.

Tentative distribution deduction (required distributions)	$19,000
DNI (excluding charitable contribution deduction)	16,000
Distribution deduction (lesser of tentative distribution deduction or DNI)	16,000

If the distributions to both Kwame and Kesha were discretionary, the $3,000 charitable contribution would be deductible by the trust and would first reduce DNI to $13,000, thereby limiting the distribution deduction to $13,000. ◀

TAX TREATMENT FOR BENEFICIARY

KEY POINT

Distributions to beneficiaries retain the character that the income has at the fiduciary level; for example, the character of rents, interest, dividends, or tax-exempt income flows through to the beneficiary.

SELF-STUDY QUESTION

Is DNI reduced by the charitable contribution deduction in calculating the portion of DNI to be included in each beneficiary's gross income?

ANSWER

DNI is not reduced by charitable contributions in determining the DNI to be included in the gross income of mandatory beneficiaries, but it is reduced in arriving at the DNI to be included in the gross income of discretionary beneficiaries.

GENERAL RULES. In general, the amount of any distributions from estates or complex trusts includible in a beneficiary's gross income equals the sum of income required to be distributed currently to the beneficiary plus any other amounts properly paid or credited, or required to be distributed (i.e., discretionary distributions) to the beneficiary during the year.[29] This general rule has three exceptions, all discussed later in this section.

Because income retains the character it has at the fiduciary level, beneficiaries do not include distributions of tax-exempt income in their gross income. Each beneficiary's distribution is deemed to consist of tax-exempt income in the proportion that total tax-exempt income bears to total DNI.[30] Thus, if 30% of DNI is from tax-exempt income, 30% of each beneficiary's distribution is deemed to consist of tax-free income.

Even in the absence of distributions of principal, mandatory payments to beneficiaries can exceed DNI because at times accounting income exceeds DNI. When the total income required to be distributed currently exceeds DNI (before reduction for the charitable contribution deduction), each beneficiary reports as gross income the following ratio of DNI attributable to taxable sources:

$$\frac{\text{Income required to be distributed currently to the beneficiary}}{\text{Aggregate income required to be distributed to all beneficiaries currently}^{31}}$$

In calculating the portion of DNI includible in the gross income of each beneficiary who receives mandatory distributions, DNI is not reduced for the charitable contribution deduction.

EXAMPLE C14-23 ▶ In the current year, Yui Trust reports net accounting income of $125,000 but DNI of only $100,000 because of certain expenses charged to principal. The trust must distribute $100,000 of income to Tai and $10,000 to Tien. It makes no discretionary distributions or charitable contributions. Because the trust's mandatory distributions exceed its DNI, the amount each beneficiary reports as gross income is as follows:

Beneficiary	*Gross Income*
Tai	$90,909 = ($100,000 ÷ $110,000) × $100,000
Tien	$9,091 = ($10,000 ÷ $110,000) × $100,000 ◀

EXCEPTION—THE TIER SYSTEM. If both principal and income are distributed, distributions will exceed income even if net accounting income and DNI are equal. If the sum of current income required to be distributed currently and all other amounts properly paid or required to be distributed (e.g., discretionary payments of income or any payments of corpus) exceed DNI, the amount taxable to each beneficiary is calculated under a tier system. Beneficiaries to whom income distributions must be made are commonly called **tier-1 beneficiaries.**[32] All other beneficiaries are known as **tier-2 beneficiaries.** An individual who receives both mandatory and discretionary payments in the same year can be both a tier-1 and a tier-2 beneficiary.

Under the tier system, tier-1 beneficiaries are the first to absorb income. The total income taxed to this group is the lesser of the aggregate mandatory distributions or DNI, which is determined without reduction for charitable contributions. If required income distributions plus all other payments exceed DNI, each tier-2 beneficiary includes in income a fraction of the excess of DNI over the income required to be distributed currently. Section 662(a)(2) states that the fraction is as follows:

$$\frac{\text{Other amounts properly paid or required to be distributed to the beneficiary}}{\text{Aggregate of amounts properly paid or required to be distributed to } \textit{all} \text{ beneficiaries}}$$

[29] Sec. 662(a).
[30] Sec. 662(b).
[31] Sec. 662(a)(1).

[32] The terms *tier-1* and *tier-2* do not appear in the IRC or Treasury Regulations.

EXAMPLE C14-24 ▶ In the current year, Eagle Trust reports net accounting income and DNI of $80,000, all from taxable sources. The trust instrument requires the trustee to distribute $30,000 of income to Holly currently. In addition, the trustee makes $60,000 of discretionary distributions, $15,000 to Holly and $45,000 to Irene. The trust pays $10,000 of the discretionary distributions from corpus. The gross income reported by each beneficiary is determined as follows.

1. Gross income from mandatory distributions:	
Lesser of:	
a. Amount required to be distributed, or	$30,000
b. DNI	80,000
Amount reportable by Holly	30,000
2. Gross income from other amounts paid:	
Lesser of:	
a. All other amounts paid, or	60,000
b. DNI minus amount required to be distributed ($80,000 − $30,000)	50,000
Amount reportable by Holly and Irene	50,000
3. Total amount reportable (1) + (2) = (3)	80,000

The portions of the $50,000 from Step 2 to be reported by each beneficiary are calculated under a pro rata approach as follows:

Holly's: $50,000 × ($15,000 ÷ $60,000) = $12,500
Irene's: $50,000 × ($45,000 ÷ $60,000) = $37,500

A recapitulation of the beneficiaries' gross income is as follows:

	Amount Reported by	
Type of Distribution	*Holly*	*Irene*
Mandatory distributions	$30,000	$ -0-
Discretionary distributions	12,500	37,500
Total	$42,500	$37,500 ◀

Tier-1 beneficiaries generally have gross income equal to their total distributions if they receive no tax-exempt interest, whereas tier-2 beneficiaries are more likely to receive a portion of their distributions tax-free. Thus, Tier-2 beneficiaries can receive more favorable tax treatment than tier-1 beneficiaries.

SELF-STUDY QUESTION

What is the ultimate effect of the separate share rule?

ANSWER

It has the effect of treating a trust or estate as two or more separate entities, each with its own DNI. This "separate" DNI is allocated to the specific beneficiary of each share of the trust or estate.

EXCEPTION—SEPARATE SHARE RULE. Some trusts and estates with more than one beneficiary can be treated as consisting of more than one entity in determining the amount of the distribution deduction and the beneficiaries' gross income.[33] In calculating the fiduciary's income tax liability, however, these trusts or estates are treated as one entity with the result that all taxable income is taxed under one rate schedule. Entities eligible for this treatment, known as the **separate share rule**, must have governing instruments requiring that distributions be made in substantially the same manner as if separate entities had been created.[34] If the separate share rule applies, the amount of the income taxable to a beneficiary can differ from the amount that otherwise would be taxable to such beneficiary. Because of this rule, beneficiaries often report lower income than the amount distributed to them.

EXAMPLE C14-25 ▶ Bart Berry created the Berry Trust for the benefit of Dale and John. According to the trust instrument, no income is to be distributed until a beneficiary reaches age 21. Moreover, income is to be divided into two equal shares. Once a beneficiary reaches age 21, the trustee may make discretionary distributions of income and principal to such beneficiary, but distributions may not exceed a beneficiary's share of the trust. Each beneficiary is to receive his remaining share of the trust assets on his thirtieth birthday. Earlier distributions of income and principal will be taken into account in determining each beneficiary's final distribution.

On January 1 of the current year, Dale reaches age 21; John is age 16. In the current year, the trust has DNI and net accounting income of $50,000, all from taxable sources. During the current year, the trustee distributes $25,000 of income (Dale's 50% share) and $80,000 of principal

[33] Sec. 663(c).

[34] Reg. Sec. 1.663(c)-3(a).

to Dale. The trustee makes no distribution of income or corpus to John. Under the separate share rule, the trust's distribution deduction and Dale's gross income inclusion cannot exceed his share of DNI, or $25,000. Dale receives the remaining $80,000 distribution tax-free. Berry Trust is taxed on John's separate share of the income (all accumulated), or $25,000. In the absence of the separate share rule, Dale would be taxed on $50,000 (the lesser of DNI or his total distributions). ◀

EXCEPTION—SPECIFIC BEQUESTS. Recall that a beneficiary is taxed on other amounts properly paid, credited, or required to be distributed,[35] subject to the constraint that the maximum amount taxed to all beneficiaries is the fiduciary's DNI. Thus, a beneficiary can be required to report gross income even though he or she receives a distribution from the principal account.

EXAMPLE C14-26 ▶ Doug died in 2001, leaving a will that bequeathed all his property to his sister Tina. During 2002, Doug's estate reports $50,000 of DNI, all from taxable sources. During 2002, the executor distributes Doug's coin collection, valued at $22,000, to Tina. The adjusted basis of the coin collection also is $22,000, its value at the date of death. The distribution of the coin collection is classified as an other amount properly paid and, even though the executor distributes no income, Tina reports $22,000 of gross income. If the coin collection's adjusted basis and FMV exceed $50,000 (DNI), Tina's gross income would be only $50,000, the DNI amount. ◀

ADDITIONAL COMMENT

The executor of an estate should carefully consider the timing of property distributions where the property being distributed is not the subject of a specific bequest. If possible, property (other than specific bequests) should be distributed in a year when the trust has little or no DNI.

On the other hand, a distribution of property does not trigger a distribution deduction at the estate level or the recognition of gross income at the beneficiary level if such property constitutes a bequest of a specific sum of money or of specific property to be paid at one time or in not more than three installments.[36] If Doug's will in Example C14-26 instead includes specific bequest language (e.g., "I bequeath my coin collection to Tina"), Tina would not report any gross income upon receiving the coin collection.

More income is generally taxed at the estate level (and less at the beneficiary level) if the decedent's will includes numerous specific bequests. If the estate has a lower marginal income tax rate than its beneficiaries' marginal tax rates, the optimal tax result is to have the income taxed to the estate because the tax liability is lower.

EXAMPLE C14-27 ▶ Dick died in 2001 and bequeathed $100,000 cash to Fred and devised his residence, valued at $300,000, to Gary. The executor distributes the cash and the residence in 2002, when the estate has $475,000 of DNI, all from taxable sources. Because the cash and residence constitute specific bequests, the estate gets no distribution deduction and the beneficiaries report no gross income. ◀

STOP & THINK *Question:* Sally is the sole beneficiary of her uncle Harry's estate. In the current year, the estate had DNI of $36,000, all from dividends and corporate interest. During the current year, the estate's executor distributed to Sally $12,200 of cash and her uncle Harry's rare book collection, valued at $5,400 on date of death and date of distribution. Uncle Harry's will made one specific bequest, the rare book collection to Sally. How much gross income should Sally report as a result of the distributions from the estate during the current year? What is the amount of the estate's distribution deduction?

Solution: Sally does not have to report gross income as a result of receiving the specific bequest of the book collection. Because Sally's cash distribution does not exceed the estate's DNI, Sally should report gross income equal to the cash distributed to her ($12,200). The estate's distribution deduction equals the amount included in Sally's gross income ($12,200). If the book collection were not a specific bequest, its distribution by the estate would be taxable to Sally because the $17,600 ($12,200 + $5,400) distributed by the estate is less than the estate's $36,000 DNI.

[35] Sec. 662(a)(2).

[36] Sec. 663(a)(1).

KEY POINT

Generally, the tax consequences of both NOLs and net capital losses are the same for estates, complex trusts, and simple trusts.

EFFECT OF A NET OPERATING LOSS

As with simple trusts, an NOL of an estate or complex trust can be carried back and carried forward. In the year the trust or estate terminates, any remaining NOL passes through to the beneficiaries who succeed to the assets. In addition, in its year of termination the estate passes through to its beneficiaries any excess of current nonoperating expenses (e.g., executor's fees) over current income. If the estate incurs NOLs over a series of years, a tax incentive exists for terminating the estate as early as possible so the beneficiaries can reap the benefit of the loss deductions.

EFFECT OF A NET CAPITAL LOSS

The tax effect of having capital losses that exceed capital gains generally is the same for estates and complex trusts as for simple trusts. As in the case of an individual taxpayer, the maximum capital loss deduction is the lesser of $3,000 or the excess of its capital losses over capital gains.[37] Simple trusts, however, receive no immediate tax benefit when capital losses exceed capital gains. Estates and complex trusts often do not distribute all their income and, thus, have taxable income against which a capital loss may be offset.

EXAMPLE C14-28 ▶ For 2001, Gold Trust reported $30,000 of net accounting income and DNI, all from taxable sources. It made discretionary distributions totaling $7,000 to Amy. Its one sale of a capital asset resulted in an $8,000 long-term capital loss. The trust deducted $3,000 of capital losses in arriving at its 2001 taxable income. The trust carries over the remaining $5,000 of capital loss to 2002. If in 2002, Gold Trust sells a capital asset for a $5,000 long-term capital gain, it will offset the $5,000 loss carryover against the $5,000 capital gain. ◀

COMPREHENSIVE ILLUSTRATION: DETERMINING A COMPLEX TRUST'S TAXABLE INCOME

The comprehensive illustration below reviews a number of points discussed earlier. A sample Form 1041 for a complex trust appears in Appendix B; it is prepared on the basis of the facts in this illustration.

BACKGROUND DATA

Ted Tims established the Cathy and Karen Stephens Trust on March 12, 1993. Its trust instrument empowers the trustee (Merchants Bank) to distribute income in its discretion to Cathy and Karen for the next 20 years. The trust will then be terminated, and the trust assets will be divided equally between Cathy and Karen, irrespective of the amount of distributions each has previously received. In other words, separate shares are not to be maintained. Under state law, capital gains are part of principal.

The 2001 income and expenses of the trust are reported below. With the exception of the information concerning distributions and payments of estimated tax, the amounts are the same as in the comprehensive illustration for a simple trust discussed previously in the chapter. As before, the holding period for the stock sold in October was four years.

	Amounts Allocable to	
	Income	*Principal*
Dividends	$30,000	
Rental income from land	5,000	
Tax-exempt interest	15,000	
Rental expenses (realtor's commissions on rental income)	1,000	

[37] Sec. 1211(b).

Trustee's fee		$ 1,200
Fee for preparation of tax return	500	
Capital gain on sale of stock		12,000
Distribution of net accounting income to:		
Cathy	14,000	
Karen	7,000	
Payments of estimated tax	5,240	3,360

TRUSTEE'S FEE

Recall that some of the trustee's fee must be allocated to tax-exempt income, with the result that this portion is nondeductible. Of the trust's $50,000 ($30,000 + $5,000 + $15,000) gross accounting income, $15,000 is from tax-exempt sources. Consequently, the nondeductible trustee's fee is $360 [($15,000 ÷ $50,000) × $1,200]. The remaining $840 of the fee is deductible, as are the $500 of tax return preparation fees.

DISTRIBUTION DEDUCTION AND DNI

Recall that the primary function of the Subchapter J rules is to provide guidance for calculating the amounts taxable to the beneficiaries and to the fiduciary. One of the crucial numbers in the process is the distribution deduction, which requires knowledge of the DNI amount. Taxable income, exclusive of the distribution deduction, is the starting point for calculating DNI and is computed as follows:

Dividends	$30,000
Rental income	5,000
Capital gain on sale of stock	12,000
Minus: Rental expenses	(1,000)
Deductible portion of trustee's fee	(840)
Fee for tax return preparation	(500)
Personal exemption	(100)
Taxable income, exclusive of distribution deduction	$44,560

DNI is calculated by adjusting taxable income, exclusive of the distribution deduction, as follows:

Taxable income, exclusive of distribution deduction	$44,560
Plus: Personal exemption	100
Minus: Capital gain on sale of stock	(12,000)
Plus: Tax-exempt interest (net of $360 of allocable expenses)	14,640
DNI	$47,300

The distribution deduction is the lesser of (1) amounts required to be distributed, plus other amounts properly paid or credited, or required to be distributed, or (2) DNI. This lesser-of amount must be reduced by tax-exempt income (net of allocable expenses). DNI, exclusive of net tax-exempt income, is calculated as follows:

DNI	$47,300
Minus: Tax-exempt income (net of $360 of allocable expenses)	(14,640)
DNI, exclusive of net tax-exempt income	$32,660

In no event may the distribution deduction exceed $32,660, the DNI, exclusive of net tax-exempt income. The DNI ceiling is of no practical significance in this example, however, because the total amount distributed is only $21,000.

ADDITIONAL COMMENT

This example dealing with a complex trust clearly illustrates the computational complexity that exists in situations with multiple categories of income and multiple beneficiaries.

Because a portion of the payments to each beneficiary is deemed to consist of tax-exempt income, the distribution deduction is less than the $21,000 distributed. Each beneficiary's share of tax-exempt income is determined by dividing DNI into categories of income. In this categorization process, rental expenses are direct expenses that must be charged against rental income, and $360 of the trustee's fees must be charged against tax-exempt income. In this example, the deductible trustee's fee and the tax return preparation fee are charged against rental income. They could, however, be charged against dividend income or pro rata against each income category. As with the simple trust illustrated earlier, total DNI of $47,300 consists of the following categories:

	Dividends	*Rents*	*Tax-Exempt Interest*	*Total*
Accounting income	$30,000	$5,000	$15,000	$50,000
Minus: Expenses:				
Trustee's fee		(840)	(360)	(1,200)
Rental expenses		(1,000)		(1,000)
Fee for tax return preparation		(500)		(500)
DNI	$30,000	$2,660	$14,640	$47,300

Because the complex trust illustration involves two beneficiaries and three categories of income, we must calculate the amount of each beneficiary's distribution that comes from each income category. These steps were not needed in the simple trust illustration because it involved only one beneficiary.

Category of Income	*Proportion of DNI*
Dividends	63.4249% = $30,000 ÷ $47,300
Rental income	5.6237% = $ 2,660 ÷ $47,300
Tax-exempt income	30.9514% = $14,640 ÷ $47,300
Total	100.0000%

As shown above, 30.9514% of each beneficiary's distribution represents tax-exempt interest and is ineligible for a distribution deduction. The amount of the distribution deduction (which cannot exceed the $32,660 DNI, exclusive of net tax-exempt income) is determined as follows:

Total amount distributed	$21,000
Minus: Net tax-exempt income deemed distributed (0.309514 × $21,000)	(6,500)
Distribution deduction	$14,500

The distributions received by the beneficiaries are deemed to consist of three categories of income in the amounts shown below.

Components of Distributions	*Cathy*	*Karen*	*Total*
Dividends (63.4249%)	$8,879	$4,440	$13,319
Plus: Rental income (5.6237%)	788	393	1,181
Gross income (69.0486%)	$9,667	$4,833	$14,500
Plus: Tax-exempt interest (30.9514%)	4,333	2,167	6,500
Total income (100%)	$14,000	$7,000	$21,000

TRUST'S TAXABLE INCOME

Once the taxable and tax-exempt distributions have been quantified, the trust's taxable income can be calculated. Table C14-3 illustrates this calculation. Unlike the simple trust situation, there is no short-cut approach to verifying taxable income for complex trusts and estates except in the years when such entities distribute all their income.

ADDITIONAL OBSERVATIONS

A few additional observations are in order concerning the Stephens Trust:

- If the entity is an estate instead of a trust, all amounts except the personal exemption are the same. The estate's personal exemption would be $600 instead of $100.

▼ **TABLE C14-3**
Comprehensive Illustration: Determining a Complex Trust's Taxable Income and Tax Liability

Gross income:	
Dividends	$30,000
Rental income	5,000
Capital gain on sale of stock	12,000
Minus: Expense deductions:	
Rental expenses	(1,000)
Deductible portion of trustee's fee	(840)
Fee for tax return preparation	(500)
Minus: Distribution deduction	(14,500)
Minus: Personal exemption	(100)
Taxable income	$30,060
Tax liability (2001 rates)[a]	$ 8,464
Minus: Estimated taxes	(8,600)
Tax owed (refunded)	($ 136)

[a]$18,060 of taxable income is taxed at the fiduciary ordinary income rates and $12,000 of long-term capital gain is taxed at the 20% maximum tax rate on capital gains.

- Assume that (1) the trust owns a building instead of land and incurs $2,000 of depreciation expense, chargeable against principal under state law, and (2) the trust instrument does not require a reserve for depreciation. Because approximately 56% of the trust's income is accumulated (i.e., $26,300 of its $47,300 DNI), $1,120 (0.56 × $2,000) of the depreciation is deductible by the trust and its taxable income is $1,120 lower. The remaining $880 (0.44 × $2,000) is deductible on the beneficiaries' returns and is divided between them according to their pro rata share of the total distributions. Cathy deducts $587 [$880 × ($14,000 ÷ $21,000)], and Karen deducts $293 [$880 × ($7,000 ÷ $21,000)]. In summary, the depreciation is deductible as follows $1,120 to the trust, $587 to Cathy, and $293 to Karen.
- If the trust instrument had mandated a reserve for depreciation equal to the depreciation expense for tax purposes, accounting income would have been reduced by the depreciation. In addition, the entire $2,000 of depreciation would have been deducted by the trust, and DNI would have been $45,300 instead of $47,300.

INCOME IN RESPECT OF A DECEDENT

OBJECTIVE 7

Recognize the significance of income in respect of a decedent

DEFINITION AND COMMON EXAMPLES

Section 691 specifies the tax treatment for specific types of income known as income in respect of a decedent. **Income in respect of a decedent (IRD)** is gross income that the decedent earned before death, but such income was not includible on the decedent's income tax return for the tax year ending with the date of his or her death or for an earlier tax year because the decedent (a cash basis taxpayer) had not collected the income. Because most individuals use the cash method of accounting, IRD generally consists of income earned, but not actually or constructively received, before death. Common examples of IRD include the following:

- Interest earned, but not received, before death
- Salary, commission, or bonus earned, but not received, before death

SELF-STUDY QUESTION

Roger, a cash method taxpayer, is a medical doctor. At the time of Roger's death, patients owe him $150,000. These accounts receivable are "property" in which Roger has an interest at the time of his death and are included in his gross estate. Why are the accounts receivable income in respect of a decedent?

ANSWER

Because they are income Roger earned while alive, but did not report as income due to his accounting method, they constitute income to his estate (or his heirs) when they are collected. Thus, they are income in respect of a decedent (IRD).

- Dividend collected after the date of death, for which the record date precedes the date of death
- Gain portion of principal collected on a pre-death installment sale

SIGNIFICANCE OF IRD

DOUBLE TAXATION. Recall from Chapter C13 that a decedent's gross estate includes property to the extent of his or her interest therein. The decedent has an interest in any income earned but not actually or constructively received before death. Thus, the decedent's gross estate includes income accrued as of the date of death. Assuming the decedent used the cash method of accounting, the decedent did not include this accrued income in gross income because he or she had not yet collected it. The income is taxed to the party (i.e., the estate or a named individual) entitled to receive it. Thus, IRD is taxed under both the transfer tax system and the income tax system. The income also is taxed twice if the decedent collects a dividend check, deposits it into his or her bank account, and dies before consuming the cash. In the latter case, the dividend is included in the decedent's individual income tax return, and the cash (from the dividend check) is included in the decedent's gross estate. The income taxes owed on the dividend income are deductible as a debt on the estate tax return.

EXAMPLE C14-29 ▶ Doug dies on July 1. Included in Doug's gross estate is an 8%, $1,000 corporate bond that pays interest each September 1 and March 1. Doug's gross estate also includes accrued interest for the period March 2 through July 1 of $27 ($1,000 × 0.08 × 4/12). On September 1, Doug's estate collects $40 of interest, of which $27 constitutes IRD. The income tax return for Doug's estate includes $40 of interest income. ◀

SELF-STUDY QUESTION

Karl receives his regular monthly paycheck on May 1 and deposits the paycheck in his savings account. He dies on May 10. He did not make any withdrawals from the account before his death. On June 1, Karl's employer pays Karl's estate one-third of Karl's monthly salary (the amount Karl had earned prior to his death on May 10). What are the tax consequences?

ANSWER

Karl's gross estate will include his savings account. Karl's final income tax return will include his salary through April 30 (i.e., his May 1 check is subject to both the income and the estate tax). The income taxes owed on the April salary are deductible as a debt on his estate tax return.

Karl's gross estate will include the one-third of his May salary. His estate also will report this amount as income. The salary is income in respect of a decedent, so the estate will receive some relief under Sec. 691(c) from the double tax.

DEDUCTIONS IN RESPECT OF A DECEDENT. Section 691(b) authorizes **deductions in respect of a decedent (DRD)**. Such deductions include trade or business expenses, expenses for the production of income, interest, taxes, depletion, etc. that are accrued before death but are not deductible on the decedent's final income tax return because the decedent used the cash method of accounting. Because some of these accrued expenses have not been paid before death, they also may be deductible as debts on the estate tax return. The accrued expenses also are deductible on the estate's income tax return when paid by the estate. Thus, a double benefit can be obtained for DRD.

EXAMPLE C14-30 ▶ Dan dies on September 20. At the time of his death, Dan owes $18,000 of salaries to the employees of his proprietorship. The executor pays the total September payroll of $29,000 on September 30. The $18,000 of accrued salaries is deductible as a debt on the estate tax return. As a trade or business (Sec. 162) expense, the salaries also constitute DRD. The $18,000 of DRD, plus any other amounts paid, is deductible on the estate's income tax return for the period of payment. ◀

SECTION 691(c) DEDUCTION. Some relief for the double taxation of IRD is provided by the Sec. 691(c) deduction. This deduction equals the federal estate taxes attributable to the net IRD included in the gross estate. The total Sec. 691(c) deduction is the excess of the decedent's actual federal estate tax over the federal estate tax that would be payable if the net IRD were excluded from the decedent's gross estate. Net IRD means IRD minus deductions in respect of a decedent (DRD). If the IRD is collected in more than one tax year, the Sec. 691(c) deduction for a particular tax year is determined by the following formula:[38]

$$\begin{array}{c}\text{Sec. 691(c)}\\ \text{deduction}\\ \text{for the year}\end{array} = \begin{array}{c}\text{Total}\\ \text{Sec. 691(c)}\\ \text{deduction}\end{array} \times \frac{\text{Net IRD included in gross income for the year}}{\text{Total Net IRD}}$$

[38] Sec. 691(c)(1).

EXAMPLE C14-31 ▶ Latoya died in 2001 with a taxable estate and estate tax base of $1 million. Assume Latoya's estate owed no state death taxes. Latoya's gross estate included $250,000 of IRD, none of which was received by her surviving spouse. Her estate had no DRD. The estate collects $200,000 of the IRD during its 2002 tax year. The Sec. 691(c) deduction for Latoya's estate for 2002 is calculated as shown below.

Actual federal estate tax liability (on base of $1 million)	$125,250
Minus: Federal estate tax on base ($750,000) determined by excluding net IRD from gross estate	(27,750)
Total Sec. 691(c) deduction	$ 97,500
Sec. 691(c) deduction available in 2002: ($200,000 ÷ $250,000) × $97,500 =	$ 78,000 ◀

NO STEP-UP IN BASIS. Most property received as the result of a decedent's death acquires a basis equal to its FMV on the date of death or the alternate valuation date. Property classified as IRD, however, retains the same basis it had in the decedent's hands.[39]

This carryover basis rule for IRD items is especially unfavorable when the decedent sells a highly appreciated asset soon before death, collects a relatively small portion of the sales price before death, and reports the sale under the installment method of accounting. For example, if the gain is 80% of the sales price, 80% of each principal payment in the post-death period will continue to be characterized as gain. If the sale instead had been postponed until after the date of death, the gain would be restricted to the post-death appreciation (if any) because the step-up in basis rules apply to the asset.

EXAMPLE C14-32 ▶ On June 3, 2002, Joel sells a parcel of investment land for $40,000. The land has a $10,000 adjusted basis in Joel's hands. The buyer pays $8,000 down and signs a $32,000 note at an interest rate acceptable to the IRS. The note is payable June 3, 2003. Joel, a cash method of accounting taxpayer, uses the installment method for reporting the $30,000 ($40,000 – $10,000) gain. The gross profit ratio is 75% ($30,000 gain ÷ $40,000 contract price). Joel dies on June 13, 2002. A gain of $6,000 (0.75 × $8,000) is reported on Joel's final individual income tax return. The estate reports a gain of $24,000 (0.75 × $32,000) on its 2003 tax return because it collects the $32,000 balance due on June 3, 2003. Had the sale contract been entered into after Joel's death, the gain would have been zero because the land's basis would have been its $40,000 FMV at the date of death. ◀

SELF-STUDY QUESTION

Roger (a cash method taxpayer) died leaving $150,000 of zero basis accounts receivable. What basis does his estate have in these accounts receivable?

ANSWER

Zero. The accounts receivable constitute IRD. If they were stepped-up in basis, they would never be subject to an income tax.

STOP & THINK *Question:* Isaac, a cash basis, calendar year taxpayer, died on May 12 of the current year. On which income tax return—Isaac's or his estate's—should the following income and expenses be reported? Assume the estate's tax year is the calendar year.

- ▶ Dividends declared in January and paid in February
- ▶ Interest income on a corporate bond that pays interest each June 30 and December 31
- ▶ Rent collected in June for a vacation home rented to tenants for the month of March, but the tenants were allowed to pay after occupying the property
- ▶ Balance due on Isaac's state income taxes for the previous year, paid in July because the return was extended
- ▶ Federal estimated income tax for the previous year that Isaac paid in January

Solution: Income received before death and deductible expenses paid before death (in this case the dividends and nothing more) should be reported on his individual return. Income received after Isaac's death, even though earned before his death, is to be reported on the estate's income tax return. The same is true for deductible expenses paid by the estate. Items to be reported on the estate's income tax return include the interest income, the rental income, and the state income taxes. The federal income taxes are not deductible on the federal income tax return of either taxpayer.

[39] Sec. 1014(c).

GRANTOR TRUST PROVISIONS

OBJECTIVE 8

Explain the effect of the grantor trust provisions

This portion of the chapter examines the provisions affecting a special type of trust known as a **grantor trust**, which is governed by Secs. 671-679. As discussed previously, income of a regular (or nongrantor) trust or an estate is taxed to the beneficiary to the extent distributed or to the fiduciary to the extent accumulated. In the case of a grantor trust, however, the trust's grantor (creator) is taxed on some or all of the trust's income even if such income is distributed to the beneficiary. In certain circumstances, a person other than the grantor or the beneficiary (e.g., a person with powers over the trust) must pay taxes on the trust's income.

PURPOSE AND EFFECT

The grantor trust rules require grantors who do not give up enough control or economic benefits when they create a trust to pay a price by being taxed on part or all of the trust's income. A grantor must report some or all of a trust's income on his or her individual tax return if he or she does not part with enough control over the trust assets or give up the right to income produced by the assets for a sufficiently long time period. For transfers after March 1, 1986, the grantor generally is taxed on the trust's income if the trust property will eventually return to the grantor or the grantor's spouse. According to the Tax Court, the grantor trust rules have the following purpose and result:

> This subpart [Secs. 671-679] enunciates the rules to be applied where, in described circumstances, a grantor has transferred property to a trust but has not parted with complete dominion and control over the property or the income which it produces. . . .[40]

Sections 671-679 use the term *treated as owner.* Section 671 specifies that when a grantor is treated as owner, the income, deductions, and credits attributable to the portion of the trust with respect to which the grantor is treated as owner are reported directly on the grantor's tax return and not on the trust's return. The fiduciary return contains only the items attributable to the portion of the trust for which the grantor is not treated as the owner.[41]

ADDITIONAL COMMENT

Many trust provisions can cause the grantor trust rules to apply. A trust need *not* be a revocable trust to be a grantor trust.

Unfortunately, the rules governing when a transfer is complete for income tax purposes (meaning the grantor avoids being taxed on the trust's income) do not agree completely with the rules concerning whether the transfer is complete for gift tax purposes or the transferred property is removed from the donor's gross estate. In certain circumstances, a donor can make a taxable gift and still be taxed on the income from the transferred property. For example, assume a donor transfers property to a trust with the income payable annually to the donor's cousin for six years and a reversion of the property to the donor at the end of the sixth year. The donor makes a gift, subject to the gift tax, of the value of a six-year income interest. Under the grantor trust rules, however, the donor continues to be taxed on the trust's income because the property reverts to the donor within too short a time period.

Retention of certain powers over property conveyed in trust can cause the trust assets to be included in the donor's gross estate even though these powers do not cause the donor to be taxed on the trust income. Assume a donor has the discretionary power to pay out or accumulate trust income until the beneficiary reaches age 21. The trust assets, including any accumulated income, are to be distributed to the beneficiary on his or her twenty-first birthday. The donor is not taxed on the trust income, but if the donor dies before the beneficiary attains age 21, the donor's gross estate will include the trust property because the donor retained control over the beneficiary's economic benefits (see discussion of Sec. 2036 in Chapter C13).

---

[40] *William Scheft,* 59 T.C. 428, at 430-431 (1972).

[41] For trusts created before March 2, 1986, the grantor may be treated as the owner with respect to the trust's capital gains but not its ordinary income because the property returns to the grantor after a period of more than ten years. In such a situation, the grantor is taxed on the capital gains and the trust and/or the beneficiary on the ordinary income.

REVOCABLE TRUSTS

The grantor of a revocable trust can control assets conveyed to the trust by altering the terms of the trust (including changing the identity of the beneficiaries) and/or withdrawing assets from the trust. Not surprisingly, Sec. 676 provides that the grantor is taxed on the income generated by a revocable trust. As Chapter C12 points out, a transfer of assets to a revocable trust is an incomplete transfer and not subject to the gift tax.

EXAMPLE C14-33 ▶ In the current year, Tom transfers property to a revocable trust and names Ann to receive the income for life and Beth to receive the remainder. The trust's income for the current year consists of $15,000 of dividends and an $8,000 long-term capital gain. The trustee distributes the dividends to Ann but retains the gain and credits it to principal. Because the trust is revocable, the dividend and capital gain income are taxed directly to Tom on his current year individual tax return. Nothing is taxed to the trust or its beneficiaries. ◀

ADDITIONAL COMMENT

A common use of the revocable trust is to avoid probate for the property held by the trust. On the death of the grantor, the trustee of the revocable trust distributes the trust property in accordance with the trust agreement. Because the trustee holds legal title to the property, he or she can distribute the property without going through the probate process.

CLIFFORD TRUSTS

Certain irrevocable trusts were subject to the grantor trust rules if, for example, the grantor had a reversionary interest that reverted (passed back) too soon. Before its amendment in 1986, Sec. 673(a) provided that the grantor was taxed on the trust's accounting income if the trust assets reverted to the grantor within ten years of the transfer date but not if the reversion date was more than ten years from the transfer date. Regardless of when the trust terminated, the grantor was always taxed on capital gains credited to principal because such gains were held for distribution to the grantor upon termination of the trust.[42] The gains were taxed in the year realized, not at the termination of the trust. If the trust period was long enough for the grantor to escape being taxed on the trust's accounting income, the trust often was referred to as a ***Clifford*** or **short-term trust.**

EXAMPLE C14-34 ▶ In June 1985, Ted transferred property to a trust whose trust instrument specifies that all of its income is payable annually to Amy for the next 18 years. At the end of 18 years, the property reverts to Ted. Amy is taxed on the trust's accounting income. Ted is taxed currently on any capital gains because he will regain the property when the trust ends. ◀

POST-1986 REVERSIONARY INTEREST TRUSTS

KEY POINT

The *Clifford,* or short-term, trust cannot be used as an income shifting device any longer. The reversion of corpus to the grantor at the end of the term of the trust now causes the trust to be treated as a grantor trust unless the reversion occurs many, many years after the funding of the trust.

The 1986 Tax Reform Act sounded the death knell for *Clifford* trusts. It amended Sec. 673(a) for transfers made after March 1, 1986 to provide that, generally, the grantor is taxed on the accounting income of the trust if he or she has a reversionary interest in either income or principal. Under Sec. 672(e), a grantor is treated as holding any interest held by his or her spouse. These rules have two exceptions.

The first exception makes the grantor trust rules inapplicable if, as of the inception of the trust, the value of the reversionary interest does not exceed 5% of the value of the trust. The second exception applies if the reversion will occur only if the beneficiary dies before reaching age 21 and the beneficiary is a lineal descendant of the grantor.

EXAMPLE C14-35 ▶ In the current year, Paul establishes a trust with income payable to his elderly parents for 15 years. The assets of the trust will then revert to Paul. The value of Paul's reversionary interest exceeds 5%. Because Paul has a reversionary interest valued at above 5% and the transfer arose after March 1, 1986, Paul is taxed currently on the trust's accounting income and capital gains. ◀

EXAMPLE C14-36 ▶ In the current year, Paul transfers property to a trust with income payable to his daughter Ruth until Ruth reaches age 21. On Ruth's twenty-first birthday, she is to receive the trust property outright. In the event Ruth dies before reaching age 21, the trust assets will revert to Paul. Paul is not taxed on the accounting income because his reversion is contingent on the death of the beneficiary (a lineal descendant) before age 21. ◀

---

[42] Sec. 677(a).

RETENTION OF ADMINISTRATIVE POWERS

Under Sec. 675, the grantor is taxed on the accounting income and gains if he or she or his or her spouse holds certain administrative powers. Such powers include, but are not limited to, the following:

- The power to purchase or exchange trust property for less than adequate consideration in money or money's worth
- The power to borrow from the trust without adequate interest or security except where the trustee (who is someone other than the grantor) is empowered under a general lending power to make loans irrespective of interest or security
- The power exercisable in a nontrustee capacity to (1) vote stock of a corporation in which the holdings of the grantor and the trust are significant from the standpoint of voting control and (2) reacquire the trust property by substituting other property of equal value.

RETENTION OF ECONOMIC BENEFITS

Section 677 taxes the grantor on the portion of the trust with respect to which the income may be

- Distributed to the grantor or his or her spouse
- Held or accumulated for future distribution to the grantor or his or her spouse
- Used to pay premiums on life insurance policies on the life of the grantor or his or her spouse

Use of trust income to provide support for a child whom the grantor is legally obligated to support also yields obvious economic benefits to the grantor. A grantor is taxed on any trust income distributed by the trustee to support people whom the grantor is legally obligated to support (e.g., children). However, the mere existence of the discretionary power to use trust income for support purposes does not cause the grantor to be taxed on the trust income. Taxation turns on whether the trust income is actually used to meet the support obligation.

The following example deals with the payment of premiums on an insurance policy on the grantor's life.

EXAMPLE C14-37 ▶ Maria is the grantor of the Martinez Trust, one of whose assets is a life insurance policy on Maria's life. The trust instrument requires that $1,000 of trust income be used to pay the insurance premiums and that the rest be distributed to Juan. Section 677 requires Maria (the grantor and insured) to be taxed on $1,000 of accounting income. The remaining income is taxed to Juan under the general trust rules. ◀

The rule concerning income held for eventual distribution to the grantor is illustrated in the next example.

EXAMPLE C14-38 ▶ Judy created a trust in January 1985 with all the income payable to Eric for 18 years. The trust assets will then revert to Judy. Section 677 taxes Judy on the capital gains provided they are credited to corpus. Eric is taxed on the accounting income because the trust was funded before March 1986 and lasts more than ten years. ◀

The next example concerns use of trust income to support the grantor's minor child.

EXAMPLE C14-39 ▶ Hal creates a trust and empowers the bank trustee to distribute income to his minor son, Louis, until the son reaches age 21. When Louis reaches age 21, the trust assets including accumulated income are to be paid over to the child. In the current year, when Louis is age 15, the trustee distributes $5,000 that is used to support Louis and $8,000 that is deposited into Louis's savings account. The remaining $12,000 of income is accumulated. Hal (the grantor) is taxed on the $5,000 used to support his son. Louis includes $8,000 in his gross income, and the trust pays tax on $12,000 less its $100 exemption. ◀

TYPICAL MISCONCEPTION

Keep in mind that the discussion in Example C14-37 covers trusts created by the grantor, who also is the insured. If the trust were created by a person other than the insured, say a parent, the income required to be used for paying life insurance premiums would not be taxed to the grantor because the insured is not the grantor or the grantor's spouse.

CONTROL OF OTHERS' ENJOYMENT

Section 674 taxes the grantor on trust income if he or she, his or her spouse, or someone without an interest in the trust (e.g., a trustee) has the power to control others' beneficial enjoyment such as by deciding how much income to distribute. Many exceptions, including one for independent trustees, exist for the general rule.

EXAMPLE C14-40 ▶ Otto is grantor and trustee of a trust over which the trustee has complete discretion to pay out the income or corpus in any amount he deems appropriate to some or all of its three beneficiaries, Kay, Fay, and May. In the current year, the trustee distributes all the income to Kay. Otto, the grantor, is taxed on the income. Kay, however, would have been taxed on the amount she received had there been an independent trustee. ◀

Under Sec. 678, an individual other than the trust's grantor or beneficiary can be required to report the trust income. The other individual is taxed on the trust income if he or she has the power under the trust instrument to vest the trust principal or the income in him- or herself, provided such power is exercisable solely by such individual.

Topic Review C14-4 summarizes the grantor trust rules.

WHAT WOULD YOU DO IN THIS SITUATION?

You are a CPA who has prepared the income tax returns for the Candy Cain Trust, an irrevocable trust, since the inception of the trust five years ago. The grantor is Able Cain, another client and the father of Candy Cain, the income beneficiary. First Bank, the trustee, is authorized to distribute income at its descretion to Candy, who is now age 17. For the current year, the trust had DNI of $15,000, all distributed to Candy to pay her medical bills incurred in an accident. All the DNI is from taxable sources. You advised Mr. Cain that he must include the $15,000 trust distribution on his individual tax return because the distribution was used to satisfy his support obligation. Mr. Cain demands that, because of how much business he has generated for you, you instead show the distribution as taxable to Candy so the income will be taxed at his daughter's 15% rate instead of at his 38.6% rate. How will you react to Mr. Cain's request?

Topic Review C14-4

Grantor Trust Rules

FACTUAL SITUATION	TAX TREATMENT
1. Trust is revocable.	Ordinary income and capital gains are taxed to grantor.
2. Irrevocable trust (funded before March 2, 1986) pays income to third-party beneficiary for more than ten years and then property reverts to grantor.	Ordinary income is taxed to beneficiary, and capital gains are taxed to grantor.
3. Same as number 2, except trust is funded on or after March 2, 1986, and the value of the reversionary interest exceeds 5% of the value of the trust.	Ordinary income and capital gains are taxed to grantor.
4. The grantor of an irrevocable trust retains administrative powers described in the IRC.	Ordinary income and capital gains are taxed to grantor.
5. The income of an irrevocable trust is disbursed to meet the grantor's obligation to support his or her children.	Ordinary income used for support is taxed to grantor.
6. The income of an irrevocable trust is disbursed to pay the premium on a life insurance policy on the life of the grantor or the grantor's spouse.	Ordinary income and capital gains are taxed to grantor to the extent they may be used to pay the premiums.

TAX PLANNING CONSIDERATIONS

ADDITIONAL COMMENT

In 2002, the first $1,850 of trust income is taxed at 15%. A complex trust pays no tax on $100 of income (because of its personal exemption) and only 15% on the next $1,850 of income. If the trust distributes income to a child under age 14 who is a dependent and has no other unearned income, the child pays no tax on the first $750 of that income and pays taxes at his or her own rate on the next $750. The rest is taxed at the parents' rates. If the child's parents are always in the top income tax bracket, non-trivial income tax savings still can be achieved by using a trust to spread income over different taxpayers. For the situation described here, a Sec. 2503(c) trust (trust for minors) is commonly used.

Many tax planning opportunities exist with respect to estates and trusts, including the ability to shift income to the fiduciary and/or the beneficiaries and the opportunity for executors or trustees of discretionary trusts to consider the tax consequences of the timing of distributions. These and other tax planning considerations are discussed below.

ABILITY TO SHIFT INCOME

Before 1987, one of the primary tax advantages of using trusts was the ability to shift income from the grantor to the trust or the beneficiary. Two changes have reduced the tax advantages of shifting income. First, the tax rate schedules for all taxpayers—but especially for fiduciaries—are very compressed. In fact, an estate or trust has only $1,850 (in 2002) of income subject to the 15% tax rate. Second, unearned income exceeding $1,500 (in 2002) of children under age 14 is taxed at the higher of the parents' or the child's tax rate, even if distributed from a trust or estate. Depending on whether the income is distributed or retained, it is taxed to the trust or the beneficiary or a portion to each. Because the trust is a separate taxpayer, income taxed to the trust is taxed under the trust's rate schedule. If the beneficiary has income from other sources, the income shifted to the beneficiary may not be taxed in the lowest tax bracket. An income tax savings nevertheless can occur whenever a portion of the shifted income is taxed at a rate lower than the rate the grantor would pay on such income.

KEY POINT

Given that one often cannot determine the exact amount of income a trust (or any other entity) has earned until after the end of the tax year, the importance of the 65-day rule for distribution planning becomes readily apparent.

TIMING OF DISTRIBUTIONS

People managing estates and discretionary trusts can reduce taxes by carefully planning the timing of distributions. From a tax standpoint, the executor or trustee should consider the beneficiary's income from other sources and make distributions in amounts that equalize the marginal tax rates of the beneficiary and the fiduciary. If the trust is a **sprinkling trust** (a discretionary trust with several beneficiaries), the trustee can accomplish tax savings for the beneficiaries by making distributions to the beneficiaries who have the lowest marginal tax rate that year. Of course, nontax reasons might require a trustee to distribute income to other beneficiaries as well. A special 65-day rule allows trustees of complex trusts and estates to treat distributions made during the first 65 days of the new tax year as if they had been made on the last day of the preceding tax year. If the trustee or executor does not make the election, the distributed income is deducted by the fiduciary and taxed to the beneficiary in the year of the actual distribution.

PROPERTY DISTRIBUTIONS

A special tax saving election is available for trusts that make noncash (property) distributions. Under the general rule affecting property distributions, the trust gets a distribution deduction equal to the lesser of the fiduciary's adjusted basis in the property or the property's FMV.[43] If the trust distributes appreciated property, the trustee can elect, however, to recognize a gain on the distribution. The gain is the excess of the property's FMV over its adjusted basis on the distribution date. If the trustee does not make the election, the trust recognizes no gain when it distributes the property.

If the trustee elects to recognize the gain, the distribution deduction equals the property's FMV. The beneficiary, in turn, takes a basis equal to the property's adjusted basis to the trust plus the gain the trust recognized on the distribution. If property likely will be sold soon after distribution, the election provision allows the trustee to choose where the appreciation will be taxed, at the trust level or the beneficiary level. If the distribution involves appreciated capital gain property, the capital gain recognized can be offset by the trust's capital loss carryovers from prior tax years.

[43] Sec. 643(d).

EXAMPLE C14-41 ▶ Todd Trust owns a number of assets, including an asset with a FMV of $35,000 and an adjusted basis of $12,000. In the current year, the trust distributes the asset to its sole beneficiary, Susan. The trust does not make any other distributions to Susan. If the trustee elects to recognize gain of $23,000, the trust receives a distribution deduction of $35,000, the FMV of the asset. Susan includes $35,000 of income in her tax return and obtains a $35,000 basis in the asset. Thus, if she sells the asset for $35,000, she will report no gain. If the trustee had not elected to recognize gain on the in-kind distribution, the distribution deduction would have been $12,000, the asset's adjusted basis. Susan's basis in the asset also would have been $12,000. ◀

CHOICE OF YEAR-END FOR ESTATES

Distributions from an estate or trust are taxed to the beneficiaries in the beneficiaries' tax year in which the fiduciary's year ends.[44] Because of the ability to defer the taxation of trust distributions to beneficiaries by choosing a noncalendar year, Congress in 1986 required all trusts (even existing fiscal-year trusts) other than tax-exempt and wholly charitable trusts to use a calendar year as their tax year.[45] Estates, however, are completely free to choose a year-end as long as the tax year does not exceed 12 months.

EXAMPLE C14-42 ▶ Molly Madison died on February 7, 2001. Madison Estate adopted a fiscal year ending January 31. During the period February 7, 2001 through January 31, 2002, Madison Estate distributes $30,000 to Bob, a calendar year beneficiary. The estate's DNI exceeds $30,000. Bob reports $30,000 of estate income on his individual return for 2002, Bob's tax year during which the estate's tax year ended. By choosing the January 31 year-end (instead of a calendar year-end), the executor postpones the taxation of income to Bob from 2001 to 2002. ◀

DEDUCTION OF ADMINISTRATION EXPENSES

Chapter C13 points out that the executor elects where to deduct administration expenses, i.e., on the estate tax return, the estate's income tax return, or some on each return. Unlike the situation for deductions in respect of a decedent, Sec. 642(g) provides that no double deduction occurs for administration expenses. Such expenses should be deducted where they will yield the greatest tax savings. Of course, if the surviving spouse receives all the decedent's property or all except for an amount equal to the exemption equivalent, deducting administration expenses on the estate tax return will produce no tax savings because the estate will owe no estate taxes.

COMPLIANCE AND PROCEDURAL CONSIDERATIONS

OBJECTIVE 9

Recognize the filing requirements for fiduciary returns

FILING REQUIREMENTS

GENERAL RULE. Every estate that has gross income of at least $600 for the tax year must file an income tax return (Form 1041-U.S. Fiduciary Income Tax Return). A trust income tax return (generally Form 1041) is required for every trust that has taxable income or has gross income of $600 or more.[46] In addition, every estate or trust that has a nonresident alien as a beneficiary must file a return.[47] A simplified trust form (Form 1041S) is available for use by simple trusts with no taxable income. This form may be prepared for simple trusts that have no capital gains or losses and have an income distribution deduction equal to the amount of income that must be distributed currently.

---

[44] Secs. 652(c) and 662(c).

[45] Sec. 645.

[46] Secs. 6012(a)(3) and (4). A special grantor trust rule, however, permits a revocable trust's income to be reported on the grantor's tax return. See Reg. Sec. 1.671-4(b).

[47] Sec. 6012(a)(5).

ETHICAL POINT

Individual beneficiaries report their share of income from trusts and estates on Schedule E of Form 1040. CPAs have a responsibility to monitor the beneficial interests that clients have in trusts and estates to prevent underreporting. Some clients may unintentionally forget to report income from a fiduciary simply because they received no cash distributions from the fiduciary during the year.

DUE DATE FOR RETURN AND TAX

The due date for fiduciary returns (Form 1041) is the same as for individuals, the fifteenth day of the fourth month following the end of the tax year.[48] If an extension is desired, Form 2758 must be filed. The extension period is four months, but an additional two-month extension may be requested.

Both trusts and estates generally must make estimated tax payments using the general rules applicable to individual taxpayers.[49] The IRC, however, exempts estates from making estimated tax payments for their first two tax years. If the fiduciary's tax liability exceeds the estimated tax payments, the balance of the tax is due on or before the due date for the return.[50] Estimated tax payments for a trust or an estate are made by using Form 1041-ES (Estimated Income Tax for Fiduciaries).

DOCUMENTS TO BE FURNISHED TO IRS

Although the executor or the trustee need not file a copy of the will or the trust instrument with the return, at times the IRS may request a copy of such documents. If the IRS makes such a request, the executor or the trustee also should transmit the following:

- A statement signed under penalty of perjury that the copy is true and complete
- A statement naming the provisions of the will or trust agreement that the executor or the trustee believes control how the income is to be divided among the fiduciary, the beneficiaries, and the grantor (if applicable)

SAMPLE SIMPLE AND COMPLEX TRUST RETURNS

Appendix B contains samples of simple and complex trust returns (Form 1041). The Appendix also illustrates completed Schedules K-1 for the reporting of distributed income, etc. to the beneficiaries. One copy of Schedule K-1 for each beneficiary is filed with Form 1041. In addition, each beneficiary receives a copy of his or her Schedule K-1, so that he or she knows the amount and type of gross income to report for the distributions received as well as other pertinent information.

The alternative minimum tax is not owed on the two sets of facts illustrated in the sample returns. When such tax is owed, the amount is reported on Schedule I of Form 1041.

PROBLEM MATERIALS

DISCUSSION QUESTIONS

C14-1 Explain to a client in laymen's language how the income of an estate or trust is subject to taxation.

C14-2 Given the nature of the tax rate schedule for trusts, what reasons exist today for creating a trust?

C14-3 List some major differences between the taxation of individuals and trusts.

C14-4 Explain to a client the significance of the income and principal categorization scheme used for fiduciary accounting purposes.

C14-5 List some common examples of principal and income items.

C14-6 A client asks about the relevance of state law in classifying items as principal or income. Explain the relevance.

C14-7 A trust from which Irene is entitled to receive only distributions of income and from which Beth will receive the remainder interest sells property at a gain. Income and corpus are classified in accordance with the Uniform Act. Will Irene receive a distribution equal to the amount of the gain? Explain.

C14-8 Refer to Question C14-7. Which taxpayer (the trust, Irene, or Beth) pays the tax on the gain?

---

[48] Sec. 6072(a).

[49] Sec. 6654(l).

[50] Sec. 6151(a).

C14-9 A trust owns some property on which depreciation is claimed. The trust distributes all of its income to its sole income beneficiary. Whose taxable income is reduced by the depreciation?

C14-10 What is the amount of the personal exemption for trusts and estates?

C14-11 A client inquires about the significance of distributable net income (DNI). Explain.

C14-12 a. Are net accounting income and DNI always the same amount?
b. If not, explain a common reason for a difference.
c. Are capital gains usually included in DNI?

C14-13 Explain how to determine the deductible portion of trustee's fees.

C14-14 Assume that a trust collects rental income and interest income on tax-exempt bonds. Will a portion of the rental expenses have to be allocated to tax-exempt income and thereby become nondeductible? Explain.

C14-15 a. Describe the short-cut approach for verifying that the amount calculated as a simple trust's taxable income is correct.
b. Can a short-cut verification process be applied with respect to trusts and estates that accumulate some of their income? Explain.

C14-16 When does the NOL of a trust or estate produce tax deductions for the beneficiaries?

C14-17 The Mary Morgan Trust, a simple trust, sells one capital asset in the current year. The sale results in a loss.
a. When will the capital loss produce a tax benefit for the trust or its beneficiary? Explain.
b. Would the result necessarily be the same for a complex trust? Explain.

C14-18 A peer states that simple trusts receive no tax benefit from a personal exemption. Is your peer correct?

C14-19 Describe the tier system for trust beneficiaries.

C14-20 Determine the accuracy of the following statement: Under the tier system, beneficiaries who receive mandatory distributions of income are more likely to be taxed on the entire distributions they receive than are beneficiaries who receive discretionary distributions.

C14-21 a. Describe to a client what income in respect of a decedent (IRD) is.
b. Describe to the client one tax disadvantage and one tax advantage that occur because of the classification of a receipt as IRD.

C14-22 Describe three situations that cause trusts to be subject to the grantor trust rules.

C14-23 A client is under the impression that the tax treatment is the same for all trusts in which the grantor has a reversionary interest. Is the client correct? Explain.

C14-24 A client is under the impression that, if the grantor trust rules apply to a trust, the grantor is always taxed on both the trust's ordinary income and its gains. Is the client correct? Explain.

C14-25 What is the benefit of the 65-day rule?

C14-26 a. When are fiduciary income tax returns due?
b. Must estates and trusts make payments of estimated income taxes?

ISSUE IDENTIFICATION QUESTIONS

C14-27 Art Rutter sold an apartment building in May 2001 for a small amount of cash and a note payable over five years. Principal and interest payments are due annually on the note in April of 2002 through 2006. Art died in August 2001. He willed all his assets to his daughter Amelia. Art's gross estate is about $2 million, and his estate tax deductions are very small. What tax issues should the executor of his estate consider with respect to reporting the sale of the building and the collection of the installments?

C14-28 For the first five months of its existence (August through December 2002), the Estate of Amy Ennis had gross income (net of expenses) of $7,000 per month. For January through July 2003, the executor estimates that the estate will have gross income (net of expenses) totaling $5,000. The estate's sole beneficiary is Amy's son, Joe, who is a calendar year taxpayer. Joe incurred a large NOL from his sole proprietorship years ago, and $34,000 of the NOL carryover remains but expires at the end of 2002. During 2002, Joe received only $5,000 of income from part-time employment. What tax issues should the executor of Amy's estate consider with respect to the reporting of the estate's income?

C14-29 Raj Kothare funded an irrevocable simple trust in May of last year. The trust benefits Raj's son for life and grandson upon the son's death. One of the assets he transferred to the trust was Webbco stock, which had a FMV on the transfer date of $35,000. Raj's basis in the stock was $39,000, and he paid no gift tax on the transfer. The stock's value has dropped to $27,000, and the trustee thinks that now (October of the current year) might be the time to sell the stock and take the loss deduction. For the current year, the trust will have $20,000 of income exclusive of any gain or loss. Raj's taxable income is approximately $15,000. What tax and non-tax issues should the trustee consider concerning the possible sale of the stock?

PROBLEMS

C14-30 *Calculation of the Tax Liability.* A trust has taxable income of $30,000 in 2002. The $30,000 includes $5,000 of long-term capital gains. What is its income tax liability? Compare this tax to the amount of tax a married individual filing a joint return would pay on the same amount of taxable income.

C14-31 *Determination of Taxable Income.* A simple trust has the following receipts and expenditures for the current year. The long-term capital gain and trustee's fees are part of principal.

Dividends	$20,000
Long-term capital gain	15,000
Trustee's fees	1,500
Distribution to beneficiary	20,000

a. What is the trust's taxable income under the formula approach of Figure C14-1?
b. What is the trust's taxable income under the short-cut approach?

C14-32 *Determination of Taxable Income.* Refer to Problem C14-31. How would your answer to Part a change if the trust in addition received $8,000 interest from tax-exempt bonds, and it distributed $28,000 instead of $20,000?

C14-33 *Determination of Taxable Income and Tax Liability.* A simple trust has the following receipts and expenditures for the current year. Assume the trust instrument is silent with respect to capital gains and that state law concerning trust accounting income follows the Uniform Act. Assume the trustee's fee is charged to income.

Dividend income	$40,000
Tax-exempt interest	9,000
Long-term capital gain	5,000
Trustee's fee	2,000
Distribution to beneficiary	47,000

a. What is the trust's taxable income under the formula approach of Figure C14-1?
b. What is the trust's tax liability?

C14-34 *Determination of Taxable Income.* During the current year, a simple trust has the following receipts and expenditures. Assume that trustee's fees are charged to income and that the Uniform Act governs for accounting.

Corporate bond interest	$60,000
Long-term capital gain	20,000
Trustee's fees	3,000

a. How much must be distributed to the beneficiary?
b. What is the trust's taxable income under the short-cut approach?

C14-35 *Determination of Distribution Deduction.* A trust has net accounting income of $24,000 and incurs a trustee's fee of $1000 in its principal account. What is its distribution deduction under the following situations:
a. It distributes $24,000, and all of its income is from taxable sources.
b. It distributes $24,000, and it has tax-exempt income (net of allocable expenses) of $2,000.
c. It distributes $10,000, and all of its income is from taxable sources.

C14-36 *Determination of Beneficiary's Income.* A trust is authorized to make discretionary distributions of income and principal to its two beneficiaries, Roy and Sandy. For the current year, it has DNI and net accounting income of $80,000, all from taxable sources. It distributes $60,000 to Roy and $40,000 to Sandy. How much gross income should each beneficiary report?

C14-37 *Determination of Beneficiary's Income.* Refer to Problem C14-36. How would your answer change if the trust instrument required that $10,000 per year be distributed to Sandy, and the trustee also made discretionary distributions of $60,000 to Roy and $30,000 to Sandy?

C14-38 ***Determination of Accounting Income and Distribution.*** A trust has the receipts and expenditures listed below for the current year. Assume the Uniform Act governs an item's classification as principal or income. What is the trust's net accounting income and the maximum distribution possible? Assume the trust cannot pay out principal.

Dividends	$12,000
Interest on tax-exempt bonds	5,000
Gain on sale of capital asset	8,000
Rental income from land	3,000
Property taxes on rental property	200
Trustee's fee charged to principal in accordance with agreement with trustees	1,200

C14-39 ***Determination of Taxable Income.*** Refer to Problem C14-38. Assume the trustee must pay out all of its income currently to its beneficiary, Julio.

a. What is the deductible portion of the trustee's fee?
b. What is the trust's taxable income exclusive of the distribution deduction?
c. What is the trust's DNI?
d. What is the trust's taxable income using the formula approach of Figure C14-1?

C14-40 ***Determination of Taxable Income.*** Refer to Problem C14-39. How would your answers change if the trust were a discretionary trust that distributes $8,000 to its beneficiary, Julio?

C14-41 ***Calculation of Deductible Expenses.*** The George Grant Trust reports the receipts and expenditures listed below. What are the trust's *deductible* expenses?

U.S. Treasury interest	$25,000
Rental income	9,000
Interest from tax-exempt bonds	6,000
Property taxes on rental property	2,000
CPA's fee for tax return preparation	800
Trustee's fee	1,900

C14-42 ***Tax Treatment of Capital Losses.*** A simple trust had a long-term capital loss of $10,000 for 2001 and a long-term capital gain of $15,000 for 2002. Its net accounting income and DNI are equal. Explain the tax treatment for the 2001 capital loss assuming the trust is in existence at the end of 2003.

C14-43 ***Tax Treatment of Capital Losses.*** Refer to Problem C14-42. How would your answer change if instead the trust were a complex trust that makes no distributions in 2001 and 2002? Assume the trust earns $8,000 of corporate bond interest income each year.

C14-44 ***Revocable Trusts.*** A revocable trust created by Amir realizes $30,000 of rental income and a $5,000 capital loss. It distributes $25,000 to Ali, its beneficiary. How much income is taxed to the trust, the grantor, and the beneficiary?

C14-45 ***Reversionary Interest Trusts.*** Holly created the Holly Marx Trust in January 2002. Starting in 2002, the trust income is payable to her adult son, Jack for 20 years. At the end of the twentieth year, the trust assets are to pass to Holly's husband. In the current year, the trust realizes $30,000 of dividend income and a $15,000 long-term capital gain. How much income is taxed to the trust, the grantor, and the beneficiary in the current year?

C14-46 ***Reversionary Interest Trusts.*** Refer to Problem C14-45. Explain how your answers would change for each independent situation indicated below:

a. At the end of the trust term, the property passes instead to Holly's nephew.
b. Holly creates the trust in October 2002 for a term of 25 years.

C14-47 ***Income in Respect of Decedent.*** The following items are reported on the first income tax return for the Ken Kimble Estate. Mr. Kimble, a cash method of accounting taxpayer, died on July 1, 2002.

Dividends	$10,000
Interest on corporate bonds	18,000
Collection on installment note from sale of investment land	24,000

The record date was June 14 for $6,000 of the dividends and October 31 for the remaining $4,000 of dividends. The bond interest is payable annually on October 1. Mr. Kimble's basis in the land was $8,000. He sold it in 2001 for a total sales and contract price of $48,000 and reported his gain under the installment method. Ignore interest on the installment note. What amount of IRD is reported on the estate's income tax return?

C14-48 *Income in Respect of Decedent.* Julie Brown died on May 29 of the current year. She was employed before her death at a gross salary of $4,000 per month. Her pay day was the last day of each month, and her employer did not pro rate her last monthly salary payment. She owned preferred stock that paid quarterly dividends of $800 per quarter each March 31, June 30, September 30, and December 31. The record date for the June dividend was June 10. Assume her estate chooses a calendar year as its tax year. What amount of gross income should be reported on the estate's first income tax return? Identify the IRD included in gross income.

C14-49 *Property Distributions.* In the current year, Maddox Trust, a complex trust, distributed an asset with a $42,000 adjusted basis and a $75,000 FMV to its sole beneficiary, Marilyn Maddox-Mason. The trustee elected to recognize gain on the distribution. Marilyn received no other distributions from the trust during the year. The distributable net income for the year for Maddox Trust was $87,000, and none of it was from tax-exempt sources.

a. What is the trust's distribution deduction?
b. On her individual income tax return, how much gross income should Marilyn report from the trust?
c. What is Marilyn's basis in the asset distributed in kind from the trust?

C14-50 *Income Recognition by Beneficiary.* Joan died April 17, 2001. Joan's executor chose a tax year for the estate that ends on March 31. The estate's only beneficiary, Kathy, reports on a calendar year. The executor of Joan's estate makes the following distributions to Kathy:

June 2001	$ 5,000
August 2001	10,000
March 2002	12,000
August 2002	14,000

The 2001 and 2002 distributions do not exceed DNI. How much income should Kathy report on her 2001 return as a result of the distributions from the estate? On her 2002 return?

COMPREHENSIVE PROBLEM

C14-51 Dana Dodson died October 31, 2001 with a gross estate of $1.7 million, debts of $20,000, and a taxable estate of $1.5 million. Dana made no adjusted taxable gifts. All of her property passed under her will to her son, Daniel Dodson. The estate chose a June 30 year-end. Its receipts and disbursements for the period ended June 30, 2002 were as follows:

Dividend income	$27,000
Interest income from corporate bonds	18,000
Interest income from tax-exempt bonds	9,000
Gain on sale of land	10,000
Executor's fee (charged to principal)	4,000
Distribution to Daniel Dodson	–0–

Of the $27,000 dividends received, $7,000 were declared October 4, 2001 with a record date of October 25 and a payment date of November 4, 2001. The corporate bonds pay interest each August 31 and February 28. The estate collected $18,000 corporate bond interest in February 2002. The tax-exempt bonds pay interest each June 30 and December 31. The estate collected $4,500 in December 2001 and $4,500 in June 2002 from the tax-exempt bonds. Dana, a cash method of accounting taxpayer, sold land in 2000 for a total gain of $60,000 and used installment reporting. She collected principal in 2000 and 2001 and reported gain of $30,000 on her 2000 return and $10,000 on her 2001 return. She collected additional principal in March 2002 and will collect a principal payment in March 2003. The gain attributable to the March 2002 and March 2003 principal collections is $10,000 per year. Ignore interest on the sale. Assume the estate owes no state estate taxes.

Calculate the following:

a. Deductible executor's fee.
b. Total IRD and IRD reported on the return for the period ended June 30, 2002.
c. Total Sec. 691(c) deduction.
d. Section 691(c) deduction deductible on the income tax return for the period ended June 30, 2002.
e. Taxable income of the estate.
f. Marginal income tax rate for the estate.

TAX STRATEGY PROBLEM

C14-52 Glorietta Trust is an irrevocable discretionary trust that Grant Glorietta funded in 1992. The discretionary income beneficiary for life is Grant's son, Gordon Glorietta (single). Gordon is a partner in a partnership in which he materially participates, and he has a large basis in his partnership interest. For 2002, the trust had $50,000 of dividend income, net of expenses, and no other income. It made no distributions to Gordon in 2002. Assume that it is now February 22, 2003, and Gordon has just learned that his share of loss from the partnership will be $72,000. Gordon has other income for 2002 of approximately $52,000. The trustee anticipates distributing $40,000 cash to Gordon before the end of February. For the last few years, Gordon's marginal tax rate was 15%. He claims the standard deduction, takes only one exemption, and files as a single individual. Discuss a tax-saving opportunity presented by this scenario. Also show a comparative analysis of the alternatives.

TAX FORM/RETURN PREPARATION PROBLEMS

C14-53 Marion Mosley created the Jenny Justice Trust in 1995 with First Bank named as trustee. For 20 years, the trust is to pay out all its income semiannually to the beneficiary, Jenny Justice. At the end of the twentieth year, the trust assets are to be distributed to Jenny's descendants. Capital gains are credited to principal, and depreciation is charged to principal. For the current year, the irrevocable trust reports the following results:

	Amounts Allocable to	
	Income	*Principal*
Rental income	$15,000	
Dividend income	27,000	
Interest on tax-exempt (non-private activity) bonds	8,000	
Long-term capital gain on sale of stock		30,000[a]
Maintenance and repairs of rental property	1,500	
Property taxes on rental property	700	
Fee for tax return preparation	500	
Trustee's fee		2,000
Depreciation		2,400
Estimated federal income taxes paid		9,000

[a] The sales price and adjusted basis are $110,000 and $80,000, respectively. Mrs. Mosley acquired the stock in 1993 and the trustee sold it in November of the current year.

Prepare a Form 1041, including any needed Schedule K-1s, for the Jenny Justice Trust. Omit pages 3 and 4 of Form 1041. The trustee's address is P.O. Box 100, Dallas, TX 75202. The identification number of the trust is 74-6224343. Jenny, whose Social Security number is 252-37-1492, resides at 2 Mountain View, Birmingham, AL 35205.

C14-54 Mark Wilson created an irrevocable trust in 1993 by transferring to it appreciated assets. Because of the unified credit, he owed no gift tax on the transfer. The trustee in its discretion is to pay out income or corpus to Doug Weldon (017-22-1344) until Doug (now age 24) becomes age 33. Then the trustee must distribute the property to Doug or his estate. The trustee is Yankee Bank, 20 State St., Boston, MA 02111. Doug resides at 38 Walden Ln., Boston, MA 02115.

During the current year, the following transactions occurred with respect to the trust:

Dividends received	$ 9,000
Rent received on raw land	1,200
Interest received from City of Salem bonds	13,000
Accountant's fee paid for prior year's return	275
Trustee's fee paid:	
Charged to income	250
Charged to corpus	400
Property taxes paid on land	140
Proceeds received from sale of stock	18,000

The stock was valued at $7,000 when transferred to the trust in 1993. Mark Wilson had paid $9,200 for the stock in 1990. The trustee distributed $5,100 to Doug and paid $4,000 of estimated federal income taxes on behalf of the trust. The City of Salem bonds are not private activity bonds. Prepare a Form 1041 and accompanying Schedule K-1 for the Mark Wilson Trust (74-9871234). Omit pages 3 and 4 of Form 1041.

C14-55 Mark Meadows funded a trust in 1994 with Merchants Bank named as trustee. He paid no gift tax on the transfer. The trustee in its discretion is to pay out income to Mark's children, Angela and Barry, for 15 years. Then the trust will terminate, and its assets, including accumulated income, will be paid to Angela and Barry in equal amounts. (Separate shares are *not* to be maintained.) In the current year, the trustee distributes $3,000 to Angela and $9,000 to Barry. The trust paid estimated federal income taxes of $15,000 and reported the following additional results for the current year.

	Amounts Allocable to	
	Income	*Principal*
Dividends	$50,000	
Interest on corporate bonds	4,000	
Interest on City of Cleveland (non-private activity) bonds	9,000	
Long-term capital loss on sale of stock		$12,000[a]
Trustee's fee		2,400
CPA's fee for tax return preparation	400	

[a] Mr. Meadows purchased the stock for $30,000 in 1990. It was valued at $44,000 when he transferred it to the trust in 1994. The trust sold the stock for $18,000 in December of the current year.

Prepare a Form 1041, including any needed Schedule K-1s, for the trust established by Mr. Meadows. Omit pages 3 and 4 of Form 1041. The trustee's address is 201 Fifth Ave., New York, NY 10017. The trust's identification number is 74-5271322. Angela (127-14-1732) and Barry (127-14-1733) reside at 3 East 246th St., Huntington, NY 11743.

CASE STUDY PROBLEMS

C14-56 Arthur Rich, a widower, is considering setting up a trust (or trusts) with a bank as trustee for his three minor children. He will fund the trust at $900,000 (or $300,000 each in the case of three trusts). A friend suggested that he might want to consider a January 31 year-end for the trusts. The friend also suggested that Arthur might want to make each trust a complex discretionary trust. Arthur is a little apprehensive about the idea of a trust that would be complex. The friend warned that trust income should not be spent on support of the children.

Required: Prepare a memorandum to the tax partner of your firm concerning the above client matter. As part of your analysis, consider the following:

a. What tax reasons, if any, can you think of for having three trusts instead of one?
b. Why do you think the friend suggested a January 31 year-end?
c. What is your reaction to the friend's suggestion about the year-end?
d. Which taxpayer, the beneficiary or the trust, is taxed on the income from a discretionary trust?
e. To what extent do trusts serve as income-shifting arrangements?
f. What can you advise Arthur concerning his apprehension about a complex trust?
g. Why did the friend warn against spending trust income for support?

C14-57 You are preparing a 2001 individual tax return for Robert Lucca, a real estate developer and long-time client. While preparing Robert's individual tax return you learn that he has income from a trust his 75-year-old father created in 2000. His 2001 income from the trust is properly reflected on a Schedule K-1 prepared by the accounting firm that prepared the trust's 2001 return. Robert prepared the trust's return for 2000, and decided that he should not be taxed on any of the trust's income because the trust distributed nothing to him. Upon reviewing Robert's copy of the trust instrument, you learn that the instrument calls for mandatory distributions of all the income to Robert every year. Assume that the trust reported only $3,300 of taxable income for 2000 and that Robert was in the highest marginal tax bracket for 2000.

a. What responsibility do you have in 2002 to correct the error made for the tax year 2000? Refer to the *Statements on Standards for Tax Services* in Appendix E.
b. Assume instead that an IRS agent has just begun to audit Robert's 2000 individual tax return. What is your responsibility if you have discovered the error on the 2000 trust return, and you are representing Robert in the audit?

TAX RESEARCH PROBLEMS

C14-58 A simple trust incurs a trustee's fee of $3,000 for the current year. Its receipts during the current year are as follows:

	Amounts Allocable to	
	Income	*Principal*
Dividends from listed stocks	$22,000	
Interest on tax-exempt (non-private activity) bonds	5,000	
Corporate distribution from a closely held firm; amount is not treated as a dividend because the firm has no earnings and profits	12,000	
Long-term capital gain on sale of land		32,000

Your manager requests that you prepare a memorandum addressing the *deductible* portion of the trustee's fee. Your manager suggests that you consider at a minimum these research sources:

- Reg. Secs. 1.652(b)-3(b) and 1.652(c)-4(e)
- Rev. Rul. 77-355, 1977-2 C.B. 82
- Rev. Rul. 80-165, 1980-1 C.B. 134

C14-59 In 2001, Bill Ames died at age 48. One of the items included in his gross estate was the principal residence where he and his widow, Lynn (age 46), lived for 20 years. Its FMV in 2001 was $200,000. In accordance with Bill's will, the residence and numerous other assets passed to a trust. Lynn is entitled to all the trust income for the rest of her life.

In 2002, the trust sells the residence for $240,000 and later that year pays $245,000 for a new house that Lynn moves into as her principal residence. Your manager asks that you draft a letter to the trustee and in the letter explain whether the trust is eligible for the nonrecognition rules for sales of principal residences.

Your manager suggests that you consider at a minimum the following research sources:

- IRC Sec. 121
- Rev. Rul. 54-583, 1954-2 C.B. 158

You should attach to the letter a list of additional relevant authorities and their citations.

C14-60 Prepare a memorandum to your manager in which you address whether the Jacobs Trust, a revocable trust funded in May 2001, must use a calendar year as its tax year. Its grantor, Joni Jacobs, has used a March 31 year-end for a number of years.

C14-61 ***Internet Research Problem.*** Your client is considering funding a trust that will contain some oil and gas properties. The trust will be governed by the rules of a state that has adopted the 1997 version of the Uniform Principal and Income Act (the 1997 Act). Your client wants to know about the allocation between the principal and income accounts of royalty income under the 1997 Act, compared with the 1962 version of the Act. Start your research by going to *http://www.law.upenn.edu/bll*. At that Web site, select "Uniform Law Research," then select "Uniform Principal and Income Act," and finally select "Final Act 1997." Consult Section 411 of the Act. Prepare a memo that addresses the client's question.

C14-62 ***Internet Research Problem.*** You are preparing for a client meeting at which the client has indicated he wants to discuss revocable trusts. Go to the Web site *http://www.financialdirect.com* and locate a discussion about revocable trusts (also known as living trusts). Summarize the points from the site about revocable (living) trusts.

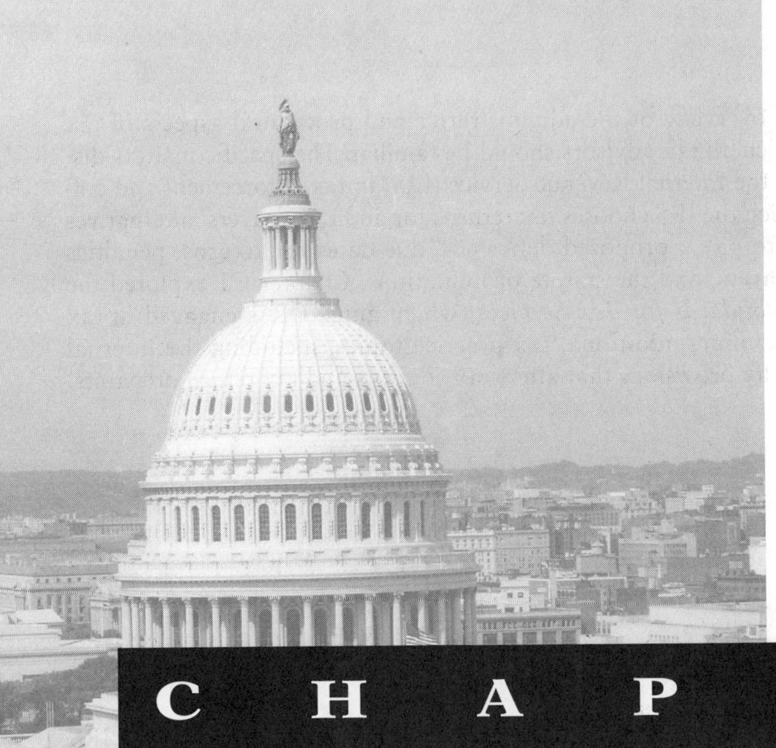

15

CHAPTER

ADMINISTRATIVE PROCEDURES

LEARNING OBJECTIVES

After studying this chapter, you should be able to

1. Understand the role of the IRS in our tax system
2. Discuss how returns are selected for audit and the alternatives available to taxpayers whose returns are audited
3. Describe the IRS's ruling process
4. Identify due dates for tax returns
5. Understand tax-related penalties generally
6. Calculate the penalty for not paying estimated taxes
7. Describe more severe penalties, including the fraud penalty
8. Understand the statute of limitations
9. Explain from whom the government may collect unpaid taxes
10. Understand the government-imposed standards for tax practitioners

CHAPTER OUTLINE

Role of the Internal Revenue Service...15-2
Audits of Tax Returns...15-3
Requests for Rulings...15-11
Due Dates...15-13
Failure-to-File and Failure-to-Pay Penalties...15-16
Estimated Taxes...15-19
Other More Severe Penalties...15-22
Statute of Limitations...15-26
Liability for Tax...15-30
Tax Practice Issues...15-31

This chapter provides an overview of the administrative and procedural aspects of tax practice, an area with which all tax advisors should be familiar. The specific matters discussed include the role of the Internal Revenue Service (IRS) in tax enforcement and collection, the manner in which the IRS chooses tax returns for audit, taxpayers' alternatives to immediately agreeing to pay a proposed deficiency, due dates for returns, penalties potentially affecting taxpayers, and the statute of limitations. Chapter C1 explored the AICPA's *Statements on Standards for Tax Services,* which guide CPAs engaged in tax practice. Chapter C15 examines additional tax practice topics, including the Internal Revenue Code (IRC) penalty provisions that affect tax advisors and tax return preparers.

ROLE OF THE INTERNAL REVENUE SERVICE

OBJECTIVE 1

Understand the role of the IRS in our tax system

The IRS is part of the Treasury Department. Its chief administrative officer is the IRS Commissioner. Overseeing the activities of the IRS is a nine-member board consisting of the Secretary of the Treasury, the IRS Commissioner, a public sector representative, and six private sector representatives. All board members are appointed by the President of the United States.

ENFORCEMENT AND COLLECTION

KEY POINT

The U.S. tax structure is based on a self-assessment system. The level of voluntary compliance actually is quite high, but one of the principal purposes of the IRS is to enforce the federal tax laws and identify taxpayers who willfully or inadvertently fail to pay their fair share of the tax burden.

One of the IRS's most significant functions is the enforcement of the tax laws.[1] The IRS is responsible for ensuring that taxpayers file returns, correctly report their tax liabilities, and pay any tax due.

The United States enjoys a high level of voluntary compliance with its tax laws. However, because some people do not comply voluntarily, the IRS must perform audits on selected taxpayers' returns and investigate nonfilers. In addition, because a number of ambiguities (gray areas) exist with respect to the proper interpretation of the tax laws, taxpayers and the IRS do not always agree on the tax treatment of transactions and events. As part of its enforcement duties, the IRS attempts to discover where taxpayers report these transactions and events differently from the way the IRS thinks they should be reported. As a later discussion points out, taxpayers who disagree with the position adopted by the IRS in auditing their returns may litigate.

The IRS must ensure that taxpayers not only report the correct tax liability, but also pay their taxes on time. For various reasons, some taxpayers file returns without paying any or all of the tax owed. The IRS's collection agents are responsible for collecting as much of the tax as possible from such persons or entities.

INTERPRETATION OF THE STATUTE

As noted in Chapter C1, the statutory language often is so vague that administrative and judicial interpretations are necessary. The IRS is charged with some of the administrative interpretations. Its most important interpretations are found in revenue rulings, revenue procedures, notices, and information releases, which are available to the general public. In addition, the IRS offers guidance to specific taxpayers in the form of letter rulings. Letter rulings, however, have no precedential value for third-party taxpayers. Each of these authorities is discussed in detail in Chapter C1.

[1] The IRS, however, does not have enforcement duties with respect to the taxes on guns and alcohol.

ORGANIZATION OF THE IRS

The IRS performs its responsibilities on a nationwide basis. It is organized *functionally* into four divisions: (1) Wage and Investment Income, (2) Small Business and Self-Employed, (3) Large and Mid-size Business, and (4) Tax Exempt (see Figure C15-1). Each division is headed by a divisional director.

The Wage and Investment Income Division has authority over individual taxpayers who report only wage and investment income. Most of these taxpayers file Forms 1040, 1040A, or 1040EZ. The Small Business and Self-Employed Division has authority over sole proprietors, individuals with supplemental income, and small corporations and partnerships. Most of these taxpayers file Forms 1065 and 1120S or Schedules C, E, and F. The Large and Mid-size Business Division has authority over corporations with assets of $5 million or more. Most of these taxpayers file Form 1120. The Tax Exempt Division has authority over tax exempt organizations, employee plans, and state and local governments. Most of these entities file forms relating to tax exempt status.

The shift to a functional mode of organization reflects Congress' desire to render the IRS more efficient and client oriented. Through this mode of organization, tax administrators can focus on their areas of technical expertise, and taxpayers can deal with the same technical experts wherever they reside.

AUDITS OF TAX RETURNS

OBJECTIVE 2

Discuss how returns are selected for audit and the alternatives available to taxpayers whose returns are audited

The IRS operates ten service centers throughout the nation, which receive and process tax returns.[2] One of the IRS's principal enforcement activities is auditing these returns. All returns are subject to some verification. One task the IRS service centers perform is checking whether amounts are properly calculated and carried from one line of a return to another. Another task is determining whether any items, such as signatures and Social Security numbers, are missing. Computers compare (or "match") by Social Security number the amounts reported on a taxpayer's return with employer- or payer-prepared documents (Forms W-2 and 1099) filed with the service center.[3] To date, however, a 100% matching of these documents with tax return information has been difficult to achieve.

If the service center detects an error in the tax liability reported on the return, it will transmit to the taxpayer a notice outlining the additional tax or refund due. If the information reported on a return is inconsistent with the information on Forms W-2 or 1099 reported by an employer or payer, the taxpayer is requested to explain the discrepancy in writing or pay some additional tax.

ADDITIONAL COMMENT

Although individual tax returns increased from 123 million to 125 million between 1998 and 1999, the number of individual returns examined *decreased* from 1.19 to 0.62 million.

PERCENTAGE OF RETURNS EXAMINED

Only a small fraction of all returns are examined. For example, for returns filed in 1999, the IRS examined only 0.49% of all individual returns, 1.12% of all C corporation returns, 0.33% of all partnership returns, 0.55% of all S corporation returns, and 0.22% of all fiduciary returns. For individuals with total positive income (i.e., gross income before losses and other deductions) of $100,000 or more, the audit rate was 0.84%, and corporations with assets of at least $250 million faced a 31.43% rate. As a result of its audit process, the IRS recommended additional taxes and penalties totaling $15.9 billion in that year.[4]

The examination percentages described above may be misleading because over half the returns filed are subject to a computerized matching in which the IRS compares the tax return information with documents (Forms 1099 and W-2) submitted by payers and

[2] IRS Service Centers are located in Andover, Massachusetts; Chamblee, Georgia; Austin, Texas; Holtsville, New York; Covington, Kentucky; Fresno, California; Kansas City, Missouri; Memphis, Tennessee; Ogden, Utah; and Philadelphia, Pennsylvania. The Chamblee, Holtsville, and Covington Service Centers are known as the Atlanta, Brookhaven, and Cincinnati Service Centers, respectively. The IRS plans to reduce the number of its service centers and centralize their operations.

[3] Form W-2 reports employees' salaries and withholding tax, and Form 1099 reports income such as interest and dividends.

[4] *Internal Revenue Service 2000 Data Book*, available for download at *http://www.irs.gov,* Tax Statistics Link, File No. 00DATABK.PDF. Examinations are done by revenue agents, tax auditors, and service center personnel.

Internal Revenue Service

Commissioner/
Deputy Commissioner

National Office Staff
HR, Finance, Communications, Etc.
1,000 IRS Employees

Chief Counsel
2,600 IRS Employees

SHARED SERVICES

Agency Wide
Shared Services
Facilities, Procurement, Etc.
4,900 IRS Employees

Agency Wide
Information
Systems Services
7,000 IRS Employees

FUNCTIONAL UNITS

Appeals
1,900 IRS Employees

Taxpayer
Advocate
Service
1,600 IRS Employees

Criminal
Investigation
4,500 IRS Employees

OPERATING DIVISIONS

Wage and
Investment Income
21,000 IRS Employees

Small Business and
Self-Employed
39,000 IRS Employees

Large and Mid-size
Business
9,500 IRS Employees

Tax Exempt
and
Government
Entities
2,800 IRS Employees

(NOTE: All numbers are approximate.)

FIGURE C15-1 ▶ IRS ORGANIZATION

Source: IRS, *Publication 3349* [Modernizing America's Tax Agency], 2000, p. 34.

employers. Because wages, interest, alimony, pensions, unemployment compensation, Social Security benefits, and other items of income are reported to the IRS by the payors, and because state income taxes, local real estate taxes, home mortgage interest, and other items of deduction are reported to the IRS by the payees, taxpayers who report only these items on their returns virtually face a 100% audit rate. According to a former Commissioner of the IRS, "[M]ore than half of the individual returns filed are simple enough so that a matching with forms filed by employers and interest payors is sufficient to insure compliance."[5]

SELECTION OF RETURNS FOR AUDIT

Returns are chosen for audit in various ways, with many being selected under the *discriminant function (DIF)* process described below. The IRS's objective in using the DIF process is to make the audit process as productive as possible by minimizing the number of audits that result in the collection of no additional taxes. The DIF process has improved the IRS's ability to select returns for audit. In recent years, the IRS failed to collect additional taxes on only about 10% to 15% of the individual returns audited by its revenue agents and tax auditors. By comparison, in the late 1960s, before the advent of the DIF program, the IRS failed to collect additional taxes in 45% to 50% of its audits.[6] Recently, the IRS began an audit approach known as the Market Segment Specialization Program (MSSP). Under the MSSP, IRS personnel develop industry expertise, and the IRS prepares MSSP audit guidelines. Examples of market segments include manufacturing, wholesale trade, retail trade (auto and boat dealers and service stations), and services (medical and health).[7] As IRS personnel become more familiar with specific industries, their ability to spot industry-specific items that taxpayers incorrectly report likely will improve.

HISTORICAL NOTE

Taxpayers have made several attempts to make the DIF variables public information. However, so far the courts have refused to require the IRS to provide such information. The basic thrust of the DIF program is that a return will be flagged if enough items on the return are out of the norm for a taxpayer in that particular income bracket.

DISCRIMINANT FUNCTION (DIF) PROGRAM. Of the individual returns audited in 1982, the IRS selected two-thirds under the DIF program. In 1999, the IRS selected only 43% under the DIF program, with the rest being selected under 12 different audit initiatives, some of which involve nonfilers, tax-shelter related write-offs, computer matches of third-party information, claims for refund, return preparers, and unallowable items.[8] The IRS began laying the groundwork for the DIF program in the mid-1960s to

- Reduce the staff and computer time necessary to screen returns
- Identify the returns most likely to contain errors
- Reduce the number of audited returns for which an examination results in little or no additional tax[9]

An assistant IRS commissioner described the DIF selection process in the following manner:

> DIF is a type of statistical analysis, using multiple variables or criteria to differentiate between two populations. For the IRS, those populations are tax returns needing examination versus those returns not needing examination. DIF essentially identifies items on tax returns having predictive power; that is, the selected items on returns in the "need to examine" group show up differently than those in the "no need to examine" group. DIF takes several items on a tax return and reduces them to a single score, which is then used as a major determinant as to whether a particular return will be examined.[10]

Returns with a relatively high DIF score have characteristics in common with returns for which the IRS earlier assessed a deficiency upon audit (e.g., the return may have reported a relatively high casualty loss or charitable contribution deduction). Because the

---

[5] Bureau of National Affairs, *BNA Daily Tax Reports,* June 20, 1984, p. G-1.

[6] Letter from Sheldon S. Cohen, former IRS Commissioner, to Representative Nancy L. Johnson, Chairman of House Ways and Means Subcommittee on Oversight Regarding the TCMP, dated July 20, 1995, reprinted in *Tax Notes Today,* August 10, 1995, Document 95 TNT 156-63.

[7] K. D. Bakhai and G. E. Bowers, "A New Era in IRS Auditing," *Florida CPA Today*, November 1994, pp. 26–30.

[8] J. L. Wedick, Jr., "Looking for a Needle in a Haystack—How the IRS Selects Returns for Audit," *The Tax Adviser,* November 1983, p. 673.

[9] Ibid., pp. 673–674.

[10] Ibid., p. 674.

WHAT WOULD YOU DO IN THIS SITUATION?

Cultural understanding and tolerance are hallmarks of modern American society. Yet in the tax sphere, are there limits to such understanding and tolerance?

Consider the case of Mr. Jung Yul Yu and his difficulties with the IRS (*U.S. v. Jung Yul Yu*, 954 F.2d 951 (3rd Cir., 1993)). Mr. Yu was born, reared, and educated as a lawyer in Korea. His employment experience included working for the Korean counterpart of the U.S. IRS. Mr. Yu immigrated to the United States at age 46 and was self-employed as a tax preparer. He became a naturalized U.S. citizen, and his tax practice flourished.

The IRS audited Mr. Yu's individual tax returns, and the audit resulted in an assessment of $27,000 in additional taxes and penalties. Mr. Yu proceeded to pay the auditing IRS agent $5,000 in return for a "no-change" letter. Unbeknownst to Mr. Yu at the time, the transaction was secretly taped. Mr. Yu was convicted of violating a U.S. law (18 USC 201(5)(1)(A)) in his attempt to bribe a government official.

At his sentencing hearing, pursuant to the U.S. Sentencing Guidelines, Mr. Yu argued that his national origin should be taken into account in determining his sentence. Mr. Yu explained that offering tax officials an "honorarium" to settle tax controversies is expected practice in Korea. Not to do so would be considered an insult to the Korean tax official's authority.

Do you believe that the $5,000 payment to the IRS agent was appropriate in these circumstances? Assume you were acting as Mr. Yu's representative. How should you have advised your client when he initially proposed to make the offer to the IRS agent?

IRS does not have the resources to audit all returns with a relatively high DIF score, IRS managers choose which of the higher scored returns should receive top priority for an audit.

The IRS has developed its DIF formulas based on information from the **Taxpayer Compliance Measurement Program (TCMP)**, discussed below. As part of its TCMP examination, the IRS classified returns into two categories: those with significant tax changes and those with minor tax changes. The only items on the tax returns used in the DIF program are those most valuable in distinguishing between returns with a significant change in taxes and those with little or no change.

ADDITIONAL COMMENT

The IRS is proposing a new national research program that will be less intrusive than the prior programs. See *The Wall Street Journal*, January 16, 2002, p. A1.

In the past, the IRS selected a small fraction of audited returns at random under the TCMP, which the IRS instigated to improve the selection process of the DIF program. Before 1994, the IRS audited about 50,000 individual returns every three years. It also conducted TCMP audits for other entities, such as corporations. In a TCMP audit, the IRS agent audited every item on the tax return. Because of budget cuts, in 1995 the IRS "indefinitely postponed" TCMP audits.[11] Thus, the data currently used in the DIF program are somewhat outdated.

The IRS also conducts what are called "financial status" or "lifestyle" audits. These audits seek to identify inconsistencies between the income that a taxpayer reports and his or her lifestyle. In the course of the audit, IRS agents review the taxpayer's overall economic situation. They may ask questions concerning where the taxpayer vacations, where his or her children go to school, and the cost and model of his or her vehicles. Although the courts generally have sanctioned the use of financial status audits, Congress has limited their use to situations in which the IRS has a reasonable indication of unreported income.

OTHER METHODS. The IRS widely uses several other methods for selecting returns for audit. Some returns are chosen because the taxpayer filed a claim for a refund of taxes paid previously, and the IRS decides to audit the tax return before refunding the requested amount. A few returns are audited because the IRS receives a tip from one taxpayer (perhaps a disgruntled former employee or ex-spouse) that another taxpayer did not file a correct return. If the IRS does collect additional taxes as a result of the audit, it is authorized to pay a reward to the individual who provided the tip. The reward is completely discretionary, although it cannot exceed 10% of the additional tax and penalties due.[12]

---

[11] "Rare Reprieve: IRS Postpones Its Superaudits," *The Wall Street Journal*, October 24, 1995, p. B1.

[12] Reg. Sec. 301.7623-1(c).

Sometimes, the process of examining the return of an entity (e.g., a corporation) will lead to an audit of a related party's return (e.g., a major stockholder).

Occasionally, the IRS investigates particular types of transactions or entities to ascertain taxpayer compliance with the tax law. As a result of these investigations, the IRS may select a number of returns for audit. For example, in 1989 the IRS examined 3,000 to 4,000 individual returns to determine whether taxpayers avoided classifying expenses as miscellaneous itemized deductions to escape the 2% floor. In 1992, the IRS cross-referenced items reported on Form 8300 (cash transactions over $10,000) with the tax returns of various businesses.[13] In 1997, the IRS investigated about 200,000 trusts (representing approximately 7% of total trust returns) to determine whether taxpayers had set them up to avoid taxes.[14]

ALTERNATIVES FOR A TAXPAYER WHOSE RETURN IS AUDITED

When the IRS notifies a taxpayer of an impending audit, the notice will indicate whether the audit is a correspondence audit, an office audit, or a field audit. In a correspondence audit, communication, such as providing documentation for a deduction or explaining why the taxpayer did not report certain income, is handled through the mail. In an office audit, the taxpayer and/or his or her tax advisor meet with an IRS employee at a nearby IRS office. The audit notice indicates which items the IRS will examine and what information the taxpayer should bring to the audit. Field examinations are common for business returns and complex individual returns. IRS officials conduct these audits either at the taxpayer's place of business or residence or at his or her tax advisor's office.

ADDITIONAL COMMENT

This special relief rule was designed to reduce the likelihood that the IRS could harass a taxpayer by repeatedly auditing a taxpayer on the same issue.

SPECIAL RELIEF RULE. A special relief rule exists for repetitive audit examinations of the same item. A taxpayer who receives an audit notice can request that the IRS suspend the examination and review whether the audit should proceed if (1) the IRS audited the taxpayer's return for the same item in at least one of the two previous years and (2) the earlier audit did not result in a change to his or her tax liability. To request the suspension, the taxpayer should call the person whose name and telephone number appear on the audit notice.

EXAMPLE C15-1 ▶ In October 2002, Tony receives notice that the IRS will audit the medical expense deduction claimed on his 2000 return. The IRS audited Tony's 1998 return with respect to medical expenses but did not assess any additional tax. Tony may request that the IRS suspend the audit of his 2000 return pending a review of whether the audit should continue. ◀

EXAMPLE C15-2 ▶ Assume the same facts as in Example C15-1 except that the IRS audited Tony's 1998 return for employee business expenses. Because that audit dealt with a different item, Tony may not ask for a suspension. ◀

ADDITIONAL COMMENT

Taxpayers should encourage the tax practitioner to handle an IRS audit. Because taxpayers usually have a limited understanding of the complexities of the tax law and its administration, having the taxpayer present at the audit generally is not a good idea.

TYPICAL MISCONCEPTION

Taxpayers should be cautious in signing a Form 870. Once this form is executed, the taxpayer no longer is permitted to administratively pursue the items under audit.

The following passages discuss taxpayers' rights during an examination of their returns.

MEETING WITH A REVENUE AGENT. Generally, the first step in the audit process is a meeting between the IRS agent and the taxpayer or the taxpayer's advisor. If the taxpayer is fortunate, the agent will agree that the return was correct as filed or, even better, that the taxpayer is entitled to a refund. In most instances, however, the agent contends that the taxpayer owes additional taxes. Taxpayers who do not agree with the outcome of their meeting may ask to meet with the agent's supervisor. A meeting with the supervisor may or may not lead to an agreement concerning the additional tax due.

Should the taxpayer agree and the agent's supervisor concur in the amount owed, the taxpayer must sign Form 870 (Waiver of Statutory Notice). This form indicates the taxpayer's agreement to waive any restrictions on the IRS's ability to assess the tax and

[13] "Tax Report," *The Wall Street Journal*, November 4, 1992, p. 1.

[14] Jacob M. Schlesinger, "IRS Cracks Down on Trusts It Believes Were Set up as Tax-Avoidance Schemes," *The Wall Street Journal*, April 4, 1997, p. A2.

consent to the IRS's collecting it. However, signing Form 870 does not preclude the taxpayer from filing a refund claim later.

If the taxpayer agrees that he or she owes additional tax and pays the tax upon signing the Form 870, interest accrues on the tax deficiency from the due date of the return through the payment date. Interest ceases to accrue 30 days after the Form 870 is signed, and the IRS charges no additional interest if the taxpayer pays the tax due within ten days of the billing date.

TECHNICAL ADVICE MEMORANDA. Occasionally, a highly technical issue with which the IRS official has had little or no experience arises in the course of the audit. Regardless of the type of audit, the official may request advice from the IRS's national office. Sometimes, the taxpayer urges the official to seek such advice. The advice is given in a Technical Advice Memorandum, which the IRS makes public in the form of a letter ruling. If the advice is favorable to the taxpayer, the agent or appeals officer must follow it. Even if the advice is pro-IRS, the official may consider the hazards of litigation in deciding whether to compromise.

APPEAL TO APPEALS DIVISION. If the taxpayer does not sign the Form 870, the IRS will send the taxpayer a report, known as a **30-day letter**, detailing the proposed changes in the taxpayer's liability and advising the taxpayer of his or her right to pursue the matter with the IRS appeals office. The taxpayer has 30 days from the date of the letter to request a conference with an IRS appeals officer.

If the audit was a field audit and the amount of additional tax plus penalties and interest in question exceeds $10,000, the taxpayer must submit a **protest letter** within the 30-day period. Only a brief written statement is necessary if the amount is between $2,501 and $10,000. An oral request is acceptable for office audits, regardless of the amount of the additional tax, penalties, and interest. If the taxpayer does not respond to the 30-day letter, the IRS will follow up with a 90-day letter, which is discussed below.

Protest letters are submitted to an officer in the appropriate IRS functional division and should include the following information:

- The taxpayer's name, address, and telephone number
- A statement that the taxpayer wishes to appeal the IRS findings to the appeals office
- A copy of the letter showing the proposed adjustments
- The tax years involved
- A list of the proposed changes with which the taxpayer disagrees
- A statement of facts supporting the taxpayer's position on any issue with which he or she disagrees
- The law or other authority on which the taxpayer relied[15]

The taxpayer must declare, under penalties of perjury, that the statement of facts is true. If the taxpayer's representative prepares the protest letter, the representative must indicate whether he or she knows personally that the statement of facts is true and correct.

KEY POINT

The appeals officer currently has the authority to settle or compromise issues with the taxpayer. To alleviate some of the workload and to make the audit process more efficient, the IRS currently is considering giving more of this settlement authority to revenue agents.

Appeals officers usually are experienced IRS personnel. Unlike IRS agents, appeals officers generally have the authority to settle (compromise) cases after considering the hazards of litigation. Their settlement authority extends to both questions of fact and questions of law. Thus, if the appeals officer believes that the IRS has approximately a 40% chance of winning in court, the appeals officer may agree to close the case if the taxpayer will pay an amount equal to 40% of the originally proposed deficiency.

In some situations, however, an appeals officer does not have settlement authority. For example, if the matter involves an appeals coordinated issue, the appeals officer must obtain concurrence or guidance from a director of appeals to reach a settlement. An **appeals coordinated issue** is an issue of wide impact or importance, frequently involving

---

[15] IRS, *Publication No. 5* [Your Appeal Rights and How to Prepare a Protest If You Don't Agree], January 1999, p. 1. A sample protest letter is contained in Robert E. Meldman and Richard J. Sideman, *Federal Taxation Practice and Procedure*, Fifth Edition, (Chicago: CCH Incorporated, 1998).

an entire industry or occupation group, for which the IRS desires consistent treatment. An example of an appeals coordinated issue is whether the taxpayer has in substance made a disposition of excess inventory and thus is entitled to claim a tax deduction for the loss on disposition.[16]

If, after the appeals conference, the taxpayer completely agrees with the IRS's position, he or she signs Form 870. However, if the appeals officer makes some concessions and the parties agree that the additional tax is less than that originally proposed, the taxpayer signs Form 870-AD (Waiver of Restrictions on Assessment and Collection). Unlike the case of a Form 870 waiver, a Form 870-AD waiver generally does not permit the taxpayer later to file a refund claim for the tax year in question. Form 870-AD is effective only if accepted by the IRS.

90-DAY LETTER

If the taxpayer and appeals officer fail to reach an agreement, or if the taxpayer does not file a written protest within 30 days of the date of the letter, the IRS issues a **90-day letter** (officially, a "Statutory Notice of Deficiency").[17] The 90-day letter specifies the amount of the deficiency; explains how the amount was calculated; and states that the IRS will assess it unless, within 90 days of the date of mailing, the taxpayer files a petition with the Tax Court.[18] During the 90-day period (and whether or not the taxpayer files the petition), the IRS may not assess the deficiency or attempt to collect it. After the 90-day period (and only if the taxpayer timely files the petition), the IRS still may not assess or collect the deficiency until the Court's decision becomes final.

LITIGATION

As mentioned earlier, taxpayer litigation can begin in one of the three trial courts: the Tax Court, a U.S. district court, or the U.S. Court of Federal Claims. After considering the time and expense of litigation, some taxpayers decide to pay the deficiency even though they believe their position is correct. Before deciding where to litigate, a taxpayer should consider the precedents, if any, of the various courts. Chapter C1 explores the issue of precedent.

TAX COURT. Taxpayers seeking to litigate in the Tax Court must file their petition with the Tax Court within 90 days of the date on which the IRS mails the Statutory Notice of Deficiency. The Tax Court strictly enforces this time limit. Before the scheduled trial date, taxpayers still may reach an agreement with the IRS. Going the Tax Court route has some advantages, including not having to pay the deficiency as a prelude to filing suit. If the amount in question does not exceed $50,000 for a given year, the taxpayer may use the informal small cases procedure, an alternative not available in other courts. A potential disadvantage of this procedure is that the taxpayer may not appeal the Court's decision.

Taxpayers must pay the additional tax, plus any interest and penalties, if they lose in Tax Court and choose not to appeal their case. In some situations, the Tax Court leaves the computation of the additional tax up to the litigating parties. When this happens, the phrase "Entered under Rule 155" appears at the end of the Tax Court's opinion.

DISTRICT COURT OR U.S. COURT OF FEDERAL CLAIMS. To litigate in either a U.S. district court or the U.S. Court of Federal Claims, the taxpayer must first pay the deficiency and then file a claim for a refund with the IRS. In all likelihood, the IRS will deny this claim on the ground that it correctly calculated the amount of the deficiency and properly assessed it. Upon notice of denial or six months after filing the claim, whichever is earlier, the taxpayer may sue the IRS for a refund. In no event, however, may the taxpayer file this lawsuit two years after the IRS has denied the claim.

---

16 *Internal Revenue Manual,* Sec. 8776.(14).

17 Upon request, the IRS may grant an extension of time for filing a protest letter.

18 Sec. 6213(a). If the notice is addressed to a person outside the United States, the time period is 150 days instead of 90.

APPEAL OF A LOWER COURT'S DECISION. Whichever party loses—the taxpayer or the IRS—may appeal the lower court's decision to an appellate court. If the case began in the Tax Court or a federal district court, the case is appealable to the circuit court of appeals for the taxpayer's geographical jurisdiction. For individuals, the taxpayer's place of residence generally determines which court of appeals has jurisdiction. In the case of corporations, the firm's principal place of business or office controls. Cases originating in the U.S. Court of Federal Claims are appealable to the Circuit Court of Appeals for the Federal Circuit; that is, all the latter cases are heard by the same circuit, irrespective of the taxpayer's residence or principal place of business.

Either the taxpayer or the government can request that the Supreme Court review an appellate court's decision. If the Supreme Court decides to hear a case, it grants **certiorari**. In any given year, however, the Supreme Court hears only a few cases dealing with tax matters.

STOP & THINK

Question: Two years ago, Pete made a large expenditure and fully deducted it in the year paid. Recently, the IRS began an audit of Pete's return for that year and contended that the expenditure is not deductible. Pete is a resident of California, which is in the Ninth Circuit. In a very similar case a few years ago, the Tax Court held that the expenditure is deductible, and the IRS did not appeal the decision. In yet another similar case litigated in a U.S. district court in California, the government initially lost but won upon appeal to the Ninth Circuit. If Pete decides to litigate, in which forum (trial court) should he bring his case, and why?

Solution: If he litigates in the Tax Court, he would not have to pay the contested tax in advance. However, under the *Golsen* Rule (see Chapter C1), the Tax Court would depart from its earlier pro-taxpayer decision and rule for the government. (Pete's case would be appealable to the Ninth Circuit, and the Ninth Circuit has adopted a pro-government position.) Because the court for his district in California would follow the Ninth Circuit precedent, he should not litigate in that court. This likely outcome would disappoint Pete if he believed that a jury would rule in his favor because only the U.S. district courts allow for jury trials. The only forum in which he possibly could win is the U.S. Court of Federal Claims. No case law that this court must follow exists because neither the Supreme Court, the Circuit Court of Appeals for the Federal Circuit, nor the U.S. Court of Federal Claims have previously ruled on the issue. (For a discussion of "forum-shopping," see Chapter C1).

BURDEN OF PROOF. In civil cases, the IRS has the burden of proving any factual issue relevant to a determination of the taxpayer's liability, provided the taxpayer meets four conditions.[19] First, the taxpayer introduces "credible evidence" regarding the issue. Credible evidence means evidence of a quality sufficient to serve as the basis of a court decision.[20] Second, the taxpayer complies with the recordkeeping and substantiation requirements of the IRC. These requirements include the proper documentation of meal and entertainment expenses (Sec. 274), charitable contributions (Sec. 170), and foreign controlled businesses (Sec. 6038). Third, the taxpayer "cooperates" with the reasonable requests of the IRS for witnesses, information, documents, meetings, and interviews. Cooperation includes providing access to, and inspection of, persons and items within the taxpayer's control. It also includes exhausting all administrative remedies available to the taxpayer.[21] Fourth, the taxpayer is either a legal person with net worth not exceeding $7 million, or a natural person.

[19] See Sec. 7491.
[20] See S. Rept. No. 105-174, 105th Cong., 1st Sess. (unpaginated).
[21] Ibid.

REQUESTS FOR RULINGS

OBJECTIVE 3

Describe the IRS's ruling process

As discussed in Chapter C1, a taxpayer can discover how the IRS views the tax treatment of a particular transaction by requesting that it rule on the transaction. The IRS will answer the request by issuing a letter ruling (sometimes referred to as a private letter ruling) to the taxpayer. A letter ruling is "a written statement issued to a taxpayer by the national office that interprets and applies the tax laws to the taxpayer's specific set of facts."[22] Letter rulings are a matter of public record, but the IRS eliminates all confidential information before making the rulings public. The IRS charges a user fee for issuing rulings, with the 2002 fees ranging from $45 for requests for identical accounting method changes to $25,000 for requests for advance pricing agreements.[23] The fee for a ruling on a proposed transaction is $6,000.

ADDITIONAL COMMENT

The information requirements for requesting a letter ruling are very precise (see Rev. Proc. 2002-1). In general, a tax professional experienced in dealing with the National Office of the IRS should be consulted. Also, a good blueprint of what should be included in a ruling request often can be found by locating an already-published letter ruling and examining its format.

INFORMATION TO BE INCLUDED IN TAXPAYER'S REQUEST

Early each calendar year, the IRS issues a revenue procedure that details how to request a letter ruling and the information that must be contained in the ruling request. Taxpayers or tax advisors should consult this procedure before requesting a ruling. Appendix B of the procedure contains a checklist the taxpayer may use to ensure that the request is in order. The IRS has issued additional detailed guidelines concerning the data to be included in the ruling request. For example, the IRS has specified what information it requires concerning the tax effects of transfers to a controlled corporation under Sec. 351. Each ruling request must contain a statement of all the relevant facts, including the following:

- Names, addresses, telephone numbers, and taxpayer identification numbers of all interested parties
- The annual accounting period and the overall accounting methods for maintaining the accounting books and filing the federal income tax returns of all interested parties
- A description of the taxpayer's business operations
- A complete statement of the business reasons for the transaction
- A detailed description of the transaction[24]

The taxpayer also should submit copies of the contracts, agreements, deeds, wills, instruments, and other documents that pertain to the transaction. The taxpayer must include an explicit statement of all the relevant facts and not merely incorporate by reference the language from the documents. The taxpayer also should indicate what confidential data should be deleted from the ruling before its release to the public.

If the taxpayer advocates a particular position, he or she must disclose the basis of this position and the authorities relied on. Even if the taxpayer is not arguing for any particular tax treatment, he or she must furnish an opinion about the tax results along with a statement of authorities supporting this opinion. In addition, the taxpayer should disclose and discuss any authorities to the contrary. The IRS suggests that, if no authorities to the contrary exist, the taxpayer should state so.

The person on whose behalf a ruling is requested should sign the following declaration: "Under penalties of perjury, I declare that I have examined this request, including accompanying documents, and to the best of my knowledge and belief, the request contains all the relevant facts relating to the request, and such facts are true, correct, and complete."[25]

---

[22] Rev. Proc. 2002-1, I.R.B. 2002-1, 1, Sec. 2.01.

[23] Rev. Procs. 2002-1, I.R.B. 2002-1, 1, Sec. 15 Appendix A and Rev. Proc. 96-53, 1996-2 C.B. 375.

[24] Rev. Proc. 2002-1, I.R.B. 2002-1, 1, Sec. 8.01. Certain revenue procedures provide a checklist of information to be included for frequently occurring transactions. See, for example, Rev. Proc. 83-59, 1983-2 C.B. 575, which includes guidelines for requesting rulings regarding a corporate formation under Sec. 351.

[25] Rev. Proc. 2002-1, I.R.B. 2002-1, 1, Sec. 8.01.

TYPICAL MISCONCEPTION

It is easy to be confused about the difference between letter rulings, which pertain to either prospective transactions or completed transactions for which a return has not yet been filed, and Technical Advice Memoranda, which pertain to completed transactions for which the return has been filed and is under audit.

WILL THE IRS RULE?

In income and gift tax matters, the IRS will rule only on proposed transactions and on completed transactions for which the taxpayer has not yet filed a return.[26] In estate tax matters, the IRS generally will not rule if the estate has filed a tax return. On the other hand, the IRS will rule on the estate tax consequences of a living person.[27] If no temporary or final Treasury Regulations have been issued for a particular statutory provision, the following policies govern the issuance of a ruling unless another IRS pronouncement holds otherwise:

- If the answer seems clear by applying the statute to the facts, the IRS will rule under the usual procedures.
- If the answer seems reasonably certain by applying the statute to the facts but not entirely free from doubt, the IRS will likewise rule.
- If the answer does not seem reasonably certain, the IRS will rule if so ruling is in the best interests of tax administration.
- If the issue cannot be readily resolved in the absence of Treasury Regulations, the IRS will not rule.[28]

The IRS will not rule on a set of alternative ways of designing a proposed transaction or on the tax consequences of hypothetical transactions. Generally, the IRS will not rule on certain issues because of the factual nature of the problem involved or for other reasons.[29]

From time to time, the IRS discloses, by means of a revenue procedure, the topics with respect to which it definitely will not rule. The list of topics is not all-inclusive; the IRS may refuse to rule on other topics whenever, in its opinion, the facts and circumstances so warrant.

SELF-STUDY QUESTION

How are letter rulings different from other IRS administrative interpretations (i.e., revenue rulings, revenue procedures, notices, and information releases)?

ANSWER

Letter rulings are written for specific taxpayers (not the general public) and have no precedential value.

According to Rev. Proc. 2002-3, the matters on which the IRS will not rule include the following:

- Whether property qualifies as the taxpayer's principal residence
- Whether compensation is reasonable in amount
- Whether a capital expenditure for an item ordinarily used for personal purposes (e.g., a swimming pool) has medical care as its primary purpose
- The determination of the amount of a corporation's earnings and profits[30]

In addition, the IRS will not rule privately on issues that it proposes to address through revenue rulings, revenue procedures, or otherwise, or that the Treasury Department proposes to address through regulations.

ADDITIONAL COMMENT

Requesting a letter ruling makes most sense for transactions that the taxpayer would not undertake without being assured of certain tax consequences. For example, certain divisive reorganizations are tax-free under Sec. 355. Taxpayers often request a ruling that a proposed transaction satisfies the intricate requirements of Sec. 355.

WHEN RULINGS ARE DESIRABLE

Private letter rulings serve to "insure" the taxpayer against adverse, after-the-fact tax consequences. They are desirable where (1) the transaction is proposed, (2) the potential tax liability is high, and (3) the law is unsettled or unclear. They also are desirable where the IRS has issued to another taxpayer a favorable ruling regarding similar facts and issues. Because only the other taxpayer may rely on the latter ruling, *this* taxpayer may seek a ruling on which he or she may confidently rely. On the other hand, private letter rulings are undesirable where the IRS has issued to another taxpayer an unfavorable ruling regarding similar facts and issues. They also are undesirable where the IRS might publicly rule on a related matter, and the taxpayer has an interest in this matter. Private letter rulings offer insight into the IRS's thinking regarding the tax treatment of proposed transactions. Although third parties may not cite them as authority for the tax consequences of their transactions, they may cite them as authority for avoiding a substantial understatement penalty (discussed elsewhere in this chapter).

---

[26] Ibid., Sec. 5.01.
[27] Ibid., Sec. 5.05.
[28] Ibid., Sec. 5.14.
[29] Ibid., Secs. 7.01 and 7.02.
[30] Rev. Proc. 2002-3, I.R.B. 2002-1, 1, Sec. 3.

DUE DATES

OBJECTIVE 4

Identify the due dates for tax returns

DUE DATES FOR RETURNS

Returns for individuals, fiduciaries, and partnerships are due on or before the fifteenth day of the fourth month following the year-end of the individual or entity.[31] C corporation and S corporation tax returns are due no later than the fifteenth day of the third month after the corporation's year-end. To be subject to reporting requirements, individuals and fiduciaries, but not corporations and partnerships, must have a minimum level of gross income during the year.[32]

EXTENSIONS

Congress realized that, in some instances, gathering the requisite information and completing the return by the designated due date is difficult. Consequently, it authorized extensions of time for filing returns. Unless the taxpayer is abroad, the extension period cannot exceed six months.[33]

INDIVIDUALS. By filing Form 4868 (Application for Automatic Extension of Time to File U.S. Individual Income Tax Return), an individual taxpayer may request an automatic extension of four months after the original due date of the return. The extension is automatic in the sense that the taxpayer need not convince the IRS that an extension is necessary. By filing Form 2688 (Application for Additional Extension of Time to File U.S. Individual Income Tax Return), the taxpayer may request an additional extension of up to two months if he or she needs additional time at the end of the four-month period. Because this latter extension is not automatic, the taxpayer must explain on the form why he or she needs more time. Even if the IRS denies the request, it often grants the taxpayer a brief grace period for filing.

EXAMPLE C15-3 ▶ Bob and Alice, his wife, are calendar year taxpayers. By filing Form 4868, they may get an automatic extension for filing their current year's return until August 15 of the following year.[34] Suppose that both have been quite ill throughout the latter year. As August 15 draws near, they may submit Form 2688 and request an additional extension until no later than October 15. They must explain their reasons for requesting an additional extension. ◀

CORPORATIONS. Corporations request an automatic extension by filing Form 7004 (Application for Automatic Extension of Time to File Corporation Income Tax Return) by the original due date of the return. Although the IRC specifies an automatic extension period of three months, Treasury Regulations and the Form 7004 instructions specify six months.[35] No additional extensions are available.

EXAMPLE C15-4 ▶ Lopez Corporation reports on a fiscal year ending March 31. The regular due date for its return is June 15. It may file Form 7004 and request an automatic six-month extension that postpones the due date until December 15. ◀

DUE DATES FOR PAYMENT OF THE TAX

Obtaining an extension merely postpones the due date for the return. It does not extend the time for paying the tax. In general, the due date for the tax payment is the same as the unextended due date for the return.[36] In addition, the first estimated tax installment for an individual taxpayer is due on the due date for the preceding year's return, and the additional payments are due two, five, and nine months later. Taxpayers who elect to let the

---

[31] Sec. 6072(a). Section 6072(c) extends the due date for returns of nonresident alien individuals to the fifteenth day of the sixth month after the end of their tax year.

[32] Secs. 6012(a)(2) and 6031(a).

[33] Sec. 6081(a).

[34] All due dates are stated in terms of the fifteenth day of the month. However, if the fifteenth falls on Saturday, Sunday, or a holiday, the due date is the next business day.

[35] Sec. 6081(b) and Reg. Sec. 1.6081-3(a).

[36] Sec. 6151(a).

TYPICAL MISCONCEPTION

Obtaining an extension defers the date by which the return must be filed, but it does *not* defer the payment date of the tax liability. Therefore, an extension for filing must be accompanied by a payment of an estimate of the taxpayer's tax liability. Computing this estimated tax liability can be difficult because much of the information necessary to complete the return may be incomplete or not yet available.

IRS compute their tax must pay it within 30 days of the date the IRS mails a notice stating the amount of tax payable.[37]

Interest accrues on any tax not paid by the return's due date. Thus, it accrues over extension periods. When individuals request an automatic extension, they should project their tax liability to the best of their ability. Any tax owed, after withholding and estimated tax payments have been subtracted from the projected amount, should be remitted with the extension request. In addition, if an extension for filing a gift tax return also is requested (on the same form), the estimated amount of gift tax liability should be remitted. Similarly, corporations should remit with their automatic extension request the amount of tax they anticipate to be due, reduced by any estimated tax already paid.

INTEREST ON TAX NOT TIMELY PAID

Any tax not paid by the original due date for the return is subject to an interest charge.[38] Taxpayers incur interest charges in four contexts.

- They file late, without having requested an extension, and pay late.
- They request an extension for filing but inaccurately estimate their tax liability and, thus, must pay some additional tax when they file their return.
- They file on time but are not financially able to pay some, or all, of the tax.
- The IRS audits their return and determines that they owe additional taxes.

RATE DETERMINATION. The IRS determines the interest rate that it charges taxpayers under rules contained in Sec. 6621. The rate varies with fluctuations in the federal short-term rate; potentially the interest rate changes at the beginning of each calendar quarter. For noncorporate taxpayers, the interest rate on both underpayments and overpayments is three percentage points higher than the federal rate. For corporate tax overpayments exceeding $10,000, the interest rate is reduced to the federal short-term rate plus one-half percentage point. For corporate underpayments exceeding $100,000, the rate is five percentage points above the federal short-term rate if the deficiency is not paid before a certain date. Rates are rounded to the nearest full percent. Applicable interest rates are as follows:

Period	*General Rate for Underpayments and Overpayments*
January 1 through March 31, 2002	6%
July 1 through December 31, 2001	7%
April 1 through June 30, 2001	8%
April 1, 2000 through March 31, 2001	9%
April 1, 1999 through March 31, 2000	8%

EXAMPLE C15-5 ▶ Ann filed her 1999 individual return in a timely manner, and the IRS audits it in March 2002. Ann is a calendar year taxpayer. The IRS contends that Ann owes $2,700 of additional taxes. Ann pays the additional taxes on March 31, 2002. Ann also must pay interest on the $2,700 deficiency for the period April 16, 2000 through March 31, 2002. The interest rate is 9% from April 16, 2000 through March 31, 2001, 8% from April 1, 2001 through June 30, 2001, 7% from July 1, 2001 through December 31, 2001, and 6% from January 1 through March 31, 2002. ◀

[37] Sec. 6151(b)(1). The special estimated tax payment rules for C corporations, S corporations, and trusts and estates are described in Chapters C3, C11, and C14, respectively, of this volume.

[38] Secs. 6601(a) and (b)(1).

HISTORICAL NOTE

Probably two of the most significant changes in tax administration have been the daily compounding of interest and tying the interest rate charged to the federal short-term rate, which has resulted in a higher rate used to calculate the interest charge than in years past. Before these two changes, taxpayers who played the "audit lottery" and took aggressive positions incurred little risk.

DAILY COMPOUNDING. Daily compounding applies to both the interest taxpayers owe to the government and the interest the government owes to taxpayers who have overpaid their taxes. The IRS has issued Rev. Proc. 95-17 containing tables to be used for calculating interest.[39] The major tax services have published these tables. In addition, software packages are available for interest calculations.

ACCRUAL PERIOD. Interest usually accrues from the original due date of the return until the date of payment. However, two important exceptions apply. First, if the IRS fails to send an individual taxpayer a notice within 18 months after the original due date or the date on which a return is timely filed, whichever is later, the accrual of interest (and penalties) will be suspended.[40] The suspension period begins on the day after the 18-month period and ends 21 days after the IRS sends the requisite notice. Second, if the IRS does not issue a notice and demand for payment within 30 days after the taxpayer signs a Form 870 (Waiver of Statutory Notice), no interest can be charged for the period between the end of the 30-day period and the date the IRS issues its notice and demand.[41] Taxpayers litigating in the Tax Court may make a deposit to reduce the interest potentially owed. If the court decides that the taxpayer owes a deficiency, interest will not accrue on the amount of the deposit.

EXAMPLE C15-6 ▶ Cindy receives an automatic extension for filing this year's return. She submits her return, along with the $700 balance she owes on this year's tax, on June 24 of the following year. She owes interest on $700 for the period April 16 of this year through June 24 of the following year. Interest is compounded daily using the interest rate for underpayments determined under Sec. 6621. ◀

EXAMPLE C15-7 ▶ After filing for an automatic extension, Hans files his 2002 return on August 15, 2003. On April 1, 2005, the IRS sends Hans a notice of deficiency in which it assesses interest. Because the IRS failed to send Hans the notice by February 15, 2005 (18 months after the date on which the return was timely filed), the accrual of interest is suspended. The suspension period begins on February 16, 2005 (the day after the 18 month period) and ends on April 21, 2005 (21 days after the IRS sends the requisite notice). ◀

EXAMPLE C15-8 ▶ Raj filed his 1999 individual return on March 17, 2000. The IRS audits the return in 2002, and on January 24, 2002, Raj signs a Form 870, on which he agrees that he owes a $780 deficiency. The IRS does not issue a notice and demand for payment until March 19, 2002. Raj pays the deficiency two days later. Raj owes interest, compounded daily at the Sec. 6621 underpayment rate, for the period April 16, 2000 through February 23, 2002. No interest can be levied for the period February 24 through March 19, 2002 because the IRS did not issue its notice and demand for payment until more than 30 days after Raj signed Form 870. ◀

ABATEMENT. The IRS does not abate interest except for unreasonable errors or delays resulting from its managerial or ministerial acts.[42] A "managerial act" involves the temporary or permanent loss of records or the exercise of judgment or discretion relating to the management of personnel.[43] A "ministerial act" involves routine procedure without the exercise of judgment or discretion.[44] A decision concerning the proper application of federal law is neither a managerial nor a ministerial act.

EXAMPLE C15-9 ▶ Omar provides documentation to an audit agent, who assures him that he will receive a copy of an audit report shortly. Before the agent has had an opportunity to act, however, the divisional manager transfers him to another office. An extended period of time elapses before the manager assigns another audit agent to Omar's case. The decision to reassign is a managerial act. The IRS may abate interest attributable to any unreasonable delay in payment resulting from this act. ◀

---

[39] Rev. Proc. 95-17, 1995-1 C.B. 556.

[40] Sec. 6404(g). Beginning in 2004, the notice must be sent within one year after the aforementioned dates.

[41] Sec. 6601(c).

[42] Sec. 6404(e).

[43] Reg. Sec. 301.6404-2(b)(1).

[44] Reg. Sec. 301.6404-2(b)(2).

EXAMPLE C15-10 ▶ Chanelle requests information from an IRS employee concerning the balance due on her current year's tax liability. The employee fails to access the most current computerized database and provides Chanelle with incorrect information. Based on this information, Chanelle pays less than the full balance due. The employee's failing to access the most current database is a ministerial act. The IRS may abate interest attributable to any unreasonable delay in payment resulting from this act. ◀

FAILURE-TO-FILE AND FAILURE-TO-PAY PENALTIES

OBJECTIVE 5

Understand tax-related penalties generally

Penalties add teeth to the accounting and reporting provisions of the Internal Revenue Code. Without them, these provisions would be mere letters on the books of the legislature—words without effect. Tax-related penalties fall into two broad categories: taxpayer and preparer. As the name suggests, taxpayer penalties apply only to taxpayers, be they individuals, corporations, estates, or trusts. Preparer penalties apply only to tax return preparers, be they firms that employ tax professionals or the professionals themselves. Within these broad categories are two distinct subcategories: civil and criminal. Civil penalties are imposed on taxpayers for failing to fulfill their accounting or reporting obligations. Criminal penalties are imposed for maliciously or willfully failing to do so. Taxpayers may raise as a defense to some penalties "reasonable cause" and a good faith belief in the correctness of their position. Sometimes, for the defense to be valid, they also must disclose this position on their tax return. This section of the text discusses two commonly encountered penalties in income, estate, and gift taxation: failure to file and failure to pay. The IRS may assess these penalties, in addition to interest, on overdue tax liabilities. Subsequent sections of the text discuss other taxpayer and preparer penalties. Topic Review C15-1 presents a summary of IRC penalty provisions. The Topic Review is provided here rather than later in the chapter to give readers a framework for following the discussion of the various penalties.

REAL-WORLD EXAMPLE

In 2000, as a result of the audit process, the IRS assessed a total of $15.9 billion in civil penalties and abated $469 million for reasonable cause.

FAILURE TO FILE

Taxpayers who do not file a return by the due date generally are liable for a penalty of 5% per month (or fraction thereof) of the net tax due.[45] A fraction of a month, even just a day, counts as a full month. The maximum penalty for failing to file is 25%. If the taxpayer receives an extension, the extended due date is treated as the original due date. In determining the net tax due (i.e., the amount subject to the penalty), the IRS reduces the taxpayer's gross tax by any taxes paid by the return's due date (e.g., withholding and estimated tax payments) and tax credits claimed on the return.[46] If any failure to file is fraudulent, the penalty rate is 15% per month with a maximum penalty of 75%.[47] For the purpose of this provision, "fraud" is defined as actual, intentional wrongdoing or the commission of an act for the specific purpose of evading a tax known or believed to be due.[48]

Penalties are not levied if a taxpayer can prove that he or she failed to file a timely return because of a reasonable cause (as opposed to willful neglect). According to Treasury Regulations, reasonable cause exists if "the taxpayer exercised ordinary business care and prudence and was nevertheless unable to file the return within the prescribed time."[49] Not surprisingly, much litigation deals with the issue of reasonable cause.

ADDITIONAL COMMENT

The most common reason given by taxpayers to support reasonable cause for failing to file a timely tax return is reliance on one's tax advisor. Other reasons include severe illness or serious accident. Reliance on a tax advisor is not always sufficient cause to obtain a waiver of the penalties.

Note that the penalty imposed for not filing on time generally is a function of the net tax due. However, a minimum penalty applies to some income tax returns.[50] Congress enacted the minimum penalty provision because of the cost to the IRS of identifying non-

[45] Sec. 6651(a).
[46] Sec. 6651(b)(1).
[47] Sec. 6651(f).
[48] *Robert W. Bradford v. CIR*, 58 AFTR 2d 86-5532, 86-2 USTC ¶9602 (9th Cir., 1996: *Chris D. Stoltzfus v. U.S.*, 22 AFTR 2d 5251, 68-2 USTC ¶9499 (3rd Cir., 1968: and *William E. Mitchell v. CIR*, 26 AFTR 684, 41-1 USTC ¶9317 (5th Cir., 1941).
[49] Reg. Sec. 301.6651-1(c)(1).
[50] Sec. 6651(a).

filers. If a taxpayer does not file an income tax return within 60 days of the due date (including any extensions), the penalty will be no less than the smaller of $100 or 100% of the tax due on the return. Taxpayers who owe no tax are not subject to the **failure-to-file penalty**. Also, the IRS may waive the penalty if the taxpayer shows reasonable cause for not filing.

EXAMPLE C15-11 ▶ Earl files his 2002 individual income tax return on July 4, 2003. Earl requested no extension and did not have reasonable cause for his late filing (but committed no fraud). Earl's 2002 return shows a balance due of $400. Under the regular rules, the late filing penalty would be $60 (0.05 × 3 months × $400). Earl's penalty is $100 because of the minimum penalty provisions applicable to his failure to file the return within 60 days of the due date. ◀

Topic Review C15-1

Overview of Penalties

Penalty	IRC Section	Applicability	Rules/Calculation	Defenses/Waiver
A. TAXPAYER—CIVIL				
Failure to file	6651(a)	All persons	*General rule:* 5% per month or fraction thereof; 25% maximum *Minimum penalty if late more than 60 days:* lesser of $100 or 100% of tax due *Fraudulent reason for not filing:* 15% per month or fraction thereof; 75% maximum	Reasonable cause, not willful neglect
Failure to pay tax	6651(a)	All persons	*General rule:* 0.5% per month or fraction thereof; 25% maximum*	Reasonable cause, not willful neglect
Failure by individual to pay estimated tax	6654	Individuals, certain estates, trusts	*General rule:* penalty at same rate as interest rate for deficiency; imposed for period between due date for estimated tax payments and earlier of payment date or due date for return	Waiver in unusual circumstances
Failure by corporation to pay estimated tax	6655	Corporations	*General rule:* penalty at same rate as interest rate for deficiency; imposed for period between due date for estimated tax payments and earlier of payment date or due date for return	—
Negligence	6662(c)	All persons	*General rule:* 20% of underpayment attributable to negligence	Reasonable cause, good faith
Substantial understatement	6662(d)	All persons	*General rule:* 20% of underpayment attributable to substantial understatement (portion for which no substantial authority and no disclosure exists)	Reasonable cause, good faith; also, substantial authority, disclosure
Civil fraud	6663	All persons	*General rule:* 75% of portion of understatement attributable to fraud.	Reasonable cause, good faith
B. TAXPAYER—CRIMINAL				
Willful attempt to evade tax	7201	All persons	*General rule:* $100,000 ($500,000 for corporations) and/or up to five years in prison	—
Willful failure to collect or pay over tax	7202	All persons	*General rule:* $10,000 and/or up to five years in prison	—
Willful failure to pay or file	7203	All persons	*General rule:* $25,000 ($100,000 for corporations) and/or up to five years in prison	—
Willfully making false or fraudulent statements	7206	All persons	*General rule:* $25,000 ($100,000 for corporations) and/or up to one year in prison	—

Topic Review C15-1 (cont.)

C. PREPARER—CIVIL				
Understatement of tax by preparer	6694(a)	Tax return preparers	*General rule:* $250	Reasonable cause, good faith; also, disclosure
Willful attempt to understate taxes	6694(b)	Tax return preparers	*General rule:* $1,000	—
Failure to furnish copy to taxpayer	6695(a)	Tax return preparers	*General rule:* $50; $25,000 maximum	Reasonable cause, not willful neglect
Failure to sign return	6695(b)	Tax return preparers	*General rule:* $50; $25,000 maximum	Reasonable cause, not willful neglect
Failure to furnish identifying number	6695(c)	Tax return preparers	*General rule:* $50; $25,000 maximum	Reasonable cause, not willful neglect
Failure to retain copy or list	6695(d)	Tax return preparers	*General rule:* $50; $25,000 maximum	Reasonable cause, not willful neglect
Failure to file correct information returns	6695(e)	Tax return preparers	*General rule:* $50 for each failure to file a return or each failure to set forth an item in a return; $25,000 maximum	Reasonable cause, not willful neglect
Improper negotiation of checks	6695(f)	Tax return preparers	*General rule:* $500 per check	—
Aiding and abetting in understatement	6701(b)	All persons	*General rule:* $1,000 ($10,000 for corporations)	—

* If the taxpayer owes both the failure-to-file and the failure-to-pay penalties for a given month, the total penalty for such month is limited to 5%.

In general, interest does not accrue on any penalty paid within ten days of the date that the IRS notifies the taxpayer of the penalty. Interest accrues under Sec. 6601(e)(2)(B) on the failure-to-file penalty, however, from the due date of the return (including any extensions) until the payment date.

FAILURE TO PAY

The **failure-to-pay penalty** is imposed at 0.5% per month (or fraction thereof).[51] The maximum penalty is 25%. The penalty is based on the gross tax shown on the return less any tax payments made and credits earned before the beginning of the month for which the penalty is calculated.[52] As with the failure-to-file penalty, the IRS may waive the failure-to-pay penalty if the taxpayer shows reasonable cause.

Because the tax is due on the original due date for the return, taxpayers who request an extension without paying 100% of their tax liability potentially owe a failure-to-pay penalty. Treasury Regulations provide some relief by exempting a taxpayer from the penalty if the additional tax due with the filing of the extended return does not exceed 10% of the tax owed for the year.[53]

EXAMPLE C15-12 ▶ Gary requests an extension for filing his 2002 individual income tax return. His 2002 tax payments include withholding of $4,500, estimated tax payments of $2,000, and $1,000 submitted with his request for an automatic extension. He files his return on June 7, 2003, showing a total tax of $8,000 and a balance due of $500. Gary is exempt from the failure-to-pay penalty because the $500 balance due does not exceed 10% of his 2002 liability (0.10 × $8,000 = $800). Had Gary's 2002 tax instead been $9,000, he would have owed an additional tax of $1,500 and a failure-to-pay penalty of $15 (0.005 × 2 months × $1,500). ◀

The 0.5% penalty increases to 1% a month, or fraction thereof, in certain circumstances. The rate is 1% for any month beginning after the earlier of

- Ten days after the date the IRS notifies the taxpayer that it plans to levy on his or her salary or property and

[51] Sec. 6651(a)(2).
[52] Sec. 6651(b)(2).
[53] Reg. Sec. 301.6651-1(c)(3) and (4).

- The day the IRS notifies and demands immediate payment from the taxpayer because it believes that collection is in jeopardy

EXAMPLE C15-13 ▶ Ginny files her 1999 individual income tax return on April 11, 2000. However, Ginny does not pay her tax liability. On October 5, 2002, the IRS notifies Ginny of its plans to levy on her property. The failure-to-pay penalty is 0.5% per month for the period April 16, 2000 through October 15, 2002. Beginning on October 16, 2002, the penalty rises to 1% per month, or fraction thereof. ◀

SELF-STUDY QUESTION

If a taxpayer does not have sufficient funds to pay his or her tax liability by the due date, should the taxpayer wait until the funds are available before filing the tax return?

ANSWER

No. He or she should file the return on a timely basis. This filing avoids the 5% per month failure-to-file penalty. The taxpayer still will owe the failure-to-pay penalty, but at least this penalty is only 0.5% per month.

Some taxpayers file on time to avoid the failure-to-file penalty even though they cannot pay the balance of the tax due. Barring a showing of reasonable cause, these taxpayers still will incur the failure-to-pay penalty. Because taxpayers who do not file a timely return are likely to owe additional taxes, they often owe both the failure-to-file and the failure-to-pay penalties.

The IRC contains a special rule for calculating the 5% per month failure-to-file penalty for periods in which the taxpayer owes both penalties. The 5% per month failure-to-file penalty is reduced by the failure-to-pay penalty.[54] Thus, the total penalties for a given month will not exceed 5%. For months when the taxpayer incurs both penalties, the failure-to-file penalty generally becomes a 4½% effective rate (0.05 − 0.005). Note, however, that no reduction occurs if the minimum penalty for failure to file applies.

EXAMPLE C15-14 ▶ Tien files her current year individual income tax return on August 5 of the following year, without having requested an extension. Her total tax is $20,000. Tien pays $15,000 in a timely manner and the $5,000 balance when she files the return. Although Tien committed no fraud, she can show no reasonable cause for the late filing and late payment. Tien's penalties are as follows:

Failure-to-pay penalty:		
$5,000 × 0.005 × 4 months		$ 100
Failure-to-file penalty:		
$5,000 × 0.05 × 4 months	$1,000	
Minus: Reduction for failure-to-pay penalty imposed for same period	(100)	900
Total penalties		$1,000 ◀

EXAMPLE C15-15 ▶ Assume the same facts as in Example C15-14 except that Tien instead pays the $5,000 balance on November 17 of the following year. The penalties are as follows:

Failure-to-pay penalty:		
$5,000 × 0.005 × 8 months (April 16 through November 17)		$ 200
Failure-to-file penalty:		
$5,000 × 0.05 × 4 months (April 16 through August 5)	$1,000	
Minus: Reduction for failure-to-pay penalty levied for April 16 through August 5 ($5,000 ×0.005 × 4 months)	(100)	900
Total penalties		$1,100 ◀

ESTIMATED TAXES

OBJECTIVE 6

Calculate the penalty for not paying estimated taxes

Individuals earning only salaries and wages generally pay their annual income tax liability through payroll withholding. The employer is responsible for remitting these withheld amounts, along with Social Security taxes, to a designated federal depository. By contrast, individuals earning other types of income, as well as C corporations, S corporations, and trusts, must estimate their annual income tax liability and prepay their taxes on a quarterly basis.[55] Estates must do the same with respect to income earned during any tax year

[54] Sec. 6651(c)(1).

[55] S corporations must pay quarterly estimated taxes on their net recognized built-in gains, passive investment income, and credit recapture amounts.

ending two years after the decedent's death.[56] Although partnerships do not pay estimated income taxes, their separate partners do if they are individuals or taxable entities. Chapters C3, C11, and C14 discuss the estimated income tax requirements for C corporations, S corporations, and fiduciaries, respectively.

PAYMENT REQUIREMENTS

Individuals should pay quarterly estimated income taxes if they have a significant amount of income from sources other than salaries and wages. The amount of each payment should be the same if this outside income accrues uniformly throughout the year. To avoid an estimated income tax penalty for the current year, individuals with AGI of $150,000 or less in the previous year should calculate each payment as follows:

Step 1: Determine the lesser of
- a. 90% of the taxpayer's regular tax, alternative minimum tax (if any), and self-employment tax for the current year, or
- b. 100% of the taxpayer's prior year regular tax, alternative minimum tax (if any), and self-employment tax if the taxpayer filed a return for the prior year and the year was not a short tax year.

Step 2: Calculate the total of
- a. Tax credits for the current year
- b. Taxes withheld on the current year's wages
- c. Overpayments of the prior year's tax liability the taxpayer requests be credited against the current year's tax

Step 3: Multiply the excess of the amount from Step 1 over the amount from Step 2 by 25%.[57]

Calendar year individual taxpayers should pay their quarterly installments on April 15, June 15, September 15, and January 15.

Individuals with AGI exceeding $150,000 ($75,000 for married filing separately) in the prior year can avoid the estimated tax penalty for the current year if they pay at least 90% of the current year's tax, or at least 112% of the prior year's tax if the prior year was 2001 (110% if the prior year was 2002 and thereafter).[58]

EXAMPLE C15-16 ▶ Mike's regular tax on his 2002 taxable income is $35,000. Mike also owes $2,000 of self-employment tax but no alternative minimum tax. Mike's 2001 total tax liability for both income and self-employment taxes was $24,000. His 2001 AGI did not exceed $150,000. Taxes withheld from Mike's wages in 2002 were $8,000. Mike did not overpay his 2001 tax or earn any 2002 credits. Mike should have made quarterly estimated tax payments of $4,000, as calculated below.

Lesser of:	90% of current year's tax (0.90 × $37,000 = $33,300) or	
	100% of prior year's $24,000 tax liability	$24,000
Minus:	Taxes withheld from 2002 wages	(8,000)
Minimum estimated tax payment to avoid penalty under general rule		$16,000
Quarterly estimated tax payments (0.25 × $16,000)		$ 4,000 ◀

ADDITIONAL COMMENT

Although it is simpler to use the amount of tax paid (or, if necessary, the applicable percentage of the amount of tax paid) in the preceding year as a safe harbor, the estimate of the current year's tax liability is preferable if the current year's tax liability is expected to be significantly less than the preceding year's tax liability.

The authority to make estimated tax payments based on the preceding year's income is especially significant for taxpayers with rising levels of income. To avoid an estimated income tax penalty, these taxpayers need to pay only an amount equal to the prior year's tax liability. Using this safe harbor eliminates the need for estimating the current year's tax liability with a high degree of accuracy.

EXAMPLE C15-17 ▶ Peter, a single calendar year taxpayer, incurs a regular tax liability of $76,000 in 2002. Peter owes no alternative minimum tax liability nor can he claim any tax credits. No overpayments of 2001

[56] For example, if the decedent's death were June 15, 2001, and the assets of the decedent's estate are not distributed by June 14, 2003, the estate must pay estimated taxes on income earned on estate assets for the tax year 2003.

[57] Secs. 6654(d), (f), and (g).

[58] Sec. 6654(d)(1)(C). Included in the definition of *individuals* are estates and trusts. Section 67(e) defines AGI for estates and trusts. (See Chapter C14.)

taxes are available to offset the 2002 tax liability. Taxes withheld evenly from Peter's wages throughout 2002 are $68,000. Peter's 2001 AGI exceeded $150,000, and his regular tax liability was $60,000. Because Peter's $17,000 of withholding for each quarter exceeds the $15,000 minimum required quarterly payments, as calculated below, he incurs no underpayment penalty.

Lesser of:	90% of current year's (0.90 × $76,000 = $68,400) or	
	112% of prior year's $60,000 tax liability	$67,200
Minus:	Taxes withheld from 2002 wages	(68,000)
Minimum estimated tax payment to avoid penalty under general rule		$ -0-

The $8,000 ($76,000 − $68,000) balance of the 2002 taxes is due on or before April 15, 2003. ◀

PENALTY FOR UNDERPAYING ESTIMATED TAXES

With the exceptions discussed in the next section, taxpayers who do not pay in the requisite amount of estimated tax by the appropriate date are subject to a penalty for underpayment of estimated taxes. The penalty is calculated at the same rate as the interest rate applicable under Sec. 6621 to late payments of tax.[59] The penalty for each quarter is calculated separately on Form 2210.

ADDITIONAL COMMENT

If a taxpayer is having taxes withheld and making estimated tax payments, a certain amount of tax planning is possible. Withholdings are deemed to have occurred equally throughout the year. Thus, disproportionately large amounts could be withheld in the last quarter to allow the taxpayer to avoid the underpayment penalty.

The amount subject to the penalty is the excess of the total tax that should have been paid during the quarter (e.g., $6,000 [$24,000 prior year's tax liability ÷ 4] in Example C15-16) over the sum of the estimated tax actually paid during that quarter on or before the installment date plus the withholding attributable to that quarter. Unless the taxpayer proves otherwise, the withholding is deemed to take place equally during each quarter. This rule creates a planning opportunity. Taxpayers who have not paid sufficient amounts of estimated tax in the first three quarters can avoid the imposition of the penalty by having large amounts of tax withheld during the last quarter.

The penalty is assessed for the time period beginning with the due date for the quarterly installment and ending on the earlier of the date the underpayment actually is paid or the due date for the return (April 15 assuming a calendar year taxpayer). The next example illustrates the computation of the underpayment penalty.

EXAMPLE C15-18 ▶ Assume the same facts as in Example C15-16 except Mike pays only $3,000 of estimated tax payments on April 15, June 17, and September 16 of 2002, and January 15 of 2003, and, for simplicity, that 10% is the Sec. 6621 underpayment rate for the entire time period. Mike files his 2002 return on March 30, 2003 and pays the $17,000 ($37,000 − $8,000 withholding − $12,000 estimated taxes) balance due at that time. Mike's underpayment penalty is determined as follows:

TYPICAL MISCONCEPTION

Many self-employed taxpayers assume they are not liable for estimated taxes if they have sufficient itemized deductions and exemptions to create zero taxable income or a taxable loss. However, a self-employment tax liability may exist even if the individual has no taxable income. Thus, taxpayers in this situation can end up with an overall tax liability and an accompanying estimated tax penalty.

	Quarter			
	First	*Second*	*Third*	*Fourth*
Amount that should have been paid ($24,000 ÷ 4)	$6,000	$6,000	$6,000	$6,000
Minus: Withholding	(2,000)	(2,000)	(2,000)	(2,000)
Estimated tax payment	(3,000)	(3,000)	(3,000)	(3,000)
Underpayment	$1,000	$1,000	$1,000	$1,000
Number of days of underpayment; ends (March 30, 2003 because earlier than April 15, 2003)	349	286	195	74
Penalty at 10% assumed annual rate for number of days of underpayment	$ 96	$ 78	$ 53	$ 20

The total penalty equals $247 ($96 + $78 + $53 + $20). The $247 penalty is not deductible. ◀

[59] Daily compounding is not applicable in calculating the penalty.

Interest is not assessed on underpayments of estimated tax.[60] However, if the entire tax is not paid by the due date for the return, interest and perhaps a failure-to-pay penalty will be levied on the unpaid amount.

EXCEPTIONS TO THE PENALTY

In certain circumstances, individuals who have not paid in the requisite amount of estimated tax nevertheless will be exempt from the underpayment penalty. The IRS imposes no penalty if the taxpayer's tax exceeds the taxes withheld from wages for the year in question by less than $1,000. Similarly, the taxpayer will not owe a penalty, regardless of the size of the underpayment, if the taxpayer owed no taxes for the prior year, the prior year consisted of 12 months, and the taxpayer was a U.S. citizen or resident alien for the entire preceding year. The Secretary of the Treasury can waive the penalty otherwise due in the case of "casualty, disaster, or other unusual circumstances" or for newly retired or disabled individuals.[61]

EXAMPLE C15-19 ▶ Paul's 2002 tax is $2,200, the same amount as his 2001 tax. His withholding tax is $1,730, and Paul does not pay any estimated taxes. Paul pays the $470 balance due on March 17, 2003. Under the general rules, Paul is subject to the underpayment penalty because he does not meet either the 90% of 2002 tax or 100% of 2001 tax minimums. However, because Paul's tax exceeds the withholding from his wages by less than $1,000, he owes no penalty for underpaying his estimated tax. ◀

Taxpayers are exempt from the underpayment penalty in still other circumstances. A discussion of all these other circumstances is beyond the scope of this text. Chapter I14 of *Prentice Hall's Federal Taxation: Individuals* and *Comprehensive* texts, however, discusses one such circumstance where the taxpayer annualizes his or her income and bases the estimated tax payment on the annualized amount.[62]

OTHER MORE SEVERE PENALTIES

OBJECTIVE 7

Describe more severe penalties, including the fraud penalty

In addition to the penalties for failure to file, failure to pay, and underpayment of estimated tax, taxpayers may be subject to other more severe penalties. These include the so-called accuracy-related penalty (applicable in several contexts) and the fraud penalty, each of which is discussed below.[63] A 20% accuracy-related penalty applies to any underpayment attributable to negligence, any substantial understatement of income tax, and several errors beyond the scope of this text. An accuracy-related penalty is not levied, however, if the government imposed the fraud penalty or if the taxpayer filed no return.

ADDITIONAL COMMENT

To shift the burden of proof to the IRS, the taxpayer must introduce credible evidence regarding a factual issue relating to his or her tax liability.

NEGLIGENCE

The accuracy-related **negligence penalty** applies whenever the IRS determines that a taxpayer has underpaid any part of his or her taxes as a result of negligence or disregard of the rules or regulations (but without intending to defraud).[64] The penalty is 20% of the underpayment attributable to negligence. Interest accrues on the negligence penalty at the rates applicable to underpayments.[65]

EXAMPLE C15-20 ▶ The IRS audits Ted's individual return and assesses a $7,500 deficiency, of which $2,500 is attributable to negligence. Ted agrees to the assessment and pays the additional tax of $7,500 the following year. Ted incurs a negligence penalty of $500 (0.20 × $2,500). ◀

---

[60] Sec. 6601(h).

[61] Sec. 6654(e).

[62] Section 6654(d)(2) allows for computation of the underpayments, if any, by annualizing income. Relief from the underpayment penalty may result from applying the annualization rules. Corporations, but not individuals, are permitted a seasonal adjustment to the annualization rules.

[63] Secs. 6662(a) and (b).

[64] Secs. 6662(b) and (c).

[65] Sec. 6601(e)(2)(B).

The IRC defines ***negligence*** as "any failure to make a reasonable attempt to comply with the provisions" of the IRC. It defines disregard of the rules or regulations as "any careless, reckless, or intentional disregard."[66] According to Treasury Regulations, a strong indication of negligence exists if the taxpayer does not include in gross income an amount of income shown on an information return or does not reasonably attempt to ascertain the correctness of a deduction, credit, or exclusion that a reasonable and prudent person would think was "too good to be true."[67]

A taxpayer is careless if he or she does not diligently try to determine the correctness of his or her position. A taxpayer is reckless if he or she exerts little or no effort to determine whether a rule or regulation exists. A taxpayer's disregard is intentional if he or she knows about the rule or regulation he or she disregards.[68]

The penalty will not be imposed for any portion of an underpayment for which the taxpayer had reasonable cause for his or her position and acted in good faith.[69] Failure to follow a regulation must be disclosed on Form 8275-R (Regulation Disclosure Statement).

EXAMPLE C15-21 ▶ The IRS audits Mario's current year individual return, and Mario agrees to a $4,000 deficiency. Mario had reasonable cause for adopting his tax return positions (which were not contrary to the applicable rules or regulations) and acted in good faith. Mario will not be liable for a penalty for negligence. ◀

ADDITIONAL COMMENT

Theoretically, penalties are designed to deter taxpayers from willfully disregarding federal tax laws. Some taxpayers have been concerned that the IRS has used the multitude of tax penalties primarily as a source of revenue. The IRS achieved this result by "stacking" penalties (i.e., applying several penalties to a single underpayment). Recent legislation has alleviated some of this concern.

SELF-STUDY QUESTION

How is an understatement different from an underpayment?

ANSWER

An underpayment can be larger than an understatement. Understatements do not include underpayments for which there was either substantial authority or adequate disclosure.

SUBSTANTIAL UNDERSTATEMENT

Taxpayers who substantially understate their income tax are liable for an accuracy-related penalty for their substantial understatements. The IRC defines a substantial understatement as an understatement of tax exceeding the greater of 10% of the tax required to be shown on the return or $5,000 (or $10,000 in the case of a C corporation).[70] Thus, this penalty does not apply unless the taxpayer understates the tax—at a minimum—by more than $5,000 (or $10,000 if a C corporation). The penalty equals 20% of the underpayment of tax attributable to the substantial understatement. It does not apply to understatements for which the taxpayer shows reasonable cause and good faith for his or her position.

UNDERSTATEMENT VERSUS UNDERPAYMENT. The amount of tax attributable to the substantial understatement may be less than the amount of the underpayment. In general, the amount of the understatement is calculated as the amount by which the tax required to be shown (i.e., the correct tax) exceeds the tax shown on the return. Because the amount of tax attributable to certain items is not treated as an understatement, the additional tax attributed to such items is not subject to the penalty. An underpayment for an item other than a tax shelter is *not* an understatement if either of the following is true:

- ▶ The taxpayer has substantial authority for the tax treatment of the item.
- ▶ The taxpayer discloses, either on the return or in a statement attached to the return, the relevant facts affecting the tax treatment of the item, and the taxpayer has a reasonable basis for such treatment.

Although neither the IRC nor Treasury Regulations define "reasonable basis," Reg. Sec. 1.6662-3(b)(3) states that a "reasonable basis" standard is significantly higher than the "not frivolous" standard that usually applies to tax preparers. The latter standard involves a tax position that is not patently improper. The taxpayer meets the adequate disclosure requirement if he or she properly completes Form 8275 and attaches it to the return, or discloses information on the return in a manner prescribed by an annual revenue procedure.[71]

---

66 Sec. 6662(c).
67 Reg. Sec. 1.6662-3(b)(1).
68 Reg. Sec. 1.6662-3(b)(2).
69 Sec. 6664(c).
70 Sec. 6662(d)(1).
71 Reg. Secs. 1.6662-4(f)(1) and (2). See Rev. Proc. 96-58, 1996-2 C.B. 390, where the Treasury Department identifies circumstances where disclosure of a position on a taxpayer's return is adequate to reduce the understatement penalty of Sec. 6662(d) and tax preparer penalties of Sec. 6694(a).

EXAMPLE C15-22 ▶ The IRS examines Val's current year individual income tax return, and Val agrees to a $9,000 deficiency, which increases her taxes from $25,000 to $34,000. Val neither made adequate disclosure concerning the items for which the IRS assessed the deficiency nor had substantial authority for her tax treatment. Thus, Val's understatement also is $9,000. This understatement is substantial because it exceeds both 10% of her correct tax liability ($3,400 = 0.10 × $34,000) and the $5,000 minimum. Val incurs a substantial understatement penalty of $1,800 (0.20 × $9,000). ◀

EXAMPLE C15-23 ▶ Assume the same facts as in Example C15-22 except Val has substantial authority for the tax treatment of an item that results in a $1,000 additional assessment. In addition, she makes adequate disclosure for a second item with respect to which the IRS assesses additional taxes of $1,500. Although Val's underpayment is $9,000, her understatement is $6,500 [$9,000 – ($1,000 + $1,500)]. This understatement is substantial because it is more than the greater of 10% of Val's tax or $5,000. However, because Val provided substantial authority and made adequate disclosure, the penalty is only $1,300 (0.20 × $6,500). ◀

ADDITIONAL COMMENT

Even though the substantial understatement penalty is a taxpayer penalty, tax preparers have a duty to make their clients aware of the potential risk of substantial understatement. In some situations, failure to do so has resulted in the client's attempting to collect the amount of the substantial understatement penalty from the preparer.

Like the negligence penalty, the substantial understatement penalty bears interest at the rate applicable to underpayments. The interest accrues from the due date of the return.

CONCEPT OF SUBSTANTIAL AUTHORITY. Treasury Regulations indicate that substantial authority

- Exists only if the weight of authorities supporting the tax treatment of an item is substantial relative to the weight of those supporting the contrary treatment, and
- Is based on an objective standard involving an analysis of law and its application to the relevant facts. This standard is more stringent than the "reasonable basis" standard that the taxpayer must meet to avoid the negligence penalty but less stringent than the "more likely than not" standard that applies to tax shelters.[72] (See discussion below.)

According to these regulations, the following are considered to be authority: statutory provisions; proposed, temporary, and final regulations; court cases; revenue rulings; revenue procedures; tax treaties; Congressional intent as reflected in committee reports and joint statements of a bill's managers; private letter rulings; technical advice memoranda; information or press releases; notices; and any other similar documents published by the IRS in the *Internal Revenue Bulletin* and the *General Explanation of the Joint Committee on Taxation* (also known as the Blue Book). Conclusions reached in treatises, periodicals, and the opinions of tax professionals are not considered to be authority. The applicability of court cases in the taxpayer's district is not taken into account in determining the existence of substantial authority. On the other hand, the applicability of court cases in the taxpayer's circuit *is* taken into account in determining the existence of substantial authority.

EXAMPLE C15-24 ▶ Authorities addressing a particular issue are as follows:

- For the government: Tax Court and Fourth Circuit Court of Appeals
- For taxpayers: U.S. District Court for Rhode Island and First Circuit Court of Appeals

The taxpayer (Tina) is a resident of Rhode Island, which is in the First Circuit. Tina would have substantial authority for a pro-taxpayer position because such a position is supported by the circuit court of appeals for Tina's geographical jurisdiction. ◀

Taxpayers should be aware that, while sparing them a substantial understatement penalty, disclosure (even with a reasonable basis for the tax treatment of the item) might raise a "red flag" that could prompt an IRS audit.

TAX SHELTERS. A different set of rules applies to tax shelter items. A *tax shelter* is any arrangement for which a significant purpose is the avoidance or evasion of federal income tax. [73] Individual understatements of these items may be reduced only if the taxpayer has,

[72] Reg. Sec. 1.6662-4(d).

[73] Sec. 6662(d)(2)(C)(iii).

in addition to substantial authority, a reasonable belief that the tax treatment of the item more likely than not was proper. *More likely than not* means a greater than 50% probability.[74] Corporate understatements of these items may not be reduced in any circumstance.

EXAMPLE C15-25 ▶ Assume the same facts as in Example C15-23 except Val's entire underpayment is due to tax shelter items, and Val does not reasonably believe the tax treatment of these items was more likely than not proper. Val's understatement is the full $9,000 because disclosure provides no relief for tax shelter items and because Val does not reasonably believe the tax treatment was more likely than not correct. Val's penalty is $1,800 (0.20 × $9,000). ◀

CIVIL FRAUD

Fraud differs from simple, honest mistakes and negligence in that it involves a deliberate attempt to deceive. Because the IRS cannot establish intent per se, it attempts to prove intent indirectly by emphasizing the taxpayer's actions. One leading authority refers to fraud cases in this manner:

> Fraud cases ordinarily involve systematic or substantial omissions from gross income or fictitious deductions or dependency claims, accompanied by the falsification or destruction of records or false or inconsistent statements to the investigating agents, especially where records are not kept by the taxpayer. The taxpayer's education and business experience are relevant.[75]

The fraud penalty equals 75% of the portion of the underpayment attributable to fraud. If the IRS establishes that any portion of an underpayment is due to fraud, the entire underpayment is treated as having resulted from fraud unless the taxpayer establishes by a preponderance of the evidence the portion that is not attributable to fraud. Like the negligence penalty, the fraud penalty bears interest.[76]

EXAMPLE C15-26 ▶ The IRS audits Ned's individual return and claims that Ned's underpayment is due to fraud. Ned agrees to the $40,000 deficiency but establishes that only $32,000 of the deficiency is attributable to fraud. The remainder results from mistakes that the IRS did not believe were due to fraud. Ned's civil fraud penalty is $24,000 (0.75 × $32,000). ◀

The fraud penalty can be imposed with respect to income, gift, and estate tax returns. If it is imposed, the negligence and substantial understatement penalties are not assessed on the portion of the underpayment attributable to fraud.[77]

With respect to a joint return, no fraud penalty can be imposed on a spouse who has not committed a fraudulent act.[78] In other words, one spouse is not liable for the other spouse's fraudulent acts.

STOP & THINK *Question:* A few years ago, Joyce filed her individual income tax return in which she reported $250,000 of taxable income. She paid all the tax shown on the return on the day she filed. She, however, fraudulently omitted an additional $100,000 of gross income and, of course, does not have substantial authority for this fraudulent omission. Moreover, she did not make a disclosure of the omitted income. If the IRS proves that Joyce committed fraud, will she be liable for both the civil fraud penalty and the substantial understatement penalty? What are the rates for the two penalties?

Solution: Because the penalties cannot be stacked, Joyce will not owe both penalties. If the IRS successfully proves fraud, she will owe a penalty of 75% of the tax due on the omitted income. She will not owe the 20% penalty for substantial understatements.

---

[74] Reg. Sec. 1.6661-5(d)(1).

[75] Boris I. Bittker and Lawrence Lokken, *Federal Taxation of Income, Estates, and Gifts* (Boston, MA: Warren, Gorham & Lamont, 1992), vol. 4, p. 114–54.

[76] Sec. 6601(e)(2)(B).

[77] Sec. 6662(b).

[78] Sec. 6663(c).

ADDITIONAL COMMENT

In fiscal 2000, the IRS initiated 3,372 criminal investigations (down from 3,952 in 1999), and it referred 2,459 for prosecution. During fiscal 2000, the IRS won 2,249 convictions, and prison sentences were handed down in 2,475 of those cases.

CRIMINAL FRAUD

Civil and criminal fraud are similar in that both involve a taxpayer's intent to misrepresent facts. They differ primarily in terms of the weight of the evidence required for conviction. Civil fraud requires proof by a preponderance of the evidence. Criminal fraud requires proof beyond a reasonable doubt. Because the latter standard is more stringent than the former, the government charges relatively few taxpayers with criminal fraud. To do so, the IRS and Justice Department must agree on the charges.

CRIMINAL FRAUD INVESTIGATIONS. The Criminal Investigation Division of the IRS conducts criminal fraud investigations. The agents responsible for the investigation are called **special agents**. Under IRS policy, at the first meeting of the special agent and the taxpayer, the special agent must

- Identify himself or herself as such
- Advise the taxpayer that he or she is the subject of a criminal investigation
- Advise the taxpayer of his or her rights to remain silent and consult legal counsel

PENALTY PROVISIONS. Sections 7201-7216 provide for criminal penalties. Three of these penalties are discussed in the following paragraphs.

Section 7201. Section 7201 provides for the assessment of a penalty against any person who "willfully attempts . . . to evade or defeat any tax." The maximum penalty is $100,000 ($500,000 for corporations), a prison sentence of up to five years, or both.

ADDITIONAL COMMENT

Any time a tax professional learns a client has engaged in activities that may constitute criminal fraud, he or she immediately should refer the client to qualified legal counsel. Counsel should then hire the accountant as a consultant. Taxpayer's communications will be confidential under the attorney–client relationship. This relationship encompasses agents of the attorney.

Section 7203. Section 7203 provides for the assessment of a penalty on any person who willfully fails to pay any tax or file a return. The maximum penalty is $25,000 ($100,000 for corporations), a prison sentence of no more than one year, or both. If the government charges the taxpayer with willfully failing to prepare a return, it need not prove that the taxpayer owes additional tax.

Section 7206. Persons other than the taxpayer can be charged under Sec. 7206. This section applies to any person who

> [W]illfully aids or assists in, or procures, counsels, or advises the preparation or presentation under, or in connection with any matter arising under the internal revenue laws, of a return, affidavit, claim, or other document, which is fraudulent or is false as to any material matter, whether or not such falsity or fraud is with the knowledge or consent of the person authorized or required to present such return, affidavit, claim, or document.[79]

What constitutes a material matter has been litigated extensively.[80] The maximum penalty under Sec. 7206 is $100,000 ($500,000 for corporations), a prison sentence of up to three years, or both. The government need not prove that the taxpayer owes additional tax.

STATUTE OF LIMITATIONS

OBJECTIVE 8

Understand the statute of limitations

The statute of limitations has the same practical implications in a tax context as in other contexts. It specifies a timeframe during which the government must assess the tax or initiate a court proceeding to collect the tax. The statute of limitations also defines the period during which a taxpayer may file a claim for a refund.

---

[79] Sec. 7206(2).

[80] See, for example, *U.S. v. Joseph DiVarco*, 32 AFTR 2d 73-5605, 73-2 USTC ¶9607 (7th Cir., 1973), wherein the court held that the source of the taxpayer's income as stated on the tax return is a material matter.

GENERAL THREE-YEAR RULE

Under the general rule of Sec. 6501(a), the statute of limitations is three years after the return is filed, regardless of whether the return is timely filed. A return filed before its due date is treated as if it were filed on the due date.[81]

EXAMPLE C15-27 ▶ Ali files his 2002 individual return on March 3, 2003. The government may not assess additional taxes for 2002 after April 17, 2006 (April 15 falls on a Saturday). If instead, Ali files his 2002 individual return on October 4, 2003, the statute of limitations for his return expires on October 4, 2006. ◀

SIX-YEAR RULE FOR SUBSTANTIAL OMISSIONS

INCOME TAX RETURNS. In the case of substantial omissions, the statute of limitations is six years after the later of the date the return is filed or the return's due date. For income tax purposes, the six-year statute is applicable if the taxpayer omits from gross income an amount exceeding 25% of the gross income shown on the return. If an item is disclosed either on the return or in a statement attached to the return, it is not treated as an omission if the disclosure is "adequate to apprise the [Treasury] Secretary of the nature and amount of such item."[82] In the case of taxpayers conducting a trade or business, gross income for purposes of the 25% omission test means the taxpayer's sales revenues (not the taxpayer's gross profit).[83] Taxpayers benefit from this special definition because it renders the 25% test applicable to a gross amount (implying a higher threshold).

EXAMPLE C15-28 ▶ Peg files her 2002 return on March 31, 2003. Her return shows $6,000 of interest from corporate bonds and $30,000 of salary. Peg attaches a statement to her return that indicates why she thinks a $2,000 receipt is nontaxable. However, because of an oversight, she does not report an $8,000 capital gain. Peg is deemed to have omitted only $8,000 rather than $10,000 (the $8,000 capital gain plus the $2,000 receipt) because she disclosed the $2,000 receipt. The $8,000 amount is 22.22% ($8,000/$36,000) of her reported gross income. Because the omission does not exceed 25% of Peg's reported gross income, the statute of limitations expires on April 17, 2006. ◀

EXAMPLE C15-29 ▶ Assume the same facts as in Example C15-28 except Peg does not make adequate disclosure of the $2,000 receipt. Thus, she is considered to have omitted $10,000 from gross income. The $10,000 amount is 27.77% ($10,000/$36,000) of her reported gross income. Therefore, the statute of limitations expires on April 15, 2009. ◀

EXAMPLE C15-30 ▶ Rita conducts a business as a sole proprietorship. Rita's 2002 return, filed on March 17, 2003, indicates sales of $100,000 and cost of goods sold of $70,000. Rita inadvertently fails to report $9,000 of interest earned on a loan to a relative. For purposes of the 25% omission test, her

WHAT WOULD YOU DO IN THIS SITUATION?

After working eight years for a large CPA firm, you begin your practice as a sole practitioner CPA. Your practice is not as profitable as you had expected, and you consider how you might attract more clients. One idea is to obtain for your clients bigger refunds than they anticipate. Your reputation for knowing tax-saving tips might grow, and your profits might increase. You think further and decide that maybe you could claim itemized deductions for charitable contributions that actually were not made and for business expenses that actually were not paid. You are aware of Sec. 7206, regarding false and fraudulent statements but think that you can avoid the "as to any material matter" stipulation by keeping the deduction overstatements relatively insubstantial. Would you try this scheme for increasing your profits? If so, do you think you would escape the scope of Sec. 7206? What ramifications might these deeds have on your standing as a CPA under the AICPA's *Statements on Standards for Tax Services* and *Code of Professional Conduct*?

---

[81] Sec. 6501(b)(1).

[82] Sec. 6501(e).

[83] Regulation Sec. 1.61-3(a) defines *gross income* as sales less cost of goods sold.

gross income is $100,000, not $30,000. The omitted interest is 9% ($9,000/$100,000) of her reported gross income. Because the $9,000 does not exceed 25% of the gross amount, the statute of limitations expires on April 17, 2006. ◀

KEY POINT

A 25% omission of gross income extends the basic statute to six years, whereas a 25% overstatement of deductions is still subject to the basic three-year statute. However, if fraud can be shown, there is no statute of limitations.

Note that the six-year rule applies only to omitted income. Thus, claiming excessive deductions will not result in a six-year statute of limitations. Moreover, if the omission involves fraud, the statute of limitations is unlimited.

GIFT AND ESTATE TAX RETURNS. A similar six-year statute of limitations applies for gift and estate tax purposes. If the taxpayer omits items that exceed 25% of the gross estate value or the total amount of gifts reported on the return, the statute of limitations expires six years after the later of the date the return is filed or the due date. Items disclosed on the return or in a statement attached to the return "in a manner adequate to apprise the [Treasury] Secretary of the nature and amount of such item" do not constitute omissions.[84] Understatements of the value of assets disclosed on the return also are not considered omissions.

EXAMPLE C15-31 ▶ John files a gift tax return for 2002 on April 1, 2003. The return reports a cash gift of $600,000. In 2002, John sells land to his son for $700,000. At the time of the sale, John thinks the land's FMV is $700,000 and does not disclose any additional amount on the gift tax return. Upon audit, the IRS determines that the FMV of the land on the sale date is $900,000. Thus, John effectively gave an additional $200,000 to his son. The $200,000 amount is 33⅓% ($200,000/$600,000) of all gifts reported. The statute of limitations expires on April 15, 2009. ◀

WHEN NO RETURN IS FILED

No statute of limitations exists if the taxpayer does not file a return.[85] Thus, the government may assess the tax or initiate a court proceeding for collection at any time.

EXAMPLE C15-32 ▶ Jill does not file a tax return for 2002. The statute of limitations never expires. Consequently, if the government discovers 20 years later that Jill did not file a return, it may assess the 2002 tax, along with penalties and interest. ◀

OTHER EXCEPTIONS TO THREE-YEAR RULE

EXTENSION OF THE THREE-YEAR PERIOD. The IRC provides other exceptions to the three-year statute of limitations rule, some of which are discussed here. The taxpayer and the IRS can mutually agree in writing to extend the statute of limitations for taxes other than the estate tax.[86] In such situations, the statute of limitations is extended until the date agreed on by the two parties. Such agreements usually are concluded when the IRS is auditing a return near the end of the statutory period. Taxpayers often agree to extending the statute of limitations because they think that, if they do not do so, the IRS will assess a higher deficiency than otherwise would have been the case. Before concluding such an agreement, the IRS must notify the taxpayer that he or she may refuse to extend the statute of limitations or may limit the extension to particular issues.

SELF-STUDY QUESTION

Should a taxpayer ever agree to extend the statute of limitations?

ANSWER

Yes. When an audit is in progress, if a taxpayer refuses to extend the limitations period, the agent may assert a deficiency for each item in question. Had the taxpayer granted an extension, perhaps many of the items in question never would have been included in the examining agent's report.

CARRYBACKS. For a year to which a net operating loss (NOL) is carried back, the statute of limitations is open until the statute expires with respect to the year in which the NOL arises.[87]

WHEN FRAUD IS PROVEN.

Deficiency and Civil Fraud Penalty. If the government successfully proves that a taxpayer filed a false or fraudulent return "with the intent to evade tax" or engaged in a "willful attempt . . . to defeat or evade tax," there is no statute of limitations.[88] In other words, the government may assess the tax or begin a court proceeding to collect the tax

---

[84] Sec. 6501(e)(2).
[85] Sec. 6501(c)(3).
[86] Sec. 6501(c)(4).
[87] Sec. 6501(h).
[88] Secs. 6501(c)(1) and (2).

and the interest thereon at any time. In addition, if the government proves fraud, it may impose a civil penalty. If it fails to prove fraud and the normal three-year statute and special six-year statute for 25% omissions have expired, it may not assess additional taxes. The fraud issue is significant in tax litigation because the burden of proving fraud is unconditionally on the government.

EXAMPLE C15-33 ▶ The IRS audits Trey's 2006 return late in 2009. It also looks at some prior years' returns and contends that Trey has willfully attempted to evade tax on his timely filed 2002 return. Trey litigates in the Tax Court, and the Court decides the fraud issue in his favor. Because the IRS did not prove fraud, it may not assess additional taxes for 2002. Had the IRS proven fraud, the statute of limitations for the 2002 return would have remained open, and the IRS could have assessed the additional taxes. ◀

ADDITIONAL COMMENT

Even though a taxpayer is home free from criminal prosecution after six years of an act or omission, he or she still is subject to civil fraud penalties if fraud is proven at any time after the six-year period.

Criminal Provisions. If taxpayers are not indicted for criminal violations of the tax law within a certain period of time, they are home free. For most criminal offenses, the maximum period is six years after the commission of the offense.[89] Taxpayers cannot be prosecuted, tried, or punished unless an indictment is made within that timeframe. The six-year period refers to the date the taxpayer commits the offense, not the date he or she files the return. Taxpayers who file fraudulent returns might commit offenses related to the returns at a subsequent date. An example of an offense that some taxpayers commit after filing a return is depositing money into a new bank account under a fictitious name.

EXAMPLE C15-34 ▶ In March 2003, Tony files a fraudulent 2002 return through which he attempts to evade tax. Before filing, Tony keeps a double set of books. In 2002, Tony deposits some funds into a bank account under a fictitious name. In 2004, he moves to another state, and on May 3, 2004, he transfers these funds to a new bank account under a different fictitious name. Depositing money into the new account is an offense relating to the fraudulent return. Provided Tony commits no additional offenses, the statute of limitations for indictment expires on May 3, 2010. ◀

REFUND CLAIMS

SELF-STUDY QUESTION

Suppose a taxpayer incorrectly includes a receipt in a tax return and then, after the statute of limitations has run for that year, correctly includes the receipt in a subsequent return. Is it equitable for the taxpayer to have to pay tax on the same income twice?

ANSWER

No. A complicated set of provisions (Secs. 1311-1314) allows, in specific situations, otherwise closed years to be opened if a position taken in an open year is inconsistent with a position taken in a closed year.

Taxpayers generally are not entitled to a refund for overpayments of tax unless they file a claim for refund by the later of three years from the date they file the return or two years from the date they pay the tax.[90] The limitations period for individuals is suspended when the individual is financially disabled. A return filed before the due date is deemed to have been filed on the due date. The due date is determined without regard to extensions. In most cases, taxpayers pay the tax concurrently with filing the return. Typically, the taxpayer files a claim for a refund in the following circumstance: the IRS has audited the taxpayer's return, has proposed a deficiency, and has assessed additional taxes. The taxpayer may have paid the additional taxes two years after the due date for the return. In such a situation, the taxpayer may file a claim for refund at any time within two years after making the additional payment (or a total of four years after the filing date). If the taxpayer does not file a claim until more than three years after the date of filing the return, the maximum refund is the amount of tax paid during the two-year period immediately preceding the date on which he or she files the claim.[91]

EXAMPLE C15-35 ▶ Pat files his 2002 return on March 11, 2003. The return shows taxes of $5,000, and Pat pays this entire amount when he files his return. He pays no additional tax. Pat must file a claim for refund by April 17, 2006. The maximum refundable amount is $5,000. ◀

EXAMPLE C15-36 ▶ Assume the same facts as in Example C15-35 except the IRS audits Pat's 2002 return, and Pat pays a $1,200 deficiency on October 3, 2005. Pat may file a claim for refund as late as October 3, 2007. If Pat files the claim later than April 17, 2006, the refund may not exceed $1,200 (the amount of tax paid during the two-year period immediately preceding the filing of the claim). ◀

---

[89] Sec. 6531.

[90] Sec. 6511(a).

[91] Under Sec. 6512, special rules apply if the IRS has mailed a notice of deficiency and if the taxpayer files a petition with the Tax Court.

LIABILITY FOR TAX

Taxpayers are primarily liable for paying their tax. Spouses and transferees may be secondarily liable, as discussed below.

OBJECTIVE 9

Explain from whom the government may collect unpaid taxes

JOINT RETURNS

Ordinarily, if spouses file a joint return, their liability to pay the tax is joint and several.[92] **Joint and several liability** means that each spouse is potentially liable for the full amount due. If one spouse fails to pay any or all of the tax, the other spouse is responsible for paying the deficiency. Joint and several liability has facilitated IRS collection efforts where one spouse absconds from the country, and the other spouse can be readily located.

VALIDITY OF JOINT RETURN. To be valid, a joint return generally must include the signatures of both spouses. However, if one spouse cannot sign because of a disability, the return still is valid if that spouse orally consents to the other spouse's signing for him or her.[93] A joint return is invalid if one spouse forces the other to file jointly.

INNOCENT SPOUSE PROVISION. Congress has provided for **innocent spouse relief** where holding one spouse liable for the taxes due from both spouses would be inequitable. Relief is available if all five of the following conditions are met:

- The spouses file a joint return.
- The return contains an understatement of tax attributable to the erroneous item(s) of an individual filing it.
- The other individual establishes that he or she neither knew nor had reason to know of any or all of the understatement.
- Based on all the facts and circumstances, holding the other individual liable for the deficiency would be inequitable.
- The other individual elects innocent spouse relief no later than two years after the IRS begins its collection efforts.

The degree of relief depends on the extent of the electing spouse's knowledge. If the spouse neither knew nor had reason to know of *an understatement,* full relief will be granted. Full relief encompasses liability for taxes, interest, and penalties attributable to the full amount of the understatement. On the other hand, if the spouse either knew or had reason to know of an understatement, but not *the extent of the understatement,* only partial relief will be granted. Partial relief encompasses liability for taxes, interest, and penalties attributable to that portion of the understatement of which the spouse was unaware.

EXAMPLE C15-37 ▶ Jim and Joy jointly filed a tax return for 2001. Joy fraudulently reported on Schedule C two expenses: one amounting to $4,000 and the other amounting to $3,000. The IRS audits the return, assesses a $2,170 deficiency, and begins its collection efforts on June 1, 2003. If (1) Jim elects innocent spouse relief no later than June 1, 2005, (2) Jim establishes that he neither knew nor had reason to know of the understatement, and (3) if holding Jim liable for the deficiency would be inequitable under the circumstances, Jim will be relieved of liability for the full $2,170 ◀

EXAMPLE C15-38 ▶ Same facts as in Example C15-37 except Jim had reason to know the $3,000 expense was fraudulent. If (1) Jim elects innocent spouse relief no later than June 1, 2005, (2) Jim establishes that he neither knew nor had reason to know the *extent* of the understatement (i.e., $7,000 as opposed to $3,000), and (3) if holding Jim liable for the full amount of the deficiency would be inequitable under the circumstances, Jim will be relieved of liability for that portion of the deficiency attributable to the $4,000 expense. ◀

[92] Sec. 6015.

[93] Reg. Sec. 1.6012-1(a)(5).

Proportional liability is liability for only that portion of a deficiency attributable to the taxpayer's separate taxable items. A joint filer incurs proportional liability if all the following conditions are met:

- The joint filer elects proportional liability within two years after the IRS begins its collection efforts.
- The electing filer is either divorced or separated at the time of the election.
- The electing filer did not reside in the same household as the other filer at any time during the 12-month period preceding the election.
- The electing filer does not have actual knowledge of any item giving rise to the deficiency.

The electing filer bears the burden of proving the amount of his or her proportional liability. The fraudulent transfer of property between joint filers immediately before the election will invalidate it.

EXAMPLE C15-39 ▶ Sam and Sue jointly filed a tax return for 2001. Sam intentionally omitted to report $8,000 in gambling winnings. Sue fraudulently deducted $1,600 in business expenses. The IRS audits the return, assesses a $3,600 deficiency, and begins its collection efforts on August 15, 2003. Sam and Sue are subsequently divorced. If Sue (1) elects innocent spouse relief no later than August 15, 2005, (2) did not reside in the same household as Sam at any time during the 12-month period preceding the election, and (3) did not actually know of Sam's omission, she will be liable for only that portion of the deficiency attributable to her fraudulent deduction. ◀

The Effect of Community Property Laws. Community property laws are ignored in determining to whom income (other than income from property) is attributable. For example, if one spouse living in a community property state wins money by gambling, the gambling income is not treated as community property for purposes of the innocent spouse provisions. If the gambling winnings are omitted from a joint return, they are deemed to be solely the income of the spouse who gambled.

TRANSFEREE LIABILITY

TYPICAL MISCONCEPTION

A taxpayer cannot escape paying taxes by transferring assets to a transferee (donee, heir, legatee, etc.) or a fiduciary (estate of the taxpayer, decedent, donor, etc.).

Section 6901 authorizes the IRS to collect taxes from persons other than the taxpayer. The two categories of persons from whom the IRS may collect taxes are transferees and fiduciaries. Transferees include donees, heirs, legatees, devisees, shareholders of dissolved corporations, parties to a reorganization, and other distributees.[94] Fiduciaries include executors and administrators of estates. In general, the statute of limitations for transferees expires one year after the statute of limitations for transferors. The transferors may be income earners in the case of income taxes, executors in the case of estate taxes, and donors in the case of gift taxes.

EXAMPLE C15-40 ▶ Lake Corporation is liquidated in the current year, and it distributes all its assets to its sole shareholder, Leo. If the IRS audits Lake's return and assesses a deficiency, Leo (the distributee) is responsible for paying the deficiency. ◀

TAX PRACTICE ISSUES

OBJECTIVE 10

Understand the government-imposed standards for tax practitioners

A number of statutes and guidelines address what constitutes proper behavior of CPAs and others engaged in tax practice.[95]

STATUTORY PROVISIONS CONCERNING TAX RETURN PREPARERS

Sections 6694-6696 impose penalties on tax return preparers for misconduct. Section 7701(a)(36) defines an income tax return preparer as a "person who prepares for com-

[94] Reg. Sec. 301.6901-1(b).

[95] Chapter C1 discusses the AICPA's *Statements on Standards for Tax Services,* which provides guidelines for CPAs engaged in tax practice. See Appendix E for a reproduction of the Statements.

KEY POINT

As evidenced by the formidable list of possible penalties, an individual considering becoming a tax return preparer needs to be aware of certain procedures set forth in the IRC.

pensation, or who employs one or more persons to prepare for compensation, any return of tax imposed by subtitle A [income tax] or any claim for refund of tax imposed by subtitle A." Preparation of a substantial portion of a return or refund claim is treated as preparation of the full return or claim. These statutory provisions do not affect preparers of estate and gift tax returns and claims for refund of such taxes.

Section 6695 imposes penalties for

- Failure to furnish the taxpayer with a copy of the return or claim ($50 per failure)
- Failure to sign a return or claim ($50 per failure)
- Failure to furnish one's identification number ($50 per failure)
- Failure to keep a copy of a return or claim or, in lieu thereof, to maintain a list of taxpayers for whom returns or claims were prepared ($50 per failure, up to a maximum of $25,000 for a return period)
- Failure to file a return disclosing the names, identification numbers, and places of work of each income tax return preparer employed ($50 per return plus $50 for each failure to set forth an item in the return)
- Endorsement or other negotiation of an income tax refund check made payable to anyone other than the preparer ($500 per check)

The first five penalties are not assessable if the preparer shows that the failure is due to reasonable cause and not willful neglect.[96]

Under Sec. 6694, a preparer will owe a $250 penalty for understating a tax liability if any portion of the understatement is due to a position that does not have a realistic possibility of being sustained on its merits. The preparer will be liable for the penalty if he or she knew, or reasonably should have known of, the position and the position either was frivolous or was not disclosed. If any portion of the understatement results from the preparer's willful attempt to understate taxes or from reckless or intentional disregard of rules or regulations, the penalty will be $1,000.

REAL WORLD EXAMPLE

In addition to these penalties, the IRS may suspend or bar a tax practitioner from practicing before the IRS. Each week the IRS publishes a list of suspended practitioners.

Regulation Sec. 1.6694-2(b)(2) states that the relevant authorities for the realistic-possibility-of-being-sustained test are the same as those that apply in the substantial authority context. The IRS "will treat a position as having a realistic possibility of being sustained on 'its merits' if a reasonable and well-informed analysis by a person knowledgeable in the tax law would lead such person to conclude that the position has approximately a one in three, or greater, likelihood of being sustained on its merits."[97]

Regulation Sec. 1.6694-3 states that preparers are considered to have willfully understated taxes if they have attempted to wrongfully reduce taxes by disregarding pertinent information. A preparer generally is deemed to have recklessly or intentionally disregarded a rule or regulation if he or she adopts a position contrary to a rule or regulation about which he or she knows or is reckless in not knowing about such rule or regulation. A preparer may adopt a position contrary to a revenue ruling if a realistic possibility exists that the position can be sustained on its merits. In addition, a preparer may depart from following a regulation without penalty if he or she has a good faith basis for challenging its validity and adequately discloses his or her position on Form 8275-R (Regulation Disclosure Statement).

STOP & THINK

Question: While preparing a client's tax return two days before the due date, Tevin comes across an item that is arguably deductible. He weighs the cost of researching whether the deduction has a realistic possibility of being sustained on its merits. He calculates that researching the issue will cost him $300 in forgone revenues and that not researching the issue will cost him $250 in preparer penalties. What should Tevin do?

Solution: Undoubtedly, Tevin should research the issue and determine whether the deduction either has a realistic possibility of being sustained on the merits or is not frivolous. If

[96] Regulation Sec. 1.6695-1(b)(5) states that, for the purpose of avoiding the failure-to-sign penalty, reasonable cause is "a cause which arises despite ordinary care and prudence exercised by the individual preparer."

[97] Reg. Sec. 1.6694-2(b).

it is not frivolous, he should disclose this position on the tax return. What is at stake here is not merely $300 in foregone revenues but also Tevin's professional reputation. His taking a position that does not meet the realistic possibility standard or that is nonfrivolous but undisclosed subjects not only him as tax preparer, but also his client as taxpayer, to penalties. If the IRS imposes a penalty on the client, the client might terminate the professional relationship with Tevin or sue Tevin for malpractice. Besides, Tevin may have miscalculated his own professional liability. If the IRS determines that Tevin recklessly or intentionally disregarded tax rules and regulations, it may impose a penalty of $1,000, not $250.

Tax preparers who offer advice relating to the preparation of a document, knowing that such advice will result in a tax understatement, will be liable for aiding and abetting in the understatement.[98] The penalty for aiding and abetting is $1,000 for advice given to noncorporate taxpayers and $10,000 for advice given to corporate taxpayers. If a preparer is assessed an aiding-and-abetting penalty, the preparer will not be assessed a Sec. 6694 preparer penalty for the same infraction.

RULES OF *CIRCULAR 230*

Treasury Department Circular 230 (or *Circular 230*) regulates the practice of attorneys, CPAs, enrolled agents, and enrolled actuaries before the IRS. Practice before the IRS includes representing taxpayers in meetings with IRS agents and appeals officers. Tax professionals who do not comply with the rules and regulations of *Circular 230* can be barred from practicing before the IRS. Such professionals are entitled to an administrative hearing before being barred.

The following rules govern the conduct of practitioners before the IRS:[99]

- ▶ If the practitioner knows that a client has not complied with federal tax laws or has made an error in or an omission from any return, the practitioner should promptly advise the client of the error or omission.[100]
- ▶ Each person practicing before the IRS is expected to exercise due diligence in preparing returns, determining the correctness of representations made to the Treasury Department, and determining the correctness of representations made to clients about tax matters.

ETHICAL POINT

In deciding whether to adopt a pro-taxpayer position on a tax return or in rendering tax advice, a tax advisor should keep in mind his or her responsibilities under the tax return preparer rules of the IRC, *Treasury Department Circular 230,* and the *Statements on Standards for Tax Services,* especially Statement No. 1. Statement No. 1 (discussed in Chapter C1 and reproduced in Appendix E) requires that a CPA have a good faith belief that the position adopted on the tax return is supported by existing law or by a good faith argument for extending, modifying, or reversing existing law.

Like Sec. 6694, *Treasury Department Circular 230* provides that a tax practitioner should always give advice or prepare a return based on a position that has a realistic possibility of being sustained on its merits or that is not frivolous and is disclosed (or, a practitioner giving advice should inform the client of the opportunity to avoid a penalty by making a disclosure). The realistic possibility standard is met if a person knowledgeable in the tax law would conclude that the position has approximately a one in three, or greater, chance of being sustained on its merits.[101] *Circular 230* also contains a detailed discussion of practices that tax professionals must follow in issuing tax shelter opinions.[102]

TAX ACCOUNTING AND TAX LAW

Accountants and lawyers frequently deal with the same issues. These issues pertain to incorporation and merger, bankruptcy and liquidation, purchases and sales, gains and losses, compensation and benefits, and estate planning. Both types of professionals are competent to practice in many of the same areas. In some areas, however, accountants are more competent than lawyers, and in other areas, lawyers are more competent than accountants. What are these areas, and where does one draw the line?

In the realm of federal taxation, achieving a clear delineation always has been difficult. When an accountant prepares a tax return, he or she invariably delves into the intricacies

[98] Sec. 6701.

[99] *Treasury Department Circular 230* (1994), Secs. 10.21 and 10.22.

[100] Section 10.21 of Prop. Reg. 111835-99 adds the additional duty of informing the client of possible corrective action and the consequences of not taking such action.

[101] Ibid., Sec. 10.34.

[102] Ibid., Sec. 10.33.

of tax law. When a lawyer gives tax advice, he or she frequently applies principles of accounting. Toward clarifying the responsibilities of each, the AICPA and American Bar Association have issued the *Statement on Practice in the Field of Federal Income Taxation.*[103] This statement denotes five areas in which CPAs and attorneys are equally competent to practice and several areas in which each is exclusively competent to practice. The areas of mutual competence are as follows:

- ▶ Preparing federal income tax returns
- ▶ Determining the tax effects of proposed transactions
- ▶ Representing taxpayers before the Treasury Department
- ▶ Practicing before the U.S. Tax Court
- ▶ Preparing claims for refunds

Areas in which an accountant is exclusively competent to practice include:

- ▶ Resolving accounting issues
- ▶ Preparing financial statements included in financial reports or submitted with tax returns
- ▶ Advising clients as to accounting methods and procedures
- ▶ Classifying transactions and summarizing them in monetary terms
- ▶ Interpreting financial results

Areas in which an attorney is exclusively competent to practice include:

- ▶ Resolving issues of law
- ▶ Preparing legal documents such as agreements, conveyances, trust instruments, and wills
- ▶ Advising clients as to the sufficiency or effect of legal documents
- ▶ Taking the necessary steps to create, amend, or dissolve a partnership, corporation, or trust
- ▶ Representing clients in criminal investigations

State bar and CPA associations have issued similar guidelines for their constituencies, and the courts generally have followed these and the national guidelines.[104]

What happens if an accountant oversteps his or her professional bounds? The transgression may constitute the **unauthorized practice of law.** The unauthorized practice of law involves the engagement, by nonlawyers, in professional activities traditionally reserved for the bar. In most states, it is actionable by injunction, damages, or both. Allegations of the unauthorized practice of law typically arise in the context of a billing dispute.[105] The CPA bills a client for professional services, and the client disputes the bill on the ground that the accountant engaged in the unauthorized practice of law. Occasionally, the court sustains the client's allegation and thus denies the accountant the amount in dispute. With this and the public interest in mind, accountants should always confine their practice to areas in which they are most competent.

ACCOUNTANT-CLIENT PRIVILEGE

According to judicial doctrine, certain communications between an attorney and a client are "privileged," i.e., nondiscoverable in the course of litigation. In 1998, Congress extended this privilege to similar communications between a federally authorized tax advisor and a client. A federally authorized tax advisor includes a certified public accountant.

The accountant-client privilege is similar to the attorney-client privilege in two respects. First, it encompasses communications for the purpose of obtaining or giving pro-

---

[103] National Conference of Lawyers and Certified Public Accountants, *Statement on Practice in the Field of Federal Income Taxation,* November 1981.

[104] See for example *Lathrop v. Donahue,* 367 U.S. 820, 81 S.Ct. 1826 (1961), *U.S. v. Gordon Buttorff,* 56 AFTR 2d 85-5247, 85-1 USTC ¶9435 (5th Cir., 1985), *Morton L. Simons v. Edgar T. Bellinger,* 643 F.2d 774, 207 U.S. App. D.C. 24 (1980), *Emilio L. Ippolito v. The State of Florida, 824 F.Supp. 1562, 1993 U.S. Dist. LEXIS 13091 (M.D. Fla., 1993), In re Application of New Jersey Society of Certified Public Accountants,* 102 N.J. 231, 507 A.2d 711 (1986).

[105] See for example, *In re Bercu,* 299 N.Y. 728, 87 N.E.2d 451 (1949), and *Agran v. Shapiro,* 46 AFTR 896, 127 Cal. App.2d 807 (App. Dept. Super. Ct., 1954).

fessional advice. Second, it excludes communications for the sole purpose of preparing a tax return. The accountant-client privilege is dissimilar in three respects. First, it is limited only to *tax* advice. Second, it may be asserted only in a noncriminal tax proceeding before a federal court or the IRS. Third, it excludes written communications between an accountant and a corporation regarding a tax shelter. A tax shelter is any plan or arrangement, a significant purpose of which is tax avoidance or evasion.

EXAMPLE C15-41 ▶ Alec, Chief Financial Officer of MultiCorp, has solicited the advice of his tax accountant, Louise, concerning a civil dispute with the IRS. Louise has advised Alec in a series of letters spanning the course of five months. An IRS appeals officer asks Louise if he can review the letters. Louise may refuse the officer's request because her professional advice was offered in anticipation of civil litigation and therefore is "privileged." ◀

EXAMPLE C15-42 ▶ Assume the same facts as in Example C15-41 except Louise sends Alec a letter concerning the foreign sales scheme. Because Louise communicates tax advice to a corporation concerning a "tax shelter" and because this communication is written, it is *not* privileged. ◀

The creation of an accountant-client privilege reflects Congress' belief that the selection of a tax advisor should not hinge on the question of privilege. It ensures that all tax advice is accorded the same protection regardless of the tax advisor's professional status.

PROBLEM MATERIALS

DISCUSSION QUESTIONS

C15-1 Describe the manner in which the IRS verifies tax returns at its service centers.

C15-2 Name some of the administrative pronouncements the IRS issues.

C15-3 a. Describe three ways in which the IRS has selected returns for audit.
b. Explain the difference between how the IRS has selected returns for audit and the scope of audit for returns selected under the DIF and TCMP procedures.

C15-4 On his individual return, Al reports salary and exemptions for himself and seven dependents. His itemized deductions consist of mortgage interest, real estate taxes, and a large loss from breeding dogs. On his individual return, Ben reports self-employment income, a large loss from a partnership, a casualty loss deduction equal to 25% of his AGI, charitable contribution deductions equal to 30% of his AGI, and an exemption for himself. Al's return indicates higher taxable income than does Ben's. Which return is more likely to be selected for audit under the DIF program? Which return was more likely to be chosen under the TCMP program? Explain your answers.

C15-5 Tom receives a notice that the IRS has decided to audit his current year return with respect to his deduction for interest expense. His return for two years ago was audited with respect to Tom's charitable contribution deduction. The IRS, however, did not assess a deficiency for the prior year return. Is any potential relief available to Tom with respect to the audit of his current year return?

C15-6 The IRS selects Brad's current year return for audit with respect to employee business expenses. Brad has just met with a revenue agent who contends that Brad owes $775 of additional taxes. Discuss briefly the alternatives available to Brad.

C15-7 What course(s) of action is (are) available to the taxpayer upon receipt of the following notices:
a. The 30-day letter?
b. The 90-day letter?
c. IRS rejection of a claim for a refund?

C15-8 List the trial courts in which a taxpayer can begin tax-related litigation.

C15-9 Why is the Tax Court widely used for litigation?

C15-10 In what situations is a protest letter necessary?

C15-11 What general types of information should be included in a request for a ruling?

C15-12 What conditions must the taxpayer meet to shift the burden of proof to the IRS?

C15-13 In what circumstances will the IRS rule on estate tax issues?

C15-14 On which of the following issues will the IRS likely issue a private letter ruling and why? In your answer, assume that no other IRS pronouncement addresses the issue and that Treasury Regulations are not required.

a. Whether the taxpayer correctly calculated a capital gain reported on last year's tax return.
b. The tax consequences of using stock derivatives in a corporate reorganization.
c. Whether a mathematical formula correctly calculates the fair market value of a stock derivative.
d. Whether the cost of an Internet course that purports to improve existing employment skills may be deducted this year as a business expense.

C15-15 Tracy wants to take advantage of a "terrific business deal" by engaging in a transaction with Homer. Homer, quite domineering and impatient, wants Tracy to conclude the transaction within two weeks and under the exact terms proposed by Homer. Otherwise, Homer will offer the deal to another party. Tracy is unsure about the tax consequences of the proposed transaction. Would you advise Tracy to request a ruling? Explain.

C15-16 Provide the following information for both individuals and corporations:
a. Due date for an income tax return assuming the taxpayer requests no extension.
b. Due date for the return assuming the taxpayer files an automatic extension request.
c. Latest possible due date for the return

C15-17 Your client wants to know whether she must file any documents for automatic extension. What do you tell her?

C15-18 A client believes that obtaining an extension for filing an income tax return would give him additional time to pay the tax at no additional cost. Is the client correct?

C15-19 Briefly explain the rules for determining the interest rate charged on tax underpayments. Is this rate the same for overpayments? In which months might the rate for underpayments change?

C15-20 Stan does not have sufficient assets in April of the current year to pay his tax liability for the previous year. However, he expects to pay the tax by August of the current year. He wonders if he should request an extension for filing instead of simply filing his return and paying the tax in August. What is your response?

C15-21 At what rate is the penalty for underpaying estimated taxes imposed? How is the penalty amount calculated?

C15-22 The IRS audited Tony's return, and Tony agreed to pay additional taxes plus the negligence penalty. Is this penalty necessarily imposed on the total additional taxes that Tony owes? Explain.

C15-23 Assume that a taxpayer owes substantial additional taxes as a result of an audit. Give two reasons why the IRS might not impose a substantial understatement penalty with respect to the additional amount owed.

C15-24 Upon audit, the IRS determines Maria's tax liability to be $40,000. She agrees to pay a $7,000 deficiency. Will she necessarily have to pay a substantial understatement penalty? Explain.

C15-25 Distinguish between circumstances that give rise to imposition of the civil fraud penalty as opposed to those that give rise to imposition of the negligence penalty.

C15-26 Distinguish between the burdens of proof the government must meet to prove civil and criminal fraud.

C15-27 Explain why the government might bring criminal tax fraud charges against a taxpayer under Sec. 7206 instead of Sec. 7201. Compare the maximum penalties under Secs. 7201, 7203, and 7206.

C15-28 In general, when does the statute of limitations expire? List four exceptions to the general rule.

C15-29 What is the purpose of the innocent spouse provisions?

C15-30 According to the IRC tax return preparer provisions, under what circumstances should a CPA sign a tax return as a preparer?

C15-31 List five penalties that, under the IRC, can be assessed against tax return preparers. Does the IRC require a CPA to verify the information a client furnishes?

C15-32 According to *Treasury Department Circular 230*, what standard should be met for a CPA to take a position on a tax return?

ISSUE IDENTIFICATION QUESTIONS

C15-33 You are preparing the tax return for Bold Corporation, which had sales of $60 million. Bold made a $1 million expenditure for which the appropriate tax treatment—deductible or capitalizable—is a gray area. Bold's Director of Federal Taxes and the Chief Financial Officer are pushing you to deduct the expenditure on the return that you are in the process of completing. What tax compliance issues should you consider in deciding whether to deduct the expenditure?

C15-34 Your client, Hank Goedert, earned $100,000 of salary and received $40,000 of dividends in the current year. His itemized deductions total $37,000. In addition, Hank received $47,000 during the year from a relative who was his former employer. You have researched whether the $47,000 should be classified as a gift or compensation and are confident that substantial authority exists for classifying the receipt as a gift. You have almost finished Hank's current year tax return. What tax compliance issues should you consider in deciding whether to report or exclude the receipt?

C15-35 The IRS audited the tax returns of Darryl Strawberry, a former major league outfielder. It contended that, between 1986 and 1990, Strawberry earned $422,250 for autograph signings, appearances, and product endorsements, but reported only $59,685. Strawberry attributed the shortfall to his receipt of cash for autograph sessions and promotional events. He allegedly concealed the cash payments in separate bank accounts unbeknownst to his CPA. What tax compliance issues regarding the alleged underreporting are pertinent?

PROBLEMS

C15-36 *Calculation of Penalties.* On August 13 of the following year, Amy files her current calendar year return and pays the amount due without having requested an extension. The tax shown on her return is $24,000. Her current year withholding tax is $15,000. Amy pays no estimated taxes and claims no tax credits on her current year return.

a. What penalties will the IRS likely impose on Amy (ignoring the penalty for underpayment of estimated taxes)? Assume Amy committed no fraud.

b. On what dollar amount, and for how many days, will Amy owe interest?

C15-37 *Calculation of Penalties.* In the preceding problem, how would your answers change if Amy instead files her return on June 18 and, on September 8 of the following year, pays the amount due, assuming her withholding tax is

a. $19,000?

b. $24,500?

c. How would your answer to Part a change if Amy requests an automatic extension?

C15-38 *Calculation of Penalties.* The taxes shown on Hu's tax returns for 2001 and 2002 were $5,000 and $8,000, respectively. Hu's withholding tax for 2002 was $5,200, and she paid no estimated taxes. Hu filed her 2002 return on March 17, 2003, but she did not have sufficient funds to pay any taxes at the time she filed her return. She paid the $2,800 balance due on June 19, 2004. Hu's AGI for 2001 did not exceed $150,000. Calculate the penalties Hu owes with respect to her 2002 tax return.

C15-39 *Calculation of Penalties.* Ted's 2002 return reported a tax liability of $1,800. Ted's withholding for 2002 was $2,200. Because of his poor memory, Ted did not file his 2002 return until May 28, 2003. What penalties (if any) does Ted owe?

C15-40 *Calculation of Penalties.* Bob, a calendar year taxpayer, files his current year individual return on July 17 of the following year without having requested an extension. His return reports an amount due of $5,100. Bob pays this amount on November 3 of the following year. What are Bob's penalties for his failure to file and his failure to pay his tax on time? Assume Bob committed no fraud.

C15-41 *Calculation of Penalties.* Carl, a calendar year taxpayer, requests an automatic extension for filing his 2002 return. By April 15, 2003, he has paid $20,000 of taxes in the form of withholding and estimated taxes. He does not pay any additional tax with his extension request. Carl files his return and pays the balance of the taxes due on June 19, 2003. For 2001 his tax liability was $19,000, and his AGI did not exceed $150,000. What penalties will Carl owe if his 2002 tax is $23,000? $20,800?

C15-42 *Determination of Interest.* Refer to the preceding problem.

a. Will Carl owe interest? If so, on what amount and for how many days?

b. Assume the applicable interest rate is 11%. Compute Carl's interest payable if his 2002 tax is $23,000. (See Rev. Proc. 95-17, 1995-1 C.B. 556, or a major tax service, for the compounding tables.)

C15-43 *Penalty for Underpayment of Estimated Taxes.* Ed's tax liability for last year was $24,000. Ed projects that his tax for this year will be $34,000. Ed is self-employed and, thus, will have no withholding. His AGI for last year did not exceed $150,000. How much estimated tax should Ed pay for this year to avoid the penalty for underpaying estimated taxes?

C15-44 *Penalty for Underpayment of Estimated Taxes.* Refer to the preceding problem. Assume that Ed expects his income for this year to decline and his tax liability for this year to be only $15,000. How much in estimated taxes, at a minimum, should Ed pay for this year? What problem will Ed encounter if he pays in the minimum amount of estimated taxes projected earlier and his income exceeds last year's because of a large capital gain in December of this year?

C15-45 *Penalty for Underpayment of Estimated Taxes.* Pam's 2001 income tax liability was $23,000. Her 2001 AGI did not exceed $150,000. On April 1, 2003, Pam, a calendar year taxpayer, files her 2002 individual return, which indicates a $30,000 income tax liability (before reduction for withholding). In addition, the return indicates self-employment taxes of $2,600. Taxes withheld from Pam's salary total $20,000; she has paid no estimated taxes.

a. Will Pam owe a penalty for not paying estimated taxes? Explain.
b. What amount (if any) per quarter is subject to the penalty? For what period will the penalty be imposed for each quarter's underpayment?
c. How would your answers to Parts a and b change if Pam's 2002 tax liability (including self-employment taxes) instead were $17,000?

C15-46 *Penalty for Underpayment of Estimated Taxes.* Amir's projected tax liability for the current year is $23,000. Although Amir has substantial dividend and interest income, he does not pay any estimated taxes. Amir's withholding for January through November of the current year is $1,300 per month. For December, he wants to increase the amount of his withholding to avoid the penalty for underpaying estimated taxes. Amir's previous year's liability (excluding withholding) is $21,000. His previous year's AGI did not exceed $150,000. What amount should Amir have withheld from his December paycheck? Explain.

C15-47 *Negligence Penalty.* The IRS audits Tan's individual return for the current year and assesses a $9,000 deficiency, $2,800 of which results from Tan's negligence. What is Tan's negligence penalty? Does the penalty bear interest?

C15-48 *Negligence Penalty.* The IRS audits Pearl's current year individual return and determines that, among other errors, she negligently failed to report dividend income of $8,000. The deficiency relating to the dividends is $2,240. The IRS argues for an additional $12,000 deficiency for various other errors that do not involve negligence. What is Pearl's negligence penalty for the $14,240 in deficiencies?

C15-49 *Substantial Understatement Penalty.* Carmen's current year individual return reports a $6,000 deduction for a questionable item not relating to a tax-shelter. Carmen does not make a disclosure regarding this item. The IRS audits Carmen's return, and she concedes to a deficiency. As a result, her tax liability increases from $20,000 to $21,860. Assume Carmen lacks substantial authority for claiming the deduction.

a. What substantial understatement penalty (if any) will be imposed?
b. Will the penalty bear interest?
c. How would your answer to Parts a and b change if the deduction instead were for $20,000, and her tax liability increased by $6,200 to $26,200?

C15-50 *Substantial Understatement Penalty.* Refer to Part c of the previous problem. Assume that Carmen discloses her position, which is not frivolous. How would your original answer change if

a. The item does not involve a tax-shelter?
b. The item does involve a tax-shelter?

C15-51 *Fraud Penalty.* Luis, a bachelor, owes $56,000 of additional taxes, all due to fraud.

a. What is the amount of the civil fraud penalty?
b. What criminal fraud penalty might be imposed under Sec. 7201?

C15-52 *Fraud Penalty.* Hal and Wanda, his wife, are in the 39.6% marginal tax bracket for the current year. Wanda fraudulently omits from their joint return $50,000 of gross income. Hal does not participate in or know about her fraudulent act. Hal, however, overstates his deductions by $10,000 because of an oversight.

a. If the government successfully proves fraud in a civil suit against Wanda, what fines and/or penalties will she owe? If Hal and Wanda establish that the overstatement is not attributable to fraud, can the government collect the civil fraud penalty from Hal?
b. If the government successfully proves fraud in a criminal suit against Wanda, what fines or penalties will she owe? Are she or Hal subject to a prison sentence?

C15-53 *Statute of Limitations.* Frank, a calendar year taxpayer, reports $100,000 of gross income and $60,000 of taxable income on his 2002 return, which he files on March 10, 2003 . He fails to report on the return a $52,000 long-term capital gain and a $10,000 short-term capital loss. When does the statute of limitations for the government's collecting the deficiency expire if

a. His omission results from an oversight?
b. His omission results from a conscious attempt to evade the tax?

C15-54 *Statute of Limitations.* Refer to the previous problem. Assume Frank commits fraud with respect to his 2002 return as late as October 7, 2004. When does the statute of limitations for indicting Frank for criminal tax fraud expire?

C15-55 *Claim for Refund.* Maria, a calendar year taxpayer, files her 2002 individual return on March 11, 2003, and on that date she pays the amount of tax due. She later discovers that she overlooked some deductions that she should have claimed on the return. By what date must she file a claim for refund?

C15-56 *Innocent Spouse Provisions.* Wilma has no income for 2002 but files a joint return with her husband, Hank. Their 2002 return reports $40,000 of gross income and AGI and $24,000 of taxable income. Hank also has $12,000 of gambling winnings (no losses) in 2002 but omits them from the return. Wilma does not know about Hank's gambling activities, much less his winnings. The IRS audits their 2002 return and assesses additional taxes. Does Wilma satisfy the tests for relief under the innocent spouse provisions?

C15-57 *Innocent Spouse Provisions.* Joe and Joan filed a joint return for the current year. They are in the 31% marginal tax bracket. Unbeknownst to Joe, Joan failed to report on the return the $8,000 value of a prize she won. She, however, used the prize to buy Joe a new boat. Does Joe meet the tests for relief under the innocent spouse provisions?

C15-58 *Unauthorized Practice of Law.* Your client, Meade Technical Solutions, proposes to merge with Dealy Cyberlabs. In advance of the merger, you (a) issue an opinion concerning the FMV of Dealy, (b) prepare pro forma financials for the merged entity to be, (c) draft Meade shareholder resolutions approving the proposed merger, (d) file a shareholder proxy statement with the U.S. Securities and Exchange Commission, and (e) advise Meade's board of directors concerning the advantages of a Type A versus a Type B reorganization. Which of these activities, if any, constitutes the unauthorized practice of law?

C15-59 *Unauthorized Practice of Law.* Your client, Envirocosmetics, recently has filed for bankruptcy. In the course of bankruptcy proceedings, you (a) prepare a plan of reorganization that alters the rights of preferred stockholders, (b) notify the Envirocosmetics' creditors of an impending bulk transfer of the company's assets, (c) review IRS secured claims against these assets, (d) restructure the company's debt by reducing its principal amount and extending its maturity, (e) advise the bankruptcy court as to how this restructuring will impact the company's NOLs. Which of these activities, if any, constitutes the unauthorized practice of law?

C15-60 *Accountant-Client Privilege* Which of the following communications between an accountant and client are privileged?

a. For tax preparation purposes only, client informs the accountant that she contributed $10,000 to a homeless shelter.
b. Client informs the accountant that he forgot to report on his tax return the $5,000 value of a prize and asks how he should correct the error.
c. Client informs the accountant that she no longer will pay alimony to her ex-husband.

C15-61 *Accountant-Client Privilege.* Which of the following communications between an accountant and client are *not* privileged?

a. In a closed-door meeting, the accountant orally advises the client to set up a foreign subsidiary to shift taxable income to a low-tax jurisdiction.
b. In a closed-door meeting, the accountant submits to the client a plan for shifting taxable income to a low-tax jurisdiction.
c. In soliciting professional advice relating to criminal fraud, the client informs the accountant that he (the client) lied to the IRS.

COMPREHENSIVE PROBLEM

C15-62 This year, Ark Corporation acquired substantially all the voting stock of BioTech Consultants, Inc. for cash. Subsequent to the acquisition, Ark's chief financial officer, Jonathan Cohen, approached Edith Murphy, Ark's tax advisor, with a question: Could

Ark amortize the "general educational skills" of BioTech's employees? Edith researched the issue but found no primary authorities on point. She did, however, find a tax journal article, co-authored by two prominent academics, that endorsed amortizing "general educational skills" for tax purposes. The article referred to numerous primary authorities that support the amortization of "technical skills," but not "general educational skills." Edith consulted these authorities directly. Based on her research, Edith in good faith advised Jonathan that Ark could amortize the "general educational skills" over a 15-year period. In so doing, has Edith met the "realistic possibility standard" of

a. The IRC?

b. The AICPA *Statements on Standards for Tax Services* (see Appendix E)?

TAX STRATEGY PROBLEM

C15-63 The IRS is disputing a deduction reported on your 2001 tax return, which you filed on April 15, 2002. On April 1, 2005, the IRS audit agent asks you to waive the statute of limitations for the entire return so as to give her additional time to obtain a Technical Advice Memorandum. The agent proposes in return for the waiver a "carrot"—the prospect of an offer in compromise—and a "stick"—the possibility of a higher penalty. Although you have substantial authority for the deduction, you consider the following alternatives: (1) waive the statute of limitations for the entire return, (2) waive the statute of limitations for the deduction only, or (3) do not waive the statute of limitations in any way, shape, or form. Which alternative should you choose, and why?

CASE STUDY PROBLEM

C15-64 A long-time client, Horace Haney, wishes to avoid currently recognizing revenue in a particular transaction. A recently finalized Treasury Regulation, however, provides that revenue should be currently recognized in such a transaction. Horace insists that you report no revenue from the transaction and, furthermore, that you make no disclosure about going against the regulation. The IRC is unclear about whether the income should be recognized currently. No relevant cases, revenue rulings, or letter rulings deal specifically with the transaction in question.

Required: Discuss whether you, a CPA, can prepare Horace's tax return and comply with his wishes. Assume that recognizing the income in question would increase Horace's tax liability by about 25%.

TAX RESEARCH PROBLEMS

C15-65 Art is named executor of the Estate of Stu Stone, his father, who died on February 3 of the current year. Art engages Larry to serve as the estate's attorney. Larry advises Art that the estate must file an estate tax return but does not mention the due date. Art, a pharmacist, has no experience in tax matters other than the preparation of his own income tax returns. Art provides Larry with all the necessary information by June 15 of the current year. On six occasions Art contacts Larry to check on the progress of the estate tax return. Each time, Larry assures Art that "everything is under control." On November 15, Art contacts Larry for the seventh time. He learns that because of a clerical oversight, the return—due on November 2 of the current year—has not been filed. Larry apologizes and says he will make sure that an associate finishes the return promptly. The return, which reports an estate tax liability of $75,200, is filed on December 7 of the current year. Your manager requests that you prepare a memorandum addressing whether the estate will owe a failure-to-file penalty. Your manager suggests that, at a minimum, you consult

- IRC Sec. 6151(a)
- *U.S. v. Robert W. Boyle,* 55 AFTR 2d 85-1535, 85-1 USTC ¶13,602 (USSC, 1985)

C15-66 Harold and Betty, factory workers who until this year prepared their own individual tax returns, purchased an investment from an investment advisor last year. They reviewed the prospectus for the investment, and the advisor explained the more complicated features to them. Early this year, they struggled to prepare their individual return for last year but, because of the investment, found it too complicated to complete. Consequently, they engaged a CPA to prepare the return for them. The CPA deducted losses from the investment against income that Harold and Betty generated from other sources. The IRS audited the return for last year and contended that the loss was not deductible. Harold and Betty, after consulting with their CPA who further considered tax consequences of the investment, agreed that the loss was not deductible and consented to paying the deficiency. The IRS also contended that the couple owes the substantial understatement penalty because they did not disclose the value of the investment on their return and did not have substantial authority for their position. Assume you are arguing on behalf of the taxpayers before the IRS and adopt the position that they should be exempted from the substantial understatement penalty. Your tax manager reminds you to consult Secs. 6662 and 6664 when conducting your research.

C15-67 Gene employed his attorney to draft identical trust instruments for each of his three minor children. Before he signs the instruments, Gene wishes to receive a ruling from the IRS concerning whether the trusts qualify for the gift tax annual exclusion. Your task is to prepare a request for a letter ruling. Each trust instrument names the Fourth City Bank as trustee and states the trust is irrevocable. It provides that, until the beneficiary reaches age 21, the trustee at its discretion is to pay income and/or principal (corpus) to the beneficiary. Upon reaching age 21, the beneficiary will have 60 days in which to request that the trust assets be paid over to him or her. Otherwise, the assets will stay in the trust until the beneficiary reaches age 35. The beneficiary also is granted a general testamentary power of appointment over the trust assets. If the beneficiary dies before the trust terminates and does not exercise his or her power of appointment (because, for example, he or she dies without a will), the trust property will be distributed to family members in accordance with state intestacy laws. The three beneficiaries are Judy (age 5), Terry (age 7), and Grady (age 11). Each trust will be funded with property valued at $100,000.

A partial list of research sources is

- IRC Secs. 2503(b) and (c)
- Reg. Sec. 25.2503-4
- Rev. Rul. 67-270, 1967-2 C.B. 349
- Rev. Rul. 74-43, 1974-1 C.B. 285
- Rev. Rul. 81-7, 1981-1 C.B. 474

C15-68 On April 10, 2001, Adam and Renee Tyler jointly filed a 2000 return that reported AGI of $68,240 ($20,500 attributable to Renee) and a tax liability of $3,050. They paid this amount in a timely fashion. On their return, the Tylers claimed a $18,405 deduction for Adam's distributive share of a partnership loss. If not for the loss, the Tylers' tax liability would have been $8,358. In the previous year, Adam had withdrawn $20,000 cash from the partnership, which he used to buy Renee a new car. Although Renee, a marketing consultant, is not active in the partnership business, she has worked for the partnership as a part-time receptionist. Adam and his partner (who incidentally is Renee's brother) failed to file a partnership return for 2000. Upon audit, the IRS discovered that the 2000 partnership records were missing. In June 2002, Adam had a heart attack. He remains in serious condition. Unable to reach Adam, the IRS sends Renee a 30-day letter proposing a $5,308 deficiency. She intends to protest. Your supervisor has asked you to write a memorandum discussing Renee's potential liabilities and defenses. In your memorandum, you should consult the following authorities:

- IRC Secs. 6013 and 6662
- *Rebecca Jo Reser v. CIR*, 79 AFTR 2d 97-2743, 97-1 USTC ¶50,416 (5th Cir., 1997)

2001 TAX TABLES AND RATE SCHEDULES

2001 Tax Table

Caution. Dependents, see the worksheet on page 33.

Use if your taxable income is less than $100,000. If $100,000 or more, use the Tax Rate Schedules.

Example. Mr. and Mrs. Brown are filing a joint return. Their taxable income on line 39 of Form 1040 is $25,300. First, they find the $25,300–25,350 income line. Next, they find the column for married filing jointly and read down the column. The amount shown where the income line and filing status column meet is $3,799. This is the tax amount they should enter on line 40 of their Form 1040.

Sample Table

At least	But less than	Single	Married filing jointly *	Married filing separately	Head of a household
		Your tax is—			
25,200	**25,250**	3,784	3,784	4,112	3,784
25,250	**25,300**	3,791	3,791	4,126	3,791
25,300	**25,350**	3,799	(3,799)	4,139	3,799
25,350	**25,400**	3,806	3,806	4,153	3,806

If line 39 (taxable income) is—		And you are—			
At least	But less than	Single	Married filing jointly *	Married filing separately	Head of a household
		Your tax is—			
0	**5**	0	0	0	0
5	**15**	2	2	2	2
15	**25**	3	3	3	3
25	**50**	6	6	6	6
50	**75**	9	9	9	9
75	**100**	13	13	13	13
100	**125**	17	17	17	17
125	**150**	21	21	21	21
150	**175**	24	24	24	24
175	**200**	28	28	28	28
200	**225**	32	32	32	32
225	**250**	36	36	36	36
250	**275**	39	39	39	39
275	**300**	43	43	43	43
300	**325**	47	47	47	47
325	**350**	51	51	51	51
350	**375**	54	54	54	54
375	**400**	58	58	58	58
400	**425**	62	62	62	62
425	**450**	66	66	66	66
450	**475**	69	69	69	69
475	**500**	73	73	73	73
500	**525**	77	77	77	77
525	**550**	81	81	81	81
550	**575**	84	84	84	84
575	**600**	88	88	88	88
600	**625**	92	92	92	92
625	**650**	96	96	96	96
650	**675**	99	99	99	99
675	**700**	103	103	103	103
700	**725**	107	107	107	107
725	**750**	111	111	111	111
750	**775**	114	114	114	114
775	**800**	118	118	118	118
800	**825**	122	122	122	122
825	**850**	126	126	126	126
850	**875**	129	129	129	129
875	**900**	133	133	133	133
900	**925**	137	137	137	137
925	**950**	141	141	141	141
950	**975**	144	144	144	144
975	**1,000**	148	148	148	148
1,000					
1,000	**1,025**	152	152	152	152
1,025	**1,050**	156	156	156	156
1,050	**1,075**	159	159	159	159
1,075	**1,100**	163	163	163	163
1,100	**1,125**	167	167	167	167
1,125	**1,150**	171	171	171	171
1,150	**1,175**	174	174	174	174
1,175	**1,200**	178	178	178	178
1,200	**1,225**	182	182	182	182
1,225	**1,250**	186	186	186	186
1,250	**1,275**	189	189	189	189
1,275	**1,300**	193	193	193	193
1,300	**1,325**	197	197	197	197
1,325	**1,350**	201	201	201	201
1,350	**1,375**	204	204	204	204
1,375	**1,400**	208	208	208	208
1,400	**1,425**	212	212	212	212
1,425	**1,450**	216	216	216	216
1,450	**1,475**	219	219	219	219
1,475	**1,500**	223	223	223	223
1,500	**1,525**	227	227	227	227
1,525	**1,550**	231	231	231	231
1,550	**1,575**	234	234	234	234
1,575	**1,600**	238	238	238	238
1,600	**1,625**	242	242	242	242
1,625	**1,650**	246	246	246	246
1,650	**1,675**	249	249	249	249
1,675	**1,700**	253	253	253	253
1,700	**1,725**	257	257	257	257
1,725	**1,750**	261	261	261	261
1,750	**1,775**	264	264	264	264
1,775	**1,800**	268	268	268	268
1,800	**1,825**	272	272	272	272
1,825	**1,850**	276	276	276	276
1,850	**1,875**	279	279	279	279
1,875	**1,900**	283	283	283	283
1,900	**1,925**	287	287	287	287
1,925	**1,950**	291	291	291	291
1,950	**1,975**	294	294	294	294
1,975	**2,000**	298	298	298	298
2,000					
2,000	**2,025**	302	302	302	302
2,025	**2,050**	306	306	306	306
2,050	**2,075**	309	309	309	309
2,075	**2,100**	313	313	313	313
2,100	**2,125**	317	317	317	317
2,125	**2,150**	321	321	321	321
2,150	**2,175**	324	324	324	324
2,175	**2,200**	328	328	328	328
2,200	**2,225**	332	332	332	332
2,225	**2,250**	336	336	336	336
2,250	**2,275**	339	339	339	339
2,275	**2,300**	343	343	343	343
2,300	**2,325**	347	347	347	347
2,325	**2,350**	351	351	351	351
2,350	**2,375**	354	354	354	354
2,375	**2,400**	358	358	358	358
2,400	**2,425**	362	362	362	362
2,425	**2,450**	366	366	366	366
2,450	**2,475**	369	369	369	369
2,475	**2,500**	373	373	373	373
2,500	**2,525**	377	377	377	377
2,525	**2,550**	381	381	381	381
2,550	**2,575**	384	384	384	384
2,575	**2,600**	388	388	388	388
2,600	**2,625**	392	392	392	392
2,625	**2,650**	396	396	396	396
2,650	**2,675**	399	399	399	399
2,675	**2,700**	403	403	403	403
2,700	**2,725**	407	407	407	407
2,725	**2,750**	411	411	411	411
2,750	**2,775**	414	414	414	414
2,775	**2,800**	418	418	418	418
2,800	**2,825**	422	422	422	422
2,825	**2,850**	426	426	426	426
2,850	**2,875**	429	429	429	429
2,875	**2,900**	433	433	433	433
2,900	**2,925**	437	437	437	437
2,925	**2,950**	441	441	441	441
2,950	**2,975**	444	444	444	444
2,975	**3,000**	448	448	448	448
3,000					
3,000	**3,050**	454	454	454	454
3,050	**3,100**	461	461	461	461
3,100	**3,150**	469	469	469	469
3,150	**3,200**	476	476	476	476
3,200	**3,250**	484	484	484	484
3,250	**3,300**	491	491	491	491
3,300	**3,350**	499	499	499	499
3,350	**3,400**	506	506	506	506
3,400	**3,450**	514	514	514	514
3,450	**3,500**	521	521	521	521
3,500	**3,550**	529	529	529	529
3,550	**3,600**	536	536	536	536
3,600	**3,650**	544	544	544	544
3,650	**3,700**	551	551	551	551
3,700	**3,750**	559	559	559	559
3,750	**3,800**	566	566	566	566
3,800	**3,850**	574	574	574	574
3,850	**3,900**	581	581	581	581
3,900	**3,950**	589	589	589	589
3,950	**4,000**	596	596	596	596
4,000					
4,000	**4,050**	604	604	604	604
4,050	**4,100**	611	611	611	611
4,100	**4,150**	619	619	619	619
4,150	**4,200**	626	626	626	626
4,200	**4,250**	634	634	634	634
4,250	**4,300**	641	641	641	641
4,300	**4,350**	649	649	649	649
4,350	**4,400**	656	656	656	656
4,400	**4,450**	664	664	664	664
4,450	**4,500**	671	671	671	671
4,500	**4,550**	679	679	679	679
4,550	**4,600**	686	686	686	686
4,600	**4,650**	694	694	694	694
4,650	**4,700**	701	701	701	701
4,700	**4,750**	709	709	709	709
4,750	**4,800**	716	716	716	716
4,800	**4,850**	724	724	724	724
4,850	**4,900**	731	731	731	731
4,900	**4,950**	739	739	739	739
4,950	**5,000**	746	746	746	746

(Continued on page 60)

* This column must also be used by a qualifying widow(er).

2001 Tax Table—*Continued* **Caution.** Dependents, see the worksheet on page 33.

If line 39 (taxable income) is—		And you are—				If line 39 (taxable income) is—		And you are—				If line 39 (taxable income) is—		And you are—			
At least	But less than	Single	Married filing jointly *	Married filing sepa-rately	Head of a house-hold	At least	But less than	Single	Married filing jointly *	Married filing sepa-rately	Head of a house-hold	At least	But less than	Single	Married filing jointly *	Married filing sepa-rately	Head of a house-hold
		Your tax is—						Your tax is—						Your tax is—			
5,000						**8,000**						**11,000**					
5,000	5,050	754	754	754	754	8,000	8,050	1,204	1,204	1,204	1,204	11,000	11,050	1,654	1,654	1,654	1,654
5,050	5,100	761	761	761	761	8,050	8,100	1,211	1,211	1,211	1,211	11,050	11,100	1,661	1,661	1,661	1,661
5,100	5,150	769	769	769	769	8,100	8,150	1,219	1,219	1,219	1,219	11,100	11,150	1,669	1,669	1,669	1,669
5,150	5,200	776	776	776	776	8,150	8,200	1,226	1,226	1,226	1,226	11,150	11,200	1,676	1,676	1,676	1,676
5,200	5,250	784	784	784	784	8,200	8,250	1,234	1,234	1,234	1,234	11,200	11,250	1,684	1,684	1,684	1,684
5,250	5,300	791	791	791	791	8,250	8,300	1,241	1,241	1,241	1,241	11,250	11,300	1,691	1,691	1,691	1,691
5,300	5,350	799	799	799	799	8,300	8,350	1,249	1,249	1,249	1,249	11,300	11,350	1,699	1,699	1,699	1,699
5,350	5,400	806	806	806	806	8,350	8,400	1,256	1,256	1,256	1,256	11,350	11,400	1,706	1,706	1,706	1,706
5,400	5,450	814	814	814	814	8,400	8,450	1,264	1,264	1,264	1,264	11,400	11,450	1,714	1,714	1,714	1,714
5,450	5,500	821	821	821	821	8,450	8,500	1,271	1,271	1,271	1,271	11,450	11,500	1,721	1,721	1,721	1,721
5,500	5,550	829	829	829	829	8,500	8,550	1,279	1,279	1,279	1,279	11,500	11,550	1,729	1,729	1,729	1,729
5,550	5,600	836	836	836	836	8,550	8,600	1,286	1,286	1,286	1,286	11,550	11,600	1,736	1,736	1,736	1,736
5,600	5,650	844	844	844	844	8,600	8,650	1,294	1,294	1,294	1,294	11,600	11,650	1,744	1,744	1,744	1,744
5,650	5,700	851	851	851	851	8,650	8,700	1,301	1,301	1,301	1,301	11,650	11,700	1,751	1,751	1,751	1,751
5,700	5,750	859	859	859	859	8,700	8,750	1,309	1,309	1,309	1,309	11,700	11,750	1,759	1,759	1,759	1,759
5,750	5,800	866	866	866	866	8,750	8,800	1,316	1,316	1,316	1,316	11,750	11,800	1,766	1,766	1,766	1,766
5,800	5,850	874	874	874	874	8,800	8,850	1,324	1,324	1,324	1,324	11,800	11,850	1,774	1,774	1,774	1,774
5,850	5,900	881	881	881	881	8,850	8,900	1,331	1,331	1,331	1,331	11,850	11,900	1,781	1,781	1,781	1,781
5,900	5,950	889	889	889	889	8,900	8,950	1,339	1,339	1,339	1,339	11,900	11,950	1,789	1,789	1,789	1,789
5,950	6,000	896	896	896	896	8,950	9,000	1,346	1,346	1,346	1,346	11,950	12,000	1,796	1,796	1,796	1,796
6,000						**9,000**						**12,000**					
6,000	6,050	904	904	904	904	9,000	9,050	1,354	1,354	1,354	1,354	12,000	12,050	1,804	1,804	1,804	1,804
6,050	6,100	911	911	911	911	9,050	9,100	1,361	1,361	1,361	1,361	12,050	12,100	1,811	1,811	1,811	1,811
6,100	6,150	919	919	919	919	9,100	9,150	1,369	1,369	1,369	1,369	12,100	12,150	1,819	1,819	1,819	1,819
6,150	6,200	926	926	926	926	9,150	9,200	1,376	1,376	1,376	1,376	12,150	12,200	1,826	1,826	1,826	1,826
6,200	6,250	934	934	934	934	9,200	9,250	1,384	1,384	1,384	1,384	12,200	12,250	1,834	1,834	1,834	1,834
6,250	6,300	941	941	941	941	9,250	9,300	1,391	1,391	1,391	1,391	12,250	12,300	1,841	1,841	1,841	1,841
6,300	6,350	949	949	949	949	9,300	9,350	1,399	1,399	1,399	1,399	12,300	12,350	1,849	1,849	1,849	1,849
6,350	6,400	956	956	956	956	9,350	9,400	1,406	1,406	1,406	1,406	12,350	12,400	1,856	1,856	1,856	1,856
6,400	6,450	964	964	964	964	9,400	9,450	1,414	1,414	1,414	1,414	12,400	12,450	1,864	1,864	1,864	1,864
6,450	6,500	971	971	971	971	9,450	9,500	1,421	1,421	1,421	1,421	12,450	12,500	1,871	1,871	1,871	1,871
6,500	6,550	979	979	979	979	9,500	9,550	1,429	1,429	1,429	1,429	12,500	12,550	1,879	1,879	1,879	1,879
6,550	6,600	986	986	986	986	9,550	9,600	1,436	1,436	1,436	1,436	12,550	12,600	1,886	1,886	1,886	1,886
6,600	6,650	994	994	994	994	9,600	9,650	1,444	1,444	1,444	1,444	12,600	12,650	1,894	1,894	1,894	1,894
6,650	6,700	1,001	1,001	1,001	1,001	9,650	9,700	1,451	1,451	1,451	1,451	12,650	12,700	1,901	1,901	1,901	1,901
6,700	6,750	1,009	1,009	1,009	1,009	9,700	9,750	1,459	1,459	1,459	1,459	12,700	12,750	1,909	1,909	1,909	1,909
6,750	6,800	1,016	1,016	1,016	1,016	9,750	9,800	1,466	1,466	1,466	1,466	12,750	12,800	1,916	1,916	1,916	1,916
6,800	6,850	1,024	1,024	1,024	1,024	9,800	9,850	1,474	1,474	1,474	1,474	12,800	12,850	1,924	1,924	1,924	1,924
6,850	6,900	1,031	1,031	1,031	1,031	9,850	9,900	1,481	1,481	1,481	1,481	12,850	12,900	1,931	1,931	1,931	1,931
6,900	6,950	1,039	1,039	1,039	1,039	9,900	9,950	1,489	1,489	1,489	1,489	12,900	12,950	1,939	1,939	1,939	1,939
6,950	7,000	1,046	1,046	1,046	1,046	9,950	10,000	1,496	1,496	1,496	1,496	12,950	13,000	1,946	1,946	1,946	1,946
7,000						**10,000**						**13,000**					
7,000	7,050	1,054	1,054	1,054	1,054	10,000	10,050	1,504	1,504	1,504	1,504	13,000	13,050	1,954	1,954	1,954	1,954
7,050	7,100	1,061	1,061	1,061	1,061	10,050	10,100	1,511	1,511	1,511	1,511	13,050	13,100	1,961	1,961	1,961	1,961
7,100	7,150	1,069	1,069	1,069	1,069	10,100	10,150	1,519	1,519	1,519	1,519	13,100	13,150	1,969	1,969	1,969	1,969
7,150	7,200	1,076	1,076	1,076	1,076	10,150	10,200	1,526	1,526	1,526	1,526	13,150	13,200	1,976	1,976	1,976	1,976
7,200	7,250	1,084	1,084	1,084	1,084	10,200	10,250	1,534	1,534	1,534	1,534	13,200	13,250	1,984	1,984	1,984	1,984
7,250	7,300	1,091	1,091	1,091	1,091	10,250	10,300	1,541	1,541	1,541	1,541	13,250	13,300	1,991	1,991	1,991	1,991
7,300	7,350	1,099	1,099	1,099	1,099	10,300	10,350	1,549	1,549	1,549	1,549	13,300	13,350	1,999	1,999	1,999	1,999
7,350	7,400	1,106	1,106	1,106	1,106	10,350	10,400	1,556	1,556	1,556	1,556	13,350	13,400	2,006	2,006	2,006	2,006
7,400	7,450	1,114	1,114	1,114	1,114	10,400	10,450	1,564	1,564	1,564	1,564	13,400	13,450	2,014	2,014	2,014	2,014
7,450	7,500	1,121	1,121	1,121	1,121	10,450	10,500	1,571	1,571	1,571	1,571	13,450	13,500	2,021	2,021	2,021	2,021
7,500	7,550	1,129	1,129	1,129	1,129	10,500	10,550	1,579	1,579	1,579	1,579	13,500	13,550	2,029	2,029	2,029	2,029
7,550	7,600	1,136	1,136	1,136	1,136	10,550	10,600	1,586	1,586	1,586	1,586	13,550	13,600	2,036	2,036	2,036	2,036
7,600	7,650	1,144	1,144	1,144	1,144	10,600	10,650	1,594	1,594	1,594	1,594	13,600	13,650	2,044	2,044	2,044	2,044
7,650	7,700	1,151	1,151	1,151	1,151	10,650	10,700	1,601	1,601	1,601	1,601	13,650	13,700	2,051	2,051	2,051	2,051
7,700	7,750	1,159	1,159	1,159	1,159	10,700	10,750	1,609	1,609	1,609	1,609	13,700	13,750	2,059	2,059	2,059	2,059
7,750	7,800	1,166	1,166	1,166	1,166	10,750	10,800	1,616	1,616	1,616	1,616	13,750	13,800	2,066	2,066	2,066	2,066
7,800	7,850	1,174	1,174	1,174	1,174	10,800	10,850	1,624	1,624	1,624	1,624	13,800	13,850	2,074	2,074	2,074	2,074
7,850	7,900	1,181	1,181	1,181	1,181	10,850	10,900	1,631	1,631	1,631	1,631	13,850	13,900	2,081	2,081	2,081	2,081
7,900	7,950	1,189	1,189	1,189	1,189	10,900	10,950	1,639	1,639	1,639	1,639	13,900	13,950	2,089	2,089	2,089	2,089
7,950	8,000	1,196	1,196	1,196	1,196	10,950	11,000	1,646	1,646	1,646	1,646	13,950	14,000	2,096	2,096	2,096	2,096

* This column must also be used by a qualifying widow(er).

(Continued on page 61)

Caution. Dependents, see the worksheet on page 33. **2001 Tax Table—*Continued***

If line 39 (taxable income) is— At least	But less than	And you are— Single	Married filing jointly *	Married filing separately	Head of a household
		Your tax is—			
14,000					
14,000	14,050	2,104	2,104	2,104	2,104
14,050	14,100	2,111	2,111	2,111	2,111
14,100	14,150	2,119	2,119	2,119	2,119
14,150	14,200	2,126	2,126	2,126	2,126
14,200	14,250	2,134	2,134	2,134	2,134
14,250	14,300	2,141	2,141	2,141	2,141
14,300	14,350	2,149	2,149	2,149	2,149
14,350	14,400	2,156	2,156	2,156	2,156
14,400	14,450	2,164	2,164	2,164	2,164
14,450	14,500	2,171	2,171	2,171	2,171
14,500	14,550	2,179	2,179	2,179	2,179
14,550	14,600	2,186	2,186	2,186	2,186
14,600	14,650	2,194	2,194	2,194	2,194
14,650	14,700	2,201	2,201	2,201	2,201
14,700	14,750	2,209	2,209	2,209	2,209
14,750	14,800	2,216	2,216	2,216	2,216
14,800	14,850	2,224	2,224	2,224	2,224
14,850	14,900	2,231	2,231	2,231	2,231
14,900	14,950	2,239	2,239	2,239	2,239
14,950	15,000	2,246	2,246	2,246	2,246
15,000					
15,000	15,050	2,254	2,254	2,254	2,254
15,050	15,100	2,261	2,261	2,261	2,261
15,100	15,150	2,269	2,269	2,269	2,269
15,150	15,200	2,276	2,276	2,276	2,276
15,200	15,250	2,284	2,284	2,284	2,284
15,250	15,300	2,291	2,291	2,291	2,291
15,300	15,350	2,299	2,299	2,299	2,299
15,350	15,400	2,306	2,306	2,306	2,306
15,400	15,450	2,314	2,314	2,314	2,314
15,450	15,500	2,321	2,321	2,321	2,321
15,500	15,550	2,329	2,329	2,329	2,329
15,550	15,600	2,336	2,336	2,336	2,336
15,600	15,650	2,344	2,344	2,344	2,344
15,650	15,700	2,351	2,351	2,351	2,351
15,700	15,750	2,359	2,359	2,359	2,359
15,750	15,800	2,366	2,366	2,366	2,366
15,800	15,850	2,374	2,374	2,374	2,374
15,850	15,900	2,381	2,381	2,381	2,381
15,900	15,950	2,389	2,389	2,389	2,389
15,950	16,000	2,396	2,396	2,396	2,396
16,000					
16,000	16,050	2,404	2,404	2,404	2,404
16,050	16,100	2,411	2,411	2,411	2,411
16,100	16,150	2,419	2,419	2,419	2,419
16,150	16,200	2,426	2,426	2,426	2,426
16,200	16,250	2,434	2,434	2,434	2,434
16,250	16,300	2,441	2,441	2,441	2,441
16,300	16,350	2,449	2,449	2,449	2,449
16,350	16,400	2,456	2,456	2,456	2,456
16,400	16,450	2,464	2,464	2,464	2,464
16,450	16,500	2,471	2,471	2,471	2,471
16,500	16,550	2,479	2,479	2,479	2,479
16,550	16,600	2,486	2,486	2,486	2,486
16,600	16,650	2,494	2,494	2,494	2,494
16,650	16,700	2,501	2,501	2,501	2,501
16,700	16,750	2,509	2,509	2,509	2,509
16,750	16,800	2,516	2,516	2,516	2,516
16,800	16,850	2,524	2,524	2,524	2,524
16,850	16,900	2,531	2,531	2,531	2,531
16,900	16,950	2,539	2,539	2,539	2,539
16,950	17,000	2,546	2,546	2,546	2,546

If line 39 (taxable income) is— At least	But less than	And you are— Single	Married filing jointly *	Married filing separately	Head of a household
		Your tax is—			
17,000					
17,000	17,050	2,554	2,554	2,554	2,554
17,050	17,100	2,561	2,561	2,561	2,561
17,100	17,150	2,569	2,569	2,569	2,569
17,150	17,200	2,576	2,576	2,576	2,576
17,200	17,250	2,584	2,584	2,584	2,584
17,250	17,300	2,591	2,591	2,591	2,591
17,300	17,350	2,599	2,599	2,599	2,599
17,350	17,400	2,606	2,606	2,606	2,606
17,400	17,450	2,614	2,614	2,614	2,614
17,450	17,500	2,621	2,621	2,621	2,621
17,500	17,550	2,629	2,629	2,629	2,629
17,550	17,600	2,636	2,636	2,636	2,636
17,600	17,650	2,644	2,644	2,644	2,644
17,650	17,700	2,651	2,651	2,651	2,651
17,700	17,750	2,659	2,659	2,659	2,659
17,750	17,800	2,666	2,666	2,666	2,666
17,800	17,850	2,674	2,674	2,674	2,674
17,850	17,900	2,681	2,681	2,681	2,681
17,900	17,950	2,689	2,689	2,689	2,689
17,950	18,000	2,696	2,696	2,696	2,696
18,000					
18,000	18,050	2,704	2,704	2,704	2,704
18,050	18,100	2,711	2,711	2,711	2,711
18,100	18,150	2,719	2,719	2,719	2,719
18,150	18,200	2,726	2,726	2,726	2,726
18,200	18,250	2,734	2,734	2,734	2,734
18,250	18,300	2,741	2,741	2,741	2,741
18,300	18,350	2,749	2,749	2,749	2,749
18,350	18,400	2,756	2,756	2,756	2,756
18,400	18,450	2,764	2,764	2,764	2,764
18,450	18,500	2,771	2,771	2,771	2,771
18,500	18,550	2,779	2,779	2,779	2,779
18,550	18,600	2,786	2,786	2,786	2,786
18,600	18,650	2,794	2,794	2,794	2,794
18,650	18,700	2,801	2,801	2,801	2,801
18,700	18,750	2,809	2,809	2,809	2,809
18,750	18,800	2,816	2,816	2,816	2,816
18,800	18,850	2,824	2,824	2,824	2,824
18,850	18,900	2,831	2,831	2,831	2,831
18,900	18,950	2,839	2,839	2,839	2,839
18,950	19,000	2,846	2,846	2,846	2,846
19,000					
19,000	19,050	2,854	2,854	2,854	2,854
19,050	19,100	2,861	2,861	2,861	2,861
19,100	19,150	2,869	2,869	2,869	2,869
19,150	19,200	2,876	2,876	2,876	2,876
19,200	19,250	2,884	2,884	2,884	2,884
19,250	19,300	2,891	2,891	2,891	2,891
19,300	19,350	2,899	2,899	2,899	2,899
19,350	19,400	2,906	2,906	2,906	2,906
19,400	19,450	2,914	2,914	2,914	2,914
19,450	19,500	2,921	2,921	2,921	2,921
19,500	19,550	2,929	2,929	2,929	2,929
19,550	19,600	2,936	2,936	2,936	2,936
19,600	19,650	2,944	2,944	2,944	2,944
19,650	19,700	2,951	2,951	2,951	2,951
19,700	19,750	2,959	2,959	2,959	2,959
19,750	19,800	2,966	2,966	2,966	2,966
19,800	19,850	2,974	2,974	2,974	2,974
19,850	19,900	2,981	2,981	2,981	2,981
19,900	19,950	2,989	2,989	2,989	2,989
19,950	20,000	2,996	2,996	2,996	2,996

If line 39 (taxable income) is— At least	But less than	And you are— Single	Married filing jointly *	Married filing separately	Head of a household
		Your tax is—			
20,000					
20,000	20,050	3,004	3,004	3,004	3,004
20,050	20,100	3,011	3,011	3,011	3,011
20,100	20,150	3,019	3,019	3,019	3,019
20,150	20,200	3,026	3,026	3,026	3,026
20,200	20,250	3,034	3,034	3,034	3,034
20,250	20,300	3,041	3,041	3,041	3,041
20,300	20,350	3,049	3,049	3,049	3,049
20,350	20,400	3,056	3,056	3,056	3,056
20,400	20,450	3,064	3,064	3,064	3,064
20,450	20,500	3,071	3,071	3,071	3,071
20,500	20,550	3,079	3,079	3,079	3,079
20,550	20,600	3,086	3,086	3,086	3,086
20,600	20,650	3,094	3,094	3,094	3,094
20,650	20,700	3,101	3,101	3,101	3,101
20,700	20,750	3,109	3,109	3,109	3,109
20,750	20,800	3,116	3,116	3,116	3,116
20,800	20,850	3,124	3,124	3,124	3,124
20,850	20,900	3,131	3,131	3,131	3,131
20,900	20,950	3,139	3,139	3,139	3,139
20,950	21,000	3,146	3,146	3,146	3,146
21,000					
21,000	21,050	3,154	3,154	3,154	3,154
21,050	21,100	3,161	3,161	3,161	3,161
21,100	21,150	3,169	3,169	3,169	3,169
21,150	21,200	3,176	3,176	3,176	3,176
21,200	21,250	3,184	3,184	3,184	3,184
21,250	21,300	3,191	3,191	3,191	3,191
21,300	21,350	3,199	3,199	3,199	3,199
21,350	21,400	3,206	3,206	3,206	3,206
21,400	21,450	3,214	3,214	3,214	3,214
21,450	21,500	3,221	3,221	3,221	3,221
21,500	21,550	3,229	3,229	3,229	3,229
21,550	21,600	3,236	3,236	3,236	3,236
21,600	21,650	3,244	3,244	3,244	3,244
21,650	21,700	3,251	3,251	3,251	3,251
21,700	21,750	3,259	3,259	3,259	3,259
21,750	21,800	3,266	3,266	3,266	3,266
21,800	21,850	3,274	3,274	3,274	3,274
21,850	21,900	3,281	3,281	3,281	3,281
21,900	21,950	3,289	3,289	3,289	3,289
21,950	22,000	3,296	3,296	3,296	3,296
22,000					
22,000	22,050	3,304	3,304	3,304	3,304
22,050	22,100	3,311	3,311	3,311	3,311
22,100	22,150	3,319	3,319	3,319	3,319
22,150	22,200	3,326	3,326	3,326	3,326
22,200	22,250	3,334	3,334	3,334	3,334
22,250	22,300	3,341	3,341	3,341	3,341
22,300	22,350	3,349	3,349	3,349	3,349
22,350	22,400	3,356	3,356	3,356	3,356
22,400	22,450	3,364	3,364	3,364	3,364
22,450	22,500	3,371	3,371	3,371	3,371
22,500	22,550	3,379	3,379	3,379	3,379
22,550	22,600	3,386	3,386	3,386	3,386
22,600	22,650	3,394	3,394	3,397	3,394
22,650	22,700	3,401	3,401	3,411	3,401
22,700	22,750	3,409	3,409	3,424	3,409
22,750	22,800	3,416	3,416	3,438	3,416
22,800	22,850	3,424	3,424	3,452	3,424
22,850	22,900	3,431	3,431	3,466	3,431
22,900	22,950	3,439	3,439	3,479	3,439
22,950	23,000	3,446	3,446	3,493	3,446

* This column must also be used by a qualifying widow(er).

(Continued on page 62)

2001 Tax Table—*Continued* **Caution.** Dependents, see the worksheet on page 33.

If line 39 (taxable income) is— At least	But less than	And you are— Single	Married filing jointly *	Married filing separately	Head of a household
		Your tax is—			
23,000					
23,000	23,050	3,454	3,454	3,507	3,454
23,050	23,100	3,461	3,461	3,521	3,461
23,100	23,150	3,469	3,469	3,534	3,469
23,150	23,200	3,476	3,476	3,548	3,476
23,200	23,250	3,484	3,484	3,562	3,484
23,250	23,300	3,491	3,491	3,576	3,491
23,300	23,350	3,499	3,499	3,589	3,499
23,350	23,400	3,506	3,506	3,603	3,506
23,400	23,450	3,514	3,514	3,617	3,514
23,450	23,500	3,521	3,521	3,631	3,521
23,500	23,550	3,529	3,529	3,644	3,529
23,550	23,600	3,536	3,536	3,658	3,536
23,600	23,650	3,544	3,544	3,672	3,544
23,650	23,700	3,551	3,551	3,686	3,551
23,700	23,750	3,559	3,559	3,699	3,559
23,750	23,800	3,566	3,566	3,713	3,566
23,800	23,850	3,574	3,574	3,727	3,574
23,850	23,900	3,581	3,581	3,741	3,581
23,900	23,950	3,589	3,589	3,754	3,589
23,950	24,000	3,596	3,596	3,768	3,596
24,000					
24,000	24,050	3,604	3,604	3,782	3,604
24,050	24,100	3,611	3,611	3,796	3,611
24,100	24,150	3,619	3,619	3,809	3,619
24,150	24,200	3,626	3,626	3,823	3,626
24,200	24,250	3,634	3,634	3,837	3,634
24,250	24,300	3,641	3,641	3,851	3,641
24,300	24,350	3,649	3,649	3,864	3,649
24,350	24,400	3,656	3,656	3,878	3,656
24,400	24,450	3,664	3,664	3,892	3,664
24,450	24,500	3,671	3,671	3,906	3,671
24,500	24,550	3,679	3,679	3,919	3,679
24,550	24,600	3,686	3,686	3,933	3,686
24,600	24,650	3,694	3,694	3,947	3,694
24,650	24,700	3,701	3,701	3,961	3,701
24,700	24,750	3,709	3,709	3,974	3,709
24,750	24,800	3,716	3,716	3,988	3,716
24,800	24,850	3,724	3,724	4,002	3,724
24,850	24,900	3,731	3,731	4,016	3,731
24,900	24,950	3,739	3,739	4,029	3,739
24,950	25,000	3,746	3,746	4,043	3,746
25,000					
25,000	25,050	3,754	3,754	4,057	3,754
25,050	25,100	3,761	3,761	4,071	3,761
25,100	25,150	3,769	3,769	4,084	3,769
25,150	25,200	3,776	3,776	4,098	3,776
25,200	25,250	3,784	3,784	4,112	3,784
25,250	25,300	3,791	3,791	4,126	3,791
25,300	25,350	3,799	3,799	4,139	3,799
25,350	25,400	3,806	3,806	4,153	3,806
25,400	25,450	3,814	3,814	4,167	3,814
25,450	25,500	3,821	3,821	4,181	3,821
25,500	25,550	3,829	3,829	4,194	3,829
25,550	25,600	3,836	3,836	4,208	3,836
25,600	25,650	3,844	3,844	4,222	3,844
25,650	25,700	3,851	3,851	4,236	3,851
25,700	25,750	3,859	3,859	4,249	3,859
25,750	25,800	3,866	3,866	4,263	3,866
25,800	25,850	3,874	3,874	4,277	3,874
25,850	25,900	3,881	3,881	4,291	3,881
25,900	25,950	3,889	3,889	4,304	3,889
25,950	26,000	3,896	3,896	4,318	3,896

If line 39 (taxable income) is— At least	But less than	And you are— Single	Married filing jointly *	Married filing separately	Head of a household
		Your tax is—			
26,000					
26,000	26,050	3,904	3,904	4,332	3,904
26,050	26,100	3,911	3,911	4,346	3,911
26,100	26,150	3,919	3,919	4,359	3,919
26,150	26,200	3,926	3,926	4,373	3,926
26,200	26,250	3,934	3,934	4,387	3,934
26,250	26,300	3,941	3,941	4,401	3,941
26,300	26,350	3,949	3,949	4,414	3,949
26,350	26,400	3,956	3,956	4,428	3,956
26,400	26,450	3,964	3,964	4,442	3,964
26,450	26,500	3,971	3,971	4,456	3,971
26,500	26,550	3,979	3,979	4,469	3,979
26,550	26,600	3,986	3,986	4,483	3,986
26,600	26,650	3,994	3,994	4,497	3,994
26,650	26,700	4,001	4,001	4,511	4,001
26,700	26,750	4,009	4,009	4,524	4,009
26,750	26,800	4,016	4,016	4,538	4,016
26,800	26,850	4,024	4,024	4,552	4,024
26,850	26,900	4,031	4,031	4,566	4,031
26,900	26,950	4,039	4,039	4,579	4,039
26,950	27,000	4,046	4,046	4,593	4,046
27,000					
27,000	27,050	4,054	4,054	4,607	4,054
27,050	27,100	4,064	4,061	4,621	4,061
27,100	27,150	4,078	4,069	4,634	4,069
27,150	27,200	4,092	4,076	4,648	4,076
27,200	27,250	4,106	4,084	4,662	4,084
27,250	27,300	4,119	4,091	4,676	4,091
27,300	27,350	4,133	4,099	4,689	4,099
27,350	27,400	4,147	4,106	4,703	4,106
27,400	27,450	4,161	4,114	4,717	4,114
27,450	27,500	4,174	4,121	4,731	4,121
27,500	27,550	4,188	4,129	4,744	4,129
27,550	27,600	4,202	4,136	4,758	4,136
27,600	27,650	4,216	4,144	4,772	4,144
27,650	27,700	4,229	4,151	4,786	4,151
27,700	27,750	4,243	4,159	4,799	4,159
27,750	27,800	4,257	4,166	4,813	4,166
27,800	27,850	4,271	4,174	4,827	4,174
27,850	27,900	4,284	4,181	4,841	4,181
27,900	27,950	4,298	4,189	4,854	4,189
27,950	28,000	4,312	4,196	4,868	4,196
28,000					
28,000	28,050	4,326	4,204	4,882	4,204
28,050	28,100	4,339	4,211	4,896	4,211
28,100	28,150	4,353	4,219	4,909	4,219
28,150	28,200	4,367	4,226	4,923	4,226
28,200	28,250	4,381	4,234	4,937	4,234
28,250	28,300	4,394	4,241	4,951	4,241
28,300	28,350	4,408	4,249	4,964	4,249
28,350	28,400	4,422	4,256	4,978	4,256
28,400	28,450	4,436	4,264	4,992	4,264
28,450	28,500	4,449	4,271	5,006	4,271
28,500	28,550	4,463	4,279	5,019	4,279
28,550	28,600	4,477	4,286	5,033	4,286
28,600	28,650	4,491	4,294	5,047	4,294
28,650	28,700	4,504	4,301	5,061	4,301
28,700	28,750	4,518	4,309	5,074	4,309
28,750	28,800	4,532	4,316	5,088	4,316
28,800	28,850	4,546	4,324	5,102	4,324
28,850	28,900	4,559	4,331	5,116	4,331
28,900	28,950	4,573	4,339	5,129	4,339
28,950	29,000	4,587	4,346	5,143	4,346

If line 39 (taxable income) is— At least	But less than	And you are— Single	Married filing jointly *	Married filing separately	Head of a household
		Your tax is—			
29,000					
29,000	29,050	4,601	4,354	5,157	4,354
29,050	29,100	4,614	4,361	5,171	4,361
29,100	29,150	4,628	4,369	5,184	4,369
29,150	29,200	4,642	4,376	5,198	4,376
29,200	29,250	4,656	4,384	5,212	4,384
29,250	29,300	4,669	4,391	5,226	4,391
29,300	29,350	4,683	4,399	5,239	4,399
29,350	29,400	4,697	4,406	5,253	4,406
29,400	29,450	4,711	4,414	5,267	4,414
29,450	29,500	4,724	4,421	5,281	4,421
29,500	29,550	4,738	4,429	5,294	4,429
29,550	29,600	4,752	4,436	5,308	4,436
29,600	29,650	4,766	4,444	5,322	4,444
29,650	29,700	4,779	4,451	5,336	4,451
29,700	29,750	4,793	4,459	5,349	4,459
29,750	29,800	4,807	4,466	5,363	4,466
29,800	29,850	4,821	4,474	5,377	4,474
29,850	29,900	4,834	4,481	5,391	4,481
29,900	29,950	4,848	4,489	5,404	4,489
29,950	30,000	4,862	4,496	5,418	4,496
30,000					
30,000	30,050	4,876	4,504	5,432	4,504
30,050	30,100	4,889	4,511	5,446	4,511
30,100	30,150	4,903	4,519	5,459	4,519
30,150	30,200	4,917	4,526	5,473	4,526
30,200	30,250	4,931	4,534	5,487	4,534
30,250	30,300	4,944	4,541	5,501	4,541
30,300	30,350	4,958	4,549	5,514	4,549
30,350	30,400	4,972	4,556	5,528	4,556
30,400	30,450	4,986	4,564	5,542	4,564
30,450	30,500	4,999	4,571	5,556	4,571
30,500	30,550	5,013	4,579	5,569	4,579
30,550	30,600	5,027	4,586	5,583	4,586
30,600	30,650	5,041	4,594	5,597	4,594
30,650	30,700	5,054	4,601	5,611	4,601
30,700	30,750	5,068	4,609	5,624	4,609
30,750	30,800	5,082	4,616	5,638	4,616
30,800	30,850	5,096	4,624	5,652	4,624
30,850	30,900	5,109	4,631	5,666	4,631
30,900	30,950	5,123	4,639	5,679	4,639
30,950	31,000	5,137	4,646	5,693	4,646
31,000					
31,000	31,050	5,151	4,654	5,707	4,654
31,050	31,100	5,164	4,661	5,721	4,661
31,100	31,150	5,178	4,669	5,734	4,669
31,150	31,200	5,192	4,676	5,748	4,676
31,200	31,250	5,206	4,684	5,762	4,684
31,250	31,300	5,219	4,691	5,776	4,691
31,300	31,350	5,233	4,699	5,789	4,699
31,350	31,400	5,247	4,706	5,803	4,706
31,400	31,450	5,261	4,714	5,817	4,714
31,450	31,500	5,274	4,721	5,831	4,721
31,500	31,550	5,288	4,729	5,844	4,729
31,550	31,600	5,302	4,736	5,858	4,736
31,600	31,650	5,316	4,744	5,872	4,744
31,650	31,700	5,329	4,751	5,886	4,751
31,700	31,750	5,343	4,759	5,899	4,759
31,750	31,800	5,357	4,766	5,913	4,766
31,800	31,850	5,371	4,774	5,927	4,774
31,850	31,900	5,384	4,781	5,941	4,781
31,900	31,950	5,398	4,789	5,954	4,789
31,950	32,000	5,412	4,796	5,968	4,796

* This column must also be used by a qualifying widow(er).

(Continued on page 63)

Caution. Dependents, see the worksheet on page 33. **2001 Tax Table—*Continued***

If line 39 (taxable income) is— At least	But less than	And you are— Single	Married filing jointly *	Married filing separately	Head of a household
		Your tax is—			
32,000					
32,000	32,050	5,426	4,804	5,982	4,804
32,050	32,100	5,439	4,811	5,996	4,811
32,100	32,150	5,453	4,819	6,009	4,819
32,150	32,200	5,467	4,826	6,023	4,826
32,200	32,250	5,481	4,834	6,037	4,834
32,250	32,300	5,494	4,841	6,051	4,841
32,300	32,350	5,508	4,849	6,064	4,849
32,350	32,400	5,522	4,856	6,078	4,856
32,400	32,450	5,536	4,864	6,092	4,864
32,450	32,500	5,549	4,871	6,106	4,871
32,500	32,550	5,563	4,879	6,119	4,879
32,550	32,600	5,577	4,886	6,133	4,886
32,600	32,650	5,591	4,894	6,147	4,894
32,650	32,700	5,604	4,901	6,161	4,901
32,700	32,750	5,618	4,909	6,174	4,909
32,750	32,800	5,632	4,916	6,188	4,916
32,800	32,850	5,646	4,924	6,202	4,924
32,850	32,900	5,659	4,931	6,216	4,931
32,900	32,950	5,673	4,939	6,229	4,939
32,950	33,000	5,687	4,946	6,243	4,946
33,000					
33,000	33,050	5,701	4,954	6,257	4,954
33,050	33,100	5,714	4,961	6,271	4,961
33,100	33,150	5,728	4,969	6,284	4,969
33,150	33,200	5,742	4,976	6,298	4,976
33,200	33,250	5,756	4,984	6,312	4,984
33,250	33,300	5,769	4,991	6,326	4,991
33,300	33,350	5,783	4,999	6,339	4,999
33,350	33,400	5,797	5,006	6,353	5,006
33,400	33,450	5,811	5,014	6,367	5,014
33,450	33,500	5,824	5,021	6,381	5,021
33,500	33,550	5,838	5,029	6,394	5,029
33,550	33,600	5,852	5,036	6,408	5,036
33,600	33,650	5,866	5,044	6,422	5,044
33,650	33,700	5,879	5,051	6,436	5,051
33,700	33,750	5,893	5,059	6,449	5,059
33,750	33,800	5,907	5,066	6,463	5,066
33,800	33,850	5,921	5,074	6,477	5,074
33,850	33,900	5,934	5,081	6,491	5,081
33,900	33,950	5,948	5,089	6,504	5,089
33,950	34,000	5,962	5,096	6,518	5,096
34,000					
34,000	34,050	5,976	5,104	6,532	5,104
34,050	34,100	5,989	5,111	6,546	5,111
34,100	34,150	6,003	5,119	6,559	5,119
34,150	34,200	6,017	5,126	6,573	5,126
34,200	34,250	6,031	5,134	6,587	5,134
34,250	34,300	6,044	5,141	6,601	5,141
34,300	34,350	6,058	5,149	6,614	5,149
34,350	34,400	6,072	5,156	6,628	5,156
34,400	34,450	6,086	5,164	6,642	5,164
34,450	34,500	6,099	5,171	6,656	5,171
34,500	34,550	6,113	5,179	6,669	5,179
34,550	34,600	6,127	5,186	6,683	5,186
34,600	34,650	6,141	5,194	6,697	5,194
34,650	34,700	6,154	5,201	6,711	5,201
34,700	34,750	6,168	5,209	6,724	5,209
34,750	34,800	6,182	5,216	6,738	5,216
34,800	34,850	6,196	5,224	6,752	5,224
34,850	34,900	6,209	5,231	6,766	5,231
34,900	34,950	6,223	5,239	6,779	5,239
34,950	35,000	6,237	5,246	6,793	5,246

If line 39 (taxable income) is— At least	But less than	And you are— Single	Married filing jointly *	Married filing separately	Head of a household
		Your tax is—			
35,000					
35,000	35,050	6,251	5,254	6,807	5,254
35,050	35,100	6,264	5,261	6,821	5,261
35,100	35,150	6,278	5,269	6,834	5,269
35,150	35,200	6,292	5,276	6,848	5,276
35,200	35,250	6,306	5,284	6,862	5,284
35,250	35,300	6,319	5,291	6,876	5,291
35,300	35,350	6,333	5,299	6,889	5,299
35,350	35,400	6,347	5,306	6,903	5,306
35,400	35,450	6,361	5,314	6,917	5,314
35,450	35,500	6,374	5,321	6,931	5,321
35,500	35,550	6,388	5,329	6,944	5,329
35,550	35,600	6,402	5,336	6,958	5,336
35,600	35,650	6,416	5,344	6,972	5,344
35,650	35,700	6,429	5,351	6,986	5,351
35,700	35,750	6,443	5,359	6,999	5,359
35,750	35,800	6,457	5,366	7,013	5,366
35,800	35,850	6,471	5,374	7,027	5,374
35,850	35,900	6,484	5,381	7,041	5,381
35,900	35,950	6,498	5,389	7,054	5,389
35,950	36,000	6,512	5,396	7,068	5,396
36,000					
36,000	36,050	6,526	5,404	7,082	5,404
36,050	36,100	6,539	5,411	7,096	5,411
36,100	36,150	6,553	5,419	7,109	5,419
36,150	36,200	6,567	5,426	7,123	5,426
36,200	36,250	6,581	5,434	7,137	5,434
36,250	36,300	6,594	5,441	7,151	5,444
36,300	36,350	6,608	5,449	7,164	5,458
36,350	36,400	6,622	5,456	7,178	5,472
36,400	36,450	6,636	5,464	7,192	5,486
36,450	36,500	6,649	5,471	7,206	5,499
36,500	36,550	6,663	5,479	7,219	5,513
36,550	36,600	6,677	5,486	7,233	5,527
36,600	36,650	6,691	5,494	7,247	5,541
36,650	36,700	6,704	5,501	7,261	5,554
36,700	36,750	6,718	5,509	7,274	5,568
36,750	36,800	6,732	5,516	7,288	5,582
36,800	36,850	6,746	5,524	7,302	5,596
36,850	36,900	6,759	5,531	7,316	5,609
36,900	36,950	6,773	5,539	7,329	5,623
36,950	37,000	6,787	5,546	7,343	5,637
37,000					
37,000	37,050	6,801	5,554	7,357	5,651
37,050	37,100	6,814	5,561	7,371	5,664
37,100	37,150	6,828	5,569	7,384	5,678
37,150	37,200	6,842	5,576	7,398	5,692
37,200	37,250	6,856	5,584	7,412	5,706
37,250	37,300	6,869	5,591	7,426	5,719
37,300	37,350	6,883	5,599	7,439	5,733
37,350	37,400	6,897	5,606	7,453	5,747
37,400	37,450	6,911	5,614	7,467	5,761
37,450	37,500	6,924	5,621	7,481	5,774
37,500	37,550	6,938	5,629	7,494	5,788
37,550	37,600	6,952	5,636	7,508	5,802
37,600	37,650	6,966	5,644	7,522	5,816
37,650	37,700	6,979	5,651	7,536	5,829
37,700	37,750	6,993	5,659	7,549	5,843
37,750	37,800	7,007	5,666	7,563	5,857
37,800	37,850	7,021	5,674	7,577	5,871
37,850	37,900	7,034	5,681	7,591	5,884
37,900	37,950	7,048	5,689	7,604	5,898
37,950	38,000	7,062	5,696	7,618	5,912

If line 39 (taxable income) is— At least	But less than	And you are— Single	Married filing jointly *	Married filing separately	Head of a household
		Your tax is—			
38,000					
38,000	38,050	7,076	5,704	7,632	5,926
38,050	38,100	7,089	5,711	7,646	5,939
38,100	38,150	7,103	5,719	7,659	5,953
38,150	38,200	7,117	5,726	7,673	5,967
38,200	38,250	7,131	5,734	7,687	5,981
38,250	38,300	7,144	5,741	7,701	5,994
38,300	38,350	7,158	5,749	7,714	6,008
38,350	38,400	7,172	5,756	7,728	6,022
38,400	38,450	7,186	5,764	7,742	6,036
38,450	38,500	7,199	5,771	7,756	6,049
38,500	38,550	7,213	5,779	7,769	6,063
38,550	38,600	7,227	5,786	7,783	6,077
38,600	38,650	7,241	5,794	7,797	6,091
38,650	38,700	7,254	5,801	7,811	6,104
38,700	38,750	7,268	5,809	7,824	6,118
38,750	38,800	7,282	5,816	7,838	6,132
38,800	38,850	7,296	5,824	7,852	6,146
38,850	38,900	7,309	5,831	7,866	6,159
38,900	38,950	7,323	5,839	7,879	6,173
38,950	39,000	7,337	5,846	7,893	6,187
39,000					
39,000	39,050	7,351	5,854	7,907	6,201
39,050	39,100	7,364	5,861	7,921	6,214
39,100	39,150	7,378	5,869	7,934	6,228
39,150	39,200	7,392	5,876	7,948	6,242
39,200	39,250	7,406	5,884	7,962	6,256
39,250	39,300	7,419	5,891	7,976	6,269
39,300	39,350	7,433	5,899	7,989	6,283
39,350	39,400	7,447	5,906	8,003	6,297
39,400	39,450	7,461	5,914	8,017	6,311
39,450	39,500	7,474	5,921	8,031	6,324
39,500	39,550	7,488	5,929	8,044	6,338
39,550	39,600	7,502	5,936	8,058	6,352
39,600	39,650	7,516	5,944	8,072	6,366
39,650	39,700	7,529	5,951	8,086	6,379
39,700	39,750	7,543	5,959	8,099	6,393
39,750	39,800	7,557	5,966	8,113	6,407
39,800	39,850	7,571	5,974	8,127	6,421
39,850	39,900	7,584	5,981	8,141	6,434
39,900	39,950	7,598	5,989	8,154	6,448
39,950	40,000	7,612	5,996	8,168	6,462
40,000					
40,000	40,050	7,626	6,004	8,182	6,476
40,050	40,100	7,639	6,011	8,196	6,489
40,100	40,150	7,653	6,019	8,209	6,503
40,150	40,200	7,667	6,026	8,223	6,517
40,200	40,250	7,681	6,034	8,237	6,531
40,250	40,300	7,694	6,041	8,251	6,544
40,300	40,350	7,708	6,049	8,264	6,558
40,350	40,400	7,722	6,056	8,278	6,572
40,400	40,450	7,736	6,064	8,292	6,586
40,450	40,500	7,749	6,071	8,306	6,599
40,500	40,550	7,763	6,079	8,319	6,613
40,550	40,600	7,777	6,086	8,333	6,627
40,600	40,650	7,791	6,094	8,347	6,641
40,650	40,700	7,804	6,101	8,361	6,654
40,700	40,750	7,818	6,109	8,374	6,668
40,750	40,800	7,832	6,116	8,388	6,682
40,800	40,850	7,846	6,124	8,402	6,696
40,850	40,900	7,859	6,131	8,416	6,709
40,900	40,950	7,873	6,139	8,429	6,723
40,950	41,000	7,887	6,146	8,443	6,737

* This column must also be used by a qualifying widow(er).

(Continued on page 64)

2001 Tax Table—*Continued* **Caution.** Dependents, see the worksheet on page 33.

If line 39 (taxable income) is— At least	But less than	And you are— Single	Married filing jointly *	Married filing separately	Head of a household
		Your tax is—			
41,000					
41,000	**41,050**	7,901	6,154	8,457	6,751
41,050	**41,100**	7,914	6,161	8,471	6,764
41,100	**41,150**	7,928	6,169	8,484	6,778
41,150	**41,200**	7,942	6,176	8,498	6,792
41,200	**41,250**	7,956	6,184	8,512	6,806
41,250	**41,300**	7,969	6,191	8,526	6,819
41,300	**41,350**	7,983	6,199	8,539	6,833
41,350	**41,400**	7,997	6,206	8,553	6,847
41,400	**41,450**	8,011	6,214	8,567	6,861
41,450	**41,500**	8,024	6,221	8,581	6,874
41,500	**41,550**	8,038	6,229	8,594	6,888
41,550	**41,600**	8,052	6,236	8,608	6,902
41,600	**41,650**	8,066	6,244	8,622	6,916
41,650	**41,700**	8,079	6,251	8,636	6,929
41,700	**41,750**	8,093	6,259	8,649	6,943
41,750	**41,800**	8,107	6,266	8,663	6,957
41,800	**41,850**	8,121	6,274	8,677	6,971
41,850	**41,900**	8,134	6,281	8,691	6,984
41,900	**41,950**	8,148	6,289	8,704	6,998
41,950	**42,000**	8,162	6,296	8,718	7,012
42,000					
42,000	**42,050**	8,176	6,304	8,732	7,026
42,050	**42,100**	8,189	6,311	8,746	7,039
42,100	**42,150**	8,203	6,319	8,759	7,053
42,150	**42,200**	8,217	6,326	8,773	7,067
42,200	**42,250**	8,231	6,334	8,787	7,081
42,250	**42,300**	8,244	6,341	8,801	7,094
42,300	**42,350**	8,258	6,349	8,814	7,108
42,350	**42,400**	8,272	6,356	8,828	7,122
42,400	**42,450**	8,286	6,364	8,842	7,136
42,450	**42,500**	8,299	6,371	8,856	7,149
42,500	**42,550**	8,313	6,379	8,869	7,163
42,550	**42,600**	8,327	6,386	8,883	7,177
42,600	**42,650**	8,341	6,394	8,897	7,191
42,650	**42,700**	8,354	6,401	8,911	7,204
42,700	**42,750**	8,368	6,409	8,924	7,218
42,750	**42,800**	8,382	6,416	8,938	7,232
42,800	**42,850**	8,396	6,424	8,952	7,246
42,850	**42,900**	8,409	6,431	8,966	7,259
42,900	**42,950**	8,423	6,439	8,979	7,273
42,950	**43,000**	8,437	6,446	8,993	7,287
43,000					
43,000	**43,050**	8,451	6,454	9,007	7,301
43,050	**43,100**	8,464	6,461	9,021	7,314
43,100	**43,150**	8,478	6,469	9,034	7,328
43,150	**43,200**	8,492	6,476	9,048	7,342
43,200	**43,250**	8,506	6,484	9,062	7,356
43,250	**43,300**	8,519	6,491	9,076	7,369
43,300	**43,350**	8,533	6,499	9,089	7,383
43,350	**43,400**	8,547	6,506	9,103	7,397
43,400	**43,450**	8,561	6,514	9,117	7,411
43,450	**43,500**	8,574	6,521	9,131	7,424
43,500	**43,550**	8,588	6,529	9,144	7,438
43,550	**43,600**	8,602	6,536	9,158	7,452
43,600	**43,650**	8,616	6,544	9,172	7,466
43,650	**43,700**	8,629	6,551	9,186	7,479
43,700	**43,750**	8,643	6,559	9,199	7,493
43,750	**43,800**	8,657	6,566	9,213	7,507
43,800	**43,850**	8,671	6,574	9,227	7,521
43,850	**43,900**	8,684	6,581	9,241	7,534
43,900	**43,950**	8,698	6,589	9,254	7,548
43,950	**44,000**	8,712	6,596	9,268	7,562
44,000					
44,000	**44,050**	8,726	6,604	9,282	7,576
44,050	**44,100**	8,739	6,611	9,296	7,589
44,100	**44,150**	8,753	6,619	9,309	7,603
44,150	**44,200**	8,767	6,626	9,323	7,617
44,200	**44,250**	8,781	6,634	9,337	7,631
44,250	**44,300**	8,794	6,641	9,351	7,644
44,300	**44,350**	8,808	6,649	9,364	7,658
44,350	**44,400**	8,822	6,656	9,378	7,672
44,400	**44,450**	8,836	6,664	9,392	7,686
44,450	**44,500**	8,849	6,671	9,406	7,699
44,500	**44,550**	8,863	6,679	9,419	7,713
44,550	**44,600**	8,877	6,686	9,433	7,727
44,600	**44,650**	8,891	6,694	9,447	7,741
44,650	**44,700**	8,904	6,701	9,461	7,754
44,700	**44,750**	8,918	6,709	9,474	7,768
44,750	**44,800**	8,932	6,716	9,488	7,782
44,800	**44,850**	8,946	6,724	9,502	7,796
44,850	**44,900**	8,959	6,731	9,516	7,809
44,900	**44,950**	8,973	6,739	9,529	7,823
44,950	**45,000**	8,987	6,746	9,543	7,837
45,000					
45,000	**45,050**	9,001	6,754	9,557	7,851
45,050	**45,100**	9,014	6,761	9,571	7,864
45,100	**45,150**	9,028	6,769	9,584	7,878
45,150	**45,200**	9,042	6,776	9,598	7,892
45,200	**45,250**	9,056	6,787	9,612	7,906
45,250	**45,300**	9,069	6,801	9,626	7,919
45,300	**45,350**	9,083	6,814	9,639	7,933
45,350	**45,400**	9,097	6,828	9,653	7,947
45,400	**45,450**	9,111	6,842	9,667	7,961
45,450	**45,500**	9,124	6,856	9,681	7,974
45,500	**45,550**	9,138	6,869	9,694	7,988
45,550	**45,600**	9,152	6,883	9,708	8,002
45,600	**45,650**	9,166	6,897	9,722	8,016
45,650	**45,700**	9,179	6,911	9,736	8,029
45,700	**45,750**	9,193	6,924	9,749	8,043
45,750	**45,800**	9,207	6,938	9,763	8,057
45,800	**45,850**	9,221	6,952	9,777	8,071
45,850	**45,900**	9,234	6,966	9,791	8,084
45,900	**45,950**	9,248	6,979	9,804	8,098
45,950	**46,000**	9,262	6,993	9,818	8,112
46,000					
46,000	**46,050**	9,276	7,007	9,832	8,126
46,050	**46,100**	9,289	7,021	9,846	8,139
46,100	**46,150**	9,303	7,034	9,859	8,153
46,150	**46,200**	9,317	7,048	9,873	8,167
46,200	**46,250**	9,331	7,062	9,887	8,181
46,250	**46,300**	9,344	7,076	9,901	8,194
46,300	**46,350**	9,358	7,089	9,914	8,208
46,350	**46,400**	9,372	7,103	9,928	8,222
46,400	**46,450**	9,386	7,117	9,942	8,236
46,450	**46,500**	9,399	7,131	9,956	8,249
46,500	**46,550**	9,413	7,144	9,969	8,263
46,550	**46,600**	9,427	7,158	9,983	8,277
46,600	**46,650**	9,441	7,172	9,997	8,291
46,650	**46,700**	9,454	7,186	10,011	8,304
46,700	**46,750**	9,468	7,199	10,024	8,318
46,750	**46,800**	9,482	7,213	10,038	8,332
46,800	**46,850**	9,496	7,227	10,052	8,346
46,850	**46,900**	9,509	7,241	10,066	8,359
46,900	**46,950**	9,523	7,254	10,079	8,373
46,950	**47,000**	9,537	7,268	10,093	8,387
47,000					
47,000	**47,050**	9,551	7,282	10,107	8,401
47,050	**47,100**	9,564	7,296	10,121	8,414
47,100	**47,150**	9,578	7,309	10,134	8,428
47,150	**47,200**	9,592	7,323	10,148	8,442
47,200	**47,250**	9,606	7,337	10,162	8,456
47,250	**47,300**	9,619	7,351	10,176	8,469
47,300	**47,350**	9,633	7,364	10,189	8,483
47,350	**47,400**	9,647	7,378	10,203	8,497
47,400	**47,450**	9,661	7,392	10,217	8,511
47,450	**47,500**	9,674	7,406	10,231	8,524
47,500	**47,550**	9,688	7,419	10,244	8,538
47,550	**47,600**	9,702	7,433	10,258	8,552
47,600	**47,650**	9,716	7,447	10,272	8,566
47,650	**47,700**	9,729	7,461	10,286	8,579
47,700	**47,750**	9,743	7,474	10,299	8,593
47,750	**47,800**	9,757	7,488	10,313	8,607
47,800	**47,850**	9,771	7,502	10,327	8,621
47,850	**47,900**	9,784	7,516	10,341	8,634
47,900	**47,950**	9,798	7,529	10,354	8,648
47,950	**48,000**	9,812	7,543	10,368	8,662
48,000					
48,000	**48,050**	9,826	7,557	10,382	8,676
48,050	**48,100**	9,839	7,571	10,396	8,689
48,100	**48,150**	9,853	7,584	10,409	8,703
48,150	**48,200**	9,867	7,598	10,423	8,717
48,200	**48,250**	9,881	7,612	10,437	8,731
48,250	**48,300**	9,894	7,626	10,451	8,744
48,300	**48,350**	9,908	7,639	10,464	8,758
48,350	**48,400**	9,922	7,653	10,478	8,772
48,400	**48,450**	9,936	7,667	10,492	8,786
48,450	**48,500**	9,949	7,681	10,506	8,799
48,500	**48,550**	9,963	7,694	10,519	8,813
48,550	**48,600**	9,977	7,708	10,533	8,827
48,600	**48,650**	9,991	7,722	10,547	8,841
48,650	**48,700**	10,004	7,736	10,561	8,854
48,700	**48,750**	10,018	7,749	10,574	8,868
48,750	**48,800**	10,032	7,763	10,588	8,882
48,800	**48,850**	10,046	7,777	10,602	8,896
48,850	**48,900**	10,059	7,791	10,616	8,909
48,900	**48,950**	10,073	7,804	10,629	8,923
48,950	**49,000**	10,087	7,818	10,643	8,937
49,000					
49,000	**49,050**	10,101	7,832	10,657	8,951
49,050	**49,100**	10,114	7,846	10,671	8,964
49,100	**49,150**	10,128	7,859	10,684	8,978
49,150	**49,200**	10,142	7,873	10,698	8,992
49,200	**49,250**	10,156	7,887	10,712	9,006
49,250	**49,300**	10,169	7,901	10,726	9,019
49,300	**49,350**	10,183	7,914	10,739	9,033
49,350	**49,400**	10,197	7,928	10,753	9,047
49,400	**49,450**	10,211	7,942	10,767	9,061
49,450	**49,500**	10,224	7,956	10,781	9,074
49,500	**49,550**	10,238	7,969	10,794	9,088
49,550	**49,600**	10,252	7,983	10,808	9,102
49,600	**49,650**	10,266	7,997	10,822	9,116
49,650	**49,700**	10,279	8,011	10,836	9,129
49,700	**49,750**	10,293	8,024	10,849	9,143
49,750	**49,800**	10,307	8,038	10,863	9,157
49,800	**49,850**	10,321	8,052	10,877	9,171
49,850	**49,900**	10,334	8,066	10,891	9,184
49,900	**49,950**	10,348	8,079	10,904	9,198
49,950	**50,000**	10,362	8,093	10,918	9,212

* This column must also be used by a qualifying widow(er).

(Continued on page 65)

Caution. Dependents, see the worksheet on page 33. **2001 Tax Table—*Continued***

If line 39 (taxable income) is— At least	But less than	And you are— Single	Married filing jointly *	Married filing sepa-rately	Head of a house-hold
		Your tax is—			
50,000					
50,000	50,050	10,376	8,107	10,932	9,226
50,050	50,100	10,389	8,121	10,946	9,239
50,100	50,150	10,403	8,134	10,959	9,253
50,150	50,200	10,417	8,148	10,973	9,267
50,200	50,250	10,431	8,162	10,987	9,281
50,250	50,300	10,444	8,176	11,001	9,294
50,300	50,350	10,458	8,189	11,014	9,308
50,350	50,400	10,472	8,203	11,028	9,322
50,400	50,450	10,486	8,217	11,042	9,336
50,450	50,500	10,499	8,231	11,056	9,349
50,500	50,550	10,513	8,244	11,069	9,363
50,550	50,600	10,527	8,258	11,083	9,377
50,600	50,650	10,541	8,272	11,097	9,391
50,650	50,700	10,554	8,286	11,111	9,404
50,700	50,750	10,568	8,299	11,124	9,418
50,750	50,800	10,582	8,313	11,138	9,432
50,800	50,850	10,596	8,327	11,152	9,446
50,850	50,900	10,609	8,341	11,166	9,459
50,900	50,950	10,623	8,354	11,179	9,473
50,950	51,000	10,637	8,368	11,193	9,487
51,000					
51,000	51,050	10,651	8,382	11,207	9,501
51,050	51,100	10,664	8,396	11,221	9,514
51,100	51,150	10,678	8,409	11,234	9,528
51,150	51,200	10,692	8,423	11,248	9,542
51,200	51,250	10,706	8,437	11,262	9,556
51,250	51,300	10,719	8,451	11,276	9,569
51,300	51,350	10,733	8,464	11,289	9,583
51,350	51,400	10,747	8,478	11,303	9,597
51,400	51,450	10,761	8,492	11,317	9,611
51,450	51,500	10,774	8,506	11,331	9,624
51,500	51,550	10,788	8,519	11,344	9,638
51,550	51,600	10,802	8,533	11,358	9,652
51,600	51,650	10,816	8,547	11,372	9,666
51,650	51,700	10,829	8,561	11,386	9,679
51,700	51,750	10,843	8,574	11,399	9,693
51,750	51,800	10,857	8,588	11,413	9,707
51,800	51,850	10,871	8,602	11,427	9,721
51,850	51,900	10,884	8,616	11,441	9,734
51,900	51,950	10,898	8,629	11,454	9,748
51,950	52,000	10,912	8,643	11,468	9,762
52,000					
52,000	52,050	10,926	8,657	11,482	9,776
52,050	52,100	10,939	8,671	11,496	9,789
52,100	52,150	10,953	8,684	11,509	9,803
52,150	52,200	10,967	8,698	11,523	9,817
52,200	52,250	10,981	8,712	11,537	9,831
52,250	52,300	10,994	8,726	11,551	9,844
52,300	52,350	11,008	8,739	11,564	9,858
52,350	52,400	11,022	8,753	11,578	9,872
52,400	52,450	11,036	8,767	11,592	9,886
52,450	52,500	11,049	8,781	11,606	9,899
52,500	52,550	11,063	8,794	11,619	9,913
52,550	52,600	11,077	8,808	11,633	9,927
52,600	52,650	11,091	8,822	11,647	9,941
52,650	52,700	11,104	8,836	11,661	9,954
52,700	52,750	11,118	8,849	11,674	9,968
52,750	52,800	11,132	8,863	11,688	9,982
52,800	52,850	11,146	8,877	11,702	9,996
52,850	52,900	11,159	8,891	11,716	10,009
52,900	52,950	11,173	8,904	11,729	10,023
52,950	53,000	11,187	8,918	11,743	10,037
53,000					
53,000	53,050	11,201	8,932	11,757	10,051
53,050	53,100	11,214	8,946	11,771	10,064
53,100	53,150	11,228	8,959	11,784	10,078
53,150	53,200	11,242	8,973	11,798	10,092
53,200	53,250	11,256	8,987	11,812	10,106
53,250	53,300	11,269	9,001	11,826	10,119
53,300	53,350	11,283	9,014	11,839	10,133
53,350	53,400	11,297	9,028	11,853	10,147
53,400	53,450	11,311	9,042	11,867	10,161
53,450	53,500	11,324	9,056	11,881	10,174
53,500	53,550	11,338	9,069	11,894	10,188
53,550	53,600	11,352	9,083	11,908	10,202
53,600	53,650	11,366	9,097	11,922	10,216
53,650	53,700	11,379	9,111	11,936	10,229
53,700	53,750	11,393	9,124	11,949	10,243
53,750	53,800	11,407	9,138	11,963	10,257
53,800	53,850	11,421	9,152	11,977	10,271
53,850	53,900	11,434	9,166	11,991	10,284
53,900	53,950	11,448	9,179	12,004	10,298
53,950	54,000	11,462	9,193	12,018	10,312
54,000					
54,000	54,050	11,476	9,207	12,032	10,326
54,050	54,100	11,489	9,221	12,046	10,339
54,100	54,150	11,503	9,234	12,059	10,353
54,150	54,200	11,517	9,248	12,073	10,367
54,200	54,250	11,531	9,262	12,087	10,381
54,250	54,300	11,544	9,276	12,101	10,394
54,300	54,350	11,558	9,289	12,114	10,408
54,350	54,400	11,572	9,303	12,128	10,422
54,400	54,450	11,586	9,317	12,142	10,436
54,450	54,500	11,599	9,331	12,156	10,449
54,500	54,550	11,613	9,344	12,169	10,463
54,550	54,600	11,627	9,358	12,183	10,477
54,600	54,650	11,641	9,372	12,197	10,491
54,650	54,700	11,654	9,386	12,212	10,504
54,700	54,750	11,668	9,399	12,227	10,518
54,750	54,800	11,682	9,413	12,243	10,532
54,800	54,850	11,696	9,427	12,258	10,546
54,850	54,900	11,709	9,441	12,273	10,559
54,900	54,950	11,723	9,454	12,288	10,573
54,950	55,000	11,737	9,468	12,304	10,587
55,000					
55,000	55,050	11,751	9,482	12,319	10,601
55,050	55,100	11,764	9,496	12,334	10,614
55,100	55,150	11,778	9,509	12,349	10,628
55,150	55,200	11,792	9,523	12,365	10,642
55,200	55,250	11,806	9,537	12,380	10,656
55,250	55,300	11,819	9,551	12,395	10,669
55,300	55,350	11,833	9,564	12,410	10,683
55,350	55,400	11,847	9,578	12,426	10,697
55,400	55,450	11,861	9,592	12,441	10,711
55,450	55,500	11,874	9,606	12,456	10,724
55,500	55,550	11,888	9,619	12,471	10,738
55,550	55,600	11,902	9,633	12,487	10,752
55,600	55,650	11,916	9,647	12,502	10,766
55,650	55,700	11,929	9,661	12,517	10,779
55,700	55,750	11,943	9,674	12,532	10,793
55,750	55,800	11,957	9,688	12,548	10,807
55,800	55,850	11,971	9,702	12,563	10,821
55,850	55,900	11,984	9,716	12,578	10,834
55,900	55,950	11,998	9,729	12,593	10,848
55,950	56,000	12,012	9,743	12,609	10,862
56,000					
56,000	56,050	12,026	9,757	12,624	10,876
56,050	56,100	12,039	9,771	12,639	10,889
56,100	56,150	12,053	9,784	12,654	10,903
56,150	56,200	12,067	9,798	12,670	10,917
56,200	56,250	12,081	9,812	12,685	10,931
56,250	56,300	12,094	9,826	12,700	10,944
56,300	56,350	12,108	9,839	12,715	10,958
56,350	56,400	12,122	9,853	12,731	10,972
56,400	56,450	12,136	9,867	12,746	10,986
56,450	56,500	12,149	9,881	12,761	10,999
56,500	56,550	12,163	9,894	12,776	11,013
56,550	56,600	12,177	9,908	12,792	11,027
56,600	56,650	12,191	9,922	12,807	11,041
56,650	56,700	12,204	9,936	12,822	11,054
56,700	56,750	12,218	9,949	12,837	11,068
56,750	56,800	12,232	9,963	12,853	11,082
56,800	56,850	12,246	9,977	12,868	11,096
56,850	56,900	12,259	9,991	12,883	11,109
56,900	56,950	12,273	10,004	12,898	11,123
56,950	57,000	12,287	10,018	12,914	11,137
57,000					
57,000	57,050	12,301	10,032	12,929	11,151
57,050	57,100	12,314	10,046	12,944	11,164
57,100	57,150	12,328	10,059	12,959	11,178
57,150	57,200	12,342	10,073	12,975	11,192
57,200	57,250	12,356	10,087	12,990	11,206
57,250	57,300	12,369	10,101	13,005	11,219
57,300	57,350	12,383	10,114	13,020	11,233
57,350	57,400	12,397	10,128	13,036	11,247
57,400	57,450	12,411	10,142	13,051	11,261
57,450	57,500	12,424	10,156	13,066	11,274
57,500	57,550	12,438	10,169	13,081	11,288
57,550	57,600	12,452	10,183	13,097	11,302
57,600	57,650	12,466	10,197	13,112	11,316
57,650	57,700	12,479	10,211	13,127	11,329
57,700	57,750	12,493	10,224	13,142	11,343
57,750	57,800	12,507	10,238	13,158	11,357
57,800	57,850	12,521	10,252	13,173	11,371
57,850	57,900	12,534	10,266	13,188	11,384
57,900	57,950	12,548	10,279	13,203	11,398
57,950	58,000	12,562	10,293	13,219	11,412
58,000					
58,000	58,050	12,576	10,307	13,234	11,426
58,050	58,100	12,589	10,321	13,249	11,439
58,100	58,150	12,603	10,334	13,264	11,453
58,150	58,200	12,617	10,348	13,280	11,467
58,200	58,250	12,631	10,362	13,295	11,481
58,250	58,300	12,644	10,376	13,310	11,494
58,300	58,350	12,658	10,389	13,325	11,508
58,350	58,400	12,672	10,403	13,341	11,522
58,400	58,450	12,686	10,417	13,356	11,536
58,450	58,500	12,699	10,431	13,371	11,549
58,500	58,550	12,713	10,444	13,386	11,563
58,550	58,600	12,727	10,458	13,402	11,577
58,600	58,650	12,741	10,472	13,417	11,591
58,650	58,700	12,754	10,486	13,432	11,604
58,700	58,750	12,768	10,499	13,447	11,618
58,750	58,800	12,782	10,513	13,463	11,632
58,800	58,850	12,796	10,527	13,478	11,646
58,850	58,900	12,809	10,541	13,493	11,659
58,900	58,950	12,823	10,554	13,508	11,673
58,950	59,000	12,837	10,568	13,524	11,687

* This column must also be used by a qualifying widow(er).

(Continued on page 66)

2001 Tax Table—*Continued* **Caution.** Dependents, see the worksheet on page 33.

59,000

If line 39 (taxable income) is— At least	But less than	And you are— Single	Married filing jointly *	Married filing separately	Head of a household
		Your tax is—			
59,000	**59,050**	12,851	10,582	13,539	11,701
59,050	**59,100**	12,864	10,596	13,554	11,714
59,100	**59,150**	12,878	10,609	13,569	11,728
59,150	**59,200**	12,892	10,623	13,585	11,742
59,200	**59,250**	12,906	10,637	13,600	11,756
59,250	**59,300**	12,919	10,651	13,615	11,769
59,300	**59,350**	12,933	10,664	13,630	11,783
59,350	**59,400**	12,947	10,678	13,646	11,797
59,400	**59,450**	12,961	10,692	13,661	11,811
59,450	**59,500**	12,974	10,706	13,676	11,824
59,500	**59,550**	12,988	10,719	13,691	11,838
59,550	**59,600**	13,002	10,733	13,707	11,852
59,600	**59,650**	13,016	10,747	13,722	11,866
59,650	**59,700**	13,029	10,761	13,737	11,879
59,700	**59,750**	13,043	10,774	13,752	11,893
59,750	**59,800**	13,057	10,788	13,768	11,907
59,800	**59,850**	13,071	10,802	13,783	11,921
59,850	**59,900**	13,084	10,816	13,798	11,934
59,900	**59,950**	13,098	10,829	13,813	11,948
59,950	**60,000**	13,112	10,843	13,829	11,962

60,000

At least	But less than	Single	Married filing jointly *	Married filing separately	Head of a household
60,000	**60,050**	13,126	10,857	13,844	11,976
60,050	**60,100**	13,139	10,871	13,859	11,989
60,100	**60,150**	13,153	10,884	13,874	12,003
60,150	**60,200**	13,167	10,898	13,890	12,017
60,200	**60,250**	13,181	10,912	13,905	12,031
60,250	**60,300**	13,194	10,926	13,920	12,044
60,300	**60,350**	13,208	10,939	13,935	12,058
60,350	**60,400**	13,222	10,953	13,951	12,072
60,400	**60,450**	13,236	10,967	13,966	12,086
60,450	**60,500**	13,249	10,981	13,981	12,099
60,500	**60,550**	13,263	10,994	13,996	12,113
60,550	**60,600**	13,277	11,008	14,012	12,127
60,600	**60,650**	13,291	11,022	14,027	12,141
60,650	**60,700**	13,304	11,036	14,042	12,154
60,700	**60,750**	13,318	11,049	14,057	12,168
60,750	**60,800**	13,332	11,063	14,073	12,182
60,800	**60,850**	13,346	11,077	14,088	12,196
60,850	**60,900**	13,359	11,091	14,103	12,209
60,900	**60,950**	13,373	11,104	14,118	12,223
60,950	**61,000**	13,387	11,118	14,134	12,237

61,000

At least	But less than	Single	Married filing jointly *	Married filing separately	Head of a household
61,000	**61,050**	13,401	11,132	14,149	12,251
61,050	**61,100**	13,414	11,146	14,164	12,264
61,100	**61,150**	13,428	11,159	14,179	12,278
61,150	**61,200**	13,442	11,173	14,195	12,292
61,200	**61,250**	13,456	11,187	14,210	12,306
61,250	**61,300**	13,469	11,201	14,225	12,319
61,300	**61,350**	13,483	11,214	14,240	12,333
61,350	**61,400**	13,497	11,228	14,256	12,347
61,400	**61,450**	13,511	11,242	14,271	12,361
61,450	**61,500**	13,524	11,256	14,286	12,374
61,500	**61,550**	13,538	11,269	14,301	12,388
61,550	**61,600**	13,552	11,283	14,317	12,402
61,600	**61,650**	13,566	11,297	14,332	12,416
61,650	**61,700**	13,579	11,311	14,347	12,429
61,700	**61,750**	13,593	11,324	14,362	12,443
61,750	**61,800**	13,607	11,338	14,378	12,457
61,800	**61,850**	13,621	11,352	14,393	12,471
61,850	**61,900**	13,634	11,366	14,408	12,484
61,900	**61,950**	13,648	11,379	14,423	12,498
61,950	**62,000**	13,662	11,393	14,439	12,512

62,000

At least	But less than	Single	Married filing jointly *	Married filing separately	Head of a household
62,000	**62,050**	13,676	11,407	14,454	12,526
62,050	**62,100**	13,689	11,421	14,469	12,539
62,100	**62,150**	13,703	11,434	14,484	12,553
62,150	**62,200**	13,717	11,448	14,500	12,567
62,200	**62,250**	13,731	11,462	14,515	12,581
62,250	**62,300**	13,744	11,476	14,530	12,594
62,300	**62,350**	13,758	11,489	14,545	12,608
62,350	**62,400**	13,772	11,503	14,561	12,622
62,400	**62,450**	13,786	11,517	14,576	12,636
62,450	**62,500**	13,799	11,531	14,591	12,649
62,500	**62,550**	13,813	11,544	14,606	12,663
62,550	**62,600**	13,827	11,558	14,622	12,677
62,600	**62,650**	13,841	11,572	14,637	12,691
62,650	**62,700**	13,854	11,586	14,652	12,704
62,700	**62,750**	13,868	11,599	14,667	12,718
62,750	**62,800**	13,882	11,613	14,683	12,732
62,800	**62,850**	13,896	11,627	14,698	12,746
62,850	**62,900**	13,909	11,641	14,713	12,759
62,900	**62,950**	13,923	11,654	14,728	12,773
62,950	**63,000**	13,937	11,668	14,744	12,787

63,000

At least	But less than	Single	Married filing jointly *	Married filing separately	Head of a household
63,000	**63,050**	13,951	11,682	14,759	12,801
63,050	**63,100**	13,964	11,696	14,774	12,814
63,100	**63,150**	13,978	11,709	14,789	12,828
63,150	**63,200**	13,992	11,723	14,805	12,842
63,200	**63,250**	14,006	11,737	14,820	12,856
63,250	**63,300**	14,019	11,751	14,835	12,869
63,300	**63,350**	14,033	11,764	14,850	12,883
63,350	**63,400**	14,047	11,778	14,866	12,897
63,400	**63,450**	14,061	11,792	14,881	12,911
63,450	**63,500**	14,074	11,806	14,896	12,924
63,500	**63,550**	14,088	11,819	14,911	12,938
63,550	**63,600**	14,102	11,833	14,927	12,952
63,600	**63,650**	14,116	11,847	14,942	12,966
63,650	**63,700**	14,129	11,861	14,957	12,979
63,700	**63,750**	14,143	11,874	14,972	12,993
63,750	**63,800**	14,157	11,888	14,988	13,007
63,800	**63,850**	14,171	11,902	15,003	13,021
63,850	**63,900**	14,184	11,916	15,018	13,034
63,900	**63,950**	14,198	11,929	15,033	13,048
63,950	**64,000**	14,212	11,943	15,049	13,062

64,000

At least	But less than	Single	Married filing jointly *	Married filing separately	Head of a household
64,000	**64,050**	14,226	11,957	15,064	13,076
64,050	**64,100**	14,239	11,971	15,079	13,089
64,100	**64,150**	14,253	11,984	15,094	13,103
64,150	**64,200**	14,267	11,998	15,110	13,117
64,200	**64,250**	14,281	12,012	15,125	13,131
64,250	**64,300**	14,294	12,026	15,140	13,144
64,300	**64,350**	14,308	12,039	15,155	13,158
64,350	**64,400**	14,322	12,053	15,171	13,172
64,400	**64,450**	14,336	12,067	15,186	13,186
64,450	**64,500**	14,349	12,081	15,201	13,199
64,500	**64,550**	14,363	12,094	15,216	13,213
64,550	**64,600**	14,377	12,108	15,232	13,227
64,600	**64,650**	14,391	12,122	15,247	13,241
64,650	**64,700**	14,404	12,136	15,262	13,254
64,700	**64,750**	14,418	12,149	15,277	13,268
64,750	**64,800**	14,432	12,163	15,293	13,282
64,800	**64,850**	14,446	12,177	15,308	13,296
64,850	**64,900**	14,459	12,191	15,323	13,309
64,900	**64,950**	14,473	12,204	15,338	13,323
64,950	**65,000**	14,487	12,218	15,354	13,337

65,000

At least	But less than	Single	Married filing jointly *	Married filing separately	Head of a household
65,000	**65,050**	14,501	12,232	15,369	13,351
65,050	**65,100**	14,514	12,246	15,384	13,364
65,100	**65,150**	14,528	12,259	15,399	13,378
65,150	**65,200**	14,542	12,273	15,415	13,392
65,200	**65,250**	14,556	12,287	15,430	13,406
65,250	**65,300**	14,569	12,301	15,445	13,419
65,300	**65,350**	14,583	12,314	15,460	13,433
65,350	**65,400**	14,597	12,328	15,476	13,447
65,400	**65,450**	14,611	12,342	15,491	13,461
65,450	**65,500**	14,624	12,356	15,506	13,474
65,500	**65,550**	14,638	12,369	15,521	13,488
65,550	**65,600**	14,653	12,383	15,537	13,502
65,600	**65,650**	14,668	12,397	15,552	13,516
65,650	**65,700**	14,683	12,411	15,567	13,529
65,700	**65,750**	14,698	12,424	15,582	13,543
65,750	**65,800**	14,714	12,438	15,598	13,557
65,800	**65,850**	14,729	12,452	15,613	13,571
65,850	**65,900**	14,744	12,466	15,628	13,584
65,900	**65,950**	14,759	12,479	15,643	13,598
65,950	**66,000**	14,775	12,493	15,659	13,612

66,000

At least	But less than	Single	Married filing jointly *	Married filing separately	Head of a household
66,000	**66,050**	14,790	12,507	15,674	13,626
66,050	**66,100**	14,805	12,521	15,689	13,639
66,100	**66,150**	14,820	12,534	15,704	13,653
66,150	**66,200**	14,836	12,548	15,720	13,667
66,200	**66,250**	14,851	12,562	15,735	13,681
66,250	**66,300**	14,866	12,576	15,750	13,694
66,300	**66,350**	14,881	12,589	15,765	13,708
66,350	**66,400**	14,897	12,603	15,781	13,722
66,400	**66,450**	14,912	12,617	15,796	13,736
66,450	**66,500**	14,927	12,631	15,811	13,749
66,500	**66,550**	14,942	12,644	15,826	13,763
66,550	**66,600**	14,958	12,658	15,842	13,777
66,600	**66,650**	14,973	12,672	15,857	13,791
66,650	**66,700**	14,988	12,686	15,872	13,804
66,700	**66,750**	15,003	12,699	15,887	13,818
66,750	**66,800**	15,019	12,713	15,903	13,832
66,800	**66,850**	15,034	12,727	15,918	13,846
66,850	**66,900**	15,049	12,741	15,933	13,859
66,900	**66,950**	15,064	12,754	15,948	13,873
66,950	**67,000**	15,080	12,768	15,964	13,887

67,000

At least	But less than	Single	Married filing jointly *	Married filing separately	Head of a household
67,000	**67,050**	15,095	12,782	15,979	13,901
67,050	**67,100**	15,110	12,796	15,994	13,914
67,100	**67,150**	15,125	12,809	16,009	13,928
67,150	**67,200**	15,141	12,823	16,025	13,942
67,200	**67,250**	15,156	12,837	16,040	13,956
67,250	**67,300**	15,171	12,851	16,055	13,969
67,300	**67,350**	15,186	12,864	16,070	13,983
67,350	**67,400**	15,202	12,878	16,086	13,997
67,400	**67,450**	15,217	12,892	16,101	14,011
67,450	**67,500**	15,232	12,906	16,116	14,024
67,500	**67,550**	15,247	12,919	16,131	14,038
67,550	**67,600**	15,263	12,933	16,147	14,052
67,600	**67,650**	15,278	12,947	16,162	14,066
67,650	**67,700**	15,293	12,961	16,177	14,079
67,700	**67,750**	15,308	12,974	16,192	14,093
67,750	**67,800**	15,324	12,988	16,208	14,107
67,800	**67,850**	15,339	13,002	16,223	14,121
67,850	**67,900**	15,354	13,016	16,238	14,134
67,900	**67,950**	15,369	13,029	16,253	14,148
67,950	**68,000**	15,385	13,043	16,269	14,162

* This column must also be used by a qualifying widow(er).

(Continued on page 67)

Caution. Dependents, see the worksheet on page 33. **2001 Tax Table**—*Continued*

If line 39 (taxable income) is—		And you are—			
At least	But less than	Single	Married filing jointly *	Married filing sepa-rately	Head of a house-hold
		Your tax is—			
68,000					
68,000	**68,050**	15,400	13,057	16,284	14,176
68,050	**68,100**	15,415	13,071	16,299	14,189
68,100	**68,150**	15,430	13,084	16,314	14,203
68,150	**68,200**	15,446	13,098	16,330	14,217
68,200	**68,250**	15,461	13,112	16,345	14,231
68,250	**68,300**	15,476	13,126	16,360	14,244
68,300	**68,350**	15,491	13,139	16,375	14,258
68,350	**68,400**	15,507	13,153	16,391	14,272
68,400	**68,450**	15,522	13,167	16,406	14,286
68,450	**68,500**	15,537	13,181	16,421	14,299
68,500	**68,550**	15,552	13,194	16,436	14,313
68,550	**68,600**	15,568	13,208	16,452	14,327
68,600	**68,650**	15,583	13,222	16,467	14,341
68,650	**68,700**	15,598	13,236	16,482	14,354
68,700	**68,750**	15,613	13,249	16,497	14,368
68,750	**68,800**	15,629	13,263	16,513	14,382
68,800	**68,850**	15,644	13,277	16,528	14,396
68,850	**68,900**	15,659	13,291	16,543	14,409
68,900	**68,950**	15,674	13,304	16,558	14,423
68,950	**69,000**	15,690	13,318	16,574	14,437
69,000					
69,000	**69,050**	15,705	13,332	16,589	14,451
69,050	**69,100**	15,720	13,346	16,604	14,464
69,100	**69,150**	15,735	13,359	16,619	14,478
69,150	**69,200**	15,751	13,373	16,635	14,492
69,200	**69,250**	15,766	13,387	16,650	14,506
69,250	**69,300**	15,781	13,401	16,665	14,519
69,300	**69,350**	15,796	13,414	16,680	14,533
69,350	**69,400**	15,812	13,428	16,696	14,547
69,400	**69,450**	15,827	13,442	16,711	14,561
69,450	**69,500**	15,842	13,456	16,726	14,574
69,500	**69,550**	15,857	13,469	16,741	14,588
69,550	**69,600**	15,873	13,483	16,757	14,602
69,600	**69,650**	15,888	13,497	16,772	14,616
69,650	**69,700**	15,903	13,511	16,787	14,629
69,700	**69,750**	15,918	13,524	16,802	14,643
69,750	**69,800**	15,934	13,538	16,818	14,657
69,800	**69,850**	15,949	13,552	16,833	14,671
69,850	**69,900**	15,964	13,566	16,848	14,684
69,900	**69,950**	15,979	13,579	16,863	14,698
69,950	**70,000**	15,995	13,593	16,879	14,712
70,000					
70,000	**70,050**	16,010	13,607	16,894	14,726
70,050	**70,100**	16,025	13,621	16,909	14,739
70,100	**70,150**	16,040	13,634	16,924	14,753
70,150	**70,200**	16,056	13,648	16,940	14,767
70,200	**70,250**	16,071	13,662	16,955	14,781
70,250	**70,300**	16,086	13,676	16,970	14,794
70,300	**70,350**	16,101	13,689	16,985	14,808
70,350	**70,400**	16,117	13,703	17,001	14,822
70,400	**70,450**	16,132	13,717	17,016	14,836
70,450	**70,500**	16,147	13,731	17,031	14,849
70,500	**70,550**	16,162	13,744	17,046	14,863
70,550	**70,600**	16,178	13,758	17,062	14,877
70,600	**70,650**	16,193	13,772	17,077	14,891
70,650	**70,700**	16,208	13,786	17,092	14,904
70,700	**70,750**	16,223	13,799	17,107	14,918
70,750	**70,800**	16,239	13,813	17,123	14,932
70,800	**70,850**	16,254	13,827	17,138	14,946
70,850	**70,900**	16,269	13,841	17,153	14,959
70,900	**70,950**	16,284	13,854	17,168	14,973
70,950	**71,000**	16,300	13,868	17,184	14,987
71,000					
71,000	**71,050**	16,315	13,882	17,199	15,001
71,050	**71,100**	16,330	13,896	17,214	15,014
71,100	**71,150**	16,345	13,909	17,229	15,028
71,150	**71,200**	16,361	13,923	17,245	15,042
71,200	**71,250**	16,376	13,937	17,260	15,056
71,250	**71,300**	16,391	13,951	17,275	15,069
71,300	**71,350**	16,406	13,964	17,290	15,083
71,350	**71,400**	16,422	13,978	17,306	15,097
71,400	**71,450**	16,437	13,992	17,321	15,111
71,450	**71,500**	16,452	14,006	17,336	15,124
71,500	**71,550**	16,467	14,019	17,351	15,138
71,550	**71,600**	16,483	14,033	17,367	15,152
71,600	**71,650**	16,498	14,047	17,382	15,166
71,650	**71,700**	16,513	14,061	17,397	15,179
71,700	**71,750**	16,528	14,074	17,412	15,193
71,750	**71,800**	16,544	14,088	17,428	15,207
71,800	**71,850**	16,559	14,102	17,443	15,221
71,850	**71,900**	16,574	14,116	17,458	15,234
71,900	**71,950**	16,589	14,129	17,473	15,248
71,950	**72,000**	16,605	14,143	17,489	15,262
72,000					
72,000	**72,050**	16,620	14,157	17,504	15,276
72,050	**72,100**	16,635	14,171	17,519	15,289
72,100	**72,150**	16,650	14,184	17,534	15,303
72,150	**72,200**	16,666	14,198	17,550	15,317
72,200	**72,250**	16,681	14,212	17,565	15,331
72,250	**72,300**	16,696	14,226	17,580	15,344
72,300	**72,350**	16,711	14,239	17,595	15,358
72,350	**72,400**	16,727	14,253	17,611	15,372
72,400	**72,450**	16,742	14,267	17,626	15,386
72,450	**72,500**	16,757	14,281	17,641	15,399
72,500	**72,550**	16,772	14,294	17,656	15,413
72,550	**72,600**	16,788	14,308	17,672	15,427
72,600	**72,650**	16,803	14,322	17,687	15,441
72,650	**72,700**	16,818	14,336	17,702	15,454
72,700	**72,750**	16,833	14,349	17,717	15,468
72,750	**72,800**	16,849	14,363	17,733	15,482
72,800	**72,850**	16,864	14,377	17,748	15,496
72,850	**72,900**	16,879	14,391	17,763	15,509
72,900	**72,950**	16,894	14,404	17,778	15,523
72,950	**73,000**	16,910	14,418	17,794	15,537
73,000					
73,000	**73,050**	16,925	14,432	17,809	15,551
73,050	**73,100**	16,940	14,446	17,824	15,564
73,100	**73,150**	16,955	14,459	17,839	15,578
73,150	**73,200**	16,971	14,473	17,855	15,592
73,200	**73,250**	16,986	14,487	17,870	15,606
73,250	**73,300**	17,001	14,501	17,885	15,619
73,300	**73,350**	17,016	14,514	17,900	15,633
73,350	**73,400**	17,032	14,528	17,916	15,647
73,400	**73,450**	17,047	14,542	17,931	15,661
73,450	**73,500**	17,062	14,556	17,946	15,674
73,500	**73,550**	17,077	14,569	17,961	15,688
73,550	**73,600**	17,093	14,583	17,977	15,702
73,600	**73,650**	17,108	14,597	17,992	15,716
73,650	**73,700**	17,123	14,611	18,007	15,729
73,700	**73,750**	17,138	14,624	18,022	15,743
73,750	**73,800**	17,154	14,638	18,038	15,757
73,800	**73,850**	17,169	14,652	18,053	15,771
73,850	**73,900**	17,184	14,666	18,068	15,784
73,900	**73,950**	17,199	14,679	18,083	15,798
73,950	**74,000**	17,215	14,693	18,099	15,812
74,000					
74,000	**74,050**	17,230	14,707	18,114	15,826
74,050	**74,100**	17,245	14,721	18,129	15,839
74,100	**74,150**	17,260	14,734	18,144	15,853
74,150	**74,200**	17,276	14,748	18,160	15,867
74,200	**74,250**	17,291	14,762	18,175	15,881
74,250	**74,300**	17,306	14,776	18,190	15,894
74,300	**74,350**	17,321	14,789	18,205	15,908
74,350	**74,400**	17,337	14,803	18,221	15,922
74,400	**74,450**	17,352	14,817	18,236	15,936
74,450	**74,500**	17,367	14,831	18,251	15,949
74,500	**74,550**	17,382	14,844	18,266	15,963
74,550	**74,600**	17,398	14,858	18,282	15,977
74,600	**74,650**	17,413	14,872	18,297	15,991
74,650	**74,700**	17,428	14,886	18,312	16,004
74,700	**74,750**	17,443	14,899	18,327	16,018
74,750	**74,800**	17,459	14,913	18,343	16,032
74,800	**74,850**	17,474	14,927	18,358	16,046
74,850	**74,900**	17,489	14,941	18,373	16,059
74,900	**74,950**	17,504	14,954	18,388	16,073
74,950	**75,000**	17,520	14,968	18,404	16,087
75,000					
75,000	**75,050**	17,535	14,982	18,419	16,101
75,050	**75,100**	17,550	14,996	18,434	16,114
75,100	**75,150**	17,565	15,009	18,449	16,128
75,150	**75,200**	17,581	15,023	18,465	16,142
75,200	**75,250**	17,596	15,037	18,480	16,156
75,250	**75,300**	17,611	15,051	18,495	16,169
75,300	**75,350**	17,626	15,064	18,510	16,183
75,350	**75,400**	17,642	15,078	18,526	16,197
75,400	**75,450**	17,657	15,092	18,541	16,211
75,450	**75,500**	17,672	15,106	18,556	16,224
75,500	**75,550**	17,687	15,119	18,571	16,238
75,550	**75,600**	17,703	15,133	18,587	16,252
75,600	**75,650**	17,718	15,147	18,602	16,266
75,650	**75,700**	17,733	15,161	18,617	16,279
75,700	**75,750**	17,748	15,174	18,632	16,293
75,750	**75,800**	17,764	15,188	18,648	16,307
75,800	**75,850**	17,779	15,202	18,663	16,321
75,850	**75,900**	17,794	15,216	18,678	16,334
75,900	**75,950**	17,809	15,229	18,693	16,348
75,950	**76,000**	17,825	15,243	18,709	16,362
76,000					
76,000	**76,050**	17,840	15,257	18,724	16,376
76,050	**76,100**	17,855	15,271	18,739	16,389
76,100	**76,150**	17,870	15,284	18,754	16,403
76,150	**76,200**	17,886	15,298	18,770	16,417
76,200	**76,250**	17,901	15,312	18,785	16,431
76,250	**76,300**	17,916	15,326	18,800	16,444
76,300	**76,350**	17,931	15,339	18,815	16,458
76,350	**76,400**	17,947	15,353	18,831	16,472
76,400	**76,450**	17,962	15,367	18,846	16,486
76,450	**76,500**	17,977	15,381	18,861	16,499
76,500	**76,550**	17,992	15,394	18,876	16,513
76,550	**76,600**	18,008	15,408	18,892	16,527
76,600	**76,650**	18,023	15,422	18,907	16,541
76,650	**76,700**	18,038	15,436	18,922	16,554
76,700	**76,750**	18,053	15,449	18,937	16,568
76,750	**76,800**	18,069	15,463	18,953	16,582
76,800	**76,850**	18,084	15,477	18,968	16,596
76,850	**76,900**	18,099	15,491	18,983	16,609
76,900	**76,950**	18,114	15,504	18,998	16,623
76,950	**77,000**	18,130	15,518	19,014	16,637

* This column must also be used by a qualifying widow(er).

(Continued on page 68)

2001 Tax Table—*Continued* **Caution.** Dependents, see the worksheet on 33.

If line 39 (taxable income) is— At least	But less than	And you are— Single	Married filing jointly *	Married filing separately	Head of a household
		Your tax is—			
77,000					
77,000	77,050	18,145	15,532	19,029	16,651
77,050	77,100	18,160	15,546	19,044	16,664
77,100	77,150	18,175	15,559	19,059	16,678
77,150	77,200	18,191	15,573	19,075	16,692
77,200	77,250	18,206	15,587	19,090	16,706
77,250	77,300	18,221	15,601	19,105	16,719
77,300	77,350	18,236	15,614	19,120	16,733
77,350	77,400	18,252	15,628	19,136	16,747
77,400	77,450	18,267	15,642	19,151	16,761
77,450	77,500	18,282	15,656	19,166	16,774
77,500	77,550	18,297	15,669	19,181	16,788
77,550	77,600	18,313	15,683	19,197	16,802
77,600	77,650	18,328	15,697	19,212	16,816
77,650	77,700	18,343	15,711	19,227	16,829
77,700	77,750	18,358	15,724	19,242	16,843
77,750	77,800	18,374	15,738	19,258	16,857
77,800	77,850	18,389	15,752	19,273	16,871
77,850	77,900	18,404	15,766	19,288	16,884
77,900	77,950	18,419	15,779	19,303	16,898
77,950	78,000	18,435	15,793	19,319	16,912
78,000					
78,000	78,050	18,450	15,807	19,334	16,926
78,050	78,100	18,465	15,821	19,349	16,939
78,100	78,150	18,480	15,834	19,364	16,953
78,150	78,200	18,496	15,848	19,380	16,967
78,200	78,250	18,511	15,862	19,395	16,981
78,250	78,300	18,526	15,876	19,410	16,994
78,300	78,350	18,541	15,889	19,425	17,008
78,350	78,400	18,557	15,903	19,441	17,022
78,400	78,450	18,572	15,917	19,456	17,036
78,450	78,500	18,587	15,931	19,471	17,049
78,500	78,550	18,602	15,944	19,486	17,063
78,550	78,600	18,618	15,958	19,502	17,077
78,600	78,650	18,633	15,972	19,517	17,091
78,650	78,700	18,648	15,986	19,532	17,104
78,700	78,750	18,663	15,999	19,547	17,118
78,750	78,800	18,679	16,013	19,563	17,132
78,800	78,850	18,694	16,027	19,578	17,146
78,850	78,900	18,709	16,041	19,593	17,159
78,900	78,950	18,724	16,054	19,608	17,173
78,950	79,000	18,740	16,068	19,624	17,187
79,000					
79,000	79,050	18,755	16,082	19,639	17,201
79,050	79,100	18,770	16,096	19,654	17,214
79,100	79,150	18,785	16,109	19,669	17,228
79,150	79,200	18,801	16,123	19,685	17,242
79,200	79,250	18,816	16,137	19,700	17,256
79,250	79,300	18,831	16,151	19,715	17,269
79,300	79,350	18,846	16,164	19,730	17,283
79,350	79,400	18,862	16,178	19,746	17,297
79,400	79,450	18,877	16,192	19,761	17,311
79,450	79,500	18,892	16,206	19,776	17,324
79,500	79,550	18,907	16,219	19,791	17,338
79,550	79,600	18,923	16,233	19,807	17,352
79,600	79,650	18,938	16,247	19,822	17,366
79,650	79,700	18,953	16,261	19,837	17,379
79,700	79,750	18,968	16,274	19,852	17,393
79,750	79,800	18,984	16,288	19,868	17,407
79,800	79,850	18,999	16,302	19,883	17,421
79,850	79,900	19,014	16,316	19,898	17,434
79,900	79,950	19,029	16,329	19,913	17,448
79,950	80,000	19,045	16,343	19,929	17,462

If line 39 (taxable income) is— At least	But less than	And you are— Single	Married filing jointly *	Married filing separately	Head of a household
		Your tax is—			
80,000					
80,000	80,050	19,060	16,357	19,944	17,476
80,050	80,100	19,075	16,371	19,959	17,489
80,100	80,150	19,090	16,384	19,974	17,503
80,150	80,200	19,106	16,398	19,990	17,517
80,200	80,250	19,121	16,412	20,005	17,531
80,250	80,300	19,136	16,426	20,020	17,544
80,300	80,350	19,151	16,439	20,035	17,558
80,350	80,400	19,167	16,453	20,051	17,572
80,400	80,450	19,182	16,467	20,066	17,586
80,450	80,500	19,197	16,481	20,081	17,599
80,500	80,550	19,212	16,494	20,096	17,613
80,550	80,600	19,228	16,508	20,112	17,627
80,600	80,650	19,243	16,522	20,127	17,641
80,650	80,700	19,258	16,536	20,142	17,654
80,700	80,750	19,273	16,549	20,157	17,668
80,750	80,800	19,289	16,563	20,173	17,682
80,800	80,850	19,304	16,577	20,188	17,696
80,850	80,900	19,319	16,591	20,203	17,709
80,900	80,950	19,334	16,604	20,218	17,723
80,950	81,000	19,350	16,618	20,234	17,737
81,000					
81,000	81,050	19,365	16,632	20,249	17,751
81,050	81,100	19,380	16,646	20,264	17,764
81,100	81,150	19,395	16,659	20,279	17,778
81,150	81,200	19,411	16,673	20,295	17,792
81,200	81,250	19,426	16,687	20,310	17,806
81,250	81,300	19,441	16,701	20,325	17,819
81,300	81,350	19,456	16,714	20,340	17,833
81,350	81,400	19,472	16,728	20,356	17,847
81,400	81,450	19,487	16,742	20,371	17,861
81,450	81,500	19,502	16,756	20,386	17,874
81,500	81,550	19,517	16,769	20,401	17,888
81,550	81,600	19,533	16,783	20,417	17,902
81,600	81,650	19,548	16,797	20,432	17,916
81,650	81,700	19,563	16,811	20,447	17,929
81,700	81,750	19,578	16,824	20,462	17,943
81,750	81,800	19,594	16,838	20,478	17,957
81,800	81,850	19,609	16,852	20,493	17,971
81,850	81,900	19,624	16,866	20,508	17,984
81,900	81,950	19,639	16,879	20,523	17,998
81,950	82,000	19,655	16,893	20,539	18,012
82,000					
82,000	82,050	19,670	16,907	20,554	18,026
82,050	82,100	19,685	16,921	20,569	18,039
82,100	82,150	19,700	16,934	20,584	18,053
82,150	82,200	19,716	16,948	20,600	18,067
82,200	82,250	19,731	16,962	20,615	18,081
82,250	82,300	19,746	16,976	20,630	18,094
82,300	82,350	19,761	16,989	20,645	18,108
82,350	82,400	19,777	17,003	20,661	18,122
82,400	82,450	19,792	17,017	20,676	18,136
82,450	82,500	19,807	17,031	20,691	18,149
82,500	82,550	19,822	17,044	20,706	18,163
82,550	82,600	19,838	17,058	20,722	18,177
82,600	82,650	19,853	17,072	20,737	18,191
82,650	82,700	19,868	17,086	20,752	18,204
82,700	82,750	19,883	17,099	20,767	18,218
82,750	82,800	19,899	17,113	20,783	18,232
82,800	82,850	19,914	17,127	20,798	18,246
82,850	82,900	19,929	17,141	20,813	18,259
82,900	82,950	19,944	17,154	20,828	18,273
82,950	83,000	19,960	17,168	20,844	18,287

If line 39 (taxable income) is— At least	But less than	And you are— Single	Married filing jointly *	Married filing separately	Head of a household
		Your tax is—			
83,000					
83,000	83,050	19,975	17,182	20,859	18,301
83,050	83,100	19,990	17,196	20,874	18,314
83,100	83,150	20,005	17,209	20,889	18,328
83,150	83,200	20,021	17,223	20,905	18,342
83,200	83,250	20,036	17,237	20,920	18,356
83,250	83,300	20,051	17,251	20,936	18,369
83,300	83,350	20,066	17,264	20,954	18,383
83,350	83,400	20,082	17,278	20,972	18,397
83,400	83,450	20,097	17,292	20,990	18,411
83,450	83,500	20,112	17,306	21,007	18,424
83,500	83,550	20,127	17,319	21,025	18,438
83,550	83,600	20,143	17,333	21,043	18,452
83,600	83,650	20,158	17,347	21,061	18,466
83,650	83,700	20,173	17,361	21,078	18,479
83,700	83,750	20,188	17,374	21,096	18,493
83,750	83,800	20,204	17,388	21,114	18,507
83,800	83,850	20,219	17,402	21,132	18,521
83,850	83,900	20,234	17,416	21,149	18,534
83,900	83,950	20,249	17,429	21,167	18,548
83,950	84,000	20,265	17,443	21,185	18,562
84,000					
84,000	84,050	20,280	17,457	21,203	18,576
84,050	84,100	20,295	17,471	21,220	18,589
84,100	84,150	20,310	17,484	21,238	18,603
84,150	84,200	20,326	17,498	21,256	18,617
84,200	84,250	20,341	17,512	21,274	18,631
84,250	84,300	20,356	17,526	21,291	18,644
84,300	84,350	20,371	17,539	21,309	18,658
84,350	84,400	20,387	17,553	21,327	18,672
84,400	84,450	20,402	17,567	21,345	18,686
84,450	84,500	20,417	17,581	21,362	18,699
84,500	84,550	20,432	17,594	21,380	18,713
84,550	84,600	20,448	17,608	21,398	18,727
84,600	84,650	20,463	17,622	21,416	18,741
84,650	84,700	20,478	17,636	21,433	18,754
84,700	84,750	20,493	17,649	21,451	18,768
84,750	84,800	20,509	17,663	21,469	18,782
84,800	84,850	20,524	17,677	21,487	18,796
84,850	84,900	20,539	17,691	21,504	18,809
84,900	84,950	20,554	17,704	21,522	18,823
84,950	85,000	20,570	17,718	21,540	18,837
85,000					
85,000	85,050	20,585	17,732	21,558	18,851
85,050	85,100	20,600	17,746	21,575	18,864
85,100	85,150	20,615	17,759	21,593	18,878
85,150	85,200	20,631	17,773	21,611	18,892
85,200	85,250	20,646	17,787	21,629	18,906
85,250	85,300	20,661	17,801	21,646	18,919
85,300	85,350	20,676	17,814	21,664	18,933
85,350	85,400	20,692	17,828	21,682	18,947
85,400	85,450	20,707	17,842	21,700	18,961
85,450	85,500	20,722	17,856	21,717	18,974
85,500	85,550	20,737	17,869	21,735	18,988
85,550	85,600	20,753	17,883	21,753	19,002
85,600	85,650	20,768	17,897	21,771	19,016
85,650	85,700	20,783	17,911	21,788	19,029
85,700	85,750	20,798	17,924	21,806	19,043
85,750	85,800	20,814	17,938	21,824	19,057
85,800	85,850	20,829	17,952	21,842	19,071
85,850	85,900	20,844	17,966	21,859	19,084
85,900	85,950	20,859	17,979	21,877	19,098
85,950	86,000	20,875	17,993	21,895	19,112

* This column must also be used by a qualifying widow(er).

(Continued on page 69)

Caution. Dependents, see the worksheet on page 33. **2001 Tax Table—*Continued***

If line 39 (taxable income) is— At least	But less than	Single	Married filing jointly *	Married filing sepa- rately	Head of a house- hold
		Your tax is—			
86,000					
86,000	86,050	20,890	18,007	21,913	19,126
86,050	86,100	20,905	18,021	21,930	19,139
86,100	86,150	20,920	18,034	21,948	19,153
86,150	86,200	20,936	18,048	21,966	19,167
86,200	86,250	20,951	18,062	21,984	19,181
86,250	86,300	20,966	18,076	22,001	19,194
86,300	86,350	20,981	18,089	22,019	19,208
86,350	86,400	20,997	18,103	22,037	19,222
86,400	86,450	21,012	18,117	22,055	19,236
86,450	86,500	21,027	18,131	22,072	19,249
86,500	86,550	21,042	18,144	22,090	19,263
86,550	86,600	21,058	18,158	22,108	19,277
86,600	86,650	21,073	18,172	22,126	19,291
86,650	86,700	21,088	18,186	22,143	19,304
86,700	86,750	21,103	18,199	22,161	19,318
86,750	86,800	21,119	18,213	22,179	19,332
86,800	86,850	21,134	18,227	22,197	19,346
86,850	86,900	21,149	18,241	22,214	19,359
86,900	86,950	21,164	18,254	22,232	19,373
86,950	87,000	21,180	18,268	22,250	19,387
87,000					
87,000	87,050	21,195	18,282	22,268	19,401
87,050	87,100	21,210	18,296	22,285	19,414
87,100	87,150	21,225	18,309	22,303	19,428
87,150	87,200	21,241	18,323	22,321	19,442
87,200	87,250	21,256	18,337	22,339	19,456
87,250	87,300	21,271	18,351	22,356	19,469
87,300	87,350	21,286	18,364	22,374	19,483
87,350	87,400	21,302	18,378	22,392	19,497
87,400	87,450	21,317	18,392	22,410	19,511
87,450	87,500	21,332	18,406	22,427	19,524
87,500	87,550	21,347	18,419	22,445	19,538
87,550	87,600	21,363	18,433	22,463	19,552
87,600	87,650	21,378	18,447	22,481	19,566
87,650	87,700	21,393	18,461	22,498	19,579
87,700	87,750	21,408	18,474	22,516	19,593
87,750	87,800	21,424	18,488	22,534	19,607
87,800	87,850	21,439	18,502	22,552	19,621
87,850	87,900	21,454	18,516	22,569	19,634
87,900	87,950	21,469	18,529	22,587	19,648
87,950	88,000	21,485	18,543	22,605	19,662
88,000					
88,000	88,050	21,500	18,557	22,623	19,676
88,050	88,100	21,515	18,571	22,640	19,689
88,100	88,150	21,530	18,584	22,658	19,703
88,150	88,200	21,546	18,598	22,676	19,717
88,200	88,250	21,561	18,612	22,694	19,731
88,250	88,300	21,576	18,626	22,711	19,744
88,300	88,350	21,591	18,639	22,729	19,758
88,350	88,400	21,607	18,653	22,747	19,772
88,400	88,450	21,622	18,667	22,765	19,786
88,450	88,500	21,637	18,681	22,782	19,799
88,500	88,550	21,652	18,694	22,800	19,813
88,550	88,600	21,668	18,708	22,818	19,827
88,600	88,650	21,683	18,722	22,836	19,841
88,650	88,700	21,698	18,736	22,853	19,854
88,700	88,750	21,713	18,749	22,871	19,868
88,750	88,800	21,729	18,763	22,889	19,882
88,800	88,850	21,744	18,777	22,907	19,896
88,850	88,900	21,759	18,791	22,924	19,909
88,900	88,950	21,774	18,804	22,942	19,923
88,950	89,000	21,790	18,818	22,960	19,937

If line 39 (taxable income) is— At least	But less than	Single	Married filing jointly *	Married filing sepa- rately	Head of a house- hold
		Your tax is—			
89,000					
89,000	89,050	21,805	18,832	22,978	19,951
89,050	89,100	21,820	18,846	22,995	19,964
89,100	89,150	21,835	18,859	23,013	19,978
89,150	89,200	21,851	18,873	23,031	19,992
89,200	89,250	21,866	18,887	23,049	20,006
89,250	89,300	21,881	18,901	23,066	20,019
89,300	89,350	21,896	18,914	23,084	20,033
89,350	89,400	21,912	18,928	23,102	20,047
89,400	89,450	21,927	18,942	23,120	20,061
89,450	89,500	21,942	18,956	23,137	20,074
89,500	89,550	21,957	18,969	23,155	20,088
89,550	89,600	21,973	18,983	23,173	20,102
89,600	89,650	21,988	18,997	23,191	20,116
89,650	89,700	22,003	19,011	23,208	20,129
89,700	89,750	22,018	19,024	23,226	20,143
89,750	89,800	22,034	19,038	23,244	20,157
89,800	89,850	22,049	19,052	23,262	20,171
89,850	89,900	22,064	19,066	23,279	20,184
89,900	89,950	22,079	19,079	23,297	20,198
89,950	90,000	22,095	19,093	23,315	20,212
90,000					
90,000	90,050	22,110	19,107	23,333	20,226
90,050	90,100	22,125	19,121	23,350	20,239
90,100	90,150	22,140	19,134	23,368	20,253
90,150	90,200	22,156	19,148	23,386	20,267
90,200	90,250	22,171	19,162	23,404	20,281
90,250	90,300	22,186	19,176	23,421	20,294
90,300	90,350	22,201	19,189	23,439	20,308
90,350	90,400	22,217	19,203	23,457	20,322
90,400	90,450	22,232	19,217	23,475	20,336
90,450	90,500	22,247	19,231	23,492	20,349
90,500	90,550	22,262	19,244	23,510	20,363
90,550	90,600	22,278	19,258	23,528	20,377
90,600	90,650	22,293	19,272	23,546	20,391
90,650	90,700	22,308	19,286	23,563	20,404
90,700	90,750	22,323	19,299	23,581	20,418
90,750	90,800	22,339	19,313	23,599	20,432
90,800	90,850	22,354	19,327	23,617	20,446
90,850	90,900	22,369	19,341	23,634	20,459
90,900	90,950	22,384	19,354	23,652	20,473
90,950	91,000	22,400	19,368	23,670	20,487
91,000					
91,000	91,050	22,415	19,382	23,688	20,501
91,050	91,100	22,430	19,396	23,705	20,514
91,100	91,150	22,445	19,409	23,723	20,528
91,150	91,200	22,461	19,423	23,741	20,542
91,200	91,250	22,476	19,437	23,759	20,556
91,250	91,300	22,491	19,451	23,776	20,569
91,300	91,350	22,506	19,464	23,794	20,583
91,350	91,400	22,522	19,478	23,812	20,597
91,400	91,450	22,537	19,492	23,830	20,611
91,450	91,500	22,552	19,506	23,847	20,624
91,500	91,550	22,567	19,519	23,865	20,638
91,550	91,600	22,583	19,533	23,883	20,652
91,600	91,650	22,598	19,547	23,901	20,666
91,650	91,700	22,613	19,561	23,918	20,679
91,700	91,750	22,628	19,574	23,936	20,693
91,750	91,800	22,644	19,588	23,954	20,707
91,800	91,850	22,659	19,602	23,972	20,721
91,850	91,900	22,674	19,616	23,989	20,734
91,900	91,950	22,689	19,629	24,007	20,748
91,950	92,000	22,705	19,643	24,025	20,762

If line 39 (taxable income) is— At least	But less than	Single	Married filing jointly *	Married filing sepa- rately	Head of a house- hold
		Your tax is—			
92,000					
92,000	92,050	22,720	19,657	24,043	20,776
92,050	92,100	22,735	19,671	24,060	20,789
92,100	92,150	22,750	19,684	24,078	20,803
92,150	92,200	22,766	19,698	24,096	20,817
92,200	92,250	22,781	19,712	24,114	20,831
92,250	92,300	22,796	19,726	24,131	20,844
92,300	92,350	22,811	19,739	24,149	20,858
92,350	92,400	22,827	19,753	24,167	20,872
92,400	92,450	22,842	19,767	24,185	20,886
92,450	92,500	22,857	19,781	24,202	20,899
92,500	92,550	22,872	19,794	24,220	20,913
92,550	92,600	22,888	19,808	24,238	20,927
92,600	92,650	22,903	19,822	24,256	20,941
92,650	92,700	22,918	19,836	24,273	20,954
92,700	92,750	22,933	19,849	24,291	20,968
92,750	92,800	22,949	19,863	24,309	20,982
92,800	92,850	22,964	19,877	24,327	20,996
92,850	92,900	22,979	19,891	24,344	21,009
92,900	92,950	22,994	19,904	24,362	21,023
92,950	93,000	23,010	19,918	24,380	21,037
93,000					
93,000	93,050	23,025	19,932	24,398	21,051
93,050	93,100	23,040	19,946	24,415	21,064
93,100	93,150	23,055	19,959	24,433	21,078
93,150	93,200	23,071	19,973	24,451	21,092
93,200	93,250	23,086	19,987	24,469	21,106
93,250	93,300	23,101	20,001	24,486	21,119
93,300	93,350	23,116	20,014	24,504	21,133
93,350	93,400	23,132	20,028	24,522	21,147
93,400	93,450	23,147	20,042	24,540	21,161
93,450	93,500	23,162	20,056	24,557	21,174
93,500	93,550	23,177	20,069	24,575	21,188
93,550	93,600	23,193	20,083	24,593	21,202
93,600	93,650	23,208	20,097	24,611	21,216
93,650	93,700	23,223	20,111	24,628	21,230
93,700	93,750	23,238	20,124	24,646	21,245
93,750	93,800	23,254	20,138	24,664	21,261
93,800	93,850	23,269	20,152	24,682	21,276
93,850	93,900	23,284	20,166	24,699	21,291
93,900	93,950	23,299	20,179	24,717	21,306
93,950	94,000	23,315	20,193	24,735	21,322
94,000					
94,000	94,050	23,330	20,207	24,753	21,337
94,050	94,100	23,345	20,221	24,770	21,352
94,100	94,150	23,360	20,234	24,788	21,367
94,150	94,200	23,376	20,248	24,806	21,383
94,200	94,250	23,391	20,262	24,824	21,398
94,250	94,300	23,406	20,276	24,841	21,413
94,300	94,350	23,421	20,289	24,859	21,428
94,350	94,400	23,437	20,303	24,877	21,444
94,400	94,450	23,452	20,317	24,895	21,459
94,450	94,500	23,467	20,331	24,912	21,474
94,500	94,550	23,482	20,344	24,930	21,489
94,550	94,600	23,498	20,358	24,948	21,505
94,600	94,650	23,513	20,372	24,966	21,520
94,650	94,700	23,528	20,386	24,983	21,535
94,700	94,750	23,543	20,399	25,001	21,550
94,750	94,800	23,559	20,413	25,019	21,566
94,800	94,850	23,574	20,427	25,037	21,581
94,850	94,900	23,589	20,441	25,054	21,596
94,900	94,950	23,604	20,454	25,072	21,611
94,950	95,000	23,620	20,468	25,090	21,627

* This column must also be used by a qualifying widow(er).

(Continued on page 70)

2001 Tax Table—*Continued* **Caution.** Dependents, see the worksheet on page 33.

If line 39 (taxable income) is— At least	But less than	And you are— Single	Married filing jointly *	Married filing sepa-rately	Head of a house-hold
		Your tax is—			
95,000					
95,000	**95,050**	23,635	20,482	25,108	21,642
95,050	**95,100**	23,650	20,496	25,125	21,657
95,100	**95,150**	23,665	20,509	25,143	21,672
95,150	**95,200**	23,681	20,523	25,161	21,688
95,200	**95,250**	23,696	20,537	25,179	21,703
95,250	**95,300**	23,711	20,551	25,196	21,718
95,300	**95,350**	23,726	20,564	25,214	21,733
95,350	**95,400**	23,742	20,578	25,232	21,749
95,400	**95,450**	23,757	20,592	25,250	21,764
95,450	**95,500**	23,772	20,606	25,267	21,779
95,500	**95,550**	23,787	20,619	25,285	21,794
95,550	**95,600**	23,803	20,633	25,303	21,810
95,600	**95,650**	23,818	20,647	25,321	21,825
95,650	**95,700**	23,833	20,661	25,338	21,840
95,700	**95,750**	23,848	20,674	25,356	21,855
95,750	**95,800**	23,864	20,688	25,374	21,871
95,800	**95,850**	23,879	20,702	25,392	21,886
95,850	**95,900**	23,894	20,716	25,409	21,901
95,900	**95,950**	23,909	20,729	25,427	21,916
95,950	**96,000**	23,925	20,743	25,445	21,932
96,000					
96,000	**96,050**	23,940	20,757	25,463	21,947
96,050	**96,100**	23,955	20,771	25,480	21,962
96,100	**96,150**	23,970	20,784	25,498	21,977
96,150	**96,200**	23,986	20,798	25,516	21,993
96,200	**96,250**	24,001	20,812	25,534	22,008
96,250	**96,300**	24,016	20,826	25,551	22,023
96,300	**96,350**	24,031	20,839	25,569	22,038
96,350	**96,400**	24,047	20,853	25,587	22,054
96,400	**96,450**	24,062	20,867	25,605	22,069
96,450	**96,500**	24,077	20,881	25,622	22,084
96,500	**96,550**	24,092	20,894	25,640	22,099
96,550	**96,600**	24,108	20,908	25,658	22,115
96,600	**96,650**	24,123	20,922	25,676	22,130
96,650	**96,700**	24,138	20,936	25,693	22,145
96,700	**96,750**	24,153	20,949	25,711	22,160
96,750	**96,800**	24,169	20,963	25,729	22,176
96,800	**96,850**	24,184	20,977	25,747	22,191
96,850	**96,900**	24,199	20,991	25,764	22,206
96,900	**96,950**	24,214	21,004	25,782	22,221
96,950	**97,000**	24,230	21,018	25,800	22,237
97,000					
97,000	**97,050**	24,245	21,032	25,818	22,252
97,050	**97,100**	24,260	21,046	25,835	22,267
97,100	**97,150**	24,275	21,059	25,853	22,282
97,150	**97,200**	24,291	21,073	25,871	22,298
97,200	**97,250**	24,306	21,087	25,889	22,313
97,250	**97,300**	24,321	21,101	25,906	22,328
97,300	**97,350**	24,336	21,114	25,924	22,343
97,350	**97,400**	24,352	21,128	25,942	22,359
97,400	**97,450**	24,367	21,142	25,960	22,374
97,450	**97,500**	24,382	21,156	25,977	22,389
97,500	**97,550**	24,397	21,169	25,995	22,404
97,550	**97,600**	24,413	21,183	26,013	22,420
97,600	**97,650**	24,428	21,197	26,031	22,435
97,650	**97,700**	24,443	21,211	26,048	22,450
97,700	**97,750**	24,458	21,224	26,066	22,465
97,750	**97,800**	24,474	21,238	26,084	22,481
97,800	**97,850**	24,489	21,252	26,102	22,496
97,850	**97,900**	24,504	21,266	26,119	22,511
97,900	**97,950**	24,519	21,279	26,137	22,526
97,950	**98,000**	24,535	21,293	26,155	22,542
98,000					
98,000	**98,050**	24,550	21,307	26,173	22,557
98,050	**98,100**	24,565	21,321	26,190	22,572
98,100	**98,150**	24,580	21,334	26,208	22,587
98,150	**98,200**	24,596	21,348	26,226	22,603
98,200	**98,250**	24,611	21,362	26,244	22,618
98,250	**98,300**	24,626	21,376	26,261	22,633
98,300	**98,350**	24,641	21,389	26,279	22,648
98,350	**98,400**	24,657	21,403	26,297	22,664
98,400	**98,450**	24,672	21,417	26,315	22,679
98,450	**98,500**	24,687	21,431	26,332	22,694
98,500	**98,550**	24,702	21,444	26,350	22,709
98,550	**98,600**	24,718	21,458	26,368	22,725
98,600	**98,650**	24,733	21,472	26,386	22,740
98,650	**98,700**	24,748	21,486	26,403	22,755
98,700	**98,750**	24,763	21,499	26,421	22,770
98,750	**98,800**	24,779	21,513	26,439	22,786
98,800	**98,850**	24,794	21,527	26,457	22,801
98,850	**98,900**	24,809	21,541	26,474	22,816
98,900	**98,950**	24,824	21,554	26,492	22,831
98,950	**99,000**	24,840	21,568	26,510	22,847
99,000					
99,000	**99,050**	24,855	21,582	26,528	22,862
99,050	**99,100**	24,870	21,596	26,545	22,877
99,100	**99,150**	24,885	21,609	26,563	22,892
99,150	**99,200**	24,901	21,623	26,581	22,908
99,200	**99,250**	24,916	21,637	26,599	22,923
99,250	**99,300**	24,931	21,651	26,616	22,938
99,300	**99,350**	24,946	21,664	26,634	22,953
99,350	**99,400**	24,962	21,678	26,652	22,969
99,400	**99,450**	24,977	21,692	26,670	22,984
99,450	**99,500**	24,992	21,706	26,687	22,999
99,500	**99,550**	25,007	21,719	26,705	23,014
99,550	**99,600**	25,023	21,733	26,723	23,030
99,600	**99,650**	25,038	21,747	26,741	23,045
99,650	**99,700**	25,053	21,761	26,758	23,060
99,700	**99,750**	25,068	21,774	26,776	23,075
99,750	**99,800**	25,084	21,788	26,794	23,091
99,800	**99,850**	25,099	21,802	26,812	23,106
99,850	**99,900**	25,114	21,816	26,829	23,121
99,900	**99,950**	25,129	21,829	26,847	23,136
99,950	**100,000**	25,145	21,843	26,865	23,152

$100,000 or over — use the Tax Rate Schedules on page 71

* This column must also be used by a qualifying widow(er).

2001 Tax Rate Schedules

Use **only** if your taxable income (Form 1040, line 39) is $100,000 or more. If less, use the **Tax Table.** Even though you cannot use the Tax Rate Schedules below if your taxable income is less than $100,000, all levels of taxable income are shown so taxpayers can see the tax rate that applies to each level.

Schedule X—Use if your filing status is **Single**

If the amount on Form 1040, line 39, is: Over—	But not over—	Enter on Form 1040, line 40	*of the amount over—*
$0	$27,050	-------- 15%	**$0**
27,050	65,550	**$4,057.50 + 27.5%**	**27,050**
65,550	136,750	**14,645.00 + 30.5%**	**65,550**
136,750	297,350	**36,361.00 + 35.5%**	**136,750**
297,350	--------	**93,374.00 + 39.1%**	**297,350**

Schedule Y-1—Use if your filing status is **Married filing jointly** or **Qualifying widow(er)**

If the amount on Form 1040, line 39, is: Over—	But not over—	Enter on Form 1040, line 40	*of the amount over—*
$0	$45,200	-------- 15%	**$0**
45,200	109,250	**$6,780.00 + 27.5%**	**45,200**
109,250	166,500	**24,393.75 + 30.5%**	**109,250**
166,500	297,350	**41,855.00 + 35.5%**	**166,500**
297,350	--------	**88,306.75 + 39.1%**	**297,350**

Dependents, see the worksheet on page 33.

Schedule Y-2—Use if your filing status is **Married filing separately**

If the amount on Form 1040, line 39, is: Over—	But not over—	Enter on Form 1040, line 40	*of the amount over—*
$0	$22,600	-------- 15%	**$0**
22,600	54,625	**$3,390.00 + 27.5%**	**22,600**
54,625	83,250	**12,196.88 + 30.5%**	**54,625**
83,250	148,675	**20,927.50 + 35.5%**	**83,250**
148,675	--------	**44,153.38 + 39.1%**	**148,675**

Schedule Z—Use if your filing status is **Head of household**

If the amount on Form 1040, line 39, is: Over—	But not over—	Enter on Form 1040, line 40	*of the amount over—*
$0	$36,250	-------- 15%	**$0**
36,250	93,650	**$5,437.50 + 27.5%**	**36,250**
93,650	151,650	**21,222.50 + 30.5%**	**93,650**
151,650	297,350	**38,912.50 + 35.5%**	**151,650**
297,350	--------	**90,636.00 + 39.1%**	**297,350**

SINGLE Persons—**MONTHLY** Payroll Period

(For Wages Paid in 2002)

If the wages are–		And the number of withholding allowances claimed is—										
At least	But less than	0	1	2	3	4	5	6	7	8	9	10
		The amount of income tax to be withheld is—										
$0	**$230**	$0	$0	$0	$0	$0	$0	$0	$0	$0	$0	$0
230	**240**	1	0	0	0	0	0	0	0	0	0	0
240	**250**	2	0	0	0	0	0	0	0	0	0	0
250	**260**	3	0	0	0	0	0	0	0	0	0	0
260	**270**	4	0	0	0	0	0	0	0	0	0	0
270	**280**	5	0	0	0	0	0	0	0	0	0	0
280	**290**	6	0	0	0	0	0	0	0	0	0	0
290	**300**	7	0	0	0	0	0	0	0	0	0	0
300	**320**	9	0	0	0	0	0	0	0	0	0	0
320	**340**	11	0	0	0	0	0	0	0	0	0	0
340	**360**	13	0	0	0	0	0	0	0	0	0	0
360	**380**	15	0	0	0	0	0	0	0	0	0	0
380	**400**	17	0	0	0	0	0	0	0	0	0	0
400	**420**	19	0	0	0	0	0	0	0	0	0	0
420	**440**	21	0	0	0	0	0	0	0	0	0	0
440	**460**	23	0	0	0	0	0	0	0	0	0	0
460	**480**	25	0	0	0	0	0	0	0	0	0	0
480	**500**	27	2	0	0	0	0	0	0	0	0	0
500	**520**	29	4	0	0	0	0	0	0	0	0	0
520	**540**	31	6	0	0	0	0	0	0	0	0	0
540	**560**	33	8	0	0	0	0	0	0	0	0	0
560	**580**	35	10	0	0	0	0	0	0	0	0	0
580	**600**	37	12	0	0	0	0	0	0	0	0	0
600	**640**	40	15	0	0	0	0	0	0	0	0	0
640	**680**	44	19	0	0	0	0	0	0	0	0	0
680	**720**	48	23	0	0	0	0	0	0	0	0	0
720	**760**	53	27	2	0	0	0	0	0	0	0	0
760	**800**	59	31	6	0	0	0	0	0	0	0	0
800	**840**	65	35	10	0	0	0	0	0	0	0	0
840	**880**	71	39	14	0	0	0	0	0	0	0	0
880	**920**	77	43	18	0	0	0	0	0	0	0	0
920	**960**	83	47	22	0	0	0	0	0	0	0	0
960	**1,000**	89	52	26	1	0	0	0	0	0	0	0
1,000	**1,040**	95	58	30	5	0	0	0	0	0	0	0
1,040	**1,080**	101	64	34	9	0	0	0	0	0	0	0
1,080	**1,120**	107	70	38	13	0	0	0	0	0	0	0
1,120	**1,160**	113	76	42	17	0	0	0	0	0	0	0
1,160	**1,200**	119	82	46	21	0	0	0	0	0	0	0
1,200	**1,240**	125	88	50	25	0	0	0	0	0	0	0
1,240	**1,280**	131	94	56	29	4	0	0	0	0	0	0
1,280	**1,320**	137	100	62	33	8	0	0	0	0	0	0
1,320	**1,360**	143	106	68	37	12	0	0	0	0	0	0
1,360	**1,400**	149	112	74	41	16	0	0	0	0	0	0
1,400	**1,440**	155	118	80	45	20	0	0	0	0	0	0
1,440	**1,480**	161	124	86	49	24	0	0	0	0	0	0
1,480	**1,520**	167	130	92	55	28	3	0	0	0	0	0
1,520	**1,560**	173	136	98	61	32	7	0	0	0	0	0
1,560	**1,600**	179	142	104	67	36	11	0	0	0	0	0
1,600	**1,640**	185	148	110	73	40	15	0	0	0	0	0
1,640	**1,680**	191	154	116	79	44	19	0	0	0	0	0
1,680	**1,720**	197	160	122	85	48	23	0	0	0	0	0
1,720	**1,760**	203	166	128	91	53	27	2	0	0	0	0
1,760	**1,800**	209	172	134	97	59	31	6	0	0	0	0
1,800	**1,840**	215	178	140	103	65	35	10	0	0	0	0
1,840	**1,880**	221	184	146	109	71	39	14	0	0	0	0
1,880	**1,920**	227	190	152	115	77	43	18	0	0	0	0
1,920	**1,960**	233	196	158	121	83	47	22	0	0	0	0
1,960	**2,000**	239	202	164	127	89	52	26	1	0	0	0
2,000	**2,040**	245	208	170	133	95	58	30	5	0	0	0
2,040	**2,080**	251	214	176	139	101	64	34	9	0	0	0
2,080	**2,120**	257	220	182	145	107	70	38	13	0	0	0
2,120	**2,160**	263	226	188	151	113	76	42	17	0	0	0
2,160	**2,200**	269	232	194	157	119	82	46	21	0	0	0
2,200	**2,240**	275	238	200	163	125	88	50	25	0	0	0
2,240	**2,280**	281	244	206	169	131	94	56	29	4	0	0
2,280	**2,320**	287	250	212	175	137	100	62	33	8	0	0
2,320	**2,360**	293	256	218	181	143	106	68	37	12	0	0
2,360	**2,400**	299	262	224	187	149	112	74	41	16	0	0
2,400	**2,440**	305	268	230	193	155	118	80	45	20	0	0
2,440	**2,480**	311	274	236	199	161	124	86	49	24	0	0

MARRIED Persons—**MONTHLY** Payroll Period

(For Wages Paid in 2002)

If the wages are–		And the number of withholding allowances claimed is—										
At least	But less than	0	1	2	3	4	5	6	7	8	9	10
		The amount of income tax to be withheld is—										
$0	$540	$0	$0	$0	$0	$0	$0	$0	$0	$0	$0	$0
540	560	1	0	0	0	0	0	0	0	0	0	0
560	580	3	0	0	0	0	0	0	0	0	0	0
580	600	5	0	0	0	0	0	0	0	0	0	0
600	640	8	0	0	0	0	0	0	0	0	0	0
640	680	12	0	0	0	0	0	0	0	0	0	0
680	720	16	0	0	0	0	0	0	0	0	0	0
720	760	20	0	0	0	0	0	0	0	0	0	0
760	800	24	0	0	0	0	0	0	0	0	0	0
800	840	28	3	0	0	0	0	0	0	0	0	0
840	880	32	7	0	0	0	0	0	0	0	0	0
880	920	36	11	0	0	0	0	0	0	0	0	0
920	960	40	15	0	0	0	0	0	0	0	0	0
960	1,000	44	19	0	0	0	0	0	0	0	0	0
1,000	1,040	48	23	0	0	0	0	0	0	0	0	0
1,040	1,080	52	27	2	0	0	0	0	0	0	0	0
1,080	1,120	56	31	6	0	0	0	0	0	0	0	0
1,120	1,160	60	35	10	0	0	0	0	0	0	0	0
1,160	1,200	64	39	14	0	0	0	0	0	0	0	0
1,200	1,240	68	43	18	0	0	0	0	0	0	0	0
1,240	1,280	72	47	22	0	0	0	0	0	0	0	0
1,280	1,320	76	51	26	1	0	0	0	0	0	0	0
1,320	1,360	80	55	30	5	0	0	0	0	0	0	0
1,360	1,400	84	59	34	9	0	0	0	0	0	0	0
1,400	1,440	88	63	38	13	0	0	0	0	0	0	0
1,440	1,480	92	67	42	17	0	0	0	0	0	0	0
1,480	1,520	96	71	46	21	0	0	0	0	0	0	0
1,520	1,560	100	75	50	25	0	0	0	0	0	0	0
1,560	1,600	106	79	54	29	4	0	0	0	0	0	0
1,600	1,640	112	83	58	33	8	0	0	0	0	0	0
1,640	1,680	118	87	62	37	12	0	0	0	0	0	0
1,680	1,720	124	91	66	41	16	0	0	0	0	0	0
1,720	1,760	130	95	70	45	20	0	0	0	0	0	0
1,760	1,800	136	99	74	49	24	0	0	0	0	0	0
1,800	1,840	142	105	78	53	28	3	0	0	0	0	0
1,840	1,880	148	111	82	57	32	7	0	0	0	0	0
1,880	1,920	154	117	86	61	36	11	0	0	0	0	0
1,920	1,960	160	123	90	65	40	15	0	0	0	0	0
1,960	2,000	166	129	94	69	44	19	0	0	0	0	0
2,000	2,040	172	135	98	73	48	23	0	0	0	0	0
2,040	2,080	178	141	103	77	52	27	2	0	0	0	0
2,080	2,120	184	147	109	81	56	31	6	0	0	0	0
2,120	2,160	190	153	115	85	60	35	10	0	0	0	0
2,160	2,200	196	159	121	89	64	39	14	0	0	0	0
2,200	2,240	202	165	127	93	68	43	18	0	0	0	0
2,240	2,280	208	171	133	97	72	47	22	0	0	0	0
2,280	2,320	214	177	139	102	76	51	26	1	0	0	0
2,320	2,360	220	183	145	108	80	55	30	5	0	0	0
2,360	2,400	226	189	151	114	84	59	34	9	0	0	0
2,400	2,440	232	195	157	120	88	63	38	13	0	0	0
2,440	2,480	238	201	163	126	92	67	42	17	0	0	0
2,480	2,520	244	207	169	132	96	71	46	21	0	0	0
2,520	2,560	250	213	175	138	100	75	50	25	0	0	0
2,560	2,600	256	219	181	144	106	79	54	29	4	0	0
2,600	2,640	262	225	187	150	112	83	58	33	8	0	0
2,640	2,680	268	231	193	156	118	87	62	37	12	0	0
2,680	2,720	274	237	199	162	124	91	66	41	16	0	0
2,720	2,760	280	243	205	168	130	95	70	45	20	0	0
2,760	2,800	286	249	211	174	136	99	74	49	24	0	0
2,800	2,840	292	255	217	180	142	105	78	53	28	3	0
2,840	2,880	298	261	223	186	148	111	82	57	32	7	0
2,880	2,920	304	267	229	192	154	117	86	61	36	11	0
2,920	2,960	310	273	235	198	160	123	90	65	40	15	0
2,960	3,000	316	279	241	204	166	129	94	69	44	19	0
3,000	3,040	322	285	247	210	172	135	98	73	48	23	0
3,040	3,080	328	291	253	216	178	141	103	77	52	27	2
3,080	3,120	334	297	259	222	184	147	109	81	56	31	6
3,120	3,160	340	303	265	228	190	153	115	85	60	35	10
3,160	3,200	346	309	271	234	196	159	121	89	64	39	14
3,200	3,240	352	315	277	240	202	165	127	93	68	43	18

APPENDIX A

TAX RESEARCH WORKING PAPER FILE

INDEX TO TAX RESEARCH FILE*

Item	Page Reference
Determine the Facts	A-2
Identify the Issues	A-2
Locate Applicable Authorities	A-2
Evaluate Authorities	A-4
Analyze the Facts in Terms of Applicable Law	A-4
Communicate Conclusions and Recommendations to Others	A-5
Memorandum-to-the-File	A-6
Client Letter	A-7

*Most accounting firms maintain a **client file** for each of their clients. Typically, this file contains copies of client letters, memoranda-to-the-file, relevant primary and secondary authorities, and billing information. In our case, the client file for Mercy Hospital would include copies of the following: (1) the September 12 letter to Elizabeth Feghali, (2) the September 9 memorandum-to-the-file, (3) IRC Sec. 119, (4) Reg. Sec. 1.119-1, (5) the *Kowalski* opinion, (6) the *Standard Federal Tax Reporter* annotation, and (7) pertinent billing information.

TAX RESEARCH FILE

As mentioned in Chapter C1 the tax research process entails six steps.

1. Determine the facts
2. Identify the issues
3. Locate applicable authorities
4. Evaluate these authorities
5. Analyze the facts
6. Communicate conclusions and recommendations to others.

Let us walk through each of these steps.

Determine the Facts Assume that we have determined the facts to be as follows:

> *Mercy Hospital maintains a cafeteria on its premises. In addition, it rents space to MacDougal's, a privately owned sandwich shop. The cafeteria closes at 8:00 p.m. MacDougal's is open 24 hours. Mercy provides meal vouchers to each of its 240 medical employees to enable them to remain on call in case of emergency. The vouchers are redeemable either at the cafeteria or at MacDougal's. Although the employees are not required to remain on or near the premises during meal hours, they generally do. Elizabeth Fegali, Mercy's Chief Administrator, has approached you with the following question: Is the value of a meal voucher includible in the employees' gross income?*

At this juncture, be sure you understand the facts before proceeding further. Remember, researching the wrong facts could produce the wrong results.

Identify the Issues Identifying the issues presupposes a minimum level of proficiency in tax accounting. This proficiency will come with time, effort, and perseverence. The central issue raised by the facts is the taxability of the meal vouchers. A resolution of this issue will hinge on the resolution of other issues raised in the course of the research.

Locate Applicable Authorities For some students, this step is the most difficult in the research process. It raises the perplexing question, "Where do I begin to look?" The answer depends on the tax resources at one's disposal, as well as one's research preferences. Four rules of thumb apply:

1. *Adopt an approach with which you are comfortable, and that you are confident will produce reliable results.*
2. *Always consult the IRC and other primary authorities.*
3. *Be as thorough as possible, taking into consideration time and billing constraints.*
4. *Make sure that the authorities you consult are current.*

One approach is to conduct a topical search. Begin by consulting the index to the Internal Revenue Code (IRC). Then read the relevant IRC section(s). If the language of the IRC is vague or ambiguous, turn to the Treasury Regulations. Read the relevant regulation section that elaborates or expounds on the IRC provision. If the language of the regulation is confusing or unclear, go to a commercial tax service. Read the relevant tax service paragraphs that explain or analyze the statutory and regulatory provisions. For references to other authorities, browse through the footnotes and annotations of the service. Then, consult these authorities directly. Finally, check the currency of the authorities consulted, with the aid of a citator or status (finding) list.

If a pertinent court decision or IRS ruling has been called to your attention, consult this authority directly. Alternatively, browse through the status (finding) list of a tax service for references to tax service paragraphs that discuss this authority. Better still, consult a citator or status list for references to court opinions or rulings that cite the authority. If you subscribe to a computerized tax service, conduct a keyword, citation, contents, or topical search. (For a discussion of these types of searches, see the computerized research supplement available for download at *www.prenhall.com/phtax*.) Then, hyperlink to the authorities cited within the text of the documents retrieved. So numerous are the approaches to tax research that one is virtually free to pick and choose. All that is required of the researcher is a basic level of skill and some imagination.

Let us adopt a topical approach to the issue of the meal vouchers. If we consult an index to the IRC, we are likely to find the heading "Meals and Lodging." Below this heading are likely to be several subheadings, some pertaining to deductions, others to exclusions. Because the voucher issue pertains to exclusions, let us peruse the latter subheadings. Most of these subheadings refer to IRC Sec. 119. If we look up this section, we will see the following passage:

Sec. 119. Meals or lodging furnished for the convenience of the employer.

> (a) **Meals and lodging furnished to employee, his spouse, and his dependents, pursuant to employment.**
> There shall be excluded from gross income of an employee the value of any meals or lodging furnished to him . . . by, or on behalf of his employer for the convenience of the employer, but only if—
>
> (1) **in the case of meals, the meals are furnished on the business premises of the employer . . .**
>
> (b) **Special rules.** For purposes of subsection (a)—
> (4) **Meals furnished to employees on business premises where meals of most employees are otherwise excludable.** All meals furnished on the business premises of an employer to such employer's employees shall be treated as furnished for the convenience of the employer if . . . more than half of the employees to whom such meals are furnished on such premises are furnished such meals for the convenience of the employer.

Section 119 appears to be applicable. It deals with meals furnished to an employee on the business premises of the employer. Our case deals with meal vouchers furnished to employees for redemption at employer-maintained and employer-rented-out facilities. But here, additional issues arise. For purposes of Sec. 119, are meal vouchers the same as "meals"? (Do not assume they are.) Are employer-maintained and employer-rented-out facilities the same as "the business premises of the employer"? (Again, do not assume they are.) And what does the IRC mean by "for the convenience of the employer"? Because the IRC offers no guidance in this respect, let us turn to the Treasury Regulations.

The applicable regulation is Reg. Sec. 1.119-1. How do we know this? Because Treasury Regulation section numbers track the IRC section numbers. Regulation Sec. 1.119-1 is the only regulation under IRC Sec. 119. If we browse through this regulation, we will find the following provision:

> (a) **Meals . . .**
> (2) **Meals furnished without a charge**
> (i) Meals furnished by an employer without charge to the employee will be regarded as furnished for the convenience of the employer if such meals are furnished for a substantial noncompensatory business reason of the employer . . .
> (ii) (a) Meals will be regarded as furnished for a substantial noncompensatory business reason of the employer when the meals are furnished to the employee during his working hours to have the employee available for emergency call during his meal period . . .
>
> (c) **Business premises of the employer.**
> (1) **In general.** For purposes of this section, the term "business premises of the employer" generally means the place of employment of the employee . . .

Based on a reading of this provision, we might conclude that the hospital meals are furnished "for the convenience of the employer." Why? Because they are furnished for a "substantial noncompensatory business reason of the employer," namely, to have the employees available for emergency call during their meal periods. They also are furnished during the employees' working hours. Moreover, under IRC Sec. 119(b)(4), if more than half the employees satisfy the "for the convenience of the employer" test, all employees will be regarded as satisfying the test. But are the meals furnished on "the business premises of the employer"? Under the regulation, the answer would depend. If the meals are furnished in the hospital cafeteria, they may be furnished on "the business premises of the employer." The hospital is the place of employment of the medical employees. The cafeteria is part of the hospital. On the other hand, if the meals are furnished at MacDougal's, they probably are not furnished on "the business premises of the employer." MacDougals's is not the place of employment of the medical employees. Nor is it a part of the hospital. Thus, Reg. Sec. 1.119-1 is enlightening with respect to two statutory terms: "for the convenience of the employer" and "the business premises of the employer." However, it is obscure with respect to the third term, "meals." Because of this obscurity, let us turn to a tax service.

Although the index to CCH's *Standard Federal Tax Reporter* does not list "meal vouchers," it does list "cash allowances in lieu of meals" as a subtopic under Meals and Lodging. Are meal vouchers the same as cash meal allowances?—perhaps so; let us see. Next to the heading "cash allowances in lieu of meals" is a reference to CCH ¶7222.59. If we look up this reference, we will find the following annotation:

¶7222.59 **Meal allowances.**—Cash meal allowances received by an employee (state trooper) from his employee were not excludible from income. *R.J. Kowalski,* SCt, 77-2 USTC ¶9748, 434 US 77.[1]

Here we discover that, in the *Kowalski* case, the U.S. Supreme Court decided that cash meal allowances received by an employee were excludible from the employee's income. Is the *Kowalski* case similar to our case? It might be. Let us find out. If we turn to paragraph 9748 of the second 1977 volume of *United States Tax Cases,* we will find the text of the *Kowalski* opinion. A synopsis of this opinion is present below.

In the mid-1970s, the State of New Jersey provided cash meal allowances to its state troopers. The state did not require the troopers to use the allowances exclusively for meals. Nor did it require them to consume their meals on its business premises. One trooper, Robert J. Kowalski, failed to report a portion of his allowance on his tax return. The IRS assessed a deficiency, and Kowalski took the IRS to court. In court, Kowalski argued that the meal allowances were excludible, because they were furnished "for the convenience of the employer." The IRS contended that the allowances were taxable because they amounted to compensation. The Supreme Court took up the case and sided with the IRS. The Court held that the IRC Sec. 119 income exclusion does not apply to cash payments; it applies only to meals in kind.[2]

For the sake of illustration, let us assume that IRC Sec. 119, Reg. Sec. 1.119-1, and the *Kowalski* case are the *only* authorities "on point." How should we evaluate them?

Evaluate Authorities IRC Sec. 119 is the key authority applicable to our case. It supplies the operative rule for resolving the issue of the meal vouchers. It is vague, however, with respect to three terms: "meals," "business premises of the employer," and "for the convenience of the employer." The principal judicial authority is the *Kowalski* case. It provides an official interpretation of the term "meals." Because the U.S. Supreme Court decided *Kowalski*, the case should be assigned considerable weight. The relevant administrative authority is Reg. Sec. 1.119-1. It expounds on the terms "business premises of the employer" and "for the convenience of the employer." Because neither the IRC nor *Kowalski* explain these terms, Reg. Sec. 1.119-1 should be accorded great weight. But what if *Kowalski* had conflicted with Reg. Sec. 1.119-1? Which should be considered more authoritative? As a general rule, high court decisions "trump" the Treasury Regulations (and all IRS pronouncements for that matter). The more recent the decision, the greater its precedential weight. Had there been no Supreme Court decision and a division of appellate authority, equal weight should have been assigned to each of the appellate court decisions.

Analyze the Facts in Terms of Applicable Law Analyzing the facts in terms of applicable law involves applying the abstractions of the law to the concreteness of the facts. It entails expressing the generalities of the law in terms of the specifics of the facts. In this process, every legal condition must be satisfied for the result prescribed by the general rule to

[1] The researcher also might read the main *Standard Federal Tax Reporter* paragraph that discusses meals and lodging furnished by the employer (CCH ¶7222.01). Within this paragraph are likely to be references to other primary authorities.

[2] At this juncture, the researcher should consult a citator to determine whether *Kowalski* is still "good law," and to locate other authorities that cite *Kowalski.*

ensue. Thus, in our case, the conditions of furnishing "meals," "on the business premises of the employer," and "for the convenience of the employer" must be satisfied for the value of the "meals" to be excluded from the employee's income.

When analyzing the facts in terms of case law, the researcher should always draw an *analogy* between case facts and client facts. Likewise, he or she should always draw a *distinction* between case facts and client facts. Remember, under the rule of precedent, a court deciding the client's case will be bound by the precedent of cases involving *similar* facts and issues. By the same token, it will *not* be bound by the precedent of cases involving *dissimilar* facts and issues.

The most useful vehicle for analyzing client facts is the memorandum-to-the-file (see page A-6). The purpose of this document is threefold: first, it assists the researcher in recalling transactions long transpired; second, it apprises colleagues and supervisors of the nature of one's research; third, it provides "substantial authority" for the tax treatment of a particular item. Let us analyze the facts of our case by way of a memorandum-to-the-file. Notice the format of this document; it generally tracks the steps in the research process itself.

Communicate Conclusions and Recommendations to Others For three practical reasons, research results always should be communicated to the client *in writing*. First, a written communication can be made after extensive revisions. An oral communication cannot. Second, in a written communication, the researcher can delve into the intricacies of tax law. Often, in an oral communication, he or she cannot. Third, a written communication reinforces an oral understanding. Alternatively, it brings to light an oral misunderstanding.

The written communication usually takes the form of a client letter (see page A-7). The purpose of this letter is two-fold: first, it apprises the client of the results of one's research; second, it recommends to the client a course of action based on these results. A sample client letter is presented below. Notice the organization of this document; it is similar to that of the memorandum-to-the-file.

Memorandum-to-the-File

Date: December 9, 20X1
From: Rosina Havacek
Re: The taxability of meal vouchers furnished by Mercy Hospital to its medical staff.

Facts
[*State only the facts that are relevant to the Issue(s) and necessary for the Analysis.*] Our client, Mercy Hospital ("Mercy"), provides meal vouchers to its medical employees to enable them to remain on emergency call. The vouchers are redeemable at Mercy's onsite cafeteria and at MacDougal's, a privately owned sandwich shop. MacDougal's rents business space from the hospital. Although Mercy does not require its employees to remain on or near it premises during their meal hours, the employees generally do. Elizabeth Fegali, Mercy's Chief Administrator, has asked us to research whether the value of the meal vouchers is taxable to the employees.

Issues
[*Identify the issue(s) raised by the Facts. Be specific.*] The taxability of the meal vouchers depends on three issues: first, whether the meals are furnished "for the convenience of the employer"; second, whether they are furnished "on the business premises of the employer"; and third, whether the vouchers are equivalent to cash.

Applicable Law
[*Discuss those legal principles that both strengthen and weaken the client's case. Because the primary authority for tax law is the IRC, begin with the IRC.*] IRC Sec. 119 provides that the value of meals is excludible from an employee's income if the meals are furnished for the convenience of, and on the business premises of the employer. [*Discuss how administrative and/or judicial authorities expound on statutory terms.*] Under Reg. Sec. 1.119-1, a meal is furnished "for the convenience of the employer" if it is furnished for a "substantial noncompensatory business reason." A "substantial noncompensatory business reason" includes the need to have the employee available for emergency calls during his or her meal period. Under IRC Sec. 119(b)(4), if more than half the employees satisfy the "for the convenience of hte employer" test, all employees will be regarded as satisfying the test. Regulation Sec. 1.119-1 defines "business premises of the employer" as the place of employment of the employee.

[*When discussing court cases, present case facts in such a way as to enable the reader to draw an analogy with client facts.*] A Supreme Court case, *Kowalski v. CIR,* 434 U.S. 77, 77-2 USTC ¶9748, discusses what constitutes "meals" for purposes of IRC Sec. 119. In *Kowalski,* the State of New Jersey furnished cash meal allowances to its state troopers to enable them to eat while on duty. It did not require the troopers to use the allowances exclusively for meals. Nor did it require them to consume their meals on its business premises. One trooper, R.J. Kowalski, excluded the value of his allowances from his income. The IRS disputed this treatment, and Kowalski took the IRS to Court. In Court, Kowalski argued that the allowances were excludible because they were furnished "for the convenience of the employer." The IRS contended that the allowances were taxable because they amounted to compensation. The U.S. Supreme Court took up the case and decided for the IRS. The Court held that the IRC Sec. 119 income exlusion does not apply to payments in cash.

Analysis
[*The Analysis should (a) apply Applicable Law to the Facts and (b) address the Issue(s). In this section, every proposition should be supported by either authority, logic, or plausible assumptions.*]

Issue 1: The meals provided by Mercy seem to be furnished "for the convenience of the employer." They are furnished to have employees available for emergency call during their meal breaks. This is a "substantial noncompensatory reason" within the meaning of Reg. Sec. 1.119-1.

Issue 2: Although the hospital cafeteria appears to be the "business premises of the employer," MacDougal's does not appear to be. The hospital is the place of employment of the medical employees. MacDougal's is not.

Issue 3: [*In applying case law to the Facts, indicate how case facts are similar to/dissimilar from client facts. If the analysis does not support a "yes-no" answer, do not give one.*] Based on the foregoing authorities, it is unclear whether the vouchers are equivalent to cash. On the one hand, they are redeemable only in meals. Thus, they resemble meals-in-kind. On the other hand, they are redeemable at more than one institution. Thus, they resemble cash. Nor is it clear whether a court deciding this case would reach the same conclusion as the Supreme Court did in *Kowalski.* In the latter case, the State of New Jersey provided its meal allowances in the form of cash. It did not require its employees to use the allowances exclusively for meals. Nor did it require them to consume their meals on its business premises. In our case, Mercy provides its meal allowances in the form of vouchers. Thus, it indirectly requires its employees to use the allowances exclusively for meals. On the other hand, it does not require them to consume their meals on its business premises.

Conclusion
[*The conclusion should (a) logically flow from the Analysis, and (b) address the Issue(s).*] Although it appears that the meals acquired by voucher in the hospital cafeteria are furnished "for the convenience of the employer" and "on the business premises of the employer," it is unclear whether the vouchers are equivalent to cash. If they *are* equivalent to cash, *or* if they are redeemed at MacDougal's, their value is likely to be taxable to the employees. On the other hand, if they are not equivalent to cash, *and* they are redeemed only in the hospital cafeteria, their value is likely to be excludible.

Professional Accounting Associates
2701 First City Plaza
Suite 905
Dallas, Texas 75019

December 12, 20X1

Elizabeth Fegali, Chief Administrator
Mercy Hospital
22650 West Haven Drive
Arlington, Texas 75527

Dear Ms. Fegali:

[*Introduction. Set a cordial tone.*] It was great to see you at last Thursday's football game. If not for that last minute fumble, the Longhorns might have taken the Big 12 Conference championship!

[*Issue/Purpose.*] In our meeting of December 6, you asked us to research whether the value of the meal vouchers that Mercy provides to its medical employees is taxable to the employees. [*Short Answer.*] I regret to inform you that if the vouchers are redeemed at MacDougal's, their value is likely to be taxable to the employees. On the other hand, if the vouchers are redeemed in the hospital cafeteria, their value is likely to be excludible from the employee's income. [*The remainder of the letter should elaborate, support, and qualify this answer.*]

[*Steps Taken in Deriving Conclusion.*] In reaching this conclusion, we consulted relevant provisions of the Internal Revenue Code ("IRC"), applicable Treasury Regulations under the IRC, and a pertinent Supreme Court case. In addition, we reviewed the documents on employee benefits that you submitted to us at our earlier meeting.

[*Facts. State only the facts that are relevant to the Issue and necessary for the Analysis.*] The facts as we understand them are as follows: Mercy provides meal vouchers to its medical employees to enable them to eat while on emergency call. The vouchers are redeemable either in the hospital cafeteria or at MacDougal's. MacDougal's is a privately owned institution that rents business space from the hospital. Although Mercy's employees are not required to remain on or near the premises during their meal hours, they generally do.

Applicable Law. State, do not interpret.] Under the IRC, the value of meals is excludible from an employee's income if two conditions are met: first, the meals are furnished "for the convenience of the employer" and second, they are provided "on the business premises of the employer." Although the IRC does not explain what is meant by "for the convenience of the employer," "business premises of the employer," and "meals," other authorities do. Specificly, the Treasury Regulations define "business premises of the employer" to be the place of employment of the employees. The regulations state that providing meals during work hours to have an employee available for emergency calls is "for the convenience of the employer." Moreover, under the IRC, if more than half the employees satisfy the "for the convenience of the employer" test, all the employees will be regarded as satisfying the test. The Supreme Court has interpreted "meals" to mean food-in-kind. The Court has held that cash allowances do not qualify as "meals."

[*Analysis. Express the generalities of Applicable Law in terms of the specifics of the Facts.*] Clearly, the meals furnished by Mercy are "for the convenience of the employer." They are furnished during the employees' work hours to have the employees available for emergency call. Although the meals provided in the hospital cafeteria appear to be furnished "on the business premises of the employer," the meals provided at MacDougal's do not appear to be. The hospital is the place of employment of the medical employees. MacDougal's is not. What is unclear is whether the meal vouchers are equivalent to food-in-kind. On the one hand, they are redeemable at more than one institution and thus resemble cash allowances. On the other hand, they are redeemable only in meals and thus resemble food-in-kind.

[*Conclusion/Recommendation.*] Because of this lack of clarity, we suggest that you modify your employee benefits plan to allow for the provision of meals-in-kind exclusively in the hospital cafeteria. In this way, you will dispel any doubt that Mercy is furnishing "meals," "for the convenience of the employer," "on the premises of the employer."

[*Closing/Follow Up.*] Please call me at 475-2020 if you have any questions concerning this conclusion. May I suggest that we meet next week to discuss the possibility of revising your employee benefits plan.

Very truly yours,
Professional Accounting Associates

By: Rosina Havacek, Junior Associate

APPENDIX B

COMPLETED TAX FORMS

Form #	Form Title	Page #
706	U.S. Estate (and Generation-Skipping Transfer) Tax Return	B-3
709	U.S. Gift (and Generation-Skipping Transfer) Tax Return	B-18
1040	U.S. Individual Income Tax Return	I2-8
1040	Schedule A—Itemized Deductions	I7-35
1040	Schedule B—Interest and Dividend Income	I3-31
1040	Schedule C—Profit or Loss From Business	I10-26
1040	Schedule D—Capital Gains and Losses	I5-34
1040	Schedule E—Supplemental Income and Loss	B-21
1040	Schedule SE—Social Security Self-Employment Tax	B-23
1040	Schedule F—Profit or Loss From Farming	B-25
1041	U.S. Fiduciary Income Tax Return (Simple Trust)	B-27
1041	U.S. Fiduciary Income Tax Return (Complex Trust)	B-32
1065	U.S. Partnership Return of Income	B-38
1120	U.S. Corporation Income Tax Return	B-46
1120	Consolidated Tax Return	B-52
1120S	U.S. Income Tax Return for an S Corporation	B-55
2106	Employee Business Expenses	I9-45
2120	Multiple Support Declaration	I2-15
2210	Underpayment of Estimated Tax by Individuals and Fiduciaries	B-63
2220	Underpayment of Estimated Tax By Corporations	B-66
4562	Depreciation and Amortization	I10-24
4626	Alternative Minimum Tax—Corporation	B-68
4684	Casualties and Thefts	I13-28
4797	Sales of Business Property	I13-26

6251	Alternative Minimum Tax—Individuals	B-71
6252	Installment Sale Income	I11-29
7004	Application for Automatic Extension of Time to File Corporation Income Tax Return	B-73
8615	Tax for Children Under Age 14 Who Have Investment Income of More Than $1,300	B-74

Note: Because of the availability of tax forms from many sources, only a limited number of forms are reprinted in this textbook. All federal forms are available from the Internal Revenue Service, either in paper form or from the IRS Web site, http://www.irs.gov

Form **706**

(Rev. November 2001)

Department of the Treasury
Internal Revenue Service

United States Estate (and Generation-Skipping Transfer) Tax Return

Estate of a citizen or resident of the United States (see separate instructions).
To be filed for decedents dying after December 31, 2000, and before January 1, 2002.
For Paperwork Reduction Act Notice, see page 25 of the separate instructions.

OMB No. 1545-0015

Part 1.—Decedent and Executor

1a Decedent's first name and middle initial (and maiden name, if any): Herman		1b Decedent's last name: Estes		2 Decedent's Social Security No.: 999 11 4444
3a Legal residence (domicile) at time of death (county, state, and ZIP code, or foreign country): Ohio		3b Year domicile established: 1935	4 Date of birth: 1917	5 Date of death: 10-13-2001
6a Name of executor (see page 4 of the instructions): John Johnson		6b Executor's address (number and street including apartment or suite no. or rural route; city, town, or post office; state; and ZIP code): 10 Main Place Dayton, OH 45347		
6c Executor's social security number (see page 4 of the instructions): 998 12 5732				
7a Name and location of court where will was probated or estate administered				7b Case number
8 If decedent died testate, check here ▶ ☒ and attach a certified copy of the will.		9 If Form 4768 is attached, check here ▶ ☐		
10 If Schedule R-1 is attached, check here ▶ ☐				

Part 2.—Tax Computation

1	Total gross estate less exclusion (from Part 5, Recapitulation, page 3, item 12)			1	1,661,900
2	Total allowable deductions (from Part 5, Recapitulation, page 3, item 23)			2	1,176,700
3	Taxable estate (subtract line 2 from line 1)			3	485,200
4	Adjusted taxable gifts (total taxable gifts (within the meaning of section 2503) made by the decedent after December 31, 1976, other than gifts that are includible in decedent's gross estate (section 2001(b)))			4	680,000
5	Add lines 3 and 4			5	1,165,200
6	Tentative tax on the amount on line 5 from Table A on page 12 of the instructions			6	413,532
7a	If line 5 exceeds $10,000,000, enter the lesser of line 5 or $17,184,000. If line 5 is $10,000,000 or less, skip lines 7a and 7b and enter -0- on line 7c	7a			
b	Subtract $10,000,000 from line 7a	7b			
c	Enter 5% (.05) of line 7b			7c	-0-
8	Total tentative tax (add lines 6 and 7c)			8	413,532
9	Total gift tax payable with respect to gifts made by the decedent after December 31, 1976. Include gift taxes by the decedent's spouse for such spouse's share of split gifts (section 2513) only if the decedent was the donor of these gifts and they are includible in the decedent's gross estate (see instructions)			9	30,650
10	Gross estate tax (subtract line 9 from line 8)			10	382,882
11	Maximum unified credit (applicable credit amount) against estate tax	11	220,550		
12	Adjustment to unified credit (applicable credit amount). (This adjustment may not exceed $6,000. See page 4 of the instructions.)	12			
13	Allowable unified credit (applicable credit amount) (subtract line 12 from line 11)			13	220,550
14	Subtract line 13 from line 10 (but do not enter less than zero)			14	162,332
15	Credit for state death taxes. Do not enter more than line 14. Figure the credit by using the amount on line 3 less $60,000. See Table B in the instructions and **attach credit evidence** (see instructions)			15	9,526
16	Subtract line 15 from line 14			16	152,806
17	Credit for Federal gift taxes on pre-1977 gifts (section 2012) (attach computation)	17			
18	Credit for foreign death taxes (from Schedule(s) P). (Attach Form(s) 706-CE.)	18			
19	Credit for tax on prior transfers (from Schedule Q)	19			
20	Total (add lines 17, 18, and 19)			20	
21	Net estate tax (subtract line 20 from line 16)			21	152,806
22	Generation-skipping transfer taxes (from Schedule R, Part 2, line 10)			22	
23	Total transfer taxes (add lines 21 and 22)			23	152,806
24	Prior payments. Explain in an attached statement	24			
25	United States Treasury bonds redeemed in payment of estate tax	25			
26	Total (add lines 24 and 25)			26	
27	Balance due (or overpayment) (subtract line 26 from line 23)			27	152,806

Under penalties of perjury, I declare that I have examined this return, including accompanying schedules and statements, and to the best of my knowledge and belief, it is true, correct, and complete. Declaration of preparer other than the executor is based on all information of which preparer has any knowledge.

John Johnson — Signature(s) of executor(s) — Date: 5-14-02

Mary Wilson — Signature of preparer other than executor — Address (and ZIP code): 100 Tower Building Austin TX 78703 — Date: 5-12-02

Cat. No. 20548R

Note: Pages not pertinent to the tax consequences are omitted.

Form 706 (Rev. 11-01)

Estate of:

Part 3—Elections by the Executor

Please check the "Yes" or "No" box for each question. (See instructions beginning on page 5.)		Yes	No
1 Do you elect alternate valuation?	1		X
2 Do you elect special use valuation? If "Yes," you must complete and attach Schedule A-1.	2		X
3 Do you elect to pay the taxes in installments as described in section 6166? If "Yes," you must attach the additional information described on page 8 of the instructions.	3		X
4 Do you elect to postpone the part of the taxes attributable to a reversionary or remainder interest as described in section 6163?	4		X

Part 4—General Information

(Note: *Please attach the necessary supplemental documents.* **You must attach the death certificate.)** *(See instructions on page 9.)*

Authorization to receive confidential tax information under Regs. sec. 601.504(b)(2)(i); to act as the estate's representative before the IRS; and to make written or oral presentations on behalf of the estate if return prepared by an attorney, accountant, or enrolled agent for the executor:

Name of representative (print or type)	State	Address (number, street, and room or suite no., city, state, and ZIP code)
John Johnson	Ohio	10 Main Place Dayton, OH 45347

I declare that I am the ☐ attorney/ ☐ certified public accountant/ ☐ enrolled agent (you must check the applicable box) for the executor and prepared this return for the executor. I am not under suspension or disbarment from practice before the Internal Revenue Service and am qualified to practice in the state shown above.

Signature	CAF number	Date	Telephone number
John Johnson	111-2222	5-14-02	(512) 444-4444

1 Death certificate number and issuing authority (attach a copy of the death certificate to this return).
1246 County Coroner

2 Decedent's business or occupation. If retired, check here ▶ ☐ and state decedent's former business or occupation.
Executive

3 Marital status of the decedent at time of death:
- ☒ Married
- ☐ Widow or widower—Name, SSN, and date of death of deceased spouse ▶
- ☐ Single
- ☐ Legally separated
- ☐ Divorced—Date divorce decree became final ▶

4a Surviving spouse's name	4b Social security number	4c Amount received (see page 9 of the instructions)
Ann Estes	555 77 9999	1,050,000

5 Individuals (other than the surviving spouse), trusts, or other estates who receive benefits from the estate (do not include charitable beneficiaries shown in Schedule O) (see instructions). For Privacy Act Notice (applicable to individual beneficiaries only), see the Instructions for Form 1040.

Name of individual, trust, or estate receiving $5,000 or more	Identifying number	Relationship to decedent	Amount (see instructions)
Johnny Estes	555-61-4107	Son	260,109
Billy Estes	556-63-4437	Son	60,109
Daughter, Dorothy Estes, receives the corpus in the special power of appointment trust created by Amelia Estes.			
All unascertainable beneficiaries and those who receive less than $5,000 ▶			
Total			320,218

Please check the "Yes" or "No" box for each question.	Yes	No
6 Does the gross estate contain any section 2044 property (qualified terminable interest property (QTIP) from a prior gift or estate) (see page 9 of the instructions)?		X

(continued on next page)

Form 706 (Rev. 11-01)

Part 4—General Information *(continued)*

Please check the "Yes" or "No" box for each question.	Yes	No
7a Have Federal gift tax returns ever been filed? If "Yes," please attach copies of the returns, if available, and furnish the following information:	X	
7b Period(s) covered: 1974, 1978, 1998 — **7c** Internal Revenue office(s) where filed: Cincinnati, Ohio		
If you answer "Yes" to any of questions 8–16, you must attach additional information as described in the instructions.		
8a Was there any insurance on the decedent's life that is not included on the return as part of the gross estate?		X
b Did the decedent own any insurance on the life of another that is not included in the gross estate?		X
9 Did the decedent at the time of death own any property as a joint tenant with right of survivorship in which **(a)** one or more of the other joint tenants was someone other than the decedent's spouse, and **(b)** less than the full value of the property is included on the return as part of the gross estate? If "Yes," you must complete and attach Schedule E		X
10 Did the decedent, at the time of death, own any interest in a partnership or unincorporated business or any stock in an inactive or closely held corporation?		X
11 Did the decedent make any transfer described in section 2035, 2036, 2037, or 2038 (see the instructions for Schedule G beginning on page 11 of the separate instructions)? If "Yes," you must complete and attach Schedule G	X	
12 Were there in existence at the time of the decedent's death:		
a Any trusts created by the decedent during his or her lifetime?		X
b Any trusts not created by the decedent under which the decedent possessed any power, beneficial interest, or trusteeship?	X	
13 Did the decedent ever possess, exercise, or release any general power of appointment? If "Yes," you must complete and attach Schedule H		X
14 Was the marital deduction computed under the transitional rule of Public Law 97-34, section 403(e)(3) (Economic Recovery Tax Act of 1981)? If "Yes," attach a separate computation of the marital deduction, enter the amount on item 20 of the Recapitulation, and note on item 20 "computation attached."		X
15 Was the decedent, immediately before death, receiving an annuity described in the "General" paragraph of the instructions for Schedule I? If "Yes," you must complete and attach Schedule I	X	
16 Was the decedent ever the beneficiary of a trust for which a deduction was claimed by the estate of a pre-deceased spouse under section 2056(b)(7) and which is not reported on this return? If "Yes," attach an explanation		X

Part 5—Recapitulation

Item number	Gross estate		Alternate value	Value at date of death
1	Schedule A—Real Estate	1		325,000
2	Schedule B—Stocks and Bonds	2		600,000
3	Schedule C—Mortgages, Notes, and Cash	3		94,250
4	Schedule D—Insurance on the Decedent's Life (attach Form(s) 712)	4		200,000
5	Schedule E—Jointly Owned Property (attach Form(s) 712 for life insurance)	5		200,000
6	Schedule F—Other Miscellaneous Property (attach Form(s) 712 for life insurance)	6		
7	Schedule G—Transfers During Decedent's Life (att. Form(s) 712 for life insurance)	7		2,650
8	Schedule H—Powers of Appointment	8		
9	Schedule I—Annuities	9		240,000
10	Total gross estate (add items 1 through 9)	10		1,661,900
11	Schedule U—Qualified Conservation Easement Exclusion	11		
12	Total gross estate less exclusion (subtract item 11 from item 10). Enter here and on line 1 of Part 2—Tax Computation	12		1,661,900

Item number	Deductions		Amount
13	Schedule J—Funeral Expenses and Expenses Incurred in Administering Property Subject to Claims	13	85,000
14	Schedule K—Debts of the Decedent	14	31,700
15	Schedule K—Mortgages and Liens	15	
16	Total of items 13 through 15	16	116,700
17	Allowable amount of deductions from item 16 (see the instructions for item 17 of the Recapitulation)	17	116,700
18	Schedule L—Net Losses During Administration	18	
19	Schedule L—Expenses Incurred in Administering Property Not Subject to Claims	19	
20	Schedule M—Bequests, etc., to Surviving Spouse	20	1,050,000
21	Schedule O—Charitable, Public, and Similar Gifts and Bequests	21	10,000
22	Schedule T—Qualified Family-Owned Business Interest Deduction	22	
23	Total allowable deductions (add items 17 through 22). Enter here and on line 2 of the Tax Computation	23	1,176,700

Form 706 (Rev. 11-01)

Estate of: Herman Estes

SCHEDULE A—Real Estate

- *For jointly owned property that must be disclosed on Schedule E, see the instructions on the reverse side of Schedule E.*
- *Real estate that is part of a sole proprietorship should be shown on Schedule F.*
- *Real estate that is included in the gross estate under section 2035, 2036, 2037, or 2038 should be shown on Schedule G.*
- *Real estate that is included in the gross estate under section 2041 should be shown on Schedule H.*
- *If you elect section 2032A valuation, you must complete Schedule A and Schedule A-1.*

Item number	Description	Alternate valuation date	Alternate value	Value at date of death
1	Personal residence, house and lot, located at 105 Elm Court, Dayton, Ohio			325,000
	Total from continuation schedules or additional sheets attached to this schedule . . .			
	TOTAL. (Also enter on Part 5, Recapitulation, page 3, at item 1.)			325,000

(If more space is needed, attach the continuation schedule from the end of this package or additional sheets of the same size.)
(See the instructions on the reverse side.)

Form 706 (Rev. 11-01)

Estate of: Herman Estes

SCHEDULE B—Stocks and Bonds

(For jointly owned property that must be disclosed on Schedule E, see the instructions for Schedule E.)

Item number	Description including face amount of bonds or number of shares and par value where needed for identification. Give 9-digit CUSIP number.	CUSIP number	Unit value	Alternate valuation date	Alternate value	Value at date of death
1	Stock in Ajax Corporation 1000 shares, $10 par value		600			600,000
	Total from continuation schedules (or additional sheets) attached to this schedule . . .					
	TOTAL. (Also enter on Part 5, Recapitulation, page 3, at item 2.)					600,000

(If more space is needed, attach the continuation schedule from the end of this package or additional sheets of the same size.)
(The instructions to Schedule B are in the separate instructions.)

Form 706 (Rev. 11-01)

Estate of: Herman Estes

SCHEDULE C—Mortgages, Notes, and Cash

(For jointly owned property that must be disclosed on Schedule E, see the instructions for Schedule E.)

Item number	Description	Alternate valuation date	Alternate value	Value at date of death
1	Checking account			19,250
2	Savings account (includes accrued interest through date of death.)			75,000
	Total from continuation schedules (or additional sheets) attached to this schedule . .			
	TOTAL. (Also enter on Part 5, Recapitulation, page 3, at item 3.)			94,250

(If more space is needed, attach the continuation schedule from the end of this package or additional sheets of the same size.)
(See the instructions on the reverse side.)

Form 706 (Rev. 11-01)

Estate of: Herman Estes

SCHEDULE D—Insurance on the Decedent's Life

You must list **all** policies on the life of the decedent and attach a Form 712 for each policy.

Item number	Description	Alternate valuation date	Alternate value	Value at date of death
1	Life insurance policy No. 123-A issued by the Life Insurance Company of Ohio Beneficiary – Johnny Estes			200,000
	Total from continuation schedules (or additional sheets) attached to this schedule . .			
	TOTAL. (Also enter on Part 5, Recapitulation, page 3, at item 4.).			200,000

(If more space is needed, attach the continuation schedule from the end of this package or additional sheets of the same size.)

(See the instructions on the reverse side.)

Form 706 (Rev. 11-01)

Estate of: Herman Estes

SCHEDULE E—Jointly Owned Property

(If you elect section 2032A valuation, you must complete Schedule E and Schedule A-1.)

PART 1.—Qualified Joint Interests—Interests Held by the Decedent and His or Her Spouse as the Only Joint Tenants (Section 2040(b)(2))

Item number	Description For securities, give CUSIP number.	Alternate valuation date	Alternate value	Value at date of death
	Land			400,000
	Total from continuation schedules (or additional sheets) attached to this schedule			
1a	Totals	**1a**		400,000
1b	Amounts included in gross estate (one-half of line **1a**)	**1b**		200,000

PART 2.—All Other Joint Interests

2a State the name and address of each surviving co-tenant. If there are more than three surviving co-tenants, list the additional co-tenants on an attached sheet.

	Name	Address (number and street, city, state, and ZIP code)
A.		
B.		
C.		

Item number	Enter letter for co-tenant	Description (including alternate valuation date if any) For securities, give CUSIP number.	Percentage includible	Includible alternate value	Includible value at date of death
		Total from continuation schedules (or additional sheets) attached to this schedule			
2b		Total other joint interests			
3		**Total includible joint interests** (add lines 1b and 2b). Also enter on Part 5, Recapitulation, page 3, at item 5			200,000

(If more space is needed, attach the continuation schedule from the end of this package or additional sheets of the same size.)
(See the instructions on the reverse side.)

Form 706 (Rev. 11-01)

Estate of: Herman Estes

SCHEDULE F—Other Miscellaneous Property Not Reportable Under Any Other Schedule

(For jointly owned property that must be disclosed on Schedule E, see the instructions for Schedule E.)
(If you elect section 2032A valuation, you must complete Schedule F and Schedule A-1.)

		Yes	No
1	Did the decedent at the time of death own any articles of artistic or collectible value in excess of $3,000 or any collections whose artistic or collectible value combined at date of death exceeded $10,000? . . . . If "Yes," submit full details on this schedule and attach appraisals.		X
2	Has the decedent's estate, spouse, or any other person, received (or will receive) any bonus or award as a result of the decedent's employment or death? . . . . If "Yes," submit full details on this schedule.		X
3	Did the decedent at the time of death have, or have access to, a safe deposit box? . . . . If "Yes," state location, and if held in joint names of decedent and another, state name and relationship of joint depositor. If any of the contents of the safe deposit box are omitted from the schedules in this return, explain fully why omitted.		X

Item number	Description For securities, give CUSIP number.	Alternate valuation date	Alternate value	Value at date of death
1				
	Total from continuation schedules (or additional sheets) attached to this schedule . .			
	TOTAL. (Also enter on Part 5, Recapitulation, page 3, at item 6.)			–0–

(If more space is needed, attach the continuation schedule from the end of this package or additional sheets of the same size.)
(See the instructions on the reverse side.)

Form 706 (Rev. 11-01)

Estate of: Herman Estes

SCHEDULE G—Transfers During Decedent's Life

(If you elect section 2032A valuation, you must complete Schedule G and Schedule A-1.)

Item number	Description For securities, give CUSIP number.	Alternate valuation date	Alternate value	Value at date of death
A.	Gift tax paid by the decedent or the estate for all gifts made by the decedent or his or her spouse within 3 years before the decedent's death (section 2035(b))	X X X X X		2,650
B.	Transfers includible under section 2035(a), 2036, 2037, or 2038:			
1				
	Total from continuation schedules (or additional sheets) attached to this schedule . .			
	TOTAL. (Also enter on Part 5, Recapitulation, page 3, at item 7.)			2,650

SCHEDULE H—Powers of Appointment

(Include "5 and 5 lapsing" powers (section 2041(b)(2)) held by the decedent.)

(If you elect section 2032A valuation, you must complete Schedule H and Schedule A-1.)

Item number	Description	Alternate valuation date	Alternate value	Value at date of death
1				
	Total from continuation schedules (or additional sheets) attached to this schedule . .			
	TOTAL. (Also enter on Part 5, Recapitulation, page 3, at item 8.)			

(If more space is needed, attach the continuation schedule from the end of this package or additional sheets of the same size.)
(The instructions to Schedules G and H are in the separate instructions.)

Form 706 (Rev. 11-01)

Estate of: Herman Estes

SCHEDULE I—Annuities

Note: *Generally, no exclusion is allowed for the estates of decedents dying after December 31, 1984 (see page 14 of the instructions).*

		Yes	No
A	Are you excluding from the decedent's gross estate the value of a lump-sum distribution described in section 2039(f)(2) (as in effect before its repeal by the Deficit Reduction Act of 1984)? . . . . If "Yes," you must attach the information required by the instructions.		X

Item number	Description Show the entire value of the annuity before any exclusions.	Alternate valuation date	Includible alternate value	Includible value at date of death
1	Qualified pension plan issued by Buckeye Corporation Beneficiary - Ann Estes - spouse			240,000
	Total from continuation schedules (or additional sheets) attached to this schedule . .			
	TOTAL. (Also enter on Part 5, Recapitulation, page 3, at item 9.)			240,000

(If more space is needed, attach the continuation schedule from the end of this package or additional sheets of the same size.)

(The instructions to Schedule I are in the separate instructions.)

Form 706 (Rev. 11-01)

Estate of: Herman Estes

SCHEDULE J—Funeral Expenses and Expenses Incurred in Administering Property Subject to Claims

Note: *Do not list on this schedule expenses of administering property not subject to claims. For those expenses, see the instructions for Schedule L.*

If executors' commissions, attorney fees, etc., are claimed and allowed as a deduction for estate tax purposes, they are not allowable as a deduction in computing the taxable income of the estate for Federal income tax purposes. They are allowable as an income tax deduction on Form 1041 if a waiver is filed to waive the deduction on Form 706 (see the Form 1041 instructions).

Item number	Description	Expense amount	Total amount
	A. Funeral expenses:	15,000	
1			
	Total funeral expenses . . . . ▶		15,000
	B. Administration expenses:		
	1 Executors' commissions—amount estimated/agreed upon/paid. (Strike out the words that do not apply.)		70,000
	2 Attorney fees—amount estimated/agreed upon/paid. (Strike out the words that do not apply.). .		
	3 Accountant fees—amount estimated/agreed upon/paid. (Strike out the words that do not apply.).		
	4 Miscellaneous expenses:	Expense amount	
	Total miscellaneous expenses from continuation schedules (or additional sheets) attached to this schedule		
	Total miscellaneous expenses . . . . ▶		

TOTAL. (Also enter on Part 5, Recapitulation, page 3, at item 13.) . . . . ▶ 85,000

(If more space is needed, attach the continuation schedule from the end of this package or additional sheets of the same size.)
(See the instructions on the reverse side.)

Form 706 (Rev. 11-01)

Estate of: Herman Estes

SCHEDULE K—Debts of the Decedent, and Mortgages and Liens

Item number	Debts of the Decedent—Creditor and nature of claim, and allowable death taxes	Amount unpaid to date	Amount in contest	Amount claimed as a deduction
1	Bank Loan (including interest accrued through date of death)	25,200		25,200
2	American Express, Visa, and Master Card credit card debts	6,500		6,500
	Total from continuation schedules (or additional sheets) attached to this schedule			
	TOTAL. (Also enter on Part 5, Recapitulation, page 3, at item 14.)			31,700

Item number	Mortgages and Liens—Description	Amount
1		
	Total from continuation schedules (or additional sheets) attached to this schedule	
	TOTAL. (Also enter on Part 5, Recapitulation, page 3, at item 15.)	

(If more space is needed, attach the continuation schedule from the end of this package or additional sheets of the same size.)
(The instructions to Schedule K are in the separate instructions.)

Form 706 (Rev. 11-01)

Estate of: Herman Estes

SCHEDULE M—Bequests, etc., to Surviving Spouse

Election To Deduct Qualified Terminable Interest Property Under Section 2056(b)(7). If a trust (or other property) meets the requirements of qualified terminable interest property under section 2056(b)(7), and

a. The trust or other property is listed on Schedule M, and

b. The value of the trust (or other property) is entered in whole or in part as a deduction on Schedule M,

then unless the executor specifically identifies the trust (all or a fractional portion or percentage) or other property to be excluded from the election, the executor shall be deemed to have made an election to have such trust (or other property) treated as qualified terminable interest property under section 2056(b)(7).

If less than the entire value of the trust (or other property) that the executor has included in the gross estate is entered as a deduction on Schedule M, the executor shall be considered to have made an election only as to a fraction of the trust (or other property). The numerator of this fraction is equal to the amount of the trust (or other property) deducted on Schedule M. The denominator is equal to the total value of the trust (or other property).

Election To Deduct Qualified Domestic Trust Property Under Section 2056A. If a trust meets the requirements of a qualified domestic trust under section 2056A(a) and this return is filed no later than 1 year after the time prescribed by law (including extensions) for filing the return, and

a. The entire value of a trust or trust property is listed on Schedule M, and

b. The entire value of the trust or trust property is entered as a deduction on Schedule M,

then unless the executor specifically identifies the trust to be excluded from the election, the executor shall be deemed to have made an election to have the entire trust treated as qualified domestic trust property.

			Yes	No
1	Did any property pass to the surviving spouse as a result of a qualified disclaimer? *If "Yes," attach a copy of the written disclaimer required by section 2518(b).*	1		X
2a	In what country was the surviving spouse born? United States			
b	What is the surviving spouse's date of birth? 3/12/40			
c	Is the surviving spouse a U.S. citizen?	2c	X	
d	If the surviving spouse is a naturalized citizen, when did the surviving spouse acquire citizenship? N/A			
e	If the surviving spouse is not a U.S. citizen, of what country is the surviving spouse a citizen? N/A			
3	**Election Out of QTIP Treatment of Annuities**—Do you elect under section 2056(b)(7)(C)(ii) **not** to treat as qualified terminable interest property any joint and survivor annuities that are included in the gross estate and would otherwise be treated as qualified terminable interest property under section 2056(b)(7)(C)? (see instructions)	3		X

Item number	Description of property interests passing to surviving spouse	Amount
1	Residence	325,000
2	Checking account	10,000
3	Savings account	75,000
4	Land, held in joint tenancy	200,000
5	Qualified pension plan	240,000
6	Trust with First Bank as Trustee	200,000
	Total from continuation schedules (or additional sheets) attached to this schedule	
4	**Total** amount of property interests listed on Schedule M (4)	1,050,000
5a	Federal estate taxes payable out of property interests listed on Schedule M (5a)	
b	Other death taxes payable out of property interests listed on Schedule M (5b)	
c	Federal and state GST taxes payable out of property interests listed on Schedule M (5c)	
d	Add items 5a, b, and c (5d)	-0-
6	Net amount of property interests listed on Schedule M (subtract 5d from 4). Also enter on Part 5, Recapitulation, page 3, at item 20 (6)	1,050,000

(If more space is needed, attach the continuation schedule from the end of this package or additional sheets of the same size.)
(See the instructions on the reverse side.)

Form 706 (Rev. 11-01)

Estate of: Herman Estes

SCHEDULE O—Charitable, Public, and Similar Gifts and Bequests

		Yes	No
1a	If the transfer was made by will, has any action been instituted to have interpreted or to contest the will or any of its provisions affecting the charitable deductions claimed in this schedule? . . . . If "Yes," full details must be submitted with this schedule.		X
b	According to the information and belief of the person or persons filing this return, is any such action planned? If "Yes," full details must be submitted with this schedule.		X
2	Did any property pass to charity as the result of a qualified disclaimer? . . . . If "Yes," attach a copy of the written disclaimer required by section 2518(b).		X

Item number	Name and address of beneficiary	Character of institution	Amount
1	American Cancer Society	Charity	10,000

Total from continuation schedules (or additional sheets) attached to this schedule		
3 Total	3	10,000
4a Federal estate tax payable out of property interests listed above	4a	
b Other death taxes payable out of property interests listed above	4b	
c Federal and state GST taxes payable out of property interests listed above	4c	
d Add items 4a, b, and c	4d	
5 Net value of property interests listed above (subtract 4d from 3). Also enter on Part 5, Recapitulation, page 3, at item 21	5	10,000

(If more space is needed, attach the continuation schedule from the end of this package or additional sheets of the same size.)
(The instructions to Schedule O are in the separate instructions.)

Form **709**

Department of the Treasury
Internal Revenue Service

United States Gift (and Generation-Skipping Transfer) Tax Return

(Section 6019 of the Internal Revenue Code) (For gifts made during calendar year 2001)

▶ See separate instructions.

OMB No. 1545-0020

2001

Part 1—General Information

1 Donor's first name and middle initial	2 Donor's last name	3 Donor's social security number
Wilma	Brown	123 45 6789
4 Address (number, street, and apartment number)		5 Legal residence (domicile) (county and state)
2 Main Street		U.S.A.
6 City, state, and ZIP code		7 Citizenship
Dalton, GA 35901		U.S.A.

		Yes	No
8	If the donor died during the year, check here ▶ ☐ and enter date of death .... , ...		
9	If you received an extension of time to file this Form 709, check here ▶ ☐ and attach the Form 4868, 2688, 2350, or extension letter		
10	Enter the total number of separate donees listed on Schedule A—count each person only once. ▶ 5		
11a	Have you (the donor) previously filed a Form 709 (or 709-A) for any other year? If the answer is "No," do not complete line 11b	X	
11b	If the answer to line 11a is "Yes," has your address changed since you last filed Form 709 (or 709-A)?		X
12	Gifts by husband or wife to third parties.—Do you consent to have the gifts (including generation-skipping transfers) made by you and by your spouse to third parties during the calendar year considered as made one-half by each of you? (See instructions.) (If the answer is "Yes," the following information must be furnished and your spouse must sign the consent shown below. **If the answer is "No," skip lines 13–18 and go to Schedule A.**)	X	
13	Name of consenting spouse Hugh Brown — 14 SSN 987-65-4321		
15	Were you married to one another during the entire calendar year? (see instructions)	X	
16	If the answer to 15 is "No," check whether ☐ married ☐ divorced or ☐ widowed, and give date (see instructions) ▶		
17	Will a gift tax return for this calendar year be filed by your spouse?	X	

18 **Consent of Spouse**—I consent to have the gifts (and generation-skipping transfers) made by me and by my spouse to third parties during the calendar year considered as made one-half by each of us. We are both aware of the joint and several liability for tax created by the execution of this consent.

Consenting spouse's signature ▶ Hugh Brown — Date ▶ 3-2-2002

Part 2—Tax Computation

Line	Description		Amount
1	Enter the amount from Schedule A, Part 3, line 15	1	342,598
2	Enter the amount from Schedule B, line 3	2	500,000
3	Total taxable gifts (add lines 1 and 2)	3	842,598
4	Tax computed on amount on line 3 (see Table for Computing Tax in separate instructions)	4	284,413
5	Tax computed on amount on line 2 (see Table for Computing Tax in separate instructions)	5	155,800
6	Balance (subtract line 5 from line 4)	6	128,613
7	Maximum unified credit (nonresident aliens, see instructions)	7	220,550 00
8	Enter the unified credit against tax allowable for all prior periods (from Sch. B, line 1, col. C)	8	68,000
9	Balance (subtract line 8 from line 7)	9	152,550
10	Enter 20% (.20) of the amount allowed as a specific exemption for gifts made after September 8, 1976, and before January 1, 1977 (see instructions)	10	
11	Balance (subtract line 10 from line 9)	11	152,550
12	Unified credit (enter the smaller of line 6 or line 11)	12	128,613
13	Credit for foreign gift taxes (see instructions)	13	
14	Total credits (add lines 12 and 13)	14	128,613
15	Balance (subtract line 14 from line 6) (do not enter less than zero)	15	-0-
16	Generation-skipping transfer taxes (from Schedule C, Part 3, col. H, Total)	16	
17	Total tax (add lines 15 and 16)	17	-0-
18	Gift and generation-skipping transfer taxes prepaid with extension of time to file	18	
19	If line 18 is less than line 17, enter **balance due** (see instructions)	19	-0-
20	If line 18 is greater than line 17, enter **amount to be refunded**	20	

Attach check or money order here.

Sign Here

Under penalties of perjury, I declare that I have examined this return, including any accompanying schedules and statements, and to the best of my knowledge and belief, it is true, correct, and complete. Declaration of preparer (other than donor) is based on all information of which preparer has any knowledge.

Signature of donor: Wilma Brown — Date: 3-2-2002

Paid Preparer's Use Only

Preparer's signature ▶ Sally Preparer — Date 3-2-2002 — Check if self-employed ▶ ☒

Firm's name (or yours if self-employed), address, and ZIP code ▶ Sally Preparer 110 Last Bank Tower, Dalton, GA 35901 — Phone no. ▶ (706) 934-5000

For Disclosure, Privacy Act, and Paperwork Reduction Act Notice, see page 12 of the separate instructions for this form. Cat. No. 16783M Form **709** (2001)

Note: Page 4 not pertinent to the tax consequences is omitted.

Form 709 (2001) Page **2**

SCHEDULE A **Computation of Taxable Gifts** (Including Transfers in Trust)

A Does the value of any item listed on Schedule A reflect any valuation discount? If the answer is "Yes," see instructions . . Yes ☐ No ☒

B ☐ ◄ Check here if you elect under section 529(c)(2)(B) to treat any transfers made this year to a qualified state tuition program as made ratably over a 5-year period beginning this year. See instructions. Attach explanation.

Part 1—Gifts Subject Only to Gift Tax. *Gifts less political organization, medical, and educational exclusions—see instructions*

A Item number	B • Donee's name and address • Relationship to donor (if any) • Description of gift • If the gift was made by means of a trust, enter trust's EIN and attach a description or copy of the trust instrument (see instructions) • If the gift was of securities, give CUSIP number	C Donor's adjusted basis of gift	D Date of gift	E Value at date of gift
1	Billy Brown, Cash	80,000	2001	80,000
2	Betsy Brown, jewelry	18,000	2001	24,000
3	Ruth Cain, remainder interest in vacation cabin (0.21196 X 100,000)	15,000	2001	21,196
4	Trust at First Bank, income to Hugh Brown for life. Remainder to Jeff Bass (QTIP Trust)	480,000	2001	600,000
	Total of Part 1 (add amounts from Part 1, column E) . . . . ►			725,196

Part 2—Gifts That are Direct Skips and are Subject to Both Gift Tax and Generation-Skipping Transfer Tax. You must list the gifts in chronological order. *Gifts less political organization, medical, and educational exclusions—see instructions. (Also list here direct skips that are subject only to the GST tax at this time as the result of the termination of an "estate tax inclusion period." See instructions.)*

A Item number	B • Donee's name and address • Relationship to donor (if any) • Description of gift • If the gift was made by means of a trust, enter trust's EIN and attach a description or copy of the trust instrument (see instructions) • If the gift was of securities, give CUSIP number	C Donor's adjusted basis of gift	D Date of gift	E Value at date of gift
1				
	Total of Part 2 (add amounts from Part 2, column E) . . . . ►			

Part 3—Taxable Gift Reconciliation

				Line	Amount
1	Total value of gifts of donor (add totals from column E of Parts 1 and 2)			1	725,196
2	One-half of items 1, 2, 3 attributable to spouse (see instructions)			2	62,598
3	Balance (subtract line 2 from line 1)			3	662,598
4	Gifts of spouse to be included (from Schedule A, Part 3, line 2 of spouse's return—see instructions) . . If any of the gifts included on this line are also subject to the generation-skipping transfer tax, check here ► ☐ and enter those gifts also on Schedule C, Part 1.			4	340,000
5	Total gifts (add lines 3 and 4)			5	1,002,598
6	Total annual exclusions for gifts listed on Schedule A (including line 4, above) (see instructions)			6	40,000
7	Total included amount of gifts (subtract line 6 from line 5)			7	962,598
	Deductions (see instructions)				
8	Gifts of interests to spouse for which a marital deduction will be claimed, based on items 4 of Schedule A	8	600,000		
9	Exclusions attributable to gifts on line 8	9	10,000		
10	Marital deduction—subtract line 9 from line 8	10	590,000		
11	Charitable deduction, based on items part 2, line 4 less exclusions	11	30,000		
12	Total deductions—add lines 10 and 11			12	620,000
13	Subtract line 12 from line 7			13	342,598
14	Generation-skipping transfer taxes payable with this Form 709 (from Schedule C, Part 3, col. H, Total)			14	
15	Taxable gifts (add lines 13 and 14). Enter here and on line 1 of the Tax Computation on page 1			15	342,598

(If more space is needed, attach additional sheets of same size.)

Form **709** (2001)

Form 709 (2001) Page **3**

SCHEDULE A Computation of Taxable Gifts *(continued)*

16 Terminable Interest (QTIP) Marital Deduction. (See instructions for line 8 of Schedule A.)

If a trust (or other property) meets the requirements of qualified terminable interest property under section 2523(f), and

a. The trust (or other property) is listed on Schedule A, and

b. The value of the trust (or other property) is entered in whole or in part as a deduction on line 8, Part 3 of Schedule A,

then the donor shall be deemed to have made an election to have such trust (or other property) treated as qualified terminable interest property under section 2523(f).

If less than the entire value of the trust (or other property) that the donor has included in Part 1 of Schedule A is entered as a deduction on line 8, the donor shall be considered to have made an election only as to a fraction of the trust (or other property). The numerator of this fraction is equal to the amount of the trust (or other property) deducted on line 10 of Part 3, Schedule A. The denominator is equal to the total value of the trust (or other property) listed in Part 1 of Schedule A.

If you make the QTIP election (see instructions for line 8 of Schedule A), the terminable interest property involved will be included in your spouse's gross estate upon his or her death (section 2044). If your spouse disposes (by gift or otherwise) of all or part of the qualifying life income interest, he or she will be considered to have made a transfer of the entire property that is subject to the gift tax (see Transfer of Certain Life Estates on page 4 of the instructions).

17 Election Out of QTIP Treatment of Annuities

☐ ◀ Check here if you elect under section 2523(f)(6) **NOT** to treat as qualified terminable interest property any joint and survivor annuities that are reported on Schedule A and would otherwise be treated as qualified terminable interest property under section 2523(f). (See instructions.) Enter the item numbers (from Schedule A) for the annuities for which you are making this election ▶

SCHEDULE B Gifts From Prior Periods

If you answered "Yes" on line 11a of page 1, Part 1, see the instructions for completing Schedule B. If you answered "No," skip to the Tax Computation on page 1 (or Schedule C, if applicable).

A Calendar year or calendar quarter (see instructions)	B Internal Revenue office where prior return was filed	C Amount of unified credit against gift tax for periods after December 31, 1976	D Amount of specific exemption for prior periods ending before January 1, 1977	E Amount of taxable gifts
1975	Atlanta, Georgia	-0-	-0-	300,000
1988	Atlanta, Georgia	68,000		200,000

1	Totals for prior periods (without adjustment for reduced specific exemption)	1	68,000	500,000
2	Amount, if any, by which total specific exemption, line 1, column D, is more than $30,000	2		-0-
3	Total amount of taxable gifts for prior periods (add amount, column E, line 1, and amount, if any, on line 2). (Enter here and on line 2 of the Tax Computation on page 1.)	3		500,000

(If more space is needed, attach additional sheets of same size.)

Form **709** (2001)

SCHEDULE E (Form 1040)

Department of the Treasury
Internal Revenue Service (99)

Supplemental Income and Loss

(From rental real estate, royalties, partnerships, S corporations, estates, trusts, REMICs, etc.)

▶ Attach to Form 1040 or Form 1041. ▶ See Instructions for Schedule E (Form 1040).

OMB No. 1545-0074

2001

Attachment Sequence No. **13**

Name(s) shown on return | **Your social security number**

Part I **Income or Loss From Rental Real Estate and Royalties** **Note.** If you are in the business of renting personal property, use **Schedule C** or **C-EZ** (see page E-1). Report farm rental income or loss from **Form 4835** on page 2, line 39.

1 Show the kind and location of each **rental real estate property:**	**2** For each rental real estate property listed on line 1, did you or your family use it during the tax year for personal purposes for more than the greater of: • 14 days **or** • 10% of the total days rented at fair rental value? (See page E-1.)		**Yes**	**No**
A		**A**		
B		**B**		
C		**C**		

		Properties A	Properties B	Properties C		Totals (Add columns A, B, and C.)
Income:						
3 Rents received	**3**				**3**	
4 Royalties received	**4**				**4**	
Expenses:						
5 Advertising	**5**					
6 Auto and travel (see page E-2)	**6**					
7 Cleaning and maintenance	**7**					
8 Commissions	**8**					
9 Insurance	**9**					
10 Legal and other professional fees	**10**					
11 Management fees	**11**					
12 Mortgage interest paid to banks, etc. (see page E-2)	**12**				**12**	
13 Other interest	**13**					
14 Repairs	**14**					
15 Supplies	**15**					
16 Taxes	**16**					
17 Utilities	**17**					
18 Other (list) ▶	**18**					
19 Add lines 5 through 18	**19**				**19**	
20 Depreciation expense or depletion (see page E-3)	**20**				**20**	
21 Total expenses. Add lines 19 and 20	**21**					
22 Income or (loss) from rental real estate or royalty properties. Subtract line 21 from line 3 (rents) or line 4 (royalties). If the result is a (loss), see page E-3 to find out if you must file **Form 6198**	**22**					
23 Deductible rental real estate loss. **Caution.** Your rental real estate loss on line 22 may be limited. See page E-3 to find out if you must file **Form 8582.** Real estate professionals must complete line 42 on page 2	**23**	( )	( )	( )		
24 **Income.** Add positive amounts shown on line 22. **Do not** include any losses					**24**	
25 **Losses.** Add royalty losses from line 22 and rental real estate losses from line 23. Enter total losses here					**25**	( )
26 **Total rental real estate and royalty income or (loss).** Combine lines 24 and 25. Enter the result here. If Parts II, III, IV, and line 39 on page 2 do not apply to you, also enter this amount on Form 1040, line 17. Otherwise, include this amount in the total on line 40 on page 2					**26**	

Schedule E (Form 1040) 2001 — Attachment Sequence No. **13** — Page **2**

Name(s) shown on return. Do not enter name and social security number if shown on other side. | **Your social security number**

Note. If you report amounts from farming or fishing on Schedule E, you must enter your gross income from those activities on line 41 below. Real estate professionals must complete line 42 below.

Part II Income or Loss From Partnerships and S Corporations

Note. If you report a loss from an at-risk activity, you **must** check either column **(e)** or **(f)** on line 27 to describe your investment in the activity. See page E-5. If you check column **(f)**, you must attach **Form 6198.**

27	**(a)** Name	**(b)** Enter **P** for partnership; **S** for S corporation	**(c)** Check if foreign partnership	**(d)** Employer identification number	Investment At Risk? **(e)** All is at risk	**(f)** Some is not at risk
A						
B						
C						
D						
E						

	Passive Income and Loss		Nonpassive Income and Loss		
	(g) Passive loss allowed (attach **Form 8582** if required)	**(h)** Passive income from **Schedule K-1**	**(i)** Nonpassive loss from **Schedule K-1**	**(j)** Section 179 expense deduction from **Form 4562**	**(k)** Nonpassive income from **Schedule K-1**
A					
B					
C					
D					
E					
28a Totals					
b Totals					

29 Add columns (h) and (k) of line 28a **29**

30 Add columns (g), (i), and (j) of line 28b . . . . . **30** ( )

31 Total partnership and S corporation income or (loss). Combine lines 29 and 30. Enter the result here and include in the total on line 40 below **31**

Part III Income or Loss From Estates and Trusts

32	**(a)** Name	**(b)** Employer identification number
A		
B		

	Passive Income and Loss		Nonpassive Income and Loss	
	(c) Passive deduction or loss allowed (attach **Form 8582** if required)	**(d)** Passive income from **Schedule K-1**	**(e)** Deduction or loss from **Schedule K-1**	**(f)** Other income from **Schedule K-1**
A				
B				
33a Totals				
b Totals				

34 Add columns (d) and (f) of line 33a **34**

35 Add columns (c) and (e) of line 33b . . . . . **35** ( )

36 Total estate and trust income or (loss). Combine lines 34 and 35. Enter the result here and include in the total on line 40 below **36**

Part IV Income or Loss From Real Estate Mortgage Investment Conduits (REMICs)—Residual Holder

37 **(a)** Name	**(b)** Employer identification number	**(c)** Excess inclusion from **Schedules Q**, line 2c (see page E-6)	**(d)** Taxable income (net loss) from **Schedules Q**, line 1b	**(e)** Income from **Schedules Q**, line 3b

38 Combine columns (d) and (e) only. Enter the result here and include in the total on line 40 below **38**

Part V Summary

39 Net farm rental income or (loss) from **Form 4835**. Also, complete line 41 below . . . **39**

40 **Total** income or (loss). Combine lines 26, 31, 36, 38, and 39. Enter the result here and on Form 1040, line 17 ▶ **40**

41 **Reconciliation of Farming and Fishing Income.** Enter your **gross** farming and fishing income reported on Form 4835, line 7; Schedule K-1 (Form 1065), line 15b; Schedule K-1 (Form 1120S), line 23; and Schedule K-1 (Form 1041), line 14 (see page E-6) . . . **41**

42 **Reconciliation for Real Estate Professionals.** If you were a real estate professional (see page E-4), enter the net income or (loss) you reported anywhere on Form 1040 from all rental real estate activities in which you materially participated under the passive activity loss rules . . **42**

SCHEDULE SE (Form 1040) Department of the Treasury Internal Revenue Service (99)	**Self-Employment Tax** ▶ **See Instructions for Schedule SE (Form 1040).** ▶ **Attach to Form 1040.**	OMB No. 1545-0074 **2001** Attachment Sequence No. **17**

Name of person with **self-employment** income (as shown on Form 1040)	Social security number of person with **self-employment** income ▶

Who Must File Schedule SE

You must file Schedule SE if:

- You had net earnings from self-employment from **other than** church employee income (line 4 of Short Schedule SE or line 4c of Long Schedule SE) of $400 or more **or**
- You had church employee income of $108.28 or more. Income from services you performed as a minister or a member of a religious order **is not** church employee income. See page SE-1.

Note. Even if you had a loss or a small amount of income from self-employment, it may be to your benefit to file Schedule SE and use either "optional method" in Part II of Long Schedule SE. See page SE-3.

Exception. If your only self-employment income was from earnings as a minister, member of a religious order, or Christian Science practitioner **and** you filed Form 4361 and received IRS approval not to be taxed on those earnings, **do not** file Schedule SE. Instead, write "Exempt–Form 4361" on Form 1040, line 53.

May I Use Short Schedule SE or Must I Use Long Schedule SE?

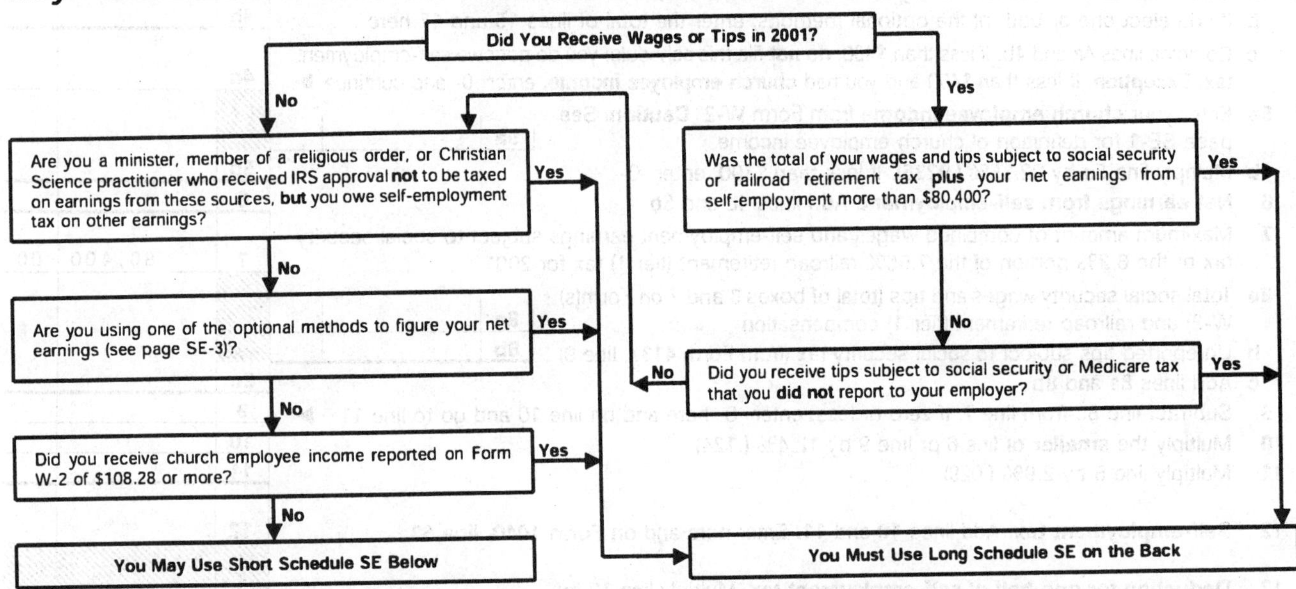

Section A—Short Schedule SE. Caution. Read above to see if you can use Short Schedule SE.

1	Net farm profit or (loss) from Schedule F, line 36, and farm partnerships, Schedule K-1 (Form 1065), line 15a	1	
2	Net profit or (loss) from Schedule C, line 31; Schedule C-EZ, line 3; Schedule K-1 (Form 1065), line 15a (other than farming); and Schedule K-1 (Form 1065-B), box 9. Ministers and members of religious orders, see page SE-1 for amounts to report on this line. See page SE-2 for other income to report	2	
3	Combine lines 1 and 2	3	
4	**Net earnings from self-employment.** Multiply line 3 by 92.35% (.9235). If less than $400, **do not** file this schedule; you do not owe self-employment tax ▶	4	
5	**Self-employment tax.** If the amount on line 4 is: • $80,400 or less, multiply line 4 by 15.3% (.153). Enter the result here and on **Form 1040, line 53.** • More than $80,400, multiply line 4 by 2.9% (.029). Then, add $9,969.60 to the result. Enter the total here and on **Form 1040, line 53.**	5	
6	**Deduction for one-half of self-employment tax.** Multiply line 5 by 50% (.5). Enter the result here and on **Form 1040, line 27** | 6 |		

Schedule SE (Form 1040) 2001 — Attachment Sequence No. **17** — Page **2**

Name of person with **self-employment** income (as shown on Form 1040)	Social security number of person with **self-employment** income ▶

Section B—Long Schedule SE

Part I Self-Employment Tax

Note. If your only income subject to self-employment tax is **church employee income,** skip lines 1 through 4b. Enter -0- on line 4c and go to line 5a. Income from services you performed as a minister or a member of a religious order **is not** church employee income. See page SE-1.

A If you are a minister, member of a religious order, or Christian Science practitioner **and** you filed Form 4361, but you had $400 or more of **other** net earnings from self-employment, check here and continue with Part I ▶ ☐

1	Net farm profit or (loss) from Schedule F, line 36, and farm partnerships, Schedule K-1 (Form 1065), line 15a. **Note.** Skip this line if you use the farm optional method. See page SE-3	**1**		
2	Net profit or (loss) from Schedule C, line 31; Schedule C-EZ, line 3; Schedule K-1 (Form 1065), line 15a (other than farming); and Schedule K-1 (Form 1065-B), box 9. Ministers and members of religious orders, see page SE-1 for amounts to report on this line. See page SE-2 for other income to report. **Note.** Skip this line if you use the nonfarm optional method. See page SE-3	**2**		
3	Combine lines 1 and 2	**3**		
4a	If line 3 is more than zero, multiply line 3 by 92.35% (.9235). Otherwise, enter amount from line 3	**4a**		
b	If you elect one or both of the optional methods, enter the total of lines 15 and 17 here	**4b**		
c	Combine lines 4a and 4b. If less than $400, **do not** file this schedule; you do not owe self-employment tax. **Exception.** If less than $400 and you had **church employee income,** enter -0- and continue ▶	**4c**		
5a	Enter your **church employee income** from Form W-2. **Caution.** See page SE-1 for definition of church employee income — **5a**			
b	Multiply line 5a by 92.35% (.9235). If less than $100, enter -0-	**5b**		
6	**Net earnings from self-employment.** Add lines 4c and 5b	**6**		
7	Maximum amount of combined wages and self-employment earnings subject to social security tax or the 6.2% portion of the 7.65% railroad retirement (tier 1) tax for 2001	**7**	80,400	00
8a	Total social security wages and tips (total of boxes 3 and 7 on Form(s) W-2) and railroad retirement (tier 1) compensation — **8a**			
b	Unreported tips subject to social security tax (from Form 4137, line 9) — **8b**			
c	Add lines 8a and 8b	**8c**		
9	Subtract line 8c from line 7. If zero or less, enter -0- here and on line 10 and go to line 11 ▶	**9**		
10	Multiply the **smaller** of line 6 or line 9 by 12.4% (.124)	**10**		
11	Multiply line 6 by 2.9% (.029)	**11**		
12	**Self-employment tax.** Add lines 10 and 11. Enter here and on **Form 1040, line 53**	**12**		
13	**Deduction for one-half of self-employment tax.** Multiply line 12 by 50% (.5). Enter the result here and on **Form 1040, line 27** — **13**			

Part II Optional Methods To Figure Net Earnings (See page SE-3.)

Farm Optional Method. You may use this method **only** if:

- Your gross farm income[1] was not more than $2,400 **or**
- Your net farm profits[2] were less than $1,733.

14	Maximum income for optional methods	**14**	1,600	00
15	Enter the **smaller** of: two-thirds (⅔) of gross farm income[1] (not less than zero) **or** $1,600. Also include this amount on line 4b above	**15**		

Nonfarm Optional Method. You may use this method **only** if:

- Your net nonfarm profits[3] were less than $1,733 and also less than 72.189% of your gross nonfarm income[4] **and**
- You had net earnings from self-employment of at least $400 in 2 of the prior 3 years.

Caution. You may use this method no more than five times.

16	Subtract line 15 from line 14	**16**		
17	Enter the **smaller** of: two-thirds (⅔) of gross nonfarm income[4] (not less than zero) **or** the amount on line 16. Also include this amount on line 4b above	**17**		

[1]From Sch. F, line 11, and Sch. K-1 (Form 1065), line 15b.
[2]From Sch. F, line 36, and Sch. K-1 (Form 1065), line 15a.
[3]From Sch. C, line 31; Sch. C-EZ, line 3; Sch. K-1 (Form 1065), line 15a; and Sch. K-1 (Form 1065-B), box 9.
[4]From Sch. C, line 7; Sch. C-EZ, line 1; Sch. K-1 (Form 1065), line 15c; and Sch. K-1 (Form 1065-B), box 9.

SCHEDULE F (Form 1040)
Department of the Treasury Internal Revenue Service (99)

Profit or Loss From Farming

▶ Attach to Form 1040, Form 1041, Form 1065, or Form 1065-B.
▶ See Instructions for Schedule F (Form 1040).

OMB No. 1545-0074
2001
Attachment Sequence No. **14**

Name of proprietor | **Social security number (SSN)**

A Principal product. Describe in one or two words your principal crop or activity for the current tax year.

B Enter code from Part IV ▶

D Employer ID number (EIN), if any

C Accounting method: (1) ☐ Cash (2) ☐ Accrual

E Did you "materially participate" in the operation of this business during 2001? If "No," see page F-2 for limit on passive losses. ☐ Yes ☐ No

Part I Farm Income—Cash Method. Complete Parts I and II (Accrual method taxpayers complete Parts II and III, and line 11 of Part I.)
Do not include sales of livestock held for draft, breeding, sport, or dairy purposes; report these sales on Form 4797.

1	Sales of livestock and other items you bought for resale	1	
2	Cost or other basis of livestock and other items reported on line 1	2	
3	Subtract line 2 from line 1	3	
4	Sales of livestock, produce, grains, and other products you raised	4	
5a	Total cooperative distributions (Form(s) 1099-PATR) 5a ____ 5b Taxable amount	5b	
6a	Agricultural program payments (see page F-2) 6a ____ 6b Taxable amount	6b	
7	Commodity Credit Corporation (CCC) loans (see page F-3):		
a	CCC loans reported under election	7a	
b	CCC loans forfeited 7b ____ 7c Taxable amount	7c	
8	Crop insurance proceeds and certain disaster payments (see page F-3):		
a	Amount received in 2001 8a ____ 8b Taxable amount	8b	
c	If election to defer to 2002 is attached, check here ▶ ☐ 8d Amount deferred from 2000	8d	
9	Custom hire (machine work) income	9	
10	Other income, including Federal and state gasoline or fuel tax credit or refund (see page F-3)	10	
11	**Gross income.** Add amounts in the right column for lines 3 through 10. If accrual method taxpayer, enter the amount from page 2, line 51 ▶	11	

Part II Farm Expenses—Cash and Accrual Method. Do not include personal or living expenses such as taxes, insurance, repairs, etc., on your home.

12	Car and truck expenses (see page F-4—also attach **Form 4562**)	12		25	Pension and profit-sharing plans	25	
13	Chemicals	13		26	Rent or lease (see page F-5):		
14	Conservation expenses (see page F-4)	14		a	Vehicles, machinery, and equipment	26a	
15	Custom hire (machine work)	15		b	Other (land, animals, etc.)	26b	
16	Depreciation and section 179 expense deduction not claimed elsewhere (see page F-4)	16		27	Repairs and maintenance	27	
				28	Seeds and plants purchased	28	
				29	Storage and warehousing	29	
17	Employee benefit programs other than on line 25	17		30	Supplies purchased	30	
				31	Taxes	31	
18	Feed purchased	18		32	Utilities	32	
19	Fertilizers and lime	19		33	Veterinary, breeding, and medicine	33	
20	Freight and trucking	20		34	Other expenses (specify):		
21	Gasoline, fuel, and oil	21		a		34a	
22	Insurance (other than health)	22		b		34b	
23	Interest:			c		34c	
a	Mortgage (paid to banks, etc.)	23a		d		34d	
b	Other	23b		e		34e	
24	Labor hired (less employment credits)	24		f		34f	

35	**Total expenses.** Add lines 12 through 34f ▶	35	
36	**Net farm profit or (loss).** Subtract line 35 from line 11. If a profit, enter on **Form 1040, line 18,** and **also** on **Schedule SE, line 1.** If a loss, you **must** go on to line 37 (estates, trusts, and partnerships, see page F-6)	36	

37 If you have a loss, you **must** check the box that describes your investment in this activity (see page F-6).
- If you checked 37a, enter the loss on **Form 1040, line 18,** and **also** on **Schedule SE, line 1.**
- If you checked 37b, you **must** attach **Form 6198.**

37a ☐ All investment is at risk.
37b ☐ Some investment is not at risk.

For Paperwork Reduction Act Notice, see Form 1040 instructions. Cat. No. 11346H **Schedule F (Form 1040) 2001**

Schedule F (Form 1040) 2001 Page **2**

Part III **Farm Income—Accrual Method** (see page F-6)
Do not include sales of livestock held for draft, breeding, sport, or dairy purposes; report these sales on Form 4797 and do not include this livestock on line 46 below.

38	Sales of livestock, produce, grains, and other products during the year				38	
39a	Total cooperative distributions (Form(s) 1099-PATR)	39a		39b Taxable amount	39b	
40a	Agricultural program payments	40a		40b Taxable amount	40b	
41	Commodity Credit Corporation (CCC) loans:					
a	CCC loans reported under election				41a	
b	CCC loans forfeited	41b		41c Taxable amount	41c	
42	Crop insurance proceeds				42	
43	Custom hire (machine work) income				43	
44	Other income, including Federal and state gasoline or fuel tax credit or refund				44	
45	Add amounts in the right column for lines 38 through 44				45	
46	Inventory of livestock, produce, grains, and other products at beginning of the year	46				
47	Cost of livestock, produce, grains, and other products purchased during the year	47				
48	Add lines 46 and 47	48				
49	Inventory of livestock, produce, grains, and other products at end of year	49				
50	Cost of livestock, produce, grains, and other products sold. Subtract line 49 from line 48*				50	
51	**Gross income.** Subtract line 50 from line 45. Enter the result here and on page 1, line 11 ▶				51	

*If you use the unit-livestock-price method or the farm-price method of valuing inventory and the amount on line 49 is larger than the amount on line 48, subtract line 48 from line 49. Enter the result on line 50. Add lines 45 and 50. Enter the total on line 51.

Part IV **Principal Agricultural Activity Codes**

Caution. File **Schedule C** (Form 1040), Profit or Loss From Business, or **Schedule C-EZ** (Form 1040), Net Profit From Business, instead of Schedule F if:

- Your principal source of income is from providing agricultural services such as soil preparation, veterinary, farm labor, horticultural, or management for a fee or on a contract basis or
- You are engaged in the business of breeding, raising, and caring for dogs, cats, or other pet animals.

These codes for the Principal Agricultural Activity classify farms by the type of activity they are engaged in to facilitate the administration of the Internal Revenue Code. These six-digit codes are based on the North American Industry Classification System (NAICS).

Select one of the following codes and enter the six-digit number on page 1, line B.

Crop Production

111100 Oilseed and grain farming
111210 Vegetable and melon farming
111300 Fruit and tree nut farming
111400 Greenhouse, nursery, and floriculture production
111900 Other crop farming

Animal Production

112111 Beef cattle ranching and farming
112112 Cattle feedlots
112120 Dairy cattle and milk production
112210 Hog and pig farming
112300 Poultry and egg production
112400 Sheep and goat farming
112510 Animal aquaculture
112900 Other animal production

Forestry and Logging

113000 Forestry and logging (including forest nurseries and timber tracts)

Form **1041** Department of the Treasury—Internal Revenue Service
U.S. Income Tax Return for Estates and Trusts **2001**

OMB No. 1545-0092

For calendar year 2001 or fiscal year beginning , 2001, and ending , 20

A Type of entity:
- ☐ Decedent's estate
- ☒ Simple trust
- ☐ Complex trust
- ☐ Grantor type trust
- ☐ Bankruptcy estate–Ch. 7
- ☐ Bankruptcy estate–Ch. 11
- ☐ Pooled income fund

B Number of Schedules K-1 attached (see instructions) ▶ 1

Name of estate or trust (If a grantor type trust, see page 10 of the instructions.) Bob Adams Trust (Simple Trust)

Name and title of fiduciary: First Bank

Number, street, and room or suite no. (If a P.O. box, see page 10 of the instructions.) Post Office Box 100

City or town, state, and ZIP code: Nashville, TN 37203

C Employer identification number: 74 : 1237211

D Date entity created: 1992

E Nonexempt charitable and split-interest trusts, check applicable boxes (see page 11 of the instructions):
- ☐ Described in section 4947(a)(1)
- ☐ Not a private foundation
- ☐ Described in section 4947(a)(2)

F Check applicable boxes: ☐ Initial return ☐ Final return ☐ Amended return ☐ Change in fiduciary's name ☐ Change in fiduciary's address

G Pooled mortgage account (see page 12 of the instructions): ☐ Bought ☐ Sold Date:

	Line	Description	No.	Amount
Income	1	Interest income	1	
	2	Ordinary dividends	2	30,000
	3	Business income or (loss) (attach Schedule C or C-EZ (Form 1040))	3	
	4	Capital gain or (loss) (attach Schedule D (Form 1041))	4	12,000
	5	Rents, royalties, partnerships, other estates and trusts, etc. (attach Schedule E (Form 1040))	5	4,000
	6	Farm income or (loss) (attach Schedule F (Form 1040)) (see below)	6	
	7	Ordinary gain or (loss) (attach Form 4797)	7	
	8	Other income. List type and amount	8	
	9	**Total income.** Combine lines 1 through 8 ▶	9	46,000
Deductions	10	Interest. Check if Form 4952 is attached ▶ ☐	10	
	11	Taxes	11	
	12	Fiduciary fees ($1,200 – $360)	12	840
	13	Charitable deduction (from Schedule A, line 7)	13	
	14	Attorney, accountant, and return preparer fees	14	500
	15a	Other deductions **not** subject to the 2% floor (attach schedule)	15a	
	b	Allowable miscellaneous itemized deductions subject to the 2% floor	15b	
	16	**Total.** Add lines 10 through 15b	16	1,340
	17	Adjusted total income or (loss). Subtract line 16 from line 9. Enter here and on Schedule B, line 1 ▶	17	44,660
	18	Income distribution deduction (from Schedule B, line 15) (attach Schedules K-1 (Form 1041))	18	32,660
	19	Estate tax deduction (including certain generation-skipping taxes) (attach computation)	19	
	20	Exemption	20	300
	21	**Total deductions.** Add lines 18 through 20 ▶	21	32,960
Tax and Payments	22	Taxable income. Subtract line 21 from line 17. If a loss, see page 17 of the instructions	22	11,700
	23	**Total tax** (from Schedule G, line 7)	23	2,160
	24	**Payments: a** 2001 estimated tax payments and amount applied from 2000 return	24a	2,600
	b	Estimated tax payments allocated to beneficiaries (from Form 1041-T)	24b	
	c	Subtract line 24b from line 24a	24c	2,600
	d	Tax paid with extension of time to file: ☐ Form 2758 ☐ Form 8736 ☐ Form 8800	24d	
	e	Federal income tax withheld. If any is from Form(s) 1099, check ▶ ☐	24e	
		Other payments: **f** Form 2439 ; **g** Form 4136 ; Total ▶	24h	
	25	**Total payments.** Add lines 24c through 24e, and 24h	25	2,600
	26	Estimated tax penalty (see page 17 of the instructions)	26	
	27	**Tax due.** If line 25 is smaller than the total of lines 23 and 26, enter amount owed	27	
	28	**Overpayment.** If line 25 is larger than the total of lines 23 and 26, enter amount overpaid	28	440
	29	Amount of line 28 to be: **a Credited to 2002 estimated tax** ▶ 440 ; **b Refunded** ▶	29	

Sign Here

Under penalties of perjury, I declare that I have examined this return, including accompanying schedules and statements, and to the best of my knowledge and belief, it is true, correct, and complete. Declaration of preparer (other than taxpayer) is based on all information of which preparer has any knowledge.

Tom Trusty — Signature of fiduciary or officer representing fiduciary | Date: 3-16-02 | EIN of fiduciary if a financial institution: 38 : 1505087

May the IRS discuss this return with the preparer shown below (see page 7)? ☒ Yes ☐ No

Paid Preparer's Use Only

Preparer's signature: Karen Certified | Date: 3-15-02 | Check if self-employed ☒ | Preparer's SSN or PTIN: 444-17-1313

Firm's name (or yours if self-employed), address, and ZIP code: Karen Certified, One Opryland Place, Nashville, TN 37204 | EIN 74 : 1234567 | Phone no. (615) 372-1900

For Paperwork Reduction Act Notice, see the separate instructions. Cat. No. 11370H Form **1041** (2001)

Line 4: Net rental income = Rental income ($5,000) – Rental expenses -- Realtor's Commissions ($1,000) = Net rental income ($4,000)

Note: Pages concerning the AMT are omitted because the trust does not owe the AMT.

Form 1041 (2001) Page **2**

Schedule A **Charitable Deduction.** Do not complete for a simple trust or a pooled income fund.

1	Amounts paid or permanently set aside for charitable purposes from gross income (see page 18)	1	
2	Tax-exempt income allocable to charitable contributions (see page 18 of the instructions)	2	
3	Subtract line 2 from line 1	3	
4	Capital gains for the tax year allocated to corpus and paid or permanently set aside for charitable purposes	4	
5	Add lines 3 and 4	5	
6	Section 1202 exclusion allocable to capital gains paid or permanently set aside for charitable purposes (see page 18 of the instructions)	6	
7	**Charitable deduction.** Subtract line 6 from line 5. Enter here and on page 1, line 13	7	None

Schedule B **Income Distribution Deduction**

1	Adjusted total income (see page 18 of the instructions)	1	44,660
2	Adjusted tax-exempt interest ($15,000 - $360)	2	14,640
3	Total net gain from Schedule D (Form 1041), line 16, column (1) (see page 19 of the instructions)	3	
4	Enter amount from Schedule A, line 4 (reduced by any allocable section 1202 exclusion)	4	
5	Capital gains for the tax year included on Schedule A, line 1 (see page 19 of the instructions)	5	
6	Enter any gain from page 1, line 4, as a negative number. If page 1, line 4, is a loss, enter the loss as a positive number	6	(12,000)
7	**Distributable net income (DNI).** Combine lines 1 through 6. If zero or less, enter -0-	7	47,300
8	If a complex trust, enter accounting income for the tax year as determined under the governing instrument and applicable local law — 8: 48,500		
9	Income required to be distributed currently	9	48,500
10	Other amounts paid, credited, or otherwise required to be distributed	10	
11	Total distributions. Add lines 9 and 10. If greater than line 8, see page 19 of the instructions	11	48,500
12	Enter the amount of tax-exempt income included on line 11	12	14,640
13	Tentative income distribution deduction. Subtract line 12 from line 11	13	33,860
14	Tentative income distribution deduction. Subtract line 2 from line 7. If zero or less, enter -0-	14	32,660
15	**Income distribution deduction.** Enter the smaller of line 13 or line 14 here and on page 1, line 18	15	32,660

Schedule G **Tax Computation** (see page 20 of the instructions)

1	**Tax:** a ☐ Tax rate schedule or ☒ Schedule D (Form 1041)	1a	2,160		
	b Tax on lump-sum distributions (attach Form 4972)	1b			
	c Alternative minimum tax (from Schedule I, line 39)	1c	-0-		
	d **Total.** Add lines 1a through 1c ▶			1d	2,160
2a	Foreign tax credit (attach Form 1116)	2a			
b	Other nonbusiness credits (attach schedule)	2b			
c	General business credit. Enter here and check which forms are attached: ☐ Form 3800 ☐ Forms (specify) ▶	2c			
d	Credit for prior year minimum tax (attach Form 8801)	2d			
3	**Total credits.** Add lines 2a through 2d ▶			3	
4	Subtract line 3 from line 1d. If zero or less, enter -0-			4	2,160
5	Recapture taxes. Check if from: ☐ Form 4255 ☐ Form 8611			5	
6	Household employment taxes. Attach Schedule H (Form 1040)			6	
7	**Total tax.** Add lines 4 through 6. Enter here and on page 1, line 23 ▶			7	2,160

Other Information

		Yes	No
1	Did the estate or trust receive tax-exempt income? If "Yes," attach a computation of the allocation of expenses. Enter the amount of tax-exempt interest income and exempt-interest dividends ▶ $ 15,000 (see below)	X	
2	Did the estate or trust receive all or any part of the earnings (salary, wages, and other compensation) of any individual by reason of a contract assignment or similar arrangement?		X
3	At any time during calendar year 2001, did the estate or trust have an interest in or a signature or other authority over a bank, securities, or other financial account in a foreign country?		X
	See page 21 of the instructions for exceptions and filing requirements for Form TD F 90-22.1. If "Yes," enter the name of the foreign country ▶		
4	During the tax year, did the estate or trust receive a distribution from, or was it the grantor of, or transferor to, a foreign trust? If "Yes," the estate or trust may have to file Form 3520. See page 21 of the instructions		X
5	Did the estate or trust receive, or pay, any qualified residence interest on seller-provided financing? If "Yes," see page 21 for required attachment		X
6	If this is an estate or a complex trust making the section 663(b) election, check here (see page 21) ▶ ☐		
7	To make a section 643(e)(3) election, attach Schedule D (Form 1041), and check here (see page 21) ▶ ☐		
8	If the decedent's estate has been open for more than 2 years, attach an explanation for the delay in closing the estate, and check here ▶ ☐		
9	Are any present or future trust beneficiaries skip persons? See page 21 of the instructions		

Line 2: Allocation of expenses: $\frac{\$15,000}{\$50,000} \times 1,200 = \$360$ of trustee's fee allocated to tax-exempt income.

Form **1041** (2001)

SCHEDULE D (Form 1041)

Department of the Treasury
Internal Revenue Service

Capital Gains and Losses

▶ Attach to Form 1041 (or Form 5227). See the separate instructions for Form 1041 (or Form 5227).

OMB No. 1545-0092

2001

Name of estate or trust: Bob Adams Trust

Employer identification number: 74 1237211

Note: *Form 5227 filers need to complete **only** Parts I and II.*

Part I **Short-Term Capital Gains and Losses—Assets Held One Year or Less**

(a) Description of property (Example, 100 shares 7% preferred of "Z" Co.)	(b) Date acquired (mo., day, yr.)	(c) Date sold (mo., day, yr.)	(d) Sales price	(e) Cost or other basis (see page 29)	(f) Gain or (Loss) (col. (d) less col. (e))
1					

Line	Description	Line	(f)
2	Short-term capital gain or (loss) from Forms 4684, 6252, 6781, and 8824	2	
3	Net short-term gain or (loss) from partnerships, S corporations, and other estates or trusts	3	
4	Short-term capital loss carryover. Enter the amount, if any, from line 9 of the 2000 Capital Loss Carryover Worksheet	4	( )
5	**Net short-term gain or (loss).** Combine lines 1 through 4 in column (f). Enter here and on line 14 below ▶	5	

Part II **Long-Term Capital Gains and Losses—Assets Held More Than One Year**

(a) Description of property (Example, 100 shares 7% preferred of "Z" Co.)	(b) Date acquired (mo., day, yr.)	(c) Date sold (mo., day, yr.)	(d) Sales price	(e) Cost or other basis (see page 29)	(f) Gain or (Loss) (col. (d) less col. (e))	(g) 28% Rate Gain or (Loss) *(see instr. below)
6 1000 shares of ABC Corporation Stock	1997	Oct. 2001	15,000	3,000	12,000	

Line	Description	Line	(f)	(g)
7	Long-term capital gain or (loss) from Forms 2439, 4684, 6252, 6781, and 8824	7		
8	Net long-term gain or (loss) from partnerships, S corporations, and other estates or trusts	8		
9	Capital gain distributions	9		
10	Gain from Form 4797, Part I	10		
11	Long-term capital loss carryover. Enter in both columns (f) and (g) the amount, if any, from line 14, of the 2000 Capital Loss Carryover Worksheet	11	( )	( )
12	Combine lines 6 through 11 in column (g)	12		
13	**Net long-term gain or (loss).** Combine lines 6 through 11 in column (f). Enter here and on line 15 below ▶	13	12,000	

*28% rate gain or loss includes **all** "collectibles gains and losses" (as defined on page 30 of the instructions) and up to 50% of the eligible gain on qualified small business stock (see page 28 of the instructions).

Part III **Summary of Parts I and II**

Line	Description	Line	(1) Beneficiaries' (see page 30)	(2) Estate's or trust's	(3) Total
14	**Net short-term gain or (loss)** (from line 5 above)	14			
15	**Net long-term gain or (loss):**				
a	28% rate gain or (loss) (from line 12 above)	15a			
b	Unrecaptured section 1250 gain (see line 17 of the worksheet on page 31)	15b			
c	Total for year (from line 13 above)	15c		12,000	12,000
16	**Total net gain or (loss).** Combine lines 14 and 15c ▶	16		12,000	12,000

Note: *If line 16, column (3), is a net gain, enter the gain on Form 1041, line 4. If lines 15c and 16, column (2), are net gains, go to Part V, and **do not** complete Part IV. If line 16, column (3), is a net loss, complete Part IV and the **Capital Loss Carryover Worksheet,** as necessary.*

Schedule D (Form 1041) 2001 Page **2**

Part IV **Capital Loss Limitation**

17	Enter here and enter as a (loss) on Form 1041, line 4, the **smaller** of: **a** The loss on line 16, column (3) **or** **b** $3,000	17	( )

If the loss on line 16, column (3), is more than $3,000, **or** *if Form 1041, page 1, line 22, is a loss, complete the* **Capital Loss Carryover Worksheet** *on page 32 of the instructions to determine your capital loss carryover.*

Part V **Tax Computation Using Maximum Capital Gains Rates** (Complete this part **only** if both lines 15c and 16 in column (2) are gains, and Form 1041, line 22 is more than zero.)

Note: *If line 15a, column (2) or line 15b, column (2) is more than zero, complete the worksheet on page 34 of the instructions to figure the amount to enter on lines 20, 27, and 38 below and skip all other lines below. Otherwise, go to line 18.*

18	Enter taxable income from Form 1041, line 22			18	11,700		
19	Enter the **smaller** of line 15c or 16 in column (2)	19	12,000				
20	If the estate or trust is filing Form 4952, enter the amount from line 4e; otherwise, enter -0- ▶	20	-0-				
21	Subtract line 20 from line 19. If zero or less, enter -0-			21	12,000		
22	Subtract line 21 from line 18. If zero or less, enter -0-			22	-0-		
23	Figure the tax on the amount on line 22. Use the 2001 Tax Rate Schedule on page 20 of the instructions					23	-0-
24	Enter the **smaller** of the amount on line 18 or $1,800			24	1,800		
	If line 24 is greater than line 22, go to line 25. Otherwise, skip lines 25 through 31 and go to line 32.						
25	Enter the amount from line 22			25	-0-		
26	Subtract line 25 from line 24. If zero or less, enter -0- and go to line 32			26	1,800		
27	Enter the estate's or trust's allocable portion of qualified 5-year gain, if any, from line 7c of the worksheet on page 33	27	-0-				
28	Enter the **smaller** of line 26 or line 27			28	-0-		
29	Multiply line 28 by 8% (.08)					29	-0-
30	Subtract line 28 from line 26			30	1,800		
31	Multiply line 30 by 10% (.10)					31	180
	If the amounts on lines 21 and 26 are the same, skip lines 32 through 35 and go to line 36.						
32	Enter the **smaller** of line 18 or line 21			32	11,700		
33	Enter the amount, if any, from line 26			33	1,800		
34	Subtract line 33 from line 32			34	9,900		
35	Multiply line 34 by 20% (.20)					35	1,980
36	Add lines 23, 29, 31, and 35					36	2,160
37	Figure the tax on the amount on line 18. Use the 2001 Tax Rate Schedule on page 20 of the instructions					37	3,577
38	**Tax on all taxable income (including capital gains).** Enter the **smaller** of line 36 or line 37 here and on line 1a of Schedule G, Form 1041					38	2,160

Schedule D (Form 1041) 2001

SCHEDULE K-1 (Form 1041)

Department of the Treasury
Internal Revenue Service

Beneficiary's Share of Income, Deductions, Credits, etc.

for the calendar year 2001, or fiscal year

beginning ...., 2001, ending ...., 20 ....

► Complete a separate Schedule K-1 for each beneficiary.

OMB No. 1545-0092

2001

☐ Amended K-1
☐ Final K-1

Name of trust or decedent's estate
Bob Adams Trust

Beneficiary's identifying number ► 389-16-4001

Estate's or trust's EIN ► 74-237211

Beneficiary's name, address, and ZIP code
Bob Adams
3 Andrew Jackson Highway
Nashville, TN 37211

Fiduciary's name, address, and ZIP code
First Bank
Post Office Box 100
Nashville, TN 37203

(a) Allocable share item		(b) Amount	(c) Calendar year 2001 Form 1040 filers enter the amounts in column (b) on:
1 Interest	1		Schedule B, Part I, line 1
2 Ordinary dividends	2	30,000	Schedule B, Part II, line 5
3 Net short-term capital gain	3		Schedule D, line 5
4 Net long-term capital gain: a Total for year	4a		Schedule D, line 12, column (f)
b 28% rate gain	4b		Schedule D, line 12, column (g)
c Qualified 5-year gain	4c		Line 4 of the worksheet for Schedule D, line 29
d Unrecaptured section 1250 gain	4d		Line 11 of the worksheet for Schedule D, line 19
5a Annuities, royalties, and other nonpassive income before directly apportioned deductions	5a		Schedule E, Part III, column (f)
b Depreciation	5b		Include on the applicable line of the appropriate tax form
c Depletion	5c		
d Amortization	5d		
6a Trade or business, rental real estate, and other rental income before directly apportioned deductions (see instructions)	6a	2,660*	Schedule E, Part III
b Depreciation	6b		Include on the applicable line of the appropriate tax form
c Depletion	6c		
d Amortization	6d		
7 Income for minimum tax purposes	7	32,660	
8 Income for regular tax purposes (add lines 1, 2, 3, 4a, 5a, and 6a)	8	32,660	
9 Adjustment for minimum tax purposes (subtract line 8 from line 7)	9		Form 6251, line 12
10 Estate tax deduction (including certain generation-skipping transfer taxes)	10		Schedule A, line 27
11 Foreign taxes	11		Form 1040, line 43 or Schedule A, line 8
12 Adjustments and tax preference items (itemize):			
a Accelerated depreciation	12a		Include on the applicable line of Form 6251
b Depletion	12b		
c Amortization	12c		
d Exclusion items	12d		2002 Form 8801
13 Deductions in the final year of trust or decedent's estate:			
a Excess deductions on termination (see instructions)	13a		Schedule A, line 22
b Short-term capital loss carryover	13b	( )	Schedule D, line 5
c Long-term capital loss carryover	13c	( )	Schedule D, line 12, columns (f) and (g)
d Net operating loss (NOL) carryover for regular tax purposes	13d	( )	Form 1040, line 21
e NOL carryover for minimum tax purposes	13e		See the instructions for Form 6251, line 20
f	13f		Include on the applicable line of the appropriate tax form
g	13g		
14 Other (itemize):			
a Payments of estimated taxes credited to you	14a		Form 1040, line 60
b Tax-exempt interest	14b	14,640	Form 1040, line 8b
c	14c		Include on the applicable line of the appropriate tax form
d	14d		
e	14e		
f	14f		
g	14g		
h	14h		

For Paperwork Reduction Act Notice, see the Instructions for Form 1041. Cat. No. 11380D Schedule K-1 (Form 1041) 2001

*$5,000 − ($1,000 + $840 + $500) = $2,660

Form **1041** Department of the Treasury—Internal Revenue Service

U.S. Income Tax Return for Estates and Trusts 2001

For calendar year 2001 or fiscal year beginning , 2001, and ending , 20 — OMB No. 1545-0092

A Type of entity:
- ☐ Decedent's estate
- ☐ Simple trust
- ☒ Complex trust
- ☐ Grantor type trust
- ☐ Bankruptcy estate–Ch. 7
- ☐ Bankruptcy estate–Ch. 11
- ☐ Pooled income fund

B Number of Schedules K-1 attached (see instructions) ▶ 2

Name of estate or trust (If a grantor type trust, see page 10 of the instructions.): Cathy and Karen Stephens Trust (Complex Trust)

Name and title of fiduciary: Merchants Bank

Number, street, and room or suite no. (If a P.O. box, see page 10 of the instructions.): 3000 Sun Plaza I

City or town, state, and ZIP code: Tampa, FL 32843

C Employer identification number: 74:5727422

D Date entity created: 3-12-93

E Nonexempt charitable and split-interest trusts, check applicable boxes (see page 11 of the instructions):
- ☐ Described in section 4947(a)(1)
- ☐ Not a private foundation
- ☐ Described in section 4947(a)(2)

F Check applicable boxes: ☐ Initial return ☐ Final return ☐ Amended return ☐ Change in fiduciary's name ☐ Change in fiduciary's address

G Pooled mortgage account (see page 12 of the instructions): ☐ Bought ☐ Sold Date:

Income	1	Interest income	1	
	2	Ordinary dividends	2	30,000
	3	Business income or (loss) (attach Schedule C or C-EZ (Form 1040))	3	
	4	Capital gain or (loss) (attach Schedule D (Form 1041))	4	12,000
	5	Rents, royalties, partnerships, other estates and trusts, etc. (attach Schedule E (Form 1040))	5	4,000
	6	Farm income or (loss) (attach Schedule F (Form 1040)) ↑ (see below)	6	
	7	Ordinary gain or (loss) (attach Form 4797)	7	
	8	Other income. List type and amount	8	
	9	**Total income.** Combine lines 1 through 8 ▶	9	46,000
Deductions	10	Interest. Check if Form 4952 is attached ▶ ☐	10	
	11	Taxes	11	
	12	Fiduciary fees ($1,200 - $360)	12	840
	13	Charitable deduction (from Schedule A, line 7)	13	
	14	Attorney, accountant, and return preparer fees	14	500
	15a	Other deductions **not** subject to the 2% floor (attach schedule)	15a	
	b	Allowable miscellaneous itemized deductions subject to the 2% floor	15b	
	16	**Total.** Add lines 10 through 15b	16	1,340
	17	Adjusted total income or (loss). Subtract line 16 from line 9. Enter here and on Schedule B, line 1 ▶	17	44,660
	18	Income distribution deduction (from Schedule B, line 15) (attach Schedules K-1 (Form 1041))	18	14,500
	19	Estate tax deduction (including certain generation-skipping taxes) (attach computation)	19	
	20	Exemption	20	100
	21	**Total deductions.** Add lines 18 through 20 ▶	21	14,600
Tax and Payments	22	Taxable income. Subtract line 21 from line 17. If a loss, see page 17 of the instructions	22	30,060
	23	**Total tax** (from Schedule G, line 7)	23	8,464
	24	**Payments: a** 2001 estimated tax payments and amount applied from 2000 return	24a	8,600
	b	Estimated tax payments allocated to beneficiaries (from Form 1041-T)	24b	
	c	Subtract line 24b from line 24a	24c	8,600
	d	Tax paid with extension of time to file: ☐ Form 2758 ☐ Form 8736 ☐ Form 8800	24d	
	e	Federal income tax withheld. If any is from Form(s) 1099, check ▶ ☐	24e	
		Other payments: **f** Form 2439 ; **g** Form 4136 ; Total ▶	24h	
	25	**Total payments.** Add lines 24c through 24e, and 24h ▶	25	8,600
	26	Estimated tax penalty (see page 17 of the instructions)	26	
	27	**Tax due.** If line 25 is smaller than the total of lines 23 and 26, enter amount owed	27	
	28	**Overpayment.** If line 25 is larger than the total of lines 23 and 26, enter amount overpaid	28	136
	29	Amount of line 28 to be: **a Credited to 2002 estimated tax** ▶ 136 ; **b Refunded** ▶	29	

Sign Here

Under penalties of perjury, I declare that I have examined this return, including accompanying schedules and statements, and to the best of my knowledge and belief, it is true, correct, and complete. Declaration of preparer (other than taxpayer) is based on all information of which preparer has any knowledge.

Fred Fidus — Signature of fiduciary or officer representing fiduciary | Date: 3-20-02 | EIN of fiduciary if a financial institution: 38:4371419

May the IRS discuss this return with the preparer shown below (see page 7)? ☒ Yes ☐ No

Paid Preparer's Use Only

Preparer's signature: Sarah Public | Date: 3-15-02 | Check if self-employed ☒ | Preparer's SSN or PTIN: 127-84-3978

Firm's name (or yours if self-employed), address, and ZIP code: Sarah Public, 200 Sun Plaza III, Tampa, FL 32843 | EIN 38:9876543 | Phone no. (813) 437-1000

For Paperwork Reduction Act Notice, see the separate instructions. Cat. No. 11370H Form **1041** (2001)

Line 4: Net Rental income
Rental income ($5,000) - Rental expenses ($1,000) = Net Rental Income ($4,000)

Note: Pages concerning the AMT are omitted because the trust does not owe the AMT.

Form 1041 (2001) Page **2**

Schedule A **Charitable Deduction.** Do not complete for a simple trust or a pooled income fund.

		Line	Amount
1	Amounts paid or permanently set aside for charitable purposes from gross income (see page 18)	1	
2	Tax-exempt income allocable to charitable contributions (see page 18 of the instructions)	2	
3	Subtract line 2 from line 1	3	
4	Capital gains for the tax year allocated to corpus and paid or permanently set aside for charitable purposes	4	
5	Add lines 3 and 4	5	
6	Section 1202 exclusion allocable to capital gains paid or permanently set aside for charitable purposes (see page 18 of the instructions)	6	
7	**Charitable deduction.** Subtract line 6 from line 5. Enter here and on page 1, line 13	7	

Schedule B **Income Distribution Deduction**

		Line	Amount
1	Adjusted total income (see page 18 of the instructions)	1	44,660
2	Adjusted tax-exempt interest (\$15,000 - \$360)	2	14,640
3	Total net gain from Schedule D (Form 1041), line 16, column (1) (see page 19 of the instructions)	3	
4	Enter amount from Schedule A, line 4 (reduced by any allocable section 1202 exclusion)	4	
5	Capital gains for the tax year included on Schedule A, line 1 (see page 19 of the instructions)	5	
6	Enter any gain from page 1, line 4, as a negative number. If page 1, line 4, is a loss, enter the loss as a positive number	6	(12,000)
7	**Distributable net income (DNI).** Combine lines 1 through 6. If zero or less, enter -0-	7	47,300
8	If a complex trust, enter accounting income for the tax year as determined under the governing instrument and applicable local law — **8** 48,500		
9	Income required to be distributed currently	9	-0-
10	Other amounts paid, credited, or otherwise required to be distributed	10	21,000
11	Total distributions. Add lines 9 and 10. If greater than line 8, see page 19 of the instructions	11	21,000
12	Enter the amount of tax-exempt income included on line 11	12	6,500
13	Tentative income distribution deduction. Subtract line 12 from line 11	13	14,500
14	Tentative income distribution deduction. Subtract line 2 from line 7. If zero or less, enter -0-	14	32,660
15	**Income distribution deduction.** Enter the smaller of line 13 or line 14 here and on page 1, line 18	15	14,500

Schedule G **Tax Computation** (see page 20 of the instructions)

1	**Tax:** a ☐ Tax rate schedule or ☐ Schedule D (Form 1041)	1a	8,464		
	b Tax on lump-sum distributions (attach Form 4972)	1b			
	c Alternative minimum tax (from Schedule I, line 39)	1c	-0-		
	d **Total.** Add lines 1a through 1c ▶			1d	8,464
2a	Foreign tax credit (attach Form 1116)	2a			
b	Other nonbusiness credits (attach schedule)	2b			
c	General business credit. Enter here and check which forms are attached: ☐ Form 3800 ☐ Forms (specify) ▶	2c			
d	Credit for prior year minimum tax (attach Form 8801)	2d			
3	**Total credits.** Add lines 2a through 2d ▶			3	
4	Subtract line 3 from line 1d. If zero or less, enter -0-			4	8,464
5	Recapture taxes. Check if from: ☐ Form 4255 ☐ Form 8611			5	
6	Household employment taxes. Attach Schedule H (Form 1040)			6	
7	**Total tax.** Add lines 4 through 6. Enter here and on page 1, line 23 ▶			7	8,464

Other Information

		Yes	No
1	Did the estate or trust receive tax-exempt income? If "Yes," attach a computation of the allocation of expenses. Enter the amount of tax-exempt interest income and exempt-interest dividends ▶ \$ 15,000 see below	X	
2	Did the estate or trust receive all or any part of the earnings (salary, wages, and other compensation) of any individual by reason of a contract assignment or similar arrangement?		X
3	At any time during calendar year 2001, did the estate or trust have an interest in or a signature or other authority over a bank, securities, or other financial account in a foreign country? See page 21 of the instructions for exceptions and filing requirements for Form TD F 90-22.1. If "Yes," enter the name of the foreign country ▶		X
4	During the tax year, did the estate or trust receive a distribution from, or was it the grantor of, or transferor to, a foreign trust? If "Yes," the estate or trust may have to file Form 3520. See page 21 of the instructions		X
5	Did the estate or trust receive, or pay, any qualified residence interest on seller-provided financing? If "Yes," see page 21 for required attachment		X
6	If this is an estate or a complex trust making the section 663(b) election, check here (see page 21) ▶ ☐		
7	To make a section 643(e)(3) election, attach Schedule D (Form 1041), and check here (see page 21) ▶ ☐		
8	If the decedent's estate has been open for more than 2 years, attach an explanation for the delay in closing the estate, and check here ▶ ☐		
9	Are any present or future trust beneficiaries skip persons? See page 21 of the instructions		X

Form **1041** (2001)

Line 1: Allocation of expense $\frac{\$15,000}{\$50,000} \times \$1,200 =$ \$360 of trustee's fee allocated to tax-exempt income.

SCHEDULE D (Form 1041)
Department of the Treasury Internal Revenue Service

Capital Gains and Losses

▶ Attach to Form 1041 (or Form 5227). See the separate instructions for Form 1041 (or Form 5227).

OMB No. 1545-0092
2001

Name of estate or trust: Cathy and Karen Stephens Trust
Employer identification number: 74:5724722

Note: *Form 5227 filers need to complete **only** Parts I and II.*

Part I Short-Term Capital Gains and Losses—Assets Held One Year or Less

(a) Description of property (Example, 100 shares 7% preferred of "Z" Co.)	(b) Date acquired (mo., day, yr.)	(c) Date sold (mo., day, yr.)	(d) Sales price	(e) Cost or other basis (see page 29)	(f) Gain or (Loss) (col. (d) less col. (e))
1					

Line	Description	(f)
2	Short-term capital gain or (loss) from Forms 4684, 6252, 6781, and 8824	
3	Net short-term gain or (loss) from partnerships, S corporations, and other estates or trusts	
4	Short-term capital loss carryover. Enter the amount, if any, from line 9 of the 2000 Capital Loss Carryover Worksheet	( )
5	**Net short-term gain or (loss).** Combine lines 1 through 4 in column (f). Enter here and on line 14 below ▶	

Part II Long-Term Capital Gains and Losses—Assets Held More Than One Year

(a) Description of property (Example, 100 shares 7% preferred of "Z" Co.)	(b) Date acquired (mo., day, yr.)	(c) Date sold (mo., day, yr.)	(d) Sales price	(e) Cost or other basis (see page 29)	(f) Gain or (Loss) (col. (d) less col. (e))	(g) 28% Rate Gain or (Loss) *(see instr. below)
6 1000 shares of ABC Corporation stock	1997	Oct. 2001	15,000	3,000	12,000	

Line	Description	(f)	(g)
7	Long-term capital gain or (loss) from Forms 2439, 4684, 6252, 6781, and 8824		
8	Net long-term gain or (loss) from partnerships, S corporations, and other estates or trusts		
9	Capital gain distributions		
10	Gain from Form 4797, Part I		
11	Long-term capital loss carryover. Enter in both columns (f) and (g) the amount, if any, from line 14, of the 2000 Capital Loss Carryover Worksheet	( )	( )
12	Combine lines 6 through 11 in column (g)		
13	**Net long-term gain or (loss).** Combine lines 6 through 11 in column (f). Enter here and on line 15 below ▶	12,000	

***28% rate gain or loss** includes **all** "collectibles gains and losses" (as defined on page 30 of the instructions) and up to 50% of the eligible gain on qualified small business stock (see page 28 of the instructions).

Part III Summary of Parts I and II

		Line	(1) Beneficiaries' (see page 30)	(2) Estate's or trust's	(3) Total
14	**Net short-term gain or (loss)** (from line 5 above)	14			
15	**Net long-term gain or (loss):**				
a	28% rate gain or (loss) (from line 12 above)	15a			
b	Unrecaptured section 1250 gain (see line 17 of the worksheet on page 31)	15b			
c	Total for year (from line 13 above)	15c		12,000	12,000
16	**Total net gain or (loss).** Combine lines 14 and 15c ▶	16		12,000	12,000

Note: *If line 16, column (3), is a net gain, enter the gain on Form 1041, line 4. If lines 15c and 16, column (2), are net gains, go to Part V, and **do not** complete Part IV. If line 16, column (3), is a net loss, complete Part IV and the **Capital Loss Carryover Worksheet,** as necessary.*

For Paperwork Reduction Act Notice, see the Instructions for Form 1041. Cat. No. 11376V **Schedule D (Form 1041) 2001**

Schedule D (Form 1041) 2001 Page 2

Part IV Capital Loss Limitation

17 Enter here and enter as a (loss) on Form 1041, line 4, the **smaller** of:
a The loss on line 16, column (3) **or**
b $3,000 . . . . . 17 ( )

If the loss on line 16, column (3), is more than $3,000, **or** *if Form 1041, page 1, line 22, is a loss, complete the* **Capital Loss Carryover Worksheet** *on page 32 of the instructions to determine your capital loss carryover.*

Part V Tax Computation Using Maximum Capital Gains Rates (Complete this part **only** if both lines 15c and 16 in column (2) are gains, and Form 1041, line 22 is more than zero.)

Note: *If line 15a, column (2) or line 15b, column (2) is more than zero, complete the worksheet on page 34 of the instructions to figure the amount to enter on lines 20, 27, and 38 below and skip all other lines below. Otherwise, go to line 18.*

18	Enter taxable income from Form 1041, line 22		18 30,060	
19	Enter the **smaller** of line 15c or 16 in column (2)	19 12,000		
20	If the estate or trust is filing Form 4952, enter the amount from line 4e; otherwise, enter -0- ▶	20 —0—		
21	Subtract line 20 from line 19. If zero or less, enter -0-		21 12,000	
22	Subtract line 21 from line 18. If zero or less, enter -0-		22 18,060	
23	Figure the tax on the amount on line 22. Use the 2001 Tax Rate Schedule on page 20 of the instructions			23 6,064
24	Enter the **smaller** of the amount on line 18 or $1,800		24 1,800	

If line 24 is greater than line 22, go to line 25. Otherwise, skip lines 25 through 31 and go to line 32.

25	Enter the amount from line 22		25	
26	Subtract line 25 from line 24. If zero or less, enter -0- and go to line 32		26	
27	Enter the estate's or trust's allocable portion of qualified 5-year gain, if any, from line 7c of the worksheet on page 33	27		
28	Enter the **smaller** of line 26 or line 27		28	
29	Multiply line 28 by 8% (.08)			29
30	Subtract line 28 from line 26		30	
31	Multiply line 30 by 10% (.10)			31

If the amounts on lines 21 and 26 are the same, skip lines 32 through 35 and go to line 36.

32	Enter the **smaller** of line 18 or line 21	32 12,000	
33	Enter the amount, if any, from line 26	33 —0—	
34	Subtract line 33 from line 32	34 12,000	
35	Multiply line 34 by 20% (.20)		35 2,400
36	Add lines 23, 29, 31, and 35		36 8,464
37	Figure the tax on the amount on line 18. Use the 2001 Tax Rate Schedule on page 20 of the instructions		37 10,756
38	**Tax on all taxable income (including capital gains).** Enter the **smaller** of line 36 or line 37 here and on line 1a of Schedule G, Form 1041		38 8,464

Schedule D (Form 1041) 2001

SCHEDULE K-1 (Form 1041)

Department of the Treasury
Internal Revenue Service

Beneficiary's Share of Income, Deductions, Credits, etc.

for the calendar year 2001, or fiscal year

beginning ...., 2001, ending ...., 20 ....

▶ Complete a separate Schedule K-1 for each beneficiary.

OMB No. 1545-0092

2001

Name of trust or decedent's estate: Cathy and Karen Stephens Trust

☐ Amended K-1
☐ Final K-1

Beneficiary's identifying number ▶ 411-36-4761

Estate's or trust's EIN ▶ 74 5727422

Beneficiary's name, address, and ZIP code:
Cathy Stephens
13 Sunny Shores
Miami Beach, FL 33131

Fiduciary's name, address, and ZIP code:
Merchants Bank
3000 Sun Plaza I
Tampa, FL 32843

(a) Allocable share item		(b) Amount	(c) Calendar year 2001 Form 1040 filers enter the amounts in column (b) on:
1 Interest	1		Schedule B, Part I, line 1
2 Ordinary dividends	2	8,879	Schedule B, Part II, line 5
3 Net short-term capital gain	3		Schedule D, line 5
4 Net long-term capital gain: a Total for year	4a		Schedule D, line 12, column (f)
b 28% rate gain	4b		Schedule D, line 12, column (g)
c Qualified 5-year gain	4c		Line 4 of the worksheet for Schedule D, line 29
d Unrecaptured section 1250 gain	4d		Line 11 of the worksheet for Schedule D, line 19
5a Annuities, royalties, and other nonpassive income before directly apportioned deductions	5a		Schedule E, Part III, column (f)
b Depreciation	5b		Include on the applicable line of the appropriate tax form
c Depletion	5c		
d Amortization	5d		
6a Trade or business, rental real estate, and other rental income before directly apportioned deductions (see instructions)	6a	788	Schedule E, Part III
b Depreciation	6b		Include on the applicable line of the appropriate tax form
c Depletion	6c		
d Amortization	6d		
7 Income for minimum tax purposes	7	9,667	
8 Income for regular tax purposes (add lines 1, 2, 3, 4a, 5a, and 6a)	8	9,667	
9 Adjustment for minimum tax purposes (subtract line 8 from line 7)	9		Form 6251, line 12
10 Estate tax deduction (including certain generation-skipping transfer taxes)	10		Schedule A, line 27
11 Foreign taxes	11		Form 1040, line 43 or Schedule A, line 8
12 Adjustments and tax preference items (itemize):			
a Accelerated depreciation	12a		Include on the applicable line of Form 6251
b Depletion	12b		
c Amortization	12c		
d Exclusion items	12d		2002 Form 8801
13 Deductions in the final year of trust or decedent's estate:			
a Excess deductions on termination (see instructions)	13a		Schedule A, line 22
b Short-term capital loss carryover	13b	( )	Schedule D, line 5
c Long-term capital loss carryover	13c	( )	Schedule D, line 12, columns (f) and (g)
d Net operating loss (NOL) carryover for regular tax purposes	13d	( )	Form 1040, line 21
e NOL carryover for minimum tax purposes	13e		See the instructions for Form 6251, line 20
f	13f		Include on the applicable line of the appropriate tax form
g	13g		
14 Other (itemize):			
a Payments of estimated taxes credited to you	14a		Form 1040, line 60
b Tax-exempt interest	14b	4,333	Form 1040, line 8b
c	14c		Include on the applicable line of the appropriate tax form
d	14d		
e	14e		
f	14f		
g	14g		
h	14h		

For Paperwork Reduction Act Notice, see the Instructions for Form 1041. Cat. No. 11380D **Schedule K-1 (Form 1041) 2001**

SCHEDULE K-1 (Form 1041)

Department of the Treasury
Internal Revenue Service

Beneficiary's Share of Income, Deductions, Credits, etc.

for the calendar year 2001, or fiscal year

beginning ...., 2001, ending ...., 20 ....

▶ Complete a separate Schedule K-1 for each beneficiary.

OMB No. 1545-0092

2001

☐ Amended K-1
☐ Final K-1

Name of trust or decedent's estate: Cathy and Karen Stephens Trust

Beneficiary's identifying number ▶ 456-78-1230

Estate's or trust's EIN ▶ 74:5727422

Beneficiary's name, address, and ZIP code:
Karen Stephens
1472 Ski Run
Vail, Colorado 74820

Fiduciary's name, address, and ZIP code:
Merchants Bank
3000 Sun Plaza I
Tampa, FL 32843

(a) Allocable share item		(b) Amount	(c) Calendar year 2001 Form 1040 filers enter the amounts in column (b) on:
1 Interest	1		Schedule B, Part I, line 1
2 Ordinary dividends	2	4,440	Schedule B, Part II, line 5
3 Net short-term capital gain	3		Schedule D, line 5
4 Net long-term capital gain: a Total for year	4a		Schedule D, line 12, column (f)
b 28% rate gain	4b		Schedule D, line 12, column (g)
c Qualified 5-year gain	4c		Line 4 of the worksheet for Schedule D, line 29
d Unrecaptured section 1250 gain	4d		Line 11 of the worksheet for Schedule D, line 19
5a Annuities, royalties, and other nonpassive income before directly apportioned deductions	5a		Schedule E, Part III, column (f)
b Depreciation	5b		Include on the applicable line of the appropriate tax form
c Depletion	5c		
d Amortization	5d		
6a Trade or business, rental real estate, and other rental income before directly apportioned deductions (see instructions)	6a	393	Schedule E, Part III
b Depreciation	6b		Include on the applicable line of the appropriate tax form
c Depletion	6c		
d Amortization	6d		
7 Income for minimum tax purposes	7	4,833	
8 Income for regular tax purposes (add lines 1, 2, 3, 4a, 5a, and 6a)	8	4,833	
9 Adjustment for minimum tax purposes (subtract line 8 from line 7)	9		Form 6251, line 12
10 Estate tax deduction (including certain generation-skipping transfer taxes)	10		Schedule A, line 27
11 Foreign taxes	11		Form 1040, line 43 or Schedule A, line 8
12 Adjustments and tax preference items (itemize):			
a Accelerated depreciation	12a		Include on the applicable line of Form 6251
b Depletion	12b		
c Amortization	12c		
d Exclusion items	12d		2002 Form 8801
13 Deductions in the final year of trust or decedent's estate:			
a Excess deductions on termination (see instructions)	13a		Schedule A, line 22
b Short-term capital loss carryover	13b	( )	Schedule D, line 5
c Long-term capital loss carryover	13c	( )	Schedule D, line 12, columns (f) and (g)
d Net operating loss (NOL) carryover for regular tax purposes	13d	( )	Form 1040, line 21
e NOL carryover for minimum tax purposes	13e		See the instructions for Form 6251, line 20
f	13f		Include on the applicable line of the appropriate tax form
g	13g		
14 Other (itemize):			
a Payments of estimated taxes credited to you	14a		Form 1040, line 60
b Tax-exempt interest	14b	2,167	Form 1040, line 8b
c	14c		Include on the applicable line of the appropriate tax form
d	14d		
e	14e		
f	14f		
g	14g		
h	14h		

For Paperwork Reduction Act Notice, see the Instructions for Form 1041. Cat. No. 11380D **Schedule K-1 (Form 1041) 2001**

Form **1065** Department of the Treasury Internal Revenue Service

U.S. Return of Partnership Income

For calendar year 2001, or tax year beginning .... , 2001, and ending ...., 20.... . ▶ See separate instructions.

OMB No. 1545-0099 **2001**

A Principal business activity: Manufacturing	Use the IRS label. Otherwise, print or type.	Name of partnership: Johns and Lawrence	D Employer identification number: 76 3456789
B Principal product or service: Furniture		Number, street, and room or suite no. If a P.O. box, see page 13 of the instructions.: 1234 University Avenue	E Date business started: 6-1-95
C Business code number: 337000		City or town, state, and ZIP code: Gainesville, FL 32611	F Total assets (see page 14 of the instructions): $ 499,484

G Check applicable boxes: (1) ☐ Initial return (2) ☐ Final return (3) ☐ Name change (4) ☐ Address change (5) ☐ Amended return

H Check accounting method: (1) ☐ Cash (2) ☒ Accrual (3) ☐ Other (specify) ▶

I Number of Schedules K-1. Attach one for each person who was a partner at any time during the tax year ▶

Caution: *Include **only** trade or business income and expenses on lines 1a through 22 below. See the instructions for more information.*

	Line			
Income	1a Gross receipts or sales	1a 869,658		
	b Less returns and allowances	1b 29,242	1c	840,416
	2 Cost of goods sold (Schedule A, line 8)		2	540,204
	3 Gross profit. Subtract line 2 from line 1c		3	300,212
	4 Ordinary income (loss) from other partnerships, estates, and trusts *(attach schedule)*		4	
	5 Net farm profit (loss) *(attach Schedule F (Form 1040))*		5	
	6 Net gain (loss) from Form 4797, Part II, line 18		6	
	7 Other income (loss) *(attach schedule)*		7	
	8 **Total income (loss).** Combine lines 3 through 7		8	300,212
Deductions (see page 15 of the instructions for limitations)	9 Salaries and wages (other than to partners) (less employment credits)		9	52,000
	10 Guaranteed payments to partners		10	36,000
	11 Repairs and maintenance		11	4,800
	12 Bad debts		12	4,000
	13 Rent		13	36,000
	14 Taxes and licenses (8,320 + 1,520)		14	9,840
	15 Interest		15	8,000
	16a Depreciation (if required, attach Form 4562)	16a 27,476		
	b Less depreciation reported on Schedule A and elsewhere on return	16b 15,000	16c	12,476
	17 Depletion **(Do not deduct oil and gas depletion.)**		17	
	18 Retirement plans, etc.		18	2,000
	19 Employee benefit programs		19	4,000
	20 Other deductions *(attach schedule)*		20	51,250
	21 **Total deductions.** Add the amounts shown in the far right column for lines 9 through 20		21	220,366
	22 **Ordinary income (loss)** from trade or business activities. Subtract line 21 from line 8		22	79,846

Sign Here

Under penalties of perjury, I declare that I have examined this return, including accompanying schedules and statements, and to the best of my knowledge and belief, it is true, correct, and complete. Declaration of preparer (other than general partner or limited liability company member) is based on all information of which preparer has any knowledge.

▶ Andrew Lawrence — Signature of general partner or limited liability company member ▶ 4-10-02 Date

May the IRS discuss this return with the preparer shown below (see instructions)? ☐ Yes ☐ No

Paid Preparer's Use Only

Preparer's signature: Michael S. Kramer	Date: 4-7-02	Check if self-employed ▶ ☒	Preparer's SSN or PTIN: 375-49-6339
Firm's name (or yours if self-employed), address, and ZIP code ▶ Michael S. Kramer 1110 McMillan Gainesville, FL 32611		EIN ▶ 59 2029763	Phone no. (352) 555-2000

For Paperwork Reduction Act Notice, see separate instructions. Cat. No. 11390Z Form **1065** (2001)

Form 1065 (2001) Page 2

Schedule A — Cost of Goods Sold (see page 18 of the instructions)

1	Inventory at beginning of year	1	64,000
2	Purchases less cost of items withdrawn for personal use	2	340,800
3	Cost of labor	3	143,204
4	Additional section 263A costs *(attach schedule)*	4	7,000
5	Other costs *(attach schedule)*	5	90,000
6	**Total.** Add lines 1 through 5	6	645,004
7	Inventory at end of year	7	104,800
8	**Cost of goods sold.** Subtract line 7 from line 6. Enter here and on page 1, line 2	8	540,204

9a Check all methods used for valuing closing inventory:
(i) ☒ Cost as described in Regulations section 1.471-3
(ii) ☐ Lower of cost or market as described in Regulations section 1.471-4
(iii) ☐ Other (specify method used and attach explanation) ▶
b Check this box if there was a writedown of "subnormal" goods as described in Regulations section 1.471-2(c) ▶ ☐
c Check this box if the LIFO inventory method was adopted this tax year for any goods *(if checked, attach Form 970)* ▶ ☐
d Do the rules of section 263A (for property produced or acquired for resale) apply to the partnership? ☒ Yes ☐ No
e Was there any change in determining quantities, cost, or valuations between opening and closing inventory? ☐ Yes ☒ No
If "Yes," attach explanation.

Schedule B — Other Information

		Yes	No
1	What type of entity is filing this return? Check the applicable box: **a** ☐ Domestic general partnership **b** ☐ Domestic limited partnership **c** ☐ Domestic limited liability company **d** ☐ Domestic limited liability partnership **e** ☐ Foreign partnership **f** ☐ Other ▶		
2	Are any partners in this partnership also partnerships?		X
3	During the partnership's tax year, did the partnership own any interest in another partnership or in any foreign entity that was disregarded as an entity separate from its owner under Regulations sections 301.7701-2 and 301.7701-3? If yes, see instructions for required attachment		X
4	Is this partnership subject to the consolidated audit procedures of sections 6221 through 6233? If "Yes," see **Designation of Tax Matters Partner** below		X
5	Does this partnership meet **all three** of the following requirements? **a** The partnership's total receipts for the tax year were less than $250,000; **b** The partnership's total assets at the end of the tax year were less than $600,000; **and** **c** Schedules K-1 are filed with the return and furnished to the partners on or before the due date (including extensions) for the partnership return. If "Yes," the partnership is not required to complete Schedules L, M-1, and M-2; Item F on page 1 of Form 1065; or Item J on Schedule K-1		X
6	Does this partnership have any foreign partners? If "Yes," the partnership may have to file Forms 8804, 8805 and 8813. See page 20 of the instructions		X
7	Is this partnership a publicly traded partnership as defined in section 469(k)(2)?		X
8	Has this partnership filed, or is it required to file, **Form 8264,** Application for Registration of a Tax Shelter?		X
9	At any time during calendar year 2001, did the partnership have an interest in or a signature or other authority over a financial account in a foreign country (such as a bank account, securities account, or other financial account)? See page 20 of the instructions for exceptions and filing requirements for Form TD F 90-22.1. If "Yes," enter the name of the foreign country. ▶		X
10	During the tax year, did the partnership receive a distribution from, or was it the grantor of, or transferor to, a foreign trust? If "Yes," the partnership may have to file Form 3520. See page 20 of the instructions		X
11	Was there a distribution of property or a transfer (e.g., by sale or death) of a partnership interest during the tax year? If "Yes," you may elect to adjust the basis of the partnership's assets under section 754 by attaching the statement described under **Elections Made By the Partnership** on page 8 of the instructions		X
12	Enter the number of Forms 8865 attached to this return ▶		

Designation of Tax Matters Partner (see page 20 of the instructions)
Enter below the general partner designated as the tax matters partner (TMP) for the tax year of this return: (Not Required)

Name of designated TMP ▶ Andrew Lawrence — Identifying number of TMP ▶ 297-63-2110
Address of designated TMP ▶ 436 N.W. 24th Ave.
Gainesville, FL 32607

Form **1065** (2001)

Form 1065 (2001) Page **3**

Schedule K **Partners' Shares of Income, Credits, Deductions, etc.**

	(a) Distributive share items		(b) Total amount
Income (Loss)	1 Ordinary income (loss) from trade or business activities (page 1, line 22)	1	79,846
	2 Net income (loss) from rental real estate activities *(attach Form 8825)*	2	
	3a Gross income from other rental activities | 3a |		
	b Expenses from other rental activities *(attach schedule)* | 3b |		
	c Net income (loss) from other rental activities. Subtract line 3b from line 3a	3c	
	4 Portfolio income (loss): a Interest income	4a	
	b Ordinary dividends	4b	1,000
	c Royalty income	4c	
	d Net short-term capital gain (loss) *(attach Schedule D (Form 1065))* (not reproduced)	4d	(2,100)
	e (1) Net long-term capital gain (loss) *(attach Schedule D (Form 1065))* (not reproduced)	4e(1)	4,500
	(2) 28% rate gain (loss) ▶ (3) Qualified 5-year gain ▶		
	f Other portfolio income (loss) *(attach schedule)*	4f	
	5 Guaranteed payments to partners	5	36,000
	6 Net section 1231 gain (loss) (other than due to casualty or theft) *(attach Form 4797)*	6	
	7 Other income (loss) *(attach schedule)*	7	
Deductions	8 Charitable contributions *(attach schedule)*	8	12,000
	9 Section 179 expense deduction *(attach Form 4562)*	9	
	10 Deductions related to portfolio income (itemize)	10	150
	11 Other deductions *(attach schedule)*	11	
Credits	12a Low-income housing credit:		
	(1) From partnerships to which section 42(j)(5) applies	12a(1)	
	(2) Other than on line 12a(1)	12a(2)	
	b Qualified rehabilitation expenditures related to rental real estate activities *(attach Form 3468)*	12b	
	c Credits (other than credits shown on lines 12a and 12b) related to rental real estate activities	12c	
	d Credits related to other rental activities	12d	
	13 Other credits	13	
Investment Interest	14a Interest expense on investment debts	14a	
	b (1) Investment income included on lines 4a, 4b, 4c, and 4f above	14b(1)	1,000
	(2) Investment expenses included on line 10 above	14b(2)	150
Self-Employment	15a Net earnings (loss) from self-employment	15a	115,846
	b Gross farming or fishing income	15b	
	c Gross nonfarm income	15c	
Adjustments and Tax Preference Items	16a Depreciation adjustment on property placed in service after 1986	16a	1,514
	b Adjusted gain or loss	16b	
	c Depletion (other than oil and gas)	16c	
	d (1) Gross income from oil, gas, and geothermal properties	16d(1)	
	(2) Deductions allocable to oil, gas, and geothermal properties	16d(2)	
	e Other adjustments and tax preference items *(attach schedule)*	16e	
Foreign Taxes	17a Name of foreign country or U.S. possession ▶		
	b Gross income from all sources	17b	
	c Gross income sourced at partner level	17c	
	d Foreign gross income sourced at partnership level:		
	(1) Passive ▶ (2) Listed categories *(attach schedule)* ▶ (3) General limitation ▶	17d(3)	
	e Deductions allocated and apportioned at partner level:		
	(1) Interest expense ▶ (2) Other ▶	17e(2)	
	f Deductions allocated and apportioned at partnership level to foreign source income:		
	(1) Passive ▶ (2) Listed categories *(attach schedule)* ▶ (3) General limitation ▶	17f(3)	
	g Total foreign taxes (check one): ▶ Paid ☐ Accrued ☐	17g	
	h Reduction in taxes available for credit *(attach schedule)*	17h	
Other	18 Section 59(e)(2) expenditures: a Type ▶ b Amount ▶	18b	18,000
	19 Tax-exempt interest income	19	
	20 Other tax-exempt income	20	
	21 Nondeductible expenses	21	6,000 *
	22 Distributions of money (cash and marketable securities)	22	
	23 Distributions of property other than money	23	28,212
	24 Other items and amounts required to be reported separately to partners *(attach schedule)*		

* $4,000 of travel and entertainment expenses disallowed and $2,000 of interest incurred to purchase tax-exempt bonds.

Form **1065** (2001)

Form 1065 (2001) Page **4**

Analysis of Net Income (Loss)

1 Net income (loss). Combine Schedule K, lines 1 through 7 in column (b). From the result, subtract the sum of Schedule K, lines 8 through 11, 14a, 17g, and 18b . . . . 1 | 107,096

2 Analysis by partner type:	(i) Corporate	(ii) Individual (active)	(iii) Individual (passive)	(iv) Partnership	(v) Exempt organization	(vi) Nominee/Other
a General partners		107,096				
b Limited partners						

Schedule L — Balance Sheets per Books (Not required if Question 5 on Schedule B is answered "Yes.")

Assets	Beginning of tax year (a)	(b)	End of tax year (c)	(d)
1 Cash		60,000		92,760
2a Trade notes and accounts receivable	25,000		24,000	
b Less allowance for bad debts	1,000	24,000	1,000	23,000
3 Inventories		64,000		104,800
4 U.S. government obligations				
5 Tax-exempt securities		200,000		200,000
6 Other current assets *(attach schedule)*		7,000		-0-
7 Mortgage and real estate loans				
8 Other investments *(attach schedule)*				
9a Buildings and other depreciable assets	151,600		151,600	
b Less accumulated depreciation	45,200	106,400	72,760	78,924
10a Depletable assets				
b Less accumulated depletion				
11 Land (net of any amortization)				
12a Intangible assets (amortizable only)				
b Less accumulated amortization				
13 Other assets *(attach schedule)*				
14 **Total** assets		461,400		499,484
Liabilities and Capital				
15 Accounts payable		26,000		19,000
16 Mortgages, notes, bonds payable in less than 1 year		4,000		4,000
17 Other current liabilities *(attach schedule)*		3,600		3,600
18 All nonrecourse loans				
19 Mortgages, notes, bonds payable in 1 year or more		130,000		119,724
20 Other liabilities *(attach schedule)*				
21 Partners' capital accounts		297,800		353,160
22 **Total** liabilities and capital		461,400		499,484

Schedule M-1 — Reconciliation of Income (Loss) per Books With Income (Loss) per Return (Not required if Question 5 on Schedule B is answered "Yes.")

1 Net income (loss) per books	83,572	6 Income recorded on books this year not included on Schedule K, lines 1 through 7 (itemize): a Tax-exempt interest $ 18,000	18,000
2 Income included on Schedule K, lines 1 through 4, 6, and 7, not recorded on books this year (itemize):		7 Deductions included on Schedule K, lines 1 through 11, 14a, 17g, and 18b, not charged against book income this year (itemize): a Depreciation $ 476	476
3 Guaranteed payments (other than health insurance)	36,000	8 Add lines 6 and 7	18,476
4 Expenses recorded on books this year not included on Schedule K, lines 1 through 11, 14a, 17g, and 18b (itemize): a Depreciation $; b Travel and entertainment $ 4,000; Interest on loans to buy tax-exempt bonds $2,000	6,000	9 Income (loss) (Analysis of Net Income (Loss), line 1). Subtract line 8 from line 5	107,096
5 Add lines 1 through 4	125,572		

Schedule M-2 — Analysis of Partners' Capital Accounts (Not required if Question 5 on Schedule B is answered "Yes.")

1 Balance at beginning of year	297,800	6 Distributions: a Cash	28,212
2 Capital contributed during year		b Property	
3 Net income (loss) per books	83,572	7 Other decreases (itemize):	
4 Other increases (itemize):			
		8 Add lines 6 and 7	28,212
5 Add lines 1 through 4	381,372	9 Balance at end of year. Subtract line 8 from line 5	353,160

Form **1065** (2001)

SCHEDULE K-1 (Form 1065)
Department of the Treasury
Internal Revenue Service

Partner's Share of Income, Credits, Deductions, etc.

▶ See separate instructions.

For calendar year 2001 or tax year beginning , 2001, and ending , 20

OMB No. 1545-0099

2001

Partner's identifying number ▶ 297-63-2110

Partnership's identifying number ▶ 76-3456789

Partner's name, address, and ZIP code
Andrew Lawrence *
436 N.W. 24th Ave.
Gainesville, FL 32607

Partnership's name, address, and ZIP code
Johns and Lawrence
1234 University Avenue
Gainesville, FL 32611

A This partner is a ☒ general partner ☐ limited partner ☐ limited liability company member

B What type of entity is this partner? ▶ Individual

C Is this partner a ☐ domestic or a ☐ foreign partner?

D Enter partner's percentage of:

	(i) Before change or termination	(ii) End of year
Profit sharing	%	50 %
Loss sharing	%	50 %
Ownership of capital	%	50 %

E IRS Center where partnership filed return: Atlanta

F Partner's share of liabilities (see instructions):
Nonrecourse . . . $
Qualified nonrecourse financing . . $
Other . . . $ 73,162

G Tax shelter registration number . . ▶ N/A

H Check here if this partnership is a publicly traded partnership as defined in section 469(k)(2) . . . . . ☐

I Check applicable boxes: (1) ☐ Final K-1 (2) ☐ Amended K-1

J Analysis of partner's capital account:

(a) Capital account at beginning of year	(b) Capital contributed during year	(c) Partner's share of lines 3, 4, and 7, Form 1065, Schedule M-2	(d) Withdrawals and distributions	(e) Capital account at end of year (combine columns (a) through (d))
148,900	0	41,786	(14,106)	176,580

		(a) Distributive share item		(b) Amount	(c) 1040 filers enter the amount in column (b) on:
Income (Loss)	1	Ordinary income (loss) from trade or business activities	1	39,923	See page 6 of Partner's Instructions for Schedule K-1 (Form 1065).
	2	Net income (loss) from rental real estate activities	2		
	3	Net income (loss) from other rental activities	3		
	4	Portfolio income (loss):			
	a	Interest	4a		Sch. B, Part I, line 1
	b	Ordinary dividends	4b	500	Sch. B, Part II, line 5
	c	Royalties	4c		Sch. E, Part I, line 4
	d	Net short-term capital gain (loss)	4d	(1,050)	Sch. D, line 5, col. (f)
	e	(1) Net long-term capital gain (loss)	4e(1)	2,250	Sch. D, line 12, col. (f)
		(2) 28% rate gain (loss)	4e(2)		Sch. D, line 12, col. (g)
		(3) Qualified 5-year gain	4e(3)		Line 4 of worksheet for Sch. D, line 29
	f	Other portfolio income (loss) *(attach schedule)*	4f		Enter on applicable line of your return.
	5	Guaranteed payments to partner	5	18,000	See page 6 of Partner's Instructions for Schedule K-1 (Form 1065).
	6	Net section 1231 gain (loss) (other than due to casualty or theft)	6		
	7	Other income (loss) *(attach schedule)*	7		Enter on applicable line of your return.
Deductions	8	Charitable contributions (see instructions) *(attach schedule)*	8	6,000	Sch. A, line 15 or 16
	9	Section 179 expense deduction	9		See pages 7 and 8 of Partner's Instructions for Schedule K-1 (Form 1065).
	10	Deductions related to portfolio income *(attach schedule)*	10	75	
	11	Other deductions *(attach schedule)*	11		
Credits	12a	Low-income housing credit:			
		(1) From section 42(j)(5) partnerships	12a(1)		Form 8586, line 5
		(2) Other than on line 12a(1)	12a(2)		
	b	Qualified rehabilitation expenditures related to rental real estate activities	12b		See page 8 of Partner's Instructions for Schedule K-1 (Form 1065).
	c	Credits (other than credits shown on lines 12a and 12b) related to rental real estate activities	12c		
	d	Credits related to other rental activities	12d		
	13	Other credits	13		

For Paperwork Reduction Act Notice, see Instructions for Form 1065. Cat. No. 11394R **Schedule K-1 (Form 1065) 2001**

* Second schedule K-1 for Stephen Johns is similar to this one but is not reproduced here.

Schedule K-1 (Form 1065) 2001 Page 2

		(a) Distributive share item		(b) Amount	(c) 1040 filers enter the amount in column (b) on:
Investment Interest	14a	Interest expense on investment debts	14a	500	Form 4952, line 1
	b	(1) Investment income included on lines 4a, 4b, 4c, and 4f	14b(1)	75	See page 9 of Partner's Instructions for Schedule K-1 (Form 1065).
		(2) Investment expenses included on line 10	14b(2)	57,923	
Self-employment	15a	Net earnings (loss) from self-employment	15a		Sch. SE, Section A or B
	b	Gross farming or fishing income	15b		See page 9 of Partner's Instructions for Schedule K-1 (Form 1065).
	c	Gross nonfarm income	15c	757	
Adjustments and Tax Preference Items	16a	Depreciation adjustment on property placed in service after 1986	16a		See page 9 of Partner's Instructions for Schedule K-1 (Form 1065) and Instructions for Form 6251.
	b	Adjusted gain or loss	16b		
	c	Depletion (other than oil and gas)	16c		
	d	(1) Gross income from oil, gas, and geothermal properties	16d(1)		
		(2) Deductions allocable to oil, gas, and geothermal properties	16d(2)		
	e	Other adjustments and tax preference items *(attach schedule)*	16e		
Foreign Taxes	17a	Name of foreign country or U.S. possession ▶			Form 1116, Part I
	b	Gross income from all sources	17b		
	c	Gross income sourced at partner level	17c		
	d	Foreign gross income sourced at partnership level:			
		(1) Passive	17d(1)		
		(2) Listed categories *(attach schedule)*	17d(2)		
		(3) General limitation	17d(3)		
	e	Deductions allocated and apportioned at partner level:			
		(1) Interest expense	17e(1)		
		(2) Other	17e(2)		
	f	Deductions allocated and apportioned at partnership level to foreign source income:			
		(1) Passive	17f(1)		
		(2) Listed categories *(attach schedule)*	17f(2)		
		(3) General limitation	17f(3)		
	g	Total foreign taxes (check one): ▶ ☐ Paid ☐ Accrued	17g		Form 1116, Part II
	h	Reduction in taxes available for credit *(attach schedule)*	17h		Form 1116, line 12
Other	18	Section 59(e)(2) expenditures: a Type ▶			See page 9 of Partner's Instructions for Schedule K-1 (Form 1065).
	b	Amount	18b	9,000	
	19	Tax-exempt interest income	19		Form 1040, line 8b
	20	Other tax-exempt income	20	3,000*	See pages 9 and 10 of Partner's Instructions for Schedule K-1 (Form 1065).
	21	Nondeductible expenses	21	28,212	
	22	Distributions of money (cash and marketable securities)	22		
	23	Distributions of property other than money	23		
	24	Recapture of low-income housing credit:			
	a	From section 42(j)(5) partnerships	24a		Form 8611, line 8
	b	Other than on line 24a	24b		

Supplemental Information

25 Supplemental information required to be reported separately to each partner *(attach additional schedules if more space is needed)*:

* $1,000 of interest expense incurred to purchase tax-exempt bonds and $2,000 of meals and entertainment expenses disallowed by Sec. 274.

FACTS FOR GENERAL PARTNERSHIP (FORM 1065)

The same basic facts presented for the Andrew Lawrence proprietorship are used for the partnership except for the following:

1. Johns and Lawrence is instead a general partnership. Andrew Lawrence and Stephen Johns are both general partners and have equal capital and profits interests. The partnership was created on June 1, 1995. Johns and Lawrence each exchanged their $100,000 of property for a 50% interest in capital and a 50% interest in profits.
2. The book income for Johns and Lawrence is presented in the attached worksheet, which reconciles book income and partnership taxable income.
3. The $18,000 salaries paid to each partner are stipulated in the partnership agreement and are treated as guaranteed payments.
4. The partnership pays federal and state employment taxes on the wages paid to employees other than the partners Johns and Lawrence. The employment tax expense is $52,000 × 0.16 = $8,320. The guaranteed payments made to Johns and Lawrence are treated as self-employment income by the two partners.
5. The partnership paid no estimated federal income taxes.
6. The $28,212 in withdrawals were paid equally to the two partners.
7. Other deductions include:

Travel	$4,000
Meals and entertainment	8,000
Minus: 50% disallowance	(4,000)
Office expenses	16,000
Transportation	10,400
General and administrative	3,000
Advertising	13,000
Miscellaneous*	850
Total	$51,250

*$150 of the miscellaneous expenses are related to the production of the dividend income and are separately stated.

8. Reconciliation of net income for the C corporation and the partnership occurs as follows:

Net income for C corporation	$63,412
Plus: Federal income taxes	14,000
Employment tax adjustment ($14,480 – $8,320)	6,160
Net income for partnership	$83,572

9. Total paid-in capital and accumulated profits were divided equally between the two partners in accordance with the actual contributions and allocation of partnership profits in the partnership agreement. Actual business operations may provide for an unequal allocation.
10. The balance sheet for Johns and Lawrence is presented on page 4 of Form 1065.

Johns and Lawrence General Partnership Reconciliation of Book and Taxable Income For Year Ending December 31, 2001

	Book Income		Adjustments		Taxable Income		Form 1065 Schedule K	
Account Name	Debit	Credit	Debit	Credit	Debit	Credit	Ordinary Income	Separately Stated Items
Sales		869,658				869,658	869,658	
Sales returns & allowances	29,242				29,242		(29,242)	
Cost of sales	540,204				540,204		(540,204)	
Dividends		1,000				1,000		1,000
Tax-exempt interest		18,000	18,000			0		18,000
Gain on stock sale		4,500				4,500		4,500
Worthless stock loss	2,100				2,100			(2,100)
Guaranteed payments[(a)]	36,000			36,000	0		(36,000)	
Other salaries	52,000				52,000		(52,000)	
Rentals	36,000				36,000		(36,000)	
Bad debts	4,000				4,000		(4,000)	
Interest:								
Working capital loans	8,000				8,000		(8,000)	
Purchase tax-exempt bonds	2,000			2,000	0			(2,000)
Employment taxes	8,320				8,320		(8,320)	
Taxes	1,520				1,520		(1,520)	
Repairs	4,800				4,800		(4,800)	
Depreciation[(b)]	12,000		476		12,476		(12,476)	
Charitable contributions	12,000				12,000			(12,000)
Travel	4,000				4,000		(4,000)	
Meals and entertainment[(c)]	8,000			4,000	4,000		(4,000)	
Meals and ent. nondeductible								(4,000)
Office expenses	16,000				16,000		(16,000)	
Advertising	13,000				13,000		(13,000)	
Transportation expense	10,400				10,400		(10,400)	
General and administrative	3,000				3,000		(3,000)	
Pension plans[(d)]	2,000				2,000		(2,000)	
Employee benefit programs[(e)]	4,000				4,000		(4,000)	
Miscellaneous	1,000				1,000		(850)	(150)
Net profit/Taxable income	83,572		23,524		107,096			
Total	893,158	893,158	42,000	42,000	875,158	875,158	79,846	

(a) Note that guaranteed payments have no net effect on taxable income. The guaranteed payments both reduce ordinary income and increase separately stated income items that are taxable.

(b) MACRS depreciation is $12,476 − $12,000 = $476

(c) 50% of the meals and entertainment expense is not deductible for tax purposes but must be separately stated on Schedules K and K-1.

(d) The pension plan expense is the same for book and tax purposes for this partnership. No pension expenses relate to pensions for the partners.

(e) The employee benefit expense is the same for book and tax purposes for this partnership. None relates to partner benefits.

Form **1120** — Department of the Treasury, Internal Revenue Service

U.S. Corporation Income Tax Return

For calendar year 2001 or tax year beginning ...., 2001, ending ...., 20 ....
▶ Instructions are separate. See page 20 for Paperwork Reduction Act Notice.

OMB No. 1545-0123 — **2001**

A Check if a:
1 Consolidated return (attach Form 851) ☐
2 Personal holding co. (attach Sch. PH) ☐
3 Personal service corp. (as defined in Temporary Regs. sec. 1.441-4T—see instructions) ☐

Use IRS label. Otherwise, print or type.

Name: Johns and Lawrence, Inc.
Number, street, and room or suite no. (If a P.O. box, see page 7 of instructions.): 1234 University Avenue
City or town, state, and ZIP code: Gainesville, FL 32611

B Employer identification number: 76 : 3457689
C Date incorporated: 6/1/95
D Total assets (see page 8 of instructions): $ 479,324

E Check applicable boxes: (1) ☐ Initial return (2) ☐ Final return (3) ☐ Name change (4) ☐ Address change

Income

Line	Description		Amount
1a	Gross receipts or sales 869,658	b Less returns and allowances 29,242	c Bal ▶ 1c: 840,416
2	Cost of goods sold (Schedule A, line 8)		540,204
3	Gross profit. Subtract line 2 from line 1c		300,212
4	Dividends (Schedule C, line 19)		1,000
5	Interest		
6	Gross rents		
7	Gross royalties		
8	Capital gain net income (attach Schedule D (Form 1120)) Not reproduced		2,400
9	Net gain or (loss) from Form 4797, Part II, line 18 (attach Form 4797)		
10	Other income (see page 8 of instructions—attach schedule)		
11	**Total income.** Add lines 3 through 10 ▶		303,612

Deductions (See instructions for limitations on deductions.)

Line	Description		Amount
12	Compensation of officers (Schedule E, line 4)		36,000
13	Salaries and wages (less employment credits)		52,000
14	Repairs and maintenance		4,800
15	Bad debts		4,000
16	Rents		36,000
17	Taxes and licenses		16,000
18	Interest		8,000
19	Charitable contributions (see page 10 of instructions for 10% limitation)		7,694
20	Depreciation (attach Form 4562)	20: 27,476	
21	Less depreciation claimed on Schedule A and elsewhere on return	21a: 15,000	21b: 12,476
22	Depletion		
23	Advertising		13,000
24	Pension, profit-sharing, etc., plans		2,000
25	Employee benefit programs		4,000
26	Other deductions (attach schedule)		38,400
27	**Total deductions.** Add lines 12 through 26 ▶		234,370
28	Taxable income before net operating loss deduction and special deductions. Subtract line 27 from line 11		69,242
29	**Less:** a Net operating loss (NOL) deduction (see page 13 of instructions)	29a	
	b Special deductions (Schedule C, line 20)	29b: 700	29c: 700

Tax and Payments

Line	Description		Amount
30	**Taxable income.** Subtract line 29c from line 28		68,542
31	**Total tax** (Schedule J, line 11)		12,136
32	**Payments:** a 2000 overpayment credited to 2001	32a	
b	2001 estimated tax payments	32b: 14,000	
c	Less 2001 refund applied for on Form 4466	32c ( ) d Bal ▶ 32d	
e	Tax deposited with Form 7004	32e	
f	Credit for tax paid on undistributed capital gains (attach Form 2439)	32f	
g	Credit for Federal tax on fuels (attach Form 4136). See instructions	32g	32h: 14,000
33	Estimated tax penalty (see page 14 of instructions). Check if Form 2220 is attached ▶ ☐		
34	**Tax due.** If line 32h is smaller than the total of lines 31 and 33, enter amount owed		
35	**Overpayment.** If line 32h is larger than the total of lines 31 and 33, enter amount overpaid		1,864
36	Enter amount of line 35 you want: **Credited to 2002 estimated tax** ▶	**Refunded** ▶	

Sign Here

Under penalties of perjury, I declare that I have examined this return, including accompanying schedules and statements, and to the best of my knowledge and belief, it is true, correct, and complete. Declaration of preparer (other than taxpayer) is based on all information of which preparer has any knowledge.

Signature of officer: Andrew Lawrence — Date: 3/15/02 — Title: Vice-President

May the IRS discuss this return with the preparer shown below (see instructions)? ☐ Yes ☐ No

Paid Preparer's Use Only

Preparer's signature: Michael Kramer — Date: 3/14/02 — Check if self-employed ☒ — Preparer's SSN or PTIN: 375 49 6339
Firm's name (or yours if self-employed), address, and ZIP code: Michael S. Kramer 1110 McMillan, Gainesville, FL 32611 — EIN 59 : 2029763 — Phone no. (352) 555-2000

Cat. No. 11450Q

Form 1120 (2001) Page 2

Schedule A Cost of Goods Sold (See page 14 of instructions.)

1	Inventory at beginning of year	1	64,000
2	Purchases	2	340,800
3	Cost of labor	3	143,204
4	Additional section 263A costs (attach schedule)	4	7,000
5	Other costs (attach schedule)	5	90,000
6	**Total.** Add lines 1 through 5	6	645,004
7	Inventory at end of year	7	104,800
8	**Cost of goods sold.** Subtract line 7 from line 6. Enter here and on line 2, page 1	8	540,204

9a Check all methods used for valuing closing inventory:

(i) ☒ Cost as described in Regulations section 1.471-3

(ii) ☐ Lower of cost or market as described in Regulations section 1.471-4

(iii) ☐ Other (Specify method used and attach explanation.) ▶

b Check if there was a writedown of subnormal goods as described in Regulations section 1.471-2(c) ▶ ☐

c Check if the LIFO inventory method was adopted this tax year for any goods (if checked, attach Form 970) ▶ ☐

d If the LIFO inventory method was used for this tax year, enter percentage (or amounts) of closing inventory computed under LIFO | 9d |

e If property is produced or acquired for resale, do the rules of section 263A apply to the corporation? ☒ Yes ☐ No

f Was there any change in determining quantities, cost, or valuations between opening and closing inventory? If "Yes," attach explanation ☐ Yes ☒ No

Schedule C Dividends and Special Deductions (See page 15 of instructions.)

		(a) Dividends received	(b) %	(c) Special deductions (a) × (b)
1	Dividends from less-than-20%-owned domestic corporations that are subject to the 70% deduction (other than debt-financed stock)	1,000	70	700
2	Dividends from 20%-or-more-owned domestic corporations that are subject to the 80% deduction (other than debt-financed stock)		80	
3	Dividends on debt-financed stock of domestic and foreign corporations (section 246A)		see instructions	
4	Dividends on certain preferred stock of less-than-20%-owned public utilities		42	
5	Dividends on certain preferred stock of 20%-or-more-owned public utilities		48	
6	Dividends from less-than-20%-owned foreign corporations and certain FSCs that are subject to the 70% deduction		70	
7	Dividends from 20%-or-more-owned foreign corporations and certain FSCs that are subject to the 80% deduction		80	
8	Dividends from wholly owned foreign subsidiaries subject to the 100% deduction (section 245(b))		100	
9	**Total.** Add lines 1 through 8. See page 16 of instructions for limitation			
10	Dividends from domestic corporations received by a small business investment company operating under the Small Business Investment Act of 1958		100	
11	Dividends from certain FSCs that are subject to the 100% deduction (section 245(c)(1))		100	
12	Dividends from affiliated group members subject to the 100% deduction (section 243(a)(3))		100	
13	Other dividends from foreign corporations not included on lines 3, 6, 7, 8, or 11			
14	Income from controlled foreign corporations under subpart F (attach Form(s) 5471)			
15	Foreign dividend gross-up (section 78)			
16	IC-DISC and former DISC dividends not included on lines 1, 2, or 3 (section 246(d))			
17	Other dividends			
18	Deduction for dividends paid on certain preferred stock of public utilities			
19	**Total dividends.** Add lines 1 through 17. Enter here and on line 4, page 1 ▶			
20	**Total special deductions.** Add lines 9, 10, 11, 12, and 18. Enter here and on line 29b, page 1 ▶			700

Schedule E Compensation of Officers (See instructions for line 12, page 1.)

Note: *Complete Schedule E only if total receipts (line 1a plus lines 4 through 10 on page 1, Form 1120) are $500,000 or more.*

(a) Name of officer	(b) Social security number	(c) Percent of time devoted to business	Percent of corporation stock owned (d) Common	(e) Preferred	(f) Amount of compensation
1 Stephen Johns	386-06-9174	100 %	50%	%	18,000
Andrew Lawrence	297-63-2110	100 %	50%	%	18,000
		%	%	%	
		%	%	%	
		%	%	%	

2	Total compensation of officers	36,000
3	Compensation of officers claimed on Schedule A and elsewhere on return	
4	Subtract line 3 from line 2. Enter the result here and on line 12, page 1	36,000

Form **1120** (2001)

Form 1120 (2001) Page 3

Schedule J **Tax Computation** (See page 16 of instructions.)

1	Check if the corporation is a member of a controlled group (see sections 1561 and 1563) . . . . ▶ ☐ **Important:** Members of a controlled group, see instructions on page 16.		
2a	If the box on line 1 is checked, enter the corporation's share of the $50,000, $25,000, and $9,925,000 taxable income brackets (in that order): (1) $ (2) $ (3) $		
b	Enter the corporation's share of: **(1)** Additional 5% tax (not more than $11,750) $ **(2)** Additional 3% tax (not more than $100,000) $		
3	Income tax. Check if a qualified personal service corporation under section 448(d)(2) (see page 17) . ▶ ☐	3	12,136
4	Alternative minimum tax (attach Form 4626)	4	
5	Add lines 3 and 4	5	
6a	Foreign tax credit (attach Form 1118) . . . 6a		
b	Possessions tax credit (attach Form 5735) . . . 6b		
c	Check: ☐ Nonconventional source fuel credit ☐ QEV credit (attach Form 8834) 6c		
d	General business credit. Check box(es) and indicate which forms are attached. ☐ Form 3800 ☐ Form(s) (specify) ▶ 6d		
e	Credit for prior year minimum tax (attach Form 8827) . . . 6e		
f	Qualified zone academy bond credit (attach Form 8860) . . . 6f		
7	**Total credits.** Add lines 6a through 6f	7	-0-
8	Subtract line 7 from line 5	8	12,136
9	Personal holding company tax (attach Schedule PH (Form 1120))	9	
10	Other taxes. Check if from: ☐ Form 4255 ☐ Form 8611 ☐ Form 8697 ☐ Form 8866 ☐ Other (attach schedule)	10	
11	**Total tax.** Add lines 8 through 10. Enter here and on line 31, page 1	11	12,136

Schedule K **Other Information** (See page 19 of instructions.)

		Yes	No
1	Check method of accounting: **a** ☐ Cash **b** ☒ Accrual **c** ☐ Other (specify) ▶		
2	See page 21 of the instructions and enter the: **a** Business activity code no. ▶ 337000 **b** Business activity ▶ Manufacturing **c** Product or service ▶ Furniture		
3	At the end of the tax year, did the corporation own, directly or indirectly, 50% or more of the voting stock of a domestic corporation? (For rules of attribution, see section 267(c).) If "Yes," attach a schedule showing: **(a)** name and employer identification number (EIN), **(b)** percentage owned, and **(c)** taxable income or (loss) before NOL and special deductions of such corporation for the tax year ending with or within your tax year.		X
4	Is the corporation a subsidiary in an affiliated group or a parent-subsidiary controlled group? If "Yes," enter name and EIN of the parent corporation ▶		X
5	At the end of the tax year, did any individual, partnership, corporation, estate, or trust own, directly or indirectly, 50% or more of the corporation's voting stock? (For rules of attribution, see section 267(c).) If "Yes," attach a schedule showing name and identifying number. (Do not include any information already entered in **4** above.) Enter percentage owned ▶ 50% *	X	
6	During this tax year, did the corporation pay dividends (other than stock dividends and distributions in exchange for stock) in excess of the corporation's current and accumulated earnings and profits? (See sections 301 and 316.) If "Yes," file **Form 5452,** Corporate Report of Nondividend Distributions. If this is a consolidated return, answer here for the parent corporation and on **Form 851,** Affiliations Schedule, for each subsidiary.		X
7	At any time during the tax year, did one foreign person own, directly or indirectly, at least 25% of **(a)** the total voting power of all classes of stock of the corporation entitled to vote or **(b)** the total value of all classes of stock of the corporation? If "Yes," enter: **(a)** Percentage owned ▶ N/A and **(b)** Owner's country ▶ N/A		X
c	The corporation may have to file **Form 5472,** Information Return of a 25% Foreign-Owned U.S. Corporation or a Foreign Corporation Engaged in a U.S. Trade or Business. Enter number of Forms 5472 attached ▶		
8	Check this box if the corporation issued publicly offered debt instruments with original issue discount . . ▶ ☐ If checked, the corporation may have to file **Form 8281,** Information Return for Publicly Offered Original Issue Discount Instruments.		
9	Enter the amount of tax-exempt interest received or accrued during the tax year ▶ $ 18,000		
10	Enter the number of shareholders at the end of the tax year (if 75 or fewer) ▶ 2		
11	If the corporation has an NOL for the tax year and is electing to forego the carryback period, check here ▶ ☐ If the corporation is filing a consolidated return, the statement required by Regulations section 1.1502-21(b)(3)(i) or (ii) must be attached or the election will not be valid.		
12	Enter the available NOL carryover from prior tax years (Do not reduce it by any deduction on line 29a.) ▶ $ None		

Note: *If the corporation, at any time during the tax year, had assets or operated a business in a foreign country or U.S. possession it may be required to attach* ***Schedule N (Form 1120),*** *Foreign Operations of U.S. Corporations, to this return. See Schedule N for details.*

* See Schedule E

Form **1120** (2001)

Form 1120 (2001) Page **4**

Schedule L — Balance Sheets per Books

Assets	Beginning of tax year (a)	Beginning of tax year (b)	End of tax year (c)	End of tax year (d)
1 Cash		60,000		72,600
2a Trade notes and accounts receivable	25,000		24,000	
b Less allowance for bad debts	(1,000)	24,000	(1,000)	23,000
3 Inventories		64,000		104,800
4 U.S. government obligations		200,000		200,000
5 Tax-exempt securities (see instructions)		7,000		
6 Other current assets (attach schedule)				
7 Loans to shareholders				
8 Mortgage and real estate loans				
9 Other investments (attach schedule)				
10a Buildings and other depreciable assets	151,600		151,600	
b Less accumulated depreciation	(45,200)	106,400	(72,676)	78,924
11a Depletable assets				
b Less accumulated depletion	( )		( )	
12 Land (net of any amortization)				
13a Intangible assets (amortizable only)				
b Less accumulated amortization	( )		( )	
14 Other assets (attach schedule)				
15 Total assets		461,400		479,324
Liabilities and Shareholders' Equity				
16 Accounts payable		26,000		19,000
17 Mortgages, notes, bonds payable in less than 1 year		4,000		4,000
18 Other current liabilities (attach schedule)		3,600		3,600
19 Loans from shareholders				
20 Mortgages, notes, bonds payable in 1 year or more		130,000		119,724
21 Other liabilities (attach schedule)				
22 Capital stock: a Preferred stock				
b Common stock	200,000	200,000		200,000
23 Additional paid-in capital				
24 Retained earnings—Appropriated (attach schedule)				
25 Retained earnings—Unappropriated		97,800		133,000
26 Adjustments to shareholders' equity (attach schedule)				
27 Less cost of treasury stock		( )		( )
28 Total liabilities and shareholders' equity		461,400		479,324

Note: *The corporation is not required to complete Schedules M-1 and M-2 if the total assets on line 15, col. (d) of Schedule L are less than $25,000.*

Schedule M-1 — Reconciliation of Income (Loss) per Books With Income per Return (See page 20 of instructions.)

1 Net income (loss) per books	63,412	7 Income recorded on books this year not included on this return (itemize): Tax-exempt interest $ 18,000	
2 Federal income tax per books	14,000		
3 Excess of capital losses over capital gains			
4 Income subject to tax not recorded on books this year (itemize):		8 Deductions on this return not charged against book income this year (itemize):	
5 Expenses recorded on books this year not deducted on this return (itemize):		a Depreciation $ 476	
a Depreciation $		b Charitable contributions $	
b Charitable contributions $ 4,306			
c Travel and entertainment $ 4,000			
Interest on loans to acquire municipal bonds 2,000	10,306	9 Add lines 7 and 8	18,476
6 Add lines 1 through 5	87,718	10 Income (line 28, page 1)—line 6 less line 9	69,242

Schedule M-2 — Analysis of Unappropriated Retained Earnings per Books (Line 25, Schedule L)

1 Balance at beginning of year	97,800	5 Distributions: a Cash	28,212
2 Net income (loss) per books	63,412	b Stock	
3 Other increases (itemize):		c Property	
		6 Other decreases (itemize):	
		7 Add lines 5 and 6	28,212
4 Add lines 1, 2, and 3	161,212	8 Balance at end of year (line 4 less line 7)	133,000

Form **1120** (2001)

FACTS FOR C CORPORATION (FORM 1120)

The same basic facts presented for the Andrew Lawrence proprietorship are used for the C corporation except for the following:

1. Andrew Lawrence and Stephen Johns are the two 50% shareholders of Johns and Lawrence, Inc., a furniture manufacturer (Business Code 337000). Johns and Lawrence is located at 1234 University Ave., Gainesville, FL 32611. Its employer identification number is 76-3456789. The following information has been gathered about the 2001 corporate tax return:

Compensation of Officers

Name	S.S. No.	Share	Title	Compensation
Stephen Johns	386-05-9174	1,000	President	$18,000
Andrew Lawrence	297-63-2110	1,000	V.P.	18,000
Total		2,000		$36,000

All salaries owed to the shareholders were paid in 2001. None of the interest or rentals is paid to the shareholders.

2. The book income for the corporation is presented in the attached worksheet, which reconciles the corporation's book income and its taxable income.

3. The company was incorporated on June 1, 1995. Each of the two officers hold one-half the stock, which they acquired on that date for a total cash and property contribution of $200,000. No change in the stockholdings has occurred since incorporation. Johns and Lawrence each devote 100% of their time to the business. No expense allowances are provided. Properly substantiated expenses, however, are reimbursed. Both officers are U.S. citizens. Johns and Lawrence is not a member of a controlled group.

4. Addresses for the officers are: Andrew Lawrence, 436 N.W. 24th Ave., Gainesville, FL 32607; Stephen Johns, 1250 N.E. 12th Ave., Gainesville, FL 32601.

5. The corporation paid estimated taxes of $14,000 for tax year 2001.

6. Other deductions include:

Travel	$ 4,000
Meals and entertainment	8,000
Minus: 50% disallowance	(4,000)
Office expenses	16,000
Transportation	10,400
General and administrative	3,000
Miscellaneous	1,000
Total	$38,400

7. The charitable contributions deduction limitation is $7,694 (see footnote b in Reconciliation worksheet on next page). A carryover of $4,306 ($12,000 – $7,694) to 2002 and the four succeeding tax years is available.

8. The $28,212 of withdrawals made by the two owners are dividends coming from the corporation's earnings and profits. They are reported as gross income on the shareholders' individual tax returns.

9. The beginning-of-the-year balance sheets for all entity forms are the same, which permits a direct comparison of the 2001 tax differences. Actually, the corporation would have reported tax differences in all prior years (1995 through 2000), which would have been included in the January 1, 2001 balance sheet. If these differences were so included, the direct comparisons would be much more difficult.

Johns and Lawrence, Inc. (C Corporation) Book Income to Taxable Income Reconciliation For Year Ending December 31, 2001

	Book Income		Adjustments		Taxable Income	
Account Name	Debit	Credit	Debit	Credit	Debit	Credit
Sales		869,658				869,658
Sales returns & allowances	29,242				29,242	
Cost of sales	540,204				540,204	
Dividends		1,000				1,000
Tax-exempt interest		18,000	18,000			0
Gain on stock sale		4,500				4,500
Worthless stock loss	2,100				2,100	
Officers' salaries	36,000				36,000	
Other salaries	52,000				52,000	
Rentals	36,000				36,000	
Bad debts	4,000				4,000	
Interest:						
Working capital loans	8,000				8,000	
Purchase tax-exempt bonds	2,000			2,000	0	
Employment taxes	14,480				14,480	
Taxes	1,520				1,520	
Repairs	4,800				4,800	
Depreciation[(a)]	12,000		476		12,476	
Charitable contributions[(b)]	12,000			4,306	7,694	
Travel	4,000				4,000	
Meals and entertainment[(c)]	8,000			4,000	4,000	
Office expenses	16,000				16,000	
Advertising	13,000				13,000	
Transportation expense	10,400				10,400	
General and administrative	3,000				3,000	
Pension plans	2,000				2,000	
Employee benefit programs	4,000				4,000	
Miscellaneous	1,000				1,000	
Federal income taxes	14,000			14,000	0	
Taxable income before spec. deds.			18,476	24,306	69,242	
Div. rec. ded. (10%-owned)[(d)]			700		700	
NOL deduction					0	
Net profit/Taxable income	63,412		5,130		68,542	
Total	893,158	893,158	24,306	24,306	875,158	875,158

(a) MACRS depreciation is $12,476 − $12,000 = $476

(b) Charitable contribution deduction limitation:

Gross income	$843,816
Minus: Deductions other than char. cont. & DRD	(766,880)
Charitable contribution base	$ 76,936
Times: 10%	× 0.10
Charitable contribution deduction	$ 7,694

(c) $8,000 × 0.50 disallowance rate = $4,000 disallowed expenses

(d) Dividends-received deduction: $1,000 × 0.70 = $700.

Form **1120** Department of the Treasury Internal Revenue Service

U.S. Corporation Income Tax Return

OMB No. 1545-0123

2001

For calendar year 2001 or tax year beginning ...., 2001, ending ...., 20....
▶ Instructions are separate. See page 20 for Paperwork Reduction Act Notice.

A Check if a:
1 Consolidated return (attach Form 851) ☒
2 Personal holding co. (attach Sch. PH) ☐
3 Personal service corp. (as defined in Temporary Regs. sec. 1.441-4T— see instructions) ☐

Use IRS label. Otherwise, print or type.

Name: Alpha Manufacturing Corp. and Subsidiaries
Number, street, and room or suite no. (If a P.O. box, see page 7 of instructions.): 820 N.W. 1st Place
City or town, state, and ZIP code: Gainesville, FL 32601

B Employer identification number: 38 : 0000001
C Date incorporated: 9-15-91
D Total assets (see page 8 of instructions): $ 3,976,492

E Check applicable boxes: (1) ☐ Initial return (2) ☐ Final return (3) ☐ Name change (4) ☐ Address change

Income

Line	Description		Amount
1a	Gross receipts or sales 6,147,000 b Less returns and allowances -0- c Bal ▶	1c	6,147,000
2	Cost of goods sold (Schedule A, line 8)	2	2,301,000
3	Gross profit. Subtract line 2 from line 1c	3	3,846,000
4	Dividends (Schedule C, line 19)	4	40,000
5	Interest	5	156,000
6	Gross rents	6	195,000
7	Gross royalties	7	
8	Capital gain net income (attach Schedule D (Form 1120))	8	67,939
9	Net gain or (loss) from Form 4797, Part II, line 18 (attach Form 4797)	9	37,080
10	Other income (see page 8 of instructions—attach schedule)	10	10,000
11	**Total income.** Add lines 3 through 10 ▶	11	4,352,019

Deductions (See instructions for limitations on deductions.)

Line	Description		Amount
12	Compensation of officers (Schedule E, line 4)	12	165,000
13	Salaries and wages (less employment credits)	13	1,356,000
14	Repairs and maintenance	14	83,000
15	Bad debts	15	48,500
16	Rents	16	179,000
17	Taxes and licenses	17	138,000
18	Interest	18	58,000
19	Charitable contributions (see page 10 of instructions for 10% limitation)	19	15,000
20	Depreciation (attach Form 4562) — 20: 246,093		
21	Less depreciation claimed on Schedule A and elsewhere on return — 21a: 77,400	21b	168,693
22	Depletion	22	
23	Advertising	23	269,140
24	Pension, profit-sharing, etc., plans	24	140,000
25	Employee benefit programs	25	105,000
26	Other deductions (attach schedule)	26	1,284,000
27	**Total deductions.** Add lines 12 through 26 ▶	27	4,009,333
28	Taxable income before net operating loss deduction and special deductions. Subtract line 27 from line 11	28	342,686
29	**Less:** a Net operating loss (NOL) deduction (see page 13 of instructions) — 29a		
	b Special deductions (Schedule C, line 20) — 29b: 32,000	29c	32,000

Tax and Payments

Line	Description		Amount
30	**Taxable income.** Subtract line 29c from line 28	30	310,686
31	**Total tax** (Schedule J, line 11)	31	104,417
32	**Payments:** a 2000 overpayment credited to 2001 — 32a		
b	2001 estimated tax payments — 32b: 146,000		
c	Less 2001 refund applied for on Form 4466 — 32c ( ) d Bal ▶ 32d: 146,000		
e	Tax deposited with Form 7004 — 32e		
f	Credit for tax paid on undistributed capital gains (attach Form 2439) — 32f		
g	Credit for Federal tax on fuels (attach Form 4136). See instructions — 32g	32h	146,000
33	Estimated tax penalty (see page 14 of instructions). Check if Form 2220 is attached ▶ ☐	33	
34	**Tax due.** If line 32h is smaller than the total of lines 31 and 33, enter amount owed	34	
35	**Overpayment.** If line 32h is larger than the total of lines 31 and 33, enter amount overpaid	35	41,583
36	Enter amount of line 35 you want: **Credited to 2002 estimated tax** ▶ **Refunded** ▶	36	41,583

Sign Here

Under penalties of perjury, I declare that I have examined this return, including accompanying schedules and statements, and to the best of my knowledge and belief, it is true, correct, and complete. Declaration of preparer (other than taxpayer) is based on all information of which preparer has any knowledge.

U.R. Stuck | 3-15-02 | President
Signature of officer | Date | Title

May the IRS discuss this return with the preparer shown below (see instructions)? ☐ Yes ☐ No

Paid Preparer's Use Only

Preparer's signature: John A. Kramer | Date: 3-15-02 | Check if self-employed ☒ | Preparer's SSN or PTIN: 241 69 3967

Firm's name (or yours if self-employed), address, and ZIP code: Kramer and Associates, 2250 NW 24th Ave Gainesville FL | EIN 01 : 0000001 | Phone no. (352) 555-5555

Form 1120—Consolidated Taxable Income Computation

Line	Title	Consolidated	Adjustments and Eliminations	1 Alpha Mfg. Corp.	2 Beta Corp.	3 Charlie Corp.	4 Delta Corp.	5 Echo Corp.
1	Gross Receipts	$6,147,000	($109,000)[1]	$1,566,000	$2,680,000	$676,000		$1,249,000
	Returns/Allowances		85,000[2]					
2	Cost Goods/Operations	(2,301,000)		(783,000)	(1,390,000)	(128,000)		–0–
3	Gross Profit	$3,846,000	($24,000)	$ 783,000	$1,290,000	$548,000	$ –0–	$1,249,000
4	Dividends (Sch. C)	40,000	(170,000)[3]	210,000				
5	Interest	156,000[5]		46,000	89,000			21,000
6	Gross Rents	195,000					$195,000	
7	Gross Royalties							
8	Capital Gain Net Income (Sch. D)	67,939		67,939				
9	Net Gain or Loss from Form 4797	37,080	(14,600) 2,920[6]	52,760	(4,000)			
10	Other Income	10,000[4]		10,000				
11	Total Income	$4,352,019	($205,680)	$1,169,699	$1,375,000	$548,000	$195,000	$1,270,000
12	Compensation of Officers	$ 165,000		$ 165,000				
13	Salaries and Wages	1,356,000		138,000	$ 240,000	$377,000	$ 36,000	$ 565,000
14	Repairs	83,000		19,000	18,000	7,000	18,000	21,000
15	Bad Debts	48,500			36,500	4,000		8,000
16	Rents	179,000		93,000	39,000	11,000		36,000
17	Taxes	138,000[4]		36,000	27,000	10,000	16,000	49,000
18	Interest	58,000		27,000			29,000[5]	2,000
19	Contributions	15,000[4]		9,000	4,000			2,000
20	Depreciation	246,093		101,900	62,930	24,370	24,043	32,850
21a	Depreciation shown elsewhere on return	(77,400)		(77,400)				
21b	Depreciation	168,693		24,500	62,930	24,370	24,043	32,850
22	Depletion	–0–						
23	Advertising	269,140			223,140	27,000		19,000
24	Pension, Profit Sharing, etc. plans	140,000		39,000	21,000	35,000		45,000
25	Employee Benefit Programs	105,000		26,000	16,000	29,000		34,000
26	Other Deductions	1,284,000[4]		409,000	401,000	72,000	49,000	353,000
27	Total Deductions	$4,009,333	$ –0–	$ 985,500	$1,088,570	$596,370	$172,043	$1,166,850

Line	Title	Consolidated	Adjustments and Eliminations	1 Alpha Mfg. Corp.	2 Beta Corp.	3 Charlie Corp.	4 Delta Corp.	5 Echo Corp.
28	Taxable Income Before NOL Dedn. and Special Deductions	$342,686	($205,680)	$184,199	$286,430	($48,370)	$22,957	$103,150
29a	NOL Deduction							
29b	Special Deductions	(32,000)	(32,000)[3]					
30	Taxable Income	$310,686	($237,680)					

Explanatory Notes

[1] The deferred intercompany profit on the sale of inventory items (intercompany item) from Alpha to Beta during 2001 was $109,000. This amount is eliminated from revenue. The deferred intercompany profit amount is reported when Beta sells the inventory outside the affiliated group or some other corresponding item occurs.

[2] Restoration of $85,000 in deferred intercompany profits arising from the sale of inventory items from Alpha to Beta in 2001 and prior years. These goods were sold outside the affiliated group in 2001. The increased intercompany profit deferral for 2001 is $24,000 ($109,000 − $85,000). This amount is reflected in the reduced gross profit amount.

[3] Intragroup dividends of $100,000 and $70,000 paid by Beta and Echo, respectively, to Alpha are an adjustment to consolidated taxable income since they were included in Alpha's separate tax return. The remaining $40,000 of dividends are from unaffiliated domestic corporations that are more than 20%-owned and eligible for an 80% dividends-received deduction (see Line 29b). A $32,000 dividends-received deduction is claimed.

[4] The supporting schedule of component items is not reproduced here.

[5] Alpha Manufacturing loaned money to Delta Corporation. Delta accrued and paid $12,000 in interest during the year. These amounts have been reported in the separate expense and income items for the individual firms.

[6] Alpha sells a truck to Beta on June 27, 2001 for $25,000. The truck (a five-year MACRS property) cost $26,000 when purchased new on June 1, 1999. Alpha claimed depreciation of $13,520 [$26,000 × (0.2000 + 0.3200)] on the truck in 1999 and 2000. Alpha claims depreciation of $2,080 ($26,000 × 0.1920 × 5/12) in 2001. Alpha claims a total of $15,600 ($13,520 + $2,080) in depreciation prior to the sale. Alpha's deferred gain (intercompany item) on the sale is $14,600 [$25,000 − ($26,000 − $15,600)]. (See Line 9, Adjustments and Eliminations.) The truck is recorded as two separate MACRS properties on Beta's tax books. Beta depreciates the original $26,000 basis for the truck using the remainder of Alpha's five-year recovery period. Depreciation on this portion of the basis is $2,912 ($26,000 × 0.1920 × 7/12) in 2001. Beta also can depreciate the second MACRS property; that is, the step-up in basis that results from the intercompany sale. Beta elects to depreciate this portion of the basis as a five-year MACRS property and claims an additional $2,920 ($14,600 × 0.2000) of depreciation in 2001. The $2,920 is the portion of the deferred gain (Sec. 1245 income) Alpha reported in 2001.

Form **1120S** Department of the Treasury Internal Revenue Service

U.S. Income Tax Return for an S Corporation

▶ **Do not file this form unless the corporation has timely filed Form 2553 to elect to be an S corporation.**

▶ **See separate instructions.**

OMB No. 1545-0130

2001

For calendar year 2001, or tax year beginning , 2001, and ending , 20

A Effective date of election as an S corporation: 6-13-95	Name: Johns and Lawrence, Inc.	C Employer identification number: 76 3456789
	Number, street, and room or suite no. (If a P.O. box, see page 11 of the instructions.): 1234 University Avenue	D Date incorporated: 6-1-95
B Business code no. (see pages 29–31): 337000	City or town, state, and ZIP code: Gainesville, FL 32611	E Total assets (see page 11): $ 493,324

Use IRS label. Otherwise, print or type.

F Check applicable boxes: (1) ☐ Initial return (2) ☐ Final return (3) ☐ Name change (4) ☐ Address change (5) ☐ Amended return

G Enter number of shareholders in the corporation at end of the tax year . . . ▶ 2

Caution: *Include **only** trade or business income and expenses on lines 1a through 21. See page 11 of the instructions for more information.*

Income	1a	Gross receipts or sales 869,658 b Less returns and allowances 29,242 c Bal ▶	1c	840,416
	2	Cost of goods sold (Schedule A, line 8)	2	540,204
	3	Gross profit. Subtract line 2 from line 1c	3	300,212
	4	Net gain (loss) from Form 4797, Part II, line 18 *(attach Form 4797)*	4	
	5	Other income (loss) *(attach schedule)*	5	
	6	**Total income (loss).** Combine lines 3 through 5 ▶	6	300,212
Deductions (see page 12 of the instructions for limitations)	7	Compensation of officers	7	36,000
	8	Salaries and wages (less employment credits)	8	52,000
	9	Repairs and maintenance	9	4,800
	10	Bad debts	10	4,000
	11	Rents	11	36,000
	12	Taxes and licenses	12	16,000
	13	Interest	13	8,000
	14a	Depreciation *(if required, attach Form 4562)* — 14a: 27,476		
	b	Depreciation claimed on Schedule A and elsewhere on return — 14b: 15,000		
	c	Subtract line 14b from line 14a	14c	12,476
	15	Depletion **(Do not deduct oil and gas depletion.)**	15	
	16	Advertising	16	13,000
	17	Pension, profit-sharing, etc., plans	17	2,000
	18	Employee benefit programs	18	4,000
	19	Other deductions *(attach schedule)*	19	38,250
	20	**Total deductions.** Add the amounts shown in the far right column for lines 7 through 19 ▶	20	226,526
	21	Ordinary income (loss) from trade or business activities. Subtract line 20 from line 6	21	73,686
Tax and Payments	22	**Tax:** a Excess net passive income tax *(attach schedule)* — 22a		
	b	Tax from Schedule D (Form 1120S) — 22b		
	c	Add lines 22a and 22b (see page 16 of the instructions for additional taxes)	22c	NONE
	23	**Payments:** a 2001 estimated tax payments and amount applied from 2000 return — 23a		
	b	Tax deposited with Form 7004 — 23b		
	c	Credit for Federal tax paid on fuels *(attach Form 4136)* — 23c		
	d	Add lines 23a through 23c	23d	NONE
	24	Estimated tax penalty. Check if Form 2220 is attached ▶ ☐	24	
	25	**Tax due.** If the total of lines 22c and 24 is larger than line 23d, enter amount owed. See page 4 of the instructions for depository method of payment ▶	25	NONE
	26	**Overpayment.** If line 23d is larger than the total of lines 22c and 24, enter amount overpaid ▶	26	
	27	Enter amount of line 26 you want: **Credited to 2002 estimated tax** ▶ **Refunded** ▶	27	

Sign Here

Under penalties of perjury, I declare that I have examined this return, including accompanying schedules and statements, and to the best of my knowledge and belief, it is true, correct, and complete. Declaration of preparer (other than taxpayer) is based on all information of which preparer has any knowledge.

Signature of officer: Andrew Lawrence | Date: 3-15-02 | Title: Vice-President

May the IRS discuss this return with the preparer shown below (see instructions)? ☒ Yes ☐ No

Paid Preparer's Use Only

Preparer's signature	Michael Kramer	Date 3-14-02	Check if self-employed ☒ Preparer's SSN or PTIN 375-49-6339
Firm's name (or yours if self-employed), address, and ZIP code	Michael S. Kramer 1110 McMillan Gainesville, FL 32611	EIN 59 2029763	Phone no. (352) 555-2000

For Paperwork Reduction Act Notice, see the separate instructions. Cat. No. 11510H Form **1120S** (2001)

Form 1120S (2001) Page 2

Schedule A Cost of Goods Sold (see page 16 of the instructions)

1	Inventory at beginning of year	1	64,000
2	Purchases	2	340,800
3	Cost of labor	3	143,204
4	Additional section 263A costs *(attach schedule)*	4	7,000
5	Other costs *(attach schedule)*	5	90,000
6	**Total.** Add lines 1 through 5	6	645,004
7	Inventory at end of year	7	104,800
8	**Cost of goods sold.** Subtract line 7 from line 6. Enter here and on page 1, line 2	8	540,204

9a Check all methods used for valuing closing inventory:

(i) ☒ Cost as described in Regulations section 1.471-3

(ii) ☐ Lower of cost or market as described in Regulations section 1.471-4

(iii) ☐ Other (specify method used and attach explanation) ▶

b Check if there was a writedown of "subnormal" goods as described in Regulations section 1.471-2(c) ▶ ☐

c Check if the LIFO inventory method was adopted this tax year for any goods *(if checked, attach Form 970)* ▶ ☐

d If the LIFO inventory method was used for this tax year, enter percentage (or amounts) of closing inventory computed under LIFO | 9d |

e Do the rules of section 263A (for property produced or acquired for resale) apply to the corporation? ☒ Yes ☐ No

f Was there any change in determining quantities, cost, or valuations between opening and closing inventory? ☐ Yes ☒ No
If "Yes," attach explanation.

Schedule B Other Information

		Yes	No
1	Check method of accounting: **(a)** ☐ Cash **(b)** ☒ Accrual **(c)** ☐ Other (specify) ▶		
2	Refer to the list on pages 29 through 31 of the instructions and state the corporation's principal: **(a)** Business activity ▶ Manufacturing **(b)** Product or service ▶ Furniture		
3	Did the corporation at the end of the tax year own, directly or indirectly, 50% or more of the voting stock of a domestic corporation? (For rules of attribution, see section 267(c).) If "Yes," attach a schedule showing: **(a)** name, address, and employer identification number and **(b)** percentage owned		X
4	Was the corporation a member of a controlled group subject to the provisions of section 1561?		X
5	Check this box if the corporation has filed or is required to file **Form 8264,** Application for Registration of a Tax Shelter ▶ ☐		
6	Check this box if the corporation issued publicly offered debt instruments with original issue discount ▶ ☐ If so, the corporation may have to file **Form 8281,** Information Return for Publicly Offered Original Issue Discount Instruments.		
7	If the corporation: **(a)** filed its election to be an S corporation after 1986, **(b)** was a C corporation before it elected to be an S corporation **or** the corporation acquired an asset with a basis determined by reference to its basis (or the basis of any other property) in the hands of a C corporation, and **(c)** has net unrealized built-in gain (defined in section 1374(d)(1)) in excess of the net recognized built-in gain from prior years, enter the net unrealized built-in gain reduced by net recognized built-in gain from prior years (see page 17 of the instructions) ▶ $		
8	Check this box if the corporation had accumulated earnings and profits at the close of the tax year (see page 17 of the instructions) ▶ ☐		

Note: *If the corporation had assets or operated a business in a foreign country or U.S. possession, it may be required to attach **Schedule N (Form 1120),** Foreign Operations of U.S. Corporations, to this return. See Schedule N for details.*

Schedule K Shareholders' Shares of Income, Credits, Deductions, etc.

Income (Loss)

(a) Pro rata share items			**(b)** Total amount
1 Ordinary income (loss) from trade or business activities (page 1, line 21)		1	73,686
2 Net income (loss) from rental real estate activities *(attach Form 8825)*		2	
3a Gross income from other rental activities	3a		
b Expenses from other rental activities *(attach schedule)*	3b		
c Net income (loss) from other rental activities. Subtract line 3b from line 3a		3c	
4 Portfolio income (loss):			
a Interest income		4a	
b Ordinary dividends		4b	1,000
c Royalty income		4c	
d Net short-term capital gain (loss) *(attach Schedule D (Form 1120S))*		4d	(2,100)
e (1) Net long-term capital gain (loss) *(attach Schedule D (Form 1120S))*		4e(1)	4,500
(2) 28% rate gain (loss) ▶ (3) Qualified 5-year gain ▶			
f Other portfolio income (loss) *(attach schedule)*		4f	
5 Net section 1231 gain (loss) (other than due to casualty or theft) *(attach Form 4797)*		5	
6 Other income (loss) *(attach schedule)*		6	

Form **1120S** (2001)

Form 1120S (2001) Page **3**

Schedule K **Shareholders' Shares of Income, Credits, Deductions, etc.** *(continued)*

Section	(a) Pro rata share items		(b) Total amount
Deductions	7 Charitable contributions *(attach schedule)*	7	12,000
	8 Section 179 expense deduction *(attach Form 4562)*	8	
	9 Deductions related to portfolio income (loss) (itemize)	9	150
	10 Other deductions *(attach schedule)*	10	
Investment Interest	11a Interest expense on investment debts	11a	
	b (1) Investment income included on lines 4a, 4b, 4c, and 4f above	11b(1)	1,000
	(2) Investment expenses included on line 9 above	11b(2)	150
Credits	12a Credit for alcohol used as a fuel *(attach Form 6478)*	12a	
	b Low-income housing credit:		
	(1) From partnerships to which section 42(j)(5) applies	12b(1)	
	(2) Other than on line 12b(1)	12b(2)	
	c Qualified rehabilitation expenditures related to rental real estate activities *(attach Form 3468)*	12c	
	d Credits (other than credits shown on lines 12b and 12c) related to rental real estate activities	12d	
	e Credits related to other rental activities	12e	
	13 Other credits	13	
Adjustments and Tax Preference Items	14a Depreciation adjustment on property placed in service after 1986	14a	1,514
	b Adjusted gain or loss	14b	
	c Depletion (other than oil and gas)	14c	
	d (1) Gross income from oil, gas, or geothermal properties	14d(1)	
	(2) Deductions allocable to oil, gas, or geothermal properties	14d(2)	
	e Other adjustments and tax preference items *(attach schedule)*	14e	
Foreign Taxes	15a Name of foreign country or U.S. possession ▶		
	b Gross income from all sources	15b	
	c Gross income sourced at shareholder level	15c	
	d Foreign gross income sourced at corporate level:		
	(1) Passive	15d(1)	
	(2) Listed categories *(attach schedule)*	15d(2)	
	(3) General limitation	15d(3)	
	e Deductions allocated and apportioned at shareholder level:		
	(1) Interest expense	15e(1)	
	(2) Other	15e(2)	
	f Deductions allocated and apportioned at corporate level to foreign source income:		
	(1) Passive	15f(1)	
	(2) Listed categories *(attach schedule)*	15f(2)	
	(3) General limitation	15f(3)	
	g Total foreign taxes (check one): ▶ ☐ Paid ☐ Accrued	15g	
	h Reduction in taxes available for credit *(attach schedule)*	15h	
Other	16 Section 59(e)(2) expenditures: a Type ▶ b Amount ▶	16b	
	17 Tax-exempt interest income	17	18,000
	18 Other tax-exempt income	18	
	19 Nondeductible expenses	19	6,000 *
	20 Total property distributions (including cash) other than dividends reported on line 22 below	20	28,212
	21 Other items and amounts required to be reported separately to shareholders *(attach schedule)*		
	22 Total dividend distributions paid from accumulated earnings and profits	22	
	23 **Income (loss).** (Required only if Schedule M-1 must be completed.) Combine lines 1 through 6 in column (b). From the result, subtract the sum of lines 7 through 11a, 15g, and 16b	23	64,936

Form **1120S** (2001)

* $4,000 travel and entertainment expenses disallowed and $2,000 of interest expenses incurred to purchase tax-exempt bonds.

Form 1120S (2001) Page **4**

Schedule L **Balance Sheets per Books**

Assets	Beginning of tax year (a)	(b)	End of tax year (c)	(d)
1 Cash		60,000		86,600
2a Trade notes and accounts receivable	25,000		24,000	
b Less allowance for bad debts	1,000	24,000	1,000	23,000
3 Inventories		64,000		104,800
4 U.S. Government obligations				
5 Tax-exempt securities		200,000		200,000
6 Other current assets *(attach schedule)*		7,000		
7 Loans to shareholders				
8 Mortgage and real estate loans				
9 Other investments *(attach schedule)*				
10a Buildings and other depreciable assets	151,600		151,600	
b Less accumulated depreciation	45,200	106,400	72,676	78,924
11a Depletable assets				
b Less accumulated depletion				
12 Land (net of any amortization)				
13a Intangible assets (amortizable only)				
b Less accumulated amortization				
14 Other assets *(attach schedule)*				
15 Total assets		461,400		493,324
Liabilities and Shareholders' Equity				
16 Accounts payable		26,000		19,000
17 Mortgages, notes, bonds payable in less than 1 year		4,000		4,000
18 Other current liabilities *(attach schedule)*		3,600		3,600
19 Loans from shareholders				
20 Mortgages, notes, bonds payable in 1 year or more		130,000		119,724
21 Other liabilities *(attach schedule)*				
22 Capital stock		200,000		200,000
23 Additional paid-in capital				
24 Retained earnings		97,800		147,000
25 Adjustments to shareholders' equity *(attach schedule)*				
26 Less cost of treasury stock		( )		( )
27 Total liabilities and shareholders' equity		461,400		493,324

Schedule M-1 **Reconciliation of Income (Loss) per Books With Income (Loss) per Return** (You are not required to complete this schedule if the total assets on line 15, column (d), of Schedule L are less than $25,000.)

1 Net income (loss) per books	77,412	5 Income recorded on books this year not included on Schedule K, lines 1 through 6 (itemize): a Tax-exempt interest $ 18,000	18,000
2 Income included on Schedule K, lines 1 through 6, not recorded on books this year (itemize):			
3 Expenses recorded on books this year not included on Schedule K, lines 1 through 11a, 15g, and 16b (itemize): a Depreciation $ b Travel and entertainment $ 4000 Interest on loans for municipal bonds $2,000	6,000	6 Deductions included on Schedule K, lines 1 through 11a, 15g, and 16b, not charged against book income this year (itemize): a Depreciation $ 476	476
		7 Add lines 5 and 6	18,476
4 Add lines 1 through 3	83,412	8 Income (loss) (Schedule K, line 23). Line 4 less line 7	64,936

Schedule M-2 **Analysis of Accumulated Adjustments Account, Other Adjustments Account, and Shareholders' Undistributed Taxable Income Previously Taxed** (see page 27 of the instructions)

	(a) Accumulated adjustments account	(b) Other adjustments account	(c) Shareholders' undistributed taxable income previously taxed
1 Balance at beginning of tax year	86,100	11,700	
2 Ordinary income from page 1, line 21	73,686		
3 Other additions	5,500 *	18,000	
4 Loss from page 1, line 21	( )		
5 Other reductions	(18,250) **	2,000)	
6 Combine lines 1 through 5	147,036		
7 Distributions other than dividend distributions	28,212		
8 Balance at end of tax year. Subtract line 7 from line 6	118,824	27,700	

* $1,000 + $4,500 = $5,500

** $12,000 + $4,000 + $150 + $2,100 = $18,250

Form **1120S** (2001)

SCHEDULE K-1 (Form 1120S)

Department of the Treasury
Internal Revenue Service

Shareholder's Share of Income, Credits, Deductions, etc.

▶ See separate instructions.

For calendar year 2001 or tax year beginning , 2001, and ending , 20

OMB No. 1545-0130

2001

Shareholder's identifying number ▶ 297-63-2110

Shareholder's name, address, and ZIP code
Andrew Lawrence *
436 N.W. 24th Avenue
Gainesville, FL 32607

Corporation's identifying number ▶ 76 3456789

Corporation's name, address, and ZIP code
Johns and Lawrence, Inc.
1234 University Avenue
Gainesville, FL 32607

A Shareholder's percentage of stock ownership for tax year (see instructions for Schedule K-1) . . . ▶ 50 %
B Internal Revenue Service Center where corporation filed its return ▶ Atlanta, GA
C Tax shelter registration number (see instructions for Schedule K-1) . . . ▶ N/A
D Check applicable boxes: (1) ☐ Final K-1 (2) ☐ Amended K-1

	(a) Pro rata share items		(b) Amount	(c) Form 1040 filers enter the amount in column (b) on:
Income (Loss)	1 Ordinary income (loss) from trade or business activities	1	36,843	See page 4 of the Shareholder's Instructions for Schedule K-1 (Form 1120S).
	2 Net income (loss) from rental real estate activities	2		
	3 Net income (loss) from other rental activities	3		
	4 Portfolio income (loss):			
	a Interest	4a		Sch. B, Part I, line 1
	b Ordinary dividends	4b	500	Sch. B, Part II, line 5
	c Royalties	4c		Sch. E, Part I, line 4
	d Net short-term capital gain (loss)	4d	<1,050>	Sch. D, line 5, col. (f)
	e (1) Net long-term capital gain (loss)	4e(1)	2,250	Sch. D, line 12, col. (f)
	(2) 28% rate gain (loss)	4e(2)		Sch. D, line 12, col. (g)
	(3) Qualified 5-year gain	4e(3)		Line 4 of worksheet for Sch. D, line 29
	f Other portfolio income (loss) *(attach schedule)*	4f		(Enter on applicable line of your return.)
	5 Net section 1231 gain (loss) (other than due to casualty or theft)	5		See Shareholder's Instructions for Schedule K-1 (Form 1120S).
	6 Other income (loss) *(attach schedule)*	6		(Enter on applicable line of your return.)
Deductions	7 Charitable contributions *(attach schedule)*	7	6,000	Sch. A, line 15 or 16
	8 Section 179 expense deduction	8		See page 6 of the Shareholder's Instructions for Schedule K-1 (Form 1120S).
	9 Deductions related to portfolio income (loss) *(attach schedule)*	9	75	
	10 Other deductions *(attach schedule)*	10		
Investment Interest	11a Interest expense on investment debts	11a		Form 4952, line 1
	b (1) Investment income included on lines 4a, 4b, 4c, and 4f above	11b(1)	500	See Shareholder's Instructions for Schedule K-1 (Form 1120S).
	(2) Investment expenses included on line 9 above	11b(2)	75	
Credits	12a Credit for alcohol used as fuel	12a		Form 6478, line 10
	b Low-income housing credit:			
	(1) From section 42(j)(5) partnerships	12b(1)		Form 8586, line 5
	(2) Other than on line 12b(1)	12b(2)		
	c Qualified rehabilitation expenditures related to rental real estate activities	12c		See pages 6 and 7 of the Shareholder's Instructions for Schedule K-1 (Form 1120S).
	d Credits (other than credits shown on lines 12b and 12c) related to rental real estate activities	12d		
	e Credits related to other rental activities	12e		
	13 Other credits	13		

For Paperwork Reduction Act Notice, see the Instructions for Form 1120S. Cat. No. 11520D **Schedule K-1 (Form 1120S) 2001**

* A second schedule K-1 for Stephen Johns is similar to this one but is not reproduced here.

Schedule K-1 (Form 1120S) 2001 — Page **2**

	(a) Pro rata share items		(b) Amount	(c) Form 1040 filers enter the amount in column (b) on:
Adjustments and Tax Preference Items	14a Depreciation adjustment on property placed in service after 1986	14a	757	See page 7 of the Shareholder's Instructions for Schedule K-1 (Form 1120S) and Instructions for Form 6251
	b Adjusted gain or loss	14b		
	c Depletion (other than oil and gas)	14c		
	d (1) Gross income from oil, gas, or geothermal properties	14d(1)		
	(2) Deductions allocable to oil, gas, or geothermal properties	14d(2)		
	e Other adjustments and tax preference items *(attach schedule)*	14e		
Foreign Taxes	15a Name of foreign country or U.S. possession ▶			Form 1116, Part I
	b Gross income from all sources	15b		
	c Gross income sourced at shareholder level	15c		
	d Foreign gross income sourced at corporate level:			
	(1) Passive	15d(1)		
	(2) Listed categories *(attach schedule)*	15d(2)		
	(3) General limitation	15d(3)		
	e Deductions allocated and apportioned at shareholder level:			
	(1) Interest expense	15e(1)		
	(2) Other	15e(2)		
	f Deductions allocated and apportioned at corporate level to foreign source income:			
	(1) Passive	15f(1)		
	(2) Listed categories *(attach schedule)*	15f(2)		
	(3) General limitation	15f(3)		
	g Total foreign taxes (check one): ▶ ☐ Paid ☐ Accrued	15g		Form 1116, Part II
	h Reduction in taxes available for credit *(attach schedule)*	15h		See Instructions for Form 1116
Other	16 Section 59(e)(2) expenditures: a Type ▶			See Shareholder's Instructions for Schedule K-1 (Form 1120S).
	b Amount	16b		
	17 Tax-exempt interest income	17	9,000	Form 1040, line 8b
	18 Other tax-exempt income	18	3,000 *	See page 7 of the Shareholder's Instructions for Schedule K-1 (Form 1120S).
	19 Nondeductible expenses	19		
	20 Property distributions (including cash) other than dividend distributions reported to you on Form 1099-DIV	20		
	21 Amount of loan repayments for "Loans From Shareholders"	21	14,106	
	22 Recapture of low-income housing credit:			
	a From section 42(j)(5) partnerships	22a		Form 8611, line 8
	b Other than on line 22a	22b		

Supplemental Information

23 Supplemental information required to be reported separately to each shareholder *(attach additional schedules if more space is needed)*:

* $1,000 of interest expense incurred to purchase tax-exempt bonds and $2,000 of meals and entertainment expenses disallowed by Sec. 274

FACTS FOR S CORPORATION (FORM 1120S)

The same basic facts presented for the Andrew Lawrence proprietorship are used for the S corporation except for the following:

1. Johns and Lawrence, Inc. made an S corporation election on June 13, 1995. The election was effective for its initial tax year.

2. The book income for Johns and Lawrence is presented in the attached worksheet, which reconciles book income and S corporation taxable income.

3. The $18,000 salaries paid to each employee are subject to the same employment tax requirements as when paid by the C corporation. The total employment taxes ($14,480) are the same as for the C corporation.

4. The S corporation paid no estimated federal income taxes.

5. The $28,212 distribution was paid equally to the two shareholders. It is not included in the shareholder's gross income but instead reduces the basis for their stock.

6. Other deductions include:

Travel	$4,000
Meals and entertainment	8,000
Minus: 50% disallowance	(4,000)
Office expenses	16,000
Transportation	10,400
General and administrative	3,000
Miscellaneous*	850
Total	$38,250

*$150 of the miscellaneous expenses are related to the production of the dividend income and are separately stated.

7. Reconciliation of net income for the C corporation and the S corporation occurs as follows:

Net income for C corporation	$63,412
Plus: Federal income taxes	14,000
Net income for S corporation	$77,412

The S corporation return can be tied back to the partnership return. The only difference between the two returns is that the S corporation pays an additional $6,160 in employment taxes with respect to the shareholder-employee salaries, as compared to the partnership's guaranteed payments. This dollar difference is reflected in the net income numbers, the ordinary income numbers, capital account balances, and total asset amounts.

8. The balance sheet for Johns and Lawrence is presented on page 4 of Form 1120S.

Johns and Lawrence, Inc. (S Corporation) Reconciliation of Book and Taxable Income For Year Ending December 31, 2001

	Book Income		Adjustments		Taxable Income		Form 1120S Schedule K	
Account Name	Debit	Credit	Debit	Credit	Debit	Credit	Ordinary Income	Separately Stated Items
Sales		869,658				869,658	869,658	
Sales returns & allowances	29,242				29,242		(29,242)	
Cost of sales	540,204				540,204		(540,204)	
Dividends		1,000				1,000		1,000
Tax-exempt interest		18,000	18,000			0		18,000
Gain on stock sale		4,500				4,500		4,500
Worthless stock loss	2,100				2,100			(2,100)
Officers salaries[a]	36,000				36,000		(36,000)	
Other salaries	52,000				52,000		(52,000)	
Rentals	36,000				36,000		(36,000)	
Bad debts	4,000				4,000		(4,000)	
Interest:								
Working capital loans	8,000				8,000		(8,000)	
Purchase tax-exempt bonds	2,000			2,000	0			(2,000)
Employment taxes	14,480				14,480		(14,480)	
Taxes	1,520				1,520		(1,520)	
Repairs	4,800				4,800		(4,800)	
Depreciation[b]	12,000		476		12,476		(12,476)	
Charitable contributions	12,000				12,000			(12,000)
Travel	4,000				4,000		(4,000)	
Meals and entertainment[c]	8,000			4,000	4,000		(4,000)	
Meals and ent. nondeductible								(4,000)
Office expenses	16,000				16,000		(16,000)	
Advertising	13,000				13,000		(13,000)	
Transportation expense	10,400				10,400		(10,400)	
General and administrative	3,000				3,000		(3,000)	
Pension plans[d]	2,000				2,000		(2,000)	
Employee benefit programs[e]	4,000				4,000		(4,000)	
Miscellaneous	1,000				1,000		(850)	(150)
Net profit/Taxable income	77,412			12,476	64,936			
Total	893,158	893,158	18,476	18,476	875,158	875,158	73,686	

[a] Salaries for the S corporation's shareholder-employees are deductible by the S corporation and are subject to the same employee taxes imposed on nonshareholder-employees.

[b] MACRS is depreciation is $12,476 − $12,000 = $476

[c] 50% of the meals and entertainment expense is not deductible for tax purposes but must be separately stated on the Schedules K and K-1.

[d] The pension plan expense is the same for book and tax purposes for this corporation. No pension expenses relate to pensions for the shareholder-employees.

[e] The employee benefit expense is the same for book and tax purposes for this corporation. None relates to shareholder-employee benefits.

Form **2210**

Department of the Treasury
Internal Revenue Service

Underpayment of Estimated Tax by Individuals, Estates, and Trusts

▶ See separate instructions.
▶ Attach to Form 1040, 1040A, 1040NR, 1040NR-EZ, or 1041.

OMB No. 1545-0140
2001
Attachment Sequence No. **06**

Name(s) shown on tax return	Identifying number

In most cases, you do not need to file Form 2210. The IRS will figure any penalty you owe and send you a bill. File Form 2210 only if one or more boxes in Part I apply to you. If you do not need to file Form 2210, you still may use it to figure your penalty. Enter the amount from Part III, line 21, or Part IV, line 37, on the penalty line of your return, but do not attach Form 2210.

Part I Reasons for Filing

Reasons for Filing—If 1a, 1b, or 1c below applies to you, you may be able to lower or eliminate your penalty. But you **must** check the boxes that apply and file Form 2210 with your tax return. If 1d below applies to you, check that box and file Form 2210 with your tax return.

1 Check whichever boxes apply (if none apply, see the text above Part I and **do not file Form 2210**):

a ☐ You request a **waiver.** In certain circumstances, the IRS will waive all or part of the penalty. See **Waiver of Penalty** on page 2 of the instructions.

b ☐ You use the **annualized income installment method.** If your income varied during the year, this method may reduce the amount of one or more required installments. See page 5 of the instructions.

c ☐ You had Federal income tax withheld from wages and, for estimated tax purposes, you treat the withheld tax as paid on the dates it was actually withheld, instead of in equal amounts on the payment due dates. See the instructions for line 23 on page 3.

d ☐ Your required annual payment (line 14 below) is based on your 2000 tax and you filed or are filing a joint return for either 2000 or 2001 but not for both years.

Part II Required Annual Payment

2	Enter your 2001 tax after credits (see page 2 of the instructions)		2
3	Other taxes (see page 2 of the instructions)		3
4	Add lines 2 and 3		4
5	Earned income credit	5	
6	Additional child tax credit	6	
7	Credit for Federal tax paid on fuels	7	
8	Add lines 5, 6, and 7		8
9	Current year tax. Subtract line 8 from line 4		9
10	Multiply line 9 by 90% (.90)	10	
11	Withholding taxes. **Do not** include any estimated tax payments on this line (see page 3 of the instructions)		11
12	Subtract line 11 from line 9. If less than $1,000, stop here; you do not owe the penalty. **Do not file Form 2210**		12
13	Enter the tax shown on your 2000 tax return (110% of that amount if the adjusted gross income shown on that return is more than $150,000, or, if married filing separately for 2001, more than $75,000). **Caution:** *See page 3 of the instructions*		13
14	**Required annual payment.** Enter the **smaller** of line 10 or line 13 **If line 11 is equal to or more than line 14, stop here; you do not owe the penalty. Do not file Form 2210 unless you checked box 1d above.**		14

Part III Short Method

Short Method (Caution: *See page 3 of the instructions to find out if you can use the short method. If you checked box* ***1b*** *or* ***1c*** *in Part I, skip this part and go to Part IV.***)**

15	Enter the amount, if any, from line 11 above	15	
16	Enter the total amount, if any, of estimated tax payments you made	16	
17	Add lines 15 and 16		17
18	**Total underpayment for year.** Subtract line 17 from line 14. If zero or less, stop here; you do not owe the penalty. **Do not file Form 2210 unless you checked box 1d above**		18
19	Multiply line 18 by .04397 (see page 3 of the instructions if you are eligible for relief due to the September 11, 2001, terrorist attacks)		19
20	• If the amount on line 18 was paid **on or after** 4/15/02, enter -0-. • If the amount on line 18 was paid **before** 4/15/02, make the following computation to find the amount to enter on line 20. Amount on line 18 × Number of days paid before 4/15/02 × .00016		20
21	**Penalty.** Subtract line 20 from line 19. Enter the result here and on Form 1040, line 71; Form 1040A, line 46; Form 1040NR, line 69; Form 1040NR-EZ, line 26; or Form 1041, line 26, **but do not file Form 2210 unless you checked one or more of the boxes in Part I above** ▶		21

Form 2210 (2001) Page 2

Part IV **Regular Method** (See page 3 of the instructions if you are filing Form 1040NR or 1040NR-EZ.)

Section A—Figure Your Underpayment		Payment Due Dates (a) 4/15/01	(b) 6/15/01	(c) 9/24/01	(d) 1/15/02
22 **Required installments.** If box 1b applies, enter the amounts from Schedule AI, line 25. Otherwise, enter 25% (.25) of line 14, Form 2210, in each column	22				
23 Estimated tax paid and tax withheld (see page 3 of the instructions). For column (a) only, also enter the amount from line 23 on line 27. If line 23 is equal to or more than line 22 for all payment periods, stop here; you do not owe the penalty. **Do not file Form 2210 unless you checked a box in Part I**	23				
Complete lines 24 through 30 of one column before going to the next column.					
24 Enter amount, if any, from line 30 of previous column	24				
25 Add lines 23 and 24	25				
26 Add amounts on lines 28 and 29 of the previous column	26				
27 Subtract line 26 from line 25. If zero or less, enter -0-. For column (a) only, enter the amount from line 23	27				
28 If the amount on line 27 is zero, subtract line 25 from line 26. Otherwise, enter -0-	28				
29 **Underpayment.** If line 22 is equal to or more than line 27, subtract line 27 from line 22. Then go to line 24 of next column. Otherwise, go to line 30 ▶	29				
30 Overpayment. If line 27 is more than line 22, subtract line 22 from line 27. Then go to line 24 of next column	30				

Section B—Figure the Penalty (Complete lines 31 through 36 of one column before going to the next column.)

			(a)	(b)	(c)	(d)
Rate Period 1	**April 16, 2001—June 30, 2001**		4/15/01	6/15/01		
	31 Number of days **from** the date shown above line 31 **to** the date the amount on line 29 was paid **or** 6/30/01, whichever is earlier	31	Days:	Days:		
	32 Underpayment on line 29 (see page 4 of the instructions) × Number of days on line 31 / 365 × .08 ▶	32	$	$		
Rate Period 2	**July 1, 2001—December 31, 2001**		6/30/01	6/30/01	9/24/01	
	33 Number of days **from** the date shown above line 33 **to** the date the amount on line 29 was paid **or** 12/31/01, whichever is earlier	33	Days:	Days:	Days:	
	34 Underpayment on line 29 (see page 5 of the instructions) × Number of days on line 33 / 365 × .07 ▶	34	$	$	$	
Rate Period 3	**January 1, 2002—April 15, 2002**		12/31/01	12/31/01	12/31/01	1/15/02
	35 Number of days **from** the date shown above line 35 **to** the date the amount on line 29 was paid **or** 4/15/02, whichever is earlier	35	Days:	Days:	Days:	Days:
	36 Underpayment on line 29 (see page 5 of the instructions) × Number of days on line 35 / 365 × .06 ▶	36	$	$	$	$

37 **Penalty.** Add all amounts on lines 32, 34, and 36 in all columns. Enter the total here and on Form 1040, line 71; Form 1040A, line 46; Form 1040NR, line 69; Form 1040NR-EZ, line 26; or Form 1041, line 26, **but do not file Form 2210 unless you checked one or more of the boxes in Part I** ▶ 37 $

Schedule AI—Annualized Income Installment Method (See pages 5 and 6 of the instructions.)

Estates and trusts, **do not** use the period ending dates shown to the right. Instead, use the following: 2/28/01, 4/30/01, 7/31/01, and 11/30/01.

Part I Annualized Income Installments

			(a) 1/1/01–3/31/01	(b) 1/1/01–5/31/01	(c) 1/1/01–8/31/01	(d) 1/1/01–12/31/01
1	Enter your adjusted gross income for each period (see instructions). (Estates and trusts, enter your taxable income without your exemption for each period.)	1				
2	Annualization amounts. (Estates and trusts, see instructions.)	2	4	2.4	1.5	1
3	Annualized income. Multiply line 1 by line 2	3				
4	Enter your itemized deductions for the period shown in each column. If you do not itemize, enter -0- and skip to line 7. (Estates and trusts, enter -0-, skip to line 9, and enter the amount from line 3 on line 9.)	4				
5	Annualization amounts	5	4	2.4	1.5	1
6	Multiply line 4 by line 5 (see instructions if line 3 is more than $66,475)	6				
7	In each column, enter the full amount of your standard deduction from Form 1040, line 36, or Form 1040A, line 22 (Form 1040NR or 1040NR-EZ filers, enter -0-. **Exception:** Indian students and business apprentices, enter standard deduction from Form 1040NR, line 35 or Form 1040NR-EZ, line 11.)	7				
8	Enter the **larger** of line 6 or line 7	8				
9	Subtract line 8 from line 3	9				
10	In each column, multiply $2,900 by the total number of exemptions claimed (see instructions if line 3 is more than $99,725). (Estates and trusts and Form 1040NR or 1040NR-EZ filers, enter the exemption amount shown on your tax return.)	10				
11	Subtract line 10 from line 9	11				
12	Figure your tax on the amount on line 11 (see instructions)	12				
13	Form 1040 filers only, complete Part II and enter your self-employment tax from line 34 below	13				
14	Enter other taxes for each payment period (see instructions)	14				
15	Total tax. Add lines 12, 13, and 14	15				
16	For each period, enter the same type of credits as allowed on Form 2210, lines 2, 5, 6, and 7 (see instructions)	16				
17	Subtract line 16 from line 15. If zero or less, enter -0-	17				
18	Applicable percentage	18	22.5%	45%	67.5%	90%
19	Multiply line 17 by line 18	19				
	Caution: *Complete lines 20–25 of one column before going to the next column.*					
20	Add the amounts in all previous columns of line 25	20				
21	Subtract line 20 from line 19. If zero or less, enter -0-	21				
22	Enter 25% (.25) of line 14 on page 1 of Form 2210 in each column	22				
23	Subtract line 25 of the previous column from line 24 of the previous column	23				
24	Add lines 22 and 23 and enter the total	24				
25	Enter the **smaller** of line 21 or line 24 here and on Form 2210, line 22 ▶	25				

Part II Annualized Self-Employment Tax

			(a)	(b)	(c)	(d)
26	Net earnings from self-employment for the period (see instructions)	26				
27	Prorated social security tax limit	27	$20,100	$33,500	$53,600	$80,400
28	Enter actual wages for the period subject to social security tax or the 6.2% portion of the 7.65% railroad retirement (tier 1) tax	28				
29	Subtract line 28 from line 27. If zero or less, enter -0-	29				
30	Annualization amounts	30	0.496	0.2976	0.186	0.124
31	Multiply line 30 by the **smaller** of line 26 or line 29	31				
32	Annualization amounts	32	0.116	0.0696	0.0435	0.029
33	Multiply line 26 by line 32	33				
34	Add lines 31 and 33. Enter the result here and on line 13 above ▶	34				

Form **2220** Department of the Treasury Internal Revenue Service

Underpayment of Estimated Tax by Corporations

▶ See separate instructions.

▶ Attach to the corporation's tax return.

OMB No. 1545-0142

2001

Name: Globe Corporation

Employer identification number: 38 1505087

Note: *In most cases, the corporation* ***does not*** *need to file Form 2220. (See Part I below for exceptions.) The IRS will figure any penalty owed and bill the corporation. If the corporation does not need to file Form 2220, it may still use it to figure the penalty. Enter the amount from line 36 on the estimated tax penalty line of the corporation's income tax return, but* ***do not*** *attach Form 2220.*

Part I Reasons for Filing—Check the boxes below that apply to the corporation. If any boxes are checked, the corporation must file Form 2220, even if it does not owe the penalty. If the box on line 1 or line 2 applies, the corporation may be able to lower or eliminate the penalty.

1 ☐ The corporation is using the annualized income installment method.

2 ☐ The corporation is using the adjusted seasonal installment method.

3 ☐ The corporation is a "large corporation" figuring its first required installment based on the prior year's tax.

Note: *The corporation also must file Form 2220 if it has a suspended research credit allowed for the current year (see the instructions for line 4) or it is an indirectly affected taxpayer (see instructions).*

Part II Figuring the Underpayment

4	Total tax (see instructions)	4	100,000
5a	Personal holding company tax (Schedule PH (Form 1120), line 26) included on line 4	5a	
b	Look-back interest included on line 4 under section 460(b)(2) for completed long-term contracts or section 167(g) for depreciation under the income forecast method	5b	
c	Credit for Federal tax paid on fuels (see instructions)	5c	
d	**Total.** Add lines 5a through 5c	5d	-0-
6	Subtract line 5d from line 4. If the result is less than $500, **do not** complete or file this form. The corporation does not owe the penalty	6	100,000
7	Enter the tax shown on the corporation's 2000 income tax return. **Caution:** *See instructions before completing this line*	7	125,000
8	Enter the **smaller** of line 6 or line 7. If the corporation must skip line 7, enter the amount from line 6	8	100,000

Line	Description		(a)	(b)	(c)	(d)
9	**Installment due dates.** Enter in columns (a) through (d) the 15th day of the 4th (***Form 990-PF filers:*** Use 5th month), 6th, 9th, and 12th months of the corporation's tax year. **Exception:** Enter October 1, 2001, instead of September 15, 2001 ▶	9	4-16-01	6-15-01	9-17-01	12-17-01
10	**Required installments.** If the box on line 1 and/or line 2 above is checked, enter the amounts from Schedule A, line 40. If the box on line 3 (but not 1 or 2) is checked, see instructions for the amounts to enter. If none of these boxes are checked, enter 25% of line 8 above in each column	10	25,000	25,000	25,000	25,000
11	Estimated tax paid or credited for each period (see instructions). For column (a) only, enter the amount from line 11 on line 15	11	16,000	16,000	16,000	16,000
	Complete lines 12 through 18 of one column before going to the next column.					
12	Enter amount, if any, from line 18 of the preceding column	12		-0-	-0-	-0-
13	Add lines 11 and 12	13		16,000	16,000	16,000
14	Add amounts on lines 16 and 17 of the preceding column	14		9,000	18,000	27,000
15	Subtract line 14 from line 13. If zero or less, enter -0-	15	16,000	7,000	-0-	-0-
16	If the amount on line 15 is zero, subtract line 13 from line 14. Otherwise, enter -0-	16		-0-	2,000	
17	**Underpayment.** If line 15 is less than or equal to line 10, subtract line 15 from line 10. Then go to line 12 of the next column. Otherwise, go to line 18	17	9,000	18,000	27,000	36,000
18	**Overpayment.** If line 10 is less than line 15, subtract line 10 from line 15. Then go to line 12 of the next column	18				

Complete Part III on page 2 to figure the penalty. If there are no entries on line 17, no penalty is owed.

For Paperwork Reduction Act Notice, see separate instructions. Cat. No. 11746L Form **2220** (2001)

Form 2220 (2001) Page **2**

Part III Figuring the Penalty

		(a)	(b)	(c)	(d)
19 Enter the date of payment or the 15th day of the 3rd month after the close of the tax year, whichever is earlier (see instructions). ***(Form 990-PF and Form 990-T filers:*** Use 5th month instead of 3rd month.)	19	6-15-01	9-17-01	12-17-01	3-15-02
20 Number of days from due date of installment on line 9 to the date shown on line 19	20	60	94	91	88
21 Number of days on line 20 after 4/15/2001 and before 7/1/2001	21	60	15	0	0
22 Underpayment on line 17 × (Number of days on line 21 / 365) × 8%	22	$ 118	$ 59	$ 0	$ 0
23 Number of days on line 20 after 6/30/2001 and before 1/1/2002	23		79	91	14
24 Underpayment on line 17 × (Number of days on line 23 / 365) × 7%	24	$	$ 273	$ 471	$ 97
25 Number of days on line 20 after 12/31/2001 and before 4/1/2002	25				74
26 Underpayment on line 17 × (Number of days on line 25 / 365) × 6%	26	$	$	$	$ 438
27 Number of days on line 20 after 3/31/2002 and before 7/1/2002	27				
28 Underpayment on line 17 × (Number of days on line 27 / 365) × *%	28	$	$	$	$
29 Number of days on line 20 after 6/30/2002 and before 10/1/2002	29				
30 Underpayment on line 17 × (Number of days on line 29 / 365) × *%	30	$	$	$	$
31 Number of days on line 20 after 9/30/2002 and before 1/1/2003	31				
32 Underpayment on line 17 × (Number of days on line 31 / 365) × *%	32	$	$	$	$
33 Number of days on line 20 after 12/31/2002 and before 2/16/2003	33				
34 Underpayment on line 17 × (Number of days on line 33 / 365) × *%	34	$	$	$	$
35 Add lines 22, 24, 26, 28, 30, 32, and 34	35	$ 118	$ 332	$ 471	$ 535

36 Penalty. Add columns (a) through (d), of line 35. Enter the total here and on Form 1120, line 33; Form 1120-A, line 29; or the comparable line for other income tax returns . . . **36** $ 1,456

***For underpayments paid after March 31, 2002:** For lines 28, 30, 32, and 34, use the penalty interest rate for each calendar quarter, which the IRS will determine during the first month in the preceding quarter. These rates are published quarterly in an IRS News Release and in a revenue ruling in the Internal Revenue Bulletin. To obtain this information on the Internet, access the IRS Web Site at **www.irs.gov**. You can also call 1-800-829-1040 to get interest rate information.

Form **2220** (2001)

Form **4626**

Department of the Treasury
Internal Revenue Service

Alternative Minimum Tax— Corporations

▶ **See separate instructions.**
▶ **Attach to the corporation's tax return.**

OMB No. 1545-0175

2001

Name: Glidden Corporation

Employer identification number: 38:1505786

1	Taxable income or (loss) before net operating loss deduction			1	128,278
2	**Adjustments and preferences:**				
a	Depreciation of post-1986 property	2a	7,500		
b	Amortization of certified pollution control facilities	2b			
c	Amortization of mining exploration and development costs	2c			
d	Amortization of circulation expenditures (personal holding companies only)	2d			
e	Adjusted gain or loss	2e	<6,918>		
f	Long-term contracts	2f			
g	Installment sales	2g			
h	Merchant marine capital construction funds	2h			
i	Section 833(b) deduction (Blue Cross, Blue Shield, and similar type organizations only)	2i			
j	Tax shelter farm activities (personal service corporations only)	2j			
k	Passive activities (closely held corporations and personal service corporations only)	2k			
l	Loss limitations	2l			
m	Depletion	2m			
n	Tax-exempt interest income from specified private activity bonds	2n			
o	Intangible drilling costs	2o			
p	Accelerated depreciation of real property (pre-1987)	2p			
q	Accelerated depreciation of leased personal property (pre-1987) (personal holding companies only)	2q			
r	Other adjustments	2r			
s	Combine lines 2a through 2r			2s	582
3	Preadjustment alternative minimum taxable income (AMTI). Combine lines 1 and 2s			3	128,860
4	**Adjusted current earnings (ACE) adjustment:**				
a	Enter the corporation's ACE from line 10 of the worksheet on page 11 of the instructions	4a	312,360		
b	Subtract line 3 from line 4a. If line 3 exceeds line 4a, enter the difference as a negative amount. See examples on page 6 of the instructions	4b	183,500		
c	Multiply line 4b by 75% (.75). Enter the result as a positive amount	4c	137,625		
d	Enter the excess, if any, of the corporation's total increases in AMTI from prior year ACE adjustments over its total reductions in AMTI from prior year ACE adjustments (see page 6 of the instructions). **Note:** *You **must** enter an amount on line 4d (even if line 4b is positive).*	4d	311,276		
e	ACE adjustment: • If you entered a positive number or zero on line 4b, enter the amount from line 4c here as a positive amount. • If you entered a negative number on line 4b, enter the smaller of line 4c or line 4d here as a negative amount.			4e	137,625
5	Combine lines 3 and 4e. If zero or less, stop here; the corporation does not owe alternative minimum tax			5	266,485
6	Alternative tax net operating loss deduction (see page 7 of the instructions)			6	-0-
7	**Alternative minimum taxable income.** Subtract line 6 from line 5. If the corporation held a residual interest in a REMIC, see page 7 of the instructions.			7	266,485

For Paperwork Reduction Act Notice, see page 10 of separate instructions. Cat. No. 12955I Form **4626** (2001)

Form 4626 (2001) Page **2**

8	Enter the amount from line 7 (alternative minimum taxable income)	8	266,485
9	**Exemption phase-out computation** (if line 8 is $310,000 or more, skip lines 9a and 9b and enter -0- on line 9c):		
a	Subtract $150,000 from line 8 (if completing this line for a member of a controlled group, see page 7 of the instructions). If zero or less, enter -0-. — **9a** 116,485		
b	Multiply line 9a by 25% (.25) — **9b** 29,121		
c	Exemption. Subtract line 9b from $40,000 (if you are completing this line for a member of a controlled group, see page 7 of the instructions). If zero or less, enter -0-.	9c	10,879
10	Subtract line 9c from line 8. If zero or less, enter -0-	10	255,606
11	Multiply line 10 by 20% (.20)	11	51,121
12	Alternative minimum tax foreign tax credit (see page 7 of the instructions)	12	
13	Tentative minimum tax. Subtract line 12 from line 11	13	51,121
14	Regular tax liability before all credits except the foreign tax credit and possessions tax credit	14	33,278
15	**Alternative minimum tax.** Subtract line 14 from line 13. If zero or less, enter -0-. Enter here and on Form 1120, Schedule J, line 4, or the appropriate line of the corporation's income tax return	15	17,843

Form **4626** (2001)

Adjusted Current Earnings Worksheet

▶ See ACE Worksheet Instructions (which begin on page 8).

1	Pre-adjustment AMTI. Enter the amount from line 3 of Form 4626				1	128,860
2	ACE depreciation adjustment:					
a	AMT depreciation		2a	32,500		
b	ACE depreciation:					
	(1) Post-1993 property	2b(1) 32,500				
	(2) Post-1989, pre-1994 property	2b(2)				
	(3) Pre-1990 MACRS property	2b(3)				
	(4) Pre-1990 original ACRS property	2b(4)				
	(5) Property described in sections 168(f)(1) through (4)	2b(5)				
	(6) Other property	2b(6)				
	(7) Total ACE depreciation. Add lines 2b(1) through 2b(6)		2b(7)	32,500		
c	ACE depreciation adjustment. Subtract line 2b(7) from line 2a				2c	-0-
3	Inclusion in ACE of items included in earnings and profits (E&P):					
a	Tax-exempt interest income		3a	15,000		
b	Death benefits from life insurance contracts		3b	100,000		
c	All other distributions from life insurance contracts (including surrenders)		3c			
d	Inside buildup of undistributed income in life insurance contracts		3d			
e	Other items (see Regulations sections 1.56(g)-1(c)(6)(iii) through (ix) for a partial list)		3e			
f	Total increase to ACE from inclusion in ACE of items included in E&P. Add lines 3a through 3e				3f	115,000
4	Disallowance of items not deductible from E&P:					
a	Certain dividends received		4a	14,000		
b	Dividends paid on certain preferred stock of public utilities that are deductible under section 247		4b			
c	Dividends paid to an ESOP that are deductible under section 404(k)		4c			
d	Nonpatronage dividends that are paid and deductible under section 1382(c)		4d			
e	Other items (see Regulations sections 1.56(g)-1(d)(3)(i) and (ii) for a partial list)		4e			
f	Total increase to ACE because of disallowance of items not deductible from E&P. Add lines 4a through 4e				4f	14,000
5	Other adjustments based on rules for figuring E&P:					
a	Intangible drilling costs		5a			
b	Circulation expenditures		5b			
c	Organizational expenditures		5c	2,500		
d	LIFO inventory adjustments		5d			
e	Installment sales		5e	52,000		
f	Total other E&P adjustments. Combine lines 5a through 5e				5f	54,500
6	Disallowance of loss on exchange of debt pools				6	
7	Acquisition expenses of life insurance companies for qualified foreign contracts				7	
8	Depletion				8	
9	Basis adjustments in determining gain or loss from sale or exchange of pre-1994 property				9	
10	**Adjusted current earnings.** Combine lines 1, 2c, 3f, 4f, and 5f through 9. Enter the result here and on line 4a of Form 4626				10	312,360

Form **6251**

Department of the Treasury Internal Revenue Service (99)

Alternative Minimum Tax—Individuals

▶ **See separate instructions.**

▶ **Attach to Form 1040 or Form 1040NR.**

OMB No. 1545-0227

2001

Attachment Sequence No. **32**

Name(s) shown on Form 1040 | **Your social security number**

Part I Alternative Minimum Taxable Income

1	If you itemized deductions on Schedule A (Form 1040), go to line 2. Otherwise, enter your standard deduction from Form 1040, line 36, here and go to line 6	1	
2	Medical and dental. Enter the **smaller** of Schedule A (Form 1040), line 4 **or** 2½% of Form 1040, line 34	2	
3	Taxes. Enter the amount from Schedule A (Form 1040), line 9	3	
4	Certain interest on a home mortgage **not** used to buy, build, or improve your home	4	
5	Miscellaneous itemized deductions. Enter the amount from Schedule A (Form 1040), line 26	5	
6	Refund of taxes. Enter any tax refund from Form 1040, line 10 or line 21	6	( )
7	Investment interest. Enter difference between regular tax and AMT deduction	7	
8	Post-1986 depreciation. Enter difference between regular tax and AMT depreciation	8	
9	Adjusted gain or loss. Enter difference between AMT and regular tax gain or loss	9	
10	Incentive stock options. Enter excess of AMT income over regular tax income	10	
11	Passive activities. Enter difference between AMT and regular tax income or loss	11	
12	Beneficiaries of estates and trusts. Enter the amount from Schedule K-1 (Form 1041), line 9	12	
13	Tax-exempt interest income from private activity bonds issued after August 7, 1986	13	

14 Other. Enter the amount, if any, for each item below and enter the total on line 14.

a Circulation expenditures		**i** Mining costs	
b Depletion		**j** Patron's adjustment	
c Depreciation (pre-1987)		**k** Pollution control facilities	
d Installment sales		**l** Research and experimental	
e Intangible drilling costs		**m** Section 1202 exclusion	
f Large partnerships		**n** Tax shelter farm activities	
g Long-term contracts		**o** Related adjustments	
h Loss limitations			

		Line	Amount	Line	Amount
				14	
15	Total adjustments and preferences. Combine lines 1 through 14	15			
16	Enter the amount from Form 1040, line 37. If less than zero, enter as a (loss)	16			
17	Enter as a positive amount any net operating loss deduction from Form 1040, line 21	17			
18	If Form 1040, line 34, is over $132,950 (over $66,475 if married filing separately) and you itemized deductions, enter the amount, if any, from line 9 of the worksheet for Schedule A (Form 1040), line 28	18	( )		
19	Combine lines 15 through 18			19	
20	Alternative tax net operating loss deduction (see page 6 of the instructions)			20	
21	**Alternative minimum taxable income.** Subtract line 20 from line 19. (If married filing separately and line 21 is more than $173,000, see page 7 of the instructions.)			21	

Part II Alternative Minimum Tax

22 Exemption amount. (If this form is for a child under age 14, see page 7 of the instructions.)

IF your filing status is . . .	**AND line 21 is not over . . .**	**THEN enter on line 22 . . .**
Single or head of household	$112,500	$35,750
Married filing jointly or qualifying widow(er)	150,000	49,000
Married filing separately	75,000	24,500

If line 21 is **over** the amount shown above for your filing status, see page 7 of the instructions. — 22

23	Subtract line 22 from line 21. If zero or less, enter -0- here and on lines 26 and 28 and stop here	23	
24	Go to Part III of Form 6251 to figure line 24 if you reported capital gain distributions directly on Form 1040, line 13, **or** you had a gain on both lines 16 and 17 of Schedule D (Form 1040) (as refigured for the AMT, if necessary). **All others:** If line 23 is $175,000 or less ($87,500 or less if married filing separately), multiply line 23 by 26% (.26). Otherwise, multiply line 23 by 28% (.28) and subtract $3,500 ($1,750 if married filing separately) from the result	24	
25	Alternative minimum tax foreign tax credit (see page 7 of the instructions)	25	
26	Tentative minimum tax. Subtract line 25 from line 24	26	
27	Enter your tax from Form 1040, line 40 (minus any tax from Form 4972 and any foreign tax credit from Form 1040, line 43)	27	
28	**Alternative minimum tax.** Subtract line 27 from line 26. If zero or less, enter -0-. Enter here and on Form 1040, line 41	28	

For Paperwork Reduction Act Notice, see page 8 of the instructions. Cat. No. 13600G Form **6251** (2001)

Form 6251 (2001) Page **2**

Part III Line 24 Computation Using Maximum Capital Gains Rates

Caution: *If you* ***did not*** *complete Part IV of Schedule D (Form 1040), see page 8 of the instructions before you complete this part.*

29	Enter the amount from Form 6251, line 23		29
30	Enter the amount from Schedule D (Form 1040), line 23, or line 9 of the Schedule D Tax Worksheet on page D-9 of the instructions for Schedule D (Form 1040), whichever applies (as refigured for the AMT, if necessary) (see page 8 of the instructions)	30	
31	Enter the amount from Schedule D (Form 1040), line 19 (as refigured for the AMT, if necessary) (see page 8 of the instructions)	31	
32	Add lines 30 and 31	32	
33	Enter the amount from Schedule D (Form 1040), line 23, or line 4 of the Schedule D Tax Worksheet on page D-9 of the instructions for Schedule D (Form 1040), whichever applies (as refigured for the AMT, if necessary) (see page 8 of the instructions)	33	
34	Enter the **smaller** of line 32 or line 33		34
35	Subtract line 34 from line 29. If zero or less, enter -0-		35
36	If line 35 is $175,000 or less ($87,500 or less if married filing separately), multiply line 35 by 26% (.26). Otherwise, multiply line 35 by 28% (.28) and subtract $3,500 ($1,750 if married filing separately) from the result		36
37	Enter the amount from Schedule D (Form 1040), line 28, or line 16 of the Schedule D Tax Worksheet on page D-9 of the instructions for Schedule D (Form 1040), whichever applies (as figured for the regular tax) (see page 8 of the instructions)	37	
38	Enter the **smallest** of line 29, line 30, or line 37. If zero, go to line 44	38	
39	Enter your qualified 5-year gain, if any, from Schedule D (Form 1040), line 29 (as refigured for the AMT, if necessary) (see page 8 of the instructions) — 39		
40	Enter the **smaller** of line 38 or line 39	40	
41	Multiply line 40 by 8% (.08)		41
42	Subtract line 40 from line 38	42	
43	Multiply line 42 by 10% (.10)		43
44	Enter the **smaller** of line 29 or line 30	44	
45	Enter the amount from line 38	45	
46	Subtract line 45 from line 44	46	
47	Multiply line 46 by 20% (.20)		47
	If line 31 is zero or blank, skip lines 48 through 51 and go to line 52. Otherwise, go to line 48.		
48	Enter the amount from line 29	48	
49	Add lines 35, 38, and 46	49	
50	Subtract line 49 from line 48	50	
51	Multiply line 50 by 25% (.25)		51
52	Add lines 36, 41, 43, 47, and 51		52
53	If line 29 is $175,000 or less ($87,500 or less if married filing separately), multiply line 29 by 26% (.26). Otherwise, multiply line 29 by 28% (.28) and subtract $3,500 ($1,750 if married filing separately) from the result		53
54	Enter the **smaller** of line 52 or line 53 here and on line 24		54

Form **6251** (2001)

Form **7004** (Rev. October 2000) Department of the Treasury Internal Revenue Service

Application for Automatic Extension of Time To File Corporation Income Tax Return

OMB No. 1545-0233

Name of corporation: Perry Corporation

Employer identification number: 38 1505286

Number, street, and room or suite no. (If a P.O. box or outside the United States, see instructions.): 1631 W. University Avenue

City or town, state, and ZIP code: Gainesville, FL 32601

Check type of return to be filed:

☐ Form 990-C	☐ Form 1120-FSC	☐ Form 1120-PC	☐ Form 1120S
☒ Form 1120	☐ Form 1120-H	☐ Form 1120-POL	☐ Form 1120-SF
☐ Form 1120-A	☐ Form 1120-L	☐ Form 1120-REIT	
☐ Form 1120-F	☐ Form 1120-ND	☐ Form 1120-RIC	

• Form 1120-F filers: Check here if the foreign corporation does not maintain an office or place of business in the United States . . . . ▶ ☐

1 **Request for Automatic Extension** (see instructions)

a **Extension date.** I request an automatic 6-month (or, for certain corporations, 3-month) extension of time until June 16, 20 03, to file the income tax return of the corporation named above for ▶ ☐ calendar year 20 ...... or ▶ ☒ tax year beginning October 1, 2001, and ending September 30, 20 02.

b **Short tax year.** If this tax year is for less than 12 months, check reason:
☐ Initial return ☐ Final return ☐ Change in accounting period ☐ Consolidated return to be filed

2 **Affiliated group members** (see instructions). If this application also covers subsidiaries to be included in a consolidated return, provide the following information:

Name and address of each member of the affiliated group	Employer identification number	Tax period

3	Tentative tax (see instructions)	3	72,000
4	**Payments and refundable credits:** (see instructions)		
a	Overpayment credited from prior year . . 4a		
b	Estimated tax payments for the tax year . . . 4b 68,000		
c	Less refund for the tax year applied for on Form 4466 . . . 4c ( ) Bal ▶	4d	68,000
e	Credit for tax paid on undistributed capital gains (Form 2439) . .	4e	
f	Credit for Federal tax on fuels (Form 4136)	4f	
5	Total. Add lines 4d through 4f (see instructions)	5	68,000
6	**Balance due.** Subtract line 5 from line 3. **Deposit this amount using the Electronic Federal Tax Payment System (EFTPS) or with a Federal Tax Deposit (FTD) Coupon** (see instructions)	6	4,000

Signature. Under penalties of perjury, I declare that I have been authorized by the above-named corporation to make this application, and to the best of my knowledge and belief, the statements made are true, correct, and complete.

E. Stephens Beeland (Signature of officer or agent) — President (Title) — 12/16/02 (Date)

For Paperwork Reduction Act Notice, see instructions. Cat. No. 13804A Form **7004** (Rev. 10-2000)

Form **8615**

Department of the Treasury
Internal Revenue Service (99)

Tax for Children Under Age 14 With Investment Income of More Than $1,500

► Attach only to the child's Form 1040, Form 1040A, or Form 1040NR.
► See separate instructions.

OMB No. 1545-0998
2001
Attachment Sequence No. **33**

Child's name shown on return | **Child's social security number**

Before you begin: If the child, the parent, or any of the parent's other children under age 14 received capital gains (including capital gain distributions) or farm income, see **Pub. 929,** Tax Rules for Children and Dependents. It explains how to figure the tax for lines 9 and 15 using the **Capital Gain Tax Worksheet** in the Form 1040 or Form 1040A instructions, or **Schedule D** or **J** (Form 1040).

A Parent's name (first, initial, and last). **Caution:** *See instructions before completing.* | **B Parent's social security number**

C Parent's filing status (check one):
☐ Single ☐ Married filing jointly ☐ Married filing separately ☐ Head of household ☐ Qualifying widow(er)

Part I Child's Net Investment Income

1	Enter the child's investment income (see instructions)	1	
2	If the child **did not** itemize deductions on Schedule A (Form 1040 or Form 1040NR), enter $1,500. If the child **did** itemize deductions, see instructions	2	
3	Subtract line 2 from line 1. If zero or less, **do not** complete the rest of this form but **do** attach it to the child's return	3	
4	Enter the child's taxable income from Form 1040, line 39; Form 1040A, line 25; or Form 1040NR, line 38	4	
5	Enter the **smaller** of line 3 or line 4. If zero, **do not** complete the rest of this form but **do** attach it to the child's return	5	

Part II Tentative Tax Based on the Tax Rate of the Parent

6	Enter the parent's taxable income from Form 1040, line 39; Form 1040A, line 25; Form 1040EZ, line 6; TeleFile Tax Record, line K; Form 1040NR, line 38; or Form 1040NR-EZ, line 14. If zero or less, enter -0-	6	
7	Enter the total, if any, from Forms 8615, line 5, of **all other** children of the parent named above. **Do not** include the amount from line 5 above	7	
8	Add lines 5, 6, and 7.	8	
9	Enter the tax on the amount on line 8 based on the **parent's** filing status above (see instructions). If the Capital Gain Tax Worksheet or Schedule D or J (Form 1040) is used, check here ► ☐	9	
10	Enter the parent's tax from Form 1040, line 40; Form 1040A, line 26, minus any alternative minimum tax; Form 1040EZ, line 11; TeleFile Tax Record, line K; Form 1040NR, line 39; or Form 1040NR-EZ, line 15. **Do not** include any tax from Form 4972 or 8814. If the Capital Gain Tax Worksheet or Schedule D or J (Form 1040) was used to figure the tax, check here ► ☐	10	
11	Subtract line 10 from line 9 and enter the result. If line 7 is blank, also enter this amount on line 13 and go to Part III	11	
12a	Add lines 5 and 7 — 12a		
b	Divide line 5 by line 12a. Enter the result as a decimal rounded to at least three places	12b	× .
13	Multiply line 11 by line 12b	13	

Part III Child's Tax—If lines 4 and 5 above are the same, enter -0- on line 15 and go to line 16.

14	Subtract line 5 from line 4 — 14		
15	Enter the tax on the amount on line 14 based on the child's filing status (see instructions). If the Capital Gain Tax Worksheet or Schedule D or J (Form 1040) is used, check here ► ☐	15	
16	Add lines 13 and 15	16	
17	Enter the tax on the amount on line 4 based on the child's filing status (see instructions). If the Capital Gain Tax Worksheet or Schedule D or J (Form 1040) is used to figure the tax, check here ► ☐	17	
18	Enter the **larger** of line 16 or line 17 here and on the child's Form 1040, line 40; Form 1040A, line 26; or Form 1040NR, line 39	18	

For Paperwork Reduction Act Notice, see page 2 of the instructions. Cat. No. 64113U Form **8615** (2001)

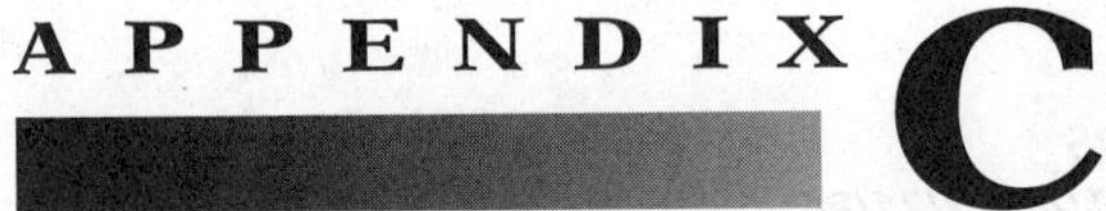

APPENDIX C

MACRS AND ACRS TABLES

ACRS, MACRS and ADS Depreciation Methods Summary

System	Characteristics	Depreciation Method: MACRS	Depreciation Method: ADS	Table No.[a] MACRS	Table No.[a] ADS
MACRS & ADS	Personal Property:				
	1. Accounting Convention	Half-year or mid-quarter	Half-year or mid-quarter[b]		
	2. Life and Method				
	a. 3-year, 5-year, 7-year, 10-year	200% DB or elect straight-line	150% DB or elect straight-line	1, 2, 3, 4, 5	10, 11[c]
	b. 15-year, 20-year	150% DB or elect straight-line	150% DB or elect straight-line[d]	1, 2, 3, 4, 5	
	3. Luxury Automobile Limitations			6	
	Real Property:				
	1. Accounting Convention	Mid-month	Mid-month		
	2. Life and Method				
	a. Residential rental property	27.5 years, straight-line	40 years straight-line	7	12
	b. Nonresidential real property	39 years, straight-line[e]	40 years straight-line	9	12

	Characteristics	ACRS	Table No.[a] ACRS
ACRS	Personal Property[f]		
	1. Accounting Convention	Half-year	
	2. Life and Method		
	a. 3-year, 5-year, 10-year, 15-year	150% DB or elect straight-line[g]	
	Real Property		
	1. Accounting Convention	First of month or Mid-month[h]	
	2. Life		
	a. 15-year property	Placed in service after 12/31/80 and before 3/16/84	16
	b. 18-year property	Placed in service after 3/15/84 and before 5/9/85	14, 15
	c. 19-year property	Placed in service after 5/8/85 and before 1/1/87	13
	3. Method		
	a. All but low-income housing	175% DB or elect straight-line	
	b. Low-income housing property	200% DB or elect straight-line	

[a] All depreciation tables in this appendix are based upon tables contained in Rev. Proc. 87-57, as amended.
[b] General and ADS tables are available for property lives from 2.5-50.0 years using the straight-line method. These tables are contained in Rev. Proc. 87-57 and are only partially reproduced here.
[c] The mid-quarter tables are available in Rev. Proc. 87-57, but are not reproduced here.
[d] Special recovery periods are assigned certain MACRS properties under the alternative depreciation system.
[e] A 31.5-year recovery period applied to nonresidential real property placed in service under the MACRS rules prior to May 13, 1993. (See Table 8)
[f] The ACRS tables for personal property are not reproduced here.
[g] Special recovery periods are required or able to be elected for personalty and realty for which a straight-line ACRS election is made. These recovery periods can be as long as 45 years.
[h] The first-of-the-month convention is used with 15-year property and 18-year real property placed in service before June 23, 1984. The mid-month convention is used with 18-year real property placed in service after June 22, 1984 and 19-year real property.

▼ **TABLE 1**

General Depreciation System—MACRS
Personal Property Placed in Service after 12/31/86
Applicable Convention: Half-year
Applicable Depreciation Method: 200 or 150 Percent Declining Balance Switching to Straight Line

If the Recover Year Is:	And the Recovery Period Is: 3-Year	5-Year	7-Year	10-Year	15-Year	20-Year
	The Depreciation Rate Is:					
1	33.33	20.00	14.29	10.00	5.00	3.750
2	44.45	32.00	24.49	18.00	9.50	7.219
3	14.81	19.20	17.49	14.40	8.55	6.677
4	7.41	11.52	12.49	11.52	7.70	6.177
5		11.52	8.93	9.22	6.93	5.713
6		5.76	8.92	7.37	6.23	5.285
7			8.93	6.55	5.90	4.888
8			4.46	6.55	5.90	4.522
9				6.56	5.91	4.462
10				6.55	5.90	4.461
11				3.28	5.91	4.462
12					5.90	4.461
13					5.91	4.462
14					5.90	4.461
15					5.91	4.462
16					2.95	4.461
17						4.462
18						4.461
19						4.462
20						4.461
21						2.231

▼ **TABLE 2**

General Depreciation System—MACRS

Personal Property Placed in Service after 12/31/86

Applicable Convention: Mid-quarter (Property Placed in Service in First Quarter)

Applicable Depreciation Method: 200 or 150 Percent Declining Balance Switching to Straight Line

If the Recovery Year Is:	And the Recovery Period Is: 3-Year	5-Year	7-Year	10-Year	15-Year	20-Year
	The Depreciation Rate Is:					
1	58.33	35.00	25.00	17.50	8.75	6.563
2	27.78	26.00	21.43	16.50	9.13	7.000
3	12.35	15.60	15.31	13.20	8.21	6.482
4	1.54	11.01	10.93	10.56	7.39	5.996
5		11.01	8.75	8.45	6.65	5.546
6		1.38	8.74	6.76	5.99	5.130
7			8.75	6.55	5.90	4.746
8			1.09	6.55	5.91	4.459
9				6.56	5.90	4.459
10				6.55	5.91	4.459
11				0.82	5.90	4.459
12					5.91	4.460
13					5.90	4.459
14					5.91	4.460
15					5.90	4.459
16					0.74	4.460
17						4.459
18						4.460
19						4.459
20						4.460
21						0.557

▼ **TABLE 3**

General Depreciation System—MACRS
Personal Property Placed in Service after 12/31/86
Applicable Convention: Mid-quarter (Property Placed in Service in Second Quarter)
Applicable Depreciation Method: 200 or 150 Percent Declining Balance Switching to Straight Line

If the Recovery Year Is:	And the Recovery Period Is: 3-Year	5-Year	7-Year	10-Year	15-Year	20-Year
	The Depreciation Rate Is:					
1	41.67	25.00	17.85	12.50	6.25	4.688
2	38.89	30.00	23.47	17.50	9.38	7.148
3	14.14	18.00	16.76	14.00	8.44	6.612
4	5.30	11.37	11.97	11.20	7.59	6.116
5		11.37	8.87	8.96	6.83	5.658
6		4.26	8.87	7.17	6.15	5.233
7			8.87	6.55	5.91	4.841
8			3.33	6.55	5.90	4.478
9				6.56	5.91	4.463
10				6.55	5.90	4.463
11				2.46	5.91	4.463
12					5.90	4.463
13					5.91	4.463
14					5.90	4.463
15					5.91	4.462
16					2.21	4.463
17						4.462
18						4.463
19						4.462
20						4.463
21						1.673

▼ **TABLE 4**

General Depreciation System—MACRS

Personal Property Placed in Service after 12/31/86

Applicable Convention: Mid-quarter (Property Placed in Service in Third Quarter)

Applicable Depreciation Method: 200 or 150 Percent Declining Balance Switching to Straight Line

If the Recovery Year Is:	And the Recovery Period Is: 3-Year	5-Year	7-Year	10-Year	15-Year	20-Year
	The Depreciation Rate Is:					
1	25.00	15.00	10.71	7.50	3.75	2.813
2	50.00	34.00	25.51	18.50	9.63	7.289
3	16.67	20.40	18.22	14.80	8.66	6.742
4	8.33	12.24	13.02	11.84	7.80	6.237
5		11.30	9.30	9.47	7.02	5.769
6		7.06	8.85	7.58	6.31	5.336
7			8.86	6.55	5.90	4.936
8			5.53	6.55	5.90	4.566
9				6.56	5.91	4.460
10				6.55	5.90	4.460
11				4.10	5.91	4.460
12					5.90	4.460
13					5.91	4.461
14					5.90	4.460
15					5.91	4.461
16					3.69	4.460
17						4.461
18						4.460
19						4.461
20						4.460
21						2.788

▼ TABLE 5

General Depreciation System—MACRS
Personal Property Placed in Service after 12/31/86
Applicable Convention: Mid-quarter (Property Placed in Service in Fourth Quarter)
Applicable Depreciation Method: 200 or 150 Percent Declining Balance Switching to Straight Line

If the Recovery Year Is:	And the Recovery Period Is: 3-Year	5-Year	7-Year	10-Year	15-Year	20-Year
	The Depreciation Rate Is:					
1	8.33	5.00	3.57	2.50	1.25	0.938
2	61.11	38.00	27.55	19.50	9.88	7.430
3	20.37	22.80	19.68	15.60	8.89	6.872
4	10.19	13.68	14.06	12.48	8.00	6.357
5		10.94	10.04	9.98	7.20	5.880
6		9.58	8.73	7.99	6.48	5.439
7			8.73	6.55	5.90	5.031
8			7.64	6.55	5.90	4.654
9				6.56	5.90	4.458
10				6.55	5.91	4.458
11				5.74	5.90	4.458
12					5.91	4.458
13					5.90	4.458
14					5.91	4.458
15					5.90	4.458
16					5.17	4.458
17						4.458
18						4.459
19						4.458
20						4.459
21						3.901

▼ TABLE 6

Luxury Automobile Limitations

	Year Automobile is Placed in Service[a]: 2000, 2001, and 2002	1999	1998	1997	1996	1995
Year 1	3,060	3,060	3,160	3,160	3,060	3,060
Year 2	4,900	5,000	5,000	5,000	4,900	4,900
Year 3	2,950	2,950	2,950	3,050	2,950	2,950
Year 4 and Each Succeeding Year	1,775	1,775	1,775	1,775	1,775	1,775

[a]For years prior to 1995, see Revenue Procedure for appropriate year.

▼ TABLE 7

General Depreciation System—MACRS
Residential Rental Real Property Placed in Service after 12/31/86
Applicable Recovery Period: 27.5 Years
Applicable Convention: Mid-month
Applicable Depreciation Method: Straight Line

If the Recovery Year Is:	And the Month in the First Recovery Year the Property Is Placed in Service Is: 1	2	3	4	5	6	7	8	9	10	11	12
	The Depreciation Rate Is:											
1	3.485	3.182	2.879	2.576	2.273	1.970	1.667	1.364	1.061	0.758	0.455	0.152
2	3.636	3.636	3.636	3.636	3.636	3.636	3.636	3.636	3.636	3.636	3.636	3.636
3	3.636	3.636	3.636	3.636	3.636	3.636	3.636	3.636	3.636	3.636	3.636	3.636
4	3.636	3.636	3.636	3.636	3.636	3.636	3.636	3.636	3.636	3.636	3.636	3.636
5	3.636	3.636	3.636	3.636	3.636	3.636	3.636	3.636	3.636	3.636	3.636	3.636
6	3.636	3.636	3.636	3.636	3.636	3.636	3.636	3.636	3.636	3.636	3.636	3.636
7	3.636	3.636	3.636	3.636	3.636	3.636	3.636	3.636	3.636	3.636	3.636	3.636
8	3.636	3.636	3.636	3.636	3.636	3.636	3.636	3.636	3.636	3.636	3.636	3.636
9	3.636	3.636	3.636	3.636	3.636	3.636	3.636	3.636	3.636	3.636	3.636	3.636
10	3.637	3.637	3.637	3.637	3.637	3.637	3.636	3.636	3.636	3.636	3.636	3.636
11	3.636	3.636	3.636	3.636	3.636	3.636	3.637	3.637	3.637	3.637	3.637	3.637
12	3.637	3.637	3.637	3.637	3.637	3.637	3.636	3.636	3.636	3.636	3.636	3.636
13	3.636	3.636	3.636	3.636	3.636	3.636	3.637	3.637	3.637	3.637	3.637	3.637
14	3.637	3.637	3.637	3.637	3.637	3.637	3.636	3.636	3.636	3.636	3.636	3.636
15	3.636	3.636	3.636	3.636	3.636	3.636	3.637	3.637	3.637	3.637	3.637	3.637
16	3.637	3.637	3.637	3.637	3.637	3.637	3.636	3.636	3.636	3.636	3.636	3.636
17	3.636	3.636	3.636	3.636	3.636	3.636	3.637	3.637	3.637	3.637	3.637	3.637
18	3.637	3.637	3.637	3.637	3.637	3.637	3.636	3.636	3.636	3.636	3.636	3.636
19	3.636	3.636	3.636	3.636	3.636	3.636	3.637	3.637	3.637	3.637	3.637	3.637
20	3.637	3.637	3.637	3.637	3.637	3.637	3.636	3.636	3.636	3.636	3.636	3.636
21	3.636	3.636	3.636	3.636	3.636	3.636	3.637	3.637	3.637	3.637	3.637	3.637
22	3.637	3.637	3.637	3.637	3.637	3.637	3.636	3.636	3.636	3.636	3.636	3.636
23	3.636	3.636	3.636	3.636	3.636	3.636	3.637	3.637	3.637	3.637	3.637	3.637
24	3.637	3.637	3.637	3.637	3.637	3.637	3.636	3.636	3.636	3.636	3.636	3.636
25	3.636	3.636	3.636	3.636	3.636	3.636	3.637	3.637	3.637	3.637	3.637	3.637
26	3.637	3.637	3.637	3.637	3.637	3.637	3.636	3.636	3.636	3.636	3.636	3.636
27	3.636	3.636	3.636	3.636	3.636	3.636	3.637	3.637	3.637	3.637	3.637	3.637
28	1.970	2.273	2.576	2.879	3.182	3.485	3.636	3.636	3.636	3.636	3.636	3.636
29	0.000	0.000	0.000	0.000	0.000	0.000	0.152	0.455	0.758	1.061	1.364	1.667

▼ TABLE 8

General Depreciation System—MACRS
Nonresidential Real Property Placed in Service after 12/31/86 and before 5/13/93
Applicable Recovery Period: 31.5 Years
Applicable Convention: Mid-month
Applicable Depreciation Method: Straight Line

If the Recovery Year Is:	And the Month in the First Recovery Year the Property Is Placed in Service Is: 1	2	3	4	5	6	7	8	9	10	11	12
	The Depreciation Rate Is:											
1	3.042	2.778	2.513	2.249	1.984	1.720	1.455	1.190	0.926	0.661	0.397	0.132
2	3.175	3.175	3.175	3.175	3.175	3.175	3.175	3.175	3.175	3.175	3.175	3.175
3	3.175	3.175	3.175	3.175	3.175	3.175	3.175	3.175	3.175	3.175	3.175	3.175
4	3.175	3.175	3.175	3.175	3.175	3.175	3.175	3.175	3.175	3.175	3.175	3.175
5	3.175	3.175	3.175	3.175	3.175	3.175	3.175	3.175	3.175	3.175	3.175	3.175
6	3.175	3.175	3.175	3.175	3.175	3.175	3.175	3.175	3.175	3.175	3.175	3.175
7	3.175	3.175	3.175	3.175	3.175	3.175	3.175	3.175	3.175	3.175	3.175	3.175
8	3.175	3.174	3.175	3.174	3.175	3.174	3.175	3.175	3.175	3.175	3.175	3.175
9	3.174	3.175	3.174	3.175	3.174	3.175	3.174	3.175	3.174	3.175	3.174	3.175
10	3.175	3.174	3.175	3.174	3.175	3.174	3.175	3.174	3.175	3.174	3.175	3.174
11	3.174	3.175	3.174	3.175	3.174	3.175	3.174	3.175	3.174	3.175	3.174	3.175
12	3.175	3.174	3.175	3.174	3.175	3.174	3.175	3.174	3.175	3.174	3.175	3.174
13	3.174	3.175	3.174	3.175	3.174	3.175	3.174	3.175	3.174	3.175	3.174	3.175
14	3.175	3.174	3.175	3.174	3.175	3.174	3.175	3.174	3.175	3.174	3.175	3.174
15	3.174	3.175	3.174	3.175	3.174	3.175	3.174	3.175	3.174	3.175	3.174	3.175
16	3.175	3.174	3.175	3.174	3.175	3.174	3.175	3.174	3.175	3.174	3.175	3.174
17	3.174	3.175	3.174	3.175	3.174	3.175	3.174	3.175	3.174	3.175	3.174	3.175
18	3.175	3.174	3.175	3.174	3.175	3.174	3.175	3.174	3.175	3.174	3.175	3.174
19	3.174	3.175	3.174	3.175	3.174	3.175	3.174	3.175	3.174	3.175	3.174	3.175
20	3.175	3.174	3.175	3.174	3.175	3.174	3.175	3.174	3.175	3.174	3.175	3.174
21	3.174	3.175	3.174	3.175	3.174	3.175	3.174	3.175	3.174	3.175	3.174	3.175
22	3.175	3.174	3.175	3.174	3.175	3.174	3.175	3.174	3.175	3.174	3.175	3.174
23	3.174	3.175	3.174	3.175	3.174	3.175	3.174	3.175	3.174	3.175	3.174	3.175
24	3.175	3.174	3.175	3.174	3.175	3.174	3.175	3.174	3.175	3.174	3.175	3.174
25	3.174	3.175	3.174	3.175	3.174	3.175	3.174	3.175	3.174	3.175	3.174	3.175
26	3.175	3.174	3.175	3.174	3.175	3.174	3.175	3.174	3.175	3.174	3.175	3.174
27	3.174	3.175	3.174	3.175	3.174	3.175	3.174	3.175	3.174	3.175	3.174	3.175
28	3.175	3.174	3.175	3.174	3.175	3.174	3.175	3.174	3.175	3.174	3.175	3.174
29	3.174	3.175	3.174	3.175	3.174	3.175	3.174	3.175	3.174	3.175	3.174	3.175
30	3.175	3.174	3.175	3.174	3.175	3.174	3.175	3.174	3.175	3.174	3.175	3.174
31	3.174	3.175	3.174	3.175	3.174	3.175	3.174	3.175	3.174	3.175	3.174	3.175
32	1.720	1.984	2.249	2.513	2.778	3.042	3.175	3.174	3.175	3.174	3.175	3.174
33	0.000	0.000	0.000	0.000	0.000	0.000	0.132	0.397	0.661	0.926	1.190	1.455

▼ TABLE 9

General Depreciation System—MACRS
Nonresidential Real Property Placed in Service after 5/12/93
Applicable Recovery Period: 39 years
Applicable Depreciation Method: Straight Line

If the Recovery Year Is:	And the Month in the First Recovery Year the Property Is Placed in Service Is: 1	2	3	4	5	6	7	8	9	10	11	12
	The Depreciation Rate Is:											
1	2.461	2.247	2.033	1.819	1.605	1.391	1.177	0.963	0.749	0.535	0.321	0.107
2-39	2.564	2.564	2.564	2.564	2.564	2.564	2.564	2.564	2.564	2.564	2.564	2.564
40	0.107	0.321	0.535	0.749	0.963	1.177	1.391	1.605	1.819	2.033	2.247	2.461

▼ TABLE 10

Alternative Depreciation System—MACRS (Partial Table)
Property Placed in Service after 12/31/86
Applicable Convention: Half-year
Applicable Depreciation Method: 150 Percent Declining Balance Switching to Straight Line

If the Recovery Year Is:	And the Recovery Period Is: 3	4	5	7	10	12
	The Depreciation Rate Is:					
1	25.00	18.75	15.00	10.71	7.50	6.25
2	37.50	30.47	25.50	19.13	13.88	11.72
3	25.00	20.31	17.85	15.03	11.79	10.25
4	12.50	20.31	16.66	12.25	10.02	8.97
5		10.16	16.66	12.25	8.74	7.85
6			8.33	12.25	8.74	7.33
7				12.25	8.74	7.33
8				6.13	8.74	7.33
9					8.74	7.33
10					8.74	7.33
11					4.37	7.32
12						7.33
13						3.66

▼ TABLE 11

Alternative Depreciation System—MACRS (Partial Table)
Property Placed in Service after 12/31/86
Applicable Convention: Half-year
Applicable Depreciation Method: Straight Line

If the Recovery Year Is:	And the Recovery Period Is: 3	4	5	7	10	12
	The Depreciation Rate Is:					
1	16.67	12.50	10.00	7.14	5.00	4.17
2	33.33	25.00	20.00	14.29	10.00	8.33
3	33.33	25.00	20.00	14.29	10.00	8.33
4	16.67	25.00	20.00	14.28	10.00	8.33
5		12.50	20.00	14.29	10.00	8.33
6			10.00	14.28	10.00	8.33
7				14.29	10.00	8.34
8				7.14	10.00	8.33
9					10.00	8.34
10					10.00	8.33
11					5.00	8.34
12						8.33
13						4.17

▼ TABLE 12

Alternative Depreciation System—MACRS
Real Property Placed into Service after 12/31/86
Applicable Recovery Period: 40 years
Applicable Convention: Mid-month
Applicable Depreciation Method: Straight Line

If the Recovery Year Is:	And the Month in the First Recovery Year the Property Is Placed in Service Is: 1	2	3	4	5	6	7	8	9	10	11	12
	The Depreciation Rate Is:											
1	2.396	2.188	1.979	1.771	1.563	1.354	1.146	0.938	0.729	0.521	0.313	0.104
2 to 40	2.500	2.500	2.500	2.500	2.500	2.500	2.500	2.500	2.500	2.500	2.500	2.500
41	0.104	0.312	0.521	0.729	0.937	1.146	1.354	1.562	1.771	1.979	2.187	2.396

▼ TABLE 13

Depreciation System—ACRS
19-Year Real Property (19-Year 175% Declining Balance)
Mid-Month Convention
Property Placed in Service after 5/8/85 and before 1/1/87

If the Recovery Year Is:	And the Month in the First Recovery Year the Property Is Placed in Service Is: 1	2	3	4	5	6	7	8	9	10	11	12
	The Depreciation Rate Is:											
1	8.8	8.1	7.3	6.5	5.8	5.0	4.2	3.5	2.7	1.9	1.1	0.4
2	8.4	8.5	8.5	8.6	8.7	8.8	8.8	8.9	9.0	9.0	9.1	9.2
3	7.6	7.7	7.7	7.8	7.9	7.9	8.0	8.1	8.1	8.2	8.3	8.3
4	6.9	7.0	7.0	7.1	7.1	7.2	7.3	7.3	7.4	7.4	7.5	7.6
5	6.3	6.3	6.4	6.4	6.5	6.5	6.6	6.6	6.7	6.8	6.8	6.9
6	5.7	5.7	5.8	5.9	5.9	5.9	6.0	6.0	6.1	6.1	6.2	6.2
7	5.2	5.2	5.3	5.3	5.3	5.4	5.4	5.5	5.5	5.6	5.6	5.6
8	4.7	4.7	4.8	4.8	4.8	4.9	4.9	5.0	5.0	5.1	5.1	5.1
9	4.2	4.3	4.3	4.4	4.4	4.5	4.5	4.5	4.5	4.6	4.6	4.7
10	4.2	4.2	4.2	4.2	4.2	4.2	4.2	4.2	4.2	4.2	4.2	4.2
11	4.2	4.2	4.2	4.2	4.2	4.2	4.2	4.2	4.2	4.2	4.2	4.2
12	4.2	4.2	4.2	4.2	4.2	4.2	4.2	4.2	4.2	4.2	4.2	4.2
13	4.2	4.2	4.2	4.2	4.2	4.2	4.2	4.2	4.2	4.2	4.2	4.2
14	4.2	4.2	4.2	4.2	4.2	4.2	4.2	4.2	4.2	4.2	4.2	4.2
15	4.2	4.2	4.2	4.2	4.2	4.2	4.2	4.2	4.2	4.2	4.2	4.2
16	4.2	4.2	4.2	4.2	4.2	4.2	4.2	4.2	4.2	4.2	4.2	4.2
17	4.2	4.2	4.2	4.2	4.2	4.2	4.2	4.2	4.2	4.2	4.2	4.2
18	4.2	4.2	4.2	4.2	4.2	4.2	4.2	4.2	4.2	4.2	4.2	4.2
19	4.2	4.2	4.2	4.2	4.2	4.2	4.2	4.2	4.2	4.2	4.2	4.2
20	0.2	0.5	0.9	1.2	1.6	1.9	2.3	2.6	3.0	3.3	3.7	4.0

▼ **TABLE 14**

Depreciation System—ACRS
18-Year Real Property (18-Year 175% Declining Balance)
Mid-Month Convention
Property Placed in Service after 6/22/84 and before 5/9/85

If the Recovery Year Is:	And the Month in the First Recovery Year the Property Is Placed in Service Is: 1	2	3	4	5	6	7	8	9	10	11	12
	The Applicable Percentage Is:											
1	9	9	8	7	6	5	4	4	3	2	1	0.4
2	9	9	9	9	9	9	9	9	9	10	10	10.0
3	8	8	8	8	8	8	8	8	9	9	9	9.0
4	7	7	7	7	7	8	8	8	8	8	8	8.0
5	7	7	7	7	7	7	7	7	7	7	7	7.0
6	6	6	6	6	6	6	6	6	6	6	6	6.0
7	5	5	5	5	6	6	6	6	6	6	6	6.0
8	5	5	5	5	5	5	5	5	5	5	5	5.0
9	5	5	5	5	5	5	5	5	5	5	5	5.0
10	5	5	5	5	5	5	5	5	5	5	5	5.0
11	5	5	5	5	5	5	5	5	5	5	5	5.0
12	5	5	5	5	5	5	5	5	5	5	5	5.0
13	4	4	4	5	4	4	5	4	4	4	5	5.0
14	4	4	4	4	4	4	4	4	4	4	4	4.0
15	4	4	4	4	4	4	4	4	4	4	4	4.0
16	4	4	4	4	4	4	4	4	4	4	4	4.0
17	4	4	4	4	4	4	4	4	4	4	4	4.0
18	4	3	4	4	4	4	4	4	4	4	4	4.0
19		1	1	1	2	2	2	3	3	3	3	3.6

▼ TABLE 15

Depreciation System—ACRS
18-Year Real Property (18-Year 175% Declining Balance)
Full-Month Convention
Property Placed in Service after 3/15/84 and before 6/23/84

If the Recovery Year Is:	And the Month in the First Recovery Year the Property Is Placed in Service Is: 1	2	3	4	5	6	7	8	9	10	11	12
	The Applicable Percentage Is:											
1	10	9	8	7	6	6	5	4	3	2	2	1
2	9	9	9	9	9	9	9	9	9	10	10	10
3	8	8	8	8	8	8	8	8	9	9	9	9
4	7	7	7	7	7	7	8	8	8	8	8	8
5	6	7	7	7	7	7	7	7	7	7	7	7
6	6	6	6	6	6	6	6	6	6	6	6	6
7	5	5	5	5	6	6	6	6	6	6	6	6
8	5	5	5	5	5	5	5	5	5	5	5	5
9	5	5	5	5	5	5	5	5	5	5	5	5
10	5	5	5	5	5	5	5	5	5	5	5	5
11	5	5	5	5	5	5	5	5	5	5	5	5
12	5	5	5	5	5	5	5	5	5	5	5	5
13	4	4	4	5	5	4	4	5	4	4	4	4
14	4	4	4	4	4	4	4	4	4	4	4	4
15	4	4	4	4	4	4	4	4	4	4	4	4
16	4	4	4	4	4	4	4	4	4	4	4	4
17	4	4	4	4	4	4	4	4	4	4	4	4
18	4	4	4	4	4	4	4	4	4	4	4	4
19			1	1	1	2	2	2	3	3	3	4

▼ TABLE 16

Depreciation System—ACRS
Full Month Convention
1. All 15-Year Real Estate (Except Low-Income Housing)
Property Placed in Service after 12/31/80 and before 3/16/84

If the Recovery Year Is:	And the Month in the First Year the Property Is Placed in Service Is: 1	2	3	4	5	6	7	8	9	10	11	12
	The Applicable Percentage Is:											
1	12	11	10	9	8	7	6	5	4	3	2	1
2	10	10	11	11	11	11	11	11	11	11	11	12
3	9	9	9	9	10	10	10	10	10	10	10	10
4	8	8	8	8	8	8	9	9	9	9	9	9
5	7	7	7	7	7	7	8	8	8	8	8	8
6	6	6	6	6	7	7	7	7	7	7	7	7
7	6	6	6	6	6	6	6	6	6	6	6	6
8	6	6	6	6	6	6	5	6	6	6	6	6
9	6	6	6	6	5	6	5	5	5	6	6	6
10	5	6	5	6	5	5	5	5	5	5	6	5
11	5	5	5	5	5	5	5	5	5	5	5	5
12	5	5	5	5	5	5	5	5	5	5	5	5
13	5	5	5	5	5	5	5	5	5	5	5	5
14	5	5	5	5	5	5	5	5	5	5	5	5
15	5	5	5	5	5	5	5	5	5	5	5	5
16	—	—	1	1	2	2	3	3	4	4	4	5

2. Low-Income Housing
Property Placed in Service after 12/31/80 and before 5/9/85[a]

If the Recovery Year Is:	And the Month in the First Year the Property Is Placed in Service Is: 1	2	3	4	5	6	7	8	9	10	11	12
	The Applicable Percentage Is:											
1	13	12	11	10	9	8	7	6	4	3	2	1
2	12	12	12	12	12	12	12	13	13	13	13	13
3	10	10	10	10	11	11	11	11	11	11	11	11
4	9	9	9	9	9	9	9	9	10	10	10	10
5	8	8	8	8	8	8	8	8	8	8	8	8
6	7	7	7	7	7	7	7	7	7	7	7	7
7	6	6	6	6	6	6	6	6	6	6	6	6
8	5	5	5	5	5	5	5	5	5	5	6	6
9	5	5	5	5	5	5	5	5	5	5	5	5
10	5	5	5	5	5	5	5	5	5	5	5	5
11	4	5	5	5	5	5	5	5	5	5	5	5
12	4	4	4	5	4	5	5	5	5	5	5	5
13	4	4	4	4	4	4	5	4	5	5	5	5
14	4	4	4	4	4	4	4	4	4	5	4	4
15	4	4	4	4	4	4	4	4	4	4	4	4
16	—	—	1	1	2	2	2	3	3	3	4	4

[a]For the period after 5/8/85, see special IRS tables (not reproduced here).

▼ **TABLE 17**

Lease Inclusion Dollar Amounts for Automobiles (Partial Table) (Other Than for Electronic Automobiles) With A Lease Term Beginning in Calendar Year 2001[a]

Fair Market Value of Automobiles		Tax Year During Lease				
Over	Not Over	1st	2nd	3rd	4th	5th and Later
$15,500	15,800	3	6	9	10	11
15,800	16,100	5	12	16	20	22
16,100	16,400	8	17	24	30	33
16,400	16,700	10	22	33	39	44
16,700	17,000	13	27	41	48	56
17,000	17,500	16	35	51	61	70
17,500	18,000	20	44	64	77	89
18,000	18,500	24	53	78	92	107
18,500	19,000	28	62	91	109	125
19,000	19,500	32	71	104	125	143
19,500	20,000	36	80	117	141	162
20,000	20,500	40	89	131	156	181
20,500	21,000	45	97	144	173	199
21,000	21,500	49	106	158	188	217
21,500	22,000	53	115	171	204	236
22,000	23,000	59	129	190	229	263
23,000	24,000	67	147	217	260	300
24,000	25,000	75	165	243	292	337
25,000	26,000	83	183	270	324	373
26,000	27,000	91	201	296	356	410
27,000	28,000	100	218	324	387	447
28,000	29,000	108	236	350	419	484
29,000	30,000	116	254	377	451	520
30,000	31,000	124	272	403	483	557
31,000	32,000	132	290	430	515	594
32,000	33,000	140	308	456	547	631
33,000	34,000	149	326	482	579	667
34,000	35,000	157	343	510	610	705
35,000	36,000	165	361	536	643	741
36,000	37,000	173	379	563	674	778
37,000	38,000	181	397	590	705	815
38,000	39,000	189	415	616	738	851
39,000	40,000	198	433	642	770	888
40,000	41,000	206	451	669	801	925
41,000	42,000	214	469	695	833	962
42,000	43,000	222	487	722	865	998
43,000	44,000	230	505	748	897	1,036
44,000	45,000	238	523	775	929	1,072
45,000	46,000	247	540	802	961	1,108
46,000	47,000	255	558	828	993	1,145
47,000	48,000	263	576	855	1,024	1,183
48,000	49,000	271	594	881	1,057	1,219
49,000	50,000	279	612	908	1,088	1,256
50,000	51,000	287	630	935	1,119	1,293
51,000	52,000	296	648	961	1,151	1,330
52,000	53,000	304	666	987	1,184	1,366
53,000	54,000	312	684	1,014	1,215	1,403
54,000	55,000	320	702	1,040	1,248	1,439

[a]Per *Rev. Proc.* 2001-19. The table for 2002 had not been released at the date of the printing.

▼ **TABLE 17 (continued)**

Fair Market Value of Automobiles		Tax Year During Lease				
Over	Not Over	1st	2nd	3rd	4th	5th and Later
$55,000	56,000	328	720	1,067	1,279	1,476
56,000	57,000	336	738	1,093	1,311	1,514
57,000	58,000	345	755	1,120	1,343	1,550
58,000	59,000	353	773	1,147	1,375	1,586
59,000	60,000	361	791	1,173	1,407	1,624

[a]Per *Rev. Proc.* 2001-19. The table for 2002 had not been released at the date of the printing.

APPENDIX D

GLOSSARY

Ability to pay A concept in taxation that holds that taxpayers be taxed according to their ability to pay such taxes, that is, taxpayers that have sufficient financial resources should pay the tax. This concept is an integral part of vertical equity.

Accountable plan A type of employee reimbursement plan that meets two tests, (1) substantiation, and (2) return of excess reimbursement. Under an accountable plan, reimbursements are excluded from the employee's gross income and the expenses are not deductible by the employee.

Accounting method The rules used to determine the tax year in which income and expenses are reported for tax purposes. Generally, the same accounting method must be used for tax purposes as is used for keeping books and records. The accounting treatment used for any item of income or expense and for specific items (e.g., installment sales and contracts) is included in this term.

Accounting period The period of time, usually 12 months, used by taxpayers to compute their taxable income. Taxpayers who do not keep records must use a calendar year. Taxpayers who do keep books and records may choose between a calendar year or a fiscal year. The accounting period election is made on the taxpayer's first filed return and cannot be changed without IRS consent. The accounting period may be less than 12 months if it is the taxpayer's first or final return or if the taxpayer is changing accounting periods. Certain restrictions upon the use of a fiscal year apply to partnerships, S corporations, and personal service corporations.

Accrual method of accounting Accounting method under which income is reported and expenses are deducted when (1) all events have occurred that fix the taxpayer's right to receive the income and (2) the amount of the item can be determined with reasonable accuracy. Taxpayers with inventories to report must use this method to report sales and purchases.

Accumulated Adjustments Account (AAA) Account that must be kept by S corporations. The cumulative total of the ordinary income or loss and separately stated items for the most recent S corporation election period.

Accumulated earnings and profits The sum of the undistributed current earnings and profits balances (and deficits) from previous years reduced by any distributions that have been made out of accumulated earnings and profits.

Accumulated earnings credit Deduction that reduces the accumulated taxable income amount. It does not offset the accumulated earnings tax on a dollar-for-dollar basis. Different rules apply for operating companies, service companies, and holding or investment companies.

Accumulated earnings tax Penalty tax on corporations other than those subject to the personal holding company tax among others. It is levied on a corporation's current year addition to its accumulated earnings balance in excess of the amount needed for reasonable business purposes and not distributed to the shareholders. This tax is intended to discourage companies from retaining excessive amounts of earnings if the funds are invested in activities that are unrelated to business needs. The tax is 39.6% of accumulated taxable income.

Accumulated taxable income The tax base for the accumulated earnings tax which is determined by taking the corporation's taxable income and increasing (decreasing) it by positive (negative) adjustments and decreasing it by the accumulated earnings credit and available dividends-paid deductions.

Accumulation distribution rules (throwback rules) Exception to the general rule that distributable net income (DNI) serves as a ceiling on the amount taxable to a beneficiary. Under the general rule, the beneficiary excludes the portion of any distribution in excess of DNI from his gross income. Accumulation distributions made by a trust are taxable to the beneficiaries in the year received.

ACE See adjusted current earnings.

Acquiescence policy IRS policy of announcing whether it agrees or disagrees with a Tax Court regular decision decided in favor of the taxpayer. Such statements are not issued for every case.

Acquisitive reorganization A transaction in which the acquiring corporation obtains all or part of the stock or assets of a target corporation.

Additional depreciation The excess of the actual amount of accelerated depreciation (or cost-recovery deductions under ACRS) over the amount of depreciation that would be deductible under the straight-line method. Such depreciation applies to Section 1250 depreciable real property acquired prior to 1987.

Adjusted gross income (AGI) A measure of taxable income that falls between gross income and taxable income. It is the income amount that is used as the basis for calculating the floor or the ceiling for numerous other tax computations.

Adjusted grossed-up basis For Sec. 338 purposes, the sum of (1) the basis of a purchasing corporation's stock interest in a target corporation plus (2) an adjustment for the target corporation's liabilities on the day following the acquisition date plus or minus (3) other relevant items.

Adjusted income from rents (AIR) This amount is equal to the corporation's gross income from rents reduced by the deductions claimed for amortization or depreciation, property taxes, interest, and rent.

Adjusted ordinary gross income (AOGI) A corporation's adjusted ordinary gross income is its ordinary gross income reduced by (1) certain expenses incurred in connection with gross income from rents, mineral, oil and gas royalties, and working interests in oil or gas wells, (2) interest received by dealers on certain U.S. obligations, (3) interest received from condemnation awards, judgments, or tax refunds, and (4) rents from certain tangible personal property manufactured or produced by the corporation.

Adjusted sales price The amount realized from the sale of a residence less any fixing-up expenses.

Adjusted taxable gift Taxable gifts made after 1976 that are valued at their date-of-gift value. These gifts affect the size of the transfer tax base at death.

Administrative interpretation Treasury Department interpretation of a provision of the Code. Such interpretations may be in the form of Treasury Regulations, revenue rulings, or revenue procedures.

Affiliated group A group consisting of a parent corporation and at least one subsidiary corporation.

Alien Individuals who are not U.S. citizens.

Alimony Payments made pursuant to divorce or separation or written agreement between spouses subject to conditions specified in the tax law. Alimony payments (as contrasted to property settlements) are deductible for AGI by the payor and are included in the gross income of the recipient.

All events test Rule holding that an accrual basis taxpayer must report an item of income (1) when all events have occurred that fix the taxpayer's right to receive the item of income and (2) when the amount of the item can be determined with reasonable accuracy. This test is not satisfied until economic performance has taken place.

Alternate valuation date The alternate valuation date is the earlier of six months after the date of death or the date the property is sold, exchanged, distributed, etc. by the estate. Unless this option is elected, the gross estate is valued at its FMV on the date of the decedent's death.

Alternative minimum tax (AMT) Tax which applies to individuals, corporations, and estates and trusts if it exceeds the taxpayer's regular tax. Most taxpayers are not subject to this tax. This tax equals the amount by which the tentative minimum tax exceeds the regular tax.

Alternative minimum taxable income (AMTI) The taxpayer's taxable income (1) increased by tax preference items and (2) adjusted for income, gain, deduction, and loss items that have to be recomputed under the AMT system.

Amount realized The amount realized equals the sum of money plus the fair market value of all other property received from the sale or other disposition of the property less any selling expenses (e.g., commissions, advertising, deed preparation costs, and legal expenses) incurred in connection with the sale.

Announcement Information release issued by the IRS to provide a technical explanation of a current tax issue. Announcements are aimed at tax practitioners rather than the general public.

Annual exclusion An exemption that is intended to relieve a donor from keeping an account of and reporting the numerous small gifts (e.g., wedding and Christmas gifts) made throughout the year. This exclusion is currently $10,000 per donee.

Annuity A series of regular payments that will continue for either a fixed period of time or until the death of the recipient. Pensions are usually paid in this way.

Appeals coordinated issue Issue over which the appeals officer must obtain a concurrence of guidance from the regional director of appeals in order to render a decision.

Applicable federal rate The rate determined monthly by the federal government which is based on the rate paid by the government on borrowed funds. The rate varies with the term of the loan. Thus, short-term loans are for a period of under three years, mid-term loans are for over three years and under nine years, and long-term loans are for over nine years.

Asset depreciation range (ADR) system of depreciation Depreciation method allowed for property placed in service before January 1, 1981. This method prescribed useful lives for various classes of assets.

Assignment of income doctrine A judicial requirement that income be taxed to the person that earns it.

At-risk basis Essentially the same amount as the regular partnership basis with the exception that liabilities increase the at-risk basis only if the partner is at-risk for such an amount.

At-risk rules These rules limit the partner's loss deductions to his at-risk basis.

Average tax rate The taxpayer's total tax liability divided by the amount of his taxable income.

Bad debt Bona fide debt that is uncollectible because it is worthless. Such debts are further characterized as "business bad debts," which give rise to an ordinary deduction, and "nonbusiness bad debts," which are treated as a short-term capital loss. A determination of whether a debt is worthless is made by reference to all the pertinent evidence (e.g., the debtor's general financial condition and whether the debt is secured by collateral). Such debts are deductible subject to certain requirements.

Bardahl formula Mathematical formula for determining the amount of working capital that a business reasonably needs for accumulated earnings tax purposes. For a manufacturing company, the formula is based on the business's operating cycle.

Bona fide debt A debt that (1) arises from a valid and enforceable obligation to pay a fixed or determinable sum of money and (2) results in a debtor-creditor relationship.

Boot Property that may not be received tax-free in certain tax-free transactions (i.e., any money, debt obligations, and so on)

Bootstrap acquisition An acquisition where an investor purchases part of a corporation's stock and then has the corporation redeem the remainder of the seller's stock.

Brother-sister controlled group This type of controlled group exists if (1) five or fewer individuals, estates, or trusts own at least 80% of the voting stock or 80% of the value of each corporation and (2) there is common ownership of more than 50% of the voting power or 50% of the value of all classes of stock.

Built-in gain A gain that accrued prior to the conversion of a C corporation to an S corporation.

Built-in gains (Sec. 1374) tax Tax on built-in gains that are recognized by the S corporation during the ten-year period commencing on the date that the S corporation election took effect.

C corporation Form of business entity that is taxed as a separate taxpaying entity. Its income is subject to an initial tax at the corporate level. Its shareholders are subject to a second tax if dividends are paid from the corporation's earnings and profits. This type of corporation is sometimes referred to as a regular corporation.

C short year That portion of an S termination year that commences on the day on which the termination is effective and continues through to the last day of the corporation's tax year.

Capital asset This category of assets includes all assets except inventory, notes and accounts receivable, and depreciable property or land used in a trade or business (e.g., property, plant, and machinery).

Capital expenditure An expenditure that adds to the value of, substantially prolongs the useful life of, or adapts the property to a new or different use qualifies as a capital expenditure.

Capital gain dividend A distribution by a regulated investment company (i.e., a mutual fund) of capital gains realized from the sale of investments in the fund. Such dividends also include undistributed capital gains allocated to the shareholders.

Capital gain Gain realized on the sale or exchange of a capital asset.

Capital gain property For charitable contribution deduction purposes, property upon which a long-term capital gain would be recognized if that property was sold at its FMV.

Capital interest An interest in the assets owned by a partnership.

Capital recovery A capital recovery amount is a deduction for depreciation or cost recovery. It is a factor in the determination of a property's adjusted basis.

Cash method of accounting Accounting method that requires the taxpayer to report income for the taxable year in which payments are actually or constructively received. Expenses are reported in the year they are paid. Most individuals and service businesses (i.e., businesses without inventories) use this method.

Cash receipts and disbursements method of accounting See Cash method of accounting.

Casualty loss Loss that arises from an identifiable event that was sudden, unexpected, or unusual (e.g., fire, storm, shipwreck, other casualty, or theft). Within certain limitations, individuals may deduct such losses from AGI. Business casualty losses are deductible for AGI.

Certiorari An appeal from a lower court (i.e., a federal court of appeals) which the U.S. Supreme Court agrees to hear. Such appeals, which are made as a writ of certiorari, are generally not granted unless (1) a constitutional issue needs to be decided or (2) there is a conflict among the lower court decisions that must be clarified.

Charitable remainder annuity trust This type of trust makes distributions to individuals for a certain time period or for life. The annual distributions are a uniform percentage (5% or higher) of the value of the trust property as valued on the date of transfer.

Charitable remainder unitrust This type of trust makes annual distributions for either a specified time period or for life. The distributions are a uniform percentage (5% or higher) of the value of the property as revalued annually.

Clifford trust A trust that is normally held for a 10-year period after which the principal reverts to the grantor. The trust accounting income is not generally taxed to the grantor.

Closed transaction Situation where the property in question (e.g., property distributed in a corporate liquidation) can be valued with reasonable certainty. The gain or loss reported on the transaction is determinable at the time the transaction occurs. See open transaction doctrine.

Closed-fact situation Situation or transaction that has already occurred.

Closely held C corporation For purposes of the at-risk rules, a C corporation in which more than 50% of the stock is owned by five or fewer individuals at any time during the last half of the corporation's tax year.

Closely held corporation A corporation that is owned by either a single individual or a small group of individuals who may or may not be family members.

Combined controlled group A group of three or more corporations which are members of a parent-subsidiary or brother-sister controlled group. In addition, at least one of the corporations must be the parent corporation of the parent-subsidiary controlled group and a member of a brother-sister controlled group.

Common law state All states other than the community property states are common law states. In such states, all assets acquired during the marriage are the property of the acquiring spouse.

Community income In any of the eight community property states, such income consists of the income from the personal efforts, investments, etc. of either spouse. Community income belongs equally to both spouses.

Community property law Law in community property states mandating that all property acquired after marriage is generally community property unless acquired by gift or inheritance. Each spouse owns a one-half interest in community property.

Community property state The eight traditional community property states (Louisiana, Texas, New Mexico, Arizona, California, Washington, Idaho, and Nevada) and Wisconsin (which adopted a similar law). These states do not follow the common law concept of property ownership.

Compensation Payment for personal services. Salaries, wages, fees, commissions, tips, bonuses, and specialized forms of compensation such as director's fees and jury's fees fall into this category. However, certain fringe benefits and some foreign-earned income are not taxed.

Completed contract method of accounting Accounting method for long-term contracts undertaken by smaller companies. Income from the contract is reported in the taxable year in which the contract is completed. The completed contract method is limited to construction contracts undertaken by smaller companies.

Consolidated tax return A single tax return filed by a group of related corporations (i.e., affiliated group).

Consolidation A form of tax-free reorganization involving two or more corporations whose assets are acquired by a new corporation. The stock, securities, and other consideration transferred by the acquiring corporation is then distributed by each target corporation to its shareholders and security holders in exchange for their stock and securities.

Constant interest rate method Used to amortize the original issue discount ratably over the life of the bond, this method determines the amount of interest income by multiplying the interest yield to maturity by the adjusted issue price.

Constructive dividend An indirect payment, or undeclared dividend, made to a shareholder without the benefit of a formal declaration usually resulting from a reclassification of a transaction by the IRS. Transactions that can produce constructive dividends include the payment of unreasonable compensation or the making of loans to shareholders.

Contributory pension plan A qualified pension plan to which employees make voluntary contributions.

Controlled group A controlled group is two or more separately incorporated businesses owned by a related group of individuals or entities. Such groups include parent-subsidiary groups, brother-sister groups, or combined groups.

Corporation A separate taxpaying entity (such as an association, joint stock company, or insurance company) that must file a tax return every year, even when it had no income or loss for the year.

Cost depletion method Calculation of the depletion of an asset (e.g., oil and gas properties) under which the asset's adjusted basis is divided by the estimated recoverable units to arrive at a per-unit depletion. This amount is then multiplied by the number of units sold to determine the cost depletion. This method may be alternated with the percentage depletion method as long as the calculation takes that into account.

Cost The amount paid for property in cash or the fair market value of the property given in exchange. The costs of acquiring the property and preparing it for use are included in the cost of the property.

Crummey trust Technique that allows a donor to set up a discretionary trust and obtain an annual exclusion. Such a trust arrangement allows the beneficiary to demand an annual distribution of the lesser of $10,000 or the amount transferred to the trust that year.

Current year's exclusion The amount of the annuity payment that is excluded from gross income. This amount is determined by multiplying the exclusion ratio by the amount received during the year.

Customs duties A federal excise tax on imported goods.

DIF See Discriminant Function Program.

Deductions for AGI Expenses one would see on an income statement prepared for financial accounting purposes, for example, compensation paid to employees, repairs to business property, and depreciation expenses. Certain nonbusiness deductions (e.g., alimony payments, moving expenses, and deductible payments to an individual retirement account (IRA) are also deductible for AGI.

Deductions from AGI Generally, deductions are allowed for certain personal expenses such as medical deductions and charitable contributions which are referred to as itemized deductions. Alternatively, individuals may deduct the standard deduction. Personal and dependency deductions are also deductions from AGI.

Deficiency dividend This type of dividend substitutes an income tax levy on the dividend payment at the shareholder level for the payment of the personal holding company tax.

Defined contribution pension plan Qualified pension plan under which a separate account is maintained for each participant and fixed amounts are contributed based upon a specific percentage-of-compensation formula. The retirement benefits are based on the value of the participant's account at the time of retirement. Defined contribution plans for self-employed individuals are referred to as *H.R. 10 plans*.

Dissolution A legal term implying that a corporation has surrendered the charter that it originally received from the state.

Distributable net income (DNI) Maximum amount of distributions taxed to the beneficiaries and deducted by a trust or estate.

Distributive share The portion of partnership taxable and nontaxable income, losses, credits, and so on that the partner must report for tax purposes.

Dividend A distribution of property made by a corporation out of its earnings and profits.

Dividends-paid deduction Distributions made out of a corporation's earnings and profits are eligible for this deduction for personal holding company tax and accumulated earnings tax purposes. The deduction is equal to the amount of money plus the adjusted basis of the nonmoney property distributed.

Dividends-received deduction This deduction attempts to mitigate the triple taxation that would occur if one corporation paid dividends to a corporate shareholder who, in turn, distributed such amounts to its individual shareholders. Certain restrictions and limitations apply to this deduction.

Divisive reorganization Transaction in which part of a transferor corporation's assets are transferred to a second, newly created corporation that is controlled by either the transferee or its shareholders.

E&P See Earnings and profits.

Economic performance test Economic performance occurs when the property or services to be provided are actually delivered.

Effective tax rate The taxpayer's total tax liability divided by his total economic income.

Employee achievement award Award given under circumstances that does not create a likelihood that it is really disguised compensation. It must be in the form of tangible personal property (other than cash) and be valued at no more than $400.

Employee stock ownership plan (ESOP) A qualified stock bonus plan or combined stock bonus plan and money purchase pension plan. ESOP's are funded by contributions of the employer's stock which are held for the employees' benefit.

Employment taxes Social security (FICA) and federal and state unemployment compensation taxes.

Entertainment expense Entertainment expenses (e.g., business meals) that are either directly related to or associated with the active conduct of a trade or business are deductible within certain limitations and restrictions. Directly related expenses are those that (1) derive a business benefit other than goodwill and (2) are incurred in a clear business setting. Expenses that are associated with the business are those that show a clear business purpose (e.g., obtaining new business) and occur on the same day the business is discussed.

Estate tax Part of the federal unified transfer tax system, this tax is based upon the total property transfers an individual makes during his lifetime and at death.

Estate A legal entity which comes into being only upon the death of the person whose assets are being administered. The estate continues in existence until the duties of the executor have been completed.

Excess depreciation See Additional depreciation.

Excess net passive income (Sec. 1375) tax Tax levied when (1) an S corporation has passive investment income for the taxable year that exceeds 25% of its gross receipts and (2) at the close of the tax year the S corporation has earnings and profits from C corporation tax years.

Excess net passive income An amount equal to the S corporation's net passive income multiplied by the fraction consisting of its passive investment income less 25% of its gross receipts divided by its passive investment income. It is limited to the corporation's taxable income.

Exclusion ratio The portion of the annuity payment that is excluded from taxation. This amount equals the investment in the contract (its cost) divided by the expected return from the annuity.

Exclusion Any item of income that the tax law says is not taxable.

Exemption equivalent That portion of the tax base that is completely free of transfer taxes as a result of the unified credit.

Expected return multiple The number of years that the annuity is expected to continue. This amount may be a stated term or for the remainder of the taxpayer's life.

Expected return The amount which a taxpayer can expect to receive from an annuity. It is determined by multiplying the amount of the annuity's annual payment by the expected return multiple.

FICA Tax withheld through the payment of payroll taxes, FICA is intended to finance social security benefits for individuals who are not self-employed. Employees and employers contribute matching amounts until a federally-set annual earnings ceiling is reached. At that time, no further contributions need be made for that year. No ceiling exists for the hospital insurance (HI) portion of the tax. Self-employed individuals are subject to self-employment tax and currently receive a *for* AGI income tax deduction equal to 50% of their self-employment tax payments.

FIFO method of inventory valuation This flow of cost method assumes that the first goods purchased will be the first goods sold. Thus, the ending inventory consists of the last goods purchased.

Failure-to-pay penalty Penalty imposed at the rate of 0.5% per month (or fraction thereof) on the amount of tax shown on the return less any tax payments made before the beginning of the month for which the penalty is being calculated. The maximum penalty is 25%.

Fair market value (FMV) The amount that would be realized from the sale of a property at a price that is agreeable to both the buyer and the seller when neither party is obligated to participate in the transaction.

Federal estate tax See estate tax.

Fiduciary accounting income The excess of accounting income over expenses for a fiduciary (i.e., an estate or trust). Excluded are any items credited to or charged against capital.

Fiduciary taxation The special tax rules that apply to fiduciaries (e.g., trusts and estates).

Fiduciary A person or other entity (e.g., a guardian, executor, trustee, or administrator) who holds and manages property for someone else.

Field audit procedure Audit procedure generally used by the IRS for corporations or individuals engaged in a trade or business and conducted at either the taxpayer's place of business or his tax advisor's office. Generally, several items on the tax return are examined.

Fiscal year An annual accounting period that ends on the last day of any month other than December. A fiscal year may be elected by taxpayers that keep books and records, such as businesses.

Fixing-up expenses Expenses incurred to assist in the sale of a residence (e.g., normal repairs and painting costs). Capital expenditures do not qualify as fixing-up expenses.

Flat tax See Proportional tax.

Foreign corporation A corporation that is incorporated under the laws of a country other than the United States.

Foreign tax credit Tax credit given to mitigate the possibility of double taxation faced by U.S. citizens, residents, and corporations earning foreign income.

Foreign-earned income An individual's earnings from personal services rendered in a foreign country.

Former passive activity An activity that was formerly considered passive, but which is not considered to be passive with respect to the taxpayer for the current year.

Forum shopping The ability to consider differing precedents in choosing the forum for litigation.

Franchise tax State tax levy sometimes based upon a weighted average formula consisting of net worth, income, and sales.

Functional-use test A test used to determine whether property is considered similar or related in service or use for purposes of involuntary conversions of property under Sec. 1033. The functional-use test requires that the replacement property be functionally the same as the converted property.

Future interest Such interests include reversions, remainders, and other interests that may not be used, owned, or enjoyed until some future date.

General business credit Special credit category consisting of tax credits commonly available to businesses. The more significant credit items are (1) the investment tax credit, (2) the targeted jobs credit, (3) the research credit, (4) the low-income housing credit, (5) the empowerment zone employment credit, (6) the disabled access credit.

General partnership A partnership with two or more partners where no partner is a limited partner.

General power of appointment Power of appointment under which the holder can appoint the property to himself, his estate, his creditors, or the creditors of his estate. Such power may be exercisable during the decedent's life, by his will, or both.

Generally accepted accounting principles (GAAP) The accounting principles that govern the preparation of financial reports to shareholders. GAAP does not apply to the tax treatment unless the method clearly reflects income. It is used only when the regulations do not specify the treatment of an item or when the regulations provide more than one alternative accounting method.

Generation-skipping transfer A disposition that (1) provides interests for more than one generation of beneficiaries who are in a younger generation than the transferor or (2) provides an interest solely for a person two or more generations younger than the transferor.

Gift tax A wealth transfer tax that applies if the property transfer occurs during a person's lifetime.

Grantor trust Trust governed by Secs. 671 through 679. The income from such trusts is taxed to the grantor even if some or all of the income has been distributed.

Grantor The transferor who creates a trust.

Gross estate The gross estate includes items to which the decedent held title at death as well as certain incomplete transfers made by the decedent prior to death.

Gross income All income received in cash, property, or services, from whatever source derived and from which the taxpayer derives a direct economic benefit.

Gross tax For income tax purposes, the amount determined by multiplying taxable income by the appropriate tax rate(s). The gross tax may also be found in the appropriate tax table for the taxpayer's filing status.

Guaranteed minimum Minimum amount of payment guaranteed to a partner. This amount is important if the partner's distributive share is less than his guaranteed minimum. See also Guaranteed payment.

Guaranteed payment Minimum amount of payment guaranteed to a partner in the form of a salary-like payment made for services provided to the partnership and interest-like payments for the use of invested capital. Guaranteed payments, which may be in the form of a guaranteed minimum amount or a set amount, are taxed as ordinary income. See also Guaranteed minimum.

H.R. 10 Plan Special retirement plan rules applicable to self-employed individuals. Such plans are often referred to as "Keogh plans."

Hedge agreement This is an obligation on the part of a shareholder-employee to repay to the corporation any portion of salary that is disallowed by the IRS as a deduction. It is also used in connection with other corporate payments to shareholder-employees (e.g., travel and entertainment expenses).

Horizontal equity A concept in taxation that refers to the notion that similarly-situated taxpayers should be treated equally under the tax law.

Hybrid method of accounting Accounting method that combines the cash and accrual methods. Under this method, taxpayers can report sales and purchases under the accrual method and other income and expense items under the cash method. See also the cash method of accounting and the accrual method of accounting.

IRS See Internal Revenue Service.

Income beneficiary Entity or individual that receives the income from a trust.

Income in respect of a decedent (IRD) Amount to which the decedent was entitled as gross income but which were not properly includible in computing his taxable income for the tax year ending with his date of death or for a previous tax year under the method of accounting employed by the decedent.

Income The economic concept of income measures the amount an individual can consume during a period and remain as well off at the end of the period as at the beginning. The accounting concept of income is a measure of the income that is realized in a transaction. The tax concept of income is close to the accounting concept. It includes both taxable and nontaxable income from any source. However, it does not include a return of capital.

Incremental A concept in taxation that described how the tax law has been changed or modified over the years. Under incrementalism, the tax law is changed or an incremental basis rather than a complete revision basis.

Indeterminate market value If the market value of the property in question cannot be determined by the usual methods, the "open transaction" doctrine may be applied and the tax consequences may be deferred until the transaction is closed. Alternatively, the property may be valued by using the fair market value of the property that is given in the exchange (e.g., the value of the services rendered).

Information Release An administrative pronouncement concerning an issue the IRS thinks the general public will be interested in. Such releases are issued in lay terms.

Innocent spouse provision This provision exempts a spouse from penalty and liability for tax if such spouse had no knowledge of nor reason to know about an item of taxable income that is in dispute.

Innocent spouse rule Rule that exempts a spouse from penalty of from liability for the tax if such spouse had no knowledge of nor reason to know about an item of community income.

Installment sale method of accounting Taxpayers may use this method of accounting to reduce the tax burden from gains on the sale of property paid for in installments. Under this method, payment of the tax is deferred until the sale proceeds are collected. This method is not applicable to sales of publicly traded property or to losses.

Installment sale Any disposition of property which involves receiving at least one payment after the close of the taxable year in which the sale occurs.

Intangible drilling and development costs (IDCs) Expenditures made by an operator for wages, fuel, repairs, hauling supplies, and so forth, incident to and necessary for the preparation and drilling of oil and gas wells.

Inter vivos trust Transfer to a trust that is made during the grantor's lifetime.

Interest The cost charged by a lender for the use of money. For example, finance charges, loan discounts, premiums, loan origination fees, and points paid by a buyer to obtain a mortgage loan are all interest expenses. The deductibility of the expense depends upon the purpose for which the indebtedness was incurred.

Interpretative Regulations Treasury Regulations that serve to broadly interpret the provisions of the Internal Revenue Code.

Interpretative Regulations Treasury Regulations that serve to interpret the provisions of the Internal Revenue Code.

Investment expenses All deductions other than interest that are directly connected with the production of investment income.

Investment interest Interest expense on indebtedness incurred to purchase or carry property held for investment (e.g., income from interest, dividends, annuities, and royalties). Interest expenses incurred from passive activities are not subject to the investment interest limitations and interest incurred to purchase or carry tax-exempt securities is not deductible. Interest incurred from passive activities is subject to the passive activity loss limitation rules.

Involuntary conversion Such a conversion occurs when property is compulsorily converted into money or other property due to theft, seizure, requisition, condemnation, or partial or complete destruction. For example, an involuntary conversion occurs when the government exercises its right of eminent domain.

Irrevocable trust Trust under which the grantor cannot require the trustee to return the trust's assets.

Itemized deductions Also known as "deductions from AGI," these personal expenditures are allowable for such items as medical expenses, state and local taxes, charitable contributions, unreimbursed employee business expenses, interest on a personal residence, and casualty and theft losses. There are specific requirements for and limitations on the deductibility of each of these items. In addition, only those taxpayers whose total itemized deductions exceed the standard deduction amount can itemize their deductions. In general, the total itemized deductions for an individual is reduced by 3% of AGI in excess of $114,700 ($57,350 for married individuals filing a separate return).

Joint income Income from jointly-held property.

Joint tenancy A popular form of property ownership that serves as a substitute for a will. Each joint tenant is deemed to have an equal interest in the property.

Judicial decisions Decision rendered by a court deciding the case that is presented to it by a plaintiff and defendant. These decisions are important sources of the tax law and can come from trial courts and appellate courts.

Keogh plan Retirement plan for self-employed individuals. This type of plan is also known as an "H.R. 10 plan."

LIFO method of inventory valuation This method assumes a last-in, first out flow of cost. It results in the lowest taxable income during periods of inflation because it shows the lowest inventory value. Price indexes are used for the valuation. The information in these indexes is grouped into groups (pools) of similar items. See also Simplified LIFO method.

LIFO recapture tax A tax imposed on a C corporation that uses the LIFO inventory method and which elects S corporation treatment. The tax is imposed in the final C corporation tax year and paid over a four-year period.

Legislative reenactment doctrine Rule holding that Congress's failure to change the wording in the Code over an extended period signifies that Congress has approved the treatment provided in the regulations.

Letter Ruling Letter rulings originate from the IRS at the taxpayer's request. They describe how the IRS will treat a proposed transaction. It is only binding on the person requesting the ruling providing the taxpayer completes the transaction as proposed in the ruling. Those of general interest are published as Revenue Rulings.

Life estate A property transfer in trust that results in the transferor reserving the right to income for life. Another individual is named to receive the property upon the transferor's death.

Like class Classes of assets defined by the Regulations that are considered to be property of a like kind for purposes of Sec. 1031. Like class property is tangible personal property that is in the same General Asset Class or the Same Product Class as other property.

Like-kind exchange A direct exchange of like-kind property. The transferred property and the received property must be held for productive use either (1) in a trade or business or (2) as an investment. Nonrecognition of gain or loss is mandatory. Certain like-kind exchanges between related parties are restricted if either party disposes of the property within two years of the exchange.

Limited liability company (LLC) A corporation that is generally taxed under the partnership rules. Although similar to an S corporation, there is no limit to (1) the number of shareholders, (2) the number of classes of stock, or (3) the types of investments in related entities.

Limited liability company A business entity that combines the legal and tax benefits of partnerships and S corporations. Generally these entities are taxed as partnerships for federal tax purposes since they do not have three or four of the "nonneutral" corporate characteristics present.

Limited liability partnership (LLP) Similar to a limited liability company, but formed under a separate state statute that generally applies to service companies.

Limited partnership A partnership where one or more of the partners is designated as a limited partner.

Liquidating distribution A distribution that (1) liquidates a partner's entire partnership interest due to retirement, death, or other business reason or (2) partially or totally liquidates a shareholder's stock interest in a corporation following the adoption of a plan at liquidation.

Liquidating distribution A distribution that liquidates a partner's entire partnership interest due to retirement, death, or other business reason. Such distributions result in a capital gain or loss to the partner whose interest is liquidated. In a corporate liquiddation, the liquidating corporation generally recognizes gains and losses on the distribution of the properties and its shareholders recognize capital gain or loss on the surrender of their stock.

Long-term capital gain (LTCG) Gain realized on the sale or exchange of a capital asset held longer than one year.

Long-term contracts Building, manufacturing, installation, and construction contracts that are not completed in the same taxable year in which they are entered into. Service contracts do not qualify as long-term contracts. See also Completed contract method of accounting.

Look-back interest Interest that is assessed on any additional tax that would have been paid if the actual total cost of the contract was used to calculate the tax rather than the estimated cost. Thus, it is applicable to any contract of portion of a contract that is accounted for under either the hybrid or percentage of completion method of accounting.

Loss corporation A corporation entitled to use a net operating loss carryover or having a net operating loss for the taxable year in which an ownership change occurs.

Majority partners The one or more partners in a partnership who have an aggregate interest in partnership profits and capital in excess of 50%.

Marginal tax rate The tax that is applied to an incremental amount of taxable income that is added to the tax base. This rate can be used to measure the tax effect of a proposed transaction. Currently, the highest marginal tax rate for individuals is 39.6%.

Marital deduction Deduction allowed for tax-free inter-spousal transfers other than those for gifts of certain terminable interests.

Market value This term refers to replacement cost under the lower of cost or market inventory method. That is, it is the price at which the taxpayer can replace the goods in question. See also Fair market value.

Material participation The level of participation by a taxpayer in an activity that determines whether the activity is either passibe or active. If a taxpayer does not meet the material participation requirements, the activity is treated as a passive activity.

Medical expense deduction Unreimbursed medical expenses incurred for medical procedures or treatments that are (1) legal in the locality in which they are performed and (2) incurred for the purpose of alleviating a physical or mental defect or illness that affects the body's structure or function are deductible from AGI. Out-of-pocket travel costs incurred while en route to a medical facility, certain capital expenditures affecting the sick person, premiums for medical insurance, and in-patient hospital care are also deductible. Certain restrictions and limitations apply to this deduction.

Memorandum decision Decision issued by the Tax Court. They deal with factual variations on matters which were decided in earlier cases.

Merger A tax-free reorganization one form of which has the acquiring corporation transfer its stock, securities, and other consideration to the target corporation in exchange for its assets and liabilities. The target corporation then distributes the consideration that it receives to its shareholders and security holders in exchange for their stock and securities.

Minimum tax credit (MTC) A tax credit allowed for the amount of alternative minimum tax that arose because of deferral and permanent adjustments and preference items. This credit may be carried over and used to offset regular tax liabilities in subsequent years.

Miscellaneous itemized deductions Certain unreimbursed employee expenses (e.g., required uniforms, travel, entertainment, and so on) fall into this category. Miscellaneous itemized deductions also include certain investment expenses, appraisal fees for charitable contributions and fees for tax return preparation. The nature of the deduction depends on whether the taxpayer is an employee or a self-employed individual.

Modified percentage of completion method A variation of the regular percentage of completion method where an election may be made to defer reporting profit from a long-term contract until at least 10% of the estimated total cost has been incurred.

Necessary expense Expense that is deductible because it is appropriate and helpful in the taxpayer's business. Such expenses must also qualify as ordinary.

Negligence penalty Penalty assessed if the IRS finds that the taxpayer has filed an incorrect return because of negligence. Generally this penalty is 20% of the underpayment attributable to negligence.

Negligence The Code defines negligence as (1) any failure to reasonably attempt to comply with the Code and (2) "careless, reckless, or intentional disregard" of the rules and regulations.

Net gift A gift upon which the donee pays the gift tax as a condition to receiving the gift.

Net investment income The excess of the taxpayer's investment income over his investment expenses. See also Investment income.

Net operating loss (NOL) A net operating loss occurs when business expenses exceed business income for any taxable year. Such losses may be carried back 3 years or carried forward 15 years to a year in which the taxpayer has taxable income. The loss is carried back first and must be deducted from years in chronological order unless a special election is made to forgo the carryback.

New loss corporation Any corporation permitted to use a net operating loss carryover after an ownership change occurs.

Ninety-day letter Officially called a Statutory Notice of Deficiency, this letter is sent when (1) the taxpayer does not file a protest letter within 30 days of receipt of the 30-day letter or (2) the taxpayer has met with an appeals officer but no agreement was reached. The letter notifies the taxpayer of the amount of the deficiency, how that amount was determined, and that a deficiency will be assessed if a petition is not filed with the Tax Court within 90 days. The taxpayer is also advised of the alternatives available to him.

Nonaccountable plan A type of employee reimbursement plan that does not meet either of the two tests for an accountable plan (see accountable plan). Under a nonaccountable plan, reimbursements are included in the employee's gross income and the expenses are deductible by the employee, subject to the 2% of AGI floor.

Nonqualified deferred compensation plan Type of plan used by employer to provide incentives or supplementary retirement benefits for executives. Such plans are not subject to the nondiscrimination and vesting rules.

Nonqualified stock option Stock option that does not meet the requirements for an incentive stock option.

Nonrecourse loan Loan for which the borrower has no liability.

Notice An interpretation by the IRS that provides quidance concerning how to interpret a statute, perhaps one recently enacted.

Office audit procedure IRS audit of a specific item on an individual's tax return. An office audit takes place at the IRS branch office.

Old loss corporation Any corporation that is allowed to use a net operating loss carryover, or which has a net operating loss for the tax year in which an ownership change occurs, and which undergoes the requisite stock ownership change.

Open transaction doctrine Valuation technique for property that can only be valued on the basis of uncertain future payments. This doctrine determines the shareholder's gain or loss when the asset is sold, collected, or able to be valued. Assets that cannot be valued are assigned a value of zero.

Open-fact or tax-planning situation Situation or transaction in which the facts have not yet occurred. In such situations, the tax advisor's task is to plan for the facts or shape them so as to produce a favorable tax result.

Open-fact situation A situation that has not yet occurred. That is, one for which the facts and events are still controllable and can be planned for.

Optional basis adjustment An elective technique that adjusts the basis for the partnership interest and the underlying assets up or down as a result of (1) distributions from the partnership to its partners, (2) sales of partnership interests by existing partners, or (3) transfers of the interest following the death of a partner.

Ordinary expense An expense that is deductible because it is reasonable in amount and bears a reasonable and proximate relationship to the income-producing activity or property.

Ordinary gross income (OGI) A corporation's ordinary gross income is its gross income reduced by (1) capital gains and (2) Sec. 1231 gains.

Ordinary income property For charitable contribution deduction purposes, any property that would result in the recognition of ordinary income if it was sold. Such property includes inventory, works of art or manuscripts created by the taxpayer, capital assets that have been held for one year or less, and Sec. 1231 property that results in ordinary income due to depreciation recapture.

Parent-subsidiary controlled group To qualify as such, a common parent must own at least 80% of the voting stock or at least 80% of the value of at least one subsidiary corporation and at least 80% of each other component member of the controlled group must be owned by other members of the controlled group.

Partial liquidation This occurs when a corporation discontinues one line of business, distributes the assets related to that business to its shareholders, and continues in at least one other line of business.

Partner A member of a partnership. The member may be an individual, trust, estate, or corporation. See also general partner and limited partner.

Partnership agreement Agreement that governs the relationship between the partners and the partnership.

Partnership interest The capital and/or profits interest in a partnership received in exchange for a contribution of properties or services (e.g., money or business equipment). The nature of a partnership interest is similar to that of corporate stock.

Partnership item Virtually all items reported by the partnership for the taxable year, including tax preference items, credit recapture items, guaranteed payments, and at-risk amounts.

Partnership ordinary income The positive sum of all partnership items of income, gain, loss, or deduction that do not have to be separately stated.

Partnership ordinary loss The negative sum of all partnership items of income, gain, loss, or deduction that do not have to be separately stated.

Partnership taxable income The sum of all taxable items among the separately stated items plus the partnership ordinary income or ordinary loss.

Partnership Syndicate, group, pool, joint venture, or other unincorporated organization which carries on a business or financial operation or venture and which has at least two partners.

Party to a reorganization Such parties include (1) corporations that result from a reorganization and (2) the corporations involved in a reorganization where one corporation acquires the stock or assets of the other corporation.

Passive activity limitation Separate limitation on the amount of losses and credits that can be claimed with respect to a passive activity.

Passive income Income from an activity that does not require the taxpayer's material involvement or participation. Thus, income from tax shelters and rental activities generally fall into this category.

Passive loss Loss generated from a passive activity. Such losses are computed separately. They may be used to offset income from other passive activities, but may not be used to offset either active income or portfolio income.

Percentage depletion method Depletion method for assets such as oil and gas that is equal to a specified percentage times the gross income from the property but which may not exceed 100% of the taxable income before depletion is deducted. Lease bonuses, advance royalties, and other amounts payable without regard to production may not be included in the calcualtion. This method is only available to small oil and gas producers and royalty owners and for certain mineral properties.

Percentage of completion method of accounting Accounting method generally used for long-term contracts under which income is reported in proportion to the amount of work that has been completed in a given year.

Permanent difference Items that are reported in taxable income but not book income or vice versa. Such differences include book income items that are nontaxable in the current year and will never be taxable and book expense items that are nondeductible in computing taxable income for the current year and will never be deductible.

Personal exemption A deduction in an amount mandated by Congress. The amount for 1997 ($2,550 for 1996) is $2,650. For years after 1989 the amount is adjusted for increases in the cost of living. An additional exemption is allowed for each individual who is a dependent. Personal and dependency exemptions are phased out for high income taxpayers.

Personal holding company (PHC) A closely held corporation (1) that is owned by five or fewer shareholders who own more than 50% of the corporation's outstanding stock at any time during the last half of its tax year and (2) whose PHC income equals at least 60% of the corporation's adjusted ordinary gross income for the tax year. Certain corporations (e.g., S corporations) are exempt from this definition.

Personal holding company income (PHCI) Twelve categories of income including the following: dividends; interest; annuities; royalties (other than minerals, oil and gas, computer software, and copyright royalties); adjusted income from rents; adjusted income from mineral, oil and gas royalties or working interests in oil and gas wells; computer software royalties; copyright royalties; produced film rents; income from personal service contracts involving a 25% or more shareholder; rental income from corporate property used by a 25% or more shareholder; and distributions from estates and trusts.

Personal interest All interest other than active business interest, investment interest, interest incurred in a passive activity, qualified residence interest, and interest incurred when paying the estate tax on an installment basis. Personal interest is currently treated as a nondeductible personal expenditure. See also Interest.

Personal service corporation (PSC) A regular C corporation whose principal activity is the performance of personal services that are substantially performed by owner-employees who own more than 10% of the value of the corporation's stock.

Personal service corporation Corporation whose principal activity is the performance of personal services.

Plan of liquidation. A written document detailing the steps to be undertaken while carrying out the complete liquidation of a corporation.

Plan of reorganization A consummated transaction that is specifically defined as a reorganization.

Pooled income fund A fund in which individuals receive an income interest for life and a charitable contribution deduction equal to the remainder interest for amounts contributed to the fund. The various individual beneficiaries receive annual distributions of income based upon their proportionate share of the fund's earnings.

Portfolio income Dividends, interest, annuities, and royalties not derived in the ordinary course of business. Gains and losses on property that produces portfolio income are included in such income.

Post-termination transition period The period of time following the termination of the S corporation election during which (1) loss and deduction carryovers can be deducted or (2) distributions of S corporation previously taxed earnings can be made tax-free.

Power of appointment The power to designate the eventual owner of a property. Such appointments may be general or specific. See also General power of appointment.

Pre-adjustment AMTI Alternative minimum taxable income determined without the adjusted current earnings adjustment and the alternative tax NOL deduction.

Pre-adjustment year For purposes of the innocent spouse provisions, the most recent tax year of the spouse ending before the date the deficiency is mailed.

Preferential dividend Dividends are preferential if (1) the amount distributed to a shareholder exceeds his ratable share of the distribution as determined by the number of shares that are owned or (2) the distribution amount for a class of stock is more or less than its rightful amount.

Preferred stock bailout A tax treatment mandated by Sec. 306 which prevents shareholders who receive nontaxable preferred stock dividends from receiving capital gain treatment upon the sale or redemption of the preferred stock.

Present interest An unrestricted right to the immediate use, possession, or enjoyment of property or the income from property (e.g., a life estate or term certain).

Previously taxed income (PTI) Income earned in a pre-1983 S corporation tax year and which was taxed to the shareholder. A money distribution of PTI can be distributed tax-free once all of a corporation's AAA balance has been distributed. See Accumulated Adjustment Account.

Primary cite The highest level official reporter which reports a particular case is called the primary cite.

Principal partner Partner who owns at least a 5% interest in the partnership's capital or profits.

Probate estate Those properties that (1) pass subject to the will or under an intestacy statute and (2) are subject to court administration are part of the probate estate.

Profit-sharing plan A qualified defined benefit plan which may be established in lieu of or in addition to a qualified pension plan. Contributions to a profit-sharing plan are usually based upon profits. Incidental benefits may or may not be included. In addition, the plan must meet certain requirements concerning determination of the amount and timing of the employer's contribution, how the employee wants to receive the employer's contribution, vesting, and forfeitures.

Profits interest Interest in the partnership's future earnings.

Progressive rate Tax that increases as the taxpayer's taxable income increases. The U.S. income tax is an example of a progressive tax.

Property settlement The division of property between spouses upon their separation or divorce.

Property tax Federal, state, or local tax levied on real and/or personal property (e.g., securities, a personal automobile).

Property Cash, tangible property (e.g., buildings and land) and intangible property (e.g., franchise rights, trademarks, and leases).

Proportional tax A method of taxation under which the tax rate is the same for all taxpayers regardless of their income. State and local sales taxes are examples of this form of tax.

Protest letter If the additional tax in question is more than $10,000 and the IRS audit was a field audit, the taxpayer must file a protest letter within 30 days. If no such letter is sent, then the IRS will follow-up with a 90-day letter. See also Ninety-day letter.

Qualified Subchapter S trusts (QSSTs) A domestic trust that owns stock in one or more S corporations and distributes (or is required to distribute) all of its income to its sole income beneficiary. The beneficiary must make an irrevocable election to be treated as the owner of the trust consisting of the S corporation stock. A separate QSST election must be made for each corporation's stock that is owned by the trust.

Qualified disclaimer Disclaimer made by a person named to receive property under a decedent's will who wishes to renounce the property and any of its benefits. Such a disclaimer must be in written form and be irrevocable. In addition, it must be made no later than 9 months after the later of the day the transfer is made or the day the recipient becomes 21 years old. The property must pass to either the decedent's spouse or another person not named by the person making the disclaimer.

Qualified joint interest If spouses are the only joint owners of a property, that property is classified as a qualified joint interest.

Qualified pension plan Pension plan that includes (1) systematic and definite payments made to a pension trust based upon actuarial methods and (2) usually provides for incidental benefits such as disability, or medical insurance benefits.

Qualified plan award Employee achievement awards given under a written plan or program that does not discriminate in favor of highly compensated employees. Such awards must be in the form of tangible personal property other than cash and be worth no more than $1,600.

Qualified residence interest Interest on an indebtedness which is secured by the taxpayer's qualified residence when it is paid or accrued. A taxpayer may have two qualified residences: a principal residence and a residence that he has personally used more than the greater of 14 days or 10% of the rental days during the year.

Qualified terminable interest property (QTIP) QTIP property is property for which a special election has been made that makes it eligible for the marital deduction. Such property must be transferred by the donor-spouse to a donee-spouse who has a qualifying interest for life. In other words, the donor does not have to grant full control over the property to his spouse.

Readily ascertainable fair market value The fair market value of nonqualified stock options can be readily ascertained where the option is traded on an established options exchange.

Realized gain or loss The gain or loss computed by taking the amount realized from a sale of property and subtracting the property's adjusted basis.

Reasonable business needs For accumulated earnings tax purposes, the amount that a prudent businessman would consider appropriate for the business's bona fide present and future needs, Sec. 303 (death tax) redemption needs, and excess business holding redemption needs.

Recapitalization A tax-free change in the capital structure of an existing corporation for a bona fide business purpose.

Recapture provision A provision requiring recapture of earlier alimony payments as ordinary income by the payor if the payments decline sharply in either the second or third year.

Recourse loan Loan for which the borrower remains liable until repayment is complete. If the loan is secured, the lender can be repaid by selling the security. Any difference in the sale amount and the loan amount must be paid by the borrower.

Recovery of basis doctrine Rule that allows taxpayers to recover the basis of an asset without being taxed. Such amounts are considered a return of capital.

Refundable credit See Tax credit.

Regressive tax A form of taxation under which the tax rate decreases as the tax base (e.g., income) increases.

Regular corporation See C corporation.

Regular decision Tax Court decision that is issued on a particular issue for the first time.

Regular tax A corporation's tax liability for income tax purposes reduced by foreign tax credits allowable for income tax purposes.

Remainder interest The portion of an interest in the property retained by a transferor who is not transferring his entire interest in a property.

Remainderman The person entitled to the remainder interest.

Replacement property Property that is acquired to replace converted property in order to retain nonrecognition of gain status. Such property must generally be functionally the same as the converted property. For example, a business machine must be replaced with a similar business machine. There are exceptions to this rule: The taxpayer-use test applies to the involuntary conversion of rental property owned by an investor; condemnations of real property held for business or investment use may be replaced by like-kind property.

Residential rental property Property from which at least 80% of the gross rental income is rental from dwelling units. Residential units include manufactured homes that are used for rental purposes, but not hotels, motels, or other establishments for transient use.

Restricted property plan Such plans are used to attract and retain key executives by giving them an ownership interest in the corporation. The income recognition rules contained in Sec. 83 govern this type of plan.

Revenue procedure Issued by the national office of the IRS and reflects the IRS's position on procedural aspects of tax practice issues. Revenue procedures are published in the Cumulative Bulletin.

Revenue ruling Issued by the national office of the IRS and reflects the IRS's interpretation of a narrow tax issue. Revenue rulings, which are published in the Cumulative Bulletin, have less weight than the Treasury Regulations.

Revenue Amounts received by the taxpayer from any source. It includes both taxable and nontaxable amounts and items that are a return of capital. Although closely related to income or gross income, differences between these items do exist.

Reverse triangular merger Type of tax-free transaction in which a subsidiary corporation is merged into a target corporation and the target corporation stays alive as a subsidiary of the parent corporation.

Reversionary interest The interest in a property that might revert back to the transferor under the terms of the transfer. If the amount of reversionary interest is 5% or less, it is not included in the gross estate.

Revocable trust Trust under which the grantor may demand that the assets be returned.

Royalties Ordinary income arising from amounts paid for the right to use property that belongs to another and is transferred for valuable consideration (e.g., a patent right where substantially all rights are transferred).

Rule against perpetuities The requirement that no property interet vest more than 21 years, plus the gestation period, after some life or lives in being at the time the interest is created.

S corporation Election that can be made by small business corporations that allows them to be taxed like partnerships rather than like C corporations. Small business corporations are those that meet the 35-shareholder limitation, the type of shareholder restrictions, and the one class of stock restriction.

S short year That portion of an S termination year that commences on the first day of the tax year and ends on the day preceding the day on which the termination is effective.

S termination year A tax year in which a termination event occurs on any day other than the first day of the tax year. It is divided into an S short year and a C short year.

Sale A transaction where one receives cash and/or the equivalent of cash, including the assumption of debt, in exchange for an asset.

Sales tax State or local tax on purchases. Generally, food items and medicines are exempt from such tax.

Section 444 election Personal service corporations, partnerships, and S corporations that are unable to otherwise elect a fiscal year, instead of their required tax year, can under Sec. 444 elect a fiscal year as their taxable year.

Secondary cite Citation to a secondary source (i.e., an unofficial reporter) for a particular case.

Section 1231 property Real or depreciable property that is (1) held for more than one year and (2) used in a trade or business. Certain property, such as inventory, U.S. government publications, copyrights, literary, musical, or artistic compositions, and letters, are excluded from this definition.

Section 1245 property Certain property subject to depreciation and, in some cases, amortization. Depreciable personal property such as equipment is Section 1245 property. However, most real property is not.

Section 1250 property Any real property that (1) is not Section 1245 property and (2) is subject to a depreciation allowance.

Section 306 stock Preferred stock that is received as a stock dividend or a part of a tax-free reorganization. Section 306 stock is subject to the special preferred stock bailout rules when sold or redeemed. See preferred stock bailouts.

Security A security includes (1) shares of stock in a corporation; (2) a right to subscribe for, or the right to receive, a share of stock in a corporation; and (3) a bond, debenture, note, or other evidence of indebtedness issued by a corporation with interest coupons or in registered form.

Separate property All property that is owned before marriage and any gifts or inheritances acquired after marriage are separate property. This distinction depends on the state of residence. However, it is possible even in community property states.

Separate share rule Rule permitting a trust with several beneficiaries to treat each beneficiary as having a separate trust interest for purposes of determining (1) the amount of the distribution deduction and (2) the beneficiary's gross income.

Severance damages Compensation for a decline in the value of the property remaining after part of the taxpayer's property is condemned. The IRS considers such damages analogous to the proceeds from property insurance.

Shifting income The process of transferring income from one family member to another. Methods for shifting income include gifts of stock or bonds to family members who are in lower tax brackets.

Short-period tax return A tax return covering a period of less than 12 months. Short period returns are commonly filed in the first or final tax year or when a change in tax year is made.

Short-term capital gain (STCG) Gain realized on the sale or exchange of a capital asset held for one year or less.

Short-term trust Trust whose period is long enough for the grantor to escape being taxed on the trust's accounting income. A *Clifford* trust is a short-term trust.

Simple trust Trust that must distribute all of its income currently and is not empowered to make a charitable contribution.

Simplified LIFO method This method of inventory valuation allows taxpayers to use a single LIFO pool rather than multiple pools. See also LIFO method.

Small cases procedure When $10,000 or less is in question for a particular year, a taxpayer may opt to have the case heard by a special commissioner rather than a Tax Court judge. The commissioner's opinion cannot be appealed and has no precedential value.

Sole proprietorship Form of business entity owned by an individual who reports all items of income and expense on Schedule C (or Schedule C-EZ) of his individual return.

Special agents The IRS agents responsible for criminal fraud investigations.

Specific write-off method of accounting Method of accounting used for bad debts. Under this method, the taxpayer deducts each bad debt individually as it becomes worthless. This is the only allowable accounting method for bad debts arising after 1986.

Spinoff A tax-free distribution in which a parent corporation distributes the stock and securities of a subsidiary to its shareholders without receiving anything in exchange.

Split-interest transfer A transfer made for both private (i.e., an individual) and public (i.e., a charitable organization) purposes.

Split-up Tax-free distribution in which a parent corporation distributes the stock or securities of two or more subsidiaries to its shareholders in exchange for all of their stock and securities in the parent corporation. The parent corporation then goes out of existence.

Splitoff Tax-free distribution in which a parent corporation distributes a subsidiary's stock and securities to some or all of its shareholders in exchange for part or all of their stock and securities in the parent corporation.

Splitting income The process of creating additional taxable entities, especially corporations, in order to reduce an individual's effective tax rate.

Sprinkling trust A discretionary trust with several beneficiaries.

Standard deduction A floor amount set by Congress to simplify the tax computation. It is used by taxpayers who do not have enough deductions to itemize. The amount of the deduction varies according to the taxpayer's filing status, age, and vision. Taxpayers who use this standard deduction are not required to keep records.

Statements on Responsibilities in Tax Practice (SRTP) Ethical standards of practice and compliance set by the Tax Division of the American Institute of Certified Public Accountants. These statements, which are not legally binding, have a great deal of influence over ethics in tax practice.

Statute of Limitations A period of time as provided by law in which a taxpayer's return may not be changed either by the IRS or the taxpayer. The Statute of Limitations is generally three years from the later of the date the tax return is filed or its due date. There is no Statute of Limitations for a fraudulent return.

Step transaction doctrine A judicial doctrine which the IRS can use to collapse a multistep transaction into a single transaction (either taxable or tax-free) in order to prevent the taxpayers from arranging a series of business transactions to obtain a tax result that is not available if only a single transaction is used.

Stock bonus plan A special type of defined benefit plan under which the employer's stock is contributed to a trust. The stock is then allocated and distributed to the participants. See also Employee stock ownership plan.

Stock dividend A dividend paid in the form of stock in the corporation issuing the dividend.

Stock option plan This category includes incentive stock options and nonqualified stock option arrangements. Such plans are used to attrack and retain key employees.

Stock redemption The acquisition by a corporation of its own stock in exchange for property. Such stock may be cancelled, retired, or held as treasury stock.

Stock rights Rights issued by a corporation to its shareholders or creditors which permits the purchase of an additional share(s) of stock at a designated exercise price with the surrender of one or more of the stock rights.

Substantially appreciated inventory This type of inventory includes (1) items held for sale in the normal course of partnership business, (2) other property which would not be considered a capital asset or Sec. 1231 property if it was sold by the partnership, and (3) any other property held by the partnership which would fall into the above classification if it was held by the selling or distributee partner.

Surviving spouse A special filing status available to widows and widowers who file a joint return for the year his or her spouse dies and for the following two years. The surviving spouse may not have remarried, must be a U.S. citizen or resident, have qualified to file a joint return for the year, and must have at least one dependent child living at home during the year.

Target corporation The corporation that transfers its assets as part of a taxable or tax-free acquisition transaction. May also be known as the acquired or transferor company.

Tax Deferred Bonds Bonds on which the interest is not subject to current taxation but is deferred to a future period of time, such as Series EE U.S. Savings Bonds.

Tax Exempt Bonds Bonds on which the interest is completely exempt from federal income taxation, such as state and municipal bonds.

Tax attributes Corporations have various tax items, such as earnings and profits, deduction and credit carryovers, and depreciation recapture potential, that are called tax attributes. The tax attributes of a target or liquidating corporation are assumed by the acquiring or parent corporation, respectively, in acquisitive reorganizations and tax-free liquidations.

Tax base The amount to which the tax rate is applied to determine the tax due. For income tax purposes, the tax base is taxable income.

Tax benefit rule Recovery of an amount in a subsequent year that produced a tax benefit in a prior year and is thus taxable to the recipient.

Tax credit Amount that can be deducted from the gross tax to arrive at the net tax due or refund due. Prepaid amounts, that is, amounts paid to the government during the year, are tax credits. Such prepaid amounts are often referred to as "refundable credits."

Tax law The tax law is comprised of the Internal Revenue Code, administrative and judicial interpretations, and the committee reports issued by the Congressional committees involved in the legislative process.

Tax matters partner (1) Partner who is designated by the partnership or (2) the gerneral partner having the largest profits interests at the close of the partnership's tax year.

Tax preference items Designated items, such as accelerated depreciation claimed on pre-1987 realty, that increase taxable income to arrive at AMTI. Unlike AMT adjustments, tax preference items do not reverse in later years and reduce AMTI.

Tax research The process of solving a specific tax-related question on the basis of both tax law sources and the specific circumstances surrounding the particular situation.

Tax services Multivolume commentaries on the tax law. Generally these commentaries contain copies of the Internal Revenue Code and the Treasury Regulations. Also included are editorial comments prepared by the publisher of the tax service, current matters, and a cross-reference to various government promulgations and judicial decisions.

Tax shelter Passive activity which may lack economic substance other than creating tax deductions and credits that enable taxpayers to reduce or eliminate the income tax liability from their regular business activities. Section 469 restricts the current use of deductions and credits arising from passive activities.

Tax treaties Bilaterals agreement entered into between two nations which address tax and other matters. Treaties provide for modifications to the basic tax laws involving residents of the two countries (e.g., reductions in the withholding rates).

Tax year The period of time (usually 12 months) selected by a taxpayer to compute their taxable income. The tax year may be a calendar year or a fiscal year. The election is made on the taxpayer's first return and cannot be changed without IRS approval. The tax year may be less than 12 months if it is the taxpayer's first or final return or if the taxpayer is changing accounting periods.

Tax A mandatory assessment levied under the authority of a political entity for the purpose of raising revenue to be used for public or governmental purposes. Such taxes may be levied by the federal, state, or local government.

Taxable income For individuals, taxable income is adjusted gross income reduced by deductions from adjusted gross income.

Taxpayer Compliance Measurement Program (TCMP) A stratified random sample used to select tax returns for audit. The program is intended to test the extent to which taxpayers are in compliance with the law.

Taxpayer-use test A test used to determine whether property is considered similar or related in service or use for purposes of involuntary conversions of property. This test is used by owner-investors (as opposed to owner-users) of property.

Technical Advice Memorandum Such memoranda are administrative interpretations issued in the form of letter ruling. Taxpayers may request them if they need guidance about the tax treatment of complicated technical matters which are being audited.

Temporary differences Items which are included in book income in the current year but which were included in taxable income in the past or will be included in the future. Book income items that are nontaxable in the current year even though they were taxed in the past or will be taxed in the future and book expenses that are not currently deductible even though that status was different in the past or will be different in the future are categorized as temporary differences.

Tentative minimum tax (TMT) Tax calculated by (1) multiplying 20% times the corporation's alternative minimum taxable income less a statutory exemption amount and (2) deducting allowable foreign tax credits.

Term certain interest A person holding such an interest has a right to receive income from property for a specified term, but does not own or hold title to such property. The property reverts to the grantor at the end of the term.

Terminable interest A property interest that ends when (1) some event occurs (or fails to occur) or (2) a specified amount of time passes.

Testamentary gift Transfer of property made at the death of the donor (i.e., bequests, devises, and inheritances).

Testamentary transfers A transferor's control or enjoyment of a property ceases at death.

Testamentary trust Trust created under the direction of a decedent's will and funded by the decedent's estate.

Testamentary Of, pertaining to, or of the nature of a testament or will.

Thirty-day letter A report sent to the taxpayer if the taxpayer does not sign Form 870 (Waiver of Statutory Notice) concerning any additional taxes assessed. The letter details the proposed changes and advises the taxpayer of his right to pursue the matter with the Appeals Office. The taxpayer then has 30 days in which to request a conference.

Throwback dividends For accumulated earnings tax and personal holding company tax purposes, these are distributions made out of current or accumulated earnings and profits in the first two and one-half months after the close of the tax year.

Tier-1 beneficiary Beneficiary to whom a distribution must be made.

Tier-2 beneficiary Beneficiary who receives a discretionary distribution.

Total economic income The amount of the taxpayer's income, including exclusions and deductions from the tax base (e.g., tax-exempt bonds), is categorized as total economic income.

Transferor corporation The corporation that transfers its assets as part of a reorganization. May also be known as acquired or target corporation.

Transportation expense The deductibility of this type of expense depends upon whether it is trade- or business-related, whether it is related to the production of income, whether the expense is employment related and therefore subject to the 2% nondeductible floor for miscellaneous itemized deductions. Commuting expenses are nondeductible. See also Travel expense.

Travel expense Such expenses include transportation, meals, and lodging incurred in the pursuit of a trade, business, or employment-related activity. There are limitations and restrictions on the deductibility of these expenses. See also Transportation expense.

Triangular reorganization A type of reorganization (i.e., Type A, B, or C) where the parent corporation uses a subsidiary corporation to serve as the acquiring corporation. See triangular merger.

Trustee An individual or institution which administers a trust for the benefit of a beneficiary.

Trustor The grantor or transferor of a trust.

Type A reorganization Type of corporate reorganization that meets the requirements of state or federal law, may take the form of a consolidation, a merger, a triangular merger, or a reverse triangular merger.

Type B reorganization Reorganization characterized by a stock-for-stock exchange. The target corporation remains in existence as a subsidiary of the acquiring corporation.

Type C reorganization A transaction that requires the acquiring corporation to obtain substantially all of the target corporation's assets in exchange for its voting stock and a limited amount of other consideration. The target corporation is generally liquidated.

Type D reorganization This type of reorganization may be either acquisitive or divisive. In the former, substantially all of the transferor corporation's assets (and possibly some or all of its liabilities) are acquired by a controlled corporation. The target corporation is liquidated. The latter involves the acquisition of the part or all of the transferor corporation's assets (and liabilities) by a controlled subsidiary corporation(s). The transferor corporation may either remain in existence or be liquidated.

Type E reorganization This type of reorganization changes the capital structure of a corporation. The corporation remains in existence.

Type F reorganization The old corporation's assets or stock are transferred to a single newly formed corporation in this type of transaction. The "old" corporation is liquidated.

Type G reorganization This type of reorganization may be either acquisitive or divisive. In either case, part or all of the target or transferor corporation's assets (and possibly some or all of its liabilities) are transferred to another corporation as part of a bankruptcy proceeding. The target or transferor corporation may either remain in existence or be liquidated.

Unfunded deferred compensation plan This type of plan is used for highly-compensated employees who wish to defer the recognition of income until future periods. Funding is generally accomplished through an escrow account for the employee's benefit.

Unified credit The unified credit enables a tax base of a certain size (i.e., the exemption equivalent) to be completely free of transfer taxes. This credit is phased out for tax bases in excess of $10,500,000 if the decedent dies after 1987. It may only be subtracted once against all of a person's transfers—throughout one's lifetime and at death. See exemption equivalent.

Unified rate schedule Progressive rate schedule for estate and gift taxes. These rates are effective for gifts made after 1976 and deaths occurring after 1976.

Unrealized receivable Right to payment for goods and services that has not been included in the owner's income because of its method of accounting.

Unreported decisions District court decisions that are not reported in official reporters. Such decisions may be reported in secondary reporters that report only tax-related cases.

Vertical equity A concept in taxation that provides that the incidence of taxation should be borne by taxpayers who have the ability to pay the tax. Taxpayers who are not similarly-situated should be treated differently under the tax law.

Voting trust An arrangement whereby the stock owned by a number of shareholders is placed under the control of a trustee for purposes of exercising the voting rights possessed by the stock. This practice increases the voting power of the minority shareholders.

Wash sale A wash sale results when the taxpayer (1) sells stock or securities and (2) purchases substantially identical stock or securities within the 61-day period extending from 30 days before the date of sale to 30 days after the date of sale.

Wealth transfer taxes Estate taxes (i.e., the tax on dispositions of property that occur as a result of the transferor's death) and gift taxes (i.e., the tax on lifetime transfers) are wealth transfer taxes.

Writ of certiorari A petition to the U.S. Supreme court to request that the Court agree to hear a case. A writ of certiorari is requested by the party (IRS or taxpayer) that lost at the Court of Appeals level.

APPENDIX E

AICPA STATEMENTS ON STANDARDS FOR TAX SERVICES NOS. 1–8 (AUGUST 2000)

PREFACE

1. Practice standards are the hallmark of calling one's self a professional. Members should fulfill their responsibilities as professionals by instituting and maintaining standards against which their professional performance can be measured. Compliance with professional standards of tax practice also confirms the public's awareness of the professionalism that is associated with CPAs as well as the AICPA.

2. This publication sets forth ethical tax practice standards for members of the AICPA: Statements on Standards for Tax Services (SSTSs or Statements). Although other standards of tax practice exist, most notably Treasury Department Circular No. 230 and penalty provisions of the Internal Revenue Code (IRC), those standards are limited in that (1) Circular No. 230 does not provide the depth of guidance contained in these Statements, (2) the IRC penalty provisions apply only to income-tax return preparation, and (3) both Circular No. 230 and the penalty provisions apply only to federal tax practice.

3. The SSTSs have been written in as simple and objective a manner as possible. However, by their nature, ethical standards provide for an appropriate range of behavior that recognizes the need for interpretations to meet a broad range of personal and professional situations. The SSTSs recognize this need by, in some sections, providing relatively subjective rules and by leaving certain terms undefined. These terms and concepts are generally rooted in tax concepts, and therefore should be readily understood by tax practitioners. It is, therefore, recognized that the enforcement of these rules, as part of the AICPA's Code of Professional Conduct Rule 201, General Standards, and Rule 202, Compliance With Standards, will be undertaken with flexibility in mind and handled on a case-by-case basis. Members are expected to comply with them.

HISTORY

4. The SSTSs have their origin in the Statements on Responsibilities in Tax Practice (SRTPs), which provided a body of advisory opinions on good tax practice. The guidelines as originally set forth in the SRTPs had come to play a much more important role than most members realized. The courts, Internal Revenue Service, state accountancy boards, and other professional organizations recognized and relied on the SRTPs as the appropriate articulation of professional conduct in a CPA's tax practice. The SRTPs, in and of themselves, had become de facto enforceable standards of professional practice, because state disciplinary organizations and malpractice cases in effect regularly held CPAs accountable for failure to follow the SRTPs when their professional practice conduct failed to meet the prescribed guidelines of conduct.

5. The AICPA's Tax Executive Committee concluded that appropriate action entailed issuance of tax practice standards that would become a part of the Institute's Code of Professional Conduct. At its July 1999 meeting, the AICPA Board of Directors approved support of the executive committee's initiative and placed the matter on the agenda of the October 1999 meeting of the Institute's governing Council. On October 19, 1999, Council approved designating the Tax Executive Committee as a standard-setting body, thus authorizing that committee to promulgate standards of tax practice. These SSTSs, largely mirroring the SRTPs, are the result.

6. The SRTPs were originally issued between 1964 and 1977. The first nine SRTPs and the Introduction were codified in 1976; the tenth SRTP was issued in 1977. The original SRTPs concerning the CPA's responsibility to sign the return (SRTPs No. 1, *Signature of Preparers*, and No. 2, *Signature of Reviewer: Assumption of Preparer's Responsibility*) were withdrawn in 1982 after Treasury Department regulations were issued adopt-

ing substantially the same standards for all tax return preparers. The sixth and seventh SRTPs, concerning the responsibility of a CPA who becomes aware of an error, were revised in 1991. The first Interpretation of the SRTPs, Interpretation 1-1, "Realistic Possibility Standard," was approved in December 1990. The SSTSs and Interpretation supersede and replace the SRTPs and their Interpretation 1-1 effective October 31, 2000. Although the number and names of the SSTSs, and the substance of the rules contained in each of them, remain the same as in the SRTPs, the language has been edited to both clarify and reflect the enforceable nature of the SSTSs. In addition, because the applicability of these standards is not limited to federal income-tax practice, the language has been changed to mirror the broader scope.

ONGOING PROCESS

7. The following Statements on Standards for Tax Services and Interpretation 1-1 to Statement No. 1, "Realistic Possibility Standard," reflect the AICPA's standards of tax practice and delineate members' responsibilities to taxpayers, the public, the government, and the profession. The Statements are intended to be part of an ongoing process that may require changes to and interpretations of current SSTSs in recognition of the accelerating rate of change in tax laws and the continued importance of tax practice to members.

8. The Tax Executive Committee promulgates SSTSs. Even though the 1999-2000 Tax Executive Committee approved this version, acknowledgement is also due to the many members whose efforts over the years went into the development of the original statements.

STATEMENT ON STANDARDS FOR TAX SERVICES NO. 1, TAX RETURN POSITIONS

INTRODUCTION

1. This Statement sets forth the applicable standards for members when recommending tax return positions and preparing or signing tax returns (including amended returns, claims for refund, and information returns) filed with any taxing authority. For purposes of these standards, a *tax return position* is (*a*) a position reflected on the tax return as to which the taxpayer has been specifically advised by a member or (*b*) a position about which a member has knowledge of all material facts and, on the basis of those facts, has concluded whether the position is appropriate. For purposes of these standards, a *taxpayer* is a client, a member's employer, or any other third-party recipient of tax services.

STATEMENT

2. The following standards apply to a member when providing professional services that involve tax return positions:

a. A member should not recommend that a tax return position be taken with respect to any item unless the member has a good-faith belief that the position has a realistic possibility of being sustained administratively or judicially on its merits if challenged.

b. A member should not prepare or sign a return that the member is aware takes a position that the member may not recommend under the standard expressed in paragraph *2a*.

c. Notwithstanding paragraph *2a*, a member may recommend a tax return position that the member concludes is not frivolous as long as the member advises the taxpayer to appropriately disclose. Notwithstanding paragraph *2b*, the member may prepare or sign a return that reflects a position that the member concludes is not frivolous as long as the position is appropriately disclosed.

d. When recommending tax return positions and when preparing or signing a return on which a tax return position is taken, a member should, when relevant, advise the taxpayer regarding potential penalty consequences of such tax return position and the opportunity, if any, to avoid such penalties through disclosure.

3. A member should not recommend a tax return position or prepare or sign a return reflecting a position that the member knows—

a. Exploits the audit selection process of a taxing authority.

b. Serves as a mere arguing position advanced solely to obtain leverage in the bargaining process of settlement negotiation with a taxing authority.

4. When recommending a tax return position, a member has both the right and responsibility to be an advocate for the taxpayer with respect to any position satisfying the aforementioned standards.

EXPLANATION

5. Our self-assessment tax system can function effectively only if taxpayers file tax returns that are true, correct, and complete. A tax return is primarily a taxpayer's representation of facts, and the taxpayer has the final responsibility for positions taken on the return.

6. In addition to a duty to the taxpayer, a member has a duty to the tax system. However, it is well established that the taxpayer has no obligation to pay more taxes than are legally owed, and a member has a duty to the taxpayer to assist in achieving that result. The standards contained in paragraphs 2, 3, and 4 recognize the members' responsibilities to both taxpayers and to the tax system.

7. In order to meet the standards contained in paragraph 2, a member should in good faith believe that the tax return position is warranted in existing law or can be supported by a good-faith argument for an extension, modification, or reversal of existing law. For example, in reaching such a conclusion, a member may consider a well-reasoned construction of the applicable statute, well-reasoned articles or treatises, or pronouncements issued by the applicable taxing authority, regardless of whether such sources would be treated as *authority* under Internal Revenue

Code section 6662 and the regulations thereunder. A position would not fail to meet these standards merely because it is later abandoned for practical or procedural considerations during an administrative hearing or in the litigation process.

8. If a member has a good-faith belief that more than one tax return position meets the standards set forth in paragraph 2, a member's advice concerning alternative acceptable positions may include a discussion of the likelihood that each such position might or might not cause the taxpayer's tax return to be examined and whether the position would be challenged in an examination. In such circumstances, such advice is not a violation of paragraph *3a*.

9. In some cases, a member may conclude that a tax return position is not warranted under the standard set forth in paragraph *2a*. A taxpayer may, however, still wish to take such a position. Under such circumstances, the taxpayer should have the opportunity to take such a position, and the member may prepare and sign the return provided the position is appropriately disclosed on the return or claim for refund and the position is not frivolous. A frivolous position is one that is knowingly advanced in bad faith and is patently improper.

10. A member's determination of whether information is appropriately disclosed by the taxpayer should be based on the facts and circumstances of the particular case and the authorities regarding disclosure in the applicable taxing jurisdiction. If a member recommending a position, but not engaged to prepare or sign the related tax return, advises the taxpayer concerning appropriate disclosure of the position, then the member shall be deemed to meet these standards.

11. If particular facts and circumstances lead a member to believe that a taxpayer penalty might be asserted, the member should so advise the taxpayer and should discuss with the taxpayer the opportunity to avoid such penalty by disclosing the position on the tax return. Although a member should advise the taxpayer with respect to disclosure, it is the taxpayer's responsibility to decide whether and how to disclose.

12. For purposes of this Statement, preparation of a tax return includes giving advice on events that have occurred at the time the advice is given if the advice is directly relevant to determining the existence, character, or amount of a schedule, entry, or other portion of a tax return.

INTERPRETATION NO. 1-1, "REALISTIC POSSIBILITY STANDARD" OF STATEMENT ON STANDARDS FOR TAX SERVICES NO. 1, TAX RETURN POSITIONS

BACKGROUND

1. Statement on Standards for Tax Services (SSTS) No. 1, *Tax Return Positions,* contains the standards a member should follow in recommending tax return positions and in preparing or signing tax returns. In general, a member should have a good-faith belief that the tax return position being recommended has a realistic possibility of being sustained administratively or judicially on its merits, if challenged. The standard contained in SSTS No. 1, paragraph *2a*, is referred to here as the realistic possibility standard. If a member concludes that a tax return position does not meet the realistic possibility standard:

a. The member may still recommend the position to the taxpayer if the position is not frivolous, and the member recommends appropriate disclosure of the position; or

b. The member may still prepare or sign a tax return containing the position, if the position is not frivolous, and the position is appropriately disclosed.

2. A *frivolous position* is one that is knowingly advanced in bad faith and is patently improper (see SSTS No. 1, paragraph 9). A member's determination of whether information is appropriately disclosed on a tax return or claim for refund is based on the facts and circumstances of the particular case and the authorities regarding disclosure in the applicable jurisdiction (see SSTS No. 1, paragraph 10).

3. If a member believes there is a possibility that a tax return position might result in penalties being asserted against a taxpayer, the member should so advise the taxpayer and should discuss with the taxpayer the opportunity, if any, of avoiding such penalties through disclosure (see SSTS No. 1, paragraph 11). Such advice may be given orally.

GENERAL INTERPRETATION

4. To meet the realistic possibility standard, a member should have a good-faith belief that the position is warranted by existing law or can be supported by a good-faith argument for an extension, modification, or reversal of the existing law through the administrative or judicial process. Such a belief should be based on reasonable interpretations of the tax law. A member should not take into account the likelihood of audit or detection when determining whether this standard has been met (see SSTS No. 1, paragraphs *3a* and 8).

5. The realistic possibility standard is less stringent than the substantial authority standard and the more likely than not standard that apply under the Internal Revenue Code (IRC) to substantial understatements of liability by taxpayers. The realistic possibility standard is stricter than the reasonable basis standard that is in the IRC.

6. In determining whether a tax return position meets the realistic possibility standard, a member may rely on authorities in addition to those evaluated when determining whether substantial authority exists under IRC section 6662. Accordingly, a member may rely on well-reasoned treatises, articles in recognized professional tax publications, and other reference tools and sources of tax analyses commonly used by tax advisers and preparers of returns.

7. In determining whether a realistic possibility exists, a member should do all of the following:

- Establish relevant background facts
- Distill the appropriate questions from those facts
- Search for authoritative answers to those questions

- Resolve the questions by weighing the authorities uncovered by that search
- Arrive at a conclusion supported by the authorities

8. A member should consider the weight of each authority to conclude whether a position meets the realistic possibility standard. In determining the weight of an authority, a member should consider its persuasiveness, relevance, and source. Thus, the type of authority is a significant factor. Other important factors include whether the facts stated by the authority are distinguishable from those of the taxpayer and whether the authority contains an analysis of the issue or merely states a conclusion.

9. The realistic possibility standard may be met despite the absence of certain types of authority. For example, a member may conclude that the realistic possibility standard has been met when the position is supported only by a well-reasoned construction of the applicable statutory provision.

10. In determining whether the realistic possibility standard has been met, the extent of research required is left to the professional judgment of the member with respect to all the facts and circumstances known to the member. A member may conclude that more than one position meets the realistic possibility standard.

SPECIFIC ILLUSTRATIONS

11. The following illustrations deal with general fact patterns. Accordingly, the application of the guidance discussed in the General Interpretation section to variations in such general facts or to particular facts or circumstances may lead to different conclusions. In each illustration there is no authority other than that indicated.

12. *Illustration 1.* A taxpayer has engaged in a transaction that is adversely affected by a new statutory provision. Prior law supports a position favorable to the taxpayer. The taxpayer believes, and the member concurs, that the new statute is inequitable as applied to the taxpayer's situation. The statute is constitutional, clearly drafted, and unambiguous. The legislative history discussing the new statute contains general comments that do not specifically address the taxpayer's situation.

13. *Conclusion.* The member should recommend the return position supported by the new statute. A position contrary to a constitutional, clear, and unambiguous statute would ordinarily be considered a frivolous position.

14. *Illustration 2.* The facts are the same as in illustration 1 except that the legislative history discussing the new statute specifically addresses the taxpayer's situation and supports a position favorable to the taxpayer.

15. *Conclusion.* In a case where the statute is clearly and unambiguously against the taxpayer's position but a contrary position exists based on legislative history specifically addressing the taxpayer's situation, a return position based either on the statutory language or on the legislative history satisfies the realistic possibility standard.

16. *Illustration 3.* The facts are the same as in illustration 1 except that the legislative history can be interpreted to provide some evidence or authority in support of the taxpayer's position; however, the legislative history does not specifically address the situation.

17. *Conclusion.* In a case where the statute is clear and unambiguous, a contrary position based on an interpretation of the legislative history that does not explicitly address the taxpayer's situation does not meet the realistic possibility standard. However, because the legislative history provides some support or evidence for the taxpayer's position, such a return position is not frivolous. A member may recommend the position to the taxpayer if the member also recommends appropriate disclosure.

18. *Illustration 4.* A taxpayer is faced with an issue involving the interpretation of a new statute. Following its passage, the statute was widely recognized to contain a drafting error, and a technical correction proposal has been introduced. The taxing authority issues a pronouncement indicating how it will administer the provision. The pronouncement interprets the statute in accordance with the proposed technical correction.

19. *Conclusion.* Return positions based on either the existing statutory language or the taxing authority pronouncement satisfy the realistic possibility standard.

20. *Illustration 5.* The facts are the same as in illustration 4 except that no taxing authority pronouncement has been issued.

21. *Conclusion.* In the absence of a taxing authority pronouncement interpreting the statute in accordance with the technical correction, only a return position based on the existing statutory language will meet the realistic possibility standard. A return position based on the proposed technical correction may be recommended if it is appropriately disclosed, since it is not frivolous.

22. *Illustration 6.* A taxpayer is seeking advice from a member regarding a recently amended statute. The member has reviewed the statute, the legislative history that specifically addresses the issue, and a recently published notice issued by the taxing authority. The member has concluded in good faith that, based on the statute and the legislative history, the taxing authority's position as stated in the notice does not reflect legislative intent.

23. *Conclusion.* The member may recommend the position supported by the statute and the legislative history because it meets the realistic possibility standard.

24. *Illustration 7.* The facts are the same as in illustration 6 except that the taxing authority pronouncement is a temporary regulation.

25. *Conclusion.* In determining whether the position meets the realistic possibility standard, a member should determine the weight to be given the regulation by analyzing factors such as whether the regulation is legislative or interpretative, or if it is inconsistent with the statute. If a member concludes that the position does not meet the realistic possibility standard, because it is not frivolous, the position may nevertheless be recommended if the member also recommends appropriate disclosure.

26. *Illustration 8.* A tax form published by a taxing authority is incorrect, but completion of the form as published provides a benefit to the taxpayer. The member knows that the taxing authority has published an announcement acknowledging the error.

27. *Conclusion.* In these circumstances, a return position in accordance with the published form is a frivolous position.

28. *Illustration 9.* A taxpayer wants to take a position that a member has concluded is frivolous. The taxpayer maintains that even if the taxing authority examines the return, the issue will not be raised.

29. *Conclusion.* The member should not consider the likelihood of audit or detection when determining whether the realistic possibility standard has been met. The member should not prepare or sign a return that contains a frivolous position even if it is disclosed.

30. *Illustration 10.* A statute is passed requiring the capitalization of certain expenditures. The taxpayer believes, and the member concurs, that to comply fully, the taxpayer will need to acquire new computer hardware and software and implement a number of new accounting procedures. The taxpayer and member agree that the costs of full compliance will be significantly greater than the resulting increase in tax due under the new provision. Because of these cost considerations, the taxpayer makes no effort to comply. The taxpayer wants the member to prepare and sign a return on which the new requirement is simply ignored.

31. *Conclusion.* The return position desired by the taxpayer is frivolous, and the member should neither prepare nor sign the return.

32. *Illustration 11.* The facts are the same as in illustration 10 except that a taxpayer has made a good-faith effort to comply with the law by calculating an estimate of expenditures to be capitalized under the new provision.

33. *Conclusion.* In this situation, the realistic possibility standard has been met. When using estimates in the preparation of a return, a member should refer to SSTS No. 4, *Use of Estimates.*

34. *Illustration 12.* On a given issue, a member has located and weighed two authorities concerning the treatment of a particular expenditure. A taxing authority has issued an administrative ruling that required the expenditure to be capitalized and amortized over several years. On the other hand, a court opinion permitted the current deduction of the expenditure. The member has concluded that these are the relevant authorities, considered the source of both authorities, and concluded that both are persuasive and relevant.

35. *Conclusion.* The realistic possibility standard is met by either position.

36. *Illustration 13.* A tax statute is silent on the treatment of an item under the statute. However, the legislative history explaining the statute directs the taxing authority to issue regulations that will require a specific treatment of the item. No regulations have been issued at the time the member must recommend a position on the tax treatment of the item.

37. *Conclusion.* The member may recommend the position supported by the legislative history because it meets the realistic possibility standard.

38. *Illustration 14.* A taxpayer wants to take a position that a member concludes meets the realistic possibility standard based on an assumption regarding an underlying nontax legal issue. The member recommends that the taxpayer seek advice from its legal counsel, and the taxpayer's attorney gives an opinion on the nontax legal issue.

39. *Conclusion.* A member may in general rely on a legal opinion on a nontax legal issue. A member should, however, use professional judgment when relying on a legal opinion. If, on its face, the opinion of the taxpayer's attorney appears to be unreasonable, unsubstantiated, or unwarranted, a member should consult his or her attorney before relying on the opinion.

40. *Illustration 15.* A taxpayer has obtained from its attorney an opinion on the tax treatment of an item and requests that a member rely on the opinion.

41. *Conclusion.* The authorities on which a member may rely include well-reasoned sources of tax analysis. If a member is satisfied about the source, relevance, and persuasiveness of the legal opinion, a member may rely on that opinion when determining whether the realistic possibility standard has been met.

STATEMENT ON STANDARDS FOR TAX SERVICES NO. 2, ANSWERS TO QUESTIONS ON RETURNS

INTRODUCTION

1. This Statement sets forth the applicable standards for members when signing the preparer's declaration on a tax return if one or more questions on the return have not been answered. The term *questions* includes requests for information on the return, in the instructions, or in the regulations, whether or not stated in the form of a question.

STATEMENT

2. A member should make a reasonable effort to obtain from the taxpayer the information necessary to provide appropriate answers to all questions on a tax return before signing as preparer.

EXPLANATION

3. It is recognized that the questions on tax returns are not of uniform importance, and often they are not applicable to the particular taxpayer. Nevertheless, there are at least two reasons why a member should be satisfied that a reasonable effort has been made to obtain information to provide appropriate answers to the questions on the return that are applicable to a taxpayer.

a. A question may be of importance in determining taxable income or loss, or the tax liability shown on the return, in which circumstance an omission may detract from the quality of the return.

b. A member often must sign a preparer's declaration stating that the return is true, correct, and complete.

4. Reasonable grounds may exist for omitting an answer to a question applicable to a taxpayer. For example, reasonable grounds may include the following:

a. The information is not readily available and the answer is not significant in terms of taxable income or loss, or the tax liability shown on the return.

b. Genuine uncertainty exists regarding the meaning of the question in relation to the particular return.

c. The answer to the question is voluminous; in such cases, a statement should be made on the return that the data will be supplied upon examination.

5. A member should not omit an answer merely because it might prove disadvantageous to a taxpayer.

6. If reasonable grounds exist for omission of an answer to an applicable question, a taxpayer is not required to provide on the return an explanation of the reason for the omission. In this connection, a member should consider whether the omission of an answer to a question may cause the return to be deemed incomplete.

STATEMENT ON STANDARDS FOR TAX SERVICES NO. 3, CERTAIN PROCEDURAL ASPECTS OF PREPARING RETURNS

INTRODUCTION

1. This Statement sets forth the applicable standards for members concerning the obligation to examine or verify certain supporting data or to consider information related to another taxpayer when preparing a taxpayer's tax return.

STATEMENT

2. In preparing or signing a return, a member may in good faith rely, without verification, on information furnished by the taxpayer or by third parties. However, a member should not ignore the implications of information furnished and should make reasonable inquiries if the information furnished appears to be incorrect, incomplete, or inconsistent either on its face or on the basis of other facts known to a member. Further, a member should refer to the taxpayer's returns for one or more prior years whenever feasible.

3. If the tax law or regulations impose a condition with respect to deductibility or other tax treatment of an item, such as taxpayer maintenance of books and records or substantiating documentation to support the reported deduction or tax treatment, a member should make appropriate inquiries to determine to the member's satisfaction whether such condition has been met.

4. When preparing a tax return, a member should consider information actually known to that member from the tax return of another taxpayer if the information is relevant to that tax return and its consideration is necessary to properly prepare that tax return. In using such information, a member should consider any limitations imposed by any law or rule relating to confidentiality.

EXPLANATION

5. The preparer's declaration on a tax return often states that the information contained therein is true, correct, and complete to the best of the preparer's knowledge and belief based on all information known by the preparer. This type of reference should be understood to include information furnished by the taxpayer or by third parties to a member in connection with the preparation of the return.

6. The preparer's declaration does not require a member to examine or verify supporting data. However, a distinction should be made between (*a*) the need either to determine by inquiry that a specifically required condition, such as maintaining books and records or substantiating documentation, has been satisfied or to obtain information when the material furnished appears to be incorrect or incomplete and (*b*) the need for a member to examine underlying information. In fulfilling his or her obligation to exercise due diligence in preparing a return, a member may rely on information furnished by the taxpayer unless it appears to be incorrect, incomplete, or inconsistent. Although a member has certain responsibilities in exercising due diligence in preparing a return, the taxpayer has the ultimate responsibility for the contents of the return. Thus, if the taxpayer presents unsupported data in the form of lists of tax information, such as dividends and interest received, charitable contributions, and medical expenses, such information may be used in the preparation of a tax return without verification unless it appears to be incorrect, incomplete, or inconsistent either on its face or on the basis of other facts known to a member.

7. Even though there is no requirement to examine underlying documentation, a member should encourage the taxpayer to provide supporting data where appropriate. For example, a member should encourage the taxpayer to submit underlying documents for use in tax return preparation to permit full consideration of income and deductions arising from security transactions and from pass-through entities, such as estates, trusts, partnerships, and S corporations.

8. The source of information provided to a member by a taxpayer for use in preparing the return is often a pass-through entity, such as a limited partnership, in which the taxpayer has an interest but is not involved in management. A member may accept the information provided by the pass-through entity without further inquiry, unless there is reason to believe it is incorrect, incomplete, or inconsistent, either on its face or on the basis of other facts known to the member. In some instances, it may be appropriate for a member to advise the taxpayer to ascertain the nature and amount of possible exposure to tax deficiencies, interest, and penalties, by contact with management of the pass-through entity.

9. A member should make use of a taxpayer's returns for one or more prior years in preparing the current return whenever feasible. Reference to prior returns and discussion of prior-year tax determinations with the taxpayer should provide information to determine the taxpayer's general tax status, avoid the omission or duplication of items, and afford a basis for the treatment of similar or related transactions. As with the examination

of information supplied for the current year's return, the extent of comparison of the details of income and deduction between years depends on the particular circumstances.

STATEMENT ON STANDARDS FOR TAX SERVICES NO. 4, USE OF ESTIMATES

INTRODUCTION

1. This Statement sets forth the applicable standards for members when using the taxpayer's estimates in the preparation of a tax return. A member may advise on estimates used in the preparation of a tax return, but the taxpayer has the responsibility to provide the estimated data. Appraisals or valuations are not considered estimates for purposes of this Statement.

STATEMENT

2. Unless prohibited by statute or by rule, a member may use the taxpayer's estimates in the preparation of a tax return if it is not practical to obtain exact data and if the member determines that the estimates are reasonable based on the facts and circumstances known to the member. If the taxpayer's estimates are used, they should be presented in a manner that does not imply greater accuracy than exists.

EXPLANATION

3. Accounting requires the exercise of professional judgment and, in many instances, the use of approximations based on judgment. The application of such accounting judgments, as long as not in conflict with methods set forth by a taxing authority, is acceptable. These judgments are not estimates within the purview of this Statement. For example, a federal income tax regulation provides that if all other conditions for accrual are met, the exact amount of income or expense need not be known or ascertained at year end if the amount can be determined with reasonable accuracy.

4. When the taxpayer's records do not accurately reflect information related to small expenditures, accuracy in recording some data may be difficult to achieve. Therefore, the use of estimates by a taxpayer in determining the amount to be deducted for such items may be appropriate.

5. When records are missing or precise information about a transaction is not available at the time the return must be filed, a member may prepare a tax return using a taxpayer's estimates of the missing data.

6. Estimated amounts should not be presented in a manner that provides a misleading impression about the degree of factual accuracy.

7. Specific disclosure that an estimate is used for an item in the return is not generally required; however, such disclosure should be made in unusual circumstances where nondisclosure might mislead the taxing authority regarding the degree of accuracy of the return as a whole. Some examples of unusual circumstances include the following:

a. A taxpayer has died or is ill at the time the return must be filed.

b. A taxpayer has not received a Schedule K-1 for a pass-through entity at the time the tax return is to be filed.

c. There is litigation pending (for example, a bankruptcy proceeding) that bears on the return.

d. Fire or computer failure has destroyed the relevant records.

STATEMENT ON STANDARDS FOR TAX SERVICES NO. 5, DEPARTURE FROM A POSITION PREVIOUSLY CONCLUDED IN AN ADMINISTRATIVE PROCEEDING OR COURT DECISION

INTRODUCTION

1. This Statement sets forth the applicable standards for members in recommending a tax return position that departs from the position determined in an administrative proceeding or in a court decision with respect to the taxpayer's prior return.

2. For purposes of this Statement, *administrative proceeding* also includes an examination by a taxing authority or an appeals conference relating to a return or a claim for refund.

3. For purposes of this Statement, *court decision* means a decision by any court having jurisdiction over tax matters.

STATEMENT

4. The tax return position with respect to an item as determined in an administrative proceeding or court decision does not restrict a member from recommending a different tax position in a later year's return, unless the taxpayer is bound to a specified treatment in the later year, such as by a formal closing agreement. Therefore, as provided in Statement on Standards for Tax Services (SSTS) No. 1, *Tax Return Positions*, the member may recommend a tax return position or prepare or sign a tax return that departs from the treatment of an item as concluded in an administrative proceeding or court decision with respect to a prior return of the taxpayer.

EXPLANATION

5. If an administrative proceeding or court decision has resulted in a determination concerning a specific tax treatment of an item in a prior year's return, a member will usually recommend this

same tax treatment in subsequent years. However, departures from consistent treatment may be justified under such circumstances as the following:

a. Taxing authorities tend to act consistently in the disposition of an item that was the subject of a prior administrative proceeding but generally are not bound to do so. Similarly, a taxpayer is not bound to follow the tax treatment of an item as consented to in an earlier administrative proceeding.

b. The determination in the administrative proceeding or the court's decision may have been caused by a lack of documentation. Supporting data for the later year may be appropriate.

c. A taxpayer may have yielded in the administrative proceeding for settlement purposes or not appealed the court decision, even though the position met the standards in SSTS No. 1.

d. Court decisions, rulings, or other authorities that are more favorable to a taxpayer's current position may have developed since the prior administrative proceeding was concluded or the prior court decision was rendered.

6. The consent in an earlier administrative proceeding and the existence of an unfavorable court decision are factors that the member should consider in evaluating whether the standards in SSTS No. 1 are met.

STATEMENT ON STANDARDS FOR TAX SERVICES NO. 6, KNOWLEDGE OF ERROR: RETURN PREPARATION

INTRODUCTION

1. This Statement sets forth the applicable standards for a member who becomes aware of an error in a taxpayer's previously filed tax return or of a taxpayer's failure to file a required tax return. As used herein, the term error includes any position, omission, or method of accounting that, at the time the return is filed, fails to meet the standards set out in Statement on Standards for Tax Services (SSTS) No. 1, *Tax Return Positions.* The term *error* also includes a position taken on a prior year's return that no longer meets these standards due to legislation, judicial decisions, or administrative pronouncements having retroactive effect. However, an error does not include an item that has an insignificant effect on the taxpayer's tax liability.

2. This Statement applies whether or not the member prepared or signed the return that contains the error.

STATEMENT

3. A member should inform the taxpayer promptly upon becoming aware of an error in a previously filed return or upon becoming aware of a taxpayer's failure to file a required return. A member should recommend the corrective measures to be taken. Such recommendation may be given orally. The member is not obligated to inform the taxing authority, and a member may not do so without the taxpayer's permission, except when required by law.

4. If a member is requested to prepare the current year's return and the taxpayer has not taken appropriate action to correct an error in a prior year's return, the member should consider whether to withdraw from preparing the return and whether to continue a professional or employment relationship with the taxpayer. If the member does prepare such current year's return, the member should take reasonable steps to ensure that the error is not repeated.

EXPLANATION

5. While performing services for a taxpayer, a member may become aware of an error in a previously filed return or may become aware that the taxpayer failed to file a required return. The member should advise the taxpayer of the error and the measures to be taken. Such recommendation may be given orally. If the member believes that the taxpayer could be charged with fraud or other criminal misconduct, the taxpayer should be advised to consult legal counsel before taking any action.

6. It is the taxpayer's responsibility to decide whether to correct the error. If the taxpayer does not correct an error, a member should consider whether to continue a professional or employment relationship with the taxpayer. While recognizing that the taxpayer may not be required by statute to correct an error by filing an amended return, a member should consider whether a taxpayer's decision not to file an amended return may predict future behavior that might require termination of the relationship. The potential for violating Code of Professional Conduct rule 301 (relating to the member's confidential client relationship), the tax law and regulations, or laws on privileged communications, and other considerations may create a conflict between the member's interests and those of the taxpayer. Therefore, a member should consider consulting with his or her own legal counsel before deciding upon recommendations to the taxpayer and whether to continue a professional or employment relationship with the taxpayer.

7. If a member decides to continue a professional or employment relationship with the taxpayer and is requested to prepare a tax return for a year subsequent to that in which the error occurred, the member should take reasonable steps to ensure that the error is not repeated. If the subsequent year's tax return cannot be prepared without perpetuating the error, the member should consider withdrawal from the return preparation. If a member learns that the taxpayer is using an erroneous method of accounting and it is past the due date to request permission to change to a method meeting the standards of SSTS No. 1, the member may sign a tax return for the current year, providing the tax return includes appropriate disclosure of the use of the erroneous method.

8. Whether an error has no more than an insignificant effect on the taxpayer's tax liability is left to the professional judgment of the member based on all the facts and circumstances known to the member. In judging whether an erroneous method of accounting has more than an insignificant effect, a member should consider the method's cumulative effect and its effect on the current year's tax return.

9. If a member becomes aware of the error while performing services for a taxpayer that do not involve tax return preparation, the member's responsibility is to advise the taxpayer of the existence of the error and to recommend that the error be discussed with the taxpayer's tax return preparer. Such recommendation may be given orally.

STATEMENT ON STANDARDS FOR TAX SERVICES NO. 7, KNOWLEDGE OF ERROR: ADMINISTRATIVE PROCEEDINGS

INTRODUCTION

1. This Statement sets forth the applicable standards for a member who becomes aware of an error in a return that is the subject of an administrative proceeding, such as an examination by a taxing authority or an appeals conference. The term *administrative proceeding* does not include a criminal proceeding. As used herein, the term *error* includes any position, omission, or method of accounting that, at the time the return is filed, fails to meet the standards set out in Statement on Standards for Tax Services (SSTS) No. 1, *Tax Return Positions*. The term *error* also includes a position taken on a prior year's return that no longer meets these standards due to legislation, judicial decisions, or administrative pronouncements having retroactive effect. However, an error does not include an item that has an insignificant effect on the taxpayer's tax liability.

2. This Statement applies whether or not the member prepared or signed the return that contains the error. Special considerations may apply when a member has been engaged by legal counsel to provide assistance in a matter relating to the counsel's client.

STATEMENT

3. If a member is representing a taxpayer in an administrative proceeding with respect to a return that contains an error of which the member is aware, the member should inform the taxpayer promptly upon becoming aware of the error. The member should recommend the corrective measures to be taken. Such recommendation may be given orally. A member is neither obligated to inform the taxing authority nor allowed to do so without the taxpayer's permission, except where required by law.

4. A member should request the taxpayer's agreement to disclose the error to the taxing authority. Lacking such agreement, the member should consider whether to withdraw from representing the taxpayer in the administrative proceeding and whether to continue a professional or employment relationship with the taxpayer.

EXPLANATION

5. When the member is engaged to represent the taxpayer before a taxing authority in an administrative proceeding with respect to a return containing an error of which the member is aware, the member should advise the taxpayer to disclose the error to the taxing authority. Such recommendation may be given orally. If the member believes that the taxpayer could be charged with fraud or other criminal misconduct, the taxpayer should be advised to consult legal counsel before taking any action.

6. It is the taxpayer's responsibility to decide whether to correct the error. If the taxpayer does not correct an error, a member should consider whether to withdraw from representing the taxpayer in the administrative proceeding and whether to continue a professional or employment relationship with the taxpayer. While recognizing that the taxpayer may not be required by statute to correct an error by filing an amended return, a member should consider whether a taxpayer's decision not to file an amended return may predict future behavior that might require termination of the relationship. Moreover, a member should consider consulting with his or her own legal counsel before deciding on recommendations to the taxpayer and whether to continue a professional or employment relationship with the taxpayer. The potential for violating Code of Professional Conduct rule 301 (relating to the member's confidential client relationship), the tax law and regulations, laws on privileged communications, potential adverse impact on a taxpayer of a member's withdrawal, and other considerations may create a conflict between the member's interests and those of the taxpayer.

7. Once disclosure is agreed on, it should not be delayed to such a degree that the taxpayer or member might be considered to have failed to act in good faith or to have, in effect, provided misleading information. In any event, disclosure should be made before the conclusion of the administrative proceeding.

8. Whether an error has an insignificant effect on the taxpayer's tax liability is left to the professional judgment of the member based on all the facts and circumstances known to the member. In judging whether an erroneous method of accounting has more than an insignificant effect, a member should consider the method's cumulative effect and its effect on the return that is the subject of the administrative proceeding.

STATEMENT ON STANDARDS FOR TAX SERVICES NO. 8, FORM AND CONTENT OF ADVICE TO TAXPAYERS

INTRODUCTION

1. This Statement sets forth the applicable standards for members concerning certain aspects of providing advice to a taxpayer and considers the circumstances in which a member has a responsibility to communicate with a taxpayer when subsequent

developments affect advice previously provided. The Statement does not, however, cover a member's responsibilities when the expectation is that the advice rendered is likely to be relied on by parties other than the taxpayer.

STATEMENT

2. A member should use judgment to ensure that tax advice provided to a taxpayer reflects professional competence and appropriately serves the taxpayer's needs. A member is not required to follow a standard format or guidelines in communicating written or oral advice to a taxpayer.

3. A member should assume that tax advice provided to a taxpayer will affect the manner in which the matters or transactions considered would be reported on the taxpayer's tax returns. Thus, for all tax advice given to a taxpayer, a member should follow the standards in Statement on Standards for Tax Services (SSTS) No. 1, *Tax Return Positions*.

4. A member has no obligation to communicate with a taxpayer when subsequent developments affect advice previously provided with respect to significant matters, except while assisting a taxpayer in implementing procedures or plans associated with the advice provided or when a member undertakes this obligation by specific agreement.

EXPLANATION

5. Tax advice is recognized as a valuable service provided by members. The form of advice may be oral or written and the subject matter may range from routine to complex. Because the range of advice is so extensive and because advice should meet the specific needs of a taxpayer, neither a standard format nor guidelines for communicating or documenting advice to the taxpayer can be established to cover all situations.

6. Although oral advice may serve a taxpayer's needs appropriately in routine matters or in well-defined areas, written communications are recommended in important, unusual, or complicated transactions. The member may use professional judgment about whether, subsequently, to document oral advice in writing.

7. In deciding on the form of advice provided to a taxpayer, a member should exercise professional judgment and should consider such factors as the following:

a. The importance of the transaction and amounts involved
b. The specific or general nature of the taxpayer's inquiry
c. The time available for development and submission of the advice
d. The technical complications presented
e. The existence of authorities and precedents
f. The tax sophistication of the taxpayer
g. The need to seek other professional advice

8. A member may assist a taxpayer in implementing procedures or plans associated with the advice offered. When providing such assistance, the member should review and revise such advice as warranted by new developments and factors affecting the transaction.

9. Sometimes a member is requested to provide tax advice but does not assist in implementing the plans adopted. Although such developments as legislative or administrative changes or future judicial interpretations may affect the advice previously provided, a member cannot be expected to communicate subsequent developments that affect such advice unless the member undertakes this obligation by specific agreement with the taxpayer.

10. Taxpayers should be informed that advice reflects professional judgment based on an existing situation and that subsequent developments could affect previous professional advice. Members may use precautionary language to the effect that their advice is based on facts as stated and authorities that are subject to change.

11. In providing tax advice, a member should be cognizant of applicable confidentiality privileges.

These Statements on Standards for Tax Services and Interpretation were unanimously adopted by the assenting votes of the twenty voting members of the twenty-one-member Tax Executive Committee.

Tax Executive Committee (1999–2000)

David A. Lifson, *Chair*
Pamela J. Pecarich, *Vice Chair*
Ward M. Bukofsky
Joseph Cammarata
Stephen R. Corrick
Anna C. Fowler
Jill Gansler
Diane P. Ilerndon
Ronald S. Katch
Allan I. Kruger
Susan W. Martin
Jeffrey A. Porter
Thomas J. Purcell, III
Jeffrey L. Raymon
Frederick II. Rothman
Barry D. Roy
Jane T. Rubin
Douglas P. Stives
Philip J. Wiesner
Claude R. Wilson, Jr.
Robert A. Zarzar

SRTP Enforceability Task Force

J. Edward Swails, *Chair*
Alan R. Einhorn
John C. Gardner
Ronald S. Katch
Michael E. Mares
Dan L. Mendelson
Daniel A. Noakes
William C. Potter

AICPA Staff

Gerald W. Padwe
Vice President
Taxation

Edward S. Karl
Director
Taxation

The AICPA gratefully acknowledges the contributions of William A. Tate, Jean L. Rothbarth, and Leonard Podolin, former chairs of the Responsibilities in Tax Practice Committee; A. M. (Tony) Komlyn and Wilber Van Scoik, former members of the Committee; and Carol B. Ferguson, AICPA Technical Manager.

Note: *Statements on Standards for Tax Services are issued by the Tax Executive Committee, the senior technical body of the Institute designated to promulgate standards of tax practice. Rules 201 and 202 of the Institute's Code of Professional Conduct require compliance with these standards.*

APPENDIX F

COMPARISON OF TAX ATTRIBUTES FOR C CORPORATIONS, PARTNERSHIPS, AND S CORPORATIONS

APPENDIX F: COMPARISON OF TAX ATTRIBUTES FOR C CORPORATIONS, PARTNERSHIPS, AND S CORPORATIONS

Tax Attribute	C Corporation	Partnership	S Corporation
I. General Characteristics			
Application of the separate entity versus conduit (flow through) concept.	*Entity:* The corporation is treated as a separate taxpaying entity. If the corporation distributes income to shareholders in the form of dividends, the shareholders are subject to a second tax on such amounts. Shareholders also are subject to a second tax if they sell their stock.	*Conduit:* The partners report their distributive share of partnership ordinary income and separately stated items on their tax returns. Most elections, such as depreciation methods, accounting period and methods, are made at the partnership level. Special tax rules apply to electing large partnerships.	*Conduit:* Similar to the partnership form of organization. However, the S corporation may be subject to tax at the corporate level on excess net passive income, or built-in gains under special circumstances.
Period of Existence.	Continues until dissolution; not effected by stock sales by shareholders.	Termination can occur by agreement, or by death, retirement, or disaffiliation of a partner.	Same as for C corporation.
Transferability of Interest.	Stock can be transferred easily; corporation may retain right to buy back shares.	Addition of new partner or transfer of partner's interest generally requires approval of other partners.	Same as for C corporation.
Liability Exposure.	Shareholders generally liable only for capital contributions.	General partners are personally, jointly, and severally liable for partnership obligations. Limited partners usually are liable only for capital contributions.	Same as for C corporation.
Management Responsibility.	Shareholders may be part of management or may hire outside management.	All general partners participate in management. Limited partners generally do not participate.	Because of limited number of shareholders, shareholders usually are part of management.
II. Election and Restrictions			
1. Restrictions on: a. Type of owners.	No restriction.	No restriction.	Limited to individuals, estates, charitable organizations, and certain kinds of trusts.
b. Number of owners.	No restriction.	No restriction.	Limited to 75 shareholders.
c. Type of entity.	Includes domestic or foreign corporations, unincorporated entities known as associations, and certain kinds of trusts. A publicly traded partnership is taxed as a corporation unless more than 90% of its income is qualifying passive income. Grandfathered publicly traded partnerships can avoid corporate taxation by paying an excise tax. Partnerships, LLCs, and proprietorships can elect to be taxed as a corporation under the check-the-box regulations.	Includes a variety of unincorporated entities including limited liability company and limited liability partnership forms. Certain joint undertakings are excluded from partnership status.	Domestic corporations and unincorporated entities (e.g., associations) are eligible. Partnerships, LLCs, and proprietorships can elect to be taxed as a corporation under the check-the-box regulations.

APPENDIX F: COMPARISON OF TAX ATTRIBUTES FOR C CORPORATIONS, PARTNERSHIPS, AND S CORPORATIONS

Tax Attribute	C Corporation	Partnership	S Corporation
d. Special tax classifications.	No restriction.	No restriction.	S corporation cannot be a Domestic International Sales Corporation, or have elected the special Puerto Rico and U.S. Possessions tax credit. Certain financial institutions and insurance companies also are ineligible.
e. Investments made by entity.	No restriction.	No restriction.	S corporation can own 80% or more of a C corporation but cannot file a consolidated tax return with the C corporation.
f. Capital structure.	No restriction.	No restriction.	Limited to a single class of stock that is outstanding. Differences in voting rights are disregarded. Special "safe harbor" rules are available for debt issues.
g. Passive interest income.	No restriction.	No restriction.	Passive investment income cannot exceed 25% of gross receipts for three consecutive tax years when the corporation also has Subchapter C E&P at the end of the year.
2. Election and shareholder consent.	No election required.	No election required.	Election can be made during the preceding tax year or first 2½ months of the tax year. Shareholders must consent to the election.
3. Termination of election.	Not applicable.	The partnership can terminate if it does not carry on any business, financial operation, or venture or if a sale or exchange of at least 50% of the profits and capital interests occurs within a 12-month period.	Occurs if one of the requirements is failed after the election is first effective or if the passive investment income test is failed for three consecutive tax years. IRS can waive invalid elections and permit inadvertent terminations not to break the S election.
4. Revocation of election.	Not applicable.	Not applicable.	Election may be revoked only by shareholders owning more than one-half of the stock. Must be made in first 2½ months of tax year or on a prospective basis.
5. New election.	Not applicable.	Not applicable.	Not permitted for five-year period without IRS consent to early reelection.

APPENDIX F: COMPARISON OF TAX ATTRIBUTES FOR C CORPORATIONS, PARTNERSHIPS, AND S CORPORATIONS

Tax Attribute	C Corporation	Partnership	S Corporation
III. Accounting Periods and Elections			
1. Taxable year.	Calendar year or fiscal year is permitted. Personal service corporations are restricted to using a calendar year unless IRS grants approval to use a fiscal year. A special election is available to use a fiscal year resulting in a three-month or less income deferral if the corporation meets a series of minimum distribution requirements.	Generally use tax year of majority or principal partners. Otherwise use of the least aggregate deferral year is required. Can use a fiscal year that has a business purpose for which IRS approval is obtained. An electing partnership may use a fiscal year resulting in a three-month or less income deferral if an additional required payment is made.	Can use a fiscal year that has a business purpose for which IRS approval is obtained. An S corporation may use a fiscal year resulting in a three-month or less income deferral if an additional required payment is made. If neither of the above applies, a calendar year must be used.
2. Accounting methods.	Elected by the corporation. Use of cash method of accounting is restricted for certain personal service corporations and C corporations having $5 million or more annual gross receipts.	Elected by the partnership. Restrictions on the use of the cash method of accounting apply to partnerships having a C corporation as a partner or that are tax shelters.	Elected by the S corporation. Restrictions on the use of the cash method of accounting apply to S corporations that are tax shelters.
IV. Taxability of Profits			
1. Taxability of profits.	Ordinary income and capital gains are taxed to the corporation. Profits are taxed a second time when distributed.	Ordinary income and separately stated income and gain items pass through to the partners at the end of the partnership's tax year whether or not distributed.	Same as partnership.
2. Allocation of profits.	Not applicable.	Based on partnership agreement. Special allocations are permitted.	Based on stock ownership on each day of the tax year. Special allocations are not permitted.
3. Character of income.	Distributed profits (including tax-exempt income) are dividends to extent of earnings and profits (E&P).	Items receiving special treatment (e.g., capital gains or tax-exempt income) pass through separately to the partner and retain same character as when earned by the partnership.	Same as partnership.
4. Maximum tax rate for earnings.	15% on the first $50,000; 25% from $50,000 to $75,000; 34% from $75,000 to $10 million. The rate is 35% for taxable income above $10 million. A 5% surcharge applies to taxable income between $100,000 and $335,000 and a 3% surcharge applies to taxable income between $15 million and $18,333,333. Special rules apply to controlled groups. Personal service corporations are taxed at a flat 35% rate.	Rates of tax applicable to noncorporate partners from 15% through 38.6% (in 2002) are levied on the income from the partnership. C corporation rates apply to corporate partners.	Same as partnership except for certain special situations where a special corporate tax applies to the S corporation.

APPENDIX F: COMPARISON OF TAX ATTRIBUTES FOR C CORPORATIONS, PARTNERSHIPS, AND S CORPORATIONS

Tax Attribute	C Corporation	Partnership	S Corporation
5. Special tax levies.	Can be subject to accumulated earnings tax, personal holding company tax, and corporate alternative minimum tax.	Not applicable.	Can be subject to built-in gains tax, excess net passive income tax, LIFO recapture tax, and investment tax credit recapture.
6. Income splitting between family members.	Only possible when earnings are distributed to shareholder. Dividends received by shareholder under age 14 are taxed at parents' marginal tax rate.	Transfer of partnership interest by gift will permit income splitting. Subject to special rules for transactions involving family members requiring payment of reasonable compensation for capital and services. Income received by partner under age 14 is taxed at parents' marginal tax rate.	Transfer of S corporation interest by gift will permit income splitting. Special rules apply to transactions involving family members requiring payment of reasonable compensation for capital and services. Income received by shareholder under age 14 is taxed at parents' marginal tax rate.
7. Sale of ownership interest.	Gain is taxed as capital gain; 50% of gain may be excluded under Sec. 1202 qualified small business stock rules. Loss is eligible for Sec. 1244 treatment.	Gain may be either ordinary income or capital gain depending on the nature of underlying partnership assets. Losses usually are capital.	Gain is capital in nature but is not eligible for special Sec. 1202 small business stock rules. Loss is eligible for Sec. 1244 treatment.
V. Treatment of Special Income, Gain, Loss, Deduction and Credit Items			
1. Capital gains and losses.	Long-term capital gains are taxed at regular tax rates. Capital losses offset capital gains; excess losses carried back three years and forward five years.	Passed through to partners (according to partnership agreement).	Passed through to shareholders (on a daily basis according to stock ownership).
2. Section 1231 gains and losses.	Eligible for long-term capital gain or ordinary loss treatment. Loss recapture occurs at the corporate level.	Passed through to partners. Loss recapture occurs at the partner level.	Same as partnership.
3. Dividends received from domestic corporation.	Eligible for 70%, 80%, or 100% dividends-received deduction.	Passed through to partners.	Same as partnership.
4. Organizational expenditures.	Amortize over 60 or more months.	Same as C corporation.	Same as partnership.
5. Charitable contributions.	Limited to 10% of taxable income.	Passed through to partners. Limitations apply at partner level.	Same as partnership.
6. Expensing of asset acquisition costs.	Limited to $24,000 in 2002.	Limited to $24,000 in 2002 for the partnership and for each partner.	Same as partnership.
7. Expenses owed to related parties.	Regular Sec. 267 rules apply to payments and sales or exchanges made to or by the corporation and certain other related parties (e.g., controlling shareholder and corporation or members of a controlled group).	Regular Sec. 267 rules can apply. Special Sec. 267 rules for passthrough entities apply to payments made by the partnership to a partner.	Same as partnership.

APPENDIX F: COMPARISON OF TAX ATTRIBUTES FOR C CORPORATIONS, PARTNERSHIPS, AND S CORPORATIONS

Tax Attribute	C Corporation	Partnership	S Corporation
8. Employment-related tax considerations.	An owner-employee may be treated as an employee for Social Security tax and corporate fringe benefit purposes. The corporate qualified pension and profit-sharing benefits available to owner-employees are comparable to the plan benefits for self-employed individuals (partners and sole proprietors).	A partner is not considered an employee of the business. Therefore, the partner must pay self-employment tax on the net self-employment income from the business. Corporate fringe benefit exclusions such as group term life insurance are not available (i.e., the premiums are not deductible by the business and are not excludable from the partner's income). Fringe benefits may be provided as nontaxable distribution or as taxable compensation.	Corporate fringe benefit exclusions generally are not available to S corporation shareholders. Fringe benefits usually are provided as nontaxable distribution or taxable compensation. S corporation shareholders may be treated as employees, however, for Social Security tax payments and qualified pension and profit sharing plan rules.
9. Tax preference items and AMT adjustments.	Subject to the corporate alternative minimum tax at the corporate level.	Passed through to partners and taxed under the alternative minimum tax rules applicable to the partner.	Same as partnership.
VI. Deductibility of Losses and Special Items			
1. Deductibility of losses.	Losses create net operating loss (NOL) that carry back two years or forward 20 years or capital loss that carry back three years or forward five years.	Ordinary losses and separately stated loss and deduction items pass through to the partners at the end of the partnership tax year. May create a personal NOL.	Same as partnership.
2. Allocation of losses.	Not applicable.	Based on partnership agreement. Special allocations are permitted.	Based on stock ownership on each day of the tax year. Special allocations are not permitted.
3. Shareholder and entity loss limitations.	Passive losses may be restricted under the passive activity limitation if the C corporation is closely held.	Limited to partner's basis for the partnership interest. Ratable share of all partnership liabilities is included in basis of partnership interest. Excess losses carry over indefinitely until partnership interest again has a basis. Subject to at risk, passive activity, and hobby loss restrictions.	Limited to shareholder's basis for the stock interest plus basis of S corporation debts to the shareholder. Excess losses carry over indefinitely until shareholder again has basis for stock or debt. Subject to the at risk, passive activity, and hobby loss restrictions.
4. Basis adjustments for debt and equity interests.	Not applicable.	Basis in partnership interest reduced by loss and deduction passthrough. Subsequent profits increase basis of partnership interest.	Basis in S corporation stock reduced by loss and deduction passthrough. Once basis of stock has been reduced to zero, any other losses and deductions reduce basis of debt (but not below zero). Subsequent net increases restore basis reductions to debt before increasing basis of stock.

Tax Attribute	C Corporation	Partnership	S Corporation
5. Investment interest deduction limitation.	Not applicable.	Investment interest expenses and income pass through to the partners. Limitation applies at partner level.	Same as partnership.
VII. Distributions			
1. Taxability of nonliquidating distributions to shareholder.	Taxable as dividends if made from current or accumulated E&P. Additional distributions first reduce shareholder's basis for stock, and distributions exceeding stock basis trigger capital gain recognition.	Tax-free unless money, money equivalents, or marketable securities received by the partner exceeds his or her basis for the partnership interest.	Tax-free if made from the accumulated adjustment account or shareholder's basis for his or her stock. Taxable if made out of accumulated E&P or after stock basis has been reduced to zero.
2. Taxability of nonliquidating distributions to distributing entity.	Gain (but not loss) recognized as if the corporation had sold the property for its FMV immediately before the distribution.	No gain or loss recognized by the partnership except when a disproportionate distribution of Sec. 751 property occurs.	Gain (but not loss) recognized and passed through to the shareholders as if the corporation had sold the property for its FMV immediately before the distribution. Gain may be taxed to the S corporation under one of the special tax levies.
3. Basis adjustment to owner's investment for distribution.	None unless the distribution exceeds E&P.	Amount of money or adjusted basis of distributed property reduces basis in partnership interest.	Amount of money or FMV of distributed property reduces basis of stock except when distribution is made out of accumulated E&P.
VIII. Other Items			
1. Tax return.	Form 1120 or 1120-A	Form 1065 (Information Return).	Form 1120S (Information Return).
2. Due date.	March 15 for calendar year C corporation.	April 15 for calendar year partnership.	March 15 for calendar year S corporation.
3. Extensions of time permitted.	Six months.	Four months.	Six months.
4. Estimated tax payments required.	Yes—April 15, June 15, September 15, and December 15 for calendar year C corporation.	No—estimated taxes are required of the partners for passed through income, etc.	Yes—Applies to built-in gains tax and excess net passive income tax.
5. Audit rules.	IRS audits corporation independently of its shareholders.	Special audit rules apply requiring audit of partnership and requiring partners to take a position consistent with the partnership tax return.	Special rules require consistent tax treatment for Subchapter S items on the corporation and shareholder returns.

APPENDIX G

CREDIT FOR STATE DEATH TAXES

IF THE ADJUSTED TAXABLE ESTATE[a] IS:	THE MAXIMUM TAX CREDIT SHALL BE:
Not over $90,000	8/10ths of 1% of the amount by which the adjusted taxable estate exceeds $40,000.
Over $90,000 but not over $140,000	$400 plus 1.6% of the excess over $90,000.
Over $140,000 but not over $240,000	$1,200 plus 2.4% of the excess over $140,000.
Over $240,000 but not over $440,000	$3,600 plus 3.2% of the excess over $240,000.
Over $440,000 but not over $640,000	$10,000 plus 4% of the excess over $440,000.
Over $640,000 but not over $840,000	$18,000 plus 4.8% of the excess over $640,000.
Over $840,000 but not over $1,040,000	$27,600 plus 5.6% of the excess over $840,000.
Over $1,040,000 but not over $1,540,000	$38,800 plus 6.4% of the excess over $1,040,000.
Over $1,540,000 but not over $2,040,000	$70,800 plus 7.2% of the excess over $1,540,000.
Over $2,040,000 but not over $2,540,000	$106,800 plus 8% of the excess over $2,040,000.
Over $2,540,000 but not over $3,040,000	$146,800 plus 8.8% of the excess over $2,540,000.
Over $3,040,000 but not over $3,540,000	$190,800 plus 9.6% of the excess over $3,040,000.
Over $3,540,000 but not over $4,040,000	$238,800 plus 10.4% of the excess over $3,540,000.
Over $4,040,000 but not over $5,040,000	$290,800 plus 11.2% of the excess over $4,040,000.
Over $5,040,000 but not over $6,040,000	$402,800 plus 12% of the excess over $5,040,000.
Over $6,040,000 but not over $7,040,000	$522,800 plus 12.8% of the excess over $6,040,000.
Over $7,040,000 but not over $8,040,000	$650,800 plus 13.6% of the excess over $7,040,000.
Over $8,040,000 but not over $9,040,000	$786,800 plus 14.4% of the excess over $8,040,000.
Over $9,040,000 but not over $10,040,000	$930,800 plus 15.2% of the excess over $9,040,000.
Over $10,040,000	$1,082,800 plus 16% of the excess over $10,040,000.

[a]Taxable estate minus $60,000.
Source: IRC Sec. 2011(b)(1).
Note: For estates of decedents dying after December 31, 2001, the maximum credit cannot exceed the following percentages of the amount determined from the above schedule:

- 75% for estates of decedents dying in 2002
- 50% for estates of decedents dying in 2003
- 25% for estates of decedents dying in 2004

For estates of decedents dying after 2004, the state tax credit will no longer be allowed.

APPENDIX H

ACTUARIAL TABLES

TRANSFERS MADE AFTER APRIL 30, 1999
EXCERPT FROM TABLE S
SINGLE LIFE REMAINDER FACTORS

	INTEREST RATE								
AGE	7%	8%	9%	10%	AGE	7%	8%	9%	10%
25	.05570	.04218	.03298	.02656	58	.28061	.24453	.21507	.19080
26	.05845	.04438	.03476	.02802	59	.29269	.25610	.22608	.20123
27	.06140	.04676	.03670	.02962	60	.30500	.26794	.23738	.21196
28	.06451	.04929	.03877	.03133	61	.31757	.28007	.24900	.22304
29	.06780	.05198	.04099	.03318	62	.33044	.29255	.26100	.23451
30	.07127	.05483	.04335	.03515	63	.34363	.30539	.27339	.24641
31	.07491	.05785	.04585	.03725	64	.35711	.31857	.28615	.25870
32	.07875	.06103	.04851	.03948	65	.37087	.33208	.29930	.27140
33	.08279	.06441	.05135	.04188	66	.38496	.34597	.31285	.28456
34	.08705	.06798	.05436	.04444	67	.39941	.36028	.32689	.29823
35	.09155	.07179	.05758	.04718	68	.41419	.37499	.34138	.31240
36	.09628	.07581	.06101	.05012	69	.42927	.39006	.35628	.32703
37	.10126	.08006	.06466	.05325	70	.44456	.40540	.37151	.34204
38	.10652	.08459	.06855	.05662	71	.46000	.42095	.38701	.35736
39	.11206	.08938	.07270	.06023	72	.47554	.43666	.40271	.37293
40	.11791	.09447	.07714	.06411	73	.49114	.45249	.41858	.38872
41	.12409	.09989	.08189	.06828	74	.50686	.46849	.43469	.40479
42	.13061	.10564	.08696	.07277	75	.52276	.48474	.45111	.42123
43	.13747	.11174	.09237	.07758	76	.53888	.50130	.46790	.43811
44	.14469	.11819	.09813	.08272	77	.55523	.51815	.48506	.45543
45	.15223	.12496	.10420	.08817	78	.57177	.53527	.50257	.47317
46	.16011	.13207	.11061	.09395	79	.58840	.55256	.52032	.49122
47	.16830	.13950	.11733	.10004	80	.60497	.56985	.53813	.50939
48	.17682	.14727	.12439	.10646	81	.62135	.58701	.55587	.52754
49	.18568	.15539	.13181	.11322	82	.63748	.60395	.57343	.54557
50	.19490	.16388	.13960	.12037	83	.65334	.62066	.59081	.56346
51	.20448	.17275	.14777	.12789	84	.66904	.63727	.60813	.58134
52	.21438	.18196	.15630	.13577	85	.68467	.65386	.62550	.59934
53	.22461	.19151	.16518	.14400	86	.70010	.67029	.64276	.61728
54	.23516	.20140	.17441	.15260	87	.71511	.68632	.66965	.63489
55	.24604	.21166	.18402	.16157	88	.72968	.70194	.67615	.65213
56	.25725	.22227	.19400	.17093	89	.74381	.71712	.69224	.66900
57	.26879	.23324	.20436	.18069					

Source: Reg. Sec. 20.2031-7(d)(7).

EXCERPT FROM TABLE B
TERM CERTAIN REMAINDER FACTORS

	INTEREST RATE			
YEARS	7.0%	8.0%	9.0%	10.0%
1	.934579	.925926	.917431	.909091
2	.873439	.857339	.841680	.826446
3	.816298	.793832	.772183	.751315
4	.762895	.735030	.708425	.683013
5	.712986	.680583	.649931	.620921
6	.666342	.630170	.596267	.564474
7	.622750	.583490	.547034	.513158
8	.582009	.540269	.501866	.466507
9	.543934	.500249	.460428	.424098
10	.508349	.463193	.422411	.385543
11	.475093	.428883	.387533	.350494
12	.444012	.397114	.355535	.318631
13	.414964	.367698	.326179	.289664
14	.387817	.340461	.299246	.263331
15	.362446	.315242	.274538	.239392
16	.338735	.291890	.251870	.217629
17	.316574	.270269	.231073	.197845
18	.295864	.250249	.211994	.179859
19	.276508	.231712	.194490	.163508
20	.258419	.214548	.178431	.148644
21	.241513	.198656	.163698	.135131
22	.225713	.183941	.150182	.122846
23	.210947	.170315	.137781	.111678
24	.197147	.157699	.126405	.101526
25	.184249	.146018	.115968	.092296

Source: Reg. Secs. 20.7520-1(a)(1) and 20.2031-7(d)(6).

APPENDIX I

INDEX OF CODE SECTIONS

1, *2-2n*, **1-9 (Figure 1-2)**, **1-25**
1(g)(7), *2-25n*
1(h), *5-16n–5-17n*
1(h)(2), *5-28n*
1(h)(3), *7-15n*
1(h)(4), *5-17n*
1.1036-1(a), *12-5n*
1.280A-2, *9-25n*
1.6662-3(b)(3), **15-23**
2(a), *2-20n*
2(b), *2-21n*
2(c), *2-22n*
8-10, **8-15**
11, **8-7**, **8-9**
11(b), **3-26**
21, *7-33*, *14-10 (Table 14-1)*, *14-11n*
21(b)(1), *14-11n*
21(c), *14-12n*
21(d)(2), *14-12n*
21(e)(1), *14-11n*
21(e)(6), *14-12n*
22, *14-10 (Table 14-1)*
22(c)(2), *14-13n*
23, *14-10 (Table 14-1)*, *14-13n*
24, *2-18*, *14-10 (Table 14-1)*, *14-10n*
24(c), *14-11n*
25, *14-10 (Table 14-1)*
25A, *14-10 (Table 14-1)*, *14-14n*
25A(b), *14-14n*
25A(c), *14-14n*
25B, *14-10 (Table 14-1)*, *14-16*
26, *14-10n*, *14-17*
26(b), **5-5**
27, *14-10 (Table 14-1)*, **3-21 (Table 3-2)**, **5-5**
29, *14-10 (Table 14-1)*, **3-21 (Table 3-2)**
30, *14-10 (Table 14-1)*, **3-21 (Table 3-2)**
30A, **3-21 (Table 3-2)**
31, *14-10 (Table 14-1)*
32, *14-10 (Table 14-1)*
32(b)(1), *14-23n*
32(c), *14-22n*
32(c)(1)(A), *14-22n*
34, **3-21 (Table 3-2)**
38, *14-19*, *14-21*, **3-21 (Table 3-2)**
38(c), *14-18n*, *14-22n*, **5-14**, **8-11n**
38(c)(2), **5-14n**
39(a), **8-11**
41, *14-10 (Table 14-1)*, *14-18–14-19*
41(c)(2), *14-19n*
41(c)(3), *14-19n*
42, *13-15n*, *14-10 (Table 14-1)*
44, *14-10 (Table 14-1)*, *14-19n*
47, *14-10 (Table 14-1)*, *14-19n*
47(a)(1), *14-19n*
47(a)(2), *14-19n*
47(c)(1)(A), *14-20n*
48, *14-10 (Table 14-1)*
48(a)(2), *14-20n*
50(c)(1), *14-20n*
51, *14-10 (Table 14-1)*, *14-20n*, *14-21*
51A, *14-10 (Table 14-1)*, *14-20n*
53, *14-6*, *14-6n*, **3-21 (Table 3-2)**, **5-14n**
55, **5-4n**, **8-10**
55(b), **5-5n**
55(b)(1), *14-2n*
55(d)(2), **5-4**
55(d)(3), *14-3n*
55(e), **5-2n**, **5-3**
55(e)(5), **5-15n**
56, **5-35**, **8-10**
56(a), **5-7n**, **11-33**
56(b)(2), *14-5n*
56(b)(2)(D), *14-5n*
56(g), **5-10**
56(g)(2), **5-9n**
56(g)(4)(A), **5-10**, **5-10n**
56(g)(4)(C)(i), **5-10n**
56(g)(4)(C)(ii), **5-10n**
56(g)(4)(D)(ii), **5-10n**
56(g)(4)(D)(iii), **5-11n**
56(g)(4)(D)(iv), **5-10n**
56(g)(4)(G), **5-11n**
56(g)(4)(I), **5-10n**
56(g)(6), **5-9n**, **5-35n**, **11-33n**
57, *14-3*, *14-3n*, **5-35**, **8-10**
57(a), **5-6n**, **11-32**
57(a)(1), *10-19n*
57(a)(7), *14-4n*
58, **8-10**
59, **8-10**
59(a), **5-15**
59(e), **5-35**
59(a)(2), **5-15n**
59(e)(4)(A), **5-35n**
59(e)(4)(B), **5-35n**
59(e)(6), **5-35**
61, *3-22*, **2-13n**, **9-10**
61(a), *2-3n*, *3-2*, *3-13*, *3-22*, *4-2*
61(a)(3), *5-2n*
61(a)(12), *4-20*
62, *6-3*, *6-3n*
62(a)(2), *9-2*
62(a)(3), *5-2n*
62(a)(15), *9-19n*
63, *2-4n*
63(c)(6), *2-12n*
66(b), *3-7n*
66(c), *3-7n*
67, *9-3–9-4*
67(c)(2), *7-28*
67(e), **14-8**, **15-20n**
68, *9-4n*, **10-32**
68-232, *10-36*
72, *9-29*, *9-29n*, *9-31*, *9-38*, **15-11**
72(e), *3-21n*
72(e)(2), *4-6n*
72(q), *4-6n*
72(t), *9-38n*
74, *3-23n*, *4-4n*, *4-7n*, *4-14*
74(b), *4-4*
74(c), *4-14n*, *4-31*
79, *4-4*, **11-34**
79(a), *4-11n*
82, *9-20*, *9-20n*
83, *9-30n*, *9-32*, **2-13n**, **9-10**
83(b), *9-32n*, *9-32–9-33*
86, *3-15n*, *3-23*, *4-4*
101, *4-4*, *4-9*, *4-9n*
101(a), *4-5n*
101(a)(2), *4-5n*
102, *4-2*, *4-4*, *4-31*, **12-2**
103, *4-4*
103(a)(1), *3-14n*
104, *4-4*, **11-34**
104(a), *4-8–4-9*
104(a)(1), *4-10*
104(a)(2), *3-25*
104(a)(3), *4-9*
105, *4-4*, **11-34**
105(a), *4-10n*
105(h)(5), *4-11n*
106, *4-4*, *4-10*, *7-6n*, **11-34**
108, *4-4*, *4-20*, **11-21**
108(b)(5), **11-14**
108(c)(3), **11-14**
108(f)(2), *4-20*
109, *3-39*, *4-31*
111, *3-26n*
117, *4-2*, *4-4*, *4-7n*, *4-23*, *9-21*, *14-14*
117(d), *4-31*
118(a), **2-28n**
119, *4-14–4-15*, **11-34**
121, *3-13n*, *4-4*, *12-2*, *12-16–12-22*, *12-25*, **14-43**
121(a), *12-16n*, *12-18n*
121(b), *12-16n*
121(c), *12-19n*
121(d)(2), *12-19n*
121(d)(3), *12-19n*
121(d)(5)(A), *12-20n*
121(d)(5)(B), *12-20n*
121(d)(6), *12-22n*
121(d)(8), *12-20n*
121(f), *12-22n*
123, *4-31*
124, *4-4*
125, *4-4*, *4-17n*, **11-34**
127, *4-17*, *9-21*, *9-21 (Table 9-3)*, *9-21n*, *14-14*, **11-34**
129, *4-4*, *4-17n*, *4-23*, *14-12*, *14-12n*, **11-34**
132, *4-4*, *4-10*, *4-12–4-13*, *4-15*, *4-23*, *9-20*, **11-34**
132(b), *4-13*
132(c), *4-13*, *4-31*
132(d), *4-13*
132(e), *4-13–4-14*
132(f), *4-13*
132(g), *9-20n*
132(j)(4), *4-13*
135, *3-28*
135(c), *3-14n*
135(c)(2)(B), *3-14n*
146(d), *3-14n*
148, *3-14n*
149(b), *3-14n*
151, **14-4**, **14-9**
151(b), *2-12n*

Entries in BOLD denote references to **Corporations**
Entries in *ITALICS* denote references to *Individuals*

151(d), *2-17n*
152, *2-13n, 2-40, 7-2n*
152(a), **1-5n**
152(b)(5), *2-16n*
152(c), *2-14n*
152(d), *2-13n*
152(e), *2-15n, 2-23n, 7-2*
162, *1-26, 4-12, 4-12n, 6-2, 6-5, 6-8, 6-49, 7-9, 7-24, 7-45, 8-13, 9-2, 9-12, 10-16, 10-18,* **1-6, 3-8n, 3-9, 4-33, 4-47, 5-17, 5-46, 9-28, 14-28**
162(a), *9-6n*, **4-13**
162(a)(1), *3-17n*
162(a)(2), *9-62*
162(c)(1), *6-12*
162(c)(3), *6-13*
162(e), *6-14*
162(g), *6-13n*
162(l), *4-10n, 6-3n*, **11-34**
162(m), *6-9*, **3-29n**
163, *7-19, 7-45*
163(a), **2-27n**
163(b), *11-22*
163(d)(3), **12-28**
163(d)(4), *11-24*
163(d)(4)(B), *7-15n*
163(d)(4)(C), *7-15n*
163(e), **2-27, 2-27n**
163(h), *7-16n*
163(h)(4)(C), *7-16n*
164, *7-9–7-11*
164(a), *5-5n*
164(a)(3), *14-17n*
164(c)(1), *7-11n*
164(f), *1-11n, 6-3n, 7-11n, 9-36, 10-10n, 10-23, 14-7n*
165, *8-3–8-4, 8-19, 8-23n, 8-25n*, **1-11, 2-32n**
165(d), *3-23n*
165(g), *8-4*, **1-11, 2-31n**
165(g)(1), *5-22*
165(g)(2), *5-22n, 8-3n*
165(g)(3), *5-22n, 8-4n*, **6-6, 6-11, 6-19n, 6-32**
165(h)(2)(A)(i), **1-9 (Figure 1-2)**
165(h)(2)(A)(ii), **1-9 (Figure 1-2)**
165(i), *8-23n*
165(l), *8-29n*
166, *8-25n*, **2-32, 2-32n, 6-11**
166(d)(1)(B), *5-15n*
167, *5-13, 10-2*
167(a), *10-2n*
167(f), *10-18*
167(f)(1), *10-17n*
167(h), **14-9**
168, *10-2, 14-20*
168(b)(2), **5-35n**
168(b)(3)(A), *13-14n*
168(b)(5), **5-35n**
168(c)(1), *10-7n*
168(d)(3), *10-5n*
168(d)(3)(B), *10-6n*
168(e)(1), *10-5n*
168(e)(2)(A), *10-8n*
168(f), *10-5n*
168(g), *10-8n*, **4-5, 5-7**
168(g)(3), **5-7**
168(g)(7), *10-8n*
168(i)(7), **2-25n, 8-16**
168(i)(7)(A), **9-10n**
169, *6-10, 10-13, 13-10n*
169(a), *13-10n*
170, *7-21, 7-36*, **1-6, 3-49, 15-10**
170(a), **3-10n**
170(b)(1)(A)(ii), **12-8n**
170(b)(1)(E), *7-22n*
170(b)(2), **3-12n**
170(d)(2), **3-12n**
170(e), *7-24n*, **3-11n**
170(e)(1)(A), *13-18n, 13-23n*
170(e)(5), **3-11n**
170(e)(6), *7-24n*
170(f)(3), *7-22n*
170(f)(8), *7-34n*
170(g), *7-21n*
171, **2-27**
172, *8-29, 8-33*, **8-24**
172(b)(1)(C), *8-33n*
172(b)(3)(C), **3-16n**
172(d)(2), *8-30n*
172(c), **3-16n**
172(d)(4)(C), *8-31n*
172(f), *8-33n*
173, **5-35**
174, *6-10n, 6-17, 10-13, 10-16n, 10-16–10-17, 11-7n, 14-18*, **5-35**
175, *6-10n*
175(a), *13-20n*
179, *6-5, 6-11, 6-17, 9-11, 10-6, 10-6n, 10-9n, 10-9–10-10, 10-12n, 10-12–10-14, 10-23, 10-30, 13-10, 13-10n, 13-20*, **3-35–3-36, 3-46, 4-5, 5-7, 9-16, 10-31–10-32, 11-48**
179(a), *13-20n*
179(b)(1), *13-20n*
179(b)(3), *10-10n*
179(d)(10), *10-10n, 13-20n*
180, 6-10n
183, *6-29–6-30, 6-32, 9-25n*, **11-22**
183(d), *6-29, 6-29n*
185, *13-10n*
188, *13-10n*
190, *6-10n, 13-10n*
193, *6-10n, 13-10n*
194, *13-10n*
194(a), *13-10n*
195, *6-15, 10-13, 10-16*, **3-9**
197, *10-13–10-16, 10-18, 10-22, 13-9*, **7-4n, 7-9–7-10**
197(a), *5-27n, 10-13n*
197(e)(3)(A), *10-18n*
197(e)(3)(A)(i), *10-18*
197(f)(1), *10-15n*
197(f)(7), *10-15n*
212, *2-4n, 6-2, 6-5, 6-7–6-8, 7-9, 7-28, 8-10n, 9-8–9-10, 9-12*, **14-7**
212(1), *9-6n*
213, *6-9, 7-3, 7-46*
213(c), *7-6n*
213(d), *7-6n*, **12-8n**
213(d)(10), *4-10n*
217, *9-18, 9-19n, 9-20*
217(d)(2), *9-47n*
217(d)(3), *9-47n*
219, *3-15n*
219(g), *9-37n*
224(a), **1-22 (Table 1-2), 3-13n**
243(a)(3), **3-14n**
243(b)(5), **3-15n**
243(c), **3-13n**
245, **3-15n**
246(b), **3-13n**
246(c)(1), **3-15n**
246A, **3-15n**
248, *6-10, 10-13*, **3-8, 5-10, 9-12, 11-15**
259, *4-8*
262, *2-4n*
263, *6-10*, **5-35**
263(c), *6-10n, 10-20n, 13-21n*
263A, *5-5, 6-11, 11-11*, **8-13, 11-51**
263A(b)(2)(B), *11-11n*
263A(f), *5-5n*
263A(f)(1)(B), *5-5n*
263A(f)(4)(B), *5-5n*
265, *6-11, 6-17*, **8-14**
265(a)(1), **14-14n**
266, *6-11, 6-17*
267, *6-25–6-28, 6-28n, 7-20, 10-10*, **1-6, 2-18, 2-33–2-34, 3-27, 4-6, 4-19, 8-34, 9-27**
267(a), *12-8n*
267(a)(1), **2-10 (Table 2-1), 2-33, 3-18–3-19, 3-26, 8-2n, 11-33**
267(a)(2), *6-28n*, **3-18–3-19, 3-27, 8-18, 11-33**
267(b), *7-20n, 8-9n*
267(b)(2), **3-18n**
267(b)(3), **8-18**
267(c)(4), *7-18n*, **1-5**
267(d), **3-19n**
267(e), *6-28n, 7-20n*, **11-33**
267(e)(3), **3-19n**
267(f)(2), **8-2n, 8-15n**
268, *13-6n*
269, **7-46–7-47, 7-49**
269A(b), *6-28n*
269A(b)(1), *8-13n*
274, *4-5, 4-12n, 6-17, 9-8, 9-12–9-14*, **15-10**
274(a)(3), *9-15n*
274(b), *4-31*
274(b)(1), *9-15n*
274(c), *9-8n*
274(d), *6-16n, 9-43n, 9-44*, **1-36**
274(h), *9-8n*
274(j), *4-14n, 9-15n*
274(k), *9-13n*
274(l)(2), *9-16n*
274(m)(3), *9-8n*
274(n), *9-12*
276(a), *6-14n*
280A, *6-31n, 6-31–6-34, 6-34 (Figure 6-4), 7-31*, **1-5**
280A(c)(1), *9-23n*
280A(c)(5), *9-25n*
280A(c)(5)(B), *6-32n*
280A(d)(1), *6-31n, 7-18, 7-18n*
280A(d)(2), *6-31n, 7-18n*
280A(d)(2)(B), *6-31n*
280A(d)(2)(C), *6-31n*
280A(e)(1), *6-32n*
280E, *6-14, 8-3*
280F, *6-17, 10-12n, 10-13*
280F(a)(2), *10-12n*
280F(b)(3), *10-11n*
280F(b)(4), *10-11n*
280F(d)(3), *10-11n*
280F(d)(4), *10-23*
280H, **3-3n, 3-4**
280H(k), *11-4n*
291, *13-14n, 13-15–13-16, 13-18*, **3-6–3-7, 6-13, 11-15**
291(a), *13-12n, 13-23n*
291(a)(1), *13-15n*
301, **4-2, 4-12, 4-18, 4-29, 4-31, 4-33, 6-21, 7-39**
301(b), **4-9n**
301(d), **4-9n, 4-10n**
302, *3-17n*, **2-29 (Table 2-3), 6-14, 7-39, 7-41n, 13-29**
302(b), **4-31, 7-18–7-19, 7-21, 7-39, 7-42**
302(b)(1), **4-23–4-25, 4-33, 7-19**
302(b)(2), **4-20–4-22, 4-25, 4-33, 7-19, 7-26, 7-40**
302(b)(3), **1-8, 4-21–4-22, 4-25, 4-28, 4-33–4-34, 4-36**
302(b)(4), **4-24, 4-30, 4-33**
302(c), **4-18n**
302(c)(2), **4-22n**
302(c)(2)(A), **1-8, 4-37n, 4-43**
302(c)(2)(C)(i), **1-8**
302(d), **4-18n, 4-33**
302(e)(1)(A), **4-24n**
302(e)(2), **4-24**
303, **2-29 (Table 2-3), 4-25–4-27, 4-33, 5-27, 5-30, 13-29**
304, **4-1, 4-30–4-33, 4-31n**
305, **4-14–4-15**

BOLD = Corporations
ITALICS = Individuals

305(a), 4-13–4-14
305(b), 2-29 (Table 2-3), 4-14–4-15
306, 1-8, 2-29 (Table 2-3), 4-28–4-30, 4-33
306(c), 4-28n
307(a), *5-11n*, 4-14n
307(b)(1), *5-11n*, 4-15n
311, 2-10 (Table 2-1), 4-27
311(a), 4-10n, 4-16n, 8-14
311(b), 7-17, 8-21, 11-27n
311(b)(2), 4-10n
312, 4-3n
312(a), 4-10n
312(a)(2), 4-11n
312(b), 4-10n
312(c), 4-10n
312(d), 4-16n
312(n)(4), 5-11n
312(n)(7), 4-27n
316(a), *3-16n*, 4-2
317, 4-16n
317(a), 4-2, 4-8n
318, *6-28n*, *8-13n*, 2-13n, 4-18–4-19, 4-22–4-23, 4-32, 4-42, 6-10, 11-33n
318(a), 4-18, 4-21, 4-23, 4-31, 4-31n
318(a)(1), 1-8, 4-22, 4-36, 7-6
318(a)(2), 7-6
318(a)(3), 7-6
331, 6-5 (Table 6-1), 6-10, 6-12, 6-14, 6-16, 6-21
331(a), 6-5
332, 6-1, 6-5 (Table 6-1), 6-7 (Table 6-2), 6-10n, 6-10–6-14, 6-13n, 6-16, 6-18–6-20, 6-32, 7-5, 7-6n
332(a), 6-10–6-11, 6-17, 6-32
332(b), 6-32
332(b)(1), 6-10n
332(b)(2), 6-11n
332(b)(3), 6-11n
334(a), 6-5 (Table 6-1), 6-6–6-7
334(b), 6-5 (Table 6-1)
334(b)(1), 6-12, 6-17
336, 6-7
336(a), 6-6, 6-7 (Table 6-2), 6-8, 6-13, 7-17
336(b), 4-10n, 6-7
336(d)(1), 6-7 (Table 6-2)
336(d)(1)(A), 6-8
336(d)(1)(B), 6-8
336(d)(2), 6-7 (Table 6-2), 6-8–6-9
336(d)(3), 6-7 (Table 6-2), 6-13
336(e), 6-13n
337, 6-1, 6-10–6-11, 6-19–6-20, 6-32, 7-5
337(a), 6-7 (Table 6-2), 6-13
337(b), 6-17
337(c), 6-13
338, 7-2, 7-3 (Table 7-1), 7-4–7-7, 7-6n, 7-10–7-11, 7-14–7-15, 7-50–7-52, 7-54–7-55, 7-62, 7-64
338(b)(1), 7-8n
338(b)(2), 7-8n
338(b)(3), 7-8n
338(b)(4), 7-8n
338(b)(6), 7-8n
338(g), 7-7n, 7-51
338(h)(2), 7-7n
338(h)(10), 7-6n
346(a), 6-14
351, *11-20*, *13-23*, 1-8, 2-11–2-28, 2-29 (Table 2-3), 2-31, 2-33–2-38, 2-41, 2-43, 4-28, 6-7 (Table 6-2), 6-8, 7-6, 7-40, 7-45, 8-4, 8-12, 10-21–10-22, 11-48, 15-11, 15-11n
351(a), 2-9, 2-10 (Table 2-1), 2-11–2-13, 2-36
351(b), 2-10 (Table 2-1), 2-12, 2-16, 2-17n, 2-24
351(d), 2-10 (Table 2-1), 2-13n
351(f), 2-10 (Table 2-1)
351(g), 2-16n
354, 7-6, 7-35, 7-35n, 7-45, 7-51
354(a), 7-18, 7-21, 7-42
354(a)(2), 7-18n
354(a)(2)(B), 7-42n
354(b)(1), 7-30n
355, 4-24, 7-6, 7-30, 7-35, 7-35n, 7-37–7-40, 7-45, 7-45n, 7-53, 7-59, 15-12
355(a), 7-38n, 7-40n
355(a)(3), 7-39n
355(b)(2), 7-40n
356, 7-6, 7-35, 7-41n, 7-59
356(a), 7-18
356(a)(2), 7-18, 7-21, 7-39n
356(b), 7-21, 7-39n
356(c), 7-39n
356(d)(2)(B), 7-18n
357, 2-21, 2-24
357(a), 2-21–2-22, 2-24, 7-21
357(b), 2-10 (Table 2-1), 2-22, 2-24, 2-34, 2-36
357(c), 2-10 (Table 2-1), 2-22–2-24, 2-34, 7-17, 7-21, 7-31, 9-7
357(c)(1)(B), 7-38n
357(c)(3), 2-23n, 2-23–2-24
358, 2-23, 7-20
358(a), 2-10 (Table 2-1), 7-21, 7-34
358(a)(1), 2-18n
358(a)(2), 2-18n
358(b)(1), 2-19n
358(d)(1), 2-21n
358(d)(2), 2-23n
361, 7-17, 7-51
361(a), 7-16n, 7-16–7-17, 7-21, 7-38n
361(b), 7-16, 7-21
361(c), 7-17n, 7-17, 7-21
361(c)(1), 7-17n, 7-38n
361(c)(2), 7-17n
361(c)(3), 7-17n
362, 2-10 (Table 2-1), 2-21n
362(a), 2-28n
362(b), 7-17, 7-21
362(c)(1), 2-30n
362(c)(2), 2-30n
368, 2-29 (Table 2-3), 7-16, 7-23, 7-26, 7-31, 7-35, 7-50, 7-53
368(a)(1), 7-15
368(a)(1)(A), 7-15, 7-23n
368(a)(1)(B), 1-6, 7-32, 7-64
368(a)(1)(C), 7-28, 7-28n, 7-30
368(a)(1)(D), 7-30n, 7-31, 7-37–7-39, 7-45
368(a)(1)(E), 7-41
368(a)(1)(F), 7-43
368(a)(1)(G), 7-35
368(a)(2)(A), 7-31
368(a)(2)(B), 7-28
368(a)(2)(C), 7-26n, 7-30
368(a)(2)(D), 7-26
368(a)(2)(G), 7-28n
368(a)(2)(H), 7-30
368(b), 7-51
368(c), 2-13, 7-26n, 7-33, 7-35n, 7-36, 7-40n
381, 6-12, 6-32, 7-46, 7-49
381(a), 6-7 (Table 6-2), 6-13n, 7-46, 11-29n
381(a)(1), 7-10n
381(c), 7-46
382, 7-34, 7-35n, 7-46–7-49, 7-53, 7-61, 8-23, 8-27, 8-27n, 8-29n, 8-29–8-31, 8-33, 8-45
382(b)(1), 7-48n
382(b)(2), 7-48n
382(b)(3), 7-49n
382(c), 7-48n
382(f), 7-48n
382(g), 7-47n
382(k)(1), 7-47n
382(k)(2), 7-47n
382(k)(3), 7-47n
383, 7-46–7-47, 7-49, 8-23, 8-29n, 8-33
384, 7-46–7-47, 7-49, 8-23, 8-29n
385, 2-26–2-27
401-416, *9-27n*
401(a), *9-28*
401(a)(17), *9-36n*
401(d), *9-36n*
401(k), *9-28n*, *9-27–9-31*, *9-61*
402(e), *9-30n*
404, *8-13n*
404(a)(3)(A), *9-30n*
404(b), 3-10n
404(h)(1), *9-41n*
404(l), *9-36n*
408(k), *9-41n*
408(p), *9-42n*
408A, *9-38n*
409(a), *9-28n*
441, 2-6n, 3-2n, 7-10
411(a), *9-29n*
441(b), 1-22 (Table 1-2)
441(i), 3-3n, 3-4n
414(q), *9-28n*
415(b)(1), *9-30n*
415(c), *9-30n*
415(c)(1), *9-36n*
422, *9-33n*
441(a), *11-27*
441(f), *11-3n*
441(g), *11-2n*
441(i)(2), *6-28n*
442, *11-4n*
443(a)(2), 3-2n
443(b)(2), *11-6n*
444, *11-4*, 3-3n, 9-14–9-15, 9-31–9-32, 11-13n, 11-13–11-14, 11-37, 11-40
446, *11-7n*, *11-36*, 3-4n, 3-48, 7-10
446(b), *6-18*
446(e), *11-27*
447, 3-4n
448, *6-20*, 3-4n, 3-48, 8-8
448(a), *11-8n*
448(b), *11-8n*
448(c), *11-8n*, 5-3
448(c)(2), 5-4
448(d), 3-22
451, *11-7n*
452, *3-28*
453, *11-7n*, *11-18*, 2-10 (Table 2-1), 8-13, 8-15
453(a), 7-4n
453(b)(2), *11-18n*
453(e), *11-21*
453(f)(6)(C), 7-19
453(h)(1)(A), 6-16n
453(i)(1), *13-19n*
453(i)(1)(B), *13-19n*
453(i)(2), *13-19n*
453(k), *11-18n*
453A(b)(2)(B), *11-21n*
453A(c), *11-21n*
453A(d), *11-20n*
453B(a), *11-20n*
460(a), *11-16n*
460(b)(3), *11-17n*
460(e), *11-16n*
461(c), *6-21*, *7-11*
461(g), *6-19n*, *7-19n*
461(h), *6-20n*, *6-21*, *11-9n*
465, 5-16n, 11-22
465(a), 3-19n, 9-25n
465(a)(1)(B), *8-12n*

465(b)(6), **9-25n**
465(c)(7), *8-13n*
469, *3-15n, 7-14, 8-7, 8-42,* **5-16n, 9-26, 10-29**
469(a)(2)(B), **3-20n**
469(a)(2)(C), **3-20n**
469(c)(1), *8-10n*
469(c)(2), *8-10n*
469(c)(6), *8-10n*
469(e)(1), *8-8n*
469(e)(2), **3-20n**
469(g), *8-8n*
469(g)(2), *8-9n*
469(h)(2), **9-26n**
469(h)(4), *8-13n*
469(i)(1), *8-15n*
469(j)(1), *8-12n*
469(j)(2), *8-13n*
469(j)(8), *8-10n*
469(k)(2), *8-13n*
471, *11-36*
471(b), *11-14n*
472(c), *11-12n*
472(d), *11-30n*
472(f), *11-13n*
474(c), *11-13n*
475, *5-14n*
475(b), *5-14n*
481, *11-27n*
481(a), *11-26, 11-27n*
481(b)(1), *11-27n*
481(b)(2), *11-27n*
481(c), *11-27n*
483, *11-22*
483(d), *11-22n*
501, **5-25, 8-3**
501(c)(2), **8-3n**
501(c)(3), *3-14, 7-24n, 7-27,* **11-40**
502, **5-25**
503, **5-25**
504, **5-25**
529, *4-8, 4-8n*
529(c)(3)(B)(v), *4-8n*
530, *9-40n, 14-14*
530(b)(1), *9-40n*
532, **5-50**
532(a), **5-24**
532(b), **5-25n**
532(c), **5-25n**
533(a), **5-25**
533(b), **5-25**
534, **5-25**
535(b), **5-31n**
535(c), **5-32n**
537, **5-27, 5-31, 5-50**
537(a), **5-30**
542(a), **5-16n, 5-50**
542(a)(2), *8-12n*, **5-16**
543(a)(1), **5-50**
543(a)(2), **5-19n**
543(a)(7), **5-20n**
543(a)(8), **5-18n**
543(b)(1), **5-17n**
543(b)(2), **5-17n**
543(b)(3), **5-17n**
544, **5-16, 5-20**
544(a)(4)(A), **5-16n**
545(b)(1), **5-21n**
545(b)(2), **5-21n**
545(b)(3), **5-21n**
545(b)(4), **5-21n**
545(b)(5), **5-22n**
547, **5-23**
547(c), **5-23n**
547(d), **5-23n**
547(e), **5-23n**
561(a), **5-22n**
561(a)(3), **5-22n**
562(a), **5-22n**
562(b), **5-22n**
562(b)(1)(B), **5-32n**
562(c), **5-22n, 5-32n**
563(a), **5-32n**
563(b), **5-22n**
564, **5-22**
565, **5-22n**
611(a), *10-19n*
611(b), **14-9**
612, *10-19n*
613(a), *10-19n*
613A(c), *10-19n*
613A(c)(7)(D), **9-15n**
616, *6-10n*, **5-35**
617, **11-14, 5-35**
617(d), **10-8**
631, *13-5*
631(a), *13-5n*
631(c), *13-6n*
631A(d)(1), *10-20n*
641(b), **14-4**
641-668, **14-5**
641-683, **14-4**
641-692, **14-2**
642(a)(1), **14-10n**
642(b), **14-4, 14-9**
642(c)(1), **14-8n**
642(e), **14-9n**
642(g), **14-35**
643(a), **14-11**
643(b), **14-5**
643(d), **14-34n**
645, **14-35n**
651, **14-13**
651(a), **14-9, 14-15n**
651(b), **14-9n, 14-15n**
652, **14-13**
652(a), **14-15n**
652(c), **14-35n**
661, **14-19**
661(a), **14-9n, 14-20**
661(c), **14-9n**
662, **14-19**
662(a), **14-9n, 14-21n**
662(a)(1), **14-21n**
662(a)(2), **14-21, 14-23n**
662(b), **14-21n**
662(c), **14-35n**
663, **14-19**
663(a)(1), **14-23n**
663(c), **14-22n**
664, **14-19**
671, **14-30**
671-679, **14-30**
672(e), **14-31**
673(a), **14-31**
674, **14-32**
675, **14-32**
676, **14-31**
677, **14-32**
677(a), **14-31n**
678, **14-33**
691, **14-27**
691(b), **14-28**
691(c), *7-9n*, **14-28–14-29, 14-40**
691(c)(1), **14-28n**
701-777, **9-2**
702, **11-15, 9-16**
702(a), **11-14, 9-16**
702(b), **9-17**
703(a), **9-16**
703(a)(2), **11-15**
703(a)(2)(F), **9-15n**
703(b), **9-15**
704, **9-18–9-19, 9-30, 10-17n, 10-29**
704(b), **9-17, 9-18n, 11-19**
704(c), **9-19, 10-3n, 10-16**
704(d), **9-24–9-26**
704(e), **9-29**
704(e)(2), **9-30n**
705, **9-23**
706, **9-12, 9-14-9-15**
706(a), **9-12**
706(b)(3), **9-13n**
706(c)(2), **10-22n**
706(d)(1), **9-18n**
707, **9-27, 9-27n**
707(a)(2)(A), **9-6**
707(a)(2)(B), **9-6**
707(b), *8-9n*, **9-26**
707(b)(1), *6-28*, **9-27**
707(b)(2), **9-27, 9-27n**
707(c), **9-26, 9-28, 9-28n**
708, **10-18, 10-23**
708(b), **10-22**
708(b)(2)(A), **10-25n**
708(b)(2)(B), **10-25n**
709(b), **9-12n**
721, **9-5, 9-10, 9-10n**
721(a), **9-6**
721(b), **9-6**
722, **9-6n, 9-8n, 10-24n**
723, **9-6n, 9-8, 10-24n**
724, **9-8–9-9, 9-9n**
724(d)(1), **9-9n**
731, **10-2–10-3, 10-3n**
731(a), **9-8n**
731(a)(1), **10-11, 10-12n**
731(a)(2), **10-12n**
731(b), **10-16n**
731(c), **10-4n**
732, **10-4n**
732(a)(2), **10-4n**
732(c), **10-4n, 10-12n**
735(a)(1), **10-7n**
735(a)(2), **10-7n**
735(b), **10-7n, 10-14n**
736(a), **2-23**
736(a)(1), **10-19n**
736(a)(2), **10-19n**
736(b), **10-19n**
737, **10-3n, 10-3–10-6, 10-16**
737(c), **10-4n**
741, **10-16**
743, **10-27**
751, **10-1–10-2, 10-7–10-11, 10-10 (Table 10-1), 10-13–10-18, 10-15 (Table 10-2), 10-17n, 10-20, 10-22, 10-26, 10-33–10-34**
751(a), **10-17n**
751(b), **10-9n**
751(c), **9-9n, 10-8n**
751(d)(2), **10-8n**
752, **9-7, 9-22**
752(a), **9-21n**
752(b), **9-21n**
754, **10-26–10-28, 10-44–10-45**
755, **10-27**
761(a), **9-2n**
761(d), **10-12n**
772, **10-31**
773(a), **10-32n**
773(b), **10-31n**
773(b)(2), **10-31n**
774(c), **10-23n, 10-33n**
775, **10-30, 10-30n**
801, **8-3, 8-3n**
852(b), *3-17n*
901, **11-14**
902, *14-17n*
904, *14-17n*
911, *2-18, 3-15n, 4-4, 14-13n, 14-17n*
911(a), *14-31n*
911(b)(1)(B), *4-18n*
911(b)(2), *4-18n*
911(d), *4-18n*
911(d)(2)(B), *4-18n*
911(e)(2), *4-18n*
931, *2-18, 3-15n*
933, *2-18, 3-15n*
1001, *8-2n*, **1-6, 2-9n, 7-17, 7-21**
1001(a), *4-3n, 5-2n*, **2-10 (Table 2-1), 7-18**
1001(c), **2-10 (Table 2-1), 6-17n, 7-11**
1012, *12-15n*, **2-10 (Table 2-1), 7-3n, 7-4n**
1014(a), *5-8n, 5-9n, 13-24n*, **7-6, 13-8n**
1014(b)(6), *5-9n*

BOLD = Corporations
ITALICS = Individuals

1014(c), **14-29n**
1014(e), **12-27n**
1015(a), *5-6n*
1015(d)(2), *5-7n*
1015(d)(6), *5-7n*
1031, *5-29, 12-2, 12-4, 12-9–12-10, 13-18,* **8-12**
1031(a), *12-2, 12-2n, 12-5n*
1031(a)(2), *12-4n*
1031(a)(2)(D), **10-20n**
1031(a)(3)(A), *12-6n*
1031(a)(3)(B), *12-6n*
1031(b), *12-2n, 12-6n*
1031(c), *12-6n*
1031(d), *12-7n*
1031(e), *12-4n*
1031(f)(1)(C), *12-8n*
1031(f)(2), *12-8n*
1031(f)(3), *12-8n*
1032, **2-10 (Table 2-1), 2-20n, 7-17, 7-21**
1033, *12-2, 12-10–12-14, 12-16, 12-20, 13-19, 13-19n*
1033(a), *12-13n*
1033(a)(1), *12-10n*
1033(a)(2), *12-12n*
1033(a)(2)(A), *12-12n–12-13n, 12-15n*
1033(a)(2)(A)(ii), *12-15n*
1033(a)(2)(B), *12-15n*
1033(a)(2)(B)(ii), *12-15n*
1033(b), *12-13n*
1033(d), *12-12n*
1033(e), *12-12n*
1033(f), *12-13n*
1033(g)(1), *12-14n*
1033(g)(2), *12-15n*
1033(g)(4), *12-15n*
1033(h)(1)(A), *12-21n*
1034, *12-17, 12-18n, 12-32*
1034(e), *12-17n*
1036, *12-5,* **7-42**
1038, *11-20n*
1060, *10-22*
1091, *6-22, 6-24*
1091(a), *6-23n*
1092(d)(1), **7-9**
1201, *5-20n*
1202, *1-14n, 5-17n, 5-17–5-19, 5-21, 8-30n, 14-4,* **2-29 (Table 2-3), 11-49–11-50**
1202(a), *4-20n,* **5-6**
1202(b)(1), *4-21n*
1202(d), *4-21n*
1202(e), *4-21n*
1211(b), *5-18n,* **14-16n, 14-24n**
1212(a), *5-20n*
1212(a)(1)(A)(ii), **8-33**
1212(b), *5-18n*
1221, *2-28, 5-13–5-14, 5-45, 8-5n, 13-5*
1221(2), *13-5n*
1222, *5-21, 5-28n,* **6-5 (Table 6-1)**
1222(11), *5-16n*
1223, *12-10n, 9-32n,* **2-10 (Table 2-1)**
1223(1), *12-9n, 5-28n, 5-29n,* **2-19n, 6-5 (Table 6-1), 7-18n, 7-20n, 7-21, 9-8n**
1223(1)(A), *12-12n*
1223(11), *5-29n*
1223(2), **2-10 (Table 2-1), 2-21n, 6-5 (Table 6-1), 9-9, 10-24n**
1223(5), *5-29n,* **4-14n, 4-15n**
1223(6), **4-15n**
1231, *5-13, 5-29, 6-5n, 7-23, 7-23n, 8-3, 8-5, 8-7, 8-22, 8-24, 10-15–10-16, 11-19, 12-9, 13-1–13-18, 13-20–13-25, 13-29, 13-34,* **1-8, 2-10 (Table 2-1), 2-17–2-20, 2-19n, 2-25, 3-7, 3-19, 3-28, 5-17, 5-17 (Table 5-1), 6-6, 8-6 (Table 8-1), 8-8, 8-12, 8-24, 8-25n, 8-32–8-33, 8-39, 9-8–9-9, 9-16, 9-18, 9-32, 10-8, 10-32, 11-14, 11-18, 11-43, 11-46, 11-48, 11-51 (Table 11-2)**
1231(a)(1), *13-2n, 13-3n*
1231(a)(2), *13-2n, 13-3n*
1231(a)(3)(A), *13-6n*
1231(a)(4)(B), *13-6n*
1231(a)(4)(C), *13-7n*
1231(b), **10-28**
1231(b)(1), *13-5n*
1231(b)(2), *13-6n*
1231(b)(3), *13-6n*
1231(b)(4), *13-6n*
1231(c)(1), *13-3n*
1231(c)(3), *13-2n*
1231(c)(4), *13-2n*
1234(a), *5-25n*
1234(b), *5-21n*
1235, *5-25–5-26*
1235(a), *5-26n*
1236, *5-14*
1237, *5-15*
1237(b)(3), *5-15n*
1239, *13-21–13-22,* **2-17n, 3-18–3-19, 3-27, 8-2n, 8-17n**
1239(a), *13-21n,* **3-19**
1239(b), **8-17n**
1239(b)(2), *13-22n*
1239(c), *13-22n*
1241, *5-27n*
1244, *1-14n, 5-14, 8-4–8-5, 8-5n, 8-7,* **2-28 (Table 2-2), 2-31–2-32, 2-32n, 6-5 (Table 6-1), 6-6, 6-9, 6-18, 7-13, 7-15, 11-4**
1244(a), *5-14n*
1244(b), *5-14n*
1244(c)(2), *8-6n*
1245, *7-23, 10-15–10-16, 11-18, 13-1–13-2, 13-5, 13-7–13-11, 13-9n–13-10n, 13-14–13-20, 13-22–13-25, 13-34,* **2-17, 2-25, 3-6–3-7, 3-11, 5-39, 6-13, 7-2, 7-5, 7-13, 7-17, 7-63, 8-17, 9-9–9-10, 9-17, 10-8, 11-18, 11-43, 11-46, 11-48**
1245(a)(2)(C), *10-15n, 13-10n*
1245(a)(3), *13-9n*
1245(a)(3)(B)(i), *13-9n*
1245(a)(3)(C), *13-10n*
1245(a)(5), *13-10n, 13-14n*
1245(a)(5)(C), *13-14n*
1245(b)(1), *13-17n*
1245(b)(2), *13-18n*
1245(b)(3), **2-17n, 2-24n, 6-13n, 7-17n, 9-10n**
1245(b)(4), *13-19n*
1245(d), *13-17n*
1250, *5-17, 5-19, 5-33, 13-1–13-2, 13-4, 13-7–13-8, 13-10–13-19, 13-22, 13-24–13-25, 13-34–13-35* **2-17, 3-6–3-7, 3-11, 3-19, 5-39, 6-13, 7-2, 7-13, 7-17, 7-62, 9-9–9-10, 10-8, 10-17n, 10-17–10-18**
1250(a)(1)(B)(i), *13-15n*
1250(a)(1)(B)(ii), *13-15n*
1250(a)(1)(B)(iii), *13-15n*
1250(a)(1)(B)(iv), *13-15n*
1250(a)(1)(B)(v), *13-14n*
1250(a)(2)(B)(v), *13-14n*
1250(a)(3), *13-11n*
1250(b)(1), *13-11n*
1250(c), *13-11n*
1250(c)(3), **2-17n**
1250(d)(1), *13-17n*
1250(d)(2), *13-18n*
1250(d)(3), **2-24n, 6-13n, 7-17n, 9-10n**
1250(d)(4), *13-19n*
1250(i), *13-17n*
1252, *13-21, 13-25,* **10-8**
1252(a)(1), *13-21n, 13-23n*
1252(a)(3), *13-21n*
1253, *5-26n, 5-26–5-27*
1253(a), *5-26n*
1253(b)(2), *5-27n*
1253(e), *5-26n*
1254, *13-25,* **10-8**
1254(a)(1), *13-21n*
1255, *13-25*
1271(a), *5-22n,* **2-27**
1271(a)(2), *5-22n*
1272, **2-27**
1272(a)(3), *5-23n*
1273, **2-27**
1273(a)(1), *5-22n*
1273(a)(3), *5-23n*
1274, *11-22–11-23,* **2-27**
1274(c)(4), *11-23n*
1274(d), **12-28**
1274A, *11-23*
1274A(c), *11-24n*
1275, **2-27**
1276(a)(1), *5-24n*
1276(b)(1), *5-24n*
1276(b)(2), *5-24n*
1278, **10-8**
1278(a)(2)(C), *5-24n*
1283, **10-8**
1301, *3-10n*
1311, **15-29**
1312, **15-29**
1313, **15-29**
1314, **15-29**
1341, *3-26n*
1361, **11-11**
1361(b)(1), **11-5n**
1361(b)(1)(A), **11-4n**
1361(b)(1)(B), **11-4n**
1361(b)(1)(C), **11-4n**
1361(c)(1), **11-4**
1361(c)(2), **11-50**
1361(c)(4), **11-6n**
1361(c)(5), **11-7**
1361(d), **11-4n**
1362, **11-8n, 11-9n**
1362(b)(2), **11-8**
1362(b)(5), **11-37n**
1362(d)(2), **11-50**
1362(e), **11-34n**
1362(e)(2), **11-11**
1362(e)(3), **11-11**
1362(e)(5)(A), **11-35n**
1362(f), **11-50**
1363(a), **5-25n**
1363(b)(2), **11-15n**
1363(b)(3), **11-15n**
1363(b)(4), **11-15n**
1363(c), **11-14n**
1363(d), **11-7**
1363(d)(3), **11-18**
1366(a), **11-14n, 11-19n**
1366(b), **11-15**
1366(d), **11-21n**
1366(d)(1), **11-21n**
1366(d)(2), **11-22n**
1366(d)(3), **11-22n**
1366(d)(3)(B), **11-23n**
1366(e), **11-23**
1367(a), **11-24n**
1367(b)(2)(B), **11-25n**
1368(b), **11-27n**
1368(d), **11-27n**
1368(e), **11-29n**
1368(e)(3), **11-36**
1371, *8-42*
1371(b), **11-15n**
1371(e), **11-31n**
1372(a), **11-33n**

1372(b), **11-33n**
1374, **11-7, 11-16–11-18, 11-17n, 11-37–11-38**
1375, **11-7, 11-10–11-11, 11-15–11-16, 11-16n, 11-17n, 11-37–11-38**
1377(a), **11-34n**
1377(a)(2), **11-20n**
1377(b)(2), **11-22**
1378(a), *11-2n*, **11-13**
1378(b), **11-13**
1396, *14-10 (Table 14-1), 14-21n*
1402(a)(12), *1-11n*
1501, **1-10n, 8-2, 8-4**
1502, **1-10, 8-2**
1503, **8-2**
1504, **3-15n, 8-2, 8-4**
1504(a), **3-27n, 8-2**
1504(a)(4), **8-3n**
1504(b), **3-27n, 8-3**
1504(c)(2)(A), **8-3n**
1561, **3-22n, 8-10**
1561(a), **3-29n**
1561(a)(2), **5-32n**
1563, **3-22n, 8-4**
1563(a)(1), **3-23n**
1563(a)(2), **3-23n**
1563(a)(3), **3-25n**
1563(c), **3-23n**
1563(d)(1), **3-23n**
1563(d)(2), **3-23n**
2001, **12-3, 13-27 (Table 13-3)**
2001(b), **13-4, 13-23n, 13-27 (Table 13-3)**
2001(b)(2), **13-4, 13-24**
2001(c), **13-4, 13-23**
2010, **13-5, 13-23, 13-27 (Table 13-3)**
2010(c), **13-23**
2011, **13-24, 13-27 (Table 13-3)**
2011(b), **13-24**
2011(f), **13-24**
2012(a), **13-24**
2013, **13-25**
2013(a), **13-25**
2014, **13-25**
2031(a), **13-46**
2032, **13-2n, 13-7**
2032(a), *5-8n*
2032(c), **13-8n**
2032A, **13-30–13-31**
2033, **13-9 (Table 13-1), 13-10, 13-13, 13-16, 13-27 (Table 13-3)**
2034, **13-10n**
2035, **13-9 (Table 13-1), 13-10, 13-17, 13-17n, 13-25, 13-27 (Table 13-3), 13-37**
2035(a), **13-10**
2035(a)(2), **13-16n**
2035(b), **13-11n**
2036, **13-9 (Table 13-1), 13-10–13-13, 13-17, 13-17n, 13-20, 13-24, 14-3n, 14-30**
2036(b)(1), **13-12n**
2036(b)(2), **13-12n**
2037, **13-9 (Table 13-1), 13-10–13-13, 13-17, 13-17n**
2038, **13-9 (Table 13-1), 13-10–13-11, 13-13, 13-17, 13-17n, 13-37, 14-3n**
2039, **13-9 (Table 13-1), 13-13, 13-27 (Table 13-3)**
2039(b), **13-14**
2040, **13-9 (Table 13-1), 13-14, 13-27 (Table 13-3)**
2040(a), **13-14n**
2040(b)(1), **13-15**
2041, **13-9 (Table 13-1), 13-15, 13-17n**
2042, **13-9 (Table 13-1), 13-10, 13-16, 13-27 (Table 13-3)**
2043, **13-17, 13-17n**
2044, **13-9 (Table 13-1), 13-17, 13-17n, 13-22**
2053, **13-18 (Table 13-2), 13-18–13-20, 13-27 (Table 13-3), 13-28–13-29, 13-35, 13-38**
2054, **13-18 (Table 13-2), 13-19–13-20, 13-28–13-29, 13-35**
2055, **13-18 (Table 13-2), 13-19, 13-27 (Table 13-3)**
2056, **13-18 (Table 13-2), 13-20n, 13-27 (Table 13-3)**
2056(b)(7), **13-22**
2056(c), **13-21**
2057, **13-18 (Table 13-2), 13-22**
2501(a), **12-7**
2501(a)(5), **12-9n**
2502(c), **12-31n**
2503(b), *1-8n, 5-7n, 5-31n*
2503(b), **12-4n, 12-16, 15-41**
2503(c), **12-17–12-18, 14-3, 14-34, 15-41**
2503(e), **12-8, 12-25**
2504(c), **12-32n**
2505, **12-6n**
2505(b), **12-7n**
2511, **13-22n**
2511(a), **12-7**
2512(b), *1-8n*
2513, **12-6, 12-22**
2513(d), **12-31n**
2514, **12-15**
2515, **13-31n**
2516, **12-9**
2518(a), **12-9**
2518(b), **12-10n**
2519, **13-17, 13-22n**
2522, **12-21**
2523(a), *1-8n*
2523(b), **12-19n**
2523(f), **12-20n**
2524, **12-18, 12-19n, 12-21**
2601, *7-9n*
2611, **13-30n**
2612(a), **13-30n**
2623, **13-31n**
2631(a), **13-31n**
2641, **13-30n**
2701, **12-13, 7-42**
2702, **12-13, 7-42**
2703, **12-13, 7-42**
2704, **12-13, 7-42**
3301, *1-11n*
3302, *1-11n*
3401, *4-23n*
3402(f)(1)(E), *14-26n*
3403, *14-25n*
4943, **5-30**
4973(b), *9-38n*
4975(e)(7), *9-28n*
6012(a)(1), *2-31n*
6012(a)(2), **3-34n, 15-13n**
6012(a)(3), **14-35n**
6012(a)(4), **14-35n**
6012(a)(5), **14-35n**
6012(c), *2-31n*
6013, *2-20n*, **15-41**
6013(d)(3), *2-30n*
6013(g), *2-20n*
6014, *14-32n*
6015, **15-30n**
6015(b), *2-30n*
6017, *14-7n*
6018, **13-35**
6018(a), *5-8n*
6019, **12-30**
6031, **10-33n**
6031(a), **15-13n**
6037, **11-37**
6037(b), **11-38n**
6038, **15-10**
6043, **6-20**
6043(a), **6-20**
6045(a), *5-36n*
6045(c), *5-36n*
6045(e)(4), *7-36n*
6072(a), *2-32n*, **14-36n, 15-13n**
6072(b), **3-35n, 11-37n**
6072(c), **15-13n**
6075(a), **13-36n**
6075(b), **12-31n**
6081(a), **13-36n, 15-13n**
6081(b), **15-13n**
6110, **1-13**
6115, *7-34n*
6151(a), **14-36n, 15-13n, 15-40**
6151(b)(1), **15-14n**
6161(a)(1), **13-28**
6161(a)(2), **13-28n**
6163, **13-28**
6166, **4-25–4-26, 13-28–13-29, 13-34–13-35**
6166(b)(1), **13-28n**
6213(a), **15-9n**
6221, **9-32n**
6222, **9-32n**
6231(a)(3), **9-32**
6231(a)(7), **9-33n**
6233, **11-38n**
6240, **10-33n**
6241, **10-33n**
6242, **10-33n**
6321, **12-39**
6404(e), **15-15n**
6404(g), **15-15n**
6501, **12-32n**
6501(a), *1-22n*, **15-27**
6501(b)(1), *1-22n*, **15-27n**
6501(c), *1-22n*
6501(c)(1), **15-28n**
6501(c)(2), **15-28n**
6501(c)(3), **15-28n**
6501(c)(4), **15-28n**
6501(c)(9), **12-32n**
6501(e), *1-22n*, **15-27n**
6501(e)(2), **15-28n**
6501(h), **15-28n**
6511(a), *1-22n*, **15-29n**
6511(d)(1), *8-34n*
6611(e), *1-22n, 14-30n*
6512, **15-29n**
6531, **15-29n**
6601, **13-36**
6601(a), **15-14n**
6601(b), **5-37**
6601(b)(1), **15-14n**
6601(c), **15-15n**
6601(e)(2)(B), **15-18, 15-22n, 15-25n**
6601(h), **15-22n**
6601(j), **13-29n**
6621, **3-32n, 3-32–3-34, 13-28, 13-28n, 15-14–15-15, 15-21**
6621(a), *1-22n*, **15-16n, 15-17**
6651(a)(1), *1-22n*
6651(a)(2), *1-22n*, **15-18n**
6651(b)(1), **15-16n**
6651(b)(2), **15-18n**
6651(c)(1), *1-22n*, **15-19n**
6651(f), *1-22n*, **15-16n**
6653, **5-37**
6654, *1-23n, 14-25n, 14-28n*, **15-17**
6654(d), **15-20n**
6654(d)(1)(C), **15-20n**
6654(d)(2), **15-22n**
6654(e), **15-22n**
6654(f), **15-20n**
6654(g), **15-20n**
6654(l), **14-36n**
6655, **3-31n, 5-37, 11-38n, 15-17**
6655(c)(2), **3-31n**
6655(d)(1), **3-48**
6655(d)(2), **11-38, 8-35**

BOLD = Corporations
ITALICS = Individuals

6655(d)(2)(B), **3-32n**
6655(e), **11-38**
6655(g), **5-37**
6655(i)(1), **3-31n**
6662, *1-23n,* **1-38, 12-32, 15-41**
6662(a), **15-22n**
6662(b), **15-22n, 15-25n**
6662(c), **15-17, 15-22n, 15-23n**
6662(d), **15-17, 15-23n**
6662(d)(1), **15-23n**
6662(d)(2)(C)(iii), **15-24n**
6662(g), **13-36n**
6662(g)(2), **12-32**
6662(h), **13-36n**
6663, *1-23n*, **15-17**
6663(c), **15-25n**
6664, **15-41**
6664(c), **15-23n**
6672, *4-23n, 14-42*
6674, *4-23n*
6682(a), *14-26n*
6694, **1-35, 15-31–15-33**
6694(a), **15-18, 15-23n**
6694(b), **15-18**
6695, **15-31–15-32**
6695(a), **15-18**
6695(b), **15-18**
6695(c), **15-18**
6695(d), **15-18**
6695(e), **15-18**
6695(f), **15-18**
6695(g), *14-33n*
6696, **15-31**
6701, **15-33n**
6701(b), **15-18**
6721, *4-23n*
6901, **15-31**
7201, **15-17, 15-26**
7202, **15-17, 15-26**
7203, **15-17, 15-26**
7204, **15-26**
7205, **15-26**
7206, **15-17, 15-26**
7206(2), **15-26n**
7207, **15-26**
7208, **15-26**
7209, **15-26**
7210, **15-26**
7211, **15-26**
7212, **15-26**
7213, **15-26**
7214, **15-26**
7215, **15-26**
7216, **15-26**
7463, **1-17n**
7491, **1-7–1-8, 15-10n**
7503, *2-32n*
7519, **9-15, 9-31–9-32, 11-13, 11-38**
7519(b), *11-4n*
7520, **12-12, 12-38, 13-7n**
7701, **1-8**
7701(a)(4), **3-2n**
7701(a)(36), **15-31**
7701(b), *2-17n*
7704, **10-28**
7704(d), **10-28**
7704(g)(3), **10-28n**
7704(c), *8-13n*
7805, **1-9–1-10**
7872, **12-28–12-29, 4-12**

1.1502-21(b)(3)(i), **8-24n**
1.1502-21(c)(2)(i), **8-28n**
1.1502-21(e), **8-24n**
1.1502-22(a)(1), **8-32n**
1.1502-22(b), **8-32n**
1.1502-24(a), **8-23n**
1.1502-26(a)(1), **8-22n**
1.1502-43, **5-50**
1.1502-75(a)(1), **8-36n**
1.1502-76(a), **8-8n**
1.1502-76(b)(1)(i), **8-7n**
1.1502-76(b)(1)(ii), **8-7n**
1.1502-76(b)(2), **8-8n**
1.1502-76(c), **8-37**
1.1502-77(a), **8-37n**
1.1502-91(a)(1), **8-29n**
1.1502-91(c), **8-29n**
1.1502-92(b)(1)(i), **8-29n**
1.1502-92(b)(1)(ii), **8-29n**
1.1502-93(a), **8-30n**
1.1502-93(d), **8-30n**
1.1502-95(b), **8-30n**
1.1563-1(a)(3), **3-25n**
1.6012-1(a)(5), **15-30n**
1.6012-2(a)(2), **3-34n, 6-20**
1.6013-1(a), *2-31n*
1.6043-1(b), **6-20**
1.6043-2(a), **6-20**
1.6043-2(b), **6-20**
1.6050H-1(f)(3), *7-18n*
1.6081-3, **11-37n, 3-35n**
1.6081-3(a), **15-13n**
1.6081-4(a)(1), *2-32n*
1.6081-4(a)(2), *2-32n*
1.6661-5(d)(1), **15-25n**
1.6662-3(b)(1), **15-23n**
1.6662-3(b)(2), **15-23n**
1.6662-4(d), **15-24n**
1.6662-4(f)(1), **15-23n**
1.6662-4(f)(2), **15-23n**
1.6655-3, **8-36**
1.6655-4(e)(3), **8-35n**
1.6694-2(b)(2), **15-32, 15-32n**
1.6694-3, **15-32**
1.6695-1(b)(5), **15-32n**
15A.453-1(c), *11-21n*
15A.453-1(d)(2)(ii)(A), *11-21n*
20.2031-1(b), **13-6n**
20.2031-2(b), **13-6n**
20.2031-2(e), **13-7n**
20.2031-5, **13-46**
20.2031-8(a), **13-14n**
20.2032-1(f), **13-8n**
20.2036-1(a), **13-12n**
20.2042-1(c)(2), **13-16n**
20.2053-2, **13-19n**
20.2055-3, **13-20n**
20.2056(e)-1(a)(6), **13-21n**
20.7520-1(a)(2), **13-7n**
25.2503-3(a), **12-17n**
25.2503-3(b), **12-17n**
25.2503-4, **15-41**
25.2511-1(a), **12-13n**
25.2511-1(h)(4), **12-14n**
25.2511-1(h)(5), **12-14n**
25.2511-1(h)(8), **12-14n**
25.2511-2(b), **12-10n, 13-46**
25.2511-2(c), **12-11n**
25.2512-1, **12-11n**
25.2512-2, **12-11n**
25.2512-6, **12-14**
25.2512-8, **12-7n**
25.2513-2(a)(1), **12-31n**
25.2701-1, **12-13n**
25.2701-2, **12-13n**
25.2701-3, **12-13n**
25.2701-4, **12-13n**
25.2701-5, **12-13n**
25.2701-6, **12-13n**
25.2702-1, **12-13n**
25.2702-2, **12-13n**
25.2702-3, **12-13n**
25.2702-4, **12-13n**
25.2702-5, **12-13n**
25.2702-6, **12-13n**
31.3401(a)(10)-1(a), *14-25n*
31.3401(a)-1(a)(2), *14-25n*
31.3401(a)-1(b)(9), *4-23n*
31.3401(c)-1(b), *9-3n*
31.3402(f)(2)-1, *14-26n*
31.3402(g)-1(a), *14-25n*
301.6031-1(e)(2), **9-31n**
301.6324-1, **12-31n**
301.6404-2(b)(1), **15-15n**
301.6404-2(b)(2), **15-15n**
301.6501(f)-1, **5-37**
301.6651-1(c)(1), **15-16n**
301.6651-1(c)(3), **15-18n**
301.6651-1(c)(4), **15-18n, 3-34n**
301.6901-1(b), **15-31n**
301.7623-1(c), **15-6n**
301.7701-1, 2, **10-21n**
301.7701-1, 3, **10-21n**

Proposed Regulations

1.168-5(b)(2)(i)(B), **2-25n**
1.168-5(b)(4)(i), **2-25n**
1.168-5(b)(7), **2-25n**
1.671-2(e), **1-22 (Table 1-2)**
1.1502-55(b), **8-10**
1.1502-55(b)(1), **8-10n**
1.1502-55(f), **8-10n**
1.1502-55(h), **8-10n**
18.1378-1, **11-13n**

Temporary Regulations

1.62-1T(e), **1-22 (Table 1-2)**
1.163-8T, *7-12n*
1.163-8T(c)(4)(ii), *7-13n*
1.163-8T(c)(4)(iv), *7-13n*
1.163-8T(c), *7-13n*
1.404(b)-1T, **3-10n**
1.444-3T(b)(1), **11-37n**
1.444-3T(b)(3), **11-37n**
1.448-1T, **3-48**
1.448-2T, **3-48**
1.469-1(e)(3)(iii), *8-10n*
1.469-5T(a), *8-11n*
1.469-5T(c), *8-11n*
1.469-5T(d), *8-12n*
1.706-1T, **9-13n**
1.7519-2T, **11-38n**

APPENDIX K

INDEX OF GOVERNMENT PROMULGATIONS

Announcements
98-1, **1-13, 1-22 (Table 1-2)**
Information Releases
86-70, **1-13**
Letter Rulings
7842068, **12-15n**
8004111, *7-3n*
8227010, *8-18n*
8544001, *8-18n*
8752010, *7-16n*
8906031, *7-16n*
8919009, *7-4n*
9237014, *9-8n*
9320003, **5-11n**
9526020, *4-7n*
200130006, **1-13**
News Releases
83-93, *7-20n*
Notices
88-74, *7-16n*, **1-22 (Table 1-2)**
89-28, *8-29n*
89-56, *7-33n*
90-25, *7-33n*
93-4, *7-36n*
98-1, **1-13**
Revenue Procedures
71-21, *3-12, 3-28, 11-15n*
72-18, *6-12n*
74-33, *11-4n*, **9-14**
77-28, **1-22 (Table 1-2)**
77-37, **2-14n, 2-15n, 7-24n, 7-26n, 7-28n, 7-30n, 7-31n, 7-44n, 7-51**
83-59, **15-11n**
84-35, **9-33n**
84-58, **1-14n**
87-15, *6-20n, 7-18n*
87-32, *11-4n*, **11-13n, 3-3n, 9-14n**
87-56, *10-5n, 10-8, 12-3*
87-57, *10-6*
89-46, *3-29n*
92-3, *12-18n*
92-12A, *7-17n*
93-27, **9-11**
94-27, *6-19n–6-20n, 7-17n–7-18n*
95-17, **15-15, 15-15n**
95-39, **8-9n**
96-58, **15-23n**
97-19, **1-12**
97-37, **1-22 (Table 1-2)**
99-49, *11-26n*
2000-22, *3-8n, 3-10, 6-20n*
2000-50, *10-17–10-18*
2001-19, *10-13n*
2001-20, *3-11*
2001-47, *9-18n*
2001-54, *9-11n*
2002-1, **15-11, 15-11n**
2002-3, **15-12, 15-12n**
Revenue Rulings
53-271, *12-13n*
54-97, *5-33n*
54-567, *2-16n*
54-583, **14-43**
55-327, *8-18n*
56-60, *5-8n*
56-602, *6-24n*
56-613, **2-13n**
57-102, *4-2n*
57-246, *14-8n*
57-344, *2-13n*
57-418, *6-16 (Figure 6-1)*
57-599, *8-18n*
58-67, *2-13n*
58-234, *5-24n–5-25n*
58-256, *11-5n*
58-419, *2-13n*
58-601, *11-27n*
59-58, *4-31*
59-60, **13-7**
59-102, *12-11n*
59-259, **2-13n**
60-31, *9-30n*
60-329, *8-18n*
61-119, *12-5n*
62-197, *8-3n*
62-210, *7-3n*
63-91, *7-4n*
63-144, *4-15, 4-15n*
63-221, *12-11n*
64-31, *12-18n*
64-162, **11-26n**
64-222, *2-14n*
64-237, *12-14n*
65-34, *2-16n*
65-185, *11-19*
65-235, **6-21n**
65-261, *5-45*
65-307, *2-13n*
66-216, *7-6n*
66-365, **7-33n**
67-270, **15-41**
67-274, **7-32n**
68-20, *4-7n*
68-37, *12-13n*
68-55, **2-17–2-18**
68-285, **7-33n**
68-348, **6-14n**
68-537, **11-26n**
68-591, *9-22n*
68-602, **6-12**
68-662, *7-29n*
69-88, *8-18n*
69-115, **4-34n**
69-240, *12-13n*
69-292, *9-23n*
69-498, *8-3n*
69-608, **4-34, 4-34n**
69-654, *12-11n*
70-50, **11-21n**
70-104, **4-46**
70-106, **6-19n**
70-140, 1970-1 C.B. 73, **7-45n**
70-598, *5-28n*
71-41, *12-15*
71-137, *12-2*
71-288, **11-21n**
71-468, *2-13n*
72-112, *8-19n*
72-224, *3-6n*
72-225, *6-24n*
72-312, *3-6n*
72-327, **7-17n**
72-593, *7-4n*
73-35, *12-13n*
73-54, **7-33n**
73-136, *7-12n*
73-156, *2-40*
73-484, **8-35n**
74-7, *12-4n*
74-33, **11-13n**
74-43, **15-41**
74-78, *9-22n*
74-144, **1-22 (Table 1-2)**
74-187, *7-12n*
74-269, **7-42n**
74-296, **4-24n**
75-3, **4-24n**
75-67, **5-20n**
75-72, **12-15n**
75-144, **11-21n**
75-168, *9-62, 9-6n*
75-170, *9-7n*
75-249, **5-20n**
75-250, **5-20n**
75-302, *7-7n, 7-31n*
75-303, *7-6, 7-7n, 7-31n*
75-330, **5-37n**
75-432, *9-62*
75-502, **4-23n**
75-521, **6-19n**
75-538, *13-37*
76-226, *9-3n*
76-255, *2-31n*
76-317, **6-11n**
76-319, *12-14*
76-364, **4-23n, 4-24**
76-541, *12-32*
77-77, *4-2*
77-282, *2-13, 2-13n*
77-298, *12-22n*
77-355, **14-43**
77-415, **7-41n**
78-39, *11-8n, 7-7n*
78-146, *12-18n*
79-10, **6-14n**
79-59, **5-21n**
79-70, **2-16n**
79-157, *13-22n*
79-174, *8-18n–8-19n*
79-175, *7-6n*
79-275, **4-24n**
79-417, *11-26*
80-45, *7-24*
80-165, **14-43**
80-177, **6-6n**
80-189, **4-32n**
80-198, **2-26n**
80-265, **1-12**
81-7, **15-41**

Entries in **BOLD** denote references to **Corporations**
Entries in *ITALICS* denote references to *Individuals*

81-25, **7-44**
81-180, *12-11n*
82-26, *12-22n*
82-74, *12-11n*
82-149, *6-13n*
82-166, *12-4n*
82-204, *5-45*
83-39, *12-23n*
83-49, *12-13n*
83-120, **7-42n**
84-15, **9-8n**
84-52, **10-20n**
84-111, **10-21n**
84-113, *9-6n*
85-48, **6-14n**
85-164, **2-19n**
86-58, **3-48**
87-22, *6-20n, 7-18n*
87-32, **11-13n**
87-41, *9-3*
87-54, **5-37n**
87-57, **9-14n, 11-13n**
87-106, *7-5n*
87-138, **1-13**
89-51, *7-22n*
91-26, **9-27n**
92-29, *6-6n, 7-29n*
92-54, **3-31n**
93-61, **7-18n, 7-26**
93-62, **7-39n**
93-72, *7-6, 7-31n*
93-86, *9-6, 9-6n*, **1-6n**
97-9, *7-3n*
97-37, *11-27n*
97-48, **11-11n**
98-1, **1-12**
98-10, **7-32n**
98-55, **11-8n**
99-7, *9-6n, 9-10n*
1998-2, **11-8n**
2000-5, **7-24, 7-24n**
2000-22, *11-7n*
2001-3, **7-51n**
2001-10, *11-7n, 11-8*
2001-58, **7-48n**
Technical Advice Memoranda
9628002, *8-42*
9801001, **1-13**
Treasury Decisions
7224, **1-11**
8756, **1-22** (Table 1-2)
Treasury Department Circular
230, **15-33, 15-33n**

APPENDIX L

INDEX OF COURT CASES

Acme Construction Co., Inc., *6-36n*
Agran v. Shapiro, **15-34n**
Amax Coal Co., Michael O. Campbell v., *14-26*
American Liberty Pipe Line Co. v. CIR, *11-36*
Andrew, Giffin A., *8-25*
Apkin, Philip, *3-28n*
Aqualane Shores, Inc. v. CIR, **2-26n, 2-34n**
Arkansas Best Corporation v. CIR, *5-14, 5-14n*
Arrowsmith, F. Donald Exr., v. CIR, *3-25n*
Arrowsmith, F. Donald, v. CIR, **6-15n**
Asjes, Jr., Everet, *12-14*
Astone, Anthony, *13-19*
Atlas Tool Co., Inc. v. CIR, **5-28n**
Ayers, Gary, *3-23n*
Azar Nut Co. v. CIR, *5-45*
Badias & Seijas, Inc., **6-21n**
Balistrieri, Joseph P., *12-11n*
Barbetti, Desio, *2-40*
Bardahl International Corp., **5-28n**
Bardahl Manufacturing Corp., **5-28n**
Bart, Stuart, *8-27n*
Bazley, J. Robert, v. CIR, **7-41n**
Bell Realty Trust, **5-50**
Bellinger, Edgar T. v. Simons, Morton L., **15-34n**
Belloff, Paul F., **1-18, 1-22 (Table 1-2)**
Berger, Ernest H., *6-36n*, **4-34n**
Berry, Henry W., *8-18n*
Berry, James E., v. Wiseman, *7-5*
Bertolini, Raymond, Trucking Co. v. CIR, *6-12*
Biscayne Bay Islands Co., *5-10*
Black Limited, E. E., v. Alsup, *11-16n*
Blair Holding Co., Inc., **5-50**
Blood Enterprises, Inc., George, *3-17n*
Bolton, Dorance D., v. CIR, *6-32n*
Bonaire Development Co. v. CIR, *6-19n, 11-8n*
Bongiovanni, John P., **2-26n**
Bonner v. City of Prichard, **1-20n**
Boston Fish Market Corporation, *4-31*
Boyle, Robert W., U.S. v., **15-40**
Bradley, M. A., Estate of, CIR v., *6-18n*
Bremerton Sun Publishing Co., **5-50**
Brumber, Loren S., *2-13n*
Bufferd, Sheldon B. v. CIR, **1-23n, 1-24n, 11-38n**
Burgess, Newton A., *7-20n*
Burnet v. Edith A. Logan, **6-15, 6-15n**
Burns, Howard F., v. U.S., *8-18n*
Buttorff, Gordon, U.S. v., **15-34n**
Byrum, Marian A., U.S. v., **1-21n**
Calhoun, Q.A., v. U.S., *11-3n*
Carey, Gerald, U.S. v., **4-34n**
Carlson, Ernest W., v. U.S., *14-42*
Carpenter, William H., *8-19n*
Cartwright, Douglas B., Executor, U.S. v., **1-10n**
Central Illinois Public Service Co. v. CIR, **1-24n**
Cesarini, Ermenegildo, v. U.S., *3-23n*
Chaitlen, Morrie, *11-36*
Chapman, Eldon S. et al., v., CIR, **7-33n, 7-64**
Chicago Stock Yards Co., Helvering v., **5-24n**
CIR v. American Liberty Pipe Line Co., *11-36*
CIR v. Rebecca Jo Reser, **15-41**
CIR v. Thor Power Tool Co., *11-36*
Clark, Donald E., v. CIR, **7-18, 7-18n**
Click, D. H., *12-32*
Cohan, George M., v. CIR, *6-16n, 6-16–6-17*
Comm v. Kikalos, *7-45*
Commerford, Patrick, U.S. v., *3-23n*
Cooney, James J., *3-10n*
Coors, Adolph, Co., *4-15*
Corn Products Refining Co. v. CIR, *5-13n, 5-13–5-14*
Correll v. U.S., *9-7n, 9-62*
Correll, O. Homer, U.S. v., **1-10n**
Costello, Edward J., *3-26*
Court Holding Co., CIR v., *1-30*
Crane, Beulah B., v. CIR, *5-3n, 8-2n*
Creative Solutions, Inc. v. U.S., *12-11n*
Crummey, D. Clifford, v. CIR, **12-18n**
Cumberland Public Service Co., U.S. v., *1-30*
Cunningham, Grace H., CIR v., *3-39*
Davis, Harold, v. U.S., *7-21n*
Davis, Kenneth C., *9-22n*
Davis, Maclin P., U.S. v., **1-21, 1-22 (Table 1-2), 4-23, 4-23n**
Dawson, Henry B., *5-9*
Day & Zimmerman, Inc., CIR v., **6-20n**
Dayton Hudson Corp. v. CIR, *11-14n*
Dean, J. Simpson, **1-18**
DeMarco, Frank, *14-19*
Demeter, Ann K., *12-18n*
Diamond, Sol, **9-10**
Diaz, Alfonso, **1-29**
Diaz, Frank, **1-29**
Diaz, Leonarda C., **1-28, 1-31**
Dibblee, Isabel, **1-30 (Figure 1-6)**
Diedrich, Victor P., v. CIR, **12-15n**
Disney, Roy O., U.S. v., *9-8*
DiVarco, Joseph, U.S. v., **15-26n**
Donahue v. Lathrop, **15-34n**
Doug-Long, Inc., **5-29n**
Drazen, Michael, *11-7*
Duarte, Henry D., **1-22 (Table 1-2), 11-23n**
Duberstein, Mose, CIR v., *4-16n*
DuPont, Pierre S., Deputy v., *6-6n, 7-12n*
Durden, Ray, *8-18n*
Eboli, Saverio, *6-19*
Eckell, Vincent W., *9-8*
Ehret-Day Co., *11-16n*
Eisner v. Myrtle H. Macomber, *3-6n, 3-16n, 3-33, 4-2*
Eisner v. Myrtle H. Macomber, **4-13, 4-13n**
Emilio L. Ippolito v. The State of Florida, **15-34n**
Evans, A. T., **7-51n**
Fairmont Homes, Inc., *6-8*
Farina, Antonino, v. McMahon, *3-23n*
Farrelly-Walsh, Inc., *5-27n*
Farrington, Ronald L., v. CIR, **2-33**
Fausner, Donald W., v. CIR, *9-9*
Fehlhaber, Robert v. CIR, **1-23n**
Fehrs, Edward J., v. U.S., **4-37, 4-37n**
Feldman, Richard L., *14-25*
First National Bank of Gainesville, Trustee, *11-26*
Flamingo Resort, Inc. v. U.S., *3-11*
Flower, Harriet C., v. U.S., *2-13n*
Flower, Harry M., *5-45*
Flushingside Realty & Construction Co., *12-12n*
Ford, Achille F., v. U.S., *5-33n*
Forest City Chevrolet, *12-11n*
Fox Chevrolet, Inc., *11-13*
France, Rose C., v. CIR, *7-3n*
Frank, Morton, *6-16 (Figure 6-1)*
Franklin, H. C., CIR v., *7-20n*
Fuchs, Frank, Estate of, v. CIR, *8-3n*
Generes, Edna, U.S. v., **2-32**
German, Jr., Harry, **1-28**
Gerstell, Robert S., *8-45*
Ginsburg, Max R., v. U.S., **10-23n**

Entries in **BOLD** denote references to **Corporations**
Entries in *ITALICS* denote references to *Individuals*

Gitlitz et al. v. Comm., **11-21**
Goldin, H.J., v. Baker, *3-24*
Goldman, Estelle, *5-45*
Golsen, Jack E., **1-21n**
Gould v. Gould, *3-18n*
Graham, Bette C., v. U.S., *13-22*
Green, Charles T., v. CIR, **1-24n**
Greene, Leonard, v. U.S., **1-20, 1-22 (Table 1-2)**
Gregg v. U.S., *8-42*
Gregory, Evelyn F., v. Helvering, **7-43n, 7-45, 7-45n**
Guito, Ralph M., Jr. v. U.S., *14-25n*
Gurvey, Gary, v. U.S., *5-27*
Haberkorn, Ronald R., *6-31n*
Haft, Robin, Trust, **4-37, 4-37n**
Hagaman v. Com., *3-17*
Hallmark Cards, Inc. v U.S., *4-31*
Hanlin, Marie, Executrix v. CIR, *6-24n*
Harrah's Club v. U.S., *10-2*
Harris, J. Wade, *13-18*
Hart Metal Products Corp. v. U.S., **5-37n**
Havemeyer, Horace, v. U.S., **13-7n**
Heininger, S. B., CIR v., *6-8n*
Heverly, Arden S., et. al., v. CIR, **7-64**
Hewitt, William, **7-51n**
Hezel, William J., *6-5*
Higgins, Eugene, v. CIR, *6-6n*
Hollman, Emanuel, *2-40*
Holsey, Joseph R., v. CIR, **4-35n**
Holt, Bill D., *8-3*
Hooper, H. M., *5-28n*
Horst, Helvering v., *3-30*
Hort, Walter M., v. CIR, *5-27n*
Howard, Jack R., *9-16*
Humphreys, Murray, v. CIR, *3-23n*
Hunt, C. L., *8-25n*
Hunter Mfg. Co., *5-22*
Huntsman, James R., v. CIR, *6-20n, 7-18n*
Hutchinson, Charles L., *8-27n*
Indopco, Inc., v. CIR, *6-10n*
Ippolito, Emilio L. v. Florida, **15-34n**
James, Eugene C., v. U.S., *3-23n*
Janss, Peter F., *9-7*
Jeanese, Inc. v. U.S., **1-10n**
Johnson, Richard E., v. Bingler, *4-7n*
Jones Co., Warren, **1-18**
Justus & Parker Co., *11-36*
Kahler, Charles F., *3-10n, 6-18n*
Keenan, W. J. Jr., v. Bowers, *8-19n*
Keller, Stephen A., v. CIR, *6-19n*
Kelley, Daniel M. v. CIR, **1-23n**
Kentucky & Indiana Terminal Railroad Co. v. U.S., *4-20*
Kimbell-Diamond Milling Co. v. CIR, **7-5, 7-5n**
King Enterprises, Inc. v. U.S., **7-19n**
Kirkpatrick, Donald O., **11-23n**
Koppers Co., Inc. v. U.S., **6-16n**
Kowalski, Robert J., CIR v., *4-15n*
Kuh, Johannes L., **1-28**
Lang Chevrolet Co., The, *3-17n*
Latchis Theatres of Keene, Inc. v. CIR, **5-50**
Lathrop v. Donahue, **15-34n**
Leavitt, Daniel, Estate of, v. CIR, **11-21n**
Lennard, Milton S., Estate of, **4-46**
Lerew, P.A., *7-46*
LeTulle, V. L. v. Scofield, **7-44n**
Levin, Samuel B., v. U.S., *6-6n*
Lewis, Nat, *9-6*
Liang, Walter K., v. CIR, *6-6n*
Liddle v. Comr., *10-36*
Liddle, Brian P., *6-10n*
Limericks, Inc. v. CIR, *3-17n*
Lindeman, Jack B., *4-14n*
London Shoe Co. v. CIR., *4-6n*
Loughlin, John O., v. U.S., *6-31n*
Lucas v. Earl, *3-30*
Lucas v. Guy C. Earl, **2-26n**
Lumpkin, James H. Jr., Estate of, v. CIR, **13-16n**
Marinello Associates, Inc., Marco S., *12-13*
Markarian, Frank, v. CIR, *2-13n*
Marshman, Homer H., CIR v., *5-3n*
Matheson, Chester, *8-35n*
Mayson Manufacturing Co. v. CIR, **4-12n**
McDaniel, David, *8-18n*
McDonald v. CIR, **1-10n**
McKenna, James P., *3-23n*
McKinney, Edith G., v. CIR, *6-32n*
McKinney, Edith G., **1-18**
McShain, John, *12-23n*
McWilliams, John P., *6-24n*
Meersman, J. P., v. U.S., *8-18n*
Melat, George R., *2-13n*
Menz, Norman W., *7-20n*
Millar, Gavin S., **11-23n**
Miller, John F., *2-13n*
Miller, William R., *8-18n*
Mizl, Daniel E., *7-3n*
Monteleone, Michele, *8-45*
Morgenstern, Joseph, *3-17n*
Morris, Homer P., *4-3n*
Morrison, James H., *7-23*
Morton L. Simons v. Edgar T. Bellinger, **15-34n**
Moss, John A., Estate of, **1-18**
Mountain Fuel Supply Co. v. U.S., *11-27*
Myron's Enterprises v. U.S., **5-28n**
Nelson Co., John A., v. Helvering, **7-44n**
Newark Morning Ledger Co. v. U.S., *10-14*
Noel, Marshall L., Estate of, CIR v., **13-16, 13-16n**
Notter, George K., *8-19n*
Nowland, Robert L., v. CIR, *4-3n*
Ohio River Collieries, *11-9*
O.H. Kruse Grain & Milling v. CIR, **2-27n**
O'Connell, Emmett J., v. U.S., *8-18n*
O'Neill, William J., Irrevocable Trust, **14-8**
Oppenheim's Inc. v. Kavanagh, *3-25n*
Orr, J. Thomas, **1-28**
Oswald, Vincent E., *6-36n*, **4-34n**
Pahl, J. G., *6-36n*
Pahl, John G., **4-34n**
Paparo, Jack, **4-23n**
Parker, James Edward, *2-13n*
Patterson, v. Williams, *9-62*
Peacock, Cassius L. III, *2-16n*
Peterson & Pegau Baking Co., *3-17n*
Picknally, Robert J., *9-22n*
Plastics Universal Corp., *6-36n*
Polacsek, R.A., *7-46*
Pollock v. FarmersU Loan & Trust Co., *1-2n*
Porter, H.K., Co., Inc., **6-32**
Powers, William J., *8-3n*
Poyner, Ernest L., v. CIR, *4-16n*
Prell, Charles M., Estate of, **13-7n**
Price, William K. III, *2-13n*
Pridemark, Inc. v. CIR, **6-16n**
Purvis, Ralph E., v. CIR, *6-6n*
Quinn, Frank D. Exec., v. CIR, *11-9n*
R. N. Smith v. U.S., *9-3n*
Raphan, Benjamin, v. U.S., **1-19**
Rebecca Jo Reser v. CIR, **15-41**
Reeves, Richard A., *3-23*
Riggs, Inc., George L., **6-19, 6-19n**
Robbins, J.H., *7-46*
Robinson, Willie C., *8-18n*
Rose, Robert M., v. CIR, *7-7n, 7-31n*
Ruddick Corp. v. U.S., **1-22 (Table 1-2)**
Russell, Edward H., v. CIR, **7-25n**
Scheft, William, **14-30n**
Schiff, Renate, v. U.S., *14-25n*
Schira, Mathias, v. CIR, *3-23n*
Schlude, Mark E., v. CIR, *3-12*
Schneider and Co., Charles, v. CIR, *6-36n*
Schwerm, Gerald, **1-28**
Selfe, Edward M., v. U.S., **11-21n**
Shaffer, Stephen R., *8-18n*
Shapiro v. Agran, **15-34n**
Sharp, Jeffrey G. v. U.S., **1-20, 1-22 (Table 1-2)**
Shauna C. Clinger, *10-36*
Simon v. Comr., *10-36*
Simon, Richard L., *6-10n*
Simons-Eastern Co. v. U.S., **5-30n**
Sirbo Holdings Inc. v. CIR, *4-31*
Smith, David, Estate of, **13-7n**
Smithgall, Charles A. v. U.S., *8-18n*
Soffron, George N. v. CIR, *5-45*
South Texas Lumber Co., CIR v., **1-10n**
Southwest Consolidated Corp., Helvering v., **7-41n**
Spaulding Bakeries, Inc., **6-32**
Speca, Gino A., v. CIR, **11-23n**
St. Charles Investment Co. v. Comm., *8-42*
Stacey, Howard, *8-18n*
Stafford, D. N., v. U.S., **2-12n, 9-6n**
Standard Fruit Product Co., *6-10n*
State Office Supply, Inc., **5-29n**
Stein, Frank, *6-24n*
Stewart, J. T. III, Trust, **6-16n**
Stewart, Spencer D., v. CIR, *12-12n*
Stiegler, Rene A. Jr., *12-19n*
Stolk, William C., v. CIR, *12-18n*
Stone, Tracy Co., Flint v., *1-2n*
Stuart, James P., *7-29*

BOLD = Corporations
ITALICS = Individuals

Sullivan, Manley S., U.S. v., *2-3n, 3-23n*
Sullivan, Neil, et al., CIR v., *6-14n*
Sun Properties, Inc. v. U.S., **2-26n, 2-34n**
Sunstein, Cass, *3-23n*
Super Food Services, Inc. v. U.S., *10-22*
Sutter, Richard A., *4-15n*
Technalysis Corp., **5-30**
Technalysis Corporation v. CIR, **5-25n**
Tellier, Walter F., CIR v., *6-7n–6-8n*
Thatcher, Wilford E., v. CIR, **2-26n**
The Donruss Company, U.S. v., **5-26, 5-26n**
Thoene, John J., *7-3n*
Thompson, Margie J., v. U.S., **1-19, 1-22 (Table 1-2)**
Thompson, William, A., Jr., *6-49*
Thompson-King-Tate, Inc. v. U.S., *11-16n*
Thor Power Tool Co. v. CIR, *11-11, 11-11n, 11-14, 11-36*
Timberlake, J. E., v. CIR, *3-17n*
Tomburello, Louis R., *4-5*
Toner, Linda M., **1-28**
Trent, John M., v. CIR, *8-27n*
Tsouprake, Ted E., v. U.S., *14-25n*
Tucker, Marvin D., *2-13n*
Tyler, Jean C., v. Tomlinson, *8-25n*
U.S. v. ———, *See* opposing party
Vila, U.S. v., *8-22*
Vogel Fertilizer Co. v. U.S., **1-21n**
Vogel Fertilizer Co., U.S. v., **1-10n**
Wagensen, F.S., *12-32*
Wall, H. F., v. U.S., **4-34n**
Wal-Mart Stores Inc. v. CIR, *11-14n*
Wassenaar, Paul R., **1-28**
Weiler, Jeffry L., *9-22n*
Weiner, L., *3-23n*
Welch, Thomas H., v. Helvering, *6-7n, 6-8n, 6-49*
Wells Lumber Co., J.W., Trust A., **1-18**
White, John P., *8-18n*
White, Layard M., *6-17n*
Whiting, Lauren, *8-18n*
Wilcox, Laird, CIR v., *3-23n*
Williams v. Patterson, *9-7n*
Williams, H.O., v. U.S., *11-36*
Wisconsin Cheeseman, Inc. v. U.S., *6-12n*
Wohlfeld, Nathan, *11-16n*
Young, Minnie K., v. CIR, *5-22n*
Yu, Jung Yul v. U.S., **15-6**
Zaninovich, Martin J., v. CIR, *6-19n, 11-8n*
Zarin, David, v. CIR, *4-20n*

APPENDIX M

SUBJECT INDEX

- Abandoned spouse, *2-22*
- Abandonment, of principal residence, *12-18–12-19*
- Accelerated cost-recovery system (ACRS)
  - alternative depreciation system, *10-8–10-9*
  - listed property, *10-10–10-13*
  - luxury automobiles, limitations on, *10-11–10-13*
  - real property, classification/recovery rates for, *10-7–10-8*
  - restrictions, *10-10–10-13*
  - straight-line method, use of, *10-8*
  - *See also* Modified ACRS, *10-1–10-13*
- Accelerated death benefits, *4-6*
- ACCESS legal data base, *1-25–1-26*
- Accountable plan, *9-16*
- Accounting for acquisitions, **7-12**
- Accounting methods
  - accrual method, *3-11–3-12*, *11-9–11-10*, **3-4–3-5**
  - affiliated groups, **8-8**
  - calendar-year requirement, *11-28*
  - cash receipts and disbursements method, *11-7–11-9*, *3-8–3-10*, **3-5**
  - change in, *11-25–11-27*
    - amount of change, *11-26–11-27*
    - reporting amount of change, *11-27*
    - voluntary changes, *11-27*
  - corporation/controlling shareholder using different methods, **3-19**
  - definition of, *11-2*
  - hybrid method, *11-10*, *3-12*, **3-5**
  - imputed interest, *11-22–11-25*
    - accrual of interest, *11-23–11-24*
    - applicable federal rate, *11-23*
    - gift, shareholder and other loans, *11-24–11-25*
  - installment sales, *11-28*
  - inventories, *11-11–11-14*, *11-28*
  - S corporations, **11-14**
  - special accounting methods, *11-15–11-22*
    - deferred payment sales, *11-21*
    - installment sales method, *11-17–11-21*
    - long-term contracts, *11-15–11-17*
  - *See also* specific methods, *3-8–3-12*, *11-1–11-28*
- Accounting periods, *11-28*, *11-2–11-7*
  - affiliated groups, **8-8**
  - C corporations, **3-2–3-4**
  - calendar-year requirement, *11-3–11-4*
  - changes in, *11-4–11-5*
    - Form 1128, Application for Change in Accounting Period, *11-5*
  - estates, **14-35**
  - 52- to 53-week year, *11-3*
  - fiscal year, *11-2*
  - partnerships, **9-12–9-15**, **9-31– 9-32**
  - periods of less than 12 months, returns for, *11-5–11-6*
  - S corporations, **11-13**, **11-37**
  - tax-planning considerations, *11-28*
  - trusts, **14-35**
  - *See also* specific methods
- Accrual method of accounting, *3-11–3-12*, *6-20–6-22*, *11-9–11-10*
  - accrual basis corporations, pledges made by, **3-10–3-11**
  - accrued compensation deductions, limitations on, **3-10**
  - affiliated groups, **8-8**
  - all-events test, *6-20–6-21*, *11-9*
  - C corporations, **3-4–3-5**
  - deductible expenses, *6-20–6-22*
  - economic performance test, *6-21*, *11-9–11-10*
  - prepaid income, *3-11–3-12*
- Accumulated adjustments account (AAA), **11-28–11-31**
- Accumulated earnings and profits (E&P), **4-3–4-8**
- Accumulated earnings tax
  - Accumulated earnings credit, **5-32–5-33**
  - accumulated taxable income, **5-31–5-33**
    - accumulated earnings credit, **5-32–5-33**
    - dividends-paid deduction, **5-32**
    - negative adjustments, **5-32**
    - positive adjustments, **5-31**
  - avoidance of, **5-36–5-37**
  - calculation of, **5-33–5-34**
  - corporations subject to, **5-24–5-25**
  - filing requirements, **5-37**
  - reasonable business needs, evidence of, **5-27–5-31**
  - tax liability, determination of, **5-31–5-33**
  - tax-avoidance motive, evidence of, **5-26**
  - tax-avoidance purpose, proving of, **5-25–5-26**
- Acquiescence policy, **1-17**
- Acquired property
  - cost of, *5-5–5-6*
    - capitalization of interest, *5-5–5-6*
    - identification problems, *5-6*
    - uniform capitalization rules, *5-5*
  - received as gift, *5-6–5-7*
    - gifts after 1921, *5-6–5-7*
      - gifts after 1976, *5-7*
  - received from decedent, *5-8–5-9*
    - basis of property, *5-8–5-9*
    - community property, *5-9*
  - *See also* Property transactions
- Acquisition indebtedness, *7-16–7-17*
- Acquisitions, **7-1**, **7-51**
  - accounting for, **7-12**
  - asset acquisitions, **7-11–7-12**
  - stock acquisitions, **7-12–7-20**
    - liquidating distributions and, **7-2–7-11**
  - tax attributes, **7-46–7-49**
    - assumption of, **7-46**
    - limitation on use of, **7-47–7-49**
  - tax consequences of, **7-11–7-14**
    - for acquiring corporation, **7-12**, **7-17–7-18**
    - for target corporation's shareholders, **7-12**, **7-18–7-20**
    - for target corporation, **7-11**, **7-16–7-18**
  - tax-free reorganization
    - tax consequences of, **7-16–7-20**
    - types of, **7-15–7-16**
  - taxable acquisitions
    - tax consequences of, **7-11–7-14**
  - taxable versus tax-free transactions, **7-11–7-14**
- Acquisitive reorganizations
  - type A reorganizations, **7-21– 7-27**
    - consolidations, **7-23–7-26**
    - mergers, **7-23–7-26**
  - type B reorganizations, **7-31–7-35**
    - advantages of, **7-34–7-35**
    - disadvantages of, **7-35**

Entries in **BOLD** denote references to **Corporations**
Entries in *ITALICS* denote references to *Individuals*

Acquisitive reorganizations (*continued*)
solely-for-voting-stock requirement, **7-32–7-33**
tax consequences of, **7-33–7-34**
triangular Type B reorganizations, **7-26–7-27**
type C reorganizations, **7-28–7-30**
advantages of, **7-29–7-30**
consideration used to effect reorganization, **7-28–7-29**
disadvantages of, **7-29–7-30**
stock distribution, **7-27**
substantially all requirement, **7-26**
tax consequences of, **7-30**
type D reorganizations, **7-30–7-31**
control requirements, **7-30–7-31**
tax consequences of, **7-31**
type G reorganizations, **7-35**
See also Divisive reorganizations; Reorganizations, **7-15, 7-21, 7-35**
Active conduct of a trade or business
Sec. 355, **7-40**
Active trade/business, interest expense, *7-13*
Adjusted basis of property
See also Basis, *5-4*
Adjusted current earnings, **5-9,–5-13**
eliminating adjustment, **5-35**
Adjusted gross income (AGI)
deductions for, *2-4–2-5*
deductions from, *2-4, 2-7–2-18*
dependency exemptions, *2-13–2-18*
itemized deductions, *2-7–2-10*
personal exemptions, *2-12*
standard deduction, *2-10–2-12*
definition of, *2-4*
state income taxes and, *1-7–1-8*
See also Gross income, *2-4*
Adjusted grossed-up basis, definition of, **7-8**
Adjusted income from rents (AIR), **5-17**
Adjusted ordinary gross income (AOGI), **5-16–5-17**
Adjusted taxable gifts, **12-4, 13-4**
valuation of, **13-4**
Adjustments, alternative minimum tax (AMT), **5-6, 5-9**
Administrative appeal procedures, *1-23*
Administrative convenience, income, *3-3–3-4*
Administrative exclusion, definition of, *4-2*
Administration expenses
as estate tax deduction, **13-18–13-19**
where to deduct, **13-35**
Administrative interpretations, **1-11–1-13**
announcements, **1-13**
citations of, **1-11**
information releases, **1-13**
letter rulings, **1-12–1-13**
notices, **1-13**
revenue procedures, **1-12**
revenue rulings, **1-11–1-12**
technical advice memoranda, **1-13**
Administrative interpretations, of tax law, *1-19*
information releases, *1-19*
letter rulings, *1-19*
revenue procedures, *1-19*
revenue rulings, *1-19*
technical advice memoranda, *1-19*
Treasury Regulations, *1-19*
Administrative powers, grantor trusts, retention of, **14-32**
Administrative procedures
audits of tax returns, **15-3–15-10**
Circular 230, **15-33**
civil fraud penalty, **15-25**
criminal fraud penalties, **15-26**
due dates, **15-13, 15-15**
estimated taxes, **15-19–15-22**
Internal Revenue Service, role of, **15-2–15-3**
negligence penalty, **15-22–15-23**
private letter rulings, requests for, **15-11–15-12**
statute of limitations, **15-26–15-29**
substantial authority, concept of, **15-24–15-25**
substantial understatement penalty, **15-23–15-25**
tax liability, **15-30–15-31**
tax practice issues, **15-31–15-33**
See also Internal Revenue Service; Statute of limitations; Tax law, **15-1, 15-33**
Adoption credit, *14-13–14-14*
Adoption expenses, *4-6–4-7*
Advance payments, annuities, *3-21*
Advances, ordinary loss deduction for, **2-32–2-33**
Affiliated corporations
worthless securities, **2-31–2-32**
Affiliated corporations, sale/exchange of securities in, *5-22*
Affiliated groups, **8-1–8-38**
compared to controlled groups, **8-4**
differences between definitions, **8-4**
definition of, **8-2, 8-4**
elections, **8-8**
accounting methods, **8-8**
tax years, **8-8**
filing requirements, **8-2**
requirements for, **8-2–8-3**
includible corporation requirement, **8-3**
stock ownership requirements, **8-2–8-3**
tax liability
alternative minimum tax liability, **8-10**
regular tax liability, **8-9–8-10**
termination of, **8-8–8-9**
effect on former members, **8-9**
good cause request to discontinue status, **8-9**
Aliens
S corporations and, **11-5**
Alimony
as gross income, *3-17–3-19*
definition of, *3-18*
recapture provisions, *3-18–3-19*
significance as income, *3-27*
All-events test, *6-20–6-21, 11-9*
Allocation of basis
basket purchase, *5-10*
common costs, *5-10–5-11*
deemed liquidation election, **7-6–7-11**
liquidation of target corporation, **7-5**
to individual assets, **7-8–7-10**
total basis for allocation, **7-8**
nontaxable stock dividends received, *5-11*
nontaxable stock rights received, *5-11–5-12*
See also Basis, *5-10–5-12*
Allocation of expenses
residential property, *6-32–6-34*
transportation expenses, *9-12*
Allocation of joint income, *3-6–3-7*
Alternate valuation date, **13-7–13-8**
definition of, **13-7**
election of, **13-36**
Alternative minimum tax (AMT), *14-2–14-7*
adjustments, *14-4–14-5*
adjusted current earnings, **5-9, 5-13**
affiliated corporations, **8-10**
alternative minimum taxable income, *14-2–14-3,* **5-4–5-14**
adjusted current earnings, **5-9–5-13**
adjustments, **5-6–5-9**
basis adjustments, **5-8**
definition of, **5-4–5-5**
disallowed losses, **5-8**
regular tax, **5-5**
statutory exemption, **5-5**
tax preference items, **5-6**
avoidance of, *14-29*
computation aspects, *14-2–14-3*
computation of, **5-2–5-15**
filing procedures, *14-32*
itemized deduction limitation, *14-4–14-5*
minimum tax credit, *14-6–14-7, 16-11–16-12*
reporting, **5-37**
S corporations, **11-32–11-33**
tax credits and, **5-14–5-15**
foreign tax credit, **5-15**
general business credit, **5-14–5-15**
minimum tax credit, **5-13–5-14**
tax preference items, *14-3–14-4*
taxpayers subject to, *14-2*
tentative minimum tax, **5-5**
trusts and estates, **14-8**
American Federal Tax Reports (AFTR) (Research Institute of America), **1-19**
Amortization
Form 4562, *10-23*
of intangible assets, *10-13–10-14*

BOLD = Corporations
ITALICS = Individuals

reporting of, *10-23*
Sec. 197 intangibles, *10-13–10-17*
Announcements, tax law, **1-13**
Annual accounting period
affiliated groups, **8-8**
C corporations, **3-2–3-4**
partnerships, **9-12–9-15, 9-31–9-32**
S corporations, **11-13, 11-37**
trusts and estates, **14-35**
Annual exclusion, gift tax
amount of, **12-16**
inter vivos gifts, **12-29**
present interest requirement, **12-16–12-18**
Crummey trust, **12-17–12-18**
special rule for trusts for minors, **12-17**
purpose of, **12-16**
result of availability of, **12-16**
Annualized income, exception, estimated taxes, **3-33–3-34**
Annuities
advance payments, *3-21*
as gross income, *3-19–3-21*
current year exclusion, *3-20*
date-of-death valuation, **13-7**
estate tax and, **13-13–13-14**
annuities not related to employment, **13-13–13-14**
exclusion ratio, *3-20*
expected return, *3-19*
gross estate, **13-13–13-14**
personal holding company income (PHCI) and, **5-18**
Antichurning rules
Sec. 338 deemed liquidation, **7-7, 7-10**
Sec. 351 corporate formation, **2-24–2-25**
Appeals Court procedures, **1-20**
Appeals Office
appeal to, **15-8–15-9**
appeals coordinated issue, **15-8–15-9**
protest letter, **15-8–15-9**
30-day letter, **15-8**
Appeals coordinated issues, **15-8–15-9**
Appreciated property
avoiding income tax on decedent's, *5-32*
donation of, *7-32–7-33*
Asset depreciation range (ADR) system, *10-8*
Asset-for-stock reorganization, Type C reorganization, **7-28–7-30**
Assets
business-use assets, *10-10–10-11*
capital assets, *2-28, 5-13–5-16, 5-30–5-31*
corporations
formation, **2-9–2-21**
tax-free reorganization, **7-16–7-41**
taxable acquisition, **7-11–7-12**
intangible assets, amortization of, *10-13–10-17*
partnerships
formation, **9-5–9-10**
personal-use assets, *10-10*
See also specific types of assets
Assignment, of income, *3-6*
Assignment of income doctrine, **2-26**
"Associated with" entertainment expenditure, *9-13–9-14*
Associations
compared to trusts, **2-8**
definition of, **2-7–2-8**
Athletic facilities, *4-13*
At-risk rules
C corporations, **3-19–3-20**
partnerships, **9-24–9-26**
S corporations, **11-22**
Attribution rules
related party transactions, **3-18–3-19**
reorganizations, **7-46–7-49**
stock redemptions, **4-18–4-20**
Audits
alternatives for taxpayers, **15-7–15-9**
appeal to Appeals Office, **15-8–15-9**
correspondence audit, **15-7**
field audit, *1-21,* **15-7**
litigation, **15-9–15-10**
appeal of lower court's decision, **15-10**
district court, **15-9**
Tax Court, **15-9**
U.S. Court of Federal Claims, **15-9**
meeting with revenue agent, **15-7–15-8**
90-day letter, **15-9**
office audit, *1-21,* **15-7**
partnerships, **9-32–9-33**
percentage of returns audited, **15-3–15-5**
S corporations, **11-39**
selection of returns for, **15-5–15-7**
discriminant function (DIF) program, **15-5–15-6**
special investigatory projects, **15-7**
Taxpayer Compliance Measurement Program, **15-6**
special relief rule, **15-7**
technical advice memoranda, **15-8**
Automobile expenses
actual expenses, *9-10–9-12*
standard mileage rate method of deduction, *9-10–9-12*
See also Transportation expenses; Travel expenses, *9-10–9-12*
Average tax rate, *1-6*
Awards
court awards, *3-24–3-25*
employee achievement awards, *4-14*
employee length of service awards, *9-15*
meritorious achievement awards, *4-7*
See also Gifts
Away-from-tax-home requirement, travel expenses, *9-6*
Bad debts
bona-fide debtor-creditor relationship, *8-24–8-25*
related-party transactions, *8-24–8-25*
business bad debts, *8-28*
discharge of indebtedness, *3-22, 4-19–4-20*
employee loans, *8-27*
nonbusiness bad debts, *8-26–8-28*
recovery of, *8-28*
tax-planning considerations, *8-34*
worthlessness of debt, *8-26*
See also Business bad debts; Discharge of indebtedness; Nonbusiness bad debts, *8-24–8-29*
Bardahl formula, **5-28, 5-30**
Bargain purchase, of corporate property, **4-13**
Bargain sales, gift tax and, **12-7**
Basis
allocation of, *5-10–5-12*
basket purchase, *5-10*
nontaxable stock dividends rights received, *5-11–5-12*
bad debts, *8-25–8-26*
corporate formation, **2-9–2-21**
documentation of, *5-33*
of acquired property, from decedent, *5-8–5-9*
of stock, wash sales, *6-22–6-25*
partnership assets, **9-8–9-9**
partnership interest, **9-8**
partnership liquidating distribution, assets received, **10-12–10-16**
property converted from personal use to business use, *5-9–5-10*
property transactions, *5-5–5-12*
corporate assets, **2-9–2-21**
shareholder's stock, **2-18–2-19**
partnership formation
S corporation stock, **11-24–11-26**
Basis adjustments
alternative minimum taxable income, **5-8**
corporate formations, **2-9–2-21**
partnerships
partnership interest, operations, **9-25**
S corporations, **11-24–11-26**
restoration of stock/debt, S corporation, **11-24–11-26**
to S corporation stock, **11-24–11-25**
to shareholder debt, **11-25–11-26**
tax-free reorganization, **7-17–7-18**
transfers
at death, **12-27**
by gift, **12-26–12-27**
Basket purchase, *5-10*
Beneficiary
complex trusts, **14-21–14-23**
separate share rule, **14-22–14-23**
specific bequests, **14-23**

Beneficiary (*continued*)
    tax treatment, **14-21–14-23**
    tier system, **14-21–14-22**
  simple trusts, tax treatment, **14-15–14-16**
Bona fide loans, to shareholders, **4-12**
Bond-for-bond exchange, Type E reorganizations, **7-42–7-43**
Bond-for-stock exchange, Type E reorganizations, **7-42**
Book income
  reconciliation to taxable income items, **3-35–3-36**
Boot
  corporate distribution, stock of controlled subsidiary, **7-35–7-41**
  corporate formation, **2-16–2-17**
  involuntary conversions, *12-10–12-16*
  like-kind exchanges, *12-2–12-10*
  tax-free reorganization, **7-16–7-20, 7-39**
    shareholder, **7-18–7-20**
    target corporation, **7-16–7-17**
Bootstrap acquisitions, **4-34**
Bribes, as expense contrary to public policy, *6-12–6-13*
Brother-sister corporations
  controlled groups, **3-23, 3-25**
  stock redemptions, **4-30–4-32**
    definition of, **4-30**
    treated as distributions, **4-31**
    treated as sales, **4-31–4-32**
Built-in gains tax, as special S corporation tax, **11-16–11-18**
Business, definition of, *6-5–6-6*
Business bad debts
  reserve method, *8-28*
  specific write-off method, *8-28*
  See also Bad debts; Discharge of indebtedness; Nonbusiness bad debts, *8-28*
Business contingencies, as reasonable business need, **5-31**
Business energy credit, *14-20*
Business enterprise acquisition, as reasonable business need, **5-28**
Business expansion, as reasonable business need, **5-28**
Business expenses, *6-4–6-16*
  business or investment requirement, *6-5*
  criteria for deductions, *6-4–6-16*
    activity engaged in for profit, *6-5–6-30*
    business investigation expenses, *6-15*
    capitalization versus expense deduction, *6-10–6-11*
    employee expenses, *9-2–9-4*
    expenses contrary to public policy, *6-12–6-14*
    expenses related to exempt income, *6-11–6-12*
    lobbying expenses, *6-14–6-15*
    necessary expense, *6-8*
    ordinary expense, *6-7–6-8*
    political contributions, *6-14–6-15*
    reasonable expense, *6-8–6-9*
  deductions/losses, *6-4–6-16*
  reporting employee expenses, *9-44*
Business income, as gross income, *3-13*
Business purpose requirement, Sec. 355, **7-41**

C corporations
  accrual method of accounting and, *3-11–3-12,* **3-4–3-5**
  check-the-box regulations, **2-8, 6-2**
  definition, **2-5**
  fringe benefits, **2-5**
  tax advantages, **2-5–2-6**
  tax attributes, **6-13–6-14, 7-46–7-49**
  tax disadvantages, **2-6**
  tax formula, *2-25,* **3-3**
  tax rates, **3-20–3-22**
  tax year, **3-2–3-4**
  See also Closely held C corporations; Corporations; S corporations, *2-25*
C short year, definition of, **11-10**
Cafeteria plans, as gross income exclusion, *4-17*
Calendar year
  C corporation
    short tax period, **3-2**
    versus fiscal year, **3-2–3-4**
  requirement, *11-28*
    C corporations, *11-28*
    partnerships, *11-2, 11-28,* **9-12–9-15, 9-31–9-32**
    personal service corporations, **3-2–3-4**
    S corporations, *11-2, 11-28,* **11-13, 11-37**
  See also Tax year
Capital assets
  dealers in securities, *5-14–5-15*
  definition of, *2-28, 5-13–5-16*
  holding period, *5-28–5-29*
    nontaxable exchange, *5-29*
    property received as gift, *5-28–5-29*
    property received from decedent, *5-29*
    receipt of nontaxable stock dividends/stock rights, *5-29*
  nonbusiness bad debt, *5-15–5-16*
  real property subdivided for sale, *5-15*
  sale/exchange, *5-21–5-27*
    franchises, *5-26–5-27*
    lease cancellation payments, *5-27*
    options, *5-24–5-25*
    patents, *5-25–5-26*
    retirement of debt instruments, *5-22–5-24*
    trademarks, *5-26–5-27*
    worthless securities, *5-22*
  securities dealers, *5-14–5-15*
  See also Assets, *2-28, 5-13–5-16, 5-30–5-31*
Capital contributions, corporations, **2-28–2-30**
  by nonshareholders, **2-30**
  by shareholders, **2-28–2-30**
Capital expenditures, definition of, *6-10–6-11*
Capital gain dividends, *3-17*
Capital gains/losses
  affiliated group members, **8-32–8-33**
  as inflation adjustment, *5-30–5-31*
  corporations
    capital loss limitation, **3-6–3-7**
  determination of, *5-2–5-5*
    realized gain or loss, *5-2–5-4*
    recognized gain or loss, *5-4–5-5*
  net gains/losses, tax treatment of, *2-28*
  netting process, *5-16–5-19*
  noncorporate taxpayers, *5-16–5-20*
  property transactions, *5-1–5-36*
    basis considerations, *5-5–5-12*
    corporate taxpayer tax treatment, *5-20–5-21*
    documentation of basis, *5-33*
    holding period, *5-28–5-29*
    noncorporate taxpayer tax treatment, *5-16–5-20*
    sale/exchange, *5-21–5-27*
  recognition, *5-2–5-3*
  reporting on Schedule, D, *5-33–5-36*
  tax treatment after 1990, *5-20*
Capital gain property, deducting contributions of, **3-11–3-12**
Capital interest, **9-10**
Capital losses, *5-18–5-20*
  corporate taxpayers, *5-20–5-21*
Capital loss property, partnerships, basis, **9-9**
Capital ownership
  family partnerships, **9-29–9-30**
    donor retained control, **9-29**
    minor donees, **9-30**
Capital recoveries, *5-4*
Capital structure
  characterization of obligations, **2-26–2-27**
  choice of, **2-26–2-30**
    debt capital, **2-27–2-28**
    equity capital, **2-28**
  See also Debt capital; Equity capital
Capitalization
  of deduction items, *6-11*
  of interest, *5-5–5-6*
  of legal fees, *6-6–6-7*
  requirements for cash-method taxpayers, *11-8–11-9*
  versus expense deduction, *6-10–6-11*
    election to deduct currently, *6-10–6-11*
    general capitalization requirements, *6-10*

BOLD = Corporations
ITALICS = Individuals

Carrybacks/carryovers
capital losses, **3-6–3-7**
charitable contributions, **3-12**
consolidated capital losses
departing group member's losses, **8-33**
SRLY rules, **8-33**
taxable income limitation, **8-33**
consolidated NOLs
Sec. 382 limitation, **8-29–8-31**
special loss limitations, SRLY rules, **8-27–8-29**
special rule for new members, **8-25–8-26**
to separate return year, **8-26–8-27**
general business credit, **5-14**
minimum tax credit, **5-13–5-14**
net operating losses, *8-33*, **3-17–3-18**
election to forgo carryback period, *8-33*
of foreign tax credits, *14-18*
passive losses, *8-8–8-9*
recomputation of taxable income in carryover year, *8-33*
Cash receipts and disbursements method of accounting, *3-8–3-10, 6-18–6-20, 11-7–11-9*
C corporations and, **3-5**
capitalization requirements, *11-8–11-9*
constructive receipt, *3-9–3-10*
corporate formation
transferor's liabilities, **2-23–2-24**
transferor's receivables, **2-26**
deductible expenses, *6-18–6-20*
prepaid expenses, *6-19*
prepaid interest, *6-19–6-20*
exceptions, *3-10*
recovery of previously deducted expenses, *3-25–3-26*
tax benefit rule, *3-26*
Casualty losses, *8-17–8-23*
as itemized deduction, *7-28*
casualty defined, *8-17–8-19*
deductible amount of, *8-19–8-20*
disaster area election, *8-23, 8-35*
exclusion of gain, *12-10–12-16, 8-21–8-22*
reporting on Form 4684, *13-25–13-28*
substantiation of loss, *8-34*
CCH Tax Court Memorandum Decisions, **1-18**
CD-ROM tax services, *1-26*
Certified public accountants (CPAs)
"good faith" belief requirement, **1-35–1-37**
knowledge of errors, **1-36–1-37**
positions on tax returns, **1-35–1-37**
procedural aspects of return preparation, **1-35–1-36**
proper behavior of, **1-35–1-37**
responsibilities, **1-35–1-37**
Charitable contributions, *7-21–7-26*
affiliated group, **8-22–8-23**
alternative minimum tax, *14-4*, **5-11**
amount of deduction, *7-21–7-26*
appreciated property, *7-32–7-33*
athletic events, *7-25*
C corporations, **3-10–3-18**
capital gain property contributions, **3-11–3-12**
donations of inventory, **3-11**
limitation, **3-12**
ordinary income property contributions, **3-11**
pledges made by accrual-basis corporation, **3-10–3-11**
sequencing of deduction calculation, **3-17–3-18**
capital gain property, *7-22–7-23*
electing to reduce contribution, *7-32*
to private nonoperating foundation, *7-22–7-23*
carryovers, application of, *7-25–7-26*
corporations
donation of inventory, *7-24*
limitation, *7-26*
pledges made by accrual-basis corporation, *7-26*
deduction limitations, *7-24–7-25*
20% limitation, *7-25*
30% limitation, *7-25*
overall 50% limitation, *7-24*
estate tax
computation of, **13-20**
split-interest transfers, **13-20**
gift tax, **12-21–12-22**
income tax savings from, **12-30**
split-interest transfers, **12-22**
transfers eligible for deduction, **12-21**
ordinary income property, *7-23–7-24*
qualifying organizations, *7-21–7-22*
reporting of, *7-33–7-36*
services, *7-24*
to private nonoperating foundation, *7-22–7-23*
Charitable remainder annuity trusts, definition of, **12-22n**
Charitable remainder unitrust, definition of, **12-22n**
Check-the-box regulations, **2-8, 6-2, 9-3**
Child and dependent care credit, *14-11–14-12, 14-31*
computation, *14-12*
dependent care assistance, *14-12*
employment-related expenses, *14-11–14-12*
Children
as dependent with unearned income, *2-23–2-25*
dependency exemptions for, *2-13–2-18*
minor children, income of, *3-8*
Circuit court of appeals, precedential value of decisions, **1-20–1-21**
Circular 230, **15-33**
Citations
administrative interpretations, **1-11–1-13**
Internal Revenue Code, **1-8**
judicial decisions, **1-14–1-24**
Treasury Regulations, **1-8–1-11**
Citators, **1-28–1-33**
Commerce Clearing House citator, **1-28–1-31**
Research Institute of America Citator, 2nd Series, **1-31–1-33**
Citizenship test, for dependency exemptions, *2-17*
Civil fraud penalty, **15-25**
when fraud is proven, **15-28–15-29**
Claim of right doctrine, *3-26–3-27*
Claims Court Reporter, **1-19**
Client letter, **1-38**
Client-oriented tax research, **1-2–1-3**
closed-fact situations, **1-2**
open-fact situations, **1-2–1-3**
Clifford trusts
Tax Reform Act (1986) and, **14-31**
grantor trust rules, **14-31**
Closed-fact situations, client-oriented tax research and, **1-2**
Closely held businesses, interests in, and deferral of estate tax payments, **13-28–13-29**
Closely held corporations
accumulated earnings tax, **5-24–5-34, 5-36–5-37**
advances, ordinary loss deduction for, **2-32–2-33**
alternative minimum tax (AMT), **5-2–5-15**
at risk rules and, **3-19–3-20, 11-22**
C corporations, *8-12–8-13*
capital structure, **2-26–2-30**
characterization of obligations, **2-26–2-27**
choice of, **2-26–2-30**
debt capital, **2-27–2-28**
equity capital, **2-28**
compensation planning for shareholder-employees, **3-28–3-29**
debt/equity regulations, **2-26–2-27**
hobby loss rules, **11-22**
investment interest expense limitations, **11-24**
material participation by, *8-13*
passive activity limitations, **3-20, 11-22**
personal holding company (PHC) tax, **5-15–5-24, 5-37**
personal service corporation, *8-13*
personal service corporation tax rates, **3-22**
special tax accounting provisions, **3-2–3-5**
taxable year, **3-2–3-4**
stock losses, ordinary loss deduction for, **2-31–2-32**
taxable year, **11-13, 11-37**

- Closely held corporations (*continued*)
  - unreasonable compensation, avoidance of, **4-33–4-34**
  - worthlessness of stock/debt obligations, **2-30–2-33**
  - *See also* C corporations
- Club dues, *9-15*
- Coal, Sec. 1231 and, *13-6*
- Collection of tax, Internal Revenue Service, role of, **15-2**
- Combined controlled groups, **3-25**
- Combined taxable income, **8-6**
- Commerce Clearing House citator, **1-28–1-31**
  - excerpt from, **1-30–1-31**
- Commissioner of Internal Revenue, *1-20*
- Common law state, **12-5**
- Community income, definition of, *3-6–3-7*
- Community property laws
  - innocent spouse provision, effect of, **15-30–15-31**
  - *See also* Divorce; Innocent spouse provision, **12-5n**
- Community property, received from decedent, *5-9*
- Community property states, **12-5**
- Compensation
  - deduction limit, publicly-held corporations, *6-8–6-9*
  - deferred compensation, *3-29*, *9-26–9-42*
  - employee compensation, as gross income, *3-13*
  - nonqualified deferred compensation plans, *9-30–9-32*
  - nontaxable compensation, employers' provision of, *9-43*
  - unreasonable compensation, *6-35–6-36*
  - *See also* specific types of compensation
- Compensation planning
  - closely held corporations, **3-28–3-29**
    - fringe benefits, **3-29**
    - salary payments, **3-28–3-29**
  - unreasonable compensation, avoidance of, **4-33–4-34**
- Completed contract method, *11-16*
- Complete liquidation
  - definition of, **6-3–6-4**
  - tax treatment, **6-2–6-14**
- Complete termination of interest
  - family attribution rules and, **4-19**
  - stock redemptions, **4-21–4-23**
- Complex trusts/estates
  - comprehensive illustration, **14-24–14-27**
  - distributable net income (DNI), determination of, **14-20**
  - distribution deduction, **14-25–14-26**
  - net capital loss effect, **14-24**
  - net operating loss effect, **14-24**
  - tax treatment for beneficiary, **14-21–14-23**
  - taxable income, **14-19, 14-24**
  - *See also* Simple trusts; Trusts
- Computer applications
  - CD-ROM tax services, *1-26*
  - tax planning, *1-25*
  - tax research, *1-25–1-26*
  - tax return preparation, *1-25*
- Computers, as tax research tool, **1-34**
- Condemnations, Sec. 1231 gains/losses resulting from, *13-6–13-7*
- Conduit approach
  - to fiduciary taxation, **14-4**
  - to partnership taxation, **9-4**
- Conference Committee, tax law and, **1-7–1-8**
- Consent dividends, **5-22**
- Conservation expenditures, Sec. 1252 recapture, *13-20–13-21*
- Consideration offset, gross estate, **13-17**
- Consolidated capital losses, **8-32–8-33**
  - carrybacks/carryforwards, **8-32, 8-33**
    - departing group member's losses, **8-33**
    - Sec. 382 limitation, **8-33**
    - SRLY rules, **8-33**
    - taxable income limitation, **8-33**
  - determining amount of gain/loss, **8-32**
  - gains/losses, **8-32**
- Consolidated net operating losses (NOLs), **8-23–8-31**
  - carrybacks/carryforwards, **8-24–8-27**
    - carryback to separate return year, **8-24–8-26**
    - carryforward to separate return year, **8-26–8-27**
  - Sec. 382 limitation, **8-29–8-31**
  - SRLY limitation, **8-27–8-29**
- Consolidated return year, definition of, **8-7n**
- Consolidated tax returns, **3-27–3-28, 8-1–8-38**
  - advantages of filing, **3-27–3-28, 8-4–8-5**
  - affiliated groups
    - definition of, **8-2–8-4**
    - tax liability, **8-9–8-10**
  - alternative minimum tax, **8-10**
  - capital gains/losses, **8-32–8-33**
    - Sec. 1231 gains/losses, **8-32**
  - charitable contributions deduction, **8-22–8-23**
  - disadvantages of filing, **3-28, 8-5**
  - dividends, **8-21–8-22**
    - consolidated dividends-received deduction, **8-21–8-22**
    - exclusion procedure, **8-21**
    - 100% dividends-received deduction election, **8-35**
  - election to file, **8-36–8-37**
  - estimated tax payments, **8-35–8-36**
  - importance of consolidated return election, **8-2**
  - intercompany transactions, **8-11–8-20**
    - other intercompany transactions, **8-18–8-20**
    - property transactions, **8-12–8-18**
  - liability for taxes due, **8-38**
  - net operating losses (NOLs), **8-23–8-31**
    - carryback to separate return year, **8-24–8-26**
    - carrybacks/carryforwards of, **8-24**
    - carryforward to separate return year, **8-26–8-27**
    - current year NOLs, **8-23–8-24**
    - Sec. 382 limitation, **8-29–8-31**
    - special loss limitations, **8-27–8-31**
    - SRLY limitation, **8-27–8-29**
  - parent corporation as agent for affiliated groups, **8-37**
  - rules, source of, **8-2**
  - tax credits, **8-10, 8-11**
    - general business credit, **8-10–8-11**
    - who can file, **8-2–8-4**
  - taxable income, **8-5–8-9**
    - affiliated group elections, **8-8**
    - income included in, **8-7–8-8**
    - termination of the affiliated group, **8-8–8-9**
  - who can file, **3-27**
- Consolidated taxable income, **8-5–8-9**
  - affiliated group elections, **8-8**
    - accounting methods, **8-8**
    - tax years, **8-8**
  - calculation of, **8-5–8-8**
  - 30-day rules, **8-8n**
- Consolidations
  - partnerships and, *10-25*
  - Type A reorganization, **7-21–7-27**
    - definition of, **7-21–7-23**
    - requirements for, **7-23–7-25**
- Constructive dividends, **4-11–4-13**
  - corporate payments for shareholder's benefit, **4-13**
  - corporate property
    - bargain purchase of, **4-13**
    - shareholder use of, **4-13**
  - definition of, **4-11**
  - gross income, *3-17*
  - intentional avoidance of dividend treatment, **4-11–4-12**
  - loans to shareholders, **4-12**
  - shareholder property, excessive compensation paid for, **4-13**
  - shareholders-employees, excessive compensation to, **3-29, 4-12–4-13**
  - unintentional constructive dividends, **4-12**
- Constructive receipt, *3-9–3-10*
- Continuity of business enterprise doctrine, **7-44–7-45**
- Continuity of interest doctrine
  - reorganizations, **7-44–7-45**
  - Sec. 355 distributions, **7-40–7-41**
- Contribution of services
  - corporate formation, **2-9–2-14**

BOLD = Corporations
ITALICS = Individuals

partnerships, **9-10–9-12**
allocating the expense deduction, **9-11**
basis adjustments, **9-11–9-12**
consequences to partnership, **9-11–9-12**
Control requirements
acquisitive Type D reorganizations, **7-30–7-31**
Sec. 351(a), **2-13–2-16**
immediately after the exchange, **2-16**
transferors of both property and services, **2-14**
transfers to existing corporations, **2-14–2-15**
Sec. 355, **7-40–7-41**
Controlled corporations, distribution of stock of
requirements, **7-40–7-41**
tax consequences
distributing corporation, **7-38–7-40**
shareholders and security holders, **7-38–7-40**
types of distributions, **7-38**
Controlled groups, **3-22–3-28**
brother-sister controlled groups, **3-23–3-25**
combined controlled groups, **3-25**
compared to affiliated groups, **8-4**
controlled group test, application of, **3-26**
definition of, **3-23**
parent-subsidiary controlled groups, **3-23**
special election, to allocate reduced tax rate benefits, **3-29–3-30**
special rules for, **3-22–3-23, 3-26–3-27**
Controlled subsidiary corporations
liquidation of, **6-10–6-12**
basis of property received, **6-12**
cancellation of stock, **6-11**
exception to gain/loss recognition rules, **6-8–6-13**
insolvent subsidiary, **6-11–6-12**
minority shareholders receiving liquidating distributions, **6-12**
recognition of gain or loss, **6-11–6-17**
requirements, **6-10–6-11**
stock ownership, **6-10–6-11**
subsidiary debt obligations, satisfaction of, **6-17**
timing of the distributions, **6-11**
Copyright, as asset, *5-13*
"Corn Products" doctrine, *5-13–5-14*
Corporate elections
accounting methods, **3-4–3-5**
accrual method, **3-4, 3-5**
affiliated group, **8-8**
cash method, **3-5**
hybrid method, **3-5**
S corporation, **11-14, 11-37**
tax year, selection of, **3-2–3-4, 8-8, 11-13, 11-37**
Corporate form
disregard of, **2-8**
Corporate property
bargain purchase of, **4-13**
shareholder use of, **4-13**
Corporate requirements, S corporations, **11-5–11-7**
Corporate stock, exchange of partnership interest for, **10-21**
Corporate taxable income
capital gains/losses, tax treatment, **3-6–3-7**
compared to individual taxable income and, **3-6**
deductions/losses, **3-6**
deductions, **3-7–3-18**
accrued compensation deductions, limitation on, **3-10**
charitable contributions, **3-10–3-12**
deduction calculations, sequencing of, **3-17–3-18**
dividends-received deduction, **3-12–3-16**
net operating losses (NOLs), **3-16–3-17**
organizational expenditures, **3-8, 3-9**
start-up expenditures, **3-9–3-10**
sales/exchanges of property, **3-6–3-7**
net capital gain, **3-6**
net capital losses, **3-6–3-7**
tax benefit recapture rule, **3-7**
Corporate taxation
controlled group rules, **3-22–3-28**
corporate elections, **3-2–3-5**
paying taxes, **3-31–3-34**
tax formula/tax rates, **3-5, 3-20–3-22**
tax liability, computation of, **3-20–3-22**
tax returns
filing requirements, **3-34**
schedules, **3-35–3-37**
types of, **3-34**
when to file, **3-35**
taxable income, computation of, **3-5–3-20**
See also C corporations, personal service corporations, S corporations, **3-1–3-34**
Corporations
accumulated earnings tax, **5-24–5-34**
alternative minimum tax (AMT), **5-2–5-15**
computation of, **5-2–5-15**
minimum tax credit, **5-13–5-14**
special AMT elections, **5-35**
tax credits and, **5-14–5-15**
capital contributions, **2-28–2-30**
by nonshareholders, **2-30**
by shareholders, **2-28–2-30**
capital gains/losses, *5-20–5-21*
charitable contributions, *7-24*, **3-10–3-18**
compared to partnerships, **2-8**
definition of, **2-8, 3-2**
disregard of corporate entity, **2-8**
dividends-received deduction, **3-12–3-16**
estimated taxes, **3-31–3-34**
extensions of due date, **3-35, 15-13**
filing requirements, **3-35**
formation of, **2-1–2-35**
legal requirements, **2-9**
tax considerations, **2-9–2-11**
net operating losses, **3-16–3-17**
nonliquidating distributions, **4-1–4-37**
tax formula/rates, *1-5, 1-7, 2-25*
tax liability computations, **3-20–3-22**
accumulated earnings tax, **5-24–5-34**
alternative minimum tax, **5-2–5-15**
personal holding company (PHC) tax, **5-15–5-24**
regular tax, **3-20–3-22**
tax payment requirements, **3-34**
tax rates, *1-4–1-7, 2-25–2-26*
tax return
filing requirements, **3-34**
schedules, **3-35–3-37**
types of, **3-35**
when to file, **3-35**
tax year, election of, **3-2–3-4**
transactions between shareholders and, **3-18–3-19**
different accounting methods used, **3-19**
gains on sale/exchange transactions, **3-19**
losses on sale/exchange transactions, **3-19**
See also C corporations; Acquisitions; Incorporation; Liquidating distributions; Nonliquidating distributions; Personal service corporations (PSCs); S corporations, **6-1, 6-21**
Correspondence audit, **15-7**
Corresponding item, **8-13**
Court system, overview of, **1-14**
Covenant not to compete
definition of, *10-15*
reporting requirements, *10-23*
Credits
accumulated earnings credit, **5-32–5-33**
alternative minimum tax, **5-13–5-15**
business energy credits, *14-20*
child and dependent care credit, *14-11–14-12, 14-31*
disabled access credit, *14-19*
earned income credit, *14-22–14-23*
Empowerment zone employment credit, *14-21–14-22*
estates, **14-10**

Credits (*continued*)
- fiduciary accounting, tax calculation formula, **14-10**
- foreign death taxes paid tax credit, estate tax, **13-25**
- foreign tax credit, *14-17–14-18, 4-18*
- general business credit, *14-9–14-10*
- minimum tax credit, *14-5,* **5-13–5-14**
- nonrefundable credits, *14-19–14-20, 14-9, 2-6*
- personal tax credits, *14-11–14-13*
  - child and dependent care credit, *14-11–14-12*
  - credit for the elderly, *14-12–14-13*
  - earned income credit, *14-22–14-23*
- rehabilitation expenditures, credit for, *14-19–14-20*
- research activities, credit for, *14-18–14-19*
- trusts, **14-10**
- unified credit, **12-4, 12-6–12-7, 12-24, 13-5, 13-23–13-24**
- work opportunity credit, *14-20–14-21*
- *See also* specific types of credit, *14-9–14-13*

Criminal fraud penalties, **15-26**
- criminal fraud investigations, **15-26**
- penalty provisions, **15-26**
  - Sec. 7201, **15-26**
  - Sec. 7203, **15-26**
  - Sec. 7206, **15-26**

Crummey trust, **12-17–12-18**

Cumulative Bulletin (C.B.), **1-12, 1-17**

Current earnings and profits (E&P), **4-3–4-6**
- adjustments to taxable income, **4-5**
- compared to accumulated earnings and profits, **4-6–4-8**
- computation of, **4-3**
- income deferred to later period, **4-4–4-5**
- income excluded from taxable income, **4-4**
- nondeductible expenses/losses in computing taxable income, **4-6**
- unallowable deductions from, **4-5–4-6**

Curtesy rights, gross estate, **13-10**

Customs duties, *1-11*

Daily compounding, of penalty interest, **15-15**

Date-of-death valuation, **13-6–13-7**
- annuities, **13-7**
- interests in firms whose stock is not publicly traded, **13-6–13-7**
- listed stocks, **13-6–13-7**
- real estate, **13-6–13-7**
- remainders, **13-7**
- reversions, **13-7**
- terms for years, **13-7**

Death benefits, employees, as gross income exclusion, *4-16*

Death of partner, **10-19–10-20**
- payments, **10-19–10-20**
- basis, **10-20**
- goodwill, **10-19–10-20**
- partnership property, **10-19**
- unrealized receivables, **10-19–10-20**

Death taxes, stock redemptions to pay for, **4-25–4-27, 13-29**

Debt
- capital, **2-27–2-28**
- issuance of debt, **2-27**
- retirement of debt instruments, *5-22–5-24*
- taxpayer's basis in, *8-25–8-26*
- unsecured debt obligations, **2-32–2-33**
- when indebtedness is satisfied, **2-27–2-28**
- when interest is paid, **2-27**
- worthlessness of, *8-26,* **2-32–2-33**
- *See also* Bad debts; Business bad debts; Equity capital; Nonbusiness bad debts

Debt-financed stock, corporations, dividends-received deduction, **3-15–3-16**

Deduction equivalent, definition of, *8-16*

Deductions for adjusted gross income, definition of, *2-4–2-5*

Deductions from adjusted gross income, definition of, *2-4*

Deductions
- AGI classification, *6-3–6-4*
- alternative minimum tax, **5-6–5-8**
- corporate taxable income
  - accrued compensation deductions, limitation on, **3-10**
  - charitable contributions, **3-10–3-12**
  - dividends-received deduction, **3-12–3-16**
  - net operating losses (NOLs), **3-16–3-17**
  - organizational expenditures, **3-8–3-9**
  - sequencing of deduction calculations, **3-17–3-18**
  - start-up expenditures, **3-9–3-10**
- criteria for deductions, *6-4–6-16*
- current earnings and profits (E&P), **4-5–4-6**
- estate tax, **13-3–13-4, 13-18–13-23**
  - administration expenses, **13-18–13-19**
  - charitable contribution deduction, **13-19–13-20**
  - debts, **13-18–13-19**
  - funeral expenses, **13-18–13-19**
  - losses, **13-19**
  - marital deduction, **13-20–13-23**
- expenses, *6-18–6-22*
  - accrual method of accounting, *6-20–6-22*
  - cash method of accounting, *6-18–6-20*
- gift tax
  - charitable contributions, **12-21, 12-22**
  - marital deduction, **12-19–12-21**
- proper substantiation requirement, *6-16–6-18, 6-37*
- special disallowance rules, *6-22–6-35*
  - hobby losses, *6-28–6-31, 6-35, 6-37*
  - home office expenses, *6-34–6-35*
  - related-party transactions, *6-25–6-28*
  - wash sales, *6-22–6-25*
- *See also* Dividends-paid deduction; Dividends-received deduction; Itemized deductions; Losses, *6-1–6-37*

Deductions in respect of a decedent (DRD), **14-28**

Deemed liquidation election
- allocation of basis, **7-8–7-10**
  - allocable basis, **7-8**
  - to individual assets, **7-8–7-10**
- deemed purchase, basis of assets following, **7-8–7-10**
- deemed sale, **7-7**
- eligible stock acquisitions, **7-6**
- grossed-up basis for stock, **7-8**
- liabilities of target corporation, **7-8**
- liquidation of target corporation, **7-5**
- Sec. 338 election, **7-6–7-7, 7-51**
- tax accounting elections for new corporation, **7-7, 7-10**
- *See also* Liquidation, **7-5–7-11**

Deferred compensation
- avoiding constructive receipt, *3-29*
- individual retirement accounts (IRAs), *9-36–9-41*
- nonqualified plans, *9-30–9-32*
- qualified plans, *9-27–9-29*
  - pension plans, *9-27*
  - profit-sharing plans, *9-28*
  - qualification requirements for, *9-28–9-29*
- self-employed individuals, *9-36*
- stock option plans, *9-32–9-35*
  - incentive stock option plans, *9-33–9-34*
  - nonqualified stock option plans, *9-34–9-35*
- tax treatment, *9-29–9-30*
  - employee retirement payments, *9-29–9-30*
  - employer contribution limitations, *9-30*
- *See also* Individual retirement accounts (IRAs); Sec. 401(k) plans; qualified pension plans; nonqualified deferred compensation plans, *3-29, 9-26–9-42*

Deferred gain
- involuntary conversions, *12-10–12-16*
- like-kind exchange, *12-2–12-10*

BOLD = Corporations
ITALICS = Individuals

sale of principal residence, *12-16–12-21*
Deferred intercompany transactions
basis and holding periods, **8-12**
deferred gain or loss,
amount/character of, **8-12**
restored gain/loss, determination of, **8-12–8-17**
See also Intercompany transactions, **8-12–8-17**
Deferred payment sales, *11-21*
Deficiency dividends, **5-23**
Defined benefit pension plan, *9-27*
Defined contribution pension plan, *9-27*
De minimis fringe benefits, *4-13, 9-13n*
De minimis rules, gift tax and, **12-28–12-29**
Demolition of property, losses from, *8-4*
Dependency exemptions, *2-5, 2-13–2-18*
citizenship test, *2-17*
definition of, *2-5*
gross income test, *2-16*
joint return test, *2-16*
phase-out of, *2-17–2-18*
qualification as dependent, *2-13–2-18*
relationship test, *2-16–2-17*
support test, *2-13–2-15*
Dependent care assistance programs, employees, as gross income exclusion, *14-12, 4-16–4-17*
Depletion, *10-18–10-20*
intangible drilling and development costs (IDCs), treatment of, *10-20*
methods, *10-18–10-20*
cost depletion method, *10-19*
percentage depletion method, *10-19–10-20*
reporting of, *10-23*
tax preference, **5-6**
Depreciation
accelerated cost-recovery system (ACRS)
restrictions, *10-10–10-13*
alternative minimum tax, **5-6–5-8**
asset depreciation range (ADR) system, *10-8*
corporate formation
computation of, transferee corporation, **2-25**
recapture of, **2-24–2-25**
earnings and profits, **4-5**
fiduciary accounting, **14-6–14-7**
Form 4562, *10-23*
modified ACRS (MACRS) rules, *10-2*
alternative depreciation system, *10-8–10-9*
conventions, *10-5–10-7*
real property, *10-7–10-8*
restrictions, *10-10–10-13*
recapture of, reorganizations, **7-17**
reporting of, *10-23*
Sec. 179 expensing election, *10-9–10-10*
See also Accelerated cost-recovery system (ACRS); Modified ACRS system; and Sec. 179, *10-1–10-13*
Device requirement, Sec. 355, **7-40**
"Directly related" entertainment expenses, *9-13*
Disabled access credit, *14-19*
Disaster losses, *8-23*
Disallowed losses, alternative minimum taxable income (AMTI), **5-8**
Discharge of indebtedness
gross income exclusion and, *4-19–4-20*
income from, as gross income, *3-22*
Disclaimers
estate tax and, **13-34**
gift tax, qualified disclaimers, **12-9–12-10**
Discounted notes, timing of interest deduction, *7-20*
Discriminant function (DIF) program, audits and, *1-21*, **15-5–15-6**
Discrimination awards, *4-9*
Disproportionate exchanges of property and stock, **2-15–2-16**
Dissolution, compared to liquidation, **6-3–6-4**
Distributable net income (DNI)
computation of, **14-11–14-12**
definition of, **14-11**
significance of, **14-10–14-11**
Distributing corporations
distribution of stock of controlled subsidiary
recognition of gain or loss, **7-38–7-40**
liquidating distributions, **6-6–6-14**
nontaxable stock dividends, effect on, **4-14–4-15**
property distributions, consequences of, **4-9–4-11**
earnings and profits, effect on, **4-10–4-11**
recognition of gain or loss, **4-10**
stock redemptions
earnings and profits, effect on, **4-27–4-28**
questions for, **4-16–4-17**
recognition of gain or loss, **4-27**
Distribution deduction
complex trusts/estates, **14-9**
determination of, **14-20**
estates, **14-9**
fiduciary accounting, calculation formula, **14-9**
trusts, **14-9**
complex trusts, **14-9**
simple trusts, **14-9**
Distribution requirement, Sec. 355, **7-40–7-41**
Distributions
C corporations
nonliquidating, **4-8–4-13**
definition of, **4-2**
reporting of, Form 5452, **4-36**
timing, of, **4-35–4-36**
stock dividends and stock rights, **4-13–4-16**
stock of controlled corporations, **7-38–7-40**
stock redemptions, **4-16–4-28, 4-30–4-32**
partnerships
liquidating, **10-12–10-16**
nonliquidating, **10-2–10-7**
S corporations, **11-27–11-31**
with accumulated earnings/profits, **11-28–11-31**
with no earnings/profits, **11-27–11-28**
tax-free reorganizations, **7-17–7-20**
shareholders and security holders, **7-18–7-20**
target corporations, **7-16–7-17**
See also Dividends; Stock distributions
District directors, IRS, *1-20*
Dividends-received deduction
Dividends
as gross income, *3-16–3-17*, **4-2**
capital gain dividends, *3-17*, **4-2–4-3**
constructive dividends, **4-11–4-13**
corporate payments for shareholder's benefit, **4-13**
corporate property, **4-13**
definition of, **4-11**
intentional avoidance of dividend treatment, **4-11–4-12**
loans to shareholders, **4-12**
shareholder property, excessive compensation paid for, **4-13**
shareholders-employees, excessive compensation to, **4-12–4-13**
unintentional constructive dividends, **4-12**
definition of, **4-2**
distributing corporation, consequences to, **4-9–4-11, 4-16, 4-27–4-28**
effect on distributing corporation, **4-10–4-11, 4-16, 4-27–4-28**
nontaxable stock dividends, **4-14–4-15**
nontaxable stock rights, **4-15**
stock of controlled subsidiary, **7-38–7-41**
stock redemptions, **4-27–4-28**
tax-free stock dividends, **4-14–4-15**
tax-free stock rights, **4-15**
taxable stock dividends, **4-16**
taxable stock rights, **4-16**
from foreign corporations, **3-15**
personal holding company income (PHCI) and, **5-18**
personal holding company tax (PHC)
consent dividends, **5-22**
current year dividends, **5-22**
deficiency dividends, **5-23**
dividend carryovers, **5-22**

Dividends (*continued*)
liquidating dividends, **5-22**
throwback dividends, **5-22**
stock dividends, *3-16–3-17*
stock redemptions, **4-16–4-32**
See also Constructive dividends
Dividends-paid deduction, **5-22–5-23, 5-32**
accumulated earnings tax, **5-33–5-34**
preferential dividends and, **5-22, 5-32**
Dividends-received deduction
affiliated groups, **8-21–8-22**
computed on consolidated basis, **8-21, 8-22**
corporations, **3-12–3-16**
affiliated group members, **3-14–3-15**
debt-financed stock, **3-15–3-16**
dividends from foreign corporations, **3-15**
general rule for, **3-13**
limitation, **3-13–3-14**
exception to, **3-14**
stock held 45 days or less, **3-15**
Divisive reorganizations
Type D reorganizations, **7-37–7-41**
asset transfer, **7-38**
business adjustments accomplished by, **7-37**
distribution of stock, **7-38–7-40**
Type G reorganizations, **7-41**
See also Acquisitive reorganizations; Reorganizations, **7-15, 7-35–7-41**
Divorce
community property laws, **12-5**
innocent spouse provision, **15-30–15-31**
property settlements, gift tax and, **12-9**
Domestic corporations, definition of, **3-2**
Donations
See also Charitable contributions, *7-21–7-26*
Donor-donee allocation of income
family S corporation, **11-23**
family partnerships, **9-30**
Double taxation
C corporations, **2-6**
estates, **14-28**
liquidating distributions, exemption from, **6-19**
partnerships, **9-5–9-6**
S corporations, **11-11**
Dower rights, gross estate, **13-10**
Due dates
corporate tax returns, **15-13, 15-14, 3-34, 3-35**
estate income tax returns, **14-36**
estate tax returns, **13-36**
extensions
corporations, **3-35, 11-37–11-38, 15-13**
estate tax return, **13-36**
fiduciaries, **14-36**
gift tax returns, **12-31**
individuals, **15-13**
partnerships, **9-31**
fiduciary returns, **14-36**
for filing individual income tax return, *2-32*
for payment of tax, **15-13–15-14**
gift tax returns, **12-31**
interest on tax not timely paid
daily compounding, **15-15**
determination of rate, **15-14**
period for which interest is imposed, **15-15**
partnerships, **9-31**
penalties, **15-16–15-19**
failure to file, **15-16–15-18**
failure to pay, **15-18–15-19**
S corporations, **11-37–11-38**
Dues, club, *9-15*

Earnings and profits (E&P), **4-3–4-8**
accumulated earnings and profits, **4-3**
current E&P, **4-3, 4-6**
current versus accumulated E&P, **4-6–4-8**
dividend distribution, effect of, **4-10, 4-16**
reporting of, **4-35–4-36**
stock redemptions, effect of, **4-27–4-28**
tax attribute carryover, **6-13–6-14, 7-46**
Earned income credit, *14-22–14-23*
Economic income, *1-6*
Economic performance test, *6-21–6-22, 11-9–11-10*
Education expenses
employees, *9-20–9-23*
general requirements for deduction, *9-21–9-23*
Educational assistance plan, *4-17*
Educational organization, definition of, **12-8**
Educational travel deductions, *9-8*
Effective tax rate, *1-6*
Elderly, tax credit for the, *14-12–14-13*
Electing large partnerships, **9-3, 9-4, 10-30–10-33**
Election by Small Business Corporation to Tax Corporation Income Directly to Shareholders (Form 2553), **11-37**
Employee achievement awards, *4-14*
Employee compensation
as gross income exclusion, *4-10–4-18*
cafeteria plans, *4-17*
dependent care, *4-16–4-17*
employee awards, *4-14*
employer-paid insurance, *4-10–4-12*
interest-free loans, *4-18*
meals/entertainment, *4-15*
meals/lodging, *4-14–4-15*
Sec. 132 benefits, *4-12–4-13*
as gross income, *3-13*
Employee death benefits, *4-16*
Employee expenses
accountable plan, *9-16*
classification of, *9-2–9-4*
unreimbursed employee expense limitations, *9-3–9-4*
education expenses, *9-20–9-23*
entertainment expenses, *9-12–9-16*
business gifts, *9-15–9-16*
business meals, *9-14–9-15*
classification of expenses, *9-13–9-14*
entertainment facilities, *9-15*
moving expenses, *9-18–9-20, 9-42*
direct moving expenses, *9-19–9-20*
distance requirement, *9-19*
employee reimbursements, *9-20, 9-42*
employment duration, *9-19, 9-42*
expense classification, *9-19*
indirect moving expenses, *9-20*
reimbursement treatment, *9-20, 9-42*
office in home, *9-23–9-47, 9-47*
general requirements for deduction, *9-23*
gross income limitations, *9-25*
reporting of, Form 8829, *6-37, 9-47*
transportation expenses, *9-9–9-12*
automobile expenses, *9-10–9-12*
definition of, *9-9–9-10*
travel expenses, *9-4–9-8*
away-from-tax-home requirement, *9-6*
business versus pleasure, *9-7–9-8*
deductibility of, *9-4–9-5*
definition of, *9-5*
foreign travel, *9-8*
See also Unreimbursed employee expenses, *9-1–9-26*
Employee fringe benefits, tax planning, *4-21–4-22*
Employee stock ownership plans (ESOPs), *9-28*
Employer identification numbers (EINs), *2-32*
Employer-employee relationship, definition of, *9-2–9-3*
Employment-related retirement benefits, gross estate, **13-14**
Employment taxes, *1-11, 14-29, 14-7–14-27*
Empowerment zones
employment credit, *14-21–14-22*
Endowment policies, income from, as gross income, *3-21*
Enforcement of tax law, Internal Revenue Service, role of, **15-2**
Entertainment expenses, *9-12–9-16*
business gifts, *9-15–9-16*
business meals, *9-14–9-15*
partial disallowance for, *9-12–9-13*
entertainment ticket limitations, *9-16*

BOLD = Corporations
ITALICS = Individuals

partial disallowance for, *9-12–9-13*
"associated with" entertainment expenditure, *9-13–9-14*
"directly related" entertainment expenses, *9-13*
substantiation of, *9-43–9-44*
Entity attribution, **4-20**
Equity capital
partnership interests, **9-2, 9-3**
stock
multiple classes of, **2-28**
tax advantages of, **2-29**
tax disadvantages of, **2-29**
worthlessness of, **2-30–2-32**
Estate Planning, **1-25**
Estate planning, selecting property to transfer at death, *5-32*
Estate tax, *1-9–1-10*
administrative expenses, where to deduct, **13-35**
alternate valuation date, **13-7–13-8**
election of, **13-36**
annuities and, **13-13–13-14**
calculation formula, **13-2–13-5**
adjusted taxable gifts, **13-4**
deductions, **13-3–13-4**
gross estate, **13-2–13-3**
comprehensive illustration, **13-25–13-27**
deductions, **13-18, 13-23**
administration expenses, **13-18–13-19**
charitable contribution deduction, **13-19– 13-20**
debts, **13-18–13-19**
funeral expenses, **13-18–13-19**
losses, **13-19**
marital deduction, **13-20–13-23**
deferral of tax payments, **13-28–13-29**
interests in closely held businesses and, **13-28–13-29, 13-34–13-35**
reasonable cause, **13-28**
remainder interests, **13-28**
reversionary interests, **13-28**
disclaimers, **13-34**
documents to be included with return, **13-36**
due date, **13-36**
exemption equivalent, **13-32**
filing requirements, **13-35–13-36**
generation-skipping transfer tax (GSTT), **13-30–13-31**
inter vivos gifts, **13-32**
life insurance, **13-16–13-17, 13-34**
liquidity, **13-28–13-30**
post-1976 gift taxes, reduction for, **13-4–13-5**
prepayments, gifts tax and, **12-30**
qualifying for installment payments, **13-34–13-35**
special use valuation, of farm realty, **13-30**
stock redemptions, to pay death taxes, **13-29**
tax base, tentative tax on, **13-4**
tax liability
computation of, **13-23–13-25**
credit for pre-1977 gift taxes, **13-24**
credit for tax on prior transfers, **13-25**
foreign death tax credit, **13-25**
state death tax credit, **13-24**
taxable estate and tax base, **13-23**
tentative tax and reduction for post-1976 gift tax, **13-23**
unified credit, **13-23–13-24**
unified credit, **13-5, 13-23–13-24**
valuation, need for documentation, **13-36**
See also Gross estate, **13-1–13-36**
Estate Tax Return (Form 706), **13-35–13-36**
Estate tax returns, substantial omissions, **15-28**
Estates, income taxation of
administration expenses deduction, **14-35**
beneficiary, tax treatment of, **14-21–14-23**
capital losses, **14-24**
credits, **14-10**
distributable net income (DNI)
computation of, **14-20**
definition of, **14-11**
significance of, **14-10, 14-11**
distribution deduction, **14-20**
documents to be furnished to IRS, **14-36**
due date, **14-36**
estimated taxes, **14-36**
expense deductions, **14-7, 14-9**
filing requirements, **14-35**
gross income, **14-7**
inception of, **14-2**
income in respect of a decedent
common examples, **14-27–14-28**
deductions in respect of a decedent, **14-28**
definition of, **14-27–14-28**
double taxation, **14-28**
(IRD), **14-27–14-29**
no step-up in basis, **14-29**
Sec. 691(c) deduction, **14-28–14-29**
significance of, **14-28–14-29**
net operating losses, **14-24**
personal exemption, **14-9–14-10, 14-20**
tax liability, **14-7–14-10**
timing of distributions, **14-34**
year-end, choice of, **14-35**
See also Trusts
Estimated taxes
affiliated groups, **8-35–8-36**
annualized income exception, **3-33–3-34**
C corporations, **3-31–3-34**
paying remaining tax liability, **3-34**
payment rules/dates, **3-31–3-32**
seasonal income exception, **3-33–3-34**
underpayment penalties, **3-32–3-33**
estates, **14-36**
individuals, **15-19–15-22**
exceptions to, **15-22**
payment requirements, **15-20–15-21**
required estimated tax payments, *14-28*
underpayment penalties, **15-21–15-22**
withholding and, *14-32*, **15-21**
partnerships, **9-32**
S corporations, **11-38–11-39**
trusts, **14-36**
Excess loss account, **8-21**
Excess net passive income tax, as special S corporation tax, **11-15–11-16**
Exchange
See also Sales/exchanges of property
definition of, *5-21*
Excise taxes, *1-11*
Exclusion ratio, annuities, *3-20*
Exclusions
from gross income, *2-3, 4-1–4-24*
awards for meritorious achievement, *4-7*
employee fringe benefits, *4-10–4-18*
foreign-earned income exclusion, *4-18–4-19*
gifts, *4-4–4-5*
income from discharge of indebtedness, *4-19–4-20*
inheritances, *4-4–4-5*
injury/sickness payments, *4-8–4-10*
life insurance proceeds, *4-5–4-6*
sale of residence, *12-19–12-21, 4-21*
scholarships/fellowships, *4-7*
selling price of property, *4-3*
unrealized income, *4-2–4-3*
gift tax, **12-16–12-18**
amount of, **12-16**
Crummey trust, **12-17–12-18**
definition of, **12-16**
present interest requirement, **12-16–12-17**
trust for minors, **12-17**
See also Annual exclusion
Exempt income, expenses related to, *6-11–6-12*
Exemption equivalent
estate tax and, **13-32**
gift tax and, **12-6**
Exemptions
dependency exemptions, *2-5, 2-13–2-18*
personal exemptions, *2-12*
Expected return, annuities, *3-19*

- Expenses
  - accrual method of accounting, deductible expenses, *6-20–6-22*
  - allocation of
    - residential property, *6-32–6-33*
    - transportation expenses, *9-9–9-12*
  - automobile expenses, *9-10–9-12*
  - business investigation expenses, *6-15*
  - cash receipts and disbursements method of accounting, deductible expenses, *6-18–6-20*
  - contrary to public policy, *6-12–6-14*
    - bribes, *6-12–6-13*
    - fines, *6-13*
    - illegal activity expenses, *6-14*
    - kickbacks, *6-12–6-13*
    - legal fees, *6-6–6-7*
    - penalties, *6-13*
  - disallowed expenses, *6-14–6-15*
    - business investigation expenses, *6-15*
    - lobbying expenses, *6-14–6-15*
    - political contributions, *6-14–6-15*
    - pre-operating/start-up costs, *6-15*
  - employee expenses, *9-1–9-26*
  - entertainment expenses, *9-12–9-16*
  - estates, **14-7–14-9**
  - fiduciary accounting, calculation formula, **14-7–14-9**
  - home office expenses, *6-34–6-35, 9-23–9-25*
  - interest expenses, *7-12–7-21*
  - investment expenses, *6-4–6-16*
  - medical expenses, *7-2–7-8*
  - moving expenses, *9-18–9-20*
  - taxpayer responsibility for, *6-16–6-18*
  - transportation expenses, *9-9–9-12*
  - travel expenses, *9-4–9-8*
  - trusts, **14-7–14-9**
  - unreimbursed employee expenses, limitations on, *9-3–9-4*
  - *See also* Deductions
- Extensions
  - of due date, **15-13**
    - C corporations, **3-35, 11-37–11-38, 15-13**
    - estate tax return, **13-36**
    - fiduciaries, **14-36**
    - gift tax return, **12-31**
    - individuals, **15-13**
    - partnerships, **9-31**
  - *See also* Due date

- Failure-to-file penalty, *1-22,* **15-16–15-18**
- Failure-to-pay penalty, *1-22,* **15-18–15-19**
- Fair market value (FMV)
  - definition of, *11-14, 5-3,* **13-6**
  - property distributions and, **14-34**
- Family attribution, **4-19**
  - complete termination of interest and, **4-21–4-23**
- Family partnerships
  - capital ownership, **9-29–9-30**
    - donor retained control, **9-29**
    - minor donees, **9-30**
  - donor-donee allocation of income, **9-30**
    - requirements for, **9-29–9-30**
- Family S corporations, **11-23**
  - *See also* Partnerships
- Farming
  - conservation expenditures, *13-20–13-21*
  - Sec. 1231 and, *13-5–13-6*
    - livestock, *13-6*
    - timber, *13-5–13-6*
    - unharvested crops/land, *13-6*
  - Sec. 1252 recapture, *13-20–13-21*
- Farm realty, special use valuation of, **13-30**
- *Federal Claims Reporter*, **1-20**
- Federal Court System, *1-19,* **1-14–1-25**
  - Appeals court procedures, **1-20**
  - District court procedures, **1-19**
  - Overview of court system, **1-14**
  - Precedential value of various decisions, **1-21–1-24**
  - Supreme Court, appeals to, **1-21**
  - Tax Court procedures, **1-14–1-18**
    - IRS acquiescence policy, **1-17**
    - Small cases procedures, **1-17**
- *Federal Income Taxation of Estates and Beneficiaries* (Ferguson et al.), **14-10n**
- Federal Insurance Contributions Act (FICA), *1-11, 1-3, 14-29, 14-7–14-25*
- *Federal Income Taxation of Estates and Beneficiaries* (Ferguson et al.), **14-10n**
- *Federal Reporter, Second Series*, **1-19n**
- *Federal Reporter, Third Series*, **1-20**
- *Federal Supplement* (F. Supp.), **1-19**
- *Federal Taxation: Research, Planning, and Procedures* (Norwood et al.), *1-24n*
- *Federal Taxation of Income, Estates, and Gifts* (Bittker), **15-25n**
- *Federal Tax Coordinator 2d* (Research Institute of America), **1-26–1-27**
- *Federal Tax Practice and Procedure* (Meldrum), **15-8n**
- Federal tax revenue, breakdown of, *1-4*
- Fellowships, exclusion from gross income, *4-7*
- Fiduciaries
  - calculation formula, **14-7–14-10**
    - credits, **14-10**
    - distribution deduction, **14-9**
    - expense deductions, **14-7–14-9**
    - gross income, **14-7**
    - personal exemption, **14-9–14-10**
  - principles of fiduciary accounting, **14-4–14-7**
    - depreciation, **14-6–14-7**
    - expenditures, **14-6**
    - income and principal, identification of, **14-4–14-5**
    - income receipts, **14-5, 14-6**
    - principal receipts, **14-6**
    - state law, effects of, **14-5**
    - terms of trust instrument, effects of, **14-5**
    - Uniform Act, **14-5–14-6**
  - *See also* Accounting, **14-1–14-36**
- Fiduciary taxation, **14-1–14-36**
  - basic principles of, **14-3–14-4**
    - conduit approach, **14-4**
    - no double taxation, **14-4**
    - similarity to rules for individuals, **14-4**
    - trusts/estates as separate taxpayers, **14-3–14-4**
- Field audit, *1-21,* **15-7**
- Filing requirements
  - affiliated groups, **8-2, 8-36–8-38**
  - alternative minimum tax, **5-37**
  - C corporations, **3-35**
  - estates
    - estate tax returns, **13-35–13-36**
    - income tax returns, **14-35**
  - gift tax returns, **12-30–12-31**
  - individuals, *14-32, 2-31–2-32*
  - personal holding company (PHC) tax, **5-37**
  - S corporations, **11-37–11-38**
  - trusts, **14-35**
- Filing status, standard deduction and, *2-10–2-12*
- Final regulations, **1-9**
- Finance charges, deductibility of, *7-12*
- Finance Committee, U.S. Senate, tax law and, **1-7**
- Financial planning, *1-24–1-25*
- Fines
  - as expense contrary to public policy, *6-13*
- Fiscal year
  - C corporation, **3-2–3-4**
  - election, *11-2–11-7*
  - estates, **14-35**
  - partnerships, **9-12–9-15, 9-31–9-32**
  - S corporations, **11-13, 11-37**
  - trusts, **14-35**
- Flat tax, *1-5*
- Flexible spending accounts, *4-17*
- Foreign death tax credit, estate tax, **13-25**
- Foreign-earned income
  - definition of, *4-18*
  - exclusion, *4-18–4-19*
- Foreign tax credit, *4-18, 14-17–14-18*
  - alternative minimum tax (AMT), **5-15**
- Foreign travel, deduction of expenses, *9-8*
- Form 1040A, *14-32–14-33, 2-32*
- Form 1040EZ, *14-32–14-33, 2-32*
- Form 1040X, *8-35, 9-47*
- Form 1040, *2-2, 2-32, 2-8–2-9, 3-29–3-32, 3-30, 5-33, 6-36, 7-36, 8-35, 9-47, 13-25*
  - Schedule A, *3-29, 3-30, 6-36, 7-33–7-36, 9-44, 13-25*
  - Schedule B, *3-29, 3-30, 3-32*
  - Schedule C, *3-30, 6-36, 7-36, 9-47, 10-23*
  - Schedule C-EZ, *9-47*

BOLD = Corporations
ITALICS = Individuals

Schedule D, *3-30, 5-33, 8-35, 11-28, 13-24–13-25*
Schedule EIC, *14-33*
Schedule E, *3-29, 3-30, 6-36, 7-36, 10-23,* **9-17, 11-38**
Schedule F, *3-30*
Schedule R, *14-32*
Schedule SE, *14-8,* **9-32**
Form 1041, **14-36**
Form 1041–ES, **14-36**
Form 1041–S, **14-35**
Form 1045, *8-35*
Form 1065, **9-17, 9-31**
Form 1065, Schedule K–1, **9-17, 9-31**
Form 1099-B, *2-32, 5-36*
Form 1099-DIV, *2-32,,* **6-20**
Form 1099-G, *2-32*
Form 1099-INT, *2-32*
Form 1099-MISC, *2-32*
Form 1099-R, *2-32*
Form 1116, *14-33*
Form 1120, **3-34–3-37, 8-36, 9-17**
Form 1120, Schedule PH, **5-37**
Form 1120–A, **3-34, 3-37**
Form 1120S, **11-37–11-38, 11-39**
Form 1120S, Schedule K–1, **11-38–11-39**
Form 1122, **8-37**
Form 1128, *11-5*
Form 1139, *8-35*
Form 2106, *3-30, 6-36n, 9-44, 10-23*
Form 2119, *12-24*
Form 2120, *2-15*
Form 2210, *14-28*
Form 2441, *14-32*
Form 2553, **11-37**
Form 2688, **15-13**
Form 2758, **14-36**
Form 3468, *14-32*
Form 3800, *14-32*
Form 3903, *3-30, 6-36n, 9-44*
Form 4562, *10-23, 9-47*
Form 4626, *14-32,* **5-37**
Form 4684, *13-24–13-25, 13-25–13-28*
Form 4782, *9-47*
Form 4797, *3-30, 11-28, 13-24–13-27, 13-25*
Form 4868, *2-32,* **15-13**
Form 5213, *6-37*
Form 5452, **4-36**
Form 6251, *14-32*
Form 6252, *11-28–11-29*
Form 7004, **3-35, 8-37, 11-37, 15-13**
Form 706, *5-33,* **13-35–13-36**
Form 709, **12-30**
Form 709A, **12-30–12-31**
Form 712, **13-36**
Form 8023, **7-51**
Form 851, **8-37**
Form 8283, *7-33, 7-36*
Form 8716, **9-31, 11-37**
Form 8752, **9-32, 11-38**
Form 8829, *6-37, 9-47*
Form 966, **6-20**
Form W-2, *2-32, 4-23, 9-44, 14-32*
Form W-4, *14-25–14-26, 14-30*
Form W-5, *14-33*
Forum shopping, precedential value of decisions and, **1-23–1-24**
Franchise tax, *1-7–1-8*
Franchises, sale/exchange of, *5-26–5-27*
Fraud
penalty for, *1-23*
when fraud is proven, **15-28–15-29**
criminal provision, **15-29**
deficiency and civil fraud penalty, **15-28–15-29**
See also Civil fraud penalty
Fringe benefits
C corporations, **2-5**
tax planning device, **3-29**
discrimination, *4-10–4-11*
S corporations, treatment of, **11-33–11-34**
See also Employee compensation
Funeral expenses, as estate tax deduction, **13-18–13-19**
Future interest, definition of, **12-17**

General business credit
affiliated groups, **8-10–8-11**
alternative minimum tax (AMT), **5-14–5-15**
claiming the credit, *14-32*
definition of, *14-9*
limitation on, *14-9–14-10*
nonrefundable credits, *14-24, 2-6*
General partner, definition of, **9-2–9-3**
General partnerships
partner's share of liabilities and, **9-22–9-23**
rights/restrictions of, **9-2–9-3**
See also Partnerships
General power of appointment, **12-15**
estate tax and, **13-15–13-16**
gift tax consequences, **12-15**
gross estate, **13-15–13-16**
Generally accepted accounting principles (GAAP), *11-11–11-12*
Generation-skipping transfer tax (GSTT), **13-30–13-31**
General Utilities doctrine, **11-16**
Gift tax, *1-8–1-9*
below market loans, **12-28–12-29**
calculation formula, **12-4–12-7**
deductions, **12-4–12-5**
determination of gifts, **12-4**
exclusions, **12-4, 12-5**
gift-splitting election, **12-5–12-6**
charitable contribution deduction, **12-18, 12-21–12-22**
comprehensive illustration, **12-25**
cumulative nature of, **12-6**
definition of, **12-2**
determination of value, **12-31–12-32**
due date, **12-31**
effect on basis, *5-7*
exclusions, **12-16–12-18**
amount of, **12-16**
present interest requirement, **12-16–12-18**
general concepts/rules, *1-8–1-9*
gift-splitting election, **12-5–12-6, 12-22–12-23, 12-31**
inter vivos gifts, **12-29–12-30**
liability computations, **12-23–12-24**
previous taxable gifts, effect of, **12-23–12-24**
unified credit, **12-24**
lifetime giving plan, basis considerations, **12-26–12-27**
marital deduction, *1-8,* **12-19–12-21**
negative aspects of gifts, **12-30**
return filing requirements, **12-30–12-31**
revocable trusts, **12-10**
retained powers, **12-10–12-11**
statute of limitations, **12-32**
statutory exemptions from, **12-8–12-10**
medical expenses payments, **12-8**
property settlements from divorce, **12-9**
qualified disclaimers, **12-9–12-10**
transfers to political organizations, **12-9**
tuition payments, **12-8**
tax liability, **12-31**
transfer consequences, **12-13–12-16**
general power of appointment, exercise of, **12-15**
joint bank accounts, **12-13–12-14**
joint tenancies, **12-14**
life insurance policies, **12-14–12-15**
net gifts, **12-15, 12-16**
transfer taxes
concept of, **12-2–12-3**
history/purpose of, **12-2–12-3**
transfers subject to, **12-7–12-16**
cessation of donor's dominion/control, **12-10–12-11**
inadequate consideration, **12-7–12-8**
unified credit, **12-4, 12-6–12-7**
unified transfer tax system, **12-3–12-4**
death tax base, impact of taxable gifts on, **12-3–12-4**
unified rate schedule, **12-3**
valuation of gifts, **12-11–12-13**
general rules, **12-11–12-12**
life estates/remainder interests, **12-12–12-13**
special valuation rules - estate freezes, **12-13**
See also Exclusions; Grantor trusts; Revocable trusts; Transfer taxes; Trusts, **12-1–12-32**
Gift tax returns, substantial omissions, **15-28**
Gifts
acquired property, *5-6–5-7*
business gifts, *9-15–9-16*
exclusion from gross income, *4-4–4-5*

Gifts (*continued*)
- holding period, *5-28–5-29*
- imputed interest, *11-24–11-25*
  - gift loans, *11-24–11-25*
- inter vivos gifts, *4-4*
- of property subject to recapture, *13-17*
- selection of property to transfer as, *5-31–5-32*
- testamentary gifts, *4-4*
- to employees, as gross income exclusion, *4-14*

"Good faith" belief requirement, certified public accountants (CPAs), **1-35–1-37**

Goodwill
- Sec. 197 intangibles, amortization of, *10-13–10-17*

Goodwill payments, at death/retirement of partner, **10-19**

Grantor trusts
- effect of, **14-30**
- provisions, **14-30–14-33**
  - *Clifford* trusts, **14-31**
  - administrative powers, retention of, **14-32**
  - control of others' enjoyment, **14-32–14-33**
  - economic benefits, retention of, **14-32**
  - post-1986 reversionary interest trusts, **14-31**
  - revocable trusts, **14-31**

Grantors, **14-2**

Gray areas, tax research, **1-4**

Gross income test, for dependency exemptions, *2-16*

Gross estate
- calculation formula for estate tax, **13-2–13-5**
- compared to probate estate, **13-9**
- estate tax calculation, **13-2–13-5**
- inclusions, **13-8–13-11**
  - annuities, **13-13–13-14**
  - consideration offset, **13-17**
  - curtesy rights, **13-10**
  - dower rights, **13-10**
  - employment-related retirement benefits, **13-14**
  - general powers of appointment, **13-15–13-16**
  - jointly owned property, **13-14–13-15**
  - life insurance, **13-16–13-17**
  - property in which decedent has interest, **13-10**
  - recipient spouse's interest in QTIP trust, **13-17–13-18**
  - transferor provisions, **13-10–13-13**
- valuation, **13-6–13-8**
  - alternate valuation date, **13-7–13-8**
  - date-of-death valuation, **13-6–13-7**

Gross income
- alimony, *3-17–3-19*
- annuities, *3-19–3-21*
- awards, *3-22–3-23*
- business income, *3-13*
- compensation, *3-13*
- constructive dividends, *3-17*
- court awards, *3-24–3-25*
- definition of, *2-3*
- discharge of indebtedness, income from, *3-22*
- dividends, *3-16–3-17*
- endowment contracts, income from, *3-21*
- estates, **14-7**
- exclusions, *4-1–4-24*
- fiduciary accounting, calculation formula, **14-7–14-8**
- filing levels, *2-31*
- gains realized from property, *3-13*
- gambling winnings, *3-22–3-23*
- illegal income, *3-23*
- inclusions, *3-1–3-29*
  - economic/accounting concepts of income, *3-2–3-3*
  - tax concept of income, *3-3–3-6*
  - to whom income is taxable, *3-6–3-8*
  - when income is taxable, *3-8–3-12*
- income passed through to taxpayer, *3-22*
- insurance proceeds, *3-24–3-25*
- interest, *3-13–3-15*
  - Series EE savings bonds exclusion, *3-14–3-15*
  - tax-exempt interest, *3-13–3-14*
- life insurance, income from, *3-21*
- pensions, *3-19–3-21*
- prizes, *3-22–3-23*
- property settlements, *3-17–3-18*
- recovery of previously deducted expenses, *3-25–3-26*
  - tax benefit rule, *3-26*
- rents, *3-15–3-16*
  - improvements by lessees, *3-15–3-16*
- royalties, *3-15–3-16*
- social security benefits, *3-23–3-24*
- substantial omission of, **15-27–15-28**
- treasure finds, *3-22–3-23*
- trusts, **14-7**
- unemployment compensation, *3-23*
- when taxable, *3-9*
- Sec. 61(a) definition, *3-2*
- *See also* Adjusted gross income (AGI), *3-13–3-27*

Grossed-up basis for stock, deemed liquidation election and, **7-8**

Group term life insurance exclusion, *4-10–4-11*

Guaranteed payments
- partnerships, **9-27–9-28**
  - determination of, **9-28**
  - fringe benefits as, **11-33–11-34**
  - guaranteed minimum, **9-28**
  - tax impact of, **9-28**

Guarantor, bad debts, *8-25*

Guarantor, S corporation loan, **11-21**

Head-of-household, *2-21–2-22*
- abandoned spouse as, *2-22–2-23*

Health insurance benefits, as gross income exclusion, *4-8–4-10*

Hedge agreements, **4-33–4-34**

Hobby losses, *6-28–6-31, 6-35, 6-37*
- deductible expenses, *6-30*
- order of deductions, *6-30–6-31*

Hobby losses, S corporation shareholders, **11-22**

Holding period
- capital assets, *5-28–5-29*
- for acquired properties, **7-18**
- for corporate formations, **2-19**
- intercompany transactions, **8-12**
- partnership interest, **9-8**
- property contributions, partnerships, **9-9**
- property transactions, *5-28–5-29*

Home equity indebtedness, *7-17*

Home office expenses
- general requirements for deduction, *9-23*
- gross income limitations, *9-25*
- reporting of, *6-37, 9-47*
- *See also* Self-employed individuals, *6-34–6-35, 9-23–9-25, 9-47*

House trailers, as principal residence, *12-18*

House-hunting trips, as indirect moving expense, *9-20*

Houseboats, as principal residence, *12-18*

H.R. 10 plans, *9-36*

Hybrid method of accounting, *11-10, 3-12*, **2-23–2-24, 3-5**

Illegal activity expenses, nondeductibility of, *6-14*

Illegal income, taxability of, *3-23*

Illegal kickbacks, *6-12–6-13*

Imputed interest, *11-22–11-25, 7-20*
- accrual of interest, *11-23–11-24*
- applicable federal rate, *11-23*
- gift, shareholder and other loans, *11-24–11-25*

Inadequate consideration
- gift tax and, **12-7–12-8**
  - bargain sales, **12-7**
  - transfers in normal course of business, **12-7–12-8**

Incentive stock option (ISO) plans, *9-33–9-34*

Includible corporation
- affiliated groups, **8-3**
- controlled group, definition of, **3-23**

Inclusions
- gross estate, **13-8–13-11**
  - annuities, **13-13–13-14**
  - comparison with probate estate, **13-9**
  - consideration offset, **13-17**
  - curtesy rights, **13-10**
  - dower rights, **13-10**
  - employee-related benefits, **13-14**

BOLD = Corporations
ITALICS = Individuals

general powers of appointment, **13-15–13-16**
jointly owned property, **13-14–13-15**
life insurance, **13-16–13-17**
property in which decedent had interest, **13-10**
recipient spouse's interest in QTIP trust, **13-17–13-18**
transferor provisions, **13-10–13-13**

Income
accounting concept of, *3-2–3-3*
allocation between married persons, *3-6–3-7*
assignment of, *3-6*
definition of, *2-3, 3-4–3-6*
economic concepts, *3-2*
economic income, *1-6*
of minor children, *3-8*
prepaid income, *3-11–3-12*
reporting of, *3-30*
tax concept of, *3-3–3-6*
administrative convenience, *3-3–3-4*
wherewithal-to-pay concept, *3-4*

Income allocations
S corporation, **11-19–11-20**
partnerships, **9-30**

Income in respect of a decedent (IRD), **14-27–14-29**
common examples, **14-27–14-28**
deductions in respect of a decedent, **14-28**
definition of, **14-27–14-28**
double taxation, **14-28**
no step-up in basis, **14-29**
Sec. 691(c) deduction, **14-28–14-29**
significance of, **14-28–14-29**

Income shifting, *3-27*
to family members, *2-28–2-29*

Income splitting
between tax entities, *2-29*
corporations and, **3-22**
family S corporation, **11-23**
family partnerships, **9-29–9-30**
lifetime gifts and, **12-29**

Income tax formula, *1-7*

Income tax returns, substantial omissions, **15-27–15-28**

Incorporation
deferring gain/loss upon, **2-12–2-26**
control requirement, **2-13–2-16**
property requirement, **2-12–2-13**
stock requirement, **2-16**
exchange of partnership interest, **10-21**
requirements for, **2-9**

Independent contractor status, versus employee status, **9-3**

Individual income tax
capital gains and losses, treatment of, *2-27–2-28, 5-16–5-20*
determination of, *2-2–2-25*
due dates for filing returns, *2-32*
filing joint or separate returns, *2-29–2-31*
forms, *2-32*
formula, *2-2–2-7*
gross tax determination, *2-19–2-25*
rate structures, *1-4–1-7*
progressive tax rate, *1-4*
proportional tax rate, *1-5*
shifting income to family members, *2-28–2-29*
who must file, *2-31*

Individual retirement accounts (IRAs), *9-36–9-41*
deductible contributions, *9-36–9-41*
nondeductible contributions, *9-38*
tax advantages, *9-38*
tax rules, *9-38–9-41*

Individual taxable income
compared to corporate taxable income, **3-6**
deductions/losses, **3-6**

Information releases, *1-19*

Information releases, tax law, **1-13**

Inheritances, exclusion from gross income, *4-4–4-5*

Injury payments, as gross income exclusion, *4-8–4-10*

Innocent spouse provision, *2-30,* **15-30–15-31**
community property laws, effect of, **15-31**
relief from tax liability, conditions to be met for, **15-30**
test for substantial understatement of tax, **15-30**

Insolvent financial institutions, deposits in, *8-28–8-29*

Insolvent subsidiary, liquidation of, **6-11–6-12**

Installment obligations, disposition of, *11-19–11-20*

Installment obligations, shareholder, liquidating distributions, **6-15–6-16**

Installment payments, qualifying an estate for, **13-34–13-35**

Installment sales, *11-17–11-21*
installment sale defined, *11-18*
recapture, *13-19–13-20*
related-party sales, *11-21*
reporting on Form 6252, *11-28–11-29*
repossession, *11-20*

Insurance
casualty losses, failure to file claim, *8-22*
employer-paid insurance, *4-10–4-12*
estate tax consequences, **13-16–13-17, 13-34**
gift tax consequences, **12-14–12-15**
health insurance benefits, as gross income exclusion, *4-8–4-10*
life insurance, *4-5–4-6*
exclusion from gross income, *4-5–4-6*
income from, *3-24–3-25*
proceeds, *4-5–4-6*
losses, *8-22–8-23*
medical insurance, *7-6–7-8*
tax treatment of, *4-11*

Intangible assets
amortization of, *10-13–10-17*
research expenditures, *10-16–10-17*
Sec. 197 intangibles, *10-13*

Intangible drilling costs (IDCs), *10-20*
capitalization versus expense election, *10-21–10-22*
definition of, *10-18*
recapture provisions, *13-21*
tax preference item, *14-3–14-4*
treatment of, *10-20*

Inter vivos gifts, **12-29–12-30**
annual exclusion, use of, **12-29**
estate tax and, **13-32**
gift in contemplation of donee-spouse's death, **12-29–12-30**
gift tax amount, removal from transfer tax base, **12-29**
income splitting, **12-29**
income tax savings, charitable gifts, **12-30**
lessening state transfer tax costs, **12-30**
post-gift appreciation, removal from tax base, **12-29**

Inter vivos trusts, **14-2**

Intercompany transactions, **8-11–8-20**
other intercompany transactions, **8-18–8-20**
property transactions, **8-12–8-17**
amount/character of deferred gain/loss, **8-12**
basis and holding period, **8-12**
restored gain/loss, determination of, **8-12–8-17**

Interest
as gross income, *3-13–3-15*
Series EE savings bonds exclusion, *3-14–3-15, 3-28–3-29*
tax-exempt interest, *3-13–3-14*
as itemized deduction, *7-12–7-21*
capitalization of, *5-5–5-6*
complete termination of, **4-21–4-23, 4-36–4-37**
debt capital, **2-27–2-28**
definition of, *7-12*
imputed interest, *11-22–11-25*
income, personal holding company income (PHCI) and, **5-18**
interest expense
acquisition indebtedness, *7-16–7-17*
active trade/business, *7-13*
classification of, *7-12–7-18*
incurred to generate tax-exempt income, *7-14*
investment interest, *7-14–7-15*
passive activity, *7-14*
personal, *7-16*
qualified residence interest, *7-16*

Interest (*continued*)
- late payment of taxes, *1-22*
- on accumulated earnings tax, **5-37**
- on late payment of tax, **15-14–15-15**
  - daily compounding, **15-15**
  - determination of rate, **15-14**
  - period for which interest is imposed, **15-15**
- on personal holding company (PHC) tax, **5-37**
- qualified terminable interest property (QTIP), **13-17–13-18**
- split-interest transfers, **12-22**
  - charitable contribution deductions and, **12-21–12-22**
  - definition of, **12-22**
  - estate tax and, **13-20**
  - example of, **12-22**
  - gift tax and, **12-22**
- timing of interest deduction, *7-19–7-20*
  - discounted notes, *7-20*
  - interest paid with loan proceeds, *7-19–7-20*
  - prepaid interest, *7-19*
- *See also* Partnership interest

Internal Revenue Bulletin (I.R.B.), **1-17**

Internal Revenue Code, *1-18, 1-3*
- as source of tax law, *1-18–1-19*
- general language of, *1-18*

Internal Revenue Code, **1-8**
- history of, **1-8**
- organizational scheme, **1-8**
- tax law and, **1-8**

Internal Revenue Service
- audits, *1-21*
  - correspondence audit, **15-7**
  - field office procedure, **15-7**
  - office audit procedure, **15-7**
  - selecting returns for, *1-21,* **15-5–15-7**
- Discriminant Function (DIF) system, *1-21*
- Discrimination Function (DIF) system, **15-5–15-6**
- enforcement procedures, *1-21*
- organization of, *1-20,* **15-3**
- role of, **15-2–15-3**
  - enforcement/collection, **15-2**
  - interpretation of statute, **15-2**
  - Interpretative regulations, *1-19*
- Taxpayer Compliance Measurement Program (TCMP), **15-6**

Interpretations, tax law, **1-7, 15-2**

Interpretative regulations, **1-10**

Inventories, *11-11–11-14*
- accounting methods, *11-11–11-14*
- donation of, *7-24,* **3-11**
- generally accepted accounting principles (GAAP), *11-11–11-12*
- inventory cost
  - determination of, *11-11–11-14*
  - "first-in, first-out", method (FIFO), *11-12*
  - "last-in, first-out" method (LIFO), *11-12–11-14*
  - lower of cost or market (LCM) method, *11-14*
  - mark-to-market method, *5-14–5-15*
- uniform capitalization rules, *11-11–11-12*
- valuation methods, *11-11–11-14*

Inventory
- partnerships, basis, **9-9**
- substantially appreciated inventory, **10-8–10-9**

Investment expenses, *6-4–6-16*
- deduction criteria, *6-4–6-16*
  - activity engaged in for profit, *6-5–6-30*
  - business/expense requirement, *6-5–6-30*
  - expenses related to exempt income, *6-11–6-12*
  - lobbying expenses, *6-14–6-15*
  - necessary expense, *6-8*
  - ordinary expense, *6-7–6-8*
  - reasonable expense, *6-8–6-9*
- trade/business versus investment classification, *6-5–6-6*

Investment interest
- interest expense, *7-14–7-15, 7-31–7-32*
- net investment income, *7-14–7-15*
- S corporation shareholders, **11-24**

Investment tax credit (ITC), *14-20*

Investments
- fixed-income investments
  - tax-exempt securities, tax preference item, *14-3–14-4*

Involuntary conversions, *12-10–12-16*
- condemnation, threat of, *12-11*
- definition of, *12-11–12-12*
- into boot, *12-12–12-13*
- into similar property, tax treatment of gain, *12-13*
- involuntary defined, *12-11–12-12*
- principal residence, *12-20–12-21*
- recapture, *13-19*
- replacement property, *12-13–12-14*
  - functional use test, *12-14*
  - replacement with like-kind property, *12-14*
  - taxpayer-use test, *12-14*
- reporting of, *12-23*
- time requirements, for replacement, *12-15–12-16*

IRS collection costs, *1-13–1-14*

IRS Letter Rulings (CCH), **1-13**

IRS rulings, *1-19*

IRS Service centers, location of, *1-20,* **15-3n**

Itemized deductions
- casualty/theft losses, *7-28*
- charitable contributions, *7-21–7-26*
  - carryovers, *7-25–7-26*
  - deduction limitations, *7-25*
  - election to reduce amount of charitable contribution, *7-32*
  - property contributions, *7-32–7-33*
  - qualifying organizations, *7-21–7-22*
  - reporting of, *7-33–7-36*
  - special rules for corporations, *7-26*
  - type of property contributed, *7-22–7-24*
- definition of, *2-4–2-5*
- interest, *7-12–7-21*
  - definition of, *7-12*
  - incurred to generate tax-exempt income, *7-14*
  - interest expense classifications, *7-12–7-18*
  - timing of deduction, *7-19–7-20*
- list of, *2-10*
- medical expenses, *7-2–7-8*
  - amount/timing of deduction, *7-6–7-8*
  - qualified expenses, *7-30–7-31, 7-3–7-6*
  - qualified individuals, *7-2–7-3*
  - reporting of, *7-33*
- miscellaneous deductions, *7-28–7-29*
  - employment-related expenses, *7-28*
  - expenses to produce income, *7-28*
  - tax return preparation fees, *7-28–7-29*
- reduction for high-income taxpayers, *7-29–7-30*
- taxes, *7-9–7-11*
  - deductible taxes, *7-9*
  - definition, *7-9*
  - reporting of, *7-36*
- *See also* specific deductions, *2-4–2-5, 2-7–2-10, 7-1–7-36*

Joint bank accounts, gift tax consequences, **12-13–12-14**

Joint returns
- filing of, *2-29–2-30*
- innocent spouse provision, *2-30*
- surviving spouse and, *2-20–2-21*
- tax liability, **15-30–15-31**
  - innocent spouse provision, **15-30–15-31**
  - validity of, **15-30**
- versus separate returns, *2-22*
- who may file, *2-19–2-20*

Joint tenancies, transfers of, gift tax consequences, **12-14**

Joint tenancy with right of survivorship, definition of, **13-14n**

Jointly owned property
- estate tax and, **13-14–13-15**
  - ownership involving only spouses, **13-15**
  - ownership involving persons other than spouses, **13-14–13-15**
- gross estate, **13-14–13-15**

Journal of Corporate Taxation, The, **1-25**

Journal of Partnership Taxation, The, **1-25**

Journal of Real Estate Taxation, The, **1-25**

BOLD = Corporations
ITALICS = Individuals

Journal of Taxation, The, **1-25**
Judicial decisions
importance of facts, **1-5–1-6**
tax law, **1-7–1-25**
Circuit Court of Appeals, **1-20**
court system, overview of, **1-14**
precedential value of decisions, **1-21–1-24**
Supreme Court, **1-21**
U.S. Court of Federal Claims, **1-19–1-20**
U.S. district courts, **1-19**
U.S. Tax Court, **1-14–1-18**
Judicial doctrines, *1-19*
reorganizations, **7-43–7-45**
business purpose requirement, **7-45**
continuity of business enterprise, **7-44–7-45**
continuity of proprietary interest, **7-41, 7-43–7-44**
step transaction doctrine, **7-45**
Judicial exclusions, definition of, *4-2*
Judicial interpretations, of tax law, *1-19*
Federal Court System, *1-19*
Judicial interpretations, tax law, **1-14–1-24**
citations, **1-11**
primary cite, **1-19**
secondary cite, **1-19**
unreported decisions, **1-19**
Federal court system, **1-14**
precedential value, **1-21–1-24**

Keogh plans, *9-36*
Key employees, employer-paid insurance, *4-10–4-12*
Kickbacks, *6-12–6-13*
Kiddie tax, *2-23–2-25*

Late payment of tax
interest on, **15-14–15-15**
determination of rate, **15-14**
period for which interest is imposed, **15-15**
See also Penalties
Law of Federal Income Taxation (Clark, Boardman, & Callaghan), **1-27**
Lease cancellation payments, *5-27*
Legal fees, as nondeductible expense, *6-6–6-7*
Legislative process, steps in, *1-18–1-20*, **1-7–1-8**
Legislative reenactment doctrine, **1-10**
Legislative regulations, *1-19*, **1-10**
Letter rulings, *1-19*
requests for, **15-11–15-12**
tax law, **1-12–1-13**
LEXIS data base, *1-25–1-26*
Life insurance, *4-5–4-6*
estate tax and, **13-16–13-17, 13-34**
exclusion from gross income, *4-5–4-6*
dividends, *4-6*
surrender of policy before death, *4-6*
incidents of ownership in policies, **13-16–13-17**
transfer of policies, gift tax consequences, **12-14–12-15**
income from, as gross income, *3-24–3-25*
LIFO method, *6-18, 11-12–11-14*
simplified LIFO method, *11-13*
Like-kind exchanges, *12-2–12-10*
basis of property received, *12-7–12-8*
boot
holding period, *12-10*
property transfers involving liabilities, *12-7*
receipt of, *12-6–12-7*
definition of, *12-2–12-5*
recapture, *13-18–13-19*
related-party transactions, *12-8–12-9*
three-party exchanges, *12-5–12-6*
Limitations
accrued compensation deductions, **3-10**
acquisitions, tax attributes, **7-47–7-49**
dividends-received deduction, exception to, **3-14**
partnerships
at-risk loss limitation, **9-24–9-25**
partner loss limitation, **9-24–9-26**
passive activity limitation, **9-26**
S corporations
investment interest limitation, **11-24**
shareholder loss limitation, **11-21–11-22**
Sec. 382 loss limitation, **7-47–7-49, 8-29–8-31**
statute of, **15-26–15-29**
Limited liability company, **10-29**
Limited liability partnerships, **2-8, 10-29–10-30**,
Limited partner, definition of, **9-3**
Limited partnerships
as tax shelter, **10-28**
exchange of interest, **10-20–10-21**
partner's share of liabilities and, **9-22–9-23**
passive activity, *8-12*
rights/restrictions of, **9-3**
See also Partnerships
Liquidating distributions
acquisition, part of, **7-2–7-11**
controlled subsidiary corporations, **6-10–6-12**
avoiding Sec. 332 nonrecognition rules, **6-19–6-20**
basis of property received, **6-12**
cancellation of stock requirement, **6-11**
debt obligations, satisfaction of, **6-17**
double tax exemption, **6-19**
effects of, **6-10–6-12**
insolvent subsidiary, **6-11–6-12**
minority shareholders receiving distributions, **6-12**
procedural consideration, **6-20–6-21**
recognition of gain or loss by liquidating corporation, **6-13**
recognition of gain or loss by shareholder, **6-7–6-13**
recognition of ordinary losses when liquidation occurs, **6-18–6-19**
requirements for shareholder tax exemption, **6-10–6-11**
stock ownership, **6-10–6-11**
tax attribute carryovers, **6-13–6-14**
timing of the distributions, **6-11**
deemed liquidation elections
adjusted grossed-up basis for stock, **7-8**
allocation of basis to individual assets, **7-8–7-10**
basis of assets after deemed sale, **7-8**
deemed sale transaction, **7-7**
election requirements, **7-11**
eligible stock acquisitions, **7-6**
liquidation of the target corporation, **7-5**
making the election, **7-6–7-7**
procedural considerations, **6-21**
tax accounting elections, **7-7–7-10**
dividends
accumulated earnings tax, **5-31–5-32**
personal holding company (PHC) tax and, **5-22, 5-36**
noncontrolled corporations
accounting method, impact of, **6-6**
basis of property received, **6-6**
character of recognized gain/loss, **6-6**
complete liquidation, definition of, **6-3–6-4**
dissolution compared to liquidation, **6-3–6-4**
distributions to related persons, **6-8**
effects of liquidating on, **6-6, 6-14**
installment obligations received by shareholders, **6-15–6-16**
liabilities assumed or acquired by shareholders, **6-7–6-8**
liquidation expenses, **6-16**
liquidation procedures, **6-20**
net operating losses (NOLs), treatment of, **6-16–6-17**
open versus closed transactions, **6-15**
ordinary losses, recognition of, **6-18–6-19**
partially liquidating distributions, **6-14–6-15**
plan of liquidation, **6-21**
procedural considerations, **6-20–6-21**

Liquidating distributions (*continued*)
- property distribution in redemption of stock, recognition of gain/loss, **6-6–6-9**
- property distribution in retirement of debt, recognition of gain/loss, **6-17**
- recognized gain/loss amount of, **6-5**
- sales with tax-avoidance purpose, **6-8–6-9**
- stock acquisition, **6-6**
- subsequent assessments against shareholders, **6-15**
- tax attributes, **6-3, 6-13–6-14**
- tax consequences, to the corporation, **6-3**
- tax consequences, to the shareholder, **6-2–6-3**
- timing the liquidation transaction, **6-18**

partnerships, **10-12–10-16, 10-33–10-34**
- basis in assets received, **10-12–10-14**
- effects on partnership, **10-12, 10-16**
- gain/loss recognition by partner, **10-14, 10-15**
- termination of partnership interest and, **10-22–10-24**

See also Deemed liquidation election

Liquidation-reincorporation transactions, **7-45**
Listed stocks, date-of-death valuation, **13-6–13-7**
Litigation
- appeal of lower court's decision, **15-10**
- district court, **15-9**
- Tax Court, **15-9**
- U.S. Court of Federal Claims, **15-9**

Livestock, Sec. 1231 and, *13-6*
Loans
- compensation loans, *11-24*
- gift loans, *11-24*
- shareholder loans, *11-24*
- tax avoidance loans, *11-24*

Loans to shareholders, as disguised dividends, **5-26**
Lobbying expenses, *6-14–6-15*
Locked-in effect, *6-27–6-28*
Long-term capital gains and losses (LTCG and LTCL), *2-28, 5-16–5-20*
Long-term care expenses, *7-5*
Long-term contracts, *11-15–11-17*
- completed contract method, *11-16*
- definition of, *11-15*
- look-back interest, *11-17*
- percentage of completion method, *11-16*

Loss corporation, **7-47**
Losses
- C corporations
  - Sec. 382 limitation, **7-47–7-49**
  - affiliated groups, **8-23, 8-31**
  - nonaffiliated, **3-6–3-7, 3-16–3-17**
- casualty/theft losses, *8-17–8-23*
  - casualty defined, *8-17–8-19*
  - deductible amount of, *8-19–8-20*
  - disaster area election, *8-35*
  - documentation of losses, *8-34*
  - limitations on personal-use property, *8-20–8-21*
  - netting casualty gains/losses on personal-use property, *8-21*
  - theft defined, *8-19*
  - when losses are deductible, *8-22–8-23*
- classification of
  - disallowance possibilities, *8-6*
  - on tax return, *8-4–8-6*
  - ordinary versus capital loss, *8-5–8-6*
- disaster losses, *8-23*
- estates, **14-16–14-17**
- hobby losses, *6-28–6-31, 6-34–6-35, 6-37*
- insurance/other reimbursements, *8-22–8-23*
- net operating losses, *8-29–8-33*
  - carryback/carryover periods, *8-33*
  - computation of, *8-30–8-33*
  - election to forgo carryback, *8-33*
  - recomputation of taxable income in carryover year, *8-33*
  - reporting the NOL, *8-35*
- partnerships, **9-24–9-26**
  - at-risk loss limitations, **9-24–9-25**
  - partner loss limitations, **9-24–9-26**
  - passive activity limitations, **9-26**
- passive losses, *8-7–8-16*
  - carryovers, *8-8–8-9*
  - computation of, *8-7–8-10*
  - credits, *8-10*
  - passive activity defined, *8-10–8-12*
  - publicly traded partnerships, *8-13–8-14*
  - real estate trades or businesses, *8-14–8-16*
  - rental real estate, *8-14–8-16*
  - taxpayers subject to passive loss rules, *8-12–8-13*
- rental real estate, *8-14–8-16*
  - active participation, *8-15*
  - limitation on deduction of loss, *8-15–8-16*
- transactions that may result in, *8-2–8-4*
  - abandoned property, *8-3*
  - confiscated property, *8-3*
  - demolition of property, *8-4*
  - expropriated property, *8-3*
  - sale/exchange of property, *8-2–8-3*
  - seized property, *8-3*
  - worthless securities, *8-35, 8-3–8-4*
- S corporations, **11-20, 11-23**
  - allocation of loss, **11-20–11-21**
  - at risk loss limitation, **11-22**
  - hobby loss rules, **11-22**
  - investment interest expense limitation, **11-24**
  - passive activity limitations, **11-22**
  - post-termination loss carryovers, **11-22–11-23**
  - shareholder loss limitations, **11-21–11-22**
- trusts, **14-16–14-17**
- *See also* Bad debts; Capital gains/losses; specific types of losses, *8-1–8-35*

Low-income housing, *13-15*
Lower of cost or market method, inventories, *11-14*
Luxury automobiles, accelerated cost recovery system (ACRS and MACRS) and, limitations on, *10-11–10-13*
- leased luxury automobiles, *10-13*

Luxury water travel, deductions for, *9-8*

Marginal tax rate, *1-4*
Marital deduction
- estate tax, **13-20–13-23**
  - passing requirement, **13-21**
  - property in gross estate, **13-21**
  - QTIP transfers, **13-22–13-23**
  - size of deduction, **13-33–3-34**
  - terminable interest rule, **13-21–13-22**
  - tests for, **13-21**
- gift tax, **12-19–12-21**
  - amount of, **12-19**
  - nondeductible terminable interests, **12-19–12-20**
  - QTIP provisions, **12-20**

Mark-to-market method, *5-14–5-15*
Market discount bonds, *5-23–5-24*
Market value, definition of, *11-14, 5-3*
Married individuals
- allocation of income between, *3-6–3-7*
- joint returns, *2-19–2-20*
- separate returns, *2-22*

Material participation
- in active trade/business, *7-13, 8-11–8-12*
- passive activity rules, *8-11–8-12*
  - by closely held corporations, *8-13*
  - by limited partnership, *8-12*
  - by personal service corporations (PSCs), *8-13*

Meals/lodging
- as gross income exclusion, *4-14–4-15*
- business meal disallowance, *9-14–9-15*

Medical expenses, *7-2–7-8*
- amount/timing of deduction, *7-6–7-8*
  - limitation on amount deductible, *7-7*
  - medical insurance reimbursements, *7-7–7-8*
  - timing of payment, *7-6–7-7*
- deductions vs. dependent care credit, *7-33*

BOLD = Corporations
ITALICS = Individuals

qualified expenses, *7-3–7-6*
capital expenditures for medical care, *7-5–7-6*
cost of living in institutions, *7-6*
deductible medical services, *7-3–7-4*
long-term care expenses, *7-5*
medical insurance premiums, *7-6*
transportation, *7-4*
qualified individuals, *7-2–7-3*
working with AGI floor, *7-30–7-31*
Medical expenses, gift tax and, **12-8**
Medical insurance
premiums, *7-6*
reimbursements, *7-7–7-8*
Medicare, tax rate, *9-3*
Meetings, travel deductions, *9-8*
Memorandum decisions, U.S. Tax Court, **1-18**
Mergers
partnerships and, **10-25**
Type A reorganizations
requirements for, **7-23–7-25**
reverse triangular mergers, **7-27**
tax consequences, **7-25–7-26**
triangular mergers, **7-26–7-27**
Minimum tax credit
individuals, *14-6–14-7*
Minimum tax credit, alternative minimum tax (AMT), **5-13–5-14**
Minimum vesting requirements, qualified pension plans, *9-29*
Minor children, income of, *3-8*
Minority shareholders, liquidating distributions and, **6-12**
Minors, present interest, special rule for trusts, **12-17**
Modified ACRS (MACRS)
alternative minimum tax, **5-7, 5-10**
corporate formations, **2-25**
earnings and profits, **4-5**
Modified ACRS (MACRS) System, *10-2*
alternative depreciation system, *10-21, 10-8–10-9*
listed property, *10-11*
luxury automobiles, limitations on, *10-11–10-13*
personal property
midquarter convention, *10-5–10-6*
year of disposition, *10-7*
real property,
classification/recovery rates for, *10-7–10-8*
residential rental property, *10-7–10-8*
restrictions, *10-10–10-12*
business-use assets, *10-10–10-11*
personal-use assets, *10-10*
recapture of excess cost-recovery deductions, *10-11*
straight-line method under, *10-8*
Moving expenses, *9-18–9-20, 9-42*
direct moving expenses, *9-19–9-20*
distance requirement, *9-19*
employer reimbursements, *9-20, 9-42*
employment duration, *9-19*
expense classification, *9-19*
indirect moving expenses, *9-20*
reporting of, *9-47*
Multiple support agreements, for medical expenses, *7-31*
Mutual funds, *3-16–3-17*

National Office, IRS, *1-20*
Natural resources
Sec. 1231 and, *13-5–13-6*
coal/domestic iron ore, *13-6*
livestock, *13-6*
timber, *13-5–13-6*
Necessary expense, *6-8*
Negligence penalty, *1-23*, **15-22–15-23**
Net accounting income, definition of, **14-5**
Net capital gain, *5-16*
long-term, *5-16*
preferential treatment for, *5-2, 5-20, 5-30–5-31*
short-term, *5-16*
Net capital losses
C corporation, **3-6–3-7**
complex trusts/estates, **14-24**
simple trusts, **14-16–14-17**
Net gains/losses, treatment of, *2-28, 5-16–5-20*
Net gifts, **12-15–12-16**
Net investment income, *7-14–7-15*
Net operating losses, *8-29–8-33*
affiliated groups, **8-23, 8-31**
carryback to separate return year, **8-24–8-26**
carrybacks/carryforwards, **8-24–8-27**
carryforward to separate return year, **8-26–8-27**
current year NOLs, **8-23–8-24**
SRLY limitation, **8-27–8-29**
Sec. 382 limitation, **8-29–8-31**
alternative minimum tax, **5-8–5-9**
C corporations, **3-16–3-17**
carryback/carryover periods, *8-33*
election to forgo carryback period, *8-33*
loss carryovers from two or more years, *8-33*
complex trusts/estates, effect of, **14-24**
computation of, *8-30–8-33*
consolidated tax returns, **8-23, 8-31**
definition of, *8-29*
earnings and profits, **4-5–4-6**
liquidating corporation, treatment of, **6-16–6-17**
obtaining the refund, *8-35*
simple trusts, **14-16**
New loss corporation, **7-47–7-48**
90-day letter, **15-9**
Nonaccountable plans, *9-16, 9-17*
Nonbusiness bad debts
advances to corporation, **2-32–2-33**
definition of, *8-26–8-27*
nonaccountable plan, *9-17*
partial worthlessness, *8-27–8-28*
tax treatment, *8-27*
See also Bad debts; Business bad debts, *5-15–5-16, 8-26–8-28*
Noncontributory pension plan, *9-27*
Noncorporate taxpayers
capital gains/losses tax treatment, *5-16–5-20*
Noncustodial parents, dependency exemptions and, *2-15*
Nondeductible terminable interests
estate tax, **13-21n**
gift tax, **12-19–12-20**
Nonliquidating distributions
active conduct of trade or business, definition of, **7-40**
complete termination of interest, **4-21–4-23, 4-36–4-37**
constructive dividends, **4-11, 4-13**
controlled corporations, stock of, **7-38–7-41**
shareholders and security holders, **7-38–7-41**
tax consequences, distributing corporation, **7-38**
not essentially equivalent to a dividend, **4-23–4-24**
partnerships, **10-2, 10-11**
basis effects of distributions, **10-4–10-7**
character of distributed property, **10-7**
holding period, **10-7**
recognition of gain, **10-2–10-4**
with Sec. 751, **10-7–10-11**
preferred stock bailouts, **4-28–4-30**
property distributions, **4-8–4-13**
spinoffs, **7-38–7-41**
split-offs, **7-38–7-41**
split-ups, **7-38–7-41**
stock dividends, **4-13–4-16**
taxable stock dividends, **4-16**
taxable stock rights, **4-16**
tax-free stock dividends, **4-14–4-15**
tax-free stock rights, **4-15**
stock redemptions, **4-16–4-28, 4-30–4-32**
attribution rules, **4-18–4-20**
bootstrap acquisitions, **4-34–4-35**
complete termination of shareholder's interest, **4-21–4-23, 4-36–4-37**
effect on distributing corporation, **4-27–4-28**
effect on shareholder, **4-17–4-18**
not essentially equivalent to a dividend, **4-23–4-24**
partial liquidations, **4-24–4-25**
preferred stock bailout, **4-28–4-30**
related corporation redemptions, **4-30–4-32**
substantially disproportionate redemptions, **4-20–4-21**
to pay death taxes, **4-25–4-27**

Nonliquidating distributions (*continued*)
stock rights, **4-13–4-16**
tax-free stock rights, **4-15**
taxable stock rights, **4-16**
timing of distributions, **4-35–4-36**
Nonqualified deferred compensation plans, *9-30–9-31*
restricted property plans, *9-31–9-32*
unfunded deferred compensation plans, *9-31*
Nonqualified stock option plans, *9-34–9-35*
taxation of, *9-34–9-35*
Nonrecognition of gain/losses
avoidance under Sec. 351, **2-33–2-34**
partnerships, formation of, **9-5–9-6**
tax-free reorganizations, **7-16**
Nonrecourse loans
definition of, **9-22**
partner's share of liabilities and, **9-22–9-23**
Nonrefundable credits, definition of, *2-6*
Nonresident aliens, head-of-household status and, *2-21*
Nonresidential real estate
Sec. 1250 recapture provisions, *13-14–13-15*
Nonshareholders, capital contributions, **2-30**
Nontaxable exchanges
holding period, *5-28–5-29*
of property, *12-1–12-24*
involuntary conversions, *12-10–12-16*
like-kind exchanges, *12-2–12-10*
sale of principal residence, *12-16–12-21*
reporting nontaxable exchanges, *12-23–12-24*
Nontaxable stock dividends received, *5-11*
Nontaxable stock rights received, *5-11–5-12*

Objectives of tax law, *1-14–1-15*
Office audit, *1-21*, **15-7**
Oil and gas property, working interest in, *8-12*
Old loss corporation, **7-47–7-48**
One class of stock requirement, S corporations, **11-5–11-7**
100% dividends-received deduction election, **8-35**
Open transaction doctrine, liquidating distributions, **6-15**
Open-fact situations, tax research, **1-2–1-3**
Option attribution, **4-20**
Optional basis adjustment, **10-26–10-28**
Options
incentive stock option (ISO) plans, *9-33–9-34*
nonqualified stock options, *9-34–9-35*
sale/exchange of, *5-24–5-25*
See also Call options, nonqualified stock option plans and stock option plans
Oral conclusions, tax research, **1-5**
Ordinary expense, *6-7–6-8*
Ordinary gross income (OGI), **5-16–5-17**
Ordinary income property
as charitable contribution, *7-23–7-24*
donation of inventory by corporation, *7-24*
corporation, deducting contributions of, **3-11**
definition of, *7-23*
Ordinary income/loss
S corporations, **11-14–11-15**
carrybacks/carryforwards when status changes, **11-15**
compared to C corporation treatment, **11-15**
deductions that cannot be claimed, **11-15**
partnerships, **9-17**
Ordinary loss
debt obligations, **2-32–2-33**
definition of, *5-22*
Sec. 1244 stock, **2-31–2-32**
Securities, worthlessness, **2-30–2-32**
versus capital loss, *8-5–8-6*
Organization forms
corporations
C corporations, **2-5–2-6**
S corporations, **2-6–2-7**
partnerships, **2-3–2-4**
sole proprietorships, **2-2–2-3**
Organizational expenditures
S corporations, **11-15**
alternative minimum tax, **5-10**
as corporate taxable income deductions, **3-8–3-9**
definition of, **3-8**
partnerships, **9-14**
Original issue discount, *5-23*, **2-27–2-28**

Parent corporation, as agent for affiliated groups, **8-37**
Parent-subsidiary corporation redemptions, **4-32**
Partial liquidations
determination made at corporate level, **4-24**
effect on shareholders, **4-24–4-25**
safe harbor, **4-24**
Partially liquidating distributions, liquidation rules, **6-14–6-15**
Partner, definition of, **9-2–9-3**
Partnership agreement, **9-17–9-18**
Partnership interest
exchange of, **10-20–10-21**
for another partnership interest, **10-20–10-21**
for corporate stock, **10-21**
incorporation, **10-21**
holding period for, **9-8**
income recognition of, **10-22**
sale of, **10-16–10-20**
impact on partnership, **10-18**
liabilities, **10-18**
Sec. 751 properties, **10-17–10-18**
transfers of, **10-22**
Partnership item, definition of, **9-32**
Partnership liabilities
effect of, **9-21–9-23**
increases/decreases in, **9-21–9-22**
partner's share of, **9-22–9-23**
Partnership property, payments at death/retirement of partner, **10-19–10-20**
Partnerships, **2-3–2-4**
check-the-box regulations, **2-8**, **9-3**
compared to corporations, **2-8**
contribution of service, **9-10–9-12**
allocation of expense deduction, **9-11**
basis adjustment, **9-11–9-12**
definition of, **2-3**
definition of, **9-2–9-3**
division of, **10-25**
electing large partnerships, **9-3–9-4**, **10-30–10-33**
elections, **9-12–9-15**
partnership's taxable year, **9-12–9-15**
estimated taxes, **9-32**
family partnerships, **9-29–9-30**
Form 1065, **9-31**
formation
tax implications of, **9-5–9-14**
fringe benefits, paid to partner, **9-27n**
general partnerships, **9-2–9-3**
IRS audit procedures, **9-32–9-33**
limited partnerships, **9-3**
liquidating distributions, **10-12–10-16**
Sec. 751 effects, **10-14–10-15**
basis in assets received, **10-12–10-14**
effects on partnership, **10-16**
gain/loss recognition by partner, **10-12**
loss limitations, **9-24–9-26**
at-risk loss limitation, **9-24–9-25**
partner loss limitation, **9-26**
passive activity limitation, **9-26**
loss recognition, timing of, **9-30–9-31**
medical insurance, **9-27n**
nonliquidating distributions, **10-2–10-7**
basis effects of distributions, **10-4–10-7**
character of distributed property, **10-7**
holding period, **10-7**
recognition of gain, **10-2–10-4**
with Sec. 751, **10-7–10-11**
operations, **9-1–9-33**
organizational expenditures, **9-14**
partner reporting of income, **9-17–9-20**
distributive share, **9-17–9-18**
partnership agreement, **9-17–9-18**

BOLD = Corporations
ITALICS = Individuals

special allocations, 9-18–9-20
varying interest rule, 9-18
partner/partnership transactions, 9-26–9-27
guaranteed payments, 9-27–9-28
sales of property, 9-26–9-27
partnership interest, 9-21–9-24
beginning basis, 9-21
partnership liabilities, effect of, 9-21–9-23
partnership reporting of income, 9-16–9-17
ordinary income, 9-17
ordinary loss, 9-17
separately stated items, 9-16–9-17
taxable income, 9-16
precontribution gain, 10-2–10-4
property contributions, 9-5–9-12
holding period for partnership interest, 9-8
holding period for property, 9-9
liabilities, 9-7–9-8
nonrecognition of gains/losses, 9-5–9-6
partner's basis in partnership interest, 9-8
precontribution gain, 10-2–10-4
recapture provisions, 9-9–9-10
recognition of gains/losses, 9-6
publicly traded partnerships, 10-28–10-29
reporting to IRS/partners, 9-31–9-32
required payments and fiscal years, *11-3–11-4*
self-employment tax, 9-32
Subchapter K, election out of, 9-2n
syndication expenditures, 9-14
tax advantages, 2-4
tax disadvantages, 2-4
tax shelter partnerships, 10-28
tax year, *11-2, 11-28,* 9-12–9-15
taxation, 9-4–9-5
distributions, 9-5
overview of, 9-4–9-5
partner's basis, 9-4–9-5
partnership profits/losses, 9-4
terminating partnership interest, 10-11–10-25
consolidations, 10-25
division of partnership, 10-25
exchange of interest, 10-20–10-21
gift of interest, 10-21
income recognition on transfer of interest, 10-22
liquidating distributions, 10-12–10-16
mergers, 10-25
retirement/death of partner, 10-19–10-20
sale of interest, 10-16–10-18
termination of partnership, 10-22–10-24
transfers of interest, 10-22
termination of, 10-22–10-24
effects, 10-23, 10-24
events causing termination, 10-22
liquidating distributions and contributions, 10-24
timing of termination, 10-23–10-24
See also Family partnerships; Limited partnerships; Oil and gas limited partnerships; Publicly traded partnerships; Special partnership issues
Party to a reorganization, definition of, 7-51
Passive activity
definition of, *8-10–8-12*
interest expense, *7-14*
limited partnerships, *8-12*
material participation, *8-11–8-12*
working interest in oil and gas property, *8-12*
Passive activity limitation rules
alternative minimum tax, 5-8
closely held C corporations, 3-20
partnerships/partners, 9-26
S corporation/shareholders, 11-22
Passive income requirement
personal holding company (PHC) tax, 5-16–5-20
S corporations, 11-36–11-37
Passive losses, *8-7–8-16*
alternative minimum tax, 5-8
carryovers
from former passive activities, *8-9*
taxable disposition of interest, *8-8–8-9*
closely held C corporations, 3-20
credits, *8-10*
identification of an activity, *8-10–8-11*
partnerships, 9-26
passive activity defined, *8-10–8-12*
passive income and, *8-8–8-10*
publicly traded partnerships, *8-13–8-14*
real estate trades or businesses, *8-14–8-16*
rental real estate, *8-14–8-16*
S corporations, 11-22
taxpayers subject to, *8-12–8-13*
Patents, sale/exchange of, *5-25–5-26*
Payment of taxes, *14-24–14-29*
C corporations, 3-31–3-34, 8-38
estates, 14-36
estimated tax payments, *14-27–14-28*
S corporations, 11-38
trusts, 14-36
withholding, *14-25–14-27*
withholding allowances/methods, *14-25–14-26*
Penalties
as nondeductible expense, *6-13*
civil fraud penalty, 15-25
criminal fraud penalties, 15-26
for failure to file, 15-16–15-18
for failure to pay, 15-18–15-19
for underpaying estimated taxes, 15-21–15-22
exceptions to, 15-22
negligence penalty, 15-22–15-23
personal holding company (PHC) tax, 5-37
substantial understatement penalty, 15-23–15-25
substantial authority, 15-24
tax shelters, 15-24–15-25
understatement versus underpayment, 15-23–15-24
summary, *1-22–1-23*
Penalty taxes
accumulated earnings tax, 5-24–5-34, 5-37
personal holding company tax, 5-15–5-24, 5-37
Pension plans, *9-27–9-28*
contributory pension plan, *9-27*
defined benefit pension plan, *9-27*
defined contribution pension plan, *9-27*
non-contributory pension plan, *9-27*
qualification of, *9-47*
types of, *9-27–9-28*
Pensions
advance payments, *3-21*
as gross income, *3-19–3-21*
determining nontaxable portion of, *3-19–3-21*
paid as annuities, *3-19–3-21*
Percentage depletion method, *10-19–10-20*
Percentage of completion method, *11-16*
Permanent differences, definition of, 3-35
Personal exemption, *2-12–2-18*
definition of, *2-5*
estates, 14-9–14-10
fiduciary accounting, calculation formula, 14-9–14-10
phase-out of, *2-17–2-18*
trusts, 14-9–14-10
Personal holding company (PHC) definition of, 5-16
Personal holding company income (PHCI)
definition of, 5-17–5-20
determination of, 5-18–5-20
personal service contracts exclusion, 5-20
rent exclusion, 5-19–5-20
See also Undistributed personal holding company income (UPHCI)
Personal holding company (PHC) tax, 5-15–5-24, 5-37
avoidance of, 5-36
changing income earned by corporation, 5-36
changing stock ownership, 5-36
liquidating the corporation, 5-36
making dividend distributions, 5-36
S corporation election, 5-36
dividend distributions, use of, 5-22–5-23

Personal holding company (PHC) tax (continued)
carryovers, **5-22**
consent dividends, **5-22**
current year dividends, **5-22–5-23**
deficiency dividends, **5-23**
liquidating dividends, **5-22**
throwback dividends, **5-22**
excluded corporations, **5-16**
filing requirements, **5-37**
interest on underpayment, **5-37**
liquidation of corporation, **5-36**
passive income requirement, **5-16–5-20**
payment of tax, **5-37**
penalties on underpayment, **5-37**
stock ownership requirement, **5-16**
tax calculation, **5-23–5-24**
Personal injury award, *4-8–4-10*
Personal interest, definition of, *7-16*
Personal property taxes, as itemized deduction, *7-10*
Personal service contracts, exclusion from PHCI, **5-20**
Personal service corporations (PSCs), *8-13*
fiscal year, **3-2–3-4**
material participation by, *8-13*
passive activity limitation, **3-20**
regular tax liability, **3-22**
Sec. 444 and, **3-2–3-4**
tax rates, **3-22**
tax year, *11-2–11-7*
Personal tax credits, *14-11–14-13*
child and dependent care credit, *14-11–14-12*
earned income credit, *14-22–14-23*
reporting of, *14-32–14-33*
tax credit for the elderly, *14-12–14-13*
Personal-use property
conversions to business use, *10-4*
limitations on, *8-20–8-21*
netting casualty gains/losses on, *8-21*
rental value, as nonincome item, *4-3*
self-help and use of, personal use property, *4-23*
Plan of liquidation, **6-21**
Points, as interest, *6-20, 7-12–7-18*
Policy-oriented research, **1-2**
Political organizations, transfers to, gift tax and, **12-9**
Pooled income fund, definition of, **12-22n**
Post-gift appreciation, *inter vivos* gifts, removal from tax base, **12-29**
Post-1976 gift taxes, reduction for, **13-4–13-5, 13-23**
Post-termination loss carryovers, S corporations, **11-22–11-23**
Power of appointment
See also General power of appointment, **12-15**
Pre-acquisition losses, offsetting of, **7-47–7-49**
Precedential value of decisions, **1-21–1-24**
Circuit Court of Appeals, **1-23**
dictum, **12-25**
forum shopping, **1-23–1-24**
Tax Court, **1-21**
U.S. Court of Federal Claims, **1-23**
U.S. District Court, **1-23**
Preferential dividends, dividends-paid deduction and, **5-22–5-32**
Preferred stock bailouts, **4-28–4-30**
nonliquidating distributions, **4-28–4-30**
Sec. 306 stock
definition of, **4-28–4-29**
dispositions of, **4-29**
Pre-1977 gift tax, credit for, **13-24**
Prepaid expenses, cash method of accounting, *6-19*
Prepaid income
accrual method of accounting and, *3-11–3-12*
tax planning and, *3-27–3-28*
Prepaid interest
cash method of accounting, *6-19–6-20*
timing of interest deduction, *7-19*
Prepayments, as tax credits, *2-6*
Present interest
Crummey trust, **12-17–12-18**
definition of, **12-17**
special rule for trusts for minors, **12-17**
Previously deducted expenses
recovery of, *3-25–3-26*
tax benefit rule, *3-26*
Primary cites, **1-19**
Principal partner, definition of, **9-13**
Principal receipts, fiduciary accounting, **14-6**
Principal residence, sale of, *12-16–12-21*
deferred gain, *12-16–12-21*
excluded gain, *12-16–12-21*
identifying principal residence, *12-22*
involuntary conversion, *12-20–12-21*
more than one residence in two-year period, *12-19*
principal residence defined, *12-18–12-19, 12-22*
property converted to business use, *12-22*
property rented prior to sale, *12-18–12-19*
realized gain, determination of, *12-17*
reporting of, *12-23–12-24*
Private activity bonds, *14-4*
Private letter ruling, **1-12–1-13**
Private nonoperating foundations
contributions to, *7-22–7-23,* **3-11**
20% limitation on capital gain property, *7-25*
Private nonoperating foundation, **3-11**
Prizes, as gross income, *3-22–3-23*
Probate estate, compared to gross estate, **13-9**
Profits interest, **9-10–9-11**
Profit-sharing plans, *9-28*
distinguishing features, *9-28*
qualification of, *9-47*
Progressive tax rate, *1-4*
Property
definition of, **4-2**
Sec. 317(a) definition, **4-8**
Sec. 351 definition, **2-12**
Property distributions
C corporations, **4-8–4-13**
consequences to distributing corporation, **4-9–4-11**
consequences to shareholders, **4-8–4-9**
estates, **14-34**
partnerships
with Sec. 751, **10-7–10-11, 10-14–10-16**
without Sec. 751, **10-2–10-7, 10-11–10-14**
S corporations
with E&P, **11-28–11-31**
without E&P, **11-27–11-28**
Property requirement, Sec. 351, **2-12**
Property settlements, as gross income, *3-18*
Property taxes, *1-11*
Property transactions
capital gains/losses, *5-1–5-36*
basis considerations, *5-5–5-12*
capital asset defined, *5-13–5-16*
corporate taxpayer tax treatment, *5-20–5-21*
determination of, *5-2–5-5*
holding period, *5-28–5-29*
noncorporate taxpayer tax treatment, *5-16–5-20*
reporting, *5-33–5-36*
sale/exchange, *5-21–5-27*
nontaxable exchanges, *12-1–12-24*
involuntary conversions, *12-10–12-16*
like-kind exchanges, *12-21, 12-2–12-10*
three-party exchanges, *12-5–12-6*
sale of principal residence, *12-16–12-21*
See also Recapture
Property transfers
like-kind exchanges, *12-21, 12-2–12-10*
recapture, *13-18–13-19*
selection of property to transfer at death, *5-32*
selection of property to transfer by gift, *5-31–5-32*
Proportional tax rate, *1-5*
Proposed regulations, **1-9**
Proprietary interest, continuity of, reorganizations, **7-43–7-44**
Protest letters, **15-8–15-9**
Publicly traded partnerships (PTPs)
definitions, **10-28**
exceptions to classification as, **10-28**
passive losses, *8-13–8-14,* **10-29**
See also Partnerships, **10-28–10-29**
Published opinions, U.S. Tax Court, **1-17–1-18**

BOLD = Corporations
ITALICS = Individuals

Punitive damages, exclusion, *4-9*

Qualified disclaimers, gift tax and, **12-9–12-10**
Qualified electric vehicle credit, *2-6*
Qualified employee discounts, *4-12–4-13*
Qualified joint interest, **13-15**
Qualified pension plans, *9-27–9-28*
  qualification requirements, *9-27*
  tax treatment employees/employers, *9-29*
    employee retirement payments, *9-29–9-30*
    employer contribution limitations, *9-30*
Qualified plan awards, *4-14*
Qualified residence
  definition of, *7-18*
  interest expense, *7-16–7-18*
Qualified Subchapter S subsidiaries, **11-6**
Qualified Subchapter S trusts (QSSTs), **11-4n, 11-4–11-5**
Qualified terminable interest property (QTIP)
  estate tax
    marital deduction and, **13-22–13-23**
    recipient spouse's interest in, **13-17–13-18**
    transfer of, **13-17–13-18**
  gift tax
    definition of, **12-20**
Qualified transportation fringes, *4-13*

Real estate
  alternative minimum tax
    as adjustment, **5-7–5-8**
    as tax preference item, **5-7**
  corporate sales, recapture, **3-7**
  date-of-death valuation, **13-6–13-7**
Real estate taxes, *1-11, 7-10–7-11*
  apportionment of, *7-10–7-11*
  as itemized deduction, *7-10–7-11*
  real property assessments for local benefits, *7-11*
Real estate trades or businesses, passive loss rules, *8-14–8-16*
Real property
  assessments for local benefits, *7-11*
  modified ACRS,
    classification/recovery rates for, *10-7–10-8*
  subdivided for sale, *5-15*
Realization, definition of, *3-2*
Realized gain/loss, *5-2–5-4*
  adjusted basis of property, *5-4*
  amount realized, *5-3*
  determination of, *5-2–5-5*
  fair market value (FMV), *5-3*
  recovery of basis doctrine, *5-4*
Reasonable business needs
  evidence of, **5-27–5-31**
    Bardahl formula, **5-28–5-30**
    no specific time limitations, **5-27**
    specific, definite, and feasible plans, **5-27**
    subsequent events, impact of, **5-27**
Reasonable cause, for deferral of estate tax payments, **13-28**
Reasonable compensation, determination of, **3-28–3-29**
Recapitalization, **7-41–7-43**
Recapture
  affiliated groups, **8-16–8-17**
  alimony, gross income, *3-17–3-19*
  avoiding depreciation recapture
    provisions, *13-23–13-24*
    nonresidential real property, *13-24*
    residential rental property, *13-23–13-24*
    transferring property at death, *13-24*
  charitable contributions, *13-18*
  corporate formation, **2-24–2-25**
  corporate sales of real estate, **3-7**
  corporations, *13-15–13-16*
  gifts of property subject to, *13-17*
  installment sales, *13-19–13-20*
  involuntary conversions, *13-19*
  like-kind exchanges, *13-18–13-19*
  of excess cost-recovery deductions, *10-11*
  partnerships, property contributions, **9-9–9-10**
  property transfers subject to at death, *13-18*
  Sec. 1245 provisions, *13-8–13-11*
  Sec. 1250 provisions, *13-11–13-16*
  tax benefit recapture rule, **3-7**
Recognized gain/loss, determination of, *5-4–5-5*
Recognition of gain/loss
  C corporations
    acquiring corporation, **7-17**
    controlled subsidiary
      corporations, liquidation of, **6-10–6-12**
    corporate formation, **2-20**
    distributing corporation, **4-10, 4-27, 6-6–6-14**
    stock distributions,
      reorganizations, **7-17**
    when property is distributed in
      redemption of stock, **6-6–6-9**
  estates, Sec. 303 redemptions, **13-29**
  partnerships
    liquidating distributions, **10-12–10-16**
    property contributions, **9-9**
  trusts, **14-34**
Recourse loans
  definition of, **9-22**
  partner's share of liabilities and, **9-22–9-23**
Recovery of basis doctrine, *5-4*
Recovery of capital principle, *4-3*
Refundable credits, definition of, *2-6*
Refund claims, statute of limitations, **15-29**
Regressive tax rate, *1-5*
Regular corporation
  See also C corporations, **2-5**
Regular decision, U.S. Tax Court, **1-14–1-17**
Regular tax liability
  affiliated groups, **8-9–8-10**
  alternative minimum tax, **5-5, 5-15**
  C corporations, **3-20–3-22**
  individuals, *14-2–14-3*
Rehabilitation expenditures
  credit for, *14-19–14-20*
Reimbursement
  automobile expenses, *9-12*
  insurance, *8-22–8-23*
  moving expenses, *9-20*
    expense classification and, *9-19*
Related corporations
  affiliated groups, **3-27–3-28, 8-2–8-4**
  controlled groups, **3-22–3-28**
  stock redemptions by, **4-30–4-32**
Related party transactions
  definition of, *13-22*
Related-party transaction rules, *6-25–6-28*
  definition of, *6-26–6-27*
  disallowed losses, *6-27–6-28*
  expense transactions, *6-28*
  sales or exchanges, *11-21*
Related party transaction rules
  expense transactions, **3-19, 11-33**
  liquidations, exceptions to
    recognition of gain/loss rules, **6-8**
  partnerships, **9-26–9-27**
  S corporations, **11-33**
  sales or exchanges, **3-19, 8-12–8-20, 11-33**
Relationship test
  for dependency exemptions, *2-16–2-17*
Remainder interest, and deferral of estate tax payments, **13-28**
Remainderman, **14-6**
Remainders, date-of-death valuation, **13-7**
Rental income expenses, adjusted ordinary gross income (AOGI) and, **5-17**
Rental real estate
  passive losses, *8-14–8-16*
  principal residence, *12-18–12-19*
  real property trades or businesses, *8-14–8-16*
Rents
  as gross income, *3-15–3-16*
  exclusion from PHCI, **5-19–5-20**
Reorganizations
  acquiring or transferee corporation, **7-17–7-18**
    basis of acquired property, **7-17–7-18**
    holding period for acquired properties, **7-18**
    recognition of gain or loss, **7-17**

Reorganizations (*continued*)
acquisitive reorganizations, **7-15, 7-21–7-35**
Type A reorganizations, **7-21–7-27**
Type B reorganizations, **7-31–7-35**
Type C reorganizations, **7-28–7-30**
Type D reorganizations, **7-30–7-31**
Type G reorganization, **7-35**
avoiding reorganization provisions, **7-50**
consideration used in reorganizations, **7-49–7-50**
divisive reorganizations, **7-15, 7-38–7-41**
Type D reorganizations, **7-38–7-41**
Type G reorganization, **7-41**
judicial restrictions on, **7-43–7-49**
business purpose requirement, **7-45**
continuity of business enterprise, **7-44–7-45**
continuity of proprietary interest, **7-43–7-44**
step transaction doctrine, **7-45**
party to a reorganization, **7-51**
plan of reorganization, **7-51**
reporting requirements, **7-51**
ruling requests, **7-51**
shareholders and security holders, **7-18–7-20**
basis of stocks/securities received, **7-20**
character of recognized gain, **7-18–7-19**
holding period of stocks/securities, **7-20**
recognition of gain or loss, **7-18**
target or transferor corporation
asset transfer, recognition of gain or loss on, **7-16**
assumption of liabilities, **7-17**
depreciation recapture, **7-17**
distribution of stock/securities, recognition of gain or loss on, **7-17**
recognition of gain, amount and character of, **7-18–7-19**
tax attributes, **7-46–7-49**
assumption of, **7-46**
limitation on use of, **7-47–7-49**
tax consequences of, **7-16–7-20**
acquiring or transferee corporation, **7-17–7-18**
shareholders and security holders, **7-18–7-20**
target or transferor corporation, **7-16–7-17**
tax-free reorganizations, types of, **7-15–7-16**
taxable transactions versus reorganizations, **7-49–7-50**
Type E reorganizations, **7-41–7-43**
Type F reorganizations, **7-43**
See also Acquisitive reorganizations; Divisive reorganizations
Repetitive audit examinations, special relief rule, **15-7**
Replacement property
involuntary conversions, *12-13–12-14*
functional use test, *12-14*
replacement with like-kind property, *12-14*
taxpayer-use test, *12-14*
principal residence, *12-16–12-19*
Repossession of property, *11-20*
Research
client-oriented research, **1-2**
closed-fact situations, **1-2**
definition, **1-2**
open fact situations, **1-2, 1-3**
steps in research process, **1-3, 1-5**
tax planning research, **1-3**
Research expenditures, *10-16–10-17, 10-23, 14-18–14-19*
computation of, *10-16–10-17*
credit for, *14-18–14-19*
deduction/amortization, *10-16–10-17*
Research Institute of America citator, **1-31–1-33**
abbreviations used in, **1-31–1-32**
excerpt from, **1-30–1-31**
information included in, **1-31**
Reserve method, business bad debts and, *8-28*
Residence, exclusion for sale, *4-21*
Residential rental property
allocation of expenses, *6-32–6-33*
definition of, *6-31–6-32*
Sec. 1250 recapture provisions, *13-11–13-16*
used for both personal/rental purposes, *6-31–6-33*
Restricted property plans, *9-31–9-32*
elections, *9-32*
Restoration of basis
S corporation debt, **11-25–11-26**
S corporation stock, **11-24–11-25**
Restored gain/loss, deferred intercompany transactions, determination of, **8-12–8-17**
Retained life estate, transfers with, **13-11–13-12**
Retirement payments, *9-29–9-30*
Return of capital distributions, **4-2**
Returns, due dates for filing, *2-32*
Returns, due dates for filing, **15-13**
Revenue Act of 1913, *1-3*
Revenue Act of 1938, Sec. 1231 and, *13-2*
Revenue Act of 1939, *1-3*
Revenue agent, meeting with for audit, **15-7–15-8**
Revenue procedures, *1-19,* **1-12**
Revenue rulings, *1-19,* **1-11–1-12**
Revenue sources, *1-3*
Reverse triangular mergers
Type A reorganizations, **7-27**
See also Triangular mergers
Reversionary interests
and deferral of estate tax payments, **13-28**
as gross estate inclusion, **13-12–13-13**
definition of, **13-12n**
Reversions, date-of-death valuation, **13-7**
Review of Taxation of Individuals, The, **1-25**
Revocable trusts
as gross estate inclusion, **13-13**
creation of, **14-3**
definition of, **14-3**
gift tax and, **12-10**
grantor trust rules, **14-31**
Royalties
as gross income, *3-15–3-16*
defined, *3-15*
Royalty income, personal holding company income (PHCI) and, **5-18**
Rule Against Perpetuities, definition of, **14-2n**
Rulings
letter rulings
definition of, **15-11**
request for, IRS decision to rule, **15-12**
information included, **15-11**
when rulings are desirable, **15-12**
tax law, **1-11–1-13**
revenue rulings, **1-11, 1-12**

S corporations
advantages of S corporation treatment, **2-6–2-7, 11-3**
alternative minimum tax (AMT) adjustments, **11-32–11-33**
basis adjustments, **11-24–11-26**
to S corporation stock, **11-24–11-25**
to shareholder debt, **11-25–11-26**
built-in gains tax, **11-16–11-18**
definition of, **2-6**
disadvantages of S corporation treatment, **2-7, 11-3–11-4**
distributions, **11-27–11-31**
corporations with accumulated earnings/profits, **11-28–11-31**
corporations with no earnings/profits, **11-27–11-28**
election of status, **11-7–11-12**
making the election, **11-8–11-9, 11-37**
estimated tax payments, **11-38–11-39**
excess net passive income tax, **11-15–11-16**
filing requirements, **11-37–11-38**
fringe benefits paid to shareholder-employees, **2-7, 11-33–11-34**
income allocation based on S corporation's accounting methods, **11-34–11-35**
increasing the benefits from S corporation losses, **11-35–11-36**
LIFO recapture tax, **11-18**

BOLD = Corporations
ITALICS = Individuals

losses
allocation of the loss, **11-20–11-21**
at-risk rules, **11-22**
hobby loss rules, **11-22**
passive activity limitation, **11-22**
shareholder loss limitation, **11-21–11-22**
operations, **11-13–11-18**
accounting method elections, **11-14**
ordinary income/loss, **11-14–11-15**
special S corporation taxes, **11-15–11-18**
taxable year, **11-13, 11-37**
passive income requirements, **11-36–11-37**
post-termination transition period, **11-22–11-23, 11-31**
qualified subchapter S subsidiaries, **11-6**
qualified subchapter S trusts, **11-4–11-5**
related party transaction rules, **11-33**
requirements, **11-4–11-7**
corporate requirements, **11-5–11-7**
shareholder requirements, **11-4–11-5**
sample S corporation tax return, **11-39**
second class of stock requirement, **11-6–11-7**
shareholder taxation, **11-19–11-23**
family S corporations, **11-23**
income allocation procedures, **11-19–11-20**
loss/deduction pass-through to shareholders, **11-20–11-23**
small business trusts, **11-5**
special taxes
LIFO recapture tax, **11-18**
built-in gains tax, **11-16–11-18**
excess net passive income tax, **11-15–11-16**
tax preference items, **11-32–11-33**
tax year, *11-28, 11-2–11-7*
required payments, *11-3–11-4*
termination of election, **11-9–11-12**
allocation of income, **11-10–11-11**
avoidance of, **11-12**
inadvertent termination, **11-11**
new election following termination, **11-11–11-12**
post-termination transition period, **11-31**
with accumulated earnings/profits, **11-28–11-31**
built-in gains tax, **11-16–11-18**
excess net passive income tax, **11-15–11-16**
money distributions, **11-28–11-31**
post-termination transition period, **11-31**
property distributions, **11-31**
termination of election, **11-31**
See also C corporations; Corporations; Ordinary income/loss; Special S corporation taxes, *2-26*, **11-1–11-39**
S short year, **11-10–11-11**
S termination year, **11-10–11-11**
Salary payments, closely held corporations, compensation planning and, **2-5, 3-28–3-29**
Salary, dependency exemption gross income test and, *2-16*
Salary reduction plans, *4-17*
Sales taxes, *1-11*
exempt items, *1-11*
Sales/exchanges of property
capital assets, *5-21–5-27*
corporate taxable income and, **3-6–3-7**
net capital gain, **3-6, 3-19**
net capital losses, **3-6–3-7, 3-19**
tax benefit recapture rule, **3-7**
partnerships
gain sales, **9-27**
loss sales, **9-27**
S corporations
built-in gains tax, **11-16–11-17**
See also Capital Assets
Schedule K–1 (Form 1041), **14-36**
Schedule K–1 (Form 1065), **9-31**
Schedule K–1 (Form 1120S), **11-39**
Schedule L (of Form 1120), **3-35**
Schedule M–1 (of Form 1120), **3-35–3-36**
Schedule M–1 (Form 1120S), **11-39**
Schedule M–2 (of Form 1120), **3-37**
Schedule M–2 (Forum 1120S), **11-39**
Scholarships
definition of, *4-7*
dependency exemption gross income test and, *2-16*
exclusion from gross income, *4-7*
Scholes, Myron and Mark Wolfson, *1-24*
Scientific research property, deducting contributions of, **3-11**
Seasonal income, exception to corporate estimated taxes, **3-33–3-34**
Sec. 102, gifts and, *4-4*
Sec. 104(a), payments for injury/sickness, *4-8–4-10*
Sec. 1221, properties not regarded as capital assets, *5-13*
Sec. 1231
gains/losses, **3-7**
Sec. 1231, gains/losses, **8-32**
Sec. 1231 property, *13-1–13-25*
history of, *13-2*
involuntary conversions, *13-6–13-7*
property, *13-5–13-6*
definition of, *13-5*
relationship to capital assets, *13-5*
reporting gains/losses on Form 4797, *13-24–13-25*
tax treatment overview, *13-3–13-4*
tax treatment procedure, *13-7–13-8*
net gains, *13-3*
net losses, *13-3–13-4*
Sec. 1237, subdividing real estate, *5-15*
Sec. 1239
depreciable property, gain on sale between related parties, *13-21–13-22*
Sec. 1244, stock
losses, *8-4, 8-5–8-6*
worthlessness of, **2-31–2-32**
Sec. 1245
corporate formation, **2-24–2-25**
partnership formation, **9-9–9-10**
property subject to, *13-9–13-11*
purpose of, *13-9–13-11*
recapture provisions, *13-8–13-11*
Sec. 1250
corporate formation, **2-24–2-25**
partnership formation, **9-9–9-10**
purpose of, *13-11*
recapture provisions, *13-11–13-16*
low-income housing, *13-15*
nonresidential real estate, *13-14–13-15*
residential rental property, *13-13*
Sec. 1250 property defined, *13-11–13-12*
Sec. 1252, conservation/land clearing expenditures, *13-20–13-21*
Sec. 1253, transfer of franchise/trademark/trade name, *5-26–5-27*
Sec. 1254, oil and gas expenditures, *13-21*
Sec. 132
employee fringe benefits, *4-12–4-13*
Sec. 179, *10-9–10-10*
employee, conduct of trade or business, *10-10n*
expensing election, *10-9–10-10*
recapture provisions, *13-20*
self-employed individuals, *10-10n*
Sec. 197 intangibles, *10-13–10-17*
Sec. 269 limitation, **7-49**
Sec. 306 stock
definition of, **4-28–4-30**
dispositions of, **4-29**
exceptions to treatment, **4-30**
redemptions of, **4-29–4-30**
See also Preferred stock bailouts
Sec. 332 liquidations, **6-10–6-12, 6-13, 6-19–6-20**
Sec. 338 deemed liquidations, **7-5–7-11, 7-51**
Sec. 351
assignment of income doctrine, **2-26**
avoidance of, **2-33–2-34**
nonrecognition of gain, **2-33–2-34**
nonrecognition of losses, **2-33–2-34**
boot, receipt of, **2-17**
computing depreciation, **2-25**
depreciation recapture, **2-24–2-25**
effect on transferee corporation, **2-20–2-21**
effect on transferors, **2-16–2-19**

- Sec. 351 (*continued*)
  - reporting requirements, **2-35**
  - requirements, **2-12**
  - shareholder's basis, computation of, **2-18–2-19**
  - transfer of multiple assets, computation of gain, **2-17–2-18**
  - transferor's holding period, **2-19**
  - transferor's liabilities, assumption of, **2-21–2-24**
  - *See also* Corporate formation; Incorporation, **2-12–2-26**
- Sec. 355
  - requirements of, **7-40–7-41**
    - active conduct of trade or business requirement, **7-40**
    - business purpose requirement, **7-41**
    - continuity of interest requirement, **7-41**
    - control requirement, **7-40**
    - device requirement, **7-40**
    - distribution requirement, **7-40–7-41**
  - tax consequences to distributing corporation, **7-38**
  - tax consequences to shareholders, **7-38–7-40**
  - *See also* Nonliquidating distributions; controlled corporations
- Sec. 381, tax attributes, **7-46–7-49**
- Sec. 382, loss limitation
  - affiliated groups, **8-29–8-31**
  - reorganizations, **7-47–7-49**
- Sec. 383 limitation, **7-49**
- Sec. 384 limitation, **7-49**
- Sec. 61, gross income, *3-13–3-27*
- Sec. 721, nonrecognition of gain, partnerships, **9-5–9-6**
- Sec. 751
  - assets defined, **10-7–10-9**
  - nonliquidating distributions with, **10-7–10-11**
    - exchange of assets and other property, **10-9–10-11**
    - substantially appreciated inventory, **10-8–10-9**
    - unrealized receivables, **10-8**
- Sec. 7872, gift tax and, **12-28–12-29**
- Secondary cites, **1-19**
- Securities
  - distribution of controlled subsidiary stock
    - basis of property received, **7-38–7-40**
    - recognition of gain, **7-38–7-40**
  - like-kind exchanges, *12-5*
  - reorganizations, recognition of gain/loss on distribution of, **7-18**
  - worthlessness of, **2-31–2-32**
  - *See also* Shareholders; Worthless securities
- Securities dealers, *5-14–5-15*
- Seized property, losses from, *8-3*
- Self-employed individuals
  - deferred compensation, *9-36*
  - defined contribution H.R. 10 plan, *9-36*
  - Keogh plans, *9-36*
  - medical insurance plans, *7-6*
  - Sec. 179 expensing election, *10-10n*
  - *See also* Home office expenses; Individual retirement accounts (IRAs)
- Self-employment tax, *14-7–14-9, 7-11*
  - partnerships, **9-32**
  - purpose of, *14-7*
  - self-employment income defined, *14-8*
- Seminar travel deductions, *9-8*
- Separate maintenance, *3-17–3-19*
- Separate property, definition of, *3-7*
- Separate returns
  - filing of, *2-29–2-30*
  - joint returns versus, *2-22*
- Separate return limitation year (SRLY) rules, **8-27–8-29**
- Separate return year, definition of, **8-7n**
- Separate share rule, trusts, **14-22–14-23**
- Separate taxable income, **8-6**
- Series EE savings bonds
  - accrued interest exclusion, *3-14–3-15*
  - reporting interest income, *3-28–3-29*
- 75-shareholder limit, S corporations and, **11-4**
- Severance damages, *12-13*
- Sex discrimination settlement, exclusion, *4-9*
- Shareholder debt
  - basis adjustments to, S corporations, **11-25–11-26**
- Shareholder-employees
  - compensation planning for, **3-28–3-29**
    - avoidance of unreasonable compensation, **4-33–4-34**
    - determination of reasonable compensation, **3-28–3-29**
    - fringe benefits, **3-29**
    - salary payments, **3-28–3-29**
- Shareholders
  - liquidating distributions, **6-5–6-16**
- Shareholders, C corporations
  - capital contributions, **2-28–2-30**
  - consequences of property distributions to, **4-9–4-11**
  - disregard of corporate form by, **2-9**
  - distribution of controlled subsidiary stock
    - basis of property received, **7-38–7-40**
    - recognition of gain, **7-38–7-40**
  - dividend distributions, *3-16–3-17,* **4-8–4-9**
  - dividends-received deduction, **3-12–3-16**
  - partial liquidations, effect on, **4-24–4-25**
  - reorganizations, tax consequences, **7-18–7-20**
  - stock redemptions
    - effect of redemption on, **4-17–4-18**
    - questions for, **4-16–4-17**
- Shareholders loans, *11-24*
- Shareholders, S corporations
  - consent to S corporation election, **11-8–11-9**
- Short tax period, **3-2**
  - short-period tax return, **3-2**
- Short-term capital gains and losses (STCG and STCL), *2-28, 5-16–5-18*
- Sickness payments, as gross income exclusion, *4-8–4-10*
- SIMPLE retirement plans, *9-42*
- Simple trusts
  - distribution deduction, **14-9**
  - taxable income
    - allocation of expenses to tax-exempt income, **14-14–14-15**
    - comprehensive illustration, **14-17–14-19**
    - distributable net income (DNI), determination of, **14-15**
    - distribution deduction, determination of, **14-15**
    - net capital loss effect, **14-16–14-17**
    - net operating loss effect, **14-16**
    - short-cut approach to proving correctness of taxable income, **14-16**
    - tax treatment for beneficiary, **14-15–14-16**
  - *See also* Complex trusts/estates; Trusts
- Simplification of tax law, attempts at, *2-28*
- Simplified employee pensions, *9-41–9-42*
- Single class of stock, S corporations, **11-5–11-7**
- Single taxpayers, *2-22*
- 65-day rule, estate tax, **14-34**
- Small business stock, exclusion, *4-20–4-21*
- Small business trusts, **11-5**
- Small cases procedures, U.S. Tax Court, **1-17**
- Smith, Adam, *1-12*
- Social objectives, tax law, *1-15*
- Social security (FICA) taxes, *1-11, 1-3, 14-29, 14-7–14-9*
- Social security benefits, *3-23–3-24*
  - dependency exemption gross income test and, *2-16*
  - dependency exemption support test and, *2-13*
  - filing status, *3-23–3-24*
- Sole proprietorships, **2-2–2-3**
  - as business form, **2-2**
  - definition of, **2-2**
  - tax advantages, **2-3**
  - tax disadvantages, **2-3**
- Solely-for-voting-stock requirement
  - Type B reorganizations, **7-31–7-35**
    - control, **7-33**
    - exceptions to, **7-32–7-33**
    - tax consequences, **7-33–7-34**

BOLD = Corporations
ITALICS = Individuals

timing of transaction, **7-33**
Sources of tax law, *1-18–1-19*
Special accounting methods
deferred payment sales, *11-21*
deferred payment sales, *11-21*
installment sales method, *See also* Installment sales, *11-17–11-21*
long-term contracts, *See also* Long-term contracts, *11-15–11-17*
Specific write-off method, bad debts, *8-28*
See also Accounting methods, *11-15–11-22*
Special agents, criminal fraud investigations, **15-26**
Special allocations
partnerships
contributed property, **9-18–9-19**
substantial economic effect, **9-19–9-20**
Special AMT elections, **5-35**
Spinoffs, **7-38–7-40**
illustration, **7-38**
recognition of gain by shareholders, **7-38–7-40**
Split-interest transfers
charitable contribution deductions and, **12-21–12-22**
definition of, **12-22**
estate tax and, **13-20**
gift tax and, **12-21–12-22**
example of, **12-22**
Split-offs, **7-38–7-40**
illustration, **7-38**
recognition of gain by shareholders, **7-38–7-40**
Split-ups, **7-38–7-40**
illustration, **7-38**
recognition of gain by shareholders, **7-38–7-40**
Sprinkling trust, **14-34**
Standard deduction, *2-10–2-12, 2-4–2-5*
Standard Federal Tax Reporter (CCH), **1-26, 1-28–1-31**
Start-up costs, definition, *6-15*
Start-up expenditures
as corporate taxable income deduction, **3-9–3-10**
examples of, **3-9**
State death tax credit, estate tax, **13-24**
State income taxes, *1-7–1-8*
as itemized deduction, *7-10*
State law, fiduciary accounting and, **14-5**
Statements on Responsibilities in Tax Practice (SRTP), **1-35–1-37**
Statute of limitations, *1-22,* **15-26–15-29**
general three-year rule, **15-27**
carrybacks, **15-28**
extension of three-year period, **15-28**
when fraud is proven, **15-28–15-29**
gift tax purposes, **12-32**
refund claims, **15-29**
six-year rule for "substantial" omissions, **15-27–15-28**
gift and estate tax returns, **15-28**
income tax returns, **15-27–15-28**
when no return is filed, **15-28**
Statutory Notice of Deficiency, **15-9**
Statutory regulations, **1-10**
Step transaction doctrine, reorganizations, **7-45**
Stock
basis rules, **8-33–8-34**
debt-financed stock, **3-15–3-16**
multiple classes of, **2-28**
tax advantages of, **2-29**
tax disadvantages of, **2-29**
worthlessness of, **2-30–2-32**
See also Sec. 306 stock
Stock acquisitions
tax-free reorganizations
basis of stock/securities received, **7-20**
holding period, **7-20**
recognition of gain/loss, **7-18**
character of, **7-18–7-19**
taxable transaction, **7-12–7-14**
See also Acquisitions
Stock bonus plans, *9-28*
Stock distributions
dividends
tax-free stock dividends, **4-14–4-15**
tax-free stock rights, **4-15**
taxable stock dividends, **4-16**
taxable stock rights, **4-16**
of controlled corporations, **7-38–7-41**
recognition of gain, **7-38–7-40**
Sec. 355 requirements, **7-40–7-41**
reorganizations
corporate recognition of gain/loss on, **7-17**
shareholder recognition of gain or loss, **7-18–7-20**
Stock dividends, *3-16–3-17*
allocation of basis, *5-11*
holding period, *5-29*
tax-free dividends, **4-14–4-15**
taxable dividends, **4-16**
Stock-for-stock exchange
Type B reorganizations, **7-31–7-35**
Type E reorganizations, **7-41–7-43**
Stock losses, ordinary loss deduction for, **2-31–2-32**
Stock option plans, *9-32–9-35*
incentive stock option (ISO) plans, *9-33–9-34*
employee requirements, *9-33–9-34*
nonqualified stock option plans, *9-34–9-35*
Stock redemptions, **4-16–4-28, 4-30–4-32**
as reasonable business need, **5-30**
attribution rules, **4-18–4-20**
entity attribution, **4-20**
family attribution, **4-19**
option attribution, **4-20**
by related corporations, **4-30–4-32**
brother-sister corporations, **4-30–4-32**
parent-subsidiary corporations, **4-32**
complete termination of interest, **4-21–4-23**
definition of, **4-16**
distributing corporation
effect on, **4-27–4-28**
E&P, effect on, **4-27–4-28**
equivalency to dividend, **4-23–4-24**
liquidating distributions, **6-5–6-14**
effects of liquidating on distributing corporation, **6-6–6-14**
effects of liquidating on shareholder, **6-5–6-16**
nonliquidating distributions, **4-16–4-28**
partial liquidations, **4-24–4-25**
determination made at corporate level, **4-24**
effect on shareholders, **4-24–4-25**
reasons for, **4-16**
Sec. 306 stock, **4-29–4-30**
shareholders
effect of redemption on, **4-17–4-18**
questions for, **4-16–4-17**
substantially disproportionate redemptions, **4-20–4-21**
to pay death taxes, **4-25–4-27**
Stock rights, *5-11–5-12*
tax-free rights, **4-15**
allocation of basis, **4-15**
holding period, **4-15**
taxable rights, **4-16**
Straight-line method (SL)
use under Modified ACRS, *10-8*
Subchapter J, purposes of, **14-5**
Subchapter K, election out of, **9-2n**
Substantial authority, concept of, **15-24**
Substantial omissions, income tax returns, **15-27–15-28**
Substantial understatement of tax, joint returns, test for, **15-30**
Substantial understatement penalty, **15-23–15-25**
substantial authority, **15-24**
tax shelters, **15-24–15-25**
understatement versus underpayment, **15-23–15-24**
Substantially all requirement, Type C reorganizations, **7-26**
Substantially appreciated inventory, **10-8–10-9**
Substantiation requirements, deduction, *6-16–6-18, 6-37*
Support test
for dependency exemptions, *2-13–2-15*
Supreme Court
appeal of lower court's decision, **15-10**
tax law decisions, **1-14–1-24**
Supreme Court Reporter (S.Ct.), **1-21**

Surviving spouse
definition of, *2-20–2-21*
joint returns and, *2-20–2-21*
Sutter rule, *4-15*
Syndication expenditures, partnerships, **9-14**

Target corporation
acquisitions of assets/stock
tax consequences for corporation, **7-11**
tax consequences for shareholders, **7-12–7-14**
definition of, **7-16n**
liquidation of, **7-2–7-4**
tax accounting elections for new target, **7-7–7-10**
Sec. 338 deemed liquidation, **7-5–7-11**
Targeted jobs credit, *14-20–14-21*
Tax Adviser, The, **1-25**
Tax attributes
acquisitions, **7-46–7-49**
assumption of, **7-46**
limitation on use of, **7-47–7-49**
carryovers, **6-13–6-14**
Tax benefit recapture rule (Sec. 291), **3-7**
Tax benefit rule, *3-26*
Tax Court Memorandum Decision (Research Institute of America), **1-18**
Tax Court of the United States Reports, **1-17–1-18**
Tax credits
affiliated groups, **8-10–8-11**
general business credit, **8-10–8-11**
alternative minimum tax (AMT), **5-13–5-15**
See also Credits
Tax law
administration of, *1-20–1-23*
administrative appeal procedures, *1-23*
audits, selection of returns for, *1-21*
enforcement procedures, *1-21*
penalties, *1-22–1-23*
statute of limitations, *1-22*
administrative interpretations, **1-11–1-13**
announcements, **1-13**
information releases, **1-13**
letter rulings, **1-12–1-13**
notices, **1-13**
revenue procedures, **1-12**
revenue rulings, **1-11–1-12**
technical advice memoranda, **1-13**
definition of, **1-1–1-2, 1-7**
enactment of, *1-18–1-20*
Internal Revenue Code, **1-8**
judicial decisions, **1-14–1-24**
Supreme Court, **1-21**
U.S. Court of Federal Claims, **1-19–1-20**
U.S. Tax Court, **1-14–1-18**
U.S. district courts, **1-19**
circuit court of appeals, **1-20**
court system, overview of, **1-14**
precedential value of decisions, **1-21–1-24**
judicial interpretations, *1-19*
legislative process, **1-7–1-8**
objectives of, *1-14–1-15*
economic objectives, *1-14*
encouragement of certain activities and industries, *1-14*
social objectives, *1-15*
sources of, *1-18–1-19*, **1-7–1-25**
administrative interpretations, *1-19*
Internal Revenue Code, *1-18–1-19*
Treasury Regulations, *1-19*
Treasury Department regulations, **1-8–1-11**
authoritative weight, **1-10**
citations, **1-11**
final regulations, **1-9**
interpretative regulations, **1-10**
proposed regulations, **1-9**
statutory regulations, **1-10**
temporary regulations, **1-9**
Tax Law Review, **1-25**
Tax liability
accumulated earnings tax, determination of, **5-31–5-33**
affiliated groups, **8-9–8-10**
alternative minimum tax liability, **8-10**
regular tax liability, **8-9–8-10**
alternative minimum tax, **5-2–5-15**
consolidated tax returns, **8-9–8-10**
corporations, **3-20–3-22**
accumulated earnings tax, **5-24–5-34**
alternative minimum tax, **5-2–5-15**
personal holding company (PHC) tax, **5-15–5-24**
regular tax, **3-20–3-22**
estates
estate tax, computation of, **13-23–13-25**
taxable estate and tax base, **13-23**
taxable estate, **13-23**
income tax, **14-7–14-10**
gift tax, **12-23–12-24, 12-31**
previous taxable gifts, **12-23–12-24**
unified credit, **12-24**
joint returns, **15-30–15-31**
innocent spouse provision, **15-30–15-31**
validity of, **15-30**
S corporations
special S corporation taxes, **11-15–11-18**
transferee liability, **15-31**
trusts, **14-7–14-10**
complex trusts, **14-19–14-24**
simple trusts, **14-13–14-17**
See also Regular tax liability
Tax Management Portfolios (Bureau of National Affairs), **1-27–1-28**
Tax matters partner, definition of, **9-33**
Tax Notes, **1-25**
Tax periodicals, **1-24–1-25**
Tax planning
accounting methods, *11-28*
accounting periods, *11-28*
alternative minimum Tax, *14-29*
bad debts, *8-34*
cash flow, *14-30*
casualty losses, *8-34*
charitable contributions, *7-32–7-33*
child and dependent care credit, *14-31*
computer applications, *1-25–1-26*
employee compensation, *4-21–4-22*
employee expenses, *9-42–9-43*
foreign earned income exclusion, *14-30–14-31*
foreign tax credits, *14-30–14-31*
general business tax credits, *14-30*
gross income exclusions, *4-21–4-23*
gross income inclusions, *3-27–3-29*
hobby losses, *6-35*
individual income tax, *2-28–2-31*
installment sales method, *11-28*
interest expense deduction, *7-31–7-32*
itemized deductions, *7-30–7-33*
like-kind exchanges, *12-21*
losses, *8-34–8-35*
medical expenses, *7-30–7-31*
moving expenses, *9-42*
net operating losses, *8-35*
nontaxable compensation, *9-43*
nontaxable exchanges, *12-21–12-22*
principal residence, sale of, *12-22*
property transactions, capital gains/losses, *5-31–5-32*
Selection of property to transfer at time of death, *5-32*
Selection of property to transfer by gift, *5-31–5-32*
self-help income, *4-23*
timing of deductions, *6-36*
underpayment penalty, *14-29–14-30*
unreasonable compensation, *6-35–6-36*
Tax practice, **15-31–15-33**
components of, *1-23–1-24*
tax compliance/procedure, *1-23*
tax planning, *1-24*
tax research, *1-23–1-24*
computer applications, *1-25–1-26*
tax research applications, *1-25–1-26*
tax return preparation, *1-25*
tax-planning applications, *1-25*
statements on responsibilities in, **1-35–1-37**
statutory provision concerning tax return preparers, **15-31–15-33**
Tax preference items
individual alternative minimum tax, *14-3–14-4*
Tax preference items, corporate alternative minimum tax, **5-6**

BOLD = Corporations
ITALICS = Individuals

Tax rate structures
- average tax rate, *1-6*
- corporate income tax rate, *1-5*
- effective tax rate, *1-6*
- individual income tax rates, *1-4–1-5*
  - progressive tax rate, *1-4*
  - proportional tax rate, *1-5*
  - regressive tax rate, *1-5*
- marginal tax rate, *1-5–1-7*

Tax rates
- definition of, *1-4–1-5, 2-5*
- self-employment tax, *14-7–14-9*

Tax Reform Act of 1986
- preferential treatment for capital gain income and, *5-2*

Tax Reform Proposals: Compliance and Tax Administration (U.S. Congress), *1-12–1-14*

Tax research, **1-1–1-38**
- citators, **1-28–1-33**
  - Commerce Clearing House Citator (CCH citator), **1-28–1-31**
  - RIA Citator, 2nd Series, **1-31–1-33**
- client-oriented tax research, **1-2**
- computers as research tool, **1-34**
- definition of, **1-2**
- end product of, **1-2**
- gray areas, **1-4**
- overview of, **1-2–1-3**
- policy-oriented tax research, **1-2**
- sample work papers and client letter, **1-38**
- steps in process, **1-3–1-5**
- tax advisors' conclusions, **1-5**
- tax periodicals, **1-24–1-25**
- tax services, **1-25–1-29**
- tax treaties, **1-24**

Tax services, **1-25–1-29**
- *CCH's Federal Tax Service*, **1-28**
- *Federal Tax Coordinator 2d*, **1-26–1-34**
- *Law of Federal Income Taxation*, **1-27**
- research of tax questions, **1-25**
- *Standard Federal Tax Reporter* (CCH service), **1-26**
- *Tax Management Portfolios*, **1-27–1-28**
- *United States Tax Reporter*, **1-25–1-26**

Tax shelters, substantial understatement penalty, **15-24–15-25**

Tax system structure
- criteria for, *1-12–1-14*

Tax treaties, **1-24**

Tax year, *11-28, 11-2–11-7*
- affiliated group elections, **8-8**
- C corporations, *11-2, 11-28*
  - annual accounting period, change in, **3-4**
  - personal service corporations, **3-2–3-4**
  - restrictions on adoption of, **3-2–3-4**
  - selection of, **3-2–3-4**
- partnerships, *11-2, 11-28,* **9-12–9-15, 9-31–9-32**
  - Sec. 706 restrictions, **9-12–9-15**
- personal service corporations (PSCs), *11-2*
- S corporations, *11-2, 11-28,* **11-13, 11-37**

Tax-deferred bonds, *3-28*

Tax-exempt obligations, *3-28*
- accrual of original issue discount, *5-23*
- interest income, *3-28*
  - dependency exemption gross income test and, *2-16*
  - interest expense incurred to generate, *7-14*
  - tax preference item, *14-3–14-4*
- private activity bonds, *14-4*

Tax-free reorganizations, **7-11–7-14, 7-15–7-49**

Tax-free stock distributions, **4-13–4-14, 7-35–7-41**

Taxable bonds, *3-28*

Taxable estate, **13-23**

Taxable income
- accumulated earnings tax and, **5-31–5-33**
  - accumulated earnings credit, **5-32–5-33**
  - dividends-paid deduction, **5-32**
  - negative adjustments, **5-32**
  - positive adjustments, **5-31**
- complex trusts/estates, **14-19–14-24**
  - comprehensive illustration, **14-24–14-27**
  - distributable net income (DNI), determination of, **14-20**
  - net capital loss effect of, **14-24**
  - net operating loss effect of, **14-24**
  - tax treatment for beneficiary, **14-21–14-23**
- corporations
  - affiliated groups, **8-7, 8-8**
  - compared to individual taxable income and, **3-6**
  - deductions, **3-7–3-18**
  - reconciliation of book income items to, **3-35–3-36**
- individuals, *2-5*
- partnerships, **9-17**
- S corporations, **11-14–11-15**
- Simple trusts, **14-13–14-17**
  - allocation of expenses to tax-exempt income, **14-14–14-15**
  - comprehensive illustration, **14-17–14-19**
  - distributable net income (DNI), determination of, **14-15**
  - exemption, **14-14**
  - net capital loss, effect of, **14-16–14-17**
  - net operating loss, effect of, **14-16**
  - short-cut approach to proving, **14-16**
  - taxation to beneficiary, **14-15–14-16**
- *See also* Corporate taxable income

Taxable interest, dependency exemption gross income test and, *2-16*

Taxable versus tax-free asset acquisitions, **7-11–7-12**
- accounting for the acquisition, **7-12**
- tax consequences, **7-11–7-12**
  - for acquiring corporation, **7-12**
  - for target corporation's shareholders, **7-12**
  - for target corporation, **7-11**

Taxable versus tax-free stock acquisitions, **7-12–7-14**
- accounting for the transaction, **7-14**
- tax consequences, **7-12–7-14**
  - for acquiring, **7-14**
  - for target corporation's shareholders, **7-14**
  - for target corporation, **7-12–7-14**

Taxation
- administration of, *1-20–1-23*
- determination of, *2-1–2-32*
- enactment of tax law, *1-18–1-20*
- objectives of, *1-14–1-15*
- tax rate structures, *1-4–1-7*
  - criteria for, *1-12–1-14*
- taxes, types of, *1-7–1-11*
- U.S. history, *1-2–1-3*
  - early periods, *1-2*
  - revenue acts, *1-3*
  - revenue sources, *1-3*
- *See also* Individual income tax, *1-1–1-26*

Taxes
- deductible taxes, *7-9*
- definition of, *7-9*
- general sales tax, *7-11*
- local income taxes, *7-10*
- nondeductible taxes, *7-9–7-10*
- payment of, *14-24–14-29*
- personal property taxes, *7-10*
- real estate taxes, *7-10–7-11*
  - apportionment of taxes, *7-10–7-11*
  - real property assessments for local benefits, *7-11*
- reporting itemized deduction, *7-36*
- state income taxes, *7-10*
- types of, *1-7–1-11*
  - customs duties, *1-11*
  - employment taxes, *1-11*
  - federal excise taxes, *1-11*
  - franchise tax, *1-7–1-8*
  - property taxes, *1-11*
  - sales taxes, *1-11*
  - state income taxes, *1-7–1-8*
  - unemployment taxes, *1-11*
  - wealth transfer taxes, *1-8–1-10*

Taxes—the Tax Magazine, **1-25**

Taxpayer Compliance Measurement Program (TCMP), audits and, **15-6**

Taxpayer identification numbers, *2-32*

- *TC Memorandum Decisions* (RIA), **1-18**
- Technical advice memoranda, *1-19*
  - audits and, **15-8**
  - tax law, **1-13**
- Temporary living expenses, as indirect moving expense, *9-20*
- Temporary regulations, **1-9**
- Tenancy by the entirety, definition of, **13-14n**
- Tentative minimum tax, definition of, **5-5**
- Term certain interest, **12-12**
- Terminable interest rule, marital deduction and, **13-21–13-22**
- Terminable interests
  - definition of, **12-19**
  - nondeductible terminable interests, characteristics of, **12-19–12-20**
  - qualified terminable interest property (QTIP), **12-20**
- Termination
  - affiliated groups, **8-8–8-9**
    - effect on former members, **8-9**
    - good cause request to discontinue status, **8-9**
  - of S corporation election, **11-9–11-12**
    - allocation of income, **11-10–11-11**
    - avoidance of, **11-12**
    - inadvertent termination, **11-11**
    - new election following termination, **11-11–11-12**
    - post-termination loss carryovers, **11-22–11-23**
  - of partnership interest, **10-22–10-24**
  - stock redemption
    - complete termination of interest, **4-21–4-23**
    - definition of, **4-21–4-23**
    - family attribution rules and, **4-21–4-23**
- Testamentary gifts, *4-4*
- Testamentary transactions, **13-2**
- Testamentary trust, **14-2**
- *The Appraisal of Real Estate* (The Appraisal Institute), **13-7n**
- *The Individual Income Tax* (Goode), *1-3n*
- *The Wealth of Nations* (Smith), *1-12*n
- Theft losses
  - as itemized deduction, *7-28*
  - deductible amount of, *8-19–8-20*
  - documentation of loss, *8-34*
  - identifiable event, *8-17–8-18*
  - measuring losses, *8-19–8-20*
  - reporting on Form 4684, *13-25–13-28*
- 30-day rules, consolidated taxable income, **8-8n**
- Three-party exchanges, of property, *12-5–12-6*
- Throwback dividends, **5-22, 5-32**
- Tickets, entertainment, limitations on, *9-16*
- Tier-1 beneficiaries, **14-21–14-22**
- Tier-2 beneficiaries, **14-21–14-22**
- Timber, Sec. 1231 and, *13-5–13-6*
- Trade, definition of, *6-5–6-6*
- Trademarks, sale/exchange of, *5-26–5-27*
- Transfer tax base, removal of gift tax amount from, **12-29**
- Transfer taxes
  - estate tax, concept of, **13-2–13-5**
  - generation-skipping transfer tax (GSTT), **13-30–13-31**
  - gift tax
    - concept of, **12-2–12-3**
    - history/purpose of, **12-2–12-3**
  - unified transfer tax system, **12-3–12-4**
    - death tax base, impact of taxable gifts on, **12-3–12-4**
    - unified credit, **12-4**
    - unified rate schedule, **12-3**
- Transfer to existing corporation, **2-14–2-15**
- Transferee corporation
  - effect of Sec. 351 on, **2-20–2-21**
  - reorganizations, **7-17–7-18**
- Transferor corporation, definition of, **7-16n**
- Transferor provisions
  - gross estate, **13-10–13-13**
    - gifts made within three years of death, **13-10–13-11**
    - gross-up rule, **13-11**
    - reversionary interests, **13-12–13-13**
    - revocable transfers, **13-13**
    - transfers with retained life estate, **13-11–13-12**
- Transferor's liabilities
  - assumption of, **2-21–2-24**
    - general rule (Sec. 357(a)), **2-21–2-22**
    - liabilities of taxpayer using cash method of accounting (Sec. 357(c)(3)), **2-23–2-24**
    - tax avoidance (Sec. 357(b)), **2-22**
- Transfers of partnership interest
  - types of transfers, **10-11, 10-25**
- Transportation expenses, *9-9–9-12*
  - automobile expenses, *9-10–9-12*
  - deductibility of, *9-9*
  - definition of, *9-9–9-10*
  - reimbursed expenses, *9-12*
  - to medical facility, *7-4*
- Travel expenses, *9-4–9-8*
  - business versus pleasure, *9-7–9-8*
  - deductibility of, *9-4–9-5*
  - definition of, *9-5*
  - foreign travel, *9-8*
  - limitations, *9-8*
  - production or collection of income, *9-4–9-6*
  - qualification requirements, *9-6*
  - substantiation of, *6-16–6-18, 9-43–9-44*
- Treasure finds, as gross income, *3-22–3-23*
- *Treasury Department Circular 230*, rules of, **15-33**
- Treasury Regulations, *1-19*, **1-8–1-11**
  - authoritative weight, **1-10**
  - citations, **1-11**
  - forms of, **1-8–1-11**
  - interpretative regulations, *1-19*, **1-10**
  - legislative regulations, *1-19*
  - statutory regulations, **1-10**
- Treble damages, as expenditure contrary to public policy, *6-13*
- Triangular reorganizations
  - Type A reorganizations, **7-26–7-27**
    - advantages of, **7-27**
    - substantially all requirement, **7-26**
  - Type B reorganizations, **7-35**
  - Type C reorganization, **7-30**
  - *See also* Reverse triangular mergers, **7-26–7-27, 7-35**
- Trustees, **14-2**
- Trusts
  - administration expense deduction, **14-35**
  - classification rules/size of exemption, **14-13–14-14**
  - compared to associations, **2-8**
  - credits, **14-10**
  - definition of, **14-2**
  - distributable net income (DNI), **14-10–14-12, 14-20**
    - computation of, **14-11–14-12, 14-15, 14-20**
    - definition of, **14-11**
    - significance of, **14-10–14-11**
  - distribution deduction, **14-9, 14-15, 14-20**
    - property distributions, **14-34**
    - 65-day rule, **14-34**
    - timing of distributions, **14-34**
  - distributions from, personal holding company income (PHCI) and, **5-18**
  - expense deductions, **14-7–14-9**
  - filing requirements, **14-35**
    - documents to be furnished to IRS, **14-36**
    - due date, **14-36**
  - grantor trust provisions, **14-30–14-33**
  - gross income, **14-7**
  - inception of, **14-2**
  - income in respect of a decedent (IRD), **14-27–14-29**
  - nontax aspects of, **14-3**
  - personal exemption, **14-9–14-10**
  - reasons for creation of, **14-3**
  - S corporations and, **11-4–11-5**
  - sample simple/complex trust returns, **14-36**
  - shift income, ability to, **14-34**
  - sprinkling trust, **14-34**
  - taxation, **14-1–14-36**
  - tax liability, **14-7–14-10**
  - tax-saving aspects of, **14-3**
  - tax treatment for beneficiary, **14-15–14-16, 14-21–14-23**
  - tax year, **14-35**

BOLD = Corporations
ITALICS = Individuals

taxable income, **14-7–14-10**
allocation of expenses to tax-exempt income, **14-14–14-15**
comprehensive illustration, **14-17–14-19, 14-24–14-27**
distribution deduction, determination of, **14-9, 14-15, 14-20**
net capital loss, effect of, **14-16–14-17, 14-24**
net operating loss, effect of, **14-16, 14-24**
short-cut approach to proving correctness of, **14-16**
See also Accumulation distribution rules; Complex trusts/estates; Grantor trusts; Simple trusts; Voting trust
Tuition payments, gift tax and, **12-8**
2% nondeductible floor, *9-3–9-4*
Type A reorganizations, **7-21–7-27**
consolidations, **7-23–7-26**
definition of, **7-23**
requirements for, **7-23–7-25**
tax consequences of, **7-25–7-26**
mergers, **7-23–7-27**
requirements for, **7-23–7-25**
reverse triangular mergers, **7-27**
tax consequences, **7-25–7-26**
triangular mergers, **7-26–7-27**
Type B reorganizations, **7-31–7-35**
advantages of, **7-34–7-35**
disadvantages of, **7-35**
solely-for-voting-stock requirement, **7-32–7-33**
control, **7-33**
exceptions to, **7-32–7-33**
timing of transaction, **7-33**
tax consequences of, **7-33–7-34**
triangular Type B reorganizations, **7-35**
Type C reorganizations, **7-28–7-30**
advantages of, **7-29–7-30**
consideration used to effect reorganization, **7-28–7-29**
disadvantages of, **7-29–7-30**
stock distribution, **7-28**
substantially all requirement, **7-28**
tax consequences of, **7-30**
Type D reorganizations, **7-30–7-31**
acquisitive Type D reorganizations, **7-30–7-31**
control requirements, **7-30–7-31**
tax consequences of, **7-31**
divisive Type D reorganization, **7-37–7-41**
requirements, **7-40–7-41**
tax consequences of, **7-37–7-40**
Type E reorganizations, **7-41–7-43**
bond-for-bond exchange, **7-42–7-43**
bond-for-stock exchange, **7-42**
stock-for-stock exchange, **7-42**
Type F reorganizations, **7-43**
Type G reorganizations
acquisitive form, **7-35**
divisive form, **7-41**

Unauthorized practice of law, **15-34**
Underpayment penalty
avoidance of, *14-29–14-30*, **15-21–15-22**
exceptions to, **15-22**
estimated taxes, *14-28*
Understatement of taxes, penalties for aiding/abetting, **15-32–15-33**
Undervaluation
of estate tax, **13-36**
of gift tax, **12-32**
Undistributed personal holding company income (UPHCI)
calculation of, **5-21–5-22**
negative adjustments, **5-22**
positive adjustments, **5-21**
See also Personal holding company income, **5-21–5-22**
Unearned income, dependents with, *2-23–2-25*
Unemployment compensation, *3-23*
Unemployment taxes, *1-11*
Unified credit, **12-4, 12-6–12-7, 12-24, 13-5, 13-23–13-24**
estate tax, **13-5, 13-23–13-24**
gift tax, **12-4, 12-6–12-7, 12-24**
Unified rate schedule, **12-3**
Unified transfer tax system, **12-3–12-4**
death tax base, impact of taxable gifts on, **12-3–12-4**
unified credit, **12-4, 12-6–12-7, 12-24**
unified rate schedule, **12-3**
Uniform Act, fiduciary accounting and, **14-5–14-6**
Uniform Limited Partnership Act (ULPA), **9-2**
Uniform Partnership Act (UPA), **9-2**
United States Board of Tax Appeals Reports, **1-23**
United States Reports, Lawyers' Edition (L. Ed.), **1-21**
United States Supreme Court Reports (U.S.), **1-21**
United States Tax Reporter (Research Institute of America), **1-25–1-26**
Unfunded deferred compensation plans, *9-31*
Unharvested crops/land, Sec. 1231 and, *13-6*
Uniform capitalization rules, cost of acquired property and, *5-5, 11-11–11-12*
Unmarried individuals, surviving spouse/head-of-household status, *2-20–2-22*
Unrealized income, as nonincome item, *4-2–4-3*
Unrealized receivables
as Sec. 751 assets, **10-8**
substantially appreciated inventory, **10-8–10-9**
partnerships, basis, **9-8–9-9**
payments for, at death/retirement of partner, **10-19**
Unreasonable compensation
hedge agreements, use of, **4-33–4-34**
See also Compensation planning
Unreasonable compensation, tax-planning considerations, *6-35–6-36*
Unreimbursed employee expenses
deductibility, *9-3–9-4*
exceptions to floor, *9-4*
limitations on, *9-3–9-4*
2% nondeductible floor, *9-3–9-4*
Unsecured debt obligations, **2-32–2-33**
U.S. Circuit Court of Appeals, **1-20**
precedential value of decisions, **1-23**
primary cites, **1-19**
secondary cites, **1-19**
U.S. Corporation Income Tax Return (Form 1120), **3-34**
U.S. Corporation Short Form Income Tax Return (Form 1120-A), **3-34**
U.S. Court of Federal Claims, **1-19–1-20**
precedential value of decisions, **1-23**
primary cites, **1-19**
secondary cites, **1-19**
U.S. district courts, **1-19**
precedential value of decisions, **1-23**
primary cites, **1-19**
secondary cites, **1-19**
unreported decisions, **1-19**
U.S. Income Tax Return for an S Corporation (Form 1120S), **11-37–11-38**
U.S. Tax Cases (USTC), **1-19**
U.S. Tax Court, **1-14–1-18**
acquiescence policy, **1-17**
history of, **1-14**
language of, **1-17**
memo decisions, **1-18**
precedential value of decisions, **1-21**
published opinions and citations, **1-17–1-18**
regular decisions, **1-14–1-17**
small cases procedures, **1-17**
Use valuation, farm realty, **13-30**

Vacation home rental, *6-31–6-33*
Valuation
of estates
adjusted taxable gifts, **13-4**
alternate valuation date, **13-7–13-8**
date-of-death valuation, **13-6–13-7**
estate tax returns, **13-36**
gross estate, **13-6–13-8**
penalty for undervaluation, **13-36**
of gifts, **12-11–12-13**
general rules, **12-11–12-12**
life estates, **12-12–12-13**
penalty for undervaluation, **12-32**
remainder interest, **12-12–12-13**

Valuation (*continued*)
of stock, deemed liquidation election and, **7-5–7-8**
Voluntary changes, in accounting methods, *11-27*
Voting trust, definition of, **11-4n**

Wage reduction plans, *4-17*
Wash sales, *6-22–6-25*
basis of stock, *6-24–6-25*
deduction of losses on, *6-22–6-25*
substantially identical stock/securities, *6-24*
Ways and Means Committee, U.S. House of Representatives, tax law and, **1-7–1-8**
Wealth transfer taxes
estate tax, *1-9–1-10*
gift tax, *1-8–1-9*
See also Estate tax; Gift tax, *1-8–1-10*
Welfare benefits, dependency exemption support test and, *2-13*
WESTLAW legal data base, **1-34**
Wherewithal-to-pay concept, *3-4*
Widow/widower, as surviving spouse, *2-20–2-21*
Withholding, *4-23–4-24, 14-25–14-27, 14-32*
allowances/methods, *14-25–14-26*
failure to withhold, *4-23–4-24*
federal income tax withheld computation, *14-27*
Work opportunity credit, *14-20–14-21*
Working capital, reasonable need of business and, **5-28–5-30**
Working condition benefits, *4-13*
Worthless securities
losses from, *8-3–8-4,* **2-31–2-32**
reporting losses from, *8-35*
ordinary loss, **2-31–2-32**
sale/exchange of, *5-22*
Worthlessness
advances to corporation, **2-32–2-33**
of stock/debt obligations, **2-30–2-32**
securities, **2-30–2-32**
unsecured debt obligations, **2-32–2-33**
ordinary loss deduction, **2-31–2-32**
Writ of certiorari, **1-14**
Written conclusions, tax research, **1-5**

Year-end, choice of
C corporation, **3-2–3-4**
partnership, **9-12–9-15**
S corporation, **11-13, 11-37**
trust's/estate's, **14-35**

BOLD = Corporations
ITALICS = Individuals